One Location, Endless Resources

Visit thinkcentral.com

Explore a whole new world of **online learning**. You will find all the components of *Holt Literature and Language Arts* in one location, including instructional resources, tracked assessments, and tools for planning and instant communication.

Easy to use

- Intuitive structure for first-time users
- Advanced options, when and if you want them
- Adjustable features to make your space suit your needs

Simple Navigation

- Find the right resources in four clicks or less
- View snapshots of
  - ✔ Your calendar
  - ✔ Assignments
  - ✔ Communication with parents and students
  - ✔ Student progress

THINK central

Use, extend, and customize

- Access pre-loaded course content, including the online textbook, assessments, remediation resources, and standard progress reports quickly and easily
- Add resources from your own files or create new ones
- Modify any resources at any time for your students

Differentiate and remediate

- Assign materials to classes, groups, or individuals for focused instruction
- Ha ... y based on ... e
- Vie ... anywhere, any

CALIFORNIA TEACHER'S EDITION

HOLT

LITERATURE AND LANGUAGE ARTS

Sixth Course

Kylene Beers
Carol Jago
Deborah Appleman
Leila Christenbury
Sara Kajder
Linda Rief

Senior Program Consultants for English-Language Development

Robin Scarcella
Mabel Rivera
Héctor Rivera

Mastering the California Standards
Reading, Writing, Listening, Speaking

HOLT, RINEHART AND WINSTON

COVER PHOTO CREDITS: (bkgd), John Kelly / The Image Bank / Getty Images; (inset), Gala Narezo / Stone / Getty Images; (cl), Sam Dudgeon / HRW Photo; (b), David Trood / Riser / Getty Images; (br), GeoStock / Photodisc / Getty Images

Printed in the United States of America

ISBN 978-0-03-099284-1

ISBN 0-03-099284-2

1 2 3 4 5 048 10 09 08

PROGRAM AUTHORS

Kylene Beers is the senior program author for *Holt Literature and Language Arts*. A former middle school teacher, she is now Senior Reading Advisor to Secondary Schools for Teachers College Reading and Writing Project at Columbia University. She is the author of *When Kids Can't Read: What Teachers Can Do* and co-editor (with Linda Rief and Robert E. Probst) of *Adolescent Literacy: Turning Promise into Practice*. The former editor of the National Council of Teachers of English (NCTE) literacy journal *Voices from the Middle*, Dr. Beers assumed the NCTE presidency in 2008. With articles in *English Journal, Journal of Adolescent and Adult Literacy, School Library Journal, Middle Matters,* and *Voices from the Middle,* she speaks both nationally and internationally as a recognized authority on struggling readers. Dr. Beers has served on the review boards of *English Journal, The ALAN Review,* the Special Interest Group on Adolescent Literature of the International Reading Association, and the Assembly on Literature for Adolescents of the NCTE. She is the 2001 recipient of the Richard W. Halley Award given by NCTE for outstanding contributions to middle school literacy.

Carol Jago is a teacher with thirty-two years of experience at Santa Monica High School in California. The author of nine books on education, she continues to share her experiences as a writer and as a speaker at conferences and seminars across the country. Her wide and varied experience in standards assessment and secondary education in general has made her a sought-after speaker. As an author, Ms. Jago also works closely with Heinemann Publishers and with the National Council of Teachers of English. Her long-time association with NCTE led to her June 2007 election to a four-year term on the council's board. During that term she will serve for one year as president of the council. She is also active with the California Association of Teachers of English (CATE) and has edited CATE's scholarly journal *California English* since 1996. Ms. Jago served on the planning committees for the 2009 NAEP Reading Framework and the 2011 NAEP Writing Framework.

Deborah Appleman is professor and chair of educational studies and director of the Summer Writing Program at Carleton College in Northfield, Minnesota. Dr. Appleman's primary research interests include adolescent response to literature, multicultural literature, and the teaching of literary theory in high school. With a team of classroom teachers, she co-edited *Braided Lives,* a multicultural literature anthology. In addition to many articles and book chapters, she is the author of *Critical Encounters in High School English: Teaching Literary Theory to Adolescents* and co-author of *Teaching Literature to Adolescents*. Her most recent book, *Reading for Themselves,* explores the use of extracurricular book clubs to encourage adolescents to read for pleasure. Dr. Appleman was a high school English teacher, working in both urban and suburban schools. She is a frequent national speaker and consultant and continues to work weekly in high schools with students and teachers.

Leila Christenbury is a former high school English teacher and currently professor of English education at Virginia Commonwealth University, Richmond. The former editor of *English Journal,* she is the author of ten books, including *Writing on Demand, Making the Journey,* and *Retracing the Journey: Teaching and Learning in an American High School.* Past president of the National Council of Teachers of English, Dr. Christenbury is also a former member of the steering committee of the National Assessment of Educational Progress (NAEP). A recipient of the Rewey Belle Inglis Award for Outstanding Woman in English Teaching, Dr. Christenbury is a frequent speaker on issues of English teaching and learning and has been interviewed and quoted on CNN and in the *New York Times, USA Today, Washington Post, Chicago Tribune,* and *US News & World Report*.

Sara Kajder, author of *Bringing the Outside In: Visual Ways to Engage Reluctant Readers* and *The Tech-Savvy English Classroom,* is an assistant professor at Virginia Polytechnic Institute and State University (Virginia Tech). She has served as co-chair of NCTE's Conference on English Education (CEE) Technology Commission and of the Society for Information Technology and Teacher Education (SITE) English Education Committee. Dr. Kajder is the recipient of the first SITE National Technology Leadership Fellowship in English Education; she is a former English and language arts teacher for high school and middle school.

Linda Rief has been a classroom teacher for twenty-five years. She is author of *The Writer's-Reader's Notebook, Inside the Writer's-Reader's Notebook, Seeking Diversity, 100 Quickwrites,* and *Vision and Voice* as well as the co-editor (with Kylene Beers and Robert E. Probst) of *Adolescent Literacy: Turning Promise into Practice*. Ms. Rief has written numerous chapters and journal articles, and she co-edited the first five years of *Voices from the Middle*. During the summer she teaches graduate courses at the University of New Hampshire and Northeastern University. She is a national and international consultant on adolescent literacy issues.

PROGRAM CONSULTANTS

Robin Scarcella is a professor at the University of California at Irvine, where she also directs the Program in Academic English/English as a Second Language. She has a Ph.D. in linguistics from the University of Southern California and an M.A. in education/second language acquisition from Stanford University. She has taught all grade levels. She has been active in shaping policies affecting language assessment, instruction, and teacher professional development. In the last four years, she has spoken to more than ten thousand teachers and administrators. She has written more than thirty scholarly articles that appear in such journals as the *TESOL Quarterly* and *Brain and Language*. Her most recent publication is *Accelerating Academic English: A Focus on the English Learner*.

Mabel Rivera is a research assistant professor at the Texas Institute for Measurement, Evaluation, and Statistics at the University of Houston. Her current research interests include the education of and prevention of reading difficulties in English-language learners. In addition, Dr. Rivera is involved in local and national service activities for preparing school personnel to teach students with special needs.

Héctor H. Rivera is an assistant professor at Southern Methodist University, School of Education and Human Development. Dr. Rivera is also the director of the SMU Professional Development /ESL Supplemental Certification Program for Math and Science Teachers of At-Risk Middle and High School LEP Newcomer Adolescents. This federally funded program develops, delivers, and evaluates professional development for educators who work with at-risk newcomer adolescent students. Dr. Rivera is also collaborating on school reform projects in Guatemala and with the Institute of Arctic Education in Greenland.

Marilyn Astore is a former teacher, principal, and county office assistant superintendent with more than 20 years of classroom experience and more than 40 years in the field of education. In her role as chair of both the California Curriculum Commission and its Reading/Language Arts/English Language Development Subject Matter Committees, she worked with other commissioners to advise the California State Board of Education on the adoption of curricular and instructional materials. She has taught teacher education classes at California State University, Sacramento; the University of San Diego; and the University of California, Davis, University Extension. Ms. Astore presents and consults on K–12 reading issues and intervention for older struggling readers.

Isabel L. Beck is professor of education and senior scientist at the University of Pittsburgh. Dr. Beck has conducted extensive research on vocabulary and comprehension and has published well over one hundred articles and several books, including *Improving Comprehension with Questioning the Author* (with Margaret McKeown) and *Bringing Words to Life: Robust Vocabulary Instruction* (with Margaret McKeown and Linda Kucan). Dr. Beck's numerous national awards include the Oscar S. Causey Award for outstanding research from the National Reading Conference and the William S. Gray Award from the International Reading Association for lifetime contributions to the field of reading research and practice.

Margaret G. McKeown is a senior scientist at the University of Pittsburgh's Learning Research and Development Center. Her research in reading comprehension and vocabulary has been published extensively in outlets for both research and practitioner audiences. Recognition of her work includes the International Reading Association's (IRA) Dissertation of the Year Award and a National Academy of Education Spencer Fellowship. Before her career in research, Dr. McKeown taught elementary school.

Amy Benjamin is a veteran teacher, literacy coach, consultant, and researcher in secondary-level literacy instruction. She has been recognized for excellence in teaching from the New York State English Council, Union College, and Tufts University. Ms. Benjamin is the author of several books about reading comprehension, writing instruction, grammar, and differentiation. Her most recent book (with Tom Oliva) is *Engaging Grammar: Practical Advice for Real Classrooms,* published by the National Council of Teachers of English. Ms. Benjamin has had a long association and leadership role with the NCTE's Assembly for the Teaching of English Grammar (ATEG).

Sandra Carsten has more than thirty-seven years of experience as a teacher and administrator in the Fresno Unified School District. She has been a leader in curriculum, instruction, and professional development and has supervised national grants. As an assistant superintendent for curriculum and instruction, she implemented standards-based programs, benchmark assessments, and protocols for monitoring student achievement. In addition, Ms. Carsten served for five years as the director of the Association of California School Administrators.

Eric Cooper is the president of the National Urban Alliance for Effective Education (NUA) and co-founder of the Urban Partnership for Literacy with the IRA. He currently works with the NCTE to support improvements in urban education and collaborates with the Council of the Great City Schools. In line with his educational mission to support the improvement of education for urban and minority students, Dr. Cooper writes, lectures, and produces educational documentaries and talk shows to provide advocacy for children who live in disadvantaged circumstances.

Harvey Daniels is a former college professor and classroom teacher, working in urban and suburban Chicago schools. Known for his pioneering work on student book clubs, Dr. Daniels is author and co-author of many books, including *Literature Circles: Voice and Choice in Book Clubs and Reading Groups* and *Best Practice: Today's Standards for Teaching and Learning in America's Schools.*

Judith L. Irvin taught middle school for several years before entering her career as a university professor. She now teaches courses in curriculum and instructional leadership and literacy at Florida State University. Dr. Irvin's many publications include *Reading and the High School Student: Strategies to Enhance Literacy* and *Integrating Literacy and Learning in the Content Area Classroom*. Her latest book, *Taking Action: A Leadership Model for Improving Adolescent Literacy,* is the result of a Carnegie-funded project and is published by the Association for Supervision and Curriculum Development.

Patrick Schwarz is professor of special education and chair of the Diversity in Learning and Development department for National-Louis University, Chicago, Illinois. He is author of *From Disability to Possibility* and *You're Welcome* (co-written with Paula Kluth), texts that have inspired teachers worldwide to reconceptualize inclusion to help all children. Other books co-written with Paula Kluth include *Just Give Him the Whale* and *Inclusion Boot-camp*. Dr. Schwarz also presents and consults worldwide through Creative Culture Consulting.

Marianne Steverson is currently president and COO of the educational services company known as Smar^{2}tel Learning Links. She has forty-two years of diversified experience in the public school sector and private educational therapy practice. She coordinates the company's in-school professional development for teachers of reading. She also manages the development of new products and methodologies. Her areas of specialization include teaching students who use African American vernacular English and teaching struggling readers.

CRITICAL REVIEWERS

Special Consultant
Deborah Keys
Research, Assessment and Accountability
Oakland Unified School District
Oakland, California

Sharon Anderson-Jones
Washington High School
Fremont Unified School District
Fremont, California

Laurel Byrd
Secondary Language Arts Academic Coach
Professional Development Academy
Hemet Unified School District
Hemet, California

Robert Chapman
Eureka High School
Eureka, California

June Gatewood
Rio Americano High School
San Juan Unified School District
Sacramento, California

Jose Ibarra-Tiznado
Basset Unified School District
La Puente, California

Jayne Nichols
Bella Vista High School
San Juan Unified School District
Fair Oaks, California

Natalie St. John
High School English Teacher
San Rafael, California

Chondra Winger
English Teacher
Elk Grove High School
Elk Grove, California

PROGRAM ADVISORS

Joyce Black-Carson
Language Arts Department Chair
Montera Middle School
Oakland, California

Dr. Julie Chan
Director, Literacy Instruction
Newport Mesa Unified School District
Costa Mesa, California

Robert Chapman
English Teacher
Eureka High School
Eureka, California

Gabrielle D'Andrea
Instructional Coach
Samuel Jackman Middle School
Sacramento, California

Jeanne Davenport
English Teacher
Lincoln Middle School
Santa Monica, California

Charlyn Earp
Reading Teacher
Mesa Verde Middle School
San Diego, California

Teisha Hase
Reading Coordinator
Oroville High School
Chico, California

Greg Johnson
English Teacher
Liberty High School
Bakersfield, California

Terry Juhl
Principal Director
Twin Ridges Elementary
North San Juan, California

Diana Lester
English Language Development Reading Coordinator
Estancia High School
Costa Mesa, California

Joanne Mitchell
President
John Marshall High School
Los Angeles, California

Fern Sheldon
Curriculum Specialist
Rowland Unified School District
Rowland Heights, California

Laura Smith
Assistant Principal
Madison Middle School
Oceanside Vista, California

Robert Valdez
AVID Core 8 Teacher
Pioneer Middle School
Tustin, California

Marsha Zandi
Language Arts Curriculum Specialist
Sweetwater Union High School
Chula Vista, California

California Minimum Course of Study

The Minimum Course of Study is designed for those teachers whose basic or advanced students can master the California English-Language Arts Content Standards without significant reteaching. The Minimum Course of Study covers what students should know and be able to do in each grade. It allows teachers to make efficient use of classroom time while ensuring student competency in mastering the standards. Note that all Minimum Course of Study selections address Reading Standard 3.5a, and that all Writing Workshops address Language Conventions Standards 1.1, 1.2, and 1.3. See the full text of these standards below.

	SELECTIONS/ FEATURES	READING, WRITING, LANGUAGE CONVENTIONS, AND LISTENING AND SPEAKING STANDARDS	
UNITS 1–6	All Minimum Course of Study Selections	**Reading Standard** **3.5** Analyze recognized works of American literature representing a variety of genres and traditions:	**a.** Trace the development of American literature from the colonial period forward.
	All Writing Workshops	**Language Conventions Standards** **1.1** Demonstrate control of grammar, diction, and paragraph and sentence structure and an understanding of English usage.	**1.2** Produce legible work that shows accurate spelling and correct punctuation and capitalization. **1.3** Reflect appropriate manuscript requirements in writing.
UNIT 1 THE ANGLO-SAXON PERIOD AND THE MIDDLE AGES 449–1485	*from* Beowulf, Parts One and Two **(C1)**	**Reading Standards** **2.2** Analyze the way in which clarity of meaning is affected by the patterns of organization, hierarchical structures, repetition of the main ideas, syntax, and word choice in the text.	**3.6** Analyze the way in which authors through the centuries have used archetypes drawn from myth and tradition in literature, film, political speeches, and religious writings (e.g., how the archetypes of banishment from an ideal world may be used to interpret Shakespeare's tragedy *Macbeth).*
	The Prologue to The Canterbury Tales **(C2)**	**Reading Standards** **3.1** Analyze characteristics of subgenres (e.g., satire, parody, allegory, pastoral) that are used in poetry, prose, plays, novels, short stories, essays, and other basic genres.	**3.3** Analyze the ways in which irony, tone, mood, the author's style, and the "sound" of language achieve specific rhetorical or aesthetic purposes or both.
		Grades 9–10 Review Standard **3.4** Determine characters' traits by what the characters say about themselves in narration,	dialogue, dramatic monologue, and soliloquy.
	Lord Randall **(C2)**	**Reading Standards** **3.1** Analyze characteristics of subgenres (e.g., satire, parody, allegory, pastoral) that are used in poetry, prose, plays, novels, short stories, essays, and other basic genres.	**3.3** Analyze the ways in which irony, tone, mood, the author's style, and the "sound" of language achieve specific rhetorical or aesthetic purposes or both.
	from Sir Gawain and the Green Knight **(C2)**	**Reading Standards** **2.2** Analyze the way in which clarity of meaning is affected by the patterns of organization, hierarchical structures, repetition of the main ideas, syntax, and word choice in the text.	**3.1** Analyze characteristics of subgenres (e.g., satire, parody, allegory, pastoral) that are used in poetry, prose, plays, novels, short stories, essays, and other basic genres.

California Minimum Course of Study

	SELECTIONS/ FEATURES	READING, WRITING, LANGUAGE CONVENTIONS, AND LISTENING AND SPEAKING STANDARDS
UNIT 1 (CONT'D)	**Writing Workshop:** Literary Analysis: Poetry	**Writing Standards** **1.1** Demonstrate an understanding of the elements of discourse (e.g., purpose, speaker, audience, form) when completing narrative, expository, persuasive, or descriptive writing assignments. **1.3** Structure ideas and arguments in a sustained, persuasive, and sophisticated way and support them with precise and relevant examples. **1.9** Revise text to highlight the individual voice, improve sentence variety and style, and enhance subtlety of meaning and tone in ways that are consistent with the purpose, audience, and genre. **2.2** Write responses to literature.
	Listening and Speaking Workshop: Presenting a Literary Analysis	**Listening and Speaking Standard** **2.3** Deliver oral responses to literature.
UNIT 2 **THE RENAISSANCE 1485–1660:** A Flourish of Genius	The Passionate Shepherd to His Love / The Nymph's Reply to the Shepherd **(C3)**	**Reading Standards** **2.2** Analyze the way in which clarity of meaning is affected by the patterns of organization, hierarchical structures, repetition of the main ideas, syntax, and word choice in the text. **3.1** Analyze characteristics of subgenres (e.g., satire, parody, allegory, pastoral) that are used in poetry, prose, plays, novels, short stories, essays, and other basic genres.
	A Valediction: Forbidding Mourning **(C3)**	**Reading Standards** **2.2** Analyze the way in which clarity of meaning is affected by the patterns of organization, hierarchical structures, repetition of the main ideas, syntax, and word choice in the text. **3.4** Analyze ways in which poets use imagery, personification, figures of speech, and sounds to evoke readers' emotions.
	The Fall of Satan *from* Paradise Lost **(C3)**	**Reading Standards** **3.3** Analyze the ways in which irony, tone, mood, the author's style, and the "sound" of language achieve specific rhetorical or aesthetic purposes or both. **3.4** Analyze ways in which poets use imagery, personification, figures of speech, and sounds to evoke readers' emotions.
	Sonnet 29 **(C4)**	**Reading Standards** **2.2** Analyze the way in which clarity of meaning is affected by the patterns of organization, hierarchical structures, repetition of the main ideas, syntax, and word choice in the text. **3.1** Analyze characteristics of subgenres (e.g., satire, parody, allegory, pastoral) that are used in poetry, prose, plays, novels, short stories, essays, and other basic genres.
	The Tragedy of Macbeth, Acts I, II, and V **(C4)**	**Reading Standards** **2.2** Analyze the way in which clarity of meaning is affected by the patterns of organization, hierarchical structures, repetition of the main ideas, syntax, and word choice in the text. **3.1** Analyze characteristics of subgenres (e.g., satire, parody, allegory, pastoral) that are used in poetry, prose, plays, novels, short stories, essays, and other basic genres.

California Minimum Course of Study **continued**

	SELECTIONS/ FEATURES	READING, WRITING, LANGUAGE CONVENTIONS, AND LISTENING AND SPEAKING STANDARDS
UNIT 2 (CONT'D)	**Writing Workshop:** Literary Research: Historical Investigation	**Writing Standards** **1.1** Demonstrate an understanding of the elements of discourse (e.g., purpose, speaker, audience, form) when completing narrative, expository, persuasive, or descriptive writing assignments. **1.3** Structure ideas and arguments in a sustained, persuasive, and sophisticated way and support them with precise and relevant examples. **1.6** Develop presentations by using clear research questions and creative and critical research strategies (e.g., field studies, oral histories, interviews, experiments, electronic sources). **1.7** Use systematic strategies to organize and record information (e.g., anecdotal scripting, annotated bibliographies). **1.9** Revise text to highlight the individual voice, improve sentence variety and style, and enhance subtlety of meaning and tone in ways that are consistent with the purpose, audience, and genre. **2.4** Write historical investigation reports.
	Listening and Speaking Workshop: Presenting a Literary	**Listening and Speaking Standard** **2.2** Deliver oral reports on historical investigations.
UNIT 3 THE RESTORATION AND THE EIGHTEENTH CENTURY 1660–1800	A Modest Proposal **(C5)**	**Reading Standards** **2.2** Analyze the way in which clarity of meaning is affected by the patterns of organization, hierarchical structures, repetition of the main ideas, syntax, and word choice in the text. **3.3** Analyze the ways in which irony, tone, mood, the author's style, and the "sound" of language achieve specific rhetorical or aesthetic purposes or both.
	from Don Quixote **(C5)**	**Reading Standard** **3.1** Analyze characteristics of subgenres (e.g., satire, parody, allegory, pastoral) that are used in poetry, prose, plays, novels, short stories, essays, and other basic genres. **Grades 9–10 Review Standard** **3.4** Determine characters' traits by what the characters say about themselves in narration, dialogue, dramatic monologue, and soliloquy.
	from A Vindication of the Rights of Woman / *from* The Education of Women / To the Ladies **(C6)**	**Reading Standards** **2.1** Analyze both the features and the rhetorical devices of different types of public documents (e.g., policy statements, speeches, debates, platforms) and the way in which authors use those features and devices. **3.3** Analyze the ways in which irony, tone, mood, the author's style, and the "sound" of language achieve specific rhetorical or aesthetic purposes or both.
	Writing Workshop: Persuasive Essay	**Writing Standards** **1.1** Demonstrate an understanding of the elements of discourse (e.g., purpose, speaker, audience, form) when completing narrative, expository, persuasive, or descriptive writing assignments. **1.3** Structure ideas and arguments in a sustained, persuasive, and sophisticated way and support them with precise and relevant examples. **1.4** Enhance meaning by employing rhetorical devices, including the extended use of parallelism, repetition, and analogy; the incorporation of visual aids (e.g., graphs, tables, pictures); and the issuance of a call for action. **1.5** Use language in natural, fresh, and vivid ways to establish a specific tone. **1.9** Revise text to highlight the individual voice, improve sentence variety and style, and enhance subtlety of meaning and tone in ways that are consistent with the purpose, audience, and genre.
	Listening and Speaking Workshop: Presenting and Analyzing Speeches	**Listening and Speaking Standards** **1.4** Use rhetorical questions, parallel structure, concrete images, figurative language, characterization, irony, and dialogue to achieve clarity, force, and aesthetic effect. **1.5** Distinguish between and use various forms of classical and contemporary logical arguments. **1.6** Use logical, ethical, and emotional appeals that enhance a specific tone and purpose. **1.7** Use appropriate rehearsal strategies to pay attention to performance details, achieve command of the text, and create skillful artistic staging. **1.9** Use research and analysis to justify strategies for gesture, movement, and vocalization, including dialect, pronunciation, and enunciation. **1.12** Identify logical fallacies used in oral addresses (e.g., attack *ad hominem*, false causality, red herring, overgeneralization, bandwagon effect).

	SELECTIONS/ FEATURES	READING, WRITING, LANGUAGE CONVENTIONS, AND LISTENING AND SPEAKING STANDARDS
UNIT 4 THE ROMANTIC PERIOD 1798–1832	The Tyger / The Lamb **(C7)**	**Reading Standard** **2.2** Analyze the way in which clarity of meaning is affected by the patterns of organization, hierarchical structures, repetition of the main ideas, syntax, and word choice in the text.
		Grades 9–10 Review Standard **3.7** Recognize and understand the significance of various literary devices, including figurative language, imagery, allegory, and symbolism, and explain their appeal.
	Lines Composed a Few Miles Above Tintern Abbey **(C7)**	**Reading Standards** **2.2** Analyze the way in which clarity of meaning is affected by the patterns of organization, hierarchical structures, repetition of the main ideas, syntax, and word choice in the text. **3.3** Analyze the ways in which irony, tone, mood, the author's style, and the "sound" of language achieve specific rhetorical or aesthetic purposes or both.
	Kubla Khan **(C7)**	**Reading Standards** **3.3** Analyze the ways in which irony, tone, mood, the author's style, and the "sound" of language achieve specific rhetorical or aesthetic purposes or both. **3.4** Analyze ways in which poets use imagery, personification, figures of speech, and sounds to evoke readers' emotions.
	The Rime of the Ancient Mariner **(C7)**	**Reading Standards** **3.1** Analyze characteristics of subgenres (e.g., satire, parody, allegory, pastoral) that are used in poetry, prose, plays, novels, short stories, essays, and other basic genres. **3.3** Analyze the ways in which irony, tone, mood, the author's style, and the "sound" of language achieve specific rhetorical or aesthetic purposes or both.
	Ozymandias **(C8)**	**Reading Standards** **2.2** Analyze the way in which clarity of meaning is affected by the patterns of organization, hierarchical structures, repetition of the main ideas, syntax, and word choice in the text. **3.3** Analyze the ways in which irony, tone, mood, the author's style, and the "sound" of language achieve specific rhetorical or aesthetic purposes or both.
	Ode on a Grecian Urn **(C8)**	**Reading Standard** **3.4** Analyze ways in which poets use imagery, personification, figures of speech, and sounds to evoke readers' emotions.
	Writing Workshop: Reflective Composition **Listening and Speaking Workshop:** Presenting a Reflective Composition	**Writing Standards** **1.1** Demonstrate an understanding of the elements of discourse (e.g., purpose, speaker, audience, form) when completing narrative, expository, persuasive, or descriptive writing assignments. **1.5** Use language in natural, fresh, and vivid ways to establish a specific tone. **1.9** Revise text to highlight the individual voice, improve sentence variety and style, and enhance subtlety of meaning and tone in ways that are consistent with the purpose, audience, and genre. **2.3** Write reflective compositions.
		Listening and Speaking Standard **2.1** Deliver reflective presentations.
UNIT 5 THE VICTORIAN PERIOD 1832–1901	The Lady of Shalott **(C9)**	**Reading Standard** **3.4** Analyze ways in which poets use imagery, personification, figures of speech, and sounds to evoke readers' emotions.
	My Last Duchess **(C9)**	**Reading Standards** **2.4** Make warranted and reasonable assertions about the author's arguments by using elements of the text to defend and clarify interpretations. **3.1** Analyze characteristics of subgenres (e.g., satire, parody, allegory, pastoral) that are used in poetry, prose, plays, novels, short stories, essays, and other basic genres.
	Sonnet 43 **(C9)**	**Reading Standards** **2.2** Analyze the way in which clarity of meaning is affected by the patterns of organization, hierarchical structures, repetition of the main ideas, syntax, and word choice in the text. **3.1** Analyze characteristics of subgenres (e.g., satire, parody, allegory, pastoral) that are used in poetry, prose, plays, novels, short stories, essays, and other basic genres.

California Minimum Course of Study **continued**

	SELECTIONS/ FEATURES	READING, WRITING, LANGUAGE CONVENTIONS, AND LISTENING AND SPEAKING STANDARDS	
UNIT 5 (CONT'D)	Dover Beach **(C10)**	**Reading Standard** **3.3** Analyze the ways in which irony, tone, mood, the author's style, and the "sound" of language achieve specific rhetorical or aesthetic purposes or both.	**3.7** Analyze recognized works of world literature from a variety of authors.
	Writing Workshop: Fictional Narrative	**Writing Standards** **1.2** Use point of view, characterization, style (e.g., use of irony), and related elements for specific rhetorical and aesthetic purposes. **1.9** Revise text to highlight the individual voice, improve sentence variety and style, and enhance	subtlety of meaning and tone in ways that are consistent with the purpose, audience, and genre. **2.1** Write fictional, autobiographical, or biographical narratives.
	Listening and Speaking Workshop: Telling a Story	**Listening and Speaking Standards** **1.9** Use research and analysis to justify strategies for gesture, movement, and vocalization, including dialect, pronunciation, and enunciation.	**2.1** Deliver reflective presentations.
UNIT 6 THE MODERN WORLD: 1900 TO THE PRESENT	On the Bottom *from* Survival in Auschwitz **(C11)**	**Reading Standards** **3.1** Analyze characteristics of subgenres (e.g., satire, parody, allegory, pastoral) that are used in poetry, prose, plays, novels, short	stories, essays, and other basic genres. **3.7** Analyze recognized works of world literature from a variety of authors.
	Blood, Sweat, and Tears **(C11)**	**Reading Standards** **2.6** Critique the power, validity, and truthfulness of arguments set forth in public documents; their appeal to both friendly and hostile audiences; and the extent to which the arguments anticipate and address reader concerns and counterclaims	(e.g., appeal to reason, to authority, to pathos and emotion). **3.3** Analyze the ways in which irony, tone, mood, the author's style, and the "sound" of language achieve specific rhetorical or aesthetic purposes or both.
	from A Room of One's Own **(C11)**	**Reading Standards** **2.5** Analyze an author's implicit and explicit philosophical assumptions and beliefs about a subject.	**3.1** Analyze characteristics of subgenres (e.g., satire, parody, allegory, pastoral) that are used in poetry, prose, plays, novels, short stories, essays, and other basic genres.
	The Hollow Men **(C12)**	**Reading Standards** **2.5** Analyze an author's implicit and explicit philosophical assumptions and beliefs about a subject.	**3.4** Analyze ways in which poets use imagery, personification, figures of speech, and sounds to evoke readers' emotions.
	The Second Coming **(C12)**	**Reading Standards** **3.2** Analyze the way in which the theme or meaning of a selection represents a view or comment on life, using textual evidence to support the claim.	**3.4** Analyze ways in which poets use imagery, personification, figures of speech, and sounds to evoke readers' emotions.
	Fern Hill **(C12)**	**Reading Standards** **3.1** Analyze characteristics of subgenres (e.g., satire, parody, allegory, pastoral) that are used in poetry, prose, plays, novels, short stories, essays, and other basic genres.	**3.3** Analyze the ways in which irony, tone, mood, the author's style, and the "sound" of language achieve specific rhetorical or aesthetic purposes or both.
	Araby **(C13)**	**Reading Standard** **3.3** Analyze the ways in which irony, tone, mood, the author's style, and the "sound" of language	achieve specific rhetorical or aesthetic purposes or both.
		Grades 9–10 Review Standard **3.3** Analyze interactions between main and subordinate characters in a literary text (e.g., internal and external conflicts, motivations, relationships,	influences) and explain the way those interactions affect the plot.

	SELECTIONS/ FEATURES	READING, WRITING, LANGUAGE CONVENTIONS, AND LISTENING AND SPEAKING STANDARDS
UNIT 6 (CONT'D)	No Witchcraft for Sale **(C13)**	**Reading Standards** **3.2** Analyze the way in which the theme or meaning of a selection represents a view or comment on life, using textual evidence to support the claim. **3.7** Analyze recognized works of world literature from a variety of authors.
	Comparing Texts: Postcolonial Literature: Games at Twilight	**Reading Standard** **3.3** Analyze the ways in which irony, tone, mood, the author's style, and the "sound" of language achieve specific rhetorical or aesthetic purposes or both.
		Grades 9–10 Review Standard **3.7** Recognize and understand the significance of various literary devices, including figurative language, imagery, allegory, and symbolism, and explain their appeal.
	Writing Workshop: Biographical Narrative	**Reading Standards** **2.1** Analyze both the features and the rhetorical devices of different types of public documents (e.g., policy statements, speeches, debates, platforms) and the way in which authors use those features and devices. **2.2** Analyze the way in which clarity of meaning is affected by the patterns of organization, hierarchical structures, repetition of the main ideas, syntax, and word choice in the text. **2.3** Verify and clarify facts presented in other types of expository texts by using a variety of consumer, workplace, and public documents.
		Writing Standards **1.1** Demonstrate an understanding of the elements of discourse (e.g., purpose, speaker, audience, form) when completing narrative, expository, persuasive, or descriptive writing assignments. **1.8** Integrate databases, graphics, and spreadsheets into word-processed documents. **1.9** Revise text to highlight the individual voice, improve sentence variety and style, and enhance subtlety of meaning and tone in ways that are consistent with the purpose, audience, and genre. **2.1** Write fictional, autobiographical, or biographical narratives. **2.6** Deliver multimedia presentations.
	Media Workshop: Analyzing and Using Media	**Listening and Speaking Standards** **1.1** Recognize strategies used by the media to inform, persuade, entertain, and transmit culture (e.g., advertisements; perpetuation of stereotypes; use of visual representations, special effects, language). **1.2** Analyze the impact of the media on the democratic process (e.g., exerting influence on elections, creating images of leaders, shaping attitudes) at the local, state, and national levels. **1.3** Interpret and evaluate the various ways in which events are presented and information is communicated by visual image makers (e.g., graphic artists, documentary filmmakers, illustrators, news photographers). **1.7** Use appropriate rehearsal strategies to pay attention to performance details, achieve command of the text, and create skillful artistic staging. **1.8** Use effective and interesting language. **1.10** Evaluate when to use different kinds of effects (e.g., visual, music, sound, graphics) to create effective productions. **1.11** Critique a speaker's diction and syntax in relation to the purpose of an oral communication and the impact the words may have on the audience. **1.12** Identify logical fallacies used in oral addresses (e.g., attack *ad hominem*, false causality, red herring, overgeneralization, bandwagon effect). **1.13** Analyze the four basic types of persuasive speech (i.e., propositions of fact, value, problem, or policy) and understand the similarities and differences in their patterns of organization and the use of persuasive language, reasoning, and proof. **1.14** Analyze the techniques used in media messages for a particular audience and evaluate their effectiveness (e.g., Orson Welles' radio broadcast "War of the Worlds"). **2.4** Deliver multimedia presentations.
RESOURCE CENTER	**The World of Work:** Workplace Reading/ Writing	**Reading Standards** **2.3** Verify and clarify facts presented in other types of expository texts by using a variety of consumer, workplace, and public documents.

California Standards Overview

The following is a correlation of *Holt Literature and Language Arts*, Sixth Course, to the *English-Language Arts Content Standards*

Written and Oral English Language Conventions are addressed in *Warriner's Handbook*, Sixth Course.

GRADES 9–10 REVIEW READING CONTINUED

Standard	Page
3.7 Recognize and understand the significance of various literary devices, including figurative language, imagery, allegory, and symbolism, and explain their appeal.	730, 734, 736, 744, 771, 829, 835, 871, 940, 1040, 1113, 1148, 1208, 1211, 1215, 1267, 1288, 1369, 1375, 1415, 1422
3.8 Interpret and evaluate the impact of ambiguities, subtleties, contradictions, ironies, and incongruities in a text.	1265, 1267
3.9 Explain how voice, persona, and the choice of a narrator affect characterization and the tone, plot, and credibility of a text.	161, 175, 557, 562, 1004, 1176, 1299, 1306
3.10 Identify and describe the function of dialogue, scene designs, soliloquies, asides, and character foils in dramatic literature.	304, 307, 1348, 1351, 1355
3.11 Evaluate the aesthetic qualities of style, including the impact of diction and figurative language on tone, mood, and theme, using the terminology of literary criticism. (Aesthetic approach)	819, 821, 943, 949
3.12 Analyze the way in which a work of literature is related to the themes and issues of its historical period. (Historical approach)	99, 110, 425, 439, 457, 477, 493, 965, 968, 1093, 1099

GRADES 9–10 REVIEW LISTENING AND SPEAKING

Standard	Page
1.9 Analyze the occasion and the interests of the audience and choose effective verbal and nonverbal techniques (e.g., voice, gestures, eye contact) for presentations.	893, 1053
2.1a Narrate a sequence of events and communicate their significance to the audience.	1307
2.3 Apply appropriate interviewing techniques: **a.** Prepare and ask relevant questions. **b.** Make notes of responses. **c.** Use language that conveys maturity, sensitivity, and respect. **d.** Respond correctly and effectively to questions. **e.** Demonstrate knowledge of the subject or organization. **f.** Compile and report responses. **g.** Evaluate the effectiveness of the interview.	991

RETEACHING OPPORTUNITIES

- **Teacher's Edition,** Reteaching Lessons
- **Universal Access: Holt Interactive Reader,** interactive readings
- **Holt Interactive Reader for English Language Development,** interactive adapted readings
- **Holt Audio Tutor,** audio support for adapted texts in English and Spanish
- **Universal Access: Differentiating Instruction,** instruction of struggling learners, English learners, and students with special needs; modified lesson plans; and leveled assessment
- ThinkCentral **Online Remediation,** diagnostic tools and individualized tutorials
- **WordSharp: An Interactive Vocabulary Tutor,** practice with academic language
- **PowerNotes,** interactive lesson presentations with activities
- **Holt Multicultural Reader,** interactive readings
- Think Central**, Student Access,** online version of the Student Edition enhanced by audio and video
- **GrammarNotes,** interactive lesson presentations with activities
- **WritingNotes,** interactive lesson presentations with activities
- **Spelling Lessons and Activities** (6–8)
- **Holt Interactive Spelling** (6–8)

HOLT

LITERATURE AND LANGUAGE ARTS

Your Road Map *to* Mastering *the* California Standards

Holt Literature and Language Arts offers a clear instructional road map for all students, with *on ramps* for strategic, benchmark, and advanced students.

Holt *Literature and Language Arts* ©2003 was the first English-Language Arts program built exclusively to align with the *Reading-Language Arts Framework for California Public Schools*. Since that time, the achievement of California students using *Holt Literature and Language Arts* ©2003 has been steadily improving. The new *Holt Literature and Language Arts* ©2010 renews its commitment to California students and teachers, with increased emphasis on vocabulary, reading, and writing and a deeper focus on the instructional needs of English learners, students with disabilities, struggling readers, and students who use African American vernacular English. Together, we will continue to work toward mastery of the California Standards for all students.

Planning Instruction

You need tools that will help you plan for all of the diverse learners in your classroom. **Resources** must be at your fingertips and foster universal access for students. In *Holt Literature and Language Arts*, sections highlighted in yellow offer a suggested minimum course of study to ensure coverage of all standards.

For more customized instruction, additional support and resources are suggested for strategic, benchmark, and advanced students.

Assessment Resources
helps you assess the progress of your students with formative and summative assessments that are easy to modify.

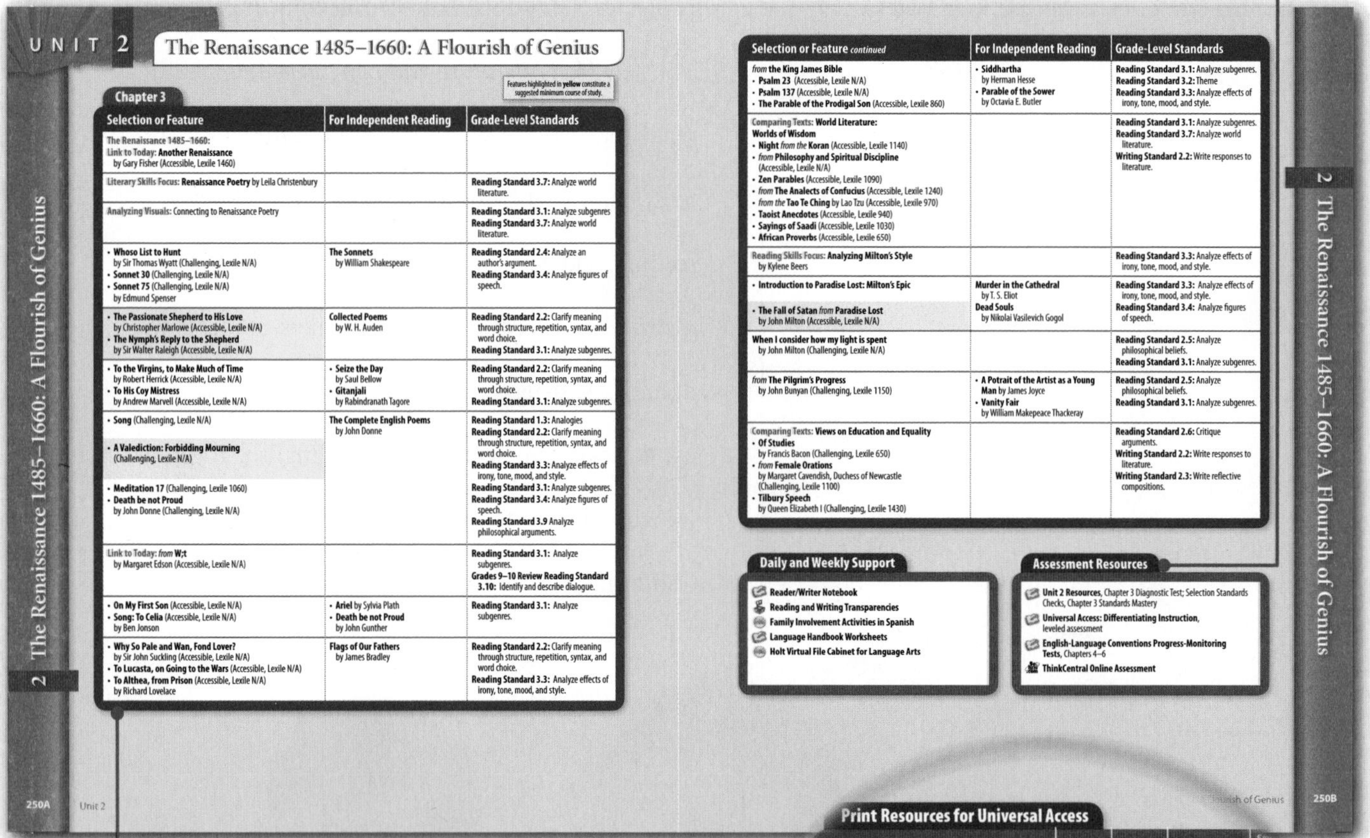

UNIT 2 The Renaissance 1485–1660: A Flourish of Genius

Features highlighted in **yellow** constitute a suggested minimum course of study.

Chapter 3

Selection or Feature	For Independent Reading	Grade-Level Standards
The Renaissance 1485–1660: Link to Today: **Another Renaissance** by Gary Fisher (Accessible, Lexile 1460)		
Literary Skills Focus: **Renaissance Poetry** by Leila Christenbury		**Reading Standard 3.7:** Analyze world literature.
Analyzing Visuals: Connecting to Renaissance Poetry		**Reading Standard 3.1:** Analyze subgenres **Reading Standard 3.7:** Analyze world literature.
• **Whoso List to Hunt** by Sir Thomas Wyatt (Challenging, Lexile N/A) • **Sonnet 30** (Challenging, Lexile N/A) • **Sonnet 75** (Challenging, Lexile N/A) by Edmund Spenser	**The Sonnets** by William Shakespeare	**Reading Standard 2.4:** Analyze an author's argument. **Reading Standard 3.4:** Analyze figures of speech.
• **The Passionate Shepherd to His Love** by Christopher Marlowe (Accessible, Lexile N/A) • **The Nymph's Reply to the Shepherd** by Sir Walter Raleigh (Accessible, Lexile N/A)	**Collected Poems** by W. H. Auden	**Reading Standard 2.2:** Clarify meaning through structure, repetition, syntax, and word choice. **Reading Standard 3.1:** Analyze subgenres.
• **To the Virgins, to Make Much of Time** by Robert Herrick (Accessible, Lexile N/A) • **To His Coy Mistress** by Andrew Marvell (Accessible, Lexile N/A)	• **Seize the Day** by Saul Bellow • **Gitanjali** by Rabindranath Tagore	**Reading Standard 2.2:** Clarify meaning through structure, repetition, syntax, and word choice. **Reading Standard 3.1:** Analyze subgenres.
• **Song** (Challenging, Lexile N/A) • **A Valediction: Forbidding Mourning** (Challenging, Lexile N/A) • **Meditation 17** (Challenging, Lexile 1060) • **Death be not Proud** by John Donne (Challenging, Lexile N/A)	**The Complete English Poems** by John Donne	**Reading Standard 1.3:** Analogies **Reading Standard 2.2:** Clarify meaning through structure, repetition, syntax, and word choice. **Reading Standard 3.3:** Analyze effects of irony, tone, mood, and style. **Reading Standard 3.1:** Analyze subgenres. **Reading Standard 3.4:** Analyze figures of speech. **Reading Standard 3.9** Analyze philosophical arguments.
Link to Today: *from* **W;t** by Margaret Edson (Accessible, Lexile N/A)		**Reading Standard 3.1:** Analyze subgenres. **Grades 9–10 Review Reading Standard 3.10:** Identify and describe dialogue.
• **On My First Son** (Accessible, Lexile N/A) • **Song: To Celia** (Accessible, Lexile N/A) by Ben Jonson	• **Ariel** by Sylvia Plath • **Death be not Proud** by John Gunther	**Reading Standard 3.1:** Analyze subgenres.
• **Why So Pale and Wan, Fond Lover?** by Sir John Suckling (Accessible, Lexile N/A) • **To Lucasta, on Going to the Wars** (Accessible, Lexile N/A) • **To Althea, from Prison** (Accessible, Lexile N/A) by Richard Lovelace	**Flags of Our Fathers** by James Bradley	**Reading Standard 2.2:** Clarify meaning through structure, repetition, syntax, and word choice. **Reading Standard 3.3:** Analyze effects of irony, tone, mood, and style.

Selection or Feature *continued*	For Independent Reading	Grade-Level Standards
from **the King James Bible** • **Psalm 23** (Accessible, Lexile N/A) • **Psalm 137** (Accessible, Lexile N/A) • **The Parable of the Prodigal Son** (Accessible, Lexile 860)	• **Siddhartha** by Herman Hesse • **Parable of the Sower** by Octavia E. Butler	**Reading Standard 3.1:** Analyze subgenres. **Reading Standard 3.2:** Theme **Reading Standard 3.3:** Analyze effects of irony, tone, mood, and style.
Comparing Texts: **World Literature: Worlds of Wisdom** • **Night** *from the* **Koran** (Accessible, Lexile 1140) • *from* **Philosophy and Spiritual Discipline** (Accessible, Lexile N/A) • **Zen Parables** (Accessible, Lexile 1090) • *from* **The Analects of Confucius** (Accessible, Lexile 1240) • *from the* **Tao Te Ching** by Lao Tzu (Accessible, Lexile 970) • **Taoist Anecdotes** (Accessible, Lexile 940) • **Sayings of Saadi** (Accessible, Lexile 1030) • **African Proverbs** (Accessible, Lexile 650)		**Reading Standard 3.1:** Analyze subgenres. **Reading Standard 3.7:** Analyze world literature. **Writing Standard 2.2:** Write responses to literature.
Reading Skills Focus: **Analyzing Milton's Style** by Kylene Beers		**Reading Standard 3.3:** Analyze effects of irony, tone, mood, and style.
• **Introduction to Paradise Lost: Milton's Epic** • **The Fall of Satan** *from* **Paradise Lost** by John Milton (Accessible, Lexile N/A)	**Murder in the Cathedral** by T. S. Eliot **Dead Souls** by Nikolai Vasilevich Gogol	**Reading Standard 3.3:** Analyze effects of irony, tone, mood, and style. **Reading Standard 3.4:** Analyze figures of speech.
When I consider how my light is spent by John Milton (Challenging, Lexile N/A)		**Reading Standard 2.5:** Analyze philosophical beliefs. **Reading Standard 3.1:** Analyze subgenres.
from **The Pilgrim's Progress** by John Bunyan (Challenging, Lexile 1150)	• **A Potrait of the Artist as a Young Man** by James Joyce • **Vanity Fair** by William Makepeace Thackeray	**Reading Standard 2.5:** Analyze philosophical beliefs. **Reading Standard 3.1:** Analyze subgenres.
Comparing Texts: **Views on Education and Equality** • **Of Studies** by Francis Bacon (Challenging, Lexile 650) • *from* **Female Orations** by Margaret Cavendish, Duchess of Newcastle (Challenging, Lexile 1100) • **Tilbury Speech** by Queen Elizabeth I (Challenging, Lexile 1430)		**Reading Standard 2.6:** Critique arguments. **Writing Standard 2.2:** Write responses to literature. **Writing Standard 2.3:** Write reflective compositions.

Daily and Weekly Support

- **Reader/Writer Notebook**
- **Reading and Writing Transparencies**
- **Family Involvement Activities in Spanish**
- **Language Handbook Worksheets**
- **Holt Virtual File Cabinet for Language Arts**

Assessment Resources

- **Unit 2 Resources**, Chapter 3 Diagnostic Test; Selection Standards Checks, Chapter 3 Standards Mastery
- **Universal Access: Differentiating Instruction**, leveled assessment
- **English-Language Conventions Progress-Monitoring Tests**, Chapters 4–6
- **ThinkCentral Online Assessment**

250A Unit 2

2 The Renaissance 1485–1660: A Flourish of Genius

250B

Print Resources for Universal Access

All Chapters	On-Level Learners	English Learners	Struggling Readers/Writers	St... Afric... Vernac...
Universal Access: Supporting Instruction in Spanish translations of selection summaries and key terms		✔		
Universal Access: Holt Interactive Writer and Speaker practice and assessment	✔	✔	✔	✔
Language and Sentence Skills Practice for Warriner's Handbook Chapters 4–8	✔			
Universal Access: Developmental Language and Sentence Skills Practice for Warriner's Handbook Chapters 4–8		✔	✔	

The **Chapter at-a-glance** chart identifies the readability and targeted skills for each selection in the chapter to help you plan for focused instruction.

Print Resources for Universal Access
help you support diverse learners whether they are struggling readers, English learners, or advanced students.

Planning Instruction

Technology Resources highlights the many digital tools that are available to support you and your students, from research to remediation.

Real Issues, Real Experts introduces authors and consultants such as Kylene Beers, Carol Jago, Isabel Beck, and Robin Scarcella, as well as master teachers who share practical suggestions for meeting the needs of your students.

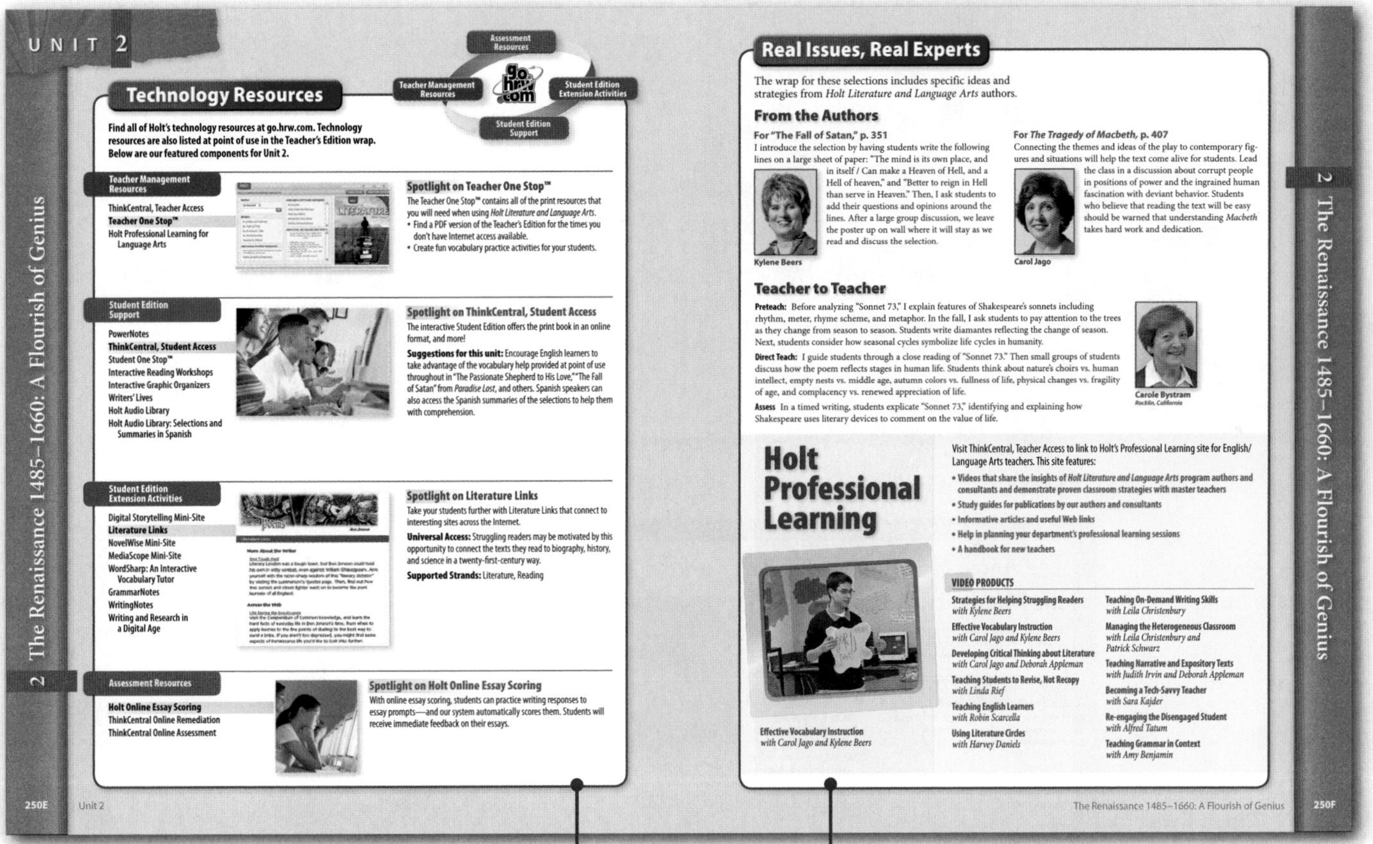

UNIT 2

Technology Resources

Assessment Resources · Teacher Management Resources · go.hrw.com · Student Edition Extension Activities · Student Edition Support

Find all of Holt's technology resources at go.hrw.com. Technology resources are also listed at point of use in the Teacher's Edition wrap. Below are our featured components for Unit 2.

Teacher Management Resources

- ThinkCentral, Teacher Access
- **Teacher One Stop™**
- Holt Professional Learning for Language Arts

Spotlight on Teacher One Stop™

The Teacher One Stop™ contains all of the print resources that you will need when using *Holt Literature and Language Arts*.

- Find a PDF version of the Teacher's Edition for the times you don't have Internet access available.
- Create fun vocabulary practice activities for your students.

Student Edition Support

- PowerNotes
- **ThinkCentral, Student Access**
- Student One Stop™
- Interactive Reading Workshops
- Interactive Graphic Organizers
- Writers' Lives
- Holt Audio Library
- Holt Audio Library: Selections and Summaries in Spanish

Spotlight on ThinkCentral, Student Access

The interactive Student Edition offers the print book in an online format, and more!

Suggestions for this unit: Encourage English learners to take advantage of the vocabulary help provided at point of use throughout in "The Passionate Shepherd to His Love," "The Fall of Satan" from *Paradise Lost*, and others. Spanish speakers can also access the Spanish summaries of the selections to help them with comprehension.

Student Edition Extension Activities

- Digital Storytelling Mini-Site
- **Literature Links**
- NovelWise Mini-Site
- MediaScope Mini-Site
- WordSharp: An Interactive Vocabulary Tutor
- GrammarNotes
- WritingNotes
- Writing and Research in a Digital Age

Spotlight on Literature Links

Take your students further with Literature Links that connect to interesting sites across the Internet.

Universal Access: Struggling readers may be motivated by this opportunity to connect the texts they read to biography, history, and science in a twenty-first-century way.

Supported Strands: Literature, Reading

Assessment Resources

- **Holt Online Essay Scoring**
- ThinkCentral Online Remediation
- ThinkCentral Online Assessment

Spotlight on Holt Online Essay Scoring

With online essay scoring, students can practice writing responses to essay prompts—and our system automatically scores them. Students will receive immediate feedback on their essays.

250E Unit 2

2 The Renaissance 1485–1660: A Flourish of Genius

Real Issues, Real Experts

The wrap for these selections includes specific ideas and strategies from *Holt Literature and Language Arts* authors.

From the Authors

For "The Fall of Satan," p. 351

I introduce the selection by having students write the following lines on a large sheet of paper: "The mind is its own place, and in itself / Can make a Heaven of Hell, and a Hell of heaven," and "Better to reign in Hell than serve in Heaven." Then, I ask students to add their questions and opinions around the lines. After a large group discussion, we leave the poster up on wall where it will stay as we read and discuss the selection.

Kylene Beers

For *The Tragedy of Macbeth*, p. 407

Connecting the themes and ideas of the play to contemporary figures and situations will help the text come alive for students. Lead the class in a discussion about corrupt people in positions of power and the ingrained human fascination with deviant behavior. Students who believe that reading the text will be easy should be warned that understanding *Macbeth* takes hard work and dedication.

Carol Jago

Teacher to Teacher

Preteach: Before analyzing "Sonnet 73," I explain features of Shakespeare's sonnets including rhythm, meter, rhyme scheme, and metaphor. In the fall, I ask students to pay attention to the trees as they change from season to season. Students write diamantes reflecting the change of season. Next, students consider how seasonal cycles symbolize life cycles in humanity.

Direct Teach: I guide students through a close reading of "Sonnet 73." Then small groups of students discuss how the poem reflects stages in human life. Students think about nature's choirs vs. human intellect, empty nests vs. middle age, autumn colors vs. fullness of life, physical changes vs. fragility of age, and complacency vs. renewed appreciation of life.

Assess In a timed writing, students explicate "Sonnet 73," identifying and explaining how Shakespeare uses literary devices to comment on the value of life.

Carole Bystram
Rocklin, California

Holt Professional Learning

Visit ThinkCentral, Teacher Access to link to Holt's Professional Learning site for English/Language Arts teachers. This site features:

- **Videos that share the insights of *Holt Literature and Language Arts* program authors and consultants and demonstrate proven classroom strategies with master teachers**
- **Study guides for publications by our authors and consultants**
- **Informative articles and useful Web links**
- **Help in planning your department's professional learning sessions**
- **A handbook for new teachers**

Effective Vocabulary Instruction
with Carol Jago and Kylene Beers

VIDEO PRODUCTS

- **Strategies for Helping Struggling Readers** *with Kylene Beers*
- **Effective Vocabulary Instruction** *with Carol Jago and Kylene Beers*
- **Developing Critical Thinking about Literature** *with Carol Jago and Deborah Appleman*
- **Teaching Students to Revise, Not Recopy** *with Linda Rief*
- **Teaching English Learners** *with Robin Scarcella*
- **Using Literature Circles** *with Harvey Daniels*
- **Teaching On-Demand Writing Skills** *with Leila Christenbury*
- **Managing the Heterogeneous Classroom** *with Leila Christenbury and Patrick Schwarz*
- **Teaching Narrative and Expository Texts** *with Judith Irvin and Deborah Appleman*
- **Becoming a Tech-Savvy Teacher** *with Sara Kajder*
- **Re-engaging the Disengaged Student** *with Alfred Tatum*
- **Teaching Grammar in Context** *with Amy Benjamin*

The Renaissance 1485–1660: A Flourish of Genius 250F

Spotlight On details key resources for each chapter.

Holt Professional Learning offers you opportunities to develop further as a teacher and gives you help with the challenges you face. An online bank of videos and a new-teacher handbook allow you to customize your professional training.

Unit Openers

Each unit is **organized around a time period,** and units fit together to create a chronological snapshot of American or British literature. Units begin by naming the chapters that fall under that particular period and introduce the overarching thematic question that unites the chapters.

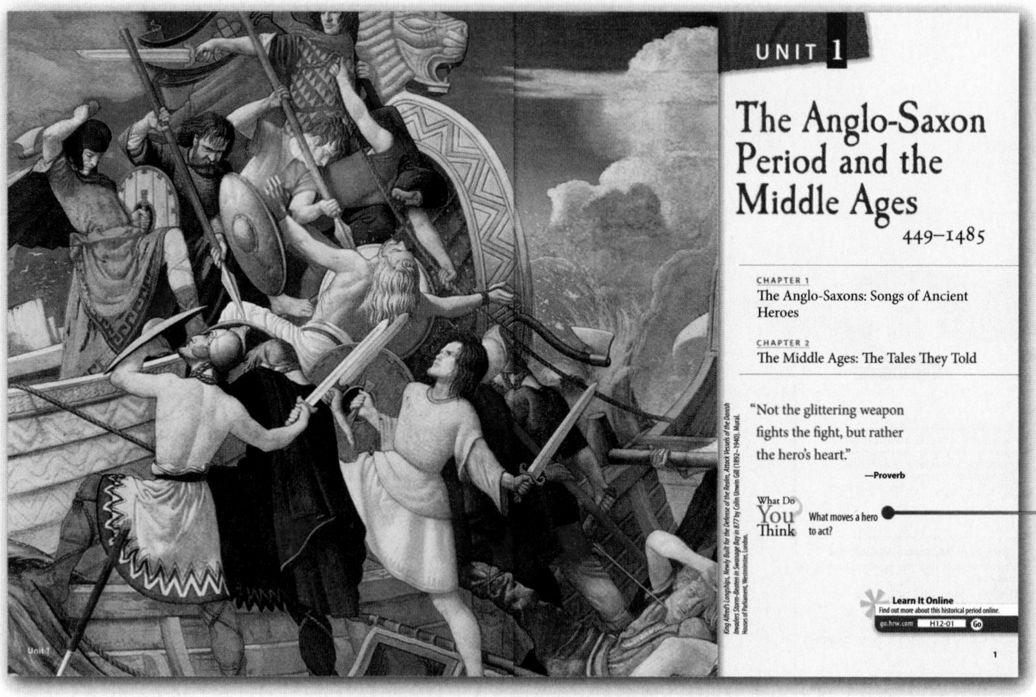

UNIT 1

The Anglo-Saxon Period and the Middle Ages
449–1485

CHAPTER 1
The Anglo-Saxons: Songs of Ancient Heroes

CHAPTER 2
The Middle Ages: The Tales They Told

"Not the glittering weapon fights the fight, but rather the hero's heart."
—Proverb

What Do You Think? What moves a hero to act?

Learn It Online
Find out more about this historical period online.
go.hrw.com H12-01 Go

King Alfred's Longships, Newly Built for the Defense of the Realm, Attack Vessels of the Danish Invaders Storm-Beaten in Swanage Bay in 877 by Colin Unwin Gill (1892–1940). Mural. Houses of Parliament, Westminster, London.

Unit 1

1

What Do You Think? poses the thematic question of the unit and creates relevance by demonstrating how the driving questions of the past remain relevant to the human condition today.

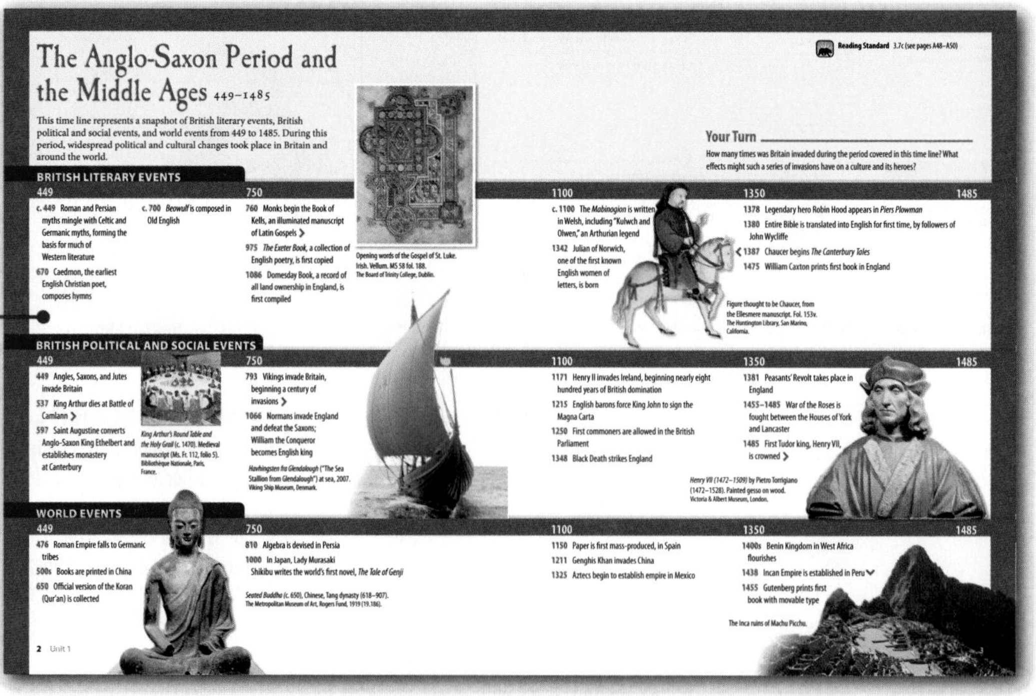

The Anglo-Saxon Period and the Middle Ages 449–1485

This time line represents a snapshot of British literary events, British political and social events, and world events from 449 to 1485. During this period, widespread political and cultural changes took place in Britain and around the world.

Reading Standard 3.7c (see pages A48–A50)

Your Turn

How many times was Britain invaded during the period covered in this time line? What effects might such a series of invasions have on a culture and its heroes?

BRITISH LITERARY EVENTS

449
- c. 449 Roman and Persian myths mingle with Celtic and Germanic myths, forming the basis for much of Western literature
- 670 Caedmon, the earliest English Christian poet, composes hymns
- c. 700 *Beowulf* is composed in Old English

750
- 760 Monks begin the Book of Kells, an illuminated manuscript of Latin Gospels
- 975 *The Exeter Book*, a collection of English poetry, is first copied
- 1086 Domesday Book, a record of all land ownership in England, is first compiled

Opening words of the Gospel of St. Luke. Irish. Vellum. MS 58 fol. 188. The Board of Trinity College, Dublin.

1100
- c. 1100 The *Mabinogion* is written in Welsh, including "Kulwch and Olwen," an Arthurian legend
- 1342 Julian of Norwich, one of the first known English women of letters, is born

1350
- 1378 Legendary hero Robin Hood appears in *Piers Plowman*
- 1380 Entire Bible is translated into English for first time, by followers of John Wycliffe
- 1387 Chaucer begins *The Canterbury Tales*
- 1475 William Caxton prints first book in England

Figure thought to be Chaucer, from the Ellesmere manuscript. Fol. 153v. The Huntington Library, San Marino, California.

BRITISH POLITICAL AND SOCIAL EVENTS

449
- 449 Angles, Saxons, and Jutes invade Britain
- 537 King Arthur dies at Battle of Camlann
- 597 Saint Augustine converts Anglo-Saxon King Ethelbert and establishes monastery at Canterbury

King Arthur's Round Table and the Holy Grail (c. 1470). Medieval manuscript (Ms. Fr. 112, folio 5). Bibliothèque Nationale, Paris, France.

750
- 793 Vikings invade Britain, beginning a century of invasions
- 1066 Normans invade England and defeat the Saxons; William the Conqueror becomes English king

Havhingsten fra Glendalough ("The Sea Stallion from Glendalough") at sea, 2007. Viking Ship Museum, Denmark.

1100
- 1171 Henry II invades Ireland, beginning nearly eight hundred years of British domination
- 1215 English barons force King John to sign the Magna Carta
- 1250 First commoners are allowed in the British Parliament
- 1348 Black Death strikes England

1350
- 1381 Peasants' Revolt takes place in England
- 1455–1485 War of the Roses is fought between the Houses of York and Lancaster
- 1485 First Tudor king, Henry VII, is crowned

Henry VII (1472–1509) by Pietro Torrigiano (1472–1528). Painted gesso on wood. Victoria & Albert Museum, London.

WORLD EVENTS

449
- 476 Roman Empire falls to Germanic tribes
- 500s Books are printed in China
- 650 Official version of the Koran (Qur'an) is collected

750
- 810 Algebra is devised in Persia
- 1000 In Japan, Lady Murasaki Shikibu writes the world's first novel, *The Tale of Genji*

Seated Buddha (c. 650), Chinese, Tang dynasty (618–907). The Metropolitan Museum of Art, Rogers Fund, 1919 (19.186).

1100
- 1150 Paper is first mass-produced, in Spain
- 1211 Genghis Khan invades China
- 1325 Aztecs begin to establish empire in Mexico

1350
- 1400s Benin Kingdom in West Africa flourishes
- 1438 Incan Empire is established in Peru
- 1455 Gutenberg prints first book with movable type

The Inca ruins of Machu Picchu.

2 Unit 1

Time lines create context for students and show the connections between history and literature.

Key Concepts

To help students grasp the unifying factors of the time period, **Key Concepts** offers students three levels of detail that show how historical events are related to the underlying social and philosophical movements that flourished during the time.

This section introduces the student to the cultural climate of the period and gives them tools to define the key characteristics of the historical period related to the literary one.

The **Key Concepts** are explored in more depth over the next pages to flesh out the summarization of the beginning graphic organizer.

The section begins with a three-column grid that shows the parallel between the **History of the Times** and the **Literature of the Times**.

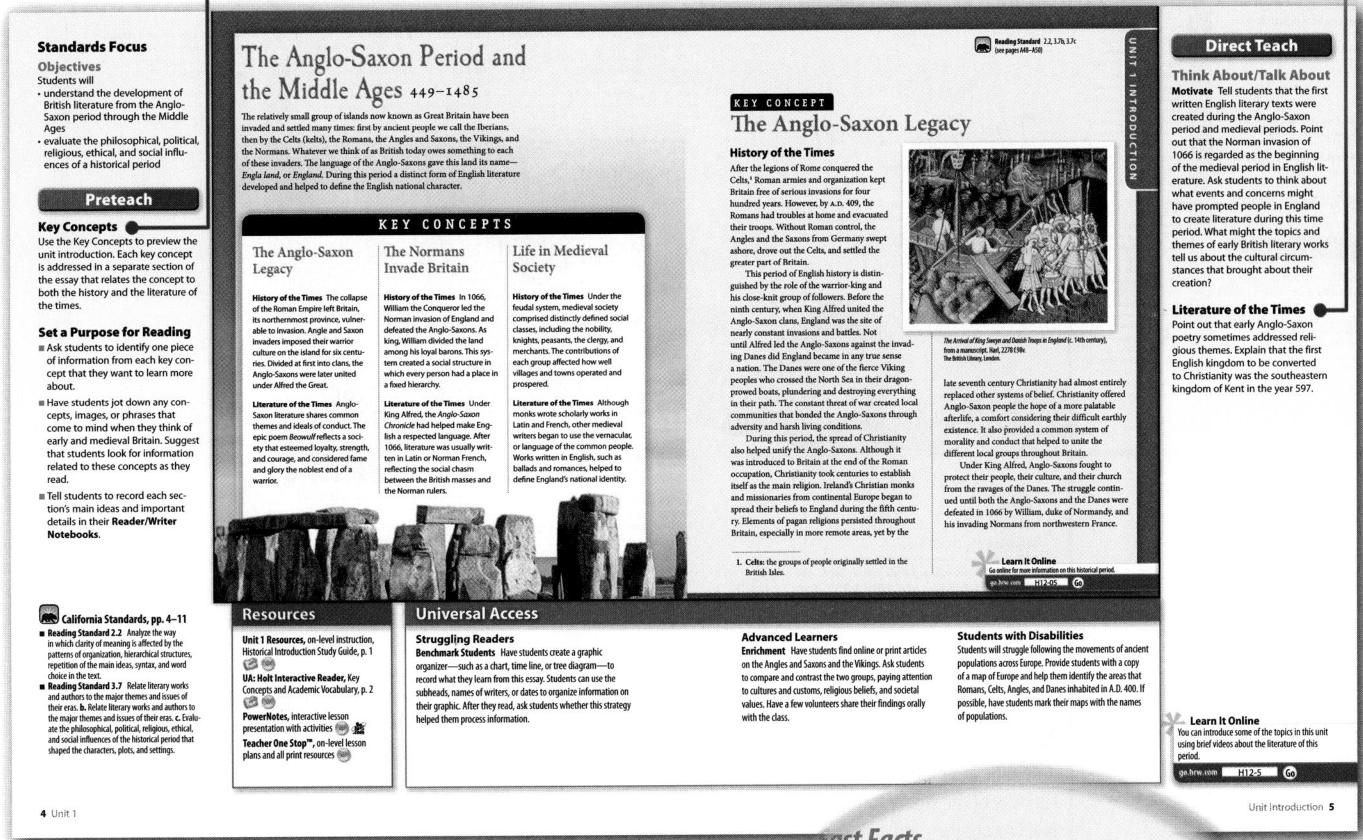
Standards Focus

Objectives
Students will
- understand the development of British literature from the Anglo-Saxon period through the Middle Ages
- evaluate the philosophical, political, religious, ethical, and social influences of a historical period

Preteach

Key Concepts
Use the Key Concepts to preview the unit introduction. Each key concept is addressed in a separate section of the essay that relates the concept to both the history and the literature of the times.

Set a Purpose for Reading
- Ask students to identify one piece of information from each key concept that they want to learn more about.
- Have students jot down any concepts, images, or phrases that come to mind when they think of early and medieval Britain. Suggest that students look for information related to these concepts as they read.
- Tell students to record each section's main ideas and important details in their **Reader/Writer Notebooks**.

California Standards, pp. 4–11
- **Reading Standard 2.2** Analyze the way in which clarity of meaning is affected by the patterns of organization, hierarchical structures, repetition of the main ideas, syntax, and word choice in the text.
- **Reading Standard 3.7** Relate literary works and authors to the major themes and issues of their eras. **b.** Relate literary works and authors to the major themes and issues of their eras. **c.** Evaluate the philosophical, political, religious, ethical, and social influences of the historical period that shaped the characters, plots, and settings.

The Anglo-Saxon Period and the Middle Ages 449–1485

The relatively small group of islands now known as Great Britain have been invaded and settled many times: first by ancient people we call the Iberians, then by the Celts (kelts), the Romans, the Angles and Saxons, the Vikings, and the Normans. Whatever we think of as British today owes something to each of these invaders. The language of the Anglo-Saxons gave this land its name—*Engla land*, or *England*. During this period a distinct form of English literature developed and helped to define the English national character.

KEY CONCEPTS

The Anglo-Saxon Legacy	The Normans Invade Britain	Life in Medieval Society
History of the Times The collapse of the Roman Empire left Britain, its northernmost province, vulnerable to invasion. Angle and Saxon invaders imposed their warrior culture on the island for six centuries. Divided at first into clans, the Anglo-Saxons were later united under Alfred the Great.	**History of the Times** In 1066, William the Conqueror led the Norman invasion of England and defeated the Anglo-Saxons. As king, William divided the land among his loyal barons. This system created a social structure in which every person had a place in a fixed hierarchy.	**History of the Times** Under the feudal system, medieval society comprised distinctly defined social classes, including the nobility, knights, peasants, the clergy, and merchants. The contributions of each group affected how well villages and towns operated and prospered.
Literature of the Times Anglo-Saxon literature shares common themes and ideals of conduct. The epic poem *Beowulf* reflects a society that esteemed loyalty, strength, and courage, and considered fame and glory the noblest end of a warrior.	**Literature of the Times** Under King Alfred, the *Anglo-Saxon Chronicle* had helped make English a respected language. After 1066, literature was usually written in Latin or Norman French, reflecting the social chasm between the British masses and the Norman rulers.	**Literature of the Times** Although monks wrote scholarly works in Latin and French, other medieval writers began to use the vernacular, or language of the common people. Works written in English, such as ballads and romances, helped to define England's national identity.

Resources

Unit 1 Resources, on-level instruction, Historical Introduction Study Guide, p. 1

UA: Holt Interactive Reader, Key Concepts and Academic Vocabulary, p. 2

PowerNotes, interactive lesson presentation with activities

Teacher One Stop™, on-level lesson plans and all print resources

Universal Access

Struggling Readers
Benchmark Students Have students create a graphic organizer—such as a chart, time line, or tree diagram—to record what they learn from this essay. Students can use the subheads, names of writers, or dates to organize information on their graphic. After they read, ask students whether this strategy helped them process information.

Advanced Learners
Enrichment Have students find online or print articles on the Angles and Saxons and the Vikings. Ask students to compare and contrast the two groups, paying attention to cultures and customs, religious beliefs, and societal values. Have a few volunteers share their findings orally with the class.

Students with Disabilities
Students will struggle following the movements of ancient populations across Europe. Provide students with a copy of a map of Europe and help them identify the areas that Romans, Celts, Angles, and Danes inhabited in A.D. 400. If possible, have students mark their maps with the names of populations.

4 Unit 1

Reading Standard 2.2, 3.7b, 3.7c (see pages A48–A50)

UNIT 1 INTRODUCTION

KEY CONCEPT

The Anglo-Saxon Legacy

History of the Times

After the legions of Rome conquered the Celts,[1] Roman armies and organization kept Britain free of serious invasions for four hundred years. However, by A.D. 409, the Romans had troubles at home and evacuated their troops. Without Roman control, the Angles and the Saxons from Germany swept ashore, drove out the Celts, and settled the greater part of Britain.

This period of English history is distinguished by the role of the warrior-king and his close-knit group of followers. Before the ninth century, when King Alfred united the Anglo-Saxon clans, England was the site of nearly constant invasions and battles. Not until Alfred led the Anglo-Saxons against the invading Danes did England became in any true sense a nation. The Danes were one of the fierce Viking peoples who crossed the North Sea in their dragon-prowed boats, plundering and destroying everything in their path. The constant threat of war created local communities that bonded the Anglo-Saxons through adversity and harsh living conditions.

During this period, the spread of Christianity also helped unify the Anglo-Saxons. Although it was introduced to Britain at the end of the Roman occupation, Christianity took centuries to establish itself as the main religion. Ireland's Christian monks and missionaries from continental Europe began to spread their beliefs to England during the fifth century. Elements of pagan religions persisted throughout Britain, especially in more remote areas, yet by the late seventh century Christianity had almost entirely replaced other systems of belief. Christianity offered Anglo-Saxon people the hope of a more palatable afterlife, a comfort considering their difficult earthly existence. It also provided a common system of morality and conduct that helped to unite the different local groups throughout Britain.

The Arrival of King Sweyn and Danish Troops in England (c. 14th century), from a manuscript. Harl, 2278 f.98v. The British Library, London.

Under King Alfred, Anglo-Saxons fought to protect their people, their culture, and their church from the ravages of the Danes. The struggle continued until both the Anglo-Saxons and the Danes were defeated in 1066 by William, duke of Normandy, and his invading Normans from northwestern France.

1. **Celts:** the groups of people originally settled in the British Isles.

Learn It Online
Go online for more information on this historical period.
go.hrw.com H12-05 Go

Direct Teach

Think About/Talk About
Motivate Tell students that the first written English literary texts were created during the Anglo-Saxon period and medieval periods. Point out that the Norman invasion of 1066 is regarded as the beginning of the medieval period in English literature. Ask students to think about what events and concerns might have prompted people in England to create literature during this time period. What might the topics and themes of early British literary works tell us about the cultural circumstances that brought about their creation?

Literature of the Times
Point out that early Anglo-Saxon poetry sometimes addressed religious themes. Explain that the first English kingdom to be converted to Christianity was the southeastern kingdom of Kent in the year 597.

Learn It Online
You can introduce some of the topics in this unit using brief videos about the literature of this period.
go.hrw.com H12-5 Go

Unit Introduction 5

Fast Facts provides an at-a-glance view of the key points from the section.

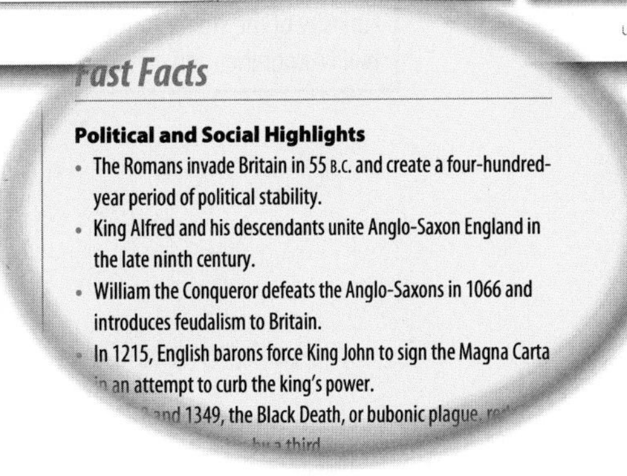
Fast Facts

Political and Social Highlights
- The Romans invade Britain in 55 B.C. and create a four-hundred-year period of political stability.
- King Alfred and his descendants unite Anglo-Saxon England in the late ninth century.
- William the Conqueror defeats the Anglo-Saxons in 1066 and introduces feudalism to Britain.
- In 1215, English barons force King John to sign the Magna Carta in an attempt to curb the king's power.
- and 1349, the Black Death, or bubonic plague,

Links to Today

Link to Today concludes the introduction to show students how the literary styles and subjects of the past find refrains in contemporary literature. Each Link to Today selection guides students to see key concepts at play in their world and serves as an accessible prelude to the literary selections that follow.

Build Background
shows students how this particular selection parallels the literature of the past and present.

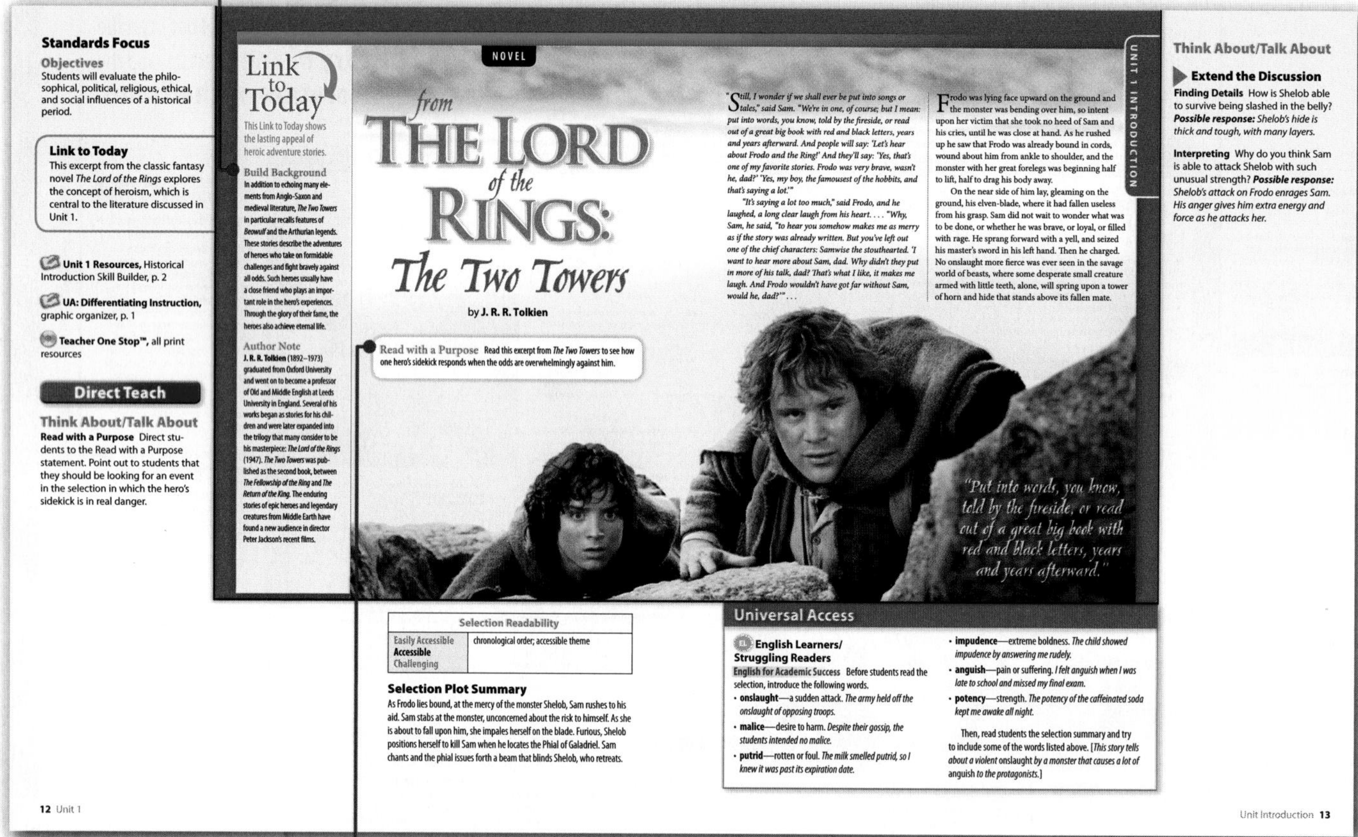

Standards Focus

Objectives
Students will evaluate the philosophical, political, religious, ethical, and social influences of a historical period.

Link to Today
This excerpt from the classic fantasy novel *The Lord of the Rings* explores the concept of heroism, which is central to the literature discussed in Unit 1.

Unit 1 Resources, Historical Introduction Skill Builder, p. 2

UA: Differentiating Instruction, graphic organizer, p. 1

Teacher One Stop™, all print resources

Direct Teach

Think About/Talk About
Read with a Purpose Direct students to the Read with a Purpose statement. Point out to students that they should be looking for an event in the selection in which the hero's sidekick is in real danger.

Link to Today

This Link to Today shows the lasting appeal of heroic adventure stories.

Build Background
In addition to echoing many elements from Anglo-Saxon and medieval literature, *The Two Towers* in particular recalls features of *Beowulf* and the Arthurian legends. These stories describe the adventures of heroes who take on formidable challenges and fight bravely against all odds. Such heroes usually have a close friend who plays an important role in the hero's experiences. Through the glory of their fame, the heroes also achieve eternal life.

Author Note
J. R. R. Tolkien (1892–1973) graduated from Oxford University and went on to become a professor of Old and Middle English at Leeds University in England. Several of his works began as stories for his children and were later expanded into the trilogy that many consider to be his masterpiece: *The Lord of the Rings* (1947). *The Two Towers* was published as the second book, between *The Fellowship of the Ring* and *The Return of the King*. The enduring stories of epic heroes and legendary creatures from Middle Earth have found a new audience in director Peter Jackson's recent films.

NOVEL

from THE LORD *of the* RINGS: *The Two Towers*

by J. R. R. Tolkien

Read with a Purpose Read this excerpt from *The Two Towers* to see how one hero's sidekick responds when the odds are overwhelmingly against him.

"Still, I wonder if we shall ever be put into songs or tales," said Sam. "We're in one, of course; but I mean: put into words, you know, told by the fireside, or read out of a great big book with red and black letters, years and years afterward. And people will say: 'Let's hear about Frodo and the Ring!' And they'll say: 'Yes, that's one of my favorite stories. Frodo was very brave, wasn't he, dad?' 'Yes, my boy, the famousest of the hobbits, and that's saying a lot.'"

"It's saying a lot too much," said Frodo, and he laughed, a long clear laugh from his heart. . . . "Why, Sam, he said, "to hear you somehow makes me as merry as if the story was already written. But you've left out one of the chief characters: Samwise the stouthearted. 'I want to hear more about Sam, dad. Why didn't they put in more of his talk, dad? That's what I like, it makes me laugh. And Frodo wouldn't have got far without Sam, would he, dad?'" . . .

Frodo was lying face upward on the ground and the monster was bending over him, so intent upon her victim that she took no heed of Sam and his cries, until he was close at hand. As he rushed up he saw that Frodo was already bound in cords, wound about him from ankle to shoulder, and the monster with her great forelegs was beginning half to lift, half to drag his body away.

On the near side of him lay, gleaming on the ground, his elven-blade, where it had fallen useless from his grasp. Sam did not wait to wonder what was to be done, or whether he was brave, or loyal, or filled with rage. He sprang forward with a yell, and seized his master's sword in his left hand. Then he charged. No onslaught more fierce was ever seen in the savage world of beasts, where some desperate small creature armed with little teeth, alone, will spring upon a tower of horn and hide that stands above its fallen mate.

UNIT 1 INTRODUCTION

"Put into words, you know, told by the fireside, or read out of a great big book with red and black letters, years and years afterward."

Think About/Talk About

Extend the Discussion
Finding Details How is Shelob able to survive being slashed in the belly? ***Possible response:*** *Shelob's hide is thick and tough, with many layers.*

Interpreting Why do you think Sam is able to attack Shelob with such unusual strength? ***Possible response:*** *Shelob's attack on Frodo enrages Sam. His anger gives him extra energy and force as he attacks her.*

Selection Readability	
Easily Accessible **Accessible** Challenging	chronological order; accessible theme

Selection Plot Summary
As Frodo lies bound, at the mercy of the monster Shelob, Sam rushes to his aid. Sam stabs at the monster, unconcerned about the risk to himself. As she is about to fall upon him, she impales herself on the blade. Furious, Shelob positions herself to kill Sam when he locates the Phial of Galadriel. Sam chants and the phial issues forth a beam that blinds Shelob, who retreats.

Universal Access

English Learners/ Struggling Readers
English for Academic Success Before students read the selection, introduce the following words.
- **onslaught**—a sudden attack. *The army held off the onslaught of opposing troops.*
- **malice**—desire to harm. *Despite their gossip, the students intended no malice.*
- **putrid**—rotten or foul. *The milk smelled putrid, so I knew it was past its expiration date.*
- **impudence**—extreme boldness. *The child showed impudence by answering me rudely.*
- **anguish**—pain or suffering. *I felt anguish when I was late to school and missed my final exam.*
- **potency**—strength. *The potency of the caffeinated soda kept me awake all night.*

Then, read students the selection summary and try to include some of the words listed above. [*This story tells about a violent* onslaught *by a monster that causes a lot of* anguish *to the protagonists.*]

12 Unit 1

Unit Introduction 13

Read with a Purpose
is designed to prompt the curiosity of the students and build comprehension.

Building Literacy

The path to student success starts with focused instruction in reading, critical thinking, and writing that is modeled, practiced, and applied. Each chapter and selection develops **strong instructional strands in the areas of literature, reading, and writing,** providing you the tools to build student literacy.

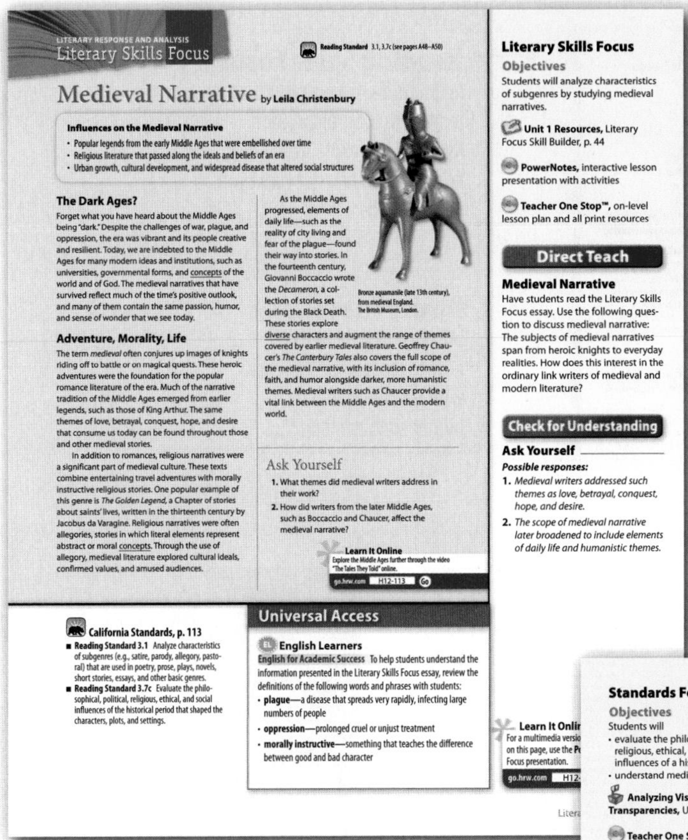

LITERARY RESPONSE AND ANALYSIS
Literary Skills Focus

Reading Standard 3.1, 3.7c (see pages A48–A50)

Medieval Narrative by Leila Christenbury

Influences on the Medieval Narrative
- Popular legends from the early Middle Ages that were embellished over time
- Religious literature that passed along the ideals and beliefs of an era
- Urban growth, cultural development, and widespread disease that altered social structures

The Dark Ages?
Forget what you have heard about the Middle Ages being "dark." Despite the challenges of war, plague, and oppression, the era was vibrant and its people creative and resilient. Today, we are indebted to the Middle Ages for many modern ideas and institutions, such as universities, governmental forms, and concepts of the world and of God. The medieval narratives that have survived reflect much of the time's positive outlook, and many of them contain the same passion, humor, and sense of wonder that we see today.

Adventure, Morality, Life
The term *medieval* often conjures up images of knights riding off to battle or on magical quests. These heroic adventures were the foundation for the popular romance literature of the era. Much of the narrative tradition of the Middle Ages emerged from earlier legends, such as those of King Arthur. The same themes of love, betrayal, conquest, hope, and desire that consume us today can be found throughout these and other medieval stories.

In addition to romances, religious narratives were a significant part of medieval culture. These texts combine entertaining travel adventures with morally instructive religious stories. One popular example of this genre is *The Golden Legend*, a Chapter of stories about saints' lives, written in the thirteenth century by Jacobus da Varagine. Religious narratives were often allegories, stories in which literal elements represent abstract or moral concepts. Through the use of allegory, medieval literature explored cultural ideals, confirmed values, and amused audiences.

As the Middle Ages progressed, elements of daily life—such as the reality of city living and fear of the plague—found their way into stories. In the fourteenth century, Giovanni Boccaccio wrote the *Decameron*, a collection of stories set during the Black Death. These stories explore diverse characters and augment the range of themes covered by earlier medieval literature. Geoffrey Chaucer's *The Canterbury Tales* also covers the full scope of the medieval narrative, with its inclusion of romance, faith, and humor alongside darker, more humanistic themes. Medieval writers such as Chaucer provide a vital link between the Middle Ages and the modern world.

Bronze aquamanile (late 13th century), from medieval England. The British Museum, London.

Ask Yourself
1. What themes did medieval writers address in their work?
2. How did writers from the later Middle Ages, such as Boccaccio and Chaucer, affect the medieval narrative?

Learn It Online
Explore the Middle Ages further through the video "The Tales They Told" online.
go.hrw.com H12-113

Literary Skills Focus
Objectives
Students will analyze characteristics of subgenres by studying medieval narratives.

Unit 1 Resources, Literary Focus Skill Builder, p. 44

PowerNotes, interactive lesson presentation with activities

Teacher One Stop™, on-level lesson plan and all print resources

Direct Teach
Medieval Narrative
Have students read the Literary Skills Focus essay. Use the following question to discuss medieval narrative: The subjects of medieval narratives span from heroic knights to everyday realities. How does this interest in the ordinary link writers of medieval and modern literature?

Check for Understanding
Ask Yourself
Possible responses:
1. *Medieval writers addressed such themes as love, betrayal, conquest, hope, and desire.*
2. *The scope of medieval narrative later broadened to include elements of daily life and humanistic themes.*

California Standards, p. 113
- Reading Standard 3.1 Analyze characteristics of subgenres (e.g., satire, parody, allegory, pastoral) that are used in poetry, prose, plays, novels, short stories, essays, and other basic genres.
- Reading Standard 3.7c Evaluate the philosophical, political, religious, ethical, and social influences of the historical period that shaped the characters, plots, and settings.

Universal Access
English Learners
English for Academic Success To help students understand the information presented in the Literary Skills Focus essay, review the definitions of the following words and phrases with students:
- plague—a disease that spreads very rapidly, infecting large numbers of people
- oppression—prolonged cruel or unjust treatment
- morally instructive—something that teaches the difference between good and bad character

Learn It Online
For a multimedia version on this page, use the Focus presentation.
go.hrw.com H12-

Literary Skills Focus begins with an engaging introduction written by one of the program authors. New terms are defined in student-friendly language with models taken from individual selections. Graphic organizers are included to support instruction. Having Literary Skills Focus is like having a "tutor in the text" to help students master literary elements.

The **Lesson Cycle** clearly delineated in the side wrap of the Teacher's Edition outlines explicit instructions and includes these steps: Preteach, Direct Teach, Check for Understanding, Assess, and Reteach.

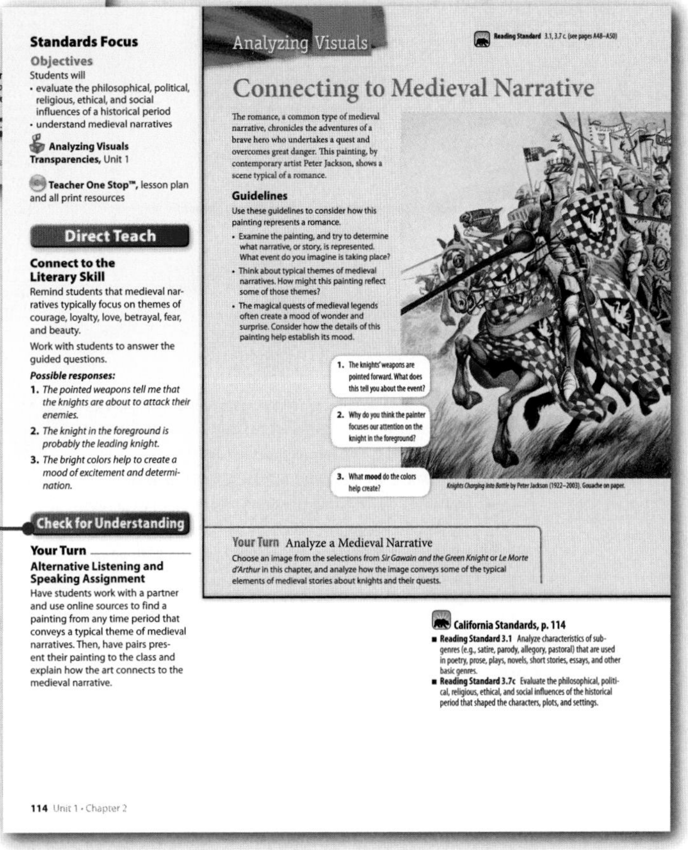

Standards Focus
Objectives
Students will
- evaluate the philosophical, political, religious, ethical, and social influences of a historical period
- understand medieval narratives

Analyzing Visuals Transparencies, Unit 1

Teacher One Stop™, lesson plan and all print resources

Direct Teach
Connect to the Literary Skill
Remind students that medieval narratives typically focus on themes of courage, loyalty, love, betrayal, fear, and beauty.
Work with students to answer the guided questions.
Possible responses:
1. *The pointed weapons tell me that the knights are about to attack their enemies.*
2. *The knight in the foreground is probably the leading knight.*
3. *The bright colors help to create a mood of excitement and determination.*

Check for Understanding
Your Turn
Alternative Listening and Speaking Assignment
Have students work with a partner and use online sources to find a painting from any time period that conveys a typical theme of medieval narratives. Then, have pairs present their painting to the class and explain how the art connects to the medieval narrative.

Analyzing Visuals

Reading Standard 3.1, 3.7c (see pages A48–A50)

Connecting to Medieval Narrative

The romance, a common type of medieval narrative, chronicles the adventures of a brave hero who undertakes a quest and overcomes great danger. This painting, by contemporary artist Peter Jackson, shows a scene typical of a romance.

Guidelines
Use these guidelines to consider how this painting represents a romance.
- Examine the painting, and try to determine what narrative, or story, is represented. What event do you imagine is taking place?
- Think about typical themes of medieval narratives. How might this painting reflect some of those themes?
- The magical quests of medieval legends often create a mood of wonder and surprise. Consider how the details of this painting help establish its mood.

1. The knights' weapons are pointed forward. What does this tell you about the event?
2. Why do you think the painter focuses our attention on the knight in the foreground?
3. What mood do the colors help create?

Knights Charging into Battle by Peter Jackson (1922–2003). Gouache on paper.

Your Turn Analyze a Medieval Narrative
Choose an image from the selections from *Sir Gawain and the Green Knight* or *Le Morte d'Arthur* in this chapter, and analyze how the image conveys some of the typical elements of medieval stories about knights and their quests.

California Standards, p. 114
- Reading Standard 3.1 Analyze characteristics of subgenres (e.g., satire, parody, allegory, pastoral) that are used in poetry, prose, plays, novels, short stories, essays, and other basic genres.
- Reading Standard 3.7c Evaluate the philosophical, political, religious, ethical, and social influences of the historical period that shaped the characters, plots, and settings.

114 Unit 1 • Chapter 2

Analyzing Visuals is an important link to literary instruction. It shows students how to use visuals to unlock meaning and better understand important literary elements.

Check for Understanding gives your students a quick opportunity for independent practice and you an opportunity for informal assessment.

Program Highlights

Support for Reading

Students need a reason to read, and they need support to read well. **Reading Skills Focus** allows you to reach all students, especially reluctant readers, with an instructive essay by Dr. Kylene Beers. New terms are defined in student-friendly language with examples from the selections. Graphic organizers support instruction.

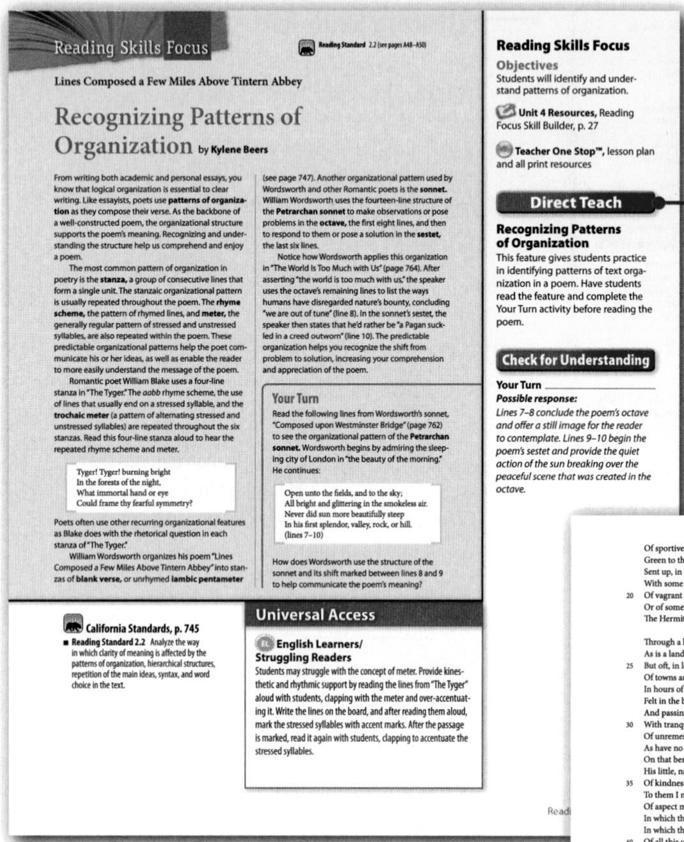

Reading Skills Focus

Reading Standard 2.2 (see pages A48–A50)

Lines Composed a Few Miles Above Tintern Abbey

Recognizing Patterns of Organization by Kylene Beers

From writing both academic and personal essays, you know that logical organization is essential to clear writing. Like essayists, poets use **patterns of organization** as they compose their verse. As the backbone of a well-constructed poem, the organizational structure supports the poem's meaning. Recognizing and understanding the structure help us comprehend and enjoy a poem.

The most common pattern of organization in poetry is the **stanza,** a group of consecutive lines that form a single unit. The stanzaic organizational pattern is usually repeated throughout the poem. The **rhyme scheme,** the pattern of rhymed lines, and **meter,** the generally regular pattern of stressed and unstressed syllables, are also repeated within the poem. These predictable organizational patterns help the poet communicate his or her ideas, as well as enable the reader to more easily understand the message of the poem.

Romantic poet William Blake uses a four-line stanza in "The Tyger." The *aabb* rhyme scheme, the use of lines that usually end on a stressed syllable, and the **trochaic meter** (a pattern of alternating stressed and unstressed syllables) are repeated throughout the six stanzas. Read this four-line stanza aloud to hear the repeated rhyme scheme and meter.

Tyger! Tyger! burning bright
In the forests of the night,
What immortal hand or eye
Could frame thy fearful symmetry?

Poets often use other recurring organizational features as Blake does with the rhetorical question in each stanza of "The Tyger."

William Wordsworth organizes his poem "Lines Composed a Few Miles Above Tintern Abbey" into stanzas of **blank verse,** or unrhymed **iambic pentameter** (see page 747). Another organizational pattern used by Wordsworth and other Romantic poets is the **sonnet.** William Wordsworth uses the fourteen-line structure of the **Petrarchan sonnet** to make observations or pose problems in the **octave,** the first eight lines, and then to respond to them or pose a solution in the **sestet,** the last six lines.

Notice how Wordsworth applies this organization in "The World Is Too Much with Us" (page 764). After asserting "the world is too much with us," the speaker uses the octave's remaining lines to list the ways humans have disregarded nature's bounty, concluding "we are out of tune" (line 8). In the sonnet's sestet, the speaker then states that he'd rather be "a Pagan suckled in a creed outworn" (line 10). The predictable organization helps you recognize the shift from problem to solution, increasing your comprehension and appreciation of the poem.

Your Turn

Read the following lines from Wordsworth's sonnet, "Composed upon Westminster Bridge" (page 762) to see the organizational pattern of the **Petrarchan sonnet.** Wordsworth begins by admiring the sleeping city of London in "the beauty of the morning." He continues:

Open unto the fields, and to the sky;
All bright and glittering in the smokeless air.
Never did sun more beautifully steep
In his first splendor, valley, rock, or hill.
(lines 7–10)

How does Wordsworth use the structure of the sonnet and its shift marked between lines 8 and 9 to help communicate the poem's meaning?

Reading Skills Focus

Objectives
Students will identify and understand patterns of organization.

Unit 4 Resources, Reading Focus Skill Builder, p. 27

Teacher One Stop™, lesson plan and all print resources

Direct Teach

Recognizing Patterns of Organization
This feature gives students practice in identifying patterns of text organization in a poem. Have students read the feature and complete the Your Turn activity before reading the poem.

Check for Understanding

Your Turn
Possible response:
Lines 7–8 conclude the poem's octave and offer a still image for the reader to contemplate. Lines 9–10 begin the poem's sestet and provide the quiet action of the sun breaking over the peaceful scene that was created in the octave.

California Standards, p. 745
■ **Reading Standard 2.2** Analyze the way in which clarity of meaning is affected by the patterns of organization, hierarchical structures, repetition of the main ideas, syntax, and word choice in the text.

Universal Access

English Learners/ Struggling Readers
Students may struggle with the concept of meter. Provide kinesthetic and rhythmic support by reading the lines from "The Tyger" aloud with students, clapping with the meter and over-accentuating it. Write the lines on the board, and after reading them aloud, mark the stressed syllables with accent marks. After the passage is marked, read it again with students, clapping to accentuate the stressed syllables.

Reading Skills Focus
helps students become stronger readers as program author Kylene Beers explains, models, and provides practice for key reading skills.

Direct Teach
provides helpful hints on how to reach your students with demonstrated techniques such as modeling.

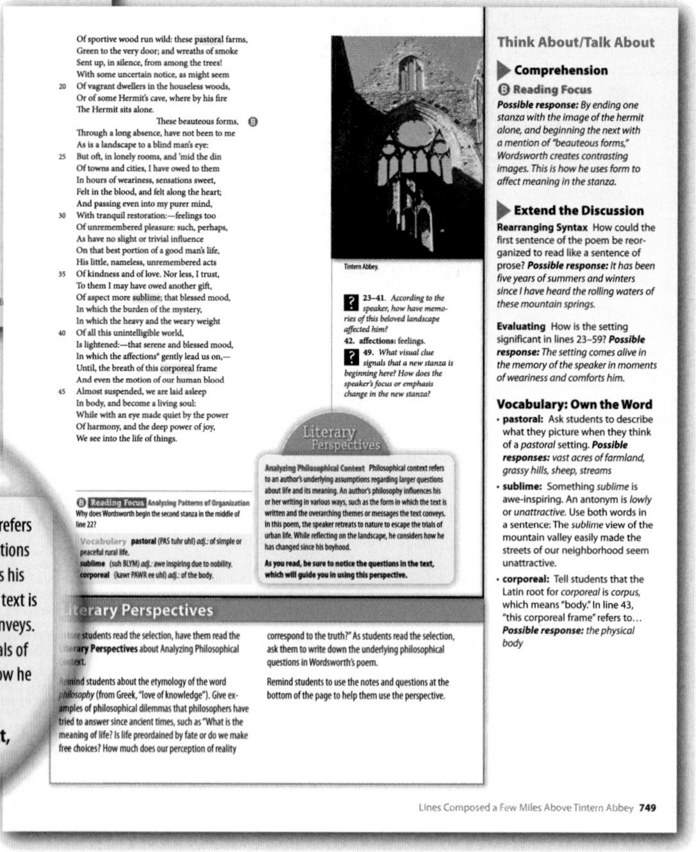

Of sportive wood run wild: these pastoral farms,
Green to the very door; and wreaths of smoke
Sent up, in silence, from among the trees!
With some uncertain notice, as might seem
Of vagrant dwellers in the houseless woods,
Or of some Hermit's cave, where by his fire
The Hermit sits alone.
These beauteous forms, B
Through a long absence, have not been to me
As is a landscape to a blind man's eye:
But oft, in lonely rooms, and 'mid the din
Of towns and cities, I have owed to them
In hours of weariness, sensations sweet,
Felt in the blood, and felt along the heart;
And passing even into my purer mind,
With tranquil restoration:—feelings too
Of unremembered pleasure: such, perhaps,
As have no slight or trivial influence
On that best portion of a good man's life,
His little, nameless, unremembered acts
Of kindness and of love. Nor less, I trust,
To them I may have owed another gift,
Of aspect more sublime; that blessed mood,
In which the burden of the mystery,
In which the heavy and the weary weight
Of all this unintelligible world,
Is lightened:—that serene and blessed mood,
In which the affections* gently lead us on,—
Until, the breath of this corporeal frame
And even the motion of our human blood
Almost suspended, we are laid asleep
In body, and become a living soul:
While with an eye made quiet by the power
Of harmony, and the deep power of joy,
We see into the life of things.

Tintern Abbey.

23–41. *According to the speaker, how have memories of this beloved landscape affected him?*
42. **affections:** feelings.
49. *What visual clue signals that a new stanza is beginning here? How does the speaker's focus or emphasis change in the new stanza?*

B **Reading Focus** Analyzing Patterns of Organization Why does Wordsworth begin the second stanza in the middle of line 22?

Vocabulary **pastoral** (PAS tuhr uhl) *adj.:* of simple or peaceful rural life.
sublime (suh BLYM) *adj.:* awe-inspiring due to nobility.
corporeal (kawr PAWR ee uhl) *adj.:* of the body.

Literary Perspectives

Analyzing Philosophical Context Philosophical context refers to an author's underlying assumptions regarding larger questions about life and its meaning. An author's philosophy influences his or her writing in various ways, such as the form in which the text is written and the overarching themes or messages the text conveys. In this poem, the speaker retreats to nature to escape the trials of urban life. While reflecting on the landscape, he considers how he has changed since his boyhood.

As you read, be sure to notice the questions in the text, which will guide you in using this perspective.

Think About/Talk About

Comprehension

B **Reading Focus**
Possible response: *By ending one stanza with the image of the hermit alone, and beginning the next with a mention of "beauteous forms," Wordsworth creates contrasting images. This is how he uses form to affect meaning in the stanza.*

Extend the Discussion
Rearranging Syntax How could the first sentence of the poem be reorganized to read like a sentence of prose? ***Possible response:*** *It has been five years of summers and winters since I have heard the rolling waters of these mountain springs.*

Evaluating How is the setting significant in lines 23–59? ***Possible response:*** *The setting comes alive in the memory of the speaker in moments of weariness and comforts him.*

Vocabulary: Own the Word
- **pastoral:** Ask students to describe what they picture when they think of a *pastoral* setting. ***Possible responses:*** *vast acres of farmland, grassy hills, sheep, streams*
- **sublime:** Something *sublime* is awe-inspiring. An antonym is *lowly* or *unattractive.* Use both words in a sentence: The *sublime* view of the mountain valley easily made the streets of our neighborhood seem unattractive.
- **corporeal:** Tell students that the Latin root for *corporeal* is *corpus,* which means "body." In line 43, "this corporeal frame" refers to… ***Possible response:*** *the physical body*

Literary Perspectives

Before students read the selection, have them read the Literary Perspectives about Analyzing Philosophical Context.

Remind students about the etymology of the word *philosophy* (from Greek, "love of knowledge"). Give examples of philosophical dilemmas that philosophers have tried to answer since ancient times, such as "What is the meaning of life? Is life preordained by fate or do we make free choices? How much does our perception of reality correspond to the truth?" As students read the selection, ask them to write down the underlying philosophical questions in Wordsworth's poem.

Remind students to use the notes and questions at the bottom of the page to help them use the perspective.

Lines Composed a Few Miles Above Tintern Abbey 749

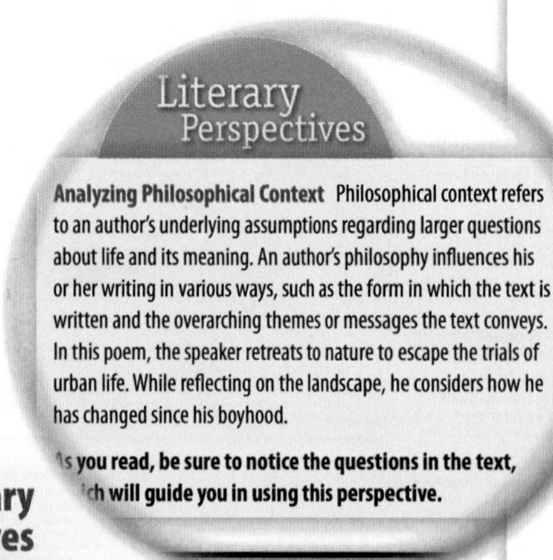

Literary Perspectives

Analyzing Philosophical Context Philosophical context refers to an author's underlying assumptions regarding larger questions about life and its meaning. An author's philosophy influences his or her writing in various ways, such as the form in which the text is written and the overarching themes or messages the text conveys. In this poem, the speaker retreats to nature to escape the trials of urban life. While reflecting on the landscape, he considers how he has changed since his boyhood.

As you read, be sure to notice the questions in the text, which will guide you in using this perspective.

Literary Perspectives
are guided-reading activities that lead students to make connections and think critically.

Preparing to Read

Each selection follows a clear instructional pattern to optimize skill development and student comprehension. While the visuals and **What Do You Think?** questions are designed to motivate students, the **Literary**, **Reading**, and **Writing Skills Focus** and **Vocabulary** reinforce the skills introduced at the beginning of the chapter. **Language Coach** gives additional help to those English learners or users of African American vernacular English who may need additional support.

What Do You Think? provides critical motivation by helping students connect and apply the selection to their lives.

Think as a Reader/Writer focuses on the reading-writing relationship by exploring the writer's craft in a text and having students apply the technique to their own writing.

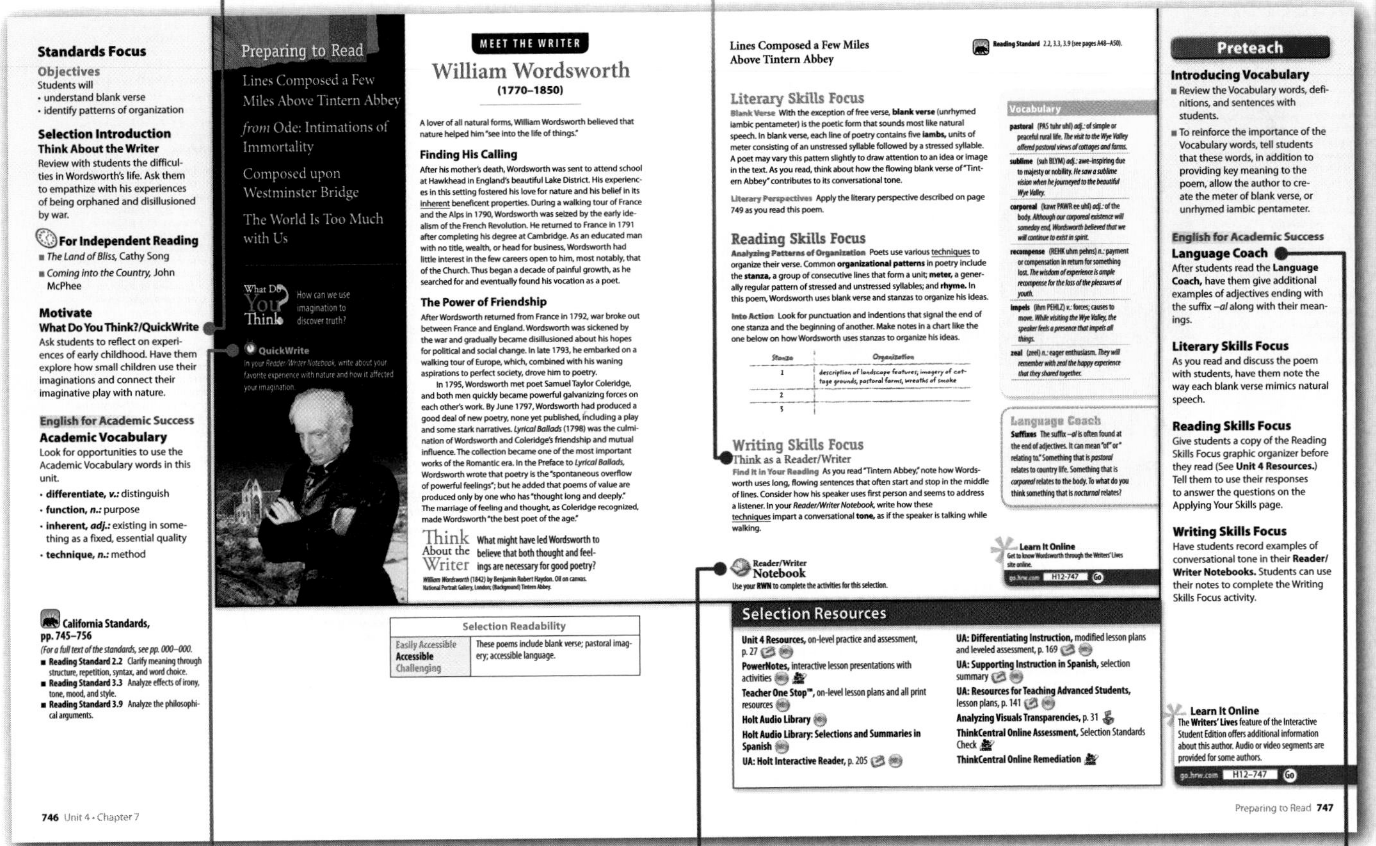

Standards Focus

Objectives
Students will
- understand blank verse
- identify patterns of organization

Selection Introduction
Think About the Writer
Review with students the difficulties in Wordsworth's life. Ask them to empathize with his experiences of being orphaned and disillusioned by war.

For Independent Reading
- *The Land of Bliss,* Cathy Song
- *Coming into the Country,* John McPhee

Motivate
What Do You Think?/QuickWrite
Ask students to reflect on experiences of early childhood. Have them explore how small children use their imaginations and connect their imaginative play with nature.

English for Academic Success
Academic Vocabulary
Look for opportunities to use the Academic Vocabulary words in this unit.
- **differentiate, *v.*:** distinguish
- **function, *n.*:** purpose
- **inherent, *adj.*:** existing in something as a fixed, essential quality
- **technique, *n.*:** method

California Standards, pp. 745–756
(For a full text of the standards, see pp. 000–000.
- **Reading Standard 2.2** Clarify meaning through structure, repetition, syntax, and word choice.
- **Reading Standard 3.3** Analyze effects of irony, tone, mood, and style.
- **Reading Standard 3.9** Analyze the philosophical arguments.

746 Unit 4 • Chapter 7

Preparing to Read

Lines Composed a Few Miles Above Tintern Abbey

from Ode: Intimations of Immortality

Composed upon Westminster Bridge

The World Is Too Much with Us

What Do You Think? How can we use imagination to discover truth?

QuickWrite
In your *Reader/Writer Notebook,* write about your favorite experience with nature and how it affected your imagination.

MEET THE WRITER

William Wordsworth (1770–1850)

A lover of all natural forms, William Wordsworth believed that nature helped him "see into the life of things."

Finding His Calling
After his mother's death, Wordsworth was sent to attend school at Hawkhead in England's beautiful Lake District. His experiences in this setting fostered his love for nature and his belief in its inherent beneficent properties. During a walking tour of France and the Alps in 1790, Wordsworth was seized by the early idealism of the French Revolution. He returned to France in 1791 after completing his degree at Cambridge. As an educated man with no title, wealth, or head for business, Wordsworth had little interest in the few careers open to him, most notably, that of the Church. Thus began a decade of painful growth, as he searched for and eventually found his vocation as a poet.

The Power of Friendship
After Wordsworth returned from France in 1792, war broke out between France and England. Wordsworth was sickened by the war and gradually became disillusioned about his hopes for political and social change. In late 1793, he embarked on a walking tour of Europe, which, combined with his waning aspirations to perfect society, drove him to poetry.

In 1795, Wordsworth met poet Samuel Taylor Coleridge, and both men quickly became powerful galvanizing forces on each other's work. By June 1797, Wordsworth had produced a good deal of new poetry, none yet published, including a play and some stark narratives. *Lyrical Ballads* (1798) was the culmination of Wordsworth and Coleridge's friendship and mutual influence. The collection became one of the most important works of the Romantic era. In the Preface to *Lyrical Ballads,* Wordsworth wrote that poetry is the "spontaneous overflow of powerful feelings"; but he added that poems of value are produced only by one who has "thought long and deeply." The marriage of feeling and thought, as Coleridge recognized, made Wordsworth "the best poet of the age."

Think About the Writer: What might have led Wordsworth to believe that both thought and feelings are necessary for good poetry?

William Wordsworth (1842) by Benjamin Robert Haydon. Oil on canvas. National Portrait Gallery, London; (Background) Tintern Abbey.

Selection Readability	
Easily Accessible **Accessible** Challenging	These poems include blank verse; pastoral imagery; accessible language.

Lines Composed a Few Miles Above Tintern Abbey

Reading Standard 2.2, 3.3, 3.9 (see pages A48–A50).

Literary Skills Focus
Blank Verse With the exception of free verse, **blank verse** (unrhymed iambic pentameter) is the poetic form that sounds most like natural speech. In blank verse, each line of poetry contains five **iambs,** units of meter consisting of an unstressed syllable followed by a stressed syllable. A poet may vary this pattern slightly to draw attention to an idea or image in the text. As you read, think about how the flowing blank verse of "Tintern Abbey" contributes to its conversational tone.

Literary Perspectives Apply the literary perspective described on page 749 as you read this poem.

Reading Skills Focus
Analyzing Patterns of Organization Poets use various techniques to organize their verse. Common **organizational patterns** in poetry include the **stanza,** a group of consecutive lines that form a unit; **meter,** a generally regular pattern of stressed and unstressed syllables; and **rhyme.** In this poem, Wordsworth uses blank verse and stanzas to organize his ideas.

Into Action Look for punctuation and indentions that signal the end of one stanza and the beginning of another. Make notes in a chart like the one below on how Wordsworth uses stanzas to organize his ideas.

Stanza	Organization
1	description of landscape features; imagery of cottage grounds, pastoral farms, wreaths of smoke
2	
3	

Writing Skills Focus
Think as a Reader/Writer
Find It in Your Reading As you read "Tintern Abbey," note how Wordsworth uses long, flowing sentences that often start and stop in the middle of lines. Consider how his speaker uses first person and seems to address a listener. In your *Reader/Writer Notebook,* write how these techniques impart a conversational **tone,** as if the speaker is talking while walking.

Vocabulary
pastoral (PAS tuhr uhl) *adj.:* of simple or peaceful rural life. *The visit to the Wye Valley offered pastoral views of cottages and farms.*
sublime (suh BLYM) *adj.:* awe-inspiring due to majesty or nobility. *He saw a sublime vision when he journeyed to the beautiful Wye Valley.*
corporeal (kawr PAWR ee uhl) *adj.:* of the body. *Although our corporeal existence will someday end, Wordsworth believed that we will continue to exist in spirit.*
recompense (REHK uhm pehns) *n.:* payment or compensation in return for something lost. *The wisdom of experience is ample recompense for the loss of the pleasures of youth.*
impels (ihm PEHLZ) *v.:* forces; causes to move. *While visiting the Wye Valley, the speaker feels a presence that impels all things.*
zeal (zeel) *n.:* eager enthusiasm. *They will remember with zeal the happy experience that they shared together.*

Language Coach
Suffixes The suffix *–al* is often found at the end of adjectives. It can mean "of" or "relating to." Something that is *pastoral* relates to country life. Something that is *corporeal* relates to the body. To what do you think something that is *nocturnal* relates?

Learn It Online
Get to know Wordsworth through the Writers' Lives site online.
go.hrw.com H12-747 Go

Reader/Writer Notebook
Use your **RWN** to complete the activities for this selection.

Selection Resources

Unit 4 Resources, on-level practice and assessment, p. 27
PowerNotes, interactive lesson presentations with activities
Teacher One Stop™, on-level lesson plans and all print resources
Holt Audio Library
Holt Audio Library: Selections and Summaries in Spanish
UA: Holt Interactive Reader, p. 205
UA: Differentiating Instruction, modified lesson plans and leveled assessment, p. 169
UA: Supporting Instruction in Spanish, selection summary
UA: Resources for Teaching Advanced Students, lesson plans, p. 141
Analyzing Visuals Transparencies, p. 31
ThinkCentral Online Assessment, Selection Standards Check
ThinkCentral Online Remediation

Preteach

Introducing Vocabulary
- Review the Vocabulary words, definitions, and sentences with students.
- To reinforce the importance of the Vocabulary words, tell students that these words, in addition to providing key meaning to the poem, allow the author to create the meter of blank verse, or unrhymed iambic pentameter.

English for Academic Success
Language Coach
After students read the **Language Coach,** have them give additional examples of adjectives ending with the suffix *–al* along with their meanings.

Literary Skills Focus
As you read and discuss the poem with students, have them note the way each blank verse mimics natural speech.

Reading Skills Focus
Give students a copy of the Reading Skills Focus graphic organizer before they read (See **Unit 4 Resources.**) Tell them to use their responses to answer the questions on the Applying Your Skills page.

Writing Skills Focus
Have students record examples of conversational tone in their **Reader/Writer Notebooks.** Students can use their notes to complete the Writing Skills Focus activity.

Learn It Online
The **Writers' Lives** feature of the Interactive Student Edition offers additional information about this author. Audio or video segments are provided for some authors.
go.hrw.com H12-747 Go

Preparing to Read 747

Reader/Writer Notebook provides students a place to record their thoughts and notes about each selection. This notebook stresses the interdependence of reading and writing.

QuickWrite/QuickTalk sparks engagement by asking for students' opinions before they read the selection.

Language Coach points out the structure, patterns, and connections of English to assist English learners and users of African American vernacular English, while also reviewing fundamentals for proficient speakers.

Instructional Support

Bold visuals combined with instructional support engage students while the annotated **Teacher's Edition** helps you plan instruction and find supporting resources.

Think About/Talk About provides options and opportunities to facilitate academic conversation.

Model the Skill

- Tell students that when a poet organizes a poem, he or she creates an **organizational pattern** that complements the content of the work.
- Point out that the stanza that comprises lines 49–57 is much shorter than other stanzas. In blank verse, **stanzas** do not have to be of a fixed length (as they do in other verse forms). Also point out that the first line of the next stanza is not a continuation of the last line of the previous stanza (as it is for every other stanza transition). Explain that the stanza contains a passionate apostrophe to nature and its comforting role in memory.

Guided Practice: Apply

Think-Pair-Share Group students in pairs, and have them discuss how the stanza breaks in the poem complement the content of the stanzas.

Think About/Talk About

Responses to Margin Questions

Lines 65–85 *He loved nature with a passionate physical intensity.*

Lines 93–102 *The presence is a spirit that connects all living things.*

If this
Be but a vain belief, yet, oh! how oft—
In darkness and amid the many shapes
Of joyless daylight; when the fretful stir
Unprofitable, and the fever of the world,
Have hung upon the beatings of my heart—
How oft, in spirit, have I turned to thee,
O sylvan° Wye! thou wanderer through the woods,
How often has my spirit turned to thee! Ⓒ
And now, with gleams of half-extinguished thought,
With many recognitions dim and faint,
And somewhat of a sad perplexity,
The picture of the mind° revives again:

Ⓒ **Reading Focus** Analyzing Patterns of Organization In meditative lyrical poetry, stanzas do not have to be fixed in length. Why do you think Wordsworth made this stanza shorter than the others? How does the speaker's focus or emphasis change in this stanza?

56. sylvan: associated with the forest or woodlands.

61. picture of the mind: primarily the picture in the mind, but also the picture the individual mind has of itself.

Analyzing Visuals

Connecting to the Text What can you infer about Wordsworth's ideas of nature from this image? How might the elements of this environment represent "all in all" to him? What does it represent to you?

Tintern Abbey in the Wye Valley.

While here I stand, not only with the sense
Of present pleasure, but with pleasing thoughts
That in this moment there is life and food
For future years. And so I dare to hope,
Though changed, no doubt, from what I was when first
I came among these hills; when like a roe°
I bounded o'er the mountains, by the sides
Of the deep rivers, and the lonely streams,
Wherever nature led: more like a man
Flying from something that he dreads, than one
Who sought the thing he loved. For nature then
(The coarser pleasures of my boyish days,
And their glad animal movements all gone by)
To me was all in all.—I cannot paint
What then I was. The sounding cataract°
Haunted me like a passion: the tall rock,
The mountain, and the deep and gloomy wood,
Their colors and their forms, were then to me
An appetite; a feeling and a love,
That had no need of a remoter charm,°
By thought supplied, nor any interest
Unborrowed from the eye.—That time is past,
And all its aching joys are now no more,
And all its dizzy raptures. Not for this
Faint° I, nor mourn nor murmur; other gifts
Have followed; for such loss, I would believe,
Abundant recompense. For I have learned
To look on nature, not as in the hour
Of thoughtless youth; but hearing oftentimes
The still, sad music of humanity,
Nor harsh nor grating, though of ample power
To chasten and subdue. And I have felt
A presence that disturbs me with the joy
Of elevated thoughts; a sense sublime
Of something far more deeply interfused,
Whose dwelling is the light of setting suns,
And the round ocean and the living air,
And the blue sky, and in the mind of man:
A motion and a spirit, that impels
All thinking things, all objects of all thought,
And rolls through all things. Therefore am I still
A lover of the meadows and the woods,

Vocabulary **recompense** (REHK uhm pehns) *n.:* payment or compensation in return for something lost.
impels (ihm PEHLZ) *v.:* forces; causes to move.

67. roe: deer.

65–85. *With a hint of nostalgia, the speaker remembers the exhilarating times he spent in nature as a youth.*

? *How would you describe the speaker's relationship to nature when he was a boy?*

76. cataract: waterfall.

81. remoter charm: appeal other than the scene itself.

86. faint: become weak; lose heart.

? **93–102.** *Re-read these lines. In your own words, what is the "presence" (line 94) that the speaker describes?*

Think About/Talk About

Comprehension

Ⓒ **Reading Focus**

Possible responses: *This stanza is specifically about the Wye Valley, and the speaker addresses the valley directly. The short stanza draws attention to this direct address.*

Extend the Discussion

Comparing and Contrasting How has the speaker's attitude changed in lines 83–91? ***Possible response:*** *Rapture has been replaced by mystical understanding.*

Determining Author's Purpose On p. 751, the speaker contrasts his views of nature as a youth with his views of nature as a mature adult. What is Wordsworth's purpose in having the speaker present this contrast? ***Possible response:*** *Wordsworth is showing the different relationships people have with nature at different points in their lives. He illustrates the calmer, more contemplative relationship one has with nature as one matures.*

Vocabulary: Own the Word

- **recompense:** Ask students, "Have you ever *recompensed* someone for some wrong or injury? Explain whom and when, and how you *recompensed* the person.
- **impels:** What, according to the poet, *impels* his thoughts? ***Possible response:*** *a motion and a spirit*

Analyzing Visuals

Connecting to the Text: *The image represents a serene and beautiful valley landscape. This can remind the reader of Wordsworth's appreciation of nature and his longing for an pure experience of nature that one can only have as a child. The presence of a church and a herd create the image of a harmonious nature.*

Real Issues, Real Experts

*Holt author **Kylene Beers** offers strategies for teaching "Lines Composed a Few Miles Above Tintern Abbey."*

To slow students down enough to enjoy this poem, begin by having students write briefly about a place they have visited as both a teen and a youngster—like a shopping mall, theater, or grandparent's house. Ask students to describe how their experiences in that place changed as they have grown older. To move into the poem, read aloud lines 1–22 to students. Next, re-read this one section and ask students to underline at least five lines (or portions of lines) they enjoyed. Then, ask students to read aloud the lines they marked. As students share their lines, one at a time in no particular order, a found poem emerges. Finally, put students in pairs and have them continue reading the poem. Some pairs may choose to read silently, and others may choose to read aloud. Have students complete a T-chart as they read that lists on one side Wordsworth's feelings about nature when he was young and on the other his feelings now that he is older.

Universal Access

Students with Disabilities

Group students into pairs. Present each pair with a prepared Venn diagram on a sheet of paper. The left circle of the Venn diagram should be titled "Young," and the right circle should be titled "Mature." Have students study p. 751 and record the speaker's differing experiences with nature. In the central circle, students should record the ways in which the speaker views nature in the same way as a youth and as a mature adult.

750 Unit 4 • Chapter 7

Lines Composed a Few Miles Above Tintern Abbey 751

Other teacher tools include **Grammar Link** mini-lessons, **Analyzing Visuals** guides, and **Real Issues, Real Experts** informational tips.

Real Issues, Real Experts

Holt author **Kylene Beers** offers strategies for teaching "Lines Composed a Few Miles Above Tintern Abbey."

To slow students down enough to enjoy this poem, begin by having students write briefly about a place they have visited a both a teen and a youngster—like a shopping mall, theater, grandparent's house. Ask students to describe how their e ences in that place changed as they have grown older. T the poem, read aloud lines 1–22 to students ction and ask students to underl

Real Issues, Real Experts shares classroom-tested and proven strategies with you as you prepare to teach your students.

Instructional Support

As you move through a lesson, annotations, such as **Model the Skill**, **Guided Practice: Apply**, and **Comprehension** and **Analysis**, support students by outlining explicit instruction. You will also find additional instructional support for advanced learners, students with disabilities, and students who use African American vernacular English.

Instructional Support

gives you options to help you plan, prepare, and execute lessons.

Guided Practice: Apply

Think as a Reader/Writer

Find It in Your Reading Call students' attention to the sentence beginning with the word "Therefore" in line 102. Ask students to identify the line on which this sentence ends [*line 111*]. Remind students that by using long sentences across many lines of verse, Wordsworth mimics natural speech in his poetry.

Use It in Your Writing Give students a topic on which to write, such as pollution in rural or urban areas. Challenge students to write one sentence that spans at least three full lines of notebook paper. Then, ask students to think about the stressed and unstressed syllables in their sentence. If they were to turn their sentence into a poem of five to seven lines, where would they break the sentence and why?

Think About/Talk About

Responses to Margin Questions

Lines 111–115 *The speaker addresses his sister, Dorothy.*

Lines 116–134 *They do not rhyme; they are addressed to another person; one line often runs in to the next line.*

Lines 121–159 *The prayer is for Dorothy. The lines can be paraphrased as follows: "When your passion matures, as mine has, and you face hardships, take comfort from memories of this place; when I'm dead, remember me—how I loved this place more because we shared it."*

And mountains; and of all that we behold
From this green earth; of all the mighty world
Of eye, and ear, —both what they half create,
And what perceive; well pleased to recognize
In nature and the language of the sense
The anchor of my purest thoughts, the nurse,
The guide, the guardian of my heart, and soul
Of all my moral being. (D)
Nor perchance,
If I were not thus taught, should I the more
Suffer my genial spirits° to decay:
For thou art with me here upon the banks
Of this fair river; thou my dearest Friend,°
My dear, dear Friend; and in thy voice I catch
The language of my former heart, and read
My former pleasures in the shooting lights
Of thy wild eyes. Oh! yet a little while
May I behold in thee what I was once,
My dear, dear Sister! and this prayer I make,
Knowing that Nature never did betray
The heart that loved her; 'tis her privilege, (E)
Through all the years of this our life, to lead
From joy to joy: for she can so inform
The mind that is within us, so impress
With quietness and beauty, and so feed
With lofty thoughts, that neither evil tongues,
Rash judgments, nor the sneers of selfish men,
Nor greetings where no kindness is, nor all
The dreary intercourse° of daily life,
Shall e'er prevail against us, or disturb
Our cheerful faith, that all which we behold
Is full of blessings. Therefore let the moon (F)
Shine on thee in thy solitary walk;
And let the misty mountain winds be free
To blow against thee: and, in after years,
When these wild ecstasies shall be matured
Into a sober pleasure; when thy mind

? 111–115. *What shift takes place in this final stanza?*

113. **suffer my genial spirits:** allow my creative powers.

115. **my dearest Friend:** Wordsworth's sister, Dorothy.

? 116–134. *What makes these lines conversational?*

? 121–159. *What prayer does the speaker make in these concluding lines? For whom is the prayer? Paraphrase the speaker's thoughts.*

131. **intercourse:** dealings; social contacts.

(D) **Literary Perspectives** Philosophical Context In lines 93–111, the speaker finds new meanings in his surroundings. What types of philosophical, spiritual, or religious meaning do you see in his words?

(E) **Literary Perspectives** Philosophical Context What might the speaker mean by "Nature never did betray / The heart that loved her" (lines 122–123)?

(F) **Literary Focus** Blank Verse Read lines 116–134 aloud, and note the rhythm of the words. How would you describe the speaker's tone here?

SOCIAL STUDIES LINK

The River Wye viewed west from Monsal Head and set in limestone dales, Bridge Peak District.

The Wye Valley

Some critics have faulted Wordsworth for painting an idyllic picture of the Wye Valley and effectively glossing over its poverty. Kenneth R. Johnson in *The Hidden Wordsworth* explains that the smoke Wordsworth saw rising through the trees was a product of the area's iron industry, which burned trees to produce charcoal for the forges. Wordsworth's suggestion that smoke "might seem" to come from "vagrant dwellers in the houseless woods" touches with extreme delicacy on a fact known to everyone who visited the abbey: that vagabonds made their living by begging from tourists. Today, the British government has designated the Wye Valley a Site of Special Scientific Interest, and the region is vigilantly protected from pollution.

Ask Yourself

Why might Wordsworth have omitted descriptions of poverty from his poem? Should knowledge about the iron industry in the Wye Valley and the beggars at the abbey change the way the poem is understood and enjoyed? Explain.

Shall be a mansion for all lovely forms,
Thy memory be as a dwelling place
For all sweet sounds and harmonies; oh! then,
If solitude, or fear, or pain, or grief,
Should be thy portion, with what healing thoughts
Of tender joy wilt thou remember me,
And these my exhortations! Nor, perchance—
If I should be where I no more can hear
Thy voice, nor catch from thy wild eyes these gleams
Of past existence—wilt thou then forget
That on the banks of this delightful stream
We stood together; and that I, so long
A worshipper of Nature, hither came
Unwearied in that service: rather say
With warmer love—oh! with far deeper zeal
Of holier love. Nor wilt thou then forget,
That after many wanderings, many years
Of absence, these steep woods and lofty cliffs,
And this green pastoral landscape, were to me
More dear, both for themselves and for thy sake!

Vocabulary **zeal** (zeel) *n.:* eager enthusiasm.

Think About/Talk About

Analysis

(D) **Literary Perspectives**
Possible response: *"Sense sublime," "deeply interfused," and "a spirit that impels all thinking things" all provide clues to Wordsworth's view of nature. These lines convey a spiritual calmness when experiencing nature. It is in spiritual calmness that one can best contemplate philosophical truths.*

(E) **Literary Perspectives**
Possible response: *Nature will not disappoint a creature that appreciates and honors her.*

(F) **Literary Focus**
Possible response: *Wordsworth varies the meter; it is not strictly iambic pentameter. There are extra unstressed syllables that create a more conversational tone.*

Social Studies Link

Ask Yourself
Possible response: *The poem deals with universal and philosophical issues such as the relationship between humans and nature and the way people's perceptions change with maturity. If Wordsworth had included descriptions of the poverty that affected the Wye Valley, the poem would have had a polemic tone that would have interfered with Wordsworth's philosophical speculation.*

Vocabulary: Own the Word

zeal: Write the word *zeal* in a center circle on the board along with its definition, "enthusiasm." Draw "spider legs" and elicit related attributes of the word from students. ***Possible responses:*** *fervor, spirit, zest, bustle, diligence, eagerness, earnestness, ardor, willingness, passion, hunger, devotion, vigor*

Universal Access

Students Who Use African American Vernacular English

English for Academic Success Read aloud lines 112–113. Point out that the phrase "If I were" uses the subjunctive mood in the past tense. Remind students that the subjunctive mood is used to express a condition that is doubtful or not factual. Tell students that when the verb *be* is used in the past subjunctive, *were* is used for all persons: *If I were taught, if he were taught,* instead of *if I was taught.* Have students create two statements in the subjunctive mood.

Reaching Reluctant Readers

Discuss with students the idea of a natural place in which people can express their true essence. Ask students to consider their own experience and tell about a place that they think stirs great emotions in them. It can be a place they visited or a place they would like to visit one day. Students can freewrite notes about the place to rearrange them in a poem of their own.

California Standards, pp. 754–756

- **Reading Standard 2.2** Analyze the way in which clarity of meaning is affected by the patterns of organization, hierarchical structures, repetition of the main ideas, syntax, and word choice in the text.
- **Reading Standard 3.2** Analyze the way in which the theme or meaning of a selection represents a view or comment on life, using textual evidence to support the claim.
- **Reading Standard 3.3** Analyze ways in which irony, tone, mood, the author's style, and the "sound" of language achieve specific rhetorical or aesthetic purposes or both.
- **Reading Standard 3.9** Analyze the philosophical arguments presented in literary works to determine whether the authors' positions have contributed to the quality of each work and the credibility of the characters. (Philosophical approach)
- **Grades 9–10 Review Reading Standard 1.1** Identify and use the literal and figurative meanings of words and understand word derivations.
- **Writing Standard 1.5** Use language in natural, fresh, and vivid ways to establish a specific tone.
- **Writing Standard 2.1** Write fictional, autobiographical, or biographical narrative. **b.** Locate scenes and incidents in specific places.
- **Writing Standard 2.3** Write reflective compositions. **a.** Explore the significance of personal experiences, events, conditions, or concerns by using rhetorical strategies (e.g., narration, description, exposition, persuasion).
- **Listening and Speaking Standard 2.3** Deliver oral responses to literature. **a.** Demonstrate a comprehensive understanding of the significant ideas of literary works.

752 Unit 4 • Chapter 7

Lines Composed a Few Miles Above Tintern Abbey 753

California Standards, pp. 754–756
- **Reading Standard 2.2** Analyze the way in which clarity o meaning is affected by the patterns of organization, hierarchical structures, repetition of the main ideas, syntax, and word choice in the text.
- **Reading Standard 3.2** Analyze the way in which the theme or meaning of a selection represents a view or comment on life using textual evidence to support the claim.
- **Reading Standard 3.3** Analyze ways in which irony, tone mood, the author's style, and the "sound" of language ach specific rhetorical or aesthetic purposes or both.
ding Standard 3.9 Analyze the philosophi in literary works to determine

Universal Access offers resources and instructional strategies for all students.

California Standards Overview highlights the standards that will be taught in the chapter.

Strategies for reaching different kinds of learners help you create learning opportunities for all students.

Program Highlights

Applying Your Skills

Applying Your Skills completes the learning cycle for each selection. The skills introduced at the beginning of the chapter conclude in a variety of activities that allow you to **Check for Understanding** and give the student an opportunity for **Independent Practice**.

Independent Practice gives students an opportunity to demonstrate the skills they have acquired.

Reading Skills Focus and **Literary Skills Focus** apply key skills practiced in the selection.

Independent Practice

Grammar Link

Your Turn

1. *The speaker responds to a landscape he has visited before, a spot above the Wye River.*
2. *The beautiful woodland place stirs deep memories.*
3. *We are studying the works of Wordsworth, the Romantic poet.*

Choices: Evaluation Criteria

Review: Homework **Determine Style**

Students compare and contrast lines of earlier poems with lines of "Tintern Abbey," referring to rhyme, meter, imagery, and poetic devices.

Connect: Timed Writing 40–50 Minutes

Students compare and contrast their experience of the place in the present with their experience of the place in the past.

Extend: Homework **Listen to Music**

- Students demonstrate understanding of how the music captures the mood of the symphony's title.
- Students write from Wordsworth's philosophical perspective.

Assess

Unit 4 Resources, Selection Standards Check, p. 30

Applying Your Skills

Lines Composed a Few Miles Above Tintern Abbey

Grammar Link

Appositives

An **appositive** is a noun or pronoun placed beside another noun or pronoun to identify or describe it. An appositive with modifiers is an **appositive phrase.**

William Wordsworth, **poet,** found his calling during the 1790s.
His poems, **some of the most influential of his time,** are still read today.

A **nonessential** or **nonrestrictive appositive** is not essential to a sentence's meaning. These appositives are set off by commas to show that they interrupt sentences that would still be clear without them.

He collaborated with Samuel Taylor Coleridge.
He collaborated with Samuel Taylor Coleridge, **another founder of English Romanticism.**

An **essential** or **restrictive appositive,** which is not set off by commas, makes the noun or pronoun it describes more specific. Without the appositive, the sentence loses essential information or meaning.

The collection appeared in 1798.
The collection ***Lyrical Ballads*** appeared in 1798.

Your Turn

Rewrite the sentences by adding the italicized words as appositives. Use commas for nonessential appositives.

1. The speaker responds to a landscape he has visited before. *(a spot on the Wye River)*
2. The place stirs deep memories. *(a beautiful woodland)*
3. We are studying the works of the romantic poet. *(William Wordsworth)*

Writing Application Write a paragraph about a friend who has had a great positive influence on you. Use

CHOICES

As you respond to the Choices, use these **Academic Vocabulary** words as appropriate: differentiate, inherent, device, technique, function.

REVIEW

Determine the Style of the Poem

The style of Romantic literature differentiates it from many earlier literary works. From what you have read of British literature, do you think "Tintern Abbey" closely resembles the poetry that preceded it, or is it innovative, representing an overt break in tradition? In a small group, hold a panel discussion, with students debating both sides of the issue.

CONNECT

Share an Experience

Timed Writing Write a short essay in which you describe a place that evokes strong memories or holds emotional meaning for you. Describe the place with specific details, and explain why the location has special significance for you.

EXTEND

Listen to Music

The preeminent German composer Ludwig van Beethoven (1770–1827) was a leading musical figure in the transition between the Classical and Romantic periods. His Symphony No. 6 in F, the *Pastoral Symphony,* is one of the great program works in music history. An ode to nature, the cheerful, melodic first movement is labeled "The Awakening of Joyful Feelings upon Arrival in the Country." Listen to this movement, and discuss how it captures the mood of the title. Then, compose a journal entry, similar to what Wordsworth might have written, commenting on Beethoven's musical homage to nature and nature's inherent effect on the human mind and emotions.

Check for Understanding

Independent Practice

Reading Skills Focus

Possible responses:

1. *He has lost his youthful passionate response to nature.*
2. *He sees a passionate, spontaneous joy in nature in her eyes.*
3. *He remembers the beauty and spiritual gifts that nature offers. He relives his experiences through his memories and through sharing the experience with his sister.*
4. *Have students focus on the content and tone of each stanza to determine the poem's pattern of organization.*

Literary Skills Focus

Possible responses:

5. *He has received maturity and a deeper understanding of nature.*
6. *He has lost his innocence and perhaps felt despair.*
7. *Nature can heal and teach by guiding someone toward a quiet place of meditation and strength.*
8. *His sister offers him a look back at his youthful relationship with nature.*
9. *The speaker realizes that nature means even more to him now than before because he has a deeper appreciation of its spiritual significance and because he has shared the experience with Dorothy. Students' responses will vary.*
10. *In lines 100–105, Wordsworth states that nature has the power to lead humans toward their truth.*
11. *Lines 30–34 and lines 114–119 are especially conversational. Wordsworth varies the number of unstressed syllables to enhance the conversational quality of the poem.*
12. *Structure, word choice, imagery, and meter contribute to the theme of nature's profound impact on humanity.*

Applying Your Skills

Reading Standard 2.2, 3.2, 3.3, 3.9 (see pages A48–A50)
Writing Standard 1.5 (see pages A51–A52)

Lines Composed a Few Miles Above Tintern Abbey

Literary Response and Analysis

Reading Skills Focus

Quick Check

1. What has the speaker lost since he first "came among these hills" (line 67)?
2. What does the speaker see in his sister that makes him more aware of what he "was once" (lines 120–121)?

Read with a Purpose

3. What benefits does the speaker derive from returning to nature? How does he come to recognize these benefits?

Reading Skills: Analyzing Patterns of Organization

4. Review your chart. How does Wordsworth use the stanzas to organize his ideas? How does the structure of the stanzas contribute to the conversational quality of the poem?

Literary Skills Focus

Literary Analysis

5. **Interpret** What "gifts" (line 86) and "abundant recompense" (line 88) does the speaker believe he has received for his "loss" (line 87)?
6. **Draw Conclusions** What does the speaker mean when he says, in line 91, that he has heard "the still, sad music of humanity"?
7. **Evaluate** In lines 109–111, the speaker calls nature "the nurse, / The guide, the guardian of my heart, and soul / Of all my moral being." How can nature heal and teach?
8. **Analyze** What role does the speaker's sister play in the poem? How does the speaker regard her involvement?
9. **Extend** Summarize and comment on the speaker's conclusion (beginning with line 102). Have you had to face losing part of your past? How did you handle the loss?
10. **Literary Perspectives** As you read, you noted Wordsworth's philosophy about nature. What assumptions about nature does he express in this poem? Support your answer with examples.

Literary Skills: Blank Verse

11. **Analyze** Find two examples from the poem that sound especially conversational in tone. How does Wordsworth's use of blank verse enhance the conversational quality of the poem?

Literary Skills Review: Theme

12. **Evaluate** The central idea or insight about human experience revealed in a work of literature is called **theme.** What is this poem's theme? What do the text's structure, word choice, or imagery reveal about the theme?

Writing Skills Focus

Think as a Reader/Writer

Use It in Your Writing In "Tintern Abbey," Wordsworth writes a deeply personal meditation in a form he and Coleridge called the "conversation poem." As you read, you noted some techniques Wordsworth uses to create a conversational tone. Using a similar conversational tone, write a poem or a brief reflective composition about a subject of your choice.

What Do You Think Now? How can experiences with nature help us think creatively about "the dreary intercourse of daily life"?

Universal Access

Struggling Writers

Provide additional scaffolding for students to complete the Writing Skills Focus activity. Review the techniques Wordsworth used to create a conversational tone. Remind them that Wordsworth varied the rhythm in lines 30–34 and in lines 114–119. Have students write a poem on a nature using the pattern of alternating stressed and unstressed syllables. Then, have them go back and add an additional unstressed syllable in two lines to create a conversational tone.

What Do You Think Now?

Brainstorm with students the ways in which nature rejuvenates them in their daily lives. Then, discuss how those experiences help them think creatively about mundane aspects of their daily routines.

Grades 9–10 Review Reading Standard 1.1 (see pages A48–A50)

Vocabulary Development

Vocabulary Check

Match the Vocabulary words with their definitions.

1. corporeal	a. forces
2. zeal	b. enthusiasm
3. impels	c. bodily
4. recompense	d. compensation
5. pastoral	e. majestic
6. sublime	f. peaceful

Vocabulary Skills: Etymology

Knowledge of **etymology,** or word origins, can be an excellent tool for understanding meaning, usage, and related words. The chart below shows the etymology of the Vocabulary words from "Tintern Abbey."

English Word	Word Origin	Original Meaning
corporeal	Latin *corporeus*	belonging to the body
impels	Latin *impellere*	*in–,* on + *pellere,* to push
pastoral	Latin *pastoralis* < *pastor*	shepherd
recompense	Latin *recompensare*	*re–,* back + *compensare,* to balance out
sublime	Latin *sublimus*	uplifted; high; lofty
zeal	Latin *zelus* < Greek *zēlos*	ardor; jealousy

Your Turn

Match the Vocabulary words with words that have similar origins. Then, write sentences that explain the similarities and differences between the two words in each pair. Consult the chart to the left and a dictionary for help.

1. corporeal	a. pastor
2. zeal	b. pension
3. impels	c. corpse
4. recompense	d. sublimation
5. pastoral	e. compel
6. sublime	f. zealot

Language Coach

Suffixes The suffix *–al,* which can mean "of" or "relating to," is often found at the end of adjectives. The suffix can be added to words that stand alone as nouns *(convention, conventional)* or to roots that cannot stand alone *(corporeal)*. Tell the meaning of each word in italics. Then, answer the questions.

1. How might *corporeal* beauty be both an advantage and a disadvantage?
2. Do poets give too much emphasis to *spiritual* concerns?
3. Does Wordsworth seem to agree with *conventional* ideas of youth and old age?
4. How can a poem produce two responses, one *emotional* and the other intellectual?

Academic Vocabulary

Write About

How does Wordsworth differentiate childhood from adulthood? Why does he say childhood functions as a state of heightened awareness?

Universal Access: Vocabulary Development

English Learners

English for Academic Success Have students find the etymology of each Academic Vocabulary word and organize their information in the vocabulary chart as shown on p. 755. Have them verbalize the relationship between the word origins to the original meanings. For example, one might say, "The word *inherent* comes from the Latin *inhaerére,* which means 'to stick.' Similarly, *inherent* refers to a quality existing or sticking onto something, or someone, permanently."

Struggling Readers

Reinforce students' understanding of the Academic Vocabulary words by discussing the meanings of related words. Have them use each word in a sentence.

- **differentiation**—the process of making something different
- **functional**—designed to be useful
- **inherently**—basically
- **technical**—of or derived from a method

Independent Practice

Vocabulary Development

Vocabulary Check

1. *c* 2. *b*
3. *a* 4. *d*
5. *f* 6. *e*

Your Turn

Possible responses:

1. c; *both refer to the body, but a* corpse *refers to a dead body.*
2. f; Zealot, *a noun, refers to a person who shows zeal.*
3. e; *both words deal with a forward drive or urge, but* compel *connotes a stronger force.*
4. b; *a* pension *is a specific kind of compensation.*
5. a; pastoral *implies the rustic scene, while a* pastor *is a religious "shepherd."*
6. d; sublimation *is the noun form of* sublime.

English for Academic Success

Language Coach

Possible responses:

1. *"of the body"; Corporeal beauty is admired and appreciated, but not lasting.*
2. *"of the spirit"; No, spiritual concerns are emphasized when necessary.*
3. *"relating to convention"; Yes. Youth reflects passion and unawareness; old age reflects maturity*
4. *"of emotion"; poetry can evoke our emotions and also pose questions for us to ponder*

English for Academic Success

Academic Vocabulary

Possible response: *Wordsworth associates childhood with a fervent and spontaneous response to the sights of nature that diminishes with age. Childhood functions as a period of heightened awareness with strong impressions on the senses.*

Comparing Texts

Comparing Texts offers students the opportunity to identify recurring themes across works, analyze the characteristics of different forms of prose, and compare and contrast points of view. Students deepen their understanding of literature and writing by exploring connections between texts.

COMPARING TEXTS: WORLD LITERATURE

Epics Across Cultures

Gilgamesh (1924) by Zabelle C. Boyajian. Gilgamesh, in search of immortality, goes to Mount Mashu, which is guarded by terrible scorpion gods who welcome him when they learn his identity.

Produced by two different cultures and composed nearly a thousand years apart, the epics *Gilgamesh* and the *Iliad* share universal themes of fear, bravery, determination, and compassion that fascinate readers today. As you read the following excerpts, consider how readers from any time and place might find meaning in these epics. After you read, you will compare the themes that connect the epics.

CONTENTS

Comparing Tex

Comparing Texts continues all the features of the single selections including Literary Skills Focus, Reading Skills Focus, Writing Skills Focus, Vocabulary study, and Language Coach.

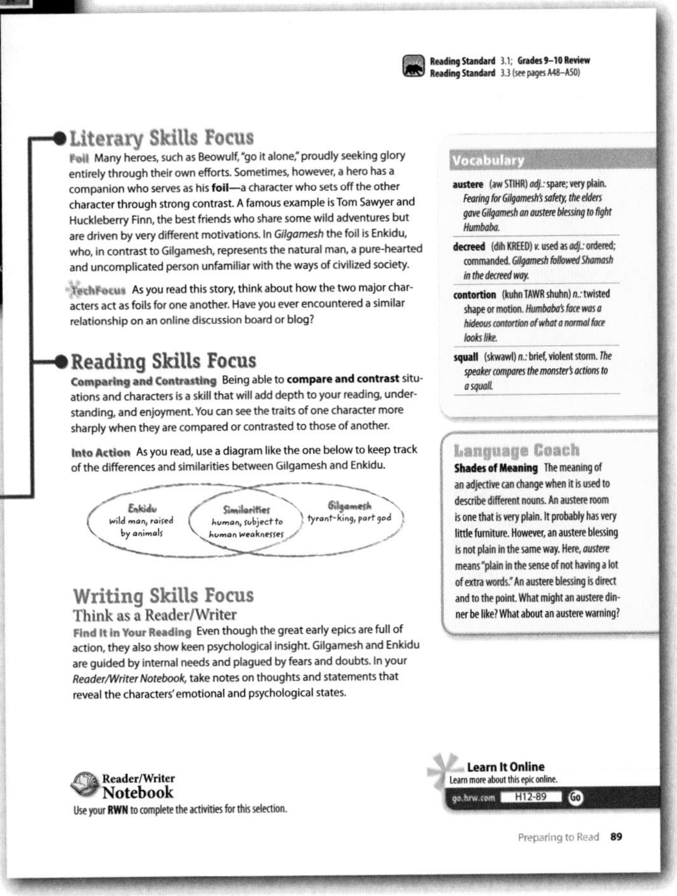

Reading Standard 3.1; **Grades 9–10 Review Reading Standard** 3.3 (see pages A48–A50)

Literary Skills Focus

Foil Many heroes, such as Beowulf, "go it alone," proudly seeking glory entirely through their own efforts. Sometimes, however, a hero has a companion who serves as his **foil**—a character who sets off the other character through strong contrast. A famous example is Tom Sawyer and Huckleberry Finn, the best friends who share some wild adventures but are driven by very different motivations. In *Gilgamesh* the foil is Enkidu, who, in contrast to Gilgamesh, represents the natural man, a pure-hearted and uncomplicated person unfamiliar with the ways of civilized society.

TechFocus As you read this story, think about how the two major characters act as foils for one another. Have you ever encountered a similar relationship on an online discussion board or blog?

Reading Skills Focus

Comparing and Contrasting Being able to **compare and contrast** situations and characters is a skill that will add depth to your reading, understanding, and enjoyment. You can see the traits of one character more sharply when they are compared or contrasted to those of another.

Into Action As you read, use a diagram like the one below to keep track of the differences and similarities between Gilgamesh and Enkidu.

Writing Skills Focus

Think as a Reader/Writer

Find It in Your Reading Even though the great early epics are full of action, they also show keen psychological insight. Gilgamesh and Enkidu are guided by internal needs and plagued by fears and doubts. In your *Reader/Writer Notebook*, take notes on thoughts and statements that reveal the characters' emotional and psychological states.

Vocabulary

austere (aw STIHR) *adj.:* spare; very plain. *Fearing for Gilgamesh's safety, the elders gave Gilgamesh an austere blessing to fight Humbaba.*

decreed (dih KREED) *v.* used as *adj.:* ordered; commanded. *Gilgamesh followed Shamash in the decreed way.*

contortion (kuhn TAWR shuhn) *n.:* twisted shape or motion. *Humbaba's face was a hideous contortion of what a normal face looks like.*

squall (skwawl) *n.:* brief, violent storm. *The speaker compares the monster's actions to a squall.*

Language Coach

Shades of Meaning The meaning of an adjective can change when it is used to describe different nouns. An austere room is one that is very plain. It probably has very little furniture. However, an austere blessing is not plain in the same way. Here, *austere* means "plain in the sense of not having a lot of extra words." An austere blessing is direct and to the point. What might an austere dinner be like? What about an austere warning?

Reader/Writer Notebook
Use your **RWN** to complete the activities for this selection.

Learn It Online
Learn more about this epic online.
go.hrw.com H12-89 Go

Preparing to Read 89

Literary Skills Focus and **Reading Skills Focus** stress the similarities and differences among selections.

Standards Review

Standards Review is the culminating activity of the chapter. **Literary**, **Informational**, **Writing**, and **Vocabulary Skills** are reviewed using new texts with a multiple-choice format and writing activities.

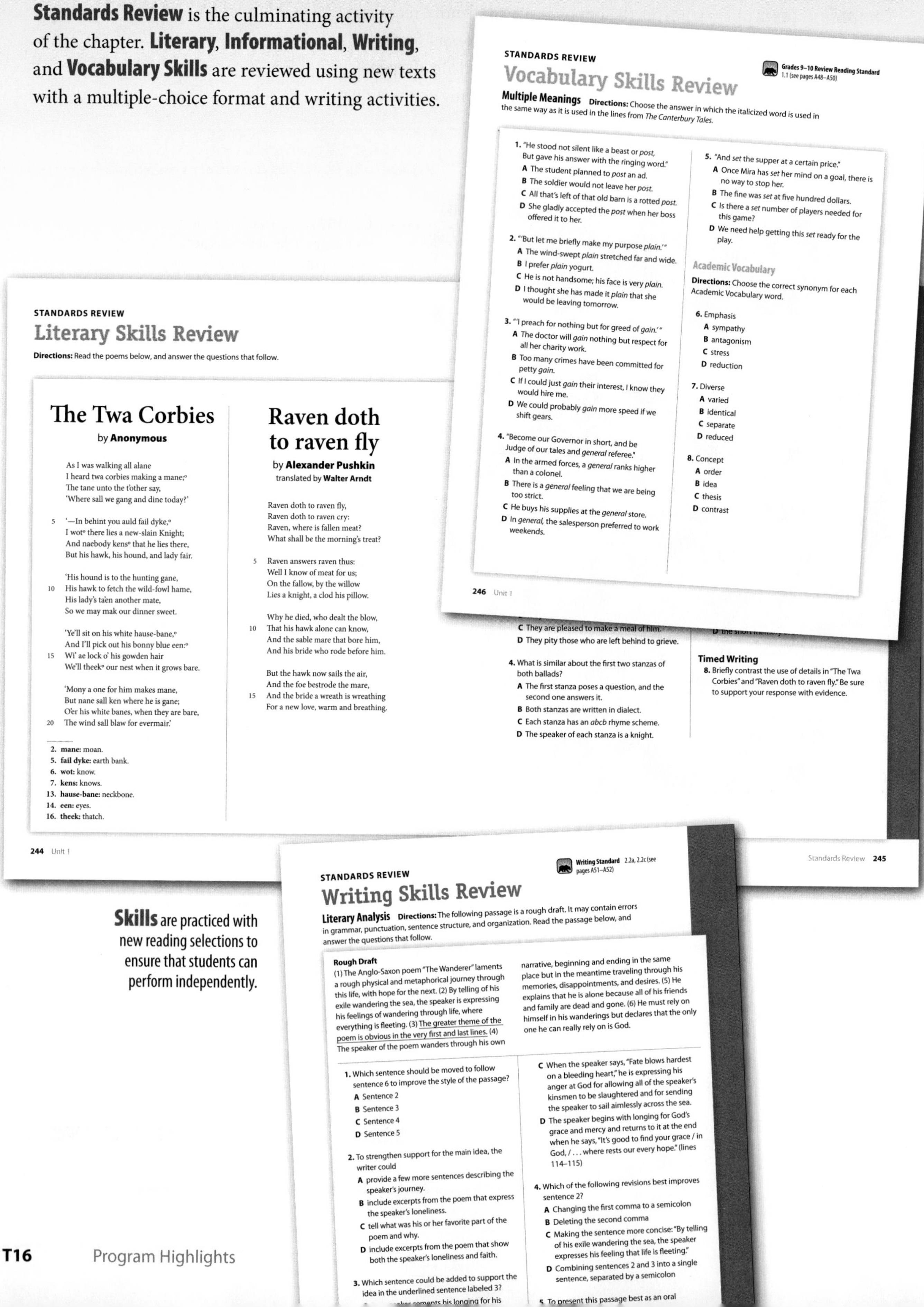

STANDARDS REVIEW

Vocabulary Skills Review

Grades 9–10 Review Reading Standard 1.1 (see pages A48–A50)

Multiple Meanings **Directions:** Choose the answer in which the italicized word is used in the same way as it is used in the lines from *The Canterbury Tales.*

1. "He stood not silent like a beast or *post,* But gave his answer with the ringing word."
   - A The student planned to *post* an ad.
   - B The soldier would not leave her *post.*
   - C All that's left of that old barn is a rotted *post.*
   - D She gladly accepted the *post* when her boss offered it to her.
2. "'But let me briefly make my purpose *plain.*'"
   - A The wind-swept *plain* stretched far and wide.
   - B I prefer *plain* yogurt.
   - C He is not handsome; his face is very *plain.*
   - D I thought she had made it *plain* that she would be leaving tomorrow.
3. "'I preach for nothing but for greed of *gain.*'"
   - A The doctor will *gain* nothing but respect for all her charity work.
   - B Too many crimes have been committed for petty *gain.*
   - C If I could just *gain* their interest, I know they would hire me.
   - D We could probably *gain* more speed if we shift gears.
4. "Become our Governor in short, and be Judge of our tales and *general* referee."
   - A In the armed forces, a *general* ranks higher than a colonel.
   - B There is a *general* feeling that we are being too strict.
   - C He buys his supplies at the *general* store.
   - D In *general,* the salesperson preferred to work weekends.
5. "And *set* the supper at a certain price."
   - A Once Mira has *set* her mind on a goal, there is no way to stop her.
   - B The fine was *set* at five hundred dollars.
   - C Is there a *set* number of players needed for this game?
   - D We need help getting this *set* ready for the play.

Academic Vocabulary

Directions: Choose the correct synonym for each Academic Vocabulary word.

6. Emphasis
   - A sympathy
   - B antagonism
   - C stress
   - D reduction
7. Diverse
   - A varied
   - B identical
   - C separate
   - D reduced
8. Concept
   - A order
   - B idea
   - C thesis
   - D contrast

246 Unit 1

STANDARDS REVIEW

Literary Skills Review

Directions: Read the poems below, and answer the questions that follow.

The Twa Corbies

by **Anonymous**

As I was walking all alane
I heard twa corbies making a mane;°
The tane unto the t'other say,
'Where sall we gang and dine today?'

'—In behint you auld fail dyke,°
I wot° there lies a new-slain Knight;
And naebody kens° that he lies there,
But his hawk, his hound, and lady fair.

'His hound is to the hunting gane,
His hawk to fetch the wild-fowl hame,
His lady's ta'en another mate,
So we may mak our dinner sweet.

'Ye'll sit on his white hause-bane,°
And I'll pick out his bonny blue een:°
Wi' ae lock o' his gowden hair
We'll theek° our nest when it grows bare.

'Mony a one for him makes mane,
But nane sall ken where he is gane;
O'er his white banes, when they are bare,
The wind sall blaw for evermair.'

2. **mane:** moan.
5. **fail dyke:** earth bank.
6. **wot:** know.
7. **kens:** knows.
13. **hause-bane:** neckbone.
14. **een:** eyes.
16. **theek:** thatch.

Raven doth to raven fly

by **Alexander Pushkin**
translated by **Walter Arndt**

Raven doth to raven fly,
Raven doth to raven cry:
Raven, where is fallen meat?
What shall be the morning's treat?

Raven answers raven thus:
Well I know of meat for us;
On the fallow, by the willow
Lies a knight, a clod his pillow.

Why he died, who dealt the blow,
That his hawk alone can know,
And the sable mare that bore him,
And his bride who rode before him.

But the hawk now sails the air,
And the foe bestrode the mare,
And the bride a wreath is wreathing
For a new love, warm and breathing.

- C They are pleased to make a meal of him.
- D They pity those who are left behind to grieve.

4. What is similar about the first two stanzas of both ballads?
   - A The first stanza poses a question, and the second one answers it.
   - B Both stanzas are written in dialect.
   - C Each stanza has an *abcb* rhyme scheme.
   - D The speaker of each stanza is a knight.

D the short ...

Timed Writing

8. Briefly contrast the use of details in "The Twa Corbies" and "Raven doth to raven fly." Be sure to support your response with evidence.

244 Unit 1

Standards Review 245

STANDARDS REVIEW

Writing Skills Review

Writing Standard 2.2a, 2.2c (see pages A51–A52)

Literary Analysis **Directions:** The following passage is a rough draft. It may contain errors in grammar, punctuation, sentence structure, and organization. Read the passage below, and answer the questions that follow.

Rough Draft

(1) The Anglo-Saxon poem "The Wanderer" laments a rough physical and metaphorical journey through this life, with hope for the next. (2) By telling of his exile wandering the sea, the speaker is expressing his feelings of wandering through life, where everything is fleeting. (3) <u>The greater theme of the poem is obvious in the very first and last lines.</u> (4) The speaker of the poem wanders through his own narrative, beginning and ending in the same place but in the meantime traveling through his memories, disappointments, and desires. (5) He explains that he is alone because all of his friends and family are dead and gone. (6) He must rely on himself in his wanderings but declares that the only one he can really rely on is God.

1. Which sentence should be moved to follow sentence 6 to improve the style of the passage?
   - A Sentence 2
   - B Sentence 3
   - C Sentence 4
   - D Sentence 5
2. To strengthen support for the main idea, the writer could
   - A provide a few more sentences describing the speaker's journey.
   - B include excerpts from the poem that express the speaker's loneliness.
   - C tell what was his or her favorite part of the poem and why.
   - D include excerpts from the poem that show both the speaker's loneliness and faith.
3. Which sentence could be added to support the idea in the underlined sentence labeled 3?
   - ... laments his longing for his ...

- C When the speaker says, "Fate blows hardest on a bleeding heart," he is expressing his anger at God for allowing all of the speaker's kinsmen to be slaughtered and for sending the speaker to sail aimlessly across the sea.
- D The speaker begins with longing for God's grace and mercy and returns to it at the end when he says, "It's good to find your grace / in God, / . . . where rests our every hope." (lines 114–115)

4. Which of the following revisions best improves sentence 2?
   - A Changing the first comma to a semicolon
   - B Deleting the second comma
   - C Making the sentence more concise: "By telling of his exile wandering the sea, the speaker expresses his feeling that life is fleeting."
   - D Combining sentences 2 and 3 into a single sentence, separated by a semicolon
5. To present this passage best as an oral ...

Skills are practiced with new reading selections to ensure that students can perform independently.

Writing Workshop

The instructional strand **Think as a Reader/Writer** culminates in the **Writing Workshop**. Students develop strategies for organizing and focusing their writing. **Preparing for Timed Writing** introduces a writing prompt and strategies students can use to practice and complete a timed-writing assignment.

Writing Workshop

Literary Analysis: Poetry

Write with a Purpose

Write an essay analyzing a poem. Your **purpose** for writing is to share your analysis and insights about the poem. Your **audience** will be your teacher and classmates and anyone else who is interested in poetry.

Think as a Reader/Writer In this collection, you have examined poems' literary elements critically and considered how these elements work together. Before you write your **poetry analysis,** read the following excerpt from Seamus Heaney's analysis of Dylan Thomas's poem "Do Not Go Gentle into That Good Night." The poem appears on page 1236.

"Do Not Go Gentle into That Good Night" fulfills its promise precisely because its craft has not lost touch with a suffered world. The villanelle[1] form, turning upon itself, advancing and retiring to and from a resolution, is not just a line-by-line virtuoso performance. Through its repetitions, the father's remoteness—and the ...

← Heaney clearly states his **thesis.**

← He explains how ...

Writing Workshop — Literary Analysis

Scoring Guide

Use the scoring guide below to evaluate your poetry analysis from the Writing Workshop or your response to the on-demand prompt on the next page.

	Literary Analysis	Organization and Focus	Sentence Structure and Vocabulary	Language Conventions
4	• demonstrates a *thoughtful, comprehensive* grasp of the text.	• accurately and coherently provides *specific* textual details and examples to support the thesis and main ideas. • demonstrates a *clear* understanding of the ambiguities, nuances, and complexities of the text. • demonstrates *thorough* comprehension of the author's use of literary and/or stylistic devices.	• provides a *variety* of sentence types and uses *precise, descriptive* language.	• contains *few, if any, errors* in the conventions of the English language. (Errors are generally first draft in nature.)
3	• demonstrates a *comprehensive* grasp of the text.	• accurately and coherently provides *general* textual details and examples to support the thesis and main ideas. • demonstrates a *general* understanding of the ambiguities, nuances, and complexities of the text. • demonstrates *general* comprehension of the author's use of literary and/or stylistic devices.	• provides a *variety* of sentence types and uses *some descriptive* language.	• may contain *some errors* in the conventions of the English language. (Errors do **not** interfere with the reader's understanding of the essay.)
2	• demonstrates a *limited* grasp of the text.	• provides *few, if any,* textual details and examples to support the thesis and main ideas. • demonstrates *limited* understanding of the ambiguities, nuances, and complexities of the text. • demonstrates *limited* comprehension of the author's use of literary and/or stylistic devices.	• provides *few, if any,* types of sentence types and *basic, predictable* language.	• may contain *several errors* in the conventions of the English language. (Errors **may** interfere with the reader's understanding of the essay.)
1	• demonstrates *minimal* grasp of the text.	• may provide **no** textual details and examples to support the thesis and main ideas. • may demonstrate **no** understanding of the ambiguities, nuances, and complexities of the text. • demonstrates *minimal* or **no** comprehension of the auth... and/or stylistic devi...	• may provide **no** sentence variety and uses *limited* vocabulary.	• may contain *serious errors* in the conventions of the English language. (Errors interfere with the reader's understanding of the essay.)

Preparing for Timed Writing

Literary Analysis

Writing Standard 1.1, 1.3, 1.9, 2.2a–e (see pages A48–A50)
Language Conventions Standard 1.1, 1.2, 1.3 (see page A53)

When responding to a literary analysis prompt, use what you have learned from reading, writing your poetry analysis, and studying the scoring guide on page 240. Use the steps below to develop a response to the following prompt.

Writing Prompt

Many pieces of literature feature a villainous character who creates conflict in the world in which he or she resides. Choose one literary villain from your reading. In an essay, explain how the villain's role is critical to the text.

Study the Prompt

Begin by reading the prompt carefully. Read it a second time, noting the requirements specified in the prompt:

Type of writing: essay
Subject: the role of the villain
Text: your choice of literary works that include a villain whose role is critical to the text

Quickly make a list of literary works that you know well that have a villain. Then determine which selection you know best. **Tip:** Spend about five minutes studying the prompt.

Plan Your Response

Once you have decided on a literary work and its villain, ask yourself these questions about his or her role:

- What background information will I need to provide about this villain and this literary work?
- What is the nature of the character's villainy?
- What are the villain's motivations?
- How does his or her evil manifest itself?
- How do the other char... villain?
- ...ehavior
- ...ugh the
- ...s on
- ...ns are

most clear. Include discussion of that scene in your essay. **Tip:** Spend about ten minutes planning your response.

Respond to the Prompt

Start writing by introducing and stating your thesis. Your thesis will be a statement about the villain's role and the theme of the literary work. Then, begin writing down the evidence that led you to your thesis. An effective way to organize your essay is chronologically, following the progression of the villain's actions. Conclude your essay with his or her final scene. As your write, think of the following points:

- Give your reader evidence from the text to support your thesis. Use short quotations if you can recall them, or retell scenes from the text.
- Elaborate on how each piece of evidence supports the thesis.
- Use the villain's final scene to conclude your essay and comment on the story's theme.

Tip: Spend about twenty minutes writing your draft.

Improve Your Response

Revising Look again at the prompt to ensure your essay fulfills the requirements. Have you explained how the villain's role relates to the author's theme? Have you used specific details from the text? Have you included details of the last scene in which the villain appears?

Proofreading Now make sure that your essay is free of errors in grammar, spelling, punctuation, and capitalization. Be certain that your edits are neat and your essay is legible.

Checking your final copy Before you turn in your final copy, read it one more time to catch any errors you may have missed and to make any finishing touches. **Tip:** Spend about five to ten minutes improving your paper.

Writing Workshop — Literary Analysis: Poetry

Peer Review

Review your draft with a peer, using this chart to check that all the contents of a poetry analysis are present and organized logically. Ensure that any suggestions you make about your partner's piece are specific. Ask your partner to clarify any suggestions he or she makes that you do not understand completely.

Evaluating and Revising

All good writers revise to make sure that their words accurately express their ideas and to improve their work. Read the evaluation questions in the left-hand column, and use the tips in the middle column to help you make revisions to your poetry analysis. Then, use the suggested techniques in the right-hand column to make any necessary revisions to your draft.

Poetry Analysis: Guidelines for Content and Organization

Evaluation Question	Tip	Revision Technique
1. Does the introduction engage the reader's interest and introduce the poem?	**Put parentheses around** the engaging opening. **Circle** the title of the poem and the name of the author.	If necessary, **add** an interest-catching opening, such as a provocative quotation or a bold statement. **Add** the name of the poem and its author.
2. Does the introduction include a thesis statement that identifies the main ideas the writer is communicating about the poem?	**Highlight** the thesis statement. **Bracket** the main ideas about the poem.	If needed, **add** a thesis statement that states your main ideas about the poem.
3. Are the major ideas clear? Do they support the thesis?	**Underline** the major ideas. **Draw an arrow** from the major points to the thesis.	**Rewrite** major ideas that are not clearly expressed. **Replace** points that don't support the thesis.
4. Do detailed and accurate references to the text support each idea?	**Draw a wavy line** under each quotation or detail from the poem.	**Add** quotations or details from the poem. **Elaborate** on how the evidence supports the point being made.
5. Is the discussion of literary elements arranged logically?	**Review** the underlined major points to make sure their arrangement is logical.	**Rearrange** major points by order of importance or chronological order.
6. Does the conclusion restate the thesis and make a closing connection about the theme of the poem?	**Highlight** the sentence restating the thesis. **Double-underline** the sentence or sentences connecting the poem to a broader theme.	**Add** a sentence that restates the thesis, or **add** a closing connection, if needed.

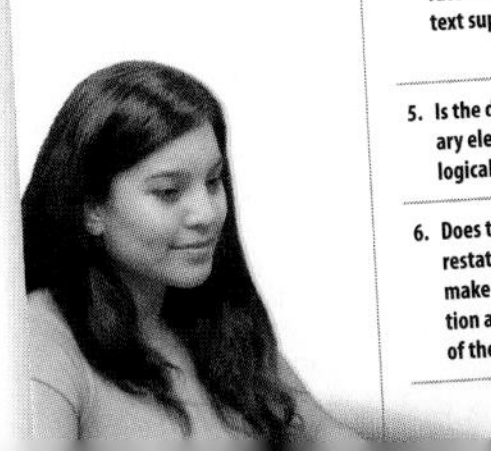

Rubrics set expectations for students and make assessment easier for teachers.

Preparing for Timed Writing gives students practice responding to prompts.

Evaluating and Revising, the most difficult aspects of writing for many students, are demonstrated by using real student papers.

Program Highlights

Program Resources *for* California Classrooms

For the Student

Think Central, Student Access includes the online version of the Student Edition, enhanced by audio, video, hyperlinked vocabulary, and point-of-use links:

- MediaScope
- Digital Storytelling
- NovelWise
- Interactive Graphic Organizers

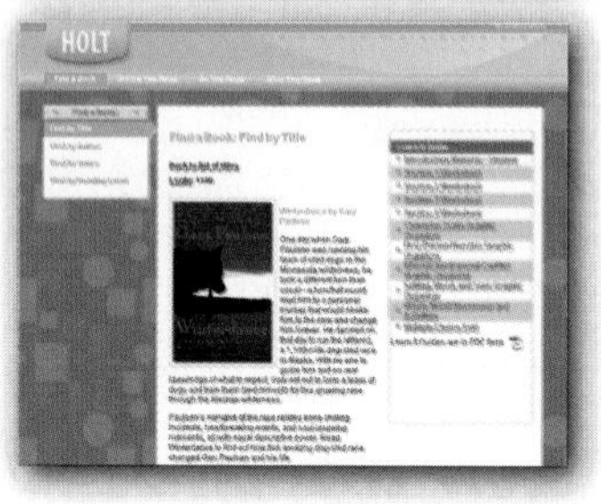

Student One Stop™ solves the backpack problem. The Student Edition, workbooks, and audio can be found on one CD-ROM.

Reader/Writer Notebook gives students a place to take notes on their reading, on vocabulary, and on writing ideas and assignments.

Lesson Planning

Teacher Edition

Think Central, Teacher Access

Teacher One Stop™ contains everything you need to plan and manage your lessons on one convenient CD-ROM, including

- *Holt OnCourse Planner*
- *ExamView® Assessment Suite*
- *Holt PuzzlePro®*
- *MindPoint®* Quiz Show
- Printable worksheets and more

Chapter Resources (Grades 6–8)

Unit Resources (Grades 9–12)

Holt Professional Learning for Language Arts offers you convenient, on-going support. Resources include

- Professional Learning Videos
- Instructional Strategies
- Training Guides
- Teacher Toolbox
- New Teacher Handbook

PowerNotes®: Instructional Presentations with Motivational Videos (CD-ROM)

GrammarNotes: Effective Grammar for Writing (CD-ROM)

WritingNotes: Process and Strategies for Effective Writing (CD-ROM)

Writing and Research in a Digital Age (CD-ROM)

Lesson Planning continued

Holt Virtual File Cabinet for Language Arts, Expanded Edition

OnCourse: Mapping Instruction provides a planning guide for using *Holt Literature and Language Arts* and *Warriner's Handbook* to ensure standards are covered.

Transition Pacing Guide is a planning calendar to help you move students from an intervention program to the basic program.

Implementation Guide for Administrators

Differentiating Instruction

Universal Access: Holt Interactive Reader

Universal Access: Holt Interactive Writer and Speaker

Universal Access: Differentiating Instruction

- Lesson Plans
- Vocabulary Practice
- Oral and Written Language Practice
- Graphic Organizers
- Leveled Progress and Summative Assessment

Universal Access: Resources for Teaching Advanced Students

Universal Access: Holt Leveled Library is a set of integrated texts and lessons designed to meet the needs of struggling, proficient, and advanced readers.

Universal Access: Supporting Instruction in Five Languages (Grades 6–8)

Universal Access: Supporting Instruction in Spanish (Grades 9–12)

Family Involvement Activities in Five Languages

Holt Pronunciation Resources

Assessment

ExamView Test Generator (on the Teacher One Stop™)

ThinkCentral Online Assessment helps you track progress with customizable reports and deliver effective intruction to all students.

ThinkCentral Online Remediation offers interactive tutorials that coach students towards mastery.

Holt Online Essay Scoring

Formal Assessment: Diagnostic, Progress Monitoring, and Summative Testing

Focus on Standards provides multiple practice opportunities in a consumable student workbook.

Preparing for the SAT and ACT (Grades 11–12)

Skill Building

Holt Six Traits for Writing

WordSharp: An Interactive Vocabulary Tutor

- Skills to Own Words walks students through the steps necessary to determine the meaning of unfamiliar words and provides scaffolded practice opportunities.
- Words You Can Use helps students internalize high-utility vocabulary, including academic language.

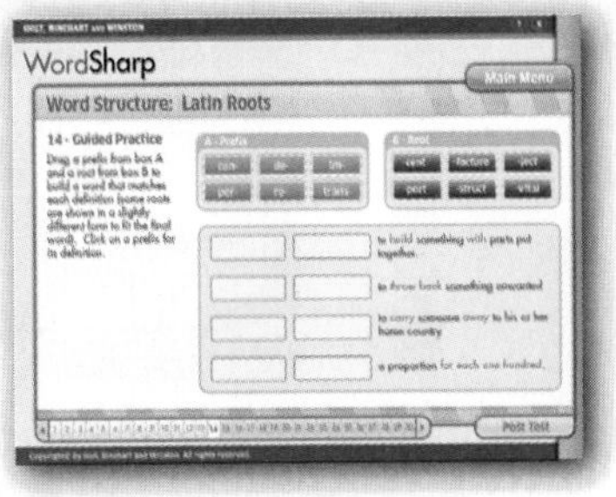

Vocabulary Development

Language Handbook Worksheets: Grammar, Usage, and Mechanics

Holt Interactive Spelling (Grades 6–8)

Spelling Lessons and Activities (Grades 6–8)

Media

Holt Audio Library provides professional readings of selections in the Student Edition.

Holt Audio Library: Selections and Summaries in Spanish

Analyzing Visuals Transparencies

Reading and Writing Transparencies include

- Proofreading Warm-ups
- Sentence Combining
- Vocabulary
- Critical Reading
- Graphic Organizers
- Daily Writing Instruction

Weekly Standards Review Transparencies provide daily/weekly standards practice.

Warriner's Handbook

Warriner's Handbook features John Warriner's unrivaled approach to grammar, usage, and mechanics to ensure mastery of language skills and conventions. Warriner developed the three-step instructional approach used in the grammar, usage, and mechanics chapter: teach students the rule, show examples of the rule, and provide immediate practice and review to reinforce the skill.

Student Edition

Teacher's Edition

Language and Sentence Skills Practice worksheets provide practice, reinforcement, and extension for *Warriner's Handbook.*

Universal Access: Developmental Language and Sentence Skills supplements *Language and Sentence Skills Practice* by providing additional instruction and practice to students who have not yet mastered key language skills.

ThinkCentral, Student Access offers convenient online access to the Student Edition.

ThinkCentral, Teacher Access provides instructional resources online.

English-Language Conventions Progress-Monitoring Tests

More Reading Choices

African American Literature

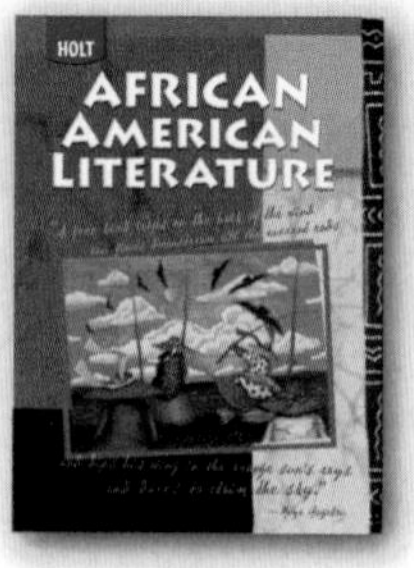

Latino Literature

Holt Multicultural Reader

Holt Leveled Library

HRW Library

Houghton Mifflin Harcourt Trade Holt, Rinehart and Winston has partnered with Houghton Mifflin Harcourt Trade to offer you additional reading options. Houghton Mifflin Harcourt Trade publishers provide high-quality, award-winning books for all ages. You will find the latest in current titles as well as beloved classics for your students and a professional library for you. For teaching materials see **www.harcourtbooks.com/ChildrenBooks/teachertools.asp**

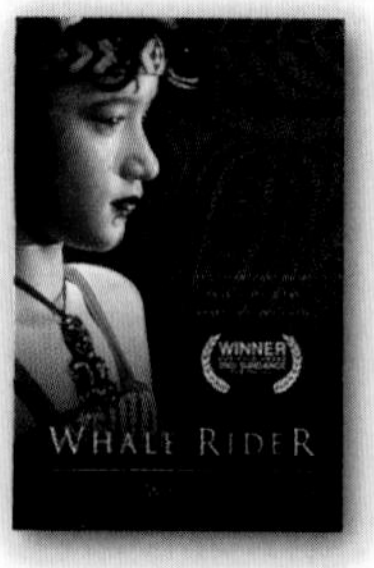

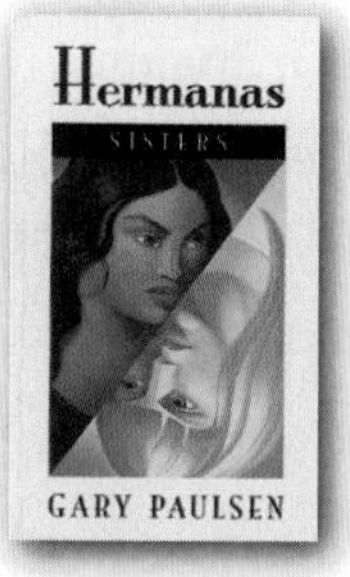

English Language Development (Grades 6–10)

This package provides one hour of daily instruction in addition to that found in the core Teacher's Edition. This instruction is connected to and consistent with the core instruction to foster student achievement in language arts. It features a balance of 1) systematic English-language instruction with strong emphasis on oral language and vocabulary development and 2) focus on language arts standards. The main goals of these materials are to build English proficiency, develop speaking and writing vocabulary for everyday and academic use, and accelerate students' transition to core curricular materials.

Newcomer Guide

- Four-week module
- Survival vocabulary and language (including obtaining necessities, making requests, and understanding instructions)
- Introduction to academic language study

Holt Interactive Reader for English Language Development (with Answer Key) Selections that form the Minimum Course of Study—with adapted text or adapted apparatus to provide additional scaffolding.

Teacher's Edition Daily lessons organized around the following strands: Build Background, Vocabulary Development, Literature and Language Study, Reading & Fluency, Writing Strategies and Applications, and Grammar and Conventions. The lessons are written to maximize student speaking and listening opportunities and to help teachers scaffold instruction for English learners.

Writing & Speaking Handbook Practice opportunities for grammar, speaking, and writing—from short writing assignments to process writing.

Holt Audio Tutor for English Language Development Audio recordings of the Minimum Course of Study selections together with side annotations; Spanish summaries and translations of annotations are also provided.

Program Resources for California Classrooms

Program Authors

from **Kylene Beers,** Senior Reading Advisor
Teachers College Reading and Writing Project
Columbia University, New York, NY

Dear Educator:

Since 2003, *Holt Literature and Language Arts* has set the benchmark for a standards-designed, not just a standards-aligned, language arts program. The achievement of California students has been significant, but there is still work to be done. To help you with that task, we have brought together a remarkable author and consultant team—people with decades of classroom experience, research experience, and expertise in helping students and teachers in diverse classrooms. We believe that in teaching all students we must first teach each student and that each student offers a promise of a better tomorrow.

Through this program, our team shares with you its collective knowledge of what works with struggling readers, English learners, students with disabilities, and those who use African American vernacular English, as well as those sometimes-overlooked populations of basic and advanced students. We contributed our time to this project because we believe that what you do and what you say to students in your classroom makes an incredible difference. We want to help you make that difference with a road map to success.

Now, please let me introduce you to the other members of our team. We are all proud to be your colleagues.

Kylene Beers

MORE ABOUT READING INSTRUCTION...

Beers, K. 2002. *When Kids Can't Read/What Teachers Can Do.* Portsmouth, NH: Heinemann.

Beers, K., R. Probst, and L. Rief, eds. 2007. *Adolescent Literacy: Turning Promise into Practice.* Portsmouth, NH: Heinemann.

Alliance for Excellent Education. 2004. *Reading Next: A Vision for Action & Research in Middle and High School Literacy.*

For more from Kylene Beers... go to thinkcentral.com.

PROGRAM AUTHORS:

Kylene Beers

Carol Jago

Deborah Appleman

Leila Christenbury

Sara Kajder

Linda Rief

Carol Jago

The book you hold now is the result of a collaborative effort of authors, consultants, editors, and classroom teachers who, together, considered the issues in language arts instruction for the twenty-first century.

As you look through the pages, you'll see the influence of Carol Jago, who constantly returned us to the backbone of this series—great literature:

"Words. Words. Words." That's all they are, yet when the words are Shakespeare's they have the power to transport readers. I want students to enjoy contemporary literature for all that it brings to their lives; but I also want them to read the classics so they can see the wine dark sea through Homer's eyes and to reflect on ways that human nature, for better and for worse, remains surprisingly constant through the ages. Great literature is a window to times and places we can never travel except on the page. With Emily Dickinson I believe that there really "is no frigate like a book to take us lands away."

Carol Jago
Teacher, Santa Monica High School, California
Director, California Reading and Literature Project, UCLA
Author, Heinemann Publishers
Board Member, National Council of Teachers of English, Los Angeles, CA

MORE ABOUT TEACHING THE CLASSICS . . .

Jago, C. 2000. *With Rigor for All: Teaching the Classics to Contemporary Students.* Portsmouth: Heinemann.

Calvino, I. 1999. *Why Read the Classics?* New York: Pantheon.

For more from Carol Jago . . . go to thinkcentral.com.

Real Issues, Real Experts

Deborah Appleman

Deborah Appleman kept us focused on why studying literature is so important. Her vision of literature instruction helped guide the entire project:

"Reading literature is one of the few school subjects that is also recreation. How, then, should teachers approach literature in ways that encourage students to both love literature and to learn from it? Although literature remains a powerful site for self-exploration, it is also an opportunity to enter textual worlds far different from one's own experiences. Our job is to teach them the critical tools that help them read closely as well as to interpret broadly."

Deborah Appleman
Professor and Chair, Educational Studies
Carlton College, Northfield, MN

MORE ABOUT TEACHING LITERATURE...

Appleman, D. 2000. *Critical Encounters in High School English.* New York: Teachers College Press.

Scholes, R. 2001. *The Crafty Reader.* New Haven: Yale University Press

For more from Deborah Appleman... go to thinkcentral.com.

Leila Christenbury

You'll note teaching tips and powerful instructional strategies that were the direct result of Leila Christenbury's efforts. Leila reminded us that great literature without effective practice of informed teachers means little...

"Even though schools are large and busy places with hundreds of students and adults interacting every day, the fact is that most teachers work alone and often feel isolated. Reaching out to other teachers, reading professional literature and going to conferences, finding and using the many resources available can open up classrooms and connect teachers to a world of effective strategies and appropriate support. This connection is crucial; the practices of informed teachers make a critical difference in student achievement."

Leila Christenbury
Professor of English Education
Virginia Commonwealth University, Richmond, VA

MORE ABOUT GOOD TEACHING...

Christenbury, L. (2006). *Making the journey: Being and becoming a teacher of English language arts.* 3rd ed. Portsmouth, NH: Heinemann.

Website: read/write/think.org

Journals: *English Journal, Voices from the Middle*

For more from Leila Christenbury... go to thinkcentral.com.

Sara Kajder

The literacy demands of the 21st century are, of course, tied to a world that is increasingly more networked, more wired, more dependent on a wide range of technology. As Sara Kajder constantly pushed us to remember,

> *"Equipping our students with 21st-century literacies means, in part, expanding the technology toolset students use as readers and writers. But that shouldn't surprise us because literacy has always been intimately tied to technology. We must teach them how to synthesize a range of texts that appear on a screen at lightning speed and communicate to authentic, global, wired audiences with the explosion of new tools, modes, and media now made readily accessible by Web 2.0."*

Sara Kajder
Assistant Professor
Virginia Polytechnic Institute and State University, Blacksburg, VA

MORE ABOUT TECHNOLOGY…

Kajder, S. 2003. *The Tech-Savvy English Classroom.* Portland, ME: Stenhouse

Alvermann, D. 2007. "Multiliterate Youth in the Time of Scientific Reading Instruction." In *Adolescent Literacy: Turning Promise into Practice* edited by K. Beers, R. Probst, and L. Rief. Portsmouth, NH: Heinemann, pp 19-26.

For more from Sara Kajder… go to thinkcentral.com.

Linda Rief

As much as I'd push us toward reading, Linda Rief would push back showing us time and again that we want students who read as a writer and write as a reader. As Linda put it,

> *"Writing, every bit as much as reading, helps our students become literate, articulate, and thoughtful citizens of the world. Reciprocal processes, both require capturing and working out meaning. When students are given opportunities to write about their reading—short, quick responses to questions—What did this reading bring to mind? What questions did it raise? How does this alter or confirm my view of the world?—our classrooms become laboratories of high-level thinking and our students become problem-solvers and producers of ideas. They move from just answering to questioning, just knowing to creating, just consuming to producing."*

Linda Rief
Instructor, University of New Hampshire
Summer Literacy Institute
Teacher, Oyster River Middle School, Durham, NH

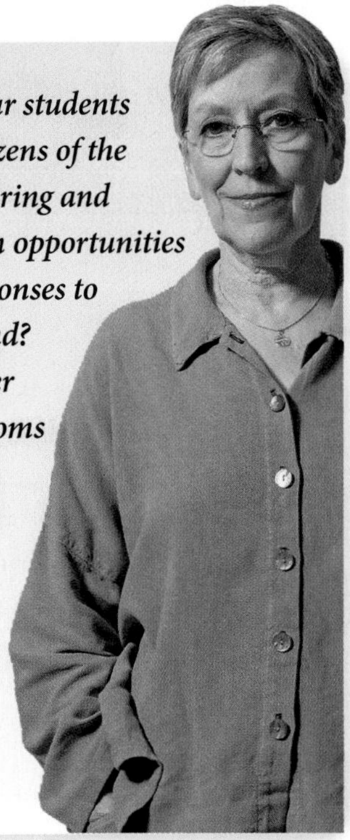

MORE ABOUT WRITING…

Rief, L. 2003. *Quickwrites.* NY: Scholastic.

Alliance for Excellent Education. 2007. *Writing Next: Effective Strategies to Improve Writing of Adolescents in Middle and High Schools.*

For more from Linda Rief… go to thinkcentral.com.

Program Consultants

Holt's program consultants come from richly varied areas of educational expertise to ensure that the program meets the disparate needs of your classroom—students who have comprehension problems or are learning English as a second language, who are visual learners, or who are disengaged. These specialists have done the research and provided the best practices to help you do the best for your students.

Comprehension

"Too many students do not leave a text with an understanding of an author's ideas. This shuts them out of rich opportunities to make contact with life lessons and human universals that literature offers, not to mention experience with the exquisite language that express such ideas."

Beck and McKeown developed an approach to comprehension called Questioning the Author that is the basis of the Read and Discuss questions in *Holt Literature and Language Arts.*

Isabel L. Beck
Professor, Department of Instruction and Learning
Senior Researcher, Learning Research and Development Center
University of Pittsburgh, PA

"Questioning the Author has been shown to be successful in supporting students to develop meaning from what they read and a coherent understanding of a text."

Students build comprehension as they read by using the sequenced questions built into *Holt Literature and Language Arts.*

Margaret McKeown
Senior Scientist, Learning Research and Development Center
University of Pittsburgh, PA

Adolescent Literacy

"For many students, the teacher is the individual most responsible for successful lives. Who can deny the power of a teacher who enables students to fall in love with learning? Academic success should be an opportunity for all, not just a gift to some."

Eric Cooper has reviewed both *Holt Literature and Language Arts* and *African American Literature.*

Eric Cooper
President for National Urban Alliance for Effective Education

For more from Real Issues, Real Experts . . . go to thinkcentral.com.

English Language Development/Academic Vocabulary

"In many cities and school districts, students who are acquiring English are the fastest growing population. Acquiring academic language, the language that is used in schools, in testing, and in scholarly discourse, is the key to success for these students."

Academic Vocabulary is introduced at the beginning of each chapter and reinforced throughout it so that students can master it.

Robin Scarcella
Director, Program in Academic English/English as a Second Language
University of California, Irvine, CA

English Language Development

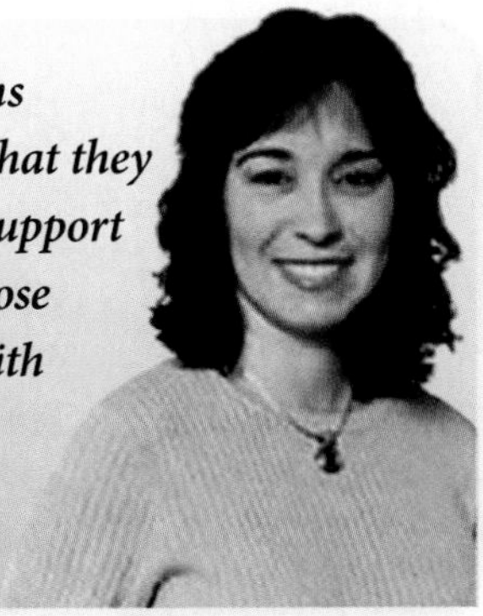

"Many students enter our classrooms without the basic skills in English that they need to be successful. We want to support teachers in meeting the needs of those students and provide a program with a literary base that is accessible to those students."

English Language Development is a program that helps students who are acquiring English to get the critical skills they need.

Mabel Rivera
Research Assistant Professor, Texas Institute for Measurement, Evaluation, and Statistics, University of Houston, TX

English Language Development

"Teaching is assisting students' performance at the Zone of Proximal Development (Tharp & Gallimore, 1988). This requires an understanding of the means for assisting students during literacy activities that are socio-culturally meaningful. My research is focused on unfolding those socio-cultural components to be used as tools for effective teaching practices."

The English Language Development Program addresses the acquisition of critical English language skills.

Hector Rivera
Assistant Professor, School of Education and Human Development
Southern Methodist University, Dallas, TX

Language-Use Instruction

"For years some educators have recognized the need to help African American vernacular English speakers gain proficiency in the use of standard English while still maintaining the undeniable "flavor and richness" of the language spoken at home."

Explicit language-use instruction is embedded throughout *Holt Literature and Language Arts* in lessons called Language Coach and Grammar Links. Notes in the Teacher's Edition extend support to meet the needs of all students.

Marianne Steverson
President and COO, Smar^{2}tel Learning Links, an educational services company

Differentiated Instruction

"When you change the way you look at your students with disabilities, the way those students look to you will change. You will see the possibilities, and in that vision, you will see the power of the inclusion."

Meeting the needs of a wide range of abilities is at the core of *Holt Literature and Language Arts,* with scaffolded instruction for the student and suggestions in the Teacher's Edition for the instructor.

Patrick Schwarz
Professor, Diversity in Learning and Development Department
National Louis University, Chicago, IL

Literature Circles

"Over the past decade, reading groups have just about doubled in the United States. For teachers trying to bring literature circles into our schools, these adult book clubs have been our implicit model—our prototype. Adult book clubs are voluntary groups of friends that create a powerful and caring community among us."

The Read On feature of *Holt Literature and Language Arts* and the *Holt Leveled Library* offer opportunities for bringing literature circles into the classroom.

Harvey Daniels
National-Louis University, Chicago, IL

For more from Real Issues, Real Experts . . . go to thinkcentral.com.

Grammar in Context

Along with diction and rhetoric, grammar is organic to the crafting of sentences and text. Writers with an awareness of grammar can make informed choices about how word order affects meaning. We can make our students better writers if we teach them to use grammatical knowledge.

The Grammar Link feature in *Holt Literature and Language Arts* offers students contextual examples drawn from the literature to help them better craft their writing.

Amy Benjamin
President of the Assembly for the Teaching of English Grammar
Consultant for National Council of Teachers
Recipient of Excellence in Teaching Awards from Tufts University and New York State English Council

Adolescent Literacy

Taking Action on Adolescent Literacy *is the title of my recently published book. It incorporates my life's work. Motivating students to engage with meaningful reading and writing in content-area classes is the key to their achievement. Improved literacy and learning must be supported by a schoolwide effort to create a literacy-rich environment for students.*

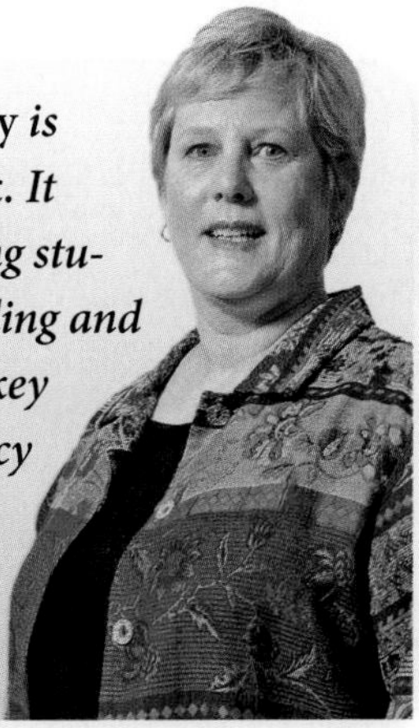

See Judith Irvin in the Professional Learning Video Reading Narrative and Expository Text.

Judith Irvin
Professor, Department of Educational Leadership and Policy
Florida State University, Tallahassee, FL

Real Issues, Real Experts

Professional Development Strategies That Work

Inspire yourself and your students with effective classroom teaching strategies

English-language arts teachers are responsible for bringing each lesson to life for their students while following the *Reading/Language Arts Framework for California Public Schools.* Holt has partnered with **Action Learning Systems** to provide professional development that includes engaging opportunities for students to establish and deepen reading comprehension skills, enhance vocabulary and concept development, and analyze the differences in text structure.

Sample Development Strategies from Action Learning Systems

Predicting with Evidence

Predicting requires students to hypothesize about what the author might discuss in the text. To hypothesize successfully, students must recall what they already know about the topic. They then read to confirm or disprove their hypotheses. This process helps students link the new information they will encounter in the reading with the information they already know. Predicting also helps students learn to use the structure of the written word. Predictions are made based on evidence from the text. Teachers model how to generate predictions based on evidence. Students need to be taught to make predictions with textual evidence.

Student Strategies for Predicting

- Access prior knowledge and experience.
- Compare what they already know with what they will learn.
- Pay close attention to whether the text is narrative or expository to see if their predictions are verified.

How to Teach It

PREPARATION

- Use a picture from the selection.

IN CLASS

- Ask, "What do you think this story is going to be about? What is your evidence?"
- Have students study the picture and write their predictions in the **Prediction** column and their evidence in the **Evidence** column.
- Ask students to share predictions and evidence with a partner. Have several share with the class.
- As students read the selection, they will continue to make predictions. Students will modify and confirm their predictions by citing textual evidence.

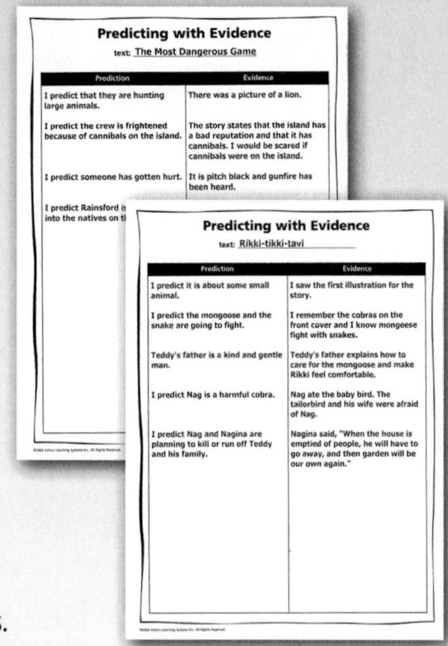

Predicting with Evidence

text: The Most Dangerous Game

Prediction	Evidence
I predict that they are hunting large animals.	There was a picture of a lion.
I predict the crew is frightened because of cannibals on the island.	The story states that the island has a bad reputation and that it has cannibals. I would be scared if cannibals were on the island.
I predict someone has gotten hurt.	It is pitch black and gunfire has been heard.
I predict Rainsford is [illegible] into the natives on t[illegible]	

Predicting with Evidence

text: Rikki-tikki-tavi

Prediction	Evidence
I predict it is about some small animal.	I saw the first illustration for the story.
I predict the mongoose and the snake are going to fight.	I remember the cobras on the front cover and I know mongeese fight with snakes.
Teddy's father is a kind and gentle man.	Teddy's father explains how to care for the mongoose and make Rikki feel comfortable.
I predict Nag is a harmful cobra.	Nag ate the baby bird. The tailorbird and his wife were afraid of Nag.
I predict Nag and Nagina are planning to kill or run off Teddy and his family.	Nagina said, "When the house is emptied of people, he will have to go away, and then garden will be our own again."

Budget Vocabulary

Budget Vocabulary is a strategy that provides continuous focus on vocabulary, especially for selections in which knowledge of vocabulary is critical for reading comprehension. The matrix can be used as a prereading activity for literary or expository text. The strategy leads to a deeper understanding of word meaning.

How to Teach It

- For the **Word** section, the teacher provides the words.
- The teacher can give the students the **Definition** or ask them to use their dictionary skills to obtain the formal definition of the word.
- For the **Related Words** section, students will use synonyms, antonyms, or words that are related by content or word structure.
- For the **Sentence** section, the teacher will specify that the sentences should be copied from the selection in which the word is introduced or used. The **Sentence** section can be used as an opportunity for students to create their own sentences to show an understanding of the word's meaning.
- The teacher will have students complete the **Visual** section and create an illustration to show their understanding of the word.

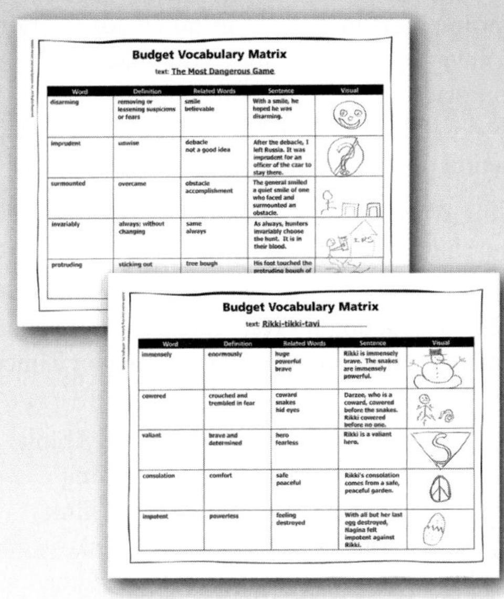

Budget Vocabulary Matrix

text: The Most Dangerous Game

Word	Definition	Related Words	Sentence	Visual
disarming	removing or lessening suspicions or fears	smile believable	With a smile, he hoped he was disarming.	
imprudent	unwise	debacle not a good idea	After the debacle, I left Russia. It was imprudent for an officer of the czar to stay there.	
surmounted	overcame	obstacle accomplishment	The general smiled a quiet smile of one who faced and surmounted an obstacle.	
invariably	always; without changing	same always	As always, hunters invariably choose the hunt. It is in their blood.	
protruding	sticking out	tree bough	His foot touched the protruding bough of	

Budget Vocabulary Matrix

text: Rikki-tikki-tavi

Word	Definition	Related Words	Sentence	Visual
immensely	enormously	huge powerful brave	Rikki is immensely brave. The snakes are immensely powerful.	
cowered	crouched and trembled in fear	coward snakes hid eyes	Darzee, who is a coward, cowered before the snakes. Rikki cowered before no one.	
valiant	brave and determined	hero fearless	Rikki is a valiant hero.	
consolation	comfort	safe peaceful	Rikki's consolation comes from a safe, peaceful garden.	
impotent	powerless	feeling destroyed	With all but her last egg destroyed, Nagina felt impotent against Rikki.	

Action Learning Systems, Inc.™

Action Learning Systems helps schools and districts focus on—and meet—their ultimate goal of increasing student achievement by offering research-based teaching strategies, training and coaching, and intervention programs. Action Learning Systems and Holt, Rinehart and Winston are working in partnership to provide exceptional professional development services to California schools.

You may download blackline masters of these instructional strategies at www.actionlearningsystems.com. Just click "Resources."

Writing Instruction in *Holt Literature and Language Arts*

Preparing Your Students for Writing Success

More than ever before, today's students need to know how to write for varied contexts and purposes: for success in academic settings, for personal expression, for interpersonal communication, for emerging digital environments, and for communication in the workplace. In *Holt Literature and Language Arts,* you will find consistent and accessible writing instruction that makes success in writing possible:

- Writing Workshops that follow a writing-process approach to developing standards-based forms of writing
- strategy instruction for responding to on-demand, or timed, writing prompts in Preparing for Timed Writing
- opportunities to observe writer's craft in Think as a Reader/Writer: Find It in Your Reading and to use elements of writer's craft in Think as a Reader/Writer: Use It in Your Writing—exemplifying the reciprocal nature of reading and writing
- professional models in each Writing Workshop to reinforce the Think as a Reader/Writer instructional strand
- in the Writing Workshops, student drafts with accompanying focused revision instruction that make revision tangible and accessible to your students
- standards-specific scoring rubrics that present the attributes of standards-based writing, incorporating the academic language students can use to discuss their own writing or provide feedback to their peers
- Timed Writing activities for writing about informational texts

An Overview of the Writing Process

The Writing Workshops in *Holt Literature and Language Arts* consistently follow a four-part writing process that guides students through the planning and development of a piece of writing.

- **Prewriting** shows students how to plan a piece of writing so that it addresses their purpose and audience. Prewriting includes strategies and graphic organizers for finding and narrowing topics, gathering information and ideas about a topic, organizing ideas and information, thinking about purpose and audience, and writing thesis statements. Prewriting also includes opportunities for peer feedback on what students are planning.
- **Drafting** guides students through organizing and shaping their composition within the structure posed by their purpose and audience. A framework provides an organizational snapshot of the type of writing students are drafting, and a Grammar Link highlights a grammatical concept central to that type of writing.
- **Evaluating and Revising** shows students how to refine and re-visit their drafts, using peer and teacher feedback. Specific, standards-based criteria provide direction for evaluating and revising the form of writing. Targeted revision lessons focus on the analysis of realistic student drafts, followed by students' application of the same revision instruction to their own writing.
- **Proofreading and Publishing** shows students how to proofread, or edit, for language conventions, using peer feedback. Proofreading is supported by an additional Grammar Link that targets common problems. Creative and appropriate publishing suggestions encourage accountability in writing for real audiences. The Writing Workshop concludes with Reflect on Your Writing, a metacognitive activity that guides students to consider what they have learned and what they can apply to other writing situations.

Providing Feedback on Students' Writing

Responding to students' writing in a timely way can be a challenge for even the most seasoned teacher. With multiple classes generating papers, the stacks can begin to mount to the ceiling. In her book *Papers, Papers, Papers* (Portsmouth, NH: Heinemann, 2005), *Holt Literature and Language Arts* author Carol Jago suggests some strategies you can use to provide focused, timely feedback to students:

- **Articulate the criteria for a writing assignment to your students *before* they write.** Then, respond to their papers with those criteria in mind. As you review your students' work, note errors or misunderstandings that crop up frequently across the class's work and target follow-up instruction to address those issues.
- **Link your comments on a current piece of writing to previous pieces students have written.** Point out individual improvements you notice as well as provide support for areas that need improvement. Your students will become aware of their own writing growth because you are commenting on it.
- **Stagger the writing assignments you give to different classes.** In this way, you will receive students' writing in manageable chunks rather than in a tidal wave. You can then budget your time to respond promptly to each class or group of students. This will give you a better chance of providing feedback in a time frame that will have an effect on student writing.
- **Determine which papers you will read.** You will likely have your students do a variety of writing in your classroom, from responses to QuickWrite activities to Choices activities to Writing Workshop compositions. Given the volume, you will find it challenging (if not impossible) to read every word they generate. Decide which writing assignments you will concentrate on to ensure that your students are mastering the writing strategies and applications standards. For example, you may choose to focus on your students' persuasive essays, rather than on their QuickWrite or What Do You Think Now? responses to a text.
- **Give your students an opportunity to provide feedback to each other.** Peer review is a strategy that enables students to see their writing as others see it, while also building accountability for providing responsible and constructive feedback. Peer-review partners or small groups can work together to improve each other's writing by using direct questions, such as, "Do you think I have enough supporting evidence?" or, "Is the title effective?" The Evaluating and Revising Guidelines in the Writing Workshops provide specific criteria for each type of writing. Students can use these guidelines as they work with their peers.

Routines *for* California Classrooms

Good habits pave the path to success. What good habits, or routines, might be put in place in California classrooms to encourage and increase academic success?

Some routines are for classroom management. The teacher who sounds a wind chime or flickers the lights to signal students to quiet down is using a classroom management routine. Other routines—academic routines—help students develop the cognitive habits that encourage academic success. For example, when you use a warm-up, you practice an academic routine in your classroom.

Twelve teacher-created and classroom-tested academic routines follow. You know your students best, so decisions about which routines to utilize and at what times are best left to you. Variations on the routines are included to provide you with options for implementation and instruction. Use the Key Questions that follow to decide on the routines best suited to your students' needs. Note that these routines promote the instructional conversations that lead to academic success for a range of students.

Key Questions

Use the questions in the right-hand column as guides for selecting, implementing, and adapting routines most appropriate for your classroom.

FOR SELECTING A ROUTINE

- Which routine will best enable my students to develop a habit that will help them be successful?
- Will I feel comfortable leading the routine on a regular basis throughout the school year?

FOR IMPLEMENTING A ROUTINE

- How will I model the routine? How often will I need to model the routine? How will the routine change (if at all) as I change instruction from standard to standard?
- What cues will I use to signal to my students that it is time to move into and out of the routine?
- What signs should I watch for in students to signal to me that they have taken ownership of the routine?
- How will I know when a routine is effective for my students?

FOR ADAPTING A ROUTINE

- Which parts of the routine are difficult for my students? Which parts are easy for them?
- How can I alter the procedure to help my students make the routine a habit? *Hint: To avoid confusion, try not to change too many parts of the routine at once.*
- Would adding or substituting a different routine help me move my students closer to academic success?

1 Activating Academic Vocabulary

WHAT IS IT?

Academic Vocabulary is the language successful readers and writers use to communicate their ideas within and across content areas. It is the language of learning and assessment. **Activating Academic Vocabulary** is the teacher's conscious and frequent use of these vocabulary words. The teacher should establish a routine in which students regularly use Academic Vocabulary in writing and speaking about the texts they are reading.

HOW DOES IT WORK?

- Teacher provides a list of Academic Vocabulary terms and definitions. (Each chapter in *Holt Literature and Language Arts* focuses on several Academic Vocabulary words that are emphasized and practiced throughout the chapter.)
- Teacher models the appropriate context and usage of each word in class discussion, instruction, and assessment.
- Students use the Academic Vocabulary words in oral discussion, written responses, and assessments.

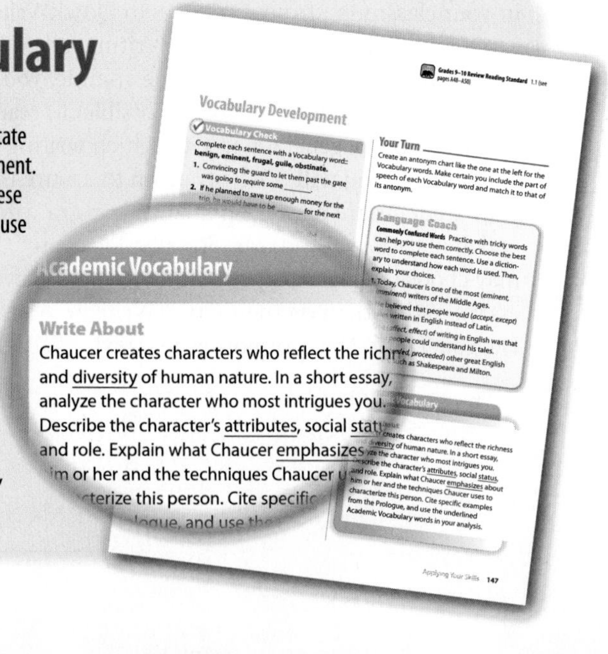

2 Three Before Me

WHAT IS IT?

Three Before Me is a routine that uses a collaborative format to improve editing in student writing.

HOW DOES IT WORK?

- Each student prepares and edits a piece of writing to bring it to final form.
- Each student asks three other students to edit his or her writing before it goes to the teacher. Students can be asked to read for one kind of error at a time or to edit the entire paper.
- Each student writer is responsible for evaluating editing suggestions and making appropriate edits to his or her writing before turning it in to the teacher.

3 Silent Sustained Reading

WHAT IS IT?

Silent Sustained Reading is a routine that extends learning time for all students by promoting independent reading for 30 minutes a day. SSR activates the positive effects of increased reading practice, including improved vocabulary acquisition, expanded background knowledge, better fluency, and contextualized practice of comprehension skills.

HOW DOES IT WORK?

- Teacher establishes a daily routine for a reading requirement of 30 minutes.
- Teacher models choosing a book appropriate for reading level and individual interests.
- Teacher institutes a chart on which students may record title, date, and number of pages read. (The *Reader/ Writer Notebook* includes a chart for this purpose.)

HINT: The clock icon accompanying For Independent Reading (with author biographies) and Read On (at the end of a chapter) signals suggestions for students' reading.

VARIATION: The Silent Sustained Reading routine may be required as homework or used in classrooms. Teachers may ask students to record new vocabulary words, respond to questions, and/or provide an oral or written summary of their reading. When reading is assigned for homework, teachers may also require parent or guardian signatures for verfication. Teachers may also use summer reading lists and community resources to further promote this routine.

4 Sticky Note Peer Review

WHAT IS IT?

Sticky Note Peer Review is a partner or small-group activity used to facilitate constructive feedback for student writing, using sticky notes.

HOW DOES IT WORK?

- In pairs or small groups, students provide constructive feedback to their peers.
- As each student in turn reads his or her paper, the other students listen, recording specific feedback on sticky notes.
- Listeners record specific words or phrases that they *liked* and that were *effective* in their classmate's piece of writing.
- On additional sticky notes, listeners record *questions* that they have about the text—especially about the need for additional information.
- On sticky notes, listeners write *suggestions* for the writer.
- It is important for students to keep each purpose separate by writing *positive* comments on one sticky note, *suggestions* on another note, and *questions* on a third note.
- Students initial their sticky notes, giving them to the writer to use for revision.
- The routine is repeated until each student has written constructive feedback for use in revision.

VARIATION: Students may use strips of paper or note cards to record their feedback.

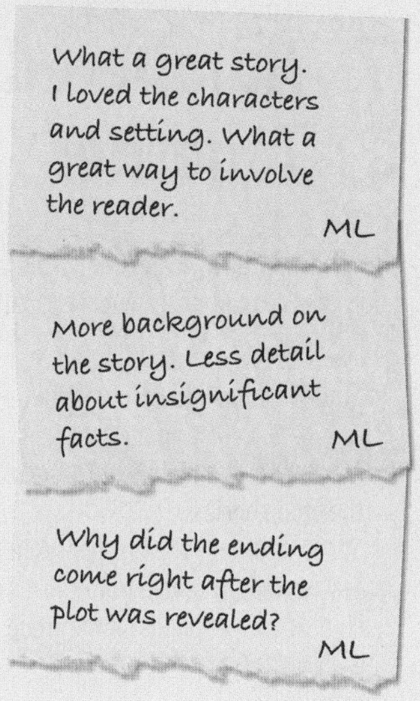

5 Think-Pair-Share

WHAT IS IT?

Think-Pair-Share is a paired student activity to promote individual accountability and collaborative thinking as preparation for class discussion.

HOW DOES IT WORK?

- Teacher poses a question to the class.
- Students think about the question individually, making notes.
- Each student partners with another student to listen,discuss, and formulate a shared response.
- Teacher calls on each or a selected student to respond to the entire class.

VARIATION: After creating a response, students in a pair may work with another pair to reach consensus before responding.

6 Pinwheel Discussion

WHAT IS IT?

Pinwheel Discussion is a group format designed to increase participation, accountability, and cooperation within small discussion groups.

HOW DOES IT WORK?

- In groups of eight, four students are seated facing in; four students are seated facing out.
- Students in the inner circle remain stationary throughout the discussion.
- Students in the outer circle move to their right after discussing each question.
- Teacher controls discussion by providing a question for each rotation.

VARIATION: Form groups of fewer than eight members as appropriate, keeping an even number of students. With a group of six, for example, three students would face in and three would face out.

7 Numbered Heads Together

WHAT IS IT?

Numbered Heads Together is a discussion format that increases individual accountability and participation within group discussions.

HOW DOES IT WORK?

- Students form into groups of four and then number off 1 – 2 – 3 – 4 within the group.
- Teacher poses a higher-order discussion question to the group or class.
- Students discuss their responses in their groups.
- Teacher calls a number from 1 to 4. That "numbered" student then responds for the group.

VARIATION: Since classrooms will be comprised of several groups, allow groups to give themselves a name such as "Bobcats" to identify their group. Teacher then calls on Bobcat #4.

HINT: Depending on how effectively a group works together, you may wish to keep the group intact for several weeks before changing its membership.

8 Three-Minute Review

WHAT IS IT?

Three-Minute Review is a routine to enhance individual accountability, active engagement, comprehension, and long-term retention of information.

HOW DOES IT WORK?

- Teacher pauses at any time during reading, lecture, or discussion.
- Teacher directs students to work independently.
- Teacher sets timer for three minutes.
- For three minutes, students re-read material, review class notes, and write clarifying questions.
- Teacher may ask, "What did you notice in your review?" or may solicit clarifying questions from student volunteers. Brief discussion and clarification follow.

VARIATION: Teacher may pose a question to guide the three-minute review period, or may direct students to write clarifying questions to be handed in. Students may also work in pairs or triads.

9 Send a Problem

WHAT IS IT?

Send a Problem is a method for keeping the pace of discussion moving in the classroom by sharing accountability among students. This routine enhances listening skills and participation.

HOW DOES IT WORK?

- Teacher poses a question during discussion and calls on a student to respond.
- Teacher waits up to 11 seconds.
- If student does not have a response, student must call on another student by name to answer the same question.
- The sending student repeats the question as he or she calls on another for assistance.
- Teacher monitors responses and can redirect or ask another question at any time.

VARIATION: If listening is a challenge for some students in your classroom, change the format to have the second student repeat the question before answering. Provide bonus points for every remembered question.

10 Jigsaw with Experts

WHAT IS IT?

Jigsaw with Experts is a collaborative approach to reading especially lengthy or difficult reading assignments.

HOW DOES IT WORK?

- Teacher divides a long or challenging reading assignment into parts—not to exceed six parts.
- Students are either assigned to or count off to match a numbered reading section.
- Students read and take notes on their section of the reading.
- Students get in small groups of three to four classmates who were assigned the same section.
- This group of "experts" discusses their section for a designated period of time, depending on the length and difficulty of the reading.
- Students then form new groups that include one representative for each section of the divided reading.
- Students discuss their respective sections and the whole piece of text for a designated amount of time.

VARIATION: Teacher may then conduct a class discussion and/or assign the entire text to be read by each student. Discussion will provide valuable background knowledge for reading the text as a whole.

11 Double-Entry Journal

WHAT IS IT?

Double-Entry Journal is a routine approach to notetaking during reading. It may be used for either in-class or independent reading. Sometimes called dialectic notetaking, a Double-Entry Journal enhances students' metacognitive skills and increases comprehension of material by having the student conduct a dialogue or conversation with the text. Individual accountability and inquiry are improved. The importance of text evidence becomes apparent in this routine.

HOW DOES IT WORK?

- Students use a notebook or journal for recording Double-Entry Journal notes. This notebook can be spiral or loose-leaf.
- Teacher models the structure of the two-column format. Each page is divided down the middle by drawing a line from top to bottom. The heading on the left side of the page is *Quotes from the Text,* and the heading on the right side is *My Notes*.
- Students record significant, important, or perplexing text passages in the left column.
- Students write their own interpretations, summaries, questions, and restatements in the right column, opposite the quoted material.

VARIATION: Teachers may provide students with a list of stems for use in the right column. Individual students may create a triple-entry journal with another student by exchanging their double-entry journals. Each student draws a line under his or her notes, and passes the journal to a partner who then responds to his or her notes.

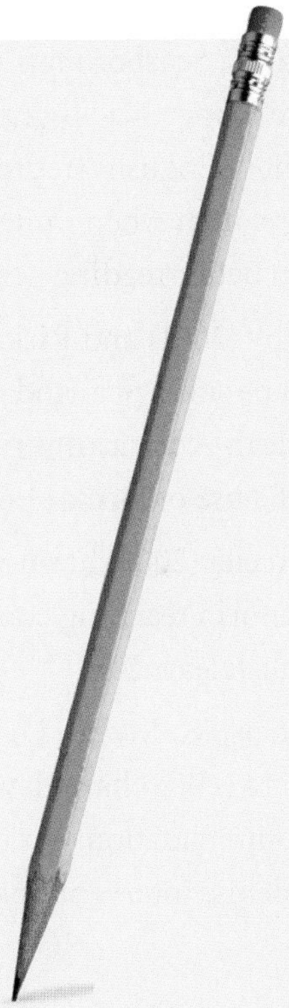

12 Reciprocal Teaching

WHAT IS IT?

Reciprocal Teaching is a method of increasing student accountability and collaborative thinking about a specific topic.

HOW DOES IT WORK?

- Teacher presents a brief lecture, facilitates a whole class discussion of a topic, or provides a reading assignment.
- Teacher presents students with a list of generic question stems.
- Students work independently to write three to five questions about the material, using the stems.
- Students do not have to be able to answer the questions they write.
- Students are grouped into learning teams of up to three students.
- Each student offers at least two questions for group discussion without duplicating another student's questions.
- Group reaches consensus on the answer to each question and finds text evidence to support it.

VARIATION: Teachers may allow students from each learning group to share their best question with the entire class. Class discussion may follow. A variety of question stems can be used to practice the instructional standards.

Linguistic Considerations for Instruction in Reading/Language Arts

Research Informing Instruction

In recent years, researchers, linguists, and educators have drawn attention to the relationship of linguistic considerations and instruction in Reading/Language Arts. Of particular interest are the acquisition and/or mastery of standard academic English as a bridge to high levels of student achievement.

- Charity, Scarborough, and Griffin (2004) have found that "higher familiarity with SE [School English] (reproducing SE features more often when imitating) was associated with better reading achievement."
- Labov (2001) and Rickford (1999) have identified phonological and grammatical features of African American vernacular English that relate to the use of formal English in academic settings.
- Scarcella (2003) has used research findings to inform teaching considerations for English learners.
- Francis, M. Rivera, Lesaux, Kieffer, and H. Rivera (2006) have developed research-based recommendations for instruction and academic interventions for English learners.

Drawing from these and other research-based recommendations, Chapter 9 of the *Reading/Language Arts Framework for California Public Schools*, "Criteria for Evaluating Instructional Materials: Kindergarten Through Grade Eight," specifies that "teacher editions must include the following features" (page 316):

"**19.** The teacher edition clearly references, explains, and provides the location of additional instructional materials and program components designed to provide extra support for students who require it (e.g., English learners, students who use African American vernacular English, struggling readers, and students with disabilities)." (page 317)

"**21.** All suggestions and procedures for meeting the instructional needs of all students are ready to use with minimum modifications to facilitate the program supporting scaffolded instruction for English learners, students with disabilities, struggling readers, and students who use African American vernacular English and providing teachers with guidance on scaffolding instruction." (page 317)

"**22.** The program provides a linguistic, contrastive analysis chart in the teacher edition that shows and explains how new or difficult sounds and features of the English language are taught and reinforced. Comparisons with the five (or more) of the most common languages in California and African American vernacular English will be incorporated as appropriate, accentuating transferable and nontransferable skills." (page 318)

How Does HLLA Address Linguistic Considerations for Instruction?

Educators using the Teacher's Edition of *Holt Literature and Language Arts* (HLLA) may have questions about the instructional support provided for English learners and students who use African American vernacular English, such as the following:

QUESTION: Why does the Teacher's Edition stress the linguistic needs of English learners and of students who use African American vernacular English?

ANSWER: Recent research-based recommendations support instruction in academic or school English (also referred to as formal English) as a pathway to academic success. The Evaluation Criteria of the *Reading/Language Arts Framework* incorporate these research-based recommendations to support teachers in effectively addressing the needs of students in these two groups who may require additional support.

QUESTION: What does this mean for students' home languages?

ANSWER: Instructional support in the Teacher's Edition is aimed at improving students' success in academic settings. At the same time, any instruction must respect students' home languages and cultures. Teachers can guide students to understand the context: that there are differences between the informal English used in conversational or home settings and the formal English used in school or workplace settings. Knowing how and when to use informal or formal English is an important skill for students in school and in the workplace.

QUESTION: How will teachers know when the Teacher's Edition includes linguistic suggestions for instruction?

ANSWER: Teachers will find instructional support for English learners and students who use African American vernacular English in the following locations:

- In the side wrap, the head **English for Academic Success** signals instructional support that focuses on the use of academic vocabulary and language.
- In the bottom wrap, the feature "Universal Access" provides scaffolding for adapting the core lesson to students' instructional needs. Point-of-use references to additional program resources are also included.
- In the side and bottom wrap, the English learner icon EL and the AAVE icon AAVE signal instruction designed to provide extra support for students who may require it.
- The following pages, T40–T47, present two charts: one, a Linguistic, Contrastive Analysis chart, and two, a chart that identifies phonological and grammatical features of African American vernacular English. These charts can help teachers identify areas of focus for instruction in academic or formal English.

Works Cited

Charity, Anne H., Hollis S. Scarborough, and Darion M. Griffin. "Familiarity with School English in African American Children and Its Relation to Early Reading Achievement." *Child Development 75* (2004): 1340-1356.

Francis, David J., Mabel Rivera, Nonie Lesaux, Michael Kieffer, and Hector Rivera. *Research-Based Recommendations for Instruction and Academic Interventions: Practical Guidelines for the Education of English Language Learners.* Houston: Center on Instruction, 2006.

Labov, William. "Applying Our Knowledge of African American English to the Problem of Raising Reading Levels in Inner-city Schools." *Sociocultural and Historical Contexts of African American English.* Ed. Sonja Lanehart. Philadelphia: Benjamins, 2001. 299-318.

Rickford, John. *African American Vernacular English: Features, Evolution, and Educational Implications.* Oxford: Blackwell, 1999.

Scarcella, Robin. *Accelerating Academic English: A Focus on the English Learner.* Oakland, CA: Regents of the University of California, 2003.

Linguistic, Contrastive Analysis

EL

The Linguistic, Contrastive Analysis chart identifies English sounds and grammatical structures that will or will not pose difficulty for users of languages other than English. Examples of how the sounds transfer or do not transfer from English to students' primary languages are included.

Phonological Features

ENGLISH	SPANISH	VIETNAMESE	CANTONESE OR MANDARIN
INITIAL CONSONANTS			
/f/ **f**an	Little difficulty.	/b/ **b**an	Little difficulty.
/v/ **v**an	/b/, /f/ **b**an, **f**an (Note: Spanish has only one sound for /b/ and /v/.)	Little difficulty.	/w/ **w**an
/th/ **th**ough	Little difficulty.	/d/ **d**oe	/d/ **d**oe (Note: /th/ does not exist.)
/th/ **th**ink	/d/ **d**ink	/d/, /z/ **d**ink, **z**ink	/d/ **d**ink
/sh/ **sh**eet	/ch/ **ch**eat (Note: /sh/ does not exist.)	/s/, /ch/ **s**eat, **ch**eat	/s/ **s**eat
/j/ **j**ar	/h/, /y/ **h**ar, **y**ar	/z/ **z**ar	Little difficulty.
/y/ **y**es	/j/ **j**es	Little difficulty.	Little difficulty.
/h/ **h**ouse	The nearest sound to /h/ in Spanish sounds like the *ch* in *Bach*.	Little difficulty.	The nearest sound to /h/ sounds like the *ch* in *Bach*.
/n/ **n**eed	Little difficulty.	Little difficulty.	/l/ **l**ead
/r/ **r**ock	/r/ rolled or trilled **R**ock	Little difficulty.	/l/ **l**ock (Note: Many speakers find /l/ and /r/ difficult to distinguish.)
/s/ **s**tudent	add /e/ before /s/ **es**tudent	Little difficulty.	Little difficulty.
/z/ **z**oo	/s/ **s**ue (Note: Initial /z/ does not exist.)	Little difficulty.	/s/ **s**ue (Note: /z/ does not exist.)
/p/, /t/, /k/ **p**ot, **t**ot, **c**ot	/b/, /d/, /g/ **b**ot, **d**ot, **g**ot	Initial /t/ in Vietnamese sounds like /d/: **d**ot.	Little difficulty.
/b/, /d/, /g/ **b**et, **d**ebt, **g**et	Initial /b/ is sometimes replaced with /v/: **v**et.	Little difficulty.	/p/, /t/, /k/ **p**et, **t**et, **k**et
MEDIAL CONSONANTS			
/zh/ mea**s**ure	/z/ me**z**ure	Little difficulty.	/z/, /sh/ me**z**ure, mea**sh**ure
/r/ ho**rr**ible	/rr/ rolled or trilled ho**R**rible	Little difficulty.	/l/ ho**l**ible

PILIPINO OR TAGALOG	HMONG	KOREAN
/p/ **p**an	/p/ **p**an	/p/ **p**an
Little difficulty.	Little difficulty.	/w/, /b/ **w**an, **b**an
/b/, /f/ **b**ow, **f**oe	/d/ **d**oe	(Note: /th/ does not exist.)
/d/ **d**ink	/d/ **d**ink	/s/ **s**ink
Little difficulty.	Little difficulty.	Little difficulty.
/y/ **y**ar	Little difficulty.	/zh/ as in rou**ge**
Little difficulty.	Little difficulty.	Little difficulty.
Little difficulty.	Little difficulty.	Little difficulty.
Little difficulty.	Little difficulty.	Little difficulty.
Little difficulty.	Little difficulty.	/l/ **l**ock (Note: /r/ does not exist.)
Little difficulty.	Little difficulty.	/sh/ **sh**tudent
/s/ **s**ue	/s/ **s**ue	/j/, /ch/ **ch**oo
/b/, /d/, /g/ **b**ot, **d**ot, **g**ot	Little difficulty.	/p/ may be replaced by /f/: **f**ought.
Little difficulty.	Little difficulty.	/b/ may be replaced by /v/: **v**et.
/z/ me**z**ure	Little difficulty.	/z/, /sh/ me**z**ure, mea**sh**ure
Little difficulty.	Little difficulty.	/l/ ho**l**ible

ENGLISH	SPANISH	VIETNAMESE	CANTONESE OR MANDARIN
FINAL CONSONANTS			
/p/, /k/, /t/ ti**p,** si**ck,** si**t**	Little difficulty.	Little difficulty.	Often dropped or replaced with a schwa sound. (Note: there are few final consonants.)
/s/ after consonant cat**s,** hat**s**	Little difficulty.	Not used in Vietnamese.	Little difficulty.
/v/ love	Usually no difficulty, but may be replaced with /b/ : lu**b**	/b/, /p/ lu**b,** lu**p**	Often deleted.
/j/ e**dg**e	/ch/ e**tch**	Often deleted.	Little difficulty.
/m/ drea**m**	/n/, /ng/ drea**n,** drea**ng**	Little difficulty.	Little difficulty.
/ng/ thi**ng**	/n/ thi**n**	Little difficulty.	/n/ thi**n**
VOWELS			
/ee/ sh**ee**p	Little difficulty.	Little difficulty.	Little difficulty.
/ih/ l**i**p	/ee/ l**ea**p	/ee/ l**ea**p	Little difficulty.
/ay/ r**ai**d	Often substitute /e/: r**e**d.	Little difficulty.	Little difficulty.
/e/ b**e**t	/ay/ b**ai**t	/a/ b**a**t	Vowel sounds might vary as a function of the surrounding consonant sounds.
/a/ c**a**t	/ah/ c**o**t	/ah/ c**o**t	/a/ does not exist; c**o**t, K**a**te, k**e**t, c**u**t. Learners might nasalize or replace with /ah/: c**o**t, /e/:b**e**t, or /u/: c**u**p. Most frequently substitute /a/ with /eh/.
/ah/ cl**o**ck	/oh/ cl**oa**k	Little difficulty.	Little difficulty.
/ah/ **a**bove	Does not exist. Often replaced by another vowel.	Little difficulty.	Does not exist. Often replaced by another vowel.
/u/ c**u**p	/ah/, /oo/ c**o**p, c**oo**p	Little difficulty.	/ah/ c**o**p
/oh/ b**oa**t	Little difficulty.	Little difficulty.	Little difficulty.
/u/ p**u**ll	/oo/ p**oo**l	/oo/ p**oo**l	/oo/ p**oo**l
/oo/ p**oo**l	Little difficulty.	Little difficulty.	Little difficulty.

	PILIPINO OR TAGALOG	HMONG	KOREAN
	Little difficulty.	/b/, /d/, /g/ ti**b**, si**d**, si**g**	Often dropped or replaced with a schwa sound. (Note: there are few final consonants.)
	Little difficulty.	Little difficulty.	Little difficulty.
	Little difficulty.	Often deleted.	Little difficulty, but may be replaced by /b/: lu**b**.
	/eh/ added at end e**dgeh**	Little difficulty.	/eh/ added at end e**dgeh**
	Little difficulty.	Little difficulty.	Little difficulty.
	/n/ thi**n**	/n/ thi**n**	/n/ thi**n**
	Little difficulty.	Little difficulty.	Little difficulty.
	/ee/ **lea**p	Little difficulty.	/ee/ **lea**p
	Little difficulty.	Little difficulty.	/eh/ r**e**d
	/ay/ b**ai**t	Little difficulty.	/ee/ b**ea**t
	/ah/ c**o**t	/ah/ c**o**t	Little difficulty.
	/oh/ cl**oa**k	Little difficulty.	/oh/ cl**oa**k (There are no long-short vowel distinctions in Korean.)
	Does not exist. Often replaced by another vowel.	Does not exist. Often replaced by another vowel.	Does not exist. Often replaced by another vowel.
	/ah/ c**o**p	Little difficulty.	/ah/ c**o**p
	Little difficulty.	/aw/ b**ou**ght	Little difficulty.
	/oo/ p**oo**l	Little difficulty.	Little difficulty.
	Little difficulty.	Little difficulty.	Little difficulty.

Grammatical Features

GRAMMAR POINT	SPANISH	VIETNAMESE	CANTONESE OR MANDARIN	PILIPINO OR TAGALOG	HMONG	KOREAN
VOWELS						
Plural Forms Nouns do not change form to show the plural in the primary language, or plurals are not used in the same way.		✔	✔		✔	✔
Possessive Forms Prepositions are either inferred or are not formed in the same way as English.	✔	✔	✔	✔	✔	✔
The word order in the primary language is different.	✔	✔	✔	✔	✔	✔
Count vs. Noncount Nouns that are count and noncount differ between English and primary language.	✔	✔	✔	✔	✔	✔
ARTICLES						
Articles are lacking, or the distinction between *a* and *the* is not paralleled in the primary language.		✔	✔	✔	✔	✔
Learners sometimes confuse the articles *a/an* with *one* since articles either do not exist in the primary language or serve a different function.		✔			✔	
PRONOUNS						
Gender of Personal Pronouns The third-person pronoun in the primary language is gender-free. The same pronoun is used where English uses masculine, feminine, and neuter pronouns, resulting in confusion of pronoun forms in English.			✔	✔	✔	
Personal Pronoun Forms The same pronoun form is used for *he/him* and *she/her,* and in some primary languages, for *I/me* and *we/us.*			✔		✔	
There is no number agreement in the primary language. In Vietnamese, plurality is never expressed.		✔	✔			
Subject pronouns may be dropped in the primary language, the verb ending supplying information on number and/or gender.	✔					
Direct objects are frequently dropped in the primary language.		✔				
A subordinate clause at the beginning of a sentence does not require a subject in the primary language.		✔	✔			✔
The redundant structure of using pronouns with subject nouns reflects "topic-comment" approach used in the primary language: The speaker mentions a topic and then makes a comment on it.	✔	✔	✔		✔	✔
It is common in the primary language to repeat nouns rather than to use pronouns.		✔	✔			✔
Possessive Forms Speakers tend to omit final *n,* creating confusion between *my* and *mine.*		✔	✔		✔	✔
VERBS						
Subject-Verb Agreement There is no subject-verb agreement in the primary language.		✔	✔	✔	✔	✔
Tense Verb forms do not change to indicate tense, or time is understood from context.		✔	✔	✔	✔	✔
Past Tense Speakers of the primary language have difficulty recognizing that a vowel shift in the middle of the verb, rather than a change in the ending of the verb, is sufficient to produce a change of tense in irregular verbs.	✔	✔	✔		✔	✔
In Negative Statements Helping verbs are not used in negative statements in the primary language.	✔		✔	✔		
Verb Tense The verb form either doesn't exist in the primary language or has a different function. Vietnamese, Hmong, Cantonese, and Mandarin do not use verbs to express time.		✔	✔	✔	✔	✔
Past Continuous In the primary language, the past continuous form can be used in contexts in which English uses the expression *used to* or the simple past.	✔			✔		
Verb as a Noun Unlike English, Cantonese does not require an infinitive marker when using a verb as a noun.			✔			
In Hmong, verbs can be connected without *and* or any other conjunction (serial verbs).					✔	

GRAMMAR POINT	SPANISH	VIETNAMESE	CANTONESE OR MANDARIN	PILIPINO OR TAGALOG	HMONG	KOREAN
VERBS CONTINUED						
Linking Verbs The verb *be* is not required in all sentences. In some primary languages, it is implied in the adjective form. In others, the concept is expressed as a verb.		✔	✔		✔	✔
Passive Voice Passive voice in the primary language does not require a helping verb.		✔	✔			✔
Transitive Verbs vs. Intransitive Verbs Verbs that do and do not take a direct object differ between English and primary language.	✔		✔	✔		
Phrasal Verbs Phrasal verbs do not exist in the primary language. There is often confusion over their meaning in English.	✔					
Have* vs. *Be Some Spanish constructions use *have* where English uses *be.*	✔					
ADJECTIVES						
Word Order Adjectives commonly come after nouns in the primary language.	✔	✔			✔	
Adjectives always come before words they modify in the primary language.			✔			
Comparison Comparative and superlative degrees are usually formed with separate words in the primary language, the equivalent of *more* and *most* in English.	✔				✔	✔
Confusion of *–ing* and *–ed* Forms The speakers of the primary language sometimes confuse these adjective forms, not distinguishing between *an interesting movie* and *an interested viewer,* for example.	✔	✔	✔	✔	✔	✔
ADVERBS						
Adverbs usually come before verbs in the primary language, and this tendency is carried over into English.			✔			
PREPOSITIONS						
English prepositions do not match the prepositions of the primary language precisely.			✔			✔
COMPLEX SENTENCES						
The primary language lacks tense markers so that matching the tenses of two verbs in one sentence correctly can be difficult. Learners may also try to analyze the tense needed in English according to meaning, which in some cases can result in the use of an incorrect tense.		✔	✔	✔	✔	✔
If* vs. *When The primary language has one expression that covers the use of English *if* and *when* for the future.				✔		
SENTENCE STRUCTURE						
The pattern in the primary language is to describe what happens first with later occurrences following. This is not an error in English, but it leads to a lack of sentence variety.			✔			
In Spanish, the phrase with the indirect object can come before the direct object.	✔					
Spanish requires double negatives in many sentence structures.	✔					
QUESTIONS						
The primary language does not use subject-verb inversion in questions.		✔	✔	✔		✔
In the primary language, word order is the same in some questions and statements, depending on the context.			✔	✔	✔	✔
In the primary language, there is no exact counterpart to the *do/did* verb in questions.	✔			✔	✔	✔
Yes/No Questions In the primary language, learners tend to answer yes by repeating the verb in question. They tend to say no by using *not* and repeating the verb.			✔		✔	
Tag Questions The primary language has no exact counterpart to a tag question, forms them differently, or does not add *do/did* to questions.		✔	✔			✔

Features of African American Vernacular English (AAVE)

AAVE

This chart identifies phonological elements and language structures of formal English that may cause difficulty for some students who use African American vernacular English.

PHONOLOGICAL ELEMENTS	FORMAL ENGLISH EXAMPLE	AAVE EXAMPLE
/th/ as in *though*	voicing /th/ in the middle and end of words: *brother, breathe*	voicing /th/ as /v/ in the middle and end of words: *brover, breave*
/th/ as in *think*	voicing /th/ in the middle and end of words: *bathroom, death*	voicing /th/ as /f/ in the middle and end of words: *bafroom, deaf*
Initial /th/ as in *this, that, the*	voicing initial /th/: *this, that, the*	voicing /d/ for initial /th/: *dis, dat, de*
/t/ in contractions	voicing of /t/ in contractions: *it's, don't*	omitting /t/ in contractions: *i's; don'*
final /g/ as in *thing*	voicing /g/ in /ihng/: *thing*	omitting /g/ in /ihng/: *thin'*
/ih/ in /ihng/	voicing /ih/ in /ihng/: *thing, bring, ring*	voicing /ang/ for /ihng/: *thang, brang, rang*
/r/ in initial consonant clusters	voicing /r/ in consonant clusters: *throw, through, brought*	omitting /r/ in consonant clusters: *th'ow, th'ough, b'ought*
final consonant clusters	voicing both sounds in final consonant clusters: *test, fist, wild, find, desk, lift*	omitting final consonant in final consonant clusters: *tes', fis', wil', fin', des', lif'*
final /r/	voicing /r/ in words with *r*-controlled vowels: *store, door, for*	omitting /r/ in words with *r*- controlled vowels: *sto', do', fo'*
final /l/ after variant vowels	voicing /l/ after variant vowels: *cool, bowl*	omitting /l/ after variant vowels: *coo', bow'*
/l/ before final /p/, /t/, /k/	voicing /l/ before final /p/, /t/, /k/: *help, belt, milk*	omitting /l/ before final /p/, /t/, /k/: *he'p, be't, mi'k*
final /uhl/	voicing final /uhl/: *people, couple, little*	omitting final /l/ in /uhl/ syllable: *peop/uh/, coup/uh/, litt/uh/*
/ih/ and /eh/ before consonants /m/ and /n/	/ih/ and /eh/ before /m/ and /n/: *him, hem; pin, pen*	voicing /ih/ for /eh/: *him for hem; pin for pen*
initial /str/	voicing initial /str/: ***str**eet*	voicing initial /str/ as /skr/: ***skr**eet*
adjacent consonants /sk/	voicing of adjacent consonants: ***ask***	transposition of adjacent consonants: ***aks***
syllable emphasis	primary stress on final syllable: *ju-LY*	primary stress on initial syllable: *JU-ly*

LANGUAGE STRUCTURES	FORMAL ENGLISH EXAMPLE	AAVE EXAMPLE
conjugating the verb *to be*	*He **is** at school. We **are** young. We **were** playing.*	*He **be** at school.* or *He at school. We **is** young. We **was** playing.*
use of *be* for habitual action	*Her mother **works** hard.*	*Her mother **be working** hard.*
subject-verb agreement	*She talks. They look.*	*She talk. They looks.*
use of verb stem as past tense	*I **finished.** He **came** down.*	*I **finish.** He **come** down.*
use of past participle form as past tense	*I **saw** the book.* or *I **had seen** the book.*	*I **seen** the book.*
use of *had* to indicate simple past	*He **sold** the car.*	*He **had sold** the car.*
past tense verbs with *–ed*	*Her cat was **called** Misty.*	*Her cat was **call** Misty.*
use of helping verbs in present tense	*She **is** coming. We **are** going.*	*She coming. We going.*
negative constructions	*He **won't ever** do that.* or *He **will never** do that. **Nobody can** do that.*	*He **won't never** do that. **Can't nobody** do that.*
plural nouns	*I have **two brothers.** It cost ten **dollars.***	*I have **two brother.** It cost ten **dollar.***
irregular plural nouns	*This is for the **children.***	*This is for the **childrens.***
/s/ in possessives between two nouns	*My **dog's** name is Buddy.*	*My **dog** name is Buddy.*
possessive pronoun *mine*	*That is **mine.***	*That is **mines.***
possessive pronoun *their*	*The girls met **their** neighbor.*	*The girls met **they** neighbor.*
/s/ in contractions	***He's** my best friend.*	***He** my best friend.*
use of articles	***a** ring; **an** apple*	***an** ring; **a** apple*
inserting *done* in verb forms	*He made the team.*	*He **done** made the team.*
double tense marking	*We **picked** that day to play.*	*We **pickted** that day to play.*
comparative forms of adjectives	*It's **better** than the other one.*	*It's **more better** than the other one.*

Contents in Brief

Standards Focus

Standards Focus

UNIT 4 The Romantic Period 1798–1832

Reading Standard 1.3, 2.2, 2.4, 3.1, 3.2, 3.3, 3.4, 3.7a–c, 3.9, Grades 9–10 Review Reading Standard 1.1, 2.5, 3.7, 3.11; Writing Standard 1.1, 1.2, 1.4, 1.5, 1.9, 2.1a, 2.1c, 2.1e, 2.2a–e, 2.3a–c, 2.4a, 2.6a, 2.6b; Language Conventions Standard 1.1, 1.2, 1.3; Listening and Speaking Standard 1.4, 1.7, 2.1a–c, 2.3a–d, Grades 9–10 Review Listening and Speaking Standard 1.9

UNIT 5 The Victorian Period 1832–1901

Reading Standard 1.2, 1.3, 2.2, 2.4, 3.1, 3.2, 3.3, 3.4, 3.7a–c, 3.9, Grades 9–10 Review Reading Standard 1.1, 1.2, 3.3, 3.11, 3.12; Writing Standard 1.2, 1.3, 1.4, 1.9, 2.1a–e, 2.2a–e, 2.3a, 2.3b; Language Conventions Standard 1.1, 1.2, 1.3; Listening and Speaking Standard 1.8a, 1.8b, 2.1a, Grades 9–10 Review Listening and Speaking Standard 1.9, 2.3a–g

UNIT 6 The Modern World 1900 to the Present

Reading Standard 1.1, 1.3, 2.1, 2.2, 2.3, 2.4, 2.5, 2.6, 3.1, 3.2, 3.3, 3.4, 3.6, 3.7a–c, 3.8, 3.9, Grades 9–10 Review Reading Standard 1.1, 1.2, 3.3, 3.4, 3.6, 3.7, 3.8, 3.9, 3.10, 3.12; Writing Standard 1.1, 1.2, 1.3, 1.4, 1.5, 1.8, 1.9, 2.1a–e, 2.2a–e, 2.3a–c, 2.6a–d; Language Conventions Standard 1.1, 1.2, 1.3; Listening and Speaking Standard 1.1, 1.2, 1.3, 1.7, 1.10, 1.11, 1.12, 1.13, 1.14, 2.1a–c, 2.3c, 2.4a–e, 2.5

RESOURCE CENTER

UNIT 1

TEACHER PLANNING GUIDE

Maps

The Anglo-Saxon Period and the Middle Ages 449–1485

"Not the glittering weapon fights the fight, but rather the hero's heart."

—Proverb

Standards Focus

Reading Standard 2.2, 3.7b, 3.7c (see pages A48–A50)

What Do You Think? What moves a hero to act?

CHAPTER 1 The Anglo-Saxons: Songs of Ancient Heroes

Standards Focus

Reading Standard 2.2, 3.1, 3.2, 3.4, 3.6, 3.7a–c; **Grades 9–10 Review Reading Standard** 1.1, 3.3, 3.12 (see pages A48–A50)

Writing Standard 1.2, 1.3, 2.2a–d (see pages A51–A52)

Comparing Texts: World Literature

Table of Contents

Standards Focus

Reading Standard 1.3, 2.2, 2.4, 2.5, 3.1, 3.3, 3.6, 3.7c, 3.8; **Grades 9–10 Review Reading Standard** 1.1, 3.4, 3.9 (see pages A48–A50)

Writing Standard 1.2, 2.1a, 2.1e, 2.2, 2.2b, 2.3a (see pages A51–A52)

Listening and Speaking Standard 1.10 (see pages A53–A55)

CHAPTER 2 The Middle Ages: The Tales They Told

Standards Focus

Reading Standard 3.7a; **Grades 9–10 Review Reading Standard 1.1 (see pages A48–A50)**

Writing Standard 1.1, 1.3, 1.9, 2.2a–e (see pages A51–A52)

Language Conventions Standard 1.1, 1.2, 1.3 (see page A53)

Listening and Speaking Standard 2.3a–e (see pages A53–A55)

UNIT 2

The Renaissance 1485–1660: A Flourish of Genius

"So much one man can do,
That does both act and know."
—Andrew Marvell

Standards Focus
Reading Standard 2.2, 3.7b, 3.7c (see pages A48–A50)

What Do You Think? How do our hearts and minds influence our actions?

Standards Focus
Reading Standard 1.2, 2.2, 2.4, 2.5, 2.6, 3.1, 3.2, 3.3, 3.4, 3.7b, 3.7c, 3.9; **Grades 9–10 Review Reading Standard** 3.10 (see pages A48–A50)
Writing Standard 1.2, 1.4, 2.1, 2.1a, 2.1c, 2.2, 2.2a–c, 2.3a, 2.3b, 2.6b (see pages A51–A52)
Listening and Speaking Standard 1.9 (see pages A53–A55)

CHAPTER 3 Love, Time, and Death

Table of Contents

Standards Focus

Reading Standard 2.2, 3.1, 3.7c; **Grades 9–10 Review Reading Standard** 3.12 (see pages A48–A50)

Writing Standard 1.2, 1.3, 2.1a–e, 2.2a–c (see pages A51–A52)

CHAPTER 4 William Shakespeare

Standards Focus
Reading Standard 3.7a; **Grades 9–10 Review Reading Standard** 1.2 (see pages A48–A50)
Writing Standard 1.1, 1.3, 1.6, 1.7, 1.9, 2.4a–e (see pages A51–A52)
Language Conventions Standard 1.1, 1.2, 1.3 (see page A53)
Listening and Speaking Standard 2.2a–d, (see pages A53–A55)

UNIT 3

The Restoration and the Eighteenth Century 1660–1800

"Good order is the foundation of all good things."
—**Edmund Burke**

Standards Focus
Reading Standard 2.2, 3.7b, 3.7c (see pages A48–A50)

What Do You Think? How can order and civilization affect human behavior?

Standards Focus
Reading Standard 1.3, 2.2, 2.4, 2.5, 3.1, 3.3, 3.7c, 3.8, 3.9; **Grades 9–10 Review Reading Standard** 1.1, 3.4, 3.9 (see pages A48–A50)
Writing Standard 1.1, 1.2, 1.5, 2.1, 2.1c, 2.1e, 2.2a–e (see pages A51–A52)
Listening and Speaking Standard 2.1a (see pages A53–A55)

CHAPTER 5 The Rise of the Novel

CHAPTER 6 Examined Lives

Standards Focus

Reading Standard 2.1, 2.2, 2.4, 2.5, 3.1, 3.2, 3.3, 3.4, 3.7a–c, 3.8, 3.9; **Grades 9–10 Review Reading Standard** 1.1 (see pages A48–A50)

Writing Standard 1.1, 1.3, 1.4, 1.5, 2.1a, 2.1c, 2.1e, 2.2a–e (see pages A51–A52)

Listening and Speaking Standard 2.3b, 2.3c (see pages A53–A55)

Standards Focus

Reading Standard 1.3, 3.7a (see pages A48–A50)

Writing Standard 1.1, 1.3, 1.4, 1.5, 1.9 (see pages A51–A52)

Language Conventions Standard 1.1, 1.2, 1.3 (see page A53)

Listening and Speaking Standard 1.4, 1.5, 1.6, 1.7, 1.9 (see pages A53–A55)

UNIT 4

TEACHER PLANNING GUIDE

The Romantic Period 1798–1832

"The divine arts of imagination: imagination, the real & eternal world of which this vegetable universe is but a faint shadow."

—William Blake

Standards Focus

Reading Standard 2.2, 3.7b, 3.7c (see pages A48–A50)

What Do You Think? How can we use imagination to discover truth?

Standards Focus

Reading Standard 1.3, 2.2, 3.1, 3.2, 3.3, 3.4, 3.7b, 3.9; **Grades 9–10 Review Reading Standard** 1.1, 3.7 (see pages A48–A50)

Writing Standard 1.1, 1.2, 1.5, 2.1a, 2.1e, 2.2a, 2.2c, 2.3a (see pages A51–A52)

Listening and Speaking Standard 1.7 (see pages A53–A55)

CHAPTER 7 Truth and Imagination

Table of Contents

Standards Focus
Reading Standard 2.2, 2.4, 3.1, 3.3, 3.4, 3.9; **Grades 9–10 Review Reading Standard** 2.5, 3.7, 3.11 (see pages A48–A50)
Writing Standard 1.2, 1.4, 1.9, 2.1a, 2.1c, 2.1e, 2.2a–e, 2.3a, 2.4a, 2.6a, 2.6b (see pages A51–A52)
Listening and Speaking Standard 1.4 (see pages A53–A55)

CHAPTER 8 The Quest for Beauty

Comparing Texts: World Literature

Standards Focus

Reading Standard 3.7a; Grades 9–10 Review Reading Standard 1.1 (see pages A48–A50)

Writing Standard 1.1, 1.5, 1.9, 2.3a–c (see pages A51–A52)

Language Conventions Standard 1.1, 1.2, 1.3 (see page A53)

Listening and Speaking Standard 2.1a–c, 2.3a–d; **Grades 9–10 Review Listening and Speaking Standard** 1.9 (see pages A53–A55)

TEACHER PLANNING GUIDE

UNIT 5

The Victorian Period 1832–1901

"For each age is a dream that is dying, / Or one that is coming to birth."
—Arthur O'Shaughnessy

Standards Focus
Reading Standard 2.2, 3.7b, 3.7c (see pages A48–A50)

What Do You Think? How can appearance be different from reality?

Standards Focus
Reading Standard 2.2, 2.4, 3.1, 3.2, 3.3, 3.4, 3.9; **Grades 9–10 Review Reading Standard** 1.1, 1.2, 3.11 (see pages A48–A50)
Writing Standard 1.2, 1.3, 1.4, 2.2a–d, 2.3a (see pages A51–A52)

CHAPTER 9 Love and Loss

UNIT 6

The Modern World 1900 to the Present

"Life spends itself in the act of transformation, dissolving, bit by bit, the world as it appeared."

—Rainer Maria Rilke

Standards Focus
Reading Standard 2.2, 3.7b, 3.7c (see pages A48–A50)

What Do You Think? How does experience shape our view of the world?

Standards Focus
Reading Standard 1.1, 1.3, 2.2, 2.5, 2.6, 3.1, 3.3, 3.4, 3.7b, 3.7c, 3.8; **Grades 9–10 Review Reading Standard** 1.1, 3.4, 3.6, 3.9, 3.12 (see pages A48–A50)
Writing Standard 1.3, 1.4, 1.5, 1.9, 2.1a, 2.1b, 2.1c, 2.2a–d, 2.3a, 2.3c (see pages A51–A52)
Listening and Speaking Standard 2.3c, 2.4a, 2.5 (see pages A53–A55)

CHAPTER 11 The World at War

CHAPTER 10 The Paradox of Progress

Standards Focus

Reading Standard 1.2, 1.3, 2.2, 2.4, 3.1, 3.2, 3.3, 3.4, 3.7a–c, 3.9; **Grades 9–10 Review Reading Standard** 1.1, 3.3, 3.12 (see pages A48–A50)

Writing Standard 1.2, 1.3, 1.9, 2.1a–d, 2.2a–e, 2.3a, 2.3b (see pages A51–A52)

Grades 9–10 Review Listening and Speaking Standard 2.3a–g (see pages A53–A55)

Standards Focus

Reading Standard 1.3, 3.7a (see pages A48–A50)

Writing Standard 1.2, 1.9, 2.1a–e (see pages A51–A52)

Language Conventions Standard 1.1, 1.2, 1.3 (see page A53)

Listening and Speaking Standard Grades 9–10 Review Listening and Speaking Standard 1.9 (see pages A53–A55)

Standards Focus

Reading Standard 1.3, 2.2, 2.4, 2.5, 3.1, 3.2, 3.3, 3.4, 3.6, 3.7c, 3.8, 3.9; **Grades 9–10 Review Reading Standard** 1.1, 1.2, 3.3, 3.4, 3.6, 3.7, 3.9, 3.10 (see pages A48–A50)

Writing Standard 1.2, 2.1b, 2.1c, 2.1e, 2.2a–e, 2.3a–c (see pages A51–A52)

CHAPTER 13 Expectation and Reality

CHAPTER 12 Modern and Contemporary Poetry

Standards Focus

Reading Standard 2.2, 2.4, 2.5, 3.1, 3.2, 3.3, 3.4, 3.9; **Grades 9–10 Review Reading Standard** 1.1, 3.7, 3.8 (see pages A48–A50)

Writing Standard 1.1, 1.3, 1.4, 1.5, 2.1a–c, 2.1e, 2.2a–d, 2.3a, 2.3b (see pages A51–A52)

Listening and Speaking Standard 2.1a–c, 2.4a–c (see pages A53–A55)

Table of Contents

Africa Emerges

Comparing Texts: World Literature

Standards Focus

Reading Standard 2.1, 2.2, 2.3, 3.7a; **Grades 9–10 Review Reading Standard** 1.1 (see pages A48–A50)

Writing Standard 1.1, 1.8, 1.9, 2.1a–e, 2.6a–d (see pages A51–A52)

Language Conventions Standard 1.1, 1.2, 1.3 (see page A53)

Listening and Speaking Standard 1.1, 1.2, 1.3, 1.7, 1.10, 1.11, 1.12, 1.13, 1.14, 2.4a–e (see pages A53–A55)

RESOURCE CENTER

Selections by Alternative Themes

Selections are listed here in alternative theme groupings.

APPEARANCE VERSUS REALITY

GOOD VERSUS EVIL

HEROES AND ANTIHEROES

HUMOR AND THE STING OF SATIRE

THE INDIVIDUAL AND SOCIETY

INNOCENCE AND EXPERIENCE

SELECTIONS BY ALTERNATIVE THEMES continued

LOSS AND DEATH

LOVE'S SORROWS, LOVE'S TRIUMPHS

OPPRESSION AND FREEDOM

PEOPLE AND NATURE

SELECTIONS BY ALTERNATIVE THEMES continued

POWER AND AMBITION

THE QUEST AND THE PERILOUS JOURNEY

THE SEARCH FOR WISDOM

THE TRANSFORMING IMAGINATION

THE WAGES OF WAR

Selections by Genre

FICTION

ALLEGORY

ANECDOTES

DEBATE

GRAPHIC NOVELS

NOVEL EXCERPTS

PARABLES

ROMANCE NARRATIVE

SHORT STORIES

DRAMA

POETRY

SELECTIONS BY GENRE continued

SELECTIONS BY GENRE continued

NONFICTION AND INFORMATIONAL TEXT

AUTOBIOGRAPHY

AXIOMS AND MAXIMS

BIOGRAPHY

DEFINITIONS

DIARY

ESSAYS

UNIT INTRODUCTIONS

LITERARY SKILLS FOCUS ESSAYS

READING SKILLS FOCUS ESSAYS

HISTORIES

LETTERS

MAGAZINE ARTICLE

MEDITATION

MEMOIRS

NEWSPAPER ARTICLES

PROVERBS

SACRED TEXTS

TRAVEL BOOK

WEB ARTICLES

PUBLIC DOCUMENTS

DEBATE

PLATFORM

POLITICAL STATEMENT

SPEECHES

Selections by Region

AFRICA

ASIA

EUROPE

GREAT BRITAIN

SELECTIONS BY REGION continued

SELECTIONS BY REGION continued

Skills, Workshops, and Features

SKILLS

LITERARY SKILLS FOCUS ESSAYS

READING SKILLS FOCUS ESSAYS

LITERARY SKILLS

Table of Contents

SKILLS, WORKSHOPS, AND FEATURES continued

READING SKILLS FOR LITERARY TEXTS

INFORMATIONAL TEXT SKILLS

VOCABULARY SKILLS

ACADEMIC VOCABULARY

Table of Contents

SKILLS, WORKSHOPS, AND FEATURES continued

LANGUAGE COACH

VOCABULARY DEVELOPMENT: VOCABULARY SKILLS

WORKSHOPS

WRITING WORKSHOPS

PREPARING FOR TIMED WRITING

LISTENING AND SPEAKING WORKSHOPS

MEDIA WORKSHOP

FEATURES

LINK TO TODAY

SKILLS, WORKSHOPS, AND FEATURES continued

ANALYZING VISUALS

CROSS-CURRICULAR LINKS

LITERARY PERSPECTIVES

GRAMMAR LINKS

READING MATTERS

STANDARDS REVIEW

THE WORLD OF WORK

WRITER'S HANDBOOK

English-Language Arts Content Standards
Grades Eleven and Twelve

Note: The following section (pages A48–A55) contains the full text of the Grades Eleven and Twelve California English-Language Arts Content Standards. Throughout the instructional pages of Holt Literature and Language Arts, Sixth Course, *California standards citation consists of domain labels and standard numbers only, with a cross-reference to the appropriate pages in this section where the full text can be found. In addition to grade-level standards, Grades Nine and Ten review standards cited in the Grade Twelve book are listed here within the relevant domains.*

READING

1.0 Word Analysis, Fluency, and Systematic Vocabulary Development

Students apply their knowledge of word origins to determine the meaning of new words encountered in reading materials and use those words accurately.

VOCABULARY AND CONCEPT DEVELOPMENT

1.1 Trace the etymology of significant terms used in political science and history. **Unit 6**

1.2 Apply knowledge of Greek, Latin, and Anglo-Saxon roots and affixes to draw inferences concerning the meaning of scientific and mathematical terminology. **Unit 2**

1.3 Discern the meaning of analogies encountered, analyzing specific comparisons as well as relationships and inferences. **Units 1, 3, 4, 5, 6**

Grades 9–10 Review

1.1 Identify and use the literal and figurative meanings of words and understand word derivations. **Units 1, 3, 4, 5, 6**

1.2 Distinguish between the denotative and connotative meanings of words and interpret the connotative power of words. **Units 2, 5, 6**

2.0 Reading Comprehension (Focus on Informational Materials)

Students read and understand grade-level-appropriate material. They analyze the organizational patterns, arguments, and positions advanced. The selections in *Recommended Readings in Literature, Grades Nine Through Twelve* illustrate the quality and complexity of the materials to be read by students. In addition, by grade twelve, students read two million words annually on their own, including a wide variety of classic and contemporary literature, magazines, newspapers, and online information.

STRUCTURAL FEATURES OF INFORMATIONAL MATERIALS

2.1 Analyze both the features and the rhetorical devices of different types of public documents (e.g., policy statements, speeches, debates, platforms) and the way in which authors use those features and devices. **Units 3, 6; Reading Matters**

COMPREHENSION AND ANALYSIS OF GRADE-LEVEL APPROPRIATE TEXT

2.2 Analyze the way in which clarity of meaning is affected by the patterns of organization, hierarchical structures, repetition of the main ideas, syntax, and word choice in the text. **Units 1, 2, 3, 4, 5, 6; Reading Matters**

2.3 Verify and clarify facts presented in other types of expository texts by using a variety of consumer, workplace, and public documents. **Unit 6; Reading Matters, World of Work**

2.4 Make warranted and reasonable assertions about the author's arguments by using elements of the text to defend and clarify interpretations. **Units 1, 2, 3, 4, 5, 6; Reading Matters**

2.5 Analyze an author's implicit and explicit philosophical assumptions and beliefs about a subject. **Units 1, 2, 3, 6; Reading Matters**

EXPOSITORY CRITIQUE

2.6 Critique the power, validity, and truthfulness of arguments set forth in public documents; their appeal to both friendly and hostile audiences; and the extent to which the arguments anticipate and address reader concerns and counterclaims (e.g., appeal to reason, to authority, to pathos and emotion). **Units 2, 6; Reading Matters**

Grades 9–10 Review

2.5 Extend ideas presented in primary or secondary sources through original analysis, evaluation, and elaboration.

3.0 Literary Response and Analysis

Students read and respond to historically or culturally significant works of literature that reflect and enhance their studies of history and social science. They conduct in-depth analyses of recurrent themes. The selections in *Recommended Readings in Literature, Grades Nine Through Twelve* illustrate the quality and complexity of the materials to be read by students.

STRUCTURAL FEATURES OF LITERATURE

3.1 Analyze characteristics of subgenres (e.g., satire, parody, allegory, pastoral) that are used in poetry, prose, plays, novels, short stories, essays, and other basic genres. **Units 1, 2, 3, 4, 5, 6**

NARRATIVE ANALYSIS OF GRADE-LEVEL-APPROPRIATE TEXT

3.2 Analyze the way in which the theme or meaning of a selection represents a view or comment on life, using textual evidence to support the claim. **Units 1, 2, 3, 4, 5, 6**

3.3 Analyze the ways in which irony, tone, mood, the author's style, and the "sound" of language achieve specific rhetorical or aesthetic purposes or both. **Units 1, 2, 3, 4, 5, 6**

3.4 Analyze ways in which poets use imagery, personification, figures of speech, and sounds to evoke readers' emotions. **Units 1, 2, 3, 4, 5, 6**

3.5 Analyze recognized works of American literature representing a variety of genres and traditions:

- **a.** Trace the development of American literature from the colonial period forward.
- **b.** Contrast the major periods, themes, styles, and trends and describe how works by members of different cultures relate to one another in each period.
- **c.** Evaluate the philosophical, political, religious, ethical, and social influences of the historical period that shaped the characters, plots, and settings.

ENGLISH-LANGUAGE ARTS CONTENT STANDARDS continued

3.6 Analyze the way in which authors through the centuries have used archetypes drawn from myth and tradition in literature, film, political speeches, and religious writings (e.g., how the archetypes of banishment from an ideal world may be used to interpret Shakespeare's tragedy *Macbeth*). **Units 1, 3, 6**

3.7 Analyze recognized works of world literature from a variety of authors:

a. Contrast the major literary forms, techniques, and characteristics of the major literary periods (e.g., Homeric Greece, medieval, romantic, neoclassic, modern). **Units 1, 2, 3, 4, 5, 6**

b. Relate literary works and authors to the major themes and issues of their eras. Units 1, 2, 3, 4, 5, 6

c. Evaluate the philosophical, political, religious, ethical, and social influences of the historical period that shaped the characters, plots, and, settings. **Units 1, 2, 3, 4, 5, 6**

LITERARY CRITICISM

3.8 Analyze the clarity and consistency of political assumptions in a selection of literary works or essays on a topic (e.g., suffrage, women's role in organized labor). (Political approach) **Units 1, 3, 6**

3.9 Analyze the philosophical arguments presented in literary works to determine whether the authors' positions have contributed to the quality of each work and the credibility of the characters. (Philosophical approach) **Units 2, 3, 4, 5, 6**

Grades 9–10 Review

3.1 Articulate the relationship between the expressed purposes and the characteristics of different forms of dramatic literature (e.g., comedy, tragedy, drama, dramatic monologue). **Unit 6**

3.3 Analyze interactions between main and subordinate characters in a literary text (e.g., internal and external conflicts, motivations, relationships, influences) and explain the way those interactions affect the plot. **Units 1, 2, 5, 6**

3.4 Determine characters' traits by what the characters say about themselves in narration, dialogue, dramatic monologue, and soliloquy. **Units 1, 2, 3, 6**

3.6 Analyze and trace an author's development of time and sequence, including the use of complex literary devices (e.g., foreshadowing, flashbacks). **Units 1, 6**

3.7 Recognize and understand the significance of various literary devices, including figurative language, imagery, allegory, and symbolism, and explain their appeal. **Units 4, 5, 6**

3.8 Interpret and evaluate the impact of ambiguities, subtleties, contradictions, ironies, and incongruities in a text. **Unit 6**

3.9 Explain how voice, persona, and the choice of a narrator affect characterization and the tone, plot, and credibility of a text. **Units 1, 3, 5, 6**

3.10 Identify and describe the function of dialogue, scene designs, soliloquies, asides, and character foils in dramatic literature. **Units 2, 6**

3.11 Evaluate the aesthetic qualities of style, including the impact of diction and figurative language on tone, mood, and theme, using the terminology of literary criticism. (Aesthetic approach). **Units 4, 5**

3.12 Analyze the way in which a work of literature is related to the themes and issues of its historical period. (Historical approach) **Units 1, 2, 5, 6**

WRITING

1.0 Writing Strategies

Students write coherent and focused texts that convey a well-defined perspective and tightly reasoned argument. The writing demonstrates students' awareness of the audience and purpose and progression through the stages of the writing process.

ORGANIZATION AND FOCUS

1.1 Demonstrate an understanding of the elements of discourse (e.g., purpose, speaker, audience, form) when completing narrative, expository, persuasive, or descriptive writing assignments. **Units 1, 2, 3, 4, 6**

1.2 Use point of view, characterization, style (e.g., use of irony), and related elements for specific rhetorical and aesthetic purposes. **Units 1, 2, 3, 4, 5, 6**

1.3 Structure ideas and arguments in a sustained, persuasive, and sophisticated way and support them with precise and relevant examples. **Units 1, 2, 3, 5, 6**

1.4 Enhance meaning by employing rhetorical devices, including the extended use of parallelism, repetition, and analogy; the incorporation of visual aids (e.g., graphs, tables, pictures); and the issuance of a call for action. **Units 2, 3, 4, 5, 6**

1.5 Use language in natural, fresh, and vivid ways to establish a specific tone. **Units 3, 4, 6**

RESEARCH AND TECHNOLOGY

1.6 Develop presentations by using clear research questions and creative and critical research strategies (e.g., field studies, oral histories, interviews, experiments, electronic sources). **Unit 2**

1.7 Use systematic strategies to organize and record information (e.g., anecdotal scripting, annotated bibliographies). **Unit 2**

1.8 Integrate databases, graphics, and spreadsheets into word-processed documents. **Unit 6; The World of Work, Writer's Handbook**

EVALUATION AND REVISION

1.9 Revise text to highlight the individual voice, improve sentence variety and style, and enhance subtlety of meaning and tone in ways that are consistent with the purpose, audience, and genre. **Units 1, 2, 3, 4, 5, 6**

2.0 Writing Applications (Genres and Their Characteristics)

Students combine the rhetorical strategies of narration, exposition, persuasion, and description to produce texts of at least 1,500 words each. Student writing demonstrates a command of standard American English and the research, organizational, and drafting strategies outlined in Writing Standard 1.0.

Using the writing strategies of grades eleven and twelve outlined in Writing Standard 1.0, students:

2.1 Write fictional, autobiographical, or biographical narratives:

- **a.** Narrate a sequence of events and communicate their significance to the audience. **Units 1, 2, 3, 4, 5, 6**
- **b.** Locate scenes and incidents in specific he characters' feelings. **Units 2, 3, 4, 5, 6**
- **d.** Pace the presentation of actions to accommodate temporal, spatial, and dramatic mood changes. **Units 2, 5, 6**
- **e.** Make effective use of descriptions of appearance, images, shifting perspectives, and sensory details. **Units 1, 2, 3, 4, 5, 6**

ENGLISH-LANGUAGE ARTS CONTENT STANDARDS **continued**

2.2 Write responses to literature:

a. Demonstrate a comprehensive understanding of the significant ideas in works or passages. **Units 1, 2, 3, 4, 5, 6**

b. Analyze the use of imagery, language, universal themes, and unique aspects of the text. **Units 1, 2, 3, 4, 5, 6**

c. Support important ideas and viewpoints through accurate and detailed references to the text and to other works. **Units 1, 2, 3, 4, 5, 6**

d. Demonstrate an understanding of the author's use of stylistic devices and an appreciation of the effects created. **Units 1, 3, 4, 5, 6**

e. Identify and assess the impact of perceived ambiguities, nuances, and complexities within the text. **Units 1, 3, 4, 5, 6**

2.3 Write reflective compositions:

a. Explore the significance of personal experiences, events, conditions, or concerns by using rhetorical strategies (e.g., narration, description, exposition, persuasion). **Units 1, 2, 4, 5, 6**

b. Draw comparisons between specific incidents and broader themes that illustrate the writer's important beliefs or generalizations about life. **Units 2, 4, 5, 6**

c. Maintain a balance in describing individual incidents and relate those incidents to more general and abstract ideas. **Units 4, 6**

2.4 Write historical investigation reports:

a. Use exposition, narration, description, argumentation, exposition, or some combination of rhetorical strategies to support the main proposition. **Units 2, 4**

b. Analyze several historical records of a single event, examining critical relationships between elements of the research topic. **Unit 2**

c. Explain the perceived reason or reasons for the similarities and differences in historical records with information derived from primary and secondary sources to support or enhance the presentation. **Unit 2**

d. Include information from all relevant perspectives and take into consideration the validity and reliability of sources. **Unit 2**

e. Include a formal bibliography. **Unit 2**

2.5 Write job applications and résumés:

a. Provide clear and purposeful information and address the intended audience appropriately. **World of Work**

b. Use varied levels, patterns, and types of language to achieve intended effects and aid comprehension. **World of Work**

c. Modify the tone to fit the purpose and audience. **World of Work**

d. Follow the conventional style for that type of document (e.g., résumé, memorandum) and use page formats, fonts, and spacing that contribute to the readability and impact of the document. **World of Work**

2.6 Deliver multimedia presentations:

a. Combine text, images, and sound and draw information from many sources (e.g., television broadcasts, videos, films, newspapers, magazines, CD-ROMs, the Internet, electronic media-generated images). **Units 4, 6**

b. Select an appropriate medium for each element of the presentation. **Units 2, 4, 6**

c. Use the selected media skillfully, editing appropriately and monitoring for quality. **Unit 6**

d. Test the audience's response and revise the presentation accordingly. **Unit 6**

WRITTEN AND ORAL ENGLISH LANGUAGE CONVENTIONS

The standards for written and oral English language conventions have been placed between those for writing and for listening and speaking because these conventions are essential to both sets of skills.

1.0 Written and Oral English-Language Conventions

Students write and speak with a command of standard English conventions.

1.1 Demonstrate control of grammar, diction, and paragraph and sentence structure and an understanding of English usage. **Units 1, 2, 3, 4, 5, 6; *Warriner's Handbook,* Sixth Course, Chapters 1, 2, 3, 4, 11, 17, 18, 19**

1.2 Produce legible work that shows accurate spelling and correct punctuation and capitalization. **Units 1, 2, 3, 4, 5, 6; *Warriner's Handbook, Sixth Course,* Chapters 12, 13, 14, 15**

1.3 Reflect appropriate manuscript requirements in writing. **Units 1, 2, 3, 4, 5, 6; *Warriner's Handbook,* Sixth Course, Manuscript Form**

LISTENING AND SPEAKING

1.0 Listening and Speaking Strategies

Students formulate adroit judgments about oral communication. They deliver focused and coherent presentations that convey clear and distinct perspectives and demonstrate solid reasoning. They use gestures, tone, and vocabulary tailored to the audience and purpose.

COMPREHENSION

1.1 Recognize strategies used by the media to inform, persuade, entertain, and transmit culture (e.g., advertisements; perpetuation of stereotypes; use of visual representations, special effects, language). **Unit 6**

1.2 Analyze the impact of the media on the democratic process (e.g., exerting influence on elections, creating images of leaders, shaping attitudes) at the local, state, and national levels. **Unit 6**

1.3 Interpret and evaluate the various ways in which events are presented and information is communicated by visual image makers (e.g., graphic artists, documentary filmmakers, illustrators, news photographers). **Unit 6**

ORGANIZATION AND DELIVERY OF ORAL COMMUNICATION

1.4 Use rhetorical questions, parallel structure, concrete images, figurative language, characterization, irony, and dialogue to achieve clarity, force, and aesthetic effect. **Units 3, 4**

1.5 Distinguish between and use various forms of classical and contemporary logical arguments, including:

- **a.** Inductive and deductive reasoning **Unit 3**
- **b.** Syllogisms and analogies **Unit 3**

1.6 Use logical, ethical, and emotional appeals that enhance a specific tone and purpose. **Unit 3**

1.7 Use appropriate rehearsal strategies to pay attention to performance details, achieve command of the text, and create skillful artistic staging. **Units 3, 4, 6**

ENGLISH-LANGUAGE ARTS CONTENT STANDARDS continued

1.8 Use effective and interesting language, including:

- **a.** Informal expressions for effect **Unit 5**
- **b.** Standard American English for clarity **Unit 5**
- **c.** Technical language for specificity **Unit 5**

1.9 Use research and analysis to justify strategies for gesture, movement, and vocalization, including dialect, pronunciation, and enunciation. **Units 2, 3**

1.10 Evaluate when to use different kinds of effects (e.g., visual, music, sound, graphics) to create effective productions. **Units 1, 6**

ANALYSIS AND EVALUATION OF ORAL AND MEDIA COMMUNICATIONS

1.11 Critique a speaker's diction and syntax in relation to the purpose of an oral communication and the impact the words may have on the audience. **Unit 6**

1.12 Identify logical fallacies used in oral addresses (e.g., attack *ad hominem,* false causality, red herring, overgeneralization, bandwagon effect). **Unit 6**

1.13 Analyze the four basic types of persuasive speech (i.e., propositions of fact, value, problem, or policy) and understand the similarities and differences in their patterns of organization and the use of persuasive language, reasoning, and proof. **Unit 6**

1.14 Analyze the techniques used in media messages for a particular audience and evaluate their effectiveness (e.g., Orson Welles' radio broadcast "War of the Worlds"). **Unit 6**

Grades 9–10 Review

1.9 Analyze the occasion and the interests of the audience and choose effective verbal and nonverbal techniques (e.g., voice, gestures, eye contact) for presentations. **Units 4, 5**

2.0 Speaking Applications (Genres and Their Characteristics)

Students deliver polished formal and extemporaneous presentations that combine traditional rhetorical strategies of narration, exposition, persuasion, and description. Student speaking demonstrates a command of standard American English and the organizational and delivery strategies outlined in Listening and Speaking Standard 1.0.

Using the speaking strategies of grades eleven and twelve outlined in Listening and Speaking Standard 1.0, students:

2.1 Deliver reflective presentations:

- **a.** Explore the significance of personal experiences, events, conditions, or concerns, using appropriate rhetorical strategies (e.g., narration, description, exposition, persuasion). **Units 3, 4, 5, 6**
- **b.** Draw comparisons between the specific incident and broader themes that illustrate the speaker's beliefs or generalizations about life. **Units 4, 6**
- **c.** Maintain a balance between describing the incident and relating it to more general, abstract ideas. **Units 4, 6**

2.2 Deliver oral reports on historical investigations:

a. Use exposition, narration, description, persuasion, or some combination of those to support the thesis. **Unit 2**

b. Analyze several historical records of a single event, examining critical relationships between elements of the research topic. **Unit 2**

c. Explain the perceived reason or reasons for the similarities and differences by using information derived from primary and secondary sources to support or enhance the presentation. **Unit 2**

d. Include information on all relevant perspectives and consider the validity and reliability of sources. **Unit 2**

2.3 Deliver oral responses to literature:

a. Demonstrate a comprehensive understanding of the significant ideas of literary works (e.g., make assertions about the text that are reasonable and supportable). **Units 1, 4**

b. Analyze the imagery, language, universal themes, and unique aspects of the text through the use of rhetorical strategies (e.g., narration, description, persuasion, exposition, a combination of those strategies). **Units 1, 3, 4**

c. Support important ideas and viewpoints through accurate and detailed references to the text or to other works. **Units 1, 3, 4, 6**

d. Demonstrate an awareness of the author's use of stylistic devices and an appreciation of the effects created. **Units 1, 4**

e. Identify and assess the impact of perceived ambiguities, nuances, and complexities within the text. **Unit 1**

2.4 Deliver multimedia presentations:

a. Combine text, images, and sound by incorporating information from a wide range of media, including films, newspapers, magazines, CD-ROMs, online information, television, videos, and electronic media-generated images. **Unit 6**

b. Select an appropriate medium for each element of the presentation. **Unit 6**

c. Use the selected media skillfully, editing appropriately and monitoring for quality. **Unit 6**

d. Test the audience's response and revise the presentation accordingly. **Unit 6**

2.5 Recite poems, selections from speeches, or dramatic soliloquies with attention to performance details to achieve clarity, force, and aesthetic effect and to demonstrate an understanding of the meaning (e.g., Hamlet's soliloquy "To Be or Not to Be"). **Unit 6**

Grades 9–10 Review

2.3 Apply appropriate interviewing techniques:

a. Prepare and ask relevant questions. **Unit 5**

b. Make notes of responses. **Unit 5**

c. Use language that conveys maturity, sensitivity, and respect. **Unit 5**

d. Respond correctly and effectively to questions. **Unit 5**

e. Demonstrate knowledge of the subject or organization. **Unit 5**

f. Compile and report responses. **Unit 5**

g. Evaluate the effectiveness of the interview. **Unit 5**

Why Be a Reader/Writer?

by **Kylene Beers**

The Journey

Once I had a college literature teacher who began each class by saying, "Enjoy the journey." After a couple of weeks, one student bravely responded to the now-routine comment with, "What journey?" The teacher just smiled and did not answer the question. We were going to have to figure *that* out for ourselves.

Years later, on a long car trip with a friend, I finally figured out what my teacher meant. About every 50 miles, my friend would ask, "Are we there yet?" It did not matter to her that we were winding our way over stunning snow-capped mountains with views of majestic waterfalls. She wanted to skip that part and *just get there!*

After hearing "Are we there yet?" one too many times, I snapped, "Enjoy the journey!!" She said, "Huh?" and I started laughing because I finally understood *exactly* what my teacher meant:

If we are only interested in doing something because of where it will get us, we miss out on too much. The journey is every bit as important as the destination.

Enjoy the journey.

Traveling via Textbook

What is the journey you ought to enjoy with a literature textbook? You know how textbooks work: There are questions to discuss, vocabulary words to learn, and essays to write.

It is easy to let finishing high school, getting into college, or landing a good job become the *reasons* why you read and write. While those are all significant things, they overlook the *critical* reason to be a reader and a writer, and that reason is only found when you remember to *enjoy the journey: Be* a reader and *be* a writer.

- Read *Beowulf* not just to answer the questions but to experience Beowulf's trials and to find out how his experiences might inform *your own.*
- Read the love poems in Chapter 3 not only to figure out the structure of a sonnet but to discover what love means *to you.*

As you write in response to the readings,

- Do not write merely to finish an assignment. Instead, write to discover when you stand in support of an author's ideas.
- Write to discover when you stand in opposition to an author's ideas.

If you read the assignments carefully, you will see they are prompts that allow you—if you let them—to discover more about *yourself and the world you live in.*

The Road Ahead

Enjoy *this* journey. My friend on the car trip never did enjoy ours—it was far easier to complain than to pause and see what was out the window. Literature offers you an amazing window to discover more about yourself and the world you live in—

- a window to worlds you might never experience
- a window to people and events, struggles and triumphs you otherwise might never know.

You just have to look.

I have great hopes that this year, more than any other year, you are open to doing just that.

Kylene Beers

Senior Author
Holt Literature and Language Arts

How to Use Your Textbook

Each time you get a new cell phone, you find it has more features than the last one. Without looking at the instructions, you may miss out on the benefits of the phone. It is the same with your textbook. This section introduces you to your book's features, so that you can be successful from the beginning.

Unit Opener

As you look at the title and dates for each unit, think about what you might know already about that time period. Think about the **quotation**. What does it suggest about the literature of the historical period? Keep the **What Do You Think?** question in mind as you go through the unit. You may find that what you think about the period and its literature evolves as you work through the unit.

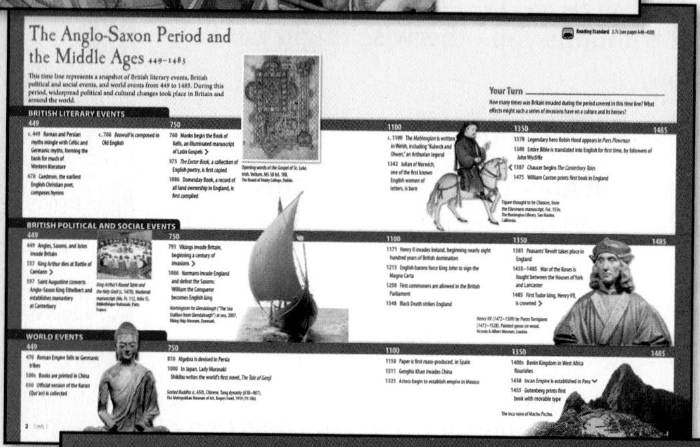

Time Line

In this book, you will study literature and events that occurred in both the recent and the distant past. The time line will help you to put it all in perspective. You will see how history and literature, including worldwide literary movements and historical events, influenced each other.

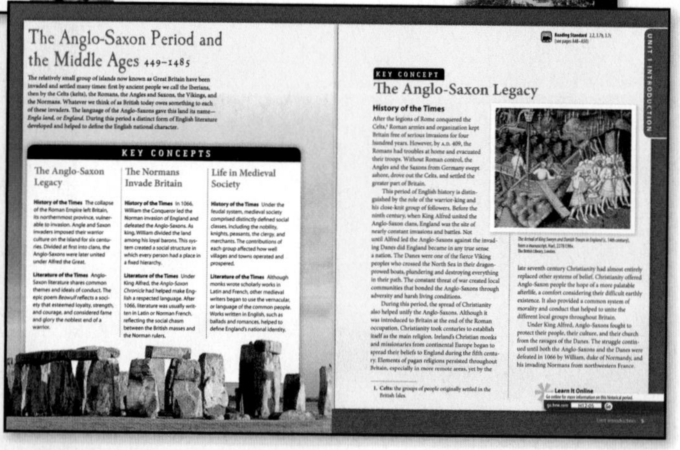

Introduction with Key Concepts

Often we say, "Cut to the chase," or, "Just give me the big picture." This is what **Key Concepts** does. For each unit, this feature provides the essentials about both the literature and the history of the time period. This understanding will be a foundation for your reading throughout the unit—how works of literature emerge in a time and place.

Link to Today

Though there has never been a century like this one in terms of instant communication, human nature has not really changed that much. Modern film makers draw on ancient epics, and modern history is influenced by past history. **Link to Today** shows the connection and the relevance between events of a particular time period and our world today.

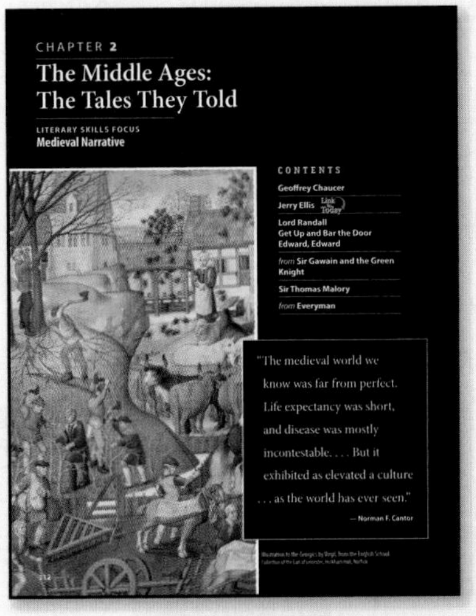

Chapter Opener

A chapter focuses on the major literary movements or literary works within the unit's time period. Each chapter opener identifies the title of the chapter—a clue to its contents—as well as a quotation that suggests a key theme or idea of the period. Try to notice the image on the opener page; consider what it suggests about the literary period.

Literary Skills Focus

The **Literary Skills Focus** gives you necessary background on the literature and the time period you are studying. Just as Japanese anime has certain styles, themes, and techniques, the literary masters of the past had a framework within which they worked. **Literary Skills Focus** helps you better understand that framework.

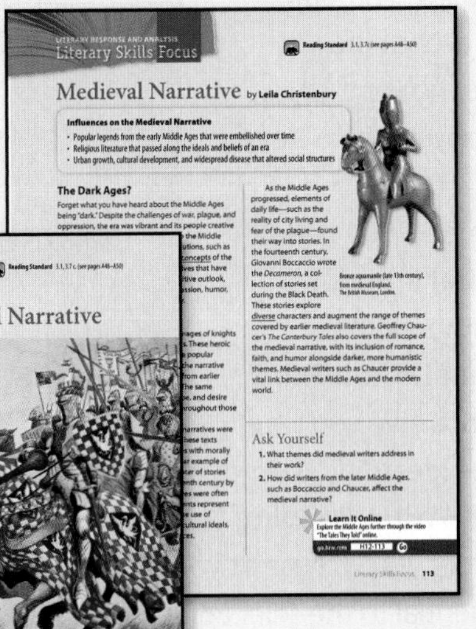

Analyzing Visuals

You are regularly immersed in images through television, magazines, street art, and billboards. Because visual media are so prevalent, you may find it challenging to think about them consciously and critically. **Analyzing Visuals** helps you apply your visual skills to images and then connect those skills to the literary works you are reading.

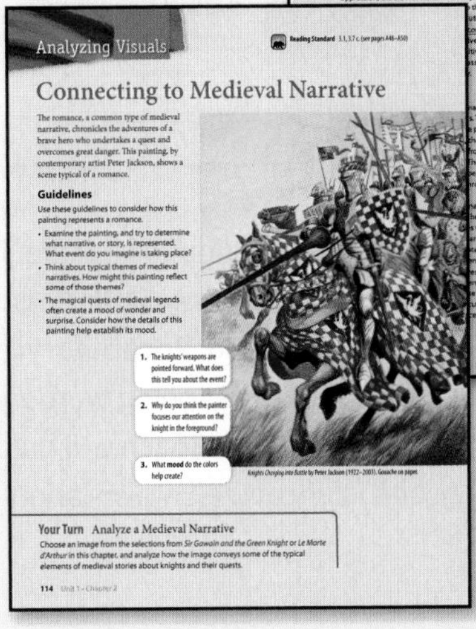

How to Use Your Textbook

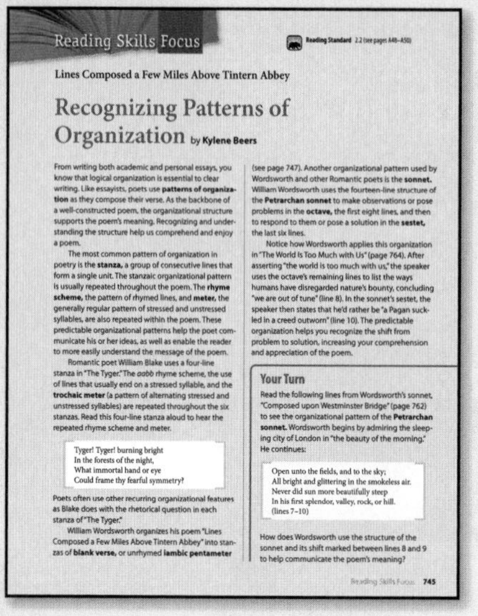

Reading Skills Focus

Reading Standard 2.2 (see pages A48–A50)

Lines Composed a Few Miles Above Tintern Abbey

Recognizing Patterns of Organization by Kylene Beers

From writing both academic and personal essays, you know that logical organization is essential to clear writing. Like essayists, poets use **patterns of organization** as they compose their verse. As the backbone of a well-constructed poem, the organizational structure supports the poem's meaning. Recognizing and understanding the structure help us comprehend and enjoy a poem.

The most common pattern of organization in poetry is the **stanza,** a group of consecutive lines that form a single unit. The stanzaic organizational pattern is usually repeated throughout the poem. The **rhyme scheme,** the pattern of rhymed lines, and **meter,** the generally regular pattern of stressed and unstressed syllables, are also repeated within the poem. These predictable organizational patterns help the poet communicate his or her ideas, as well as enable the reader to more easily understand the message of the poem.

Romantic poet William Blake uses a four-line stanza in "The Tyger." The *aabb* rhyme scheme, the use of lines that usually end on a stressed syllable, and the **trochaic meter** (a pattern of alternating stressed and unstressed syllables) are repeated throughout the six stanzas. Read this four-line stanza aloud to hear the repeated rhyme scheme and meter.

Tyger! Tyger! burning bright
In the forests of the night,
What immortal hand or eye
Could frame thy fearful symmetry?

Poets often use other recurring organizational features as Blake does with the rhetorical question in each stanza of "The Tyger."

William Wordsworth organizes his poem "Lines Composed a Few Miles Above Tintern Abbey" into stanzas of **blank verse,** or unrhymed **iambic pentameter** (see page 747). Another organizational pattern used by Wordsworth and other Romantic poets is the **sonnet.** William Wordsworth uses the fourteen-line structure of the **Petrarchan sonnet** to make observations or pose problems in the **octave,** the first eight lines, and then to respond to them or pose a solution in the **sestet,** the last six lines.

Notice how Wordsworth applies this organization in "The World Is Too Much with Us" (page 764). After asserting "the world is too much with us," the speaker uses the octave's remaining lines to list the ways humans have disregarded nature's bounty, concluding "we are out of tune" (line 8). In the sonnet's sestet, the speaker then states that he'd rather be "a Pagan suckled in a creed outworn" (line 10). The predictable organization helps you recognize the shift from problem to solution, increasing your comprehension and appreciation of the poem.

Your Turn

Read the following lines from Wordsworth's sonnet, "Composed upon Westminster Bridge" (page 762) to see the organizational pattern of the **Petrarchan sonnet.** Wordsworth begins by admiring the sleeping city of London in "the beauty of the morning." He continues:

Open unto the fields, and to the sky;
All bright and glittering in the smokeless air.
Never did sun more beautifully steep
In his first splendor, valley, rock, or hill.
(lines 7–10)

How does Wordsworth use the structure of the sonnet and its shift marked between lines 8 and 9 to help communicate the poem's meaning?

Reading Skills Focus 745

Reading Skills Focus

Sometimes reading selections written in the past seems a little like trying to read something in another language that you barely know. **Reading Skills Focus** gives you the keys to unlock the text. Is the word order changed in this poem? How did the writer use imagery to help the reader visualize the story in his mind? How is the sentence structure different from what we see in today's literature?

Literary Selection Pages

Preparing to Read

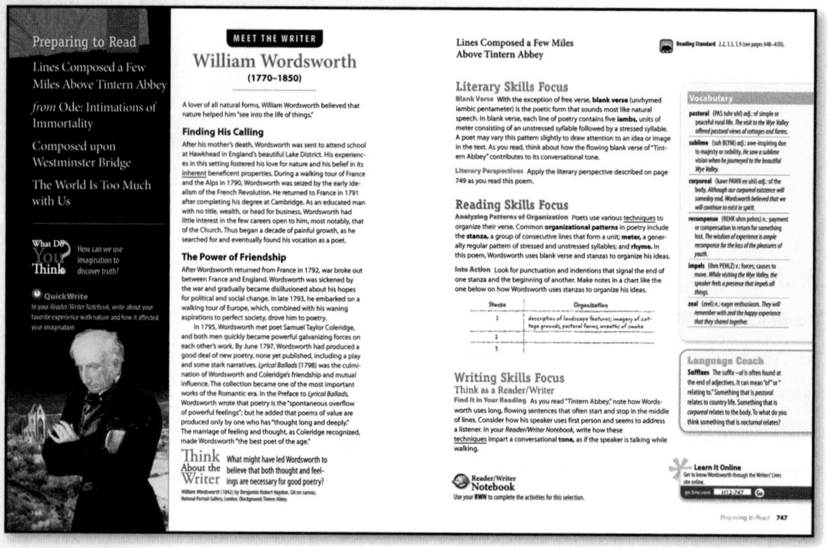

Preparing to Read

Lines Composed a Few Miles Above Tintern Abbey

from Ode: Intimations of Immortality

Composed upon Westminster Bridge

The World Is Too Much with Us

What Do You Think? How can we use imagination to discover truth?

QuickWrite
In your *Reader/Writer Notebook,* write about your favorite experience with nature and how it affected your imagination.

MEET THE WRITER

William Wordsworth

(1770–1850)

A lover of all natural forms, William Wordsworth believed that nature helped him "see into the life of things."

Finding His Calling

After his mother's death, Wordsworth was sent to attend school at Hawkhead in England's beautiful Lake District. His experiences in this setting fostered his love for nature and his belief in its inherent beneficent properties. During a walking tour of France and the Alps in 1790, Wordsworth was seized by the early idealism of the French Revolution. He returned to France in 1791 after completing his degree at Cambridge. As an educated man with no title, wealth, or head for business, Wordsworth had little interest in the few careers open to him, most notably, that of the Church. Thus began a decade of painful growth, as he searched for and eventually found his vocation as a poet.

The Power of Friendship

After Wordsworth returned from France in 1792, war broke out between France and England. Wordsworth was sickened by the war and gradually became disillusioned about his hopes for political and social change. In late 1793, he embarked on a walking tour of Europe, which, combined with his waning aspirations to perfect society, drove him to poetry.

In 1795, Wordsworth met poet Samuel Taylor Coleridge, and both men quickly became powerful galvanizing forces on each other's work. By June 1797, Wordsworth had produced a good deal of new poetry, none yet published, including a play and some stark narratives. *Lyrical Ballads* (1798) was the culmination of Wordsworth and Coleridge's friendship and mutual influence. The collection became one of the most important works of the Romantic era. In the Preface to *Lyrical Ballads,* Wordsworth wrote that poetry is the "spontaneous overflow of powerful feelings"; but he added that poems of value are produced only by one who has "thought long and deeply." The marriage of feeling and thought, as Coleridge recognized, made Wordsworth "the best poet of the age."

Think About the Writer: What might have led Wordsworth to believe that both thought and feelings are necessary for good poetry?

William Wordsworth (1842) by Benjamin Robert Haydon. Oil on canvas. National Portrait Gallery, London; (Background) Tintern Abbey.

Lines Composed a Few Miles Above Tintern Abbey

Reading Standard 2.2, 3.3, 3.9 (see pages A48–A50).

Literary Skills Focus

Blank Verse With the exception of free verse, **blank verse** (unrhymed iambic pentameter) is the poetic form that sounds most like natural speech. In blank verse, each line of poetry contains five **iambs,** units of meter consisting of an unstressed syllable followed by a stressed syllable. A poet may vary this pattern slightly to draw attention to an idea or image in the text. As you read, think about how the flowing blank verse of "Tintern Abbey" contributes to its conversational tone.

Literary Perspectives Apply the literary perspective described on page 749 as you read this poem.

Reading Skills Focus

Analyzing Patterns of Organization Poets use various techniques to organize their verse. Common **organizational patterns** in poetry include the **stanza,** a group of consecutive lines that form a unit; **meter,** a generally regular pattern of stressed and unstressed syllables; and **rhyme.** In this poem, Wordsworth uses blank verse and stanzas to organize his ideas.

Into Action Look for punctuation and indentions that signal the end of one stanza and the beginning of another. Make notes in a chart like the one below on how Wordsworth uses stanzas to organize his ideas.

Stanza	Organization
1	description of landscape features; imagery of cottage grounds, pastoral farms, wreaths of smoke
2	
3	

Writing Skills Focus

Think as a Reader/Writer

Find It in Your Reading As you read "Tintern Abbey," note how Wordsworth uses long, flowing sentences that often start and stop in the middle of lines. Consider how his speaker uses first person and seems to address a listener. In your *Reader/Writer Notebook,* write how these techniques impart a conversational **tone,** as if the speaker is talking while walking.

Reader/Writer Notebook

Use your **RWN** to complete the activities for this selection.

Vocabulary

pastoral (PAS tuhr uhl) *adj.:* of simple or peaceful rural life. *The visit to the Wye Valley offered pastoral views of cottages and farms.*

sublime (suh BLYM) *adj.:* awe-inspiring due to majesty or nobility. *He saw a sublime vision when he journeyed to the beautiful Wye Valley.*

corporeal (kawr PAWR ee uhl) *adj.:* of the body. *Although our corporeal existence will someday end, Wordsworth believed that we will continue to exist in spirit.*

recompense (REHK uhm pehns) *n.:* payment or compensation in return for something lost. *The wisdom of experience is ample recompense for the loss of the pleasures of youth.*

impels (ihm PEHLZ) *v.:* forces; causes to move. *While visiting the Wye Valley, the speaker feels a presence that impels all things.*

zeal (zeel) *n.:* eager enthusiasm. *They will remember with zeal the happy experience that they shared together.*

Language Coach

Suffixes The suffix *–al* is often found at the end of adjectives. It can mean "of" or "relating to." Something that is *pastoral* relates to country life. Something that is *corporeal* relates to the body. To what do you think something that is *nocturnal* relates?

Learn It Online
Get to know Wordsworth through the Writers' Lives site online.

go.hrw.com H12-747 Go

Preparing to Read 747

Before you do anything important, such as playing the big game, going on a date, or taking a trip, you prepare. Do you have everything you need to make the venture successful? **Preparing to Read** ensures that you have the essential elements you need. **Meet the Writer** introduces you to the author of the selection. **What Do You Think?** and **QuickWrite** give you ways to connect the ideas and themes of the literary selection to your life. The **Literary Skills Focus, Reading Skills Focus,** and **Writing Skills Focus** present the skills you will use as you read the selection. **Vocabulary** lists the words essential to the selection's meaning, besides being words you should add to your own active vocabulary. **Language Coach** will guide you through the complex rules and large vocabulary of the English language.

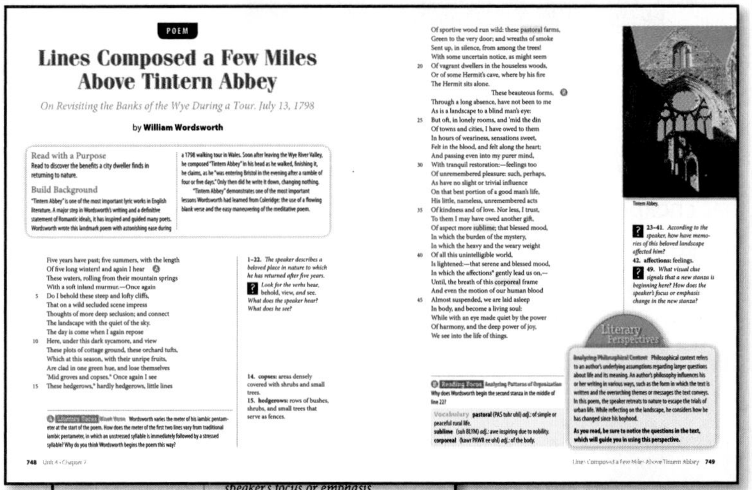

Selection

Which songs, movies, or stories from today do you think will captivate people fifty or even five hundred years from now? The few that survive will be the ones that help us grasp what it means to be human. The selections in this textbook are those universal ones that have survived. **Read with a Purpose** gives you a goal for your reading. **Build Background** provides any information you may need as context for the selection.

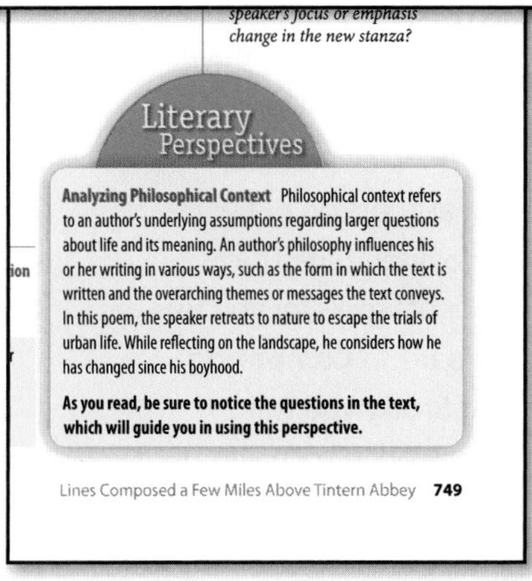

Literary Perspectives

Whether you are male or female, rich or poor, native or new to the U.S. influences how you see things. These same factors affect how authors write as well as how you read a piece of literature. **Literary Perspectives** helps you become aware of different perspectives, or lenses, for looking at literature to get a more complete view.

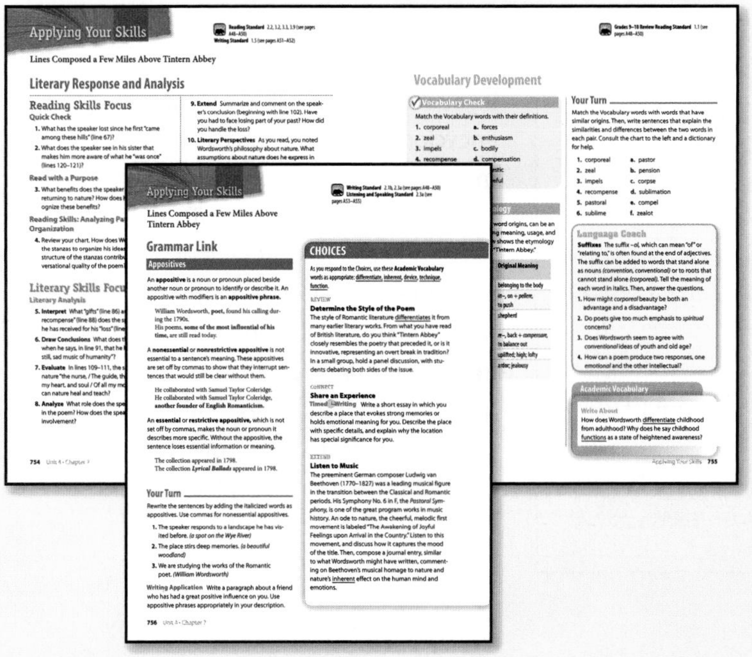

Applying Your Skills

Athletes, musicians, and artists all practice long and hard to perfect their skills. Games, performances, or exhibitions give them a venue for applying their skills. **Applying Your Skills** gives you the opportunity to apply the reading, literary and vocabulary skills you learned about before reading and then practiced throughout the selection. It shows how you are mastering the skills in each selection.

How to Use Your Textbook

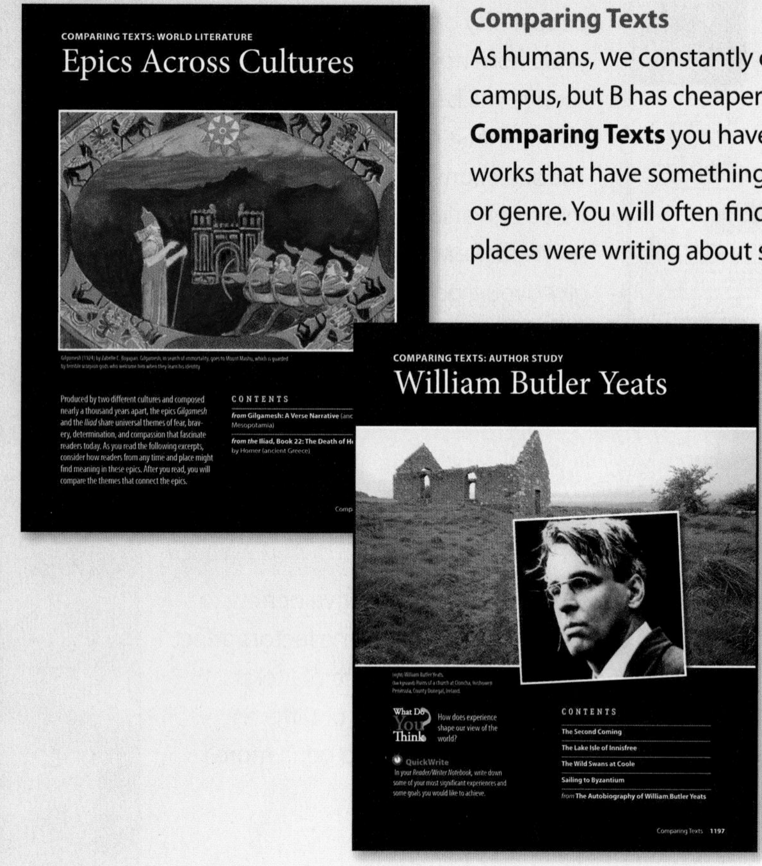

Comparing Texts

As humans, we constantly compare. College A has the prettiest campus, but B has cheaper tuition, and C is closer to home. In **Comparing Texts** you have an opportunity to compare several works that have something in common such as a subject, theme, or genre. You will often find that writers in very different times and places were writing about similar things.

Comparing Texts: Author Study

When you hear a band that you like, do you ever want to listen to their earlier CDs to compare what they sound like? The same applies to authors. Great authors do not write just one work of literature. They write a number of works for you to read and compare. In **Comparing Texts: Author Study** you will explore several works by one author to make deeper connections as you read.

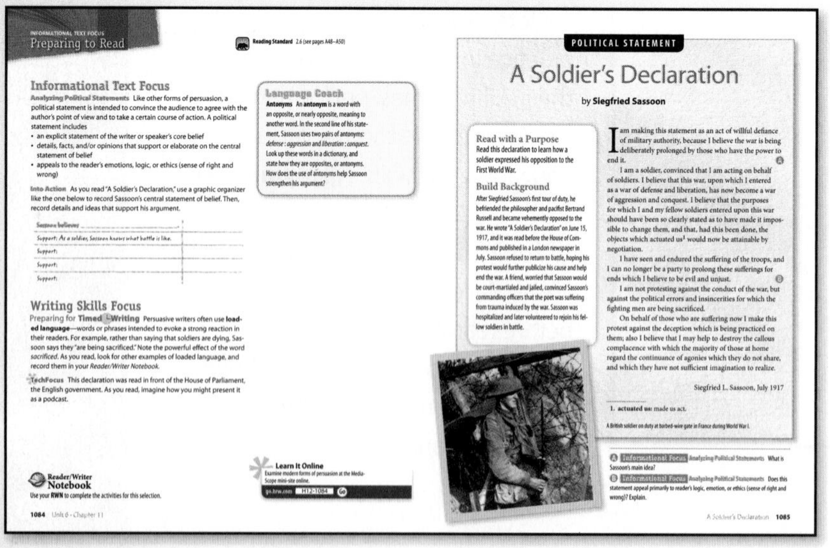

Informational Text Focus

If you have ever read an online encyclopedia or a technical manual, you have been reading informational text. The skills you need for this type of reading are different from the ones you use for literary text. **Informational Text Focus** helps you gain the skills that will enable you to be a more successful reader in daily life and on standardized tests.

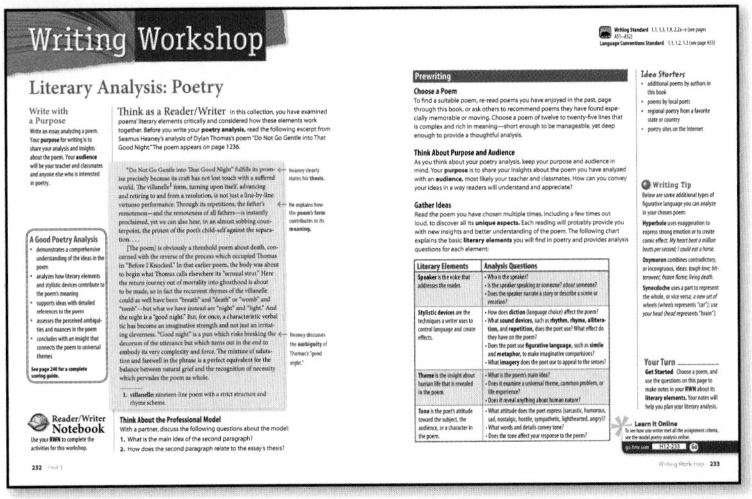
Writing Workshop

Literary Analysis: Poetry

Writing Workshop

As you look forward to work, technical training, or college, you may wonder whether you will leave writing behind in high school. The answer is most definitely "no." Any further education or career will require that you write, probably more than you have the past eleven or twelve years. **Writing Workshops** prepare you for that writing by helping you think through a piece of writing from the glimmer of an idea to the final version.

Preparing for Timed Writing

Have you ever nervously sat with a blank sheet of paper, trying to respond to a writing prompt, while the clock ticks ominously? **Preparing for Timed Writing** helps you practice for on-demand, or timed, writing so that you can realize your dreams of success.

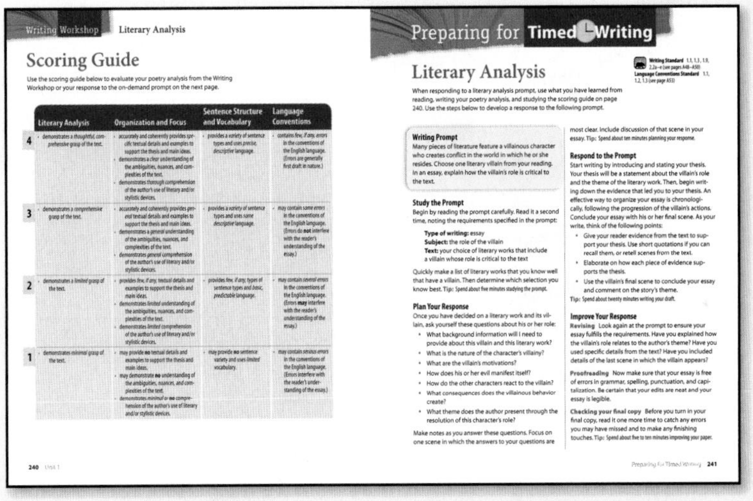
Scoring Guide

Preparing for Timed Writing

Literary Analysis

Literary Skills Review

The Twa Corbies

Raven doth to raven fly

Standards Review

Does the thought of taking a standardized test make you break out into a cold sweat? **Standards Review** can reduce your anxiety by giving you the practice you need to feel more confident during testing.

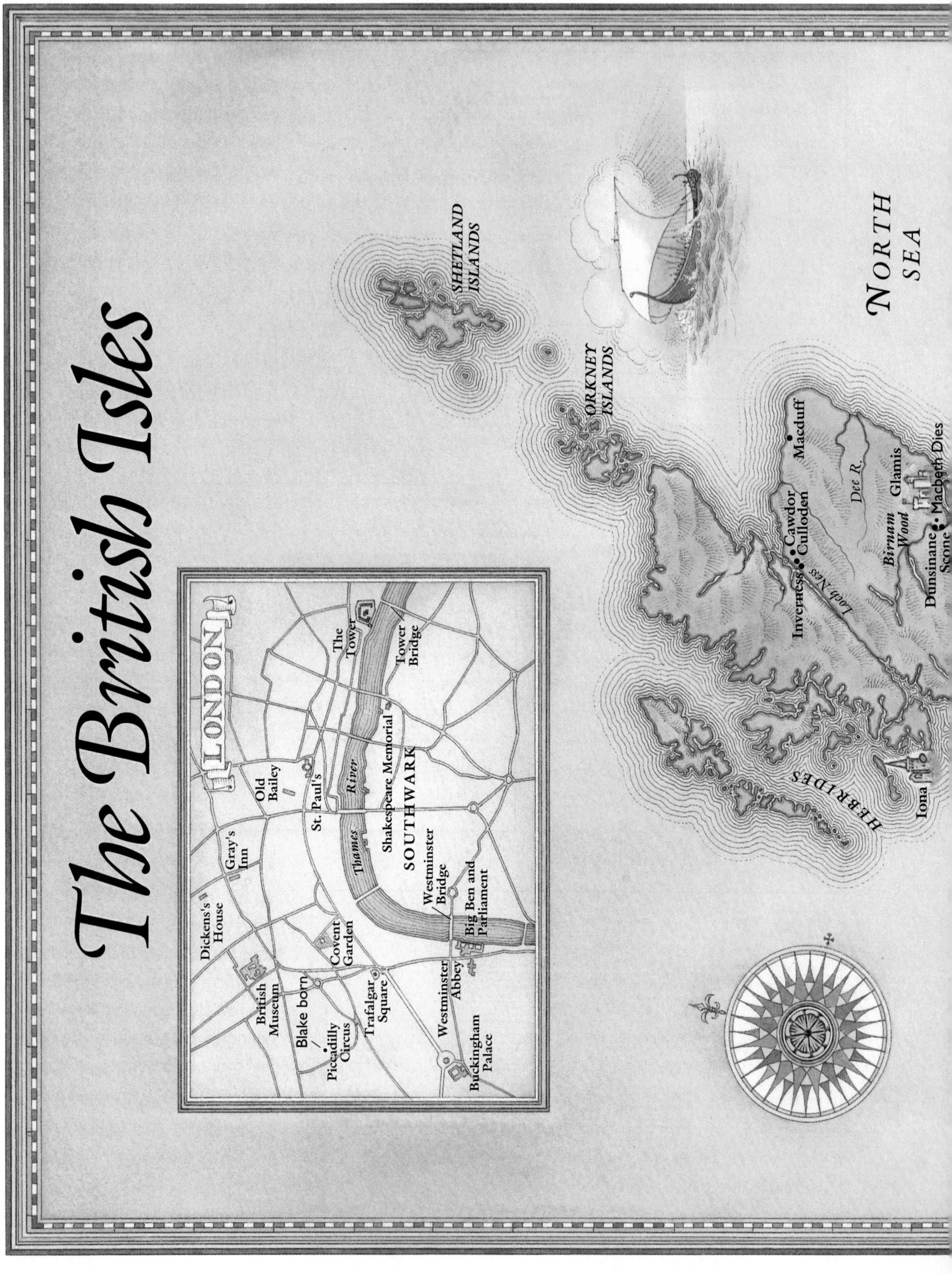
The British Isles
LONDON
Dickens's House
Gray's Inn
Old Bailey
British Museum
Blake born
Piccadilly Circus
Covent Garden
St. Paul's
The Tower
Tower Bridge
Trafalgar Square
Thames River
Shakespeare Memorial
SOUTHWARK
Westminster Bridge
Big Ben and Parliament
Westminster Abbey
Buckingham Palace
SHETLAND ISLANDS
ORKNEY ISLANDS
NORTH SEA
HEBRIDES
Iona
Inverness
Cawdor
Culloden
Loch Ness
Macduff
Dee R.
Glamis
Birnam Wood
Dunsinane
Scone
Macbeth Dies

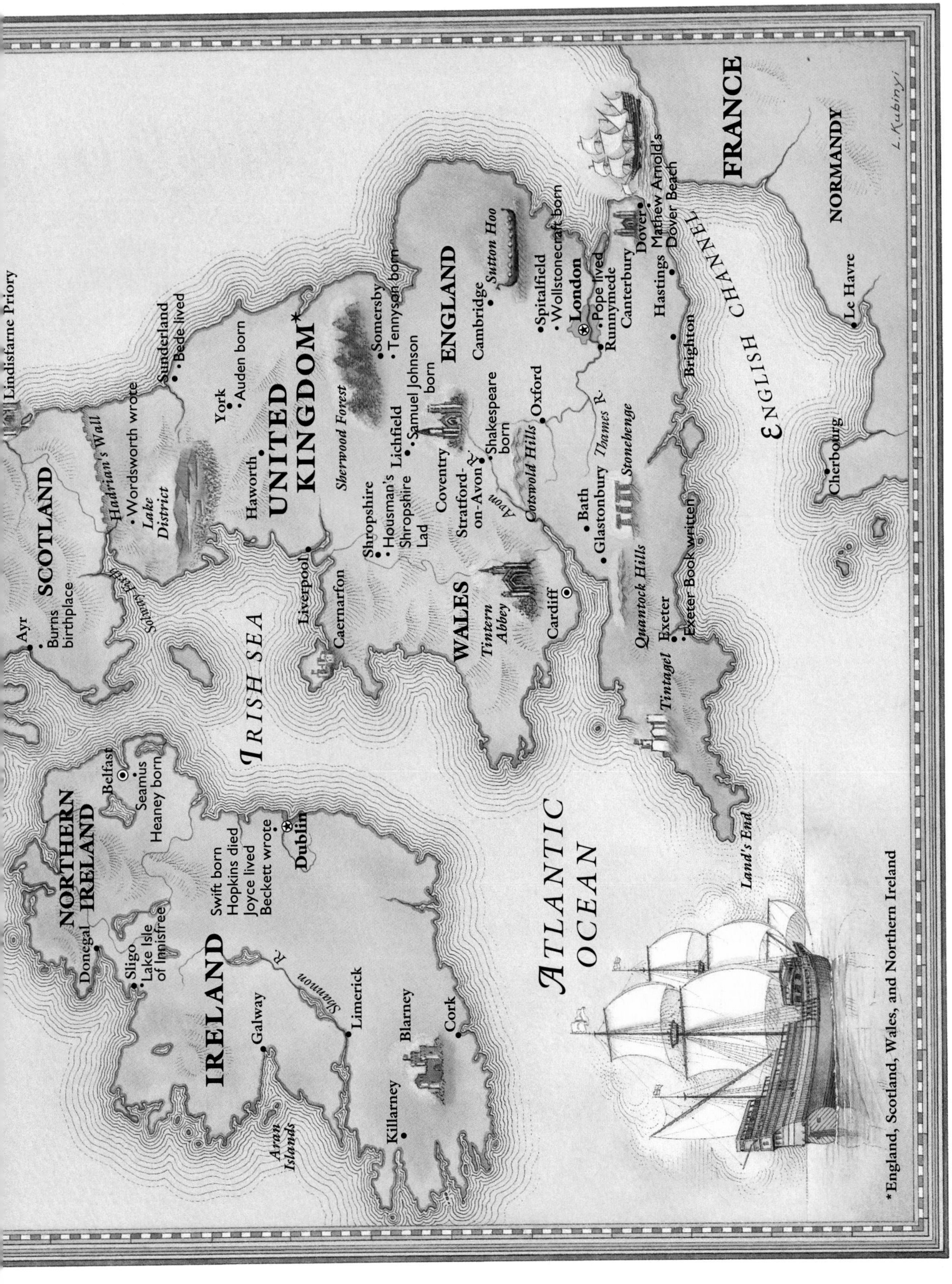

SCOTLAND
Lindisfarne Priory
Ayr
Burns birthplace
Solway Firth
Hadrian's Wall
Wordsworth wrote
Lake District
Sunderland
Bede lived
York
Auden born
Haworth
UNITED KINGDOM*
Sherwood Forest
Somersby
Tennyson born
ENGLAND
Sutton Hoo
Cambridge
Liverpool
Caernarfon
Shropshire
Housman's Shropshire Lad
Lichfield
Samuel Johnson born
Coventry
Stratford-on-Avon
Shakespeare born
Avon R.
Oxford
Cotswold Hills
Thames R.
Spitalfield
Wollstonecraft born
London
Pope lived
Runnymede
Canterbury
Dover
Mathew Arnold's Dover Beach
WALES
Tintern Abbey
Cardiff
Bath
Glastonbury
Stonehenge
Quantock Hills
Exeter
Exeter Book written
Tintagel
Land's End
Hastings
Brighton
ENGLISH CHANNEL
FRANCE
NORMANDY
Le Havre
Cherbourg
IRISH SEA
NORTHERN IRELAND
Belfast
Seamus Heaney born
Donegal
Sligo
Lake Isle of Innisfree
Dublin
Swift born
Hopkins died
Joyce lived
Beckett wrote
IRELAND
Galway
Shannon R.
Limerick
Blarney
Cork
Killarney
Aran Islands
ATLANTIC OCEAN
L. Kubinyi
*England, Scotland, Wales, and Northern Ireland

Map of
NORTH AMERICA
Canada
Toronto
Atwood lives
United States
St. Louis
Eliot born
ATLANTIC OCEAN
CARIBBEAN SEA
St. Lucia
Walcott born
Trinidad and Tobago
PACIFIC OCEAN
SOUTH AMERICA
Chile
Linares Province
Neruda born
Argentina
Buenos Aires
Borges writes

Literary Maps

The Anglo-Saxon Period and The Middle Ages 449–1485

Features highlighted in **yellow** constitute a suggested minimum course of study.

Chapter 1

Selection or Feature	For Independent Reading	Grade-Level Standards
The Anglo-Saxon Period and the Middle Ages 449–1485 **Link to Today:** *from* **The Lord of the Rings: The Two Towers** by J. R. R. Tolkien (Accessible, Lexile 1110)		
Literary Skills Focus: The Epic Tradition by David Adams Leeming		**Reading Standard 3.6:** Archetypes **Reading Standard 3.7:** Contrasting literary forms
Reading Skills Focus: Paraphrasing by Kylene Beers		**Reading Standard 2.2:** Clarify meaning through structure, repetition, syntax, and word choice.
• *from* **Beowulf, Part One** translated by Burton Raffel (Challenging, Lexile N/A) • *from* **Beowulf, Part Two** translated by Seamus Heaney (Challenging, Lexile N/A)	• **The Tombs of Atuan** by Ursula K. Le Guin • **Crusader** by Edward Bloor	**Reading Standard 2.2:** Clarify meaning through structure, repetition, syntax, and word choice. **Reading Standard 3.6:** Archetypes
Link to Today: *from* **The Collected Beowulf** by Gareth Hinds (Challenging, Lexile 1100)		**Reading Standard 3.1:** Analyze subgenres **Reading Standard 3.6:** Archetypes
from **The Exeter Book** Anonymous (Challenging, Lexile N/A) • **The Seafarer** translated by Burton Raffel • **The Wife's Lament** translated by Richard Hamer • **The Wanderer** translated by Burton Raffel • **Anglo-Saxon Riddles** translated by Burton Raffel	**How to Read a Poem** by Edward Hirsch	**Reading Standard 2.2:** Clarify meaning through structure, repetition, syntax, and word choice. **Reading Standard 3.1:** Analyze subgenres **Reading Standard 3.2:** Theme
from **A History of the English Church and People** by Bede, translated by Leo Sherley-Price (Challenging, Lexile 1140)	• **The Inferno** by Dante • **Body and Soul** by Frank Conroy	**Reading Standard 3.7:** Relate works to themes and issues of period.
Comparing Texts: World Literature: Epics Across Cultures • *from* **Gilgamesh: A Verse Narrative** retold by Herbert Mason (Accessible, Lexile N/A) • The **Iliad** *from* **Book 22: The Death of Hector** by Homer, translated by Robert Fagles (Challenging, Lexile N/A)	• **The Places in Between** by Rory Stewart • **The King Must Die** by Mary Renault • **Troy** by Adéle Geras • **Herpes: A Novel** by Robert Cormier	**Reading Standard 3.1:** Analyze subgenres **Reading Standard 3.4:** Analyze figures of speech **Grades 9–10 Review Reading Standard 3.3:** Analyze interactions between characters **Writing Standard 2.2:** Understanding significant ideas

Daily and Weekly Support

- **Reader/Writer Notebook**
- **Reading and Writing Transparencies**
- **Family Involvement Activities in Spanish**
- **Language Handbook Worksheets**
- **Holt Virtual File Cabinet for Language Arts**

Assessment Resources

- **Unit 1 Resources**, Chapter 1 Diagnostic Test; Selection Standards Checks, Chapter 1 Standards Mastery
- **Universal Access: Differentiating Instruction**, leveled assessment
- **Formal Assessment**, Entry-Level Test
- **English-Language Conventions Progress-Monitoring Tests**, Chapters 1–2
- **ThinkCentral Online Assessment**

Chapter 2

Selection or Feature	For Independent Reading	Grade-Level Standards
Literary Skills Focus: **Medieval Narrative** by Leila Christenbury		**Reading Standard 3.1:** Analyze subgenres. **Reading Standard 3.7:** Analyze world literature.
Analyzing Visuals: Connecting to Medieval Narrative		**Reading Standard 3.1:** Analyze subgenres. **Reading Standard 3.7:** Analyze world literature.
Reading Skills Focus: **Analyzing Style** by Kylene Beers		**Reading Standard 3.3:** Analyze effects of irony, tone, mood, and style.
from **The Canterbury Tales** by Geoffrey Chaucer (Accessible, Lexile N/A) • **The Prologue** • *from* **The Pardoner's Tale** • *from* **The Wife of Bath's Tale**	**A River Sutra** by Gita Mehta	**Reading Standard 2.5:** Analyze philosophical beliefs. **Reading Standard 3.1:** Analyze subgenres. **Reading Standard 3.3:** Analyze effects of irony, tone, mood, and style. **Reading Standard 3.8:** Analyze political assumptions. **Grades 9–10 Review Reading Standard 3.4:** Characters' traits **Grades 9–10 Review Reading Standard 3.9:** Narrator's voice and persona
Link to Today: *from* **Walking to Canterbury** by Jerry Ellis (Accessible, Lexile 1250)		**Reading Standard 2.2:** Clarity of ideas
• **Lord Randall** Anonymous (Challenging, Lexile N/A) • **Get Up and Bar the Door** by Anonymous (Challenging, Lexile N/A) • **Edward, Edward** by Anonymous (Challenging, Lexile N/A)	**Cambodian Folk Stories from the Gatiloke** by Muriel P. Carrison	**Reading Standard 3.1:** Analyze subgenres. **Reading Standard 3.3:** Analyze effects of irony, tone, mood, and style.
from **Sir Gawain and the Green Knight** translated by John Gardner (Challenging, Lexile 870)	• **Narcissus and Goldmund** by Hermann Hesse • **Ivanhoe** by Sir Walter Scott	**Reading Standard 2.2:** Clarify meaning through structure, repetition, syntax, and word choice. **Reading Standard 3.1:** Analyze subgenres
from **Le Morte d'Arthur** by Sir Thomas Malory, retold by Keith Baines (Accessible, Lexile 1090)	• **Sun Dancing** by Geoffrey Moorhouse • **The Story of King Arthur and His Knights** by Howard Pyle	**Reading Standard 2.2:** Clarify meaning through structure, repetition, syntax, and word choice. **Reading Standard 3.6:** Archetypes
from **Everyman** Anonymous (Challenging, Lexile N/A)	• **A Midsummer Night's Dream** by William Shakespeare • **Tales from Shakespeare** by Charles and Mary Lamb	**Reading Standard 2.4:** Analyze an author's arguments. **Reading Standard 3.1:** Analyze subgenres.

Daily and Weekly Support

- **Reader/Writer Notebook**
- **Reading and Writing Transparencies**
- **Family Involvement Activities in Spanish**
- **Language Handbook Worksheets**
- **Holt Virtual File Cabinet for Language Arts**

Assessment Resources

- **Unit 1 Resources**, Chapter 2 Diagnostic Test; Selection Standards Checks, Chapter 2 Standards Mastery
- **Universal Access: Differentiating Instruction**, leveled assessment
- **Formal Assessment**, Progress Monitoring Test 1
- **English Language Conventions Progress-Monitoring Tests**, Chapters 2–3
- **ThinkCentral Online Assessment**

Mastering the Skills

Selection or Feature	Grade-Level Standards
Writing Workshop: Literary Analysis: Poetry	**Writing Standard 1.1:** Understand elements of discourse. **Writing Standard 1.3:** Structure and support ideas and arguments. **Writing Standard 1.9:** Revise text. **Writing Standard 2.2:** Responses to literature
Preparing for Timed Writing	**Writing Standard 1.1:** Understand elements of discourse.
Listening and Speaking Workshop: Presenting a Literary Analysis	**Listening and Speaking Standard 2.3:** Deliver oral responses to literature.
Standards Review: Literary Skills Review Vocabulary Skills Review Writing Skills Review	**Reading Standard 3.7:** Analyze recognized works of literature from a variety of authors. **Grades 9–10 Review Reading Standard 1.1:** Literal and figurative meanings of words **Writing Standard 2.2:** Write responses to literature.

Print Resources for Universal Access

Unit 1 • Chapter 1

	On-Level Learners	English Learners	Struggling Readers	Students Who Use African American Vernacular English	Advanced Learners	Students with Disabilities
Unit 1 Resources practice and assessment for selections and features in Chapter 1	✔				✔	
Universal Access: Holt Interactive Reader interactive readings for *from* Beowulf, Part One and Part Two		✔	✔	✔		✔
Universal Access: Differentiating Instruction modified lesson plans and leveled assessment for *from* Beowulf, Part One and Part Two		✔	✔	✔		✔
Universal Access: Resources for Teaching Advanced Students lesson plans for *from* Beowulf, Part One and Part Two					✔	

Print Resources for Universal Access

Unit 1 • Chapter 2

	On-Level Learners	English Learners	Struggling Readers	Students Who Use African American Vernacular English	Advanced Learners	Students with Disabilities
Unit 1 Resources practice and assessment for selections and features in Chapter 2	✔				✔	
Universal Access: Holt Interactive Reader interactive readings for The Prologue *from* The Canterbury Tales, Lord Randall, *from* Sir Gawain and the Green Knight		✔	✔	✔		✔
Universal Access: Differentiating Instruction modified lesson plans and leveled assessment for The Prologue *from* The Canterbury Tales, Lord Randall, *from* Sir Gawain and the Green Knight		✔	✔	✔		✔
Universal Access: Resources for Teaching Advanced Students lesson plans for The Prologue *from* The Canterbury Tales, Lord Randall, *from* Sir Gawain and the Green Knight					✔	

Print Resources for Universal Access

All Chapters

	On-Level Learners	English Learners	Struggling Readers/Writers	Students Who Use African American Vernacular English	Advanced Learners	Students with Disabilities
Universal Access: Supporting Instruction in Spanish translations of selection summaries and key terms		✔				
Universal Access: Holt Interactive Writer and Speaker practice and assessment	✔	✔	✔	✔	✔	✔
Language and Sentence Skills Practice for Warriner's Handbook Chapters 1–4	✔				✔	
Universal Access: Developmental Language and Sentence Skills Practice for Warriner's Handbook Chapters 1–4		✔	✔	✔		✔

Technology Resources

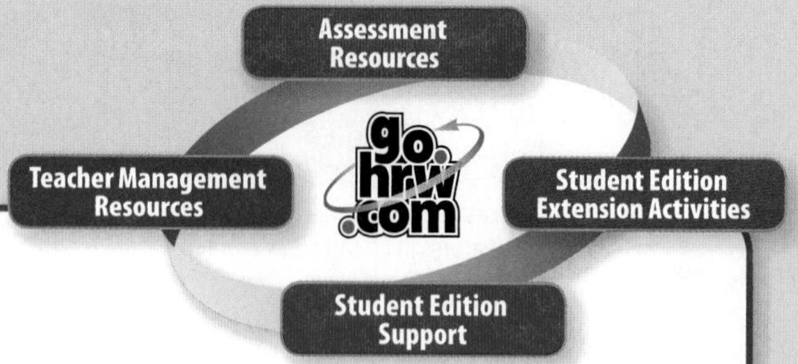

Find all of Holt's technology resources at go.hrw.com. Technology resources are also listed at point of use in the Teacher's Edition wrap. Below are our featured components for Unit 1.

Teacher Management Resources

- ThinkCentral, Teacher Access
- Teacher One Stop™
- Holt Professional Learning for Language Arts

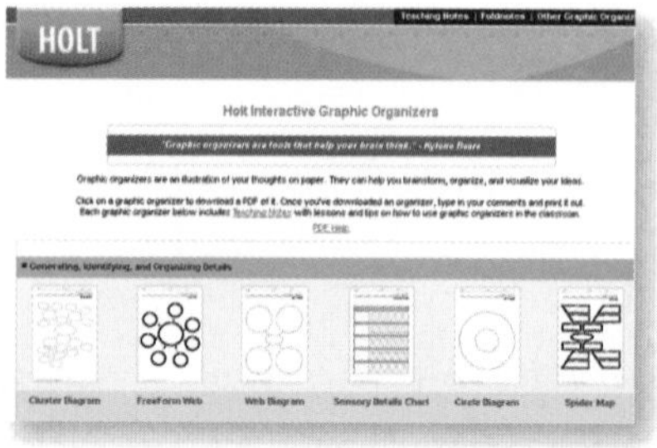

Spotlight on ThinkCentral, Teacher Access

All of the unit's resources are available on ThinkCentral, Teacher Access:

- Suggest students use the interactive Venn diagram when comparing the excerpts from *Gilgamesh* and from the *Iliad*.
- Play the audio recordings of "Lord Randall," "Get Up and Bar the Door," and "Edward, Edward" so students can hear these ballads brought to life.

Student Edition Support

- **PowerNotes**
- ThinkCentral, Student Access
- Student One Stop™
- Interactive Reading Workshops
- Interactive Graphic Organizers
- Writers' Lives
- Holt Audio Library
- Holt Audio Library: Selections and Summaries in Spanish

Spotlight on PowerNotes

Help your students build background for and motivate them to read the excerpts from *Beowulf*, from *The Canterbury Tales*: The Prologue, "Lord Randall," and *Sir Gawain and the Green Knight* through the PowerNotes videos.

Universal Access: Struggling Readers will particularly benefit from the background information these videos provide.

Supported Strands: Vocabulary, Reading, Literature, Writing

Available on DVD-ROM as well as on go.hrw.com.

Student Edition Extension Activities

- Digital Storytelling Mini-Site
- **GrammarNotes**
- NovelWise Mini-Site
- MediaScope Mini-Site
- WordSharp: An Interactive Vocabulary Tutor
- WritingNotes
- Writing and Research in a Digital Age
- Literature Links

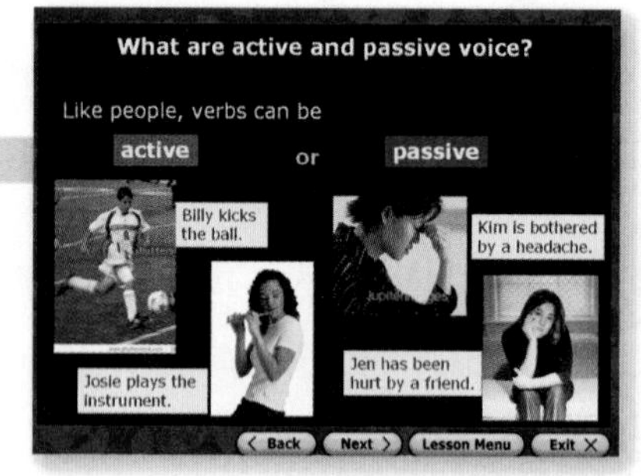

Spotlight on GrammarNotes

These customizable PowerPoint presentations provide student-friendly, interactive instruction on basic grammar concepts—and help students connect grammar with writing and literature.

Universal Access: English learners and struggling writers can benefit from the presentation "Using Active Voice and Passive Voice" when writing essays or the literary analysis in this unit's Writing Workshop.

Supported Strand: Writing

Assessment Resources

- **ThinkCentral Online Assessment**
- Holt Online Essay Scoring
- ThinkCentral Online Remediation

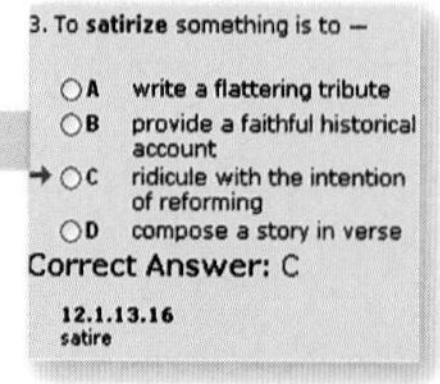
3. To **satirize** something is to —

- A write a flattering tribute
- B provide a faithful historical account
- C ridicule with the intention of reforming
- D compose a story in verse

Correct Answer: C

12.1.13.16
satire

Spotlight on ThinkCentral Online Assessment

Find the Chapters 1–2 Diagnostic Tests and Standards Mastery here, correlated to standards covered in this unit. The individualized diagnostic reporting will let you see exactly which concepts in this unit for which each student will need extra help.

Real Issues, Real Experts

The wrap for these selections includes specific ideas and strategies from *Holt Literature and Language Arts* authors.

From the Authors

For *Beowulf*, p. 23

When teaching *Beowulf*, I begin by explaining that each of the heroic episodes is self-contained and the epic itself book-ended with funerals. When students understand how a story "works," they can relax into their reading.

Carol Jago

For *The Canterbury Tales*, p. 122

A careful reading of Chaucer's "Prologue," can be an investigation of life in fourteenth-century England and the motives that animated it. Like detectives scrutinizing people on a street corner, your students need to separate appearances from truth.

Deborah Appleman

For Analyzing Poetry, p. 232

When we ask students to write about literature, we should ask them to approach their exploratory analysis with an attitude. This investigatory posture may help students expand their analysis and complicate—in a good way—their understanding of a text.

Leila Christenbury

Teacher to Teacher

Preteach Before reading the selections in this unit, I define the "life relevancy" words *history, psychology, philosophy, sociology* and *theology.* Then, I show short clips from films like *Star Wars or The Lord of the Rings* and ask students to identify examples of each word in the film. After students have identified examples, I have my them work in groups to research and explain the term "monomyth."

Direct Teach Have students continue working in groups while reading the selections from *Beowulf.* Then, have students complete a "Life Relevancy Word" and "Elements of the Monomyth" graphic organizers and research the biographies and stories of real-life modern heroes.

Assess Ask students to create multimedia or poster presentations demonstrating parallels between the legendary and real-life heroes. Encourage them to explain how their common elements reflect the human experience.

Matt Rehling
Huntington Beach, California

Holt Professional Learning

Visit ThinkCentral, Teacher Access to link to Holt's Professional Learning site for English/ Language Arts teachers. This site features:

- Videos that share the insights of *Holt Literature and Language Arts* program authors and consultants and demonstrate proven classroom strategies with master teachers
- Study guides for publications by our authors and consultants
- Informative articles and useful Web links
- Help in planning your department's professional learning sessions
- A handbook for new teachers

Re-engaging the Disengaged Student
with Alfred Tatum

VIDEO PRODUCTS

Strategies for Helping Struggling Readers
with Kylene Beers

Effective Vocabulary Instruction
with Carol Jago and Kylene Beers

Developing Critical Thinking about Literature
with Carol Jago and Deborah Appleman

Teaching Students to Revise, Not Recopy
with Linda Rief

Teaching English Learners
with Robin Scarcella

Using Literature Circles
with Harvey Daniels

Teaching On-Demand Writing Skills
with Leila Christenbury

Managing the Heterogeneous Classroom
with Leila Christenbury and Patrick Schwarz

Teaching Narrative and Expository Texts
with Judith Irvin and Deborah Appleman

Becoming a Tech-Savvy Teacher
with Sara Kajder

Re-engaging the Disengaged Student
with Alfred Tatum

Teaching Grammar in Context
with Amy Benjamin

UNIT 1

Unit Objectives

- Students will read excerpts from *Beowulf, Gilgamesh,* and the *Iliad* and will learn the characteristics of epic poetry and of the archetypal hero.
- Students will learn about Anglo-Saxon values and the distinct characteristics of Anglo-Saxon poetry by reading examples of Anglo-Saxon elegies, riddles, and historical poems.
- Students will learn how the Norman invasion influenced early medieval English society, its language, and its literature.
- Students will read excerpts from *Sir Gawain and the Green Knight* and *Le Morte d'Arthur* as examples of romance narratives.
- Students will analyze Geoffrey Chaucer's use of imagery, irony, and characterization in excerpts from *The Canterbury Tales*.

Analyzing Visuals

Tell students that the creator of the painting is British. King Alfred was eventually victorious in the battle against the Danes.

Extension Activity What can you tell from the painting about King Alfred's enduring image? ***Responses will vary.*** *The warriors are painted to look proud and fearless. The painting does not dwell on the violence but instead emphasizes the king's heroic stateliness.*

Unit Resources

On Course: Mapping Instruction

Unit 1 Resources

Warriner's Handbook
- Chapter 1, Parts of Speech Overview
- Chapter 2, The Parts of a Sentence

Teacher One Stop™

Formal Assessment, Progress Monitoring Test

English-Language Conventions Progress-Monitoring Tests

ThinkCentral Online Assessment

Holt Virtual File Cabinet for Language Arts, grammar, reading, and vocabulary resources

Holt Pronunciation Resources
- Phoneme Sounds and Spellings
- Support for Speakers of African American Vernacular English

ThinkCentral Online Remediation

Direct Teach

Teach the Time Line

Give students 5–10 minutes to study the time line. Then, ask the following questions:

- What did the Saxons, Vikings, and Normans have in common? ***Possible response:*** *At different times, each of these groups invaded Britain.*
- Which three entries on the time line show the relationship between early English literature and religious tradition? ***Possible response:*** *c. 670, Caedmon, the earliest English Christian poet, composes hymns; 760, Monks begin the Book of Kells, an illuminated manuscript of Latin Gospels; 1380, entire Bible is translated into English for first time, by followers of John Wycliffe.*
- How did the social role of ordinary British citizens change during the thirteenth century? ***Possible response:*** *Beginning in the middle of the thirteenth century, commoners were allowed to become members of the British Parliament.*

The Anglo-Saxon Period and the Middle Ages 449–1485

This time line represents a snapshot of British literary events, British political and social events, and world events from 449 to 1485. During this period, widespread political and cultural changes took place in Britain and around the world.

Opening words of the Gospel of St. Luke. Irish. Vellum. MS 58 fol. 188. The Board of Trinity College, Dublin.

BRITISH LITERARY EVENTS

449

c. 449 Roman and Persian myths mingle with Celtic and Germanic myths, forming the basis for much of Western literature

670 Caedmon, the earliest English Christian poet, composes hymns

c. 700 *Beowulf* is composed in Old English

750

760 Monks begin the Book of Kells, an illuminated manuscript of Latin Gospels >

975 *The Exeter Book*, a collection of English poetry, is first copied

1086 Domesday Book, a record of all land ownership in England, is first compiled

BRITISH POLITICAL AND SOCIAL EVENTS

449

449 Angles, Saxons, and Jutes invade Britain

537 King Arthur dies at Battle of Camlann >

597 Saint Augustine converts Anglo-Saxon King Ethelbert and establishes monastery at Canterbury

King Arthur's Round Table and the Holy Grail (c. 1470). Medieval manuscript (Ms. Fr. 112, folio 5). Bibliothèque Nationale, Paris, France.

750

793 Vikings invade Britain, beginning a century of invasions >

1066 Normans invade England and defeat the Saxons; William the Conqueror becomes English king

Havhingsten fra Glendalough ("The Sea Stallion from Glendalough") at sea, 2007. Viking Ship Museum, Denmark.

WORLD EVENTS

449

476 Roman Empire falls to Germanic tribes

500s Books are printed in China

650 Official version of the Koran (Qur'an) is collected

750

810 Algebra is devised in Persia

1000 In Japan, Lady Murasaki Shikibu writes the world's first novel, *The Tale of Genji*

Seated Buddha (c. 650), Chinese, Tang dynasty (618–907). The Metropolitan Museum of Art, Rogers Fund, 1919 (19.186).

California Standards, pp. 2–3

- **Reading Standard 3.7c** Evaluate the philosophical, political, religious, ethical, and social influences of the historical period that shaped the characters, plots and settings.

Universal Access

EL English Learners/ Struggling Readers

English for Academic Success Read through each section of the time line with students and clarify the following words and phrases that may impede students' understanding.

- **British Literary Events:** *mingle, basis, illuminated manuscript, compiled, Arthurian*
- **British Political and Social Events:** *converts, monastery, domination, barons, commoners, Black Death*
- **World Events:** *devised, mass-produced, establish, flourishes*

Use a map to help students understand the geographic origins of specific cultures, such as Roman, Saxon, Persian, Celtic, Germanic, and Norman. When possible, connect these terms to modern countries.

King Alfred's Longships, Newly Built for the Defense of the Realm, Attack Vessels of the Danish Invaders Storm-Beaten in Swanage Bay in 877 by Colin Unwin Gill (1892–1940). Mural. Houses of Parliament, Westminster, London.

UNIT 1

The Anglo-Saxon Period and the Middle Ages

449–1485

CHAPTER 1
The Anglo-Saxons: Songs of Ancient Heroes

CHAPTER 2
The Middle Ages: The Tales They Told

"Not the glittering weapon fights the fight, but rather the hero's heart."

—**Proverb**

What Do You Think? What moves a hero to act?

Learn It Online
Find out more about this historical period online.
go.hrw.com H12-01 Go

1

The Quotation

- Explain to students that while the origins of this proverb are not precisely known, the proverb reflects Anglo-Saxon culture in its emphasis on valor in battle. The word "heart" represents the quality of courage.
- Anglo-Saxon culture, influenced by early Roman tradition as well as the beliefs of invading Germanic tribes, valued physical strength and heroism. These traits were honored in legends about supremely courageous and powerful heroes, retold both orally and in writing.

Routines for California Classrooms

For ideas on classroom practices and approaches to grouping, see the discussion of routines on pages T34–T37 of this Teacher's Edition.

What Do You Think?

What moves a hero to act?

- Have students draw connections between the unit question, the proverb, and the situations about which they write. Ask students how they define heroism and how people might act heroically in situations that do not involve physical battle.
- Have students write for 3–5 minutes in their **Reader/Writer Notebooks** about a situation in which they or someone they know acted heroically.
- Refer students to the time line on the next page to help them think about how historical events influenced Anglo-Saxon perspectives on heroism.

Real Issues, Real Experts: Professional Learning

Spotlight on . . .
Motivation and Vocabulary Videos

Works such as *Beowulf* and *The Canterbury Tales* challenge students with archaic vocabulary and perceived irrelevance to modern life. To help you overcome these challenges, consider the suggestions you'll find in these videos:

In ***Re-engaging the Disengaged Student***, **Alfred Tatum**, an expert on culturally responsive education, discusses ways to make reading tasks relevant to students.

Effective Vocabulary Instruction, featuring Holt authors **Carol Jago** and **Kylene Beers**, details a three-pronged approach that will help students take ownership of their vocabulary development.

Each video is accompanied by printable articles, planning materials, and a training guide for supervisors. For these resources and more, visit **Holt Professional Learning** by going to this page in **ThinkCentral, Teacher Access.**

Learn It Online
You can introduce some of the topics in this unit using brief videos about the literature of this period.
go.hrw.com H12-1 Go

Standards Focus

Objectives

Students will

- understand the development of British literature from the Anglo-Saxon period through the Middle Ages
- evaluate the philosophical, political, religious, ethical, and social influences of a historical period

Preteach

Key Concepts

Use the Key Concepts to preview the unit introduction. Each key concept is addressed in a separate section of the essay that relates the concept to both the history and the literature of the times.

Set a Purpose for Reading

- Ask students to identify one piece of information from each key concept that they want to learn more about.
- Have students jot down any concepts, images, or phrases that come to mind when they think of early and medieval Britain. Suggest that students look for information related to these concepts as they read.
- Tell students to record each section's main ideas and important details in their **Reader/Writer Notebooks**.

The Anglo-Saxon Period and the Middle Ages 449–1485

The relatively small group of islands now known as Great Britain have been invaded and settled many times: first by ancient people we call the Iberians, then by the Celts (kelts), the Romans, the Angles and Saxons, the Vikings, and the Normans. Whatever we think of as British today owes something to each of these invaders. The language of the Anglo-Saxons gave this land its name—*Engla land,* or *England.* During this period a distinct form of English literature developed and helped to define the English national character.

KEY CONCEPTS

The Anglo-Saxon Legacy

History of the Times The collapse of the Roman Empire left Britain, its northernmost province, vulnerable to invasion. Angle and Saxon invaders imposed their warrior culture on the island for six centuries. Divided at first into clans, the Anglo-Saxons were later united under Alfred the Great.

Literature of the Times Anglo-Saxon literature shares common themes and ideals of conduct. The epic poem *Beowulf* reflects a society that esteemed loyalty, strength, and courage, and considered fame and glory the noblest end of a warrior.

The Normans Invade Britain

History of the Times In 1066, William the Conqueror led the Norman invasion of England and defeated the Anglo-Saxons. As king, William divided the land among his loyal barons. This system created a social structure in which every person had a place in a fixed hierarchy.

Literature of the Times Under King Alfred, the *Anglo-Saxon Chronicle* had helped make English a respected language. After 1066, literature was usually written in Latin or Norman French, reflecting the social chasm between the British masses and the Norman rulers.

Life in Medieval Society

History of the Times Under the feudal system, medieval society comprised distinctly defined social classes, including the nobility, knights, peasants, the clergy, and merchants. The contributions of each group affected how well villages and towns operated and prospered.

Literature of the Times Although monks wrote scholarly works in Latin and French, other medieval writers began to use the vernacular, or language of the common people. Works written in English, such as ballads and romances, helped to define England's national identity.

California Standards, pp. 4–11

- **Reading Standard 2.2** Analyze the way in which clarity of meaning is affected by the patterns of organization, hierarchical structures, repetition of the main ideas, syntax, and word choice in the text.
- **Reading Standard 3.7** Relate literary works and authors to the major themes and issues of their eras. **b.** Relate literary works and authors to the major themes and issues of their eras. **c.** Evaluate the philosophical, political, religious, ethical, and social influences of the historical period that shaped the characters, plots, and settings.

Resources

Unit 1 Resources, on-level instruction, Historical Introduction Study Guide, p. 1

UA: Holt Interactive Reader, Key Concepts and Academic Vocabulary, p. 2

PowerNotes, interactive lesson presentation with activities go.hrw.com

Teacher One Stop™, on-level lesson plans and all print resources

Universal Access

Struggling Readers

Benchmark Students Have students create a graphic organizer—such as a chart, time line, or tree diagram—to record what they learn from this essay. Students can use the subheads, names of writers, or dates to organize information on their graphic. After they read, ask students whether this strategy helped them process information.

Reading Standard 3.7c (see pages A48–A50)

Your Turn

How many times was Britain invaded during the period covered in this time line? What effects might such a series of invasions have on a culture and its heroes?

1100 **1350** **1485**

c. 1100 The *Mabinogion* is written in Welsh, including "Kulwch and Olwen," an Arthurian legend

1342 Julian of Norwich, one of the first known English women of letters, is born

1378 Legendary hero Robin Hood appears in *Piers Plowman*

1380 Entire Bible is translated into English for first time, by followers of John Wycliffe

1387 Chaucer begins *The Canterbury Tales*

1475 William Caxton prints first book in England

Figure thought to be Chaucer, from the Ellesmere manuscript. Fol. 153v. The Huntington Library, San Marino, California.

1100 **1350** **1485**

1171 Henry II invades Ireland, beginning nearly eight hundred years of British domination

1215 English barons force King John to sign the Magna Carta

1250 First commoners are allowed in the British Parliament

1348 Black Death strikes England

1381 Peasants' Revolt takes place in England

1455–1485 War of the Roses is fought between the Houses of York and Lancaster

1485 First Tudor king, Henry VII, is crowned

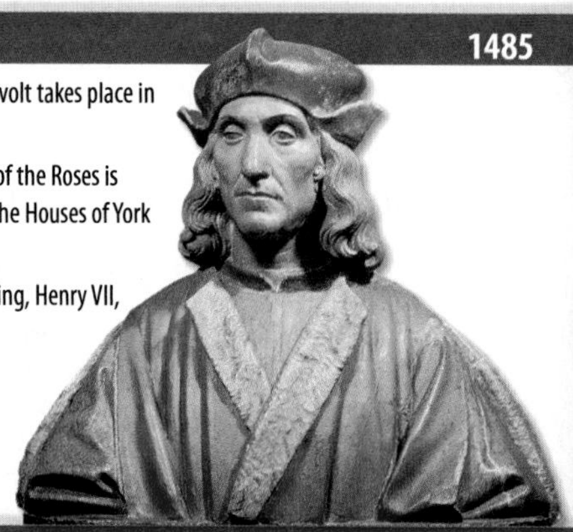

Henry VII (1472–1509) by Pietro Torrigiano (1472–1528). Painted gesso on wood. Victoria & Albert Museum, London.

1100 **1350** **1485**

1150 Paper is first mass-produced, in Spain

1211 Genghis Khan invades China

1325 Aztecs begin to establish empire in Mexico

1400s Benin Kingdom in West Africa flourishes

1438 Incan Empire is established in Peru

1455 Gutenberg prints first book with movable type

The Inca ruins of Machu Picchu.

Advanced Learners

Acceleration Point out that the first English translation of the Bible did not appear until 1380, and no book was printed in England until approximately 1475. Tell students that in feudal England, illiteracy was quite prevalent; literacy was limited to the wealthy and the clergy. Have students hold group discussions evaluating the importance of the aforementioned events.

Students with Disabilities

Tell students that the three time lines show events from the years A.D. 449–1485. Explain that students can compare events on the three time lines by reading the page vertically. Model connecting an event on the time line of British literature to contemporary historical events. You might say: "In 760, monks began creating the Book of Kells. Around that time, Vikings began to invade Britain, and algebra was invented in Persia."

Check for Understanding

Your Turn

Have students talk with a partner about how the repeated invasions of Britain might have influenced early English literature's emphasis on warfare and heroism. Then, have partners share their opinions with the rest of the class.

Explore the Time Line

Enrichment The following activity offers options for students to explore the literary, political, social, and world events presented on the time line.

Group Activity Explain to students that Anglo-Saxon literature often focuses on the adventures of a hero, and that some legendary heroes in fiction were inspired by historical figures.

- Divide the class into two groups. Assign each group a legendary hero to research: King Arthur or Robin Hood.
- Have each group research its assigned topic, focusing on these questions: Are the legends about this hero clearly based on fact? If so, how closely does literature follow historical reality?
- As students research their topic, remind them to relate their research to the unit question: What moves a hero to act?
- Have groups orally report their findings to the class. Remind them to discuss how events or conditions moved a hero to act.

Think About/Talk About

Literature of the Times

According to the Anglo-Saxon historian Bede, Caedmon was prompted to write his first hymn—nine lines of poetry praising the Christian god—by a command given to him by a stranger in a dream. Although Caedmon allegedly continued to write throughout his life, "Caedmon's Hymn" is his only surviving text.

Comprehension Check

Possible response: *The Roman evacuation of troops from Britain in the early fifth century allowed the Angles and Saxons to invade the British provinces.*

Literature of the Times

When the Anglo-Saxons invaded Britain, they introduced a traditional Germanic ethos that celebrated the warrior and his exploits. Little evidence survives of Anglo-Saxon oral poetry, which was primarily used for telling stories and reciting magic. True English literature did not develop until Caedmon, an illiterate cowherd, began composing his own religion-inspired poetry in his native tongue. Before the sixth century there is no evidence that the Anglo-Saxons composed anything in their own language.

When Old English poetry did finally blossom, it became distinctive in several ways. Alliteration, or the use of repeated consonant sounds, gives the poetry a musical quality. Bards[2]—whom the Anglo-Saxons called *scops* (skahps)—relied on sound devices to help them remember their tales, and they repeated phrases and images that audiences would expect and understand. Single ideas are often repeated throughout a poem to create a layered effect in which each appearance adds a new depth of meaning to the whole. The *kenning*, a metaphor expressed as a compound noun—such as "whale-path" for the sea—is also Anglo-Saxon in origin and represents the literature's unique power of description.

For the Anglo-Saxons, creating poetry was as important as fighting, hunting, farming, or loving. For the non-Christian Anglo-Saxons, whose religion offered no hope of an afterlife, only fame and its commemoration in poetry could provide a defense against death. Perhaps this explains why the Anglo-Saxon bards, gifted with the skill to preserve fame in the collective memory, were honored members of society.

Many people consider the epic poem *Beowulf* to be the shining star of Old English literature. It was composed during the early eighth century, first recorded in writing nearly three hundred years later, and printed in 1815. The only surviving manuscript is from around the year 1000. In meter, style, and theme *Beowulf* adheres to the Germanic heroic tradition, yet it represents the core values of Anglo-Saxon culture. Another example of Anglo-Saxon literature is *The Exeter Book*, the largest collection of Old English poetry in existence. It was first compiled in writing around 975, includes nearly one hundred riddles, and exhibits other, diverse styles of early poetry.

Historical poems were another important genre of the time. These poems served as a historical record and were collected in the *Anglo-Saxon Chronicle*, a chronological account of events that begins with the Anglo-Saxon period and extends to Norman-controlled England. The seven manuscripts remain a primary source of early English history.

2. **bards:** poets, often also singers.

Comprehension Check

What event led to the Anglo-Saxon invasion of the British provinces?

Fast Facts

Political and Social Highlights

- The Romans invade Britain in 55 B.C. and create a four-hundred-year period of political stability.
- King Alfred and his descendants unite Anglo-Saxon England in the late ninth century.
- William the Conqueror defeats the Anglo-Saxons in 1066 and introduces feudalism to Britain.
- In 1215, English barons force King John to sign the Magna Carta in an attempt to curb the king's power.
- In 1348 and 1349, the Black Death, or bubonic plague, reduces England's population by a third.

Literary Highlights

- The brooding fatalism of pagan Anglo-Saxon culture gives the first British epic, *Beowulf,* its melancholy tone and stress on earthly heroism.
- The bards, or *scops,* ensure stories have an important position in early British culture.
- Christian monks copy ancient manuscripts, preserving classical and Anglo-Saxon texts.
- Chivalry gives rise to a new form of literature, the romance.

Secondary Source

The Historian's View

Here is how a modern historian, C. Warren Hollister, describes King Alfred the Great: "Like all successful leaders of the age, Alfred was an able warrior. But more than that, he was a brilliant, imaginative organizer who systematized military recruitment and founded the English navy, seeing clearly that Christian Europe could not hope to drive back the Vikings without challenging them on the seas. He filled his land with fortresses which served both as defensive strongholds and as places of sanctuary for the agrarian population in time of war. . . Alfred clarified and rationalized the laws of his people, enforced them strictly, and ruled with an authority such as no Anglo-Saxon king had exercised before his time.

"King Alfred was also a scholar and a patron of learning. . . . By Alfred's time, Latin—the key to classical Christian culture—was almost unknown in England. [He] gathered scholars from far and wide—England, Wales, the continent—and set them to work

Reading Standard 2.2, 3.7b, 3.7c (see pages A48–A50)

KEY CONCEPT

The Anglo-Saxon Legacy

History of the Times

After the legions of Rome conquered the Celts,[1] Roman armies and organization kept Britain free of serious invasions for four hundred years. However, by A.D. 409, the Romans had troubles at home and evacuated their troops. Without Roman control, the Angles and the Saxons from Germany swept ashore, drove out the Celts, and settled the greater part of Britain.

This period of English history is distinguished by the role of the warrior-king and his close-knit group of followers. Before the ninth century, when King Alfred united the Anglo-Saxon clans, England was the site of nearly constant invasions and battles. Not until Alfred led the Anglo-Saxons against the invading Danes did England became in any true sense a nation. The Danes were one of the fierce Viking peoples who crossed the North Sea in their dragon-prowed boats, plundering and destroying everything in their path. The constant threat of war created local communities that bonded the Anglo-Saxons through adversity and harsh living conditions.

During this period, the spread of Christianity also helped unify the Anglo-Saxons. Although it was introduced to Britain at the end of the Roman occupation, Christianity took centuries to establish itself as the main religion. Ireland's Christian monks and missionaries from continental Europe began to spread their beliefs to England during the fifth century. Elements of pagan religions persisted throughout Britain, especially in more remote areas, yet by the late seventh century Christianity had almost entirely replaced other systems of belief. Christianity offered Anglo-Saxon people the hope of a more palatable afterlife, a comfort considering their difficult earthly existence. It also provided a common system of morality and conduct that helped to unite the different local groups throughout Britain.

Under King Alfred, Anglo-Saxons fought to protect their people, their culture, and their church from the ravages of the Danes. The struggle continued until both the Anglo-Saxons and the Danes were defeated in 1066 by William, duke of Normandy, and his invading Normans from northwestern France.

The Arrival of King Sweyn and Danish Troops in England (c. 14th century), from a manuscript. Harl, 2278 f.98v.
The British Library, London.

1. **Celts:** the groups of people originally settled in the British Isles.

Learn It Online
Go online for more information on this historical period.
go.hrw.com H12-05 Go

Direct Teach

Think About/Talk About

Motivate Tell students that the first written English literary texts were created during the Anglo-Saxon period and medieval periods. Point out that the Norman invasion of 1066 is regarded as the beginning of the medieval period in English literature. Ask students to think about what events and concerns might have prompted people in England to create literature during this time period. What might the topics and themes of early British literary works tell us about the cultural circumstances that brought about their creation?

Literature of the Times

Point out that early Anglo-Saxon poetry sometimes addressed religious themes. Explain that the first English kingdom to be converted to Christianity was the southeastern kingdom of Kent in the year 597.

Advanced Learners

Enrichment Have students find online or print articles on the Angles and Saxons and the Vikings. Ask students to compare and contrast the two groups, paying attention to cultures and customs, religious beliefs, and societal values. Have a few volunteers share their findings orally with the class.

Students with Disabilities

Students will struggle following the movements of ancient populations across Europe. Provide students with a copy of a map of Europe and help them identify the areas that Romans, Celts, Angles, and Danes inhabited in A.D. 400. If possible, have students mark their maps with the names of populations.

Learn It Online
You can introduce some of the topics in this unit using brief videos about the literature of this period.
go.hrw.com H12-5 Go

Think About/Talk About

Literature of the Times

Tell students that a morality play is a form of drama in which moral lessons are taught by characters who represent qualities such as Truth, Faith, or Vice. Morality plays were usually performed by semi-professional actors.

Link to Today

Women's Rights Go Wrong

This feature explains that women living in medieval England had far fewer rights than English women living hundreds of years earlier during the Anglo-Saxon period.

1. Ask these questions to help students build background: How have men and women sometimes been treated differently under the law? What legal rights do you think British women did or did not have during the Anglo-Saxon period and the medieval period?
2. After students have read the feature, ask them what changes might have caused medieval women to have fewer rights than their predecessors.
3. Finally, ask students to respond to the **Ask Yourself** question. Use students' responses to spark class discussion.
4. Encourage interested students to do further research on the history of women's rights in Britain.

Comprehension Check

Possible response: *The social hierarchy established under feudalism created thousands of knights whose duty was to serve their king.*

William maintained the efficient systems of government established by the Anglo-Saxons but centralized power under his own rule. To complement the Anglo-Saxons' more democratic and artistic tendencies, the Normans brought administrative ability, an emphasis on law and order, and cultural unity. William also began to replace the English nobility with Normans, modified the expectations for the behavior of the elites, and created great class divisions that oppressed the Anglo-Saxons.

Literature of the Times

The Norman conquest not only displaced the English aristocracy but also ousted the English vernacular.[4] William's rule made Norman French the language of the state. Old English became obsolete and began to disappear from the laws and literature. French—and Latin in the monasteries—would remain the official language until the Hundred Years' War, when two English kings (Edward III and Henry V) claimed the right to the French throne during the fourteenth and fifteenth centuries.

The learning boom of the twelfth and thirteenth centuries resulted in an array of literature. *The Book of Kings* is the oldest significant example of Anglo-Norman prose. Bibles and gospels created in monasteries are still celebrated for their brilliant illuminated manuscripts, which were all done by hand. Poems like *The Voyage of St. Brendan,* religious allegories such as *Castle of Love*, many morality plays, and even biographies were created during this time.

Comprehension Check

How was William the Conqueror able to form such a powerful army following his victory in 1066?

4. **vernacular:** a native language; the everyday language used by most people of a certain country or place.

Link to Today

Women's Rights Go Wrong

It is hard to imagine a time when women were to enjoy fewer rights in the future than they did at present, but such a time came in England of the Middle Ages. Women in Anglo-Saxon England actually fared *better* than their later medieval counterparts. Despite a culture that emphasized warfare and masculine strength, women had more rights in Anglo-Saxon society than they did after the Norman Conquest.

Evidence from wills first used during the later Anglo-Saxon period shows that women inherited and held property—even after marriage. With his proposal, a prospective husband had to offer *morgengifu*, or "morning-gift," of money and land directly to the woman. After marriage the wife had personal control over these assets. Christianity offered women opportunities for education and power. Some became nuns or abbesses: for example, Hild (614–680), the abbess of Whitby (in present-day Yorkshire), accumulated an immense library and turned Whitby into a center of learning.

Medieval women, in contrast, had few individual rights. They held no political power within a militaristic system and were considered subservient to their male relatives. Their social rank was entirely contingent on their father's or husband's position, and they were responsible for child care and housekeeping regardless of their class. Some women experienced temporary power when their husbands were away on business or at war, but they were expected to abdicate their leadership positions the moment the men returned.

Ask Yourself

How do women's roles today compare to their roles during the Anglo-Saxon and medieval periods?

Cross-Curricular Connection

HISTORY: The Bayeux Tapestry

- Tell students that the Bayeux Tapestry, an embroidered band of linen named for the French town where it was discovered, is a piece of medieval artwork that depicts the Norman invasion of England.
- The tapestry shows the events of the Norman Conquest in chronological order, ending with the retreat of King Harold's English troops at the Battle of Hastings in 1066.
- Not much is known of the tapestry's specific origin. It was probably created around the year 1092, and it may have been commissioned by a French bishop named Odo, who was William's half-brother.
- The tapestry's borders are decorated with figures and scenes. Some of these scenes are related to the tapestry's main narrative, but others are depictions of Aesop's fables and other tales popular in the medieval period.

KEY CONCEPT

UNIT 1 INTRODUCTION

The Normans Invade Britain

History of the Times

In 1051, William, duke of Normandy, paid Britain's King Edward a visit. William claimed that during this visit, the king—who had no children—promised William the English throne. As Edward was dying, however, he announced that his kingdom should go to Harold, the British earl of Wessex. This betrayal, imagined or not, spurred William to lead an invasion of England by Normans in 1066.

At the Battle of Hastings, Harold was killed by a chance arrow. William, convinced of his fate, proclaimed himself ruler of England. The new king was crowned on Christmas Day, 1066.

Native revolts against Norman leadership continued until 1071, but William smothered the opposition by rapidly building castles throughout the land. The establishment of a social system called feudalism[3]—which creates a hierarchy of rulers under one lord—further secured William's reign. It also provided him with a network of thousands of knights sworn to serve him, the most powerful European army of the time.

3. **feudalism:** feudal system; the social, economic, and political system of Europe in the Middle Ages. Under this system, individuals gave military and other services to their overlords in return for protection and land. The ultimate overlord was the king.

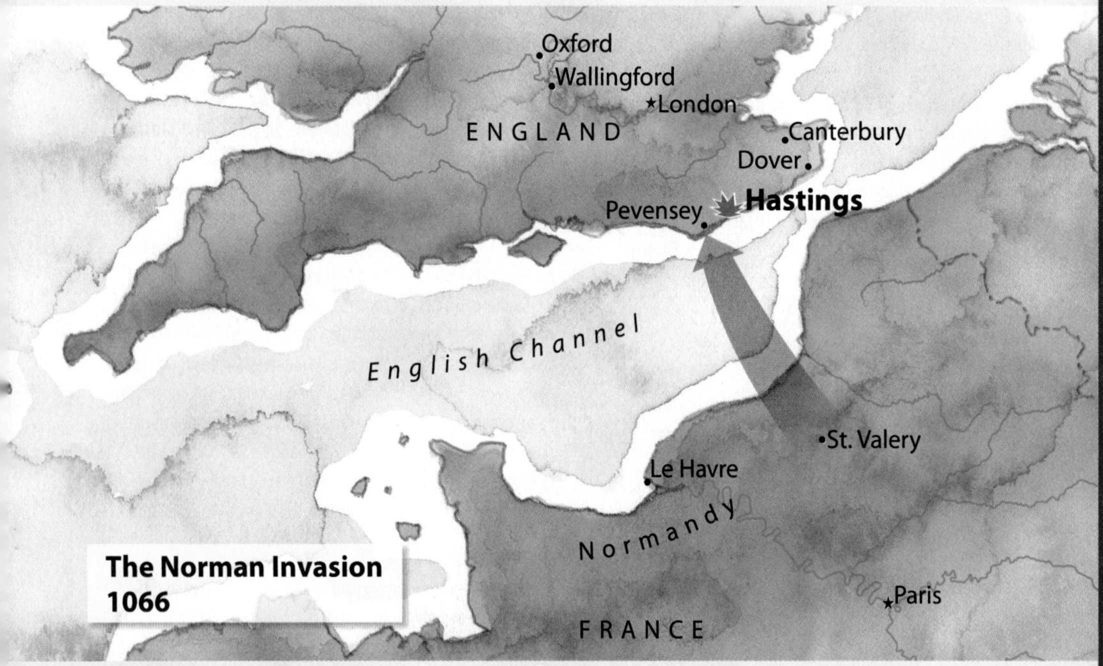

William and his army set sail near St. Valery and Le Havre in the Norman region of France, moved across the English Channel, and invaded Britain at Pevensey. About two weeks later, on October 14, 1066, the Normans defeated Harold at the Battle of Hastings. The subsequent battles at Oxford, Canterbury, and Wallingford helped secure the Normans' control of the region.

Think About/Talk About

History of the Times

Although students may think of castles as essentially English, the first castles in England were built by the Normans in the years following their invasion of England. One of the castles built by William's followers was the Tower of London, which later became an infamous prison and place of execution.

teaching Latin and translating Latin classics into the Anglo-Saxon language. . . . Alfred's intellectual revival . . . was a salvage operation rather than an outburst of originality. He was both modest and accurate when he described himself as one who wandered through a great forest collecting timber with which others could build."

From *Medieval Europe: A Short History, 3rd Edition*, by C. Warren Hollister. Copyright © 1964, 1968, 1974 by John Wiley & Sons, Inc.

Analyzing Visuals

Extension Activity Ask students to make inferences on the reason the town of Hastings is designated with a different symbol and font style. ***Possible response:*** *The map highlights the most significant battle. Hastings was the town in which William, duke of Normandy, defeated the English army and proclaimed himself ruler of England. The subsequent battles served to strengthen William's dominion.*

Think About/Talk About

Literature of the Times

Tell students that *Le Morte d'Arthur* tells the story of the legendary King Arthur and his Knights of the Round Table. While Arthur may not have been a historical king, references to his legend have been found in records written as early as A.D. 600. However, Sir Thomas Malory's retelling of Arthur's story is the one on which most subsequent versions are based.

Comprehension Check

Possible response: *The themes of morality and chivalry that run through much of medieval English literature reflect contemporary concerns about moral and religious instruction as well as the ideal of courtly love.*

Social mobility was nearly impossible in the Middle Ages. Regardless of how hard a merchant worked or how much money an artisan earned, social status remained fixed. Hope resided only in apprenticing a talented son to a more respected vocation or marrying a daughter "up" to a husband from a higher class.

Literature of the Times

A particular literature emerged from the turbulent history of England at this time. The works of Julian of Norwich and Sir Thomas Malory, along with the products of monasteries and universities, reflect a culture interested in the moral instruction of its population. Chaucer's *The Canterbury Tales* satirizes social classes and institutions with the story of a group of pilgrims[6] traveling to the city of Canterbury. Another important work of medieval moral literature is *The Book of Margery Kempe.* Kempe, an illiterate religious mystic and spiritualist, dictated her autobiography to two clerks in a span of four years in the 1430s. The drama *Everyman,* which explores the fate of the human soul in a realistic fashion not often achieved by morality plays of the time, is another work of moral instruction.

Perhaps the most distinctive form of literature from this time period deals with the ideal of courtly love—the concept that a knight's bravery and nobility could be increased by his pure adoration of a lady. The romance narrative is a medieval genre that celebrates the adventures of a brave knight or other hero who has to overcome danger for the love of a noble lady or some other high ideal. Courtly love supported the medieval concept of chivalry, a system of social codes and ideals governing the behavior of knights and gentlewomen and guided by allegiance to an overlord. Perhaps the most famous-romance narratives are *Sir Gawain and the Green Knight* and Malory's *Le Morte d'Arthur.*

Comprehension Check

Describe the trends in English literature during the Middle Ages. Were they reflective of life at the time?

6. **pilgrims:** those who travel to a shrine or holy place as a religious act.

Seated King, The Lewis Chessmen (about A.D. 1150–1200). Found on the Isle of Lewis, Outer Hebrides, Scotland. The chess pieces consist of elaborately worked walrus ivory and whale's teeth in the forms of seated kings and queens. >
The British Museum, London.

Universal Access

Advanced Learners

Acceleration Point out that Chaucer's *Canterbury Tales* present members of different social classes in a satirical light; that is, the tales lightly poke fun at people's flaws.

Divide the class into groups of three. Have each group member use print or online sources to research one of the three major medieval social classes: clergy, noblemen, and laborers. Ask students: Why would a writer satirize this group? What flaws (real or perceived) would motivate someone to criticize this group?

Have students discuss their findings with the other members of their groups and write a brief (one-page) response to the questions.

KEY CONCEPT

Life in Medieval Society

History of the Times

Medieval society was dependent on the contributions of a diverse group of people. Priests held an elevated status and were responsible for the administration of the sacraments,[5] which could not be performed by any other member of the population. Knights were noblemen responsible for combat and strong leadership of their followers. The bulk of society consisted of laborers: peasants, who owned their land, and serfs, who did not. Their responsibilities were to farm the land and pledge loyalty to their feudal overlords. A great proportion of the teaching and learning in society occurred in the monasteries and convents of religious orders; these organizations were also social service institutions, functioning as orphanages and hospitals.

Villages, built around castles, were where most Europeans lived during the Middle Ages. The village was the fundamental social and economic center of medieval society. Town life was clearly different from rural life, but the lifestyles were dependent on each other. The majority of merchants and artisans lived in villages. Townspeople viewed themselves as having more freedom and opportunity for artistic expression. Rural laborers, on the other hand, were yoked to the land, and, in the case of serfs, were little more than slaves to their overlords.

---

5. **sacraments:** any of certain Christian rites, such as baptism or the Eucharist.

Analyzing Visuals

Connecting to the Text What does this painting reveal about life in the Middle Ages?

The Month of September from the Grimani Breviary by the Master of the Grimani Breviary (fl. 1515).
Biblioteca Marciana, Venice, Italy.

Think About/Talk About

History of the Times

Tell students that serfs, also called "villeins" in medieval England, were people who worked for lords and were, in some ways, considered the lords' "property." Serfdom began to disappear in England in the fourteenth century, when a labor shortage caused by the Black Death made it easier for workers to demand fair payment for their services.

- While the original version of the tapestry is now displayed in Bayeux, France, a group of British women who believed that England should also have a copy of the artifact worked to create an accurate replica of the tapestry. The English replica, which was completed in 1886, is now on display in Reading, England.

Analyzing Visuals

Connecting to the Text: *In the foreground, the artist represents rural laborers working in the garden and transporting goods, possibly to the castle in the background. The painting depicts the lives of rural laborers in the Middle Ages, and also highlights the distance that existed between the peasants and their feudal lords, whose power is symbolized by the imposing castle that stands out in the distance.*

Standards Focus

Objectives

Students will evaluate the philosophical, political, religious, ethical, and social influences of a historical period.

Link to Today

This excerpt from the classic fantasy novel *The Lord of the Rings* explores the concept of heroism, which is central to the literature discussed in Unit 1.

Unit 1 Resources, Historical Introduction Skill Builder, p. 2

UA: Differentiating Instruction, graphic organizer, p. 1

Teacher One Stop™, all print resources

Direct Teach

Think About/Talk About

Read with a Purpose Direct students to the Read with a Purpose statement. Point out to students that they should be looking for an event in the selection in which the hero's sidekick is in real danger.

Link to Today

This Link to Today shows the lasting appeal of heroic adventure stories.

Build Background

In addition to echoing many elements from Anglo-Saxon and medieval literature, *The Two Towers* in particular recalls features of *Beowulf* and the Arthurian legends. These stories describe the adventures of heroes who take on formidable challenges and fight bravely against all odds. Such heroes usually have a close friend who plays an important role in the hero's experiences. Through the glory of their fame, the heroes also achieve eternal life.

Author Note

J. R. R. Tolkien (1892–1973) graduated from Oxford University and went on to become a professor of Old and Middle English at Leeds University in England. Several of his works began as stories for his children and were later expanded into the trilogy that many consider to be his masterpiece: *The Lord of the Rings* (1947). *The Two Towers* was published as the second book, between *The Fellowship of the Ring* and *The Return of the King.* The enduring stories of epic heroes and legendary creatures from Middle Earth have found a new audience in director Peter Jackson's recent films.

NOVEL

from THE LORD *of the* RINGS: *The Two Towers*

by **J. R. R. Tolkien**

Read with a Purpose Read this excerpt from *The Two Towers* to see how one hero's sidekick responds when the odds are overwhelmingly against him.

Selection Readability	
Easily Accessible **Accessible** Challenging	chronological order; accessible theme

Selection Plot Summary

As Frodo lies bound, at the mercy of the monster Shelob, Sam rushes to his aid. Sam stabs at the monster, unconcerned about the risk to himself. As she is about to fall upon him, she impales herself on the blade. Furious, Shelob positions herself to kill Sam when he locates the Phial of Galadriel. Sam chants and the phial issues forth a beam that blinds Shelob, who retreats.

April, calendar miniature from the *Très Riches Heures du Duc de Berry* (1416), (Engagement scene. In the background, the Chateau de Dourdan), by the Limbourg Brothers. Ms.65, f .4v.
Musée Condé, Chantilly, France.

Wrap Up

Talk About . . .

The Anglo-Saxon heroes were exclusively male, but Celtic history and mythology record some powerful female warriors. How do these ancient views of heroism compare with contemporary ideas of greatness? With a partner or in a small group, discuss the ways in which individuals gain fame and fortune today. Try to use each Academic Vocabulary word listed below at least once in your discussion.

Write About . . .

Geoffrey Chaucer sought to teach, but he also wanted to entertain. What examples of books or movies can you think of that are both entertaining and instructive? Do you think this combination is effective? Explain.

Academic Vocabulary for Unit 1

Talking and Writing About Literature
Academic Vocabulary is the language you use to write and talk about literature. Use these words to discuss the literature you will read in this unit. These words will be underlined throughout the unit.

concept (KAHN sehpt) *n.:* notion or idea. *The concept of courtly love was a theme repeated throughout medieval literature.*

diverse (duh VURS) *adj.:* varied. *A person of diverse interests can talk on many subjects.*

emphasis (EHM fuh sihs) *n.:* stress; importance. *When writing the essay, give special emphasis to examples from the story.*

status (STAT uhs) *n.:* social or professional rank. *What was the status of women in medieval society?*

attribute (uh TRIHB yoot) *v.:* regard as being caused by something. *We attribute the core values of* Beowulf *to the Anglo-Saxon tradition.*

Your Turn
Copy the Academic Vocabulary list into your *Reader/Writer Notebook.* Try to use the words as you outline the main ideas of the selections in the chapter that follows.

Check for Understanding

Talk About...
Students might explain that although ancient heroes tended to be known for their physical feats or their skill in battle, today's notions of personal greatness encompass a much broader range of talents and skills. They might also mention that today, as in the past, people's heroic accomplishments are often remembered through oral and written narrative.

Write About...
Students might mention that when a reader is entertained by a book, he or she might be more receptive to the educational messages that the book contains. If an educational text is dry or dull, people might stop reading it before they learn what the author wants to teach.

PowerNotes, Academic Vocabulary lesson and activities

go.hrw.com **WordSharp: An Interactive Vocabulary Tutor,** more practice with academic language

Academic Vocabulary

Talking and Writing About Literature
English for Academic Success Write the following questions on the board. Tell students these are the kinds of questions they will encounter on standardized tests. Discuss the word meanings and then have students use the historical introduction to answer the questions.

- What **concept** comforted many Anglo-Saxon people who converted to Christianity? ***Possible response:*** *Anglo-Saxons were comforted by the concept of an afterlife.*
- In the **diverse** medieval society, which class had the least rights? ***Possible response:*** *Serfs were at the bottom of the social pyramid. They were laborers who did not own land.*
- What was the **emphasis** of romance narrative? ***Possible response:*** *Romance narrative dealt primarily with the ideal of courtly love.*
- How did the Norman Conquest affect the **status** of the English language in Britain? ***Possible response:*** *Old English lost its status as the primary spoken and written language when the Normans declared French to be the official state language.*

Chapter Objectives

- Students will learn about elements of the epic genre by reading excerpts from the epic poems *Beowulf, Gilgamesh,* and the *Iliad.*
- Students will develop an appreciation for elegiac poetry by studying selections from *The Exeter Book.*
- Students will develop deeper connections to the text by retelling parts of the selections.
- Students will analyze the historical contexts of literary works.
- Students will compare and contrast themes and values in the literature of different cultures.

The Quotation

Tell students that the epic poems tell of the great deeds of superhuman heroes in ancient history. Ask what they think the author means by the phrase "weave a net of words." ***Possible response:*** *The author means that the proud old soldiers would tell stories of long-ago battles. These exciting stories would draw in listeners. The words are like a fishing net that ensnares listeners.*

Analyzing Visuals

Extension Activity Look closely at the image on p. 16. In what way is the image related to the quote? ***Possible response:*** *The tapestry is a visual representation of the old soldiers' stories woven in a net of words.*

CHAPTER **1**

The Anglo-Saxons: Songs of Ancient Heroes

LITERARY SKILLS FOCUS

The Epic Tradition

CONTENTS

"And sometimes a proud old soldier
Who had heard songs of the ancient heroes
And could sing them all through, story after story,
Would weave a net of words."

—**from *Beowulf,* translated by Burton Raffel**

Norman calvary attacks a hill defended by Saxon infantry.
Bayeux Tapestry, embroidery (11th century).
Musée de la Tapisserie, Bayeux, France.

Chapter 1

California Standards Overview

- **Reading Standard 2.2** Analyze the way in which clarity of meaning is affected by the patterns of organization, hierarchical structures, repetition of the main ideas, syntax, and word choice in the text.
- **Reading Standard 3.1** Analyze characteristics of subgenres (e.g., satire, parody, allegory, pastoral) that are used in poetry, prose, plays, novels, short stories, essays, and other basic genres.
- **Reading Standard 3.2** Analyze the way in which the theme or meaning of a selection represents a view or comment on life, using textual evidence to support the claim.
- **Reading Standard 3.4** Analyze ways in which poets use imagery, personification, figures of speech, and "sounds" to evoke readers' emotions.
- **Reading Standard 3.6** Analyze the way in which authors through the centuries have used archetypes drawn from myth and tradition in literature, film, political speeches, and religious writings (e.g., how the archetype of banishment from an ideal world may be used to interpret Shakespeare's tragedy *Macbeth*).
- **Reading Standard 3.7** Analyze recognized works of world literature from a variety of authors: **a.** Contrast the major literary forms, techniques, and characteristics of the major literary forms (e.g., Homeric Greece, medieval, romantic, neoclassic, modern.) **b.** Relate literary works and authors to the major themes and issues of their eras. **c.** Evaluate the philosophical, political, religious, ethical, and social influences of the historical period that shaped the characters, plots and settings.
- **Grades 9–10 Review Reading Standard 3.3** Analyze interactions between main and subordinate characters in a literary text (e.g., internal and external conflicts, motivations, relationships, influence) and explain the way those interactions affect the plot.
- **Grades 9–10 Review Reading Standard 3.12** Analyze the way in which a work of literature is related to the themes and issues of its historical period. (Historical approach).
- **Writing Standard 2.2a** Demonstrate a comprehensive understanding of the significant ideas in works or passages. **2.2b** Analyze the use of imagery, language, and universal themes, and unique aspects of the text. **2.2c** Support important ideas and viewpoints through accurate and detailed references to the text and to other works.

"Galadriel!" he said faintly, and then he heard voices far off but clear: the crying of the Elves as they walked under the stars in the beloved shadows of the Shire, and the music of the Elves as it came through his sleep in the Hall of Fire in the house of Elrond.

Gilthoniel A Elbereth!

And then his tongue was loosed and his voice cried in a language which he did not know:

A Elbereth Gilthoniel
o menel palan-diriel,
le nallon sí di'nguruthos!
A tiro nin, Fanuilos!

And with that he staggered to his feet and was Samwise the hobbit, Hamfast's son, again.

"Now come, you filth!" he cried. "You've hurt my master, you brute, and you'll pay for it. We're going on; but we'll settle with you first. Come on, and taste it again!"

As if his indomitable[2] spirit had set its potency in motion, the glass blazed suddenly like a white torch in his hand. It flamed like a star that leaping from the firmament sears the dark air with intolerable light. No such terror out of heaven had ever burned in Shelob's face before. The beams of it entered into her wounded head and scored it with unbearable pain, and the dreadful infection of light spread from eye to eye. She fell back beating the air with her forelegs, her sight blasted by inner lightnings, her mind in agony. Then turning her maimed head away, she rolled aside and began to crawl, claw by claw, toward the opening in the dark cliff behind.

Sam came on. He was reeling like a drunken man, but he came on. And Shelob cowed at last, shrunken in defeat, jerked and quivered as she tried to hasten from him. She reached the hole, and squeezing down, leaving a trail of green-yellow slime, she slipped in, even as Sam hewed a last stroke at her dragging legs. Then he fell to the ground.

Shelob was gone; and whether she lay long in her lair, nursing her malice and her misery, and in slow years of darkness healed herself from within, rebuilding her clustered eyes, until with hunger like death she spun once more her dreadful snares in the glens of the Mountains of Shadow, this tale does not tell.

2. **indomitable:** incapable of being defeated.

Ask Yourself

1. **Read with a Purpose** In this episode, Sam comes to Frodo's rescue without thinking about the danger he risks to himself. Would you describe his actions as courageous or reckless or both? Explain your answer.
2. Tolkien emphasizes the role of a hero's friend or kinsman when he writes "Frodo wouldn't have got far without Sam, would he, dad?" Do you think that a hero's power is inherent to the individual or does it sometimes depends on the courage of his or her companions?
3. What kinds of skills, knowledge, and weapons does the hero use in this excerpt? Do you think that a hero should use just his or her body in a challenge against all odds, or is it acceptable to use weapons or tools?

Think About/Talk About

Extend the Discussion

Summarizing Review the Read with a Purpose statement on p. 12. What overwhelming odds does Sam face in this excerpt, and how does he respond? Summarize the events of the selection in a few sentences. ***Possible response:*** *Sam fights a creature that is much bigger and stronger than he is. He defeats the creature using skill and bravery.*

Making Judgments Re-read the last paragraph. Do you like the way the author ends this story? Why or why not? ***Possible responses:*** *Yes, not knowing what happened to Shelob adds suspense and mystery to the story. No, I do not like the way the author ends the story. It is too open-ended. I think Tolkien should have told us explicitly what happened to Shelob after the fight.*

Ask Yourself

Possible responses:

1. *I think Sam's actions are more courageous than reckless. It is his instinct to rush to his friend's defense, even when he is putting himself in harm's way. Sam seems to care more about Frodo than about himself and will do anything to save him.*
2. *Many heroes rely on the help of companions. Few people are so powerful or courageous that they can consistently act heroically, with no support from others.*
3. *Sam uses a sword and the Phial of Galadriel during his battle with Shelob, but he also relies on his own skill and strength. I think it is perfectly acceptable to use tools and weapons when you face incredible odds. In some cases, they may be your only chance of succeeding.*

Think About/Talk About

Extend the Discussion

Finding Details How does the Phial of Galadriel help Sam? ***Possible response:*** *It helps give him renewed strength and hope. It also shines a bright light that blinds Shelob.*

Determining Author's Purpose Why do think the author describes Shelob's thoughts and feelings in addition to Sam's? ***Possible response:*** *By describing Shelob's thoughts, the author gives the reader more insight into Sam and Frodo's enemy. The foe is not simply a lumbering beast; her fierce emotions and cunning make her all the more dangerous.*

The Lord of the Rings: The Return of the King (2003). Sean Astin and Elijah Wood.

Disturbed as if out of some gloating dream by his small yell she turned slowly the dreadful malice of her glance upon him. But almost before she was aware that a fury was upon her greater than any she had known in countless years, the shining sword bit upon her foot and shore away the claw. Sam sprang in, inside the arches of her legs, and with a quick upthrust of his other hand stabbed at the clustered eyes upon her lowered head. One great eye went dark.

Now the miserable creature was right under her, for the moment out of the reach of her sting and of her claws. Her vast belly was above him with its putrid light, and the stench of it almost smote[1] him down. Still his fury held for one more blow, and before she could sink upon him, smothering him and all his little impudence of courage, he slashed the bright elven-blade across her with desperate strength.

But Shelob was not as dragons are, no softer spot had she save only her eyes. Knobbed and pitted with corruption was her age-old hide, but ever thickened from within with layer on layer of evil growth. The blade scored it with a dreadful gash, but those hideous folds could not be pierced by any strength of men, not though Elf or Dwarf should forge the steel or the hand of Beren or of Túrin wield it. She yielded to the stroke, and then heaved up the great bag of her belly high above Sam's head. Poison frothed and bubbled from the wound. Now splaying her legs she drove her huge bulk down on him again. Too soon. For Sam still stood upon his feet, and dropping his own sword, with both hands he held the elven-blade point upwards, fending off that ghastly roof; and so Shelob, with the driving force of her own cruel will, with strength greater than any warrior's hand, thrust herself upon a bitter spike. Deep, deep it pricked, as Sam was crushed slowly to the ground.

No such anguish had Shelob ever known, or dreamed of knowing, in all her long world of wickedness. Not the doughtiest soldier of old Gondor, nor the most savage Orc entrapped, had ever thus endured her, or set blade to her beloved flesh. A shudder went through her. Heaving up again, wrenching away from the pain, she bent her writhing limbs beneath her and sprang backwards in a convulsive leap.

Sam had fallen to his knees by Frodo's head, his senses reeling in the foul stench, his two hands still gripping the hilt of the sword. Through the mist before his eyes he was aware dimly of Frodo's face, and stubbornly he fought to master himself and to drag himself out of the swoon that was upon him. Slowly he raised his head and saw her, only a few paces away, eyeing him, her beak drabbling a spittle of venom, and a green ooze trickling from below her wounded eye. There she crouched, her shuddering belly splayed upon the ground, the great bows of her legs quivering, as she gathered herself for another spring—this time to crush and sting to death: no little bite of poison to still the struggling of her meat; this time to slay and then to rend.

Even as Sam himself crouched, looking at her, seeing his death in her eyes, a thought came to him, as if some remote voice had spoken, and he fumbled in his breast with his left hand, and found what he sought: cold and hard and solid it seemed to his touch in a phantom world of horror, the Phial of Galadriel.

1. **smote:** struck, as in combat.

Cross-Curricular Connection

LITERATURE: J.R.R. Tolkien

Born out of Tolkien's love of myths, *The Hobbit,* a story about a hobbit on a quest for treasure, was published with pictures drawn by Tolkien himself in 1937. Originally meant to entertain his four children, the book captured the attention of many readers. So in 1954, Tolkien published a kind of sequel, *The Lord of the Rings,* the acclaimed story of the One Ring that must be destroyed before the Dark Lord, Sauron, uses it for his evil purposes. By the end of the 20th century, the three-part novel had sold more than 50 million copies in 30 languages. The film series based on the books also became widely popular and successful.

"Still, I wonder if we shall ever be put into songs or tales," said Sam. "We're in one, of course; but I mean: put into words, you know, told by the fireside, or read out of a great big book with red and black letters, years and years afterward. And people will say: 'Let's hear about Frodo and the Ring!' And they'll say: 'Yes, that's one of my favorite stories. Frodo was very brave, wasn't he, dad?' 'Yes, my boy, the famousest of the hobbits, and that's saying a lot.'"

"It's saying a lot too much," said Frodo, and he laughed, a long clear laugh from his heart. . . . "Why, Sam, he said, "to hear you somehow makes me as merry as if the story was already written. But you've left out one of the chief characters: Samwise the stouthearted. 'I want to hear more about Sam, dad. Why didn't they put in more of his talk, dad? That's what I like, it makes me laugh. And Frodo wouldn't have got far without Sam, would he, dad?'" . . .

Frodo was lying face upward on the ground and the monster was bending over him, so intent upon her victim that she took no heed of Sam and his cries, until he was close at hand. As he rushed up he saw that Frodo was already bound in cords, wound about him from ankle to shoulder, and the monster with her great forelegs was beginning half to lift, half to drag his body away.

On the near side of him lay, gleaming on the ground, his elven-blade, where it had fallen useless from his grasp. Sam did not wait to wonder what was to be done, or whether he was brave, or loyal, or filled with rage. He sprang forward with a yell, and seized his master's sword in his left hand. Then he charged. No onslaught more fierce was ever seen in the savage world of beasts, where some desperate small creature armed with little teeth, alone, will spring upon a tower of horn and hide that stands above its fallen mate.

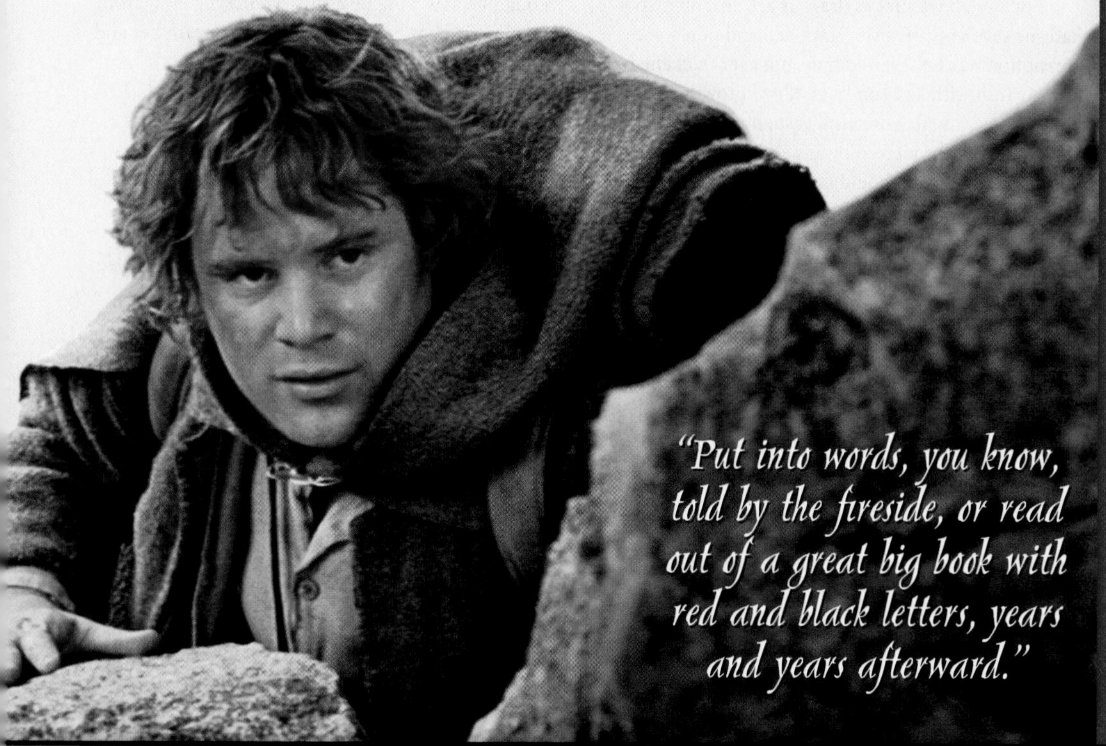

"Put into words, you know, told by the fireside, or read out of a great big book with red and black letters, years and years afterward."

Think About/Talk About

Extend the Discussion

Finding Details How is Shelob able to survive being slashed in the belly? ***Possible response:*** *Shelob's hide is thick and tough, with many layers.*

Interpreting Why do you think Sam is able to attack Shelob with such unusual strength? ***Possible response:*** *Shelob's attack on Frodo enrages Sam. His anger gives him extra energy and force as he attacks her.*

Universal Access

EL English Learners/ Struggling Readers

English for Academic Success Before students read the selection, introduce the following words.

- **onslaught**—a sudden attack. *The army held off the onslaught of opposing troops.*
- **malice**—desire to harm. *Despite their gossip, the students intended no malice.*
- **putrid**—rotten or foul. *The milk smelled putrid, so I knew it was past its expiration date.*
- **impudence**—extreme boldness. *The child showed impudence by answering me rudely.*
- **anguish**—pain or suffering. *I felt anguish when I was late to school and missed my final exam.*
- **potency**—strength. *The potency of the caffeinated soda kept me awake all night.*

Then, read students the selection summary and try to include some of the words listed above. [*This story tells about a violent* onslaught *by a monster that causes a lot of* anguish *to the protagonists.*]

Check for Understanding

Ask Yourself

Possible responses:

1. *Epics transmit a culture's history, values, and traditions from one generation to the next. Epic heroes embody a human ideal.*
2. *In the* Harry Potter *series, the main character performs superhuman deeds and is changed in the process.*

Learn It Online
For a multimedia version of the instruction found on this page, use the **PowerNotes** Literary Skills Focus presentation.

go.hrw.com H12-18 Go

be said that there is but one archetypal mythic hero whose life has been replicated in many lands by many, many people. A legendary hero is usually the founder of something—the founder of a new age, the founder of a new religion, the founder of a new city, the founder of a new way of life. In order to found something new, one has to leave the old and go in quest of the seed idea, a germinal idea that will have the potentiality of bringing forth that new thing.

As in our own journey through life, there are often trials and obstacles that stand between the hero and his or her goals. Like Beowulf, we must fight our own Grendels and dragons—our inner and outer demons—sometimes all alone. It is the epic hero's belief in himself, his own powers, and his cherished values, that make success possible in the face of challenges.

The Epic Lives On

Today, the epic tradition thrives in our own popular culture. In movies, comic books, fantasy novels, television shows, and video games, we meet a diverse array of larger-than-life, often superhuman characters—both male and female—whom we recognize as descendants of the ancient epic heroes. The archetype endures because it continues to be a universal and relevant symbol for some of the most deeply held values of humankind. In Beowulf's journey from self-seeking adventure to heroic but humble death, in Gilgamesh's transition from arrogant king to returning pilgrim, and in Achilles' passage from pouting adolescent to experienced warrior, we find a dramatic record of the personal and collective human quest.

Ask Yourself

1. Why are epics so important to a culture?
2. Think of a modern-day epic that you enjoy. How do you relate to it? How is it like ancient epics?

Itur-Shamagen, king of Mari, in prayer (2800–2300 B.C.). Sumerian. National Museum, Damascus, Syria.

Learn It Online
Try the *PowerNotes* version of this lesson online.

go.hrw.com H12-18 Go

Universal Access

Advanced Learners

Acceleration Give students an opportunity to deepen their understanding of the epic poem by comparing the epic hero to protagonists from books they have read and movies they have seen. Ask students to think of a protagonist who does not have the qualities of an epic hero. Then, ask them to think about which protagonists from books or films most resemble epic heroes.

Reading Standard 3.6, 3.7a (see pages A48–A50)

The Epic Tradition by David Adams Leeming

Characteristics of an Epic

- Long narrative poem about a quest, told in formal, elevated language
- Larger-than-life hero who embodies the values of a particular culture
- Incredible plot involving large-scale events
- Mix of myth, legend, and history that often includes gods and goddesses as characters

A Bridge from the Past to the Future

"I teach kings the history of their ancestors," declares the narrator of the African epic *Sundiata,* "for the world is old, but the future springs from the past." These words can be applied to epics from all times and places, for an epic—a long narrative poem about the exploits of a national hero—is a bridge from the past to the future. Epics carry a culture's history, values, and traditions from one generation to the next. Although epics may vary across different cultures or times, the epic tradition remains a constant social feature—where there are people, there are epics, retelling the triumphs and trials of life.

The Epic Hero

Whereas old religious stories, or myths, explain the origins and deeds of gods, the epic tradition reflects the human need to understand ourselves and bridge the gap between the human and the divine. A special kind of godlike human being, the epic hero, satisfies this need. Beowulf and other epic heroes, such as Achilles and Gilgamesh, carry the status and power of the gods within themselves but are also subject to the joys and hardships of the human condition.

While the heroes of the Anglo-Saxon *Beowulf,* the Mesopotamian *Gilgamesh,* and the Greek *Iliad* all embody the particular values of their cultures, we also find these values distilled in a single figure, the heroic **archetype,** the model that is somehow familiar to people of all places and times. In expressing the universal human quest for knowledge and understanding, this epic hero represents the core of the epic tradition.

Viking ship of war. Anglo-Saxon manuscript illumination (c. 1025-1050). Ms. Cotton Tiberius. BV, part I, fol.40v. The British Library, London.

When asked why there are so many hero stories in mythology, Joseph Campbell, one of the twentieth century's foremost interpreters of myths and archetypes, said, "Because that's what's worth writing about." According to Campbell,

> There is a certain typical hero sequence of actions which can be detected in stories from all over the world and from many periods of history. Essentially, it might even

Literary Skills Focus

Objectives

Students will

- analyze the archetype of the epic hero
- compare the literary forms of major literary periods

Unit 1 Resources, Literary Focus Skill Builder, p. 5

PowerNotes, interactive lesson presentation with activities

Teacher One Stop™, on-level lesson plan and all print resources

Direct Teach

A Bridge from the Past to the Future

- Review the Literary Skills Focus. Then, use the following prompt to discuss the qualities of an epic hero.
- Epic heroes represent the values of a culture. Discuss with students the qualities an epic hero might have in today's culture.

California Standards, pp. 17–18

- **Reading Standard 3.6** Analyze the way in which authors through the centuries have used archetypes drawn from myth and tradition in literature, film, political speeches, and religious writings (e.g., how the archetype of banishment from an ideal world may be used to interpret Shakespeare's tragedy *Macbeth*).
- **Reading Standard 3.7a** Contrast the major literary forms, techniques, and characteristics of the major literary forms (e.g., Homeric Greece, medieval, romantic, neoclassic, modern.)

Universal Access

English Learners

Ask students to think of epic heroes they know of or could imagine from their own cultures. If someone were to write an epic poem about a larger-than-life hero, how would this hero embody the values of their cultures? What kinds of deeds would they accomplish? What personality traits would they possess?

Standards Focus

Objectives

Students will
- understand the archetype of the epic hero drawn from myth and tradition
- paraphrase a text

Selection Introduction

Think About the Epic

Ask students to think of a time when they felt riveted by a story someone was telling.

For Independent Reading

- *The Tombs of Atuan,* Ursula K. Le Guin
- *Crusader,* Edward Bloor

Motivate

What Do You Think?/QuickWrite

Use the QuickWrite to have students reflect on contemporary heroes. Have students share with a partner the qualities they think a hero should possess, then have them record their responses in their **Reader/Writer Notebooks.**

English for Academic Success

Academic Vocabulary

Look for opportunities to use the Academic Vocabulary words in this unit.
- **attribute, *v.*:** regard as being caused by something
- **concept, *n.*:** notion or idea
- **emphasis, *n.*:** stress; importance

California Standards, pp. 20–53

- **Reading Standard 2.2** Analyze the way in which clarity of meaning is affected by the patterns of organization, hierarchical structures, repetition of the main ideas, syntax, and word choice in the text.
- **Reading Standard 3.6** Analyze the way in which authors through the centuries have used archetypes drawn from myth and tradition in literature, film, political speeches, and religious writings (e.g., how the archetype of banishment from an ideal world may be used to interpret Shakespeare's tragedy *Macbeth*).

Preparing to Read

from Beowulf

What Do You Think? What moves a hero to act?

QuickWrite

Think about a hero you know or have read about. In your *Reader/Writer Notebook,* write down a list of situations in which a person can rise above his or her place in life to become a hero.

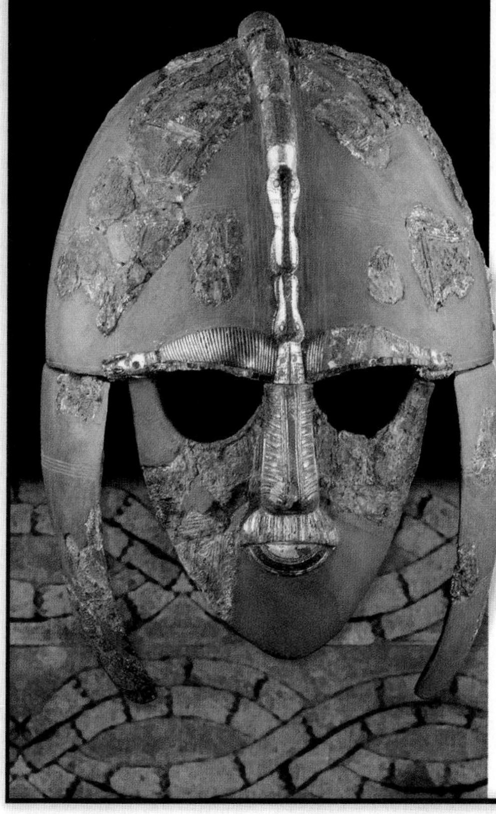

INTRODUCTION

Beowulf, one of the most important and exciting epics of Western literature, features monsters, gory battles, and a brave hero.

A Classic of the Epic Tradition

Originally an oral epic, *Beowulf* was handed down with changes and embellishments from one minstrel to another. The first great work of English national literature, *Beowulf* is a celebration of the epic hero. As such, it uses a host of traditional **motifs,** or recurring elements, associated with heroic literature all over the world.

The epic tells of Beowulf (his name may mean "bear"), a Geat from Sweden who crosses the sea to Denmark in a quest to defend the Herot mead-hall and rescue King Hrothgar's people from the demonic monster Grendel. Beowulf demonstrates his bravery and strength by fighting alone and with his friend Wiglaf, and gains eternal fame through battle.

The Sources of *Beowulf*

Compared to the Homerian epics, *Beowulf* is short—approximately 3,200 lines. It was composed in Old English, probably in the northeastern part of England sometime between 700 and 750, but depicts the world of the early sixth century. Much of the poem's material is based on early Celtic and Scandinavian folk legends. Because of its geographical descriptions and emphasis on Christian elements, it has been assumed that the poet who wrote the version we know today was a Northumbrian monk.

The only surviving manuscript of *Beowulf* dates from the year 1000 and is now in the British Museum in London. Burned and stained, it was discovered in the eighteenth century. Somehow it had survived Henry VIII's destruction of the monasteries two hundred years earlier.

Part One of the text you are about to read is from Burton Raffel's popular 1963 translation of the epic. Part Two is from the Irish poet Seamus Heaney's award-winning (and bestselling) translation of the work, published in 2000.

Think About the Epic *Beowulf* was originally an oral tale. What kinds of stories can be shared today by means other than books? How does telling a story out loud keep it alive?

Helmet (7th century) from the ship-burial at Sutton Hoo. Anglo-Saxon. Suffolk, England. The British Museum, London.

Selection Readability	
Easily Accessible Accessible **Challenging**	complex syntax; difficult vocabulary; epic poem

Reading Standard 2.2 (see pages A48–A50)

from Beowulf

Paraphrasing by Kylene Beers

An efficient way of checking your own understanding of what you are reading is to paraphrase, or put into your own words, what you have read. Paraphrasing is actually a harder skill than memorizing a portion of a text, for memorization doesn't require comprehension. Rather, putting what you have read into your own words means you have determined what the author means and now can explain it in your own way. When you paraphrase what you have read, you keep the author's intent but use language that is your own.

The author of *Beowulf* uses poetic language to share ideas about events, characters, and beliefs. The original audiences of this epic poem would have been familiar with the hero and his adventures, as well as with the conventions of style. Although this style makes the poem beautiful, it can sometimes be difficult for a modern reader to understand. **Paraphrasing** is a good way to capture the meaning of the poem's details.

Your Turn

Read the following lines from an early passage of *Beowulf*, "The Monster Grendel" (lines 5–14).

> The poet's clear songs, sung
> Of the ancient beginnings of us all, recalling
> The Almighty making the earth, shaping
> These beautiful plains marked off by oceans,
> Then proudly setting the sun and moon
> To glow across the land and light it;
> The corners of the earth were made lovely
> with trees
> And leaves, made quick with life, with each
> Of the nations who now move on its face.
> And then
> As now warriors sang of their pleasure.

To paraphrase this passage, first look for words that represent people, places, and things (nouns) that you recognize. Record them *in order* in the column marked "Nouns." Then, read again and identify the actions or verbs that seem to go with these nouns. Note any words or phrases that complement or are related to each group of nouns and verbs. See the examples in the chart below.

Nouns	Verbs	Phrases
poet	sung	songs of the beginnings
Almighty	making	the earth, sun, moon
Corners of earth	were made	

Re-read each group of words in the chart, and then re-read the original passage. Using your chart, create the paraphrase by putting the text into your own words. It might look something like this:

> People told stories of the beginning of life when God created the earth, oceans, and sky, making them beautiful. We still celebrate that time.

Notice that a paraphrase is shorter than the original and combines repetitions into a single statement. As you read *Beowulf* or any other challenging text, use this process of paraphrasing when you come to a passage that seems unclear.

Learn It Online
Learn paraphrasing through *PowerNotes*. Find the multimedia version of this lesson online.
go.hrw.com H12-19 Go

Reading Skills Focus

Objectives

Students will use paraphrasing or retelling as a strategy for comprehension.

Unit 1 Resources, Reading Focus Skill Builder, p. 6

Teacher One Stop™, on-level lesson plan and all print resources

Direct Teach

Paraphrasing

This essay gives students practice in paraphrasing to check comprehension as they read the often difficult text in Beowulf. Have students read the essay and complete the Your Turn charting activity before they read the epic.

Check for Understanding

Your Turn

Ask students to compare and discuss their paraphrases in small groups. Have them comment on whether they successfully condensed repetitive words and phrases in the original text.

Learn It Online
For a multimedia version of the instruction found on this page, use the **PowerNotes** Reading Skills Focus presentation.
go.hrw.com H12-19 Go

California Standards, p. 19

- **Reading Standard 2.2** Analyze the way in which clarity of meaning is affected by the patterns of organization, hierarchical structures, repetition of the main ideas, syntax, and word choice in the text.

Universal Access

English Learners/ Struggling Readers

English for Academic Success Have student pairs create a Nouns, Verbs, Phrases chart, putting the following words in the correct column and order: *Hrothgar's men, monster, demon, lived, stirred, Grendel, haunted, moors and marshes, made his home, hell, spawned, slime.* Then, have students read lines 15–20 of the epic poem on pp. 23–24. Guide students in paraphrasing: Instruct students to think of different ways of expressing the verbs and phrases, offering examples such as *awoke and moved about* for *stirred.*

Reading Standard 2.2, 3.6 (see pages A48–A50)

Literary Skills Focus

Archetype: The Epic Hero An **archetype** is a very old imaginative pattern that appears in literature of different cultures and time periods. An archetype can be a character, a plot, an image, or a setting. One character archetype is the **epic hero,** the main character of a myth or long narrative poem. These heroes personify the values of the societies that create them, but as archetypes, they also embody universal ideals.

Reading Skills Focus

Paraphrasing Poetry often uses literary devices and unconventional word order to enhance the rhythmic and musical qualities of its language. Paraphrasing can help you comprehend particularly difficult poetic passages. To paraphrase a passage, first group nouns, verbs, and phrases that support an idea. Then, rewrite the passage in your own words.

Into Action As you read, identify lines containing nouns, verbs, and phrases that describe the epic hero Beowulf and his actions. Use a chart like the one below to list these nouns, verbs, and phrases in these passages.

Nouns / Pronouns	Verbs	Phrases
my duty	was	to go to the Danes
I	drove / chased	giants
I	swam	hunting monsters

Writing Skills Focus

Think as a Reader/Writer

Find It in Your Reading Although much of the epic progresses in narrative, the main characters deliver speeches to each other, establishing their credentials, their heritage, and their intentions. In your *Reader/Writer Notebook,* make notes about what characterizes these speeches.

TechFocus As you read *Beowulf,* think how its characters are similar to those you have met in modern TV shows, movies, and video games.

Reader/Writer Notebook

Use your **RWN** to complete the activities for this selection.

Vocabulary

reparation (rehp uh RAY shuhn) *n.:* payment to make up for a wrong or injury. *Hrothgar's warriors could expect no reparation from Grendel for the crimes he committed against them.*

reprisal (rih PRY zuhl) *n.:* punishment in return for an injury. *Grendel's mother attacked Herot as a reprisal for Beowulf's killing of her son.*

loathsome (LOHTH suhm) *adj.:* very hateful; disgusting. *The details of Grendel's attacks on the Geats are loathsome.*

vehemently (VEE uh muhnt lee) *adv.:* violently. *Roaring in anger, the she-wolf struck vehemently at Beowulf.*

infallible (ihn FAL uh buhl) *adj.:* unable to fail or be wrong. *The dragon's mortal blow showed that Beowulf was not an infallible hero.*

extolled (ehk STOHLD) *v.:* praised. *The Geats extolled their fallen king by constructing a great memorial to him.*

Language Coach

Connotations Some words have similar meanings but different **connotations,** the emotions or ideas evoked when you use a certain word. *Extol* means "to praise" but has particularly strong positive connotations. If you *extol* someone's good qualities, you praise them with great enthusiasm. Similarly, *loathsome* has stronger connotations than *hateful*. Saying something is *loathsome* is a powerful way to say it really disgusts you.

Learn It Online

Find Beowulf in the twenty-first century online.

go.hrw.com H12-21 Go

Selection Resources

Unit 1 Resources, on-level practice and assessment, p. 7

PowerNotes, interactive lesson presentation with activities

Teacher One Stop™, on-level lesson plans and all print resources

Holt Audio Library

Holt Audio Library: Selections and Summaries in Spanish

UA: Holt Interactive Reader, p. 3

UA: Differentiating Instruction, modified lesson plans and leveled assessment, p. 2

UA: Resources for Teaching Advanced Students, lesson plans, p. 57

UA: Supporting Instruction in Spanish, selection summary

ThinkCentral Online Assessment, Selection Standards Check

ThinkCentral Online Remediation

Preteach

Introducing Vocabulary

- Read aloud the Vocabulary words, definitions, and sample sentences. Then, use this activity to check students' understanding.
- To reinforce the importance of the Vocabulary words, tell students that these words help shape the protagonist as an epic hero. Explain that absolute terms such as *infallible* are often applied to the epic hero, whereas very negative terms such as *loathsome* will often identify the epic hero's antagonist.

English for Academic Success
Language Coach

After reading the **Language Coach,** write the following word groups on the board:

1: *appreciate, favor, adore, revere*

2: *angry, furious, raging, upset*

Have students discuss the different connotations among the words in each group. Then, ask students to use each word in a sentence.

Literary Skills Focus

As you read and discuss the selection with students, have them note values that the epic hero stands for.

Reading Skills Focus

Give students a copy of the graphic organizer before they read. Tell them to use their responses to answer the questions on the Applying Your Skills page.

Writing Skills Focus

As students read, have them use their **Reader/Writer Notebooks** to record notes about the speeches delivered by characters. Students can use their notes to complete the Writing Skills Focus activity.

Learn It Online

The **PowerNotes** presentation for this lesson includes a short video that introduces the selection. The video is also available on the online version of this page.

go.hrw.com H12-21 Go

Teacher Preparation
Selection Plot Summary

For twelve years, the monster Grendel has preyed upon the warriors loyal to Hrothgar, king of the Danes. Word of their plight has spread to many nations. Beowulf, a powerful warrior from the land of the Geats (Sweden), visits Hrothgar in the Danes' mead-hall, Herot, to offer his help. After boasting of his past achievements and evoking envy and scorn from one of Hrothgar's men, Beowulf vows to fight Grendel without weapons.

That night, Grendel attacks, killing one Geat. Beowulf's men find themselves powerless, their weapons useless. Beowulf rips off Grendel's arm, mortally wounding him, and Grendel retreats to the swamps near Herot. The Danes and Geats celebrate Beowulf's heroism and rejoice at Grendel's defeat.

Furious at her son's death, Grendel's mother attacks Herot. Armed, Beowulf swims to the bottom of the lake where she lives. Because his sword cannot penetrate the monster's hide, Beowulf fights her with his bare hands. Ultimately he kills her with a magical sword, "hammered by giants," that hangs in her underwater lair. He then finds Grendel's body and beheads it to avenge Grendel's victims.

Real Issues, Real Experts

Holt author ***Carol Jago*** *offers strategies for teaching* Beowulf.

Maybe the reason some students do not seem to have the "reading skills" we think necessary for negotiating a classic like *Beowulf* is that we are not teaching them very well. I am not speaking here about teaching students how to read but rather about teaching students how stories work. In our urgency to abandon the lecture format, literature teachers may have adopted too passive a role. Clearly we want to make genuine student response the cornerstone of our classrooms, but withholding information about how a story works may make it impossible for some students to have any response at all.

Take *Beowulf,* for example. I begin our reading of the epic by outlining *Beowulf's* three "agons"—the hero's engagement with three monsters: Grendel, Grendel's mother, and the dragon. Each of the heroic episodes is self-contained and the epic itself book-ended with funerals. When students understand how a story "works,"

EPIC

from Beowulf

Part One

translated by **Burton Raffel**

Read with a Purpose

Read to discover the qualities that the Anglo-Saxons considered heroic.

Building Background

The epic poem *Beowulf* was composed in the Anglo-Saxon period following the fall of the Roman Empire. The story concerns a brave and strong hero who hears tales of a fearsome beast that has laid waste to a kingdom of Danes. Note how the history and ancestry of each character is emphasized throughout the epic.

The Monster Grendel

I

. . . A powerful monster, living down
In the darkness, growled in pain, impatient
As day after day the music rang
Loud in that hall,° the harp's rejoicing
Call and the poet's clear songs, sung
Of the ancient beginnings of us all, recalling
The Almighty making the earth, shaping
These beautiful plains marked off by oceans,
Then proudly setting the sun and moon
To glow across the land and light it;
The corners of the earth were made lovely with trees
And leaves, made quick with life, with each
Of the nations who now move on its face. And then
As now warriors sang of their pleasure:
So Hrothgar's men lived happy in his hall
Till the monster stirred, that demon, that fiend,
Grendel, who haunted the moors, the wild

4. hall: guest-hall or mead-hall. (Mead is a fermented drink made from honey, water, yeast, and malt.) The hall was a central gathering place where Anglo-Saxon warriors could feast, listen to a bard's stories, and sleep in safety.

Analyzing Visuals

Connecting to the Text Notice the ship's ornate carvings and vibrant colors on page 22. How might the decoration serve a warlike, as well as aesthetic, function?

(opposite) *Visitors from Overseas* by Nikolai Roerich (1874–1947). Tretyakov Gallery, Moscow, Russia.

they can relax into their reading unworried about how the section before them fits within the whole.

If you are a Beowulf fan like me, you may be excited to hear that Beowulf scholar Benjamin Bagby has re-created and recorded a live performance of the poem as it could have been experienced one thousand years ago. Singing about honor and glory, strength and guts, kings and gold, Bagby performs Beowulf in Old English and accompanies himself on an Anglo-Saxon harp.

Direct Teach

Think About/Talk About

Read with a Purpose Have students read and reflect on the Read with a Purpose statement. Remind students that since Beowulf is the hero of this epic poem, they should think about and write down the words and phrases that describe him. Tell students to pay special attention to adjectives describing Beowulf and to opinions that other characters and the narrator express about him.

Extend the Discussion

Summarizing What were the poet's songs about? ***Possible response:*** *The poet sang of the beginning of things: the earth and seas, all that was given life by God.*

Interpreting What phrases on the first page of the selection provide the best evidence of Grendel's evil nature? ***Possible response:*** *Line 16 defines Grendel as "that demon, that fiend." Lines 1–2 tell he is from a place "down / In the darkness."*

Analyzing Visuals

Connecting to the Text: *The decorations may distinguish the ship from others as a warship. They may also identify the country to which the ship belongs, which would aid the ships in recognizing their comrades, allies, and enemies.*

Model the Skill

- Provide students with copies of the Reading Skills Focus graphic organizer for *Beowulf*. (See **Unit 1 Resources**.)
- Model how to use the graphic organizer to paraphrase a passage. Read lines 64–72 aloud. Tell students to look for the nouns, verbs, and phrases that describe the action. The characters mentioned are Hrothgar and Grendel. Other important words and phrases are *misery, savage war,* and *seeking no peace.*
- Explain that these words can be used to paraphrase the lines as follows: *Hrothgar's sorrow for Grendel's evil deeds was soon known everywhere. Everyone knew there was no stopping the monster's slaughter.* Point out to students that the paraphrase is shorter than the original text.

Guided Practice: Apply

Guide students in filling out their graphic organizer. Help them find nouns, verbs, and phrases that will help them to paraphrase, as below.

Nouns	Verbs	Phrases
Grendel	went up	to Herot
Hrothgar's sorrow	leaped	the seas

Think About/Talk About

Responses to Margin Questions

Lines 53–58 *Hrothgar's men are afraid for their lives.*

Lines 59–64 *Grendel's reign of terror has lasted for twelve years.*

Lines 79–89 *It shows how desperately Hrothgar needs a hero like Beowulf.*

Marshes, and made his home in a hell
Not hell but earth. He was spawned in that slime, (A)
Conceived by a pair of those monsters born
Of Cain,° murderous creatures banished
By God, punished forever for the crime
Of Abel's death. The Almighty drove
Those demons out, and their exile was bitter,
Shut away from men; they split
Into a thousand forms of evil—spirits
And fiends, goblins, monsters, giants,
A brood forever opposing the Lord's
Will, and again and again defeated.

2

Then, when darkness had dropped, Grendel
Went up to Herot, wondering what the warriors
Would do in that hall when their drinking was done.
He found them sprawled in sleep, suspecting
Nothing, their dreams undisturbed. The monster's
Thoughts were as quick as his greed or his claws:
He slipped through the door and there in the silence
Snatched up thirty men, smashed them
Unknowing in their beds, and ran out with their bodies,
The blood dripping behind him, back
To his lair, delighted with his night's slaughter.
At daybreak, with the sun's first light, they saw
How well he had worked, and in that gray morning
Broke their long feast with tears and laments
For the dead. Hrothgar, their lord, sat joyless
In Herot, a mighty prince mourning
The fate of his lost friends and companions,
Knowing by its tracks that some demon had torn
His followers apart. He wept, fearing
The beginning might not be the end. And that night
Grendel came again, so set
On murder that no crime could ever be enough,
No savage assault quench his lust
For evil. Then each warrior tried
To escape him, searched for rest in different
Beds, as far from Herot as they could find,
Seeing how Grendel hunted when they slept. (B)
Distance was safety; the only survivors

21. Cain: Grendel is the offspring of one of the descendants of Cain, a son of Adam and Eve. Cain killed his brother, Abel, and became the first murderer. He was eternally cursed by God and, according to legend, fathered all the evil beings that plague humankind: monsters, demons, and evil spirits.

Silver bowl (7th century). Sutton Hoo ship burial, Suffolk, England.
The Granger Collection, N.Y.

? **53–58.** *Why do none of Hrothgar's men challenge Grendel?*

(A) **Literary Focus** **Epic Hero** Epic heroes embody the values of the societies that create them. What values can you identify in the lines you have read so far?

(B) **Literary Focus** **Epic Hero** Epic heroes perform great deeds. What do you think Beowulf's great deed will be?

Universal Access

EL English Learners

English for Academic Success Ask students to read aloud lines 30–89 with a partner. Then, have them respond to the following questions. To what being does Hrothgar attribute the merciless slaughter of his men? What character trait of Grendel is given emphasis in lines 66–72? In your opinion, does Grendel show respect for Hrothgar's status? Explain.

✔ See **UA: Differentiating Instruction** for strategies for teaching English learners.

Struggling Readers

Have students read pp. 24–25 silently. Then, write the following paraphrase on the board: *Grendel did not try to hurt God. Grendel did not love.* Ask students to find the lines that are paraphrased in the displayed sentences. [*lines 82–85*] Then, have them suggest how they could add clarity to the original meaning of the lines. [*Grendel, even during the night, would never attempt to hurt king Hrothgar, whose position was divinely appointed. Grendel could never understand God's love.*]

So mankind's enemy continued his crimes.

Were those who fled him. Hate had triumphed.
        So Grendel ruled, fought with the righteous,
One against many, and won; so Herot
Stood empty, and stayed deserted for years,
Twelve winters of grief for Hrothgar, king
Of the Danes, sorrow heaped at his door
By hell-forged hands. His misery leaped **C**
The seas, was told and sung in all
Men's ears: how Grendel's hatred began,
How the monster relished his savage war
On the Danes, keeping the bloody feud
Alive, seeking no peace, offering
No truce, accepting no settlement, no price
In gold or land, and paying the living
For one crime only with another. No one
Waited for reparation from his plundering claws:
That shadow of death hunted in the darkness,
Stalked Hrothgar's warriors, old
And young, lying in waiting, hidden
In mist, invisibly following them from the edge
Of the marsh, always there, unseen.
        So mankind's enemy continued his crimes,
Killing as often as he could, coming
Alone, bloodthirsty and horrible. Though he lived
In Herot, when the night hid him, he never
Dared to touch king Hrothgar's glorious
Throne, protected by God—God,
Whose love Grendel could not know. But Hrothgar's
Heart was bent. The best and most noble
Of his council debated remedies, sat
In secret sessions, talking of terror
And wondering what the bravest of warriors could do.
And sometimes they sacrificed to the old stone gods,
Made heathen vows, hoping for Hell's
Support, the Devil's guidance in driving
Their affliction off. That was their way,
And the heathen's only hope, Hell
Always in their hearts, knowing neither God

? **59–64.** *How long has Grendel's reign of terror lasted?*

? **79–89.** *Why does the poem include this background information about Grendel and Hrothgar?*

C **Reading Focus** **Paraphrasing** When you read an epic poem, paraphrasing can be an effective tool to help you comprehend a passage. Paraphrase lines 59–64 in a few sentences.

Vocabulary **reparation** (rehp uh RAY shuhn) *n.:* payment to make up for a wrong or injury.

Advanced Learners

Acceleration Remind students that the original text of *Beowulf* was composed in Old English, which is very different from the language we speak today. Tell students that the history of English is divided into three periods: Old English, Middle English, and Modern English. This translation uses Modern English but uses elevated diction and poetic devices. Have students modernize the poem further by rewriting a brief section using contemporary language and sentence structure.

Students with Disabilities

Students may benefit by drawing an event of the epic. Direct students to look for details to illustrate as they read lines 18–21, 30–34, and 41–44. Then, have students compare their drawings, discussing the similarities and differences. Display the drawings around the classroom to help stimulate interest and facilitate comprehension.

✔ See **UA: Differentiating Instruction** for strategies for teaching students with disabilities.

Think About/Talk About

Comprehension

C Reading Focus

Possible response: *For twelve years, Grendel fought and won alone against righteous men. Grendel's powerful hands brought great sorrow to Hrothgar.*

Analysis

A Literary Focus

Possible response: *Lines 1–20 introduce the values of friendship among men, gratefulness to God as the Almighty Creator of the earth, and camaraderie among warriors.*

B Literary Focus

Possible response: *Beowulf's great deed will be to free Hrothgar's kingdom from the monster Grendel.*

Extend the Discussion

Making Inferences What is the most likely reason Grendel never dares to touch Hrothgar's throne? ***Possible response:*** *According to lines 83–84, Hrothgar's throne is protected by God. Maybe Grendel is not powerful enough to attack it.*

Speculating According to lines 88–99, what actions did Hrothgar's noblest men take to try to defeat the monster? How does the narrator seem to view these actions? ***Possible responses:*** *They sat in secret meetings, discussing what the bravest warriors would do. They offered sacrifices to the stone gods and made heathen vows. The writer seems to disapprove of their "heathen" attempts to solve their problem, saying that their actions prevented them from knowing God's presence.*

Vocabulary: Own the Word

reparation: Tell students the root word for *reparation* is *reparāre,* which in Latin means "to repair." When you make *reparations,* you are making amends for a wrong or injury. Have students think of a time when they had to make *reparation* for a wrong.

Guided Practice: Apply

Think as a Reader/Writer

Find It in Your Reading Point out to students that *Beowulf* makes frequent references to the ancestry of its characters. Explain that ancestry is linked to character traits, as in the introduction of Grendel in lines 16–29.

Use It in Your Writing Have students write a two- or three-line description of an imaginary, modern superhero. Ask students to introduce the hero's qualities by explaining his or her origins.

Think About/Talk About

Build Background: Medieval Armor

Tell students that the mail shirt was composed of as many as twenty thousand small iron rings riveted or welded shut, creating a mesh-net effect. It protected against stray arrows or spears. The mail shirt continued to be worn as the main body armor until the fourteenth century.

Extend the Discussion

Finding Details In lines 116–119, why do the wise men agree to let Beowulf sail to help Hrothgar? ***Possible response:*** *The wise men do not worry about Beowulf's safety because the omens for his mission are good.*

Interpreting In line 105, why is Hrothgar's sorrow described as "bitter and fresh"? ***Possible response:*** *The sorrow is bitter because Hrothgar feels powerless against Grendel's fury. It is also fresh because the monster has attacked continually for twelve years, so the king's pain is constantly renewed.*

Eagle shield ornament (7th century), from the Sutton Hoo ship burial, Suffolk, England.
The British Museum, London.

Nor His passing as He walks through our world, the Lord
Of Heaven and earth; their ears could not hear
His praise nor know His glory. Let them
Beware, those who are thrust into danger,
Clutched at by trouble, yet can carry no solace
In their hearts, cannot hope to be better! Hail
To those who will rise to God, drop off
Their dead bodies, and seek our Father's peace!

3

So the living sorrow of Healfdane's son°
Simmered, bitter and fresh, and no wisdom
Or strength could break it: That agony hung
On king and people alike, harsh
And unending, violent and cruel, and evil.
In his far-off home Beowulf, Higlac's
Follower° and the strongest of the Geats—greater
And stronger than anyone anywhere in this world—
Heard how Grendel filled nights with horror
And quickly commanded a boat fitted out,
Proclaiming that he'd go to that famous king,
Would sail across the sea to Hrothgar,
Now when help was needed. None **(D)**
Of the wise ones regretted his going, much
As he was loved by the Geats: The omens were good,
And they urged the adventure on. So Beowulf
Chose the mightiest men he could find,

104. Healfdane's son: Hrothgar.

109–110. Higlac's follower: Higlac is Beowulf's uncle and feudal lord.

(D) Literary Focus **Epic Hero** What qualities of the epic hero are conveyed in lines 109–116?

Universal Access

Struggling Readers

Strategic Students Assist students in understanding the archetype of the epic hero.

1. Have students consider the hero's reputation. What did his hometown think of him? How is this a heroic quality?
2. Have students point out which quality of the hero is noted by the "great king of the Danes," in line 128? Why is this quality important? What does it reveal about the culture and society of that time?

Advanced Learners

Acceleration Challenge students to make inferences about how Hrothgar and Beowulf are alike in some ways and different in others. Ask them to share their observations, paraphrasing lines from the text to support their views.

✔ See **UA: Resources for Teaching Advanced Students** for strategies for teaching advanced learners.

The bravest and best of the Geats, fourteen
In all, and led them down to their boat;
He knew the sea, would point the prow°
Straight to that distant Danish shore. . . .

Beowulf arrives in Denmark and is directed to Herot, the mead-hall of King Hrothgar. The king sends Wulfgar, one of his thanes (or feudal lords), to greet the visitors.

The Arrival of the Hero

4

. . . Then Wulfgar went to the door and addressed
The waiting seafarers with soldier's words:
"My lord, the great king of the Danes, commands me
To tell you that he knows of your noble birth
And that having come to him from over the open
Sea you have come bravely and are welcome.
Now go to him as you are, in your armor and helmets,
But leave your battle-shields here, and your spears,
Let them lie waiting for the promises your words
May make." (E)
Beowulf arose, with his men
Around him, ordering a few to remain
With their weapons, leading the others quickly
Along under Herot's steep roof into Hrothgar's
Presence. Standing on that prince's own hearth,
Helmeted, the silvery metal of his mail shirt°
Gleaming with a smith's° high art, he greeted
The Danes' great lord:
"Hail, Hrothgar!
Higlac is my cousin° and my king; the days
Of my youth have been filled with glory. Now Grendel's
Name has echoed in our land: Sailors
Have brought us stories of Herot, the best
Of all mead-halls, deserted and useless when the moon
Hangs in skies the sun had lit,
Light and life fleeing together.
My people have said, the wisest, most knowing
And best of them, that my duty was to go to the Danes'
Great king. They have seen my strength for themselves, (F)

123. prow: front part of a boat.

139. mail shirt: armored garment made of interlocking metal rings.
140. smith's: metalworker's.
142. cousin: any relative.

(E) **Literary Focus** **Epic Hero** How do Wulfgar's words show Beowulf's heroic qualities?

(F) **Literary Focus** **Epic Hero** Beowulf says that he has come to kill Grendel. What proof does he offer here that he is the right hero for the job?

Think About/Talk About

Analysis

(D) Literary Focus

Possible response: *The qualities of the epic hero conveyed in lines 109–116 are as follows: noble heritage, unsurpassed strength, strong leadership, and the capacity for quick, decisive action.*

(E) Literary Focus

Possible response: *Wulfgar honors Beowulf's "noble birth" and praises him for his bravery. Noble heritage and bravery are fundamental traits of the epic hero.*

(F) Literary Focus

Possible response: *Beowulf has proven his value by killing many enemies, chasing giants away from the earth, and hunting monsters in the ocean.*

Extend the Discussion

Finding Details How did Beowulf get word of Grendel's attacks on Herot Hall? ***Possible response:*** *Beowulf heard about Grendel and Herot from the stories that sailors told and spread through his land.*

Tone In lines 142–153, what tone does Beowulf use when first speaking to Hrothgar? ***Possible response:*** *Beowulf's tone is respectful. He speaks to the king of the Danes with deference and praise for his kingdom.*

Students with Disabilities

Have students re-read lines 104–108. Point out that many words are used to describe the sorrow Hrothgar experiences for the death of his men. Ask students to read the lines carefully and use context clues to understand unfamiliar words such as *agony.* Then, have them write all the words in lines 104–108 that are related to the idea of sorrow. Explain that studying a group of words that have similar meanings or pertain to similar situations is an effective way to build the vocabulary needed to paraphrase a text.

AAVE Students Who Use African American Vernacular English

English for Academic Success Tell students that singular nouns, such as "Grendel's Name" in lines 143–144, take the verb form *has*, not *have.* Plural nouns such as "my people" in line 49, on the other hand, use *have*. Ask students to point out other subjects that use *has* or *have* in lines 141–151 and read aloud the subject-verb combinations. Remind students that the subject of an action in one line may not be on the same line, so students should look to previous lines.

Think About/Talk About

Literary Connection

Tell students that Beowulf boasts to Hrothgar of all his extraordinary deeds and bravery demonstrated through the killing of great monsters. Modern readers sometimes consider boasting offensive; however, boasting is a tradition of epic poetry. Odysseus frequently boasts in the *Odyssey.* In the world of *Beowulf,* boasting serves as both an implicit promise to help and a presentation of credentials.

▶ Extend the Discussion

Finding Details In lines 160–174, what request does Beowulf have for Hrothgar? ***Possible response:*** *Beowulf wants to confront Grendel with his bare hands, accompanied by some of his men.*

Characterization What does Beowulf's request to Hrothgar say about Beowulf's heroism? ***Possible responses:*** *Beowulf does not want to have an unfair advantage over Grendel, who fights with no weapons. He has the courage to face the monster with no special protection. His words convey his bravery as well as his respect for Hrothgar, who has lost so many men to Grendel.*

Responses to Margin Questions

Lines 180–185 *Grendel will devour Beowulf, so there will be no body left to bury.*

Lines 191–207 *Hrothgar may wish to point out that Beowulf is honoring his father's debt to Hrothgar.*

Have watched me rise from the darkness of war,
Dripping with my enemies' blood. I drove
Five great giants into chains, chased
All of that race from the earth. I swam
In the blackness of night, hunting monsters
Out of the ocean, and killing them one
By one; death was my errand and the fate
They had earned. Now Grendel and I are called
Together, and I've come. Grant me, then,
Lord and protector of this noble place,
A single request! I have come so far,
Oh shelterer of warriors and your people's loved friend,
That this one favor you should not refuse me—
That I, alone and with the help of my men,
May purge all evil from this hall. I have heard,
Too, that the monster's scorn of men
Is so great that he needs no weapons and fears none.
Nor will I. My lord Higlac
Might think less of me if I let my sword
Go where my feet were afraid to, if I hid
Behind some broad linden shield:° My hands
Alone shall fight for me, struggle for life
Against the monster. God must decide (G)
Who will be given to death's cold grip.
Grendel's plan, I think, will be
What it has been before, to invade this hall
And gorge his belly with our bodies. If he can,
If he can. And I think, if my time will have come,
There'll be nothing to mourn over, no corpse to prepare
For its grave: Grendel will carry our bloody
Flesh to the moors, crunch on our bones,
And smear torn scraps of our skin on the walls
Of his den. No, I expect no Danes
Will fret about sewing our shrouds,° if he wins.
And if death does take me, send the hammered
Mail of my armor to Higlac, return
The inheritance I had from Hrethel,° and he
From Wayland.° Fate will unwind as it must!"

5

Hrothgar replied, protector of the Danes:
"Beowulf, you've come to us in friendship, and because
Of the reception your father found at our court.
Edgetho had begun a bitter feud,

(G) Literary Focus Epic Hero To what does Beowulf attribute the outcome of the epic battle?

Runic mount with animal's head (8th century). Anglo-Saxon. Biting head, probably part of the binding of a scabbard for a seax (Anglo-Saxon weapon or hunting knife). M&ME (1869–10,1).
The British Museum, London.

172. linden shield: shield made from wood of the linden tree.

? 180–185. *Why will Hrothgar not have to hold a funeral if Beowulf dies?*

185. shrouds: cloths used to wrap a body for burial.
188. Hrethel: Beowulf's grandfather, former king of the Geats.
189. Wayland: a smith celebrated for his skill in making swords and mail shirts.

? 191–207. *What do you think causes Hrothgar to make this speech, reminding Beowulf of the time he helped Beowulf's father? What is the probable effect of these words on Beowulf?*

Developing Oral Fluency

Use pp. 28–29 to explain to students the importance of paying attention to punctuation when reading aloud. Point out the long sentences in the selection, and note that the text is divided into short phrases and sentences through the use of commas and semicolons. Model for students a fluent reading of a long sentence, such as the one beginning on line 199 and ending on line 204.

Small-Group Activity Have students work in small groups to read aloud the first section of *Beowulf* (pp. 23–26). Ask them to share parts of the section so that everyone has a chance to read aloud. Students should strive for a clear and expressive reading. For this reason, remind them to pay special attention to the selection's punctuation.

✔ See the **Oral Language Skill Builder** in **UA: Differentiating Instruction.**

Killing Hathlaf, a Wulfing warrior:°
Your father's countrymen were afraid of war,
If he returned to his home, and they turned him away.
Then he traveled across the curving waves
To the land of the Danes. I was new to the throne,
Then, a young man ruling this wide
Kingdom and its golden city: Hergar,
My older brother, a far better man
Than I, had died and dying made me,
Second among Healfdane's sons, first
In this nation. I bought the end of Edgetho's
Quarrel, sent ancient treasures through the ocean's
Furrows to the Wulfings; your father swore
He'd keep that peace. My tongue grows heavy,
And my heart, when I try to tell you what Grendel
Has brought us, the damage he's done, here
In this hall. You see for yourself how much smaller
Our ranks have become, and can guess what we've lost
To his terror. Surely the Lord Almighty
Could stop his madness, smother his lust! **H**
How many times have my men, glowing
With courage drawn from too many cups
Of ale, sworn to stay after dark
And stem that horror with a sweep of their swords.
And then, in the morning, this mead-hall glittering
With new light would be drenched with blood, the benches
Stained red, the floors, all wet from that fiend's
Savage assault—and my soldiers would be fewer
Still, death taking more and more.
But to table, Beowulf, a banquet in your honor:
Let us toast your victories, and talk of the future."
Then Hrothgar's men gave places to the Geats,
Yielded benches to the brave visitors,
And led them to the feast. The keeper of the mead
Came carrying out the carved flasks,
And poured that bright sweetness. A poet
Sang, from time to time, in a clear
Pure voice. Danes and visiting Geats
Celebrated as one, drank and rejoiced.

194. Wulfing warrior: The Wulfings were a Germanic tribe. Hrothgar's queen might have been a Wulfing.

Bronze stag atop ceremonial scepter (7th century A.D.) from the Sutton Hoo ship burial, Suffolk, England.
The British Museum, London.

H **Reading Focus** **Paraphrasing** In your own words, paraphrase these lines about Grendel's influence.

Think About/Talk About

Comprehension

H Reading Focus

Possible response: *Grendel has carried out much destruction in the hall. Look at how much our numbers have been reduced! Guess what we have lost through his acts of madness and eagerness to kill!*

Analysis

G Literary Focus

Possible response: *Beowulf believes his victory or defeat is up to fate.*

Extend the Discussion

Characterization How would you describe Hrothgar after his reply to Beowulf in lines 191–224? ***Possible response:*** *Hrothgar was once a strong king and loyal to his allies, but now he seems old and weak. His grief over the deaths of his warriors at Grendel's hands shows that he is a compassionate ruler.*

Reaching Reluctant Readers

Motivate students' interest in the selection by helping them connect to the text. Ask students to think about a situation where they were in a position to help a relative, friend, or neighbor in need:

- How did they act in this situation? Did they immediately offer their assistance, or did they hesitate because of a lack of confidence in their abilities?
- Have students consider their motivations for offering help. Were their motivations purely unselfish? What did they have to gain or lose from this opportunity?

Model the Skill

- Model **paraphrasing** using lines 239–245. For example, you might mention that reading these lines for the first time could be confusing.
- Students might start by reading slowly and then paraphrasing what they have read. Unferth says that Beowulf and Brecca had a swimming match. Unferth says they risked their lives, so it must have been a dangerous match. In line 244, Unferth says that the old, wise officials warned Beowulf not to swim, but that Beowulf was too prideful to listen.

Guided Practice: Apply

Read-Talk-Write Group students in pairs to review Beowulf's version of the story, paying attention to key nouns, verbs, and phrases. Have them complete the Nouns, Verbs, Phrases chart. Ask students to take turns paraphrasing a few lines at a time. Ask volunteers to share their paraphrases with the class.

Think About/Talk About

Build Background: Herot Hall

Archaeologists have confirmed that Herot was built of wood held together with iron bands. The gabled roof was overlaid with gold, and the floor was inlaid. Herot means *hart* or *stag*. The hart was an Anglo-Saxon symbol of kinship.

Response to Margin Question

Lines 239–252 *Beowulf was not risking his life for any particular cause; it was just a competition for the sake of adventure.*

Unferth's Challenge

6

Unferth spoke, Ecglaf's son,
Who sat at Hrothgar's feet, spoke harshly
And sharp (vexed by Beowulf's adventure,
By their visitor's courage, and angry that anyone
In Denmark or anywhere on earth had ever
Acquired glory and fame greater
Than his own):
"You're Beowulf, are you—the same
Boastful fool who fought a swimming
Match with Brecca, both of you daring
And young and proud, exploring the deepest
Seas, risking your lives for no reason
But the danger? All older and wiser heads warned you
Not to, but no one could check such pride.
With Brecca at your side you swam along
The sea-paths, your swift-moving hands pulling you
Over the ocean's face. Then winter
Churned through the water, the waves ran you
As they willed, and you struggled seven long nights
To survive. And at the end victory was his,
Not yours. The sea carried him close
To his home, to southern Norway, near
The land of the Brondings, where he ruled and was loved,
Where his treasure was piled and his strength protected
His towns and his people. He'd promised to outswim you:
Bonstan's son° made that boast ring true.
You've been lucky in your battles, Beowulf, but I think
Your luck may change if you challenge Grendel,
Staying a whole night through in this hall,
Waiting where that fiercest of demons can find you."
Beowulf answered, Edgetho's great son:
"Ah! Unferth, my friend, your face
Is hot with ale, and your tongue has tried
To tell us about Brecca's doings. But the truth
Is simple: No man swims in the sea
As I can, no strength is a match for mine.
As boys, Brecca and I had boasted—
We were both too young to know better—that we'd risk
Our lives far out at sea, and so
We did. Each of us carried a naked
Sword, prepared for whales or the swift

? **239–252.** *Why might Unferth think that Beowulf is ashamed of having taken part in the swimming race?*

257. Bonstan's son: Brecca.

Anglo-Saxon gold buckle (7th century) from the Sutton Hoo ship burial, Suffolk, England. The British Library, London.

Literary Focus **Epic Hero** An epic hero represents the ideal of his society. Here, however, Unferth challenges Beowulf's bravery. How do you think he feels about Beowulf?

Universal Access

EL English Learners

English for Academic Success Have students demonstrate understanding of the syntax and word choice by paraphrasing lines 286–291 in their own words. To guide them in this skill, draw a chart on the board with the headings: Key Words, Nouns, and Verbs. Explain that in paraphrasing, students can retain a few key words from the text. For instance, in these lines, students may want to keep the words *claws, heart,* and *sword.* Ask students to brainstorm nouns that they could use to replace the nouns in the text and list the nouns that students call out on the board. For instance, students may suggest *creature* or *beast* for "monster," *floor* for "bottom," and *destiny* for "fate." Then, have them brainstorm alternative verbs. Encourage students to refer to a thesaurus during this exercise if they have difficulty coming up with words. Remind them not to choose words that are unfamiliar to them, however.

✔ See **UA: Differentiating Instruction** for strategies for teaching English learners.

"A monster seized me, drew me swiftly toward the bottom."

Sharp teeth and beaks of needlefish.
He could never leave me behind, swim faster
Across the waves than I could, and I
Had chosen to remain close to his side. **J**
I remained near him for five long nights,
Until a flood swept us apart;
The frozen sea surged around me,
It grew dark, the wind turned bitter, blowing
From the north, and the waves were savage. Creatures
Who sleep deep in the sea were stirred
Into life—and the iron hammered links
Of my mail shirt, these shining bits of metal
Woven across my breast, saved me
From death. A monster seized me, drew me
Swiftly toward the bottom, swimming with its claws
Tight in my flesh. But fate let me
Find its heart with my sword, hack myself
Free; I fought that beast's last battle,
Left it floating lifeless in the sea.

7

"Other monsters crowded around me,
Continually attacking. I treated them politely,
Offering the edge of my razor-sharp sword.
But the feast, I think, did not please them, filled
Their evil bellies with no banquet-rich food,
Thrashing there at the bottom of the sea; **K**
By morning they'd decided to sleep on the shore,
Lying on their backs, their blood spilled out
On the sand. Afterwards, sailors could cross
That sea-road and feel no fear; nothing
Would stop their passing. Then God's bright beacon
Appeared in the east, the water lay still,
And at last I could see the land, wind-swept
Cliff-walls at the edge of the coast. Fate saves
The living when they drive away death by themselves!
Lucky or not, nine was the number
Of sea-huge monsters I killed. What man,
Anywhere under Heaven's high arch, has fought

Saxon brooch (early 6th century) discovered at Mitcham, South London. Gold leaf on wood. Museum of London, UK.

J **Literary Focus** **Epic Hero** What is Beowulf's explanation for not leaving Brecca far behind? What heroic quality does this suggest?

K **Literary Focus** **Epic Hero** How does the language of Beowulf's speech emphasize Beowulf's calm, confident (and perhaps arrogant) nature?

Think About/Talk About

Analysis

I Literary Focus

Possible response: *If Unferth needs to challenge Beowulf's bravery, he most likely feels threatened or jealous.*

J Literary Focus

Possible response: *Beowulf claims Brecca was not a strong swimmer, so he decided to stay and protect him, which was a display of Beowulf's bravery and compassion.*

K Literary Focus

Possible response: *Beowulf describes the monsters attacking him in a nonchalant manner, as if to suggest that defending himself against them was effortless.*

Extend the Discussion

Finding Details What "feast" does Beowulf offer to the other sea monsters in line 294? ***Possible response:*** *Beowulf serves them the edge of his sword.*

Evaluating A challenge to a hero made by a character of inferior status, like Unferth, is a common motif in epic poetry. How does Unferth's challenge build suspense? ***Possible response:*** *Unferth's challenge raises a question in readers' minds about Beowulf's ability to defeat Grendel.*

Struggling Readers

Students might have trouble differentiating Unferth's swimming match story from the story of Beowulf slaying Grendel. Give students a copy of the story from the **UA: Holt Interactive Reader,** and have students use a pencil to mark where the swimming match story begins and ends. Then, help students understand how the story affects readers' interpretation of the rest of the text. As they read, encourage students to ask themselves: "What does the story of the swimming match tell me about Beowulf? How is that related to his upcoming battle with Grendel?"

Advanced Learners

Acceleration After Unferth attempts to shame Beowulf with the story of the swimming match, Beowulf counters with his version of the story. The truth of the story is never disclosed as there are no witnesses. Ask students to consider whether Beowulf lost the swimming match to Brecca or closely guarded Brecca and then killed a few sea monsters after a storm separated them. Divide students into two groups, and have them collect evidence for either Beowulf's or Brecca's version of the story and engage in a formal debate for the class.

Think About/Talk About

Literary Connection

Tell students that attending a banquet or party before departing for a quest seems to be a recurring element in epics. Ask students if they can think of other famous epics that feature a party scene before the beginning of a long journey. For example, Frodo attends a village feast in the first book of the *Lord of the Rings* series, *The Fellowship of the Ring*.

▶ Extend the Discussion

Summarizing What explanation does Beowulf give for Grendel continuing to attack the hall in lines 325–334? ***Possible response:*** *Beowulf suggests that Grendel would not attack if Unferth and the Danes were strong enough to fight him.*

Characterization In lines 344–345, how do the banquet guests respond to Beowulf's speech? ***Possible response:*** *The guests are happy; they laugh and toast each other.*

Response to Margin Question

Lines 323–334 *Beowulf responds to Unferth's challenge by revealing that Unferth murdered his brothers and is destined for hell.*

In such darkness, endured more misery, or been harder
Pressed? Yet I survived the sea, smashed
The monsters' hot jaws, swam home from my journey.
The swift-flowing waters swept me along
And I landed on Finnish soil. I've heard
No tales of you, Unferth, telling
Of such clashing terror, such contests in the night!
Brecca's battles were never so bold;
Neither he nor you can match me—and I mean
No boast, have announced no more than I know
To be true. And there's more: You murdered your brothers,
Your own close kin. Words and bright wit
Won't help your soul; you'll suffer hell's fires,
Unferth, forever tormented. Ecglaf's
Proud son, if your hands were as hard, your heart
As fierce as you think it, no fool would dare
To raid your hall, ruin Herot
And oppress its prince, as Grendel has done.
But he's learned that terror is his alone,
Discovered he can come for your people with no fear
Of reprisal; he's found no fighting, here,
But only food, only delight.
He murders as he likes, with no mercy, gorges
And feasts on your flesh, and expects no trouble,
No quarrel from the quiet Danes. Now
The Geats will show him courage, soon
He can test his strength in battle. And when the sun
Comes up again, opening another
Bright day from the south, anyone in Denmark
May enter this hall: That evil will be gone!" **L**
    Hrothgar, gray-haired and brave, sat happily
Listening, the famous ring-giver sure,
At last, that Grendel could be killed; he believed
In Beowulf's bold strength and the firmness of his spirit.
    There was the sound of laughter, and the cheerful clanking
Of cups, and pleasant words. Then Welthow,
Hrothgar's gold-ringed queen, greeted
The warriors; a noble woman who knew
What was right, she raised a flowing cup
To Hrothgar first, holding it high
For the lord of the Danes to drink, wishing him
Joy in that feast. The famous king
Drank with pleasure and blessed their banquet.

L **Reading Focus** **Paraphrasing** How would you paraphrase the story up to this point?

Vocabulary **reprisal** (rih PRY zuhl) *n.:* punishment in return for an injury.

? **323–334.** *What is Beowulf's final response to Unferth's challenge?*

Book I, from the *Beowulf* graphic novel, featuring the Francis Gummere verse translation.

Universal Access

Struggling Readers

Benchmark Students Read aloud lines 320–327 to the class. Explain that in these lines, Beowulf points out Unferth's failings after he gives his own account of the swimming match with Brecca. Ask students how these lines highlight the strengths and virtues of the epic hero, Beowulf. To help students sort out their thoughts, have them draw a Venn diagram in which they list the differences and similarities between the two characters. Have students verbally summarize their differences and similarities in a few sentences.

Ask students to consider whether Beowulf's criticism of Unferth is justified. Do students think more or less of Beowulf as an epic hero as a result of his verbal charge?

✔ Invite students to read the selection in interactive format in **UA: Holt Interactive Reader.**

Then Welthow went from warrior to warrior,
Pouring a portion from the jeweled cup
For each, till the bracelet-wearing queen
Had carried the mead-cup among them and it was Beowulf's
Turn to be served. She saluted the Geats'
Great prince, thanked God for answering her prayers,
For allowing her hands the happy duty
Of offering mead to a hero who would help
Her afflicted people. He drank what she poured,
Edgetho's brave son, then assured the Danish
Queen that his heart was firm and his hands
Ready:
"When we crossed the sea, my comrades
And I, I already knew that all
My purpose was this: to win the good will
Of your people or die in battle, pressed
In Grendel's fierce grip. Let me live in greatness
And courage, or here in this hall welcome
My death!" (M)
Welthow was pleased with his words
His bright-tongued boasts; she carried them back
To her lord, walked nobly across to his side.
The feast went on, laughter and music
And the brave words of warriors celebrating
Their delight. Then Hrothgar rose, Healfdane's
Son, heavy with sleep; as soon
As the sun had gone, he knew that Grendel
Would come to Herot, would visit that hall
When night had covered the earth with its net
And the shapes of darkness moved black and silent
Through the world. Hrothgar's warriors rose with him.
He went to Beowulf, embraced the Geats'
Brave prince, wished him well, and hoped
That Herot would be his to command. And then
He declared:
"No one strange to this land
Has ever been granted what I've given you,
No one in all the years of my rule.
Make this best of all mead-halls yours, and then
Keep it free of evil, fight
With glory in your heart! Purge Herot
And your ship will sail home with its treasure-holds full." . . . (N)

Shoulder clasp (7th century A.D.), from the Sutton Hoo ship burial, Suffolk, England. The British Museum, London.

(M) **Literary Focus** **Epic Hero** What does Beowulf's speech reveal about his character?

(N) **Reading Focus** **Paraphrasing** What verbs in lines 385–391 could help you paraphrase Hrothgar's speech?

Cross-Curricular Connection

HISTORY: *Comitatus*

In lines 364–370, Beowulf expresses an idea that is somewhat similar to the either-or thinking of Patrick Henry's "Give me liberty or give me death," and Tennyson's "Theirs not to reason why, / Theirs but to do and die." For an Anglo-Saxon warrior, life was an either-or situation: Life without loyalty or courage was worse than death. According to the Anglo-Saxon code of the *comitatus,* warriors must defend their lord to the death. Thus, a true hero would worry more about showing fear or being disloyal than about dying.

Whole-Class Activity Have students name and discuss modern incarnations of this "do or die" philosophy, which are sometimes heard from firefighters or astronauts.

Think About/Talk About

Comprehension

(L) Reading Focus

Possible response: *A demonic creature came up to Herot and mercilessly slaughtered the sleeping men. Their ruler Hrothgar despaired as Grendel continued to fill his hunger for blood. In a distant land, the hero of the Geats, Beowulf, heard about Grendel's rampages and came to Herot with his followers, declaring he would fight Grendel with his hands. When his abilities were challenged by Unferth, Beowulf defended himself and revealed the true account of the swimming race with Brecca, explaining that his struggle with monstrous creatures had made him lose the race. After pointing out that Unferth had murdered his brothers, Beowulf declared that the Geats would deal with Grendel and rid the hall of evil.*

(N) Reading Focus

Possible response: *The verbs* keep, fight, purge, *and* sail *help to paraphrase Hrothgar's promise of a reward if Beowulf is victorious.*

Analysis

(M) Literary Focus

Possible response: *Beowulf shows his dedication and heroism by vowing to honor the Danes or die trying.*

Extend the Discussion

Symbolism What could the offering of mead to the king and Beowulf and the other warriors, as described in lines 345–363, symbolize for the Danes? ***Possible response:*** *It could symbolize a blessing or a delivering of strength for the upcoming battle.*

Vocabulary: Own the Word

reprisal: A *reprisal* is an act of revenge; a near antonym is *leniency.* Use both words in a sentence. ***Possible response:*** *We knew the Bulldogs would not show us leniency; in fact, we anticipated a reprisal from our rival team after our championship win last year.*

Think About/Talk About

Literary Connection

Many cultures have produced poems that celebrate their heroes and express their values and customs. In *Beowulf,* these cultural values include the following:

- honoring courage over long life
- enjoying feasts, stories, and music
- viewing life fatalistically, even within the Christian tradition
- admiring physical strength more than intelligence
- valuing loyalty to the lord or king above all

Extend the Discussion

Finding Details According to lines 409–414, what does Grendel feel when he sees the hall that he is about to attack? ***Possible response:*** *As Grendel approaches the hall, he is pleased and eager to attack the sleeping soldiers.*

Determining Author's Purpose At the beginning of the section titled "The Battle with Grendel," Grendel emerges from a swamp to attack Herot. Why does the author choose to have Grendel come from a swamp? ***Possible response:*** *Grendel comes out of the swamp because it furthers his image as the antihero. Swamps are disgusting and damp, a fitting place for a vile creature like Grendel to reside. The mist of the "misty hills and bogs" (392–93) also shroud Grendel in mystery, much in the same way that smoke is used to mystify the villains of horror stories and films.*

The feast ends. Beowulf and his men take the place of Hrothgar's followers and lie down to sleep in Herot. Beowulf, however, is wakeful, eager to meet his enemy.

The Battle with Grendel

8

Out from the marsh, from the foot of misty
Hills and bogs, bearing God's hatred,
Grendel came, hoping to kill
Anyone he could trap on this trip to high Herot. (O)
He moved quickly through the cloudy night,
Up from his swampland, sliding silently
Toward that gold-shining hall. He had visited Hrothgar's
Home before, knew the way—
But never, before nor after that night,
Found Herot defended so firmly, his reception
So harsh. He journeyed, forever joyless,
Straight to the door, then snapped it open,
Tore its iron fasteners with a touch,
And rushed angrily over the threshold.
He strode quickly across the inlaid
Floor, snarling and fierce: His eyes
Gleamed in the darkness, burned with a gruesome
Light. Then he stopped, seeing the hall
Crowded with sleeping warriors, stuffed
With rows of young soldiers resting together.
And his heart laughed, he relished the sight,
Intended to tear the life from those bodies
By morning; the monster's mind was hot
With the thought of food and the feasting his belly
Would soon know. But fate, that night, intended (P)
Grendel to gnaw the broken bones
Of his last human supper. Human
Eyes were watching his evil steps,
Waiting to see his swift hard claws.
Grendel snatched at the first Geat
He came to, ripped him apart, cut
His body to bits with powerful jaws,
Drank the blood from his veins, and bolted
Him down, hands and feet; death
And Grendel's great teeth came together,

The Battersea Shield, Iron Age (350–50 B.C.). The British Museum, London.

(O) **Literary Focus** **Epic Hero** How do these lines show us that Grendel is the opposite of the epic hero?

(P) **Reading Focus** **Paraphrasing** What words in lines 402–415 could you omit if you wrote a paragraph paraphrasing this visit to Herot?

Reaching Reluctant Readers

Refer students back to the What Do You Think question on p. 20. Point out to students that "Higlac's follower" in line 440 is Beowulf, and that before he tightens his grip on Grendel, he remembers the "final boast" he had made earlier. Ask students why this might have motivated him the most to go through with his plan to defeat Grendel.

Have students think of a similar situation where they had boasted in front of others of their abilities or talents or possessions. How did they follow up on these boasts? If they had the opportunity again to make a public boast, would they do it? Why or why not?

CULTURE LINK

Eric Owens as Grendel in production of *Grendel* (Los Angeles).

Grendel

It is often said that "history is written by the victors," and for that reason, it is important to think objectively when we read literary and historical narratives. Like history, literature can be revised to exhibit a point of view different from that of the original author. In literature, revisionism often becomes apparent when popular stories are retold from the perspective of the antagonist, the character or force that opposes the main character. The musical *Wicked,* for example, based on the novel by Gregory Maguire, spins a new story for the wicked witch from *The Wizard of Oz* by showcasing her character's rich history prior to the beginning of the movie. John Gardner takes a similar approach in his novel *Grendel*—later turned into an opera—which retells the epic of *Beowulf* from Grendel's point of view.

Ask Yourself

Based on your reading of "The Monster Grendel," think about what Grendel's personal reasons might have been for attacking Herot over the years. Was it truly mindless evil that drove him to murder? What could justify his slaughter of Hrothgar's people?

Snapping life shut. Then he stepped to another
Still body, clutched at Beowulf with his claws,
Grasped at a strong-hearted wakeful sleeper
—And was instantly seized himself, claws
Bent back as Beowulf leaned up on one arm.
That shepherd of evil,° guardian of crime,
Knew at once that nowhere on earth
Had he met a man whose hands were harder;
His mind was flooded with fear—but nothing Ⓠ
Could take his talons and himself from that tight
Hard grip. Grendel's one thought was to run
From Beowulf, flee back to his marsh and hide there:
This was a different Herot than the hall he had emptied.
But Higlac's follower remembered his final
Boast and, standing erect, stopped
The monster's flight, fastened those claws
In his fists till they cracked, clutched Grendel
Closer. The infamous killer fought
For his freedom, wanting no flesh but retreat,

Ⓠ **Literary Focus** **Epic Hero** How do we know that Beowulf is greater than the Danes?

432. shepherd of evil: a kenning for Grendel. The **kenning,** a metaphor made of compound words, is a staple of Anglo-Saxon literature. Simple kennings are compound words formed from two common nouns: *sky-candle* for sun, *battle-dew* for blood. More complex kennings are formed with compound adjectives and nouns. A ship became a *foamy-throated ship,* then a *foamy-throated sea-stallion,* and finally a *foamy-throated sea-stallion of the whale-road.* In their original language, kennings are usually written as simple compounds without hyphens or spaces between the words. In translation, kennings are often hyphenated, written as possessives (*wolf of wounds*), or written as prepositional phrases (*shepherd of evil*).

Think About/Talk About

Comprehension

Ⓟ Reading Focus

Possible response: *The words that could be omitted would be the repetitions describing Grendel's state of mind: "his heart laughed," and "the monster's mind was hot."*

Analysis

Ⓠ Literary Focus

Possible response: *Grendel is described as bearing God's hatred, in contrast to a hero who bears God's graces.*

Ⓠ Literary Focus

Possible response: *Grendel has torn apart countless Danes, but he encounters something new in Beowulf. Unlike the Danes, Beowulf has strong hands and fights back against Grendel.*

Extend the Discussion

Comparing and Contrasting In lines 432–448, how does Grendel's reaction to the battle differ from Beowulf's? ***Possible response:*** *Grendel becomes fearful during the battle and tries to flee, while Beowulf remains brave and confident during the fight.*

Synthesizing As Beowulf fights the monster, Grendel tries to run back to his swamp. In lines 440–444, why does Beowulf refuse to let the monster run away, never to return to Herot? ***Possible response:*** *It is not enough for Beowulf to simply scare off the monster and protect the town; Beowulf must exhibit his unwavering bravery and might by slaying Grendel.*

Universal Access

Students with Disabilities

In "The Monster Grendel" and "The Battle with Grendel," it is up to the reader to interpret the subtle descriptions in the text and develop a vision of Grendel.

Activity Working in small groups, have students create representations of the monster Grendel. Students should refer to the text for clues about Grendel's appearance to help them develop the image. Their representations can be hand drawings, collages, or computer-generated images. Groups should then share their images with the class.

Culture Link

Ask Yourself

Possible response: *Grendel was trying to sleep when he was awoken by the humans' music. When he approached the hall, he found them asleep. He was angry that they were able to sleep and he was not, and perhaps he also felt isolated and resentful of their camaraderie and contentment.*

Guided Practice: Apply

Think as a Reader/Writer

Find It in Your Reading Explain to students that a kenning is a phrase used in place of a noun. Kennings are used quite often in Anglo-Saxon literature. Point out the phrase "that night's fierce work," a kenning for *battle* in line 509. Tell students to look for more examples of kennings as they read.

Use It in Your Writing Have students select a noun in *Beowulf* and write two or three kennings to replace it.

Think About/Talk About

Responses to Margin Questions

Lines 467–472 *Beowulf represents humanity and its virtues; Grendel represents hatred and the powers of darkness. The kennings used to describe Grendel—shepherd of evil, guardian of crime, and the infamous killer, for example—serve to highlight the distinction.*

Lines 514–517 *He hangs the monster's arm from Herot's rafters. The act is a gesture of triumph and an assurance to everyone at Herot that Grendel will trouble the hall no more.*

Lines 522–533 *The steaming, boiling water of the lake, suggesting the fires of hell, evokes the image of Grendel slowly bleeding to death. Finally, Grendel dies "in murky darkness."*

Desiring nothing but escape; his claws
Had been caught, he was trapped. That trip to Herot
Was a miserable journey for the writhing monster!
The high hall rang, its roof boards swayed,
And Danes shook with terror. Down
The aisles the battle swept, angry
And wild. Herot trembled, wonderfully
Built to withstand the blows, the struggling
Great bodies beating at its beautiful walls;
Shaped and fastened with iron, inside
And out, artfully worked, the building
Stood firm. Its benches rattled, fell
To the floor, gold-covered boards grating
As Grendel and Beowulf battled across them.
Hrothgar's wise men had fashioned Herot
To stand forever; only fire,
They had planned, could shatter what such skill had put
Together, swallow in hot flames such splendor
Of ivory and iron and wood. Suddenly
The sounds changed, the Danes started
In new terror, cowering in their beds as the terrible
Screams of the Almighty's enemy sang
In the darkness, the horrible shrieks of pain
And defeat, the tears torn out of Grendel's
Taut throat, hell's captive caught in the arms
Of him who of all the men on earth
Was the strongest. (R)

9

That mighty protector of men
Meant to hold the monster till its life
Leaped out, knowing the fiend was no use
To anyone in Denmark. All of Beowulf's
Band had jumped from their beds, ancestral
Swords raised and ready, determined
To protect their prince if they could. Their courage
Was great but all wasted: They could hack at Grendel (S)
From every side, trying to open
A path for his evil soul, but their points
Could not hurt him, the sharpest and hardest iron
Could not scratch at his skin, for that sin-stained demon

? **467–472.** *Earlier in the epic it was explained that Grendel is a descendant of Cain, who was cursed by God. In what ways is this battle between Grendel and Beowulf really a battle between good and evil? What details in the description of the battle make this clear?*

(R) **Literary Focus** **Epic Hero** What details in lines 449–471 demonstrate Beowulf's superhuman strength?

(S) **Reading Focus** **Paraphrasing** How would you paraphrase the reasons that Beowulf's men can't harm Grendel?

Word-Attack Skills Mini-Lesson

English for Academic Success Tell students that breaking words with prefixes and suffixes into their component parts is often a good strategy for decoding unfamiliar words, but with some words, this strategy can lead to mispronunciations. Use the word *infamous* (l. 444) as an example. It is made up of the prefix *in-* and the adjective *famous,* but it is not pronounced like a combination of *in* and *famous.* The stress shifts to the first syllable, and the word is pronounced *IN fuh muhs.*

Explain that these shifts in stress often account for pronunciations that are different from what students might expect. In other instances, words with similar spellings are pronounced differently. Use the word *weary* as an example. Someone unfamiliar with the word might think it was a combination of *wear* and the suffix *-y* and read it as *WAIR ee* instead of *WEER ee.*

Had bewitched all men's weapons, laid spells
That blunted every mortal man's blade.
And yet his time had come, his days
Were over, his death near; down
To hell he would go, swept groaning and helpless
To the waiting hands of still worse fiends.
Now he discovered—once the afflictor **T**
Of men, tormentor of their days—what it meant
To feud with Almighty God: Grendel
Saw that his strength was deserting him, his claws
Bound fast, Higlac's brave follower tearing at
His hands. The monster's hatred rose higher,
But his power had gone. He twisted in pain,
And the bleeding sinews deep in his shoulder
Snapped, muscle and bone split
And broke. The battle was over, Beowulf
Had been granted new glory: Grendel escaped,
But wounded as he was could flee to his den,
His miserable hole at the bottom of the marsh,
Only to die, to wait for the end
Of all his days. And after that bloody
Combat the Danes laughed with delight.
He who had come to them from across the sea,
Bold and strong-minded, had driven affliction
Off, purged Herot clean. He was happy,
Now, with that night's fierce work; the Danes
Had been served as he'd boasted he'd serve them; Beowulf,
A prince of the Geats, had killed Grendel,
Ended the grief, the sorrow, the suffering
Forced on Hrothgar's helpless people
By a bloodthirsty fiend. No Dane doubted
The victory, for the proof, hanging high
From the rafters where Beowulf had hung it, was the monster's
Arm, claw and shoulder and all.

10

And then, in the morning, crowds surrounded
Herot, warriors coming to that hall
From faraway lands, princes and leaders
Of men hurrying to behold the monster's
Great staggering tracks. They gaped with no sense
Of sorrow, felt no regret for his suffering,
Went tracing his bloody footprints, his beaten
And lonely flight, to the edge of the lake

T Reading Focus Paraphrasing In your own words, describe how Beowulf defeats Grendel.

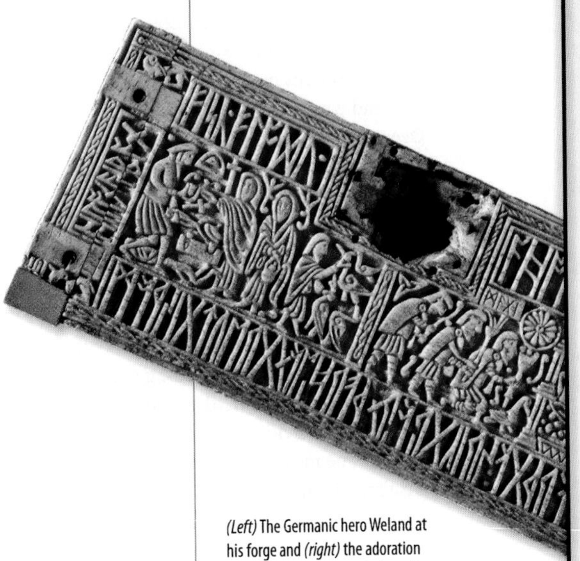

(Left) The Germanic hero Weland at his forge and *(right)* the adoration of the Magi (8th century), from the Franks casket. Whalebone.
The British Museum, London.

? 514–517. *How does Beowulf prove his victory over Grendel? Why might he do this?*

? 522–533. *What has happened to Grendel?*

Think About/Talk About

Comprehension

S Reading Focus

Possible response: *Grendel put a spell on all mortal men's weapons so they could not harm him.*

T Reading Focus

Possible response: *Beowulf rips Grendel's arm from his shoulder, defeating the beast. Grendel escapes, but only to die in his den.*

Analysis

R Literary Focus

Possible response: *Beowulf has "harder" hands than anyone else whom Grendel has met, and he is holding on to Grendel with a grip that cracks the mighty monster's claws.*

Extend the Discussion

Archetype of the Epic Hero As this episode in the story ends, what details remind us that Beowulf is a hero of epic proportions, able to represent the Anglo-Saxon people and their values? ***Possible response:*** *By rescuing the Danes from evil, Beowulf has fulfilled his promise and attained new glory.*

Activity Display these words that appear to be base words with prefixes or suffixes. Have students tell if a word does [D] or does not [DN] sound like a combination of its parts.

1. tormentor — torment + or [*DN*]
2. inventor — invent + or [*DN*]
3. peaceable — peace + able [*D*]
4. omnipresent — omni + present [*D*]
5. omnipotent — omni + potent [*DN*]

Developing Oral Fluency

Use lines 473–517 to demonstrate to students how to read poetry stanzas. First, read some of the lines as if they were written in paragraph form. Then, read all the lines as a poem in verse. Ask students to identify the difference between the two readings. How did pauses and stresses differ between the two readings? How does the second reading resemble a song?

Paired Activity Ask students to take turns reading the selected lines. Instruct one student to read and the other student to listen to ensure that he or she is correctly modeling the teacher's reading.

Model the Skill

- Review the **archetype of an epic hero**. Explain that an archetype is a classic example of a person or thing that usually serves as a model for subsequent examples. For instance, Shakespeare's Romeo and Juliet are the archetypal example of a doomed young couple in love. Ask students if they can name other fictional characters who could be considered archetypes. ***Possible response:*** *Superman is the archetype of a modern fictional superhero.*
- Tell students that in this selection Beowulf serves as an **archetype of an epic hero**. Read aloud lines 570–582. Explain that in these lines, Beowulf jumps into the lake to battle Grendel's mother in her hellish lair. Beowulf's fearless pursuit and his determination to rid the people of this dangerous monster exemplify his heroism.

Guided Practice: Apply

Think-Pair-Share Group students in pairs, and have them read the rest of "The Monster's Mother." Have students note examples of heroism in this section. Then, ask students to participate in a class discussion comparing Beowulf to modern heroes such as police officers or soldiers.

Think About/Talk About

Response to Margin Question

Lines 570–594 *Fully armed, Beowulf descends to the bottom of the lake—a journey that takes hours. No ordinary man could stay underwater that long. In addition, when Beowulf finds himself in the monster's lair, he is bathed in a supernatural light that protects him.*

Where he'd dragged his corpselike way, doomed
And already weary of his vanishing life.
The water was bloody, steaming and boiling
In horrible pounding waves, heat
Sucked from his magic veins; but the swirling
Surf had covered his death, hidden
Deep in murky darkness his miserable
End, as hell opened to receive him.
Then old and young rejoiced, turned back
From that happy pilgrimage, mounted their hard-hooved
Horses, high-spirited stallions, and rode them
Slowly toward Herot again, retelling
Beowulf's bravery as they jogged along.
And over and over they swore that nowhere
On earth or under the spreading sky
Or between the seas, neither south nor north,
Was there a warrior worthier to rule over men.
(But no one meant Beowulf's praise to belittle
Hrothgar, their kind and gracious king!) . . .

Grendel's monstrous mother, in grief for her son, next attacks Herot, and in her dripping claws she carries off one man—Hrothgar's closest friend. The monster also carries off Grendel's arm, which Beowulf had hung high from the rafters. Beowulf is awakened and called for again. In one of the most famous verses in the epic, the old king describes where Grendel and his mother live.

II

. . . "They live in secret places, windy (U)
Cliffs, wolf-dens where water pours
From the rocks, then runs underground, where mist
Steams like black clouds, and the groves of trees
Growing out over their lake are all covered
With frozen spray, and wind down snakelike
Roots that reach as far as the water
And help keep it dark. At night that lake
Burns like a torch. No one knows its bottom,
No wisdom reaches such depths. A deer,
Hunted through the woods by packs of hounds,
A stag with great horns, though driven through the forest
From faraway places, prefers to die
On those shores, refuses to save its life

Purse lid, from the Sutton Hoo ship burial (c. 625–30 A.D.). Gold, garnets, and millefiori glass. The British Library, London.

(U) **Literary Focus** **Epic Hero** How does this description of Grendel's home differ from other descriptions of the lair in the epic?

Universal Access

English Learners

English for Academic Success Students might be unfamiliar with some of the vocabulary, especially words no longer in common use. Point out that *Beowulf* includes many words that refer to obsolete items and concepts, such as *mail.* Tell students to use context clues to try to figure out the meaning of words they do not recognize. Note, for instance, that if they do not know what *murky* means in line 532, they might be able to infer its meaning from the surrounding words, such as *hidden* and *darkness.* Point out the connection between *pilgrimage* (line 535) and *pilgrim.* Remind students that some words have multiple meanings and that they may be confused by recognizable words that have additional meanings they do not know. Note, for instance, that *host* (line 586) has multiple meanings. Ask students to explain the meaning of *host,* and ask them if they know of additional meanings (e.g., the organism on which a parasite lives). Tell students that *host* in line 586 means *multitude.*

In that water. It isn't far, nor is it
A pleasant spot! When the wind stirs
And storms, waves splash toward the sky,
As dark as the air, as black as the rain
That the heavens weep. Our only help,
Again, lies with you. Grendel's mother
Is hidden in her terrible home, in a place
You've not seen. Seek it, if you dare! Save us,
Once more, and again twisted gold,
Heaped-up ancient treasure, will reward you
For the battle you win!" **V**

"Twisted gold, heaped-up ancient treasure, will reward you for the battle you win!"

Carrying the sword Hrunting, Beowulf goes to the lake where Grendel's mother has her underwater lair. Then, fully armed, he dives to the depths of this watery hell.

The Monster's Mother

12

. . . He leaped into the lake, would not wait for anyone's
Answer; the heaving water covered him
Over. For hours he sank through the waves;
At last he saw the mud of the bottom.
And all at once the greedy she-wolf
Who'd ruled those waters for half a hundred
Years discovered him, saw that a creature
From above had come to explore the bottom
Of her wet world. She welcomed him in her claws,
Clutched at him savagely but could not harm him,
Tried to work her fingers through the tight
Ring-woven mail on his breast, but tore
And scratched in vain. Then she carried him, armor
And sword and all, to her home; he struggled
To free his weapon, and failed. The fight
Brought other monsters swimming to see
Her catch, a host of sea beasts who beat at
His mail shirt, stabbing with tusks and teeth
As they followed along. Then he realized, suddenly,
That she'd brought him into someone's battle-hall,

V **Reading Focus** **Paraphrasing** How would you describe what Hrothgar is asking Beowulf to do in lines 563–569?

? **570–594.** *Describe how Beowulf comes to the lair of Grendel's mother. What details remind you that Beowulf is not an ordinary man?*

Think About/Talk About

Comprehension

V Reading Focus

Possible response: *Hrothgar is asking Beowulf to save the Danes again by finding and killing Grendel's mother, who is still a threat.*

Analysis

U Literary Focus

Possible response: *Grendel's home is associated with images of windy cliffs, secret dens, swirling mists, and a burning, bottomless lake that strikes fear in animals. By contrast, Grendel's home in the beginning of the epic was described only as a dark, hellish moor.*

Extend the Discussion

Archetype of the Epic Hero Reread lines 534–544. Why is it noteworthy that people are "retelling Beowulf's bravery" as they return to Herot? ***Possible response:*** *In "retelling Beowulf's bravery," the characters in the story do what the epic poem itself does to honor a hero. Through this storytelling, the poet emphasizes the role of epic poems in rewarding heroes by establishing and preserving a glorious reputation for them.*

Cross-Curricular Connection

ART: Anglo-Saxon Artistry

The Anglo-Saxons' artistry was confirmed by the 1939 discovery of a burial mound at Sutton Hoo in East Anglia. Believed to be the burial site of a King Raedwald, Sutton Hoo yielded silver and gold and thousands of intricately mounted garnets. Before this find, scholars had doubted that Anglo-Saxon artisans were capable of creating the magnificent treasures described in Beowulf. Yet, as Rupert Bruce-Mitford of the British Museum writes, the Sutton Hoo objects "reveal . . . a completely unexpected school of art, and a supreme one. It is pagan Saxon art in its final flower, overloaded, but not decadent. The gold jewelry is brimming with novel and daring ideas. It shows an overflowing exuberance and displays the highest level of craftsmanship, excelling anything known in this medium from the rest of Europe in its era."

Think About/Talk About

Build Background: Christian Parallels

Tell students that critics who trace Christian parallels in the epic suggest that the light that blazes when Grendel's mother dies indicates God's favor upon Beowulf. Similarly, Beowulf's immersion in the lake is seen as a kind of baptism—a type of purification before he achieves his goal.

Extend the Discussion

Drawing Conclusions What does Beowulf accomplish by cutting the head off of Grendel's already dead body? ***Possible response:*** *Grendel's death is not enough to repay Beowulf and the Danes for the suffering he caused. In severing the monster's head, Beowulf seeks to dishonor Grendel, exact from him symbolic repayment for his crimes, and prove to others that Grendel is dead.*

Responses to Margin Questions

Lines 607–632 *The suspense lies in the back-and-forth nature of the struggle: First, Beowulf seems to have the advantage, and then Grendel's mother does. Beowulf's success seems most in doubt when the monster pins him down. He is saved by his chain-mail shirt and by the grace of God.*

Lines 648–665 *Beowulf's final revenge occurs when he beheads the body of Grendel. The story is resolved when Grendel's body twitches and then lies still, presumably dead.*

And there the water's heat could not hurt him,
Nor anything in the lake attack him through
The building's high-arching roof. A brilliant
Light burned all around him, the lake
Itself like a fiery flame.
Then he saw
The mighty water witch, and swung his sword,
His ring-marked blade, straight at her head;
The iron sang its fierce song,
Sang Beowulf's strength. But her guest (W)
Discovered that no sword could slice her evil
Skin, that Hrunting could not hurt her, was useless
Now when he needed it. They wrestled, she ripped
And tore and clawed at him, bit holes in his helmet,
And that too failed him; for the first time in years
Of being worn to war it would earn no glory;
It was the last time anyone would wear it. But Beowulf
Longed only for fame, leaped back
Into battle. He tossed his sword aside,
Angry; the steel-edged blade lay where
He'd dropped it. If weapons were useless he'd use
His hands, the strength in his fingers. So fame
Comes to the men who mean to win it
And care about nothing else! He raised
His arms and seized her by the shoulder; anger
Doubled his strength, he threw her to the floor.
She fell, Grendel's fierce mother, and the Geats'
Proud prince was ready to leap on her. But she rose
At once and repaid him with her clutching claws,
Wildly tearing at him. He was weary, that best
And strongest of soldiers; his feet stumbled
And in an instant she had him down, held helpless.
Squatting with her weight on his stomach, she drew
A dagger, brown with dried blood and prepared
To avenge her only son. But he was stretched
On his back, and her stabbing blade was blunted
By the woven mail shirt he wore on his chest.
The hammered links held; the point
Could not touch him. He'd have traveled to the bottom of the earth,
Edgetho's son, and died there, if that shining
Woven metal had not helped—and Holy (X)

(W) **Literary Focus** **Epic Hero** What metaphor is used to describe the sound of Beowulf's sword?

(X) **Literary Focus** **Epic Hero** What is the role of supernatural forces in the success of the hero's journey?

? 607–632. *What details in this description of the battle between Grendel's mother and Beowulf add to your suspense about the outcome? At what point do you think Beowulf may not be successful? What saves him?*

"Sigurd's Helmet" (7th century) from a pre-Viking grave at Vendel.
Upplandsmuseet, Uppsala, Sweden.

Universal Access

Advanced Learners

Acceleration Point out that the words *sang* and *song* in lines 597–598 provide more than a colorful substitute for more literal language. Ask students to explain why it is particularly fitting in this context to say that Beowulf's sword *sang.* [*The epic poem is a kind of song, one that ensures the fame of the hero whose exploits it celebrates; Beowulf is fighting for fame, and his sword is singing out as an extension of his inherent strength.*]

Reaching Reluctant Readers

Point out parallels between epic poems like *Beowulf* and contemporary movies and novels featuring superheroes or epic adventures, such as *X-Men* or *Lord of the Rings.* Ask students if there are details in the description of Beowulf's battle with Grendel's mother that remind them of fight scenes in films they have seen. Ask them to comment on the description of Grendel's mother unexpectedly rising back up in lines 615–617 or *squatting* on Beowulf in line 621. Have students explain the dramatic effect of such details.

God, who sent him victory, gave judgment
For truth and right, Ruler of the Heavens,
Once Beowulf was back on his feet and fighting.

13

Then he saw, hanging on the wall, a heavy
Sword, hammered by giants, strong
And blessed with their magic, the best of all weapons
But so massive that no ordinary man could lift
Its carved and decorated length. He drew it
From its scabbard, broke the chain on its hilt,°
And then, savage, now, angry
And desperate, lifted it high over his head
And struck with all the strength he had left,
Caught her in the neck and cut it through,
Broke bones and all. Her body fell
To the floor, lifeless, the sword was wet
With her blood, and Beowulf rejoiced at the sight. **Y**
The brilliant light shone, suddenly,
As though burning in that hall, and as bright as Heaven's
Own candle, lit in the sky. He looked
At her home, then following along the wall
Went walking, his hands tight on the sword,
His heart still angry. He was hunting another
Dead monster, and took his weapon with him
For final revenge against Grendel's vicious
Attacks, his nighttime raids, over
And over, coming to Herot when Hrothgar's
Men slept, killing them in their beds,
Eating some on the spot, fifteen
Or more, and running to his loathsome moor
With another such sickening meal waiting
In his pouch. But Beowulf repaid him for those visits,
Found him lying dead in his corner,
Armless, exactly as that fierce fighter
Had sent him out from Herot, then struck off
His head with a single swift blow. The body
Jerked for the last time, then lay still. . . . **Z**

638. scabbard . . . hilt: A scabbard is a case that holds the blade of a sword; a hilt is a sword's handle.

? **648–665.** *What is Beowulf's final revenge against Grendel? What action of Beowulf's provides a resolution, or wrapping up, of the episode?*

Y Reading Focus Paraphrasing Lines 633–645 describe Beowulf killing Grendel's mother. What images in this description are essential to paraphrasing it?

Z Literary Focus Epic Hero What role do violence and the battle play in creating a hero's image?

Vocabulary **loathsome** (LOHTH suhm) *adj.:* very hateful; disgusting.

Think About/Talk About

Comprehension

Y Reading Focus

Possible response: *He lifts his sword and cuts off her head. The essential details are the weapon that he used and which part of the monster's body was hit.*

Analysis

W Literary Focus

Possible response: *The sound of his sword is described as a "fierce song."*

X Literary Focus

Possible response: *Beowulf's relation to the supernatural sets him apart from others. Supernatural forces help him defeat supernatural enemies.*

Z Literary Focus

Possible response: *Violence is essential to the hero's image because the hero is defined by valor in battle. The hero responds to violence and also initiates it. The hero is celebrated for ruthlessness and the ability to destroy enemies.*

Vocabulary: Own the Word

loathsome: Waiting for several hours in traffic is a *loathsome* situation. Wet, dirty socks have a *loathsome* smell. Heavy rain is *loathsome* weather. Have students describe a situation they find *loathsome.*

Monitor Students' Comprehension

Guide the class in answering these comprehension questions.

1. What protects Beowulf from the first attack by Grendel's mother? [*He is protected by the ring-woven mail, or armor, that he wears.*]
2. Why does Beowulf go hunting for Grendel's dead body? [*He seeks further revenge for the death and destruction Grendel brought upon the Danes.*]
3. What obstacle does Beowulf face in his confrontation with Grendel's mother? [*Beowulf's sword is useless against the monster.*]

California Standards, p. 42

- **Reading Standard 2.2** Analyze the way in which clarity of meaning is affected by the patterns of organization, hierarchical structures, repetition of the main ideas, syntax, and word choice in the text.
- **Reading Standard 3.2** Analyze the way in which theme or meaning of a selection represents a view or comment on life, using textual evidence to support the claim.
- **Reading Standard 3.6** Analyze the way in which authors through the centuries have used archetypes drawn from myth and tradition in literature, film, political speeches, and religious writings (e.g., how the archetype of banishment from an ideal world may be used to interpret Shakespeare's tragedy *Macbeth*).
- **Writing Standard 1.2** Use point of view, characterization, style (e.g., use of irony), and related elements for specific rhetorical and aesthetic purposes.

Check for Understanding

Independent Practice

Reading Skills Focus

Possible responses:

1. *Beowulf has a duty to help Hrothgar, who helped his father.*
2. *Unferth envies Beowulf for having won greater fame.*
3. *Grendel's mother attacks Herot to avenge the death of her son and retrieve his severed arm.*
4. *Anglo-Saxon society valued military valor, family lineage, courage, loyalty, and an honorable reputation.*
5. *Responses will reflect students' charts.*

Literary Skills Focus

Possible responses:

6. *Grendel lives in the dark (line 2), attacks at night (line 30), and is described as a "shadow of death" (line 74). By associating Grendel with death and darkness, the poem causes us to fear him.*
7. *Beowulf battles Grendel in Hrothgar's hall, his home territory, and an environment suited for humans; he fights Grendel's mother in her underwater lair, and he uses his superhuman abilities to survive.*
8. *Beowulf battles Grendel unarmed to make it a fair fight and show his trust in God. Grendel's imperviousness to weapons suggests that his evil must be destroyed by divine intervention.*
9. *Grendel's mother and her flaming underwater lair represent an evil greater than Grendel alone: the primordial source of evil, the evil that begets evil.*
10. *Beowulf's heroic qualities inspire awe but make him hard to relate to as a fellow human being.*
11. *Universal themes include the importance of having an honorable reputation, the clash between good and evil, and the righteousness of seeking vengeance.*

Applying Your Skills

Reading Standard 2.2, 3.2, 3.6 (see pages A48–A50)
Writing Standard 1.2 (see pages A51–A52)

from **Beowulf, Part One**

Literary Response and Analysis

Reading Skills Focus

Quick Check

1. Besides seeking fame and glory, why does Beowulf go to help Hrothgar and the Danes?
2. Why does Unferth challenge Beowulf?
3. Why does Grendel's mother attack Herot?

Read with a Purpose

4. Based on your observations of Beowulf's heroic qualities, what impression do you have of Anglo-Saxon society?

Reading Skills: Paraphrasing

5. As you read, you listed nouns, verbs, and phrases that describe Beowulf or his actions. Now, add another column in which you paraphrase each passage. How does paraphrasing help you see how Beowulf fits the archetype of the epic hero?

Nouns / Pronouns	Verbs	Phrases / Objects	Paraphrases
my duty	was	to go to the Danes	
I	drove /chased	giants	
I	swam	hunting monsters	

Literary Skills Focus

Literary Analysis

6. **Analyze** Identify images of Grendel that associate him with death or darkness. How are these images supposed to make you feel about Grendel?
7. **Interpret** The battle with Grendel and the battle with Grendel's mother take place in very different settings. How do these two settings differ?
8. **Evaluate** How does Beowulf's insistence that he fight without a weapon illustrate the concept of an epic hero?
9. **Extend** A common occurrence in myths and legends is the hero's discovery of an evil greater than the one he has set out to destroy. Often this greater evil is a creator or parent archetype. What greater evil does Beowulf discover? How does this greater evil fit the creator archetype?

Literary Skills: Epic Hero

10. **Evaluate** How do Beowulf's heroic qualities affect your feelings about his overall character? Is it easy or difficult to relate to him? Explain.

Literary Skills Review: Universal Themes

11. **Analyze** A **universal theme** is one that occurs in literature from many different cultures around the world and throughout time. What universal themes can you find in *Beowulf*?

Writing Skills Focus

Think as a Reader/Writer

Use It in Your Writing Review your notes about the characteristics of the speeches Beowulf and the others make. Imitating the style of the epic, write a speech of ten or more lines delivered by Beowulf at the end of Part One.

What Do You Think Now? What is the main cause for Beowulf's heroic actions in Part One? Do you think his motive will be the same in Part Two?

Universal Access

Struggling Writers

Some students may need additional scaffolding to complete the Writing Skills Focus activity. Before they write Beowulf's speech, have students read aloud Beowulf's words to Hrothgar in lines 141–189 with a partner. Instruct students to write a brief description of the tone, language, and character of Beowulf while they read as prewriting to their own speech.

What Do You Think Now?

To help students answer these questions, have small groups discuss their views about Beowulf's motives in Part One and their expectations for Part Two. Then, ask the groups to share their views with the class.

EPIC

from Beowulf

Part Two

translated by **Seamus Heaney**

Read with a Purpose Read to discover how Beowulf rises to the heroic challenges before him.

Beowulf carries Grendel's head to King Hrothgar and then returns gift-laden to the land of the Geats, where he succeeds to the throne. After fifty winters pass, Beowulf, now an old man, faces his final task: He must fight a dragon who, angry because a thief has stolen a jeweled cup from the dragon's hoard of gold, is laying waste to the Geats' land. Beowulf and eleven warriors are guided to the dragon's lair by the thief who stole the cup. For Beowulf the price of this last victory will be great.

The Final Battle

14

Then he addressed each dear companion
one final time, those fighters in their helmets, Ⓐ
resolute and high-born: "I would rather not
use a weapon if I knew another way
to grapple with the dragon and make good my boast
as I did against Grendel in days gone by.
But I shall be meeting molten venom

Ⓐ **Literary Focus** **Epic Hero** Read Beowulf's speech that begins on this page. How is King Beowulf different from the younger Beowulf who defeated Grendel?

The Prow/The Oseberg Viking Ship. Museum of Cultural History, University of Oslo, Norway.

Teacher Preparation

Selection Plot Summary

Beowulf has reigned for many years as king of the Geats. A dragon, seeking revenge for a theft, has threatened the Geats' land. Beowulf and a band of his warriors vow to battle the dragon. The battle proves to be Beowulf's last. His sword cannot penetrate the dragon's thick hide, and the dragon gains the advantage in battle, threatening him with his fiery breath. Beowulf is stoic in this crisis, but his men flee. Only Wiglaf remains with him. Wiglaf and Beowulf kill the dragon, and Wiglaf brings the dragon's treasure hoard to the king. Dying, Beowulf leaves the treasure to his people and bestows his armor—and the mantle of leadership—onto Wiglaf. Wiglaf agrees to build a memorial barrow for Beowulf, where Beowulf's ashes are placed after his death.

Direct Teach

Think About/Talk About

Read with a Purpose Tell students to think about how a person's life experience affects his or her attitude. Have students think about the differences they might see in Beowulf's character now that he is older and presumably wiser.

Analysis

Ⓐ Literary Focus

Possible response: *King Beowulf appears less brash and confident than did his younger self.*

Universal Access

EL English Learners

English for Academic Success Students may not recognize the meaning of some words. Provide students with the following definitions of potentially unfamiliar words. Then, have them paraphrase the lines on page 43.

- **addressed**—to speak directly to
- **resolute**—determined
- **grapple**—to wrestle
- **molten**—melted; liquefied by heat
- **venom**—poison

Struggling Readers

Couple each student with an advanced learner to practice the reading skill of paraphrasing. As they read, students should track lines that they consider especially challenging. After they have read the selection, students should go back and paraphrase the difficult lines with the help of an advanced learner. Advanced learners should be careful not to give away the correct interpretation too easily; instead, they should challenge their fellow students to interpret context clues in the text.

Model the Skill

- Tell students that many Anglo-Saxon words have **affixes**. An affix is an additional element placed at the beginning (prefix) or end (suffix) of a word.
- Write the selection word *infallible* on the board, and underline the first two letters.
- Tell students that the affix *in-* implies a negative meaning, so *infallible* means *not fallible*, or *not able to fail*. Knowing this can help students figure out the meaning of words such as *inalienable* and *incapacitate*.

Guided Practice: Apply

Ask students to think of other words that start with the prefix *in-*. Write them on the board along with their meanings.

Think About/Talk About

Response to Margin Question

Lines 709–720 *Grendel and his mother are freakish, brutal monsters. The dragon, however, is an archetypal figure that emerges from the bowels of earth and dominates the air with its flames. Translator Seamus Heaney says that the dragon appears less a physical opponent than an embodiment of "wyrd," or fate.*

in the fire he breathes, so I go forth
in mail-shirt and shield. I won't shift a foot
when I meet the cave-guard: what occurs on the wall
between the two of us will turn out as fate,
overseer of men, decides. I am resolved.
I scorn further words against this sky-borne foe.

"Men at arms, remain here on the barrow,° (B)
safe in your armour, to see which one of us
is better in the end at bearing wounds
in a deadly fray. This fight is not yours,
nor is it up to any man except me
to measure his strength against the monster
or to prove his worth. I shall win the gold
by my courage, or else mortal combat,
doom of battle, will bear your lord away."

Then he drew himself up beside his shield.
The fabled warrior in his warshirt and helmet

679. barrow (BAR oh): hill.

(B) **Literary Focus** **Epic Hero** How does Beowulf's resignation to his fate <u>emphasize</u> his deep responsibility to his people?

West Stow Saxon village reconstruction, Suffolk, England.

Universal Access

English Learners

English for Academic Success Read aloud the sentence "Hate was ignited" (line 704) and write it on the board. Circle the word *hate*. Tell students that in sentences using a passive voice, unlike active sentences, the subject of the sentence (*hate*) is receiving the action. The person or thing that is doing the "igniting" is not as important as what is being "ignited." Point out that the passive voice is constructed by using a form of the verb *be* and a past participle, usually ending in *-ed*.

Advanced Learners

Enrichment Have groups of students discuss the relationship between King Beowulf and his companions. Ask them to consider what they have learned about Anglo-Saxon society and the role of the king. Have students compare the relationship between Anglo-Saxon kings and their warriors to today's relationship between the president of the United States and the military. Encourage students to research this relationship before drawing conclusions. Ask students to present their conclusions to the class.

Unyielding, the lord of his people loomed by his tall shield, sure of his ground.

trusted in his own strength entirely
and went under the crag. No coward path.
Hard by the rock-face that hale veteran,
a good man who had gone repeatedly
into combat and danger and come through,
saw a stone arch and a gushing stream
that burst from the barrow, blazing and wafting
a deadly heat. It would be hard to survive **C**
unscathed near the hoard, to hold firm
against the dragon in those flaming depths.
Then he gave a shout. The lord of the Geats
unburdened his breast and broke out
in a storm of anger. Under grey stone
his voice challenged and resounded clearly.
Hate was ignited. The hoard-guard recognized
a human voice, the time was over
for peace and parleying.° Pouring forth
in a hot battle-fume, the breath of the monster
burst from the rock. There was a rumble under ground.
Down there in the barrow, Beowulf the warrior
lifted his shield: the outlandish thing
writhed and convulsed and vehemently
turned on the king, whose keen-edged sword,
an heirloom inherited by ancient right,
was already in his hand. Roused to a fury,
each antagonist struck terror in the other.
Unyielding, the lord of his people loomed
by his tall shield, sure of his ground,
while the serpent looped and unleashed itself.
Swaddled in flames, it came gliding and flexing
and racing towards its fate. Yet his shield defended **D**
the renowned leader's life and limb
for a shorter time than he meant it to:
that final day was the first time

706. parleying: discussing.

709–720. The image of a lone hero standing up to a fire-breathing dragon or other giant monster is one of the most archetypal images in Western heroic literature.

? *How does the dragon compare with Grendel and Grendel's mother?*

C Reading Focus Paraphrasing How would you reword the poetic diction in this sentence (lines 692–697)?

D Reading Focus Paraphrasing Rewrite lines 708–720 to explain what goes wrong in Beowulf's confrontation with the dragon.

Vocabulary vehemently (VEE uh muhnt lee) *adv.:* violently.

Think About/Talk About

Comprehension

C Reading Focus

Possible response: *Standing firm next to the rock, the strong veteran who had fought and succeeded many times saw a stone arch and a deadly-hot stream that burst from the barrow.*

D Reading Focus

Possible response: *As the ground shook, Beowulf held up his shield and the violently twisting beast faced the warrior and his ancient and sharp sword. They were enraged and furious, and as Beowulf stood his ground, the dragon, blazing with fire, slid towards him. The shield, however, did not last long enough to protect him, and for the first time he was denied victory.*

Analysis

B Literary Focus

Possible response: *Beowulf is willing to battle to the death against the dragon. He is no longer fighting for his own honor and glory. His maturity and selflessness are apparent in his willingness to risk his life for the sake of his people.*

Extend the Discussion

Archetype of the Epic Hero How do lines 723–725 foreshadow the downfall of an epic hero? ***Possible response:*** *Lines 723–725 tell about a "final day" in which Beowulf fails to attain the glory he deserves. The word "final" indicates that this is Beowulf's last battle.*

Vocabulary: Own the Word

vehemently: Demonstrate a person *vehemently* denying an accusation. Then demonstrate someone calmly denying an accusation. Have students stand at their desks and demonstrate both reactions.

Students with Disabilities

To check students' comprehension of the main ideas, have them verbalize their understanding by completing the following blanks with their own words.

1. Beowulf feels ______ about the battle before he goes to meet the dragon.
2. Beowulf relied only on ______ during battle.
3. The dragon stirred when he heard ______.
4. Beowulf held a ______, an heirloom that he had been given.

AAVE Students Who Use African American Vernacular English

English for Academic Success Students may be used to the informal expression *ain't* instead of the formal contractions *is not, am not,* and *are not.* Write the following on the board: "This fight is not yours." Underline *is not.* Tell students that in formal English, the correct expression is *isn't,* or *is not,* and not *ain't.* Have them compose sentences each using the expressions *is not, am not,* and *are not.* Ask students to share their sentences with the class.

Think About/Talk About

Literary Connection

Remind students that before it was ever written down, *Beowulf* was meant to be heard. Devices of sound, therefore, are an important part of its storytelling style. In his translation, Seamus Heaney often uses words whose sounds imitate or suggest their meaning—that is, onomatopoeia. Point out words such as *slashed* (line 728).

Extend the Discussion

Analyzing Details In lines 727–736, what is the best evidence that fate is abandoning Beowulf? ***Possible response:*** *His sword does not strike as effectively as it did in previous battles.*

Making Inferences In lines 746–749, why do you think Beowulf's men flee from battle? ***Possible response:*** *They see the beast steadily gaining an advantage over their powerful king and realize that Beowulf is going to lose the fight. Terrified that the dragon will attack them, they run into the woods, hoping the dragon cannot find them there.*

Responses to Margin Questions

Lines 737–741 *It appears that Beowulf is about to die.*

Lines 746–749 *Beowulf's men panic and run for their lives.*

Gundestrup cauldron.
National Museum of Denmark.

when Beowulf fought and fate denied him
glory in battle. So the king of the Geats
raised his hand and struck hard
at the enamelled scales, but scarcely cut through:
the blade flashed and slashed yet the blow
was far less powerful than the hard-pressed king
had need of at that moment. The mound-keeper
went into a spasm and spouted deadly flames:
when he felt the stroke, battle-fire
billowed and spewed. Beowulf was foiled°
of a glorious victory. The glittering sword,
infallible before that day,
failed when he unsheathed it, as it never should have.
For the son of Ecgtheow, it was no easy thing
to have to give ground like that and go
unwillingly to inhabit another home
in a place beyond; so every man must yield
the leasehold of his days.

It was not long
until the fierce contenders clashed again.
The hoard-guard took heart, inhaled and swelled up
and got a new wind; he who had once ruled
was furled° in fire and had to face the worst.
No help or backing was to be had then
from his high-born comrades; that hand-picked troop
broke ranks and ran for their lives
to the safety of the wood. But within one heart

733. foiled: prevented.

? **737–741.** *What are you led to believe about Beowulf's ultimate fate?*

745. furled: rolled up.

? **746–749.** *How do Beowulf's men react to the sight of the dragon gaining victory over Beowulf?*

Vocabulary **infallible** (ihn FAL uh buhl) *adj.:* unable to fail or be wrong.

Cross-Curricular Connection

HISTORY: Thanes

In Anglo-Saxon society, the king was surrounded by trusted warriors and lords called thanes. *Thane* was an honorific that distinguished warriors who were close to the king. The title was hereditary but could also be acquired through merit. A warrior who became a thane received a gift of land from the king. A thane could receive orders only from the king and was expected to follow the king into war. The loyalty and respect between the king and his thanes was fundamental within Anglo-Saxon culture.

Small-Group Activity Ask students to compare and contrast the Anglo-Saxon values of trust, loyalty, and respect to American values in today's political culture. What qualities of a presidential candidate would most likely obtain the people's approval and help the candidate get elected into office?

sorrow welled up: in a man of worth
the claims of kinship cannot be denied.

15

His name was Wiglaf, a son of Weohstan's,
a well-regarded Shylfing warrior
related to Aelfhere. When he saw his lord
tormented by the heat of his scalding helmet,
he remembered the bountiful gifts bestowed on him,
how well he lived among the Waegmundings,
the freehold° he inherited from his father before him.
He could not hold back: one hand brandished
the yellow-timbered shield, the other drew his sword— . . . (E)

Sad at heart, addressing his companions,
Wiglaf spoke wise and fluent words:
"I remember that time when mead was flowing,
how we pledged loyalty to our lord in the hall,
promised our ring-giver we would be worth our price,
make good the gift of the war-gear,
those swords and helmets, as and when
his need required it. He picked us out
from the army deliberately, honoured us and judged us
fit for this action, made me these lavish° gifts—
and all because he considered us the best
of his arms-bearing thanes.° And now, although (F)
he wanted this challenge to be one he'd face
by himself alone—the shepherd of our land,
a man unequaled in the quest for glory
and a name for daring—now the day has come
when this lord we serve needs sound men

758. freehold: estate.

770. lavish (LAV ihsh): extravagant.

772. thanes (thaynz): in Anglo-Saxon England, a group of men who held land of the king in exchange for military service.

(E) **Reading Focus** **Paraphrasing** Paraphrase these lines about Wiglaf.

(F) **Literary Focus** **Epic Hero** Epic heroes almost always have a weakness or fatal flaw that causes of their downfall. What might Beowulf's weakness be?

Norse chessmen, from a Viking hoard, Isle of Lewis, the Outer Hebrides, Scotland.
The British Museum, London.

Cross-Curricular Connection

MUSIC: Lament for Beowulf

It is not surprising that American composer Howard Hanson (1896–1981) wrote a composition inspired by *Beowulf*, for he frequently wrote music that drew on his Scandinavian heritage. Hanson even called his first symphony the *Nordic*, as a tribute to his Swedish immigrant parents.

Whole-Class Activity After students read the selection from *Beowulf*, have them listen to Hanson's *Lament for Beowulf* and decide to which event or events in the epic the music applies. Then, ask them to write a paragraph exploring the connections between the music and the poem.

Think About/Talk About

Comprehension

(E) Reading Focus

Possible response: *His name was Wiglaf, son of Weohstan, a highly regarded warrior. When Wiglaf saw his lord afflicted by the heat of the helmet, he remembered all the gifts he received from his lord, how well he lived among the Waegmundings, the estate he inherited from his father. Wiglaf could not resist: with one hand he brandished his shield; with the other he drew his sword.*

Analysis

(F) Literary Focus

Possible response: *Beowulf's weakness is trusting too much in his fellow warriors. He relies on them at a critical point in battle, only to have them all flee when he needs them most.*

Extend the Discussion

Cause and Effect In lines 754–761, what prompts Wiglaf to talk to his companions? ***Possible response:*** *Wiglaf remembers all the gifts received by the king and those received by his father. He also remembers the happy life he led under Beowulf's rule.*

Archetype of the Epic Hero Does Wiglaf possess the characteristics of an epic hero? What evidence in the text supports your opinion? ***Possible response:*** *Yes, although Wiglaf is not boastful or arrogant, he displays the qualities of an epic hero. He refuses to abandon his king like the other warriors. He also gives an eloquent speech to convince his companions to return to the battle.*

Vocabulary: Own the Word

infallible: Remind students that the prefix *in–* means "not." An *infallible* person does not have faults. Ask students to applaud in order to indicate how much they would like to be described as *infallible*. ***Possible response:*** *Students applaud loudly because they want to be thought of as unfailing and never in the wrong.*

Model the Skill

- Review the **archetype of an epic hero**. Explain that the Anglo-Saxons focused less on the after-life than on the personal glory or fame that lasted long after a hero's death. Tell students that when a hero died, Anglo-Saxons would have praised the hero's accomplishments and exemplary character, and they would hold dear the hero's memory.
- Tell students that the ultimate role of an epic hero is to leave something of lasting value to his culture. Read aloud lines 802–809. Point out that these lines state that Beowulf has left his people wealth and has set an example of selfless courage.

Guided Practice: Apply

Think-Pair-Share Ask students to work in pairs and write a eulogy for Beowulf. Have them include details from the text that show how he made positive contributions to his people. Have each pair share its eulogy with the class.

Think About/Talk About

Response to Margin Question

Lines 810–816 *He wishes for his thanes to build him a barrow that passing ships might see so that he will be remembered.*

to give him their support. Let us go to him,
help our leader through the hot flame
and dread of the fire. As God is my witness,
I would rather my body were robed in the same
burning blaze as my gold-giver's body
than go back home bearing arms.
That is unthinkable, unless we have first
slain the foe and defended the life
of the prince of the Weather-Geats. I well know
the things he has done for us deserve better.
Should he alone be left exposed
to fall in battle? We must bond together,
shield and helmet, mail-shirt and sword."

Together Beowulf and the young Wiglaf kill the dragon, but the old king is fatally wounded. Beowulf, thinking of his people, asks to see the monster's treasure. Wiglaf enters the dragon's cave and finds a priceless hoard of jewels and gold.

16

. . . Wiglaf went quickly, keen to get back,
excited by the treasure; anxiety weighed
on his brave heart, he was hoping he would find
the leader of the Geats alive where he had left him
helpless, earlier, on the open ground.
So he came to the place, carrying the treasure,
and found his lord bleeding profusely,
his life at an end; again he began
to swab his body. The beginnings of an utterance
broke out from the king's breast-cage.
The old lord gazed sadly at the gold.

"To the everlasting Lord of All,
to the King of Glory, I give thanks
that I behold this treasure here in front of me,
that I have been thus allowed to leave my people
so well endowed on the day I die. (G)
Now that I have bartered my last breath
to own this fortune, it is up to you
to look after their needs. I can hold out no longer.
Order my troop to construct a barrow
on a headland on the coast, after my pyre has cooled.
It will loom on the horizon at Hronesness

? **810–816.** *Why is constructing a memorial important to Beowulf?*

(G) **Literary Focus** **Epic Hero** The death of a hero or other important characters in literature often includes a symbolic passing on of duties. In these lines, how does Beowulf pass on his heroic status? What do these items represent?

Universal Access

EL English Learners

English for Academic Success Ask students to point out the predominant verb tense on this page. [*simple past tense*] Remind them that the simple past tense of a verb is formed by adding *–ed* to the simple present form of the verb. Mention that some verbs do not follow this rule, and they are called irregular verbs. Ask students to find the irregular verbs on this page and write these verbs next to their simple present form. [*cut, had, went, took, broke,* and *ran*.]

Advanced Learners

Enrichment After reviewing the traits of an epic hero with the class, ask students to create their own modern epic hero. Divide students into pairs, and have them write a poem in which they introduce their character's moral strengths and weaknesses. Ask for volunteers to read their poems aloud. Then, have the class discuss what heroic traits each character possesses.

and be a reminder among my people—
so that in coming times crews under sail
will call it Beowulf's Barrow, as they steer
ships across the wide and shrouded waters."

Then the king in his great-heartedness unclasped
the collar of gold from his neck and gave it
to the young thane, telling him to use
it and the warshirt and the gilded helmet well.

"You are the last of us, the only one left
of the Waegmundings. Fate swept us away,
sent my whole brave high-born clan
to their final doom. Now I must follow them."
That was the warrior's last word.
He had no more to confide. The furious heat
of the pyre would assail° him. His soul fled from his breast
to its destined place among the steadfast ones.

Wiglaf berates the faithless warriors who did not go to the aid of their king. With sorrow the Geats cremate the corpse of their greatest king. They place his ashes, along with all of the dragon's treasure, in a huge burial tower by the sea, where it can be seen by voyagers.

827. assail (uh SAYL): attack.

17

Then twelve warriors rode around the tomb,
chieftains' sons, champions in battle,
all of them distraught, chanting in dirges,
mourning his loss as a man and a king.
They extolled his heroic nature and exploits
and gave thanks for his greatness; which was the proper thing,
for a man should praise a prince whom he holds dear
and cherish his memory when that moment comes
when he has to be convoyed from his bodily home.
So the Geat people, his hearth companions,
sorrowed for the lord who had been laid low.
They said that of all the kings upon the earth (H)
he was the man most gracious and fair-minded,
kindest to his people and keenest to win fame.

Knights on their mounts, The Lewis Chessmen (about A.D. 1150–1200). Isle of Lewis, the Outer Hebrides, Scotland.
The British Museum, London.

(H) **Literary Focus** **Epic Hero** According to the final lines of the poem, what qualities make Beowulf a great hero?

Vocabulary **extolled** (ehk STOHLD) *v.:* praised.

Think About/Talk About

Analysis

(G) Literary Focus

Possible responses: *Beowulf passes his duties on to Wiglaf, who stays with him until the end. Beowulf asks Wiglaf to take care of the people's needs and gives him a golden collar, a war shirt, and a gilded helmet. These are all symbols of kingship, and by giving them to Wiglaf, Beowulf is naming the young warrior as the next king.*

(H) Literary Focus

Possible response: *Beowulf was thought to be the kindest, most gracious king his people had known. He was just and fair in his rule, and he was always interested in performing great deeds for glory.*

Vocabulary: Own the Word

extolled: Write the word *extolled* in a center circle on the board with the definition "praised." Draw spider legs from the center circle, asking students to add attributes to the semantic web. ***Possible responses:*** *celebrated, lauded, acclaimed, hailed, cheered*

Monitor Students' Comprehension

Guide the class in answering these comprehension questions.

1. Why does Beowulf bring his weapon to battle the dragon? [*He needs protection against the dragon's venom and fire.*]
2. How does the dragon react to Beowulf's attack? [*The dragon is scared, but fights violently against the hero.*]
3. How does Beowulf reward Wiglaf's courage and loyalty? [*He gives him his gold collar, his war shirt, and his helmet.*]

California Standards, pp. 50–53

- **Reading Standard 2.2** Analyze the way in which clarity of meaning is affected by the patterns of organization, hierarchical structures, repetition of the main ideas, syntax, and word choice in the text.
- **Reading Standard 3.4** Analyze ways in which poets use imagery, personification, figures of speech, and sound to evoke readers' emotions.
- **Reading Standard 3.6** Analyze the way in which authors through the centuries have used archetypes drawn from myth and tradition in literature, film, political speeches, and religious writings (e.g., how the archetype of banishment from an ideal world may be used to interpret Shakespeare's tragedy *Macbeth*).
- **Grades 9–10 Review Reading Standard 1.1** Identify and use the literal and figurative meanings of words and understand word derivations.
- **Writing Standard 1.2** Use point of view, characterization, style (e.g., use of irony, and related elements for specific rhetorical and aesthetic purposes.
- **Writing Standard 2.1** Write fictional, autobiographical, or biographical narratives.
- **Listening and Speaking Standard 2.4** Deliver multimedia presentations.

Check for Understanding

Independent Practice

Reading Skills Focus

Possible responses:

1. *A thief stole a jeweled cup from the dragon's hoard.*
2. *Beowulf plans to take his eleven strongest warriors and call the dragon out to battle.*
3. *Wiglaf scolds his fellow soldiers because they abandoned their king during battle.*
4. *He performed great deeds and was gracious, fair-minded, and brave—all qualities of an epic hero. Yes, I feel the Anglo-Saxons truly appreciated positive qualities in their heroes and encouraged people to make constructive contributions to society.*
5. *Have students add a column to their graphic organizer and fill in the column with ideas about the relationship between the style of the passage and the mood of the passage.*

Literary Skills Focus

Possible responses:

6. *The dragon is described as outlandish, writhing, convulsing, and swaddled in flames. The dragon may symbolize Beowulf's death.*
7. *Grendel wages war for bloodlust; the dragon, for revenge. Their instincts relate to Beowulf's motivation as a young man and as an old king.*
8. *Beowulf was doomed from the beginning.*
9. *Yes, Beowulf would be able to defeat the monsters no matter what method he used because he is the hero of the poem. No; trickery is not an attribute of an epic hero.*
10. *Ask each group of students to share at least one alliterative passage.*

Applying Your Skills

Reading Standard 2.2, 3.4, 3.6 (see pages A48–A50)
Writing Standard 1.2 (see pages A51–A52)

from Beowulf, Part Two

Literary Response and Analysis

Reading Skills Focus

Quick Check

1. Why does the dragon wreak havoc upon Beowulf's land and people?
2. What is Beowulf's strategy in fighting the dragon?
3. Why does Wiglaf scold his fellow soldiers after Beowulf's death?

Read with a Purpose

4. How did Beowulf rise to the heroic challenges he had to face in Part Two? Has your impression of Anglo-Saxon society changed because of Beowulf's heroic qualities?

Reading Skills: Paraphrasing

5. While reading Part Two, you paraphrased the passages that were difficult to understand. Using a chart like the one below, chart the development of your paraphrases. Write about how the style of each passage contributed to the mood and meaning of the passage.

Passage Line Numbers	Difficult Words in Passage	Re-arrange Word Order	Para-phrase	Relation-ship of Style and Meaning

Literary Skills Focus

Literary Analysis

6. **Analyze** What details does the poet use to describe the dragon? Keeping those details in mind, explain what the dragon might symbolize as Beowulf's final foe.

7. **Interpret** Grendel and the dragon wage war for different reasons. What are these reasons? How are these different motivations related to the underlying themes of the epic?

8. **Extend** Was there any way for Beowulf to defeat the dragon, or was he doomed from the start?

Literary Skills: Epic Hero

9. **Analyze** If Beowulf had a different set of heroic traits, such as great intelligence, could he still have been able to defeat the monsters? Explain.

Literary Skills Review: Alliteration

10. **Extend** The repetition of the same or similar consonant sounds in words that are close together is called **alliteration.** Look back on the selection to find passages rich in alliteration. Read these passages aloud to help you fully appreciate the importance of the sound of the epic. Form a group, and assign roles for each reader to demonstrate the dramatic qualities of the epic.

Writing Skills Focus

Think as a Reader/Writer

Use It in Your Writing Continuing to imitate the style of the speeches in the epic, write a ten-line speech delivered by one of the warriors, extolling Beowulf's greatness.

What Do You Think Now? How does Beowulf's motivation change from Part One to Part Two? How would you describe his personality in Part Two as opposed to that in Part One?

Universal Access

Struggling Writers

Some students may need additional scaffolding to write in the style of the speeches in the epic. Have them create a list of accomplishments and traits of Beowulf mentioned in the epic that they can include in their speech. For example, the list might include *gracious, fair-minded, kind, glorious, unequaled in bravery and greatness, one who persevered in battle until vanquishing the beast,* etc.

What Do You Think Now?

Have students form small groups to discuss their views about Beowulf's motives in Parts One and Two. Ask them to cite examples from the text to support their assertions. Have the groups share their views with the class.

Applying Your Skills

from Beowulf, Parts One and Two

Grades 9–10 Review Reading Standard 1.1 (see pages A48–A50)

Vocabulary Development

Vocabulary Check

Match the Vocabulary words with their definitions.

1. reparation	**a.** disgusting
2. loathsome	**b.** perfect
3. reprisal	**c.** penalty
4. vehemently	**d.** intensely
5. infallible	**e.** compensation
6. extolled	**f.** acclaimed

Vocabulary Skills: Prefixes and Suffixes

Prefixes are word parts attached to the beginning of a word, and **suffixes** are word parts attached to the end of a word. Most prefixes and suffixes alter a word's meaning or part of speech. However, some suffixes, also called inflectional endings, simply change a word's number or tense. For example, *–ed* changes a verb to the past tense, and *–s* turns a singular noun into a plural one. The table below contains examples of some common prefixes and suffixes.

Prefix or Suffix	Function / Meaning	Example
–ed	changes verb's form to past tense	planted
–ly	turns an adjective into an adverb	slowly
ex–	"out or out of; beyond; from"	exhale
in–	"not"	incapable
re–	"again; back; backward"	return
–tion	turns a verb into a noun	visualization
–some	"causes"	troublesome

Your Turn

Use the chart to help you complete the items below.

1. Use the suffix *–tion* to turn a verb into a noun.
2. Explain the difference in meaning between *infallible* and *fallible.*
3. *Reprehend* is a verb meaning "to blame." Its Latin root means "to pull back." Which Vocabulary word has the same root as *reprehend?*
4. Write a sentence using the present-tense form of *extolled.*
5. Without using a dictionary, write the definition of *expel.* Hint: Its root, *pellere,* means "to push."

Language Coach

Connotations A word's **connotations** are the ideas, emotions, or thoughts you associate with the word. A word might have strong positive or negative connotations. One way to notice a word's connotations is to imagine replacing it with another word. Describe how the meaning of each sentence changes when you alternate using the words below in parentheses.

1. The poem (*praises, extols*) the deeds of a great hero.
2. A (*hateful, loathsome*) monster attacked Beowulf and his men.
3. Beowulf struck (*strongly, vehemently*) at his enemy.
4. The hero's (*reprisal, vengeance*) was harsh.

Academic Vocabulary

Talk About

Some observers believe that the concept of a hero forever changed after the September 11, 2001, attacks. Acts of heroism were attributed to a much more diverse group of men and women. In a small group, discuss your ideas about how one achieves hero status in America.

Universal Access: Vocabulary Development

English Learners

English for Academic Success Encourage students to gain more familiarity with the Academic Vocabulary by having them discuss these questions in groups:

- Discuss the advantages of knowing people from diverse backgrounds.
- Give examples of titles that people might attach to names to indicate status.
- Why might people attribute a downturn in the economy to the poor decisions by government officials?
- Explain why many schools in the U.S. need to address diverse learners.
- At which points in U.S. or world history did the concept of racial equality invite conflict?
- How might a speaker place an emphasis on a particular aspect of a topic?

✔ See the **Academic and Selection Vocabulary Skill Builder** in **UA: Differentiating Instruction.**

Independent Practice

Vocabulary Development

Vocabulary Check

1. *e* **2.** *a*
3. *c* **4.** *d*
5. *b* **6.** *f*

Your Turn

1. *acclaim, acclamation*
2. Fallible *means "imperfect; able to be wrong."* Infallible *means "unable to be wrong."*
3. *reprisal*
4. *Esther* extols *the beauty of neoclassical Renaissance paintings in her letter about visiting the museum.*
5. Expel *means "to push out."*

go.hrw.com **WordSharp: An Interactive Vocabulary Tutor,** more practice with academic language

English for Academic Success

Language Coach

Possible responses:

1. *The word* extol *refers to a higher degree of praise.*
2. *The word* loathsome *is mostly used to describe something revolting;* hateful *refers to something that is despised.*
3. *The adverb* vehemently *has a more intense and violent connotation than* strongly.
4. *The word* reprisal *refers to retaliation, so* vengeance *has a stronger, more powerful connotation.*

English for Academic Success

Academic Vocabulary

Possible response: *Hero* status *is still reserved for the most elite men and women, but the* concept *incorporates a* diverse *group. Heroes can be Olympic athletes or cell biologists. They are people who protect, but they are also people who display values that we admire—courage, loyalty, and perseverance.*

Independent Practice
Vocabulary Development

Your Turn

Anglo-Saxon Prefixes:

- *a–* *apart*
- *be–* *begrudge*
- *for–* *forgive*
- *mis–* *mistake*
- *over–* *overburden*
- *un–* *unlikely*

Anglo-Saxon Suffixes:

- *–en* *wooden*
- *–dom* *freedom*
- *–ful* *joyful*
- *–hood* *childhood*
- *–ish* *babyish*
- *–less* *thoughtless*
- *–like* *womblike*
- *–ly* *saintly*
- *–ness* *happiness*
- *–some* *worrisome*
- *–ward* *windward*
- *–y* *wordy*

Applying Your Skills

from **Beowulf, Parts One and Two**

Grades 9–10 Review Reading Standard 1.1 (see pages A48–A50)

Vocabulary Development

Vocabulary Skills: Anglo-Saxon Words and Word Parts

English has borrowed words from most of the world's languages, but many words in our basic vocabulary come to us from **Anglo-Saxon,** or Old English. The following are descendants of Old English words:

- the names of numbers ("one" from *an,* "two" from *twa,* "three" from *threo,* "four" from *feower*)
- words designating family relations ("father" from *faeder,* "mother" from *moder,* "son" from *sunu,* "daughter" from *dohtor*)
- names for parts of the body ("heart" from *heorte,* "foot" from *fot*)
- common, everyday things and activities ("apple" from *aeppel,* "hound" from *hund,* "weave" from *wefan*)

Many conventions in the English language can also be traced back to Anglo-Saxon times. Making nouns plural by adding *s* and creating possessives by adding *'s* come to us from Old English. Old English has given us the vowel changes in some irregular verbs, like *sing, sang, sung* (*singen, sang, sungen*) and the regular *–ed* (and sometimes *–t*) endings for the past tense and past participles of regular verbs (as in *healed, has healed*). The word endings we use to create degrees of comparison between adjectives (as in *darker, darkest*) are also Anglo-Saxon in origin.

Anglo-Saxon has contributed many important word parts—prefixes and suffixes—to the English language. Some of these affixes change the tense, person, or number of a word—often a verb. Others change the entire meaning of a word and its part of speech.

Your Turn

List examples of modern English words that use each of the Anglo-Saxon affixes shown on this page.

Prefixes from Anglo-Saxon	Meanings	Examples
a–	in; on; of; up; to	ashore, aside, atop
be–	around; about; treat as	behind, before, befriend
for–	away; off; from	forsake, forget
mis–	badly; not; wrongly	misspell, misjudge
over–	above; excessive	overtake, oversee
un–	not; reverse of	untrue, unknown

Suffixes from Anglo-Saxon	Meanings	Examples
–en	made of; like	golden, molten
–dom	state; rank; condition	wisdom, kingdom
–ful	full of; marked by	wonderful, useful
–hood	state; condition	neighborhood, childhood
–ish	suggesting; like	selfish, childish
–less	lacking; without	hopeless, helpless
–like	like; similar	dreamlike, childlike
–ly	like; characteristic of	friendly, cowardly
–ness	quality; state	kindness, tenderness
–some	apt to; showing	meddlesome, tiresome
–ward	in the direction of	forward, skyward
–y	showing; suggesting	wavy, hilly, salty

Universal Access: Vocabulary Development

EL English Learners

English for Academic Success Display these additional prefixes and suffixes for students along with their meanings:

- *im–:* not
- *–ess:* female
- *–ence, ency:* "state of"
- *–ant:* agent

Then, have students work in groups of three to four to brainstorm examples for each category, without any reference aids. After students have finished, ask groups to call out their list of words to compare results among groups. Encourage students to brainstorm as many words as possible, using only words that are familiar to them.

✔ See the **Academic and Selection Vocabulary Skill Builder** in **UA: Differentiating Instruction.**

Reading Standard 3.6 (see pages A48–A50)
Writing Standard 2.1 (see pages A51–A52)
Listening and Speaking Standard 2.4 (see pages A53–A55)

Grammar Link

Subject-Verb Agreement

Proper subject-verb agreement is essential to writing coherent, meaningful sentences but isn't always easy to recognize. Although you can often identify the correct verb form by listening to what "sounds" right, in some cases the answer isn't so clear. Consider this incorrectly written sentence:

Neither Beowulf nor his subjects *mourns* the death of Grendel.

The singular form *mourns* is incorrect because when a **compound subject** containing a singular and a plural subject is joined by *or* or *nor,* the verb agrees with the subject closer to the verb. Consider another example of tricky subject-verb agreement:

Twenty dollars is the price of a ticket to the opera *Grendel.*

The plural form *is* is used because in this context twenty dollars is thought of as a single unit.

Your Turn

Write the correct verb forms for these sentences.

1. Herot's joy or laughter (anger/angers) Grendel.
2. One hundred dollars (was/were) found throughout the auditorium.
3. Either Beowulf or his soldiers (march/marches) to the barrow to battle the dragon.

Writing Application Review drafts in your *Reader/Writer Notebook* to determine if you have errors in subject-verb agreement. Change verb forms as necessary to correct your sentences.

CHOICES

As you respond to the Choices, use these **Academic Vocabulary** words as appropriate: attribute, concept, diverse, emphasis, status.

REVIEW

Compare Heroic Qualities

Group Discussion Although translated from Old English, *Beowulf* is considered one of the first great epics of the English language. How do Beowulf's heroic qualities compare to the qualities of heroes from other myths, such as Hercules? What do these heroic qualities emphasize about the values of each culture? In a group, discuss heroes from various cultures and compare them to Beowulf.

CONNECT

Make a Documentary

TechFocus In a group, plan and create a documentary about various epic heroes, including Beowulf and similar modern characters. Cast students to play the part of each epic hero; others can play interviewers, sidekicks, or even villains. Make sure your documentary examines why each epic hero is important to his or her society, as well as how the heroes are similar and different. If you have access to a video camera, film your documentary; if not, perform it live for your class.

EXTEND

Write a Sequel

Pretend that Beowulf did not die in his battle with the dragon. What might the great warrior-king do next? Write a story or outline of Beowulf's continuing adventures in a world of monsters and villains. Where would he travel? Whom and what would he fight? To what would you attribute his downfall?

Learn It Online
Practice Vocabulary skills with *WordSharp.*
go.hrw.com H12-53 Go

Independent Practice

Grammar Link

Your Turn

1. *angers*
2. *was*
3. *march*

Choices: Evaluation Criteria

Review: Homework
Compare Heroic Qualities
Students compare the qualities of the epic hero Beowulf to the qualities of other heroes.

Connect: Homework
Make a Documentary
Students develop a documentary that examines why different epic heroes are important to society and how they are similar or different.

Extend: Homework
Write a Sequel
The sequel maintains the style and tone of *Beowulf.*

Assess

Unit 1 Resources, Selection Standards Check, p. 11

ThinkCentral Online Assessment, Selection Standards Check

Teacher One Stop™, editable Selection Standards Check

Reteach

For a lesson reteaching **archetypes,** see **Reteaching Lessons,** p. 1449S.

ThinkCentral Online Remediation

Learn It Online
WordSharp: An Interactive Vocabulary Tutor provides additional support for vocabulary development. Multimedia tutorials show students how to apply vocabulary skills to unfamiliar words—and how to make those words their own.
go.hrw.com H12-53 Go

Universal Access: Grammar Link

English Learners

English for Academic Success To help students understand subject-verb agreement, explain that a subject is a noun or pronoun (a person, place, or thing) that the sentence is about and a verb is an action word to which the subject is connected. The subject and verb of a sentence must "agree" in number. If the subject is singular, the verb must be singular. If the subject is plural, the verb must be plural. This is called subject-verb agreement. Remind students of the rules about subject-verb agreement using forms of the verb *to be.* If a subject is singular, students should use *am* or *is,* and if the subject is plural, they should use *are.* Display the two sentences below for students. Ask them to look at the two sentences and change the verbs so that they agree with the subjects.

- I is taking the test. [*I am taking the test.*]
- Ellen and Jose is finished. [*Ellen and Jose are finished.*]

✔ For more practice with subject-verb agreement, see **Warriner's Handbook, GrammarNotes,** and **Language Handbook Worksheets.**

Standards Focus

Objectives

Students will
- analyze the archetype of the epic hero
- respond to graphics and graphic novels

Motivate

What Do You Think?/QuickWrite

Use the QuickWrite to have students consider what prompts a person to take action against an injustice. Ask a few students to give examples of times they wanted to right a wrong. Then, have students write in their **Reader/Writer Notebooks**, referencing personal experiences to support their responses.

Literary/Reading/Writing Skills Focus

- As you read and discuss the selection with students, have students record how visual images convey Beowulf's heroic qualities.
- Give students a copy of the Reading Skills Focus graphic organizer before they read. (See **Unit 1 Resources.**)
- Have students note graphic details and the use of color to illustrate action and characters in their **Reader/Writer Notebooks**. Students can use their notes to complete the Writing Skills Focus activity.

California Standards, pp. 54–59

- **Reading Standard 3.1** Analyze characteristics of subgenres (e.g., satire, parody, allegory, pastoral) that are used in poetry, prose, plays, novels, short stories, essays, and other basic genres.
- **Reading Standard 3.6** Analyze the way in which authors through the centuries have used archetypes drawn from myth and tradition in literature, film, political speeches and religious writings (e.g., how the archetype of banishment from an ideal world may be used to interpret Shakespeare's tragedy *Macbeth*).

Preparing to Read

Reading Standard 3.1, 3.6 (see pages A48–A50)

Link to Today

This Link to Today gives a classic new life with mood-drenched images.

from The Collected Beowulf

by **Gareth Hinds**

Reader/Writer Notebook

Use your **RWN** to complete the activities for these selections.

What Do You Think? What moves a hero to act?

QuickWrite

Think about a time when you or someone you know wanted to right a wrong that had been done. Did you or the other person take action? What happened? Record your thoughts in your *Reader/Writer Notebook.*

Literary Skills Focus

Archetype: The Epic Hero The **archetype** of the **epic hero** has endured for thousands of years in serious literature and in popular culture. Today's comic books and graphic novels are particularly well suited to showing the exploits of these larger-than-life heroes who overcome great obstacles, including formidable foes and threatening monsters.

Reading Skills Focus

Responding to Graphic Novels Graphic novels employ a variety of visual tools to tell a story. In *The Collected Beowulf,* Gareth Hinds uses contrasting colors, separate panels, close-up pictures that display characters' emotions, and images of groups of characters. Even the text, which appears in an old-fashioned script against multicolored backgrounds, adds a visual dimension to the story. As you read, use a chart like the one below to note how images help convey Beowulf's heroic qualities.

Heroic Quality	Image
bravery	close-up of Beowulf's face as he moves forward with sword

Writing Skills Focus

Think as a Reader/Writer

Find It in Your Reading Illustrators of previously published stories such as the *Beowulf* epic make choices about which scenes to depict visually and how to present them. As you read, use your *Reader/Writer Notebook* to comment on the graphic details and the range of colors Hinds uses to illustrate the action and the characters.

Selection Readability	
Easily Accessible Accessible **Challenging**	historical context; complex poetry quote; unfamiliar vocabulary

Selection Summary

This episode of Beowulf takes place just after Beowulf defeated Grendel. He is diving down to battle Grendel's mother in her underwater lair.

GRAPHIC NOVEL

Link to Today

The graphic novel excerpt from *The Collected Beowulf* explores the imagery and values of Beowulf through a contemporary point of view.

Direct Teach

Think About/Talk About

Extend the Discussion

Graphic Novel Before reading, look carefully at the typeface, or shape of the letters, on the page. What does the typeface tell you about the story even before you begin to read? What is the most likely reason for this choice? ***Possible response:*** *The typeface seems to mimic medieval lettering. Even before I start reading, I can tell the story takes place a very long time ago. The artist is representing the story in a modern format, but the typeface reminds the reader that the epic poem* Beowulf *was written hundreds of years ago.*

Selection Resources

Unit 1 Resources, on-level practice and assessment, p. 8

Teacher One Stop™, on-level lesson plans and all print resources

Holt Audio Library

Holt Audio Library: Selections and Summaries in Spanish

UA: Differentiating Instruction: graphic organizer, p. 8

UA: Supporting Instruction in Spanish selection summary

ThinkCentral Online Assessment, Selection Standards Check

ThinkCentral Online Remediation

Model the Skill

- Review the **archetype of an epic hero**. Explain that an archetype can be displayed in text and in pictures or photographs.
- Tell students that in this graphic novel, the image of Beowulf serves as an archetype of an epic hero. Direct students to the picture of Beowulf swimming to the hellish lair of Grendel's mother. Beowulf's facial expression appears to be fearless, and there is determination in his eyes. His clothing and weapons suggest he is prepared for battle. This image exemplifies his heroism.

Guided Practice: Apply

Think-Pair-Share Group students in pairs, and have them compare the picture of Beowulf on p. 56 to the picture of Aeschere on p. 57. Ask them to discuss how the differences between these two pictures support the analysis of Beowulf as the epic hero of the tale. Then ask pairs to share their comparisons with the whole class.

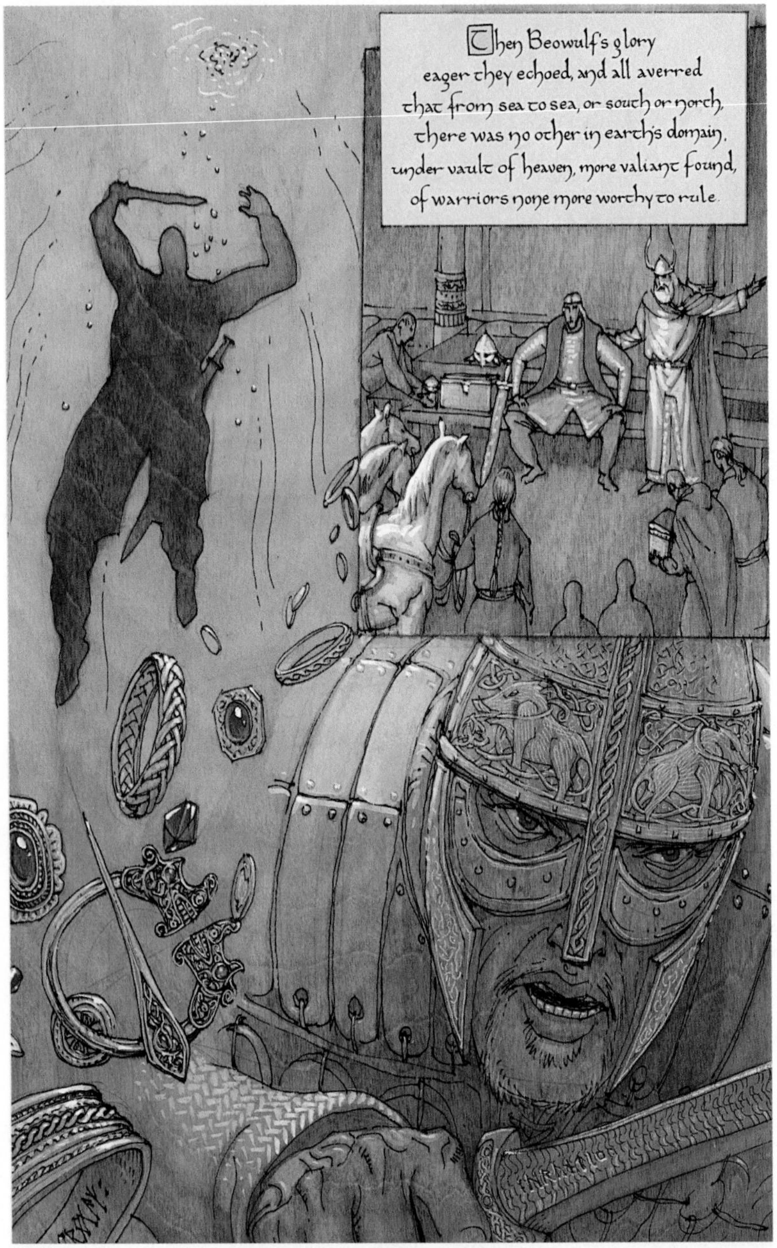

Universal Access

EL English Learners

English for Academic Success Students might have trouble following the captions within the panel, given the use of unfamiliar words and complex sentences. For this reason, it might be helpful for them to use the knowledge they have already acquired reading excerpts from *Beowulf*. Have students think about what they already know about the plot, and then have them discuss which part of the story is narrated in the graphic novel. Finally, have them paraphrase the captions.

Struggling Readers

Strategic Students Guide students in responding to the graphics. In small groups, have students study the shadowy figure of Beowulf on p. 56, swimming toward the bottom of the sea. Ask them to guess what Beowulf is wearing, what weapons he is carrying, and his fearless attitude. Then, have students look to the smaller panel set in the darker-colored background. How do we know that the figure in the middle is Beowulf? What does this image seem to be revealing about him as a hero? Have groups share their responses.

Think About/Talk About

Extend the Discussion

Graphic Novel Often in graphic novels, parts of a story are told solely through images. On this page, what parts of the story of Beowulf can you recognize? ***Possible response:*** *On this page, Grendel's arm is hanging in the doorway, the soldiers are settling down to sleep after the long battle, and Grendel's mother comes and takes Hrothgar's friend away.*

Students with Disabilities

Students may find the highly visual graphic novel to be more accessible than a text-based story. Give these readers some time to connect with the events as they unfold in pictures. Then, ask them to connect the words on the page to the action they see depicted in the images. After students have spent time interpreting the images, ask them if they have any questions about the story that the images do not answer. Challenge students to locate answers to their questions in the text.

Compare and Contrast

Ask students to compare the storytelling methods of the graphic novel of *Beowulf* to the text-based novel.

- **Similarities** Both follow Beowulf on his quest. Both engage the reader in the tale of an epic hero.
- **Differences** The text-based novel tells the reader exactly what is going on in the story. The graphic novel invites readers to use their imagination to interpret the tale and "fill in" the details of what happens. The text-based novel relies on the reader to visualize the scene; the graphic novel relies on the reader to interpret the dialogue.

Think About/Talk About

Extend the Discussion

Finding Details When he speaks the phrase "better friends to avenge than fruitlessly mourn them," what is Beowulf suggesting to King Hrothgar? ***Possible response:*** *Beowulf means that mourning alone is not going to accomplish anything. He is suggesting that the best way to honor Aeschere's death is to go into battle against Grendel's mother and seek revenge for her terrible deed.*

Evaluating Which character from Beowulf do you think is represented in each of the images shown here? How can you tell? ***Possible response:*** *I can tell from his clothing and helmet that the figure at the far left is Hrothgar. I can infer from the sword in the figure's hand that the character floating downward is Beowulf. I think the dead figure at the far right is Aeschere. Aeschere is killed by Grendel's mother, and the footprints leading toward the body seem to be hers.*

Monitor Students' Comprehension

To check students' understanding of the archetype of the epic hero, ask them to explain the qualities of the epic hero conveyed by Beowulf's close-up on p. 56. ***Possible response:*** *Beowulf is throwing himself into battle, and he looks focused and fearless. Courage and focus are two qualities of the epic hero.*

California Standards, p. 59

- **Reading Standard 3.1** Analyze characteristics of subgenres (e.g., satire, parody, allegory, pastoral) that are used in poetry, prose, plays, novels, short stories, essays, and other basic genres.
- **Reading Standard 3.6** Analyze the way in which authors through the centuries have used archetypes drawn from myth and tradition in literature, film, political speeches and religious writings (e.g., how the archetypes of banishment from an ideal world may be used to interpret Shakespeare's tragedy *Macbeth*).
- **Grades 9–10 Review Reading Standard 3.6** Analyze and trace an author's development of time and sequence, including the use of complex literary devices.
- **Writing Standard 2.2** Write responses to literature: **d.** Demonstrate an understanding of the author's use of stylistic devices and an appreciation of the effects created.

Standards Focus

Objectives

Students will
- identify the main idea of the text
- analyze characteristics of subgenres, such as the elegy

Selection Introduction

Think About the Poems

Before students answer, have them think about what they have learned so far about Anglo-Saxon culture, religion, and traditions.

For Independent Reading

*How to Read a Poem,** Edward Hirsch

HRW LIBRARY *This title is available in the HRW library.

Motivate

What Do You Think?/QuickWrite

Pair students and have them brainstorm and discuss important losses in their lives and what they write about in a riddle.

English for Academic Success

Academic Vocabulary

Look for opportunities to use the Academic Vocabulary word in this unit.

- **concept, *n.*:** notion or idea

California Standards, pp. 60–73

- **Reading Standard 3.1** Analyze characteristics of subgenres (e.g., satire, parody, allegory, pastoral) that are used in poetry, prose, plays, novels, short stories, essays, and other basic genres.
- **Reading Standard 3.2** Analyze the way in which the theme or meaning of a selection represents a view or comment on life, using textual evidence to support the claim.

Preparing to Read

The Seafarer
The Wife's Lament
The Wanderer
Anglo-Saxon Riddles

What Do You Think? What moves a hero to act?

QuickWrite

Quickly record some ideas for a poem of loss and for a riddle in your *Reader/Writer Notebook.*

INTRODUCTION

The Exeter Book, a manuscript of Anglo-Saxon poems dating from around the middle of the tenth century, is the largest of four important collections of Anglo-Saxon poetry that have survived to the present time.

Anglo-Saxon Poetry Preserved

Containing more than thirty poems and ninety riddles, *The Exeter Book* is something of a riddle itself. Although Bishop Leofric gave the manuscript to the cathedral at Exeter (a city in southwest England) in the eleventh century, no one knows where the manuscript originated. Some of the book's leaves have been damaged by fire and, as a result, the readability of the texts has been affected. There are signs that the book's cover had been used as a chopping board, and some pages are marked by beer stains. Today, however, its "songs"—written down by monks in about 975—are our chief source of Anglo-Saxon poetry.

Poems of Loss and Puzzles for Pleasure

The dominant mood in Anglo-Saxon poetry is **elegiac,** or mournful. As you have seen in *Beowulf,* this sense of sadness over the grimness and fleetingness of earthly life occurs in the heroic epic. This mournfulness also has a place in several Old English fragments in which the speaker laments the passing of better days and greater glories. The three lyrics that follow, "The Seafarer," "The Wife's Lament," and "The Wanderer," are all elegies that have common themes including exile, a long journey, and the loss of something or someone.

Despite the grim tone of much Anglo-Saxon literature, the light tone of Anglo-Saxon riddles shows that people in those days liked to be entertained just as we do today. The compilation of riddles in *The Exeter Book* is the earliest known in England and provides clever, imaginative puzzles for its readers to solve. Their authorship and composition dates are unknown. Although some can be traced to Latin originals, the Old English riddles often differ significantly from Latin prototypes; the Old English riddles are "literary games" rather than "merely exercises in metaphor."

Think About the Poems What do the different types of literature found in *The Exeter Book* tell you about the Anglo-Saxon people?

The viking ship of King Harold II (detail) sailing against the ship of his half-brother King Olaf II of Norway in 1030 (c. 1375). Fresco from a Danish church. The Granger Collection, N.Y.

Selection Readability	
Easily Accessible Accessible **Challenging**	These poems include complex syntax; abstract symbolism; difficult vocabulary; longer stanzas.

Applying Your Skills

Reading Standard 3.1, 3.6; Grades 9–10 Review Reading Standard 3.6 (see pages A48–A50)
Writing Standard 2.2d (see pages A51–A52)

from The Collected Beowulf

Literary Response and Analysis

Reading Skills Focus

Quick Check

1. At what point in the narrative of *Beowulf* does this episode take place?
2. Toward what is Beowulf diving?
3. On the last page of the selection, why is the figure on the left covering his face with his hand?

Reading Skills: Responding to Graphic Novels

4. As you read, you used a chart to note images that demonstrate Beowulf's heroic qualities. Now, review the notes in your chart, and add a column listing the effects each scene creates.

Heroic Quality	Image	Effects
bravery	close-up of Beowulf's face as he moves forward with sword	shows his determination to kill his foe

Literary Skills Focus

Literary Analysis

5. **Interpret** In the scene presented on page 57, the artist uses one color to show the events narrated by the words on the page and another color to depict an event that happens later in the epic. How does the use of color help you make sense of the visual elements on the page?
6. **Draw Conclusions** This excerpt depicts a scene that is summarized in the *Beowulf* epic poem that you read. How does the graphic excerpt contribute to your overall understanding of *Beowulf?*

Literary Skills: The Epic Hero

7. **Evaluate** In this excerpt, triumphant language appears against the mysterious, frightening imagery of Beowulf's dive. How does this contrast affect your understanding of the scene? What does it suggest about Beowulf as a hero?
8. **Interpret** In a small group, create a list of epic heroes from poems, books, movies, graphic novels, and comics. How do these heroes resemble Beowulf? How are they different? What drives them to act? What makes their actions heroic?

Literary Skills Review: Sequence of Action

9. **Analyze** The **sequence of action** refers to how chronological events are presented in a narrative. How are the different panels in this excerpt like and unlike sequential events in a narrative text?

Writing Skills Focus

Think as a Reader/Writer

Use It in Your Writing Look back at the notes you took in your *Reader/Writer Notebook* about the details and colors Hinds uses to bring *Beowulf* to life visually. Choose a single page from the excerpt reprinted here, and write a paragraph explaining how details and color enhance both character and action in the narrative.

What Do You Think Now This graphic novel makes Grendel's mother inescapably frightening. Does that change your impression of Beowulf's courage?

Universal Access

Struggling Writers

Provide additional scaffolding for students by having them create a chart with two columns and two rows. The columns should be titled "details" and "color," and the rows should be labeled "character" and "action." Demonstrate filling out the space corresponding to "details" and "character" by pointing out that, for p. 58, the grave expressions of the figures on the left emphasize their emotional reaction to the death of their friend. Have students work in pairs to complete the chart before writing a paragraph on their own.

	details	color
character	add an emotional dimension	
action		shows sequence of actions

Check for Understanding

Independent Practice

Reading Skills Focus

Possible responses:

1. *It takes place just after Beowulf defeats Grendel.*
2. *He is diving toward Grendel's mother.*
3. *The figure seems to be Hrothgar. Grendel's mother took his closest friend, and Hrothgar is desperate.*
4. *Ask students to think about the mood conveyed by each panel (fear, courage, sadness, expectation, etc.).*

Literary Skills Focus

Possible responses:

5. *The different colors help keep the timing of the events in order.*
6. *The graphic excerpt emphasizes the violence and terror described in the original epic.*
7. *The contrast suggests that Beowulf has superhuman courage and abilities. He is stronger than all other men and is not afraid of fighting.*
8. *Have students consider the qualities and quests of epic heroes before compiling their list.*
9. *They are like a narrative in that the story moves forward from page to page. They are different because the images within a panel are not always set sequentially left to right, as the words on a page would be.*

What Do You Think Now?

Ask students to think about their impressions of Beowulf as they read the epic poem and compare it with their present impressions.

Teacher Preparation

Selection Summary

The speaker in this elegy is a sailor who has endured many hard winters on the cold northern seas. Yet the sea has a powerful attraction for him, and he prefers its rigors to the comforts of life on land in an age that no longer produces brave and generous heroes. In fact, the sea is used as a powerful metaphor for life itself. The poem ends with a Christian exhortation to love God.

Direct Teach

Think About/Talk About

Read with a Purpose Have students read the Read with a Purpose statement. Remind them that elegies usually focus on mourning or loss and the way it affects a person's perspective.

Extend the Discussion

Comparing and Contrasting What two ways of life is the seafarer contrasting? ***Possible response:*** *The seafarer contrasts the loneliness, harshness, and coldness of life at sea to the conviviality, warmth, and intimacy of life on land.*

Evaluating In what ways do the opening lines suggest an elegy? ***Possible response:*** *They convey a sense of suffering and pain; they also may suggest a loss of youth and hopelessness.*

POEM

The Seafarer

translated by **Burton Raffel**

Read with a Purpose

As you read the next three poems, discover how the speakers reflect not only on loss but also on life.

Build Background

The speaker of this poem is an old sailor who has drifted through many winters on the ice-cold seas of life. Some interpreters of the poem have suggested that the poem is an allegory—a story with a literal meaning and a symbolic meaning—about the journey of life. Seafaring symbolizes the suffering necessary in the Christian way of life—the seafarer chooses the ascetic life, severe and without worldly pleasures, as a path to salvation.

This tale is true, and mine. It tells
How the sea took me, swept me back
And forth in sorrow and fear and pain,
Showed me suffering in a hundred ships,
In a thousand ports, and in me. It tells
Of smashing surf when I sweated in the cold
Of an anxious watch, perched in the bow
As it dashed under cliffs. My feet were cast
In icy bands, bound with frost,
With frozen chains, and hardship groaned
Around my heart. Hunger tore
At my sea-weary soul. No man sheltered
On the quiet fairness of earth can feel
How wretched I was, drifting through winter
On an ice-cold sea, whirled in sorrow,
Alone in a world blown clear of love,
Hung with icicles. The hailstorms flew.
The only sound was the roaring sea,
The freezing waves. The song of the swan
Might serve for pleasure, the cry of the sea-fowl,
The death-noise of birds instead of laughter,
The mewing of gulls instead of mead.°
Storms beat on the rocky cliffs and were echoed
By icy-feathered terns° and the eagle's screams;
No kinsman could offer comfort there,

22. mead: a beverage made from fermented honey and water.

24. terns (turnz): seabirds related to gulls.

Vocabulary **wretched** (REHCH ihd) *adj.:* miserable; unhappy.

Universal Access

English Learners

English for Academic Success Remind students to use context clues to figure out the meaning of unfamiliar words. Model using context clues to figure out the meaning of *surf* in line 6. You might say: "The poem is about a mariner. He tells about the difficulties experienced at sea. One context clue is the word *smashing*. What can 'smash' in the sea? Maybe *surf* means *wave*. If I look in the dictionary, I find out that *surf* is the foam formed by a wave when it crashes upon the shore."

Struggling Readers

Model for students how to understand the characteristics of an elegy. Read aloud lines 11–17, putting an emphasis on words that reveal the speaker's troubles and sorrow, such as *hunger* and *sea-weary*. You might say: "I know that an elegy is a poem that grieves over some kind of loss. As I look over these lines, I notice it says the speaker is 'sea-weary,' 'wretched,' 'cold,' and feeling lonely. These lines tell me that the seafarer is lamenting about his lonely, miserable time at sea." Ask students to look for other details that support this conclusion.

The Seafarer / The Wife's Lament / The Wanderer

Literary Skills Focus

Elegy An **elegy** is a type of poem that mourns a person's death or laments something lost. The speakers in "The Seafarer" and "The Wanderer" yearn for a peace they used to know, while the speaker in "The Wife's Lament" mourns her separation from her exiled husband.

Reading Skills Focus

Identifying Theme The **theme** is the central idea or insight about human experience expressed in a work of literature. Although the elegies from *The Exeter Book* were composed more than a thousand years ago, they have themes that are still relevant to our lives today. To identify these themes, pay close attention to the poems' descriptive details. Key details provide clues to the poets' ideas about life and the messages they wish to convey.

Into Action As you read each poem, use a chart like the one below to keep track of significant words and details. Add as many circles as you need. After you read, you will fill in the middle circle with the poem's theme.

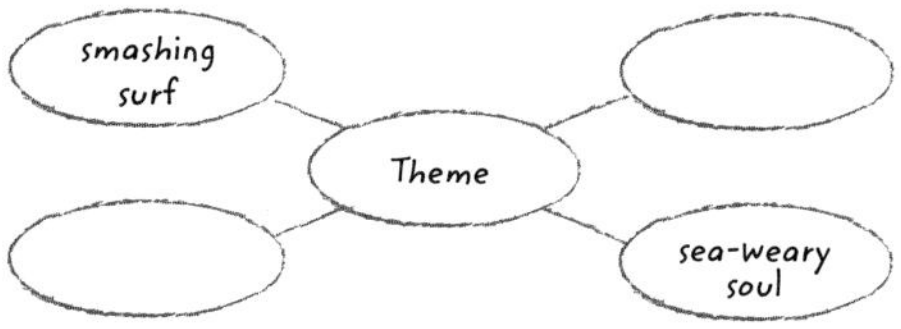

Writing Skills Focus

Think as a Reader/Writer

Find It in Your Reading Writers of elegies use words and images that help create a sad, mournful mood. As you read, record in your *Reader/Writer Notebook* words and images that contribute to the sorrowful mood of these three elegies.

Vocabulary

wretched (REHCH ihd) *adj.:* miserable; unhappy. *Harsh conditions made the sailor's life wretched.*

desolation (dehs uh LAY shuhn) *n.:* grief; loneliness. *The sailor felt desolation after losing his friends.*

ravenous (RAV uh nuhs) *adj.:* very hungry. *The sailor says his spirit is ravenous and cannot be satisfied.*

demeanor (dih MEE nuhr) *n.:* the way in which a person behaves. *His pleasant demeanor hid his bad intentions.*

gloat (gloht) *v.:* feel or express great, often malicious, self-satisfaction or pleasure. *A wise warrior does not gloat about his victories.*

Language Coach

Related Words When you learn a new word, you may be able to learn related words that contain the same basic word part. The word *desolation* is a noun that means "loneliness." When you remove the *–ion* ending, you can find the verb and adjective *desolate.* What do you think *desolate* means? *Wretched* is an adjective that means "miserable." What do you think the noun *wretch* means?

Learn It Online
Find an interactive word web to use as you read.
go.hrw.com H12-61 Go

Reader/Writer Notebook
Use your **RWN** to complete the activities for these selections.

Selection Resources

Unit 1 Resources, on-level practice and assessment, p. 14

Teacher One Stop™, on-level lesson plans and all print resources

Holt Audio Library

Holt Audio Library: Selections and Summaries in Spanish

UA: Differentiating Instruction: graphic organizer, p. 9

UA: Supporting Instruction in Spanish, selection summary

ThinkCentral Online Assessment, Selection Standards Check

ThinkCentral Online Remediation

Preteach

Introducing Vocabulary

- Review the Vocabulary words, definitions, and sentences with students.
- To reinforce students' understanding of the Vocabulary words, tell them that these words can help them understand the purpose of an elegy. Elegies usually have a *wretched* speaker whose *demeanor* suggests he is experiencing *desolation.* The speaker may feel emotionally starved or *ravenous,* and others may *gloat* at his misfortunes.

English for Academic Success

Language Coach

Have students read the **Language Coach** and work in pairs to answer the questions. ***Possible responses:*** *Desolate—lonely; wretch—an unhappy or miserable person.*

Literary Skills Focus

As you read and discuss the elegies with students, stop to compare and contrast the speakers' feelings of loss with expressions of grief in modern poems and songs.

Reading Skills Focus

Give students a copy of the Reading Skills Focus graphic organizer before they read. (See **Unit 1 Resources.**) Tell them to use their notes to answer the questions on the Applying Your Skills page.

Writing Skills Focus

Have students record words and images that illustrate the mood of the elegy in their **Reader/Writer Notebooks.** Students can use their notes to complete the Writing Skills Focus activity.

Learn It Online
Introduce students to **Interactive Graphic Organizers**—tools for generating and organizing details, determining main ideas, drawing conclusions, comparing and contrasting ideas, and other key skills.
go.hrw.com H12-61 Go

Model the Skill

- Tell students that the **theme** is a broad message about life that the selection conveys. Explain that paying attention to details about the speaker and setting is one way to understand the theme of a poem.
- Tell students the theme of this elegy is the speaker's isolation and hopelessness. Write the word *hopelessness* at the center of the word web and add related details such as "vanished" (line 86), "pleasures are dead" (line 86), and "glory is tarnished" (line 88).

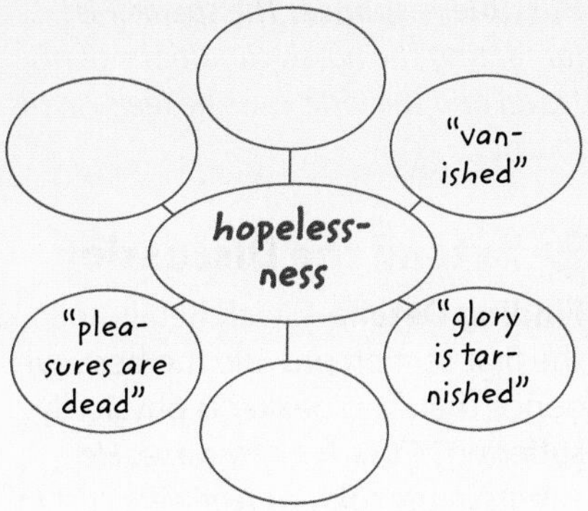

Guided Practice: Apply

Think-Pair Share Have students create their word webs in assigned pairs, finding additional details that develop the elegy's theme.

Think as a Reader/Writer

Find It in Your Reading Direct students to line 46. Remind students that this subjective detail discloses the speaker's feelings of loneliness at sea and in life.

Use It in Your Writing Tell students to write two to three sentences describing a place that makes them feel lonely. Ask students to use vivid imagery and metaphors to convey their feelings effectively.

So born to greatness, so bold with his youth,
Grown so brave, or so graced by God,
That he feels no fear as the sails unfurl,
Wondering what Fate has willed and will do.
No harps ring in his heart, no rewards,
No passion for women, no worldly pleasures,
Nothing, only the ocean's heave;
But longing wraps itself around him.
Orchards blossom, the towns bloom,
Fields grow lovely as the world springs fresh,
And all these admonish that willing mind
Leaping to journeys, always set
In thoughts traveling on a quickening tide.
So summer's sentinel, the cuckoo, sings
In his murmuring voice, and our hearts mourn
As he urges. Who could understand,
In ignorant ease, what we others suffer
As the paths of exile stretch endlessly on?
And yet my heart wanders away,
My soul roams with the sea, the whales'
Home,° wandering to the widest corners
Of the world, returning ravenous with desire,
Flying solitary, screaming, exciting me
To the open ocean, breaking oaths **C**
On the curve of a wave. Thus the joys of God
Are fervent with life, where life itself
Fades quickly into the earth. The wealth
Of the world neither reaches to Heaven nor remains.
No man has ever faced the dawn
Certain which of Fate's three threats
Would fall: illness, or age, or an enemy's
Sword, snatching the life from his soul.
The praise the living pour on the dead
Flowers from reputation: plant
An earthly life of profit reaped
Even from hatred and rancor, of bravery
Flung in the devil's face, and death
Can only bring you earthly praise
And a song to celebrate a place
With the angels, life eternally blessed
In the hosts of Heaven. The days are gone
When the kingdoms of earth flourished in glory;

Boat with three sailors landing on whale while it swallows fish (13th century). Ashmole 1511, folio 86 v. Bodleian Library, Oxford.

59-60. whales' home: a kenning for "the sea." In Anglo-Saxon poetry, a **kenning** is a metaphorical phrase or compound word used to name a person, place, thing, or event indirectly.

C **Literary Focus** **Elegy** What is the speaker trying to find?

Vocabulary **ravenous** (RAV uh nuhs) *adj.:* very hungry.

Developing Oral Fluency

Whole-Class Activity The layout of the poem can make it hard for students to read the lines smoothly. To help students improve their oral fluency, have them read a section of the poem aloud in a group. Choose a section, and tell students to take turns reading a sentence aloud in their group. Have students first read the section to themselves and ask for help with any words they have trouble pronouncing or understanding. While each student reads, ask other students to highlight or circle the words that were pronounced incorrectly, and after the student has finished reading, have the other students give their feedback.

Universal Access

EL English Learners

Monitor students' understanding of the selection by encouraging them to orally respond to the selection. Have students use the pattern, "In lines x–y, the speaker believes/acknowledges/feels that ______." For example: "In lines 106–108, the speaker believes the godless die quickly, while the humble are strengthened by heaven's angels."

To a soul left drowning in desolation. **A**
And who could believe, knowing but
The passion of cities, swelled proud with wine
And no taste of misfortune, how often, how wearily,
I put myself back on the paths of the sea.
Night would blacken; it would snow from the north;
Frost bound the earth and hail would fall,
The coldest seeds. And how my heart
Would begin to beat, knowing once more
The salt waves tossing and the towering sea!
The time for journeys would come and my soul
Called me eagerly out, sent me over
The horizon, seeking foreigners' homes. **B**
But there isn't a man on earth so proud,

Stormy skies over Bamburgh Castle, Northumberland, England.

A **Literary Focus** **Elegy** An elegy mourns or laments the loss of something. What does the speaker seem to be lamenting in the first section?

B **Reading Focus** **Identifying Theme** How does the speaker describe himself in lines 30–38? What do these descriptions imply about the poem's theme?

Vocabulary **desolation** (dehs uh LAY shuhn) *n.:* grief; loneliness.

Advanced Learners

Acceleration Have students dispute or support the following statement: "'The Seafarer' contains both Christian and non-Christian elements." As students prepare their responses, remind them to use precise words and lines from the poem to support their opinions.

Students with Disabilities

Students might have trouble reading a poem without a clear plot. Before students read the poem, explain that "The Seafarer" describes the thoughts and feelings of a sailor. Have students brainstorm problems and fears that a sailor might have, and ask them to keep in mind that the sailor in this poem lived in an era with rudimentary technology. Discuss with students what they expect the poem will be about.

Think About/Talk About

Comprehension

B Reading Focus

Possible responses: *The speaker describes himself as a relentless traveler who cannot resist the call of the sea. This mirrors the speaker's idea that human existence is ruled by fate and that life is an inevitable journey towards death.*

Analysis

A Literary Focus

Possible response: *The speaker is lamenting the harsh conditions of his travel and the loneliness he feels on his journey.*

Extend the Discussion

Finding Details Which details in the first section provide the best evidence that the speaker is physically suffering? ***Possible response:*** *He sweats in the cold; his feet were cast in icy bands; hunger tore at his soul.*

Interpreting Why does the seafarer return to the ocean time after time despite his loneliness? ***Possible response:*** *He may feel more at home on the sea than on land.*

Vocabulary: Own the Word

- **wretched:** Ask students to applaud as an indicator of how much they would want to be in a *wretched* state. ***Possible response:*** *Students do not applaud and explain that they would not want to be unhappy.*
- **desolation:** Draw a circle around the word *desolation*. Ask students to look up the word in a thesaurus and volunteer answers for the "spider legs" that extend from the center. ***Possible responses:*** *isolation, waste, bleakness, devastation, forlornness*

Teacher Preparation

Selection Summary

"The Wife's Lament" relates the speaker's longing for her husband, from whom she has been separated for mysterious reasons. The speaker of this poem is a wife who is suffering in exile from her husband and people. The first part of the poem suggests that the wife married into an enemy clan that has not received her in a friendly manner. She accuses her husband's family of plotting to separate her and her husband. Her husband may have committed a crime because he is sent to a distant place, and the wife is banished to a forest where she lives alone. There, the wife mourns the loss of her husband and home. She ends her lament believing that her husband feels grief just as she does.

Direct Teach

Think About/Talk About

Read with a Purpose Have students read the Read with a Purpose statement. Point out that the speaker is mourning the loss of her husband and the loss of her community. Have students note adjectives, imagery, and other clues that reveal the speaker's feelings.

Extend the Discussion

Finding Details In lines 18–21, how does the speaker describe her husband? ***Possible response:*** *The husband was an unlucky, troubled man who probably had criminal tendencies but nevertheless appeared cheerful.*

Tone How would you describe the tone of this poem? ***Possible response:*** *The tone is one of desperation and distress.*

POEM

The Wife's Lament

translated by **Richard Hamer**

Read with a Purpose

Read to discover examples of the speaker's feelings of isolation and exile.

Build Background

The ties of kinship were such an important part of life during the Anglo-Saxon period that the threat of becoming isolated from one's community was almost unbearable. The speaker of this elegy mourns the loss of her husband and what he represents—security, comfort, and safety—although it is not clear why she has lost his favor or why she is a "friendless exile." The speaker may have been married to her husband in order to end a dispute between clans, and if the dispute were rekindled, she would have been separated from her husband and banished. Another interpretation is that the husband, too, has turned against her. Whatever the cause of her isolation, her grief represents the universal concept of loss and loneliness.

I sing this song about myself, full sad,
My own distress, and tell what hardships I
Have had to suffer since I first grew up,
Present and past, but never more than now;
I ever suffered grief through banishment.°
For since my lord departed from this people
Over the sea, each dawn have I had care
Wondering where my lord may be on land.
When I set off to join and serve my lord,
A friendless exile in my sorry plight,
My husband's kinsmen plotted secretly
How they might separate us from each other
That we might live in wretchedness apart
Most widely in the world: and my heart longed.
In the first place my lord had ordered me
To take up my abode° here, though I had
Among these people few dear loyal friends;
Therefore my heart is sad. Then had I found
A fitting man, but one ill-starred,° distressed,
Whose hiding heart was contemplating crime,
Though cheerful his demeanor. We had vowed
Full many a time that naught° should come between us

5. banishment: living in exile.

16. take up my abode: make this a home.

19. ill-starred: unfortunate.

22. naught: nothing.

Vocabulary **demeanor** (dih MEEN uhr) *n.:* the way in which a person behaves.

Universal Access

English Learners

English for Academic Success Read aloud lines 1–18 to students. Explain the meanings of terms such as *kinsmen* and *plight.* Then, help them identify key details in the poem by instructing them to find the answers to the following questions after they read the lines again with a partner: What is the speaker's mood in these lines? Who is her "lord"? What is the speaker lamenting? Invite volunteers to share their responses with the class.

Struggling Readers

Strategic Students Demonstrate the skill of recognizing the theme of the poem by saying: "I notice that the poem repeats words such as *sad* in lines 1 and 18, *yearn* or *long* in lines 14, 30, and 55, and *banishment* in lines 5 and 39. I also notice the key details such as the speaker's separation and exile from her husband, her in-laws' plotting, and her *joyless* isolation on the sea. I might conclude that the poet views life as one marked by loneliness and in need of loving relationships."

Now there are no rulers, no emperors,
No givers of gold, as once there were,
When wonderful things were worked among them
And they lived in lordly magnificence.
Those powers have vanished, those pleasures are dead.
The weakest survives and the world continues,
Kept spinning by toil. All glory is tarnished.
The world's honor ages and shrinks.
Bent like the men who mold it. Their faces
Blanch° as time advances, their beards
Wither and they mourn the memory of friends.
The sons of princes, sown in the dust. **D**
The soul stripped of its flesh knows nothing
Of sweetness or sour, feels no pain,
Bends neither its hand nor its brain. A brother
Opens his palms and pours down gold
On his kinsman's grave, strewing his coffin
With treasures intended for Heaven, but nothing
Golden shakes the wrath of God
For a soul overflowing with sin, and nothing
Hidden on earth rises to Heaven.
We all fear God. He turns the earth,
He set it swinging firmly in space,
Gave life to the world and light to the sky.
Death leaps at the fools who forget their God.
He who lives humbly has angels from Heaven
To carry him courage and strength and belief.
A man must conquer pride, not kill it,
Be firm with his fellows, chaste for himself,
Treat all the world as the world deserves,
With love or with hate but never with harm,
Though an enemy seek to scorch him in hell,
Or set the flames of a funeral pyre°
Under his lord. Fate is stronger
And God mightier than any man's mind.
Our thoughts should turn to where our home is,
Consider the ways of coming there,
Then strive for sure permission for us
To rise to that eternal joy,
That life born in the love of God
And the hope of Heaven. Praise the Holy
Grace of Him who honored us,
Eternal, unchanging creator of earth. Amen.

91. blanch: turn pale.

Viking Oseberg stem/stern.

114. funeral pyre (FYOO nuhr uhl pyr): pile (usually of wood) on which a dead body is burned. *See* the burial of Beowulf, page 49.

D **Reading Focus** **Identifying Theme** What details does the poet use to describe the past and the present?

Think About/Talk About

Comprehension

D Reading Focus

Possible response: *The seafarer speaks about the glorious and generous rulers of the past as opposed to a modern age without emperors and "givers of gold." The only survivors of the past are pale, withered men mourning the loss of their friends.*

Analysis

C Literary Focus

Possible response: *The speaker is trying to find a sense of peace.*

Extend the Discussion

Drawing Conclusions In lines 55–57, the speaker asks the question, "Who could understand, in ignorant ease, what we others suffer as the paths of exile stretch endlessly on?" What does the phrase "paths of exile" refer to? ***Possible responses:*** *the open sea; the life of a religious person*

Interpreting Though the beginning of the poem describes the hardship and sacrifice of being a seafarer, lines 58–64 describe a different relationship with the sea. What shift in the speaker's feelings is expressed here? ***Possible responses:*** *The speaker describes being drawn to the sea. The speaker is "ravenous with desire" for the open ocean.*

Vocabulary: Own the Word

ravenous: Remind students that the connotation of *ravenous* is extremely hungry. You might say: "We got hungry around lunch time, but after fasting for lunch and dinner, we became *ravenous*." Ask students to create a pair of related statements showing how being *ravenous* is more intense than being hungry.

Cross-Curricular Connection

HISTORY: Old English

Old English, also called Anglo-Saxon, was the language used in England until the middle of the eleventh century. There are four dialects of Old English: Mercian, Kentish Northumbrian, and West Saxon. West Saxon was the dialect used by the politically powerful in Wessex, a region located in the southern part of England, where King Alfred the Great ruled during the ninth century. The first period of significant literary activity occurred during King Alfred's reign; therefore, most Old English works are written in the West Saxon dialect.

Small-Group Activity Have students work in small groups to research the literary activities during King Alfred's reign. What was his attitude toward learning? What kinds of literary works were produced during the period? What role did he play in the history of Old English literature?

HSS Analysis Skills: HI 4

But death alone, and nothing else at all. **A**
All that has changed, and it is now as though
Our marriage and our love had never been,
And far or near forever I must suffer
The feud of my beloved husband dear.
So in this forest grove they made me dwell,
Under the oak-tree, in this earthy barrow.°
Old is this earth-cave, all I do is yearn.
The dales are dark with high hills up above,
Sharp hedge surrounds it, overgrown with briars,
And joyless is the place. Full often here
The absence of my lord comes sharply to me.
Dear lovers in this world lie in their beds,
While I alone at crack of dawn must walk
Under the oak-tree round this earthy cave,
Where I must stay the length of summer days,
Where I may weep my banishment and all
My many hardships, for I never can
Contrive to set at rest my careworn heart,
Nor all the longing that this life has brought me.
A young man always must be serious,
And tough his character; likewise he should
Seem cheerful, even though his heart is sad
With multitude of cares. All earthly joy
Must come from his own self. Since my dear lord
Is outcast, far off in a distant land,
Frozen by storms beneath a stormy cliff
And dwelling in some desolate abode
Beside the sea, my weary-hearted lord
Must suffer pitiless anxiety.
And all too often he will call to mind
A happier dwelling. Grief must always be
For him who yearning longs for his beloved. **B**

29. barrow: mound of earth.

A Literary Focus **Elegy** What specific words in lines 1–23 help you identify this poem as an elegy?

B Reading Focus **Identifying Theme** What do the last two lines reveal about the poem's theme?

Detail of Anglo-Saxon sarcophagus lid found in crypt of St. Mary's Church in Wirksworth, Derbyshire, England.

Think About/Talk About

Comprehension

B Reading Focus

Possible response: *The desperate longing of the wife connects with the poem's themes of loneliness and banishment.*

Analysis

A Literary Focus

Possible response: *distress, suffer, grief, exile, plight, wretchedness, longed.*

Extend the Discussion

Finding Sequence of Events Point out that the wife moves back and forth in time throughout the poem. At what point does the wife finish speaking of the past and begin to focus on the present? ***Possible response:*** *Starting in line 24, when she speaks of "now," she contemplates her losses in the present.*

Interpreting In lines 43–55, how does the wife try to redeem her husband's memory? ***Possible responses:*** *She tries to justify her husband's actions by reasoning that he, like any young man, has to be serious and tough to get through life. She also affirms that his cheerfulness masks his inner sadness.*

Vocabulary: Own the Word

demeanor: Ask students to describe the wife's *demeanor* as it is suggested in the poem. ***Possible responses:*** *lonely, confused, wistful*

Advanced Learners

Enrichment Invite students to think of other works of literature in which a main character is outcast or lost in a foreign culture. Then, have them write a short essay comparing that character's experience with the speaker's experience in "The Wife's Lament."

Compare and Contrast

Ask students to compare "The Wife's Lament" to "The Seafarer."

- **Similarities** Both poems are elegies. Both speakers are mourning a loss and feel lonely.
- **Differences** One speaker is a man, and the other is a woman. One is mourning the loss of a way of life, and the other is mourning the loss of a person. The sorrow of one speaker is caused by the fate given to him by God, and the sorrow of the other speaker is caused by the acts of her kinsmen.

Teacher Preparation

Selection Summary

Part of the Old English oral tradition, "The Wanderer" is a mournful elegy that ends with a twist. The speaker is a warrior who recalls a battle in which his friends, family, and lord are killed. He conveys an overwhelming sense of sadness as he recalls details of "this dark twisted life" in which "Fortune vanishes, friendship vanishes . . . And all the earth rolls into emptiness." The tone is sorrowful, and the details of battle and loss are timeless. "Wisdom is slow and comes but late," the speaker admits, but the poem ends abruptly on a hopeful and religious note. Some scholars believe the last lines were added later, since their tone is so different from the rest of the poem.

Direct Teach

Think About/Talk About

Read with a Purpose Direct students to read the Read with a Purpose statement. Remind students that authors sometimes use metaphors to describe a feeling or experience. Have students take note of details in the selection that describe the speaker's journey at sea. Point out that these details may also be metaphors for his journey through life.

Comprehension

A Reading Focus

Possible response: *The speaker describes himself as lonely and sad. His heart is full of grief because he is lost and without a home.*

Analysis

B Literary Focus

Possible response: *The speaker is lamenting the loss of his home, his people, and his lord.*

POEM

The Wanderer

translated by **Burton Raffel**

Read with a Purpose

Read to discover how the speaker uses his story of wandering in the sea as a metaphor for wandering through life.

Build Background

Early Anglo-Saxon poetry often used Christian symbolism to explain the harsh conditions of life in the earthly world. In this poem, the speaker is literally on a journey across the frigid ocean. He is symbolically on the journey through a life filled with isolation, pain, and suffering. As with all journeys, however, the speaker of "The Wanderer" looks forward to coming home—in this case, to a safe harbor and a restful afterlife.

This lonely traveler longs for grace,
For the mercy of God; grief hangs on
His heart and follows the frost-cold foam
He cuts in the sea, sailing endlessly,
Aimlessly, in exile. Fate has opened
A single port: memory. He sees
His kinsmen slaughtered again, and cries:
"I've drunk too many lonely dawns,
Gray with mourning. Once there were men
To whom my heart could hurry, hot
With open longing. They're long since dead.
My heart has closed on itself, quietly
Learning that silence is noble and sorrow
Nothing that speech can cure. Sadness
Has never driven sadness off;
Fate blows hardest on a bleeding heart. **A**
So those who thirst for glory smother
Secret weakness and longing, neither
Weep nor sigh nor listen to the sickness
In their souls. So I, lost and homeless,
Forced to flee the darkness that fell
On the earth and my lord. **B**
Leaving everything,
Weary with winter I wandered out
On the frozen waves, hoping to find

A **Reading Focus** **Identifying Theme** How does the speaker describe himself?

B **Literary Focus** **Elegy** What is the speaker lamenting?

Universal Access

English Learners

English for Academic Success Before students read the selection, remind them that words formed by a verb and the suffix *–er* refer to people who perform an action. Explain that wanderer means "one who wanders." For the same reason, the word *traveler* used in line 1 means "one who travels." Tell students that the title of the poem relates to the theme in that the wanderer is wandering because he is searching for something. Ask students to read the poem to discover what the wanderer is searching to find. *[peace, God's grace, joy]*

Struggling Readers

Guide students in understanding the symbolism in the poem to facilitate their understanding of key details. Have students create a two-column chart. In the first column, have students work with an advanced learner in pairs to discuss and record lines from the selection that describe elements of the speaker's physical journey. In the second column, have them record lines that symbolize the speaker's journey through life. Have pairs share their responses with the class.

Think About/Talk About

Extend the Discussion

Drawing Conclusions In lines 8–22, the speaker describes how he is alone on his journey. What probably happened to all his friends? ***Possible responses:*** *They are gone; they are long since dead.*

Interpreting In line 16, what does the speaker mean by saying, "Fate blows hardest on a bleeding heart?" How does this idea affect his journey? ***Possible responses:*** *Life is harder on those who show sadness. The speaker must keep his feelings to himself and smother his secret weakness and longing.*

Advanced Learners

Acceleration Remind students that elegies were sometimes used to help the writer heal through self-expression. Ask students to take the point of view of the protagonist from "The Seafarer," "The Wife's Lament," or "The Wanderer" and write a journal entry describing his or her situation. Ask students to use current language in their writing and refer to details from the poem.

Students with Disabilities

Students might have trouble following the long sentences that make up this poem. Divide students in pairs and have them read five to ten lines at a time. Have them paraphrase the lines. Ask them to summarize in one sentence what happens in each part of the poem and write the sentence in their **Reader/Writer Notebooks**. Tell students to use the sentences to create a summary of the entire poem.

Model the Skill

- Tell students that **elegies** are mostly meditative. That means they present the speaker's philosophical views and provide thorough insight into the speaker's emotional state.
- Read lines 24–32 aloud. Explain that in these lines, the speaker describes himself as a lonely character who is fated to experience eternal exile. Point out that he is constantly remembering his past, which is dominated by loss and grief. The idea of an existence spent longing for what is lost forever is in accord with the usual themes of elegiac poems.

Guided Practice: Apply

Turn-and-Talk As students read the poem, ask them to take notes about the wanderer's view of life and death and about his emotional state. Then, have students discuss in pairs how the thoughts and emotions they have recorded reflect the hopelessness and sadness that are characteristic of elegies.

Think About/Talk About

Extend the Discussion

Drawing Conclusions In lines 34–49, how does the speaker remember his lord? ***Possible response:*** *The speaker has tender memories of his lord: he remembers feasts and his lord's aid.*

Recognizing Rhetorical Devices In lines 54–55, the speaker states, "How loathsome become the frozen waves to a weary heart." What do you think the waves are a metaphor for? ***Possible response:*** *Waves may be a metaphor for the pain, hardship, and misfortune in the world, conditions of human existence that renew themselves every day.*

A place, a people, a lord to replace
My lost ones. No one knew me, now,
No one offered comfort, allowed
Me feasting or joy. How cruel a journey
I've traveled, sharing my bread with sorrow
Alone, an exile in every land,
Could only be told by telling° my footsteps.
For who can hear: "friendless and poor,"
And know what I've known since the long cheerful nights
When, young and yearning, with my lord I yet feasted
Most welcome of all. That warmth is dead.
He only knows who needs his lord
As I do, eager for long-missing aid;
He only knows who never sleeps
Without the deepest dreams of longing.
Sometimes it seems I see my lord,
Kiss and embrace him, bend my hands
And head to his knee, kneeling as though
He still sat enthroned, ruling his thanes.°
And I open my eyes, embracing the air,
And see the brown sea-billows heave,
See the sea birds bathe, spreading
Their white-feathered wings, watch the frost
And the hail and the snow. And heavy in heart
I long for my lord, alone and unloved.
Sometimes it seems I see my kin
And greet them gladly, give them welcome,
The best of friends. They fade away,
Swimming soundlessly out of sight,
Leaving nothing. **C**
How loathsome become
The frozen waves to a weary heart.
In this brief world I cannot wonder
That my mind is set on melancholy,
Because I never forget the fate
Of men, robbed of their riches, suddenly
Looted by death—the doom of earth,
Sent to us all by every rising
Sun. Wisdom is slow, and comes
But late. He who has it is patient;
He cannot be hasty to hate or speak,
He must be bold and yet not blind,
Nor ever too craven,° complacent, or covetous,

32. telling: here, "counting."

44. thanes (thaynz): people who, in exchange for their military service, held land of a king or lord.

68. craven (KRAY vuhn): cowardly or weak.

C **Literary Focus** **Elegy** What images help create a sad, elegiac mood in lines 29–55?

Word-Attack Skills Mini-Lesson

English for Academic Success Call students' attention to the different pronunciations of the letters *th* as exemplified by the words *the* and *theory*. Explain that the two different sounds are defined as "voiced" (*the*) or "voiceless" (*theory*) based on whether they allow an emission of voice. Have students pronounce the two words and, at the same time, touch their throat to see which word allows their voice to emerge. Then, ask students to find all the words on pp. 70–71 that contain the letters *th* (*the, them, there, warmth, enthroned, thanes, bathe, white-feathered, loathsome, wealth*). Ask students to draw a two-column chart with the columns labeled "Voiced" and "Voiceless." Help students place each word in the correct column. [Voiced: *the, them, there, bathe, white-feathered;* Voiceless: *warmth, enthroned, thanes, loathsome, wealth*]

Analyzing Visuals

Connecting to the Text What images can you find in "The Wanderer" that correspond to details in this photograph? How do these images and details contribute to the mood of the work?

Nor ready to gloat before he wins glory.
The man's a fool who flings his boasts
Hotly to the heavens, heeding his spleen°
And not the better boldness of knowledge.
What knowing man knows not the ghostly,
Wastelike end of worldly wealth:
See, already the wreckage is there,
The windswept walls stand far and wide,
The storm-beaten blocks besmeared with frost,
The mead-halls° crumbled, the monarchs thrown down
And stripped of their pleasures. The proudest of warriors
Now lie by the wall: some of them war

Vocabulary **gloat** (gloht) *v.:* feel or express great, often malicious, self-satisfaction or pleasure.

71. spleen: archaic use meaning "whim."

78. mead-halls: Mead is an alcoholic drink made from honey and water; a mead-hall was a gathering place, usually in the home of a king or a lord.

Think About/Talk About

Analysis

Ⓒ Literary Focus

Possible response: *The images of frozen waves, white-feathered birds, frost, and snow create a sad mood.*

Extend the Discussion

Finding Details How does the speaker describe the "wastelike ending of worldly wealth"? ***Possible response:*** *He envisions crumbled cities and monarchs stripped of their reign and pleasures. He sees nothing but desolate walls and wounded warriors.*

Making Judgments How do you think the speaker feels at the end of the poem? Is he still lamenting? ***Possible response:*** *He feels that everything ultimately turns to waste; cities will crumble, monarchies will end, and warriors will eventually die.*

Vocabulary: Own the Word

gloat: Demonstrate a person's facial expression when *gloating* over something. Ask one or two students to also demonstrate a *gloating* expression.

Cross-Curricular Connection

HISTORY: Kinship and Exile

A fundamental value of Anglo-Saxon society was kinship. Kinship refers to the relationship individuals had with members of their families and with their leaders. Kinship was also fundamental to Anglo-Saxon law, and those whose families were attacked could expect legal reparation. Given the importance of kinship, exile was considered one of the worst punishments that could be inflicted on a member of the Anglo-Saxon society. The sense of hopelessness of exile is evident in the elegies of *The Exeter Book* and in other works of the same period, such as *Beowulf.*

Analyzing Visuals

Connecting to the Text: *The photograph shows an icy and deserted shore. The water reminds the reader of the "frozen waves" (line 25) sailed by the wanderer. The barren landscape can also represent the "ghostly, wastelike end of worldly wealth" in which all human struggle is forgotten. The images and details suggest a physically and emotionally cold atmosphere.*

Think About/Talk About

Comprehension

D Reading Focus

Possible response: *Earthly pleasures like fortune, friendship, and love are doomed to extinction. All human concerns and joys are destined to pass and throw the earth "into emptiness."*

Extend the Discussion

Drawing Conclusions What is the speaker's view of pleasures and glory of life (line 108)? ***Possible response:*** *The speaker says that the pleasures of life will be humbled by the passing of time.*

Interpreting What do the questions in lines 90–98 tell about the speaker's view of the fate of mankind? ***Possible response:*** *The speaker seems to believe that the great struggles and glories of the past have no meaning in the face of death. Everything is bound to decay and to be forgotten.*

Destroyed; some the monstrous sea bird
Bore over the ocean; to some the old wolf
Dealt out death; and for some dejected
Followers fashioned an earth-cave coffin.
Thus the Maker of men lays waste
This earth, crushing our callow mirth,°
And the work of old giants stands withered and still.

He who these ruins rightly sees,
And deeply considers this dark twisted life,
Who sagely remembers the endless slaughters
Of a bloody past, is bound to proclaim,
"Where is the war steed? Where
is the warrior? Where is his warlord?
Where now the feasting-places?
Where now the mead-hall pleasures?
Alas, bright cup! Alas, brave knight!
Alas, you glorious princes! All gone,
Lost in the night, as you never had lived,
And all that survives you a serpentine wall,
Wondrously high, worked in strange ways.
Mighty spears have slain these men,
Greedy weapons have framed their fate.
These rocky slopes are beaten by storms,
This earth pinned down by driving snow,
By the horror of winter, smothering warmth
In the shadows of night. And the north angrily
Hurls its hailstorms at our helpless heads.
Everything earthly is evilly born,
Firmly clutched by a fickle Fate.
Fortune vanishes, friendship vanishes,
Man is fleeting, woman is fleeting,
And all this earth rolls into emptiness." **D**

So says the sage in his heart,
sitting alone with his thought.
It's good to guard your faith,
nor let your grief come forth
Until it cannot call
for help, nor help but heed
The path you've placed before it.
It's good to find your grace
In God, the heavenly rock
where rests our every hope.

86. callow mirth (KAL oh murth): immature laughter.

D Reading Focus Identifying Theme What do the descriptions of earthly pleasures and concerns reveal about the poem's theme?

California Standards, p. 73

- **Reading Standard 3.1** Analyze characteristics of subgenres (e.g., satire, parody, allegory, pastoral) that are used in poetry, prose, plays, novels, short stories, essays, and other basic genres.
- **Reading Standard 3.2** Analyze the way in which the theme or meaning of a selection represents a view or comment on life, using textual evidence to support the claim.
- **Reading Standard 3.3** Analyze the ways in which irony, tone, mood, the author's style, and the "sound" of language achieve specific rhetorical or aesthetic purposes or both.
- **Writing Standard 2.2** Write responses to literature: **d.** Demonstrate an understanding of the author's use of stylistic devices and an appreciation of the effects created.

Applying Your Skills

Reading Standard 3.1, 3.2, 3.3 (see pages A48–A50)
Writing Standard: 2.2d (see pages A51–A52)

The Seafarer / The Wife's Lament / The Wanderer

Literary Response and Analysis

Reading Skills Focus

Read with a Purpose

1. In what ways do the three poems reflect upon life as well as loss?

Reading Skills: Identifying Theme

2. Look back at the charts you made to record key details from the poems. Write the theme of each poem in the middle circle. How are these themes relevant to people's concerns today?

Vocabulary Check

Match each Vocabulary word with its definition.

3. demeanor — a. very hungry
4. desolation — b. miserable
5. gloat — c. the way in which a person behaves
6. ravenous — d. loneliness
7. wretched — e. feel malicious self-satisfaction

Literary Skills Focus

Literary Analysis

8. **Analyze** "The Seafarer" in lines 64–66 connects seafaring with religion. What is the speaker's attitude toward life on earth?

9. **Extend** In line 88 of "The Seafarer," the speaker says, "All glory is tarnished." Does this idea apply to today's heroes and to present-day life? Explain.

10. **Evaluate** Describe the place where the speaker in "The Wife's Lament" is forced to live. What words and images emphasize its desolation?

11. **Analyze** What images of winter does the speaker in "The Wanderer" use? How do these images contribute to the poem's mood?

12. **Compare and Contrast** Compare and contrast the experiences of the three speakers.

Literary Skills: Elegy

13. **Analyze** How do the contrasting descriptions of past and present contribute to the elegiac quality of each of these three poems?

Literary Skills Review: Tone

14. **Analyze** The attitude a writer takes toward the reader, a subject, or a character is **tone.** Writers convey tone through word choice and details. Describe the tone of each poem. Support your analysis with examples from the texts.

Writing Skills Focus

Think as a Reader/Writer

Use It in Your Writing Review your QuickWrite about what you would lament if you were writing an elegy. Using one of the poems as a model, create a speaker and write an elegy filled with mournful images that laments the loss of something important.

What Do You Think Now? Can an everyday person be a hero? Explain.

Universal Access

Struggling Writers

To provide additional scaffolding for students to complete the Writing Skills Focus activity, write the following sentence starters on the board for students to incorporate in their poems:

I long for my . . .
How loathsome is/are . . .
Where is the . . . ? Where now the . . . ?
Alas, . . . ! Alas, . . . !
So say the wise in their heart, . . .

Remind students to write in the first-person point of view.

What Do You Think Now?

Have students refer back to the cause of each speaker's sadness. Ask students if they think confronting one's sadness is a heroic act. Ask them to support their responses with examples from the text or their own lives.

Check for Understanding

Independent Practice

Reading Skills Focus

Possible responses:

1. *The speakers compare their own personal losses to the mortality of all living things.*
2. *Have students tie in their key words and phrases to a main idea for each poem.*

Vocabulary Check

3. *c* 4. *d*
5. *e* 6. *a*
7. *b*

Literary Skills Focus

Possible responses:

8. *Life on earth is short, but life with God is joyous and eternal.*
9. *Yes, even today's heroes and present-day life are doomed to be forgotten.*
10. *She lives in an "earth-cave" in a dark forest. The words* old, dark, sharp, overgrown with briars, *and* joyless *emphasize the desolation of the place.*
11. *The images of frozen waves, frost, snow, white-feathered wings, and hailstorms contribute to the desolate mood.*
12. *Each speaker experiences loss and isolation. In "The Wife's Lament," the speaker mourns the loss of her husband, while the other speakers mourn the loss of the past.*
13. *The grief for the loss of past joys and glories gives the poem a sad, melancholy mood.*
14. *All poems have a sad, elegiac tone. "The Seafarer" mourns the passing of ancient glory with words such as* dead *and* vanished. *"The Wife's Lament" displays a desperate tone in describing her sense of abandonment. In "The Wanderer," the feeling of hopelessness is brought to new heights.*

Preteach

English for Academic Success

Language Coach

Ask students to comment on the meanings of other words beginning with the prefix *ex–*, such as *exclude, exhale*, and *external*. Point out how these words can be transformed into their antonyms by replacing *ex–* with *in–*. Then, have students answer the **Language Coach** question. [Abundance *means "a very large quantity of something." If you have an* abundance *of something, you have so much that it is "overflowing."*]

Literary Skills Focus

As you read and discuss the selection with students, have them note examples of personification in the selections.

Reading Skills Focus

Give students a copy of the Reading Skills Focus graphic organizer before they read. (See **Unit 1 Resources.**) Tell them to use their responses to answer the questions on the Applying Your Skills page.

Writing Skills Focus

Have students record helpful as well as misleading clues in their **Reader/Writer Notebooks.** Students can use their notes to complete the Writing Skills Focus activity.

Learn It Online

The online version of this selection includes audio support to engage all students and to help struggling readers with reading comprehension and vocabulary.

go.hrw.com H12-74 Go

Preparing to Read

Reading Standard 2.2, 3.1 (see pages A48–A50)

Anglo-Saxon Riddles

Literary Skills Focus

Riddles A **riddle** is a puzzling question posed as a problem to be solved. The following Anglo-Saxon riddles **personify,** or give human qualities to, the common things being described, and the descriptions include other figurative language such as metaphors and similes. Often, the personified object assumes the first-person point of view and describes itself.

Reading Skills Focus

Using Context Clues A piece of writing consists of related details. These details, or **clues,** combine to form the **context** of the selection. When taken out of context, some details may lead in the wrong direction or no longer make sense. By considering the details as a whole, you can decipher the author's meaning. When you solve riddles, it is especially important to consider how each clue relates to other clues.

Into Action As you read each riddle, list clues in a context-clue chart like the one below. When you finish reading, use your chart to solve the riddle.

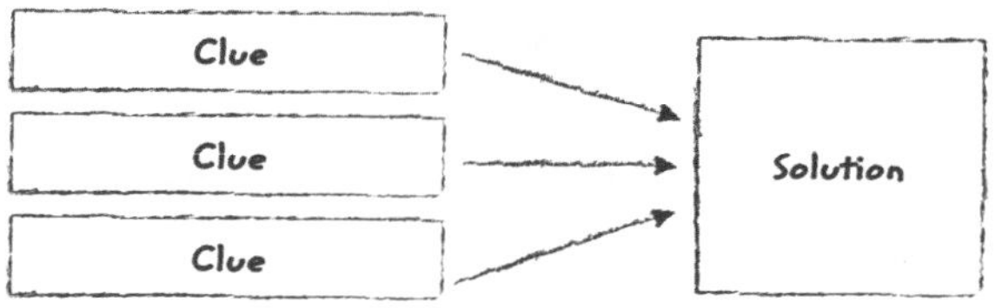

Writing Skills Focus

Think as a Reader/Writer

Find It In Your Reading A **riddle** is a series of clues that both confuse and inform the reader. As you read, pay attention to how some clues might lead you in the wrong direction. In your *Reader/Writer Notebook,* note words and phrases that lead you in the right direction and others that distract you.

Language Coach

Etymology Knowing some word origins can help you figure out unfamiliar words. The Latin prefix *ex–* means "away from." In Riddle 1, the speaker says something "drives me into exile." You can use the meaning of the prefix *ex–* to help you understand the word *exile,* which means "being forced to live away from your own home." The word *abundance* in Riddle 32 comes from the Latin word for "overflowing." How does that meaning help you understand *abundance*?

Reader/Writer Notebook

Use your **RWN** to complete the activities for these selections.

Learn It Online

Listen for clues in the audio readings of these riddles online.

go.hrw.com H12-74 Go

Selection Resources

Unit 1 Resources, on-level practice and assessment, p. 15

Teacher One Stop™, on-level lesson plans and all print resources

Holt Audio Library

Holt Audio Library: Selection and Summaries in Spanish

UA: Supporting Instruction in Spanish, selection summary

ThinkCentral Online Assessment, Selection Standards Check

California Standards, pp. 74–79

- **Reading Standard 2.2** Analyze the way in which clarity of meaning is affected by the patterns of organization, hierarchical structures, repetition of the main ideas, syntax, and word choice in the text.
- **Reading Standard 3.1** Analyze characteristics of subgenres (e.g., satire, parody, allegory, pastoral) that are used in poetry, prose, novels, short stories, essays, and other basic genres.

VERSE RIDDLES

Anglo-Saxon Riddles

translated by **Burton Raffel**

Read with a Purpose
As you read the next three poems, try to discover the everyday objects or occurrences that are being described.

Build Background
The word *riddle* comes from an Old English word meaning "opinion" or "advice." Riddles exist in many ancient languages, including Sanskrit, Hebrew, Arabic, Persian, Greek, and Latin, as well as Old English. The Anglo-Saxon riddles that follow have been preserved in *The Exeter Book* and are believed to be the oldest riddles in the English language.

Riddle 1

How many men are so knowing, so wise,
That their tongues can tell Who drives me into exile,
Swells me brave and strong and fierce,
Sends me roaring across the earth,
Wild and cruel, burning men's homes,
Wrecking their palaces? Smoke leaps up,
Gray like a wolf, and all the world
Crackles with the sounds of pain and death.
When I shake forests, uproot peaceful
Groves, clouds cover me; exalted
Powers hurl me far and wide.
What once protected the world, sheltered
Men, I bear on my back, bodies
And souls whirled in the mist. Where
Am I swallowed down, and what is my name? **A**

Rough Sea with Wreckage (c. 1840) by J.M.W. Turner (1775-1851). Oil on canvas.
Clore Collection, Tate Gallery, London.

A **Literary Focus** **Riddles** What images are conveyed by lines 3 and 4 and by lines 9 and 10?

Universal Access

EL English Learners

English for Academic Success Remind students that this Anglo-Saxon riddle is written in the first-person point of view, using personal pronouns such as *I* and *my*. In pairs, have one student read the poem aloud and substitute the first-person pronouns with second-person pronouns. Then, have the partner read the poem aloud, substituting the first-person pronouns with third-person pronouns. Ask students why most riddles assume the first-person point of view.

Struggling Readers

Assist students in using context clues to solve the riddle. Remind students to consider all the details together in order to solve the riddle. Have students read the riddle to themselves silently several times, then ask them to complete the blanks to help them decipher the meaning of the riddle: What can be driven into exile, expands in ______ and ______, burns and wrecks structures, causes smoke to ______, shakes ______, is covered by ______, is hurled "far and wide," whirls ______, and is never consumed?

Teacher Preparation

Selection Summaries

These three riddles, translated from Old English by Burton Raffel, are from *The Exeter Book,* the largest existing collection of Anglo Saxon poetry. Among its 131 pages are about 90 playful riddles of various lengths. Their solutions include swords, onions, ink, and bookworms. Riddle 1 is full of imagery of smoke, fire, shaking and uprooting; its solution is wind. The solution of Riddle 12 calls men to battlefields and drinking halls: a horn. Riddle 30 describes a useful yet armless creature whose belly delivers abundance: a sailing ship.

Direct Teach

Think About/Talk About

Read with a Purpose Have students read the Read with a Purpose statement. Remind them that Anglo-Saxon riddles often describe everyday objects to which the reader can easily relate. This makes it easier for the reader to find the solution of the riddle.

Analysis

A Literary Focus

Possible response: *The images describe the actions of a natural force. In line 3–4 this force is destructive, but in lines 9–10, it is mild.*

Extend the Discussion

Paraphrasing Restate lines 12–13 in your own words. ***Possible response:*** *That which used to protect men and the world is now in my hands.*

Point of View Which point of view is used in this riddle? What is the effect? ***Possible responses:*** *The riddle is written from the first-person point of view. This gives the object human qualities, which makes the riddle more entertaining.*

Model the Skill

- Provide students with copies of the Reading Skills Focus graphic organizer for "Anglo-Saxon Riddles." (See **Unit 1 Resources.**)
- Explain that the main characteristic of riddles is the presence of both helpful and misleading clues. All clues are logically connected to the object, but certain clues present unusual connections that lead the reader astray.
- Model adding an inference to the graphic organizer. Invite students to consider lines 13–19 and the many hints that the mysterious object has produced a sound. In line 17, the object reveals that it has a voice, and in the lines that follow, it mentions singing in the night.

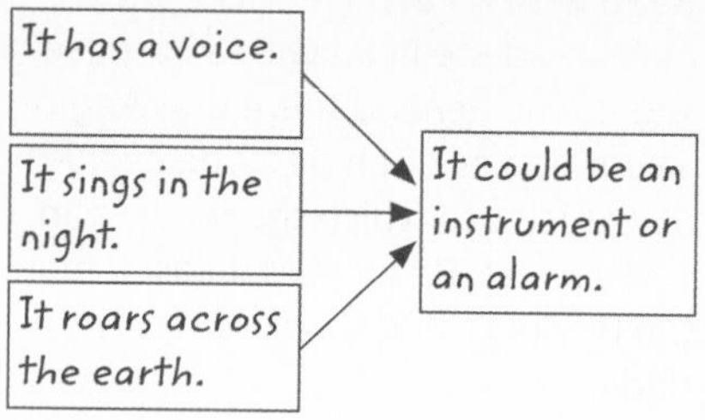

Guided Practice: Apply

Have students add more clues to the graphic organizer and make their own inferences about the identity of the object.

Think as a Reader/Writer

Find It in Your Reading Point out that many details in the riddle refer to physical qualities of the object ("warrior's weapon," "headless"), whereas others make references to the effect the object has on people's lives ("I've been filled to the depth of my heart by girls with glittering bracelets"). Explain that these contrasting clues help prevent the reader from arriving at the solution too easily.

Use It in Your Writing Ask students to write two clues to describe a school bell. Have students provide a helpful clue and an obscure one.

Universal Access

Struggling Readers

Model using context clues to decipher the author's meaning. You might say: "Line 1 tells me that the object can be used as a weapon, so I will note this in my graphic organizer. Lines 2–3 say it can be decorated, and lines 4–5 reveal that it makes a sound calling men to war. Lines 5–7 continue the association of this object to war, while lines 8–9 reveal that this object is also used by girls perhaps for a festive occasion. All the clues so far hint that the object is some kind of instrument used in war. I will keep reading for confirmation."

Advanced Learners

Enrichment Explain that a good riddle is both challenging to solve and enjoyable to read. Have students look around the classroom and choose an object to write a riddle about. Have students use at least three literary devices, such as personification, similes, and metaphors, to make their riddles entertaining. Have students read their work to the class and ask their classmates to try to solve the riddles.

Riddle 14

I was a warrior's weapon, once.
Now striplings° have woven silver wires,
And gold, around me. Men have kissed me,
And I've called a field of laughing comrades
To war and death. I've crossed borders
On galloping steeds, and crossed the shining
Water, riding a ship. I've been filled
To the depth of my heart by girls with glittering
Bracelets, and I've lain along the bare
Cold planks, headless, plucked and worn. **B**
They've hung me high on a wall, bright
With jewels and beautiful, and left me to watch
Their warriors drinking. Mounted troops
Have carried me out and opened my breast
To the swelling wind of some soldier's lips.
My voice has invited princes to feasts
Of wine, and has sung in the night to save
What savage thieves have stolen, driving them
Off into darkness. Ask my name.

2. striplings: young men.

B Reading Focus **Using Context Clues** What objects might be used both by soldiers in battle and by young girls?

(Opposite) The Devonshire hunting tapestries. Detail of boar and bear hunt with man with horn (1424–1450). Inv.: T204–1957. Victoria & Albert Museum, London.

Analyzing Visuals

Connecting to the Text What image in this fifteenth-century tapestry fits the clues in the riddle?

Think About/Talk About

Comprehension

B Reading Focus

Possible response: *metal objects, musical instruments*

Extend the Discussion

Drawing Conclusions Which lines help make clear that the poem describes a musical instrument? ***Possible responses:*** *Lines 4–5 describe how the poem's speaker "called a field of laughing comrades to war and death." In lines 16–17, the speaker asserts, "My voice has invited princes to feasts of wine, and has sung in the night."*

Interpreting What is the speaker's attitude toward the adventures described in the poem? ***Possible response:*** *The speaker seems to take pleasure in recounting past voyages, scenes of battle, and celebrations.*

Students with Disabilities

Students may gain a better understanding of the imagery in the riddles after they are provided with the solution. After discussing the possible solutions with the class, ask students to go back to the riddles and find all the clues that point to the solution. Ask them to write three sentences about each riddle [*The solution of Riddle 14 could be a horn because it is used on ships and produces a sound.*]

Analyzing Visuals

Connecting to the Text: *The man at the center of the tapestry is holding a horn. The horn could fit the clues in the riddle, because a horn is used in war ("warrior's weapon"), is brought to the lips and blown into ("opened my breast to the swelling wind of some soldier's lips"), and is used to ward off robbers ("has sung in the night to save what savage thieves have stolen").*

Think About/Talk About

Comprehension

Ⓒ Reading Focus

Possible response: *The object may be a ship, because it sails the sea and resembles a foot.*

Extend the Discussion

Drawing Conclusions In Riddle 32, which details best support the idea that the object described is a human invention? ***Possible responses****: In lines 3–4, the object is described as "made for motion."*

Figurative Language What kind of figurative speech is predominant in Riddle 32? ***Possible responses:*** *The riddle contains many examples of personification. In line 3, it is evident that the riddle is about an inanimate object ("ingenious thing"), but the riddle attributes human qualities and characteristics to it. The object has a foot, ribs, a mouth, and a belly.*

Riddle 32

Our world is lovely in different ways,
Hung with beauty and works of hands.
I saw an ingenious thing, made
For motion, slide against the sand,
Shrieking as it went. It walked swiftly
On its only foot, this odd-shaped monster,
Traveled in an open country without
Seeing, without arms, or hands,
With many ribs, and its mouth in its middle.
Its work is useful, and welcome, for it loads
Its belly with food, and brings abundance
To men, to poor and to rich, paying
Its tribute year after year. Solve
This riddle, if you can, and unravel its name. Ⓒ

Ⓒ **Reading Focus** **Using Context Clues** What objects can you think of that are "made for motion" and have an odd shape that resembles a single "foot"?

California Standards, p. 79

- **Reading Standard 2.2** Analyze the way in which clarity of meaning is affected by the patterns of organization, hierarchical structures, repetition of the main ideas, syntax, and word choice in the text.
- **Reading Standard 3.1** Analyze characteristics of subgenres (e.g., satire, parody, allegory, pastoral) that are used in poetry, prose, plays, novels, short stories, essays, and other basic genres.
- **Reading Standard 3.3** Analyze the ways in which irony, tone, mood, the author's style, and the "sound" of language achieve specific rhetorical or aesthetic purposes or both.
- **Writing Standard 2.2** Write responses to literature: **d.** Demonstrate an understanding of the author's use of stylistic devices and an appreciation of the effects created.

Applying Your Skills

Reading Standard 2.2, 3.1, 3.3 (see pages A48–A50)
Writing Standard 2.2d (see pages A51–A52)

Anglo-Saxon Riddles

Literary Response and Analysis

Reading Skills Focus

Quick Check

1. Name some activities in which the speaker in Riddle 1 has participated.
2. How does the speaker of Riddle 14 describe himself?
3. How does the speaker of Riddle 32 describe the world?

Read with a Purpose

4. Why might someone bother to write a riddle about an everyday object or occurrence?

Reading Skills: Using Context Clues

5. As you read, you used charts to list clues. Now, review the clues for each riddle. What do you conclude is the solution for each riddle?

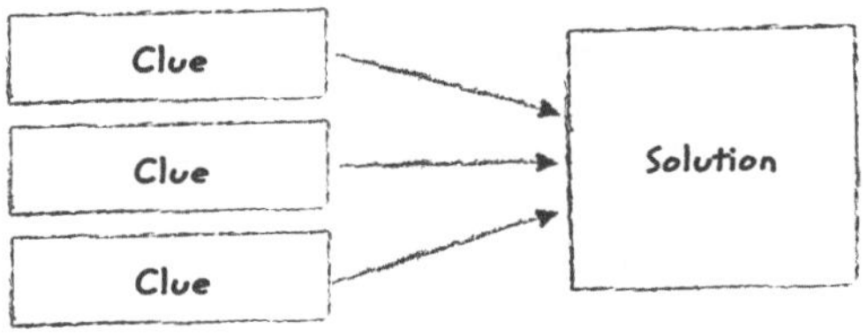

Literary Skills Focus

Literary Analysis

6. **Analyze** How does personification add to the overall effect of the Anglo-Saxon riddles?
7. **Analyze** Find examples of vivid verbs and verb forms in the riddles. What effect do they have?
8. **Hypothesize** Why do you think myths of classical antiquity contain riddles for heroes to solve?
9. **Extend** J.R.R. Tolkien, who wrote *The Lord of the Rings,* included this riddle in *The Hobbit:*

   This thing all things devours:
   Birds, beasts, trees, flowers;
   Gnaws iron, bites steel;
   Grinds hard stones to meal;
   Slays king, ruins town,
   And beats high mountain down.

   What is the solution?

Literary Skills: Riddle

10. **Analyze** In your *Reader/Writer Notebook,* you noted how the riddles confuse and mislead the reader. Select one of the Anglo-Saxon riddles, and explain how the author misleads the reader. Provide examples from the text.

Literary Skills Review: Alliteration

11. **Analyze** Authors use alliteration to create a musical quality and to unify and emphasize features in their writing. **Alliteration** is the repetition of similar consonant sounds that are near each other. "Sally sells seashells" is an example of alliteration because the *s* sound is repeated. What examples can you find of alliteration in the Anglo-Saxon riddles, and what are their effects?

Writing Skills Focus

Think as a Reader/Writer

Use It in Your Writing Using the riddles as a model, write your own riddle with clues leading to the solution as well as distractions leading away from it.

What Do You Think Now People have been enjoying riddles for thousands of years. What do you think explains their continuing popularity?

Universal Access

Struggling Writers

To complete the Writing Skills Focus, provide additional scaffolding for students by having them brainstorm names and words that are associated with the object they are writing about. Then, ask them to write sentences using those words. Remind them that they should not mention the object, but should use a pronoun instead.

What Do You Think Now?

Before they respond to the question, ask students to consider why people enjoy solving puzzles.

Assess

Unit 1 Resources,
Selection Standards Check, p. 18

ThinkCentral Online Assessment,
Selection Standards Check

Check for Understanding

Independent Practice

Reading Skills Focus

Possible responses:

1. *The speaker has participated in burning people's homes, shaking forests, and uprooting peaceful groves.*
2. *He describes himself as a useful object on ships as well as an ornament.*
3. *The world is lovely for its variety of natural beauties and inventive objects.*
4. *The goal might be to entertain the reader with unusual descriptions of familiar objects.*
5. *Tell students to review the context clues they have written and to underline the most important ones.*

Literary Skills Focus

Possible responses:

6. *The descriptions become easier for the reader to relate to.*
7. *Vivid verbs include "swells me brave," "wrecking their palaces," "souls whirled in the mist" in Riddle 1; "woven silver wires," "opened my breast," in Riddle 14; and "shrieking," "walked swiftly," and "loads its belly" in Riddle 32. These vivid details help entertain, but also mislead, the reader.*
8. *They are entertaining for both the reader and the writer.*
9. *Responses will vary. Students might eventually suggest "time" because time slowly brings everything to an end.*
10. *Riddle 32 describes the object as a living creature, but in fact, it is an inanimate object.*
11. *The following lines include alliteration: Line 3 of Riddle 1 ("Swells me brave and strong and fierce"); line 15 of Riddle 14 ("The swelling wind of some soldier's lips"); and lines 4–5 of Riddle 32 ("slides against the sand, shrieking").*

Standards Focus

Objectives

Students will

- evaluate the philosophical, political, religious, and social influences of a historical period
- relate works to historical context

Selection Introduction

Think About the Writer

Before students answer the question, have them think about how Bede's work was received among his contemporaries.

For Independent Reading

- *The Inferno,* Dante
- *Body and Soul*, Frank Conroy

Motivate

What Do You Think?/QuickWrite

Use the QuickWrite to discuss with students simple acts of kindness as well as extraordinary acts of charity and self-sacrifice.

English for Academic Success

Academic Vocabulary

Look for opportunities to use the Academic Vocabulary words in this unit.

- **diverse,** ***adj.:*** varied
- **emphasis,** ***n.:*** stress; importance
- **status,** ***n.:*** social or professional rank

California Standards, pp. 80–86

- **Reading Standard 3.7** Relate literary works and authors to the major themes and issues of their eras. **b.** Analyze recognized works of world literature from a variety of authors. **c.** Evaluate the philosophical, political, religious, ethical, and social influences of the historical period that shaped the characters, plots and settings.

Preparing to Read

from A History of the English Church and People

What Do You Think? What moves a hero to act?

QuickWrite

How can an ordinary person have a positive impact on the lives of others? In your *Reader/Writer Notebook,* write a paragraph explaining your thoughts.

The Fuller Brooch, Anglo-Saxon (late 9th century).
The British Museum, London.

MEET THE WRITER

Bede

(c. 673–735)

Bede was the earliest English historian and the first significant prose writer.

The Simple Life

Bede, a monk, was known in his own day as a person of great scholarship and learning. His diverse writings include grammatical handbooks, biographies, commentaries on books of the Bible, homilies, and verse.

The title "Venerable" was added to his name in recognition of his status and reputation for wisdom, humility, and scholarship. He seems to have traveled little and spent most of his life, beginning at the age of seven, at the monastery of Jarrow.

Our knowledge of Bede's life comes mainly from his scriptural commentaries that were found in many monastic libraries throughout western Europe. He began using B.C. and A.D. to describe dates—a method of dating that has now been used for centuries.

Early Classics

Bede completed works in three main categories: scientific, spiritual, and historical. He worked on everything from chronologies to hymns. Bede's *A History of the English Church and People,* originally written in Latin, was translated into Old English during the reign of King Alfred the Great. It quickly became a classic that helped the people of the emerging English nation take pride in their past. The *History* itself is more than a chronicle of events. It also contains legends, lives of saints, local traditions, and stories. From Bede's history we can see a fairly accurate picture of Anglo-Saxon daily life.

A selection from the *History,* "Caedmon of Whitby" tells of a miracle in the life of the first known English religious poet. Much like the scops, or professional poets of the time who celebrated the heroic deeds of their royal patrons, Caedmon celebrates the glorious works of God.

Think About the Writer If Bede were alive today, what kinds of people might he write about? Explain.

Selection Readability	
Easily Accessible Accessible **Challenging**	historical context; complex poetry quote; unfamiliar vocabulary

Reading Standard 3.7b, 3.7c (see pages A48–A50)

Literary Skills Focus

Setting The **setting** is the time and place in which a work of fiction or nonfiction takes place. It can also reflect a culture's beliefs and expectations for behavior. Bede establishes the importance of religion in people's lives to emphasize how Caedmon's verses inspired awe.

Reading Skills Focus

Understanding Historical Context To better understand some nonfiction, you should consider the **historical context** in which it was written. Historical context refers to the issues, living conditions, and values of a period in history. In a different historical context, Caedmon's ability might have been viewed as either suspect or unimportant.

Into Action While reading the selection, find evidence in the text that describes life in late seventh-century Anglo-Saxon society. As you read, take notes in a chart like the one below to record details that relate to Bede's historical context.

Issues	Living Conditions	Values	Other Facts
		religious devotion	

Writing Skills Focus

Think as a Reader/Writer

Find It in Your Reading Authors of nonfiction use facts, statistics, examples, and anecdotes to support the points they are making. In this excerpt, Bede uses an **anecdote,** or little story, to support the point he makes in the first paragraph—that Caedmon receives his gift from God. As you read, pay attention to how the anecdote contains the elements of a story in a very compressed form.

Vocabulary

singularly (SIHNG gyuh luhr lee) *adv.:* extraordinarily; unusually. *Bede's historical record is a singularly good one.*

frivolous (FRIHV uh luhs) *adj.:* silly or unimportant. *His serious nature prevented him from singing anything frivolous.*

profane (proh FAYN) *adj.:* irreverent; not associated with religious matters. *As a religious person, the young man would not write anything that was profane.*

secular (SEHK yuh luhr) *adj.:* not belonging to a religious order; worldly. *Before joining the monastery, Caedmon lived a secular life.*

doctrine (DAHK truhn) *n.:* teachings of the church. *Church doctrine is sometimes communicated with song.*

Language Coach

Antonyms A secular view focuses on issues in the world; a religious view focuses on spiritual issues. *Secular* and *religious* are antonyms—they have opposite meanings. What other Vocabulary word is also an antonym for *religious?* Does this word have exactly the same meaning as *secular?* Explain.

Learn It Online
Get to know the Vocabulary words inside and out online.

go.hrw.com H12-81 Go

Reader/Writer Notebook
Use your **RWN** to complete the activities for this selection.

Selection Resources

Unit 1 Resources, on-level practice and assessment, p. 27

Teacher One Stop™, on-level lesson plans and all print resources

Holt Audio Library

Holt Audio Library: Selections and Summaries in Spanish

UA: Differentiating Instruction: graphic organizer, p. 10

UA: Supporting Instruction in Spanish, selection summary

ThinkCentral Online Assessment, Selection Standards Check

ThinkCentral Online Remediation

Preteach

Introducing Vocabulary

- Review the Vocabulary words, definitions, and sentences with students.
- To reinforce students' understanding of the Vocabulary words, tell students that these words can help them understand the historical period in which Bede lived. Bede composed a *singularly* popular historical document that taught Church doctrine with the intent of dissuading people from *frivolous* or *profane* behavior.

English for Academic Success

Language Skills Coach

After reading the **Language Coach,** have students provide two antonyms each for *singularly, frivolous,* and *profane.* Then, ask students to compare the meanings of the words in each antonyms pair.

Literary Skills Focus

After you read and discuss the selection with students, have them verbally describe the scene during which Caedmon sings to the abbess.

Reading Skills Focus

Give students a copy of the Reading Skills Focus graphic organizer before they read. (See **Unit 1 Resources.**) Tell them to use their responses to answer the questions on the Applying Your Skills page.

Writing Skills Focus

As they read the anecdote, have students note elements of a story in their **Reader/Writer Notebooks.** Students can use their notes to complete the Writing Skills Focus activity.

Learn It Online
Send students to **Word Watch** for audio pronunciations, synonyms and antonyms, and brief histories of word origins.

go.hrw.com H12-81 Go

Teacher Preparation

Selection Summary

In this excerpt from *A History of the English Church and People*, Bede tells of Caedmon, now regarded as the first English religious poet. As a young man, Caedmon lives an unremarkable life as a lay brother in a monastery. He shows no interest in poetry, preferring to leave a feast rather than sing poems. One night, a visitor comes to him in a dream and asks him to "sing about the creation of all things." Caedmon obeys. Upon waking, he shares his songs with others at the monastery and joins the religious order. He studies the events of sacred history and relates them in his songs.

Direct Teach

Think About/Talk About

Read with a Purpose Have students read the Read with a Purpose statement. Point out the key phrase in the statement: "inspires awe." As students read the selection, have them record instances from the text in which people are awed by Caedmon's devotional poetry. Have students think about why they reacted with praise and astonishment.

Comprehension

A Reading Focus

Possible response: *From these lines, the reader can learn how Anglo-Saxon people socialized. The author describes feasts to which guests were invited to entertain each other with music and songs. The use of the word "sometimes" implies that this kind of celebration was fairly common.*

HISTORY

from

A History of the English Church and People

by **Bede**

translated by **Leo Sherley-Price**

Read with a Purpose

Read to discover why Caedmon's ability to create beautiful verse inspires awe.

Build Background

Considered to be the first English religious poet, Caedmon of Whitby was an illiterate herdsman who communicated religious thought and beliefs in verse, or poetic form. Caedmon's Hymn praises God by using some of the same elements used in heroic verse forms.

Caedmon of Whitby

In this monastery of [Whitby] lived a brother singularly gifted by God's grace. So skillful was he in composing religious and devotional songs that, when any passage of Scripture[1] was explained to him by interpreters, he could quickly turn it into delightful and moving poetry in his own English tongue. These verses of his have stirred the hearts of many folk to despise the world and aspire to heavenly things. Others after him tried to compose religious poems in English, but none could compare with him; for he did not acquire the art of poetry from men or through any human teacher but received it as a free gift from God. For this reason he could never compose any frivolous or profane verses; but only such as had a religious theme fell fittingly from his devout lips. He had followed a secular occupation until well advanced in years without ever learning anything about poetry. Indeed it sometimes happened at a feast that all the guests in turn would be invited to sing and entertain the company; then, when he saw the harp coming his way, he would get up from table and go home. **A**

On one such occasion he had left the house in which the entertainment was being held and went

1. **passage of Scripture:** a passage from the Bible.

A **Reading Focus** **Understanding Historical Context** What can we learn about everyday Anglo-Saxon life from reading these lines?

Vocabulary **singularly** (SIHNG gyuh luhr lee) *adv.:* extraordinarily; unusually.
frivolous (FRIHV uh luhs) *adj.:* silly or unimportant.
profane (proh FAYN) *adj.:* irreverent; not associated with religious matters.
secular (SEHK yuh luhr) *adj.:* not belonging to a religious order; worldly.

Universal Access

English Learners

English for Academic Success Ask students to describe what the selection reveals about setting and historical context by using these sentence starters:

1. We learn from this excerpt that Anglo-Saxon life involved . . .
2. The verses that Caedmon sings in his dream seem to emphasize . . .
3. The sentence "These verses of his have stirred the hearts of many folk to despise the world . . ." reveals that Caedmon's culture valued . . .

Struggling Readers

Guide students in understanding historical context. Direct students to the end of p. 82, and read aloud the sentence "On one such occasion . . ." Point out the part of the sentence "it was his duty that night to look after the beasts." Tell students that they might infer from these details that conditions in that time were not entirely safe and secure, otherwise, Caedmon wouldn't have to be guarding the beasts. Point out also that his culture probably valued responsibility, as it was his [Caedmon's] duty to stand watch that night.

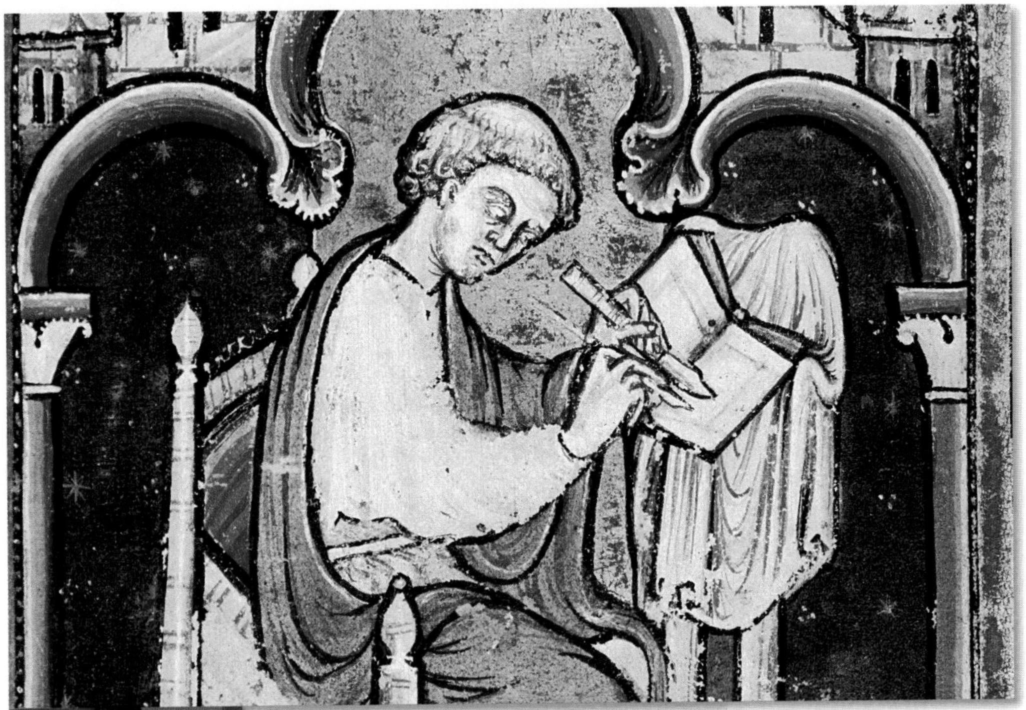

Analyzing Visuals

Connecting to the Text The brightly colored, embellished images in medieval manuscripts were called illuminations (from the Latin word *illuminare,* meaning "to light up") because of the glow created by the gold and silver. How does this illustration help you understand the setting and historical context of Bede's *History*?

A tonsured, seated scribe (probably Bede) writing, from *Life of Saint Cuthbert* (12th c.), Durham. Yates Thompson 26, f.2. The British Library, London.

out to the stable, where it was his duty that night to look after the beasts. There when the time came he settled down to sleep. Suddenly in a dream he saw a man standing beside him who called him by name. "Caedmon," he said, "sing me a song." "I don't know how to sing," he replied. "It is because I cannot sing that I left the feast and came here." The man who addressed him then said: "But you shall sing to me." "What should I sing about?" he replied. "Sing about the Creation of all things," the other answered. And Caedmon immediately began to sing verses in praise of God the Creator that he had never heard before, and their theme ran thus: **B**

Praise we the Fashioner now of Heaven's fabric,
The majesty of his might and his mind's wisdom,
Work of the world-warden, worker of all wonders,
How he the Lord of Glory everlasting,
Wrought first for the race of men Heaven as a
rooftree,
Then made he Middle Earth to be their mansion.

This is the general sense, but not the actual words that Caedmon sang in his dream; for verses, however masterly, cannot be translated literally from one

B **Literary Focus** **Setting** What does this paragraph emphasize about life in this period?

Think About/Talk About

Analysis

B Literary Focus

Possible response: *This paragraph emphasizes details about daily life and a typical person's duties during the Anglo-Saxon period. Caedmon spends the night in a stable to look after the horses.*

Extend the Discussion

Recognizing Philosophical Assumptions On page 83, Bede notes that "verses, however masterly, cannot be translated literally from one language to another without losing much of their beauty and dignity." What can this tell you about Bede's philosophical assumptions regarding the transcription of the word of God? ***Possible response:*** *Bede likely believes that all human transcriptions of God's words, whether sung in verse or written down, are crude representations of the true dignity of the word of God.*

Analyzing Visuals

Connecting to the Text: *The seated scribe in the illumination seems to be writing under divine inspiration. The glowing colors emphasize the inspirational role that Christian religion was meant to have in Bede's time.*

Vocabulary: Own the Word

- **singularly:** Ask students to name ways in which a person would be *singularly* gifted by God's grace.
- **frivolous:** Ask students to demonstrate making a *frivolous* gesture.
- **profane:** *Profane* means irreligious; a synonym is *irreverent.* Use both words in a sentence. *His profane comments clearly displayed his irreverence for the establishment.*
- **secular:** Ask students to list examples of *secular* concerns. ***Possible responses:*** *one's status in society, finances, food, clothing, shelter*

Advanced Learners

Acceleration Introduce students to the term *hagiography.* Explain that this term refers to the literature recounting the lives of the Christian saints; however, it also includes biographical materials about other people considered saintly or blessed, such as Caedmon. Ask students to think about how this excerpt is, or is not, a good example of hagiography.

Students with Disabilities

To help students understand historical context, help them brainstorm differences between daily life in Anglo-Saxon times and today (technology, science, religion, recreational activities, etc.).

Think About/Talk About

Analysis

Ⓒ Literary Focus

Possible response: *The setting tells about the importance of religion in Anglo-Saxon life and the role that preaching and oral tradition had during that period.*

Extend the Discussion

Synthesizing What religious purpose do Caedmon's poems have? ***Possible response:*** *They were intended to inspire people to live more devout lives.*

Vocabulary: Own the Word

doctrine: When a person is *indoctrinated,* it means they are instructed in a teaching or *doctrine.* Ask students what methods might be used to *indoctrinate* children of an idea.

Monitor Students' Comprehension

Guide the class in answering these comprehension questions.

1. Describe the role of religious poetry in the Anglo-Saxon period. [*Oral tradition was the primary means of sharing information, so religious poetry must have been an effective tool to teach Christian beliefs.*]
2. What did the abbess offer Caedmon after she became convinced of his extraordinary gift? [*She offered him admission into the community of brothers in the monastery.*]
3. Name three subjects Caedmon sings about during his time at the monastery. [*Caedmon sings about Israel's exodus from Egypt, the Lord's Resurrection, and the teaching of the Apostles.*]

language into another without losing much of their beauty and dignity. When Caedmon awoke, he remembered everything that he had sung in his dream, and soon added more verses in the same style to a song truly worthy of God.

Early in the morning he went to his superior, the reeve,[2] and told him about this gift that he had received. The reeve took him before the abbess,[3] who ordered him to give an account of his dream and repeat the verses in the presence of many learned men, so that a decision might be reached by common consent as to their quality and origin. All of them agreed that Caedmon's gift had been given him by our Lord. And they explained to him a passage of Scriptural history or doctrine and asked him to render it into verse if he could. He promised to do this, and returned next morning with excellent verses as they had ordered him. The abbess was delighted that God had given such grace to the man, and advised him to abandon secular life and adopt the monastic state.[4] And when she had admitted him into the Community as a brother, she ordered him to be instructed in the events of sacred history. So Caedmon stored up in his memory all that he learned, and like one of the clean animals chewing the cud, turned it into such melodious verse that his delightful renderings turned his instructors into auditors. He sang of the Creation of the world, the origin of the human race, and the whole story of Genesis. He sang of Israel's exodus from Egypt, the entry into the Promised Land, and many other events of Scriptural history. He sang of the Lord's Incarnation,[5] Passion,[6] Resurrection,[7] and Ascension into Heaven,[8] the coming of the Holy Spirit, and the teaching of the Apostles. He also made many poems on the terrors of the Last Judgment, the horrible pains of Hell, and the joys of the Kingdom of Heaven. In addition to these, he composed several others on the blessings and judgments of God, by which he sought to turn his hearers from delight in wickedness and to inspire them to love and do good. For Caedmon was a deeply religious man, who humbly submitted to regular discipline and hotly rebuked all who tried to follow another course. And so he crowned his life with a happy end. Ⓒ

When Caedmon awoke, he remembered everything that he had sung in his dream, and soon added more verses . . . to a song truly worthy of God.

2. **reeve:** the manager of an estate; here, the steward in charge of the monastery.
3. **abbess** (AB ihs): the superior nun of a monastery for nuns and monks.
4. **monastic state:** Caedmon was originally a lay brother, a nonclergy member, attached to the monastery. Here, the abbess is inviting him to become a full-fledged member of the monastery by taking special vows and participating in the singing of the choir.
5. **Incarnation** (ihn kahr NAY shuhn): appearance in human form.
6. **Passion:** refers to the suffering of Jesus Christ.
7. **Resurrection** (rehz uh REHK shuhn): the condition of being restored to life after dying.
8. **Ascension into Heaven:** after his resurrection, Jesus Christ is said to have risen into heaven.

Vocabulary **doctrine** (DAHK truhn) *n.:* teachings of the church.

Ⓒ **Literary Focus** **Setting** How does the setting contribute to the reader's understanding of the historical context?

California Standards, pp. 85–86

- **Reading Standard 3.3** Analyze the ways in which irony, tone, mood, the author's style, and the "sound" of language achieve specific rhetorical or aesthetic purposes or both.
- **Reading Standard 3.7** Relate literary works and authors to the major themes and issues of their eras. **b.** Analyze recognized works of world literature from a variety of authors. **c.** Evaluate the philosophical, political, religious, ethical, and social influences of the historical period that shaped the characters, plots and settings.
- **Grades 9–10 Review Reading Standard 1.1** Identify and use the literal and figurative meanings of words and understand word derivations.
- **Writing Standard 1.3** Structure ideas and arguments in a sustained, persuasive, and sophisticated way and support them with precise and relevant examples.

Applying Your Skills

Reading Standard 3.3, 3.7b, 3.7c (see pages A48–A50)
Writing Standard 1.3 (see pages A51–A52)

from A History of the English Church and People

Literary Response and Analysis

Reading Skills Focus

Quick Check

1. What was Caedmon's gift?
2. Why did Caedmon leave the party?
3. What was the topic of Caedmon's first poem?
4. Why does the abbess urge Caedmon to become a monk?

Read with a Purpose

5. Why were people so moved by Caedmon's verse?

Reading Skills: Analyzing Historical Context

6. While reading, you noted how seventh-century Anglo-Saxon life was described. Review your chart, considering what it reveals about the historical context. Why did the people value Caedmon's ability and see it as a miracle?

Issues	Living Conditions	Values	Other Facts
		religious devotion	

Literary Skills Focus

Literary Analysis

7. **Interpret** Since so few people were educated, a strong oral tradition developed over time. **Oral tradition** consists of stories and histories passed by word of mouth from one generation to the next. What clues in the selection tell you that Caedmon's story is an example of oral tradition?
8. **Evaluate** How do Caedmon's social standing and depth of knowledge change after he receives his gift from God? Cite passages from the selection to support your response.
9. **Analyze** Scholars believe that Bede's historical records are very reliable, but a certain amount of bias still exists. Evaluate the text, and identify examples of bias.
10. **Interpret** What religious purpose did Caedmon's poem's have? How were they useful for religious instruction?

Literary Skills: Setting

11. **Analyze** How does the setting emphasize the awe-inspiring quality of Caedmon's verse?

Literary Skills Review: Tone

12. **Analyze** The attitude a writer takes toward the reader, a subject, or a character or person described in the text is **tone.** What is Bede's tone in this selection about Caedmon?

Writing Skills Focus

Think as a Reader/Writer

Use It in Your Writing Review the anecdote in paragraph 2 that supports Bede's point. Write a statement of your own about something you have observed, for example, that *speed causes traffic accidents,* and support it with an anecdote.

What Do You Think Now? How does Caedmon use his gifts to inspire others?

Check for Understanding

Independent Practice

Reading Skills Focus

Possible responses:

1. *His gift was to transform events of sacred history into inspiring verse.*
2. *He was embarrassed by his inability to sing.*
3. *The poem was about God as creator of all things.*
4. *She thinks he should use his talent for the church.*
5. *Caedmon's verse was especially beautiful and inspiring.*
6. *Have students review their notes on the values of Caedmon's society before answering the question.*

Literary Skills Focus

Possible responses:

7. *The selection tells about "auditors" or "hearers," which means Caedmon's gift was an example of oral tradition.*
8. *Caedmon progresses from a lowly lay brother to a full-fledged member of the monastic community. When Bede writes that Caedmon's "delightful renderings turned his instructors into auditors," he shows that Caedmon was highly honored within the monastery.*
9. *There are many instances in which the author openly praises Caedmon. Caedmon's verse is described as "melodious" and "delightful." This indicates the author's bias toward Christian spirituality.*
10. *The poems aimed at inspiring Christian faith in the listeners. The poetic form also made it easier for the listener to remember the content of Caedmon's verse.*
11. *At the time in which the events took place, religion was of great importance, as was oral tradition.*
12. *Bede's tone is solemn and celebratory.*

Universal Access

Struggling Writers

Give students ideas for statements by writing the following examples on the board. Students can choose one or come up with their own:

- Practice makes perfect.
- One kind, unselfish act breeds another.

Then, provide additional scaffolding for students by having them create a brief outline of their anecdote. Remind students that they should outline events in chronological order.

What Do You Think Now?

Before students answer the What Do You Think Now question, have them refer back to the topics of Caedmon's devotional songs as described in the last paragraph of the selection.

Independent Practice
Vocabulary Development

Vocabulary Check

1. *c* **2.** *e*
3. *d* **4.** *a*
5. *b*

Your Turn

Possible response: *All the words in the word bank are of Latin origin. In the seventh century, when Bede was writing, Anglo-Saxon society was shifting from paganism to Christianity. Education during that period was provided solely by the church. Therefore, religious words became common in the language.*

English for Academic Success

Language Coach

1. *c* **2.** *c*
3. *a* **4.** *a*

English for Academic Success

Academic Vocabulary

Possible response: *In this selection, Bede recounts the story of Caedmon, whose religious verse inspired diverse listeners of his time. Bede emphasizes beliefs held by the Anglo-Saxon society through Caedmon's songs and through Caedmon's disciplined life.*

Assess

Unit 1 Resources, Selection Standards Check, p. 24

ThinkCentral Online Assessment, Selection Standards Check

Teacher One Stop™, editable Selection Standards Check

Applying Your Skills

Grades 9–10 Review Reading Standard 1.1 (see pages A48–A50)

from **A History of the English Church and People**

Vocabulary Development

Vocabulary Check

Match the Vocabulary words with their definitions.

1. singularly **a.** worldly
2. frivolous **b.** beliefs
3. profane **c.** uniquely
4. secular **d.** irreverent
5. doctrine **e.** silly

Vocabulary Skills: Etymology

The English language was not always the language we hear and read today. It has evolved over many centuries and has been influenced by different periods in history. It has also borrowed words from other languages. We can trace many words back to their original form and use by means of **etymology,** or the study of word origins.

Many of the words in the selection from Bede's *History* reflect the influence of other languages on English. Other words reflect the growth of Christianity in England. Notice the origins of the words below from the modern translation of Bede's *History.* Though the spellings of the words have changed, note how the words were originally used.

English Word	Word Origin	Original Meaning
devout	Old French *devot,* from Latin *devotus*	(Old French) devoted, (Latin) to vow
compose	French *composer* from French *poser* and Latin *componere*	(French) to form (Latin) to put together, arrange
translate	Latin *translatus*	carried over, transferred
dignity	Old French *dignete,* from Latin *dignitas, dignus*	(Old French) high rank, (Latin) worth, worthy

Your Turn

Some of the Vocabulary words reflect the influence of Christianity during Bede's time. Using a dictionary, look up the origins of each Vocabulary word. Make a list to show the origin of each word. Why do you think religious words were so important to the people of the Anglo-Saxon period?

Language Coach

Antonyms Words with opposite meanings are called **antonyms.** Some examples of antonym pairs are *good/bad, calm/nervous, young/old.* Read each word and the three answer choices. Write the letter of the antonym for each word.

1. profane
a. wicked **b.** ridiculous **c.** religious

2. frivolous
a. playful **b.** angry **c.** serious

3. singularly
a. commonly **b.** rarely **c.** fondly

4. secular
a. spiritual **b.** strange **c.** free

Academic Vocabulary

Write About

The writings of Bede depict a diverse representation of the Anglo-Saxon populace. In a short paragraph, explain how his writing emphasizes beliefs and values important to all the citizens. Be sure to cite specific examples from the text and use the underlined Academic Vocabulary words in your response.

Universal Access: Vocabulary Development

English Learners

English for Academic Success Inform students that they can research word origins in the dictionary. Explain that word origins, or etymologies, usually appear in brackets or in double brackets in the dictionary entry. The languages of origin are usually abbreviated. For example, *L* refers to Latin, *O.E.* refers to Old English, and *Fr.* refers to French.

Activity Ask students to flip through the pages of a dictionary to study examples of etymologies. Then, have them research the etymology of the following words:

- *camera* (from M.L. *camera,* meaning *vaulted chamber*)
- *Saturday* (from O.E. *Sæternes,* meaning *Saturn*)
- *itinerant* (from L. *iter,* meaning *journey*)
- *etymology* (from Gk. *etymon,* meaning *true sense*)

✔ See the **Academic and Selection Vocabulary Skill Builder** in **UA: Differentiating Instruction.**

Epics Across Cultures

Gilgamesh (1924) by Zabelle C. Boyajian. Gilgamesh, in search of immortality, goes to Mount Mashu, which is guarded by terrible scorpion gods who welcome him when they learn his identity.

Produced by two different cultures and composed nearly a thousand years apart, the epics *Gilgamesh* and the *Iliad* share universal themes of fear, bravery, determination, and compassion that fascinate readers today. As you read the following excerpts, consider how readers from any time and place might find meaning in these epics. After you read, you will compare the themes that connect the epics.

CONTENTS

Standards Focus

Objectives

Students will
- analyze the epic genre and the archetype of the epic hero
- understand the use of a foil

English for Academic Success

Academic Vocabulary

Look for opportunities to use the Academic Vocabulary words in this unit.

- **attribute, *v.*:** regard as being caused by something
- **concept, *n.*:** notion or idea
- **diverse, *adj.*:** varied
- **emphasis, *n.*:** stress; importance
- **status, *n.*:** social or professional rank

Analyzing Visuals

Extension Activity Ask students to identify and describe elements of the epic poem in this illustration of *Gilgamesh*. ***Possible response:*** *This image depicts the hero Gilgamesh being welcomed by scorpion gods. This image reflects the characteristics of the epic because epic poems revolve around a heroic character who performs supernatural deeds and deals with monsters and demons.*

Selection Introduction
Think About the Epic
Before students answer the question, have them think about what they have learned about Gilgamesh's origins and about the hero's qualities and flaws.

For Independent Reading
- *The Places in Between*,* Rory Stewart
- *The King Must Die*, Mary Renault

HRW LIBRARY *This title is available in the HRW library.

Motivate
What Do You Think?/QuickWrite
Have students use their **Reader/ Writer Notebooks** to write a paragraph about what they saw and did during their adventure and how they felt afterwards.

Preparing to Read

from Gilgamesh

What Do You Think? What moves a hero to act?

QuickWrite

This story is thousands of years old, but its two main characters are best friends who experience the same desire for excitement that people do today. In your *Reader/Writer Notebook,* write briefly about an adventure you have had with a friend.

INTRODUCTION

Gilgamesh reveals much about the ancient Mesopotamians' sometimes pessimistic view of life, but it also emphasizes the sensitivity and humanity of an ancient people—like us in their joys, sorrows, and strivings.

A Mesopotamian Epic
Like most epics, Gilgamesh is based on at least a grain of truth. Many scholars believe that Gilgamesh was an actual king who reigned over the city-state of Uruk, in Sumer, sometime between 2700 and 2500 B.C. Over the centuries, Gilgamesh became a legendary figure, rather like King Arthur in Europe. Tales of Gilgamesh's exploits grew and were probably recited in verse for centuries before they were recorded in writing. The earliest written fragments date from about 2000 B.C. Later the epic was reworked by writers from the Sumerian, Babylonian, and Assyrian cultures. Some scholars believe the epic was put into its most complete form in 1300 B.C.

The Original Epic Hero?
The Gilgamesh of the epic is a superhuman hero, two parts god and one part human. In many ways it is his human weaknesses rather than his superhuman powers that make him so interesting. He is the leader of his people and builder of a great city, yet he has excessive pride. Refusing to accept death—"the common lot of man"—Gilgamesh embarks on a quest for immortality. With superhuman strength, courage, and persistence, he confronts obstacles along the way, but ultimately he must contend with human limitations.

Gilgamesh may be the original epic hero. Versions of his epic have been found as far north as the Black Sea, as far south as Jerusalem, and from the Mediterranean coast eastward to the Persian Gulf. Many of the epic's images, events, and characters, including Gilgamesh himself, are **archetypes—**patterns that appear in literature across cultures and throughout the ages. The frequency of these patterns suggests their basis in fundamental, and even primordial, shared human experience.

Think About the Epic What might be the reason that superhuman Gilgamesh has to contend with human limitations in the end?

A hero (Gilgamesh?) taming a young lion. Relief from the palace of Sargon II (8th century B.C.), Khorsabad, Iraq. The Louvre, Paris, France.

California Standards, pp. 88–97
- **Reading Standard 3.1** Analyze characteristics of subgenres (e.g., satire, parody, allegory, pastoral) that are used in poetry, prose, plays, novels, short stories, essays, and other basic genres.
- **Grades 9–10 Review Reading Standard 3.3** Analyze interactions between main and subordinate characters in a literary text (e.g., internal and external conflicts, motivations, relationships, influence) and explain the way those interactions affect the plot.

Selection Readability	
Easily Accessible Accessible **Challenging**	epic poem; unfamiliar context; abstract symbolism; archaic vocabulary; archaic syntax

Reading Standard 3.1; Grades 9–10 Review
Reading Standard 3.3 (see pages A48–A50)

Literary Skills Focus

Foil Many heroes, such as Beowulf, "go it alone," proudly seeking glory entirely through their own efforts. Sometimes, however, a hero has a companion who serves as his **foil**—a character who sets off the other character through strong contrast. A famous example is Tom Sawyer and Huckleberry Finn, the best friends who share some wild adventures but are driven by very different motivations. In *Gilgamesh* the foil is Enkidu, who, in contrast to Gilgamesh, represents the natural man, a pure-hearted and uncomplicated person unfamiliar with the ways of civilized society.

TechFocus As you read this story, think about how the two major characters act as foils for one another. Have you ever encountered a similar relationship on an online discussion board or blog?

Reading Skills Focus

Comparing and Contrasting Being able to **compare and contrast** situations and characters is a skill that will add depth to your reading, understanding, and enjoyment. You can see the traits of one character more sharply when they are compared or contrasted to those of another.

Into Action As you read, use a diagram like the one below to keep track of the differences and similarities between Gilgamesh and Enkidu.

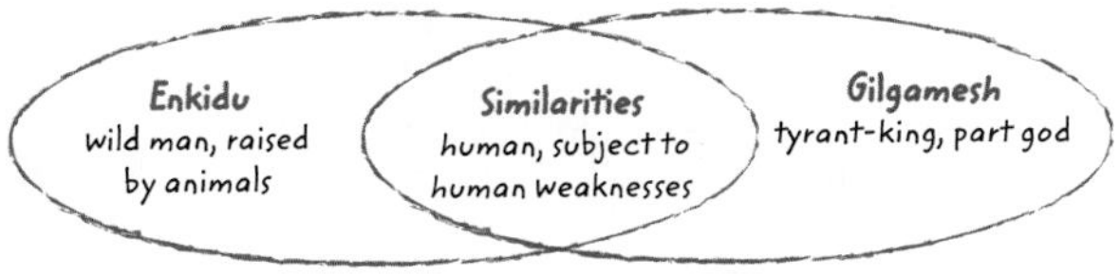

Writing Skills Focus

Think as a Reader/Writer

Find It in Your Reading Even though the great early epics are full of action, they also show keen psychological insight. Gilgamesh and Enkidu are guided by internal needs and plagued by fears and doubts. In your *Reader/Writer Notebook,* take notes on thoughts and statements that reveal the characters' emotional and psychological states.

Reader/Writer Notebook
Use your **RWN** to complete the activities for this selection.

Vocabulary

austere (aw STIHR) *adj.:* spare; very plain. *Fearing for Gilgamesh's safety, the elders gave Gilgamesh an austere blessing to fight Humbaba.*

decreed (dih KREED) *v.* used as *adj.:* ordered; commanded. *Gilgamesh followed Shamash in the decreed way.*

contortion (kuhn TAWR shuhn) *n.:* twisted shape or motion. *Humbaba's face was a hideous contortion of what a normal face looks like.*

squall (skwawl) *n.:* brief, violent storm. *The speaker compares the monster's actions to a squall.*

Language Coach

Shades of Meaning The meaning of an adjective can change when it is used to describe different nouns. An austere room is one that is very plain. It probably has very little furniture. However, an austere blessing is not plain in the same way. Here, *austere* means "plain in the sense of not having a lot of extra words." An austere blessing is direct and to the point. What might an austere dinner be like? What about an austere warning?

Learn It Online
Learn more about this epic online.
go.hrw.com H12-89 Go

Comparing Texts Resources

Unit 1 Resources, on-level practice and assessment, p. 21

Teacher One Stop™, on-level lesson plans and all print resources

Holt Audio Library

Holt Audio Library: Selections and Summaries in Spanish

UA: Differentiating Instruction: graphic organizer, p. 11

UA: Supporting Instruction in Spanish selection summary

ThinkCentral Online Assessment, Selection Standards Check

ThinkCentral Online Remediation

Preteach

Introducing Vocabulary

Read aloud the Vocabulary words, definitions, and sample sentences. Then, use this activity to check students' understanding.

1. Describe the characteristics of an **austere** location.
2. List things that can be **decreed**.
3. Explain the effects of **contortion** on an object.
4. Compare a **squall** to a rain shower.

English for Academic Success

Language Coach

After students read the **Language Coach,** have them think about the different meanings between a *contorted* facial expression and a *contorted* body. [*A contorted expression is strangely distorted; a contorted body is twisted.*]

Literary Skills Focus

As you read and discuss the selection with students, have them pay attention to how Gilgamesh and Enkidu communicate with each other.

Reading Skills Focus

Give students a copy of the Reading Skills Focus graphic organizer before they read. (See **Unit 1 Resources.**) Tell them to use their responses to answer the questions on the Applying Your Skills page.

Writing Skills Focus

Have students record words related to their understanding of Gilgamesh's and Enkidu's thoughts and feelings in their **Reader/Writer Notebooks.** Students can use their notes to complete the Writing Skills Focus activity.

Learn It Online
The online version of this selection includes audio support to engage all students and to help struggling readers with reading comprehension and vocabulary.
go.hrw.com H12-89 Go

Teacher Preparation

Selection Plot Summary

In this excerpt, Gilgamesh decides to fight the evil Humbaba, servant of the gods. The elders of Uruk urge him on even though Gilgamesh's close friend Enkidu warns him of the risk. Gilgamesh and Enkidu travel through a forest and spend the night there, frightened and dreaming of phantoms and the death they may face. Gilgamesh awakens and chops down a cedar. The giant Humbaba then approaches them. Although Humbaba injures Enkidu, the men ultimately defeat the giant. Just as Gilgamesh raises his ax for the deathblow, Humbaba begs for mercy. He promises to serve Gilgamesh as he once served the gods, but Enkidu warns his friend not to trust Humbaba. With a brief flash of regret, Gilgamesh beheads Humbaba.

Direct Teach

Think About/Talk About

Read with a Purpose Have students read the Read with a Purpose statement. Point out that the statement asks to analyze the characters' "attitudes toward each other." As you read the selection, have students note the way characters behave with each other. Ask students to pay attention to the tone the characters use and the phrases that express their feelings for one another.

EPIC

from Gilgamesh

A Verse Narrative

retold by **Herbert Mason**

Read with a Purpose

Read to discover what Gilgamesh's and Enkidu's attitudes toward each other reveal about their characters.

Build Background

Craving an adventure that will bring them fame, close friends Gilgamesh and Enkidu plan a journey to the cedar forest. There they will confront the monstrous and evil guardian of the forest, the giant Humbaba. As this part of the story opens, Gilgamesh is speaking to Enkidu, trying to relieve his fears of meeting the monster.

Sumerian ruins at Uruk.

Universal Access

English Learners

English for Academic Success Have students think about prefixes that transform a word into its antonym, or opposite. Ask students to look for examples of words with such prefixes on the first page of the selection (*immoral, discourage,* and *impatient*) and define each word. Ask students to describe the character of Gilgamesh using one or two of these words, and then have them write a sentence describing Enkidu using the antonyms of the words.

Struggling Readers

Strategic Students To help students read Gilgamesh, discuss the use of the foil in literature. Explain that readers frequently analyze relationships between characters. Remind students that a foil is a character who highlights the main character's traits through comparison or contrast, and who may be similar to or different from the main character. Ask students, "Who is the foil? Is the foil like or unlike the main character?"

Why are you worried about death?
Only the gods are immortal anyway,
Sighed Gilgamesh.
What men do is nothing, so fear is never
Justified. What happened to your power
That once could challenge and equal mine?
I will go ahead of you, and if I die
I will at least have the reward
Of having people say: He died in war
Against Humbaba. You cannot discourage me
With fears and hesitations.
I will fight Humbaba,
I will cut down his cedars.
Tell the armorers to build us two-edged swords
And double shields and tell them
I am impatient and cannot wait long. **A**

Thus Gilgamesh and Enkidu went
Together to the marketplace
To notify the Elders of Uruk

A **Literary Focus** **Foil** How does Gilgamesh's opening speech to Enkidu show that Enkidu is his foil?

Think About/Talk About

Analysis

A Literary Focus

Possible response: *Gilgamesh is anxious to go into an extremely dangerous battle. In his speech, Gilgamesh rejects Enkidu's reasons for hesitating. This contrast highlights Gilgamesh's fearlessness.*

Extend the Discussion

Finding Details In the first stanza, what reason for fighting Humbaba does Gilgamesh give? ***Possible response:*** *He wants to prove that his people should not fear Humbaba.*

Synthesizing How would you summarize Gilgamesh's attitude toward death? ***Possible response:*** *Unlike the gods, all humans die; your actions are not important, so fear of losing your life is not justified. However, if you die in battle against a worthy enemy, you will be remembered and praised.*

Advanced Learners

Acceleration Point out that the epic hero has flaws and limitations. Ask students to consider Gilgamesh's strengths and weaknesses and how they are balanced by Enkidu's character traits. Ask students to discuss with the class how the balance between the characters serves the plot.

Students with Disabilities

Have students write two adjectives that describe Gilgamesh and Enkidu, respectively. Then, ask them to write a sentence describing each character using the adjectives. Then, instruct students to combine the two sentences using a transition to connect the sentences. Suggest transitions such as *similarly, however,* or *on the other hand.*

Model the Skill

- Review the idea that a **foil** highlights important traits of the main character and may balance the main character's actions with opposite or tempering actions.
- Read aloud lines 60–63. Tell students that this passage illustrates a twist in the story. A role reversal occurs at this point. Enkidu now acts as a supporter and encourager of a reluctant Gilgamesh. Gilgamesh has become the hesitant and fearful character, while Enkidu has become the more confident and determined character.

Guided Practice: Apply

Turn-and-Talk Ask students to read lines 69–73. Have students work in pairs to discuss the different reactions of Enkidu and Gilgamesh in the impending battle with Humbaba.

Think as a Reader/Writer

Find It in Your Reading Point out that in lines 80–86, Gilgamesh and Enkidu have very different responses to the danger posed by Humbaba. Enkidu is paralyzed by fear, while Gilgamesh is strengthened by it.

Use It in Your Writing Imagine you are writing a short story about a hero and his or her foil. The two characters come across a mysterious cave. Write two or three sentences describing each character's reactions to the mystery. Be sure to use the actions of your foil to contrast the actions of your main character.

Who were meeting in their senate.
They too were talking of Humbaba,
As they often did,
Edging always in their thoughts
Toward the forbidden.

The one you speak of, Gilgamesh addressed them,
I now must meet. I want to prove
Him not the awesome thing we think he is
And that the boundaries set up by gods
Are not unbreakable. I will defeat him
In his cedar forest. The youth of Uruk
Need this fight. They have grown soft
And restless. **B**

The old men leaned a little forward
Remembering old wars. A flush burned on
Their cheeks. It seemed a little dangerous
And yet they saw their king
Was seized with passion for this fight.
Their voices gave the confidence his friend
Had failed to give; some even said
Enkidu's wisdom was a sign of cowardice.
You see, my friend, laughed Gilgamesh,
The wise of Uruk have outnumbered you.

Amidst the speeches in the hall
That called upon the gods for their protection,
Gilgamesh saw in his friend that pain
He had seen before and asked him what it was
That troubled him.

Enkidu could not speak. He held his tears
Back. Barely audibly he said:
It is a road which you have never traveled. **C**

The armorers brought to Gilgamesh his weapons
And put them in his hand. He took his quiver,
Bow and ax, and two-edged sword,
And they began to march.

Gilgamesh between two demigods supporting the sun. Detail from a stone monument (9th century B.C.), Tell Halaf, Syria. Archaeological Museum, Aleppo, Syria.

B **Reading Focus** **Comparing and Contrasting** How does Gilgamesh compare with the youth of Uruk?

C **Reading Focus** **Comparing and Contrasting** What is the difference in Gilgamesh's and Enkidu's moods in this scene? Whose mood does the assembly seem to share?

Universal Access

Struggling Readers

Strategic Students Ask students to draw a Venn diagram and categorize the actions of Gilgamesh and Enkidu. Tell them to write actions taken by only Gilgamesh in the left section, by only Enkidu in the right section, and by both Gilgamesh and Enkidu in the center section. Ask them to look for patterns in their diagram after they have finished. [*Students may note that the actions taken by only Gilgamesh are opposed to those taken by only Enkidu; the characters balance each other out.*]

AAVE Students Who Use African American Vernacular English

English for Academic Success Give students practice in voicing the /r/ sound. Students may pronounce *brought* (l. 51) and *before* (l. 93) incorrectly by omitting the /r/ sound. Remind students that in formal English, the words are pronounced as (braht), and (bee FOHR).

✔ For additional instruction and strategies, see **Holt Pronunciation Resources** and **ThinkCentral, Teacher Access.**

The Elders gave their austere blessing
And the people shouted: Let Enkidu lead,
Don't trust your strength, he knows the forests,
The one who goes ahead will save his friend.
May Shamash° bring you victory. . . .

After three days they reached the edge
Of the forest where Humbaba's watchman stood.
Suddenly it was Gilgamesh who was afraid,
Enkidu who reminded him to be fearless.
The watchman sounded his warning to Humbaba.
The two friends moved slowly toward the forest gate.

When Enkidu touched the gate his hand felt numb,
He could not move his fingers or his wrist,
His face turned pale like someone's witnessing a death,
He tried to ask his friend for help
Whom he had just encouraged to move on,
But he could only stutter and hold out
His paralyzed hand.
It will pass, said Gilgamesh.
Would you want to stay behind because of that?
We must go down into the forest together.
Forget your fear of death. I will go before you
And protect you. Enkidu followed close behind
So filled with fear he could not think or speak.
Soon they reached the high cedars.

They stood in awe at the foot
Of the green mountain. Pleasure
Seemed to grow from fear of Gilgamesh.
As when one comes upon a path in woods
Unvisited by men, one is drawn near
The lost and undiscovered in himself;
He was revitalized by danger.
They knew it was the path Humbaba made.
Some called the forest "Hell," and others "Paradise";
What difference does it make? said Gilgamesh.
But night was falling quickly
And they had no time to call it names,
Except perhaps "The Dark,"
Before they found a place at the edge of the forest
To serve as shelter for their sleep.

59. Shamash (SHAH mahsh): god associated with the sun and human laws.

Vocabulary **austere** (aw STIHR) *adj:* spare; very plain.

Think About/Talk About

Comprehension

B Reading Focus

Possible response: *Gilgamesh is fearless and strong compared to the soft and restless youth of Uruk.*

C Reading Focus

Possible responses: *Gilgamesh is confident and secure, while Enkidu is fearful and troubled. The assembly shares in Gilgamesh's mood.*

Extend the Discussion

Comparing and Contrasting In lines 25–42, how are the Elders of Uruk different from Enkidu? ***Possible response:*** *While Enkidu has reservations, the Elders are able to recognize their king's enthusiasm for the fight, and they support Gilgamesh wholeheartedly.*

Evaluating On page 93, how do Gilgamesh and Enkidu support each other? What does this reveal about their friendship? ***Possible responses:*** *When one is afraid, the other encourages him. Although they may disagree, they ultimately will always support each other.*

Vocabulary: Own the Word

austere: Ask students what their classroom would look like if it were described as *austere.* ***Possible responses:*** *dark, no posters or pictures on the wall, no student work posted, no books or supplies on shelves*

Cross-Curricular Connection

HISTORY: Mesopotamia

Show students a map of southwestern Asia, where the epic of Gilgamesh is set. Tell students that the name *Mesopotamia* comes from ancient Greek and means *between rivers.* Mesopotamia was the region between the rivers Tigris and Euphrates, where the Sumer, Assyrian, and Babylonian civilizations flourished. Today, the region is shared among Syria, Turkey, and Iraq. Mesopotamia, now considered the birthplace of civilization, yielded great accomplishments in architecture, administration, mathematics, astronomy, and literature.

Activity Have small groups research the accomplishments of one of the three ancient Mesopotamian civilizations and present their research to the class.

Think About/Talk About

Literary Connection

Point out that many ancient cultures believed in the interpretations of dreams. In fact, dreams were often believed to have prophetic powers. This may lead the reader to make predictions about the destiny of the two protagonists.

Extend the Discussion

Drawing Conclusions How does Enkidu feel about Gilgamesh's dreams? How does he choose to answer his friend's question? ***Possible response:*** *Enkidu thinks that Gilgamesh's dreams foreshadow Enkidu's death. Still, he decides to reassure Gilgamesh of victory against Humbaba, and chooses not to express his own fears.*

Theme Enkidu's fear and pain during the night are exacerbated by having to face them alone, as Gilgamesh is sleeping. What theme recurs in this passage? ***Possible response:*** *the importance of friendship; people are stronger together than they are alone.*

It was a restless night for both. One snatched
At sleep and sprang awake from dreams. The other
Could not rest because of pain that spread
Throughout his side. Enkidu was alone
With sights he saw brought on by pain
And fear, as one in deep despair
May lie beside his love who sleeps
And seems so unafraid, absorbing in himself the phantoms
That she cannot see—phantoms diminished for one
When two can see and stay awake to talk of them
And search out a solution to despair,
Or lie together in each other's arms,
Or weep and in exhaustion from their tears
Perhaps find laughter for their fears.
But alone and awake the size and nature
Of the creatures in his mind grow monstrous,
Beyond resemblance to the creatures he had known
Before the prostitute° had come into his life. **D**

He cried aloud for them to stop appearing over him
Emerging from behind the trees with phosphorescent° eyes
Brought on by rain. He could not hear his voice
But knew he screamed and could not move his arms
But thought they tried to move
As if a heavy weight he could raise
Or wriggle out from underneath
Had settled on his chest,
Like a turtle trapped beneath a fallen branch,
Each effort only added to paralysis.
He could not make his friend, his one companion, hear.

Gilgamesh awoke but could not hear
His friend in agony, he still was captive to his dreams
Which he would tell aloud to exorcise:°
I saw us standing in a mountain gorge,
A rockslide fell on us, we seemed no more
Than insects under it. And then
A solitary graceful man appeared
And pulled me out from under the mountain.
He gave me water and I felt released. **E**

Clay mask of Humbaba (c. 1800–1600 B.C.). From Sippar, southern Iraq.
British Museum, London.

112. the prostitute: The first human Enkidu ever met. Before meeting her, he believed he was an animal, not a human.
114. phosphorescent (fahs fuh REHS uhnt): giving off light.

126. exorcise: to drive out.

D **Literary Focus** **Foil** What effect does the detailed description of Enkidu's suffering have on the portrayal of Gilgamesh, who is sleeping off and on?

E **Reading Focus** **Comparing and Contrasting** How do Gilgamesh and Enkidu handle their anxieties differently?

Universal Access

Struggling Readers

Benchmark Students Have students read lines 95–112. Remind students that a foil is one who causes the main character to stand out because of his or her contrasting traits or actions. Point out the contrast in lines 95–96. One character is "snatching at sleep" while the other cannot sleep because of fear and deep despair. Tell students that here, anxious Enkidu, is acting as a foil for the sleeping Gilgamesh, highlighting Gilgamesh's ability to control his fears.

Advanced Learners

Acceleration Have students work in small groups to research the plot of *Gilgamesh* up to the events described in the selection. Ask them to pay special attention to the evolution of the characters of Gilgamesh and Enkidu and the birth of their friendship. Ask students to write a dialogue between the two characters in which they tell about their past. After they have finished, have them read their dialogues to the class. Ask other students to comment on both strengths and weaknesses.

Tomorrow you will be victorious,
Enkidu said, to whom the dream brought chills
(For only one of them, he knew, would be released)
Which Gilgamesh could not perceive in the darkness
For he went back to sleep without responding
To his friend's interpretation of his dream.

Did you call me? Gilgamesh sat up again.
Why did I wake again? I thought you touched me.
Why am I afraid? I felt my limbs grow numb
As if some god passed over us drawing out our life.
I had another dream:
This time the heavens were alive with fire, but soon
The clouds began to thicken, death rained down on us,
The lightning flashes stopped, and everything
Which rained down turned to ashes.
What does this mean, Enkidu?

That you will be victorious against Humbaba,
Enkidu said, or someone said through him
Because he could not hear his voice
Or move his limbs although he thought he spoke,
And soon he saw his friend asleep beside him.

At dawn Gilgamesh raised his ax
And struck at the great cedar.
When Humbaba heard the sound of falling trees,
He hurried down the path that they had seen
But only he had traveled. Gilgamesh felt weak
At the sound of Humbaba's footsteps and called to Shamash
Saying, I have followed you in the way decreed;
Why am I abandoned now? Suddenly the winds
Sprang up. They saw the great head of Humbaba
Like a water buffalo's bellowing down the path,
His huge and clumsy legs, his flailing arms
Thrashing at phantoms in his precious trees.
His single stroke could cut a cedar down
And leave no mark on him. His shoulders,
Like a porter's° under building stones,
Were permanently bent by what he bore;
He was the slave who did the work for gods
But whom the gods would never notice.

168. porter's: A porter is a person who carries things for other people.

Vocabulary **decreed** (dih KREED) *v.* used as *adj.:* ordered; commanded.

Think About/Talk About

Comprehension

E Reading Focus

Possible response: *Gilgamesh is able to relieve his fears by sharing them with Enkidu. Enkidu instead keeps his fears to himself, which increases his anxiety.*

Analysis

D Literary Focus

Possible response: *It highlights Gilgamesh's ability to control part of his anxiety. Unlike Enkidu, the hero is able to get some sleep.*

Extend the Discussion

Paraphrasing In lines 113–123, what image is used to describe Enkidu's paralyzing fear? ***Possible response:*** *Enkidu is compared to a turtle trapped under a fallen branch, struggling to escape but getting more and more stuck at every attempt.*

Interpreting In the last stanza of this page, what detail provides a clue to the reader that Humbaba had a difficult existence? ***Possible response:*** *At the end of the selection, Humbaba is described as a slave of the gods. This information gives the reader insight about the psychological state of the giant.*

Vocabulary: Own the Word

decreed: *Decree* is the noun form of *decreed.* A *decree* is an authoritative order. President Abraham Lincoln *decreed* the abolition of slavery in the Emancipation Proclamation. Ask students to name other *decrees* in the past or in the present.

Students with Disabilities

Students might have trouble understanding where dialogue begins and ends in this selection. Divide students into pairs, and ask them to mark with sticky notes when dialogue starts and ends in the selection. Ask them to transcribe a few lines from the selection in their **Reader/Writer Notebooks** and add quotation marks.

Developing Oral Fluency

Use the dialogue between Gilgamesh and Enkidu (lines 127–133 and 139–149) to demonstrate to students how to read with expression. Explain that fluent readers read with intonation and expression because they focus on content and punctuation.

Small-Group Activity Divide students into groups of three. Ask students to re-read the dialogue between Gilgamesh and Enkidu on pp. 94–95. Then, ask them to each take a role (Gilgamesh, Enkidu, and the narrator) and to read the verses with intonation and expression.

Think About/Talk About

Analysis

(F) Literary Focus

Possible responses: *Enkidu is the one who is first involved in the battle, while Gilgamesh is paralyzed by fear. In the end, Enkidu is the one who urges Gilgamesh to strike the lethal blow to Humbaba.*

Extend the Discussion

Making Judgments What does Gilgamesh's final reaction to Humbaba's plea for life show about his priorities? ***Possible response:*** *Although he loves power, he loves Enkidu more.*

Vocabulary: Own the Word

- **contortion:** How safe would you feel floating on a sea that was in *contortion?* ***Possible response:*** *Not safe at all; the boat could possibly flip over on a contorting sea.*
- **squall:** Help students connect to the word personally. Ask them what they would do if they were caught outside during a *squall.*

Monitor Students' Comprehension

Guide the class in answering these comprehension questions.

1. Why do the Elders of Uruk agree to Gilgamesh's plan even though it is dangerous? [*They are encouraged by Gilgamesh's passionate speech.*]
2. How does Enkidu's body language show his anxiety in the selection? [*He barely speaks, he trembles, and he cannot move.*]
3. After reading the selection, how would you describe Gilgamesh's character? [*He is fearless and sometimes reckless. He also shows loyalty to his friend.*]

Monstrous in his contortion, he aroused
The two almost to pity.
But pity was the thing that might have killed.
It made them pause just long enough to show
How pitiless he was to them. Gilgamesh in horror saw
Him strike the back of Enkidu and beat him to the ground
Until he thought his friend was crushed to death.
He stood still watching as the monster leaned to make
His final strike against his friend, unable
To move to help him, and then Enkidu slid
Along the ground like a ram making its final lunge
On wounded knees. Humbaba fell and seemed
To crack the ground itself in two, and Gilgamesh,
As if this fall had snapped him from his daze,
Returned to life
And stood over Humbaba with his ax
Raised high above his head watching the monster plead
In strangled sobs and desperate appeals
The way the sea contorts under a violent squall.
I'll serve you as I served the gods, Humbaba said;
I'll build you houses from their sacred trees.

Enkidu feared his friend was weakening
And called out: Gilgamesh! Don't trust him! (F)
As if there were some hunger in himself
That Gilgamesh was feeling
That turned him momentarily to yearn
For someone who would serve, he paused;
And then he raised his ax up higher
And swung it in a perfect arc
Into Humbaba's neck. He reached out
To touch the wounded shoulder of his friend,

And late that night he reached again
To see if he was yet asleep, but there was only
Quiet breathing. The stars against the midnight sky
Were sparkling like mica° in a riverbed.
In the slight breeze
The head of Humbaba was swinging from a tree.

206. **mica** (MY kuh): kind of thin, crystalline mineral.

(F) Literary Focus Foil How are Gilgamesh's and Enkidu's traditional roles reversed in this scene? What effect does this reversal have on their roles as hero and foil?

Vocabulary **contortion** (kuhn TAWR shuhn) *n.:* twisted shape or motion.
squall (skwawl) *n.:* brief, violent storm.

California Standards, p. 97

- **Reading Standard 3.1** Analyze characteristics of subgenres (e.g., satire, parody, allegory, pastoral) that are used in poetry, prose, plays, novels, short stories, essays, and other basic genres.
- **Reading Standard 3.6** Analyze the way in which authors through the centuries have used archetypes drawn from myth and tradition in literature, film, political speeches, and religious writings (e.g., how the archetype of banishment from an ideal world may be used to interpret Shakespeare's tragedy *Macbeth*).
- **Grades 9–10 Review Reading Standard 3.3** Analyze interactions between main and subordinate characters in a literary text (e.g., internal and external conflicts, motivations, relationships, influence) and explain the way those interactions affect the plot.
- **Writing Standard 1.2** Use point of view, characterization, style (e.g., use of irony), and related elements for specific rhetorical and aesthetic purposes.

Applying Your Skills

Reading Standard 3.1, 3.6; **Grades 9–10 Review**
Reading Standard 3.3 (see pages A48–A50)
Writing Standard 1.2 (see pages A51–A52)

from Gilgamesh

Literary Response and Analysis

Reading Skills Focus

Quick Check

1. How do the elders of Uruk respond to Gilgamesh?
2. Summarize the battle with Humbaba. Do events unfold as Gilgamesh anticipated? Explain.

Read with a Purpose

3. What do you learn about Gilgamesh's strengths and weaknesses by contrasting him with his foil, Enkidu?

Reading Skills: Comparing and Contrasting

4. As you read, you compared and contrasted Gilgamesh and Enkidu. Now, add to your diagram, noting how Gilgamesh and Enkidu's differences and similarities advance the plot of the epic.

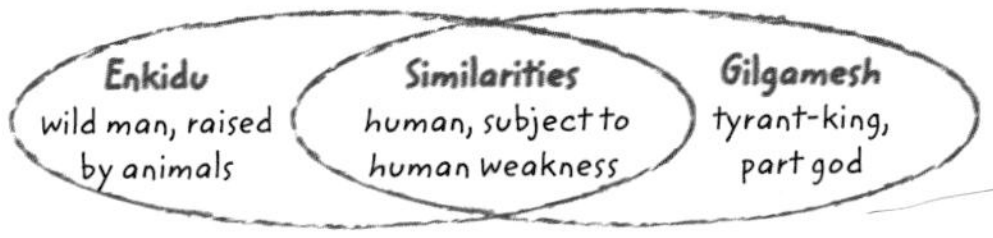

Vocabulary Check

Match each Vocabulary word to its definition.

5. austere	**a.** twisted shape or motion
6. decreed	**b.** brief, violent storm
7. contortion	**c.** spare; very plain
8. squall	**d.** ordered; commanded

Literary Skills Focus

Literary Analysis

9. **Analyze** How do Gilgamesh and Enkidu help each other on their adventure? Are there any ways in which they hurt each other?
10. **Interpret** Enkidu associates Humbaba with death. How does Gilgamesh characterize Humbaba? What is Humbaba's relationship with the gods?
11. **Extend** Is Gilgamesh a hero worthy of unqualified admiration? What lessons, if any, do you think he still needs to learn if he is to be a true epic hero?

Literary Skills: Foil

12. **Evaluate** Enkidu is a foil of Gilgamesh. How is Humbaba a foil for both Gilgamesh and Enkidu?

Literary Skills Review: Epic Hero

13. **Compare and Contrast** To fulfill his quest, an **epic hero** must typically overcome great obstacles. How is Gilgamesh like and unlike the epic hero Beowulf? What elements of Gilgamesh's battle with Humbaba are similar to Beowulf's battles with his monsters?

Writing Skills Focus

Think as a Reader/Writer

Use It in Your Writing Imagine what Gilgamesh or Enkidu is thinking and feeling in the hours before he confronts Humbaba. Write an interior monologue that expresses what one hero is thinking. Use the first-person pronoun.

What Do You Think Now? What is the most powerful force moving Gilgamesh to act against Humbaba in the end?

Universal Access

Struggling Writers

To complete the Writing Skills Focus activity, provide additional scaffolding for students by displaying on the board a list of issues and concerns that one hero is thinking about. The list might include:

- whether the hero will come out of the fight alive
- whether the hero has enough strength and resources to overcome Humbaba
- whether the hero's companion will stay at his side or leave him
- what the hero's dream is foretelling about the fight
- how the hero will be able to stand his ground

Tell students to address these concerns in their interior monologue. Remind students to write in the first person.

Check for Understanding

Independent Practice

Reading Skills Focus

Possible responses:

1. *The elders agree to his plan.*
2. *Humbaba initially strikes Enkidu, which is not what Gilgamesh expected. Gilgamesh is frozen in shock.*
3. *Gilgamesh encourages Enkidu to fight but is terrified when he thinks Enkidu is in danger.*
4. *Ask students to consider different reactions that Gilgamesh and Enkidu display in different situations.*

Vocabulary Check

5. *c* **6.** *d*
7. *a* **8.** *b*

Literary Skills Focus

Possible responses:

9. *They always encourage and defend each other. Sometimes their encouragement does not reflect their true feelings.*
10. *Unlike Enkidu, Gilgamesh is not afraid of Humbaba. He thinks the monster is too proud and that people should not fear Humbaba.*
11. *Students may say that Gilgamesh is too thoughtless to be admirable. He needs to learn humility.*
12. *Humbaba shows cowardice by offering to be a slave.*
13. *Both are brave, strong, and nobly born, and both seek fame and glory. Gilgamesh is more defiant of the gods and depends on his friend Enkidu, whereas Beowulf is mainly self-sufficient. Each severs the head of his opponent.*

What Do You Think Now?

Ask students to consider the character's feelings and thoughts before killing Humbaba and identify the strongest motivator for his action.

Selection Introduction

Think About the Writer

Before students answer the question, have them think about the forms of entertainment available to people in Homer's time compared to those available today. Ask students to consider why artists were so important in Greek society between 900 and 700 B.C.

For Independent Reading

- *Troy,** Adèle Geras
- *Heroes: A Novel,* Robert Cormier

HRW LIBRARY *This title is available in the HRW library.

Motivate

What Do You Think?/QuickWrite

Have students think about a person in their lives whom they find honorable. Start a group discussion of the qualities that students think can most benefit society. Ask students to write their thoughts in their **Reader/Writer Notebooks.**

Preparing to Read

from the Iliad, Book 22: The Death of Hector

What Do You Think? What moves a hero to act?

QuickWrite

In the *Iliad,* characters such as Achilles and Hector strive for *arête,* or personal honor and excellence. In their eyes it is honorable to fight bravely for one's king and comrades, and dishonorable to seek personal safety when others are threatened. What do honor and personal excellence mean to you? Take notes on your own and other contemporary ideals of honor and how they compare to *arête.*

Homer (9th–8th century B.C.). Marble bust. Museo Capitolino, Rome.

MEET THE WRITER

Homer and the *Iliad*

(c. 900–700 B.C.)

Europe's first and most enduring epics, the *Iliad* and the *Odyssey,* were composed sometime between 900 and 700 B.C. by Homer, about whom little is known. He was probably a native of the Greek district of Ionia on the western coast of Asia Minor. Homer belonged to a class of bards who played a vital role in Greek society, serving as historians and entertainers.

Homer's Epic Conventions

Features of Homer's work were so widely imitated in later written epics that they became recognizable characteristics, or conventions, of the epic genre. Many of these conventions originated in the oral tradition that gave birth to the *Iliad.* Oral poets used formulas that allowed them to summarize past events or sketch characters quickly. Conventions include the invocation, or formal plea to the gods for aid; *in medias res,* the technique of beginning the story in the middle of the action and using flashbacks; epic similes, which are extended, elaborate comparisons; and the stock epithet, a descriptive adjective or phrase repeatedly used with—or in the place of—a noun or proper name.

The Legend of the Trojan War

The *Iliad* and the *Odyssey* tell stories about the heroes and events of the Trojan War, a war that, according to Greek myth, was triggered by a beauty contest. Three goddesses—Hera, Athena, and Aphrodite—competed for a golden apple that was inscribed "To the Fairest." The gods chose Paris, a mortal, to judge the contest. Each goddess offered Paris a bribe for his vote. Paris accepted Aphrodite's bribe—Helen, the world's most beautiful woman and the wife of King Menelaus of Sparta. Paris abducted Helen and sailed for Troy. Outraged, Greek chieftains united to attack Troy. The conflict continued for ten years before the Greeks sacked the city and recaptured Helen.

The *Iliad* opens as the Trojan War enters its tenth year. The poem revolves around Achilles, the bravest Greek warrior, and his enemy Hector, the warrior-prince of Troy. In Book 22, the conflict between the two antagonists reaches its tragic climax.

Think About the Writer Homer was both historian and entertainer. What kind of job might enable him to serve both of those functions in modern society?

California Standards, pp. 98–111

- **Reading Standard 3.4** Analyze ways in which poets use imagery, personification, figures of speech, and "sounds" to evoke readers' emotions.
- **Grades 9–10 Review Reading Standard 3.12** Analyze the way in which a work of literature is related to the themes and issues of its historical period. (Historical approach).

Selection Readability	
Easily Accessible **Accessible** Challenging	unfamiliar setting; unfamiliar characters; historical context; epic poem

Reading Standard 3.4; Grades 9–10 Review
Reading Standard 3.12 (see pages A48–A50)

Literary Skills Focus

Epic Simile One of the most important features of the *Iliad* is Homer's use of **epic similes** (also called **Homeric similes**). These complex comparisons extend over many lines and use the words *like* and *as* to compare heroic actions to everyday events. In this excerpt, Achilles, in pursuit of Hector, is compared to a hunting dog. By using the familiar image of a hunt, Homer makes it easy for his audience to imagine Achilles racing after Hector in a relentless frenzy.

Literary Perspectives Apply the literary perspective described on page 103 as you read this epic.

Reading Skills Focus

Visualizing Imagery Writers use imagery to help their audiences visualize, or picture, the events in a story. Before you can **visualize imagery,** you have to understand the words and ideas that convey it. You will need to pay close attention to descriptive words and the pictures they create.

Into Action As you read, use a chart like the one below to keep track of powerful imagery from epic similes in the text. In column 1, be sure to note the line numbers for each example you find.

Line Numbers	Descriptive Words	Resulting Image
Lines 1–6	"swift Achilles . . . coursing Hector, nonstop / as a hound" hunts "a fawn"	simile creates image of powerful dog relentlessly hunting vulnerable fawn

Writing Skills Focus

Think as a Reader/Writer

Find It in Your Reading Homer's heroes are driven by a desire for personal honor. As you read the *Iliad*, look for clues about what things Achilles, Hector, and Homer consider honorable. In your *Reader/Writer Notebook*, record particular words that convey their attitudes.

Reader/Writer Notebook

Use your **RWN** to complete the activities for this selection.

Vocabulary

groveling (GRAHV uhl ihng) *v.* used as *adj.:* crawling; begging; humiliating oneself. *The groveling Apollo was unable to convince Zeus to save Hector.*

gallant (GAL uhnt) *adj.:* noble; brave. *Risking his life for the sake of his dead son, gallant Priam crossed the enemy lines in the dark.*

scourge (skurj) *n.:* cause of serious trouble. *Hector calls Achilles, who has been his people's deadliest enemy, the scourge of the Trojans.*

fawning (FAWN ihng) *v.:* used as *adj.:* cringing and pleading. *Desperate to retrieve Hector's body, the fawning father wept at Achilles' feet.*

Language Coach

Verbs Used as Adjectives A verb expresses an action; an adjective describes a noun or a pronoun. Verbs with an *–ing* ending can sometimes be used as adjectives. **Verb:** The soldier was *groveling* to save his life. **Adjective:** The *groveling* soldier crawled on his knees. What does the verb *fawn* mean? How can it be used as a verb? as an adjective?

Learn It Online
Learn more about this epic online.
go.hrw.com H12-99 Go

Comparing Texts Resources

Unit 1 Resources, on-level practice and assessment, p. 33

Teacher One Stop™, on-level lesson plans and all print resources

Holt Audio Library

Holt Audio Library: Selections and Summaries in Spanish

UA: Differentiating Instruction: graphic organizer, p. 11

UA: Supporting Instruction in Spanish, selection summary

ThinkCentral Online Assessment, Selection Standards Check

ThinkCentral Online Remediation

Preteach

Introducing Vocabulary

- Review the Vocabulary words, definitions, and sentences with students.
- To reinforce the importance of the Vocabulary words, tell students the words help the author compare the characters' actions to everyday images. Hector is described as a *gallant* captain, whose fate cannot be changed despite any amount of *groveling* by Phoebus, leaving him as a *fawning* dog at the feet of Achilles, the *scourge* of the Trojans.

English for Academic Success

Language Coach

Have students use the word *fawning* as a verb in one sentence and as an adjective in another sentence. Then, have them think of other verbs with an *–ing* ending that can be used as adjectives.

Literary Skills Focus

As you read and discuss the selection with students, have them note how epic similes are sustained throughout the selection.

Reading Skills Focus

Give students a copy of the Reading Skills Focus graphic organizer before they read. (See **Unit 1 Resources.**) Tell them to use their responses to answer the questions on the Applying Your Skills page.

Writing Skills Focus

As you read and discuss the selection with students, have them record clues about Achilles' and Hector's concept of honor in their **Reader/Writer Notebooks.** Students can use their notes to complete the Writing Skills Focus activity.

Learn It Online
The online version of this selection includes audio support to engage all students and to help struggling readers with reading comprehension and vocabulary.
go.hrw.com H12-99 Go

Teacher Preparation
Selection Plot Summary
The Trojan forces have retreated into the city, but Hector remains alone waiting to challenge the mighty Greek warrior Achilles. Achilles approaches at a run, raging at Hector's disrespectful treatment of the body of Patroclus, Achilles' friend; Hector loses his courage and flees. As Achilles pursues Hector, they circle the walls of Troy three times. Zeus, king of the gods, favors Hector, but Athena, goddess of wisdom, is on the side of the Greeks. The Greeks strike the Trojan down. The dying Hector begs Achilles to return his body to his parents for honorable burial, but Achilles refuses. The Greeks gloat and stab Hector's dead body numerous times. His anger still unappeased, Achilles ties the body by the ankles to the back of his chariot and drives back to the Greek lines.

EPIC

the Iliad

from Book 22: The Death of Hector

by **Homer**

translated by **Robert Fagles**

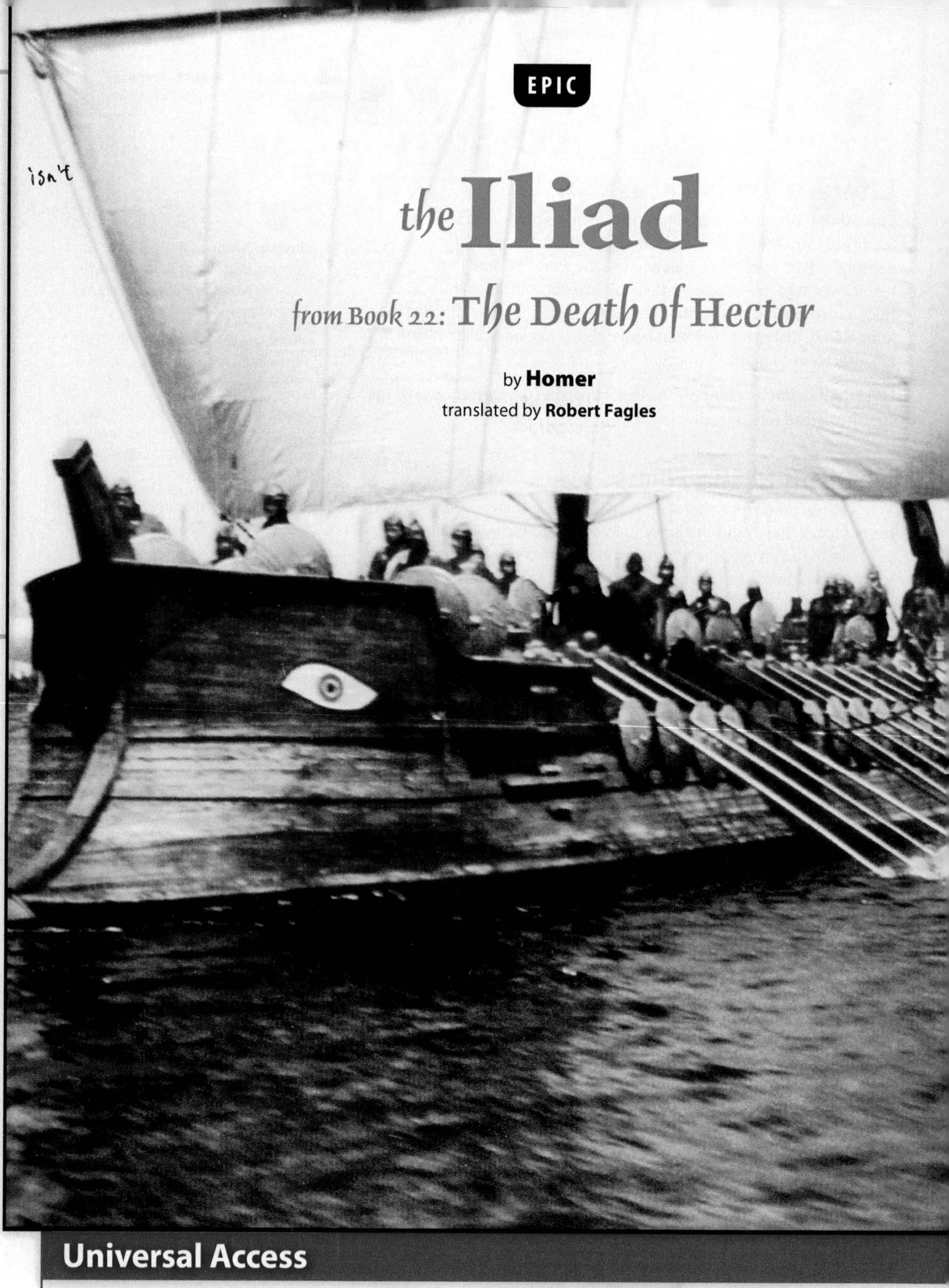

Universal Access

English Learners
English for Academic Success Help students visualize the events of the poem by clarifying the description of each character. Students may be unfamiliar with words such as *shield, lance, spear,* or *armor.* Show students pictures of each object and its corresponding name in English. To enrich the discussion, encourage students to explain meanings of borrowings from other languages that they recognize in the selection.

Struggling Readers
Struggling Students Model visualizing imagery for students. As students read lines 25–33, point that the descriptive words, "gripping the beam [of the scales] mid-haft . . . and down went Hector's day of doom, dragging him down to the strong House of Death" bring to mind the image of an object—representing Hector's life—falling helplessly into a dark pit, where all the dead end up. Ask students to point out lines that help them picture what is happening.

Read with a Purpose

Read to discover how Homer feels about a hero's power over his own fate.

Build Background

As the *Iliad* begins, the war between the Greeks and the Trojans has been at a stalemate for nearly ten years. Each army has fought bravely, and each has received the help of the gods. The god Apollo assists Hector and the Trojans, and the goddess Athena aids Achilles and the Greeks (also referred to as the Achaeans or the Argives). Prior to the events in the excerpt that follows, Hector has killed Patroclus, Achilles' dearest friend, and has stripped the corpse of its armor, leaving the body exposed and unburied. Because the Greeks believed a soul could not rest until certain burial rites had been performed, Achilles is enraged at Hector and seeks revenge.

The Characters in the *Iliad*

The Greeks

Achilles (uh KIHL eez): son of a mortal king, Peleus, and the sea goddess Thetis; king of the Myrmidons; mightiest of the Greek warriors.

Patroclus (puh TROH kluhs): Greek warrior and dearest friend of Achilles.

The Trojans

Hector (HEHK tuhr): son of King Priam and Queen Hecuba; commander of the Trojan forces.

Paris (PAR ihs): son of King Priam and Queen Hecuba; also known as Alexandros.

Priam (PRY uhm): king of Troy; father of Hector and Paris.

Gods and Goddesses

Apollo (uh PAHL oh): god of poetry, music, and prophecy; often referred to only as the son of Zeus and Leto, the daughter of Titans. Apollo sides with the Trojans.

Athena (uh THEE nuh): goddess of wisdom. Athena takes the Greeks' side in the conflict.

Zeus (zoos): father-god. Zeus remains more or less neutral throughout the conflict.

Advanced Learners

Enrichment Have students discuss the idea of heroes in the *Iliad.* Point out that Achilles is a hero to the Greeks, but he is a villain to the Trojans. Have students take note of the events that occur in this selection and any previous events referenced. Then, ask students to write a newspaper article reporting the death of Hector. The article should be written from the point of view of either the Trojans or the Greeks.

Students with Disabilities

Students might have trouble reading this selection without background information from the previous sections of the epic poem. Familiarize students with the storyline by giving them a brief description of each character and the major events leading up to the beginning of the selection. This will help students visualize the events that occur in this selection.

Direct Teach

Talk About/Think About

Read with a Purpose Have students read the Read with a Purpose statement. Point out that the concepts of "power" and "fate" are addressed repeatedly throughout the poem. Have students note details regarding the characters' power to control their own fate.

Build Background: Epic Poetry

Explain to students that Homer's other masterpiece the *Odyssey* takes place in the aftermath of the events of the *Iliad.* The ten-year siege of Troy finally over, Odysseus, one of the Greek generals, sets out for his home on the island of Ithaca. The poem relates his fantastic adventures on the long voyage home. Odysseus tangles with the Sirens, the Cyclops, the witch Calypso, and the sea god Poseidon, among others; loses his ship and all his men; and is washed ashore before finally making it home to his wife and son in Ithaca. Tell students that the English word *odyssey,* meaning *an epic journey,* comes from the name Odysseus.

Model the Skill

- Provide students with copies of the Reading Skills Focus graphic organizer. (See **Unit 1 Resources**.)
- Model using **visualization of imagery** as a strategy for comprehension. Direct students' attention to lines 1–14. Explain that Achilles, in these lines, is compared to a hound that is relentlessly hunting a fawn, which represents Hector. Next, model tracing the descriptive words from the text that help readers visualize this epic simile. Tell that two words that describe Achilles are *swift* and *coursing*, and they help establish the comparison of Achilles to a hound.

Line Numbers	Descriptive Words	Resulting Image
1–14	swift, coursing	Achilles is compared to an unyielding hound trailing his enemy.

Guided Practice: Apply

Turn-and-Talk Ask student pairs to identify and discuss other verbs used to indicate Achilles' speed and determination. (Students are likely to identify verbs such as *hunting, nosing, rush, intercept,* and *sprinting*.)

Think About/Talk About

Responses to Margin Questions

Lines 25–31 *Zeus places Achilles' and Hector's fates of death upon his sacred golden scales. The judgment goes against the Trojan: Hector's fate goes down, indicating that his time has come to die.*

Lines 34–52 *Athena tells Achilles she is going to persuade Hector to fight him face to face. Athena makes Hector believe that she is Deiphobus, coming to help him fight Achilles. In this way, she persuades him to turn and fight Achilles.*

As this excerpt opens, the exhausted Trojans take refuge behind their city walls, but Hector remains outside the gates. As Achilles races toward Troy, Hector's parents urge their son to come inside the walls, to safety. But after an inner struggle, Hector decides to fight to the death. As Achilles nears, Hector panics and flees in fear. An epic chase around the walls of Troy begins. Looking down from Mount Olympus, Zeus considers granting Apollo his wish and saving Hector from death. Athena protests vehemently, however, and Zeus grants the battle to her. Athena races down from Olympus to help Achilles, her favorite. Hector's fate is sealed.

And swift Achilles kept on coursing Hector, nonstop
as a hound in the mountains starts a fawn from its lair,
hunting him down the gorges, down the narrow glens
and the fawn goes to ground, hiding deep in brush
but the hound comes racing fast, nosing him out
until he lands his kill. So Hector could never throw
Achilles off his trail, the swift racer° Achilles—
time and again he'd make a dash for the Dardan Gates,°
trying to rush beneath the rock-built ramparts, hoping
men on the heights might save him, somehow, raining spears
but time and again Achilles would intercept him quickly,
heading him off, forcing him out across the plain
and always sprinting along the city side himself—
endless as in a dream . . . **A**
when a man can't catch another fleeing on ahead
and he can never escape nor his rival overtake him—
so the one could never run the other down in his speed
nor the other spring away. And how could Hector have fled
the fates of death so long? How unless one last time,
one final time Apollo had swept in close beside him,
driving strength in his legs and knees to race the wind?
And brilliant Achilles shook his head at the armies,
never letting them hurl their sharp spears at Hector—
someone might snatch the glory, Achilles come in second.
But once they reached the springs for the fourth time,
then Father Zeus held out his sacred golden scales:

7. swift racer: a stock epithet for Achilles.

8. Dardan Gates: gates of Troy. Dardania, a city built near the foot of Mount Ida, became part of Troy.

A **Literary Focus** **Epic Simile** Which simile emphasizes Achilles' speed?

Menelaus and Hector fighting over the body of the Trojan Euphorbos (c. 600 B.C.).
The British Museum, London.

Cross-Curricular Connection

MUSIC: Oral History

The word *Iliad* means *a song about Ilium,* which is another name for the city of Troy. During the seventh century B.C., the story of the *Iliad* was told through song. People called poet-singers read the work in dramatic fashion to audiences. Poet-singers performed at public events such as athletic competitions, religious festivals, and community feasts. This form of storytelling was an important part of Greek social and cultural life.

Activity Have students look through the poem for the section that they think audiences would find most exciting. Ask for a volunteer to read the section in dramatic fashion as a poet-singer would.

in them he placed two fates of death that lays men low—
one for Achilles, one for Hector breaker of horses°—
and gripping the beam mid-haft the Father raised it high
and down went Hector's day of doom, dragging him down
to the strong House of Death—and god Apollo left him. **B**
Athena rushed to Achilles, her bright eyes gleaming,
standing shoulder-to-shoulder, winging orders now:
"At last our hopes run high, my brilliant Achilles—
Father Zeus must love you—
we'll sweep great glory back to Achaea's fleet,
we'll kill this Hector, mad as he is for battle!
No way for him to escape us now, no longer—
not even if Phoebus the distant deadly Archer°
goes through torments, pleading for Hector's life,
groveling over and over before our storming Father Zeus.
But you, you hold your ground and catch your breath
while I run Hector down and persuade the man
to fight you face-to-face."
So Athena commanded
and he obeyed, rejoicing at heart—Achilles stopped,
leaning against his ashen spearshaft barbed in bronze.
And Athena left him there, caught up with Hector at once,
and taking the build and vibrant voice of Deiphobus°
stood shoulder-to-shoulder with him, winging orders:
"Dear brother, how brutally swift Achilles hunts you—
coursing you round the city of Priam in all his
lethal speed!
Come, let us stand our ground together—beat him
back."

"Deiphobus!"—Hector, his helmet flashing,
called out to her—
"dearest of all my brothers, all these warring years,
of all the sons that Priam and Hecuba produced!
Now I'm determined to praise you all the more,
you who dared—seeing me in these straits—
to venture out from the walls, all for *my* sake,
while the others stay inside and cling to safety."

? **25–31.** *How does Zeus decide the fates of Hector and Achilles? What is the final judgment?*

28. breaker of horses: a stock epithet for Hector.

? **34–52.** *What does Athena tell Achilles she is going to do? How does Athena trick Hector?*

39. deadly Archer: a stock epithet.

48. Deiphobus (dee IHF uh buhs): one of Hector's brothers.

Literary Perspectives

Analyzing Historical Context A literary work's historical context is everything that was happening when the work was written, including the social, cultural, and political climate. Thinking about key elements of ancient Greek culture will help you interpret Homer's enduring epic. For example, the Greeks believed that each person had an assigned fate, called a *moira,* and that the boundaries of that fate should not be challenged. They felt that one should try to bear the limitations of the human condition with dignity and proper pride. A Greek hero should gain as much fame and glory as possible within the boundaries of his *moira.* Going beyond those boundaries invariably brings divine vengeance. The *Iliad* presents many examples of a character's hubris (arrogance resulting from excessive pride) leading to his downfall. Achilles succumbs to hubris when he sulkily refuses to return to battle. This hubris, combined with his friend Patroclus's own hubris over his triumph in a battle, leads to Patroclus's death. As you read, look for instances when the characters discuss or react to their fate. Think about how the idea of *moira* and hubris relate to Hector's death.

As you read, be sure to notice the questions in the text, which will guide you in using this perspective.

B Reading Focus **Visualizing Imagery** What image does Homer use to show that Zeus is deciding the fates of Hector and Achilles?

Vocabulary **groveling** (GRAHV uhl ihng) *v.* used as *adj.:* crawling; begging; humiliating oneself.

Think About/Talk About

Comprehension

B Reading Focus

Possible response: *Homer uses the image of "sacred golden scales" to show how Zeus decides the fates of Hector and Achilles.*

Analysis

A Literary Focus

Possible response: *In the opening of the book, Achilles chases Hector "as a hound in the mountains starts a fawn from its lair."*

Extend the Discussion

Identifying Cause and Effect In the opening of the selection, Hector is chased by Achilles. Why is Hector unable to retreat behind the walls of Troy? ***Possible responses:*** *Achilles is too fast, and Hector cannot outrun him; Achilles heads him off and forces him into the open plain.*

Evaluating In line 35 Athena states, "Father Zeus must love you" when speaking to Achilles. How important is it to these characters to have the love of Zeus on their side? ***Possible response:*** *It is very important. Zeus is the father of all gods and the most powerful. He decides the fate of all mortals.*

Vocabulary: Own the Word

groveling: Remind students that *groveling* means "begging or humiliating oneself." Ask students to explain why Phoebus might *grovel* for Hector's life. ***Possible response:*** *He might grovel, or beg, because he is desperate to save Hector and does not know of any other way to appeal to Zeus's sense of humanity.*

Developing Oral Fluency

Whole-Class Activity The layout of the poem can make it hard for students to read the lines smoothly. To help students improve their oral fluency, have them read the poem as a play. Assign the lines of Achilles, Hector, and Athena to students, and also choose someone to serve as the narrator for lines that are not spoken by characters. Assign different students to read parts every few pages so more students can participate.

✔ See the **Oral Language Skill Builder** in **UA: Differentiating Instruction.**

Literary Perspectives

Have students read the **Literary Perspectives** about Analyzing Historical Context. Point out that lines 26–31 reveal the gods have already decided on the fate of the two warriors. Ask them to note places in the text where Hector's hubris leads to his end and places where Hector seems to acknowledge his fate. Have them also consider how Achilles takes advantage of Athena's help to prove his glory. Would Achilles have acted differently without Athena's promise of victory? Explain.

Remind students to use the notes and questions at the bottom of the page to help them use the perspective.

Guided Practice: Apply

Think as a Reader/Writer

Find It in Your Reading Direct students to lines 136–139, in which Hector explains that he would like to die with honor. He states that he wants to go down "in some great clash of arms that even men to come will hear of down the years."

Use It in Your Writing Tell students to write three sentences describing this "great clash of arms" in a way that portrays Hector as an honorable warrior.

Think About/Talk About

Responses to Margin Questions

Lines 73–79 *Hector vows to stand and fight. He believes he has the support of his brother and is ready to accept whatever fate may bring.*

Lines 78–98 *Hector has offered to make a pact with Achilles that the victor will return the other man's body to his comrades for honorable burial. Achilles refuses because he says that Hector is too dishonorable to make pacts with.*

Lines 106–117 *Hector's words suggest that the success or failure of mortals often depends on the favor of the gods. Hector is unaware that Athena is present in the form of Deiphobus to help Achilles.*

Lines 123–139 *Hector realizes that the gods have taken Achilles' side and that he, Hector, is about to die at the hands of the Greek. Hector decides to die while engaged in a glorious struggle against Achilles.*

The goddess answered quickly, her eyes blazing,
"True, dear brother—how your father and mother both
implored me, time and again, clutching my knees,
and the comrades round me begging me to stay!
Such was the fear that broke them, man for man,
but the heart within me broke with grief for you.
Now headlong on and fight! No letup, no lance spared!
So now, now we'll *see* if Achilles kills us both
and hauls our bloody armor back to the beaked ships
or *he* goes down in pain beneath your spear."

Athena luring him on with all her immortal cunning—
and now, at last, as the two came closing for the kill
it was tall Hector, helmet flashing, who led off:
"No more running from you in fear, Achilles!
Not as before. Three times I fled around
the great city of Priam—I lacked courage then
to stand your onslaught. Now my spirit stirs me
to meet you face-to-face. Now kill or be killed!
Come, we'll swear to the gods, the highest witnesses—
the gods will oversee our binding pacts. I swear
I will never mutilate you—merciless as you are—
if Zeus allows me to last it out and tear your life away.
But once I've stripped your glorious armor, Achilles,
I will give your body back to your loyal comrades.
Swear you'll do the same." **C**
                                        A swift dark glance
and the headstrong runner answered, "Hector, stop!
You unforgivable, you . . . don't talk to me of pacts.
There are no binding oaths between men and lions—
wolves and lambs can enjoy no meeting of the minds—
they are all bent on hating each other to the death.
So with you and me. No love between us. No truce **D**
till one or the other falls and gluts with blood
Ares who hacks at men behind his rawhide shield.
Come, call up whatever courage you can muster.
Life or death—now prove yourself a spearman,
a daring man of war! No more escape for you—
Athena will kill you with my spear in just a moment.
Now you'll pay at a stroke for all my comrades' grief,
all you killed in the fury of your spear!"

? **73–79.** *What does Hector vow? Why does he now have courage?*

? **78–98.** *What pact has Hector offered Achilles? Why does Achilles refuse the pact?*

Athena in armor. Silver tetradrachm of Ptolemy I (c. 324–323 B.C.).
Fitzwilliam Museum, Cambridge, England.

C **Literary Perspectives** **Historical Context** What does Hector's pact suggest about how Greeks valued the treatment of the human body after death?

D **Reading Focus** **Visualizing Imagery** What insulting image does Achilles present to Hector by comparing Hector and himself to lambs and wolves?

Universal Access

EL English Learners

English for Academic Success Direct students to the phrase "bent on" in line 89. Explain to students that this idiom means *to be set on [doing something]* or *to be determined [to do something]*. Ask students what Achilles is "bent on" doing in these lines. [*Achilles is determined to hate Hector until either of them dies.*] Point out to students that the epic simile is used again when Achilles believes there can be no agreement between them because they are like the wolf and lamb.

Struggling Readers

Strategic Students Help students look for descriptive words that create mental pictures as they read. Using a ruler as a prop, demonstrate the action of poising and hurling. Tell students that *seething* means "to be violently excited." Read aloud lines 118–124. Then, read the lines aloud again, this time asking students to close their eyes and picture the actions of the scene. Ask students what images came to their minds and which words helped to create those images.

With that,
shaft poised, he hurled and his spear's long shadow flew
but seeing it coming glorious Hector ducked away,
crouching down, watching the bronze tip fly past
and stab the earth—but Athena snatched it up
and passed it back to Achilles
and Hector the gallant captain never saw her.
He sounded out a challenge to Peleus' princely son:
"You missed, look—the great godlike Achilles!
So you knew nothing at all from Zeus about my death—
and yet how sure you were! All bluff, cunning with words,
that's all you are—trying to make me fear you,
lose my nerve, forget my fighting strength.
Well, you'll never plant your lance in my back
as I flee *you* in fear—plunge it through my chest
as I come charging in, if a god gives you the chance!
But now it's for you to dodge *my* brazen spear—
I wish you'd bury it in your body to the hilt.
How much lighter the war would be for Trojans then
if you, their greatest scourge, were dead and gone!"

Shaft poised, he hurled and his spear's long shadow flew
and it struck Achilles' shield—a dead-center hit—
but off and away it glanced and Hector seethed,
his hurtling spear, his whole arm's power poured
in a wasted shot. He stood there, cast down . . .
he had no spear in reserve. So Hector shouted out
to Deiphobus bearing his white shield—with a ringing shout
he called for a heavy lance—
but the man was nowhere near
him, vanished—
yes and Hector knew the truth in his heart
and the fighter cried aloud, "My time has come!
At last the gods have called me down to death.
I thought he was at my side, the hero Deiphobus—
he's safe inside the walls, Athena's tricked me blind.
And now death, grim death is looming up beside me,
no longer far away. No way to escape it now. This,
this was their pleasure after all, sealed long ago—
Zeus and the son of Zeus, the distant deadly Archer—
though often before now they rushed to my defense.
So now I meet my doom. Well let me die—

Vocabulary **gallant** (GAL uhnt) *adj:* noble; brave.
scourge (skurj) *n.:* cause of serious trouble.

106–117. Hector is emboldened by Achilles' unsuccessful attack.

? *What do Hector's words suggest about the relationship between mortals and gods? Of what is Hector unaware?*

? **123–139.** *What truth does Hector now realize? What does he decide to do?*

Think About/Talk About

Comprehension

D Reading Focus

Possible response: *By using the imagery of lambs and wolves, Achilles suggests that he is strong like a wolf, while Hector is weak like a lamb.*

Analysis

C Literary Perspectives

Possible response: *Hector's pact suggests that the Greeks honored the deceased by celebrating them with determined burial rites.*

Extend the Discussion

Finding Details How does Athena, disguised as Deiphobus, convince Hector to fight Achilles face to face? ***Possible response:*** *Deiphobus tells Hector that he has come to help even though their parents begged him not to and reassures Hector that he will be behind him.*

Vocabulary: Own the Word

- **gallant:** A *gallant* person is daring and courageous; an antonym is *cowardly.* Use both words in a sentence: The *gallant* Hector hurled his spear at his foe while his cowardly brothers watched from afar.
- **scourge:** Who was the *scourge* of the Trojans and why? ***Possible response:*** *Achilles, with his superior fighting and leadership abilities, was making it difficult for the Trojans to gain an advantage in the war.*

Students with Disabilities

Guide students in understanding the use of the epic simile. Ask students to list adjectives that describe the perceptiveness and pace of hunting dogs. Then have them list adjectives that describe the pace of a small animal being chased, such as rabbit or raccoon, being chased by dogs. Instruct students to use two adjectives from their first list to describe Achilles in a sentence. Then, tell them to use two adjectives from their second list to describe Hector in a sentence.

Compare and Contrast

Ask students to compare and contrast the characters of Achilles and Hector.

- **Similarities** Both are leaders of their people. Each wants to be honorable. They receive help from gods. Both are greedy for glory. They act as though they were godlike.
- **Differences** Achilles is sure of himself, while Hector is not confident in his ability to win the battle. Achilles is headstrong, and Hector is merciful. Achilles has a deep hatred for Hector, while Hector is indifferent toward Achilles.

Think About/Talk About

Literary Connection

Tell students that Achilles' anger has been described as extreme and intemperate, but in lines 185–186, the hero says he wishes that his rage could be even greater so that he could eat Hector's raw flesh. Achilles believes that Hector's crime against Patroclus is so horrible that no punishment is too barbaric.

Build Background: Burial Rites

A dead Greek or Trojan warrior was dressed in white and laid out so his troops could pay their respects by circling the bier and lamenting. The body was then burned on a massive funeral pyre along with sacrificial offerings of bulls, sheep, goats, and jars of honey and oil.

Extend the Discussion

Epic Simile What does the simile in lines 139–144 imply about Hector's attitude in the face of death?

Possible response: *Now that his death is assured, Hector shows heroic bravery. Instead of being the pursued, Hector swoops eagerly upon his pursuer.*

Responses to Margin Questions

Lines 156–165 *Achilles drives his spear through Hector's throat, the one spot unprotected by Patroclus's armor.*

Lines 175–182 *Hector pleads that Achilles give his body back to Hector's Trojan friends, who will ensure that it receives the funeral rites proper for a great hero.*

Lines 183–194 *Achilles spurns Hector's plea with anger and tells him, "The dogs and birds will rend you—blood and bone!"*

but not without struggle, not without glory, no,
in some great clash of arms that even men to come
will hear of down the years!"
And on that resolve
he drew the whetted sword that hung at his side,
tempered, massive, and gathering all his force
he swooped like a soaring eagle
launching down from the dark clouds to earth
to snatch some helpless lamb or trembling hare. **E**
So Hector swooped now, swinging his whetted sword
and Achilles charged too, bursting with rage, barbaric,
guarding his chest with the well-wrought blazoned shield,
head tossing his gleaming helmet, four horns strong
and the golden plumes shook that the god of fire
drove in bristling thick along its ridge.
Bright as that star amid the stars in the night sky,
star of the evening, brightest star that rides the heavens,
so fire flared from the sharp point of the spear Achilles
brandished high in his right hand, bent on Hector's death, **F**
scanning his splendid body—where to pierce it best?
The rest of his flesh seemed all encased in armor,
burnished, brazen—*Achilles'* armor that Hector stripped
from strong Patroclus when he killed him—true,
but one spot lay exposed,
where collarbones lift the neckbone off the shoulders,
the open throat, where the end of life comes quickest—*there*
as Hector charged in fury brilliant Achilles drove his spear
and the point went stabbing clean through the tender neck
but the heavy bronze weapon failed to slash the windpipe—
Hector could still gasp out some words, some last reply . . .
he crashed in the dust—
godlike Achilles gloried over him:
"Hector—surely you thought when you stripped Patroclus' armor
that you, you would be safe! Never a fear of me—
far from fighting as I was—you fool!
Left behind there, down by the beaked ships
his great avenger waited, a greater man by far—
that man was I, and I smashed your strength! And you—
the dogs and birds will maul you, shame your corpse
while Achaeans bury my dear friend in glory!"

156–165. Here we are reminded that Hector is wearing Achilles' old armor. Achilles had given the armor to his dear friend Patroclus, whom Hector had killed.

? *How does Achilles mortally wound Hector?*

E **Literary Focus** **Epic Simile** To what is Hector compared as he runs toward Achilles?

F **Reading Focus** **Visualizing Imagery** What descriptive words does Homer use to create a vivid image of Achilles' charge?

Word-Attack Skills Mini-Lesson

English for Academic Success Use the selection word *groveling* to explore the sounds of vowels that precede the letter *v*. Explain that the number of consonant letters that follow a vowel can signal whether the vowel sound is short or long. Pronounce the words *blazoned* and *blizzard*. In *blazoned*, the vowel sound is long: *BLAY zuhnd*. In *blizzard*, it is short: *BLIHZ uhrd*. Explain that in a word like *groveling*, however, the single *v* is not a clue that the first vowel sound is long because the consonant *v* is rarely doubled in English words. Compare the initial vowel sounds in *graven* and *gravel*.

Activity In each set, two words have the same vowel sound in the first syllable; the other has a different sound. Have students identify the word with the different vowel sound.

1. haversack	haven	havoc
2. craven	davenport	bravery
3. hover	shovel	clover
4. maverick	gravity	gravy
5. ravel	raven	ravenous
6. savory	savage	scavenge

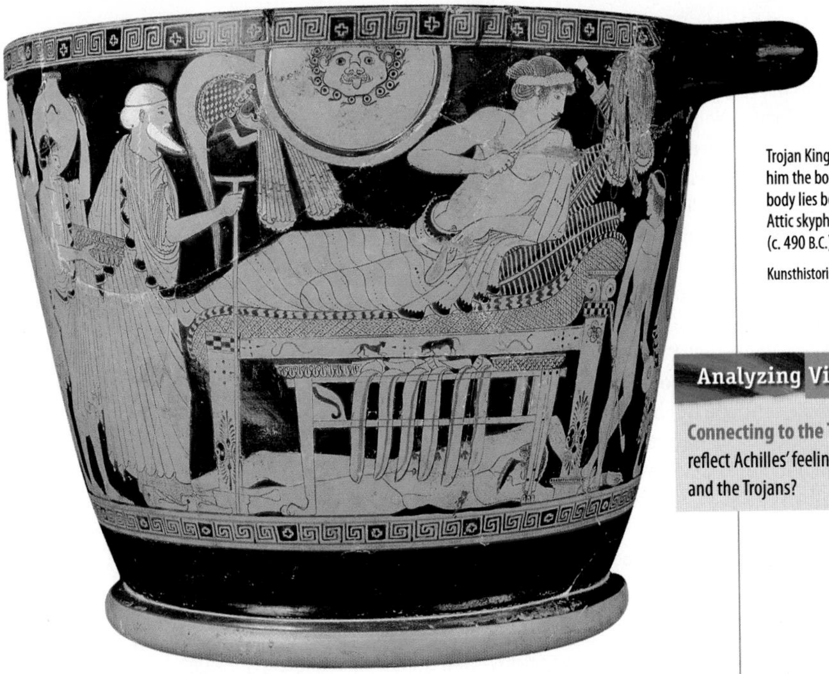

Trojan King Priam begs Achilles to give him the body of Hector, his slain son. Hector's body lies beneath Achilles' bed. Red-figured Attic skyphos (drinking vessel) from Caere (c. 490 B.C.).

Kunsthistorisches Museum, Vienna.

Analyzing Visuals

Connecting to the Text How does this image reflect Achilles' feelings and attitude toward Hector and the Trojans?

Struggling for breath, Hector, his helmet flashing,
said, "I beg you, beg you by your life, your parents—
don't let the dogs devour me by the Argive ships!
Wait, take the princely ransom of bronze and gold,
the gifts my father and noble mother will give you—
but give my body to friends to carry home again,
so Trojan men and Trojan women can do me honor
with fitting rites of fire once I am dead."

Staring grimly, the proud runner Achilles answered,
"Beg no more, you fawning dog—begging me by my parents!
Would to god my rage, my fury would drive me now
to hack your flesh away and eat you raw—
such agonies you have caused me! Ransom?
No man alive could keep the dog-packs off you,
not if they haul in ten, twenty times that ransom
and pile it here before me and promise fortunes more—
no, not even if Dardan Priam should offer to weigh out
your bulk in gold! Not even then will your noble mother
lay you on your deathbed, mourn the son she bore . . .
The dogs and birds will rend you—blood and bone!"

175–182. This exchange between Hector and Achilles emphasizes the importance the Greeks and Trojans placed on a proper burial. Without "fitting rites," both men believed, the soul of the departed would never find rest.

? *What does Hector plead?*

? **183–194.** *How does Achilles react to Hector's plea?*

Vocabulary **fawning** (FAWN ihng) *v.* used as *adj.:* cringing and pleading.

Think About/Talk About

Comprehension

F Reading Focus

Possible response: *Homer uses descriptive words such as* barbaric, gleaming, golden, bristling, *and* bright *to create a vivid image of Achilles' charge.*

Analysis

E Literary Focus

Possible response: *As he runs toward Achilles, Hector is compared to a soaring eagle swooping down from the dark clouds to the earth to snatch some helpless lamb or trembling hare.*

Extend the Discussion

Finding Details As Hector struggles to breathe in lines 175–182, what does he offer to Achilles in exchange for the return of his body to the Trojan people? ***Possible response:*** *He offers him his princely ransom of bronze and gold from his father and mother.*

Making Inferences In lines 167–168, Achilles states, "Hector—surely you thought when you stripped Patroclus' armor that you, you would be safe! Never a fear of me—." Do you think Hector still fears Achilles? ***Possible response:*** *Yes, Hector begs for his life.*

Vocabulary: Own the Word

fawning: Ask students to answer the following questions:

- What might a *fawning* person do or say to win someone's favor?
- Why might a person be *fawning* over someone?
- How do dogs act when they are *fawning* on their masters?

Universal Access

AAVE Students Who Use African American Vernacular English

English for Academic Success Reinforce formal English patterns of past tense verbs. Read aloud from the second part of line 139 ("And on . . .") to the end of line 140. Draw students' attention to the verbs *drew.* Some students may be tempted to read it as "he drawn." Explain that "he drew" is appropriate because the actions of Achilles and Hector in the passage are written in the simple past tense, so the *drew* is in the simple past tense form of *draw,* not *drawn.*

Analyzing Visuals

Connecting to the Text: *The image on the drinking vessel shows old King Priam standing at the foot of Achilles' bed, asking for Achilles' permission to give his son a proper burial. Achilles' face, however, is turned away from the king: his defiant posture reflects his contempt toward Hector and the Trojans.*

Model the Skill

- Review the literary concept of a **foil.** Remind students that one character is the foil of another character when the qualities of one bring out contrasting qualities of the other.
- Tell students that in lines 195–209, Hector's acceptance of his fate and serious warning about Achilles' day of doom is set off by Achilles' prideful victory. Also point out to students that Achilles remains hardened toward Hector and the Trojans to the end by not honoring Hector's wish to return his body to his family, and instead stabbing it repeatedly and dragging it on the dust behind his chariot. Indicate to students that throughout the excerpt, Achilles remains bitter and hardened in his heart toward Hector, who does not share a similarly strong resentment toward his foe.

Guided Practice: Apply

Think-Pair-Share Ask students to, with a partner, go back to the previous pages they have read and look for other contrasting characteristics between Hector and Achilles. Have pairs share their findings with the rest of the class.

Think About/Talk About

Responses to Margin Questions

Lines 212–218 *The Greek soldiers marvel at the physical beauty of Hector, and they gloat and stab his body numerous times as a sign of disrespect.*

Lines 242–253 *Hector's body is transported from the scene of death by being dragged behind Achilles' chariot. Most students will say that they feel pity for Hector, and some may say that they also feel disgust for Achilles.*

At the point of death, Hector, his helmet flashing,
said, "I know you well—I see my fate before me.
Never a chance that I could win you over . . .
Iron inside your chest, that heart of yours.
But now beware, or my curse will draw god's wrath
upon your head, that day when Paris and lord Apollo—
for all your fighting heart—destroy you at the Scaean Gates!"°

Death cut him short. The end closed in around him.
Flying free of his limbs
his soul went winging down to the House of Death,
wailing his fate, leaving his manhood far behind,
his young and supple strength. But brilliant Achilles
taunted Hector's body, dead as he was, "Die, die!
For my own death, I'll meet it freely—whenever Zeus
and the other deathless gods would like to bring it on!"

With that he wrenched his bronze spear from the corpse,
laid it aside and ripped the bloody armor off the back. **G**

200–201. Paris . . . Gates: Hector is foretelling Achilles' ultimate fate. Achilles will later be slain by Paris, who will shoot an arrow into Achilles' heel, the only vulnerable part of his body.

G Reading Focus **Visualizing Imagery** What descriptive verbs paint the gruesome image of this scene?

Achilles and Hector. Scene from the *Iliad*. Crater by Berlin Painter (490 B.C.).

Universal Access

Struggling Readers

Students may have a hard time using visualization to help them comprehend the poem if they are struggling to comprehend the text. Have students read lines 210–222. Have the class break into small groups and ask them to practice demonstrating the actions in these lines. One student should practice reading aloud, while the other students in the group can practice acting out the roles of Achilles, Hector, and the "other sons of Achaea." Then, have groups act out their roles in front of the class while the lines are read.

Advanced Learners

Enrichment While each character in the poem strives to be a hero, each also has significant vulnerabilities: Achilles' heel and Hector's throat. Have students look through the poem to find other vulnerabilities or weaknesses in each character. In small groups, have students compare these attributes to a weakness in themselves that could be considered their own Achilles' heel.

And the other sons of Achaea, running up around him,
crowded closer, all of them gazing wonder-struck
at the build and marvelous, lithe beauty of Hector.
And not a man came forward who did not stab his body,
glancing toward a comrade, laughing: "Ah, look here—
how much softer he is to handle now, this Hector,
than when he gutted our ships with roaring fire!"

Standing over him, so they'd gloat and stab his body.
But once he had stripped the corpse the proud runner Achilles
took his stand in the midst of all the Argive troops
and urged them on with a flight of winging orders:
"Friends—lords of the Argives, O my captains!
Now that the gods have let me kill this man
who caused us agonies, loss on crushing loss—
more than the rest of all their men combined—
come, let us ring their walls in armor, test them,
see what recourse the Trojans still may have in mind.
Will they abandon the city heights with this man fallen?
Or brace for a last, dying stand though Hector's gone?
But wait—what am I saying? Why this deep debate?
Down by the ships a body lies unwept, unburied—
Patroclus . . . I will never forget him,
not as long as I'm still among the living
and my springing knees will lift and drive me on.
Though the dead forget their dead in the House of Death,
I will remember, even there, my dear companion.
Now,
come, you sons of Achaea, raise a song of triumph!
Down to the ships we march and bear this corpse on high—
we have won ourselves great glory. We have brought
magnificent Hector down, that man the Trojans
glorified in their city like a god!"
So he triumphed
and now he was bent on outrage, on shaming noble Hector.
Piercing the tendons, ankle to heel behind both feet,
he knotted straps of rawhide through them both,
lashed them to his chariot, left the head to drag
and mounting the car, hoisting the famous arms° aboard,
he whipped his team to a run and breakneck on they flew,
holding nothing back. And a thick cloud of dust rose up
from the man they dragged, his dark hair swirling round
that head so handsome once, all tumbled low in the dust—
since Zeus had given him over to his enemies now
to be defiled in the land of his own fathers.

212–218. Achilles' comrades gather around the great warrior and the body of his victim.
? *What do the Greek soldiers do to Hector's body?*

Sarcophagus depicting Priam begging Achilles for the body of his son Hector. Marble.

242–253. Achilles' wrath is so great that he cannot stop at merely killing Hector.
? *How is Hector's body transported from the scene of death? How do you feel as you read this description?*

247. famous arms: Hector's armor.

Think About/Talk About

Comprehension

G Reading Focus

Possible response: *The descriptive verbs that create the gruesome image are* wrenched *and* ripped.

Extend the Discussion

Making Inferences Re-read lines 242–253. How do you think the poet feels about the shaming of Hector's body? ***Possible response:*** *The poet describes the scene as an "outrage," and uses the word* defiled, *so it seems he disapproves of Achilles' actions.*

Monitor Students' Comprehension

Guide the class in answering these comprehension questions.

1. Why was Achilles so determined to defeat Hector? [*He wanted to avenge the death of Patroclus, a close friend.*]
2. What characteristics of Hector's brother, Deiphobus, does Athena take on to fool Hector? [*She takes on Deiphobus's build and his vibrant voice.*]
3. Which ultimate humiliation does Achilles inflict on Hector's corpse? [*Achilles does not give Hector a proper burial, but drags the hero's body with his chariot.*]

California Standards, pp. 110–111

- **Reading Standard 3.1** Analyze characteristics of subgenres (e.g., satire, parody, allegory, pastoral) that are used in poetry, prose, plays, novels, short stories, essays, and other basic genres.
- **Reading Standard 3.4** Analyze ways in which poets use imagery, personification, figures of speech, and "sounds" to evoke readers' emotions.
- **Reading Standard 3.7** Analyze recognized works of world literature from a variety of authors. **b.** Relate literary works and authors to the major themes and issues of their eras. **c.** Evaluate the philosophical, political, religious, ethical, and social influences of the historical period that shaped the characters, plots and settings.
- **Grades 9–10 Review Reading Standard 3.3** Analyze interactions between main and subordinate characters in a literary text (e.g., internal and external conflicts, motivations, relationships, influence) and explain the way those interactions affect the plot.
- **Grades 9–10 Review Reading Standard 3.12** Analyze the way a work of literature is related to the themes and issues of its historical period. (Historical approach)
- **Writing Standard 2.2** Write responses to literature: **a.** Demonstrate a comprehensive understanding of the significant ideas in works or passages. **b.** Analyze the imagery, language, universal themes, and unique aspects of the text. **c.** Support important ideas and viewpoints through accurate and detailed references to the text and to other works.
- **Listening and Speaking Standard 2.3** Deliver oral responses to literature: **c.** Support important ideas and viewpoints through accurate and detailed references to the text or to other works.

Check for Understanding

Independent Practice

Reading Skills Focus

Possible responses:

1. *Athena*
2. *Zeus weighs Hector's and Achilles' fates on a golden scale; Hector's fate is pulled downward towards death, his fate.*
3. *He is avenging Patroclus' death.*
4. *Hector's pride led to his death by causing him to ignore his parents' advice. Or, both Hector's character and his fate were instrumental in his doom.*
5. *Have students visualize the similes.*

Vocabulary Check

6. *groveling–dejected; Someone who is overly humble is groveling.*
7. *scourge–menace; Something that brings evil is a scourge.*
8. *fawning–pleading; Someone who flatters unctuously is fawning.*

Literary Skills Focus

Possible responses:

9. *It is both; It celebrates the heroes of war, but ultimately heroes are brought down by the brutality.*
10. *When an American soldier dies in a foreign land, the body is brought back home for a proper burial.*
11. *It suggests Greek wartime culture left the outcome to the strength of the warriors and to fate.*
12. *Epic similes help the reader visualize the scene.*
13. *Achilles' tenacious drive for revenge makes Hector seem spiritless and weak. Hector's desire to make a pact makes him honorable, while Achilles' refusal makes him seem ruthless.*

What Do You Think Now?

Have students compare the two characters' motivation and decide which of the two is more heroic.

Applying Your Skills

Reading Standard 3.4; **Grades 9–10 Review**
Reading Standard 3.3, 3.12 (see pages A48–A50)
Writing Standard 2.2a (see pages A51–A52)

from the Iliad, Book 22: The Death of Hector

Literary Response and Analysis

Reading Skills Focus

Quick Check

1. Who deceives Hector for Achilles' sake?
2. Why does Zeus decline to save Hector?
3. Why does Achilles deny Hector's dying request?

Read with a Purpose

4. Homer explores the relationship between *moira* (fate) and character. Is Hector doomed by his noble character, by fate, or by both?

Reading Skills: Visualizing Imagery

5. As you read, you noted specific, powerful images within epic similes as well as the words that described them. Now, record how the image helped you understand the epic simile.

Line Numbers	Descriptive Words	Resulting Image	How It Clarifies the Simile
Lines 1–6	"swift Achilles . . . coursing Hector, nonstop / as a hound" hunts "a fawn"	simile creates image of powerful dog relentlessly hunting vulnerable fawn	shows Achilles' determination to terrify, exhaust, and capture Hector

Vocabulary Check

Use the chart for **gallant** as a model as you make charts for the other three Vocabulary words.

Word	Meaning	Example
gallant	noble; brave	Someone who suffers without complaining is gallant.

6. groveling **7.** scourge **8.** fawning

Literary Skills Focus

Literary Analysis

9. **Evaluate** The *Iliad* is primarily a war epic. Does the *Iliad* condemn war's brutality, celebrate the heroism that war can inspire, or evenly examine both? Provide examples from the text.
10. **Extend** Hector requests that his body be left unmutilated and returned to his parents for burial. What events in wars today, or in movies or stories about war, show that we have the same concern for the bodies of our soldiers?
11. **Literary Perspectives** No other warriors try to interfere in the battle between Hector and Achilles. What does this fact suggest about ancient Greek values and wartime culture?

Literary Skills: Epic Simile

12. **Analyze** How do Homer's epic similes make straightforward action—a chase, a confrontation, and a death match—seem more heroic?

Literary Skills Review: Foil

13. **Analyze** A **foil** is a character who, by contrast, emphasizes the qualities of another character. How are Achilles and Hector foils for each other?

Writing Skills Focus

Think as a Reader/Writer

Use It in Your Writing Write an essay about two characters with contrasting views of honor. Show how each feels about what is and is not honorable.

What Do You Think Now? Do you think Achilles' behavior after Hector's death is heroic? Explain.

Universal Access

Struggling Writers

To complete the Writing Skills Focus, provide additional scaffolding for students by having them create T-charts. The left side should be labeled with one character's name, and the right side should have the other character's name. As students jot notes in each column, have them address each character's definition of honor, the kinds of motivations that are honorable, and actions and causes that are honorable. Remind students to use textual evidence to support each character's viewpoints. Display the following chart on the board as an example to help students begin:

Hector	Achilles
it's honorable to return the body of one's opponent to the family for proper burial	taking revenge on one's friend, even in a brutal manner, is honorable

COMPARING TEXTS
Wrap Up

Reading Standard 3.1, 3.7b, 3.7c (see pages A48–A50)
Writing Standard 2.2a–c (see pages A51–A52)
Listening and Speaking Standard 2.3c (see pages A53–A55)

from Gilgamesh: A Verse Narrative
from the Iliad: The Death of Hector

Writing Skills Focus
Analyzing Literary Criticism

The critic David Denby made this statement about the ethos, or attitudes and ethical beliefs, of the Greek and Trojan warriors of Homer's *Iliad:*

> Accepting death in battle as inevitable, the Greek and Trojan aristocrats of the *Iliad* experience the world not as pleasant or unpleasant, nor as good and evil, but as glorious or shameful.

Write an essay in which you analyze Denby's statement as it relates to either the *Iliad* or *Gilgamesh*. You will be either agreeing with Denby's perspective or disagreeing with it. To support your analysis, use specific evidence from the selection you choose to write about.

Plan Your Essay Answering the following questions may help you plan your essay.

- Why do epic heroes see their behavior in absolutes: good/evil; glorious/shameful?
- What is the role of fate in this belief?
- What is the role of a violent and uncertain world as the context for these beliefs?

Create a Thesis Statement Your thesis statement will articulate your perspective on the relationship between Denby's observation and your own analysis of either the *Iliad* or *Gilgamesh*. Here are two sample thesis statements for this essay:

Denby's observation that the aristocrats of the Iliad view the world as either glorious or shameful is equally true for the way Gilgamesh interacts with the world.

Denby's assertion that the Greek and Trojan aristocrats of the Iliad view the world as either glorious or shameful is not correct.

Support Your Analysis Supporting points are needed to develop an effective analysis. Use paraphrased and direct quotations from the text to support these points.

CHOICES

As you respond to the Choices, use these **Academic Vocabulary** words as appropriate: attribute, concept, diverse, emphasis, status.

REVIEW

Compare and Contrast Epics Across Cultures
In a small group, review the battle scenes from the three epics you have read. Discuss how the battle scenes in the *Iliad* compare with those in *Beowulf* and *Gilgamesh*. How does each epic hero respond to the sometimes fatal violence he faces in battle? Are the heroes equally heroic in their behaviors?

CONNECT

Connect a Common Theme
Timed Writing Friendship is an important theme in both the *Iliad* and *Gilgamesh*. Achilles is fiercely loyal to Patroclus, and *Gilgamesh* stands by Enkidu to face the worst possible danger. In an essay, explain the motivations and outcomes of the friendships of these epic heroes. Use specific references to the text to support your analysis.

EXTEND

Characterize a Foil
TechFocus Both *Gilgamesh* and the *Iliad* contain a set of characters that act as foils to one another: Gilgamesh and Enkidu; Achilles and Hector. With a partner, bring the foils from one of the epics alive by creating a written dialogue that might appear online on a blog or discussion board. You should each take on the persona of one of the characters from the epic you choose and then develop a discussion in which your comments help reveal the attributes of your foil. Think carefully how you can use written statements to emphasize your character's personality and the way in which it contrasts with your foil's.

Universal Access

Struggling Writers
Some students may need additional scaffolding to complete the Writing Skills Focus activity. Have students look for two instances in the text that they could use to prove or disprove David Denby's statement. Remind them that they can refer to either the *Iliad, Gilgamesh,* or both. Tell them to look for passages that address glory and fame or shame and humiliation. Before students write their essay, have them compose an outline that includes their thesis and at least two supporting points, with each point including direct quotations or paraphrases from the text.

Independent Practice

Choices: Evaluation Criteria

Review: Homework
Compare and Contrast Epics Across Cultures
Students compare the battle scene and heroes in the *Iliad* to other epic poems.

Connect: Timed Writing 40–50 Minutes
- Essay discusses motivations and outcomes of the friendships of the epic heroes.
- Essay includes specific references to text.

Extend: Homework
Characterize a Foil
- Students compare the traits and qualities of foils from *Gilgamesh* with foils from the *Iliad*.
- Dialogues reveal character's personality and differences with the character's foil.

Assess

Unit 1 Resources, Selection Standards Check, pp. 30, 33

go.hrw.com **ThinkCentral Online Assessment,** Selection Standards Check

Teacher One Stop™, editable Selection Standards Check

Reteach

To reteach **archetypes,** see **Reteaching Lessons,** p. 1449S.

go.hrw.com **ThinkCentral Online Remediation**

CHAPTER 2

The Middle Ages: The Tales They Told

LITERARY SKILLS FOCUS

Medieval Narrative

CONTENTS

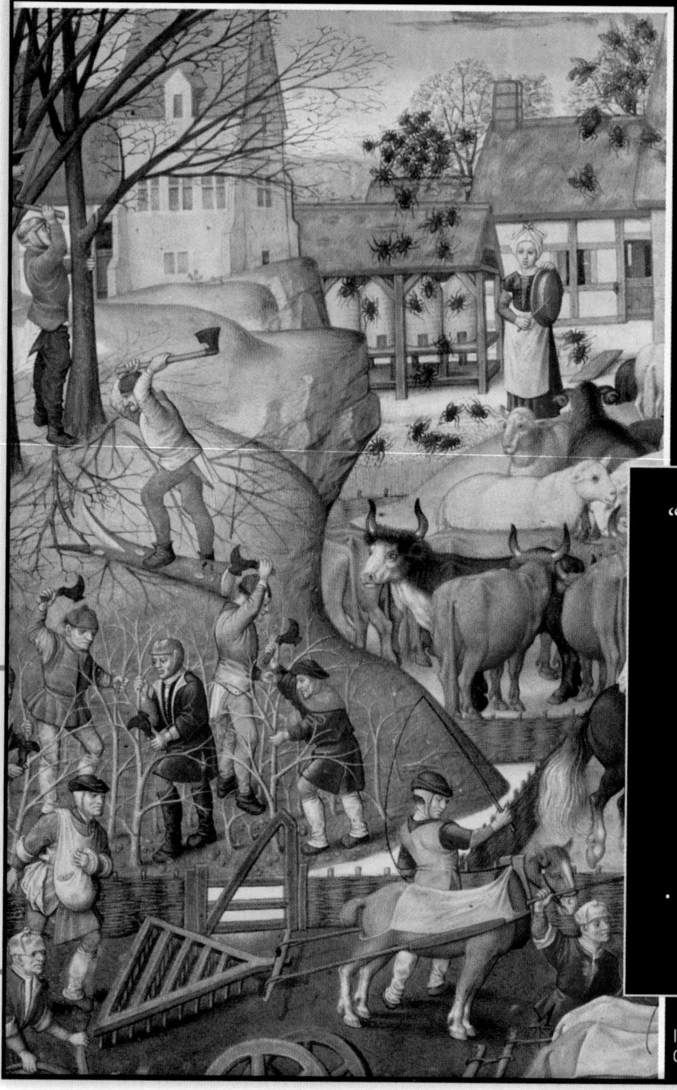

"The medieval world we know was far from perfect. Life expectancy was short, and disease was mostly incontestable. . . . But it exhibited as elevated a culture . . . as the world has ever seen."

— **Norman F. Cantor**

Illustration to the *Georgics* by Virgil, from the English School. Collection of the Earl of Leicester, Holkham Hall, Norfolk.

Chapter Objectives

- Students will learn about elements of medieval narrative, including romances and religious allegories, by reading selected ballads and selections from *The Canterbury Tales, Le Morte d'Arthur, Sir Gawain and the Green Knight,* and *Everyman.*
- Students will refine their skills of literary analysis through focused attention to key stylistic details.
- Students will learn how to approach a writing test that calls for a response to literature.
- At the end of the unit, students will write a literary analysis and present it orally.

The Quotation

Inform students that this quotation is from *Civilizations of the Middle Ages* by Norman F. Cantor, a professor at New York University. This quote shows the contradictory nature of the Middle Ages: daily life was in many ways brutal; yet amidst this hardship, a refined culture flourished.

Analyzing Visuals

Extension Activity How is the image related to the quotation? ***Possible response:*** *It depicts ordinary people at work, reminding us of aspects of medieval life that receive little attention in medieval literature until late in the Middle Ages.*

Chapter 2

California Standards Overview

- **Reading Standard 2.2** Analyze the way in which clarity of meaning is affected by patterns of organization, hierarchical structures, repetition of the main ideas, syntax, and word choice in the text.
- **Reading Standard 2.4** Make warranted and reasonable assertions about the author's arguments by using elements of the text to defend and clarify interpretations.
- **Reading Standard 2.5** Analyze an author's implicit and explicit philosophical assumptions and beliefs about a subject.
- **Reading Standard 3.1** Analyze characteristics of subgenres (e.g., satire, parody, allegory, pastoral) that are used in poetry, prose, plays, novels, short stories, essays, and other basic genres.
- **Reading Standard 3.3** Analyze the ways in which irony, tone, mood, the author's style, and the "sound" of language achieve specific rhetorical or aesthetic purposes or both.
- **Reading Standard 3.6** Analyze the way in which authors through the centuries have used archetypes drawn from myth and tradition in literature, film, political speeches, and religious writings (e.g., how the archetypes of banishment from an ideal world may be used to interpret Shakespeare's tragedy *Macbeth*.)
- **Reading Standard 3.7 c.** Evaluate the philosophical, political, religious, ethical, and social influences of the historical period that shaped the characters, plots, and settings.
- **Reading Standard 3.8** Analyze the clarity and consistency of political assumptions in a selection of literary works or essays on a topic (e.g., suffrage, women's role in organized labor) (Political approach).
- **Grades 9–10 Review Reading Standard 3.4** Determine characters' traits by what the characters say about themselves in narration, dialogue, dramatic monologue, and soliloquy.
- **Grades 9–10 Review Reading Standard 3.9** Explain how voice, persona, and the choice of a narrator affect characterization and the tone, plot, and credibility of a text.

Reading Standard 3.1, 3.7c (see pages A48–A50)

Medieval Narrative by Leila Christenbury

Influences on the Medieval Narrative

- Popular legends from the early Middle Ages that were embellished over time
- Religious literature that passed along the ideals and beliefs of an era
- Urban growth, cultural development, and widespread disease that altered social structures

Bronze aquamanile (late 13th century), from medieval England.
The British Museum, London.

The Dark Ages?

Forget what you have heard about the Middle Ages being "dark." Despite the challenges of war, plague, and oppression, the era was vibrant and its people creative and resilient. Today, we are indebted to the Middle Ages for many modern ideas and institutions, such as universities, governmental forms, and concepts of the world and of God. The medieval narratives that have survived reflect much of the time's positive outlook, and many of them contain the same passion, humor, and sense of wonder that we see today.

Adventure, Morality, Life

The term *medieval* often conjures up images of knights riding off to battle or on magical quests. These heroic adventures were the foundation for the popular romance literature of the era. Much of the narrative tradition of the Middle Ages emerged from earlier legends, such as those of King Arthur. The same themes of love, betrayal, conquest, hope, and desire that consume us today can be found throughout those and other medieval stories.

In addition to romances, religious narratives were a significant part of medieval culture. These texts combine entertaining travel adventures with morally instructive religious stories. One popular example of this genre is *The Golden Legend,* a Chapter of stories about saints' lives, written in the thirteenth century by Jacobus da Varagine. Religious narratives were often allegories, stories in which literal elements represent abstract or moral concepts. Through the use of allegory, medieval literature explored cultural ideals, confirmed values, and amused audiences.

As the Middle Ages progressed, elements of daily life—such as the reality of city living and fear of the plague—found their way into stories. In the fourteenth century, Giovanni Boccaccio wrote the *Decameron*, a collection of stories set during the Black Death. These stories explore diverse characters and augment the range of themes covered by earlier medieval literature. Geoffrey Chaucer's *The Canterbury Tales* also covers the full scope of the medieval narrative, with its inclusion of romance, faith, and humor alongside darker, more humanistic themes. Medieval writers such as Chaucer provide a vital link between the Middle Ages and the modern world.

Ask Yourself

1. What themes did medieval writers address in their work?
2. How did writers from the later Middle Ages, such as Boccaccio and Chaucer, affect the medieval narrative?

Learn It Online
Explore the Middle Ages further through the video "The Tales They Told" online.
go.hrw.com H12-113 Go

Literary Skills Focus

Objectives

Students will analyze characteristics of subgenres by studying medieval narratives.

Unit 1 Resources, Literary Focus Skill Builder, p. 44

PowerNotes, interactive lesson presentation with activities

Teacher One Stop™, on-level lesson plan and all print resources

Direct Teach

Medieval Narrative

Have students read the Literary Skills Focus essay. Use the following question to discuss medieval narrative: The subjects of medieval narratives span from heroic knights to everyday realities. How does this interest in the ordinary link writers of medieval and modern literature?

Check for Understanding

Ask Yourself

Possible responses:

1. *Medieval writers addressed such themes as love, betrayal, conquest, hope, and desire.*
2. *The scope of medieval narrative later broadened to include elements of daily life and humanistic themes.*

California Standards, p. 113

- **Reading Standard 3.1** Analyze characteristics of subgenres (e.g., satire, parody, allegory, pastoral) that are used in poetry, prose, plays, novels, short stories, essays, and other basic genres.
- **Reading Standard 3.7c** Evaluate the philosophical, political, religious, ethical, and social influences of the historical period that shaped the characters, plots, and settings.

Universal Access

English Learners

English for Academic Success To help students understand the information presented in the Literary Skills Focus essay, review the definitions of the following words and phrases with students:

- **plague**—a disease that spreads very rapidly, infecting large numbers of people
- **oppression**—prolonged cruel or unjust treatment
- **morally instructive**—something that teaches the difference between good and bad character

Learn It Online
For a multimedia version of the instruction found on this page, use the **PowerNotes** Literary Skills Focus presentation.
go.hrw.com H12-113 Go

Standards Focus

Objectives

Students will

- evaluate the philosophical, political, religious, ethical, and social influences of a historical period
- understand medieval narratives

Analyzing Visuals Transparencies, Unit 1

Teacher One Stop™, lesson plan and all print resources

Direct Teach

Connect to the Literary Skill

Remind students that medieval narratives typically focus on themes of courage, loyalty, love, betrayal, fear, and beauty.

Work with students to answer the guided questions.

Possible responses:

1. *The pointed weapons tell me that the knights are about to attack their enemies.*
2. *The knight in the foreground is probably the leading knight.*
3. *The bright colors help to create a mood of excitement and determination.*

Check for Understanding

Your Turn

Alternative Listening and Speaking Assignment

Have students work with a partner and use online sources to find a painting from any time period that conveys a typical theme of medieval narratives. Then, have pairs present their painting to the class and explain how the art connects to the medieval narrative.

Analyzing Visuals

Reading Standard 3.1, 3.7 c. (see pages A48–A50)

Connecting to Medieval Narrative

The romance, a common type of medieval narrative, chronicles the adventures of a brave hero who undertakes a quest and overcomes great danger. This painting, by contemporary artist Peter Jackson, shows a scene typical of a romance.

Guidelines

Use these guidelines to consider how this painting represents a romance.

- Examine the painting, and try to determine what narrative, or story, is represented. What event do you imagine is taking place?
- Think about typical themes of medieval narratives. How might this painting reflect some of those themes?
- The magical quests of medieval legends often create a mood of wonder and surprise. Consider how the details of this painting help establish its mood.

1. The knights' weapons are pointed forward. What does this tell you about the event?
2. Why do you think the painter focuses our attention on the knight in the foreground?
3. What **mood** do the colors help create?

Knights Charging into Battle by Peter Jackson (1922–2003). Gouache on paper.

Your Turn Analyze a Medieval Narrative

Choose an image from the selections from *Sir Gawain and the Green Knight* or *Le Morte d'Arthur* in this chapter, and analyze how the image conveys some of the typical elements of medieval stories about knights and their quests.

California Standards, p. 114

- **Reading Standard 3.1** Analyze characteristics of subgenres (e.g., satire, parody, allegory, pastoral) that are used in poetry, prose, plays, novels, short stories, essays, and other basic genres.
- **Reading Standard 3.7c** Evaluate the philosophical, political, religious, ethical, and social influences of the historical period that shaped the characters, plots, and settings.

Reading Standard 3.3 (see pages A48–A50)

The Prologue to The Canterbury Tales

Analyzing Style: Key Details by Kylene Beers

Say It with Style

There are as many ways to say something as people can think of words to say it. An author's style is the particular way he or she says or describes something in writing. Many authors have a distinctive style: curt and to the point, exaggerated, or highly descriptive.

It is likely that as a reader you already know which styles you prefer over others. An author's choices ultimately determine style, as he or she answers questions such as "How will I describe something?" and "What details will I use?" Analyzing significant descriptions and details in a writer's style can help you gain insight into what the writer is trying to express.

All in the Details

The Prologue from Chaucer's *The Canterbury Tales* is a collection of character sketches that vividly describe different individuals and their lives. To avoid getting lost in such stylistically rich literature, focus on the key details. By determining how the reader will understand the descriptions, **key details** can reveal significant insights about the characters, the setting, or the plot. Analyzing how something is described can also reveal the feelings of the author or speaker.

For example, Chaucer opens the Prologue with a description of rain. The description's key details define the tone and reveal how his speaker views the April showers.

> When in April the sweet showers fall
> And pierce the drought of March to the root, and all
> The veins are bathed in liquor of such power
> As brings about the engendering of the flower.

We know that the speaker is clearly admiring the rain through the set-up of the description. The second and fourth lines present fairly straightforward descriptions of drought ending and flowers growing. The first and third lines, however, include details that reveal the speaker's perspective on the rain. In the first line, the speaker describes the showers as *sweet,* and in the third line he describes the veins as *bathed.* If you imagine changing just two words, replacing *sweet* with *dark,* and *bathed* with *drowned,* you see how the tone and meaning are affected by the key details.

Your Turn

Read the following passage about the Knight's character from the Prologue. Analyze the description with a partner, and discuss how each of you perceives the Knight. Which key details affect your view of the Knight? Which details are most revealing about the Knight's character?

> Speaking of his equipment, he possessed
> Fine horses, but he was not gaily dressed.
> He wore a fustian[1] tunic stained and dark
> With smudges where his armor had left mark;
> Just home from service, he had joined our ranks
> To do his pilgrimage and render thanks.

1. **fustian** (FUHS chuhn): made of coarse cloth woven from linen and cotton.

Learn It Online
Find a *PowerNotes* interactive introduction to analyzing style online.
go.hrw.com H12-115 Go

Reading Skills Focus

Objectives

Students will analyze style.

Unit 1 Resources, Reading Focus Skill Builder, p. 45

Teacher One Stop™, on-level lesson plan and all print resources

Direct Teach

Analyzing Style: Key Details

This essay gives students practice in analyzing style using key details. Have students read the essay and complete the Your Turn activity before they begin *The Canterbury Tales.*

Check for Understanding

Independent Practice

Your Turn

Ask students to discuss their perceptions of the Knight with a partner. Have partners compare with another pair of students their views of the Knight and discuss which details reveal the most about the Knight's character. [*Since he owns fine horses, he seems to be well off. His stained clothing indicates that he is dedicated to his duty and does not overemphasize his looks in order to impress others. The last line tells me he is devout and honorable, as he intends to "render thanks."*]

California Standards, p. 115

- **Reading Standard 3.3** Analyze the ways in which irony, tone, mood, the author's style, and the "sound" of language achieve specific rhetorical or aesthetic purposes or both.

Universal Access

Struggling Readers

Remind students that details are vivid, memorable words that help readers picture what is happening. Important details can tell you more about a character or situation, while less important details may be there only to add interest in the story. Just like a detective, readers have to decide which details are most important and can help them draw new conclusions, and which details merely add color to the story.

Learn It Online
For a multimedia version of the instruction found on this page, use the **PowerNotes** Reading Skills Focus presentation.
go.hrw.com H12-115 Go

Standards Focus

Objectives

Students will

- analyze the ways in which the author's style achieves specific rhetorical and aesthetic purposes
- determine characters' traits by what the characters say about themselves

Selection Introduction

Think About the Writer

To help students respond to the question, ask them to summarize what they learned about Chaucer's life from the Meet the Writer selection on pp. 116–117. Then, ask them to think about how Chaucer's family background and life experiences may have helped and inspired him as a writer. Ask them to comment, for instance, on the possible significance of his travels—what might he have learned by spending time in France and Italy? Ask them to also consider what insights Chaucer may have gained through his varied work experiences: as a page in the household of a prominent family, as a soldier, as an ambassador, as a justice of the peace, and as a member of Parliament.

For Independent Reading

A River Sutra, Gita Mehta

Preparing to Read

The Canterbury Tales

What Do You Think? What moves a hero to act?

QuickWrite

If you wanted to write a story about a pilgrimage, what sorts of characters would you include, and where would they go? Write two paragraphs in your *Reader/Writer Notebook* explaining your choices.

MEET THE WRITER

Geoffrey Chaucer

(c. 1343–1400)

Geoffrey Chaucer, using everyday language of the times, brings to life diverse characters from medieval society.

The Father of English Poetry

Geoffrey Chaucer made the English language respectable. Often hailed as the father of English poetry, he composed his works in the English vernacular, or everyday language, at a time when the languages of literature, science, diplomacy, and religion were Latin and French. Before Chaucer, many people thought that English couldn't possibly convey the nuances and complexities of serious literature.

A Privileged Place

Chaucer was born into a middle-class family in London in the early 1340s, not long after the beginning of the Hundred Years' War between England and France. His father was a wine merchant who had enough money to provide his son with some education. The young Chaucer read a great deal and had some legal training. He became a page to a prominent family and received the finest training in good manners. As he advanced in his career, he became attached to several noble patrons.

Chaucer was captured in France while serving as a soldier during the Hundred Years' War and was of sufficiently high social status to have the king contribute to his ransom. Although details of his personal life are sparse, we know that he married a woman named Philippa and had at least two children. On several occasions he was sent to Europe as the king's ambassador. In 1367, he was awarded the first of several pensions for his services to the Crown. (On April 23, 1374, he was granted the promise of a daily pitcher of wine.) In 1385, he was appointed justice of the peace in the county of Kent and later became a member of Parliament. Despite his government responsibilities, between 1374 and 1386 Chaucer composed several great allegorical poems, including *House of Fame* and *Parliament of Fowls*, and his love story *Troilus and Criseyde*.

Geoffrey Chaucer (1400) by unknown artist.
National Portrait Gallery, London.
(background) Warrior's Chapel, Canterbury Cathedral, Kent, England.

Outside Influences

In 1372 and 1378, Chaucer traveled in Italy, where he was very likely influenced by the poems of Dante and Petrarch and by the stories of Giovanni Boccaccio. Chaucer's *The Canterbury Tales* (c. 1387–1400) shares attributes of Boccaccio's collection of tales, the *Decameron* (c. 1348–1353). Both use a framing device within which the characters tell their tales, and both include tales based on similar plots.

Chaucer began writing *The Canterbury Tales* in 1387, during a period of unemployment when his patron was out of the country. Despite the fact that he never completed all the stories (perhaps because, some speculate, he felt that he had lost his ability to find rhymes), the collection is considered one of the greatest works in the English language. Even *The Canterbury Tales'* Prologue alone, in which each traveler is described, is sufficient to place Chaucer in the company of later giants such as Shakespeare and Milton.

Personality in Poetry

The greatness of *The Canterbury Tales* lies in Chaucer's language and the strength of spirit and personality that it effuses. John Gardner, one of Chaucer's many biographers, offers a tribute to Chaucer's lasting power:

> In a dark, troubled age, as it seems to us, he was a comfortable optimist, serene, full of faith. For all his delight in irony—and all his poetry has a touch of that—he affirmed this life, to say nothing of the next, from the bottom of his capacious heart. Joy—satisfaction without a trace of sentimental simple-mindedness—is still the effect of Chaucer's poetry and of Chaucer's personality as it emerges from the poems.

The date on Chaucer's tombstone reads October 25, 1400, but it is uncertain how he died or even if that is his correct death date. (His tombstone was erected by an admirer in 1556.) Chaucer was, quite fittingly, the first of many English writers to be buried in the famous Poets' Corner of Westminster Abbey in London. "The Father of English poetry," notes Nevill Coghill, "lies in his family vault."

Portrait of Geoffrey Chaucer (c. 1342/43–1400), from the Ellesmere manuscript (15th century).
Huntington Library and Art Gallery, San Marino, California.

Think About the Writer Although the details of Chaucer's life are obscure, the colorful nature of his work is certain. What kind of life must a person lead to characterize others so richly?

Learn It Online
Find out more about Chaucer online.
go.hrw.com H12-117 Go

Motivate

What Do You Think?/QuickWrite

Explain that a pilgrimage is a journey to a place believed to be holy or a utopia reflecting what the pilgrim seeks. Remind students that they may have read stories about pilgrimages (such as *The Alchemist* and *The Grapes of Wrath*). Ask students why people in stories go on a pilgrimage. Ask about the problems and surprises they might encounter, such as unusual people who help or hinder them. Have them describe the starkly different characters they imagine would be traveling together. Then, have students record their ideas in their **Reader/Writer Notebooks**.

English for Academic Success

Academic Vocabulary

Look for opportunities to use the Academic Vocabulary words in this unit.

- **attribute, *n.*:** a quality or characteristic
- **concept, *n.*:** notion or idea
- **diverse, *adj.*:** varied
- **emphasis, *n.*:** stress; importance
- **status, *n.*:** social or professional rank

Selection Readability	
Easily Accessible **Accessible** Challenging	Excerpts from *The Canterbury Tales* include complex syntax, abstract symbolism, difficult vocabulary, longer poem stanzas.

Learn It Online
The enhanced author biography offers more information on the life of the author as well as Holt's interactive resources pertaining to the author.
go.hrw.com H12-117 Go

Direct Teach

Think About/Talk About

Preparing for a Journey

- Tell students that Chaucer's *The Canterbury Tales* is widely read and studied today because it paints a vivid, detailed portrait of life during the Middle Ages.
- Ask students to think about other ways that historians learn about the people of the past. Which sources provide the most accurate and complete information?
- Have students consider how historians of the future will learn about the people of our time. What will they study to learn about us? What artifacts will be the most informative? What artifacts might be misleading?

INTRODUCTION TO *The Canterbury Tales*

Through its wide range of characters and rich collection of stories, *The Canterbury Tales* creates a snapshot of medieval society. In this work, Chaucer brings together a group of people with varied backgrounds and beliefs and uses them to explore different aspects of life in the Middle Ages. The characters are joined in a common quest: a pilgrimage, or religious journey, from London to the shrine of the martyr Saint Thomas à Becket at Canterbury Cathedral. The group travels on horseback along their fifty-five-mile trek to Canterbury, a popular destination for pilgrims during Chaucer's time. During their pilgrimage, the characters tell each other stories that provide readers with a vivid view of the medieval world.

Preparing for a Journey

Chaucer begins his *Tales* with a general Prologue, which he uses to describe the spring setting and introduce the characters. Spring represents more than just the usual time for the start of pilgrimages in Chaucer's day—it is also a rich symbol of new life and a reawakening. In this opening, the pilgrim narrator, whom many consider to be Chaucer himself, sketches distinct, individual portraits of his fellow pilgrims. Through these portraits, Chaucer illuminates all classes of life in the Middle Ages. Nevill Coghill, one of Chaucer's translators, says this about the Prologue:

> In all literature there is nothing that touches or resembles the Prologue. It is the concise portrait of an entire nation, high and low, old and young, male and female, lay and clerical, learned and ignorant, rogue and righteous, land and sea, town and country, but without extremes.

The Prologue takes place on the eve of the pilgrimage, as these characters first encounter each other at the Tabard Inn in Southwark, a borough in the south of London. Although most medieval inns provided only barebones accommodations, they still served as a welcome oasis during rugged travels. The pilgrims spend their evening basking in the hospitality of the inn's host, who concludes their festivities by proposing a storytelling contest as a way to pass the time along their journey to Canterbury. This proposal sets up the *Tales'* frame story—the main story of their pilgrimage that surrounds the individual stories told by the travelers.

Chaucer's Canterbury Pilgrims (1810) engraved and published by William Blake (1757–1827). Private collection.

Universal Access

EL English Learners

English for Academic Success Before students read the selection, introduce the following words:

- **pilgrimage**—a religious journey to a holy place; re-awakening; a rebirth or new start
- **oasis**—a haven from a troubling or trying situation
- **translation**—a version in another language that has an equivalent meaning to the original
- **penance**—an act of religious devotion performed to show sorrow for committing a sin

A Classic Medieval Narrative

Chaucer's *Tales* works as a brilliant depiction of his society, a timeless exploration of human nature, and a classic example of a medieval quest narrative. The poem's quest—the pilgrimage to Canterbury—begins with images of spring and awakening, winds its way through the territory of penance and death, and concludes with the Parson's reflections on eternal life. Although the *Tales* remains unfinished, the arc of this quest mirrors the spiritual renewal that the pilgrims themselves are seeking at the shrine of Saint Thomas à Becket. Because much of what these characters seek and ponder remains relevant to people today, the *Tales* presents a medieval narrative that still illuminates human nature in the modern world.

Middle English Pronunciation Guide

The version of *The Canterbury Tales* included in this book is a translation into Modern English by Nevill Coghill. Chaucer's original text was written in Middle English, an older version of the English language that was spoken during the medieval era. Although Coghill's translation reflects the spirit of Chaucer's text, you might try to read some of the *Tales* in the wonderfully musical original. Using the guide on the right to help you, practice speaking some of the lines from the opening passage that appears on the next page in the original Middle English.

Brief Pronunciation Guide to Middle English

Vowels

a: *ah,* as in *father.*
ai, ay, ei, ey: *ay,* as in *pay.*
au, aw: *ow,* as in *house.*
i: *ee,* as in *me.*
oo, o: *oh,* as in *oat.*
u: *oo,* as in *who.*
ee: *ay,* as in *pay.* For example, *eek* is pronounced *ayk.*
e: at times *ay;* also sometimes *eh,* as in *men.*
e: When it is the final letter, *e* in Middle English is a separate syllable sounded like a final *uh;* for example, *soote* (which also uses the *"oo"* rule mentioned above) rhymes with *soda.* However, when the final *e* precedes a word that starts with a vowel or an *h,* it is not sounded. In "droghte of March," the final *e* in *droghte* is silent.

Consonants

g: hard *g,* as in *go,* except before *e* or *i* (in words borrowed from French), where it is sounded like *zh* or *j,* as in *garage. Pilgrimage* rhymes with *garage.*
gh: like a German *ch. Knight* is pronounced *k-nee-hkt.*
–tion, –cial: The *t* and *c* in these letter combinations are not blended with the *i* as they are in Modern English (as in the words *condition* and *special*). The *i* is sounded as a separate syllable. Therefore, in Middle English *special* would have three syllables: SPEH see al (*c* has the sound of *s* when it comes before *i*). *Condition* would have four syllables: kahn dee see AHN.

Think About/Talk About

A Classic Medieval Narrative

- *The Canterbury Tales* remains relevant to readers throughout the centuries because people continue to relate to the ideals and themes of medieval times.
- Ask students to think about the medieval themes and ideals addressed in the Literary Skills Focus essay on p. 113 and discuss which ideals they relate to personally. How do they seek an enlightened view of their world? Which themes are more or less relevant today?

Middle English Pronunciation Guide

- Explain to students that languages evolve and change over time. Make sure students understand the difference between Old English and Middle English. Old English, dating from the period before the Norman invasion in 1066, bears little resemblance to Modern English. Middle English, however, includes many words that a Modern English speaker could understand.
- Guide students in reviewing and using the guidelines in the "Brief Pronunciation Guide to Middle English." Model pronouncing the vowel and consonant sounds for students.

Cross-Curricular Connection

SOCIAL STUDIES: Plotting the Pilgrims' Journey

Have students research the places mentioned in *The Canterbury Tales* in an atlas. Have students work in small groups to make a map showing the area. Then, have students plot the fifty-five-mile pilgrimage of the characters on the map. Have them include symbols depicting important landmarks, such as the inn and the pilgrims' destination, the Canterbury Cathedral.

HSS Analysis Skills: CS 3

Think About/Talk About

Literary Connection

- Explain that *The Canterbury Tales* is written in iambic pentameter, a meter that imitates the natural rhythm of spoken English. Shakespeare also utilizes iambic pentameter, as students will see later. An iamb is made up of one unstressed syllable and one stressed syllable (da-DUM). Iambic pentameter uses five of these iambic feet on one line (pentameter) for a total of ten syllables (da-DUM, da-DUM, da-DUM, da-DUM, da-DUM).
- Point out that many of Chaucer's lines actually have eleven syllables. In these cases, an extra unstressed syllable appears at the end of the line, creating a weak or soft ending.
- Have students practice using iambic pentameter in pairs. Have one person relay a sentence in iambic pentameter, keeping track of the stressed and unstressed syllables. Then, have the partner respond with another sentence in iambic pentameter. Because this meter models natural speech, students should be able to use it while still speaking naturally.
- Play the CD recording of the first eighteen lines of the Prologue in Middle English from the **Holt Audio Library.** Have students perform a choral reading of a few lines.

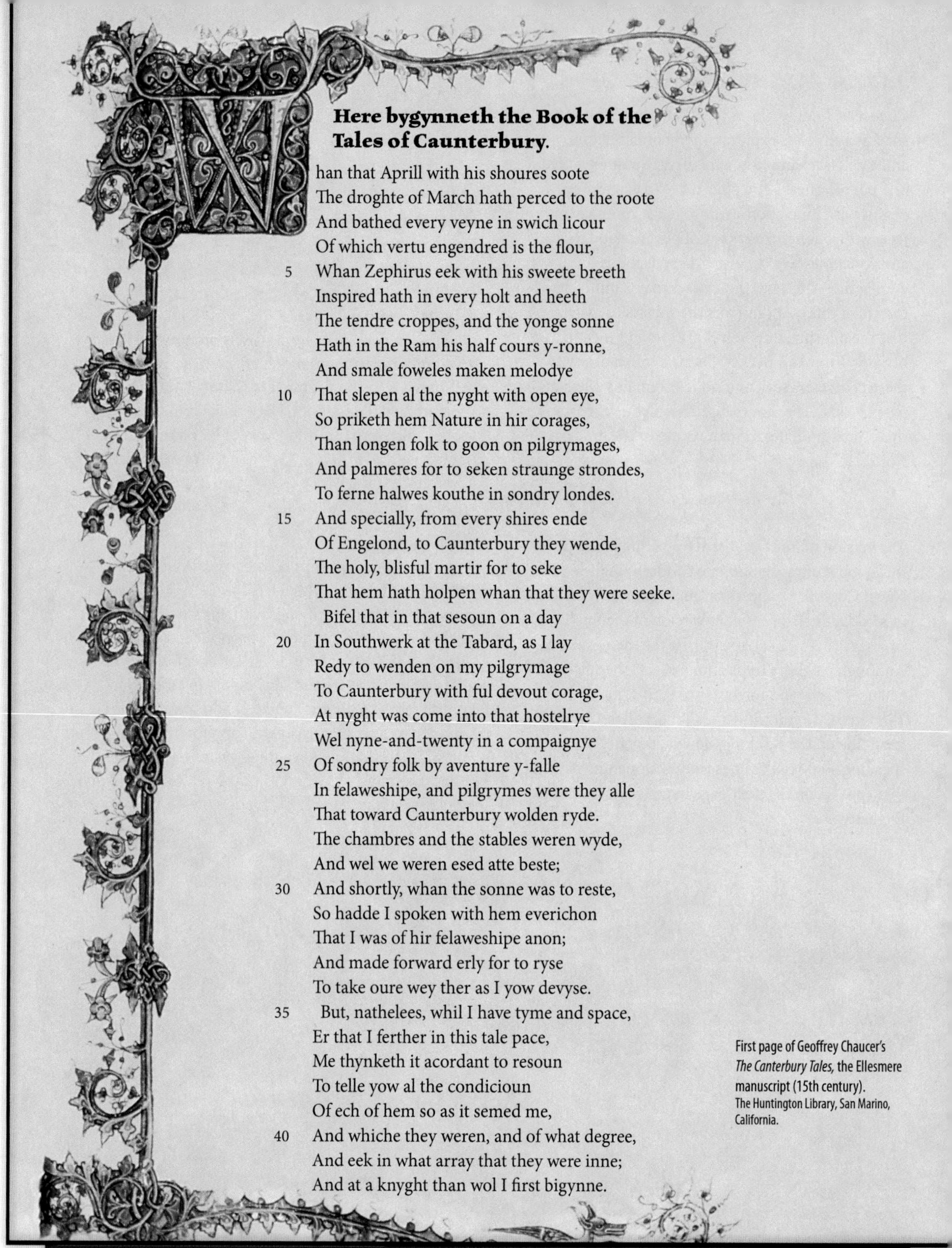

Here bygynneth the Book of the Tales of Caunterbury.

Whan that Aprill with his shoures soote
The droghte of March hath perced to the roote
And bathed every veyne in swich licour
Of which vertu engendred is the flour,
Whan Zephirus eek with his sweete breeth
Inspired hath in every holt and heeth
The tendre croppes, and the yonge sonne
Hath in the Ram his half cours y-ronne,
And smale foweles maken melodye
That slepen al the nyght with open eye,
So priketh hem Nature in hir corages,
Than longen folk to goon on pilgrymages,
And palmeres for to seken straunge strondes,
To ferne halwes kouthe in sondry londes.
And specially, from every shires ende
Of Engelond, to Caunterbury they wende,
The holy, blisful martir for to seke
That hem hath holpen whan that they were seeke.
Bifel that in that sesoun on a day
In Southwerk at the Tabard, as I lay
Redy to wenden on my pilgrymage
To Caunterbury with ful devout corage,
At nyght was come into that hostelrye
Wel nyne-and-twenty in a compaignye
Of sondry folk by aventure y-falle
In felaweshipe, and pilgrymes were they alle
That toward Caunterbury wolden ryde.
The chambres and the stables weren wyde,
And wel we weren esed atte beste;
And shortly, whan the sonne was to reste,
So hadde I spoken with hem everichon
That I was of hir felaweshipe anon;
And made forward erly for to ryse
To take oure wey ther as I yow devyse.
But, nathelees, whil I have tyme and space,
Er that I ferther in this tale pace,
Me thynketh it acordant to resoun
To telle yow al the condicioun
Of ech of hem so as it semed me,
And whiche they weren, and of what degree,
And eek in what array that they were inne;
And at a knyght than wol I first bigynne.

First page of Geoffrey Chaucer's *The Canterbury Tales,* the Ellesmere manuscript (15th century).
The Huntington Library, San Marino, California.

Selection Resources

Unit 1 Resources, on-level practice and assessment, pp. 46, 52, 58

PowerNotes, interactive lesson presentations with activities

Teacher One Stop™, on-level lesson plans and all print resources

Holt Audio Library

Holt Audio Library: Selections and Summaries in Spanish

UA: Holt Interactive Reader, p. 23

UA: Differentiating Instruction, modified lesson plans and leveled assessment, p. 17

UA: Resources for Teaching Advanced Students, lesson plans, p. 61

UA: Supporting Instruction in Spanish, selection summary

Analyzing Visuals Transparencies, p. 1

ThinkCentral Online Assessment

ThinkCentral Online Remediation

Preparing to Read

Reading Standard 3.1, 3.3; **Grades 9–10 Review Reading Standard** 3.4 (see pages A48–A50)

The Prologue to The Canterbury Tales

Literary Skills Focus

Characterization/Frame Story Writers reveal a character's personality through **characterization.** In the Prologue to *The Canterbury Tales,* Chaucer describes the main characters' appearances, actions, and thoughts to create vivid and realistic portraits. The Prologue takes place the night before the group's journey and serves as a frame story for the characters' individual stories that follow thereafter. While Chaucer uses the **frame story,** a story that contains other stories, to unite his travelers' tales, the tales themselves also have thematic unity.

Reading Skills Focus

Analyzing Style: Key Details With twenty-nine pilgrims to introduce in the Prologue, Chaucer could not develop any one character at great length. Instead, he provides a few well-chosen details that make each character stand out vividly. Identifying **key details** concerning these characters can help you determine what Chaucer thinks about his characters and their experiences. Note that these details may undermine what the characters think of themselves or would like others to think about them.

Into Action As you read, use a chart like the one below to note one or two key details about the main characters in the Prologue. Briefly describe what you think each detail emphasizes about the character.

Main Character	Key Detail	What Detail Emphasizes
the Knight	"He had done nobly in his sovereign's war / And ridden into battle" (lines 47–48)	It tells us he's a brave man, a strong warrior, and someone of great experience.

Writing Skills Focus

Think as a Reader/Writer

Find It in Your Reading Describing each character's appearance is one method of **characterization** used by Chaucer. As you read, consider how Chaucer describes each character's physical appearance. In your *Reader/Writer Notebook,* take notes on the different types of physical details.

Vocabulary

eminent (EHM uh nuhnt) *adj.:* great; of high standing. *After a lifetime of glorious battles, he was the most eminent knight in the kingdom.*

benign (bih NYN) *adj.:* kind; gracious. *Even when the family was late with the rent, the benign Franklin did not harass them.*

guile (gyl) *n.:* sly dealings; skill in deceiving. *The thief used his guile to steal things before his victims could notice.*

obstinate (AHB stuh niht) *adj.:* unreasonably stubborn. *An obstinate man, the Pardoner will never admit his stubborn nature.*

frugal (FROO guhl) *adj.:* thrifty; careful with money. *The Host finds it difficult to be frugal; he likes to be generous with his money.*

Language Coach

Commonly Confused Words It is easy to confuse words that have similar sounds. *Eminent,* for example, is an adjective that describes someone or something of high standing. *Imminent* is an adjective that means "about to happen." What is the difference between an imminent leader and an eminent leader?

Learn It Online
Journey back to the time of *The Canterbury Tales* with this video introduction online.

go.hrw.com H12-121 Go

Reader/Writer Notebook
Use your **RWN** to complete the activities for this selection.

California Standards, pp. 121–148

- **Reading Standard 3.1** Analyze characteristics of subgenres (e.g., satire, parody, allegory, pastoral) that are used in poetry, prose, plays, novels, short stories, essays, and other basic genres.
- **Reading Standard 3.3** Analyze the ways in which irony, tone, mood, the author's style, and the "sound" of language achieve specific rhetorical or aesthetic purposes or both.
- **Grades 9–10 Review Reading Standard 3.4** Determine characters' traits by what the characters say about themselves in narration, dialogue, dramatic monologue, and soliloquy.

Preteach

Introducing Vocabulary

- Review the Vocabulary words, definitions, and sentences with students.
- To reinforce the importance of the Vocabulary words, tell students that these words describe the characters in *The Canterbury Tales.* In medieval England, *eminent* people of the nobility were admired along with *benign* members of the clergy. Conversely, people who were *obstinate* or *frugal,* or who used deception and *guile,* were scorned.

English for Academic Success

Language Coach

After students read the **Language Coach,** have them discuss with a partner the answer to the question. [*An eminent leader is a great or high-ranking leader, while an imminent leader is one who is about to come to power.*] For more practice with commonly confused words, have students discuss the difference between the word *guile* and the verb *beguile.*

Literary Skills Focus

As you read and discuss the selection with students, have them note how the author makes use of a frame story to collect the characters' tales.

Reading Skills Focus

Give students a copy of the Reading Skills Focus graphic organizer before they read. Tell them to use their responses to answer the question on the Applying Your Skills page.

Writing Skills Focus

Have students record the characters' physical details in their **Reader/Writer Notebooks.** Students can use their notes to complete the Writing Skills Focus activity.

Learn It Online
The **PowerNotes** presentation for this lesson includes a short video that introduces the selection. The video is also available on the online version of this page.

go.hrw.com H12-121 Go

Teacher Preparation

Selection Plot Summary

The Prologue to *The Canterbury Tales* begins with a description of the onset of spring. According to the narrator, this is the time of year when many people choose to make a pilgrimage. During his own pilgrimage, the narrator finds himself staying at an inn when a group of twenty-nine travelers arrive for the evening. The narrator joins the group and then begins the task of describing each of the travelers in detail. The narrator focuses on physical descriptions as he highlights each member of the party. As the group finishes their supper, the Host of the tavern addresses the group. He proposes, as a form of amusement during their journey, a challenge to each member of the group to tell the best tale. The Host appoints himself as the judge and invites himself along on the pilgrimage. In the morning, the Host wakes the members of the party and they make their way to Canterbury. As the Prologue closes, the Host declares that the person who draws the shortest straw will be the first to tell his or her tale.

Direct Teach

Think About/Talk About

Read with a Purpose Have students read the Read with a Purpose statement. Tell students to take note of the appearance, occupation, and manners of the characters in the Prologue. Have students record their observations as they read.

Response to Margin Question

Lines 1–18 *People long to go on pilgrimages.*

NARRATIVE POEM

THE PROLOGUE TO *The Canterbury Tales*

by **Geoffrey Chaucer**

translated by **Nevill Coghill**

Read with a Purpose

Read to discover how Chaucer uses a collection of diverse individuals to create a vibrant picture of medieval culture and society.

Build Background

The Canterbury Tales is a group of stories told by the characters as they travel together to visit the shrine of Saint Thomas à Becket in Canterbury. The Prologue sets up the purpose of their journey, introduces all of the characters, and provides a detailed description of each member of the group. Written at the end of the fourteenth century, the poem provides a rich view of life during Chaucer's time.

John Lydgate and the Canterbury Pilgrims Leaving Canterbury, from *Troy Book and the Siege of Thebes,* a volume of Lydgate's poems (1412–1422).
The British Library, London. MS Royal 18 D 11, fol. 148.

Real Issues, Real Experts

*Holt author **Deborah Appleman** offers strategies for teaching the Prologue to* The Canterbury Tales.

In any time and place, it seems, we judge people by familiar measures: the way they dress, the things they own, their manner of speech, and the things they choose to tell us. Many of us pride ourselves on our ability to see the truth beneath appearances and to discern the real character of those we meet. The keener and more detailed the observations we make, the more we fancy ourselves successful students of humanity.

The "General Prologue" to *The Canterbury Tales* is filled with both astute and subtle observations of those who will become its cast of characters. Through a brilliant series of sketches, Chaucer reveals a group of pilgrims one at a time to his audience, and each sketch creates a dominant impression by which we might know the people whose tales we will eventually hear. The details of these sketches include social class markers, personal foibles and fetishes, and, in a clearly ironic tone, a series of hints as to the real nature of each pilgrim.

THE PROLOGUE

When in April the sweet showers fall
And pierce the drought of March to the root, and all
The veins are bathed in liquor of such power
As brings about the engendering of the flower,
When also Zephyrus° with his sweet breath
Exhales an air in every grove and heath
Upon the tender shoots, and the young sun
His half-course in the sign of the *Ram*° has run,
And the small fowl are making melody
That sleep away the night with open eye
(So nature pricks them and their heart engages)
Then people long to go on pilgrimages
And palmers° long to seek the stranger strands
Of far-off saints, hallowed in sundry lands,
And specially, from every shire's end
Of England, down to Canterbury they wend°
To seek the holy blissful martyr, quick
To give his help to them when they were sick.
  It happened in that season that one day
In Southwark, at *The Tabard,* as I lay
Ready to go on pilgrimage and start
For Canterbury, most devout at heart,
At night there came into that hostelry°
Some nine and twenty in a company
Of sundry folk happening then to fall
In fellowship, and they were pilgrims all
That towards Canterbury meant to ride. Ⓐ

1–18. These lines consist of a single, long sentence that is built on this structure: "When *x* occurs, then *y* happens."

? *According to the narrator, what do people long to do when spring brings new life?*

5. Zephyrus (ZEF uh ruhs): in Greek mythology, god of the west wind.

8. Ram: Aries, first sign of the zodiac. The time is mid-April.

13. palmers: people who wore palm fronds to show that they had visited the Holy Land.

16. wend: go; travel.

23. hostelry: inn. The Tabard is a lodging place.

Ⓐ **Literary Focus** **Frame Story** How do lines 1–27 foreshadow the frame story about many different characters?

Think About/Talk About

Analysis

Ⓐ Literary Focus

Possible response: *The narrator mentions seeing a large group of people who were all traveling to the same place. This sets the stage for a frame story, as the narrator will incorporate all of these characters into the story.*

Extend the Discussion

Summarizing What is described in the first ten lines of the Prologue? ***Possible response:*** *The poem begins with descriptions of the blooming flowers, the gentle wind, the young sun, and the cautious fowl.*

Making Inferences In these first lines of the Prologue, the narrator includes himself in the story. What characteristics about the narrator can you infer from these opening lines? ***Possible response:*** *The narrator is very eloquent; he may be a poet or storyteller; in line 21, the narrator discloses that he is about to go on a pilgrimage, so we can infer that he has religious beliefs.*

A careful reading of Chaucer's "Prologue," then, can be an investigation of life in fourteenth-century England and the motives that animated it. Chaucer's pilgrims have chosen their own ways of revealing themselves, and the narrator of the "Prologue" has carefully encoded for us a catalog of their characteristics. Like detectives scrutinizing people on a street corner, your students need to separate appearances from truth.

Model the Skill

- Provide students with copies of the Reading Skills Focus graphic organizer for the Prologue to *The Canterbury Tales.* (See **Unit 1 Resources**.)
- Tell students that in a long introduction, the writer must provide key details that stand out and are easy for the reader to visualize and remember.
- Model adding a key detail to the graphic organizer. Direct students to read lines 61–62. Tell them to include the direct key quote in the second column of their graphic organizer and then describe what the quote illustrates about the Knight's character in the third column.

Character	Example	Meaning
Knight	For all along the Mediterranean coast/ He had embarked with many a noble host.	The Knight is well-traveled and well-respected among his peers.

Guided Practice: Apply

Ask students to read lines 81–102, the Squire's introduction. Guide students as they discuss the key details they read. Then, ask the students to complete a new row in their graphic organizer.

Think About/Talk About

Response to Margin Question

Lines 87–102 *The Squire, a strong, talented, and handsome lad, fights valiantly, speaks and sings eloquently, and seeks adventure. He embodies the concept of chivalry in his devotion to his lady, his bravery, his courtly skills, and his courtesy and humility.*

The rooms and stables of the inn were wide:
They made us easy, all was of the best.
And, briefly, when the sun had gone to rest,
I'd spoken to them all upon the trip
And was soon one with them in fellowship,
Pledged to rise early and to take the way
to Canterbury, as you heard me say.
But none the less, while I have time and space,
Before my story takes a further pace,
It seems a reasonable thing to say
What their condition was, the full array
Of each of them, as it appeared to me,
According to profession and degree,
And what apparel they were riding in;
And at a Knight I therefore will begin.

The Knight, from *The Canterbury Tales* by Geoffrey Chaucer, the Ellesmere manuscript. The Huntington Library, San Marino, CA.

The Knight

There was a *Knight,* a most distinguished man,
Who from the day on which he first began
To ride abroad had followed chivalry,
Truth, honor, generousness, and courtesy.
He had done nobly in his sovereign's war
And ridden into battle, no man more,
As well in Christian as in heathen° places,
And ever honored for his noble graces.
When we took Alexandria,° he was there.
He often sat at table in the chair
Of honor, above all nations, when in Prussia.
In Lithuania he had ridden, and Russia,
No Christian man so often, of his rank.
When, in Granada, Algeciras sank
Under assault, he had been there, and in
North Africa, raiding Benamarin;
In Anatolia he had been as well
And fought when Ayas and Attalia fell,
For all along the Mediterranean coast
He had embarked with many a noble host.
In fifteen mortal battles he had been
And jousted for our faith at Tramissene
Thrice in the lists, and always killed his man.
This same distinguished knight had led the van
Once with the Bey of Balat, doing work
For him against another heathen Turk; **B**

43. Note that italics will designate each new character as that character is introduced.
As you read, you might wish to create a list of all the characters introduced in the Prologue.

49. heathen: pagan. Chaucer uses the term to mean "non-Christian."
51. Alexandria: city in Egypt captured by the Crusaders in 1365. In the next few lines, Chaucer is indicating the Knight's distinguished and extensive career.

B Reading Focus **Analyzing Key Details** What qualities does the Knight possess that differ from those you might expect to find in a veteran soldier?

Universal Access

EL English Learners

English for Academic Success Explain that a *prologue* is an introductory passage that may accompany a novel, play, or long poem, and that it gives details about characters and settings. Ask students what information they expect to find out by reading the Prologue to *The Canterbury Tales.*

✔ See the **English Language Skill Builder** in **UA: Differentiating Instruction.**

Struggling Readers

Benchmark Students To help students identify key details and understand what the details emphasize about the characters, tell students to pay close attention to the physical description of the Knight as you read lines 75–80 aloud. Point out that Chaucer describes the Knight's tunic as "stained and dark / with smudges." Explain that this description reveals that the Knight is a plain, modest man who cares little about impressing others. As students continue to read, encourage them to question what the details reveal about the characters.

His only care was study, and indeed
He never spoke a word more than was need,
Formal at that, respectful in the extreme,
Short, to the point, and lofty in his theme.
A tone of moral virtue filled his speech
And gladly would he learn, and gladly teach. G

The Lawyer

A *Sergeant at the Law* who paid his calls,
Wary and wise, for clients at St. Paul's°
There also was, of noted excellence.
Discreet he was, a man to reverence,
Or so he seemed, his sayings were so wise.
He often had been Justice of Assize
By letters patent,° and in full commission.
His fame and learning and his high position
Had won him many a robe and many a fee.
There was no such conveyancer° as he;
All was fee-simple° to his strong digestion,
Not one conveyance could be called in question.
Though there was nowhere one so busy as he,
He was less busy than he seemed to be.
He knew of every judgment, case, and crime
Ever recorded since King William's time.
He could dictate defenses or draft deeds;
No one could pinch a comma from his screeds°
And he knew every statute off by rote.
He wore a homely parti-colored° coat,
Girt with a silken belt of pin-stripe stuff;
Of his appearance I have said enough.

The Franklin

There was a *Franklin*° with him, it appeared;
White as a daisy-petal was his beard.
A sanguine° man, high-colored and benign,
He loved a morning sop of cake in wine.
He lived for pleasure and had always done,
For he was Epicurus'° very son,
In whose opinion sensual delight
Was the one true felicity in sight.

G **Reading Focus** **Analyzing Key Details** Which details in the sketch of the Oxford Cleric match the stereotype of the poor student?

Vocabulary **benign** (bih NYN) *adj.:* kind; gracious.

? **295–318.** *In what ways is the Oxford Cleric significantly different from the Nun, the Monk, and the Friar?*

320. St. Paul's: London cathedral. Lawyers often met outside it to discuss their cases when courts were closed.
325. letters patent: letters from the king permitting people to act as judges at the Assizes, court sessions held periodically.

328. conveyancer: person who draws up documents transferring ownership of land. The Lawyer is transferring the ownership to himself.
329. fee-simple: absolute ownership of real property; in other words, he took absolute possession of everything.
336. screeds: tiresome, lengthy writings.
338. parti-colored: multi-colored.

341. franklin: well-to-do land-owner who is not of the nobility.
343. sanguine: ruddy complexioned. In Chaucer's day this was considered a sign of a cheerful temperament; today the word signifies optimism.
346. Epicurus': Epicurus (341–270 B.C.), an ancient Greek philosopher, taught that the goal of life is pleasure, which is achieved through virtue and moderation. Most people came to think of Epicureans as pleasure seekers.

Think About/Talk About

Comprehension

G Reading Focus

Possible response: *The Oxford Cleric's worn clothing and habit of borrowing from friends plays into modern stereotypes of poor college students.*

Extend the Discussion

Making Generalizations Which attributes make the Lawyer successful? ***Possible responses:*** *He is eloquent and seems wise; he is crafty and has an excellent memory for legal precedent.*

Interpreting How does the description of the Merchant's tone and demeanor reveal that he is a hypocrite? ***Possible response:*** *The Merchant sits high on his horse as if he is a powerful businessman and brags about his success even though his business is doing poorly. He insists that the country needs police at sea to protect his goods from pirates, while he himself is a debtor.*

Vocabulary: Own the Word

benign: To help students understand the word *benign,* help them make a personal connection to the word. Ask: "Would you like to be described as *benign?* Explain why or why not."

Developing Oral Fluency

To help student improve their oral fluency and enunciation, have students pay close attention to the emphasis they place on the last word in each line. Select one description to review with the class. Model for students how to emphasize some of the words in order to keep the rhyme scheme flowing smoothly. You might say: "When reading the description of the Lawyer, I know that after I read the word *excellence* in line 321, I must emphasize the same *–ence* sound found in the word *reverence* in line 322.

Group Activity As a group, have students read the selected description aloud, emphasizing the last word of each line. Ask students to practice putting the correct emphasis on each pair of end rhymes.

✔ See **UA: Differentiating Instruction** for practice passages for developing oral fluency.

Model the Skill

- Review the concept of **characterization**. Explain to students that good writers allow characters to reveal themselves through their actions, thoughts, and appearances. Explain that in many cases, the reader comes away with a very different opinion of the character than the character has of him- or herself.
- Read lines 386–388 aloud to students. Tell students that these lines characterize the guildsmen's wives. However, readers must read between the lines to figure out whether the guildsmen's wives would characterize themselves this way, or if the characterization carries with it some judgment by the narrator.
- Point out to students that lines 386–388 are not complimentary of the guildsmen's wives. Tell students that these lines reveal that the wives desperately want their husbands to succeed because of their own desire for status. The narrator has inserted his own judgment into the characterization of the wives.

Guided Practice: Apply

Have students read the description of the Cook on p. 133. Ask them to identify orally words and phrases that characterize the Cook. Record these descriptive words on the board. Then, guide students in a discussion to determine whether the narrator's opinion of the character has colored the description.

Think About/Talk About

Response to Margin Question

Lines 371–388 *The reader learns more about the guildsmen's wives who are ambitious for their husbands because of their own status seeking and vanity.*

As noted as St. Julian° was for bounty
He made his household free to all the County.
His bread, his ale were finest of the fine
And no one had a better stock of wine.
His house was never short of bake-meat pies,
Of fish and flesh, and these in such supplies
It positively snowed with meat and drink
And all the dainties that a man could think.
According to the seasons of the year
Changes of dish were ordered to appear.
He kept fat partridges in coops, beyond,
Many a bream and pike were in his pond.
Woe to the cook unless the sauce was hot
And sharp, or if he wasn't on the spot!
And in his hall a table stood arrayed
And ready all day long, with places laid.
As Justice at the Sessions° none stood higher;
He often had been Member for the Shire.°
A dagger and a little purse of silk
Hung at his girdle, white as morning milk.
As Sheriff he checked audit, every entry.
He was a model among landed gentry.

349. St. Julian: patron saint of hospitality.
365. Justice at the Sessions: judge at a court meeting.
366. Member for the Shire: county representative in Parliament.

The Franklin, from *The Canterbury Tales* by Geoffrey Chaucer, the Ellesmere manuscript
The Huntington Library, San Marino, CA.

The Guildsmen

A *Haberdasher,*° *a Dyer, a Carpenter,*
A *Weaver,* and a *Carpet-maker* were
Among our ranks, all in the livery°
Of one impressive guild-fraternity.
They were so trim and fresh their gear would pass
For new. Their knives were not tricked out with brass
But wrought with purest silver, which avouches°
A like display on girdles and on pouches.
Each seemed a worthy burgess,° fit to grace
A guild-hall with a seat upon the dais.
Their wisdom would have justified a plan
To make each one of them an alderman;°
They had the capital and revenue,
Besides their wives declared it was their due.
And if they did not think so, then they ought;
To be called *"Madam"* is a glorious thought,
And so is going to church and being seen
Having your mantle carried, like a queen. (H)

371. haberdasher: seller of men's clothing and accessories.
373. livery: traditional uniform associated with a particular trade.
377. avouches: guarantees.
379. burgess: citizen.
382. alderman: head of a guild and therefore a member of the town council.

? **371–388.** *What characters do you learn more about in these lines: the guildsmen or their wives? Explain.*

(H) **Literary Focus** **Characterization** How are the guildsmen's wives characterized in this section?

Universal Access

English Learners/ Struggling Readers

English for Academic Success Explain to students that Chaucer uses many multiple-meaning words in his descriptions of the characters. Read the following line aloud to students: "The nicer rules of conscience he ignored" (line 408). Ask students to define the word *nice*. Students will most likely mention that *nice* means "pleasant and kind." Tell students that the word *nice* actually has several meanings, including "subtle, requiring discernment." Guide students in using this definition of *nice* to interpret line 408. [*The Skipper did not adhere to societal rules or was unable to distinguish between right and wrong.*]

The Cook

They had a *Cook* with them who stood alone
For boiling chicken with a marrow-bone,
Sharp flavoring-powder and a spice for savor.
He could distinguish London ale by flavor,
And he could roast and seethe and broil and fry,
Make good thick soup, and bake a tasty pie.
But what a pity—so it seemed to me,
That he should have an ulcer on his knee.
As for blancmange,° he made it with the best.

The Skipper

There was a *Skipper* hailing from far west;
He came from Dartmouth, so I understood.
He rode a farmer's horse as best he could,
In a woollen gown that reached his knee.
A dagger on a lanyard° falling free
Hung from his neck under his arm and down.
The summer heat had tanned his color brown,
And certainly he was an excellent fellow.
Many a draught of vintage, red and yellow,
He'd drawn at Bordeaux, while the trader snored.
The nicer rules of conscience he ignored.
If, when he fought, the enemy vessel sank,
He sent his prisoners home; they walked the plank. **I**
As for his skill in reckoning his tides,
Currents, and many another risk besides,
Moons, harbors, pilots, he had such dispatch
That none from Hull to Carthage was his match.
Hardy he was, prudent in undertaking;
His beard in many a tempest had its shaking,
And he knew all the havens as they were
From Gottland to the Cape of Finisterre,
And every creek in Brittany and Spain;
The barge he owned was called *The Maudelayne.*

The Doctor

A *Doctor* too emerged as we proceeded;
No one alive could talk as well as he did
On points of medicine and of surgery,
For, being grounded in astronomy,
He watched his patient closely for the hours
When, by his horoscope, he knew the powers

397. blancmange (bluh MOHNZH): French for "white food." In Chaucer's day blancmange was a sweet dish made from diced chicken, milk, sugar, and almonds.

402. lanyard: cord.

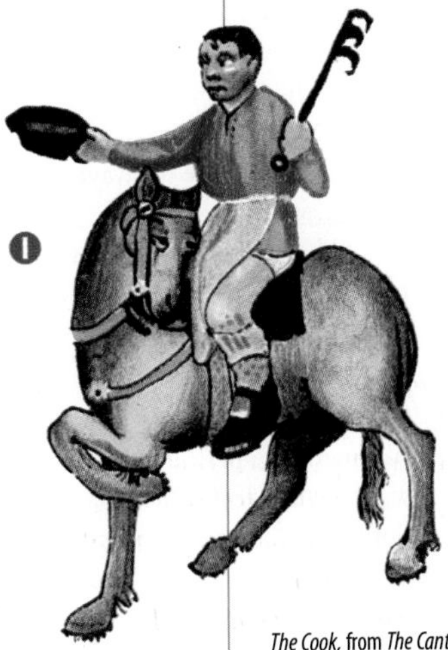

The Cook, from *The Canterbury Tales* by Geoffrey Chaucer, the Ellesmere manuscript.
The Huntington Library, San Marino, CA.

I Reading Focus **Analyzing Key Details** Lines 408–410 reveal an important detail about the Skipper. What does "sent his prisoners home" actually mean?

Think About/Talk About

Comprehension

I Reading Focus

Possible response: *The Skipper "sent his prisoners home" by making them walk the plank. "Home" in this instance is used as a metaphor for death or the afterlife.*

Analysis

H Literary Focus

Possible response: *The guildsmen's wives are concerned with wealth and social status. Each wishes her husband were an alderman and dreams of being respected and admired.*

Extend the Discussion

Rereading How is the Franklin characterized in this section? ***Possible responses:*** *The Franklin is described as a cheerful person who opens his home and food to others. The narrator describes him as "a model among landed gentry," indicating approval of the Franklin's generosity.*

Evaluating The section on the guildsmen describes five men and their wives very briefly. Why do you think the narrator has chosen to group these characters together? ***Possible responses:*** *The narrator seems to regard the guildsmen as interchangeable. Neither the guildsmen nor their wives have noteworthy attributes. The minimal description implies that these characters will have minor roles in the main text.*

Advanced Learners

Acceleration Create semantic differential scales to have students understand and analyze the characteristics of the Franklin. Have students write down opposing adjectives (jovial/grouchy; parsimonious/liberal; powerful/ineffective). Ask students to decide how much of each trait the Franklin possesses and to write a sentence to express their opinion.

For more information about the Scales strategy, see this page in ***ThinkCentral, Teacher Access.***

Think About/Talk About

Build Background: The Black Death

"Pestilences" refers to the bubonic plague—the Black Death that struck Europe in the mid-fourteenth century. Medieval doctors were unable to understand, much less stop, the process of infection, but apparently were quite willing to accept payment for trying.

Build Background: Tithes

Parishioners in the Middle Ages, not unlike today, paid a tithe to the Church consisting of one-tenth of their income. Chaucer's narrator is probably referring to this custom when he describes the Parson's reluctance to "extort a fee." The Parson is patient and understanding; he would rather give to the poor than take money from them.

Extend the Discussion

Finding Details Describe the doctor's diet, according to lines 445–447. ***Possible response:*** *He did not indulge himself in the pleasures of food but consumed only what was healthy for the body.*

Making Inferences What does the Wife of Bath's behavior, described in lines 459–462, reveal about her character? ***Possible responses:*** *Her pride and irritability are not particularly admirable qualities; a medieval audience would consider pride and anger among the seven deadly sins.*

Responses to Margin Questions

Lines 451–454 *He got his gold from treating widespread diseases.*

Lines 455–486 *She may fit the stereotype of a loud, pushy, rich lady.*

Of favorable planets, then ascendent,
Worked on the images for his dependent.
The cause of every malady you'd got
He knew, and whether dry, cold, moist, or hot;°
He knew their seat, their humor and condition.
He was a perfect practicing physician.
These causes being known for what they were,
He gave the man his medicine then and there.
All his apothecaries° in a tribe
Were ready with the drugs he would prescribe
And each made money from the other's guile;
They had been friendly for a goodish while. J
He was well-versed in Aesculapius° too
And what Hippocrates and Rufus knew
And Dioscorides, now dead and gone,
Galen and Rhazes, Hali, Serapion,
Averroes, Avicenna, Constantine,
Scotch Bernard, John of Gaddesden, Gilbertine.
In his own diet he observed some measure;
There were no superfluities° for pleasure,
Only digestives, nutritives and such.
He did not read the Bible very much.
In blood-red garments, slashed with bluish gray
And lined with taffeta, he rode his way;
Yet he was rather close as to expenses
And kept the gold he won in pestilences.
Gold stimulates the heart, or so we're told.
He therefore had a special love of gold.

The Wife of Bath

A worthy *woman* from beside *Bath* city
Was with us, somewhat deaf, which was a pity.
In making cloth she showed so great a bent
She bettered those of Ypres and of Ghent.°
In all the parish not a dame dared stir
Towards the altar steps in front of her,
And if indeed they did, so wrath was she
As to be quite put out of charity.
Her kerchiefs were of finely woven ground;°
I dared have sworn they weighed a good ten pound,
The ones she wore on Sunday, on her head.

430. dry . . . hot: People of the time believed that one's physical and mental conditions were influenced by the balance of four major humors, or fluids, in the body—blood (hot and wet); yellow bile (hot and dry); phlegm (cold and wet); and black bile (cold and dry).

435. apothecaries: pharmacists.

439. Aesculapius: in Greek and Roman mythology, the god of medicine. The names that follow were early Greek, Roman, Middle Eastern, and medieval medical authorities.

446. superfluities: excesses.

? **451–454.** *How did the Doctor get his gold?*

458. Ypres . . . Ghent: Flemish centers of the wool trade.

463. ground: type of cloth.

J **Literary Focus** **Characterization** How does the description of the Doctor's dealings in lines 435–438 change how he is characterized?

Vocabulary **guile** (gyl) *n.:* sly dealings; skill in deceiving.

Universal Access

English Learners

English for Academic Success In order for students to get a clear grasp of the characters, it is important for them to understand the adjectives Chaucer uses to describe the travelers. Record some of the key adjectives Chaucer uses to describe the Parson: *renown, patient, benign, devout,* and *diligent.* Point out to Spanish-speaking students that many of these adjectives have a Spanish cognate (*renombre, paciente, benigno, devoto,* and *diligente*). Have students use their knowledge of the definition of the Spanish cognates to better understand the Parson. Encourage students as they read to look for words that are similar to those in their native language.

Struggling Readers

Model for students the reading skill of analyzing key details. For example, you might say, "When I read, I know a detail is important if it tells me something I need to remember. In lines 455–456, the details that stand out are *worthy, somewhat deaf,* and *pity*. These details tell me that the Wife of Bath's poor hearing is an imperfection. I will start to look for more imperfections in her."

Her hose were of the finest scarlet red
And gartered tight; her shoes were soft and new.
Bold was her face, handsome, and red in hue.
A worthy woman all her life, what's more
She'd had five husbands, all at the church door,
Apart from other company in youth;
No need just now to speak of that, forsooth.
And she had thrice been to Jerusalem,
Seen many strange rivers and passed over them;
She'd been to Rome and also to Boulogne,
St. James of Compostella and Cologne,
And she was skilled in wandering by the way.
She had gap-teeth,° set widely, truth to say.
Easily on an ambling horse she sat
Well wimpled° up, and on her head a hat
As broad as is a buckler or a shield;
She had a flowing mantle that concealed
Large hips, her heels spurred sharply under that.
In company she liked to laugh and chat
And knew the remedies for love's mischances,
An art in which she knew the oldest dances.

The Parson

A holy-minded man of good renown
There was, and poor, the *Parson* to a town,
Yet he was rich in holy thought and work. (K)
He also was a learned man, a clerk,
Who truly knew Christ's gospel and would preach it
Devoutly to parishioners, and teach it.
Benign and wonderfully diligent,
And patient when adversity was sent
(For so he proved in much adversity)
He hated cursing to extort a fee,
Nay rather he preferred beyond a doubt
Giving to poor parishioners round about
Both from church offerings and his property;
He could in little find sufficiency.
Wide was his parish, with houses far asunder,
Yet he neglected not in rain or thunder,
In sickness or in grief, to pay a call
On the remotest, whether great or small,
Upon his feet, and in his hand a stave.°

(K) **Reading Focus** **Analyzing Key Details** How do the details contained in these opening lines contrast with the descriptions of the previous religious figures—the Nun, the Monk, and the Friar?

? **455–486.** *Does the Wife of Bath evoke any comic female stereotypes? Explain.*

478. gap-teeth: In Chaucer's time, gap-teeth on a woman were considered a sign of boldness and were said to indicate an aptitude for love and travel.

480. wimpled: A wimple is a linen covering for the head and neck.

The Parson, from *The Canterbury Tales* by Geoffrey Chaucer, the Ellesmere manuscript.
The Huntington Library, San Marino, CA.

505. stave: staff.

Think About/Talk About

Comprehension

(K) Reading Focus

Possible response: *The details in the opening lines show that the Parson, unlike the Nun, the Monk, and the Friar, has all the qualities a person living in the medieval era would expect in a religious figure.*

Analysis

(J) Literary Focus

Possible response: *The Doctor seems to be a caring physician, but these lines reveal that he is in collusion with the pharmacists and is corrupt.*

Extend the Discussion

Breaking Down Difficult Text
According to lines 487–489, how was the Parson simultaneously rich and poor? ***Possible response:*** *The parson was poor in worldly goods but rich in good deeds and holy thoughts.*

Evaluating Which words in lines 490–494 show the narrator's attitude toward the Parson? ***Possible responses:*** *The narrator speaks about the Parson in positive terms: the words* learned, truly, devoutly, benign, wonderfully diligent, *and* patient *catalog the Parson's many virtues. Through the narrator's sincere, positive description, the author reveals that his purpose is to portray an upright member of the clergy.*

Vocabulary: Own the Word

guile: When someone uses *guile,* he or she uses trickery or deceit. What does the Doctor's use of *guile* suggest about him? ***Possible response:*** *He is greedy and dishonest; he prescribes medicines and gets a kickback from the apothecaries.*

Advanced Learners

Acceleration Remind students that the pilgrims' descriptions are conveyed by a narrator who is not entirely impartial. By characterizing his fellow travelers and revealing his opinion of each pilgrim, the narrator implicitly characterizes himself. Have small groups discuss what the descriptions on these pages reveal about the character of the narrator. Ask students: "If there were a stanza in the introduction that described the narrator, what might it say?"

Students with Disabilities

To help students complete the Reading Skills Focus graphic organizer, first introduce students to the concept of determining what key details emphasize by providing familiar examples that students might experience in everyday life. For example, have students imagine they heard a story about a person who saved a child from drowning. Explain that this key detail about the person lets them know that the person is heroic and brave. As students read, help them record key details about each traveler. Work with them to identify what the details emphasize about the traveler.

Model the Skill

- Review the concept of **characterization**. Explain to students that writers use characterization to unveil distinctive physical features, behavior, or nature of a character.
- Have students read aloud the description of the Parson that begins on p. 135 and concludes on p. 136. Tell students that in the portrait of the Parson, the narrator includes many details that present the Parson in idealized terms, as he did with the Knight. You might say: "The narrator says the Parson is a 'noble example to his sheep' and 'a holy-minded man of good renown.' Based on this description, I can tell that the Parson lives according to a high moral standard and is respected by many."

Guided Practice: Apply

Have students read the description of the Miller and work in pairs to identify words and phrases that characterize this pilgrim. Then, have pairs compare and contrast the characterization of the Parson and the Miller. Guide students in a discussion about how the narrator portrays these characters. Ask them to comment on the fact that these descriptions, unlike the descriptions of the other characters, are completely positive or negative.

Think About/Talk About

Responses to Margin Questions

Lines 539–555 *They are both poor, hardworking, honest, pious, and devoted to helping their neighbors. The narrator clearly approves of the Plowman because he makes no disparaging or ironic remarks about him.*

Lines 568–575 *No. He is compared to a sow or fox, a spade, an old sow's ear, and a furnace door. These comparisons suggest that he is wily, uncouth, dirty, brutish, and fierce.*

This noble example to his sheep° he gave
That first he wrought, and afterward he taught;
And it was from the Gospel he had caught
Those words, and he would add this figure too,
That if gold rust, what then will iron do?
For if a priest be foul in whom we trust
No wonder that a common man should rust;
And shame it is to see—let priests take stock—
A shitten shepherd and a snowy flock.
The true example that a priest should give
Is one of cleanness, how the sheep should live.
He did not set his benefice to hire°
And leave his sheep encumbered in the mire
Or run to London to earn easy bread
By singing masses for the wealthy dead,
Or find some Brotherhood and get enrolled.°
He stayed at home and watched over his fold
So that no wolf should make the sheep miscarry.
He was a shepherd and no mercenary.°
Holy and virtuous he was, but then
Never contemptuous of sinful men,
Never disdainful, never too proud or fine,
But was discreet in teaching and benign.
His business was to show a fair behavior
And draw men thus to Heaven and their Savior,
Unless indeed a man were obstinate;
And such, whether of high or low estate,°
He put to sharp rebuke, to say the least.
I think there never was a better priest.
He sought no pomp or glory in his dealings,
No scrupulosity had spiced his feelings.
Christ and His Twelve Apostles and their lore
He taught, but followed it himself before.

The Plowman

There was a *Plowman* with him there, his brother;
Many a load of dung one time or other
He must have carted through the morning dew.
He was an honest worker, good and true,
Living in peace and perfect charity,
And, as the gospel bade him, so did he,
Loving God best with all his heart and mind
And then his neighbor as himself, repined

506. sheep: his parishioners.

517. He . . . benefice to hire: He did not hire someone else to perform his duties.

521. find . . . enrolled: He did not take a job as a paid chaplain to a guild.

524. mercenary: someone who will agree to do anything for money.

532. estate: rank; social standing.

? **539–555.** *How is the Plowman like his brother, the Parson? How can you tell that the narrator approves of him?*

Vocabulary **obstinate** (AHB stuh niht) *adj.:* unreasonably stubborn.

Developing Oral Fluency

Small-Group Activity Have students work in small groups to prepare to read aloud passages from the Prologue. You might assign a different character to each group and suggest that each group divide the character's lines evenly among its members. Each student should have at least two practice readings with a partner before reading his or her assigned lines to the class. Remind students to play close attention to the way the passage is punctuated. Doing so will enable them to convey its meaning more accurately and smoothly.

At no misfortune, slacked for no content,
For steadily about his work he went
To thrash his corn, to dig or to manure
Or make a ditch; and he would help the poor
For love of Christ and never take a penny
If he could help it, and, as prompt as any,
He paid his tithes in full when they were due
On what he owned, and on his earnings too.
He wore a tabard smock° and rode a mare. L
There was a *Reeve,*° also a *Miller,* there,
A College *Manciple*° from the Inns of Court,
A papal *Pardoner*° and, in close consort,
A Church-Court *Summoner,*° riding at a trot,
And finally myself—that was the lot.

The Miller

The *Miller* was a chap of sixteen stone,°
A great stout fellow big in brawn and bone.
He did well out of them, for he could go
And win the ram at any wrestling show.
Broad, knotty, and short-shouldered, he would boast
He could heave any door off hinge and post,
Or take a run and break it with his head.
His beard, like any sow or fox, was red
And broad as well, as though it were a spade;
And, at its very tip, his nose displayed
A wart on which there stood a tuft of hair
Red as the bristles in an old sow's ear.
His nostrils were as black as they were wide.
He had a sword and buckler at his side,
His mighty mouth was like a furnace door.
A wrangler and buffoon, he had a store
Of tavern stories, filthy in the main.
His was a master-hand at stealing grain.
He felt it with his thumb and thus he knew
Its quality and took three times his due—
A thumb of gold, by God, to gauge an oat!°
He wore a hood of blue and a white coat.
He liked to play his bagpipes up and down
And that was how he brought us out of town.

The Miller, from *The Canterbury Tales* by Geoffrey Chaucer, the Ellesmere manuscript. The Huntington Library, San Marino, CA.

555. tabard smock: short jacket.
556. reeve: serf who was the steward of a manor. A reeve saw that the estate's work was done and that everything was accounted for.
557. manciple: minor employee whose principal duty was to purchase provisions for a college or law firm.
558. pardoner: minor member of the Church who bought and sold pardons for sinners.
559. summoner: low-ranking officer who summoned people to appear in Church court.
561. sixteen stone: 224 pounds.

? **568–575.** *Do any of the comparisons that the narrator makes flatter the character of the Miller? Explain.*

581. thumb . . . oat: In other words, he pressed on the scale with his thumb to increase the weight of the grain.

L **Literary Focus** **Characterization** To which other character is the Plowman very similar? Why is this similarity unsurprising?

Think About/Talk About

Analysis

L Literary Focus

Possible responses: *The Plowman's virtues are similar to the Parson's. Both are hardworking, honest people. This is not surprising because they are brothers.*

Extend the Discussion

Monitoring Your Reading How did the Miller steal grain? ***Possible response:*** *The Miller used his thumb to press on the scale so that the resulting measurement was three times greater than the actual weight of the grain.*

Speculating Why do you think Chaucer introduces the Miller right after the Plowman? What does this say about the nature of these characters? ***Possible responses:*** *The Miller is the exact opposite of the honest, peaceable Plowman. The Miller is an earthy, ugly cheat and thief. Placing these descriptions so close together emphasizes the Plowman's virtue and the Miller's lack thereof.*

Vocabulary: Own the Word

obstinate: Remind students that the connotation of *obstinate* is "unreasonably stubborn." For example, you might say "The stubborn baby finally gave in to his mother's demands, but the *obstinate* child adamantly refused to give in to his mother."

Cross-Curricular Connection

LITERATURE: Chaucer's Naïve Narrator

Explaining the role of the naïve narrator, David Williams says that the irony we perceive "is produced by a kind of flash of communication we get with Chaucer the Author over the head of Pilgrim Chaucer. The author catches our eye, so to speak, and winks." But when the narrator describes the Parson, that irony disappears: "In contrast to the corrupt Monk, . . . the Parson . . . is the epitome of simple virtue, a credit to his profession and a witness to man's moral perfectibility. The Narrator lists his virtues with an unusual reverence, and the complete absence of irony suggests that for once, at least, Pilgrim Chaucer and Chaucer the Author see things in exactly the same way."

Think About/Talk About

Build Background: The Reeve

A reeve was a manager of an estate. It was his job to inspect everything and impose fines if he found anything amiss. Like the Manciple, Chaucer's Reeve uses his skills to cheat his employer by pocketing the money his efficient management has saved. Yet the auditor cannot catch him cheating because he is clever enough to make his account books come out right.

Extend the Discussion

Finding Details What does the narrator mention as quite remarkable about the Manciple? ***Possible response:*** *Although he could neither read nor write, he understood the market far better than the lawyers he worked for.*

Characterization How does the Reeve treat the serfs and others beneath him? ***Possible response:*** *He is hard on them, always trying to catch them cheating, and so they fear him.*

Response to Margin Question

Lines 641–666 *His physical appearance is disgusting, and so is his character. The boils and pimples on his face symbolize his inner corruption and moral decay, which cannot be cleaned up or cured. Lines 665–666 are ironic because the Summoner is clearly neither noble nor kind.*

The Manciple

The *Manciple* came from the Inner Temple;°
All caterers might follow his example
In buying victuals; he was never rash
Whether he bought on credit or paid cash.
He used to watch the market most precisely
And got in first, and so he did quite nicely.
Now isn't it a marvel of God's grace
That an illiterate fellow can outpace
The wisdom of a heap of learned men?
His masters—he had more than thirty then—
All versed in the abstrusest° legal knowledge,
Could have produced a dozen from their College
Fit to be stewards in land and rents and game
To any Peer in England you could name,
And show him how to live on what he had
Debt-free (unless of course the Peer were mad)
Or be as frugal as he might desire,
And make them fit to help about the Shire
In any legal case there was to try;
And yet this Manciple could wipe their eye.°

The Manciple, from *The Canterbury Tales*, the Ellesmere manuscript. The Huntington Library, San Marino, CA.

585. Inner Temple: one of the four legal societies in London composing the Inns of Court. Only the Inns were permitted to license lawyers.
595. abstrusest: most complex; hardest to understand.

The Reeve

The *Reeve* was old and choleric° and thin;
His beard was shaven closely to the skin,
His shorn hair came abruptly to a stop
Above his ears, and he was docked° on top
Just like a priest in front; his legs were lean,
Like sticks they were, no calf was to be seen.
He kept his bins and garners° very trim;
No auditor could gain a point on him.
And he could judge by watching drought and rain
The yield he might expect from seed and grain.
His master's sheep, his animals and hens,
Pigs, horses, dairies, stores, and cattle-pens
Were wholly trusted to his government.
He had been under contract to present
The accounts, right from his master's earliest years.
No one had ever caught him in arrears.°
No bailiff,° serf, or herdsman dared to kick,
He knew their dodges, knew their every trick;
Feared like the plague he was, by those beneath.

604. wipe their eye: outdo them. This medieval idiom means something like "steal their thunder" or "show them up."
605. choleric: having too much choler, or yellow bile, and (supposedly) thus bad-tempered.
608. docked: clipped short.
611. garners: granaries.
620. in arrears: behind schedule in repaying debts.
621. bailiff: here, farm manager.

Vocabulary **frugal** (FROO guhl) *adj.:* thrifty; careful with money.

Universal Access

EL English Learners

Have students create word webs for both the Reeve and the Summoner. Have students re-read each segment of text and find words and phrases that describe each character's appearance. Ask students to rate each word with either a plus or a minus to indicate whether they think Chaucer meant the description to be positive or negative. At the end, have them tally the results for each character.

Struggling Readers

Have students re-read line 646 ("Children were afraid when he appeared"). Explain that writers sometimes include summary sentences like this one to help readers understand the author's purpose. Then, have students re-read lines 641–653. Have them list at least three things they read about the Summoner's appearance in those lines that would make children afraid.

He had a lovely dwelling on a heath,
Shadowed in green by trees above the sward.°
A better hand at bargains than his lord,
He had grown rich and had a store of treasure
Well tucked away, yet out it came to pleasure
His lord with subtle loans or gifts of goods,
To earn his thanks and even coats and hoods.
When young he'd learnt a useful trade and still
He was a carpenter of first-rate skill.
The stallion-cob° he rode at a slow trot
Was dapple-gray and bore the name of Scot.
He wore an overcoat of bluish shade
And rather long; he had a rusty blade
Slung at his side. He came, as I heard tell,
From Norfolk, near a place called Baldeswell.
His coat was tucked under his belt and splayed.
He rode the hindmost of our cavalcade. Ⓜ

The Reeve, detail from *The Canterbury Tales* by Geoffrey Chaucer.
The Huntington Library, San Marino, CA.

The Summoner

There was a *Summoner* with us at that Inn,
His face on fire, like a cherubim,°
For he had carbuncles.° His eyes were narrow,
He was as hot and lecherous as a sparrow.
Black scabby brows he had, and a thin beard.
Children were afraid when he appeared.
No quicksilver, lead ointment, tartar creams,
No brimstone, no boracic, so it seems,
Could make a salve that had the power to bite,
Clean up, or cure his whelks° of knobby white
Or purge the pimples sitting on his cheeks.
Garlic he loved, and onions too, and leeks,
And drinking strong red wine till all was hazy.
Then he would shout and jabber as if crazy,
And wouldn't speak a word except in Latin
When he was drunk, such tags as he was pat in;
He only had a few, say two or three,
That he had mugged up out of some decree;
No wonder, for he heard them every day.
And, as you know, a man can teach a jay°
To call out "Walter" better than the Pope.
But had you tried to test his wits and grope
For more, you'd have found nothing in the bag.
Then *"Questio quid juris"*° was his tag.

625. sward: lawn.
633. stallion-cob: stocky male riding horse.

642. cherubim: in medieval art, a little angel with a rosy face.
643. carbuncles: pus-filled skin inflammations, similar to boils.

650. whelks: pus-filled sores.

? **641–666.** *How does the Summoner's physical appearance (lines 642–651) match his inner character? How do you know that Chaucer is being ironic in lines 665–666?*

660. jay: type of bird.

664. *Questio quid juris:* Latin for "I ask what point of the law [applies]." The Summoner uses this phrase to stall and dodge the issue.

Ⓜ **Literary Focus** **Characterization** Based on this sketch, what is the narrator's opinion of the Reeve?

Think About/Talk About

Analysis

Ⓜ Literary Focus
Possible responses: *The narrator does not seem to approve of the Reeve, but his description shows a grudging respect. The Reeve is bad-tempered but also shrewder than his employer; he is an effective manager.*

Extend the Discussion

Rereading Line 611 explains that the Reeve "kept his bins and garners very trim." How does the physical description of the Reeve in lines 605–610 also show him to be "very trim"? ***Possible responses:*** *He has no beard and he keeps his hair very short. His legs are thin, like sticks, with no calf to be seen. He is as trim as his bins.*

Interpreting The Summoner knows only a few Latin phrases. How would you explain the metaphor in lines 662–663? ***Possible responses:*** *The Summoner's wits, or mind, are being compared to a bag. The metaphor is saying that if you looked inside his mind trying to find more knowledge of Latin, you would find it empty.*

Vocabulary: Own the Word

frugal: Someone who is *frugal* is thrifty and careful with money. When might it be necessary for a person to be *frugal* like the Manciple? ***Possible responses:*** *when they are saving up to buy something special; when they have been spending too much money*

Advanced Learners

Acceleration Challenge students to make inferences about how the Manciple and the Reeve are alike, especially with regard to their business acumen and management skills. Ask students to share their observations, paraphrasing lines from the text to support their views.

Think About/Talk About

Literary Connection

Read aloud lines 705–706. Tell students that the Middle English identifies this relic as a Veronica—a handkerchief belonging to Saint Veronica, said to show the image of Jesus's face because she had wiped his brow with it while he carried the cross.

Extend the Discussion

Comparing and Contrasting Read lines 695–711, which provide a physical description of the Pardoner. How is his appearance similar to, or different from, the Summoner's appearance? ***Possible response:*** *The Pardoner is not as physically repulsive as the Summoner. He has long blonde hair and smooth, hairless skin.*

Making Judgments Judging from the description in lines 695–711, what is the narrator's opinion of the Pardoner? ***Possible response:*** *The narrator sees him as silly and effeminate; he does not have a high opinion of the Pardoner.*

Responses to Margin Questions

Lines 689–704 *These are all unappealing images that make him seem unwholesome and repugnant.*

Lines 714–734 *People are susceptible to the Pardoner's flattery and his skill at oratory.*

Lines 740–744 *He will report on the rest of the pilgrimage as it happened, that is, chronologically.*

He was a noble varlet° and a kind one,
You'd meet none better if you went to find one.
Why, he'd allow—just for a quart of wine—
Any good lad to keep a concubine
A twelvemonth and dispense him altogether!
And he had finches of his own to feather:°
And if he found some rascal with a maid
He would instruct him not to be afraid
In such a case of the Archdeacon's curse
(Unless the rascal's soul were in his purse)
For in his purse the punishment should be.
"Purse is the good Archdeacon's Hell," said he.
But well I know he lied in what he said;
A curse should put a guilty man in dread,
For curses kill, as shriving brings, salvation.
We should beware of excommunication.
Thus, as he pleased, the man could bring duress
On any young fellow in the diocese.
He knew their secrets, they did what he said.
He wore a garland set upon his head
Large as the holly-bush upon a stake
Outside an ale-house, and he had a cake,
A round one, which it was his joke to wield
As if it were intended for a shield. (N)

665. varlet: scoundrel.

670. finches . . . feather: taking care of his own interests.

The Summoner, from *The Canterbury Tales,* by Geoffrey Chaucer, the Ellesmere manuscript. The Huntington Library, San Marino, CA.

The Pardoner

He and a gentle *Pardoner* rode together,
A bird from Charing Cross of the same feather,
Just back from visiting the Court of Rome.
He loudly sang *"Come hither, love, come home!"*
The Summoner sang deep seconds° to this song,
No trumpet ever sounded half so strong.
This Pardoner had hair as yellow as wax,
Hanging down smoothly like a hank of flax.
In driblets fell his locks behind his head
Down to his shoulders which they overspread;
Thinly they fell, like rat-tails, one by one.
He wore no hood upon his head, for fun;
The hood inside his wallet had been stowed,
He aimed at riding in the latest mode;
But for a little cap his head was bare
And he had bulging eye-balls, like a hare.
He'd sewed a holy relic° on his cap;

? **689–704.** *How do such details as "yellow as wax," "driblets," "like rat-tails," and "bulging eye-balls, like a hare" affect the way you feel about the Pardoner?*

693. deep seconds: harmonies.

705. relic: remains of a saint.

(N) **Literary Focus** **Characterization** What final impression of the Summoner is created through the description in lines 684–688?

Cross-Curricular Connection

SOCIAL STUDIES: Relics

Relics are body parts or other objects associated with a saint or other holy figure or event. Saying a prayer while holding a relic was thought to bring an indulgence, or respite from the suffering a person would have to undergo in Purgatory before reaching Heaven. Relics were highly valued in medieval society, not only by pilgrims but also by the churches and shrines where they were kept. Sometimes one church would steal relics from another in hopes of attracting more pilgrims. Once a pilgrim reached a holy site, he or she would try to buy a relic to bring home (like a souvenir). Relics owned by laypeople were usually kept in reliquaries in the form of necklaces or rings. Many relics were fake—like the pig's bones the Pardoner is passing off as saint's bones—yet they were easy to sell to credulous people.

His wallet lay before him on his lap,
Brimful of pardons° come from Rome, all hot.
He had the same small voice a goat has got.
His chin no beard had harbored, nor would harbor,
Smoother than ever chin was left by barber.
I judge he was a gelding, or a mare.
As to his trade, from Berwick down to Ware
There was no pardoner of equal grace,
For in his trunk he had a pillow-case
Which he asserted was Our Lady's veil.
He said he had a gobbet° of the sail
Saint Peter had the time when he made bold
To walk the waves, till Jesu Christ took hold.
He had a cross of metal set with stones
And, in a glass, a rubble of pigs' bones.
And with these relics, any time he found
Some poor up-country parson to astound,
In one short day, in money down, he drew
More than the parson in a month or two, (O)
And by his flatteries and prevarication°
Made monkeys of the priest and congregation.
But still to do him justice first and last
In church he was a noble ecclesiast.°
How well he read a lesson or told a story!
But best of all he sang an Offertory,°
For well he knew that when that song was sung
He'd have to preach and tune his honey-tongue
And (well he could) win silver from the crowd.
That's why he sang so merrily and loud.
  Now I have told you shortly, in a clause,
The rank, the array, the number, and the cause
Of our assembly in this company
In Southwark, at that high-class hostelry
Known as *The Tabard,* close beside *The Bell.*
And now the time has come for me to tell
How we behaved that evening; I'll begin
After we had alighted at the Inn,
Then I'll report our journey, stage by stage,
All the remainder of our pilgrimage.
But first I beg of you, in courtesy,
Not to condemn me as unmannerly
If I speak plainly and with no concealings
And give account of all their words and dealings,

707. pardons: small strips of parchment with papal seals attached. They were sold as indulgences (pardons for sins), with the proceeds supposedly going to a religious house.

716. gobbet: fragment.

? **714–734.** *These lines depict the Pardoner as a scam artist. If this is the case, why do people fall for his tricks?*

725. prevarication: telling lies.

728. ecclesiast: practitioner of Church ritual.

730. Offertory: hymn sung while offerings are collected in church.

The Pardoner, from *The Canterbury Tales* by Geoffrey Chaucer, the Ellesmere manuscript. The Huntington Library, San Marino, CA.

? **740–744.** *How will the narrator organize the rest of his narrative?*

(O) **Reading Focus** **Analyzing Key Details** Why do you think the poet chooses to include a comparison to the Parson here?

Think About/Talk About

Comprehension

(O) Reading Focus

Possible response: *The comparison with the Parson reminds readers that the Parson and the Pardoner are almost exact opposites.*

Analysis

(N) Literary Focus

Possible response: *The reader's final impression of the Summoner is that he is foolish and pretentious, even a buffoon.*

Extend the Discussion

Finding Details According to lines 714–726, how does the Pardoner supplement his income? ***Possible response:*** *He sells worthless trinkets that he claims are holy relics, such as scraps of cloth that supposedly came from the sail of St. Peter's ship.*

Speculating In line 665, the narrator describes the Summoner as "noble" and "kind." What is ironic about this description? What does this use of irony suggest about the narrator? ***Possible responses:*** *This description suggests that the Summoner is kind and noble because the terms of his bribery and blackmail are reasonable. The narrator's sarcastic description tells us that he has a sense of humor and reminds us that we cannot take his words at face value.*

Compare and Contrast

Ask students to compare and contrast the Summoner and the Pardoner.

- **Similarities** The Summoner and the Pardoner are both associated with the church. The Summoner calls people to appear before a church court. The Pardoner sells pardons for sinners. Both figures are seriously flawed in ways that affect their performance of their duties. The Summoner drinks too much and speaks nonsense when he is drunk. The Pardoner cons the gullible by misrepresenting trash as sacred relics.
- **Differences** The Summoner is a pretentious but harmless fool when he drinks. The Pardoner, however, intentionally and wickedly takes advantage of people.

Think About/Talk About

Extend the Discussion

Rereading In lines 759–760, what justification does the narrator offer for presenting the tales exactly as they were told to him? ***Possible response:*** *He notes that Jesus Christ spoke directly and plainly in Scripture, and His words were not indecent.*

Recognizing Rhetorical Devices How sincere is the narrator when he claims, in lines 763–766, that he is not sharp enough to remember the proper order for the tales—that is, to begin by presenting the tales told by people of highest social rank? What is the narrator's—or Chaucer's—purpose in saying he is "short of wit"? ***Possible responses:*** *The narrator is not being sincere. His previous descriptions of the pilgrims showed that he is extremely conscious of people's social class; his ability to recall every detail about them shows that he has a sharp memory. He could probably tell the tales in the "proper" order if he wanted to. I think Chaucer, as the author, just wants an excuse to present the tales in whatever order he likes.*

Response to Margin Question

Lines 745–766 *He is apologizing for being about to speak frankly, relating everything the pilgrims said and did, even if their words were offensive.*

Analyzing Visuals

Connecting to the Text Why does the painter use contrasting colors in the dress of the pilgrims? How might different colors be used to suggest different character traits?

Using their very phrases as they fell.
For certainly, as you all know so well,
He who repeats a tale after a man
Is bound to say, as nearly as he can,
Each single word, if he remembers it,
However rudely spoken or unfit,
Or else the tale he tells will be untrue,
The things pretended and the phrases new.
He may not flinch although it were his brother,
He may as well say one word as another.
And Christ Himself spoke broad in Holy Writ,
Yet there is no scurrility° in it,
And Plato says, for those with power to read,
"The word should be as cousin to the deed."
Further I beg you to forgive it me
If I neglect the order and degree
And what is due to rank in what I've planned.
I'm short of wit as you will understand.

? **745–766.** *What is the narrator apologizing for in advance?*

760. scurrility: indecency.

Analyzing Visuals

Connecting to the Text: *The contrasting colors in the dress of the pilgrims emphasize their varying backgrounds and personalities. Dark colors could suggest that the pilgrim is religious or conservative; bright, flashy colors suggest a character of wealth or pretension; white-colored clothing might suggest purity.*

Universal Access

Advanced Learners

Enrichment Encourage students to read at least one of the pilgrims' portraits in the original Middle English. *The Riverside Chaucer* and *The Canterbury Tales Complete*, both edited by Larry D. Benson, present the original text with excellent glosses.

Canterbury Pilgrims by Alfred George Webster (fl. 1876–1917).
Lincolnshire County Council, Usher Gallery, Lincoln, UK.

The Host

Our *Host* gave us great welcome; everyone
Was given a place and supper was begun.
He served the finest victuals you could think,
The wine was strong and we were glad to drink.
A very striking man our Host withal,
And fit to be a marshal in a hall.
His eyes were bright, his girth a little wide;
There is no finer burgess in Cheapside.°
Bold in his speech, yet wise and full of tact,
There was no manly attribute he lacked,
What's more he was a merry-hearted man.
After our meal he jokingly began
To talk of sport, and, among other things (P)
After we'd settled up our reckonings,
He said as follows: "Truly, gentlemen,
You're very welcome and I can't think when
—Upon my word I'm telling you no lie—
I've seen a gathering here that looked so spry,

774. Cheapside: district of medieval London.

(P) **Literary Focus** **Characterization** What do you learn about the Host in lines 771–779? How do you think the narrator feels about the Host? Explain.

Think About/Talk About

Analysis

(P) Literary Focus

Possible responses: *Readers learn that the Host is a fine, good-looking, almost commanding person with a sense of humor and every good quality one would want to see in a person. The narrator clearly thinks highly of the Host because of these qualities.*

Extend the Discussion

Making Predictions Based on the descriptions of each pilgrim in the preceding pages, what sorts of tales do you think they might tell? ***Possible responses:*** *The Nun might tell a romantic tale about members of the nobility. The Knight and Squire might tell tales of battles or other adventures. The Parson will probably tell a moral parable.*

Determining Author's Purpose Why do you think Chaucer introduces the Host at this point in the poem? ***Possible responses:*** *The narrator has introduced all the characters one by one. Now Chaucer is ready to move on to the next part of the poem, where the characters tell their tales. The introduction of the Host, who proposes the storytelling competition, provides a transition between the Prologue and the pilgrims' tales.*

Cross-Curricular Connection

LITERATURE: *The Decameron*

Tell students that *The Canterbury Tales* was inspired by a classic of the Italian literature, Giovanni Boccaccio's *The Decameron*. Written in the middle of the fourteenth century, *The Decameron* begins with ten characters who retire to the countryside to escape the plague that was raging in Florence. They remain isolated for ten days, and every day each of them must tell a story to the others.

Think About/Talk About

Literary Connection

Tell students that the Host, the landlord of the Tabard, is later identified as Harry Bailey. Though based on a real London innkeeper of that name, the character of the Host is nevertheless a literary creation. As students read this section of the Prologue, ask them to look for ways in which Chaucer directly and indirectly characterizes the Host.

Extend the Discussion

Finding Details In lines 804–807, how do the pilgrims react to the Host's proposal? ***Possible response:*** *They accept his proposal without any complaints. They seem to feel that agreeing to the Host's proposal is easier than rejecting it.*

Synthesizing In line 792, what does the Host assume about the travelers? ***Possible response:*** *The Host assumes they would not mind having some fun along the way to Canterbury.*

Responses to Margin Questions

Lines 781–803 *He is a cheerful person who enjoys the company of others and whom people enjoy being around.*

Lines 811–829 *The Host will choose the best tale—the most enjoyable and morally instructive one—and the prize will be a free supper at the tavern, paid for by all the other pilgrims. Anyone who refuses to tell a tale will have to pay the entire cost of the journey.*

No, not this year, as in this tavern now.
I'd think you up some fun if I knew how.
And, as it happens, a thought has just occurred
To please you, costing nothing, on my word.
You're off to Canterbury—well, God speed!
Blessed St. Thomas answer to your need!
And I don't doubt, before the journey's done
You mean to while the time in tales and fun.
Indeed, there's little pleasure for your bones
Riding along and all as dumb as stones.
So let me then propose for your enjoyment,
Just as I said, a suitable employment.
And if my notion suits and you agree
And promise to submit yourselves to me
Playing your parts exactly as I say
Tomorrow as you ride along the way,
Then by my father's soul (and he is dead)
If you don't like it you can have my head!
Hold up your hands, and not another word."
  Well, our opinion was not long deferred,
It seemed not worth a serious debate;
We all agreed to it at any rate
And bade him issue what commands he would.
"My lords," he said, "now listen for your good,
And please don't treat my notion with disdain.
This is the point. I'll make it short and plain.
Each one of you shall help to make things slip
By telling two stories on the outward trip
To Canterbury, that's what I intend,
And, on the homeward way to journey's end
Another two, tales from the days of old;
And then the man whose story is best told,
That is to say who gives the fullest measure
Of good morality and general pleasure,
He shall be given a supper, paid by all,
Here in this tavern, in this very hall,
When we come back again from Canterbury.
And in the hope to keep you bright and merry
I'll go along with you myself and ride
All at my own expense and serve as guide.
I'll be the judge, and those who won't obey°
Shall pay for what we spend upon the way.
Now if you all agree to what you've heard
Tell me at once without another word,
And I will make arrangements early for it."
  Of course we all agreed, in fact we swore it
Delightedly, and made entreaty° too

? 781–803. *What do words like* fun *(line 786),* pleasure *(line 793), and* enjoyment *(line 795) suggest about the Host's character?*

Figure thought to be Chaucer, detail from *The Canterbury Tales* by Geoffrey Chaucer.
The Huntington Library, San Marino, CA.

? 811–829. *Summarize the rules the Host proposes for the storytelling competition. What is the prize? Who will be the judge?*

825. those who won't obey: refers to those who won't play the game of telling a story when it's their turn. Lines 853–854 further clarify their penalty: Those who won't obey must pay the cost of the entire journey.

831. entreaty: urgent request.

Universal Access

Struggling Readers

Have students work in pairs to compile a list of key characteristics of Chaucer's characters. Each pair should choose three characters and create a list of four to five character traits for each. Students should choose traits that are telling, such as facial features or good or bad qualities.

Activity Match each pair with another pair. One pair should read the list of traits to the other pair and ask them to name the characters they are describing. For example, the words *noble, well dressed, generous, brave,* and *chivalrous* would most likely describe the Knight. Pairs should then switch roles once they have named all three characters.

That he should act as he proposed to do,
Become our Governor in short, and be
Judge of our tales and general referee,
And set the supper at a certain price.
We promised to be ruled by his advice
Come high, come low; unanimously thus
We set him up in judgment over us.
More wine was fetched, the business being done;
We drank it off and up went everyone
To bed without a moment of delay.
Early next morning at the spring of day
Up rose our Host and roused us like a cock,
Gathering us together in a flock,
And off we rode at slightly faster pace
Than walking to St. Thomas' watering-place;
And there our Host drew up, began to ease
His horse, and said, "Now, listen if you please,
My lords! Remember what you promised me.
If evensong and matins will agree°
Let's see who shall be first to tell a tale.
And as I hope to drink good wine and ale
I'll be your judge. The rebel who disobeys,
However much the journey costs, he pays.
Now draw for cut° and then we can depart;
The man who draws the shortest cut shall start." Q

850. if . . . agree: in other words, if you feel the same way in the evening (at evensong, or evening prayers) as you do in the morning (at matins, or morning prayers).
855. draw for cut: in other words, draw straws.

Q **Literary Focus** **Frame Story** Why are lines 848–856 an important element of the frame story of *The Canterbury Tales*?

Think About/Talk About

Analysis

Q Literary Focus

Possible responses: *These lines provide a direct transition between the Prologue and the actual tales. Readers are acquainted with the pilgrims and have started forming opinions about them; now readers are ready to judge the pilgrims' stories.*

Extend the Discussion

Making Judgments In lines 825–826, the Host announces he will be the judge of the pilgrims' tales. What do you think makes the Host especially qualified to be the judge? ***Possible responses:*** *The Host was the one who proposed the idea; he has no relation to any of the other pilgrims.*

Monitor Students' Comprehension

Guide the class in answering these comprehension questions.

1. During which month do people "long to go on pilgrimages"? [*April*]
2. Which of the pilgrims described by the narrator are women? [*the Prioress and the Wife of Bath*]
3. What plan does the Host propose to the pilgrims? [*Each pilgrim will tell two stories on the way to Canterbury and two more on the return trip.*]

California Standards, pp. 146–148

- **Reading Standard 3.1** Analyze characteristics of subgenres (e.g., satire, parody, allegory, pastoral) that are used in poetry, prose, plays, novels, short stories, essays, and other basic genres.
- **Reading Standard 3.3** Analyze the ways in which irony, tone, mood, the author's style, and the "sound" of language achieve specific rhetorical or aesthetic purposes or both.
- **Grades 9–10 Review Reading Standard 1.1** Identify and use the literal and figurative meanings of words and understand word derivations.
- **Grades 9–10 Review Reading Standard 3.3** Analyze interactions between main and subordinate characters in a literary text (e.g., internal and external conflicts, motivations, relationships, influences) and explain the way those interactions affect the plot.
- **Grades 9–10 Review Reading Standard 3.4** Determine characters' traits by what the characters say about themselves in narration, dialogue, dramatic monologue, and soliloquy.
- **Writing Standard 2.1b** Locate scenes and incidents in specific places.
- **Writing Standard 2.2** Write responses to literature. **b.** Analyze the imagery, language, universal themes, and unique aspects of the text. **c.** Support important ideas and viewpoints through accurate and detailed references to the text and to other works.
- **Writing Standard 2.3b** Draw comparisons between specific incidents and broader themes that illustrate the writer's important beliefs or generalizations about life.
- **Listening and Speaking Standard 2.1a** Explore the significance of personal experiences, events, conditions, or concerns, using appropriate rhetorical strategies (e.g., narration, description, exposition, persuasion).

Check for Understanding

Independent Practice

Reading Skills Focus

Possible responses:

1. *April is the beginning of spring and represents nature's rebirth.*
2. *The narrator is at an inn and is joined by twenty-nine pilgrims headed for Canterbury.*
3. *He does not preach for money.*
4. *He promises a free meal to the best storyteller.*
5. *very important—it determined one's income and social status*
6. *Ask students how the key details contribute to their opinions.*

Literary Skills Focus

Possible responses:

7. *Merchant—hypocrisy; Franklin—the gentry's excesses; Doctor—greed; Miller—dishonesty*
8. *The Cleric is serious about his studies; the Monk does not study. The Parson and the Plowman live according to their principles.*
9. *He idealizes the Knight, Oxford Cleric, Parson, and Plowman.*
10. *He values honesty, modesty, and piety. He condemns cheating.*
11. *The Yeoman is described as neat to indicate his skills as a woodsman; the Knight's worn clothing suggests a simple man; the Host's bright eyes and girth suggest affability and cheerfulness.*
12. *The reader has met all of the pilgrims and has begun to judge them. The frame story explains the rules of the game.*
13. *The Parson and the Pardoner are the most striking opposites. The Parson sincerely cares about his parishioners; the Pardoner uses religion for his selfish aims.*

What Do You Think Now?

To help students answer the question, have them review key details recorded about the Host in their graphic organizer and look for context clues that reveal his motivation.

Applying Your Skills

Reading Standard 3.1, 3.3; **Grades 9–10 Review Reading Standard** 3.3, 3.4 (see pagesA48–A50)
Writing Standard 2.2 (see pages A51–A52)

The Prologue to The Canterbury Tales

Literary Response and Analysis

Reading Skills Focus

Quick Check

1. How does the April setting help motivate the travelers to go on their journey?
2. Where is the narrator at the beginning of the Prologue? Who joins him, and why?
3. Why is the Parson so poor?
4. How does the Host encourage the travelers to tell their stories?

Read with a Purpose

5. How important do you think someone's occupation was in medieval society?

Reading Skills: Analyzing Style: Key Details

6. In your chart, you recorded key details Chaucer uses to describe each main character. Add a new column in which you describe how and why each detail made you feel a certain way about the character.

Main Character	Key Detail	What Detail Emphasizes	What It Makes You Feel
the Knight	"He had done nobly in his sovereign's war / And ridden into battle"	He's a brave man, a strong warrior, and someone of great experience.	I admire him because he was willing to risk his life for the people of his kingdom.

Literary Skills Focus

Literary Analysis

7. **Analyze** What aspects of medieval society does Chaucer satirize in his portrayals of the Merchant, Franklin, Doctor, and Miller?
8. **Compare and Contrast** Some of the poem's characters contrast strikingly with each other, and others display strong similarities. Choose a contrasting pair and a similar pair. Explain the differences and similarities in each pair.
9. **Evaluate** Which pilgrims does Chaucer idealize?
10. **Interpret** What do the narrator's descriptions of others reveal about his biases and values?

Literary Skills: Characterization

11. **Evaluate** Chaucer uses physical details to reveal character. Describe three pilgrims whose inner natures are revealed by their appearance.

Literary Skills: Frame Story

12. **Analyze** Describe the Prologue's frame story and how it sets up the rest of the *Tales.*

Literary Skills Review: Foil

13. **Make Judgments** A **foil** is a character who emphasizes another character's qualities by sharp contrast. Which two characters are the most striking opposites? How do they act as foils for each other?

Writing Skills Focus

Think as a Reader/Writer

Use It in Your Writing Chaucer's descriptions create strong impressions of each character's appearance. Write a paragraph describing the appearance of a fictional character. Use details that reveal characteristics, such as status, habits, self-image, and inner nature.

What Do You Think Now? What motivated the Host to join the group of travelers and serve as their leader?

Universal Access

Struggling Writers

To complete the Writing Skills Focus, provide additional scaffolding for students by having them create a character web. Have students draw a circle in the center of a piece of paper. Then, have students draw five to six boxes around the circle. Have students draw lines connecting the central circle to each of the surrounding boxes. Tell students to write the name of the character they plan to describe in the circle. Encourage them to write words and phrases that describe the character in the boxes. Students can use their webs to help them write their descriptive paragraphs.

✔ See **UA: Differentiating Instruction** for strategies for teaching struggling writers.

Grades 9–10 Review Reading Standard 1.1 (see pages A48–A50)

Vocabulary Development

Vocabulary Check

Complete each sentence with a Vocabulary word:: **benign, eminent, frugal, guile, obstinate.**

1. Convincing the guard to let them past the gate was going to require some ________.
2. If he planned to save up enough money for the trip, he would have to be ________ for the next couple of months.
3. Even though the players were right, the bullheaded coach was too ________ to agree with them.
4. His long tenure and impressive collection of awards made him the university's ________ professor.
5. She was sympathetic to others' troubles, and she approached everyone with a ________ attitude.

Vocabulary Skills: Antonyms

Antonyms are words that are have opposite meanings, such as *smooth* and *rough*. Antonyms are also usually the same part of speech. For example, although the noun *sorrow* and the adjective *joyful* are associated with contrasting ideas, they are not antonyms. An antonym for *sorrow* would be another noun, such as *joy*. The following chart shows pairs of antonyms and their parts of speech.

Word	Part of Speech	Antonym
seller	*noun*	buyer
yell	*verb*	whisper
mournful	*adjective*	cheerful
rapidly	*adverb*	slowly

Your Turn

Create an antonym chart like the one at the left for the Vocabulary words. Make certain you include the part of speech of each Vocabulary word and match it to that of its antonym.

Language Coach

Commonly Confused Words Practice with tricky words can help you use them correctly. Choose the best word to complete each sentence. Use a dictionary to understand how each word is used. Then, explain your choices.

1. Today, Chaucer is one of the most (*eminent, imminent*) writers of the Middle Ages.
2. He believed that people would (*accept, except*) tales written in English instead of Latin.
3. One (*affect, effect*) of writing in English was that more people could understand his tales.
4. He (*preceded, proceeded*) other great English writers, such as Shakespeare and Milton.

Academic Vocabulary

Write About

Chaucer creates characters who reflect the richness and diversity of human nature. In a short essay, analyze the character who most intrigues you. Describe the character's attributes, social status, and role. Explain what Chaucer emphasizes about him or her and the techniques Chaucer uses to characterize this person. Cite specific examples from the Prologue, and use the underlined Academic Vocabulary words in your analysis.

Independent Practice

Vocabulary Development

Vocabulary Check

1. *guile*
2. *frugal*
3. *obstinate*
4. *eminent*
5. *benign*

Your Turn

Possible responses:

eminent (*adj.*)—obscure

benign (*adj.*)—malevolent

guile (*n.*)—honesty

obstinate (*adj.*)—compliant

frugal (*adj.*)—extravagant

English for Academic Success

Language Coach

Possible responses:

1. *eminent, meaning "notable"*
2. *accept, meaning "receive"*
3. *effect, meaning "consequence"*
4. *preceded, meaning "came before"*

English for Academic Success

Academic Vocabulary

Possible responses: *Essays should include a description of the person's characteristics, social status, role, and key attributes that Chaucer emphasizes as well as the methods Chaucer uses to characterize the person.*

Universal Access: Vocabulary Development

English Learners

English for Academic Success Some students may need to review the concept of antonyms before completing the Your Turn activity. Explain to students that there are two types of antonyms—polar antonyms and scalar antonyms. Polar antonyms have no middle ground. The word pairs *boy/girl* and *right/wrong* are polar antonyms. Scalar antonyms allow for gradations of meaning between them. The words *happy* and *sad* are scalar antonyms. Point out to students that many of the Vocabulary words have scalar antonyms, not polar antonyms. Encourage students to use a thesaurus to help them complete the exercise.

✔ See the **Academic and Selection Vocabulary Skill Builder** in **UA: Differentiating Instruction.**

Independent Practice

Grammar Link

Your Turn

1. *The Host is enjoying a rowdy tale.*
2. *The pilgrims will be conversing on their way to Canterbury tomorrow.*
3. *The guildsmen were hoping to advance in society.*
4. *The Oxford Cleric will be returning to Oxford after this trip to Canterbury.*

Choices: Evaluation Criteria

Review: Timed Writing 40–50 Minutes

Students write an essay that explores Chaucer's view of social class.

Connect: Homework
Write a Frame Story

Students assign diverse qualities and roles to travelers.

Extend: Homework
Tell Your Own Story

Students include key details describing people and events.

Assess

Unit 1 Resources, Selection Standards Check, p. 49

go.hrw.com **ThinkCentral Online Assessment,** Selection Standards Check

Teacher One Stop™, editable Selection Standards Check

Reteach

go.hrw.com **ThinkCentral Online Remediation**

Learn It Online

The **Digital Storytelling** mini-site shows students how to take a personal experience and craft it into a short film—complete with music, images, and special effects.

go.hrw.com H12-148 Go

Applying Your Skills

Writing Standard 2.1b, 2.2b–c, 2.3b (see pages A51–A52)
Listening and Speaking Standard 2.1a (see pages A53–A55)

The Prologue to The Canterbury Tales

Grammar Link

Progressive Form of Verbs

Each verb has a **progressive form,** which expresses a continuing action or state of being. The progressive form consists of the appropriate tense of the verb *be* plus the *–ing* form of a verb. Progressive forms exist for present, present perfect, past, past perfect, future, and future perfect verbs.

I am traveling to Canterbury.
PRESENT PROGRESSIVE

The page has been playing his lute all day.
PRESENT PERFECT PROGRESSIVE

They were telling tales to entertain each other.
PAST PROGRESSIVE

The Wife of Bath had been telling us a story.
PAST PERFECT PROGRESSIVE

We will be deciding the winner on the way back.
FUTURE PROGRESSIVE

By the time the trip ends, they will have been traveling for days. FUTURE PERFECT PROGRESSIVE

Your Turn

Rewrite the following sentences using a progressive form of a verb.

1. The Host enjoys a rowdy tale.
2. The pilgrims will converse on their way to Canterbury tomorrow.
3. The guildsmen hoped to advance in society.
4. The Oxford Cleric will return to Oxford after this trip to Canterbury.

Writing Application When might it make sense to use the progressive form of verbs in your writing? Experiment by replacing the verbs with the progressive form in a paragraph you have already written.

CHOICES

As you respond to the Choices, use these **Academic Vocabulary** words as appropriate: attribute, concept, diverse, emphasis, status.

REVIEW

Define Past Lives

Timed Writing Chaucer's descriptions of the pilgrims correspond to the strict classifications of social status observed in the Middle Ages. Choose two of the pilgrims that represent distinctly different social classes. Explain in an essay how Chaucer's portraits of the individuals convey his feelings about the social classes each represents. Use textual evidence to support your response.

CONNECT

Write a Frame Story

Write your own prologue to a modern frame story. Set your story in an airport or bus station or on a tour or pilgrimage. You might establish your frame by featuring characters who are stranded by a storm or waiting for rescue from an accident. Select a narrator, and describe the travelers with diverse characteristics, roles, and professions. Emphasize attributes that reveal characters' inner natures.

EXTEND

Tell Your Own Story

By the Prologue's end, the Host has convinced everyone to tell a story. What story might you tell in such a competition? Think of an event from your own life that might make an entertaining story, and write notes to help you recall the key details. Outline your notes, and practice telling your story. Then, tell your story to the whole class or in a small group.

Learn It Online

Tell your story in a twenty-first-century form—through a digital story. Learn how online.

go.hrw.com H12-148 Go

Universal Access: Grammar Link

EL English Learners

English for Academic Success To help students understand the progressive form of verbs, write these sentences on the board.

- I am taking a trip this summer.
- I will be taking a trip this summer.
- I have been taking a trip this summer.
- I was taking a trip this summer.

Ask students to read and think about the differences in each sentence. Review the progressive verb forms and ask them to indicate which progressive form is used in each sentence.

Then, ask students to correct the verb tense in the following sentences:

1. I will be traveling for the past several weeks. [*have been traveling*]
2. We were talking for days by the time we get there. [*will have been talking*]

✔ For more practice with progressive verbs, see **Warriner's Handbook, GrammarNotes,** and **Language Handbook Worksheets.**

Reading Standard 2.5, 3.3 (see pages A48–A50)

from The Pardoner's Tale

Literary Skills Focus

Verbal and Situational Irony A discrepancy between appearance and reality is called **irony.** Chaucer uses irony throughout *The Canterbury Tales.* **Situational irony** occurs when what actually happens is the opposite of what is expected. **Verbal irony** occurs when someone says one thing but really means something else. The contrast seen in the Pardoner, who preaches against vice and should be helping people, but in reality is selfish and corrupt, creates both situational and verbal irony.

Reading Skills Focus

Drawing Conclusions When you **draw a conclusion,** you form a concept that is based on the text but not explicitly stated. In "The Pardoner's Tale," characters refer to Death as if he is an actual person. By noticing, however, how events are described, you can conclude that Death represents an idea.

Into Action As you read, record your conclusions in the first column of a chart like the one below. In the second column, explain how the text supports those conclusions.

Conclusion	How Conclusion Is Supported
Death is the idea or presence of death, not an actual person.	The characters speak of Death as a character, so we expect to meet him as a character. However, we never see him personified.

Writing Skills Focus

Think as a Reader/Writer

Find It in Your Reading "The Pardoner's Tale" is filled with devious characters, and what they say is often very different from what they actually mean. As you read, notice the **verbal irony** that results from this contrast between a character's words and meaning. In your *Reader/Writer Notebook,* record the examples of verbal irony that you find most interesting.

TechFocus As you read, think about the different ways you encounter stories in the modern world.

Vocabulary

avarice (AV uhr ihs) *n.:* uncontrolled desire for wealth. *His avarice led him to seek riches at the expense of others.*

abominable (uh BAHM uh nuh buhl) *adj.:* disgusting; hateful. *Poisoning the friend who trusted him was an abominable act.*

adversary (AD vuhr sehr ee) *n.:* enemy; opponent. *Sin should have been the Pardoner's adversary, but it seemed to be one of his closest friends.*

pallor (PAL uhr) *n.:* paleness. *Death is traditionally pictured with a sickening pallor.*

absolve (ab SAHLV) *v.:* forgive; make free from blame. *After the man confesses his sins, the Pardoner should absolve him.*

Language Coach

Forms of Words The word *absolve* is a verb that means "to forgive." It is related to the noun *absolution,* which means "forgiveness." Notice that the *v* changes to a *u* in the noun form. How can you follow the same pattern and change the verbs *solve* and *revolve* into nouns? What do the new words mean?

Learn It Online
Delve deeper into the Vocabulary words with Word Watch online.

go.hrw.com H12-149 Go

Reader/Writer Notebook
Use your **RWN** to complete the activities for this selection.

California Standards, pp. 149–160

- **Reading Standard 2.5** Analyze an author's implicit and explicit philosophical assumptions and beliefs about a subject.
- **Reading Standard 3.3** Analyze the ways in which irony, tone, mood, the author's style, and the "sound" of language achieve specific rhetorical or aesthetic purposes or both.

Preteach

Introducing Vocabulary

Use this activity to check students' understanding of the Vocabulary words.

1. Explain why a person of **avarice** would have difficulty being satisfied with little.
2. Tell how the weather can be **abominable.**
3. Explain how two **adversaries** might behave toward each other.
4. List two situations that might induce **pallor.**
5. Explain how someone who has been **absolved** of a sin feels.

English for Academic Success

Language Coach

After students read the **Language Coach,** have them discuss their answers to the questions with a partner. [*solution—explanation or answer; revolution—a single cycle or turn*]

Literary Skills Focus

As you read the selection with students, have them note instances of situational and verbal irony.

Reading Skills Focus

Give students a copy of the Reading Skills Focus graphic organizer before reading. (See **Unit 1 Resources.**) Have them use their responses to answer questions on the Applying Your Skills page.

Writing Skills Focus

Have students record interesting examples of verbal irony in their **Reader/Writer Notebooks.** Students can use their notes to complete the Writing Skills Focus activity.

Learn It Online
Send students to **Word Watch** for audio pronunciations, synonyms and antonyms, and brief histories of word origins.

go.hrw.com H12-149 Go

Teacher Preparation

Selection Plot Summary

"The Pardoner's Tale" begins with the Pardoner's simple statement of his main idea that greed, particularly for wealth, is the root of all evil. He launches into the narrative of three young men who are living a wild life. The men discover a fortune in coins under an oak tree. They decide it is important to protect their wealth, and so they send one man into town to fetch wine and bread while the other two guard the pile. The guards plot to kill him for his share, but the man running the errand is just as greedy, and he poisons their wine. The two guards kill him, and then die after drinking the wine. The Pardoner declares that greed was their downfall, but immediately tries to sell his relics to those assembled to listen to him. Ironically, he is as greedy as the men in his story.

Universal Access

English Learners

Make sure students understand the role of a pardoner in the Middle Ages. Explain that he was a clergyman who traveled around hearing confessions and granting forgiveness for sins. While pardoners were forbidden by the Church to accept money for their services, Chaucer implies that many of them did. Point out that in this tale students will find many ironic discrepancies between what characters expected to happen and what actually does happen, and between what "The Pardoner's Tale" teaches and the way the Pardoner behaves.

Struggling Readers

Students will find the irony within the tale the Pardoner tells easier to grasp than the overall irony Chaucer intends. Suggest that students return to the Pardoner's Prologue after they have read and understood the narrative of the three young men who find Death under the oak tree. Once they have worked through the story's irony, their understanding of irony can be applied to the Pardoner himself.

NARRATIVE POEM

FROM *The Pardoner's Tale*

by **Geoffrey Chaucer**

translated by **Nevill Coghill**

The Pardoner, detail from *The Canterbury Tales* by Geoffrey Chaucer. The Huntington Library, San Marino, CA.

Read with a Purpose

Read to discover how Chaucer uses the Pardoner's tale to explore the impulses that lead people to be destructive.

Build Background

In the medieval Church, a pardoner was a clergyman with the power to forgive sins and grant indulgences, the Church's relief from temporal and purgatorial punishments for sins. Forgiving sins and granting indulgences were powers the pope bestowed upon the clergy to spiritually benefit believers. Such benefits were not supposed to be bought and sold, but greedy clergy sometimes took advantage of people's fear of punishment and demanded money. Some, like Chaucer's Pardoner, kept the money for themselves.

FROM *The Pardoner's Prologue*

"But let me briefly make my purpose plain;
I preach for nothing but for greed of gain
And use the same old text, as bold as brass,
Radix malorum est cupiditas.°
And thus I preach against the very vice
I make my living out of—avarice.
And yet however guilty of that sin
Myself, with others I have power to win
Them from it, I can bring them to repent;
But that is not my principal intent. **A**
Covetousness° is both the root and stuff
Of all I preach. That ought to be enough.
"Well, then I give examples thick and fast
From bygone times, old stories from the past.

4. *Radix malorum est cupiditas* (RAH dihks mah LOH rum ehst koo PIH dih tahs): Latin: literally, "The root of evil is desire" (1 Timothy 6:10). The Pardoner has been telling the pilgrims about his preaching methods.

11. covetousness: quality of craving wealth or possessions; greed.

A **Reading Focus** **Drawing Conclusions** Why does the Pardoner admit he preaches to make a personal profit?

Vocabulary **avarice** (AV uhr ihs) *n.:* uncontrolled desire for wealth.

(Opposite) The Knight and the Squire from "The Pardoner's Prologue" of *The Canterbury Tales* by Harry Mileham (1873–1957).

Direct Teach

Think About/Talk About

Read with a Purpose Have students read the Read with a Purpose statement. Ask what impulses might lead people to destructiveness.

Comprehension

A Reading Focus

Possible responses: *He is so immoral he is proud of his vice; he may be carried away with his own cleverness in telling his tale.*

Extend the Discussion

Summarizing Summarize the first 12 lines. ***Possible response:*** *Lines 1–12 introduce the Pardoner as a greedy man who makes no secret of his own vice.*

Characterization What language does the Pardoner speak in line 4? ***Possible response:*** *He speaks Latin, the language of the Roman Catholic Church.*

Vocabulary: Own the Word

avarice: Help students understand the word *avarice* has a negative connotation because of the extreme nature of one's desire for wealth. Ask students to list actions of someone who exhibits *avarice.*

Advanced Learners

Enrichment In the Pardoner's Prologue, the Pardoner immediately reveals himself to be guilty of the sin he preaches against. Have students work alone or in pairs to think of three contemporary professions and a strong belief or code of behavior that each of the professions upholds. Ask students to identify an action that a person practicing each profession could do that would be considered ironic.

Students with Disabilities

Divide students into pairs, and ask them to take turns reading the tales in segments, stopping briefly to retell the main events to their partners. You might suggest they stop and summarize after lines 102, 161, 199, 230, 274, 290, and 332. Monitor partners' discussions to make sure that students have a clear understanding of the main ideas and details included in "The Pardoner's Tale."

Think About/Talk About

Build Background: The Seven Deadly Sins

In medieval times, people were keenly concerned about the seven deadly sins: pride, avarice, lust, anger, gluttony, envy, and sloth. According to the Church, these sins brought eternal damnation unless the sinner confessed and obtained a pardon. In the opening lines of "The Pardoner's Tale," the Pardoner acknowledges that his own vices include avarice, sloth, and perhaps gluttony and lust.

Literary Connection

Explain that most of Chaucer's tales are based on older stories. The earliest known version of "The Pardoner's Tale" is found in the Hindu collection *Vedabbha Jātaka*.

Extend the Discussion

Rereading How does the Pardoner describe his life in lines 25–31? ***Possible response:*** *He extorts money from the rich and the poor without guilt, and he spends it on personal enjoyment.*

Evaluating What is significant about the way the Pardoner begins to describe the three young men in his story? ***Possible response:*** *He is very much like the young men in his tale, even though he is very critical of them.*

A yokel° mind loves stories from of old,
Being the kind it can repeat and hold.
What! Do you think, as long as I can preach
And get their silver for the things I teach,
That I will live in poverty, from choice?
That's not the counsel of my inner voice!
No! Let me preach and beg from kirk° to kirk
And never do an honest job of work,
No, nor make baskets, like St. Paul, to gain
A livelihood. I do not preach in vain.
There's no apostle I would counterfeit;
I mean to have money, wool and cheese and wheat
Though it were given me by the poorest lad
Or poorest village widow, though she had
A string of starving children, all agape.°
No, let me drink the liquor of the grape
And keep a jolly wench in every town!
"But listen, gentlemen; to bring things down
To a conclusion, would you like a tale?
Now as I've drunk a draft of corn-ripe ale,
By God it stands to reason I can strike
On some good story that you all will like.
For though I am a wholly vicious° man
Don't think I can't tell moral tales. I can!
Here's one I often preach when out for winning;
Now please be quiet. Here is the beginning."

15. yokel: rustic; of the country.

21. kirk: Scottish for "church."

29. agape: open-mouthed.

37. vicious: here, possessing many faults.

The Pardoner's Tale

In Flanders once there was a company
Of youngsters haunting vice and ribaldry,°
Riot and gambling, stews and public-houses
Where each with harp, guitar, or lute carouses,°
Dancing and dicing° day and night, and bold
To eat and drink far more than they can hold,
Doing thereby the devil sacrifice
Within that devil's temple of cursed vice,
Abominable in superfluity,
With oaths so damnable in blasphemy°
That it's a grisly thing to hear them swear.
Our dear Lord's body they will rend and tear.°. . .
It's of three rioters° I have to tell
Who, long before the morning service bell,
Were sitting in a tavern for a drink.

42. ribaldry: vulgar language or humor.
44. carouses: drinks and celebrates noisily.
45. dicing: gambling (throwing dice).

50. blasphemy: mockery of God.

52. Our . . . tear: Their oaths refer to "God's arms" and "God's blessed bones."
53. rioters: people living a wild, unrestrained lifestyle.

Vocabulary **abominable** (uh BAHM uh nuh buhl) *adj.:* disgusting; hateful.

Universal Access

EL English Learners

English for Academic Success Students may struggle to understand Chaucer's use of archaic language. Read aloud line 43 on p. 152. Explain to students that today, the word *riot* is associated with the uprising of a mob, but here the word means "wild living." Stews were brothels. Public-houses were places where liquor was sold. As students continue reading the tale, have them record words they have trouble understanding and look them up in a print or online dictionary.

Struggling Readers

Strategic Students To help students read "The Pardoner's Tale," model the reading skill of drawing conclusions. You might say: "In "The Pardoner's Prologue," the Pardoner mentions that he is a greedy, immoral person. However, in the opening lines of his tale, he describes the rioters as abominable and ribald. Using this information, I can draw the conclusion that the Pardoner is a hypocritical person. He condemns others for committing the same sins he himself confesses to executing."

And as they sat, they heard the hand-bell clink
Before a coffin going to the grave;
One of them called the little tavern-knave°
And said "Go and find out at once—look spry!—
Whose corpse is in that coffin passing by;
And see you get the name correctly too."
"Sir," said the boy, "no need, I promise you;
Two hours before you came here I was told.
He was a friend of yours in days of old,
And suddenly, last night, the man was slain,
Upon his bench, face up, dead drunk again.
There came a privy° thief, they call him Death,
Who kills us all round here, and in a breath
He speared him through the heart, he never stirred.
And then Death went his way without a word.
He's killed a thousand in the present plague,°
And, sir, it doesn't do to be too vague
If you should meet him; you had best be wary.
Be on your guard with such an adversary,
Be primed to meet him everywhere you go,
That's what my mother said. It's all I know."
The publican° joined in with, "By St. Mary,
What the child says is right; you'd best be wary,
This very year he killed, in a large village
A mile away, man, woman, serf at tillage,°
Page in the household, children—all there were.
Yes, I imagine that he lives round there.
It's well to be prepared in these alarms,°
He might do you dishonor." "Huh, God's arms!"
The rioter said, "Is he so fierce to meet?
I'll search for him, by Jesus, street by street.
God's blessed bones! I'll register a vow!
Here, chaps! The three of us together now,
Hold up your hands, like me, and we'll be brothers
In this affair, and each defend the others,
And we will kill this traitor Death, I say! **B**
Away with him as he has made away
With all our friends. God's dignity! Tonight!"
They made their bargain, swore with appetite,
These three, to live and die for one another
As brother-born might swear to his born brother.
And up they started in their drunken rage

58. tavern-knave: serving boy.

67. privy: archaic usage meaning "secretive; furtive."

71. present plague: the Black Death, which killed nearly one third of the population of England during the mid-fourteenth century.

77. publican: tavern keeper; from *public house,* a tavern or inn.

80. tillage: working the land.

83. alarms: here, anxious times.

B Literary Focus Irony Why is it ironic that the rioters vow as brothers to kill Death? Would you categorize this irony as verbal or situational?

Vocabulary **adversary** (AD vuhr sehr ee) *n.:* enemy; opponent.

Think About/Talk About

Analysis

B Literary Focus

Possible responses: *Under normal circumstances, Death kills humans, but in this case, humans are attempting to kill Death. I would categorize this as verbal irony because the vow itself is contradictory.*

Extend the Discussion

Identifying Cause and Effect What effect does seeing a coffin pass in the street have on the three young men? ***Possible response:*** *It makes them angry and encourages them to seek out and kill Death.*

Moral Tale What explicit advice is being offered in lines 73–82? What moral lesson is implied? ***Possible responses:*** *Do not forget that the threat of death is always close at hand. Live virtuously because you cannot escape death and the punishment for sin that comes after death.*

Vocabulary: Own the Word

- **abominable:** The connotation of *abominable* is that a person has disgustingly bad behavior. Why does the Pardoner describe the rioters as *abominable*? ***Possible responses:*** *They riot, gamble, and use vulgar language; they mock God.*
- **adversary:** Point out to students that some synonyms for *adversary* are *enemy, foe, opponent,* and *rival.* Ask students to explain why running into an *adversary* might cause someone's complexion to become pale. ***Possible response:*** *Meeting an enemy unexpectedly might cause anyone to turn pale with fear.*

Advanced Learners

Enrichment Ask students to visit the library or media center to research the location of Flanders, the setting of "The Pardoner's Tale." Ask them to determine whether the Pardoner's portrait of life in Flanders in medieval times is accurate. They may be surprised to learn about the pastimes available to young men in this time period. As a group, have them prepare a mini-lesson in which they present their findings to the class. Encourage them to employ visual as well as verbal descriptions for their mini-lesson.

Students with Disabilities

Chaucer's narrative poem can be daunting even for the most proficient reader. As students read the poem, remind them to pay close attention to the glosses in the side margins. Explain that these glosses provide important information and definitions that will aid students' understanding of the text. When students come across a difficult word or phrase, encourage them to check the glosses before consulting a dictionary or other source.

Model the Skill

- Provide students with copies of the Reading Skills Focus graphic organizer for "The Pardoner's Tale." (See **Unit 1 Resources**.)
- Tell students that to **draw a conclusion**, readers must use evidence from the text and combine it with personal observations and prior knowledge.
- Model adding a conclusion to the graphic organizer. Read aloud lines 105–109. Explain that in these lines, the narrator introduces a new character. This is an old man who seems to know about the intentions of the three young men. He also says that Death will not kill him, so it seems this man is a supernatural being. Readers know that the Pardoner is telling a story with a moral, so maybe this character is Death itself, advising the three young men not to challenge destiny.

Conclusion	How Conclusion Is Supported
The old man is Death himself.	He knows a lot about the young men; he says Death cannot kill him.

Guided Practice: Apply

Have students continue reading through line 177. Ask students to draw a conclusion about the rioters, the golden florins, and the old man's words. Students should add their conclusion and evidence to the chart.

And made towards this village which the page
And publican had spoken of before.
Many and grisly were the oaths they swore,
Tearing Christ's blessed body to a shred;
"If we can only catch him, Death is dead!"
When they had gone not fully half a mile,
Just as they were about to cross a stile,°
They came upon a very poor old man
Who humbly greeted them and thus began,
"God look to you, my lords, and give you quiet!"
To which the proudest of these men of riot
Gave back the answer, "What, old fool? Give place!
Why are you all wrapped up except your face?
Why live so long? Isn't it time to die?"
The old, old fellow looked him in the eye
And said, "Because I never yet have found,
Though I have walked to India, searching round
Village and city on my pilgrimage,
One who would change his youth to have my age
And so my age is mine and must be still
Upon me, for such time as God may will.
"Not even Death, alas, will take my life;
So, like a wretched prisoner at strife
Within himself, I walk alone and wait
About the earth, which is my mother's gate,°
Knock-knocking with my staff from night to noon
And crying, 'Mother, open to me soon!
Look at me, mother, won't you let me in?
See how I wither, flesh and blood and skin!
Alas! When will these bones be laid to rest?
Mother, I would exchange—for that were best—
The wardrobe in my chamber, standing there
So long, for yours! Aye, for a shirt of hair°
To wrap me in!' She has refused her grace,
Whence comes the pallor of my withered face. **C**
"But it dishonored you when you began
To speak so roughly, sir, to an old man,
Unless he had injured you in word or deed.
It says in holy writ,° as you may read,
'Thou shalt rise up before the hoary° head
And honor it.' And therefore be it said,
'Do no more harm to an old man than you,

104. stile: steps used for climbing over a wall.

122. mother's gate: The old man refers to Death as a mother, her house surrounded by a gate (the earth). Thus, "mother's gate" is the entrance to a grave.

130. shirt of hair: Coarse shirts of woven horsehair were worn as penance. Here, the old man refers to such a shirt to be used to wrap his body for burial.

136. holy writ: the Bible.
137. hoary: white.

C **Reading Focus** **Drawing Conclusions** Who is this old man? What might he represent, or what purpose might he serve in the story?

Vocabulary **pallor** (PAL uhr) *n.:* paleness.

Universal Access

EL English Learners

English for Academic Success Students may struggle to understand the informal language usage that the narrator employs in "The Pardoner's Tale." Read aloud line 180 on p. 155. Explain to students that the word *chaps,* meaning "fellows" or "boys" (today we might say "guys"), is an example of informal language. Although occasionally used in American English, the word is most frequently used in British English. (The word *chaps* is the translator's, not Chaucer's.)

Struggling Readers

Strategic Students These students must be able to follow what happens in the Pardoner's narrative before they will be able to extract its moral or understand its ironies. To help students track the plot, show them how to construct a time line illustrating the chain of events that leads to the rioters' deaths. Write in the first event for them: "Rioters decide to kill Death." Then, have students work on their own.

Being now young, would have another do
When you are old'—if you should live till then.
And so may God be with you, gentlemen,
For I must go whither I have to go."
"By God," the gambler said, "you shan't do so,
You don't get off so easy, by St. John!
I heard you mention, just a moment gone,
A certain traitor Death who singles out
And kills the fine young fellows hereabout.
And you're his spy, by God! You wait a bit.
Say where he is or you shall pay for it,
By God and by the Holy Sacrament!
I say you've joined together by consent
To kill us younger folk, you thieving swine!"
"Well, sirs," he said, "if it be your design
To find out Death, turn up this crooked way
Towards that grove, I left him there today
Under a tree, and there you'll find him waiting.
He isn't one to hide for all your prating.°
You see that oak? He won't be far to find.
And God protect you that redeemed mankind,
Aye, and amend° you!" Thus that ancient man.
At once the three young rioters began
To run, and reached the tree, and there they found
A pile of golden florins° on the ground,
New-coined, eight bushels of them as they thought.
No longer was it Death those fellows sought, **D**
For they were all so thrilled to see the sight,
The florins were so beautiful and bright,
That down they sat beside the precious pile.
The wickedest spoke first after a while.
"Brothers," he said, "you listen to what I say.
I'm pretty sharp although I joke away.
It's clear that Fortune has bestowed this treasure
To let us live in jollity and pleasure.
Light come, light go! We'll spend it as we ought.
God's precious dignity! Who would have thought
This morning was to be our lucky day?
"If one could only get the gold away,
Back to my house, or else to yours, perhaps—
For as you know, the gold is ours, chaps—
We'd all be at the top of fortune, hey?
But certainly it can't be done by day.
People would call us robbers—a strong gang,
So our own property would make us hang.

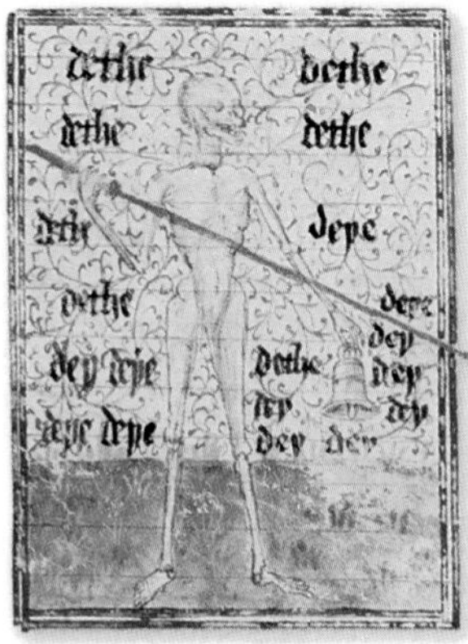

Death with his Spear, from "The Pardoner's Tale." MS Douce 322, fol. 19v. The Bodleian Library, University of Oxford.

158. prating: chattering.

161. amend: improve.

164. florins: coins worth twenty-four pence. *Pence* is the British plural of *penny.*

The Three Living, the Three Dead, from the *French Psalter and Prayer Book of Bonne of Luxembourg, Duchess of Normandy* (before 1349), probably by Jean Le Noir, his daughter Bourgot, and his workshop.
The Metropolitan Museum of Art, NY, The Cloisters Collection 1969 (69.86) 69.86, folio 321v–322r.

D **Literary Focus** **Irony** What is ironic about the rioters' discovery?

Think About/Talk About

Comprehension

C Reading Focus

Possible responses: *He may be Death. He may be an angel or just an old man looking for Death.*

Analysis

D Literary Focus

Possible response: *The young men did not find Death, but they probably have found the instrument of their own death in the gold coins.*

Extend the Discussion

Characterization Is the old man sincere? Why or why not? ***Possible responses:*** *Yes, he is sincere because he blesses the young men's efforts. No, he is not sincere; the old man knows the young men have undertaken an impossible task. The old man's message is false.*

Evaluating In lines 155–156, the old man points the three young men in the direction of Death. Is the Death the young men seek an actual character? What clues in the reading support your response? ***Possible responses:*** *The young men think he is a person, and they run toward where Death is, which makes it seem as if they think they will find an actual person. They do not find a person, so Death does not seem to be an actual character.*

Vocabulary: Own the Word

pallor: Ask students to list things that might cause a person to have an unhealthy *pallor* in his or her face. ***Possible responses:*** *lack of food or proper nutrition; dehydration; extremely hot weather; seasickness*

Cross-Curricular Connection

ART: Picture the Tale

Group Activity Assign one of the following sections of "The Pardoner's Tale" to a group of students: lines 53–93, 94–132, 133–177, 178–217, 218–263, 264–290. Direct students to recreate the story visually on paper; they can draw freehand or cut and paste pictures. Also, ask students to add speech balloons, captions, or other text as needed. Groups should divide duties up among members, but you should require that a written summary of each member's contribution be handed in with the final product. When all groups are finished, have each group present its section of the tale, in order, to the rest of the class. Ask other class members to make one positive comment and one suggestion for improvement to each group. Finally, have all groups revise their presentations based on the comments they received. Each group's final product can be displayed on a bulletin board.

Guided Practice: Apply

Think as a Reader/Writer

Find It in Your Reading Point out that lines 202, 216, and 217 contain examples of verbal irony, where the speaker's words do not reflect the speaker's true intentions. Tell students that even though the speaker claims to be trustworthy, his devious scheme to kill the youngest already demonstrates that he is not.

Use It in Your Writing Ask students to write a few sentences in which a speaker's words contradict his actions.

Think About/Talk About

Literary Connection

Explain that, at the end of p. 157, the Pardoner describes the working of the Devil. The young man has already fallen into sin through drunkenness. As a result, God allows the Devil (the Fiend) to lure the young man further into evil. Inform students that, according to Christian theology, God does not cause evil but allows people to be tempted by it.

No, we must bring this treasure back by night
Some prudent way, and keep it out of sight.
And so as a solution I propose
We draw for lots and see the way it goes;
The one who draws the longest, lucky man,
Shall run to town as quickly as he can
To fetch us bread and wine—but keep things dark°—
While two remain in hiding here to mark
Our heap of treasure. If there's no delay,
When night comes down we'll carry it away,
All three of us, wherever we have planned."
He gathered lots and hid them in his hand
Bidding them draw for where the luck should fall.
It fell upon the youngest of them all,
And off he ran at once towards the town.
As soon as he had gone the first sat down
And thus began a parley° with the other:
"You know that you can trust me as a brother;
Now let me tell you where your profit lies;
You know our friend has gone to get supplies
And here's a lot of gold that is to be
Divided equally among us three.
Nevertheless, if I could shape things thus
So that we shared it out—the two of us—
Wouldn't you take it as a friendly act?"
"But how?" the other said. "He knows the fact
That all the gold was left with me and you;
What can we tell him? What are we to do?"
"Is it a bargain," said the first, "or no?
For I can tell you in a word or so
What's to be done to bring the thing about."
"Trust me," the other said, "you needn't doubt
My word. I won't betray you, I'll be true."
"Well," said his friend, "you see that we are two,
And two are twice as powerful as one.
Now look; when he comes back, get up in fun
To have a wrestle; then, as you attack,
I'll up and put my dagger through his back
While you and he are struggling, as in game;
Then draw your dagger too and do the same.
Then all this money will be ours to spend,
Divided equally of course, dear friend.
Then we can gratify our lusts and fill
The day with dicing at our own sweet will." **E**

191. keep things dark: do it in secret.

201. parley: discussion.

E Literary Focus **Irony** Why is this discussion between the two rioters ironic? Is this verbal or situational irony?

Developing Oral Fluency

Whole-Class Activity Encourage students to prepare an oral reading of the tale to help them follow its intricate narrative structure.

Have them begin by working together in groups of three or four to decide who is speaking in each major segment of the selection. Help them discover that the Pardoner speaks the Prologue and narrates the tale in which specific characters, such as the publican and the rioters, engage in dialogue. Have the students come together as a class, mark these instances of dialogue within the tale (alert them to look for quotation marks), and choose individuals to read the exact words of each other's characters. Finally, call their attention to the final thirteen lines of the selection, and make sure they understand that this is a return to the frame story in which the general narrator is speaking.

After students have prepared their script, have them rehearse reading aloud with attention to expressiveness.

✔ See the **Oral Language Skill Builder** in **UA: Differentiating Instruction.**

Analyzing Visuals

Connecting to the Text Briefly describe what is happening in this illustration. What irony does this scene convey?

The Pardoner's Tale: The Three Rogues Search in the Woods for Death (1907) by Walter Appleton Clark.

Thus these two miscreants° agreed to slay
The third and youngest, as you heard me say.
The youngest, as he ran towards the town,
Kept turning over, rolling up and down
Within his heart the beauty of those bright
New florins, saying, "Lord, to think I might
Have all that treasure to myself alone!
Could there be anyone beneath the throne
Of God so happy as I then should be?"
And so the Fiend,° our common enemy,
Was given power to put it in his thought
That there was always poison to be bought,
And that with poison he could kill his friends.
To men in such a state the Devil sends
Thoughts of this kind, and has a full permission
To lure them on to sorrow and perdition;°
For this young man was utterly content
To kill them both and never to repent.
And on he ran, he had no thought to tarry,
Came to the town, found an apothecary°
And said, "Sell me some poison if you will,

229. **miscreants:** criminals; literally, "unbelievers."

238. **Fiend:** the devil.

244. **perdition:** damnation.

248. **apothecary:** druggist. Formerly, apothecaries made and prescribed medications.

Think About/Talk About

Analysis

E Literary Focus

Possible responses: *They claim to be acting as brothers while they are plotting to betray the youngest rioter. Their conversation is an example of verbal irony.*

Extend the Discussion

Drawing Conclusions In line 194, why does one young man suggest that the three wait until the cover of night to transport their gold? ***Possible responses:*** *The characters might wait until nightfall to keep the fortune a secret from others who live as these men do. The man making the suggestion will be able to kill the others without being seen and caught.*

Character Motivation What is the man really trying to accomplish in sending off only one man? ***Possible responses:*** *He is trying to gain a larger share of the fortune. He is trying to get one of the other men alone so he can kill him or plot with him.*

Analyzing Visuals

Connecting to the Text: *The three Rogues are cautiously walking in the woods at night, searching for Death. The irony is that Death is with them, following the Rogues.*

Universal Access

AAVE Students Who Use African American Vernacular English

English for Academic Success Some students may struggle with the usage of *is* versus *are* according to the rules of formal English. Point out how, in the lines 218–219 on p. 156, one of the rioters says "You see that we *are* two / And two *are* twice as powerful as one." Tell students that in casual conversations they might be tempted to say these lines in the following manner: "You see that we *is* two, / And two *is* twice as powerful as one." Explain to students that in formal English, *are* is the appropriate form of *to be* for the subjects *you, we,* and *they; is* accompanies the subjects *he, she,* and *it.* Have students write three sentences about the characters in "The Pardoner's Tale" using *is* and *are* correctly.

✔ For additional instruction and strategies, see **Think-Central, Teacher Access.**

Model the Skill

- Review the concept of **irony**. Explain that even though the Pardoner warns his audience that immoral behavior will get them in trouble, he does not follow his own advice. You might ask: "What is something the Pardoner says is bad, even though he practices it?" [*hoarding wealth/greed*]
- Tell students that we can also identify situational irony by observing what the characters think is going on as opposed to what is actually happening. Read from line 275, beginning with "Why make a sermon of it?. . ." Point out how the two men kill the other man for his share of the treasure. Explain that each man plotted to kill the others, and all of them succeeded. However, this is ironic, because the success of their evil plans results in their death.

Guided Practice: Apply

Think-Pair-Share Have students read line 275, and guide them as they discuss the irony in the narrator's words. ***Possible response:*** *"The Pardoner's Tale" is an exemplum, or moral anecdote, of the kind frequently used in sermons. The Pardoner is saying he will not make a sermon of his tale. However, that is what he intends to do for his own gain.*

Think About/Talk About

Literary Connection

Read aloud lines 272–273. Point out that the phrase "the devil's clay" is an apposition to the subject. This is an example of direct characterization, yet it is essentially a metaphor. Explain that the rioter's character was molded, like clay, by the Devil. He is like clay: changeable, easily manipulated, and without moral integrity.

I have a lot of rats I want to kill
And there's a polecat too about my yard
That takes my chickens and it hits me hard;
But I'll get even, as is only right,
With vermin that destroy a man by night." **F**
The chemist answered, "I've a preparation
Which you shall have, and by my soul's salvation
If any living creature eat or drink
A mouthful, ere° he has the time to think,
Though he took less than makes a grain of wheat,
You'll see him fall down dying at your feet;
Yes, die he must, and in so short a while
You'd hardly have the time to walk a mile,
The poison is so strong, you understand."
This cursed fellow grabbed into his hand
The box of poison and away he ran
Into a neighboring street, and found a man
Who lent him three large bottles. He withdrew
And deftly poured the poison into two.
He kept the third one clean, as well he might,
For his own drink, meaning to work all night
Stacking the gold and carrying it away.
And when this rioter, this devil's clay,
Had filled his bottles up with wine, all three,
Back to rejoin his comrades sauntered° he.
Why make a sermon of it? Why waste breath?
Exactly in the way they'd planned his death
They fell on him and slew him, two to one.
Then said the first of them when this was done,
"Now for a drink. Sit down and let's be merry,
For later on there'll be the corpse to bury."
And, as it happened, reaching for a sup,
He took a bottle full of poison up
And drank; and his companion, nothing loth,°
Drank from it also, and they perished both.
There is, in Avicenna's° long relation
Concerning poison and its operation,
Trust me, no ghastlier section to transcend
What these two wretches suffered at their end.
Thus these two murderers received their due,
So did the treacherous young poisoner too. . . .
"One thing I should have mentioned in my tale,
Dear people. I've some relics in my bale°
And pardons too, as full and fine, I hope,

258. ere: before.

Pilgrims on the road to Canterbury, Trinity Chapel Miracle Window, Canterbury Cathedral, England. Stained glass.

274. sauntered: strolled.

283. loth: reluctant; unwilling; alternative spelling of *loath*.

285. Avicenna's: Avicenna (A.D. 980–1037), a famous Islamic philosopher and doctor, wrote several medical books.

292. relics in my bale: Relics are objects considered holy because of association with a saint—hair, bones, teeth, or clothing. A *bale* is a bundle of goods. In the Middle Ages, many relics were faked.

F **Literary Focus** **Irony** What is ironic about the reason the young man gives for buying the poison?

Universal Access

Struggling Readers

Strategic Students As students read the tale, encourage students to have their own dialogue with the text. Suggest that students write down their questions, predictions, and emotional reactions to as many lines or sections as possible. Then, have them share their notes with a partner and work with that partner to answer questions and compare responses.

Students with Disabilities

Students may have trouble with the quick switch from the Pardoner's narrative to the tale of the Pardoner. Have them read to line 290 and stop. Make sure they understand clearly what happened to each of the three friends and help them see how they were caught up in their own foolishness. This will help students understand the larger picture when they read the last forty-eight lines.

As any in England, given me by the Pope. **G**
If there be one among you that is willing
To have my absolution° for a shilling°
Devoutly given, come! and do not harden
Your hearts but kneel in humbleness for pardon;
Or else, receive my pardon as we go.
You can renew it every town or so
Always provided that you still renew
Each time, and in good money, what is due.
It is an honor to you to have found
A pardoner with his credentials sound
Who can absolve you as you ply the spur°
In any accident that may occur.
For instance—we are all at Fortune's beck°—
Your horse may throw you down and break your neck.
What a security it is to all
To have me here among you and at call
With pardon for the lowly and the great
When soul leaves body for the future state!
And I advise our Host here to begin,
The most enveloped of you all in sin.
Come forward, Host, you shall be the first to pay,
And kiss my holy relics right away.
Only a groat.° Come on, unbuckle your purse!"
"No, no," said he,° "not I, and may the curse
Of Christ descend upon me if I do! . . ."

The Pardoner said nothing, not a word;
He was so angry that he couldn't speak.
"Well," said our Host, "if you're for showing pique,°
I'll joke no more, not with an angry man."
The worthy Knight immediately began,
Seeing the fun was getting rather rough,
And said, "No more, we've all had quite enough.
Now, Master Pardoner, perk up, look cheerly!
And you, Sir Host, whom I esteem so dearly,
I beg of you to kiss the Pardoner.
"Come, Pardoner, draw nearer, my dear sir.
Let's laugh again and keep the ball in play."°
They kissed, and we continued on our way.

296. absolution: forgiveness. **shilling:** coin worth twelve pence.

305. ply the spur: In today's terms, this idiom means something like "rev it up" or "put on speed." It refers to the action of a rider digging his spurs into a horse to make it go faster.
307. beck: summons; in other words, subject to Fortune's will.

317. groat: silver coin worth four pence.
318. he: the Host.

322. pique: resentment and ill humor.

331. keep the ball in play: continue.

G Reading Focus **Drawing Conclusions** Do you think the Pardoner's relics are authentic or fake? Explain your reasoning.

Vocabulary **absolve** (ab SAHLV) *v.:* forgive; make free from blame.

Think About/Talk About

Comprehension

G Reading Focus
Possible responses: *Fake. The Pardoner is a dishonest man interested in making money for himself.*

Analysis

F Literary Focus
Possible responses: *He wants it for "vermin that destroy a man by night." Ironically, the "vermin" he plans to kill are planning to "destroy a man"—him. In addition, the young man fits his own definition of vermin.*

Extend the Discussion

Characterization What insights into the characters of the Pardoner, the Host, and the Knight are revealed in lines 313–332? ***Possible responses:*** *The Pardoner is ready to insult others, but loses his temper when someone sees through him. The Host reveals himself to be not easily fooled or intimidated in his contempt for the Pardoner. The Knight views himself as a beneficent superior, intervening between his inferiors to smooth over conflicts and assuage hard feelings.*

Vocabulary: Own the Word

absolve: Remind students that *absolve* means "forgive." Ask the following question: "Have you ever had to *absolve* someone? Explain when and why you *absolved* that person."

Monitor Students' Comprehension

Guide the class in answering these comprehension questions.

1. What vow do the rioters make in the beginning of the tale? [*They vow to find and destroy Death.*]
2. Where does the old man tell the rioters to look for Death? [*under a nearby oak tree*]
3. What was the rioter's plan for the gold? [*The younger rioter will go to town while the other two stay with the treasure. Each rioter had a plan to steal the gold from the others.*]

California Standards, p. 160

- **Reading Standard 2.5** Analyze an author's implicit and explicit philosophical assumptions and beliefs about a subject.
- **Reading Standard 3.3** Analyze the ways in which irony, tone, mood, the author's style, and the "sound" of language achieve specific rhetorical or aesthetic purposes or both.
- **Writing Standard 1.2** Use point of view, characterization, style (e.g., use of irony), and related elements for specific rhetorical and aesthetic purposes.

Check for Understanding

Independent Practice

Reading Skills Focus

Possible responses:

1. *He says he is corrupt and greedy.*
2. *They want to kill him.*
3. *The Pardoner's moral is that greed can lead to death. Chaucer's moral may be to beware of hypocrites.*
4. *Ask students to share reasons why they may have changed their minds after reviewing conclusions.*

Vocabulary Check

5. *someone self-centered*
6. *on the team you're playing against*
7. *no*
8. *It is opposite in meaning.*
9. *to free him or her from blame*

Literary Skills Focus

Possible responses:

10. *Chaucer satirizes greedy clerics who deceive the faithful.*
11. *Yes; the Pardoner is an example of someone who does not practice what he preaches.*
12. *Some may be familiar with the saying "Money is the root of all evil" and agree with it. Others may feel pride is the most basic sin.*
13. *The rioters seek to kill Death but instead find gold under a tree, which ironically brings about their death (situational). The rioters plan to split the gold but secretly scheme to kill the others (verbal).*
14. *Line 123: "from night to noon" shows that the old man is tireless in his wanderings; Line 168: "beautiful and bright" describes the pile of money that sways the young men; Line 325: "rather rough" suggests the seriousness of the action.*

What Do You Think Now?

Tell students to consider the personalities of the rioters, the rioters' motivation, and the characteristics that make a good leader.

Applying Your Skills

Reading Standard 2.5, 3.3 (see pages A48–A50)
Writing Standard 1.2 (see pages A51–A52)

from The Pardoner's Tale

Literary Response and Analysis

Reading Skills Focus

Quick Check

1. How does the Pardoner describe himself in the Prologue to his tale?
2. Why are the three rioters looking for Death?

Read with a Purpose

3. What moral does the Pardoner want us to draw from his tale? What moral does Chaucer want us to draw from "The Pardoner's Tale"?

Reading Skills: Drawing Conclusions

4. Review the conclusions you recorded as you read. Sometimes what you read later will contradict your earlier conclusions. Record whether or not you agree with your initial conclusions, and explain any changes you make.

Conclusion	How Conclusion Is Supported	Reviewing the Conclusion
Death is the idea or presence of death, not an actual person.	The characters speak of Death as a character, so we expect to meet him as a character. However, we never see him personified.	The description in the tavern of the man's death makes me wonder, but I still think Death is just symbolic in this poem.

Vocabulary Check

Demonstrate your knowledge of Vocabulary words by answering the following questions.

5. Who is more likely to act out of **avarice:** someone self-centered or someone charitable?
6. Is your **adversary** on your team or on the team you are playing against?
7. Is it **abominable** to help someone in need?
8. How is blushing related to **pallor?**
9. What does it mean to **absolve** someone from blame?

Literary Skills Focus

Literary Analysis

10. **Evaluate** What attributes of medieval society (and human nature in general) do you think Chaucer is satirizing in "The Pardoner's Tale"?
11. **Extend** Do people with the Pardoner's ethics exist today—in all sorts of professions? Explain.
12. **Analyze** Is greed or desire the root of all evil? Discuss the Pardoner's moral.

Literary Skills: Verbal and Situational Irony

13. **Analyze** Use evidence from the tale to explain the ending's verbal and situational irony.

Literary Skills Review: Alliteration

14. **Analyze** In each of the first three lines from "The Pardoner's Prologue," Chaucer uses **alliteration,** the repetition of the same consonant sounds in words close to each other. Identify and explain three other examples of alliteration in the poem.

Writing Skills Focus

Think as a Reader/Writer

Use It in Your Writing Verbal irony can occur when one character deceives another. Write a short scene with dialogue in which a character misleads another by saying one thing but meaning something else.

What Do You Think Now

After finding the gold, the "wickedest" young man takes the lead and devises a plan for the group. Why do the other two agree to follow his lead?

Assess

Unit 1 Resources,
Selection Standards Check, p. 55

go.hrw.com **ThinkCentral Online Assessment,**
Selection Standards Check

Teacher One Stop™,
editable Selection Standards Check

Universal Access

Struggling Writers

Some students may need additional scaffolding to complete the Writing Skills Focus activity. Before they write their scenes, give students a modern-day example of verbal irony. Give students the following scenario: "When a friend asks you how you liked spending three hours cleaning your room, you might answer, 'It was just great.' You both know that was not the case, of course." Discuss with students some other examples of verbal irony. After students have a grasp of the concept, give them time to write their scenes of dialogue.

Preparing to Read

Reading Standard 3.8; **Grades 9–10 Review Reading Standard** 3.4, 3.9 (see pages A48–A50)

from The Wife of Bath's Tale

Literary Skills Focus

Narrator The **narrator,** the teller of the story, has a distinct voice or character that is revealed through the story's subject matter, tone, and language. The narrator may be the author speaking or may be a character or persona created by the author. Chaucer masterfully matches his narrators and their stories: The Wife of Bath reveals as much about herself as she does about medieval society or women's desires. However, we cannot be sure that her views are those of Chaucer or of the majority of women in her day.

Literary Perspectives Apply the literary perspective described on page 163 as you read this narrative poem.

Reading Skills Focus

Interpreting Character We can **interpret characters** by noting details about them. While some characters are elusive, the Wife of Bath is not: She clearly expresses her ideas about women, men, and marriage.

Into Action As you read, use a chart like the one below to note details of the Wife's views on women, marriage, and true gentility. How do her views help you understand her role as a narrator and her story selection?

Topics	Details
Women	"A woman wants...sovereignty / Over her husband . . . he must not be above her."
Marriage	
Goodness / True Gentility	

Writing Skills Focus

Think as a Reader/Writer

Find It In Your Reading As you read, take notes in your *Reader/Writer Notebook* on how the Wife reveals her nature through **details** and **tone** and where she interrupts her story to give her own opinion.

Reader/Writer Notebook

Use your **RWN** to complete the activities for this selection.

Vocabulary

disperses (dihs PURS ihz) *v.:* breaks up and scatters. *The party disperses at the end of the trip.*

bequest (bih KWEHST) *n.:* gift left through a will. *The Wife of Bath wants a rich and sickly husband who can leave her widowed with a large bequest.*

prowess (PROW ihs) *n.:* outstanding ability. *The Wife rode quite comfortably and showed great prowess on the horse.*

temporal (TEHM puhr uhl) *adj.:* limited to this world; not spiritual. *Material goods are only temporal, but love endures forever.*

pestilence (PEHS tuh luhns) *n.:* plague. *The Wife of Bath believes the greatest pestilence to married women is cheap and long-lived husbands.*

Language Coach

Noun Endings The endings *–ence* and *–ance* usually tell you that a word is a noun. Nouns name people, places, or things, including intangible things, such as *independence, resistance,* and *nonsense.* Which listed Vocabulary word has an ending that indicates it is a noun?

Learn It Online

Hear the Wife of Bath—or an actor playing her—tell you this tale online.

go.hrw.com H12-161 Go

California Standards, pp. 161–177

- **Reading Standard 3.8** Analyze the clarity and consistency of political assumptions in a selection of literary works or essays on a topic (e.g., suffrage, women's role in organized labor) (Political approach).
- **Grades 9–10 Review Reading Standard 3.4** Determine characters' traits by what the characters say about themselves in narration, dialogue, dramatic monologue, and soliloquy.
- **Grades 9–10 Review Reading Standard 3.9** Explain how voice, persona, and the choice of a narrator affect characterization and the tone, plot, and credibility of a text.

Preteach

Introducing Vocabulary

- Review the Vocabulary words, definitions, and sentences with students.
- To reinforce the importance of the Vocabulary words, tell students that many of these words relate to the value system against which the Wife of Bath argues in her story. Her story rejects the notion that *prowess* is determined by the *bequests* that a person receives or by that person's *temporal* wealth.

English for Academic Success

Language Coach

After students read the **Language Coach,** tell them that the Vocabulary word *pestilence* has an ending that indicates it is a noun. Then, ask students to name additional abstract nouns ending in *–ence* or *–ance.* [*competence, eminence, confidence, instance, pittance*]

Literary Skills Focus

As you read and discuss the selection with students, have them note the voice and character of the narrator.

Reading Skills Focus

Give students a copy of the Reading Skills Focus graphic organizer before they read. (See **Unit 1 Resources.**) Tell them to use their responses to answer the questions on the Applying Your Skills page.

Writing Skills Focus

Have students note the Wife's nature that comes out through her tone and details in their **Reader/Writer Notebooks**. Students can use their notes to complete the Writing Skills Focus activity.

Learn It Online

The online version of this selection includes audio support to engage all students and to help struggling readers with reading comprehension and vocabulary.

go.hrw.com H12-161 Go

Teacher Preparation
Selection Plot Summary

The Wife of Bath tells the pilgrims a legend from the days of King Arthur. After a knight rapes a maiden, he is sentenced to death, but the queen informs him that if he can discover "the thing that women most desire," his life will be spared. The Knight sets off on a quest to discover women's greatest desire, but after a year, he has still not found the answer to his question.

On his way home, however, the Knight meets a foul-looking old crone who tells him that she will give him the information he seeks if he will grant her the first thing she asks for. The Knight agrees, and the old woman tells him that women most desire power over their husbands. The Knight saves his own life by repeating this information to the queen, but the old woman immediately demands that the Knight marry her, and the Knight reluctantly agrees.

The woman then offers the Knight a choice: She can be either a beautiful, faithless wife or an ugly, faithful wife. Remembering the lesson that the woman taught him, the Knight allows her to make the choice, and she rewards him by becoming young, beautiful, and faithful.

NARRATIVE POEM

FROM

The Wife of Bath's Tale

by **Geoffrey Chaucer**

translated by **Nevill Coghill**

Read with a Purpose

Read to discover the nature of women according to the Wife of Bath.

Build Background

In this tale, the Wife explores the relationship between men and women with her winding story about a knight's unusual quest. Like many of the stories in *The Canterbury Tales,* the Wife's tale works much like a fable, using its characters and plot to reveal human nature.

Direct Teach

Think About/Talk About

Read with a Purpose Have a volunteer read the Read with a Purpose statement. Ask students to paraphrase the sentence and to identify its key concept. Remind students that the morals conveyed in *The Canterbury Tales* often represented the universal truths of Chaucer's time. Have students keep track of places in the text that support a moral teaching.

Universal Access

EL English Learners

Encourage English learners to rely on punctuation marks to follow who is speaking. Remind them that quotation marks indicate dialogue, or the exact words of a speaker. Call attention also to Chaucer's use of rhyming couplets throughout the poem and to the jaunty rhythms that their use creates.

✔ See the **English Language Skill Builder** in **UA: Differentiating Instruction.**

Struggling Readers

Benchmark Students Point out to students that the tale begins with dialogue between the Pardoner and the Wife of Bath. Remind students that dialogue can reveal information about a character's personality and beliefs. Read aloud lines 7–21. Tell students that these lines show that the Wife of Bath claims to know a lot about marriage and is educated enough to have read Ptolemy. As students continue to read, encourage them to look for instances in which the Wife of Bath digresses from her tale and inserts her own ideas and opinions.

Save for his wife, there was not one that knew.
He loved her best, and trusted in her too.
He begged her not to tell a living creature
That he possessed so horrible a feature.
And she—she swore, were all the world to win,
She would not do such villainy and sin
As saddle her husband with so foul a name;
Besides to speak would be to share the shame.
Nevertheless she thought she would have died
Keeping this secret bottled up inside;
It seemed to swell her heart and she, no doubt,
Thought it was on the point of bursting out.
Fearing to speak of it to woman or man,
Down to a reedy marsh she quickly ran
And reached the sedge.° Her heart was all on fire
And, as a bittern° bumbles in the mire,
She whispered to the water, near the ground,
"Betray me not, O water, with thy sound!
To thee alone I tell it: It appears
My husband has a pair of ass's ears!

147. sedge: grasslike plant.

148. bittern: type of wading bird.

Analyzing Visuals

Connecting to the Text In this staging of *The Canterbury Tales,* what do the costumes and props convey about the tone and emphasis of the production and the status and diversity of the characters?

Analyzing Visuals

Connecting to the Text: *The costumes accurately reproduce the clothing in the English Middle Ages. The audience will definitely be able to recognize the various characters and immediately associate the social status each character belongs to. The employment of hobby-horses suggests that the characters will not be taken too seriously, which means that the representation will maintain the light-hearted and ironic tone of the original literary work.*

Think About/Talk About

Analysis

E Literary Focus

Possible response: *The Wife of Bath is emphasizing the difference between what women think of themselves and what they want other people to think.*

Extend the Discussion

Drawing Conclusions Based on lines 119–126, what does the Wife of Bath think about the nature of most women? ***Possible response:*** *She thinks that women like to be thought of as good and sinless, but they are not. For example, they cannot keep a secret.*

Synthesizing In lines 119–126, the Wife of Bath calls women vicious and indiscreet. Why might she choose the tale of Midas to illustrate this claim? ***Possible responses:*** *In this tale, Midas's wife fails to keep his secret, costing her husband his dignity. The Wife of Bath might use this to show that women break vows as the Knight in her tale broke codes of chivalry.*

Think About/Talk About

Literary Connection

Point out that students will encounter some of the archaic language used here in other early English literature. Examples include *nay* in line 168, *ere* in line 170, *lo* in line 171, and *alack* in line 181. Tell students that *nay* means "no" and *ere* means "before." *Lo* is an expression of surprise or wonder, meaning "look"; *alack* is an expression of dismay, meaning "alas."

Extend the Discussion

Finding Details In lines 181–189, what agreement do the Knight and old woman reach? ***Possible response:*** *The woman agrees to help the Knight in his quest, and he agrees, on his honor, to do whatever she next requires of him.*

Character Motivation Lines 33–38 introduced an otherworldly "fairy-tale" setting in the distant past. Re-read lines 166–175. What does the Wife of Bath want her listeners to understand about the old crone? ***Possible response:*** *The Wife of Bath uses supernatural events to imply that the crone may be more than she appears; she probably has special powers.*

Ah! My heart's well again, the secret's out!
I could no longer keep it, not a doubt."
And so you see, although we may hold fast
A little while, it must come out at last,
We can't keep secrets; as for Midas, well,
Read Ovid for his story;° he will tell. (F)
This knight that I am telling you about
Perceived at last he never would find out
What it could be that women loved the best.
Faint was the soul within his sorrowful breast,
As home he went, he dared no longer stay;
His year was up and now it was the day.
As he rode home in a dejected mood
Suddenly, at the margin° of a wood,
He saw a dance upon the leafy floor
Of four and twenty ladies, nay, and more.
Eagerly he approached, in hope to learn
Some words of wisdom ere he should return;
But lo! Before he came to where they were,
Dancers and dance all vanished into air!
There wasn't a living creature to be seen
Save one old woman crouched upon the green.
A fouler-looking creature I suppose
Could scarcely be imagined. She arose
And said, "Sir knight, there's no way on from here.
Tell me what you are looking for, my dear,
For peradventure° that were best for you;
We old, old women know a thing or two."
"Dear Mother," said the knight, "alack the day!
I am as good as dead if I can't say
What thing it is that women most desire;
If you could tell me I would pay your hire."
"Give me your hand," she said, "and swear to do
Whatever I shall next require of you
—If so to do should lie within your might—
And you shall know the answer before night."
"Upon my honor," he answered, "I agree." (G)
"Then," said the crone, "I dare to guarantee
Your life is safe; I shall make good my claim.
Upon my life the queen will say the same.

158. Read Ovid. . .story: In Ovid's version, it is Midas's barber, not his wife, who tells the secret to a hole in the ground. Reeds grow up from the spot and whisper the secret whenever the wind rustles them.

166. margin: edge.

179. peradventure: perhaps.

(F) **Reading Focus** **Interpreting Character** What does this digression say about the Wife of Bath's nature?

(G) **Literary Perspectives** **Analyzing Political Context** Why is it significant that the old woman holds the answer to the knight's question?

Literary Perspectives

Have students read lines 214–218. Point out to students that in these lines, the Knight suggests that a woman wants to be equal to her husband and desires to have power over him so that he will bend to her will. Explain that people living during Chaucer's time adhered closely to the laws and rules defined in the Bible. Tell students that the Bible definitely states that a woman is to be subject to her husband. Religious persons living during the 1300s would have been horrified to hear the Wife of Bath deny the words from the Bible.

Activity Have students evaluate the Wife of Bath's feminist perspective. Does she differ from feminist thinkers today? If so, how?

Show me the very proudest of them all
In costly coverchief or jeweled caul°
That dare say no to what I have to teach.
Let us go forward without further speech."
And then she crooned her gospel in his ear
And told him to be glad and not to fear.
  They came to court. This knight, in full array,
Stood forth and said, "O Queen, I've kept my day
And kept my word and have my answer ready."
  There sat the noble matrons and the heady
Young girls, and widows too, that have the grace
Of wisdom, all assembled in that place,
And there the queen herself was throned to hear
And judge his answer. Then the knight drew near
And silence was commanded through the hall.
  The queen gave order he should tell them all
What thing it was that women wanted most.
He stood not silent like a beast or post,
But gave his answer with the ringing word
Of a man's voice and the assembly heard:
  "My liege° and lady, in general," said he,
"A woman wants the self-same sovereignty°
Over her husband as over her lover,
And master him; he must not be above her.
That is your greatest wish, whether you kill
Or spare me; please yourself. I wait your will."
  In all the court not one that shook her head
Or contradicted what the knight had said;
Maid, wife, and widow cried, "He's saved his life!" **H**
  And on the word up started the old wife,
The one the knight saw sitting on the green,
And cried, "Your mercy, sovereign lady queen!
Before the court disperses, do me right!
'Twas I who taught this answer to the knight,
For which he swore, and pledged his honor to it,
That the first thing I asked of him he'd do it,
So far as it should lie within his might.
Before this court I ask you then, sir knight,
To keep your word and take me for your wife;
For well you know that I have saved your life.
If this be false, deny it on your sword!"
  "Alas!" he said, "Old lady, by the Lord

194. coverchief . . . caul: women's headgear. The coverchief covered the entire head; the caul, a small, netted cap, was sometimes ornamented.

213. liege: lord.
214. sovereignty: power.

The Knight and the Old Lady. Ms Douce 195, folio 105r. The Bodleian Library, University of Oxford.

H Literary Focus **Narrator** How does the narrator create suspense in this moment of the story?

Vocabulary **disperses** (dihs PURS ihz) *v.:* breaks up and scatters.

Developing Oral Fluency

Group Activity Divide the class into groups of five students. Have the groups practice reading lines 159–233. Speakers in each group may include three narrators, a knight, and the old woman. Remind students that the Wife of Bath tells the story to many listeners. Encourage students to engage their listeners by varying the tone of their voice, including hand gestures, and inserting dramatic pauses appropriately. Have students present their interpretations to the class. At the end of each presentation, lead the class in a discussion about what was effective during their reading. Ask the listeners what they think the group could do to improve their oral presentations in the future.

Think About/Talk About

Comprehension

F Reading Focus

Possible response: *She is well-versed in ancient literature and does not always agree with what other people think.*

Analysis

G Literary Perspectives

Possible responses: *The old woman is described as unattractive; she is probably not someone who the knight would normally be drawn to. It is significant that the old woman holds the answer to the knight's question because she most likely has little experience with men and would not be the person the reader would expect to hold the answer.*

H Literary Focus

Possible responses: *The narrator creates suspense by reminding the reader that the Knight's life is at stake. While other women in the kingdom agree with the Knight's answer, the queen does not speak, so his life may still be in danger.*

Extend the Discussion

Irony The Wife of Bath describes the Knight's presentation to the court as "the ringing word / Of a man's voice" in lines 211–212. Why is this situation ironic? ***Possible response:*** *The Knight's "ringing" voice presents words that are not his own to the court; they are the words of a wise old woman.*

Vocabulary: Own the Word

disperses: Ask students what might cause a crowd to *disperse* in a quick manner. ***Possible responses:*** *a fire alarm; a thunderstorm; any type of potential danger.* What would it look like when a crowd *disperses* quickly? ***Possible responses:*** *people running, pushing others out of the way*

Model the Skill

- Model **interpreting character** by reading to understand the character's beliefs.
- Read lines 309–314 aloud. Tell students that the old woman reveals what she believes through her word choice. If students do not understand the lines, they can paraphrase them first: "If noble behavior were passed down through genetics, could the descendants stop being noble? If not, then noble people would never do evil." Students may notice that she makes a logical argument using "If . . . then."
- Tell students that this type of argument is commonly used to try to persuade people. The old woman is trying to persuade the knight that being of noble blood does not make him a good person.

Guided Practice: Apply

Have students read the knight's reaction to the old woman in lines 274–279. Ask students to identify orally what they can infer about the knight's character based on his reaction. [*The knight is shallow and egotistical as he places too much emphasis on rank and appearance.*] Ask students to contrast the knight in the Wife's Tale with the Knight on the pilgrimage to Canterbury.

I know indeed that such was my behest,°
But for God's love think of a new request,
Take all my goods, but leave my body free."
"A curse on us," she said, "if I agree!
I may be foul, I may be poor and old,
Yet will not choose to be, for all the gold
That's bedded in the earth or lies above,
Less than your wife, nay, than your very love!"
"My love?" said he. "By heaven, my damnation!
Alas that any of my race and station
Should ever make so foul a misalliance!"°
Yet in the end his pleading and defiance
All went for nothing, he was forced to wed.
He takes his ancient wife and goes to bed.
Now peradventure some may well suspect
A lack of care in me since I neglect
To tell of the rejoicings and display
Made at the feast upon their wedding-day.
I have but a short answer to let fall;
I say there was no joy or feast at all,
Nothing but heaviness of heart and sorrow.
He married her in private on the morrow
And all day long stayed hidden like an owl,
It was such torture that his wife looked foul.
Great was the anguish churning in his head
When he and she were piloted to bed;
He wallowed° back and forth in desperate style.
His ancient wife lay smiling all the while;
At last she said "Bless us! Is this, my dear,
How knights and wives get on together here?
Are these the laws of good King Arthur's house?
Are knights of his all so contemptuous?
I am your own beloved and your wife,
And I am she, indeed, that saved your life;
And certainly I never did you wrong.
Then why, this first of nights, so sad a song?
You're carrying on as if you were half-witted
Say, for God's love, what sin have I committed?
I'll put things right if you will tell me how."
"Put right?" he cried. "That never can be now!
Nothing can ever be put right again!
You're old, and so abominably plain,
So poor to start with, so low-bred to follow;
It's little wonder if I twist and wallow!
God, that my heart would burst within my breast!"
"Is that," said she, "the cause of your unrest?"
"Yes, certainly," he said, "and can you wonder?"

235. behest: command; order.

245. misalliance: here, a marriage that is unsuitable or inappropriate.

261. wallowed: tossed and turned.

Medieval knight on horseback, from medieval collection of Minnelieder.

Universal Access

EL English Learners

English for Academic Success Lines 282–321 of the old woman's long argument use elevated, often legalistic language that may be difficult for English learners to understand. Clarify the meanings of the following terms: *gentle* (meaning "noble"), *arrogance, bequeath, bequest, bade, prowess, temporal, gentility, implanted, lineage, vice,* and *villainy.*

Struggling Readers

Lines 282–321 may pose problems for struggling readers. Have students work together in groups to break the text up into manageable chunks and work together to apply strategies to improve their comprehension, such as paraphrasing or changing inverted word order to normal word order. For instance, lines 282–284 can be paraphrased, "If you showed me a little courtesy, I could soon fix your problem."

"I could set right what you suppose a blunder,
That's if I cared to, in a day or two,
If I were shown more courtesy by you.
Just now," she said, "you spoke of gentle birth,
Such as descends from ancient wealth and worth.
If that's the claim you make for gentlemen
Such arrogance is hardly worth a hen.
Whoever loves to work for virtuous ends,
Public and private, and who most intends
To do what deeds of gentleness he can,
Take him to be the greatest gentleman.
Christ wills we take our gentleness from Him,
Not from a wealth of ancestry long dim,
Though they bequeath their whole establishment
By which we claim to be of high descent.
Our fathers cannot make us a bequest
Of all those virtues that became them best
And earned for them the name of gentlemen,
But bade us follow them as best we can.
"Thus the wise poet of the Florentines,
Dante° by name, has written in these lines,
For such is the opinion Dante launches:
'Seldom arises by these slender branches
Prowess of men, for it is God, no less,
Wills us to claim of Him our gentleness.'
For of our parents nothing can we claim
Save temporal things, and these may hurt and maim.
"But everyone knows this as well as I;
For if gentility were implanted by
The natural course of lineage° down the line,
Public or private, could it cease to shine
In doing the fair work of gentle deed?
No vice or villainy could then bear seed.
"Take fire and carry it to the darkest house
Between this kingdom and the Caucasus,°
And shut the doors on it and leave it there,
It will burn on, and it will burn as fair
As if ten thousand men were there to see,
For fire will keep its nature and degree,
I can assure you, sir, until it dies.
"But gentleness, as you will recognize,
Is not annexed in nature to possessions.

302. Dante: Dante Alighieri (1265–1321), Italian poet who wrote *The Divine Comedy.*

311. lineage: ancestry.

316. Caucasus: mountain range in southeastern Europe, between the Black Sea and the Caspian Sea; in other words, far away.

Vocabulary **bequest** (bih KWEHST) *n.:* gift left through a will.
prowess (PROW ihs) *n.:* outstanding ability.
temporal (TEHM puhr uhl) *adj.:* limited to this world; not spiritual.

Advanced Learners

Enrichment Have students re-read lines 282–321 and respond to the question, "Is the Wife of Bath conveying her opinions through the old woman's voice? If so, how?" On one sheet of paper, each student should write a short response using evidence from the text to support his or her answer. Students should exchange papers with a partner and respond to each other's response. When students are finished, ask them to share highlights of their silent debate with the class. Stress the importance of supporting opinions with textual evidence.

Students with Disabilities

Students should re-read lines 282–321. Assign each student one of those lines to paraphrase. Model how to paraphrase with several of the remaining lines. Explain to students that paraphrasing means "restating a line in your own words." Paraphrasing helps you better understand what you read. When students have completed their paraphrase, have them read their lines in order to complete the paraphrased speech by the old woman. Have students line up in order around the room and read their paraphrased lines aloud.

Think About/Talk About

Extend the Discussion

Breaking Down Difficult Text
Re-read lines 289–292, paying close attention to the actions the old woman describes. Restate in your own words what the old woman says about who is a true gentleman. ***Possible response:*** *She says that virtuous actions, not noble ancestry, are what mark a true gentleman.*

Recognizing Rhetorical Devices
What is the old woman's purpose in referring to Dante in lines 301–308? Is this an effective means of argument? Why or why not? ***Possible responses:*** *The old woman refers to Dante to show that she is not the only person who thinks noble origins are not what makes a person noble. It is an effective argument because she is quoting someone who was probably a respected writer in her time.*

Vocabulary: Own the Word

- **bequest:** Ask students to name things that a father might leave in a *bequest* to his children. ***Possible responses:*** *money; cherished personal belongings; clothes; a house*
- **prowess:** Remind students that *prowess* means "outstanding ability." To help students personally connect to the Vocabulary word, ask the following question: "Have you ever shown *prowess* on an athletic field? Explain when and how you showed *prowess* while playing a sport."
- **temporal:** Remind students that *temporal* means "limited to this world; not spiritual." Ask students to explain what the narrator means when she says that "*temporal* things . . . hurt and maim." ***Possible response:*** *Too many possessions distract a person from attaining wisdom and pursuing salvation.*

Think About/Talk About

Literary Connection

Point out that lines 353–358 express a rather simple idea about poverty in a complex way. The old woman is saying that God himself chose a life of poverty, so poverty should not be criticized as shameful.

Extend the Discussion

Drawing Conclusions According to lines 335–340, what is the source of gentility? ***Possible response:*** *Gentility comes from God, not from ancestry.*

Interpreting Why does the woman differentiate between two types of poverty (worldly and spiritual) in lines 353–367? What is she implying by making this distinction? ***Possible responses:*** *She wants to convey to the Knight that a person may be rich in spirit despite having few material possessions. She is also implying that the Knight is spiritually poor.*

Men fail in living up to their professions;°
But fire never ceases to be fire.
God knows you'll often find, if you inquire,
Some lording° full of villainy and shame.
If you would be esteemed for the mere name
Of having been by birth a gentleman
And stemming from some virtuous, noble clan,
And do not live yourself by gentle deed
Or take your father's noble code and creed,
You are no gentleman, though duke or earl.
Vice and bad manners are what make a churl.°
"Gentility is only the renown
For bounty that your fathers handed down,
Quite foreign to your person, not your own;
Gentility must come from God alone.
That we are gentle comes to us by grace
And by no means is it bequeathed with place.
"Reflect how noble (says Valerius)°
Was Tullius surnamed Hostilius,°
Who rose from poverty to nobleness.
And read Boethius,° Seneca° no less, **I**
Thus they express themselves and are agreed:
'Gentle is he that does a gentle deed.'
And therefore, my dear husband, I conclude
That even if my ancestors were rude,
Yet God on high—and so I hope He will—
Can grant me grace to live in virtue still,
A gentlewoman only when beginning
To live in virtue and to shrink from sinning.
"As for my poverty which you reprove,
Almighty God Himself in whom we move,
Believe, and have our being, chose a life
Of poverty, and every man or wife
Nay, every child can see our Heavenly King
Would never stoop to choose a shameful thing.
No shame in poverty if the heart is gay,
As Seneca and all the learned say.
He who accepts his poverty unhurt
I'd say is rich although he lacked a shirt.
But truly poor are they who whine and fret
And covet what they cannot hope to get.
And he that, having nothing, covets not,
Is rich, though you may think he is a sot.°
"True poverty can find a song to sing.

324. professions: promises.

327. lording: young lord.

334. churl: ill-mannered person.

341. Valerius: Roman writer who collected historical anecdotes that public speakers could use.

342. Tullius surnamed Hostilius: legendary king of Rome who rose from humble origins.

344. Boethius (c. A.D. 480–c. 524): Roman philosopher. In his *Consolation of Philosophy,* he argues that rank is no guarantee of honorable conduct.
Seneca (c. 4 B.C.–A.D. 65): Roman philosopher whose works were popular in the Middle Ages.

366. sot: fool.

I **Reading Focus** **Interpreting Character** What is the old woman's purpose in mentioning all of these famous figures?

Universal Access

AAVE Students Who Use African American Vernacular English

English for Academic Success Tell students that applying the formal English rules of subject-verb agreement can get complicated when a sentence contains a compound subject, particularly if the two subjects differ in number. For example, on p. 172, the speaker uses the following sentence: "Vice and bad manners are what make a churl." The subject of the sentence is "vice and bad manners." The first subject *Vice* is singular, while the second subject *bad manners* is plural. Explain to students that when two subjects are joined by *and,* the plural verb is most often used. However, when a singular subject and a plural subject are joined by *or* or *nor,* the verb agrees with the subject nearer the verb. Write the following sentences on the board and have students work collaboratively to determine whether the subject and verb agree and discuss why: *Neither the Host nor the pilgrims wants to lose the contest. The Wife of Bath and the Nun lack certain virtues.* Have students read aloud the corrected sentences.

Juvenal° says a pleasant little thing:
'The poor can dance and sing in the relief
Of having nothing that will tempt a thief.'
Though it be hateful, poverty is good,
A great incentive to a livelihood,
And a great help to our capacity
For wisdom, if accepted patiently.
Poverty is, though wanting in estate,
A kind of wealth that none calumniate.°
Poverty often, when the heart is lowly,
Brings one to God and teaches what is holy,
Gives knowledge of oneself and even lends
A glass by which to see one's truest friends.
And since it's no offense, let me be plain;
Do not rebuke my poverty again.
"Lastly you taxed me, sir, with being old.
Yet even if you never had been told
By ancient books, you gentlemen engage
Yourselves in honor to respect old age.
To call an old man 'father' shows good breeding,
And this could be supported from my reading.
"You say I'm old and fouler than a fen.°
You need not fear to be a cuckold,° then.
Filth and old age, I'm sure you will agree,
Are powerful wardens over chastity.
Nevertheless, well knowing your delights,
I shall fulfill your worldly appetites.
"You have two choices; which one will you try?
To have me old and ugly till I die,
But still a loyal, true, and humble wife
That never will displease you all her life,
Or would you rather I were young and pretty
And chance your arm what happens in a city
Where friends will visit you because of me,
Yes, and in other places too, maybe.
Which would you have? The choice is all your own."
The knight thought long, and with a piteous groan
At last he said, with all the care in life,
"My lady and my love, my dearest wife,
I leave the matter to your wise decision.
You make the choice yourself, for the provision
Of what may be agreeable and rich
In honor to us both, I don't care which;
Whatever pleases you suffices° me." (J)

(J) **Reading Focus** **Interpreting Character** What does this response reveal about the knight?

368. Juvenal (c. A.D. 60–c. 140): Roman satirist.

376. calumniate: slander.

389. fen: swamp.

390. cuckold: man whose wife has cheated on him.

411. suffices: satisfies.

Think About/Talk About

Comprehension

(I) Reading Focus

Possible responses: *The old woman mentions these figures because their authority adds weight to her argument; she wants to show the Knight that she is educated and intelligent.*

(J) Reading Focus

Possible responses: *In the course of the story, he has changed his values; he has become less shallow and arrogant and is now a thoughtful person who remembers advice he has been given. By deferring to his wife, he acknowledges that she has won the debate.*

Extend the Discussion

Finding the Main Idea Re-read lines 353–388. What are the two main points the old woman develops in this portion of her argument? ***Possible response:*** *Her main points are that there is no shame in poverty and that age should be respected.*

Persuasion As the speech progresses, the woman uses logical appeals to persuade the knight of her point of view. What logical argument does she use in lines 389–394? How effective is it? ***Possible responses:*** *She points out that if she really is as old and ugly as the knight says, at least he can be sure that she will be faithful. This is effective because she is using the knight's own arguments against him.*

Reaching Reluctant Readers

Have students respond to the question, "Would you rather have a partner who was old and ugly, but faithful and true, or would you rather have a young, attractive partner who might be unfaithful and disloyal? Why?" Have students jot down their ideas in their **Reader/Writer Notebooks** and then discuss their responses within groups of three or five students. Students should then share their viewpoints and supporting arguments with the class.

Think About/Talk About

Extend the Discussion

Figurative Language How effective is the use of figurative language in lines 429–431? ***Possible response:*** *The Wife states that the Knight's heart is bathing and melting in his wife's love; this effectively shows the couple's happiness.*

Vocabulary: Own the Word

pestilence: Remind students that a *pestilence* is a plague or epidemic. Ask students to describe whom the Wife of Bath hopes will receive a *pestilence.* ***Possible response:*** *She hopes that Jesus sends old, stingy, or domineering husbands a fatal disease.*

Monitor Students' Comprehension

Guide the class in answering these comprehension questions.

1. What does the Pardoner admit to the Wife of Bath? [*He confesses he was to marry this year and no longer wants a wife.*]
2. According to the Wife of Bath, why shouldn't a husband reprove his wife for her faults? [*Because he has so many faults of his own.*]
3. Summarize the tale of Midas in a few sentences. [*Midas grew ass's ears and only his wife knew. She vowed to keep a secret but broke that vow and told the grasses in the marsh.*]

"And have I won the mastery?" said she,
"Since I'm to choose and rule as I think fit?"
"Certainly, wife," he answered her, "that's it."
"Kiss me," she cried. "No quarrels! On my oath
And word of honor, you shall find me both,
That is, both fair and faithful as a wife;
May I go howling mad and take my life
Unless I prove to be as good and true
As ever wife was since the world was new!
And if to-morrow when the sun's above
I seem less fair than any lady-love,
Than any queen or empress east or west,
Do with my life and death as you think best.
Cast up the curtain, husband. Look at me!"
And when indeed the knight had looked to see,
Lo, she was young and lovely, rich in charms.
In ecstasy he caught her in his arms,
His heart went bathing in a bath of blisses
And melted in a hundred thousand kisses,
And she responded in the fullest measure
With all that could delight or give him pleasure.
So they lived ever after to the end
In perfect bliss; and may Christ Jesus send
Us husbands meek and young and fresh in bed,
And grace to overbid them when we wed.
And—Jesu hear my prayer!—cut short the lives
Of those who won't be governed by their wives;
And all old, angry niggards of their pence,°
God send them soon a very pestilence!

439. niggards of their pence: stingy with their money.

Vocabulary **pestilence** (PEHS tuh luhns) *n.:* plague.

California Standards, pp. 175–177

- **Reading Standard 1.3** Discern the meaning of analogies encountered, analyzing specific comparisons as well as relationships and inferences.
- **Reading Standard 3.0** Students read and respond to historically or culturally significant works of literature that reflect and enhance their studies of history and social science. They conduct in-depth analyses of recurrent themes.
- **Reading Standard 3.3** Analyze the way in which irony, tone, mood, the author's style, and the "sound" of language achieve specific rhetorical or aesthetic purposes or both.
- **Reading Standard 3.7b** Relate literary works and authors to the major themes and issues of their eras.
- **Reading Standard 3.8** Analyze the clarity and consistency of political assumptions in a selection of literary works or essays on a topic (e.g., suffrage, women's role in organized labor). (Political approach)
- **Grades 9–10 Review Reading Standard 3.4** Determine characters' traits by what the characters say about themselves in narration, dialogue, dramatic monologue, and soliloquy.
- **Grades 9–10 Review Reading Standard 3.9** Explain how voice, persona, and the choice of a narrator affect characterization and the tone, plot, and credibility of a text.
- **Writing Standard 1.2** Use point of view, characterization, style (e.g., use of irony) and related elements for specific rhetorical and aesthetic purposes.
- **Writing Standard 2.2c** Support important ideas and viewpoints through accurate and detailed references to the text and to other works.
- **Listening and Speaking Standard 2.3c** Support important ideas and viewpoints through accurate and detailed references to the text or to other works.

Applying Your Skills

Reading Standard 3.3, 3.8; Grades 9–10 Review
Reading Standard 3.4, 3.9 (see pages A48–A50)
Writing Standard 1.2 (see pages A51–A52)

from The Wife of Bath's Tale

Literary Response and Analysis

Reading Skills Focus

Quick Check

1. Identify (a) the knight's crime; (b) his original punishment; and (c) his second punishment.
2. What payment for her help does the old woman demand? What is the knight's response?
3. What final choice does the old woman offer the knight? How does he respond?

Read with a Purpose

4. Does the Wife of Bath's tale describe the characteristics she values in women? Why or why not?

Reading Skills: Interpreting Character

5. As you read, you noted details that reveal the Wife's opinions. Add a column to your chart, and explain how her views define her as a narrator.

Topics	Details	How Her Views Define Her as a Narrator
Women	"A woman wants...sovereignty / Over her husband... he must not be above her."	
Marriage		
Goodness / True Gentility		

Literary Skills Focus

Literary Analysis

6. **Draw Conclusions** Why do you think the queen takes a special interest in the knight's case?
7. **Evaluate** What does the Wife of Bath's character show about Chaucer's views on women?
8. **Analyze** During the Wife's story, the poet hints at, or **foreshadows,** the old woman's transformation. Explain how Chaucer sets up this twist in the story, and cite evidence in the text.
9. **Literary Perspectives** How does the Wife of Bath's perspective on women contrast with the political status of women in her day? How does her perspective fit into the political structure of today's society?

Literary Skills: Narrator

10. **Evaluate** Consider what the Wife, as narrator, says about people's perceptions of women's desires. What do you think of these proposals?

Literary Skills Review: Irony

11. **Analyze** A contrast or discrepancy between what is said and what is really meant, or between what is expected and what really happens is **irony.** The knight's quest—forced upon him by the queen—is to find out what women want. What irony do you see in this punishment?

Writing Skills Focus

Think as a Reader/Writer

Use It in Your Writing As you read, you noted aspects of the Wife's narration, such as her word choices, tone, and subject matter. Now, write a brief story of your own with a first-person narrator. Reveal your narrator's attributes through your word choices, tone, and subject matter.

What Do You Think Now? Why do you think the knight agrees at the end of the story to let the old woman decide their fate together?

Check for Understanding

Independent Practice

Reading Skills Focus

Possible responses:

1. *Crime—forcing himself on a woman sexually. Original punishment—death. Second punishment—also death, unless he can find what women most desire.*
2. *She demands that he marry her. He pleads with her to ask him for anything else but that.*
3. *She asks if he'd rather she were old and ugly, but faithful, or young and beautiful, but possibly unfaithful. He tells her to decide.*
4. *Yes; by criticizing women as hypocritical, the Wife of Bath offers her own view on what she values in women: honesty.*
5. *Help students connect the Wife's views to her character.*

Literary Skills Focus

Possible responses:

6. *As a woman in power, she wants to avenge the wrong suffered by another woman in her kingdom.*
7. *It shows that Chaucer saw women as individuals.*
8. *The Wife mentions dancing fairies early in the tale. Before the Knight meets the old woman in the wood, he sees dancing women.*
9. *Her ideas were heretical in Chaucer's time, while they would not be as politically subversive today.*
10. *People's perceptions of women's desires vary. Some think women desire wealth, some freedom, others honor, and still others, flattery.*
11. *It is ironic that a man whose interactions with women were all based on what he wanted should have to save his life by finding out what women want.*

Universal Access

Struggling Writers

Some students may need additional scaffolding to complete the Writing Skills Focus activity. Before they write their stories with a first-person narrator, have them work in pairs to discuss how the Wife of Bath's narration revealed information about her character. Then, have students think about what attributes they want their own narrator to have. Have students brainstorm with their partners to create a list of words that would help convey the attributes of their character.

What Do You Think Now?

Have students refer back to the last four stanzas of the tale in which the Knight describes his rationale for his decision.

Independent Practice
Vocabulary Development

Vocabulary Check
1. *after*
2. *given*
3. *athlete*
4. *everyday*
5. *A single insect is not, but many insects could be.*

Your Turn
1. *prowess*
2. *pestilence*
3. *disperse*
4. *temporal*
5. *bequest*

English for Academic Success

Language Coach
Possible responses: *Nouns—defiance, arrogance, pestilence, evidence. Adjectives—evident, defiant, pestilent, arrogant.*

English for Academic Success

Academic Vocabulary
Possible response: *Students should explain how the outcome of the Wife of Bath's tale can be attributed to the knight's final understanding of women. Students might argue that the status of men and women in medieval society was different from today because women were then expected to adhere to a certain code of behavior that implied submissiveness.*

Applying Your Skills

Reading Standard 1.3 (see pages 000–000)

from The Wife of Bath's Tale

Vocabulary Development

✓ Vocabulary Check
Answer the following questions about Vocabulary words.

1. Do rain clouds **disperse** before or after a storm?
2. If something is a **bequest**, is it given or taken away?
3. Who is more likely to have physical **prowess,** an athlete or a professor?
4. Are **temporal** things sacred or everyday?
5. Is an insect an example of **pestilence?**

Vocabulary Skills: Analogies
In word analogies, the relationship between one pair of words is similar to the relationship between another pair of words. For example:

LETTER : ENVELOPE :: hand : glove

In other words, a *letter* is to an *envelope* as a *hand* is to a *glove*. How are the paired items similarly related? *A letter goes into an envelope as a hand goes into a glove.*

Common relationships in analogies include whole/part or part/whole; cause and effect; synonyms; and antonyms. Study the examples in the chart below.

Relationship Type	Example	Explanation
Part to whole	cow : herd	A cow is part of a herd.
Cause and Effect	lightning : forest fire	Lightning can cause a forest fire.
Synonyms	rough : coarse	These two words have similar meanings.
Antonyms	rough : smooth	These two words have opposite meanings.

Your Turn
In each of the examples below, choose the Vocabulary word that best completes the analogy.

1. BLUNDERER : INABILITY :: expert : _______
2. RAIN : FLOOD :: virus : _______
3. HOT : COLD :: _______ : collect
4. ETERNAL : IMMORTAL :: _______ : mortal
5. AGREEMENT : CONTRACT :: _______ : will

Language Coach
Noun Endings The ending of a word often indicates whether it is a noun or an adjective. Words that end in *–ance* and *–ence* are usually nouns, which name people, places, or things. Words that end in *–ant* and *–ent* are usually adjectives, which can describe nouns. Sort the following words into a chart like the one below. Then, use each word in a sentence.

defiance arrogance evident defiant
pestilence evidence pestilent arrogant

Nouns	Adjectives

Academic Vocabulary
Talk About
Consider how the knight initially gets into trouble and how things turn out for him. Do you find the conclusion satisfying? Is the outcome attributed to an adequate transformation in the knight? How does the tale reflect the status of men and women in medieval society? Explain.

Universal Access: Vocabulary Development

EL English Learners
English for Academic Success Have students practice analogies with objects that they see around the class (for example, pen : notebook : : marker : board). Divide students into pairs, and ask them to come up with three to five analogies about other objects and to write a sentence illustrating each analogy, such as "I use the pen to write on the notebook like I use the marker to write on the board."

Then, ask students to read the following analogies and write down the relationship between the two pairs of words.

Example: disperse : scatter : : assemble : gather / The definition of disperse is to scatter, just as the definition of assemble is to gather.

- land : bequest :: money : reward
- praise : criticism :: prowess : inability
- temporal : earthly :: puzzling : difficult
- variation : uniformity :: health : pestilence

✓ See the **Academic and Selection Vocabulary Skill Builder** in **UA: Differentiating Instruction.**

Reading Standard 3.7b (see pages A48–A50)
Writing Standard 2.2c (see pages A51–A52)
Listening and Speaking Standard 2.3c (see pages A53–A55)

CHOICES

As you respond to the Choices, use these **Academic Vocabulary** words as appropriate: attribute, concept, diverse, emphasis, status.

REVIEW

Listen to the Women

During his quest, the knight receives many responses to his query about women. Review the Wife's description of the women's opinions. Note what these responses have in common and how they differ. What does this passage convey about the relationship between men and women? about the status of women? In a small group, discuss your interpretations of this passage.

Get in Touch with Midas

In the middle of her tale, the Wife tells a story about Midas. Review Midas's story, and consider these questions: Why do you think the Wife tells this story? Is the story more about Midas's vanity or his wife's ability to keep a secret? Are his wife's actions a betrayal even though she did not tell a person? Write an essay explaining your opinions with supporting details from the text.

CONNECT

Seek Out Chivalry

During Chaucer's time, knights were expected to adhere to the ideals of chivalry, and much of the period's literature explores this concept. Online or in the library, research the medieval code of chivalry. Consider these questions: How does the Wife's story explore these ideals? How does the knight's behavior follow or contradict the chivalric code? After completing your research, discuss in a small group how the chivalric code relates to the Wife's tale.

Find the Past in the Present

TechFocus In Chaucer's time, the way an ordinary person was most likely to encounter a story was through oral narratives. Make a list of all the ways that you could read, see, or hear a story today (for example, a magazine article, a song, a commercial). Then, retell "The Wife of Bath's Tale" using one of these modern methods. What are the advantages and disadvantages of expressing a story in this modern form?

EXTEND

Take Your Turn at Teaching

In the Wife's story, the queen challenges the knight to answer a question to save himself. Recall a wrongdoer from something else you've read. Think of a question to ask the wrongdoer to help him or her understand his or her error. Write down what the character did wrong, what your question is, and why you chose the question. In a small group, discuss your character's situations and questions and whether they might help someone learn or change.

Create a Character

In the Wife's tale, the old woman explores the discrepancy between appearance and reality and how people come to misjudge each other. Write a character sketch describing someone whose appearance does not reflect the nature of his or her character. Explain why the character's appearance may be misleading about his or her personality. Create a picture, collage, or computer graphic representing the differences between the character's physical and internal qualities.

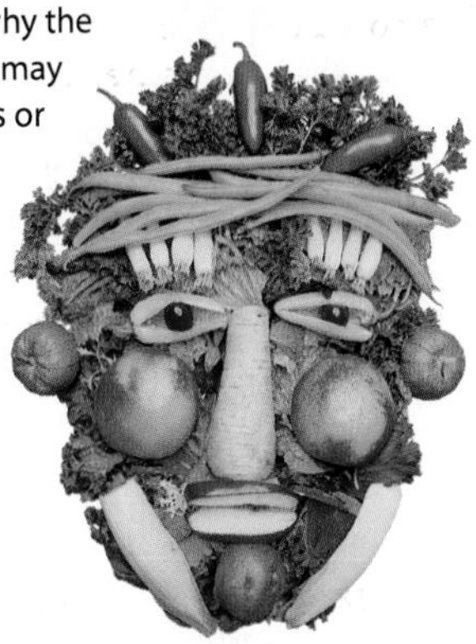

Independent Practice

Choices: Evaluation Criteria

Review: Homework
Listen to the Women

- Students identify similarities and differences in the opinions.
- Students' interpretations are supported by textual evidence.

Review: Homework
Get in Touch with Midas

Students clearly state their opinion of the wife's actions.

Connect: Homework
Seek Out Chivalry

Students' responses demonstrate their understanding of the code of chivalry.

Connect: Homework
Find the Past in the Present

Students retell a modern version of "The Wife of Bath's Tale."

Extend: Homework
Take Your Turn at Teaching

- Questions address the wrongdoer's action.
- Discussion is focused on helping someone change.

Extend: Homework
Create a Character

- Character sketch includes many details about appearance.
- Students address the discrepancy between physical and internal qualities.

Assess

Unit 1 Resources,
Selection Standards Check, p. 61

go.hrw.com **ThinkCentral Online Assessment,**
Selection Standards Check

Teacher One Stop™,
editable Selection Standards Check

Reteach

go.hrw.com **ThinkCentral Online Remediation**

Standards Focus

Objectives

Students will analyze the way in which clarity of meaning is affected by patterns of organization, such as comparing and contrasting.

Motivate

What Do You Think?/QuickWrite

Have students write for ten minutes about a hero who is significant for a particular country. Students should explain that hero's motivations.

Preteach

Introducing Vocabulary

Use this activity to check students' understanding.

1. List ideas that might be **ingrained** in the minds of arrogant people.
2. Name a performance that would **entice** you to go to the theater.
3. Describe a situation that might **perplex** you.
4. Name three historical figures who are considered **notorious**.
5. List ingredients you might need to **concoct** a dessert.

Informational Text/Writing Skills Focus

- Give students a copy of the Informational Text Focus graphic organizer before they read. (See **Unit 1 Resources**.) Tell them to use their responses to answer the questions on the Applying Your Skills page.
- Have students record cultural items of medieval and modern periods in their **Reader/Writer Notebooks.**

INFORMATIONAL TEXT FOCUS

Preparing to Read

Reading Standard 2.2 (see pages A48–A50)

Link to Today

from Walking to Canterbury

What Do You Think? What moves a hero to act?

QuickWrite

Like Chaucer's pilgrims, people today often travel to a place important to their family, culture, or country. In your *Reader/Writer Notebook,* write about an important place that you would like to visit.

Informational Text Focus

Comparing and Contrasting A popular topic in nonfiction writing is the exploration of the past. Such works often provide a fresh perspective on historic people, places, and events by **comparing** and **contrasting** them to the contemporary world. Reflecting on these comparisons can help you identify common elements across time, as well as the differences between past and present.

Into Action As you read, use a chart like the one below to note some of the main similarities and differences between medieval London and modern London as described by the author.

Similarities	Differences
Both are bustling places crowded with people.	Modern London has many more types of transportation available.

Writing Skills Focus

Preparing for Timed Writing The author of *Walking to Canterbury* describes modern London with imagery that creates a panorama of the sights, sounds, and smells of the city today. Use your *Reader/Writer Notebook* to record the most vivid images.

Vocabulary

ingrained (ihn GRAYND) *v.* used as *adj.:* deeply and firmly fixed in one's nature or being. *Some of the same feelings of the medieval town have become ingrained in modern London's atmosphere.*

enticing (ehn TYS ihng) *v.* used as *adj.:* attracting by arousing hopes or desires; tempting. *The promise of adventure on the journey was enticing.*

perplexed (puhr PLEHKSD) *v.:* troubled with doubt; puzzled. *The author's appearance clearly perplexed the customs agent.*

notorious (noh TAWR ee uhs) *adj.:* well known because of something bad; having a bad reputation. *The original inn where the pilgrims stayed was notorious for its shady clientele.*

concocted (kahn KAHKT ihd) *v.* used as *adj.:* prepared (food or drink) by mixing various ingredients. *While hiking, he enjoyed a dinner concocted from his small supply of food.*

Language Coach

Roots The Latin root *perplexus* means "tangled." How does the meaning of the root help you understand one of the listed words?

Reader/Writer Notebook

Use your **RWN** to complete the activities for this selection.

California Standards, pp. 178–183

- **Reading Standard 2.2** Analyze the way in which clarity of meaning is affected by patterns of organization, hierarchical structures, repetition of the main ideas, syntax, and word choice in the text.

Selection Readability	
Easily Accessible **Accessible** Challenging	familiar syntax; accessible vocabulary

Selection Summary

This article describes the beginning of one man's modern-day pilgrimage from London to Canterbury, England.

Link to Today

This Link to Today gives a new perspective on the idea of a pilgrimage.

Read with a Purpose

Read to discover how the author uses his own journey to explore the ways in which a historical setting can change over time.

Build Background

Geoffrey Chaucer's famous work *The Canterbury Tales* follows a group of characters along their religious journey from London to Canterbury in fourteenth-century England. In the book *Walking to Canterbury,* contemporary author Jerry Ellis describes his own journey along the same path to Canterbury. Using the poem as his guide, Ellis examines Chaucer's setting from a modern perspective.

TRAVEL BOOK

from Walking to Canterbury

by **Jerry Ellis**

When I presented my passport to the immigration officer at Heathrow Airport,[1] she studied me as if I were an international oddity. I wore tennis shoes, a blue cotton shirt, a brown leather jacket, and jeans. My hat was stained from years of sun, rain, and sweat. Dove and blue jay feathers stuck from one side of the hat, while a rattlesnake rattle rode snug in the back of the band. My backpack bulged with clothes, a camera, a journal, cooking utensils, a tent, toiletries, and personal items.

"On a hike?" she said, taking a closer look at the rattlesnake rattle.

"A pilgrimage," I said, hoping that the trek would be charged with extraordinary experiences. "From London to Canterbury. I plan to do it in the same amount of time it took medieval pilgrims. Seven days."

She now seemed all the more intrigued with my attire, which was notably different from that of a pilgrim in the Middle Ages. The only thing I had in common with Chaucer's pilgrims[2] was my hat.

Like mine, decorated with feathers and the snake's rattle, which I had collected on my walks, a pilgrim would have worn a big floppy hat, decorated with badges or shells to offer proof of his journeys. He might also have worn a "sclavein," which was a long, russet-colored tunic with big sleeves,

1. **Heathrow Airport:** an airport located near London, England.
2. **Chaucer's pilgrims:** the characters in Chaucer's poem *The Canterbury Tales.*

Pilgrimage to St. Aldhelm's Chapel, St. Aldhelm's Head, Dorset, U.K.

Selection Resources

Unit 1 Resources, on-level practice and assessment, p. 64

Teacher One Stop™, on-level lesson plans and all print resources

Holt Audio Library: Selections and Summaries in Spanish

UA: Differentiating Instruction, graphic organizer, p. 21

UA: Supporting Instruction in Spanish, selection summary

Analyzing Visuals Transparencies, p. 4

ThinkCentral Online Assessment, Selection Standards Check

Link to Today

Like *The Canterbury Tales,* this article describes the experiences of a traveler in England.

Direct Teach

Think About/Talk About

Read with a Purpose Have students read the Read with a Purpose statement. Then, ask them to think of some of the ways that England might have changed since Chaucer's time.

Extend the Discussion

Comparing and Contrasting What is the only item of clothing that the author says he has in common with a pilgrim in the Middle Ages? ***Possible response:*** *He says that the only thing he has in common is his hat.*

Speculating What do you think is the author's reason for going on a pilgrimage to Canterbury? ***Possible responses:*** *He wanted to know what traveling to Canterbury was like for medieval pilgrims; he wanted to have a better understanding of why they made the journey long ago.*

Model the Skill

- Model for students adding additional information to the Informational Text Focus graphic organizer. Provide students with copies of the graphic organizer for the excerpt from "Walking to Canterbury." (See **Unit 1 Resources**.)
- Tell students that after noting details about modern and medieval London, they can begin noting differences. Modern London has trains, subways, airplanes, in-line skating, cars, phone booths, computers, and televisions. None of these items existed in medieval London.

Similarities	Differences
Both modern and medieval London were busy with activity.	Modern London is noisier—sounds from a nearby park, televisions, cars . . .

Guided Practice: Apply

Read-Talk-Write Have students work in pairs to look for and discuss additional similarities and differences between medieval and modern London. Ask students to add their thoughts to the graphic organizer.

sometimes patched with crosses. A soft pouch, a "scrip," would have hung from a leather belt strung over his shoulder. The pouch was small, to indicate that the pilgrim had little money or none at all. A rosary of beads might have dangled from his arm or neck, and he could have carried a wooden staff with a metal toe. Leather shoes probably covered his feet.

The pilgrim's dress was symbolic as well as practical. The staff defended the traveler against wild dogs and wolves, which represented the Devil. It also served as a third leg and suggested the Trinity[3] as well as the wood of the Cross. The tunic, similar to the clothes Jesus wore, reflected the pilgrim's humanity. The medieval imagery became so ingrained into the British psyche that Sir Walter Raleigh used it two hundred years later in his poem "His Pilgrimage": **A**

> Give me my scallop shell of quiet
> My staff of faith to walk upon;
> My scrip of joy, immortal diet;
> My bottle of salvation;
> My gown of glory, hopes true gauge,
> And thus I'll take my pilgrimage.

Dressed in my modern pilgrim attire, I took a train from the airport to Victoria Station in London and there boarded the tube (British for subway) to Russell Square near the British Museum to look for an affordable bed-and-breakfast for the night. The sun was setting, and the streets smelled of Indian curry, Chinese food, and fish-and-chips. Red phone booths stood like monuments on the sidewalk, where two men wearing double-length hair rocked their hips as each paraded with a blaring boom box on his shoulder. A bobbie (British for cop) at the corner motioned for two sleek black taxis to hurry on, and three teenagers on Rollerblades played follow the leader as the first jumped over a garbage can. No rain fell, but so many people carried umbrellas that it seemed a Mary Poppins party simmered in the approaching night's pot. My mouth watered just to walk new streets, and enchanting British accents fell on my ears like notes of an exotic song being born in the very air I breathed.

A pub's window revealed two women throwing darts, and the sound of a whacked tennis ball erupted from a small park. Images on televisions flickered inside shadowy apartments, and somewhere down an alley a car shrieked. The enticing smell of perfume from a woman strolling in front of me lingered as a lone jet streaked the sky, its red wing lights blinking. The sights and sounds of modern London were in sharp contrast to the Middle Ages.

In the 1300s, if a renegade medieval serf[4] could cross the Thames[5] into London and stay here one year and a day without being caught by his lord, he became a free man. The city itself occupied only one square mile then. About thirty-five thousand people populated London, and they ranged from ragged serfs and students to members of the craft guilds (like carpenters and weavers), clergymen, and nobles. **B** Regardless of whether they survived on scraps of cabbage snatched from the common marketplace or dined on roasted pigs in rooms hung with tapestries, all of the populace lived surrounded by the smell of open sewers. At sundown all were also locked within London when the walled city closed its gates. . . . .

Night had fallen when I checked into a third-story room at the Avalon Hotel, overlooking a grove of trees in a public park. A lone figure strummed a guitar as he

3. **the Trinity:** the Christian "Holy Trinity" of God the Father, the Son (Jesus), and the Holy Spirit.
4. **serf:** a peasant in the feudal system who ranked between a freeman and a slave.
5. **Thames:** a major river that flows through southern England and runs through London.

A **Informational Focus** **Comparing and Contrasting** How is what the author is carrying different from what the pilgrims carried?

B **Informational Focus** **Comparing and Contrasting** How are these elements of medieval London similar to those of a modern city?

Vocabulary **ingrained** (ihn GRAYND) *v.* used as *adj.:* deeply and firmly fixed in one's nature or being.
enticing (ehn TYS ihng) *v.* used as *adj.:* attracting by arousing hopes or desires; tempting.

Universal Access

EL English Learners

English for Academic Success Help students compare and contrast elements of medieval and modern London by clarifying modern culture references in the selection. Explain that "fish-and-chips" is a meal that includes fried fish with French fries and that "Mary Poppins" is a fictional character in literature and film who could fly while holding her magic umbrella. Have students scan the section for other cultural references that they do not understand. Ask students to find one key word in the text that may help explain the reference.

Struggling Readers

To help students read "Walking to Canterbury," model the reading skill of comparing and contrasting. You might say: "The speaker notices many sights and sounds in modern London that would not be present in medieval London." Work with students to note details in the article about London in the present and London in the past.

Chaucer's Canterbury Pilgrims, Tabard Inn by Edward Henry Corbould.

"Give me my scallop shell of quiet
My staff of faith to walk upon;
My scrip of joy, immortal diet;
My bottle of salvation;
My gown of glory, hopes true gauge,
And thus I'll take my pilgrimage."
—Sir Walter Raleigh

Pilgrim Badges (tin-lead alloy), by English School. Museum of London.

(*above*) Sign for The George Inn in Southwark, a public house in London, England. (*right*) University of Kent, Canterbury, Great Britain.

Modern-day Canterbury

Compare and Contrast

Ask students to compare "Walking to Canterbury" with the selections from Chaucer's *Canterbury Tales* (pp. 118–174).

- **Similarities** Both texts describe a time and place in England and focus on a pilgrimage between London and Canterbury.
- **Differences** The text of the article is prose, while the text of *The Canterbury Tales* is in rhymed verse.

Challenge students to use the painting and photos on p.181 to compare and contrast the appearance of London streets during medieval and modern times.

- **Similarities** Both are filled with businesses; some of the architecture still looks the same.
- **Differences** The modern streets are paved; the medieval streets are dirt; there are electric lights, and the buildings look more kempt in modern London.

Think About/Talk About

Comprehension

A Informational Focus

Possible responses: *The pilgrims had far fewer items; they did not carry cameras, tents, or camping gear. Many of the objects carried by medieval pilgrims had religious significance.*

B Informational Focus

Possible responses: *Modern cities are also very crowded. The population of modern cities includes people with little or no money, very wealthy people, workers, students, and religious leaders.*

Extend the Discussion

Drawing Conclusions In the second paragraph on p. 180, the author refers to "the British psyche." What does he mean by this term? ***Possible response:*** *The phrase "British psyche" refers to ideas and feelings rooted in the nation's history that still play an important role in the thinking and behavior of many British people.*

Interpreting In Sir Walter Raleigh's poem "The Pilgrimage," the speaker states that he needs his "scrip of joy," "bottle of salvation," and "gown of glory" for his pilgrimage. What practical items do you think the speaker could be referring to? Why are they important to him? ***Possible responses:*** *The "scrip of joy" could be religious verses; "the bottle of salvation" could be water or holy wine; the "gown of glory" could be his clothing. They are important because they represent his religious faith, the central reason for his journey.*

Vocabulary: Own the Word

- **ingrained:** Remind students that *ingrained* means "deeply and firmly fixed in one's nature or being." What does the narrator say has become *ingrained* in the British psyche? [*medieval imagery*]
- **enticing:** Ask students to name things that a cat might find *enticing*. ***Possible responses:*** *a ball of yarn; kitty litter; shoestrings; a furry rug*

Think About/Talk About

Comprehension

C Informational Focus

Possible response: *A guest in medieval times would have seen and heard pigeons and live music, but not cars or benches.*

D Informational Focus

Possible response: *Southwark had brothels, cheap hotels, and pickpockets in those times. Today it is filled with shops and offices.*

E Informational Focus

Possible responses: *He uses the Thames to show the historical continuity between medieval period and modern times. Although the manufactured world has changed rapidly, some aspects of the natural world have stayed the same.*

Vocabulary: Own the Word

- **perplexed:** Remind students that *perplexed* means "troubled with doubt." Ask students the following question: "Have you ever been *perplexed* when talking to a friend? Explain when and why you felt *perplexed* when talking to a friend."
- **notorious:** Ask students to name some *notorious* characters from literature or history. ***Possible responses:*** *Grendel; Grendel's mother; Modred, Macbeth, Julius Caesar, Napoleon*
- **concocted:** Ask students to describe something unusual or interesting they have *concocted* in the past.

Monitor Students' Comprehension

Guide the class in answering these comprehension questions.

1. How is the narrator's lodging different from the lodging of most medieval pilgrims? [*Pilgrims did not lodge in private rooms, but in monasteries or on the floor of inns.*]
2. What has happened to the Tabard Inn of *The Canterbury Tales*? [*It burned down centuries before the narrator's pilgrimage.*]

perched atop a bench near the tallest tree. A car horn sounded, and two cooing pigeons fluttered from my windowsill. **C**

My tiny room, reached by a narrow flight of squeaky wooden stairs, smelled of freshly ground coffee, which perplexed me until I discovered that the bag of Guatemalan in my backpack had spilled. The bathroom was across the hall, but my room had a washbasin, hot and cold water, and a mirror on the wall. A television, receiving only three channels, sat atop a table next to a chest of drawers. Two cups, decorated with hand-painted red tulips, rested on the table with a porcelain pot and tea bags. Though as modest as my budget, the room felt cozy, safe, and warm. The £25 (about $40) for the night included a full breakfast, one I planned to make good use of before embarking on my pilgrimage the next morning.

Most medieval pilgrims sought food and shelter in monasteries, where the monks gave freely and, when they obeyed the Benedictine rule,[6] even washed the travelers' feet. But often there were more pilgrims than there was room, and the pilgrims were forced to sleep outside on the ground or in an inn, where as many as three or four people shared a bed for a penny apiece—a whole day's wages. Such medieval inns were infested with rats and fleas, and innkeepers were notorious for serving spoiled food and cheating their patrons. Robbery was easily committed after putting a pilgrim to sleep with a drugged drink, concocted by mixing equal parts of seed of henbane, darnel, black poppy, and dried bryony root, which were pounded into a powder and added to ale.

The characters in *The Canterbury Tales* gathered in Tabard Inn the night before beginning their pilgrimage, and within minutes of checking into my hotel room, I took a subway to the site of the inn. It was located in Southwark, which was a red-light district in the Middle Ages. Today it is a collection of shops, pubs, and offices. **D**

A real place in the Middle Ages near the foot of London Bridge, Tabard Inn burned centuries ago. Now only a plaque in a stone wall informs passersby of its existence.

Just up the street a sign designating The George pictured a knight in armor on horseback slaying a dragon. The Globe Theatre[7] was only blocks away down by the river, and Shakespeare himself frequented The George, the only pub in the same block where the Tabard Inn once stood. . . .

Back on the streets, I started walking to my hotel. Big Ben's giant hands told time in the near distance, and Westminster Abbey towered against the night with its heavenly steeples. The Thames reflected moonlight as the tide shifted, just as it had done when Chaucer lived here. **E**

6. **Benedictine rule:** the standard code of conduct for monks living in monasteries, written by Saint Benedictine in the sixth century.

7. **Globe Theatre:** London theater where William Shakespeare presented his plays during his lifetime.

C Informational Focus **Comparing and Contrasting** In what ways is this scene similar to what a guest in a medieval inn might have experienced? In what ways is it different?

D Informational Focus **Comparing and Contrasting** According to the author, how has Southwark changed since the Middle Ages?

E Informational Focus **Comparing and Contrasting** What is the author using the Thames to represent or symbolize here?

Vocabulary **perplexed** (puhr PLEHKSD) *v.:* troubled with doubt; puzzled.
notorious (noh TAWR ee uhs) *adj.:* well known because of something bad; having a bad reputation.
concocted (kahn KAHKT ihd) *v.* used as *adj.:* prepared (food or drink) by mixing a variety of ingredients.

California Standards, p. 183

- **Reading Standard 2.2** Analyze the way in which clarity of meaning is affected by patterns of organization, hierarchical structures, repetition of the main ideas, syntax, and word choice in the text.
- **Writing Standard 2.2b** Analyze the use of imagery, language, universal themes, and unique aspects of the text.
- **Listening and Speaking Standard 1.10** Evaluate when to use different kinds of effects (e.g., visual, music, sound, graphics) to create effective productions.

Applying Your Skills

Reading Standard 2.2 (see pages A48–A50)
Listening and Speaking 1.10 (see pages A53–A55)
Writing Standard 2.2b (see pages A51–A52)

from Walking to Canterbury

Analyze Informational Texts

Informational Text Focus

Quick Check

1. Why does the author at first seem unusual to the immigration officer?
2. What kinds of scents does the author encounter while walking the streets of London?
3. Where did most medieval pilgrims seek lodging? Why was this usually their first choice?
4. What became of the real Tabard Inn from Chaucer's *Tales*?

Read with a Purpose

5. How does the author try to make his first night in London similar to the pilgrims' night before their journey?

Informational Skills: Comparing and Contrasting

6. Look back at the chart in which you recorded the main similarities and differences between medieval London and modern London. Overall, do you think the author believes that the two eras have more similarities than differences, or just the opposite? Explain your response.

Vocabulary Check

Match each Vocabulary word with its antonym.

7. ingrained — a. unknown
8. enticing — b. superficial
9. perplexed — c. disassembled
10. notorious — d. repulsed
11. concocted — e. clarified

Text Analysis

12. **Interpret** What does the attire of the medieval pilgrims reflect about their interests and beliefs?
13. **Analyze** How does the author use his walk from the tube to the Avalon Hotel to depict modern London?
14. **Evaluate** In this passage, the author mixes medieval history with the recounting of his travels in London. Is this an effective storytelling method, or does jumping back and forth make it more difficult to follow his story? Explain.

Listening and Speaking

15. **Extend** Think about a journey you would like to take. Where would you go? What would you bring? Prepare a multi-media presentation in which you describe a significant journey. Use a variety of effects (visual, music, sound, graphics) to make your production effective.

Writing Skills Focus

Timed Writing In a paragraph, discuss how the author of *Walking to Canterbury* uses imagery to depict a modern, bustling London. Be sure to support your response with evidence from the text.

What Do You Think Now?

How does the author's motivation for his journey to Canterbury compare to the original pilgrims' reasons for taking the journey? Support your response with evidence from the text.

Universal Access

Struggling Writers

English for Academic Success To complete the Writing Skills Focus activity, provide additional scaffolding for students by having them create T-charts. On the left side, have them list at least four images that the author includes in *Walking to Canterbury*. For example, they might note the following image from p. 180: "the streets smelled of Indian curry, Chinese food, and fish-and-chips." On the right side, have them describe what the image shows about London. The image noted above suggests that London is a multicultural and diverse city. Remind students that they should note images that set modern-day London apart from the London of medieval times.

Image	What It Shows
"the streets smelled of Indian curry, Chinese food, and fish-and-chips"	London is a multicultural and diverse city.

Check for Understanding

Independent Practice

Informational Text Focus

Possible responses:

1. *He is wearing casual clothes and carrying a large overstuffed pack filled with camping gear.*
2. *Chinese and Indian food, fish and chips, and a woman's perfume*
3. *Monasteries; these places were free and safe.*
4. *It burned down centuries ago.*
5. *He visits some of the places where the pilgrims might have been on the night before their journey.*
6. *Students' explanations of the similarities and differences will vary.*

Vocabulary Check

7. *b* **8.** *d*
9. *e* **10.** *a*
11. *c*

Possible responses:

12. *The pilgrims' attire shows that they were focused on the spiritual side of their lives. They carried very few possessions and little or no money. Most of what they carried was for practical or religious uses.*
13. *He describes many of the sights, sounds, and smells that he encounters along the way.*
14. *The structure of the essay gives the reader a good sense of how the two time periods are alike and different.*
15. *Students should create a multimedia presentation in which they describe a journey they would like to take. Students should note where they want to go and what they plan to bring.*

What Do You Think Now?

Tell students to consider the religious nature of the author's trip and that of the original pilgrims. Remind students to use information from the article to support their points of view.

Standards Focus

Objectives

Students will
- analyze the ways in which irony, tone, mood, the author's style, and diction achieve specific rhetorical and aesthetic purposes
- analyze characteristics of subgenres, such as ballads

Selection Introduction

Think About the Ballads

Before students answer the question, have them think about a contemporary song that reflects the culture and attitudes of their generation.

For Independent Reading

Cambodian Folk Stories from the Gatiloke, Muriel P. Carrison

Motivate

What Do You Think?/QuickWrite

Have students identify songs that tell about people's lives. Discuss each song with students, asking them to tell whether the song shows heroism or human failure.

English for Academic Success

Academic Vocabulary

Look for opportunities to use the Academic Vocabulary words in this unit.
- **diverse, *adj.*:** varied
- **emphasis, *n.*:** stress; importance
- **status, *n.*:** social or professional rank

California Standards, pp. 184–193

- **Reading Standard 3.1** Analyze characteristics of subgenres (e.g., satire, parody, allegory, pastorals) that are used in poetry, prose, plays, novels, short stories, essays, and other basic genres.
- **Reading Standard 3.3** Analyze the way in which irony, tone, mood, the author's style, and the "sound" of language achieve specific rhetorical or aesthetic purposes or both.

Preparing to Read

Lord Randall
Get Up and Bar the Door
Edward, Edward

What Do You Think? What moves a hero to act?

QuickWrite

Think of songs you know that tell stories about heroism, such as heroic people, actions, or qualities. Choose the song you know best, and retell it in your own words in your *Reader/Writer Notebook.*

INTRODUCTION

Ballads

Using a strong beat and repetition, ballads are a type of story passed from performer to performer, from generation to generation.

Poetry of the People

In the Middle Ages, just as today, certain forms of entertainment tended toward the sensational. Like today's popular music, medieval ballads were the poetry of the people, and their subjects were predictably popular—domestic tragedy, false love, true love, the absurdity in husband-wife relationships, and the supernatural. Unlike today's music, ballads were not copyrighted by a composer but were passed down orally from singer to singer.

Song and Dance

We often associate popular songs with dancing. The word *ballad* is in fact derived from an Old French word meaning "dancing song." Although the English ballads' connection with dance has been lost, it is clear from their meter and structure that the original ballads were composed to be accompanied by music.

The meter of the old ballads is characterized by a strong, simple beat. The verse forms are relatively uncomplicated and have a primitive freshness that appeals to a general, rather than to an elitist, audience. Only later, in the era of literary ballads (more sophisticated poems that artfully evoked the atmosphere of the originals), did the rhyme scheme (*abcb*) and meter of the ballad stanza become standard.

The ballads as we know them today probably took their form in the fifteenth century, but they were not printed until Sir Thomas Percy published a number of them in 1765. Inspired by Percy, Sir Walter Scott and others traveled around the British Isles and copied down such folk songs from the people who still sang them. These ballads represent the rich history of the time.

Think About the Ballads Think about popular songs today as well as songs you might know from when your parents were growing up. How do popular songs or ballads reflect the culture and attitudes of a particular era?

Young musician, from14th century manuscript of *De Musica* by Anicius Boetius (c. 450-524). Folio 47R. Biblioteca Nazionale, Naples.

Selection Readability	
Easily Accessible Accessible **Challenging**	These poems include historical context, complex poetry, unfamiliar vocabulary.

Reading Standard 3.1, 3.3 (see pages A48–A50)

Literary Skills Focus

Ballad **Ballads** are songs or songlike poems that tell stories in simple, rhythmic language. Virtually every ballad includes certain predictable features, including sensational or tragic subject matter, omitted details, supernatural events, and a **refrain**—a repeated word, line, or group of lines.

Reading Skills Focus

Understanding Purpose Although we do not know who composed these ballads, we can still determine the **purpose** from details in the text. We can look at details such as dialogue, images, or repetition. In "Lord Randall," for example, the mother repeats "my son" and "my handsome young man" in each stanza. We can see that she loves her boy and that she is upset about his behavior. We can also guess that the purpose of this ballad is to share a tragic event with the listeners. The author of "Get Up and Bar the Door," in contrast, wants to share a humorous tale. We learn this purpose from details found at the very beginning of the ballad: This story will take place during a holiday inside a home full of comforting food.

Into Action As you read, use a chart like the one below to record details that help you determine the purposes of the ballads.

	"Lord Randall"	"Get Up and Bar the Door"	"Edward, Edward"
Details	mother's pleading tone		
Purpose:	to move to sadness		

Writing Skills Focus

Think as a Reader/Writer

Find It in Your Reading Repetition is an essential feature of ballads. **Incremental repetition**—a phrase or sentence that is repeated with a new element each time—helps advance the story until the climax is reached. As you read, pay special attention to the use of repetition in each ballad.

TechFocus As you read these ballads, think about what a music video version of them might look like.

Language Coach

Anglo-Saxon Roots Many English words have changed their spelling and pronunciation since the Middle Ages. For example, the modern pronoun *you* was commonly written as *ye*. Today's English verb *have* was written often as *hae*. What familiar words can you discover in these words from the Middle Ages: *gat, nae, wi, sae, doun, mither*?

Reader/Writer Notebook

Use your **RWN** to complete the activities for these selections.

Learn It Online

Explore Internet links for these ballads online.

go.hrw.com H12-185 Go

Preteach

English for Academic Success

Language Coach

Have students search the ballads on the following pages for the words common to the Middle Ages introduced in the **Language Coach.** Challenge students to use the context of the ballad to figure out the meaning of the words. [*got, no, with, so, down, mother*]

Literary Skills Focus

As you read the selection with students, ask students to note characteristics of the ballad.

Reading Skills Focus

Give students a copy of the Reading Skills Focus graphic organizer before they read. (See **Unit 1 Resources.**) Tell them to use their responses to answer the questions on the Applying Your Skills page.

Writing Skills Focus

Have students record phrases or sentences that are repeated throughout each ballad in their **Reader/Writer Notebooks**. Students can use their notes to complete the Writing Skills Focus activity.

Selection Resources

Unit 1 Resources, on-level practice and assessment p. 69

PowerNotes, interactive lesson presentation with activities

Teacher One Stop™, on-level lesson plans and all print resources

Holt Audio Library

Holt Audio Library: Selections and Summaries in Spanish

UA: Holt Interactive Reader, p. 47

UA: Differentiating Instruction, modified lesson plans and leveled assessment, p. 22

UA: Resources for Teaching Advanced Students, lesson plans, p. 65

UA: Supporting Instruction in Spanish, selection summary

ThinkCentral Online Assessment, Selection Standards Check

ThinkCentral Online Remediation

Learn It Online

Literature Links direct students to pre-screened Web sites offering more information related to a selection.

go.hrw.com H12-185 Go

Teacher Preparation
Selection Summary
In "Lord Randall," the protagonist has returned from hunting in the woods, tired and weary, and would like his mother to make his bed so that he can lie down because he knows he will soon be dead.

Direct Teach

Think About/Talk About
Read with a Purpose Remind students that the ballad is set in the Middle Ages. Point out the words "wild wood." Ask students to think about how perceptions of nature have changed throughout history. Then, have students discuss why nature might have been perceived as a "wild" place in the Middle Ages.

Comprehension
B Reading Focus

Possible responses: *Lord Randall admits that he is poisoned and is dying. The purpose of the ballad may be to tell the tragic tale of a mother losing her son.*

Analysis
A Literary Focus

Possible responses: *Lord Randall's mother has a repeated concern for her son, her "handsome young man." Lord Randall repeats his request for his mother to "make my bed soon," for he wants to lie down because he is "weary wi' hunting."*

BALLAD

LORD RANDALL

Read with a Purpose
Read this ballad to discover what happened to Lord Randall in the "wild wood."

Build Background
This ballad is sung in diverse versions in several countries. The basic story varies little, but Randall is variously known as Donald, Randolph, Ramsay, Ransome, and Durango. Sometimes his last meal consists of fish, sometimes snakes. The dialect of the version below is Scottish. This ballad, like many others, is sung entirely as a conversation in a question-and-answer format that builds suspense.

"O where hae ye been, Lord Randall, my son?
O where hae ye been, my handsome young man?"
"I hae been to the wild wood; mother, make my bed soon,
For I'm weary wi' hunting, and fain° wald lie down."

"Where gat ye your dinner, Lord Randall, my son?
Where gat ye your dinner, my handsome young man?"
"I din'd wi' my true-love; mother, make my bed soon,
For I'm weary wi' hunting, and fain wald lie down." **A**

"What gat ye to° your dinner, Lord Randall, my son?
What gat ye to your dinner, my handsome young man?"
"I gat eels boil'd in broo;° mother, make my bed soon,
For I'm weary wi' hunting, and fain wald lie down."

"What became of your bloodhounds, Lord Randall, my son?
What became of your bloodhounds, my handsome young man?"
"O they swell'd and they died; mother, make my bed soon,
For I'm weary wi' hunting, and fain wald lie down."

"O I fear ye are poison'd, Lord Randall, my son!
O I fear ye are poison'd, my handsome young man!"
"O yes! I am poison'd; mother, make my bed soon,
For I'm sick at the heart, and I fain wald lie down." **B**

4. fain: gladly.

9. gat ye to: did you have for.
11. broo: archaic form of "broth."

A Literary Focus **Ballad** What lines here could be considered a refrain?

B Reading Focus **Understanding Purpose** What does Lord Randall's response to his mother's suspicion tell you about the purpose of the ballad?

Universal Access

English Learners
English for Academic Success Help students with the Scottish dialect of this ballad. Begin by rephrasing the first line: "Where have you been, Lord Randall, my son?" Then, help students rephrase the fourth line. Point out that an apostrophe can indicate one or more missing letters, as in *wi'* for *with* (line 4) or *din'd* for *dined* (line 7). Encourage students to rephrase as they read, and assist them when necessary.

Struggling Readers
Students might have trouble understanding the author's purpose in the ballad. Remind them that the purpose of a ballad is to tell a story. Model for students the reading skill of understanding purpose by pointing out repetition in the ballad. You might say: "When I read this selection, I look carefully at the repeated words, lines, or phrases. The repetition of words and phrases helps me understand the author's purpose."

✔ See **UA: Differentiating Instruction** for strategies for teaching struggling readers.

Man riding a horse, hunting with a hawk, (detail) from the *Bedford Hours* calendar page for May (1414-1423) by the Workshop of the Master of the Duke of Bedford, Paris.
The British Library, f.5 Add.18850.

HEALTH LINK

Deadly Dining

Medieval diners did not have the modern conveniences of refrigeration and hygiene that we have come to expect. In fact, food poisoning was a common experience during the Middle Ages. The son in "Lord Randall" and the faithful hunting dogs who share his supper suffer from an acute gastrointestinal illness after eating eels. King Henry I (1068–1135) defied his doctor's orders and ate a fatal meal at his hunting lodge in St. Denis-le-Fermont, near Gisors. Pope Martin IV (1281–1285) probably also died after eating a meal of eels or lampreys with wine, a dish so associated with him that Dante identified him with eternal gluttony in *The Divine Comedy.*

Ask Yourself

What are some other consequences of improper hygiene and refrigeration?

Think About/Talk About

Extend the Discussion

Drawing Conclusions What observations does Lord Randall's mother make that lead her to conclude that her son is poisoned? ***Possible responses:*** *She sees that he is weary and wants to lie down. When she asks where his hounds have gone, she discovers they are dead.*

Making Judgments There are many questions and answers that are repeated throughout the selection. How does this affect the way you read and perceive the ballad? ***Possible responses:*** *It gives the ballad a rhythmic quality that grows more and more intense as the situation is revealed. The rhythm of the ballad builds suspense for the reader.*

Health Link

Ask Yourself

Possible responses: *Improper hygiene and lack of refrigeration led to extreme illness and even death. If tainted food was distributed over a large area, it could lead to an epidemic. Have students discuss issues related to improper hygiene in modern society.*

Advanced Learners

Acceleration Have students discuss the reflection of culture in "Lord Randall." Remind students that some of the details in the ballad are changed when it is told in different countries and dialects. Have students rewrite a section of this ballad as if these events took place in modern culture. Then, have students discuss the differences between the original ballad and their own.

✔ See **UA: Resources for Teaching Advanced Students** for strategies for teaching advanced learners.

Students with Disabilities

After they read each ballad, introduce students to the Sketch to Stretch strategy. Have students make a drawing of their interpretation of the text, and below their sketches, have them add a sentence that explains their interpretation with support from the text.

go.hrw.com *For more about the Sketch to Stretch strategy, see this page in* ***ThinkCentral, Teacher Access.***

Teacher Preparation

Selection Summary

"Get Up and Bar the Door" is about a husband and wife who bicker over who will get up and bar (lock) the door.

Direct Teach

Think About/Talk About

Read with a Purpose Remind students that ballads are written for different purposes. Some are laments (for example, Lord Randall), and others are humorous. Ask students to think about the author's purpose for writing this ballad. Then, have them discuss who they think will win the argument: the goodman or the goodwife.

Analysis

A Literary Focus

Possible response: *The characters, setting, and main problem or conflict are all introduced in the first three stanzas. The main characters are a husband and wife. The setting is in their home. The conflict is caused by the open door.*

Extend the Discussion

Finding Details In the beginning of the ballad, what reason does the wife give for not wanting to bar the door? ***Possible response:*** *She is busy cooking and doing housework.*

Synthesizing What does the interaction between the goodman and goodwife in the first four stanzas suggest about their relationship? ***Possible responses:*** *The goodman is lazy and wants his wife to do everything; the goodwife is annoyed with her husband; both are extremely stubborn toward each other.*

BALLAD

GET UP AND BAR THE DOOR

Read with a Purpose
Read to discover who wins the "battle of the sexes" in this ballad of medieval England.

Build Background
The story in this ballad exists in many versions in Europe, Asia, and the Middle East—perhaps illustrating the universal theme sometimes called the battle of the sexes. *Goodman* and *goodwife* are terms that were commonly applied to married men and women, something like *Mr.* and *Mrs.* today. The story takes place around November 11, Martinmas, or the feast of Saint Martin of Tours, which was usually celebrated with a big meal.

It fell about the Martinmas time,
And a gay time it was then,
When our goodwife got puddings° to make,
And she's boild them in the pan.

The wind sae cauld blew south and north,
And blew into the floor;
Quoth our goodman to our goodwife,
"Gae out and bar the door."

"My hand is in my hussyfskap,°
Goodman, as ye may see;
An° it should nae be barrd this hundred year,
It's no be barrd for me." **A**

They made a paction tween them twa,
They made it firm and sure,
That the first word whaeer should speak,
Should rise and bar the door.

Then by there came two gentlemen,
At twelve o clock at night,
And they could neither see house nor hall,
Nor coal nor candle-light.

3. puddings: soft foods usually for special occasions; during this time, often meaning sausages.

9. hussyfskap: archaic word meaning "household chores."
11. an: archaic form of "if."

A Literary Focus **Ballad** What story elements are introduced in these first three stanzas?

Developing Oral Fluency

Group Activity The unfamiliar language in the ballad can make it hard for students to read the lines smoothly. To help students improve their oral fluency, first have students read the ballad silently. Ask them to think about how they would pronounce the unfamiliar words. Then, have students read the selection aloud as a group. Repeat this process until students develop a rhythm and are able to read the lines smoothly. Model proper pronunciation as necessary.

✔ See the **UA: Differentiating Instruction** for practice passages for developing oral fluency.

"Now whether is this a rich man's house,
Or whether it is a poor?"
But neer a word ane° o them speak,
For barring of the door.

And first they ate the white puddings,
And then they ate the black;
Tho muckle° thought the goodwife to hersel,
Yet neer a word she spake.

Then said the one unto the other,
"Here, man, tak ye my knife;
Do ye tak aff the auld man's beard,
And I'll kiss the goodwife."

"But there's nae water in the house,°
And what shall we do than?"
"What ails ye at the pudding-broo,°
That boils into the pan?"

O up then started our goodman,
An angry man was he:
"Will ye kiss my wife before my een,
And scad° me wi pudding-bree?"°

Then up and started our goodwife,
Gied three skips on the floor:
"Goodman, you've spoken the foremost word,
Get up and bar the door." Ⓑ

23. ane: archaic form of "one."

27. muckle: archaic form of "much."

33. but . . . house: He probably wants water to soften the husband's beard.
35. What . . . pudding-broo: What's wrong with using the pudding broth?
40. scad: archaic form of "scald." **pudding-bree:** *Bree* is archaic form of "broth."

Ⓑ **Reading Focus** **Understanding Purpose** What clues to the comic nature of this ballad are given in the final stanza?

January, from the *Da Costa Book of Hours* (c. 1515) by Simon Bening (1483–1561), Flemish (Bruges). MS. 399, f.2v. The Pierpont Morgan Library, NY.

Think About/Talk About

Comprehension

Ⓑ Reading Focus
Possible response: *The wife was willing to sacrifice her home, possessions, and dignity to win the argument.*

Extend the Discussion

Paraphrasing In line 31, one man tells the other to cut off the goodman's beard. How does he suggest doing this in the lines that follow? ***Possible response:*** *by soaking his beard in the pudding broth and cutting it off with a knife*

Making Judgments Think about the series of events that occur in this ballad. What seem to be the priorities of the goodman and goodwife? ***Possible responses:*** *Both would rather have strangers come into their home and eat their food than lose an argument; the goodman would rather lose the argument than be humiliated by the strangers; the goodwife's priority is to win the argument.*

Cross-Curricular Connection

HISTORY: Marriage in the Middle Ages

During the Middle Ages, marriage could be used as a way to connect clans, settle disputes, and expand the social influence of a family. Men were usually significantly older than their wives. The bride's family often offered the groom money, or a dowry, to cover the cost of living for his new wife. Although separation of husband and wife was allowed, divorce was not accepted by the church during this time.

HSS Analysis Skills: HI 3

Teacher Preparation

Selection Summary

"Edward, Edward" is a discussion between a mother and her son about why the son's sword is covered in blood. The son finally confesses that he has killed his father and now must exile himself.

Direct Teach

Think About/Talk About

Read with a Purpose Have students read the Read with a Purpose statement. Then, have students predict what has happened to Edward.

Comprehension

Ⓐ Reading Focus

Possible response: *The image of blood dripping from Edward's sword implies that this is a tragic ballad.*

Ⓑ Reading Focus

Possible response: *Edward's mother does not believe him. She already has a feeling that he killed his father, and she wants to hear him admit to it.*

BALLAD

EDWARD, EDWARD

Read with a Purpose

Read this ballad to discover why Edward has blood on his sword.

Build Background

Like "Lord Randall," this tragic ballad exists in similar versions in different countries. Sir Thomas Percy, who in the 1760s compiled many popular ballads, found the same characters in a Swedish ballad and noted that a different version appeared with the title "Son Davie, Son Davie."

"Why does your brand sae drop wi' blude,° Ⓐ
Edward, Edward?
Why does your brand sae drop wi' blude,
And why sae sad gang ye,° O?"—
"O I hae kill'd my hawk sae gude,°
Mither, mither;
O I hae kill'd my hawk sae gude,
And I had nae mair° but he, O."

"Your hawk's blude was never sae red,
Edward, Edward;
Your hawk's blude was never sae red,
My dear son, I tell thee, O."—
"O I hae kill'd my red-roan steed,
Mither, mither;
O I hae kill'd my red-roan steed,
That erst° was sae fair and free, O."

"Your steed was auld,° and ye hae got mair,
Edward, Edward;
Your steed was auld, and ye hae got mair;
Some other dule ye dree,° O."— Ⓑ
"O I hae kill'd my father dear,
Mither, mither;
O I hae kill'd my father dear,
Alas, and wae is me, O!"

1. brand . . . blude: sword so drip with blood.

4. gang ye: go you.

5. gude: good.

8. nae mair: no more.

16. erst: before.

17. auld: old.

20. dule ye dree: grief you suffer.

Ⓐ **Reading Focus** **Understanding Purpose** What clues to the tragic nature of this ballad are given in the first sentence?

Ⓑ **Reading Focus** **Understanding Purpose** Why does Edward's mother mention that his hawk's blood was not so red and his steed was old and not his only horse?

Universal Access

EL English Learners/ Struggling Readers

English for Academic Success Students may have a hard time understanding the key details in the ballad without a clear understanding of some unfamiliar words. Before students read this selection, introduce the following words.

- **mither**—mother. *The mither questioned her son.*
- **fair**—beautiful. *The horse's shiny coat was very fair.*
- **steed**—horse. *He rode his steed through the forest.*
- **penance**—self-punishment. *The man went into exile as penance for his crime.*
- **yonder**—some distance away. *The town was close to his home, but the sea was located yonder.*
- **curse**—an inflicted power that can cause harm. *The son was cursed by the death of his father.*

Then, have students read the ballad. Remind them to recall the meaning of these words to help them understand the ballad's key details.

"And whatten penance will ye dree° for that,
Edward, Edward?
Whatten penance will ye dree for that?
My dear son, now tell me, O."—
"I'll set my feet in yonder boat,
Mither, mither;
I'll set my feet in yonder boat,
And I'll fare over the sea, O."

"And what will ye do wi' your tow'rs and your ha',°
Edward, Edward?
And what will ye do wi' your tow'rs and your ha',
That were sae fair to see, O?"—
"I'll let them stand till they doun fa',°
Mither, mither;
I'll let them stand till they doun fa',
For here never mair maun° I be, O."

"And what will ye leave to your bairns° and your wife,
Edward, Edward?
And what will ye leave to your bairns and your wife,
When ye gang owre the sea, O?"—
"The warld's room: let them beg through life,
Mither, mither;
The warld's room: let them beg through life;
For them never mair will I see, O."

"And what will ye leave to your ain° mither dear,
Edward, Edward?
And what will ye leave to your ain mither dear,
My dear son, now tell me, O?"—
"The curse of hell frae me sall ye bear,°
Mither, mither;
The curse of hell frae me saw
Sic counsels° ye gave to me, O!" **C**

25. Whatten . . . dree: What punishment for sin will you suffer?

33. ha': hall; that is, ancestral home.

37. doun fa': fall down.

40. maun: must.

41. bairns: children.

49. ain: own.
53. frae me sall ye bear: you will carry for me.
56. sic counsels: such advice.

C Literary Focus **Ballad** What is the surprise ending here?

The Sin of Worldly Vanities (c. 1300–c. 1320). The consequences of worldly vanities such as hunting and hawking are shown here as a rider with his hawk and hound is approached by a devil. One of a set illustrating the temptations, from poems by Matfre Ermengau. British Library, London.

Think About/Talk About

Analysis

C Literary Focus

Possible response: *The surprise at the end reveals that the mother asked her son to kill his father.*

Extend the Discussion

Finding Sequence of Events After Edward admits to killing his father, what does he say he will do for his penance? ***Possible response:*** *He is going into exile and will sail away in a boat.*

Character Motivation Edward tells his mother that she will receive his curse because she advised him to kill his father. What do you think the mother's motives were for convincing her son to kill his father? ***Possible response:*** *She planned to receive all his possessions.*

California Standards, pp. 192–193

- **Reading Standard 3.1** Analyze characteristics of subgenres (e.g., satire, parody, allegory, pastorals) that are used in poetry, prose, plays, novels, short stories, essays, and other basic genres.
- **Reading Standard 3.3** Analyze the way in which irony, tone, mood, the author's style, and the "sound" of language achieve specific rhetorical or aesthetic purposes or both.
- **Writing Standard 1.2** Use point of view, characterization, style (e.g., use of irony), and related elements for specific rhetorical and aesthetic purposes.
- **Writing Standard 1.6** Develop presentations by using clear research questions and creative and critical research strategies (e.g., field studies, oral histories, interviews, experiments, electronic sources).
- **Writing Standard 2.1** Write fictional, autobiographical, or biographical narratives.
- **Listening and Speaking Standard 2.3d** Demonstrate an awareness of the author's use of stylistic devices and an appreciation of the effects created.
- **Listening and Speaking Standard 2.4a** Combine text, images, and sound by incorporating information from a wide range of media, including films, newspapers, magazines, CD-ROMs, online information, television, videos, and electronic media-generated images.

Check for Understanding

Independent Practice

Reading Skills Focus

Possible responses:

1. *He was hunting in the wild woods.*
2. *They argue about who should shut the door. Their pact is that whoever speaks first has to "get up and bar the door."*
3. *She asks what he plans to do with his belongings and his land.*
4. *All three ballads seem to view life as unpredictable and violent.*
5. *Ask students to add another column to record the details that are the most powerful and significant.*

Literary Skills Focus

Possible responses:

6. *He eats poisonous eels.*
7. *Most students will suspect Lord Randall's lover. Questions might be: How did the dogs die? Does Lord Randall actually die? Is the person who poisoned him ever identified and punished?*
8. Dear *is not used in a sincere way. This could imply that the relationship between Edward and his mother is not a loving one.*
9. *They are both very stubborn.*
10. *It gives the ballads rhythm; it builds suspense in the stories.*
11. *In "Lord Randall," you suspect that he is just tired, but he is actually dying. In "Get Up and Bar the Door," you expect it to be a tragedy, but it has a comedic ending. In "Edward, Edward," you expect Edward's mother to be upset about her husband's death, but learn the murder was her idea.*

What Do You Think Now?

Ask students to explain how the popularity of the selected ballads could make these everyday characters be perceived as heroes. Have students think about other examples of everyday people who have become heroes through exposure from the media.

Applying Your Skills

Reading Standard 3.1, 3.3 (see pages A48–A50)
Writing Standard 1.2 (see pages A51–A52)

Ballads

Literary Response and Analysis

Reading Skills Focus

Quick Check

1. Where has Lord Randall been while away from his home?
2. In "Get Up and Bar the Door," what do the husband and wife argue about? What pact do they make?
3. What is the response of Edward's mother when he announces that he killed his father?

Read with a Purpose

4. What common view of life is represented in the three ballads?

Reading Skills: Understanding Purpose

5. While you read the ballads, you made note of details in the text that gave you clues to the author's purpose. Now that you have finished reading, review your conclusions. Then, add a row to your chart and identify, for each ballad, the most powerful and significant detail that led to your interpretation of the ballad's purpose.

	"Lord Randall"	"Get Up and Bar the Door"	"Edward, Edward"
Details:	mother's pleading tone		
Purpose:	to move to sadness		
Most powerful and significant detail:			

Literary Skills Focus

Literary Analysis

6. **Infer** How did Lord Randall become ill?
7. **Analyze** Typical of ballads, "Lord Randall" ends with only half the story told. Why do you suppose the young man's lover has poisoned him? What other questions regarding the plot are left unanswered?
8. **Interpret** How is the word *dear* used differently by Edward and his mother in "Edward, Edward"? How do you interpret this difference?
9. **Make Judgments** In "Get Up and Bar the Door," what does the battle between the goodwife and goodman reveal about their characters?

Literary Skills: Ballad

10. **Compare** Questions and answers are often used by ballad authors. How does the series of questions and answers move the narratives of "Lord Randall" and "Edward, Edward" forward?

Literary Skills Review: Irony

11. **Evaluate** The contrast between what is expected and what really happens is called **irony.** How is each of these ballads ironic?

Writing Skills Focus

Think as a Reader/Writer

Use It in Your Writing Review your notes on the use of repetition in each ballad. Using one of the ballads as a model, write a dialogue (it may or may not be a ballad) that uses repetition, including incremental repetition, to build to a climax and create a surprise ending. Use quotations to indicate who is speaking.

What Do You Think Now? How can a popular song turn an everyday person into a hero?

Universal Access

Struggling Writers

English for Academic Success Some students may need additional scaffolding to complete the Writing Skills Focus activity. Before they write their own dialogues or ballads, have them work in pairs to re-read "Get Up and Bar the Door" as a dialogue between two characters. Direct students to note the way in which the author lets the reader knows who is speaking by the use of speech tags and punctuation. Have students note the repetition used in the ballad and discuss how they might use the same technique in a dialogue of their own.

Reading Standard 3.1 (see pages A48–A50)
Writing Standard 1.6, 2.1 (see pages A51–A52)
Listening and Speaking Standard 2.3d, 2.4a (see pages A53–A55)

CHOICES

As you respond to the Choices, use the **Academic Vocabulary** words as appropriate: attribute, concept, diverse, emphasis, status.

REVIEW

Identify Modern Ballads

With a partner, write down all the characteristics of ballads that you've learned in class and from reading the selections (the use of repetition, dialogue, and so on). Search the Internet for ballad lyrics on a specific topic appropriate for what you are studying in class—for example, "modern ballad lyrics" or "modern English ballad lyrics." Use your list as a guide for judging whether or not songs you find are ballads.

Compare Interpretations

Suppose that everything Edward predicts in "Edward, Edward" comes true. Create an illustration of the situation two years after the conversation in the ballad takes place. Emphasize elements that speak to each prediction Edward makes. Compare and contrast your interpretations with those of a classmate.

CONNECT

Understand Purpose

Timed Writing Ballads depict the culture that produced them. In an essay, explain at least three characteristics of medieval English life as it is depicted in the ballads in this unit. Cite examples from the ballads to support your analysis.

Create a Music Video

TechFocus In a small group, create a music video to accompany one of these ballads. Search for a recording of the ballad you choose, or perform your own. Then, find or film images to go along with the ballad. Use the images to reveal your impressions of the ballad. Show your video to your class, and discuss how what your group created was similar to or different from how others visualized the ballad.

EXTEND

Perform a Ballad

Group Activity The comic "Get Up and Bar the Door" is just one example of how ballads handle the battle of the sexes. In a small group, find the ballad "The Old Man Who Lived in the Woods" (available in *A Treasury of New England Folklore* by B. A. Botkin) or a slightly different version called "Father Grumble" (located in *Folk Songs of the American People* edited by Alan Lomax). At what point in this new ballad do you know who's going to win the battle? How does this ballad use repetition to create humor? Use these insights as you decide how to sing the ballad, and perform it as a group for your class.

Lost, Josh Holloway, Yunjin Kin, "The Whole Truth," March 22, 2006.

Write News Stories

The simplicity and shortness of most ballads mean they focus on the big picture. Transform one of the ballads you read into a news story for the front page of a newspaper, and add realistic details that fit and fill out the narrative. Get together with members of your class, and arrange the stories to form a front page.

Independent Practice

Choices: Evaluation Criteria

Review: Homework
Identify Modern Ballads
- Students decide if the piece they found is a ballad.
- Students show a clear understanding of the characteristics of a ballad.

Review: Homework
Compare Interpretations
Students draw details from each of Edward's predictions.

Connect: Timed Writing 40–50 Minutes
Students use examples to support the three characteristics of medieval English life.

Connect: Homework
Create a Music Video
- Students draw a connection between medieval and modern culture.
- Groups compare and contrast videos to those of other groups

Extend: Homework
Perform a Ballad
Students show a clear understanding of the characteristics of a ballad.

Extend: Homework
Write News Stories
- Story makes connections between medieval and modern culture.
- Story follows structure and format of a news article.

Assess

Unit 1 Resources, Selection Standards Check, p. 70

ThinkCentral Online Assessment, Selection Standards Check

Teacher One Stop™, editable Selection Standards Check

Reteach

ThinkCentral Online Remediation

Standards Focus

Objectives

Students will

- analyze the way in which clarity of meaning is affected by patterns of organization, such as cause and effect
- analyze characteristics of subgenres such as the medieval romance narrative

Selection Introduction

Think About the Poem

Before students answer, have them think about the elements of a medieval romance, such as a hero who overcomes obstacles, and then provide contemporary examples.

For Independent Reading

- *Narcissus and Goldmund,* Hermann Hesse
- *Ivanhoe,* Sir Walter Scott

Motivate

What Do You Think?/QuickWrite

Use the QuickWrite to have students think about the internal struggles ordinary people contend with when they try to make good decisions.

English for Academic Success

Academic Vocabulary

Look for opportunities to use the Academic Vocabulary words in this unit.

- **attribute, *n.*:** a quality or characteristic
- **concept, *n.*:** notion or idea
- **diverse, *adj.*:** varied
- **emphasis, *n.*:** stress; importance

Preparing to Read

from Sir Gawain and the Green Knight

What Do You Think? What moves a hero to act?

QuickWrite

Many heroes are tempted on their journeys. For example, Sir Gawain is tempted to steal from his host. In your *Reader/Writer Notebook,* write about why you think people may be tempted to steal.

Suit of armor made for Christian I (1560–91) of Saxony (c. 1590) by Anton Peffenhauser (c. 1525–1602).

INTRODUCTION

About nine hundred years ago Chrétien de Troyes, a French court poet, began to craft tales of knightly adventures focusing on the exploits of King Arthur and the Knights of the Round Table. During the second half of the twelfth century, Chrétien invented the style of narrative that is known today as **Arthurian romance.**

Not Just a Love Story

The medieval **romance** is a long narrative of prose or poetry that tells the adventures of a hero on a quest for something valuable. Love can play a role in Arthurian romance, but the hero is the focus. Because the romance hero is bound by the code of chivalry, which emphasizes loyalty to his lord and service to those who are oppressed, many romances are about seeking justice and helping people in need. The romance hero almost always encounters a series of trials, sometimes with dragons or supernatural beings such as witches or fairies. Today the term *romance* means any story that presents a happier, more perfect, or more heroic world.

Gawain the Gallant

One of the most famous Arthurian romances is *Sir Gawain and the Green Knight,* an anonymous narrative probably written around 1375. At this time, the ideals of knightly conduct were beginning to fade, and the poem is filled with romantic conventions that cling to those concepts.

As the poem opens, King Arthur and his knights are celebrating Christmas in Camelot. Suddenly, an enormous green stranger armed with a huge ax rides into the hall where the knights are dining. He challenges any knight to hit him immediately and says that he will return the hit after a year and a day. Gawain, the best of the knights, accepts the terms and beheads the challenger. The Green Knight calmly picks up his own head, repeats his challenge, and gallops off with his head in his hand. The following selection tells what happens when Gawain encounters the Green Knight on the appointed day.

Think About the Poem What contemporary story or movie can you think of that fits most of the criteria for a medieval romance?

California Standards, pp. 194–205

- **Reading Standard 2.2** Analyze the way in which clarity of meaning is affected by patterns of organization, hierarchical structures, repetition of the main ideas, syntax, and word choice in the text.
- **Reading Standard 3.1** Analyze characteristics of subgenres (e.g., satire, parody, allegory, pastoral) that are used in poetry, prose, plays, novels, short stories, essays, and other basic genres.

Selection Readability	
Easily Accessible Accessible **Challenging**	historical context; complex narrative poem; unfamiliar vocabulary

Reading Standard 2.2, 3.1 (see pages A48–A50)

Literary Skills Focus

The Romance The medieval **romance** narrative, which can be prose or poetry, features an idealized hero who undertakes a quest and overcomes danger for the sake of a noble lady or high ideal. The hero faces trials and adventures, often encountering supernatural or magical beings. Arthurian romance includes stories of Camelot and King Arthur's Knights of the Round Table.

Reading Skills Focus

Understanding Cause and Effect A **cause** is the event that makes something happen. An **effect** is the result of that event. Recognizing causes and effects will help you understand the relationship between events in a narrative. Sometimes one action follows another but is not caused by it. Two events that are wrongly labeled as cause and effect create a **logical fallacy.**

Into Action As you read, use a diagram like the one below to record a cause for each of the important events of the selection. Be sure not to create incorrect relationships, or logical fallacies.

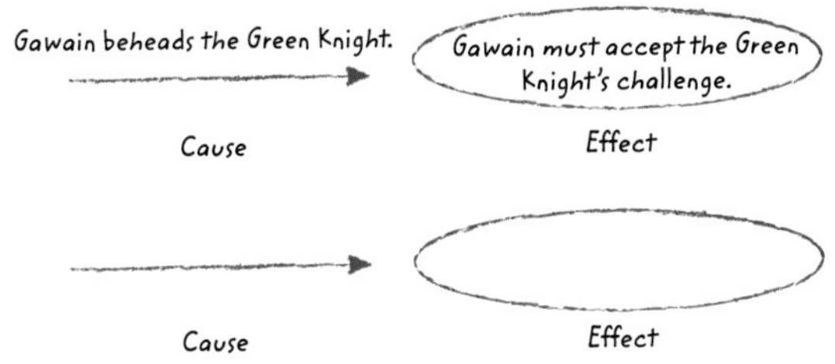

Writing Skills Focus

Think as a Reader/Writer

Find It in Your Reading Writers often use **imagery** to share their ideas with readers. A writer might present a visual picture of a dream, for example, to share a character's innermost feelings in a dramatic way. As you read, note in your *Reader/Writer Notebook* passages in the selection in which imagery helps you understand and "experience" the romance hero's challenges.

Reader/Writer Notebook

Use your **RWN** to complete the activities for this selection.

Vocabulary

whetting (HWEHT ihng) *v.* used as *adj.:* sharpening a blade on a stone made for the purpose. *He sharpened the blade on a whetting stone.*

daunted (DAWNT ihd) *v.:* made to lose courage. *Gawain had never before been daunted by anything.*

shied (shyd) *v.:* shrank or flinched away. *Gawain shied from the blow of the ax.*

efficacious (ehf uh KAY shuhs) *adj.:* effective or useful. *Gawain's brave and boastful voice proves to be efficacious in his confrontation with the Green Knight.*

covetousness (KUHV uh tuhs nihs) *n.:* desire for what belongs to others. *Gawain accused himself of covetousness.*

Language Coach

Past-Tense Verbs Most verbs add the *–ed* ending to show action in the past. Verbs that end in *y* change the *y* to *i* before adding *–ed.* The verb *shied* is the past-tense form of the verb *shy*. What other Vocabulary word ends in *–ed*?

Learn It Online

Find interactive cause-and-effect graphic organizers online.

go.hrw.com H12-195 Go

Selection Resources

Unit 1 Resources, on-level practice and assessment p. 73

PowerNotes, interactive lesson presentation with activities

Teacher One Stop™, on-level lesson plans and all print resources

Holt Audio Library

Holt Audio Library: Selections and Summaries in Spanish

UA: Holt Interactive Reader, p. 53

UA: Differentiating Instruction, modified lesson plans and leveled assessment, p. 26

UA: Resources for Teaching Advanced Students, lesson plans, p. 68

UA: Supporting Instruction in Spanish, selection summary

Analyzing Visuals Transparencies, p. 7

ThinkCentral Online Assessment, Selection Standards Check

ThinkCentral Online Remediation

Preteach

Introducing Vocabulary

- Review the Vocabulary words, definitions, and sentences with students.
- To reinforce students' understanding of the Vocabulary words, tell students that these words can help them understand Sir Gawain's challenge. Explain that he was an *efficacious* fighter who rarely *shied* from danger or became *daunted* by an opponent. However, Sir Gawain is faced with feelings of *covetousness* and must overcome temptation to maintain his knightly honor.

English for Academic Success

Language Coach

After students read the **Language Coach,** ask them to give other examples of past-tense verb forms that change a *y* to an *i* and add *-ed.* ***Possible responses:*** *tried, allied, applied, babied, bullied*

Literary Skills Focus

As you read and discuss the selection with students, tell them that often in the medieval romance narrative, the hero's actions cause some result that is meant to teach the character—and the reader—a lesson.

Reading Skills Focus

Give students a copy of the Reading Skills Focus graphic organizer before they read. Tell them to use their responses to answer the questions on the Applying Your Skills page.

Writing Skills Focus

Have students record lines that conjure up images in their **Reader/Writer Notebooks.**

Learn It Online

If your students need help organizing a paper [or extra reading support for informational text], introduce them to **Interactive Graphic Organizers**—tools for generating and organizing ideas, comparing and contrasting, and other key skills.

go.hrw.com H12-195 Go

Teacher Preparation
Selection Plot Summary
When Sir Gawain arrives at the Green Chapel (as he agreed to do a year and a day before), he hears the sound of an ax being sharpened. When the Green Knight bursts forth with a terrible weapon, Gawain bows his head to take the blow. The Green Knight raises his ax twice to test Gawain's courage, and with a third blow barely nicks him. Then the Green Knight reveals himself as the man who gave Gawain hospitality and ordered his wife to tempt Gawain. The Green Knight accuses Gawain of cheating by accepting the green sash from his wife, an accusation that makes Gawain blush and cry with remorse. Finally, the Green Knight concedes that Gawain has repented and spares his life.

Direct Teach
Think About/Talk About
Read with a Purpose Have student read the Read with a Purpose statement. Tell students to pay attention to elements that threaten to prevent Gawain from keeping his promise.

Analysis
(A) Literary Focus

Possible responses: *The scenery described in lines 1–8 has the romance elements of being a "strange, wild place," rocky and rugged, meaning the terrain may be enchanted or supernatural. The place is not beautiful, not easy to travel, and poses a challenge for Gawain, the hero, alone in the strange landscape.*

NARRATIVE POEM

from Sir Gawain and the Green Knight

translated by **John Gardner**

Read with a Purpose
Read this selection from an Arthurian romance to find out if Gawain keeps his promises.

Build Background
Gawain has come upon a mysterious castle, where for three days he is tempted by the absent lord's wife. On the last day he accepts more than just her kisses and takes a magical green sash that she claims will protect him from harm. Gawain leaves the castle with the green sash wrapped around his armor, intent on finding the Green Chapel and the dreaded Green Knight. He is certain he is headed for his death.

He put his spurs to Gringolet,° plunged down the path,
Shoved through the heavy thicket grown up by the woods
And rode down the steep slope to the floor of the valley;
He looked around him then—a strange, wild place,
And not a sign of a chapel on any side
But only steep, high banks surrounding him,
And great, rough knots of rock and rugged crags
That scraped the passing clouds, as it seemed to him. (A)
He heaved at the heavy reins to hold back his horse
And squinted in every direction in search of the Chapel,
And still he saw nothing except—and this was strange—
A small green hill all alone, a sort of barrow,°
A low, smooth bulge on the bank of the brimming creek
That flowed from the foot of a waterfall,
And the water in the pool was bubbling as if it were boiling.
Sir Gawain urged Gringolet on till he came to the mound
And lightly dismounted and made the reins secure
On the great, thick limb of a gnarled and ancient tree;
Then he went up to the barrow and walked all around it,
Wondering in his wits what on earth it might be.
It had at each end and on either side an entrance,
And patches of grass were growing all over the thing,
And all the inside was hollow—an old, old cave
Or the cleft of some ancient crag, he couldn't tell which
it was.

1. **Gringolet:** Gawain's horse.

12. **barrow:** grave mound.

(A) **Literary Focus** **The Romance** How does this scenery fit in with the elements of the romance?

Universal Access

English Learners
English for Academic Success To help students visualize the action of the selection, ask students to find the action verbs in the text. Explain that while the text uses some common, ordinary verbs, such as *went* and *walked,* many of the verbs specifically convey an action, such as *plunged, heaved, squinted*, and *urged*. Ask students to find synonyms for each verb they encounter.

✔ See **UA: Differentiating Instruction** for strategies for teaching English learners.

Struggling Readers
Tell students that asking *why* questions will help them understand cause-and-effect relationships in the epic poem *Sir Gawain and the Green Knight*. You might say: "As I read, I ask *why* questions such as 'Why did Gawain plunge down the path?' and 'Why is Gawain looking for the Green Knight?' Making cause-and-effect connections helps me understand the purpose of the text and clarifies the storyline."

✔ See **UA: Differentiating Instruction** for strategies for teaching struggling readers.

Sir Gawain and the Green Knight. Illustration by William McLaren.

"Whoo, Lord!" thought the knight,
"Is *this* the fellow's place?
Here the Devil might
Recite his midnight mass. **B**

"Dear God," thought Gawain, "the place is deserted enough!
And it's ugly enough, all overgrown with weeds!
Well might it amuse that marvel of green
To do his devotions here, in his devilish way! **C**
In my five senses I fear it's the Fiend himself
Who's brought me to meet him here to murder me.
May fire and fury befall this fiendish Chapel,
As cursed a kirk° as I ever yet came across!"
With his helmet on his head and his lance in hand
He leaped up onto the roof of the rock-walled room
And, high on that hill, he heard, from an echoing rock
Beyond the pool, on the hillside, a horrible noise.
Brrrack! It clattered in the cliffs as if to cleave them,
A sound like a grindstone grinding on a scythe!°
Brrrack! It whirred and rattled like water on a mill wheel!
Brrrrrack! It rushed and rang till your blood ran cold.

B Reading Focus **Understanding Cause and Effect** In these two stanzas, Gawain describes a disturbing and frightening place. What causes him to stay in such a place?

C Literary Focus **The Romance** What particular convention, or element, of romances does Gawain's description of whom—or what—he expects to meet call to mind?

Analyzing Visuals

Connecting to the Text In this painting, who appears to take the role of the romantic hero? What other elements of the romance can you find in this painting?

37. kirk: Scottish word for "church."

43. scythe: long-handled cutting tool.

Think About/Talk About

Comprehension

B Reading Focus

Possible responses: *Gawain stays in the landscape because he chose to accept a challenge from the Green Knight. As a result, Gawain's honor depends on his ability to keep his word and confront the Green Knight, even if he has to risk his life. Gawain's journey is about honor, not survival.*

Analysis

C Literary Focus

Possible response: *Gawain's enemy, the "Fiend," has the romance element of being supernatural. The romance foe is larger than life, with mythic strength, who presents a challenge seemingly beyond human capacity to overcome.*

Analyzing Visuals

Connecting to the Text: *The hero appears to be the man in the blue robe standing just right of the center of the painting. All other onlookers seem to fear the man on the horse except for the one man who stands to challenge him. The small details in the painting portray the lavish pageantry of the Middle Ages and the custom of a festive banquet with royal guests, courtiers, and musicians.*

Advanced Learners

Enrichment Ask students to think of present-day romances from comic books, adventure films, and television shows that share the characteristics of *Sir Gawain and the Green Knight.* Students should identify works with evocative settings, supernatural events, and often ambiguous conflicts between good and evil. Challenge students to point out the similarities and differences between their examples and the reading.

✔ See **UA: Resources for Teaching Advanced Students** for strategies for teaching advanced learners.

Students with Disabilities

Although students are reading only a part of the story of Gawain, the excerpt has a strong plotline. Model the creation of a plot diagram, identifying each part. As students read, have them create a plot diagram that shows the conflict, the main events, the climax, and the resolution. Explain to students that creating a plot diagram will help them identify cause-and-effect relationships between the events of the story. After students finish reading, have them use their completed diagrams to summarize the story and show how events are connected to one another.

Model the Skill

- Provide students with copies of the Reading Skills Focus graphic organizer for *Sir Gawain and the Green Knight*. (See **Unit 1 Resources**.)
- Tell students that medieval romance narratives often tell the story of a hero's quest. During these quests, the hero encounters obstacles. His actions determine the outcome of his quest.
- Model adding a cause-and-effect relationship from the narrative to the graphic organizer. Direct students to re-read lines 106–110. Tell them that these lines illustrate a cause-and-effect relationship. Tell them that Sir Gawain looks up at the ax as the Green Knight swings it down. Sir Gawain's action is a cause. The effect of his action is that the Green Knight begins to mock him for showing fear.

Guided Practice: Apply

Guide students in filling out one item in the cause and effect chart, as below. Guide students to see the relationship between the events.

Cause	Effect
The Green Knight mocks Sir Gawain.	Sir Gawain gains courage.

And then: "Oh God," thought Gawain, "it grinds, I think,
For me—a blade prepared for the blow I must take
as my right!
God's will be done! But here!
He may well get his knight,
But still, no use in fear;
I won't fall dead of fright!"

And then Sir Gawain roared in a ringing voice,
"Where is the hero who swore he'd be here to meet me?
Sir Gawain the Good is come to the Green Chapel!
If any man would meet me, make it now,
For it's now or never, I've no wish to dawdle here long."
"Stay there!" called someone high above his head,
"I'll pay you promptly all that I promised before."
But still he went on with that whetting noise a while,
Turning again to his grinding before he'd come down.
At last, from a hole by a rock he came out into sight,
Came plunging out of his den with a terrible weapon,
A huge new Danish ax to deliver his blow with,
With a vicious swine of a bit bent back to the handle,
Filed to a razor's edge and four foot long,
Not one inch less by the length of that gleaming lace.
The great Green Knight was garbed as before,
Face, legs, hair, beard, all as before but for this:
That now he walked the world on his own two legs,
The ax handle striking the stone like a walking-stave.°
When the knight came down to the water he would not wade
But vaulted across on his ax, then with awful strides
Came fiercely over the field filled all around
with snow.
Sir Gawain met him there
And bowed—but none too low!
Said the other, "I see, sweet sir,
You go where you say you'll go!

"Gawain," the Green Knight said, "may God be your guard!
You're very welcome indeed, sir, here at my place;
You've timed your travel, my friend, as a true man should.
You recall the terms of the contract drawn up between us:
At this time a year ago you took your chances,
And I'm pledged now, this New Year, to make you my payment. **D**

Gawain, directed by Di Trevis.

71. walking-stave: walking stick or staff.

D **Reading Focus** **Understanding Cause and Effect** The Green Knight is going to give Gawain an ax blow to the back of his neck. What do you expect the result to be?

Vocabulary **whetting** (HWEHT ihng) *v.* used as *adj.:* sharpening a blade on a stone made for the purpose.

Developing Oral Fluency

Use the dialogue in *Sir Gawain and the Green Knight* on pp. 198–199 to help students illustrate the drama of the poem when reading aloud. Point out that Gawain may use a different tone of voice when he speaks to himself than when he calls to the Green Knight.

Whole-Class Activity Assign students the reading roles of Sir Gawain, the Green Knight, and narrators. As a class, read pages 198–199 aloud. Be sure to take turns so more students have a chance to participate. Remind students that when they read aloud, they provide an interpretation of the meaning of the poem with the tone of their voice. Ask them to notice the different interpretations of their fellow classmates.

And here we are in this valley, all alone,
And no man here to part us, proceed as we may;
Heave off your helmet then, and have here your pay;
And debate no more with me than I did then
When you severed my head from my neck with a single swipe."
"Never fear," said Gawain, "by God who gave
Me life, I'll raise no complaint at the grimness of it;
But take your single stroke, and I'll stand still
And allow you to work as you like and not oppose
you here."
He bowed toward the ground
And let his skin show clear;
However his heart might pound,
He would not show his fear.

Quickly then the man in the green made ready,
Grabbed up his keen-ground ax to strike Sir Gawain;
With all the might in his body he bore it aloft
And sharply brought it down as if to slay him;
Had he made it fall with the force he first intended
He would have stretched out the strongest man on earth.
But Sir Gawain cast a side glance at the ax
As it glided down to give him his Kingdom Come,°
And his shoulders jerked away from the iron a little,
And the Green Knight caught the handle, holding it back,
And mocked the prince with many a proud reproof:°
"You can't be Gawain," he said, "who's thought so good,
A man who's never been daunted on hill or dale! E
For look how you flinch for fear before anything's felt!
I never heard tell that Sir Gawain was ever a coward!
I never moved a muscle when *you* came down;
In Arthur's hall I never so much as winced.
My head fell off at my feet, yet I never flickered;
But you! You tremble at heart before you're touched!
I'm bound to be called a better man than you, then,
my lord."
Said Gawain, "I shied once:
No more. You have my word.
But if my head falls to the stones
It cannot be restored.

"But be brisk, man, by your faith, and come to the point!

107. his Kingdom Come: life after death.

110. reproof: rebuke; scolding.

E **Literary Focus** **The Romance** What does Gawain's glance reveal about him?

Vocabulary **daunted** (DAWNT ihd) *v.:* made to lose courage.
shied (shyd) *v.:* shrank or flinched away.

Think About/Talk About

Comprehension

D Reading Focus

Possible response: *Even though all the elements are in place for Gawain to be killed, and Gawain himself expects to be killed, the hero of epic poetry does not usually die. The pleasurable suspense in reading a romance adventure comes from not knowing how the hero will conquer the enemy or escape the predicament.*

Analysis

E Literary Focus

Possible responses: *Because he thinks he will be beheaded, Gawain may have lost his nerve at the last second. His glance at the blade may reveal his fear of death, or perhaps his hope, even to the end, of finding a way to save his own life.*

Vocabulary: Own the Word

- **whetting:** In the text, *whetting* is used as an adjective: a *whetting* noise. What kind of sound is made when a person is *whetting* a knife? What effect would that sound have on a listener? ***Possible responses:*** *The sound is like a slapping sound. It might make someone fearful.*
- **daunted:** Demonstrate the body language of a person who is *daunted* by a task they have to complete. Then, ask one or two students to act like they are *daunted* by the task of walking to the door.
- **shied:** Remind students that *shied* means "shrank or flinched away." To help students personally connect to the Vocabulary word, ask the following question: "Have you ever *shied* away from something you really wanted to do? Explain when and why you *shied* away from an activity in which you wanted to take part."

Cross-Curricular Connection

HISTORY: Knightly Armor

In the Middle Ages, a knight wore heavy armor and carried many pounds worth of weaponry made of wood and metal. The armor was hot and cumbersome. It took multiple squires and pages to dress a knight in the various layers of clothing before the ridge armor was applied. The sword and the lance were the medieval knight's main weapons. Knights also used smaller weapons such as daggers, cleavers, and axes as they were best for piercing chain mail during person-to-person combat. Because the identities of the knights were concealed inside the armor, they would paint elaborate designs on their chests or shields to avoid killing their fellow comrades.

Guided Practice: Apply

Think as a Reader/Writer

Find It in Your Reading In lines 150–160, it becomes apparent that Sir Gawain's quest will not end as he expected. Point out to students that the surprise twist at this point in the story depends on our limited point of view—we know only what Sir Gawain knows.

Use It in Your Writing After reading lines 150–183, have students revisit lines 150–160 and rewrite them from the Green Knight's point of view.

Think About/Talk About

Literary Connection

Triples appear in many fairy tales and medieval romances. Here, the Green Knight prepares to make the third stroke, signaling the climax of the story.

Extend the Discussion

Finding Details How does the narrator describe the way Gawain stands as he waits to be struck by the Green Knight's ax? ***Possible response:*** *Gawain stands as "still as a stone;" and as strong as a tree "wedged in rocky ground by a hundred roots."*

Interpreting In lines 140–145, how does Sir Gawain turn the tables on the Green Knight? ***Possible response:*** *Gawain is now the one taunting the Green Knight by claiming that the knight is actually the "cringing coward." Gawain challenges the Green Knight to stop his threats and follow through with his blow.*

Deal out my doom if you can, and do it at once,
For I'll stand for one good stroke, and I'll start no more
Until your ax has hit—and that I swear."
"Here goes, then," said the other, and heaves it aloft
And stands there waiting, scowling like a madman;
He swings down sharp, then suddenly stops again,
Holds back the ax with his hand before it can hurt,
And Gawain stands there stirring not even a nerve;
He stood there still as a stone or the stock of a tree
That's wedged in rocky ground by a hundred roots. **F**
O, merrily then he spoke, the man in green:
"Good! You've got your heart back! Now I can hit you.
May all that glory the good King Arthur gave you
Prove efficacious now—if it ever can—
And save your neck." In rage Sir Gawain shouted,
"*Hit* me, hero! I'm right up to here with your threats!
Is it *you* that's the cringing coward after all?"
"Whoo!" said the man in green, "he's wrathful, too!
No pauses, then; I'll pay up my pledge at once,
I vow!"
He takes his stride to strike
And lifts his lip and brow;
It's not a thing Gawain can like,
For nothing can save him now!

He raises that ax up lightly and flashes it down,
And that blinding bit bites in at the knight's bare neck—
But hard as he hammered it down, it hurt him no more
Than to nick the nape of his neck, so it split the skin;
The sharp blade slit to the flesh through the shiny hide,
And red blood shot to his shoulders and spattered the ground.
And when Gawain saw his blood where it blinked in the snow
He sprang from the man with a leap to the length of a spear;
He snatched up his helmet swiftly and slapped it on,
Shifted his shield into place with a jerk of his shoulders,
And snapped his sword out faster than sight; said boldly—
And, mortal born of his mother that he was,
There was never on earth a man so happy by half—
"No more strokes, my friend; you've had your swing!
I've stood one swipe of your ax without resistance;
If you offer me any more, I'll repay you at once
With all the force and fire I've got—as you

Sir Gawain and the Green Knight (detail) by William McLaren.

F **Reading Focus** **Understanding Cause and Effect** Why does the Green Knight stop his ax before it hits Gawain?

Vocabulary **efficacious** (ehf uh KAY shuhs) *adj.:* effective or useful.

Universal Access

EL English Learners

English for Academic Success Some students may experience difficulty understanding certain phrases with the poem. Idioms, in particular, may prohibit students from comprehending the text. Point out the idiom used by the Green Knight in line 137: "You've got your heart back!" Explain that the Green Knight uses this idiom to mean that Gawain still has the courage to fight back. Have students read on to find out why Gawain's renewed courage makes the Green Knight happy.

AAVE Students Who Use African American Vernacular English

English for Academic Success Some students may struggle with forming or identifying the past tenses of verbs in formal English. Explain that in "Sir Gawain and the Green Knight," the author includes the past tenses of regular and irregular verbs, such as *considered* and *studied* on p. 201 and *kept, spoke,* and *stood* on pp. 200–201. Tell students that many regular verbs change to formal English past tense simply by adding *–ed* to

will see. (G)
I take one stroke, that's all,
For that was the compact we
Arranged in Arthur's hall;
But now, no more for me!"

The Green Knight remained where he stood, relaxing on his ax—
Settled the shaft on the rocks and leaned on the sharp end—
And studied the young man standing there, shoulders hunched,
And considered that staunch° and doughty° stance he took,
Undaunted yet, and in his heart he liked it;
And then he said merrily, with a mighty voice—
With a roar like rushing wind he reproved the knight—
"Here, don't be such an ogre on your ground!
Nobody here has behaved with bad manners toward you
Or done a thing except as the contract said.
I owed you a stroke, and I've struck; consider yourself
Well paid. And now I release you from all further duties.
If I'd cared to hustle, it may be, perchance, that I might
Have hit somewhat harder, and then you might well be cross!
The first time I lifted my ax it was lighthearted sport,
I merely feinted and made no mark, as was right,
For you kept our pact of the first night with honor
And abided by your word and held yourself true to me,
Giving me all you owed as a good man should. (H)
I feinted a second time, friend, for the morning
You kissed my pretty wife twice and returned me the kisses;
And so for the first two days, mere feints, nothing more
severe.
A man who's true to his word,
There's nothing he needs to fear;
You failed me, though, on the third
Exchange, so I've tapped you here.

"That sash you wear by your scabbard° belongs to me;
My own wife gave it to you, as I ought to know.
I know, too, of your kisses and all your words
And my wife's advances, for I myself arranged them.
It was I who sent her to test you. I'm convinced
You're the finest man that ever walked this earth.
As a pearl is of greater price than dry white peas,
So Gawain indeed stands out above all other knights.
But you lacked a little, sir; you were less than loyal;

175. staunch: steadfast; stubborn. **doughty:** courageous.

199. scabbard: carrying case that covers the blade of a sword; sheath.

(G) **Reading Focus** **Understanding Cause and Effect** What causes Gawain to be able to survive the Green Knight's stroke?

(H) **Reading Focus** **Understanding Cause and Effect** To what does the Green Knight attribute his actions?

Think About/Talk About

Comprehension

(F) Reading Focus

Possible response: *The Green Knight claims that he wanted to test Gawain's steadiness and see if he was as courageous as King Arthur had boasted he was.*

(G) Reading Focus

Possible response: *Because Gawain demonstrated honesty, loyalty, and courage—qualities of a hero—the Green Knight did not hit Gawain.*

(H) Reading Focus

Possible response: *The Green Knight explains that Gawain's ability to keep a promise and reject his wife's advances caused him to deliver two false blows. He gave one minor cut because Gawain accepted the green sash.*

Extend the Discussion

Paraphrasing What does the Green Knight reveal in his speech, lines 179–206, that Gawain did not know? ***Possible response:*** *Gawain did not know that the Green Knight asked his wife to test Gawain.*

Character Motivation Why did the Green Knight secretly test Gawain, as he confesses in lines 201–202? ***Possible response:*** *The Green Knight wanted to discover for himself if Gawain was as noble a knight as he seemed and as Arthur claimed.*

Vocabulary: Own the Word

efficacious: The root word for *efficacious* is *efficere,* which is Latin and means "accomplish." Someone who is *efficacious* is effective in accomplishing a task. Have students make a list of things that are *efficacious* in fighting the common cold.

the ending. Irregular verbs do not follow these patterns, but can be acquired by making note of the formal English versions of past tenses of irregular verbs when they read. Have students provide either the formal or informal English past tenses of the following verbs, while you supply the opposite form for comparison: *leap, walk, ring, cheer, fight.*

✔ For additional instruction and strategies, see **Think-Central, Teacher Access.**

Advanced Learners

Acceleration Introduce these students to the *post hoc fallacy*—the logical fallacy of assuming that because something happens after something else, it must have happened because of the first event. (The *post hoc fallacy* is also referred to as *"post hoc, ergo propter hoc"*—literally "after this, therefore because of this.") Challenge students to locate a passage in the text in which a quick read might make someone think a cause-and-effect relationship exists, but a closer read reveals the cause-and-effect relationship to be a fallacy.

Think About/Talk About

Comprehension

J Reading Focus

Possible response: *The Green Knight befriends Gawain because he is impressed with the way Gawain takes responsibility for his actions and repairs and compensates for faults and weaknesses within himself.*

Analysis

I Literary Focus

Possible response: *Gawain is angry with himself for hedging even the least bit; by dishonorably accepting the green sash, he thought he might save his life rather than depend entirely on his own resources.*

Extend the Discussion

Synthesizing What role does the Green Knight ultimately serve for Gawain? ***Possible responses:*** *The Green Knight is Gawain's teacher, mentor, and now an ally, a friend. He also acts as Sir Gawain's conscience.*

Vocabulary: Own the Word

covetousness: Remind students that *covetousness* means "desire for what belongs to others." Ask students to explain what Gawain says about *covetousness* in the poem. ***Possible response:*** *He says that covetousness should be cursed and suggests that this trait destroys a person's virtue.*

But since it was not for the sash itself or for lust
But because you loved your life, I blame you less."
Sir Gawain stood in a study° a long, long while,
So miserable with disgrace that he wept within,
And all the blood of his chest went up to his face
And he shrank away in shame from the man's gentle words.
The first words Gawain could find to say were these:
"Cursed be cowardice and covetousness both,
Villainy and vice that destroy all virtue!"
He caught at the knots of the girdle° and loosened them
And fiercely flung the sash at the Green Knight.
"There, there's my fault! The foul fiend vex it!
Foolish cowardice taught me, from fear of your stroke,
To bargain, covetous, and abandon my kind,
The selflessness and loyalty suitable in knights;
Here I stand, faulty and false, much as I've feared them,
Both of them, untruth and treachery; may they see sorrow
and care!
I can't deny my guilt;
My works shine none too fair!
Give me your good will
And henceforth I'll beware." (I)

At that, the Green Knight laughed, saying graciously,
"Whatever harm I've had, I hold it amended
Since now you're confessed so clean, acknowledging sins
And bearing the plain penance of my point;
I consider you polished as white and as perfectly clean
As if you had never fallen since first you were born.
And I give you, sir, this gold-embroidered girdle,
For the cloth is as green as my gown. Sir Gawain, think
On this when you go forth among great princes;
Remember our struggle here; recall to your mind
This rich token. Remember the Green Chapel. (J)
And now, come on, let's both go back to my castle
And finish the New Year's revels° with feasting and joy,
not strife,
I beg you," said the lord,
And said, "As for my wife,
She'll be your friend, no more
A threat against your life."

210. stood in a study: stood thinking deeply.

217. girdle: a sash worn as a belt.

Gawain, directed by Di Trevis.

242. revels: festivities, often as part of a celebration.

I Literary Focus **The Romance** Why is Gawain so angry with himself?

J Reading Focus **Understanding Cause and Effect** What is the effect of Gawain's choice to take the blow, of his confession, and of his apology?

Vocabulary **covetousness** (KUHV uh tuhs nihs) *n.:* desire for what belongs to others.

California Standards, pp. 203–205

- **Reading Standard 2.2** Analyze the way in which clarity of meaning is affected by patterns of organization, hierarchical structures, repetition of the main ideas, syntax, and word choice in the text.
- **Reading Standard 3.1** Analyze characteristics of subgenres (e.g., satire, parody, allegory, pastoral) that are used in poetry, prose, plays, novels, short stories, essays, and other basic genres.
- **Grades 9–10 Review Reading Standard 1.1** Identify and use the literal and figurative meanings of words and understand word derivations.
- **Grades 9–10 Review Reading Standard 3.3** Analyze interactions between main and subordinate characters in a literary text (e.g., internal and external conflicts, motivations, relationships, influences) and explain the way those interactions affect the plot.
- **Writing Standard 2.2d** Demonstrate an understanding of the author's use of stylistic devices and an appreciation of the effects created.
- **Writing Standard 2.3a** Explore the significance of personal experiences, events, conditions, or concerns by using rhetorical strategies (e.g., narration, descriptions, expositions, persuasion.)
- **Listening and Speaking Standard 2.3b** Analyze the imagery, language, universal themes, and unique aspects of the text through the use of rhetorical strategies (e.g., narration, description, persuasion, exposition, a combination of those strategies.)
- **Listening and Speaking Standard 2.4a** Combine text, images, and sound by incorporating information from a wide range of media, including films, newspapers, magazines, CD-ROMs, online information, television, videos, and electronic media-generated images.

Applying Your Skills

Reading Standard 2.2, 3.1; Grades 9–10 Review Reading Standard 3.3 (see pages A48–A50)
Writing Standard 2.3a (see pages A51–A52)

from Sir Gawain and the Green Knight

Literary Response and Analysis

Reading Skills Focus

Quick Check

1. Why did Sir Gawain go to the Green Chapel?
2. What reasons did Sir Gawain have to be concerned about the outcome of the meeting?
3. What prevents Gawain's death?

Read with a Purpose

4. Does Gawain keep his promises?

Reading Skills: Understanding Cause and Effect

5. As you read *Sir Gawain and the Green Knight,* you noted effects and their causes. Now, review your conclusions. Add more arrows to your diagrams, and identify which effects had multiple causes.

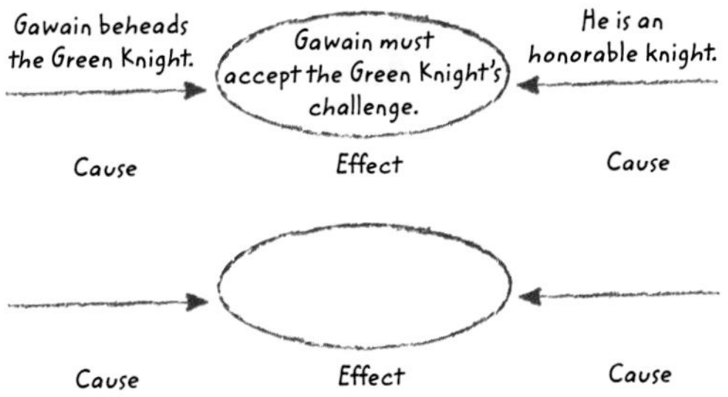

Literary Skills Focus

Literary Analysis

6. **Draw Conclusions** What images make the setting of the confrontation seem demonic?
7. **Evaluate** The Green Knight believes that Gawain has restored himself completely by his confession of his fault and acceptance of the blow. Do you agree? Explain.
8. **Make Judgments** How would you describe the writer's **tone**—or attitude—in this tale? Is he entirely serious, or do you find moments of humor? Find passages in the text to support your answer.
9. **Extend** What meaning will the gift Gawain receives have for him in the future?

Literary Skills: The Romance

10. **Interpret** How is Gawain a superhuman romance hero? How is he weak or flawed, just as an ordinary person might be? Cite details from the poem to support your response.

Literary Skills Review: Climax

11. **Draw Conclusions** The **climax** of a story is the point when the major conflict reaches its greatest moment of tension—the resolution is unknown, but the end is in sight. What do you think is the climax of this story?

Writing Skills Focus

Think as a Reader/Writer

Use It in Your Writing Review your notes on how the poem uses imagery to convey Gawain's challenges. Write a short paragraph about a time when you or someone you know faced a challenge. Use imagery to make your description come alive for your readers.

What Do You Think Now How does the chivalric code of honor and heroism affect Gawain?

Universal Access

Struggling Writers

English for Academic Success To complete the Writing Skills Focus activity, provide additional scaffolding for students by having them create a list of vivid images that will help describe their experience. Encourage students to write three main headings on their papers: Sight, Sound, and Touch. Under each heading, have students include images that appeal to that particular sense. As students write their descriptive paragraphs, have them use their lists to help them include images in their writing.

What Do You Think Now?

Ask students to consider the motivations behind Gawain's words and actions throughout the selection.

Check for Understanding

Independent Practice

Reading Skills Focus

Possible responses:

1. *He goes there to fulfill his promise to the Green Knight.*
2. *The Green Knight was going to behead him. The setting of the Chapel itself suggested doom.*
3. *his noble qualities*
4. *Yes, Gawain meets the Green Knight at the exact time and place specified to allow him one undefended stroke.*
5. *Ask students to add more arrows to their diagram to identify which effects have multiple causes.*

Literary Skills Focus

Possible responses:

6. *The deep valley is rocky and craggy with water that looks like it is boiling.*
7. *Yes, Gawain's confession shows responsibility and repentance. No, Gawain might make the same mistake again in the future.*
8. *Some of the Green Knight's speeches were humorous, for example in line 179, he tells Gawain that if he cut his head off, Gawain would have a right to complain.*
9. *The girdle might have magical protective powers. It is also proof of their bond of friendship.*
10. *As a hero, Gawain faces a supernatural creature and willingly faces death to keep his word. As a human, he gives in to temptation, flinches at an ax swing, and bemoans his weaknesses.*
11. *The climax is the first time the Green Knight swings the ax.*

Independent Practice

Vocabulary Development

Vocabulary Check

1. *c* **2.** *d*
3. *a* **4.** *e*
5. *b*

Your Turn

whetting: *sharpening*

synonym: *honing / antonym: dulling*

daunted: *frightened*

synonym: *intimidated / antonym: courageous*

shied: *drew back, as if afraid*

synonym: *shrank / antonym: asserted*

covetousness: *excessive desire*

synonym: *greed / antonym: selflessness*

English for Academic Success

Language Coach

Possible responses:

1. *shy—to draw back*
2. *ply—to use*
3. *pry—to inquire about; to separate*
4. *comply—to go along with*
5. *deny—to refuse*
6. *supply—to provide*

English for Academic Success

Academic Vocabulary

Possible responses: *The modern concept of a hero is most often someone who has faced and overcome seemingly insurmountable obstacles in life. Certain attributes they might possess are perseverance, courage, adventurousness, and integrity. Heroes in diverse cultures might vary according to how the cultures value physical versus mental strength, or accomplishments versus character.*

Learn It Online

WordSharp: An Interactive Vocabulary Tutor provides additional support for vocabulary development. Multimedia tutorials show students how to apply vocabulary skills to unfamiliar words—and how to make those words their own.

go.hrw.com H12-204 Go

Applying Your Skills

Grades 9–10 Review Reading Standard Reading Standard 1.1 (see pages A48–A50)

from Sir Gawain and the Green Knight

Vocabulary Development

Vocabulary Check

Match the Vocabulary words with their synonyms.

1. whetting	**a.** flinched
2. daunted	**b.** envy
3. shied	**c.** sharpening
4. efficacious	**d.** made afraid
5. covetousness	**e.** effective

Vocabulary Skills: Map Meanings

A word map can help you learn a word's relationship to other words. You can use word maps to identify a word's **synonyms,** which are words with similar meanings, and **antonyms,** which are words with opposite meanings. When you know a word's synonyms and antonyms, you can use them in your writing. Here is a sample word map:

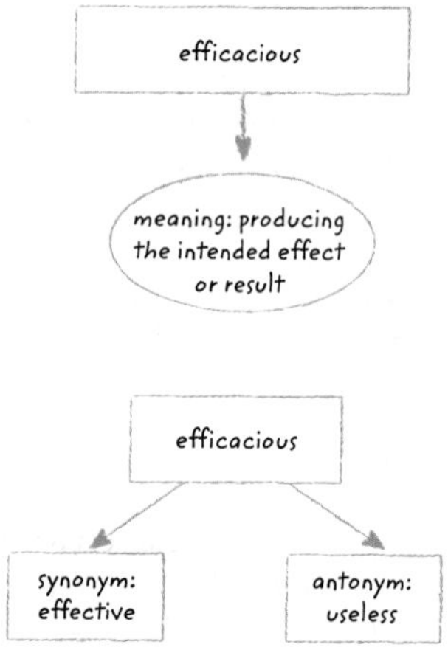

Your Turn

For each of the other Vocabulary words, create a word map like the one in the left-hand column. Not every Vocabulary word will have an antonym.

Language Coach

Past-Tense Verbs Follow spelling rules to help you recognize verbs. Most verbs add *–ed* to form the past tense. If the verb ends in *y*, the *y* is changed to *i* before adding *–ed*. For example: *cried* is the past tense of the verb *cry*. Write the present-tense form of each verb below. Then, define each word or look up its meaning in a dictionary.

1. shied	**4.** complied
2. plied	**5.** denied
3. pried	**6.** supplied

Academic Vocabulary

Talk About

In a small group, discuss the modern concept of a hero. What qualities do we attribute to heroes? How might qualities vary among diverse cultures? What qualities are universal? What might be a modern hero's quest, and what form would the tests of the hero's honor or courage take?

Learn It Online

Find out more about synonyms with *WordSharp*.

go.hrw.com H12-204 Go

Universal Access: Vocabulary Development

EL English Learners

English for Academic Success While students may understand the meaning of a word, they may need additional practice in identifying synonyms and antonyms for a word. Pair students with a proficient English speaker; then, have them engage in an instructional conversation in which they determine synonyms and antonyms for the following words from "Sir Gawain and the Green Knight." Encourage students to find the words in the poem and use the context to help them with this exercise.

- plunged (line 1)
- devilish (line 33)
- coward (line 114)
- vow (line 145)

✔ See the **Academic and Selection Vocabulary Skill Builder** in **UA: Differentiating Instruction.**

Writing Standard 2.2d (see pages A51–A52)
Listening and Speaking Standard 2.3b, 2.4a (see pages A53–A55)

Grammar Link

Transitive and Intransitive Verbs

A **transitive** verb has a direct object—a word or word group that tells who or what receives the action of the verb. You could say, "I studied my geometry notes for an hour." In this sentence, *studied* is transitive because it has a direct object: *my geometry notes.* In contrast, an **intransitive** verb does not have a direct object. You could say, "Luis also studied for an hour." Here, *studied* is intransitive because it has no direct object. When you want to decide whether a verb is transitive or intransitive, look at the entire sentence for a clue. If you are still not sure whether a verb is transitive or intransitive, look in a dictionary. Most dictionaries group the definitions of verbs according to whether the verbs are used transitively *(v.t.)* or intransitively *(v.i.)*.

Your Turn

Identify each italicized verb below as transitive or intransitive.

1. "It *whirred* and *rattled* like water on a mill wheel!"
2. "Sir Gawain *met* him there
   And *bowed.*"
3. "And his shoulders *jerked* away from the iron a little,
   And the Green Knight *caught* the handle."
4. "Said Gawain, 'I *shied* once:
   No more.'"
5. "He *takes* his stride to strike
   And *lifts* his lip and brow."

Writing Application Select a paragraph you have written, and identify the verbs as either transitive or intransitive.

CHOICES

As you respond to the Choices, use these **Academic Vocabulary** words as appropriate: attribute, concept, diverse, emphasis, status.

REVIEW

Set the Scene

TechFocus At the beginning of this selection, the sights and sounds Gawain encounters fill him with foreboding. In a short multimedia presentation, create your own representation of what Gawain saw and heard. You can use still images combined with sound, create an animation, or film a live scenario.

CONNECT

Present a Romance

Modern tales of quests feature many elements of the medieval romance. With a partner, select a contemporary tale told in a movie, television show, book, or other medium that reflects the elements of romance. You might consider the genres of adventure (such as the Indiana Jones series) and space quests (such as the Star Wars series). Make an oral presentation to the class in which you show the relevant scene and *emphasize* how it reflects elements of romance. Explain the similarities and differences between *Sir Gawain and the Green Knight* and your contemporary example.

EXTEND

Write a Parody

Group Activity The strong elements of romance make it ripe for **parody**—a work that makes fun of another work by imitating some aspect of the writer's style. With a group, brainstorm ways in which you can parody a medieval or Arthurian romance. Think carefully about setting, characters, and plot as you work. Your parody can take the form of a prose narrative, a poem, skit, play, video, or recorded song or ballad.

Independent Practice

Grammar Link

Your Turn

1. *Both are intransitive.*
2. *transitive/intransitive*
3. *intransitive/transitive*
4. *intransitive*
5. *Both are transitive.*

Choices: Evaluation Criteria

Review: Homework
Set the Scene

- Students compose a scene that appeals to the five senses.
- Students demonstrate a close and accurate reading of the text.

Connect: Homework
Present a Romance

- Students use the elements of the medieval romance as a set of criteria to compare *Sir Gawain and the Green Knight* and a modern romance.
- Students' comparisons reflect an in-depth reading of *Sir Gawain and the Green Knight.*

Extend: Homework
Write a Parody

- Parodies show an understanding of the characters' personalities represented in the original text.
- Parodies mimic the style and tone of a medieval romance.

Universal Access: Grammar Link

English Learners

English for Academic Success Remind students that transitive verbs have a direct object, while intransitive verbs do not have a direct object. Tell students that a direct object answers the question "Whom?" or "What?" after a transitive verb. Write the following sentences on the board.

The knight **invited** the warriors to join him in battle. (Invited whom? The warriors)

The soldier **destroyed** whatever got in his path. (Destroyed what? Whatever got in his path)

Model for students asking the questions "Whom?" or "What?" to determine whether a verb is transitive or intransitive.

To give students additional practice on transitive and intransitive verbs, ask them to rewrite these sentences to make the intransitive verbs transitive.

1. The ax struck the third time.
2. They finished triumphantly.
3. The knight forgave graciously.

✔ For more practice with transitive and intransitive verbs, see **Warriner's Handbook, GrammarNotes,** and **Language Handbook Worksheets.**

Assess

Unit 1 Resources, Selection Standards Check, p. 76

go.hrw.com **ThinkCentral Online Assessment,** Selection Standards Check

Teacher One Stop™, editable Selection Standards Check

Reteach

go.hrw.com **ThinkCentral Online Remediation**

Standards Focus

Objectives

Students will analyze the archetype of the romance hero.

Selection Introduction

Think About the Writer

Have students think of literary heroes who stand for love or valor in ancient epics. [Beowulf, Gilgamesh, Hector and Achilles from the *Iliad*].

For Independent Reading

- *Sun Dancing,** by Geoffrey Moorhouse
- *The Story of King Arthur and His Knights,* Howard Pyle

HRW LIBRARY *This title is available in the HRW library.

Motivate

What Do You Think?/QuickWrite

Before students answer the QuickWrite, ask them to define and describe a hero in their **Reader/ Writer Notebooks.**

English for Academic Success

Academic Vocabulary

Look for opportunities to use the Academic Vocabulary words in this unit.

- **attribute, *n.:*** quality; characteristic
- **concept, *n.:*** notion or idea
- **emphasis, *n.:*** stress; importance
- **status, *n.:*** social or professional rank

California Standards, pp. 206–215

- **Reading Standard 2.2** Analyze the way in which clarity of meaning is affected by patterns of organization, hierarchical structures, repetition of the main ideas, syntax, and word choice in the text.
- **Reading Standard 3.6** Analyze the way in which authors through the centuries have used archetypes drawn from myth and tradition in literature, film, political speeches, and religious writings (e.g., how the archetypes of banishment from an ideal world may be used to interpret Shakespeare's tragedy *Macbeth.*)

Preparing to Read

from Le Morte d'Arthur

What Do You Think? What moves a hero to act?

QuickWrite

Why must every hero have an antagonist or enemy? Would the hero be considered heroic without an enemy? Write your ideas in your *Reader/Writer Notebook.*

Tournament of Knights of the Round Table watched by King Arthur and Queen Guinevere, from 15th-century French manuscript of *Le roman du roi Arthur et les compagnons de la Table Ronde (Book of King Arthur and the Knights of the Round Table)* by Chrétien de Troyes (died c. 1183). Biblioteca Nazionale, Turin.

MEET THE WRITER

Sir Thomas Malory

(c. 1405–1471)

The historical identity of Sir Thomas Malory is a mystery that has puzzled scholars and historians for centuries.

Mysterious Malory

All we know for sure about Malory is that he was a knight familiar with chivalric romances who was writing in the years 1469–1470. There was more than one Sir Thomas Malory at the time, but it is generally presumed that an imprisoned knight from Warwickshire is the Malory on the manuscript. This Malory served in France during the Hundred Years' War and apparently fought at the siege of Calais in 1436. He was elected to Parliament at least once.The record of this war hero also includes a series of arrests for theft, burglary, and assault, including the robbing of an abbey in which he allegedly broke down eighteen doors and roughed up the monks. However, since there is no record of any trials or convictions, the accusations against Malory may have been politically motivated.

A Fascination with King Arthur

The Arthur in Malory's work is not the historical sixth-century general who helped his fellow Britons defend themselves against the invading Saxons. Rather, Malory's Arthur is a consolidation of later legends that developed in England and on the Continent. Using Celtic and Continental sources, Malory created a mythic Arthur who later became the very embodiment of British values.

Coming as it does at the end of the fifteenth century, Malory's work serves as a kind of swan song to the feudal order of the Middle Ages with its castles, knights, and chivalric codes. Malory's readers lived in a different world. Cities were growing, and money and competition were replacing the old feudal ways of barter and mutual obligation. With the death of the ideal King Arthur, Malory is recording the death of the entire way of life that the legendary King Arthur represents.

Think About the Writer What other literary heroes of any time period might have attracted Malory's interest?

Selection Readability	
Easily Accessible **Accessible** Challenging	simple dialogue; accessible theme

Reading Standard 2.4, 3.1 (see pages A48–A50)

Literary Skills Focus

Allegory An **allegory** is a story in which characters, plot events, and settings stand for abstract or moral concepts. Allegorical stories operate on two levels of meaning: a surface level and a deeper, below-the-surface level. Because the main purpose of allegories is to instruct, the surface story is a way of conveying a symbolic story with an important moral lesson. Authors of allegories often use personification to give human form to abstract concepts and qualities.

Reading Skills Focus

Making Critical Judgments When you read, you should take note of the characters and events and make judgments about them. **Making critical judgments** will help you understand the allegorical purpose and meaning of *Everyman.* In an allegory, the actions and words of the characters have symbolic meaning.

Into Action As you read, record the actions of each character as each responds to Everyman's request. From these actions, form a critical judgment about the characters.

Character	Action	My Judgment
Everyman		
Death		
Fellowship	Refuses to go on the journey	Will not risk death for Everyman

Writing Skills Focus

Think as a Reader/Writer

Find It in Your Reading As you read the excerpt from *Everyman,* pay close attention to the writer's use of **personification.** In your *Reader/Writer Notebook,* write down examples of how giving human qualities to concepts like fellowship and knowledge helps achieve the story's allegorical purpose.

Vocabulary

reverence (REHV uhr uhns) *n.:* feeling of great respect and awe. *Life should be treated with reverence.*

transitory (TRAN suh tawr ee) *adj.:* impermanent. *Material goods are only transitory.*

reckoning (REHK uh nihng) *n.:* calculation; accounting. *Everyman wonders if he will be ready for the final reckoning of his life.*

lechery (LEHCH uhr ee) *n.:* indulgence in lust. *Lechery is most disturbing in those who have sworn to avoid it.*

commendable (kuh MEHN duh buhl) *adj.:* deserving of admiration. *Everyman's quest to live a moral life is commendable.*

Language Coach

Suffixes A suffix comes at the end of a word and often changes its part of speech. *Commend* is a verb that means "to praise or admire." When you add the suffix *–able,* you get the adjective *commendable,* which means "deserving of admiration." Identify the verb you in each of these adjectives: *lovable, predictable, imaginable, comparable.* What does each adjective mean?

Learn It Online
Let voice actors bring this play excerpt to life for you.
go.hrw.com H12-217 Go

Reader/Writer Notebook
Use your **RWN** to complete the activities for this selection.

Selection Resources

Unit 1 Resources, on-level practice and assessment, p. 85

Teacher One Stop™, on-level lesson plans and all print resources

Holt Audio Library

Holt Audio Library: Selections and Summaries in Spanish

UA: Differentiating Instruction, graphic organizer, p. 30

UA: Supporting Instruction in Spanish, selection summary

ThinkCentral Online Assessment, Selection Standards Check

ThinkCentral Online Remediation

Preteach

Introducing Vocabulary

- Read aloud the Vocabulary words and sample sentences. Then, use this activity to check students' understanding.
- Tell students that these words support the play as allegory. The words *reverence, reckoning,* and *lechery* take on religious and moral connotations.

English for Academic Success

Language Coach

Have students reinforce their understanding of adjectives ending in *–able* by creating sentences containing those words. [*A better outcome can be imagined, so it is "imaginable."*]

Literary Skills Focus

As you read and discuss the selection with students, have them think about the abstract concepts that the characters, events, and settings might represent.

Reading Skills Focus

Give students a copy of the Reading Skills Focus graphic organizer before they read. Tell them to use their responses to answer the questions on the Applying Your Skills page.

Writing Skills Focus

Have students record examples of personification in their **Reader/Writer Notebooks.** Students can use their notes to complete the Writing Skills Focus activity.

Learn It Online
The online version of this selection includes audio support to engage all students and to help struggling readers with reading comprehension and vocabulary.
go.hrw.com H12–217 Go

Teacher Preparation
Selection Plot Summary
God is disappointed by Everyman's focus on earthly life and possessions. God feels that Everyman has lost sight of what is truly important in life. Everyman is told by Death of his impending reckoning with God, when he will be held accountable for his actions on Earth. Everyman, afraid of his reckoning with God, calls on his acquaintances to guide him. At first, they each agree to help until they find out his journey ends in death. In the end, only Good Deeds stays with him to his grave.

Direct Teach

Think About/Talk About
Read with a Purpose Have students read the Read with a Purpose statement. As students read the selection, have them note how Everyman's words, actions, and experiences represent those of all human beings.

Literary Connection
Tell students that because morality plays were performed in public, the script used vernacular language so all members of the audience would understand the play.

Universal Access

English Learners
Have students work with a partner to summarize small portions of text as they read to help them gather the meaning before moving on. Tell students to develop an outline of the story as they decipher each portion of the text. Remind them to refer to their outline as they work through the activities at the end of the selection.

Struggling Readers
To help students understand characterization, model the reading skill of making critical judgments. You might say: "When I read, I can make judgments about the characters. This will help me better understand the story and the author's purpose. For instance, Messenger's opening lines show that his motivation is to gain the audience's attention." Encourage students as they read to ask themselves, "What do I know about the characters? What seems to motivate them in this story?"

MORALITY PLAY

from Everyman

Read with a Purpose
Read to identify how Everyman represents all human beings.

Build Background
Typical of its time period, *Everyman* is written mainly in rhyming couplets, and the stage directions are much simpler than those of modern plays. The emphasis is not on action as much as it is on the speeches and dialogues of the play.

Characters

Messenger
God
Death
Everyman
Fellowship
Kindred
Cousin
Goods
Good Deeds
Knowledge
Confession
Beauty
Strength
Discretion
Five-Wits
Angel
Doctor

Here beginneth a treatise how the High Father of Heaven sendeth Death to summon every creature to come and give account of their lives in this world, and is in manner of a moral play.

[*Enter* MESSENGER.]

Messenger.
I pray you all give your audience,
And hear this matter with reverence,
By figure a moral play.
The *Summoning of Everyman* called it is,
That of our lives and ending shows
How transitory we be all day.
The matter is wonder precious,
But the intent of it is more gracious

Vocabulary **reverence** (REHV uhr uhns) *n.:* feeling of great respect and awe.
transitory (TRAN suh tawr ee) *adj.:* impermanent.

Think About/Talk About

Extend the Discussion

Paraphrasing In the first line of dialogue, what does Messenger mean by "I pray you all give your audience"? ***Possible response:*** *He means he hopes the audience will pay close attention to what they are about to hear.*

Determining Author's Purpose
What was the author's purpose in having a messenger appear at the beginning of the play? ***Possible response:*** *The writer wanted to clearly state the intention of the play—to morally educate the listeners—and to draw in their full attention from the beginning.*

Vocabulary: Own the Word

- **reverence:** Have students applaud to show how much they would like to be viewed with *reverence* by their peers. ***Possible response:*** *Students applaud loudly because they want to be admired and respected by their peers.*
- **transitory:** Ask students to name things that are *transitory.* ***Possible responses:*** *life; daylight; childhood*

Advanced Learners

Acceleration Have students research other morality plays. Ask them to compare and contrast other medieval morality plays such as *The Castle of Perseverance* and *Condemnation des banquets* with *Everyman*. Discuss the common themes of allegories and how they differ from the types of plays audiences are used to seeing today.

Students with Disabilities

To help students understand the twofold nature of allegory, have them discuss the character of Fellowship in this excerpt. Have them use a dictionary to help them define the word *fellowship.* [*friendly association with people who share one's interests*] Then, have them explain how someone would demonstrate this characteristic. Then, ask them to identify whom and what the character of Fellowship shows companionship to.

Model the Skill

- Provide students with copies of the Reading Skills Focus graphic organizer for "Everyman" (See **Unit 1 Resources**) or ask them to use a piece of their own paper.
- Model for students how to use the Reading Skills Focus graphic organizer to record critical judgments about characters. Tell students that the actions and words of the character named Messenger have symbolic meaning. Messenger introduced the play by explaining that human life is fleeting, and that sins that seem enjoyable during life cause anguish after death.

Character	My Judgment
Messenger	Alerts the audience that life is fleeting

Guided Practice: Apply

Listen-and-Talk Ask student pairs to discuss the allegorical message in the words of God on pp. 220–221. [*The author is using the character of God to criticize the moral decadence and lack of faith in contemporary medieval society.*] Have students add *God* to the Reading Skills Focus graphic organizer and record their thoughts in the column headed "My Judgment."

Think About/Talk About

Extend the Discussion

Allegory What are "pride, covetise, wrath, and lechery," and why does God mention them in line 37? ***Possible responses:*** *These are four of the seven deadly sins—pride, covetousness, wrath, and lechery. The character of God mentions these as examples of sins that people commit unthinkingly or even regard as "commendable." He wants to show that people have forgotten about living moral lives.*

And sweet to bear away.
The story saith: Man, in the beginning
Look well, and take good heed to the ending,
Be you never so gay.
You think sin in the beginning full sweet,
Which in the end causeth the soul to weep,
When the body lieth in clay.
Here shall you see how fellowship and jollity,
Both strength, pleasure, and beauty,
Will fade from thee as flower in May.
For ye shall hear how our Heaven-King
Calleth Everyman to a general reckoning. **A**
Give audience and hear what he doth say.

[*Exit* MESSENGER.—*Enter* GOD.]

God.

I perceive, here in my majesty,
How that all the creatures be to me unkind,
Living without dread in worldly prosperity.
Of ghostly sight the people be so blind,
Drowned in sin, they know me not for their God.
In worldly riches is all their mind:
They fear not my righteousness, the sharp rod;
My law that I showed, when I for them died
They forget clean, and shedding of my blood red.
I hanged between two, it cannot be denied:
To get them life I suffered to be dead.°
I healed their feet, with thorns hurt was my head.
I could do no more than I did, truly— **B**
And now I see the people do clean forsake me.
They use the seven deadly sins damnable,
As pride, covetise,° wrath, and lechery
Now in the world be made commendable.
And thus they leave of angels the heavenly company.
Every man liveth so after his own pleasure,
And yet of their life they be nothing sure.
I see the more that I them forbear,
The worse they be from year to year:
All that liveth appaireth° fast.

For ye shall hear how our Heaven-King calleth Everyman to a general reckoning.

29–32. when I for them died …I suffered to be dead: God is referring here to the crucifixion of Jesus.

37. covetise: avarice.

44. appaireth: degenerates.

A **Literary Focus** **Allegory** What does the character Everyman symbolize?

B **Reading Focus** **Making Critical Judgments** Why does God sound frustrated?

Vocabulary **reckoning** (REHK uh nihng) *n.:* calculation; accounting.
lechery (LEHCH uhr ee) *n.:* indulgence in lust.
commendable (kuh MEHN duh buhl) *adj.:* deserving of admiration.

Reaching Reluctant Readers

Have students discuss in small groups their opinions of the character Everyman. Pose the following questions to get them started: "If you were in Everyman's situation, who would you turn to first? Why? What do you think this person's reaction would be if he or she found out you were faced with death? How are the people you would turn to like, or unlike, the allegorical characters in the play?" Encourage students to explain their points of view and compare and contrast their thoughts with those of other group members.

Therefore I will, in all the haste,
Have a reckoning of every man's person. **C**
For, and I leave the people thus alone
In their life and wicked tempests,
Verily they will become much worse than beasts;
For now one would by envy another up eat.
Charity do they all clean forgeet.
I hoped well that every man
In my glory should make his mansion,
And thereto I had them all elect.
But now I see, like traitors deject,
They thank me not for the pleasure that I to them meant,
Nor yet for their being that I them have lent.
I proffered the people great multitude of mercy,
And few there be that asketh it heartily.
They be so cumbered° with worldly riches
That needs on them I must do justice—
On every man living without fear.
Where art thou, Death, thou mighty messenger?

[*Enter* DEATH.]

Death.
Almighty God, I am here at your will,
Your commandment to fulfill.

God.
Go thou to Everyman,
And show him, in my name,
A pilgrimage he must on him take,
Which he in no wise° may escape;
And that he bring with him a sure reckoning
Without delay or any tarrying.

Death.
Lord, I will in the world go run over all,
And cruelly out-search both great and small.

[*Exit* GOD.]

Everyman will I beset that liveth beastly
Out of God's laws, and dreadeth not folly.
He that loveth riches I will strike with my dart,
His sight to blind, and from heaven to depart
Except that Almsdeeds° be his good friend—
In hell for to dwell, world without end.
Lo, yonder I see Everyman walking:

60. cumbered: encumbered.

69. wise: ways.

78. almsdeeds: good deeds.

C **Reading Focus** **Making Critical Judgments** What does God plan to do?

Developing Oral Fluency

Group Activity Have students practice using academic vocabulary with one another in an instructional discussion. Divide students in groups of three or four and have each group brainstorm three or four challenging questions to ask another group. Tell students that the questions should be based on the text of pages 228–229. Approve the questions that students generate before allowing students to present them to another group. Tell students that they can focus on vocabulary as well as details in the play. Encourage students to use words and phrases from the following list: *interpret, express an opinion, paraphrase, predict, define, describe, infer,* and *explain.*

Think About/Talk About

Comprehension

B Reading Focus

Possible response: *God feels that He tried to do all he could to show people the right way to live and guide them to eternal life, including coming to earth as Christ and dying for humanity's sins.*

C Reading Focus

Possible response: *God plans to hold each person accountable for what he or she does.*

Analysis

A Literary Focus

Possible response: *Everyman symbolizes humanity. The author of the play believes that all human beings are eventually called before God to be judged, just as Everyman is.*

Vocabulary: Own the Word

- **reckoning:** Ask students what Everyman might hope for God to say at his final *reckoning.* ***Possible response:*** *He probably hopes that God will say that he [Everyman] has lived a great, honorable life.*
- **lechery:** Draw a word web on the board and write the word *lechery* in the center circle. Have students provide synonymous words and phrases to the web. ***Possible responses:*** *lewdness; carnality; raunchiness; debauchery; lustfulness*
- **commendable:** Remind students that *commendable* means "deserving of admiration." The verb form is *commend* and the noun form is *commendation*. To help students personally connect to the Vocabulary word, ask the following question: "Have you ever received a *commendation*? Have you been *commended* for an accomplishment?"

Model the Skill

- Model for students how to understand the use of **allegory**. Remind students that an allegory is a story in which elements such as characters and settings have a secondary meaning that is more important than what is literally stated in the text. An allegory uses symbols to describe a situation in unusual and vivid terms.
- Read aloud lines 103–112. Explain that Death, sent by God, is inviting Everyman to a journey from which he cannot come back. The allegorical meaning of the journey is death, which is unavoidable and irreversible. Next, Death talks about God's judgment, and about the fact that Everyman will have no support. This serves to give the allegory a religious meaning. According to the Christian religion, people die alone and must take responsibility for their actions before God.

Guided Practice: Apply

Have students read and discuss lines 119–123, in which Everyman says Death has come unexpectedly and then tries to bribe Death to put their journey off. Ask students to think about the allegorical meaning of Everyman's response and share their ideas orally with the class.

Full little he thinketh on my coming; **D**
His mind is on fleshly lusts and his treasure,
And great pain it shall cause him to endure
Before the Lord Heaven-King.

[*Enter* EVERYMAN.]

Everyman, stand still! Whither art thou going
Thus gaily? Hast thou thy Maker forgeet?

Everyman.
Why askest thou?
Why wouldest thou weet?°

Death.
Yea, sir, I will show you:
In great haste I am sent to thee
From God out of his majesty.

Everyman.
What! sent to me?

Death.
Yea, certainly.
Though thou have forgot him here,
He thinketh on thee in the heavenly sphere,
As, ere we depart, thou shalt know.

Everyman.
What desireth God of me?

Death.
That shall I show thee:
A reckoning he will needs have
Without any longer respite.

Everyman.
To give a reckoning longer leisure I crave.
This blind° matter troubleth my wit.

Death.
On thee thou must take a long journey:
Therefore thy book of count with thee thou bring,
For turn again thou cannot by no way.
And look thou be sure of thy reckoning,
For before God thou shalt answer and shew°
Thy many bad deeds and good but a few—
How thou hast spent thy life and in what wise,
Before the Chief Lord of Paradise.
Have ado that we were in that way,°
For weet thou well, thou shalt make none attornay.°

88. Why wouldest thou weet: What do you want?

102. blind: obscure.

107. shew: archaic form of *showed.*

111. Have ado . . . in that way: Let's see about making that journey.

112. For weet . . . none attornay: You know you will have no support.

D **Literary Focus** **Allegory** Everyman is not aware of God's presence. What does this tell us about Everyman's moral state?

Universal Access

EL English Learners

English for Academic Success English learners may have trouble grasping the message of the allegory if they do not recognize the meanings of the character names. As they read through the play, have these students write a key in their notebooks with the character name at left and a more familiar synonym at right (for example, they might write "Friendship" next to "Fellowship"). Allow students to refer to these characters with the more familiar names as they discuss their understanding of the reading.

Struggling Readers

Students may find it difficult to keep up with the shifting dialogue in this play. Have students work in pairs. Each student should read a part aloud, with one student reading the part of Everyman and the other student reading the part of Death. Tell students to read aloud lines 85–102, and then ask them to discuss what they read with their partner.

Everyman.
Full unready I am such reckoning to give.
I know thee not. What messenger art thou?

Death.
I am Death that no man dreadeth,°
For every man I 'rest,° and no man spareth;
For it is God's commandment
That all to me should be obedient.

Everyman.
O Death, thou comest when I had thee least in mind.
In thy power it lieth me to save:
Yet of my good will I give thee, if thou will be kind,
Yea, a thousand pound shalt thou have—
And defer this matter till another day. **E**

Death.
Everyman, it may not be, by no way.
I set nought by gold, silver, nor riches,
Nor by pope, emperor, king, duke, nor princes,
For, and I would receive gifts great,
All the world I might get.
But my custom is clean contrary:
I give thee no respite. Come hence, and not tarry! . . .

Everyman.
O wretched caitiff!° Whither shall I flee
That I might 'scape this endless sorrow?
Now, gentle Death, spare me till tomorrow,
That I may amend me
With good advisement.

Death.
Nay, thereto I will not consent,
Nor no man will I respite,
But to the heart suddenly I shall smite,
Without any advisement. **F**
And now out of thy sight I will me hie:
See thou make thee ready shortly,
For thou mayst say this is the day
That no man living may 'scape away.

[*Exit* DEATH.]

Everyman.
Alas, I may well weep with sighs deep:

115. that no man dreadeth: that dreads no man.
116. 'rest: arrest.

131. caitiff: coward.

E **Literary Focus** **Allegory** Why does Everyman think he can make a deal with Death?

F **Reading Focus** **Making Critical Judgments** Why does Death not permit Everyman to bargain with him?

Think About/Talk About

Comprehension

F Reading Focus

Possible response: *Death does not permit Everyman to bargain with him because Death's task was given to him by God, and no worldly goods can equal the importance of completing God's commands.*

Analysis

D Literary Focus

Possible response: *This tells us that Everyman probably did not consider God when making choices in his life. Religion and morality are not major concerns for him.*

E Literary Focus

Possible response: *Everyman thinks he can make a deal with Death because that is how he is used to handling his everyday problems. Earthly problems can sometimes be solved by spending money; he does not yet realize that money cannot solve this problem.*

Extend the Discussion

Monitoring Your Reading What does Death mean by saying "I give thee no respite" in line 130? ***Possible response:*** *Death is telling Everyman that he will not make an exception for him. Death will make sure Everyman completes his journey as God intended.*

Making Judgments How would this story be different if Everyman were able to convince Death to take his money and leave him alone? ***Possible response:*** *Part of the message of the morality play is that no amount of money can buy escape from death or forgiveness for your sins. If Everyman could convince Death to go away, then the message would be completely different.*

Advanced Learners

Acceleration After reading pp. 222–223, have students compose a modernized, short dialogue between Everyman and Death. Tell students they should include Death's message from God to Everyman and Everyman's response to the message. Ask them to include vivid details to describe Everyman's emotions.

Students with Disabilities

Have students re-read Everyman's lines on pp. 222–223. Ask them to describe his emotions and inner thoughts at certain points of his conversation with Death. Have students express their thoughts using the formula: "In line(s) [xx], Everyman appears to be feeling [adjective] when Death . . ." Give students the following example: "In lines 87–88, Everyman appears to be annoyed when Death stops him and asks where he thinks he is going."

Guided Practice: Apply

Think as a Reader/Writer

Find It in Your Reading Point out to students that Fellowship is another example of the author's use of personification in his writing.

Use It in Your Writing Have students write a short poem or paragraph using personification. Encourage them to use the personification to give a deeper meaning to teach a lesson.

Think About/Talk About

Extend the Discussion

Finding Details Whom does Everyman turn to first for help? ***Possible response:*** *Everyman goes to Fellowship for help.*

Making Predictions How do you think Fellowship will react when he finds out Everyman's journey ends in death? ***Possible response:*** *Fellowship will probably stay with Everyman for a while and then turn away. Even though he cares for Everyman, he will probably not want to give his life up to accompany Everyman to the end of his journey.*

Now have I no manner of company
To help me in my journey and me to keep.
And also my writing is full unready—
How shall I do now for to excuse me?
I would to God I had never be geet!°
To my soul a full great profit it had be.
For now I fear pains huge and great.
The time passeth: Lord, help, that all wrought!
For though I mourn, it availeth nought.
The day passeth and is almost ago:
I wot° not well what for to do.
To whom were I best my complaint to make?
What and I to Fellowship thereof spake,°
And showed him of this sudden chance?
For in him is all mine affiance,°
We have in the world so many a day
Be good friends in sport and play.
I see him yonder, certainly.
I trust that he will bear me company.
Therefore to him will I speak to ease my sorrow.

[*Enter* FELLOWSHIP.]

Well met, good Fellowship, and good morrow!

Fellowship.
Everyman, good morrow, by this day!
Sir, why lookest thou so piteously?
If anything be amiss, I pray thee me say,
That I may help to remedy.

Everyman.
Yea, good Fellowship, yea:
I am in great jeopardy.

Fellowship.
My true friend, show to me your mind.
I will not forsake thee to my life's end
In the way of good company.

Everyman.
That was well spoken, and lovingly!

Fellowship.
Sir, I must needs know your heaviness.
I have pity to see you in any distress.
If any have you wronged, ye shall revenged be,
Though I on the ground be slain for thee,
Though that I know before that I should die.

Everyman.
Verily, Fellowship, gramercy.°

149. geet: born.

155. wot: know.

157. spake: archaic form of *spoke.*

159. affiance: trust.

181. Verily . . . gramercy: Truly . . . thank you.

Developing Oral Fluency

Read a section of dialogue aloud, modeling appropriate expression, tone, and pacing for students.

Whole-Class Activity Choose students to play the parts of Everyman and Fellowship.

- Have the students act out the play, mimicking the tone and expressions they expect Everyman and Fellowship to have.
- Ask other members of the class if they interpreted Everyman and Fellowship's tone differently, and allow students time to explore what these different interpretations might mean for the overall message of the play.

✔ See the **Oral Language Skill Builder** in **UA: Differentiating Instruction.**

Death and Man II (1911) by Egon Schiele (1890–1918).
Museum Leopold, Vienna, Austria.

Analyzing Visuals

Connecting to the Text In what way does this image represent the concept of "Everyman" through form and color?

Fellowship.
Tush! by thy thanks I set not a stree.°
Show me your grief and say no more.

Everyman.
If I my heart should to you break,
And then you to turn your mind fro me,
And would not me comfort when ye hear me speak,
Then should I ten times sorrier be.

Fellowship.
Sir, I say as I will do, indeed.

Everyman.
Then be you a good friend at need.
I have found you true herebefore.

Fellowship.
And so ye shall evermore.
For, in faith, and thou go to hell,
I will not forsake thee by the way.

Everyman.
Ye speak like a good friend. I believe you well.
I shall deserve it, and I may.

Fellowship.
I speak of no deserving, by this day!
For he that will say and nothing do

182. stree: straw.

Think About/Talk About

Extend the Discussion

Finding Details What does Everyman seem to be worrying about in lines 184–187? ***Possible response:*** *Everyman seems to be worrying that Fellowship will turn his back on him once he hears what his problem is.*

Interpreting It takes quite a bit of convincing for Everyman to describe his problem to Fellowship. Why do you think this is so? ***Possible response:*** *Deep down, Everyman knows that Fellowship will betray him. He tries to tell Fellowship how hurt he will be if Fellowship leaves him, but in the end, he knows Fellowship will not be able to keep his promises.*

Cross-Curricular Connection

LITERATURE: The Origin of *Everyman*

Everyman's author is unknown; however, the play was most likely written toward the end of the fifteenth century. Although it is thought to be the translation of a Flemish play, it is also possible that *Everyman* was written first. Historians have verified four versions of the Everyman story from that time period, but two of them are incomplete.

Analyzing Visuals

Connecting to the Text: *The painting represents Death and Man in a very stylized manner. Death and Man resemble each other and carry no characteristic that would identify them. In this painting, Death holds onto the Man in an embrace. This can remind the reader of the play's idea that every man must face death alone, and that death is the only inescapable reality in people's lives.*

Think About/Talk About

Extend the Discussion

Finding Details Why does Fellowship abandon Everyman after promising not to forsake him? ***Possible response:*** *He learns that Everyman had been approached by Death, becomes afraid, and perhaps wants to delay meeting death.*

Speculating Why do you think it is so important for Everyman to have Fellowship with him on his journey? ***Possible response:*** *Everyman is desperate for companionship because he is terrified of where he will end up and needs the supporting presence of a friend.*

Is not worthy with good company to go.
Therefore show me the grief of your mind,
As to your friend most loving and kind.

Everyman.
I shall show you how it is:
Commanded I am to go a journay,
A long way, hard and dangerous,
And give a strait count,° without delay,
Before the high judge Adonai.°
Wherefore I pray you bear me company,
As ye have promised, in this journay.

Fellowship.
That is matter indeed! Promise is duty— **G**
But, and I should take such a voyage on me,
I know it well, it should be to my pain.
Also it maketh me afeard, certain.
But let us take counsel here, as well we can—
For your words would fear° a strong man.

Everyman.
Why, ye said, if I had need,
Ye would me never forsake, quick ne° dead,
Though it were to hell, truly.

Fellowship.
So I said, certainly,
But such pleasures be set aside, the sooth to say.
And also, if we took such a journay,
When should we again come?

Everyman.
Nay, never again, till the day of doom.

Fellowship.
In faith, then will not I come there!
Who hath you these tidings brought?

Everyman.
Indeed, Death was with me here.

Fellowship.
Now by God that all hath bought,°
If Death were the messenger,
For no man that is living today
I will not go that loath journay—
Not for the father that begat me!

Everyman.
Ye promised otherwise, pardie.°

204. strait count: strict account.

205. Adonai: Hebrew name for God.

213. fear: frighten.

215. ne: nor.

225. bought: redeemed.

230. pardie: by God.

When should we again come? Nay, never again, till the day of doom.

G Reading Focus **Making Critical Judgments** What does the statement "promise is duty" mean?

Word-Attack Skills Mini-Lesson

English for Academic Success Write the selection words *Knowledge* and *know* on the board. Tell students that consonants that precede the letter *n* at the beginning of a word are often silent, but in a few instances both the consonant and the *n* are sounded.

Activity Have students identify whether the initial consonant is voiced in the following words. After they complete the activity, ask students, "What general rule can be applied to words that begin with a consonant and the letter *n*?" [*Consonants that precede the letter n are silent except when the consonant is the letter s.*]

1. gnaw [*silent*]
2. snare [*voiced*]
3. pneumonia [*silent*]
4. knelt [*silent*]
5. snore [*voiced*]
6. mnemonic [*silent*]
7. knob [*silent*]
8. gnostic [*silent*]
9. knock [*silent*]
10. snorkeling [*voiced*]

Fellowship.
I wot well I said so, truly.
And yet, if thou wilt eat and drink and make good cheer,
Or haunt to women the lusty company,
I would not forsake you while the day is clear,
Trust me verily! . . .

Everyman.
Whither away, Fellowship? Will thou forsake me?

Fellowship.
Yea, by my fay!° To God I betake thee.

Everyman.
Farewell, good Fellowship! For thee my heart is sore.
Adieu forever—I shall see thee no more.

Fellowship.
In faith, Everyman, farewell now at the ending:
For you I will remember that parting is mourning. . . .
[*Exit* FELLOWSHIP.]

[Kindred, Cousin, and Goods also decline to go with Everyman. Good Deeds offers to help but cannot walk. Good Deeds calls on Knowledge, who offers to go with Everyman and be his guide. Knowledge leads Everyman to Confession. After Everyman confesses his sins and gives penance, Good Deeds is able to walk and accompany Everyman. Then Everyman calls on Discretion, Strength, Beauty, and Five-Wits to help him. On the advice of Five-Wits and Knowledge, Everyman goes to a priest to receive holy sacraments. When Everyman returns, Beauty and Strength depart. Discretion, Five-Wits, Knowledge, and Good Deeds remain.]

Everyman.
I had weened° surer I should you have found.
He that trusteth in his Strength
She him deceiveth at the length.
Both Strength and Beauty forsaketh me—
Yet they promise, me fair and lovingly.

Discretion.
Everyman, I will after Strength be gone:
As for me, I will leave you alone.

Everyman.
Why Discretion, will ye forsake me?

Discretion.
Yea, in faith, I will go from thee.
For when Strength goeth before,
I follow after evermore.

237. fay: faith.

242. weened: supposed.

Think About/Talk About

Comprehension

G Reading Focus

Possible response: *The statement "promise is duty" means that a promise is something you must follow through on.*

Extend the Discussion

Finding Details In what instances would Fellowship have gone on a journey with Everyman? Re-read lines 213–235 to help you with your response. ***Possible response:*** *Fellowship would go with Everyman only if Everyman were on a journey that was fun, such as a journey to get food and drink or to meet women.*

Making Judgments Of the characters who Everyman approaches, who do you think is the best acquaintance to have and why? ***Possible response:*** *I think Knowledge is the best one to have because it is important to have a good understanding of a problem in order to figure it out.*

Think About/Talk About

▶ Extend the Discussion

Finding Details Which character vows to stick by Everyman through death? Which characters turn their backs on him? ***Possible response:*** *Good Deeds promises to stay with Everyman. Discretion and Five-Wits abandon him.*

Symbolism One by one, Everyman's friends leave him to his fate. Think about the order in which the friends appear and then leave Everyman. What is the significance of the order in which they leave him? ***Possible response:*** *Everyman seems to lose his allegorical friends in the same order that people lose certain things in life as they age. He loses fellowship first, then his family, then his possessions, and finally his senses, such as hearing and sight.*

Everyman.
Yet I pray thee, for the love of the Trinity,
Look in my grave once piteously.

Discretion.
Nay, so nigh will I not come.
Farewell everyone!

[*Exit* DISCRETION.]

Everyman.
O all thing faileth save God alone—
Beauty, Strength, and Discretion.
For when Death bloweth his blast
They all run fro me full fast. **H**

Five-Wits. **I**
Everyman, my leave now of thee I take.
I will follow the other, for here I thee forsake.

Everyman.
Alas, then may I wail and weep,
For I took you for my best friend. **J**

Five-Wits.
I will no longer thee keep.
Now farewell, and there an end!

[*Exit* FIVE-WITS.]

Everyman.
O Jesu, help, all hath forsaken me!

Good Deeds.
Nay, Everyman, I will bide with thee:
I will not forsake thee indeed;
Thou shalt find me a good friend at need.

Everyman.
Gramercy, Good Deeds! Now may I true friends see.
They have forsaken me every one—
I loved them better than my Good Deeds alone.
Knowledge, will ye forsake me also?

Knowledge.
Yea, Everyman, when ye to Death shall go,
But not yet, for no manner of danger.

Everyman.
Gramercy, Knowledge, with all my heart!

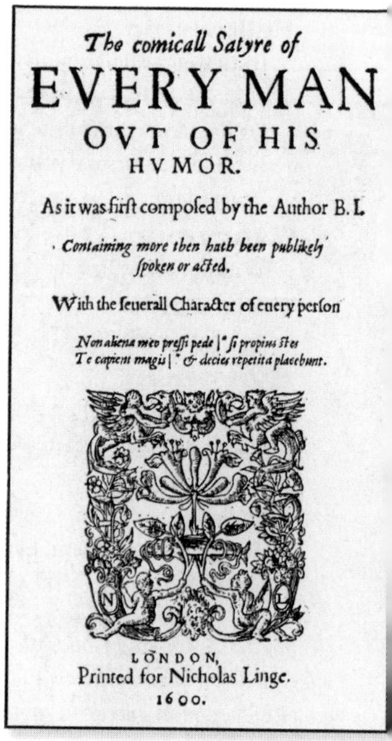
The comicall Satyre of
EVERY MAN
OVT OF HIS
HVMOR.
As it was first composed by the Author B. I.
Containing more then hath been publikely spoken or acted.
With the seuerall Character of euery person.
Non aliena meo pressi pede | *si propius stes
Te capient magis | * & decies repetita placebunt.
LONDON,
Printed for Nicholas Linge.
1600.

Frontispiece of 1600 edition.

H **Reading Focus** **Making Critical Judgments** What change does Everyman begin to experience? What causes this change?

I **Literary Focus** **Allegory** What would you expect a character called Five-Wits to symbolize?

J **Literary Focus** **Allegory** Why might Five-Wits have been Everyman's "best friend"?

Universal Access

EL English Learners

English for Academic Success Often students are so focused on the text at hand that they forget to look at notes in the margins or foot of a page. Point out that words with a margin note are marked by a symbol to denote a clarification or meaning. Remind students to use these margin notes to help them better understand the text as they read.

Struggling Readers

Have students trace Everyman's encounters with other characters and the changes in his character as a result of his encounters. Tell students to construct a chart with two columns, one labeled "Event," and the other labeled "Change." Have students write down three key events or encounters in the play and next to each encounter write what Everyman learned or the change that he went through.

Knowledge.
Nay, yet will I not depart from hence depart
Till I see where ye shall become.°

Everyman.
Methink, alas, that I must be gone
To make my reckoning and my debts pay,
For I see my time is nigh spent away.
Take example, all ye that this do hear or see,
How they that I best loved do forsake me,
Except my Good Deeds that bideth truly.

Good Deeds.
All earthly things is but vanity. (K)
Beauty, Strength, and Discretion do man forsake,
Foolish friends and kinsmen that fair spake—
All fleeth save Good Deeds, and that am I.

Everyman.
Have mercy on me, God most mighty,
And stand by me, thou mother and maid, holy Mary! (L)

Good Deeds.
Fear not: I will speak for thee. (M)

Everyman.
Here I cry God mercy!

Good Deeds.
Short our end, and 'minish° our pain.
Let us go, and never come again.

Everyman.
Into thy hands, Lord, my soul I commend:
Receive it, Lord, that it be not lost.
As thou me boughtest, so me defend,
And save me from the fiend's boast,
That I may appear with that blessed host
That shall be saved at the day of doom.
In manus tuas,° of might's most
Forever *commendo spiritum meum.*°

[Everyman *and* Good Deeds *descend into the grave.*]

Knowledge.
Now hath he suffered that we all shall endure,

279. where ye shall become: what shall become of you.

294. 'minish: lessen.

302. *in manus tuas:* Latin, meaning "into your hands" (speaking to God).
303. *commendo spiritum meum:* Latin, meaning "I commend my spirit."

(K) **Literary Focus** **Allegory** What are "earthly things" here?

(L) **Reading Focus** **Critical Judgments** Why does Everyman ask God to have mercy on him?

(M) **Literary Focus** **Allegory** What does it mean when Good Deeds assures Everyman that he will speak for him?

Think About/Talk About

Comprehension

(H) Reading Focus

Possible response: *He starts to realize that those he thought were his true friends were really not.*

(L) Reading Focus

Possible response: *Everyman asks God to have mercy on him because he feels he has repented.*

Analysis

(I) Literary Focus

Possible response: *I would expect a character called Five-Wits to symbolize Everyman's five senses.*

(J) Literary Focus

Possible response: *Five-Wits may have been Everyman's "best friend" because the five senses accompany us everywhere and allow us to keep in contact with the outside world.*

(K) Literary Focus

Possible response: *Beauty, Strength, and Discretion are the "earthly things."*

(M) Literary Focus

Possible response: *Everyman wants Good Deeds to speak for him so that God will recognize Everyman's virtuous characteristics.*

Advanced Learners

Acceleration Have students discuss the possible purpose of the characters named Kindred, Cousin, and Goods. Ask them to relate these characters to the concepts they symbolize and infer the reasons each of these characters turned Everyman down when Everyman approached them to discuss his journey.

Students with Disabilities

Have students create their own posters advertising a modern showing of the play. Provide students with a sample poster to give them design ideas. Have them include an illustration of a scene from the play or their visual interpretation of the play's themes. Ask students to present their posters to the class.

Think About/Talk About

Comprehension

O Reading Focus

Possible response: *It means that, one cannot go back and make amends after meeting Death; it must be done before one dies.*

Analysis

N Literary Focus

Possible response: *The virtue is Good Deeds.*

Extend the Discussion

Interpreting What does the Doctor mean in line 320 when he says "And forsake Pride, for he deceiveth you in the end"? ***Possible response:*** *The Doctor means that pride is false pride; no amount of pride will help someone on his or her journey at the end of life.*

Speculating What do you think Everyman's afterlife is like? Why? ***Possible response:*** *I think he ended up going to Heaven because the Angel says "Here above thou shalt go" and seems to be rejoicing at Everyman's repentance.*

Monitor Students' Comprehension

Guide the class in answering these comprehension questions.

1. What did God perceive of man at the beginning of the play? [*Man lived without fear of God and thought only of worldly riches.*]
2. When is Good Deeds able to walk with Everyman? [*after Everyman confesses and gives penance*]
3. Where does Everyman most likely end up? [*in Heaven*]

The Good Deeds shall make all sure.
Now hath he made ending,
Methinketh that I hear angels sing
And make great joy and melody
Where Everyman's soul received shall be.

Angel.

[*within*] Come, excellent elect spouse to Jesu!°
Here above thou shalt go
Because of thy singular virtue. (N)
Now the soul is taken the body fro,
Thy reckoning is crystal clear:
Now shalt thou into the heavenly sphere—
Unto the which all ye shall come
That liveth well before the day of doom.

[*Enter* DOCTOR.]

Doctor.

This memorial men may have in mind:
Ye hearers, take it of worth, old and young,
And forsake Pride, for he deceiveth you in the end.
And remember Beauty, Five-Wits, Strength, and Discretion,
They all at the last do Everyman forsake,
Save his Good Deeds there doth he take—
But beware, for and they be small,
Before God he hath no help at all—
None excuse may be there for Everyman.
Alas, how shall he do than?
For after death amends may no man make, (O)
For then mercy and pity doth him forsake.
If his reckoning be not clear when he doth come,
God will say, *"Ite, maledicti, in ignem eternum!"*°
And he that hath his account whole and sound,
High in heaven he shall be crowned,
Unto which place God bring us all thither,
That we may live body and soul togither.
Thereto help, the Trinity!
Amen, say ye, for saint charity.

(N) **Literary Focus** **Allegory** What is the singular virtue to which the Angel refers?

(O) **Reading Focus** **Making Critical Judgments** What might it mean that "after death amends may no man make"?

310. elect . . . Jesu!: the soul.

And forsake Pride, for he deceiveth you in the end.

331. *Ite, maledicti, in ignem eternum:* Latin, meaning "Go, cursed ones, into the eternal fire!"

California Standards, p. 231

- **Reading Standard 2.4** Make warranted and reasonable assertions about the author's arguments by using elements of the text to defend and clarify interpretations.
- **Reading Standard 3.1** Analyze characteristics of subgenres (e.g., satire, parody, allegory, pastoral) that are used in poetry, prose, plays, novels, short stories, essays, and other basic genres.
- **Grades 9–10 Review Reading Standard 3.4** Determine characters' traits by what the characters say about themselves in narration, dialogue, dramatic monologue, and soliloquy.
- **Writing Standard 1.2** Use point of view, characterization, style (e.g., use of irony), and related elements for specific rhetorical and aesthetic purposes.
- **Writing Standard 2.1e** Make effective use of descriptions of appearances, images, shifting perspectives, and sensory details.

Applying Your Skills

Reading Standard 2.4, 3.1; Grades 9–10 Review
Reading Standard 3.4 (see pages A48–A50)
Writing Standard 1.2, 2.1e (see pages A51–A52)

from Everyman

Literary Response and Analysis

Reading Skills Focus

Quick Check

1. Who sends Death to Everyman?
2. What does Everyman do first after meeting with Death?
3. Who stays with Everyman until he dies?

Read with a Purpose

4. What is the author saying about the nature and fate of every human being?

Reading Skills: Making Critical Judgments

5. When you read, you took note of the characters' actions and made judgments about them. Add another column to your chart. In it, explain the allegorical meaning of each character.

Character	Actions	My Judgment	Allegorical Meaning
Everyman			
Death			
Fellowship	Refuses to go on the journey	Will not risk death for Everyman	

Vocabulary Check

Match each Vocabulary word to its definition.

6. reverence
7. transitory
8. reckoning
9. lechery
10. commendable

a. impermanent
b. deserving of admiration
c. indulgence in lust
d. feeling of great respect and awe
e. calculation; accounting

Literary Skills Focus

Literary Analysis

11. **Evaluate** Why do Strength, Beauty, Discretion, and Five-Wits leave Everyman in the order that they do?
12. **Interpret** What is the reason for Doctor's speech at the end of the play? Why is it significant that the speaker is a doctor? Explain.

Literary Skills: Allegory

13. **Analyze** How does the personification of abstract concepts and qualities help convey the moral lesson of this allegory? Explain.

Literary Skills Review: Characterization

14. **Make Judgments** The process by which the writer reveals the personality of a character is called **characterization**. How is Death characterized in *Everyman*? How is this portrayal similar to or different from your expectations for such a character who represents death?

Writing Skills Focus

Think as a Reader/Writer

Use It in Your Writing As you read, you noted how the author of *Everyman* uses personification to create allegorical meaning. Write a short allegory—just a few paragraphs—in which you **personify** abstract concepts to teach a moral lesson.

What Do You Think Now Is Everyman a hero in this play? Why or why not?

Check for Understanding

Independent Practice

Reading Skills Focus

Possible responses:

1. *God sends Death to Everyman.*
2. *He tries to put Death off, and then goes to Fellowship for help.*
3. *Good Deeds*
4. *The author is saying that after death each person will be held accountable for their actions.*
5. *Students should add the column "Allegorical Meaning" to their graphic organizers.*

Vocabulary Check

6. *d* 7. *a*
8. *e* 9. *c*
10. *b*

Literary Skills Focus

Possible responses:

11. *They leave in the order that a person will lose these things as he or she ages.*
12. *The Doctor's speech acts as a warning for those that may doubt the story of Everyman. It is significant that the speaker is a doctor because people may be more inclined to believe what he has to say.*
13. *Personification helps convey the moral lesson because as we read the play, we can imagine having a meeting with these ideas and think more deeply about how they affect our lives.*
14. *In this play, Death is seen as an ally of God; he is doing God's work. Typically, a character representing death is portrayed as evil or a servant of the devil.*

What Do You Think Now?

When giving their responses, have students cite examples from the play to support their opinion.

Universal Access

Struggling Writers

English for Academic Success Some students may need additional scaffolding to complete the Writing Skills Focus activity. Before they write their allegories, ask students to brainstorm two or more allegorical characters. Tell students that they may borrow some of the characters from "Everyman." Have students write a short description of each character. Remind students that each character should play a role in demonstrating and teaching a moral lesson.

Assess

Unit 1 Resources, Selection Standards Check, p. 88

ThinkCentral Online Assessment, Selection Standards Check

Teacher One Stop™, editable Selection Standards Check

Standards Focus

Objectives

Students will

- utilize various prewriting strategies
- analyze a poem

Preteach

Write with a Purpose Read aloud the essentials of a good poetry analysis to guide students' understanding of this type of writing. Also refer students to the scoring guide on p. 240 for more information on poetry analysis that they can use throughout the workshop.

Direct Teach

Model the Skill

Think as a Reader/Writer Use the professional model on this page and others in the unit to provide examples of the elements of a good poetry analysis. Point out the way the Heaney model explains the significance of form and word choice.

Think About the Model

Possible responses:

1. *The main idea of the second paragraph is that the poem delivers a complex message about death, addressing both its positive and its negative aspects.*
2. *The second paragraph's main idea relates to the thesis by providing examples of language that exemplifies Dylan Thomas's poetic craft.*

Writing Workshop

Literary Analysis: Poetry

Write with a Purpose

Write an essay analyzing a poem. Your **purpose** for writing is to share your analysis and insights about the poem. Your **audience** will be your teacher and classmates and anyone else who is interested in poetry.

Think as a Reader/Writer

In this collection, you have examined poems' literary elements critically and considered how these elements work together. Before you write your **poetry analysis,** read the following excerpt from Seamus Heaney's analysis of Dylan Thomas's poem "Do Not Go Gentle into That Good Night." The poem appears on page 1236.

"Do Not Go Gentle into That Good Night" fulfills its promise precisely because its craft has not lost touch with a suffered world. The villanelle[1] form, turning upon itself, advancing and retiring to and from a resolution, is not just a line-by-line virtuoso performance. Through its repetitions, the father's remoteness—and the remoteness of all fathers—is instantly proclaimed, yet we can also hear, in an almost sobbing counterpoint, the protest of the poet's child-self against the separation. . . .

← Heaney clearly states his **thesis.**

← He explains how the **poem's form** contributes to its **meaning.**

[The poem] is obviously a threshold poem about death, concerned with the reverse of the process which occupied Thomas in "Before I Knocked." In that earlier poem, the body was about to begin what Thomas calls elsewhere its "sensual strut." Here the return journey out of mortality into ghosthood is about to be made, so in fact the recurrent rhymes of the villanelle could as well have been "breath" and "death" or "womb" and "tomb"—but what we have instead are "night" and "light." And the night is a "good night." But, for once, a characteristic verbal tic has become an imaginative strength and not just an irritating cleverness. "Good night" is a pun which risks breaking the decorum of the utterance but which turns out in the end to embody its very complexity and force. The mixture of salutation and farewell in the phrase is a perfect equivalent for the balance between natural grief and the recognition of necessity which pervades the poem as whole.

← Heaney discusses the **ambiguity** of Thomas's "good night."

1. **villanelle:** nineteen-line poem with a strict structure and rhyme scheme.

A Good Poetry Analysis

- demonstrates a comprehensive understanding of the ideas in the poem
- analyzes how literary elements and stylistic devices contribute to the poem's meaning
- supports ideas with detailed references to the poem
- assesses the perceived ambiguities and nuances in the poem
- concludes with an insight that connects the poem to universal themes

See page 240 for a complete scoring guide.

Reader/Writer Notebook

Use your **RWN** to complete the activities for this workshop.

Think About the Professional Model

With a partner, discuss the following questions about the model:

1. What is the main idea of the second paragraph?
2. How does the second paragraph relate to the essay's thesis?

California Standards, pp. 232–240

- **Writing Standard 1.1** Demonstrate an understanding of the elements of discourse (e.g. purpose, speaker, audience, form) when completing narrative, expository, persuasive or descriptive writing assignments.
- **Writing Standard 1.3** Structure ideas and arguments in a sustained persuasive and sophisticated way and support them with precise and relevant examples
- **Writing Standard 1.9** Revise text to highlight the individual voice, improve sentence variety and style, and enhance subtlety of meaning and tone in ways that are consistent with the purpose, audience, and genre.
- **Writing Standard 2.2** Write responses to literature: **a.** Demonstrate a comprehensive understanding of the significant ideas in works or passages. **b.** Analyze the use of imagery, language, universal themes and unique aspects of the text. **c.** Support important ideas and viewpoints through accurate and detailed references to the text and to other works **d.** Demonstrate an understanding of the author's use of stylistic devices and an appreciation of the effects created **e.** Identify and assess the impact of perceived ambiguities, nuances, and complexities within the text.

Writing Workshop Resources

UA: Holt Interactive Writer and Speaker, practice and assessment, p. 37

UA: Differentiating Instruction, modified lesson plans, p. 37

WritingNotes, interactive lesson presentations with activities

GrammarNotes, interactive lesson presentations with activities

Writing Standard 1.1, 1.3, 1.9, 2.2a–e (see pages A51–A52)
Language Conventions Standard 1.1, 1.2, 1.3 (see page A53)

Prewriting

Choose a Poem

To find a suitable poem, re-read poems you have enjoyed in the past, page through this book, or ask others to recommend poems they have found especially memorable or moving. Choose a poem of twelve to twenty-five lines that is complex and rich in meaning—short enough to be manageable, yet deep enough to provide a thoughtful analysis.

Think About Purpose and Audience

As you think about your poetry analysis, keep your purpose and audience in mind. Your **purpose** is to share your insights about the poem you have analyzed with an **audience,** most likely your teacher and classmates. How can you convey your ideas in a way readers will understand and appreciate?

Gather Ideas

Read the poem you have chosen multiple times, including a few times out loud, to discover all its **unique aspects.** Each reading will probably provide you with new insights and better understanding of the poem. The following chart explains the basic **literary elements** you will find in poetry and provides analysis questions for each element:

Literary Elements	Analysis Questions
Speaker is the voice that addresses the reader.	• Who is the speaker? • Is the speaker speaking *to* someone? *about* someone? • Does the speaker narrate a story or describe a scene or emotion?
Stylistic devices are the techniques a writer uses to control language and create effects.	• How does **diction** (language choice) affect the poem? • What **sound devices,** such as **rhythm, rhyme, alliteration,** and **repetition,** does the poet use? What effect do they have on the poem? • Does the poet use **figurative language,** such as **simile** and **metaphor,** to make imaginative comparisions? • What **imagery** does the poet use to appeal to the senses?
Theme is the insight about human life that is revealed in the poem.	• What is the poem's main idea? • Does it examine a universal theme, common problem, or life experience? • Does it reveal anything about human nature?
Tone is the poet's attitude toward the subject, the audience, or a character in the poem.	• What attitude does the poet express (sarcastic, humorous, sad, nostalgic, hostile, sympathetic, lighthearted, angry)? • What words and details convey tone? • Does the tone affect your response to the poem?

Idea Starters

- additional poems by authors in this book
- poems by local poets
- regional poetry from a favorite state or country
- poetry sites on the Internet

Writing Tip

Below are some additional types of figurative language you can analyze in your chosen poem:

Hyperbole uses exaggeration to express strong emotion or to create comic effect: *My heart beat a million beats per second; I could eat a horse.*

Oxymoron combines contradictory, or incongruous, ideas: *tough love; bittersweet; frozen flame; living death.*

Synecdoche uses a part to represent the whole, or vice versa: *a new set of wheels (wheels* represents "car"*); use your head (head* represents "brain"*).*

Your Turn

Get Started Choose a poem, and use the questions on this page to make notes in your **RWN** about its **literary elements.** Your notes will help you plan your literary analysis.

Learn It Online
To see how one writer met all the assignment criteria, see the model poetry analysis online.

go.hrw.com H12-233 Go

Guided Practice: Apply

Choose a Poem

- Have students locate poems in reliable sources such as a textbook or an anthology edited by a respected poet or poetry scholar. Explain to students that poems found in many popular magazines, written by acquaintances, or printed in vanity anthologies (in which the author pays to have work published) may not stand up to serious analysis.
- Have students form groups and brainstorm a checklist with criteria for a good poem. Record students' ideas on the board to create a class checklist. Then, have students use the checklist to help them choose a poem for analysis.

Think About Purpose and Audience

- Have students identify and list audiences who would read their poems and jot down a few notes about the audience's background knowledge of poetry analysis.
- After students have identified potential audiences, ask students to identify their writing purpose and how it would change if the audience changed.

Your Turn

Get Started Give students a few minutes of silence to think before they begin brainstorming. Tell them to highlight parts of the poem that provide answers to the analysis questions and make notes in the margins about what each highlighted phrase communicates to them.

Writing and Research in a Digital Age, interactive lesson presentations with activities

Teacher One Stop™, on-level lesson plans and all print resources

Holt Six Traits for Writing, rubrics, prompts, and sample papers

Language and Sentence Skills Practice

UA: Developmental Language and Sentence Practice

Language Handbook Worksheets, p. 126

Formal Assessment, Progress Monitoring Test 1

ThinkCentral Online Assessment, Writing Workshop Test

ThinkCentral Online Remediation

Holt Online Essay Scoring

Learn It Online
Interactive Writer's Models in the **Interactive Student Edition** provide annotated sample essays along with writing tips and strategies.

go.hrw.com H12-233 Go

Guided Practice: Apply

Create a Thesis Statement

Have students answer the following questions about their poems: Do one or two literary elements stand out as more interesting or significant than others? What overall effect do the elements create? Then, encourage students to use their answers to create a thesis statement for their analysis.

Gather Supporting Evidence

- Remind students that they should write about the one or two most significant elements in the poem. This means that they should focus on the elements that matter most to the poem's overall effect rather than the elements that simply appear most often.
- Have students discuss their poems with a partner. Encourage students to identify the most important literary elements in their poems. Then, have students use their discussion to help them fill out an evidence chart similar to the one on p. 234.

Your Turn

Complete Your Analysis Have students complete the **Your Turn** as independent practice. Students can use graphic organizers to organize their ideas from brainstorming. Encourage students to create several graphic organizers for different ideas and then assess which poetic elements are most worthy of analysis.

Choose a Topic

Once you have an understanding of the significant ideas in the poem and how the literary elements help communicate those ideas, you can decide which of the literary elements are most significant. To determine which elements to include as the **topic** of your analysis, consider these questions:

- What elements are most critical to the poem you chose?
- What elements do you feel dominate the poem?
- What elements best support the author's intentions in writing the poem?

Create a Thesis Statement

Next, write a **thesis statement—**one or two sentences that identify the poem's key elements and summarize your insights about how they work together to create meaning. As you write your thesis statement, remember:

- Your thesis statement is essentially a one- or two-sentence preview of what you are going to examine, discuss, and prove in your poetry analysis.
- Be flexible—your thesis statement will probably change as you write and revise your drafts.

Gather Supporting Evidence

Your analysis must support each of your major points with **textual evidence** from the poem—direct quotations and details from the poem expressed in your own words. You must **elaborate,** or explain thoroughly, how each piece of evidence supports the point you are making. You can add depth to your analysis by elaborating on how the **ambiguities, nuances,** and **complexities** make the poem rich and meaningful.

- **Ambiguities** are words or lines that can be interpreted in more than one way or that have more than one meaning. For example, in the professional model on page 232, Seamus Heaney elaborates on the ambiguity of Dylan Thomas's "good night," which can be either a simple farewell or a very solemn final goodbye.
- **Complexities** result when a poem is rich in meaning and requires some thought to understand or interpret. Heaney points out that Thomas's poem both criticizes fathers for their remoteness and mourns their loss.
- **Nuances** are changes in the tone or meaning of the poem. "Do Not Go Gentle into That Good Night" begins with rage that turns to sorrow and desperation as the speaker turns his attention from the more general *wise, good, wild,* and *grave* men to the specific man—the speaker's dying father.

As you gather your evidence, create a chart like the one below.

Literary Element	Quotation or Detail	Elaboration
1.		
2.		
3.		

Your Turn

Complete Your Analysis Using the instructions on this page, complete your personal analysis of the poem—your ideas about how its elements work together to create meaning. Write your ideas in your **RWN.** You will base your literary analysis on these ideas.

Poetry Analysis Writing Prompts

Students can choose their own poetry analysis idea or use one of the following prompts to write an analysis.

Music Analyze song lyrics that have poetic qualities. Make sure that the lyrics have literary elements, such as ambiguities, nuances, and complexities that will create a thought-provoking analysis.

World Languages If you speak a different language, analyze a poem written in that language as well as its English translation. Discuss any differences you find in the analysis.

Drafting

Organize and Draft Your Analysis

Your essay's focus will help you determine how to organize your ideas.

- If your essay focuses on a single literary element, you may want to use **chronological order,** tracing the development of the element from its first appearance in the poem to its last.
- If your essay focuses on two or more literary elements, you may want to organze them by **order of importance,** discussing the elements from most significant to least, or vice versa.

Use your prewriting notes and the **Writer's Framework** to the right to draft your analysis.

Framework of a Poetry Analysis

Introduction
- Start with an attention-grabbing quotation or bold statement.
- Introduce the poem's title and author.
- State your thesis, including the key elements you will discuss.

Body
- Organize literary elements in chronological order or by order of importance.
- Discuss each literary element.
- Provide textual evidence for each element, and elaborate.

Conclusion
- Restate your thesis.
- Summarize your main points.
- Show how the poem relates to broader themes in life.

Writing Tip

When discussing poetry, use the **literary present tense.** For example, on page 232, Seamus Heaney writes "the father's remoteness . . . **is** instantly proclaimed. . . ." and "what Thomas **calls** elsewhere . . ." Even though Dylan Thomas has been dead for several decades, Heaney uses the present tense to talk about what Thomas continues to do through his writing.

Grammar Link Punctuating Poetry Quotations

Because your poetry analysis will include direct quotations from the poem, follow these guidelines for **quoting poetry.** Look at these examples:

Quoting words or phrases (less than a line): Punctuate as needed in your sentence.

> Thomas repeats the phrase "dying of the light."

Quoting one line: Punctuate the line as needed in your sentence, keeping the original capitalization and punctuation of the line.

> A good example of Thomas's use of assonance is the long *i* sound in "Good men, the last wave by, crying how bright."

Quoting more than one line: Use a slash (/) with a space on both sides to show where one line stops and the next starts.

> Thomas's mixed feelings toward death are present in the poem's last stanza: "And you, my father, there on the sad height, / Curse, bless, me now with your fierce tears, I pray."

Your Turn

Draft Your Poetry Analysis

Using the notes from prewriting and the **Writer's Framework,** create your first draft. Remember to do the following:
- Clearly state your **thesis.**
- Think of **main points** that prove your thesis.
- Support your main points with **evidence** from the poem.
- **Elaborate** on your evidence.

Guided Practice: Apply

Outline Your Analysis

Remind students that their analysis should include an introduction, body, and conclusion. Point out that each literary element mentioned, as well as each example from the text, should support their thesis. If a particular element or quotation does not clearly relate to the thesis, students should question whether it is relevant to the paper.

Grammar Link

For practice, have students write a few sentences incorporating quotations from the poem they are analyzing. Ask them to correctly incorporate:

- a phrase
- one line
- a quotation of more than one line

Warriner's Handbook, Sixth Course, pp. 365–369

Your Turn

Draft Your Poetry Analysis Ask students to complete the **Your Turn** as independent practice. Remind students to use their graphic organizer as they begin writing. Suggest that students use every other line as they write their drafts so they can more easily revise drafts later.

Real Issues, Real Experts

*Holt author **Leila Christenbury** offers strategies for helping students to analyze literature in writing.*

Much of the advice we often give students about analyzing and writing about literature asks them to show closure, to make forceful points about their final conclusions. While this is often appropriate, we can also ask students to take a questioning or exploratory attitude. This more tentative, investigatory posture may help students expand their analysis and complicate—in a good way—their understanding of a text.

In their reading of the literature and also in their analysis and writing, we can ask students to do the following :
- Consider possible alternatives. What could the author have added or deleted? How would this change the meaning?
- Look for repeated patterns and breaks the pattern. What does the repetition or deviation indicate?
- Begin their writing with a question rather than an assertion and keep in mind that the analysis may not so much answer that question as explore it.

Model the Skill

- Using a student draft on a transparency, model how to use the questions, tips, and revision techniques suggested in the chart. You might use a student's poetry analysis or a poetry analysis of your own creation to evaluate and revise using the steps in the chart.
- Ask volunteers to demonstrate using each of the steps on their own poetry analyses.

Peer Review

Before students meet with their partners, remind them to always begin by saying something positive about the draft. Their focus should be to improve weak areas and point out strong ones, not simply to find things that are wrong.

Holt Six Traits for Writing, rubrics, prompts, and sample papers

Peer Review

Review your draft with a peer, using this chart to check that all the contents of a poetry analysis are present and organized logically. Ensure that any suggestions you make about your partner's piece are specific. Ask your partner to clarify any suggestions he or she makes that you do not understand completely.

Evaluating and Revising

All good writers revise to make sure that their words accurately express their ideas and to improve their work. Read the evaluation questions in the left-hand column, and use the tips in the middle column to help you make revisions to your poetry analysis. Then, use the suggested techniques in the right-hand column to make any necessary revisions to your draft.

Poetry Analysis: Guidelines for Content and Organization

Evaluation Question	Tip	Revision Technique
1. Does the introduction engage the reader's interest and introduce the poem?	**Put parentheses around** the engaging opening. **Circle** the title of the poem and the name of the author.	If necessary, **add** an interest-catching opening, such as a provocative quotation or a bold statement. **Add** the name of the poem and its author.
2. Does the introduction include a thesis statement that identifies the main ideas the writer is communicating about the poem?	**Highlight** the thesis statement. **Bracket** the main ideas about the poem.	If needed, **add** a thesis statement that states your main ideas about the poem.
3. Are the major ideas clear? Do they support the thesis?	**Underline** the major ideas. **Draw an arrow** from the major points to the thesis.	**Rewrite** major ideas that are not clearly expressed. **Replace** points that don't support the thesis.
4. Do detailed and accurate references to the text support each idea?	**Draw a wavy line** under each quotation or detail from the poem.	**Add** quotations or details from the poem. **Elaborate** on how the evidence supports the point being made.
5. Is the discussion of literary elements arranged logically?	**Review** the underlined major points to make sure their arrangement is logical.	**Rearrange** major points by order of importance or chronological order.
6. Does the conclusion restate the thesis and make a closing connection about the theme of the poem?	**Highlight** the sentence restating the thesis. **Double-underline** the sentence or sentences connecting the poem to a broader theme.	**Add** a sentence that restates the thesis, or **add** a closing connection, if needed.

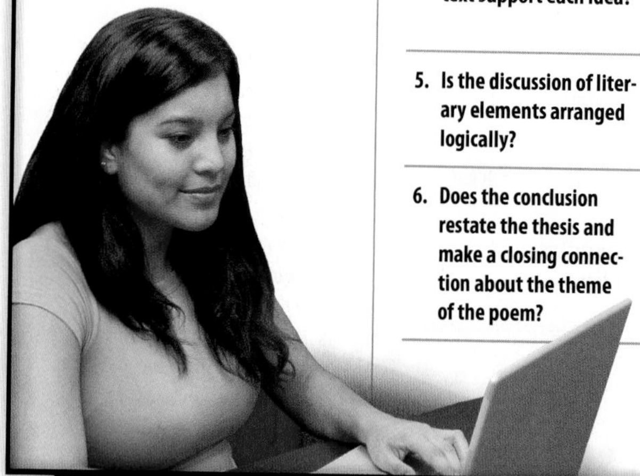

Real Issues, Real Experts

Holt Professional Learning for Language Arts

To watch videos on teaching **revision, grammar,** and **on-demand writing skills** featuring Linda Rief, Amy Benjamin, and Leila Christenbury, go to this page in **ThinkCentral, Teacher Access.**

Universal Access

EL English Learners

Give students the following sentence starters to use in their analyses:

"One technique the poet uses is . . ."

"An example of this technique is . . ."

"The effect of this technique is . . ."

Explain vocabulary as needed.

Read this student's draft with comments on its structure; note the suggestions for how it could be made even stronger. The poem this student analyzes appears on the right.

Missing the Sea
by Derek Walcott

Something removed roars in the ears of this house,
Hangs its drapes windless, stuns mirrors
Till reflections lack substance.

Some sound like the gnashing of windmills ground
To a dead halt;
A deafening absence, a blow.

It hoops this valley, weighs this mountain,
Estranges gesture, pushes this pencil
Through a thick nothing now,

Freights cupboards with silence, folds sour laundry
Like the clothes of the dead left exactly
As the dead behaved by the beloved,

Incredulous, expecting occupancy.

Student Draft

Absence and Loss in "Missing the Sea"

by Robert Scott, Sea View High School

Born in 1930 on the island of Saint Lucia, and later living in Jamaica and Trinidad, the poet Derek Walcott reveals the influence of countless sailors in his poem "Missing the Sea." The speaker laments the terrible emptiness of a house when occupied by a person who loves the freedom of the sea.

The poem's speaker expresses his loss in images of sound or absence of the sound of the wind. The wind is an effective synecdoche (using parts to represent the whole) because it represents attributes associated with the sea: water, salt, and vastness. Although absent from the house, this wind becomes "something removed [that] roars in the ears of this house." Strong verbs ("roars," "hangs," "stuns") describe a wind so strong it "weighs this mountain." Every image is harsh. Even those that emphasize the silence at the same time create a grating noise, "sound like the gnashing of windmills ground / To a dead halt." An oxymoron is also used to illustrate its power: "A deafening absence, a blow." It is this absent force that propels the sailor-poet to write his lament: "pushes this pencil." The present state of the housebound speaker is "thick nothing now," emphasizing the negative and empty conditions through alliteration.

Robert's introduction identifies the **poet** and **poem** but does not have a clear **thesis statement.**

Robert uses **direct quotations** from the poem to support his ideas.

His analysis includes **figurative language: synecdoche** and **oxymoron.**

MINI-LESSON How to Write a Thesis Statement

Although Robert's essay introduces the poet and poem, it does not have a clear **thesis statement.** His thesis statement should connect the literary elements (images of absence and loss) to the meaning of the poem (the expression of the agony of the land-bound sailor). Each of the supporting points in his essay should, then, directly support his thesis.

Robert's Revision of Paragraph 1

The speaker laments the terrible emptiness of a house when occupied by a person who loves the freedom of the sea. ^ In "Missing the Sea," Walcott uses images of absence and loss to express the agony of a shore-bound sailor.

Your Turn

Revise Your Thesis Statement Read your draft, and then ask yourself,

- Could my thesis be stated more clearly?
- Is my thesis supported by the rest of my essay, or does my evidence support a different thesis?

Guided Practice: Apply

Student Draft

Model reading the Student Draft and the annotations in blue, and explain that the yellow highlighting illustrates the student's language choices. Explain that a mini-lesson follows with helpful information about ways to improve this draft as well as their own.

Mini-Lesson

How to Write a Thesis Statement

- Explain that the student writer has revised his opening paragraph by creating a thesis statement that summarizes the point he intends to prove. Ask students to comment on the clarity of this statement.
- Suggest that students share their thesis statement with a partner to inquire whether the main points are understandable and explicit.

Your Turn

Revise Your Thesis Statement As students complete the **Your Turn,** tell them to find two pieces of evidence in their compositions that support the thesis. If they cannot find two such pieces of evidence, tell them to think about whether their paper actually supports and develops a different thesis and to revise the thesis, if necessary.

Struggling Writers

After students have written their thesis statement for their analysis, have them trade their statements with a partner. Have students evaluate their partner's thesis statement. Ask students to make sure the statement connects the literary elements to the meaning of the poem. Encourage students to give their partner feedback about how they might be able to improve their statement. Students may refer to the revision of the Student Draft on p. 237.

Students with Disabilities

Allow students to create a chart instead of paragraphs for their analysis. The chart should have columns labeled "Literary Element," "Examples," and "Effect." Have the students explain the chart in an oral presentation to the class or to a small group.

Guided Practice: Apply

Student Draft

- Explain that the Student Draft is continued and completed on this page. Again the draft is annotated and highlighted for the students.
- Read the draft and annotations aloud and discuss.

Mini-Lesson

How to Conclude an Analysis

- Tell students to make sure their analysis end with some insight that readers can apply to future reading or to their own lives.
- Explain to students that offering an insight at the end of a composition helps readers understand the composition's purpose.

Your Turn

Conclude Your Analysis As students work with a partner to complete the **Your Turn,** have them think about what insight they should add to their drafts and where it should be placed for maximum effect. Remind them that they should also restate the thesis in different words.

Student Draft *continues*

The essay is arranged **chronologically,** moving from the poem's beginning to its end.

In the last full stanza, Walcott uses the images of objects found in the house (silent cupboards and "sour laundry"), again using synecdoche. The lack of sound is emphasized with the cupboard, and the negative sensory images continue with the laundry.

Instead of a direct quotation, Robert **paraphrases** and **elaborates** on the content of the last stanza.

These domestic images grow even stronger through the simile of the clothes of the dead. The deceased person's clothes are left exactly as in life. So too, the memory of the sea occupies the mind of the speaker, exactly as it did when he lived on the sea. He expects the sound of the wind but is left bereft and incredulous at its absence, just as one would feel looking at the clothes of a loved one who has passed away; the living, remaining person expresses his grief at the sight, just as the poem's speaker expresses his loss. By comparing the absence of the wind to the death of a loved one, Walcott emphasizes the depth of his passion and longing for the sea.

Robert's analysis ends without an effective **conclusion.**

MINI-LESSON How to Conclude an Analysis

A poetry analysis must arrive at a definite conclusion, and not simply end with the last line of the poem. At the conclusion, readers should feel as if the analysis is complete, that all the ideas discussed have been tied together neatly. An effective conclusion echoes the thesis statement, summarizes the key points, and leaves readers with a final thought that offers some insight readers can apply to their own experiences or future reading.

Robert concludes his analysis with his examination of the poem's last stanza. To improve his essay, he decides to add another paragraph in order to leave readers with a final thought and a sense of closure.

Robert's Draft of Paragraph 4

By comparing the absence of the wind to the death of a loved one, Walcott emphasizes the depth of his passion and longing for the sea.

Robert's Revision of Paragraph 4

By comparing the absence of the wind to the death of a loved one, Walcott emphasizes the depth of his passion and longing for the sea.

^¶ Although many readers have not experienced a sailor's life, most have suffered the personal loss of something or someone cherished. In "Missing the Sea," Derek Walcott uses concrete images and strong figurative language to exemplify the universality of losing what you love most.

Your Turn

Conclude Your Analysis

- Re-read your analysis. Do you have an effective closing paragraph?
- Does your conclusion address the thesis and leave the reader with an insight and a new perspective?

Universal Access

EL English Learners

English for Academic Success Introduce students to vocabulary and phrases that will help them conclude their composition. Suggest that students consider the following transitions for use in their compositions:

- therefore
- in contrast
- despite the fact
- contrary to the belief
- consequently

AAVE Students Who Use African American Vernacular English

English for Academic Success Point out the fourth paragraph of the Student Draft on p. 238 that begins "These domestic images." Ask students to record some of the verbs in the paragraph in their **Reader/Writer Notebooks:** *grow, are, occupies, expects, expresses.* Tell students that the writer of the draft is using the literary present. Explain to students that one helpful definition of literature is that it is "news that stays news," that is,

Proofreading and Publishing

Proofread

You have worked hard to express your literary insights. Now you need to **proofread,** or **edit,** your final draft one last time before you make your final copy.

> **Grammar Link Using Quotation Marks**
>
> Always use **quotation marks** to enclose direct quotations. Many of the quotations in your poetry analysis will be only parts, or fragments, of a line or sentence. If the quotation is obviously a fragment, it can begin with a lowercase letter.
>
> In the last full stanza, Walcott uses the images of objects found in the house (silent cupboards and "sour laundry"), again using synecdoche.
>
> If the quoted fragment is at the end of the sentence in which it appears, the end punctuation for the sentence is often inside the closing quotation mark, as shown in this example:
>
> An oxymoron is also used to illustrate its power: "A deafening absence, a blow."
>
> Remember these additional rules:
>
> - Commas and periods are placed *inside* the closing quotation mark; question marks and exclamation points are placed *inside* the closing quotation mark only if the quotation is a question or an exclamation.
> - Semicolons, colons, and dashes are placed *outside* the closing quotation mark. Question marks and exclamation points are placed *outside* the closing quotation mark if the sentence (not the quotation) is a question or an exclamation.

Publishing

Share the knowledge and insight you have gained from writing your analysis. Here are some ideas for publishing your work:

- Create and distribute a poetry pamphlet. Include graphics, background information, the poem, and your analysis. Before distributing pamphlets on school grounds, obtain approval from your school's administration.
- Recite your poem at a poetry slam, and share your insights about the poem with your audience. For more on **reciting literature,** see page 242.

Reflect on the Process In your **RWN,** write a short response to each of the following questions:

1. How did writing an analysis improve your understanding of the poem?
2. What parts of your analysis will you apply to other poems?
3. How will your literary analysis relate to other kinds of writing?

Proofreading Tip

Ask a classmate to help you by reading your analysis backward, one sentence at a time, making sure that each sentence is structured and punctuated correctly.

Submission Ideas

- Web sites
- scholarly journals
- poetry magazines

Your Turn

Proofread and Publish

Proofread your essay for errors in organization as well as in grammar, usage, and mechanics. As you proofread, note in particular the punctuation of quotations from the poem. Correct any errors you find. Then, publish your essay to share your insights.

Guided Practice: Apply

Proofreading

Integrating with Grammar, Usage, and Mechanics If students make errors in using quotation marks as they are proofreading, send them to the Punctuation chapters in **Warriner's Handbook.**

Grammar Link

- Tell students to read their final drafts and circle all the quotations in their analyses.
- Have students check that each quotation is surrounded by quotation marks, that it is capitalized correctly, and that any end punctuation is inside the quotes.

Publishing

Brainstorm with students additional ways to publish their poetry analyses.

Reflect on the Process

Have students reflect on their writing process as well as their final product. Challenge them to reflect metacognitively about how they can improve and apply what they have learned.

Your Turn

Proofread and Publish Have students highlight or underline the revisions and submit their drafts with their final poetry analyses so that you can make sure they are following the revision guidelines on p. 236.

writing will always offer insight into the human condition and should be written about in the present tense. Have students re-read their analyses. Encourage them to circle the verbs they use in their compositions and make sure these verbs are in their present-tense form.

Advanced Learners

Acceleration Suggest that students use the library or Internet to search for an analysis of their poem in a scholarly journal. Have students compare their analysis to that of a respected scholar and note any similarities or differences in interpretation. Have students imagine they are presenting their analysis to the scholarly writer when constructing their conclusion.

Guided Practice: Apply

Scoring Guide

- Tell students that the best way to understand scoring guides is to use them to score actual writing.
- Distribute a copy of a composition with the student's name removed, and work as a class to evaluate the composition. Ask students to score their own compositions and then write a brief paragraph using the language of the scoring guide to explain the reasons for the score.

Holt Six Traits for Writing, rubrics, prompts, and sample papers

Assess

UA: Holt Interactive Writer and Speaker, literary analysis analytical scales and rubrics, p. 37

ThinkCentral Online Assessment, Writing Workshop Test

Teacher One Stop™, editable Writing Workshop Test

Reteach

ThinkCentral Online Remediation

California Standards, pp. 240–241

- **Writing Standard 1.1** Demonstrate an understanding of the elements of discourse (e.g. purpose, speaker, audience, form) when completing narrative, expository, persuasive or descriptive writing assignments.

Scoring Guide

Use the scoring guide below to evaluate your poetry analysis from the Writing Workshop or your response to the on-demand prompt on the next page.

	Literary Analysis	Organization and Focus	Sentence Structure and Vocabulary	Language Conventions
4	• demonstrates a *thoughtful, comprehensive* grasp of the text.	• accurately and coherently provides *specific* textual details and examples to support the thesis and main ideas. • demonstrates a *clear* understanding of the ambiguities, nuances, and complexities of the text. • demonstrates *thorough* comprehension of the author's use of literary and/or stylistic devices.	• provides a *variety* of sentence types and uses *precise, descriptive* language.	• contains *few, if any, errors* in the conventions of the English language. (Errors are generally first draft in nature.)
3	• demonstrates a *comprehensive* grasp of the text.	• accurately and coherently provides *general* textual details and examples to support the thesis and main ideas. • demonstrates a *general* understanding of the ambiguities, nuances, and complexities of the text. • demonstrates *general* comprehension of the author's use of literary and/or stylistic devices.	• provides a *variety* of sentence types and uses *some descriptive* language.	• may contain *some errors* in the conventions of the English language. (Errors do **not** interfere with the reader's understanding of the essay.)
2	• demonstrates a *limited* grasp of the text.	• provides *few, if any,* textual details and examples to support the thesis and main ideas. • demonstrates *limited* understanding of the ambiguities, nuances, and complexities of the text. • demonstrates *limited* comprehension of the author's use of literary and/or stylistic devices.	• provides *few, if any,* types of sentence types and *basic, predictable* language.	• may contain *several errors* in the conventions of the English language. (Errors **may** interfere with the reader's understanding of the essay.)
1	• demonstrates *minimal* grasp of the text.	• may provide **no** textual details and examples to support the thesis and main ideas. • may demonstrate **no** understanding of the ambiguities, nuances, and complexities of the text. • demonstrates *minimal* or **no** comprehension of the author's use of literary and/or stylistic devices.	• may provide **no** sentence variety and uses *limited* vocabulary.	• may contain *serious errors* in the conventions of the English language. (Errors interfere with the reader's understanding of the essay.)

Poetry Analysis Writing Prompts

Students can use the writing prompt in the Student Edition or one of the following prompts.

- Many poems and other works of literature use an image, such as water or a particular color, as a symbol. Students may choose a symbol in a poem or story and explain how the author uses it and why it is important to the work.
- Suggest to students that they write about the style of a poem or other work of literature. What makes the way the words are presented unusual? What seems to be the reason for the author's style choices, and what is their effect?
- Suggest that students write a composition about the theme of a poem or other work of literature. How does the author present the theme? Students should consider how other elements in the work affect the theme.

Preparing for Timed Writing

Literary Analysis

Writing Standard 1.1, 1.3 , 1.9, 2.2a–e (see pages A48–A50)
Language Conventions Standard 1.1, 1.2, 1.3 (see page A53)

When responding to a literary analysis prompt, use what you have learned from reading, writing your poetry analysis, and studying the scoring guide on page 240. Use the steps below to develop a response to the following prompt.

Writing Prompt
Many pieces of literature feature a villainous character who creates conflict in the world in which he or she resides. Choose one literary villain from your reading. In an essay, explain how the villain's role is critical to the text.

Study the Prompt
Begin by reading the prompt carefully. Read it a second time, noting the requirements specified in the prompt:

Type of writing: essay
Subject: the role of the villain
Text: your choice of literary works that include a villain whose role is critical to the text

Quickly make a list of literary works that you know well that have a villain. Then determine which selection you know best. **Tip:** Spend about five minutes studying the prompt.

Plan Your Response
Once you have decided on a literary work and its villain, ask yourself these questions about his or her role:

- What background information will I need to provide about this villain and this literary work?
- What is the nature of the character's villainy?
- What are the villain's motivations?
- How does his or her evil manifest itself?
- How do the other characters react to the villain?
- What consequences does the villainous behavior create?
- What theme does the author present through the resolution of this character's role?

Make notes as you answer these questions. Focus on one scene in which the answers to your questions are most clear. Include discussion of that scene in your essay. **Tip:** Spend about ten minutes planning your response.

Respond to the Prompt
Start writing by introducing and stating your thesis. Your thesis will be a statement about the villain's role and the theme of the literary work. Then, begin writing down the evidence that led you to your thesis. An effective way to organize your essay is chronologically, following the progression of the villain's actions. Conclude your essay with his or her final scene. As your write, think of the following points:

- Give your reader evidence from the text to support your thesis. Use short quotations if you can recall them, or retell scenes from the text.
- Elaborate on how each piece of evidence supports the thesis.
- Use the villain's final scene to conclude your essay and comment on the story's theme.

Tip: Spend about twenty minutes writing your draft.

Improve Your Response
Revising Look again at the prompt to ensure your essay fulfills the requirements. Have you explained how the villain's role relates to the author's theme? Have you used specific details from the text? Have you included details of the last scene in which the villain appears?

Proofreading Now make sure that your essay is free of errors in grammar, spelling, punctuation, and capitalization. Be certain that your edits are neat and your essay is legible.

Checking your final copy Before you turn in your final copy, read it one more time to catch any errors you may have missed and to make any finishing touches. **Tip:** Spend about five to ten minutes improving your paper.

Standards Focus

Objectives
Students will learn the elements of writing a poetry analysis.

Direct Teach

Study the Prompt
Before students begin writing, encourage them to answer the following questions:

1. What is my time limit?
2. What are the key skills assessed in the scoring guide?
3. Who is my audience?
4. What is my purpose?

Plan Your Response
Remind students that the literary analysis scoring guide emphasizes thoughtful, creative analysis of the work. Tell students that they should ask themselves these questions to evaluate their writing as they work on their drafts: Have I said something new and interesting about the work? Do I explain my ideas clearly?

Improve Your Response
Point out that the scoring guide also emphasizes developing ideas thoroughly. Remind students to focus on supporting any claims they make.

Assess

Use the scoring guide on p. 240 to assess students' compositions.

Universal Access

English Learners
Ask students to highlight with a marker the elements of the work that they discuss in their compositions. Then, ask them to underline the statements that prove what they say about each element. Do they have sufficient evidence for the claims they make?

Struggling Writers
Ask students to review their work and pay attention to the way they use examples. Do they fully explain why each example they use is important? What could be added to make each example's importance clearer to the reader?

Standards Focus

Objectives

Students will deliver an oral response to literature.

Preteach

Speak with a Purpose Ask students to think about a time when they were engaged while someone was delivering a speech. Have them address the following questions and freewrite their responses: What was the situation? Was the subject matter important to you?

Direct Teach

Model the Skill

Adapt Your Analysis

Model for students how to create an introduction that grabs the attention of an audience. You might suggest that students speaking about "The Pardoner's Tale" perform a dramatic reading of a scene or use a familiar English saying to introduce the idea that greed leads only to destruction. For example, "There's an old saying: 'Greed is a permanent slavery.' In 'The Pardoner's Tale,' the three thieves prove that excessive greed can lead to a person's demise."

Guided Practice: Apply

As students plan their introductions, have them search for a quote that connects to their thesis or find a section of text to perform. Have them share their ideas with a partner.

California Standards, pp. 242–243

- **Listening and Speaking Standard 2.3** Deliver oral responses to literature: **a.** Demonstrate a comprehensive understanding of the significant ideas of literary works (e.g., make assertions about the text that are reasonable and supportable). **b.** Analyze the imagery, language, universal themes, and unique aspects of the text through the use of rhetorical strategies (e.g., narration, description, persuasion, exposition, a combination of those strategies). **c.** Support important ideas and viewpoints through accurate and detailed references to the text or to other works. **d.** Demonstrate an awareness of the author's use of stylistic devices and an appreciation of the effects created. **e.** Identify and assess the impact of perceived ambiguities, nuances, and complexities within the text.

Presenting a Literary Analysis

Speak with a Purpose

Adapt your literary analysis as an oral presentation, and share it with your class.

Think as a Reader/Writer When you write, you have to think as a reader and determine how to make your thoughts and ideas clear to your audience. As a speaker, you must also be aware of your audience. When you adapt a piece of writing into an oral presentation, you have to determine how to convey your ideas effectively without simply reading your words out loud.

Reading and writing about poetry probably helped you learn more about that genre. Now, you can share your understanding with your classmates by adapting your essay for an oral presentation.

Adapt Your Analysis

Adapt the Text

Writing your literary analysis was the hard part. Now, with a few basic adaptations to your essay, you can create a dynamic and interesting presentation. The organization of your presentation can be the same as that used in your essay: You just need to add some interesting features to captivate your audience.

Grabbing the attention of your audience is critical. The **introduction** to an oral presentation must be more dramatic than your written introduction. Some of this drama will arise from the way you present and verbalize your introduction, but it is also important to add a few extra touches, such as beginning your introduction with one of the unique aspects of the work you are discussing. When speaking about "The Wife of Bath's Tale," for example, you might mention Geoffrey Chaucer's use of a strong and very liberated woman as his main character. Another way to get your listener's attention is with a dramatic interpretation of lines from the poem. End your introduction with a strong but simple thesis statement that leaves listeners with a clear idea about the poem, the literary elements, and/or the author whose works you plan to discuss.

The **body** of your oral presentation should cover the main points of your essay. Elaborate on the evidence just as you did in your essay. Explain for your listeners the effects of stylistic devices that the authors use, such as imagery. To help listeners understand your analysis, include many lines from the poem. Be sure to add additional explanations of any events or passages that are difficult to understand (**complexities**), have multiple interpretations (**ambiguities**), or show subtle shades of meaning (**nuances**).

The **conclusion** of an oral presentation, like the conclusion of a written work, serves as a wrap-up of your ideas. To leave a lasting impression on your listeners, make your conclusion memorable. You can use a rhetorical question, repetition, or parallelism when restating your thesis. Consider framing your final observation in terms of universal themes. For example, a universal theme in the works of Chaucer and Tolkien is that of good versus evil. To exemplify the points you made, consider ending with a dynamic quotation from the poem.

Reader/Writer Notebook

Use your **RWN** for completing the activities in this workshop.

Resources

UA: Holt Interactive Writer and Speaker, practice and assessment, p. 121

UA: Differentiating Instruction, modified lesson plans, p. 39

Teacher One Stop™, on-level lesson plans and all print resources

Listening and Speaking Standard 2.3a–e (see pages A53–A55)

Rehearse and Deliver Your Analysis

Speak Naturally

To speak effectively, you must sound as natural and as relaxed as possible. Instead of memorizing your presentation, use the following steps to help you speak extemporaneously.

Step 1 Make concise notes on notecards.

Step 2 In your notes, write down key words and phrases about the main points of your analysis.

Step 3 Include reminders of specific points you want to make in your presentation.

Step 4 Carefully copy the quotations and lines from the work you will be presenting, and be certain you can read them.

Step 5 Arrange your notecards in the right order for a smooth presentation.

Polish Your Presentation

Merely standing still and staring straight ahead will not make your presentation effective. Use the following techniques to deliver an engaging presentation.

- **Pronunciation and Enunciation** It is easy to be nervous when speaking to a group, so focus on pronouncing words correctly. Speak clearly (enunciate), and speak at a natural pace so each word is understandable.
- **Emphasis and Pauses** To get your main points across to your audience, change your tone and volume for emphasis. Pausing is also an effective way to emphasize something you have just said. It allows your listeners time to digest a point you made and lends suspense to a point you are about to make.
- **Facial Expressions and Gestures** Change your facial expressions as you deliver your presentation. A blank face is like a monotone speaking tone; it almost guarantees that your audience will tune out. Although many of us do not use hand gestures when speaking casually, in oral presentations, relaxed gestures can help emphasize our words and make the presentation seem more natural. Moving around further helps keep your audience's attention.
- **Eye Contact** Continually make eye contact with members of your audience. Eye contact will engage your listeners and convey that the message you are sharing is one they need to hear.

Rehearse

Rehearse your presentation to practice these techniques and to become thoroughly familiar with the content of your presentation. If possible, present your response to an audience of friends and family and ask them for feedback.

A Good Oral Presentation

- sounds natural and relaxed, not memorized
- is delivered in a natural-sounding voice
- is rehearsed to perfect the content and delivery of the presentation

Speaking Tip

Use standard American English when you deliver your presentation. Avoid slang and colloquialisms in an oral response to literature. Your listeners could misunderstand your language or your message.

Model the Skill

Polish Your Presentation

If students struggle with the concept of using facial expressions and gestures in their speech, explain that they use nonverbal communication in everyday conversations. Take part in a conversation with a volunteer about things you like and dislike.

Guided Practice: Apply

Ask the class to take note of gestures, facial expressions, and body language used during this conversation. Have students find places in their presentation to use nonverbal techniques to communicate their message to their audience.

Teaching Tip

Rehearse and Present Encourage students who are having difficulty to record a dress rehearsal on audiotape or videotape. This will allow those who are anxious about performing to increase their confidence through focused practice, and to evaluate and refine details of their recitation that need further work.

English for Academic Success

Remind students to use formal English when presenting their analysis. Pair students with a proficient speaker who can read over the presentation and point out where the student has used informal English.

Assess

Independent Practice

UA: Holt Interactive Writer and Speaker, Literary Analysis Evaluation Guide, p. 121

Universal Access

English Learners

Give English learners extra time to practice their enunciation and pronunciation.

- After reading through their speech, have students pair up.
- Have students provide a copy of their speech to their partner. Then, have them perform their speech for their partner.
- Listeners should underline the words that the speaker mispronounces or does not enunciate.
- Students should continue to practice their speeches, paying attention to the words their partners underlined.

Struggling Learners

Some students may not yet be ready to present their speeches in front of their classmates. Have each student deliver the speech in front of the entire class, but if it is clear that a student's performance is affected by anxiety or embarrassment, give him or her the option to deliver the speech in front of only you. Combine the two performance grades into one grade that reflects the attempt to speak in front of the class.

Standards Focus

Objectives

Students will compare and contrast works of major literary periods.

Literary Skills Review

Review

If necessary, use the following questions to guide students in their reading before they answer the questions at the end of the review.

Main Idea

What is the main idea that is shared by the poems? ***Possible response:*** *They both are about birds that go to feed on a dead knight.*

Theme

What elegiac theme is shared by the poems? ***Possible response:*** *All glory is bound to pass and be forgotten.*

Major Details

Which details in the poems indicate that the knight has been forgotten? ***Possible response:*** *In both poems, the knight's lady has gone with another man, and his hound dog and hawk are back hunting on their own.*

Test-Taking Tip

Before taking a test, get a full night's rest and a healthy breakfast. If you are tired or hungry during the test, you may be distracted.

California Standards, pp. 244–245

- **Reading Standard 3.7a** Contrast the major literary forms, techniques, and characteristics of the major literary periods (e.g., Homeric Greece, medieval, romantic, neoclassic, modern).

STANDARDS REVIEW

Literary Skills Review

Directions: Read the poems below, and answer the questions that follow.

The Twa Corbies

by **Anonymous**

As I was walking all alane
I heard twa corbies making a mane;°
The tane unto the t'other say,
'Where sall we gang and dine today?'

'—In behint you auld fail dyke,°
I wot° there lies a new-slain Knight;
And naebody kens° that he lies there,
But his hawk, his hound, and lady fair.

'His hound is to the hunting gane,
His hawk to fetch the wild-fowl hame,
His lady's ta'en another mate,
So we may mak our dinner sweet.

'Ye'll sit on his white hause-bane,°
And I'll pick out his bonny blue een:°
Wi' ae lock o' his gowden hair
We'll theek° our nest when it grows bare.

'Mony a one for him makes mane,
But nane sall ken where he is gane;
O'er his white banes, when they are bare,
The wind sall blaw for evermair.'

2. mane: moan.
5. fail dyke: earth bank.
6. wot: know.
7. kens: knows.
13. hause-bane: neckbone.
14. een: eyes.
16. theek: thatch.

Raven doth to raven fly

by **Alexander Pushkin**
translated by **Walter Arndt**

Raven doth to raven fly,
Raven doth to raven cry:
Raven, where is fallen meat?
What shall be the morning's treat?

Raven answers raven thus:
Well I know of meat for us;
On the fallow, by the willow
Lies a knight, a clod his pillow.

Why he died, who dealt the blow,
That his hawk alone can know,
And the sable mare that bore him,
And his bride who rode before him.

But the hawk now sails the air,
And the foe bestrode the mare,
And the bride a wreath is wreathing
For a new love, warm and breathing.

Resources for Skills and Standards Review

Unit 1 Resources, Unit Standards Mastery, Unit Vocabulary Review, p. 94

UA: Differentiating Instruction, below-level Chapter Standards Mastery

Teacher One Stop™, editable Chapter Standards Mastery

Focus on the Standards with CAHSEE Support

Preparing for the SAT and ACT

ThinkCentral Online Assessment, Chapter Standards Mastery

ThinkCentral Online Remediation

Holt Online Essay Scoring

1. In "The Twa Corbies," which of the following *most* helps you realize that the corbies are birds?
   - **A** "I heard twa corbies making a mane."
   - **B** "'Ye'll sit on his white hause-bane."
   - **C** "We'll theek our nest when it grows bare."
   - **D** "So we may mak our dinner sweet."

2. In "The Twa Corbies," the lady reacts to the Knight's death by
   - **A** taking another mate.
   - **B** killing his hawk and hound.
   - **C** becoming grief-stricken.
   - **D** searching for him forever.

3. In "The Twa Corbies," what is the attitude of the corbies toward the dead Knight?
   - **A** They regret that he died so young.
   - **B** They believe he will be remembered forever.
   - **C** They are pleased to make a meal of him.
   - **D** They pity those who are left behind to grieve.

4. What is similar about the first two stanzas of both ballads?
   - **A** The first stanza poses a question, and the second one answers it.
   - **B** Both stanzas are written in dialect.
   - **C** Each stanza has an *abcb* rhyme scheme.
   - **D** The speaker of each stanza is a knight.

5. What does the third stanza of "Raven doth to raven fly" imply about how the knight died?
   - **A** He fell off his horse.
   - **B** He was slain by an enemy.
   - **C** His bride poisoned him.
   - **D** He died in a hunting accident.

6. Unlike "The Twa Corbies," the last stanza of "Raven doth to raven fly" emphasizes
   - **A** the knight's decay.
   - **B** the lady's lack of grief.
   - **C** the corbies' meal.
   - **D** the hound's hunting activities.

7. A theme common to both ballads is
   - **A** the beauty of nature.
   - **B** the peacefulness of death.
   - **C** the importance of friendship.
   - **D** the short memory of survivors.

Timed Writing

8. Briefly contrast the use of details in "The Twa Corbies" and "Raven doth to raven fly." Be sure to support your response with evidence.

Assess

Answers and Explanations

1. ***C*** *Nest defines corbies as "birds."*
2. ***A*** *Ta'en sounds like taken, which is found in A.*
3. ***C*** *The corbies remark how they will eat him and then use his hair for their nests.*
4. ***A*** *Both ask a question in the first stanza, answering it in the second.*
5. ***B*** *The "blow" given to the knight was likely dealt by an enemy.*
6. ***B*** *The last stanza of the poem mentions that the bride is awaiting a new love, which shows that she is not grieving for the knight.*
7. ***D*** *Both ballads mention the knight's lover who has quickly moved on after his death, showcasing the brevity of love.*

Timed Writing

8. *"Raven doth to raven fly" makes a statement about the instability of love, while "The Twa Corbies" focuses on the ease at which the knight is forgotten and left to be eaten by the birds.*

Reteach

go.hrw.com **ThinkCentral Online Remediation**

Word-Attack Skills Mini-Lesson

Review Use the activities below to check students' grasp of the word-attack skills taught in this unit.

Activity Have students assign the label *s* to words in which the *u* is silent and the label *w* to words in which it stands for /w/.

guide [s]	guilty [s]	guy [s]
guess [s]	plague [s]	guardian [s]
acquire [w]	disguise [s]	aquarium [w]

Activity Display these words that appear to be base words with prefixes or suffixes. Have students tell if a word does [D] or does not [DN] sound like a combination of its parts.

1. director — direct + *–or* [DN]
2. tracker — track + *–er* [D]
3. traceable — trace + *–able* [DN]

Activity Ask students to determine in which of these words the *th* is voiceless.

<u>Thane</u>	these	<u>through</u>
<u>length</u>	thou	loathing

Vocabulary Skills Review

Assess

Answers and Explanations

1. **C** *In A, post means "announce." In B and D, post means "position." In C, post means "pole," which is how it is used in the lines from the poem.*
2. **D** *In A, plain means "area." In B and C, plain means "simple." In D, plain means "clear," just like in the lines form the poem.*
3. **B** *In the lines from the poem, gain is used as a noun. In A, C, and D, gain is used as a verb. Gain is used as a noun in B.*
4. **B** *In the lines from the poem, general means "not specialized." In A, general refers to a military rank. In C, general means "miscellaneous." D uses general to mean "usually."*
5. **B** *In the lines from the poem, set means "establish." In C and D, set is used as a noun. In A, set means "harden." In B, set means "fix or establish."*

Academic Vocabulary

6. *c* **7.** *a* **8.** *b*

Reteach

go.hrw.com ThinkCentral Online Remediation

California Standards, p. 246

- **Grades 9–10 Review Reading Standard**
  1.1 Identify and use the literal and figurative meanings of words and understand word derivations.

STANDARDS REVIEW

Grades 9–10 Review Reading Standard 1.1 (see pages A48–A50)

Vocabulary Skills Review

Multiple Meanings **Directions:** Choose the answer in which the italicized word is used in the same way as it is used in the lines from *The Canterbury Tales.*

1. "He stood not silent like a beast or *post,*
But gave his answer with the ringing word."

A The student planned to *post* an ad.
B The soldier would not leave her *post.*
C All that's left of that old barn is a rotted *post.*
D She gladly accepted the *post* when her boss offered it to her.

2. "'But let me briefly make my purpose *plain.*'"

A The wind-swept *plain* stretched far and wide.
B I prefer *plain* yogurt.
C He is not handsome; his face is very *plain.*
D I thought she has made it *plain* that she would be leaving tomorrow.

3. "'I preach for nothing but for greed of *gain.*'"

A The doctor will *gain* nothing but respect for all her charity work.
B Too many crimes have been committed for petty *gain.*
C If I could just *gain* their interest, I know they would hire me.
D We could probably *gain* more speed if we shift gears.

4. "Become our Governor in short, and be
Judge of our tales and *general* referee."

A In the armed forces, a *general* ranks higher than a colonel.
B There is a *general* feeling that we are being too strict.
C He buys his supplies at the *general* store.
D In *general,* the salesperson preferred to work weekends.

5. "And *set* the supper at a certain price."

A Once Mira has *set* her mind on a goal, there is no way to stop her.
B The fine was *set* at five hundred dollars.
C Is there a *set* number of players needed for this game?
D We need help getting this *set* ready for the play.

Academic Vocabulary

Directions: Choose the correct synonym for each Academic Vocabulary word.

6. Emphasis
A sympathy
B antagonism
C stress
D reduction

7. Diverse
A varied
B identical
C separate
D reduced

8. Concept
A order
B idea
C thesis
D contrast

Vocabulary Review

Use this activity to assess whether students have retained the unit Vocabulary. Ask students to choose the sentence from each pair that uses the word correctly.

1. a. *The master's reprisal of his apprentice exposed the apprentice as unfit to be a blacksmith.*
   b. *After being thrown off his horse, the knight sought reprisal by hitting the horse with his whip.* [√]
2. a. *The judge ordered that the prosecutor receive reparation from the defendant for her mistreatment.* [√]
   b. *The defendant's medical condition affected her reparation system, making hard labor dangerous.*
3. a. *The movie scene depicting the bloody battle was loathsome.* [√]
   b. *The loathsome man placed a personals advertisement in the local newspaper.*
4. a. *The infallible hero survived the attack.* [√]
   b. *The destruction caused by the storm was infallible.*
5. a. *The vehemently spider crept towards the fly.*
   b. *The starving wanderer vehemently devoured the berries he found at the edge of the forest.* [√]

STANDARDS REVIEW

Writing Skills Review

Writing Standard 2.2a, 2.2c (see pages A51–A52)

Literary Analysis **Directions:** The following passage is a rough draft. It may contain errors in grammar, punctuation, sentence structure, and organization. Read the passage below, and answer the questions that follow.

Rough Draft

(1) The Anglo-Saxon poem "The Wanderer" laments a rough physical and metaphorical journey through this life, with hope for the next. (2) By telling of his exile wandering the sea, the speaker is expressing his feelings of wandering through life, where everything is fleeting. (3) The greater theme of the poem is obvious in the very first and last lines. (4) The speaker of the poem wanders through his own narrative, beginning and ending in the same place but in the meantime traveling through his memories, disappointments, and desires. (5) He explains that he is alone because all of his friends and family are dead and gone. (6) He must rely on himself in his wanderings but declares that the only one he can really rely on is God.

1. Which sentence should be moved to follow sentence 6 to improve the style of the passage?

A Sentence 2

B Sentence 3

C Sentence 4

D Sentence 5

2. To strengthen support for the main idea, the writer could

A provide a few more sentences describing the speaker's journey.

B include excerpts from the poem that express the speaker's loneliness.

C tell what was his or her favorite part of the poem and why.

D include excerpts from the poem that show both the speaker's loneliness and faith.

3. Which sentence could be added to support the idea in the underlined sentence labeled 3?

A The speaker cements his longing for his kinsmen when he cries, "Alas, you glorious princes! All gone, / Lost in the night, as you never had lived." (lines 95–96)

B The speaker begins by saying that what he wants is grace and mentions God and God's laying waste to the earth throughout the poem.

C When the speaker says, "Fate blows hardest on a bleeding heart," he is expressing his anger at God for allowing all of the speaker's kinsmen to be slaughtered and for sending the speaker to sail aimlessly across the sea.

D The speaker begins with longing for God's grace and mercy and returns to it at the end when he says, "It's good to find your grace / in God, / . . . where rests our every hope." (lines 114–115)

4. Which of the following revisions best improves sentence 2?

A Changing the first comma to a semicolon

B Deleting the second comma

C Making the sentence more concise: "By telling of his exile wandering the sea, the speaker expresses his feeling that life is fleeting."

D Combining sentences 2 and 3 into a single sentence, separated by a semicolon

5. To present this passage best as an oral presentation, the writer should

A pause to emphasize important ideas.

B make eye contact as he or she speaks.

C rehearse thoroughly before presenting the speech.

D do all of the above.

Writing Skills Review

Assess

Answers and Explanations

1. B *Sentence 3 disrupts the order and flow of the paragraph. It discusses a separate theme in the poem. A, C, and D discuss the theme of wandering.*

2. D *Loneliness and faith are mentioned in the analysis, and textual evidence would support the author's claims. A would not strengthen the writer's main idea. B supports only part of the main idea. C is not relevant for the purposes of this assignment.*

3. D *A supports the idea of the speaker being lonely. B supports the speaker's faith. C supports the speaker's anger. D supports the theme emerging at the poem's beginning and end.*

4. C *C is the most clear and concise version of the sentence. A uses the semicolon inappropriately. B and D take away coherence.*

5. D *Eye contact (B) should be made to engage the audience. Rehearsing thoroughly (C) helps increase the speaker's confidence. Pausing (A) is a useful tool while delivering an oral presentation.*

Reteach

go.hrw.com **ThinkCentral Online Remediation**

Application Homework

Song Analysis

Have students use what they have learned in this workshop to analyze a popular or favorite song. Students should obtain a copy of the lyrics of the song but should consider the musical aspect when delving into their analysis. With approval, students can play their song for the class before presenting their song analysis in an oral presentation.

Extension

Relating Poetry to Life

Poems often relate to the hardships and joys in our own lives, which is why many people turn to poetry for inspiration during these times. Have students select a poem that they feel relates to a personal life experience. Students should analyze the poem, incorporating the poem's relevance to their real-life experience into the essay. Evidence to support their thesis should come from the text of the poem and their own personal experience.

California Standards, p. 247

- **Writing Standard 2.2** Write responses to literature: **a.** Demonstrate a comprehensive understanding of the significant ideas in works or passages. **c.** Support important ideas and viewpoints through accurate and detailed references to the text and to other works.

Read On

If students enjoyed the themes and topics explored in this unit, you might recommend these titles for independent reading.

Assessment Options

The following projects can help you evaluate and assess your students' outside work. Videotapes or audiotapes of completed projects may be included in students' portfolios.

Explore Point of View

Drawing inspiration from John Gardner's novel, rewrite a story from the point of view of another character. Consider how a different character may interpret the events of the story. Turn your adaptation into a short story, poem, or play.

Re-create a Medieval Castle

Using the book *The Medieval Castle*, construct a scale model of a medieval castle. Show how the weapons, clothes, food, and lives of medieval castle dwellers were different from today's. Be creative when choosing your materials. Some common household items can be transformed into medieval relics with just a touch of imaginative thinking.

Read On

For Independent Reading

FICTION

Grendel

How does it feel to be the most dreaded monster in the world? In John Gardner's contemporary novel, the ancient tale of *Beowulf* is retold from the perspective of Grendel, who shows there is more to him than his frightening appearance. Through flashbacks and stories wrought with painstaking detail, he chronicles the forces that have shaped his identity and provides insight into the motivation behind his violent actions. After searching for meaning and questioning the heroic values that depend upon his own demise, Grendel still falls in defeat—but with his own ending to tell.

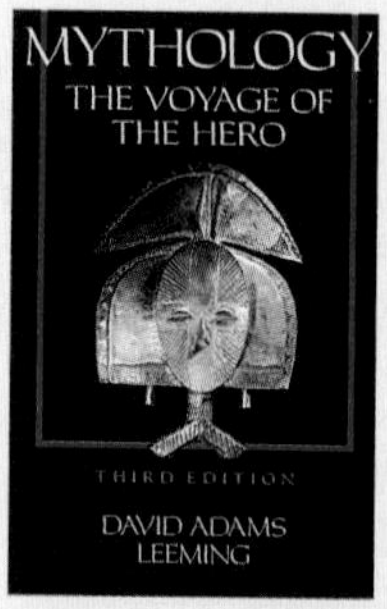

FOLKLORE/MYTHOLOGY

Mythology: The Voyage of the Hero

With narratives from English, Chinese, African, Indian, Indonesian, and Navajo cultures, David Adams Leeming's anthology demonstrates the diversity and universality of mythic tales. The collection, which explores both the hero and the heroine, is arranged by the universal hero's typical rites of passage, such as birth, quest, death, and rebirth. Philosophical and sociological influences on the meaning of myth and hero are considered in Leeming's examination of these enduring tales.

NONFICTION

The Medieval Castle

What was life really like inside a fortress? This book provides an in-depth look at everyday life in peace and war for residents of medieval castles. It also explores the effect of the castle in medieval society and the types of warfare that resulted from it. As Philip Warner describes the weapons, clothes, food, and leisure pastimes of the inhabitants of these magnificent structures, he creates a vivid portait of the medieval castle dwellers themselves, and shows us what they have in common with people today.

DRAMA

Becket

In *The Canterbury Tales*, a motley crew of determined pilgrims travels to the shrine of Saint Thomas à Becket. This French play by Jean Anouilh, translated into English, explores the relationship between Becket and King Henry II, who in 1162 appointed Becket Archbishop of Canterbury. A once cordial relationship between the two men deteriorates when Becket refuses to serve the king over God. Becket finds himself in the midst of fierce opposition, which ultimately drives him to make the sacrifice that earns him his sainthood.

Word Counts and Readabilities of Read On Books

Fiction	Estimated Word Counts	Readability
Grendel	50,700	Easily Accessible
Becket	30,081	Accessible
The Hobbit and *The Lord of the Rings*	112,400	Accessible
Mythology: The Voyage of the Hero	119,400	Accessible
Murder in the Cathedral	13,889	Challenging

FICTION

The Hobbit *and* The Lord of The Rings

J. R. R. Tolkien's *Lord of the Rings* is a three-volume fantasy epic that recounts the Great War of the Ring and the ending of the Third Age of Middle-Earth. The hobbit Frodo is called upon to embark on a dangerous mission: to destroy the One Ring by casting it into Mount Doom. To do so, Frodo and a brave group of companions must travel to the realm of the Dark Lord. *The Hobbit* (precursor to *The Ring* trilogy) follows Bilbo Baggins, Frodo's uncle, on a hazardous quest to recover stolen treasure from a dragon.

NONFICTION

Stonehenge Complete

Stonehenge, a prehistoric ruin of massive stone blocks, stands in a circle on a desolate plain in central southern England. The mysteries of Stonehenge will probably never be solved, but writers, mystics, and scholars continue to speculate about how and why Stonehenge was built and who built it. In this lavishly illustrated book, Christopher Chippindale explores the many theories about builders (Romans, Merlin, Druids) and their possible motivations (religious, astronomical, agricultural) for erecting this ancient monument.

NONFICTION

A Distant Mirror

Life in the Middle Ages included its fair share of harrowing events: the Little Ice Age, which froze the Baltic Sea and shortened the growing season; the bubonic plague, which killed more than one third of the population; and the battle between the English and French at Poitiers, in which the arrows of the English archers were so thick they darkened the sky. There were also the concerns of day-to-day life: what to wear, whom to marry, how to pay taxes, where to speak English instead of French, and when to travel. Barbara Tuchman explains all this and more in great detail.

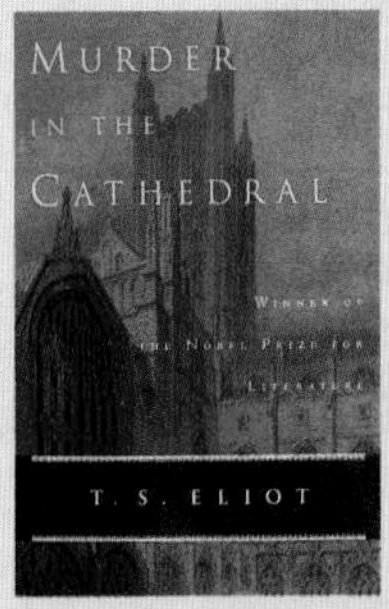

DRAMA

Murder in the Cathedral

Culminating in the brutal assassination of Archbishop Thomas à Becket in Canterbury Cathedral on December 29, 1170, T. S. Eliot's poetic play recounts the internal struggles of Becket in his conflict with King Henry II over the role of the Church in England. Written in the 1930s, as Fascists gained power in Europe, the play seeks to warn its audience about the propensity of political power and ideologies to undermine religious, ethical, and moral principles.

Learn It Online
Explore novels—and find tips for choosing, reading, and studying novels—on *NovelWise*.
go.hrw.com H12-249 Go

Nonfiction	Estimated Word Counts	Readability
The Medieval Castle	60,905	Accessible
Stonehenge Complete	26,508	Accessible
A Distant Mirror	255,819	Accessible

Assessment Options

Write a Myth

Using the mythic tales depicted in *Mythology: The Voyage of the Hero* as a guide, write your own myth. Replicate the themes highlighted in David Adams Leeming's work that pertain to the hero's rites of passage. Give your myth a contemporary twist by focusing on modern rites of passage.

Put On a Play

Be the director of a performance of Jean Anouilh's play *Becket*. Design the set, pick out the costumes, and cast the play. Pick up hints from the play to help with your set design. Research the clothing worn during the play's time period to help with costume design. Choose modern film and television stars to play the parts, but give support for your choices. Compile all your designs and research into a portfolio to present to the class.

Learn It Online
The **NovelWise** mini-site includes instruction on choosing, reading, and analyzing novels; it also contains a catalogue of book summaries, study guides, teaching guides, and PowerPoint presentations.
go.hrw.com H12–249 Go

The Renaissance 1485–1660: A Flourish of Genius

Features highlighted in **yellow** constitute a suggested minimum course of study.

Chapter 3

Selection or Feature	For Independent Reading	Grade-Level Standards
The Renaissance 1485–1660: **Link to Today: Another Renaissance** by Gary Fisher (Accessible, Lexile 1460)		
Literary Skills Focus: Renaissance Poetry by Leila Christenbury		**Reading Standard 3.7:** Analyze world literature.
Analyzing Visuals: Connecting to Renaissance Poetry		**Reading Standard 3.1:** Analyze subgenres **Reading Standard 3.7:** Analyze world literature.
• **Whoso List to Hunt** by Sir Thomas Wyatt (Challenging, Lexile N/A) • **Sonnet 30** (Challenging, Lexile N/A) • **Sonnet 75** (Challenging, Lexile N/A) by Edmund Spenser	**The Sonnets** by William Shakespeare	**Reading Standard 2.4:** Analyze an author's argument. **Reading Standard 3.4:** Analyze figures of speech.
• **The Passionate Shepherd to His Love** by Christopher Marlowe (Accessible, Lexile N/A) • **The Nymph's Reply to the Shepherd** by Sir Walter Raleigh (Accessible, Lexile N/A)	**Collected Poems** by W. H. Auden	**Reading Standard 2.2:** Clarify meaning through structure, repetition, syntax, and word choice. **Reading Standard 3.1:** Analyze subgenres.
• **To the Virgins, to Make Much of Time** by Robert Herrick (Accessible, Lexile N/A) • **To His Coy Mistress** by Andrew Marvell (Accessible, Lexile N/A)	• **Seize the Day** by Saul Bellow • **Gitanjali** by Rabindranath Tagore	**Reading Standard 2.2:** Clarify meaning through structure, repetition, syntax, and word choice. **Reading Standard 3.1:** Analyze subgenres.
• **Song** (Challenging, Lexile N/A) • **A Valediction: Forbidding Mourning** (Challenging, Lexile N/A) • **Meditation 17** (Challenging, Lexile 1060) • **Death be not Proud** by John Donne (Challenging, Lexile N/A)	**The Complete English Poems** by John Donne	**Reading Standard 1.3:** Analogies **Reading Standard 2.2:** Clarify meaning through structure, repetition, syntax, and word choice. **Reading Standard 3.3:** Analyze effects of irony, tone, mood, and style. **Reading Standard 3.1:** Analyze subgenres. **Reading Standard 3.4:** Analyze figures of speech. **Reading Standard 3.9** Analyze philosophical arguments.
Link to Today: *from* **W;t** by Margaret Edson (Accessible, Lexile N/A)		**Reading Standard 3.1:** Analyze subgenres. **Grades 9–10 Review Reading Standard 3.10:** Identify and describe dialogue.
• **On My First Son** (Accessible, Lexile N/A) • **Song: To Celia** (Accessible, Lexile N/A) by Ben Jonson	• **Ariel** by Sylvia Plath • **Death be not Proud** by John Gunther	**Reading Standard 3.1:** Analyze subgenres.
• **Why So Pale and Wan, Fond Lover?** by Sir John Suckling (Accessible, Lexile N/A) • **To Lucasta, on Going to the Wars** (Accessible, Lexile N/A) • **To Althea, from Prison** (Accessible, Lexile N/A) by Richard Lovelace	**Flags of Our Fathers** by James Bradley	**Reading Standard 2.2:** Clarify meaning through structure, repetition, syntax, and word choice. **Reading Standard 3.3:** Analyze effects of irony, tone, mood, and style.

Selection or Feature *continued*	For Independent Reading	Grade-Level Standards
from **the King James Bible** • **Psalm 23** (Accessible, Lexile N/A) • **Psalm 137** (Accessible, Lexile N/A) • **The Parable of the Prodigal Son** (Accessible, Lexile 860)	• **Siddhartha** by Herman Hesse • **Parable of the Sower** by Octavia E. Butler	**Reading Standard 3.1:** Analyze subgenres. **Reading Standard 3.2:** Theme **Reading Standard 3.3:** Analyze effects of irony, tone, mood, and style.
Comparing Texts: **World Literature: Worlds of Wisdom** • **Night** *from the* **Koran** (Accessible, Lexile 1140) • *from* **Philosophy and Spiritual Discipline** (Accessible, Lexile N/A) • **Zen Parables** (Accessible, Lexile 1090) • *from* **The Analects of Confucius** (Accessible, Lexile 1240) • *from the* **Tao Te Ching** by Lao Tzu (Accessible, Lexile 970) • **Taoist Anecdotes** (Accessible, Lexile 940) • **Sayings of Saadi** (Accessible, Lexile 1030) • **African Proverbs** (Accessible, Lexile 650)		**Reading Standard 3.1:** Analyze subgenres. **Reading Standard 3.7:** Analyze world literature. **Writing Standard 2.2:** Write responses to literature.
Reading Skills Focus: **Analyzing Milton's Style** by Kylene Beers		**Reading Standard 3.3:** Analyze effects of irony, tone, mood, and style.
• **Introduction to Paradise Lost: Milton's Epic** • **The Fall of Satan** *from* **Paradise Lost** by John Milton (Accessible, Lexile N/A)	**Murder in the Cathedral** by T. S. Eliot **Dead Souls** by Nikolai Vasilevich Gogol	**Reading Standard 3.3:** Analyze effects of irony, tone, mood, and style. **Reading Standard 3.4:** Analyze figures of speech.
When I consider how my light is spent by John Milton (Challenging, Lexile N/A)		**Reading Standard 2.5:** Analyze philosophical beliefs. **Reading Standard 3.1:** Analyze subgenres.
from **The Pilgrim's Progress** by John Bunyan (Challenging, Lexile 1150)	• **A Potrait of the Artist as a Young Man** by James Joyce • **Vanity Fair** by William Makepeace Thackeray	**Reading Standard 2.5:** Analyze philosophical beliefs. **Reading Standard 3.1:** Analyze subgenres.
Comparing Texts: **Views on Education and Equality** • **Of Studies** by Francis Bacon (Challenging, Lexile 650) • *from* **Female Orations** by Margaret Cavendish, Duchess of Newcastle (Challenging, Lexile 1100) • **Tilbury Speech** by Queen Elizabeth I (Challenging, Lexile 1430)		**Reading Standard 2.6:** Critique arguments. **Writing Standard 2.2:** Write responses to literature. **Writing Standard 2.3:** Write reflective compositions.

Daily and Weekly Support

- **Reader/Writer Notebook**
- **Reading and Writing Transparencies**
- **Family Involvement Activities in Spanish**
- **Language Handbook Worksheets**
- **Holt Virtual File Cabinet for Language Arts**

Assessment Resources

- **Unit 2 Resources**, Chapter 3 Diagnostic Test; Selection Standards Checks, Chapter 3 Standards Mastery
- **Universal Access: Differentiating Instruction**, leveled assessment
- **English-Language Conventions Progress-Monitoring Tests**, Chapters 4–6
- go.hrw.com **ThinkCentral Online Assessment**

Features highlighted in **yellow** constitute a suggested minimum course of study.

Chapter 4

Selection or Feature	For Independent Reading	Grade-Level Standards
Literary Skills Focus: Shakespeare's Sonnets and Plays by Leila Christenbury		**Reading Standard 3.1** Analyze subgenres. **Reading Standard 3.7:** Analyze world literature.
• **Sonnet 18** (Challenging, Lexile N/A) • **Sonnet 29** (Challenging, Lexile N/A) • **Sonnet 30** (Challenging, Lexile N/A) • **Sonnet 71** (Challenging, Lexile N/A) • **Sonnet 73** (Challenging, Lexile N/A) • **Sonnet 116** (Challenging, Lexile N/A) • **Sonnet 130** (Challenging, Lexile N/A) by William Shakespeare	• **Loving Will Shakespeare** by Carolyn Meyer	**Reading Standard 2.2:** Clarify meaning through structure, repetition, syntax, and word choice. **Reading Standard 3.1:** Analyze subgenres.
Reading Skills Focus: Using Questioning to Monitor Reading by Kylene Beers		**Reading Standard 2.2:** Clarify meaning through structure, repetition, syntax, and word choice.
The Tragedy of Macbeth by William Shakespeare (Challenging, Lexile N/A) • **Act I** • **Act II** • **Act III** • **Act IV** • **Act V**		**Reading Standard 2.2:** Clarify meaning through structure, repetition, syntax, and word choice. **Reading Standard 3.1:** Analyze subgenres. **Grades 9–10 Review Reading Standard 3.12** Analyze the way literature is related to themes and issues of its historical period.
Link to Today: *from* **Macbeth: The Graphic Novel** adapted by Arthur Byron and cover illustrated by Tony Leonard Tamai (Challenging, Lexile 590)		**Reading Standard 3.1:** Analyze subgenres.

Mastering the Skills

Selection or Feature	Grade-Level Standards
Writing Workshop: Literary Research: Historical Investigation	**Writing Standard 1.1:** Understand elements of discourse. **Writing Standard 1.3:** Structure and support ideas and arguments . **Writing Standard 1.6:** Develop presentations. **Writing Standard 1.7:** Organize information. **Writing Standard 1.9:** Revise text. **Writing Standard 2.4:** Write historical investigative reports.
Preparing for Timed Writing	**Writing Standard 1.1:** Understanding elements of discourse.
Listening and Speaking Workshop: Presenting a Literary Research Paper	**Listening and Speaking Standard 2.2** Deliver oral reports.
Standards Review: Literary Skills Review Vocabulary Skills Review Writing Skills Review	**Reading Standard 3.7** Contrast literary forms. **Grades 9–10 Review Reading Standard 1.2** Denotative and connotative meanings **Writing Standard 2.4:** Write historical investigation reports.

Daily and Weekly Support

- **Reader/Writer Notebook**
- **Reading and Writing Transparencies**
- **Family Involvement Activities in Spanish**
- **Language Handbook Worksheets**
- **Holt Virtual File Cabinet for Language Arts**

Assessment Resources

- **Unit 2 Resources**, Chapter 4 Diagnostic Test; Selection Standards Checks, Chapter 4 Standards Mastery
- **Universal Access: Differentiating Instruction**, leveled assessment
- **Formal Assessment**, Progress Monitoring Test 2
- **English-Language Conventions Progress-Monitoring Tests**, Chapters 7–8
- **ThinkCentral Online Assessment**

Print Resources for Universal Access

Unit 2 • Chapters 3–4

	On-Level Learners	English Learners	Struggling Readers	Students Who Use African American Vernacular English	Advanced Learners	Students with Disabilities
Unit 2 Resources practice and assessment for selections and features in Chapter 3 and Chapter 4	✔				✔	
Universal Access: Holt Interactive Reader interactive readings for Minimum-Course-of-Study selelctions		✔	✔	✔		✔
Universal Access: Differentiating Instruction modified lesson plans and leveled assessment for Minimum-Course-of-Study selelctions		✔	✔	✔		✔
Universal Access: Resources for Teaching Advanced Students lesson plans for Minimum-Course-of-Study selelctions					✔	

Print Resources for Universal Access

All Chapters

	On-Level Learners	English Learners	Struggling Readers/Writers	Students Who Use African American Vernacular English	Advanced Learners	Students with Disabilities
Universal Access: Supporting Instruction in Spanish translations of selection summaries and key terms		✔				
Universal Access: Holt Interactive Writer and Speaker practice and assessment	✔	✔	✔	✔	✔	✔
Language and Sentence Skills Practice for Warriner's Handbook Chapters 4–8	✔				✔	
Universal Access: Developmental Language and Sentence Skills Practice for Warriner's Handbook Chapters 4–8		✔	✔	✔		✔

Technology Resources

Assessment Resources

Teacher Management Resources

Student Edition Extension Activities

Student Edition Support

Find all of Holt's technology resources at go.hrw.com. Technology resources are also listed at point of use in the Teacher's Edition wrap. Below are our featured components for Unit 2.

Teacher Management Resources

- ThinkCentral, Teacher Access
- **Teacher One Stop™**
- Holt Professional Learning for Language Arts

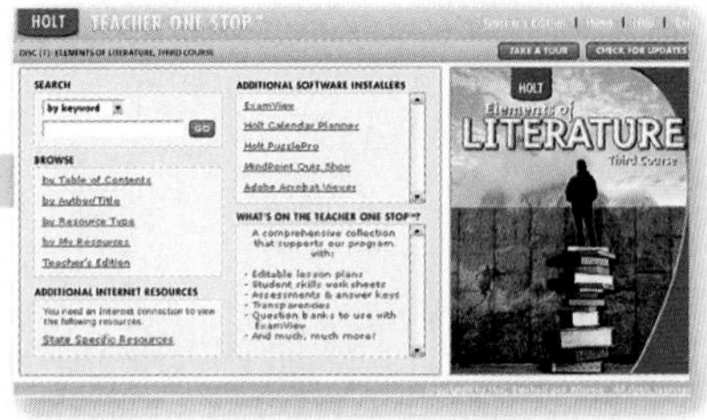

Spotlight on Teacher One Stop™

The Teacher One Stop™ contains all of the print resources that you will need when using *Holt Literature and Language Arts*.

- Find a PDF version of the Teacher's Edition for the times you don't have Internet access available.
- Create fun vocabulary practice activities for your students.

Student Edition Support

- PowerNotes
- **ThinkCentral, Student Access**
- Student One Stop™
- Interactive Reading Workshops
- Interactive Graphic Organizers
- Writers' Lives
- Holt Audio Library
- Holt Audio Library: Selections and Summaries in Spanish

Spotlight on ThinkCentral, Student Access

The interactive Student Edition offers the print book in an online format, and more!

Suggestions for this unit: Encourage English learners to take advantage of the vocabulary help provided at point of use throughout in "The Passionate Shepherd to His Love," "The Fall of Satan" from *Paradise Lost*, and others. Spanish speakers can also access the Spanish summaries of the selections to help them with comprehension.

Student Edition Extension Activities

- Digital Storytelling Mini-Site
- **Literature Links**
- NovelWise Mini-Site
- MediaScope Mini-Site
- WordSharp: An Interactive Vocabulary Tutor
- GrammarNotes
- WritingNotes
- Writing and Research in a Digital Age

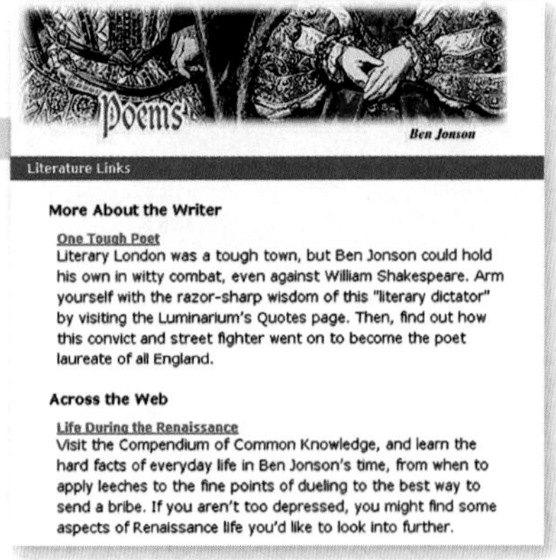

Poems

Ben Jonson

Literature Links

More About the Writer

One Tough Poet

Literary London was a tough town, but Ben Jonson could hold his own in witty combat, even against William Shakespeare. Arm yourself with the razor-sharp wisdom of this "literary dictator" by visiting the Luminarium's Quotes page. Then, find out how this convict and street fighter went on to become the poet laureate of all England.

Across the Web

Life During the Renaissance

Visit the Compendium of Common Knowledge, and learn the hard facts of everyday life in Ben Jonson's time, from when to apply leeches to the fine points of dueling to the best way to send a bribe. If you aren't too depressed, you might find some aspects of Renaissance life you'd like to look into further.

Spotlight on Literature Links

Take your students further with Literature Links that connect to interesting sites across the Internet.

Universal Access: Struggling readers may be motivated by this opportunity to connect the texts they read to biography, history, and science in a twenty-first-century way.

Supported Strands: Literature, Reading

Assessment Resources

- **Holt Online Essay Scoring**
- ThinkCentral Online Remediation
- ThinkCentral Online Assessment

Spotlight on Holt Online Essay Scoring

With online essay scoring, students can practice writing responses to essay prompts—and our system automatically scores them. Students will receive immediate feedback on their essays.

Real Issues, Real Experts

The wrap for these selections includes specific ideas and strategies from *Holt Literature and Language Arts* authors.

From the Authors

For "The Fall of Satan," p. 351

I introduce the selection by having students write the following lines on a large sheet of paper: "The mind is its own place, and in itself / Can make a Heaven of Hell, and a Hell of heaven," and "Better to reign in Hell than serve in Heaven." Then, I ask students to add their questions and opinions around the lines. After a large group discussion, we leave the poster up on wall where it will stay as we read and discuss the selection.

Kylene Beers

For *The Tragedy of Macbeth,* p. 407

Connecting the themes and ideas of the play to contemporary figures and situations will help the text come alive for students. Lead the class in a discussion about corrupt people in positions of power and the ingrained human fascination with deviant behavior. Students who believe that reading the text will be easy should be warned that understanding *Macbeth* takes hard work and dedication.

Carol Jago

Teacher to Teacher

Preteach: Before analyzing "Sonnet 73," I explain features of Shakespeare's sonnets including rhythm, meter, rhyme scheme, and metaphor. In the fall, I ask students to pay attention to the trees as they change from season to season. Students write diamantes reflecting the change of season. Next, students consider how seasonal cycles symbolize life cycles in humanity.

Direct Teach: I guide students through a close reading of "Sonnet 73." Then small groups of students discuss how the poem reflects stages in human life. Students think about nature's choirs vs. human intellect, empty nests vs. middle age, autumn colors vs. fullness of life, physical changes vs. fragility of age, and complacency vs. renewed appreciation of life.

Assess In a timed writing, students explicate "Sonnet 73," identifying and explaining how Shakespeare uses literary devices to comment on the value of life.

Carole Bystram
Rocklin, California

Holt Professional Learning

Visit ThinkCentral, Teacher Access to link to Holt's Professional Learning site for English/Language Arts teachers. This site features:

- **Videos that share the insights of *Holt Literature and Language Arts* program authors and consultants and demonstrate proven classroom strategies with master teachers**
- **Study guides for publications by our authors and consultants**
- **Informative articles and useful Web links**
- **Help in planning your department's professional learning sessions**
- **A handbook for new teachers**

Effective Vocabulary Instruction
with Carol Jago and Kylene Beers

VIDEO PRODUCTS

Strategies for Helping Struggling Readers
with Kylene Beers

Effective Vocabulary Instruction
with Carol Jago and Kylene Beers

Developing Critical Thinking about Literature
with Carol Jago and Deborah Appleman

Teaching Students to Revise, Not Recopy
with Linda Rief

Teaching English Learners
with Robin Scarcella

Using Literature Circles
with Harvey Daniels

Teaching On-Demand Writing Skills
with Leila Christenbury

Managing the Heterogeneous Classroom
with Leila Christenbury and Patrick Schwarz

Teaching Narrative and Expository Texts
with Judith Irvin and Deborah Appleman

Becoming a Tech-Savvy Teacher
with Sara Kajder

Re-engaging the Disengaged Student
with Alfred Tatum

Teaching Grammar in Context
with Amy Benjamin

UNIT 2

Unit Objectives

- Students will read examples of Marlowe's pastorals, Donne's metaphysical poetry, and Shakespeare's sonnets.
- Students will learn how the age of exploration, the printing press, and humanism influenced education, society, religion, and literature.
- Students will read excerpts from the Bible and *Paradise Lost* as examples of religious poetry.
- Students will analyze the characteristics of tragedy in Shakespeare's *Macbeth*.
- At the end of the unit, students will report and present literary research.

Analyzing Visuals

Use the online textbook to project this image for viewing. Explain to students that this painting shows objects representative of the highest achievements of Renaissance learning.

Extension Activity Which arts and disciplines are represented in this painting? ***Possible responses:*** *On the upper shelf, the celestial globe and the other instruments may represent astronomy. The lute on the bottom shelf represents music. The globe on the bottom shelf may represent physics or geography.*

Unit Resources

On Course: Mapping Instruction

Unit 2 Resources

Warriner's Handbook

- Chapter 4, The Clause
- Chapter 5, Agreement
- Chapter 6, Using Pronouns Correctly
- Chapter 7, Clear Reference
- Chapter 8, Using Verbs Correctly

Teacher One Stop™

Formal Assessment, Progress Monitoring Test 2

English-Language Conventions Progress-Monitoring Tests

ThinkCentral Online Assessment

Holt Virtual File Cabinet for Language Arts, grammar, reading, and vocabulary resources

Holt Pronunciation Resources

- Phoneme Sounds and Spellings
- Support for Speakers of African American Vernacular English

ThinkCentral Online Remediation

The French Ambassadors of King Henry II at the Court of the English King Henry VIII (detail) by Hans Holbein the Younger (1497–1543). National Gallery, London.

UNIT 2

THE RENAISSANCE:

A Flourish of Genius

1485–1660

CHAPTER 3
Love, Time, and Death

CHAPTER 4
William Shakespeare

"So much one man can do,
That does both act and know."

—Andrew Marvell

What Do You Think? How do our hearts and minds influence our actions?

Learn It Online
Find out more about this historical period online.
go.hrw.com H12-251 Go

Real Issues, Real Experts: Professional Learning

Spotlight on . . .
Motivation and Vocabulary Videos

Works such as Milton's *Paradise Lost* challenge students learning English as a foreign language. To help them, consider the suggestions you'll find in these videos:

In *Managing the Heterogeneous Classroom*, **Leila Christenbury** and **Patrick Schwarz** provide tips on managing the classroom, flexible grouping, and inclusion of students with special needs.

In *Teaching English Learners*, Holt author **Robin Scarcella** shares proven strategies that will help you advance your students' English language development as well as their understanding of the content you teach.

Each video is accompanied by printable articles, planning materials, Web links, and a training guide for supervisors. For these resources and more, visit **Holt Professional Learning** by going to this page in **ThinkCentral, Teacher Access.**

The Quotation

- Explain to students that this quotation is from "An Horatian Ode upon Cromwell's Return from Ireland," written in 1650 by Andrew Marvell, one of the greatest metaphysical poets. The ode addresses Oliver Cromwell, lord protector of England, Scotland, and Ireland during the Commonwealth.
- Tell students the quote expresses Marvell's admiration for a remarkable leader who firmly believed in religious toleration and was instrumental in restoring England's status as a powerful European force.

Routines for California Classrooms

For ideas on classroom practices and approaches to grouping, see the discussion of routines on pages T34–T37 of this Teacher's Edition.

What Do You Think?

How do our hearts and minds influence our actions?

- Have students draw connections between the unit question, the quotation, and the situation about which they write. Ask students to explain how knowledge of the past can have an effect on actions in the present. Have them give examples.
- Have students write for three to five minutes in their **Reader/Writer Notebooks** about a situation in which their feelings or knowledge of something influenced their behavior or actions.
- Refer students to the time line on the next page to help them think about how historical events changed peoples' views on individual freedom.

Learn It Online
You can introduce some of the topics in this unit using brief videos about the literature of this period.
go.hrw.com H12–251 Go

Direct Teach

Teach the Time Line

Give students five to ten minutes to study the time line. Then, ask the following questions:

- Which two events directly challenged the religious and political authority of the Roman Catholic Church? ***Possible response:*** *Henry VIII's self-appointed position as head of the Church of England and Martin Luther's role in bringing about the Protestant Reformation*
- Which events demonstrate advancements in scientific thought? ***Possible response:*** *Copernicus's theory that planets orbit the sun and Galileo's use of a telescope*
- From what year could literate British individuals be informed of national and world events? ***Possible response:*** *1621, when publication of newspapers began in London*

California Standards, pp. 252–253

- **Reading Standard 3.7** Analyze recognized works of world literature from a variety of authors: **c.** Evaluate the philosophical, political, religious, ethical, and social influences of the historical period that shaped the characters, plots, and settings.

THE RENAISSANCE:

A Flourish of Genius

1485–1660

This time line represents a snapshot of British literary events, British political and social events, and world events from 1485 to 1660. This period is known as the Renaissance—a cultural revolution marked by scientific progress and artistic and literary achievement.

BRITISH LITERARY EVENTS

1485

c. 1516 Thomas More's *Utopia* is published >

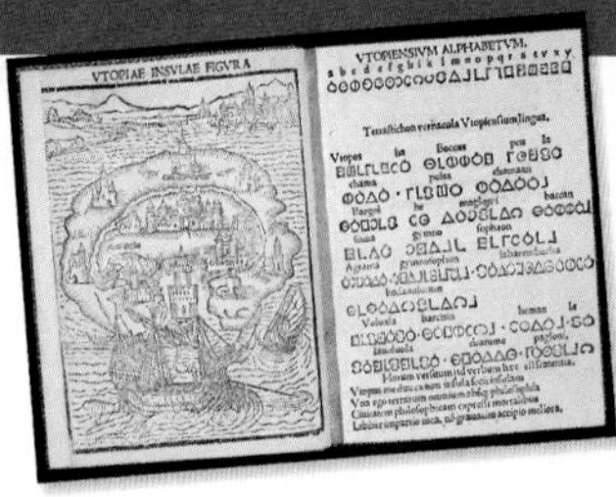

Apud inclyta Basileam (1518), by Ambrosius Holbein.
The New York Public Library.

1530

1538 Book-licensing laws are implemented in England

1557 *Tottel's Miscellany,* a collection of poetry, including poems by Wyatt and Surrey, is published

1564 William Shakespeare is born

Elizabeth I, Armada Jewel by Nicholas Hilliard (1547–1619).
Victoria & Albert Museum, London.

BRITISH POLITICAL AND SOCIAL EVENTS

1485

1485 Richard III is defeated and killed in battle; Henry Tudor becomes King Henry VII

1492 Henry VII rejects all historic rights to French territory

1530

1534 Henry VIII declares himself head of the Church of England through the Act of Supremacy >

1558 Elizabeth I is crowned Queen of England

Henry VIII, from the original returns transcripts and *Valor Ecclesiaticus* (1535).
National Archives, London.

WORLD EVENTS

1485

1492 Columbus reaches the Americas >

1517 Martin Luther begins the Protestant Reformation

1517 First Africans are taken to the Americas as slaves

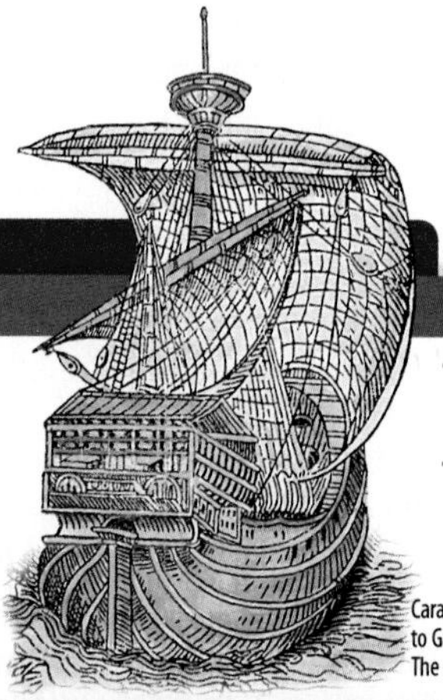

Caravel from the illustrated edition of the Colombus letter to Gabriel Sanchez (1493).
The Granger Collection, NY.

1530

1543 Nicolaus Copernicus issues theory that planets orbit the sun

1572 Montaigne begins to compose the essays

Universal Access

English Learners/Struggling Readers

English for Academic Success Read each section of the time line with students, and clarify the following words and phrases that may impede their understanding.

- **British Literary Events:** *Utopia, licensing, implemented, tragical*
- **British Political and Social Events:** *defeated, supremacy, crowned, charter, assassinate, founded, beheaded, expelled, readmitted, restored*
- **World Events:** *Reformation, slaves, issues, theory, orbits, compose, presides, Pilgrims, expels, establish, settlement*

Reading Standard 3.7c (see pages A48–A50)

Your Turn

With a partner, choose two British literary events from this time line. Then, locate British or world events that might be related to these literary events. In a short paragraph, explain the connection between the historical events and the literary events.

1590 **1620** **1660**

1590 Edmund Spenser publishes first three books of *The Faerie Queene*

1604 Marlowe's *The Tragical History of Doctor Faustus* is published

1605–1606 Shakespeare writes *King Lear* and *Macbeth* ›

1610–1611 John Donne writes *Holy Sonnets*

1611 King James Bible is published

1621 Publication of newspapers begins in London

1658 Milton begins writing *Paradise Lost*

Ian Holm as "King Lear." National Theatre (1997).

1590 **1620** **1660**

1600 Elizabeth I awards a charter to the British East India Company, opening British trade with Asia

1605 Guy Fawkes and others attempt to blow up Parliament and assassinate James I in the failed Gunpowder Plot

1607 First English colony is founded in Jamestown, Virginia

1642–1651 English Civil Wars

1649 Charles I is beheaded

1653–1658 Oliver Cromwell rules England as Lord Protector ›

1655 Jewish people, expelled in 1290, are readmitted to England

1660 Charles II is restored to the throne

Crown of Oliver Cromwell (17th century) by English School. Fitzwilliam Museum, University of Cambridge, UK.

1590 **1620** **1660**

1566–1590 Mogul ruler Akbar presides over a Golden Age in what is now India

1609 Galileo is the first person to study the sky with a telescope ›

1620 Pilgrims on the *Mayflower* land at Plymouth Rock, Massachusetts

1639 Japan expels all Europeans except the Dutch

1649 Taj Mahal, in Agra, India, is completed

1652 Dutch traders establish a settlement in South Africa

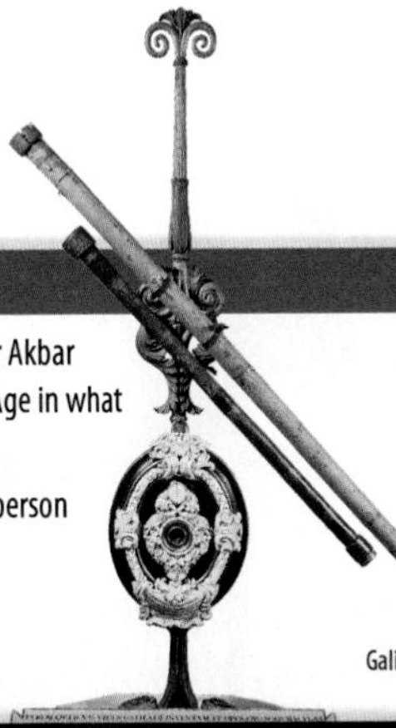

Galileo's Telescope.

Check for Understanding

Your Turn

Have students discuss with a partner how a British or world event might have led to or influenced the two literary events. Then, have partners share their opinions with the rest of the class.

Explore the Time Line Independent Practice

Enrichment The following activity offers options for students to explore the literary, political and social, and world events presented on the time line.

Paired Activity Explain to students that as the corruption in the Roman Catholic Church grew, many scholars, religious figures, and political leaders expressed disapproval.

- Divide the class into pairs. Have each pair read an excerpt of *The Praise of Folly* by Erasmus.
- Have partners come up with answers to the following question as they read: What institution is attacked in several aspects and how?
- As students research their topic, ask them to consider how the unit question—how our hearts and minds influence our actions—links ideas put forth in *The Praise of Folly* and the Protestant Reformation.
- Have groups present their work to the class. Remind them to discuss how the Reformation and Erasmus's writings are related.

Advanced Learners

Enrichment Have students research accounts of their own or someone else's family immigration and create a time line tracing the events leading up to the family's departure from the native country, arrival to America, and events caused by arrival. Ask students to trace the path taken by the family on a world map. Then, have students give a brief oral report on their time lines and maps.

Students with Disabilities

Tell students that the three time lines show events from the years 1485–1660. Explain that students can compare events on the three time lines by reading the page vertically. Model how to connect an event on the time line of British literature to events in British and world history. You might say: "In 1516, Thomas More finished writing *Utopia*. Around that time, the first Africans were forced to go to America as slaves."

Standards Focus

Objectives

Students will

- understand the development of British literature during the Renaissance era
- evaluate the philosophical, political, religious, ethical, and social influences of a historical period

Preteach

Key Concepts

Use the Key Concepts to preview the unit introduction. Each key concept is addressed in a separate section of the essay that relates the concept to both the history and the literature of the times.

Set a Purpose for Reading

- Ask students to identify one piece of information from each key concept that they want to learn more about.
- Have students jot down any concepts, images, or phrases that come to mind when they think of Britain during the Renaissance era. Suggest that students look for information related to these concepts as they read.
- Tell students to record the main ideas and important details from each key concept in their **Reader/Writer Notebooks.**

California Standards, pp. 254–261

- **Reading Standard 2.2** Analyze the way in which clarity of meaning is affected by the patterns of organization, hierarchical structures, repetition of the main ideas, syntax, and word choice in the text.
- **Reading Standard 3.7** Analyze recognized works of world literature from a variety of authors: **b.** Relate literary works and authors to the major themes and issues of their eras. **c.** Evaluate the philosophical, political, religious, ethical, and social influences of the historical period that shaped the characters, plots, and settings.

THE RENAISSANCE: A Flourish of Genius

1485–1660

The Renaissance era in Europe and in England was marked by a change in the way people thought about themselves and the world. No longer content with the fixed religious beliefs of the Middle Ages, people became more involved in expanding their knowledge of history, art, science, and especially the classic texts of ancient Greece and Rome. The Roman Catholic Church was challenged on a number of fronts. By the end of the sixteenth century, the Church had lost its position as the supreme moral and political power in Europe.

KEY CONCEPTS

The Beginnings of Tudor Rule

History of the Times Henry Tudor defeated the Yorkist king Richard III at Bosworth Field and established the Tudor dynasty, which ruled for 118 years. Under Henry Tudor the middle class gained more power, commerce expanded, and the country prospered.

Literature of the Times The invention of the printing press in Germany spread throughout Europe. Literacy increased, and Europe experienced a creative rebirth of the arts.

The Protestant Reformation

History of the Times Henry VIII declared himself head of the English church when the pope refused to annul Henry's marriage to Catherine of Aragon. Great social and religious upheaval swept across England.

Literature of the Times The Renaissance encouraged individual curiosity and creativity. During this time, bold new thoughts, beautiful poetry, and powerful dramatic works emerged.

England's Greatest Monarch

History of the Times Henry VIII was succeeded by his sickly son Edward. His two daughters, Mary and Elizabeth, ultimately changed English history. To this day, Elizabeth I is generally considered England's greatest ruler.

Literature of the Times The Renaissance was a golden age for literature. Poetry and drama flourished alongside religious allegory and philosophical works.

Main gatehouse of Hampton Court Palace, London.

Resources

Unit 2 Resources, on-level instruction, Historical Introduction Study Guide, p. 1

UA: Holt Interactive Reader, Key Concepts and Academic Vocabulary, p. 71

PowerNotes, interactive lesson presentation with activities

Teacher One Stop™, on-level lesson plans and all print resources

Universal Access

EL English Learners/Struggling Readers

English for Academic Success To help students understand the information presented on p. 254 of the Unit Introduction, review the definitions of the following phrases with students.

- **fixed religious beliefs**—"unchangeable religious teaching"
- **challenged on a number of fronts**—"attacked in several points or aspects"
- **upheaval ensued**—"disorder took place as a result"
- **flourished alongside**—"grew in number along with"

Reading Standard 2.2, 3.7b, 3.7c (see pages A48–A50)

UNIT 2 INTRODUCTION

KEY CONCEPT

The Beginnings of Tudor Rule

History of the Times

The transition from the medieval period to the modern period took place primarily during the reign of the Tudors. When the Tudor line eventually ended in 1603, many modern institutions had replaced medieval ones.

Henry Tudor was a Welsh nobleman who seized the throne after the long struggle known as the Wars of the Roses. Once in power in 1485, Henry submitted his claim to Parliament, which granted him the title of king but not by hereditary right. To strengthen his position and place the Tudor line on a secure foundation, Henry married Elizabeth of York, the daughter of Edward IV, and dealt swiftly with the pretenders[1] who claimed a right to the throne.

Aware that he needed the support of the people, Henry acted to ensure peace with foreign powers. He also expanded commerce, giving his support to the English merchant class and reducing the power of the nobles. He awarded offices to men from the middle class who were loyal to him, and guaranteed Tudor law throughout the country.

By the time Henry died in 1509, England had changed considerably. The land was prosperous, the people were moderately united, and the throne was protected. The new king, Henry VIII, would mostly battle with the Church for authority and worry about producing an heir for England.

1. **pretenders:** individuals who claim to be rightful heirs to a position of power, but whose claim is largely denied.

Analyzing Visuals

Connecting to the Text The title of this painting is *The Family of Henry VIII: An Allegory of the Tudor Succession.* Consider that an allegory operates on both a literal level and a symbolic level. What elements in the painting do you think might symbolize Tudor succession?

The Family of Henry VIII: An Allegory of the Tudor Succession (c. 1570–1575) by Lucas de Heere (1534–1584). Oil on panel. National Museum and Gallery of Wales, Cardiff.

Learn It Online
Go online to learn more about this historical period.
go.hrw.com H12-255 Go

Direct Teach

Think About/Talk About

Motivate Tell students that the historical period known as the Renaissance is generally believed to have begun in Italy, in the fourteenth century. As artists, scientists, and musicians were venturing into new realms of discovery and expression, writers in England drew inspiration from their Greek predecessors to write epic tales of heroism and adventure. What might the topics and themes found in British literature during this period tell us about the cultural environment in which they were written?

Analyzing Visuals

Connecting to the Text: *Henry VIII sits enthroned at the center, symbolizing the authority he wielded in his reign. Mary Tudor and Philip II are pictured standing next to an armed soldier, who symbolizes violence and war, while Elizabeth is pictured near figures representing peace and wealth, characteristic of her reign.*

Advanced Learners

Acceleration Explain that the Bible was the first book printed by Johannes Gutenberg using the printing press. Ask students to discuss why this innovation was such an important milestone in the production of books. Then, have students think about the following questions: Why was translating the Bible into English so significant in the political arena? What did it imply about the church's tradition of interpreting the Bible for people?

Students with Disabilities

Have students imagine a world without books, newspapers, magazines, or anything else in print. How would information spread within a nation or across the world? Ask students to picture a class in which students have no books to read from, and silent reading is not an option—everything is read aloud by the teacher or a student. If students want to study a passage, they would have to copy it down word for word from the board. How would the pace of their lessons and the degree of students' interest in the lessons differ?

Learn It Online
For a multimedia introduction to the key concepts covered in this unit, use the **PowerNotes** Unit 2 presentation.
go.hrw.com H12-255 Go

Think About/Talk About

Literature of the Times

Sir Thomas More's *Utopia* analyzes the social, economic, penal, and moral issues of England in dialogue form. These issues include religious discrimination, private ownership, poverty, and social instability. The term *utopia* is derived from the Greek words *ou*, or "not," and *topos*, or "place." Thus, *utopia* can be translated as "no-place land," where social and moral problems are nonexistent.

Comprehension Check

Possible response: *He eliminated other claimants to the throne, weakened the political power and influence of the nobles, secured Tudor law, and sought peace with foreign powers, gaining the people's support.*

Literature of the Times

The fifteenth century was a key period for the growth of literacy in England. William Caxton introduced the printing press to the country in 1485, the same year that Henry Tudor took the throne.

Humanism was a major influence on English literature during this time. This intellectual movement looked not only to the Bible but also to Latin and Greek scholarship for wisdom and knowledge. Humanists combined classical ideals with traditional Christian thought to teach people how to live and rule. The foremost humanist in England was unquestionably Sir Thomas More, who wrote *Utopia* (1516), a famous treatise on human society. Hundreds of writers have imitated or parodied *Utopia*, which has provided us with a useful adjective for describing impractical social schemes: *utopian*. More himself, however, was far from impractical; he rose to the very top of his profession, was knighted, and became one of the king's chief ministers.

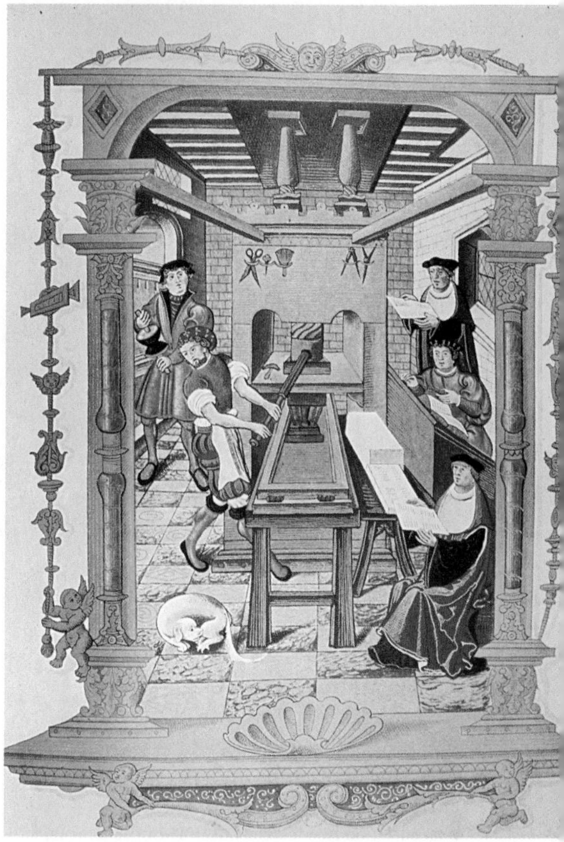

Printing press (16th century).
Bibliothèque Nationale, Paris, France.

Comprehension Check

How did Henry Tudor increase the authority of the monarchy?

Fast Facts

Political and Social Highlights

- The Protestant Reformation begins in England in 1534, when King Henry VIII rejects the authority of the pope in Rome and declares himself head of the English Church.
- In 1553, Mary Tudor becomes queen and restores the pope's power in England.
- Elizabeth I assumes the throne in 1558 and reestablishes the Church of England.
- In 1588, the Royal Navy defeats the Spanish Armada.

Literary Highlights

- Humanists use Latin and Greek classics along with the Bible to answer fundamental questions about life.
- In 1611, the King James Bible is published.
- Dramas, including the plays of William Shakespeare, are the greatest literary achievement of the English Renaissance.

Secondary Source

More's Conflict with King Henry VIII

Historian Francis Hackett offers this assessment of Thomas More's motivations for opposing King Henry VIII: "The conflict between Henry and Thomas More was a conflict of civilizations, a conflict of principles, a conflict of wills. A new ferment, that of nationalism and commerce and the possibilities of economic individualism, was beginning to work in society, and was breaking up the medieval mind. Thomas More had been a humanist...; he had criticized Rome until he saw that it was in danger of falling and in its collapse dragging down the precious spiritual tradition of a society governed from above. But when this danger was present, when the alternative to the papal religion of Christ, which Luther assailed, was the willfulness of Henry... then More forgot his zeal to reform the Church in a greater zeal to love his master, to praise him, and to serve him."

KEY CONCEPT

The Protestant Reformation

History of the Times

Henry VIII, who reigned from 1509 to 1547, is perhaps most famous for his six wives. The fates of these women are summarized in a jingle:

Divorced, beheaded, died,
Divorced, beheaded, survived.

Like his father, Henry VIII knew that a male heir was essential to securing the throne. His first wife, Catherine of Aragon, had failed to give him a son after twenty-four years of marriage. (Her sole surviving child was a daughter, Mary.) Henry appealed to Pope Clement VII to annul his marriage or to declare that it was never a proper union. Henry claimed that because Catherine had originally been married to his older brother Arthur—for five months before Arthur died—she could not rightfully be married to Henry. (It was against Church law to marry a dead sibling's spouse.) Because the original marriage between Catherine and Arthur had itself been annulled on the grounds that it was never consummated (so Henry could marry Catherine), Clement refused to grant a second annulment. If Henry's new annulment were granted, a great dilemma would be created for the Church, for the original annulment would therefore have been based on a lie. Further pressure from Catherine's powerful nephew, the king of Spain, also prompted Clement to reject Henry's request.

Portrait of Henry VIII (c.1525–1530) by English School (16th century).

In response, Henry appointed a new archbishop of Canterbury, who obligingly granted the annulment. In 1534, Henry finalized the break from Rome by declaring himself head of the English Church. He seized the vast and wealthy resources of the Catholic Church in England, and filled his treasury with the profit he made from selling off Church land.

Henry's decision to overthrow the Catholic Church in England was widely supported. The financial demands of the Church on the English people incited resentment, and corruption was widespread among the clergy. New religious ideas, specifically those of Martin Luther, were being debated, and change was inevitable. Henry's assertion, however, that he was the head of the Church of England was not tolerated universally, and many subjects remained faithful to the pope. The most famous of these was Henry's own friend, Sir Thomas More, author of *Utopia* and then lord chancellor of England. For his protests against Henry's claim to religious authority, More was beheaded in 1535.

Cross-Curricular Connection

HISTORY: Martin Luther

Following his graduation from the University of Erfurt, Martin Luther took up the study of law, but he suddenly abandoned the study several weeks later on July 17, 1505, to his father's disappointment. After surviving a violent thunderstorm, Luther vowed to devote his life to the monastery if he survived, and he took steps to fulfill this vow. Even as a monk, however, Luther continued his schooling, this time studying theology, and received his doctorate in 1512.

It was in 1518 that Luther made his own revelation about the Christian understanding of the doctrine of salvation. Luther's assertion that salvation came about solely through God's grace, not of a combination of humans' good works and God's grace, contradicted traditional theological views. When Luther was ordered to recant his views, he refused, saying, "Here I stand. I can do no other. God help me. Amen." Following his excommunication, he went into hiding and began work on translating the New Testament into the German vernacular, one of his greatest achievements.

Think About/Talk About

History of the Times

- Tell students that Catherine was first wedded at age sixteen to Arthur, son of Henry VII, for political reasons. Six months after the wedding, Arthur died. Eight years later, she married Henry VIII and gave birth to a stillborn daughter; experienced a miscarriage; and had two sons who died young and one daughter, Mary. Catherine was forty-two when Henry VIII sought an annulment.
- Martin Luther is credited with beginning the Protestant Reformation, in which people moved away from the Catholic Church. His religious beliefs were based on the understanding that salvation is predestined, and decided only by God. Other faiths developed from these views of Christianity such as Lutheran, Anglican, Calvinist, and Anabaptist. These followers became known as Protestants.

Think About/Talk About

Literature of the Times

The aim of humanist teaching, as poet John Milton summarized in "Of Education," was not to produce scholars, but to prepare students to "perform justly, skillfully, and magnanimously all the offices, both private and public, of peace and war."

Link to Today

Timepieces Across Time

This feature emphasizes the importance of human innovation with the example of the modern clock in the Renaissance that has evolved to today's various methods of telling time.

1. Ask this question to help students build background: How did the innovations of the Renaissance era influence the literature?
2. After students have read the feature, ask them how timekeeping devices evolved to become smaller.
3. Finally, ask students to respond to the **Ask Yourself** question. Use students' responses to spark class discussion.
4. Encourage students to do further research on the history of the clock or another device.

Comprehension Check

Possible responses: *The English people were financially burdened by the Church and fed up with corruption in the Church clergy. By breaking with Rome, England could become a stronger global influence, politically and culturally.*

After Henry's marriage to Catherine was declared invalid, he married Anne Boleyn, who bore a daughter, Elizabeth. Henry had Anne beheaded because she did not give him sons, and then married Jane Seymour, his third wife. She died giving birth to Henry's son, Edward. All three of Henry's children had different mothers.

Despite the controversies of his thirty-eight-year reign, Henry left an important legacy. He created the Royal Navy, which is credited with protecting England from foreign invasion. He also helped England spread its political power, language, and literature over the globe. Henry was a true Renaissance man—a poet, musician, athlete, hunter, and supporter of humanistic learning. Much of what we recall about Henry VIII—his tendency to send friends and wives to the chopping block—stemmed from his desperate desire to have a male heir. He died without knowing that Elizabeth, the child he ignored because she was female, would become England's greatest ruler.

Literature of the Times

The Renaissance had started in Italy in the fourteenth century and began to flourish in England after Henry VIII ascended to the throne. The Tudors, whose claim to the throne through Henry VII was based more on successful warfare than divine right and established bloodline, needed to distinguish themselves socially and politically as rightful English rulers. They also required a class of cultivated officials who would remain loyal to them. Supporting the growth of humanism allowed Tudor monarchs to accomplish both goals, as well as to patronize the development of English literature.

Humanist scholars wrote in Latin, but gradually English writers began to use the vernacular[2] and started translating Greek and Roman classics into English. Henry VIII authorized the translation of the Bible into English.

Comprehension Check

Why was Henry VIII's decision to overthrow the Church so widely embraced? What did he gain from breaking with Rome?

2. **vernacular:** native language.

Link to Today

Timepieces Across Time

Do you tell time by wearing a watch, checking a clock, or looking at your cell phone? In the last century, remarkable innovations have been made in temporal technologies. The Renaissance was also a period of great advances in timekeeping. While many types of clocks existed in the ancient world, the Renaissance saw the first development of modern clocks. Clocks first appeared in town centers, usually in church towers: England's oldest surviving clock, which dates from around 1386, is on Salisbury Cathedral. Before the invention of revolving hands, clocks announced themselves audibly, clanging out the hour, day and night. As individuals increasingly sought to use time to regulate their lives, clocks became privately owned possessions. As technology became more refined, timepieces became more common, more portable, and much smaller. Soon almost everyone felt the need to wear or carry a personal clock. Furthermore, as clocks proliferated, so did references to time and timekeeping in literature.

Clock made for the tower in Salisbury Cathedral (1386) by English School. Wiltshire, UK.

Ask Yourself

What can we learn about human beings by studying the history of inventions?

Cross-Curricular Connection

SCIENCE: The Scientific, or "Baconian," Method

Information for students:

- The scientific method is a strategy used to observe phenomena by experimentation, reasoning, and the formulation of hypotheses.
- First called the Baconian method, after Francis Bacon, an English philosopher, it was proposed in Bacon's book *Novum Organum,* or "New Instrument."
- Bacon believed that inductive reasoning, rather than deductive reasoning, should be used in acquiring and correcting knowledge.
- Bacon sought to change the approach to science used in the Middle Ages, saying, "Men have sought to make a world from their own conception . . . , but if, instead of doing so, they had consulted experience and observation, they would have the facts and not opinions to reason about, and might have ultimately arrived at the knowledge of the laws which govern the material world."

Standards Focus

Objectives

Students will evaluate the philosophical, political, religious, ethical, and social influences of a historical period.

Link to Today

This article describes the role of the printing press in the Renaissance and how today the Internet is bringing about another "Renaissance."

Unit 2 Resources, Historical Introduction Skill Builder, p. 1

UA: Differentiating Instruction, graphic organizer, p. 54

Teacher One Stop™, lesson plan and all print resources

Direct Teach

Think About/Talk About

Read with a Purpose Direct students to the Read with a Purpose statement. Tell students that they should think about how the Internet allows people to use their creativity and share their ideas with others, just as the printing press and better ink in Shakespeare's world improved access to ideas.

WEB ARTICLE

File Edit View Favorites Tools Help

Back Forward Stop Refresh Home Search Favorites History Mail Print

Address http://www.etimes.com Go

Link to Today

This Link to Today claims that, thanks to the Internet, we are currently living in the midst of another Renaissance.

Read with a Purpose

Read to see what makes your world as creative as that of Shakespeare.

Build Background

Leon Battista Alberti, an accomplished thinker and artist of the Renaissance, first put forth the idea of the Renaissance man. Alberti wrote that "a man can do all things if he will," including achievements in the fields of art, science, and sports. The idea of the Renaissance man follows from humanism, a philosophy that places humans at the center of the universe and encourages the development of human knowledge and excellence.

Another Renaissance?

by **Gary Fisher**

Electronic Engineering Times

It must have been exciting to live during the Renaissance. This period, beginning in the fourteenth century, saw perhaps the most significant growth of literature, technology and the arts in history to that time. Particular advances, such as the development of printing and oil-based inks, permitted large numbers of individuals not only to see and to even own works produced by creative minds, but to produce and distribute their own work for others to see and judge.

And produce they did.

Interior of a Printing Shop (1632) by Matthaeus Merian the Elder (1593–1650).

Selection Readability	
Easily Accessible **Accessible** Challenging	chronological order; accessible theme

Selection Summary

This essay posits the idea that, with the growth of the Internet, we are in the midst of a revolution in technology and opportunity comparable to the Renaissance in the fourteenth century. Fisher suggests that we "may be standing in the midst of another 'Renaissance,'" in which millions are taking advantage of the global audience computers offer. "Who will be the next DaVinci?" Fisher asks in conclusion: likely someone online.

Literature of the Times

The defeat of the Armada was an impetus[5] for Renaissance writers, for with this victory Elizabeth had confirmed the national identity of her kingdom. Writers celebrated her as a beloved symbol of peace, security, and prosperity, frequently dedicating their works to her. She also appeared mythologically as Cynthia, Diana, Gloriana, and the Faerie Queene in a host of literary works. The sixteenth century saw a great deal of publishing, and, particularly in the 1590s, an astounding outpouring of manuscripts.

Elizabeth's court became the center of a literary culture that included many gifted writers and courtiers who wrote only for a select circle of friends. Edmund Spenser, who considered himself a professional writer, published his masterpiece *The Faerie Queene* and dedicated it to Elizabeth. Even in the reign of James, poets like John Donne did not seek to have their work published.

The greatest literary achievement of the Renaissance in England is its body of dramatic work. The plays of Shakespeare and his contemporaries were written for public theaters rather than for aristocratic patrons. The last great writer of the English Renaissance is John Milton, who lived past the period of the Commonwealth and into the Restoration.

Comprehension Check

Describe the historical and literary impact of the defeat of the Spanish Armada.

5. **impetus:** a catalyst; a cause for action.

(*opposite*) *Elizabeth I, Armada Jewel* (cover) by Nicholas Hilliard (1547–1619). Victoria & Albert Museum, London.

Wrap Up

Talk About...

Discuss the merits of a monarchy versus a democracy. Which form of government makes the most sense to you? Use each Academic Vocabulary word **listed below** at least once in your discussion.

Write About...

The invention of the printing press and the Internet changed the world. Write a paragraph comparing the influence of the printing press on society since its invention in the fifteenth century and the influence of the Internet on contemporary society.

Academic Vocabulary for Unit 2

Talking and Writing About Literature

Academic Vocabulary is the language you use to talk and write about literature. Use these words to discuss the literature you read in this unit. These words will be underlined throughout the unit.

established (ehs TAB lihsht) *v.:* set up; caused to happen. *Henry VII established the Tudor bloodline.*

ensure (ehn SHOOR) *v.:* tomake certain. *During his reign, Henry VII acted to ensure that the Tudor line would continue.*

widespread (WYD sprehd) *adj.:* occurring over a wide area. *Henry had widespread support for his decision to overthrow the Church in England.*

controversies (KAHN truh vur seez) *n.:* lengthy disagreement. *Despite its controversies, Henry's reign saw great achievements.*

contradiction (kahn truh DIHK shuhn) *n.:* statement in opposition to another; inconsistency. *The Catholic Church felt it would be a contradiction to annul Henry VIII's marriage to Catherine.*

Your Turn

Copy the Academic Vocabulary words into your *Reader/Writer Notebook.* Try to use the Academic Vocabulary words as you outline the key events of the period, and as you answer the questions about the literature in the unit.

Think About/Talk About

Literature of the Times

Tell students that *The Faerie Queene*, written by Edmund Spenser and published in 1596, is an allegorical work consisting of six books based on knightly virtues: holiness, temperance, chastity, friendship, justice, and courtesy. Queen Elizabeth is portrayed as Gloriana, the Faerie Queene, and represents Glory.

Comprehension Check

Possible response: *The Armada's defeat secured England's place in the world and determined the main language of North America.*

Check for Understanding

Talk About . . .

Some students might note that a democracy gives the people an opportunity to be a part of the political process, while a monarchy gives absolute power to a single individual. Students will be likely to mention that a democracy makes the most sense to them because it is the form of government with which they have personal experience.

Write About . . .

Students might mention that while the printing press stored knowledge efficiently and spread knowledge at a quick pace, the Internet quickened communication around the globe and provided more "space" to store knowledge.

PowerNotes, Academic Vocabulary lesson and activities

go.hrw.com **WordSharp: An Interactive Vocabulary Tutor,** more practice with academic language

Academic Vocabulary

Talking and Writing About Literature

English for Academic Success Present the following questions to students. Tell students that these are the kinds of questions they will encounter on standardized tests. Discuss the meaning of the words; then, have students use the historical introduction to answer the questions.

- Who **established** the Church of England for the second time to bring peace to England? ***Possible response:*** *Elizabeth I established the Church of England again after Mary had attempted to do away with it.*
- How did Elizabeth **ensure** her political authority throughout her reign? ***Possible response:*** *Elizabeth ensured her position of authority by refusing to marry.*
- What sentiment was **widespread** in England when Mary Tudor married? ***Possible response:*** *There was widespread anger and discontentment because Mary wedded a ruler from Spain, which England loathed.*

Think About/Talk About

History of the Times

Tell students that in 1588, the Spanish Armada was the largest fleet of ships that had ever been assembled; consequently, the Spanish expected to defeat the English fleet, which was composed of fewer and smaller ships. The English ships, however, were faster, so the English strategy was to scatter the Spanish fleet in order to gain an advantage. The English set ablaze eight small frigates and sailed them into the Armada, thereby scattering the alarmed Spanish ships and forcing them to retreat.

La Volta, a Renaissance dance (16th century).

and lived under house arrest as a royal exile in England. Because Elizabeth was childless, Mary had a claim to the English crown. When Elizabeth had Mary beheaded in 1588, Philip of Spain—irritated by Elizabeth's refusal to marry him as much as by the execution of another Catholic ally—found reason to invade England. He subsequently sent the Spanish Armada, a fleet of warships, to conquer England, which ultimately destroyed the Armada with the help of some strong storms in the Irish Sea. Without this victory, Spain may well have conquered Britain and later occupied North America.

In 1603, Elizabeth was succeeded by James VI of Scotland, her second cousin and the son of Mary Stuart. As James I, he reigned until 1625, leaving behind a weakened crown for his despotic son, Charles I, who was beheaded in 1649. England was governed by Parliament,and the Puritan leader Oliver Cromwell until 1660. When Charles II emerged from exile to assume power, the Renaissance was ending, and England was a different country.

Compare and Contrast

Point out that the dominant characteristics of the English Renaissance differed from those of the Italian Renaissance. Divide the class into pairs. Have one student in each pair focus on the highlights of the English Renaissance and the other focus on achievements in the Italian Renaissance. Ask each student to use print or online sources to research his or her topic. Students should consider this question: What major similarities and differences can be found between the English Renaissance and the Italian Renaissance? Have students discuss their findings with their partners and write a one-page response to the question.

KEY CONCEPT

England's Greatest Monarch

UNIT 2 INTRODUCTION

History of the Times

Elizabeth I, *Armada Portrait* (1588) by Marcus Gheeraerts the Younger.

Elizabeth I—possibly the most brilliant monarch in English history—inherited the kingdom only after her brother, Edward VI, died of tuberculosis[3] and her sister, "Bloody" Mary, died of a fever.

Edward VI's reign was short and uneventful. Crowned at age nine, Edward, though intelligent, was controlled for the remaining six years of his life by manipulative relatives. Mary, however, was a far more formidable force. A devout Catholic, she wanted to avenge the wrongs committed against her mother and her Church. When she took the throne in 1553, Mary restored power to English Catholics. She earned the name Bloody Mary for executing Protestants at the stake. Her support waned when she married Philip II, king of Spain, at a time when fear and hatred of Spain were escalating. Because Mary died childless, her sister Elizabeth succeeded to the throne.

Elizabeth's first task was to restore law and order to a kingdom torn by fierce religious feuds. Elizabeth reestablished the Church of England and refused to acknowledge the pope's authority. As a result, she was excommunicated, that is to say, officially expelled from the Roman Catholic Church. Because Elizabeth knew that taking a husband would put her under male authority, she eluded marriage for her entire reign despite much external pressure. When Parliament begged her to marry, she said, "I am your anointed Queen. I will never be by violence constrained to do anything." She remained "the Virgin Queen," from which the American colony Virginia got its name.

Elizabeth foiled several plots against her life, some of which were engineered by her cousin Mary Stuart, Queen of Scots, also a direct descendant of Henry VII. Mary Stuart, who was a Catholic, was deposed[4] from her throne in Protestant Scotland,

3. **tuberculosis:** a contagious and eventually fatal lung disease.

4. **deposed:** removed from power, dethroned.

Think About/Talk About

History of the Times

The indignation and anger aimed at Queen Mary I by her subjects during the persecution of 283 Protestants stemmed not from the fact that the persecution took place—other Tudors had also executed people for heresy. However, in her efforts to restore Catholicism to England, Mary began executing not only religious figures, but also ordinary members of the public. Most of the executions that took place throughout her reign were of commoners, a travesty that enraged the general public.

- Bacon is also known for his saying, "knowledge is power."
- Upon meeting Bacon, Queen Elizabeth recognized his quick intellect and called him "the young Lord Keeper."

Small-Group Activity Have students discuss in small groups different ways in which they have used the scientific method. Ask them to consider examples not only from their science classes but from other parts of their lives as well.

Edit View Favorites Tools Help

Forward Stop Refresh Home Search Favorites History Mail Print

http://www.etimes.com Go

The printing presses of the printers Plantin-Moretus in Antwerp.
Museum Plantin-Moretus, Antwerp, Belgium.

During the Renaissance, in brilliant contrast to an age in which literature and art required a wealthy patron to achieve any hope of a wide audience, it became possible for almost anyone who could learn the necessary skills and acquire access to the required technology to see their ideas—the results of their creative talents—spread to the four winds.

Much of the work, of course, was produced for personal satisfaction, and much for limited distribution among very specific audiences—societies, guilds[1] and members of other groups were sometimes united by little more than their published works. For all, the technologies of the Renaissance suddenly transformed the ability to read and write from the specialized domain of clerics[2] into a skill useful to anyone, and gave anyone "touched by the muse"[3] an outlet for their creative works.

1. **guilds:** associations of artists or craftsmen, organized to maintain standards and to protect the interests of their members.
2. **clerics:** members of the clergy such as priests and monks.
3. **muse:** goddess who inspires a poet or artist. "Touched by the muse" means inspired by a creative force.

Think About/Talk About

Extend the Discussion

Finding Details Who did artists and writers depend on for their audience before the Renaissance? ***Possible response:*** *They looked to wealthy patrons to serve as their main audience.*

Making Inferences After reading the second paragraph, what can you infer about the social effect printing technology had on the world? ***Possible response:*** *Before the Renaissance, most works were published or handwritten for personal enjoyment, but today people print in practically every field for a variety of purposes. Publishing works was once a specialized skill, but today it can be done by almost anyone.*

Universal Access

EL English Learners/ Struggling Readers

English for Academic Success Before students read the selection, introduce the following words.

- **advances**—improvement. *Technological advances over the past century have not been insignificant.*
- **harness**—to put to use. *By harnessing their brainpower, the group came up with all the answers to the math problems.*
- **synthesize**—to combine parts. *The poem synthesized rhyme, alliteration, and imagery.*
- **illiterate**—unable to read and write. *After a few months, the hardworking student was no longer illiterate and could read just about anything.*

Then, ask questions that contain one of the words and challenge students to respond using the word.

Think About/Talk About

Extend the Discussion

Monitoring Reading How does the writer define a "Renaissance man"? ***Possible response:*** *A "Renaissance man" is described as a person who is familiar with the current ideas and technologies and who builds upon these ideas to form his or her own.*

Speculating Why might people prefer electronic communication to non-electronic communication, or vice versa? ***Possible responses:*** *Electronic communication is quick, convenient, and less costly. However, people might prefer the alternative method because it is more personal to the receiver and is not dependent on electricity and computers.*

File Edit View Favorites Tools Help

Back Forward Stop Refresh Home Search Favorites History Mail Print

Address http://www.etimes.com

Link to Today

Perhaps the most significant effect of the Renaissance was the widespread access it opened to ideas. One of the most persistent concepts we still associate with the period is that of "Renaissance men," individuals who harnessed the technologies and creative energy of the time to put most of the current body of knowledge at their fingertips. These people wrote, but just as importantly they read and corresponded with others, building on that interaction and exchange of ideas to synthesize and develop their own.

We may be standing in the midst of another "Renaissance." Computers, the Internet and other forms of online communications, and a widespread spirit of creativity have come together during our time to give anyone with the desire to connect a worldwide audience for their talents, and millions are taking advantage of the opportunity. Many whose fifth-grade teachers might have considered them both illiterate and devoid of artistic talent are today busily learning to organize and publish the products of their creative energies in electronic form, daring to offer their ideas to a potential audience of millions.

"The Gathering," the world's largest convention of computer enthusiasts. Hamar, Norway.

Universal Access

Advanced Learners

Enrichment Tell students to compose a visual or essay illustrating an imaginary figure who would exemplify today's "Renaissance man or woman." Before students begin, have them consider the person's skills, talents, interests, and accomplishments. As they present their Renaissance person in class, have students compare each student's definition of a Renaissance person today.

Cross-Curricular Connection

HISTORY: The Renaissance Man

Working in small groups, have students prepare a brief report on a Renaissance figure. Choices can include Leone Battista Alberti, Blaise Pascal, Gottfried Leibniz, or Johann Wolfgang von Goethe. Students should give a brief background of the person, including family and education, as well as achievements, talents, and interests. Students should then present their reports to the class.

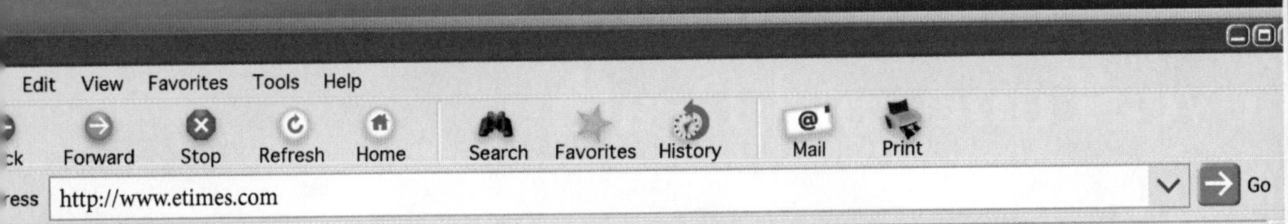

The Proportions of the Human Body (1996) by Electros aka Babis Vekri.

The age of the **Renaissance person** may have returned; the sum of human thought and knowledge, from classical literature to the most recent discoveries of science, can be literally at the fingertips of anyone with the desire to master the skills and a little technology. The spirit of the Renaissance seems also to be returning; just as the "men of arts and letters"[4] of that former era were willing—sometimes even eager—to correspond with those interested in their ideas, many of today's leading philosophers, writers and researchers participate in electronic discussion groups and gladly respond to thoughtful e-mail.

Who will be the next Da Vinci, the next Bacon, the next Jefferson?[5] It's very possible they're online today.

4. **letters:** literature and other written forms of communication.
5. **Da Vinci:** Leonardo da Vinci (1452–1519), Italian artist and scientist; **Bacon:** Francis Bacon (1561–1626), British statesman and philosopher; **Jefferson:** Thomas Jefferson (1743–1846), American statesman and philosopher. Da Vinci, Bacon, and Jefferson are all considered Renaissance men.

Ask Yourself

1. **Read with a Purpose** According to Gary Fisher, what does our world today have in common with the Renaissance?
2. How did Renaissance technology affect reading and writing?
3. What specific features distinguished the Renaissance from prior ages?
4. Why might someone disagree with Fisher that "the sum of human thought and knowledge . . . can be literally at the fingertips of anyone with the desire to master the skills and a little technology"? Explain.

Think About/Talk About

Extend the Discussion

Finding Details Why does the writer believe that the age of the "Renaissance man" has returned? ***Possible response:*** *Virtually all knowledge, from ancient times to the present, is easily accessible to anyone who can operate a computer and has access to the Internet.*

Speculating Describe the "Renaissance men" of today. What skills or abilities would they possess? ***Possible responses:*** *Today's "Renaissance man"—or woman—would be someone who is gifted in several areas at once and is able to connect and articulate ideas in his or her areas of expertise as well as areas with which he or she is less familiar. A Renaissance man or woman is an innovative thinker who reflects upon what the future will have in store for humanity.*

Ask Yourself

Possible responses:

1. *Our world today is similar to the Renaissance because scholars and thinkers can interact with one another more easily, we have easy access to human knowledge, and we can display our creative works to a wider audience.*
2. *Renaissance technology increased the number of people who could read and write, made written work widely available, and encouraged people to freely express their creativity.*
3. *The Renaissance stood out from previous ages as a period characterized by open communication and correspondence among leading philosophers, thinkers, artists, and writers, a spirit of innovation and creativity, and improved accessibility to ideas.*
4. *Someone might disagree with Fisher's statement because not all human knowledge is necessarily available at our fingertips. There is still much information that can be accessed only in print format. Also, some knowledge is exclusive because it is meant for only certain groups, such as governmental or business organizations.*

Chapter Objectives

- Students will analyze characteristics of pastoral poems.
- Students will read and study examples of *carpe diem* poetry and metaphysical poetry.
- Students will develop an appreciation for subgenres of prose, including parables.
- Students will analyze Milton's style by reading an excerpt from *Paradise Lost.*
- Students will compare and contrast themes across different cultures.

The Quotation

Tell students that the literary skills focus for Chapter 3 is Renaissance poetry, which reflects humanistic thinking. Ask students what they think the author means by the phrase "That man who dwells upon himself, . . . rests in his true centre." ***Possible response:*** *The author, John Donne, means that when man knows himself well, he is focused and centered.*

Analyzing Visuals

Extension Activity In what way is the image related to the words of John Donne? ***Possible response:*** *The image reveals the helplessness of a human against supernatural forces. Humans are small and frail and at the mercy of higher powers.*

CHAPTER **3**

Love, Time, and Death

LITERARY SKILLS FOCUS

Renaissance Poetry

Fall of the Rebel Angels by Pieter Brueghel the Elder.
Musée d'Art Ancien, Musées Royaux des Beaux-Arts, Brussels, Belgium.

CONTENTS

"Man is but earth; 'Tis true; but earth is the centre. That man who dwells upon himself, who is always conversant in himself, rests in his true centre."

—John Donne

Chapter 3

California Standards Overview

- **Reading Standard 2.2** Analyze the way in which clarity of meaning is affected by the patterns of organization, hierarchical structures, repetition of the main ideas, syntax, and word choice in the text.
- **Reading Standard 2.4** Make warranted and reasonable assertions about the author's arguments by using elements of the text to defend and clarify interpretations.
- **Reading Standard 2.5** Analyze an author's implicit and explicit philosophical beliefs and assumptions about a subject.
- **Reading Standard 2.6** Critique the power, validity, and truthfulness of arguments set forth in public documents; their appeal to both friendly and hostile audiences; and the extent to which the arguments anticipate and address reader concerns and counterclaims (e.g., appeal to reason, to authority, to pathos and emotion).
- **Reading Standard 3.1** Analyze characteristics of subgenres (e.g., satire, parody, allegory, pastoral) that are used in poetry, prose, plays, novels, short stories, essays, and other basic genres.
- **Reading Standard 3.2** Analyze the way in which the theme or meaning of a selection represents a view or comment on life, using textual evidence to support the claim.
- **Reading Standard 3.3** Analyze the ways in which irony, tone, mood, the author's style, and the "sound" of language achieve specific rhetorical or aesthetic purposes or both.
- **Reading Standard 3.4** Analyze ways in which poets use imagery, personification, figures of speech, and sounds to evoke readers' emotions.
- **Reading Standard 3.7** Analyze recognized works of world literature from a variety of authors: **b.** Relate literary works and authors to the major themes and issues of their eras. **c.** Evaluate the philosophical, political, religious, ethical, and social influences of the historical period that shaped the characters, plots, and settings.
- **Reading Standard 3.9** Analyze the philosophical arguments presented in literary works to determine whether the authors' positions have contributed to the quality of each work and the credibility of the characters (Philosophical approach).

LITERARY RESPONSE AND ANALYSIS
Literary Skills Focus

Reading Standard 3.7c (see pages A48–A50)

Renaissance Poetry by Leila Christenbury

Influences on Renaissance Poetry

- Humanism, a belief in the central worth and dignity of human beings
- A new interest in ancient Greek and Roman writings, including drama and poetry
- Italian verse forms, including the sonnet
- Powerful patrons of the arts, such as Elizabeth I

The Renaissance's explosion of faith in the preeminence of the individual is often seen as the turning point between the Middle Ages and the modern world. Such confidence found a fitting outlet in poetry.

The Spirit of the Age

During the Renaissance (a term meaning "rebirth") people began to see life in an entirely new way. In the Middle Ages, people had been taught to focus not on the pleasures of this world but on the rewards of the next. With the surge of new ideas in the Renaissance, people began to question the beliefs of the past. Writers created poems that focused on their own lives, their relationships, and the physical world around them.

The widespread belief in personal ability and the potential of the individual has its roots in **humanism,** an intellectual movement in which writers and artists sought to synthesize the lessons of Latin and Greek classics with the teachings of Christianity. Humanism grew into a powerful philosophical and educational trend that shaped much Renaissance art and philosophy. Drawing on ideas from the ancient Greeks and Romans, Renaissance writers became optimistic about the power of human thought and action. They wanted to educate others and cultivate the ability of individuals to understand the natural world and live virtuously.

The humanist focus on the classics had a strong influence on Renaissance poetry. Poets admired the elaborate poetic patterns of ancient writers who composed poems that followed complicated rules regarding subject matter, line length, and **rhyme scheme.**

The Development of the Sonnet

In addition to imitating classical forms of poetry, Renaissance poets expressed their ideas in the **sonnet,** a verse form that had developed in Italy during the late Middle Ages. The word *sonnet* is derived from the Italian word *sonetto,* meaning "little sound or song." A sonnet is a fourteen-line lyric poem, which is written in **iambic pentameter** and adheres to one of several strict rhyme schemes. In Italy, the sonnet form was perfected by Francesco Petrarca (1304–1374), known in English as Petrarch. Petrarch believed that the sonnet, with its brevity and musical rhymes, was a perfect medium for the expression of emotion, especially love. An example of the form he popularized, called the **Italian,** or **Petrarchan sonnet,** is on p. 400.

The Petrarchan sonnet has two parts: an eight-line section called the octave, with a rhyme scheme of *abbaabba,* followed by a six-line section called the sestet, with a rhyme scheme of *cdecde* or *cdcdcd.* Typically, the octave establishes the speaker's situation, and the sestet resolves, draws conclusions about, or expresses a reaction to that situation. The transition from octave to sestet is called the **turn.** Like many literary terms, the *turn* is a metaphor; the speaker is, figuratively speaking, turning from one thought to another.

During the English Renaissance, Sir Thomas Wyatt, a diplomat in the court of King Henry VIII, translated some of Petrarch's sonnets and wrote a few of his own, slightly modifying the Italian form. Building on Wyatt's modifications, Henry Howard, Earl of Surrey, changed the rhyme scheme of the Italian sonnet to adapt it to the rhyme-poor English language. Surrey's

Literary Skills Focus

Objectives

Students will understand the influences of a historical period on a literary genre.

Unit 2 Resources, Literary Focus Skill Builder, p. 5

PowerNotes, interactive lesson presentation with activities

Teacher One Stop™, on-level lesson plan and all print resources

Direct Teach

Renaissance Poetry

Have students read the Literary Skills Focus essay. Then, use the following question to help students develop greater understanding of influences on Renaissance poetry.

Renaissance poets drew inspiration from ancient Greek and Roman writings and from Christianity as well. How did writers synthesize ideas from both sources without contradicting pagan or Christian ideas?

California Standards, pp. 267–268

- **Reading Standard 3.7** Analyze recognized works of world literature from a variety of authors: **c.** Evaluate the philosophical, political, religious, ethical, and social influences of the historical period that shaped the characters, plots, and settings.

Check for Understanding

Ask Yourself

Possible responses:

1. *Classical literature provided Greek and Roman themes; Renaissance poets emulated patterns, line length, and rhyme schemes of ancient poets.*
2. *Renaissance people wrote poetry to entertain friends. Upper-class men and women learned to write and sing poetry to be respected and admired. During Elizabeth's reign, her court celebrated poetry with music and drama.*

LITERARY RESPONSE AND ANALYSIS

Literary Skills Focus

innovations distinguished the English sonnet from the Italian sonnet. The English sonnet ultimately became known as the Shakespearean sonnet because William Shakespeare used it with such distinction.

Although the Shakespearean sonnet adheres to the fixed requirement of fourteen iambic pentameter lines, its organization differs from that of a Petrarchan sonnet. While a Petrarchan sonnet uses the octave and sestet to pose a question and answer or a problem and solution, a Shakespearean sonnet is divided into three quatrains, or groups of four lines, and a couplet, which consists of two lines. The three quatrains express related ideas and the couplet sums up the poet's message. The turn, or shift in thought, often occurs at the third quatrain or at the couplet. The Shakespearean sonnet's rhyme scheme is *abab cdcd efef gg.*

Edmund Spenser developed a third type of sonnet, accordingly called the Spenserian sonnet. Like the Shakespearean sonnet, the Spenserian sonnet has three quatrains and a couplet, but it uses an interlocking rhyme scheme: *abab bcbc cdcd ee.* This rhyme scheme reinforces the relationship of ideas between the quatrains and helps emphasize the closing comment in the couplet.

Poetry and Society

Social life among the upper classes required men and women to know many forms of poetry. To be popular and well received, you had to able to write in verse and sing it, too—sometimes accompanying yourself on a stringed instrument. This trend was greatly influenced by the remarkable wit and literary skills of Elizabeth I, who wrote and admired good poetry. Her courtiers often wrote verses in her honor, and her court was noted for its dramatic presentations and music. Other people imitated court behavior, writing to appear more learned or fashionable, or simply for their own enjoyment. Poetry during the Renaissance was woven into people's lives and, for the literate, represented an important aspect of the everyday world—much as music and lyrics are an integral part of our world today.

Analyzing Visuals

Connecting to the Text What do the activities of each of the three subjects in the painting suggest about the Renaissance lifestyle?

Three Musicians by the Master of the Half-Figures (fl. c. 1500–1533). Tempera on panel.

Ask Yourself

1. How did the rediscovery of classical literature shape Renaissance poetry?
2. How did people use poetry during the Renaissance?

Learn It Online

Learn about Renaissance poetry through *PowerNotes.*

go.hrw.com H12-268 Go

Analyzing Visuals

Connecting to the Text: *By showing three beautiful and young women studying music, this painting reflects the belief in the importance and capabilities of the individual. It also depicts the pleasures of this world.*

Universal Access

Advanced Learners

Enrichment Challenge students to compare poetic influences of the Renaissance with those of today. Ask students to compare topics and themes of Renaissance poetry—such as love, nature, the country, and virtue—to topics of modern music. Have students write a short essay on how at least three of the topics or themes are reflected in today's music and lyrics.

Learn It Online

For a multimedia version of the instruction found on this page, use the **PowerNotes** Literary Skills Focus presentation.

go.hrw.com H12-268 Go

Reading Standard 3.1, 3.7c (see pages A48–A50)

Connecting to Renaissance Poetry

Renaissance poetry celebrates individuals, their relationships, and their natural surroundings. This image is an early Renaissance illumination, or illustration, of a medieval story about courtly love—a topic that continued to be popular during the Renaissance.

Guidelines

Use these guidelines to consider how this illumination expresses ideas typical of Renaissance poetry.

- How does the **setting** reflect ideas associated with Renaissance poetry?
- What event appears to be taking place?
- To what social class do the people belong? How can you tell?

1. What is occurring at the center of the illumination? What Renaissance value does this scene reflect?
2. What are the people in the foreground doing? What can you determine about their relationship?
3. Examine the depiction of nature, and describe the relationship of the people to the natural world.

Lutenist and singers in a garden, from *Roman de la Rose* (c. 1490–1500). The British Library, London.

Your Turn Analyze Renaissance Poetry

Choose another image in this chapter, and write a short paragraph explaining how it reflects some of the themes of Renaissance poetry.

California Standards, p. 269

- **Reading Standard 3.1** Analyze characteristics of subgenres (e.g., satire, parody, allegory, pastoral) that are used in poetry, prose, plays, novels, short stories, essays, and other basic genres.
- **Reading Standard 3.7** Analyze recognized works of world literature from a variety of authors: **c.** Evaluate the philosophical, political, religious, ethical, and social influences of the historical period that shaped the characters, plots, and settings.

Universal Access

English Learners

English for Academic Success Tell students that the word *illumination* is derived from the Latin *illuminare,* meaning "to throw into light," from *in–* and *lumen* (light). Originally, the word *illuminate* meant "to decorate written material with gold, silver, or bright colors."

Standards Focus

Objectives

Students will analyze elements of Renaissance poetry in an illumination.

Analyzing Visuals Transparencies, Unit 2

Teacher One Stop™, lesson plan and all print resources

Direct Teach

Connect to the Literary Skill

Tell students that this illumination reflects themes of Renaissance poetry through the actions and costumes of the figures.

Work with students to answer the guided questions:

Possible responses:

1. *People are engaging in a leisurely activity as they listen to the lyre, accompanied by a female vocalist sitting by the musician. This scene reflects the Renaissance values of individual abilities and the embracing of nature.*
2. *The couple in the foreground is holding hands. They seem to be having some kind of an intimate moment before the lady enters the courtyard.*
3. *The people in this illumination seem to be one with nature as they comfortably enjoy their activities in an outdoor setting.*

Check for Understanding

Your Turn

Alternative Listening and Speaking Assignment

Have students work with a partner to find a Renaissance painting on the Internet. Have them use the guidelines to analyze the visual for Renaissance values. Then, have them present their analysis of the painting to the class.

Standards Focus

Objectives

Students will

- understand characteristics of the speaker
- draw inferences

Selection Introduction

Think About the Writers

Have students brainstorm names of influential contemporary musicians and screenwriters. Then, have them explain why each one is considered to be an innovator.

For Independent Reading

The Sonnets, William Shakespeare

Motivate

What Do You Think?/QuickWrite

Have students analyze a poem or story in which one character describes his or her love for another. Then, have students record how the character expresses his or her love.

English for Academic Success

Academic Vocabulary

Look for opportunities to use the Academic Vocabulary words in this unit.

- **contradiction, *n.*:** statement in opposition to another
- **established, *v.*:** set up; caused to happen

California Standards, pp. 270–275

- **Reading Standard 2.4** Make warranted and reasonable assertions about the author's arguments by using elements of the text to defend and clarify interpretations.
- **Reading Standard 3.4** Analyze ways in which poets use imagery, personification, figures of speech, and sounds to evoke readers' emotions.

Preparing to Read

SIR THOMAS WYATT

Whoso List to Hunt

EDMUND SPENSER

Sonnet 30
Sonnet 75

What Do You Think How do our hearts and minds influence our actions?

QuickWrite

Declare your love (real or imagined) for another person in a short piece of writing. What words will best convey your feelings of love? Record your work in your *Reader/Writer Notebook.*

Sir Thomas Wyatt (c. 1540), after Hans Holbein the Younger. National Portrait Gallery, London.

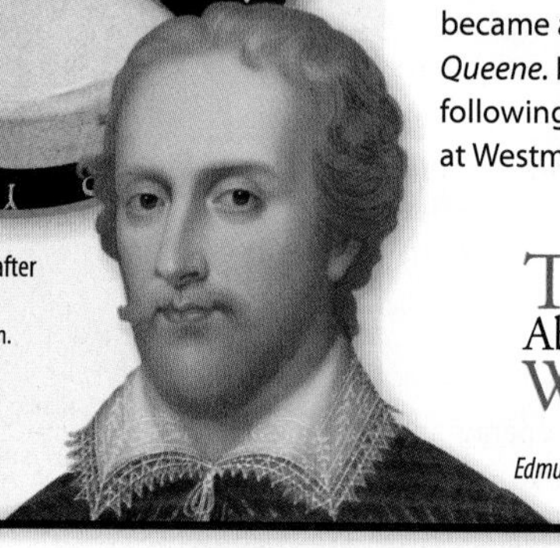

Edmund Spenser by Henry Bone.

MEET THE WRITER

Sir Thomas Wyatt
(1503–1542)

Sir Thomas Wyatt is remembered today as a literary innovator. Before Wyatt, English poetry was essentially medieval in subject, style, and form. Wyatt brought the Italian sonnet to England, where it soon became established as a staple of Elizabethan lyric poetry.

A courtier and diplomat, Thomas Wyatt served as an ambassador to Henry VIII. He may have been in love with Anne Boleyn, future queen and mother of Elizabeth I. Several of Wyatt's works are thought to have been written in her honor.

Like most courtiers, Wyatt did not publish his poems, and circulated his works chiefly among his friends. The first book to feature Wyatt's sonnets was published fifteen years after his death.

Edmund Spenser
(1552–1599)

Edmund Spenser was one of the most influential poets of his day. His major works include *The Shepheardes Calendar,* a series of pastoral poems that combine many different forms and meters, and *The Faerie Queene,* the longest epic poem in the English language. Spenser invented a sonnet form based on an intricate pattern of rhymes, called the Spenserian sonnet, and a special stanza form called the Spenserian stanza. Both influenced later poets.

Spenser attended Cambridge University as a "sizar," or poor scholar. When he served as personal secretary to the earl of Leicester, he met Sir Philip Sidney, another gifted poet, to whom he dedicated *The Shepheardes Calendar.* Later, Spenser became a landowner in Ireland, where he wrote *The Faerie Queene.* His castle burned in 1598, and he died in London the following year. He is buried next to Chaucer in the Poets' Corner at Westminster Abbey.

Think About the Writers Wyatt and Spenser are considered innovators. What writers or musicians today are creating new forms and influencing other artists?

Selection Readability	
Easily Accessible Accessible **Challenging**	These sonnets include unfamiliar situation; poetic language; abstract ideas.

Reading Standard 2.4, 3.4 (see pages A48–A50)

Literary Skills Focus

Speaker The **speaker** is the voice that addresses the reader in a poem. The speaker may be the poet or a created character whose voice and concerns do not necessarily reflect those of the poet. The speaker may even be an animal or an inanimate object. Even if a poem uses the pronoun *I*, readers cannot assume that the speaker is the poet.

Reading Skills Focus

Drawing Inferences Forming logical conclusions from details in a text and from your own experiences is known as **drawing inferences.** As you read, look for clues, such as images, word choice, and shifts in tone, which will help you better understand an author's message.

Into Action In these poems, contrasting images can help you draw inferences about the speakers and the poems' messages. When reading the selections, take note of the contrasting, or contradictory images. Using a chart like the one below for each sonnet, record the lines and the contrasting words you find. Be sure to note verbs as well as nouns.

Lines	Contrasting Words
"My love is like to ice, and I to fire;"	ice and fire

Writing Skills Focus

Think as a Reader/Writer

Find It in Your Reading As you read these three poems, pay attention to the structure of each **sonnet.** Note that Wyatt uses the Petrarchan form while Spenser uses his own modification of the English sonnet, known as the Spenserian sonnet. Keep track of each poem's stanza structure and rhyme scheme. Where does the turn, or shift in thought, occur in each sonnet? Answer these questions in your *Reader/Writer Notebook*.

Language Coach

Multiple Meanings The word *vain* can mean "not likely to be successful." Wyatt describes a hunt that is "in vain" because the hunter is not likely to catch the hunted. In Sonnet 75, Spenser describes a man who acts "in vain" in writing his love's name in the sand. The poet also plays with the other meaning of *vain,* which is "proud." What does it mean when a "vain man" acts "in vain"?

Reader/Writer Notebook

Use your **RWN** to complete the activities for these selections.

Learn It Online

Listen to these poems read aloud online.

go.hrw.com H12-271 Go

Preteach

English for Academic Success

Language Coach

Ask students to think of all the meanings of the word *cold* and different ways the word can be used. Then, have them look for the multiple meanings of the word in a dictionary. How does Spenser use the word in Sonnet 30?

Literary Skills Focus

As you read and discuss the selection with students, have them consider the speaker's views.

Reading Skills Focus

Give students a copy of the Reading Skills Focus graphic organizer before they read. (See **Unit 2 Resources.**) Tell them to use their responses to answer the questions on the Applying Your Skills page.

Writing Skills Focus

Have students jot down notes on the structure of the sonnet in their **Reader/Writer Notebooks.** Students can use their notes to complete the Writing Skills Focus activity.

Selection Resources

Unit 2 Resources, on-level practice and assessment, p. 7

Teacher One Stop™, on-level lesson plans and all print resources

Holt Audio Library

Holt Audio Library: Selections and Summaries in Spanish

UA: Differentiating Instruction, graphic organizer, p. 55

UA: Supporting Instruction in Spanish, selection summary

ThinkCentral Online Assessment, Selection Standards Check

ThinkCentral Online Remediation

Learn It Online

The online version of this selection includes audio support to engage all students and to help struggling readers with reading comprehension and vocabulary.

go.hrw.com H12-271 Go

Teacher Preparation

Selection Summary

"Whoso List to Hunt" uses a hunt metaphor to describe a man pursuing a woman, whom he compares to a deer. The speaker is tired of the chase, and he invites others to take it up. He uses a classical allusion to warn others that their prey (probably Anne Boleyn), like Caesar's deer, is claimed by a powerful ruler (probably Henry VIII). The speaker ends by warning that this woman is wild although she looks tame.

Direct Teach

Think About/Talk About

Read with a Purpose Have students read the Read with a Purpose statement. Tell students to pay attention to words and phrases that indicate the speaker's feelings.

Comprehension

B Reading Focus

Possible response: *The woman in the sonnet probably held a very high place in society to adorn herself with such precious jewels.*

Analysis

A Literary Focus

Possible response: *The speaker uses irony to describe himself as a losing suitor. The truth is the woman is unattainable.*

Analyzing Visuals

Connecting to the Text: *She is covered in gems and jewels, which makes her appear to be of high status, just like the woman in the poem. Both the woman in the portrait and the woman in the poem are attractive.*

SONNET

Whoso List to Hunt

by **Sir Thomas Wyatt**

Read with a Purpose

Read to discover the speaker's feelings about the creature he pursues.

Build Background

As a courtier, Wyatt was expected to compose songs, battle for the king, dance, joust in tournaments, and carry on intrigues with the ladies. According to traditional gossip, this poem is about Wyatt's longing for Anne Boleyn, a beautiful young woman at court. When he realized that King Henry VIII also fancied Anne, Wyatt gave up the pursuit to whoever else wanted to "hunt" her. In the poem below, it is thought that the deer with the jeweled collar refers to Anne.

Whoso list° to hunt, I know where is an hind,°
But as for me, alas, I may no more.
The vain travail° hath wearied me so sore
I am of them that farthest cometh behind. **A**
Yet may I, by no means, my wearied mind
Draw from the deer, but as she fleeth afore,
Fainting I follow. I leave off therefore,
Since in a net I seek to hold the wind.

Who list her hunt, I put him out of doubt,°
As well as I, may spend his time in vain.
And graven with diamonds in letters plain
There is written, her fair neck round about,
"*Noli me tangere,* for Caesar's I am,
And wild for to hold, though I seem tame." **B**

1. whoso list: whoever desires. **hind:** female deer.
3. travail: hard work.
9. put him out of doubt: assure him.

A Literary Focus **Speaker** The speaker places himself last in the hunt. What does this say about his view of himself?

B Reading Focus **Drawing Inferences** What can you infer from the image of diamonds?

Analyzing Visuals

Connecting to the Text How well does this portrait of Anne Boleyn represent the woman described in the poem? Explain.

Anne Boleyn (16th century) by an unknown artist. Oil on panel. National Portrait Gallery, London.

Universal Access

EL English Learners

English for Academic Success Students may have trouble understanding the unfamiliar words and inverted sentences in "Whoso List to Hunt." Read lines 1–4, rephrasing inverted sentences and substituting easier words for more difficult ones, such as *hopeless* for *vain.* Remind students that the "hunt" the speaker speaks of refers to his pursuit of a lady's affections. Based on the first four lines, ask students to describe how the speaker feels about his chance of success in this pursuit.

Struggling Readers

Ask students to work in groups to paraphrase "Whoso List to Hunt." Then, ask them to use evidence from the sonnet to discuss the relationship between the speaker and the woman he loves. Encourage students to consider whether the speaker and the woman were very close, or whether they were allowed to spend much time together. Have students organize their inferences in a two-column table. In the first column, students will list facts from the sonnet. In the second column, they will list their inferences based on facts.

SONNET

Sonnet 30

by **Edmund Spenser**

Read with a Purpose
Read to learn why the speaker thinks love can bend the rules of nature.

Build Background
This sonnet was part of a larger group of sonnets known as the *Amoretti* ("little love poems"), published in 1595. Spenser wrote these sonnets to his wife, Elizabeth. The poems are about their courtship.

My love is like to ice, and I to fire;
How comes it then that this her cold so great
Is not dissolved through my so hot desire,
But harder grows the more I her entreat? Ⓐ
Or how comes it that my exceeding heat
Is not delayed° by her heart frozen cold,
But that I burn much more in boiling sweat,
And feel my flames augmented manifold?°
What more miraculous thing may be told
That fire which all thing melts, should harden ice,
And ice which is congealed° with senseless cold,
Should kindle fire by wonderful device?°
Such is the power of love in gentle mind,
That it can alter all the course of kind.° Ⓑ

6. **delayed:** tempered.

8. **augmented manifold:** increased in many ways.

11. **congealed:** thickened.
12. **device:** trick.

14. **kind:** nature.

Ⓐ **Literary Focus** **Speaker** Why do you think the speaker asks direct questions of the reader?

Ⓑ **Reading Focus** **Drawing Inferences** Note the turn, or shift in thought, in the final couplet. Based on this shift, what can you infer about the poet's message?

Teacher Preparation
Selection Summary
In Sonnet 30, the speaker compares his love for a woman to fire and her rejection of his love to ice. The sonnet develops a paradox, concluding that in the case of love, the rules of nature are suspended.

Direct Teach

Think About/Talk About
Read with a Purpose Have students read the Read with a Purpose statement. Tell students to write down instances in which the speaker mentions physical laws or phenomena.

Comprehension
Ⓑ Reading Focus

Possible response: *After wondering about the "miraculous" transformations in her beloved and in himself, the speaker finally explains that love is to blame for subverting the laws of nature. The message is that love follows its own rules.*

Analysis
Ⓐ Literary Focus

Possible response: *He is entreating his audience to help him understand the paradox he is contemplating.*

Extend the Discussion
Making Inferences How does the final couplet explain the feelings between the speaker and the loved woman? ***Possible response:*** *The obstinate love of the speaker and the equally obstinate rejection by the woman seem to be evidence that love is so powerful that it can alter physical laws.*

Advanced Learners
Acceleration Have students discuss Wyatt's sonnet according to the historical context. Ask students to make inferences about the role of Wyatt in the court of Henry VIII and the relationship between the poet and the king. Have students research Wyatt, Anne Boleyn, and King Henry VIII in an encyclopedia in the library or online. Then, have students share their inferences with the class, using supporting evidence from their sources.

Students with Disabilities
As students read the poem, "Whoso List to Hunt" for the third or fourth time, have them look for hunting images. Ask students what emotions the speaker is feeling, and which words or phrases give clues to the speaker's sentiments. Have students describe how they might feel if they were hunting for an animal that kept escaping. Would they give up easily? Why or why not?

Teacher Preparation

Selection Summary

In Sonnet 75, the speaker describes writing his beloved's name in the sand and seeing the waves wash it away twice. When she protests that it is futile to try to immortalize anything mortal, he promises to make her name and their love live forever through his verse.

Direct Teach

Think About/Talk About

Read with a Purpose Have students read the Read with a Purpose statement. Tell them to pay attention to the dialogue between the speaker and the woman.

Comprehension

A Reading Focus

Possible response: *This expression indicates that the speaker wrote the name of his beloved a second time.*

C Reading Focus

Possible response: *He believes her virtues are so remarkable they need immortal fame.*

Analysis

B Literary Focus

Possible response: *The two voices heighten the contrast between the high expectations of love and the disappointments brought by reality.*

Extend the Discussion

Finding Details In Sonnet 75, why does the woman complain the speaker is vain? ***Possible response:*** *She believes it is vain to try to transform an ephemeral thing into something permanent.*

Imagery What image does the author use to represent love's impermanence? ***Possible response:*** *Spencer uses the image of waves washing away the name of his beloved from the sand.*

SONNET

SONNET 75

by **Edmund Spenser**

Read with a Purpose
Read to discover what happens in the exchange between the speaker and the woman he loves.

Build Background
In this sonnet, Spenser uses the image of the sea and its eternal tides to emphasize the cyclical nature of life and the immortality brought by his poetry.

One day I wrote her name upon the strand,°
But came the waves and washèd it away;
Again I wrote it with a second hand, **A**
But came the tide, and made my pains his prey.
"Vain man," said she, "that doest in vain assay,°
A mortal thing so to immortalize,
For I myself shall like to this decay,
And eke° my name be wipèd out likewise." **B**
"Not so," quod° I, "let baser things devise°
To die in dust, but you shall live by fame:
My verse your virtues rare shall eternize,
And in the heavens write your glorious name.
Where whenas death shall all the world subdue,
Our love shall live, and later life renew." **C**

1. **strand:** beach.

5. **assay:** try.

8. **eke:** also.

9. **quod:** said. **devise:** plan.

A Reading Focus **Drawing Inferences** What does "second hand" mean?

B Literary Focus **Speaker** Why do you think Spenser uses two voices in this poem?

C Reading Focus **Drawing Inferences** In the poem, the male speaker wants to immortalize his love. Why does he think she is worthy of fame?

California Standards, p. 275

- **Reading Standard 2.4** Make warranted and reasonable assertions about the author's arguments by using elements of the text to defend and clarify interpretations.
- **Reading Standard 3.4** Analyze ways in which poets use imagery, personification, figures of speech, and sounds to evoke readers' emotions.
- **Writing Standard 2.1** Write fictional, autobiographical, or biographical narratives: **a.** Narrate a sequence of events and communicate their significance to the audience.

Reading Standard 2.4, 3.4 (see pages A48–A50)
Writing Standard 2.1a (see pages A51–A52)

Whoso List to Hunt / Sonnet 30 / Sonnet 75

Literary Response and Analysis

Reading Skills Focus

Quick Check

1. What might the deer represent in "Whoso List to Hunt"?
2. What is the "miraculous thing" in Sonnet 30?
3. In Sonnet 75, how does the poet plan to immortalize his love?

Read with a Purpose

4. What do the speakers' ideas about romantic love have in common?

Reading Skills: Drawing Inferences

5. Add a third column to the chart you made about contrasting images. List inferences these images help you draw about the speakers and messages.

Lines	Contrasting Words	Inferences I Can Draw
"My love is like to ice, and I to fire;"	ice and fire	The speaker and his love are opposites, or she doesn't love him at all.

Literary Skills Focus

Literary Analysis

6. **Interpret** In "Whoso List to Hunt," what warning does the speaker give? What image shows that the speaker considers the chase hopeless?
7. **Analyze** What **paradoxes,** or contradictions that are actually true, can you find in Sonnet 30?
8. **Evaluate** In what sense has the love of the two people in Sonnet 75 survived today?
9. **Summarize** In your own words, write brief prose summaries of two of the three sonnets. Describe each sonnet's mood, scene, and story.
10. **Extend** Some attitudes concerning love and men and women have changed since these sonnets were written. Do you think the speakers' feelings are still relevant? Cite details from the poems to explain your response.

Literary Skills: Speaker

11. **Synthesize** All three sonnets have male speakers. How might the sonnets change if they had female speakers?

Literary Skills Review: Metaphor

12. **Analyze** One of the most common figures of speech is **metaphor,** a comparison between two unlike things without the use of a connective word such as *like* or *as*. Write down at least one metaphor from each poem. How do these metaphors contribute to the poems' meanings?

Writing Skills Focus

Think as a Reader/Writer

Use It in Your Writing As you read, you took notes on the structure of each sonnet. Where does the turn, or shift in thought, occur ? In your *Reader/Writer Notebook,* write a sonnet that explains a situation or expresses a problem and then comments on that situation or states a solution to the problem.

What Do You Think Now? How is each of these sonnets an expression of the heart and the mind?

Universal Access

Struggling Writers

Some students may need additional scaffolding to complete the Writing Skills Focus activity. Review the sonnet form, demonstrating how each line is composed in iambic pentameter. Tell students that Spenser's sonnets consist of three quatrains and a couplet, and that they follow the rhyme scheme *abab bcbc cdcd ee.* Ask students to write six sentences in which they discuss the problem, and then have them state their comment or solution in one sentence. When students have finished, have them use two lines for each sentence and reword the lines to conform to the rhyme pattern *abab bcbc cdcd ee.* Remind students that their poems should show a clear shift in thought before the last two lines.

Check for Understanding

Independent Practice

Reading Skills Focus

Possible responses:

1. *the woman loved by the speaker*
2. *fire's inability to melt ice and ice's inability to quench fire*
3. *He will write a poem about her.*
4. *Each tells how passionate love is met by a cold response.*
5. *Have students add a column of inferences drawn from the contrasts in the sonnets they read.*

Literary Skills Focus

Possible responses:

6. *The speaker warns that the woman is not obtainable. "Since in a net I cannot hold the wind" conveys hopelessness.*
7. *Ice and fire are coexisting without changing properties.*
8. *It survives today in the form of the sonnet itself.*
9. *Have students consider mood, scene, and story in their summaries.*
10. *The speakers' feelings are still relevant because love may still be one-sided, with one person feeling more strongly than the other.*
11. *If the sonnets were written from the women's points of view, we might have a clearer idea of why these women were less enthusiastic than their suitors.*
12. *In lines 7 and 8 of "Whoso List to Hunt," the speaker resolves to give up his pursuit of his love, "Since in a net I seek to hold the wind." He is comparing his pursuit to a task as hopeless as catching the wind in a net. The metaphor makes the meaning more clear.*

What Do You Think Now?

Have students consider the feelings and thoughts expressed in the sonnets they just read.

Standards Focus

Objectives

Students will

- analyze the characteristics of pastoral poems
- understand inverted word order

Selection Introduction

Think About the Writers

With students, discuss the personalities of the writers based on their adventurous lives. Ask students to think about what kind of poetry could stem from an adventurous life.

For Independent Reading

Collected Poems, W. H. Auden

Motivate

What Do You Think?/QuickWrite

Have students think about a book, film, or TV show that portrayed an ideal romantic escape. Did they enjoy it? Why or why not?

English for Academic Success

Academic Vocabulary

Look for opportunities to use the Academic Vocabulary words in this unit.

- **controversies, *n.*:** lengthy disagreement
- **ensure, *v.*:** to make happen
- **established, *v.*:** caused to happen
- **widespread, *adj.*:** occurring over a wide area

California Standards, pp. 276–281

- **Reading Standard 2.2** Analyze the way in which clarity of meaning is affected by the patterns of organization, hierarchical structures, repetition of the main ideas, syntax, and word choice in the text.
- **Reading Standard 3.1** Analyze characteristics of subgenres (e.g., satire, parody, allegory, pastoral) that are used in poetry, prose, plays, novels, short stories, essays, and other basic genres.

Preparing to Read

CHRISTOPHER MARLOWE

The Passionate Shepherd to His Love

SIR WALTER RALEIGH

The Nymph's Reply to the Shepherd

What Do You Think? How do our hearts and minds influence our actions?

QuickWrite

In your *Reader/Writer Notebook,* explain why the idea of romantic escape is so appealing to human beings of any time period.

Reputed portrait of Christopher Marlowe (1585) by French School. Oil. The Master and Fellows of Corpus Christi College, Cambridge, England.

Sir Walter Raleigh (c. 1585) by Nicholas Hilliard. National Portrait Gallery, London.

MEET THE WRITER

Christopher Marlowe

(1564–1593)

Playwright, poet, brawler, and spy, Christopher Marlowe was the rebel of the Elizabethan writers. In 1587, he began doing espionage for England, but his government affiliation did not keep him on the right side of the law. He was arrested in 1593 on charges of making scandalous and controversial speeches. Days before the court date, Marlowe died instantly from a stab wound sustained in a brawl. While his assailant was acquitted on grounds of self-defense, it is possible that the testimony was fabricated and Marlowe was assassinated for political reasons.

Marlowe's best-known play is *The Tragicall History of Dr. Faustus,* the story about a man who bargains with Satan. Marlowe's heroes are driven, power-hungry men who refuse to recognize their own limits as humans or their responsibilities to others. To express these themes, Marlowe created wild and soaring poetry, like nothing heard before on the stage.

Sir Walter Raleigh

(1552–1618)

Handsome, arrogant, and dashing, Sir Walter Raleigh was a colorful figure in a very colorful era. His powerful poems reflect the courage of a man who was ready to accept his fate without self-pity.

Raleigh, who called himself a "seafaring man, a soldier, a courtier," was a favorite of Queen Elizabeth I. After Elizabeth died, however, his enemies convicted him of treason on trumped-up evidence and sentenced him to death.

Even in prison, Raleigh dreamed of a final expedition to South America. In 1617, still under a death sentence, he was granted this last voyage. It was a disaster. His men attacked a Spanish settlement, and the Spanish king pressed King James to execute Raleigh. Raleigh's words upon seeing the executioner's ax reflect both his courage and wit: "This is a sharp medicine, but it is a physician for all diseases."

Think About the Writers What effect do you think Marlowe's and Raleigh's adventures might have had on their poetry?

Selection Readability	
Easily Accessible **Accessible** Challenging	The poems include familiar vocabulary; accessible theme; stanzas.

The Passionate Shepherd to His Love/
The Nymph's Reply to the Shepherd

Reading Standard 2.2, 3.1 (see pages A48–A50)

Literary Skills Focus

Pastoral Poems Marlowe's "The Passionate Shepherd to His Love" is a **pastoral,** a poem depicting country life in idealized terms. In pastoral poems, handsome shepherds and beautiful nymphs live in harmony with nature. Absent are harsh and gritty images of rural labor. Sometimes called an **antipastoral,** Raleigh's "The Nymph's Reply to the Shepherd" mocks the pastoral poem's idyllic, idealistic descriptions of rural life.

Reading Skills Focus

Understanding Inverted Word Order Inversion, or **inverted word order,** is the rearrangement of standard word order in a phrase or sentence. The normal word order in English is subject, verb, and then object or complement: *We will read poetry.* Inverted word order reverses the word order: *Poetry we will read.* Inversion can affect **tone,** by emphasizing a particular word or idea. Poets may invert word order so that a line fits the poem's meter or rhyme scheme.

Into Action When you read a phrase or sentence with inverted word order, restate it in normal order to understand it better. For each poem, use a chart like the one below to record phrases and sentences in inverted word order and to rewrite them in normal word order.

Inverted Word Order	Normal Word Order
"And we will all the pleasures prove"	And we will prove all the pleasures.
"wool / Which from our pretty lambs we pull,"	

Writing Skills Focus

Think as a Reader/Writer

Find It in Your Reading A **refrain** is a repeated word, phrase, line, or group of lines. Refrains are used to establish rhythm, build suspense, or emphasize key words or ideas. As you read the poems, note in your *Reader/Writer Notebook* the refrains and their effects.

TechFocus As you read these poems, consider how modern writers might use images and sound effects to complement their words.

Vocabulary

melodious (muh LOH dee uhs) *adj.:* producing pleasant sounds. *The shepherd awoke to the melodious sounds of the birds.*

fragrant (FRAY gruhnt) *adj.:* sweet smelling. *We walked with the lambs through a meadow of fragrant grass and flowers.*

embroidered (ehm BROY duhrd) *v.* used as *adj.:* ornamented with needlework or as if with needlework. *She wore a beautiful dress embroidered with flowers.*

folly (FAHL ee) *n.:* foolishness. *It would be folly for a shepherd to play all the time and never work.*

Language Coach

Suffixes When you add the suffix *–ous* to the noun *melody,* you get the adjective *melodious.* Notice that the *y* changes to *i* when you add this suffix. Explain the meanings of the following adjectives and tell how they were formed from nouns: *mysterious, envious, industrious, rigorous, scandalous.*

Learn It Online
Plunge into these poems with a video introduction online.
go.hrw.com H12-277 Go

Reader/Writer Notebook
Use your **RWN** to complete the activities for these selections.

Selection Resources

Unit 2 Resources, on-level practice and assessment, p. 11

PowerNotes, interactive lesson presentation with activities

Teacher One Stop™, on-level lesson plans and all print resources

Holt Audio Library

Holt Audio Library: Selections and Summaries in Spanish

UA: Holt Interactive Reader, p. 73

UA: Differentiating Instruction, modified lesson plans and leveled assessment, p. 56

UA: Resources for Teaching Advanced Students, lesson plans, p. 81

UA: Supporting Instruction in Spanish, selection summary

ThinkCentral Online Assessment,. Selection Standards Check

ThinkCentral Online Remediation

Preteach

Introducing Vocabulary

- Read aloud the Vocabulary words, definitions, and sample sentences. Then, use this activity to check students' understanding.
- To reinforce the importance of the Vocabulary words, tell students that these words support the pastoral idyll that the poets want to create. *Melodious, fragrant,* and *embroidered* conjure up ideal images of country life, and even *folly* has a lighthearted tone.

English for Academic Success

Language Coach

Ask students to brainstorm other suffixes that transform the noun form of a word into the adjective form. [*–able: capable; –ic: poetic; –ive: festive*]

Literary Skills Focus

As you read and discuss the selection with students, have them note descriptions idealizing rural life.

Reading Skills Focus

Give students a copy of the Reading Skills Focus graphic organizer before they read. (See **Unit 2 Resources.**) Tell them to use their responses to answer the questions on the Applying Your Skills page.

Writing Skills Focus

Have students use their **Reader/Writer Notebooks** to note the refrains in the poems and describe their effects. Students can use their notes to complete the Writing Skills Focus activity.

Learn It Online
The **PowerNotes** presentation for this lesson includes a short video that introduces the poems. The video is also available on the online version of this page.
go.hrw.com H12-277 Go

Teacher Preparation

Selection Summary

In "The Passionate Shepherd to His Love," a shepherd describes the beauty of life in the country to his beloved to persuade her to go live with him.

Direct Teach

Think About/Talk About

Read with a Purpose Have students read the Read with a Purpose statement. Ask students to focus on the promises made by the shepherd to persuade his beloved to go live with him.

Comprehension

A Reading Focus

Possible response: *He inverts the word order to maintain the rhyme scheme.*

Analysis

B Literary Focus

Possible responses: *Gold buckles, coral clasps, and amber studs are precious items that are hardly in a shepherd's budget.*

Extend the Discussion

Repetition What is the effect of the repetition of line 1 at the end of the fifth and last stanzas? ***Possible response:*** *The repetition creates a pleasant, song-like rhythm and emphasizes the speaker's urgency to have his beloved go with him.*

Expressing an Opinion Do you find the speaker persuasive? Why or why not? ***Possible responses:*** *No, the life he depicts is unrealistic; yes, his vision is sensitive and passionate.*

POEM

The Passionate Shepherd to His Love

by **Christopher Marlowe**

Read with a Purpose

Read to find out what promises the shepherd makes to his beloved.

Build Background

Seventeenth-century London was growing rapidly. At the beginning of the century, the city's population swelled to 220,000 and pollution was an increasing problem. Not far from the city's borders lay the countryside, a refuge from the trials of urban life. Perhaps it is not surprising then that city dwellers enjoyed and sought out pastoral poetry, music, and painting.

Probably the most famous of the English pastorals, Marlowe's poem is also part of the *carpe diem* tradition, a call to "seize the day" by living life to the fullest. This poem has often been set to music, and several poets have written answers or sequels to it. Sir Walter Raleigh's reply is the most famous.

Young Man Leaning Against a Tree, miniature by Nicholas Hilliard (1585–1595). Victoria & Albert Museum, London.

Come live with me, and be my love,
And we will all the pleasures prove° **A**
That valleys, groves, hills, and fields,
Woods, or steepy mountain yields.

And we will sit upon the rocks,
Seeing the shepherds feed their flocks
By shallow rivers, to whose falls
Melodious birds sing madrigals.°

And I will make thee beds of roses,
And a thousand fragrant posies,
A cap of flowers, and a kirtle,°
Embroidered all with leaves of myrtle.

A gown made of the finest wool
Which from our pretty lambs we pull,
Fair linèd slippers for the cold,
With buckles of the purest gold.

A belt of straw and ivy buds,
With coral clasps and amber studs,
And if these pleasures may thee move,
Come live with me, and be my love. **B**

The shepherd swains° shall dance and sing
For thy delight each May morning.
If these delights thy mind may move,
Then live with me, and be my love.

2. prove: experience.
8. madrigals: complicated songs for several voices.
11. kirtle: archaic word meaning "dress," "gown," or "skirt."

21. swains: young boys.

A Reading Focus **Understanding Inverted Word Order** Why does Marlowe invert the word order in line 2?

B Literary Focus **Pastoral Poems** What promised gifts seem least likely to be possessed by real shepherds?

Vocabulary **melodious** (muh LOH dee uhs) *adj.:* producing pleasant sounds.
fragrant (FRAY gruhnt) *adj.:* sweet smelling.
embroidered (ehm BROY duhrd) *v.* used as *adj.:* ornamented with needlework or as if with needlework.

Universal Access

Struggling Readers

Strategic Students After students read each stanza for the third or fourth time, have them complete a two-column chart listing pastoral images in the first column and the thoughts, emotions, and feelings evoked by each image in the second column. Then, ask them to look over their responses in the second column and share with the class their overall impressions from the poem as a whole.

✔ See **UA: Differentiating Instruction** for strategies for teaching struggling readers.

Advanced Learners

Acceleration The sweet madrigals of the English Renaissance complement the themes in "The Passionate Shepherd to His Love." Students might find examples of songs and airs by Renaissance composers such as Thomas Tallis, Orlando Gibbons, John Dowland, and William Byrd. Have them analyze how the lyrics, the sounds of the instruments (lute and viol), and the tunes evoke the pastoral atmosphere expressed by Marlowe.

✔ See **UA: Resources for Teaching Advanced Students** for strategies for teaching advanced learners.

POEM

The Nymph's Reply to the Shepherd

by **Sir Walter Raleigh**

Read with a Purpose
Read the following poem to see if the nymph accepts the shepherd's offer.

If all the world and love were young,
And truth in every shepherd's tongue,
These pretty pleasures might me move **A**
To live with thee and be thy love.

But Time drives flocks from field to fold,°
When rivers rage and rocks grow cold,
And Philomel° becometh dumb; **B**
The rest complains of cares to come.

The flowers do fade, and wanton° fields
To wayward winter reckoning yields;
A honey tongue, a heart of gall°
Is fancy's spring, but sorrow's fall.

Thy gowns, thy shoes, thy beds of roses,
Thy cap, thy kirtle, and thy posies.
Soon break, soon wither, soon forgotten,
In folly ripe, in reason rotten.

Thy belt of straw and ivy buds,
Thy coral clasps and amber studs,
All these in me no means can move
To come to thee and be thy love.

But could youth last and love still breed,
Had joys no date, nor age no need,
Then these delights my mind might move
To live with thee and be thy love.

5. fold: pen where sheep are kept in winter.
7. Philomel: the nightingale.
9. wanton: luxuriant.
11. gall: bitter substance.

The Hireling Shepherd (1851) by William Holman Hunt.
Manchester Art Gallery, UK.

A Reading Focus **Understanding Inverted Word Order** How would the rhyme and meter of the poem be affected if this line were in normal word order?

B Literary Focus **Pastoral Poems** What season does the speaker describe in this stanza? Why does she use such harsh language in her description?

Vocabulary **folly** (FAHL ee) *n.:* foolishness.

Teacher Preparation

Selection Summary

In "The Nymph's Reply to the Shepherd," a nymph ridicules a shepherd's promises of love by painting a realistic view of the effect of time on passionate love.

Direct Teach

Think About/Talk About

Read with a Purpose Have students read the Read with a Purpose statement. Ask students to focus on the nymph's tone to figure out her reaction to the shepherd.

Comprehension

A Reading Focus

Possible response: *"Move" would no longer form a near rhyme with "love."*

Analysis

B Literary Focus

Possible response: *She describes winter and creates harsh images to counter the shepherd's ideal images of spring.*

Vocabulary: Own the Word

- **melodious:** Ask students to think of other creatures or things that produce *melodious* sounds. ***Possible responses:*** *cell phones, crickets*
- **fragrant:** *Fragrance* is a noun form of *fragrant.* A perfume or cologne is a *fragrance.* A *fragrance* is also defined as a pleasant, sweet smell. Ask students to describe *fragrances* that remind them of their childhood.
- **embroidered:** Ask students to list other kinds of decorations that a dress might be *embroidered* with. ***Possible responses:*** *glittering jewels, flowers, lace*
- **folly:** Tell students that the root word for *folly* is *follis,* Latin for "windbag" or "fool." A person characterized by *folly* lacks common sense and understanding.

California Standards, pp. 280–281

- **Reading Standard 2.2** Analyze the way in which clarity of meaning is affected by the patterns of organization, hierarchical structures, repetition of the main ideas, syntax, and word choice in the text.
- **Reading Standard 3.1** Analyze characteristics of subgenres (e.g., satire, parody, allegory, pastoral) that are used in poetry, prose, plays, novels, short stories, essays, and other basic genres.
- **Reading Standard 3.3** Analyze the ways in which irony, tone, mood, the author's style, and the "sound" of language achieve specific rhetorical or aesthetic purposes or both.
- **Writing Standard 2.2** Write responses to literature: **a.** Demonstrate a comprehensive understanding of the significant ideas in works or passages.
- **Listening and Speaking Standard 2.3** Deliver oral responses to literature: **b.** Analyze the imagery, language, universal themes, and unique aspects of the text through the use of rhetorical strategies (e.g., narration, description, persuasion, exposition, a combination of those strategies).

Check for Understanding

Reading Skills Focus

Possible responses:

1. *She will enjoy sitting and watching the shepherds work. She will lie on beds of roses and have a hat of flowers. She will also receive a fine gown and slippers.*
2. *She accuses the shepherd of lying.*
3. *The nymph believes that the items the shepherd gives her will break or become damaged over time.*
4. *The shepherd promises her a life of leisure and finery. The nymph finds these promises unrealistic.*
5. *Ask students to note the effects on rhyme, rhythm, and meter.*

Vocabulary Check

6. *c* **7.** *d*

8. *a* **9.** *b*

Literary Skills Focus

Possible responses:

10. *Idealized images of valleys, hills, woods, and rivers fit the definition of pastoral poetry. The nymph mocks these by portraying them in the harshness of winter.*
11. *The shepherd is more persuasive because he is moved by passion. The nymph is more persuasive because she is realistic.*
12. *The literature of the Renaissance celebrated a life in harmony with nature. This is apparent in the idyllic beauty of the countryside presented in this poem.*
13. *Marlowe's tone is seductive and idealistic. Raleigh's tone is mocking and suspicious.*

Applying Your Skills

Reading Standard 2.2, 3.1, 3.3 (see pages A48–A50)
Writing Standard 2.2a (see pages A51–A52)

The Passionate Shepherd to His Love
The Nymph's Reply to the Shepherd

Literary Response and Analysis

Reading Skills Focus

Quick Check

1. In "The Passionate Shepherd," what pleasant entertainment does the shepherd offer his love?
2. In line 2 of "The Nymph's Reply," what does the nymph accuse the shepherd of doing?
3. According to the nymph, what will happen to the shepherd's lovely gifts?

Read with a Purpose

4. Describe the promises that the shepherd makes. How would the nymph describe the promises?

Reading Skills: Understanding Inverted Word Order

5. As you read, you rewrote lines that use inverted word order. Now, add a column to each poem's chart and explain the effects created by the inverted word order. Note that there may be several effects.

Inverted Word Order	Normal Word Order	Effect in Poem
"And we will all the pleasures prove"	And we will prove all the pleasures.	1. maintains rhyme with line above
"wool / Which from our pretty lambs we pull,"		

Vocabulary Check

Choose the synonym for each Vocabulary word.

6. melodious	**a.** ornamented
7. fragrant	**b.** foolishness
8. embroidered	**c.** pleasant sounding
9. folly	**d.** sweet smelling

Literary Skills Focus

Literary Analysis

10. **Compare and Contrast** What details in "The Passionate Shepherd to His Love" enable it to be categorized as pastoral poetry? How does the description of rural life in "The Nymph's Reply" mock the first poem's idealistic details?
11. **Evaluate** How persuasive are the shepherd and the nymph as they make their cases? With whom are you more inclined to agree? Why?

Literary Skills: Pastoral Poetry

12. **Interpret** How does the description of the pastoral world in "The Passionate Shepherd" reflect the Renaissance view of country life?

Literary Skills Review: Tone

13. **Analyze** The attitude a writer takes toward the reader or the subject is called **tone.** What is Raleigh's tone in "The Nymph's Reply"? How does his tone compare to Marlowe's?

Writing Skills Focus

Think as a Reader/Writer

Use It in Your Writing Review how the poems' speakers repeat words, phrases, and lines to emphasize their arguments. In your *Reader/Writer Notebook,* write a poem or song in which you use a refrain to persuade your readers to think in a certain way.

What Do You Think Now Whose poem is influenced more by the heart, and whose poem is influenced more by the mind?

What Do You Think Now?

Ask students to review the poems and focus on the tone used by the two speakers. Have students think about which of the two speakers is more emotional and which is more rational.

Universal Access

Struggling Writers

Some students may need additional scaffolding to complete the Writing Skills Focus activity. Have students begin by choosing a topic and considering what they want to say about the topic. Tell them to express this thought in a refrain of 1–2 lines. As students write their poem or song, tell them to repeat the refrain to reinforce the idea of the refrain throughout their writing.

Writing Standard 2.2a (see pages A51–A52)
Listening and Speaking Standard 2.3b (see pages A53–A55)

Grammar Link

Sentence Fragments and Run-on Sentences

A **sentence fragment** is a word group that does not express a complete thought. Some fragments are **phrase fragments,** which lack either a subject or a verb: *Herding the sheep.* Others are **subordinate clauses,** which have a subject and verb but do not express a complete thought on their own: *While they herded the sheep.* To correct a fragment, add the missing part: *While they herded the sheep, the shepherds sang.*

A **run-on sentence** is two or more complete sentences run together as one. Many run-ons are **comma splices,** two or more complete thoughts linked only with a comma: *The clouds dispersed, the moonlight revealed the sheep.* Other run-ons, called **fused sentences,** lack punctuation or a connecting word between the thoughts: *The clouds dispersed the moonlight revealed the sheep.* You can correct a run-on in three ways:

1. Use periods or semicolons to divide the sentences. *The clouds dispersed. The moonlight revealed the sheep.*
2. Use a comma and a coordinating conjunction. *The clouds dispersed,* ***and*** *the moonlight revealed the sheep.* (coordinating conjunction)
3. Make one sentence the subordinate clause of the other: ***When the clouds dispersed,*** *the moonlight revealed the sheep.* (subordinate clause)

Your Turn

Identify and correct the fragments and run-ons.

1. Although the shepherd offers a leisurely life.
2. The nymph's response to the shepherd's words?
3. Flowers bloom birds sing.
4. Still, winter comes, icy rain falls.

Writing Application Review a piece of writing in your *Reader/Writer Notebook* for fragments and run-on sentences. Correct any you find by using the three methods described above.

CHOICES

As you respond to the Choices, use these **Academic Vocabulary** words as appropriate: establish, ensure, widespread, controversy, contradiction.

REVIEW

Accept the Offer

Write a formal letter from the nymph to the shepherd in which she accepts his request to be his love. In your letter, explain why the nymph has changed her mind. What kind of life does she hope to have with the shepherd? What conditions must the shepherd meet to ensure that she will join him? Use details from both poems to develop your letter.

CONNECT

Advertise the Pastoral Life

TechFocus Marlowe's poem reads almost like an advertisement for rural life. With a partner, convert this poem into a commercial or print advertisement that the shepherd might have created. If you make a commercial, use images and sounds to accompany Marlowe's words. Use persuasive techniques to encourage your viewers to consider the widespread benefits of country life. How do you think the nymph might have responded if given this advertisement?

EXTEND

Stage a Debate

Group Activity In a small group, use reason, evidence, and persuasive techniques to prepare an argument that either states it is better to live solely for today, as the shepherd claims to do, or to plan and work for the future, as the nymph advises. Choose a debater to act as the shepherd or the nymph to present each group's argument.

Universal Access: Grammar Link

English Learners

English for Academic Success Explain to students that a semicolon can be used occasionally to separate two independent clauses that have their own subject and verb. Display these sentences on the board:

- The nymph rejected his offer; and made him sad.
- The nymph rejected his offer; he walked away sadly.

Tell students that the first sentence is incorrect because the second clause is not independent. Both clauses on each side of the semicolon should be complete sentences and have a similar idea or meaning.

Ask students to examine a short story or a novel and trace instances in which the semicolon is used. Then, ask them to write a short paragraph in which they use this punctuation at least twice.

✔ For more practice with sentence fragments and run-on sentences, see **Warriner's Handbook, GrammarNotes** and **Language Handbook Worksheets.**

Independent Practice

Grammar Link

Your Turn

1. *The shepherd offers a leisurely life.*
2. *What was the nymph's response to the shepherd's words?*
3. *Flowers bloom; birds sing.*
4. *Still, winter comes and icy rain falls.*

Choices: Evaluation Criteria

Review: Homework
Accept the Offer

- The letter includes details and information from the poems.
- The conditions placed by the nymph agree with her personality as it emerges from Raleigh's poem.

Connect: Homework
Advertise the Pastoral Life

- Students use media and persuasive techniques to convey a pastoral message.
- Students consider the nymph's response to the message.

Extend: Homework
Stage a Debate

- Students take a clear side with either the shepherd or the nymph.
- The arguments present solid supporting ideas.

Assess

Unit 2 Resources, Selection Standards Check, p. 14

ThinkCentral Online Assessment, Selection Standards Check

Teacher One-Stop™, editable Selection Standards Check

Reteach

To reteach **poetic devices,** see **Reteaching Lessons,** pp. 1449Q–1449R.

ThinkCentral Online Remediation

Standards Focus

Objectives

Students will

- analyze the characteristics of *carpe diem* poetry
- use paraphrasing or retelling to add clarity to meaning

Selection Introduction

Think About the Writers

Before students answer the question, have them think of some reasons why, in a time of political turmoil, *carpe diem* poets might have wanted readers to "seize the day."

For Independent Reading

- *Seize the Day,* Saul Bellow
- *Gitanjali,* Rabindranath Tagore

Motivate

What Do You Think?/QuickTalk

Ask students to think of a time someone told them to make the most of their youth. What reasons did he or she give for this advice? Did this advice come from their heart or their mind?

English for Academic Success

Academic Vocabulary

Look for opportunities to use the Academic Vocabulary words in this unit.

- **contradiction, *n.*:** statement in opposition to another
- **established, *v.*:** caused to happen

California Standards, pp. 282–287

- **Reading Standard 2.2** Analyze the way in which clarity of meaning is affected by the patterns of organization, hierarchical structures, repetition of the main ideas, syntax, and word choice in the text.
- **Reading Standard 3.1** Analyze characteristics of subgenres (e.g., satire, parody, allegory, pastoral) that are used in poetry, prose, plays, novels, short stories, essays, and other basic genres.

Preparing to Read

ROBERT HERRICK

To the Virgins, to Make Much of Time

ANDREW MARVELL

To His Coy Mistress

What Do You Think? How do our hearts and minds influence our actions?

QuickTalk

Do you think the drive to make the most of one's youth comes from the heart or the mind? Discuss your responses in a small group.

Robert Herrick, after the frontispiece to Herrick's *Hesperides* (1648).

Andrew Marvell (c. 1655-1660) by unknown artist. National Portrait Gallery, London.

MEET THE WRITER

Robert Herrick

(1591–1674)

Robert Herrick wrote some of his best poems while he was the vicar of Dean Prior in Devonshire, in the West Country. Herrick's lyrical poetry covers a wide range; he composed poems in imitation of the Latin love poets as well as wrote about his small house, his cat, his spaniel, or whatever else came into his mind. Herrick's poems create a portrait of "Merrie England," a timeless, idealized pastoral state full of innocent pleasures. Behind the innocent guise of his pastoral poetry, however, often lurk Herrick's particular, and sometimes contradictory, political views.

Herrick's stay in Dean Prior abruptly ended in 1647 with the arrival of Cromwell's army, which seized his parish and replaced him with a more puritanical clergyman. He spent the next thirteen years in London, where he published a poetry collection called *Hesperides,* a title from classical mythology that alludes to the treasures within Herrick's work. When Charles II was restored to power, so was Herrick, who lived on at Dean Prior until his death.

Andrew Marvell

(1621–1678)

Andrew Marvell's poems capture much of what is admirable in Renaissance lyric poetry. His poems display precision, sophistication, and lightness of touch. Educated at Cambridge, Marvell traveled through much of Europe as a young man. He managed to move between political parties through the upheaval of the Civil Wars, befriending pro-Puritan John Milton as well as several supporters of the royal family. From 1659 until his death, he served in Parliament, establishing sufficient influence with the Royalists to save Milton's life after the Restoration.

Marvell's poetry was largely unpublished during his lifetime but was read and circulated among his friends. His work demonstrates an artistic control of language that appears at once to be graceful and complex.

Think About the Writers How might political turmoil have influenced these poets to write poetry that calls on readers to live life to the fullest?

Selection Readability	
Easily Accessible **Accessible** Challenging	These poems include short stanzas; familiar theme; familiar language.

To the Virgins, to Make Much of Time / To His Coy Mistress

Reading Standard 2.2, 3.1 (see pages A48–A50)

Literary Skills Focus

Carpe Diem Sprung from the pen of the classical Latin poet Horace, ***carpe diem*** (literally "seize the day") is an admonition to "make the most of your life while you can." The *carpe diem* theme became increasingly popular in Renaissance English poetry, and "To the Virgins, to Make Much of Time" and "To His Coy Mistress" are some of the greatest and most famous examples. As you read, look for each speaker's warning to young women who ignore the advice to "seize the day."

Reading Skills Focus

Paraphrasing Readers **paraphrase** when they restate in their own words something they have read. Paraphrasing helps you clarify or simplify what you are reading. To paraphrase, pause after a paragraph, an important scene, or a stanza, and reword what you have just read.

Into Action While reading "To the Virgins, to Make Much of Time," take a moment after reading each stanza to paraphrase what the speaker has said. Use a chart like the one below to write your paraphrases. Continue this for "To His Coy Mistress." This poem has no stanzas, but you can pause to paraphrase after every sentence or complete thought.

Stanzas/Lines	My Paraphrase
Herrick, Stanza 1	Enjoy the pleasures of today while you can. Time moves on; like flowers, these pleasures will soon fade.

Writing Skills Focus

Find It in Your Reading Writers, especially poets, use **figurative language**—language that describes one thing in terms of another—to communicate ideas effectively. Herrick and Marvell, for instance, use **personification,** a kind of metaphor in which a nonhuman thing or quality is talked about as if it were human. As you read, look for examples of personification, and think about how it helps establish the *carpe diem* theme.

Language Coach

Word Origins The word *coy* comes from a Latin root that means "quiet." The meaning of *coy* has evolved such that today *coy* describes a specific kind of quietness, one that is cold, aloof, and inaccessible. As the meaning of the word deepened over time, *coyness* was used to describe a reluctance to make a commitment. Choose another word from one of the poems, and trace its origins.

Reader/Writer Notebook

Use your **RWN** to complete the activities for these selections.

Learn It Online

Let a voice actor bring these poems alive for you.

go.hrw.com H12-283 Go

Selection Resources

Unit 2 Resources, on-level practice and assessment p. 17

Teacher One Stop™, on-level lesson plans and all print resources

Holt Audio Library

Holt Audio Library: Selections and Summaries in Spanish

UA: Differentiating Instruction, graphic organizer, p. 59

UA: Supporting Instruction in Spanish, selection summary

Analyzing Visuals Transparencies, p. 10

ThinkCentral Online Assessment, Selection Standards Check

ThinkCentral Online Remediation

Preteach

English for Academic Success

Language Coach

Ask students to use a dictionary or other source to find the origins and other derivations and their meanings of the words *quiet* and *prime*.

Literary Skills Focus

As you read and discuss the selection with students, have them note the speaker's warning to those who fail to "seize the day."

Reading Skills Focus

Give students a copy of the Reading Skills Focus graphic organizer before they read. (See **Unit 2 Resources.**) Tell them to use their responses to answer the questions on the Applying Your Skills page.

Writing Skills Focus

Have students record examples of personification in their **Reader/Writer Notebooks.** Students can use their notes to complete the Writing Skills Focus activity.

Learn It Online

The online version of these poems includes audio support to engage all students and to help struggling readers with reading comprehension and vocabulary.

go.hrw.com H12-283 Go

Teacher Preparation
Selection Summary
In "To the Virgins, to Make Much of Time," the speaker warns that time flies and youth fades. For these reasons, he says, young women should marry quickly—before losing the chance.

Direct Teach

Think About/Talk About
Read with a Purpose Have students read the Read with a Purpose statement. Point out that the statement asks them to "identify the reasons the speaker gives to 'seize the day.'"

Comprehension
Ⓐ Reading Focus

Possible response: *"Live fully while you are young enough to enjoy it."*

Analysis
Ⓑ Literary Focus

Possible responses: *sunset; rosebuds; flowers dying*

Extend the Discussion
Audience Whom does the author address in this poem? ***Possible response:*** *The author addresses virgins who are young and need to live their life while they still can.*

Carpe Diem According to the final stanza, what will happen to young women who do not follow the poem's advice? ***Possible response:*** *The consequence of not living life to the fullest while young will be to never wed.*

POEM

To the Virgins, to Make Much of Time

by **Robert Herrick**

Read with a Purpose
Read this poem to identify the reasons the speaker gives to "seize the day."

Build Background
Herrick and Marvell both used a graceful and polished style to write about love, pleasure, and honor. Herrick, a priest, addresses all young women in "To the Virgins, to Make Much of Time," while Marvell argues that even immoral behavior while alive is preferable to being good but dead.

Gather ye rosebuds while ye may, Ⓐ
  Old Time is still a-flying;
And this same flower that smiles today,
  Tomorrow will be dying.

The glorious lamp of heaven, the sun,
  The higher he's a-getting,
The sooner will his race be run,
  And nearer he's to setting.

That age is best which is the first,
  When youth and blood are warmer;
But being spent, the worse, and worst
  Times still° succeed the former.

Then be not coy,° but use your time;
  And while ye may, go marry:
For having lost but once your prime,
  You may forever tarry.° Ⓑ

Spring (1595) by Lucas van Valckenborch. Private Collection.

12. still: always.

13. coy: cold; inaccessible; aloof.

16. tarry: delay; linger.

Ⓐ **Reading Focus** **Paraphrasing** How would you restate this famous opening line in your own words?

Ⓑ **Literary Focus** ***Carpe Diem*** What images does the speaker draw from the natural world to describe how quickly one's youth passes?

Universal Access

EL English Learners
Remind students that *carpe diem* means "to live or enjoy today to the fullest." Point out that in the first two stanzas, the poet assigns human qualities to nonhuman things to set forth the theme of *carpe diem*. Have students read the first two stanzas, and in pairs, retell what is happening in each stanza. Then, ask each pair to think of their own examples of something in nature that demonstrates the "seize the day" idea.

Advanced Learners
Acceleration Have students compare the poem's *carpe diem* message with the worldview in this political epigram by Herrick:

Moderation

In things a moderation keep,
Kings ought to shear, not skin, their sheep.

POEM

To His Coy Mistress

by **Andrew Marvell**

Read with a Purpose
Read to discover how this speaker is like the speaker of Herrick's poem, and how he is different.

Had we but world° enough, and time,
This coyness,° Lady, were no crime.
We would sit down, and think which way
To walk, and pass our long love's day.
Thou by the Indian Ganges' side
Shouldst rubies find; I by the tide
Of Humber° would complain.° I would
Love you ten years before the Flood,°
And you should, if you please, refuse
Till the conversion of the Jews.°
My vegetable° love should grow
Vaster than empires and more slow;
An hundred years should go to praise
Thine eyes, and on thy forehead gaze;
Two hundred to adore each breast,
But thirty thousand to the rest;
An age at least to every part,
And the last age should show your heart.
For, Lady, you deserve this state,°
Nor would I love at lower rate. **A**
But at my back I always hear
Time's wingèd chariot hurrying near;
And yonder all before us lie
Deserts of vast eternity.
Thy beauty shall no more be found,
Nor, in thy marble vault, shall sound
My echoing song; then worms shall try
That long-preserved virginity,
And your quaint honor turn to dust,
And into ashes all my lust:

1. world: geographical space.
2. coyness: reluctance to make a commitment.
7. Humber: muddy river in Marvell's hometown of Hull; here, ironically compared to the grand Ganges in India. **complain:** utter complaints about not being loved.
8. Flood: Biblical flood, described in Genesis.
10. conversion of the Jews: Christians once believed that all Jews would be converted to Christianity immediately before the Last Judgment.
11. vegetable: plantlike; having the power to grow very large, like oak trees.
19. state: ceremony.

A Reading Focus **Paraphrasing** Paraphrase what the speaker says he would do to demonstrate his love, if he had all the time in the world.

Universal Access

EL English Learners

English for Academic Success Point out to students that the word *quaint* in line 29 refers to the meaning "odd in a charming way." Explain that *quaint* can also mean "skillfully made," and the word is derived from the Latin word *cognōscere,* meaning "to know." Other words that are derived from this Latin word are *cognition,* meaning "knowledge," and *recognize,* meaning "to identify."

Advanced Learners

Acceleration Divide students into groups of three or four, and have them compose a rap centering on the *carpe diem* theme in iambic pentameter. Have each student in a group contribute at least two lines that rhyme. Thus, the poem should have the rhyme scheme *aabbccddeeff*, and so forth. Have groups present their raps in front of the class.

Teacher Preparation

Selection Summary

In "To His Coy Mistress," the speaker uses hyperbole to describe the extreme lengths to which he would go to express his love if only there were time enough to do so.

Direct Teach

Think About/Talk About

Read with a Purpose Have students read the Read with a Purpose statement. Point out that the statement asks them to discover the differences and similarities between the speakers of the two poems.

Comprehension

A Reading Focus

Possible response: *sit; think about walking to pass the day; complain about not being loved; spend years convincing her to love him; his love growing slow like a vegetable; spending many years praising her eyes, forehead, breasts, and the rest of her*

Extend the Discussion

Figurative Language What figure of speech does the speaker use to show the intensity of his feelings in lines 3–20? ***Possible response:*** *hyperbole, or overstatement*

Personification How is time personified in lines 21–22? ***Possible response:*** *Time is depicted as a winged charioteer pursuing the speaker.*

Think About/Talk About

Analysis

B Literary Focus

Possible responses: *The speaker says it is private in the grave, but no one embraces there. The idea of embracing in the grave supports the idea of seizing every opportunity.*

Extend the Discussion

Finding Details On this page, what are some things that the speaker says about time? How does the speaker feel about time? ***Possible responses:*** *It is "slow-chapped," and it devours life; the speaker fears time.*

Carpe Diem In the last two lines, how does the speaker's suggestion to make the sun "run" support the *carpe diem* theme? ***Possible response:*** *He says that they cannot make time stand still, but they can make the most of the time they have.*

Analyzing Visuals

Connecting to the Text: *The young man in the painting appears to be making a marriage proposal to the lady, thus reflecting the poem's theme to "seize the day" before it is too late, and before the beauty of the lady fades with time.*

The Month of July (detail of a couple) (c. 1400) by Italian School. Fresco.
Castello del Buonconsiglio, Trent, Italy.

Analyzing Visuals

Connecting to the Text "To His Coy Mistress" is one of the most famous invitations to love in English literature. How does the body language of the subjects express some of the poem's ideas?

The grave's a fine and private place,
But none, I think, do there embrace.
  Now therefore, while the youthful hue
Sits on thy skin like morning dew,
And while thy willing soul transpires°
At every pore with instant fires,
Now let us sport us while we may,
And now, like amorous birds of prey,
Rather at once our time devour
Than languish in his slow-chapped° power.
Let us roll all our strength and all
Our sweetness up into one ball,
And tear our pleasures with rough strife
Through the iron gates of life;
Thus, though we cannot make our sun
Stand still, yet we will make him run. **B**

35. transpires: breathes out.

40. slow-chapped: slow-jawed. Time is seen as consuming life.

B Literary Focus ***Carpe Diem*** What is humorous about the speaker's description of the grave in lines 31–32? How does this use of humor support the *carpe diem* theme?

California Standards, p. 287

- **Reading Standard 2.2** Analyze the way in which clarity of meaning is affected by the patterns of organization, hierarchical structures, repetition of the main ideas, syntax, and word choice in the text.
- **Reading Standard 3.1** Analyze characteristics of subgenres (e.g., satire, parody, allegory, pastoral) that are used in poetry, prose, plays, novels, short stories, essays, and other basic genres.
- **Reading Standard 3.4** Analyze ways in which poets use imagery, personification, figures of speech, and sounds to evoke readers' emotions.
- **Writing Standard 2.3** Write reflective compositions: **a.** Explore the significance of personal experiences, events, conditions, or concerns by using rhetorical strategies (e.g., narration, description, exposition, persuasion).

Applying Your Skills

Reading Standard 2.2, 3.1, 3.4 (see pages A48–A50)
Writing Standard 2.3a (see pages A51–A52)

To the Virgins, to Make Much of Time
To His Coy Mistress

Literary Response and Analysis

Reading Skills Focus

Quick Check

1. According to both speakers, what occurs when someone's youth has passed?
2. According to Herrick's speaker, what may happen to a woman who refuses to fall in love?
3. Of what "crime" does the speaker in Marvell's poem accuse his love?

Read with a Purpose

4. Why, according to the speakers in the poems, should young women "seize the day"?

Reading Skills: Paraphrasing

5. As you read, you paraphrased sections of each poem to check your comprehension of the poet's ideas. Now, add a new column to your chart for each poem. Explain how the particular line or stanza supports the *carpe diem* theme.

Stanzas/Lines	My Paraphrase	Support for Theme
Herrick, Stanza 1	Enjoy the pleasures of today while you can. Time moves on; like flowers, these pleasures will soon fade.	Gives a direct command, doesn't waste time getting to the point, which is what "act before it's too late" is all about.

Literary Skills Focus

Literary Analysis

6. **Infer** What can you infer about the speakers' attitudes toward marriage from these poems?
7. **Evaluate** The sun appears in both "To the Virgins" (line 5) and "To His Coy Mistress" (line 45). How does each poet use the image of the sun?
8. **Compare and Contrast** Herrick, in "To the Virgins," and Marvell, in "To His Coy Mistress," have similar objectives but different approaches. Is one poet more persuasive than the other? How are their arguments similar and different?
9. **Extend** How would you describe the tone of each poem's speaker? Are their warnings to "seize the day" motivated purely by good intentions?

Literary Skills: *Carpe Diem*

10. **Interpret** How does the advice the speakers give reflect the *carpe diem* theme?

Literary Skills Review: Hyperbole

11. **Analyze** Marvell uses both **hyperbole**—extreme exaggeration, or overstatement—as well as understatement in his argument. Identify examples of each device. Then, explain how each contributes to the poem's exploration of the subjects of youth/beauty and age/death.

Writing Skills Focus

Think as a Reader/Writer

Use It in Your Writing Review how the poems' speakers use personification to describe how short and sweet youth, and even all of life, can be. Then, use personification to write a paragraph in your *Reader/Writer Notebook* in which you describe what it is like to be young. In your writing, you might personify youth, time, or some other abstract aspect of life, such as death or aging.

What Do You Think Now? Does *carpe diem* appeal more to the mind or to the heart?

Check for Understanding

Independent Practice

Reading Skills Focus

Possible responses:

1. *They start dying.*
2. *She will lose her chance forever.*
3. *He accuses her of coyness.*
4. *They do not have a lot of time and will not be young forever.*
5. *Instruct students to discuss how the lines or stanzas support the carpe diem theme.*

Literary Skills Focus

Possible responses:

6. *One should marry while young.*
7. *Herrick uses the sun to warn that life is finite; Marvell uses it to challenge his mistress to join him in outrunning time.*
8. *Students should think about whether one poet is more persuasive than the other, and compare their arguments.*
9. *Herrick's speaker is more fatherly, urging young women to live their lives and to marry young. The speaker of Marvell's poem has different intentions: he is trying to convince a specific woman to "seize the day" with him.*
10. *The speakers tell their respective audiences to live in the present or they will regret it in the future.*
11. *In lines 13–14, the speaker claims that if he had the time, he would devote one hundred years to admiring his lover's eyes, which is a hyperbole. In lines 27–28, he provides an understatement when he describes worms taking his lover's virginity—the worms are devouring the entire corpse, not just the corpse's honor.*

What Do You Think Now?

Have students discuss whether *carpe diem* poetry appeals more to the mind or the heart and why they think so. Ask students, "Which part of you relates to *carpe diem,* your mind or your heart? What stops you from seizing the day?"

Universal Access

Struggling Writers

To help students complete the Writing Skills Focus activity, have them use Marvell's personification of time as a model to personify time in a different way while still showing that time catches up quickly. Ask them to brainstorm human characteristics they might associate with time, such as the capabilities to see, move, and hear.

Assess

Unit 2 Resources, Selection Standards Check, p. 18

go.hrw.com **ThinkCentral Online Assessment,** Selection Standards Check

Teacher One Stop™, editable Selection Standards Check

Standards Focus

Objectives

Students will
- analyze the characteristics of metaphysical poetry
- understand the use of tone and onomatopoeia
- understand the use of paradox
- identify the main idea of the text
- identify comparison-contrast organization

Selection Introduction

Think About the Writer

Have students list contrasts and contradictions in Donne's life. For instance, he was a brilliant thinker but was denied an Oxford degree.

For Independent Reading

The Complete English Poems, John Donne

Motivate

What Do You Think?/QuickWrite

Ask students how someone might retain a bond with someone who has passed away.

English for Academic Success

Academic Vocabulary

Look for opportunities to use this Academic Vocabulary words in this unit.

- **contradiction, *n.*:** statement in opposition to another
- **ensure, *v.*:** to make certain
- **established, *v.*:** set up; caused to happen

California Standards, pp. 288–303

- **Reading Standard 2.2** Analyze the way in which clarity of meaning is affected by the patterns of organization, hierarchical structures, repetition of the main ideas, syntax, and word choice in the text.
- **Reading Standard 3.1** Analyze characteristics of subgenres (e.g., satire, parody, allegory, pastoral) that are used in poetry, prose, plays, novels, short stories, essays, and other basic genres.

Preparing to Read

Song
A Valediction: Forbidding Mourning
Meditation 17
Death be not proud

What Do You Think? How do our hearts and minds influence our actions?

QuickWrite

When people have a close bond, can they ever really be separated—even by death? Record your thoughts in your *Reader/Writer Notebook.*

John Donne (1572–1631).

MEET THE WRITER

John Donne
(1572–1631)

As a brash young man, Donne wrote worldly, cynical lyrics; as a reverent preacher, he composed magnificent sermons and sacred poetry. His writings reflect a complex individuality.

A Life of Contrasts

Though now considered the foremost metaphysical poet, Donne never wished to be known publicly as a poet. Born a Catholic, Donne aspired in his youth to be a courtier. He was later appointed to one of the highest positions in the Anglican Church and established himself as a great preacher.

At age twelve, Donne was already studying at Oxford. Because of his religion, he was barred from taking a degree, so he returned to London to study law. The man known as "Jack" Donne, a handsome, well-dressed youth who devoted mornings to reading and afternoons to socializing, soon emerged. One friend described him as "a great visitor of ladies, a great frequenter of plays, a great writer of . . . [metaphorical] verses."

Undone Ambitions

After many adventures, including two naval expeditions, Donne became secretary to Thomas Egerton, lord keeper of the great seal. This post might have been the start of a brilliant government career; however, in 1601, Donne sparked controversy when he married seventeen-year-old Anne More. Marriage with a minor, without her father's consent, was a serious crime. Anne's father had Donne jailed and dismissed from his position.

Although Donne was not in prison long, he was never able to recover his position. For years, he and Anne had to live off the bounty of friends and relatives. In the early 1600s, Donne continued to write poetry in private and prose for the public. He now wrote against the Church of Rome and became known as an important defender of the Church of England. In 1615, James I persuaded Donne to become a clergyman. His theatrical sermons soon won him advancement in the Church, and he rose to be dean of St. Paul's, the principal cathedral of England, in London.

Think About the Writer How might Donne's contrasting life experiences have influenced and enriched his writings?

Selection Readability	
Easily Accessible Accessible **Challenging**	These selections include historical context; complex narrative poem; unfamiliar vocabulary.

Teacher Preparation

Selection Summary

In this poem, the speaker urges his wife to behave with dignity when they part. The couple's love is described as a union of soul that cannot be broken by distance.

Direct Teach

Think About/Talk About

Read with a Purpose Have students read the Read with a Purpose statement. Ask students to focus on the speaker's explanation for the unbreakable bond between two people in love.

Comprehension

A Reading Focus

Possible response: *Natural disasters on Earth more closely affect humans than disruptions in planetary movements, even if those disruptions occur on a larger scale. Donne's point is that the love between the speaker and his wife is so exalted that minor disruptions, such as a temporary separation, cannot truly affect it.*

Extend the Discussion

Finding the Main Idea What main point does Donne express in the second stanza? ***Possible response:*** *Do not express to others outward, dramatic emotions about the death of a loved one.*

Making Inferences Why does the speaker urge his wife to part from him quietly? ***Possible response:*** *It would spoil the sacredness of their love to display their feelings publicly.*

POEM

A Valediction: Forbidding Mourning

by **John Donne**

Read with a Purpose

Read to discover the speaker's attitude about being separated from his lover.

Build Background

A valediction is a farewell. Izaak Walton, an acquaintance of Donne, claimed that this poem was written when Donne was called away to France on a diplomatic mission. His wife, pregnant at the time, did not want him to leave, but he felt obligated to the mission's leader, Sir Robert Drury. Two days after arriving in Paris, Donne had a vision, which he described to Sir Robert: "I have seen my dear wife pass twice by me through this room, with her hair hanging about her shoulders, and a dead child in her arms." A messenger from England brought the news that "Mrs. Donne . . . after a long and dangerous labor . . . [had given birth to] a dead child" on the very day Donne had the vision.

As virtuous men pass mildly away,
 And whisper to their souls, to go,
Whilst some of their sad friends do say,
 The breath goes now, and some say, no:

So let us melt, and make no noise,
 No tear-floods, nor sigh-tempests move,
'Twere profanation° of our joys
 To tell the laity° our love.

Moving of th' earth° brings harms and fears,
 Men reckon what it did and meant,°
But trepidation of the spheres,°
 Though greater far, is innocent.° **A**

Dull sublunary° lovers' love
 (Whose soul° is sense°) cannot admit
Absence, because it doth remove
 Those things which elemented° it.

7. profanation: lack of reverence or respect.
8. laity: laypersons; here, those unable to understand the "religion" of true love.
9. moving of th' earth: earthquake.
10. meant: "What does it mean?" was a question usually asked of any unusual phenomenon.
11. trepidation of the spheres: irregularities in the movements of remote heavenly bodies.
12. innocent: unobserved and harmless compared with earthquakes.
13. sublunary: under the moon, therefore subject to change.
14. soul: essence. **sense:** the body with its five senses; that is, purely physical rather than spiritual.
16. elemented: constituted; composed.

A Reading Focus **Recognizing Comparisons and Contrasts** How do the movements of Earth and the other planets differ?

Vocabulary **virtuous** (VUR choo uhs) *adj.:* moral; righteous. **reckon** (REHK uhn) *v.:* estimate; consider.

Differentiating Instruction

EL English Learners

Have students practice completing the following sentences in pairs, then ask them to share their sentences with the class: In stanza 3, the poet compares _____ to _____. In stanza 6, the poet likens _____ to _____. The poet makes a comparison between _____ and _____ in stanza 7. The poet then makes a comparison between _____ and _____ in the last stanza.

✔ See **UA: Differentiating Instruction** for strategies for teaching English learners.

Advanced Learners

Enrichment Ask students to imagine they are leaving a loved one behind for a long, possibly dangerous journey. Have students write their own "valediction" in a brief letter. Have students include at least three comparisons that involve surprising and unusual objects to describe their emotions.

✔ See **UA: Resources for Teaching Advanced Students** for strategies for teaching advanced learners.

Preparing to Read

A Valediction: Forbidding Mourning

Reading Standard 2.2, 3.4 (see pages A48–A50)

Literary Skills Focus

Metaphysical Conceits The metaphysical poets were known for their intellectual and often unexpected comparisons. A **metaphysical conceit** is an elaborate, clever figure of speech that makes connections between two things that are startlingly different. "A Valediction: Forbidding Mourning" contains the most famous of all metaphysical conceits, a comparison of lovers to the two prongs of a drafter's compass.

Reading Skills Focus

Recognizing Comparisons and Contrasts A **comparison** looks at similarities; a **contrast** considers differences. Comparison and contrast may be used to help structure a poem. Analyze the comparisons and contrasts in each stanza of this poem. For example, in stanza 1, the speaker compares parting from his lover to souls passing from virtuous men at death. In stanza 2, the speaker contrasts the quiet parting of the lovers with a tumultuous parting marked by floods of tears and tempestuous sighs.

Into Action As you read, use a chart like the one below to record the comparisons and contrasts in the poem.

Comparisons	Contrasts
the way virtuous men die / the way the lovers should part	the quiet way the lovers will part / floods and tempests

Writing Skills Focus

Think as a Reader/Writer

Find It in Your Reading Donne's poetry includes ideas and images from scholarly disciplines and from everyday life. In your *Reader/Writer Notebook*, note the unusual images and metaphors that Donne employs.

Vocabulary

virtuous (VUR choo uhs) *adj.*: moral; righteous. *Donne implies that virtuous men need not fear death because their souls will go to heaven.*

reckon (REHK uhn) *v.*: estimate; consider. *When confronted with a puzzling phenomenon, humans often reckon its cause and significance.*

endure (ehn DOOR) *v.*: undergo; bear. *Many people are forced to endure loneliness when separated from those they love.*

Language Coach

Latin Roots *Endure* comes from the Latin root that means "to harden." To *endure* something difficult is to make yourself hard against it. The same root appears in these words: *enduring, durable, unendurable*. How does the Latin root affect the meaning of each word?

Learn It Online
Prepare to read this poem the multimedia way—through *PowerNotes* online.

go.hrw.com H12-291 Go

Reader/Writer Notebook
Use your **RWN** to complete the activities for this selection.

California Standards, pp. 291–295

- **Reading Standard 2.2** Analyze the way in which clarity of meaning is affected by the patterns of organization, hierarchical structures, repetition of the main ideas, syntax, and word choice in the text.
- **Reading Standard 3.4** Analyze ways in which poets use imagery, personification, figures of speech, and sounds to evoke readers' emotions.

Preteach

Introducing Vocabulary

- Review the Vocabulary words, definitions, and sentences with students.
- To reinforce the importance of the Vocabulary words, tell students that these words support Donne's use of metaphysical conceits. For instance, he compares the parting of two lovers to the dying of *virtuous* men.

English for Academic Success

Language Coach

Have students look up in a dictionary the Latin root word of *reckon* and compare the meaning of the root to the meaning of the word. Tell them to repeat this exercise with *virtuous*.

Literary Skills Focus

As you read and discuss the selection with students, have them note examples of extended, unlikely comparisons.

Reading Skills Focus

Give students a copy of the Reading Skills Focus graphic organizer before they read. (See **Unit 2 Resources.**) Tell them to use their responses to the answer questions on the Applying Your Skills page.

Writing Skills Focus

Have students record examples of images that are unusual for poetry in their **Reader/Writer Notebooks**. Students can use their notes to complete the Writing Skills Focus activity.

Learn It Online
For a multimedia version of the instruction on this page, use the **PowerNotes** introduction to this selection

go.hrw.com H12–291 Go

Teacher Preparation

Selection Summary

The speaker uses imagery and hyperbole to argue that there are no women who can be both beautiful and faithful.

Direct Teach

Think About/Talk About

Read with a Purpose Have students read the Read with a Purpose statement. Ask them to pay attention to the tone of Donne's poem. Is it reasonable, bitter, or sarcastic?

Comprehension

B Reading Focus

Possible response: *Donne argues that women cannot be both beautiful and faithful.*

Analysis

A Literary Focus

Possible response: *The commands are absurd and impossible; the images are startling and unfamiliar.*

C Literary Focus

Possible response: *Donne exaggerates when he states that even if a reader finds a faithful woman, she will be unfaithful before the speaker has a chance to meet her—even if he has to travel only a short distance to do so.*

Vocabulary: Own the Word

- **advance:** A general might *advance* his troops in battle. The director of a company might *advance* an employee's position. A businessman might *advance* his interests. What do these three examples have in common?
- **pilgrimage:** Ask students: Why might someone go on a *pilgrimage?* How might *pilgrimages* today differ from *pilgrimages* in the Middle Ages? Ask students how the noun *pilgrim* helps them understand the word *pilgrimage.*

POEM

Song

by **John Donne**

Read with a Purpose

Read to discover one man's attitude about the possibility of finding a faithful woman.

Build Background

Unlike the multitude of Renaissance songs idealizing women, the following song by Donne satirizes women using hyperbole, or gross exaggeration. As you read this poem, imagine a lover who has fallen for the "perfect woman" one too many times, and, as a result, now has a cynical view of all women.

Go, and catch a falling star,
  Get with child a mandrake° root,
Tell me, where all past years are,
  Or who cleft° the devil's foot,
Teach me to hear mermaids singing,
Or to keep off envy's stinging,
    And find
    What wind
Serves to advance an honest mind. **A**

If thou be'st born to strange sights,
  Things invisible to see,
Ride ten thousand days and nights,
  Till age snow white hairs on thee,
Thou, when thou return'st, wilt tell me
All strange wonders that befell thee,
    And swear
    Nowhere
Lives a woman true, and fair. **B**

If thou find'st one, let me know,
  Such a pilgrimage were sweet;
Yet do not, I would not go,
  Though at next door we might meet,
Though she were true, when you met her,
And last, till you write your letter,
    Yet she
    Will be
False, ere I come, to two, or three. **C**

2. **mandrake:** plant whose forked root is said to resemble a human being's torso and legs.
4. **cleft**: split.

Kjosfoss, Norway.

A Literary Focus **Metaphysical Poetry** How would you describe the imagery used in the commands in the first stanza?

B Reading Focus **Identifying the Main Idea** What main idea does the speaker express in lines 16–18?

C Literary Focus **Metaphysical Poetry** What example of hyperbole appears in the last six lines of the poem?

Vocabulary **advance** (ad VANS) *v.:* bring forward; promote. **pilgrimage** (PIHL gruh mihj) *n.:* journey.

Universal Access

Struggling Readers

To help students read "Song," model the reading skill of identifying the main idea. You might say: "The main idea is what a text is mostly about. In some poems, like this one, the final lines of each stanza state the main idea. While I read, I think about the main idea of each stanza. Then, I put those ideas together to find the overall idea of the poem." Encourage students to ask themselves, "What are the poem's stanzas about? How do the stanzas work together to develop a single main idea?"

Students with Disabilities

Help students paraphrase the text by breaking it down into small parts. Ask them to come up with a sentence to summarize each part and transcribe it in their **Reader/Writer Notebooks.** After they have successfully paraphrased the poem, ask students to identify the main idea based on their paraphrases.

Reading Standard 2.2, 3.1 (see pages A48–A50)

Song

Literary Skills Focus

Metaphysical Poetry The term **metaphysical poetry** has been applied to the work of John Donne, Andrew Marvell, and other seventeenth-century poets whose detached, intellectual style sharply contrasts with the emotional extravagance of most of the Elizabethan love poets who preceded them. Metaphysical poetry is known for its startling **imagery,** intricate figures of speech, irregular **meter,** sheer verbal wit, philosophical musings, and references to esoteric fields of knowledge.

Reading Skills Focus

Identifying the Main Idea The **main idea** of a text is the central thought or message that the writer communicates. In metaphysical poetry, the main idea often focuses on the poet's thoughts on an intellectual or philosophical problem. Donne's "Song" presents the poet's opinion on whether or not it is possible to find a beautiful, yet faithful, woman.

Into Action As you read, use a chart like the one below to summarize each stanza of the poem and note each stanza's images.

Stanza	Summary	Images
Stanza 1	The speaker asks the reader to complete several impossible and absurd tasks.	catching a falling star; mandrake root; the devil's cleft foot; singing mermaids

Writing Skills Focus

Think as a Reader/Writer

Find It in Your Reading In "Song," Donne uses **hyperbole,** or exaggeration, to illustrate how difficult it is to find a beautiful, faithful woman. As you read, take notes in your *Reader/Writer Notebook* on Donne's use of exaggerated images.

TechFocus As you read, think about what personal experiences in Donne's life might have contributed to these poems.

Vocabulary

advance (ad VANS) *v.:* bring forward; promote. *What habits advance learning and build character?*

pilgrimage (PIHL gruh mihj) *n.:* journey. *The poem's speaker doubts the success of a pilgrimage to find a faithful woman.*

Language Coach

Connotation Some words have strong connotations—ideas that people often think of automatically when they hear the word. A *pilgrimage* is a journey with a special significance. The connotations of the word are religious because most pilgrimages are journeys to holy places. Why might a poet decide to use a word with religious connotations in a nonreligious poem?

Learn It Online
Learn more about Donne's life online.

go.hrw.com H12-289 Go

Reader/Writer Notebook
Use your **RWN** to complete the activities for this selection.

Selection Resources

Unit 2 Resources, on-level practice and assessment, pp. 21, 27, 33

PowerNotes, interactive lesson presentation with activities

Teacher One Stop™, on-level lesson plans and all print resources

Holt Audio Library

Holt Audio Library: Selections and Summaries in Spanish

UA: Holt Interactive Reader, p. 81

UA: Differentiating Instruction, modified lesson plans and leveled assessment, p. 60

UA: Resources for Teaching Advanced Students, lesson plans, p. 84

UA: Supporting Instruction in Spanish, selection summary

ThinkCentral Online Assessment

ThinkCentral Online Remediation

Preteach

Introducing Vocabulary

- Review the Vocabulary words, definitions, and sentences with students.
- To reinforce the importance of the Vocabulary words, tell students that these words support Donne's use of imagery, common in metaphysical poetry.

English for Academic Success

Language Coach

Have students brainstorm other ideas they associate with the word *pilgrimage.* ***Possible response:*** *The word* pilgrimage *carries such ideas as self-discovery and faith. A poet may include this word to evoke the emotions and senses that are associated with these ideas.*

Literary Skills Focus

As you read and discuss the selection with students, have them note examples of the characteristics of metaphysical poetry.

Reading Skills Focus

Give students a copy of the Reading Skills Focus graphic organizer before they read. (See **Unit 2 Resources.**) Tell them to use their responses to answer the questions on the Applying Your Skills page.

Writing Skills Focus

Have students record examples of hyperbole in their **Reader/Writer Notebooks.** Students can use their notes to complete the Writing Skills Focus activity.

Learn It Online
The enhanced author biography offers more information on the life of the author as well as Holt's interactive resources pertaining to the author.

go.hrw.com H12–289 Go

But we by a love, so much refined,
That ourselves know not what it is,
Interassurèd of the mind,
Care less eyes, lips, and hands to miss.

Our two souls therefore, which are one,
Though I must go, endure not yet
A breach°, but an expansion,
Like gold to airy thinness beat. **B** **C**

If they be two, they are two so
As stiff twin compasses are two,
Thy soul the fixed foot, makes no show
To move, but doth, if th' other do. **D**

And though it in the center sit,
Yet when the other far doth roam,
It leans, and hearkens after it,
And grows erect, as that comes home.

Such wilt thou be to me, who must
Like th' other foot, obliquely° run;
Thy firmness° makes my circle just,°
And makes me end, where I begun.

23. breach: break; split.

34. obliquely: off course.

35. firmness: fidelity.

just: perfect. A circle symbolizes perfection, hence wedding rings.

B **Literary Focus** **Metaphysical Conceits** What makes the comparison in line 24 a metaphysical conceit?

C **Reading Focus** **Recognizing Comparisons and Contrasts** What comparison does Donne use in the sixth stanza to express the separation of the lovers' souls?

D **Literary Focus** **Metaphysical Conceits** What makes the use of the word *circle* in the final two lines such a perfect word choice at the end of this poem?

Vocabulary **endure** (ehn DOOR) *v.:* undergo; bear.

Analyzing Visuals

Connecting to the Text How does a stained-glass image of lovers blend two different sorts of imagery? What aspects of this image convey a mood and theme similar to those of the poem?

From *King Rene's Honeymoon* series (1862) by William Morris. Stained glass. Morris, Marshall, Faulkener & Co. Victoria & Albert Museum, London.

Think About/Talk About

Comprehension

C Reading Focus

Possible response: *The souls are compared to a lump of gold beaten thinner than paper. Their separation does not resemble a division but instead an expansion into a thin golden foil.*

Analysis

B Literary Focus

Possible response: *It compares human souls to gold that is beaten into a thin sheet. The poet uses an unusual extended comparison to show that the lovers' souls are not harmed by their separation.*

D Literary Focus

Possible response: *Like perfect love, a circle has no beginning and no end. It is continuous and everlasting. The circle evokes not only the compass image but also the orbit of the heavenly bodies, which Donne refers to earlier.*

Analyzing Visuals

Connecting to the Text: *Stained glass images usually depict religious themes. In this case, the stained glass portrays a couple in amorous behavior. Similarly, the poem elevates the speaker's love for his wife with lofty images of spiritual love.*

Vocabulary: Own the Word

- **virtuous:** A *virtuous* person is righteous and morally upright; the antonym of *virtuous* is *wicked* or *unethical.* Use both words in a sentence: A *virtuous* leader is highly respected for his or her integrity and character; a *wicked* leader is not trusted nor esteemed by his or her followers.
- **reckon:** Have students complete this sentence after reading stanza 3: Men *reckoned* what . . . meant.
- **endure:** Ask students: "Have you ever *endured* a serious injury or illness in your life? Explain when and how you *endured* the pain."

California Standards, pp. 294–295

- **Reading Standard 2.2** Analyze the way in which clarity of meaning is affected by the patterns of organization, hierarchical structures, repetition of the main ideas, syntax, and word choice in the text.
- **Reading Standard 3.1** Analyze characteristics of subgenres (e.g., satire, parody, allegory, pastoral) that are used in poetry, prose, plays, novels, short stories, essays, and other basic genres.
- **Reading Standard 3.4** Analyze ways in which poets use imagery, personification, figures of speech, and sounds to evoke readers' emotions.
- **Listening and Speaking Standard 2.4** Deliver multimedia presentations: **a.** Combine text, images, and sound by incorporating information from a wide range of media, including films, newspapers, magazines, CD-ROMs, online information, television, videos, and electronic media-generated images.

Check for Understanding

Independent Practice

Reading Skills Focus

Possible responses:

1. *In the first poem, the speaker is bitter and cynical about love. In the second poem, the speaker is tender and affectionate.*
2. *Have students relate images to the main idea.*
3. *Have students describe the emotions revealed through the comparisons and contrasts.*

Vocabulary Check

4. *b* **5.** *e* **6.** *a*
7. *d* **8.** *c*

Literary Skills Focus

Possible responses:

9. *The contrast between "true" and "false" highlights the disparity between the nonexistent ideal woman and women as they really are, according to Donne.*
10. *When things melt, they may blend together, just as the lovers' souls are blended.*
11. *The commands in the first stanza, "ten thousand days and nights" in line 12, and the exaggeration in lines 25–27 are used to make the speaker's points.*
12. *Donne compares two lovers to the two needles of a compass; one moves in tandem with the other. The image suggests the unchangeable connection between the lovers.*
13. *Like the mermaids' song, love that seems appealing might tempt a person to doom.*

Applying Your Skills

Reading Standard 2.2, 3.1, 3.4 (see pages A48–A50)

Song

A Valediction: Forbidding Mourning

Literary Response and Analysis

Reading Skills Focus

Read with a Purpose

1. Contrast the tones of the two poems.

Reading Skills: Identifying the Main Idea

2. Review your chart for "Song." In a new column, state each stanza's main idea, and explain how the images in the stanza support the main idea.

Stanza	Summary	Images	How Images Support Main Idea
Stanza 1	The speaker asks the reader to complete several impossible and absurd tasks.	catching a falling star; mandrake root; the devil's cleft foot; singing mermaids	shows the impossibility of finding a beautiful and faithful woman

Reading Skills: Recognizing Comparisons and Contrasts

3. Review your chart on comparisons and contrasts in "A Valediction" and add a column in which you describe the emotions expressed by the comparisons and contrasts you identified.

Vocabulary Check

Match the Vocabulary words with their synonyms.

4. advance	**a.** moral; righteous
5. pilgrimage	**b.** promote
6. virtuous	**c.** undergo; bear
7. reckon	**d.** consider; estimate
8. endure	**e.** journey

Literary Skills Focus

Literary Analysis

9. **Analyze** Donne uses the word *true* twice in "Song," then ends with the word *false.* How does this contrast affect the meaning of the poem?
10. **Interpret** In "Valediction," line 5, how is the image of melting relevant to the poem?

Literary Skills: Metaphysical Poetry

11. **Evaluate** In "Song," what hyperbole does the speaker use?

Literary Skills: Metaphysical Conceits

12. **Analyze** Explain the conceit in lines 25–36 of "A Valediction" and what it suggests about love.

Literary Skills Review: Allusion

13. **Analyze** A reference to something from literature, history, or other familiar cultural areas is an **allusion.** "Song" alludes to the mythological mermaid singing that lures sailors to crash their ships. What does this allusion signify in "Song"?

Writing Skills Focus

Think as a Reader/Writer

Use It in Your Writing Review your notes on Donne's use of unusual, exaggerated images to convey ideas. In your *Reader/Writer Notebook,* write a paragraph in which you use hyperbole and unusual comparisons to describe an impossible goal.

What Do You Think Now

How can positive thinking influence our feelings and actions?

What Do You Think Now?

Have students consider how our attitudes toward a situation can change not only the outcome, but also our feelings and behavior. Ask students to think of an event during which they felt positive. Did their optimism changed their behavior? How?

Universal Access

Struggling Writers

Some students may need additional scaffolding to complete the Writing Skills Focus activity. Ask students to write about the goal of finding their soul mate. Have them write about difficulties and setbacks they might encounter during their search. Then, ask them to take some of their ideas and incorporate hyperbole by exaggerating the descriptions in their sentences. Encourage them to also incorporate an unusual comparison. Have students weave their sentences into a paragraph.

Reading Standard 3.4 (see pages A48–A50)
Listening and Speaking Standard 2.4a (see pages A53–A55)

Grammar Link

Direct and Indirect Objects

A **complement** is a word or word group that completes the meaning of a verb. A **direct object** is a complement that tells who or what receives the verb's action or shows the result of the action. A direct object may be a noun, pronoun, or word group that functions as a noun. To find a direct object, ask "whom?" or "what?" after a transitive verb. A direct object may be compound.

John Donne wrote **poems.**
He also wrote **meditations** and **sermons.**

An **indirect object** is a complement that often appears in sentences containing direct objects and that tells to whom or to what (or for whom or for what) the action of a transitive verb is done. An indirect object may be a noun, a pronoun, or a word group that functions as a noun. An indirect object may be compound.

In "Valediction" the speaker tells the **woman** goodbye.
Friends gave **Donne** and **his wife** financial support.

Your Turn

Identify each direct and indirect object in the following sentences.

1. Metaphysical poets revolutionized poetry.
2. Most Renaissance poets gave readers sweet, musical verse.
3. Donne based the rhythms and sounds of his poems on spoken English.

Writing Application Write a paragraph describing an activity or event. Include at least five direct objects and two indirect objects in your description.

CHOICES

As you respond to the Choices, use these **Academic Vocabulary** words as appropriate: establish, ensure, widespread, controversy, contradiction.

REVIEW

Create a Visual Image

Images fill "Song" and "A Valediction." Choose one of these images, and incorporate it into a painting, drawing, or other artwork. Ensure that your design establishes the connection between the image and the ideas it represents. For example, how could a painting contain the elements of a compass and represent the souls of two lovers?

CONNECT

Document the Story Behind the Poem

TechFocus What real events might have affected Donne's views as they are represented in "Song" and "A Valediction"? Research Donne's life to see what he experienced during the times he wrote the poems. In a small group, prepare a documentary script explaining your findings. Dramatize events, or cast group members as "experts" to explore Donne's motives. If you cannot videotape your documentary, perform it live for your class.

World map from the *Portolan Atlas of the World* (c. 1540) by Battista Agnese of Venice. Royal Geographic Society, London.

EXTEND

Explain a Worldview

Partner Activity During the Renaissance many people thought Earth was the center of the universe. With a partner, research the Elizabethan worldview reflected in the imagery of "A Valediction." Create a poster with visuals and text explaining how Donne uses Renaissance cosmology in the poem.

Universal Access: Grammar Link

English Learners

English for Academic Success Use this lesson to reinforce the standard English use of direct and indirect objects. While the students are watching, drop a book on the floor. Then, write this sentence on the board, with the verb, *dropped,* underlined:

- The teacher dropped the book.

Tell students that the direct object of this sentence is the person, place, or thing that receives the action of the verb. What was dropped? [*the book*]

Next, hand the book to a student and write this sentence on the board, with the verb, *gave,* underlined:

- The teacher gave the book to the student.

Tell students that the indirect object of this sentence is to whom or to what the verb is done. To whom or to what did the teacher give the book? [*the student*]

✔ For more practice with direct and indirect objects, see **Warriner's Handbook, GrammarNotes,** and **Language Handbook Worksheets.**

Independent Practice

Grammar Link

Your Turn

1. direct object: *poetry*
2. direct object: *sweet, musical verse;* indirect object: *readers*
3. direct object: *the rhythms and sounds*

Choices: Evaluation Criteria

Review: Homework
Create a Visual Image
Students' artwork illustrates an interpretation of a specific passage from John Donne's work.

Connect: Homework
Document the Story Behind the Poem
Students use reliable sources and reference them both in-text and in a works cited page.

Extend: Homework
Explain a Worldview
- Students demonstrate an understanding of the Renaissance worldview.
- Students explain how Donne incorporated Renaissance cosmological views in his poems.

Assess

Unit 2 Resources, Selection Standards Check, pp. 24, 30

go.hrw.com **ThinkCentral Online Assessment,** Selection Standards Check

Teacher One Stop™, editable Selection Standards Check

Reteach

go.hrw.com **ThinkCentral Online Remediation**

Preteach

Introducing Vocabulary

Review the Vocabulary words, definitions, and sample sentences with students. Then, use this activity to check students' understanding.

1. Explain what happens when a fire **diminishes** in intensity.
2. List three causes of **affliction** in the life of a student.
3. Give an example of **tribulation** that a person might experience during a major catastrophe like a flood.
4. Name a profession that involves **contemplation.**

English for Academic Success

Language Coach

Possible responses: *Contemplate becomes contemplation by dropping the "e" and adding "-ion." Similar words include participate/participation, suspend/suspension, and ascend/ascension.*

Literary Skills Focus

As you read and discuss the selection with students, have them record images, words, and details that illustrate the tone.

Reading Skills Focus

Give students a copy of the Reading Skills Focus graphic organizer before they read. (See **Unit 2 Resources.**) Tell them to use their responses to answer the questions on the Applying Your Skills page.

Writing Skills Focus

Have students record instances of the bell as an image in their **Reader/Writer Notebooks.** Students can use their notes to complete the Writing Skills Focus activity.

Learn It Online

Word Watch provides an audio pronunciation of each word, plus synonyms, antonyms, the word used in a sentence, and a brief history of the word's origin.

go.hrw.com H12-296 Go

Preparing to Read

Reading Standard 2.2, 3.3 (see pages A48–A50)

Meditation 17

Literary Skills Focus

Tone In literature, **tone** reflects an author's attitude toward the reader, a subject, or a character. Identifying tone can help you figure out the author's **purpose** and the work's **theme.** Spoken language has vocal inflections as well as nonverbal signals such as facial expressions that help the listener determine the speaker's tone. A writer achieves similar effects through words, images, and details. In "Meditation 17," Donne writes on the significance of the tolling bell: "As therefore the bell that rings . . . calls not upon the preacher only, but upon the congregation to come; so this bell calls us all." The tone of this sentence is serious and melancholy.

Reading Skills Focus

Recognizing Patterns of Organization The organization of Donne's "Meditation 17" is based on several metaphors that develop the theme that everyone is part of a common humanity.

Into Action As you read, use a chart like the one below to record each metaphor. Then show how Donne extends or develops the metaphor.

Metaphor	Development
Humanity is a book and God is the author.	Each person is a chapter in the book. When a person dies, his or her chapter is translated into the afterlife. God rebinds the pages for the Library, or heaven.

Writing Skills Focus

Think as a Reader/Writer

Find It in Your Reading The tolling bell that begins the meditation with its ringing continues to ring throughout the piece. The bell image acts as the connecting thread for the various sections and is a constant reminder that Donne is talking about death. As you read, note instances of the bell image. How does it function as a transition from one section of the text to another?

TechFocus Imagine the music that might accompany the following two selections by Donne.

Vocabulary

diminishes (duh MIHN ihsh ehz) *v.:* makes smaller; lessens; reduces. *Grief arising from death diminishes over time for some mourners but not Donne.*

affliction (uh FLIHK shuhn) *n.:* suffering; something that causes distress or hardship. *Donne believes affliction brings humans closer to God.*

tribulation (trihb yuh LAY shuhn) *n.:* great trouble or misery. *Donne believes that trial and tribulation can benefit a person.*

contemplation (kahn tuhm PLAY shuhn) *n.:* deep thought; meditation. *Ringing church bells triggers Donne's contemplation of his own mortality.*

Language Coach

Suffixes When you add the suffix *–tion* to the verb *afflict*, you get the noun *affliction*. What verb can you find in the noun *contemplation*? Explain how the spelling of the verb changes when you add the suffix *–tion*. Name three other verbs that become nouns when this suffix is added.

Reader/Writer Notebook

Use your **RWN** to complete the activities for this selection.

Learn It Online

Explore these Vocabulary words further through Word Watch online.

go.hrw.com H12-296 Go

California Standards, pp. 296–299

- **Reading Standard 2.2** Analyze the way in which clarity of meaning is affected by the patterns of organization, hierarchical structures, repetition of the main ideas, syntax, and word choice in the text.
- **Reading Standard 3.3** Analyze the ways in which irony, tone, mood, the author's style, and the "sound" of language achieve specific rhetorical or aesthetic purposes or both.

MEDITATION

Meditation 17

by **John Donne**

Read with a Purpose

Read to discover how recognizing another person's suffering can help us through difficult times.

Build Background

In 1624, prompted by a serious illness, Donne wrote a series of meditations—thoughtful reflections on a particular theme. The opening of "Meditation 17" refers to the practice in Donne's time of ringing church bells to announce the death of a church member.

Nunc lento	Now, this bell tolling softly
sonitu dicunt,	for another, says to me,
Morieris.	Thou must die. **A**

Perchance he for whom this bell tolls, may be so ill, as that he knows not it tolls for him; and perchance I may think myself so much better than I am, as that they who are about me, and see my state, may have caused it to toll for me, and I know not that. The Church is catholic, universal, so are all her actions; all that she does belongs to all. When she baptizes a child, that action concerns me; for that child is thereby connected to that Head[1] which is my Head too, and engrafted into that body, whereof I am a member. And when she buries a man, that action concerns me: All mankind is of one Author, and is one volume; when one man dies, one chapter is not torn out of the book, but translated[2] into a better language; and every chapter must be so translated; God employs several translators; some pieces are translated by age, some by sickness, some by war, some by justice; but God's hand is in every translation; and his hand shall bind up all our scattered leaves[3] again, for that Library where every book shall lie open to one another: As therefore the bell that rings to a sermon, calls not upon the preacher only, but upon the congregation to come; so this bell calls us all: but how much more me, who am brought so near the door by this sickness. **B** There was a contention as far as a suit[4] (in which both piety and dignity, religion

1. **Head:** Christ.
2. **translated:** spiritually carried across from one realm to another.
3. **leaves:** pages.
4. **contention . . . suit:** argument that went as far as a lawsuit.

A Literary Focus **Tone** How do these lines affect the tone of the meditation?

B Reading Focus **Recognizing Patterns of Organization** Donne has introduced the idea of God as Author. How is this idea developed through these following lines?

Funeral Effigy of John Donne, St. Paul's Cathedral, London.

Universal Access

Struggling Readers

Benchmark Students Guide students in understanding the writer's use of tone in this selection. Ask students what topic is mentioned in the opening lines of the selection and why the writer might have included those lines. As they continue reading, instruct students to ask themselves what attitude the writer seems to set forth concerning the topic they identified in the beginning of the selection. Ask students to identify three words that contribute to the writer's tone.

Students with Disabilities

Ask students to compare how people view death today to how people viewed death four hundred years ago, when the life expectancy in England was about thirty-five years. Have students freewrite for one minute on the topic of death. After reading the selection, have students compare their meditations on death to those thoughts expressed by Donne.

Teacher Preparation

Selection Summary

Donne uses a series of analogies to illustrate that all humans are creatures of God. The author also states that affliction can secure the sufferer a place in heaven.

Direct Teach

Think About/Talk About

Read With a Purpose Have students read the Read with a Purpose statement. Ask them why some people choose to remain ignorant of another's suffering. Ask students how they respond when witnessing another's suffering.

Comprehension

B Reading Focus

Possible response: *God both oversees the translation of the chapters, or people's lives, and rebinds the pages for final opening in the Library, or heaven.*

Analysis

A Literary Focus

Possible response: *By introducing the concept that we all must die, Donne establishes a somber, almost reverent tone at the beginning of his meditation.*

Extend the Discussion

Metaphysical Conceit What metaphysical conceit does Donne present after stating that all of humanity is a book authored by God? ***Possible response:*** *He states that each person is a chapter of the book and is translated into a better language after death.*

Think About/Talk About

Comprehension

Ⓒ Reading Focus

Possible response: *He uses the metaphor of continents. Each person is part of the whole of humanity, just as a piece of ground is part of a continent. The loss of one person, or one piece of earth, affects the whole.*

Analysis

Ⓓ Literary Focus

Possible response: *Donne's tone shows his strength of conviction. His final lines echo the imagery of his opening lines, bringing the meditation full circle.*

Extend the Discussion

Determining Author's Purpose
What does Donne want his readers to be more aware of with both his metaphors? ***Possible response:*** *He wants his readers to be more aware of their own mortality.*

Vocabulary: Own the Word

- **diminishes:** Have students brainstorm attributes that would go on each spider leg of a semantic web for this word. ***Possible responses:*** *shrink, contract, wane, reduce, decrease*
- **affliction:** Ask students to list examples of an emotional *affliction*. ***Possible responses:*** *stress, anxiety, depression, anger, grief, broken heart*
- **tribulation:** Remind students that *tribulation* connotes "serious hardship." You might say: "Babysitting those naughty kids is troublesome, but having to raise disobedient kids for life is a *tribulation*." Ask students to create a pair of related statements that show how *tribulation* is more serious than trouble.
- **contemplation:** Demonstrate the posture of a person who is in *contemplation*. Ask a few students to stay seated at their desks and demonstrate.

and estimation,[5] were mingled), which of the religious orders should ring to prayers first in the morning; and it was determined, that they should ring first that rose earliest. If we understand aright the dignity of this bell that tolls for our evening prayer, we would be glad to make it ours, by rising early, in that application, that it might be ours, as well as his, whose indeed it is. The bell doth toll for him that thinks it doth; and though it intermit[6] again, yet from that minute, that that occasion wrought upon him, he is united to God. Who casts not up his eye to the sun when it rises? but who takes off his eye from a comet when that breaks out?[7] Who bends not his ear to any bell, which upon any occasion rings? but who can remove it from that bell, which is passing a piece of himself out of this world?

No man is an island, entire of itself; every man is a piece of the continent, a part of the main;[8] if a clod be washed away by the sea, Europe is the less, as well as if a promontory were, as well as if a manor of thy friends or of thine own were; any man's death diminishes me, because I am involved in mankind; and therefore never send to know for whom the bell tolls; it tolls for thee. Ⓒ Neither can we call this a begging of misery or a borrowing of misery, as though we were not miserable enough of ourselves, but must fetch in more from the next house, in taking upon us the misery of our neighbors. Truly it were an excusable covetousness if we did; for affliction is a treasure, and scarce any man hath enough of it. No man hath affliction enough that is not matured, and ripened by it, and made fit for God by that affliction. If a man carry treasure in bullion, or in a wedge of gold, and have none coined into current monies, his treasure will not defray[9] him as he travels. Tribulation is treasure in the nature of it, but it is not current money in the use of it, except we get nearer and nearer our home, Heaven, by it. Another man may be sick too, and sick to death, and this affliction may lie in his bowels, as gold in a mine, and be of no use to him; but this bell, that tells me of his affliction, digs out, and applies that gold to me; if by this consideration of another's danger I take mine own into contemplation, and so secure myself by making my recourse[10] to my God, who is our only security. Ⓓ

5. **estimation:** self-esteem.
6. **intermit:** cease.
7. **comet . . . out:** Comets were regarded as signs of disaster to come.
8. **main:** mainland.
9. **defray:** pay for.
10. **making my recourse:** turning for aid.

Now, this bell tolling softly for another, says to me, Thou must die.

The Bells of Rostov (1983) by Sergei Chepik. Courtesy of the artist.

Ⓒ **Reading Focus** **Recognizing Patterns of Organization** How does the famous quotation "No man is an island, entire of itself" clarify the idea that we are all connected to each other?

Ⓓ **Literary Focus** **Tone** How would you describe the tone of the last lines of the meditation?

Vocabulary **diminishes** (duh MIHN ihsh ehz) *v.:* makes smaller; lessens; reduces.
affliction (uh FLIHK shuhn) *n.:* suffering; something that causes distress or hardship.
tribulation (trihb yuh LAY shuhn) *n.:* great trouble or misery.
contemplation (kahn tuhm PLAY shuhn) *n.:* deep thought; meditation.

California Standards, p. 299

- **Reading Standard 2.2** Analyze the way in which clarity of meaning is affected by the patterns of organization, hierarchical structures, repetition of the main ideas, syntax, and word choice in the text.
- **Reading Standard 3.3** Analyze the ways in which irony, tone, mood, the author's style, and the "sound" of language achieve specific rhetorical or aesthetic purposes or both.
- **Writing Standard 2.3** Write reflective compositions:
  a. Explore the significance of personal experiences, events, conditions, or concerns by using rhetorical strategies (e.g., narration, description, exposition, persuasion).

Reading Standard 2.2, 3.3 (see pages A48–A50)
Writing Standard 2.3a (see pages A51–A52)

Meditation 17

Literary Response and Analysis

Reading Skills Focus

Read with a Purpose

1. According to Donne, how can the suffering of one person benefit others?

Reading Skills: Recognizing Patterns of Organization

2. Review your notes about Donne's use of metaphor in "Meditation 17." Add a column to your chart, and summarize the main idea of each comparison.

Metaphor	Development	Main Idea
Humanity is a book, and God is the author.	Each person is a chapter in the book. When a person dies, his or her chapter is translated into the afterlife. God rebinds the pages for the Library, or heaven.	All people are interconnected because God made them.

Vocabulary Check

Match each Vocabulary word with its synonym.

3. diminishes — a. thought
4. affliction — b. misery
5. tribulation — c. lessens
6. contemplation — d. suffering

Literary Skills Focus

Literary Analysis

7. **Interpret** How are the comparisons in the meditation examples of a metaphysical conceit?
8. **Analyze** Which images best support Donne's point that all people are connected?
9. **Evalute** What do you think of Donne's opinion that suffering can bring good?

Literary Skills: Tone

10. **Analyze** Using the text to support your answer, choose a word to describe the meditation's tone.

Literary Skills Review: Onomatopoeia

11. **Evaluate** The use of words whose sounds suggest or imitate their meaning is called **onomatopoeia.** Where does onomatopoeia appear in the meditation? What is its effect?

Writing Skills Focus

Think as a Reader/Writer

Use It in Your Writing You noted how Donne uses the bell image to connect the sections and to affect the piece's tone and organization. Use a recurring image in your own writing. Choose a sound, such as waves on the shore, cars on the highway, or ambulance sirens, and use it as your starting point for writing your own meditation. Return to the image at least twice, and be sure to end your piece with it.

What Do You Think Now? Donne says that suffering can be valuable. How might you act differently in a difficult situation if you could think of suffering as an opportunity rather than a challenge?

For CHOICES see page 303.

Universal Access

Struggling Writers

Some students may need additional scaffolding to complete the Writing Skills Focus activity. Help students brainstorm by having them create a spider web diagram with a description of their chosen image in the center circle. Have them think of the tone of their meditation based on the image and write a brief description of the tone on one of the legs. For example, if the image is cars on a highway, the tone might be frenzied or hurried. Then, have them state the symbolic meaning of their image on another leg. The meaning of the image of cars on a highway might be that time is short. Ask them to fill out three to four legs that expand upon the meaning of the image. Encourage them to include metaphors, similes, and additional images.

Check for Understanding

Independent Practice

Reading Skills Focus

Possible responses:

1. *People can see suffering as a reminder that pain and death will also come to them. It can also give them an opportunity to turn to God.*
2. *Ask students to consider what idea Donne is trying to illustrate through each metaphor.*

Vocabulary Check

3. *c* 4. *d*
5. *b* 6. *a*

Literary Skills Focus

Possible responses:

7. *Donne's comparisons, such as humans' lives and books, and people and continents, are highly dissimilar, thus serving as metaphysical conceits.*
8. *The line "no man is an island" has poetic resonance and clear imagery, making it highly memorable.*
9. *It takes courage to embrace his profound attitude. People who have suffered can attest to it; those who have not may shy away from it.*
10. *The tone of this piece is powerful. Donne references the cycle of life, God, and struggle.*
11. *Onomatopoeia appears in the use of the word "toll." The word suggests the sound of a bell, especially since Donne chooses to repeat the word, reminding the reader that a bell tolls not once, but several times.*

What Do You Think Now?

Ask students to reflect on the idea that painful experiences can improve and strengthen our values.

Preteach

Introducing Vocabulary

- Review the Vocabulary words, definitions, and sentences with students.
- To reinforce the importance of the Vocabulary words, tell students that these words show the conventional view of death, which Donne contradicts in his poem.

English for Academic Success

Language Coach

Ask students what the word *stroke* in line 12 might be mistaken to mean, and what it means in context. ***Possible response:*** Stroke *might be mistaken to mean an "obstructed blood vessel;" in context it means "a blow or strike."*

Literary Skills Focus

As you read and discuss the selection with students, have them note the development of paradoxes in "Death be not proud."

Writing Skills Focus

Have students use their **Reader/Writer Notebooks** to record examples of ideas or images that seem contradictory. Students can use their notes to complete the Writing Skills Focus activity.

Learn It Online
The enhanced author biography offers more information on the life of the author as well as Holt's interactive resources pertaining to the author.
go.hrw.com H12-300 Go

Preparing to Read

Reading Standard 3.4, 3.9 (see pages A48–A50)

Death be not proud

Literary Skills Focus

Paradox A **paradox** is a statement that at first glance seems impossible or illogical: "The child is father of the man." When examined more closely, a paradox expresses a deeper truth than was first apparent: "What we are as adults is very much influenced by our childhood experiences." Many writers use paradox to express things in life that seem contradictory yet are true. In "Death be not proud," Donne uses a paradox to communicate his belief that the death of a person's body leads to one's eternal life. Paradoxes capture our attention and force us to think more deeply about something we might otherwise take for granted.

Literary Perspectives Apply the literary perspective described on page 301 as you read this poem.

Writing Skills Focus

Think as a Reader/Writer

Find It in Your Reading Like a riddle, a paradox invites you to look beneath the surface of the words and search for a hidden meaning. As you read "Death be not proud," use your *Reader/Writer Notebook* to keep track of ideas or images that you find contradictory. To help organize your notes, record the contradictory text in the left column; and in the right column, explain why it seems contradictory.

Contradictory text	Why it seems contradictory

Vocabulary

dreadful (DREHD fuhl) *adj.:* terrible; causing fear. *The speaker does not think death is dreadful because he believes in life after death.*

desperate (DEHS puhr iht) *adj.:* driven by hopelessness; moved to use extreme means to try to escape frustration and loss. *Desperate men may fear, court, or cause death.*

Language Coach

Commonly Confused Words When Donne describes "desperate men," he refers to men who are reckless because they have no hope. They feel *desperation*, anxiety brought on by a great sense of urgency. Take care not to confuse the word *desperate* with *disparate*, which means "unalike" or "not similar."

Learn It Online
Find out more about Donne, his work, and his world through these Internet links online.
go.hrw.com H12-300 Go

Reader/Writer Notebook
Use your **RWN** to complete the activities for this selection.

California Standards, pp. 300–303

- **Reading Standard 3.4** Analyze ways in which poets use imagery, personification, figures of speech, and sounds to evoke readers' emotions.
- **Reading Standard 3.9** Analyze the philosophical arguments presented in literary works to determine whether the authors' positions have contributed to the quality of each work and the credibility of the characters (Philosophical approach).

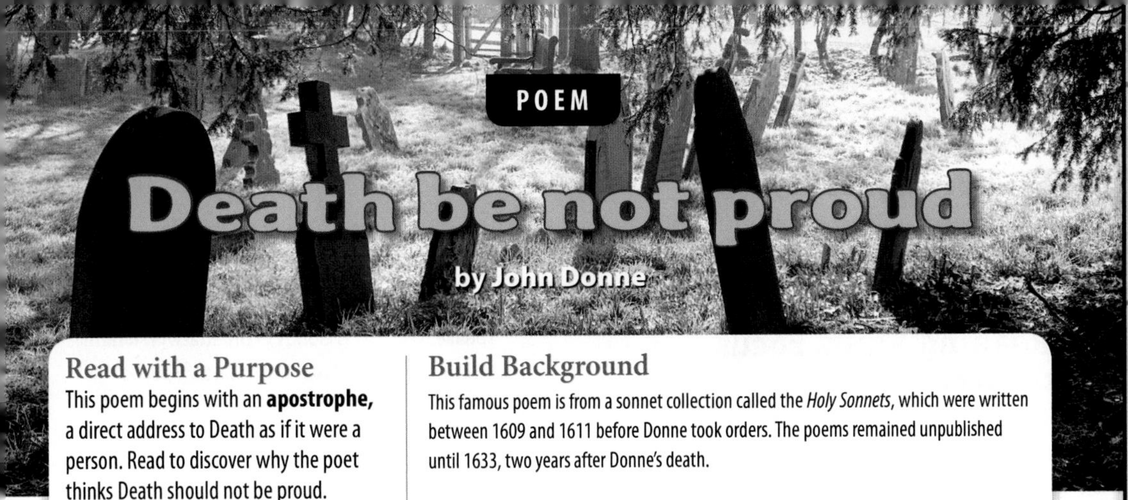

POEM

Death be not proud

by John Donne

Read with a Purpose

This poem begins with an **apostrophe,** a direct address to Death as if it were a person. Read to discover why the poet thinks Death should not be proud.

Build Background

This famous poem is from a sonnet collection called the *Holy Sonnets*, which were written between 1609 and 1611 before Donne took orders. The poems remained unpublished until 1633, two years after Donne's death.

Death be not proud, though some have callèd thee
Mighty and dreadful, for thou art not so,
For those whom thou think'st thou dost overthrow,
Die not, poor Death, nor yet canst thou kill me.
From rest and sleep, which but thy pictures° be,
Much pleasure,° then from thee, much more must flow, **A**
And soonest our best men with thee do go,
Rest of their bones, and soul's delivery.°
Thou art slave to fate, chance, kings, and desperate men,
And dost with poison, war, and sickness dwell,
And poppy,° or charms° can make us sleep as well,
And better than thy stroke; why swell'st° thou then?
One short sleep past, we wake eternally,
And death shall be no more; Death, thou shalt die. **B**

5. pictures: images. A sleeping person can resemble a dead person.
6. much pleasure: That is, rest and sleep give much pleasure.
8. rest . . . delivery: Death gives the body rest and delivers the soul from the bondage of the body.
11. poppy: opium.
charms: magic; hypnotism.
12. swell'st: swell with pride.

A Literary Focus **Paradox** How does Donne explain that Death causes pleasure?

B Literary Perspectives **Analyzing Philosophical Context** The speaker personifies Death, addressing it as if it were a person. What does this action indicate about the poet's philosophical stance toward Death?

Vocabulary **dreadful** (DREHD fuhl) *adj.:* terrible; causing fear.
desperate (DEHS puhr iht) *adj.:* driven by hopelessness; moved to use extreme means to try to escape frustration and loss.

Literary Perspectives

Analyzing Philosophical Context Philosophical context refers to an author's underlying assumptions about life and its meaning, for *philosophy* refers to the conscious search for truth. An author's personal philosophy influences various aspects of a literary text, including the credibility of its characters, its literary form, and its overarching themes or messages. Death is one of the most common themes in Donne's poetry. How does "Death be not proud" reflect Donne's struggle with the meaning of life and death?

As you read, be sure to notice the questions in the text, which will guide you in using this perspective.

Literary Perspectives

After students read the selection, have them read the **Literary Perspectives** about Analyzing Philosophical Context. Have students read the philosophical arguments presented in the poem, and then ask them to consider an alternate philosophy of life and death and how it might be expressed in a poem. How might the tone, theme, and major points differ from those of Donne's poem? Would Donne still confront Death in a similar manner?

Remind students to use the notes and questions at the bottom of the page to help them use the perspective.

Guide students in answering the **Literary Perspectives** question on this page. Explain to students that the question is asking them to think about how the speaker's action of confronting Death in person reveals the beliefs the poet may have about Death. Ask students, "What is the author's tone in his direct address to Death? What does he want to demonstrate about his attitude toward Death by speaking to it?"

Teacher Preparation

Selection Summary

The speaker sneers at Death because the soul never actually dies and is delivered in Death to eternal life.

Direct Teach

Think About/Talk About

Read with a Purpose Ask students to think of films, books, or other sources in which Death is personified.

Analysis

A Literary Focus

Possible response: *Death is often portrayed as a state of peaceful rest and eternal sleep. In that way, it offers the promise of pleasure.*

B Literary Perspectives

Possible response: *Perhaps the speaker personifies death in order to see death not as a state of being but as something he can confront, wrestle with, and enter into a relationship with. He sees death as a fleeting point to get past and move beyond.*

Extend the Discussion

Interpreting In line 11, why is death compared to opium and magic? ***Possible response:*** *They all cause people to lose consciousness.*

Paradox Why, in the terms of this poem, does Death not actually kill those whom it thinks it kills? ***Possible responses:*** *There is an afterlife; death is a transitional state; the spirit of a person goes on living.*

Vocabulary: Own the Word

- **dreadful:** A rainy and windy day is *dreadful* weather. A *dreadful* place is the sewer.
- **desperate:** Ask students: "Have you ever been *desperate* about getting something? Explain what you were *desperate* for and why."

Check for Understanding

Independent Practice

Reading Skills Focus

Possible responses:

1. *Death can bring sleep and rest as well as release from suffering.*
2. *Desperate people can cause their own deaths through suicide.*
3. *Death does not kill anyone. It is a slave to "fate, chance, kings, and desperate men."*

Vocabulary Check

4. *being chased by a vicious dog*
5. *a person who has lost his job*

Literary Skills Focus

Possible responses:

6. *He assumes Death is proud, that Death takes cruel enjoyment from killing people.*
7. *The speaker's tone is defiant. He challenges Death.*
8. *In death, people look like they are asleep. Death must be restful, peaceful oblivion, like sleep.*
9. *The speaker starts with a stern warning to Death, moves on to insincere sympathy and ridicule of Death, drops to a hushed tone, and ends with a striking judgment of Death.*
10. *He sees death as a brief but perhaps frightening, dreadful passage that leads to new life.*
11. *The resolution is that people die but wake to eternal life, so ultimately Death itself dies.*
12. *Death is a doorway to the afterlife.*

Applying Your Skills

Reading Standard 3.2, 3.4, 3.9 (see pages A48–A50)
Writing Standard 2.3a (see pages A51–A52)

Death be not proud

Literary Response and Analysis

Reading Skills Focus

Quick Check

1. What pleasures can Death bring?
2. How is Death a slave to desperate men?

Read with a Purpose

3. According to the poem, what are the reasons Death should not be proud?

Vocabulary Check

Answer the questions about the Vocabulary words.

4. Which experience might you describe as **dreadful,** being chased by a vicious dog or being startled by a sudden noise?
5. Which person is more likely to feel **desperate,** the one who has failed a quiz or the one who has lost his job?

Literary Skills Focus

Literary Analysis

6. **Infer** What does the speaker assume about Death's self-image?
7. **Analyze** How would you describe the tone of this poem? What attitude does the speaker take toward Death?
8. **Interpret** According to the poem, how are rest and sleep like Death? What point does Donne make by using this comparison?
9. **Evaluate** As the sonnet develops, how does the speaker shift the grounds of his attack on death?
10. **Literary Perspectives** An important part of one's philosophy toward life is, ironically, one's philosophy toward death. How would you summarize the poet's attitude toward death, as conveyed in this poem?

Literary Skills: Paradox

11. **Analyze** How does the sonnet resolve its paradoxes: that those who die do not die and that Death itself will die?

Literary Skills Review: Theme

12. **Infer** The central idea or insight about human experience revealed in a work of literature is called **theme.** Some themes are stated directly, but most are implied. Write a sentence expressing the theme of "Death be not proud."

Writing Skills Focus

Think as a Reader/Writer

Use It in Your Writing As you read the poem, you noted ideas and images that seemed contradictory. Now, choose one of these contradictions. Using it as a starting point, write an essay or meditation in your *Reader/Writer Notebook* that brings out the meaning behind the paradox.

What Do You Think Now? Many people feel powerless when confronted by death. Do you think Donne is able to regain some kind of power over his own mortality in these poems? Explain.

What Do You Think Now?

Tell students to refer to specific examples from Donne's writing that demonstrate how the speaker does or does not regain power over death.

Universal Access

Struggling Writers

Some students may need additional scaffolding to complete the Writing Skills Focus activity. Help students think about a paradox by considering the different meanings of similar words or phrases. For example, for the phrase "Death, thou shalt die," students might explain what is meant by "thou shalt die" and contrast the meaning of "die" with the meaning of "Death." To help students understand the paradoxes ask them the following questions: What does Donne mean when he says that those who die do not die? How is it possible for Death itself to die?

Reading Standard 3.6 (see pages A48–A50)
Writing Standard 2.1a, 2.3a (see pages A51–A52)
Listening and Speaking Standard 2.3d (see pages A53–A55)

Meditation 17
Death be not proud

CHOICES

As you respond to the Choices, use these **Academic Vocabulary** words as appropriate: contradiction, controversy, ensure, establish, widespread.

REVIEW

Compare and Contrast

In "Death be not proud," Donne personifies Death. How does Donne's treatment compare with that of the personified Death in Chaucer's "The Pardoner's Tale" (see page 151)? In an essay compare and contrast the two portrayals of death. Consider Death's character and power and how people respond to Death. Cite examples from both texts to support your points.

Death, the Grim Reaper (c. 1468–1506) from the Office of the Dead, The Mirandola Hours. Add. 50002. Folio No: 85. The British Library, London.

Make a Time Line

During Donne's lifetime, the religious and political landscape of England was in constant upheaval. With a partner, research the life of John Donne as well as the political and cultural events that took place during his lifetime. Who was in power? What was the source of tension between the Roman Catholic and Anglican churches? What was going on in the rest of the world? Create a time line that puts Donne's work in historical and cultural perspective.

CONNECT

Write a Script

Though written by the same person, "Meditation 17" and "Death be not proud" have different voices. Imagine a conversation between the speakers in the two works. Establish the topic and whether the topic is a debate or agreement; then write a dialogue that re-creates the conversation.

Think About Rituals

The tolling of church bells has traditionally been part of a religious funeral. For many people, rituals and customs are an important part of grieving. What rituals are commonly used to mark the death of a loved one? With a partner, discuss ways that people in our society approach funerals. What kinds of choices must be made when a person dies? How do our different cultural backgrounds influence these choices?

EXTEND

Swap Forms

Timed Writing Think about your own experiences with loss of life or death. Perhaps these experiences are through the media or they are far more personal, involving family and friends. In an expository essay, explain your experience and how it has affected your thinking and your behavior.

Set It to Music

TechFocus With a partner, choose a passage from either "Meditation 17" or "Death be not proud." Using instruments, computer software, or your voices, compose music that expresses the passage's emotions. You may set the words from your passage to the music, or read the passage aloud as an introduction. Share your composition with your classmates.

California Standards, pp. 302–303

- **Reading Standard 3.2** Analyze the way in which the theme or meaning of a selection represents a view or comment on life, using textual evidence to support the claim.
- **Reading Standard 3.4** Analyze ways in which poets use imagery, personification, figures of speech, and sounds to evoke readers' emotions.
- **Reading Standard 3.6** Analyze the way in which authors through the centuries have used archetypes drawn from myth and tradition in literature, film, political speeches, and religious writings.
- **Reading Standard 3.9** Analyze the philosophical arguments presented in literary works to determine whether the authors' positions have contributed to the quality of each work and the credibility of the characters.
- **Writing Standard 2.1** Write fictional, autobiographical, or biographical narratives: **a.** Narrate a sequence of events and communicate their significance to the audience.
- **Writing Standard 2.3** Write reflective compositions: **a.** Explore the significance of personal experiences, events, conditions, or concerns by using rhetorical strategies (e.g., narration, description, exposition, persuasion).
- **Listening and Speaking Standard 2.3** Deliver oral responses to literature: **d.** Demonstrate an awareness of the author's use of stylistic devices and an appreciation of the effects created.

Independent Practice

Choices: Evaluation Criteria

Review: Homework
Compare and Contrast
Students consistently use point-by-point or block format to compare and contrast.

Review: Homework
Make a Time Line
Students connect events on the time line to Donne's writing.

Connect: Homework
Write a Script
Students' dialogues express the two different voices present in the selections and establish a topic.

Connect: Homework
Think about Rituals
Students discuss the topic frankly while respecting each other's opinions and experiences.

Extend: Timed Writing 40–50 Minutes
Students follow the form and structure of an expository essay.

Extend: Homework
Set It to Music
Students explain how the music they chose or created reflects the mood of the passage.

Assess

Unit 2 Resources, Selection Standards Check, p. 36

go.hrw.com **ThinkCentral Online Assessment,** Selection Standards Check

Teacher One Stop™, editable Selection Standards Check

Reteach

go.hrw.com **ThinkCentral Online Remediation**

Standards Focus

Objectives

Students will
- understand dialogue and its function
- analyze the author's style

Motivate

What Do You Think?/QuickWrite

Have students analyze an art, sport, or other activity that is important to them. Ask students to write for five minutes about what drives them to pursue this interest.

Preteach

Introducing Vocabulary

1. Explain why you might adopt a **veneer** of composure.
2. Explain the effect of **insufficient** evidence in a trial.
3. List enterprises for which one needs to be **valiant**.
4. Name one way to **vanquish** an army.

English for Academic Success

Language Coach

Have students brainstorm other words with the prefix *-in*, meaning "not." [*indifferent, inaccurate*]

Literary/Reading/Writing Skills Focus

- Have students note how the writer develops plot and character through dialogue.
- Give students a copy of the Reading Skills Focus graphic organizer before they read. (See **Unit 2 Resources.**)
- Have students record points of direction in their **Reader/Writer Notebooks.**

Learn It Online

The online version of this selection includes audio support to engage all students and to help struggling readers with reading comprehension and vocabulary.

go.hrw.com H12-304 Go

Preparing to Read

Reading Standard 3.3; **Grades 9–10 Review Reading Standard** 3.10 (see pages A48–A50)

Link to Today

from W;t

What Do You Think

How do our hearts and minds influence our actions?

QuickWrite

Think about a sport, activity, or type of art that is important to you. What draws you to it? Write a paragraph that describes this activity and its importance.

Literary Skills Focus

Dialogue The majority of what we know about a play's characters is based on what they say or do. **Dialogue,** the directly quoted words of people speaking to one another, bears the burden of plot exposition, pacing, and character development. Even for a talented writer, creating dialogue that sounds natural and accomplishes these goals is a challenge.

Reading Skills Focus

Analyzing Style Playwrights give their characters unique voices by varying speaking **styles**—phrasing, choice of words, and pacing.

Into Action Describe the dialogue in this scene, focusing on each speaker's style and the emotions expressed by the dialogue.

	Vivian	E. M.
Speaking style	hesitant; easily interrupted	
Emotional Expression		angry; dislikes Vivian's essay

Writing Skills Focus

Think as a Reader/Writer

Find It in Your Reading As you read, note the ways in which the writer "directs" the action of the play, including stage directions, references to action in the dialogue, and punctuation.

Reader/Writer Notebook

Use your **RWN** to complete the activities for this selection.

Vocabulary

veneer (vuh NIHR) *n.:* surface appearance or show. *To understand a poem by Donne, you need more than a veneer of scholarship.*

insufficient (ihn suh FIHSH uhnt) *adj.:* not enough. *Analytical methods that might work for the writing of other poets are insufficient for understanding Donne.*

valiant (VAL yuhnt) *adj.:* brave; courageous. *"Death be not proud" depicts a valiant struggle with death.*

vanquish (VANG kwihsh) *v.:* defeat in battle or conflict. *Donne believed that through faith we can vanquish death.*

Language Coach

Related Words The Latin prefix *in–* means "non or not," so *insufficient* means "not sufficient" or "not enough." Without this prefix, *sufficient* simply means "enough." What do you think the related verb *suffice* means? What about the adverb *sufficiently?*

Learn It Online

Listen to Edson's dialogue with the audio version of this excerpt.

go.hrw.com H12-304 Go

California Standards, pp. 304–307

- **Reading Standard 3.3** Analyze the ways in which irony, tone, mood, the author's style, and the "sound" of language achieve specific rhetorical or aesthetic purposes or both.
- **Grades 9–10 Review Reading Standard 3.10** Identify and describe the function of dialogue, scene designs, soliloquies, asides, and character foils in dramatic literature.

Selection Readability	
Easily Accessible **Accessible** Challenging	familiar context; conversational; familiar genre

Selection Summary

A professor accuses a student of sloppy workmanship in a paper she wrote about "Death be not proud." The professor insists upon close reading of the authentic edition of the poem and discusses her belief that much of Donne's meaning is revealed by the way he capitalized and punctuated the sonnet.

DRAMA

from W;t

by **Margaret Edson**

Link to Today

This link to today emphasizes the significance of little things.

Read with a Purpose

Read to discover why the professor believes so strongly in her way of reading a poem.

Build Background

Margaret Edson's Pulitzer Prize–winning play *W;t* tells the story of Vivian Bearing, an English professor who has devoted her career to studying John Donne's *Holy Sonnets.* At the beginning of the play, Bearing has been diagnosed with terminal cancer. In this scene, a flashback to Bearing's college days, she recalls a confrontational meeting with one of her English literature professors (E. M. Ashford) about Donne's Holy Sonnet Six, or "Death be not proud."

Author Note

Margaret Edson (1961–) considers herself first and foremost a teacher, even though she won much acclaim for her first play, *W;t.* Born in Washington, D.C., Edson's educational background is in Renaissance history and English literature, but her writing has also been influenced by her professional experiences, including the two years she spent working in a cancer ward for AIDS patients. Edson drew from this experience when she wrote *W;t* in 1991.

E.M. Please sit down. Your essay on Holy Sonnet Six, Miss Bearing, is a melodrama, with a veneer of scholarship unworthy of you—to say nothing of Donne. Do it again. **A**

Vivian. I, ah . . . **B**

E.M. You must begin with a text, Miss Bearing, not with a feeling.

Death be not proud, though some have called thee
Mighty and dreadfull, for, thou art not soe.

You have entirely missed the point of the poem, because, I must tell you, you have used an edition of the text that is inauthentically punctuated. In the Gardner edition—

Vivian. That edition was checked out of the library—

E.M. Miss Bearing! **C**

Vivian. Sorry.

E.M. You take this too lightly, Miss Bearing. This is Metaphysical Poetry, not The Modern Novel. The standards of scholarship and critical reading which one would apply to any other text are simply insufficient. The effort must be total for the results to be meaningful. Do you think the punctuation of the last line of this sonnet is merely an insignificant detail?

The sonnet begins with a valiant struggle with death, calling on all the forces of intellect and drama to vanquish the enemy. But it is ultimately about overcoming the seemingly insuperable barriers separating life, death, and eternal life.

A Reading Focus **Analyzing Style** What is the tone of E. M.'s opening lines?

B Literary Focus **Dialogue** Why do Vivian's words trail off?

C Reading Focus **Analyzing Style** What does E. M. communicate by exclaiming "Miss Bearing!"?

Vocabulary **veneer** (vuh NIHR) *n.:* surface appearance or show.
insufficient (ihn suh FIHSH uhnt) *adj.:* not enough
valiant (VAL yuhnt) *adj.:* brave; courageous.
vanquish (VANG kwihsh) *v.:* defeat in battle or conflict.

Link to Today

This drama exhibits how seemingly insignificant details can mean the difference between life and death.

Direct Teach

Think About/Talk About

Comprehension

A Reading Focus

Possible response: *The tone is disappointment; E. M. believes that Vivian's essay could be much better.*

C Reading Focus

Possible response: *E. M. communicates that Vivian has rudely interrupted her with a poor excuse.*

Analysis

B Literary Focus

Possible response: *Vivian's words trail off because she is uncertain.*

Extend the Discussion

Making Inferences Is Vivian's apology sincere? ***Possible response:*** *Vivian's apology is not sincere. She does not care about the subject matter as much as E. M.*

Vocabulary: Own the Word

- **veneer:** Have students complete the sentence: *E. M. accused Vivian of writing with a veneer of . . . in her essay.*
- **insufficient:** What, according to E. M. was *insufficiently* applied to Vivian's essay? ***Possible response:*** *Vivian's essay showed an insufficient application of critical reading and scholarship.*
- **valiant:** Ask students to applaud as an indicator of how much they would want to be described as *valiant.* ***Possible response:*** *Students applaud loudly because they want to be thought of as brave and noble.*
- **vanquish:** The root word for *vanquish* is *vincere,* Latin for "to overcome." When you *vanquish* your opponent, you are victorious.

Selection Resources

Unit 2 Resources, on-level practice and assessment, p. 39

Teacher One Stop™, on-level lesson plans and all print resources

Holt Audio Library

Holt Audio Library: Selections and Summaries in Spanish

UA: Differentiating Instruction, graphic organizer, p. 64

UA: Supporting Instruction in Spanish, selection summary

ThinkCentral Online Assessment, Selection Standards Check

ThinkCentral Online Remediation

Think About/Talk About

Analysis

D Literary Focus

Possible response: *Vivian would probably give another insincere apology; she still has no emotional connection to the text, which she discovers later in life.*

Extend the Discussion

Irony Why might Vivian recall E. M.'s interpretation of the poem at the end of the selection? ***Possible response:*** *Sick with terminal cancer, Vivian looks for a way to face her approaching death. The version of the line punctuated by a comma offers less drama but more comfort.*

Monitor Students' Comprehension

Guide the class in identifying these statements about the selection as either true or false.

1. E. M. prefers modern novels to Donne's poetry. [*F*]
2. The punctuation of one line can change the meaning of the entire poem. [*T*]
3. Donne's Holy Sonnet Six is ultimately about celebrating life. [*F*]

In the edition you chose, this profoundly simple meaning is sacrificed to hysterical punctuation:

And Death—*capital D*—shall be no more—*semicolon!*

Death—*capital D—comma*—thou shalt die—*exclamation point!*

If you go in for this sort of thing, I suggest you take up Shakespeare.

Gardner's edition of the Holy Sonnets returns to the Westmoreland manuscript source of 1610—not for sentimental reasons, I assure you, but because Helen Gardner is a *scholar.* It reads:

And death shall be no more, *comma,* Death thou shalt die.

[*As she recites this line, she makes a little gesture at the comma.*]

Nothing but a breath—a comma—separates life from life everlasting. It is very simple really. With the original punctuation restored, death is no longer something to act out on a stage, with exclamation points. It's a comma, a pause.

This way, the *uncompromising* way, one learns something from this poem, wouldn't you say? Life, death. Soul, God. Past, present. Not insuperable barriers, not semicolons, just a comma. D

Nothing but a breath—a comma—separates life from life everlasting.

D Literary Focus **Dialogue** What do you think Vivian might say if she were given a few more lines in this scene?

California Standards, p. 307

- **Reading Standard 3.3** Analyze the ways in which irony, tone, mood, the author's style, and the "sound" of language achieve specific rhetorical or aesthetic purposes or both.
- **Grades 9–10 Review Reading Standard 3.3** Analyze interactions between main and subordinate characters in a literary text (e.g., internal and external conflicts, motivations, relationships, influences) and explain the way those interactions affect the plot.
- **Grades 9–10 Review Reading Standard 3.10** Identify and describe the function of dialogue, scene designs, soliloquies, asides, and character foils in dramatic literature.
- **Writing Standard 2.1** Write fictional, autobiographical, or biographical narratives.

Applying Your Skills

Reading Standard 3.3; **Grades 9–10 Review Reading Standard** 3.3, 3.10 (see pages A48–A50)
Writing Standard 2.1 (see pages A51–A52)

from W;t

Literary Response and Analysis

Reading Skills Focus

Quick Check

1. What does E. M. think is "the point" of Donne's sonnet? Explain your answer.
2. Why does E. M. regard the Gardner edition of Donne's Holy Sonnets as superior?

Read with a Purpose

3. Why is the punctuation of the last line of Donne's sonnet so important to the professor? Explain.

Reading Skills: Analyzing Style

4. As you read, you noted speaking styles and emotions in the dialogue. Now, add a row to your chart briefly describing each character.

	Vivian	E. M.
Speaking style	hesitant; easily interrupted	
Emotional Expression		angry; dislikes Vivian's essay
Character	shy; uncertain	

Vocabulary Check

Match each Vocabulary word with its antonym.

5. veneer — a. cowardly
6. insufficient — b. surrender
7. valiant — c. depth
8. vanquish — d. excessive

Literary Skills Focus

Literary Analysis

9. **Draw Conclusions** What is E. M.'s opinion of the modern novel? How do you know?
10. **Evaluate** How important is punctuation? Do you think the difference between a semicolon and a comma is that important? Explain.

Literary Skills: Dialogue

11. **Analyze** What kind of behavior does the dialogue suggest for E. M.? Defend your answer by quoting from her part of the dialogue.

Literary Skills Review: Conflict

12. **Evaluate** A struggle between opposing forces inside a person is **internal conflict. External conflict** is a struggle between people, between a person and a force of nature, or between a person and society. Does this scene have an internal conflict, an external conflict, or both? Explain.

Writing Skills Focus

Think as a Reader/Writer

Use It in Your Writing While you read the poem, you noted strategies Edson used to "direct" the play. Now, work in a small group to write the dialogue for a short scene between two people. Add necessary stage directions in brackets. Use italics and punctuation to help the actors know how to perform each line.

What Do You Think Now? In this selection, the professor is passionate even about details of punctuation. Think of an activity you are passionate about. Why are even the details significant to you?

Check for Understanding

Independent Practice

Reading Skills Focus

Possible responses:

1. *E. M. believes that Donne's sonnet is about "overcoming the seemingly insuperable barriers separating life, death, and eternal life."*
2. *E. M. believes that Gardner wrote a superior edition because she is a scholar.*
3. *The professor is passionate about the message of the sonnet, which changes with a single change in punctuation.*
4. *Ask students to consider how verbal and emotional expression can help readers analyze character.*

Vocabulary Check

5. *c* 6. *d*
7. *a* 8. *b*

Literary Skills Focus

Possible responses:

9. *E. M. does not like the modern novel; she believes more effort is needed to read metaphysical poetry, making it superior.*
10. *Poems have short lines, so any decision the poet makes is extremely important. The difference between a comma and a semicolon is the difference between a full stop and a pause.*
11. *E. M.'s assertiveness in the line "This way, the uncompromising way, one learns something from this poem," suggests E. M.'s passion for this subject.*
12. *E. M. is struggling to help Vivian see the little things in life, an external conflict. Vivian is also struggling internally to look at poetry differently.*

What Do You Think Now?

Have students imagine that someone is belittling their favorite activity. Ask them to consider how that would make them feel and how they would defend that activity.

Universal Access

Struggling Writers

Some students may need additional scaffolding to complete the Writing Skills Focus activity. Before students begin to write their dialogues, direct them to the stage directions in the text. As they write their dialogues, instruct them to write in stage directions frequently before or after each line of dialogue to indicate how the line is performed. Remind them that they can use italics in a character's line to indicate emphasis. If students need additional help with the dialogue, allow them to work with a partner to create a verbal exchange before writing.

Assess

Unit 2 Resources,
Selection Standards Check, p. 42

go.hrw.com ThinkCentral Online Assessment,
Selection Standards Check

Teacher One Stop™,
editable Selection Standards Check

Standards Focus

Objectives

Students will understand the characteristics of lyric poetry.

Selection Introduction

Think About the Writer

Have students contrast a writer's motivation, drive, and quality of work when writing to compete versus writing for oneself.

For Independent Reading

- *Ariel,* Sylvia Plath
- *Death be Not Proud,* John Gunther

Motivate

What Do You Think?/QuickTalk

Have students think of stories they have read or seen on TV or film of writers who allow or keep their feelings from influencing their work.

English for Academic Success

Academic Vocabulary

Look for opportunities to use the Academic Vocabulary words in this unit.

- **contradiction, *n.*:** statement in opposition to another
- **controversies, *n.*:** lengthy disagreements
- **established, *v.*:** caused to happen
- **ensure, *v.*:** to make certain
- **widespread, *adj.*:** occurring on a wide area

California Standards, pp. 308–313

- **Reading Standard 3.1** Analyze characteristics of subgenres (e.g., satire, parody, allegory, pastoral) that are used in poetry, prose, plays, novels, short stories, essays, and other basic genres.

Preparing to Read

On My First Son
Song: To Celia

What Do You Think? How do our hearts and minds influence our actions?

QuickTalk

In a small group, discuss a piece of literature you have read or seen enacted in the media that closely resembles the author's feelings about that topic. How does knowing the author's feelings affect you as the reader or viewer?

Canon, with circular staves and rose at center. British Library, London, Roy 11 E XI f.2v.

MEET THE WRITER

Ben Jonson
(1572–1637)

If his friend William Shakespeare had never existed, Jonson would probably be regarded as the chief dramatist of the age.

A Complete Londoner

Jonson overcame humble beginnings to create tragedies and comedies for the public theater, to devise masques (dramatic performances including music and lavish costumes) for the court of James I, and to be honored as poet laureate in 1616.

As a boy, Jonson met the headmaster of the elite Westminster School in London, who enrolled the boy at Westminster at his own expense. There Jonson studied Latin and Greek and learned a poetic trick he would use for the rest of his life—to write poems in prose before turning them into verse.

Jonson joined the army and fought the Spanish at Flanders—while the two armies watched, he engaged in single combat with the Spanish champion and killed him. Back in England he became a playwright and an actor. He had two brushes with the law: Once he killed a fellow actor in a duel, and once he went to jail for insulting Scotland in a play. At the Mermaid Tavern he held combats of wit with Shakespeare and others.

Writer and Literary Dictator

In 1616, Jonson astonished the reading public by publishing plays and poems under the title *Works*—a label traditionally used for intellectual subjects such as theology and history. He believed that poems and plays are serious works of art, as serious in their own way as theology and history and as worthy of high regard.

At the height of his career, Jonson was a sort of literary dictator—opinionated and quick-tempered but admired by a number of younger writers, known as "the tribe of Ben" or "the sons of Ben." They stood by an elderly, poor, and neglected Jonson whose blunt manner had ensured him many enemies. Jonson was buried near Chaucer in the Poets' Corner of Westminster Abbey. His inscription reads: "O rare Ben Jonson."

Think About the Writer Jonson was famous for his rivalry with Shakespeare. How might this competition have influenced his work?

Benjamin Jonson (early 17th century) after Abraham van Blyenberch. National Portrait Gallery, London.

Selection Readability	
Easily Accessible **Accessible** Challenging	These poems include accessible theme; accessible vocabulary.

Reading Standard 3.1 (see pages A48–A50)

Literary Skills Focus

Lyrics A **lyric,** from the Greek word *lurikos,* from *lura,* meaning "lyre," is a poem that imaginatively and melodically expresses a speaker's personal thoughts and feelings. Among the early Greeks, the lyric expressed the emotion of an individual singer accompanied by a lyre, a stringed harp-like instrument. Generally the lyric poem no longer has musical accompaniment, but it conveys melody through the musical effects of language, such as **rhyme**, **rhythm**, **alliteration**, and **onomatopoeia**. It also remains distinguished by subjectivity, emotion, and imagination. The lyric's forms are varied. One of its most expressive forms is the **sonnet**. Other forms of lyrics are elegies, odes, and songs.

Ben Jonson wrote some of the finest lyrics in the English language, several of which appear in his plays and masques. Note the musical effects in the two poems included here. In addition to end rhyme, look for other techniques of repetition that create verbal music.

Writing Skills Focus

Think as a Reader/Writer

Find It in Your Reading Throughout "On My First Son" and "Song: To Celia," Jonson uses descriptive words and phrases to reveal his speakers' feelings. Some of these descriptive words and phrases are metaphors; others contain imagery. As you read the poems, create a chart in your *Reader/Writer Notebook* to record particular lines and examples. In the far right column, record how these lines of descriptive phrases evoke a particular feeling.

Line #	Example	Feeling expressed or evoked
1	"Drink to me only with thine eyes"	tender and warmhearted devotion

Reader/Writer Notebook

Use your **RWN** to complete the activities for these selections.

Vocabulary

lament (luh MEHNT) *v.:* mourn or grieve for. *Jonson laments his son's death.*

misery (MIHZ uh ree) *n.:* wretchedness; suffering. *The plague brought misery to many people in England.*

pledge (plehj) *v.:* solemnly promise. *The speaker will pledge his love to Celia.*

divine (dih VYN) *adj.:* of or like God or a god; given or inspired by God. *The speaker is so in love with Celia that he thinks she is divine.*

Language Coach

Parts of Speech Some words can be used as different parts of speech. The verb *lament* means "to mourn or grieve for." The same word can also be used as a noun. A lament is an expression of grief or sorrow. What other Vocabulary words can be used as different parts of speech? What do they mean?

Learn It Online

Get the inside story on the Vocabulary words through Word Watch online.

go.hrw.com H12-309 Go

Preteach

Introducing Vocabulary

- Review the Vocabulary words, definitions, and sentences with students.
- To reinforce students' understanding of the Vocabulary words, explain to students that these words convey intense emotions and have strong connotations. Jonson was in *misery* and penned a *lament* for his deceased son. He also made a *pledge* to the *divine* object of his love for eternity.

English for Academic Success

Language Coach

Possible responses: pledge, *as a noun, means "an oath;"* divine *as a verb means" to guess."* Have students list other examples of words that can be used as different parts of speech.

Literary Skills Focus

As you read and discuss the selection with students, have them list characteristics of lyrics in each of the works.

Writing Skills Focus

Have students record descriptive details that reveal the speaker's emotions in their **Reader/Writer Notebooks.** Students can use their notes to complete the Writing Skills Focus activity.

Learn It Online

Send students to **Word Watch** for audio pronunciations, synonyms and antonyms, and brief histories of word origins.

go.hrw.com H12-309 Go

Selection Resources

Unit 2 Resources, on-level practice and assessment, p. 45

Teacher One Stop™, on-level lesson plans and all print resources

Holt Audio Library

Holt Audio Library: Selections and Summaries in Spanish

UA: Differentiating Instruction, graphic organizer, p. 65

UA: Supporting Instruction in Spanish, selection summary

ThinkCentral Online Assessment, Selection Standards Check

ThinkCentral Online Remediation

Teacher Preparation
Selection Summary
"On My First Son" begins with a farewell to a dead son. The speaker consoles himself with the thought that his son is now free of the pains of living and of growing old. He concludes with a vow never again to "like too much" what he loves.

Direct Teach

Think About/Talk About
Read with a Purpose Have a student volunteer read the Read with a Purpose statement. Ask students to discuss types of grief; grief can come from the loss of a person, material goods, ideas, or beliefs. Ask students what types of emotions are associated with the death of a loved one or the loss of love. As students read the selection, note words that convey emotions associated with grief and love.

▶ Analysis
Ⓐ Literary Focus
Possible response: *The sound of s slows the reader's pace and emphasizes the idea that Jonson finds hope in his son's escape from the evils of the world and from growing old.*

Analyzing Visuals
Connecting to the Text: *The boy represented in the visual could be the same age as Ben Jonson's son at the time of his death.*

POEM

On My First Son

by **Ben Jonson**

Read with a Purpose
Read this poem to understand how a father grieves over his son's death.

Build Background
This poem is about Ben Jonson's son Benjamin, who died of the plague on his seventh birthday. Jonson wrote "On My First Son" as a farewell to his child. The name *Benjamin* in Hebrew means "child of the right hand" and, ironically, connotes a "lucky, clever child." The **epigraph,** or inscription that appears on a grave, is in quotation marks at the end of the poem.

Farewell, thou child of my right hand,° and joy;
  My sin was too much hope of thee, loved boy:
Seven years thou wert lent to me, and I thee pay,°
  Exacted° by thy fate, on the just° day.
Oh, could I lose all father° now! for why
  Will man lament the state he should envy—
To have so soon 'scaped world's and flesh's rage, Ⓐ
  And if no other misery, yet age?
Rest in soft peace, and asked, say, "Here doth lie
  Ben Jonson his best piece of poetry;
For whose sake henceforth all his vows be such
  As what he loves may never like too much."

1. child of my right hand: The name Benjamin in Hebrew means "child of the right hand."
3. thee pay: pay with you, give you back.
4. exacted: forced. **just:** exact. Loans were often made for exactly seven years.
5. father: sense of fatherhood; the need to mourn like a father.

Portrait of a Boy (panel) by Robert Peake the Elder.

Ⓐ Literary Focus **Lyrics** What lyrical effect does the use of alliteration create in this line?

Vocabulary **lament** (luh MEHNT) *v.*: mourn or grieve for.
misery (MIHZ uh ree) *n.*: wretchedness; suffering.

Analyzing Visuals
Connecting to the Text How might this child represent Jonson's "best piece of poetry"?

Universal Access

Struggling Readers
Model understanding how descriptive words and phrases convey emotion. Read aloud lines 1–5. You might say: "In the first two lines, the speaker expresses his attachment to his son. In lines 3–4, the phrase 'I thee pay,' expresses a quiet acceptance on the father's part of his son's death. The speaker then becomes more expressive with his grief in line 5 as he laments being a father." Ask students to re-read the rest of the poem and note what the speaker seems to be feeling in each line. Ask them to identify the words that convey the feelings.

Advanced Learners
Acceleration Ask students to identify the main motifs in each poem. Have them find words and phrases that indicate the mood of each poem while concentrating on each motif. Ask students: How does motif convey theme? Have students discuss the question with a partner, supporting their responses with evidence from the texts.

POEM

Song: To Celia

by **Ben Jonson**

Read with a Purpose

Read to discover how the speaker uses surprising comparisons to describe his love.

Build Background

"Song: To Celia" celebrates the rejuvenating powers of love. It is associated with a famous tune that many people still know. Thomas Arne (1710–1778), who also wrote the British national anthem, composed music for Jonson's poem and titled it "Drink to Me Only with Thine Eyes."

Drink to me only with thine eyes,
And I will pledge with mine;
Or leave a kiss but in the cup,
And I'll not look for wine. Ⓐ
The thirst that from the soul doth rise
Doth ask a drink divine;
But might I of Jove's nectar° sup,
I would not change° for thine.
I sent thee late a rosy wreath,
Not so much honoring thee
As giving it a hope, that there
It could not withered be.
But thou thereon didst only breathe,
And sent'st it back to me;
Since when it grows, and smells, I swear,
Not of itself but thee.

7. **Jove's nectar:** Jove, more commonly called Jupiter, is the supreme god in Roman mythology. Nectar was the drink that kept the gods immortal.
8. **change:** exchange.

Gathering Rosebuds by John William Waterhouse (1849-1917).

Ⓐ **Literary Focus** **Lyrics** What grammatical structures are repeated in the first four lines? What lyrical effect does this parallelism create?

Vocabulary **pledge** (plehj) *v.:* solemnly promise.
divine (dih VYN) *adj.:* of or like God or a god; given or inspired by God.

Teacher Preparation
Selection Summary

In "Song: To Celia," the speaker praises a woman, saying that he prefers her kiss to wine and would not exchange it even for a drink that would make him immortal.

Direct Teach

Think About/Talk About

Analysis

Ⓐ Literary Focus

Possible response: *The writer uses imperative sentences ("Drink to me . . . / Or leave a kiss . . .). This parallelism conveys the strength of the speaker's emotions since imperatives are strong sentences.*

Extend the Discussion

Paradox What paradox does Jonson present about the wreath? What deeper truth might this suggest? ***Possible response:*** *By claiming that the wreath is now growing rather than fading, the poet is suggesting that the woman rejuvenates him.*

Vocabulary: Own the Word

- **lament:** Write *lament* in a circle on the board along with the definition, "to mourn." Then, draw spider legs and elicit from students related attributes. ***Possible responses:*** *bewail, sorrow, grief, bemoan*
- **misery:** Ask students: "Have you ever cheered up a friend who was in *misery*? Explain who, when and how you encouraged the person."
- **pledge:** Ask students to identify a common *pledge* that many people make. ***Possible responses:*** *the Pledge of Allegiance, wedding vows*
- **divine:** Tell students that the connotation of *divine* is "unusually lovely." You might say: "The tenor vocalist had a lovely voice, but the soprano's voice was *divine.*" Ask students to create a pair of statements showing how *divine* is stronger than *nice* or *lovely.*

California Standards, pp. 312–313

- **Reading Standard 3.1** Analyze characteristics of subgenres (e.g., satire, parody, allegory, pastoral) that are used in poetry, prose, plays, novels, short stories, essays, and other basic genres.
- **Reading Standard 3.4** Analyze ways in which poets use imagery, personification, figures of speech, and sounds to evoke readers' emotions.
- **Reading Standard 3.7** Analyze recognized works of world literature from a variety of authors: **b.** Relate literary works and authors to the major themes and issues of their eras.
- **Writing Standard 1.1** Demonstrate an understanding of the elements of discourse (e.g., purpose, speaker, audience, form) when completing narrative, expository, persuasive, or descriptive writing assignments.
- **Writing Standard 2.2** Write responses to literature: **a.** Demonstrate a comprehensive understanding of the significant ideas in works or passages. **b.** Analyze the use of imagery, language, universal themes, and unique aspects of the text. **c.** Support important ideas and viewpoints through accurate and detailed references to the text and to other works.
- **Listening and Speaking Standard 2.3** Deliver oral responses to literature.

Check for Understanding

Independent Practice

Reading Skills Focus

Possible responses:

1. *His sin was hoping too much for his son's survival.*
2. *He compares his son to a loan.*
3. *The speaker asks to be left a kiss.*
4. *The speaker sends a rose wreath.*
5. *Filial love and romantic love.*

Vocabulary Skills Check

6. *c* **7.** *d*

8. *a* **9.** *b*

Literary Skills Focus

Possible responses:

10. *The tone is emotional and sorrowful.*
11. *The dead no longer suffer, but the living suffer the loss of the dead and of life.*
12. *In this metaphor, Jonson compares his son to a seven-year loan that has come due; that is, Jonson sees his son as being "on loan" to him from God. This metaphor suggests that Jonson takes a somewhat fatalistic view of life in which all events are ordained by God.*
13. *He thirsts for her, and even if he were offered immortality, he would choose his love.*
14. *the speaker's heart*
15. *In "On My First Son," Jonson despairs but recognizes that his son no longer suffers. In "Song: To Celia," the impression is of desperation and unconditional love.*
16. *"On My First Son":* aabbccddeeff; *"Song: To Celia":* abcbabcbdefedefe. *Though the poems are not visually separated into stanzas, they have a stanza-like pattern.*

Applying Your Skills

Reading Standard 3.1, 3.4 (see pages A48–A50)
Writing Standard 2.2 (see pages A51–A52)

On My First Son / Song: To Celia

Literary Response and Analysis

Reading Skills Focus

Quick Check

1. What is the speaker's sin in "On My First Son"?
2. To what does the speaker of "On My First Son" compare his son?
3. What does the speaker of "Song: To Celia" ask his beloved to leave for him in a cup?
4. What does the speaker of "Song: To Celia" send to his beloved?

Read with a Purpose

5. What different kinds of love are described in the poems "On My First Son" and "Song: To Celia"?

Vocabulary Check

Match the Vocabulary words with their synonyms.

6. lament	**a.** promise
7. misery	**b.** godly; godlike
8. pledge	**c.** mourn; grieve
9. divine	**d.** distress; suffering

Literary Skills Focus

Literary Analysis

10. **Interpret** How would you describe the **tone** of "On My First Son"?
11. **Draw Conclusions** In "On My First Son," why does Jonson say we might envy the dead?
12. **Analyze** Explain the metaphor Jonson uses in lines 3–4 of "On My First Son." What does this comparison say about how Jonson views life?
13. **Infer** In "Song: To Celia," how does the speaker use the idea of drinking a cup of wine to praise his lady?
14. **Hypothesize** What might the wreath represent to the speaker in "Song: To Celia"?

Literary Skills: Lyric

15. **Analyze** A lyric expresses a speaker's personal thoughts and feelings. Describe the emotional impression created by each poem.

Literary Skills Review: Rhyme Scheme

16. **Analyze** The pattern of rhymed lines in a poem is called its **rhyme scheme**. Describe the rhyme scheme in each poem. Give each new rhyme a new letter of the alphabet. What do you discover about the rhymes in Jonson's poems?

Writing Skills Focus

Think as a Reader/Writer

Use It in Your Writing While you read, you noticed how Jonson uses descriptive language to reveal feelings about the son or the beloved. Using descriptive language, write a poem in your *Reader/Writer Notebook* about someone or something vital to you.

What Do You Think Now? How does love lead us to a deeper understanding of ourselves and our role in the world?

What Do You Think Now?

Have students refer back to the poems when thinking about events that deepen one's understanding and perspective of the world. Ask students to consider how gain or loss of love can change one's understanding of their place in the world.

Universal Access

Struggling Writers

Some students may need additional scaffolding to complete the Writing Skills Focus activity. Invite students to begin writing by creating a list of emotions that they associate with the subject of their lyric. Then, ask students to develop short sentences that explain their emotions. Have students rework the sentences into a poem.

Teacher Preparation

Selection Summary

In "To Althea, from Prison," the speaker talks of the nature of confinement versus liberty and asserts that although he is in jail, he is spiritually and imaginatively free.

Direct Teach

Think About/Talk About

Read with a Purpose Explain to students that Cavalier poets were known for their polished and elegant lyrics. As the students read the selection, ask them to look for details that display Cavalier ideas.

Comprehension

Ⓒ Reading Focus

Possible response: *Both have the freedom to go where they wish, which the speaker lacks. Both, however, lack freedoms that the speaker has: The fish cannot experience camaraderie; the winds cannot commit to a principle.*

Analysis

Ⓐ Literary Focus

Possible responses: *The words* unconfined *and* liberty *refer to freedom. The words* tangled *and* fettered *refer to imprisonment. They set up the paradox by displaying the speaker's feelings of freedom while in prison.*

Ⓑ Literary Focus

Possible response: *The first stanza sets up an image of the speaker being happy and free when he thinks of his beloved Althea.*

POEM

To Althea, from Prison

by **Richard Lovelace**

Read with a Purpose
Read to discover how this poem illustrates Cavalier ideals.

Build Background
On two different occasions, Lovelace was imprisoned for his loyalty to the English king. Lovelace was said to be a handsome man with many admirers, but whether or not this poem is autobiographical remains a mystery.

When Love with unconfinèd wings
  Hovers within my gates,
And my divine Althea brings
  To whisper at the grates;
When I lie tangled in her hair
  And fettered to her eye,
The gods that wanton° in the air
  Know no such liberty. Ⓐ Ⓑ

When flowing cups run swiftly round,
  With no allaying Thames,°
Our careless heads with roses bound,
  Our hearts with loyal flames;
When thirsty grief in wine we steep,
  When healths and drafts go free,°
Fishes that tipple° in the deep
  Know no such liberty.

When, like committed linnets,° I
  With shriller throat shall sing
The sweetness, mercy, majesty,
  And glories of my King;°
When I shall voice aloud how good
  He is, how great should be,
Enlargèd winds that curl the flood
  Know no such liberty. Ⓒ

Stone walls do not a prison make,
  Nor iron bars a cage:
Minds innocent and quiet take
  That for an hermitage.°
If I have freedom in my love,
  And in my soul am free,
Angels alone, that soar above,
  Enjoy such liberty.

7. **wanton:** frolic.
10. **allaying Thames:** the wine is not diluted with water from the Thames, a river that flows through London.
14. **healths and drafts go free:** generously toasting one another's health and drinking.
15. **tipple:** to drink too much alcohol; here, the fish "get drunk" on water.
17. **committed linnets:** caged birds.
20. **my King:** Charles I, king of England from 1625 to 1649.
28. **hermitage:** a quiet, secluded retreat.

Ⓐ **Literary Focus** **Diction** Find two words in the first stanza that refer to freedom and two words that refer to imprisonment. How do they set up a **paradox,** or an apparent contradiction that is actually true?

Ⓑ **Literary Focus** **Diction** How do the words from the first stanza contribute to the joyful or passionate atmosphere?

Ⓒ **Reading Focus** **Comparing and Contrasting** Why does the speaker compare himself to fishes and the winds?

California Standards, p. 319

- **Reading Standard 2.2** Analyze the way in which clarity of meaning is affected by the patterns of organization, hierarchical structures, repetition of the main ideas, syntax, and word choice in the text.
- **Reading Standard 3.3** Analyze the ways in which irony, tone, mood, the author's style, and the "sound" of language achieve specific rhetorical or aesthetic purposes or both.
- **Writing Standard 2.1** Write fictional, autobiographical, or biographical narratives: **c.** Describe with concrete sensory details the sights, sounds, and smells of a scene and the specific actions, movements, gestures, and feelings of the characters; use interior monologue to depict the characters' feelings.

POEM

To Lucasta, on Going to the Wars

by **Richard Lovelace**

Read with a Purpose

Read to determine the speaker's attitude toward war.

Build Background

The English Civil Wars are the backdrop for this poem, which takes the form of a lover's farewell to his beloved. The poem is famous for applying the language of love and courtship to warfare.

Tell me not, sweet, I am unkind,
  That from the nunnery°
Of thy chaste breast and quiet mind
  To war and arms I fly.

True, a new mistress now I chase,
  The first foe in the field;
And with a stronger faith embrace
  A sword, a horse, a shield. **A**

Yet this inconstancy is such
  As you too shall adore;
I could not love thee, dear, so much,
  Loved I not honor more. **B**

2. **nunnery:** a building where nuns live; here, used as a metaphor for a pure, safe place.

La Belle Dame Sans Merci (1902) by Sir Frank Dicksee (1853–1928). Bristol City Museum and Art Gallery, U.K.

Analyzing Visuals

Connecting to the Text Discuss how the image relates to the tone and mood of the poem.

A **Literary Focus** **Diction** Which words in this stanza contribute to its sad, melancholy tone?

B **Reading Focus** **Comparing and Contrasting** How does the treatment of love in these final lines differ from the lighthearted approach taken in "Why So Pale and Wan, Fond Lover?"

Vocabulary **chaste** (chayst) *adj.:* pure or modest in nature.
embrace (ehm BRAYS) *v.:* accept readily; adopt.
inconstancy (ihn KAHN stuhn see) *n.:* changeability.

Advanced Learners

Acceleration Inform students that while "Why So Pale and Wan, Fond Lover?" is generally viewed as one man speaking to another, it is possible the poet is talking to himself. Have students form groups of four and start a discussion supporting this interpretation. Tell groups to find evidence in the text to support their claim.

Analyzing Visuals

Connecting to the Text: *The painting represents a man in his armor as he looks lovingly at a beautiful woman. The situation reminds the reader of the content of "To Lucasta, on Going to the Wars," which is about a soldier bidding farewell to his beloved. The painting's ethereal and romantic atmosphere perfectly relates to the tone of Lovelace's poem.*

Teacher Preparation

Selection Summary

In "To Lucasta, on Going to the Wars," a man addresses his beloved directly and explains why he must leave her and go to war. His metaphors connect love and war.

Direct Teach

Think About/Talk About

Read with a Purpose Have students read the Read with a Purpose statement. Ask students to look for details that reveal the speaker's feelings about war.

Comprehension

B Reading Focus

Possible response: *The treatment of love is much more intense because it concerns the love that one shares with another person.*

Analysis

A Literary Focus

Possible response: *"Mistress," "foe," and "a sword, a horse, a shield," represent the things that are taking the speaker away from his love.*

Vocabulary: Own the Word

- **wan:** Ask students to explain why the young lover in the poem is so pale and *wan.* [*He is feeling faint from his lovesickness.*]
- **mute:** Ask students why the young lover was *mute.* [*He was shy.*]
- **chaste:** Tell students *chastity* is the noun form of *chaste.* Someone who makes a vow of *chastity* vows to avoid all sexual contact.
- **embrace:** Tell students that *embrace* has a stronger connotation than accept. For instance, "I accept your criticism, but I *embrace* your praise."
- **inconstancy:** Remind students that *constant* means "steadfast." The prefix *in–* changes this meaning. Ask students for examples of things in nature that are *inconstant* or exhibit *inconstancy.*

Teacher Preparation

Selection Summary

In "Why So Pale and Wan, Fond Lover?," the speaker addresses a man who is pining for the love of a woman who is indifferent to him. In a series of rhetorical questions, the speaker advises the young man to drop his futile suit.

Direct Teach

Think About/Talk About

Read with a Purpose Have a student read the Read with a Purpose statement. Ask students to discuss the kind of advice someone would give to a young man in love. As students read the selection, ask them to note elements of advice.

Analysis

A Literary Focus

Possible response: *The word "fond" means foolish, so the speaker thinks the young lover is a fool. The speaker tells the lover to quit because his actions are unwise.*

Extend the Discussion

Paraphrasing Reword lines 3–4 to ease understanding. ***Possible response:*** *"When your good looks have no effect on her, will a glum face be more attractive?"*

Mood In what way does the poem go from lighthearted teasing to angry impatience? ***Possible response:*** *The poem begins by the speaker gently teasing the young lover, saying that he will never win his lady's love if he does not speak. The speaker then ends the poem with a mild curse by stating that if the woman will not love the young man then "the devil take her!"*

POEM

Why So Pale and Wan, Fond Lover?

by **Sir John Suckling**

Read with a Purpose
Read to discover the speaker's advice to a young man in love.

Build Background
One convention of Renaissance love poetry is that young men suffer from unrequited love. Part of this convention is that the women who are the objects of admiration show no pity or interest. The speaker in this poem addresses someone who is suffering, a fond, or foolish, lover who looks "pale and wan."

Why so pale and wan, fond lover?
  Prithee,° why so pale?
Will, when looking well can't move her,
  Looking ill prevail? (A)
  Prithee, why so pale?

Why so dull and mute, young sinner?
  Prithee, why so mute?
Will, when speaking well can't win her,
  Saying nothing do't?
  Prithee, why so mute?

Quit, quit, for shame; this will not move,
  This cannot take her.
If of herself she will not love,
  Nothing can make her:
  The devil take her!

2. prithee: contraction of "I pray thee"; I ask you.

Henry Percy, 9th Earl of Northumberland (c. 1595) by Nicholas Hilliard (1547–1619).
Fitzwilliam Museum, University of Cambridge, U.K.

(A) Literary Focus Diction What words reveal the speaker's attitude toward the lover?

Vocabulary **wan** (wahn) *adj.:* faint or weak.
mute (myoot) *adj.:* not speaking; silent.

Universal Access

English Learners

English for Academic Success To help students with archaic language and syntax of these poems, pair them with more-proficient English speakers. Before students begin reading, go over the vocabulary words with each pair to be sure students understand the new terms.

✔ See the **English Language Skill Builder** in **UA: Differentiating Instruction.**

Struggling Readers

Guide students in comparing and contrasting literary works. Tell students that the speaker in "Why So Pale," observing the young man's lack of initiative, takes on an instructive, almost critical tone, while the speaker in "To Lucasta" seems apologetic as he explains his need to go to war and fight for honor. Ask students to think about what message each poet may be trying to communicate and to contrast the two themes.

Why So Pale and Wan, Fond Lover? / To Lucasta, on Going to the Wars / To Althea, from Prison

Reading Standard 2.2, 3.3 (see pages A48–A50)

Literary Skills Focus

Diction A writer's or speaker's choice of words is called **diction**. Diction can be formal, informal, colloquial, poetic, ornate, plain, abstract, or concrete. Diction depends on the writer's subject, purpose, and audience. **Connotations**—meanings, associations, and emotions attached to words—are an important aspect of diction. Some words, for example, are suited to informal conversations but are inappropriate in a formal speech. Diction is an essential element of **style**. Diction is a critical element in conveying an author's tone or attitude about a subject.

Reading Skills Focus

Comparing and Contrasting Comparing and contrasting literary works can help you better understand each one. When you **compare and contrast**, you focus on how important elements are similar and different.

Into Action As you read, compare the persons being addressed, the speakers themselves, the images employed, and the tone and themes conveyed. Record your observations using a chart like the one below.

Elements for comparing/contrasting	"Why So Pale . . ."	"To Lucasta . . ."	"To Althea . . ."
person addressed	a man in love	a woman the speaker loves	a woman the speaker loves
speaker			
images			
tone			
theme			

Writing Skills Focus

Think as a Reader/Writer

Find It in your Reading **Imagery** is language that appeals to the five senses—sight, sound, taste, smell, and touch. Most imagery is visual—it establishes pictures in the reader's mind. Some images appeal to more than one sense. As you read, use your *Reader/Writer Notebook* to record some of the images, the words the authors choose to convey them, and the senses to which they appeal.

Reader/Writer Notebook

Use your **RWN** to complete the activities for these selections.

Vocabulary

wan (wahn) *adj.:* faint or weak. *Lovesickness has made the young man wan.*

mute (myoot) *adj.:* not speaking; silent. *Normally talkative, he has become mute as he dreams of the woman he loves.*

chaste (chayst) *adj.:* pure or modest in nature. *The man loves the woman's gentle, chaste nature.*

embrace (ehm BRAYS) *v.:* accept readily; adopt. *The soldiers patriotically embrace their solemn duty.*

inconstancy (ihn KAHN stuhn see) *n.:* changeability. *The soldier explains his inconstancy to his love: He must leave her to serve his country.*

Language Coach

Homonyms Words that have the same pronunciation but not the same spelling are called **homonyms**. Homonyms have different meanings and some homonym pairs include verbs in the past tense. The homonym of *chaste* (meaning "pure") is the past-tense verb *chased*, which means "ran after." Spell a homonym for each of these words: *guessed, discussed, leased, missed, passed.*

Learn It Online

Hear these poems read aloud online.

go.hrw.com H12-315 Go

Selection Resources

Unit 2 Resources, on-level practice and assessment, p. 50

Teacher One Stop™, on-level lesson plans and all print resources

Holt Audio Library

Holt Audio Library: Selections and Summaries in Spanish

UA: Differentiating Instruction, graphic organizer, p. 65

UA: Supporting Instruction in Spanish, selection summary

ThinkCentral Online Assessment, Selection Standards Check

ThinkCentral Online Remediation

Preteach

Introducing Vocabulary

- Review the Vocabulary words, definitions, and sentences with students.
- To reinforce students' understanding of the Vocabulary words, explain that the diction in these works usually has a melancholy tone in which the main characters are saddened and sometimes *wan* or *mute*. Suckling and Lovelace both *embrace* the *inconstancy* of life and draw inspiration from their emotions.

English for Academic Success

Language Coach

After students read the **Language Coach,** have students think of homonyms of *pale* and *dear.* [*pail, deer*]

Literary Skills Focus

As you read and discuss the selection with students, have them compare and contrast diction between the poets.

Reading Skills Focus

Give students a copy of the Reading Skills Focus graphic organizer before they read. (See **Unit 2 Resources.**) Tell them to use their responses to answer the questions on the Applying Your Skills page.

Writing Skills Focus

Have students record examples of imagery in their **Reader/Writer Notebooks.** Students can use their notes to complete the Writing Skills Focus activity.

Learn It Online

The online version of this selection includes audio support to engage all students and to help struggling readers with reading comprehension and vocabulary.

go.hrw.com H12-315 Go

Standards Focus

Objectives

Students will

- understand diction and word choice
- compare and contrast literary works

Selection Introduction

Think About the Writers

Have students compare the different political environments that may have influenced the careers of Suckling and Lovelace to the political situations during which the earlier courtiers lived.

Motivate

What Do You Think?/QuickWrite

Have students consider the emotions associated with "burn out" and "fade away." Ask them to write about whether or not a person whose actions are driven by their heart would agree it is "Better to burn out than to fade away."

For Independent Reading

Flags of Our Fathers, James Bradley

English for Academic Success

Academic Vocabulary

Look for opportunities to use the Academic Vocabulary words in this unit.

- **contradiction, *n.*:** inconsistency
- **established, *v.*:** caused to happen

California Standards, pp. 314–319

- **Reading Standard 2.2** Analyze the way in which clarity of meaning is affected by the patterns of organization, hierarchical structures, repetition of the main ideas, syntax, and word choice in the text.
- **Reading Standard 3.3** Analyze the ways in which irony, tone, mood, the author's style, and the "sound" of language achieve specific rhetorical or aesthetic purposes or both.

Preparing to Read

SIR JOHN SUCKLING

Why So Pale and Wan, Fond Lover?

RICHARD LOVELACE

To Lucasta, on Going to the Wars

To Althea, from Prison

What Do You Think? How do our hearts and minds influence our actions?

QuickWrite

Write about the saying "Better to burn out than to fade away." Do you agree? Does it relate more to decisions prompted by the heart or the mind?

Sir John Suckling (c. 1640) after Sir Anthony Van Dyck.
National Portrait Gallery, London.

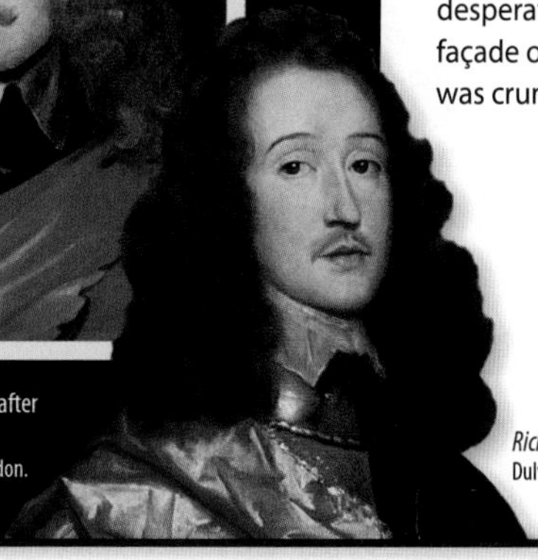

Richard Lovelace, attributed to William Dobson.
Dulwich Picture Gallery, London.

MEET THE WRITER

Sir John Suckling

(1609–1642)

Sir John Suckling was born rich, but he lost his fortune through gambling and extravagant living. When war broke out, he raised a company of one hundred men, outfitted in scarlet coats and white doublets, to fight for the king. He plotted to deliver one of the king's chief advisors from imprisonment in the Tower of London. However, the plot was discovered, and Suckling was forced to flee to France. There, at the age of thirty-three, he died. Historians are not sure whether he took his own life or was murdered.

Suckling's poetry belongs to the Cavalier school, so named for its writers who were Royalists or supporters of the king. His poetry was witty, charming, and graceful, earning him the praise of being "natural, easy Suckling."

Richard Lovelace

(1618–1657)

Like his fellow Cavalier poets, Richard Lovelace (pronounced LUHV lehs) came from a wealthy family. His good looks and elegant manners created a stir when he was at Oxford University. After Oxford, Lovelace became a favorite courtier to King Charles and Queen Henrietta Maria. Lovelace became an ardent Royalist and, when the Civil Wars broke out, he fought bravely for King Charles. He was imprisoned twice by the opposing Parliamentary forces. Like Suckling, he lost all his wealth and land, and he died in poverty at age thirty-nine.

Lovelace's work is considered to be more serious than Suckling's. The poetry is tinged with a slight element of desperation and melancholy—suggesting that beneath a façade of gallantry and elegance, the careless, aristocratic life was crumbling away.

Think About the Writer How do these courtier-poets' careers compare with those of earlier courtiers such as Wyatt and Raleigh?

Selection Readability	
Easily Accessible **Accessible** Challenging	These poems include accessible context; accessible theme; short poetry lines.

Reading Standard 3.7b (see pages A48–A50)
Writing Standard 1.1, 2.2a–c (see pages A51–A52)
Listening and Speaking Standard 2.3 (see pages A53–A55)

Grammar Link

Imperative Mood

When a verb is used to express a direct command, a request, or an instruction, it is considered to be in the **imperative mood**:

Try another approach.
Enclose a stamped, self-addressed envelope.

The imperative is used with the second person. The subject is usually not expressed but is understood to be *you.* The command "Go to the board" means "(You) go to the board." The *you* is implied, not stated expressly.

In poetry, an apostrophe often begins with an imperative verb. An **apostrophe** is a figure of speech in which something that is absent is addressed as if it were present and could answer. An apostrophe can add immediacy or excitement to a poem. John Donne uses an apostrophe in his sonnet "Death be not proud" when he addresses Death as if it were a person. There, the verb *be* is in the imperative mood.

Your Turn

Identify the imperative mood in these lines by circling the imperative verbs. Not all lines will have imperative verbs.

1. "My sin was too much hope of thee, loved boy"
2. "Rest in soft peace"
3. "Drink to me only with thine eyes"
4. "Or leave a kiss but in the cup"
5. "It could not withered be"

Writing Application Write a short speech in which you try to persuade someone to do something—for example, to vote, to volunteer for a cause, or to help fund a project. In your speech, use some imperative verbs to help give force to your argument.

CHOICES

As you respond to the Choices, use these **Academic Vocabulary** words as appropriate: contradiction, controversy, ensure, establish, widespread.

REVIEW

Analyze Imperative Mood and Apostrophe

Both poems include striking examples of the imperative mood and of apostrophe. Write a comparison-contrast essay analyzing the effect of the imperative mood and apostrophe on tone in the two poems.

Ben Jonson Pub, UK.

CONNECT

Explore Jonson's Influence

Timed Writing A group of writers met regularly with Jonson at London taverns. This "tribe of Ben" included Robert Herrick, Thomas Carew, John Suckling, and Richard Lovelace. Jonson established standards for clarity and precision in writing. In an essay, explain Jonson's influence on one of the poets in the group. Cite examples from both poets to support your points.

EXTEND

Make Music

The British composer Thomas Arne set Jonson's "Song: To Celia" to music in a composition titled "Drink to Me Only with Thine Eyes." Find a recording of this song, using library resources or an online search. Listen to the music, and re-read the poem. Then, re-read "On My First Son," and compose music that interprets it. Record your song, and play it for your classmates. Explain how you created your melody and what you hope to convey with it.

Independent Practice

Grammar Link

Your Turn

1. *no imperative verb*
2. *Rest*
3. *Drink*
4. *Leave*
5. *no imperative verb*

Choices: Evaluation Criteria

Review: Homework

Analyze Imperative Mood and Apostrophe

- Students give examples of imperative mood and of apostrophe from the text.
- Students express how imperative mood and apostrophe affects the tone in both poems.

Research: Timed Writing 40–50 Minutes

Students draw a connection between the writer's and Jonson's work.

Extend: Homework

Make Music

- The song conveys the subject matter of the poem.
- Students should describe the process of creating the new melody.

Assess

Unit 2 Resources, Selection Standards Check, p. 47

ThinkCentral Online Assessment, Selection Standards Check

Teacher One-Stop™, editable Selection Standards Check

Reteach

ThinkCentral Online Remediation

Universal Access: Grammar Link

EL English Learners

English for Academic Success Tell students that they can recognize imperative verbs by the absence of the pronoun *you*. Explain that *you* is implied when using the imperative. Add that sentences in which the imperative is used end either with a period or an exclamation point. The period is mostly used for requests or mild commands. An exclamation point is used for strong, urgent commands.

Give students the following examples:

1. Please send me the photographs.
2. Call me in two hours.
3. Don't go that way!
4. Take me with you!

For more practice with the imperative mood, see **Warriner's Handbook**, **GrammarNotes,** and **Language Handbook Worksheets.**

Applying Your Skills

Reading Standard 2.2, 3.3 (see pages A48–A50)
Writing Standard 2.1c (see pages A51–A52)

Why So Pale and Wan, Fond Lover?
To Lucasta, on Going to the Wars
To Althea, from Prison

Literary Response and Analysis

Reading Skills Focus

Quick Check

1. In "Why So Pale and Wan," how has the woman responded to the man?
2. In "To Lucasta," who is the "new mistress"?
3. In "To Althea," who is admired for being "good" and "great"?

Read with a Purpose

4. What does the speaker conclude in each poem?

Reading Skills: Comparing and Contrasting

5. Now that you have noted the poems' similarities and differences, write a paragraph about how diction affects these similarities and differences.

Vocabulary Check

Answer the questions about the Vocabulary words.

6. Would a **wan** smile be a big grin?
7. Is a person keeping a secret likely to be **mute** about it?
8. Would a **chaste** person lie and cheat?
9. Is a person set in his ways likely to **embrace** change?
10. Would it seem reasonable to accuse a traitor of **inconstancy**?

Literary Skills Focus

Literary Analysis

11. **Analyze** In "Why So Pale and Wan," what advice does the speaker give the pale lover? What is the speaker's **tone**, or attitude toward his subject? How does his tone change? How does it differ from the tone of Lovelace's two poems?
12. **Analyze** In "To Lucasta," what metaphors of love are used to describe war? What do you think of these romantic ways of talking about war?
13. **Infer** The speaker in "To Lucasta" implies two paradoxes: that his inconstancy (line 9) is really constancy; and that to be loyal he must be disloyal. How can these contradictions be true?
14. **Interpret** In "To Althea" what do the paradoxical lines "Stone walls do not a prison make, / Nor iron bars a cage" suggest about the idea of freedom?

Literary Skills: Diction

15. **Analyze** How is each poet's **diction** suited to his subject? Explain your reasoning, and support it with examples from the text.

Literary Skills Review: Refrain

16. **Analyze** A **refrain** is a word, phrase, line, or group of lines repeated to create rhythm and suspense and to organize and emphasize ideas. What are the poems' refrains and their effects?

Writing Skills Focus

Think as a Reader/Writer

Use It in Your Writing The imagery used by Lovelace and Suckling appeals to many of the senses. Write a poem describing a place you know well. Use adjectives that appeal to the senses to describe your place.

What Do You Think Now? How might trying to achieve an impossible goal affect a person's life?

Universal Access

Struggling Writers

Some students may need additional scaffolding to complete the Writing Skills Focus activity. Invite students to begin writing by creating short sentences about the physical characteristics of their location. Then, ask students to describe how they feel when they see or experience these characteristics. Have students incorporate these feelings in their description. Remind students to include sensory details that appeal to sight, hearing, smell, taste, and touch.

What Do You Think Now?

Ask the students how failure to reach their goal because of unexpected interference could affect their outlook on life.

Assess

Unit 2 Resources,
Selection Standards Check, p. 53

Check for Understanding

Independent Practice

Reading Skills Focus

Possible responses:

1. *She is indifferent to the man.*
2. *War is the speaker's new mistress.*
3. *King Charles I is good and great.*
4. *A man's ability to love is powerful.*
5. *Have students consider how the diction affects similarities and differences between the poems.*

Vocabulary Check

6. *no* 7. *yes*
8. *no* 9. *no*
10. *yes*

Literary Skills Focus

Possible responses:

11. *He tells the lover to forget the woman. The tone goes from caring to annoyed to disgusted. In "Lucasta," the tone is confident; in "Althea," it is accepting.*
12. *He uses "mistress" to refer to the army; "chase" for his battlefield foe; "embrace" for his allegiance to the military; and "inconstancy" for his departing from Lucasta for battle. Using romantic language omits the horrors of war.*
13. *He says that a man cannot be loyal to a woman if he does not honor other commitments.*
14. *Stone walls and iron bars cannot imprison a mind. He feels free because he can still love Althea and praise his king.*
15. *In "Pale," the speaker uses words such as "can't move her" to show his love is unrequited. In "Lucasta," the speaker uses metaphors to show emotion. In "Althea," the speaker repeats "liberty" to convey that freedom is a state of mind.*
16. *In "Pale," the repeating questions emphasize the lover's foolishness. "Love" repeats in "Lucasta" to reinforce the speaker's two love's. In "Althea," the repetition of "liberty" emphasizes the idea of freedom.*

Standards Focus

Objectives

Students will

- analyze the use of parallelism and metaphor and their effects
- understand archaic language

Selection Introduction

Think About the Translation

Have students think about the purpose and challenges of translating.

For Independent Reading

- *Siddhartha,* Hermann Hesse
- *Parable of the Sower,* Octavia E. Butler

Motivate

What Do You Think?/QuickWrite

Before students complete the QuickWrite, have them write in their **Reader/Writer Notebooks** examples of a story or a song giving guidance for people's lives. Have students write about how a story or song might influence one's heart or mind.

English for Academic Success

Academic Vocabulary

Look for opportunities to use the Academic Vocabulary words in this unit.

- **contradiction, *n.*:** statement in opposition to another
- **controversies, *n.*:** lengthy disagreements
- **ensure, *v.*:** to make certain
- **established, *v.*:** set up; caused to happen
- **widespread, *adj.*:** occurring over a wide area

Preparing to Read

from the King James Bible

What Do You Think? How do our hearts and minds influence our actions?

QuickWrite

How can stories and songs help guide people through life? Write a paragraph or two explaining your thoughts.

Title page from the King James Bible (1611). Printed by Robert Barker, London.
The Pierpont Morgan Library, NY.

King James I of England and Scotland.
Schloss Ambras, Innsbruck, Austria.

INTRODUCTION

The King James Bible
(1611)

One of the first acts of James I after he was crowned king of England was to sponsor a new translation of the Bible.

A Masterpiece by a Committee

There were many translations of the Bible available, but King James and others disliked the interpretive comments included in the existing translations. Moreover, Renaissance scholarship had made people more historically minded and sensitive to textual inaccuracies. The king appointed a team of clergymen to work on the translation. Seven years later, after a final review by a committee of bishops, the translation was published. It has been known variously as the King James Bible, because James sponsored it; as the Authorized Version, because the Anglican Church authorized its use; and simply as the English Bible, for its widespread influence on the civilization and literature of the English-speaking world.

A Lasting Presence

If English-speaking people living before our time read anything, they read the English Bible. And if they did not read, they regularly heard the Bible read in church. For nearly four centuries, most writers in English have been influenced, consciously or unconsciously, by the English Bible. They have quoted it, echoed it, paraphrased it, alluded to it, imitated it, and retold its fascinating stories.

Everyday English is full of words and phrases from the English Bible: "lovingkindness," "tender mercy," "long-suffering," "the patience of Job." We "cast pearls before swine" and "wait until the eleventh hour before acting." Many Biblical words (such as *scapegoat)* are so embedded in our language that we use them without knowing we are using Biblical language.

Think About the Translation If you had the chance to pick any book and translate it into another language, which book and language would you choose? Why?

320

California Standards, pp. 320–330

- **Reading Standard 3.1** Analyze characteristics of subgenres (e.g., satire, parody, allegory, pastoral) that are used in poetry, prose, plays, novels, short stories, essays, and other basic genres.
- **Reading Standard 3.3** Analyze the ways in which irony, tone, mood, the author's style, and the "sound" of language achieve specific rhetorical or aesthetic purposes or both.

Reading Standard 3.1, 3.3 (see pages A48–A50)

Literary Skills Focus

Parallelism The repetition of words, phrases, or sentences that have the same grammatical structure or restate a similar idea is called **parallelism**. Here is an example of parallelism from Psalm 98 of the King James Bible:

Let the floods clap their hands,
Let the hills be joyful together.

Often found in literature meant to be sung or recited, parallelism establishes a sense of rhythm, balance, and order.

Reading Skills Focus

Understanding Archaic Language Old-fashioned language that is no longer used except in special situations is **archaic language**. Several verb forms in the psalms are archaic. For example, the ending *-eth* is the archaic equivalent of the modern third-person present-tense *-s* ending: *maketh/makes.*

Into Action As you read, use a chart like the one below to record each archaic verb in the psalms. Change each verb to the form that is in use today.

Psalm and Line Numbers	Archaic Verbs	Contemporary Forms
Psalm 23, Line 2	maketh	makes

Writing Skills Focus

Think as a Reader/Writer

Find It in Your Reading Psalm 23 contains several **metaphors**—figures of speech that compare two unlike things without using a connective word such as *like, as, than,* or *resembles.* As you read, note in your *Reader/Writer Notebook* the metaphors used for *God.*

Language Coach

Latin Roots The adjective *captive* means "held by force." It comes from a Latin root that means "to take hold of." The adjective *capable*, which means "able to do something well," comes from the same root. Here, the root refers to taking hold of something in a figurative sense. Someone who is capable is "able to hold much." The verb *incapacitate* includes the same Latin root. What do you think it means?

Reader/Writer Notebook

Use your **RWN** to complete the activities for these selections.

Learn It Online

Learn more about the King James Bible through these Internet links.

go.hrw.com H12-321 Go

Preteach

English for Academic Success

Language Coach

Have students read the **Language Coach.** Ask students to look up the Latin root of the word *raze* in a dictionary or other source. Have them connect the root to the meaning of the word.

Literary Skills Focus

As you read and discuss the selection with students, have them note examples of parallelism.

Reading Skills Focus

Give students a copy of the graphic organizer before they read. (See **Unit 2 Resources.**) Tell them to use their responses to answer the questions on the Applying Your Skills page.

Writing Skills Focus

Have students record metaphors used for *God* in their **Reader/Writer Notebooks.** Students can use their notes to complete the Writing Skills Focus activity.

Selection Resources

Unit 2 Resources, on-level practice and assessment, p. 56

Teacher One Stop™, on-level lesson plans

Holt Audio Library

Holt Audio Library: Selections and Summaries in Spanish

UA: Differentiating Instruction, graphic organizer, p. 66

UA: Supporting Instruction in Spanish, selection summary

ThinkCentral Online Assessment

Selection Readability

Easily Accessible / **Accessible** / Challenging	These selections include accessible vocabulary; accessible theme; simple sentence structure.

Learn It Online

Literature Links direct students to pre-screened Web sites offering more information related to a selection.

go.hrw.com H12–321 Go

Teacher Preparation

Selection Summary

Psalm 23 displays extended metaphors to describe faith in God. The speaker first compares God to a shepherd. Then the speaker speaks of being welcomed into the house of God.

Direct Teach

Think About/Talk About

Read with a Purpose Have students discuss the idea of trust and how it can relate to religious faith. Ask students to look for instances in the selection in which the author shows his belief that human existence is in the hands of God.

Comprehension

B Reading Focus

Possible response: *You prepare a table for me in plain sight of my enemies.*

Analysis

A Literary Focus

Possible response: *The repeated structure is the subject-verb-object pattern: "He maketh me," "He leadeth me," and "He restoreth my soul."*

Extend the Discussion

Speculating What kinds of experiences might be described as "walk[ing] through the valley of the shadow of death"? ***Possible responses:*** *dealing with a life-threatening illness or injury; living with depression; being a victim of a violent crime*

PSALM

Psalm 23

from the KING JAMES BIBLE

Read with a Purpose

Read this psalm to discover how the speaker expresses trust in God.

Build Background

Psalm 23 may be the best-known religious poem in the Western world. It is a song of trust that affirms the speaker's confidence in God. The poem uses two extended metaphors and its imagery reflects the pastoral way of life of the Israelite people.

The Lord is my shepherd; I shall not want.
He maketh me to lie down in green pastures:
He leadeth me beside the still waters.
He restoreth my soul:
He leadeth me in the paths of righteousness for his name's sake.° **A**
Yea, though I walk through the valley of the shadow of death,
I will fear no evil: For thou art with me;
Thy rod and thy staff° they comfort me.
Thou preparest a table before me in the presence of mine
enemies: **B**
Thou anointest my head with oil;° my cup runneth over.
Surely goodness and mercy shall follow me all the days of my life:
And I will dwell in the house of the Lord forever.

5. his name's sake: not because the speaker has earned it, but for the glory of God.

8. thy rod and thy staff: The shepherd's tools: the first to defend the sheep from enemies; the second to guide the sheep.

10. anointest my head with oil: a custom to show respect or hospitality.

A Literary Focus Parallelism What grammatical structure is repeated in lines 2–5 to develop the metaphor in line 1? How does the repetition enhance the psalm's message?

B Reading Focus Understanding Archaic Language This line includes several archaic expressions. Restate the line's meaning in modern English.

Ivory carving of herders, Germany.

Universal Access

Struggling Readers

Strategic Students Some students may struggle to recognize the use of parallelism in this selection. Explain that they should look for repeating words or phrases, particularly at the beginning of lines. Read aloud the last four lines of Psalm 137. Ask students to identify the words that are repeated. ["Happy shall he be, that . . ."] Point out that while the ending of lines 18 and 20 do not repeat word for word, they use the same grammatical pattern ("that rewardeth," "that taketh") and are therefore parallel.

Students with Disabilities

Tell students that one of the main ideas in Psalm 23 is comfort, and one of the main ideas in Psalm 137 is homesickness. Explain that homesickness can be more about people and way of life, not just a place. Ask students to think about what brings them or other people comfort, or a time when they or someone they know felt homesick. Ask students to write about or discuss their emotions with a partner.

PSALM

Psalm 137

from the KING JAMES BIBLE

Read with a Purpose

Read to discover the speaker's feelings about being separated from his homeland.

Build Background

This psalm connects directly to the history of the people of Israel. In the sixth century B.C., King Nebuchadnezzar of Babylon conquered Jerusalem. Many Israelites were sent to Babylon, where they were held as captives. This lament over a remembered home has been recited by many captives in the centuries since it was first sung.

By the rivers of Babylon, there we sat down, yea, we wept,
When we remembered Zion.°
We hanged our harps
Upon the willows in the midst thereof.
For there they that carried us away captive required of us a song;
And they that wasted us required of us mirth, **A**
Saying, "Sing us one of the songs of Zion."
How shall we sing the Lord's song
In a strange land?
If I forget thee, O Jerusalem,
Let my right hand forget her cunning.
If I do not remember thee,
Let my tongue cleave° to the roof of my mouth;
If I prefer not Jerusalem above my chief joy. **B**
Remember, O Lord, the children of Edom° in the day of
Jerusalem;
Who said, "Raze it,° raze it, even to the foundation thereof."
O daughter of Babylon,° who art to be destroyed;
Happy shall he be, that rewardeth thee
As thou hast served us.
Happy shall he be, that taketh
And dasheth thy little ones against the stones.

2. Zion: a hill in Jerusalem that is often a symbol for the whole of Israel.

13. cleave: adhere; stick.

15. children of Edom: The Edomites, neighbors of the Israelites, rejoiced when the Israelites' kingdom was conquered and most of its population was deported.

16. Raze it: Level it to the ground.

17. daughter of Babylon: the Babylonian people.

A Literary Focus Parallelism How does the parallelism in lines 5–6 help us to understand the speaker's sorrow?

B Literary Focus Parallelism What structure is repeated in lines 10–14? How does this repetition help you understand the speaker's feelings?

Teacher Preparation

Selection Summary

The speaker of Psalm 137 expresses mournfulness, resolution, anger, and finally, vengefulness. The natural images of water and willows suggest weeping, loss, and longing, and the setting is "a strange land" far from home.

Direct Teach

Think About/Talk About

Read with a Purpose Have students discuss the feelings caused by being away from home. Ask students to discuss their own experiences, or try to imagine how someone would feel when forced to leave his or her home.

Analysis

A Literary Focus

Possible response: *Both lines contain "they that . . . required of us . . . ," emphasizing the speaker's sorrow for his captivity and his being forced to sing in a strange land.*

B Literary Focus

Possible response: *"If I . . . / Let my . . . " This repetition emphasizes the speaker's emotions because the consequences of his forgetfulness are dire.*

Extend the Discussion

Identifying Tone What is the tone of lines 11–21, and why might the tone be important to the psalm's meaning? ***Possible response:*** *The tone is angry, joyful, and vengeful. The tone is important because it sends the message that the speaker has been wronged and believes that the Lord will right the wrongs against him.*

California Standards, p. 324

- **Reading Standard 3.1** Analyze characteristics of subgenres (e.g., satire, parody, allegory, pastoral) that are used in poetry, prose, plays, novels, short stories, essays, and other basic genres.
- **Reading Standard 3.3** Analyze the ways in which irony, tone, mood, the author's style, and the "sound" of language achieve specific rhetorical or aesthetic purposes or both.
- **Reading Standard 3.4** Analyze ways in which poets use imagery, personification, figures of speech, and sounds to evoke readers' emotions.
- **Writing Standard 2.1** Write fictional, autobiographical, or biographical narratives: **c.** Describe with concrete sensory details the sights, sounds, and smells of a scene and the specific actions, movements, gestures, and feelings of the characters; use interior monologue to depict the characters' feelings.

Universal Access

Advanced Learners

Enrichment Have students research the historical context of the poem. Have them place the date of the events in the poem, and ask them to research the Babylonian rulers who captured and enslaved the Israelites. Then, ask them to write a brief paragraph summarizing their findings and have them share the major points in their paragraph with the class. Does this new knowledge of the historical background affect their understanding of the speaker's emotions? Why or why not?

Check for Understanding

Independent Practice

Reading Skills Focus

Possible responses:

1. *God is always with him.*
2. *a song from the Israelites; they were in a strange land*
3. *The people who take revenge on the Babylonians for the Israelites will be rewarded.*
4. *Psalm 23 expresses emotions such as love and trust. Psalm 137 expresses sorrow and anger.*
5. *Ask students to write down phrases, not just the archaic pronouns.*

Literary Skills Focus

Possible response:

6. *a shepherd and a host in a home; comfort and warmth*
7. *Lines 6, 7, and 9 suggest that life has dangers.*
8. *It changes the mood from formal to personal and intimate.*
9. *Homesickness is conveyed strongly in lines 1–2 and 10–14, as is revenge in lines 15–21. Some students may be appalled by the violent image.*
10. *Psalm 137 would have special meaning for any group facing literal or figurative captivity. Its continuing relevance resides in the emotions expressed—love of one's homeland and a desire to see wrongs avenged.*
11. *Parallelism as in lines 2–5 gives the poem a sing-song quality.*
12. *The image of the shepherd conveys peace. The image of the harps hanging on a willow conveys sorrow.*

Applying Your Skills

Reading Standard 3.1, 3.3, 3.4 (see pages A48–A50)
Writing Standard 2.1c (see pages A51–A52)

Psalm 23 / Psalm 137

Literary Response and Analysis

Reading Skills Focus

Quick Check

1. Why is the speaker of Psalm 23 unafraid?
2. In Psalm 137, what did the captors request? Why is the speaker reluctant to participate in their request?
3. What do lines 18–19 in Psalm 137 mean?

Read with a Purpose

4. What different emotions do the speakers of these psalms express?

Reading Skills: Understanding Archaic Language

5. You noted archaic verbs in the psalms. Now, make a chart for archaic pronouns. The personal pronoun *thou* is the archaic form of the second-person singular pronoun *you*. *Thy* is the possessive form for *your*. *Thee* is the objective form for *you*.

Psalms and Line Numbers	Archaic Pronouns	Contemporary Forms
Psalm 23, Line 7	thou	you

Literary Skills Focus

Literary Analysis

6. **Analyze** What metaphors are used to portray God in Psalm 23? What feelings do they evoke?
7. **Interpret** Which lines in Psalm 23 hint at the idea that life is a perilous journey?
8. **Analyze** In Psalm 23 how does the shift from speaking about God in the third person to speaking to God in the second person affect the psalm's tone?
9. **Evaluate** What emotions does the speaker express in Psalm 137? Which lines convey these emotions? How do you react to the psalm's final line?
10. **Extend** On what occasions might Psalm 137 be sung? What relevance might the text have for people today?

Literary Skills: Parallelism

11. **Analyze** These psalms have no rhyme or meter, yet they are often praised for their literary beauty. How does the use of parallelism enhance the poems' lyrical quality? Use examples from the text to support your answer.

Literary Skills Review: Imagery

12. **Analyze** Language that appeals to the senses is called **imagery**. Identify examples of imagery in the two psalms, and analyze their effects.

Writing Skills Focus

Think as a Reader/Writer

Use It in Your Writing Review the use of metaphor in Psalm 23. In your *Reader/Writer Notebook,* write a ten-line poem in which you convey someone's positive qualities through descriptive metaphors.

What Do You Think Now? Do these songs come from the heart or mind of the speaker, or both? Explain.

For **CHOICES** *see page 330.*

What Do You Think Now?

Have students choose one line from each psalm that comes from the speakers' hearts and one line that comes from the speakers' minds.

Universal Access

Struggling Writers

To provide additional scaffolding for students who have difficulty completing the Writing Skills Focus activity, ask them to think of someone they adore or respect greatly. To what kind of figure might they compare this person—A coach? A doctor? An angel? Tell students to think of the characteristics and functions of these kinds of figures as they use the figures to describe their person's positive qualities.

Reading Standard 3.1, 3.2 (see pages A48–A50)

The Parable of the Prodigal Son

Literary Skills Focus

Parable A **parable** is a short, allegorical story that teaches a moral or religious lesson about life. In an **allegory** the characters, settings, and events stand for abstract or moral concepts. Because symbols can be interpreted in multiple ways, even a brief allegory can yield more than one meaning. The parables in the Gospels are attributed to Jesus. In "The Parable of the Prodigal Son" the father is (literally) a parent to his sons and is (symbolically) a parent to all who seek forgiveness and a fresh start.

Reading Skills Focus

Drawing Inferences About Theme The central idea about human experience revealed in a work is its **theme**. A parable's theme is tied to its allegorical structure. On a literal level, this story is about two sons, an inheritance, and a loving father. On a symbolic level, the parable carries messages about God, sin, and forgiveness. To state the theme, you need to understand how the symbolic level is related to the literal meaning.

Into Action As you read, use a chart like the one below. Identify the parable's literal features, such as characters, events, and settings, and make an educated guess about each feature's symbolic meaning.

Literal Features of the Parable	Symbolic Meaning
father's gift to his sons	God's gifts to humanity

Language Coach

Synonyms Synonyms are words with similar meanings. However, two synonyms usually do not have exactly the same meaning. Here is a list of synonyms for the word *prodigal:*

- wasteful
- reckless
- extravagant
- uncontrolled

What is the meaning of each word? Which one do you think is the best synonym for *prodigal?* Why?

Writing Skills Focus

Think as a Reader/Writer

Find It in Your Reading The **settings** in this story are each established more by characters and events than by a physical description. In your *Reader/Writer Notebook,* record the elements that indirectly reveal the settings and note how they help give each setting an allegorical meaning.

Learn It Online
Listen to this parable online.
go.hrw.com H12-325 Go

Reader/Writer Notebook
Use your **RWN** to complete the activities for this selection.

Preteach

English for Academic Success

Language Coach

Have students read the **Language Coach.** Ask students to brainstorm synonyms for the word *devour* and differentiate between the meanings of the synonyms and the word. Which synonyms are closest to the meaning of *devour*?

Literary Skills Focus

As you read and discuss the selection with students, have them note characters, settings, and events that stand for moral concepts.

Reading Skills Focus

Give students a copy of the Reading Skills Focus graphic organizer before they read. (See **Unit 2 Resources.**) Tell them to use their responses to answer the questions on the Applying Your Skills page.

Writing Skills Focus

Have students record details that reveal the settings in their **Reader/Writer Notebooks.** Students can use their notes to complete the Writing Skills Focus activity.

California Standards, pp. 325–330

- **Reading Standard 3.1** Analyze characteristics of subgenres (e.g., satire, parody, allegory, pastoral) that are used in poetry, prose, plays, novels, short stories, essays, and other basic genres.
- **Reading Standard 3.2** Analyze the way in which the theme or meaning of a selection represents a view or comment on life, using textual evidence to support the claim.

Selection Resources

Unit 2 Resources, on-level practice and assessment, p. 57

Teacher One Stop™, on-level lesson plans and all print resources

Holt Audio Library

Holt Audio Library: Selections and Summaries in Spanish

UA: Supporting Instruction in Spanish, selection summary

ThinkCentral Online Assessment, Selection Standards Check

Learn It Online
The online version of this selection includes audio support to engage all students and to help struggling readers with reading comprehension and vocabulary.
go.hrw.com H12–325 Go

Teacher Preparation

Selection Summary

In "The Parable of the Prodigal Son," a farmer has two sons. The younger son requests his inheritance, goes out into the world, and squanders the money. Because the younger son is now poor, he finds work tending another man's pigs. To assuage his hunger, he begins to eat the pigs' food. The younger son decides to return to his father. When his father sees the younger son in the distance, he rejoices and slaughters his best calf for a feast. Jealous, the older brother asks his father to explain his actions. The father states that all he owns belongs to his eldest, but the younger son who was lost is now found.

PARABLE

The Parable of the Prodigal Son

from the KING JAMES BIBLE

Read with a Purpose
Read this parable to discover how characters can represent ideas such as forgiveness and sin.

Build Background
This story is about inheritance, justice, and fairness. In ancient Israel, the oldest son in a family usually inherited a major share of his father's wealth and became the head of the family upon his father's death. Note that the word *prodigal*—which never occurs in the story—means "recklessly extravagant" and "wasteful" but also "abundantly generous."

And he[1] said, A certain man had two sons:

And the younger of them said to his father, Father, give me the portion of goods that falleth to me. And he divided unto them his living.

And not many days after the younger son gathered all together, and took his journey into a far country, and there wasted his substance with riotous living.

And when he had spent all, there arose a mighty famine in that land; and he began to be in want.

And he went and joined himself to a citizen of that country; and he sent him into his fields to feed swine.[2] **A**

And he would fain have filled his belly with the husks that the swine did eat: and no man gave unto him.

And when he came to himself, he said, How many hired servants of my father's have bread enough and to spare, and I perish with hunger!

I will arise and go to my father, and will say unto him, Father, I have sinned against heaven, and before thee,

1. **he:** Jesus.

2. **swine:** pigs. The ancient Israelites considered swine ritually taboo, or unclean, and they avoided any contact with them. Tending pigs would have been considered degrading work.

A **Literary Focus** **Parable** What might the settings of "a far country" and "fields to feed swine" symbolize?

Direct Teach

Think About/Talk About

Read with a Purpose Have students read the Read with a Purpose statement. Then, have students brainstorm definitions of forgiveness and sin. Lead a class discussion about how characters or people can show these ideas through their actions.

Analysis

A Literary Focus

Possible responses: *These settings might symbolize that the story could take place anywhere. The parable also begins much like a fairy tale (Long ago and far away).*

Extend the Discussion

Interpreting The father allows the younger son to waste his hard-earned money. Why might the father let the younger son make a poor decision? ***Possible response:*** *The father loves his son unconditionally, and he wants his son to realize and fix his own mistakes.*

Universal Access

EL English Learners

English for Academic Success Before students read the parable, clarify words that may be difficult for them.

goods—possessions. *The father divided all his goods equally among his three sons.*

substance—wealth. *The woman desired to live with substance and sought rich men.*

riotous—wild, uncontrolled. *The boy's constant riotous behavior got him expelled.*

fain—gladly. *We would have fain missed class.*

Struggling Readers

Strategic Students To help students read the parable, model the reading skill of making inferences about theme. You might say: "When I read a parable, I look at the characters' roles. I ask myself as I read, 'What human quality might this character represent? How is the character's role tied in to the overall message of the story?'"

Think About/Talk About

Extend the Discussion

Finding Details Why did the younger son envy the swine? ***Possible response:*** *They had more food to eat than he did.*

Parable Who might the father symbolize in this parable? ***Possible response:*** *God*

Analyzing Visuals

Connecting to the Text: *Rejoicing and merrymaking over the reunion of father and son are represented by the central figures and the pleased people in the background. The bright colors might represent the son's restoration and enlightenment and the people's jubilance.*

The Prodigal Son by Marc Chagall (1887–1985).

Analyzing Visuals

Connecting to the Text Which elements of the parable can you identify in this image? What do the colors represent?

Advanced Learners

Acceleration Have students freewrite about modern parables and allegories they have seen alluded to in popular culture. Then, challenge them to create their own parable or allegory that incorporates a theme. Remind students to allow the actions and words of the characters to speak for themselves; they should communicate a concept by showing, not telling.

Students with Disabilities

Ask students to study the visual shown on p. 327. Have them describe the mood or atmosphere of the painting. Ask them to explain how the details contribute to this mood. Then, have them create their own visual depicting the scene in which the prodigal son finds himself penniless. Encourage them to use colors to convey a certain mood. Have them describe the mood of their scene in a few sentences below their drawings.

Think About/Talk About

Comprehension

C Reading Focus

Possible response: *It tells us that those who are lost and then found are more cause for rejoicing than those who never doubt their faith.*

Analysis

B Literary Focus

Possible responses: *The words and actions of the younger son are of a person who has recognized his wrong-doing and feels sorry for it. He might represent sinners against God.*

Extend the Discussion

Parable What human quality does the older son represent? ***Possible responses:*** *envy; resentfulness; self-righteousness*

Monitor Students' Comprehension

Guide the class in answering these True-False questions.

1. The father refuses his younger son's request for money. [*F*]
2. Upon his return the younger son asks to be regarded as a servant. [*T*]
3. The older son orders that a feast be prepared for his brother. [*F*]

And am no more worthy to be called thy son: make me as one of thy hired servants. **B**

And he arose, and came to his father. But when he was yet a great way off, his father saw him, and had compassion, and ran, and fell on his neck, and kissed him.

And the son said unto him, Father, I have sinned against heaven, and in thy sight, and am no more worthy to be called thy son.

But the father said to his servants, Bring forth the best robe, and put it on him; and put a ring on his hand, and shoes on his feet:

And bring hither the fatted calf, and kill it; and let us eat, and be merry:

For this my son was dead, and is alive again; he was lost, and is found. And they began to be merry.

Now his elder son was in the field: and as he came and drew nigh to the house, he heard music and dancing.

And he called one of the servants, and asked what these things meant.

And he said unto him, Thy brother is come; and thy father hath killed the fatted calf, because he hath received him safe and sound.

And he was angry, and would not go in: therefore came his father out, and entreated him.

And he answering said to his father, Lo, these many years do I serve thee, neither transgressed I at any time thy commandment: and yet thou never gavest me a kid,[3] that I might make merry with my friends:

But as soon as this thy son was come, which hath devoured thy living with harlots,[4] thou hast killed for him the fatted calf.

And he said unto him, Son, thou art ever with me, and all that I have is thine.

It was meet that we should make merry, and be glad: for this thy brother was dead, and is alive again; and was lost, and is found. **C**

—Luke 15:11–32

3. **kid:** baby goat.

4. **harlots:** prostitutes.

B Literary Focus **Parable** How would you characterize the words and actions of the younger son? What or whom might the son represent?

C Reading Focus **Drawing Inferences About Theme** What does the father's reply tell you about the theme of the parable?

California Standards, pp. 329–330

- **Reading Standard 3.1** Analyze characteristics of subgenres (e.g., satire, parody, allegory, pastoral) that are used in poetry, prose, plays, novels, short stories, essays, and other basic genres.
- **Reading Standard 3.2** Analyze the way in which the theme or meaning of a selection represents a view or comment on life, using textual evidence to support the claim.
- **Grades 9–10 Review Reading Standard 3.4** Determine characters' traits by what the characters say about themselves in narration, dialogue, dramatic monologue, and soliloquy.
- **Writing Standard 1.2** Use point of view, characterization, style, (e.g., use of irony), and related elements for specific rhetorical and aesthetic purposes.
- **Writing Standard 2.2** Write responses to literature: **b.** Analyze the use of imagery, language, universal themes, and unique aspects of the text. **d.** Demonstrate an understanding of the author's use of stylistic devices and an appreciation of the effects created.
- **Listening and Speaking Standard 1.10** Evaluate when to use different kinds of effects (e.g., visual, music, sound, graphics) to create effective productions.

Reading Standard 3.1, 3.2; Grades 9–10 Review Reading Standard 3.4 (see pages A48–A50)
Writing Standard 1.2 (see pages A51–A52)

The Parable of the Prodigal Son

Literary Response and Analysis

Reading Skills Focus

Quick Check

1. How did the younger son get his money? How does he lose it?
2. Why does the younger son return home?
3. How does the father greet the returning son?
4. Why does the older brother become angry?

Read with a Purpose

5. How do the father and his sons represent ideas of forgiveness and sin?

Reading Skills: Drawing Inferences About Theme

6. Now that you have interpreted the symbolic meaning of the parable's characters, settings, and events, record your inferences about the parable's theme in a new column of your chart.

Literal Features of the Parable	Symbolic Meaning	Inferences About Theme
father's gift to his sons	God's gifts to humanity	God gives everyone gifts.

Literary Skills Focus

Literary Analysis

7. **Summarize** In your own words, summarize the older brother's complaints.
8. **Analyze** Why did the father not discipline the older son for his attitude toward his brother?
9. **Make Judgments** At the end of the parable, whose position do you understand better, that of the father or that of the older son? Why?
10. **Analyze** The word *prodigal* usually means "recklessly extravagant or wasteful," but it can also mean "lavish" and "abundant." Which characters could be called prodigal? Why?
11. **Extend** To what contemporary situations could the parable apply?

Literary Skills: Parable

12. **Analyze** Parables use allegories to teach a moral lesson. On a literal level, what might be the message of "The Prodigal Son?" What is the message on a symbolic level?

Literary Skills Review: Characterization

13. **Analyze** A writer's method of revealing characters' personalities is called **characterization**. Writers reveal their characters by letting us hear how they speak, by describing their appearance, actions, thoughts, and feelings, and by telling us directly what they are like. Which characterization techniques are used in this parable? Why are these techniques particularly well suited to teaching a moral lesson?

Writing Skills Focus

Think as a Reader/Writer

Use It in Your Writing The setting in "The Parable of the Prodigal Son" is established more through references to people and events than by direct description. In your *Reader/Writer Notebook,* write a brief story in which you convey the setting without directly describing it.

What Do You Think Now

Which characters in this story were influenced by their hearts? Which were influenced by their minds?

Check for Understanding

Independent Practice

Reading Skills Focus

Possible responses:

1. *He asked for his inheritance. He spent it on frivolous things.*
2. *He is hungry and repents of his behavior.*
3. *He gives a feast in his honor.*
4. *He does not understand why he has never had a feast in his honor.*
5. *The father represents forgiveness by his welcome to the prodigal son. The sons represent sins because they either abandon the father's home or allow feelings of envy.*
6. *Have students think about how the allegorical meaning of the features relate to the theme.*

Literary Skills Focus

Possible responses:

7. *He has done everything his father has asked of him and has never been shown the love the father shows the younger son.*
8. *The father wants the elder son to understand why the younger son's return is an occasion for much rejoicing.*
9. *The elder son, because I would be jealous too.*
10. *the younger son, because he wasted money; the father, because he gives his son a feast*
11. *The parable could apply to a child who feels that he or she is not appreciated, or to anyone who makes a bad choice or mistake.*
12. *It might say that sinners who repent are dearer to God than those who never question their faith. Forgiveness is never too late for repentant sinners.*
13. *It uses both unmarked dialogue and the characters' actions to show readers what the characters are like. These techniques are well suited to parables because actions speak louder than words.*

Universal Access

Struggling Writers

Guide students using additional scaffolding to help them complete the Writing Skills Focus activity. Some students may struggle to make indirect descriptions. Invite students to first think of a setting and brainstorm possible events and the kinds of people associated with the setting. Then, have them start writing their short story. Tell them to incorporate details describing the people and events they brainstormed.

What Do You Think Now?

Have students refer back to the interaction between the father and the eldest son on p. 328 before answering the question.

Independent Practice

Grammar Link

Your Turn

1. *Psalm 23 may be better known than any other psalm.*
2. *He is less likely to forgive than his father.*

Choices: Evaluation Criteria

Review: Timed Writing 40–50 Minutes

Students demonstrate understanding of both versions' rhythm, connotation, and musicality.

Connect: Homework
Judge Music for the Psalms

- Students search the Internet for appropriate sources of music referencing Psalm 23.
- Students connect the meaning of Psalm 23 to the music of Schubert and Rutter.

Extend: Homework
Evaluate Prodigal Images

Paragraphs display understanding of how the image represents the parable's ideas and conveys a moral lesson.

Assess

Unit 2 Resources, Selection Standards Check, p. 58

ThinkCentral Online Assessment, Selection Standards Check

Teacher One-Stop™, editable Selection Standards Check

Reteach

To reteach **theme and meaning,** see **Reteaching Lessons,** pp. 1449M–1449N.

ThinkCentral Online Remediation

Applying Your Skills

Writing Standard 2.2b, 2.2d (see pages A41–A52)
Listening and Speaking Standard 1.10 (see pages A53–A55)

Psalm 23 / Psalm 137
The Parable of the Prodigal Son

Grammar Link

Using Modifiers Correctly

Use the comparative form when comparing two things. Use the superlative form when comparing more than two things.

SUPERLATIVE FORM: The King James Bible was the *most scholarly* Biblical translation of its time.

COMPARATIVE FORM: Later scholars revised the King James Bible in the 1880s to make it *more accurate, more consistent, and more modern.*

Include the word *other* or *else* when you are comparing one member of a group with the rest of the group.

The King James Bible stands with Shakespeare as an exemplar of English when the language was *more flexible and eloquent* than at any *other* time.

Avoid using double comparisons. A double comparison results from using two comparative forms (usually *–er* and *more*) or using two superlative forms (usually *–est* and *most*) to modify the same word.

NONSTANDARD: Shakespeare's works display a vocabulary almost three times *more broader* than the vocabulary of the King James Bible.

STANDARD: Shakespeare's works display a vocabulary almost three times *broader* than the vocabulary of the King James Bible.

Your Turn

Correct the comparative and superlative forms below.

1. Psalm 23 may be better known than any psalm.
2. He is less likelier to forgive than his father.

Writing Application Write a paragraph in which you use comparative and superlative forms to compare and contrast your subject with other things.

CHOICES

As you respond to the Choices, use these **Academic Vocabulary** words as appropriate: contradiction, controversy, ensure, establish, widespread.

REVIEW

Compare and Contrast Translations

Timed Writing In an essay, compare and contrast the following lines from other translations of Psalm 23 with the King James translation, lines 3 and 10.

- He leads me to water in places of repose; …You anoint my head with oil; my drink is abundant.
- He … leads me beside the waters of peace; …Thou hast richly bathed my head with oil, and my cup runs over.

Consider the variations in connotation, rhythm, and musicality, and cite examples from the three translations in your essay.

CONNECT

Judge Music for the Psalms

Use the Internet to find musical recordings of Franz Schubert's and John Rutter's music for Psalm 23. Play recordings for your classmates, and discuss how the music enhances the psalm's meaning.

Prodigal Son. Stained glass (1952) by Einar Forseth, Oretoro, Sweden. Victoria & Albert Museum, London: Inv.: E356-1956.

EXTEND

Evaluate Prodigal Images

Using the Internet or art books, find a work of art that illustrates "The Parable of the Prodigal Son." Then, write a brief essay in which you analyze how the art's visual images establish a tone, represent the parable's ideas, and help convey a moral lesson. Use examples from the artwork and from the parable to support your analysis.

Universal Access: Grammar Link

English Learners

English for Academic Success Tell students that when they compare the qualities of two items to an equal degree, they should use the form:

_______ is as _______ as _______.

For example:

1. Your issues are just as important as mine.
2. The brown fox is just as fast as my white rabbit.
3. Her room felt as hot as a sauna!

Have students come up with three examples of their own in which they compare two items to an equal degree.

For more practice using modifiers, see **Warriner's Handbook, GrammarNotes,** and **Language Handbook Worksheets.**

COMPARING TEXTS: WORLD LITERATURE

Worlds of Wisdom

Ascent of Muhammad to Heaven on Buraq. Nizami, Khamsa. Safavid Dynasty (1539-43). Gouache, ink, and gold on paper. British Library, London, Ms. Or. 2265, fol. 195a.

From age to age, people have wrestled with the same fundamental questions about life. Every society creates its own "wisdom literature"—poems, stories, and sayings that provide guidance on everything from rearing children to preparing for the afterlife.

CONTENTS

Comparing Texts Resources

Unit 2 Resources, on-level practice and assessment, p. 62

Teacher One Stop™, on-level lesson plans and all print resources

Holt Audio Library

Holt Audio Library: Selections and Summaries in Spanish

UA: Differentiating Instruction, graphic organizer, p. 67

UA: Supporting Instruction in Spanish, selection summary

ThinkCentral Online Assessment, Selection Standards Check

ThinkCentral Online Remediation

Overview

Students will read "wisdom literature" from cultures around the world, including excerpts from the Koran, from the Bhagavad-Gita, the *Analects* of Confucius, and the *Tao Te Ching*, as well as Zen parables, Taoist anecdotes, sayings of Saadi, and African proverbs. Students will learn the characteristics of didactic literature, which conveys moral lessons by addressing questions of good and evil and exploring the consequences of good and bad behavior.

Standards Focus

Objectives

Students will

- understand didactic literature
- recognize and compare themes that cross cultures
- evaluate the philosophical, religious, ethical, and social influences of a historical period

English for Academic Success

Academic Vocabulary

Look for opportunities to use the Academic Vocabulary words in this unit.

- **contradiction, *n.*:** inconsistency
- **controversies, *n.*:** lengthy disagreement
- **ensure, *v.*:** to make certain
- **established, *v.*:** set up
- **widespread, *adj.*:** occurring over a wide area

Analyzing Visuals

Extension Activity Ask students to study the image to identify possible elements related to good and evil. ***Possible response:*** *In this image, the prophet Muhammad is accompanied by angels, and they all represent God. There are images of flame, reminiscent of ideas about punishment after death, and representing evil.*

Preteach

English for Academic Success

Language Coach

Have students read the **Language Coach**. Tell students that the word *moral* comes from the Latin *mōrālis*, meaning "custom." Ask them to relate the Latin meaning to the definition of "moral." [*"Moral" refers to rules of proper conduct. Some customs or manners are viewed as proper conduct.*]

Literary Skills Focus

As you read and discuss the selection with students, have them note characteristics of didactic literature.

Reading Skills Focus

Give students a copy of the Reading Skills Focus graphic organizer before the read. (See **Unit 2 Resources**.) Tell them to use their responses to answer the questions on the Applying Your Skills page.

Writing Skills Focus

Have students record metaphors in their **Reader/Writer Notebooks.** Student can use their notes to complete the Writing Skills Focus activity.

California Standards, pp. 332–344

- **Reading Standard 3.1** Analyze characteristics of subgenres (e.g., satire, parody, allegory, pastoral) that are used in poetry, prose, plays, novels, short stories, essays, and other basic genres.
- **Reading Standard 3.7** Analyze recognized works of world literature from a variety of authors: **b.** Relate literary works and authors to the major themes and issues of their eras.

Preparing to Read

Reading Standard 3.1, 3.7b (see pages A48–A50)

Worlds of Wisdom

Literary Skills Focus

Didactic Literature Literature that is meant to instruct, give advice, or convey a philosophical or moral message is known as **didactic literature**. Much wisdom literature comes in the form of sacred texts. Secular works such as proverbs, fables, anecdotes, folk tales, and maxims can also serve as didactic literature. Most didactic literature ultimately comes from an oral tradition.

Reading Skills Focus

Comparing Ideas Across Cultures Even in cultures that seem very different, didactic literature frequently addresses similar questions: What is good, and what is evil? What are the consequences of good and bad behavior? The answers to these questions are often similar as well. For example, good is rewarded, and evil is punished.

Into Action As you read, note the major characteristics and the messages of each selection.

Selection	Characteristics	Messages
from Koran	Sacred text; repetition, parallelism; serious, commanding tone	Charitable acts done in God's name lead to salvation.
from Bhagavad-Gita	Sacred text from epic poem in form of dialogue; parallelism; serious tone	Self-discipline and detachment from the material world lead to serenity.

Writing Skills Focus

Think as a Reader/Writer

Find It in Your Reading Didactic literature often uses **metaphor** as a tool to clarify ideas and engage the reader's imagination. A metaphor is a figure of speech that makes a comparison between two unlike things without the use of specific words of comparison such as *like* or *as*. As you read, notice how the writers use metaphors in these selections.

Language Coach

Word Origins A **parable** is a short story that illustrates a religious or moral lesson. The origin of the word *parable* highlights the idea that a parable makes a comparison. A story or idea is told in terms of something else. The word *parable* comes from the Greek words meaning "beside" and "throw." A parable is "thrown beside," or compared with, another topic. The audience for the parable must interpret this comparison to get the point of the parable.

Reader/Writer Notebook

Use your **RWN** to complete the activities for these selections.

Learn It Online

Explore the Worlds of Wisdom further with these Internet links.

go.hrw.com H12-332 Go

Selection Readability	
Easily Accessible **Accessible** Challenging	These selections include familiar syntax; accessible theme.

SACRED TEXT

Night *from the* Koran

translated by **N. J. Dawood**

Read with a Purpose

Read this excerpt from the Koran to discover some guiding principles of faith.

Build Background

The word *Koran (qu'ran)* is Arabic for "recitation." Followers of Islam believe that the Koran—first written down in Arabic in the middle of the seventh century—contains God's revelation to the prophet Muhammad through the angel Gabriel. The Koran declares that Allah is the one all-powerful God who created the world. Allah is merciful and compassionate, but he is also the God of Judgment Day. Each of the Koran's 114 chapters—called *suras*—begins, "In the Name of Allah, the Compassionate, the Merciful."

In the Name of Allah, the Compassionate, the Merciful

By the night, when she lets fall her darkness, and by the radiant day! By Him that created the male and the female, your endeavors have different ends!

For him that gives in charity and guards himself against evil and believes in goodness, We shall smooth the path of salvation; but for him that neither gives nor takes and disbelieves in goodness, We shall smooth the path of affliction. When he breathes his last, his riches will not avail him. **A**

It is for Us to give guidance. Ours is the life of this world, Ours the life to come. I warn you, then, of the blazing fire, in which none shall burn save the hardened sinner, who denies the truth and gives no heed. But the good man who purifies himself by almsgiving[1] shall keep away from it: and so shall he that does good works for the sake of the Most High only, not in recompense[2] for a favor. Such men shall be content. **B**

Leaf from a Qur'an manuscript (11th century). Eastern kufic calligraphy, 40.164.2a.
Rogers Fund (1940). The Metropolitan Museum of Art.

1. **almsgiving:** performing deeds of charity.
2. **recompense:** repayment.

A Literary Focus **Didactic Literature** How does this paragraph instruct people to behave?

B Reading Focus **Comparing Ideas Across Cultures** In this paragraph, what similarities do you notice between Islam and other religions you might have read about or might know?

Universal Access

English Learners

English for Academic Success The translations of some wisdom literature contain formal diction. Make sure students know the meaning of *endeavors* (undertakings), *affliction* (suffering), *heed* (notice), *sage* (wise person), *sensuous* (of the five senses), *brooding* (thinking about obsessively) and *mused* (reflected).

Advanced Learners

Enrichment Have students choose a recurring theme in wisdom literature and compare and contrast the ways in which the message is conveyed in various writings including the Bible.

Students with Disabilities

Inform students that the Koran is a sacred text and is considered didactic literature because it includes teachings on how people should treat one another. Ask students if they can think of any other literary works that give readers advice on how to treat others.

Teacher Preparation

Selection Summary

The excerpt begins by identifying God as the creator of all. It then gives moral directives on living a holy life. The speaker in the last two paragraphs appears to be God, who promises salvation to those who practice charity and believe in goodness. Affliction is promised to those who fail to give and to believe.

Direct Teach

Think About/Talk About

Read with a Purpose Ask students to explain the meaning of a guiding principle of faith. As students read the selection, have them take note of the instructions the text gives.

Comprehension

B Reading Focus

Possible response: *Like Christianity and Judaism, Islam emphasizes the importance of faith and charity.*

Analysis

A Literary Focus

Possible response: *It instructs people to be generous, avoid evil, and believe in goodness.*

Extend the Discussion

Analyzing Theme Point out that the word *gives* is repeated multiple times in paragraphs 2 and 3. How does the selection connect giving to faith? ***Possible response:*** *Those who believe in goodness give freely to charity. They trust God will give them guidance and happiness.*

Learn It Online

For a multimedia version of the instruction on this page, use the **PowerNotes** introduction to this selection.

go.hrw.com H12-333 Go

Teacher Preparation

Selection Summary

Krishna counsels Arjuna to give up desires, for when one forgoes the sensual pleasures, one's insight is true.

Direct Teach

Think About/Talk About

Read with a Purpose Have students read the Read with a Purpose statement. Ask them what kind of guidance they think a warrior might need.

Analysis

A Literary Focus

Possible response: *Wisdom is a special gift that can be gained only through self-discipline.*

Extend the Discussion

Finding Details According to lines 1–4, what is to be gained by giving up desire? ***Possible response:*** *insight and the peace of self-acceptance*

Didactic Literature Why, in line 23, does Krishna describe the senses as "bewildering"? ***Possible response:*** *The senses inflame feelings such as anger, fear, and desire. These feelings cause confusion by disturbing and distracting the mind.*

SACRED TEXT

from Philosophy and Spiritual Discipline

from the Bhagavad-Gita

translated by **Barbara Stoler Miller**

Read with a Purpose

Read this excerpt from an ancient poem to discover what advice a god can give to a warrior.

Build Background

The Bhagavad-Gita, or "Song of the Lord," is part of what may be the longest poem ever written—a Hindu epic called the *Mahabharata*. It influenced Mahatma Gandhi (1869–1948), the charismatic social reformer who led India to independence from Britain in 1947. The Gita consists of a dialogue between Arjuna and his charioteer, Krishna. In this excerpt, Krishna, an earthly embodiment of a major god, and the warrior Arjuna argue just before a great battle with Arjuna's relatives. Krishna urges Arjuna to fulfill his *dharma* (sacred duty) by waging battle, but Arjuna hesitates to fight members of his family.

Lord Krishna

When he gives up desires in his mind,
is content with the self within himself,
then he is said to be a man
whose insight is sure, Arjuna.

When suffering does not disturb his mind,
when his craving for pleasures has vanished,
when attraction, fear, and anger are gone,
he is called a sage whose thought is sure.

When he shows no preference
in fortune or misfortune
and neither exults nor hates,
his insight is sure.

When, like a tortoise retracting
its limbs, he withdraws his senses
completely from sensuous objects,
his insight is sure.

Sensuous objects fade
when the embodied self abstains from food;
the taste lingers, but it too fades
in the vision of higher truth.

Even when a man of wisdom
tries to control them, Arjuna,
the bewildering senses
attack his mind with violence. A

A **Literary Focus** Didactic Literature What is Lord Krishna's attitude toward wisdom?

Universal Access

EL English Learners

English for Academic Success Students might have trouble with the unusual sentence structure in lines 1–20. To help them understand the context and recognize the sentence pattern, explain that the pronoun *he* in line 1 means "a person" and point out that the first four sentences of the selection resemble definitions. To illustrate, offer this example:

"Students are called seniors when they are in their last year of high school."

Point out that this sentence consists of a main clause followed by a *when* clause; whereas, the sentences in lines 1–20 of the selection each begin with a *when* clause. Note that the sentences in the selection have an unusual word order.

Controlling them all,
with discipline he should focus on me;
when his senses are under control,
his insight is sure.

Brooding about sensuous objects
makes attachment to them grow;
from attachment desire arises,
from desire anger is born. B

From anger comes confusion;
from confusion memory lapses;
from broken memory understanding is lost;
from loss of understanding, he is ruined. C

But a man of inner strength
whose senses experience objects
without attraction and hatred,
in self-control, finds serenity.

B Literary Focus **Didactic Literature** What is Krishna saying in this stanza about the relationship between material objects and anger?

C Reading Focus **Comparing Ideas Across Cultures** According to Krishna, what is the worst thing that can happen to a person? According to the excerpt from the Koran, what is the worst thing that could happen to a person?

Arjuna and His Charioteer Lord Krishna Confront Karna (1820) India.
Edith H. Bell Fund (1975).Philadelphia Museum of Art.

Analyzing Visuals

Connecting to the Text Discuss the relationship between the image and the text. Consider the background information about the text. How does the image reflect the message and tone of the text? How might the image seem ironic or paradoxical in relation to the text?

Think About/Talk About

Comprehension

C Reading Focus

Possible responses: *For Krishna, it is losing understanding, which means losing serenity. In the excerpt from the Koran, it is disbelieving in goodness and refusing charity, for these are sins punished by fire.*

Analysis

B Literary Focus

Possible response: *Material objects foster dependence and desire, and these feelings breed anger.*

Extend the Discussion

Monitoring Reading What are the characteristics of the "inner strength" preached by Lord Krishna? ***Possible response:*** *"Inner strength" is the capability to control the senses and get rid of attachment to material things.*

Interpreting Why does Lord Krishna state that a person's insight becomes "sure" once senses are under control? ***Possible response:*** *Human thinking is influenced by emotions. If people manage to control their feelings, their understanding will not be misled.*

Universal Access

Struggling Readers

To assist students in understanding the message of this ancient poem, guide them in summarizing the main idea in each stanza. Call on a volunteer to read aloud the first stanza. Ask them to summarize the main point in the stanza into a question-answer format. For example, in lines 1–4, Lord Krishna advises Arjuna on insightfulness. The question might be, "How does a person gain true insight?" and the answer, "By desiring nothing." Ask students to repeat this exercise for the rest of the stanzas.

Analyzing Visuals

Connecting to the Text: *The text stresses discipline over emotion and personal needs. The image portrays Arjuna confronting Karna despite his hesitation over going to war. While the text emphasizes the importance of detachment from worldly desires, the image ironically portrays two armies fighting over the control of a kingdom, which represents a worldly desire.*

Teacher Preparation
Selection Summary

In each of these parables, an individual encounters a Zen master, who is depicted as a teacher. The Zen masters in these parables do not directly convey wisdom or advice, but instead indirectly offer insight by speaking and acting in enigmatic ways that prompt people to think and guide them to discover wisdom themselves. In particular, the Zen masters use surprise as a means to teach; by responding to people's behavior and questions in startling and puzzling ways, the masters lead people to reassess their assumptions and gain a broader perspective.

Direct Teach

Think About/Talk About

Read with a Purpose Have students read the Read with a Purpose statement. Ask them to describe their understanding of the word *philosophy.* As students read the selection, have them take note of details that point to the underlying philosophy of Zen Buddhism.

PARABLES

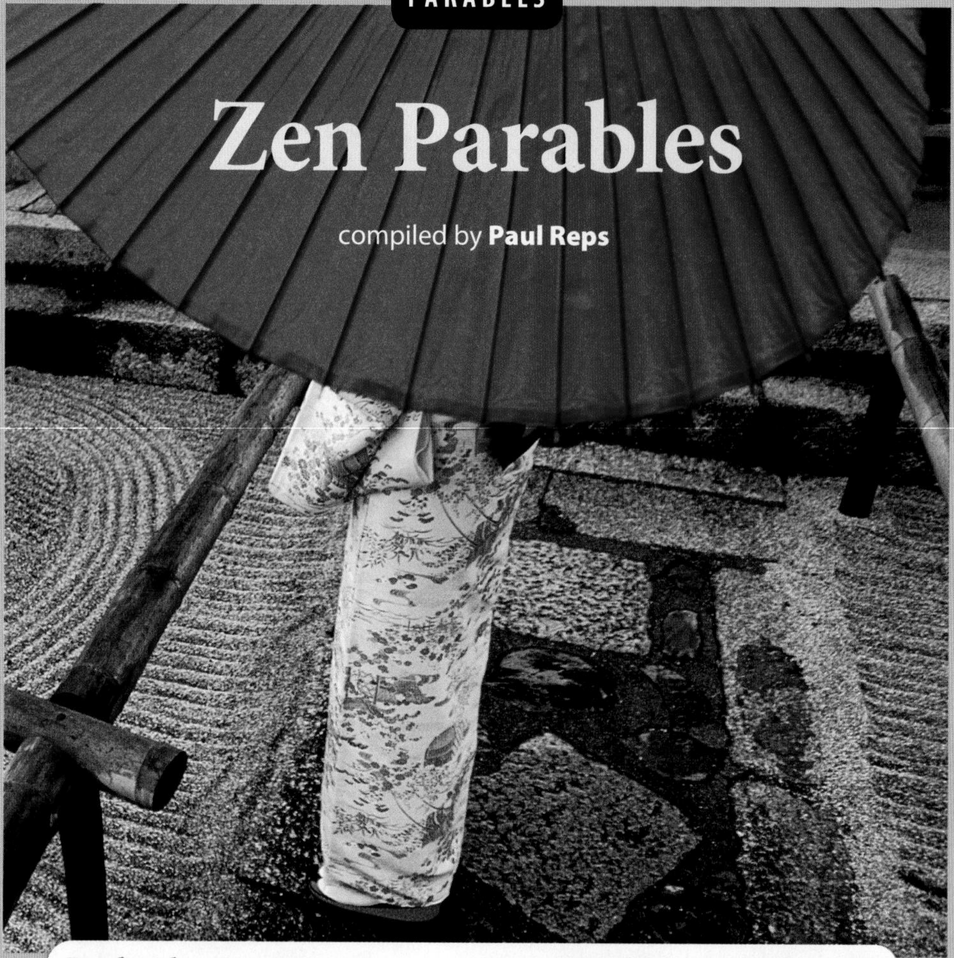

Zen Parables

compiled by **Paul Reps**

Read with a Purpose

Read to discover the philosophy that underlies Zen Buddhism.

Build Background

The Zen parables illustrate the insights of Zen Buddhism. The object of Zen is to free the mind of everyday, conventional logic through meditation. Instead of imparting facts in a clear and logical way, the Zen master first tries to confuse his students, to force them to abandon all preconceived notions of what knowledge is. He might ask a nonsensical question that has no answer, such as "What is the sound of one hand clapping?" This technique prepares students to understand the lessons inherent in the deceptively simple **parables**, or brief allegorical stories.

Compare and Contrast

Have students compare and contrast the aesthetics of style. All the wisdom literature in this unit, including the Bible, has been translated from the original. Have students compare the aesthetic appeal of the King James translation of Psalms 23 and 137 with that of the translation of the Bhagavad-Gita. Encourage them to compare techniques used in each (such as parallelism) as well as the overall effect on the reader.

The Moon Cannot Be Stolen

Ryokan, a Zen master, lived the simplest kind of life in a little hut at the foot of a mountain. One evening a thief visited the hut only to discover there was nothing in it to steal.

Ryokan returned and caught him. "You may have come a long way to visit me," he told the prowler, "and you should not return empty-handed. Please take my clothes as a gift."

The thief was bewildered. He took the clothes and slunk away.

Ryokan sat naked, watching the moon. "Poor fellow," he mused, "I wish I could give him this beautiful moon." **A**

Temper

A Zen student came to Bankei and complained: "Master, I have an ungovernable temper. How can I cure it?"

"You have something very strange," replied Bankei. "Let me see what you have."

"Just now I cannot show it to you," replied the other.

"When can you show it to me?" asked Bankei.

"It arises unexpectedly," replied the student.

"Then," concluded Bankei, "it must not be your own true nature. If it were, you could show it to me at any time. When you were born, you did not have it, and your parents did not give it to you. Think that over."

The Gates of Paradise

A soldier named Nobushige came to Hakuin, and asked: "Is there really a paradise and a hell?"

"Who are you?" inquired Hakuin.

"I am a samurai," the warrior replied.

"You, a soldier!" exclaimed Hakuin. "What kind of ruler would have you as his guard? Your face looks like that of a beggar."

Nobushige became so angry that he began to draw his sword, but Hakuin continued: "So you have a sword! Your weapon is probably much too dull to cut off my head."

As Nobushige drew his sword, Hakuin remarked: "Here open the gates of hell!"

At these words the samurai, perceiving the master's discipline, sheathed his sword and bowed.

"Here open the gates of paradise," said Hakuin.

The First Principle

When one goes to Obaku temple in Kyoto, he sees carved over the gate the words "The First Principle." The letters are unusually large, and those who appreciate calligraphy[1] always admire them as being a masterpiece. They were drawn by Kosen two hundred years ago.

When the master drew them he did so on paper, from which workmen made the larger carving in wood. As Kosen sketched the letters, a bold pupil was with him who had made several gallons of ink for the calligraphy and who never failed to criticize his master's work.

"That is not good," he told Kosen after the first effort.

"How is that one?"

"Poor. Worse than before," pronounced the pupil. **B**

Kosen patiently wrote one sheet after another until eighty-four First Principles had accumulated, still without the approval of the pupil.

Then, when the young man stepped outside for a few moments, Kosen thought: "Now is my chance to escape his keen eye," and he wrote hurriedly, with a mind free from distraction:

"The First Principle."

"A masterpiece," pronounced the pupil.

1. **calligraphy:** the art of beautiful handwriting.

A Literary Focus Didactic Literature What is the master trying to teach the thief?

B Reading Focus Comparing Ideas Across Cultures How does the master's attitude toward the pupil compare to Krishna's attitude toward Arjuna in the Bhagavad-Gita?

Think About/Talk About

Comprehension

B Reading Focus

Possible response: *The relationship between Krishna and Arjuna is more hierarchical; Krishna is an indisputable authority. In the Zen parable, the master respects his student almost to a fault.*

Analysis

A Literary Focus

Possible response: *Stealing is pointless because that which is truly valuable—like the moon, or the gift of another's generosity—cannot be stolen.*

Extend the Discussion

Theme In "Temper," what does Bankei mean when he says that the student's "ungovernable temper" is not his true nature? ***Possible response:*** *His temper is not an unalterable aspect of his being, but rather something he can change.*

Monitoring Reading What life message is contained in the fourth parable? ***Possible response:*** *The message is that anger is hell, and a disciplined life is paradise.*

Developing Oral Fluency

Small-Group Activity Have students work in groups of three or four to practice reading aloud "The First Principle" or "The Gates of Paradise;" assign one student to read the Zen master's part, another to read the words of the student or soldier, and one or two students to read the part of the narrator. Encourage them to read with expression and act out the scene. To conclude the activity, ask one or two groups to perform for the rest of the class. Ask students to comment on what they liked about their peers' dramatizations of the parable.

Universal Access

Advanced Learners

Enrichment Divide students in groups, and have them choose the wisdom literature of a culture other than England in the seventeenth century. Have them research the time and place in which the literature was written. Ask students to research images and representations, maps, and other resources they can add to their research. Have students present their findings to the class.

Teacher Preparation

Selection Summary

These three analects teach that knowledge is realizing what you do not know, that you can learn something from every person, and that a saying with universal application is "Never do to others what you would not like them to do to you."

Direct Teach

Think About/Talk About

Read with a Purpose Have students read the Read with a Purpose statement. Then, ask them to describe different attitudes people might have toward learning.

Comprehension

B Reading Focus

Possible responses: *It sounds like the Golden Rule: "do unto others as you would have them do unto you." It is a core teaching of many cultures because the behavior it commands is essential to civilized society.*

Analysis

A Literary Focus

Possible response: *You can learn from everyone; even fools have lessons to offer.*

Extend the Discussion

Didactic Literature In the first paragraph, what advice does the Master give on the importance of recognizing when you do not know something? ***Possible response:*** *Knowledge is being able to recognize what you know and what you do not know.*

MAXIMS

from The Analects of Confucius

translated and annotated by **Arthur Waley**

Read with a Purpose
Read these brief statements, or **maxims**, to discover Confucius's attitude toward learning.

Build Background
Confucius, who established an important and lasting Chinese philosophical system, left no written works. After his death around 479, his disciples gathered his sayings in a collection known as *The Analects*—"selected sayings." Here, Confucius describes a concept called *chung-yung*, or "the golden mean," that emphasizes virtues such as loyalty, obedience, integrity, and obligation to one's parents and ancestors.

The Master said, "Yu, shall I teach you what knowledge is? When you know a thing, to recognize that you know it, and when you do not know a thing, to recognize that you do not know it. That is knowledge."

The Master said, "Even when walking in a party of no more than three I can always be certain of learning from those I am with. There will be good qualities that I can select for imitation and bad ones that will teach me what requires correction in myself." **A**

Tzu-kung asked, saying, "Is there any single saying that one can act upon all day and every day?" The Master said, "Perhaps the saying about consideration: 'Never do to others what you would not like them to do to you.'" **B**

Statue of Confucius, Chinatown, New York.

A Literary Focus **Didactic Literature** What lesson is Confucius teaching here?

B Reading Focus **Comparing Ideas Across Cultures** Where did you first hear of a similar concept? Why do you think this concept appears in so many different cultures?

Universal Access

EL English Learners

English for Academic Success Explain to students that a homonym is a word that has the same pronunciation, or sound, as another word but has a different meaning or spelling, such as *two* and *too.* Point out to students that *principle* means "fundamental truth" and that the homonym *principal* may mean "most important" or "head of a school."

Students with Disabilities

To help students keep track of the different philosophies and cultures covered in this group of selections, have them draw a web as they read. In the center balloon, they should put the words "Wisdom Literature." Each balloon extending from the center balloon should contain the name of a work or an author. Each balloon extending from the title or author balloon should summarize an important teaching of that philosophy.

SACRED TEXT

from the Tao Te Ching

by **Lao Tzu**

translated by **Stephen Mitchell**

Read with a Purpose

Read to discover how the philosophy of Taoism finds wisdom in nature.

Build Background

The *Tao Te Ching*, or "Classic of the Way of Power," is a book of sayings and poems that teach the nature of Taoism. It is attributed to Lao Tzu, who, according to legend, was born as an old, bearded, white-haired man and lived to the age of 160. Broadly defined, Taoism consists of the joyful acceptance of life and a willingness to yield to the natural world, becoming one with it.

The supreme good is like water,
which nourishes all things without trying to.
It is content with the low places that people
disdain.
Thus it is like the Tao.

In dwelling, live close to the ground.
In thinking, keep to the simple.
In conflict, be fair and generous.
In governing, don't try to control. **A**
In work, do what you enjoy.
In family life, be completely present.

When you are content to be simply yourself
and don't compare or compete,
everybody will respect you. **B**

Lao-Tzu on His Buffalo (18th century) by Chinese School. Bibliothèque Nationale, Paris.

A **Literary Focus** **Didactic Literature** What is this saying about how to be a good leader?

B **Reading Focus** **Comparing Ideas Across Cultures** Compare these three lines with the first four lines in the excerpt from the Bhagavad-Gita. How is the focus of these passages similar?

Teacher Preparation

Selection Summary

In this selection from the *Tao Te Ching*, Lao Tzu suggests water provides a good model for wise conduct. Like water, he advises, people should be satisfied to occupy low places and inconspicuously benefit all.

Direct Teach

Think About/Talk About

Read with a Purpose Have students read the Read with a Purpose statement. Then, ask them to think about how nature might serve as a source of wisdom.

Comprehension

B Reading Focus

Possible response: *Both passages emphasize the value of being satisfied with who you are.*

Analysis

A Literary Focus

Possible response: *Lao Tzu suggests a good leader does not seek to exercise total power over those he governs.*

Extend the Discussion

Simile Why does Lao Tzu compare good conduct to water? ***Possible response:*** *Water is powerful because it is necessary for life, but it is unobtrusive and adaptable because it is transparent and fluid.*

Didactic Literature How might a ruler govern and not control, as suggested in line 8? ***Possible response:*** *A ruler should be a model, not an enforcer, of morality.*

Cross-Curricular Connection

HISTORY: Lao Tzu and Confucius

Lao Tzu's biographer recounts a meeting between his subject and Confucius. Lao Tzu counseled Confucius to rid himself of excessive enthusiasm, arrogance, and other traits of no use to his "true self." Confucius was so struck by Lao Tzu's wisdom that he told his disciples, "the dragon is beyond my knowledge; it ascends into the heaven on the cloud and the wind. Today I have seen Lao Tzu, and he is like a dragon!"

Universal Access

Struggling Readers

Strategic Students Model for students how to compare the characteristics of didactic literature across cultures. You might say: "I notice that the selections from the sacred text *Tao Te Ching* is written in a poetic form, involves only one speaker, and contains parallelism in the second stanza. *The Analects,* on the other hand, is in prose form and includes repetition and dialogue. Both have a serious tone."

Teacher Preparation

Selection Summary

"Gold, Gold" tells of a man so eager for gold that he steals some before many witnesses, blindly overlooking the fact that he is sure to be caught. "A Clever Judge" relates how a judge tricks a thief into revealing himself.

Direct Teach

Think About/Talk About

Read with a Purpose As students read the Read with a Purpose statement, ask them to name clever or unwise characters from well-known stories or folklore.

Comprehension

Ⓐ Reading Focus

Possible response: *This anecdote confirms Lord Krishna's warning that "brooding about sensuous objects" causes ruinous confusion.*

Analysis

Ⓑ Literary Focus

Possible response: *Guilt makes people fearful that their misdeeds will be exposed, and fear makes guilty people vulnerable to discovery.*

Extend the Discussion

Didactic Literature How can the first anecdote be read as an allegory? In other words, what might the thief and gold symbolize? ***Possible response:*** *The thief might stand for anyone in the throes of an obsession. The gold could be any object of desire—love, good grades, or recognition.*

ANECDOTES

Taoist Anecdotes

translated and edited by **Moss Roberts**

Read with a Purpose
Read to discover what makes certain characters either clever or unwise.

Build Background
Followers of Taoism have long used **anecdotes,** or brief stories, to convey their philosophy indirectly. The stories are intended to impart the spiritual teachings of Taoism, with its focus on oneness with the world and the unchangeable nature of the Way.

Gold, Gold

Many, many years ago there was a man of the land of Ch'i who had a great passion for gold. One day at the crack of dawn he went to the market—straight to the gold dealers' stalls, where he snatched some gold and ran. The market guards soon caught him. "With so many people around, how did you expect to get away with it?" a guard asked.

"When I took it," he replied, "I saw only the gold, not the people." Ⓐ

—Lieh Tzu

A Clever Judge

In the days when Ch'en Shu-ku was a magistrate[1] in Chienchou, there was a man who had lost an article of some value. A number of people were arrested, but no one could discover exactly who the thief was. So Shu-ku laid a trap for the suspects. "I know of a temple," he told them, "whose bell can tell a thief from an honest man. It has great spiritual powers."

The magistrate had the bell fetched and reverently enshrined in a rear chamber. Then he had the suspects brought before the bell to stand and testify to their guilt or innocence. He explained to them that if an innocent man touched the bell it would remain silent, but that if the man was guilty it would ring out.

Then the magistrate led his staff in solemn worship to the bell. The sacrifices concluded, he had the bell placed behind a curtain, while one of his assistants secretly smeared it with ink. After a time he took the suspects to the bell and had each one in turn extend his hands through the curtain and touch the bell. As each man withdrew his hands, Shu-ku examined them. Everyone's hands were stained except for those of one man, who confessed to the theft under questioning. He had not dared touch the bell for fear it would ring. Ⓑ

—Chang Shih-nan

Moral Teaching for Shop Boys, Giving Good and Bad Examples of Behavior (1857) by Utagawa Kuniyoshi. Oriental & African Studies Library, University of London.

1. **magistrate:** judge.

Ⓐ **Reading Focus** **Comparing Ideas Across Cultures** How does the message of this passage compare to Lord Krishna's argument from the Bhagavad-Gita?

Ⓑ **Literary Focus** **Didactic Literature** What does this anecdote tell you about the effects of fear and guilt?

Universal Access

English Learners

Ask students to recite proverbs, aphorisms, axioms, or maxims in their native language and to express them, if they can, in English. Have students identify any similarities between the selections they read and sayings from their native culture.

Struggling Readers

Tell students that summarizing the main teaching of each text in one or two sentences will help them compare the teachings across cultures. For example, "Gold, Gold" basically demonstrates what happens when a person is so obsessed with a material possession that he loses his awareness of his surroundings since his mind is captivated by it. Point out that the Bhagavad-Gita warns the warrior that attachment to objects eventually leads to confusion, loss of understanding, and ruin. Thus, "Gold, Gold" provides the perfect example of what would happen if the warrior did not heed Lord Krishna's advice.

MAXIMS

Sayings of Saadi

translated by **Idries Shah**

Read with a Purpose
Read to understand how Saadi uses animals to teach lessons that humans can use.

Build Background
The poet Saadi lived in thirteenth-century Persia (now Iran). He followed Sufism (SOO fihz uhm), a sect of Islam that believes humans can transcend the physical world through proper philosophy and practice. Even today, Sufis are not attached to belongings and places, and they are not driven by concerns of time, money, or achievement. They concentrate instead on walking the *tariqah,* or path toward the Divine Nature. The path comprises repentance, abstinence, renunciation, poverty, patience, gratitude, and acceptance.

The Unfed Dervish

When I see the poor dervish[1] unfed
My own food is pain and poison to me. **A**

Information and Knowledge

However much you study, you cannot know
without action.
A donkey laden with books is neither an
intellectual nor a wise man.
Empty of essence, what learning has he—
Whether upon him is firewood or book?

The Elephant Keeper

Make no friendship with an elephant keeper
If you have no room to entertain an elephant. **B**

Safety and Riches

Deep in the sea are riches beyond compare.
But if you seek safety, it is on the shore.

The Fox and the Camels

A fox was seen running away in terror. Someone asked what was troubling it. The fox answered:

"They are taking camels for forced labor."

"Fool!" he was told, "the fate of camels has nothing to do with you, who do not even look like one." "Silence!" said the fox, "for if an intriguer were to state that I was a camel, *who* would work for my release?"

1. **dervish:** Muslim monk dedicated to a life of poverty.

A Reading Focus **Comparing Ideas Across Cultures** How is Saadi's attitude here similar to or different from the Zen master's in "The Moon Cannot Be Stolen"?

B Literary Focus **Didactic Literature** How does the humor in this proverb make it effective for teaching about friendships?

Portrait of a Sufi (17th century), Adil Shahi period (1490–1686). 57.51.30. Bequest of Cora Timken Burnett (1956). The Metropolitan Museum of Art.

Teacher Preparation

Selection Summary

Saadi offers advice through proverbs and fables that vividly illustrate the wisdom of his teachings, sometimes using animals as examples.

Direct Teach

Think About/Talk About

Read with a Purpose Have students read the Read with a Purpose statement. Ask them to develop an argument for or against using animals as examples in didactic literature.

Comprehension

A Reading Focus

Possible response: *Both show compassion. The Zen master feels sympathy for the thief unable to appreciate the moon. Saadi empathizes with the monk who lacks food.*

Analysis

B Literary Focus

Possible response: *The humor encourages honesty and tolerance of human frailty, making the lesson about friendship easier to accept.*

Extend the Discussion

Theme In "Information and Knowledge," what does the donkey laden with books represent? ***Possible response:*** *Learning that is not put to use through action is no more valuable to a person than a load of books is to a donkey.*

Universal Access

Advanced Learners

Enrichment Like "The Parable of the Prodigal Son" from the King James Bible, the Taoist anecdotes teach lessons. Have students compare and contrast the form and content of "The Parable of the Prodigal Son" with one or both of the Taoist anecdotes. Their comparison of form might explore character development, allegory, plot development, and development of theme. The comparison of content might focus on the teachings and what they reveal about each belief system.

Students with Disabilities

Ask students to compose their own saying using the sayings of Saadi as a model. If they were going to teach on the topic of hard work versus laziness, which animals would they use as models (besides an ant and a grasshopper)? How would they demonstrate that irresponsibility and carelessness yield no rewards?

Teacher Preparation

Selection Summary

These African proverbs are single-sentence expressions of general truths. Most use vivid images or analogies to illustrate their points.

Direct Teach

Think About/Talk About

Read with a Purpose Have students read the Read with a Purpose statement. Point out that all literature reflects, in some way, the culture and region from which it originates. Ask students to list features of the African landscape or culture that they expect to see reflected in African proverbs.

Comprehension

B Reading Focus

Possible responses: *No matter how hard you try, you cannot change your nature.*

Analysis

A Literary Focus

Possible response: *"It is easy to despise what you cannot get."*

Extend the Discussion

Tracing Recurring Themes How is the proverb: "The frog wanted to be as big as the elephant, and burst" related to the proverb from the Democratic Republic of Congo (Zaire)? ***Possible response:*** *The proverb from Zaire suggests that it is impossible to change one's essential nature. This proverb suggests that it is dangerous to try to change one's nature.*

PROVERBS

African Proverbs

compiled by **Charlotte** and **Wolf Leslau**

Read with a Purpose

Read to discover how the proverbs of a region reflect its landscape and culture.

Build Background

In the oral literatures of Africa, **proverbs** represent a poetic form that achieves great depth of meaning using very few words. In cultures without written language, proverbs function as the distilled essence of people's values and knowledge. They are used to entertain, settle legal disputes, resolve ethical dilemmas, and teach children the philosophy of their people. The following proverbs are from Ashanti, the Democratic Republic of the Congo, and Ethiopia. Ashanti, known for its gold and its bright kente cloth, is located in the rainforests of central Ghana. The Democratic Republic of the Congo is a country of many great rivers and is bordered by the Atlantic Ocean and Lake Tanganyika. Ethiopia, in the Horn of Africa, is one of the oldest civilizations in the world. This region has a dramatic landscape of desert, mountains, and fertile plateau savannahs.

Only when you have crossed the river, can you say the crocodile has a lump on his snout. —*Ashanti*

When a man is wealthy, he may wear an old cloth. —*Ashanti*

The ruin of a nation begins in the homes of its people. —*Ashanti*

He who cannot dance will say: "The drum is bad." **A** —*Ashanti*

It is the fool's sheep that break loose twice. —*Ashanti*

No one tests the depth of a river with both feet. —*Ashanti*

Wood may remain ten years in the water, but it will never become a crocodile. **B** —*Zaire*

Evil enters like a needle and spreads like an oak tree. —*Ethiopia*

The witness of a rat is another rat. —*Ethiopia*

The frog wanted to be as big as the elephant, and burst. —*Ethiopia*

When the heart overflows, it comes out through the mouth. —*Ethiopia*

When spider webs unite, they can tie up a lion. —*Ethiopia*

Confiding a secret to an unworthy person is like carrying grain in a bag with a hole. —*Ethiopia*

I have a cow in the sky, but cannot drink her milk. —*Ethiopia*

If you offend, ask for pardon; if offended, forgive. —*Ethiopia*

A fool and water will go the way they are diverted. —*Ethiopia*

Headpiece in the form of a crocodile (20th century) West African. Indianapolis Museum of Art.

A Literary Focus **Comparing Ideas Across Cultures** Does this remind you of any common sayings from your everyday life?

B Reading Focus **Didactic Literature** What lesson is this simple proverb teaching about trying to be something you are not?

California Standards, p. 343

- **Reading Standard 3.1** Analyze characteristics of subgenres (e.g., satire, parody, allegory, pastoral) that are used in poetry, prose, plays, novels, short stories, essays, and other basic genres.
- **Reading Standard 3.3** Analyze the ways in which irony, tone, mood, the author's style, and the "sound" of language achieve specific rhetorical or aesthetic purposes or both.
- **Reading Standard 3.7** Analyze recognized works of world literature from a variety of authors: **b.** Relate literary works and authors to the major themes and issues of their eras.
- **Writing Standard 2.3** Write reflective compositions: **b.** Draw comparisons between specific incidents and broader themes that illustrate the writer's important beliefs or generalizations about life.

Reading Standard 3.1, 3.3, 3.7b (see pages A48–A50)
Writing Standard 2.3b (see pages A51–A52)

Worlds of Wisdom

Literary Response and Analysis

Reading Skills Focus

Quick Check

1. In the Zen parable "Temper," what conclusion does master Bankei draw about the student's "ungovernable temper"?
2. In the Taoist anecdote "A Clever Judge," how does the thief get caught?
3. What is the message of Saadi's saying "Safety and Riches"?

Read with a Purpose

4. What do these examples of didactic literature tell you about how people seek wisdom?

Reading Skills: Comparing Ideas Across Cultures

5. As you read, you noted major characteristics of each piece of wisdom literature and summarized each message. Now compare and contrast the form and content of the messages.

Selection	Characteristics	Messages	Similarities and Differences
from the Koran	Sacred text; repetition, parallelism; serious, commanding tone	Charitable acts done in God's name lead to salvation.	Charity's role in salvation; belief in afterlife; punishment in afterlife
from the Bhagavad-Gita	Sacred text from epic poem in form of dialogue; parallelism; serious tone	Self-discipline and detachment from the material world lead to serenity	Focus on self-discipline and detachment; no discussion of charity or afterlife

Literary Skills Focus

Literary Analysis

6. **Contrast** Describe one important difference between the Hindu philosophy described by Krishna and the ideas described in the excerpt from the Koran.
7. **Evaluate** Which excerpt do you think teaches most effectively? Explain your answer.
8. **Analyze** According to Saadi's saying "Information and Knowledge," what is the difference between information and knowledge?
9. **Extend** Explain how three of these pieces of literature might directly relate to our lives today.

Literary Skills: Didactic Literature

10. **Interpret** Which selection teaches in the most direct, or explicit, way? Which selection is most indirect in its approach?

Literary Skills Review: Tone

11. **Compare** The attitude of a writer toward the subject or audience is called **tone**. Choose two selections and compare their tones. How does the tone affect each selection's message?

Writing Skills Focus

Think as a Reader/Writer

Use It in Your Writing As you read, you noted the use of metaphors. Create several instructive and entertaining proverbs of your own, and add them to your *Reader/Writer Notebook.*

What Do You Think Now What does didactic literature teach about how our hearts and minds influence our actions?

Check for Understanding

Independent Practice

Reading Skills Focus

Possible responses:

1. *The student's temper is not something inherent to his nature so he can learn to control it if he wishes.*
2. *He gets caught by avoiding a bell that would supposedly test his guilt.*
3. *With great riches comes great risk.*
4. *Many people seek wisdom through those who are wiser than themselves.*
5. *Ask students to list similarities and differences found among the messages' content and form.*

Literary Skills Focus

Possible responses:

6. *Hindu philosophy emphasizes the role of the individual in attaining serenity. The Koran stresses the role of God in helping believers achieve salvation.*
7. *The Zen parables teach most effectively because they encourage reflection.*
8. *Information is simply facts. Knowledge is the ability to use facts in a meaningful way.*
9. *Responses will vary; all of them are relevant today.*
10. *The Analects of Confucius are most direct; the Zen parables are most indirect.*
11. *Tone in the Bhagavad-Gita is very serious, while the tone in "The Elephant Keeper" is very humorous. The tone affects the magnitude of the message. A message with a serious tone may seem more important.*

Universal Access

Struggling Writers

Some students may need additional scaffolding to complete the Writing Skills Focus activity. Suggest that students think of and write down a few proverbs first. Allow students to use a resource book of proverbs, if necessary. Then, have them replace the characters or elements in their proverbs with animals or elements found in nature. Remind them that they can include humor in their proverbs.

What Do You Think Now?

Ask students to consider first the philosophies underlying the various sayings in each selection. Have them cite specific teachings that connect the heart and mind to the action.

Check for Understanding

Independent Practice

What Do You Think Now?
To help students respond to the question, tell them to cite specific examples to support their claims. Tell them to acknowledge examples that counter their own arguments.

Assess

Unit 2 Resources, Selection Standards Check, p. 63

ThinkCentral Online Assessment, Selection Standards Check

Teacher One Stop™, editable Selection Standards Check

Reteach

ThinkCentral Online Remediation

COMPARING TEXTS
Wrap Up

Writing Standard 2.2a–c (see pages A51–A52)

World Literature: Worlds of Wisdom

Writing Skills Focus

Writing a Comparison-Contrast Essay

All of the selections you have just read deal with issues of morality. Which of the authors express similar views? How is each author's argument unique? Which pieces express attitudes toward life that you find surprising, baffling, contradictory, controversial, or in conflict with your own views and beliefs? Which pieces strike you as accurately reflecting your beliefs? Write an essay in which you compare the views on morality expressed in two or three of the selections.

Prewriting

To start writing, consider the following points:

- How is the issue of morality discussed in the selections? Which selections focus more on behavior in this world? Which focus more on an afterlife?
- How does each author reveal opinions on morality? What viewpoints does the author include? (Are they the author's own viewpoints, or the viewpoints of others?)
- Which selections did you find most convincing, and why?

Gather Details

Create an H-chart to record your ideas about the two or three selections you choose to compare. In the center of the H, record the main similarity. Then, write the title of each selection you have chosen at the top of the H. Record your notes about each selection. Then, examine the notes looking for other similarities and differences. From your notes, develop a thesis statement that includes the similarities and the points of difference that you can support with text evidence in an essay.

Drafting

Since you are writing a comparison-contrast essay, use the point-by-point method, using at least one body paragraph to develop the basis of similarity. Then continue with similarities or move to differences in the selections you have chosen to analyze.

Point-by-Point Method

Topic Sentence/Paragraph
•Selection 1
•Selection 2
Topic Sentence/Paragraph
•Selection 1
•Selection 2

Revising and Editing

- Read your paper. Identify your thesis. Have you proven the thesis in the rest of your paper? Do you return to it in the closing paragraph?
- Add text evidence if each point is not supported.
- Proofread your essay and correct any errors in spelling, mechanics, and usage. Use details and examples from the texts to support your ideas, and make sure that your essay has a clear structure from beginning to end.

An effective comparison- contrast essay

- clearly states in the opening paragraph what is being compared and contrasted
- uses a thesis statement to convey the main idea
- has an effective and logical organization that includes similarities and differences
- cites and explains text passages to support ideas
- contains no errors in spelling, punctuation, and grammar

What Do You Think Now? Do you think these pieces of wisdom literature appeal more to the heart or to the mind as a means of teaching people how to live? Explain.

Universal Access

Struggling Writers

Some students may need additional scaffolding. Tell students that creating an H-chart will help them know what to argue in their thesis. Display this H-chart as a guide:

Bhagavad-Gita		Tao Te Ching
• addresses warrior	• how to gain wisdom	• refers to nature
	• self-contentment	

California Standards, p. 344

- **Writing Standard 2.2** Write responses to literature: **a.** Demonstrate a comprehensive understanding of the significant ideas in works or passages. **b.** Analyze the use of imagery, language, universal themes, and unique aspects of the text. **c.** Support important ideas and viewpoints through accurate and detailed references to the text and to other works.

Reading Skills Focus

The Fall of Satan *from* Paradise Lost

Reading Standard 3.3 (see pages A48–A50)

Analyzing Milton's Style by Kylene Beers

Analyzing an author's style in a work of literature can sometimes feel artificial. Why pick a poem apart? If you approach this process with a sense of exploration, you will see that analysis can improve your comprehension of a complex text by sending you back to the poem to re-read passages and by focusing your attention on the literary tools the poet has employed.

It is common for readers to be intimidated by Milton's style when they first encounter it. As it grows more familiar to you, however, you will begin to follow the meaning of the text. You will discover a story that overflows with fantastic imagery, epic drama, and profound ideas. Through his unique use of language, Milton elevates his poem into the realm of the sacred and gives its voice an air of divine authority.

Careful reading and re-reading of challenging passages is the key to getting the most out of Milton's work. For example, many modern readers are challenged by the numerous references, called **allusions,** to classic literature, Christian theology, and Renaissance culture within Milton's work. Use the footnotes to think about these references, and then re-read the passages with new knowledge.

Below is an excerpt from the opening of *Paradise Lost* and some accompanying footnotes. Read the lines and the footnotes, and then read the lines again.

> Restore us, and regain the blissful seat,
> Sing, Heavenly Muse, that on the secret top
> Of Oreb, or of Sinai,[1] didst inspire
> That shepherd,[2] who first taught the chosen seed[3]

If you do not understand the Biblical allusion, you might not understand the comparison in these lines.

1. **Oreb . . . Sinai:** names for the mountain where Moses received God's inspiration.
2. **shepherd:** Moses, a Jewish prophet.
3. **chosen seed:** the Hebrews.

However, once it is clear that Milton is comparing himself to Moses, and his words to Moses' reception of the word of God, you can understand that Milton wants his poem to feel divinely inspired. Re-read the lines one more time. Does the language seem clearer now than when you initially encountered it?

You can use the same strategy of reading and re-reading to better understand passages with challenging syntax or inverted word order. Milton often uses unusual sentence structure, placing sentence parts in unexpected places. In these cases, first locate the sentence's subject and verb to find out who is doing what.

Your Turn

In this excerpt from *Paradise Lost,* the speaker poses a question throughout six lines. Examine the text carefully, and briefly **paraphrase**—restate in your own words—the speaker's basic question.

> Say first, for Heaven hides nothing from thy view,
> Nor the deep tract of Hell, say first what cause
> Moved our grand parents[1] in that happy state,
> Favored of Heaven so highly, to fall off
> From their Creator, and transgress his will
> For one restraint,[2] lords of the world besides?[3]

1. **grand parents:** Adam and Eve.
2. **one restraint:** the command not to eat of the fruit of the tree of knowledge. 3. **besides:** in every other way.

Learn It Online
For more on Milton's style, see *PowerNotes.*
go.hrw.com H12-345 Go

Reading Skills Focus

Objectives

Students will understand an author's style.

Unit 2 Resources, Reading Focus Skill Builder, p. 6

Teacher One Stop™, lesson plans and all print resources

Direct Teach

Analyzing Milton's Style

This feature gives students practice in analyzing the style John Milton used in *Paradise Lost.* Have students read the feature and complete the Your Turn activity before reading the poem.

Check for Understanding

Independent Practice

Your Turn

Possible response: *Neither heaven nor hell can hide anything from you. So tell me, what caused Adam and Eve, who were once so highly favored, to break God's only command so that He had to expel them from the Garden of Eden? They had everything, so why couldn't they follow that one rule?*

California Standards, p. 345

- **Reading Standard 3.3** Analyze the ways in which irony, tone, mood, the author's style, and the "sound" of language achieve specific rhetorical or aesthetic purposes or both.

Universal Access

English Learners

English for Academic Success Work with students to help them master difficult words in the Reading Skills Focus essay. Some students may not understand the meaning of words such as *analyzing, exploration, intimidated, epic drama, profound, accompanying, footnotes, syntax,* and *inverted.* Define each word in simple language and provide an example as students encounter each word. Point out to students that knowing the meaning of these words will help them understand how to analyze Milton's style.

Learn It Online
For a multimedia version of the instruction found on this page, use the **PowerNotes** Reading Skills Focus presentation.
go.hrw.com H12-345 Go

Standards Focus

Objectives

Students will understand and analyze an author's style.

Selection Introduction

Think About the Writer

- Before students answer the question, explain that Milton wrote many papers about politics and was, for a time, active in government. Because Milton's beliefs were highly unorthodox within Puritan society, he risked his life by expressing his views in his writings.
- While students are formulating their answer to the question, have them think about the risks that many people take when expressing their political views. Have them consider modern forms of art and literature that express unorthodox ideologies. Then have students ask themselves if these art forms have had any impact on their own political beliefs.

Preparing to Read

The Fall of Satan *from* Paradise Lost

When I consider how my light is spent

What Do You Think

How do our hearts and minds influence our actions?

QuickWrite

Do you think an uneducated person can be as accomplished a poet as an educated one? What might an uneducated person be able to bring to poetry that an educated person might not? Write an entry in your *Reader/Writer Notebook* that answers these questions.

John Milton (c. 1629) by unknown artist. National Portrait Gallery, London.

MEET THE WRITER

John Milton

(1608–1674)

Like Chaucer and Shakespeare, Milton is one of the towering figures of English literature.

The Scholar Poet

John Milton showed an early talent for languages, mastering the ancient languages of Latin, Greek, and Hebrew, and achieving fluency in many European tongues. After attaining distinction during his education at Cambridge University, Milton spent six years at his father's country house, where he read ancient and modern writing and became thoroughly acquainted with the Bible. During this period of private study, he wrote poetry, including *Lycidas*, an elegy for a Cambridge classmate. In 1638, Milton left England for two years of travel in Europe. When he returned, England was soon to be ravaged by civil war.

Political Career

In the 1640s, an ongoing struggle between King Charles and his Parliament came to a head. A believer in the Puritan cause, Milton engaged in the paper warfare that accompanied the conflict and started publishing controversial prose works—some of them very elaborate and a few of them very insulting—in support of the Parliamentary party. Although Milton shared some Puritan ideas and attitudes, such as a dislike of kings and bishops, he also differed greatly from orthodox thinking in other important ways. For example, he advocated divorce for incompatible married couples and argued that the press should be free from government censorship and interference. Although we take these freedoms for granted today, most people in the seventeenth century—particularly most Puritans—would have considered them dangerously radical.

Milton served in the government under Oliver Cromwell, who ruled England as lord protector after the Parliamentary party had won the Civil Wars and executed King Charles. As Latin secretary to the Council of State, Milton was responsible for translating all correspondence with foreign countries, as Latin was then the language of diplomacy.

In his later years, Milton's eyesight began to fail. By 1652, he could only distinguish day from night; by the age of forty-four, before he had finished his life's work, Milton was totally blind.

Selection Readability	
Easily Accessible Accessible **Challenging**	The selections by John Milton contain serious subject matter; complex syntax; abstract symbolism; epic poem.

A Change of Leadership

Milton believed that the ideal government was a republic in which the most capable, intelligent, and virtuous men would be established as leaders. In 1660, the cause for which he had worked twenty years became totally discredited; the English restored to power the son of their dead king and crowned him King Charles II. Milton was stripped of his possessions and arrested as a traitor. Fortunately, thanks to influential friends such as Andrew Marvell, Milton was allowed to go into retirement rather than to the scaffold. From that point forward, he lived in seclusion with his three daughters and his third wife (his first two wives and only son had died). By reading aloud to him, his daughters enabled Milton to carry on the studies he thought necessary for a poet.

Milton's First Meeting with Mary Powell, Accompanied by her Brother (1862) by Alfred Rankley.

The Road to *Paradise Lost*

Being a poet, in Milton's view, meant imitating the great writers of antiquity: the epic poets Homer and Virgil and the Greek dramatists Aeschylus, Sophocles, and Euripides. Because those writers chose subjects drawn from their own nations' histories, Milton considered various English subjects for his works, especially King Arthur and the knights of the Round Table. After years of thinking and reading, however, Milton decided that King Arthur's exploits were mainly fictitious, and so he settled on subjects drawn from the Bible.

Milton began publishing his writing while still at Cambridge. Even after his retirement from politics, and before the Restoration of Charles II, Milton continued to write political pamphlets about education, freedom of the press, divorce, and religion. He also worked simultaneously on the epic that would become *Paradise Lost*.

A Profound Work of Art

Milton published *Paradise Lost* twice: first in a ten-book version in 1667 and then in twelve books in 1674, the year of his death. Throughout his life he composed many different plans for the epic, and even once thought of it as a tragedy with Satan—the fallen archangel turned chief devil—as its protagonist. In the finished poem, Satan remains very conspicuous. The first two books are devoted mainly to him (he appears frequently in Books III–X), and Milton lavishes on Satan some of his most glorious writing. Thus, it's unsurprising that many readers regard Satan as the hero of the poem. The poet and artist William Blake asserted that Milton was "of the Devil's party without knowing it."

This argument is convincing, however, only to those who concentrate on certain parts of the poem and ignore the remainder. Although the setting of the poem alternates between Hell and Heaven, the most important action takes place on Earth, where the first human beings, Adam and Eve, are given the choice of obeying or disobeying God. They choose to disobey and, having done so, they accept their punishment and make the best of the life that is left to them. They are the heroes of Milton's epic, and, in some ways, they represent us all.

Think About the Writer Milton was closely involved in the political scene of his time. What role do you think literature and the arts should take in political or social debates?

For Independent Reading

- *Murder in the Cathedral,* T. S. Eliot
- *Dead Souls,* Nikolai Vasilevich Gogol

Motivate

What Do You Think?/QuickWrite

Have students think about the question and consider how an artist's work is influenced by his or her educational and emotional experiences. Ask them to discuss things that people do out of love, hate, fear, or pride. Point out that uneducated as well as educated writers have communicated emotions through poetry. Ask students to think about what might be the advantage for an educated poet in expressing his or her emotions. Have students consider this point when using their **Reader/Writer Notebooks.**

English for Academic Success

Academic Vocabulary

Look for opportunities to use the Academic Vocabulary words in this unit.

- **contradiction, *n.*:** statement in opposition to another; inconsistency
- **controversies, *n.*:** lengthy disagreement
- **established, *v.*:** set up; caused to happen
- **widespread, *adj.*:** occurring over a wide area

Selection Resources

Unit 2 Resources, on-level practice and assessment, p. 66

PowerNotes, interactive lesson presentation with activities

Teacher One Stop™, on-level lesson plans and all print resources

Holt Audio Library

Holt Audio Library: Selections and Summaries in Spanish

UA: Holt Interactive Reader, p. 87

UA: Differentiating Instruction, modified lesson plans and leveled assessment, p. 68

UA: Supporting Instruction in Spanish, selection summary, p. 87

UA: Resources for Teaching Advanced Students, lesson plans

Analyzing Visuals Transparencies, p. 13

ThinkCentral Online Assessment

Direct Teach

Think About/Talk About

Setting a Grand Stage

- Give students examples of epics that begin with invocations. Explain that the purpose of an invocation is to show how the voice of a divine being is speaking through the poet. Thus these invocations serve to invest the work with greater importance or moral authority.
- Tell students that Homer's *Iliad* begins "Sing, goddess, the anger of Peleus's son Achilles." The opening words of his *Odyssey* are "Sing in me, Muse, and through me tell the story." Ask interested students to read the opening invocations of Homer's epics in their entirety and to compare them with Milton's invocation at the beginning of *Paradise Lost.* You might also suggest that they read the invocations of Virgil's *Aeneid* and Dante's *Divine Comedy* and compare them with Milton's opening lines.

Introduction to *Paradise Lost*

Milton's Epic

When Milton wrote *Paradise Lost*, his intent was clear: to create literature's greatest epic poem. His allusions to Homer, Virgil, Dante, and a host of lesser epic poets leave no doubt that Milton wanted *Paradise Lost* to encompass and also surpass all previous epics. Milton asserts this bold ambition at the very beginning of the poem, describing its content as "things unattempted yet in prose or rhyme" (line 16). Unlike an **oral epic** or a **primary epic** such as *Beowulf,* which is performed by generations of storytellers, *Paradise Lost* is a **literary epic,** the product of an individual writer.

Milton plants *Paradise Lost* firmly in the epic tradition by following the standard conventions of the form. He begins with an invocation to the Muse; he starts the action *in media res* ("in the middle of things"); and he writes in an elevated style on a grand subject. Milton's unique style and the cosmic scale of his subject help distinguish his poem from earlier literary epics. Milton's epic does not deal with earthly matters, and instead tells a story from the dawn of Creation, depicting a conflict between good and evil. In *Paradise Lost,* the battle is not fought between people, but between Satan and God. Milton's style matches the grandeur of this story. He combines ornate language, complex syntax, blank verse, multiple allusions, and elaborate comparisons called **epic similes.** The result is a text rich in beauty, power and drama, very much the epic masterpiece that Milton so passionately hoped to create.

The Angel Michael Binding Satan (c. 1850) by William Blake.
Harvard University Art Museums, Fogg Art Museum. Gift of W. A. White (1915).

Setting a Grand Stage

Paradise Lost begins in a manner that is traditional for epics: the speaker invokes the Muse and states the subject of the poem. The Muse is traditionally one of the nine Greek goddesses of inspiration. In "invoking" the Muse, the speaker essentially asks the divine being to speak through the poet. In *Paradise Lost,* Milton

Universal Access

Struggling Readers

Check students' comprehension of the introduction to Milton's epic. Have them discuss their responses to the questions below and then share with the class:

- How does a literary epic differ from an oral or primary epic?
- List some characteristics of Milton's style that distinguishes this epic from others.
- What is Milton's explanation of the existence of evil? Does he blame God? Explain.

Advanced Learners

Enrichment Divide students into groups of three or four and have them read a pamphlet by John Milton on themes such as politics, religion, divorce, and freedom. Have students discuss how Milton's ideas can be applicable today, if they are at all. Have students present the results of their discussion to the class.

uses the first sixteen lines—which are one long, complex sentence—to invoke the Muse. Grammatically, the sentence begins in line 6 with the command "Sing, Heavenly Muse." To understand what he wants the Muse to sing about, we must move back to line 1, which is a reference to Adam and Eve's "first disobedience" against God in the Garden of Eden. This story of the act of disobedience, expulsion from Paradise, and the possibility of redemption is what Milton wants the Muse to relate through him. He completes the statement of his subject in lines 24–26, in which he boldly declares that he is going to "justify the ways of God to men." This declaration is Milton's great argument, or theme.

Posing an Ancient Question

If evil exists in a universe ruled by God, why does God allow that evil to exist? This question is what Milton feels he must explain. In exploring this question, the poet attempts to resolve a dilemma that has puzzled people throughout the ages. Milton asserts that God is not responsible for these evils. As he points out in the first few lines, it was Adam and Eve's own disobedient actions that "Brought death into the world, and all our woe" (line 3). Milton argues that Adam and Eve were given a choice—good or evil—and provided with the freedom to make their own decision. According to the poet, it was their choice that allowed evil and its consequences to be unleashed on the world.

Adam and Eve's fateful choice is commonly referred to in Christian theology as the *original sin,* but readers do not need to accept this traditional explanation of evil in order to enjoy the poem or find it thought provoking. The poem is rich enough to provide support for many different interpretations.

Bringing Hope to the Struggle

In "The Fall of Satan" at the beginning of *Paradise Lost,* Milton depicts Satan just after he has been banished to Hell. According to the poem, God purposely decides to let Satan escape and establish himself on Earth so that goodness can triumph. Milton argues that goodness can only be true goodness if it results from a struggle to overcome evil. Therefore, by releasing Satan to do his evil work, God gives human beings

A Dungeon Horrible (1979) by Terrance Lindall.
Williamsburg Art and Historical Center, and the Yuko Nii Foundation.

something to fight against, a struggle that can allow them to be redeemed. Milton's view of life is heroic and optimistic. He suggests that Adam and Eve's tragic loss of Paradise actually enabled a greater beauty to emerge: the grace of human beings engaged in a noble struggle against darkness. The Archangel Michael tells Adam and Eve how to live in their new imperfect world. Practice good deeds, he says, and patience, temperance, faith, and love, and

> then wilt thou be not loath
> To leave this Paradise, but shalt possess
> A Paradise within thee, happier far.
> —Book XII, lines 585–587

Think About/Talk About

Bringing Hope to the Struggle

Explain to students that the idea that Adam and Eve's fall from grace ultimately benefited humanity stems from John Milton's personal religious views. Explain that Milton frequently disagreed with the established religious doctrine of his time. Throughout his life, the poet meditated about religion and the role of institutionalized churches, which he often denounced in tracts. His treatise *On Christian Doctrine,* written between 1655 and 1660, could not be published in England because of its heretical content. In this work, Milton deviated from the dogma of the Holy Trinity and rejected the Ten Commandments. In his view, the only precept Christians needed to follow was Christ's commandment to love one another.

Cross-Curricular Connection

HISTORY: English Rule in the 1600s

It could be said that the English Civil War was fought over the question of what type of rule the country would have. Some people wanted a hereditary monarchy, while others wanted to be ruled by the larger, elected body of citizens known as Parliament. During Milton's lifetime, power swung back and forth between various monarchs and Parliament. It was not until after his death that Parliament finally was established as the ruling body for the nation. This took place in 1689 after King James II abdicated the throne. William and Mary became the king and queen, ruling jointly with Parliament. That same year the Bill of Rights was passed. It stated the rights of English citizens and set rules about who could govern.

Preteach

Introducing Vocabulary

- Review the Vocabulary words, definitions, and sentences with students.
- To reinforce the importance of the Vocabulary words, tell students that the words are related in tone and meaning. They are all about some aspect of struggle and misery. In *Paradise Lost,* Milton shows the *contention* between the forces of good and evil, as *impetuous* human beings are tempted to *transgress* against God but wish to avoid the *infernal desolation* of hell.

English for Academic Success

Language Coach

Have students read the **Language Coach**. Have students find multiple meanings of *desolation* and use each meaning in a sentence.

Literary Skills Focus

As you read and discuss the selection with students, have them pay attention to diction, syntax, and meter.

Reading Skills Focus

Give students a copy of the Reading Skills Focus graphic organizer before they read. (See **Unit 2 Resources**.) Tell them to use their responses to answer the questions on the Applying Your Skills page.

Writing Skills Focus

Have students record epic similes in their **Reader/Writer Notebooks.** Student can use their notes to complete the Writing Skills Focus activity.

Learn It Online

The **PowerNotes** presentation for this lesson includes a short video that introduces the selection. The video is also available on the online version of this page.

go.hrw.com H12-350 Go

Preparing to Read

Reading Standard 3.3, 3.4 (see pages A48–A50)

The Fall of Satan *from* Paradise Lost

Literary Skills Focus

Style The way in which writers use language to express ideas is called **style.** An author's style is closely connected to **diction,** or word choice, and **syntax,** or sentence construction. Milton writes in **blank verse** (unrhymed iambic pentameter), the form Shakespeare uses in his plays. With the exception of free verse, blank verse reflects the natural rhythm of English speech more than any other form. Milton also uses **epic similes,** extended comparisons that draw parallels between dissimilar things.

Reading Skills Focus

Analyzing Milton's Style Milton includes many references to the Bible and to classical literature. The footnotes will help you with unfamiliar names and terms. Use **context clues** for unfamiliar words. Because Milton's constructions do not always follow the standard subject-verb-object order, analyze long sentences by **paraphrasing** them in your own words.

Into Action Use a chart like the one below to note the phrases or lines that you find challenging and paraphrase them in your own words.

Difficult lines	Paraphrase
Him the Almighty Power Hurled headlong flaming from the ethereal sky With hideous ruin and combustion down To bottomless perdition (44–47)	Almighty God (subject) threw (verb) Satan headfirst from Heaven (ethereal sky) in a streak of flames and debris, to a bottomless pit of suffering (perdition).

Writing Skills Focus

Think as a Reader/Writer

Find It in Your Reading Milton's **epic similes** enhance his descriptions of Satan and Hell. As you read, list them in your *Reader/Writer Notebook.*

TechFocus In line 74, Milton describes Earth as the center of ten concentric spheres. How can you learn more about the study of astronomy in Milton's day? Discuss ways to investigate this topic with classmates.

Vocabulary

transgress (trans GREHS) *v.:* sin against; violate a limit. *He roused the others to fight and transgress God's will.*

infernal (ihn FUR nuhl) *adj.:* hellish; fiendish. *Humanity is prey to the whims of the infernal demons.*

contention (kuhn TEHN shuhn) *n.:* struggle. *The angels were in contention for power.*

impetuous (ihm PEHCH oo uhs) *adj.:* forceful; violent. *The impetuous angels tried to take over heaven but were driven out.*

desolation (dehs uh LAY shuhn) *n.:* utter misery; extreme loneliness. *Satan vows to lead humans into a state of desolation.*

Language Coach

Multiple Meanings When Milton uses the word *impetuous* in this selection, it means "forceful." The same word can often mean "acting rashly, without considering the consequences." Similarly, *contention* can refer to a struggle or to the opinion a person forms as part of an argument. Explain how both meanings are used in this sentence: *It is my contention that contention between people is inevitable.*

Reader/Writer Notebook

Use your **RWN** to complete the activities for this selection.

Learn It Online

Meet this famous poem with a video introduction.

go.hrw.com H12-350 Go

California Standards, pp. 346–362

- **Reading Standard 3.3** Analyze the ways in which irony, tone, mood, the author's style, and the "sound" of language achieve specific rhetorical or aesthetic purposes or both.
- **Reading Standard 3.4** Analyze ways in which poets use imagery, personification, figures of speech, and sounds to evoke readers' emotions.

EPIC POEM

The Fall of Satan

from *Paradise Lost*

by **John Milton**

Read with a Purpose

Read to discover how Satan is depicted with good and evil characteristics.

Build Background

At the opening of *Paradise Lost,* Milton states that his intention is to "justify the ways of God to men." He seeks to illuminate the consequences of Adam's action, that is to say, the misuse of reason and free will and its effect on all succeeding generations of human beings. After the invocation, the action starts *in medias res* ("in the middle of things"). The rebellious angels led by Satan have been defeated and thrown into Hell. Milton vividly depicts Satan and the horrors of Hell.

Of man's first disobedience, and the fruit
Of that forbidden tree, whose mortal taste
Brought death into the world, and all our woe,
With loss of Eden, till one greater Man°
Restore us, and regain the blissful seat,
Sing, Heavenly Muse,° that on the secret top
Of Oreb, or of Sinai,° didst inspire
That shepherd,° who first taught the chosen seed°
In the beginning how the Heavens and Earth
Rose out of Chaos; or if Sion hill°
Delight thee more, and Siloa's brook° that flowed
Fast by the oracle of God, I thence
Invoke thy aid to my adventurous song,
That with no middle flight intends to soar
Above the Aonian mount,° while it pursues
Things unattempted yet in prose or rhyme. **A**
And chiefly thou, O Spirit,° that dost prefer
Before all temples the upright heart and pure,
Instruct me, for thou know'st; thou from the first
Wast present, and with mighty wings outspread
Dove-like sat'st brooding on the vast abyss
And mad'st it pregnant: what in me is dark

? **1–16.** *Paraphrase the first sentence of the epic. What will the subject of Milton's story be? (See lines 1–5.)*

4. one greater Man: Christ.
6. Heavenly Muse: Urania, muse of astronomy and sacred poetry. Milton hopes to be inspired by Urania, just as Moses was inspired to receive God's word for the Hebrews.
7. Oreb . . . Sinai: names for the mountain where Moses received God's inspiration.
8. shepherd: Moses. **chosen seed:** the Hebrews.
10. Sion hill: Zion, a hill near Jerusalem.
11. Siloa's brook: stream that flowed past the Temple, "the oracle of God," on Mount Zion.
15. Aonian mount: in Greek mythology, Mount Helicon, the home of the Muses.
17. Spirit: Holy Spirit; divine inspiration.

A **Reading Focus** **Analyzing Milton's Style** How would you describe Milton's sentence structure in these opening lines?

Universal Access

EL English Learners

English for Academic Success Model figuring out the meanings of unfamiliar words using context clues. Direct students to lines 20–23. Suggest that students paraphrase the lines and then replace the unknown word with a blank. Remind students that when they paraphrase, they should translate the difficult phrases into simpler grammatical constructions using vocabulary they know.

Write on the board, "with wings stretched out, sitting like a dove, ______ing on the huge ________, causing it to 'be with child,' so that the darkness became light."

Tell students that lines 20–23 seem to say the gentle Spirit is situated in such a way on some kind of vast space as to cause it to become "pregnant." Thus, *brooding* might refer to an activity that helps produce offspring, and *abyss* might refer to a dark space or hole.

Teacher Preparation

Selection Plot Summary

In this excerpt from *Paradise Lost,* the author first asks the muse to help him tell how the serpent, or Satan, tempted Adam and Eve to disobey God, which caused them to fall from grace. Then Milton describes how Satan led a group of rebellious angels to defy God. The rebels lost and so were thrown into Hell. Satan declares that he would rather rule in Hell than serve in Heaven.

Direct Teach

Think About/Talk About

Read with a Purpose Have them record instances from the text in which Milton uses details to develop the character of Satan. Point out that they should pay close attention to how Satan appears, what he says, and what he does.

Comprehension

A Reading Focus

Possible response: *The opening lines use a complex sentence structure. The first sentence lasts for 16 lines, and subjects, objects, and verbs are not in their usual order.*

Extend the Discussion

Milton's Style What is the effect of the elaborate and lengthy sentence in lines 1–16? ***Possible response:*** *It forces the reader to give weight to each word, to see how all the words fit together.*

Response to Margin Question

Lines 1–16 *Paraphrase: Tell me, about humanity's first sin and the forbidden fruit that made humans mortal and miserable over the loss of Eden, until a better man came along to save us all. Milton's subject is original sin and its causes and consequences.*

Model the Skill

- Provide students with copies of the Reading Skills Focus graphic organizer for "The Fall of Satan" from *Paradise Lost.*
- Read lines 44–49 aloud. Then, reread the lines, using the definitions in the notes when possible. Redo the word order to make the text clearer. For example, you might want to place "Who durst defy the Omnipotent to arms" after "him" (line 44).

Difficult Lines	Paraphrase
(44–49) Him the Almighty Power / Hurled headlong flaming from the ethereal sky / With hideous ruin and combustion down / To bottomless perdition, there to dwell / In adamantine chains and penal fire / Who durst defy the Omnipotent to arms.	God threw the one who dared challenge him [Satan] down from Heaven to eternal damnation, to dwell in Hell in chains and fire.

Guided Practice: Apply

Turn-and-Talk Ask students to compare the paraphrased text to the original and discuss how paraphrasing does not imply a literal translation of a text into modern English.

Think About/Talk About

Responses to Margin Questions

Lines 26 *Milton's purpose is to prove to humans that God's treatment of them is consistent with his goodness.*

Lines 52–56 *He is tormented by the loss of eternal paradise and the prospect of eternal torment.*

Illumine, what is low raise and support;
That to the height of this great argument
I may assert Eternal Providence,
And justify the ways of God to men.
  Say first, for Heaven hides nothing from thy view,
Nor the deep tract of Hell, say first what cause
Moved our grand parents° in that happy state,
Favored of Heaven so highly, to fall off
From their Creator, and transgress his will
For one restraint,° lords of the world besides?°
Who first seduced them to that foul revolt?
The infernal Serpent;° he it was, whose guile,
Stirred up with envy and revenge, deceived
The mother of mankind, what time his pride
Had cast him out from Heaven, with all his host
Of rebel angels, by whose aid aspiring
To set himself in glory above his peers,°
He trusted to have equaled the Most High,
If he opposed; and with ambitious aim
Against the throne and monarchy of God,
Raised impious war in Heaven and battle proud
With vain attempt. Him the Almighty Power **B**
Hurled headlong flaming from the ethereal° sky
With hideous ruin and combustion down
To bottomless perdition,° there to dwell
In adamantine° chains and penal° fire,
Who durst° defy the Omnipotent to arms.
Nine times the space that measures day and night
To mortal men, he with his horrid crew
Lay vanquished, rolling in the fiery gulf,
Confounded though immortal. But his doom
Reserved him to more wrath; for now the thought
Both of lost happiness and lasting pain
Torments him; round he throws his baleful eyes,
That witnessed huge affliction and dismay
Mixed with obdurate° pride and steadfast hate.
At once as far as angels ken° he views
The dismal situation waste and wild:
A dungeon horrible on all sides round
As one great furnace flamed, yet from those flames

? **26.** *According to line 26, what is Milton's purpose? State this purpose in your own words.*

29. grand parents: Adam and Eve.

32. one restraint: the command not to eat of the fruit of the tree of knowledge. **besides:** in every other way.

34. Serpent: Milton is referring to Satan's final form.

39. peers: equals; the other archangels.

45. ethereal: heavenly.

47. perdition: damnation.

48. adamantine (ad uh MAN tihn): unbreakable. **penal:** punishing.

49. durst: dared.

52–56. Milton explains that the archangel Satan, jealous of God's power, has rebelled against the Almighty and thus been expelled from Heaven. The action of the poem begins at this point, *in medias res* ("in the middle of things"), the customary starting point of classical epics.

? *What most torments Satan in Hell?*

58. obdurate: stubborn; unrepentant.

59. ken: range of view.

B **Reading Focus** **Analyzing Milton's Style** What is Milton describing in lines 37–44?

Vocabulary **transgress** (trans GREHS) *v.:* sin against; violate a limit.
infernal (ihn FUR nuhl) *adj.:* hellish; fiendish.

Real Issues, Real Experts

*Holt author **Kylene Beers** offers strategies for teaching "The Fall of Satan."*

To introduce "The Fall of Satan," I make a list of characters (on chart paper or a transparency) that students will meet. Much like a playbill tells viewers when actors appear in the play, I show students at what lines they will meet those characters. Next, I have students mark (with Post-It notes or by jotting down line numbers) the following chunks of text: lines 1–26; 27–83; 84–127; 128–155; 156–191; 192–241; 242–end. I tell students each chunk carries the epic further along and they might want to read each chunk a couple of times before moving to the next chunk.

Next, I read aloud lines 1–26. We discuss this section using the think-pair-share strategy. Students first write briefly about what has happened in this first section; then, with one other student, they share what they think has happened; finally, they share their thoughts with the class.

The Great Day of His Wrath (1857) colored engraving by John Martin. Private collection.

Analyzing Visuals

Connecting to the Text How do contrasts between light and dark contribute to the emotional atmosphere surrounding Satan's expulsion from Heaven?

No light, but rather darkness visible
Served only to discover sights of woe,
Regions of sorrow, doleful shades, where peace
And rest can never dwell, hope never comes
That comes to all; but torture without end
Still urges,° and a fiery deluge, fed
With ever-burning sulfur unconsumed:
Such place Eternal Justice had prepared
For those rebellious, here their prison ordained
In utter darkness, and their portion set
As far removed from God and light of Heaven
As from the center thrice to the utmost pole.° **C**
O how unlike the place from whence they fell!
There the companions of his fall, o'erwhelmed
With floods and whirlwinds of tempestuous fire,
He soon discerns, and weltering° by his side
One next himself in power, and next in crime,
Long after known in Palestine, and named

68. still urges: always afflicts.

74. center . . . pole: three times the distance from Earth, or "center," to the outermost point in the universe. In Milton's cosmos, Earth is the center of ten concentric spheres.

78. weltering: rolling about.

C Literary Focus Style Notice Milton's use of words with contrasting meanings in lines 61–74. What effect do these contrasts create?

After we have worked through this chunk, students continue reading on their own. I tell students they might find the following tips helpful:

- First, they should read aloud the most troublesome parts.
- Next, they should read with a reading partner. With the reading partner, students should stop occasionally and discuss the images Milton is creating, footnotes, and confusing parts, and then offer summaries of what they are reading. If they want to use the think-pair-share format like we did with lines 1–26, then they should combine with one other group to share.
- Finally, while they should re-read sections that are confusing, they should also keep moving forward. Reading partnerships should keep a list of questions that remain unanswered for full-class discussion as they move forward.

Think About/Talk About

Comprehension

B Reading Focus

Possible response: *Milton describes how Satan decided he was better than the other archangels and unsuccessfully challenged the power of God.*

Analysis

C Literary Focus

Possible response: *The contrasting meanings emphasize the extreme difference between the darkness and pain of Hell and the bliss of Heaven.*

Extend the Discussion

Milton's Style In lines 66 and 67, Milton says that in Hell "hope never comes that comes to all." What does this phrase mean? ***Possible response:*** *The phrase most likely means that everyone who is not in Hell has hope at some point, but those in Hell will never have any hope at all.*

Analyzing Visuals

Connecting to the Text: *The contrasts between light and dark emphasize the dramatic results of Satan's expulsion, in which he perpetually remains engulfed in darkness, horror, and pain.*

Vocabulary: Own the Word

- **transgress:** Tell students that a noun form of *transgress* is *transgressor*. A *transgressor* is someone who violates a law or command.
- **infernal:** Tell students the root word for *infernal* is *infernus,* which is Latin for "lower." Something *infernal* is related to the underworld or hell. Have students think of an example of an *infernal* punishment.

Think About/Talk About

Literary Connection

Point out to students that in line 104, Milton uses the phrase "in dubious battle." Explain that John Steinbeck, the author *Of Mice and Men*, used these words as a title for a novel about a struggle between migrant farm workers and farmers in California. Steinbeck also featured a quotation from *Paradise Lost* at the beginning of this work.

Responses to Margin Questions

Lines 93–124 *Satan speaks of his "Innumerable force of spirits armed" and of the two "powers" engaging "in dubious battle." Although he speaks of Heaven as a lost "field," Satan refers to God as a "grand Foe" in an "eternal war," suggesting that he does not concede final defeat.*

Lines 143–145 *Beelzebub admits that God is almighty and implies submission to him; Satan acknowledges God's power but vows never to repent.*

Lines 156–168 *Satan vows never to do good, to thwart any effort by God to do good, and to turn anything good into evil. His intention is the essence of evil in that his commitment to evil is uncompromising.*

Beelzebub.° To whom the Arch-Enemy,
And then in Heaven called Satan,° with bold words
Breaking the horrid silence thus began:
"If thou beest he—but O how fallen! how changed
From him, who in the happy realms of light
Clothed with transcendent brightness didst outshine
Myriads though bright—if he whom mutual league,
United thoughts and counsels, equal hope
And hazard in the glorious enterprise,
Joined with me once, now misery hath joined
In equal ruin: into what pit thou seest
From what height fallen! so much the stronger proved
He with his thunder;° and till then who knew
The force of those dire arms? Yet not for those,
Nor what the potent Victor in his rage
Can else inflict, do I repent or change,
Though changed in outward luster, that fixed mind
And high disdain, from sense of injured merit, **D**
That with the Mightiest raised me to contend,
And to the fierce contention brought along
Innumerable force of spirits armed
That durst dislike his reign, and, me preferring,
His utmost power with adverse power opposed
In dubious battle on the plains of Heaven,
And shook his throne. What though the field be lost?
All is not lost; the unconquerable will,
And study° of revenge, immortal hate,
And courage never to submit or yield:
And what is else not to be overcome?
That glory never shall his wrath or might
Extort from me. To bow and sue for grace
With suppliant° knee, and deify his power
Who from the terror of this arm so late
Doubted° his empire, that were low indeed,
That were an ignominy and shame beneath
This downfall; since by fate the strength of gods
And this empyreal substance° cannot fail,
Since through experience of this great event,
In arms not worse, in foresight much advanced,
We may with more successful hope resolve
To wage by force or guile eternal war

81. Beelzebub (bee EHL zuh buhb): next in power to Satan; described as prince of the devils in Matthew 12:24.

82. Satan: Hebrew for "adversary; opposer."

93. He . . . thunder: God.

93–124. In this speech, Satan claims that although he has been defeated by God (the "potent Victor"), he will not surrender.

? *What details in Satan's speech show that he sees himself and God as the generals of two opposing armies? What is Satan's attitude toward his defeat?*

107. study: pursuit.

112. suppliant: humble.

114. doubted: archaic word meaning "feared for."

117. empyreal (ehm PIHR ee uhl) **substance:** heavenly (and therefore indestructible) substance of which all angels (including Satan) are made.

D **Literary Focus Style** Lines 94–98 illustrate nonstandard syntax. The subject of the sentence occurs in the middle of the sentence (the *I* in line 96). Re-read these lines carefully; what does Satan say he will not do?

Vocabulary **contention** (kuhn TEHN shuhn) *n.:* struggle.

Universal Access

English Learners

To help students paraphrase Milton's difficult syntax, pair them with more advanced students whose first language is English. Advise them to focus on identifying subjects and verbs in Milton's long sentences.

✔ See **UA: Differentiating Instruction** for strategies for teaching English learners.

Struggling Readers

Remind students that they can analyze the long and unusual sentence structure of the poem by using the Reading Skills Focus graphic organizer. Help them identify the subject and verb in long sentences. Model how to do this for lines 143–146. For example, you might say, "As I read, I realize that the subject of this sentence is the word *he* in line 143. Reading the words in parentheses, I realize that these words describe the subject. When I go on, I find that the verb is *have left* and appears after the parentheses."

Irreconcilable to our grand Foe,
Who now triumphs, and in the excess of joy
Sole reigning holds the tyranny of Heaven."
So spake the apostate° Angel, though in pain,
Vaunting° aloud, but racked with deep despair;
And him thus answered soon his bold compeer:°
"O Prince, O Chief of many thronèd Powers,
That led the embattled Seraphim° to war
Under thy conduct, and in dreadful deeds
Fearless, endangered Heaven's perpetual King,
And put to proof his high supremacy,
Whether upheld by strength, or chance, or fate; **E**
Too well I see and rue the dire event,°
That with sad overthrow and foul defeat
Hath lost us Heaven, and all this mighty host
In horrible destruction laid thus low,
As far as gods and heavenly essences
Can perish: for the mind and spirit remains
Invincible, and vigor soon returns,
Though all our glory extinct, and happy state
Here swallowed up in endless misery.
But what if he our Conqueror (whom I now
Of force° believe almighty, since no less
Than such could have o'erpowered such force as ours)
Have left us this our spirit and strength entire
Strongly to suffer and support our pains,
That we may so suffice° his vengeful ire,
Or do him mightier service as his thralls°
By right of war, whate'er his business be,
Here in the heart of Hell to work in fire,
Or do his errands in the gloomy deep?
What can it then avail,° though yet we feel
Strength undiminished, or eternal being
To undergo eternal punishment?"
Whereto with speedy words the Arch-Fiend replied:
"Fallen Cherub, to be weak is miserable,
Doing or suffering:° But of this be sure,
To do aught° good never will be our task,
But ever to do ill our sole delight,
As being the contrary to his high will
Whom we resist. If then his providence
Out of our evil seek to bring forth good,
Our labor must be to pervert that end,

125. apostate: guilty of abandoning one's beliefs. Satan is apostate.
126. vaunting: boasting.
127. compeer: companion; equal. Now Beelzebub speaks.
129. Seraphim: highest order of angels.

134. event: archaic word meaning "outcome."

? **143–145.** *What does Beelzebub admit about God? How is his attitude different from Satan's?*

144. of force: of necessity.
148. suffice: archaic for "satisfy."
149. thralls: slaves.

153. avail: be of help or advantage.

? **156–168.** *What does Satan vow? In what ways might this be considered the essence of evil?*

158. doing or suffering: whether active or passive.
159. aught: anything; whatever.

E Reading Focus **Analyzing Milton's Style** The formality of lines 128–133 adds to the exalted tone of Milton's style. What does Beelzebub reveal in these lines?

Advanced Learners

Acceleration Explain that Satan's polished rhetoric and rousing oratory are major factors in his appeal. The reader may abhor Satan's worldview but still be impressed by his eloquence.

Activity Ask students to discuss why they think Satan is sometimes persuasive despite the evil and incorrectness of his ideas. Have them refer to specific places in the text during the discussion.

Think About/Talk About

Comprehension

E Reading Focus

Possible response: *Beelzebub reveals that he feels allegiance toward Satan but is very aware of God's supremacy.*

Analysis

D Literary Focus

Possible response: *Satan says that he will not repent of his actions or change his evil ways. Though God has defeated him, he still feels a sense of disdainful superiority.*

Extend the Discussion

Paraphrasing Restate the meaning of lines 139–142. ***Possible response***: *Even though our glory and eternal happiness are forever lost, our strength, mind, and spirit remain strong.*

Interpreting What does Beelzebub mean in lines 137–141 when he describes himself and Satan as "laid thus low, / As far as gods and heavenly essences / Can perish: for the mind and spirit remains / Invincible, and vigor soon returns, / Though all our glory extinct"? What is his attitude toward their defeat? ***Possible responses***: *Beelzebub's attitude toward their defeat is complicated. He feels that God has brought them as low as possible, and the glory they hoped to have is gone. On the other hand, he feels that their spirits are still vigorous and undefeated.*

Vocabulary: Own the Word

contention: A *contention* is struggle or strife; the antonym is *accord* or *harmony*. Use both words in a sentence. For example: Satan's rebellion against God led to a fierce *contention* while the loyal heavenly forces stayed in accord with God.

Model the Skill

- Remind students that **epic similes** are a form of comparison that runs longer than a usual simile.
- Use lines 192–202 to model for students the skill of analyzing epic similes. Explain that in these lines, Milton is comparing Satan to the Titans and other giants of Greek mythology and Biblical stories. Point out that Milton uses this epic simile to stress Satan's ugliness and colossal size.

Guided Practice: Apply

Read-Talk-Write Have students reread lines 192–225 and consider how the epic similes emphasize the stateliness of the character of Satan. Ask students to discuss how the similes and other details develop the character. Have them write one paragraph about their conclusions.

Think as a Reader/Writer

Find It in Your Reading Point out lines 180–185 and the words and phrases that Satan uses to describe Hell, such as "dreary plain," "wild," "void of light," and "livid flames."

Use It in Your Writing Ask students to write two or three lines in which they describe a familiar landscape using sensory details.

Think About/Talk About

Response to Margin Question

Lines 214–220 *God will allow Satan to do evil. However, God will respond by showering humanity with kindness and mercy—even when human beings are tempted by Satan—while inflicting severe punishment on Satan himself.*

And out of good still° to find means of evil;
Which oftimes may succeed, so as perhaps
Shall grieve him, if I fail not, and disturb
His inmost counsels from their destined aim.
But see the angry Victor° hath recalled
His ministers of vengeance and pursuit
Back to the gates of Heaven; the sulfurous hail
Shot after us in storm, o'erblown hath laid
The fiery surge, that from the precipice
Of Heaven received us falling, and the thunder,
Winged with red lightning and impetuous rage,
Perhaps hath spent his shafts, and ceases now
To bellow through the vast and boundless deep.
Let us not slip° the occasion, whether scorn
Or satiate° fury yield it from our Foe.
Seest thou yon dreary plain, forlorn and wild,
The seat of desolation, void of light,
Save what the glimmering of these livid flames
Casts pale and dreadful? Thither let us tend
From off the tossing of these fiery waves,
There rest, if any rest can harbor there,

165. still: always.

169. angry Victor: God.

178. slip: lose.
179. satiate: satisfied.

Vocabulary **impetuous** (ihm PEHCH oo uhs) *adj.:* forceful; violent.
desolation (dehs uh LAY shuhn) *n.:* utter misery; extreme loneliness.

ART LINK

The Fall of the Rebel Angels by Gustave Doré, from Book I of John Milton's *Paradise Lost.*

Illustrations of *Paradise Lost*

The rich imagery of Milton's epic has tempted many artists, some of whom are also considered visionaries. English poet William Blake (1757–1827) responded to Milton's writing in 12 intense watercolor illustrations that reflect his own mystical ideas and mercurial passions. French artist Gustave Doré (1832–1883) presented a very different vision of Milton's world in 40 highly detailed engravings that gave the poem's religious figures a more solid presence in the observable world. Twentieth-century philosopher and painter Terrance Lindall (1944–) created a series of surrealist illustrations that included such startling images as lizard-like demons, floating eyes, and a magical woman with snakes for legs.

Ask Yourself

What attracts artists to Milton's poem? What kind of artwork inspired by Milton's visions and themes might you create?

Art Link

Ask Yourself

Possible responses: *Artists are attracted to Milton's vivid depictions of Satan and hell. His use of epic similes aids in visualization of the characters and setting, while an in-depth exploration of the tensions between good and evil evoke an emotional response. Milton's themes might inspire some to create artwork on a large-scale such as a canvas wall painting or fresco.*

Universal Access

Students with Disabilities

Before students paraphrase specific sections of the epic, provide them with an outline that summarizes the major developments in the epic. Have them match the lines in the poem that pertain to each major idea in the outline so that when they paraphrase specific lines they can keep the big picture in mind.

✔ See **UA: Differentiating Instruction** for strategies for teaching students with disabilities.

And reassembling our afflicted powers,
Consult how we may henceforth most offend
Our Enemy, our own loss how repair,
How overcome this dire calamity,
What reinforcement we may gain from hope,
If not, what resolution from despair."
  Thus Satan talking to his nearest mate
With head uplift above the wave, and eyes
That sparkling blazed; his other parts besides,
Prone on the flood, extended long and large,
Lay floating many a rood,° in bulk as huge
As whom the fables name of monstrous size,
Titanian or Earth-born, that warred on Jove,
Briareos or Typhon,° whom the den
By ancient Tarsus held, or that sea-beast
Leviathan,° which God of all his works
Created hugest that swim the ocean stream:
Him haply slumbering on the Norway foam,
The pilot of some small night-foundered° skiff,
Deeming some island, oft, as seamen tell,
With fixèd anchor in his scaly rind
Moors by his side under the lee, while night
Invests° the sea, and wishèd morn delays:
So stretched out huge in length the Arch-Fiend lay
Chained on the burning lake; nor ever thence **F**
Had risen or heaved his head, but that the will
And high permission of all-ruling Heaven
Left him at large to his own dark designs,
That with reiterated crimes he might
Heap on himself damnation, while he sought
Evil to others, and enraged might see
How all his malice served but to bring forth
Infinite goodness, grace, and mercy shown
On man by him seduced, but on himself
Treble confusion, wrath, and vengeance poured.
  Forthwith upright he rears from off the pool
His mighty stature; on each hand the flames
Driven backward slope their pointing spires, and rolled
In billows, leave in the midst a horrid vale. **G**
Then with expanded wings he steers his flight
Aloft, incumbent° on the dusky air

196. rood: old unit of measure varying locally from about six to eight yards.

198–199. Titanian . . . Typhon: In an epic simile, Milton compares Satan to the Titans and giants of Greek mythology. Briareos, a hundred-handed giant, helped Zeus (Jove) battle the Titans. Typhon, a hundred-headed serpent-monster from Cilicia (near Tarsus), attacked heaven and was imprisoned by Zeus.

201. Leviathan: biblical sea monster, either a reptile or a whale.

204. night-foundered: overtaken by night.

208. invests: covers.

214–220. Milton reminds his readers that Satan remains at the mercy of God and that God plans to use Satan's evil to bring good into the world.

? *Why has God left Satan "to his own dark designs"? Paraphrase what Milton says in lines 214–220.*

226. incumbent: lying.

F Literary Focus Style In lines 192–210, Milton employs epic similes to describe Satan lying on the lake of fire. To what is Satan being compared, and what do the comparisons suggest about Satan?

G Reading Focus Analyzing Milton's Style In lines 221–238, Milton uses vivid language to depict Satan. What impression do the comparisons create?

Think About/Talk About

Comprehension

G Reading Focus

Possible response: *These lines create the impression that Satan is as powerful as a volcanic eruption, fiery and dangerous, and that although he has been defeated, he is still a force to be reckoned with.*

Analysis

F Literary Focus

Possible responses: *Satan is being compared to the epic figures of Greek mythology who fought against the power of Zeus, the most important Greek god. Milton also compares Satan to a huge sea monster. These comparisons suggest that Satan is enormously large and powerful.*

Extend the Discussion

Finding Details What does Satan propose to do in lines 187–189? ***Possible response:*** *Satan proposes regrouping his forces and determining how best to continue to fight against God and how to overcome their defeat.*

Style How does Milton shift the reader's visual vantage point in lines 192–196? ***Possible response:*** *Milton shifts from a focus on Satan's head to a view of the fallen angel's enormous body.*

Vocabulary: Own the Word

- **impetuous:** *Impetuous* is violent and forceful; the antonym is *calm* or *cautious*. Use both words in a sentence. The *impetuous* waves finally became calm after the tornado had passed.
- **desolation:** Have students finish the following sentence after reading lines 180–185: *Satan called his resting place a "seat of desolation" because. . . .*

Word-Attack Skills Mini-Lesson

English for Academic Success Remind students that *ea* and *ee* are two ways to spell the sound /ee/. Have students think of words that illustrate these letter-sound relationships and write them on the board. [*eat, easy, heal, team, bee, seed*] Display the following selection words: *ethereal, vengeance, Beelzebub.* Discuss the sounds of *ea* or *ee* in each word.

In *ethereal, ea* stands for two vowel sounds, /ee/ and the unstressed vowel sound /uh/: (ih THIHR ee uhl). In *vengeance,* the letters *ea* together stand for /uh/: (VEHN juhns). The *e* after the *g* gives that letter its soft sound. In Beelzebub, *ee* stands for /ee/ and /eh/: (bee EHL zuh buhb).

Activity Have students identify the two words in each set in which the letters *ea* or *ee* stand for the same sound or sounds. Students may consult a dictionary.

1. empyreal	realm	arboreal
2. subterranean	protean	vengeance
3. creature	miscreant	pancreas
4. reestablished	fenugreek	seest

Think About/Talk About

Comprehension

Ⓗ Reading Focus

Possible responses: *Milton is saying that Satan and Beelzebub—and human beings—can control how they perceive their surroundings. They can turn a terrible circumstance into something very good or a good circumstance into something very bad. Milton's style makes these lines memorable because he makes his point quickly and powerfully by juxtaposing in one sentence the two phrases: "Heaven of Hell" and "Hell of Heaven."*

Extend the Discussion

Making Connections How does the saying "Misery loves company" apply to lines 264–270? ***Possible response:*** *Satan is eager to rally his forces so that they can share with him "their part / In this unhappy mansion." He needs their support to pursue revenge and may also believe that sharing his torment with others will make it more bearable.*

Monitor Students' Comprehension

Guide the class in answering these comprehension questions.

1. What does Milton state is his intention in writing *Paradise Lost?* [*to justify the ways of God to men*]
2. Why has Satan ended up in Hell? [*Satan challenged the power of God and lost the battle.*]
3. How does Hell appear in the poem? How does it compare to Heaven, the place where Satan and Beelzebub formerly lived? [*Hell is desolate, fiery, dark, wild, forlorn, a place with no hope; Heaven is the opposite of Hell, full of light, a paradise.*]

That felt unusual weight, till on dry land
He lights, if it were land that ever burned
With solid, as the lake with liquid fire;
And such appeared in hue, as when the force
Of subterranean wind transports a hill
Torn from Pelorus,° or the shattered side
Of thundering Etna,° whose combustible
And fueled entrails thence conceiving fire,
Sublimed° with mineral fury, aid the winds,
And leave a singèd bottom all involved°
With stench and smoke: such resting found the sole
Of unblest feet. Him followed his next mate,
Both glorying to have scaped the Stygian° flood
As gods, and by their own recovered strength,
Not by the sufferance° of supernal° power.
"Is this the region, this the soil, the clime,"
Said then the lost Archangel, "this the seat
That we must change for Heaven, this mournful gloom
For that celestial light? Be it so, since he
Who now is sovereign can dispose and bid
What shall be right: farthest from him is best,
Whom reason hath equaled, force hath made supreme
Above his equals. Farewell, happy fields,
Where joy forever dwells! Hail, horrors! hail,
Infernal world! and thou, profoundest° Hell,
Receive thy new possessor; one who brings
A mind not to be changed by place or time.
The mind is its own place, and in itself
Can make a Heaven of Hell, a Hell of Heaven. Ⓗ
What matter where, if I be still the same,
And what I should be, all but less than he
Whom thunder hath made greater? Here at least
We shall be free; the Almighty hath not built
Here for his envy, will not drive us hence:
Here we may reign secure, and in my choice
To reign is worth ambition, though in Hell:
Better to reign in Hell than serve in Heaven.
But wherefore let we then our faithful friends,
The associates and copartners of our loss,
Lie thus astonished° on the oblivious° pool,
And call them not to share with us their part
In this unhappy mansion, or once more
With rallied arms to try what may be yet
Regained in Heaven, or what more lost in Hell?"

232. Pelorus: headland in Sicily, Italy; now called Cape Faro.
233. Etna: volcano in Sicily, Italy.
235. sublimed: vaporized.
236. involved: enveloped.

239. Stygian (STIHJ ee uhn): of or like the river Styx; infernal, hellish. In Greek mythology, the river Styx encircles the underworld.
241. sufferance: permission.
supernal: heavenly.

251. profoundest: lowest; deepest.

266. astonished: dazed.
oblivious: causing forgetfulness.

Ⓗ **Reading Focus** **Analyzing Milton's Style** Paraphrase lines 254–255. How does Milton's style make these lines memorable?

California Standards, pp. 359–362

- **Reading Standard 1.2** Apply knowledge of Greek, Latin, and Anglo-Saxon roots and affixes to draw inferences concerning the meaning of scientific and mathematical terminology.
- **Reading Standard 3.3** Analyze the ways in which irony, tone, mood, the author's style, and the "sound" of language achieve specific rhetorical or aesthetic purposes or both.
- **Reading Standard 3.4** Analyze ways in which poets use imagery, personification, figures of speech, and sounds to evoke readers' emotions.
- **Writing Standard 2.2** Write responses to literature: **a.** Demonstrate a comprehensive understanding of the significant ideas in works or passages.
- **Writing Standard 2.3** Write reflective compositions: **a.** Explore the significance of personal experiences, events, conditions, or concerns by using rhetorical strategies (e.g., narration, description, exposition, persuasion). **b.** Draw comparisons between specific incidents and broader themes that illustrate the writer's important beliefs or generalizations about life.
- **Writing Standard 2.4** Write historical investigation reports: **b.** Analyze several historical records of a single event, examining critical relationships between elements of the research topic.

Applying Your Skills

Reading Standard 3.3, 3.4 (see pages A48–A50)
Writing Standard 2.2a (see pages A51–A52)

The Fall of Satan *from* Paradise Lost

Literary Response and Analysis

Reading Skills Focus

Quick Check

1. In the poem's opening, what does the speaker ask of the Heavenly Muse? Why?
2. With whom does Satan discuss his plans?
3. Near the end of the excerpt, what shows that Satan has fully accepted living in Hell?

Read with a Purpose

4. In what ways might Satan be seen as heroic?

Reading Skills: Analyzing Milton's Style

5. As you read, you analyzed some of the poem's challenging lines. Review these lines and your restatement of what Milton is saying. Add another column to your chart, and analyze the elements of style in the lines you paraphrased.

Difficult Lines	Paraphrase	Analysis of Style
Him the Almighty Power Hurled headlong flaming from the ethereal sky With hideous ruin and combustion down To bottomless perdition (44–47)	Almighty God (subject) threw (verb) Satan, head-first from Heaven (ethereal sky) in a streak of flames and debris, to a bottomless pit of suffering (perdi-tion).	Inversion: sentence begins with Him (object) followed by Almighty Power (subject) Grand diction: ethereal, perdition Alliteration: hurled headlong, hideous Vivid visual imagery: headlong flaming; bottomless perdition

Literary Skills Focus

Literary Analysis

6. **Interpret** Re-read the description of Hell in lines 53–74. How is Hell both a psychological state and a physical place?
7. **Analyze** A famous phrase in this poem is the description of Hell in line 63 as "darkness visible." This phrase is an **oxymoron,** a figure of speech that relies on **paradox,** or a self-contradictory idea. Why is this an effective image?
8. **Evaluate** How effective is Milton in creating a setting that is terrifying and an embodiment of evil? Explain your answer using textual details.

Literary Skills: Style

9. **Interpret** How does Milton create the elevated, epic style that gives *Paradise Lost* its power?

Literary Skills Review: Dramatic Irony

10. **Draw Conclusions** When the reader knows something that a character does not, **dramatic irony** is occurring. In lines 210–220 the speaker says that despite Satan's power and grandeur, the devil is still subject to God's purposes. How do these lines contribute to the dramatic irony in Satan's assertion of freedom in lines 242–270?

Writing Skills Focus

Think as a Reader/Writer

Use It in Your Writing Milton's epic similes of Satan and Hell add depth to the poem through their wealth of details. Write an epic simile of your own, describing the larger-than-life nature of something that would not normally be seen in an extraordinary way.

What Do You Think Now?

Is Milton's Satan influenced more by his heart or mind? What governs his actions?

Check for Understanding

Independent Practice

Reading Skills Focus

Possible responses:

1. *He asks for help in writing his poem, "adventurous song," so that he will fulfill his purpose of justifying God's ways to humankind.*
2. *with Beelzebub*
3. *He claims he would rather rule in Hell than serve in Heaven.*
4. *Despite his terrible defeat at the hands of God, Satan vows never to change his course. He is strong in physical strength and spirit.*
5. *Students should describe the order of subjects, verbs, and objects and show how the diction and imagery contribute to the poem's style.*

Literary Skills Focus

Possible responses:

6. *Hell is at once physically desolate, dismal, fiery, and dark. Satan is also tormented psychologically by pride, pain, and revenge.*
7. *This image increases the sense of confusion that meets Satan's eyes.*
8. *Very effectively—Milton uses vivid language to describe the place where Satan has landed, making allusions to terrible winds and erupting volcanoes. He describes the utter desolation and calls it a "dungeon horrible" and a "great furnace" filled with "liquid fire."*
9. *Milton's word choice, imagery, and sentence structure create an epic style. He uses complex sentences filled with references to the Bible and Greek and Roman mythology. He creates epic similes to compare the events in the story to other great works of literature.*
10. *Whatever he thinks or says, as long as Satan is subject to God, he is not really free.*

Universal Access

Struggling Writers

Guide students with additional scaffolding to help them complete the Writing Skills Focus activity. Have students think of a professional athlete, musician, or actor whom they admire. Before students write their epic simile, ask them to create a T-chart listing the person's qualities and traits in the left column. In the right column, have them take the quality or trait on the left and expand or exaggerate it to make it larger-than-life. Encourage students to use a thesaurus and include heroic details.

What Do You Think Now

Ask students to consider whether Satan's actions result from his reasoning and rationality or whether they are spurred by his emotions.

Independent Practice
Vocabulary Development
Vocabulary Check

1. *c* **2.** *e*
3. *d* **4.** *a*
5. *b*

Your Turn

Possible responses:

transgress*—trans, "to cross"—to break a rule or law, which is similar to the idea of stepping across a boundary or law*

infernal*—infernus, "hell"—"something very bad or relating to hell*

contention*—contendere, "to stretch with force or stretch vigorously"—to fight or struggle to get something*

impetuous*—impetus, a form of impetere, "to attack"—to act quickly, without thinking; to have violence, passion, or great force*

desolation*—desolatus, "deserted"—utter misery or extreme loneliness, which is similar to being completely deserted*

English for Academic Success
Language Coach

Tell students that it is often a good idea to figure out the part of speech represented by the word before determining its meaning in context.

Possible responses:

1. *c*
2. *b*
3. *a*
4. *d*

English for Academic Success
Academic Vocabulary

Possible responses: *Students analyze the contradictions in the character of Satan, described by Milton as stately and impressive. Students will make inferences about why this representation is controversial.*

Applying Your Skills

Reading Standard 1.2 (see pages A48–A50)

The Fall of Satan *from* Paradise Lost

Vocabulary Development

Vocabulary Check

Choose the Vocabulary word that best completes each sentence.

a. transgress **c.** contention **e.** desolation
b. infernal **d.** impetuous

1. They were the best two teams in the league, so everyone assumed they would be in ______ for the championship.
2. As all of his companions started slowly disappearing, ______ began to set in.
3. The rushing, ______ waters tore through the canyon.
4. His commander had drawn the line, and to ______ it would be a serious mistake.
5. They all felt as though they might melt under the blistering heat of that ______ summer.

Vocabulary Skills: Etymologies

Exploring **etymologies,** or word origins, can provide a deeper understanding of how a word is used in a text. Particularly in a complex work like *Paradise Lost,* researching the etymologies of words can give you greater understanding of a text's meaning.

Let us see how etymologies work. In line 81, Milton introduces Beelzebub. The name Beelzebub comes from Hebrew words meaning "god of flies." Literally, he is the "lord of filth." The word is also connected to *baal,* a false god or idol. Knowing this etymology gives the reader a deeper understanding of Milton's purpose.

Your Turn

Use a dictionary to explore the etymologies of the Vocabulary words. Use the chart in the next column to list each Vocabulary word, its origin, and the relationship of the word's current meaning to its etymology.

Word	Etymology	Relationship between word and etymology
transgress		

Language Coach

Multiple Meanings Words often have more than one meaning. Notice how the word is used in a sentence to decide which meaning is intended. In the sentences that follow, choose the correct meaning of the word:

impetuous a. *(adj.)* forceful; violent; b. *(adj.)* acting rashly, without considering the consequences

contention c. *(n.)* struggle; d. *(n.)* opinion as made as part of an argument

1. The heated discussion led to *contention* among the angels.
2. Do you think Satan made an *impetuous* decision without thinking about its impact?
3. The *impetuous* enemies fought in a sweeping battle.
4. It is Satan's *contention* that he will never surrender.

Academic Vocabulary

Write About

The depiction of Satan in *Paradise Lost* is controversial because certain virtues he possesses suggest that Milton seeks to establish him as the epic's hero. Write a short paragraph examining the contradiction that occurs when an "evil" character like Satan becomes admirable to the reader. Consider how Milton ensures that readers objectively consider Satan's point of view.

Universal Access: Vocabulary Development

EL English Learners

English for Academic Success Students may need additional help in recognizing which meaning is intended in a sentence. Pair students with proficient English speakers. Instruct them to engage in instructional dialogue in which they work through the following sentences, deciding on which meaning is used.

- Following the tragic accident, the victim's relatives felt utter **desolation**.
- After years of neglect and natural disasters, the land had long been abandoned and remained in a state of **desolation**.
- He **transgressed** the boundaries of proper conduct when he walked out on a serious conversation.
- The priest wondered if the woman had truly repented her **transgressions**.

✔ See the **Academic and Selection Vocabulary Skill Builder** in **UA: Differentiating Instruction.**

Reading Standard 1.2 (see pages A48–A50)

Vocabulary Skills: Scientific and Mathematical Words Derived from Greek and Latin

Many of the scientific and mathematical terms that we use today are derived from ancient Greek and Latin, the classical languages that were rediscovered during the Renaissance. Developing a knowledge of Greek and Latin roots and affixes can help you understand complex scientific and mathematical words.

Words are built on a base, or **root,** which contains the core of the word's meaning. The root *bio,* for instance, comes from a Greek word meaning "life." The words *biorhythm, biome,* and *biodegradable* contain this root. These words also contain **affixes**—word parts added to the beginning (prefixes) or end (suffixes) of a root to modify its meaning. For example, by adding the **suffix** *-logy,* meaning "study of," to the root *bio,* the word *biology*—"the study of life"—is formed. The **prefix** *micro* added to *biology* creates the word *microbiology,* "the study of very small [*microscopic*] life-forms."

Study these charts to learn some Greek and Latin word parts common to scientific and mathematical terms.

Greek and Latin Roots	Meaning	Examples
anthro– / andro–	human	anthropology; android
geo–	earth	geography; geology
hydr–, hydro–	water	hydrogen; hydration
iso–	alike; equal	isosceles; isometric
patho–	disease	pathology
psyche–	mind	psychology

Greek and Latin Affixes	Meaning	Examples
anti–	against	antibiotic; antidote
–gen–	something that produces or is produced	generate; oxygen; hydrogen
hemi–	half	hemisphere
hypo–	under; below	hypodermic
meta–	change; over	metamorphosis
–osis	state; condition	mitosis; symbiosis
sub–	under	subtract

Your Turn

The words below are scientific terms that have Greek or Latin origins. Using these charts and your own word knowledge, guess at each word's meaning. Identify which word parts helped you to guess the word's meaning. Then, look up the words in a dictionary and check your guesses. If your guess is incorrect, explain how the actual definition differs from yours.

1. anthropomorphic
2. aerobiology
3. pathogen
4. psychopathology
5. metamorphosis
6. suborbital

Independent Practice

Your Turn

Possible responses:

1. **anthropomorphic:** *related to human beings, perhaps something about the shape or form of human beings*

   Definition: "giving human traits to things that are not human"
2. **aerobiology:** *the study of life in the air*

   Definition: "the study of things that are in the air, such as polluting agents or germs"
3. **pathogen:** *something that produces a disease*

   Definition: "something that can cause an illness"
4. **psychopathology:** *the study of diseases of the mind*

   Definition: "the study of mental disorders"
5. **metamorphosis:** *a change in the state or condition of something*

   Definition: "a complete change in how something looks"
6. **suborbital:** *below the level of orbiting*

   Definition: "making less than a single orbit around the earth"

Independent Practice

Grammar Link

Your Turn

After the rocks were pushed aside, the men tried pushing the truck, which was heavier than they thought. When they were exhausted, Jim gathered the men. He pulled out a watch that he had been carrying in his pocket. When it got late, the darkness would begin.

Choices: Evaluation Criteria

Review: Homework
Plot for Inspiration
Students' epics are organized in three sections that address the setback, the hero's emotional reaction, and the resulting action.

Connect: Homework
Explore the Cosmos
Students use research to show how Copernicus, Galileo, and Newton advanced the field of astronomy.

Extend: Homework
Describe the View from the Middle
The description shows how entering the scene at a climactic, highly emotional moment affects the writers' perception of people in the scene.

Assess

Unit 2 Resources, Selection Standards Test, p. 69

go.hrw.com **ThinkCentral Online Assessment,** Selection Standards Check

Teacher One-Stop™, editable Selection Standards Check

Reteach

To reteach **author's style,** see **Reteaching Lessons,** pp. 1449O–1449P.

go.hrw.com **ThinkCentral Online Remediation**

Applying Your Skills

Writing Standard 2.3a, 2.3b, 2.4b (see pages A51–A52)

Grammar Link

Adjective Clauses and Adverb Clauses

To combine choppy sentences, use adjective and adverb clauses. An **adjective clause** is a subordinate clause that modifies a noun or pronoun. It usually begins with a **relative pronoun**—*who, whom, whose, which,* or *that*—or a **relative adverb**—*where* or *when.*

An **adverb clause** is a subordinate clause that modifies a verb, an adjective, or an adverb. It tells how, when, where, why, to what extent, or under what condition. An adverb clause begins with a **subordinating conjunction:** *after, although, because, if, since, when.*

In the example below, four choppy sentences are combined into one longer sentence by using both an adjective and an adverb clause.

Without subordinate clauses
The captain gave the signal. This started the soldiers running. They ran to the cave. It was dark and wet inside.

adverb clause
When the captain gave the signal, the soldiers ran to the cave, which was dark and wet inside.
adjective clause

In the sentence above, the adjective and adverb clauses add information about the soldiers.

Your Turn

Rewrite the following paragraph by combining the ideas through the use of adjective and adverb clauses. Try to vary sentence structure and avoid repetition.

First the rocks were moved aside. Then men tried pushing the truck. The truck was heavier than they thought. Jim gathered the men. They were exhausted. He pulled out a watch. He had been carrying the watch in his pocket. The darkness would begin. It would begin when it got late.

Writing Application Choose a paragraph you previously wrote, and, whenever possible, condense the shorter sentences by using adjective and adverb clauses.

CHOICES

As you respond to the Choices, use these **Academic Vocabulary** words as appropriate: establish, ensure, widespread, controversy, contradiction.

REVIEW

Plot for Inspiration
In *Paradise Lost,* Satan refuses to accept his defeat and uses it to fuel his desire for revenge. Although Satan is motivated by evil, in real life people often use setbacks as positive inspiration. Think of a story that follows this pattern, and outline the plot of an epic based on the story. In your outline, divide the epic into three sections. In the first, include details of the person's defeat or setback; in the second, include the person's reaction to the setback; in the third, include what the person is inspired to do.

CONNECT

Explore the Cosmos
TechFocus Three of the most famous astronomers of all time—Copernicus, Galileo, and Newton—lived during the Renaissance. Conduct research to learn what widespread advances they made in the field of astronomy. Then, design a Web page providing facts and images showing how people perceived the universe at the time Milton wrote *Paradise Lost.*

EXTEND

Describe the View from the Middle
Paradise Lost begins its narrative *in media res,* or in the middle of the action. Review the passage beginning at line 53, when Satan just has just been cast into Hell. Beginning to read at this point feels like walking into the room in the middle of an argument—you meet the characters in a moment of high emotion. Recall a time when you stepped into the middle of an intense discussion or a strange circumstance. Describe the scene from your point of view and explain how you think entering in the middle affected your perception of the people involved.

Universal Access: Grammar Link

EL English Learners

English for Academic Success Tell students that their sentences in a paragraph will flow more smoothly when they begin a few sentences with an adverb clause instead of the traditional, subject-verb clause. Have students change the following clauses into an adverb clause by inserting a subordinating conjunction (*after, although, because, if, since, when, as, before, rather than, as soon as, whenever, while*). Then, have them complete the sentence.

1. He released the prisoner, . . .
2. She opened the window, . . .
3. The noise reached her ears, . . .
4. The sea monster roared, . . .
5. It rained all day, . . .
6. We called the police, . . .

✔ For more practice with adjective and adverb clauses, see **Warriner's Handbook, GrammarNotes,** and **Language Handbook Worksheets.**

Reading Standard 2.5, 3.4 (see pages A48–A50)

When I consider how my light is spent

Literary Skills Focus

Allusion An **allusion** is a reference to a statement, person, place, event, or thing from literature, history, religion, mythology, politics, or popular culture. Literary works frequently allude to past literary classics: Hemingway's novel *For Whom the Bell Tolls* takes its title from a work by John Donne. In ordinary conversation, allusions frequently take the form of **eponyms,** whereby the name of a famous person known for a particular attribute is substituted for that attribute. For example, we may call an intelligent person an Einstein or a good baseball player a Babe Ruth.

Reading Skills Focus

Analyzing Author's Purpose Milton felt that his role as a poet was a divine calling. In the sonnet on his blindness, he struggles to understand and accept his condition as part of God's plan. Notice how the structure of his sonnet conforms to his purpose of serving God. In the first part of the sonnet, he asks a question. In the last six lines, he receives his answer.

Into Action As you read, use a chart to state the problem that Milton tries to resolve. Then, fill in the answer that comes after the turn in line 8.

Problem	Resolution
The speaker doesn't know how he can serve God because he is blind. He fears that he will be unable to use his one talent, writing. How can he continue to serve God if light (sight) is denied?	

Writing Skills Focus

Think as a Reader/Writer

Find It in Your Reading Recognizing allusions as you read can help broaden your understanding of a text. In your *Reader/Writer Notebook,* note any allusions that you encounter as you read the poem.

Language Coach

Word Origins Some words develop their meanings because they sound like what they describe. The word *murmur* means "something spoken very softly or unclearly." When you say the word aloud, you can hear that the word itself can sound soft and unclear. Explain how the sound of the these words relates to their meanings: *mumble, rattle, gobble, chitchat*.

Reader/Writer Notebook

Use your **RWN** to complete the activities for this selection.

Learn It Online

Listen to this sonnet read aloud online.

go.hrw.com H12-363 Go

Preteach

English for Academic Success

Language Coach

Have students read the **Language Coach**. Ask students to brainstorm other words that sound like what they describe. [*tinkle, chime, hiss, squeak, groan, hush*]

Literary Skills Focus

As you read and discuss the selection with students, have them note examples of allusion.

Reading Skills Focus

Give students a copy of the Reading Skills Focus graphic organizer before they read. (See **Unit 2 Resources.**) Tell them to use their responses to answer the questions on the Applying Your Skills page.

Writing Skills Focus

Have students record allusions in their **Reader/Writer Notebooks.** Student can use their notes to complete the Writing Skills Focus activity.

California Standards, pp. 363–365

- **Reading Standard 2.5** Analyze an author's implicit and explicit philosophical assumptions and beliefs about a subject.
- **Reading Standard 3.4** Analyze ways in which poets use imagery, personification, figures of speech, and sounds to evoke readers' emotions.

Selection Resources

Unit 2 Resources, on-level practice and assessment, p. 72

Teacher One Stop™, on-level lesson plans

Holt Audio Library

Holt Audio Library: Selections and Summaries in Spanish

UA: Differentiating Instruction, graphic organizer, p. 71

UA: Supporting Instruction in Spanish, selection summary

ThinkCentral Online Assessment, go.hrw.com

Learn It Online

The online version of this selection includes audio support to engage all students and to help struggling readers with reading comprehension and vocabulary.

go.hrw.com H12-363 Go

Teacher Preparation

Selection Summary

In this poem, Milton grieves for his lost sight and expresses his fear that he will never use his abilities as he had hoped to. However, he finds consolation in the thought that patiently bearing his burden and waiting to serve God will advance the divine plan as much as completing the heroic works of which he dreamed.

Direct Teach

Think About/Talk About

Read with a Purpose Have students read the Read with a Purpose statement. Tell them that as they read, they should identify the problem that the speaker faces that has brought him to a turning point.

Comprehension

B Reading Focus

Possible response: *Milton understands that his plight of blindness, while very difficult for him, is "mild." This may mean that it is mild compared to the afflictions of many other people, or that it is mild because he knows God is completely good.*

Analysis

A Literary Focus

Possible response: *The Biblical allusions reinforce the idea that Milton is considering what it means to serve God.*

California Standards, p. 365

- **Reading Standard 2.5** Analyze an author's implicit and explicit philosophical assumptions and beliefs about a subject.
- **Reading Standard 3.3** Analyze the ways in which irony, tone, mood, the author's style, and the "sound" of language achieve specific rhetorical or aesthetic purposes or both.
- **Reading Standard 3.4** Analyze ways in which poets use imagery, personification, figures of speech, and sounds to evoke readers' emotions.
- **Writing Standard 1.4** Enhance meaning by employing rhetorical devices, including the extended use of parallelism, repetition, and analogy; the incorporation of visual aids (e.g., graphs, tables, pictures); and the issuance of a call for action.

POEM

When I consider how my light is spent

by **John Milton**

Read with a Purpose
Read to discover how the speaker faces a turning point in his life.

Build Background
"When I consider how my light is spent," sometimes titled "On His Blindness," dramatizes the loss of sight Milton experienced in middle age. Long before he accomplished his life's work, Milton was almost completely blind. Deeply religious and believing firmly in man's accountability to God, Milton asks in the first part of the sonnet, "How can I continue to do the work that God expects of me?" He proposes an answer in the remainder of the sonnet.

When I consider how my light is spent
  Ere° half my days in this dark world and wide,
  And that one talent° which is death to hide (A)
  Lodged with me useless, though my soul more bent
To serve therewith my Maker, and present
  My true account, lest He returning chide,
  "Doth God exact day-labor, light denied?"
  I fondly° ask. But Patience, to prevent
That murmur, soon replies, "God doth not need
  Either man's work or His own gifts. Who best
  Bear His mild yoke, they serve Him best. His state (B)
Is kingly: Thousands° at His bidding speed,
  And post o'er land and ocean without rest;
  They also serve who only stand and wait."

2. ere: before.
3. talent: reference to the parable of the talents (Matthew 25:14–30), in which a servant is scolded for burying his one talent, or coin, in the earth instead of putting it to good use.
8. fondly: foolishly.
12. thousands: of angels.

A Literary Focus **Allusion** Milton uses Biblical allusions throughout his work. How does his use of allusion help to reveal his purpose?

B Reading Focus **Analyzing Author's Purpose** Milton's phrase "mild yoke" refers to the burdens that a person must bear in life. Why might he refer to his blindness as a merely a "mild yoke" here, rather than as something more difficult to handle?

John Milton Composing Poetry (19th century) by Leon Bortarel. Private collection.

Universal Access

Struggling Readers

Model for students how to fill out their Reading Skills Focus graphic organizers. Point out that line 8 signals a turn with the word "But." Line 9 confirms the turn because Patience "replies" to his question in line 7 by saying that God does not need the results of the speaker's labor and work, since everything man produces is God's ("His") anyway. Line 11 reassures the speaker that serving is also accomplished when people simply bear their burdens in life. Students should note this resolution in their graphic organizers.

Applying Your Skills

Reading Standard 2.5, 3.3, 3.4 (see pages A48–A50)
Writing Standard 1.4 (see pages A51–A52)

When I consider how my light is spent

Literary Response and Analysis

Reading Skills Focus

Quick Check

1. What frustration or disappointment does Milton express in the poem's first two lines?
2. To what famous religious parable does Milton allude in the first part of the sonnet?
3. By the end of the poem, how has Milton decided to respond to his worries?

Read with a Purpose

4. The tone of the poem changes about halfway through, around line 8. How does Milton's attitude in the second half compare with his attitude in the first half?

Reading Skills: Analyzing Author's Purpose

5. While you read, you analyzed the structure of Milton's poem. Now, return to your chart and add another column explaining how the sonnet's structure suits Milton's purpose.

Problem	Resolution	Milton's Purpose
The speaker doesn't know how he can serve God because he is blind. He fears that he will be unable to use his one talent, writing. How can he continue to serve God if light (sight) is denied?	He realizes that God does not need man's work. He can best serve God by bearing his burdens with patience and maintaining his faith.	

Literary Skills Focus

Literary Analysis

6. **Analyze** In line 8, what do you think Milton means when he says that "Patience" replies to his question?
7. **Make Judgments** In the opening line, how does Milton's metaphor give us insight into how he perceives his blindness?
8. **Evaluate** In fourteen lines, Milton experiences a significant change in his point of view. Do you think this change is convincing or do you suspect that Milton still has doubts? Explain your opinion and support it with evidence from the text.

Literary Skills: Allusion

9. **Infer** Early in the sonnet, Milton alludes to a Biblical parable. How does this reference explain Milton's anxiety in the first half of the poem?

Literary Skills Review: Rhyme Scheme

10. **Evaluate** The pattern of rhymed lines in a poem is called its **rhyme scheme.** How does the rhyme scheme of Milton's sonnet reinforce his ideas?

Writing Skills Focus

Think as a Reader/Writer

Use It in Your Writing Allusions range from direct quotations to minor hints to characters or events in another literary work. In your *Reader/Writer Notebook*, write a paragraph about a problem or event in your life and include at least two literary allusions.

What Do You Think Now? In this sonnet, is Milton more influenced by his heart or his mind? Explain.

Check for Understanding

Independent Practice

Reading Skills Focus

Possible responses:

1. *He has gone blind before half his life is over.*
2. *the Biblical parable of the talents*
3. *He recognizes that God does not need him to write; he can serve God by simply obeying His will.*
4. *In the first half, he questions whether he can truly serve God if he, a writer, is blind. In the second half, he speaks in the voice of Patience. He realizes God does not need anything from him other than his faith.*
5. *Ask students to show how the structure of the poem supports each point of view in the poem.*

Literary Skills Focus

Possible responses:

6. *Milton has come to have a more accepting perspective of his fate.*
7. *The metaphor is a literal reference to how being blind leaves him in darkness, but also shows that he feels as if his life ("my light") is used up.*
8. *Milton seems not to accept his fate entirely. He still believes what he said in line 3—it is "death to hide" his talent.*
9. *The parable describes a man who wastes a coin (a talent). Milton fears he will also be wasting his talent and will be scolded by God.*
10. *The first half is eight lines, two sets of lines rhymed abba. The second is six lines, two sets rhymed abc. This unifies each section and makes one different from the other, reinforcing the two ideas of the poem.*

What Do You Think Now?

Have students individually create a Venn diagram of aspects of Milton's work influenced by his heart, those influenced by his mind, and aspects that are influenced by both.

Struggling Writers

Some students may need additional scaffolding to complete the Writing Skills Focus activity. Ask students to first create a list of literary characters or events. Suggest that students use at least one direct quotation and one hint in their paragraphs. Help them start off their list by displaying possible allusions on the board:

- **Biblical:** the parable of the Prodigal Son, Psalm 23, Armageddon
- **Folk/fairy tales:** Cinderella, Jack and the Beanstalk
- **Greek or Roman mythology:** Hercules, Medusa, Achilles
- **Political quotes:** Martin Luther King, Jr., Winston Churchill, John F. Kennedy
- **Literary figures**: Romeo and Juliet, Macbeth, Hamlet, Scrooge, Odysseus

Standards Focus

Objectives

Students will
- analyze characteristics of allegory
- analyze a writer's beliefs

Selection Introduction

Think About the Writer

Have students think about why Bunyan was imprisoned. Ask students to consider the subject and purpose of the writings he completed during his time in prison.

For Independent Reading

- *A Portrait of the Artist as a Young Man,* James Joyce
- *Vanity Fair,* William Makepeace Thackeray

Motivate

What Do You Think?/QuickTalk

Have students consider how emotions and reason affect what we do. Discuss with students circumstances that might prompt a person to take a strong and perhaps unpopular stand.

English for Academic Success

Academic Vocabulary

Look for opportunities to use the Academic Vocabulary words in this unit.

- **controversies, *n.*:** lengthy disagreement
- **established, *v.*:** set up

California Standards, pp. 366–372

- **Reading Standard 2.5** Analyze an author's implicit and explicit philosophical assumptions and beliefs about a subject.
- **Reading Standard 3.1** Analyze characteristics of subgenres (e.g., satire, parody, allegory, pastoral) that are used in poetry, prose, plays, novels, short stories, essays, and other basic genres.

Preparing to Read

from The Pilgrim's Progress

What Do You Think? How do our hearts and minds influence our actions?

QuickTalk

Think about a time when you stood up for something in which you believed. What did you learn about yourself as a result? In a small group, discuss how other people's rules (fair or unfair) have helped you determine what is important to you. Record your thoughts in your *Reader/Writer Notebook.*

John Bunyan (1683) from *The Pilgrim's Progress.*
Rare Book & Special Collection Library, Sidney University.

MEET THE WRITER

John Bunyan

(1628–1688)

John Bunyan came from humble beginnings, originally working as a tinker, a maker and mender of pots and pans. Despite being impoverished and poorly educated, he wrote a book that for many years was second only to the Bible as the most widely read book among English readers: *The Pilgrim's Progress from This World to That Which Is to Come* (1678), commonly called *The Pilgrim's Progress.* Over time it has become established as one of the best-known allegories in English.

Unyielding Faith

As a young soldier in the Parliamentary army during the English Civil Wars, Bunyan met many Christians who questioned the authority of the Anglican Church. Anglicans called them Nonconformists or Dissenters. After an intense spiritual struggle, Bunyan joined a Nonconformist Puritan sect and began preaching for a Baptist congregation. Because England had no monarch during this time (1649–1660), Puritan religious sects like the Baptists flourished. When the monarchy was restored, however, so were laws against Dissenters.

Amidst much controversy, Bunyan defied these laws. In 1660, he was arrested for preaching without a license and imprisoned for twelve years. While in prison, Bunyan wrote about his inner life in *Grace Abounding to the Chief of Sinners* (1666). He recorded how God's grace had transformed him from an obscure, sinful man to a preacher. During his second confinement in 1677, he finished *The Pilgrim's Progress,* which traced the life journey of Christian, an allegorical character. The story's popularity led Bunyan to publish a sequel that depicts Christian's wife and children. Several phrases in our language originated in Bunyan's allegory, including "Vanity Fair," "the house beautiful," and "the slough of despond."

Released from prison again after the laws against Dissenters were relaxed, Bunyan returned to preaching, attracting thousands of listeners. King Charles II himself expressed astonishment that a tinker could draw such crowds.

Think About the Writer How do you think Bunyan's time in prison shaped his faith?

Selection Readability	
Easily Accessible Accessible **Challenging**	historical context; complex syntax; unfamiliar vocabulary

Reading Standard 2.5, 3.1 (see pages A48–A50)

Literary Skills Focus

Allegory An **allegory** is a story in which the characters, settings, and events stand for abstract or moral concepts. An allegory can be read on one level for its literal meaning and on a second level for its symbolic meaning. One of the best-known allegories in the English language is Bunyan's *The Pilgrim's Progress.* It recounts the journey of a character named Christian as he travels through an earthly world toward the spiritual world. The dual levels of storytelling are reflected in the names of the people, places, and events in the story.

Reading Skills Focus

Making Generalizations About a Writer's Beliefs A **generalization** is a statement that can be supported by different kinds of evidence. The episode of Vanity Fair depicts a town fair on market day. What beliefs can you infer from the narrator's attitude toward the merchandise, diversions, and people at Vanity Fair? Use this evidence to draw generalizations about the writer's beliefs.

Into Action As you read, use a chart like the one below to note the many examples of vanity in this allegory. What kinds of things, people, or behaviors does Bunyan's dreaming narrator consider to be vain?

Types of Things	Types of People	Types of Actions
Houses	Jugglers	Theft

Writing Skills Focus

Think as a Reader/Writer

Find It in Your Reading The jury described by Bunyan's narrator represents a long list of vices. As you read, notice the qualities and behaviors attributed to the members of the jury. In your *Reader/Writer Notebook,* list the vices represented by the jury and note their negative characteristics as described or suggested by the narrator.

TechFocus Use a computer drawing program to create illustrations that represent three of the characters in *The Pilgrim's Progress.* Compare your illustrations with those of your classmates. Discuss how visual clues can help clarify the representations Bunyan is making in his allegory.

Reader/Writer Notebook

Use your **RWN** to complete the activities for this selection.

Vocabulary

reproachfully (rih PROHCH fuhl ee) *adv.:* accusingly. *The crowd yelled reproachfully at the two travelers.*

confounded (kahn FOWN dihd) *v.* used as *adj.:* confused. *The citizens of Vanity were confounded after observing the behavior of Christian and Faithful.*

malice (MAL ihs) *n.:* active ill will; spite. *The townspeople acted with malice toward Christian and Faithful.*

implacable (ihm PLAK uh buhl) *adj.:* unyielding. *Faithful faced an implacable man on the jury.*

respite (REHS piht) *n.:* postponement; reprieve. *Christian was granted a respite when he was sent to prison instead of being killed.*

Language Coach

Prefixes The prefix *im–*, meaning "not," is often attached to words that begin with *p. Implacable* is a common English word that means "impossible to please." *Placable* was once a common word that meant "easily pleased" but today is rarely used. What new words can you form by adding the *im–* prefix to these words: *passive, partial, personal, possibility?*

Learn It Online
Advance your vocabulary with Word Watch.
go.hrw.com H12-367 Go

Selection Resources

Unit 2 Resources, on-level practice and assessment, p. 76

Teacher One Stop™, on-level lesson plans and all print resources

Holt Audio Library

Holt Audio Library: Selections and Summaries in Spanish

UA: Differentiating Instruction, graphic organizer, p. 72

UA: Supporting Instruction in Spanish, selection summary

ThinkCentral Online Assessment, Selection Standards Check

ThinkCentral Online Remediation

Preteach

Introducing Vocabulary

Use this activity to check students' understanding.

1. The visitors were ______ by the impropriety of the townspeople. [*confounded*]
2. The pilgrims were given no ______ from temptation. [*respite*]
3. Instead of being shown kindness, the men were treated with ______. [*malice*]
4. The ______ jurors stared coldly at the man on trial. [*implacable*]
5. John Bunyan wrote ______ about the evils in society. [*reproachfully*]

English for Academic Success

Language Coach

Have students read the **Language Coach**. Ask students to brainstorm two other words with the prefix *im–*, meaning "not." [*immoral, immodest*]

Literary Skills Focus

As you read and discuss the selection with students, have them note people, places, and events that stand for abstract concepts.

Reading Skills Focus

Give students a copy of the Reading Skills Focus graphic organizer before they read. (See **Unit 2 Resources.**) Tell them to use their responses to answer the questions on the Applying Your Skills page.

Writing Skills Focus

Have students record the jury's negative attributes in their **Reader/Writer Notebooks.** Students can use their notes to complete the Writing Skills Focus activity.

Learn It Online
Send students to **Word Watch** for audio pronunciations, synonyms and antonyms, and brief histories of word origins.
go.hrw.com H12-367 Go

Teacher Preparation

Selection Plot Summary

Beelzebub and his minions, in *The Pilgrim's Progress,* have set up Vanity Fair on the road to the Celestial City to tempt people with pleasures and delights. When Faithful and Christian reach the fair, they are arrested because they shunned the town's allurements. Faithful is tortured and put to death. Christian escapes and meets another companion, Hopeful, who accompanies him to the Celestial City, which they enter in honor as righteous believers.

Direct Teach

Think About/Talk About

Read with a Purpose Have students read the Read with a Purpose statement. Point out that the key words in the statement are "journey" and "salvation." As students read the selection, have them note important details about the journey.

Analysis

A Literary Focus

Possible response: *This paragraph implies that humans have always been plagued by vanity; the problem is long-standing.*

Extend the Discussion

Finding Details According to the fourth and fifth paragraphs, what kinds of activities take place at Vanity Fair? ***Possible response:*** *There are witless activities such as games and plays as well as criminal activities such as thefts, murders, and adulteries.*

Analyzing Details In the third paragraph, why does the narrator trace the establishment of Vanity Fair to Beelzebub, Apollyon, and Legion, over 5,000 years ago? ***Possible response:*** *In Christian doctrine, these three figures represent evil. Tracing the history back 5,000 years shows that the sins depicted are age-old sins.*

ALLEGORY

from The Pilgrim's Progress

by **John Bunyan**

Read with a Purpose

Read to discover how one man's journey can reflect humanity's salvation.

Build Background

Bunyan's narrator in *The Pilgrim's Progress* recounts a dream in which a man named Christian travels from the City of Destruction to the Celestial City. At this point in the story, Christian and his companion, Faithful, enter a town called Vanity in which the local fair, or outdoor market, is in full swing. In Bunyan's day, merchants from all over Europe would sell goods at such fairs, where the buying and selling would be accompanied by eating, drinking, and general merriment. Bunyan had little formal education but studied the Bible on his own, and, accordingly, his writing style reflects the King James Version of the Bible.

Then I saw in my dream that when they were got out of the wilderness they presently saw a town before them, and the name of that town is Vanity; and at the town there is a fair kept called Vanity-Fair. It is kept all the year long; it beareth the name of Vanity-Fair, because the town where 'tis kept is lighter than vanity; and also, because all that is there sold, or that cometh thither, is Vanity. As is the saying of the wise, *All that cometh is vanity.*

This Fair is no new erected business, but a thing of ancient standing; I will show you the original of it. **A**

Almost five thousand years agone, there were pilgrims walking to the Celestial City, as these two honest persons are; and Beelzebub, Apollyon, and Legion,[1] with their companions, perceiving by the path that the Pilgrims made that their way to the City lay through this town of Vanity, they contrived here to set up a fair; a fair wherein should be sold of all sorts of vanity, and that it should last all the year long. Therefore at this Fair are all such merchandise sold, as houses, lands, trades, places, honours, preferments,[2] titles, countries, kingdoms, lusts, pleasures, and delights of all sorts, as whores, bawds, wives, husbands, children, masters, servants, lives, blood, bodies, souls, silver, gold, pearls, precious stones, and what not.

And moreover, at this Fair there is at all times to be seen jugglings, cheats, games, plays, fools, apes, knaves, and rogues, and that of all sorts.

Here are to be seen too, and that for nothing, thefts, murders, adulteries, false-swearers, and that of a blood-red colour.

And as in other fairs of less moment there are the several rows and streets under their proper names, where such and such wares are vended: so here likewise, you have the proper places, rows, streets (*viz.*[3] countries and kingdoms), where the wares of this Fair are soonest to be found: here is the Britain Row, the French Row, the Italian Row, the Spanish Row, the German Row, where several sorts of vanities are to be

1. **Beelzebub:** Satan. **Apollyon:** the angel of the bottomless pit in the book of Revelation. **Legion:** unclean spirits or devils.
2. **preferments:** appointments to political or religious positions.
3. **viz.:** namely.

A **Literary Focus** **Allegory** What does this paragraph say about the relationship of people to vanity?

Universal Access

English Learners

English for Academic Success To explain the importance of names in this allegory, have students make a list of each character's name before reading the excerpt. Ask students to write a few words expressing their understanding of the character's name and any predictions they might have about the characters based on his or her name. For example: *Mr. Cruelty—mean, causes pain.* Allow students to use a dictionary to look up the meanings of any words they do not know.

Struggling Readers

To help students understand *The Pilgrim's Progress,* model the reading skill of making generalizations about the writer's beliefs. You might say: "In an allegory, the narrator usually speaks for the writer. So when the narrator states that Beelzebub, or the devil, started Vanity Fair, you can make the generalization that Bunyan views the world as a place of temptation and that the devil will do his best to entice every person that passes through it."

Analyzing Visuals

Connecting to the Text Note how circular shapes give a sense of motion to the map of the pathway to Jerusalem. What does the orientation of the picture's features say about the significance of Vanity Fair?

Plan of the road from the City of Destruction to the Celestial City (19th century), from *The Pilgrim's Progress* by William Blake.

sold. But as in other fairs, some one commodity is as the chief of all the fair, so the ware of Rome and her merchandise is greatly promoted in this Fair: only our English nation, with some others, have taken a dislike thereat.[4]

Now, as I said, the way to the Celestial City lies just through this town, where this lusty Fair is kept; and he that will go to the City, and yet not go through this town, must needs go out of the world. The Prince of Princes himself, when here, went through this Town[5] to his own country, and that upon a fair-day too. Yea, and as I think it was Beelzebub, the chief lord of this Fair, that invited him to buy of his vanities; yea, would have made him lord of the Fair, would he but have done him reverence as he went through the town. Yea, because he was such a person of honour, Beelzebub had him from street to street, and showed him all the kingdoms of the world in a little time, that he might if possible allure that Blessed One, to cheapen[6] and buy some of his vanities. But he had no

4. **the ware of Rome . . . a dislike thereat:** reference to the Church of Rome, and the Church of England's separation from it. Rome is the center of the Catholic Church's hierarchy.

5. **The Prince of Princes . . . Town:** reference to the temptation of Christ (Matthew 4:11–11).
6. **cheapen:** ask the price of.

Think About/Talk About

Extend the Discussion

Finding Details What did Beelzebub seek from the Prince of Princes? ***Possible response:*** *He wanted the Prince of Princes to honor and revere him.*

Allegory Why must Christian pass through Vanity Fair? ***Possible response:*** *The character represents every ordinary Christian who must face temptation and reject worldly pleasures to gain entry into heaven.*

Analyzing Visuals

Connecting to the Text: *The etching shows the temptations that Christian must face and overcome during his life before finally reaching the "Celestial City", or Heaven. Vanity Fair is the temptation that lies the closest to Celestial City, signifying that everybody must struggle with vanity, sooner or later.*

Advanced Learners

Enrichment Challenge students to read parts of Dante Alighieri's *Divine Comedy,* the medieval poem that consists of the *Inferno, Purgatorio,* and *Paradiso.* Have them compare and contrast Dante's themes, characters, style, and tone to those of John Bunyan.

Students with Disabilities

Have students further explore the temptations of Vanity Fair. Ask students to create an advertisement flyer that would entice travelers to stop at Vanity Fair. Remind students that they should use information from the selection regarding the types of merchandise and events that occur at the fair.

Model the Skill

Model for students the reading skill of **making a generalization about a writer's beliefs.** Read the fifth paragraph of p. 370 aloud. Explain to students that Christian and Faithful demonstrate the virtue of not prioritizing worldly wealth by ignoring the merchandisers who offer them various wares. Tell students that Bunyan viewed materialism and possessions as temptations that distracted people from God.

Guided Practice: Apply

Think-Pair-Share Have students form pairs and discuss the author's beliefs about the jury. What is the significance of the jurors' names? What is the narrator's attitude toward the jury? Have pairs share their thoughts with the class.

Think as a Reader/Writer

Find It in Your Reading Point out the names of the members of the jury. Discuss the personal qualities that names such as "Mr. Hate-light" and "Mr. Malice" stand for.

Use It in Your Writing Have students make up two original allegorical names of people who are opposites. Then, have them write a few lines of dialogue between the two characters that show they hold opposite beliefs and values.

Think About/Talk About

Literary Connection

Tell students that William Makepeace Thackeray used Bunyan's term for a corrupt and worldly place as the title of a book, *Vanity Fair,* which depicts a venal and materialistic society.

mind to the merchandise, and therefore left the town without laying out so much as one farthing upon these vanities. This Fair therefore is an ancient thing, of long standing, and a very great Fair. **B**

Now these pilgrims, as I said, must needs go through this Fair: well, so they did; but behold, even as they entered into the Fair, all the people in the Fair were moved, and the town itself as it were in a hubbub about them; and that for several reasons: for,

First, the pilgrims were clothed with such kind of raiment as was diverse from the raiment of any that traded in that Fair. The people therefore of the Fair made a great gazing upon them: Some said they were fools, some they were bedlams,[7] and some "They are outlandish-men."[8]

Secondly, and as they wondered at their apparel so they did likewise at their speech; for few could understand what they said; they naturally spoke the language of Canaan;[9] but they that kept the Fair, were the men of this world: so that from one end of the Fair to the other, they seemed barbarians each to the other.

Thirdly, but that which did not a little amuse the merchandisers was that these pilgrims set very light by all their wares, they cared not so much as to look upon them; and if they called upon them to buy, they would put their fingers in their ears, and cry, *Turn away mine eyes from beholding vanity;* and look upwards, signifying that their trade and traffic was in Heaven.

One chanced mockingly, beholding the carriages of the men, to say unto them, "What will ye buy?" but they, looking gravely upon him, said, "We buy the truth." At that there was an occasion taken to despise the men the more; some mocking, some taunting, some speaking reproachfully, and some calling upon others to smite them. At last things came to a hubbub and great stir in the Fair; insomuch that all order was confounded. Now was word presently brought to the great one of the Fair, who quickly came down and deputed some of his most trusty friends to take these men into examination about whom the Fair was almost overturned. . . .

The townspeople at Vanity Fair are immediately suspicious of Christian and Faithful, and they arrest the two pilgrims and bring them to trial. Three witnesses, Envy, Superstition, and Pick-thank, a favor-seeker, testify against Faithful. His fate is turned over to a jury of townspeople.

Then went the jury out, whose names were Mr. Blind-man, Mr. No-good, Mr. Malice, Mr. Love-lust, Mr. Live-loose, Mr. Heady, Mr. High-mind, Mr. Enmity, Mr. Liar, Mr. Cruelty, Mr. Hate-light, and Mr. Implacable, who every one gave in his private verdict against him among themselves, and afterwards unanimously concluded to bring him in guilty before the Judge. And first Mr. Blind-man, the foreman, said, "I see clearly that this man is an heretic." **C**

Then said Mr. No-good, "Away with such a fellow from the earth." "Ay," said Mr. Malice, "for I hate the very looks of him." Then said Mr. Love-lust, "I could never endure him." "Nor I," said Mr. Live-loose, "for he would always be condemning my way." "Hang him, hang him," said Mr. Heady. "A sorry scrub," said Mr. High-mind. "My heart riseth against him," said Mr. Enmity. "He is a rogue," said Mr. Liar. "Hanging is too good for him," said Mr. Cruelty. "Let's dispatch him out of the way," said Mr. Hate-light. Then said Mr. Implacable, "Might I have all the world given me, I could not be reconciled to him, therefore let us forthwith bring him in guilty of death." And so they did, therefore he was presently condemned to be had from the place where he was, to the place from whence he came, and there to be put to the most cruel death that could be invented.

7. **bedlams:** mental patients from Bethlehem Hospital, the notorious hospital for the insane in London.
8. **outlandish-men:** foreigners.
9. **Canaan:** Promised Land. The "language of Canaan" is the language of the Bible.

B Reading Focus Making Generalizations About a Writer's Beliefs What fundamental beliefs of Bunyan's can you infer from his attitude toward "vanity," "merchandise," and "all the kingdoms of the world"?

C Literary Focus Allegory Why is Mr. Blind-man's name allegorical? Why is his statement ironic?

Vocabulary **reproachfully** (rih PROHCH fuhl ee) *adv.:* accusingly.
confounded (kahn FOWN dihd) *v.* used as *adj.:* confused.
malice (MAL ihs) *n.:* active ill will; spite.
implacable (ihm PLAK uh buhl) *adj.:* unyieldiing.

Developing Oral Fluency

Use the first paragraph on p. 368 of *Pilgrim's Progress* to explain to students the importance of paying attention to sentence structure when reading long "periodic" sentences aloud. Note that the text is divided into short phrases and sentences through the use of commas and semicolons. Note also that a single short sentence, such as "All that cometh is vanity," takes on a very emphatic tone due to its placement among these longer sentences.

Small-Group Activity Have students work in small groups to read this paragraph aloud clearly and expressively. Have students listen to each other's readings and critique each other's performance. Remind them to maintain a properly serious, almost mystical, tone when relating the narrator's dream.

✔ See the **Oral Language Skill Builder** in **UA: Differentiating Instruction**.

They therefore brought him out to do with him according to their law; and first they scourged him, then they buffeted him, then they lanced his flesh with knives; after that they stoned him with stones, then pricked him with their swords; and last of all they burned him to ashes at the stake. Thus came Faithful to his end. D

Now, I saw that there stood behind the multitude a chariot and a couple of horses, waiting for Faithful, who (so soon as his adversaries had dispatched him) was taken up into it, and straightway was carried up through the clouds, with sound of trumpet, the nearest way to the Celestial Gate. But as for Christian, he had some respite, and was remanded back to prison; so he there remained for a space: but he that over-rules all things, having the power of their rage in his own hand, so wrought it about that Christian for that time escaped them, and went his way. . . .

Christian continues on his journey and finds another companion, the convert Hopeful. After more trials and tests of faith, the two reach their long-awaited destination: the Gates of the Celestial City.

Now I saw in my dream, that these two men went in at the Gate; and lo, as they entered they were transfigured, and they had raiment put on that shone like gold. There was also that met them with harps and crowns, and gave them to them, the harp to praise withal, and the crowns in token of honour. Then I heard in my dream, that all the bells in the City rang again for joy; and that it was said unto them, *"Enter ye into the joy of your Lord."* I also heard the men themselves, that they sang with a loud voice, saying, *"Blessing, honour, glory, and power, be to him that sitteth upon the throne, and to the Lamb for ever and ever."*

Now just as the Gates were opened to let in the men, I looked in after them; and behold, the City shone like the sun, the streets also were paved with gold, and in them walked many men with crowns on their heads, palms in their hands, and golden harps to sing praises withal.

D Reading Focus Making Generalizations About a Writer's Beliefs What is Bunyan suggesting by providing these details of Faithful's death? What do we learn about Bunyan's own views from these details?

Vocabulary respite (REHS piht) *n.:* postponement; reprieve.

CULTURE LINK

Romola Garay and Jonathan Rhys-Meyers in *Vanity Fair* (2004).

Vanity Fair

John Bunyan painted an image of Vanity Fair so powerful that the term *Vanity Fair* earned a place in the dictionary, where it is defined as "a place or scene of ostentation or empty, idle amusement and frivolity." The term was later used by William Makepeace Thackeray as the title for his 1847 satiric novel about selfish members of London society who follow their own desires. Throughout the years, the term retained its strength, but it began to have more favorable connotations by 1860 when *Vanity Fair* became the title of a British society magazine. Condé Nast then bought the name and launched the twentieth-century version of *Vanity Fair* magazine, a publication focused on contemporary society, celebrities, and style.

Ask Yourself

Think about the definition of the word *vanity*. Why was Vanity Fair such an effective name for Bunyan's fictional market? Explain.

California Standards, p. 372

- **Reading Standard 2.5** Analyze an author's implicit and explicit philosophical assumptions and beliefs about a subject.
- **Reading Standard 3.1** Analyze characteristics of subgenres (e.g., satire, parody, allegory, pastoral) that are used in poetry, prose, plays, novels, short stories, essays, and other basic genres.
- **Reading Standard 3.7** Analyze recognized works of world literature from a variety of authors: **c.** Evaluate the philosophical, political, religious, ethical, and social influences of the historical period that shaped the characters, plots, and settings.
- **Writing Standard 2.3** Write reflective compositions: **a.** Explore the significance of personal experiences, events, conditions, or concerns by using rhetorical strategies (e.g., narration, description, exposition, persuasion).

Think About/Talk About

Comprehension

B Reading Focus

Possible response: *The Blessed One has no interest in what Beelzebub offers. This shows Bunyan's belief that attaining salvation is more important than obtaining material goods.*

D Reading Focus

Possible responses: *Bunyan is suggesting that Faithful died as a martyr. Bunyan clearly considers Faithful's death noble.*

Analysis

C Literary Focus

Possible responses: *Mr. Blind-man's name could stand for impartial justice, but in this case it may stand for ignorance. The irony lies in his claim that he says he can "clearly see" that Faithful is a heretic.*

Culture Link

Ask Yourself

Possible responses: *"Vanity" means "excessive pride in oneself or one's appearance." "Vanity Fair" is an apt title for a shallow, worldly place full of idle amusement.*

Vocabulary: Own the Word

- **reproachfully:** Ask students to give an example of a *reproachful* comment a merchandiser would make to the pilgrims.
- **confounded:** Ask a few students to demonstrate being *confounded* by something.
- **malice:** Tell students that the root word for *malice* is *malus,* Latin for "bad." When you harbor *malice* towards someone, you are bitter towards them.
- **implacable:** Have students applaud if they would not mind pleading before an *implacable* judge.
- **respite:** Have students complete the sentence: Because Christian had *respite,* he was not . . . .

Check for Understanding

Independent Practice

Reading Skills Focus

Possible responses:

1. *to Celestial City*
2. *They are transfigured, given fine clothes, and welcomed with honor.*
3. *They must be strong-willed and steadfast in order to face and pass tests of faith.*
4. *Ask students to add notes to each column, explaining how each item represents some aspect of vanity.*

Vocabulary Check

5. *e* **6.** *d*
7. *a* **8.** *b*
9. *c*

Literary Skills Focus

Possible responses:

10. *When the Prince of Princes passed through Vanity Fair, Beelzebub tried to tempt him with kingdoms and other fine offers, but he bought nothing and left.*
11. *The jury condemns Faithful because he is a heretic. He does not share their beliefs in the worth of the vanities. Allegorically, he represents faith, which cannot coexist with sin.*
12. *Biblical language such as "Turn away mine eyes from beholding vanity" expresses the eternal truths that Bunyan believes in. Common speech, as in the jury statements, expresses the thoughts of sinners.*
13. *Bunyan shows Faithful being carried up through the clouds, which represent the Heaven that awaits faithful Christians.*
14. *Vanity Fair as a setting puts temptation in the path of all who enter.*

What Do You Think Now?

Have students explain the source of the characters' convictions and strength of purpose.

Applying Your Skills

Reading Standard 2.5, 3.1, 3.7c (see pages A48–A50)
Writing Standard 2.3a (see pages A51–A52)

from The Pilgrim's Progress

Literary Response and Analysis

Reading Skills Focus

Quick Check

1. Where are Christian and Faithful traveling?
2. What happens to Christian and Hopeful when they reach their final destination?

Read with a Purpose

3. What traits are necessary for humans (such as Christian, Faithful, and Hopeful) to reach the Celestial City, or salvation?

Reading Skills: Making Generalizations About a Writer's Beliefs

4. While reading, you made lists of the vices that the narrator cites as examples of vanity. Now, return to your chart, and add notes to each column, explaining how each item represents some aspect of vanity.

Types of Things	Types of People	Types of Actions
Houses—people build fancy houses to show off	Jugglers—people care too much about entertainment	Theft—people are greedy and will take what isn't theirs

Vocabulary Check

Match the Vocabulary words with their definitions.

5. reproachfully	**a.** spite
6. confounded	**b.** unyielding
7. malice	**c.** postponement
8. implacable	**d.** confused
9. respite	**e.** accusingly

Literary Skills Focus

Literary Analysis

10. Summarize In your own words, summarize the paragraph that describes the visit of the Prince of Princes to the town.

11. Draw Conclusions What do you think is the primary reason the jury sentences Faithful to death?

12. Analyze Bunyan incorporates both Biblical language and common speech into his writing. Identify examples of common speech in the text. Then, identify examples of Biblical language. Why does Bunyan use each type of speech?

Literary Skills: Allegory

13. Evaluate How do Bunyan's final paragraphs reinforce the idea that the Celestial City represents heaven and salvation?

Literary Skills Review: Setting

14. Hypothesize The time and location in which a story takes place is its **setting.** How does the setting of Vanity Fair influence the actions of the characters?

Writing Skills Focus

Think as a Reader/Writer

Use It in Your Writing Bunyan uses his description of the fair and jury to list various vices. Write a one-page description of a modern-day place or event. Include references to at least two modern virtues or vices.

What Do You Think Now

How do the hearts and minds of Christian, Faithful, and Hopeful influence their actions in this selection?

Assess

Unit 2 Resources,
Selection Standards Check, p. 79

go.hrw.com ThinkCentral Online Assessment,
Selection Standards Check

Teacher One Stop™,
editable Selection Standards Check

Universal Access

Struggling Writers

Some students may need additional scaffolding to complete the Writing Skills Focus activity. Before students begin writing, have them make a list of the various vices mentioned in the selection. Remind students that the modern-day place or events should be a reasonable setting for the particular vices they incorporate into their writing.

COMPARING TEXTS

Views on Education and Equality

Saint Magdalen Reading. Master Female Half Figures. Inv. 2156. Louvre, Paris.

The essay, debate, and speech in this section show Renaissance views on the value of education. Sir Francis Bacon's essay praises formal education, which was unavailable to most people and particularly to women. The debate by Margaret Cavendish and the speech by Queen Elizabeth I express the views of women who were as intellectually accomplished as their male peers. Compare the views in all three selections and consider the relationship between education and equality today.

CONTENTS

Overview

Students will read excerpts on the themes of education and equality, taken from the writings of three Renaissance figures: Sir Francis Bacon, Margaret Cavendish (Duchess of Newcastle), and Queen Elizabeth I. Students will analyze the arguments of each writer and explore how the writers present evidence to support their main arguments. Students will also compare and contrast the writers' ideas about education.

Standards Focus

Objectives

Students will
- analyze arguments
- evaluate the philosophical, political, religious, ethical and social influences of a historical period

English for Academic Success

Academic Vocabulary

Look for opportunities to use the Academic Vocabulary words.
- **controversies,** ***n.:*** lengthy disagreement
- **established,** ***v.:*** set up

Analyzing Visuals

Tell students that this painting dates back to the Renaissance period.

Extension Activity Ask students to discuss how femininity is portrayed in this painting. ***Possible responses:*** *Mary Magdalene appears calm and beautiful, dignified and serene. She is peacefully reading at her writing desk. This painting presents an ideal of an educated, refined, yet modest woman.*

Comparing Texts Resources

Unit 2 Resources, on-level practice and assessment, p. 82

Teacher One Stop™, on-level lesson plans and all print resources

Holt Audio Library

Holt Audio Library: Selections and Summaries in Spanish

UA: Differentiating Instruction, graphic organizer, p. 73

UA: Supporting Instruction in Spanish, selection summary

Analyzing Visuals Transparencies, p. 16

ThinkCentral Online Assessment, Selection Standards Check

ThinkCentral Online Remediation

Preteach

Introducing Vocabulary

Read aloud the Vocabulary words, definitions, and sample sentences. Then, use this activity to check students' understanding.

1. List ways a person can behave like a **sloth**.
2. Explain how someone can speak with **affectation.**
3. List the advantages of studying with **diligence.**
4. Explain how laziness is an **impediment** to success.
5. Name a reason a soldier could be accused of **treachery**.
6. Give an example of an **industrious** animal.

English for Academic Success

Language Coach

After reading the **Language Coach**, have students provide antonyms for *impediment* and *treachery*. [*benefit, loyalty*]

Informational Text Focus

Give students a copy of the Informational Text Focus graphic organizer before they read. (See **Unit 2 Resources.**) Tell them to use their responses to answer the questions on the Applying Your Skills page.

Writing Skills Focus

Have students note the authors' use of metaphors and similes in their **Reader/Writer Notebooks.** Students can use their responses to complete the Writing Skills Focus activity.

Learn It Online

Send students to **Word Watch** for audio pronunciations, synonyms and antonyms, and brief histories of word origins.

go.hrw.com H12-374 Go

INFORMATIONAL TEXT FOCUS

Preparing to Read

Reading Standard 2.6 (see pages A48–A50)

Of Studies / *from* Female Orations
Tilbury Speech

Informational Text Focus

Analyzing Arguments Speech or writing that uses logic to try to change the way people think is called an **argument.** A good argument is stated clearly and is supported by details, examples, or reasons. Any debate, real or fictional, requires each side to analyze the specific points of the opposing side. Contrasting ideas and arguments are often presented in a **parallel structure.** The repetition of words, phrases, or sentences that have a similar grammatical structure is **parallelism.**

Into Action As you read each selection, focus on how each author uses parallelism in presenting arguments. For each work, make a chart like the one below. Note the main arguments that are established. Then, write down a few examples of parallelism.

Selection	"Of Studies"
Main Arguments	Learning and studying helps us think clearly and judge wisely.
Instances of Parallelism	1. 2. 3.

Writing Skills Focus

Preparing for Timed Writing In your *Reader/Writer Notebook,* record **metaphors** and **similes** you encounter in the following selections. Note the persuasive appeal of these figures of speech.

TechFocus As you read, consider your own opinion on the value of education. Think about what and how you learn in school and in other environments. How might you express your opinions in a blog?

Vocabulary

sloth (slawth) *n.:* laziness; idleness. *Bacon argues against sloth or inactivity.*

affectation (af ehk TAY shuhn) *n.:* artificial behavior designed to impress others. *Elizabeth's speech comes across as sincere, without a trace of affectation.*

diligence (DIHL uh juhns) *n.:* carefulness. *Bacon recommends diligence in reading.*

impediment (ihm PEHD uh muhnt) *n.:* obstacle; stumbling block. *The author argues that being female is not an impediment to learning.*

industrious (ihn DUHS tree uhs) *adj.:* hard-working. *Women have been industrious in their efforts to prove that they are capable.*

treachery (TREHCH uhr ee) *n.:* breaking of faith; betrayal of trust. *Many of Bacon's readers seem to think that educating women is a form of treachery against men.*

Language Coach

Antonyms *Slothful* and *industrious* are antonyms, words with opposite meanings. Which Vocabulary word above is an antonym for *carelessness?*

Reader/Writer Notebook

Use your **RWN** to complete the activities for these selections.

Learn It Online

Expand your Vocabulary with Word Watch.

go.hrw.com H12-374 Go

California Standards, pp. 373–383

- **Reading Standard 2.6** Critique the power, validity, and truthfulness of arguments set forth in public documents; their appeal to both friendly and hostile audiences; and the extent to which the arguments anticipate and address reader concerns and counterclaims (e.g., appeal to reason, to authority, to pathos and emotion).

ESSAY

Of Studies

by **Francis Bacon**

Read with a Purpose

Read this essay to discover the author's attitude toward reading and study.

Build Background

A true Renaissance man, Francis Bacon (1561–1626) was involved in politics, science, law, architecture, literature, and economics. Bacon's *Essays,* his best-known literary works, are intended to help people get ahead in life. Bacon was the first Englishman to use the word *essay* to designate a brief discourse in prose, and borrowed the word from the French writer Michel de Montaigne.

Bacon's essays are written in a terse, compact style that demands a reader's full attention. His essay on the value of studies brims with specific proposals and bold assertions. Take note of the details, examples, and reasons that Bacon uses to establish his arguments and persuade his readers.

Studies serve for delight, for ornament, and for ability. Their chief use for delight is in privateness and retiring;[1] for ornament, is in discourse; and for ability, is in the judgment and disposition[2] of business. For expert men can execute, and perhaps judge of particulars, one by one; but the general counsels, and the plots and marshaling of affairs, come best from those that are learned. To spend too much time in studies is sloth; to use them too much for ornament is affectation; to make judgment wholly by their rules is the humor[3] of a scholar. They perfect nature and are perfected by experience; for natural abilities are like natural plants that need pruning by study; and studies themselves do give forth directions too much at large, except they be bounded in by experience. Crafty men contemn[4] studies; simple men admire them; and wise men use them: For they teach not their own use; but that is a wisdom without them[5] and above them, won by observation. Read not to contradict and confute;[6] nor to believe and take for granted; nor to find

Sir Francis Bacon, Viscount of St. Albans (17th century) by Paul van Somer.

1. **privateness and retiring:** privacy and leisure.
2. **disposition:** thoughtful placement.
3. **humor:** temperament.
4. **contemn:** despise.
5. **without them:** separate from them; outside them.
6. **confute:** dispute.

Vocabulary **sloth** (slawth) *n.:* laziness; idleness.
affectation (af ehk TAY shuhn) *n.:* artificial behavior designed to impress others.

Teacher Preparation

Selection Summary

"Of Studies" stresses the proper value and uses of learning. For example, the best experts are the learned; study and experience need to be balanced against each other; the wise use learning for their own benefit; each kind of study and activity has its value; and math, philosophy, and law improve defects of the mind.

Direct Teach

Think About/Talk About

Read with a Purpose Have students read the Read with a Purpose statement. Ask them to track instances in which the author expresses opinions rather than facts.

Extend the Discussion

Finding Details According to the first paragraph, how can learned people benefit society? ***Possible response:*** *They are better than others in offering good advice and conducting their affairs.*

Interpreting According to Francis Bacon, why must education go hand in hand with practical experience? ***Possible response:*** *Without experience, education would be a lazy exercise in affectation. Education needs to be applied to everyday life to be advantageous.*

Vocabulary: Own the Word

- **sloth:** Ask students if they agree with Bacon's opinion that "spending too much time in studies" is *sloth,* and have them explain their responses.
- **affectation:** Display the word *affectation* inside a circle on the board, and include the definition "a show." Then, draw "spider legs" and have students add attributes to the web. ***Possible responses:*** *pretense, artificiality, mannerism, airs, deception*

Universal Access

EL English Learners

English for Academic Success Provide support for students in recognizing and understanding the use of parallelism. Write the sentence: *To spend too much time in studies . . . of a scholar" on the board.* Ask students, "What grammatical structure seems to repeat throughout this sentence?" Students should point out, *To (do an action) . . . is . . . (descriptive word or phrase).* Confirm that students recognize "them" and "their" as referring to "studies." Have them paraphrase the sentence in their own words.

Selection Readability	
Easily Accessible Accessible **Challenging**	These selections include historical context; core ideas; unfamiliar vocabulary.

Think About/Talk About

Analysis

Ⓐ Informational Focus

Possible response: *According to Bacon, if people do not write, consult others, or read, they must have, respectively, a good memory, the ability to think quickly, or great cunning or shrewdness, so as to give the impression that they know more than they actually do.*

Extend the Discussion

Finding Details According to the author, what is the advantage in reading about a wide variety of subjects? ***Possible response:*** *Different genres benefit the mind in different ways, making the reader wiser, wittier, more subtle, and graver.*

Interpreting Why does Bacon recommend studying mathematics, philosophy, and the law? ***Possible response:*** *He recommends these studies for the effect they have on a person's thinking: they refine one's thought processes, making them more disciplined.*

Vocabulary: Own the Word

- **diligence:** Ask students to demonstrate writing or reading a book *diligently.*
- **impediment:** A synonym for *impediment* is *obstacle.* Use both words in a sentence. One of the major *impediments* for struggling learners is motivation; without this obstacle, learners would understand more quickly.

Monitor Students' Comprehension

Guide the class in answering the following True-False questions.

1. Bacon believes you can feel secure if you make judgments based only on what you have studied. [*F*]
2. Bacon says that you do not need to read every book thoroughly. [*T*]
3. In Bacon's view, mental pursuits are superior to physical ones, such as walking and riding. [*F*]

talk and discourse; but to weigh and consider. Some books are to be tasted, others to be swallowed, and some few to be chewed and digested: That is, some books are to be read only in parts; others to be read, but not curiously; and some few to be read wholly, and with diligence and attention. Some books also may be read by deputy, and extracts made of them by others; but that would be only in the less important arguments, and the meaner sort of books; else distilled books are like common distilled waters,[7] flashy[8] things. Reading maketh a full man; conference a ready man; and writing an exact man. And therefore, if a man write little, he had need have a great memory; if he confer little, he had need have a present wit;[9] and if he read little, he had need have much cunning, to seem to know that he doth not. Ⓐ

Histories make men wise; poets witty; the mathematics subtle; natural philosophy deep; moral grave; logic and rhetoric able to contend. *Abeunt studia in mores.*[10] Nay, there is no stond[11] or impediment in the wit but may be wrought out by fit studies: like as diseases of the body may have appropriate exercises. Bowling is good for the stone and reins;[12] shooting for the lungs and breast; gentle walking for the stomach; riding for the head; and the like. So if a man's wit be wandering, let him study the mathematics; for in demonstrations, if his wit be called away never so little, he must begin again: If his wit be not apt to distinguish or find differences, let him study the Schoolmen;[13] for they are *cymini sectores:*[14] If he be not apt to beat over[15] matters, and to call one thing to prove and illustrate another, let him study the lawyers' cases; so every defect of the mind may have a special receipt.[16]

---

7. **common distilled waters:** homemade remedies.
8. **flashy:** superficial; empty.
9. **present wit:** ability to think fast.
10. ***Abeunt . . . mores:*** Latin for "Studies help to form character," from *Heroides* by Ovid (43 B.C.–c. A.D.17).
11. **stond:** obstruction.
12. **stone and reins:** archaic form of "kidney stones and the kidneys."
13. **schoolmen:** medieval philosophers.
14. ***cymini sectores:*** Latin for "hairsplitters"; literally, dividers of the cumin seed.
15. **beat over:** thoroughly discuss.
16. **receipt:** remedy.

Ⓐ Informational Focus Analyzing Arguments Bacon lists three things in this passage that make a person complete. What difficulties result if a man lacks any of the three, or does them "little"?

Vocabulary **diligence** (DIHL uh juhns) *n.:* carefulness.
impediment (ihm PEHD uh muhnt) *n.:* obstacle; stumbling block.

A Still Life of Books (detail) by Charles E. Bizet d'Annonay (17th century). Musée de l'Ain, Bourg-en-Bresse, France.

Universal Access

Struggling Readers

Strategic Students To help students read "Of Studies," model the informational skill of analyzing arguments. You might say, "When I read a persuasive essay, I look for explicit and implicit details that tell about the message the author wants to convey. Then, I consider what ideas the author opposes." Ask students, "What ideas is the author presenting? What opposing ideas is the author rejecting?"

Students with Disabilities

To help students understand the argument presented in "Of Studies," explain that the author of the selection is discussing the best reasons for people to get an education. Explain that a good argument presents evidence and opinions to support a particular idea. Have students create a chart with two columns titled "Reasons" and "Support." As students read, they can use the chart to record reasons and supporting details in order to understand how the essay is organized.

DEBATE

from Female Orations

by **Margaret Cavendish, Duchess of Newcastle**

Read with a Purpose
Read to discover how one author uses debate to express different views on the roles of men and women.

Build Background
Margaret Cavendish (1623–1673) wrote *Female Orations* as a fictional debate between women representing a range of viewpoints on the role of women in society. Cavendish, an eccentric gentlewoman, had both access to education and the freedom to write about what she pleased. Cavendish openly tackles controversial topics such as the situation of women in a male-dominated society. Her writings offer insight into the complexities of the cultural and political climate women experienced in the mid-seventeenth century.

I

Ladies, gentlewomen, and other inferior women, but not less worthy: I have been industrious to assemble you together, and wish I were so fortunate as to persuade you to make frequent assemblies, associations, and combinations amongst our own sex, that we may unite in prudent counsels, to make ourselves as free, happy, and famous as men; whereas now we live and die as if we were produced from beasts, rather than from men; for men are happy, and we women are miserable; they possess all the ease, rest, pleasure, wealth, power, and fame; whereas women are restless with labor, easeless with pain, melancholy for want of pleasures, helpless for want of power, and die in oblivion, for want of fame. Nevertheless, men are so unconscionable and cruel against us that they endeavor to bar us of all sorts of liberty, and will not suffer us freely to associate amongst our own sex; but would fain[1] bury us in their houses or beds, as in a grave. The truth is, we live like bats or owls, labor like beasts, and die like worms. **A**

Margaret Cavendish, Duchess of Newcastle by Samuel Cooper.
Collection of the Duke of Buccleuch & Queensberry, KT.

1. **fain:** eagerly; gladly.

A **Informational Focus** **Analyzing Arguments** What is the function of the parallel structure within the long sentence that opens this paragraph?

Vocabulary **industrious** (ihn DUHS tree uhs) *adj.:* hardworking.

Universal Access

EL English Learners

English for Academic Success Have students read these definitions of potentially difficult words in *Female Orations* and then compose sentences using them.

- **inferior**—less important or worthy
- **industrious**—diligent, hardworking
- **prudent**—wise
- **oblivion**—state of being forgotten or unknown
- **unconscionable**—without conscience or principles, dishonorable

AAVE Students Who Use African American Vernacular English

English for Academic Success Remind students that in formal English, the subject and verb must always agree. Read aloud the sentence portions, "for men are happy, and we women are miserable" and "whereas women are restless with labor." As you read, stress the verb *are,* which agrees with the plural subjects *men* and *women.* Remind students that formal English uses the construction *men and women are,* not *men and women is.*

Teacher Preparation
Selection Summary

The first debater in *Female Orations* states that men have taken away women's freedom. The second speaker thinks that men do not take women seriously. The third speaker believes that men are better than women. The final speaker states that women are, overall, superior to men.

Direct Teach

Think About/Talk About

Read with a Purpose Have students read the Read with a Purpose statement. Then, direct their attention to the title "Female Orations." Point out that the work presents the differing viewpoints of several characters. Ask students to predict what male and female roles the author will discuss and what her actual point of view is.

Analysis

A Informational Focus
Possible response: *The parallel structure in this passage helps highlight the comparisons between men and women in a way that stresses opposites.*

Extend the Discussion

Identifying Details What is the first speaker's opinion on the situation of women? ***Possible response:*** *The speaker thinks women are exploited and lead a life of misery.*

Speculating What do you think motivates the first speaker's statements? ***Possible response:*** *The speaker feels frustrated about women's role in society because women are both isolated and subjugated.*

Vocabulary: Own the Word

industrious: Ask: "Why might assembling her audience require *industriousness* on Cavendish's part?" ***Possible response:*** *Women in her day were reluctant to discuss or discouraged from discussing controversial issues.*

Think About/Talk About

Literary Connection

Cavendish may have been familiar with translations of Dante's *Divine Comedy* (written in the early 1300s). The orator's reference to the first speaker as a possible "guide" to lead women out of the "hell of subjection" may be an allusion to Dante's famed guides, Virgil and Beatrice, who conduct Dante through Hell and Purgatory and into Paradise.

Extend the Discussion

Comparing and Contrasting How is the last speaker's salutation to readers different from the others? ***Possible response:*** *The last speaker does not address her remarks to "other inferior women," as the other speakers did.*

Determining Author's Purpose
Why do you think Cavendish used four fictional speakers to present different views of women's situation? ***Possible response:*** *She probably wanted to show that women did not necessarily agree about the proper roles of men and women. By using four speakers, Cavendish shows that she can see many sides of the argument.*

II

Ladies, gentlewomen, and other inferior women: The lady that spoke to you hath spoken wisely and eloquently, in expressing our unhappiness; but she hath not declared a remedy, or showed us a way to come out of our miseries; but, if she could or would be our guide, to lead us out of the labyrinth[2] men have put us into, we should not only praise and admire her, but adore and worship her as our goddess: but alas! men, that are not only our tyrants but our devils, keep us in the hell of subjection, from whence I cannot perceive any redemption or getting out; we may complain and bewail our condition, yet that will not free us; we may murmur and rail against men, yet they regard not what we say. In short, our words to men are as empty sounds; our sighs, as puffs of winds; and our tears, as fruitless showers; and our power is so inconsiderable, that men laugh at our weakness. B

III

Ladies, gentlewomen, and other inferior women: The former orations were exclamations against men, repining[3] at their condition and mourning for our own; but we have no reason to speak against men, who are our admirers and lovers; they are our protectors, defenders, and maintainers; they admire our beauties, and love our persons; they protect us from injuries, defend us from dangers, are industrious for our subsistence, and provide for our children; they swim great voyages by sea, travel long journeys by land, to get us rarities and curiosities; they dig to the center of the earth for gold for us; they dive to the bottom of the sea for jewels for us: they build to the skies houses for us: they hunt, fowl, fish, plant, and reap for food for us. All which, we could not do ourselves; and yet we complain of men, as if they were our enemies, whenas[4] we could not possibly live without them, which shows we are as ungrateful as inconstant. But we have more reason to murmur against Nature, than against men, who hath made men more ingenious, witty, and wise than women; more strong, industrious, and laborious than women; for women are witless and strengthless, and unprofitable creatures, did they not bear children.

Wherefore, let us love men, praise men, and pray for men; for without men, we should be the most miserable creatures that Nature hath made or could make. . . .

Several other viewpoints are expressed as the debate continues in parts IV–VI. Part VII, which follows, is the last section of the debate. C

2. **labyrinth:** maze.
3. **repining:** complaining.
4. **whenas:** while on the other hand.

B **Informational Focus** **Analyzing Arguments** How would you summarize the argument of this speaker?

C **Informational Focus** **Analyzing Arguments** How does the argument of this speaker differ from those of the previous two?

Analyzing Visuals

Connecting to the Text Examine the painting and the title on this book cover. After reading the excerpts from *Female Orations,* why do you think Margaret Cavendish would have been called "Mad Madge" during her lifetime?

Universal Access

Advanced Learners

Acceleration Instruct students to prepare for a debate to present in the next class session. Have students prepare to discuss the role of women in society today compared to their role at the time when Cavendish wrote these orations. Ask students to use parallelism to make their arguments more engaging.

Students with Disabilities

Explain to students that an argument persuades people to believe someone's ideas or to take a particular action. Before students read a section, have them skim the section and pick three familiar words that they think may be important to the speaker's argument. After students read, have them discuss how the words they chose were or were not important in making the argument convincing. For instance, students may note that the word *remedy* reinforces the speaker's point that women need a solution to their dire situation of helplessness.

VII

Noble ladies, honorable gentlewomen, and worthy female-commoners: The former oratoress's speech was to persuade us out of ourselves and to be that which Nature never intended us to be, to wit, masculine. But why should we desire to be masculine, since our own sex and condition is far the better? For if men have more courage, they have more danger; and if men have more strength, they have more labor than women have; if men are more eloquent in speech, women are more harmonious in voice; if men be more active, women are more graceful; if men have more liberty, women have more safety; for we never fight duels nor battles; nor do we go long travels or dangerous voyages; we labor not in building nor digging in mines, quarries, or pits, for metal, stone, or coals; neither do we waste or shorten our lives with university or scholastical studies, questions, and disputes; we burn not our faces with smiths' forges or chemists' furnaces; and hundreds of other actions which men are employed in; for they would not only fade the fresh beauty, spoil the lovely features, and decay the youth of women, causing them to appear old, when they are young; but would break their small limbs, and destroy their tender lives. Wherefore women have no reason to complain against Nature or the god of Nature, for although the gifts are not the same as they have given to men, yet those gifts they have given to women are much better; for we women are much more favored by Nature than men, in giving us such beauties, features, shapes, graceful demeanor, and such insinuating[5] and enticing attractives, that men are forced to admire us, love us, and be desirous of us; insomuch that rather than not have and enjoy us, they will deliver to our disposals their power, persons, and lives, enslaving themselves to our will and pleasures; also, we are their saints, whom they adore and worship; and what can we desire more than to be men's tyrants, destinies, and goddesses? (D)

5. **insinuating:** suggesting something in an indirect way.

(D) **Informational Focus** **Analyzing Arguments** How does Cavendish use parallelism on a larger scale in this last argument?

Think About/Talk About

Comprehension

(B) Informational Focus

Possible response: *She can find no remedy for women's plight because men do not take women's complaints seriously. She views the situation as hopeless.*

Analysis

(C) Informational Focus

Possible response: *The third speaker defends men and does not believe they are women's enemies. She believes that nature has made women "witless and strengthless, and unprofitable creatures" except for their role in child-bearing.*

(D) Informational Focus

Possible response: *The last speaker uses parallelism to state an argument against women and then refute it, supporting the position that women are more favored by nature than men and that men, in truth, willingly enslave themselves "to our will and pleasures."*

Analyzing Visuals

Connecting to the Text: *She might have been called "Mad Madge" because she dared to freely express her views of femininity, some of which opposed the views of her time.*

Monitor Students' Comprehension

To check students' understanding of the selection, ask them to explain why, according to the last speaker, women have no reason to complain. [*The speaker claims that women are so much more favorably endowed by nature that men are forced to admire them.*]

Compare and Contrast

Ask students to compare and contrast Francis Bacon's view of education in "Of Studies" with the ideas presented by the last speaker in Margaret Cavendish's *Female Orations.*

- **Similarities** Neither writer seems concerned with ensuring a better education for women.
- **Differences** Bacon is a man of his times who champions the importance of learning but does not suggest that women receive the same education as men. Cavendish's speaker does not seem to value education at all. She states, "neither do we waste or shorten our lives with university or scholastical studies, questions, and disputes." She seems happy that women are not expected to be educated.

Teacher Preparation
Selection Summary

In "Tilbury Speech," Queen Elizabeth states her love for her people and announces her determination to protect her kingdom until death.

Direct Teach

Think About/Talk About

Build Background: Elizabeth I on Film

The life of Elizabeth I has been dramatized in films including *Fire Over England* (1936), *The Sea Hawk* (1940), *The Private Lives of Elizabeth and Essex* (1939), *The Virgin Queen* (1955), *Shakespeare in Love* (1998), *Elizabeth* (1998), and *Elizabeth: The Golden Age* (2007).

Extend the Discussion

Paraphrasing At the beginning of the speech, what does Elizabeth say she was warned about? ***Possible response:*** *She was warned about arming her troops, for fear of treachery.*

Making Inferences When Elizabeth says "Let tyrants fear," what does she want listeners to infer about her? ***Possible response:*** *She probably wants them to infer that, unlike her enemies, she is not a tyrant. Thus, she can trust her people, and her people can trust her.*

SPEECH

Tilbury Speech

by **Queen Elizabeth I**

Read with a Purpose

Read this speech to discover how Elizabeth summons loyalty and courage in her subjects.

Build Background

Queen Elizabeth I (reigned 1558–1603) wrote poems, letters, prayers, sermons, and translations, and, at the same time, governed the country, conducted foreign policy, fostered the arts, and dedicated herself fervently to the newly established religion of her realm. She also wrote masterful speeches and political addresses. One of her best-known orations is the Tilbury Speech, given in 1588 before news of the destruction of the Spanish Armada reached England. With this speech, Elizabeth aimed to rouse her land forces to defend England against Spanish invasion.

Helen Mirren, Jeremy Irons, and Hugh Dancy in *Elizabeth I* (2005).

Universal Access

English Learners

English for Academic Success Have students carefully read the first sentence of the selection. Have them use the dictionary to find the meaning of any unfamiliar words, and then ask them to discuss how the Queen is trying to persuade her people. Have students find instances of repetition in those lines and discuss the effect of repetition on the entire speech.

Struggling Readers

Explain to students that, to understand an author's argument, it is important to understand the author's point of view and values. Have students consider the words, "for my God, for my kingdom, for my people, my honor, and my blood." Have students discuss the fact that the Queen is ready to live or die for these things. Include in the discussion how the value system of the Queen and her people, *God*, *kingdom*, *people*, *honor*, and *blood* are related.

The Arrival of Queen Elizabeth I at Tilbury; and the Defeat of the Spanish Armada (17th century), left hand panel, by English School. St. Faith's Church, Gaywood, Norfolk, UK.

My loving people: We have been persuaded by some that are careful of our safety to take heed how we commit ourself to armed multitudes for fear of treachery, but I assure you I do not desire to live to distrust my faithful and loving people. Let tyrants fear. I have always so behaved myself that, under God, I have placed my chiefest strength and safeguard in the loyal hearts and goodwill of my subjects. And therefore I am come amongst you, as you see, at this time, not for my recreation and disport,[1] but being resolved in the midst and heat of the battle to live or die amongst you all, to lay down for my God, and for my kingdom, and for my people, my honor and my blood, even in the dust. **A** I know I have the body but of a weak and feeble woman, but I have the heart and stomach of a king—and of a king of England too—and think foul scorn that Parma, or Spain, or any prince of Europe should dare to invade the borders of my realm. To which, rather than any dishonor shall grow by me, I myself will take up arms, I myself will be your general, judge, and rewarder of every one of your virtues in the field. I know already for your forwardness you have deserved rewards and crowns, and we do assure you, in the word of a prince, they shall be duly paid you. **B**

1. **disport:** pleasant diversion; entertainment.

A **Informational Focus** **Analyzing Arguments** How does Elizabeth's use of parallelism create a relationship between God, England, and the English people?

B **Informational Focus** **Analyzing Arguments** How would you summarize the argument of this speaker?

Vocabulary **treachery** (TREHCH uhr ee) *n.:* breaking of faith; betrayal of trust.

Think About/Talk About

Comprehension

B Informational Focus

Possible response: *Her argument could be summarized as follows: "I trust in your loyalty, and I am ready to sacrifice myself for my kingdom. I know your valor as warriors and I promise you the rewards you have earned."*

Analysis

A Informational Focus

Possible response: *Elizabeth's use of parallelism links God, her kingdom, her people, her honor, and her blood into a single vision of what she is willing to fight for.*

Extend the Discussion

Finding Details What reason does Elizabeth give for coming to Tilbury? ***Possible response:*** *She says that she came to Tilbury to reassure her people that she will do whatever is necessary to defend them.*

Interpreting Why does Elizabeth mention her physical weaknesses? ***Possible responses:*** *She wants her subjects to trust in her strength even though she is a woman. By assuring them that she has "the heart and stomach of a king," she hopes to inspire their confidence.*

Vocabulary: Own the Word

treachery: Ask students to give an example of an act of *treachery* in a political context. ***Possible response:*** *pretending to be loyal to one's nation while acting as a spy for another nation*

Monitor Students' Comprehension

To check students' understanding of the selection, ask them to explain how Elizabeth throws a sop to those who regard women as weak while asserting her own power. [*She admits that her body is less strong than a man's but claims that her courage and spirit are those of a king.*]

California Standards, pp. 382–383

- **Reading Standard 2.6** Critique the power, validity, and truthfulness of arguments set forth in public documents; their appeal to both friendly and hostile audiences; and the extent to which the arguments anticipate and address reader concerns and counterclaims (e.g., appeal to reason, to authority, to pathos and emotion).
- **Writing Standard 2.2** Write responses to literature: **a.** Demonstrate a comprehensive understanding of the significant ideas in works or passages. **b.** Analyze the use of imagery, language, universal themes, and unique aspects of the text. **c.** Support important ideas and viewpoints through accurate and detailed references to the text and to other works.
- **Writing Standard 2.3** Write reflective compositions: **a.** Explore the significance of personal experiences, events, conditions, or concerns by using rhetorical strategies (e.g., narration, description, exposition, persuasion).
- **Writing Standard 2.6** Deliver multimedia presentations: **b.** Select an appropriate medium for each element of the presentation.
- **Listening and Speaking Standard 1.9** Use research and analysis to justify strategies for gesture, movement, and vocalization, including dialect, pronunciation, and enunciation.
- **Listening and Speaking Standard 2.2** Deliver oral reports on historical investigations: **a.** Use exposition, narration, description, persuasion, or some combination of those to support the thesis.

Check for Understanding

Independent Practice

Informational Text Focus

Possible responses:

1. *Elizabeth says that she is their ruler and will be their "general, judge, and rewarder."*
2. *The first speakers address readers as "Ladies, gentlewomen, and other inferior women." The final speaker replaces the third phrase with "worthy female-commoners."*
3. *Students should support their opinions using evidence from the selection.*
4. *Have students consider the main point expressed by each author. Then, have them consider which aspects of the argument are best supported by the parallelism.*

Vocabulary Check

5. *d* **6.** *c*
7. *b* **8.** *a*
9. *f* **10.** *e*

Possible responses:

11. *Bacon, as a person of his time, might not have thought to include women. However, his ideas are just as valid when applied to women as to men.*
12. *There are touches of humor in all the statements. However, the humor could also be masking an underlying truth that women of the time had no real power and were expected to be subservient.*
13. *Monarchs in Queen Elizabeth's time were expected to be men, and women were regarded as the physically and mentally weaker sex. She needs to prove that she is a man's equal.*
14. *Have students practice presenting the speech in small groups so that the other groups members can give feedback on the speaker's volume, gestures, and voice inflections.*

INFORMATIONAL TEXT FOCUS

Applying Your Skills

Reading Standard 2.6 (see pages A48–A50)
Listening and Speaking Standard 1.9 (see pages A53–A55)
Writing Standard 2.6b (see pages A51–A52)

Of Studies / *from* Female Orations
Tilbury Speech

Analyze Informational Texts

Informational Text Focus

Quick Check

1. What does Elizabeth say to assert her power?
2. How do the different speakers address their audience in Cavendish's debate?

Read with a Purpose

3. Each selection presents different attitudes about education and gender. Which writer's ideas are closest to yours? Explain.

Informational Skills: Analyzing Arguments

4. Return to the charts in which you recorded the main arguments and instances of parallelism. Now add a new row, analyzing how each use of parallelism directly supports the speaker's argument.

Selection	"Of Studies"
Main Arguments	Learning and studying helps us think clearly and judge wisely.
Instances of Parallelism	1. 2. 3.
How Parallelism Supports the Argument	

Vocabulary Check

Match each Vocabulary word to its synonym.

5. affectation	**a.** obstacle
6. treachery	**b.** laziness
7. sloth	**c.** betrayal
8. impediment	**d.** artificiality
9. diligence	**e.** hardworking
10. industrious	**f.** care

Text Analysis

11. Evaluate Do you think Francis Bacon intended to use the word *man* throughout "Of Studies" to refer just to men, or to any human being?

12. Compare Review the excerpts from Cavendish's *Female Orations.* Characterize the speaker of each section. Are all the speakers meant to be serious, or are some of them trying for humor?

13. Infer In the Tilbury Speech, Elizabeth says that she has the body of "a weak and feeble woman" but "the heart and stomach of a king." What inferences can you draw about gender assumptions during her time?

Listening and Speaking

14. Extend Although Queen Elizabeth's Tilbury Speech is a carefully crafted piece of writing, it was written to be spoken and heard. Make a photocopy of this speech. Then, read it aloud several times, underlining words and phrases your voice emphasizes as you speak. Practice the speech, using gestures to reinforce what you emphasize with your voice. Consider sharing your reading with your class.

Writing Skills Focus

Timed Writing In one or two paragraphs, briefly discuss the persuasive appeal of metaphors and similes in the selections by Francis Bacon, Margaret Cavendish, and Queen Elizabeth I. Be sure to support your response with specific evidence from the texts.

What Do You Think Now? What changes did each side hope to achieve by fighting the Civil War? Do you think these changes could have been accomplished in a peaceful way? Explain.

What Do You Think Now?

Direct students' attention to the part of the selection "On Studies" in which Bacon states, "Crafty men contemn studies; simple men admire them; and wise men use them." Have students think about details in the selection that support these words.

Universal Access

Struggling Writers

Provide additional scaffolding to guide students in the Writing Skills Focus activity. Have them prewrite by working in groups and first listing the metaphors and similes found in each selection. Ask them also to summarize the main point of each essay. Then, have them individually consider how the metaphors and similes strengthened the main point of each speaker.

Writing Standard 2.2a–c, 2.3a (see pages A51–A52)
Listening and Speaking Standard 2.2a (see pages A53–A55)

Of Studies / *from* Female Orations
Tilbury Speech

Writing Skills Focus

Write a Comparison-Contrast Essay

The selections you have just read all address controversial issues of education and gender equality. Which of the selections express similar views? How is each argument unique? Write an essay in which you compare the points of view on education and gender equality expressed in two of the selections. Before you begin writing, consider the following points:

1. How are the issues of education and gender equality combined in the selections? Which selection focuses more on education? Which focuses more on equality?
2. How does the writer or speaker reveal his or her opinion on education and/or equality? Are things directly stated, or are they implied? What viewpoints are included, and whose viewpoints are they?
3. Which selection did you find most convincing as an argument, and why?

Use details and examples from the texts to support your ideas, and make sure that your essay has a clear structure.

Review the elements of a successful comparison-contrast essay.

An effective comparison- contrast essay should

- clearly state what is being compared and contrasted in the opening paragraph
- use a thesis statement to establish the main idea
- be organized logically and effectively
- include quotations or references to text passages to support ideas
- include a conclusion that restates the thesis and demonstrates how it has been proved
- contain few or no errors in spelling, punctuation, and grammar

CHOICES

As you respond to the Choices, use these **Academic Vocabulary** words as appropriate: contradiction, controversy, ensure, establish, widespread.

REVIEW

Evaluate Education

Write an essay of your own in response to Bacon's reflections on studies. Your response may range from total disagreement to total approval of his ideas. Include examples and experiences from real life to support your response.

CONNECT

Write a Blog

TechFocus Write your own blog about the value of your education, both inside and outside school. Use personal anecdotes, images, and links to enhance your blog. (You can write your blog on paper if you do not have access to the Internet.) Then, ask two or three friends to read your blog and post responses to it.

EXTEND

Women in Renaissance Society

Research Activity The debates in *Female Orations* present various viewpoints from fictional women of the time. What impression do you get from these debates about women's lives in seventeenth-century Europe? Do some outside research on the role of women in Renaissance society, and compare your findings to the portrayal Cavendish presents in her debates. Present your results to the class.

What Do You Think Now? Each of the writers in this section bases opinions on personal experience. How do you think people form their opinions about equality and education today?

Independent Practice

Choices:
Evaluation Criteria

Review: Homework
Evaluate Education

- Students agree or disagree with Bacon's reflections on studies.
- Students relate real-life examples and experiences to support or refute Bacon.

Connect: Homework
Write a Blog

- Blogs address the beneficial uses of education inside and outside school.
- Students' blogs include personal anecdotes, images, links, and comments from other students.

Extend: Homework
Women in Renaissance Society

- Students present their impressions of the lives of seventeenth-century European women.
- Students compare the ideas in *Female Orations* with their own research findings.

Assess

Unit 2 Resources, Selection Standards Check, p. 85

go.hrw.com **ThinkCentral Online Assessment,** Selection Standards Check

Teacher One Stop™, editable Selection Standards Check

Reteach

To reteach **analyzing arguments,** see **Reteaching Lessons**, pp. 1449F–1449H.

go.hrw.com **ThinkCentral Online Remediation**

Universal Access

Struggling Writers

Have students work with a partner and choose two selections for the comparison-contrast essay. Instruct students pairs to identify, discuss, and record their answers to the questions 1 and 2 in a Venn diagram. Suggest that students answer question 3 on their own in their concluding paragraphs. Ask students to refer to the completed Venn diagrams while they are writing their essays independently.

What Do You Think Now?

Have students consider whether people today base their opinion on their personal experiences or on other sources. How would they prepare a debate on equality and education today? What information would they present in their argument?

Chapter Objectives

- Students will learn about characteristics of sonnets by reading a selection of Shakespeare's sonnets.
- Students will analyze the characteristics of tragedy by reading *The Tragedy of Macbeth* in its entirety.
- As they read *The Tragedy of Macbeth*, students will examine tone, irony, and the use of foil in the tragedy.

The Quotation

Tell students that Ben Jonson (1572–1637) was a rival author and friend of William Shakespeare (1564–1616). Shakespeare allegedly acted in Jonson's play, *Every Man In His Humour,* in 1598 at the Globe Theatre. The quotation comes from Jonson's poem of praise, "To the Memory of my Beloved Master William Shakespeare, and What He Hath Left Us." The poem introduced the First Folio of Shakespeare's works, published posthumously in 1623.

Analyzing Visuals

Extension Activity This photograph is of a recreation of the Globe Theatre. Point out to students how the audience stands before the stage and some audience members have boxes looking down toward the stage. Tell students to refer to the photograph when they read the description of the Globe in the essay. Ask them to point out aspects of the theater that are seen in the photograph and that the photograph does not portray.

CHAPTER **4**

William Shakespeare

LITERARY SKILLS FOCUS

Shakespeare's Sonnets and Plays

A Midsummer Night's Dream, Globe Theatre.

CONTENTS

"Soul of the Age!
The applause,
delight, the wonder
of our stage."

—**Ben Jonson**

Chapter 4

California Standards Overview

- **Reading Standard 2.2** Analyze the way in which clarity of meaning is affected by the patterns of organization, hierarchical structures, repetition of the main ideas, syntax, and word choice in the text.
- **Reading Standard 3.1** Analyze characteristics of subgenres (e.g., satire, parody, allegory, pastoral) that are used in poetry, prose, plays, novels, short stories, essays, and other basic genres.
- **Grades 9–10 Review Reading Standard 3.1** Analyze the way in which a work of literature is related to the themes and issues of its historical period. (Historical approach)
- **Writing Standard 1.3** Structure ideas and arguments in a sustained, persuasive, and sophisticated way and support them with precise and relevant examples.
- **Writing Standard 2.2** Write responses to literature: **a.** Demonstrate a comprehensive understanding of the significant ideas in works or passages. **b.** Analyze the use of imagery, language, universal themes, and unique aspects of the text. **c.** Support important ideas and viewpoints through accurate and detailed references to the text and to other works.
- **Writing Standard 2.3b** Draw comparisons between specific incidents and broader themes that illustrate the writer's important beliefs or generalizations about life.

Reading Standard 3.1, 3.7c (see pages A48–A50)

Shakespeare's Sonnets and Plays

by **Leila Christenbury**

Characteristics of Shakespeare's Sonnets and Plays

- Reflect influences from mythology and ancient history
- Primarily use iambic pentameter
- Display an immense range of human emotions
- Represent cornerstones of centuries of English literature

The Sonnets of Shakespeare

William Shakespeare lived for just over fifty years, but he created some of the most influential literature ever written in English. Shakespeare's work still fascinates us: His characters are complex, his ideas are illuminating, and his language is as precise as it is poetic. Whether writing about love or ambition, marriage or murder, Shakespeare produced poems and plays that engage, entertain, and sustain us.

Even if Shakespeare had written no plays, his reputation as a poet, as the author of the *Sonnets,* would have been immense. Published in 1609, his series of 154 sonnets features a male speaker and a recurring subject: love. Beyond these points there is little agreement and widespread debate among critics concerning the sonnets. Is the sonnets' speaker a dramatic character invented by Shakespeare, like Romeo or Hamlet, or is the speaker the poet himself? The speaker does refer to himself as "Will" a few times, as well as makes puns on his name, but what evidence exists to prove that all the sonnets are spoken by this Will?

If the sonnets are, in fact, about the real man Shakespeare, then who are the real people behind the characters in the sonnets: the beloved young man who may be the subject of either many of the first 126 sonnets, or of some of the later sonnets? Who is the rival poet referred to in several sonnets? Are the speaker, fair young man, dark lady, and other poet the only four characters, or are there others?

Is the order in which the sonnets were originally published (probably without Shakespeare's consent) the intended sequence? Could they be rearranged to tell a more coherent story? *Should* they be rearranged?

These issues continue to generate controversy among critics. There is consensus, however, about the undeniable artistic merit of the sonnets. With great style and emotion, these poems express profound observations about important human experiences.

The Shakespearean Sonnet's Form

As established by the rules of the sonnet form, each of Shakespeare's sonnets has a formal organization and a logical organization of ideas.

As discussed on page 268, the **Shakespearean sonnet** is a fourteen-line poem that uses **iambic pentameter,** has three quatrains followed by a final couplet, and adheres to a strict rhyme scheme. The iambic pentameter meter consists of five iambs. Iambs are **metrical feet,** or units of measure, in which one unstressed syllable is followed by one stressed syllable. The Shakespearean sonnet's **rhyme scheme** is *abab cdcd efef gg.*

The logical organization of ideas in Shakespeare's sonnet varies from poem to poem. Sonnet 18 (page 391), for example, offers a twist on the standard love poem, in which the attributes of a loved one are compared to something—in this case, a summer's day. The first two quatrains present the imperfections of the summer's day rather than the more standard recitation of the loved one's perfect qualities. As often happens in Shakespeare's sonnets, the **turn,** a shift in focus or thought, occurs at the beginning of the third quatrain in line 9.

The Rise of the Renaissance Theater

The English had been writing and performing plays for centuries before the Renaissance. Most scholars believe that early medieval drama originated in the ceremonies of the Roman Catholic liturgy. Eventually, drama moved out of the churches and into the marketplaces, where in the 1300s and 1400s various workers'

Literary Skills Focus

Objectives

Students will

- understand the characteristics of Shakespearean sonnets and plays
- understand the philosophical, political, religious, ethical, and social influences of a historical period

Unit 2 Resources, Literary Focus Skill Builder, p. 93

PowerNotes, interactive lesson presentation with activities

Teacher One Stop™, on-level lesson plan and all print resources

Direct Teach

The Sonnets of Shakespeare

The Literary Skills Focus essay introduces students to Shakespeare's sonnets and plays. As students read the essay, have them write questions they have in their **Reader/Writer Notebooks.** Then, discuss the questions as a class before students complete the Your Turn activity.

Universal Access

Struggling Readers

Have students create a *5W* chart or Reporter's Formula for the information contained in the section "The Sonnets of Shakespeare." Have students trace in the text what, who, why, when, and where a certain event happened. In this case, the event is the writing of sonnets by playwright and poet William Shakespeare in seventeenth-century England. Explain to students that a *5W* chart is a great tool to understand different aspects of a historical period, such as politics, philosophy, religion, or ethics.

California Standards, pp. 385–387

- **Reading Standard 3.1** Analyze characteristics of subgenres (e.g., satire, parody, allegory, pastoral) that are used in poetry, prose, plays, novels, short stories, essays, and other basic genres.
- **Reading Standard 3.7c** Evaluate the philosophical, political, religious, ethical, and social influences of the historical period that shaped the characters, plots, and settings.

Shakespeare's Plays

- Ask students to consider what other theater work Shakespeare did besides writing plays. [*He staged productions, found actors, and arranged their parts.*]
- Have students think about Shakespeare's interest in the business of theater and what his interest suggests about his personality.

The Globe

The name of the Globe was probably inspired by the burden Hercules was often depicted bearing on his shoulders. Building the Globe from the demolished theater in 1599 could well have seemed a Herculean feat to Shakespeare and his friends.

guilds staged cycles of plays that dramatized the history of the human race.

Although religious themes were still important, dramatic productions eventually became less about religion. Several types of plays were written and produced before the Renaissance: **miracle** and **mystery plays** taught people stories from the Bible and saints' lives, and **morality plays** provided instruction on how to live and die according to Christian principles. Beginning in the 1500s, a new type of play called an **interlude** developed. Interludes were one-act plays, some of them indistinguishable from moralities, others rowdy and farcical. With the advent of interludes, playwrights stopped being anonymous. Even before the new humanist learning emerged, there were strong dramatic traditions with which the great Renaissance playwrights were familiar.

Shakespeare's Plays

Written mostly in the 1590s, Shakespeare's early plays were some of his most performed and admired. This immensely varied group contains a history play about a deformed usurper who becomes the king of England (*Richard III*), a rowdy farce about mistaken identity (*The Comedy of Errors*), a blood-and-thunder tragedy (*Titus Andronicus*), and a poetic tragedy about ill-fated lovers (*Romeo and Juliet*).

In the late 1590s, Shakespeare entered a period of great prosperity. Elizabeth I was near the end of her reign when Shakespeare completed his cycle of plays about England during the Wars of the Roses: *Richard II*, both parts of *Henry IV*, and *Henry V*. He also wrote one of his most frequently performed tragedies, *Julius Caesar*, the magical comedy *A Midsummer Night's Dream*, and the darker comedy *A Merchant of Venice*.

As the seventeenth century began, Shakespeare was writing his greatest tragedies: *Hamlet*, *Othello*, *King Lear*, *Macbeth*, and *Antony and Cleopatra*. These plays are preoccupied with evil, violence, and death, but there is no evidence that Shakespeare himself was unhappy or depressed when he wrote them. Happily for us, Shakespeare's productivity was at its peak during the years 1600–1607.

Although we might think of Shakespeare as primarily a writer, we must remember that he was the consummate man of the theater, a man of business and action. He staged productions, managed the playhouse, and coordinated the actors. He had to provide good parts in every play for the principal performers in his company. His actors often played more than one character in a play, so he had to arrange for doubling or even tripling of roles. He planned his scenes carefully so that nobody would ever have to be onstage in two different roles at the same time.

Shakespeare also had to work within the conventions of the Renaissance stage. For example, there were no female actors during Shakespeare's time, so he worked to establish female characters that were accessible to the male actors playing these roles. Shakespeare's expertise with the page and the stage made him a complete man of the drama *and* theater.

The Globe

By the mid-sixteenth century, the art of drama in England was three centuries old, but the idea of housing it in a permanent building was new. Even after theaters had been built, plays were still performed in improvised spaces—particularly when acting companies toured the provinces or played in the large houses of royalty and nobility. The first public theater, called the Theater, in London was built in 1576. When the Theater was demolished in 1599, the timbers were used to build the Globe.

The Globe is probably the most famous public theater from Shakespeare's time, because Shakespeare's company owned it. Many of Shakespeare's plays were first performed in the Globe. Unfortunately, the original theater was destroyed by fire in 1613, and plans for the Globe have not survived. Most scholars agree that the depiction of the Globe by C. Walter Hodges is accurate. According to Hodges, the theater had three main sections: the building proper, the stage, and the tiring house, or backstage area. The main building, a wooden structure three stories high and roughly circular in shape, surrounded a spacious yard open to the sky. The public theater housed an amazingly large crowd: three

Universal Access

Advanced Learners

Enrichment Have students choose one aspect they find interesting about Shakespeare's life and writings and conduct some online research. Have them take a few notes and present their notes to the class in an informal presentation.

Students with Disabilities

Divide students into small groups to learn through a jigsawing technique. Have each small group read a small section of the Literary Skills Focus essay. One person in the group should take notes about the most important points of the section. When the small groups have finished reading, have one member of each group present the most important points of the section to the rest of the class. Students should take notes on the presentations in their **Reader/Writer Notebooks.**

Reading Standard 3.1, 3.7c (see pages A48–A50)

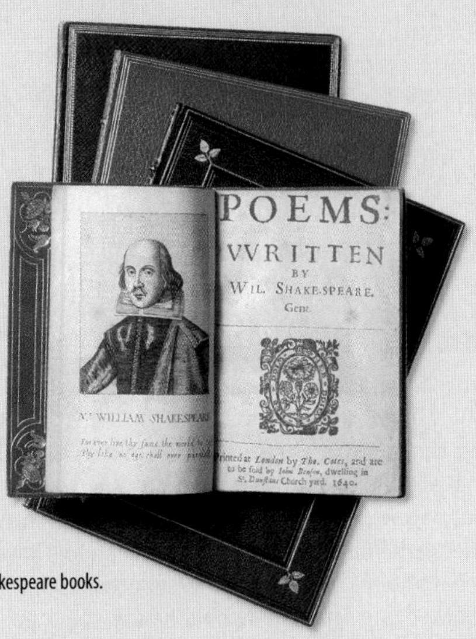

Shakespeare books.

thousand, according to two contemporary accounts.

The stage projected halfway out into the yard, so actors performed very close to the audience. The actors were highly trained and were expected to be able to sing, dance, wrestle, fence, and clown.

Special effects were also in high demand. Audiences loved to see witches or devils emerge through the trapdoor in the stage, which everybody knew led down to Hell, just as everybody knew that the ceiling over part of the stage represented Heaven.

The third section of the theater was the tiring house, a tall building that contained machinery and dressing rooms and provided a two-story back wall for the stage. A gallery was contained above this wall and a curtained space lay below. In the gallery, the audience could sit, musicians could perform, and parts of the play could be staged. At any given time, the gallery might serve as Macbeth's tower or the perch of the mysterious players in *The Taming of the Shrew.* The curtained area below the gallery was used mainly for "discoveries" of things hidden from the audience until the proper time.

Although the Globe Theater (rebuilt after the 1613 fire) was closed down in 1642, a full-scale model of the original was constructed in 1997. American actor and director Sam Wanamaker spearheaded the recontruction project, which took nearly ten years to complete. Today, the new Globe Theater (or, as it is called,"Shakespeare's Globe Theater") houses a professional theater company, historical exhibits, and an education center.

The Power of Imagination

Renaissance audiences took for granted that whatever happens on the stage is make-believe. When the people in the audience saw actors carrying lanterns, they knew it was night, even though the sun was shining brightly overhead. A few bushes became a forest. Furthermore, often instead of seeing a scene, they heard it described, as when Shakespeare has a character exclaim over a sunrise:

But look, the morn in russet mantle clad
Walks o'er the dew of yon high eastward hill.
—*Hamlet,* Act I, Scene 1, lines 166–167

Music for the Masses

When people went to the London theater, they expected not only to see a play but also to hear music. Trumpets announced the beginning of a play and important arrivals and departures within the drama. Although most of the original music has been lost, Shakespeare's works include a great variety of sad, happy, comic, and thoughtful songs that advance the play's action, help establish a scene's mood, or reveal character.

Ask Yourself

1. What are the required elements of the Shakespearean sonnet?
2. How were outdoor settings created on the Renaissance stage?

Learn It Online
Try the *PowerNotes* version of this lesson.
go.hrw.com H12-387 Go

Music for the Masses

- Available musical instruments in the Renaissance included the viol (a stringed instrument), the virginal (a small harpsichord held in the lap), the recorder (a flute-like instrument), the cornet (a trumpet-like cylinder of ivory and wood with finger holes like those on a recorder), the sackbut (an early trombone), and a double-reed instrument called the hautboy (HO boy), or oboe.
- Have student use interactive resources to research the appearance and the sound of Renaissance instruments. If possible, play recorded music from leading British composer of the Renaissance, William Byrd.

Check for Understanding

Ask Yourself

Possible responses:

1. *The Shakespearean sonnet consists of three quatrains on a related theme, followed by a couplet. There is a shift in theme at the start of the third quatrain, and the final couplet provides closure or sums up the message.*
2. *Descriptions of outdoor settings were written into a play's dialogue so audiences could imagine them. Also, simple props were used to imply to audiences that the scene was taking place outdoors.*

Learn It Online
For a multimedia version of the instruction on this page, check out the **PowerNotes** Literary Skills Focus presentation.
go.hrw.com H12-387 Go

Standards Focus

Objectives

Students will

- understand the characteristics of Shakespearean sonnets
- use text structure to understand meaning

Motivate

What Do You Think?/QuickWrite

Use the QuickWrite to have students think about how love is portrayed in novels, films, and television shows today. Ask students to think of common plotlines or problems they see in romantic or dramatic films. Work with them to map out a generic plotline for a typical romantic movie. Ask them to write in their **Reader/Writer Notebooks** about why love is such a universal, timeless subject.

English for Academic Success

Academic Vocabulary

Look for opportunities to use the Academic Vocabulary words in this unit.

- **contradiction, *n.*:** opposition between two things or statements
- **controversy, *n.*:** a dispute or disagreement that is usually public
- **ensure, *v.*:** to make sure; guarantee
- **establish, *v.*:** to bring about
- **widespread, *adj.*:** common; prevalent

MEET THE WRITER

William Shakespeare

(1564–1616)

What Do You Think? How do our hearts and minds influence our actions?

QuickWrite

Think of someone you know or have read about who was in love. Did love make the person see the world more clearly, or did it cloud his or her vision? Explain your answer in a paragraph in your *Reader/Writer Notebook.*

Every literate person has heard of Shakespeare, the author of more than thirty-six remarkable plays and more than 150 poems.

The Early Years

"The Bard" was born in Stratford-on-Avon, a prosperous market town in England, and was christened in the parish church on April 26, 1564. His parents came from respected families in the area, and, as a young man, Shakespeare probably attended the King's New School. He may have become a teacher; however, because his plays demonstrate knowledge of many diverse fields, some people have speculated he may have held a number of different occupations.

At eighteen, Shakespeare married Anne Hathaway. They had three children: a daughter, Susanna, and twins, Hamnet and Judith. In 1587, Shakespeare moved to London for a career in the theater.

A Life in the Theater

In the late 1590s, near the end of Elizabeth I's reign, Shakespeare completed his cycle of plays about England during the Wars of the Roses: *Richard II,* both parts of *Henry IV,* and *Henry V.* Also in this period he wrote the tragedy *Julius Caesar* and the comedies most frequently performed today, such as *A Midsummer Night's Dream* and *The Merchant of Venice.* He also wrote or rewrote *Hamlet,* the tragedy that, of all his works, has provoked the most varied and controversial interpretations from critics, scholars, and actors.

By 1592, Shakespeare was active in the London scene, writing and performing in a theater troupe called the Lord Chamberlain's

Statue of William Shakespeare (19th century) by English School.

A Shakespeare Time Line

Anne Hathaway Shakespeare (17th century). The Granger Collection, NY.

1560 — 1585

c. 1564 Born in Stratford-on-Avon

1582 Married Anne Hathaway

1587 Leaves family and moves to London; begins career in dramatic arts

Selection Readability	
Easily Accessible Accessible **Challenging**	Shakespeare's sonnets include historical context; complex narrative poems; unfamiliar vocabulary.

Preteach

Introducing Vocabulary

Read aloud the Vocabulary words and sample sentences. Then, use this activity to check students' understanding.

1. Describe the characteristics of a **temperate** climate.
2. Explain how people may react when they are met with **scorn**.
3. Tell when you would **summon** your friends.
4. Explain when you might be **surly**.
5. List two objects that can **expire**.
6. List some effects of **impediments**.
7. Name something that **reeks**.

English for Academic Success

Language Coach

Give students an opportunity to answer the **Language Coach** questions and discuss their responses. ***Possible responses:*** *Shakespeare used the verb* reeks *because he wanted to emphasize how bad the scent was. The vivid verbs that describe the actions* call, die, *and* refuse *are* summon, expire, *and* scorn, *respectively.*

Literary Skills Focus

As you read and discuss the selection, have students note how each sonnet adheres to or deviates from the standard sonnet structure.

Reading Skills Focus

Give students a copy of the Reading Skills Focus graphic organizer before they read. (See **Unit 2 Resources.**)

Writing Skills Focus

Have students record metaphors in their **Reader/Writer Notebooks**.

Learn It Online

The online version of this selection includes audio support to engage all students and to help struggling readers with reading comprehension and vocabulary.

go.hrw.com H12-390 Go

Preparing to Read

Reading Standard 2.2, 3.1 (see pages A48–A50)

Sonnets 18, 29, 30, 71, 73, 116, and 130

Literary Skills Focus

Shakespearean Sonnets The **Shakespearean sonnet** is fourteen lines with three four-line units, called **quatrains;** a final two-line unit, called a **couplet;** and the **rhyme scheme** *abab cdcd efef gg.* The **meter,** or rhythmic pattern, is **iambic pentameter,** with each line consisting of five iambs. An **iamb** is an unstressed syllable followed by a stressed syllable.

Reading Skills Focus

Using Text Structure to Understand Meaning The organization of thought in a Shakespearean sonnet usually corresponds to its structure. The three quatrains often express related ideas, and the couplet summarizes the message. As you read, look for the **turn,** or shift in thought, in each sonnet. Does it occur at the beginning of the third quatrain, in the final couplet, or in a different place? Can the couplet be considered a second turn?

Into Action Track each sonnet's train of thought and corresponding turn or turns.

Poem	Turn, or Shift in Thought
Sonnet 18	In line 9, focus shifts from nature's faults to the beloved
Sonnet 29	

Writing Skills Focus

Think as a Reader/Writer

Find It in Your Reading Shakespeare's sonnets are characterized by their clever **metaphors**—comparisons between two unlike things. As you read, record Shakespeare's metaphors in your *Reader/Writer Notebook.*

TechFocus As you read these sonnets, think about the different ways in which modern people send messages to their loved ones.

Vocabulary

temperate (TEHM puhr iht) *adj.:* moderate. *The temperate woman was much admired for her self-restraint.*

scorn (skawrn) *v.:* refuse; reject by showing contempt. *The young man scorns the idea of marrying beneath his class.*

summon (SUHM uhn) *v.:* call. *By concentrating, she can summon childhood memories.*

surly (SUR lee) *adj.:* unfriendly; sullen. *The surly dog even bit his loving master.*

expire (ehk SPYR) *v.:* die; come to an end. *The soldier feared he would expire in battle.*

impediments (ihm PEHD uh muhnts) *n.:* obstacles; obstructions. *The many impediments to their union discouraged the couple.*

reeks (reeks) *v.:* has a strong, bad smell. *The kitchen reeks whenever the cook burns the bread.*

Language Coach

Connotations Good writers choose vivid verbs to create strong images. These verbs have stronger connotations—associated ideas—than neutral verbs. In one sonnet, Shakespeare describes an odor that *reeks.* Why might he have chosen this verb instead of a more neutral word, such as *smells?* Which Vocabulary words are vivid verbs that describe these actions: *call, die, refuse?*

Reader/Writer Notebook

Use your **RWN** to complete the activities for these selections.

Learn It Online

Hear a professional actor read these sonnets online.

go.hrw.com H12-390 Go

California Standards, pp. 390–400

- **Reading Standard 2.2** Analyze the way in which clarity of meaning is affected by the patterns of organization, hierarchical structures, repetition of the main ideas, syntax, and word choice in the text.
- **Reading Standard 3.1** Analyze characteristics of subgenres (e.g., satire, parody, allegory, pastoral) that are used in poetry, prose, plays, novels, short stories, essays, and other basic genres.

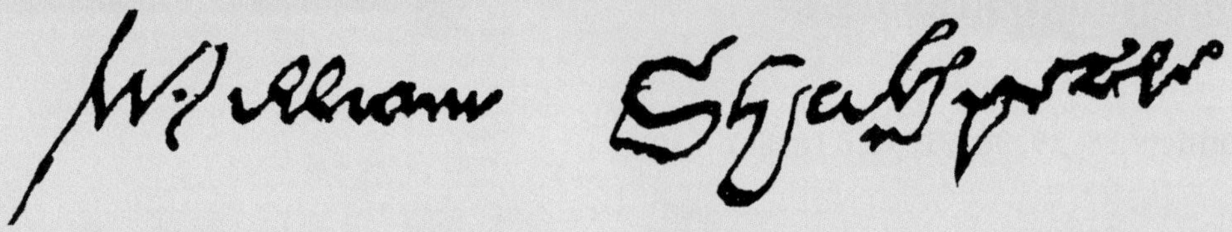

Men. He stayed with this group—though its name changed—until his retirement, enjoying the patronage of noblemen and royalty. Six of his plays were performed at the court of Queen Elizabeth; in fact, according to an old tradition, she asked him to write *The Merry Wives of Windsor* because she wanted to see the merry old knight John Falstaff in love.

Shakespeare achieved widespread success under Elizabeth's successor, James I. As the troupe's patron, James renamed it the King's Men, gave it license to perform anywhere in the British realm, raised its salaries, and appointed its highest members, including Shakespeare, to serve as grooms of the royal chamber.

The Twilight Years

Shakespeare seems to have retired to Stratford around 1610, although he continued to write for the London stage. His last English history play, *Henry VIII,* contained a tribute to the late queen. During the play's first performance in June 1613, the firing of the cannon at the end of Act I set the Globe's thatched roof on fire, and the building burned to the ground. No injuries were recorded, although a bottle of ale had to be poured on a man whose breeches were burning.

Shakespeare's last recorded visit to London was made in November 1614. He probably spent most of the last two years of his life in Stratford. He died on April 23, 1616, and was buried under the floor of Stratford Church. His epitaph is a warning not to move his remains to the churchyard—a common practice in his time to make room for the newly deceased:

Good friend, for Jesus' sake forbear
To dig the dust enclosèd here!
Blest be the man that spares these stones,
And curst be he that moves my bones.

Think About the Writer Because he lacked a university education, some critics question whether Shakespeare is the author of all his works. How essential do you think education would have been for writing his works?

Key Elements of Shakespeare's Writing

- Plays written in **blank verse,** which is unrhymed **iambic pentameter**
- Sonnets written in **rhymed iambic pentameter**
- Striking **metaphors** and poetic turns of phrase
- Heartbreaking **tragedies** and uproarious **comedies**
- Profound insights into human nature

Selection Introduction

Think About the Writer

An ongoing scholarly debate over the authorship of Shakespeare's plays began about 150 years after his death. Several contemporary authors, such as Sir Francis Bacon, Christopher Marlowe, and Edward de Vere, have been suggested as the actual authors, although there is little evidence to support these claims. Ask students to discuss, with a partner or in small groups, the implications the debate has for historical research.

For Independent Reading

*Loving Will Shakespeare,** Carolyn Meyer

HRW LIBRARY *This title is available in the HRW library.

1590s Writes many of his plays, including *Henry V, Romeo and Juliet, A Midsummer Night's Dream,* and *The Merchant of Venice*

1594 Joins dramatic company, the Lord Chamberlain's Men, which includes tragic actor Richard Burbage and clown Will Kemp

Anonymous Portrait of Richard Burbage (17th century), by English School. Dulwich Picture Gallery, London.

1603 The Lord Chamberlain's Men perform for King James; with the king's patronage, company name becomes the King's Men

1590 — 1600 — 1616

1592 Achieves success in London theater; from this point forward his work is well documented

1610 Retires and moves back to Stratford; continues to help manage the Globe and Blackfriars theaters

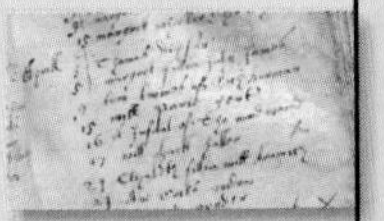

1616 Dies on April 23 in Stratford; buried beneath Stratford Church

Selection Resources

- **Unit 2 Resources,** on-level practice and assessment, p. 95
- **PowerNotes,** interactive lesson presentation with activities
- **Teacher One Stop™,** on-level lesson plans and all print resources
- **Holt Audio Library**
- **Holt Audio Library: Selections and Summaries in Spanish**
- **UA: Holt Interactive Reader,** p. 105
- **UA: Differentiating Instruction,** modified lesson plans and leveled assessment, p. 80
- **UA: Resources for Teaching Advanced Students,** lesson plans, p. 90
- **UA: Supporting Instruction in Spanish,** selection summary
- **ThinkCentral Online Assessment,** Selection Standards Check
- **ThinkCentral Online Remediation**

SONNET

Sonnet 18

by **William Shakespeare**

Read with a Purpose
Read to discover how the speaker feels about trying to describe his beloved's beauty.

Build Background
In the Northern Hemisphere, summer begins on June 21, the day of the summer solstice. Shakespeare probably used the word *summer* in Sonnet 18 to mean "spring and summer," as evidenced by his reference to the "buds of May."

Shall I compare thee to a summer's day?
Thou art more lovely and more temperate.
Rough winds do shake the darling buds of May,
And summer's lease hath all too short a date.
Sometime too hot the eye of heaven shines,
And often is his gold complexion dimmed;
And every fair from fair sometime declines,
By chance, or nature's changing course untrimmed.
But thy eternal summer shall not fade, Ⓐ
Nor lose possession of that fair thou owest,
Nor shall Death brag thou wander'st in his shade
When in eternal lines to time thou grow'st.
So long as men can breathe, or eyes can see,
So long lives this, and this gives life to thee. Ⓑ

Summer (1895), by Walter Crane.

Ⓐ **Literary Focus** **Shakespearean Sonnets** How does the ninth line provide a different view of the sonnet's central theme?

Ⓑ **Reading Focus** **Using Text Structure to Understand Meaning** What new idea is introduced in the last two lines? What does Shakespeare mean when he uses the word *this*?

Vocabulary **temperate** (TEHM puhr iht) *adj.:* moderate.

Universal Access

English Learners/ Struggling Readers

English for Academic Success Help students understand the figurative language and imagery by translating words and phrases they may not be able to visualize. For example:

- line 2: "temperate"—even-tempered, mild; the metaphor compares climate to a person's disposition.
- line 4: "summer's lease"—summer's duration; Shakespeare compares the season's length to a lease or temporary contract.
- line 5: "the hot eye of heaven"—the sun
- line 6: "his gold complexion dimmed"—when the sun is behind clouds.

Teacher Preparation

Selection Summary

In Sonnet 18, the narrator compares his lover to a summer's day using metaphors and purports that, unlike a summer day, his lover's beauty will never fade.

Direct Teach

Think About/Talk About

Read with a Purpose Before students read Sonnet 18, ask them how they remember the beauty of someone they love.

Comprehension

Ⓑ Reading Focus

Possible response: *The couplet shifts focus to the poet, stating that his writing will immortalize the beloved. "This" refers to the poem.*

Analysis

Ⓐ Literary Focus

Possible response: *The first two quatrains describe how nature's beauty fades. Line 9 begins with the transition "But," which indicates a change in theme and states that the beauty of the speaker's love will never fade.*

Extend the Discussion

Speculating What is the meaning of the repetition at the beginning of the lines in the final couplet? ***Possible response:*** *The repetition of "so long" creates a pleasant musical rhythm but also makes a comparison that states the immortality of the sonnet's subject.*

Vocabulary: Own the Word

temperate: Ask students the following question to test their knowledge of the Vocabulary word: How might you expect someone with a *temperate* demeanor to behave? ***Possible response:*** *I would expect him or her to be calm and mild-mannered.*

Teacher Preparation

Selection Summary

In Sonnet 29, the speaker feels depressed, but states that his love brings him joy.

Direct Teach

Think About/Talk About

Read with a Purpose After they read the Read with a Purpose statement, ask students if they, or someone they know, has ever felt self-pity.

Comprehension

B Reading Focus

Possible responses: *Line 9 begins a change in mood with the transitional word* Yet. *In line 10, the poet thinks about the person he loves, to whom he addresses the poem, and his mood improves.*

Analysis

A Literary Focus

Possible response: *He is "in disgrace," which may refer to how he is publicly seen by others. He appeals to heaven and then curses it while he wallows in self-pity.*

Analyzing Visuals

Connecting to the Text: *The sonnets of Shakespeare describe nature as mostly benign and delicate. In Sonnet 18, for example, the beauty of the speaker's beloved is evoked through the image of "darling buds of May."*

SONNET

Sonnet 29

by **William Shakespeare**

Read with a Purpose

Read this sonnet to discover how Shakespeare's speaker motivates himself when he feels unworthy.

Build Background

Even famous writers have their bad days. In this sonnet, the speaker describes a time when he feels depressed, jealous, and frustrated. He goes on to tell how he regains his confidence and creativity.

When, in disgrace with Fortune and men's eyes,
I all alone beweep my outcast state,
And trouble deaf heaven with my bootless° cries,
And look upon myself and curse my fate, **A**
Wishing me like to one more rich in hope,
Featured like him, like him° with friends possessed,
Desiring this man's art,° and that man's scope,°
With what I most enjoy contented least;
Yet in these thoughts myself almost despising,
Haply° I think on thee, and then my state,
Like to the lark° at break of day arising
From sullen earth, sings hymns at heaven's gate;
For thy sweet love remembered such wealth brings
That then I scorn to change my state with kings. **B**

3. bootless: useless; futile.

5–6. one . . . him . . . him: three men whom the speaker envies.

7. art: literary ability. **scope:** power.

10. haply: by chance.

A Literary Focus **Shakespearean Sonnets** What problems does the speaker describe in the first quatrain?

B Reading Focus **Using Text Structure to Understand Meaning** What prompts a change in the speaker's mood? Where in the sonnet does this shift occur?

Vocabulary **scorn** (skawrn) *v.:* refuse; reject by showing contempt.

Analyzing Visuals

Connecting to the Text Note the contrast between the subject's elaborate formal dress and his natural surroundings. In what ways do the sonnets of Shakespeare comment on natural and environmental beauty?

Sir Brooke Boothby (1781), by Joseph Wright of Derby. Tate Gallery, London.

Universal Access

English Learners

Help students identify with the speaker. Ask them to imagine a time when they have felt like the speaker—sad, far from someone they love, unable to sleep, or alone with their thoughts. As students read the poem in that frame of mind, ask them to write notes about what they relate to most in the poems and why.

✔ See **UA: Differentiating Instruction** for strategies for teaching English learners.

Struggling Readers

Model using text structure to understand meaning in Sonnet 29. You might say: "When I read a Shakespearean sonnet, I try to break the sonnet into quatrains and couplets and analyze the main idea of each. The first quatrain states the speaker's problem; the second quatrain tells what the speaker hopes for. The third quatrain brings the 'turn,' and the final couplet usually resolves the problem, often with humor."

✔ See **UA: Differentiating Instruction** for strategies for teaching struggling readers.

SONNET

Sonnet 30

by **William Shakespeare**

Read with a Purpose
Read this sonnet to understand how the speaker overcomes feelings of loss and regret.

Build Background
Shakespeare begins this sonnet with a strikingly original metaphor. Periods of quiet meditation are called **sessions,** as though they were court trials in which one's thoughts come to the bar of justice to hear their cases tried. (*Sessions* is a British legal term that refers to minor court cases.)

When to the sessions of sweet silent thought
I summon up remembrance of things past,
I sigh the lack of many a thing I sought,
And with old woes new wail° my dear time's waste.°
Then can I drown an eye (unused to flow)
For precious friends hid in death's dateless° night,
And weep afresh love's long since canceled woe,
And moan th' expense° of many a vanished sight.°
Then can I grieve at grievances foregone, Ⓐ
And heavily from woe to woe tell° o'er
The sad account of fore° bemoanèd moan,
Which I new pay as if not paid before.
But if the while I think on thee, dear friend,
All losses are restored and sorrows end. Ⓑ

4. **new wail:** again lament. **my . . . waste:** the damage that time has done to things dear to me.
6. **dateless:** endless.
8. **expense:** loss. **vanished sight:** things gone, such as dead friends.
10. **tell:** count.
11. **fore:** already.

Ⓐ **Literary Focus** **Shakespearean Sonnets** What sorrows trouble the speaker in the second quatrain?

Ⓑ **Reading Focus** **Using Text Structure to Understand Meaning** How does the speaker's attitude change in the final couplet?

Vocabulary **summon** (SUHM uhn) *v.:* call.

The Happy Lovers, by Gustav Courbet (1844). Musée des Beaux-Arts, Lyon, France.

Teacher Preparation
Selection Summary
In Sonnet 30, the narrator remembers the past with sorrow and regret; in the last couplet, he says the memories of his friend are joyful.

Direct Teach

Think About/Talk About
Read with a Purpose Tell students to read the Read with a Purpose statement. Ask them how they or someone else overcame loss and regret, and why it was or was not difficult.

Comprehension
Ⓑ Reading Focus
Possible response: *Though he does not say why, the speaker abruptly stops grieving when he thinks again of the one to whom he addresses the poem.*

Analysis
Ⓐ Literary Focus
Possible response: *bereavement at the death of friends; regret for lost love*

Extend the Discussion
Evaluating What is the effect of the sibilance of the consonants in lines 1–4? ***Possible response:*** *Sibilance tends to slow the words down. The sound is soft and hushed, like a whisper. It adds to the gentle, melancholy tone.*

Vocabulary: Own the Word
- **scorn:** Tell students that some synonyms for the word *scorn* are *belittle, contempt,* and *disdain.* Remind students that synonyms often have different shades of meaning. Ask students to arrange the words on a continuum in order from positive to negative. ***Possible response:*** *belittle, scorn, disdain, contempt*
- **summon:** Ask students to explain what the speaker of Sonnet 30 *summons.* ***Possible response:*** *memories of things and times past*

California Standards, p. 394
- **Reading Standard 2.2** Analyze the way in which clarity of meaning is affected by the patterns of organization, hierarchical structures, repetition of the main ideas, syntax, and word choice in the in the text.
- **Reading Standard 3.1** Analyze characteristics of subgenres (e.g., satire, parody, allegory, pastoral) that are used in poetry, prose, plays, novels, short stories, essays, and other basic genres.
- **Reading Standard 3.3** Analyze the ways in which irony, tone, mood, the author's style, and the "sound" of language achieve specific rhetorical or aesthetic purposes or both.
- **Writing Standard 1.2** Use point of view, characterization, style (e.g., use of irony), and related elements for specific rhetorical and aesthetic purposes.

Check for Understanding

Independent Practice

Reading Skills Focus

Possible responses:

1. *In each sonnet, he expresses why he needs his beloved and how his beloved lifts his spirits.*
2. *Sonnets 29 and 30 share the same themes: thinking of a loved one can ameliorate sorrow about the past and departed loved ones.*

Vocabulary Check

3. *b*
4. *c*
5. *a*

Literary Skills Focus

Possible response:

6. *At the peak of summer's beauty, its natural elements destroy it.*
7. *In both poems, the despondent speaker is restored by thinking of someone he loves.*
8. *Starting with line 1 in Sonnet 30, the speaker uses dry, emotionless legal language to describe his sorrow—for example, the words* summon, canceled, expense, grievances, *and* account.
9. *In Sonnet 30, the turn that usually comes at line 9 does not come until line 13, lengthening the time it takes the speaker to recover from his morose state.*
10. *Beginning with the word* Shall, *Sonnet 18 repeats* sh *in* shake, shines, short, complexion, possession, *and* shade. *The repetition gives the poem a slow, hushed sensuality.*

Applying Your Skills

Reading Standard 2.2, 3.1, 3.3 (see pages A48–A50)
Writing Standard 1.2 (see pages A51–A52)

Sonnets 18, 29, and 30

Literary Response and Analysis

Reading Skills Focus

Read with a Purpose

1. What is the speaker's attitude toward his loved one in each of these sonnets?

Reading Skills: Using Text Structure to Understand Meaning

2. As you read, you tracked the turn, or shift in thought, in each sonnet. Now, use clues from the turn and couplet to determine the overall theme.

Poem	Turn, or Shift in Thought	Theme
Sonnet 18	In line 9, focus shifts from nature's thoughts to the beloved	Art that describes love can make love eternal.
Sonnet 29		

Vocabulary Check

Match each Vocabulary word with its antonym.

3. scorn — a. extreme
4. summon — b. appreciate
5. temperate — c. dismiss

Literary Skills Focus

Literary Analysis

6. **Interpret** In the first two quatrains of Sonnet 18, what are the speaker's feelings about summer?
7. **Compare and Contrast** What similarities can you find in the main ideas in Sonnets 29 and 30?
8. **Evaluate** Shakespeare's sonnets use **conceits,** elaborate figures of speech that draw a surprising connection between two seemingly dissimilar things. In these sonnets, which conceit makes the most unexpected comparison? Explain.

Literary Skills: Shakespearean Sonnets

9. **Analyze** Shakespeare adheres to basic sonnet structure, but he plays with the rules. For example, one quatrain may not contain a complete thought, or the turn may not occur on a single line. Find an example of Shakespeare's deviation from structure, and explain its effect.

Literary Skills Review: Alliteration

10. **Extend** The repetition of consonant sounds in words close to one another, **alliteration,** increases a poem's musical effects and the connection between words. Find an example of alliteration in the sonnet and tell how it contributes to the poem's sound and meaning.

Writing Skills Focus

Think as a Reader/Writer

Use It in Your Writing As you read, you recorded Shakespeare's metaphors. Choose one or two that you found particularly powerful. What is unexpected and striking about the comparisons? Now, write out several metaphors that you could use in a poem.

What Do You Think Now? In each sonnet, how do the speaker's emotions affect how he thinks about the world?

For CHOICES see page 400.

Universal Access

Struggling Writers

Some students may need additional scaffolding to complete the Writing Skills Focus activity. To help students create effective, vivid metaphors, invite them first to consider a noun referring to a fundamental human emotion (i.e., love, friendship, respect). Then, ask students to use free-association to think about objects that they link to that emotion. Have students choose one word to create a metaphor and write one sentence to explain it.

What Do You Think Now?

Tell students to reference the poems in response to the question. Tell them to list the emotions the speaker expresses, either overtly or by implication. (For example, he never says he is lonely, though it seems he is.) Then, tell them to look for clues in the poem about his world outlook—for example, his belief, in Sonnet 29, that others have it better than he does.

SONNET

Sonnet 71

by **William Shakespeare**

Read with a Purpose
Read this sonnet to learn how the speaker wants his beloved to act after his death.

Build Background
In several of his sonnets, Shakespeare emphasizes the age difference between the speaker and his lover. The speaker is often portrayed as older than his beloved and will presumably die first.

No longer mourn for me when I am dead
Than you shall hear the surly sullen bell
Give warning to the world that I am fled
From this vile world, with vilest worms to dwell. **A**
Nay, if you read this line, remember not
The hand that writ it; for I love you so **B**
That I in your sweet thoughts would be forgot
If thinking on me then should make you woe.
O, if, I say, you look upon this verse
When I, perhaps, compounded am with clay,
Do not so much as my poor name rehearse,
But let your love even with my life decay,
Lest the wise world should look into your moan
And mock you with me after I am gone.

A Reading Focus **Using Text Structure to Understand Meaning** What poetic device does Shakespeare use in lines 4–5 to emphasize the idea of a vile world?

B Literary Focus **Shakespearean Sonnets** How do the speaker's tone and focus shift in line 6?

Vocabulary **surly** (SUR lee) *adj.:* bad-tempered; unfriendly.

St. Catherine's Parish Church, Eskdale Cumbria, England.

Universal Access

Struggling Readers

Struggling Students Remind students that Shakespearean sonnets often have a turn, or a shift in focus and thought. Explain to students that in Sonnet 71, the shift in mood is more subtle than in the preceding sonnets. Have students read lines 1–5 of the sonnet. Encourage students to record the negative words that Shakespeare uses in these lines [*vile, sullen, surly, worms, mourn*]. Then, have students read the next four lines. Point out the words *love* and *sweet thoughts.* Tell students that in these lines, Shakespeare's tone has shifted. He moves from discussing the bitter negativity about both life and death to deep tenderness toward his beloved.

As students continue to read Shakespeare's sonnets, encourage them to examine the diction used in the poems. Doing so may help them identify where the turn occurs.

Teacher Preparation

Selection Summary

The speaker alternates between bitterness and tenderness, urging his lover not to mourn his death. He hopes to shield his beloved from grief and from others' snide comments about their relationship.

Direct Teach

Think About/Talk About

Read with a Purpose Before students read Sonnet 71, tell them to anticipate what the speaker will ask his beloved to do after his death.

Comprehension

A Reading Focus

Possible response: *Worms are often a metaphor or symbol for death. The speaker also uses alliteration, repeating the* v *and* w *sounds. The words* worms *and* world *share the same vowel sound.*

Analysis

B Literary Focus

Possible response: *In line 6, he describes whom the speaker should not remember and begins to profess his love.*

Extend the Discussion

Evaluating What is the speaker's tone? Does he seem resigned to his death or saddened by it? ***Possible response:*** *His tone is sorrowful, somber, and serious, as if he dreads rather than accepts death.*

Vocabulary: Own the Word

surly: Demonstrate the facial expression of someone who has a *surly* attitude. Then, ask one or two students to stand at their desks and demonstrate.

Teacher Preparation
Selection Summary
In Sonnet 73, the speaker describes aging, using images of autumn, twilight, ruins, and a dying fire. He reflects that his impending death makes him even dearer to his younger lover.

Direct Teach

Think About/Talk About
Read with a Purpose Have students read the Read with a Purpose statement. Before they read Sonnet 73, ask students what problems and concerns aging poses.

Comprehension
A Reading Focus
Possible response: *Lines 5 and 9 are parallel; they use the same structure of "In me thou see'st . . ." Each line is followed with three lines of descriptive imagery.*

Analysis
B Literary Focus
Possible response: *In the first twelve lines, the speaker compares himself to things that fade or die: the trees in autumn, a day that is turning to night, and a dying fire. The turn occurs in line 13, when the speaker notes that his beloved loves him all the more knowing they have little time left together.*

Extend the Discussion
Meter What meter do you hear in Sonnet 73? ***Possible response:*** *The sonnet is written in the standard iambic pentameter used for sonnets.*

SONNET

Sonnet 73

by **William Shakespeare**

Read with a Purpose
Read this sonnet to see how the speaker's aging affects his beloved.

Build Background
As in Sonnet 71, the speaker of Sonnet 73 dwells on the fact that he is growing older. Each quatrain creates and develops a different metaphor for aging.

That time of year thou mayst in me behold
When yellow leaves, or none, or few, do hang
Upon those boughs which shake against the cold,
Bare ruined choirs° where late the sweet birds sang.
In me thou see'st the twilight of such day
As after sunset fadeth in the west,
Which by and by black night doth take away,
Death's second self, that seals up all in rest.
In me thou see'st the glowing of such fire, **A**
That on the ashes of his youth doth lie
As the deathbed whereon it must expire,
Consumed with that which it was nourished by.°
  This thou perceivest, which makes thy love more strong,
  To love that well which thou must leave ere long. **B**

4. choirs: parts of a church or cathedral in which services are held. The landscape of Shakespeare's England was dotted with church ruins, a result of Henry VIII's destruction of monasteries.

12. consumed . . . nourished by: choked by the ashes of the wood that once fed its flame.

A Reading Focus **Using Text Structure to Understand Meaning** What parallel structures does Shakespeare use to introduce each metaphor for age and death?

B Literary Focus **Shakespearean Sonnets** Find the turn, or shift in thought, in this sonnet. What does the speaker tell his beloved in the final couplet?

Vocabulary **expire** (ehk SPYR) *v.:* die; come to an end.

Universal Access

EL English Learners
English for Academic Success Shakespeare's archaic vocabulary and diction will challenge English learners and may impede them from being able to understand the meaning of the sonnets. You might ease students into each sonnet by first guiding them in identifying, pronouncing, and defining the rhyming phrases at the end of the lines. Then, pair students with a proficient English speaker. Have them read each sonnet aloud and work together to paraphrase each quatrain and couplet. Discuss students' ideas after they have read each sonnet.

Struggling Readers
Explain to students that in Sonnet 116, Shakespeare makes allusions to images with which they may be unfamiliar. For example, in lines 7–8, Shakespeare uses the image of Polaris to convey the idea that love remains constant just as a ship relies on the North Star to guide its course. Point out that in lines 9–10, the speaker alludes to the medieval image of time as the grim reaper, who cuts off life with the sweep of a sickle. Explain that understanding these allusions will help them understand the train of thought in the sonnet.

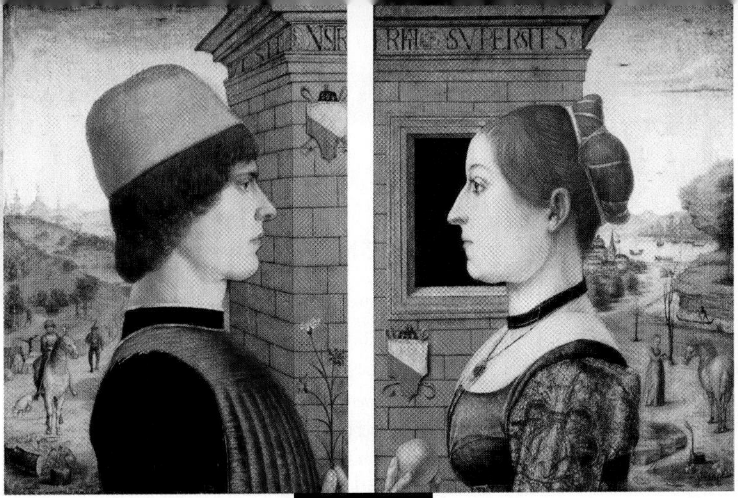

Members of the Gozzadini family, Emilian School (15th century). The Metropolitan Museum of Art, Robert Lehman Collection, 1975.1.96.

SONNET

Sonnet 116

by **William Shakespeare**

Read with a Purpose

Read to discover the speaker's feelings about the constancy of love.

Build Background

In this sonnet, Shakespeare asserts that true love is firm against all "impediments." *Impediments* is a word taken from the wedding ceremony of the Church of England: "If any of you know cause or just impediment why these persons should not be joined together . . ."

Let me not to the marriage of true minds
Admit impediments. Love is not love
Which alters when it alteration finds,
Or bends with the remover to remove. **A**
Oh no! It is an ever-fixèd mark°
That looks on tempests and is never shaken.
It is the star to every wandering bark,°
Whose worth's unknown, although his height be taken.°
Love's not Time's fool, though rosy lips and cheeks
Within his bending sickle's compass° come.
Love alters not with his brief hours and weeks,
But bears it out° even to the edge of doom.
If this be error and upon me proved,
I never writ, nor no man ever loved. **B**

5. mark: seamark; a prominent object onshore that serves as a guide to sailors.
7. bark: boat.
8. height be taken: altitude measured to determine a ship's position.
10. compass: range; reach.
12. bears it out: survives.

A Reading Focus **Using Text Structure to Understand Meaning** What argument, or thesis, does Shakespeare establish in the first quatrain?

B Literary Focus **Shakespearean Sonnets** What does the speaker conclude in the final couplet?

Vocabulary **impediments** (ihm PEHD uh muhnts) *n. pl.:* obstacles; obstructions.

Teacher Preparation
Selection Summary

In Sonnet 116, the speaker offers an idealistic definition of love: Love stands constant despite the passage of time or the fading of beauty. If he is wrong, he claims, then he is not a writer and no one ever loved.

Direct Teach

Think About/Talk About

Read with a Purpose Ask the class to define the quality of constancy. Guide their thinking by asking them how constancy might be important in love and other endeavors.

Comprehension

A Reading Focus

Possible response: *True love never changes even if everything else in the world is changing.*

Analysis

B Literary Focus

Possible response: *The speaker is confident in his assertion. If he were wrong, it would mean nothing he believed as true ever existed—that he never wrote (which he has) and that no one has ever loved (which is impossible).*

Vocabulary: Own the Word

- **expire:** Remind students that *expire* means "come to an end." Read the following sentence aloud to students and have them complete the sentence: "Because my gym membership was about to *expire*. . . ." ***Possible response:*** *I decided to renew it right away.*
- **impediments:** Ask students what *impediments* might affect a student's performance on a test. ***Possible responses:*** *loud noises; lack of studying; a ticking clock*

Advanced Learners

Enrichment Challenge students to compare and contrast Sonnets 18 and 73 and to use the poems' text as their only source. Have them share their notes with a partner, in small groups, or as a class. Then, have students discuss the similarities and differences in their ideas and observations about the sonnets.

AAVE Students Who Use African American Vernacular English

English for Academic Success Some students may have difficulty with *'s* that indicates a singular possessive, such as *Time's fool.* They may omit the pronunciation of the *'s* in speaking and not include it in writing. Write on the board: "_______ sickle cuts down youth." Ask students how this sentence should begin. Then, ask a volunteer to read the sentence aloud. Have students look for other examples of *'s* in Shakespeare's sonnets and practice reading the line aloud to a partner. Walk around the classroom to monitor students' pronunciation of the possessives.

✔ For additional instruction and strategies, see **Holt Pronunciation Resources** and **ThinkCentral, Teacher Access.**

Teacher Preparation

Selection Summary

The speaker of Sonnet 130 describes the object of his love with humorous frankness: She is far from the idealized damsel of conventional love poems; instead, she is an ordinary mortal. Yet, he stresses, he can love such a woman as much as he scorns hackneyed poetic conventions.

Direct Teach

Think About/Talk About

Read with a Purpose After students read the Read with a Purpose statement, ask them to discuss with a partner how images of men and women are idealized today.

Comprehension

B Reading Focus

Possible response: *She is not idealized. The speaker describes her as having ungainly features.*

Analysis

A Literary Focus

Possible response: *It does not matter to the speaker that she does not have superficial beauty; he loves her anyway.*

Extend the Discussion

Determining Author's Purpose

What, in your opinion, was Shakespeare's purpose in writing Sonnet 130? ***Possible response:*** *His purpose might have been to amuse readers by mocking trite conceits, or to affirm that love exists between real—not idealized—men and women.*

Vocabulary: Own the Word

reeks: Remind students that *reeks* means that something "has a strong, bad smell." Ask students to name a food that *reeks.* ***Possible responses:*** *brussels sprouts; tuna fish; cheese*

SONNET

Sonnet 130

by **William Shakespeare**

Read with a Purpose

Read this sonnet to see how and why the speaker shuns describing his mistress in unconventional ways.

Build Background

In this sonnet, Shakespeare ridicules the fashionable, exaggerated metaphors some of his fellow poets were using to describe the women they loved: "Your eyes are suns that set me on fire, your cheeks are roses, your breasts are white as snow." These overwrought metaphors, known as **conceits,** are traceable to Petrarch, but by 1600 they had become tiresome or laughable due to excessive use. Note that in Renaissance usage, the word *mistress* simply meant "girlfriend."

My mistress' eyes are nothing like the sun,
Coral is far more red than her lips' red.
If snow be white, why then her breasts are dun,°
If hairs be wires, black wires grow on her head.
I have seen roses damasked,° red and white,
But no such roses see I in her cheeks.
And in some perfumes is there more delight
Than in the breath that from my mistress reeks,
I love to hear her speak, yet well I know
That music hath a far more pleasing sound.
I grant I never saw a goddess go,
My mistress, when she walks, treads on the ground. **A**
And yet, by Heaven, I think my love as rare
As any she belied° with false compare. **B**

3. **dun:** dull, grayish brown.

5. **damasked:** marked or streaked in two colors.

14. **belied:** misrepresented.

A Literary Focus **Shakespearean Sonnets** What is unusual about the speaker's description of his beloved in this sonnet?

B Reading Focus **Using Text Structure to Understand Meaning** How does the final couplet clarify the speaker's attitude toward his mistress?

Vocabulary **reeks** (reeks) *v.:* has a strong, bad smell.

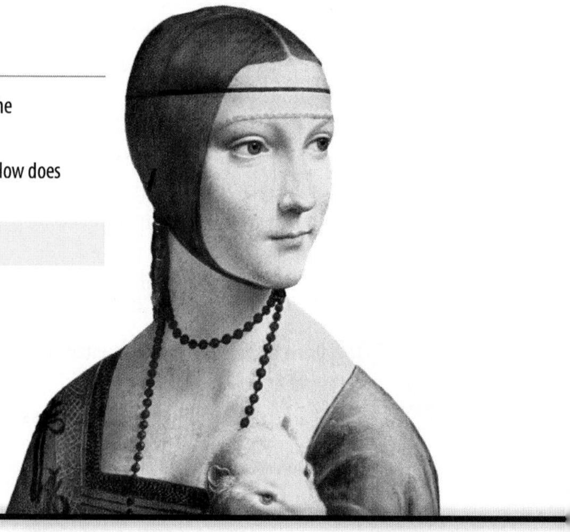

The Lady with the Ermine, by Leonardo da Vinci (1496). Czartoryski Museum, Krakow, Poland.

California Standards, pp. 399–400

- **Reading Standard 2.2** Analyze the way in which clarity of meaning is affected by the patterns of organization, hierarchical structures, repetition of the main ideas, syntax, and word choice in the text.
- **Reading Standard 3.1** Analyze characteristics of subgenres (e.g., satire, parody, allegory, pastoral) that are used in poetry, prose, plays, novels, short stories, essays, and other basic genres.
- **Reading Standard 3.3** Analyze the ways in which irony, tone, mood, the author's style, and the "sound" of language achieve specific rhetorical or aesthetic purposes or both.
- **Writing Standard 2.2** Write responses to literature: **b.** Analyze the use of imagery, language, universal themes, and unique aspects of the text.
- **Writing Standard 2.6** Deliver multimedia presentations: **a.** Combine text, images, and sound and draw information from many sources (e.g., television broadcasts, videos, films, newspapers, magazines, CD-ROMs, the Internet, electronic media-generated images).
- **Listening and Speaking Standard 2.3** Deliver oral responses to literature: **b.** Analyze the imagery, language, universal themes, and unique aspects of the text through the use of rhetorical strategies (e.g., narration, description, persuasion, exposition, a combination of those strategies).

Applying Your Skills

Reading Standard 2.2, 3.1, 3.3 (see pages A48–A50)
Writing Standard 2.2b (see pages A51–A52)

Sonnets 71, 73, 116, and 130

Literary Response and Analysis

Reading Skills Focus

Read with a Purpose

1. According to the speaker in these poems, what effects do time and nature have on love?

Reading Skills: Using Text Structure to Understand Meaning

2. As you read, you noted the location of the turn in each of the sonnets. Now, add your conclusions about theme and the details that support those conclusions.

Poem	Turn, or Shift in Thought	Theme	Supporting Details
Sonnet 71			
Sonnet 73			

Vocabulary Check

Match each Vocabulary word with its synonym.

3. surly — a. sullen
4. reeks — b. hindrances
5. impediments — c. perish
6. expire — d. stinks

Literary Skills Focus

Literary Analysis

7. **Analyze** In Sonnet 71, is the speaker sincere when he calls the world *wise?* Explain.
8. **Interpret** In Sonnet 73, how does the speaker's age affect his beloved?
9. **Compare and Contrast** How do the sentiments expressed in Sonnets 116 and 130 differ?
10. **Evaluate** Which sonnet expresses the most profound thoughts about love? Which has the greatest emotional impact? Use details in your answer.

Literary Skills: Shakespearean Sonnets

11. **Analyze** Shakespeare adheres to the basic sonnet structure but plays with the rules. Give an example of something he does that is unexpected in one of these four sonnets. What is the effect of the deviation?

Literary Skills Review: Tone

12. **Analyze** The writer's attitude toward the subject or the reader is called **tone.** Compare and contrast the tones of these four sonnets.

Writing Skills Focus

Think as a Reader/Writer

Use It in Your Writing What metaphors are used to describe love in Sonnet 116? How do these metaphors express the poem's theme? Using your own metaphors, write a short essay about the fleetingness or the permanence of love.

What Do You Think Now? In each sonnet, how do the speaker's emotions affect how he thinks about the world?

Check for Understanding

Independent Practice

Reading Skills Focus

Possible responses:

1. *He declares that time and nature have no effect on true love; however, he fears change and dying.*
2. *Have students make their conclusions about theme in each sonnet based on details.*

Vocabulary Check

3. *a* 4. *d*
5. *b* 6. *c*

Literary Skills Focus

Possible response:

7. *The near rhyme of vile in line 4 with wise may be an intended echo. The speaker does not respect critics' opinions but acknowledges their power.*
8. *The speaker thinks his beloved sees his youth fading and fears that their time together will soon come to an end.*
9. *Sonnet 116 speaks of abstract love with reverence; Sonnet 130 describes the woman he loves humorously.*
10. *Sonnet 130 criticizes a superficial social convention; Sonnet 116 expresses a profound belief about love.*
11. *In Sonnet 73, the speaker does not turn the argument until the couplet. The sonnet's resolution is abrupt, with little space for elaboration.*
12. *The tone in Sonnet 71 and Sonnet 73 is serious and gloomy in contrast to the assertive tone of Sonnet 116 and Sonnet 130.*

Universal Access

Struggling Writers

Some students may need additional scaffolding to complete the Writing Skills Focus activity. Tell students that the main idea of Sonnet 116 is the eternity of love. Explain that in the poem, Shakespeare uses two metaphors to help convey this idea. Before students write their essays, have them work in pairs to identify the metaphors Shakespeare uses. [*It is an ever-fixed mark (line 5); It is the star to every wandering bark (line 7)*] Have students discuss these metaphors in pairs. Then, have them use their ideas to help them write their essays.

What Do You Think Now?

As students think about the question, tell them to consider Shakespeare's ultimate purpose for writing each sonnet. Ask students to articulate what message he intended to convey.

Independent Practice

Choices: Evaluation Criteria

Review: **Homework**
Compare Petrarch and Shakespeare

- Students demonstrate clear understanding of the structure of the sonnet.
- Students demonstrate understanding of the themes of each sonnet.
- Students identify similar and different elements in Petrarchan and Shakespearean sonnet.

Connect: **Homework**
Compose Modern Messages

- Students' choices are supported by their background knowledge and their study of the sonnets.
- Students can provide solid rationale for the choices they make.

Extend: **Homework**
Sing a Song of Shakespeare

- Students' ideas demonstrate originality.
- Students' work respectfully acknowledges their audience.

Applying Your Skills

Reading Standard 2.2, 3.1 (see pages A48–A50)
Writing Standard 2.2b, 2.6a (see pages A51–A52)
Listening and Speaking Standard 2.3b (see pages A53–A55)

Sonnets 71, 73, 116, and 130

CHOICES

As you respond to the Choices, use these **Academic Vocabulary** words as appropriate: establish, ensure, widespread, controversy, contradiction.

REVIEW

Compare Petrarch and Shakespeare

Unlike the Shakespearean sonnet, the Petrarchan sonnet is divided into an eight-line octave and a six-line sestet. In a Petrarchan sonnet, the turn or shift usually occurs on or near the ninth line. Read Sonnet 42 by Petrarch. Write a brief essay comparing his sonnet to one of Shakespeare's. Consider the structure of the poems as well as the language, imagery, themes, and poetic devices.

Sonnet 42

by **Petrarch**

The spring returns, the spring wind softly
  blowing *a*
Sprinkles the grass with gleam and glitter of
  showers, *b*
Powdering pearl and diamond, dripping with
  flowers, *b*
Dropping wet flowers, dancing the winters going; *a*
The swallow twitters, the groves of midnight are
  glowing *a*
With nightingale music and madness; the sweet
  fierce powers *b*
Of love flame up through the earth; the seed-soul
  towers *b*
And trembles; nature is filled to overflowing . . . *a*
The spring returns, but there is no returning *c*
Of spring for me. O heart with anguish burning! *c*
She that unlocked all April in a breath *d*
Returns not . . . And these meadows, blossoms,
  birds *e*
These lovely gentle girls—words, empty words *e*
As bitter as the black estates of death! *d*

—translated by Joseph Auslander

CONNECT

Compose Modern Messages

TechFocus Many of these sonnets function as messages from the speaker to a loved one. Today, people can send personal messages through various avenues, such as e-mail, voice mail, songs, and greeting cards. Choose two of the sonnets, and re-create their messages in one of these modern forms. Present your revised message to your class. Which form do you think is more effective at establishing and conveying its message? Which form is more powerful? Why do you think so?

EXTEND

Sing a Song of Shakespeare

Over the years, setting Shakespeare's poems to music has become a widespread practice. Choose two of your favorite sonnets from this collection, and search for melodies for each. If you can, write original music for them. Alternatively, you can pick famous existing melodies that you feel express the tone and mood of the sonnet. Play the melodies for your class, enlisting the help of a musical classmate to sing for you. Explain why you picked those particular sonnets and melodies and why you feel they express the mood of Shakespeare's poems.

Chateau de Chaumont Tapestry Set (16th century), by French School, 19600.176.3.
The Cleveland Museum of Art, Leonard C. Hanna, Jr. Fund.

Learn It Online
Find out how media literate you are online.
go.hrw.com H12-400 Go

Assess

Unit 2 Resources, Selection Standards Check, p. 98

ThinkCentral Online Assessment, Selection Standards Check

Teacher One Stop™, editable Selection Standards Check

Reteach

ThinkCentral Online Remediation

Learn It Online
For an in-depth look at media literacy, direct students to the **MediaScope** mini-site, which shows students how to create, analyze, and critique media.
go.hrw.com H12-400 Go

Reading Standard 2.2 (see pages A48–A50)

Using Questioning to Monitor Reading by Kylene Beers

When we say someone is lost in a book, we usually mean that he or she is totally absorbed by a good story. It is also possible to get lost in a book in quite a different way if—for one reason or another—you are confused about what the text means.

Some texts are more challenging than others to read. Works written in a different culture or time period often use unfamiliar settings, expressions, and archaic vocabulary. Use the footnotes provided to explain the meanings of words that are unfamiliar to you.

When a text is written in poetic verse, the meter (iambic pentameter in the case of Shakespeare's *Macbeth*) can be intimidating. Remember that iambic pentameter imitates the natural rhythm of human speech; when a section is confusing, read it aloud.

In addition to using footnotes and reading aloud, read the summary provided for each scene. Also, read the stage directions. Both will provide you with background information and context that you need.

Even with these aids, sometimes you need to ask yourself questions when you feel lost in a challenging text. For example, read the following excerpt from Act I, Scene 2 of *Macbeth*.

> **Malcolm:** This is the sergeant
> Who like a good and hardy soldier fought
> 'Gainst my captivity. Hail, brave friend!
> Say to the king the knowledge of the broil
> As thou didst leave it.

The stage directions and summary for the scene explain that Malcolm is with King Duncan and a bleeding captain fresh from the battlefield. The footnote defines *broil* as "quarrel." Using these clues, you can form a good question: What is Malcolm asking the wounded soldier (whom he calls *sergeant*) to do? The answer is that Malcolm asks him to give the king current information about the battle.

Let us use this technique again with this passage from Act I, Scene 3 (lines 39–43).

> **Banquo:** What are these
> So withered, and so wild in their attire,
> That look not like th' inhabitants o' th' earth,
> And yet are on't? Live you, or are you aught
> That man may question?

The summary and scene directions tell you that Banquo and Macbeth have met three witches. Using clues from the text ("withered, and wild"; they "look not like" inhabitants of the earth), you can infer that Banquo is asking whether or not the witches are real.

Your Turn

Read this passage from Act I, Scene 3, and then ask yourself questions to monitor your understanding. Which of your own questions can you answer?

> **Ross:**
> And for an earnest of a greater honor,
> He bade me, from him, call thee Thane of Cawdor;
> In which addition, hail, most worthy thane!
> For it is thine.

Learn It Online
For more information on this historical period see
go.hrw.com H12-401 Go

Reading Skills Focus

Objectives

Students will learn how to use questioning to monitor reading comprehension.

Unit 2 Resources, Reading Focus Skill Builder, p. 94

Teacher One Stop™, on-level lesson plan and all print resources

Direct Teach

Using Questioning to Monitor Reading

This feature gives students practice in using questioning to monitor reading in *Macbeth*, a Shakespearean tragedy written in poetic verse that presents challenging content. Have students read the feature and complete the Your Turn activity before reading the tragedy.

Check for Understanding

Your Turn

Ask students to consider what they know about thanes from previous selections. [*Students may ask, "Who ordered the pledge?" and "Why is this pledge given to Macbeth?" Students may answer that the king is the only one who dispenses honorary titles, such as that of thane. The King awards Macbeth the title of thane for his success in battle.*]

Universal Access

English Learners/ Struggling Readers

English for Academic Success Begin by telling students about "stage directions." Explain that stage directions are instructions that tell the actors how they should move on the stage, or that tell about the look of the stage when a scene opens. Add that stage directions are written in italics and appear between brackets. Remind students that stage directions contain precious information for the understanding of a play.

California Standards, p. 401

- **Reading Standard 2.2** Analyze the way in which clarity of meaning is affected by the patterns of organization, hierarchical structures, repetition of the main ideas, syntax, and word choice in the text.

Learn It Online
You can introduce some of the topics in this unit using brief videos about the literature of this period.
go.hrw.com H12-401 Go

Standards Focus

Objectives

Students will
- understand characteristics of a tragedy
- use questioning to monitor reading comprehension

English for Academic Success

Academic Vocabulary

Look for opportunities to use the Academic Vocabulary words in this unit.

- **contradiction, *n.*:** statement in opposition to another; inconsistency
- **controversies, *n.*:** lengthy disagreement
- **ensure, *v.*:** to make certain
- **established, *v.*:** set up; caused to happen
- **widespread, *adj.*:** occurring over a wide area

Direct Teach

Think About/Talk About

Build Background: Inspiration for Macbeth

During a visit to Oxford in August 1606, King James enjoyed a show that featured three sibyls reciting Latin verses containing prophesies to Banquo, James's ancestor and the founder of the house of Stuart. About six weeks later, Shakespeare and his company came to Oxford. Some scholars believe that, upon hearing of the king's favorable reaction to the entertainment, he decided to write *Macbeth*.

Introduction to THE TRAGEDY of MACBETH

Sources of the Play

Shakespeare's play *Macbeth* conforms to the general rule of Renaissance tragedies that states that the drama had to be about real people whose deeds are recorded in history. (Renaissance comedies, on the other hand, concerned the imaginary doings of fictitious characters.) Shakespeare took the main events of Macbeth's career as king of Scotland (1040–1057) from Raphael Holinshed's *Chronicles of England, Scotland, and Ireland* (1577), Shakespeare's source for historical material for many of his plays.

Ellen Terry as Lady Macbeth (1885-1886), by John Singer Sargent. Tate Gallery, London.

There are striking differences, however, between Shakespeare's account of Macbeth and Holinshed's. The historical Macbeth had a much more legitimate claim to King Duncan's throne than did the Macbeth of Shakespeare. The historical Macbeth gained the throne with the help of other nobles dissatisfied with King Duncan, and he ruled rather successfully. In contrast, Shakespeare's Macbeth has no supporters except his wife, whose strong and ambitious nature Shakespeare develops from a brief moment in history. Furthermore, in the play, the reign of Macbeth and his wife brings nothing but violence and disaster to Scotland.

One explanation for these changes to Holinshed's story is that Shakespeare wanted to explore—from a safe distance—the events and attitudes of his own time. Contemporary audiences have all but lost sight of the scandal that was a backdrop for the play: the Gunpowder Plot of 1605, in which several Catholic zealots plotted to blow up King James I and his Protestant Parliament. Garry Wills, a professor and political columnist, says that for its Elizabethan audience, *Macbeth* was a thriller. (According to Wills, the Gunpowder Plot would compare to a plan to bomb the U.S. Capitol building during a presidential address.) The threat to an anointed king, and the perceived evil behind it, was relived in Macbeth's imperilment of the social order in a Scotland of the distant past.

Shakespeare altered his source text, in ways both small and large, in order to pay homage to his own king and country; his changes were intended for an audience of his particular moment in history. If King James, the patron of Shakespeare's company, ever saw the play, it must have pleased him. Since he had recently survived the Gunpowder Plot, James was especially interested in attacks on kings; he always defended the idea that he ruled by divine right. Moreover, James was a Scot and claimed to be a direct descendant of Banquo, to whom the third witch says, "Thou shalt get kings, though thou be none." For these reasons, scholars have long considered *Macbeth* a play written for a command performance at court, despite having no direct evidence. James reportedly refused to sit through long plays, and this royal shortcoming has even been used to explain the fact that *Macbeth* is one of Shakespeare's shortest plays.

We can also say that Shakespeare made many changes in Holinshed's story because Shakespeare was much more interested in psychological truth than in historical fact. In this sense, *Macbeth* is also about *real* people, men and women tempted by ambition and power, caught up in a web of wants and needs. In playing out these real feelings and desires, Shakespeare's *Macbeth* transcends the historical Macbeth and gives us a portrait and a play for all times. As the critic Sylvan Barnet notes, "When one reads or sees *Macbeth,* one cannot help feeling that one is experiencing a re-creation or representation of what a man is, in the present, even in the timeless."

Three Witches, by Johann Heinrich Fuessli, oil on canvas. Royal Shakespeare Theater Collection, London.

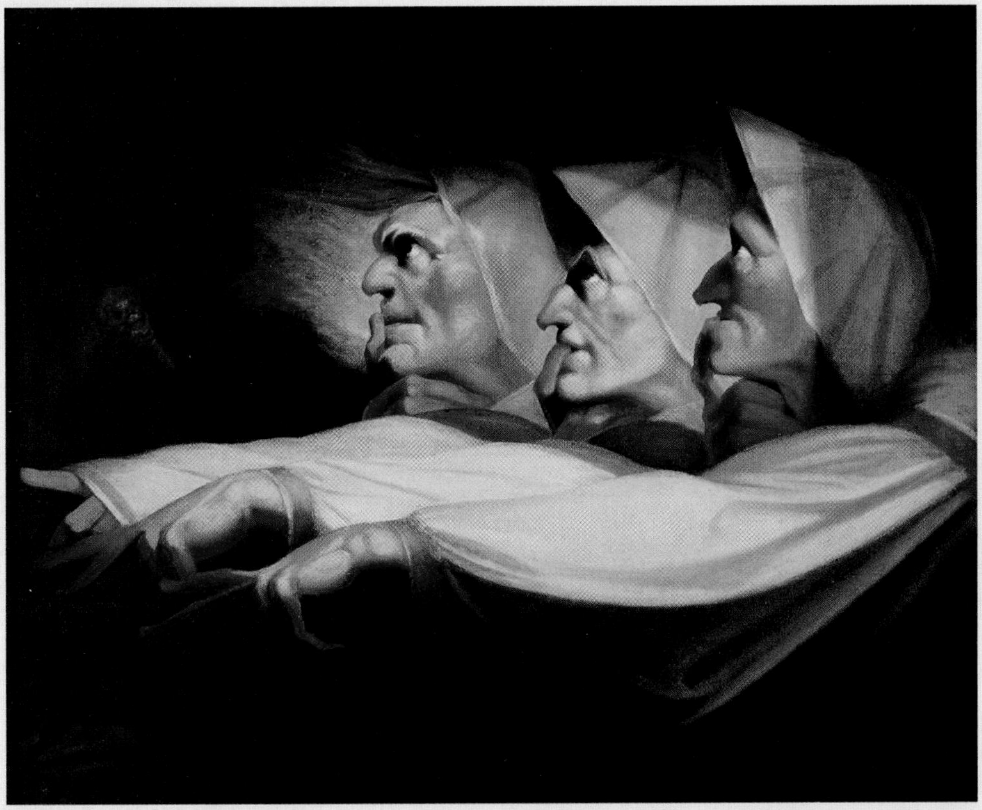

Think About/Talk About

Build Background: The History Behind Macbeth

Some critics believe that Shakespeare consulted Buchanan's *History of Scotland* while writing the play, because elements of Macbeth's characterization are more similar to this account than they are to Holinshed's. Other possible sources include Seneca's *Medea* and Aeschylus's *Agamemnon*.

Monitor Students' Comprehension

To check students' understanding of the connection between James I and *Macbeth*, ask them to explain what the Gunpowder Plot of 1605 has to do with the play. [*The Gunpowder Plot was an attempt by Catholics to kill James, the reigning king, who was a Protestant.* Macbeth *is not about the Gunpowder Plot, but about Macbeth's comparable efforts to wrest power from a legitimate king. Shakespeare's* Macbeth *explores the societal implications of this treasonous act.*]

Selection Resources

Unit 2 Resources, on-level practice and assessment, p. 101

PowerNotes, interactive lesson presentation with activities

Teacher One Stop™, on-level lesson plans and all print resources

Holt Audio Library

Holt Audio Library: Selections and Summaries in Spanish

UA: Holt Interactive Reader, p. 109

UA: Differentiating Instruction, modified lesson plans and leveled assessment, p. 84

UA: Resources for Teaching Advanced Students, lesson plans, p. 93

UA: Supporting Instruction in Spanish, selection summary

ThinkCentral Online Assessment, Selection Standards Check

ThinkCentral Online Remediation

Preteach

English for Academic Success

Language Coach

Have students use two different meanings of the word *strange* in a sentence. Then, have students share their sentences with the class. Challenge the listening students to figure out the definition of the word *strange* based on its context in the sentence.

Literary Skills Focus

As you read and discuss the selection with students, have them note actions and dialogue that provide evidence about Macbeth's tragic flaw.

Reading Skills Focus

Give students a copy of the Reading Skills Focus graphic organizer before they read. (See **Unit 2 Resources**.) Tell them to use their responses to answer the questions on the Applying Your Skills page.

Writing Skills Focus

Ask students to record how a character's speech, thoughts, actions, and appearance reveals his or her personality in their **Reader/Writer Notebooks.** Students can use their notes to complete the Writing Skills Focus activity.

Learn It Online

The **PowerNotes** presentation for this lesson includes a short video that introduces the selection. The video is also available on the online version of this page.

go.hrw.com H12-404 Go

Preparing to Read

Reading Standard 2.2, 3.1; **Grades 9–10 Review Reading Standard** 3.12 (see pages A48–A50)

The Tragedy of Macbeth, Act I

Literary Skills Focus

Tragedy A **tragedy** is a story in which a heroic character dies or comes to another unhappy end. The main character in most tragedies is dignified, courageous, and often high ranking. The downfall of the character occurs because of a **tragic flaw**—a character weakness or error in judgment—or because of circumstances beyond his or her control. The tragic hero usually gains wisdom by the end of the story.

Literary Perspectives Apply the literary perspective described on page 407 as you read this play.

Reading Skills Focus

Using Questioning to Monitor Reading Because it was written four centuries ago, *Macbeth* contains language and ideas that may be unfamiliar to you. As you read the play, you can clarify your understanding by pausing to ask yourself questions.

Into Action As you read, use a chart like the one below to follow the development of the plot. Record one question for every major scene.

Act, Scene, Line	Questions I Have
Act I, Scene 1, line 10	What might the witches mean by something both "foul" and "fair"?

Writing Skills Focus

Think as a Reader/Writer

Find It in Your Reading In your *Reader/Writer Notebook,* record how Shakespeare reveals his characters through their speech, thoughts, actions, and appearance.

TechFocus As you read *Macbeth,* take notes on how you imagine the setting for each scene. Think about how you could convey the setting in a media presentation.

Language Coach

Multiple Meanings Repeated words can carry many shades of meaning. The adjective *strange* is used sixteen times in *Macbeth;* the adverb *strangely* appears twice. *Strange* can have several meanings:

- not normal or ordinary; odd
- not previously experienced
- hard to explain
- out of place
- coming from another place; alien

When you read this word, pause to consider which meaning is being used. Ask yourself: Why might Shakespeare have repeated *strange* so frequently in *Macbeth?*

(Opposite)
Liev Schreiber and Jennifer Ehle star in Moises Kaufman's production of *Macbeth,* at the Delacorte Theater in NY (June 13th, 2006).

Reader/Writer Notebook
Use your **RWN** to complete the activities for this selection.

Learn It Online
Meet Macbeth through this video introduction.
go.hrw.com H12-404 Go

California Standards, pp. 404–495

- **Reading Standard 2.2** Analyze the way in which clarity of meaning is affected by the patterns of organization, hierarchical structures, repetition of the main ideas, syntax, and word choice in the text.
- **Reading Standard 3.1** Analyze characteristics of subgenres (e.g., satire, parody, allegory, pastoral) that are used in poetry, prose, plays, novels, short stories, essays, and other basic genres.
- **Grades 9–10 Review Reading Standard 3.12** Analyze the way in which a work of literature is related to the themes and issues of its historical period. (Historical approach)

DRAMA

THE TRAGEDY of MACBETH

by WILLIAM SHAKESPEARE

Read with a Purpose

Read to discover what tragic flaw ensures Macbeth's downfall.

Build Background

Some of the strongest and most widespread ideas about tragedy come from the Greek philosopher Aristotle. Aristotle observed that tragic drama of his time centered on a hero—usually of high status—who possesses a tragic flaw. As a result of this flaw, the hero's choices bring about personal and universal catastrophes. Shakespeare's tragedies are written in this ancient tradition, but with attention to his own audience.

For example, in Shakespeare's time, audiences would have expected special effects in his plays. Thunder, produced by rolling cannonballs in the area above the stage, and lightning would have set the mood in the first scene, when witches might have made their appearance from a trapdoor on the stage.

Selection Readability	
Easily Accessible Accessible **Challenging**	historical context; archaic vocabulary; challenging sentence structure; iambic pentameter

Direct Teach

Think About/Talk About

Read with a Purpose Explain to students that a character's tragic flaw is a quality that is not always inherently bad but becomes dangerous when taken to extremes. For example, ambition can be a positive quality. However, excessive ambition, which in Macbeth's case leads him to murder, can destroy someone.

THE TRAGEDY of MACBETH

CHARACTERS

Duncan, king of Scotland
Malcolm, **Donalbain** } his sons
Macbeth, **Banquo**, **Macduff**, **Lennox**, **Ross**, **Menteith**, **Angus**, **Caithness** } noblemen of Scotland
Fleance, son to Banquo
Siward, earl of Northumberland, general of the English forces
Young Siward, his son
Seyton, an officer attending on Macbeth
Son to Macduff
An English Doctor
A Scottish Doctor
A Porter
An Old Man
Three Murderers
Lady Macbeth
Lady Macduff
A Gentlewoman attending on Lady Macbeth
Hecate
Witches
Apparitions
Lords, Officers, Soldiers, Attendants, and Messengers

Setting: Scotland; England

Glamis Castle, Angus, Scotland. Macbeth is referred to as the thane, or lord, of Glamis. The castle is believed by some to be the fictional setting for the play.

Teacher Preparation

Selection Plot Summary

Act 1 begins as three cackling witches plan to meet Macbeth on the heath as he returns from battle. Then, a captain reports to King Duncan of Scotland that Macbeth has killed the traitor Macdonwald in battle. Another lord reports that Macbeth and Banquo have forced the invading Norwegians to surrender. Unknown to Macbeth, Duncan condemns to death the present Thane of Cawdor for treason and awards Macbeth his title. Macbeth and Banquo meet three witches who make three predictions: that Macbeth will be Thane of Cawdor; that Macbeth will be king; and that Banquo will beget kings. Ross and Angus, two noblemen, arrive to tell Macbeth he has been made Thane of Cawdor. The news causes Macbeth to take the witches' prophecies seriously, and he begins to consider murdering King Duncan. At Inverness, Lady Macbeth reads a letter from Macbeth relaying the witches' prophecies. Fearing Macbeth is too softhearted to do what he must to become king, she resolves to use her power over him to steel his will. When she learns the king will visit their castle that night, Lady Macbeth sees it as the perfect opportunity to murder him. King Duncan arrives at Macbeth's castle. The king comments with dramatic irony on the pleasant atmosphere surrounding Macbeth's home.

Universal Access

EL English Learners

To help students visualize the setting and action and to understand the main conflict of the tragedy, encourage them to watch one of the film versions of the play before reading it. Also, read the summary of each scene aloud before assigning it.

✔ See **UA: Differentiating Instruction** for strategies for teaching English learners.

Struggling Readers

Tell students that as they read this play, they will take notes throughout their reading about the qualities that define Macbeth as a tragic hero. As students read, help them use a chart or other organized format to note the character traits, motives, and actions that make Macbeth a tragic hero. Ask students to write down their ideas about Macbeth's traits, motives, and actions. Then, discuss the characteristics of a tragedy using their notes.

✔ See **UA: Differentiating Instruction** for strategies for teaching struggling readers.

Act I

Scene 1. *An open place.*

Thunder and lightning. Enter three WITCHES.

First Witch.
When shall we three meet again?
In thunder, lightning, or in rain?
Second Witch.
When the hurlyburly's done,
When the battle's lost and won.
Third Witch.
That will be ere the set of sun.
First Witch.
Where the place?
Second Witch. Upon the heath.
Third Witch.
There to meet with Macbeth.
First Witch.
I come, Graymalkin.°
Second Witch.
Paddock° calls.
Third Witch. Anon!°
All.
Fair is foul, and foul is fair.
Hover through the fog and filthy air. Ⓐ [*Exeunt.*]

8. Graymalkin: the first witch's attendant or familiar, a gray cat.
9. Paddock: a toad, the second witch's familiar. **Anon!:** Soon!

Ⓐ **Literary Focus** **Tragedy** What elements in the first scene lay the foundation for the tragedy to come?

Literary Perspectives

Analyzing Historical Context Knowledge of the ideas and events of Shakespeare's time can help you understand *Macbeth's* themes of bloodshed, violence, and political turmoil. Perhaps the most important historical event surrounding *Macbeth* was the ascension of a new monarch in charge of the British Isles. James I, king of Britain and Shakespeare's patron when *Macbeth* was written, had ruled Scotland since he was an infant. His path to ruling all of Britain was not direct, for he followed in the footsteps of his ancestors, assuming the throne when Queen Elizabeth I died childless in 1603. Political struggles had taxed Britain for centuries, and Henry VIII had overthrown the religious system as well as killed two wives in the pursuit of a male heir. Because of this unrest, English citizens had a strong belief in the need for social order and a fear of the disorder that could result from an abuse of power.

As you read, be sure to notice the questions in the text, which will guide you in using this perspective.

Think About/Talk About

Analysis

Ⓐ Literary Focus

Possible response: *The witches' connection with Macbeth and the turnaround of what is natural ("Fair is foul, and foul is fair") lay the foundation for the tragedy.*

Extend the Discussion

Theme The rhymed couplet in lines 10–11 is the witches' most famous utterance. What theme does it introduce? ***Possible response:*** *It introduces the theme that appearances are deceiving; good and evil become blurred. The couplet also signals a change of scene, because the witches utter the lines just before they exit the stage.*

Literary Perspectives

Before students read the selection, have them read the **Literary Perspectives** about Analyzing Historical Context. Focus on the political culture of a society run by an absolute monarch, such as England during the reign of Henry VIII (1509–1547) or Elizabeth I (1558–1603). Explain how society depended on a stable monarchy. Parliament and the nobility derived their powers and titles from the monarch. Instability—such as the conflict between Henry VIII and the Catholic Church—could cause unease and unrest.

Remind students to use the notes and questions at the bottom of the page to help them use the perspective.

Think About/Talk About

Literary Connection

Tell students that blood is mentioned more than one hundred times in the play. As they read, ask students to think about its significance as an image and to consider whether it has different meanings at different points in the drama.

Responses to Margin Questions

Line 7 *The captain would gasp from weakness but speak urgently to convey the good news.*

Line 23 *Macbeth slashed Macdonwald from navel to jaws, beheaded him, and displayed his head on a pole on the battlements.*

Line 35 *The captain is speaking ironically, saying that Macbeth and Banquo were not daunted by the new assault from such a weak enemy; he may also be speaking in an admiring tone.*

Line 44 *Students may come to see Duncan as overly trusting and naïve, or as a strong king who placed his confidence in the wrong person.*

Scene 2. *A camp.*

Alarum within.° *Enter* KING DUNCAN, MALCOLM, DONALBAIN, LENNOX, *with* ATTENDANTS, *meeting a bleeding* CAPTAIN.

King.
What bloody man is that? He can report,
As seemeth by his plight, of the revolt
The newest state.
Malcolm. This is the sergeant
Who like a good and hardy soldier fought
'Gainst my captivity. Hail, brave friend!
Say to the king the knowledge of the broil°
As thou didst leave it.
Captain. Doubtful it stood,
As two spent swimmers, that do cling together
And choke their art.° The merciless Macdonwald—
Worthy to be a rebel for to that
The multiplying villainies of nature
Do swarm upon him—from the Western Isles°
Of kerns and gallowglasses° is supplied;
And Fortune, on his damnèd quarrel smiling,
Showed like a rebel's whore: but all's too weak:
For brave Macbeth—well he deserves that name—
Disdaining Fortune, with his brandished steel,
Which smoked with bloody execution,
Like valor's minion° carved out his passage
Till he faced the slave;
Which nev'r shook hands, nor bade farewell to him,
Till he unseamed him from the nave to th' chops,°
And fixed his head upon our battlements.
King.
O valiant cousin! Worthy gentleman!
Captain.
As whence the sun 'gins his reflection°
Shipwracking storms and direful thunders break,
So from that spring whence comfort seemed to come
Discomfort swells. Mark, King of Scotland, mark:
No sooner justice had, with valor armed,
Compelled these skipping kerns to trust their heels
But the Norweyan° lord, surveying vantage,°
With furbished arms and new supplies of men,
Began a fresh assault.
King. Dismayed not this

Alarum within: trumpets offstage.

6. **broil:** quarrel.

? **Staging the Play**
7. *The captain is bloody and could be carried in or supported by others. How would he speak his lines?*

9. **choke their art:** hinder each other's ability to swim.

12. **Western Isles:** a region of western Scotland comprising the Outer Hebrides.

13. **kerns and gallowglasses:** lightly armed Irish soldiers and heavily armed soldiers.

19. **minion:** favorite.

22. **unseamed . . . chops:** split him from navel to jaws.

? 23. *Notice that this horrible action is described by a messenger, not shown onstage. What did Macbeth do to the rebellious Macdonwald?*

25. **'gins his reflection:** rises.

31. **Norweyan:** Norwegian. **surveying vantage:** seeing an opportunity.

Real Issues, Real Experts

Holt author ***Carol Jago*** *offers suggestions for teaching* Macbeth.

If there has ever been a Golden Age for English teachers when we could turn to *Macbeth*, assign Act I for homework, and begin class with "So what did you think?" I missed it. In the 32 years I have spent in high school classrooms, I never taught such a class.

I'm not complaining; I simply think teenagers need more help and prodding to make Shakespeare come alive. The fact that students cannot read the play on their own does not mean that they should not read it. In order to make the play "real," I try to show students how Macbeth struggles with the same temptation leaders have grappled with throughout history—the corrupting influence of power.

Working through the play together, I invite students to think about Macbeth in contemporary terms: What do you think about Lady Macbeth's influence on her husband? Is breaking a law for the first time harder than doing it for a second or third time? Can leaders become out-of-touch with reality? How does this happen? Why?

Our captains, Macbeth and Banquo? **B**

Captain. Yes;

As° sparrows eagles, or the hare the lion.
If I say sooth,° I must report they were
As cannons overcharged with double cracks;
So they doubly redoubled strokes upon the foe.
Except° they meant to bathe in reeking wounds,
Or memorize another Golgotha,° **C**
I cannot tell—
But I am faint; my gashes cry for help.

King.
So well thy words become thee as thy wounds;
They smack of honor both. Go get him surgeons.

[*Exit* CAPTAIN *attended.*]

[*Enter* ROSS *and* ANGUS.]

Who comes here?

Malcolm. The worthy Thane° of Ross.

Lennox.
What a haste looks through his eyes! So should he look
That seems to° speak things strange.

Ross. God save the king!

King.
Whence cam'st thou, worthy thane?

Ross. From Fife, great king;
Where the Norweyan banners flout the sky
And fan our people cold.
Norway himself,° with terrible numbers, **D**
Assisted by that most disloyal traitor
The Thane of Cawdor, began a dismal conflict;
Till that Bellona's bridegroom,° lapped in proof,°
Confronted him with self-comparisons,°
Point against point, rebellious arm 'gainst arm,
Curbing his lavish° spirit: and, to conclude,
The victory fell on us.

King. Great happiness!

35. As: no more than.

? **35.** *This line can be delivered in several ways. How do you imagine the captain speaks it?*

36. sooth: truth.

39. Except: unless.

40. memorize another Golgotha: make the place as memorable as Golgotha, where Christ was crucified.

? **44.** *Duncan can be portrayed in several ways: as a strong but aging king, as a frail old man, or as a kind but foolish old man who fails to understand what is happening. As the play goes on, decide how you interpret Duncan's character.*

45. Thane: Scottish title of nobility.

47. seems to: seems about to.

51. Norway himself: that is, the king of Norway.

54. Bellona's bridegroom: Bellona is the goddess of war. Macbeth, who is a great soldier, is called her mate. **lapped in proof:** clad in armor.

55. self-comparisons: countermovements.

57. lavish: insolent; rude.

B **Reading Focus** **Using Questioning to Monitor Reading** This line closely links Macbeth and Banquo, yet the title of the play is *The Tragedy of Macbeth*. What questions does this raise for you about the relationship between these two characters?

C **Literary Perspectives** **Analyzing Historical Context** What does this reference to Golgotha tell you about the religious beliefs of the time?

D **Literary Perspectives** **Analyzing Historical Context** What traditional relationship between rulers and the military—quite different from what we expect today—is revealed in both the Scottish and the Norwegian approach to warfare in this scene?

Think About/Talk About

Comprehension

B Reading Focus

Possible responses: *What kind of man is Banquo? Will he be Macbeth's friend, rival, or both?*

Analysis

C Literary Perspectives

Possible response: *It was a predominantly Christian society. People used events from the Bible as reference points for understanding and describing the events of their own time.*

D Literary Perspectives

Possible response: *Traditionally, members of the nobility and even rulers personally led their troops into battle.*

Extend the Discussion

Making Predictions What do you expect will happen to Macbeth and Banquo when they return? ***Possible response:*** *King Duncan will probably reward them in some way for their bravery.*

Making Inferences What do lines 49–58 help you infer about the Thane of Cawdor? How is he different from Macbeth and Banquo? ***Possible responses:*** *The Thane of Cawdor was a "most disloyal traitor" to his king. Macbeth and Banquo are right and honorable.*

I used the word *work* intentionally. Teachers err when we tell students that Shakespeare is fun, not because it cannot be. The mistake is with suggesting that reading *Macbeth* will be as easy as watching the latest television drama. I tell students that what we are about to do will be hard, but that I promise to be there to help at every step along the way.

Model the Skill

- Provide students with copies of the Reading Skills Focus graphic organizer for "Macbeth, Act 1." (See **Unit 2 Resources**.)
- Tell students that **questioning** is a useful tool **to monitor understanding** of a text. As students read, they should record their questions about characters and plot. Explain that they should also try to answer their own questions as they proceed with their reading.
- Model adding a question to the graphic organizer. Read lines 14–26 on p. 411 aloud. Tell students they might wonder what the witches are doing in this scene. Do the witches' words show concern about Macbeth? What does sleeplessness have to do with their curse? Explain that they should keep these questions in mind and look to see whether they are answered in the text.

Act, Scene, Line	Questions I Have
Act I, Scene 3, Lines 14–26	Do the witches' words show concern about Macbeth? What does sleeplessness have to do with their curse?

Guided Practice: Apply

Ask students to exchange their questions and discuss possible responses as they read the rest of the act.

Think About/Talk About

Response to Margin Question

Line 67 *The king would say these lines enthusiastically; he is proud to bestow this honor.*

Peter Lindford as Macbeth and Gerard Logan as Banquo.

Ross. That now
Sweno, the Norways' king, craves composition;°
Nor would we deign him burial of his men
Till he disbursèd, at Saint Colme's Inch,°
Ten thousand dollars to our general use.
King.
No more that Thane of Cawdor shall deceive **E**
Our bosom interest:° go pronounce his present° death,
And with his former title greet Macbeth.
Ross.
I'll see it done.
King.
What he hath lost, noble Macbeth hath won. **F** [*Exeunt.*]

59. composition: peace terms.

61. Saint Colme's Inch: island off the coast of Scotland.

64. bosom interest: heart's trust. **present:** immediate.

? **Staging the Play**
67. *As you read, notice how later events relate to the king's words. How would you have him say these lines?*

E **Reading Focus** **Using Questioning to Monitor Reading** King Duncan states that he was deceived by the Thane of Cawdor. What questions does this raise for you about Duncan's personality?

F **Literary Focus** **Tragedy** What evidence in this scene supports the idea of Macbeth as a high-ranking, dignified, and courageous man?

Universal Access

Advanced Learners

Enrichment As students read the play, ask them to compare it to other plays, stories, and movies in which ambition leads a character astray. Have students consider the following: the nature of ambition, the actions taken by the character to satisfy this ambition, the influence of other characters, the outcome, and the underlying tone. Students may revisit these ideas for any long-term projects they complete after reading *Macbeth*.

Students with Disabilities

The complex language and syntax of *Macbeth* will make it difficult for students to follow the plot. Before students read *Macbeth*, give them an overview of the main events of the play. Invite students to ask questions until they show an adequate understanding of the plot. If possible, have them draw an outline of the play that they can use as a reference as they read.

✔ See **UA: Differentiating Instruction** for strategies for teaching students with disabilities.

Scene 3. *A heath.*

Thunder. Enter the three WITCHES.

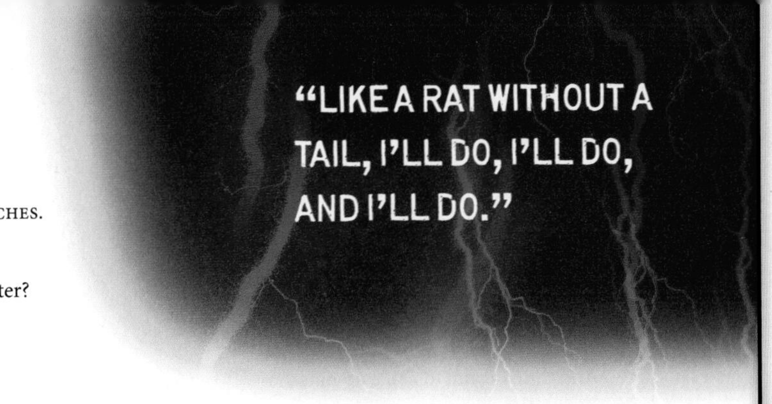

First Witch.
Where hast thou been, sister?

Second Witch.
Killing swine.

Third Witch.
Sister, where thou?

First Witch.
A sailor's wife had chestnuts in her lap,
And mounched, and mounched, and mounched. "Give me," quoth I.
"Aroint thee,° witch!" the rump-fed ronyon° cries.
Her husband's to Aleppo gone, master o' th' *Tiger:*
But in a sieve° I'll thither sail,
And, like a rat without a tail,
I'll do, I'll do, and I'll do.

Second Witch.
I'll give thee a wind.

First Witch.
Th' art kind.

Third Witch.
And I another.

First Witch.
I myself have all the other;
And the very ports they blow,°
All the quarters that they know
I' th' shipman's card.°
I'll drain him dry as hay:
Sleep shall neither night nor day
Hang upon his penthouse lid;°
He shall live a man forbid:°
Weary sev'nights nine times nine
Shall he dwindle, peak,° and pine:
Though his bark cannot be lost,
Yet it shall be tempest-tossed.
Look what I have.

Second Witch.
Show me, show me.

First Witch.
Here I have a pilot's thumb,
Wracked as homeward he did come.

[*Drum within.*]

6. Aroint thee: begone. **rump-fed ronyon:** fat-rumped, scabby creature.
8. But in a sieve: Witches were believed to have the power to sail in sieves.

15. ports they blow: harbors they blow into.
17. card: compass.

20. penthouse lid: eyelid.
21. forbid: cursed.

23. peak: grow pale.

Think About/Talk About

Comprehension

E Reading Focus

Possible response: *It raises these questions: What acts does he consider deceitful? Is Duncan too trusting? Does he often act out of anger?*

Analysis

F Literary Focus

Possible response: *Macbeth and Banquo are compared to eagles and lions, animals that are traditionally considered proud, noble, and fierce. Macbeth is called the groom of the goddess of war; he has defeated and beheaded the traitor Cawdor.*

Extend the Discussion

Breaking Down Difficult Text
Re-read lines 19–23. What troubles will the first witch visit upon the man she refers to here? ***Possible response:*** *She will curse him so he cannot sleep and will become pale and weary.*

Figurative Language What does the phrase "his bark cannot be lost" suggest about the witches' powers? ***Possible responses:*** *The metaphor suggests that the witches do not have ultimate control over people's lives or decisions. They cannot take the sailor's life and soul unless he surrenders to evil.*

Universal Access

EL English Learners

English for Academic Success Remind students that context often provides clues to the meaning of words. (1) The unfamiliar word might be defined in an appositive, as in "Sweno, the Norways' king." (2) Words with similar or contrasting meanings might point to the word's definition, as in "fair is foul, and foul is fair." (3) The sentences surrounding the unfamiliar word might give a clue.

Activity Ask students to choose three words from Act I whose meaning they are unsure of and to use context clues to guess at the meaning of each. Have them check their guesses in a dictionary. Explain to students that this activity will help them better understand the plot of *Macbeth.*

Think About/Talk About

Literary Connection

Tell students that prophecies from Greek mythology were often cloaked in paradox in order to subtly foreshadow dramatic events in the story. The witches' puzzling paradoxes come out of a long soothsaying tradition.

Responses to Margin Questions

Line 38 *Macbeth has not heard these lines before but is unknowingly echoing the witches' comment. Although the weather is foul, with thunder, lightning, and fog, and the brutality of the battlefield is also foul, Macbeth's success has made the day "fair" to him.*

Line 39 *Banquo might step back and reach for his sword or raise his hand to ward them off. He might gasp or sound surprised as he completes his casual question only to be confronted by the strange trio.*

Line 51 *Macbeth is startled. He might show fear through his facial expressions or a gesture of surprise. Banquo is addressing the witches.*

Line 61 *Banquo asks the witches to foretell his future, too, if they can.*

Line 71 *Macbeth's tone might be puzzled, intrigued, or entranced—or perhaps all three.*

Stage direction *Banquo seems to be puzzled and dismisses the witches as fantasies. Macbeth is eager to hear more.*

Third Witch.
A drum, a drum!
Macbeth doth come.

All.
The weird sisters, hand in hand,
Posters° of the sea and land,
Thus do go about, about:
Thrice to thine, and thrice to mine,
And thrice again, to make up nine.
Peace! The charm's wound up.

[*Enter* MACBETH *and* BANQUO.]

Macbeth.
So foul and fair a day I have not seen. (G)

Banquo.
How far is't called to Forres?° What are these
So withered, and so wild in their attire,
That look not like th' inhabitants o' th' earth,
And yet are on't? Live you, or are you aught
That man may question? You seem to understand me,
By each at once her choppy° finger laying
Upon her skinny lips. You should° be women,
And yet your beards forbid me to interpret
That you are so.

Macbeth. Speak, if you can: what are you?

First Witch.
All hail, Macbeth! Hail to thee, Thane of Glamis!

Second Witch.
All hail, Macbeth! Hail to thee, Thane of Cawdor!

Third Witch.
All hail, Macbeth, that shalt be king hereafter!

Banquo.
Good sir, why do you start, and seem to fear (H)
Things that do sound so fair? I' th' name of truth,
Are ye fantastical, or that indeed
Which outwardly ye show? My noble partner

33. Posters: travelers.

? **38.** *What words is Macbeth echoing here? Why, given the weather, does Macbeth think the day is "fair"?*

39. Forres: town in northeastern Scotland and site of King Duncan's castle.

? **Staging the Play**
39. *What should Banquo do as he sees the witches? How should his voice change between the words* Forres *and* What?

44. choppy: chapped; sore.

45. should: must.

? **51.** *Banquo's words give a clue as to how Macbeth reacts to the witches. What is Macbeth doing? When Banquo asks, "Are ye fantastical," whom is he addressing?*

(G) **Reading Focus** **Using Questioning to Monitor Reading** This line echoes the witches' line in Act I, Scene 1, line 10. What questions does it bring up for you about Macbeth and the witches?

(H) **Literary Focus** **Tragedy** Why might a high-ranking noble—who is related to the king ("cousin"; Act I, Scene 1, line 24) and presumably in line for the throne—"start, and seem to fear" when he hears the prediction that he will, in fact, become king?

Literary Perspectives

Students may feel that the inclusion of witches in the play adds a fictional element to the otherwise historically-based play. Explain to students that in the sixteenth and seventeenth centuries, many European Christians believed in witchcraft. James I of England became convinced of the existence of witches when the alleged North Berwick witches claimed responsibility for a storm that nearly sank his honeymoon ship, an act similar to those described by the witches in Scene 3. Macbeth's belief in the witches and their prophecies was not unusual for the people living during his time.

You greet with present grace and great prediction
Of noble having and of royal hope,
That he seems rapt withal:° to me you speak not.
If you can look into the seeds of time,
And say which grain will grow and which will not,
Speak then to me, who neither beg nor fear
Your favors nor your hate.

First Witch. Hail!

Second Witch. Hail!

Third Witch. Hail!

First Witch.
Lesser than Macbeth, and greater.

Second Witch.
Not so happy,° yet much happier.

Third Witch.
Thou shalt get° kings, though thou be none.
So all hail, Macbeth and Banquo! **I**

First Witch.
Banquo and Macbeth, all hail!

Macbeth.
Stay, you imperfect° speakers, tell me more:
By Sinel's death I know I am Thane of Glamis;
But how of Cawdor? The Thane of Cawdor lives,
A prosperous gentleman; and to be king
Stands not within the prospect of belief,
No more than to be Cawdor. Say from whence
You owe° this strange intelligence?° Or why
Upon this blasted heath you stop our way
With such prophetic greeting? Speak, I charge you. **J**

[WITCHES *vanish.*]

Banquo.
The earth hath bubbles as the water has,
And these are of them. Whither are they vanished?

57. rapt withal: entranced by it.

? **61.** *What does Banquo ask the witches?*

66. happy: lucky.

67. get: beget.

70. imperfect: unfinished.

? **Elements of Drama**
71. *Sinel is Macbeth's father. What do you think Macbeth's tone is here? Is he overeager? or just casually curious?*

76. owe: own; have. **intelligence:** information.

? **Staging the Play**
Stage direction: *The witches on Shakespeare's stage would have vanished through the trapdoor. Is Banquo, in his next speech, intrigued or disturbed? How does Macbeth feel?*

I **Reading Focus** **Using Questioning to Monitor Reading** Macbeth and Banquo are again linked, this time by the witches. What questions does this second connection raise?

J **Literary Perspective** **Analyzing Historical Context** The portrayal of the witches reveals beliefs about witches in Shakespeare's time. What traits are displayed here?

Think About/Talk About

Comprehension

G Reading Focus

Possible responses: *It brings up these questions: What do the witches have planned for Macbeth? Will he be cursed with sleeplessness?*

I Reading Focus

Possible responses: *It raises these questions: How will Banquo and Macbeth's relationship change by the end of the play? How would Banquo react to being lower in rank than Macbeth?*

Analysis

H Literary Focus

Possible response: *The witches' words may reflect Macbeth's own secret hopes.*

J Literary Perspectives

Possible response: *This line indicates that witches have the gift of prophecy and know the future.*

Extend the Discussion

Comparing and Contrasting How would you compare Macbeth's and Banquo's ambitions? ***Possible responses:*** *Although they both get good news from the witches, Macbeth seems far more swept up by the witches' predictions, indicating that he is an ambitious man. Banquo seems more self-possessed.*

Cross-Curricular Connection

LANGUAGE: Word Origins

Draw students' attention to line 32 ("The weird sisters, hand in hand"). Explain that *weird* derives from the Old English word *wyrd*, meaning "fate" or "destiny." The *Oxford English Dictionary* notes that the use of the word, in its plural form, refers to the Fates, three goddesses that decided over human lives.

Activity Have students research the etymology of the word *weird* and its variations through time. Students can use the dictionary or Internet resources for their research.

Think About/Talk About

Literary Connection

Explain that asides such as the one at the beginning of p. 415 let the audience know Macbeth's and Banquo's thoughts without the other characters being aware of them.

Extend the Discussion

Paraphrasing What does Ross tell Macbeth in lines 104–107 that Macbeth does not yet know? ***Possible response:*** *Ross formally tells Macbeth that King Duncan has made him Thane of Cawdor.*

Making Judgments In lines 79–85, Macbeth and Banquo react differently to the witches' sudden departure. What do their reactions reveal about them? ***Possible response:*** *Macbeth is sorry they left; he seems eager to hear more about his future. Banquo, in contrast, wonders whether he and Macbeth are insane and imagined the encounter. He is cautious.*

Responses to Margin Questions

Line 117 *He might sound eager, exultant, or determined. His mood might be one of glee or wonder.*

Line 126 *He warns Macbeth that the witches may plan to harm him.*

Stage direction *Macbeth might come downstage and face the audience, while the other characters remain upstage, engaged in conversation. The "swelling act" (line 128) suggests the stately music that heralds a king.*

Macbeth.
Into the air, and what seemed corporal° melted
As breath into the wind. Would they had stayed!

Banquo.
Were such things here as we do speak about?
Or have we eaten on the insane root°
That takes the reason prisoner?

Macbeth.
Your children shall be kings.

Banquo. You shall be king.

Macbeth.
And Thane of Cawdor too. Went it not so?

Banquo.
To th' selfsame tune and words. Who's here?

[*Enter* ROSS *and* ANGUS.]

Ross.
The king hath happily received, Macbeth,
The news of thy success; and when he reads°
Thy personal venture in the rebels' fight,
His wonders and his praises do contend
Which should be thine or his. Silenced with that,
In viewing o'er the rest o' th' selfsame day,
He finds thee in the stout Norweyan ranks,
Nothing afeard of what thyself didst make,
Strange images of death.° As thick as tale
Came post with post,° and every one did bear
Thy praises in his kingdom's great defense,
And poured them down before him.

Angus. We are sent
To give thee, from our royal master, thanks;
Only to herald thee into his sight,
Not pay thee.

Ross.
And for an earnest° of a greater honor,
He bade me, from him, call thee Thane of Cawdor;
In which addition,° hail, most worthy thane!
For it is thine.

Banquo. What, can the devil speak true?

Macbeth.
The Thane of Cawdor lives: why do you dress me
In borrowed robes?

Angus. Who was the thane lives yet,
But under heavy judgment bears that life
Which he deserves to lose. Whether he was combined
With those of Norway, or did line° the rebel

81. corporal: corporeal (bodily; physical).

84. insane root: henbane, believed to cause insanity.

90. reads: considers.

96–97. Nothing . . . death: killing, and not being afraid of being killed.

98. post with post: messenger with a message.

104. earnest: pledge.

106. addition: title.

112. line: support.

Compare and Contrast

Ask students to compare and contrast Macbeth's and Banquo's responses to the prophecies.

- **Similarities** Both characters have been promised honors. Macbeth will receive further titles and will become king. Banquo will become the father of kings. Initially, neither sees how these prophecies could come true.
- **Differences** Banquo is quicker to link the promises to the devil and see the potential harm if they come to pass. He fears that the witches' words can take "the reason prisoner." He is interested in the witches' predictions but does not display the intense interest Macbeth does. The witches' words leave Macbeth "rapt withal" (line 57)—implying that their words captivate him by feeding his ambitions. When Ross appears to deliver the king's good news, Macbeth is again "rapt" (line 142). He wonders if he will even have to lift a hand. "Chance may crown me, / Without my stir" (lines 143–144). Banquo, on the other hand, still refers to the witches as "instruments of darkness" (line 124).

With hidden help and vantage, or that with both
He labored in his country's wrack, I know not;
But treasons capital,° confessed and proved,
Have overthrown him.

Macbeth (*aside*). Glamis, and Thane of Cawdor:
The greatest is behind. (*To* ROSS *and* ANGUS.) Thanks for your pains.
(*Aside to* BANQUO.) Do you not hope your children shall be kings,
When those that gave the Thane of Cawdor to me
Promised no less to them?

Banquo (*aside to* MACBETH). That, trusted home,°
Might yet enkindle you unto the crown,°
Besides the Thane of Cawdor. But 'tis strange:
And oftentimes, to win us to our harm,
The instruments of darkness tell us truths,
Win us with honest trifles, to betray 's (K)
In deepest consequence.
Cousins,° a word, I pray you.

Macbeth (*aside*). Two truths are told
As happy prologues to the swelling act
Of the imperial theme.—I thank you, gentlemen.—
(*Aside.*) This supernatural soliciting
Cannot be ill, cannot be good. If ill,
Why hath it given me earnest of success,
Commencing in a truth? I am Thane of Cawdor:
If good, why do I yield to that suggestion
Whose horrid image doth unfix my hair
And make my seated heart knock at my ribs,
Against the use of nature? Present fears
Are less than horrible imaginings.
My thought, whose murder yet is but fantastical, (L)
Shakes so my single° state of man that function
Is smothered in surmise, and nothing is
But what is not.°

Banquo. Look, how our partner's rapt.

Macbeth (*aside*).
If chance will have me king, why, chance may crown me, (M)
Without my stir.

115. capital: deserving death.

? 117. Behind *here means "to follow." How should this important aside be spoken? What is Macbeth's mood?*

120. trusted home: trusted all the way.
121. enkindle . . . crown: arouse in you the ambition to become king.

? 126. *How does this speech show Banquo as part of the conscience of the play?*

127. Cousins: This word is used frequently by Shakespeare to mean "fellows" or "relatives" of some sort.

? Staging the Play
Stage direction: *A character's private comments on what is happening, asides, are spoken for the benefit of the audience. When a character is delivering an aside, the director or the playwright must arrange for the others onstage to be involved in some way so that it would be natural for them not to notice the character delivering the aside. Where should Macbeth go onstage to deliver this important aside? Where are Banquo, Angus, and Ross?*

140. single: unaided; weak.
141–142. nothing . . . not: Nothing is real to me except my imaginings.

(K) Literary Focus Tragedy What do Banquo's words about the witches indicate about Macbeth's fate?

(L) Reading Focus Using Questioning to Monitor Reading Macbeth describes different paths to the throne. What questions can you ask to determine his fears and concerns?

(M) Reading Focus Using Questioning to Monitor Reading This last speech seems to contradict the previous one. What questions can you ask to clarify his motives?

Universal Access

Advanced Learners

Acceleration Shakespeare's use of imagery in *Macbeth* is brilliant, commenting on and reinforcing the character, plot, atmosphere, and theme. Divide students into five groups, letting each group choose one of the following motifs:

- blood
- clothing
- light and darkness
- sickness and health
- unnatural events in nature that mirror human evil

Have each group follow its motif through the play, identifying pertinent lines. Once groups have compiled their lists, have them analyze how the images contribute to the atmosphere, foreshadow or echo plot events, and reveal the characters' inner feelings. Challenge students to connect their motif to the concept of a tragic flaw. Ask students to analyze what their motif reveals about Macbeth and his flaws.

Think About/Talk About

Comprehension

(L) Reading Focus

Possible responses: *What will happen to Macbeth if he takes these different paths? What is the "horrid image" he is thinking of?*

(M) Reading Focus

Possible responses: *How far will he go to support his ambitions? Is he willing to wait passively for the throne, or will he take action to attain it?*

Analysis

(K) Literary Focus

Possible response: *The witches, as "instruments of darkness," may be telling the truth about some things but will ultimately betray Macbeth.*

Extend the Discussion

Tragedy What are the two ways Macbeth imagines he could become king? ***Possible response:*** *He could become king by murdering Duncan or by waiting to see if chance brings him to the throne.*

Model the Skill

- Remind students that paraphrasing involves restating a portion of text in your own words. Explain that two techniques they can use to paraphrase Shakespeare are to replace pronouns or unfamiliar words or phrases, and to break up long sentences into shorter sentences.
- Read aloud Malcolm's words in lines 2–5. Paraphrase the first sentence: "My lord, they're not back yet." Then paraphrase the second clause: "However, I spoke with someone who saw Cawdor die." Explain that you will begin a new sentence to paraphrase the text that follows: "He reported that Cawdor openly admitted his treasons."

Guided Practice: Apply

Ask students to select another passage of 3–5 lines to paraphrase. Have students discuss their paraphrases together.

Think About/Talk About

Responses to Margin Questions

Line 145 *He compares Macbeth's honors to new clothes, not yet broken in. Banquo's mood is calm because he dismisses the witches' comments; Macbeth's mood is excited because he believes the witches.*

Line 8 *Cawdor ended his life more nobly than he lived it.*

Line 12 *Duncan has revealed his weakness—he is too trusting and not a good judge of character. Ironically, even as Duncan is acknowledging his mistake about the previous Thane of Cawdor, he is making the same mistake about Macbeth.*

Banquo. New honors come upon him,
Like our strange° garments, cleave not to their mold
But with the aid of use.

Macbeth (*aside*). Come what come may,
Time and the hour runs through the roughest day.

Banquo.
Worthy Macbeth, we stay upon your leisure.

Macbeth.
Give me your favor.° My dull brain was wrought
With things forgotten. Kind gentlemen, your pains
Are registered where every day I turn
The leaf to read them. Let us toward the king.
(*Aside to* BANQUO.) Think upon what hath chanced, and at more time,
The interim having weighed it, let us speak
Our free hearts each to other.

Banquo. Very gladly.

Macbeth.
Till then, enough. Come, friends. [*Exeunt.*]

145. strange: new.

? **145.** *To what does Banquo compare Macbeth and his new honors? Is Banquo's mood different from Macbeth's?*

149. favor: pardon.

Scene 4. *Forres. The palace.*

Flourish.° *Enter* KING DUNCAN, LENNOX, MALCOLM, DONALBAIN, *and* ATTENDANTS.

King.
Is execution done on Cawdor? Are not
Those in commission yet returned?

Malcolm. My liege,
They are not yet come back. But I have spoke
With one that saw him die, who did report
That very frankly he confessed his treasons,
Implored your highness' pardon and set forth
A deep repentance: nothing in his life
Became him like the leaving it. He died (N)
As one that had been studied in his death
To throw away the dearest thing he owed°
As 'twere a careless trifle.

King. There's no art
To find the mind's construction in the face:

Flourish: of trumpets.

? **8.** *What does this famous line mean: "nothing in his life / Became him like the leaving it"?*

10. owed: owned.

? **Elements of Drama**
12. *What irony do you detect here? What does Duncan fail to realize about another face?*

(N) **Reading Focus** **Using Questioning to Monitor Reading** Shakespeare might have described Cawdor's death in many different ways. What questions do you have about Shakespeare's decision to describe the traitor's death as honorable?

Universal Access

Struggling Readers

Strategic Students Remind students that a character's tragic flaw is his or her weakness or error in judgment. Tell students that most often they will have to make inferences about a character's tragic flaw. However, sometimes a character's flaw may be revealed through his or her dialogue. Read lines 12–15 of Scene 4 aloud to students. Guide students in interpreting these lines. You might say: "In these lines, Duncan is revealing his weakness to Malcolm. He explains that he is unable to distinguish appearance from reality and he cannot read people's characters. I think that Duncan's inability to determine whether a person is trustworthy will lead to his downfall." As students continue to read, have them be on the lookout for dialogue that reveals information about the character's flaws.

Macbeth (Peter Lindford) with King Duncan (Daid Pearson), Ludlow Festival, England.

He was a gentleman on whom I built
An absolute trust.

[*Enter* MACBETH, BANQUO, ROSS, *and* ANGUS.]

O worthiest cousin!
The sin of my ingratitude even now
Was heavy on me: thou art so far before,
That swiftest wing of recompense is slow
To overtake thee. Would thou hadst less deserved,
That the proportion° both of thanks and payment
Might have been mine! Only I have left to say,
More is thy due than more than all can pay.

Macbeth.
The service and the loyalty I owe,
In doing it, pays itself.° Your highness' part
Is to receive our duties: and our duties
Are to your throne and state children and servants;
Which do but what they should, by doing everything
Safe toward° your love and honor.

King. Welcome hither.

19. proportion: greater amount.

23. pays itself: is its own reward.

27. Safe toward: safeguarding.

Think About/Talk About

Comprehension

N Reading Focus

Possible responses: *Does Shakespeare intend Cawdor's repentance to be a commentary on Macbeth's possible treason? Is his repentance an example of "fair" becoming "foul" and "foul" becoming "fair"? Does Shakespeare not intend for Cawdor to be the main villain in this play?*

Extend the Discussion

Drawing Conclusions In lines 13–14, what seems to upset Duncan the most about Cawdor's treason? ***Possible response:*** *Duncan trusted Cawdor, and Cawdor betrayed that trust.*

Speculating What might Macbeth make of the words in lines 20–21? ***Possible responses:*** *With his imagination so worked up, Macbeth might construe this as a promise of the throne; he might appreciate Duncan's deep gratitude.*

Developing Oral Fluency

Use Malcolm's speech (Scene 4, lines 2–11) to explain to students the importance of the interplay between the poetry's rhythm and the sentence structure when reading Shakespeare aloud. Begin by noting where sentences begin and end (often mid-line), making the thought carry over naturally into the next line of verse. Point out the lack of end rhyme, making this flow of ideas sound very natural to the ear.

Small-Group Activity Have students work in small groups to do a choral reading of Malcolm's speech. Have them divide the speech into short, meaningful segments that successive readers could shape into a single, unified speech in the manner of some choral-style commercials. Students should strive for a clear and expressive reading.

✔ See **UA: Differentiating Instruction** for practice passages for developing oral fluency.

Think About/Talk About

Build Background: Tanistry

Duncan is violating two laws by naming Malcolm his successor: first, a law prohibiting a minor from succeeding to the throne; second, the law of tanistry, in effect from 843 to 1058 (coinciding with the end of Macbeth's reign), which said that no son of a king on the throne could succeed his father directly. Tanistry required the first ranking adult of the nearest branch of the family to succeed the king (as Macbeth does in the play). Then, succession would revert to the original branch of the family, so that the line of succession alternated between the branches of the royal family.

Responses to Margin Questions

Line 32 *Some might think Macbeth, will behave honorably; others may be suspicious of his sincerity. The king hugs Banquo, but gives Macbeth the title of Thane of Cawdor and speaks to him with greater admiration and respect. Macbeth may feel that Duncan is treating him as an equal.*

Line 35 *wiping away tears of joy*

Line 43 *his son Malcolm*

Line 53 *In l. 50, Macbeth speaks of literal darkness, and in l. 51, he speaks of the darkness in his heart.*

Stage direction *She may be reading lines with varying emphasis and using her facial expressions to show excitement and craftiness.*

Line 13 *Lady Macbeth may keep the letter literally close to her heart as she keeps its contents secret. She is addressing the absent Macbeth. The phrase "milk of human kindness" hints at sensitivity, like the tenderness of a mother nursing her infant.*

Line 26 *the king's crown*

Line 36 *She may be speaking figuratively of the raven as a symbol of death, or she may be referring to the messenger who brings news that bodes ill for Duncan.*

I have begun to plant thee, and will labor
To make thee full of growing. Noble Banquo,
That hast no less deserved, nor must be known
No less to have done so, let me enfold thee
And hold thee to my heart.

Banquo. There if I grow,
The harvest is your own.

King. My plenteous joys,
Wanton in fullness, seek to hide themselves
In drops of sorrow. Sons, kinsmen, thanes,
And you whose places are the nearest, know,
We will establish our estate upon
Our eldest, Malcolm, whom we name hereafter
The Prince of Cumberland: which honor must
Not unaccompanied invest him only,
But signs of nobleness, like stars, shall shine
On all deservers. From hence to Inverness,°
And bind us further to you.

Macbeth.
The rest is labor, which is not used for you.°
I'll be myself the harbinger,° and make joyful
The hearing of my wife with your approach;
So, humbly take my leave.

King. My worthy Cawdor!

Macbeth (*aside*).
The Prince of Cumberland! That is a step
On which I must fall down, or else o'erleap,
For in my way it lies. Stars, hide your fires;
Let not light see my black and deep desires:
The eye wink at the hand;° yet let that be
Which the eye fears, when it is done, to see. [*Exit.*]

King.
True, worthy Banquo; he is full so valiant,
And in his commendations° I am fed;
It is a banquet to me. Let's after him,
Whose care is gone before to bid us welcome.
It is a peerless kinsman. [*Flourish. Exeunt.*]

Scene 5. *Inverness. Macbeth's castle.*

Enter Macbeth's wife, LADY MACBETH, *alone, with a letter.*

Lady Macbeth (*reads*). "They met me in the day of success; and I have learned by the perfect'st report they have more in

32. *You know Macbeth's thoughts. How do you feel about him as the king lavishes praise on him? Is the king's reception of Banquo even warmer? How might Macbeth react here?*

35. *There is a clue in this line that shows how much the king is moved. What is the king doing as he says the words "drops of sorrow"?*

42. Inverness: Macbeth's castle.

43. *Who is to inherit Duncan's crown?*

44. The rest . . . you: When rest is not used for you, it is labor.

45. harbinger: sign of something to come.

52. wink . . . hand: be blind to the hand's deed.

53. *Where in this speech do we begin to hear Macbeth talk in terms of darkness?*

55. his commendations: praises of him.

Glamis Castle, Angus, Scotland.

Literary Focus **Tragedy** How do you think Macbeth would have reacted to this news had he not met the witches and heard their prophecy?

Universal Access

Struggling Readers

Model the skill of using questioning to monitor reading. You might say: "There is a lot happening in this play, so I often have to use questioning to make sure I understand what is going on." Read aloud from the beginning of Scene 5 through the end of Macbeth's letter at line 13. You might say: "I want to make sure I understand this letter, so I'll ask, 'What is Macbeth's purpose in writing to Lady Macbeth?' The answer is that he wants to encourage her by telling her of the witches' prophecy."

Advanced Learners

Enrichment Explain to students that Macbeth is torn between his loyalty to his kinsman and his desire to be king. Have students think about the conflicting feelings that Macbeth is experiencing. Have students write a short monologue in which they take the role of Macbeth and express their inner fears and torments in their own words.

them than mortal knowledge. When I burned in desire to question them further, they made themselves air, into which they vanished. Whiles I stood rapt in the wonder of it, came missives° from the King, who all-hailed me 'Thane of Cawdor'; by which title, before, these weird sisters saluted me, and referred me to the coming on of time, with 'Hail, king that shalt be!' This have I thought good to deliver thee, my dearest partner of greatness, that thou mightst not lose the dues of rejoicing, by being ignorant of what greatness is promised thee. Lay it to thy heart, and farewell."

Glamis thou art, and Cawdor, and shalt be
What thou art promised. Yet do I fear thy nature;
It is too full o' th' milk of human kindness
To catch the nearest way. Thou wouldst be great,
Art not without ambition, but without
The illness° should attend it. What thou wouldst highly,
That wouldst thou holily; wouldst not play false,
And yet wouldst wrongly win. Thou'dst have, great Glamis,
That which cries, "Thus thou must do" if thou have it;
And that which rather thou dost fear to do
Than wishest should be undone. Hie thee hither,
That I may pour my spirits in thine ear,
And chastise with the valor of my tongue
All that impedes thee from the golden round
Which fate and metaphysical° aid doth seem
To have thee crowned withal. **P**

[*Enter* MESSENGER.]

What is your tidings?

Messenger.
The king comes here tonight.

Lady Macbeth. Thou'rt mad to say it!
Is not thy master with him, who, were't so,
Would have informed for preparation?

Messenger.
So please you, it is true. Our thane is coming.
One of my fellows had the speed of him,°
Who, almost dead for breath, had scarcely more
Than would make up his message.

Lady Macbeth. Give him tending;
He brings great news. [*Exit* MESSENGER.]
The raven himself is hoarse

P Reading Focus **Using Questioning to Monitor Reading** What questions do you have about Lady Macbeth's analysis of her husband's personality?

? Staging the Play
Stage direction: *As you picture Lady Macbeth reading this letter, try to imagine what she would be doing onstage and what her mood would be, especially at the words "Thane of Cawdor."*

6. missives: messengers.

? **13.** *What does Lady Macbeth do with the letter? Whom is she addressing here with "thou" and "thy"? How would you explain "th' milk of human kindness"?*

18. illness: wickedness; evil nature.

? **26.** *What do you guess the "golden round" is?*

27. metaphysical: supernatural.

33. had . . . him: had more speed than he did.

? **36.** *Who is the raven she refers to as being hoarse? Why does she call him a raven?*

Think About/Talk About

Comprehension

P Reading Focus

Possible responses: *What evidence does Lady Macbeth have to support her claims about Macbeth's weakness in character? He seems ruthless on the battlefield; will he also be ruthless in pursuing his desire to be king?*

Analysis

O Literary Focus

Possible response: *Macbeth would probably have accepted Duncan's decision without resentment, pleased to have been recently named Thane of Cawdor. He might have been happy for Malcolm as well, but because of the witches' prophecy, he is now envious.*

Extend the Discussion

Summarizing Summarize Lady Macbeth's assessment of her husband's character after she reads his letter. ***Possible response:*** *Lady Macbeth thinks that Macbeth is ambitious but too kindhearted to seize the quickest route to the throne. He will be reluctant to do evil. She wants him to do whatever needs to be done, even if it frightens him, to make the glorious prophecy come true.*

Evaluating How do Lady Macbeth's views of good and evil come to light in her speech in lines 13–20? ***Possible response:*** *Lady Macbeth sees evil as a necessary component of ambition. She seems even more ambitious than her husband and prizes power over all other values. To her, personal morality is an obstacle to be overcome, not a force that should guide one's actions.*

Cross-Curricular Connection

SOCIAL STUDIES: Witchcraft

Shakespeare was writing about witches for an audience obsessed by witchcraft. People of the time believed that witches were linked to the devil and that they preyed not only on people's souls but also on dead bodies not buried in consecrated ground. Today, certain cultures still believe in beings who use supernatural powers for wicked ends.

Discuss with students how other writers and film directors have portrayed witches, such as those in fairy tales like *Snow White*, or in movies such as *The Wizard of Oz*, or in plays such as *The Crucible*. Ask how these portrayals compare with that of the three witches in *Macbeth*.

Model the Skill

- Review the structure of a **tragedy**. Explain how inside and outside forces inexorably draw a tragic hero to his or her downfall. Ask students to name at least one external force that appears to be drawing Macbeth toward a tragic end. [*the witches' prophecy; the Thane of Cawdor's execution*]
- Read aloud lines 35–52, in which Lady Macbeth prays to become "unsexed" so that she can carry out the murder. Explain to students that Lady Macbeth represents another external force who will ruin Macbeth.

Guided Practice: Apply

Think-Pair-Share Ask students to discuss and identify other inner and external forces that condemn Macbeth to his tragic fate. ***Possible responses:*** *Macbeth's ambition; Duncan's trust in him; Macbeth's envy of Malcolm*

Think About/Talk About

Responses to Margin Questions

Line 52 *She has prayed that her finest womanly qualities be made "foul." She would like to be able to act as strong and stoic as a man.*

Line 57 *Their reunion suggests real passion. A director might have them embrace and gaze into each other's eyes.*

Line 69 *Macbeth may be impressed by her fervor, eager to pursue the enterprise, or eager for reassurance that all will be well.*

Line 9 *Though readers know evil lurks within, the visitors remark how pleasant the castle is. This dramatic irony illustrates the paradox "Fair is foul, and foul is fair." Lady Macbeth probably pretends to be pleased and flattered by the royal visit.*

That croaks the fatal entrance of Duncan
Under my battlements. Come, you spirits
That tend on mortal° thoughts, unsex me here,
And fill me, from the crown to the toe, top-full
Of direst cruelty! Make thick my blood,
Stop up th' access and passage to remorse,
That no compunctious visitings of nature°
Shake my fell° purpose, nor keep peace between
Th' effect and it! Come to my woman's breasts,
And take my milk for gall,° you murd'ring ministers,°
Wherever in your sightless° substances
You wait on nature's mischief! Come, thick night,
And pall° thee in the dunnest° smoke of hell,
That my keen knife see not the wound it makes,
Nor heaven peep through the blanket of the dark,
To cry "Hold, hold!" Q

[*Enter* MACBETH.]

Great Glamis! Worthy Cawdor!
Greater than both, by the all-hail hereafter!
Thy letters have transported me beyond
This ignorant present, and I feel now
The future in the instant.

Macbeth. My dearest love,
Duncan comes here tonight.

Lady Macbeth. And when goes hence?

Macbeth.
Tomorrow, as he purposes.

Lady Macbeth. O, never
Shall sun that morrow see!
Your face, my thane, is as a book where men
May read strange matters. To beguile the time,°
Look like the time; bear welcome in your eye,
Your hand, your tongue: look like th' innocent flower,
But be the serpent under't. He that's coming
Must be provided for: and you shall put
This night's great business into my dispatch;°
Which shall to all our nights and days to come
Give solely sovereign sway and masterdom.

Macbeth.
We will speak further.

Lady Macbeth. Only look up clear.°
To alter favor ever is to fear.°
Leave all the rest to me. [*Exeunt.*]

Q **Reading Focus** **Using Questioning to Monitor Reading** What questions can you ask about Lady Macbeth's role in Macbeth's downfall?

39. mortal: deadly.

43. compunctious . . . nature: natural feelings of compassion.
44. fell: savage.
46. gall: a bitter substance; bile. **murd'ring ministers:** agents of murder.
47. sightless: invisible.
49. pall: cover with a shroud, a burial cloth. **dunnest:** darkest.

? **52.** *How has Lady Macbeth reinforced the witches' statement: "Fair is foul, and foul is fair"?*

? **Staging the Play**
57. *Is their passion for each other as great as their passion for power? If you feel it is, how might a director illustrate it here?*

61. beguile the time: deceive those around you.

66. dispatch: management.

69. clear: undisturbed.
? **69.** *How is Macbeth feeling?*
70. To alter . . . fear: To show an altered face is dangerous.

Sean Bean and Samantha Bond in the production of *Macbeth* at the Albery Theatre, St. Martins Lane, London.

Scene 6. *Before Macbeth's castle.*

Hautboys° and torches. Enter KING DUNCAN, MALCOLM, DONALBAIN, BANQUO, LENNOX, MACDUFF, ROSS, ANGUS, *and* ATTENDANTS.

King.
This castle hath a pleasant seat;° the air
Nimbly and sweetly recommends itself
Unto our gentle senses.

Banquo. This guest of summer,
The temple-haunting martlet,° does approve°
By his loved mansionry° that the heaven's breath
Smells wooingly here. No jutty,° frieze,
Buttress, nor coign of vantage,° but this bird
Hath made his pendent bed and procreant° cradle.
Where they most breed and haunt, I have observed
The air is delicate.

[*Enter* LADY MACBETH.]

King. See, see, our honored hostess!

Hautboys: oboes.

1. **seat:** situation; setting.

4. **martlet:** bird that builds nests in churches. **approve:** prove.

5. **mansionry:** nest (dwelling).

6. **jutty:** projection.

7. **coign of vantage:** advantageous corner (of the castle).

8. **procreant:** breeding.

? Elements of Drama
9. *This scene contrasts strongly with the previous one. Again, what irony do you detect as Duncan admires the castle? How do you imagine Lady Macbeth acts as she now enters to greet her guests?*

Think About/Talk About

Comprehension

Ⓠ Reading Focus

Possible responses: *What is Lady Macbeth asking in this speech? How does she plan to help Macbeth become king?*

Extend the Discussion

Tragedy What role do you think Lady Macbeth will play in Macbeth's downfall? ***Possible response:*** *She will provoke Macbeth into doing the evil deed that will lead to his tragic downfall. If he shows any reluctance, she will goad him on.*

Evaluating How does the exchange between Duncan and Banquo at the beginning of Scene 6 evoke the audience's sympathy? ***Possible response:*** *This dialogue points out the trust that Duncan is placing in the Macbeths. Because it is clear that Duncan suspects no ill will, and because the audience knows that the Macbeths are planning his murder, the audience feels sympathetic toward Duncan.*

Universal Access

Students with Disabilities

Paraphrase for students the advice that Lady Macbeth gives to her husband. You might say: "To deceive those around you, behave like them in a way that fits the situation. Have your face and behavior seem innocent, but be cruel deep inside." Discuss with them how Macbeth might feel about deceiving Duncan, especially when the king has always expressed affection for Macbeth.

Advanced Learners

Acceleration Have students re-read line 58 on p. 420 and discuss as many interpretations of this line as possible. [*Macbeth's line could imply that even though Duncan plans to leave tomorrow, Macbeth and his wife will prevent it. Lady Macbeth follows up on the idea with her metaphorical statement that "never / Shall sun that morrow see," implying that Duncan will not be alive the following day. Students may also interpret Macbeth's line as an innocent statement, in which case Lady Macbeth is the first to suggest the murder.*] After students have shared their interpretations, have them discuss what tragic flaw this line might reveal about Macbeth.

Think About/Talk About

Extend the Discussion

Figurative Language What comparison is Macbeth making in Scene 7, lines 25–28 of his soliloquy? ***Possible response:*** *Macbeth compares his intent to commit murder to a horse; instead of a spur, he has ambition. However, like an inept rider, he may overleap or vault over the horse and fall to the other side.*

Characterization How would you describe Duncan's character? ***Possible response:*** *Duncan has some positive qualities, such as his appreciativeness, kindness, courtesy, and generosity. However, he also has negative traits, such as foolishness and gullibility.*

Responses to Margin Questions

Line 31 *Perhaps Duncan and Lady Macbeth join hands and move offstage, or the king may kiss her hand.*

Line 1 *He is afraid of the consequences of the murder; he has obligations as Duncan's kinsman, subject, and host; he is motivated by ambition, not by hatred of Duncan or dissatisfaction with Duncan's rule.*

Line 26 *Some students may say yes; without ambition, there is no reason for Macbeth to kill Duncan. Others may say no; Lady Macbeth acts as a spur.*

The love that follows us sometime is our trouble,
Which still we thank as love. Herein I teach you
How you shall bid God 'ield° us for your pains
And thank us for your trouble.

Lady Macbeth. All our service
In every point twice done, and then done double,
Were poor and single business to contend
Against those honors deep and broad wherewith
Your majesty loads our house: for those of old,
And the late dignities heaped up to them,
We rest your hermits.°

King. Where's the Thane of Cawdor?
We coursed° him at the heels, and had a purpose
To be his purveyor:° but he rides well,
And his great love, sharp as his spur, hath holp° him
To his home before us. Fair and noble hostess,
We are your guest tonight.

Lady Macbeth. Your servants ever
Have theirs, themselves, and what is theirs, in compt,°
To make their audit at your highness' pleasure,
Still° to return your own.

King. Give me your hand.
Conduct me to mine host: we love him highly,
And shall continue our graces toward him.
By your leave, hostess. *[Exeunt.]*

Scene 7. Macbeth's castle.

Hautboys. Torches. Enter a SEWER,° *and diverse* SERVANTS *with dishes and service, and pass over the stage. Then enter* MACBETH.

Macbeth.
If it were done when 'tis done, then 'twere well
It were done quickly. If th' assassination
Could trammel up the consequence, and catch,
With his surcease,° success; that but this blow
Might be the be-all and the end-all—here,
But here, upon this bank and shoal of time,
We'd jump the life to come. But in these cases Ⓡ
We still have judgment here; that we but teach
Bloody instructions, which, being taught, return
To plague th' inventor: this even-handed justice
Commends th' ingredients of our poisoned chalice
To our own lips. He's here in double trust:

Ⓡ **Literary Focus Tragedy** What does Macbeth reveal that he believes about his fate?

13. **'ield:** reward.

20. **We rest your hermits:** We'll remain dependents who will pray for you.
21. **coursed:** chased.
22. **purveyor:** advance man.
23. **holp:** helped.

26. **in compt:** in trust.

28. **Still:** always.

? 31. *How do you imagine the scene ends?*

sewer: butler.

? 1. *In this speech, one of Shakespeare's great soliloquies, Macbeth voices his indecision and possibly reveals his conscience. A* ***soliloquy*** *is a meditative kind of speech in which a character, alone on stage and usually pretending that the audience is not present, thinks out loud. The audience is meant to understand that the speaker tells the truth freely and openly, however discreditable that truth may be. What are Macbeth's conflicts here?*

4. **his surcease:** Duncan's death.

Universal Access

Advanced Learners

Acceleration Have students re-read lines 10–12 of Scene 7. Ask students to discuss how the idea of justice is present in the tragedy. Encourage students to ask themselves: "How do Macbeth and Lady Macbeth view justice? How is justice administered in the play? What might be the author's idea of justice?" Have students consider the theme of justice as they read the rest of the tragedy. Students may choose to use a note-taking structure that allows them to track the theme of justice and other themes as they are introduced throughout the play.

First, as I am his kinsman and his subject,
Strong both against the deed; then, as his host,
Who should against his murderer shut the door,
Not bear the knife myself. Besides, this Duncan
Hath borne his faculties° so meek, hath been
So clear° in his great office, that his virtues
Will plead like angels trumpet-tongued against
The deep damnation of his taking-off;°
And pity, like a naked newborn babe,
Striding the blast, or heaven's cherubin horsed
Upon the sightless couriers° of the air,
Shall blow the horrid deed in every eye,
That° tears shall drown the wind. I have no spur
To prick the sides of my intent, but only
Vaulting ambition, which o'erleaps itself
And falls on th' other——

[*Enter* LADY MACBETH.]

How now! What news?

Lady Macbeth.
He has almost supped. Why have you left the chamber?

Macbeth.
Hath he asked for me?

Lady Macbeth. Know you not he has?

Macbeth.
We will proceed no further in this business:
He hath honored me of late, and I have bought
Golden opinions from all sorts of people,
Which would be worn now in their newest gloss,
Not cast aside so soon.

Lady Macbeth. Was the hope drunk
Wherein you dressed yourself? Hath it slept since?
And wakes it now, to look so green° and pale
At what it did so freely? From this time
Such I account thy love. Art thou afeard
To be the same in thine own act and valor
As thou art in desire? Wouldst thou have that
Which thou esteem'st the ornament of life,°
And live a coward in thine own esteem,
Letting "I dare not" wait upon° "I would,"
Like the poor cat i' th' adage?°

Macbeth. Prithee, peace!
I dare do all that may become a man;
Who dares do more is none.

Lady Macbeth. What beast was't then
That made you break° this enterprise to me?

17. faculties: powers.
18. clear: clean.

20. taking-off: murder.

23. sightless couriers: winds.

25. That: so that.

? **26.** *Macbeth says he has no spur to prick the sides of his intent. Is that true?*

37. green: sickly.

42. ornament of life: crown.

44. wait upon: follow.
45. poor . . . adage: a saying about a cat who wants fish but won't wet its paws.

48. break: disclose; reveal.

Guided Practice

Analysis

R Literary Focus

Possible response: *Macbeth is here evaluating the risks and consequences of his actions. He seems to believe that fate is ultimately determined by his choices.*

Extend the Discussion

Finding Details What does Macbeth state as his reason for backing out of the plan to kill Duncan in lines 31–34? ***Possible response:*** *Macbeth says that the glory of his new position makes killing the king unnecessary.*

Interpreting What does Lady Macbeth mean by her words to her husband in lines 35–45? What is she trying to accomplish here? ***Possible responses:*** *She is challenging Macbeth by implying that he is too cowardly to attain the crown. She is trying to shame him into fulfilling their plan to kill Duncan.*

Reaching Reluctant Readers

Students may be resistant to the unfamiliar language in Shakespeare. Check students' comprehension with the following activity.

- Have students form groups of three. Explain they are King Duncan's trusted servants and that they suspect Macbeth and his wife are plotting to murder the king.
- Point out to students that their letter must contain solid evidence in order to convince the unsuspecting king that his newly honored Thane is plotting treason. Tell students they should gather evidence from the text of the play.
- Groups will draw evidence from Act I that casts suspicion on Macbeth. Evidence can include facts (actual events from Act I), audio evidence (incriminating speeches), and psychological testimony (any changes in Macbeth's behavior). Remind students that as they collect evidence, they should also record the specific scene and lines from which they obtained the evidence.
- At the conclusion of the class period, each group can present its letter while the other groups comment on its credibility and persuasive strength.

Think About/Talk About

Comprehension

T Reading Focus

Possible response: *How much control does Lady Macbeth have in the relationship?*

Analysis

S Literary Focus

Possible response: *She thinks that he is weak and feminine.*

Responses to Margin Questions

Line 54 *She challenges Macbeth's manliness. The words "We fail?" could be spoken with irony or disbelief. Speaking the line as a statement would convey the meaning, "If we fail, we fail, but we should at least make the attempt."*

Line 72 *She plans to give the guards wine to make them unconscious, after which she and Macbeth will kill Duncan and frame the guards for the murder.*

Line 81 *He should pause and speak grimly or with determination.*

Line 82 *The line echoes the line "Fair is foul, and foul is fair" in that the mask of a fair face conceals a foul heart.*

Monitor Students' Comprehension

Guide the class in answering these questions.

1. In Act I, Scene I, why does Duncan give Macbeth a new title? [*to reward him for his brave service*]
2. Whom does Duncan name as Prince of Cumberland? [*his son Malcolm*]
3. In the final scene of this act, what is the conflict between Macbeth and his wife? [*whether to kill Duncan*]

When you durst do it, then you were a man;
And to be more than what you were, you would
Be so much more the man. Nor time nor place S
Did then adhere,° and yet you would make both.
They have made themselves, and that their fitness now
Does unmake you. I have given suck, and know
How tender 'tis to love the babe that milks me:
I would, while it was smiling in my face,
Have plucked my nipple from his boneless gums,
And dashed the brains out, had I so sworn as you
Have done to this.

Macbeth. If we should fail?

Lady Macbeth. We fail?
But° screw your courage to the sticking-place,°
And we'll not fail. When Duncan is asleep—
Whereto the rather shall his day's hard journey
Soundly invite him—his two chamberlains
Will I with wine and wassail° so convince,°
That memory, the warder of the brain,
Shall be a fume, and the receipt of reason
A limbeck only:° when in swinish sleep
Their drenchèd natures lie as in a death,
What cannot you and I perform upon
Th' unguarded Duncan, what not put upon
His spongy officers, who shall bear the guilt
Of our great quell?

Macbeth. Bring forth men-children only;
For thy undaunted mettle° should compose
Nothing but males. Will it not be received,
When we have marked with blood those sleepy two
Of his own chamber, and used their very daggers,
That they have done't?

Lady Macbeth. Who dares receive it other,
As we shall make our griefs and clamor roar
Upon his death?

Macbeth. I am settled, and bend up
Each corporal agent to this terrible feat.
Away, and mock the time° with fairest show:
False face must hide what the false heart doth know. T

[Exeunt.]

52. adhere: suit.

? **54.** *How does Lady Macbeth try to intimidate her husband in this speech? Watch what she says about herself in the next lines. There has been some question as to whether "We fail?" (line 59) should be a question. How does the meaning change if the line is spoken as a statement?*

60. But: only. **sticking-place:** the notch in a crossbow.

64. wassail: drinking. **convince:** overcome.

66–67. the receipt . . . only: The reasoning part of the brain would become like a limbeck (or still), distilling only confused thoughts.

? **72.** Quell *is "murder." What are Lady Macbeth's plans?*

73. mettle: spirit.

81. mock the time: deceive the world.

? **Staging the Play**
81. *Should Macbeth pause here? How should these key words be spoken?*

? **82.** *How is this yet another echo of the witches' words in Scene 1?*

S Literary Focus Tragedy Lady Macbeth argues that following through with his murderous plans would make Macbeth more of a man. Based on these lines, what does she think of her husband?

T Reading Focus Using Questioning to Monitor Reading As Act I ends, Lady Macbeth has, at least for the moment, the upper hand in the argument. What questions about their relationship does this raise for you?

California Standards, p. 425

- **Reading Standard 2.2** Analyze the way in which clarity of meaning is affected by the patterns of organization, hierarchical structures, repetition of the main ideas, syntax, and word choice in the text.
- **Reading Standard 3.1** Analyze characteristics of subgenres (e.g., satire, parody, allegory, pastoral) that are used in poetry, prose, plays, novels, short stories, essays, and other basic genres.
- **Reading Standard 3.4** Analyze ways in which poets use imagery, personification, figures of speech, and sounds to evoke readers' emotions.
- **Grades 9–10 Review Reading Standard 3.12** Analyze the way in which a work of literature is related to the themes and issues of its historical period. (Historical approach).
- **Writing Standard 2.1** Write fictional, autobiographical, or biographical narratives: **c.** Describe with concrete sensory details the sights, sounds, and smells of a scene and the specific actions, movements, gestures, and feelings of the characters; use interior monologue to depict the characters' feelings.

Applying Your Skills

Reading Standard 2.2, 3.1, 3.4; **Grades 9–10 Review**
Reading Standard 3.12 (see pages A48–A50)
Writing Standard 2.1c (see pages A51–A52)

The Tragedy of Macbeth
Act I

Literary Response and Analysis

Reading Skills Focus

Quick Check

1. What does the king determine to do for Macbeth? Why?
2. What do the witches predict for Banquo and Macbeth in Scene 3?

Read with a Purpose

3. What flaw pushes Macbeth from his stunning victory toward a tragic downfall?

Reading Skills: Using Questions to Monitor Reading

4. While reading Act I, you recorded questions that you had about the text. Now, add another column, record your answers, and note how you found those answers.

Act, Scene, Line	Questions I Have	My Answers
Act I, Scene 1, line 10	What might the witches mean by something both "foul" and "fair"?	Being king is "fair," but murder is "foul," and the whole thing is confusing for Macbeth, who is unsure what to do.

Literary Skills Focus

Literary Analysis

5. **Analyze** How can Banquo be both "lesser than Macbeth, and greater"?
6. **Interpret** How does Banquo's reaction to the witches differ from Macbeth's? What do you think Macbeth's reaction suggests about his character?
7. **Evaluate** What conflict does Macbeth experience after he hears the witches' prophecy?
8. **Make Judgments** In Scene 7, lines 31–35, Macbeth presents an argument to Lady Macbeth for abandoning their plot. What do these lines indicate about what he really values?
9. **Literary Perspectives** English citizens in Shakespeare's time believed in the need for social order. What evidence can you find that Macbeth himself believes in order despite his "vaulting ambition"?

Literary Skills: Tragedy

10. **Interpret** Which characteristics of a tragic hero does Macbeth possess and Banquo lack?

Literary Skills Review: Paradox

11. **Extend** A **paradox** is an apparent contradiction that is actually true. The witches' prediction that Banquo will be "lesser than Macbeth, and greater" is a paradox. Find other examples of paradox in Act I, and explain the hidden truths they reveal.

Writing Skills Focus

Think as a Reader/Writer

Use It in Your Writing As you read Act I, you noted how Shakespeare reveals his characters' personalities through their speech, thoughts, actions, and appearance. Now, write a description of any character's thoughts as he or she struggles to make an important decision. Try to use your character's words and thoughts to reveal his or her personality.

What Do You Think Now? In Act I, how does Macbeth respond to the impulses of his heart and mind?

For more activities see page 494–495.

Universal Access

Struggling Writers

Some students may need additional scaffolding to complete the Writing Skills Focus activity. Give students a definite character and a problem they can develop. For example, they could examine the inner struggle of a student running for class president who is considering tarnishing his or her opponent's reputation in order to win the election. Ask students to identify with the character to evaluate the pros and cons of the situation and to make inferences about his or her emotional state.

What Do You Think Now?

Ask students to think about the conflicts that Macbeth faces in Act I. Ask students, "What are the conflicting values with which Macbeth struggles? How does this struggle make Macbeth seem more or less realistic?"

Assess

Unit 2 Resources,
Selection Standards Check, p. 102

Check for Understanding

Independent Practice

Reading Skills Focus

Possible responses:

1. *The king decides to give Cawdor's title to Macbeth as a reward for saving the nation.*
2. *They predict that Macbeth will become king and that Banquo's children will be kings.*
3. *His tragic flaw is ambition.*
4. *Have students share their questions and discuss how they found the correct answers.*

Literary Skills Focus

Possible responses:

5. *Banquo is lesser than Macbeth because he will not be king, but greater because his descendants will rule.*
6. *Banquo is not afraid of the prophecy, but Macbeth seems shaken. Macbeth's reaction suggests that he is insecure and easily manipulated.*
7. *Macbeth does not know whether fate will lead him to the crown or whether he will have to intervene.*
8. *He values loyalty and honor.*
9. *Macbeth acknowledges that Duncan is a good king in Scene 7, lines 16–20.*
10. *Macbeth has a tragic flaw. While Banquo is content that his children will be kings, Macbeth's ambition is setting him on a dangerous course.*
11. *In line 131 of Scene 3, Macbeth says the witches' prophecy "cannot be ill, cannot be good." This reveals Macbeth's conflicted response to the prophecy. He cannot deny his delight at the thought of becoming king, but at the same time, he is horrified to find himself wishing for Duncan's death.*

Teacher Preparation

Selection Plot Summary

Act II begins with Macbeth agonizing over his impending deed—the murder of Duncan. Lady Macbeth scolds him for his squeamish hesitancy, yet she herself feels ambivalent, saying that she would kill Duncan herself, except that he looks like her father. After Macbeth kills Duncan, Lady Macbeth smears the sleeping servants with Duncan's blood, leaving the daggers in the servants' hands. The next morning those in the castle discover that Duncan is dead. Macbeth kills the servants, seemingly out of revenge for Duncan's murder, but really to protect himself. Lady Macbeth pretends to faint in horror at the king's murder. Duncan's sons, Malcolm and Donalbain, fearing they will be murdered next, flee to England and Ireland respectively. Their disappearance causes Macduff to suspect them of killing their father.

Direct Teach

Think About/Talk About

Responses to Margin Questions

Stage direction *Fleance is Banquo's son. Earlier, the witches told Banquo that he would beget kings—perhaps this son will become a king one day. There is no indication that Macbeth and Lady Macbeth have children other than Lady Macbeth's reference to having nursed a baby.*

Line 24 *He may wish to find out if Banquo would support his claim if Duncan died naturally, or to find out, in general, what Banquo is thinking. Students might say Macbeth's motives are self-serving.*

Line 32 *The bell signals the moment when Macbeth and Lady Macbeth will enact their plan.*

Line 41 *He draws his own dagger to compare it to the imaginary one.*

Act II

Scene 1. *Inverness. Court of Macbeth's castle.*

Enter BANQUO, *and* FLEANCE, *with a torch before him (on the way to bed).*

Banquo.
How goes the night, boy?

Fleance.
The moon is down; I have not heard the clock.

Banquo.
And she goes down at twelve

Fleance. I take't, 'tis later, sir.

Banquo.
Hold, take my sword. There's husbandry° in heaven.
Their candles are all out. Take thee that too.
A heavy summons° lies like lead upon me, **A**
And yet I would not sleep. Merciful powers,
Restrain in me the cursèd thoughts that nature
Gives way to in repose! **B**

[*Enter* MACBETH, *and a* SERVANT *with a torch.*]

Give me my sword!
Who's there?

Macbeth.
A friend.

Banquo.
What, sir, not yet at rest? The king's a-bed:
He hath been in unusual pleasure, and
Sent forth great largess to your offices:°
This diamond he greets your wife withal,
By the name of most kind hostess; and shut up°
In measureless content. **C**

Macbeth. Being unprepared,
Our will became the servant to defect,°
Which else should free have wrought.

? **Staging the Play**
Stage direction: *Who is Fleance? What would you remember of the witches' prophecy when you see him here? Do we know if Macbeth and his wife have any children?*

4. **husbandry:** economizing (that is, putting out the lights to save money on candles).
6. **summons:** call to sleep.

14. **largess to your offices:** gifts to your servants' quarters.
16. **shut up:** concluded.

18. **to defect:** to insufficient preparations.

A **Literary Focus** **Tragedy** The first scene of Act I established a dark, ominous mood for the tragedy with the appearance of the witches in a thunderstorm. How do the first lines of Act II contribute to the mood?

B **Literary Focus** **Tragedy** Based on these lines, what does Banquo fear?

C **Reading Focus** **Using Questioning to Monitor Reading** Duncan's generosity suggests that he remains ignorant of Macbeth's character and thoughts. What questions arise about how his failing leadership contributes to Macbeth's ambition?

Universal Access

EL English Learners/ Struggling Readers

English for Academic Success Direct students to line 12. Tell students that today people say someone is "in bed," not "a-bed." Explain that a few forms are still used with the introductory *a* that means "on" or "in," such as *aloft*, which means "high up, at the top of." Ask students to think of other examples and their definitions. [*atop*—"on top of something"; *aboard*—"on board"; *aflutter*—"fluttering"; *aloud*—"out loud"]

Advanced Learners

Enrichment Although the play may de-emphasize the murder of Duncan by placing it offstage, remind students that Macbeth is about to take a human life. Ask them to think about Duncan, who is about to be murdered in his sleep, and to jot down a few notes describing their thoughts about him as a king and as a human being. Ask students to share their ideas with the class.

Banquo. All's well.
I dreamt last night of the three weird sisters:
To you they have showed some truth.
Macbeth. I think not of them.
Yet, when we can entreat an hour to serve,
We would spend it in some words upon that business,
If you would grant the time.
Banquo. At your kind'st leisure.
Macbeth.
If you shall cleave to my consent, when 'tis,°
It shall make honor for you.
Banquo. So° I lose none
In seeking to augment it, but still keep
My bosom franchised° and allegiance clear,°
I shall be counseled. **D**
Macbeth. Good repose the while!
Banquo.
Thanks, sir. The like to you!
[*Exit* BANQUO, *with* FLEANCE.]
Macbeth.
Go bid thy mistress, when my drink is ready,
She strike upon the bell. Get thee to bed.
[*Exit* SERVANT.]
Is this a dagger which I see before me,
The handle toward my hand? Come, let me clutch thee.
I have thee not, and yet I see thee still.
Art thou not, fatal vision, sensible°
To feeling as to sight, or art thou but
A dagger of the mind, a false creation,
Proceeding from the heat-oppressèd brain?
I see thee yet, in form as palpable°
As this which now I draw.
Thou marshal'st me the way that I was going;
And such an instrument I was to use.
Mine eyes are made the fools o' th' other senses,
Or else worth all the rest. I see thee still;
And on thy blade and dudgeon° gouts° of blood,
Which was not so before. There's no such thing.
It is the bloody business which informs°
Thus to mine eyes. Now o'er the one half-world
Nature seems dead, and wicked dreams abuse°
The curtained sleep; witchcraft celebrates
Pale Hecate's° offerings; and withered murder,

D Literary Focus Tragedy In the conversation between Macbeth and Banquo, to what does the pronoun *it* refer?

? 24. *This is the second time Macbeth has suggested he and Banquo talk. Do you think he might want to confide in Banquo? Does he want Banquo to side with him? How would you characterize his motives?*

25. cleave . . . 'tis: join my cause, when the time comes.
26. So: provided that.
28. franchised: free (from guilt). **clear:** clean.

? 32. *What is to happen upon the ringing of the bell?*

36. sensible: perceptible to the senses.

40. palpable: obvious.

? Staging the Play
41. *This soliloquy is a key moment in revealing Macbeth's character. What does Shakespeare have Macbeth do at this moment?*

46. dudgeon: hilt. **gouts:** large drops.
48. informs: gives shape.

50. abuse: deceive.

52. Hecate's: Hecate (HEHK uh tee) is the goddess of sorcery.

Think About/Talk About

Comprehension

C Reading Focus

Possible responses: *Why does Duncan trust Macbeth to this extent? How might Duncan's character encourage Macbeth's ambition?*

Analysis

A Literary Focus

Possible response: *The night is dark; there is no moon. Banquo and Fleance are unable to sleep. These details set an ominous tone.*

B Literary Focus

Possible response: *Banquo fears he will have nightmares.*

D Literary Focus

Possible response: *The pronoun* it *refers to an alliance between Macbeth and Banquo.*

Extend the Discussion

Drawing Conclusions Study lines 12–17. What is Banquo's impression of Duncan and Macbeth's relationship? ***Possible response:*** *Banquo mentions the extravagant gifts Duncan has given his host. He thinks they have a close and loyal relationship.*

Making Inferences What can you infer about Macbeth's feelings from the imagery used in line 46? ***Possible response:*** *He is realizing the seriousness and gravity of what he plans to do.*

Students with Disabilities

Tell students that in lines 33–64, Macbeth delivers a soliloquy, or a speech delivered while alone that allows a character's thoughts and ideas to be conveyed to the audience. To help students break down this important soliloquy, read it aloud. Then guide the group in a line-by-line analysis, asking students to paraphrase every few lines. As you analyze the speech, encourage students to discuss what they learn about Macbeth's state of mind. [*His anxiety about the murder he plans to commit is making him unbalanced.*] Explain to students that the soliloquy foreshadows Macbeth's tragic fall, which will occur later in the play.

Model the Skill

Model for students how to use the Reading Skills Focus graphic organizer. Ask students to read lines 26–29 in Act II, Scene 2. Explain that if they are a little confused by what Macbeth is feeling, they should mark the scene in the chart and fill in questions that address the things they are uncertain about.

Act, Scene, Line	Questions I Have
Act II, Scene 2, Lines 26–29	Is Macbeth feeling remorseful? What does he mean by 'hangman hands'?

Guided Practice: Apply

Ask students to create five new questions about the content of pp. 428–429.

Think About/Talk About

Responses to Margin Questions

Line 64 *A person might feel horror, revulsion, or suspense.*

Line 3 *You would hear an owl shrieking. The grooms are "them" and Macbeth is "He."*

Line 13 *She might speak with remorse, tenderness, or surprise at her own inability to overcome her emotions. If she is not feeling remorse, then at least she shows a more vulnerable side of her character.*

Line 33 *Yes, the words "must not" and "make us mad" suggest that she is fighting to control a troubled soul; no, she is just trying to calm Macbeth down.*

Line 41 *Banquo said that he tried not to sleep in order to avoid evil dreams. Since first imagining Duncan's murder, Macbeth has been stuck in time, at the moment of the murder.*

Alarumed° by his sentinel, the wolf,
Whose howl's his watch, thus with his stealthy pace,
With Tarquin's° ravishing strides, towards his design
Moves like a ghost. Thou sure and firm-set earth,
Hear not my steps, which way they walk, for fear
Thy very stones prate of my whereabout,
And take the present horror from the time,
Which now suits with it.° Whiles I threat, he lives:
Words to the heat of deeds too cold breath gives. **E**

[*A bell rings.*]

I go, and it is done: the bell invites me.
Hear it not, Duncan, for it is a knell
That summons thee to heaven, or to hell.

[*Exit.*]

Scene 2. Macbeth's castle.

Enter LADY MACBETH.

Lady Macbeth.
That which hath made them drunk hath made me bold;
What hath quenched them hath given me fire. Hark! Peace!
It was the owl that shrieked, the fatal bellman,
Which gives the stern'st good-night.° He is about it.
The doors are open, and the surfeited grooms
Do mock their charge with snores. I have drugged their possets,°
That death and nature do contend about them,
Whether they live or die.

Macbeth *(within).* Who's there? What, ho?

Lady Macbeth.
Alack, I am afraid they have awaked.
And 'tis not done! Th' attempt and not the deed
Confounds° us. Hark! I laid their daggers ready;
He could not miss 'em. Had he not resembled
My father as he slept, I had done't.

[*Enter* MACBETH.]

My husband!

Macbeth.
I have done the deed. Didst thou not hear a noise?

Lady Macbeth.

E **Reading Focus** **Using Questioning to Monitor Reading** Macbeth's speech is a combination of hallucination, imagery, allusion, and fact. What questions could you ask to clarify the meaning of his words?

53. Alarumed: called to action.

55. Tarquin's: Tarquin was a Roman tyrant who raped a woman named Lucrece.

60. now suits with it: now seems suitable to it.

? Staging the Play
64. *What should the audience be feeling as Macbeth exits?*

? **3.** *What sound would you hear at this point? In this soliloquy, who are the "them," and who is "He"?*

4. stern'st good-night: The owl's call is supposed to portend death. The bellman was a person who rang a bell outside a condemned person's cell the night before his execution to warn him to confess his sins.

6. possets: bedtime drinks.

11. Confounds: ruins.

? Staging the Play
13. *How should Lady Macbeth say this last line, which reveals why the plans have changed? Do you think she is beginning to show remorse?*

Glamis Castle, Angus, Scotland.

Developing Oral Fluency

Paired Activity Group students in pairs. One student will read the part of Macbeth, the other the part of Lady Macbeth. Have students practice reading Scene 2 aloud, focusing on expression and pacing. Remind students what a critical moment this is in the lives of Macbeth and Lady Macbeth. Pairs can volunteer to present their scene to the class.

✔ See the **UA: Differentiating Instruction** for practice passages for developing oral fluency.

I heard the owl scream and the crickets cry.
Did not you speak?
Macbeth. When?
Lady Macbeth. Now.
Macbeth. As I descended?
Lady Macbeth. Ay.
Macbeth. Hark!
Who lies i' th' second chamber?
Lady Macbeth. Donalbain.
Macbeth. This is a sorry sight. (F)
Lady Macbeth.
A foolish thought, to say a sorry sight.
Macbeth.
There's one did laugh in 's sleep, and one cried "Murder!"
That they did wake each other. I stood and heard them.
But they did say their prayers, and addressed them
Again to sleep.
Lady Macbeth. There are two lodged together.
Macbeth.
One cried "God bless us!" and "Amen" the other,
As they had seen me with these hangman's hands:
List'ning their fear, I could not say "Amen,"
When they did say "God bless us!"
Lady Macbeth. Consider it not so deeply.
Macbeth.
But wherefore could not I pronounce "Amen"?
I had most need of blessing, and "Amen"
Stuck in my throat.
Lady Macbeth. These deeds must not be thought
After these ways; so, it will make us mad.
Macbeth.
Methought I heard a voice cry "Sleep no more!
Macbeth does murder sleep"—the innocent sleep,
Sleep that knits up the raveled sleave° of care,
The death of each day's life, sore labor's bath,
Balm of hurt minds, great nature's second course,°
Chief nourisher in life's feast——
Lady Macbeth. What do you mean?
Macbeth.
Still it cried "Sleep no more!" to all the house:
"Glamis hath murdered sleep, and therefore Cawdor
Shall sleep no more: Macbeth shall sleep no more."

(F) **Literary Focus** **Tragedy** The sentence breaks and interruptions in the middle of these lines create a choppy effect. Why is this effect appropriate for Macbeth and Lady Macbeth's conversation?

Falcon Square, Inverness City.

? 33. *Is Lady Macbeth fighting for control here?*

36. **raveled sleave:** tangled thread.

38. **second course:** sleep (the less substantial first course is food).

? 41. *Who else complained about sleep? In what way has Glamis "murdered sleep"?*

Think About/Talk About

Comprehension

(E) Reading Focus

Possible responses: *Why is Macbeth comparing himself to Tarquin? What request does he make to the "firm-set earth" and why?*

Analysis

(F) Literary Focus

Possible response: *The effect mimics the panic felt by the couple.*

Extend the Discussion

Finding Details In lines 9–10, what does Lady Macbeth fear will ruin their plan—and thus lead to the ruin of her and Macbeth? ***Possible response:*** *If the guards awaken before Macbeth murders Duncan and see Macbeth attempting to kill him, they will be discovered and punished for plotting against him.*

Figurative Language Identify the metaphors that describe sleep in lines 34–39. ***Possible response:*** *a knitter who untangles the threads of care; the death of the life of each day; a bath that soothes a laborer; an ointment that heals the mind; the body's greatest need after food*

Universal Access

EL English Learners

English for Academic Success Some students may struggle to understand Shakespeare's odd use of sentence constructions in *Macbeth*. Direct students' attention to line 21 on p. 429: "A foolish thought, to say a sorry sight." Point out that this is a shortened version of "It is a foolish thought to say that this is a sorry sight." To give students practice in understanding lines with difficult sentence construction, have students read line 29. Encourage students to work in pairs to interpret Lady Macbeth's line. [*Do not consider it so deeply.*]

Struggling Readers

Tell students that because *Macbeth* is a tragedy, they know that the tragic hero Macbeth will eventually die or be met with some type of tragic end. Explain to students that as they read the play, they should look for clues and details that foreshadow Macbeth's fall. You might say: "In lines 62–64, Macbeth says that the bell tolls for Duncan. However, I can also infer that the bell that summons King Duncan to heaven or hell also announces Macbeth's journey to damnation." As students continue to read, encourage them to make a list of details that warn of Macbeth's demise.

Guided Practice: Apply

Think as a Reader/Writer

Find It in Your Reading Point out Macbeth's emotional state in lines 56–62. Tell students that Macbeth is describing his bewilderment and confusion over his murderous actions; he is expressing his guilt by saying even "great Neptune's ocean" could not wash the blood from his hands.

Use It in Your Writing Tell students to write two more sentences in Macbeth's voice that creatively portray his sense of guilt and horror through the use of simile, metaphor, or imagery.

Think About/Talk About

Responses to Margin Questions

Line 46 *It is Duncan's blood. They are cleaning up after the murder. She is probably shocked that Macbeth removed the murder weapons, which could implicate him. They may have been in his belt or sleeve.*

Line 63 *Her hands are bloody, but she appears confident.*

Line 71 *He is acting lost and dazed.*

Stage direction *He might wish it could awaken his soul or conscience; or, he might wish he could awaken to a state of grace.*

Stage direction *The Porter might fumble with the gates or keys, pantomime the people he is imagining, put his hands over his ears, or pretend to do his own knocking.*

Lady Macbeth.
Who was it that thus cried? Why, worthy thane,
You do unbend your noble strength, to think
So brainsickly of things. Go get some water,
And wash this filthy witness from your hand.
Why did you bring these daggers from the place?
They must lie there: go carry them, and smear
The sleepy grooms with blood.

Macbeth. I'll go no more.
I am afraid to think what I have done;
Look on 't again I dare not.

Lady Macbeth. Infirm of purpose!
Give me the daggers. The sleeping and the dead **G**
Are but as pictures. 'Tis the eye of childhood
That fears a painted devil. If he do bleed,
I'll gild the faces of the grooms withal,
For it must seem their guilt. *[Exit. Knock within.]*

Macbeth. Whence is that knocking?
How is't with me, when every noise appalls me?
What hands are here? Ha! They pluck out mine eyes!

? **Staging the Play**
46. *What is the "filthy witness"? What actions are the couple engaged in here? In the next line, Lady Macbeth discovers the daggers. Why is she so alarmed at seeing them in her husband's hands? How could Macbeth have been carrying them so they were previously not visible?*

G **Reading Focus** **Using Questioning to Monitor Reading** Act II contains a number of links between sleep and death. What might you ask yourself to clarify why Shakespeare makes this connection?

Helen Baxendale as Lady Macbeth (1997).

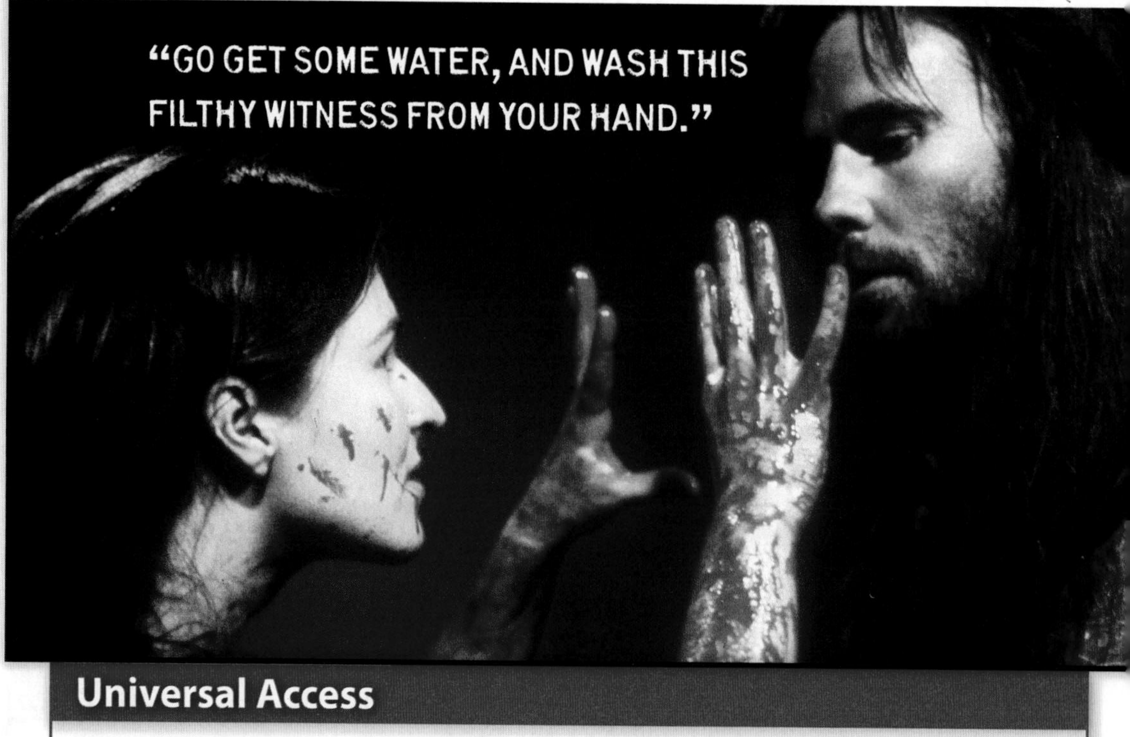

Universal Access

Struggling Readers

Students may benefit from reading *Macbeth* aloud with a partner. As students read together, ask them to pause at the end of each page to raise any questions they might have about the text. Encourage pairs to work together to figure out the answers to each other's questions. Remind students that they might not be able to answer all their questions immediately. Instead, tell students that they may have to continue reading to find the answers they are seeking.

Advanced Learners

Acceleration Ask students how the imagery in lines 57–62 concerning blood and water in Macbeth's speech contrasts with that in Lady Macbeth's speech. [*Macbeth believes that "all great Neptune's ocean" could not clean his hands, while Lady Macbeth claims "a little water clears us of this deed."*] Have students discuss the significance of this difference.

✔ See **UA: Resources for Teaching Advanced Students** for strategies for teaching advanced learners.

Will all great Neptune's ocean wash this blood
Clean from my hand? No; this my hand will rather
The multitudinous seas incarnadine,°
Making the green one red.

[*Enter* LADY MACBETH.]

Lady Macbeth.
My hands are of your color, but I shame
To wear a heart so white. (*Knock.*) I hear a knocking
At the south entry. Retire we to our chamber.
A little water clears us of this deed:
How easy is it then! Your constancy
Hath left you unattended.° (*Knock.*) Hark! more knocking.
Get on your nightgown, lest occasion call us
And show us to be watchers.° Be not lost (H)
So poorly in your thoughts.

Macbeth.
To know my deed, 'twere best not know myself.

[*Knock.*]

Wake Duncan with thy knocking! I would thou couldst! (I)
[*Exeunt.*]

Scene 3. *Macbeth's castle.*

Enter a PORTER. *Knocking within.*

Porter. Here's a knocking indeed! If a man were porter of hell gate, he should have old° turning the key. (*Knock.*) Knock, knock, knock! Who's there, i' th' name of Beelzebub?° Here's a farmer, that hanged himself on th' expectation of plenty. Come in time! Have napkins enow° about you; here you'll sweat for 't. (*Knock.*) Knock, knock! Who's there, in th' other devil's name? Faith, here's an equivocator,° that could swear in both the scales against either scale; who committed treason enough for God's sake, yet could not equivocate to heaven. O, come in, equivocator. (*Knock.*) (J) Knock, knock, knock! Who's there? Faith, here's an English

61. incarnadine: make red.

? **63.** *Based on this speech, what does Lady Macbeth look like?*

67–68. Your . . . unattended: Your firmness has deserted you.

70. watchers: that is, up late.

? **71.** *How is Macbeth behaving?*

? **Staging the Play**
Stage direction: *In the theater, this sharp, loud knocking is frightening. In the next line, what might Macbeth wish the knocking could awake in himself?*

? **Staging the Play**
Stage direction: *Note that the Porter is drunk. What would he be doing during this long speech while the knocking persists?*

2. have old: grow old.
3. Beelzebub: the Devil.

5. enow: enough.

7. equivocator: The Porter means a Jesuit, a member of the Society of Jesus, a religious order. (Jesuits were believed by some to use false arguments in their zeal for souls.)

(H) **Literary Focus** **Tragedy** The actions that constitute the murder and its coverup are not told in sequence. Make a list, in the correct order, of what Macbeth and Lady Macbeth did.

(I) **Reading Focus** **Using Questioning to Monitor Reading** Now that Macbeth has murdered Duncan, what questions can you ask to understand Macbeth's current state of mind?

(J) **Literary Perspectives** **Analyzing Historical Context** These lines refer to the failed Gunpowder Plot, a conspiracy to blow up King James and Parliament. What significance would this reference have had for Shakespeare's audience in the early seventeenth century?

Think About/Talk About

Comprehension

(G) Reading Focus
Possible response: *How are sleep and death alike?*

(I) Reading Focus
Possible responses: *How does Macbeth feel about his action? How will he pull himself together in time?*

Analysis

(H) Literary Focus
Possible response: *They drugged the servants, Macbeth committed the murder, he carried the daggers out with him, Lady Macbeth brought them back, Lady Macbeth smeared blood on the servants, Lady Macbeth returned to Macbeth, the two retired to wash their hands.*

(J) Literary Perspectives
Possible response: *The reference has political significance just as a reference to an assassination attempt would have today.*

Extend the Discussion

Irony In lines 63–64 and 67–68, why is Lady Macbeth's criticism of her husband ironic? ***Possible response:*** *It is ironic that she is being so stern with him when she herself was unable to commit the murder.*

Cross-Curricular Connection

HISTORY: The Gunpowder Plot

In his book *Witches & Jesuits*, historian Gary Wills outlines the basic facts of the Gunpowder Plot of 1605. This plot greatly shocked Protestants of the time.

"A cell of papists—the 'enemy within' of that time, directed from Rome by skulking Jesuits—had trundled keg after keg of gunpowder into a vault under parliament. A munitions expert named Guy Fawkes was discovered with the detonating materials, ready to ignite the fuse (train) when the King was addressing his Parliament, in the presence of the Prince, his heir, and all leading members of his court. The Parliament—all the Lords Spiritual and Temporal, the leading justices, and members of Commons—would be consumed in a particularly horrible way." Some critics believe that the Porter's speech is filled with references to the Jesuit priest, Father Henry Garnett, who was implicated in the Gunpowder Plot in November 1605 and hanged as a traitor. Garnett used the assumed name *Farmer* and defended equivocation as just.

Think About/Talk About

Responses to Margin Questions

Line 36 *They are about to discover the body of Duncan and the bloodied grooms.*

Line 47 *Macbeth must be sick with anxiety. As he says the first two words, he realizes that they are a lie, so he amends his statement. His correction could make him appear nervous.*

Line 54 *Unnatural winds and voices, screeching owls, and earthquakes parallel the unnatural death of Duncan.*

Line 55 *Macbeth might speak as if he were simply agreeing with Lennox but with a sidelong glance at his wife. His tone might indicate a trace of fatigue or remorse.*

Line 63 *Macduff speaks of the king as if he were a sacred building, or temple, that it is a sacrilege to attack. This image reflects the Elizabethan belief that kings were divinely anointed.*

tailor come hither for stealing out of a French hose:° come in, tailor. Here you may roast your goose.° (*Knock.*) Knock, knock; never at quiet! What are you? But this place is too cold for hell. I'll devil-porter it no further. I had thought to have let in some of all professions that go the primrose way to th' everlasting bonfire. (*Knock.*) Anon, anon! (*Opens an entrance.*) I pray you, remember the porter.

[*Enter* MACDUFF *and* LENNOX.]

Macduff.
Was it so late, friend, ere you went to bed,
That you do lie so late?

Porter. Faith, sir, we were carousing till the second cock:° and drink, sir, is a great provoker of three things.

Macduff. What three things does drink especially provoke?

Porter. Marry, sir, nose-painting, sleep, and urine. Lechery, sir, it provokes and unprovokes; it provokes the desire, but it takes away the performance: therefore much drink may be said to be an equivocator with lechery: it makes him and it mars him; it sets him on and it takes him off; it persuades him and disheartens him; makes him stand to and not stand to; in conclusion, equivocates him in a sleep, and giving him the lie, leaves him.

Macduff. I believe drink gave thee the lie° last night.

Porter. That it did, sir, i' the very throat on me: but I requited him for his lie, and, I think, being too strong for him, though he took up my legs sometime, yet I make a shift to cast° him.

Macduff. Is thy master stirring? (K)

[*Enter* MACBETH.]

Our knocking has awaked him; here he comes.

Lennox.
Good morrow, noble sir.

Macbeth. Good morrow, both.

Macduff.
Is the king stirring, worthy thane?

Macbeth. Not yet.

Macduff.
He did command me to call timely° on him:
I have almost slipped the hour.

Macbeth. I'll bring you to him.

Macduff.

(K) **Literary Focus** **Tragedy** Why would Shakespeare focus on the Porter just after the murder of the king?

12. French hose: tightfitting stocking.
13. goose: iron used by a tailor for pressing.

21. second cock: about 3:00 A.M.

32. gave thee the lie: pun meaning "called you a liar" and "stretched you out, lying in bed."
35. cast: here, a pun meaning "to cast in plaster" and "to vomit" (cast out).

? **36.** *All the time this humorous bantering is going on, what do we know these king's men are about to discover?*

40. timely: early.

Glamis Castle, Angus, Scotland.

Compare and Contrast

Have students compare and contrast the Porter's speech in lines 24–31 with Lennox's speech in lines 48–54.

- **Similarities** Both speeches are held in a conversation with another person. They are both eight lines long. They both foreshadow a problem with the king.
- **Differences** The rhythm of Lennox's speech is in iambic pentameter, while the Porter's does not use a regular rhythm. Lennox's speech is written in poetry form, while the Porter's is in prose. The Porter's speech is casual and humorous, while Lennox's is formal and serious.

I know this is a joyful trouble to you;
But yet 'tis one.

Macbeth.
The labor we delight in physics° pain.
This is the door.

Macduff. I'll make so bold to call,
For 'tis my limited service.°

[*Exit* MACDUFF.]

Lennox.
Goes the king hence today?

Macbeth. He does: he did appoint so.

Lennox.
The night has been unruly. Where we lay,
Our chimneys were blown down, and, as they say,
Lamentings heard i' th' air, strange screams of death,
And prophesying with accents terrible
Of dire combustion° and confused events
New hatched to th' woeful time: the obscure bird
Clamored the livelong night. Some say, the earth
Was feverous and did shake.

Macbeth. 'Twas a rough night.

Lennox.
My young remembrance cannot parallel
A fellow to it.

[*Enter* MACDUFF.]

Macduff.
O horror, horror, horror! Tongue nor heart
Cannot conceive nor name thee.

Macbeth and Lennox. What's the matter?

Macduff.
Confusion now hath made his masterpiece.
Most sacrilegious murder hath broke ope
The Lord's anointed temple,° and stole thence (L)
The life o' th' building.

Macbeth. What is't you say? The life?

Lennox.
Mean you his majesty?

Macduff.
Approach the chamber, and destroy your sight
With a new Gorgon:° do not bid me speak;
See, and then speak yourselves. Awake, awake!

[*Exeunt* MACBETH *and* LENNOX.]

(L) Literary Perspectives **Analyzing Historical Context** What Renaissance belief about the relationship of the king to the divine is expressed through this speech?

44. physics: cures.

46. limited service: appointed duty.

? **47.** *How must Macbeth be feeling?*

52. combustion: tumult; uproar.

? **54.** *In Elizabethan times, people often believed that nature mirrored terrible things happening to human beings, especially to kings. How did this weather mirror what was happening to the king in Macbeth's castle?*

? **Staging the Play**
55. *This single line is full of irony. How might Macbeth say it?*

62. Lord's anointed temple: body of the king.

? **63.** *How would you explain Macduff's metaphors?*

66. Gorgon: creature from Greek mythology whose face could turn an onlooker to stone.

Think About/Talk About

Analysis

(K) Literary Focus

Possible response: *Shakespeare wanted to create comic relief. He also needs to give Macbeth time to wash up before Macduff enters.*

(L) Literary Perspectives

Possible response: *People of that time believed that the king was directly connected to God.*

Extend the Discussion

Irony What is ironic about Macduff's use of the word *timely* in line 40? ***Possible response:*** *Far from being timely, Macduff's arrival is too late to save the king.*

Figurative Language In line 64, what metaphor does Macduff use that allows Lennox to assume he is talking about the king? ***Possible response:*** *Macduff's reference to the "Lord's anointed temple" would be more obvious to Lennox than it would to us today.*

Cross-Curricular Connection

HISTORY: The Elizabethan World

The Elizabethans thought the universe extended in a great chain beginning with God and extending down to the lowliest insects and worms. Everything in this chain had a place, reflecting a natural order. Harmony in heaven mirrored harmony in nature and in the political and social world. When this order was disrupted, the structure of the universe broke down. Audiences therefore were probably not surprised when Duncan's killing led to disturbances in nature.

Model the Skill

- Model for students how to use **questioning to monitor their understanding** of the play.
- Read lines 115–118 aloud. Explain that Donalbain's words to Malcolm could be confusing at first. Point out that immediately after this exchange, the two decide to flee. Students can address the difficult parts by asking questions such as, "What does Donalbain mean by 'our fate, hid in an auger-hole, / May rush, and seize us?' What is Donalbain fearful of? Does line 118 mean they have not had the chance to shed tears and should find the time to? Or does it mean they should not mourn yet?"

Guided Practice: Apply

Turn-and-Talk Ask students to write down a few questions on their own and then exchange their questions with a partner to try to find a likely response. When they have read the whole act, have students check again their questions and responses.

Think About/Talk About

Responses to Margin Questions

Line 82 *She must play the part seriously, expressing the surprise and horror that such a deed merits.*

Line 94 *Some students may say that "as it seemed" suggests that Lennox is not fully convinced. Others may argue that Lennox's line, "No man's life was to be trusted with them" is as good as an indictment.*

Ring the alarum bell. Murder and treason!
Banquo and Donalbain! Malcolm! Awake!
Shake off this downy sleep, death's counterfeit,
And look on death itself! Up, up, and see
The great doom's image! Malcolm! Banquo!
As from your graves rise up, and walk like sprites,
To countenance° this horror. Ring the bell.

[*Bell rings. Enter* LADY MACBETH.]

Lady Macbeth.
What's the business,
That such a hideous trumpet calls to parley°
The sleepers of the house? Speak, speak!
Macduff. O gentle lady,
'Tis not for you to hear what I can speak:
The repetition, in a woman's ear,
Would murder as it fell.

[*Enter* BANQUO.]

O Banquo, Banquo!
Our royal master's murdered.
Lady Macbeth. Woe, alas!
What, in our house?
Banquo. Too cruel anywhere.
Dear Duff, I prithee, contradict thyself,
And say it is not so.

[*Enter* MACBETH, LENNOX, *and* ROSS.]

Macbeth.
Had I but died an hour before this chance,
I had lived a blessèd time; for from this instant
There's nothing serious in mortality:°
All is but toys. Renown and grace is dead,
The wine of life is drawn, and the mere lees°
Is left this vault° to brag of.

[*Enter* MALCOLM *and* DONALBAIN.]

Donalbain.
What is amiss?
Macbeth. You are, and do not know't.
The spring, the head, the fountain of your blood
Is stopped; the very source of it is stopped.
Macduff.
Your royal father's murdered.
Malcolm. O, by whom?

74. countenance: be in keeping with.

76. parley: conference of war.

Staging the Play
82. *The emphasis on Lady Macbeth's gentleness and fairness when we know the foulness underneath might well merit a snicker from the audience. The snicker might be expected to grow into a laugh when she says, "What, in our house?" These are difficult moments to act. How do you think Lady Macbeth should be behaving?*

87. mortality: life.

89. lees: dregs.
90. vault: pun on "wine vault" and the "vault of heaven."

94. *Macbeth and Lady Macbeth might well look at each other at this moment. Does Lennox draw the conclusion they intended: that the servants killed Duncan?*

Universal Access

English Learners

English for Academic Success Have students choose words to include on working English vocabulary lists. Check the lists to help students focus on more common words rather than obscure, archaic, or high-level words.

✔ See the **English Language Skill Builder** in **UA: Differentiating Instruction**.

Struggling Readers

To help students read *Macbeth*, model the reading skill of questioning to monitor reading. Use lines 75–120 as an example. You might say: "As I read lines 75–120, I ask myself questions about the reactions of each of the characters when they hear about the murder of the king. This will help with my comprehension of the text. I wonder, does Banquo immediately suspect Macbeth of the murder? How significant is Macduff's character to the rest of the play? Do Donalbain and Malcolm now fear for their lives?"

Model the Skill

Model understanding the characteristics of **tragedy**. Read aloud lines 20–35. Point out to students that in these lines, Hecate informs the witches of her plan to deceive Macbeth into a false perception of security and safety. Tell students that in a tragedy, outside forces can sometimes contribute to the tragic hero's downfall.

Guided Practice: Apply

Turn-and-Talk Group students in pairs to look for other scenes in which outside forces intervened to help turn Macbeth against his better judgment. Have students discuss whether Macbeth's tragic decisions can be attributed to outside forces.

Think About/Talk About

Extend the Discussion

Finding Details According to Hecate in lines 27–29, what shall draw Macbeth "on to his confusion"? ***Possible response:*** *Hecate says that she will create artificial spirits that Macbeth will see and that will lead him to his ruin.*

Interpreting What tone of voice do you think Lennox uses in lines 6–7 when he remarks that people may say Fleance killed Banquo? ***Possible response:*** *He would speak these lines in a bitter, sarcastic tone of voice to emphasize the absurdity of the idea that Fleance killed Banquo. Lennox knows this explanation is ridiculous; without accusing Macbeth directly, he is making it clear that he suspects Macbeth of the murders.*

And at the pit of Acheron°
Meet me i' th' morning: thither he
Will come to know his destiny.
Your vessels and your spells provide,
Your charms and everything beside.
I am for th' air; this night I'll spend
Unto a dismal and a fatal end:
Great business must be wrought ere noon.
Upon the corner of the moon
There hangs a vap'rous drop profound;°
I'll catch it ere it come to ground:
And that distilled by magic sleights°
Shall raise such artificial sprites°
As by the strength of their illusion

15. Acheron: river of Hades.

24. profound: heavy.

26. sleights: arts.

27. artificial sprites: spirits created by magic arts.

Josette Simon (Witch) in *Macbeth.* Barbican Theatre, London (1983).

Universal Access

AAVE Students Who Use African American Vernacular English

English for Academic Success Some students may struggle with the pronunciation of the *th* digraph as in *this, that,* or *father.* For instance, students might voice the *th* letter combination as /d/, /f/, or /v/ in informal English. Tell students that in formal English, however, the *th* combination is pronounced /th/. Have students locate the words *that, their, think, thoughts,* and *things* on p. 455. Have students practice voicing the /th/ required in formal English by repeating the following words as a class after you: *death, farther, everything, thanks, this, there.*

✔ For additional instruction and strategies, see **Holt Pronunciation Resources** and **ThinkCentral, Teacher Access.**

Macbeth.
How say'st thou, that Macduff denies his person
At our great bidding?

Lady Macbeth. Did you send to him, sir?

Macbeth.
I hear it by the way,° but I will send:
There's not a one of them but in his house
I keep a servant fee'd.° I will tomorrow,
And betimes° I will, to the weird sisters:
More shall they speak, for now I am bent° to know
By the worst means the worst. For mine own good
All causes° shall give way. I am in blood
Stepped in so far that, should I wade no more,
Returning were as tedious as go o'er.
Strange things I have in head that will to hand,
Which must be acted ere they may be scanned.° (N)

Lady Macbeth.
You lack the season of all natures,° sleep.

Macbeth.
Come, we'll to sleep. My strange and self-abuse°
Is the initiate fear that wants hard use.°
We are yet but young in deed. *[Exeunt.]*

Scene 5. *A witches' haunt.*

Thunder. Enter the three WITCHES, *meeting* HECATE.

First Witch.
Why, how now, Hecate! you look angerly.

Hecate.
Have I not reason, beldams° as you are,
Saucy and overbold? How did you dare
To trade and traffic with Macbeth
In riddles and affairs of death;
And I, the mistress of your charms,
The close contriver° of all harms,
Was never called to bear my part,
Or show the glory of our art?
And, which is worse, all you have done
Hath been but for a wayward son,
Spiteful and wrathful; who, as others do,
Loves for his own ends, not for you.
But make amends now: get you gone,

130. by the way: incidentally.

132. fee'd: that is, paid to spy.
133. betimes: quickly.
134. bent: determined.

136. causes: considerations.

? **140.** *Does the prospect of a new adventure animate Macbeth? Or is he spent and exhausted?*

140. may be scanned: can be examined.

141. season . . . natures: seasoning (preservative) of all living creatures.

142. self-abuse: delusion.

143. initiate . . . use: beginner's fear that lacks hardening practice.

? **144.** *How might Lady Macbeth react to this last line?*

? **Scene 5.** Macbeth *was published in the first folio in 1623, seven years after Shakespeare's death. Some people think that this scene was written by someone else because the play was short and needed fleshing out. After you read the scene, decide if you think it "sounds" like the rest of the play.*

2. beldams: hags.

7. close contriver: secret inventor.

(N) **Literary Focus** **Tragedy** What new information about Macbeth's state of mind is revealed in this speech?

the groups to share their examples and explain what aspects of the stories and the heroes can be considered tragic. Ask students to comment on what tragic flaws their heroes exhibit and how these heroes do or do not resemble Macbeth. Students may take notes on the discussion to refer to later when they complete any culminating activities for the unit.

Think About/Talk About

Comprehension

(M) Reading Focus

Possible responses: *What is Macbeth's true condition? Has he completely lost his senses? What will Lady Macbeth do if he has? How will she continue the deception and protect herself? How much do the other lords know or suspect of Macbeth's dark deeds?*

Analysis

(N) Literary Focus

Possible response: *Macbeth reveals that he is determined to know what is going to happen, however bad it is. He feels that he has done so much evil that he cannot turn back. In the last line of the speech, he shows that he will act on impulse without thinking about potential consequences.*

Extend the Discussion

Drawing Conclusions What conclusions is Macbeth drawing about Macduff in lines 129–132? ***Possible response:*** *This is the second time that Macduff has refused to attend a ceremony (the first one was Macbeth's coronation). Macbeth must realize by now that Macduff suspects him of Duncan's murder.*

Interpreting What do the last lines of Scene 4, in which Macbeth characterizes himself as a beginner, suggest regarding his descent into evil? ***Possible response:*** *Macbeth blames his instability on the fact that he has little previous experience committing evil deeds. He believes that his anxiety will pass as he gains more experience, which suggests that he will continue on his destructive path.*

Think About/Talk About

Responses to Margin Questions

Line 108 *Despite all the brave talk, Macbeth does not seem very brave at all. As he utters the words, "I am a man again," he may feel relief that the ghost has disappeared, along with anxiety about having lost control of himself. His words are probably an attempt to reassure himself as well as his wife and guests.*

Line 110 *The other guests would most likely continue the meal, talk among themselves, and remark on Macbeth's odd behavior. Because travel was slower and more difficult at that time, the guests most likely planned to spend the night at Inverness. They would probably feel anxious and uneasy about staying there, given the disturbance they have just witnessed.*

Line 117 *Lady Macbeth says that Macbeth is getting worse and worse. The actor should show this deterioration in some physical manner, such as unsteadiness on his feet or putting his face into his hands.*

Line 122 *Students should describe how Macbeth would deliver the speech and explain why. They may state that Macbeth should deliver the speech slowly because he is describing his own undoing. Alternatively, if he is still feeling unsettled, his speech may be faster to reflect his nervousness. His mood is desperate and dark.*

Line 140 *Macbeth seems spent and exhausted.*

Line 144 *Lady Macbeth should realize that Macbeth is implying that there will be more murders at their hands. She may shake her head in sorrow and dismay.*

Scene 5 *The lines here differ markedly from the blank verse (unrhymed iambic pentameter) of most of the play. From line 2 on, it is written in rhymed couplets. Students may argue that this suggests the work of another author.*

Only it spoils the pleasure of the time.

Macbeth.
What man dare, I dare.
Approach thou like the rugged Russian bear,
The armed rhinoceros, or th' Hyrcan° tiger;
Take any shape but that, and my firm nerves°
Shall never tremble. Or be alive again,
And dare me to the desert° with thy sword.
If trembling I inhabit then, protest me
The baby of a girl.° Hence, horrible shadow!
Unreal mock'ry, hence! [*Exit* GHOST.]
Why, so: being gone,
I am a man again. Pray you, sit still.

Lady Macbeth.
You have displaced the mirth, broke the good meeting,
With most admired° disorder. Ⓜ

Macbeth. Can such things be,
And overcome us° like a summer's cloud,
Without our special wonder? You make me strange
Even to the disposition that I owe,°
When now I think you can behold such sights,
And keep the natural ruby of your cheeks,
When mine is blanched with fear.

Ross. What sights, my lord?

Lady Macbeth.
I pray you, speak not: he grows worse and worse;
Question enrages him: at once, good night.
Stand not upon the order of your going,°
But go at once.

Lennox. Good night; and better health
Attend his majesty!

Lady Macbeth. A kind good night to all!

[*Exeunt* LORDS.]

Macbeth.
It will have blood, they say: blood will have blood.
Stones have been known to move and trees to speak;
Augurs and understood relations° have
By maggot-pies and choughs and rooks brought forth°
The secret'st man of blood. What is the night?°

Lady Macbeth.
Almost at odds with morning, which is which.

101. Hyrcan: of Hyrcania (near the Caspian Sea).
102. nerves: sinews.
104. desert: lonely place.
105–106. If . . . girl: If then I tremble, proclaim me a baby girl.

? Staging the Play
108. *How "brave" should Macbeth appear to be with all the "brave" talk in these lines? What is his mood when he says, "I am a man again"?*

110. admired: amazing.

? **110.** *Lady Macbeth and her husband converse in private again. What would the other guests be doing?*

111. overcome us: come over us.
112–113. You . . . owe: You make me wonder what my nature is.

? Staging the Play
117. *What clue here would tell the actor playing Macbeth how he should behave?*

119. Stand . . . going: Do not insist on departing in the order of your rank.

? Staging the Play
122. *Read this speech carefully, and decide how Macbeth would deliver it: slowly? quickly? What is his mood?*

124. Augurs . . . relations: auguries (omens) and comprehended reports.
125. By . . . forth: by magpies, crows, and rooks (telltale birds) revealed.
126. What . . . night: What time of night is it?

Ⓜ **Reading Focus** **Using Questioning to Monitor Reading** Based on Macbeth's behavior here, Lady Macbeth decides that the plan is beginning to unravel. What questions does her decision to break up the party raise for you?

Universal Access

Struggling Readers

Some students may have questions about the meaning of Macbeth's speech in lines 99–109. Begin by reviewing the glosses as a class. Then, read aloud short sections of the text. Have students listen carefully and then summarize to a partner what they have heard. As students explain what they think is taking place, discuss their responses and help them correct any misunderstandings.

Advanced Learners

Acceleration Point out to students that Shakespeare wrote other tragedies, including *Romeo and Juliet, Othello,* and *Hamlet.* Explain that the early Greeks wrote tragedies and that there are modern tragedies as well. These dramas share variations on the theme that through fate or a tragic flaw, one or more characters will come to a terrible end. Have students work in groups to list other examples of heroes from popular culture or classical literature who could be considered tragic. Ask

Imposters to° true fear, would well become
A woman's story at a winter's fire,
Authorized° by her grandam. Shame itself!
Why do you make such faces? When all's done,
You look but on a stool.

Macbeth. Prithee, see there!
Behold! Look! Lo! How say you?
Why, what care I? If thou canst nod, speak too.
If charnel houses° and our graves must send
Those that we bury back, our monuments
Shall be the maws of kites.° [*Exit* GHOST.]

Lady Macbeth. What, quite unmanned in folly?

Macbeth.
If I stand here, I saw him.

Lady Macbeth. Fie, for shame!

Macbeth.
Blood hath been shed ere now, i' th' olden time,
Ere humane statute purged the gentle weal;°
Ay, and since too, murders have been performed
Too terrible for the ear. The time has been
That, when the brains were out, the man would die,
And there an end; but now they rise again,
With twenty mortal murders on their crowns,°
And push us from our stools. This is more strange
Than such a murder is.

Lady Macbeth. My worthy lord,
Your noble friends do lack you.

Macbeth. I do forget.
Do not muse at me, my most worthy friends;
I have a strange infirmity, which is nothing
To those that know me. Come, love and health to all!
Then I'll sit down. Give me some wine, fill full.

[*Enter* GHOST.]

I drink to th' general joy o' th' whole table,
And to our dear friend Banquo, whom we miss;
Would he were here! To all and him we thirst,°
And all to all.°

Lords. Our duties, and the pledge.

Macbeth.
Avaunt! and quit my sight! Let the earth hide thee!
Thy bones are marrowless, thy blood is cold;
Thou hast no speculation° in those eyes
Which thou dost glare with.

Lady Macbeth. Think of this, good peers,
But as a thing of custom; 'tis no other.

64. to: compared with.

66. Authorized: vouched for.

? Staging the Play
68. *What could the actor playing Banquo do here in mockery of Macbeth?*

? Elements of Drama
70. *What action is Macbeth engaged in here? What is his tone?*

71. charnel houses: vaults containing bones.

72–73. our . . . kites: Our tombs shall be the bellies of rapacious birds.

? **75.** *To whom is Macbeth talking?*

76. purged . . . weal: cleansed the state and made it gentle.

81. mortal . . . crowns: deadly wounds on their heads.

? **85.** *What impression is Macbeth trying to create?*

91. thirst: desire to drink.

92. all to all: Let everybody drink to everybody.

? **93.** *Whom is Macbeth addressing now? According to this speech, what might the ghost be doing?*

95. speculation: sight.

Think About/Talk About

Analysis

Literary Focus

Possible response: *Macbeth is now seeing ghosts. While he was previously quite anxious and fearful, he had not yet begun to hallucinate. The scene shows how his sanity and grasp of reality are beginning to deteriorate.*

Extend the Discussion

Drawing Conclusions What is Lady Macbeth's attitude toward Macbeth in lines 60–68? ***Possible response:*** *Lady Macbeth is angry and does not believe that there is a ghost. She accuses Macbeth of being a coward, a man who is afraid of something that does not exist.*

Interpreting What does Lady Macbeth mean when she says in lines 67–68 "When all's done, you look but on a stool?" ***Possible response:*** *She means that there is just an empty seat where Macbeth thinks he sees Banquo's ghost.*

Cross-Curricular Connection

SOCIAL STUDIES: Debate

Whole-Class Activity Stage a philosophical debate in your classroom. Have students take sides on this question: "Does history repeat itself?" Encourage students to locate events in the play that have occurred in history. Divide the students on each side into smaller groups for developing supporting arguments. Have each group's spokesperson present one supporting argument to the class.

Think About/Talk About

Responses to Margin Questions

Line 37 *Lady Macbeth is upset with Macbeth for not welcoming the guests in proper fashion.*

Stage direction *The ghost should appear on stage to make its presence more believable. He should appear grotesque, with bloody gashes, to fully convey the horror of Macbeth's act.*

Line 46 *Macbeth sees the ghost of Banquo sitting in Macbeth's chair.*

Line 49 *Macbeth should ask this question with accusatory terror in his voice, reflecting his increasing paranoia. He is speaking to his guests.*

Line 51 *The ghost is shaking his head at Macbeth, accusing him. Nobody else can see it. The others should be acting confused by Macbeth's words and actions.*

Line 53 *It is unlikely that this has been true since his youth. He is an acclaimed warrior who could not have been as successful in battle if he were prone to fits of imagination. Lady Macbeth is most likely saying this to calm the guests.*

Line 58 *She has pulled him away from the guests.*

Line 68 *He might glower at Macbeth, shake his head, or make threatening gestures.*

Line 70 *He is pointing to the ghost, possibly turning to Lady Macbeth for confirmation of what he sees. He may speak in a despairing tone or in a mocking manner.*

Line 75 *He seems to be talking to himself. He is clearly not talking to the ghost, who has exited.*

Line 85 *Macbeth is trying to create the impression that nothing is seriously wrong with him.*

Line 93 *Macbeth is addressing Banquo's ghost, who stares accusingly at him.*

[*Enter the* GHOST OF BANQUO, *and sits in Macbeth's place.*]

Macbeth. Sweet remembrancer!°
Now good digestion wait on appetite,
And health on both!
Lennox. May't please your highness sit.
Macbeth.
Here had we now our country's honor roofed,°
Were the graced person of our Banquo present—
Who may I rather challenge for unkindness
Than pity for mischance!°
Ross. His absence, sir,
Lays blame upon his promise. Please't your highness
To grace us with your royal company?
Macbeth.
The table's full.
Lennox. Here is a place reserved, sir.
Macbeth.
Where?
Lennox.
Here, my good lord. What is't that moves your highness?
Macbeth.
Which of you have done this?
Lords. What, my good lord?
Macbeth.
Thou canst not say I did it. Never shake
Thy gory locks at me.
Ross.
Gentlemen, rise, his highness is not well. (L)
Lady Macbeth.
Sit, worthy friends. My Lord is often thus,
And hath been from his youth. Pray you, keep seat.
The fit is momentary; upon a thought°
He will again be well. If much you note him,
You shall offend him and extend his passion.°
Feed, and regard him not.—Are you a man?
Macbeth.
Ay, and a bold one, that dare look on that
Which might appall the devil.
Lady Macbeth. O proper stuff!
This is the very painting of your fear.
This is the air-drawn dagger which, you said,
Led you to Duncan. O, these flaws° and starts,

37. remembrancer: reminder.

? **37.** *Lady Macbeth has summoned her husband to her area of the stage. How would you describe her mood?*

? ***Stage direction:*** *The ghost is crucial to this scene. Should the ghost be imagined? Or should it actually appear onstage? If so, how should it look?*

40. our . . . roofed: our nobility under one roof.

42–43. Who . . . mischance: whom I hope I may reprove because he is unkind rather than pity because he has encountered an accident.

? **46.** *When Macbeth says this line, what does he see?*

? **Staging the Play**
49. *How should Macbeth ask this question? Whom should he address?*

? **Staging the Play**
51. *According to Macbeth's speech here, what is the ghost doing? Does anyone else see the ghost? How should the others be acting?*

? **53.** *Do you think this statement is true? Or is Lady Macbeth desperately trying to cover for her husband?*

55. upon a thought: as quick as a thought.

57. extend his passion: lengthen his fit.

? **Staging the Play**
58. *Where do you think Lady Macbeth has taken her husband so that she can whisper this intimidating line?*

63. flaws: gusts; outbursts.

(L) **Literary Focus** **Tragedy** How does this scene mark the beginning of Macbeth's actual deterioration?

Reaching Reluctant Readers

Ask students: "What is causing Macbeth to lose his nerve and perhaps even his sanity? I think he is losing his nerve because of his guilt for what he has done and his fear of being found out." Ask students how guilt can affect the way people act, and have them discuss their own or other people's experiences with guilt. Talk about how hard it can be to get rid of guilty feelings, even when the cause for these feelings may be relatively minor. Then, as students read, tell them to keep in mind that guilt and fear are driving Macbeth to behave in a peculiar fashion.

Whole as the marble, founded° as the rock,
As broad and general as the casing air:°
But now I am cabined, cribbed,° confined, bound in
To saucy° doubts and fears.—But Banquo's safe?

First Murderer.
Ay, my good lord: safe in a ditch he bides,
With twenty trenchèd° gashes on his head,
The least a death to nature.

Macbeth. Thanks for that.
(*Aside.*) There the grown serpent lies; the worm° that's fled
Hath nature that in time will venom breed,
No teeth for th' present. Get thee gone. Tomorrow
We'll hear ourselves° again. [*Exit* FIRST MURDERER.]

Lady Macbeth. My royal lord,
You do not give the cheer.° The feast is sold
That is not often vouched, while 'tis a-making,
'Tis given with welcome. To feed were best at home;°
From thence, the sauce to meat° is ceremony;
Meeting were bare without it.

22. founded: firmly based.
23. broad . . . casing air: unconfined as the surrounding air.
24. cribbed: penned up.
25. saucy: insolent.
27. trenchèd: trenchlike.
29. worm: serpent.
32. hear ourselves: talk it over.
33. cheer: sense of cordiality.
33–35. The feast . . . home: The feast seems sold (not given) when the host fails to welcome the guests. Mere eating is best done at home.
36. meat: food.

Act III/IV: The Banquet. Derek Jacobi (rear) as Macbeth. Royal Shakespeare Company (1993).

Cross-Curricular Connection

LITERATURE: Shakespeare's Art of Name-Calling

"Dunghill groom," "serpent's egg," "valiant flea," and "false caterpillar" are just a few of the insults Shakespeare's characters hurl at one another. Shakespeare is a master of the art of name-calling. His characters often use dog imagery in their insults as Macbeth does in the scene with the murderers. Here are some additional dog-related insults Shakespeare uses in other plays: "common cry of curs," "butcher's cur," "cut-throat dog," "thou mongrel beef-witted lord," "puppy-headed monster," and "false hound."

Whole-Class Activity Briefly discuss the damaging effects of insults on the person toward whom the insults are directed. As students read the rest of the play, ask them to keep a two-column chart of the insults used by various characters. Students should record the speaker and the insult in the first column and use the second column to jot down notes about the purpose of the insult and the recipient's reaction. You might want to play the various parts of Act III aloud as part of this activity. Then, have students choose an insult from the play and analyze why it is effective in its context.

Think About/Talk About

Analysis

K Literary Focus

Possible response: *This speech would seem to disprove the theory. If Macbeth had been one of the murderers, he would have already known that Fleance had escaped. Macbeth seems surprised by this. The fit to which he refers is the very tense and fearful state in which he has lived since murdering Duncan. On the other hand, when Macbeth says "Here comes my fit again," he might be saying that he was already very upset when Fleance escaped, and now he has to feel those emotions again.*

Extend the Discussion

Finding Details In line 26, where does the First Murderer say that Banquo lies? ***Possible response:*** *The First Murderer says that Banquo lies in a ditch.*

Interpreting Who or what is the "worm that's fled" in line 29? What does Macbeth fear? ***Possible response:*** *The "worm that's fled" refers to Fleance. Macbeth is afraid that at some point in the future, Fleance will become the sire of kings instead of Macbeth.*

Guided Practice: Apply

Think as a Reader/Writer

Find It in Your Reading Have students read the aside spoken by Macbeth in lines 21–25. Point out that the asides allow the audience to know what is going on in the character's mind. Asides also inform the audience of what is happening in the play that other characters should not know about.

Use It in Your Writing Have students write a brief dialogue and include an aside of a few lines about a forthcoming event or intent.

Think About/Talk About

Extend the Discussion

Interpreting In line 15, Macbeth says to the Murderer, "'Tis better thee without than he within." What does Macbeth mean? ***Possible response:*** *Macbeth is saying that he would rather see blood on the face of the murderer than have Banquo be alive with blood left within his body.*

Responses to Margin Questions

Line 22 *Macbeth has acquired Cawdor and the throne, and although he has aroused suspicion, he is apparently without open opposition. Fleance's escape is his first clear failure.*

Line 2 *The subjects become aware around Act III, Scene 4, lines 48–58.*

Line 20 *He would act surprised, horrified, or angry.*

First Murderer.
Well, let's away and say how much is done. [*Exeunt.*]

Scene 4. *The palace.*

Banquet prepared. Enter MACBETH, LADY MACBETH, ROSS, LENNOX, LORDS, *and* ATTENDANTS.

Macbeth.
You know your own degrees;° sit down:
At first and last, the hearty welcome.

Lords.
Thanks to your majesty.

Macbeth.
Oneself will mingle with society°
And play the humble host.
Our hostess keeps her state,° but in best time
We will require° her welcome.

Lady Macbeth.
Pronounce it for me, sir, to all our friends,
For my heart speaks they are welcome.

[*Enter* FIRST MURDERER.]

Macbeth.
See, they encounter° thee with their hearts' thanks.
Both sides are even: here I'll sit i' th' midst:
Be large in mirth; anon we'll drink a measure°
The table round. (*Goes to* FIRST MURDERER.) There's blood
upon thy face.

First Murderer.
'Tis Banquo's then.

Macbeth.
'Tis better thee without than he within.°
Is he dispatched?

First Murderer. My lord, his throat is cut;
That I did for him.

Macbeth. Thou art the best o' th' cutthroats.
Yet he's good that did the like for Fleance;
If thou didst it, thou art the nonpareil.

First Murderer.
Most royal sir, Fleance is 'scaped.

Macbeth (*aside*).
Then comes my fit again: I had else been perfect, (K)

(K) **Literary Focus** **Tragedy** Some people have argued that Macbeth was the Third Murderer. How does this speech support or contradict that theory? Explain your answer.

? Elements of Drama
22. *This scene, so essential to the play, is often called the play's turning point or technical climax. What have been Macbeth's good fortunes so far?*

1. degrees: ranks.

? Elements of Drama
2. *This crucial scene is often called the dramatic climax of the play; it is tremendously exciting when staged well. Notice where Macbeth's subjects become aware of his capacity for irrational behavior.*

4. society: the company.

6. keeps her state: remains seated in her chair of state.

7. require: request.

10. encounter: meet.

12. measure: goblet.

15. thee . . . within: outside you than inside him.

? Staging the Play
20. *How would Macbeth react to this line?*

Universal Access

Advanced Learners

Enrichment After reading the end of Act III, Scene 3, students may have questions about how Fleance was able to escape the clutches of the three murderers. Tell students that the Third Murderer also has been identified as a supporter of Banquo and his son. This camp argues that Fleance—especially on foot—would never have been able to escape three grown men without "insider" help. The Third Murderer is the one who accuses the other of blowing out the torch, so perhaps he really is Fleance's secret helper. Ask students to re-read this section of the play and express their opinion of this theory.

Third Murderer. Macbeth.

Second Murderer.
He needs not our mistrust; since he delivers
Our offices and what we have to do
To the direction just.°

First Murderer. Then stand with us.
The west yet glimmers with some streaks of day.
Now spurs the lated° traveler apace
To gain the timely inn, and near approaches
The subject of our watch.

Third Murderer. Hark! I hear horses.

Banquo (*within*). Give us a light there, ho!

Second Murderer. Then 'tis he. The rest
That are within the note of expectation°
Already are i' th' court.

First Murderer. His horses go about.

Third Murderer.
Almost a mile: but he does usually—
So all men do—from hence to th' palace gate
Make it their walk.

[*Enter* BANQUO *and* FLEANCE, *with a torch.*]

Second Murderer.
A light, a light!

Third Murderer. 'Tis he.

First Murderer. Stand to't.

Banquo.
It will be rain tonight.

First Murderer. Let it come down.

[*They set upon* BANQUO.]

Banquo.
O, treachery! Fly, good Fleance, fly, fly, fly!
[*Exit* FLEANCE.]
Thou mayst revenge. O slave!
[*Dies.*]

Third Murderer.
Who did strike out the light?

First Murderer. Was't not the way?°

Third Murderer.
There's but one down; the son is fled. (J)

Second Murderer.
We have lost best half of our affair.

? **1.** *The identity of the Third Murderer is not made clear. Whom would you name as possible suspects?*

2–4. He needs . . . just: We need not mistrust him (the Third Murderer) since he describes our duties exactly according to our directions.

6. lated: belated.

10. within . . . expectation: on the list of expected guests.

Statue at Glamis Castle.

19. way: thing to do.

? **Staging the Play**
19. *What might the murderers be doing as the light goes out?*

? **Staging the Play**
21. *Disposal of bodies is always a problem for directors of Shakespeare's plays. How would you have Banquo's body carried off? By whom?*

(J) **Literary Focus** **Tragedy** How does the Third Murderer differ from the other murderers? Was Macbeth wise to send him?

Think About/Talk About

Analysis

(I) Literary Focus

Possible response: *Macbeth is now trying to protect Lady Macbeth from knowing about all the terrible things he is doing. Macbeth is taking more initiative and, consequently, is becoming more isolated. This isolation will contribute to his downfall.*

(J) Literary Focus

Possible response: *The Third Murderer seems to know more about the ways of the castle (such as walking the final mile) and, in particular, about Banquo's habits. It is difficult to say whether Macbeth was wise to send the Third Murderer. Perhaps not, since the murderers were unable to kill both Banquo and Fleance. It is even possible that the Third Murderer put the light out and let Fleance escape.*

Extend the Discussion

Finding Details In lines 12–14, what does the Third Murderer tell the others about how riders approach the palace? ***Possible response:*** *He tells the other murderers that riders get off their horses and walk the last mile.*

Drawing Conclusions Why is line 17 a turning point for Macbeth? ***Possible response:*** *Even though readers do not know how things will end, Fleance's escape means that the prophecy about Banquo can still come true. Moreover, this is the first time that Macbeth has been openly thwarted, so it may foreshadow a reversal of momentum in the play.*

Universal Access

Struggling Readers

Benchmark Students Pair struggling readers with more proficient readers. After students have read each scene, have them discuss what they have read with their partner. Encourage pairs to ask questions of one another to help them clarify their understanding of the text. Have students write down any questions that they are unable to answer due to lack of information or understanding of the text. After pairs have discussed, invite students to share any pending questions they have with the entire class. Work with the class to answer their remaining questions.

Model the Skill

Model understanding the archetype of the **tragic hero**. Read lines 45–56 aloud. Tell students that Macbeth is choosing to keep his plans of murder hidden from his wife and is asking the night to conceal the actions. This tells the audience that Macbeth is succumbing, without hesitation, to his evil desires and ambitions, paving the road for his own downfall.

Guided Practice: Apply

Read-Talk-Write Group students in pairs to re-read the end of Scene 2 and discuss the different view they now hold of Macbeth, compared to their views at the beginning of Act I. Ask students to write down their thoughts on the pace of Macbeth's transformation, whether they see it as gradual or sudden.

Think About/Talk About

Responses to Margin Questions

Line 35 *Lady Macbeth speaks with urgency and fear. She is worried about Macbeth's state of mind.*

Line 1 *Perhaps he is a messenger sent by Macbeth or one of Macbeth's officers. He cannot be Macbeth himself because he is with his banquet guests when one of the murderers reports back to him, and he appears genuinely shocked when he hears that Fleance escaped.*

Line 19 *As the light goes out, the murderers might be attacking Banquo.*

Line 21 *The murderers could carry Banquo offstage. Alternatively, the director could wait until the scene changes and darken the stage, at which time the actor playing Banquo could walk off in the dark.*

Gentle my lord, sleek° o'er your rugged° looks;
Be bright and jovial among your guests tonight.

Macbeth.
So shall I, love; and so, I pray, be you:
Let your remembrance apply to Banquo;°
Present him eminence,° both with eye and tongue:
Unsafe the while, that we must lave°
Our honors in these flattering streams
And make our faces vizards° to our hearts,
Disguising what they are.

Lady Macbeth. You must leave this.

Macbeth.
O, full of scorpions is my mind, dear wife!
Thou know'st that Banquo, and his Fleance, lives.

Lady Macbeth.
But in them nature's copy's not eterne.°

Macbeth.
There's comfort yet; they are assailable.
Then be thou jocund. Ere the bat hath flown
His cloistered flight, ere to black Hecate's summons
The shard-borne° beetle with his drowsy hums
Hath rung night's yawning peal, there shall be done
A deed of dreadful note.

Lady Macbeth. What's to be done?

Macbeth.
Be innocent of the knowledge, dearest chuck,° ❶
Till thou applaud the deed. Come, seeling° night,
Scarf up° the tender eye of pitiful day,
And with thy bloody and invisible hand
Cancel and tear to pieces that great bond
Which keeps me pale! Light thickens, and the crow
Makes wing to th' rooky° wood.
Good things of day begin to droop and drowse,
Whiles night's black agents to their preys do rouse.
Thou marvel'st at my words: but hold thee still;
Things bad begun make strong themselves by ill:
So, prithee, go with me. *[Exeunt.]*

Scene 3. *Near the palace.*

Enter three MURDERERS.

First Murderer.
But who did bid thee join with us?

❶ **Literary Focus** **Tragedy** How has the relationship between Lady Macbeth and Macbeth changed? How does this change help develop Macbeth's character as a tragic hero?

27. sleek: smooth. **rugged:** furrowed.

30. Let . . . Banquo: That is, focus your thoughts on Banquo.
31. eminence: honors.
32. lave: wash.
34. vizards: masks.

? Staging the Play
35. *With what degree of urgency must Lady Macbeth say this line?*

38. nature's copy's not eterne: That is, they will not live forever.

42. shard-borne: carried on scaly wings.

45. chuck: chick (a term of endearment).
46. seeling: eye-closing; blinding.
47. Scarf up: blindfold.

51. rooky: full of rooks, or crows.

Universal Access

EL English Learners

English for Academic Success Students may have difficulty understanding what Shakespeare means when he writes phrases such as "vizards to our hearts, / Disguising what they are" (lines 34–35). Point out that the gloss for *vizards* explains that the word means "masks." Then, tell students that Macbeth is saying that he and Lady Macbeth must not reveal the true feelings of their hearts. Encourage students to refer to glosses when they have questions about what they are reading.

I'll call upon you straight. Abide within.
It is concluded: Banquo, thy soul's flight,
If it find heaven, must find it out tonight. [*Exeunt.*]

Scene 2. *The palace.*

Enter LADY MACBETH *and a* SERVANT.

Lady Macbeth.
Is Banquo gone from court?

Servant.
Ay, madam, but returns again tonight.

Lady Macbeth.
Say to the king, I would attend his leisure
For a few words.

Servant. Madam, I will. [*Exit.*]

Lady Macbeth. Nought's had, all's spent,
Where our desire is got without content:
'Tis safer to be that which we destroy
Than by destruction dwell in doubtful joy.

[*Enter* MACBETH.]

How now, my lord! Why do you keep alone,
Of sorriest fancies your companions making,
Using those thoughts which should indeed have died
With them they think on? Things without° all remedy
Should be without regard: what's done is done. (H)

Macbeth.
We have scorched° the snake, not killed it:
She'll close° and be herself, whilst our poor malice°
Remains in danger of her former tooth.
But let the frame of things disjoint,° both the worlds° suffer,
Ere we will eat our meal in fear, and sleep
In the affliction of these terrible dreams
That shake us nightly: better be with the dead,
Whom we, to gain our peace, have sent to peace,
Than on the torture of the mind to lie
In restless ecstasy.° Duncan is in his grave;
After life's fitful fever he sleeps well.
Treason has done his worst: nor steel, nor poison,
Malice domestic,° foreign levy,° nothing,
Can touch him further.

Lady Macbeth. Come on.

(H) **Reading Focus** **Using Questioning to Monitor Reading** Lady Macbeth's response is based on her interpretation of Macbeth's thoughts. What questions do you have about her insight into his mind?

? **140.** *What has Macbeth arranged with the murderers? What is his mood here? Does Lady Macbeth have any part in arranging these next murders?*

? **7.** *What reversal of attitudes takes place here?*

11. without: beyond.

? **Staging the Play**
12. *This scene can be played in several ways. Is Lady Macbeth hostile to her husband and angry with him? Or can she be shown to have some tenderness in this scene?*

13. scorched: slashed.

14. close: heal. **malice:** enmity; hatred.

16. frame of things disjoint: universe collapse. **worlds:** heaven and earth.

22. ecstasy: frenzy.

25. Malice domestic: domestic war (civil war). **foreign levy:** exaction of tribute by a foreign country.

? **Staging the Play**
26. *What do you picture the couple doing in this scene? Are they sitting together? Are they close, or is there a distance between them?*

Think About/Talk About

Comprehension

(F) Reading Focus

Possible responses: *What has the Second Murderer just told Macbeth? Is there anything more Macbeth wants to hear from either man?*

(H) Reading Focus

Possible responses: *Does Lady Macbeth really know what Macbeth is going through? Does she know about Banquo? What is she feeling about the changes in Macbeth?*

Analysis

(G) Literary Focus

Possible response: *Having already murdered the king, Macbeth has become more willing to commit murder, even to kill a young, inexperienced rival. He will do anything to keep Banquo's heirs from becoming heirs to the throne he now considers his own.*

Extend the Discussion

Evaluating How is the motif of sleeplessness highlighted in lines 17–26? ***Possible response***: *Macbeth sleeps fitfully and has terrible dreams, while Duncan is at peace. This reinforces the idea that Macbeth "murdered sleep."*

examples from their own experiences or from other people's experience. Following their discussion, students can add their ideas to their notes for future reference.

Students with Disabilities

Put up a large sheet of paper on which students can write questions for other students to answer. Periodically check to make sure that misconceptions are cleared up. Leave some time at the beginning or end of each class to discuss the posted questions and answers and to allow students to add or answer questions. In a different colored ink, write "Anything New?" next to interpretations that may change as students encounter additional information in the text. Remind them that as new clues surface, they must rethink or expand their interpretations. (For example, speculation about Lady Macbeth's children must also take into account Act IV, Scene 3, l. 216, which students have not yet read.)

Think About/Talk About

Extend the Discussion

Interpreting Macbeth says in lines 122–123 that he will "wail his fall / Who I myself struck down." What does he mean? ***Possible responses:*** *Macbeth means that after he has Banquo killed, he will act as if he cared about him as a close friend. Outwardly, he will grieve for his death.*

Responses to Margin Questions

Line 126 *Macbeth argues that for political reasons he must appear unblemished and retain the goodwill of his and Banquo's mutual friends.*

Line 140 *Macbeth has arranged with the murderers to kill Banquo and Fleance. Macbeth's mood is determined and somber. It does not seem that Lady Macbeth had anything to do with arranging these murders.*

Line 7 *Realizing that they must now live with fear and suspicion, Lady Macbeth is beginning to believe that the throne is not worth the price of murder. Macbeth is becoming hardened and blinded by his ambition. He sees murder as the only way to stay in power.*

Line 12 *Lady Macbeth could be frustrated and angry with Macbeth. This would seem likely because she does not want Macbeth to jeopardize what they have gained from their deeds.*

Line 26 *If Macbeth and his wife are seen as being emotionally close, they may touch each other as they move about. But if they are understood to be drifting apart—Lady Macbeth complains that he keeps to himself—they may avoid touching or stand far apart.*

Hath so incensed that I am reckless what
I do to spite the world.
First Murderer. And I another
So weary with disasters, tugged with fortune,
That I would set° my life on any chance,
To mend it or be rid on't.
Macbeth. Both of you
Know Banquo was your enemy.
Both Murderers. True, my lord.
Macbeth.
So is he mine, and in such bloody distance°
That every minute of his being thrusts
Against my near'st of life:° and though I could
With barefaced power sweep him from my sight
And bid my will avouch° it, yet I must not,
For° certain friends that are both his and mine,
Whose loves I may not drop, but wail his fall
Who I myself struck down: and thence it is
That I to your assistance do make love,
Masking the business from the common eye
For sundry weighty reasons.
Second Murderer. We shall, my lord,
Perform what you command us.
First Murderer. Though our lives— **F**
Macbeth.
Your spirits shine through you. Within this hour at most
I will advise you where to plant yourselves,
Acquaint you with the perfect spy° o' th' time,
The moment on't; for't must be done tonight,
And something° from the palace; always thought°
That I require a clearness:° and with him—
To leave no rubs° nor botches in the work—
Fleance his son, that keeps him company,
Whose absence is no less material to me
Than is his father's, must embrace the fate **G**
Of that dark hour. Resolve yourselves apart:°
I'll come to you anon.
Murderers. We are resolved, my lord.
Macbeth.

113. set: risk.

116. distance: quarrel.

118. near'st of life: vital spot.

120. avouch: justify.
121. For: because of.

? **126.** *How does Macbeth justify to the murderers the fact that he has to ask them to kill Banquo?*

130. perfect spy: exact information.
132. something: some distance. **thought:** remembered.
133. clearness: freedom from suspicion.
134. rubs: flaws.

138. apart: alone (make up your minds by yourselves).

Glamis Castle, Angus, Scotland.

F **Reading Focus** **Using Questions to Monitor Reading** Macbeth apparently cuts off the First Murderer's speech. What questions do you have about this exchange?

G **Literary Focus** **Tragedy** In Act III, Scene 1, lines 54–55, Macbeth says of Banquo, "There is none but he / Whose being I do fear." Later that scene, lines 135–136, Macbeth says to the murderers, "Fleance his son, that keeps him company, / Whose absence is no less material to me / Than is his father's." How has Macbeth's view of murder changed since he killed Duncan?

Universal Access

EL English Learners

Have students work with partners. Have each pair choose a short passage from the play. Tell them to read the passage aloud and then briefly summarize in their **Reader/Writer Notebooks** what they think is happening in the passage. After each partner has written a short summary, have them talk about whether their summaries are accurate. Encourage students to discuss what led up to the events in the passage they chose.

Advanced Learners

Enrichment Have students hold a small-group discussion about the character of Macbeth at this point in the play. Point out that Macbeth is king and, in theory, should be able to do whatever he wants. Ask students to discuss whether Macbeth has any choice in his actions and to explain why or why not. Have them make suggestions for ways that he could act differently or try to change the murderous course upon which he has set. Then, have students discuss how one's actions can limit future choices or broaden them. Ask students to provide

[*Enter* SERVANT *and* TWO MURDERERS.]

Now go to the door, and stay there till we call.

[*Exit* SERVANT.]

Was it not yesterday we spoke together?

Murderers.
It was, so please your highness.

Macbeth. Well then, now
Have you considered of my speeches? Know
That it was he in the times past, which held you
So under fortune,° which you thought had been
Our innocent self: this I made good to you
In our last conference; passed in probation° with you,
How you were borne in hand,° how crossed; the instruments,°
Who wrought with them, and all things else that might
To half a soul° and to a notion° crazed
Say "Thus did Banquo."

First Murderer. You made it known to us.

Macbeth.
I did so; and went further, which is now
Our point of second meeting. Do you find
Your patience so predominant in your nature,
That you can let this go? Are you so gospeled,°
To pray for this good man and for his issue,
Whose heavy hand hath bowed you to the grave
And beggared yours forever?

First Murderer. We are men, my liege.

Macbeth.
Ay, in the catalogue ye go for° men;
As hounds and greyhounds, mongrels, spaniels, curs,
Shoughs, water-rugs° and demi-wolves, are clept°
All by the name of dogs: the valued file°
Distinguishes the swift, the slow, the subtle,
The housekeeper, the hunter, every one
According to the gift which bounteous nature
Hath in him closed,° whereby he does receive
Particular addition, from the bill°
That writes them all alike: and so of men.
Now if you have a station in the file,
Not i' th' worst rank of manhood, say't,
And I will put that business in your bosoms
Whose execution takes your enemy off,
Grapples you to the heart and love of us,
Who wear our health but sickly in his life,°
Which in his death were perfect.

Second Murderer. I am one, my liege,
Whom the vile blows and buffets of the world

? **Staging the Play**
74. *What do you imagine the murderers would be like: the all-too-common "hit men" of contemporary movies? Or could they simply be officers who have a grudge against Banquo? (They have been portrayed in many ways.)*

77–78. held you / So under fortune: kept you from good fortune.
80. probation: review.
81. borne in hand: deceived. **instruments:** tools.
83. soul: brain. **notion:** mind.

88. gospeled: so meek from reading the Gospel (of Jesus).

? **91.** *What techniques is Macbeth using on the murderers?*

92. go for: pass as.

94. Shoughs, water-rugs: shaggy dogs and long-haired water dogs. **clept:** called.
95. valued file: classification by valuable traits.

99. closed: enclosed.
100. bill: list.

107. Who wear . . . life: who are "sick" while he (Banquo) still lives.

Think About/Talk About

Analysis

E Literary Focus

Possible response: *In this passage, Macbeth still appears to be fair though he is truly foul. He has also learned that although the witches said he would be king, the "foul" side of their prediction is that Banquo will produce a line of kings.*

Extend the Discussion

Finding Details With whom is Macbeth speaking in lines 74–109? ***Possible response:*** *Macbeth is speaking to two men whom he has hired to murder Banquo and Fleance.*

Speculating In lines 75–84, Macbeth tells the murderers that Banquo is the person who has kept them from good fortune. Why would he say this? Is he telling the truth? Why or why not? ***Possible response:*** *Macbeth wants to convince the murderers to hate Banquo enough to kill him. He is not telling the truth because he has become morally corrupt and because he will continue to lie until he attains his desire.*

Universal Access

EL English Learners

English for Academic Success Explain that pronoun referents do not always precede the pronoun. As a result, students may not always know to whom a pronoun refers until they read a few more lines. Read aloud the following line: "That it was he in the times past, which held you" (line 77). You might say: "In this line, Macbeth uses the pronoun *he* but has not yet mentioned the subject to which this pronoun refers. If I continue reading through line 84, I understand that the pronoun *he* refers to Banquo."

Struggling Readers

Strategic Students To help students focus on the plot, have them keep a time line of the key events that take place. Remind students that a time line lists events in chronological order. Pause periodically to review with the class what has happened so far in the play or discuss any questions they may have about events or characters in the play.

Model the Skill

- Model how to use the Reading Skills Focus graphic organizer to monitor reading (See **Unit 2 Resources.**)
- Read lines 65–72. Point out to students that Banquo's "issue" in line 65 is actually his sons. Tell students that when **using questioning to monitor reading**, they should focus on analyzing a character's inner thoughts and behavior. For lines 65–72, one could ask what speaking tone would most likely be reflected by Macbeth. Since Macbeth is acknowledging the darkness in his mind and enmity between him and other persons, he seems to be speaking in a half-embittered, half-fearful tone.

Guided Practice: Apply

Have students read p. 443 and write questions that address Macbeth's mood and tone.

Think About/Talk About

Responses to Margin Questions

Line 63 *An "unlineal hand" is one that produces no offspring or heirs to the throne. In this case, barren means "to be unable to have children." The scepter is traditionally a symbol of a king's power. Therefore, a "barren scepter" means that though Macbeth is king, he may have no children to gain the throne.*

Line 72 *He believes that Banquo's heirs, not his own, will become kings. He is angry that he has sold his own soul so that another man's sons can become kings. Macbeth has given up his peace of mind and his honor.*

Line 74 *Some students will suggest that these men are officers who bear a personal grudge against Banquo.*

Line 91 *Macbeth convinces the murderers that Banquo is to blame for their troubles. He attacks their manhood by accusing them of being the lowest type of dog.*

To act in safety. There is none but he
Whose being I do fear: and under him
My genius is rebuked,° as it is said **E**
Mark Antony's was by Caesar. He chid the sisters,
When first they put the name of king upon me,
And bade them speak to him; then prophetlike
They hailed him father to a line of kings.
Upon my head they placed a fruitless crown
And put a barren scepter in my gripe,
Thence to be wrenched with an unlineal hand,
No son of mine succeeding. If't be so,
For Banquo's issue have I filed° my mind;
For them the gracious Duncan have I murdered;
Put rancors° in the vessel of my peace
Only for them, and mine eternal jewel°
Given to the common enemy of man,°
To make them kings, the seeds of Banquo kings!
Rather than so, come, fate, into the list,°
And champion me to th' utterance!° Who's there?

56. genius is rebuked: guardian spirit is cowed.

? **63.** *What is an "unlineal hand"? What is a "barren scepter"? What now is bothering Macbeth?*

65. filed: defiled; dirtied.
67. rancors: bitter enmity.
68. eternal jewel: immortal soul.
69. common enemy of man: Satan.
71. list: battle.
72. champion me to th' utterance: fight against me till I give up.

? **72.** *In this important soliloquy, why exactly is Macbeth so angry? How does this compare to the previous soliloquy?*

E Literary Focus Tragedy How does this passage develop the theme "Fair is foul, and foul is fair"?

Analyzing Visuals

Connecting to the Text How do we know which character is Macbeth in this photo? How is his character represented differently than the other male characters?

(standing, right) Cathy Owen (Lady Macbeth) and Peter Lindford (Macbeth). Ludlow Festival, UK (2001).

Developing Oral Fluency

Paired Activity Assign pairs of students to read a passage aloud. One student should ask questions that arise during the reading, and the other should answer as many of them as possible. Have them reverse roles after an assigned number of lines. At the end of each passage, both students should summarize what they understand in a short paragraph and list their unanswered questions.

✔ See the **Oral Language Skill Builder** in **UA: Differentiating Instruction.**

Analyzing Visuals

Connecting to the Text: *We can tell that the character standing on the right is Macbeth because his red clothing stands out. The other men are dressed in less vivid colors, and their bodies are faced towards him, giving him prominence in the scene. His posture and gestures suit those of a host, while the others are sitting or standing as guests would.*

Banquo.
As far, my lord, as will fill up the time
'Twixt this and supper. Go not my horse the better,°
I must become a borrower of the night
For a dark hour or twain.

Macbeth. Fail not our feast.

Banquo.
My lord, I will not.

Macbeth.
We hear our bloody cousins are bestowed°
In England and in Ireland, not confessing
Their cruel parricide, filling their hearers
With strange invention.° But of that tomorrow, **C**
When therewithal we shall have cause of state
Craving us jointly.° Hie you to horse. Adieu,
Till you return at night. Goes Fleance with you?

Banquo.
Ay, my good lord: our time does call upon 's. **D**

Macbeth.
I wish your horses swift and sure of foot,
And so I do commend you to their backs.
Farewell. [*Exit* BANQUO.]
Let every man be master of his time
Till seven at night. To make society
The sweeter welcome, we will keep ourself
Till supper-time alone. While° then, God be with you!

[*Exeunt* LORDS *and all but* MACBETH *and a* SERVANT.]

Sirrah, a word with you: attend° those men
Our pleasure?

Attendant.
They are, my lord, without the palace gate.

Macbeth.
Bring them before us. [*Exit* SERVANT.]
To be thus° is nothing, but° to be safely thus—
Our fears in Banquo stick deep,
And in his royalty of nature reigns that
Which would be feared. 'Tis much he dares;
And, to° that dauntless temper° of his mind,
He hath a wisdom that doth guide his valor

25. Go not my horse the better: unless my horse goes faster than I expect.

29. are bestowed: have taken refuge.

32. invention: lies.

34. us jointly: our joint attention.

? **42.** *Notice that Macbeth uses the "royal we"; that is, he speaks of himself as "we," as a representative of all the people.*

43. While: until.

44. attend: await.

48. thus: king. **but:** unless.

52. to: added to. **temper:** quality.

C **Literary Focus** **Tragedy** What is Macbeth trying to accomplish when he says that his "bloody cousins" have fled to England and Ireland?

D **Reading Focus** **Using Questioning to Monitor Reading** In the conversation with Banquo, Macbeth wants to know Banquo's plans. What questions do you have about Macbeth's curiosity?

Think About/Talk About

Comprehension

D Reading Focus

Possible responses: *Why does Macbeth want to know Banquo's plans? What is Macbeth plotting to do? Would he really kill Banquo? How has the witches' prophecy influenced Macbeth's actions?*

Analysis

C Literary Focus

Possible response: *Macbeth is trying to make people think that the cousins have killed their father.*

Extend the Discussion

Drawing Conclusions Why is Macbeth especially curious about Banquo's plans? ***Possible response:*** *Macbeth is plotting against Banquo.*

Making Judgments Why has Banquo done nothing about his suspicions of Macbeth, despite his vow to fight against malice in Act II, Scene 3, lines 120–126? ***Possible response:*** *Banquo might suspect Macbeth but cannot prove anything, so he thinks it best to play along with him. However, in line 36, his disgust for Macbeth is apparent in his desire to leave quickly.*

Advanced Learners

Acceleration Have students work in groups to analyze Macbeth's thoughts and motivations in Act III. Have one member of the group record these observations. Then, have students collaborate to write a psychological profile of Macbeth, answering the following questions:

- Is guilt causing him to hallucinate, or does he really see things others do not?
- Why does he plot additional murders?

Students should cite specific lines to support their theories.

Students with Disabilities

To help students with disabilities read and understand the play, you may want to play a sound recording or video of all or parts of Act III of *Macbeth* before students read. Or, you may want to have students read a scene first and then view a film. As students view the video, have them take notes about what stands out to them and what they might look for as they read.

Teacher Preparation
Selection Plot Summary

Act III of *Macbeth* opens with Banquo voicing his suspicion that Macbeth has murdered Duncan. Banquo rides with Fleance away from the castle during the afternoon, but Macbeth meets with two men and instructs them to kill Banquo and Fleance. Lady Macbeth asks Macbeth to be merry at dinner. The murderers kill Banquo as he returns to the castle, but Fleance escapes. At dinner, Macbeth sees Banquo's ghost. Lady Macbeth makes excuses and sends everyone home. Macbeth says he will visit the witches. Hecate says that her magic will bring about Macbeth's ruin. Lennox and a lord discuss the growing opposition to Macbeth and say that Macduff has gone to England to join Malcolm.

Direct Teach

Think About/Talk About

Analysis

A Literary Perspectives

Possible response: *King James ruled during Shakespeare's time, so Shakespeare might have wanted to portray Banquo as a heroic person.*

B Literary Focus

Possible response: *Banquo is the first to speak in both acts. The mood at the beginning of both acts is dark and fearful. In Act II, Macbeth is preparing to murder Duncan. At the beginning of Act III, Duncan and the servants are dead.*

Responses to Margin Questions

Line 10 *Banquo is troubled and thoughtful; he is suspicious that Macbeth has helped the prophecies along. Because they did come true, however, he is hopeful about the witches' prediction concerning him and his descendants.*

Line 42 *He probably wants others to think he will be alone so they do not suspect that he has set up a secret meeting.*

Act III

Scene 1. *Forres. The palace.*

Enter BANQUO.

Banquo.
Thou hast it now: king, Cawdor, Glamis, all,
As the weird women promised, and I fear
Thou play'dst most foully for't. Yet it was said **A**
It should not stand° in thy posterity,
But that myself should be the root and father
Of many kings. If there come truth from them—
As upon thee, Macbeth, their speeches shine—
Why, by the verities on thee made good,
May they not be my oracles as well
And set me up in hope? But hush, no more! **B**

[*Sennet° sounded. Enter* MACBETH *as king,* LADY MACBETH, LENNOX, ROSS, LORDS, *and* ATTENDANTS.]

Macbeth.
Here's our chief guest.
Lady Macbeth. If he had been forgotten,
It had been as a gap in our great feast,
And all-thing° unbecoming.
Macbeth.
Tonight we hold a solemn supper, sir,
And I'll request your presence.
Banquo. Let your highness
Command upon me, to the which my duties
Are with a most indissoluble tie
For ever knit.
Macbeth.
Ride you this afternoon?
Banquo. Ay, my good lord.
Macbeth.
We should have else desired your good advice
(Which still° hath been both grave and prosperous°)
In this day's council; but we'll take tomorrow.
Is't far you ride?

4. **stand:** continue.

? 10. *How would you describe Banquo's mood?*

Sennet: trumpet.

13. **all-thing:** altogether.

21. **still:** always. **grave and prosperous:** weighty and profitable.

A Literary Perspectives **Analyzing Historical Context** King James claimed to be a direct descendant of Banquo. How might that claim have affected Shakespeare's portrayal of Banquo in these lines?

B Literary Focus **Tragedy** Compare the beginning lines of Acts II and III. What is similar? What has changed?

Universal Access

EL English Learners

English for Academic Success To help students comprehend Act III, make sure that they understand all the words. Explain the meaning of words such as *play'dst, posterity, verities, unbecoming,* and *indissoluble.* Then, have students re-read text to see if they understand its meaning. Invite students to explain difficult text to a partner. Answer any questions students might have.

✔ See the **English Language Skill Builder** in **UA: Differentiating Instruction.**

Struggling Readers

Model the reading skill of using questioning to monitor reading. You might say: "Before I read this section of Macbeth, I re-read my notes about Act II to prepare myself for questions I might have. I read an interaction between characters and ask myself if I understood what I read. If I don't, I skim the page to find where I got lost. Then, I re-read the section. If I still do not understand, I take some notes about it." Encourage students to ask themselves, "Do I understand what's happening in this scene? What can I do to understand what's going on?"

Applying Your Skills

Reading Standard 2.2, 3.1, 3.4; **Grades 9–10 Review** Reading Standard 3.12 (see pages A48–A50) Writing Standard 2.1a, 2.1c (see pages A51–A52)

The Tragedy of Macbeth
Act II

Literary Response and Analysis

Reading Skills Focus

Quick Check

1. Describe Macbeth's vision at the end of Scene 1.
2. What reason does Macbeth give for killing Duncan's two guards?
3. Where do Malcolm, Donalbain, Ross, and Macduff go at the end of the act, and why?

Read with a Purpose

4. How does Macbeth's flaw continue to push him toward a tragic ending?

Reading Skills: Using Questions to Monitor Reading

5. While reading Act II, you recorded questions that you had about the text. Continue the answers you added to your chart after Act I.

Act, Scene, Line	Questions I have	My Answers
Act II, Scene 2, line 46	What is the "filthy witness"?	It is the blood all over Macbeth's hands (lines 45, 46); blood doesn't lie, but it is messy, and so is their crime—a dirty truth.

Literary Skills Focus

Literary Analysis

6. **Analyze** Who suspects Macbeth? Support your answer with lines from Act II.
7. **Interpret** What message do you think Lady Macbeth wants her fainting spell to convey?
8. **Evaluate** The end of this act does not give us a feeling of justice. Why do you think Shakespeare ends Act II where he did?
9. **Extend** What hints can you find in Act II that suggest the fate of Macbeth and Lady Macbeth?
10. **Literary Perspectives** Why do you think Shakespeare chose not to show the murder of Duncan directly to his audience?

Literary Skills: Tragedy

11. **Analyze** How does Shakespeare continue to use Banquo to emphasize Macbeth's tragic flaw?

Literary Skills Review: Motifs

12. **Extend** A **motif** is a word, image, metaphor, or idea that occurs repeatedly in a work of literature. Two important motifs in *Macbeth* are the image of blood and the idea of sleep. What examples of these motifs can you find in Act II?

Writing Skills Focus

Think as a Reader/Writer

Use It in Your Writing Although most of *Macbeth* is in **blank verse,** or unrhymed iambic pentameter, Shakespeare occasionally varies this pattern. Look back at the Porter's speech in Scene 3. You may have noticed that the Porter—a character of low status—does not speak in verse at all. Notice other ways that Shakespeare differentiates the Porter's speech from the speech of other characters. Then, write a brief dialogue between a serious character and a comic one. Use specific language to establish their personalities.

What Do You Think Now? In Act II, how does Macbeth respond to the impulses of his heart and mind?

For more activities see pages 494–495.

Check for Understanding

Independent Practice

Reading Skills Focus

Possible responses:

1. *Macbeth sees a dagger before him with its handle toward him. At one point, drops of blood appear on it.*
2. *He says he was so furious at Duncan's death that he had to.*
3. *Malcolm and Donalbain go to England and Ireland, respectively, to avoid Duncan's fate. Macduff goes to Fife. Ross goes to Scone to attend Macbeth's coronation.*
4. *His ambition has led him to kill Duncan; he kills again to cover his tracks.*
5. *Students should answer the questions written in their Reading Skills Focus graphic organizers.*

Literary Skills Focus

Possible responses:

6. *Macduff seems to suspect Macbeth since he questions Macbeth's motives for killing the servants in line 101 of Scene 3.*
7. *She wants her fainting spell to convey her horror and frailty, making her appear innocent.*
8. *It is like a false ending because for the time being, Macbeth seems to have succeeded.*
9. *Macbeth says in Scene 3 that he no longer sees a reason to live. Lady Macbeth says that they had better not reflect on their deed.*
10. *Keeping the murder offstage increases the mystery. It also makes the audience feel more gentle toward Macbeth than they would if they witnessed the murder.*
11. *Shakespeare contrasts Banquo with Macbeth. Banquo is determined to find justice. He does not have ulterior motives.*
12. *Examples of blood: Scene 2: lines 45–49, 54–55, 59–62. Examples of sleep: Scene 1: lines 5–7; Scene 2: lines 12–13, 22–25, 34–42, 52–53; Scene 3: lines 70–71.*

Universal Access

Struggling Writers

Some students may need additional scaffolding to complete the Writing Skills Focus activity. Have students discuss how a serious character's speech might differ from a comic character's speech. Record students' responses on the board. Students might note that a serious character will most likely speak in a formal tone and use complete sentences, while a comic character will use slang and might speak in fragments or use figurative language. Encourage students to use these ideas as they write their dialogue between the two characters.

What Do You Think Now?

Have students refer back to all of Macbeth's actions and justifications. Have students review these actions and decide if Macbeth made them using his heart or his mind.

Assess

Unit 2 Resources,
Selection Standards Check, p. 104

Think About/Talk About

Comprehension

Q Reading Focus

Possible responses: *Why does Macduff want to go to Fife? What will Ross do in Scone?*

Analysis

R Literary Focus

Possible response: *Shakespeare most likely chose to end the scene this way because the Old Man's words may foreshadow events or warn that, by attending the coronation, Ross and other Macbeth supporters are opportunistic or hypocritical—trying to "make good of bad, and friends of foes." The line is appropriate not only because the Old Man is disturbed by recent events but also because it reinforces the theme of reversal, of "fair is foul."*

Extend the Discussion

Figurative Language In line 38, what warning does Macduff convey by using the clothing metaphor? ***Possible response:*** *He hints that with Macbeth as king instead of Duncan, their new situations ("robes") may not suit them as well as their old ones did.*

Monitor Students' Comprehension

Guide the class in answering these comprehension questions.

1. How does Duncan die? [*Macbeth stabs him.*]
2. Why does Lady Macbeth refuse to murder Duncan? [*The sleeping Duncan reminds her of her father.*]
3. In Scene 4, whom does Macduff suspect of Duncan's murder? [*Macduff says that Malcolm and Donalbain are suspected, but he does not attend Macbeth's coronation, possibly because he suspects Macbeth.*]

[*Enter* MACDUFF.]

Here comes the good Macduff.
How goes the world, sir, now?

Macduff. Why, see you not?

Ross.
Is't known who did this more than bloody deed?

Macduff.
Those that Macbeth hath slain.

Ross. Alas, the day!
What good could they pretend?°

Macduff. They were suborned:°
Malcolm and Donalbain, the king's two sons,
Are stol'n away and fled, which puts upon them
Suspicion of the deed.

Ross. 'Gainst nature still.
Thriftless° ambition, that will ravin up°
Thine own life's means!° Then 'tis most like
The sovereignty will fall upon Macbeth.

Macduff.
He is already named,° and gone to Scone°
To be invested.°

Ross. Where is Duncan's body?

Macduff.
Carried to Colmekill,°
The sacred storehouse of his predecessors
And guardian of their bones.

Ross. Will you to Scone?

Macduff.
No, cousin, I'll to Fife.

Ross. Well, I will thither. Q

Macduff.
Well, may you see things well done there. Adieu,
Lest our old robes sit easier than our new!

Ross.
Farewell, father.

Old Man.
God's benison° go with you, and with those
That would make good of bad, and friends of foes! R

[*Exeunt omnes.*]

Chapel Stained Glass. Glamis Castle, Angus, Scotland.

24. pretend: hope for. **suborned:** bribed.

28. Thriftless: wasteful. **ravin up:** greedily devour.

29. own life's means: parent.

31. named: elected. **Scone** (skoon).

32. invested: installed as king.

33. Colmekill: Iona Island, the ancient burying place of Scottish kings. (It was founded by St. Colm.)

40. benison: blessing.

Q Reading Focus **Using Questioning to Monitor Reading** The act's last bit of dialogue concerns Ross's and Macduff's plans. What questions might you ask to better understand their plans?

R Literary Focus **Tragedy** Why do you think Shakespeare ends the act with the Old Man's statement?

California Standards, p. 439

- **Reading Standard 2.2** Analyze the way in which clarity of meaning is affected by the patterns of organization, hierarchical structures, repetition of the main ideas, syntax, and word choice in the text.
- **Reading Standard 3.1** Analyze characteristics of subgenres (e.g., satire, parody, allegory, pastoral) that are used in poetry, prose, plays, novels, short stories, essays, and other basic genres.
- **Reading Standard 3.4** Analyze ways in which poets use imagery, personification, figures of speech, and sounds to evoke readers' emotions.
- **Grades 9–10 Review Reading Standard 3.12** Analyze the way in which a work of literature is related to the themes and issues of its historical period. (Historical approach).
- **Writing Standard 2.1** Write fictional, autobiographical, or biographical narratives: **a.** Narrate a sequence of events and communicate their significance to the audience. **c.** Describe with concrete sensory details the sights, sounds, and smells of a scene and the specific actions, movements, gestures, and feelings of the characters; use interior monologue to depict the characters' feelings.

The Alarm (Act II), Macbeth *production at the Princess's Theatre* (1901), by Anonymous. Victoria & Albert Museum, London.

Analyzing Visuals

Connecting to the Text Note the vibrant, almost festive, colors used in the depiction of the soldiers in *Macbeth*. What might the artist be suggesting about warfare and battle?

Is't night's predominance,° or the day's shame,
That darkness does the face of earth entomb,
When living light should kiss it?
Old Man. 'Tis unnatural,
Even like the deed that's done. On Tuesday last
A falcon, tow'ring in her pride of place,°
Was by a mousing° owl hawked at and killed.
Ross.
And Duncan's horses—a thing most strange and certain—
Beauteous and swift, the minions° of their race,
Turned wild in nature, broke their stalls, flung out,°
Contending 'gainst obedience, as they would make
War with mankind.
Old Man. 'Tis said they eat° each other.
Ross.
They did so, to th' amazement of mine eyes,
That looked upon't.

8. predominance: astrological supremacy.

12. tow'ring . . . place: soaring at her summit.

13. mousing: usually mouse-eating.

15. minions: darlings.

16. flung out: lunged wildly.

18. eat: ate.

Think About/Talk About

Analysis

Ⓞ Literary Focus

Possible response: *He allows his wife to pressure him into killing Duncan. Her comments about courage and fear affected his feelings of manliness.*

Ⓟ Literary Perspectives

Possible response: *King James had recently survived the Gunpowder Plot.*

Extend the Discussion

Comparing and Contrasting In the beginning of Scene 4, how does the dialogue between the Old Man and Ross compare to Lennox's speech in lines 48–55? ***Possible response:*** *Like Lennox, Ross and the Old Man present evidence that disorders in nature are mirroring the unnatural death of the king, supporting the Elizabethan idea that the murder is a disruption of natural law.*

Imagery What does the image of Banquo standing in "the great hand of God" suggest about his intent? ***Possible response:*** *Banquo intends to stand on the side of righteousness in fighting the "treasonous malice" that killed Duncan. It also suggests that he believes the murder has not been avenged yet—in other words, he suspects that the grooms were not guilty.*

Analyzing Visuals

Connecting to the Text: *The painting shows a night scene in front of a castle crowded with soldiers. The artist's vivid use of color in the soldiers' armor suggests the intensity and drama of battle and the disruptive nature of warfare.*

Model the Skill

- Model for students the skill of analyzing characteristics of a **tragedy** by helping them to understand metaphors.
- Read aloud lines 12–13. Tell students that in these lines, the old man talks about a falcon being killed by a mousing owl. Explain that this is an unnatural phenomenon. Shakespeare is using the birds as metaphors for the unnatural death of a great man, Duncan, by a lesser man or men.

Guided Practice: Apply

Ask students how the image of Duncan's horses gone wild and cannibalizing each other in lines 14–18 serves as a metaphor for Macbeth. ***Possible response:*** *Macbeth, too, has been the minion of his race as the savior of his country. He, too, has turned wild, broken out of his rank, and destroyed one of his own.*

To know it further. Fears and scruples° shake us.
In the great hand of God I stand, and thence
Against the undivulged pretense° I fight
Of treasonous malice.

Macduff. And so do I.

All. So all.

Macbeth.
Let's briefly° put on manly readiness,
And meet i' th' hall together. (O)

All. Well contented.

[*Exeunt all but* MALCOLM *and* DONALBAIN.]

Malcolm.
What will you do? Let's not consort with them.
To show an unfelt sorrow is an office°
Which the false man does easy. I'll to England.

Donalbain.
To Ireland, I; our separated fortune
Shall keep us both the safer. Where we are
There's daggers in men's smiles; the near in blood,
The nearer bloody. (P)

Malcolm. This murderous shaft that's shot
Hath not yet lighted, and our safest way
Is to avoid the aim. Therefore to horse;
And let us not be dainty of° leave-taking,
But shift away. There's warrant° in that theft
Which steals itself° when there's no mercy left.

[*Exeunt.*]

Scene 4. *Outside Macbeth's castle.*

Enter ROSS *with an* OLD MAN.

Old Man.
Threescore and ten I can remember well:
Within the volume of which time I have seen
Hours dreadful and things strange, but this sore° night
Hath trifled former knowings.°

Ross. Ha, good father,
Thou seest the heavens, as troubled with man's act,
Threatens his bloody stage. By th' clock 'tis day,
And yet dark night strangles the traveling lamp:°

123. scruples: suspicions.

125. undivulged pretense: hidden purpose.

127. briefly: quickly.

130. office: function.

138. dainty of: fussy about.
139. warrant: justification.
140. steals itself: steals oneself away.

3. sore: grievous.
4. trifled former knowings: made trifles of former experiences.

7. traveling lamp: sun.

(O) **Literary Focus** **Tragedy** Macbeth refers to "manly readiness" in Act II, Scene 3, line 127, suggesting that masculine strength will be important for catching the murderers. How do Macbeth's ideas about masculine qualities affect his behavior in the play?

(P) **Literary Perspectives** **Analyzing Historical Context** Why would these words have had special meaning for King James?

Reaching Reluctant Readers

Have students construct a visual image to explore the Elizabethan idea of a disruption in the natural order of things. Ask students to think of an unnatural event that could have also taken place in the scene. Perhaps the castle is infested with a hoard of insects, or a room holding caged birds would become chaos as birds struggle to escape and fly about their cages restlessly. Encourage students to be creative in their illustrations, and remind them that their drawings should clearly depict an unnatural aspect of a scene.

Lennox.

Those of his chamber, as it seemed, had done't:
Their hands and faces were all badged° with blood;
So were their daggers, which unwiped we found
Upon their pillows. They stared, and were distracted.
No man's life was to be trusted with them.

Macbeth.

O, yet I do repent me of my fury,
That I did kill them.

Macduff. Wherefore did you so?

Macbeth.

Who can be wise, amazed, temp'rate and furious,
Loyal and neutral, in a moment? No man.
The expedition° of my violent love
Outrun the pauser, reason. Here lay Duncan,
His silver skin laced with his golden blood,
And his gashed stabs looked like a breach in nature
For ruin's wasteful entrance: there, the murderers,
Steeped in the colors of their trade, their daggers
Unmannerly breeched with gore.° Who could refrain,°
That had a heart to love, and in that heart
Courage to make 's love known? Ⓜ

Lady Macbeth. Help me hence, ho! Ⓝ

Macduff.

Look to the lady.

Malcolm (*aside to* DONALBAIN). Why do we hold our tongues,
That most may claim this argument for ours?°

Donalbain (*aside to* MALCOLM).

What should be spoken here,
Where our fate, hid in an auger-hole,°
May rush, and seize us? Let's away:
Our tears are not yet brewed.

Malcolm (*aside to* DONALBAIN). Nor our strong sorrow
Upon the foot of motion.°

Banquo. Look to the lady.

[LADY MACBETH *is carried out.*]

And when we have our naked frailties hid,°
That suffer in exposure, let us meet
And question° this most bloody piece of work,

96. badged: marked.

104. expedition: haste.

110. Unmannerly breeched with gore: unbecomingly covered with blood, as if wearing red trousers. **refrain:** check oneself.

114. That . . . ours: who are the most concerned with this topic.

116. auger-hole: unsuspected place.

118–119. Our tears . . . motion: We have not yet had time for tears nor to express our sorrows in action.

120. naked frailties hid: poor bodies clothed.
122. question: discuss.

Ⓜ **Reading Focus** **Using Questioning to Monitor Reading** What questions could you ask to help you understand the various characters' eulogies?

Ⓝ **Reading Focus** **Using Questioning to Monitor Reading** What questions do you have about Lady Macbeth's plan in this scene?

Think About/Talk About

Comprehension

Ⓜ Reading Focus

Possible responses: *Does Macbeth still feel a sense of loyalty towards Duncan? What does he mean by "breach in nature"?*

Ⓝ Reading Focus

Possible responses: *Is Lady Macbeth convincing in her surprise? Is any of her grief real?*

Extend the Discussion

Finding Details What is Lady Macbeth's first reaction to the news of the king's death? ***Possible response:*** *She asks if the murder had occurred in their house.*

Imagery Macbeth says that Duncan had "silver skin" and "golden blood," implying Duncan's royal and saintly qualities. Why does Macbeth use such extravagant imagery to describe Duncan's death? ***Possible response:*** *Macbeth's pretentious eloquence is meant to cover up his insincerity; his anxiety and guilt make him ramble on inappropriately.*

Advanced Learners

Acceleration Have students identify a particular passage in the play that they found most confusing or had the most questions about. Encourage students to rewrite this passage using the conventions of drama but updating the language to make it more accessible for a modern audience. Students should work to clarify any hard-to-comprehend parts of the text. After students have reworked their passages, invite them to share their writing with the class. Have the class discuss whether the new passage is an improvement upon Shakespeare's words.

Students with Disabilities

To help them visualize events, have students do a sketch exercise, drawing images that relate to an assigned passage. Have them share their drawings with the class and discuss thematic links, conclusions, generalizations, or cause-and-effect relationships that the images help them see. Ask students to explain how creating their sketches helped them understand any confusing parts of the play or helped them answer any questions they had about the text.

Shall draw him on to his confusion.°
He shall spurn fate, scorn death, and bear
His hopes 'bove wisdom, grace, and fear:
And you all know security°
Is mortal's chiefest enemy. **O** [*Music and a song.*]
Hark! I am called; my little spirit, see,
Sits in a foggy cloud and stays for me.
[*Exit.*]

[*Sing within,* "Come away, come away," *etc.*]

First Witch.
Come, let's make haste; she'll soon be back again.
[*Exeunt.*]

Scene 6. *The palace.*

Enter LENNOX *and another* LORD.

Lennox.
My former speeches have but hit your thoughts,°
Which can interpret farther. Only I say
Things have been strangely borne.° The gracious Duncan
Was pitied of Macbeth: marry, he was dead.
And the right-valiant Banquo walked too late;
Whom, you may say, if't please you, Fleance killed,
For Fleance fled. Men must not walk too late.
Who cannot want the thought,° how monstrous
It was for Malcolm and for Donalbain
To kill their gracious father? Damnèd fact!°
How it did grieve Macbeth! Did he not straight,
In pious rage, the two delinquents tear,
That were the slaves of drink and thralls° of sleep?
Was not that nobly done? Ay, and wisely too;
For 'twould have angered any heart alive
To hear the men deny't. So that I say **P**
He has borne all things well: and I do think
That, had he Duncan's sons under his key—
As, an 't° please heaven, he shall not—they should find
What 'twere to kill a father. So should Fleance.
But, peace! for from broad words,° and 'cause he failed

29. confusion: ruin.

32. security: overconfidence.

1. My . . . thoughts: My recent words have only coincided with what you have in your mind.
3. borne: managed.

8. cannot . . . thought: cannot help thinking.
10. fact: evil deed.

13. thralls: slaves.

19. an 't: if it.

21. for . . . words: because of frank talk.

O Reading Focus **Using Questioning to Monitor Reading** What questions can you ask to determine what draws Macbeth "on to his confusion"?
P Literary Focus **Tragedy** What does Lennox suggest about Macbeth?

Think About/Talk About

Comprehension

O Reading Focus
Possible responses: *Who or what are the spirits that will draw Macbeth to his ruin? In what ways is Macbeth overconfident?*

Analysis

P Literary Focus
Possible response: *Lennox suggests in subtle ways that he is suspicious of Macbeth. Even though he describes Macbeth's killing the guards as "nobly done" in line 14, he follows with "and wise too." The latter phrase could imply that Macbeth was wise to kill the guards before they could deny killing the king.*

Extend the Discussion

Summarizing Summarize the major points of Hecate's speech.
Possible response: *Hecate, queen of the witches, berates the weird sisters for leaving her out of their previous encounters with Macbeth. She promises to marshal magic forces to ensure Macbeth's ruin.*

Interpreting What does Lennox mean in line 7 when he cautions that "Men must not walk too late?"
Possible response: *He means that they are living in a very dangerous time when nobody is safe from treachery. "To walk late" is to risk death, which is what happened to Banquo.*

Universal Access

Advanced Learners

Acceleration Tell students that Hecate's speech in Scene 5 reveals information about Macbeth's tragic flaw and the qualities that will cause him to continue down a destructive path. Have students re-read Hecate's speech and analyze it to determine what information they learn about Macbeth and his character. After students read the speech, have them share their ideas with the class. [*Students may note that Hecate implies that Macbeth's tragic flaw—ruthless ambition—has drawn him "on to his confusion." Students may also mention that Hecate believes that Macbeth's overconfidence will ultimately lead to his destruction.*]

Think About/Talk About

Analysis

Q Literary Perspectives

Possible response: *In Shakespeare's time, the throne was passed from parent to child. Shakespeare was writing for an audience that lived under this type of succession.*

R Literary Focus

Possible response: *Macbeth would be very angry and fearful at Macduff's refusal, knowing that Macduff represents a very real threat to Macbeth's rule.*

Response to Margin Question

Line 49 *The lords have grown so suspicious about Macbeth's motive for silencing the grooms and placing blame on those who have fled that they support Malcolm and Macduff, who are working in England to raise an army against Macbeth.*

Monitor Students' Comprehension

Guide the class in answering these comprehension questions.

1. Why does Macbeth think he has to kill Banquo and Fleance? [*He wants to prevent the witches' prophecy about Banquo's descendants from coming true.*]
2. Who is Hecate? [*She is the queen of the witches.*]
3. How does Lady Macbeth deal with Macbeth's strange behavior? [*She pretends that his behavior, though odd, has been a lifelong affliction that is of no real significance.*]

His presence at the tyrant's feast, I hear,
Macduff lives in disgrace. Sir, can you tell
Where he bestows himself?

Lord. The son of Duncan,
From whom this tyrant holds the due of birth,° (Q)
Lives in the English court, and is received
Of the most pious Edward° with such grace
That the malevolence of fortune nothing
Takes from his high respect.° Thither Macduff
Is gone to pray the holy king, upon his aid°
To wake Northumberland° and warlike Siward;°
That by the help of these, with Him above
To ratify the work, we may again
Give to our tables meat, sleep to our nights,
Free from our feasts and banquets bloody knives,
Do faithful homage and receive free° honors:
All which we pine for now. And this report
Hath so exasperate the king that he
Prepares for some attempt of war.

Lennox. Sent he to Macduff?

Lord.
He did: and with an absolute "Sir, not I," (R)
The cloudy° messenger turns me his back,
And hums, as who should say "You'll rue the time
That clogs° me with this answer."

Lennox. And that well might
Advise him to a caution, t' hold what distance
His wisdom can provide. Some holy angel
Fly to the court of England and unfold
His message ere he come, that a swift blessing
May soon return to this our suffering country
Under a hand accursed!

Lord. I'll send my prayers with him.

[*Exeunt.*]

25. due of birth: birthright.

27. Edward: Edward the Confessor (reigned 1042–1066).

28–29. nothing . . . respect: does not diminish the high respect in which he is held.

30. upon his aid: to aid him (Malcolm).

31. To wake Northumberland: that is, to arouse the people in Northumberland, an English county near Scotland. **Siward:** Earl of Northumberland.

36. free: freely granted.

41. cloudy: disturbed.

43. clogs: burdens.

? Elements of Drama
49. *This is basically an "information" scene. Can you summarize what it tells you about the plot?*

Q Literary Perspectives **Analyzing Historical Context** In the time of Macbeth, Scottish laws prevented lineal succession (from parent to child) of the throne. Instead, rule was passed between families. In light of the historical situation in Shakespeare's time, why might Shakespeare have changed this concept?

R Literary Focus **Tragedy** Given how Macbeth's plans develop in this act, how would you expect him to respond to Macduff's refusal?

California Standards, p. 457

- **Reading Standard 2.2** Analyze the way in which clarity of meaning is affected by the patterns of organization, hierarchical structures, repetition of the main ideas, syntax, and word choice in the text.
- **Reading Standard 3.1** Analyze characteristics of subgenres (e.g., satire, parody, allegory, pastoral) that are used in poetry, prose, plays, novels, short stories, essays, and other basic genres.
- **Reading Standard 3.3** Analyze the ways in which irony, tone, mood, the author's style, and the "sound" of language achieve specific rhetorical or aesthetic purposes or both.
- **Grades 9–10 Review Reading Standard 3.12** Analyze the way in which a work of literature is related to the themes and issues of its historical period. (Historical approach).
- **Writing Standard 2.1** Write fictional, autobiographical, or biographical narratives: **c.** Describe with concrete sensory details the sights, sounds, and smells of a scene and the specific actions, movements, gestures, and feelings of the characters; use interior monologue to depict the characters' feelings. **e.** Make effective use of descriptions of appearance, images, shifting perspectives, and sensory details.

Applying Your Skills

Reading Standard 2.2, 3.1, 3.3; Grades 9–10 Review
Reading Standard 3.12 (see pages A48–A50)
Writing Standard 2.1c, 2.1e (see pages A51–A52)

The Tragedy of Macbeth
Act III

Literary Response and Analysis

Reading Skills Focus

Quick Check

1. Macbeth publicly announces that he will be alone until dinner. What does he really do during this time?
2. Why does Macbeth refuse to sit in the chair that is offered to him at dinner?
3. Where is Macduff during Act III? Why?

Read with a Purpose

4. How does Shakespeare portray Macbeth's tragic flaw in this act?

Reading Skills: Using Questions to Monitor Reading

5. While reading Act III, you continued to record your questions about the text. Now, record and explain your answers.

Act, Scene, Line	Questions I Have	My Answers
Act III, Scene 2, lines 16–26	Why is Macbeth talking about Duncan as if he envies the dead king?	Suffering from nightmares (lines 18, 19), Macbeth wishes his distress would end.

Literary Skills Focus

Literary Analysis

6. **Analyze** In Act I, Lady Macbeth attacks Macbeth's masculinity and thereby convinces him to murder Duncan. How does the question of manhood come up in Act III?
7. **Analyze** How do lines 27–34 in Act III, Scene 2 express the "foul is fair" theme?
8. **Interpret** When the two murderers explain their criminal behavior, what do we learn about them?
9. **Interpret** The events during the dinner entrance (Act III, 4, 1–2) and exit (lines 119–120) are quite different. Why is this difference significant?
10. **Evaluate** How does Macbeth's situation at the end of Act III compare to his situation at the end of Act II? Explain your answer.
11. **Literary Perspectives** Why does Shakespeare portray Banquo as a good man and good father?

Literary Skills: Tragedy

12. **Analyze** In Act III, we see a darker side of Macbeth. When does he reach a turning point that ensures his tragic end? Provide examples from the text.

Literary Skills Review: Irony

13. **Analyze** There are several types of irony. **Verbal irony** occurs when someone says one thing but means something quite different. **Situational irony** occurs when what happens is the opposite of what is expected. **Dramatic irony** occurs when the audience or reader knows something important that a character does not. Give examples of each type of irony from Act III.

Writing Skills Focus

Think as a Reader/Writer

Use It in Your Writing In your *Reader/Writer Notebook*, you noted Shakespeare's use of characterization. Find an example in Act III where other characters describe Macbeth. Use this example as a model to write your own brief scene in which two characters describe a third character who is not present.

What Do You Think Now? In Act III, how does Macbeth respond to the impulses of his heart and mind?

For more activities see pages 494–495.

Universal Access

Struggling Writers

Some students may need additional scaffolding to complete the Writing Skills Focus activity. Have students brainstorm ways in which a speaker's diction and tone of voice can reveal information about another character. Students may want to include discussion of the character's actions, which will help them respond with an appropriate tone. As students write their dialogue, encourage them to use stage directions and adjectives that help reveal clues about the absent person's character.

What Do You Think Now?

Have students identify decisions that Macbeth makes in Act III. Then, have them decide whether Macbeth uses his mind or his heart to make each decision. Remind students to consider the consequences of each action Macbeth takes or does not take.

Assess

Unit 2 Resources,
Selection Standards Check, p. 106

Check for Understanding

Independent Practice

Reading Skills Focus

Possible responses:

1. *He meets with the murderers.*
2. *He sees Banquo's ghost there.*
3. *Macduff has gone to England to help Malcolm overthrow Macbeth.*
4. *Macbeth's ambition makes him willing to do anything to keep the throne, including killing Banquo.*
5. *Students should support their answers with textual evidence.*

Literary Skills Focus

Possible responses:

6. *Macbeth insists "I am a man again" when he recovers from the fit of terror provoked by his vision of Banquo's ghost.*
7. *Lady Macbeth tells Macbeth to look jovial despite his unease. Macbeth reminds her to praise the murdered Banquo, stating that they must use their faces to hide what is in their hearts.*
8. *Plagued by misfortune, they are willing to do anything.*
9. *At first, Macbeth chats easily, but in the end, he barely speaks. Lady Macbeth tells everyone to leave.*
10. *At the end of Act II, Macbeth has been named king. By the end of Act III, he has murdered Banquo. Guilt tears him apart despite his desperate wish to stay in power.*
11. *Shakespeare contrasts Banquo's goodness with Macbeth's evil. Banquo is a father, so his heirs will become kings after his death.*
12. *Macbeth's turning point is when he sends murderers to kill Banquo and Fleance, which quickly leads to the deterioration of his sanity.*
13. *Verbal: Lennox suspects Macbeth but says "he has borne all things well" (III.6.17). Situational: The dinner is supposed to solidify Macbeth's power but causes his guests to doubt him. Dramatic: Macbeth says he wishes Banquo were present, when the audience knows he had Banquo killed.*

Teacher Preparation
Selection Plot Summary

Act IV of *Macbeth* begins as the three witches concoct a foul brew and chant over a caldron. Macbeth enters and demands to know the future. The witches show him three apparitions that warn him of the threat of Macduff and the continuation of Banquo's royal line. The witches vanish, and Lennox enters to tell Macbeth that Macduff has fled to England. Macbeth resolves to murder Lady Macduff and her children. Meanwhile, Macduff secures aid from Malcolm and forms an army to fight Macbeth's forces. Ross enters to tell Macduff his family has been murdered. Turning his grief into anger, Macduff prays to meet Macbeth in battle.

Direct Teach

Think About/Talk About

Extend the Discussion

Interpreting The ingredients the witches use probably reflect beliefs prevalent in Elizabethan England. Why else might this disgusting recipe be appropriate? ***Possible response:*** *The witches are in league with evil, and the recipe reflects their wickedness.*

Response to Margin Question

Stage direction *The witches might act gleeful, focused, or serious.*

Act IV

Scene 1. *A witches' haunt.*

Thunder. Enter the three WITCHES.

First Witch.
Thrice the brinded° cat hath mewed.

Second Witch.
Thrice and once the hedge-pig° whined.

Third Witch.
Harpier° cries, 'Tis time, 'tis time.

First Witch.
Round about the caldron go:
In the poisoned entrails throw.
Toad, that under cold stone
Days and nights has thirty-one
Swelt'red venom sleeping got,°
Boil thou first i' th' charmèd pot.

All.
Double, double, toil and trouble;
Fire burn and caldron bubble.

? Staging the Play
Stage direction: *This scene usually begins in darkness. In Shakespeare's day, the caldron might have risen through the trapdoor. How would you have the witches act: gleeful? lamenting?*

1. **brinded:** brindled.

2. **hedge-pig:** hedgehog.

3. **Harpier:** an attendant spirit like Graymalkin and Paddock in Act I, Scene 1.

8. **Swelt'red . . . got:** venom sweated out while sleeping.

The Witches, The Royal Opera, Covent Garden, London (2002).

Universal Access

EL English Learners/ Struggling Readers

English for Academic Success Before students read the scene, introduce the following words.

- ***entrails***—*intestines.* The soldier fell as his entrails spilled out of the wound.
- ***venom***—*poison produced by animals.* The snakebite surprisingly contained no venom.
- ***caldron***—*a large kettle.* The witches chanted and danced around the boiling caldron.
- ***toil***—*hard and continuous work.* After toiling in the fields all day, the farmer sat down to a hearty supper.
- ***blaspheming***—*to speak disrespectfully of something sacred.* The man was removed from the church when he disrupted the service by shouting blasphemies against God.

Then, ask students to try to use at least four of the words in separate sentences using their own words.

Second Witch.
Fillet° of a fenny° snake,
In the caldron boil and bake;
Eye of newt and toe of frog,
Wool of bat and tongue of dog,
Adder's fork° and blindworm's° sting,
Lizard's leg and howlet's° wing,
For a charm of pow'rful trouble,
Like a hell-broth boil and bubble.

All.
Double, double, toil and trouble;
Fire burn and caldron bubble.

Third Witch.
Scale of dragon, tooth of wolf,
Witch's mummy,° maw and gulf°
Of the ravined° salt-sea shark,
Root of hemlock digged i' th' dark,
Liver of blaspheming Jew,
Gall of goat, and slips of yew
Slivered in the moon's eclipse,
Nose of Turk and Tartar's lips,
Finger of birth-strangled babe
Ditch-delivered by a drab,°
Make the gruel thick and slab:°
Add thereto a tiger's chaudron,°
For th' ingredients of our caldron.

All.
Double, double, toil and trouble;
Fire burn and caldron bubble. **A**

Second Witch.
Cool it with a baboon's blood,
Then the charm is firm and good.

[*Enter* HECATE *and the other three* WITCHES.]

Hecate.
O, well done! I commend your pains;
And every one shall share i' th' gains:
And now about the caldron sing,
Like elves and fairies in a ring,
Enchanting all that you put in.

[*Music and a song:* "Black Spirits," *etc.*]

[*Exeunt* HECATE *and the other three* WITCHES.]

12. Fillet: slice. **fenny:** from a swamp.

16. fork: forked tongue. **blindworm's:** legless lizard's.
17. howlet's: owl's.

23. Witch's mummy: mummified flesh of a witch. **maw and gulf:** stomach and gullet.
24. ravined: ravenous.

31. drab: harlot.
32. slab: slimy.
33. chaudron: entrails.

A Literary Focus Tragedy Compare the beginnings of Acts I and IV. What is similar? What has changed?

Think About/Talk About

Analysis

A Literary Focus

Possible response: *Both acts open with the three witches and attendant spirits with thunder in the background. However, the state of the kingdom has changed. In Act I the kingdom was in good hands, but in Act IV the once-orderly realm has become disorderly following Duncan's murder.*

Extend the Discussion

Finding Details What three signs inform the witches that it is time for them to do evil? ***Possible response:*** *The three signs are: the mewing of a cat, the whining of a hedgehog, and the cry of Harpier.*

Imagery How is the state of the kingdom under Macbeth's rule reflected in the images of dismemberment in lines 26–30? ***Possible response:*** *The kingdom is torn by dissension because of Macbeth's evil deeds.*

Advanced Learners

Acceleration Remind students that like Act I, Act IV also opens with a scene that includes the three witches. Have students revisit the opening scene of Act I. Then, ask students to create a Venn diagram in which they compare the opening scenes of the two acts. How have the witches changed? How are they the same? How has their perception of Macbeth changed? After students complete their diagrams, have them share their ideas with a partner. Then, have them consider why the witches' scenes are integral to the plot of the play.

Students with Disabilities

Have students choose a section of the play that makes a strong impact on them, and ask them to write their thoughts about it on a note card. Then, have students share their passages and comments with the class. Ask students to explain the passage in detail to help other students who may have had difficulty with this particular passage. Encourage other students to ask questions of the presenter to help them clarify their own understanding of the passage.

Model the Skill

- Review with students the characteristics of a **tragedy**. Remind students that the hero has a tragic flaw that ultimately leads to his or her downfall.
- Read lines 71–72 aloud. Remind students that the hero must eventually face the consequences of his tragic flaw. Tell students that these lines foreshadow tragic events for Macbeth because Macbeth is warned about Macduff, which hints that his inevitable downfall will come at Macduff's hands.

Guided Practice: Apply

Turn-and-Talk Ask students to think about how events have not progressed as smoothly as Macbeth had planned. Ask students to discuss how foiled plans have exacerbated Macbeth's tragic flaw.

Think About/Talk About

Responses to Margin Questions

Scene sections *Possible divisions are (1) chanting around the caldron, (2) Macbeth's appearance, (3) the three apparitions, (4) the show of eight kings, and (5) Macbeth's talk with Lennox.*

Line 61 *Students who recall Hecate's line in Act III, Scene 5 may say that Macbeth is not a full participant in evil. Students who focus on Act IV, Scene I may say that the witches now identify him as "something wicked."*

Line 67 *They are tossing ingredients into the boiling caldron and muttering incantations while speaking with Macbeth.*

Line 71 *The apparition speaks to warn Macbeth that Macduff could defeat him. The helmet suggests that the defeat might occur in battle.*

Second Witch.
By the pricking of my thumbs,
Something wicked this way comes:
Open, locks,
Whoever knocks!

[*Enter* MACBETH.]

Macbeth.
How now, you secret, black, and midnight hags! (B)
What is't you do?
All. A deed without a name.
Macbeth.
I conjure you, by that which you profess,
Howe'er you come to know it, answer me:
Though you untie the winds and let them fight
Against the churches; though the yesty° waves
Confound° and swallow navigation up;
Though bladed corn be lodged° and trees blown down;
Though castles topple on their warders' heads;
Though palaces and pyramids do slope°
Their heads to their foundations; though the treasure
Of nature's germens° tumble all together,
Even till destruction sicken,° answer me
To what I ask you. (C)
First Witch. Speak.
Second Witch. Demand.
Third Witch. We'll answer.
First Witch.
Say, if th' hadst rather hear it from our mouths,
Or from our masters?
Macbeth. Call 'em, let me see 'em.
First Witch.
Pour in sow's blood, that hath eaten
Her nine farrow;° grease that's sweaten°
From the murderer's gibbet° throw
Into the flame.
All. Come, high or low,
Thyself and office° deftly show!

[*Thunder.* FIRST APPARITION: *an Armed Head.*°]

Macbeth.
Tell me, thou unknown power——

(B) **Literary Focus** **Tragedy** How has Macbeth's attitude toward the witches changed since his earlier encounters with them?

(C) **Literary Focus** **Tragedy** How has Macbeth's attitude about risk changed?

? *This exciting scene has five major sections, each with its own intensity. See if you can identify them when you are finished.*

53. yesty: foamy.
54. Confound: destroy.
55. bladed . . . lodged: grain in the ear be beaten down.
57. slope: bend.

59. nature's germens: seeds of all life.
60. sicken: sicken at its own work.

? **Staging the Play**
61. *These exchanges are spoken rapidly. Do the witches now see Macbeth as a participant in evil?*

65. farrow: young pigs.
sweaten: sweated.
66. gibbet: gallows.

? **67.** *What are the witches doing during this scene?*

68. office: function.
Armed Head: helmeted head.

Analyzing Visuals

Connecting to the Text How does the image on the opposite page illustrate Macbeth's relationship with the witches?

Reaching Reluctant Readers

Have students consider how a director might set up this scene onstage. Discuss the answers to the following questions as a class.

1. How might the "Armed Head" have appeared onstage? If you were the production manager, what would you suggest to make the "Armed Head" resemble an apparition?
2. How would the apparition's words sound? Loud, deep, and intimidating? Soft, eerie, and mysterious?
3. What would you have the witches do during the appearance of the apparition?
4. How do you think an audience in Shakespeare's day would have reacted to the apparition, compared to an audience today?

First Witch. He knows thy thought:
Hear his speech, but say thou nought.

First Apparition.
Macbeth! Macbeth! Macbeth! Beware Macduff!
Beware the Thane of Fife. Dismiss me: enough.

[*He descends.*]

Macbeth.
Whate'er thou art, for thy good caution thanks:
Thou hast harped° my fear aright. But one word more—

First Witch.
He will not be commanded. Here's another, **D**
More potent than the first.

? **71.** *Why does the "Armed Head" deliver this message? How does the form of the apparition support the warning the apparition gives?*

74. harped: hit upon; struck the note of.

D **Literary Focus** **Tragedy** Why does Macbeth hope to control the witches?

The Witches (*left-right:* Katy Behean, Josette Simon, Lesley Sharp) with Macbeth (Bob Peck). RSC/Barbican Theatre, London (1983).

Analyzing Visuals

Connecting to the Text: *The witches in the visual are standing over Macbeth, who is visibly under their influence. Their act of allowing Macbeth to "see" or "not see" future events is illustrated by their action of covering his eyes with their hands. It appears that they are giving him supernatural insight into the future or weaving their evil powers to play with his mind.*

Think About/Talk About

Analysis

B Literary Focus

Possible response: *Although he is still entranced by their words, he now regards them as evil and expresses revulsion when he calls them "midnight hags."*

C Literary Focus

Possible response: *Macbeth is no longer afraid of any risks he might incur; he is obsessed and determined to meet his own needs quickly.*

D Literary Focus

Possible response: *Macbeth seeks to control the witches so he can gather information from the apparitions. He is frustrated that they vanish before revealing everything he wants to know.*

Extend the Discussion

Monitoring Your Reading What is Macbeth's "fear" mentioned in line 74? ***Possible response:*** *This line emphasizes that Macduff is a threat because both the witches and Macbeth identify him as an enemy.*

Tragedy To fulfill his ambition, Macbeth has upset the social order by killing Duncan. What is he unable to control? Where in the play was this previously demonstrated? ***Possible responses:*** *He cannot control the supernatural world of spirits. This was demonstrated earlier by his inability to make the witches elaborate on their prophecies or to get rid of Banquo's ghost.*

Think About/Talk About

Literary Connection

Tell students that critic Cleanth Brooks believes that the "bloody" (stage direction above line 77) and "crowned" (stage direction at line 86) apparitions of children that Macbeth sees are symbols of "the future which Macbeth would like to control." Other critics feel the apparitions represent certain people, specifically Macduff and Malcolm.

Responses to Margin Questions

Line 82 *The message seems to mean no one can harm Macbeth, but the wording is unusual and may be some sort of riddle.*

Line 93 *Macbeth will not be defeated until Birnam Wood marches on his castle at Dunsinane. Since the second and third prophecies seem impossible to fulfill, Macbeth must feel untouchable and hence be exultant.*

Line 102 *Macbeth is consumed by the desire to know whether Banquo's descendants will inherit his throne. His tone might change from exultation to desperation, since he wants to know this very badly.*

[*Thunder.* SECOND APPARITION: *a Bloody Child.*]

Second Apparition.
Macbeth! Macbeth! Macbeth!
Macbeth.
Had I three ears, I'd hear thee.
Second Apparition.
Be bloody, bold, and resolute! Laugh to scorn
The pow'r of man, for none of woman born
Shall harm Macbeth. [*Descends.*]
Macbeth.
Then live, Macduff: what need I fear of thee?
But yet I'll make assurance double sure,
And take a bond of fate.° Thou shalt not live;
That I may tell pale-hearted fear it lies,
And sleep in spite of thunder.

? **82.** *Macbeth takes the child's message to mean he need not fear Macduff. Nonetheless, why should the Second Apparition's message be approached with caution?*

84. take . . . fate: get a guarantee from fate (that is, he will kill Macduff and thus will compel fate to keep its word).

Greg Hicks as Macbeth *(2nd right)* stars with *(left-right)* Meg Fraser, Louise Bagay, and Ruth Gemmell as the Three Witches in the Royal Shakespeare Company production of *Macbeth* at the Royal Shakespeare Theatre, Stratford-upon-Avon.

Universal Access

English Learners

English for Academic Success Define a compound adjective for students (two or more words linked by a hyphen so that they become a single adjective). Have students find three compound adjectives on pp. 462–463 (*pale-hearted, lion-mettled, earth-bound*). Ask students to define the word parts of each compound adjective first before defining the compound adjective as a whole. Ask students to come up with two of their own compound adjectives to describe events or people in *Macbeth*.

Struggling Readers

To help students understand details and ideas in this scene, have students ask themselves questions while reading. Point out in lines 110–111, the witches decide to show Macbeth the answer to his question even though they told him to not seek answers. Students may wonder why they change their minds so quickly. The answer to the question may be found in line 110. It hints that Macbeth will see things that will not please him. Since the witches plan for his ruin, they probably

[*Thunder.* THIRD APPARITION: *a Child Crowned, with a tree in his hand.*]

What is this,
That rises like the issue° of a king,
And wears upon his baby-brow the round
And top of sovereignty?°

All. Listen, but speak not to't.

Third Apparition.
Be lion-mettled, proud, and take no care
Who chafes, who frets, or where conspirers are:
Macbeth shall never vanquished be until
Great Birnam Wood to high Dunsinane Hill
Shall come against him. [*Descends.*]

Macbeth. That will never be.
Who can impress° the forest, bid the tree
Unfix his earth-bound root? Sweet bodements,° good!
Rebellious dead, rise never, till the Wood
Of Birnam rise, and our high-placed Macbeth
Shall live the lease of nature,° pay his breath
To time and mortal custom.° Yet my heart
Throbs to know one thing. Tell me, if your art
Can tell so much: shall Banquo's issue ever
Reign in this kingdom? **E**

All. Seek to know no more. **F**

Macbeth.
I will be satisfied.° Deny me this,
And an eternal curse fall on you! Let me know.
Why sinks that caldron? And what noise° is this?

[*Hautboys.*]

First Witch. Show!
Second Witch. Show!
Third Witch. Show!
All.
Show his eyes, and grieve his heart;
Come like shadows, so depart!

87. issue: offspring.

88–89. round . . . sovereignty: that is, crown.

? 93. *What does the Third Apparition prophesy? What must be Macbeth's mental state at this point?*

95. impress: conscript; draft.

96. bodements: prophecies.

99. lease of nature: natural life span.

100. mortal custom: natural death.

? **Elements of Drama** 102. *What is Macbeth's mood? How might his tone change when he asks about Banquo's issue, or children?*

104. satisfied: that is, fully informed.

106. noise: music.

E Literary Focus Tragedy Macbeth's deepest desire has changed over time. First, he just wished to remove Duncan; then, he wanted Banquo dead because he thought Banquo was suspicious of him. What does he want now?

F Reading Focus Using Questioning to Monitor Reading The witches tell Macbeth that he should "seek to know no more" (Act IV, Scene 1, line 103). Since they have (seemingly) been cooperating with Macbeth, what questions would help you clarify this apparent change in their approach?

Think About/Talk About

Comprehension

F Reading Focus

Possible responses: *Why do the witches discourage Macbeth from seeking to know any more? Are they trying to help him or trick him? Is his future so awful that he should not try to find out about it?*

Analysis

E Literary Focus

Possible response: *He desperately wants to know whether Banquo's descendants will rule Scotland. He may also want Banquo's children dead so they will not be a threat to him.*

Extend the Discussion

Drawing Conclusions Why does Macbeth want to kill Macduff despite the prophecy that no man "born of woman" can harm Macbeth? What conclusion can you draw about his state of mind? ***Possible response:*** *Macbeth will kill Macduff to ensure that fate cannot trick him, because he does not completely trust the apparition. He will try to hold onto his power through any means necessary. His judgment is deteriorating, because killing more people will make his kingdom even more unstable.*

Characterization Macbeth suddenly starts to speak in couplets, whereas previously he used them mainly to end a scene. What might account for this change? ***Possible response:*** *Macbeth is so influenced by the witches that he begins to speak in rhyme as they do.*

advised Macbeth not to ask more questions, knowing it would only tempt him more. Ask students to write down a question they have about this scene. Then, have students re-read the scene and attempt to answer their own question.

Advanced Learners

Acceleration Have students form small groups, and ask them to write questions about the strange relationship between Macbeth and the witches. Ask them to focus on how the witches take advantage of Macbeth. [*Students might ask: How is Macbeth made a victim here? How are the witches' schemes going as planned? What makes it easy for them to have their way with him?*] Then, have group members discuss the answers to each other's questions.

Think About/Talk About

Responses to Margin Questions

Stage direction *Banquo smiles at Macbeth and gestures to indicate that the eight kings are his descendants.*

Line 124 *Banquo still has bloody gashes. Macbeth must be furious and confused that despite the three promising prophecies, Banquo will win in the end.*

Line 136 *Lennox's entrance marks the sudden return of reality and sanity. It changes the focus of suspense, redirecting the audience's attention to the thanes' increasing suspicions. Lennox tells Macbeth that Macduff has fled to England to raise an army to fight against him.*

Stage direction *The scene might take place in a bedroom or living room to make the ensuing violence more personal and wrenching.*

[*A show of eight* KINGS *and* BANQUO, *last* KING *with a glass*° *in his hand.*]

Macbeth.
Thou art too like the spirit of Banquo. Down!
Thy crown does sear mine eyelids. And thy hair,
Thou other gold-bound brow, is like the first.
A third is like the former. Filthy hags!
Why do you show me this? A fourth! Start,° eyes!
What, will the line stretch out to th' crack of doom?°
Another yet! A seventh! I'll see no more.
And yet the eighth° appears, who bears a glass
Which shows me many more; and some I see
That twofold balls and treble scepters° carry: (G)
Horrible sight! Now I see 'tis true;
For the blood-boltered° Banquo smiles upon me,
And points at them for his.° What, is this so?

First Witch.
Ay, sir, all this is so. But why
Stands Macbeth thus amazedly?
Come, sisters, cheer we up his sprites,°
And show the best of our delights:
I'll charm the air to give a sound,
While you perform your antic round,°
That this great king may kindly say
Our duties did his welcome pay.

[*Music. The* WITCHES *dance, and vanish.*]

Macbeth.
Where are they? Gone? Let this pernicious hour
Stand aye accursèd in the calendar!
Come in, without there!

[*Enter* LENNOX.] (H)

Lennox. What's your grace's will?

Macbeth.
Saw you the weird sisters?

Lennox. No, my lord.

Macbeth.
Came they not by you?

Lennox. No indeed, my lord.

? **Staging the Play**
Stage direction: *A parade of eight Stuart kings passes before Macbeth. These are the kings of Banquo's line. The last king, Banquo, holds up a mirror* (glass) *to suggest an infinite number of descendants. According to the next speech, how does Banquo act toward Macbeth?*

116. Start: that is, from the sockets.
117. crack of doom: blast (of a trumpet) at Doomsday.
119. eighth: King James I of England (the present king).
121. twofold . . . scepters: coronation emblems.
123. blood-boltered: matted with blood.
124. his: his descendants.

? **124.** *What does Banquo look like? What must be Macbeth's mental state now?*

127. sprites: spirits.
130. antic round: grotesque, circular dance.

? **Elements of Drama**
136. *How would the mood onstage change as Lennox appears? What crucial information does he give Macbeth?*

(G) **Literary Perspectives** **Analyzing Historical Context** How does this final apparition symbolically honor James I?

(H) **Literary Focus** **Tragedy** Why do you think Lennox is still attending Macbeth?

Word-Attack Skills Mini-Lesson

English for Academic Success Use the word *accurséd* in l. 133 to introduce the pronunciation of *–ed* when it is stressed in certain words. Explain that *–ed* is found at the end of a past tense verb. Thus, the *–ed* can be stressed in some instances and not in others, depending on a slight shift in meaning. Illustrate this using the word *learned.* When the last syllable is stressed, the word is used as an adjective, synonymous with *educated* or *accomplished.* When the last syllable is not stressed, the word is used as the past tense of the verb *to learn.*

Activity Have students practice pronouncing the underlined words with a stress on the last syllable.

1. The police spent several minutes interrogating their latest arrest, an alleged burglar.
2. The well-endowed lady left a huge inheritance for her ten beloved grandchildren.
3. He ran for the finish line with dogged determination.
4. The learned scholar impressed the audience when he correctly answered the one-million-dollar question.
5. The farmers were grateful when the blessed rain fell.

Macbeth.
Infected by the air whereon they ride,
And damned all those that trust them! I did hear
The galloping of horse.° Who was't came by?

Lennox.
'Tis two or three, my lord, that bring you word
Macduff is fled to England. **I**

Macbeth. Fled to England?

Lennox.
Ay, my good lord.

Macbeth *(aside).*
Time, thou anticipat'st° my dread exploits.
The flighty purpose never is o'ertook
Unless the deed go with it.° From this moment
The very firstlings of my heart° shall be
The firstlings of my hand. And even now,
To crown my thoughts with acts, be it thought and done:
The castle of Macduff I will surprise;°
Seize upon Fife; give to th' edge o' th' sword
His wife, his babes, and all unfortunate souls
That trace him in his line.° No boasting like a fool;
This deed I'll do before this purpose cool: **J**
But no more sights!—Where are these gentlemen?
Come, bring me where they are. [*Exeunt.*]

140. horse: horses (or horsemen).

144. anticipat'st: foretold.
145–146. The flighty . . . it: The fleeting plan is never accomplished unless an action accompanies it.
147. firstlings . . . heart: that is, first thoughts, impulses.
150. surprise: attack suddenly.

153. trace . . . line: are of his lineage.

Scene 2. *Macduff's castle.*

Enter Macduff's wife LADY MACDUFF, *her* SON, *and* ROSS.

Lady Macduff.
What had he done, to make him fly the land?

Ross.
You must have patience, madam.

Lady Macduff. He had none:
His flight was madness. When our actions do not,
Our fears do make us traitors.

Ross. You know not
Whether it was his wisdom or his fear.

? **Staging the Play**
Stage direction: *In many productions, the mood of this scene contrasts dramatically with the previous scenes of horror. How would you stage this domestic scene to suggest the vulnerability of Lady Macduff and her children?*

Glamis Castle, Angus, Scotland.

I **Reading Focus** **Using Questioning to Monitor Reading** Lennox tells Macbeth something he apparently does not know: Macduff's location. What questions can you ask to clarify Lennox's motives?

J **Literary Focus** **Tragedy** How does Macbeth's attitude here differ from his response to the murders of Banquo and Fleance?

Developing Oral Fluency

Mixed-Ability Group Activity Create mixed-ability groups with four to five students in a group. Then, read all or part of Act IV aloud as a class. Have each group share the role of one character. They may decide that they will take turns in a certain order, that each group member will read a certain number of lines, or that members will use a preset signal when they are ready for the next member to take over. Have groups meet in a scheduled practice period in which readers having difficulty can get help from other group members. While reading aloud, encourage students to infuse their lines with drama when the dialogue invites it.

Think About/Talk About

Comprehension

I Reading Focus

Possible responses: *Why does Lennox inform Macbeth of Macduff's whereabouts? Is he still loyal because Macbeth is the king, or because he is afraid of Macbeth? Does he anticipate that Macbeth will have Macduff's family killed?*

Analysis

G Literary Perspectives

Possible response: *The final apparition points to James I, King of Scotland and England, as indicated by the multiple coronation emblems carried by the eighth king.*

H Literary Focus

Possible responses: *Lennox is afraid to leave; he is waiting for more substantial proof; he is a spy in Macbeth's castle.*

J Literary Focus

Possible response: *Macbeth was upset and fearful when he heard of Fleance's escape. But here he shows no sign of fear, only determination.*

Extend the Discussion

Irony Why are Macbeth's words in lines 138–140 ironic? ***Possible response:*** *Macbeth himself trusts the witches, so he is damning himself.*

Speculating Why might Macduff have fled without telling his wife? ***Possible response:*** *Macduff might have fled so that anyone trying to find out where he was would be unable to get any information from her. Alternatively, he may have put his duty to his country before his family.*

Model the Skill

- Remind students that they can **monitor their comprehension by asking questions** while reading the text.
- Point out the dialogue between Lady Macduff and her son. Ask students why they think Lady Macduff insists that her husband is dead, yet her son does not believe her.
- Tell students that they can find clues to the answer in lines 6–14. In these lines, Lady Macduff is clearly angry with her husband for leaving his family. She acts as though he was dead in her eyes for abandoning his family. Her son is not angry with his father and hopes he is still alive.

Guided Practice: Apply

Have students write down a few questions they have about Act IV, Scene 2. Pair students with a partner and have them attempt to answer each other's questions. If students are unable to come up with an answer, ask them to share the question with the whole class.

Think About/Talk About

Responses to Margin Questions

Line 17 *Ross might extend his hands as if pleading. He might lower his voice or look over his shoulder.*

Line 30 *He might kiss Lady Macduff's cheek or hand and tousle the boy's hair. Ross may be younger than Lady Macduff.*

Line 31 *She might act betrayed by her husband's flight and afraid of the general chaos; or, she might conceal her fear for her son's sake.*

Lady Macduff.
Wisdom! To leave his wife, to leave his babes,
His mansion and his titles,° in a place
From whence himself does fly? He loves us not;
He wants the natural touch:° for the poor wren,
The most diminutive of birds, will fight,
Her young ones in her nest, against the owl.
All is the fear and nothing is the love;
As little is the wisdom, where the flight
So runs against all reason.
Ross. My dearest coz,°
I pray you, school° yourself. But, for your husband,
He is noble, wise, judicious, and best knows
The fits o' th' season.° I dare not speak much further:
But cruel are the times, when we are traitors
And do not know ourselves; when we hold rumor
From what we fear,° yet know not what we fear,
But float upon a wild and violent sea
Each way and move. I take my leave of you.
Shall not be long but I'll be here again.
Things at the worst will cease,° or else climb upward

7. titles: possessions.

9. wants . . . touch: that is, lacks natural affection for his wife and children.

14. coz: cousin.
15. school: control.

? Staging the Play
17. *How could Ross show his fear in line 17?*
17. fits . . . season: disorders of the time.
19–20. hold . . . fear: believe rumors because we fear.

24. cease: cease worsening.

Child actor in *Macbeth,* Royal Shakespeare Company (1993).

Universal Access

Advanced Learners

Acceleration Have students work in groups of four or five to define the word *traitor.* They might wish to use a graphic organizer, such as a cluster map, to organize their thoughts. Then, have them debate the following question: How might someone be a traitor to his or her country? Before students read Scene 2, ask the groups to speculate on how Lady Macduff will feel about her husband's leaving Scotland. After they read the scene, have the groups discuss whether they accept Lady Macduff's definition of a traitor as one "who swears and lies." Is Macduff a traitor, or is there another explanation for his behavior? Finally, have students compare the behavior of Macduff and Macbeth. Who is more of a traitor? Why?

To what they were before. My pretty cousin,
Blessing upon you! (K)

Lady Macduff.
Fathered he is, and yet he's fatherless.

Ross.
I am so much a fool, should I stay longer,
It would be my disgrace° and your discomfort.
I take my leave at once. (L) [*Exit* Ross.]

Lady Macduff. Sirrah,° your father's dead:
And what will you do now? How will you live?

Son.
As birds do, mother.

Lady Macduff. What, with worms and flies?

Son.
With what I get, I mean; and so do they.

Lady Macduff.
Poor bird! thou'dst never fear the net nor lime,°
The pitfall nor the gin.°

Son.
Why should I, mother? Poor birds they are not set for.
My father is not dead, for all your saying.

Lady Macduff.
Yes, he is dead: how wilt thou do for a father?

Son. Nay, how will you do for a husband?

Lady Macduff. Why, I can buy me twenty at any market.

Son. Then you'll buy 'em to sell° again.

Lady Macduff.
Thou speak'st with all thy wit, and yet, i' faith,
With wit enough for thee.°

Son.
Was my father a traitor, mother?

Lady Macduff. Ay, that he was.

Son. What is a traitor?

Lady Macduff. Why, one that swears and lies.°

Son. And be all traitors that do so?

Lady Macduff. Every one that does so is a traitor, and must be hanged.

Son. And must they all be hanged that swear and lie?

Lady Macduff. Every one.

Son. Who must hang them?

Lady Macduff. Why, the honest men.

(K) **Literary Focus** **Tragedy** What has changed in Ross's behavior?

(L) **Reading Focus** **Using Questioning to Monitor Reading** Ross offers several reasons for why he should leave (Act IV, Scene 2, lines 28–30). What questions would you ask to explain his behavior?

29. It . . . disgrace: That is, I would weep.

30. Sirrah: here, an affectionate address to a child.

? Staging the Play
30. *In taking his leave, how would Ross show affection for Lady Macduff and her young son? Would you have Ross be younger or older than Lady Macduff?*

? Staging the Play
31. *How would you have Lady Macduff act in this scene: frightened? bitter? loving? resigned?*

34. lime: birdlime (smeared on branches to catch birds).

35. gin: trap.

41. sell: betray.

43. for thee: for a child.

47. swears and lies: takes an oath and breaks it.

Think About/Talk About

Comprehension

(L) Reading Focus

Possible responses: *Why does Ross leave the family so quickly? Does he expect Macduff to be killed? If so, is he worried that Lady Macduff will realize this?*

Analysis

(K) Literary Focus

Possible response: *Ross seems afraid at first. Then he becomes resigned, reasoning that the situation will soon reach its worst point, after which it can only improve.*

Extend the Discussion

Imagery How is the bird mentioned in line 34 a fitting image for Macduff's son? ***Possible responses:*** *The image of the innocent, trapped bird makes the boy seem defenseless and vulnerable. It is also a reminder that Macbeth has resolved to trap Macduff's family in their home.*

Cross-Curricular Connection

ART: Props and Scenery

Ask students to describe which prop or piece of scenery used in *The Tragedy of Macbeth* has captured their imagination up to this point: the witches' caldron, the castle, the imaginary dagger, the banquet room, or another object.

Group Activity Have students work in groups of four to create this prop or piece of scenery for the play. Each group should assign a role to each of its members: an artist (to design the piece), a production manager (to oversee the collection of necessary building materials), and workers (to build, paint, and erect the prop or piece). Students should present their prop or piece of scenery to the class and briefly explain why they chose that object and what is its role in the tragedy.

Think About/Talk About

Extend the Discussion

Comparing and Contrasting How does Macduff's son express his cynicism toward the world? How does his mother express hers? ***Possible response:*** *He believes there are more "liars and swearers" than honest men in the world. His mother mentions in lines 71–73 that evil deeds are often esteemed, and good deeds lead to harm.*

Theme How do Lady Macduff's words reflect the "Fair is foul, and foul is fair" theme? ***Possible response:*** *There is no escape in a world where evil acts are rewarded and good acts are overlooked.*

Responses to Margin Questions

Line 69 *Lady Macbeth has been upset by Macbeth's mood swings, wild imagination, and emotional distance from her. However, there has been no evidence that she has initiated any action, so she probably has not sent the messenger. Lady Macduff looks for some way to flee and asks what she has done. She soon recalls, however, that under Macbeth's rule innocence and goodness are of no value.*

Line 75 *The boy might try to protect his mother—perhaps he steps in front of her to shield her. Lady Macduff might try to block her son from the murderer's path. Perhaps they both back away.*

Son. Then the liars and swearers are fools; for there are liars
and swearers enow° to beat the honest men and hang up them.
Lady Macduff. Now, God help thee, poor monkey! But
how wilt thou do for a father?
Son. If he were dead, you'd weep for him. If you would not, it
were a good sign that I should quickly have a new father.
Lady Macduff. Poor prattler, how thou talk'st!

[*Enter a* MESSENGER.]

Messenger.
Bless you, fair dame! I am not to you known,
Though in your state of honor I am perfect.°
I doubt° some danger does approach you nearly:
If you will take a homely° man's advice,
Be not found here; hence, with your little ones.
To fright you thus, methinks I am too savage;
To do worse to you were fell° cruelty,
Which is too nigh your person. Heaven preserve you!
I dare abide no longer. [*Exit* MESSENGER.]
Lady Macduff. Whither should I fly?
I have done no harm. But I remember now
I am in this earthly world, where to do harm
Is often laudable, to do good sometime
Accounted dangerous folly. Why then, alas,
Do I put up that womanly defense,
To say I have done no harm?—What are these faces?

[*Enter* MURDERERS.] Ⓜ

Murderer.
Where is your husband?
Lady Macduff.
I hope, in no place so unsanctified
Where such as thou mayst find him.
Murderer. He's a traitor.
Son.
Thou li'st, thou shag-eared° villain!
Murderer. What, you egg!

[*Stabbing him.*]

Young fry° of treachery!
Son. He has killed me, mother:

55. enow: enough.

62. in . . . perfect: That is, I am fully informed of your honorable rank.
63. doubt: fear.
64. homely: plain.

67. fell: fierce.

Elements of Drama
69. *Some readers think that Lady Macbeth has sent this messenger. Is there any support for this theory? Would it be typical of her character? What must Lady Macduff do when she hears this terrible message?*

Staging the Play
75. *What would Lady Macduff and her son do as they see the murderers enter the room?*

79. shag-eared: hairy-eared.

80. fry: spawn.

Ⓜ **Reading Focus** **Using Questioning to Monitor Reading** The stage direction in this scene reads "Enter Murderers," without numbering them or giving further identification. What questions does this raise for you?

Cross-Curricular Connection

LITERATURE: Holinshed's Chronicles
Shakespeare's story outline is usually thought to be based on Raphael Holinshed's historical account of King Duncan and Macbeth. The following excerpt is found in Volume V of Holinshed's *Chronicles of England, Scotland, and Ireland:* "Immediatlie then, being aduertised whereabout Makduffe went, he [Macbeth] came hastily with a great power into Fife, and foorthwith besieged the castell where Makduffe dwelled, trusting to haue found him therein. They that kept the house, without anie resistance opened the gates, and suffered him to enter, mistrusting none euill. But neuerthelesse Makbeth most cruellie caused the wife and children of Makduffe, with all other whom he found in that castell, to be slaine. Also he confiscated the goods of Makduffe, proclamed him traitor, and confined him out of all parts of his realme; but Makduffe was alreadie escaped out of danger, and gotten into England vnto Malcolme Cammore, to trie what purchase hée might."

Glamis Castle, Angus, Scotland.

Run away, I pray you! [*Dies.*]

[*Exit* LADY MACDUFF, *crying* "Murder!" *followed by* MURDERERS.]

Scene 3. *England. Before the king's palace.*

Enter MALCOLM *and* MACDUFF.

Malcolm.
Let us seek out some desolate shade, and there
Weep our sad bosoms empty.

Macduff. Let us rather
Hold fast the mortal° sword, and like good men
Bestride our down-fall'n birthdom.° Each new morn
New widows howl, new orphans cry, new sorrows
Strike heaven on the face, that° it resounds
As if it felt with Scotland and yelled out
Like syllable of dolor.° Ⓝ

Malcolm. What I believe, I'll wail;
What know, believe; and what I can redress,

3. mortal: deadly.
4. Bestride . . . birthdom: protectively stand over our native land.
6. that: so that.
8. Like . . . dolor: similar sound of grief.

Ⓝ **Literary Focus** **Tragedy** How does Macduff describe the expanded scope of Macbeth's destruction in these lines?

Think About/Talk About

Comprehension

Ⓜ Reading Focus

Possible responses: *How many murderers were there, and who were they? Were they eager to kill the family or were they reluctantly acting under orders?*

Analysis

Ⓝ Literary Focus

Possible response: *He says that every day brings more widows, orphans, and sorrows, so that it seems that heaven itself must be lamenting the country's turmoil.*

Extend the Discussion

Responding to the Text How do you feel about Lady Macduff and her son? ***Possible response:*** *Students will probably find relief in these two guiltless characters and admire their close relationship. Some may enjoy their witty banter but worry about their safety.*

Evaluating How does the arrival of the messenger in line 61 elevate tension? ***Possible response:*** *The audience is probably glad that Lady Macduff and her son have a chance to escape since they know what Macbeth plans to do to them. They probably hope that the family gets away successfully.*

Think About/Talk About

Literary Connection

Tell students that, in keeping with Holinshed's *Chronicle,* Shakespeare has Malcolm charge himself with lust, avarice, and deceit. "Shakespeare is showing the nature of royalty by describing the opposite," says critic Kenneth Muir.

Responses to Margin Questions

Line 14 *Neither Malcolm nor Macduff knows that Macbeth has already had Macduff's family killed.*

Line 37 *Depending upon the interpretation of Malcolm, the actor might play the role as if he were disheartened, resigned, offended, or angry.*

Line 57 *Macduff says that no one, not even a devil from hell, is worse than Macbeth. He believes any other ruler would be preferable.*

Line 66 *By discussing his imaginary vices, Malcolm can see how much Macduff will tolerate. Malcolm seems to be trying to see whether Macduff is loyal to Scotland or loyal to Macbeth.*

Line 84 *Malcolm must convince Macduff that all these allegations about himself are true, yet somehow let the audience know that he is merely testing Macduff. An ironic delivery might not convince Macduff; a serious delivery might elicit a more concerned response.*

As I shall find the time to friend,° I will.
What you have spoke, it may be so perchance.
This tyrant, whose sole° name blisters our tongues,
Was once thought honest:° you have loved him well;
He hath not touched you yet. I am young; but something
You may deserve of him through me;° and wisdom°
To offer up a weak, poor, innocent lamb
T' appease an angry god. (O)

Macduff.
I am not treacherous.

Malcolm. But Macbeth is.
A good and virtuous nature may recoil
In° an imperial charge. But I shall crave your pardon;
That which you are, my thoughts cannot transpose:°
Angels are bright still, though the brightest° fell:
Though all things foul would wear° the brows of grace,
Yet grace must still look so.°

Macduff. I have lost my hopes.

Malcolm.
Perchance even there where I did find my doubts.
Why in that rawness° left you wife and child,
Those precious motives, those strong knots of love,
Without leave-taking? I pray you,
Let not my jealousies° be your dishonors,
But mine own safeties. You may be rightly just°
Whatever I shall think.

Macduff. Bleed, bleed, poor country:
Great tyranny, lay thou thy basis° sure,
For goodness dare not check° thee: wear thou thy wrongs;
The title is affeered.° Fare thee well, lord:
I would not be the villain that thou think'st
For the whole space that's in the tyrant's grasp
And the rich East to boot.

Malcolm. Be not offended:
I speak not as in absolute fear of you.
I think our country sinks beneath the yoke;
It weeps, it bleeds, and each new day a gash
Is added to her wounds. I think withal°
There would be hands uplifted in my right;°
And here from gracious England° have I offer
Of goodly thousands: but, for° all this,
When I shall tread upon the tyrant's head,
Or wear it on my sword, yet my poor country

10. to friend: to be friendly, favorable.
12. sole: very.
13. honest: good.

? Elements of Drama
14. *What great irony would the audience feel upon hearing this line, given what has just taken place in the previous scene?*

15. deserve . . . me: that is, earn by betraying me to Macbeth. **wisdom:** it may be wise.
19–20. recoil / In: give way under.
21. transpose: transform.
22. the brightest: Lucifer, the angel who led the revolt of the angels and was thrown out of heaven; Satan.
23. would wear: desire to wear.
24. so: like itself.
26. rawness: unprotected condition.
29. jealousies: suspicions.
30. rightly just: perfectly honorable.
32. basis: foundation.
33. check: restrain.
34. affeered: legally confirmed.

? Staging the Play
37. *This speech might present a problem for the actor playing Macduff because it does not clearly relate to what has preceded it. It seems too grand and philosophical at this point in the play. How would you have the actor deliver this speech?*

41. withal: moreover.
42. in my right: on behalf of my claim.
43. England: the king of England.
44. for: despite.

(O) **Literary Focus** **Tragedy** What does Malcolm seem to suspect about Macbeth and Macduff? Why is this suspicion ironic?

Universal Access

EL English Learners

English for Academic Success Direct students to line 58. Point out the words *luxurious* and *avaricious.* Tell students that words ending in *–ous* or *–ious* act as adjectives. Ask them who is being described as *luxurious* and *avaricious.* [*Macbeth*] Have students work with a partner to look for other words that end in *–ious* or *–ous.* [*virtuous,* line 19; *gracious,* line 43, *malicious,* line 59; *spacious,* line 71; *pernicious,* line 85] Ask them to look up the meaning of each and then have them compose a sentence using each of the adjectives.

Struggling Readers

Direct students' attention to lines 66–76 on p. 471. You might say: "In this scene, I know that Macduff and Malcolm are discussing Macbeth's reign. After reading these lines, I have the following question: What does Malcolm mean when he says 'Boundless intemperance in nature is a tyranny'? I know that Malcolm is referring to Macbeth's behavior. As I continue reading, I see the words 'vulture' and 'devour.' I think that Malcolm is describing Macbeth's ruthless reign and his desire to gain the throne by any means necessary."

Shall have more vices than it had before,
More suffer, and more sundry ways than ever,
By him that shall succeed.

Macduff. What should he be?

Malcolm.
It is myself I mean, in whom I know
All the particulars° of vice so grafted°
That, when they shall be opened,° black Macbeth
Will seem as pure as snow, and the poor state
Esteem him as a lamb, being compared
With my confineless harms.°

Macduff. Not in the legions
Of horrid hell can come a devil more damned
In evils to top Macbeth.

Malcolm. I grant him bloody,
Luxurious,° avaricious, false, deceitful,
Sudden,° malicious, smacking of every sin
That has a name: but there's no bottom, none,
In my voluptuousness:° your wives, your daughters,
Your matrons and your maids, could not fill up
The cistern of my lust, and my desire
All continent° impediments would o'erbear,
That did oppose my will. Better Macbeth
Than such an one to reign.

Macduff. Boundless intemperance
In nature° is a tyranny; it hath been
Th' untimely emptying of the happy throne,
And fall of many kings. But fear not yet
To take upon you what is yours: you may
Convey° your pleasures in a spacious plenty,
And yet seem cold, the time° you may so hoodwink.
We have willing dames enough. There cannot be
That vulture in you, to devour so many
As will to greatness dedicate themselves,
Finding it so inclined.

Malcolm. With this there grows
In my most ill-composed affection° such
A stanchless° avarice that, were I king,
I should cut off the nobles for their lands,
Desire his jewels and this other's house:
And my more-having would be as a sauce
To make me hunger more, that I should forge
Quarrels unjust against the good and loyal,
Destroying them for wealth.

Macduff. This avarice
Sticks deeper, grows with more pernicious root
Than summer-seeming° lust, and it hath been

"NOT IN THE LEGIONS OF HORRID HELL CAN COME A DEVIL MORE DAMNED IN EVILS TO TOP MACBETH."

51. particulars: special kinds. **grafted:** engrafted.
52. opened: in bloom (that is, revealed).

55. confineless harms: unbounded evils.

? **57.** *How has Macduff responded to this speech?*

58. Luxurious: lecherous.
59. Sudden: violent.

61. voluptuousness: lust.

64. continent: restraining.

? **66.** *Why do you think Malcolm is drawing attention to his vices? What could he hope to accomplish?*

67. nature: man's nature.

71. Convey: secretly manage.
72. time: here, people.

77. ill-composed affection: evilly compounded character.
78. stanchless: never ending.

? **Staging the Play**
84. *How do you imagine Malcolm delivering this speech? How could his delivery affect Macduff's response?*

86. summer-seeming: youthful, or transitory.

Think About/Talk About

Analysis

Literary Focus

Possible response: *Malcolm suspects that Macduff may betray him to Macbeth. This is ironic because at one point Macduff suspected Malcolm of murdering Duncan.*

Extend the Discussion

Finding Details What kind of image of Scotland is created in lines 39–41? What scene does this image recall? ***Possible response:*** *Scotland is likened to a stabbed woman, who is weeping and bleeding, and who is wounded again every day. This scene recalls the murder of Lady Macduff.*

Analyzing Details In lines 32–37, what is Macduff about to do? Why? ***Possible response:*** *Macduff is preparing to leave. He sees that Malcolm does not trust him, so he thinks there is no hope of saving Scotland now. There cannot be an alliance between the thanes who oppose Macbeth and the rightful kin (Malcolm) because Malcolm is too nervous to trust anyone.*

Advanced Learners

Enrichment Have students compare and contrast the internal and external conflicts in *Macbeth,* such as Macbeth's reluctance to kill Duncan versus Lady Macbeth's determination to commit the murder, or Lady Macbeth's inner turmoil after Duncan's death versus Macbeth's increasing ease with murder, as evidenced by his reaction to the deaths of Banquo and Macduff's family. Then, have students compare and contrast these conflicts with conflicts found in other novels they have read. Students should write a brief essay discussing their conclusions.

Students with Disabilities

Remind students that a cause makes something happen and an effect is what happens as a result of that cause. Although an author may state the cause and its effect, more often readers must infer the probable cause or effect. To do this, they should use prior knowledge and experience of how things happen. Encourage students to use a graphic organizer, such as a story map, to identify as many effects as possible resulting from Duncan's murder. In some cases, students may indicate a chain reaction where an effect becomes a cause that leads to yet another effect.

Think About/Talk About

Extend the Discussion

Evaluating Why is Macduff unable to tolerate Malcolm's last confession, although he has accepted Malcolm's previous flaws? ***Possible response:*** *Although lust and avarice might exist in men who are otherwise sufficiently moral to rule, Malcolm, in his last statement, denies that he has any moral virtues and suggests that his rule would cause chaos and strife. To Macduff, this probably sounds too much like Macbeth's rule.*

Responses to Margin Questions

Line 114 *Malcolm drops his sinful, arrogant air and speaks in his normal, gentle tone. Macduff has shown that he is completely loyal to Scotland, disgusted by Macbeth's actions, and repulsed by the vices that Malcolm claimed to have possessed.*

Line 137 *There should be a fairly sharp, uncomfortable pause before "Why are you silent?" Most students will feel he probably speaks in a matter-of-fact way because he realizes that he has stunned Macduff.*

The sword of our slain kings.° Yet do not fear.
Scotland hath foisons to fill up your will
Of your mere own.° All these are portable,°
With other graces weighed.

Malcolm.
But I have none: the king-becoming graces,
As justice, verity, temp'rance, stableness,
Bounty, perseverance, mercy, lowliness,
Devotion, patience, courage, fortitude,
I have no relish of° them, but abound
In the division of each several crime,°
Acting it many ways. Nay, had I pow'r, I should
Pour the sweet milk of concord into hell,
Uproar° the universal peace, confound
All unity on earth. **P**

Macduff. O Scotland, Scotland!

Malcolm.
If such a one be fit to govern, speak:
I am as I have spoken.

Macduff. Fit to govern!
No, not to live. O nation miserable!
With an untitled° tyrant bloody-sceptered,
When shalt thou see thy wholesome days again,
Since that the truest issue of thy throne
By his own interdiction° stands accursed,
And does blaspheme his breed?° Thy royal father
Was a most sainted king: the queen that bore thee,
Oft'ner upon her knees than on her feet,
Died° every day she lived. Fare thee well!
These evils thou repeat'st upon thyself
Hath banished me from Scotland. O my breast,
Thy hope ends here! **Q**

Malcolm. Macduff, this noble passion,
Child of integrity, hath from my soul
Wiped the black scruples,° reconciled my thoughts
To thy good truth and honor. Devilish Macbeth
By many of these trains° hath sought to win me
Into his power; and modest wisdom° plucks me
From over-credulous haste: but God above

87. sword . . . kings: the cause of death to our kings.
88–89. foisons . . . own: enough abundance of your own to satisfy your covetousness.
portable: bearable.

95. relish of: taste for.
96. division . . . crime: variations of each kind of crime.

99. Uproar: put into a tumult.

104. untitled: having no right to the throne.

107. interdiction: curse; exclusion.
108. breed: ancestry.

111. Died: that is, prepared for heaven.

? Elements of Drama
114. *How might the tone change here? How has Macduff proved himself?*

116. scruples: suspicions.

118. trains: plots.
119. modest wisdom: prudence.

P **Reading Focus** **Using Questioning to Monitor Reading** This very dense exchange between Macbeth and Malcolm contains many archaic terms. What questions could help you summarize each character's words?

Q **Literary Focus** **Tragedy** How does Macduff's harsh judgment of Malcolm suggest problems for Macbeth?

The roof of Glamis Castle, Angus, Scotland.

Cross-Curricular Connection

HISTORY: Siward, Earl of Northumbria

Siward, an English nobleman, lived during the eleventh century and married into the Northumbrian house. Certain sources report that this marriage created a distant relation to Duncan, thus also making him a relation of Malcolm. According to a historical source, following the defeat of King Duncan in 1040 by Macbeth, the young Malcolm was sent to Northumbria and put under the care of Siward, who trained him as well. Siward became a famous general to Edward the Confessor, and in 1053 Siward led 10,000 English soldiers against Scotland. Before Siward died, he expressed disappointment that he could not be killed on the battlefield.

Deal between thee and me! For even now
I put myself to° thy direction, and
Unspeak mine own detraction;° here abjure
The taints and blames I laid upon myself,
For° strangers to my nature. I am yet
Unknown to woman, never was forsworn,
Scarcely have coveted what was mine own,
At no time broke my faith, would not betray
The devil to his fellow, and delight
No less in truth than life. My first false speaking
Was this upon myself. What I am truly,
Is thine and my poor country's to command:
Whither indeed, before thy here-approach,
Old Siward, with ten thousand warlike men,
Already at a point,° was setting forth.
Now we'll together, and the chance of goodness
Be like our warranted quarrel!° Why are you silent? **R**

Macduff.
Such welcome and unwelcome things at once
'Tis hard to reconcile.

[*Enter a* DOCTOR.]

Malcolm.
Well, more anon. Comes the king forth, I pray you?

Doctor.
Ay, sir. There are a crew of wretched souls
That stay° his cure: their malady convinces
The great assay of art;° but at his touch,
Such sanctity hath heaven given his hand,
They presently amend.°

Malcolm. I thank you, doctor.

[*Exit* DOCTOR.]

Macduff.
What's the disease he means?

Malcolm. 'Tis called the evil:°
A most miraculous work in this good king,
Which often since my here-remain in England
I have seen him do. How he solicits heaven,
Himself best knows: but strangely visited° people,
All swoll'n and ulcerous, pitiful to the eye,

122. to: under.
123. detraction: slander.

125. For: as.

135. at a point: prepared.
136–137. the chance . . . quarrel: May our chance of success equal the justice of our cause.

? Staging the Play
137. *Where should Malcolm pause in this line? Should he act puzzled, or matter-of-fact?*

142. stay: await.
142–143. convinces . . . art: defies the efforts of medical science.

145. presently amend: immediately recover.

146. evil: scrofula, called "the king's evil" because it allegedly could be cured by the king's touch.

150. strangely visited: oddly afflicted.

R Reading Focus Using Questioning to Monitor Reading Malcolm has withheld the good news that Siward and ten thousand men are ready to fight Macbeth. What questions can explain this omission?

Universal Access

Advanced Learners

Acceleration Point out to students that in this scene, Malcolm and Macduff learn more information about Macbeth's treachery. Encourage students to analyze the conversation between Malcolm and Macduff. Then, ask student pairs to discuss the following questions: How do you think Malcolm and Macduff will respond to Macbeth's actions? What role do you think these two men will play in Macbeth's tragic downfall? After pairs have answered the questions, have them share their ideas with the class.

Think About/Talk About

Comprehension

P Reading Focus

Possible responses: *What are "verity" and "temperance," and how are these qualities connected to being a good king? Why does Malcolm believe he is unfit to rule Scotland?*

R Reading Focus

Possible responses: *Why did Malcolm fail to inform Macduff right away that an army was ready to fight Macbeth? Was he testing Macduff's loyalty? Was he trying to see whether Macduff would side with him even if no one else did?*

Analysis

Q Literary Focus

Possible response: *Macduff unequivocally states that someone with many vices is not fit to rule. He values morality and will not be loyal to a tyrant. He must be disgusted with Macbeth's criminal acts and ready to turn against him.*

Extend the Discussion

Comparing and Contrasting What difference between Malcolm and Duncan do lines 114–120 highlight? ***Possible response:*** *By lying about himself in order to test Macduff, Malcolm shows that he is cautious, crafty, and able to discern Macduff's true character—unlike Duncan, who was deceived twice by traitors.*

Making Judgments In lines 138–139, Macduff is puzzled. Should he trust Malcolm? Why or why not? ***Possible response:*** *He should trust Malcolm. Even though Malcolm has manipulated Macduff, he must be telling the truth about planning to attack Macbeth. After all, Malcolm must want to avenge his father.*

Model the Skill

- Model understanding the **tragic hero** by analyzing his foil. Explain to students that a **foil** is a character who sets off another character by strong contrast.
- Explain to students how Edward the Confessor, the king of England, serves as a foil for Macbeth in this scene. You might say that not only does Edward the Confessor's touch heal instead of harm, but he also can foresee the future. The people living under his rule enjoy many blessings instead of murders and crimes.

Guided Practice: Apply

Have students read lines 147–159. Then ask them to discuss, with a partner, the specific differences between life in England under the rule of Edward the Confessor and life in Scotland under the control of Macbeth.

Think About/Talk About

Responses to Margin Questions

Stage direction *Students may guess that Ross relates the news that Macduff's family has been murdered.*

Line 176 *He would probably look away, hoping that Macduff will not look in his eyes and guess the truth.*

Line 179 *For Macduff, "peace" means that his family is well. For Ross, it means the peace that comes with death.*

Line 203 *We see it by the look of grief on his face and the tone of his voice.*

The mere° despair of surgery, he cures,
Hanging a golden stamp° about their necks,
Put on with holy prayers: and 'tis spoken,
To the succeeding royalty he leaves
The healing benediction. With this strange virtue°
He hath a heavenly gift of prophecy,
And sundry blessings hang about his throne
That speak° him full of grace. Ⓢ

[*Enter* ROSS.]

Macduff. See, who comes here?
Malcolm.
My countryman; but yet I know him not.
Macduff.
My ever gentle° cousin, welcome hither.
Malcolm.
I know him now: good God, betimes° remove
The means that makes us strangers!
Ross. Sir, amen.
Macduff.
Stands Scotland where it did?
Ross. Alas, poor country!
Almost afraid to know itself! It cannot
Be called our mother but our grave, where nothing°
But who knows nothing is once seen to smile;
Where sighs and groans, and shrieks that rent the air,
Are made, not marked;° where violent sorrow seems
A modern ecstasy.° The dead man's knell
Is there scarce asked for who, and good men's lives
Expire before the flowers in their caps,
Dying or ere they sicken.
Macduff. O, relation
Too nice,° and yet too true!
Malcolm. What's the newest grief?
Ross.
That of an hour's age doth hiss the speaker;°
Each minute teems° a new one.
Macduff. How does my wife?
Ross.
Why, well.
Macduff. And all my children?
Ross. Well too.

152. mere: utter.
153. stamp: coin.

156. virtue: power.

159. speak: proclaim.

? *Stage direction: Ross is Macduff's countryman. What news do you anticipate he brings with him?*

161. gentle: noble.

162. betimes: quickly.

166. nothing: no one.

169. marked: noticed.
170. modern ecstasy: ordinary emotion.

173–174. relation / Too nice: tale too accurate.

175. That . . . speaker: The report of the grief of an hour ago is hissed as stale news.
176. teems: gives birth to.

? **176.** *Does Ross look at Macduff while speaking this line, or does he turn away?*

Ⓢ **Literary Perspectives** **Analyzing Historical Context** These lines refer to Edward the Confessor, king of England from 978 to 1016. Edward was believed to be capable of healing people by touching them. Why do you think Shakespeare mentions him here?

Universal Access

EL English Learners

English for Academic Success Explain to students that a pun is a play on words; Shakespeare often used puns in his works. A pun draws its humor from a word that has multiple meanings or from words or expressions that sound alike but have different meanings. For example, in line 206, Ross may be punning on the word *deer.* He describes the family as having been slaughtered like deer; the murder victims were also *dear* to Macduff.

Struggling Readers

Guide the students in paraphrasing lines 181–188. This will help them answer any questions they have in their Reading Skills Focus graphic organizer. Have students write out the lines double-spaced on loose-leaf paper. Ask them to look up the meanings of any words they are not familiar with, or read the definitions in the footnotes, and write the definition of the word near or above it. Then have them paraphrase the passage, line by line, in their own words.

Macduff.
The tyrant has not battered at their peace?
Ross.
No; they were well at peace when I did leave 'em.
Macduff.
Be not a niggard of your speech: how goes't?
Ross.
When I came hither to transport the tidings,
Which I have heavily° borne, there ran a rumor
Of many worthy fellows that were out;°
Which was to my belief witnessed° the rather,
For that I saw the tyrant's power° afoot.
Now is the time of help. Your eye in Scotland
Would create soldiers, make our women fight,
To doff their dire distresses.
Malcolm. Be't their comfort
We are coming thither. Gracious England hath
Lent us good Siward and ten thousand men;
An older and a better soldier none
That Christendom gives out.°
Ross. Would I could answer
This comfort with the like! But I have words
That would° be howled out in the desert air,
Where hearing should not latch° them.
Macduff. What concern they?
The general cause or is it a fee-grief
Due to some single breast?°
Ross. No mind that's honest
But in it shares some woe, though the main part
Pertains to you alone.
Macduff. If it be mine,
Keep it not from me, quickly let me have it.
Ross.
Let not your ears despise my tongue forever,
Which shall possess them with the heaviest sound
That ever yet they heard.
Macduff. Humh! I guess at it.
Ross.
Your castle is surprised;° your wife and babes
Savagely slaughtered. To relate the manner,
Were, on the quarry° of these murdered deer,
To add the death of you.
Malcolm. Merciful heaven!
What, man! Ne'er pull your hat upon your brows;
Give sorrow words. The grief that does not speak
Whispers the o'er-fraught heart,° and bids it break.

? **179.** *What is the double meaning of this line?*

182. heavily: sadly.
183. out: up in arms.
184. witnessed: attested.
185. power: army.

192. gives out: reports.

194. would: should.
195. latch: catch.
196–197. fee-grief . . . breast: that is, personal grief belonging to an individual.

? **Staging the Play**
203. *Macduff's pain becomes visible. How should we see it?*

204. surprised: suddenly attacked.
206. quarry: heap of slaughtered game.

210. Whispers . . . heart: whispers to the overburdened heart.

Think About/Talk About

Analysis

Literary Perspectives

Possible response: *Shakespeare might mention Edward as a healer to give the public the idea that their king, James, desires to meet the people's needs. Also, by presenting the King of England as a healer in the play, Shakespeare emphasizes the evil and destruction occurring under Macbeth's rule in Scotland.*

Extend the Discussion

Evaluating What do you think of the way Ross breaks the bad news to Macduff? ***Possible response:*** *It is similar to the way Macduff gently tries to break the news of Duncan's death to Lady Macbeth in Act II, except that she not only already knew about it but had planned the murder. Here, Macduff deserves the sensitivity Ross uses. Even though Ross lied earlier, it is easy to understand why it was hard for Ross to tell the truth. His reluctance to deliver the news also builds suspense.*

Figurative Language Point out that lines 201–203 is an example of synecdoche—the use of part of something to stand for the whole. What does "your ears" in line 201 stand for? [*you*] "My tongue?" [*me*] What is the literal meaning of this line? ***Possible response:*** *Please do not hate me for what I am about to tell you.*

Advanced Learners

Acceleration Remind students how in Act III, Scene 4, line 25, the sentence "Banquo's safe" represented a kind of wordplay. The word was indeed used to describe how Banquo had been murdered successfully, and how his body was "safe in a ditch." Ask students to locate another example of this type of wordplay on this page. [*Line 179, "No, they were well at peace when I did leave him."*]

Students with Disabilities

Model the Think-Aloud strategy for students. Read lines 164–167 aloud. You might say: "I understand that Scotland is a land of grief and violence, in contrast to England." Have students read lines 176–177 and make a comment, identify comprehension problems, or make a prediction.

go.hrw.com For more about the Think Aloud strategy, see **Think-Central, Teacher Access.**

Think About/Talk About

Analysis

Literary Focus

Possible response: *Macbeth's lineage will never continue since he has no children—unlike Banquo, whose descendants will rule Scotland. Macduff also cannot fully avenge his family's murder because Macbeth can never know the pain of losing one's child.*

Responses to Margin Questions

Line 211 *He could cry out in distress or try to master his feelings by speaking in a normal tone.*

Line 216 If *Macduff refers to Macbeth, he might speak with pain and scorn. If he refers to Malcolm, he might be reminding himself of the reason for Malcolm's lack of understanding, and his tone might be less harsh.*

Line 220 *Malcolm urges Macduff to act on his feelings. At the beginning of the scene, Malcolm's desire to take time to grieve for his father suggests that he would not criticize Macduff for his desire to grieve.*

Monitor Students' Comprehension

Guide the class in answering these comprehension questions.

1. When the Second Witch says, "Something wicked this way comes," to whom is she referring? [*She is referring to Macbeth.*]
2. According to the Second Apparition, who cannot harm Macbeth? [*Macbeth cannot be harmed by anyone born of woman.*]
3. How does Malcolm test Macduff's loyalty to Scotland? [*Malcolm pretends to be more evil and ruthless than Macbeth.*]

Macduff.
My children too?
Ross. Wife, children, servants, all
That could be found.
Macduff. And I must be from thence!
My wife killed too?
Ross. I have said.
Malcolm. Be comforted.
Let's make us med'cines of our great revenge,
To cure this deadly grief.
Macduff.
He has no children. All my pretty ones?
Did you say all? O hell-kite!° All?
What, all my pretty chickens and their dam°
At one fell swoop?
Malcolm.
Dispute° it like a man.
Macduff. I shall do so;
But I must also feel it as a man.
I cannot but remember such things were,
That were most precious to me. Did heaven look on,
And would not take their part? Sinful Macduff,
They were all struck for thee! Naught° that I am,
Not for their own demerits but for mine
Fell slaughter on their souls. Heaven rest them now!
Malcolm.
Be this the whetstone of your sword. Let grief
Convert to anger; blunt not the heart, enrage it.
Macduff.
O, I could play the woman with mine eyes,
And braggart with my tongue! But, gentle heavens,
Cut short all intermission;° front to front°
Bring thou this fiend of Scotland and myself;
Within my sword's length set him. If he 'scape,
Heaven forgive him too!
Malcolm. This time goes manly.
Come, go we to the king. Our power is ready;
Our lack is nothing but our leave.° Macbeth
Is ripe for shaking, and the pow'rs above
Put on their instruments.° Receive what cheer you may.
The night is long that never finds the day. [*Exeunt.*]

? **Staging the Play**
211. *How full, or soft, a voice would you have Macduff use in this line?*

? **Staging the Play**
216. *How would Macduff say this line: "He has no children"?*

217. hell-kite: hellish bird of prey.
218. dam: mother.

? **220.** *Is Malcolm being critical or encouraging here?*

220. Dispute: counter.

225. Naught: wicked.

232. intermission: interval. **front to front:** forehead to forehead (that is, face to face).

237. Our lack . . . leave: We need only to take our leave.
239. Put . . . instruments: arm themselves.

Literary Focus **Tragedy** Macduff could be referring to either Malcolm or Macbeth in this line. Why might it be significant that Macbeth has no children?

California Standards, p. 477

- **Reading Standard 2.2** Analyze the way in which clarity of meaning is affected by the patterns of organization, hierarchical structures, repetition of the main ideas, syntax, and word choice in the text.
- **Reading Standard 3.1** Analyze characteristics of subgenres (e.g., satire, parody, allegory, pastoral) that are used in poetry, prose, plays, novels, short stories, essays, and other basic genres.
- **Grades 9–10 Review Reading Standard 3.3** Analyze interactions between main and subordinate characters in a literary text (e.g., internal and external conflicts, motivations, relationships, influence) and explain the way those interactions affect the plot.
- **Grades 9–10 Review Reading Standard 3.12** Analyze the way in which a work of literature is related to the themes and issues of its historical period. (Historical approach).
- **Writing Standard 2.1** Write fictional, autobiographical, or biographical narratives: **b.** Locate scenes and incidents in specific places. **c.** Describe with concrete sensory details the sights, sounds, and smells of a scene and the specific actions, movements, gestures, and feelings of the characters; use interior monologue to depict the characters' feelings. **d.** Pace the presentation of actions to accommodate temporal, spatial, and dramatic mood changes.

Applying Your Skills

Reading Standard 2.2, 3.1; Grades 9–10 Review Reading Standard 3.3, 3.12 (see pages A48–A50)
Writing Standard 2.1b, 2.1c, 2.1d (see pages A51–A52)

The Tragedy of Macbeth
Act IV

Literary Response and Analysis

Reading Skills Focus

Quick Check

1. What does Macbeth ask the witches, and how do they respond?
2. At the end of Scene 1, what does Macbeth vow? How does he fulfill his vow in Scene 2?
3. According to Macduff and Malcolm in Scene 3, how has Macbeth's reign affected Scotland?

Read with a Purpose

4. How does Macbeth show more than one tragic flaw in Act IV?

Reading Skills: Using Questions to Monitor Reading

5. As you read, you recorded your questions about Act IV. Now, record and explain your answers.

Act, Scene, Line	Questions I Have	My Answers
Act IV, Scene 1, line 81	Why does the Second Apparition tell Macbeth no one can harm him, if the first told him to fear Macduff?	This may be a riddle that will lead to his tragic end. Macbeth has already fulfilled the witches' Act I prophecies.

Literary Skills Focus

Literary Analysis

6. **Interpret** How does Macbeth explain the meaning of the first three apparitions?
7. **Analyze** How has Macbeth's moral character deteriorated since he last met the witches?
8. **Analyze** Have the witches caused any of the changes in Macbeth's moral character? Explain.
9. **Make Judgments** In Scene 3, Malcolm deliberately lies to Macduff. What does this behavior, and the reason for it, reveal about his character?
10. **Literary Perspectives** What does the conversation between Macduff and Malcolm in Scene 3 imply about the qualities that Shakespeare's audience would have considered acceptable—and unacceptable—in a king?

Literary Skills: Tragedy

11. **Analyze** In Act IV, what does Macbeth do that seems to ensure his tragic downfall?

Literary Skills Review: Foil

12. **Analyze** A **foil** is a character who sets off another character by sharp contrast. Banquo serves as a foil for Macbeth. How are Macduff or Malcolm foils to Macbeth?

Writing Skills Focus

Think as a Reader/Writer

Use It in Your Writing Review your notes about Macbeth's conversation with the witches in Scene 1. Although Macbeth normally speaks in **blank verse,** in lines 94–106 he speaks in rhymed couplets—the speaking pattern of the witches. This shift reveals that Macbeth is becoming as sinister as the witches. In your *Reader/Writer Notebook,* write a short scene in which one character begins to imitate another character's way of speaking.

What Do You Think Now? In Act IV, how does Macbeth respond to the impulses of his heart and mind?

Check for Understanding

Independent Practice

Reading Skills Focus

Possible responses:

1. *Macbeth wants to know if he will remain in power and if Banquo's heirs will rule. The witches let the apparition answer with prophecies and show him a procession of Banquo's descendants.*
2. *Macbeth vows to strike Macduff's family and then has Lady Macduff and her son killed.*
3. *Macbeth's reign has wounded Scotland and created disorder.*
4. *He is ruthless, overly ambitious, and deceitful.*
5. *Students should use their knowledge of characters and plot to ask and answer as many questions as possible.*

Literary Skills Focus

Possible responses:

6. *He believes that no one can come against him or defeat him in battle in the end.*
7. *Previously a hero in battle, he is now a murderer and a traitor.*
8. *The witches set up a chain of evil events, but Macbeth acted out of his own free will. They did not alter his character.*
9. *Malcolm tests Macduff's loyalty because he is wise and wary, not easily fooled like his father.*
10. *The conversation implies that Shakespeare's audience would not think favorably of the king that Malcolm initially pretended to be. They would have wanted a virtuous king.*
11. *Macbeth kills Macduff's family.*
12. *Macduff serves as a foil for Macbeth by staying loyal to his country and fighting for good, not evil. Malcolm is a foil in that he pretends to be corrupt but reveals his good intentions, while Macbeth pretends to be good but is corrupt.*

Universal Access

Struggling Writers

Some students may need additional scaffolding to complete the Writing Skills Focus activity. Have students re-examine ll. 94–103 in Scene 1. Have students note how, like the witches, Macbeth begins to speak in rhymed couplets. Tell students before writing their scene to first create a character who speaks in a unique manner. For example, the character might rhyme every line or use excessive amounts of slang. Have students decide what kind of speaking pattern they want to include in their dialogue.

What Do You Think Now?

Have students refer back to all of Macbeth's actions and justifications in Act IV. Have students review these actions and decide whether Macbeth made them using his heart or his mind.

Assess

Unit 2 Resources,
Selection Standards Check, p. 108

Teacher Preparation
Selection Plot Summary

In Act V of *Macbeth*, while Macbeth gathers his men to fight Malcolm, Lady Macbeth is left alone in the castle at Dunsinane. She thinks about the atrocities Macbeth has committed at her command and of his own will; the guilt drives her mad and she dies. Macbeth thinks himself indestructible, but is killed by Macduff, who is not "woman born." Malcolm is hailed as the new king as the play draws to a close.

Direct Teach

Think About/Talk About

Analysis

Ⓐ Literary Focus

Possible response: *Lady Macbeth sleeps but is unable to escape her daily life, which is a horrific nightmare, even in her dreams.*

Ⓑ Literary Focus

Possible response: *Hand washing has appeared in Act II, Scene 2, when Lady Macbeth tells Macbeth to wash his hands. Now, Lady Macbeth frequently washes her hands, and the activity is now an obsession. The evil acts she has committed make her feel perpetually dirty.*

Responses to Margin Questions

Line 28 *She checks them, and upon finding an invisible spot of blood, tries to wash it off.*

Line 35 *Duncan's blood*

Line 37 *Macduff*

Line 43 *She sniffs an imaginary spot on one hand.*

Line 55 *Macbeth*

Scene 1. *Dunsinane. In the castle.*

Enter a DOCTOR *of physic and a waiting* GENTLEWOMAN.

Doctor. I have two nights watched with you, but can perceive no truth in your report. When was it she last walked?

Gentlewoman. Since his majesty went into the field, I have seen her rise from her bed, throw her nightgown upon her, unlock her closet,° take forth paper, fold it, write upon't, read it, afterwards seal it, and again return to bed; yet all this while in a most fast sleep.

Doctor. A great perturbation in nature, to receive at once the benefit of sleep and do the effects of watching!° In this slumb'ry agitation, besides her walking and other actual performances,° what, at any time, have you heard her say? Ⓐ

Gentlewoman. That, sir, which I will not report after her.

Doctor. You may to me, and 'tis most meet° you should.

Gentlewoman. Neither to you nor anyone, having no witness to confirm my speech.

[*Enter* LADY MACBETH, *with a taper.*]

Lo you, here she comes! This is her very guise,° and, upon my life, fast asleep! Observe her; stand close.°

Doctor. How came she by that light?

Gentlewoman. Why, it stood by her. She has light by her continually. 'Tis her command.

Doctor. You see, her eyes are open.

Gentlewoman. Ay, but their sense° are shut.

Doctor. What is it she does now? Look, how she rubs her hands.

Gentlewoman. It is an accustomed action with her, to seem thus washing her hands: I have known her continue in this a quarter of an hour. Ⓑ

Lady Macbeth. Yet here's a spot.

Doctor. Hark! she speaks. I will set down what comes from her, to satisfy° my remembrance the more strongly.

Lady Macbeth. Out, damned spot! Out, I say! One: two: why, then 'tis time to do't. Hell is murky. Fie, my lord, fie! A soldier,

5. closet: chest.

9. effects of watching: deeds of one awake.

10–11. actual performances: deeds.

13. meet: suitable.

16. guise: custom.

17. close: hidden.

22. sense: powers of sight.

? Staging the Play
28. *After setting down the taper on a table, what does Lady Macbeth do with her hands?*

30. satisfy: confirm.

Ⓐ **Literary Focus** **Tragedy** How does the idea of unnatural sleep contribute to the play's tragic themes?

Ⓑ **Literary Focus** **Tragedy** Where has the subject of hand washing arisen previously? What do Lady Macbeth's actions tell us about the nature of evil?

Universal Access

EL English Learners

To help students understand the content of the selection, have them skim the text to get a general idea of its content. Ask students to point out what they think are key words in the text. Explain that a good reader uses key words as clues to interpret unfamiliar words and complex sentences.

✔ See **UA: Differentiating Instruction** for strategies for teaching English learners.

Struggling Readers

Benchmark Students As they read Act V of *Macbeth*, encourage students to record details in the play that reveal Macbeth and Lady Macbeth as tragic characters. As the play draws to the end, have students focus on the signs of the characters' downfall. Ask students to discuss their notes with the class.

✔ Invite students to read the selection in interactive format in **UA: Holt Interactive Reader.**

and afeard? What need we fear who knows it, when none can call our pow'r to accompt?° Yet who would have thought the old man to have had so much blood in him?

Doctor. Do you mark that?

Lady Macbeth. The Thane of Fife had a wife. Where is she now? What, will these hands ne'er be clean? No more o' that, my lord, no more o' that! You mar all with this starting.

Doctor. Go to,° go to! You have known what you should not.

Gentlewoman. She has spoke what she should not, I am sure of that. Heaven knows what she has known.

Lady Macbeth. Here's the smell of the blood still. All the perfumes of Arabia will not sweeten this little hand. Oh, oh, oh!

Doctor. What a sigh is there! The heart is sorely charged.°

Gentlewoman. I would not have such a heart in my bosom for the dignity° of the whole body.

Doctor. Well, well, well——

Gentlewoman. Pray God it be, sir.

Doctor. This disease is beyond my practice.° Yet I have known those which have walked in their sleep who have died holily in their beds.

Lady Macbeth. Wash your hands; put on your nightgown; look not so pale! I tell you yet again, Banquo's buried. He cannot come out on 's° grave.

Doctor. Even so?

Lady Macbeth. To bed, to bed! There's knocking at the gate.

34. to accompt: to account.

? **35.** *What does she think is still on her hands?*

? **37.** *Who is the Thane of Fife?*

40. Go to: an exclamation.

? **Staging the Play**
43. *What does this line suggest?*

45. charged: burdened.

47. dignity: worth; rank.

50. practice: professional skill.

55. on 's: of his.

? **55.** *To whom does she think she is speaking here?*

Sally Dexter as Lady Macbeth, Queens Theatre, Shaftsbury Avenue (1999).

Think About/Talk About

Extend the Discussion

Finding Details Re-read Lady Macbeth's dialogue from lines 31–56. Which phrases reveal her role in the murder(s)? ***Possible response:*** *Lines 34–35: "who would have / thought the old man to have had so much blood in him?"; line 43: "Here's the smell of the blood still."; line 54: "I tell you yet again, Banquo's buried."*

Determining Author's Purpose The doctor and the gentlewoman express pity for Lady Macbeth in lines 45–47. Why do you think Shakespeare has them do so? ***Possible response:*** *Shakespeare wants the audience to pity the guilt-torn sleepwalker and not view her as completely evil.*

Advanced Learners

Acceleration Have students consider the decision-making process that leads to Macbeth's downfall. Starting with the decision of whether to believe the witches' initial predictions, they should trace the path Macbeth follows from one decision to another. Ask students to speculate about how Macbeth's fate might have differed if, for example, he had decided not to murder Duncan. Encourage students to share their ideas with the class.

✔ See **UA: Resources for Teaching Advanced Students** for strategies for teaching advanced learners.

Learners with Diverse Needs

Have students apply the Somebody Wanted But So strategy. Create the chart with the headings: "Somebody," "Wanted," "But," and "So." Have students add the characters of Macbeth and Lady Macbeth under "Somebody." Then, help them fill in the "Wanted" column [*They wanted to gain power and secure it from outside threats*]. After they have read the selection, help students fill the last two columns.

go.hrw.com For more about the Somebody Wanted But So strategy, see **ThinkCentral, Teacher Access.**

Guided Practice: Apply

Think as a Reader/Writer

Find It in Your Reading Point out to students that Macbeth now feels "his title / Hang loose about him" (lines 20–21) in a simile that demeans himself. Explain that Macbeth's deeds have corrupted his rule and turned him into a tyrant. Encourage students to find more evidence of this change.

Use It in Your Writing Have students write an effective simile that illustrates a dramatic change in a person's status.

Think About/Talk About

Extend the Discussion

Finding Details In lines 63–69, what is the doctor's advice to the gentlewoman regarding Lady Macbeth? ***Possible response:*** *The doctor wants the gentlewoman to watch Lady Macbeth constantly.*

Imagery Point out the images of illness used to represent evil. What does the doctor mean when he talks about "infected minds" in line 63? ***Possible response:*** *He refers to the characters' guilty consciences.*

Responses to Margin Questions

Line 59 *She thinks she hears knocking at the gate, as in Act II, Scene 2. She leaves the stage in frantic haste.*

Line 5 *It was mentioned in the third prophecy by the three witches.*

Come, come, come, come, give me your hand! What's done
cannot be undone. To bed, to bed, to bed! (C)
[*Exit* LADY MACBETH.]

Doctor. Will she go now to bed?
Gentlewoman. Directly.
Doctor.
Foul whisp'rings are abroad. Unnatural deeds
Do breed unnatural troubles. Infected minds
To their deaf pillows will discharge their secrets.
More needs she the divine° than the physician. (D)
God, God forgive us all! Look after her;
Remove from her the means of all annoyance,°
And still° keep eyes upon her. So good night.
My mind she has mated° and amazed my sight:
I think, but dare not speak.
Gentlewoman. Good night, good doctor.
[*Exeunt.*]

? Staging the Play
59. *Once again there is a sudden dramatic change. What echo from the past bring about this change? How do you think Lady Macbeth leaves the stage?*

65. divine: priest.
67. annoyance: injury.
68. still: continuously.
69. mated: baffled.

Scene 2. *The country near Dunsinane.*

Drum and colors. Enter MENTEITH, CAITHNESS, ANGUS, LENNOX, SOLDIERS.

Menteith.
The English pow'r° is near, led on by Malcolm,
His uncle Siward and the good Macduff. (E)
Revenges burn in them; for their dear° causes
Would to the bleeding and the grim alarm°
Excite the mortified° man.
Angus. Near Birnam Wood
Shall we well meet them; that way are they coming.
Caithness.
Who knows if Donalbain be with his brother?
Lennox.
For certain, sir, he is not. I have a file°
Of all the gentry: there is Siward's son,
And many unrough° youths that even now
Protest° their first of manhood.
Menteith. What does the tyrant?

1. pow'r: army.
3. dear: heartfelt.
4. alarm: call to arms.
5. mortified: half dead.

? **5.** *Where have you heard about Birnam Wood before?*

8. file: list.
10. unrough: beardless.
11. Protest: assert.

(C) **Literary Focus** **Tragedy** Lady Macbeth recounts not only the crimes she committed with Macbeth but also those crimes he committed himself. Identify each of these crimes.

(D) **Literary Perspectives** **Analyzing Historical Context** What do the doctor's words imply about Renaissance Christian beliefs?

(E) **Literary Focus** **Tragedy** Macbeth has moved from being a ruler to being a tyrant. How does this contrast with the leadership of those who rise against him?

Developing Oral Fluency

Use Scene II to give students practice in reading plays with expression. Remind students that side notes to the text explain some of the more difficult words and phrases. Fluent readers use these notes to express emotions in their voices as they read. Also, remind students that punctuation marks and capital letters within sentences give readers clues about when to pause, when to stress certain words or phrases, and when to make changes in intonation. If some students do not understand some of the words used in the passage, encourage them to ask questions or use a dictionary. Understanding the words will guide them in choosing which intonation is most effective.

Group Activity Place students into groups of four or allow them to pair up themselves.

- Model reading lines 12–16 twice. You are your intonation; you can read these lines angrily or matter-of-factly.

Independent Practice

Literary Skills Focus

Possible responses:

1. *At the beginning of the play, his flaw is that he is too ambitious. Eventually, Macbeth becomes obsessed with power.*
2. *Lady Macbeth begins as a strong character but goes mad.*
3. *At the beginning of the play, the Macbeths seem to have a partnership: they share the same ambitions. Gradually, Lady Macbeth grows more helpless (I.5.53–55), and Macbeth grows more determined.*
4. *The play seems to make the statement that a thirst for power can be a person's downfall. As long as Macbeth was content with his place, good things happened to him. However, once he tried to seize the throne, he invited only disaster.*
5. *The historical perspective gave more depth to my understanding of Macbeth. In particular, the fact that the play may have reminded Shakespeare's audience of a real-life plot to murder a king makes me able to read this play as a thriller.*
6. *For as long as Macbeth seems to be struggling with his plot to kill Duncan, I have some sympathy for him. I lost sympathy for him when he had Banquo killed and later had Macduff's family killed.*
7. *Student responses should accurately identify the archetype of the fall and should also relate this knowledge to events in Macbeth.*

Grammar Link

Your Turn

1. *The Jacobean period began in 1603 with King James I's reign.*
2. *The play alludes to Edward the Confessor, a king of England.*
3. *The Witches are ruled by Hecate, the Queen of the Night.*

Applying Your Skills

Reading Standard 3.1, 3.6; **Grades 9–10 Review Reading Standard** 3.12 (see pages A48–A50)

The Tragedy of Macbeth
Acts I–V

Literary Response and Analysis

Literary Skills Focus

Literary Analysis

1. **Analyze** What is Macbeth's tragic flaw at the play's start? How does it change?
2. **Analyze** How does Lady Macbeth evolve?
3. **Interpret** How does the relationship between Macbeth and Lady Macbeth change? Why? Use examples from the text to support your ideas.
4. **Infer** What is the play's strongest lesson about human nature? Explain your answer with examples from the text.
5. **Literary Perspectives** As you read, you considered how historical context shaped Shakespeare's writing of *Macbeth*. Explain how this perspective affected your interpretation of the play. How did it influence your understanding of characters, plot events, or scenes? How might you have approached the text differently without any historical background information?

Literary Skills: Tragedy

6. **Analyze** The philosopher Aristotle argued that a bad man cannot be the principal character of a tragedy. Does Shakespeare ensure that you retain sympathy for Macbeth? Did you lose sympathy for Macbeth? If so, where?

Literary Skills Review: Archetype

7. **Analyze** An **archetype** is a pattern that appears in literature across cultures and throughout the ages. An archetype may be a character, plot, image, or setting. A familiar pattern from the Bible is the archetype of the fall, in which someone is banished from an ideal world because of a sin or great failing. Explain how the archetype of the fall is developed in *Macbeth*.

Grammar Link

Combining Sentences by Inserting Words and Phrases

No matter what type of writing you do, you will want your writing to be clear, effective, and interesting. Short sentences can be effective, but too many of them make writing choppy. You can combine these sentences in various ways. One approach is to take a key word from one sentence and insert it into another. (You may have to alter the form of the word, such as by changing a noun to an adjective.) Here is an example:

> *Macbeth* is one of Shakespeare's plays. *Macbeth* is a tragedy.
> *Macbeth* is one of Shakespeare's tragic plays.

Drop *Macbeth is a,* and change *tragedy* to *tragic* to combine the sentences.

You can also combine sentences by turning a short sentence into a phrase and inserting it into another sentence. Here is an example:

> Have you read *The Tragedy of Macbeth*? It was written by William Shakespeare.
> Have you read *The Tragedy of Macbeth* by William Shakespeare?

The circled words mean the same thing, so you can drop *It,* delete *was written,* and insert the phrase *by William Shakespeare* into the first sentence.

Your Turn

Combine each pair of sentences by adapting a key word or phrase from one and adding it to the other.

1. The Jacobean period began in 1603. The Jacobean period began with King James I's reign.
2. The play alludes to Edward, a king of England. Edward was called "the Confessor."
3. The witches are ruled by the Queen of the Night. The Queen of the Night is Hecate.

Universal Access: Grammar Link

EL English Learners/ Struggling Readers

English for Academic Success Some students may find it easier to combine sentences that address familiar subject matter. Have students work on the following sentences as an alternative activity:

1. Barry finished his homework. Barry put his homework in his backpack. [*Barry finished his homework and put it in his backpack.*]
2. Kim's dog is friendly. Kim's dog is a beagle. [*Kim's dog is a friendly beagle.*]
3. Someone had opened the window. The window was dirty. [*Someone had opened the dirty window.*]
4. Tina arrived ten minutes after the bell rang. It was her first day at school. [*Tina arrived ten minutes after the bell rang on her first day at school.*]

✔ For more practice with combining sentences, see **Warriner's Handbook, GrammarNotes,** and **Language Handbook Worksheets.**

Applying Your Skills

Reading Standard 2.2, 3.1, 3.4; Grades 9–10 Review
Reading Standard 3.12 (see pages A48–A50)
Writing Standard 2.1c, 2.1d (see pages A51–A52)

The Tragedy of Macbeth
Act V

Literary Response and Analysis

Reading Skills Focus

Quick Check

1. Why, according to the Doctor, is Lady Macbeth walking in her sleep?
2. When does Lady Macbeth die?
3. How does Birnam Wood come to Dunsinane?
4. What happens to Macbeth? Who becomes king?

Read with a Purpose

5. How do Macbeth's flaws lead to his tragic end?

Reading Skills: Using Questions to Monitor Reading

6. As you read, you recorded your questions about Act V. Now, record and explain your answers.

Act, Scene, Line	Questions I Have	My Answers
Act V, Scene 1, line 12	Why won't the Gentlewoman tell the doctor what she's heard Lady Macbeth say?	The woman may be afraid to report what she knows because she fears for her life.

Literary Skills Focus

Literary Analysis

7. **Analyze** Why do you think Shakespeare has Lady Macbeth walk in her sleep? How is this scene related to the remarks Macbeth makes in Act II, Scene 2, just after he kills Duncan?
8. **Make Judgments** Act V contains the play's **climax,** the most emotional and suspenseful part of the action and the moment when the characters' conflict is finally resolved. Which part of Act V do you consider the climax? Explain.
9. **Make Judgments** Shakespeare gave most of his tragic heroes impressive dying speeches that say something significant about their own life and death. Although Shakespeare didn't give such a speech to Macbeth, which speech in the play would serve best as his dying speech? Explain.
10. **Extend** In Act V, Macbeth says that life "is a tale / Told by an idiot, full of sound and fury, / Signifying nothing." Do you agree or disagree? Explain.
11. **Literary Perspectives** How does the ending of *Macbeth* meet the expectations of Shakespeare's Renaissance audience—including King James?

Literary Skills: Tragedy

12. **Analyze** Is Macbeth's downfall caused solely by a tragic flaw, or do other factors also help bring him to a tragic end? Explain.

Literary Skills Review: Imagery

13. **Analyze** Language that appeals to the senses—sight, hearing, smell, taste, and touch—is called **imagery.** Identify two images in Act V, and analyze how they contribute to the play's mood.

Writing Skills Focus

Think as a Reader/Writer

Use It in Your Writing As you read, you noted how Shakespeare reveals his characters' personalities through their actions. What does Macbeth's final action reveal about him? Write a brief dramatic scene in which a character refuses to give up when facing great danger. Let your character's actions show his or her true nature. You may include stage directions.

What Do You Think Now? In Act V, how does Macbeth respond to the impulses of his heart and mind?

Check for Understanding

Independent Practice

Reading Skills Focus

Possible responses:

1. *She sleepwalks because she feels guilty for her dishonorable deeds.*
2. *She dies shortly after the English soldiers appear at Dunsinane.*
3. *Malcolm's soldiers carry pieces of the forest up to Dunsinane as camouflage.*
4. *Macduff kills Macbeth and Malcolm becomes king.*
5. *He was overconfident he could not be harmed; if he had fled when the soldiers attacked, he might not have been killed by Macduff.*
6. *Students should ask and answer questions about circumstances motivating characters to act or speak a certain way.*

Literary Skills Focus

Possible responses:

7. *Her sleepwalking shows she does indeed feel guilty for her actions. Macbeth, after killing Duncan, thought he heard a voice saying "Macbeth does murder sleep."*
8. *It could be when Macduff and Macbeth fight and Macbeth dies.*
9. *His speech near the end of Scene 8 could be his dying speech; he says he will not give in despite the odds.*
10. *Life may be short, but we can still make a difference in the world.*
11. *The ending helps show that people can never get away with regicide; when the right king is enthroned, order is present.*
12. *His downfall is mostly caused by greed and overconfidence, though the witches did help foster these negative traits.*
13. *One image is that of life as a player on the stage, strutting for an hour and then gone. This leads to a hopeless mood. Another image is blood that Lady Macbeth feels is on her hands—she feels permanently guilty about her misdeeds, furthering the dark mood.*

Universal Access

Struggling Writers

Some students may need additional scaffolding to complete the Writing Skills Focus activity. Have students think about a fearless, stubborn character in books they have read or films they have seen. Ask them to write a dramatic scene that recounts an event in which the character proved his or her fearlessness and stubbornness. Ask students to include stage directions to indicate the character's movement on the stage.

What Do You Think Now?

Remind students that Shakespeare reveals his characters through their speech, thoughts, actions, and appearances. Have students discuss how Macbeth's character is revealed by how he responds to his thoughts and desires.

Think About/Talk About

Comprehension

P Reading Focus

Possible response: *How does Siward and Malcolm's response to Young Siward's death compare to Macduff and Malcolm's response to the death of Macduff's household?*

Analysis

Q Literary Perspectives

Possible response: *The return of order to the kingdom should accompany the restoration of the divinely appointed ruler.*

Responses to Margin Questions

Line 53 *Malcolm exhibits great concern for each missing man and promises posthumous honor for young Siward. Old Siward, satisfied his son died bravely facing the enemy, says no further honor is necessary.*

Stage direction *relieved; gracious; moved; jubilant*

Line 75 *Students may suggest that Malcolm lead the way and that the others follow in order of rank.*

Monitor Students' Comprehension

Guide the class in answering these comprehension questions.

1. Why does Lady Macbeth keep washing her hands? [*She feels dirty after helping to murder innocent people and wants to feel clean again.*]
2. At the end of the play, what happens to Young Siward? [*He tried to fight Macbeth but died. He is hailed as a hero.*]
3. What happens to most of Macbeth's soldiers? [*They fight on Malcolm's side, leading to a swift surrender by Macbeth's castle.*]

And so his knell is knolled.
Malcolm. He's worth more sorrow,
And that I'll spend for him.
Siward. He's worth no more:
They say he parted well and paid his score:°
And so God be with him! Here comes newer comfort. **P**

[*Enter* MACDUFF, *with Macbeth's head.*]

Macduff.
Hail, king! for so thou art: behold, where stands
Th' usurper's cursèd head. The time is free.°
I see thee compassed° with thy kingdom's pearl,
That speak my salutation in their minds,
Whose voices I desire aloud with mine:
Hail, King of Scotland!
All. Hail, King of Scotland!

[*Flourish.*]

Malcolm.
We shall not spend a large expense of time
Before we reckon with your several loves,°
And make us even with you. My thanes and kinsmen,
Henceforth be earls, the first that ever Scotland
In such an honor named. What's more to do,
Which would be planted newly with the time°—
As calling home our exiled friends abroad
That fled the snares of watchful tyranny,
Producing forth the cruel ministers°
Of this dead butcher and his fiendlike queen,
Who, as 'tis thought, by self and violent hands°
Took off her life—this, and what needful else
That calls upon us,° by the grace of Grace
We will perform in measure, time, and place:°
So thanks to all at once and to each one,
Whom we invite to see us crowned at Scone. **Q**

[*Flourish. Exeunt omnes.*]

52. parted . . . score: departed well and settled his account.

? Elements of Drama
53. *What character traits does Malcolm show in this scene? How is old Siward like a military man to the end?*

55. The time is free: The world is liberated.

56. compassed: surrounded.

? Staging the Play
Stage direction: *Macduff enters with Macbeth's head on a pole. A great shout is heard. What is Macduff's tone in the next speech?*

61. reckon . . . loves: reward the devotion of each of you.

64–65. What's . . . time: what else must be done that should be newly established in this age.

68. ministers: agents.

70. self . . . hands: her own violent hands.

72. calls upon us: demands my attention.

73. in . . . place: fittingly, at the appropriate time and place.

? Staging the Play
75. *Scone is a village in Scotland. For centuries, all Scottish kings were crowned in Scone on the Stone of Destiny. The stone was taken to England in 1296 and was returned to Scotland, to Edinburgh Castle, in 1996. How would you have the characters exit? Who would exit last?*

P Reading Focus **Using Questioning to Monitor Reading** The exchange between Siward and Malcolm recalls the conversation between Macduff and Malcolm after the news of the death of Macduff's family reached them (Act IV, Scene 3, lines 220–235). What can you ask yourself to explain this connection?

Q Literary Perspectives **Analyzing Historical Context** Why would the restoration of order be important to Shakespeare's audience?

California Standards, p. 493

- **Reading Standard 2.2** Analyze the way in which clarity of meaning is affected by the patterns of organization, hierarchical structures, repetition of the main ideas, syntax, and word choice in the text.
- **Reading Standard 3.1** Analyze characteristics of subgenres (e.g., satire, parody, allegory, pastoral) that are used in poetry, prose, plays, novels, short stories, essays, and other basic genres.
- **Reading Standard 3.4** Analyze ways in which poets use imagery, personification, figures of speech, and sounds to evoke readers' emotions.
- **Grades 9–10 Review Reading Standard 3.12** Analyze the way in which a work of literature is related to the themes and issues of its historical period. (Historical approach).
- **Writing Standard 2.1** Write fictional, autobiographical, or biographical narratives: **c.** Describe with concrete sensory details the sights, sounds, and smells of a scene and the specific actions, movements, gestures, and feelings of the characters; use interior monologue to depict the characters' feelings. **d.** Pace the presentation of actions to accommodate temporal, spatial, and dramatic mood changes.

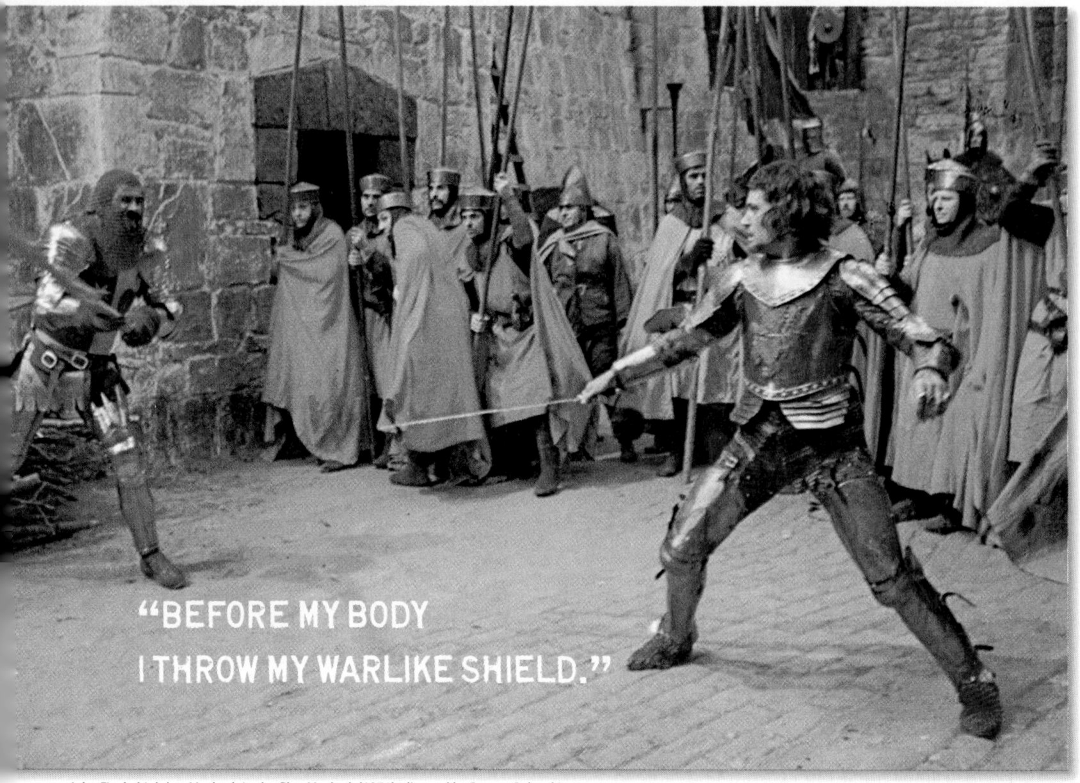

John Finch *(right)* as Macbeth in the film *Macbeth* (1971), directed by Roman Polanski.

Ross.
Your son, my lord, has paid a soldier's debt:
He only lived but till he was a man;
The which no sooner had his prowess confirmed
In the unshrinking station° where he fought,
But like a man he died.
Siward. Then he is dead?
Ross.
Ay, and brought off the field. Your cause of sorrow
Must not be measured by his worth, for then
It hath no end.
Siward. Had he his hurts before?
Ross.
Ay, on the front.
Siward. Why then, God's soldier be he!
Had I as many sons as I have hairs,
I would not wish them to a fairer death:

42. unshrinking station: that is, place at which he stood firmly.

Think About/Talk About

Analysis

Ⓞ Literary Focus

Possible response: *Macbeth refuses to give up or be affected by Malcolm's threats. Despite the enormous odds against him, Macbeth intends to try his best, which makes his inevitable failure even more tragic.*

Extend the Discussion

Comparing and Contrasting What earlier event in the play is mirrored in lines 39–43? ***Possible response:*** *The event in lines 39–43 mirrors the beheading of Macdonwald by Macbeth (the traitor beheaded by the loyal Scot). Also, the murder of a king (Macbeth) in order to restore order mirrors the murder of a king (Duncan), an action that has destroyed order.*

Evaluating Is Macbeth the typical tragic hero? Why? ***Possible responses:*** *Yes; Macbeth is an honorable nobleman who falls as a result of a tragic flaw. No; he is a brutal person from the start and a "butcher," as Malcolm calls him.*

- "Schiudi, inferno" ("Open your maw, O Hell!")—chorus mourning Duncan's murder
- "Ah! La paterna mano" ("Ah, this is father's hand")—Macduff mourns his family's murder
- "Una macchia è qui tuttora" ("A stain is still here")—Lady Macbeth's sleepwalking scene

Model the Skill

Model **analyzing the characteristics of a tragic hero**. Explain how, as the play progresses, it becomes harder to empathize with Macbeth. His tragic, yet human, emotions of ambition and guilt are now replaced with stubbornness, paranoia, and violence for violence's sake. Even when Macbeth finds himself alone against everybody else, he is ready to attack and kill Macduff.

Guided Practice: Apply

Ask students to discuss in detail how Macbeth goes through a process of dehumanization throughout the play. Have students hypothesize the greatest cause of his dehumanization.

Think About/Talk About

Response to Margin Question

Line 16 *As the prophecy predicts, Macduff was not "of woman born" in the natural way but was delivered by Caesarean section.*

With thy keen sword impress° as make me bleed:
Let fall thy blade on vulnerable crests;°
I bear a charmèd life, which must not yield
To one of woman born.

Macduff. Despair° thy charm,
And let the angel° whom thou still hast served
Tell thee, Macduff was from his mother's womb
Untimely ripped.

Macbeth.
Accursèd be that tongue that tells me so,
For it hath cowed my better part of man!°
And be these juggling fiends no more believed,
That palter° with us in a double sense;
That keep the word of promise to our ear,
And break it to our hope. I'll not fight with thee.

Macduff.
Then yield thee, coward,
And live to be the show and gaze o' th' time:°
We'll have thee, as our rarer monsters° are,
Painted upon a pole,° and underwrit,
"Here may you see the tyrant."

Macbeth. I will not yield,
To kiss the ground before young Malcolm's feet,
And to be baited° with the rabble's curse.
Though Birnam Wood be come to Dunsinane,
And thou opposed, being of no woman born,
Yet I will try the last. Before my body
I throw my warlike shield. Lay on, Macduff;
And damned be him that first cries "Hold, enough!" (O)

[Exeunt, fighting. Alarums.]

[Reenter fighting, and MACBETH *slain. Exit* MACDUFF, *with* MACBETH. *Retreat and flourish.° Enter, with drum and colors,* MALCOLM, SIWARD, ROSS, THANES, *and* SOLDIERS.*]*

Malcolm.
I would the friends we miss were safe arrived.

Siward.
Some must go off;° and yet, by these I see,
So great a day as this is cheaply bought.

Malcolm.
Macduff is missing, and your noble son.

10. impress: make an impression on.
11. vulnerable crests: heads that can be wounded.

13. Despair: despair of.
14. angel: that is, fallen angel; fiend.

? **16.** *What is the meaning of lines 15–16? How do they relate to the prophecy?*

18. better . . . man: manly spirit.

20. palter: equivocate.

24. gaze . . . time: spectacle of the age.
25. monsters: freaks.
26. Painted . . . pole: pictured on a banner set by a showman's booth.

29. baited: assailed (like a bear by dogs).

Retreat and flourish: trumpet call to withdraw, and fanfare.

36. go off: die (theatrical metaphor).

(O) **Literary Focus** **Tragedy** To arouse pity for a fallen tragic hero, the playwright must remind the audience of the hero's potential for greatness. How do these lines accomplish that purpose?

Cross-Curricular Connection

MUSIC: Verdi's Opera

Giuseppe Verdi (1813–1901) revolutionized Italian opera with masterpieces such as *Aida, Rigoletto, Il Trovatore,* and *La Traviata.* An admirer of Shakespeare's plays, he drew on them for inspiration for his fine operas: *Otello, Falstaff,* and *Macbeth*. Verdi's *Macbeth* is famous in the music world for its rousing choruses, strong characterization, and high drama—the last two qualities are not at all a surprise, given the source. *Macbeth* premiered in Florence, Italy, in 1847.

Activity After students have finished reading Macbeth, play these highlights from Verdi's opera and have students guess, based on the mood of the music, which of the following scenes or incidents Verdi is attempting to capture:

- "Mi si affaccia un pugnal?" ("Is this a dagger appearing before me?")—Macbeth's dagger scene

If thou be'st slain and with no stroke of mine,
My wife and children's ghosts will haunt me still.
I cannot strike at wretched kerns,° whose arms
Are hired to bear their staves.° Either thou, Macbeth, (N)
Or else my sword, with an unbattered edge,
I sheathe again undeeded.° There thou shouldst be;
By this great clatter, one of greatest note
Seems bruited.° Let me find him, Fortune!
And more I beg not. [*Exit. Alarums.*]

[*Enter* MALCOLM *and* SIWARD.]

Siward.
This way, my lord. The castle's gently rend'red:°
The tyrant's people on both sides do fight;
The noble thanes do bravely in the war;
The day almost itself professes° yours,
And little is to do.

Malcolm. We have met with foes
That strike beside us.°

Siward. Enter, sir, the castle. [*Exeunt. Alarum.*]

17. kerns: foot soldiers.
18. staves: spears.

20. undeeded: that is, having done nothing.
22. bruited: reported.

24. gently rend'red: surrendered without a struggle.

27. itself professes: declares itself.

29. That . . . us: that is, who deliberately miss us.

Scene 8. *Another part of the field.*

Enter MACBETH.

Macbeth.
Why should I play the Roman fool, and die
On mine own sword? Whiles I see lives,° the gashes
Do better upon them.

[*Enter* MACDUFF.]

Macduff. Turn, hell-hound, turn!

Macbeth.
Of all men else I have avoided thee.
But get thee back! My soul is too much charged°
With blood of thine already.

Macduff. I have no words:
My voice is in my sword, thou bloodier villain
Than terms can give thee out!°

[*Fight. Alarum.*]

Macbeth. Thou losest labor:
As easy mayst thou the intrenchant° air

2. Whiles . . . lives: so long as I see living men.

5. charged: burdened.

8. terms . . . out: words can describe you.

9. intrenchant: incapable of being cut.

(N) **Literary Focus** **Tragedy** How does Macduff's motivation to fight contrast with Macbeth's?

Think About/Talk About

Analysis

(M) Literary Focus
Possible response: *Macbeth is caught like a trapped animal. He has nowhere to run and must face the consequences of his actions.*

(N) Literary Focus
Possible response: *Macduff fights eagerly to avenge the death of his wife and children; whereas, Macbeth fights out of ambition for power.*

Extend the Discussion

Identifying Cause and Effect What motivates Macbeth to say, "My soul is too much charged / With blood of thine already"? ***Possible response:*** *Macbeth now feels guilty about murdering Macduff's family.*

Analyzing Character At the beginning of Scene 7, Macbeth compares himself to a bear tied to a stake, which was a sport in Shakespearean time. What does this comparison reveal about his state of mind? ***Possible response:*** *Macbeth feels utterly trapped, like the bear whose chain limits its movements and prevents it from using its strength to its advantage.*

Advanced Learners

Enrichment Have students choose either the character of Macbeth or Lady Macbeth and write an introduction as if they were introducing that character as the guest speaker at a banquet. Tell students that the introduction must focus on their character's tragic flaw(s). Remind students that the introductions can be serious or humorous. Have students deliver their introductions in a formal manner. Encourage them to dramatize their brief speech with appropriate pauses, inflection, and enunciation.

Students with Disabilities

Read aloud Scene 7, lines 14–23. Explain that a tyrant is a ruler who governs ignoring his subjects' will. Add that tyrants are known to use military force to secure their power and defy possible threats. Ask students what makes Macbeth a tyrant. Remind them finally that Macbeth became a tyrant because of his ambition, but that he was initially a respected and loyal leader.

✔ See **UA: Differentiating Instruction** for strategies for teaching students with disabilities.

Think About/Talk About

Literary Connection

Tell students that in Scene 8, lines 1–3, Macbeth is saying that he does not wish to die like the Roman leaders Brutus and Cassius, who killed themselves with their own swords rather than face defeat.

Extend the Discussion

Summarizing What happens in Scene 6? ***Possible response:*** *Upon reaching the front of Macbeth's castle, Malcolm orders his troops to throw down their camouflage and attack. Siward and his son are to lead, with Malcolm and Macduff in reserve.*

Figurative Language In what way are the trumpets "clamorous harbingers of blood and death"? ***Possible response:*** *The trumpets lead the soldiers into battle, where the men face shedding their blood and possibly dying.*

Response to Margin Question

Line 4 *Macbeth clings to the prophecy, which he interprets as meaning no living person can harm him since everyone is born of a woman.*

Siward. Fare you well.
Do we° but find the tyrant's power° tonight,
Let us be beaten, if we cannot fight.
Macduff.
Make all our trumpets speak; give them all breath,
Those clamorous harbingers of blood and death.
[*Exeunt. Alarums continued.*]

7. **Do we:** if we do. **power:** forces.

Scene 7. *Another part of the field.*

Enter MACBETH.

Macbeth.
They have tied me to a stake; I cannot fly,
But bearlike I must fight the course.° What's he (M)
That was not born of woman? Such a one
Am I to fear, or none.

2. **course:** bout; round. (He has in mind an attack of dogs or men upon a bear chained to a stake.)

? 4. *What is Macbeth desperately clinging to now?*

[*Enter* YOUNG SIWARD.]

Young Siward.
What is thy name?
Macbeth. Thou'lt be afraid to hear it.
Young Siward.
No; though thou call'st thyself a hotter name
Than any is in hell.
Macbeth. My name's Macbeth.
Young Siward.
The devil himself could not pronounce a title
More hateful to mine ear.
Macbeth. No, nor more fearful.
Young Siward.
Thou liest, abhorrèd tyrant; with my sword
I'll prove the lie thou speak'st.

[*Fight, and* YOUNG SIWARD *slain.*]

Macbeth. Thou wast born of woman.
But swords I smile at, weapons laugh to scorn,
Brandished by man that's of a woman born. [*Exit.*]

[*Alarums. Enter* MACDUFF.]

Macduff.
That way the noise is. Tyrant, show thy face!

(M) **Literary Focus** **Tragedy** What does the image of Macbeth as a captive animal show us about his situation?

Coat of Armor at Glamis Castle, Angus, Scotland.

Universal Access

English Learners

Encourage students to return to earlier acts and identify lines that they understand differently now that they are more accustomed to Shakespearean language and understand the general plot.

✔ See **UA: Differentiating Instruction** for strategies for teaching English learners.

Struggling Readers

To help students understand the differences and similarities between characters in the play, have them use a scale or comparison grid to rate characters on their traits, such as deciding who is more loyal, Macbeth or Macduff.

✔ See **UA: Differentiating Instruction** for strategies for teaching struggling readers.

Thou com'st to use thy tongue; thy story quickly!

Messenger.
Gracious my lord,
I should report that which I say I saw,
But know not how to do't.

Macbeth. Well, say, sir.

Messenger.
As I did stand my watch upon the hill,
I looked toward Birnam, and anon, methought,
The wood began to move.

Macbeth. Liar and slave! **L**

Messenger.
Let me endure your wrath, if't be not so.
Within this three mile may you see it coming;
I say a moving grove.

Macbeth. If thou speak'st false,
Upon the next tree shalt thou hang alive,
Till famine cling° thee. If thy speech be sooth,°
I care not if thou dost for me as much.
I pull in resolution,° and begin
To doubt° th' equivocation of the fiend
That lies like truth: "Fear not, till Birnam Wood
Do come to Dunsinane!" And now a wood
Comes toward Dunsinane. Arm, arm, and out!
If this which he avouches° does appear,
There is nor flying hence nor tarrying here.
I 'gin to be aweary of the sun,
And wish th' estate° o' th' world were now undone.
Ring the alarum bell! Blow wind, come wrack!
At least we'll die with harness° on our back. *[Exeunt.]*

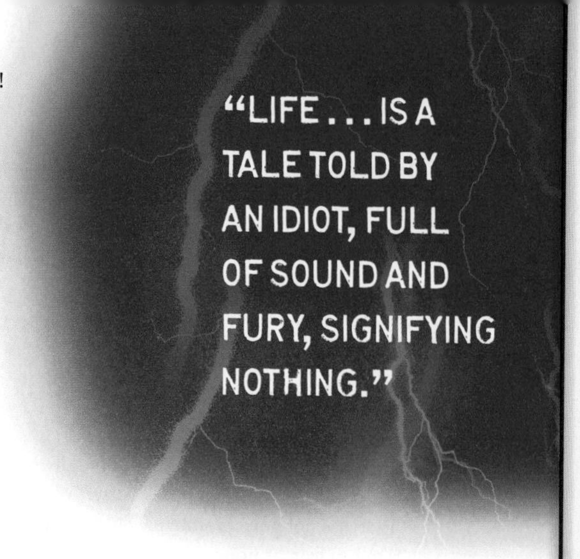

40. cling: wither. **sooth:** truth.

42. pull in resolution: restrain confidence.

43. doubt: suspect.

47. avouches: asserts.

50. th' estate: the orderly condition.

52. harness: armor.

? **Elements of Drama**
52. *Macbeth ends the scene in a state of great emotion. How would you characterize his mental state?*

Scene 6. *Dunsinane. Before the castle.*

Drum and colors. Enter MALCOLM, SIWARD, MACDUFF, *and their* ARMY, *with boughs.*

Malcolm.
Now near enough. Your leavy° screens throw down,
And show like those you are. You, worthy uncle,
Shall, with my cousin, your right noble son,
Lead our first battle.° Worthy Macduff and we°
Shall take upon 's what else remains to do,
According to our order.°

1. leavy: leafy.

4. battle: battalion. **we:** Malcolm uses the "royal we."

6. order: plan.

L **Literary Focus** **Tragedy** Why does Macbeth respond so violently to the Messenger's report?

Think About/Talk About

Analysis

K **Literary Focus**

Possible response: *When Macduff learned about the death of his wife, his reaction expressed desperation and rage. Macbeth's reaction lacks Macduff's energy. The king is already lost in gloomy meditations on the meaning of life, and the death of Lady Macbeth is accepted as an inevitable occurrence.*

L **Literary Focus**

Possible response: *The witches prophesied to Macbeth that he would be killed when the "Great Birnam Wood" would have moved to his castle. The king dismissed that omen as impossible, but now he is considering that his end might be near because Malcolm's camouflaged soldiers look as if the wood is coming to Dunsinane.*

Extend the Discussion

Monitoring Your Reading How does Macbeth react to the news of the moving wood? ***Possible response:*** *Macbeth first accuses the messenger of lying and then begins to panic. He knows that he will die when "Birnam Wood do come to Dunsinane".*

Analyzing Details Why does Macbeth care that he and his men will "die with harness on our back" (line 52)? ***Possible response:*** *Honor is very important to Macbeth and his men; it is an honorable death to fall fighting in battle.*

Cross-Curricular Connection

SOCIAL STUDIES: Military Strategies

Some students may wish to explore the military strategies in the text and in *Holinshed's Chronicles*. They might explore the use of camouflage, siege tactics, castle defense, various armor and weapons, or even the use of bagpipes and trumpets for military battle calls. Ask students to research their topic and give an oral report on their findings. Interested students can compare and contrast battle tactics in Macbeth's time with those used today.

Analyzing Visuals

Connecting to the Text: *The artist is trying to communicate how Lady Macbeth's treacherous actions have caused her to go mad. She cannot bear to think about what she has done and must push it from her mind. Some students might think the artist is trying to convey what a callous, unfeeling individual she is.*

Think About/Talk About

Building Background: Battle at Dunsinane Hill

Tell students that in 1054, Siward, Earl of Northumbria, led an invasion of Scotland. At the time, Macbeth was king of Scotland. The outcome of the battle was that part of southern Scotland came under Malcolm's possession, while Macbeth survived the fight. Macbeth died three years later in a battle, defeated by the English.

Extend the Discussion

Summarizing What is Macbeth's view of human existence according to lines 23–28? ***Possible response:*** *Macbeth views human existence as a pointless struggle that culminates in death.*

Tragedy How do Macbeth's words in lines 17–28 characterize him as a tragic hero? ***Possible response:*** *In those lines, Macbeth declares his life, and the lives of all humans, as insignificant. He is admitting his own defeat as a human being. Ultimate defeat always characterizes the destiny of tragic heroes.*

Response to Margin Question

Line 52 *Macbeth is near despair. Realizing that it matters little whether he remains in the castle or goes out, he resolves to die fighting.*

Analyzing Visuals

Connecting to the Text Note the blank, unemotional quality of Lady Macbeth's visage. What do you think the artist is trying to communicate about her character?

Lady Macbeth, by Odilon Redon, pastel drawing.

Seyton.
The queen, my lord, is dead.
Macbeth.
She should° have died hereafter;
There would have been a time for such a word.°
Tomorrow, and tomorrow, and tomorrow
Creeps in this petty pace from day to day,
To the last syllable of recorded time;
And all our yesterdays have lighted fools
The way to dusty death. Out, out, brief candle!
Life's but a walking shadow, a poor player
That struts and frets his hour upon the stage
And then is heard no more. It is a tale
Told by an idiot, full of sound and fury,
Signifying nothing. (K)

[*Enter a* MESSENGER.]

17. **should:** inevitably would.
18. **word:** message.

(K) **Literary Focus** **Tragedy** Compare Macbeth's and Macduff's reactions to the death of their wives. What does this contrast tell us about Macbeth's downfall?

Universal Access

AAVE Students Who Use African American Vernacular English

English for Academic Success Some students may struggle with the correct use of the verb "to be" when forming contractions. Explain that in formal English, when using a contraction to describe how someone or something is, the subject must be followed by an apostrophe and the letter *s*, to stand for *is*. Direct students to line 24 on p. 486, "Life's but a walking shadow." Explain that this statement represents formal English use of *to be* in a contraction: *Life is* but a walking shadow; *Life's* but a walking shadow. Have students practice forming contractions using: *he is mad; she is upset with him; Macbeth is ruthless.* After students complete this task, have volunteers write their answers on the board.

✔ For additional instruction and strategies, see **Think-Central, Teacher Access.**

Keeps still in Dunsinane, and will endure°
Our setting down before't.
Malcolm. 'Tis his main hope,
For where there is advantage to be given°
Both more and less° have given him the revolt,
And none serve with him but constrainèd things
Whose hearts are absent too.
Macduff. Let our just censures
Attend the true event,° and put we on
Industrious soldiership.
Siward. The time approaches,
That will with due decision make us know
What we shall say we have and what we owe.°
Thoughts speculative their unsure hopes relate,
But certain issue strokes must arbitrate:°
Towards which advance the war.° [*Exeunt, marching.*]

9. endure: allow.

11. advantage . . . given: afforded an opportunity.
12. more and less: high and low.

14–15. just . . . event: true judgments await the actual outcome.

18. owe: own. The contrast is between "what we shall say we have" and "what we shall really have."
20. certain . . . arbitrate: The definite outcome must be decided by battle.
21. war: army.

Scene 5. *Dunsinane. Within the castle.*

Enter MACBETH, SEYTON, *and* SOLDIERS, *with drum and colors.*

Macbeth.
Hang out our banners on the outward walls.
The cry is still "They come!" Our castle's strength
Will laugh a siege to scorn. Here let them lie
Till famine and the ague° eat them up.
Were they not forced° with those that should be ours,
We might have met them dareful,° beard to beard,
And beat them backward home.

[*A cry within of women.*]

What is that noise?

Seyton.
It is the cry of women, my good lord. [*Exit.*]

Macbeth.
I have almost forgot the taste of fears:
The time has been, my senses would have cooled
To hear a night-shriek, and my fell° of hair
Would at a dismal treatise° rouse and stir
As life were in't. I have supped full with horrors.
Direness, familiar to my slaughterous thoughts,
Cannot once start° me.

[*Enter* SEYTON.]

Wherefore was that cry?

4. ague: fever.
5. forced: reinforced.
6. met them dareful: that is, met them on the battlefield boldly.

? Staging the Play
7. *Macbeth should contrast with Malcolm now. How should Macbeth be acting?*

11. fell: pelt.
12. treatise: story.

15. start: startle.

Think About/Talk About

Analysis

J Literary Focus
Possible response: *Malcolm is encouraging every soldier to take some tree branches and stay hidden, hoping that this will make Macbeth think there are fewer soldiers than there actually are. Macbeth is going to underestimate the enemy, which might lead to his downfall.*

Extend the Discussion

Finding Details At the beginning of Scene 5, what is Macbeth's attitude regarding Malcolm's soldiers? ***Possible response:*** *Macbeth thinks that his castle is strong enough to withstand any attack by them. He thinks that the soldiers will die of famine and fever.*

Figurative Language To what "disease" is Macbeth referring in line 51? ***Possible response:*** *He calls the rebellious thanes and their English allies a disease and recommends purging the land.* What is ironic about his metaphor? ***Possible response:*** *The audience knows, even if Macbeth does not, that Macbeth is the sickness in the land, and that he is calling for his own demise.*

Advanced Learners

Enrichment Point out that the story of *Macbeth* has existed for many years and has been reinterpreted many times. Have students research different versions of the *Macbeth* story and create a presentation for the class detailing the similarities and differences between Shakespeare's original story and the other versions. Some suggestions for interpretations are Akira Kurosawa's *Kumonosojoo (Throne of Blood)* and Vishal Bharadwaj's *Maqbool.*

Students with Disabilities

Have students predict who will win the battle based on the advantages of each side. Instruct students to draw a chart with two columns and two rows, listing Macbeth's advantages and disadvantages in the first row and first and second columns, respectively, and Malcolm's advantages and disadvantages in the second row and first and second columns, respectively. Ask students which side possesses more advantages and which possesses the fewer disadvantages.

Model the Skill

Model understanding the **archetype of the tragic hero**. Read lines 1–4 of Scene 5 aloud. You might say: "In these lines, Macbeth is preparing for the arrival of Malcolm's troops. I read that Macbeth is ready for the fight, though he is not preparing to leave the castle, because he says 'our castle's strength / Will laugh a siege to scorn.' This tells me that Macbeth is brave, but he does not see his own tragic end. Obstinacy is a trait that can be found in tragic heroes."

Guided Practice: Apply

Ask students to read the rest of p. 487 and find other instances in which Macbeth shows his obstinacy at challenging fate. Have students discuss their thoughts with a partner, and then write a short paragraph about obstinacy as a tragic flaw in Macbeth.

Responses to Margin Questions

Line 56 *Some possibilities are disgust, irritation, arrogance, self-pity, concern for the country, and whimsy.*

Line 60 *He seems to be fortifying his failing courage with false hopes based on the enigmatic words of the apparitions.*

Line 5 *Each soldier is to cut a leafy branch and carry it in front of him as camouflage so that Macbeth's scouts will not see the advancing army.*

Line 7 *In contrast to Malcolm's calm forcefulness and determination, Macbeth could act bitter and scornful and show false bravery.*

Macbeth.
Throw physic° to the dogs, I'll none of it.
Come, put mine armor on. Give me my staff.
Seyton, send out.—Doctor, the thanes fly from me.—
Come, sir, dispatch.° If thou couldst, doctor, cast
The water° of my land, find her disease
And purge it to a sound and pristine health,
I would applaud thee to the very echo,
That should applaud again.—Pull't off, I say.—
What rhubarb, senna, or what purgative drug,
Would scour these English hence? Hear'st thou of them?
Doctor.
Ay, my good lord; your royal preparation
Makes us hear something.
Macbeth. Bring it° after me.
I will not be afraid of death and bane°
Till Birnam Forest come to Dunsinane.
Doctor (*aside*).
Were I from Dunsinane away and clear,
Profit again should hardly draw me here. [*Exeunt.*]

47. physic: medical science.

50. dispatch: hurry.

50–51. cast / The water: literally, analyze the urine.

? **56.** *Lines 47–56 express various emotions. What different feelings is Macbeth experiencing?*

58. it: the armor.

59. bane: destruction.

? **60.** *Is Macbeth truly courageous here? Or is he merely coasting on a kind of false bravery enabled by the witches' prophecies?*

Scene 4. *Country near Birnam Wood.*

Drum and colors. Enter MALCOLM, SIWARD, MACDUFF, *Siward's son* YOUNG SIWARD, MENTEITH, CAITHNESS, ANGUS, *and* SOLDIERS, *marching.*

Malcolm.
Cousins, I hope the days are near at hand
That chambers will be safe.°
Menteith. We doubt it nothing.°
Siward.
What wood is this before us?
Menteith. The Wood of Birnam.
Malcolm.
Let every soldier hew him down a bough
And bear't before him. Thereby shall we shadow
The numbers of our host, and make discovery°
Err in report of us.
Soldiers. It shall be done. J
Siward.
We learn no other but° the confident tyrant

2. That . . . safe: that a man will be safe in his bedroom.
nothing: not at all.

? **Staging the Play**
5. *Describe what the soldiers are to do here and why.*

6. discovery: Macbeth's scouts.

8. no other but: nothing but that.

J **Literary Focus** **Tragedy** What does Malcolm's command indicate about Macbeth's fate?

Universal Access

English Learners

English for Academic Success Tell students that the adjective *speculative* in line 19 follows the noun it modifies, and the subject *thoughts* is far removed from the verb *relate*. Ask students to translate this sentence into standard word order. [*Speculative thoughts relate their unsure hopes*.] Explain that Siward is saying that "strokes," or fighting, will settle the issues that the thanes and Malcolm are speculating about now.

Struggling Readers

Have students create a character web both for Macbeth and Malcolm. Have students re-read Scene 4, lines 1–14, and Scene 5, lines 1–15. Tell them to trace adjectives that refer to these characters throughout the scene as well as important statements the characters make. Ask students to transcribe each adjective in the character webs. Ask students to look up other words in the thesaurus or dictionary that they think would describe Macbeth and Malcolm.

Macbeth.
Take thy face hence. [*Exit* SERVANT.]
Seyton!—I am sick at heart,
When I behold—Seyton, I say!—This push°
Will cheer me ever, or disseat° me now.
I have lived long enough. My way of life
Is fall'n into the sear,° the yellow leaf,
And that which should accompany old age,
As honor, love, obedience, troops of friends,
I must not look to have; but, in their stead,
Curses not loud but deep, mouth-honor, breath,
Which the poor heart would fain deny, and dare not. **H**
Seyton!

[*Enter* SEYTON.]

Seyton.
What's your gracious pleasure?
Macbeth. What news more?
Seyton.
All is confirmed, my lord, which was reported.
Macbeth.
I'll fight, till from my bones my flesh be hacked.
Give me my armor.
Seyton. 'Tis not needed yet.
Macbeth.
I'll put it on.
Send out moe° horses, skirr° the country round.
Hang those that talk of fear. Give me mine armor.
How does your patient, doctor?
Doctor. Not so sick, my lord,
As she is troubled with thick-coming fancies
That keep her from her rest.
Macbeth. Cure her of that.
Canst thou not minister to a mind diseased,
Pluck from the memory a rooted sorrow,
Raze out° the written troubles of the brain,
And with some sweet oblivious° antidote
Cleanse the stuffed bosom of that perilous stuff
Which weighs upon the heart?
Doctor. Therein the patient
Must minister to himself. **I**

20. push: effort.
21. disseat: unthrone (with wordplay on *cheer,* pronounced *chair*).
? **22.** *What is Macbeth's mood now?*
23. sear: withered.
35. moe: more. **skirr:** scour.
? **37.** *Who is the doctor's patient?*
42. Raze out: erase.
43. oblivious: causing forgetfulness.

H Literary Focus Tragedy Some argue that Macbeth shows increased insight here; others believe he is merely acknowledging reality. With which position do you agree, and why?
I Reading Focus Using Questioning to Monitor Reading Macbeth demands a cure for Lady Macbeth. What questions would help you identify what she needs?

Think About/Talk About

Comprehension

I Reading Focus
Possible responses: *What is actually wrong with Lady Macbeth? Are there any drugs that can cure what ails her?*

Analysis

F Literary Focus
Possible response: *Macbeth seeks to be a hero, but he has been corrupted by greed and power; he has become a villain detested by even his own people.*

G Literary Focus
Possible response: *He does not have fear because he thinks that there is no such thing as a man "not born of woman."*

H Literary Focus
Possible response: *Macbeth finally assesses his situation and shows insight into his true character; he sees what will happen to him and does not fear death.*

Extend the Discussion

Drawing Conclusions Re-read lines 18–28. What conclusion can you draw about Macbeth's readiness to face the English soldiers? ***Possible response:*** *Macbeth seems to anticipate his own death, but he remains fast in his desire to die a warrior.*

Characterization What do the disjointed speech of Macbeth in lines 30–37 of p. 483 reveal about his state of mind? ***Possible response:*** *He is agitated due to his impending demise.*

Cross-Curricular Connection

SCIENCE: Medieval Medicine

Although some doctors in the Middle Ages were well trained and had studied the writings of such Greek physician as Hippocrates, the majority relied on folk remedies. Various herbs and poultices were an essential part of the practice. For instance, egg whites were used to relieve digestive problems and marigolds to reduce fever. Purgative drugs, or drugs designed to cleanse the system, included dandelions, rhubarb, and senna. When Lady Macbeth becomes ill, Macbeth calls a doctor and encourages him to use these remedies on her.

Activity Ask students to investigate medical practices in the mid-eleventh century. What training did doctors need? What aliments were they most often called upon to treat? How effective were their treatments?

Model the Skill

Model for students adding questions to the Reading Skills Focus graphic organizer. For example, in Act V, Scene 3, lines 16–17, they can ask: "What might Macbeth mean when he tells the soldier 'Those linen cheeks of thine / Are counselors to fear'?"

Act, Scene, Line	Questions I Have
Act V, Scene III, line 16–17	What does Macbeth mean by "linen cheeks" being "counselors to fear"?

Guided Practice: Apply

After students read, ask them to discuss which questions are prompted by Macbeth's contradictory behavior.

Think About/Talk About

Responses to Margin Questions

Line 22 *Students may be confused by the contradiction between line 21, in which Macbeth seems to think there is a possibility his case may succeed, and line 22, in which he sounds defeated and perhaps fatalistic.*

Line 37 *Lady Macbeth*

Caithness. Well, march we on,
To give obedience where 'tis truly owed.
Meet we the med'cine° of the sickly weal,°
And with him pour we, in our country's purge,
Each drop of us.°
Lennox. Or so much as it needs
To dew° the sovereign° flower and drown the weeds.
Make we our march towards Birnam. (F)

[*Exeunt, marching.*]

27. med'cine: that is, Malcolm. **weal:** commonwealth.
29. Each . . . us: that is, every last drop of our blood.
30. dew: bedew; water (and thus make grow). **sovereign:** royal; also, remedial.

Scene 3. *Dunsinane. In the castle.*

Enter MACBETH, DOCTOR, *and* ATTENDANTS.

Macbeth.
Bring me no more reports; let them fly all!
Till Birnam Wood remove to Dunsinane
I cannot taint° with fear. What's the boy Malcolm? (G)
Was he not born of woman? The spirits that know
All mortal consequences° have pronounced me thus:
"Fear not, Macbeth; no man that's born of woman
Shall e'er have power upon thee." Then fly, false thanes,
And mingle with the English epicures.
The mind I sway° by and the heart I bear
Shall never sag with doubt nor shake with fear.

[*Enter* SERVANT.]

The devil damn thee black, thou cream-faced loon!°
Where got'st thou that goose look?
Servant.
There is ten thousand——
Macbeth. Geese, villain?
Servant. Soldiers, sir.
Macbeth.
Go prick thy face and over-red° thy fear,
Thou lily-livered boy. What soldiers, patch?°
Death of° thy soul! Those linen° cheeks of thine
Are counselors to fear. What soldiers, whey-face?
Servant.
The English force, so please you.

3. taint: become infected.
5. mortal consequences: future human events.
9. sway: move.
11. loon: fool.
14. over-red: cover with red.
15. patch: fool.
16. of: upon. **linen:** pale.

(F) **Literary Focus** **Tragedy** Here, the Scottish thanes discuss joining forces with Malcolm. Is Macbeth's impending fall that of a tragic hero, or is he a villain?

(G) **Literary Focus** **Tragedy** In these lines, how does Macbeth explain his irrational behavior?

Universal Access

Advanced Learners

Enrichment Have students form groups of two or three and discuss the changes in Macbeth and Lady Macbeth since the murder of Duncan. How does Lady Macbeth deal with Duncan's murder in her mind now, in contrast to before? Are students more sympathetic toward Lady Macbeth now that she is weakened? How has Macbeth changed? What has led to his increasing aggressiveness and confidence? Ask groups to share their thoughts with the class and compare responses.

SCIENCE LINK

Cynthia Makris (Lady Macbeth) Savonlinna Opera Festival, Finland (2001).

Hand Washing

Being named after someone is usually an honor, though perhaps not if that "someone" is Lady Macbeth. At the University of Toronto and Northwestern University, researchers have found that people who have done something wrong often have an uncontrollable urge to clean themselves. This phenomenon is called the Macbeth Effect.

The connection between moral and physical cleanliness is widespread in both ancient and contemporary societies. Immoral behavior may be considered "dirty," and for many religions physical cleanliness is associated with virtuousness. In the King James Bible (Psalm 51:2), for example, salvation is associated with cleanliness: "Wash me thoroughly from mine iniquity, / and cleanse me from my sin."

Apparently, even pretending to be immoral has its consequences. The actor Liev Schreiber, who played Macbeth in New York in 2006, reported that although actors typically do not use the theater showers after a play, actors lined up to use them after performances of *Macbeth.* It may have been the effect of the humidity and summer heat; or, perhaps it was an example of the Macbeth Effect in action!

Ask Yourself

How does knowing that Shakespeare's portrayal of guilty behavior was proved to be accurate four hundred years later affect your understanding of the play?

Caithness.
Great Dunsinane he strongly fortifies.
Some say he's mad; others, that lesser hate him,
Do call it valiant fury: but, for certain,
He cannot buckle his distempered° cause
Within the belt of rule.°
Angus. Now does he feel
His secret murders sticking on his hands;
Now minutely revolts upbraid° his faith-breach.
Those he commands move only in command,
Nothing in love. Now does he feel his title
Hang loose about him, like a giant's robe
Upon a dwarfish thief.
Menteith. Who then shall blame
His pestered° senses to recoil and start,
When all that is within him does condemn
Itself for being there?

15. distempered: swollen with disease.

16. rule: self-control.

18. minutely revolts upbraid: rebellions every minute rebuke.

23. pestered: tormented.

Think About/Talk About

Analysis

C Literary Focus

Possible response: *Lady Macbeth and her husband got King Duncan's guards drunk, killed the king, and blamed it on the guards. Macbeth also has Banquo killed and tries to have his son, Fleance, killed. He also has Macduff's wife and children killed.*

D Literary Perspectives

Possible response: *Renaissance Christians believe that a priest could cure what ails Lady Macbeth when the physician cannot.*

E Literary Focus

Possible response: *Macbeth has become a tyrant, but Macduff appears to be a true leader, respected by his men.*

Extend the Discussion

Drawing Conclusions At the beginning of Scene 2, how do Macbeth's men feel about their king? ***Possible response:*** *They no longer love him—they follow his command but do not really support him any more.*

Making Judgments What do you think that "He cannot belt his distempered cause / Within the belt of rule" (lines 15–16) refers to? ***Possible response:*** *Macbeth appears to have gone mad. He cannot control himself; his bloodlust and his desire to be king rule over him.*

- Next, have each group act out the scene. Tell students to focus on reading expressively both to the audience and to the appropriate character.
- Conclude the activity by discussing how the punctuation and expression in the lines can help the audience understand what is happening in the play.

✔ See **UA: Differentiating Instruction** for practice passages for developing oral fluency.

Science Link

Ask Yourself

Possible response: *The play seems more relevant to real life now, since people today still have the same response to committing an unethical deed.*

Writing Standard 2.4b–d (see pages A51–A52)
Listening and Speaking Standard 2.3b, 2.4a–c (see pages A53–A55)

CHOICES

As you respond to the Choices, use these **Academic Vocabulary** words as appropriate: establish, ensure, widespread, controversy, contradiction.

REVIEW

Create a Time Line

Using the Internet or books from the library, find out more about the widespread social and political unrest in England during the fifteenth, sixteenth, and early seventeenth centuries. Create a time line showing important disruptions, battles, and changes in the monarchy. Then, write two paragraphs explaining how these events would have affected a Renaissance audience's interpretation of *Macbeth.*

Write a Character Sketch

Timed Writing *Macbeth* is full of vivid characters, both static (or unchanging) and dynamic (changing). Static characters, like the witches, serve a plot purpose but do not undergo any type of growth themselves; dynamic characters, like Lady Macbeth, change throughout the course of the play. Select one dynamic character from *Macbeth,* and write a brief essay analyzing the significance of the character's changes. Be sure to include a discussion of how and when the character changes, and support your argument with evidence from the play.

CONNECT

Connect to Critical Commentary

Shakespeare has been the focus of many scholarly books, magazines, and critical reviews over the centuries. Pick a theme in the play that interests you—such as the role of women, the power of fate and the supernatural, or a historical controversy—and, using the Internet and books from the library, research what scholars have to say on your topic. Find at least three sources of scholarly opinions, and then write a brief report that discusses your findings.

Connect to the Stage

Group Activity *Macbeth* has been performed in many different ways over the centuries. A number of versions have been made into movies that range from strictly Shakespearean-style productions to modern-day or futuristic adaptations. There is even a famous version of *Macbeth* set in feudal Japan. With a small group, head to the library to find a movie version of *Macbeth.* Watch it with your group, and then put together a presentation in which you display how the movie is different from the original script and what effect you think this difference has on the story overall. If the movie is a strict interpretation with few differences, focus your presentation on how the actors handle Shakespeare's stage directions and famous lines.

EXTEND

Create a Visual

Macbeth presents a wide range of human emotions, from the witches' calculated evil, to Macduff's grief for his family, to the Porter's comic banter. Create a collage, painting, or drawing that explores the emotional range of the play. In keeping with the contrasts, show characters at moments when they feel very different emotions. You might show the emotional range of one character or the contrasting emotions of several. Present your visual to the class. Explain your imagery and choice of emotions.

Set the Scene

TechFocus Shakespeare says very little about scenery in the text of *Macbeth.* Consequently, modern producers are at liberty to set the stage in whatever way will help create the tragic mood. How would you design the set? Pick an act from *Macbeth,* and create a slide show or PowerPoint presentation showing how you would set each scene in the act. Practice your presentation, and then deliver it to your class.

Independent Practice

Choices: Evaluation Criteria

Review: Homework
Create a Time Line
Time line reflects adequate research.

Review: Timed Writing 40–50 Minutes
Analysis of character is supported with evidence from the text.

Connect: Homework
Connect to Critical Commentary
Report refers to three sources.

Connect: Homework
Connect to the Stage
Presentation discusses differences and their effect on the story.

Extend: Homework
Create a Visual
Images are used to show emotions.

Extend: Homework
Set the Scene
Students describes the set in detail.

Assess

Unit 2 Resources, Selection Standards Check, p. 110

go.hrw.com **ThinkCentral Online Assessment,** Selection Standards Check

Reteach

go.hrw.com **ThinkCentral Online Remediation**

California Standards, pp. 494–495

- **Reading Standard 3.1** Analyze characteristics of subgenres (e.g., satire, parody, allegory, pastoral) that are used in poetry, prose, plays, novels, short stories, essays, and other basic genres.
- **Reading Standard 3.6** Analyze the way in which authors through the centuries have used archetypes drawn from myth and tradition in literature, film, political speeches, and religious writings (e.g., how the archetypes of banishment from an ideal world may be used to interpret Shakespeare's tragedy *Macbeth*).
- **Grades 9–10 Review Reading Standard 3.12** Analyze the way in which a work of literature is related to the themes and issues of its historical period. (Historical approach).
- **Writing Standard 2.4** Write historical investigation reports: **b.** Analyze several historical records of a single event, examining critical relationships between elements of the research topic. **c.** Explain the perceived reason or reasons for the similarities and differences in historical records with information derived from primary and secondary sources to support or enhance the presentation. **d.** Include information from all relevant perspectives and take into consideration the validity and reliability of sources.
- **Listening and Speaking Standard 2.3** Deliver oral responses to literature: **b.** Analyze the imagery, language, universal themes, and unique aspects of the text through the use of rhetorical strategies (e.g., narration, description, persuasion, exposition, a combination of those strategies).
- **Listening and Speaking Standard 2.4** Deliver multimedia presentations: **a.** Combine text, images, and sound by incorporating information from a wide range of media, including films, newspapers, magazines, CD-ROMs, online information, television, videos, and electronic media-generated images. **b.** Select an appropriate medium for each element of the presentation. **c.** Use the selected media skillfully, editing appropriately and monitoring for quality.

Standards Focus

Objectives

Students will

- understand and analyze the characteristics of tragedy
- respond to graphics

Motivate

What Do You Think?/QuickTalk

Use the QuickTalk to spark a discussion on how emotions can be represented graphically. Ask students to give examples of graphic novels, paintings, ads, and other illustrations that convey strong emotions.

Literary Skills Focus

As you read and discuss the selection with students, have them note examples of tragic plot lines they have read or watched in books, films, or on television.

Reading Skills Focus

Give students a copy of the Reading Skills Focus graphic organizer before they read. (See **Unit 2 Resources.**) Tell them to use their responses to answer the questions on the Applying Your Skills page.

Writing Skills Focus

Have students record graphic details in their **Reader/Writer Notebooks.** Students can use their notes to complete the Writing Skills Focus activity.

Learn It Online

Literature Links direct students to pre-screened Web sites offering more information related to a selection.

go.hrw.com H12-496 Go

Link to Today

This Link to Today gives Shakespeare's classic a fresh visual update.

from Macbeth: The Graphic Novel

adapted by Arthur Byron Cover

illustrated by Tony Leonard Tamai

Reader/Writer Notebook

Use your **RWN** to complete the activities for this selection.

Reading Standard 3.1 (see pages A48–A50)

What Do You Think How do our hearts and minds influence our actions?

QuickTalk With a partner, discuss the advantages of seeing a text, particularly a play, represented as a graphic novel.

Literary Skills Focus

Tragedy Tales of murderous ambition are widespread outside the pages of Shakespeare's tragedies. Similar stories abound in operas, movies, and even graphic novels. In this excerpt, murder and tragedy translate well into the larger-than-life fantasy world of powerful dragon lords.

Reading Skills Focus

Responding to Graphic Novels Adapted graphic novels make numerous changes to original sources in order to ensure the visual appeal and momentum. In *Macbeth: The Graphic Novel* the author-illustrator team Arthur Byron Cover and Tony Leonard Tamai use very short pieces of Shakespeare's dialogue and rely on the graphic elements to convey the bulk of the action.

Into Action As you read, think about the changes that this combination of words and images creates for *Macbeth.* Make a list like the one below of visual details that enhance the story for you.

Visual Detail	*How the Detail Enhances the Story*
Banquo has a goatee and unruly hair.	*The details make it easy to identify him in each frame.*

Writing Skills Focus

Think as a Reader/Writer

Find It in Your Reading As you read, notice the graphic details used to illustrate the text. In your *Reader/Writer Notebook,* take notes about images that convey emotion.

Learn It Online

Explore other ways that this classic play lives on in the twenty-first century through these Internet links.

go.hrw.com H12-496 Go

California Standards, pp. 496–502

- **Reading Standard 3.1** Analyze characteristics of subgenres (e.g., satire, parody, allegory, pastoral) that are used in poetry, prose, plays, novels, short stories, essays, and other basic genres.

Selection Readability	
Easily Accessible Accessible **Challenging**	multiple themes; higher-level vocabulary

Selection Summary

This excerpt from a graphic adaptation of *Macbeth* takes place right before the murder of King Duncan. Macbeth is roaming restlessly in the castle, and runs into Banquo and Fleance. Banquo restates Duncan's love for Macbeth and tells him that the king has gone to sleep. Once alone again, Macbeth follows an imaginary dagger into Duncan's room.

Link to Today

This graphic rendition of *Macbeth* presents the first scene of Act II, focusing on Macbeth's mindset before the murder of Duncan.

Direct Teach

Think About/Talk About

Extend the Discussion

Making Inferences Based on what you read in *Macbeth,* who do you think the three figures on the right-bottom corner are? ***Possible response:*** *The three figures are wearing masks and cloaks, and one of them is holding a crystal ball. They could be representing the three witches whose prophecies stir Macbeth's ambition.*

Analyzing Graphics How is the character of Macbeth represented on the cover of this graphic novel? ***Possible response:*** *Macbeth is represented here as a strong warrior with a defiant attitude. This image shows Macbeth in the latter part of the tragedy, in which violence and thirst of power prevail over doubt and guilt.*

Selection Resources

Unit 2 Resources, on-level practice and assessment, p. 113

Teacher One Stop™, on-level lesson plans

Holt Audio Library: Selections and Summaries in Spanish

UA: Differentiating Instruction, graphic organizer, p. 95

UA: Supporting Instruction in Spanish, selection summary

ThinkCentral Online Assessment, Selection Standards Check go.hrw.com

Model the Skill

- Provide students with copies of the Reading Skills Focus graphic organizer for *Macbeth: The Graphic Novel.* (See **Unit 2 Resources.**)
- Model the skill of **responding to graphics.** Ask students to skim pp. 498–499. Tell them to focus on the visual detail they notice first. Explain that the illustrations on these pages set the scene as well as catch the reader's interest in the story. Each panel uses details, character expressions, and text to move the story along.
- Remind students what is happening in this scene. Macbeth's expression is troubled. The lines drawn in the background emphasize Macbeth's figure. This page concentrates on what Macbeth is doing and thinking. On the next page, what he is doing and where he is going is important, so the illustrator emphasizes the background and Macbeth's movement.

Visual Detail	How the Detail Enhances the Story
Macbeth's expression is troubled.	This helps reveal Macbeth's internal conflict.

Guided Practice: Apply

Group students in pairs to discuss pp. 498–499. Ask them to use their graphic organizer to take notes on images and details. Then, have students write down any changes they would make and why their changes would make the illustrations more effective. Give pairs the option to sketch out the suggestions they have for improving the pages and panels. After student pairs have completed their work, ask volunteers to share with the whole class.

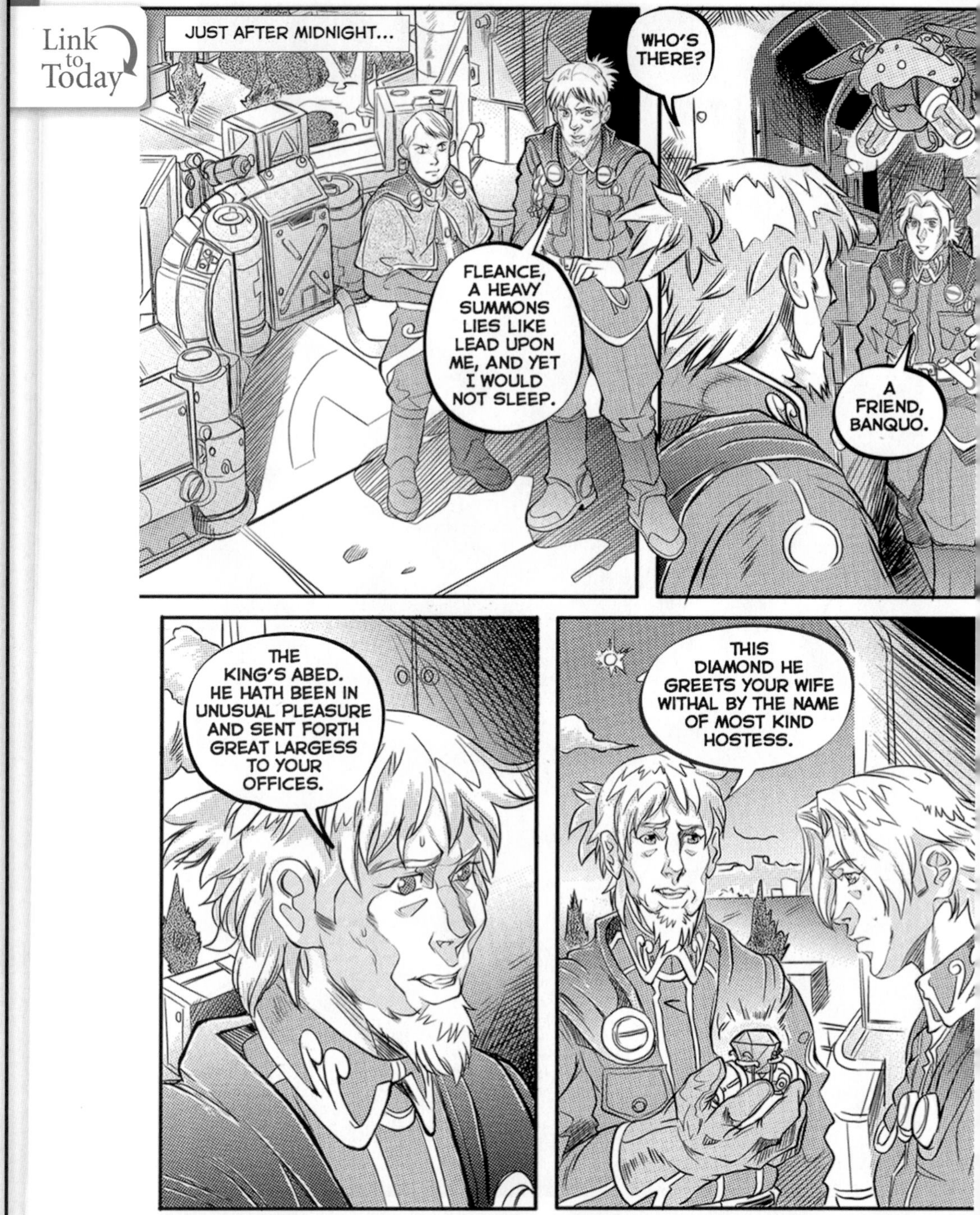

Universal Access

English Learners

English for Academic Success Help students use elements in the illustrations as context clues to understand unfamiliar words and archaic language. Point students to the word *largess* in the second frame. Explain that, in order to understand the word, they should look at the big diamond that is being given to Duncan in the third frame. Tell them that *largess* means "generosity."

Struggling Readers

Assist students with analyzing the graphics as they read. Instruct students to ask themselves, "Which event from Shakespeare's *Macbeth* is illustrated here? What can I infer about the characters by their expressions and gestures? What is the mood of the frames?"

Think About/Talk About

Extend the Discussion

Analyzing Graphics In the last frame of p. 499, what does the shadow on Macbeth's face symbolize? ***Possible response:*** *Macbeth is beginning to hallucinate and will soon murder his king. The shadow emphasizes the character's anxiety and evil resolve.*

Character Motivations In the first frame of p. 499, what does Banquo's body language reveal about his feelings for Macbeth? ***Possible response:*** *Banquo is touching Macbeth's shoulder while recalling the strange meeting they both had with the three witches. This gestures hints at the friendship and closeness between Banquo and Macbeth that existed at the beginning of the play.*

Advanced Learners

Acceleration Have students discuss the setting of *Macbeth: The Graphic Novel* and why Shakespeare's play can be relevant in a science-fiction setting.

Activity Divide students into groups and ask them to write a short synopsis for a movie about Macbeth set in contemporary times. Have them focus on the characters and their relationship with the modern world. Each group will present its synopsis to the rest of the class for discussion.

Students with Disabilities

Prepare a "shuffled outline" made by numbered sentences that describe each of the frames in random order. Ask students to look carefully at each frame of the selection, and then locate the appropriate description in the outline. Finally, have students rewrite the sentences in the correct order.

Think About/Talk About

Extend the Discussion

Setting How is the setting of this graphic novel different from Shakespeare's play? ***Possible response:*** *Whereas the original play is set in eleventh-century Scotland, this graphic novel is set in a futuristic world. The tall buildings, the seemingly refined technology, and the space suits worn by the characters are all elements of science fiction.*

Analyzing Graphics How does Macbeth's expression convey his inner feelings? ***Possible response:*** *On p. 500, in the first frame, Macbeth's expression is one of worry. However, as he reflects on his inner feelings, his worry turns to anger in the second frame.*

Link to Today

Compare and Contrast

Ask students to compare and contrast the graphic novel excerpt with Act II Scene 1 of Shakespeare's play *Macbeth.* To help students compare the texts, have them consider the following questions:

- How is the scene in the graphic novel similar to the scene in the original play? [*Both scenes include similar dialogue; however, the graphic novel does not include every line that is included in the original play. The action in both scenes in the same; Macbeth encounters Banquo and Fleance outside and then Macbeth imagines a dagger before he kills Duncan.*]
- How do the scenes differ? [*The graphic novel does not include stage directions; the reader must use the images to see the action.*]
- Which genre do you think best conveys the action in the scene? [*The graphic novel best conveys the action in the scene. The drawings allow the reader to see the character's facial expressions and the reader can get a better sense of Macbeth's anguish over his decision to kill Duncan.*]

Think About/Talk About

Extend the Discussion

Finding Details Which details in the frame explain why the guards are sleeping soundly? ***Possible response:*** *The guards are sleeping next to a table covered with leftover and empty wine glasses. The guards must have drunk enough to fall into a deep sleep.*

Analyzing Graphics How does the noise of the dagger shown in the third frame of p. 500 emphasize the text? ***Possible response:*** *In that frame, Macbeth is reaching for the dagger. The clinking sound indicates that the dagger is no longer an imaginary one.*

California Standards, p. 502

- **Reading Standard 3.1** Analyze characteristics of subgenres (e.g., satire, parody, allegory, pastoral) that are used in poetry, prose, plays, novels, short stories, essays, and other basic genres.
- **Reading Standard 3.3** Analyze the ways in which irony, tone, mood, the author's style, and the "sound" of language achieve specific rhetorical or aesthetic purposes or both.
- **Writing Standard 2.1** Write fictional, autobiographical, or biographical narratives: **a.** Narrate a sequence of events and communicate their significance to the audience.

Check for Understanding

Independent Practice

Reading Skills Focus

Possible response:

1. *He is anxious and unable to sleep. He probably foresees Macbeth's evil deed after the witches' prophecy.*
2. *He is reaching for an imaginary dagger that he has been seeing since he left Banquo and Fleance.*
3. *Macbeth goes toward Duncan's room and, finding the guards fast asleep, enters and gets ready to kill the sleeping king.*
4. *Ask students to compare plot events and details in both selections.*

Literary Skills Focus

Possible response:

5. *The original play allowed more space for character development by recounting Macbeth's reasoning. Shortening the dialogue, however, does speed up the pace of the story.*
6. *The diamond gives a concrete representation of Duncan's generosity.*
7. *This version shows a helpless king caught in his sleep. This adds to the gravity of the murder.*
8. *The setting has a magic component that makes it easier to represent the play's supernatural elements.*
9. *A color version could have represented more vividly the emotional content of the story.*

What Do You Think Now?

Have students mention visual details they noted in their **Reader/Writer Notebooks** that helped to depict Macbeth's inner conflict. Ask them to give reasons why they believe his conflict is based on emotional struggle, wrestling of thoughts, or both.

Applying Your Skills

Reading Standard 3.1, 3.3 (see pages A48–A50)
Writing Standard 2.1a (see pages A51–A52)

from **Macbeth: The Graphic Novel**

Literary Response and Analysis

Reading Skills Focus

Quick Check

1. What is Banquo's mood in the opening frame? Explain.
2. In the first frame on the third page, Macbeth's hands are depicted in the foreground, grasping at something. What is he reaching for?
3. Summarize the action on the last page.

Reading Skills: Responding to Graphic Novels

4. Look over your chart of visual details and how they enhance the story. Then, write a short paragraph summarizing the difference between reading Shakespeare's play and reading this graphic version of the story. Use your chart for examples and support.

Visual Detail	How the Detail Enhances the Story
Banquo has a goatee and unruly hair.	The details make it easy to identify him in each frame.

Literary Skills Focus

Literary Analysis

5. **Analyze** Identify one advantage and one disadvantage of shortening Shakespeare's dialogue for this graphic novel. Explain.
6. **Interpret** Readers of Shakespeare usually take Banquo's diamond as a metaphor for Lady Macbeth's role as hostess. Why do you think the illustrator chose to show a real diamond in the graphic version of the scene? Explain.
7. **Interpret** The last page of this excerpt depicts Macbeth on his way to murdering Duncan—an action that takes place offstage in Shakespeare's play. What advantage does the addition of this action offer to readers of the graphic novel? Explain.

Literary Skills: Tragedy

8. **Evaluate** This graphic novel moves Shakespeare's tragedy to a dragon-riding world in the distant future. How does the change of setting affect the story? Explain.

Literary Skills Review: Mood

9. **Evaluate** The **mood** in a work of literature is the atmosphere or feeling it creates for a reader. How might the mood of this graphic novel change if all the frames were depicted in color instead of black and white? Explain.

Writing Skills Focus

Think as a Reader/Writer

Use It in Your Writing Look back at the notes you took in your *Reader/Writer Notebook* about graphic details used to convey characters' emotions and the words they accompany. Using the illustrations in the graphic novel as your guide, rewrite the dialogue for one page. Create new captions to express the emotions that are visually depicted in each frame.

What Do You Think Now? In the frames devoted to Macbeth's soliloquy about an invisible dagger, how does the graphic novel depict his internal conflict? Is he experiencing a conflict of the heart or of the mind? Or both? Explain.

Universal Access: Grammar Link

Struggling Writers

To complete the Writing Skills Focus activity, provide additional scaffolding for students by having them create T-charts. On the left side, have them list the characters included in the scene. For example, they might want to begin with the character of Banquo because he speaks first in the graphic novel. On the right side, have them make a list of adjectives or phrases that describe how the characters feel in the scene. Students might note that Banquo is "anxious," "preoccupied with terrible thoughts," and "unable to sleep." After students have completed their charts, have them use their notes to write new dialogue for the characters.

Character	Character's Feelings
Banquo	anxious; preoccupied with terrible thoughts; unable to sleep

Writing Standard 1.3, 2.2a–c (see pages A51–A52)

Author Study: William Shakespeare

Writing Skills Focus

Write a Comparison-Contrast Essay

Choose two of Shakespeare's sonnets, two characters from *Macbeth,* or two passages from *Macbeth* that show a striking similarity or a revealing contrast. Write an essay in which you compare and contrast your choices, focusing on Shakespeare's language, tone, or theme. Consider one of the following approaches for your essay:

- Compare and contrast Sonnets 18 and 116. What is the poet's attitude toward love in these sonnets, and what belief does he reveal about the power of the written word?
- Compare and contrast Sonnets 29 and 30. What kind of problem does each sonnet present, what is the poet's attitude toward the problem, and how does the final couplet resolve the problem?
- Compare and contrast Sonnets 71 and 73. What kind of attitude does each sonnet express toward aging and death? How does the poet convey his attitude?
- Compare and contrast Sonnets 18 and 130. What methods does the poet use to describe his beloved, and what kind of thematic statement does he make about love?
- Compare and contrast Macbeth and Lady Macbeth in a single act of *Macbeth.* What traits do you see in them, and how does Shakespeare reveal these traits? You might wish to focus on a single revealing scene for this essay.
- Compare and contrast two of Macbeth's soliloquies. What does he reveal about himself in each soliloquy, and how does Shakespeare use language to convey Macbeth's character?
- Compare and contrast Lady Macbeth in Act I and Act V of *Macbeth.* What kind of language does she use in each act, and what does her language reveal about her character?

Guidelines for a Comparison-Contrast Essay

The following guidelines will ensure a successful essay:

- Begin by introducing the two subjects of your essay. If your essay focuses on two sonnets, consider a brief overview of the Shakespearean sonnet. Then, briefly introduce each sonnet by letting your reader know the situation and theme.
- Close your introduction with a thesis statement that explicitly identifies the similarities and/or differences you intend to discuss in the body of your essay.
- Follow one of the two proven methods for a comparison-contrast essay: (1) Devote a section of your essay to each major point you want to make. Discuss first one subject and then the next. If your subjects are Sonnets 18 and 116, you will discuss Sonnet 18 first for each part of your paper. (2) Divide the body of your paper into two major sections—one for each subject. If your subjects are Sonnets 18 and 116, you will discuss all the points you wish to make about Sonnet 18 before moving on to Sonnet 116.
- Use quotations from Shakespeare to illustrate the point you are trying to make.
- Conclude by discussing what your comparison and contrast reveals about Shakespeare as a writer or about human nature.

What Do You Think Now?

Do you think that Shakespeare's work was influenced more by his heart or his mind? Explain your answer, and cite examples from his work.

Independent Practice

What Do You Think Now?

Ask students to think about examples in which Shakespeare seems more concerned with human feelings than philosophical reasoning. Have students compare and discuss each example and create their opinions based on their discussion.

Assess

Unit 2 Resources, Selection Standards Check, pp. 114, 116

ThinkCentral Online Assessment, Selection Standards Check

Teacher One Stop™, editable Selection Standards Check

Reteach

For a lesson reteaching **irony, tone, and author's style,** see **Reteaching Lessons,** pp. 1449O–1449P.

ThinkCentral Online Remediation

Universal Access

Struggling Writers

Some students may need additional scaffolding to complete the Writing Skills Focus activity. Give students a definite topic to focus their compare-and-contrast essay on. Ask students to focus on Sonnets 29 and 30 and compare the problems and solutions presented in both. Have students create a chart in which they note problems and solutions, and then have them develop their essay based on their notes.

California Standards, p. 503

- **Writing Standard 1.3** Structure ideas and arguments in a sustained, persuasive, and sophisticated way and support them with precise and relevant examples.
- **Writing Standard 2.2** Write responses to literature: **a.** Demonstrate a comprehensive understanding of the significant ideas in works or passages. **b.** Analyze the use of imagery, language, universal themes, and unique aspects of the text. **c.** Support important ideas and viewpoints through accurate and detailed references to the text and to other works.

Standards Focus

Objectives

Students will learn prewriting, drafting, and revising techniques for writing a literary research paper.

Preteach

Write with a Purpose Read aloud the essentials of a good literary research paper to guide students' understanding of this type of writing. Refer students to the scoring guide on p. 516 for more information on reporting literary research that they can use throughout the workshop.

Direct Teach

Model the Skill

Think as a Reader/Writer Use the professional model on this page and others in the unit to provide examples of the elements of a good literary research paper. Point out how the Auden model gives background information about the literary work as well as other relevant historical information.

Think About the Model

Possible responses:

1. *It gives examples of how well the play follows literary conventions of the Renaissance.*
2. *The author should expand on how the history of courtly love is important to writing a "perfect" play.*

Writing Workshop

Literary Research: Historical Investigation

Write with a Purpose

Write a formal research paper on a topic that links literature and historical investigation. Your **purpose** for writing is to convey the results of your research to your **audience**—your teacher and classmates.

A Good Literary Research Paper

- asserts a proposition about a text's historical and cultural relevance
- provides relevant and precise examples to support the proposition
- uses rhetorical strategies to support the proposition.
- uses valid and reliable sources for information
- demonstrates the use of critical research strategies
- includes a formal bibliography

See page 516 for a complete scoring guide.

Reader/Writer Notebook

Use your **RWN** to complete the activities for this workshop.

Think as a Reader/Writer

In this workshop, you will investigate a particular connection between history and literature. Before you write your **literary research paper,** read the twentieth-century poet W. H. Auden's examination of Shakespeare's play *Love's Labour's Lost.*

Love's Labour's Lost is not the greatest of Shakespeare's plays, but it is one of the most perfect. Its subject, education and culture, is interesting. The forms of culture it deals with are those prevalent in Shakespeare's time and include neo-Platonic humanism,[1] courtly manners, courtly love,[2] and Euphuism.[3] All humanism and learning is made fun of in the play, all social life is made fun of, all art is made fun of—it is not specific satire. The play begins with the scheme of four young men to found a kind of neo-Platonic academy. They already have a certain education in social manners. . . .

← Auden clearly states his **thesis.**

← He provides **background information** about the play.

[*Auden discusses neo-Platonic humanism and courtly manners in the paragraphs omitted here.*]

The courtly manners in the play are also affected by the medieval and Renaissance traditions of courtly love, which began with the Troubadours in eleventh-century Provence and were codified in the thirteenth century by Andreas Capellanus in a Latin work, *De Arte Honeste Amandi.* Andreas stipulated a number of rules of courtly love. First, the lovers must not be married. They must endure great difficulties in the achievement of their love, and must be jealous of a rival, which is undesirable in marriage, but is an essential proof of courtly love. Finally, the beloved noble lady must be treated as God.

← Auden traces the historical origin of courtly love.

1. **neo-Platonic humanism:** belief that through the study of human life, people can reach a oneness with God.
2. **courtly manners, courtly love:** refined behavior expected of people in the royal court.
3. **Euphuism:** overly ornate Elizabethan literary style.

Think About the Professional Model

With a partner, discuss the following questions about the model:

1. How does paragraph 2 help support the writer's thesis?
2. What else could he add to paragraph 2 to better support its main idea?

California Standards, pp. 504–516

- **Writing Standard 1.1** Demonstrate an understanding of the elements of discourse (e.g., purpose, speaker, audience, form) when completing narrative, expository, persuasive, or descriptive writing assignments.
- **Writing Standard 1.3** Structure ideas and arguments in a sustained persuasive and sophisticated way and support them with precise and relevant examples.
- **Writing Standard 1.6** Develop presentations by using clear research questions and creative and critical research strategies.
- **Writing Standard 1.7** Use systematic strategies to organize and record information (e.g., anecdotal scripting, annotated bibliographies).
- **Writing Standard 1.9** Revise text to highlight the individual voice, improve sentence variety and style, and enhance subtlety of meaning and tone in ways that are consistent with the purpose, audience, and genre.
- **Writing Standard 2.4a** Use exposition, narration, description, argumentation, exposition or some combination of rhetorical strategies to support the main proposition. **d.** Include information from all relevant perspectives and take into consideration the validity and reliability of sources. **e.** Include a formal bibliography.

Writing Workshop Resources

UA: Holt Interactive Writer and Speaker, practice and assessment, p. 50

UA: Differentiating Instruction, modified lesson plans, p. 103

WritingNotes, interactive lesson presentations with activities

GrammarNotes, interactive lesson presentations with activities

Writing and Research in a Digital Age, interactive lesson presentations with activities

Writing Standard 1.1, 1.3, 1.6, 1.7, 1.9, 2.4a, 2.4d, 2.4e (see pages A51–A52)
Language Conventions Standard 1.1, 1.2, 1.3 (see page A53)

Prewriting

Choose a Research Topic

Literary research is a labor-intensive process that can be rewarding for what you can learn about a literary subject. If a topic does not immediately come to mind, search your textbook, and record a list of several authors and works that intrigue you. Use the Internet and general reference works to do preliminary research on the authors and works in your list. Then, choose a general topic.

To decide on an appropriate historical approach to your topic, review the information provided in your textbook (especially the unit introductions), or ask your school's librarian or media specialist to direct you to appropriate resources. Here are some sample topics, appropriate for literary and historical investigation:

- How accurately *Beowulf* reflects the history and culture of the ancient Germanic tribes who populate its pages
- How Geoffrey Chaucer's life as a civil servant in fourteenth-century England influenced his writing
- How the writing of John Stuart Mill or Charles Dickens influenced social and economic reforms of the Victorian period

Narrow your subject so that you can cover it adequately. Keep challenging yourself to be more specific by asking yourself increasingly specific questions.

Make a Research Plan

Develop a list of research questions by using the *5W-How?* method: Answer the questions *Who? What? When? Where? Why?* and *How?* The following are questions one writer asked to investigate Shakespeare's source for *Julius Caesar:*

- Who was Julius Caesar?
- What account of Caesar's life did Shakespeare use as his model?
- When did the original historical events take place?
  —How do they reflect themes that were important to Shakespeare's audience?
- Where does the action of the play occur?
  —Why would the historical setting have meaning for Shakespeare's audience?
- Why was the audience interested in what happened after the death of a strong ruler?
- How did Shakespeare's audience view Caesar and his assassins?

Think About Purpose and Audience

As you plan your literary research paper, think about your purpose and audience. Your **purpose** is to convey the results of your research to your **audience**—usually your teacher and classmates. What does your audience already know about the literary work, author, and historical period? What will you need to explain?

Idea Starters

- favorite authors
- favorite works of literature
- favorite historical time period

Writing Tip

Begin your research with what you know and what interests you. Expand on your knowledge and interests by using your school's library or media center. Many schools subscribe to online databases designed to support literary and historical investigations. Ask your librarian or media specialist how to use these valuable research tools and how best to use the Internet for preliminary research on the questions that interest you.

Your Turn

Get Started While making notes in your **RWN,** choose a research **topic** and develop **research questions** to guide your investigation. Keep your **purpose** and **audience** in mind as you look for answers to your research questions.

Learn It Online
For an example of a complete, double-spaced literary research paper, go online.
go.hrw.com H12-505 Go

Teacher One Stop™, on-level lesson plans and all print resources

Holt Six Traits for Writing, rubrics, prompts, and sample papers

Language and Sentence Skills Practice,

UA: Developmental Language and Sentence Practice

Language Handbook Worksheets, p.126

Formal Assessment, Progress Monitoring Test 2

ThinkCentral Online Assessment, Writing Workshop Test

ThinkCentral Online Remediation

Holt Online Essay Scoring

Guided Practice: Apply

Choose a Research Topic

- Suggest that students make a list of five favorite books they have read in school or major works that they have read on their own.
- Have students make a semantic web for each of the books they listed, including everything they know about the book that they think might be worth researching or analyzing. Students should use their webs to choose which work would be the best topic for a literary research paper.

Think About Purpose and Audience

- Have students identify and list audiences who would read their literary research papers.
- After students have identified potential audiences, ask students to identify their writing purpose and how it would change if the audience changed.

Your Turn

Get Started Point out to students that some of the questions will probably yield more interesting answers than others. They should not spend all their time on questions like "who" and "what" if "why" and "how" questions will generate better topics for research.

Learn It Online
Interactive Writer's Models on the Interactive Student Edition provide annotated sample essays along with writing tips and strategies.
go.hrw.com H12-505 Go

Guided Practice: Apply

Begin Research

- Discuss with students how they can tell whether a resource, particularly an Internet resource, is reliable. Some telltale signs of an unreliable resource are typos, grammatical mistakes, and flashy graphics with minimal content. Students should also look for information about when the site was last updated. If it has not been updated within the past year, the information may be out of date.
- You may want to encourage students to look for information from both primary and secondary sources. Remind students that primary sources include personal journals, photographs, interviews, or any other information provided by a first-hand observer. Secondary sources include historical analyses, biographies, newspaper reports, or any information told from a second-hand perspective.

Your Turn

Begin Your Research Have students complete the **Your Turn** as independent practice. After students make their list of resources, have them rank each source according to its usefulness and reliability. Point out that students should avoid using resources from the bottom of the list.

Writing Tip
Check the **reliability** and **validity** of your sources. A source is reliable and valid when its information is accurate and its ideas are presented objectively. Be careful when selecting Internet sources. Make sure that the site is sponsored by a trustworthy organization that has some expertise in the field.

Begin Research

Start your search for answers to your research questions by consulting general reference works or by doing keyword searches using an online search engine. Ask your school's librarian how to find works that will give an **overview** of your topic. An adequate overview will enable you to explore a variety of both print and nonprint sources. Use the chart below as a general resource guide.

Information Sources	
Library Sources	**What to Look For**
Library or online catalog	Books, records, audiotapes, videotapes, and digital media
Readers' Guide to Periodical Literature	Magazines and some journal articles, indexed by subject and author
Indexes to newspapers, essays, and articles	Articles from major newspapers, such as *The New York Times*; possibly local newspapers
Specialized reference books and CD-ROMs	Encyclopedias of special subjects, such as *Contemporary Authors*; biographical references, such as *Current Biography*
Online databases, microfilm, and microfiche	Collections of specialized material, such as literary criticism; indexes to major newspapers; back issues of some newspapers and magazines
Community Resources	**What to Look For**
Internet and online services	Articles, interviews, pictures, video and audio recordings
Museums, historical societies, and government offices	Exhibits, experts, and records
Schools and colleges	Libraries, experts, exhibits, and special collections
TV and radio; video stores	Documentary and instructional programs and videos

Research Guidelines As you seek sources, keep these guidelines in mind:

- **Balance primary and secondary sources. Primary sources** include firsthand, original information, such as letters, autobiographies, historical documents, and works of literature and art. **Secondary sources** consist of information derived from, or about, primary sources or other secondary sources. Examples include reference works, documentary films, biographies, and history books.
- **Cover all relevant perspectives.** Your literary research paper will be an original **synthesis,** or combination, of information you gather from research, the conclusions you draw from that research information, and your own insights into the topic. Look for sources that reveal the perspectives of a variety of literary and historical authorities on your subject.

Your Turn

Begin Your Research Refer to the research questions in your **RWN** as you look at sources to find the information you need. Then, make a list of sources that might have useful and relevant information.

Literary Research Paper Writing Prompts

Students can choose their own literary research paper idea or use one of the following prompts to write a paper.

Social Studies Choose a novel with a historical setting. Research and discuss whether the setting, language, and events included in the novel are historically accurate.

Science Choose a science fiction novel that includes references to scientific phenomena. Research the science behind the story and discuss its purpose and importance in the novel.

Psychology Write a research paper about an interesting character from a literary work. Research information from the field of psychology that may explain the motivation and reasoning behind the character's behavior.

Record Sources

Keep track of your source information; it will later be included in a *Bibliography* in your paper. For each source, make a **source card,** like the one below.

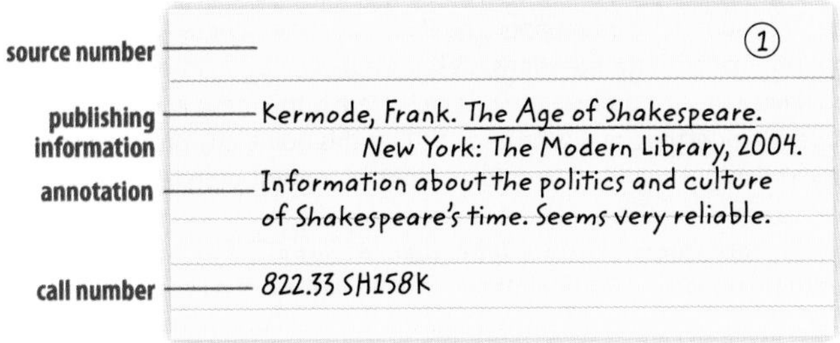

Research, and Take Notes

Now you are ready to search for specific information to answer your research questions. As you take notes, use the following guidelines to decide how to record each piece of information—direct quotation, paraphrase, or summary:

- **Direct Quotation** When a passage is phrased in a memorable way or if you want to capture its technical accuracy, quote the author directly and exactly, word for word. Enclose the passage in quotation marks.
- **Paraphrase** Paraphrasing means that you completely rewrite a passage, using your own words and style. A paraphrase is usually about the same length as the original.
- **Summary** When you want to use the main ideas presented in a passage, summarize the information. A typical summary is highly condensed—much shorter than the original passage.

Avoid **plagiarizing,** or failing to give credit to an author whose words or ideas you have used. When you paraphrase or summarize, be sure to completely rewrite the original passages. Simply subsituting synonyms for some of the words from your source is insufficient. See page 509 for information on giving credit by documenting your sources. The following is a sample **notecard:**

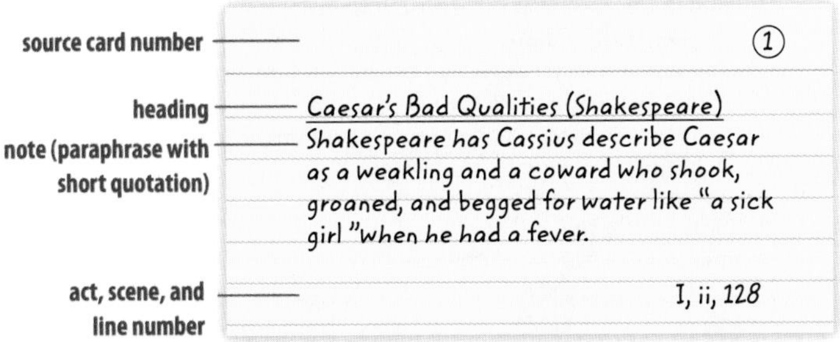

Writing Tip

- Number your sources. Use the number, rather than the author and title, when you take notes from a given source.
- Record all publishing information (author, title, city, publisher, and date). This workshop uses the Modern Language Association (MLA) format, but your teacher may prefer another.
- Annotate each card with a short note about the contents of the source and your evaluation of it.
- Note the call number or location of the source. This information will save you time if you need to return to the source later.

Your Turn

Cite Sources, and Take Notes
Create **source cards,** using the correct format, for each source you use. Skim your sources for information you can use in your essay. When you find relevant information, write it on a **notecard** like the one on this page.

Guided Practice: Apply

Record Sources

Emphasize to students the importance of recording accurate information on their source cards, as these will be students' main resource when they create their *Bibliography*. Students should pay close attention to the spelling of authors' names and the correct punctuation of the source titles.

Research, and Take Notes

Help students understand the difference between a direct quotation, paraphrase, and summary by working with the following quote from Ernest Hemingway: "All modern American literature comes from one book by Mark Twain called *Huckleberry Finn.*"

Direct quotation: Novelist Ernest Hemingway once stated, "All modern American literature comes from one book by Mark Twain called *Huckleberry Finn.*"

Paraphrase: Novelist Ernest Hemingway felt that Mark Twain's *Huckleberry Finn* had a significant influence on the development of American literature.

Summary: Earnest Hemingway believed Mark Twain was an influential American author.

Your Turn

Cite Sources, and Take Notes Have students complete the **Your Turn** as independent practice. Encourage students to use a large binder clip or folder to keep their note cards organized.

Universal Access

English Learners

English for Academic Success Review difficult academic vocabulary words in the text, including *primary, secondary, periodical, historical,* and *database.*

Struggling Writers

Model looking up information related to students' topics in resources students might have difficulty using, such as online databases and specialized reference books.

Advanced Learners

Enrichment Challenge students to assess the advantages and disadvantages of using each of the library sources listed on p. 506. Then, have students present their assessment to the class and suggest ways to overcome or avoid the disadvantages of certain sources.

Guided Practice: Apply

Write a Thesis Statement

- Point out to students that there are many possible thesis statements for the same topic and that their thesis statements may change as their research progresses.
- Ask students to refer to their notes and think about the most significant topic or idea addressed throughout their research. Students can use this information to help them write a thesis statement.

Make an Outline

- Have students talk with a partner about which organizational structure would best suit the ideas they plan to address in their paper—chronological order, logical order, or order of importance.
- Some students may not find a formal outline useful. Allow those students to use a graphic organizer, such as a flow chart, to organize their ideas. Remind students to include the main idea, supporting ideas, evidence, and details in their organizer.

Writing Tip

Analyze your information to see if it is relevant and useful.

- Divide your notes into categories based on their headings. Do more research for headings for which you do not have enough information. Discard notes that turn out to be irrelevant to your topic.
- Analyze your notes for consistency. If sources do not agree on the facts, evaluate each source, and use information from the one that is more reliable and valid.
- If two reliable and valid sources disagree on an important point, consider presenting this difference as part of your paper.

Drafting

Write a Thesis Statement

Your **thesis statement** is a sentence or two identifying the main idea that you intend to support in your paper. The thesis statement, or proposition, answers your original research questions, stating your conclusion about the information you have analyzed during your research. Here is the thesis statement for the student model that begins on page 512. At this point, any proposition is preliminary. You might change it later for reasons of content or style.

Shakespeare wanted to show his audience that all three main characters—Caesar, Brutus, and Mark Antony—are a mixture of good and evil.

Make an Outline

Develop an outline by arranging your notecards according to your main-idea headings. Rearrange the headings until you have an order that makes sense. You will probably use a combination of organizational patterns—chronological order, order of importance, and logical order—for both your main ideas and your specific examples and supporting details.

- **Chronological order** can be used to discuss events in an author's or character's life in the order in which the events occurred.
- **Order of importance** can be used to discuss main ideas about an author's work. The most important idea is often discussed last for greatest effect.
- **Logical order** groups ideas by the relationships among them. Cause-effect and comparison-contrast are common examples.

Organizing your notes and creating a **formal outline** simplify the process of writing your paper in its final form. Your outline can also serve as a table of contents for the finished paper. Look at this partial outline of the student model:

I. Introduction
  A. Shakespeare's source
  B. Thesis statement
II. Plutarch: Shakespeare's source
  A. Historian and biographer
  B. Lives of Noble Grecians and Romans
    1. Shows good and bad in historical figures
    2. Demonstrates admiration of Caesar
III. Shakespeare's challenge: depicting the bad in Caesar
  A. Audience was inclined to see him as good
    1. Belief in monarchy as system of government
    2. Belief in the divine right of kings
  B. Exaggerations of Caesar's frailties
    1. Acts like "a sick girl"
    2. Falls down in the marketplace

Universal Access

EL English Learners

English for Academic Success Introduce students to unfamiliar words or phrases they may encounter when developing an outline.

- **organizational pattern** – the way in which something is put into order or grouped
- **logical order** – an order based on a clear pattern of thought
- **theory** – a set of ideas used to explain something
- **citation** – a reference to an original source

Struggling Writers

Go over how to format an outline with students. Make sure they understand that the Roman numerals are the main points, and the letters are points that support the main points. Work with students to rewrite the sample outline in paragraph form to help them see the transition from one step of the writing process to the next.

✔ See **UA: Differentiating Instruction** for strategies for teaching struggling writers.

Document Sources

To **document** a paper means to identify the sources for the information in your paper. In general, document all quotations; all theories, ideas, and opinions other than your own; all data from surveys, research studies, and interviews; and all facts and statistics. Do not document common knowledge—information that can be found in several sources or standard reference works.

Place **parenthetical citations** (sources enclosed in parentheses) within the body of your paper as close as possible to the information they document. These citations direct readers to more complete information in the *Bibliography*, located at the end of the paper. The chart below gives some guidelines.

Guidelines for Parenthetical Documentation

Type of Source	Content of Citation and Example
Sources with one author	Author's last name and a page number, if any: (Kermode 32)
Sources with more than one author	Authors' last names and page number: (Wells and Johnson 322) If more than three, use first author's last name and *et al.* (and others): (Anderson et al. 313)
Same source, two citations	Author's last name and page numbers, if any: (Bullough 37, 39)
Multivolume sources	Author's last name, volume, and page number: (Prucha 2: 214)
Sources with a title only	Title (often abbreviated) and page number: (Lives 38)
Literary sources published in many editions	Author's last name, title, and division references (act, scene, canto, book, chapter, part, and line numbers) in place of page numbers: (Shakespeare, JC 1.2.128) (Note: JC abbreviates Julius Caesar.)
Indirect sources	Abbreviation *qtd. in* (quoted in) before source: (qtd. in Morrow 29)

Grammar Link Punctuating Parenthetical Citations

Here are some rules for adding parenthetical citations to your paper:

- Place citations ***after*** the closing quotation mark.
- Place citations ***before*** punctuation (such as periods) at the end of sentences.

Cassius describes Caesar as "a sick girl" (Shakespeare, JC 1.2.128).

One exception to these rules is **block quotations**—quotations that run more than four lines, which are indented and do not have quotation marks. Instead, place *all* citations *after* the end punctuation.

Difficult battles, long and swift
marches, coarse diet, hard work, and sleeping in the open
field conditioned him against his diseases. (McFarland, Graves, and Graves 233)

Writing Tip

If you have clearly indicated the author and title of your source in the text leading up to a citation, you do not need to list that information in your parenthetical citation.
For example:
In *Shakespeare's Canary,* Kuemmel and Lanier make very clear the Bard's love of songbirds (34).

Your Turn

Write Your Draft Using your **outline** as a guide, write the first draft of your literary research paper. Remember to write a **thesis statement,** or **proposition,** and **document** your sources, using **parenthetical citations.**

Guided Practice: Apply

Document Sources

Help students evaluate what information is common knowledge and what information needs to be documented. Inform students that the statement, "The famous play *Romeo and Juliet* was written by the English writer William Shakespeare," would not need to be cited because that information is familiar to most people. However, details about when the play was first performed or which actors have played the role of Romeo's friend Mercutio are not common knowledge. These details would need to be cited. Tell students if they are ever in doubt about whether information is common knowledge, it should be cited.

Grammar Link

For practice, have students choose three quotes from their research that were gathered from different types of sources. Students should correctly punctuate the quotes in parenthetical citations, following the guidelines in the chart on this page.

Warriner's Handbook, Sixth Course, pp. 549–550

Your Turn

Write Your Draft Ask students to complete the **Your Turn** as independent practice. Remind them to add citations whenever they use someone else's ideas, regardless of whether they use direct quotes. Suggest that students use every other line as they write their drafts so that revisions can be made more easily.

Advanced Learners

Enrichment Challenge students to rewrite the outline using chronological order or order of importance. Ask students to assess which organization they believe fits the material best, and why.

Guided Practice: Apply

Assemble the *Bibliography*

- Explain to students that a working bibliography would include all the sources they encountered in their research, while a Works Cited list includes only the sources they cited in parenthetical documentation in the body of their research paper. To assemble the Works Cited list, have students alphabetize their source cards and then remove cards for sources they did not cite in their paper.
- Ask students to consider whether each source meets each of the Four R's: whether it is relevant, recent, reliable, and representative. Have students fill out a Four R chart like the one below with a row for each resource and a column for each of the Four R's.

Source	Relevant?	Recent?
1		
2		
3		

Reliable?	Representative?

- You may want to point out to students the footnoting capabilities of most word-processing programs. These features can save time and frustration.

Reference Note

For more on **formatting,** or the ***Works Cited* list,** see the model on page 514.

Writing Tip

The list of *Works Cited* is a type of *Bibliography:* the list of sources you actually *cite* in your research paper. By contrast, a *Bibliography* includes *all* the sources you *consulted* in researching your topic.

Writing Tip

For a complete version of a research paper, log on to the Interactive Student Edition at go.hrw.com and go to page 512.

Assemble the *Bibliography* or *Works Cited*

The *Bibliography,* or list of *Works Cited*, the final section of your paper, lists all the sources—both print and nonprint—that you used in your paper. The following sample entries are a reference for preparing your *Bibliography,* or list of *Works Cited.* Notice that you include page numbers only for sources that are part of a larger work, such as an essay in a book of essays.

Sample *Bibliography,* or *Works Cited* Entries

Standard Reference Works If an author is credited in a standard reference work, cite that person's name first in an entry. Otherwise, the title of the book or article appears first. You do not need to cite the editor. Page and volume numbers are not needed if the work alphabetizes entries. For common reference works, use only the edition (if listed) and the year of publication.

Print Encyclopedia Article

"Plutarch." The World Book Encyclopedia. 2006 ed.

Books

One Author

Kermode, Frank. The Age of Shakespeare. New York: The Modern Library, 2004.

Two or More Authors

Kuemmel, Scott, and Terry Lanier. Shakespeare's Canary. New York: Harcourt, 2009.

For four or more authors, list the first author followed by *et al.*

Selections Within Books

From a Book of Works by Several Authors

Bullough, Geoffrey. "Julius Caesar and Plutarch." Twentieth Century Interpretations of Julius Caesar. Ed. Leonard F. Dean. New Jersey: Prentice, 1968. 90–94.

Articles from Magazines, Newspapers, and Journals

From a Monthly or Quarterly Magazine

Morrow, Lance. "Plutarch's Exemplary Lives." Smithsonian 1 July 2004: 107–111.

From a Daily Newspaper

Jones, Chris. "Shaw Festival Debuts in Chicago Shakespeare's New Season." Chicago Tribune 18 Apr. 2007: E4.

Other Sources

Film or Video Recording

Julius Caesar. Dir. Mankiewicz. 1953. DVD. Warner Home Video, 2006.

Material Accessed Through the Internet

Jackson, Dana. From History to the Stage: An Account of Shakespeare's Adaptation of Julius Caesar. 2000. Shakespeare Online. 25 Sept. 2009 <www.shakespeare-online.com/essays/fromhistorytostage.html>.

Interviews

Keeling, Nichole. Telephone interview. 20 Sept. 2009.

E-mail Message or Personal Letter

Trahn, Linda. E-mail to the author. 27 Sept. 2009.

Universal Access

EL English Learners

English for Academic Success Inform students that a *Bibliography* is also sometimes referred to as an *appendix.* Explain to them that the term *bibliography* refers only to printed materials, while the term *appendix* can refer to any additional matter located at the end of a book or document. Inform students that *bibliography* is the most appropriate term to use for this section of their paper.

Struggling Writers

Ask students to summarize aloud what they have learned about how to create a *Bibliography* to discover if any of it has been difficult for them to understand. Correct any misconceptions.

Advanced Learners

Enrichment Have students write a notecard for each source they used that tells the advantages and disadvantages of the source. Keep the cards so that other students can reference them as good examples.

Evaluating and Revising

Use the guidelines in the following chart to evaluate and revise the content and organization of your paper. Ask yourself the questions in the left-hand column, and then use the tips in the middle column. Finally, use the revision techniques suggested in the right-hand column as necessary.

Literary Research Paper: Guidelines for Content and Organization

Evaluation Question	Tip	Revision Technique
1. Does the introduction hook the reader's attention, give background information, and clearly state the thesis, or proposition?	**Circle** the hook, **underline** background information, and **bracket** the thesis statement, or proposition.	**Add** a quotation or interesting detail to hook readers. **Add** necessary background. **Add** a thesis statement, or proposition.
2. Does the body include only main ideas and supporting details that are relevant to the thesis?	With a colored marker, **highlight** the main ideas. **Number** supporting details for each.	**Delete** irrelevant ideas and details. **Add** details to support ideas with fewer than three supporting details.
3. Are facts and ideas stated mainly in your own words?	**Star** sentences containing direct quotations. If more than one third of the sentences are starred, revise.	**Replace** unnecessary direct quotations with paraphrases and summaries.
4. Are sources credited when necessary? Are citations correctly placed and punctuated?	**Place check marks** by material that came from outside sources and requires documentation.	**Add** parenthetical citations. **Correct** placement and punctuation of citations.
5. Does the conclusion restate the thesis?	**Bracket** the restatement of the thesis.	**Add** a sentence or two restating the thesis.
6. Is the list of *Works Cited* complete and correctly formatted?	**Compare** citations that have checks with the entries in your list of *Works Cited*.	**Add** *Works Cited* entries, and **revise** incorrectly formatted entries.

Peer Review

Ask a peer to use the evaluation questions and tips in the chart to the left to evaluate your draft and suggest revisions. Make notes about your partner's observations and suggestions.

Model the Skill

- Using a student draft on a transparency, model how to use the questions, tips, and revision techniques suggested in the chart. You might use a student's paper or a paper of your own creation to evaluate and revise using the steps in the chart.
- Ask volunteers to demonstrate using each of the steps on their own essays.

Peer Review

At the beginning of the peer review session, have each student ask his or her partner to identify the main idea of his or her paper. This will help focus students' reading of each other's drafts.

Holt Six Traits for Writing, rubrics, prompts, and sample papers

Students with Disabilities

Some students may become easily frustrated with the attention to detail that writing a *Bibliography* entails. Suggest students use a composition program that will automatically arrange their source information into a standard format such as MLA or APA style. Students must enter their source information into an on-screen form, which will prompt them if they neglect to note required data.

Guided Practice: Apply

Student Draft

- Explain that the Student Draft on this page is the first half of a literary research paper written by the student whose outline appeared on p. 508.
- Model reading the draft and the annotations in blue. Explain that a mini-lesson follows with helpful information about ways for students to improve this draft as well as their own writing.

Mini-Lesson

Providing Background Information

- Explain that the student writer has revised her opening by adding background information that will make the essay's introduction clear to readers who have not researched this topic.
- Remind students to write their paper with the assumption that the reader is not familiar with the topic. Point out that students should briefly state any information that is essential for understanding.

Your Turn

Provide Background Information

Before students complete the **Your Turn,** suggest that they jot down basic background information that they have learned from their research. Then, students should consider whether this information is important for their readers to know.

Read the following portions of a student draft, and note the comments on its strengths and the suggestions for improvement.

Student Draft

Shakespeare's Caesar

by Susan Chang, Reagan High School

Susan's **opening statement** is vague. →

Her **thesis statement** is clear. →

When Shakespeare wrote *Julius Caesar,* he made some changes. By looking at these changes, we can tell something about Shakespeare's purpose. The changes show that Shakespeare wanted to show his audience that all three main characters—Caesar, Brutus, and Mark Antony—are a mixture of good and evil.

To contrast Shakespeare's portrayal of Caesar, Susan **summarizes** Plutarch's view. →

Plutarch was a Greek historian and biographer. He wrote *Lives* not so much to record history as to show how the moral character—both good and bad—shaped the lives and destinies of the famous people he wrote about. His biography clearly shows admiration for Caesar, whom he portrays as a natural-born orator, great soldier and general, and statesman who was beloved by his soldiers and people.

MINI-LESSON Providing Background Information

Susan's opening statement is vague. Readers may ask, "What did Shakespeare change?" Writers sometimes incorrectly assume that the reader is as familiar with their topic as they are. To ensure readers can follow your historical research, include background information that will be necessary for the average reader, that is, someone who has *not* done the same amount of research on the topic as you. Susan added background information to help readers understand the changes she is going to discuss.

Susan's Revision of Paragraph 1

Most people know that Shakespeare's play Julius Caesar is based on history. What many people don't know is that he took the story from a particular source: Plutarch's Lives of Noble Grecians and Romans. Most of the events—and even some of the language—in Shakespeare's play is the same as in Plutarch's account. ^However, w~~W~~hen Shakespeare wrote *Julius Caesar,* he ^did make ~~made~~ some changes. By looking at these changes, we can tell something about Shakespeare's purpose.

Your Turn

Provide Background Information Read your draft, and ask yourself whether you give your readers sufficient information about the following:

- the writer
- the writer's sources
- the writer's time and place
- the literary work

Real Issues, Real Experts

Holt Professional Learning for Language Arts

To watch videos on teaching **revision, grammar,** and **on-demand writing skills** featuring Linda Rief, Amy Benjamin, and Leila Christenbury, go to this page in **ThinkCentral, Teacher Access.**

Student Draft *continues*

Shakespeare faced a challenge in depicting the evil in Caesar. Many English people of the Renaissance believed that kings and queens ruled by divine right, so they were horrified by the kingly ruler's assassination (Jackson). To keep his audience from siding entirely with Caesar, Shakespeare had to show him in a worse light than Plutarch did. For instance, Plutarch describes Caesar's weaknesses but makes clear that he overcame them to do great deeds.

> In spite of his brave fighting and displays of energy, Caesar was physically weak. He was subject to epilepsy, and his slender physique and soft white skin made his courage and perseverance unusually remarkable. Difficult battles, long and swift marches, coarse diet, hard work, and sleeping in the open field conditioned him against his diseases. (McFarland, Graves, and Graves 233)

In contrast, Shakespeare exaggerates Caesar's frailties. He has Cassius describe Caesar as a weakling and a coward who shook, groaned, and begged for water like "a sick girl "when he had a fever (1.2.128). Despite the fact that these words come from Cassius, who is not always reliable, they still color the audience's opinion of Caesar. Shakespeare follows this information by having Casca report that at the marketplace, "Caesar fell down and foamed at the mouth and was speechless" (1.2.250–251). Shakespeare paints Caesar not as a man who overcame illness but as a man who feared and gave in to it. The Caesar of the play may be powerful, but he is also a hypocrite who pretends to a valor he lacks. This hypocrisy makes his death seem less tragic and his assassins less clearly in the wrong.

← Susan states a **main idea** and then gives **supporting details.** She uses a **parenthetical citation** to credit an online **source** without page numbers.

← She quotes a long passage from a source, using **block quotation style,** but introduces the quotation incorrectly.

← Because the text clearly states that the quotations come from Shakespeare and *Julius Caesar,* Susan does not need to include the author or title in this paragraph's citations.

MINI-LESSON Introducing Quotations

Quotations should not disrupt the flow of your paper. Introduce them gracefully either with an introductory sentence followed by a colon or by weaving them in—making them a part of your sentence. Susan corrected her introduction to the block quotation.

Susan's Revision of Paragraph 3

light than Plutarch did. For instance, Plutarch describes Caesar's weaknesses but makes clear that he overcame them to do great deeds:

> In spite of his brave fighting and displays of energy, Caesar was physically weak. He was subject to epilepsy, and his slender physique and soft white skin made his courage and perseverance unusually remarkable. . . .

Susan *correctly* weaves this quotation into her sentence, as indicated by the boldface type:

> He has Cassius describe Caesar as a weakling and a coward who shook, groaned, and begged for water like **"a sick girl"** when he had a fever. . . .

Your Turn

Introduce Quotations Read your draft, making sure the introduction of quotations does not interrupt the flow of your paper and ideas. Ask a peer to review your draft and to suggest ways to introduce your quotations more smoothly.

Guided Practice: Apply

Student Draft

- Explain that the Student Draft is continued and completed on this page. Again the draft is annotated for the students.
- Read the draft and annotations aloud and discuss. Refer students to the revision techniques on p. 511. Ask students to comment on the student's success in revising this paper.

Mini-Lesson Introducing Quotations

- Explain that the student writer has revised her paragraph by introducing the block quotation correctly.
- Remind students to pay attention to the punctuation of quotations. They should usually use commas or colons to lead into quotes.

Your Turn

Introduce Quotations Have students highlight or underline the quotations in their partner's papers and rate how well the quotation is introduced on a scale of 1–5, 5 being the best. Then have students consider revising quotes that their partner scored as a 3 or below.

Universal Access

EL English Learners

Some students from different cultural or language backgrounds may feel the urge to add too much background information to their papers if they are anxious about their lack of familiarity with a topic. Have those students partner with native-speaking students and ask for suggestions about what information is unnecessary because it is already familiar to most readers.

✔ See **UA: Differentiating Instruction** for strategies for teaching English learners.

AAVE Students Who Use African American Vernacular English

English for Academic Success Point out the first full sentence in the student's revision on p. 513. Tell students that in formal writing, the subject and verb of a sentence must agree. Explain that the subject of the sentence—*Plutarch*—agrees with the verbs in the sentence—*describes* and *makes*. Remind students that they should add *s* to verbs used with third-person subjects. Have students complete the following sentence with the correct form of the verb *learn:* John ___ in school each day. [*learns*]

Guided Practice: Apply

Student Draft

Explain that the *Bibliography* for the Student Draft is on this page. Have students compare this *Bibliography* to the citations on the previous pages. Ask students to comment on the student's success with the assignment.

Student Draft *continues*

In her conclusion, Susan restates her thesis. →

By showing Caesar, Brutus, and Mark Antony each as a blending of good and evil traits, Shakespeare makes the story of Caesar's assassination a story of the human struggle with our internal faults and failings. Caesar's arrogance and love of power first arouse Brutus's concern for the republic and then lead Caesar to ignore the warnings that would have saved him. Brutus's simple, trusting nature leads him to overlook the dishonorable agendas of his co-conspirators and misread the mood of the people. Finally, Mark Antony's nobility in avenging Caesar is tainted with cynical self-interest. None of the play's main characters are blameless, but each has a measure of nobility.

Writing Tip

Notice how the writer uses these rules for formatting her *Works Cited*. Make sure to follow them when making your own.

- *Works Cited* pages usually begin on a separate page.
- The title *Works Cited* is centered above the list of sources.
- Each source entry begins on a separate line.
- The first line of the entry is left aligned; additional lines have a hanging indent of a half inch.
- Sources are sorted alphabetically by authors' last names. Sources with no author are sorted by title.
- If an author is cited for more than one source, his or her name appears only in the first entry. Additional entries use three hyphens (---) in place of the author's name.

Works Cited

Bullough, Geoffrey. "Julius Caesar and Plutarch." Twentieth Century Interpretations of Julius Caesar. Ed. Leonard F. Dean. Englewood Cliffs, NJ: Prentice Hall, 1968.

"Caesar, Julius." Encyclopedia Britannica. 2007. Encyclopedia Britannica Online. 25 Sept. 2009 <http://www.britannica.com/eb/article-9000074>.

Delaney, Bill. "Shakespeare's Julius Caesar." The Explicator Summer 2002: 188.

Jackson, Dana. From History to the Stage: An Account of Shakespeare's Adaptation of Julius Caesar. 2000. Shakespeare Online. 28 Sept. 2009 <http://www.shakespeare-online.com/essays/fromhistorytostage.html>.

Kermode, Frank. The Age of Shakespeare. New York: The Modern Library, 2004.

McFarland, John W., and Pleasant and Audrey Graves, eds. Lives from Plutarch. New York: Random House, 1966.

Morrow, Lance. "Plutarch's Exemplary Lives." Smithsonian 1 July 2004: 107–111.

"Plutarch." The World Book Encyclopedia. 2006 ed.

Shakespeare, William. Julius Caesar. Ed. S. F. Johnson. New York: Penguin Books, 1960.

Universal Access

EL English Learners/ Struggling Writers

English for Academic Success Introduce students to MLA style abbreviations they may be confused by when developing their *Bibliography*.

- **U** – University, *U of Illinois*
- **P** – Press, *Walt Whitman P*
- **UP** – University Press, *Johns Hopkins UP*
- **ed** – edition, *2005 ed.*
- **Ed** – edited by, *Ed. Antonio Begani*

Advanced Learners

Acceleration Challenge students to work together and combine their papers to create a literary "mini-magazine" for the class. Have students create three "departments": one in charge of organizing the papers; one to edit the papers for proper form and fit; and one to work on the production process, including how to efficiently print, bind, and create a cover for the collection of works. Then, students should work together develop a name, cover concept, and introduction for their "mini-magazine."

Proofreading and Publishing

Proofreading

Do not allow careless errors in grammar, usage, and mechanics to destroy your credibility. **Proofread,** or **edit,** your paper carefully to be sure that you have followed the **conventions** of standard American English.

Grammar Link **Punctuating Quotations**

When weaving a quotation into your text, you must sometimes add words or phrases to make the quotation clearer to readers. When you add to a quotation, you must place your addition in brackets ([ ]). At other times, you may want to quote some—but not all—of a writer's words so that you can better get at the main idea you are pointing out to your reader. When you leave words or phrases out of a quotation, you must replace them with ellipses (. . .).

Susan wove a quotation into her first draft but punctuated it incorrectly, possibly misleading readers about what Shakespeare's lines actually say. She revised her quotation to indicate where she added and deleted text.

> Shakespeare follows this information by having Casca report that at the marketplace "[Caesar] fell down . . . and foamed at the mouth and was speechless" (1.2.250–251).

Publishing

Consider these publishing ideas to share your hard work and insight:

- Ask your school librarian or media specialist to make your work available in the library or media center.
- Offer to present the paper to another class—an English class or possibly a history class. You may wish to conduct additional research to find interesting and relevant audio and video support.
- Work collaboratively with your classmates to create a Web site that features your research findings. Include a space for reader feedback, if your teacher and school allow it.

Reflect on the Process Consider what you have learned about the topic, the research and writing processes, and yourself as a writer. In your **RWN,** write short responses to these questions**:**

1. What questions did your research answer that you had not asked or anticipated? Describe them.
2. What passage in your paper was the most effective combination of research and conclusions drawn from the research? Why?

Proofreading Tip

Proofreading partners need to be honest, so that they can address a paper's strengths and weaknesses. However, try to be tactful, for it can be hard to receive criticism on something into which you have put so much effort.

- Start with positive comments ("I liked the way that you . . ." or "I can tell you have put a lot of thought into . . .").
- Provide specific suggestions ("Your introduction could use more background because I didn't understand . . .") rather than vague judgments ("This introduction was terrible!").

Your Turn

Proofread and Publish

As you proofread your draft, check all your quotations against the texts from which they originate. If you have added or deleted words or phrases, make sure you have correctly used brackets and ellipses. When you are finished, make a final copy of your paper, and publish it.

Guided Practice: Apply

Proofreading

Integrating with Grammar, Usage, and Mechanics If students make errors in punctuating quotations as they are proofreading, send them to the Punctuation chapters in **Warriner's Handbook.**

Grammar Link

For practice, have students choose two quotes from their resources. For each quote, students should write a sentence using part of the quote and add some introductory text, punctuating the sentence so that it flows smoothly.

Publishing

Brainstorm with students additional ways to publish their literary research papers.

Reflect on the Process

Have students reflect on their writing process as well as their final product. Challenge them to reflect metacognitively about how they can improve and apply what they have learned.

Your Turn

Proofread and Publish If students have omitted any words from a quote and replaced them with brackets or ellipses, have them read those quotes aloud to ensure that the quote still sounds like a smooth and uninterrupted thought.

Guided Practice: Apply

Scoring Guide

- Tell students that the best way to understand scoring guides is to use them to score actual writing.
- Distribute a copy of an essay with the student's name removed and work as a class to evaluate the essay. Ask students to score their own essays and then write a brief paragraph using the language of the scoring guide to explain the reasons for their score.

Holt Six Traits for Writing, rubrics, prompts, and sample papers

Assess

UA: Holt Interactive Writer and Speaker, expository essay analytical scales and rubrics, p. 50

ThinkCentral Online Assessment, Writing Workshop Test

Teacher One Stop™, editable Writing Workshop Test

Reteach

ThinkCentral Online Remediation

Scoring Guide

Use the scoring guide below to evaluate your literary research paper from the Writing Workshop or your response to the on-demand prompt on the next page.

	Expository Writing	Organization and Focus	Sentence Structure and Vocabulary	Language Conventions
4	• provides a *meaningful* thesis that is responsive to the writing task.	• *thoroughly* supports the thesis and main ideas with *specific* details and examples. • demonstrates a *clear* sense of audience. • demonstrates a *consistent* tone and focus, and illustrates a *purposeful* control of organization.	• provides a *variety* of sentence types and uses *precise, descriptive* language.	• contains *few, if any, errors* in the conventions of the English language. (Errors are generally first draft in nature.)
3	• provides a thesis that is *responsive* to the writing task.	• supports the thesis and main ideas with details and examples. • demonstrates a *general* sense of audience. • demonstrates a *consistent* tone and focus and illustrates a control of organization.	• provides a *variety* of sentence types and uses *some descriptive* language.	• may contain *some errors* in the conventions of the English language. (Errors do **not** interfere with the reader's understanding of the essay.)
2	• provides a thesis or main idea that is *related* to the writing task.	• supports the thesis or main idea(s) with *limited* details and/or examples. • demonstrates *little* or **no** sense of audience. • demonstrates an *inconsistent* tone and focus; and illustrates *little, if any,* control of organization.	• provides *few, if any,* types of sentence types and basic, *predictable* language.	• may contain *several errors* in the conventions of the English language. (Errors **may** interfere with the reader's understanding of the essay.)
1	• may provide a *weak* thesis or main idea that is related to the writing task.	• *fails* to support the thesis or main ideas with details and/or examples. • may demonstrate **no** sense of audience. • demonstrates a *lack* of tone and focus; and illustrates **no** control of organization.	• may provide **no** sentence variety and uses *limited* vocabulary.	• may contain *serious errors* in the conventions of the English language. (Errors interfere with the reader's understanding of the essay.)

California Standards, pp. 516–517

- **Writing Standard 1.1** Demonstrate an understanding of the elements of discourse (e.g. purpose, speaker, audience, form) when completing narrative, expository, persuasive or descriptive writing assignments.
- **Writing Standard 1.3** Structure ideas and arguments in a sustained persuasive and sophisticated way and support them with precise and relevant examples.
- **Writing Standard 1.6** Develop presentations by using clear research questions and creative and critical research strategies.
- **Writing Standard 1.7** Use systematic strategies to organize and record information (e.g., anecdotal scripting, annotated bibliographies).
- **Writing Standard 1.9** Revise text to highlight the individual voice, improve sentence variety and style, and enhance subtlety of meaning and tone in ways that are consistent with the purpose, audience, and genre.
- **Writing Standard 2.4a** Use exposition, narration, description, argumentation, exposition or some combination of rhetorical strategies to support the main proposition. **d.** Include information from all relevant perspectives and take into consideration the validity and reliability of sources. **e.** Include a formal bibliography.

Expository Writing Prompts

Students can use the writing prompt in the Student Edition or one of the following prompts.

- Suggest to students that they write an essay about the best way to make a decision. Students should choose whether it is best to make decisions quickly or spend a long time thinking about them, and use literature they have read to support their positions.
- Suggest to students that they write an essay about how good ideas can go too far. Students should use evidence from literature they have read to support their ideas.

Preparing for Timed Writing

Expository Essay

Writing Standard 1.1, 1.3, 1.6, 1.7, 1.9, 2.4a, 2.4d, 2.4e (see pages A51–A52)
Language Conventions Standard 1.1, 1.2, 1.3 (see page A53)

When responding to an expository prompt, use what you have learned from reading, writing your literary research paper, and studying the scoring guide on page 516. Use the steps below to develop a response to the following prompt.

Writing Prompt
Although ambition can be a good thing, too much ambition can be harmful both to the ambitious individual and to others. Write an essay explaining the harmful effects of excessive ambition.

Study the Prompt
Read the prompt carefully. Then, read it a second time, underlining words that will help you approach the prompt effectively: *ambition, harmful effects, individual,* and *others*. The prompt asks you to explain, which means you will be answering two questions in your essay: *why?* and *how?* The *why?* question asks you to explain the reasons the ambition was harmful. *How?* asks you to show the harmful effects of the ambition. **Tip:** Spend about five minutes studying the prompt.

Plan Your Response
Decide quickly if you will use a personal example of ambition and its effects or if you will use hypothetical examples, drawing supporting details from your reading or other media. Try to be as specific as possible.

When you decide on the examples you will use, ask and answer the following questions:

- What is the evidence of the ambition?
- Who or what did this ambition affect?
- What was the result of the ambition?
- Why was it harmful? How? To whom?
- What did you and others learn as a result?

Using your answers, draw a conclusion, and write a **thesis statement** about ambition's harmful effects. **Tip:** Spend about ten minutes planning your response.

Respond to the Prompt
Begin writing to start the flow of ideas. You might begin by defining *ambition* in your own words and then introducing your thesis statment. Include a brief scene to illustrate your definition. In the body text, explain the reasons *why* ambition is harmful and relate the reasons to your definition. For each harmful effect, provide examples of *how* it is harmful. In your conclusion, relate what your essay says about ambition and human nature in general. **Tip:** Spend about twenty minutes writing your draft.

Improve Your Response
Revising Check your response against the prompt. Does your response explain that too much ambition can be harmful and demonstrate its harmful effects to the ambitious person and to others? Have you used specific examples to illustrate the harmful effects? Have you restated your thesis in the conclusion? Have you thought about lessons learned?

Proofreading Take a few minutes to edit your response to correct errors in grammar, usage, and mechanics. Check your usage of two key words that you will likely use in your essay:

- *Affect* is a verb that means "to influence."
  Praise can *affect* your self-image.
- *Effect* is a noun that means "the result of an action."
  The *effect* of his pride was loneliness.

Be certain that your paper is legible and neat and that any edits are easy to read.

Checking Your Final Copy Finally, read your response once more before you turn it in. You may catch an important mistake or think of the perfect last sentence! **Tip:** Save five or ten minutes to improve your paper.

Standards Focus

Objectives
Students will learn the elements of writing an expository essay.

Direct Teach

Study the Prompt
Before students begin writing, encourage them to answer the following questions:

1. What is my time limit?
2. What are the key skills assessed in the scoring guide?
3. Who is my audience?
4. What is my purpose?

Plan Your Response
Remind students that the scoring guide emphasizes the importance of a clear thesis and thoughtful ideas. Tell students they should use controlled language when expressing their thesis and ideas.

Improve Your Response
Point out that the scoring guide emphasized the development of ideas. Encourage students to develop their ideas completely with examples, details, and explanations.

Assess

Use the scoring guide on p. 516 to assess student's essays.

Universal Access

Struggling Writers
Ask students to think about characters they have encountered in previous readings that have suffered from excessive ambition (for example, the protagonist of Shakespeare's *The Tragedy of Macbeth*). Have students consider the disastrous effect excessive ambition had on these characters and how it ultimately resulted in their demise.

✔ See **UA: Differentiating Instruction** for strategies for teaching struggling writers.

Students with Disabilities
To help students create an outline for their essay, have them write down questions that are implicit in the prompt. Have students transcribe the following questions: What is ambition? In which situations do people usually experience ambition? Can ambition be too intense and possibly harmful? Ask students to write notes to answer these question and organize their thoughts into an outline.

✔ See **UA: Differentiating Instruction** for strategies for teaching students with disabilities.

Standards Focus

Objectives

Students will interpret literary texts when preparing oral interpretations.

Preteach

Speak with a Purpose Ask students to think about a time when someone was speaking or delivering a speech.

- Ask students what makes an oral presentation interesting. Have them consider both content and delivery.
- Brainstorm with students effective speeches that students might have seen on shows, films, or plays.

Direct Teach

Model the Skill

Adapt Your Literary Research Paper

Model how to adapt a literary research paper into an oral presentation. Explain that the first step is to think about their audience. Students might ask themselves: What information does an audience need to understand my speech?

Guided Practice: Apply

Have students imagine they are going to adapt their paper for a specific audience. Ask them to work in pairs to decide what they might do to adapt their speech for this audience.

Presenting a Literary Research Paper

Speak with a Purpose

Adapt your literary research paper for an oral presentation, and then share it with your class.

Think as a Reader/Writer Scholars in fields such as science, history, literature, and anthropology publish their research in scholarly or professional journals. You have probably encountered such writings in your research. These same scholars also make oral presentations of their research at professional conferences. In this workshop, you will do the same: transform your written report into an oral presentation for your peers.

Adapt Your Literary Research Paper

Simple and Clear

Reading a paper is quite different from listening to a presentation. As readers, we have the opportunity to go back and re-read to eliminate any confusion. Listeners do not have that opportunity. When adapting a written work into an oral presentation, it is important to think about what parts you may need to simplify and clarify for your audience. It is also important to hold your audience's attention with speaking techniques and interesting content. Use some of these tips to adjust the content:

- Grab your audience's interest by using an intriguing fact or a powerful quotation in your introduction.
- Teach your audience about your main idea by stating your thesis clearly and repeating certain points for emphasis.
- End your presentation with a powerful conclusion. Your conclusion should be as engaging as your introduction. Restate your thesis, and finish with a compelling quotation or anecdote.
- Simplify vocabulary, and break up longer sentences into shorter ones.
- Inform and entertain your audience by using exposition, narration, and description.
- Share as much information from primary and secondary sources as you can during the time allotted for your presentation.
- Do not cite sources except to identify the author of important quotations, facts, or ideas. In your introduction, let your audience know your report is drawn from a variety of sources.

Reader/Writer Notebook

Use your **RWN** to complete the activities for this workshop.

Resources

UA: Holt Interactive Writer and Speaker, practice and assessment, p. 125

UA: Differentiating Instruction, modified lesson plans, p. 105

Teacher One Stop™, on-level lesson plans and all print resources

California Standards, pp. 518–519

- **Listening and Speaking Standard 2.2** Deliver oral reports on historical investigations. **a.** Use exposition, narration, description, persuasion, or some combination of those to support the thesis. **b.** Analyze several historical records of a single event, examining critical relationships between elements of the research topic. **c.** Explain the perceived reason or reasons for the similarities and differences by using information derived from primary and secondary sources to support or enhance the presentation. **d.** Include information on all relevant perspectives and consider the validity and reliability of sources.

Listening and Speaking Standard 2.2a–d (see pages A53–A55)

Deliver Your Literary Research Paper

Speaking Formally

When you are giving a presentation about a topic you know well, plan to deliver it extemporaneously. Instead of memorizing your presentation, rehearse it until you are thoroughly familiar with your material. Make notecards with reminders of important points and the full text of quotations. Number your notecards, and keep them in order. As you rehearse your presentation, maintain a formal, objective tone suitable to serious research. When you become comfortable with your material, allow yourself to vary your phrasing. Do not read your presentation from your notes; instead, use your notecards to guide you.

Using Visuals

If possible, enhance your presentation with visuals such as charts, graphs, photographs, or exhibits. Visuals should be large enough for the entire audience to see and should also make a relevant contribution to your presentation. Think carefully about how you want to incorporate your visuals. Practice using them when you rehearse.

Preparation Is Key

After you have adapted the content of your paper, made your notecards, and determined how you want to use visuals, you will need to get comfortable with your presentation. To make sure you are well prepared, videotape your presentation, practice in front of a mirror, or present your report to your family or friends. As you rehearse, work to perfect the content of your report and use the following tips to improve your delivery.

- Speak clearly, using standard American English. Avoid using overly technical terms and slang.
- Modulate your voice to emphasize important points.
- Pause before points you want to emphasize. Pause also to give your audience time to absorb information.
- Use natural, relaxed gestures, and make eye contact with your audience.

Before You Begin

You are now prepared to give a successful oral presentation of your literary research paper. If you feel anxious or unprepared, re-read the advice presented above. Remember, too, that the more times you rehearse, the more comfortable with your presentation you will become.

A Good Oral Presentation

- follows a clear, step-by-step plan
- uses effective verbal and nonverbal speaking techniques
- uses visuals appropriately
- exhibits confidence and enthusiasm
- reveals that care and practice went into planning and rehearsing the presentation

Speaking Tip

If you have speaker's anxiety, take several slow, deep breaths just before your presentation. Then, look for friendly faces in the audience and make eye contact with them. If you lose your place, pause and use your notecards to get started again.

Model the Skill

Deliver Your Literary Research Paper

Remind students that visual aids can enhance their presentations and help their audience better understand the topic. Model using a visual aid to discuss a specific topic, such as population growth in your state. As you discuss the topic, show students a bar graph or line graph that provides more information about the topic.

Guided Practice: Apply

Ask student pairs to brainstorm ideas for visuals to include in their presentations. After students brainstorm, give them an opportunity to create their visual aid.

Teaching Tip

Practice Makes Perfect Have students exchange their research papers with a peer. Then, have each student perform an oral presentation of a section of his or her peer's speech. As the student who wrote the original paper studies the section that has been modified, the other student delivers a short speech based on that section. The listener should jot down comments about the effectiveness of the modifications.

English for Academic Success

Remind students to use formal English when presenting their research paper. They should use informal English, such as slang, only when a character is speaking and only if slang is the appropriate form for the character.

Universal Access

EL English Learners

Have English learners pair up to perfect the delivery of their presentations. Keeping a copy of their presentation for themselves, have students provide a copy to their partner. Then, ask students to listen as their partner reads their speech. Have students take notes on how their partner pronounces difficult words, keeps pace, and emphasizes key words in the speech.

Struggling Learners

Offer the following suggestions to struggling learners for the visual element of their presentations:

- an image slideshow
- a poster with related images or diagrams
- a video clip
- a handmade diagram
- a handout with important statistics, quotes, or points

Assess

UA: Holt Literature Writer and Speaker, Literary Research Evaluation Guide

Standards Focus

Objectives

Students will compare works from different literary periods.

Literary Skills Review

Review

If necessary, use the following questions to guide students in their reading before they answer the questions at the end of the review.

Plot

What are the poems mainly about? ***Possible response:*** *The speaker in both poems addresses the woman he loves and imagines her as an old woman remembering the love they shared and the time that passed.*

Theme

How is the theme of the first poem different from that of the second poem? ***Possible response:*** *Ronsard ends his poem with an exhortation to enjoy youth while it lasts. Yeats's poem has a somber ending, telling about the melancholy view that old lovers have toward their past joys.*

Test-Taking Tip

When you read, look up the meanings of unfamiliar words in the dictionary. You will increase your chances of knowing unfamiliar words during a test-taking situation when reference material is not accessible.

California Standards, pp. 520–521

- **Reading Standard 3.7** Analyze recognized works of world literature from a variety of authors. **a.** Contrast the major literary forms, techniques, and characteristics of the major literary periods (e.g., Homeric Greece, medieval, romantic, neoclassic, modern).

STANDARDS RVIEW

Literary Skills Review

Comparing Literature **Directions:** Read the poems below, and answer the questions that follow.

When You Are Old

by **Pierre de Ronsard**
translated by **Humbert Wolfe**

When you are old, at evening candle-lit
beside the fire bending to your wool,
read out my verse and murmur, "Ronsard writ
this praise for me when I was beautiful."

And not a maid but, at the sound of it,
though nodding at the stitch on broidered stool,
will start awake, and bless love's benefit
whose long fidelities bring Time to school.

I shall be thin and ghost beneath the earth
by myrtle shade in quiet after pain,
but you, a crone,° will crouch beside the hearth
mourning my love and all your proud disdain.
And since what comes tomorrow who can say?
Live, pluck the roses of the world today.

11. crone: old woman.

When You Are Old

by **William Butler Yeats**

When you are old and grey and full of sleep,
And nodding by the fire, take down this book,
And slowly read, and dream of the soft look
Your eyes had once, and of their shadows deep;

How many loved your moments of glad grace,
And loved your beauty with love false or true,
But one man loved the pilgrim soul in you,
And loved the sorrows of your changing face;

And bending down beside the glowing bars,
Murmur, a little sadly, how Love fled
And paced upon the mountains overhead
And hid his face amid a crowd of stars.

Resources for Skills and Standards Review

Unit 2 Resources, Unit Standards Mastery, Unit Vocabulary Review, p. 119

UA: Differentiating Instruction, below-level Chapter Standards Mastery

Teacher One Stop™, editable Chapter Standards Mastery

Focus on Standards with CAHSEE Support

Preparing for the SAT and ACT

ThinkCentral Online Assessment, Chapter Standards Mastery

ThinkCentral Online Remediation

Holt Online Essay Scoring

Reading Standard 3.7a (see pages A48–A50)

1. The speaker in both poems is asking the woman he is addressing to imagine that she
   - **A** is happy in her solitude.
   - **B** is still beautiful in old age.
   - **C** has not been forgotten.
   - **D** is old and reading his poetry.

2. The last two lines of Ronsard's poem are an example of the literary theme known as
   - **A** *carpe diem*.
   - **B** caesura.
   - **C** metaphysical conceit.
   - **D** kenning.

3. What do the last two lines of Ronsard's poem reveal about the speaker's purpose in addressing the woman?
   - **A** He wishes to get even with her for rejecting him.
   - **B** He is trying to persuade her to give in to his advances now.
   - **C** He wishes to immortalize her in a love poem.
   - **D** He is trying to stop her from pursuing him.

4. The roses in the last line of Ronsard's poem symbolize
   - **A** broken promises.
   - **B** flowers.
   - **C** worldly pleasures.
   - **D** compliments.

5. Ronsard's poem is an example of which poetic form?
   - **A** Shakespearean sonnet
   - **B** literary epic
   - **C** Petrarchan sonnet
   - **D** ballad

6. What emotion do both poets hope to evoke in the women they are addressing?
   - **A** pity
   - **B** revenge
   - **C** regret
   - **D** joy

7. How does the attitude toward time expressed in Ronsard's poem reflect Renaissance attitudes on that subject?
   - **A** Ronsard's speaker is acutely aware of the brevity of youth, beauty, and earthly life.
   - **B** Ronsard's speaker is focused on the afterlife rather than earthly life.
   - **C** Ronsard's speaker feels he has enough time to accomplish what he wants in life.
   - **D** Ronsard's speaker expects that time inevitably will bring greater happiness.

Timed Writing

8. In a short essay, compare and contrast these two poems. Focus on tone and the methods the poets use to convey tone.

Assess

Answers and Explanations

1. **D** *In Yeats's poem, the speaker asks the woman to "murmur . . . sadly" (10), so A is incorrect. In Ronsard's poem, the speaker refers to her as beautiful in the past, not in the present (B). In both, the speaker imagines that he is gone, not the woman (C).*
2. **A** *The lines describe living for the moment, or carpe diem.*
3. **B** *The speaker wants the woman to marry him now.*
4. **C** *The theme would suggest that the rose symbolizes opportunities that should be seized.*
5. **A** *The sonnet (A) has the rhyme scheme* abab abab cdcd ee.
6. **C** *They are not begging to be pitied (A). Revenge is too fierce an emotion for aspiring lovers (B). Both realize that joy may come, but it is not the immediate emotion they hope to create (D).*
7. **A** *The speaker knows that earthly life will not last (A), so he encourages the woman to seize the day.*

Timed Writing

8. *Both poets use words connoting death. In the Ronsard poem, the use of mourning in line 12 suggests having love taken away prematurely. In the Yeats's poem, love flees and hides among the stars (lines 10–12). Personifying love and using words associated with death creates a sorrowful tone.*

Word-Attack Skills Mini-Lesson

English for Academic Success

Review Use these activities below to check students' grasp of the word-attack skills taught in this unit.

Activity Have students decide which of the underlined words in each sentence is pronounced as a two- or three-syllable word.

1. The puppy fetched a wretched old doll. [*wretched*]
2. He dragged the ragged toy by a tattered ear across the floor. [*ragged*]
3. Yipping and pouncing, he waged playful war on the aged bear. [*aged*]
4. Then he shoved the beloved plaything under the coach. [*beloved*]

Activity Have students read the following words and state the number of syllables heard in each one.

1. beatific [4]
2. beanery [3]
3. rearrangement [4]
4. spirea [3]
5. zealot [2]
6. preamble [4]

Reteach

go.hrw.com ThinkCentral Online Remediation

Vocabulary Skills Review

Assess

Answers and Explanations

1. ***B*** *Contemplation does not suggest any negative or positive effects, but merely deep thought.*
2. ***C*** *The speaker is frustrated by being confounded, suggesting that it is negative.*
3. ***C*** Insinuated *is used to mean "speculated falsely," which is negative.*
4. ***C*** *Tribulation suggests hardship. The outcome is not positive or neutral.*
5. ***A*** *Diligence leads to a positive end, so it is neither neutral nor negative.*
6. ***C*** *Treachery is committed by a villain, which makes it neither positive nor neutral.*
7. ***C*** Transgression *refers to an infringement of a law, so it has a negative connotation.*

Academic Vocabulary

8. ***A*** *The word* widespread *refers to something that occurs on a large scale.*
9. ***C*** *The word* controversial *means "causing debate or argument."*

Reteach

go.hrw.com ThinkCentral Online Remediation

California Standards, p. 522

- **Grades 9–10 Review Reading Standard**
  1.2 Distinguish between the denotative and connotative meanings of words and interpret the connotative power of words.

STANDARDS REVIEW

Grades 9–10 Review Reading Standard 1.2 (see pages A48–A50)

Vocabulary Skills Review

Denotation and Connotation **Directions:** A word's **denotation** is its dictionary definition. **Connotation,** by contrast, refers to a word's emotional overtones—positive, negative, or neutral. Read each of the following short passages, and identify the connotation of the italicized word as positive, neutral, or negative.

1. John was deep in *contemplation* about which college to attend. Calmly, he gave the decision his complete attention.
A positive
B neutral
C negative

2. The puzzle *confounded* me. The situation was so frustrating that I had to ask two friends for help.
A positive
B neutral
C negative

3. An envious rival *insinuated* that I had not earned my good grades honestly. I was so insulted!
A positive
B neutral
C negative

4. This country experienced severe *tribulation* over the assassination of President John F. Kennedy. There are few things worse for a nation than the violent loss of a leader.
A positive
B neutral
C negative

5. Barb's *diligence* and attention to detail paid off when she took first prize in the science fair.
A positive
B neutral
C negative

6. The villain's *treachery* was a powerful, frighteningly realistic part of the movie.
A positive
B neutral
C negative

7. Many drivers think of speeding as a minor *transgression*, but even a minor violation of the speed limit can cause a fatal accident.
A positive
B neutral
C negative

Academic Vocabulary

Directions: Choose the best definition for the italicized word in each sentence.

8. Macbeth's excessive ambition leads to *widespread* violence.
A occurring in many places
B happening too often
C malicious
D politically motivated

9. The six marriages of Henry VIII made him a *controversial* figure not only in England but in all of Europe.
A unpopular
B deplorable
C subject to disagreement or argument
D subject to ridicule

Vocabulary Review

Use this activity to assess whether students have retained the unit Vocabulary. Ask students to choose the word from the box that fits the content of each sentence.

fragrant	endure	pledge	scorn	surly

1. The bread had a ______ smell as it came out of the oven. [*fragrant*]
2. The soldiers made a ______ of loyalty to their country. [*pledge*]
3. After I was caught cheating, I was met with contempt and ______. [*scorn*]
4. Paul is a great runner who can ______ the steepest paths. [*endure*]
5. The ______ waiter dropped the bread on the table and stormed away. [*surly*]

STANDARDS REVIEW

Writing Standard 2.4a–e (see pages A51–A52)

Writing Skills Review

Write a Historical Research Paper **Directions:** The following passage is a rough draft. It may contain errors in grammar, punctuation, sentence structure, and organization. Read the passage below, and answer the questions that follow.

Rough Draft

(1) The Globe Theater experienced a great many problems in its first few years of existence. (2) First, the theater was closed during plague epidemics in 1603 and 1609. (3) Then, in 1613 it was destroyed by a fire that broke out during a performance of *Henry VIII*. (4) It was rebuilt the following year and flourished for over twenty-eight years. (5) In 1642, the Puritans closed the theater because they believed that plays were the work of the devil. (6) The theater was torn down in 1644 to make room for tenement housing. (7) The exact location of the theater was unknown until 1989, when parts of its original foundation were found beneath Anchor Terrace on Park Street.

1. Which of these transitions could be added to the beginning of sentence 5?
   - **A** However,
   - **B** As a result,
   - **C** For example,
   - **D** Consequently,

2. Which of the following facts would improve a reader's understanding of the time frame?
   - **A** The Globe experienced five major setbacks during its time.
   - **B** The Globe was built in 1599.
   - **C** Citizens were not happy about the theater's location.
   - **D** The Globe was built by the Burbage family.

3. Which statement would appropriately develop one of the paragraph's supporting facts?
   - **A** The Globe was located in Southwark, on the south bank of the Thames River.
   - **B** If the theater had lasted through Cromwell's Puritan administration, it might have survived well into the next century.
   - **C** Fire broke out at the end of the first act of *Henry VIII*, when the firing of a cannon set the thatched roof of the theater ablaze.
   - **D** The original theater was only in use for forty-five years, yet its place as home for Shakespeare's plays made it immortal.

4. Which of the following sources would most likely include additional information on the early history of the Globe?
   - **A** a copy of *Henry VIII*
   - **B** architectural drawings of the Globe Theater
   - **C** a book about the history of London in the 1600s
   - **D** a critical study of Shakespeare's plays

5. Which of the following would be the BEST way to clarify the underlined words in the sentence labeled 1?
   - **A** many foreseeable challenges
   - **B** many diverse mishaps
   - **C** many insurmountable obstacles
   - **D** many unexpected conveniences

6. During an oral presentation of this passage, the speaker should —
   - **A** pause to emphasize important ideas
   - **B** avoid making eye contact in order to focus on the message
   - **C** stand perfectly still while talking
   - **D** speak softly so others may practice their presentations

Writing Skills Review

Assess

Answers and Explanations

1. ***A*** *Sentence 5 is not a result (B), example (C), or consequence (D) of sentence 4. It is a contrast with sentence 4, so A is correct.*
2. ***B*** *C and D are not related to time. A does not give any new information. B would improve the reader's understanding of the time frame.*
3. ***C*** *A, B, and D do not develop any of the paragraph's supporting facts. C develops the fact in sentence 3, which supports the main idea in sentence 1.*
4. ***B*** *A and D would not directly address the Globe. C is too broad and may not have information on the theater. B would provide insight into the design and function of the theater.*
5. ***A*** *B and C are already mentioned in this paragraph. D does not relate to the Globe. A is related but would present new information.*
6. ***A*** *A would help facilitate the audience's understanding and retain their interest. B, C, and D would not.*

Reteach

go.hrw.com **ThinkCentral Online Remediation**

Application **Homework**

Literature and Current Events

Have students use the research and documentation skills they have learned in this workshop to investigate a connection between current events and a piece of literature. Students may investigate connections between a modern novel, short story, or poem, and recent news articles. As they did in the workshop, students should provide a works cited page and follow MLA guidelines. Tasks may be divided between homework and class work.

Extension

Publish Findings in a Documentary

Students should form groups with classmates who have explored a similar theme or piece of literature to create a documentary-style video on their joint topic. In their videos, students should assume the roles of experts when delivering interviews or pointing out findings others have made on the topic. Encourage students to incorporate creative elements such as reenactments, on-site locations, and different media.

California Standards, p. 523

- **Writing Standard 2.4** Write historical investigation reports: **a.** Use exposition, narration, description, argumentation, or some combination of rhetorical strategies to support the main proposition. **b.** Analyze several historical records of a single event, examining critical relationships between elements of the research topic. **c.** Explain the perceived reason or reasons for the similarities and differences in historical records with information derived from primary and secondary sources to support or enhance the presentation. **d.** Include information from all relevant perspectives and take into consideration the validity and reliability of sources. **e.** Include a formal bibliography.

Read On

If students enjoyed the themes and topics explored in this unit, you might recommend these titles for independent reading.

A Note on Web Sites

Web sites and online material change continually and without notice. Holt cannot ensure the accuracy or appropriateness of these materials. Students, teachers, and guardians should assume responsibility for checking all online materials. The sites described on these Read On pages are well established and have been developed for—and in some cases, by—students.

Assessment Options

The following projects can help you evaluate and assess your students' outside work. Videotapes or audiotapes of completed projects may be included in students' portfolios.

Zen and the Art of Surviving Senior Year

After reading *Zen and the Art of Motorcycle Maintenance,* ask students to explore the philosophy behind successfully completing high school. Have them consider questions posed by Robert Pirsig as they relate to battling senioritis, graduating, and preparing for college.

Read On

For Independent Reading

FICTION

Mary, Bloody Mary

The story of Mary Tudor's childhood reads like a classic fairy tale. A princess who was to inherit the throne of England, she is suddenly banished by her father, Henry VIII, then abused by an evil stepmother (who has enchanted her father), and finally, forced to care for her baby stepsister, who inherits Mary's right to the throne. Told in the voice of the young Mary, this novel by Carolyn Meyer explores the history and intrigue of the dramatic rule of Henry VIII and its venomous effect on Mary who, when she becomes Queen of England, is called Bloody Mary for good reason.

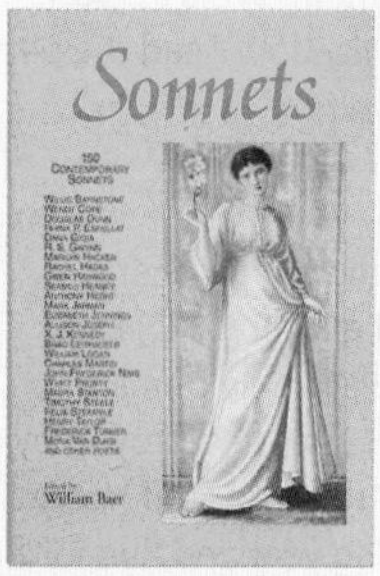

POETRY

Sonnets: 150 Contemporary Sonnets

The poetic form made famous by Shakespeare is making a comeback. This wide-ranging collection of contemporary sonnets showcases the beauty and power of the sonnet structure as employed by some of our most celebrated living poets, including Seamus Heaney, Marilyn Hacker, and Wyatt Prunty. Exploring subjects as diverse as nature, movies, family, politics, and school, these poems show that the sonnet is making its mark on twenty-first-century literature.

NONFICTION

Zen and the Art of Motorcycle Maintenance: An Inquiry into Values

What is the nature of the universe? What is our place in it? Robert Pirsig describes a cross-country road trip, during which the author tours two thousand years of Western philosophy. Focusing on questions that intrigued Francis Bacon and John Milton, Pirsig invites the reader to consider his or her own place in a rapidly changing world.

NONFICTION

Mary, Queen of Scots

Antonia Fraser's goal in this detailed biography is to separate the facts from the fiction surrounding Mary, Queen of Scots, whose life makes most fictional thrillers seem tame. As an infant, she becomes Queen of Scotland and at six years old is sent to live in France as a pawn to secure a Scot-French Catholic alliance against Protestant England. Her French husband dies, and her second husband is murdered. She then marries the man responsible for his murder. The Pope severs relations with Mary, and she is deposed. Frantically hoping for help from Elizabeth, she flees to England.

Word Counts and Readabilities of Read On Books

Fiction	Estimated Word Counts	Readability
Mary, Bloody Mary	46,771	Easily Accessible
Sonnets: 150 Contemporary Sonnets	18,743	Accessible
Hamlet	29,551	Challenging
Rosencrantz and Guildenstern Are Dead	22,975	Accessible
Cyrano De Bergerac	36,944	Accessible

DRAMA

Hamlet

"To be or not to be—that is the question." Often considered Shakespeare's greatest tragedy, *Hamlet* follows the obsession of a young man plagued by his father's death. After a visit from his father's ghost, Hamlet, the prince of Denmark, becomes determined to seek justice at any cost, and a catastrophic chain of events that shatters the royal court soon follows. Shakespeare's masterpiece features some of the most famous and emotionally wrenching soliloquies and poetry in the history of theater.

DRAMA

Rosencrantz and Guildenstern Are Dead

This play turned Tom Stoppard into an overnight sensation. Stoppard took two minor characters from *Hamlet* and made them the center of a play that deals with the illusion of reality, the nature of identity, and how much or how little control we have over an inevitable destiny. The play is both comic and tragic, and although we know the outcome, Stoppard keeps us in suspense until the final lines. This is a play that you will be thinking about for days after you read or see it.

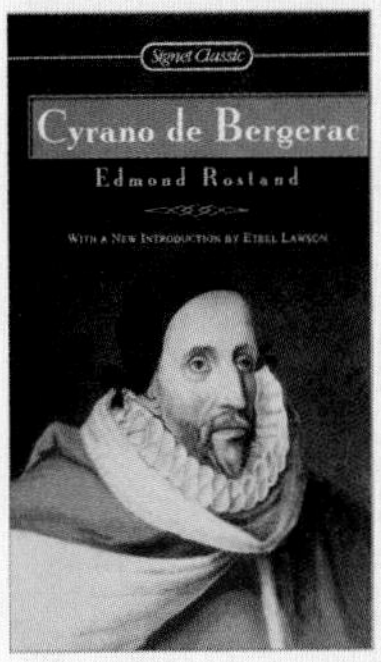

DRAMA

Cyrano de Bergerac

Edmond Rostand used the famous 17th-century French playwright, soldier, and swordsman Cyrano de Bergerac as the inspiration for this boisterous tragicomedy. Cyrano is brilliant, witty (he can compose a poem in the middle of a duel), brave, and hopelessly in love with the beautiful, intelligent Roxane. Fearful of rejection because of his extremely long nose, he can confess his love for Roxane only by putting words into the mouth of Christian, the handsome young man she loves. This love triangle takes readers through one plot twist after another without a dull moment.

WEB SITE

Folger Shakespeare Library

Thou brave tiger-booted wafer-cake! Thou yeasty lily-livered hedge-pig! Learn to distinguish a Shakespearean compliment from a Shakespearean insult. Hear and see audio-video clips with acting tips on expressing anger, amazement, sorrow, love. Check out the radio documentary "Shakespeare Is a Black Woman." Read sonnets written by high-school students. Find out more about Shakespeare's life and work, and follow the links to all things Shakespeare at the Folger Shakespeare Library Web site.

Learn It Online
Explore novels with *NovelWise*.
go.hrw.com H12-525 Go

Nonfiction	Estimated Word Counts	Readability
Zen and the Art of Motorcycle Maintenance: An Enquiry into Values	68,900	Accessible
Mary, Queen of Scots	248,781	Challenging
Folger Shakespeare Library	Web site	Accessible

Assessment Options

Explore a Character

Have students create a visual representation of a character from *Hamlet.* Ask students to create a drawing, painting, sculpture, or collage that reflects the actions, words, and thoughts of the character in the play. Ask them to present their representation to the class and be prepared to defend their choices with evidence from the text.

Film Review

Have students watch the 1990 film version of *Rosencrantz and Guildenstern are Dead* and write a review of the film, comparing and contrasting the filmed version with the written version.

The True Cyrano

Ask students to write and present an oral presentation on the real Cyrano de Bergerac, comparing and contrasting the real person to the fictional character.

Stage a Scene

Have students who read *Mary, Bloody Mary* collaborate to bring an event described in the book to life. Tell students to plan and stage the scene based on details from the book as well as from their imagination. Remind students that they should portray Mary as she is portrayed in the book.

Learn It Online
For more assessment options, see the **Digital Storytelling Mini-site** and the Project-Based Learning Mini-site.
go.hrw.com H12–525 Go

The Restoration and the Eighteenth Century 1660–1800

Chapter 5

Features highlighted in **yellow** constitute a suggested minimum course of study.

Selection or Feature	For Independent Reading	Grade-Level Standards
The Restoration and Eighteenth Century 1660–1800 **Link to Today: 1 Dead in Attic** by Chris Rose (Accessible, Lexile 1020)		
Literary Skills Focus: The Rise of the Novel by Leila Christenbury		**Reading Standard 2.2:** Clarify meaning through structure, repetition, syntax, and word choice. **Reading Standard 3.1:** Analyze subgenres. **Reading Standard 3.7:** Analyze world literature.
Analyzing Visuals: Connecting to Novels		**Reading Standard 3.1:** Analyze subgenres. **Reading Standard 3.7:** Analyze world literature.
from **The Diary of Samuel Pepys** by Samuel Pepys (Challenging, Lexile 1550)	**The Diary of a Young Girl** by Anne Frank	**Reading Standard 3.1:** Analyze subgenres. **Reading Standard 2.4:** Analyze an author's arguments.
Link to Today: Diary of Samuel Pepys Weblog by Tom Regan (Accessible, Lexile 1590)		**Reading Standard 2.2:** Clarify meaning through structure, repetition, syntax, and word choice.
from **A Journal of the Plague Year** by Daniel Defoe (Challenging, Lexile 1460)	• **The Barbary Plague: The Black Death in Victorian San Francisco** by Marilyn Chase • **The Plague** by Albert Camus	**Reading Standard 1.3:** Analogies **Reading Standard 3.3:** Analyze effects of irony, tone, mood, and style. **Grades 9–10 Review** **Reading Standard 3.9:** Narrator's voice and persona
• *from* **Gulliver's Travels (Part 1: A Voyage to Lilliput)** (Accessible, Lexile 1320) • *from* **Gulliver's Travels (Part 2: A Voyage to Brobdingnag)** (Accessible, Lexile 1490) by Jonathan Swift	• **Hatred, Bigotry, and Prejudice: Definitions, Causes, and Solutions** by Robert Baird, ed. • **The Hitchhiker's Guide to the Galaxy** by Douglas Adams	**Reading Standard 2.5:** Analyze philosophical beliefs. **Reading Standard 3.3:** Analyze effects of irony, tone, mood, and style. **Grades 9–10 Review** **Reading Standard 1.1:** Literal and figurative meanings
Reading Skills Focus: Recognizing Persuasive Techniques by Kylene Beers		**Reading Standard 2.2:** Clarify meaning through structure, repetition, syntax, and word choice.
A Modest Proposal by Jonathan Swift (Accessible, Lexile 1850)		**Reading Standard 2.2:** Clarify meaning through structure, repetition, syntax, and word choice. **Reading Standard 3.3:** Analyze effects of irony, tone, mood, and style. **Reading Standard 3.8** Analyze political assumptions. **Reading Standard 3.9:** Analyze philosophical arguments.
Comparing Texts: World Literature: Satirical Novels • *from* **Candide** by Voltaire (Accessible, Lexile 1050) • *from* **Don Quixote** by Miguel de Cervantes (Accessible, Lexile 1460)	• **Animal Farm** by George Orwell • **My World and Welcome to It** by James Thurber • **The Three Musketeers** by E. R. Escober	**Reading Standard 3.1:** Analyze subgenres. **Reading Standard 3.3:** Analyze effects of irony, tone, mood, and style. **Grades 9–10 Review** **Reading Standard 3.4:** Analyze figures of speech. **Writing Standard 2.2:** Write responses to literature.

Daily and Weekly Support

- **Reader/Writer Notebook**
- **Reading and Writing Transparencies**
- **Family Involvement Activities in Spanish**
- **Language Handbook Worksheets**
- **Holt Virtual File Cabinet for Language Arts**

Assessment Resources

- **Unit 3 Resources**, Chapter 5 Diagnostic Test; Selection Standards Checks, Chapter 5 Standards Mastery
- **Universal Access: Differentiating Instruction**, leveled assessment
- **English-Language Conventions Progress-Monitoring Tests**, Chapters 8–9
- **ThinkCentral Online Assessment**

Chapter 6

Selection or Feature	For Independent Reading	Grade-Level Standards
Literary Skills Focus: Form and Function in the Age of Reason by Leila Christenbury		**Reading Standard 3.7:** Analyze world literature.
• **Heroic Couplets** (Accessible, Lexile N/A) • *from* **An Essay on Man** (Accessible, Lexile N/A) by Alexander Pope	• **Candide** by Francois Voltaire • **Cyrano de Bergerac** by Edmund Rostand	**Reading Standard 2.5:** Analyze philosophical beliefs. **Reading Standard 3.4:** Analyze figures of speech.
Reading Skills Focus: Identifying Tone by Kylene Beers		**Reading Standard 3.3:** Analyze effects of irony, tone, mood, and style.
from **The Rape of the Lock** by Alexander Pope (Accessible, Lexile N/A)		**Reading Standard 3.1:** Analyze subgenres. **Reading Standard 3.3:** Analyze effects of irony, tone, mood, and style. **Grades 9–10** **Review Reading Standard 1.1:** Literal and figurative meanings
from **A Dictionary of the English Language** by Samuel Johnson (Accessible, Lexile 1250)	• **The Education of Robert Nifkin** by Daniel Pinkwater	**Reading Standard 2.2:** Clarify meaning through structure, repetition, syntax, and word choice.
Link to Today: ***from*** **The Meaning of Everything** by Simon Winchester (Accessible, Lexile 1500)	• **Something to Declare** by Julia Alverez • **Growing Up Asian American** by Marta Hong	**Reading Standard 2.4:** Analyze an author's arguments.
from **The Life of Samuel Johnson** by James Boswell (Accessible, Lexile 1250)	**Autobiography of Mark Twain** by Mark Twain	**Reading Standard 3.1:** Analyze subgenres. **Reading Standard 3.2:** Theme **Reading Standard 3.3:** Analyze effects of irony, tone, mood, and style.
Elegy Written in a Country Churchyard by Thomas Gray (Challenging, Lexile N/A)	**Novemberland: Selected Poems, 1956–1993** by Gunter Grass	**Reading Standard 2.2:** Clarify meaning through structure, repetition, syntax, and word choice. **Reading Standard 3.1:** Analyze subgenres.
Comparing Texts: Views on Women's Rights • *from* **A Vindication of the Rights of Woman** by Mary Wollstonecraft (Accessible, Lexile 1520) • *from* **The Education of Women** by Daniel Defoe (Accessible, Lexile 970) • *from* **To the Ladies** by Mary, Lady Chudleigh (Accessible, Lexile N/A)	• **The Seneca Falls Inheritance** by Miriam Monfredo • **Restless Spirit: The Life and Work of Dorothea Lange** by Elizabeth Partridge	**Reading Standard 3.1:** Analyze subgenres. **Reading Standard 3.3** Analyze effects of irony, tone, mood, and style. **Reading Standard 3.8:** Analyze political assumptions. **Writing Standard 1.1:** Understand elements of discourse. **Writing Standard 1.3:** Structure and support ideas and arguments.

Daily and Weekly Support

- **Reader/Writer Notebook**
- **Reading and Writing Transparencies**
- **Family Involvement Activities in Spanish**
- **Language Handbook Worksheets**
- **Holt Virtual File Cabinet for Language Arts**

Assessment Resources

- **Unit 3 Resources**, Chapter 6 Diagnostic Test; Selection Standards Checks, Chapter 6 Standards Mastery
- **Universal Access: Differentiating Instruction**, leveled assessment
- **Formal Assessment**, Midyear Summative Test
- **English-Language Conventions Progress-Monitoring Tests**, Chapters 9–10
- **ThinkCentral Online Assessment**

Mastering the Skills

Selection or Feature	Grade-Level Standards
Writing Workshop: Persuasive Essay	**Writing Standard 1.1:** Understanding elements of discourse . **Writing Standard 1.3:** Structure and support ideas and arguments. **Writing Standard 1.4:** Applying rhetorical devices. **Writing Standard 1.5:** Establish tone. **Writing Standard 1.9:** Revise text.
Preparing for Timed Writing	**Writing Standard 1.1:** Understanding elements of discourse.
Listening and Speaking Workshop: Presenting and Analyzing Speeches	**Listening and Speaking Standard 1.4:** Use rhetorical questions, parallel structure, concrete images, figurative language, characterization, irony, and dialogue. **Listening and Speaking Standard 1.5:** Use logical arguments. **Listening and Speaking Standard 1.6:** Use logical, ethical, and emotional appeals. **Listening and Speaking Standard 1.7:** Use rehearsal strategies.
Standards Review: Literary Skills Review Vocabulary Skills Review Writing Skills Review	**Reading Standard 3.7:** Contrast literary works. **Reading Standard 1.3:** Analogies **Writing Standard 1.9:** Revise text.

Print Resources for Universal Access

Unit 3 • Chapter 5

	On-Level Learners	English Learners	Struggling Readers	Students Who Use African American Vernacular English	Advanced Learners	Students with Disabilities
Unit 3 Resources practice and assessment for selections and features in Chapter 5	✔				✔	
Universal Access: Holt Interactive Reader interactive readings for A Modest Proposal and *from* Don Quixote		✔	✔	✔		✔
Universal Access: Differentiating Instruction modified lesson plans for A Modest Proposa and *from* Don Quixote		✔	✔	✔		✔
Universal Access: Resources for Teaching Advanced Students lesson plans for A Modest Proposal and *from* Don Quixote					✔	

Print Resources for Universal Access

Unit 3 • Chapter 6

	On-Level Learners	English Learners	Struggling Readers	Students Who Use African American Vernacular English	Advanced Learners	Students with Disabilities
Unit 3 Resources practice and assessment for selections and features in Chapter 6	✔				✔	
Universal Access: Holt Interactive Reader interactive readings for *from* A Vindication of the Rights of Woman, *from* The Education of Women, To		✔	✔	✔		✔
Universal Access: Differentiating Instruction modified lesson plans for *from* A Vindication of the Rights of Woman, *from* The Education of Women, To		✔	✔	✔		✔
Universal Access: Resources for Teaching Advanced Students lesson plans for *from* A Vindication of the Rights of Woman, *from* The Education of Women, To the Ladies					✔	

Print Resources for Universal Access

All Chapters

	On-Level Learners	English Learners	Struggling Readers/Writers	Students Who Use African American Vernacular English	Advanced Learners	Students with Disabilities
Universal Access: Supporting Instruction in Spanish translations of selection summaries and key terms		✔				
Universal Access: Holt Interactive Writer and Speaker practice and assessment	✔	✔	✔	✔	✔	✔
Language and Sentence Skills Practice for Warriner's Handbook Chapters 8–10	✔				✔	
Universal Access: Developmental Language and Sentence Skills Practice for Warriner's Handbook Chapters 8–10		✔	✔	✔		✔

Technology Resources

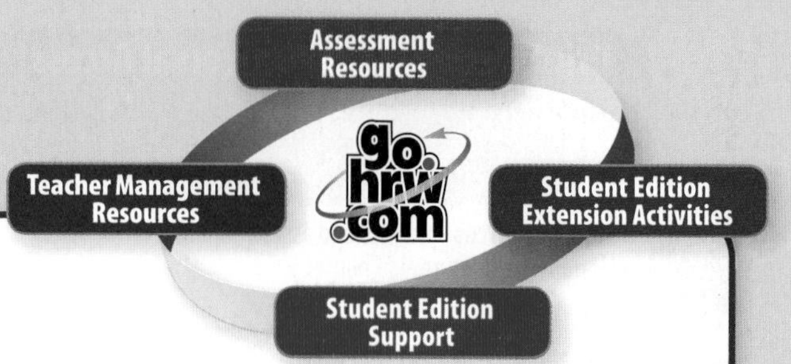

Find all of Holt's technology resources at go.hrw.com. Technology resources are also listed at point of use in the wrap; below are our featured components for Unit 3.

Teacher Management Resources

ThinkCentral, Teacher Access
Teacher One Stop™
Holt Professional Learning for Language Arts

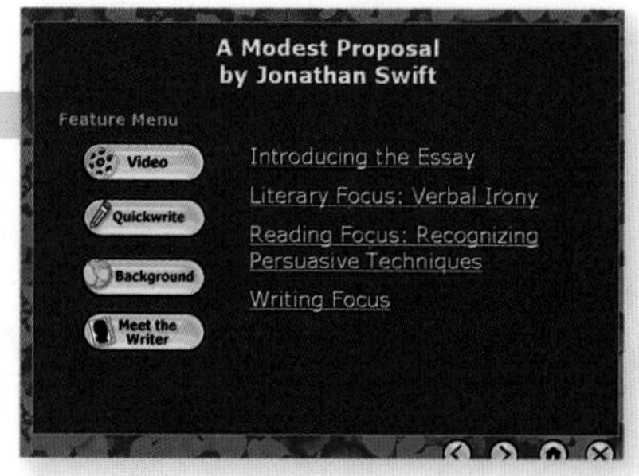

Spotlight on ThinkCentral, Teacher Access

All of the unit's resources are available on the online Teacher's Edition. Online suggestions:

- Use the **PowerNotes** presentations for *A Modest Proposal, Don Quixote*, *A Vindication of the Rights of Women*, and the other minimum course of study selections in this unit.

Student Edition Support

PowerNotes
ThinkCentral, Student Access
Student One Stop™
Interactive Reading Workshops
Interactive Graphic Organizers
Writers' Lives
Holt Audio Library
Holt Audio Library: Selections and Summaries in Spanish

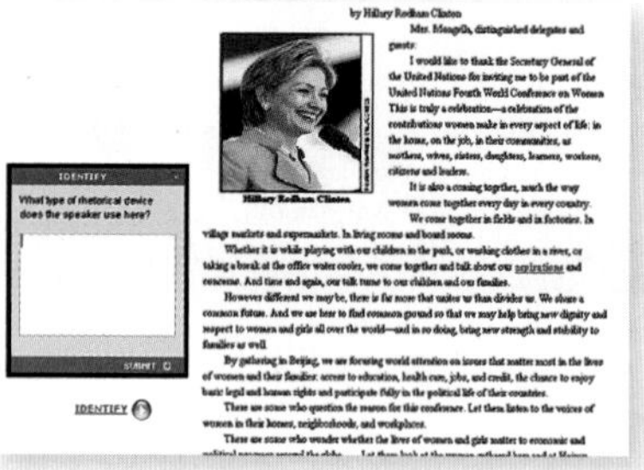

Spotlight on Interactive Reading Workshops

Give your students more practice with recognizing persuasive techniques through this interactive reading workshop. Students can answer pop-up questions, and their answers will be reported to you.

Universal Access: Struggling readers will benefit from this additional, motivational practice.

Supported Strands: Reading, Vocabulary

Student Edition Extension Activities

Digital Storytelling Mini-Site
NovelWise Mini-Site
MediaScope Mini-Site
WordSharp: An Interactive Vocabulary Tutor
GrammarNotes
WritingNotes
Writing and Research in a Digital Age
Literature Links

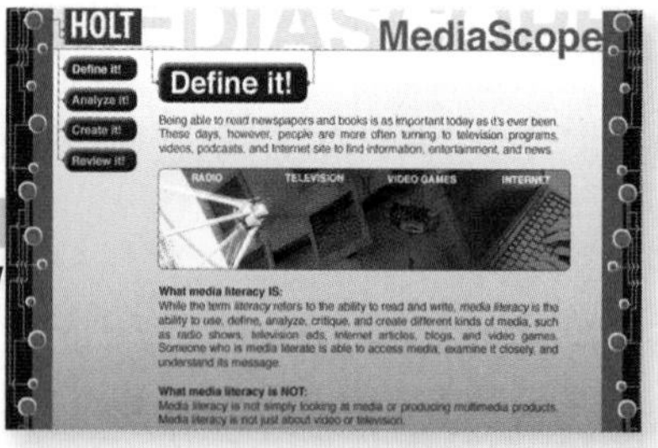

Spotlight on MediaScope Mini-Site

Help students understand and learn how to analyze modern methods of persuasive techniques through the MediaScope site.

Universal Access: English learners may benefit from the opportunity to break down media.

Supported Strand: Writing

Assessment Resources

ThinkCentral Online Assessment
Holt Online Essay Scoring
ThinkCentral Online Remediation

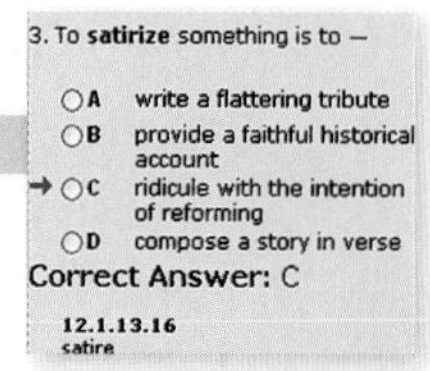

Spotlight on ThinkCentral Online Assessment

Preview and assign the Chapters 5–6 Diagnostic Tests and Standards Mastery here.

Real Issues, Real Experts

The wrap for these selections includes specific ideas and strategies from *Holt Literature and Language Arts* authors.

From the Authors

For *A Modest Proposal* p. 581

Despite having been published almost 300 years ago, *A Modest Proposal* still has the power to shock. Students can outline the logical structure that Swift uses and list examples of offensive language (*breeders, savages, popish,* etc.). They could also discuss what current national or international situation is outrageous enough to inspire a contemporary *Modest Proposal* and what similarly dire events could be seen as analogous to the eighteenth-century Irish crisis.

Leila Christenbury

For Writing Workshop: Persuasive Essay p. 685

One approach I have used to help my students find lively topics for persuasive essays has been to start with the newspaper. Most newspapers will furnish teachers with free copies just for the asking. Give students a copy of a newspaper and ask them to scan the headlines for news stories that pique their interest. Have students clip these articles for future reference. After about 20 minutes, ask students to turn and talk to a partner about one idea they have for an opinion piece.

Carol Jago

Teacher to Teacher

Charlyn Earp
San Diego, California

Preteach: To discuss the various modes of writing that writers of this literary period used to convey their ideas, I bring to class examples of essays, poems (haiku to epic), plays, short stories, and cartoons. I choose some examples with similar topics to demonstrate the various ways to express the same idea. I work with students to list all the modes on the board. Then, we discuss the author's purpose for writing each one.

Direct Teach: Pairs of students peruse as many of the examples as possible. Students then identify the purpose for each piece and compare and contrast pieces.

Assess: Partners decide on an idea they would like to share with the class. They use two different writing modes to express their idea. We publish these by posting them in the room and having students discuss each other's work and the impact of each mode.

Holt Professional Learning

Visit ThinkCentral, Teacher Access to link to Holt's Professional Learning site for English/Language Arts teachers. This site features:

- **Videos that share the insights of *Holt Literature and Language Arts* program authors and consultants and demonstrate proven classroom strategies with master teachers**
- **Study guides for publications by our authors and consultants**
- **Informative articles and useful Web links**
- **Help in planning your department's professional learning sessions**
- **A handbook for new teachers**

Developing Critical Thinking About Literature
with Carol Jago and Deborah Appleman

VIDEO PRODUCTS

Strategies for Helping Struggling Readers
with Kylene Beers

Effective Vocabulary Instruction
with Carol Jago and Kylene Beers

Developing Critical Thinking about Literature
with Carol Jago and Deborah Appleman

Teaching Students to Revise, Not Recopy
with Linda Rief

Teaching English Learners *with Robin Scarcella*

Using Literature Circles
with Harvey Daniels

Teaching On-Demand Writing Skills
with Leila Christenbury

Managing the Heterogeneous Classroom
with Leila Christenbury and Patrick Schwarz

Teaching Narrative and Expository Texts
with Judith Irvin and Deborah Appleman

Becoming a Tech-Savvy Teacher
with Sara Kajder

Re-engaging the Disengaged Student
with Alfred Tatum

Teaching Grammar in Context
with Amy Benjamin

UNIT 3

Unit Objectives

- Students will read excerpts from Samuel Pepys's *Diary,* Defoe's *A Journal of the Plague Year*, and Swift's *Gulliver's Travels* to learn about the rise of the novel in English literature.
- Students will learn to identify the characteristics of parody and satire, and they will compare excerpts from the novels *Candide* and *Don Quixote*.
- Students will learn how England's departure from Puritan rule led to the Restoration period, a time during which reason and order dominated literary and philosophical thinking.
- Students will read excerpts from *An Essay on Man*, *The Rape of the Lock*, and *A Modest Proposal* as examples of literature from the Age of Reason.
- Students will read differing views on women's rights, including excerpts from *A Vindication of the Rights of Women*, *The Education of Women*, and *To the Ladies*.
- At the end of the unit, students will write and present a persuasive essay.

Analyzing Visuals

Extension Activity Ask students to explain how the mansion in the photograph complements the quotation. ***Responses will vary.*** *The symmetrical structure of the mansion and the gardens conveys the idea of "good order."*

Unit Resources

On Course: Mapping Instruction

Unit 3 Resources

Warriner's Handbook
- Chapter 8, Using Verbs Correctly
- Chapter 9–10, Using Modifiers

Teacher One Stop™

Formal Assessment, Midyear Summative Test

English-Language Conventions Progress-Monitoring Tests

ThinkCentral Online Assessment

Holt Virtual File Cabinet for Language Arts, grammar, reading, and vocabulary resources

Holt Pronunciation Resources
- Phoneme Sounds and Spellings
- Support for Speakers of African American Vernacular English

ThinkCentral Online Remediation

Aerial view of Holkham Hall and gardens, home of Lord Leicester. Norfolk, UK.

UNIT 3

The Restoration and the Eighteenth Century

1660–1800

CHAPTER 5
The Rise of the Novel

CHAPTER 6
Examined Lives

"Good order is the foundation of all good things."

—Edmund Burke

What Do You Think? How can order and civilization affect human behavior?

Learn It Online
Find out more about this historical period online.
go.hrw.com H12-527 Go

Real Issues, Real Experts: Professional Learning

Spotlight on . . .
Motivation and Vocabulary Videos

Analyzing works such as *Gulliver's Travels* pose many challenges to students. To help you overcome these challenges, consider the suggestions you'll find in these videos:

Carol Jago and Deborah Appleman, in *Developing Critical Thinking About Literature*, discuss vocabulary development in three ways: preteaching selection vocabulary, teaching academic vocabulary, and teaching students skills to acquire new vocabulary independently.

Becoming a Tech-Savvy Teacher, featuring Holt author **Sara Kajder** demonstrates ways to use technology to improve instruction as a new way of addressing skills.

For these resources and more, visit **Holt Professional Learning** by going to this page in **ThinkCentral, Teacher Access.**

The Quotation

- Tell students that Edmund Burke was born in 1729 and died in 1797. Burke was a political writer who periodically served in the British government. Explain that he was well known as someone who spoke up for people who were treated unfairly at the hands of powerful governments or companies.
- Though Burke believed that Britain had the right to hold colonies, he also cautioned against taking advantage of them. As reflected in the quote, he believed that basic social institutions had to be preserved. Burke supported change and reform, but not revolution. For this reason, he did not support the French Revolution.

Routines for California Classrooms

For ideas on classroom practices and approaches to grouping, see the discussion of routines on pages T34–T37 of this Teacher's Edition.

What Do You Think?

How can order and civilization affect human behavior?

- Have students discuss what life might be like without social order. Ask students to consider how social order results from an agreement among people. Conversely, ask them to think about times when governments impose order on others.
- Have students write about a situation in which social order might be absent. Ask them to explain what the consequences might be.
- Direct students to the time line to help them think about how historical events influenced British perspectives on order and reason.

Learn It Online
The *Best of All Possible Worlds* video is a brief, fast-paced introduction to the various forms that literature takes in the Neoclassical period.
go.hrw.com H12–527 Go

Direct Teach

Teach the Time Line

Give students five to ten minutes to study the time line. Then, ask the following questions:

- Which two works of British literature are concerned with human rights? ***Possible response:*** *Jonathan Swift's* A Modest Proposal *and Mary Wollstonecraft's* A Vindication of the Rights of Woman.
- What three significant scientific advances took place in British history between 1660 and 1800? ***Possible response:*** *Sir Isaac Newton published* Mathematical Principles of Natural Philosophy, *James Watt invented the steam engine, and Edward Jenner developed a vaccination for smallpox.*
- What did China, Spain, and Russia have in common based on events in the World Events time line? ***Possible response:*** *The three nations were all expanding their territories.*

California Standards, pp. 528–529

- **Reading Standard 3.7** Analyze recognized works of world literature from a variety of authors: **c.** Evaluate the philosophical, political, religious, ethical, and social influences of the historical period that shaped the characters, plots, and settings.

The Restoration and the Eighteenth Century 1660–1800

This time line represents a snapshot of British literary events, British political and social events, and world events from 1660 to 1800. During this time, England saw the monarchy restored and Protestant succession secured. An interest in rationality emerged and the arts flourished.

BRITISH LITERARY EVENTS

1660

1660 Samuel Pepys begins his diary

1660s London theaters reopen after being closed by Puritans; actresses appear onstage for the first time

1668 John Dryden is named poet laureate of England

1678 John Bunyan publishes Part 1 of *The Pilgrim's Progress*

1680

1709 Richard Steele starts *The Tatler*, an early newspaper; he and Joseph Addison start *The Spectator* in 1711

Sir Richard Steele (1711) by Sir Godfrey Kneller. The Granger Collection.

1712 Alexander Pope publishes part of his mock epic, *The Rape of the Lock*

1719 Daniel Defoe publishes *Robinson Crusoe*

1729 Jonathan Swift publishes *A Modest Proposal,* protesting English treatment of the Irish poor

BRITISH POLITICAL AND SOCIAL EVENTS

1660

1660 Charles II assumes the British throne, beginning the Restoration

1665 More than 68,000 Londoners die from the plague

1666 The Great Fire of London destroys much of the city

Illustration of Sir Isaac Newton and his telescope.

1680

1687 Sir Isaac Newton publishes *Mathematical Principles of Natural Philosophy,* establishing scientific laws of motion and gravity

1689 Glorious (Bloodless) Revolution; James II, a Catholic, is succeeded by Protestant monarchs William and Mary

1690 John Locke publishes an *Essay Concerning Human Understanding,* a landmark of rationalist philosophy

1695 The Penal Laws and the Test Act of 1673 deprive Catholics of civil rights

1707 England, Scotland, and Wales are unified politically as Great Britain

WORLD EVENTS

1660

1661–1715 Louis XIV rules in France, the center of cultural influence for the time

1660s Moliere stages *The School for Wives, Tartuffe,* and *The Misanthrope* to scandal and acclaim in Paris

1670s Ashanti Empire is formed in Africa

1675 King Philip's War erupts between colonists and Native Americans in New England

1680

1700s Spain establishes colonies in South America, Mexico, and the Philippines

1721 Russian ruler Peter the Great takes over Sweden as he expands the Russian Empire

Peter the Great Defeating the Swedes at Poltava in 1709 (1764). Tapestry.

Universal Access

English Learners/ Struggling Readers

English for Academic Success Read each section of the time line with students and clarify the following words and phrases that may impede their understanding.

- **British Literary Events:** *poet laureate, periodical, elegy, influential, vindication, prophetic, lyrical*
- **British Political and Social Events:** *assumes, plague, succeeded, monarchs, motion, gravity, deprive, rationalist, economic, vaccination*
- **World Events:** *influence, scandal, acclaim, czarina, symphony, deciphering, hieroglyphs*

Reading Standard 3.7c (see pages A48–A50)

Your Turn

In a small group, review the time line, and discuss which British literary, political, and social events probably had the most impact on other cultures, including American culture.

1740 — **1780** — **1800**

1740 Samuel Richardson publishes *Pamela, or Virtue Rewarded*

1751 Thomas Gray writes *Elegy Written in a Country Churchyard,* one of the most influential English poems

1755 Samuel Johnson publishes his *Dictionary of the English Language*

1773 Oliver Goldsmith writes the comedy of manners *She Stoops to Conquer*

1791 James Boswell's *The Life of Samuel Johnson* is published

1792 Mary Wollstonecraft publishes *A Vindication of the Rights of Woman*

1793 William Blake begins work on his prophetic books and introduces his personal mythology

1798 William Wordsworth and Samuel Taylor Coleridge publish early Romantic work *Lyrical Ballads*

1740 — **1780** — **1800**

1754 Seven Years' War ends; Britain controls most territories throughout North America

1765 James Watt invents steam engine, which powers Industrial Revolution ›

1775 War with American colonies begins

1776 Adam Smith's early economic work *Wealth of Nations* appears

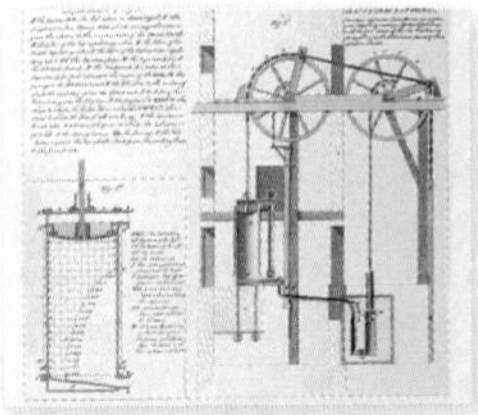

Patent drawing by James Watt of a steam engine.

1780 British put down Irish nationalist rebellion

1798 Edward Jenner develops smallpox vaccine ›

Edward Jenner Performing the First Vaccination Against Smallpox in 1796 (1879) by Gaston Melingue. Academie Nationale de Medicine, Paris, France.

1740 — **1780** — **1800**

1742 George Frideric Handel's *Messiah* is first performed in Dublin, Ireland

1759 Voltaire's *Candide* is published

1762 Catherine the Great becomes czarina of Russia; expands Russian Empire into Poland

1765 Mozart writes *Symphony No. 1* at age nine

1780s Slave trade peaks in Africa

1789 French Revolution begins

1799 Rosetta Stone, the key to deciphering Egyptian hieroglyphs, is discovered in Egypt ›

The Rosetta Stone (196 B.C.), from Fort St. Julien, el-Rashid (Rosetta), Egypt, British Museum, London.

Advanced Learners

Enrichment As you discuss the time line, draw students' attention to Richard Steele and the periodical *The Tatler*. Explain that Steele and another writer, Joseph Addison, wrote essays in *The Tatler* and later created the daily newspaper *The Spectator*. Both of these publications contained influential writings of the day aimed at reforming public manners and morals. The two men also impacted the development of the essay as a form of writing. Have students find out more about *The Tatler* or *The Spectator* by reading selections from either publication in print or online media.

Students with Disabilities

Tell students that the three time lines show events from the years 1660–1800. Explain that students can compare events on the three time lines by reading the page vertically. Model how to connect an event on the British literature time line to contemporary events in British and world history. You might say: "Around 1660, Samuel Pepys began his diary and London theaters were reopened. At about that same time, Louis XIV ruled in France and the Ashanti Empire in Africa was being formed."

Check for Understanding

Your Turn

Tell students that they should be able to identify which British literary, political, and social events had the most impact on other cultures and why.

Explore the Time Line

Enrichment The following activity offers options for students to explore the literary, political, social, and world events presented on the time line.

Group Activity Point out to students that British politics had a strong influence on literature.

- Divide the class into small groups. Have each group choose either the Puritans or Charles II to learn how each influenced literature.
- Have each group research its assigned topic, focusing on these questions: In what ways did government policies and attitudes influence literature? What is the relationship between a society's government and the literature its writers produce?
- As students research their topic, remind them to relate their research to the unit question: How can order and civilization affect human behavior?
- Have groups present their findings to the class. Remind students to discuss how order and civilization affect human behavior.

Standards Focus

Objectives

Students will evaluate the philosophical, political, religious, ethical, and social influences of a historical period.

Preteach

Key Concepts

Use the Key Concepts to preview the unit introduction. Each key concept is addressed in a separate section of the essay that relates the concept to both the history and the literature of the times.

Set a Purpose for Reading

- Ask students to identify one piece of information from each key concept about which they want to learn more.
- Have students jot down references to philosophical, political, religious, ethical, and social influences during the Restoration period. Suggest that students create a chart to organize their notes.
- Tell students to record each section's main ideas and important details in their **Reader/Writer Notebooks.**

The Restoration and the Eighteenth Century

1660–1800

The Restoration followed nearly twenty years of civil war and Puritan rule. The Church of England regained its power, and ushered in a sophisticated age of taste, refinement, and luxury. Reaction to the Roman Catholicism of James II brought about the Glorious Revolution of 1688, and Protestant succession to the throne of England was secured. In literature, the genius of the age was satire, addressed chiefly to the educated and leisured classes. A growing base of middle-class readers encouraged new forms of popular literature.

KEY CONCEPTS

Order and Reason

History of the Times With the restoration of the monarchy, stability returned to England after years of war. Fire and disease ravaged London in the 1660s, but by the middle of the eighteenth century, calm and order reigned. A new scientific and rational age emerged.

Literature of the Times Theater reflected the life of the upper classes. Satirists attacked the immorality and bad taste of the age. Journalism began. Writers of the neoclassical school revived standards of order and balance found in the classical literature of ancient Rome.

Social Classes

History of the Times The social order of England was based on a class system, with the hereditary nobility at the top and a large impoverished class at the bottom. Toward the end of the period, the Industrial Revolution was creating overcrowded slums and wretched working conditions.

Literature of the Times On the stage, comedies of manners appealed to men and women of fashion. Writers were still dependent on patrons, but this system gave way to large numbers of professional writers who created works for the middle classes.

Values and Beliefs

History of the Times The labels *Age of Enlightenment* and *Age of Reason* reveal how people viewed themselves. Religious views were influenced by the philosophy of rationalism. A movement called deism proposed that God could be discovered through the use of reason and the observation of nature.

Literature of the Times Writers used satire to expose moral corruption and commercialism. Journalists also advocated reforms. At the end of the period, focus shifted from elegance, taste, and reason toward emotional expression.

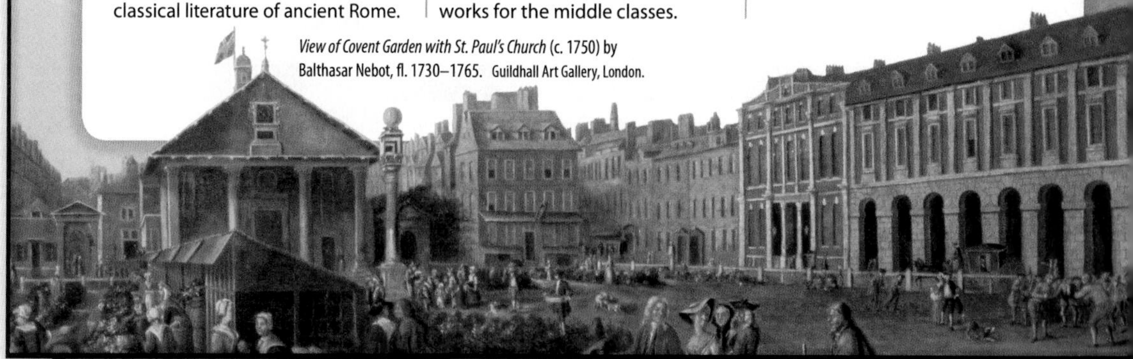

View of Covent Garden with St. Paul's Church (c. 1750) by Balthasar Nebot, fl. 1730–1765. Guildhall Art Gallery, London.

California Standards, pp. 530–535

- **Reading Standard 2.2** Analyze the way in which clarity of meaning is affected by the patterns of organization, hierarchical structures, repetition of the main ideas, syntax, and word choice in the text.
- **Reading Standard 3.7** Analyze recognized works of world literature from a variety of authors: **b.** Relate literary works and authors to the major themes and issues of their eras. **c.** Evaluate the philosophical, political, religious, ethical, and social influences of the historical period that shaped the characters, plots, and settings.

Resources

Unit 3 Resources, on-level instruction, Historical Introduction Study Guide, p. 1

UA: Holt Interactive Reader, Key Concepts and Academic Vocabulary, p. 147

PowerNotes, interactive lesson presentation with activities go.hrw.com

Teacher One Stop™, on-level lesson plans and all print resources

Universal Access

EL English Learners/ Struggling Readers

To help students retain the facts in this essay, have them generate two comprehension questions for every page of text. Have students jot down notes in response. Then, have small groups of students take turns answering the questions orally. Clarify confusing points.

Reading Standard 2.2, 3.7b, 3.7c (see pages A48–A50)

UNIT 3 INTRODUCTION

KEY CONCEPT

Order and Reason

History of the Times

In 1660, after twenty years of civil war and Puritan dictatorship, England was ready for stability and the return of Charles II. Five years later, London suffered an outbreak of plague, and the Great Fire of 1666 destroyed much of the city. By the middle of the 1700s, however, England had reached a time of peace and calm. The Glorious Revolution of 1688 that enabled William and Mary to take the throne occurred without bloodshed. During this era, Parliament became more powerful, and a two-party political system emerged.

This period of order allowed Britain's great thinkers to excel in their fields. Because at the time rational thought was considered the most powerful way to approach the world, this era is often called the Enlightenment or the Age of Reason. The work of Sir Isaac Newton and others fostered the concept that the universe was a perfect mechanism, set in motion by God, that could be understood through observation and reason. Many fields benefited from this new way of thinking.

Literature of the Times

Literature in the Restoration was influenced by French classical ideas and preferences. An emphasis on brilliance and cleverness, known as **wit,** is characteristic of literature written for the privileged classes. Satire became a dominant form in the works of English writers such as Alexander Pope and Jonathan Swift.

Writers who worked in the neoclassic tradition used forms imitating the Latin classics. For this reason, the age has also been called the Augustan Age after the Roman emperor Augustus, who was a patron of writers and artists. Pope adopted the classic epic form for his mock epic, *The Rape of the Lock.* He used the traditional literary devices found in serious epics to compose his comic narrative poem. Augustan poets are also known for their preference for public themes. Not until the end of the period did a new kind of poetry expressing private themes appear.

Comprehension Check

How do the labels *Age of Reason*, *Enlightenment*, and *Augustan Age* summarize this period?

Fast Facts

Political and Social Highlights

- Charles II is restored to the throne in 1660, ushering in an era of stability.
- William and Mary assume the throne in 1689, securing Protestant succession.
- Great Britain is formed in 1707 when Scotland and Wales are politically aligned with England.
- War erupts between Britain and the American colonies in 1775.

Literary Highlights

- After closure by Puritan leaders in 1642, theaters reopen in the 1660s, paving the way for Restoration dramatists.
- Alexander Pope and Jonathan Swift write accomplished satires in verse and in prose.
- A new profession, journalism, emerges.
- The novel finds an audience in the middle class. *Robinson Crusoe* (1719) by Daniel Defoe may be the first English novel.

Learn It Online
Go online for information on this historical period.
go.hrw.com H12-531 Go

Direct Teach

Think About/Talk About

Motivate Tell students that restoration of the monarchy, which people saw as the natural order of things, inspired a period of rationalism in philosophy and literature. Ask students to consider ways that political and social conditions in a society can influence all types of literature. To support their ideas, have students offer examples from different times and places.

History of the Times

Tell students that the Bloodless Revolution was an important step in an ongoing process in which power shifted back and forth between a British king or queen and the people represented by the Parliament.

Literature of the Times

Point out that the social conditions of the eighteenth century prompted some writers to create satires and essays aimed at awakening the public to the harsh treatment of the poor or discrimination against women. Authors such as Jonathan Swift and Mary Wollstonecraft hoped that their writing would bring about changes in society.

Comprehension Check

Possible response: *The labels* Age of Reason, Enlightenment, *and* Augustan Age *give the impression of a time that is governed by rational thought, a quest for knowledge, and a desire for stability.*

Advanced Learners

Acceleration Have students discuss in small groups how novels have changed since the 1700s. Tell them to include examples for each suggested change. Students could focus on how novels now include genres such as mystery, fantasy, and science fiction. Students might also discuss changes in how authors use dialogue or plot structure.

Students with Disabilities

Initiate an instructional discussion with students by having them complete the blanks:

- The restoration of the monarchy brought to England a sense of ______.
- Literature during the Restoration criticized ______.
- Most of the population of England was concentrated near the ______ of the class system.
- This period is also referred to as ______ and ______.

Learn It Online
You can introduce some of the topics in this unit using brief videos about the literature of this period.
go.hrw.com H12-531 Go

Think About/Talk About

History of the Times

- In 1696, a tax was instituted on windows, which prompted many people to block up their windows to avoid the tax. Blocking windows created stagnant air and a lack of light. Space and air seemed luxuries that only the rich could afford.
- Although medical science had begun to develop, superstition still marked the treatment of the sick in the early part of the eighteenth century. For example, smallpox was commonly treated with a black powder made by burning thirty to forty live toads. Bleeding served as a remedy for most ailments. As odd as it might seem today, the connection between dirt and disease had not yet been made by the medical profession.

Literature of the Times

Tell students that Jonathan Swift once remarked, "Satire is a sort of glass wherein beholders do generally discover everybody's face but their own."

KEY CONCEPT

Social Classes

History of the Times

When Charles II returned from exile in France, he brought with him the lavish and leisured culture of the French aristocrats. Formal and artificial fashions included makeup, powdered wigs, and elaborate clothing. The upper classes attended balls, dances, plays, gambling soirees, and dinner parties. They retreated to seaside spas during the summer, spent the social season in town, and lived intermittently at their country houses. Change in fashion, however, was inevitable, and by the end of the eighteenth century, the period of elegance and excess was coming to an end.

During this same time, the indigent suffered from bad health, inadequate living conditions, and a lack of education. Excrement littered the city streets, rapidly spreading disease. Tenements in London, where entire families could live in a single rat-infested room, were overcrowded and filthy. Poor people often died young; at one point, 74 percent of children in London died before they turned five.

Children were expected to work, and abuse was common. Industrialization transformed towns into gritty manufacturing centers. As merchants grew rich, lower-class workers were left behind. Charities and the government offered little help, and debtors who were unable to pay their bills were frequently sent to prison.

Because physicians practiced medicine almost exclusively with the rich, little was known about the illnesses of the poor. Lack of personal hygiene contributed to their general state of bad health.

Literature of the Times

After the return of Charles II, English writers were receptive to French wit and French literary taste. The literary form that had the greatest success during the period following the Restoration was the drama, which reflected the sophistication of Charles's court.

The first half of the eighteenth century was memorable for the satire of Alexander Pope and

Link to Today

Political Cartoons and Caricatures

Satire was not confined to writers during the eighteenth century. Visual artists were also sharp social critics. William Hogarth (1697–1764) satirized contemporary life in his paintings and engravings.

Earthly Airbus by Alen Lauzan Falcon.

One form of visual satire with a long history is the political cartoon. Today, political cartoons appear in newspapers and magazines. They often include **caricatures**—portraits that exaggerate notable physical characteristics of a person. The leading caricaturist of the eighteenth century was the Englishman James Gillray (1756–1815), who ridiculed George III and the French Revolution. His work continues to influence today's satirists.

As an art form, caricature dates back to the fifteenth and sixteenth centuries. Italian artists Leonardo da Vinci and Annibale Carracci produced portraits of public figures with exaggerated physical features to satirize ridiculous behavior. During the Protestant Reformation, Martin Luther used editorial cartoons as a way for illiterate peasants to understand his criticisms of the Catholic Church.

Political cartoons and caricatures are still meaningful. They use visual appeal and humor to entertain and comment on social and political conditions. Just look at the editorial pages of today's newspapers—you'll see a brand of satire that echoes James Gillray and the 1700s.

Ask Yourself

With a partner, analyze William Hogarth's engraving on the next page. What is being satirized? What is the message?

Cross-Curricular Connection

HISTORY: Cromwell and Charles II

One reason Charles II was restored to power was the failures of Oliver Cromwell's rule. Cromwell had begun by taking democratic measures: He abolished the monarchy and the House of Lords, instituted the commonwealth (a republican form of government), and oversaw the drafting of a constitution for England. Beset with problems, however, Cromwell set aside the constitution and imposed military rule. He also instituted a strict Puritan morality, which made illegal such leisure-time activities as attending the theater.

The stress of governing England weighed heavily on Cromwell. In 1658, not long before he died, he told Parliament, "I would have been glad to have lived under my woodside, and to have kept a flock of sheep, rather than to have undertaken this government."

Jonathan Swift and the essays of Richard Steele and Joseph Addison. All of these writers proclaimed the need for traditional values and saw in literature a means of asserting good sense and controlling folly and vice. These writers did not hesitate to criticize their own upper-class audience. Pope's mock epic, *The Rape of the Lock,* ridiculed the lifestyle of the aristocracy by treating a petty quarrel as an epic battle.

The Enraged Musician (1741) by William Hogarth.

The dominant literary figure during the second half of the eighteenth century was Samuel Johnson, considered the most learned man of his day. Johnson represents a transition from the Augustan period to the Romantic period. He is responsible for the first comprehensive dictionary of the English language, which became the basis for all subsequent English dictionaries.

By the middle of the century, new genres were becoming popular with a growing middle-class readership. Women as well as men were in the ranks of new readers. The familiar periodical essay made its appearance in the *Tatler* and later in the *Spectator.*

The novel had differentiated itself from travel narratives and journalistic writing. Writers were creating longer fictional works that often were filled with adventures. Daniel Defoe's *Robinson Crusoe,* a series of fictional letters written by a shipwrecked sailor, is considered by some to be the first English novel. Experiments in prose fiction resulted in other early novels such as Henry Fielding's raucous *Tom Jones,* Samuel Richardson's tragic *Clarissa,* and Laurence Sterne's hilarious hodge-podge *The Life and Opinions of Tristram Shandy, Gentleman.* Women writers also entered the literary arena for the first time and in large numbers, led by Aphra Behn, Eliza Haywood, and Fanny Burney.

Comprehension Check

How did the different social and economic classes in English society lead to the development of various types of literature?

Primary Source

Locke on Religious Tolerance

In 1690, early in the reign of William and Mary, John Locke published *A Letter Concerning Tolerance*. In this treatise, he presented what seemed at the time a radical idea: that people's religious beliefs are their private business and not matters in which a government should involve itself. He wrote: "If a Roman Catholick believe that to be really the body of Christ, which another man calls bread, he does no injury thereby to his neighbour. If a Jew do not believe the New Testament to be the word of God, he does not thereby alter any thing in men's civil rights. If a Heathen doubt both Testaments, he is not therefore to be punished as a pernicious citizen. The power of the magistrate, and the estates of the people, may be equally secure, whether any man believe these things or not. . . . [T]he business of laws is not to provide for the truth of opinions, but for the safety and security of the Commonwealth, and of every particular man's goods and persons."

Think About/Talk About

Link to Today

Political Cartoons and Caricatures

This feature explains how artists during the eighteenth century satirized contemporary life.

1. Ask these questions to help students build background: What are examples of political cartoons today? Where would you most likely find political cartoons?
2. After students have read the feature, ask them to discuss how images can increase the impact of a satirical statement.
3. Encourage students to focus on the images and words the cartoonist emphasizes. Have students identify what stands out to them.
4. Have students discuss how satirists today use broadcast media and the Internet to satirize the world around them.

Comprehension Check

Possible responses: *Writers began for the first time to address the concerns and ideals of the growing middle class. Also, journalistic writing gave way to a consumerist enjoyment of literature.*

Think About/Talk About

History of the Times

Tell students that during the exile of the royal court in France, Charles II became addicted to the theater. After lifting the ban on theater, Charles and his brother James patronized companies of actors. Boys and men no longer acted female roles. The new theater had female actors, and the new plays emphasized the sexual relations of men and women in unsentimental and unromantic ways.

Link to Today
The Coffeehouse Awakening

This feature explains that coffeehouses became very popular in Restoration England.

1. Ask these questions to help students build background: Why might so many coffeehouses have opened after Charles II began to go to the theater? How was his attitude different from previous kings?
2. After students have read the feature, ask them to consider which places today have become settings for discussions and debates.
3. Have students consider the physical space of a coffee shop. What furniture would it have? What colors would it use to decorate? How does one's physical surroundings promote discussion?
4. Encourage interested students to do further research on the history of coffee shops in their neighborhoods.

KEY CONCEPT

Values and Beliefs

History of the Times

Church and state were tightly interwoven during the Restoration and the eighteenth century. When Charles II began his rule in 1660, he immediately reopened the theaters, which had been closed by Puritan leaders in 1642 because the Puritans believed plays were immoral. Theatergoing again became popular, and for the first time women were allowed to perform on stage.

Although Charles was a Protestant, his brother and heir, James II, was Roman Catholic. British leaders, who recalled both the Catholic backlash of Bloody Mary Tudor and the strict Puritanism of Cromwell's dictatorship, feared a monarch who favored alliances with the Catholic powers of Europe. For that reason, Parliament expelled James in the Glorious Revolution (so called because it occurred without any bloodshed) and offered the monarchy to his Protestant daughter, Mary, and her Dutch husband, William of Orange. They accepted, ruling equally as William III and Mary II. The Anglican Church was the official church of England.

Although William and Mary were a safe choice for a Parliament fearing religious turmoil, they were not a choice that provided religious freedom. William and Mary and succeeding monarchs restricted the rights of Catholics, Puritans, and others who did not belong to the Church of England. The Test Act of 1673 deprived Catholics of the right to hold office, and the Penal Laws of 1695 withheld civil rights from Irish Catholics. Persecution of religious minorities continued well into the eighteenth century.

The rise of rationalism in the eighteenth century created another form of spirituality called **deism,** a belief system based on reason and the observation of nature. Deists, such as Isaac Newton and John Locke, believed a creator had set an orderly universe in motion and then allowed it to run its own course without divine intervention. Although many intellectuals embraced deism, Christianity continued to dominate Europe, as it had in the Middle Ages and the Renaissance.

Literature of the Times

The Anglican Church dominated religious life as the state religion. Protestants who remained outside the Anglican Church were known as Dissenters. Like Roman Catholics, they were subject to various civil restrictions. Prominent writers of this period were Roman Catholics and Dissenters.

John Dryden, a Catholic, was England's poet laureate for nearly twenty years, but he had to resign his post in 1688 when Catholics were denied public office following the expulsion of James II.

Link to Today

The Coffeehouse Awakening

In many urban areas today, a coffeehouse appears on almost every corner. Coffeehouses have become popular spots for refreshment, relaxation, conversation, and reading.

Charles Dickens Coffee House in London, England.

Coffeehouses were also exceedingly popular in Restoration England. In fact, 3,000 coffeehouses opened in London after Charles II was restored to the throne. The times were more lighthearted after years of dour Puritan rule, and the Age of Reason promoted lively philosophical and intellectual debates, which often occurred in those coffeehouses.

Ask Yourself

How might you design a coffeehouse today that promotes philosophical and intellectual discussions?

Cross-Curricular Connection

POLITICS: The Test Act

Point out that the Test Act of 1673 deprived Catholics in England of the right to hold public office and that other laws discriminated against non-Anglican populations.

Group Activity Divide the class into groups of four. Within these groups, have pairs of students use online and print sources to learn about laws in American history that deprived specific groups of people the right to vote or hold office. Have students consider these questions:

- What groups of people have been deprived of basic political rights in our history?
- In what ways did the social order in the United States fail the population as a whole?
- What happened to change these situations?

Have students discuss in their groups what they learned. Ask each group to write a brief composition that responds to the questions.

HSS Analysis Skills: CS 1, HI 1, 4

King William III and Queen Mary III (18th century). Eg. 2572. Folio No: 16. British Museum, London.

Alexander Pope's Roman Catholic faith excluded him from a university education and a public position despite his prodigious talents.

Because Daniel Defoe was a Presbyterian, he was not permitted to attend Oxford or Cambridge. He reacted to the religious intolerance of his time by writing *The Shortest Way with Dissenters,* which reduced the position of the authorities to absurdity. Defoe pretended to support the Anglican policy against Dissenters. The authorities at first took his writing literally, but when they discovered that he was actually being ironic, they decided to punish him. He was arrested, tried, and sentenced to three appearances in the pillory. While crowds usually further degraded criminals in the pillory by throwing rotten vegetables and rocks at them, in this case, a group of Defoe's friends sang a satiric song he had composed, threw flowers at him, and cheered him for defying the government.

Comprehension Check

What influence did religion and morality have during this era, which is sometimes called the Age of Satire?

Wrap Up

Talk About . . .

With a partner, discuss what injustices or follies satirists are likely to ridicule. Try to use each **Academic Vocabulary** word at least once in your discussion.

Write About . . .

Alexander Pope said "Satire's my weapon." How effective is satire compared to other weapons of criticism? Explain your response in two paragraphs.

Academic Vocabulary for Unit 3

Talking and Writing About Literature

Academic Vocabulary is the language you use to write and talk about literature. Use these words to discuss the works you read in this unit. These words are underlined throughout the unit.

approach (uh PROHCH) *n.:* way of addressing something. *The satiric approach sometimes exaggerates a flaw to ridicule it.*

convince (kuhn VIHNS) *v.:* persuade; cause to believe. *Writers of satire try to convince readers to correct social problems.*

dominate (DAHM uh nayt) *v.:* hold a commanding position. *What philosophies dominate the Age of Reason?*

enhance (ehn HANS) *v.:* improve the quality of. *Pope's skillful epic similes enhance the mock epic,* The Rape of the Lock.

participate (pahr TIHS uh payt) *v:* take part in. *William and Mary restricted the rights of Catholics to participate in government.*

Your Turn

Copy the Academic Vocabulary list into your *Reader/Writer Notebook*. Then, use the information you have learned from the unit introduction to write a sentence for each word, discussing some aspect of English literature from 1660 to 1800.

Check for Understanding

Talk About . . .

Students might begin by brainstorming examples of satire in their society (political satire, vignettes). Encourage students to identify themes or topics of satire. Students may note that many satirists focus on those who have power over others and treat them unfairly. Students might also note that satirists target aspects of culture they deem silly or immoral.

Write About . . .

Students might argue that satire is very effective because it can be witty and subtle as well as caustic and rebellious. Some may say that satire is not as effective as direct statements of fact backed up with evidence. Students should give examples to support their ideas. Examples might come from the Restoration as well as from contemporary American culture.

Comprehension Check

Possible responses: *Religion and morality had a very strong influence on the era. Religious affiliation affected people's right to speak out and to be educated. The government discriminated against those who were not Anglicans. Many writers wrote about some aspect of religion or religious practice.*

PowerNotes, Academic Vocabulary lesson and activities

go.hrw.com **WordSharp: An Interactive Vocabulary Tutor,** more practice with academic language

Academic Vocabulary

Talking and Writing About Literature

English for Academic Success Display the following questions to students. Tell students these are the kinds of questions they will encounter on standardized tests. Discuss the meaning of the words, and have students use the historical introduction to answer the questions.

- What **approach** to writing ridiculed the manners of the time? ***Possible response:*** *Satire was a style of writing that ridiculed the manners of the time.*
- What was Jonathan Swift trying to **convince** his readers to believe when he wrote *A Modest Proposal*? ***Possible response:*** *Swift was trying to convince his readers that the British should treat the poor of Ireland more fairly.*
- How does wit **enhance** a satirist's writing? ***Possible response:*** *Wit can enhance a satirist's writing by making it more clever and therefore more entertaining to read. Humor can make harsh criticism more acceptable to the reader.*

Standards Focus

Objectives

Students will evaluate the philosophical, political, religious, ethical, and social influences of a historical period.

Link to Today

Like many of the selections in Unit 3, this article about New Orleans three months after Hurricane Katrina presents firsthand observations about culture and society.

Unit 3 Resources, Historical Introduction Skill Builder, p. 1

UA: Differentiating Instruction, graphic organizer, p. 12

Teacher One Stop™, lesson plan and all print resources

Direct Teach

Think About/Talk About

Read with a Purpose Direct students to the Read with a Purpose statement. Ask students to note the author's considerations and emotions after the devastation of New Orleans by Hurricane Katrina.

Extend the Discussion

Speculating Why does the narrator often visit the areas that were devastated by Katrina? ***Possible response:*** *He wants to keep the tragedy of Hurricane Katrina fresh in his mind.*

Link to Today

This Link to Today provides contemporary insight into how people cope with a massive disaster.

Read with a Purpose

Read to see how one New Orleans resident reacted to the devastation of Hurricane Katrina.

Build Background

Hurricane Katrina slammed New Orleans and the Gulf Coast in August 2005, leaving more than 1,800 people dead and thousands homeless. It was one of the most destructive and costly natural disasters in United States history. This column appeared on November 17, 2005, less than three months after Katrina hit.

Author Note

Chris Rose (1960–) is a columnist for the New Orleans *Times-Picayune* newspaper, where he writes on a variety of subjects, including New Orleans life and entertainment. He was named a finalist for a Pulitzer Prize for his post-Katrina columns, which are collected under the title *1 Dead in Attic.* He was born in Washington, D.C. and graduated from the University of Wisconsin.

NEWSPAPER ARTICLE

1 Dead in Attic

by CHRIS ROSE

The New Orleans *Times-Picayune*

I live on The Island,[1] where much has the appearance of Life Goes On. Gas stations, bars, pizza joints, joggers, strollers, dogs, churches, shoppers, neighbors, even garage sales. Sometimes trash and mail service, sometimes not. It sets to mind a modicum of complacency that maybe everything is all right.

But I have this terrible habit of getting into my car every two or three days and driving into the Valley Down Below, that vast wasteland below sea level that was my city, and it's mind-blowing A) how vast it is and B) how wasted it is.

My wife questions the wisdom of my frequent forays into the massive expanse of blown-apart lives and property that local street maps used to call Gentilly, Lakeview, the East and the Lower 9th. She fears that it contributes to my unhappiness and general instability and I suspect she is right. Perhaps I should just stay on the stretch of safe, dry land Uptown where we live and try to move on, focus on pleasant things, quit making myself miserable, quit reliving all those terrible things we saw on TV that first week.

That's advice I wish I could follow, but I can't. I am compelled for reasons that are not entirely clear to me. And so I drive. I drive around and try to figure out those Byzantine[2] markings and symbols that the cops and the National Guard[3] spray-painted on all the houses around here, cryptic communications that tell the story of who or what was or wasn't inside the house when the floodwater rose to the ceiling.

In some cases, there's no interpretation needed. There's one I pass on St. Roch Avenue in the 8th Ward at least once a week. It says: "1 Dead in Attic." That certainly sums up the situation. No mystery there. It's spray-painted there on the front of the house and it probably will remain spray-painted there for weeks, months, maybe years, a perpetual reminder of the untimely passing of a citizen, a resident, a New Orleanian. One of us.

1. **The Island:** a part of New Orleans that escaped flooding.
2. **Byzantine:** complex, intricate, and confusing.
3. **National Guard:** the reserve militia of each state of the United States.

Selection Readability	
Easily Accessible **Accessible** Challenging	familiar language; accessible theme; accessible genre

Selection Summary

This column is an obituary for a nameless person who perished in the New Orleans flood in 2005. Because police spray-painted "1 Dead in Attic" on a house, the author uses it to comment on how poorly the city has dealt with its tragedy. The column ends with an image of Indian Mardi Gras costumes tacked to doors, an eerie reminder of the city's once vibrant spirit.

(Above) Houses flooded by Hurricane Katrina, New Orleans, September 2005. *(Left)* View of London during the Great Fire, which started on September 2, 1666.

You'd think some numerical coding could have conveyed this information on this house, so that I—we all—wouldn't have to drive by places like this every day and be reminded: "1 Dead in Attic."

I have seen plenty of houses in worse shape than the one where 1 Dead in Attic used to live, houses in Gentilly and the Lower 9th that yield the most chilling visual displays in town: low-rider shotgun rooftops with holes that were hacked away from the inside with an ax, leaving small, splintered openings through which people sought escape. Imagine if your life came to that point, and remained there, on display, all over town for us to see, day after day.

Amazingly, those rooftops are the stories with happy endings. I mean, they got out, right? But where are they now? Do you think they have trouble sleeping at night?

The occasional rooftops still have painted messages: "HELP US." I guess they had paint cans in their attic. And an ax, like Margaret Orr and Aaron Broussard[4] always told us we should have if we weren't going to evacuate. Some people thought Orr and Broussard were crazy. Alarmists. Extremists. Well, maybe they are crazy. But they were right.

Perhaps 1 Dead in Attic should have heeded this advice. But judging from the ages on the

4. **Margaret Orr and Aaron Broussard:** a New Orleans weather forecaster and the president of Jefferson Parish, which includes part of New Orleans.

Think About/Talk About

Extend the Discussion

Monitoring Your Reading What do the houses look like in Gentilly and the Lower 9th Ward? ***Possible response:*** *They have signs painted on their roofs and gaping holes in the roofs from which people escaped the flood.*

Irony Re-read paragraph 4 on p. 537. Identify the type of irony concerning the allusion to Orr and Broussard, and explain why the irony occurs. ***Possible responses:*** *The irony is situational. Few people believed the warnings from Orr and Broussard about possible floods and did not take necessary precautions. In the end, those who did not prepare for the worst made a terrible mistake.*

Universal Access

English Learners

English for Academic Success Before students read, introduce the following words:

- **modicum**—a small amount. *The young man showed only a modicum of interest when he attended the lecture.*
- **cryptic**—mysterious or hidden. *Julie's cryptic note confused Sam and Louise.*
- **perpetual**—happening again and again. *After the perpetual forty-day rain, the valley flooded.*
- **grieved**—mourned. *Margaret grieved for many years after her husband died.*
- **raucous**—loud or boisterous. *The neighbors demanded that the raucous noise from the backyard cease immediately.*
- **reveled**—celebrated. *When Josephine was able to return to her house, she reveled in the sheer pleasure of being home once again.*

Challenge students to write a paragraph using at least three of these words.

Think About/Talk About

Extend the Discussion

Finding Details What does the author imagine 1 Dead in Attic might be like, according to the third full paragraph? ***Possible response:*** *He thinks that 1 Dead in Attic might have been someone he knew or met, but he will never know.*

Making Inferences What can you infer about the author's emotions based on the questions he asks in the left column about 1 Dead in Attic? Whom does 1 Dead in Attic represent? ***Possible response:*** *The questions Rose poses shows that he wants to know who the person is, whether the person had a family, and what the person might have been like when he or she was alive. 1 Dead in Attic represents all the unknown deaths caused by the flooding.*

Link to Today

state's official victims list, he or she was probably up in years. And stubborn. And unafraid. And now a statistic.

I wonder who eventually came and took 1 Dead in Attic away. Who knows? Hell, with the way things run around here—I wonder if anyone has come to take 1 Dead in Attic away. And who claimed him or her? Who grieved over 1 Dead in Attic and who buried 1 Dead in Attic?

Mardi Gras Indian headdress, New Orleans, 2005.
Eliot Kamenitz ©2007 The Times-Picayune Publishing Co.

Was there anyone with him or her at the end and what was the last thing they said to each other? How did 1 Dead in Attic spend the last weekend in August of the year 2005? What were their plans? Maybe dinner at Mandich on St. Claude?[5] Maybe a Labor Day family reunion in City Park—one of those raucous picnics where everybody wears matching T-shirts to mark the occasion and they rent a DJ and a SpaceWalk and a couple of guys actually get there the night before to secure a good, shady spot?

I wonder if I ever met 1 Dead in Attic. Maybe in the course of my job or maybe at a Saints[6] game or maybe we once stood next to each other at a Mardi Gras[7] parade . . . . 1 Dead in Attic could have been my mail carrier, a waitress at my favorite restaurant or the guy who burglarized my house a couple years ago. Who knows?

My wife, she's right. I've got to quit just randomly driving around. This can't be helping anything. But I can't stop. I return to the Valley Down Below over and over, looking for signs of progress in all that muck, some sign that things are getting better, that things are improving, that we don't all have to live in a state of abeyance forever but—you know what? I just don't see them there.

I mean, in the 8th Ward, tucked down there behind St. Roch Cemetery, life looks pretty much like it did when the floodwater first receded 10 weeks ago, with lots of cars pointing this way and that, kids' yard toys caked in mire, portraits of despair, desolation and loss. And hatchet holes in rooftops.

But there's something I've discovered about the 8th Ward in this strange exercise of mine: Apparently, a lot of Mardi Gras Indians[8] are from there. Or were from there; I'm not sure what the proper terminology is. On several desolate streets that I drive down, I see where some folks have returned to a few of the homes and they haven't bothered to put their

5. **Mandich on St. Claude:** a famous New Orleans restaurant.
6. **Saints:** New Orleans Saints, a professional football team.
7. **Mardi Gras:** a season of carnival in New Orleans, which occurs before Lent begins.
8. **Mardi Gras Indians:** in New Orleans, members of African American organizations, called tribes, that wear elaborate costumes and parade on Mardi Gras day.

Cross-Curricular Connection

MUSIC: Mardi Gras Bands

In small groups, have students use print and online sources to research the music of Mardi Gras bands, particularly that of different groups of Mardi Gras Indians. Encourage students to identify and find out about the history of popular Mardi Gras songs. Students can obtain sound clips to use as musical examples from various online sources. Once students have completed their research, have each group give a brief report that includes musical examples.

furniture and appliances out on the curb—what's the point, really?—but they have retrieved their tattered and muddy Indian suits and sequins and feathers and they have nailed them to the fronts of their houses.

The colors of these displays is startling because everything else in the 8th is gray. The streets, the walls, the cars, even the trees. Just gray. So the oranges and blues and greens of the Indian costumes are something beautiful to behold, like the first flowers to bloom after the fallout. I don't know what the significance of these displays is, but they hold a mystical fascination for me. They haunt me, almost as much as the spray paint on the front of a house that says 1 Dead in Attic. They look like ghosts hanging there. They are reminders of something. Something very New Orleans.

Do these memorials mean these guys—the Indians—are coming back? I mean, they have to, don't they? Where else could they do what they do? And—maybe this is a strange time to ask—but who are these guys, anyway? Why do they do what they do with all those feathers and beads that take so much time and money to make? What's with all the Big Chief and Spy Boy[9] role-playing?

As many times as I have reveled in their rhythmic, poetic and sometimes borderline absurd revelry in the streets of our city, I now realize that if you asked me to explain the origins and meaning of the Mardi Gras Indians—I couldn't do it. I have no clue. And that makes me wish I'd been paying more attention for the past 20 years. I could have learned something.

I could have learned something about a people whose history is now but a sepia mist over back-of-town streets and neighborhoods that nobody's ever heard of and where nobody lives and nothing ever happens anymore; a freeze frame still life in the air, a story of what we once were.

9. **Big Chief and Spy Boy:** two of the ranks of New Orleans Indians. Spy Boy leads the procession for a tribe, and Big Chief is the head.

Ask Yourself

1. **Read with a Purpose** After reading these comments, how would you describe the author's state of mind as he drove the streets of New Orleans in the months after Hurricane Katrina? Explain.
2. The author's neighborhood was not badly damaged by the hurricane, and he could have stayed away from New Orleans' devastated areas. Why, then, did he make a point of driving the damaged neighborhoods? Explain.
3. Where did the author get the title for this article, and why do you think he focuses so much of the essay on this phrase? Explain.
4. How did the costumes of Mardi Gras Indians attract the author's attention, and how did they affect his state of mind as he thought about New Orleans and the hurricane? Explain.
5. In this article's conclusion, the author wishes he had been paying more attention in the decades before Hurricane Katrina. Explain why.

Think About/Talk About

Extend the Discussion

Finding Details According to the second paragraph, why do the colors of the Mardi Gras Indian costumes seem so startling to the author?
Possible response: *The colors are so startling because the background of the neighborhood after the flood is so gray and colorless.*

Tone In the first paragraph, the author says that it is pointless for people in the 8th Ward to put their appliances and furniture out on the curb. What does this paragraph indicate about the author's tone?
Possible responses: *The author's words indicate that nobody is picking up any of these items and that the items would just sit out on the curb for an indeterminate amount of time. This anecdote tells me that the author is depressed and overwhelmed by all the destruction and that he thinks nothing can be done to help the situation.*

Ask Yourself

Possible responses:

1. *The author is upset; he is miserable about what has happened to his city and obsessed with going back and viewing the worst areas. Though he knows that viewing the destruction makes him feel bad, he cannot stop driving around.*
2. *He thinks about the people who died and what their lives might have been like. Driving around also leads him to voice regrets, such as his lack of interest in the Mardi Gras Indians.*
3. *The title comes from a house that has been spray-painted during the flood to indicate that there was a dead person in the attic. The phrase evokes a stark and powerful image of one person's terrible fate during the destruction of the city. The author uses the phrase to symbolize his emotions and the emotions of the city after the flood.*
4. *The costumes are nailed to the front of houses in the 8th Ward. They are beautifully and brightly colored and stand out against the gray background of the devastated neighborhood. They strike the author as having mystical significance because they look like ghosts that remind him of "something very New Orleans."*
5. *The author realizes that the Indians are an important part of the history and culture of the city that may be lost now. He wishes he had learned about them while they were still living there.*

Chapter Objectives

- Students will learn about the rise of the novel by analyzing the characteristics of novels by Samuel Pepys, Daniel Defoe, and Jonathan Swift.
- Students will connect themes and characteristics of the first novel rise to modern literary genres such as weblogs.

The Quotation

Tell students that the Literary Skills Focus of Chapter 5 is the birth and development of the novel, a literary form that describes human events and emotions with a degree of realism that had not been attempted before. Ask students to explain how Austen's words apply to novels they read. ***Possible response:*** *Novels often describe in detail the emotional lives of a multitude of characters. To achieve this difficult goal, the author needs to have a deep understanding of human nature and scrupulous writing skills.*

Analyzing Visuals

Extension Activity What does this painting suggest about the prevalence of the novel in the eighteenth century home? ***Possible response:*** *The child in the painting is reading, so novels were probably accessible to young people. However, the child and the man are well-dressed, which suggests that only the upper-class had access to novels.*

CHAPTER **5**

The Rise of the Novel

LITERARY SKILLS FOCUS

The Rise of the Novel

The Reverend Randall Burroughs and his Son Ellis by Johann Joseph Zoffany.
Louvre, Paris, France.

CONTENTS

> "'Oh! it is only a novel!' . . . or, in short, only some work in which the most thorough knowledge of human nature, the happiest delineation of its varieties, the liveliest effusions of wit and humour are conveyed to the world in the best chosen language."
>
> — **Jane Austen, *Northanger Abbey***

Chapter 5

California Standards Overview

- **Reading Standard 2.2** Analyze the way in which clarity of meaning is affected by the patterns of organization, hierarchical structures, repetition of the main ideas, syntax, and word choice in the text.
- **Reading Standard 2.4** Make warranted and reasonable assertions about the author's arguments by using elements of the text to defend and clarify interpretations.
- **Reading Standard 2.5** Analyze an author's implicit and explicit philosophical assumptions and beliefs about a subject.
- **Reading Standard 3.1** Analyze characteristics of subgenres (e.g., satire, parody, allegory, pastoral) that are used in poetry, prose, plays, novels, short stories, essays, and other basic genres.
- **Reading Standard 3.3** Analyze the ways in which irony, tone, mood, the author's style, and the "sound" of language achieve specific rhetorical or aesthetic purposes or both.
- **Reading Standard 3.7** Analyze recognized works of world literature from a variety of authors: **c.** Evaluate the philosophical, political, religious, ethical, and social influences of the historical period that shaped the characters, plots, and setting.
- **Reading Standard 3.8** Analyze the clarity and consistency of political assumptions in a selection of literary works or essays on a topic (e.g., suffrage, women's role in organized labor) (Political approach).
- **Reading Standard 3.9** Analyze the philosophical arguments presented in literary works to determine whether the authors' positions have contributed to the quality of each work and the credibility of the characters. (Philosophical approach)
- **Grades 9–10 Review Reading Standard 3.4** Determine characters' traits by what the characters say about themselves in narration, dialogue, dramatic monologue, and soliloquy.
- **Grades 9–10 Review Reading Standard 3.9** Explain how voice, persona, and the choice of a narrator affect characterization and the tone, plot, and credibility of a text.

LITERARY RESPONSE AND ANALYSIS

Literary Skills Focus

Reading Standard 2.2, 3.1, 3.7c (see pages A48–A50)

The Rise of the Novel by Leila Christenbury

Influences on the Rise of the Novel

- Tradition of narratives, allegories, and satires
- New interest in biographies and journals as historical documents
- Increases in leisure time and literacy rates

What Is New About the Novel?

The novel is a long fictional prose narrative; it is literature that tells a story. In this chapter, you will read excerpts from some of the precursors to novels, such as *The Diary of Samuel Pepys*, and from some of the earliest examples of novels, such as *Gulliver's Travels.* If the word *novel* means "new," we are led to ask: What exactly was new about this form of writing?

Compared with stories from earlier times, the emerging novels conveyed a sense of realism. The **protagonist,** or main character, of a novel differed from the superhuman or godlike persons in myths and epics such as *Beowulf* and the brave and noble figures in romances such as *Le Morte d'Arthur*. The novel's main character could be anyone—a person's nobility, wealth, or education might become part of the plot, but the lack of these advantages did not keep a character out of the story's spotlight. Early novels told the stories of many different kinds of lives.

A novel's plot followed the adventures and misadventures of the hero or heroine and the characters he or she encountered. Some early critics of the novel mused that the novel failed to offer adequate moral instruction for readers. Samuel Johnson, an eighteenth-century writer and notable creator of *A Dictionary of the English Language,* commenting on the new fiction, worried that readers might develop sympathy for rascally heroes: "As we accompany them through their adventures with delight, and are led by degrees to interest ourselves in their favour . . . we lose the abhorrence of their faults, because they do not hinder our pleasure." Then as now, most readers read novels for fun. Much as movies today are usually intended to entertain their audiences, early novels used intriguing plots to provide enjoyment for readers.

Newspapers, Diaries, and Travel Writing

Early novels grew out of several different sources—many of which were nonfiction. Readers had tasted the excitement of scandalous urban gossip in the newspapers. The growing popularity of diaries and epistolary correspondence created an audience that expected intimate details. This development also created a desire for insight into characters' motivations, hopes, and fears. The growth in trade between England and countries throughout the world created popular interest in other countries and cultures and particularly in travel logs. Early novel writers used elements from all these genres to lend excitement, alternative voices, and energy to their writing. In this chapter, you will read an excerpt from an actual diary and an excerpt from a fictional journal written to seem like an actual diary.

Early Novelists

Although the English novel did not emerge until the eighteenth century, writers in other parts of the world experimented with forms similar to the novel centuries earlier. The Greek *Daphnis and Chloe* (third century) can be considered a novel, as can *The Tale of Genji,* a vast chronicle of court life written in about 1000 by Murasaki Shikibu, a lady-in-waiting to the Japanese empress Akito. In Europe, the novel first emerged with the publication of Miguel Cervantes' *Don Quixote.*

California Standards, pp. 541–542

- **Reading Standard 2.2** Analyze the way in which clarity of meaning is affected by the patterns of organization, hierarchical structures, repetition of the main ideas, syntax, and word choice in the text.
- **Reading Standard 3.1** Analyze characteristics of subgenres (e.g., satire, parody, allegory, pastoral) that are used in poetry, prose, plays, novels, short stories, essays, and other basic genres.
- **Reading Standard 3.7** Analyze recognized works of world literature from a variety of authors: **c.** Evaluate the philosophical, political, religious, ethical, and social influences of the historical period that shaped the characters, plots, and setting.

Literary Skills Focus

Objectives

Students will

- understand the philosophical, political, religious, ethical, and social influences of a historical period
- understand the rise of the novel

Unit 3 Resources, Literary Focus Skill Builder, p. 5

PowerNotes, interactive lesson presentation with activities

Teacher One Stop™, on-level lesson plan and all print resources

Direct Teach

What Is New About the Novel?

- Tell students that the ancestors of the novel include the epic of ancient times and the romance of the Middle Ages: Both are long tales of highly fictionalized (if not wholly imaginary) adventures. Over time and across cultures, other kinds of long stories developed, including the picaresque story, in which the adventures of some happy rascal are chronicled and, usually, satirized. Yet, none of these forms had either the plot structure (conflict, rising action, climax, and resolution) or the character development associated with the novel today.
- Ask students to briefly describe the characters, plot, and setting of novels they have read. Begin the discussion by briefly mentioning novels many students may have read, such as *To Kill a Mockingbird* or *The Red Badge of Courage*. Ask students to compare these works with elements of earlier kinds of fiction, such as epic poetry.

Early Novelists

- Tell students about Henry Fielding's *Tom Jones* (1749), a masterpiece of British literature that chronicles the life of Tom, a foundling raised with a squire's son who is always trying to get Tom into trouble. When the two become rivals for the attention of the daughter of a neighboring squire, Tom is banished. He finds himself in a series of picaresque—occasionally bawdy—adventures.
- Ask students to explain which characteristics of the plot of *Tom Jones* make it an example of an early novel.

Check for Understanding

Ask Yourself

Possible responses:

1. *We can relate to a character who exhibits human strengths and weaknesses, overcomes obstacles, and experiences the same triumphs and failures we do.*
2. *Many protagonists have embodied a particular element of evil; for example, protagonists can be thieves, assassins, or murderers. Sometimes these characters are glorified, especially in film.*

Learn It Online

The **NovelWise** mini-site includes instruction on choosing, reading, and analyzing novels; it also contains a catalogue of book summaries, study guides, teaching guides, and PowerPoint presentations.

go.hrw.com H12-542 Go

LITERARY RESPONSE AND ANALYSIS

Literary Skills Focus

Drawing on the traditions of regal chivalric romances, only to satirize them via a bumbling but well-intentioned protagonist, Cervantes ultimately created a new textual structure through the hybridization of tragic and comic forms.

Lady Aphra Behn's *Oroonoko, or the History of the Royal Slave* (1688) is called by some the first English novel and by others a "protonovel." A combination of fiction, history, and travelogue, it presents a realistic account of the British slave trade. Daniel Defoe's *Robinson Crusoe* (1719), the loosely structured narrative of the courage and ingenuity of a castaway and his Man Friday, is labeled by other critics as the first English novel. Nearly all readers agree, however, that Samuel Richardson's book *Pamela* (1740) is a novel. Richardson (1689–1761) was perhaps the first novelist to explore in great detail the emotional life of his characters, especially his heroines (in *Pamela* and *Clarissa*).

The novels of the prominent eighteenth-century novelist Henry Fielding (1707–1754) are crammed with rough and rowdy incidents, and though Fielding makes his characters seem good, they are never soft or sentimental. Fielding's rollicking novel *Tom Jones* has even been made into an Oscar-winning movie, proof that his high-spirited characters are still fresh and funny today. Laurence Sterne (1713–1768) produced the landmark fictional autobiography *Tristram Shandy,* an experimental novel which, despite the efforts of many imitators, remains uniquely whimsical.

These novels of Sterne, Richardson, Behn, and others tell us about life at a particular time and help us understand that the joys and disappointments of human experience transcend time periods.

Tom Jones (1963), starring Susannah York, Hugh Griffith, Albert Finney.

Ask Yourself

1. Why might the hero of a novel appeal more to readers than a godlike or noble hero from a myth or epic poem?
2. To what extent do you think Johnson's observation—that we lose disgust for the moral flaws of main characters because we enjoy reading about them—applies to us as modern novel-readers or moviegoers?

Learn It Online

Find out more about novels, and scope out modern novels, on the *NovelWise* site.

go.hrw.com H12-542 Go

Universal Access

English Learners

Initiate an academic discussion with students by having them classify each factor as a political, religious, ethical, or social influence on the novel.

- England's expansion of trade relations with other countries around the world
- An increase in leisure time and activities
- A growing popularity of urban gossip and diaries
- A growing literacy rate

Struggling Readers

Test students' understanding of major details in the essay. Instruct students to construct a web diagram. Tell them to write "The Rise of the Novel" in the center circle. Then, have them draw seven straight lines extending outward from the center circle. After students read each paragraph, ask them to record the major detail of each paragraph on one of the lines. After students have finished, ask volunteers to read aloud one of the major details and have the other students identify the paragraph in which the detail is found.

Analyzing Visuals

Reading Standard 3.1, 3.7c (see pages A48–A50)

Connecting to Novels

Early novels, which could be satirical and more realistic than previous fictional writings, told the stories of many different types of lives. This etching from the eighteenth century has several characteristics in common with the first novels.

Guidelines

An etching is an image produced by carving a picture or design on a metal plate and then pressing that plate onto paper. Use the guidelines below to consider how this etching reflects concerns of the novel.

- What satirical elements do you see in this etching?
- How are the people portrayed? Would you say the etching is realistic or not realistic? Explain.
- How do both the etching and the text beneath it convey a sense of plot?

1. Who or what are the heads at the left of the etching? What are they saying and why?

2. How do the relative sizes of the people and objects express the artist's **point of view?**

3. **Irony,** a contrast between expectation and reality, is characteristic of **satire.** What ironic elements can you find?

Midas Transmuting All into Gold Paper, published by Hannah Humphrey (1797).
Courtesy of Warden and Scholars of New College, Oxford.

Your Turn Analyze Satire

Choose a satirical image or a cartoon from this unit, and discuss with a partner how the image displays some satirical elements.

Standards Focus

Objectives

Students will analyze satirical characteristics in an etching.

Analyzing Visuals Transparencies, Unit 3

Teacher One Stop™, lesson plan and all print resources

Direct Teach

Connect to the Literary Skill

Tell students that authors of satirical vignettes usually exaggerate the characteristics of the subject they represent. The exaggeration combines a comic effect with the more serious criticisms of the satirized subject.

Work with students to answer the guided questions.

Possible responses:

1. *The heads, representing Whigs, are whispering "Midas has ears" to point out the prime minister's ridiculousness.*
2. *The figures below the bank appear small and powerless compared to the huge gold safe.*
3. *William Pitt, pictured as Midas, emits paper money when his stomach is full of gold coins. The figures on the right proclaim England's state of prosperity when England is in trouble.*

Check for Understanding

Your Turn

Alternative Listening and Speaking Assignment

Have students work with a partner to find a political cartoon in a newspaper or Web site and analyze what satirical elements might be present. Then, have them give an oral presentation, explaining their findings to the class.

California Standards, p. 543

- **Reading Standard 3.1** Analyze characteristics of subgenres (e.g., satire, parody, allegory, pastoral) that are used in poetry, prose, plays, novels, short stories, essays, and other basic genres.
- **Reading Standard 3.7** Analyze recognized works of world literature from a variety of authors: **c.** Evaluate the philosophical, political, religious, ethical, and social influences of the historical period that shaped the characters, plots, and settings.

Universal Access

Struggling Readers

Inform students that this political cartoon, published during William Pitt's leadership, satirized the Bank of England's creation of bank notes during a financial crisis, when England's supply of gold was low. Have students identify the following elements in the cartoon:

- French revolutionaries leaping into the sky
- Tory putti declaring the "Prosperous state of British Finances"
- a small fleet of ships leaving Brest harbor
- customers making a run on the bank

Standards Focus

Objectives

Students will
- analyze characteristics of subgenres, such as a diary
- evaluate an author's credibility

Selection Introduction

Think About the Writer

No one would ever know about an incident as small as the theater spitting if Pepys had not recorded it. Ask students to brainstorm small, specific events that happen to them that might have a surprising importance as they go about their daily lives.

For Independent Reading

The Diary of a Young Girl, Anne Frank

Motivate

What Do You Think?/QuickTalk

Use the QuickTalk to have students think about the differences between the reactions of people who were directly involved in a modern-day disaster or tragedy and the reactions of people who read about the incident from far away. Have students write ideas in their **Reader/Writer Notebooks.**

English for Academic Success

Academic Vocabulary

Look for opportunities to use the Academic Vocabulary words in this unit.
- **convince, *v.*:** persuade; cause to believe
- **enhance, *v.*:** improve the quality of
- **participate, *v.*:** take part in

Preparing to Read

from The Diary of Samuel Pepys

What Do You Think? How can order and civilization affect human behavior?

QuickTalk

Think about a natural disaster, such as a fire or damaging storm, that you have read about or experienced. How did people respond to the challenge? In a small group, discuss the disaster as well as people's response to it.

Portrait of Samuel Pepys (1666) by John Hayls (fl. 1651–76). Oil on canvas. National Portrait Gallery, London.

MEET THE WRITER

Samuel Pepys
(1633–1703)

From 1660 to 1669, Samuel Pepys (pronounced "peeps") kept a private diary about life and events in London.

The Curious Londoner

Pepys was a hardworking, accomplished naval administrator whose constant desire to learn and to participate in new experiences led him to explore the cultural and intellectual life of London. Music, art, literature, science, mathematics, the theater—Pepys enjoyed them all. He was the confidant of the kings Charles II and James II, and he counted among his friends many of London's influential architects, artists, mathematicians, and scientists. His diary reflects his broad interests and endless curiosity.

Historians find the *Diary* useful because Pepys was a firsthand observer of seventeenth-century life, both public and private. In 1660, he took part in bringing the exiled king Charles II back to England. He witnessed joyous occasions such as Charles's coronation in 1661 and disasters such as the plague of 1665 and the Great Fire of 1666. He recorded these significant public happenings in his diary along with trivial personal experiences. For example, on one occasion he wrote: "I went to . . . the theater, where I saw again *The Lost Lady,* which doth please me better than before. And here, I sitting behind in a dark place, a lady spat backward upon me by mistake, not seeing me. But after seeing her to be a very pretty lady, I was not troubled at all." The *Diary* is full of unexpected little anecdotes such as this one.

The Diary Goes Public

Housed at Cambridge University since 1723, Pepys's diary, which fills six 282-page notebooks in shorthand, is the longest intimate eyewitness account of life in seventeenth-century London. Its contents remained unknown until the shorthand was first transcribed in 1825. A complete transcription of the most intimate parts was not published until the 1970s and 1980s.

Think About the Writer What events or aspects of daily life in your city might intrigue a curious person such as Samuel Pepys?

California Standards, pp. 544–549
- **Reading Standard 2.4** Make warranted and reasonable assertions about the author's arguments by using elements of the text to defend and clarify interpretations.
- **Reading Standard 3.1** Analyze characteristics of subgenres (e.g., satire, parody, allegory, pastoral) that are used in poetry, prose, plays, novels, short stories, essays, and other basic genres.

Selection Readability	
Easily Accessible Accessible **Challenging**	humorous; accessible vocabulary and theme; familiar genre

Reading Standard 2.4, 3.1 (see pages A48–A50)

Literary Skills Focus

Diary A **diary** is a record a person keeps of feelings, impressions, and events. Diaries are usually written for the writer's eyes only. Pepys intended his diary to be private—at least during his lifetime. He wrote it in shorthand and encoded especially personal passages in a mix of Spanish, Latin, and French. However, because Pepys carefully preserved his diary and willed it, along with other books, to Cambridge University, it is likely he imagined that someone, someday, would read his entries.

Reading Skills Focus

Evaluating an Author's Credibility Pepys witnessed some of the events he wrote about in his diary, and heard and recorded information about others. How do these methods of obtaining information affect his **credibility,** or believability? In this excerpt, Pepys relates not only facts about the Great Fire of London but also his opinions and emotional reactions. Think about his statements and his sources of information as you evaluate his credibility.

Into Action Use a chart to analyze Pepys's statements. Record the source of his information for each statement, and note whether it is a fact, an opinion, or an emotional response.

Statement About the Fire	Source of the Information	Fact, Opinion, or Emotional Response?
Pepys saw the fire far off and was not worried.	Pepys is an eyewitness; he also hears about the fire from Jane.	The fire is a fact, but Pepys also feels relief that it is far off.

Writing Skills Focus

Think as a Reader/Writer

Find It in Your Reading A skillful observer, Pepys provides hundreds of snapshots of life in London. His entries are not a carefully constructed narrative but rather a series of quick descriptions of what he saw, thought, and felt. Notice details that make Pepys's account a valuable historical and engaging personal record. In your *Reader/Writer Notebook,* record details that you think are effective, and explain why you chose them.

Vocabulary

lamentable (luh MEHN tuh buhl) *adj.:* deserving of or inspiring sorrow. *Pepys regarded the fire's destruction as lamentable.*

flinging (FLIHNG ihng) *v.:* throwing forcefully. *The people were flinging their possessions into the river to protect them from the fire.*

quench (kwehnch) *v.:* put out; extinguish. *Londoners were unable to quench the fire before it destroyed four-fifths of the city.*

combustible (kuhm BUHS tuh buhl) *adj.:* easy to set on fire; fast-burning. *Built of wood and crowded against each other on narrow streets, the houses of London were highly combustible.*

dismayed (dihs MAYD) *v.:* upset; alarmed. *News that the fire was out of control and had burned hundreds of houses dismayed the people of London.*

Language Coach

Suffixes The suffixes *–able* and *–ible* can change verbs to adjectives. *Lament* is a verb that means "to show sorrow." When you add the suffix *–able*, you form the adjective *lamentable*, which means "deserving of or inspiring sorrow." Which Vocabulary word includes the *–ible* suffix? What related verb do you get if you remove the suffix? What does the verb mean?

Learn It Online
Listen to this diary with the audio version online.
go.hrw.com H12-545 Go

Reader/Writer Notebook
Use your **RWN** to complete the activities for this selection.

Selection Resources

Unit 3 Resources, on-level practice and assessment, p. 7

Teacher One Stop™, on-level lesson plans and all print resources

Holt Audio Library

Holt Audio Library: Selections and Summaries in Spanish

UA: Differentiating Instruction, graphic organizer, p. 121

UA: Supporting Instruction in Spanish, selection summary

Analyzing Visuals Transparencies, p. 19

ThinkCentral Online Assessment, Selection Standards Check

ThinkCentral Online Remediation

Preteach

Introducing Vocabulary

Read aloud the Vocabulary words, definitions, and sample sentences. Then, use this activity to check students' understanding.

1. Name a **lamentable** situation that afflicts the current state of affairs.
2. Name an emotion that can have you **flinging** an object away.
3. Describe a way to **quench** one's thirst.
4. List materials that are **combustible.**
5. Explain which kind of news may leave people **dismayed.**

English for Academic Success

Language Coach

After students read the **Language Coach,** have them brainstorm five adjectives ending in *–able* and *–ible,* and ask them to note the related verb in each. Point out that some *–able* and *–ible* words, such as *culpable,* do not contain related verbs.

Literary Skills Focus

As you read and discuss the selection with students, have them note elements that characterize the selection as a diary (dates, tone, feelings, and impressions).

Reading Skills Focus

Give students a copy of the Reading Skills Focus graphic organizer before they read. (See **Unit 3 Resources.**)

Writing Skills Focus

Have students record effective details about life in London in the time of Pepys in their **Reader/Writer Notebooks**. Students can use their notes to complete the Writing Skills Focus activity.

Learn It Online
The online version of this selection includes audio support to engage all students and to help struggling readers with reading comprehension and vocabulary.
go.hrw.com H12-545 Go

Teacher Preparation

Selection Summary

In this selection, Samuel Pepys describes the emotional and physical devastation caused by the Great Fire of London. He illustrates his travels from one part of town to another, during which he sees people he knows trying to save their belongings and livelihoods.

Direct Teach

Think About/Talk About

Read with a Purpose Have students read the Read with a Purpose statement. Ask them to consider how calamities can affect our emotional state as well as our behavior. As they read, ask students to consider whether Pepys's emotional and practical reactions are ever contradictory.

Analysis

A Literary Focus

Possible response: *Pepys inserts personal statements about people he knows and for whom he cares in his narrative of the fire. He weaves factual information and personal opinions together.*

Extend the Discussion

Style Consider the sentence on p. 546 that begins with "About seven rose again . . ." What effect does Pepys's habit of omitting words from sentences have on his style? ***Possible responses:*** *It makes his writing informal and fast paced; it makes his ideas more difficult to follow.*

DIARY

from The Diary of Samuel Pepys

by **Samuel Pepys**

Read with a Purpose

Read this diary entry to observe Pepys's emotional and practical reactions to the Great Fire.

Build Background

The Great Fire of London started in the house of the king's baker on September 2, 1666. Strong eastern winds fanned it into the city's streets, where it burned until September 5, when it was finally contained and extinguished. The fire razed a large part of the city. It destroyed many city buildings, dozens of churches, a cathedral, and about 13,000 houses, leaving many Londoners homeless.

September 2, 1666

The First Day of the Great Fire of London

Lord's Day. Some of our maids sitting up late last night to get things ready against our feast today, Jane called us up, about three in the morning, to tell us of a great fire they saw in the City. So I rose, and slipped on my nightgown and went to her window, and thought it to be on the back-side of Mark Lane at the furthest; but being unused to such fires as followed, I thought it far enough off, and so went to bed again and to sleep. About seven rose again to dress myself, and there looked out at the window and saw the fire not so much as it was, and further off. So to my closet[1] to set things to rights after yesterday's cleaning. By and by Jane comes and tells me that she hears that above three hundred houses have been burned down tonight by the fire we saw, and that it was now burning down all Fish Street by London Bridge. So I made myself ready presently, and walked to the Tower[2] and there got up upon one of the high places, Sir. J. Robinson's little son going up with me; and there I did see the houses[3] at that end of the bridge all on fire, and an infinite great fire on this and the other side of the end of the bridge—which, among other people, did trouble me for poor little Michell and our Sarah[4] on the bridge. So down, with my heart full of trouble, to **A** the Lieutenant of the Tower, who tells me that it begun this morning in the King's baker's house in Pudding Lane, and that it hath burned down St. Magnes Church and most part of Fish Street already. So I down to the waterside and there got a boat and through bridge, and there saw a lamentable fire. Poor Michell's house, as far as the Old Swan,[5] already burned that way and the fire running further, that in a very little

1. **closet:** private room.
2. **Tower:** Tower of London, close to Pepys's house.
3. **houses:** shops and dwellings built on London Bridge.
4. **Sarah:** maid whom Mrs. Pepys discharged on December 5, 1662. Pepys wrote: "The wench cried, and I was ready to cry too."
5. **Michell's house . . . Old Swan:** Betty Michell, a former sweetheart of Pepys, lost her house in the fire. The Old Swan was a tavern on Thames Street, near London Bridge.

A Literary Focus Diary How do these lines show us both a factual recording of events and Pepys's personal opinion about those facts?

Vocabulary **lamentable** (luh MEHN tuh buhl) *adj.:* deserving of or inspiring sorrow.

Universal Access

Struggling Readers

To help students read "The Diary of Samuel Pepys," model the reading skill of evaluating an author's credibility. Explain that as students read a selection, they should ask whether the author's statements represent facts or opinions. Encourage students to ask themselves as they read, "Does this statement represent a fact or an opinion? How can I tell?" When students encounter an opinion, ask them to look in the selection for facts that support that opinion.

Students with Disabilities

Explain that a diary is made up of entries that usually tell about events that happened on one day. Explain that the diary entry on pp. 546–547 begins with a date, and point out how the details in the entry describe events that happened on this date. Then, read the first two sentences of the selection aloud and explain that entry is written from a first-person point of view. Explain that this selection is a diary about a fire that ignited in London a long time ago. Ask students to make inferences about what the diary might describe.

Check for Understanding

Independent Practice

Informational Text Focus

Possible responses:

1. *Ten years; the entries are being published in real time.*
2. *hyperlinks to familiar terms, additional annotations by readers, further links to more detailed information*
3. *Readers can suggest links to articles that will provide more information and share comments.*
4. *Reading the printed version might be overwhelming; reading the online version will take longer, but will allow readers to interact with the text.*
5. *Among the similarities, students' notes should include that weblogs and diaries provide a first-person account of daily occurrences. Among the differences, students should point out that weblogs are written for public consumption and that diaries are not meant to be public.*
6. *Three contemporaries of Stephen King are Paul Auster, Tom Clancy, and Anne Rice.*
7. *Yes, you might find them in an archive surveying the history of graphic novels.*
8. *yes*
9. *Oil consumption may decrease due to the discovery of alternative fuels.*
10. *soundtracks and cinematography*
11. *The existence and popularity of the Pepys Web site argues that seemingly old-fashioned text appeals to modern audiences.*
12. *No, Pepys never meant for his personal entries to be published. Yes, the contents of Pepys's diary serve as valuable historical information that should be shared.*
13. *Responses will vary.*
14. *Students will analyze how freedom of speech applies to weblogs' content.*

INFORMATIONAL TEXT FOCUS

Applying Your Skills

Reading Standard 2.2 (see pages A48–A50)
Listening and Speaking Standard 2.1a (see pages A53–A55)
Writing Standard 2.2 (see pages A51–A52)

Diary of Samuel Pepys Weblog

Analyze Informational Texts

Informational Text Focus

Quick Check

1. How long will it take Gyford to publish all of Pepys's diary on the Internet? Why?
2. What features enhance the diary for visitors to the Weblog?
3. How can readers actively participate in the project?

Read with a Purpose

4. The published version of Pepys's diary fills nine thick volumes. How do online readers of the diary experience the text differently than someone reading a printed edition?

Informational Skills: Comparing and Contrasting

5. Look at the Venn diagram in which you noted similarities and differences between diaries and Weblogs. Now, write a paragraph responding to the following question: Are diaries and blogs more similar or more different? Explain.

Vocabulary Check

Use the Vocabulary word to answer each question.

6. Who are three **contemporaries** of your favorite author?
7. Would you ever find comic books in an **archive**? Why or why not?
8. Are life's **mundanities** usually predictable?
9. Will the world's **consumption** of oil increase or decrease in fifty years? Why?
10. In your favorite film, what effects **complemented** the script?

Text Analysis

11. **Interpret** What does the author mean when he says that the Pepys Weblog "makes a compelling argument that oldies often remain goodies"?
12. **Evaluate** Pepys did not write his diary for publication. Do you think that publishing his private writings is justified? Why or why not?
13. **Extend** Suggest how another text from an earlier era might be presented on the Internet. Describe advantages and disadvantages of your proposal.

Listening and Speaking

14. **Analyze** Because a Weblog is open to millions of Internet users, critics have questioned the wisdom of posting uncensored thoughts. With a trusted adult, discuss whether people should limit what they post on personal blogs. Then, discuss the question with a small group in your class, and share the group's conclusions with the class.

Writing Skills Focus

Timed Writing Write a paragraph in which you explain what motivated Phil Gyford to create this site. Use examples from the article to support your conclusions.

What Do You Think Now?

How might reading Pepys's diary as part of an online community enhance a reader's understanding of both the seventeenth century and today's world?

Universal Access

Struggling Writers

Some students may need additional scaffolding to complete the Writing Skills Focus activity. Students might have difficulty writing a paragraph that explains Gyford's primary goal for creating the weblog. Have students discuss why any author might choose to publish their work. Then, have them revisit the article to locate reasons why Gyford chose to publish Pepys's diary as a weblog. Encourage students to write three to five sentences explaining his purpose.

What Do You Think Now?

Have students consider how the content of comments by online readers will affect Gyford's weblog as well as Pepys's original writing. Ask them to think about how modern perspectives will affect the interpretation of Pepys's diary.

While the diary is already available online in bulk form (enter "Pepys" into the search engine at Project Gutenberg),[6] few would have the stamina to plow through even significant chunks of a 10-year diary at a single sitting. In the weblog format, the work is infinitely more digestible, and also gives visitors the chance to experience the entries in "real-time" (or should that be "shifted-time?"), reading a February 1 entry on February 1. Ⓑ

But unlike the typical weblog, which is created for public consumption, Pepys never expected anyone to read his writings (at least while he was alive), so the work is entirely free of self-censorship and includes all the author's petty jealousies, insecurities, and infidelities. (This candid honesty in part contributed to the fact that the diary was only published in its entirety in 1970, as it took a few hundred years for some of the author's more "adult" entries to be considered fit for public consumption.) Ⓒ

Not content to simply copy and paste an existing work into his website, Gyford has also complemented the original content with abundant hyperlinks to more detailed information. So, if in your explorations you come across but can't quite place the name "Greatorex," a linked page will introduce him as a prominent mathematical instrument maker. Mentions of geographic locations are linked to an interactive map of London. Ⓓ

Each day's entry also has its own URL (so you can quickly pick up where you left off) and a collection of Annotations added by site visitors offering general comments, additional historical tidbits, and occasional reader-suggested links to more detailed information. A "TrackBack" feature collects more reader-suggested links, and the entire diary to date is available through an onsite archive.

The only question now is, can you commit to 10 years of regular visits?

The Diary of Samuel Pepys can be found at http://www.pepysdiary.com/.

6. **Project Gutenberg**: Named for the fifteenth-century inventor of the printing press, this Internet site offers free access to more than 22,000 electronic texts.

Tower of London.

Internet

Ⓑ **Informational Focus** **Comparing and Contrasting** What is the difference between "real-time" and "shifted-time"?

Ⓒ **Informational Focus** **Comparing and Contrasting** What phrase does the author use to introduce a contrast between Weblogs and Pepys's diary?

Ⓓ **Informational Focus** **Comparing and Contrasting** How does the use of hyperlinks compare with using footnotes in a printed book?

Vocabulary **consumption** (kuhn SUHMP shuhn) *n.:* use.
complemented (KAHM pluh mehnt ihd) *v.:* made more complete by adding something.
archive (AHR kyv) *n.:* collection of documents or other data.

Think About/Talk About

Comprehension

Ⓐ Informational Focus

Possible response: *The author points out that Pepys achieved many intentional goals, including founding the Navy and working as a bureaucrat. He was an unintentional historian because his diary has become a valuable historical source.*

Ⓑ Informational Focus

Possible response: *"Real-time" refers to events that unfold in the same time as the events being described. "Shifted-time" refers to the idea that readers read the events in real-time while their time frame is shifted forward.*

Ⓒ Informational Focus

Possible response: *The phrase "but unlike" introduces the contrast.*

Ⓓ Informational Focus

Possible response: *Hyperlinks and footnotes serve the same purpose: to explain unfamiliar terms or provide more information.*

Vocabulary: Own the Word

- **contemporaries:** Ask students to name *contemporaries* of Shakespeare. ***Possible responses:*** *Christopher Marlowe, James I, Sir Walter Raleigh*
- **consumption:** Ask students why people might want to share their private thoughts in weblogs meant for public *consumption.*
- **complemented:** Ask students to name a pair of items that *complement* one another. ***Possible response:*** *shoes and socks*
- **archive:** Tell students the root word for *archive* is *archeion,* which in Greek means "official documents." Have students explain why a government office might have an *archive.*

California Standards, pp. 554–555

- **Reading Standard 2.2** Analyze the way in which clarity of meaning is affected by the patterns of organization, hierarchical structures, repetition of the main ideas, syntax, and word choice in the text.
- **Reading Standard 3.4** Analyze ways in which poets use imagery, personification, figures of speech, and sounds to evoke readers' emotions.
- **Writing Standard 2.2** Write responses to literature: **a.** Demonstrate a comprehensive understanding of the significant ideas in works or passages. **b.** Analyze the use of imagery, language, universal themes, and unique aspects of the text. **c.** Support important ideas and viewpoints through accurate and detailed references to the text and to other works. **d.** Demonstrate an understanding of the author's use of stylistic devices and an appreciation of the effects created. **e.** Identify and assess the impact of perceived ambiguities, nuances, and complexities within the text.
- **Listening and Speaking 2.1a** Explore the significance of personal experiences, events, conditions, or concerns, using appropriate rhetorical strategies.
- **Listening and Speaking 2.3** **a.** Demonstrate a comprehensive understanding of the significant ideas of literary works. **b.** Analyze the imagery, language, universal themes, and unique aspects of text through the use of rhetorical strategies. **c.** Support important ideas and viewpoints through accurate and detailed references to the text or to other works. **d.** Demonstrate an awareness of the author's use of stylistic devices and an appreciation of the effects created. **e.** Identify and assess the impact of perceived ambiguities, nuances, and complexities within the text.

Model the Skill

- To help students read "Diary of Samuel Pepys Weblog," model the reading skill of identifying **comparison-contrast organization**.
- Provide students with copies of the Informational Text Focus graphic organizer for "Diary of Samuel Pepys Weblog." (See **Unit 3 Resources**.)
- Tell students that, as they read the selection, they should take note of all the similarities and differences that the author presents about diaries and weblogs in the graphic organizer. For example, one similarity between the two is that "both detail everyday events of life."

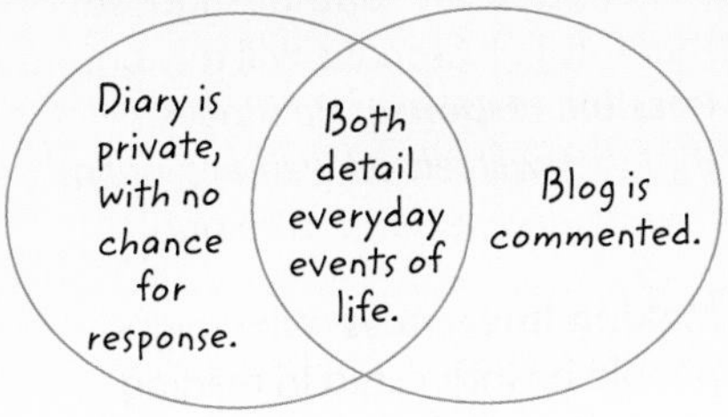

Guided Practice: Apply

Turn-and-Talk Ask students to reflect on the differences and similarities between Pepys's diary and Gyford's weblog and discuss them. Ask them to base their discussion on the information about the features of Gyford's weblog as it is described in the selection.

Old London bridge, detail from *Vischer's London* (17th century).

This site will almost certainly become the most comprehensive example of the first-person historical account available on the Web. Webmaster Phil Gyford has taken *The Diary of Samuel Pepys*—a diary that spans 10 years of the 17th century—and set himself the task of presenting it over the next 10 years as a Weblog. The first great modern bureaucrat, founder of the professional navy, and through his diary, one of history's greatest unintentional historians, Pepys was a friend to such contemporaries as Isaac Newton[2] and Christopher Wren,[3] and even spent a bit of time in the Tower of London.[4] (But then again, who didn't?) His diary's entries, beginning on January 1st of 1660, include such day-to-day routines as government committees, parliamentary debates, and river outings, as well as such historic events as the coronation of Charles II after the dissolution of the Commonwealth, the "Black Death" of 1665,[5] and the Great Fire of London in 1666. **A**

2. **Isaac Newton**: English scientist, mathematician, and philosopher (1643–1727).
3. **Christopher Wren**: English architect; designer of fifty-three London churches, including St. Paul's Cathedral (1632–1723).
4. **Tower of London**: Fortress in London, often used as a prison for those of high status. Pepys was imprisoned in May 1679 for suspicion of treason. He was released two months later, and the charges were dropped the following year.
5. **"Black Death" of 1665**: Between late 1664 and 1666, bubonic plague killed perhaps more than 75,000 people in London, up to one-fifth of the city's population.

A Informational Focus Comparing and Contrasting How does the author contrast Pepys's intentional and unintentional accomplishments?

Vocabulary contemporaries (kuhn TEHM puh rehr eez) *n.:* people living during the same time period; peers.

Internet

Universal Access

Struggling Readers

Strategic Students Before students read the selection, make sure they understand what a weblog is. Then, ask students to brainstorm characteristics of diaries and weblogs. Ask them to consider the tone, style, audience, and purpose of both genres. This will help students recognize similarities and differences between the two genres as they read the selection. Ask students to give examples of famous diaries and weblogs they have read or heard about.

Advanced Learners

Acceleration Ask students to complete their graphic organizer comparing and contrasting different literary elements such as style, tone, theme, relevant details, and author's credibility. Ask students to use the characteristics listed in their Venn diagram to think about other examples of books that could be adapted to a weblog format.

WEB ARTICLE

Link to Today

This Link to Today describes how a seventeenth-century text has been reformatted as an Internet blog.

Read with a Purpose

Read to discover how Pepys's writings have found a new life in an online environment.

Build Background

When Samuel Pepys began writing the private diary he would continue for ten years, London was a thriving city. About 500,000 people lived in and around the city, and it was the center of England's political, business, and entertainment worlds. Pepys sought out contact with his fellow Londoners and took full advantage of the city's intellectual resources.

File Edit View Favorites Tools Help

Back Forward Stop Refresh Home

Address Go

Diary of Samuel Pepys WEBLOG

by Tom Regan, *csmonitor.com*

HALIFAX, NOVA SCOTIA—Thanks to weblogs, online forums, and personal websites, future historians (near future, anyway) are likely to have access to an overabundance of first-hand accounts of the mundanities of daily life, as well as world-changing events. Of course, there's no reason that the same tools can't be adapted to serve observations made before the invention of the Internet—or moveable type,[1] for that matter—and the following example makes a compelling argument that oldies often remain goodies.

1. **moveable type**: metal letters and punctuation used to print text; invented by Johannes Gutenberg around 1450.

Vocabulary **mundanities** (muhn DAN uh teez) *n.*: commonplace events of daily life.

The Tower of London.

Link to Today

This article tells how one man has incorporated Samuel Pepys's seventeenth-century diary into the format of today's weblog.

Direct Teach

Think About/Talk About

Read with a Purpose Now that they have read an excerpt of Pepys's diary, ask students to think about whether his writing is suited for a weblog.

Extend the Discussion

Finding Details What types of sources does the author suggest that future historians will rely on? ***Possible response:*** *He suggests that they will rely on weblogs, online forums, and personal Web sites.*

Making Inferences Why might people be interested in reading about the mundanities of daily life? ***Possible responses:*** *People might find comfort in knowing that most people's lives are not that different from their own; people find it interesting to take a glimpse into others' private thoughts and lives.*

Vocabulary: Own the Word

mundanities: *Mundanities* are "commonplace events of daily life." A near antonym is *rarities.* Use both in a sentence: Seeing a dog wander the street is among the *mundanities* of daily life, but seeing an elephant in the street is a rarity.

Selection Resources

Unit 3 Resources, on-level practice and assessment, p. 13

Teacher One Stop™, on-level lesson plans

Holt Audio Library: Selections and Summaries in Spanish

UA: Differentiating Instruction, graphic organizer, p. 122

UA: Supporting Instruction in Spanish, selection summary

ThinkCentral Online Assessment, Selection Standards Check

ThinkCentral Online Remediation

California Standards, pp. 550–555

- **Reading Standard 2.2** Analyze the way in which clarity of meaning is affected by the patterns of organization, hierarchical structures, repetition of the main ideas, syntax, and word choice in the text.

Standards Focus

Objectives

Students will identify comparison-contrast organization.

Motivate

What Do You Think?/QuickWrite

Ask students to compare readers of blogs and diaries. Have them consider how different audiences inspire different purposes and styles.

Preteach

Introducing Vocabulary

Read aloud the Vocabulary words, definitions, and sample sentences. Then, ask students to write synonyms for each of the following words, choosing from the Vocabulary words.

1. utilization [*consumption*]
2. tediousness [*mundanities*]
3. records [*archive*]
4. balanced [*complemented*]
5. equals [*contemporaries*]

English for Academic Success

Language Coach

Ask students to read the **Language Coach.** Have students find the origin of the word *domain. [from the Latin word* dominus, *or "lord."*]

Informational Text/ Writing Skills Focus

- Give students a copy of the Informational Text Focus graphic organizer before they read.
- Have students note the process that Gyford followed for the blog in their **Reader/Writer Notebooks.**

Learn It Online

If your student needs help organizing a paper [or extra reading support for informational text], introduce them to **Interactive Graphic Organizers**—tools for generating and organizing ideas, comparing and contrasting, and other key skills.

go.hrw.com H12-550 Go

INFORMATIONAL TEXT FOCUS

Preparing to Read

Reading Standard 2.2 (see pages A48–A50)

Link to Today

Diary of Samuel Pepys Weblog

What Do You Think

How can order and civilization affect human behavior?

QuickWrite

Do you keep a journal, diary, or blog? What motivates people to write these daily accounts? With a small group, discuss at least three advantages to keeping a record of your thoughts and activities.

Informational Text Focus

Comparing and Contrasting Articles often follow a **comparison-contrast** organization to present ideas about two or more topics. A writer compares topics by explaining what they have in common and contrasts them by explaining how they are different. In this article, Tom Regan compares Pepys's famous seventeenth-century diary with today's Internet blogs.

Into Action As you read, use a Venn diagram like the one below to note similarities and differences between diaries and Weblogs. The central region identifies features that both topics share. The outer regions list ways in which they differ.

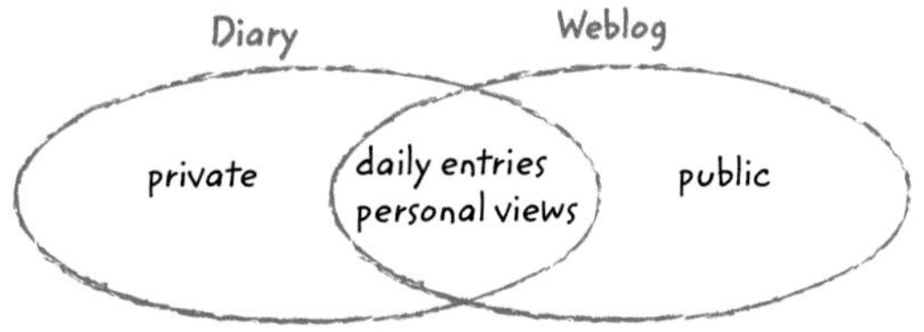

Writing Skills Focus

Preparing for Timed Writing Regan's article describes an online project that will take ten years to complete. Launching such a long-term project requires determination and a strong motivation. As you read, use your *Reader/Writer Notebook* to record clues that help you understand why Phil Gyford created this Web site.

TechFocus As you read the article, think about other ways modern technology might bring Pepys's diary to life.

Vocabulary

mundanities (muhn DAN uh teez) *n.:* commonplace events of daily life. *If you focus only on life's mundanities, you will not experience its glories.*

contemporaries (kuhn TEHM puh rehr eez) *n.:* people living during the same time period; peers. *Pepys and his contemporaries probably would have been amazed by modern media, such as the Internet.*

consumption (kuhn SUHMP shuhn) *n.:* use. *Public consumption of newspapers often increases during a scandal.*

complemented (KAHM pluh mehnt ihd) *v.:* made more complete by adding something. *The writer complemented his article with detailed illustrations.*

archive (AHR kyv) *n.:* collection of documents or other data. *The archive includes the writer's letters, journals, and books.*

Language Coach

Commonly Confused Words It is easy to confuse the verbs *complement*, meaning "to accompany" and *compliment*, meaning "to praise." In your *Reader/Writer Notebook*, write two sentences using each verb.

Reader/Writer Notebook

Use your **RWN** to complete the activities for this selection.

Learn It Online

Check out an interactive Venn diagram online.

go.hrw.com H12-550 Go

Selection Readability	
Easily Accessible Accessible Challenging	familiar context; accessible vocabulary; familiar syntax

Selection Summary

In this article, Tom Regan discusses how Web site designer Phil Gyford has turned Samuel Pepys's diary into a weblog. Gyford's site is complete with explanatory footnotes that enhance understanding of the text. Visitors can also view comments from all over the world—and add their own. An international community of readers echoes and discusses Pepys's daily musings.

Grades 9–10 Review Reading Standard 1.1 (see pages A48–A50)

Vocabulary Development

Vocabulary Check

Match the Vocabulary words with their definitions.

1. lamentable	a. flammable
2. flinging	b. pitiable
3. quench	c. upset
4. combustible	d. throwing
5. dismayed	e. putout

Vocabulary Skills: Synonyms

Were you able to match the Vocabulary words and definitions above correctly? If so, you know some synonyms for those words. The term *synonym* comes from a Greek word combining the meanings "similar" and "name." **Synonyms** are words that have the same or nearly the same meaning. Synonyms often reflect subtle differences or shades of meaning. English is a language rich with synonyms. When you write, you can explore synonyms to vary your writing or to choose the word that communicates exactly what you mean.

Consider the word *flinging*. One synonym is *throwing*. But what other synonyms can you find for *flinging*? You can use a dictionary or thesaurus to complete a word web to show some synonyms for *flinging*.

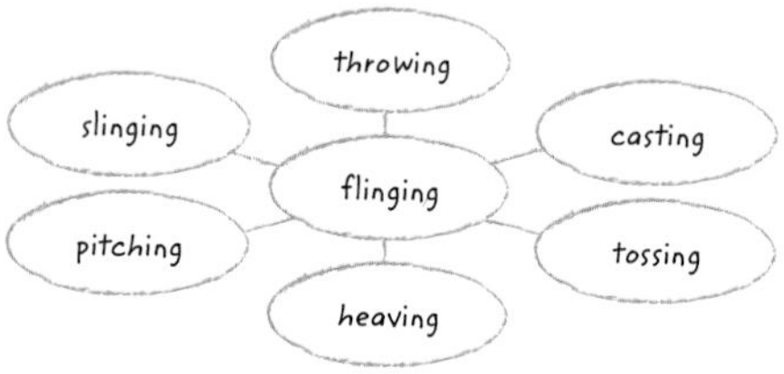

Each of these choices conveys a similar idea with a different shade of meaning. Understanding those shades of meaning helps you choose a word to say something specific or exact. For example, *throwing* is a general synonym for *flinging*. *Flinging* suggests throwing forcefully, *heaving* suggests throwing with effort, *tossing* suggests throwing casually, and *pitching* suggests throwing carefully.

Your Turn

Use a dictionary or thesaurus to find synonyms for the Vocabulary words. Create a word web for each word. Then, use a synonym from each web to replace the Vocabulary words in the following sentences. Discuss with a partner whether changing the word alters the sentence's meaning.

1. He is *flinging* the papers into the trash.
2. *Quench* the fire before you go to bed.
3. News of the tragedy *dismayed* us.

Language Coach

Suffixes You can form adjectives from some verbs by adding the suffixes *–able* or *–ible*, which mean "worthy of" or "capable of." Create adjectives by combining the verbs and suffixes listed below. Then, tell the meaning of each adjective.

1. combust + *–ible*
2. respect + *–able*
3. access + *–ible*
4. manage + *–able*

Academic Vocabulary

Write About

Consider how keeping a diary might enhance your life and help you participate in life more fully. Then, write a paragraph to convince a friend to keep a diary.

For **CHOICES** see page 555.

Universal Access: Vocabulary Development

English Learners

English for Academic Success Teach students how to look for synonyms in a print or online dictionary or thesaurus.

- Have them look up the vocabulary words in each reference book, and discuss the differences between the words and their synonyms.
- Ask them to transcribe the synonyms of the Academic Vocabulary words *enhance, participate, dominate,* and *convince.*
- Have them discuss variations in the meaning of each Academic Vocabulary word they looked up.
- Tell students that they should keep a thesaurus handy especially during writing so that they can think of specific words instead of repeating the same, familiar words.

✔ See the **Academic and Selection Vocabulary Skill Builder** in **UA: Differentiating Instruction.**

Independent Practice

Vocabulary Development

Vocabulary Check

1. *b* **2.** *d*
3. *e* **4.** *a*
5. *c*

Your Turn

Possible responses:

1. *tossing; stuffing; throwing*
2. *douse; drench; soak; put out*
3. *devastated; concerned; appalled; disheartened*

English for Academic Success

Language Coach

Possible responses:

1. *combustible—capable of catching fire*
2. *respectable—worthy of respect*
3. *accessible—capable of being reached*
4. *manageable—capable of being managed or controlled*

English for Academic Success

Academic Vocabulary

Possible response: *Keeping a diary enhances people's lives by helping them consider their actions each day of their lives. People can participate in life more fully because writing diary entries increases their awareness of how they are reacting to things and growing through changes. Students' paragraphs should convince a friend to keep a diary by listing several advantages and examples from personal experience.*

Assess

Unit 3 Resources, Selection Standards Check, p. 10

ThinkCentral Online Assessment, Selection Standards Check

Teacher One Stop™, editable Selection Standards Check

Check for Understanding

Independent Practice

Reading Skills Focus

Possible responses:

1. *It began in the king's baker's house on Pudding Lane and spread due to drought.*
2. *He learned about it from Pepys's account.*
3. *He thought houses should be torn down so the fire would have nothing to burn.*
4. *Pepys was alarmed, but acted quickly in reporting the incident to the king so measures could be taken.*
5. *Remind students to evaluate the author's credibility by thinking about what possible emotions could have interfered with a factual account of the fire.*

Literary Skills Focus

Possible responses:

6. *Pepys shows initiative and a sincere interest in assessing the fire's damage by suggesting solutions to the king.*
7. *Pepys is observant and level-headed; he takes responsibility for helping during a disaster.*
8. *Pepys does not describe the sounds of London during the fire, how long the fire lasted, and how it was finally extinguished.*
9. *The entries appear in chronological order. This structure is effective because the diarist can re-read to find the order of events. Pepys probably wanted to record events exactly as he remembered them.*
10. *Pepys's diction is precise and objective for the most part, but it ventures into being emotional at times. His language becomes sentimental when he sees human and animal hardship, as in the phrases "poor pigeons" and "poor little Mitchell and our Sarah."*

Applying Your Skills

Reading Standard 2.2, 2.4, 3.1 (see pages A48–A50)
Writing Standard 2.1c, 2.1e (see pages A51–A52)

from The Diary of Samuel Pepys

Literary Response and Analysis

Reading Skills Focus

Quick Check

1. Where did the fire start, and what caused it to spread through London?
2. How did the king learn about the extent of the fire?
3. What did Pepys think should be done to stop the fire? Why?

Read with a Purpose

4. When Pepys realized the extent of the fire, what were his emotional and practical responses?

Reading Skills: Evaluating an Author's Credibility

5. You analyzed Pepys's statements about the fire. Now, evaluate Pepys's credibility. Review your chart, and consider the author's purpose, audience, background, attitude toward his subject, and any bias you think he might have. Do you find Pepys's account credible? Why? When might an eyewitness account not be credible?

Statement About the Fire	Source of the Information	Fact, Opinion, or Emotional Response?
Pepys saw the fire far off and was not worried.	Pepys is an eyewitness; he also hears about the fire from Jane.	The fire is a fact, but Pepys also feels relief that it is far off.

Literary Skills Focus

Literary Analysis

6. **Draw Conclusions** What do you learn about Pepys from his movements during the fire?
7. **Infer** What can you infer about Pepys's character from the concerns he expresses during the fire?
8. **Analyze** Pepys probably wrote this entry after, not as, the fire took place. What details appear to be omitted from his description of the fire?

Literary Skills: Diary

9. **Analyze** How is this diary entry organized? Why is this structure effective for a diarist?

Literary Skills Review: Diction

10. **Interpret** A writer's choice of words is called **diction.** Writers choose words depending on their audience, subject, and purpose. Diction may be simple or flowery, concrete or abstract, modern or old-fashioned, general or specific, casual or formal. How would you describe Pepys's diction? Give examples to support your answer.

Writing Skills Focus

Think as a Reader/Writer

Use It in Your Writing Now that you have seen how details can enrich an account in a diary, use the same technique to write a diary entry about an event in your own life. What would you like to remember about the event? Include details to show what you saw, thought, and felt.

What Do You Think Now? Disasters can create chaos and disorder. How did the people of London, including Pepys, respond to the fire that disrupted their lives?

Universal Access

Struggling Writers

Have students discuss with a partner two events they might want to write about. As one student tells what they remember about each event, the partner should record to see the amount of detail that the student provides about each event. After both students have shared two events and details, they can choose to write on the event that generated more details. Tell students to individually construct a three-column chart in which they record in greater detail the sights, feelings, and thought about the event. Have them refer to their charts as they write.

What Do You Think Now?

Have students point out specific details in the texts to show how Pepys and others in London responded to the fire.

time it got as far as the Steelyard while I was there. Everybody endeavoring to remove their goods, and flinging into the river or bringing them into lighters[6] that lay off. Poor people staying in their houses as long as till the very fire touched them, and then running into boats or clambering from one pair of stair by the waterside to another. And among other things, the poor pigeons I perceive were loath to leave their houses, but hovered about the windows and balconies till they were some of them burned, their wings, and fell down.

Having stayed, and in an hour's time seen the fire rage every way, and nobody to my sight endeavoring to quench it, but to remove their goods and leave all to the fire; and having seen it get as far as the Steelyard, and the wind mighty high and driving it into the City, and everything, after so long a drought, proving combustible, even the very stones of churches, and among other things, the poor steeple by which pretty Mrs.—lives, and whereof my old schoolfellow Elborough is parson, taken fire in the very top and there burned till it fall down—I to Whitehall with a gentleman with me who desired to go off from the Tower to see the fire in my boat—to Whitehall, and there up to the King's closet in the chapel, where people came about me and I did give them an account dismayed them all; and word was carried in to the King, so I was called for and did tell the King and Duke of York what I saw, and that unless his Majesty did command houses to be pulled down, nothing could stop the fire. . . . **B**

6. **lighters:** large, open barges.

B Reading Focus **Evaluating an Author's Credibility** How does knowing that Pepys will speak with the king make his account more credible?

Vocabulary **flinging** (FLIHNG ihng) *v.:* throwing forcefully.
quench (kwehnch) *v.:* put out; extinguish.
combustible (kuhm BUHS tuh buhl) *adj.:* easy to set on fire; fast-burning.
dismayed (dihs MAYD) *v.:* upset; alarmed.

The Great Fire of London, September 1666, with Ludgate and Old St. Paul's (c. 1670). Oil on canvas. Yale Center for British Art, Paul Mellon Collection, USA.

Think About/Talk About

Comprehension

B Reading Focus

Possible response: *Pepys's conversation with the king either shows that the writer is an important person or that the king is very accessible to his people. Pepys saw the fire itself, and he was in the king's chambers recommending how to quench the flames.*

Extend the Discussion

Style Note that the paragraph that begins with "Having stayed . . . " consists of a single sentence. What effect does this long, packed sentence have? ***Possible responses:*** *It conveys the great urgency Pepys felt; it shows how his mind was racing; it creates an almost unbearable tension; it suggests there was no revision of the writing, which is characteristic of a diary.*

Vocabulary: Own the Word

- **lamentable:** To *lament* (verb form) means to mourn or grieve. A *lament* (noun form) can also be an elegy or mournful song. Ask students to give an example of a *lamentable* situation.
- **flinging:** Demonstrate the posture of a person who is *flinging* a pebble into a lake. Ask one or two students to stand at their desks and demonstrate.
- **quench:** Ask students to complete the following sentence: Pepys observed that, instead of trying to *quench* the fire, people . . .
- **combustible:** Ask students to list examples of highly *combustible* substances. ***Possible responses:*** *explosives, fireworks, lighter fluid, aerosol sprays, matches*
- **dismayed:** Write *dismayed* in a center circle on the board, with the definition "upset." Have students add synonyms to the semantic web. ***Possible responses:*** *appalled, horrified, daunted, disconcerted, surprised, shocked*

California Standards, pp. 548–549

- **Reading Standard 2.2** Analyze the way in which clarity of meaning is affected by the patterns of organization, hierarchical structures, repetition of the main ideas, syntax, and word choice in the text.
- **Reading Standard 2.4** Make warranted and reasonable assertions about the author's arguments by using elements of the text to defend and clarify interpretations.
- **Reading Standard 3.1** Analyze characteristics of subgenres (e.g., satire, parody, allegory, pastoral) that are used in poetry, prose, plays, novels, short stories, essays, and other basic genres.
- **Grades 9–10 Review Reading Standard 1.1** Identify and use the literal and figurative meanings of words and understand word derivations.
- **Writing Standard 2.1** Write fictional, autobiographical, or biographical narratives: **c.** Describe with concrete sensory details the sights, sounds, and smells of a scene and the specific actions, movements, gestures, and feelings of the characters; use interior monologue to depict the characters' feelings. **e.** Make effective use of descriptions of appearance, images, shifting perspectives, and sensory details.

Reading Standard 2.2, 3.4 (see pages A48–A50)
Writing Standard 2.2a–e (see pages A51–A52)
Listening and Speaking 2.3a–e (see pages A53–A55)

CHOICES

As you respond to the Choices, use these **Academic Vocabulary** words as appropriate: approach, convince, dominate, enhance, participate.

REVIEW

Compare Diary and Blog

With a partner, use the Internet to visit the Web site where Phil Gyford is posting Samuel Pepys's diary in Weblog form. Find an entry that interests you, and read it closely. Click on some of the links in the entry. Discuss with your partner how this experience differs from reading a printed diary entry like the one on page 546. Then, read the comments that blog visitors have added to the diary entry. Discuss this experience with your partner. How does it enhance your appreciation of what Pepys wrote in the entry itself?

CONNECT

Log On

Use a search engine to locate Gyford's blog. Read the current entries posted, and then participate further by adding a comment, perhaps to explain a word or reference in the entry or to answer another reader's question. You may also wish to ask a question of your own and see how others respond.

Publish Pepys in a Modern Format

TechFocus Phil Gyford brought Pepys's diary into the modern age by transforming it into a blog. What other forms might a modern version of the diary take? In a small group, turn Pepys's diary entry on pages 546–547 into another form in which a modern person might share a similar personal experience: for example, a digital story, a video diary, or even a series of cell-phone text messages. Share your updated version of Pepys's diary with your class.

EXTEND

Discuss the Diary and Poem

British poet John Dryden wrote a poem about the year 1666 in London, including the excerpt below about the Great Fire. Read the stanzas closely that depict the panic triggered by the spreading fire. With a small group, discuss the following question: How does Dryden's imagery enhance what you learned about the fire from Pepys (pages 546–547)?

from **Annus Mirabilis: The Year of Wonders**

At length the crackling noise and dreadful blaze
  Call'd up some waking lover to the sight;
And long it was ere he the rest could raise,
  Whose heavy eyelids yet were full of night.

The next to danger, hot pursued by fate,
  Half-clothed, half-naked, hastily retire:
And frighted mothers strike their breasts too late,
  For helpless infants left amidst the fire.

Their cries soon waken all the dwellers near;
  Now murmuring noises rise in every street:
The more remote run stumbling with their fear,
  And in the dark men jostle as they meet.

Analyze Depictions of the Great Fire

Timed Writing Study the painting of the Great Fire of London on page 547. How does it add to what you learned from the Pepys diary entry and the Dryden stanzas above? Write an essay responding to the following question: Which of the three depictions of the fire is the most effective, and why? Cite examples.

Independent Practice

Choices: Evaluation Criteria

Review: Homework
Compare Diary and Blog

Students show understanding of the strengths and possible weaknesses of both genres.

Connect: Homework
Log On

Students' comments demonstrate a close reading of the blog entry.

Connect: Homework
Publish Pepys in a Modern Format

Students demonstrate how their modern version creatively uses current technology to present Pepys's diary in another form.

Extend: Homework
Discuss the Diary and Poem

Students exhibit understanding of the imagery in Dryden's poem and connect the imagery to Pepys's account of the fire.

Extend: Timed Writing 40–50 Minutes

Students give detailed examples and reasons in their responses and show understanding of details in each representation.

Assess

Unit 3 Resources, Selection Standards Check, pp. 10, 16

ThinkCentral Online Assessment, Selection Standards Check

Teacher One Stop™, editable Selection Standards Check

Reteach

ThinkCentral Online Remediation

Standards Focus

Objectives

Students will
- understand narrative voice
- make critical judgments

Selection Introduction

Think About the Writer

Have students identify current media trends similar to the topics that interested Defoe, for example, journalism.

For Independent Reading

- *The Barbary Plague: The Black Death in Victorian San Francisco,* Marilyn Chase
- *The Plague,* Albert Camus

Motivate

What Do You Think?/QuickWrite

Tell students they can refer to news sources to respond to the QuickWrite. They may want to do some research online, talk to an adult, or compare ideas with each other before writing the paragraph in their **Reader/Writer Notebooks.**

English for Academic Success

Academic Vocabulary

Look for opportunities to use the Academic Vocabulary words in this unit.

- **approach,** ***n.:*** way of addressing something
- **enhance,** ***v.:*** improve the quality of

California Standards, pp. 556–563

- **Reading Standard 3.3** Analyze the ways in which irony, tone, mood, the author's style, and the "sound" of language achieve specific rhetorical or aesthetic purposes or both.
- **Grades 9–10 Review Reading Standard 3.9** Explain how voice, persona, and the choice of a narrator affect characterization and the tone, plot, and credibility of a text.

Preparing to Read

from A Journal of the Plague Year

What Do You Think? How can order and civilization affect human behavior?

QuickWrite

Do you keep a journal, diary, or blog? What motivates people to write these daily accounts? With a small group, discuss three advantages to keeping a record of your thoughts and activities.

Daniel Defoe. Colored engraving after Michiel van der Gucht. The Granger Collection, New York.

MEET THE WRITER

Daniel Defoe

(1660–1731)

A skillful journalist and pamphleteer, Defoe wrote hundreds of works. We remember Defoe chiefly for the writing he produced late in life, *Robinson Crusoe* and *Moll Flanders,* books we now consider early examples of the realistic English novel.

A Crowded Career

Defoe had a complicated career and was at various times a tradesman, a political agent, a reformer, and a journalist. Born Daniel Foe, he added the aristocratic prefix *De* to his name when he was about thirty-five. As a Dissenter, a Nonconformist who did not belong to the Anglican Church, Defoe was barred from attending Oxford or Cambridge University. Nevertheless, he received an excellent education at a Dissenters' academy. As a merchant dealing in wool, real estate, diving bells, and other commodities, he made and lost fortunes. He participated in politics, sometimes offending the government, at other times serving as a spy or propagandist. Throughout these experiences, he wrote frequently—altogether over five hundred works, in prose and verse, including a news pamphlet, *The Review,* which he published three times a week for over seven years. He addressed a broad range of subjects, including the choosing of a wife, the history of the devil, and the manufacture of glass.

Fiction or Nonfiction?

Defoe penned his best-known tales after years of writing as a journalist. Though fiction, *Robinson Crusoe, Moll Flanders,* and *A Journal of the Plague Year* appear to be true autobiographical accounts. Defoe's plain, vigorous style suits his characters and subject matter well. He uses idiomatic English and fills his stories with detailed practical knowledge. For *A Journal of the Plague Year,* presented as an eyewitness account of the London plague of 1665, Defoe sought convincing details in reports, pamphlets, mortality records, and sermons from the time of the plague, and in the memories of his uncle, Henry Foe (perhaps the H. F. who narrates the journal). A masterpiece, the *Journal* is a realistic work of fiction that grips readers even today.

Think About the Writer What current or recent events might appeal to Defoe as sources for a fictional journal or a realistic novel?

Selection Readability	
Easily Accessible Accessible **Challenging**	historical context; complex syntax; unfamiliar vocabulary

Reading Standard 3.3; **Grades 9–10 Review**
Reading Standard 3.9 (see pages A48–A50)

Literary Skills Focus

Narrative Voice A **narrator** is the storyteller in a work of fiction. *A Journal of the Plague Year* has a first-person narrator who sees and participates in the events described. The narrator's voice or character is revealed through the subject matter, the tone, and the narrator's language.

Less personal and intimate than a diary, a **journal** is a record of events kept regularly by a person who sees or takes part in the events. The words *journalism* and *journal* are related. Like newspapers, journals report facts. Journals also record the writer's reaction to events. As you read, think about how you would describe the narrator's voice. What does he think about his subject, and how does he express his thoughts?

Reading Skills Focus

Making Critical Judgments Defoe creates a character, H. F., to report his experiences of the plague. As you read, you will critically judge this character's nature, beliefs, and credibility. To judge critically is not to correct or complain about a work; rather, it is to analyze what the narrator says and how, when, and why he says it.

Into Action Use a chart like the one below to note what details the narrator relates, whether they are facts or reactions, and why the narrator chooses to include them.

Detail H. F. Relates	Fact or Reaction?	Why H. F. Includes the Detail
how the plague spread	H. F. thinks it's a fact.	to inform but also to build credibility

Writing Skills Focus

Think as a Reader/Writer

Find It in Your Reading Defoe uses dialogue to capture what H. F. overhears in Bell Alley. In your *Reader/Writer Notebook,* note details in the dialogue and the description surrounding the dialogue that make the passage vivid. How does Defoe's use of dialogue and description of what H. F. hears affect the account and its narrative voice?

Vocabulary

infect (ihn FEHKT) *v.:* spread a disease to. *Londoners believed contact with the sick could infect the healthy.*

proportion (pruh PAWR shuhn) *n.:* ratio; relative amount. *The proportion of Londoners sick with the plague decreased as people fled to the country.*

consequently (KAHN suh kwehnt lee) *adv.:* as a result of something. *H. F. had to go to his brother's house in the city; consequently, he passed houses where people were sick.*

credible (KREHD uh buhl) *adj.:* believable. *The journal's many details of London life during the plague make the account credible.*

torment (TAWR mehnt) *n.:* great pain. *What torment the survivors of the plague suffered as they grieved lost friends!*

quarantine (KWAWR uhn teen) *n.:* enforced isolation of ill people to prevent the spread of sickness. *Placing people in quarantine did not stop the spread of plague because rats carried the disease.*

Language Coach

Word Origins The word *quarantine* comes from the Italian word for *forty*. In the fourteenth century, there was a rule in Italy that ships from other nations had to wait forty days before they could unload passengers or cargo. What might have inspired this rule? How does this word origin help you remember the meaning of *quarantine?*

Learn It Online
Use Word Watch online to meet these Vocabulary words the interactive way.
go.hrw.com H12-557 Go

Reader/Writer Notebook
Use your **RWN** to complete the activities for this selection.

Selection Resources

Unit 3 Resources, on-level practice and assessment, p. 18

Teacher One Stop™, on-level lesson plans and all print resources

Holt Audio Library

Holt Audio Library: Selections and Summaries in Spanish

UA: Differentiating Instruction, graphic organizer, p. 123

UA: Supporting Instruction in Spanish, selection summary

Analyzing Visuals Transparencies, p. 22

ThinkCentral Online Assessment, Selection Standards Check

ThinkCentral Online Remediation

Preteach

Introducing Vocabulary

Use this activity to check students' understanding.

1. Name two diseases that **infect** people.
2. Guess the **proportion** of teachers to students in your school.
3. Tell about a major decision you made and what happened **consequently**.
4. List elements that make online resources **credible**.
5. Describe the feelings that stem from **torment**.
6. Name a situation in which people would be placed in **quarantine**.

English for Academic Success

Language Coach

After students read the **Language Coach**, give them other examples of word origins. [Infect *comes from the Latin root* infectus, *meaning "spoiled, stained."*]

Literary Skills Focus

As you read and discuss the selection with students, have them note instances in which the author's voice is most evident.

Reading Skills Focus

Give students a copy of the Reading Skills Focus graphic organizer before they read. (See **Unit 3 Resources**.) Tell them to use their responses to answer the questions on the Applying Your Skills page.

Writing Skills Focus

Have students record vivid details in dialogue and descriptions in their **Reader/Writer Notebooks**. Students can use their notes to complete the Writing Skills Focus activity.

Learn It Online
Send students to **Word Watch** for audio pronunciations, synonyms and antonyms, and brief histories of word origins.
go.hrw.com H12-557 Go

Teacher Preparation

Selection Summary

These excerpts are from Daniel Defoe's retrospective account of the bubonic plague that ravaged London in 1665, killing tens of thousands and instilling in survivors a terror of contagion. Although the work presents itself as nonfiction, it is a fictional account. The episodes here focus on what the narrator sees in his daily walks around plague-infected London—people dying, fleeing, and mourning.

Direct Teach

Think About/Talk About

Read with a Purpose Have students read the Read with a Purpose statement. Then, ask them to look in the selection for details that tell about how the bubonic plague changed daily life in London.

Analysis

A Literary Focus

Possible response: *The narrator associates his expertise with that of doctors and explains the process of the disease as if he were teaching it to readers. His tone is certain and assured.*

Extend the Discussion

Evaluating Why do you think Defoe chose to have H. F. include numerical data in his account? Provide examples from the text to support your answer. ***Possible responses:*** *H. F. mentions details such as the number of people whom one person could infect and the average time period from the first appearance of symptoms to the victim's death. These details show the reader that H. F. is well-informed; they also serve to convey the magnitude and severity of the plague.*

NOVEL

from A Journal of the Plague Year

by **Daniel Defoe**

Read with a Purpose

Read to learn how the fear of infectious disease and death can affect daily life.

Build Background

A Journal of the Plague Year is set in 1665, during the last terrible visitation of the bubonic plague in London. (Pepys survived and recorded the event in his *Diary*.) When Defoe published his work in 1722, the plague had reappeared in Europe, reaching Marseilles in France. Fearful that merchant ships would bring infection to England, the English government placed a temporary embargo on shipping. Although nearly sixty years had been enough time for the English to lose their fear of the plague, Defoe's *Journal*—possibly published at his government's request—reminded them of its terrors. The *Journal*'s narrator identifies himself only as "H. F.," a citizen of London.

1. The Infection Spreads

Here the opinion of the physicians agreed with my observation afterward, namely, that the danger was spreading insensibly, for the sick could infect none but those that came within reach of the sick person; but that one man who may have really received the infection and knows it not, but goes abroad and about as a sound person, may give the plague to a thousand people, and they to greater numbers in proportion, and neither the person giving the infection or the persons receiving it know anything of it, and perhaps not feel the effects of it for several days after. **A**

For example, many persons in the time of this visitation never perceived that they were infected till they found to their unspeakable surprise, the tokens come out upon them; after which they seldom lived six hours; for those spots they called the tokens were really gangrene spots, or mortified flesh[1] in small knobs as broad as a little silver penny, and hard as a piece of callus or horn; so that, when the disease was come up to that length, there was nothing could follow but certain death; and yet, as I said, they knew nothing of their being infected, nor found themselves so much as out of order, till those mortal[2] marks were upon them. But everybody must allow that they were infected in a high degree before, and must have been so some time, and consequently their breath, their sweat, their very clothes, were contagious for many days before. . . .

2. Dismal Scenes

I had some little obligations, indeed, upon me to go to my brother's house, which was in Coleman Street[3]

1. **gangrene . . . flesh:** decay of soft tissues from a blockage of blood flow.
2. **mortal:** fatal.
3. **Coleman Street:** This place and other places Defoe names are all within the old City of London, unless otherwise noted.

A Literary Focus **Narrative Voice** How does H. F. lend his own narrative voice authority in this paragraph?

Vocabulary **infect** (ihn FEHKT) *v.:* spread a disease to.
proportion (pruh PAWR shuhn) *n.:* ratio; relative amount.
consequently (KAHN suh kwehnt lee) *adv.:* as a result of something.

Universal Access

English Learners

English for Academic Success Read sections of "A Journal of the Plague Year" aloud as students follow along in their books. Point out and explain idiomatic expressions, such as "goes . . . about." Remind students to read the annotations for information about unfamiliar terms and vocabulary.

Struggling Readers

Strategic Students To help students read the journal, model the reading skill of making critical judgments. Explain that making critical judgments means to question the significance and purpose of the author's statements. For example, in the first sentence of the selection, the narrator claims that physicians agree with his observation about the spreading of the plague. This statement is made to state the narrator's credibility.

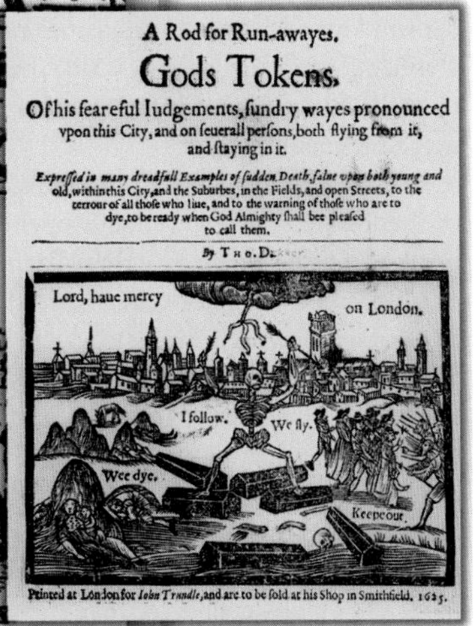

A Rod for Run-awayes.

Gods Tokens.

Of his feareful Iudgements, sundry wayes pronounced vpon this City, and on seuerall persons, both flying from it, and staying in it.

Expressed in many dreadfull Examples of sudden Death, falne vpon both young and old, within this City, and the Suburbes, in the Fields, and open Streets, to the terrour of all those who liue, and to the warning of those who are to dye, to be ready when God Almighty shall bee pleased to call them.

By Tho. D

Printed at London for *Iohn Trundle*, and are to be sold at his Shop in Smithfield. 1625.

God's Tokens, A Rod for Runaways (1625). Woodcut.

Analyzing Visuals

Connecting to the Text
How do the images and captions convey the terror and magnitude of the plague Defoe describes in the selection?

Aspects of the Great Plague of London (1665).
The Granger Collection, New York.

Think About/Talk About

Extend the Discussion

Summarizing Summarize how the plague manifested itself physically. ***Possible response:*** *The plague caused small, hard gangrene spots to appear on the skin.*

Speculating Why does Defoe assume a first-person viewpoint even though he was not an eyewitness to the plague? ***Possible response:*** *Defoe probably wants to make the Journal seem convincing and personal.*

Analyzing Visuals

Connecting to the Text: *The upper images depict people evacuating London by the masses, conveying the magnitude of the plague. "Hell" awaits the dead that are spilling out of carts.*

Vocabulary: Own the Word

- **infect**: Ask students: "Has your computer ever been *infected* with a virus? Explain when and how it got *infected*. What other kinds of *infections* are you familiar with?"
- **proportion:** If *proportion* refers to the quota or percentage of parts to the whole, ask students what Defoe means when he uses the word *proportion* to discuss the spread of the plague.
- **consequently:** Tell students that while *consequently* does not have a negative connotation, the noun form of the word *consequence* does. For example: "You must be prepared to deal with the *consequences* of not studying for today's test." Ask students to write a sentence that uses both *consequently* and *consequence.*

Advanced Learners

Enrichment Discuss with students the ways in which today's print and broadcast media blend news reporting with entertainment. Ask students for specific examples. Encourage them to reflect on how this blending of elements affects our perceptions of news events. Then, ask them to compare the strategies Defoe uses in his "Journal" with those they have observed in contemporary media.

Students with Disabilities

Read aloud the first paragraph of the selection to introduce the concept of author's voice. Ask whether the author sounds calm, enraged, amused, sad, or critical. Explain that students should pay attention to word choice or diction to determine the author's voice. Challenge students to infer the author's purpose based on his voice.

Model the Skill

- Provide students with copies of the Reading Skills Focus graphic organizer for "A Journal of the Plague Year." (See **Unit 3 Resources**.)
- Read aloud the paragraph on p. 560 that begins with, "Just in Bell Alley, . . ." Point out how the narrator describes particularly dreary scenes of the plague and how he often expresses his own personal feelings about those scenes. For example, he retells the tragic story of a merchant who takes his life, presumably because of his fear of the plague. Explain that the narrator probably wants to show the tragic consequences of the plague, and that he might want to show the reader his close involvement with the events he narrates.

Detail H. F. Relates	Fact or Reaction?
A merchant has committed suicide.	H. F. presents it as fact.

Why H. F. Includes the Detail:

to inform readers and show his involvement with the events

Guided Practice: Apply

Turn-Pair-Share Have students discuss other instances in which H. F. retells particularly tragic events. Ask them to discuss why the narrator might prefer to retell specific anecdotes rather than describe the broad effects of the plague on the population of London.

parish and which he had left to my care, and I went at first every day, but afterward only once or twice a week.

In these walks I had many dismal scenes before my eyes, as particularly of persons falling dead in the streets, terrible shrieks and screechings of women, who, in their agonies, would throw open their chamber windows and cry out in a dismal, surprising manner. It is impossible to describe the variety of postures in which the passions of the poor people would express themselves.

Passing through Tokenhouse Yard, in Lothbury, of a sudden a casement[4] violently opened just over my head, and a woman gave three frightful screeches, and then cried, "Oh! death, death, death!" in a most inimitable[5] tone, and which struck me with horror and a chillness in my very blood. There was nobody to be seen in the whole street, neither did any other window open, for people had no curiosity now in any case, nor could anybody help one another, so I went on to pass into Bell Alley. **B** **C**

Just in Bell Alley, on the right hand of the passage, there was a more terrible cry than that, though it was not so directed out at the window; but the whole family was in a terrible fright, and I could hear women and children run screaming about the rooms like distracted, when a garret[6] window opened and somebody from a window on the other side the alley called and asked, "What is the matter?" upon which, from the first window, it was answered, "Oh Lord, my old master has hanged himself!" The other asked again, "Is he quite dead?" and the first answered, "Ay, ay, quite dead; quite dead and cold!" This person was a merchant and a deputy alderman, and very rich. I care not to mention the name, though I knew his name too, but that would be an hardship to the family, which is now flourishing again.

4. **casement:** hinged window.
5. **inimitable:** difficult or impossible to imitate.
6. **garret:** attic.

B Literary Focus Narrative Voice In what tone does H. F. report the terrible sights he encounters as he walks about the city? How does this tone help create narrative voice?

C Reading Focus Making Critical Judgments Comment on or expand upon H. F.'s explanation for the absence of a reaction from anyone else to the cries of the woman at Tokenhouse Yard.

But this is but one; it is scarce credible what dreadful cases happened in particular families every day. People in the rage of the distemper, or in the torment of their swellings, which was indeed intolerable, running out of their own government,[7] raving and distracted, and oftentimes laying violent hands upon themselves, throwing themselves out at their windows, shooting themselves, etc.; mothers murdering their own children in their lunacy,[8] some dying of mere grief as a passion, some of mere fright and surprise without any infection at all, others frighted into idiotism and foolish distractions, some into despair and lunacy, others into melancholy madness.

The pain of the swelling was in particular very violent, and to some intolerable; the physicians and surgeons may be said to have tortured many poor creatures even to death. The swellings in some grew hard, and they applied violent drawing plasters or poultices[9] to break them, and if these did not do they cut and scarified[10] them in a terrible manner. In some those swellings were made hard partly by the force of the distemper and partly by their being too violently drawn, and were so hard that no instrument could cut them, and then they burnt them with caustics,[11] so that many died raving mad with the torment, and some in the very operation. In these distresses, some, for want of help to hold them down in their beds, or to look to them, laid hands upon themselves as above. Some broke out into the streets, perhaps naked, and would run directly down to the river if they were not stopped by the watchman or other officers, and plunge themselves into the water wherever they found it.

It often pierced my very soul to hear the groans and cries of those who were thus tormented, but of the two this was counted the most promising particular in the whole infection, for if these swellings

7. **out of their own government:** unable to control themselves.
8. **lunacy:** madness.
9. **drawing plasters or poultices:** hot packs used to soften sores and draw infection to the skin's surface.
10. **scarified:** punctured.
11. **caustics:** chemicals that can burn or eat away flesh.

Vocabulary **credible** (KREHD uh buhl) *adj.:* believable.
torment (TAWR mehnt) *n.:* great pain.

Reaching Reluctant Readers

Have students take on the role of London's city officials in 1665. Have them discuss the effects of the epidemic and devise an emergency plan to cope with these effects and minimize the spread of the disease. Students should base their discussion on what they have learned about the bubonic plague in Defoe's "Journal." Ask students to organize their plan in a chart in which they list emerging problems and possible solutions. Then, have students compare and contrast counteraction in Defoe's time with their solutions.

Universal Access

AAVE Students Who Use African American Vernacular English

English for Academic Success Read aloud the last sentence in the second full paragraph on p. 560. Point out the single negative word used in each clause: *nobody, neither, no,* and *nor.* Tell students to avoid double negatives; for example, students might want to write "There wasn't nobody," "neither did no other window," and "people had no curiosity now in no case." Remind students that in formal English, only one negative word is used in a thought.

could be brought to a head, and to break and run, or, as the surgeons call it, to digest, the patient generally recovered; whereas those who, like the gentlewoman's daughter, were struck with death at the beginning, and had the tokens come out upon them, often went about indifferent easy till a little before they died, and some till the moment they dropped down, as in apoplexies[12] and epilepsies is often the case. Such would be taken suddenly very sick, and would run to a bench or bulk,[13] or any convenient place that offered itself, or to their own houses if possible, as I mentioned before, and there sit down, grow faint, and die. This kind of dying was much the same as it was with those who die of common mortifications,[14] who die swooning, and, as it were, go away in a dream. Such as died thus had very little notice of their being infected at all till the gangrene was spread through their whole body; nor could physicians themselves know certainly how it was with them till they opened their breasts or other parts of their body and saw the tokens. **D**

3. Escape from Quarantine

I remember one citizen who, having thus broken out of his house in Aldersgate Street or thereabout, went along the road to Islington;[15] he attempted to have gone in at the Angel Inn, and after that the White Horse, two inns known still by the same signs, but was refused; after which he came to the Pied Bull, an inn also still continuing the same sign. He asked them for lodging for one night only, pretending to be going into Lincolnshire,[16] and assuring them of his being very sound and free from the infection, which also at that time had not reached much that way.

They told him they had no lodging that they could spare but one bed up in the garret, and that they could spare that bed for one night, some drovers being expected the next day with cattle; so, if he would accept of that lodging, he might have it, which he did. So a servant was sent up with a candle with him to show him the room. He was very well dressed, and looked like a person not used to lie in a garret; and when he came to the room he fetched a deep sigh, and said to the servant, "I have seldom lain in such a lodging as this." However, the servant assuring him again that they had no better, "Well," says he, "I must make shift; this is a dreadful time; but it is but for one night." So he sat down upon the bedside, and bade the maid, I think it was, fetch him up a pint of warm ale. Accordingly the servant went for the ale, but some hurry in the house, which perhaps employed her other ways, put it out of her head, and she went up no more to him.

The next morning, seeing no appearance of the gentleman, somebody in the house asked the servant that had showed him upstairs what was become of him. She started. "Alas!" says she, "I never thought more of him. He bade me carry him some warm ale, but I forgot." Upon which, not the maid, but some other person was sent up to see after him, who, coming into the room, found him stark dead and almost cold, stretched out across the bed. His clothes were pulled off, his jaw fallen, his eyes open in a most frightful posture, the rug of the bed being grasped hard in one of his hands, so that it was plain he died soon after the maid left him; and 'tis probable, had she gone up with the ale, she had found him dead in a few minutes after he sat down upon the bed. The alarm was great in the house, as anyone may suppose, they having been free from the distemper till that disaster, which, bringing the infection to the house, spread it immediately to other houses round about it. . . . **E**

12. **apoplexies:** strokes.
13. **bulk:** archaic word for a low stall projecting from a wall or storefront.
14. **mortifications:** archaic word for gangrene.
15. **Islington:** suburb north of London.
16. **Lincolnshire:** county on the east coast of England.

D Literary Focus **Narrative Voice** What emotions does H. F. convey as he lists the effects of the plague on the people? What might his purpose in conveying these emotions be?

Vocabulary **quarantine** (KWAWR uhn teen) *n.:* enforced isolation of ill people to prevent the spread of sickness.

E Reading Focus **Making Critical Judgments** In this entry, rather than describing numerous cases of suffering, H. F. tells at length the story of one man. What does H. F. gain by changing his approach in this passage?

Think About/Talk About

Comprehension

C Reading Focus

Possible response: *Because the plague was so widespread, people became numb to each other's suffering. Those who were still healthy could not risk catching the disease by helping anyone or even having contact with the sick. An added effect of the plague's horror might have been intense isolation.*

E Reading Focus

Possible response: *The long, detailed anecdote captures the reader's attention and encourages the reader to identify with the desperation that each community affected by the plague experienced.*

Analysis

B Literary Focus

Possible responses: *The narrator's tone is competent and detached for the most part, although the recounting of particularly disturbing events prompts him to express his feelings. The reader might think that H. F. is knowledgeable and close to the tragedy he describes.*

D Literary Focus

Possible response: *The detailed description of gruesome or heartbreaking scenes has the effect of shocking the readers and makes them sympathize with the horrific scenarios created by the plague.*

Vocabulary: Own the Word

- **credible:** Tell students that a noun form of *credible* is *credibility.* A person's *credibility* refers to whether the person can be believed.
- **torment:** Remind students that the connotation of *torment* is great mental or physical pain. You might say: "Taking the difficult history test was painful, but the possibility of failing the class left me in *torment.*"
- **quarantine:** The citizen who escaped from the *quarantine* posed a danger to places that were free of infection because . . . .

California Standards, pp. 562–563

- **Reading Standard 1.3** Discern the meaning of analogies encountered, analyzing specific comparisons as well as relationships and inferences.
- **Reading Standard 3.3** Analyze the ways in which irony, tone, mood, the author's style, and the "sound" of language achieve specific rhetorical or aesthetic purposes or both.
- **Grades 9–10 Review Reading Standard 3.9** Explain how voice, persona, and the choice of a narrator affect characterization and the tone, plot, and credibility of a text.
- **Writing Standard 2.1** Write fictional, autobiographical, or biographical narratives.

Check for Understanding

Independent Practice

Reading Skills Focus

Possible response:

1. *The plague caused "tokens" or gangrene spots.*
2. *He has work to do in his brother's house.*
3. *Doctors punctured the tokens to drain them or applied harsh chemicals to heal them.*
4. *She forgets about it.*
5. *Fear makes people stay away from each other. The fear sparks H. F's curiosity.*
6. *Ask students to consider what is the most likely effect of the information presented by the narrator on the reader.*

Literary Skills Focus

Possible responses:

7. *Students may note that the level of detail makes the "Journal" seem more authentic and personal. Defoe's journalistic viewpoint heightens the immediacy and emotional impact of the narrator's experience and gives the reader what appears to be a firsthand glimpse of the horror and devastation wrought by the plague.*
8. *H. F. may think the escaped man selfishly infected others to care for his own comfort.*
9. *"Morbid curiosity" is a fascination with horrific details of death and suffering. Yes. Today, television news and reality shows sometimes play to the audiences' morbid curiosity about tragic events that happen in other people's lives.*
10. *In a time when so many died and no one hoped to live on, H. F. expressed amazement that anyone, including himself, survived.*
11. *The author strives to maintain immediacy and sensationalism in his writing. If the "Journal" had been written during the plague, the narrator's tone would have probably sounded less composed.*

Applying Your Skills

Reading Standard 3.3; **Grades 9–10 Review Reading Standard** 3.9 (see pages A48–A50)
Writing Standard 2.1 (see pages A51–A52)

from **A Journal of the Plague Year**

Literary Response and Analysis

Reading Skills Focus

Quick Check

1. What were the symptoms of the plague?
2. Why does H. F. risk infection to go into the city?
3. What attempts were made to cure people?
4. Why doesn't the maid take ale to the lodger?

Read with a Purpose

5. How does the fear of infectious disease affect many Londoners? How does it affect H. F.?

Reading Skills: Making Critical Judgments

6. Defoe's description of the plague in London appears to be nonfiction but is actually historical fiction. As you read, you recorded and analyzed details. In a new column of your chart, judge whether the detail increases the journalistic (nonfiction) tone of the entries, builds the fictional story of the entries, or both.

Detail H. F. Relates	Fact or Reaction?	Why H. F. Includes the Detail	Nonfiction and Fiction
how the plague spread	H. F. thinks it's a fact.	to inform but also to build credibility	nonfiction—This detail sounds clinical and scientific and makes the entry sound serious, like a report.

Literary Skills Focus

Literary Analysis

7. **Analyze** What effect does Defoe create by using the first-person point of view? Cite examples from the text to support your response.
8. **Infer** What can you infer about H. F.'s opinion of the man who escaped from quarantine?
9. **Extend** What is meant by "morbid curiosity"? Does H. F. possess this kind of curiosity? Where does morbid curiosity appear in modern life?

Literary Skills: Narrative Voice

10. **Analyze** H. F. concludes his journal with these lines: "A dreadful plague in London was / In the year sixty-five, / Which swept an hundred thousand souls / Away; yet I alive!" What amazement does H. F. express toward his subject in these lines?

Literary Skills Review: Tone

11. **Analyze** How might the journal's **tone,** the writer's attitude toward the events he is recounting, have been different if the work actually had been written during the London plague?

Writing Skills Focus

Think as a Reader/Writer

Use It in Your Writing You have noted how Defoe uses dialogue and the description surrounding the dialogue to make an account vivid and to shape the narrative voice. Now, write your own narrative paragraph about an important event in your life. Use vivid descriptions and interesting, expressive dialogue.

What Do You Think Now? What might have been the response of Londoners to the inability of city physicians and authorities to treat suffering victims or stop the spread of the plague?

Universal Access

Struggling Writers

Some students may need additional scaffolding to complete the Writing Skills Focus activity. Have students brainstorm events that involved a memorable conversation or dialogue. Have them write the dialogues first, then think about how the dialogue started and how it was resolved before writing their narrative paragraphs.

What Do You Think Now?

Tell students to reference relevant sections of Defoe's writing as they respond to the question. Ask them to draw on their knowledge of modern attitudes toward medical practitioners and the health care system to make inferences about the likely public response to the ineffectiveness of physicians and city officials.

Reading Standard 1.3 (see pages A48–A50)

Vocabulary Development

Vocabulary Check

Match the Vocabulary words with their definitions.

1. infect — a. isolation for health reasons.
2. proportion — b. sicken; contaminate
3. consequently — c. convincing; likely
4. credible — d. therefore; thus
5. torment — e. suffering
6. quarantine — f. ratio

Vocabulary Skills: Analogies

In a word **analogy,** the relationship between the first pair of words is the same as the relationship between the second pair of words. Look at the pair of words below:

GREEN LIGHT : GO :: RED LIGHT : STOP

This is an abbreviated way of saying:

A green light has the same relationship to the action of going as a red light has to the action of stopping.

The analogy form shows the relationship and allows you to extend the analogy to another similar idea:

GREEN LIGHT : GO :: RED LIGHT : STOP :: YELLOW LIGHT : PREPARE TO STOP

Analogies help you learn new vocabulary because they show you how words are related to other words that you already know. Here's another example:

CREDIBLE : BELIEVABLE :: CREDULOUS : BELIEVING

You know that *credible* and *believable* are synonyms, and you can see that *credulous,* having the same root as *credible,* probably has a meaning related to *credible.* This analogy confirms your guess: *Credulous* has the same relationship to *believing* as *credible* has to *believable:* They are synonyms.

Your Turn

For each Vocabulary word, construct an analogy to broaden your understanding of the word. Analogies can point out many kinds of relationships: similarities and differences, actors and actions, tools and uses, synonyms and antonyms, and so on. Complete the table below, using a variety of relationships. Be prepared to explain the relationship each analogy demonstrates.

word	:	word	::	word	:	word

Language Coach

Word Origins Choose the phrase you think describes the origin of each word below. Check your answers with a dictionary.

1. torment
   a. from the Latin word for *twist*
   b. from the Latin word for *wind*
2. infect
   a. from the Latin word for *move*
   b. from the Latin word for *spoil*
3. credible
   a. from the Latin word for *trust*
   b. from the Latin word for *true*

Academic Vocabulary

Talk About

With a partner, compare modern approaches to infectious disease with the responses Defoe records. What factors enhance our modern understanding of disease?

Independent Practice

Vocabulary Development

Vocabulary Check

1. *b* 2. *f*
3. *d* 4. *c*
5. *e* 6. *a*

Your Turn

infect : contaminate :: infection : contamination

proportion : ratio :: portion : part

consequently : as a result :: consequence : result

credible : believable :: credentials : authority

torment : pain :: torture : to cause pain

quarantine : to isolate :: quarters : separate rooms

English for Academic Success

Language Coach

1. *a*
2. *b*
3. *a*

English for Academic Success

Academic Vocabulary

Possible response: *Modern approaches to infectious diseases include practices such as vaccination and sterilization and are the result of many years of research and discoveries. Modern advances in research and technology enhance our understanding of disease.*

Assess

Unit 3 Resources, Selection Standards Check, p. 21

ThinkCentral Online Assessment, Selection Standards Check

Teacher One Stop™, editable Selection Standards Check

Universal Access: Vocabulary Development

English Learners

English for Academic Success To help students practice with analogies, give them examples that relate to their daily lives. Ask them to come up with analogies for the following words:

1. singer : audience :: [*teacher : class*]
2. bicycle : bell :: [*car : horn*]
3. breakfast : morning :: [*dinner : evening*]
4. book : chapter :: [*Web site : Web page*]

Then, have students orally explain the relationship between the following analogies:

1. drizzle : storm :: drip : pour [*degree*]
2. dog : canine :: cat : feline [*type*]
3. slice : loaf :: foot : body [*part to whole*]
4. calm : hectic :: soft : loud [*antonyms*]

✔ See the **Academic and Selection Vocabulary Skill Builder** in **UA: Differentiating Instruction.**

Standards Focus

Objectives

Students will

- understand situational irony
- analyze author's purpose

Selection Introduction

Think About the Writer

Remind students that as dean of St. Patrick's Cathedral in Dublin, Jonathan Swift belonged to the upper-middle class. However, he was also very aware of the plight of the Irish poor, who would have passed his door every day.

For Independent Reading

- *Hatred, Bigotry, and Prejudice: Definitions, Causes, and Solutions,* Robert Baird, ed.
- *The Hitchhiker's Guide to the Galaxy,* Douglas Adams

Motivate

What Do You Think?/QuickWrite

Ask students to discuss the characteristics of a highly civilized society. (Students may name characteristics such as democratic ideals, support of personal rights, social equality, easily accessible education, an efficient legal system, etc.). Have students brainstorm examples of social problems at a national and local level that conflict with their ideal of civilization. Tell them to write their thoughts in their **Reader/Writer Notebooks.**

English for Academic Success

Academic Vocabulary

Look for opportunities to use the Academic Vocabulary words in this unit.

- **approach,** ***n.:*** way of addressing something
- **convince,** ***v.:*** persuade; cause to believe
- **enhance,** ***v.:*** improve the quality of
- **participate,** ***v.:*** take part in

Preparing to Read

from Gulliver's Travels

A Modest Proposal

What Do You Think

How can order and civilization affect human behavior?

QuickWrite

Think about social problems in your community or in the world in general. In your *Reader/Writer Notebook,* write down a list of social problems that you consider to be most in need of attention.

Jonathan Swift (c. 1718) by Charles Jervas. Oil on canvas. National Portrait Gallery, London.

MEET THE WRITER

Jonathan Swift

(1667–1745)

Jonathan Swift is the principal prose writer of the early eighteenth century and England's greatest satirist. He once said that the secret of good prose is "proper words in proper places." He is a master of precise and clear writing.

Both Irish and English

Jonathan Swift was born in Dublin, Ireland, to English parents. His father died seven months before his birth, at which time Swift was abducted by his nurse. He spent three years in England before being returned to Ireland, where he was cared for by his uncle. He regarded himself as more English than Irish.

After studying at Trinity College, Dublin, Swift went to England, where he worked as a private secretary to Sir William Temple, a distant relative, writer, and wealthy statesman. Swift hoped his relationship to Temple would enhance his own chances for a political career in England, but that never came to pass. Eventually Swift received a master's degree from Oxford University and was ordained a priest. Although he wanted to be made an English bishop, the only appointment he could get was back in Ireland as the dean of St. Patrick's Cathedral in Dublin. Swift returned to his native city, was installed as dean, and held that office for the remaining thirty years of his life.

National Hero

Swift did not write for fame or money. His aim in writing was to improve human conduct, to make people more decent and humane toward one another. *Gulliver's Travels* (1726) attacks many different varieties of human misbehavior, vice, and folly. Swift's experiences in Ireland gave him firsthand knowledge of the abject poverty and suffering of the lower classes. Swift even became an Irish patriot in his pamphlets, defending the Irish against the oppressive policies of their English rulers. In *A Modest Proposal* (1729), his most famous pamphlet, he uses irony to offer an outrageous solution to Irish poverty.

Think About the Writer How do you think Swift's ties to both England and Ireland influenced his perspective on the social issues of his time?

California Standards, pp. 564–578

- **Reading Standard 2.5** Analyze an author's implicit and explicit philosophical assumptions and beliefs about a subject.
- **Reading Standard 3.3** Analyze the ways in which irony, tone, mood, the author's style, and the "sound" of language achieve specific rhetorical or aesthetic purposes or both.

Selection Readability	
Easily Accessible **Accessible** Challenging	These selections include humorous language; accessible vocabulary; accessible theme.

Reading Standard 2.5, 3.3 (see pages A48–A50)

from Gulliver's Travels

Literary Skills Focus

Situational Irony When what actually happens is the opposite of what is expected or appropriate, we say that **situational irony** occurs. "The Necklace," a short story by Guy de Maupassant, contains a famous example of situational irony: A man and a woman struggle for years to pay for an expensive diamond necklace they have lost only to discover that it was made of paste. Situational irony, which is often accompanied by surprise, reminds us that life is unpredictable.

Reading Skills Focus

Analyzing an Author's Purpose Swift uses **satire** to make fun of human weakness, vice, and folly, hoping to motivate his readers to change themselves and society. In "A Voyage to Lilliput," his target is political institutions. For example, the politicians in Lilliput obtain their positions by dancing on a tightrope. What does this say about Swift's opinion of politicians? of his country's political system?

Into Action As you read, use a chart like the one below. List important events, actions, or images in the first column. In the second column, explain what Swift is suggesting through each event, action, or image.

Event, Action, Image	Institution	Satirical Point
Gulliver is entertained by rope dancers.	politics	These political leaders "danced" around issues instead of solving the country's problems.

Writing Skills Focus

Think as a Reader/Writer

Find It in Your Reading In *Gulliver's Travels,* Swift uses **satire** to expose the follies and vices of human behavior. As you read, take note of the words and images he uses to emphasize the extremes he sees in people, and record them in your *Reader/Writer Notebook.*

Vocabulary

conjectured (kuhn JEHK chuhrd) *v.:* reasoned; guessed. *When Gulliver first saw a Lilliputian, he conjectured that the rest of the population must be about the same size.*

quelled (kwehld) *v.:* subdued. *The troops quelled the civil uprising of the protesters.*

schism (SKIHZ uhm) *n.:* division. *The disagreement caused a schism between Lilliput and Blefuscu.*

copious (KOH pee uhs) *adj.:* wordy; profuse. *Gulliver gave the King and Queen a copious amount of information about England.*

odious (OH dee uhs) *adj.:* hateful; offensive. *Despite Gulliver's efforts to be likable, the King still called him an "odious vermin."*

Language Coach

Verb Tenses When learning a verb in the past tense, be sure also to learn the present tense form. *Conjecture,* the present tense of *conjectured,* takes a *–d* to form the past tense. However, *quell* (the present tense of *quelled*) takes an *–ed* to form the past tense.

Learn It Online
Find out more about Jonathan Swift with this online biography.

go.hrw.com H12-565 Go

Reader/Writer Notebook
Use your **RWN** to complete the activities for this selection.

Selection Resources

Unit 3 Resources, on-level practice and assessment, p. 24

Teacher One Stop™, on-level lesson plans and all print resources

Holt Audio Library

Holt Audio Library: Selections and Summaries in Spanish

UA: Differentiating Instruction, graphic organizer, p. 124

UA: Supporting Instruction in Spanish, selection summary

ThinkCentral Online Assessment, Selection Standards Check

ThinkCentral Online Remediation

Preteach

Introducing Vocabulary

Use this activity to check students' understanding.

1. List aspects of your personality that might be **conjectured** by someone who analyzed your hobbies.
2. Explain how a student's anxiety before a test can be **quelled**.
3. Name an event that might cause a **schism** within a political party.
4. Explain why surveys require a **copious** amount of information.
5. Name an **odious** activity you must perform regularly.

English for Academic Success

Language Coach

Have students read the **Language Coach**. Remind students that the present progressive tense of the word *conjecture* is *conjecturing,* and have them use it in a sentence.

Literary Skills Focus

As you read and discuss the selection with students, have them note occurrences of situational irony by examining surprising or unpredictable events.

Reading Skills Focus

Give students a copy of the Reading Skills Focus graphic organizer before they read. (See **Unit 3 Resources**.) Tell them to use their responses to answer the questions on the Applying Your Skills page.

Writing Skills Focus

Have students record key words and images that describe characters in their **Reader/Writer Notebooks.**

Learn It Online
The enhanced author biography offers more information on the life of the author as well as Holt's interactive resources pertaining to the author.

go.hrw.com H12-565 Go

Teacher Preparation
Selection Plot Summary

In "A Voyage to Lilliput," from Part 1 of *Gulliver's Travels,* a shipwrecked Gulliver is held captive by a race of six-inch-tall humans who feed him and bring him to court. There, he observes what high officials must do to attain their positions and discusses with the emperor the political and religious controversies that cause tension in society. In "A Voyage to Brobdingnag", Gulliver finds himself in a country of giants where he and his countrymen back home are mocked for their insignificance and vices.

Direct Teach

Think About/Talk About

Read with a Purpose Have students read the Read with a Purpose statement. Point out that Swift wants readers to consider the contradictions of human nature. In "A Voyage to Lilliput," Swift puts humanity under the microscope of his scrutiny. In "A Voyage to Brobdingnag," Swift puts Gulliver and his own society under the microscope.

Extend the Discussion

Finding the Main Idea Whom has Swift chosen to narrate the story, and where has he placed this character? ***Possible response:*** *Swift is using a traveler named Gulliver, who, at the moment, is lying on his back, tied down and able to "see nothing except the sky."*

Irony What is ironic about the fact that Gulliver's captors are armed? ***Possible response:*** *Their tiny bows and arrows are useless against such a huge enemy.*

NOVEL

from Gulliver's Travels

from Part 1: A Voyage to Lilliput

by **Jonathan Swift**

Read with a Purpose

Read to discover what Gulliver's travels reveal about human nature.

Build Background

Swift's best-known work, *Gulliver's Travels,* was published anonymously in 1726 under the original title of *Travels into Several Remote Nations of the World.* The narrator, Lemuel Gulliver, is a well-meaning but simple Englishman who describes innocently whatever he sees. Gulliver is aptly named, for a *gull* was a term for someone easily duped, or gullible. It is up to the reader to see the truths that Gulliver misses.

The first voyage, describing the visit to Lilliput, opens with an account of Gulliver's early life: his birth, parentage, and scholarship. After studying medicine, Gulliver becomes a ship's doctor and embarks on a long voyage; when the ship breaks up in a storm somewhere in the South Pacific, he manages to swim ashore and, exhausted, falls into a deep sleep.

I lay down on the grass, which was very short and soft, where I slept sounder than ever I remember to have done in my life, and, as I reckoned, above nine hours; for when I awaked, it was just daylight. I attempted to rise, but was not able to stir: For as I happened to lie on my back, I found my arms and legs were strongly fastened on each side to the ground; and my hair, which was long and thick, tied down in the same manner. I likewise felt several slender ligatures[1] across my body, from my armpits to my thighs. I could only look upward; the sun began to grow hot, and the light offended my eyes. I heard a confused noise about me, but in the posture I lay, could see nothing except the sky.

In a little time I felt something alive moving on my left leg, which advancing gently forward over my breast, came almost up to my chin; when bending my eyes downward as much as I could, I perceived it to be a human creature not six inches high, with a bow and arrow in his hands, and a quiver at his back. In the meantime, I felt at least forty more of the same kind (as I conjectured) following the first. I was in the utmost astonishment, and roared so loud, that they all ran back in a fright; and some of them, as I was afterward told, were hurt with the falls they got by leaping from my sides upon the ground. However, they soon returned, and one of them, who ventured so far as to get a full sight of my face, lifting up his hands and eyes

1. **ligatures:** ties or bonds.

Vocabulary **conjectured** (kuhn JEHK chuhrd) *v.:* reasoned; guessed.

Universal Access

English Learners

English for Academic Success Some students might experience difficulty understanding certain words or phrases commonly used in the English language in Jonathan Swift's time. Clarify terms such as *reckon* (suppose), *whereupon* (at which), *whereof* (of what, of which), and *till* (until). Explain to students that when the letter *a* appears before words such as *a-groaning,* it acts as a preposition meaning "on," "into," "in," "to," or "toward." Other examples are *afoot, ashore,* and *afar.*

Struggling Readers

Model the reading skill of understanding the author's purpose. You might say: "When I read the opening paragraph on p. 566, I notice that the author is describing a man tied to the ground. I read the second paragraph. I discover that the man is a prisoner—but a prisoner of creatures who are just six inches tall. I remember that the introduction calls the story a satire. Satire is written for the purpose of entertaining, but writers also use satire to motivate readers to change."

by way of admiration, cried out in a shrill, but distinct voice, *Hekinah degul:*[2] The others repeated the same words several times, but then I knew not what they meant. I lay all this while, as the reader may believe, in great uneasiness: At length, struggling to get loose, I had the fortune to break the strings, and wrench out the pegs that fastened my left arm to the ground; for, by lifting it up to my face, I discovered the methods they had taken to bind me, and at the same time with a violent pull, which gave me excessive pain, I a little loosened the strings that tied down my hair on the left side, so that I was just able to turn my head about two inches. But the creatures ran off a second time, before I could seize them; whereupon there was a great shout in a very shrill accent, and after it ceased, I heard one of them cry aloud, *Tolgo phonac;* when in an instant I felt above an hundred arrows discharged on my left hand, which pricked me like so many needles; and besides, they shot another flight into the air, as we do bombs in Europe, whereof many, I suppose, fell on my body (though I felt them not), and some on my face, which I immediately covered with my left hand. When this shower of arrows was over, I fell a-groaning with grief and pain, and then striving again to get loose, they discharged another volley larger than the first, and some of them attempted with spears to stick me in the sides; but, by good luck, I had on me a buff jerkin,[3] which they could not pierce. I thought it the most prudent method to lie still, and my design was to continue so till night, when, my left hand being already loose, I could easily free myself: And as for the inhabitants, I had reason to believe I might be a match for the greatest armies they could bring against me, if they were all of the same size with him that I saw. But fortune disposed otherwise of me. **A**

2. **Hekinah degul:** This and other examples of the Lilliputian language are mainly nonsense words.

3. **buff jerkin:** short, close-fitting leather jacket, often without sleeves.

A Literary Focus **Situational Irony** What is ironic about the soldiers' actions toward Gulliver?

Television production of *Gulliver's Travels.*

Think About/Talk About

Analysis

A Literary Focus

Possible response: *Gulliver's great size would let him escape from the soldiers with ease, but the soldiers persist in trying to keep Gulliver captive.*

Extend the Discussion

Drawing Conclusions In the second paragraph of the selection, what are some clues that the creatures are like human beings? ***Possible response:*** *The creatures sound like an organized army, with tactics and a plan.*

Satire Satire is criticism mixed with humor. What is humorous so far? ***Possible responses:*** *The presence of a huge Gulliver and impossibly tiny Lilliputians; the way Gulliver is tied down and shot at; the silly, made-up language.*

Vocabulary: Own the Word

conjectured: Gulliver *conjectured* that there were at least forty-one tiny human creatures walking on him because . . . ***Possible response:*** *He could only feel them, he could not see them.*

Advanced Learners

Acceleration Have students decide what a twenty-first century version of "A Voyage to Lilliput" could satirize. Then have them write a sketch or prepare a storyboard for a sketch that would bring Swift's vision to today's world.

Students with Disabilities

To help students understand satire, explain that satire pokes fun at the way a society behaves. Pair students with other learners to help them understand what is happening in each scene Swift describes. Have them identify scenes they find funny and explain why. Then have them explain what serious point Swift might be trying to make.

✔ See **UA: Differentiating Instruction** for a graphic organizer to scaffold instruction for students with disabilities.

Model the Skill

- Tell students that one way to identify **satire** is to look for elements that seem comical or absurd.
- Read aloud the last paragraph on p. 569, in which the narrator describes his conversation with a Lilliputian official.
- Point out that the lofty titles given to the emperor and his messenger ("His Imperial Majesty," "His Excellency") sharply contrast with their puny size. Remind students that Gulliver has just mused about hurling forty or fifty Lilliputians to the ground. Although the official refuses to grant Gulliver his liberty, Gulliver could break his bonds if he chose. Explain that the contrast shows political officials as somewhat ridiculous, with an exaggerated sense of their own importance.

Guided Practice: Apply

Turn-and-Talk Have students continue to read the story with a partner. Tell them to note other situations that strike them as funny or absurd. Ask student pairs to share their findings. Challenge them to determine what Swift is satirizing in each instance.

Think as a Reader/Writer

Find It in Your Reading Point out the amount of food that Gulliver can eat at one sitting. Discuss his appetite from the point of view of a Lilliputian watching him eat and drink. What human vice might Swift be satirizing?

Use It in Your Writing Have students write two or three sentences from the point of view of the Lilliputians as they watch Gulliver gorge himself. Ask students to suggest the onlookers' surprise by including vivid vocabulary that mimics the narrator's.

When the people observed I was quiet, they discharged no more arrows; but, by the noise increasing, I knew their numbers were greater; and about four yards from me, over against my right ear, I heard a knocking for above an hour, like that of people at work; when turning my head that way, as well as the pegs and strings would permit me, I saw a stage erected, about a foot and a half from the ground, capable of holding four of the inhabitants, with two or three ladders to mount it: From whence one of them, who seemed to be a person of quality, made me a long speech, whereof I understood not one syllable. But I should have mentioned, that before the principal person began his oration, he cried out three times, *Langro dehul san* (these words and the former were afterward repeated and explained to me). Whereupon immediately about fifty of the inhabitants came and cut the strings that fastened the left side of my head, which gave me the liberty of turning it to the right, and of observing the person and gesture of him who was to speak. He appeared to be of a middle age, and taller than any of the other three who attended him, whereof one was a page who held up his train, and seemed to be somewhat longer than my middle finger; the other two stood one on each side to support him. He acted every part of an orator, and I could observe many periods of threatenings, and others of promises, pity, and kindness.

I answered in a few words, but in the most submissive manner, lifting up my left hand, and both my eyes to the sun, as calling him for a witness; and being almost famished with hunger, having not eaten a morsel for some hours before I left the ship. I found the demands of nature so strong upon me, that I could not forbear showing my impatience (perhaps against the strict rules of decency) by putting my finger frequently on my mouth, to signify that I wanted food. The *Hurgo*[4] (for so they call a great lord, as I afterward learnt) understood me very well. He descended from the stage, and commanded that several ladders should be applied to my sides, on which above an hundred of the inhabitants mounted and walked toward my mouth, laden with baskets full of meat,[5] which had been provided and sent thither by the King's orders, upon the first intelligence he received of me. I observed there was the flesh[6] of several animals, but could not distinguish them by the taste. There were shoulders, legs, and loins, shaped like those of mutton, and very well dressed, but smaller than the wings of a lark. I ate them by two or three at a mouthful, and took three loaves at a time, about the bigness of musket bullets. They supplied me as fast as they could, showing a thousand marks of wonder and astonishment at my bulk and appetite. **B**

I then made another sign that I wanted drink. They found by my eating, that a small quantity would not suffice me; and being a most ingenious people, they slung up with great dexterity one of their largest hogsheads,[7] then rolled it toward my hand, and beat out the top; I drank it off at a draft, which I might well do, for it hardly held half a pint, and tasted like a small wine of Burgundy, but much more delicious. They brought me a second hogshead, which I drank in the same manner, and made signs for more, but they had none to give me. When I had performed these wonders, they shouted for joy, and danced upon my breast, repeating several times as they did at first, *Hekinah degul.* They made me a sign that I should throw down the two hogsheads, but first warned the people below to stand out of the way, crying aloud, *Borach mivola,* and when they saw the vessels in the air, there was an universal shout of *Hekinah degul.* I confess I was often tempted, while they were passing backward and forward on my body, to seize forty or fifty of the first that came in my reach, and dash them against the ground. But the remembrance of what I had felt, which probably might not be the worst they could do, and the

4. ***Hurgo:*** This Lilliputian word is perhaps a partial anagram (a word formed by rearranging the letters of another word) of the English word *rogue.* It would be characteristic of Swift to call a "great lord" a rogue.

5. **meat:** food.
6. **flesh:** meat.
7. **hogsheads:** barrels.

B **Literary Focus** **Situational Irony** What is ironic about the Lilliputians feeding Gulliver?

Universal Access

AAVE Students Who Use African American Vernacular English

English for Academic Success Ask students to read aloud portions of the second full paragraph on p. 568, telling them to pay attention to plural nouns, the voicing of *l* at ends of words such as *shoulders* and *rules,* and words with *–ed* endings.

✔ For additional instruction and strategies, see **Holt Pronunciation Resources** and **ThinkCentral, Teacher Access.**

Cross-Curricular Connection

SOCIAL SCIENCE: Visual Satire

Explain to students that caricature is a form of visual satire in which an artist distorts the appearance of a subject to convey his or her personal qualities and to make a point.

Small-Group Activity Ask groups of students to compile a collection of political cartoons, categorize them by subject, and analyze the techniques used by the artists. Encourage students to create their own satirical cartoons based on politics or on some issue of current interest in your school.

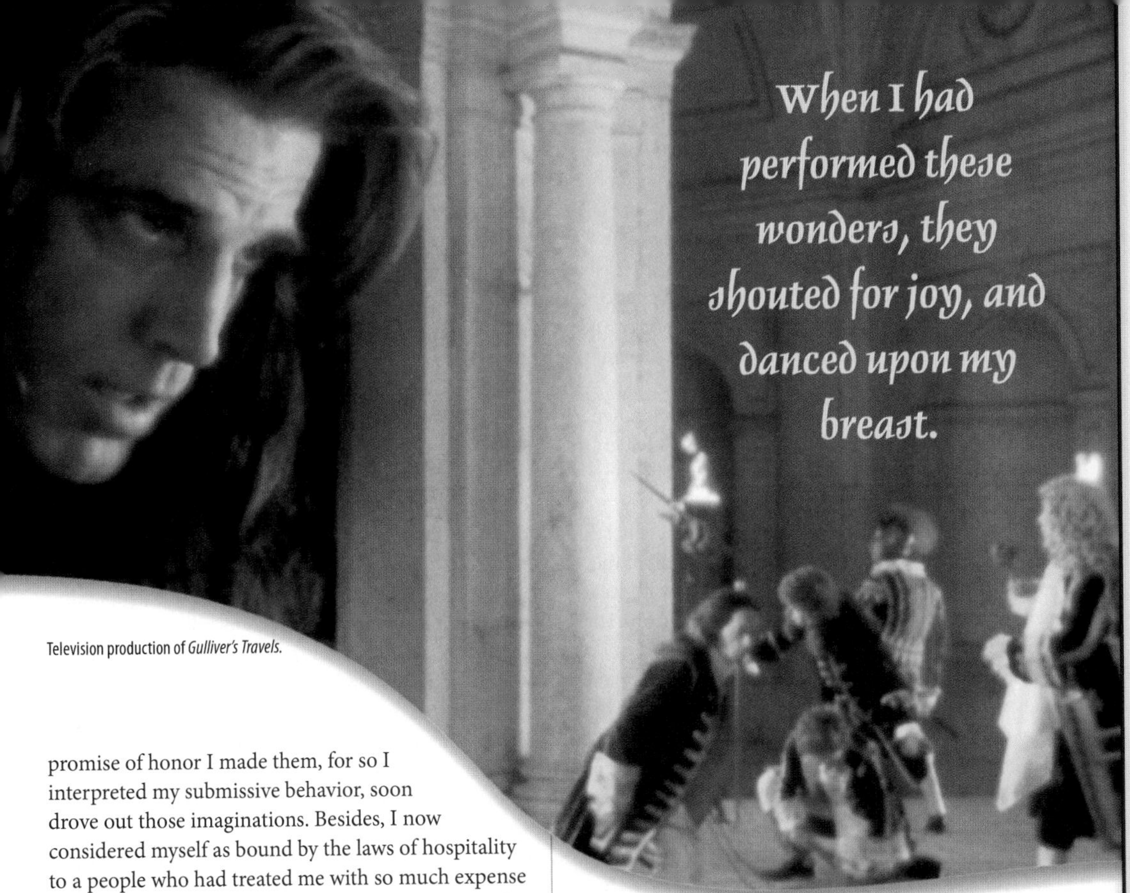

Television production of *Gulliver's Travels.*

promise of honor I made them, for so I interpreted my submissive behavior, soon drove out those imaginations. Besides, I now considered myself as bound by the laws of hospitality to a people who had treated me with so much expense and magnificence. However, in my thoughts, I could not sufficiently wonder at the intrepidity of these diminutive mortals, who durst venture to mount and walk on my body, while one of my hands was at liberty, without trembling at the very sight of so prodigious a creature as I must appear to them. **C**

After some time, when they observed that I made no more demands for meat, there appeared before me a person of high rank from his Imperial Majesty. His Excellency, having mounted on the small of my right leg, advanced forward up to my face, with about a dozen of his retinue. And producing his credentials under the Signet Royal,[8] which he applied close to my eyes, spoke about ten minutes, without any signs of anger, but with a kind of determinate resolution; often pointing forward, which, as I afterward found, was toward the capital city, about half a mile distant, whither it was agreed by his Majesty in council that I must be conveyed. I answered in few words, but to no purpose, and made a sign with my hand that was loose, putting it to the other (but over his Excellency's head for fear of hurting him or his train) and then to my own head and body, to signify that I desired my liberty. It appeared that he understood me well enough, for he shook his head by way of disapprobation, and held his hand in a posture to show that I must be carried as a prisoner. However, he made other

8. **Signet Royal:** royal seal that marks official documents.

C **Reading Focus** **Analyzing an Author's Purpose**
Gulliver imagines himself hurting the Lilliputians but restrains himself. What point might Swift be making here?

Developing Oral Fluency

Model reading part of the selection aloud to students. As you do, discuss ways to use pitch, volume, pauses, body language, and eye contact with the audience to achieve fluency and add dramatic effect. Discuss how students can use expression and tone of voice to convey their interpretation of the narrator's attitude towards a particular character.

Paired Activity Have students work in pairs to practice their own oral reading skills in selected passages. After they have practiced a few times, have them present their readings to the whole class. If time allows, ask students to write a paragraph about the parts of the oral reading they found difficult and why.

✔ See the **Oral Language Skill Builder** in **UA: Differentiating Instruction.**

Think About/Talk About

Comprehension

C Reading Focus
Possible response: *Swift might be suggesting that it is human nature to want to strike back at those who have harmed you but that the impulse should be restrained. He may be saying that if people would think for a moment before choosing violence, a lot of needless pain could be avoided.*

Analysis

B Literary Focus
Possible response: *Gulliver has been treated as an enemy, tied down, and shot at, but now that he is hungry, the Lilliputians are generously rushing to serve him; they are behaving in a civilized manner toward Gulliver, despite the threat he poses to them.*

Extend the Discussion

Finding Details On p. 569, what does Gulliver mean by saying that he wonders at the "intrepidity of these diminutive mortals"? ***Possible response:*** *He is surprised by the courage shown by the small Lilliputians, who venture around Gulliver's mouth without fear.*

Satire What is the author's attitude toward the leader or king's speech? ***Possible response:*** *Swift is making fun of the speech, which seems to include a whole range of emotions and messages (and therefore, probably says not much at all). It seems more important for the king or leader to act "every part of an orator" than to actually say something meaningful.*

Think About/Talk About

Extend the Discussion

Finding Details Which detail in the second paragraph of p. 570 best supports the idea that the Lilliputians still did not trust Gulliver completely? ***Possible response:*** *The Lilliputians poured a sleeping potion into Gulliver's wine to make sure he would sleep and not escape.*

Evaluating Do you find Gulliver's ability to communicate through sign language convincing? Why or why not? ***Possible responses:*** *His ability to communicate hunger and thirst is convincing because the nonverbal messages for these states seem fairly universal. His ability to communicate more abstract qualities, such as sincerity, is less convincing because there are no universal gestures for these, and Gulliver is a complete stranger to the Lilliputian culture.*

signs to let me understand that I should have meat and drink enough, and very good treatment. Whereupon I once more thought of attempting to break my bonds; but again, when I felt the smart of their arrows, upon my face and hands, which were all in blisters, and many of the darts still sticking in them, and observing likewise that the number of my enemies increased, I gave tokens[9] to let them know that they might do with me what they pleased. Upon this, the *Hurgo* and his train withdrew, with much civility and cheerful countenances.

Soon after I heard a general shout, with frequent repetitions of the words, *Peplom selan,* and I felt great numbers of people on my left side relaxing the cords to such a degree, that I was able to turn upon my right, and to ease myself with making water; which I very plentifully did, to the great astonishment of the people, who conjecturing by my motions what I was going to do, immediately opened to the right and left on that side, to avoid the torrent which fell with such noise and violence from me. But before this, they had daubed my face and both my hands with a sort of ointment very pleasant to the smell, which in a few minutes removed all the smart of their arrows. These circumstances, added to the refreshment I had received by their victuals and drink, which were very nourishing, disposed me to sleep. I slept about eight hours, as I was afterward assured; and it was no wonder, for the physicians, by the Emperor's order, had mingled a sleeping potion in the hogshead of wine. . . . **D**

My gentleness and good behavior had gained so far on the Emperor and his court, and indeed upon the army and people in general, that I began to conceive hopes of getting my liberty in a short time. I took all possible methods to cultivate this favorable disposition. The natives came by degrees to be less apprehensive of any danger from me. I would sometimes lie down, and let five or six of them dance on my hand. And at last the boys and girls would venture to come and play at hide-and-seek in my hair. I had now made a good progress in understanding and speaking their language. The Emperor had a mind one day to entertain me with several of the country shows, wherein they exceed all nations I have known, both for dexterity and magnificence. I was diverted with none so much as that of the rope dancers,[10] performed upon a slender white thread, extended about two foot, and twelve inches from the ground. Upon which I shall desire liberty, with the reader's patience, to enlarge a little.

This diversion is only practiced by those persons who are candidates for great employments, and high favor, at court. They are trained in this art from their youth, and are not always of noble birth, or liberal education. When a great office is vacant, either by death or disgrace (which often happens), five or six of those candidates petition the Emperor to entertain his Majesty and the court with a dance on the rope, and whoever jumps the highest without falling, succeeds in the office. Very often the chief ministers themselves are commanded to show their skill, and to convince the Emperor that they have not lost their faculty. Flimnap, the Treasurer, is allowed to cut a caper on the straight rope, at least an inch higher than any other lord in the whole empire. I have seen him do the summerset[11] several times together upon a trencher fixed on the rope, which is no thicker than a common packthread[12] in England. My friend Reldresal, principal Secretary for Private Affairs, is, in my opinion, if I am not partial, the second after the Treasurer; the rest of the great officers are much upon a par. **E**

These diversions are often attended with fatal accidents, whereof great numbers are on record. I myself have seen two or three candidates break a limb. But the danger is much greater when the ministers themselves are commanded to show their dexterity; for, by contending to excel themselves and their fellows, they strain so far, that there is hardly one of them who hath

9. **gave tokens:** signaled.

10. **rope dancers:** tightrope dancers.

11. **summerset:** somersault.

12. **packthread:** twine.

D **Reading Focus** **Analyzing an Author's Purpose** What might be Swift's purpose for including this humorous scene?

E **Reading Focus** **Analyzing an Author's Purpose** Gulliver is impressed by the officeholders' rope-dancing skills instead of by their skills as government ministers. What might Swift be telling the reader about politicians?

Cross-Curricular Connection

HISTORY: The Objects of Swift's Caricatures

The emperor may be a spoof on King George I, who was on the throne of England when Swift was writing *Gulliver's Travels.* Flimnap is probably a caricature of Sir. Robert Walpole, the Whig Prime Minister, and Reldresal is perhaps Lord Charles Townshend, the secretary of state. Walpole and Townshend were leading figures in George I's government.

Assuming that Swift is referring to life in England in the second full paragraph that starts on p. 571, the "two mighty evils" that exist from an Anglican point of view are the domestic threat of Roman Catholicism and the international threat of France, England's traditional enemy.

not received a fall, and some of them two or three. I was assured that a year or two before my arrival, Flimnap would have infallibly broke his neck, if one of the King's cushions, that accidentally lay on the ground, had not weakened the force of his fall.

There is likewise another diversion, which is only shown before the Emperor and Empress, and first minister, upon particular occasions. The Emperor lays on the table three fine silken threads of six inches long. One is blue, the other red, and the third green. These threads are proposed as prizes for those persons whom the Emperor hath a mind to distinguish by a peculiar mark of his favor. The ceremony is performed in his Majesty's great chamber of state, where the candidates are to undergo a trial of dexterity very different from the former, and such as I have not observed the least resemblance of in any other country of the Old or the New World. The Emperor holds a stick in his hands, both ends parallel to the horizon, while the candidates advancing one by one, sometimes leap over the stick, sometimes creep under it backward and forward several times, according as the stick is advanced or depressed. Sometimes the Emperor holds one end of the stick, and his first minister the other; sometimes the minister has it entirely to himself. Whoever performs his part with most agility, and holds out the longest in leaping and creeping, is rewarded with the blue-colored silk; the red is given to the next, and the green to the third, which they all wear girt[13] twice round about the middle; and you see few great persons about this court, who are not adorned with one of these girdles. . . .

One morning, about a fortnight after I had obtained my liberty, Reldresal, principal Secretary (as they style him) of Private Affairs, came to my house attended only by one servant. He ordered his coach to wait at a distance, and desired I would give him an hour's audience; which I readily consented to, on account of his quality and personal merits, as well as of the many good offices he had done me during my solicitations at court. I offered to lie down, that he might the more conveniently reach my ear; but he chose rather to let me hold him in my hand during our conversation. He began with compliments on my liberty, said he might pretend to some merit in it; but, however, added, that if it had not been for the present situation of things at court, perhaps I might not have obtained it so soon. "For," said he, "as flourishing a condition as we appear to be in to foreigners, we labor under two mighty evils: a violent faction at home, and the danger of an invasion by a most potent enemy from abroad. As to the first, you are to understand, that for about seventy moons past there have been two struggling parties in this empire, under the names of *Tramecksan* and *Slamecksan,* from the high and low heels on their shoes, by which they distinguish themselves. It is alleged indeed, that the high heels are most agreeable to our ancient constitution: But however this be, his Majesty hath determined to make use of only low heels in the administration of the government, and all offices in the gift of the Crown, as you cannot but observe; and particularly, that his Majesty's Imperial heels are lower at least by a *drurr* than any of his court; (*drurr* is a measure about the fourteenth part of an inch). The animosities between these two parties run so high, that they will neither eat nor drink, nor talk with each other. We compute the *Tramecksan,* or High-Heels, to exceed us in number; but the power is wholly on our side. We apprehend his Imperial Highness, the Heir to the Crown, to have some tendency toward the High-Heels; at least we can plainly discover one of his heels higher than the other, which gives him a hobble in his gait. Now, in the midst of these intestine[14] disquiets, we are threatened with an invasion from the island of Blefuscu, which is the other great empire of the universe, almost as large and powerful as this of his Majesty. For as to what we have heard you affirm, that there are other kingdoms and states in the world inhabited by human creatures as large as yourself, our philosophers are in much doubt, and would rather conjecture that you dropped from the moon, or one of the stars; because it is certain, that an hundred mortals of your bulk would, in a short time, destroy all the fruits and cattle of his Majesty's dominions. Besides, our histories of six thousand moons make no mention of any other regions, than the two great empires of Lilliput and Blefuscu. Which two mighty powers have, as I was going to tell you, been engaged in a most obstinate war for six and thirty

13. **girt:** encircled.

14. **intestine:** internal.

Think About/Talk About

Comprehension

D Reading Focus

Possible response: *Swift may include the scene simply for the sake of humor or for the sake of mocking the coarseness of everyday behavior.*

E Reading Focus

Possible responses: *Swift may be implying that politicians have a primary duty to please or impress their masters, no matter how humiliating the task. He may also be suggesting that the government's activities are as irrelevant as the tightrope dance.*

Extend the Discussion

Monitoring Your Reading What are "two mighty evils" that Reldresal states the Lilliputian people labor under? ***Possible response:*** *The evils are a violent faction at home, between the Tramecksan and Slamecksan political parties, and the danger of an invasion by foreign enemies.*

Irony What is humorous about the description of Gulliver's interaction with the Lilliputians in the third paragraph on p. 570? What are the implications of this humor? ***Possible responses:*** *The idea that the Lilliputians are dancing on Gulliver's hands and playing hide-and-seek in his hair is ludicrous. These details show the innocence on both sides; both Gulliver and the Lilliputians are playing, and some trust has developed between them.*

Describing the differences between the High-Heels and the Low-Heels and, on p. 572, the Big-Endians and the Small-Endians, Swift might be satirizing the conflict between the Anglicans and the Catholics, high-church Anglicans and low-church Anglicans, the nobility and the bureaucrats, the Royalists and the Parliamentarians, or the Whigs and the Tories.

Universal Access

EL English Learners/ Struggling Readers

English for Academic Success Explain to students that one way to ridicule something is through the use of puns, or wordplay. Direct students' attention to the use of the word *fall* at the beginning of p. 571 ("had not weakened the force of his fall"). Tell students that *fall* could mean an actual fall or a figurative fall from favor or grace. Ask students to consider alternative meanings of words throughout the selection.

Model the Skill

- Model the skill of understanding **situational irony**. Have students read the first paragraph on p. 572. Tell students that, when looking for situational irony, they should look for situations with unexpected outcomes.
- Point out to students that the beginning of this paragraph states that the present emperor's grandfather once accidentally cut his finger while breaking an egg.
- Explain that the situational irony is that the emperor based a major decision on a meaningless coincidence; his edict about how to break eggs has resulted in war.

Guided Practice: Apply

Read-Talk-Write Have students work in pairs to review the first paragraph on p. 572 and look for other examples of situational irony. Then, ask students to write a short paragraph summarizing the situation but have them change the result so that it is no longer ironic.

moons past. It began upon the following occasion. It is allowed on all hands, that the primitive way of breaking eggs[15] before we eat them, was upon the larger end: But his present Majesty's grandfather, while he was a boy, going to eat an egg, and breaking it according to the ancient practice, happened to cut one of his fingers. Whereupon the Emperor his father published an edict, commanding all his subjects, upon great penalties, to break the smaller end of their eggs. The people so highly resented this law, that our histories tell us there have been six rebellions raised on that account; wherein one Emperor lost his life, and another his crown. These civil commotions were constantly fomented by the monarchs of Blefuscu; and when they were quelled, the exiles always fled for refuge to that empire. It is computed, that eleven thousand persons have, at several times, suffered death, rather than submit to break their eggs at the smaller end. Many hundred large volumes have been published upon this controversy: But the books of the Big-Endians have been long forbidden, and the whole party rendered incapable by law of holding employments. During the course of these troubles, the emperors of Blefuscu did frequently expostulate by their ambassadors, accusing us of making a schism in religion, by offending against a fundamental doctrine of our great prophet Lustrog, in the fifty-fourth chapter of the Brundrecal (which is their Alcoran).[16] This, however, is thought to be a mere strain upon the text, for the words are these: *That all true believers shall break their eggs at the convenient end;* and which is the convenient end, seems, in my humble opinion, to be left to every man's conscience, or at least in the power of the chief magistrate to determine. Now the Big-Endian exiles have found so much credit in the Emperor of Blefuscu's court, and so much private assistance and encouragement from their party here at home, that a bloody war has been carried on between the two empires for six and thirty moons with various success; during which time we have lost forty capital ships, and a much greater number of smaller vessels, together with thirty thousand of our best seamen and soldiers; and the damage received by the enemy is reckoned to be somewhat greater than ours. However, they have now equipped a numerous fleet, and are just preparing to make a descent upon us; and his Imperial Majesty, placing great confidence in your valor and strength, has commanded me to lay this account of his affairs before you." **F**

I desired the Secretary to present my humble duty to the Emperor, and to let him know, that I thought it would not become me, who was a foreigner, to interfere with parties; but I was ready, with the hazard of my life, to defend his person and state against all invaders.

15. **primitive way of breaking eggs:** The English eat a boiled egg by standing it up in an egg cup, cutting off one end with a knife, and scooping out the contents with a spoon.
16. **Alcoran:** archaic English name for the Koran, the sacred book of Islam.

F **Reading Focus** **Analyzing an Author's Purpose** What is ironic about the argument between the Big-Endians and the rest of the Lilliputians?

Vocabulary **quelled** (kwehld) *v.:* subdued.
schism (SKIHZ uhm) *n.:* division.

Analyzing Visuals

Connecting to the Text Consider the two perspectives in Part I, that of the Lilliputian and that of Gulliver, as exemplified in this photograph. In what ways does the presence of each subject affect the overall composition of the photograph? Try looking at the photograph again, but this time alternate covering either Gulliver or the Lilliputian with your hand. How do your impressions of the photograph and the text change when you alternate perspectives?

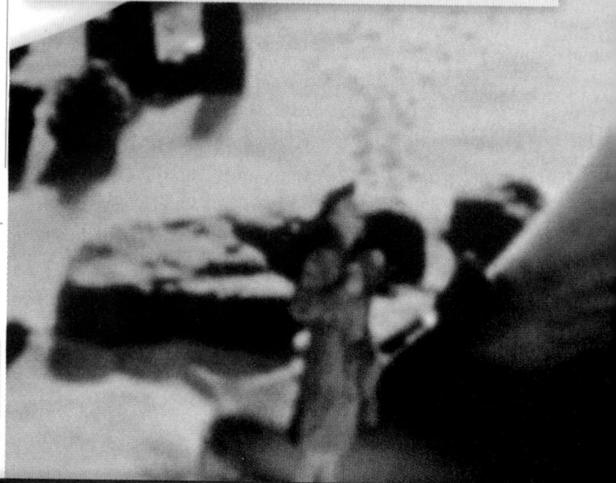

Universal Access

Students with Disabilities

Point out that most of the paragraphs in this selection are quite long and may be difficult for students to follow. Have students imagine they are editors marking up a manuscript of this story, and ask them where they might insert paragraph breaks, for instance, with the paragraph that begins "One morning, . . ." on p. 571. Encourage students to summarize each of their new "paragraphs" in a sentence or two.

Analyzing Visuals

Connecting to the Text: *The presence of both subjects causes the overall composition to have an imbalanced quality. The Lilliputian's presence suggests huge cliffs are in the background, while Gulliver's presence suggests the "cliffs" are actually rocks. Covering Gulliver in the photograph would lessen the sense of vulnerability of the Lilliputian. Without the Lilliputian, Gulliver does not appear to possess an advantage in size and strength.*

Think About/Talk About

See Student Edition p. 572 for the question that relates to the following answer.

Comprehension

F Reading Focus

Possible response: *It is ironic that a disagreement about something as seemingly insignificant as which end of an egg to crack could lead to such consequences as thousands of deaths, civil war, and war with another nation.*

Extend the Discussion

Finding Details What is Reldresal's opinion on the correct way to break eggs? ***Possible response:*** *Since the Alcoran states that "all true believers break their eggs at the convenient end," Reldresal believes that it is up to every man's conscience to determine which end an egg should be broken.*

Interpreting Why does Swift make a point of linking the Big-Endian controversies with religious strife? ***Possible response:*** *He is alluding to one of the major conflicts of his time. The rift between Catholics and Protestants caused similar dissent within England and between Protestant England and Catholic France and Spain. Swift may be implying that religious differences are not significant enough to justify bloodshed.*

Vocabulary: Own the Word

- **schism:** A *schism* is a split; the antonym is *accord.* Use both words in a sentence. A *schism* is caused by disagreement; accord results from agreement.
- **quelled:** Ask students to describe how policemen might *quell* a riot. ***Possible response:*** *throwing tear gas, arresting the leaders*

Universal Access

EL English Learners

English for Academic Success Point out that Swift, throughout this selection, makes frequent use of semicolons. Tell students that in their own writing, they should avoid using semicolons frequently, and only use them occasionally. Remind them that semicolons join two complete and related thoughts, and have them write an example of a sentence that correctly uses the semicolon.

Struggling Readers

Some students may have trouble gleaning the major details from the long sentences in this selection. Suggest that they find the answers to the following questions as they read p. 572: Why did the Emperor publish an edict and what did it require? How did people react to the law? Who frequently stirred up commotion? What did the emperors of Blefuscu claim the Lilliputian Emperor was offending? Who were the Big-Endians?

Model the Skill

- Model applying the skill of **analyzing an author's purpose.** Point out that in the first selection, the Lilliputians provide the most occasions for satire. During his voyage to Brobdingnag, it is Gulliver's words that are used to satirize England.
- Read aloud the end of the first paragraph of p. 574 ("And thus he continued on, while my color came and went several times..."). Point out how Gulliver, after having descried the king as an extremely intelligent and perceptive man, now reacts with anger to any criticism made about his native country. This gives the author the possibility of having the king of Brobdingnag express reasonable and severe criticism of the politics of England, while hiding himself behind Gulliver's patriotism.

Guided Practice: Apply

Turn-and-Talk Have students continue to read the story with a partner. Tell them to note other instances where the author uses Gulliver's words to satirize England. Ask student pairs to share their findings.

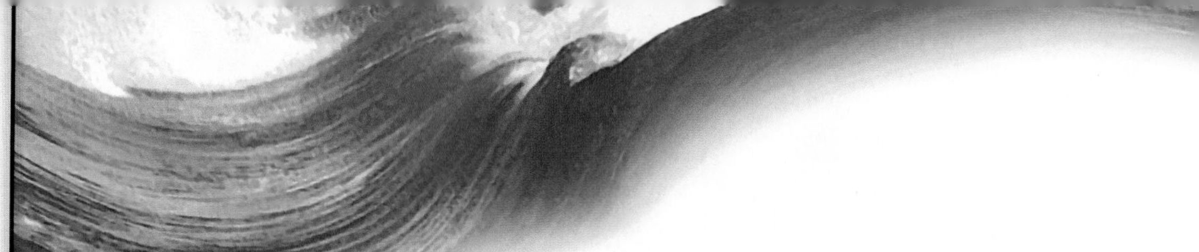

from Part 2: A Voyage to Brobdingnag

On his second voyage, Gulliver finds himself in Brobdingnag (BRAHB dihng nag), *a country Swift locates in Alaska. Here everything is twelve times larger than in England. The situation in Part I is now reversed, and Gulliver discovers what it is like to be an insignificant, timid creature among giants. At court he tries to impress the king and queen with his importance and the importance of England and its civilization. Although its inhabitants look like large and ugly brutes, Brobdingnag is a kind of utopia, a model society with an enlightened and benevolent king. Note how the king treats Gulliver despite his opinion of Gulliver's size and civilization.*

It is the custom that every Wednesday (which, as I have before observed, was their Sabbath) the King and Queen, with the royal issue of both sexes, dine together in the apartment of his Majesty, to whom I was now become a favorite; and at these times my little chair and table were placed at his left hand, before one of the saltcellars.[1] This prince took a pleasure in conversing with me, inquiring into the manners, religion, laws, government, and learning of Europe; wherein I gave him the best account I was able. His apprehension was so clear, and his judgment so exact, that he made very wise reflections and observations upon all I said. But, I confess, that after I had been a little too copious in talking of my own beloved country, of our trade, and wars by sea and land, of our schisms in religion, and parties in the state; the prejudices of his education prevailed[2] so far, that he could not forbear taking me up in his right hand, and stroking me gently with the other, after an hearty fit of laughing, asked me, whether I were a Whig or a Tory.[3] Then turning to his first minister, who waited behind him with a white staff, near as tall as the mainmast of the *Royal Sovereign,*[4] he observed how contemptible a thing was human grandeur, which could be mimicked by such diminutive insects as I. "And yet," said he, "I dare engage, those creatures have their titles and distinctions of honor, they contrive little nests and burrows, that they call houses and cities; they make a figure in dress and equipage;[5] they love, they fight, they dispute, they cheat, they betray." And thus he continued on, while my color came and went several times, with indignation to hear our noble country, the mistress of arts and arms, the scourge of France, the arbitress of Europe, the seat of virtue, piety, honor, and truth, the pride and envy of the world, so contemptuously treated. **A**

But as I was not in a condition to resent injuries, so, upon mature thoughts, I began to doubt whether I were injured or no. For, after having been accustomed several months to the sight and converse of

1. **saltcellars:** dishes of salt.
2. **prevailed:** predominated; held sway.
3. **Whig . . . Tory:** the two chief political parties of eighteenth-century Great Britain.
4. ***Royal Sovereign:*** one of the largest British warships of Swift's age. A white staff is the symbol of the office of the British treasurer.
5. **equipage:**carriage and horses with servants.

Vocabulary **copious** (KOH pee uhs) *adj.:* wordy; profuse.

A **Reading Focus** **Analyzing an Author's Purpose** What is Swift's attitude toward the king? What details tell you this?

Universal Access

English Learners

English for Academic Success Ask students to re-read carefully the words that Gulliver uses to describe his country at the end of the first paragraph. Explain that nouns or phrases that follow a noun to better explain its meaning are called *appositives.* Ask students to consider Swift's satirical intent in the novel, and to discuss whether these appositives can be ironic.

✔ See the **English Language Skill Builder** in **UA: Differentiating Instruction.**

Struggling Readers

Have students use points of the discussion between Gulliver and the king ("the manners, religion, laws, government, and learning of Europe") as categories for a web chart. Ask students to use the web chart to track what Swift is satirizing in this segment of "A Voyage to Brobdingnag." Then, ask students to discuss their conclusions.

✔ See **UA: Differentiating Instruction** for a graphic organizer to scaffold instruction for struggling readers.

Independent Practice

Vocabulary Development

Vocabulary Check

1. *considered*
2. *political party*
3. *angry*
4. *satisfied*
5. *repelled*

Your Turn

quelled: antonym: *fomented*

The agreement quelled one rebellion but fomented a worse one.

schism: antonym: *union*

The schism between East and West led to a union between West and South.

conjectured: antonym: *knew*

Jason conjectured that the river was over the next hill, but the scout knew that it was farther away.

odious: antonym: *delightful*

Children often consider broccoli odious, but adults find it delightful.

English for Academic Success

Language Coach

Possible responses:

1. *conjecture—an opinion formed on the basis of incomplete information*
2. *dispose—get rid of by throwing away*
3. *interpret—explain the meaning of*
4. *convey—make something known or understandable to someone*
5. *determine—decide firmly upon something*

English for Academic Success

Academic Vocabulary

Possible response: *Gulliver's traveling enhances his understanding of his own world because he starts to consider different perspectives on government and morals. Gulliver's approach to people changes, and he is no longer blind to the vices and weaknesses of England.*

Assess

Unit 3 Resources, Selection Standards Check, p. 27

Applying Your Skills

from Gulliver's Travels

Grades 9–10 Review Reading Standard 1.1 (see pages A48–A50)

Vocabulary Development

Vocabulary Check

Answer these questions to test your knowledge of the Vocabulary words.

1. If you have **conjectured** something, has it been considered or purchased?
2. Are you more likely to see a **schism** in a political party or at a tea party?
3. If your opinions and rights are **quelled,** are you likely to be happy or angry?
4. Will you be satisfied or hungry after **copious** amounts of food?
5. Are you repelled or attracted by things that are **odious** to you?

Vocabulary Skills: Antonyms

An **antonym** is a word that has the opposite or nearly the opposite meaning of another word. An unabridged dictionary may list antonyms as well as synonyms for certain words. Familiarity with a word's antonym can help us better understand the word's meaning in the following ways:

- By contrasting qualities and meanings, we can form a more complete picture of what a word does and does not represent.
- Using antonyms in everyday speaking and writing adds a level of depth and interest to our language.
- Knowing antonyms allows us to give expression to one of the undeniable and intriguing facts of life—the existence of opposites.

Your Turn

In a chart like the one below, list antonyms for the Vocabulary words. Then, write a sentence using each Vocabulary word and its antonym.

Vocabulary Word	Antonym	Sentence Using Both Words
copious	meager	The critic took copious notes about the play but gave it very meager praise.
quelled		
schism		
conjectured		
odious		

Language Coach

Verb Tenses When you read a verb in the past tense, take time to identify the present-tense form. For regular verbs, you will remove *-ed* or *-d* from the past-tense form. Write and define the present tense for each of the following past-tense verbs.

1. conjectured
2. disposed
3. interpreted
4. conveyed
5. determined

Academic Vocabulary

Talk About

With a partner, discuss how Gulliver's travels enhance his understanding of his world. How does his approach to people change after meeting and participating in cultures different from his own?

Universal Access: Vocabulary Development

English Learners

English for Academic Success Ask students to create a two-column chart whose columns are labeled, "Lilliputians" and "Brobdingnagians." Ask them to write characteristics of the Lilliputians under the appropriate title and then research each characteristic's antonym in a thesaurus. Have them transcribe the antonym in the "Brobdingnagians" column only if it applies to the Brobdingnagians. Have them follow the same process for the Brobdingnagians, listing additional characteristics and then transcribing antonyms that apply to the Lilliputians.

✔ See the **Academic and Selection Vocabulary Skill Builder** in **UA: Differentiating Instruction.**

Applying Your Skills

Reading Standard 2.5,3.1, 3.3 (see pages A48–A50)
Writing Standard 2.1c (see pages A51–A52)

from Gulliver's Travels

Literary Response and Analysis

Reading Skills Focus

Quick Check

1. How does Gulliver feel he is treated by the Lilliputians?
2. How does the Brobdingnagian king regard Gulliver's home country?
3. After several months with the Brobdingnagians, how does Gulliver feel about himself?

Read with a Purpose

4. How is what the reader learns about human nature different from what Gulliver learns?

Reading Skills: Understanding the Author's Purpose

5. Review the chart you prepared before reading. Now add another column to your chart, noting how each example supports the author's purpose in the work as a whole.

Event; Action, Image	Institution	Satirical Point	Author's Purpose
Gulliver is entertained by rope dancers.	Politics	These political leaders "danced" around issues instead of solving the country's problems.	This example targets the use of influence and favoritism in political appointments.

Literary Skills Focus

Literary Analysis

6. **Summarize** Write a description of what happens to Gulliver in either Part I or Part II.
7. **Interpret** How would you describe Swift's **tone,** or his attitude toward the Lilliputians? toward the Brobdingnagians? What words or passages support your answer?
8. **Analyze** Is there any relationship between the physical size of the Lilliputians and the Brobdingnagians and the way Swift wants us to evaluate their behavior? Does size **symbolize** moral value? Explain.

Literary Skills: Situational Irony

9. **Draw Conclusions** How does Swift's use of situational irony help you understand his opinion about events in his own time period?

Literary Skills Review: Satire

10. **Make Judgments** Writing that attacks or ridicules the shortcomings of people or institutions in an attempt to bring about change is called **satire.** How is *Gulliver's Travels* effective as a satire?

Writing Skills Focus

Think as a Reader/Writer

Use It in Your Writing Previously, you noted the words and images Swift uses to emphasize the extremes he sees in people. Using your *Reader/Writer Notebook* and similar words and images, create your own character sketch of another extreme character that Gulliver might encounter on his journeys.

What Do You Think Now? How do the social orders in Lilliput and Brobdingnag affect the behavior of their inhabitants?

Check for Understanding

Independent Practice

Reading Skills Focus

Possible responses:

1. *Gulliver feels he is treated well; he is fed and given his freedom.*
2. *He regards it as corrupt and full of "ignorance, idleness, and vice."*
3. *He feels that he is smaller than he actually is.*
4. *The reader learns from Gulliver's flaws as well as the flaws of those with whom he interacts.*
5. *Remind students that the purpose of satire is to expose vice to heal society. Have them consider the vices exposed in the selection.*

Literary Skills Focus

Possible responses:

6. *Gulliver was lost at sea and ended up on the island of Lilliput, where citizens are only six inches tall. There he was held captive but ultimately set free. While on the island, he learned about the disgrace of the Lilliputian government.*
7. *The tone of the passages about Lilliput is bitter, but humorous; this is displayed in the passage involving the rope dancers. The tone in passages about Brobdingnag is primarily bitter, as in the passage involving the flies.*
8. *Size symbolizes moral value. The Lilliputians are tiny but warlike and arrogant. The giants in Brobdingnag live in harmony.*
9. *Swift's use of situational irony shows that he feels many events and situations of his time were at best absurd, and at worst, the exact opposite of what should be.*
10. Gulliver's Travels *is an effective satire because Swift examines this imaginary society at its best and at its worst, which prompts readers to look at the good and bad aspects of their own society.*

Universal Access

Struggling Writers

Some students may need additional scaffolding to complete the Writing Skills Focus activity. Invite students to work in groups and think about a possible character sketch of a public figure. Have students brainstorm vivid and comical details that emphasize extremes in their subject's looks, behavior, and beliefs. Then, tell students to compose the character sketch individually.

What Do You Think Now?

Suggest that the warlike nature of Lilliput's leaders makes all Lilliputians warlike; whereas, the leaders of Brobdingnag reject the vileness of humanity. Ask students to reflect on the history and customs of these two peoples to answer the question effectively.

Think About/Talk About

Comprehension

C Reading Focus

Possible response: *Swift uses Gulliver's physical size to symbolize his insignificance and, by extension, England's insignificance.*

Analysis

B Literary Focus

Possible response: *Gulliver sees himself as brave, but in reality he is only fighting off flies. He is present for the queen's amusement.*

Extend the Discussion

Evaluating How does Swift make sure the reader understands that the king's words express the author's thoughts about England? ***Possible responses:*** *The king is portrayed as a wise man. Gulliver's answers to the king are not transcribed, which means that the author wants the reader to consider the king's critical standpoint more than Gulliver's passionate, but naïve, patriotic defense.*

Monitor Students' Comprehension

Guide the class in answering these comprehension questions.

1. What test do the candidates for high office in Lilliput have to undergo? [*They must rope-dance.*]
2. Explain how the war between Lilliput and Blefuscu began. [*The Emperor of Lilliput commanded his subjects to break eggs at the small end, but some subjects rebelled and Blefuscu gave them sanctuary.*]
3. What do English people think of themselves according to Gulliver? [*They think of themselves as noble, creative, powerful, and honorable.*]

would sometimes alight upon my victuals, and leave their loathsome excrement or spawn behind, which to me was very visible, though not to the natives of that country, whose large optics were not so acute as mine in viewing smaller objects. Sometimes they would fix upon my nose or forehead, where they stung me to the quick, smelling very offensively, and I could easily trace that viscous[10] matter, which our naturalists tell us enables those creatures to walk with their feet upward upon a ceiling. I had much ado to defend myself against these detestable animals, and could not forbear starting when they came on my face. It was the common practice of the dwarf to catch a number of these insects in his hand, as schoolboys do among us, and let them out suddenly under my nose, on purpose to frighten me, and divert the Queen. My remedy was to cut them in pieces with my knife as they flew in the air, wherein my dexterity was much admired. . . . **B**

He [the King] was perfectly astonished with the historical account I gave him of our affairs during the last century, protesting it was only an heap of conspiracies, rebellions, murders, massacres, revolutions, banishments; the very worst effects that avarice, faction, hypocrisy, perfidiousness, cruelty, rage, madness, hatred, envy, lust, malice, and ambition, could produce.

His Majesty, in another audience, was at the pains to recapitulate the sum of all I had spoken; compared the questions he made with the answers I had given; then taking me into his hands, and stroking me gently, delivered himself in these words, which I shall never forget, nor the manner he spoke them in.

"My little friend Grildrig,[11] you have made a most admirable panegyric[12] upon your country. You have clearly proved that ignorance, idleness, and vice, are the proper ingredients for qualifying a legislator: that laws are best explained, interpreted, and applied by those whose interest and abilities lie in perverting, confounding, and eluding them. I observe among you some lines of an institution, which in its original might have been tolerable, but these half erased, and the rest wholly blurred and blotted by corruptions. It doth not appear from all you have said, how any one perfection[13] is required toward the procurement of any one station among you; much less that men are ennobled on account of their virtue, that priests are advanced for their piety or learning, soldiers for their conduct or valor, judges for their integrity, senators for the love of their country, or counselors for their wisdom. As for yourself (continued the King), who have spent the greatest part of your life in traveling, I am well disposed to hope you may hitherto have escaped many vices of your country. But by what I have gathered from your own relation, and the answers I have with much pains wringed and extorted from you, I cannot but conclude the bulk of your natives to be the most pernicious[14] race of little odious vermin that nature ever suffered to crawl upon the surface of the earth." **C**

10. **viscous:** sticky.

11. **Grildrig:** the Brobdingnagians' name for Gulliver.
12. **panegyric:** speech full of praise.
13. **perfection:** here, virtue.
14. **pernicious:** wicked; extremely harmful.

B Literary Focus **Situational Irony** Although Gulliver bravely defends himself against the gigantic flies, the queen calls him a coward. Why don't the Brobdingnagians admire Gulliver's bravery?

C Reading Focus **Analyzing an Author's Purpose** Why might Swift use physical size to illustrate Gulliver's feelings about himself and his society?

California Standards, pp. 577–578

- **Reading Standard 2.5** Analyze an author's implicit and explicit philosophical assumptions and beliefs about a subject.
- **Reading Standard 3.1** Analyze characteristics of subgenres (e.g., satire, parody, allegory, pastoral) that are used in poetry, prose, plays, novels, short stories, essays, and other basic genres.
- **Reading Standard 3.3** Analyze the ways in which irony, tone, mood, the author's style, and the "sound" of language achieve specific rhetorical or aesthetic purposes or both.
- **Grades 9–10 Review Reading Standard 1.1** Identify and use the literal and figurative meanings of words and understand word derivations.
- **Writing Standard 2.1** Write fictional, autobiographical, or biographical narratives: **c.** Describe with concrete sensory details the sights, sounds, and smells of a scene and the specific actions, movements, gestures, and feelings of the characters; use interior monologue to depict the characters' feelings.

this people, and observed every object upon which I cast my eyes, to be of proportionable magnitude, the horror I had first conceived from their bulk and aspect was so far worn off, that if I had then beheld a company of English lords and ladies in their finery and birthday clothes,[6] acting their several parts in the most courtly manner, of strutting, and bowing, and prating;[7] to say the truth, I should have been strongly tempted to laugh as much at them as this King and his grandees[8] did at me. Neither indeed could I forbear smiling at myself, when the Queen used to place me upon her hand toward a looking glass, by which both our persons appeared before me in full view together; and there could be nothing more ridiculous than the comparison; so that I really began to imagine myself dwindled many degrees below my usual size. . . .

I was frequently rallied[9] by the Queen upon account of my fearfulness, and she used to ask me whether the people of my country were as great cowards as myself. The occasion was this: The kingdom is much pestered with flies in summer; and these odious insects, each of them as big as a Dunstable lark, hardly gave me any rest while I sat at dinner, with their continual humming and buzzing about my ears. They

6. **birthday clothes:** new outfits worn on a royal's birthday.
7. **prating:** talking pompously.
8. **grandees:** important persons; from the Spanish *grande*.

9. **rallied:** teased.

Vocabulary **odious** (OH dee uhs) *adj.*: hateful; offensive.

Television production of *Gulliver's Travels*.

Think About/Talk About

Comprehension

A Reading Focus

Possible responses: *Gulliver says the king is a person of great wisdom and extreme courtesy; Swift portrays him as a person who is curious, intelligent, and generous, but he is also mocking and insensitive.*

Extend the Discussion

Finding Details In the first column on p. 575, which words help to create a negative impression of the English lords and ladies? ***Possible response:*** *The words "strutting" and "prating" have negative connotations. Those words are used to denote the arrogance of the English nobility.*

Satire How does the prince belittle Gulliver and England on p. 574? ***Possible response:*** *The prince calls Gulliver an insect and comments on the ridiculousness of the intrigue and bickering in such a small, insignificant country as England. He makes the English sound like ants or little rodents that make their nests and scurry about mindlessly.*

Vocabulary: Own the Word

- **copious:** Ask students to talk about a time they fell asleep during a *copious* lecture.
- **odious:** Tell students to applaud softly, loudly, or not at all to indicate how much they would like to be thought of as *odious.* ***Possible response:*** *Students do not applaud because they would not want to thought of as disgusting.*

Advanced Learners

Enrichment Challenge students to learn more about the word *utopia,* the name of an imaginary island in a book of the same name written by Sir. Thomas More in 1516. The word, from Greek, means "no place." Have students suggest the kind of culture and society Jonathan Swift might consider a utopia.

Students with Disabilities

To monitor students' understanding of the selection, have them create a Venn diagram in which they compare and contrast Lilliputians to the inhabitants of Brobdingnag. Ask them to add details about the inhabitants of Brobdingnag as they read. For example, students might write as the first detail about Brobdingnag that the king seems wise and is most likely unconcerned about petty matters.

Reading Skills Focus

A Modest Proposal

Reading Standard 2.2 (see pages A48–A50).

Recognizing Persuasive Techniques

by **Kylene Beers**

Warning! If you read Jonathan Swift's *A Modest Proposal* or Voltaire's *Candide* without recognizing persuasive techniques, you will miss the whole point. Swift and Voltaire seek not only to entertain their readers; each also wants readers to believe that his views are correct.

What makes you believe someone? Is it that he or she shows you convincing evidence? Is it that you like the person? The most effective persuasive writers combine a variety of techniques to convince you to accept their messages.

Three major types of appeals are used in effective persuasive writing. In a **logical appeal,** an author supports an argument through reason, facts, and statistics. In an **emotional appeal,** an author uses moving language and vivid descriptions to arouse strong feelings in readers. Lastly, in an **ethical appeal,** an author establishes credibility, sharing his or her own experiences, qualifications, and motivations, to gain readers' confidence and support.

Sometimes Swift uses logic to address the problem of poverty and starvation. In the following passage, note his use of logical supporting evidence.

> Supposing that one thousand families in this city, would be constant customers for infants' flesh, besides others who might have it at merry meetings, particularly weddings and christenings, I compute that Dublin would take off annually about twenty thousand carcasses, and the rest of the kingdom (where probably they will be sold somewhat cheaper) the remaining eighty thousand.

Swift is, of course, being ironic in his suggestion that babies should be sold as meat, but his appeal to logic is clear. He mentions actual numbers, specific situations, and real places to give his argument credibility.

Your Turn

Look at the following sentences from *A Modest Proposal.* Using the questions as a guide, identify the type of appeal in each example.

In sentence 1, what scene is described and what effect does the author hope it will have on the reader? What language evokes an emotional appeal?

> It is a melancholy object to those, who walk through this great town, or travel in the country, when they see the streets, the roads, and cabin doors, crowded with beggars of the female sex, followed by three, four, or six children, all in rags, and importuning every passenger for an alms.

In sentence 2, why does the author mention that he has spent many years thinking about this subject? What appeal is he using when his cites his experience?

> As to my own part, having turned my thoughts, for many years, upon this important subject, and maturely weighed the several schemes of other projectors, I have always found them grossly mistaken in their computation.

Learn It Online

Explore modern persuasive techniques on the MediaScope mini-site.

go.hrw.com H12-579 Go

Reading Skills Focus

Objectives

Students will understand persuasive techniques (logical, emotional, and ethical appeals).

Unit 3 Resources, Reading Focus Skill Builder, p. 6

Teacher One Stop™, lesson plan and all print resources

Direct Teach

Recognizing Persuasive Techniques

This feature gives students practice in recognizing persuasive techniques in the satirical work, "A Modest Proposal," which tries to persuade the reader to agree to a peculiar plan. Have students read the feature and complete the Your Turn activity before reading the selection.

Check for Understanding

Your Turn

Possible responses:

1. *Sentence 1 describes streets crowded with destitute female beggars and their children. Through the word "melancholy" and the phrase "all in rags," Swift uses emotional appeal to generate pity and concern in the reader.*
2. *Swift establishes the credibility of his research by using ethical appeal.*

Universal Access

Struggling Readers

Have students create a proposal about one aspect of their school that they would like to change, or an improvement they would like to implement. Ask them to write one sentence for each kind of persuasive technique analyzed in the Reading Skills Focus essay.

California Standards, p. 579

- **Reading Standard 2.2** Analyze the way in which clarity of meaning is affected by the patterns of organization, hierarchical structures, repetition of the main ideas, syntax, and word choice in the text.

Learn It Online

For additional support analyzing media, students can go to the **MediaScope** site to analyze other types of media, such as a Web page, a TV news story, a political TV ad, and a print advertisement.

go.hrw.com H12-579 Go

Preteach

Introducing Vocabulary

1. Explain why food is a form of **sustenance**.
2. Explain how people can react to a **prodigious** storm.
3. Describe the typical afternoon of a **scrupulous** student.
4. Explain why newspapers would **censure** a tax raise.
5. Name an **expedient** to improve the quality of the air.
6. Explain why an audience might have difficulty comprehending a speaker who **digressed** during a speech.
7. List reasons that cause **animosities** between friends.

English for Academic Success

Language Coach

After students read the **Language Coach**, have pairs practice pronouncing each word correctly.

Literary Skills Focus

As you read and discuss the selection with students, have them note instances of verbal irony.

Reading Skills Focus

Give students a copy of the Reading Skills Focus graphic organizer. (See **Unit 3 Resources.**) Tell them to use their responses to answer the questions on the Applying Your Skills page.

Writing Skills Focus

Have students record in their **Reader/Writer Notebooks** places in the text that indicate the essay's nature as satire. Students can use their notes to complete the Writing Skills Focus activity.

Learn It Online
The **PowerNotes** presentation for this lesson includes a short video that introduces the selection. The video is also available on the online version of this page.

go.hrw.com H12-580 Go

Preparing to Read

A Modest Proposal

Reading Standard 2.2, 3.3, 3.8, 3.9 (see pages A48–A50)

Literary Skills Focus

Verbal Irony Sometimes writers and speakers use words that mean the opposite of what they really seem to be saying. **Verbal irony** is a contrast between what is said and what is really meant. Saying "thanks a lot" to someone who refuses to help you is an example of verbal irony. In speech, you can often recognize verbal irony by a person's tone of voice. In writing, the voice of the speaker is revealed in the choice of words and details.

Literary Perspective Apply the literary perspectives described on page 582 as you read this selection.

Reading Skills Focus

Recognizing Persuasive Techniques An effective persuasive message appeals to an audience on many levels. In a **logical appeal,** an author supports a position with evidence, whereas in an **emotional appeal,** an author uses language and descriptions to arouse strong feelings. In an **ethical appeal,** an author establishes himself or herself as a reliable and trustworthy source.

Into Action Use a chart like the one below to keep track of some of the persuasive techniques in this essay. When you encounter a persuasive appeal, write down its page number or line, and a brief paraphrase. Check the appropriate column to indicate the type of appeal.

Page	Example	Logical	Emotional	Ethical
581	In the first paragraph the speaker describes the sad sight of crowds of beggars asking for help.		✓	

Writing Skills Focus

Think as a Reader/Writer

Find It in Your Reading As you read, use your *Reader/Writer Notebook* to make note of the places in the text that most clearly indicate this essay's nature as satire.

TechFocus Choose an ad from television or the Internet and note the persuasive qualities that you believe make the ad effective or not.

Reader/Writer Notebook
Use your **RWN** to complete the activities for this selection.

Vocabulary

sustenance (SUHS tuh nuhns) *n.:* food or provisions needed to support life. *Poor mothers beg for sustenance for their children.*

prodigious (proh DIHJ uhs) *adj.:* huge; very great. *A prodigious number of children grow up in poverty.*

scrupulous (SKROO pyoo luhs) *adj.:* extremely careful in deciding what is right or wrong. *Some scrupulous people might object that these proposals are too cruel.*

censure (SEHN shuhr) *v.:* express disapproval of. *People who censure these proposals should suggest an alternative.*

expedient (ehk SPEE dee uhnt) *n.:* way of getting something; a means for achieving an end. *An expedient has been proposed, but there is no hope of putting it into practice.*

digressed (dy GREHSD) *v.:* wandered away from the subject. *I have digressed and will return to discussing the crux of my proposal.*

animosities (an ih MAHS uh teez) *n. pl.:* hostilities; violent hatreds or resentments. *If political animosities are allowed to continue, we will not find a useful solution.*

Language Coach

Stressed Syllables Read the Vocabulary words aloud to become familiar with how they sound. Which syllables are accented?

Learn It Online
Meet *A Modest Proposal* through this video introduction online.

go.hrw.com H12-580 Go

California Standards, pp. 580–590

- **Reading Standard 2.2** Analyze the way in which clarity of meaning is affected by the patterns of organization, hierarchical structures, repetition of the main ideas, syntax, and word choice in the text.
- **Reading Standard 3.3** Analyze the ways in which irony, tone, mood, the author's style, and the "sound" of language achieve specific rhetorical or aesthetic purposes or both.
- **Reading Standard 3.8** Analyze the clarity and consistency of political assumptions in a selection of literary works or essays on a topic.
- **Reading Standard 3.9** Analyze the philosophical arguments presented in literary works to determine whether the authors' positions have contributed to the quality of each work and the credibility of the characters.

Selection Readability	
Easily Accessible **Accessible** Challenging	historical context; complex poetry quote; unfamiliar vocabulary

ESSAY

A Modest Proposal

by **Jonathan Swift**

FOR PREVENTING THE CHILDREN OF POOR PEOPLE IN IRELAND FROM BEING A BURDEN TO THEIR PARENTS OR COUNTRY, AND FOR MAKING THEM BENEFICIAL TO THE PUBLIC

Read with a Purpose
Read to discover who will benefit from Swift's proposal.

Build Background
In this essay, Swift does not write in his own voice but rather uses a **persona,** that of a "projector" who is an economic planner. Swift pretends to be objective, sensible, even sensitive and kind. The difference between the essay's sober, straightforward style and its appalling content, however, gives the proposal its ironic force. At times, Swift seems to drop the persona and speak in his own voice, expressing his fury and indignation.

It is a melancholy object to those, who walk through this great town,[1] or travel in the country, when they see the streets, the roads, and cabin doors, crowded with beggars of the female sex, followed by three, four, or six children, all in rags, and importuning every passenger for an alms.[2] These mothers instead of being able to work for their honest livelihood, are forced to employ all their time in strolling, to beg sustenance for their helpless infants, who, as they grow up either turn thieves for want of work, or leave their dear native country to fight for the Pretender[3] in Spain, or sell themselves to the Barbadoes.[4]

I think it is agreed by all parties, that this prodigious number of children, in the arms, or on the backs, or at the heels of their mothers, and frequently of their fathers, is in the present deplorable state of the kingdom, a very great additional grievance; and therefore whoever could find out a fair, cheap, and easy method of making these children sound and useful members of the commonwealth would deserve so well of the public, as to have his statue set up for a preserver of the nation.

1. **town:** Dublin.
2. **importuning . . . alms:** begging passersby for a handout.
3. **the Pretender:** Some Irishmen who left their country due to poverty went to fight for James Francis Edward Stuart (1688–1766), son of England's last Catholic king, the deposed James II. He was known as the "Pretender" because he kept trying to gain the throne.
4. **sell . . . Barbadoes:** Some Irish went to the West Indies to work as indentured servants.

Vocabulary **sustenance** (SUHS tuh nuhns) *n.:* food or provisions needed to support life.
prodigious (proh DIHJ uhs) *adj.:* huge; very great.

View of Old Chapel Lane or High Street in Skibbereen, Ireland.
The Granger Collection, NY.

Selection Resources

Unit 3 Resources, on-level practice and assessment, p. 30

PowerNotes, interactive lesson presentation with activities

Teacher One Stop™, on-level lesson plans and all print resources

Holt Audio Library

Holt Audio Library: Selections and Summaries in Spanish

UA: Holt Interactive Reader, p. 149

UA: Differentiating Instruction, modified lesson plans and leveled assessment, p. 125

UA: Supporting Instruction in Spanish, selection summary

UA: Resources for Teaching Advanced Students, lesson plans, p. 115

ThinkCentral Online Assessment, Selection Standards Check

ThinkCentral Online Remediation

Teacher Preparation
Selection Summary
In *A Modest Proposal,* Swift makes an outrageous proposal that he ironically calls "modest." He suggests that Irish babies be slaughtered and sold to the gentry as food as a way of relieving their parents of a financial burden while adding variety to the diet of the nobility. Irish poor children could be fattened up and fed to Ireland's rich landowners. This plan would combat overpopulation, spare families the cost of raising children, and improve the lives of the wealthy. The speaker gives supporting facts and suggests recipes for the meat.

Direct Teach

Think About/Talk About
Read with a Purpose Have students read the Read with a Purpose statement. Then, direct their attention to the Build Background statement and discuss Swift's persona and the reasons Swift might want to use this literary device to present his ideas. Remind students that Swift's essay is both persuasive and ironic in intent.

Extend the Discussion
Multiple Meanings Have students define the word *modest* in the title of the essay. Students may think of modesty only in relation to decency or shyness about one's body. Ask them to use the dictionary to find other meanings. ***Possible response:*** *not bold; limited in size, amount, or scope*

Vocabulary: Own the Word
- **sustenance:** Tell students the verb form of *sustenance* is *sustain.* A person is *sustained* by constant nourishment.
- **prodigious:** Ask students to name something they would want in *prodigious* amounts. ***Possible responses:*** *allowance money, school vacations, friends*

Model the Skill

- Provide students with copies of the Reading Skills Focus graphic organizer for *A Modest Proposal.* (See **Unit 3 Resources**.)
- Tell students that recognizing **persuasive techniques** helps the reader maintain an objective outlook toward the text. To determine what kind of appeal the author uses, students can consider whether the author is quoting facts, using emotional language, or boasting about his or her credentials.
- Model tracking persuasive techniques in the graphic organizer. You might say: "In the second paragraph, the author states that his method will put an end to voluntary abortion. He defines the practice as 'horrid' and as a sacrifice of 'innocent babies.' These definitions are evidence of an ethical appeal—the author's plan would eliminate abortion and infanticide. They can also be interpreted as emotional appeal, as the author tries to stir disgust and disdain in the reader."

Page	Example
582	In the third paragraph, the author states that his method will put an end to voluntary abortion.

Logical	Emotional	Ethical
	√	√

Guided Practice: Apply

Think-Pair-Share Group students in pairs to continue reading for other examples of persuasive technique through logical, emotional, or ethical appeal. Ask student pairs to share their findings with the rest of the class.

But my intention is very far from being confined to provide only for the children of professed beggars; it is of a much greater extent, and shall take in the whole number of infants at a certain age, who are born of parents in effect as little able to support them, as those who demand our charity in the streets.

As to my own part, having turned my thoughts, for many years, upon this important subject, and maturely weighed the several schemes of other projectors, I have always found them grossly mistaken in their computation. It is true a child, just dropped from its dam,[5] may be supported by her milk, for a solar year with little other nourishment, at most not above the value of two shillings, which the mother may certainly get, or the value in scraps, by her lawful occupation of begging, and it is exactly at one year old that I propose to provide for them, in such a manner, as, instead of being a charge upon their parents, or the parish, or wanting food and raiment[6] for the rest of their lives, they shall, on the contrary, contribute to the feeding and partly to the clothing of many thousands. **A**

There is likewise another great advantage in my scheme, that it will prevent those voluntary abortions, and that horrid practice of women murdering their bastard children, alas! too frequent among us, sacrificing the poor innocent babes, I doubt, more to avoid the expense, than the shame, which would move tears and pity in the most savage and inhuman breast. **B**

The number of souls in Ireland being usually reckoned one million and a half, of these I calculate there may be about two hundred thousand couples whose wives are breeders, from which number I subtract thirty thousand couples, who are able to maintain their own children, although I apprehend there cannot be so many under the present distresses of the kingdom, but this being granted, there will remain an hundred and seventy thousand breeders. I again subtract fifty thousand for those women who miscarry, or whose children die by accident, or disease within the year. There only remain an hundred and twenty thousand children of poor parents annually born: The question therefore is, how this number shall be reared, and provided for, which, as I have already said, under the present situation of affairs, is utterly impossible by all the methods hitherto proposed, for we can neither employ them in handicraft, or agriculture; we neither build houses (I mean in the country) nor cultivate land: They can very seldom pick up a livelihood by stealing until they arrive at six years old, except where they are of towardly parts,[7] although, I confess they learn the rudiments much earlier, during which time, they can however be properly looked upon only as probationers,[8] as I have been informed by a principal gentleman in the county of Cavan,[9] who protested to me, that he never knew above one or two instances under the age of six, even in

5. **dam:** mother (ordinarily used only for animals).
6. **raiment:** clothing.

7. **of towardly parts:** exceptionally advanced for their age.
8. **they can . . . probationers:** Children younger than six are apprentices in the profession of stealing.
9. **Cavan:** inland county in Ireland that is remote from Dublin.

Literary Perspectives

Analyzing Credibility in Literature When the way a story is told does not match what we know about the person telling it, we may question the narrator's credibility. Consider the fact that *A Modest Proposal* is not narrated purely by its author, for in it Swift uses a persona, that of a learned, judicious economic planner who seems to care sincerely for the Irish poor. How does that persona's inconceivable and preposterous proposal affect his (and Swift's) credibility? Why might Swift have intentionally created this effect?

Analyzing Political Context Literary texts are influenced by the particular worldview of the author, whether it is his or her political perspective, gender, or social class. Explore the way Swift represents the disparity between rich and poor in *A Modest Proposal.* How does he convey to his audience the urgency of this issue? **As you read, be sure to notice the questions in the text that will guide you in using each perspective.**

A Reading Focus **Recognizing Persuasive Techniques** How does Swift use an ethical appeal in this paragraph?

B Reading Focus **Recognizing Persuasive Techniques** What kind of persuasive appeal is the author using in this paragraph? How does the word choice enhance the effectiveness of the appeal?

Literary Perspectives

Before students read the selection, have them read the **Literary Perspectives** about Analyzing Credibility in Literature and Analyzing Political Context.

Ask them to discuss how the impact and effectiveness of the essay would change if the speaker had written in a serious, non-ironic one, directly stating his observations and opinions of the needs of the poor and the corruption of the wealthy.

Remind students to use the notes and questions at the bottom of the page to help them use each perspective.

a part of the kingdom so renowned for the quickest proficiency in that art. **C**

I am assured by our merchants, that a boy or girl, before twelve years old, is no saleable commodity, and even when they come to this age, they will not yield above three pounds, or three pounds and half a crown at most on the exchange, which cannot turn to account[10] either to the parents or the kingdom, the charge of nutriment and rags having been at least four times that value.

I shall now therefore humbly propose my own thoughts, which I hope will not be liable to the least objection.

I have been assured by a very knowing American[11] of my acquaintance in London, that a young healthy child well nursed is at a year old a most delicious, nourishing, and wholesome food, whether stewed, roasted, baked, or boiled, and I make no doubt that it will equally serve in a fricassee, or ragout.[12]

I do therefore humbly offer it to public consideration, that of the hundred and twenty thousand children, already computed, twenty thousand may be reserved for breed, whereof only one-fourth part to be males, which is more than we allow to sheep, black cattle, or swine, and my reason is that these children are seldom the fruits of marriage, a circumstance not much regarded by our savages; therefore one male will be sufficient to serve four females. That the remaining hundred thousand may at a year old be offered in sale to the persons of quality, and fortune, through the kingdom, always advising the mother to let them suck plentifully in the last month, so as to render them plump, and fat for a good table. A child will make two dishes at an entertainment for friends, and when the family dines alone, the fore or hind quarter will make a reasonable dish, and seasoned with a little pepper or salt will be very good boiled on the fourth day, especially in winter.

I have reckoned upon a medium, that a child just born will weigh twelve pounds, and in a solar year if tolerably nursed increaseth to twenty-eight pounds.

I grant this food will be somewhat dear,[13] and therefore very proper for landlords, who, as they have already devoured[14] most of the parents, seem to have the best title to the children.

Infant's flesh will be in season throughout the year, but more plentiful in March, and a little before and after, for we are told by a grave author,[15] an eminent French physician, that fish being a prolific diet, there are more children born in Roman Catholic countries about nine months after Lent, than at any other season, therefore reckoning a year after Lent, the markets will be more glutted than usual, because the number of popish infants, is at least three to one in this kingdom, and therefore it will have one other collateral advantage by lessening the number of papists[16] among us.

I have already computed the charge of nursing a beggar's child (in which list I reckon all cottagers,[17] laborers, and four-fifths of the farmers) to be about two shillings per annum,[18] rags included, and I believe no gentleman would repine to give ten shillings for the carcass of a good fat child, which, as I have said will make four dishes of excellent nutritive meat, when he hath only some particular friend, or his own family to dine with him. Thus the squire will learn to be a good landlord, and grow popular among his tenants, the mother will have eight shillings net profit, and be fit for work until she produceth another child.

Those who are more thrifty (as I must confess the times require) may flay[19] the carcass; the skin of

10. **turn to account:** be profitable.
11. **American:** To Swift's readers this label would have suggested a barbaric person.
12. **fricassee, or ragout** (frihk uh SEE, ra GOO): different kinds of meat stew.
13. **dear:** expensive.
14. **devoured:** made poor by charging high rents.
15. **grave author:** The French satirist François Rabelais produced works that are comic rather than "grave."
16. **popish . . . papists:** derogatory terms for Roman Catholics.
17. **cottagers:** tenant farmers.
18. **per annum:** per year.
19. **flay:** remove the skin of.

C Literary Focus **Verbal Irony** What is the "art" that Swift is referring to? What is ironic about the way the author discusses this topic?

Real Issues, Real Experts

Holt author ***Leila Christenbury*** *offers strategies for teaching* A Modest Proposal.

A Modest Proposal is extreme sport, a model of hate speech and racism, and at its angry center it advocates the breaking of one of humankind's most powerful taboos. Modern students would be quite challenged to write their own *A Modest Proposal*; the text in content and tone is complex, and the subject matter is particularly unique. Yet, students can certainly outline the logical structure that Swift uses in *A Modest Proposal* as well as list his offensive language ("breeders," "savages," "popish"). They could also discuss, from their perspective, what current national or international situation is outrageous enough to inspire a contemporary *A Modest Proposal*. Have students consider the following question: What similarly dire event or events could be seen as analogous to the eighteenth-century Irish crisis, to whom, and why?

Direct Teach

Think About/Talk About

Comprehension

A Reading Focus

Possible response: *He proposes a solution that will dramatically alleviate poverty among infants.*

B Reading Focus

Possible responses: *He is making an emotional appeal to save the children from being killed by their mothers. "Horrid," "murdering," "poor innocent," and "alas!" add emotional distress and desperation to the appeal.*

Analysis

C Literary Focus

Possible responses: *The "art" is the art of theft. It is ironic because theft is illegal.*

Extend the Discussion

Drawing Conclusions What horrible plan is the author "humbly" proposing? ***Possible response:*** *The author is proposing that children be sold as meat. Swift clarifies his ideas by having the speaker repeat several synonyms for cooked—"stewed," "roasted," "baked," and "boiled".*

Interpreting In the last paragraph, what attitudes toward Catholics is Swift satirizing? ***Possible responses:*** *He is satirizing the belief that a Catholic child is less valuable than a Protestant one. He is also satirizing Protestants' desire to get rid of Catholics for conceiving children during Lent, a time when people should practice abstinence.*

Model the Skill

- Review the concept of **verbal irony** with students. Tell students that verbal irony is often delivered through a careful choice of tone. Read aloud the third paragraph of p. 584, beginning with "A very worthy person . . ." You might say: "The tone in this paragraph is self-effacing and polite. The discrepancy between the speaker's genteel tone and the horrific proposal shocks readers while reminding them of Swift's true purpose—to criticize inhuman attitudes toward the poor."
- Then read the part of the paragraph that describes the quality of adolescents' meat. You might say: "Note how the speaker describes the meat of young boys. His word choice and tone seem to belong to a serious argument, but we know that he is using irony."

Guided Practice: Apply

Turn-and-Talk Have students continue their analysis of the author's word choice and irony on pp. 584–585. Ask student pairs to share their conclusions.

Think About/Talk About

Build Background

Point out that the struggle between Catholics and Protestants in Ireland continues today. Explain that during the 1500s and 1600s, all the English monarchs (with the exception of James II) took measures to suppress Catholicism in Ireland. At the same time, they seized a great deal of Irish land and gave it to English settlers. As a result, Irish Catholics became strongly united—and strongly anti-English. Still, by 1704, Catholics were not allowed to purchase or inherit land or to serve in the Irish Parliament or army.

which, artificially dressed, will make admirable gloves for ladies, and summer boots for fine gentlemen. **D**

As to our city of Dublin, shambles[20] may be appointed for this purpose, in the most convenient parts of it, and butchers we may be assured will not be wanting, although I rather recommend buying the children alive, and dressing them hot from the knife,[21] as we do roasting pigs. **E**

A very worthy person, a true lover of his country, and whose virtues I highly esteem, was lately pleased, in discoursing on this matter, to offer a refinement upon my scheme. He said, that many gentlemen of this kingdom, having of late destroyed their deer, he conceived that the want of venison might be well supplied by the bodies of young lads and maidens, not exceeding fourteen years of age, nor under twelve, so great a number of both sexes in every country being now ready to starve, for want of work and service:[22] and these to be disposed of by their parents if alive, or otherwise by their nearest relations. But with due deference to so excellent a friend, and so deserving a patriot, I cannot be altogether in his sentiments, for as to the males, my American acquaintance assured me from frequent experience, that their flesh was generally tough and lean, like that of our schoolboys, by continual exercise, and their taste disagreeable, and to fatten them would not answer the charge. Then as to the females, it would, I think with humble submission, be a loss to the public, because they soon would become breeders themselves: And besides it is not improbable that some scrupulous people might be apt to censure such a practice (although indeed very unjustly) as a little bordering upon cruelty, which, I confess, hath always been with me the strongest objection against any project, how well soever intended.

But in order to justify my friend, he confessed that this expedient was put into his head by the famous Sallmanaazor,[23] a native of the island Formosa, who came from thence to London, above twenty years ago, and in conversation told my friend, that in his country when any young person happened to be put to death, the executioner sold the carcass to persons of quality, as a prime dainty, and that, in his time, the body of a plump girl of fifteen, who was crucified for an attempt to poison the emperor, was sold to his imperial majesty's prime minister of state, and other great mandarins[24] of the court, in joints[25] from the gibbet,[26] at four hundred crowns. Neither indeed can I deny, that if the same use were made of several plump young girls in this town, who, without one single groat[27] to their fortunes, cannot stir abroad without a chair,[28] and appear at the playhouse, and assemblies in foreign fineries, which they never will pay for; the kingdom would not be the worse.

Some persons of a desponding spirit are in great concern about that vast number of poor people, who are aged, diseased, or maimed, and I have been desired to employ my thoughts what course may be taken, to ease the nation of so grievous an encumbrance. But I am not in the least pain upon that matter, because it is very well known, that they are every day dying, and rotting, by cold, and famine, and filth, and vermin,[29] as fast as can be reasonably expected. And as to the younger laborers they are now in almost as hopeful a

20. **shambles:** slaughterhouses.
21. **dressing them hot from the knife:** killing the infant only moments before cooking it.
22. **service:** employment as servants.
23. **Sallmanaazor:** George Psalmanazar (c. 1679–1763) was a Frenchman who pretended to be from Formosa, or modern Taiwan, and wrote a fraudulent account of it.
24. **mandarins:** Chinese officials.
25. **joints:** large cuts of meat, including the bone.
26. **gibbet:** wooden frame used for hanging criminals.
27. **groat:** fourpence, or a very small sum.
28. **chair:** sedan chair; a covered seat carried by servants.
29. **vermin:** pests such as lice, fleas, and bedbugs.

D Literary Focus **Analyzing Political Context** Note how the speaker uses language usually associated with descriptions of animals. Why does the speaker talk of the children of the poor as if they were livestock?

E Reading Focus **Recognizing Persuasive Techniques** When the speaker suggests "dressing" children "hot from the knife," what effect does he expect his word choice to create?

Vocabulary **scrupulous** (SKROO pyoo luhs) *adj.:* extremely careful in deciding what is right or wrong.
censure (SEHN shuhr) *v.:* express disapproval of.
expedient (ehk SPEE dee uhnt) *n.:* way of getting something; a means for achieving an end.

Universal Access

EL English Learners

Have students work with partners to paraphrase passages. When they paraphrase, have them take into account the kind of appeal—emotional, logical, or ethical—the passage is intended to make. Remind students of the irony that underlies Swift's words; often, he means the opposite of what the words literally say.

✔ See **UA: Differentiating Instruction** for strategies for teaching English learners.

Struggling Readers

To help students read *A Modest Proposal,* model the reading skill of recognizing appeals to emotion, logic, and ethics. You might say: "When I read this selection, I ask myself questions to determine the kind of appeal that the author uses." Encourage students as they read to ask themselves: "Is the author flaunting facts and numbers? Is the author trying to stir feelings in the reader? Is the author showing off his credentials?"

✔ See **UA: Differentiating Instruction** for strategies for teaching struggling readers.

condition. They cannot get work, and consequently pine away for want of nourishment, to a degree, that if at any time they are accidentally hired to common labor, they have not strength to perform it, and thus the country and themselves are in a fair way of being soon delivered from the evils to come. F

I have too long digressed, and therefore shall return to my subject. I think the advantages by the proposal which I have made are obvious and many as well as of the highest importance.

For first, as I have already observed, it would greatly lessen the number of papists, with whom we are yearly overrun, being the principal breeders of the nation, as well as our most dangerous enemies, and who stay at home on purpose with a design to deliver the kingdom to the Pretender, hoping to take their advantage by the absence of so many good Protestants,[30] who have chosen rather to leave their country, than stay at home, and pay tithes[31] against their conscience, to an idolatrous Episcopal curate.

Secondly, the poorer tenants will have something valuable of their own, which by law may be made liable to distress,[32] and help to pay their landlord's rent, their corn and cattle being already seized, and money a thing unknown.

Thirdly, whereas the maintenance of an hundred

---

30. **good Protestants:** used ironically to mean bad Protestants because they object to the Church of Ireland's bishops and regard them as "idolatrous."
31. **tithes:** monetary gifts to the church equivalent to one tenth of each donor's income.
32. **distress:** The money from the sale of their children may be seized by their landlords as payment for debt.

F **Literary Focus** **Verbal Irony** What is ironic about the use of the word *hopeful* in this paragraph?

Vocabulary **digressed** (dy GREHSD) *v.:* wandered away from the subject.

Bridget O'Donnell with her children during the 19th century potato famine. (Inset) Searching for potatoes during the Great Potato Famine (1846–1847, Ireland. The Granger Collection, N.Y.

Word-Attack Skills Mini-Lesson

English for Academic Success Point out that deciding which syllable to stress is one of the main challenges in reading longer and more sophisticated words. Use the selection word *idolatrous* (p. 585) as a starting point for a discussion of differences in the pronunciation of related words. Write *idolatrous* on the board, and ask students to identify the base word, *idol*. Compare the stressed syllables in the two words. In *idol*, the first syllable is the stressed syllable (Y duhl). In *idolatrous* the second syllable—which is unstressed in the base word, *idol*, is stressed (y DOL uh truhs).

Activity Have students identify the most heavily stressed syllable in each of these words.

1. expedient	expedite	expedition
2. scruple	scrupulous	scrupulosity
3. family	familiar	familial
4. propose	proposal	proposition
5. oblige	obligate	obligatory

Think About/Talk About

Comprehension

E Reading Focus

Possible response: *Swift is hoping for "shock value"; the thought of treating children like roasted pigs should horrify readers.*

Analysis

D Literary Focus

Possible response: *The speaker mocks the view that children of the poor have less value than children of the wealthy, thus he compares them to domesticated animals valued only for their work efforts.*

F Literary Focus

Possible response: *Swift means that the young laborers are anything but hopeful.*

Extend the Discussion

Drawing Conclusions Based on the first paragraph, what is the plight of young adults in Ireland in Swift's time? ***Possible response:*** *Young laborers cannot find employment, and for that reason they are undernourished. Even if they eventually find a job, they are too weak to perform.*

Vocabulary: Own the Word

- **scrupulous:** Have students fill out a semantic web for *scrupulous.* [*exact, strict, painstaking, particular*]
- **censure:** Tell students that *censure* comes from the Latin *censura,* meaning "judgment." When you *censure* a law or practice, you are criticizing it.
- **expedient:** Remind students that *expedient* connotes something useful in a situation, but not always morally acceptable. You might say: "It would be *expedient* for the management to lay off a few workers." Ask students to create a sentence using this connotation of *expedient.*
- **digressed:** Demonstrate giving a talk on one topic and *digressing.* Ask one or two students to demonstrate using other topics.

Model the Skill

- Explain to students that a word's **denotation** corresponds to its dictionary definition. A word's **connotation** refers instead to the feelings and associations connected with it.
- Read aloud the paragraph that begins with "Sixthly . . ."
- Explain that the word *settlement*, when used to refer to someone's work life, usually has a positive connotation. Someone who is *settled* usually has a steady job. In the selection, the positive connotation of the word is used ironically. The children will receive "settlement for life," or until they become meat on the tables of the wealthy.

Guided Practice: Apply

Turn-and-Talk Ask students to discuss which words or phrases would be more realistic than *settlement*. ***Possible responses:*** *massacre, extermination*

Think as a Reader/Writer

Find It in Your Reading Point out how the author uses a calm, deferential tone to introduce the most horrifying proposal.

Use It in Your Writing Ask students to write two or three sentences in which they pretend to agree with the speaker's proposal as a solution to contemporary problems. Ask them to use a tone similar to Swift's to introduce the proposal.

thousand children, from two years old, and upwards, cannot be computed at less than ten shillings apiece per annum, the nation's stock will be thereby increased fifty thousand pounds per annum, besides the profit of a new dish, introduced to the tables of all gentlemen of fortune in the kingdom, who have any refinement in taste, and the money will circulate among ourselves, the goods being entirely of our own growth and manufacture. **G**

Fourthly, the constant breeders, besides the gain of eight shillings sterling per annum, by the sale of their children, will be rid of the charge of maintaining them after the first year.

Fifthly, this food would likewise bring great custom to taverns, where the vintners[33] will certainly be so prudent as to procure the best receipts[34] for dressing it to perfection, and consequently have their houses frequented by all the fine gentlemen, who justly value themselves upon their knowledge in good eating, and a skillful cook, who understands how to oblige his guests will contrive to make it as expensive as they please.

Sixthly, this would be a great inducement to marriage, which all wise nations have either encouraged by rewards, or enforced by laws and penalties. It would increase the care and tenderness of mothers toward their children, when they were sure of a settlement for life to the poor babes, provided in some sort by the public to their annual profit instead of expense, we should soon see an honest emulation[35] among the married women, which of them could bring the fattest child to the market, men would become as fond of their wives, during the time of their pregnancy, as they are now of their mares in foal, their cows in calf, or sows when they are ready to farrow,[36] nor offer to beat or kick them (as is too frequent a practice) for fear of a miscarriage.

Many other advantages might be enumerated. For instance, the addition of some thousand carcasses in our exportation of barreled beef. The propagation of swine's flesh, and improvement in the art of making good bacon, so much wanted among us by the great destruction of pigs, too frequent at our tables, which are no way comparable in taste, or magnificence to a well-grown, fat yearling child, which roasted whole will make a considerable figure at a Lord Mayor's feast, or any other public entertainment. But this, and many others I omit being studious of brevity.

Supposing that one thousand families in this city, would be constant customers for infants' flesh, besides others who might have it at merry meetings, particularly weddings and christenings, I compute that Dublin would take off annually about twenty thousand carcasses, and the rest of the kingdom (where probably they will be sold somewhat cheaper) the remaining eighty thousand. **H**

I can think of no one objection, that will possibly be raised against this proposal, unless it should be urged that the number of people will be thereby much lessened in the kingdom. This I freely own, and it was indeed one principal design in offering it to the world. I desire the reader will observe, that I calculate my remedy for this one individual kingdom of Ireland, and for no other that ever was, is, or, I think, ever can be upon earth. Therefore let no man talk to me of other expedients: *Of taxing our absentees*[37] *at five shillings a pound; of using neither clothes, nor household furniture, except what is of our own growth and manufacture; of utterly rejecting the materials and instruments that promote foreign luxury; of curing the expensiveness of pride, vanity, idleness, and gaming*[38] *in our women; of introducing a vein of parsimony,*[39] *prudence, and temperance; of learning to love our country, wherein we differ even from Laplanders, and the*

33. **vintners:** wine merchants.
34. **receipts:** recipes.
35. **emulation:** competition.
36. **farrow:** produce piglets.
37. **absentees:** English landowners who refused to live on their Irish property.
38. **gaming:** gambling.
39. **parsimony:** thriftiness; economy.

G **Literary Perspective** **Analyzing Credibility in Literature** What might you assume about the background of the speaker, given his discussion of Irish children in economic and monetary terms?

H **Reading Focus** **Recognizing Persuasive Techniques** What kind of persuasive appeal is used in this paragraph? What is also ironic about this appeal—in particular, with the mention of "christenings"?

Cross-Curricular Connection

HISTORY: "Colonial" Ireland

During this period, England treated Ireland like a colony, plundering its resources and then selling the Irish the goods made from those resources. During Swift's time, important goals for Ireland were to circulate money within its borders and to grow its own goods.

Paired Activity Ask students to research with a partner Ireland in the seventeenth and eighteenth centuries, in particular, the impact of England's political and economic treatment of Ireland on the Irish. Have them report their findings in an oral presentation.

HSS Analysis Skills: HI 4

inhabitants of Topinamboo;[40] *of quitting our animosities, and factions,*[41] *nor act any longer like the Jews, who were murdering one another at the very moment their city*[42] *was taken; of being a little cautious not to sell our country and consciences for nothing; of teaching landlords to have at least one degree of mercy toward their tenants. Lastly of putting a spirit of honesty, industry, and skill into our shopkeepers, who, if a resolution could now be taken to buy only our native goods, would immediately unite to cheat and exact*[43] *upon us in the price, the measure, and the goodness, nor could ever yet be brought to make one fair proposal of just dealing, though often and earnestly invited to it.* **I**

Therefore I repeat, let no man talk to me of these and the like expedients, till he hath at least a glimpse of hope, that there will ever be some hearty and sincere attempt to put them in practice.

But as to myself, having been wearied out for many years with offering vain, idle, visionary thoughts, and at length utterly despairing of success, I fortunately fell upon this proposal, which as it is wholly new, so it hath something solid and real, of no expense and little trouble, full in our own power, and whereby we can incur no danger in disobliging England. For this kind of commodity will not bear exportation, the flesh being of too tender a consistence, to admit a long continuance in salt, although perhaps I could name a country,[44] which would be glad to eat up our whole nation without it.

After all I am not so violently bent upon my own opinion, as to reject any offer, proposed by wise men, which shall be found equally innocent, cheap, easy, and effectual. But before something of that kind shall be advanced in contradiction to my scheme, and offering a better, I desire the author, or authors will be pleased maturely to consider two points. First, as things now stand, how they will be able to find food and raiment for a hundred thousand useless mouths and backs. And secondly, there being a round million of creatures in human figure, throughout this kingdom, whose whole subsistence[45] put into a common stock would leave them in debt two millions of pounds sterling, adding those who are beggars by profession to the bulk of farmers, cottagers, and laborers, with their wives and children, who are beggars in effect; I desire those politicians, who dislike my overture, and may perhaps be so bold to attempt an answer, that they will first ask the parents of these mortals, whether they would not at this day think it a great happiness to have been sold for food at a year old, in the manner I prescribe, and thereby have avoided such a perpetual scene of misfortunes, as they have since gone through, by the oppression of landlords, the impossibility of paying rent without money or trade, the want of common sustenance, with neither house nor clothes to cover them from inclemencies of weather, and the most inevitable prospect of entailing the like, or great miseries, upon their breed forever.

I profess in the sincerity of my heart that I have not the least personal interest in endeavoring to promote this necessary work, having no other motive than the public good of my country, by advancing our trade, providing for infants, relieving the poor, and giving some pleasure to the rich. I have no children, by which I can propose to get a single penny; the youngest being nine years old, and my wife past childbearing. **J**

40. **Laplanders . . . Topinamboo:** Lapland is a region encompassing some parts of northern Europe, and Topinamboo is a region of Brazil. Swift suggests that if Brazilians and Laplanders can love their seemingly inhospitable lands, the Irish should love Ireland.
41. **factions:** political groups that work against the interests of other groups.
42. **their city:** Jerusalem, which the Roman emperor Titus destroyed in A.D. 70 while Jewish factions fought one another.
43. **exact:** force payment.
44. **a country:** England.
45. **subsistence:** all means of keeping alive; possessions.

I Reading Focus **Recognizing Persuasive Techniques** What objection does the speaker anticipate? What counterargument does he make?

Vocabulary **animosities** (an ih MAHS uh teez) *n. pl.*: hostilities; violent hatreds or resentments.

J Literary Focus **Verbal Irony** How is the speaker's claim that he hasn't "the least personal interest" ironic?

Think About/Talk About

Comprehension

H Reading Focus

Possible responses: *The numbers that he cites show that the speaker is appealing to logic. Serving infants' flesh at christenings, which, in the Catholic tradition, occur shortly after birth, is especially ironic because it is so macabre.*

I Reading Focus

Possible responses: *The objection is that the population of the kingdom will go down. He responds by explaining that he writes only about Ireland.*

Analysis

G Literary Perspectives

Possible response: *Students might assume that the speaker is well educated in economics.*

J Literary Focus

Possible response: *It is ironic because Swift is very interested in improving the lot of the poor.*

Vocabulary: Own the Word

animosities: *Animosity* is enmity or hostility; an antonym is *friendship.* Use both words in a sentence. The bitter argument between the two boys produced *animosity* and consequently ended their friendship.

California Standards, pp. 588–590

- **Reading Standard 2.2** Analyze the way in which clarity of meaning is affected by the patterns of organization, hierarchical structures, repetition of the main ideas, syntax, and word choice in the text.
- **Reading Standard 3.3** Analyze the ways in which irony, tone, mood, the author's style, and the "sound" of language achieve specific rhetorical or aesthetic purposes or both.
- **Reading Standard 3.8** Analyze the clarity and consistency of political assumptions in a selection of literary works or essays on a topic (e.g., suffrage, women's role in organized labor) (Political approach).
- **Reading Standard 3.9** Analyze the philosophical arguments presented in literary works to determine whether the authors' positions have contributed to the quality of each work and the credibility of the characters (Philosophical approach).
- **Grades 9–10 Review Reading Standard 1.2** Distinguish between the denotative and connotative meanings of words and interpret the connotative power of words.
- **Writing Standard 1.1** Identify and use the literal and figurative meanings of words and understand word derivations.
- **Writing Standard 2.2** Write responses to literature: **a.** Demonstrate a comprehensive understanding of the significant ideas in works or passages. **b.** Analyze the use of imagery, language, universal themes, and unique aspects of the text. **c.** Support important ideas and viewpoints through accurate and detailed references to the text and to other works.
- **Writing Standard 2.6** Deliver multimedia presentations: **a.** Combine text, images, and sound and draw information from many sources (e.g., television broadcasts, videos, films, newspapers, magazines, CD-ROMs, the Internet, electronic media-generated images). **b.** Select an appropriate medium for each element of the presentation. **c.** Use the selected media skillfully, editing appropriately and monitoring for quality.

Check for Understanding

Independent Practice

Reading Skills Focus

Possible responses:

1. *Its purpose is to reform a system that disregards the poor.*
2. *He means the exact opposite: England should alleviate the poverty of the Irish people.*
3. *The persona lets Swift write in a seemingly dispassionate tone.*
4. *According to the speaker, his plan would (1) reduce the number of Catholics, (2) give the poor an asset, (3) aid the economy and introduce a new food, (4) decrease the time "breeders" have to raise children, (5) improve taverns' business, and (6) encourage marriage.*
5. *Sentences should reflect understanding of the overall effect of each appeal on the essay.*

Literary Skills Focus

Possible responses:

6. *Examples are "breeders (p. 582); "saleable commodity" (p. 583); "dressing them . . . like roast pigs" (p. 584). This language emphasizes the inhumane condition of the Irish poor.*
7. *One expedient is taxing absentee English landowners. This expedient is probably dismissed because the wealthy will never comply with extra taxes.*
8. *The delay makes his proposal seem like a reasonable idea.*
9. *Each perspective motivates the reader to seek the real message that Swift is trying to convey.*
10. *Readers could misinterpret the irony, as some in Swift's day actually did. However, outrage could also lead readers to find another more acceptable solution to poverty in Ireland.*
11. *The Protestants will profit and the Irish Catholics will suffer.*
12. *Swift's tone is very bitter. The expedients the writer rejects (pp. 586–587) are solutions that Swift would recommend.*

Applying Your Skills

Reading Standard 2.2, 3.3, 3.8, 3.9 (see pages A48–A50)
Writing Standard 1.1 (see pages A51–A52)

A Modest Proposal

Literary Response and Analysis

Reading Skills Focus

Quick Check

1. How would you state the purpose of this essay? Whom or what is Swift trying to reform?
2. What is the speaker's real meaning when he asserts that England will not mind if Ireland kills and eats its babies?
3. How does assuming the persona of an economic planner help Swift achieve his purpose?

Read with a Purpose

4. In your own words, list the six advantages of the speaker's proposal. Who would benefit or suffer from the proposal?

Reading Skills: Recognizing Persuasive Techniques

5. As you read *A Modest Proposal,* you recorded some logical, emotional, and ethical appeals. Refer to your chart to write a few sentences explaining how Swift uses each type of appeal to make his points in the essay as a whole.

Literary Skills Focus

Literary Analysis

6. **Analyze** One technique used to deny people rights is language that dehumanizes them. List several examples of dehumanizing language that Swift uses (ironically) about the Irish.
7. **Summarize** Before writing this pamphlet, Swift had recommended many of the "other expedients" he lists. In your own words, summarize some of the other proposals, and explain why the speaker ultimately dismisses them.
8. **Hypothesize** Swift doesn't reveal his plan until later in the essay. What is the effect of this delay?
9. **Literary Perspectives** While reading the proposal, you have considered the writing from both credibility and political perspectives. How do these contexts individually and collectively contribute to how you perceive Swift's argument?

Literary Skills: Verbal Irony

10. **Evaluate** Is Swift's use of irony effective, or does it risk being taken seriously by readers who might be outraged by his apparent cruelty?
11. **Analyze** Swift lists several advantages of his proposal. Who really profits from these "advantages"? Who actually suffers?

Literary Skills Review: Tone

12. **Analyze** A writer's attitude toward a subject or the reader is called tone. How would you describe Swift's tone in *A Modest Proposal?*

Writing Skills Focus

Think as a Reader/Writer

Use It in Your Writing Using your notes and experience reading *A Modest Proposal,* write a short satire with a created persona who attempts to solve one of today's problems. Share your satirical essay with classmates.

What Do You Think Now

How can injustices hide behind the appearance of civilization?

Universal Access

Struggling Writers

Some students may need additional scaffolding to complete the Writing Skills Focus activity. Have students work in small groups and brainstorm a list of political and social issues they might satirize in their essay. Ask them to consider possible "solutions." After students have finished brainstorming and each has chosen an issue to address, have them create a three-column chart in which they list examples of persuasive appeal (emotional, ethical, and logical) as a prewriting exercise to their essay.

What Do You Think Now?

Have students discuss the present international situation and the wealth that is enjoyed in some countries. Ask students to reflect on the political, social, and psychological reasons why wealthy nations often do not intervene to aid struggling countries.

Grades 9–10 Review Reading Standard 1.2 (see pages A48–A50)

Vocabulary Development

Vocabulary Check

Match each Vocabulary word with its synonym.

1. animosities	a. nourishment
2. censure	b. huge
3. digressed	c. careful
4. expedient	d. criticize
5. prodigious	e. wandered
6. scrupulous	f. hatreds
7. sustenance	g. means

Vocabulary Skills: Connotation and Intensity

In addition to a word's literal, dictionary meaning, or **denotation,** a word has **connotations,** the emotional ideas and feelings that people may connect to it. Words can have positive, negative, or neutral connotations. Look at the line scale below. The words have a similar literal meaning, but their connotations vary depending on the context in which they are used.

Positive	Neutral	Negative
youthful	young	immature

Words can also differ in terms of **intensity,** or degree of strength, as the line scale below depicts.

High Intensity		Low Intensity
adore	love	like

Your Turn

Read each example, and use the line scales as tools to answer the questions.

1. "And besides it is not improbable that some **scrupulous** people might be apt to **censure** such a practice (although indeed very unjustly) as a little bordering upon cruelty."

   What word with a negative connotation could you substitute for *scrupulous?* What word of higher intensity could you use for *censure?*

2. "I think it is agreed by all parties, that this **prodigious** number of children . . . is . . . a very great additional grievance."

   What word of lesser intensity could be substituted for *prodigious?*

3. "therefore reckoning a year after Lent, the markets will be more **glutted** than usual . . ."

   What is the connotation of the word *glutted?*

Language Coach

Stressed Syllables When pronouncing words of three, four, and five syllables, you must decide which syllable receives the stress. Words such as *scrupulous* and *sustenance* have a stress on the first syllable, while *expedient* and *prodigious* have a stress on the second syllable. *Animosities* has a main stress on the third syllable, with a softer stress on the first syllable. Practice saying these words aloud to get a feel for the placement of stress.

Academic Vocabulary

Talk About

With a partner, discuss how you would approach a good friend if you wanted to convince him or her that the status quo should be changed.

Universal Access: Vocabulary Development

English Learners

English for Academic Success To build confidence in students' pronunciation skills, use this exercise to give them additional practice. Display the words below on the board. Read each word aloud, and have students repeat each word that is pronounced. Then, ask them to identify which syllable is stressed in each word.

- melancholy [*first syllable*]
- deplorable [*second syllable*]
- temperance [*first syllable*]
- commodity [*second syllable*]
- parsimony [*first syllable*]
- endeavoring [*second syllable*]

✔ See the **Academic and Selection Vocabulary Skill Builder** in **UA: Differentiating Instruction.**

Independent Practice

Vocabulary Development

Vocabulary Check

1. *f* **2.** *d*
3. *e* **4.** *g*
5. *b* **6.** *c*
7. *a*

Your Turn

Possible responses:

1. *scrupulous: fastidious, fussy, picky; censure: condemn, denounce*
2. *large*
3. *The word "glutted" means "overstocked" or "exceeding demand."*

go.hrw.com **WordSharp: An Interactive Vocabulary Tutor,** more practice with academic language

English for Academic Success

Language Coach

Suggest that students say the words aloud or under their breath so that they can hear the stresses. It may help to exaggerate the stresses at first so that the stress is clear to the ear. Have students look up *animosity* in the dictionary to observe how primary and secondary stress is marked in the phonetic spelling.

English for Academic Success

Academic Vocabulary

Possible response: *If I wanted to convince a friend that the status quo should be changed, I would approach my friend with a proposal and outline who would benefit from my proposal and how.*

Independent Practice

Grammar Link

Your Turn

1. *A woman who cannot provide for her children is forced to resort to begging.*
2. *Many children learn to steal the things that they need to live.*
3. *C*
4. *Neither a landowner nor a tenant could object to a proposal that would only benefit him or her.*

Choices: Evaluation Criteria

Review: Homework
Understand Irony in Language

- Students present accurate paraphrases of Swift's work.
- Students clearly explain the workings of ironic reasoning.

Connect: Timed Writing 40–50 Minutes

Essay cites information from the text to support main ideas.

Extend: Homework
Create Another "Modest" Proposal

- The proposals contain vivid details and surprising ideas.
- Students point clearly to an issue.

Assess

Unit 3 Resources, Selection Standards Check, p. 33

go.hrw.com **ThinkCentral Online Assessment,** Selection Standards Check

Teacher One Stop™, editable Selection Standards Check

Reteach

For lessons reteaching **irony, tone, and author's style**, see **Reteaching Lessons,** pp. 1449O–1449P.

go.hrw.com **ThinkCentral Online Remediation**

Applying Your Skills

A Modest Proposal

Reading Standard 3.3 (see pages A48–A50)
Writing Standard 2.2a–c, 2.6a–c (see pages A51–A52)

Grammar Link

Pronoun and Antecedent Agreement

A **pronoun** usually takes the place of a noun or another pronoun. **Antecedents** are the words to which pronouns refer. Pronouns should agree with, or match, their antecedents in number and gender. Look at the sentences below.

1. Give Tasha her book.
2. The cats are meowing for their dinner.
3. Either Luis or Jake has left his jacket.

In the first example, the singular, feminine pronoun *her* agrees with the feminine antecedent *Tasha.* In the second example, the plural pronoun *their* agrees with the plural antecedent cats. The third example demonstrates how the singular pronoun *his* should be used when *or* or *nor* connects two singular subjects of the same gender, in this case, masculine.

Your Turn

The following sentences may contain pronouns that do not agree with their antecedents. If a pronoun is incorrect, replace it with the correct pronoun. If the pronoun is correct, write *C.*

1. A woman who cannot provide for their children is forced to resort to begging.
2. Many children learn to steal the things that he or she need to live.
3. Poor tenants will profit from this proposal since they will have money to pay their rents.
4. Neither a landowner nor a tenant could object to a proposal that would only benefit him.

Writing Application Choose a piece of your own writing, and check to make sure that all pronouns agree with their antecedents. Mark any errors you find, and rewrite for clarity and correctness.

CHOICES

As you respond to the Choices activities, use these **Academic Vocabulary** words as appropriate: approach, convince, dominate, enhance, participate.

REVIEW

Understand Irony in Language

Class Presentation With a partner, return to some of the most ironic passages of *A Modest Proposal.* Work together to analyze and paraphrase Swift's sentences. Then, present your findings to the class. Explain how his outlandish logic would be offensive if taken at face value.

CONNECT

Explain Irish Living Conditions

Timed Writing Using *A Modest Proposal* as the primary source, write an expository essay about the living conditions of the Irish poor in the early 1700s. Use evidence from the text to support your analysis.

EXTEND

Create Another "Modest" Proposal

TechFocus Create a "modest" proposal of your own. Choose a modern social or political problem, and propose an outrageous solution. Your proposal should take an idea to its most ridiculous extent in order to highlight the seriousness of the problem. Instead of writing a pamphlet as Swift did, create a podcast in which you try to convince your viewers to agree with your solution.

Universal Access: Grammar Link

English Learners

English for Academic Success Remind students that when the antecedent is a word such as *anyone, anybody, someone, neither, something, someone, everyone,* or *everybody,* the pronoun should be singular. Explain that if the antecedent can be either feminine or masculine, students should use expressions such as *he or she* or *his or her* to keep the text free of gender bias. You may want to point out that use of the expression *he or she* has arisen in fairly recent times. After the feminist movement of the 1970s, people made a great effort to avoid the use of masculine pronouns to refer to both males and females.

✔ For more practice with pronoun and antecedent agreement, see **Warriner's Handbook, Grammar-Notes,** and **Language Handbook Worksheets.**

COMPARING TEXTS : WORLD LITERATURE

Satirical Novels

Baron Munchausen (John Neville) next to Turkish soldiers in a scene from *The Adventures of Baron Munchausen* (1988).

In *Candide,* considered a great work of French literature, Voltaire criticizes his contemporaries, European culture, and humanity itself. In *Don Quixote,* a Spanish masterwork written over a century earlier, Cervantes makes fun of medieval romances, stories in which a chivalric knight rides forth on a grand quest in the name of a beautiful maiden. As you read the excerpts from these novels, note the targets of the authors' criticism and the techniques used by the authors. In what ways does the content of each novel reveal the author's culture and background?

CONTENTS

Standards Focus

Objectives

Students will
- analyze the characteristics of satire and parody
- draw inferences about character
- write a comparison-contrast essay

English for Academic Success

Academic Vocabulary

Look for opportunities to use the Academic Vocabulary words in this unit.
- **approach, *n.*:** way of addressing
- **convince, *v.*:** cause to believe
- **dominate, *v.*:** command
- **enhance, *v.*:** improve the quality of
- **participate, *v.*:** take part in

Analyzing Visuals

Tell students that this is a scene from the movie *The Adventures of Baron Munchausen,* which recounts a sort of tall tale of the fantastical adventures of Baron Munchausen.

Extension Activity What aspects of the nobility does this scene seem to satirize? ***Possible response:*** *The characters are dressed in extremely refined clothes. The characters are wearing precious jewelry, fine lacy cuffs, and ermine robes. The scene may poke fun at excessive luxury, here brought to its absurd extreme.*

Direct Teach

Neither Nice nor Neutral: The Purposes of Satire

Tell students that while the Romans are said to have invented satire, its roots go back to the Greek comedies of Aristophanes, which range from broad farce to elegant wit. The two outstanding satirists of the Roman period are Horace and Juvenal. Horace's satires are full of good humor and forgiveness; Juvenal's satires bitterly criticize a society preoccupied with luxury and depravity.

INTRODUCTION

THE STING OF SATIRE

by **Robert DeMaria, Jr.**

A **satire** is a piece of writing designed to make its readers feel critical—of themselves, of their fellow human beings, of their society. Some satires, like Alexander Pope's *The Rape of the Lock,* are intended to make us laugh at human foolishness and weakness; these satires are good-natured and laugh-provoking. Other satires, like Swift's *A Modest Proposal,* may make us laugh, but it is often a bitter kind of laughter, arising from anger and indignation at human vices and crimes.

Neither Nice nor Neutral: The Purposes of Satire

No matter how humorous a satire may be, its ultimate purpose is most often serious: Satirists are dissatisfied with the status quo, and want to change things. Instead of giving constructive advice, though, satirists focus solely on what is wrong with the world and its inhabitants. They use exaggeration to make folly, vice, and vanity appear ridiculous and therefore unattractive. We must not expect satirists to be objective or neutral, to present both sides of a question, or to show the good and bad traits of a character. Instead, we must understand that satire is fueled by extravagant exaggeration and wild generalization: Lawyers are greedy, politicians are corrupt, scholars are boring. Satirists make fun of vicious, selfish, mean-spirited people in the hope that we will see aspects of ourselves in such people and mend our ways. Thus, satirists perform an important function in society: They expose errors and absurdities that we no longer notice because custom and familiarity have blinded us to them.

The Uses of Satire

Satire is the most prevalent of all literary forms, appearing in fiction, nonfiction, poetry, and drama. It is also one of the oldest. In its crudest form, invective (another word for name-calling) satire is probably as old as civilization. The more formal satire found in the literature of the West was mostly influenced by ancient Greek and Roman writers.

The Royal Academy Exhibition by Thomas Rowlandson.

Universal Access

English Learners

Have students review the information in the essay by writing an outline that covers these topics, including the following: a definition of satire, the purposes of satire, some examples of satire, a definition of parody, the age of satire in Europe, and the fate of satire. As students read, have them fill in the outline with information about each topic.

Struggling Readers

To help students read the essay, model the skill of using a chart to understand the main idea. You might say: "I'll make a two-column chart to keep track of the important ideas in this essay. In the left column, I'll list social conditions that encourage satire. In the right column, I'll list social conditions that discourage satire. Whenever the author discusses how social conditions affect satire, I'll write the social condition in the appropriate column."

Throughout history, satire has traditionally thrived whenever repressive governments are in power and their obvious corruptions can be ridiculed. Times of prosperity and indulgence, when reckless spending and greed prevail—when upper classes "sup" while the lower classes starve—are likewise eras when satirists flourish.

Scathing Humor: The Weapon of the Satirist

One of the most useful techniques available to the satirist is parody, a mocking imitation of a writer's style or of a particular genre. Often, the style being parodied is applied to a trivial subject. Pope's *The Rape of the Lock,* for example, parodies the epic style to describe the theft of a lock of hair. Likewise, Miguel de Cervantes's *Don Quixote* parodies the chivalric romance, finding its satire in the incongruity that arises from the clash between the romantic and the real. Parody can only be used successfully by writers who are familiar with many works of literature and who understand and appreciate style.

Mick Jagger by Petar Pismestrovic.

The Great Age of Satire

Satire thrived across western Europe, beginning early in Italy and cropping up later in Spain, most famously in Cervantes's parody of medieval romances, *Don Quixote* (1605). Throughout his comic novel, Cervantes ridicules the often tangled and confusing passages that are hallmarks of chivalric romances. The narrator tells us that Don Quixote read so many romances that "his brain dried up." Many passages from such tales are so convoluted that "Aristotle himself would not have been able to understand them, even if he had been resurrected for that sole purpose." Wickedly, Cervantes quotes literally from a tale by a sixteenth-century writer whose language is so exaggerated that Cervantes does not need to embellish it further: "The reason of the unreason that afflicts my reason, in such a manner weakens my reason that I with reason lament me of your comeliness."

The great age of Western satire began in the latter half of the seventeenth century and lasted until the middle of the eighteenth century—a time of great social stability, especially in England and France.

The Fate of Satire: Make Way for Romanticism

At the end of the eighteenth century, the American Revolution, the French Revolution, and several other events shattered the peaceful climate that had thus far prevailed. Most European governments became less restrictive, and the sort of oppositional temper that marks satire and parody became harder for writers to invoke. Amid the efforts to build new nations, satire and parody gave way to attempts to recapture the grandeur of the old epics and romances. Human nature was celebrated as naturally good and noble rather than criticized as inherently corrupt and mean.

While some later writers, such as Lord Byron and Charles Dickens, did write masterful satirical works, people, for the most part, sought to glorify the achievements of their cultures. The Romantic lyric, the extended elegy, and the epic narrative became the most popular literary forms in the West in the early part of the nineteenth century. Too much critical honesty finally seemed to be more than society could bear. As one character in Molière's play *The Misanthrope* says:

> "In certain cases, it would be uncouth
> And most absurd to speak the naked truth;
> With all respect for your exalted notions,
> It's often best to veil one's true emotions.
> Wouldn't the social fabric come undone
> If we were wholly frank with everyone?"

Scathing Humor: The Weapon of the Satirist

Explain that the prototype of medieval chivalric romances is the Arthurian legend. Review with students some of the major conventions of medieval romances: courtly love, the virtuous hero, the journey, and supernatural beings. Then, point out that it is not the Arthur legend that Cervantes is parodying, but the host of imitators the Arthurian legend spawned.

The Fate of Satire: Make Way for Romanticism

Born Jean Baptiste Poquelin in 1622, Molière became an actor, director, administrator, and playwright. In addition to other works, he produced twelve satirical full-length comedies that are considered among the most incisive satires of all time. His gallery of satiric characters includes Tartuffe the religious hypocrite, Jourdain the social climber, Harpagon the miser, and Argan the hypochondriac.

Advanced Learners

Enrichment Voltaire wrote *Candide* almost fifty years after Pope wrote *The Rape of the Lock*. Have students research English society in the early years of the eighteenth century and French society in the mid-eighteenth century. Direct them to focus on the economic and political stability of these two societies and their general worldviews. What are some similarities and differences between the two societies?

Students with Disabilities

To help students understand the definition of a parody, have them look at an example of a parody on video. Have students view, for instance, a parody of the story of Robin Hood in the film *Robin Hood: Men in Tights* (1993). As they view the video clip, ask students to look for typical elements in the original story that are mocked or ridiculed.

Selection Introduction

Think About the Writer

Explain that Voltaire criticized many who treated others unjustly. He often satirized people in power, whether leaders of the noble class, the military, or religious institutions. Have students write for five minutes. Ask students to identify examples of injustice in today's world that Voltaire might criticize. Use students' examples to prompt discussion.

For Independent Reading

- *Animal Farm,* George Orwell
- *My World and Welcome to It,* James Thurber

Motivate

What Do You Think/QuickTalk

Have students identify social injustices that exist today. Tell them to first consider events that are taking place in other parts of the world. Then, have them look closer to home and identify social problems in their own community. Have students suggest new ways that communities might work together to solve problems. Have students record their suggestions in their **Reader/Writer Notebooks.**

California Standards, pp. 594–601

- **Reading Standard 3.1** Analyze characteristics of subgenres (e.g., satire, parody, allegory, pastoral) that are used in poetry, prose, plays, novels, short stories, essays, and other basic genres.
- **Reading Standard 3.3** Analyze the ways in which irony, tone, mood, the author's style, and the "sound" of language achieve specific rhetorical or aesthetic purposes or both.

Preparing to Read

from Candide

What Do You Think How can order and civilization affect human behavior?

QuickTalk
What social injustices exist today? With a small group, discuss how people in your community or in the country are working to solve these problems.

Voltaire (after 1718) by Nicholas de Largilliere. Oil on canvas. Musée de la Ville de Paris, Musée Carnavalet, Paris, France.

MEET THE WRITER

Voltaire
(1694–1778)

François-Marie Arouet, better known by his pen name, Voltaire, was a soldier who fought with words. As a satirist, philosopher, historian, dramatist, and poet, Voltaire wrote works that criticized the wastefulness of war, the intolerance of organized religion, and society's indifferent approach toward the plight of the poor.

A Dangerous Mind

Born in Paris to middle-class parents, Voltaire studied law for a time but soon gave it up to become a writer. His reputation was quickly established based on his classical tragedies and political satires. Voltaire's sharp words were not always well received, however, and a violent encounter with an offended nobleman left Voltaire battered, bruised, and imprisoned. He was exiled to England in 1726.

In London, Voltaire met Jonathan Swift and Alexander Pope and was deeply influenced by the works of Bacon, Newton, and Locke. When Voltaire returned to Paris, he wrote philosophical essays about how people live and work according to their moral principles. Once again, the nobility was not amused. Voltaire's most formidable work, "Essay on the Morals and the Spirit of the Nations from Charlemagne to Louis XIII," was banned, and the controversial author was forced to flee Paris.

The Practical Life

Of Voltaire's numerous romances and tales, *Candide* is his most famous and enduring. Voltaire had little patience for theory and idle speculation. His emphasis on modest but practical action is reflected in the last page of *Candide*: "Let us work without arguing . . . it's the only way to make life endurable."

Although Voltaire lived much of his later life near the French-Swiss border, he died in Paris at the age of eighty-three on a visit to see his last play produced. He was refused a Christian burial, but his remains were interred in Paris with great ceremony thirteen years later.

Think About the Writer What injustices of today's world would Voltaire criticize? Explain.

Wewelsburg Castle, Germany.

Selection Readability	
Easily Accessible **Accessible** Challenging	humorous; accessible vocabulary and theme; familiar genre

Reading Standard 3.1, 3.3 (see pages A48–A50)

Literary Skills Focus

Satire The type of writing known as **satire** ridicules the shortcomings of human beings or institutions in order to bring about change. Satires often try to convince the reader to do or believe something by showing the opposing view as absurd, vicious, or inhumane. Writers use exaggeration, irony, understatement, ridiculous situations, and many other tools to create satire. As you read, learn about Voltaire's beliefs by noting the objects of Voltaire's satire and whether his commentary is gentle or vicious.

Reading Skills Focus

Analyzing an Author's Style An author's **style** is the distinctive way he or she uses language. A style can be casual or formal, plain or elaborate, concrete or abstract, and so on. Elements of style include word choice, syntax, and use of imagery and figurative language. As you read, notice how Voltaire's style enhances his satire.

Into Action As you read, use a chart like the one below to find examples of Voltaire's style. Then, write a brief assessment of each example.

Element of Style	Example	Assessment
Word Choice	Describes Pangloss as an "oracle" and Candide as "little."	Fancy word emphasizes Pangloss's scholarly nature; simple word emphasizes Candide's innocence.
Syntax		
Figurative Language		
Imagery		

Writing Skills Focus

Think as a Reader/Writer

Find It in Your Reading To create effective satire, writers use a variety of tools, including outrageous exaggerations and bizarre statements that are delivered as if they make sense. While reading *Candide,* use your *Reader/Writer Notebook* to track how Voltaire uses these two particular tools of satire within the dialogues between characters.

Reader/Writer Notebook

Use your **RWN** to complete the activities for this selection.

Vocabulary

endowed (ehn DOWD) *v.* used as *adj.:* provided with. *Candide, endowed with a simple, trusting nature, ventures into the world.*

rendered (REHN duhrd) *v.:* made; caused to be. *The baroness's extreme weight rendered her more respectable to the people of Westphalia.*

candor (KAN duhr) *n.:* honesty; directness. *Innocent Candide reacts to life's unfortunate situations with great candor.*

pensive (PEHN sihv) *adj.* reflective; thoughtful. *Dr. Pangloss's philosophy inspired Cunegonde and made her feel deeply pensive.*

vivacity (vy VAS uh tee) *n.:* liveliness; energetic spirit. *Candide expresses his love for Cunegonde with enthusiasm and vivacity.*

Language Coach

The Sounds of *C* Use the pronunciation guides to read the Vocabulary words. In which word does the letter *c* have the sound of /k/? In which word does the same letter have the sound of /s/? Notice what vowel follows the letter *c* in each word. Can you make a general pronunciation rule based on what you notice?

Learn It Online

Get to know the Vocabulary words inside and out through Word Watch.

go.hrw.com H12-595 Go

Comparing Texts Resources

Unit 3 Resources, on-level practice and assessment, p. 36

Teacher One Stop™, on-level lesson plans and all print resources

Holt Audio Library

Holt Audio Library: Selections and Summaries in Spanish

UA: Differentiating Instruction, graphic organizer, p. 128

UA: Supporting Instruction in Spanish, selection summary

ThinkCentral Online Assessment, Selection Standards Check

ThinkCentral Online Remediation

Preteach

Introducing Vocabulary

Ask students to use the appropriate Vocabulary word to complete the following sentences.

1. The ______ of the exuberant dancers was evident to everyone in the audience. [*vivacity*]
2. After losing the game, Johan was in a ______ mood. [*pensive*]
3. Felicity was well known among her friends for her ______ and willingness to be frank. [*candor*]
4. When the flood waters peaked, the building had six feet of water in it and was ______ useless. [*rendered*]
5. The college was ______ with a large amount of land. [*endowed*]

English for Academic Success

Language Coach

Possible response: *C is pronounced /k/ in* candor *and pronounced /s/ in* vivacity. *If an* i *or an* e *follows the* c, *it is pronounced /s/, and if any other letter follows the* c, *it is pronounced /k/.*

Literary Skills Focus

As you read and discuss the selection with students, have them take notes about the subjects of Voltaire's satire.

Reading Skills Focus

Give students a copy of the Reading Skills Focus graphic organizer before they read. (See **Unit 3 Resources.**) Tell them to use their responses to answer the questions on the Applying Your Skills page.

Writing Skills Focus

Have students record instances of exaggeration and bizarre statements in their **Reader/Writer Notebooks.** Students can use their notes to complete the Writing Skills Focus activity.

Learn It Online

Send students to **Word Watch** for audio pronunciations, synonyms, antonyms, and brief histories of word origins.

go.hrw.com H12-595 Go

Teacher Preparation

Selection Plot Summary

In this excerpt from the first two chapters of *Candide,* the reader meets the main character, Candide, who is growing up on the estate of Baron Thunder-ten-tronckh. When Candide is caught expressing amorous interest in the baroness's daughter, Cunegonde, he is expelled from the estate. At first he wanders aimlessly, but he is soon captured by the Bulgarians, impressed into military service, and severely punished after his attempt at desertion.

Direct Teach

Think About/Talk About

Read with a Purpose Have students read the Read with a Purpose statement. Tell them that as they read, they should pay close attention to Candide's words and note ways in which Candide is honest no matter what the circumstances.

NOVEL

from CANDIDE

by **Voltaire** translated by **Richard Aldington**

Read with a Purpose

Candide's name comes from the word *candor,* meaning "honesty" or "directness." Read to discover how Candide lives up to his name.

Build Background

In this excerpt, Voltaire satirizes the nobility, the military, and the ideas of German philosopher Gottfried Leibniz. Leibniz claimed that a rational God had created a rational world in which everything has a place and a purpose. Voltaire's Dr. Pangloss directly echoes Leibniz every time he proclaims, "In the best of all possible worlds, . . . all is for the best."

Wewelsburg Castle, Germany

Daniel Evans (Candide) and Alex Kelley (Cunegonde) in *Candide.*

Universal Access

English Learners

To help students understand *Candide*, point out and explain the footnotes that accompany the text. To check their comprehension of the story, read the first paragraph aloud and ask the following questions: Who owns the castle? [*Baron Thunder-ten-tronckh*] Why was the youth named Candide? [*He was very honest and simple-minded.*] Why would Candide's mother never marry his father? [*He did not have good enough breeding for her.*]

Struggling Readers

To help students read *Candide*, model the reading skill of analyzing an author's style. You might say: "When I read a novel, I notice how the author creates a style with word choice, sentence structure, images, and figurative language. I notice whether the style is relaxed and casual or formal. I look to see if the author uses words that are hard to understand and note any elements that make the style unique." As students read, have them ask themselves: "How does Voltaire use language to satirize the society in which he lives?"

CHAPTER I

How Candide was brought up in a noble castle and how he was expelled from the same

In the castle of Baron Thunder-ten-tronckh in Westphalia[1] there lived a youth, endowed by Nature with the most gentle character. His face was the expression of his soul. His judgment was quite honest and he was extremely simple-minded; and this was the reason, I think, that he was named Candide. Old servants in the house suspected that he was the son of the Baron's sister and a decent honest gentleman of the neighborhood, whom this young lady would never marry because he could only prove seventy-one quarterings,[2] and the rest of his genealogical tree was lost, owing to the injuries of time. The Baron was one of the most powerful lords in Westphalia, for his castle possessed a door and windows. His Great Hall was even decorated with a piece of tapestry. The dogs in his stableyards formed a pack of hounds when necessary; his grooms were his huntsmen; the village curate was his Grand Almoner.[3] They all called him "My Lord," and laughed heartily at his stories. The Baroness weighed about three hundred and fifty pounds, was therefore greatly respected, and did the honors of the house with a dignity which rendered her still more respectable. Her daughter Cunegonde, aged seventeen, was rosy-cheeked, fresh, plump, and tempting. The Baron's son appeared in every respect worthy of his father. The tutor Pangloss[4] was the oracle of the house, and little Candide followed his lessons with all the candor of his age and character. Pangloss taught metaphysico-theologo-cosmolonigology.[5] He proved admirably that there is no effect without a cause and that in this best of all possible worlds, My Lord the Baron's castle was the best of castles and his wife the best of all possible Baronesses. "'Tis demonstrated," said he, "that things cannot be otherwise; for, since everything is made for an end, everything is necessarily for the best end. Observe that noses were made to wear spectacles; and so we have spectacles. Legs were visibly instituted to be breeched, and we have breeches. Stones were formed to be quarried and to build castles; and My Lord has a very noble castle; the greatest Baron in the province should have the best house; and as pigs were made to be eaten, we eat pork all the year round; consequently, those who have asserted that all is well talk nonsense; they ought to have said that all is for the best." Candide listened attentively and believed innocently; for he thought Mademoiselle Cunegonde extremely beautiful, although he was never bold enough to tell her so. He decided that after the happiness of being born Baron of Thunder-ten-tronckh, the second degree of happiness was to be Mademoiselle Cunegonde; the third, to see her every day; and the fourth to listen to Doctor Pangloss, the greatest philosopher of the province and therefore of the whole world. One day when Cunegonde was walking near the castle, in a little

1. **Westphalia:** region in western Germany noted for its excellent ham. In a letter to his niece, Voltaire described Westphalia as "vast, sad, sterile, detestable."
2. **quarterings:** divisions on a coat of arms or family tree. Seventy-one is an absurdly high number, tracing a person's genealogy over two thousand years.
3. **Grand Almoner:** member of a noble household responsible for allotting charity to the poor.
4. **Pangloss:** Greek for "all tongue."
5. **metaphysico-theologo-cosmolonigology:** This nonsense term is a satirical poke at the philosopher Leibniz and his followers, especially the embedded syllable *–nig–*, which is a shortened form of *nigaud*, the French word for "simpleton."

A Literary Focus Satire What technique of satire does Voltaire use to describe Candide's genealogy?

B Reading Focus Analyzing an Author's Style What words does Voltaire use to describe Cunegonde? How does this word choice affect your image of her?

Vocabulary **endowed** (ehn DOWD) *v.* used as *adj.:* provided with.
rendered (REHN duhrd) *v.:* made; caused to be.
candor (KAN duhr) *n.:* honesty; directness.

Think About/Talk About

Comprehension

B Reading Focus

Possible responses: *Voltaire describes Cunegonde as "seventeen, rosy-cheeked, fresh, plump, and tempting." Voltaire portrays her as an innocent, but attractive young woman, who could easily tempt a young man.*

Analysis

A Literary Focus

Possible response: *Voltaire is exaggerating about the need for nobles to marry carefully into "good" families.*

Extend the Discussion

Satire In the middle of the third paragraph, Pangloss states his philosophy. What are elements that contribute to Voltaire's satire of philosophers and the humor of the text? ***Possible response***: *Voltaire includes absurd conclusions such as "noses were made for spectacles, and so we have spectacles . . . as pigs were made to be eaten, we eat pork all the year round."*

Vocabulary: Own the Word

- **endowed:** Tell students the root word for *endowed* is *dōtāre,* Latin for "to provide with a dowry." A person might be *endowed* with a source of income, a talent, or quality. Ask students with what quality or talent they have been naturally *endowed.*
- **rendered:** Ask students to give an example of a situation *rendering* them helpless. ***Possible responses:*** *being locked in a room, getting lost on the highway with no map or cell phone, being cornered by a fierce dog*
- **candor:** Tell students that *candid* is an adjective form of *candor.* A *candid* person is honest and sincere. Have students construct a sentence using the word *candid.*

Advanced Learners

Enrichment Have students research the philosophical beliefs of Gottfried Leibniz in small groups. Tell them to address the following questions and present their findings to the class.

- What specific aspects of this branch of philosophy does Voltaire satirize?
- Based on their findings, what conjectures can students make about Pangloss's role in the selection as a whole?
- What does Voltaire seem to believe about the philosophical beliefs of Leibniz?

Students with Disabilities

Students may benefit from drawing descriptions of characters in the passage. Direct students to look for details as they read about the Baroness, her daughter, and Candide. Then, have students compare their drawings, discussing the similarities and differences. Display the drawings around the classroom to help stimulate interest and facilitate comprehension.

Model the Skill

- Provide students with copies of the Reading Skills Focus graphic organizer for "Candide." (See **Unit 3 Resources**.)
- To help students analyze Voltaire's writing, model the reading skill of **analyzing the author's style**.
- You might tell students: "As I read, I am going to use the chart to record elements of Voltaire's style. I have been noticing that the author often uses exaggeration, so I am going to write 'exaggeration' in the left column of the chart under 'Element of Style.' When I read the description of Candide's capture and punishment, I notice examples of exaggeration: the amount of strokes he receives, the choice offered to him by the judges, his punishment, and his recovery. Now I will write these items in the chart in the second column under 'Example.' Then, I will use the information I have written to assess Voltaire's style: exaggeration can make the satire more humorous and effective."

Element of Style	Example	Assessment
Exaggeration	strokes, choice offered by the judges, punishment, recovery	Exaggeration can make the satire more humorous and effective.

Guided Practice: Apply

QuickWrite Use the QuickWrite to help students connect with the reading material. As students complete their charts, remind them to look for elements of Voltaire's writing that make this work different from other works they have read; these differences indicate elements of style of satirical writing. Have students write for five minutes about the unique nature of Voltaire's writing.

wood which was called The Park, she observed Doctor Pangloss in the bushes, giving a lesson in experimental physics to her mother's waiting-maid, a very pretty and docile brunette. Mademoiselle Cunegonde had a great inclination for science and watched breathlessly the reiterated experiments she witnessed; she observed clearly the Doctor's sufficient reason, the effects and the causes, and returned home very much excited, pensive, filled with the desire of learning, reflecting that she might be the sufficient reason of young Candide and that he might be hers. On her **C** way back to the castle she met Candide and blushed; Candide also blushed. She bade him good morning in a hesitating voice; Candide replied without knowing what he was saying. Next day, when they left the table after dinner, Cunegonde and Candide found themselves behind a screen; Cunegonde dropped her handkerchief, Candide picked it up; she innocently held his hand; the young man innocently kissed the young lady's hand with remarkable vivacity, tenderness, and grace; their lips met, their eyes sparkled, their knees trembled, their hands wandered. Baron Thunder-ten-tronckh passed near the screen, and, observing this cause and effect, expelled Candide from the castle by kicking him in the backside frequently and hard. Cunegonde swooned; when she recovered her senses, the Baroness slapped her in the face; and all was in consternation[6] in the noblest and most agreeable of all possible castles. **D**

6. **consternation:** bewilderment; dismay.

C Reading Focus **Analyzing an Author's Style** What techniques does Voltaire use to disguise Pangloss's improper activities in the bushes?

D Literary Focus **Satire** How does Voltaire use irony to ridicule the Baron's family?

Vocabulary
pensive (PEHN sihv) *adj.* reflective; thoughtful.
vivacity (vy VAS uh tee) *n.:* liveliness; energetic spirit.

Chapter II

What happened to Candide among the Bulgarians

Candide, expelled from the earthly paradise, wandered for a long time without knowing where he was going, turning up his eyes to Heaven, gazing back frequently at the noblest of castles which held the most beautiful of young Baronesses; he lay down to sleep supperless between two furrows in the open fields: It snowed heavily in large flakes. The next morning the shivering Candide, penniless, dying of cold and exhaustion, dragged himself toward the neighboring town, which was called Waldberghoff-trarbk-dikdorff. He halted sadly at the door of an inn. Two men dressed in blue noticed him. "Comrade," said one, "there's a well-built young man of the right height."[7] They went up to Candide and very civilly invited him to dinner. "Gentlemen," said Candide with charming modesty, "you do me a great honor, but I have no money to pay my share." "Ah, sir," said one of the men in blue, "persons of your figure and merit never pay anything; are you not five feet five tall?" "Yes, gentlemen," said he,

7. **height:** Voltaire is making fun of the recruiting practices of the "King of the Bulgarians"—Voltaire's satiric name for King Frederick the Great of Prussia—who chose and organized soldiers according to their height.

Daniel Evans as Candide; Alex Kelley as Cunegonde.

Word-Attack Skills Mini-Lesson

English for Academic Success Explain that in reading *Candide*, students must identify combining forms and affixes to read the long, invented word *meta-physico-theologo-cosmolonigology*. Model using this strategy with the less-challenging word *interminable*. Write the word *interminable* on the board, and explore how the word can be divided into parts. Identifying its parts as the prefix *inter–*, the base word *mine*, and the suffix *–able* results in an incorrect understanding of the word's meaning and an incorrect pronunciation: (ihn tur MUHN uh buhl). The word must instead be recognized as the prefix *in–* added to the adjective *terminable*, which is related to the verb *terminate*: (ihn TUR muh nuh buhl).

Activity Have students identify the components of these words—prefix, suffix, and base word.
intramural [*intra– + mural*]
extradition [*extra– + diction*]
reallocation [*re– + allocate + –ion*]
contrapuntal [*contra– + punt + –al*]
retrospective [*retro– + spect + –ive*]
protolithic [*proto- + lith + -ic*]

bowing, "that is my height." "Ah, sir, come to table; we will not only pay your expenses, we will never allow a man like you to be short of money; men were only made to help each other." "You are in the right," said Candide, "that is what Doctor Pangloss was always telling me, and I see that everything is for the best." They begged him to accept a few crowns,[8] he took them and wished to give them an IOU, they refused to take it, and all sat down to table. "Do you not love tenderly ..." "Oh, yes," said he. "I love Mademoiselle Cunegonde tenderly." "No," said one of the gentlemen. "We were asking if you do not tenderly love the King of the Bulgarians." "Not a bit," said he, "for I have never seen him." "What! He is the most charming of kings, and you must drink his health." "Oh, gladly, gentlemen." And he drank. "That is sufficient," he was told. "You are now the support, the aid, the defender, the hero of the Bulgarians, your fortune is made, and your glory assured." They immediately put irons on his legs and took him to a regiment. He was made to turn to the right and left, to raise the ramrod and return the ramrod, to take aim, to fire, to march double time, and he was given thirty strokes with a stick; the next day he drilled not quite so badly, and received only twenty strokes; the day after, he only had ten and was looked on as a prodigy[9] by his comrades. **E** Candide was completely mystified and could not make out how he was a hero. One fine spring day he thought he would take a walk, going straight ahead, in the belief that to use his legs as he pleased was a privilege of the human species as well as of animals. He had not gone two leagues[10] when four other heroes, each six feet tall, fell upon him, bound him, and dragged him back to a cell. He was asked by his judges whether he would rather be thrashed thirty-six times by the whole regiment or receive a dozen lead bullets at once in his brain. Although he protested that men's wills are free and that he wanted neither one nor the other, he had to make a choice; by virtue of that gift of God which is called liberty, he determined to run the gauntlet[11] thirty-six times and actually did so twice. There were two thousand men in the regiment. That made four thousand strokes which laid bare the muscles and nerves from his neck to his backside. As they were about to proceed to a third turn, Candide, utterly exhausted, begged as a favor that they would be so kind as to smash his head; he obtained this favor; they bound his eyes and he was made to kneel down. At that moment the King of the Bulgarians came by and inquired the victim's crime, and as this King was possessed of a vast genius, he perceived from what he learned about Candide that he was a young metaphysician[12] very ignorant in worldly matters, and therefore pardoned him with a clemency[13] which will be praised in all newspapers and all ages. An honest surgeon healed Candide in three weeks with the ointments recommended by Dioscorides.[14] He had already regained a little skin and could walk when the King of the Bulgarians went to war with the King of the Abares.[15] **F**

8. **crowns:** units of money.
9. **prodigy:** someone gifted from childhood with an exceptional quality or talent.
10. **leagues:** units of distance equal to about three miles.
11. **run the gauntlet:** run between two rows of soldiers who strike the victim with clubs or other weapons.
12. **metaphysician:** philosopher who studies the nature of reality and the origin and structure of the universe.
13. **clemency:** tendency to be merciful when deciding a punishment.
14. **Dioscorides:** Greek army physician who wrote a treatise on medicine in the first century. Even in Voltaire's day, Dioscorides' work was out-of-date.
15. **Abares:** that is, the French, who fought against the "Bulgarians," or Prussians, in the Seven Years' War (1756–1763).

E Literary Focus **Satire** What element of satire does Voltaire use to make fun of the military?

F Reading Focus **Analyzing an Author's Style** How does Voltaire use understatement to satirize Candide's "walk" and subsequent arrest?

Think About/Talk About

Comprehension

C Reading Focus

Possible response: *He describes their activities as a kind of science experiment and uses scientific and philosophic terms instead of actually describing what is taking place.*

F Reading Focus

Possible response: *Voltaire describes Candide's capture, sentencing, and very horrible punishment in matter-of-fact terms, as if he were describing a mundane series of events.*

Analysis

D Literary Focus

Possible response: *The final sentence of the chapter is ironic because Voltaire says that the castle is the "noblest and most agreeable" and yet "all is in consternation."*

E Literary Focus

Possible response: *Voltaire exaggerates the intensity of the training and also makes Candide become a respected soldier so quickly that it seems like a joke.*

Extend the Discussion

Satire How does the Biblical allusion at the end of Chapter I and at the beginning of Chapter II contribute to the satire? ***Possible response:*** *The allusion to the expulsion from the Garden of Eden makes Candide's offense seem silly and unimportant, and it makes his punishment seem grossly unfair.*

Vocabulary: Own the Word

- **pensive:** Ask students to demonstrate the facial expression of a person who is *pensive.*
- **vivacity:** Write *vivacity: "lively spirit"* in the center of a circle on the board. Have students contribute attributes to the semantic web. ***Possible responses:*** *animation, vigor, fervor, high spirits, enthusiasm, ardor*

California Standards, pp. 600–601

- **Reading Standards 3.1** Analyze characteristics of subgenres (e.g., satire, parody, allegory, pastoral) that are used in poetry, prose, plays, novels, short stories, essays, and other basic genres.
- **Reading Standards 3.3** Analyze the ways in which irony, tone, mood, the author's style, and the "sound" of language achieve specific rhetorical or aesthetic purposes or both.
- **Reading Standards 3.6** Analyze the way in which authors through the centuries have used archetypes drawn from myth and tradition in literature, film, political speeches, and religious writings (e.g., how the archetypes of banishment from an ideal world may be used to interpret Shakespeare's tragedy *Macbeth*).
- **Grades 9–10 Review Reading Standard 1.1** Identify and use the literal and figurative meanings of words and understand word derivations.
- **Writing Standards 1.5** Use language in natural, fresh, and vivid ways to establish a specific tone.

Check for Understanding

Independent Practice

Reading Skills Focus

Possible responses:

1. *He acquired his name because of his honesty and simple-minded nature.*
2. *There is no effect without a cause, and this is the best of all possible worlds.*
3. *He is punished for walking away.*
4. *He seems to believe that the world is all for the best no matter what happens.*
5. *Ask students to consider which human vice or weakness the author mocks in each example.*

Literary Skills Focus

Possible responses:

6. *Some politicians say it is all for the best when they cannot solve a problem; some clergy say it is all for the best when they cannot explain why bad things happen; some teachers say it is all for the best when students fail because students will try harder next time.*
7. *Voltaire wants to test Candide's optimistic outlook on life.*
8. *Institutions such as the military prevent people from exercising free will.*
9. *Voltaire most likely wanted to change the structure of society in which power and money were in the hands of a few privileged individuals. He wanted people to have more freedom.*
10. *Candide is thrown into an unfamiliar world in which he faces dangers without really knowing how to cope. At this point Candide has yet to achieve enlightenment, though it could be said that in his positive outlook he carries a certain degree of enlightenment wherever he goes.*

Applying Your Skills

Reading Standard 3.1, 3.3, 3.6 (see pages A48–A50)
Writing Standard 1.5 (see pages A48–A50)

from Candide

Literary Response and Analysis

Reading Skills Focus

Quick Check

1. How did Candide acquire his name?
2. Explain Doctor Pangloss's philosophy.
3. Why is Candide punished by the Bulgarian army?

Read with a Purpose

4. How does Candide react to his difficulties?

Reading Skills: Analyzing Author's Style

5. As you read, you assessed examples of Voltaire's style. Now add a column to your chart in which you explain how each element of his style enhances the satire of the novel.

Element of Style	Example	Assessment	How It Enhances Satire
Word Choice	Describes Pangloss as an "oracle" and Candide as "little."	Fancy word emphasizes Pangloss's scholarly nature; simple word emphasizes Candide's innocence.	Describing Pangloss as an oracle creates humor since his philosophy turns out to be foolish.
Syntax			
Figurative Language			
Imagery			

Literary Skills Focus

Literary Analysis

6. **Analyze** Do people like Doctor Pangloss exist in today's world of education, politics, or religion?
7. **Evaluate** Based on what you've read of *Candide,* why do you think Voltaire sends Candide through such a damaging series of trials and tribulations?
8. **Interpret** As Chapter II illustrates, Candide suffers every time he exercises what he believes to be his free will. According to Voltaire, what forces get in the way of a person's exercise of free will?

Literary Skills: Satire

9. **Infer** Part of the purpose of satire is to bring about a change in an institution or way of life. What changes do you think Voltaire wanted to influence in French society by writing *Candide*?

Literary Skills Review: Archetype

10. **Compare** An **archetype** is a pattern that has appeared in literature across cultures and times. A common archetype is the journey: A hero is thrust into a strange world to face dangers and wonders. How does this excerpt from *Candide* express the archetype of the journey?

Writing Skills Focus

Think as a Reader/Writer

Use It in Your Writing Review your notes on how Voltaire creates satire. In your *Reader/Writer Notebook,* write a brief dialogue between two characters that uses exaggeration and bizarre statements to create an ironic tone.

What Do You Think Now? How does social order affect the characters in *Candide*?

Universal Access

Struggling Writers

Some students may need additional scaffolding to complete the Writing Skills Focus activity. Before students write, have them choose a social issue such as health insurance, poverty, immigration, or the education system. Ask them to express in a sentence or two what aspect of the problem they plan to mock or exaggerate in their dialogue before writing their dialogues.

What Do You Think Now?

Ask students how the social order in which Candide lived led to his expulsion from the castle and how the military institution changed his life.

Grades 9–10 Review Reading Standard 1.1 (see pages A48–A50)

Vocabulary Development

Vocabulary Check

Match the Vocabulary words with their definitions.

1. endowed a. liveliness
2. rendered b. thoughtful
3. candor c. innocence in manner
4. pensive d. made
5. vivacity e. provided with

Vocabulary Skills: Etymology

In some ways, words are like people—they have ancestors and descendants, sisters and brothers, even distant relatives. Knowing a word's **etymology,** or origin and history, will not only help you understand the word itself, but can help you learn definitions of related words without having to find them in a dictionary.

Review the following chart to see how some English words passed into the language from Latin. Also note related words in the third column.

Word	Etymology	Related Words
quarter	Latin *quartus,* "four"	quartering, quarterly, quartet
provide	Latin *pro–,* "before" + *videre,* "to see"	provider, provident, providence
office	Latin *officium,* "duty, service"	official, officer, officiate
prodigy	Latin *prodigium,* "an omen"	prodigious, prodigiously

Your Turn

Make a chart like the one on the left. Then, use a dictionary to list the etymology and related words for each Vocabulary word.

Language Coach

The Sounds of *C* The letter *c* can have the sound of /k/ or /s/. When a *c* is followed by *a, o,* or *u,* it usually has the /k/ sound. When it is followed by *i* or *e,* it usually has the /s/ sound.Use a chart like the one below to classify each of the following words: *cosmos, reticent, civility, incognito, campaign, recipient, incumbent, despicable, sincerely, recurring.*

/k/ sound	/s/ sound

Academic Vocabulary

Write About

What techniques did Voltaire use to convince readers that society needed to change? How could the same approach be used today?

Independent Practice

Vocabulary Development

Vocabulary Check

1. *e* **2.** *d* **3.** *c* **4.** *b* **5.** *a*

Your Turn

Sample response:

endowed: *Latin* en– *"to cause to be" and* dotare *"to bestow or give"*; dowry, dower, dowager

English for Academic Success

Language Coach

[/k/ sound: cosmos, incognito, campaign, incumbent, despicable, recurring; /s/ sound: reticent, civility, recipient, sincerely]

English for Academic Success

Academic Vocabulary

Possible response: *Voltaire used satire to expose and mock society's shortcomings. The same approach could convince readers today that society needs to change through political cartoons, movies, and Web sites.*

Assess

Unit 3 Resources, Selection Standards Check, p. 39

ThinkCentral Online Assessment, Selection Standards Check

Teacher One-Stop™, editable Selection Standards Check

Reteach

ThinkCentral Online Remediation

Universal Access: Vocabulary Development

English Learners

English for Academic Success To help students appreciate how the study of etymology can clarify the meaning of words, have them practice with researching etymons of names such as school subjects. Help students research the etymology of the words below.

- biology, physics
- astronomy, astrology
- geometry, calculus, algebra, statistics
- geography, history, anthropology
- literature, bibliography
- orchestra, athletics

Have students create a chart like the one on p. 601 to list etymologies and related words.

✔ See the **Academic and Selection Vocabulary Skill Builder** in **UA: Differentiating Instruction.**

Selection Introduction

Think About the Writer

Have students write for five minutes. Ask them to identify genres of literature that Cervantes might parody if he were alive today. Possible genres could include romance, fantasy, science fiction, and spy stories.

For Independent Reading

- *The Three Musketeers,* Alexandre Dumas
- *A Connecticut Yankee in King Arthur's Court,* Mark Twain

Motivate

What Do You Think?/QuickWrite

Before students respond to the QuickWrite question, ask them to discuss the pace at which styles, ideas, customs, and technology change in today's world. Have students identify examples to support their ideas. Point out that the pace of change was much slower in previous centuries. Have students respond to the question in their **Reader/Writer Notebooks.** Students should explain why out-of-date items can seem funny.

Preparing to Read

from Don Quixote

What Do You Think? How can order and civilization affect human behavior?

QuickWrite

Think of a book, movie, or TV show that made you laugh because it represented ideas, fashions, or styles that were out of date. Why do we consider these things funny? Write your response in your *Reader/Writer Notebook.*

Miguel de Cervantes (17th century) by Juan de Jaurequi y Aguilar.

MEET THE WRITER

Miguel de Cervantes

(1547–1616)

Unlike his famous protagonist, Miguel de Cervantes fought in many battles and survived many real adventures. He is best remembered, however, for his hilarious novel *Don Quixote,* now considered a cornerstone of Western literature, about a fictional gentleman's imaginary exploits.

Cervantes the Prisoner

In 1569, the young Cervantes, seeing no opportunities at home, joined the army and was wounded at the Battle of Lepanto in 1571. Cervantes hoped to be promoted to an army captain after the war, but he was captured by a band of Barbary pirates. After five years of enslavement in Algeria, Cervantes returned to Spain in 1580 with no hope of resuming his military career. Over the years he worked as a playwright, bureaucrat, and tax collector before landing in jail for failure to pay his debts.

According to legend, Cervantes was in jail when he was struck with the idea for *Don Quixote.* Don Quixote is a poor, aging landowner who reads nothing but romantic tales of chivalry. Teetering on the edge of madness, the old man becomes convinced that he is a knight-errant, even though the age of knights is long past.

Quixote the Conqueror

The Ingenious Gentleman Don Quixote of La Mancha was a smash hit when it was published in 1605. Translations into French and English appeared within ten years.

Despite his book's widespread success, Cervantes remained poor. At the time, authors were at the mercy of publishers and were seldom able to retain the copyrights on their books, a situation that was common until the nineteenth century. *Don Quixote's* publisher, not Cervantes, reaped the lion's share of the book's profits. Cervantes died in poverty on April 22, 1616—one day before Shakespeare. He left the world a comic masterpiece that earned him the title "father of the modern novel."

Think About the Writer *Don Quixote* is a parody of medieval romances. If Cervantes were alive today, what literary genre might he parody? Why?

California Standards, pp. 602–610

- **Reading Standard 3.1** Analyze characteristics of subgenres (e.g., satire, parody, allegory, pastoral) that are used in poetry, prose, plays, novels, short stories, essays, and other basic genres.
- **Grades 9–10 Review Reading Standard 3.4** Determine characters' traits by what the characters say about themselves in narration, dialogue, dramatic monologue, and soliloquy.

Selection Readability	
Easily Accessible **Accessible** Challenging	familiar syntax; simple dialogue; accessible vocabulary; familiar genre

Reading Standard 3.1; Grades 9–10 Review
Reading Standard 3.4 (see pages A48–A50)

Literary Skills Focus

Parody A **parody** is an imitation of a work of literature, art, or music for amusement or instruction. Parodies often borrow characteristics of the original work and transfer them to a ridiculous subject. Writers take this approach by using exaggeration, verbal irony (saying one thing and meaning another), incongruity (purposefully pairing things that don't belong together), and humorous imitation. Cervantes's object of parody in *Don Quixote* is the medieval romance, which featured chivalrous knights on epic quests, often to win the love of a beautiful noblewoman.

Reading Skills Focus

Drawing Inferences About Character A **character** is an individual in a story or play. Although sometimes writers tell us directly what a character is like, other times we must draw inferences about a character by paying attention to the character's words, appearance, actions, thoughts and feelings, and effect on other characters.

Into Action As you read, use a chart like the one below to note examples of the characters' words and behavior. In the second column, write down the inference you draw from each example.

Words and Behaviors	Inference About Character
"'...it is a great service to God to remove so accursed a breed from the face of the earth.'" (Don Quixote's words)	Quixote believes he is a servant of God on a divine mission.
"Sancho upon his donkey . . ." (Sancho's actions)	

Writing Skills Focus

Think as a Reader/Writer

Find It in Your Reading Throughout the novel, Cervantes uses **exaggeration** to create parody. For example, Quixote does not just call out to the windmills, he shouts "at the top of his lungs." As you read, use your *Reader/Writer Notebook* to note how Cervantes uses exaggeration to create his master parody.

TechFocus As you read this selection, think about contemporary parodies you've seen on television, in movies, or on the Internet.

Reader/Writer Notebook

Use your **RWN** to complete the activities for this selection.

Vocabulary

vile (vyl) *adj.:* evil; disgusting. *Don Quixote vows to rid the world of the vile giants.*

succor (SUHK uhr) *v.:* to help in time of distress. *Quixote prays that his beloved Dulcinea will succor him as he takes on the great giants.*

enmity (EHN muh tee) *n.:* hostility. *Quixote believes that a powerful magician who bears enmity for him is responsible for turning the giants back into windmills.*

flaccid (FLAS ihd) *adj.:* limp; flabby. *Their water bag had gone flaccid, indicating they would need to find water soon.*

disposition (dihs puh ZIHSH uhn) *n.:* natural qualities of personality. *Sancho Panza claims that he has a gentle and peaceful disposition.*

Language Coach

Homonyms English has many words that sound the same but are spelled differently. These are called **homonyms.** For example, *vile,* an adjective that means "evil," is a homonym of *vial,* a small glass bottle. In what kind of story or movie might someone find a vile vial?

Learn It Online
Let this online video introduction set you off into the world of Don Quixote.
go.hrw.com H12-603 Go

Comparing Texts Resources

Unit 3 Resources, on-level practice and assessment, p. 42
PowerNotes, interactive lesson presentations with activities
Teacher One Stop™, on-level lesson plans and all print resources
Holt Audio Library
Holt Audio Library: Selections and Summaries in Spanish
UA: Holt Interactive Reader, p. 165
UA: Differentiating Instruction, modified lesson plans and leveled assessment, p. 129
UA: Resources for Teaching Advanced Students, lesson plans, p. 118
UA: Supporting Instruction in Spanish, selection summary
Analyzing Visuals Transparencies, p. 25
ThinkCentral Online Assessment, Selection Standards Check
ThinkCentral Online Remediation

Preteach

Introducing Vocabulary

Use this activity to check students' understanding.

1. Name something that you think smells **vile**.
2. Name a community organization whose volunteers **succor** others.
3. Suggest two ways people can avoid provoking their neighbor's **enmity**.
4. How would you try to revive a **flaccid** houseplant?
5. Suggest a nickname for someone with a cheerful **disposition**.

English for Academic Success

Language Coach

Tell students that homonyms are words that sound alike, but are spelled differently. [*A fairy tale may have a vile vial.*]

Literary Skills Focus

As you read the selection with students, have them note the author's use of parody.

Reading Skills Focus

Give students a copy of the Reading Skills Focus graphic organizer before they read. (See **Unit 3 Resources.**) Tell them to use their inferences to answer the questions on the Applying Your Skills page.

Writing Skills Focus

Have students use their **Reader/Writer Notebooks** to record instances of exaggeration. Students can use their notes to complete the Writing Skills Focus activity.

Learn It Online
The **PowerNotes** presentation for this lesson includes a short video that introduces the selection. The video is also available on the online version of this page.
go.hrw.com H12-603 Go

Teacher Preparation
Selection Plot Summary

In this excerpt from Chapter 8 of *Don Quixote,* the hero, whose quest for adventures has been inspired by his reading of medieval romances, fearlessly engages in "righteous warfare" with windmills that he perceives as "lawless giants." Badly battered by the first windmill's whirling vanes, Don Quixote brushes off the outcome of the encounter as "the fortunes of war" and attributes to a non-existent magician the change of the "giants" into windmills. Aching but undeterred, he remounts the equally battered Rocinante and rides on in search of more adventures, the loyal Sancho Panza at his side.

Direct Teach

Think About/Talk About

Read with a Purpose Have students read the Read with a Purpose statement. Tell them that as they read, they should pay attention to when Don Quixote gets into trouble. Then, they should consider how Quixote's wild imagination has contributed to his problems.

NOVEL

from Don Quixote

by **Miguel de Cervantes**

translated by **Samuel Putnam**

Read with a Purpose

Read to discover why Don Quixote's imagination is an "affliction."

Build Background

Don Quixote is a middle-aged gentleman who spends all his time reading books about chivalry. Quixote's obsessive reading sends him close to madness when he comes to believe that he himself is a knight-errant. He takes down the family's rusty armor and names his bony old nag Rocinante. He chooses a country girl named Aldonza Lorenzo as his fair lady and renames her Dulcinea del Toboso. As he sets out to right the injustices in the world, he rides alongside his trusty squire, a poor farmer named Sancho Panza. The excerpt you are about to read from Chapter 8 relates what happens when Don Quixote and Sancho catch sight of thirty or forty windmills.

Metal sculpture of Don Quixote beside windmills in Spain.

Universal Access

English Learners

English for Academic Success Remind students that Don Quixote imagines himself as a knight-errant. As such, he carries a shield and a lance, a fourteen-foot wooden spear tipped with steel that was used for jousting or tilting with the enemy. Point out Cervantes' word choice that would typically be found in knights' tales: *valorous, righteous, vile, succor,* and *peril.*

✔ See **UA: Differentiating Instruction** for strategies for teaching English learners.

Struggling Readers

To help students read *Don Quixote*, model the reading skill of drawing inferences about character. You might say: "Reading this excerpt from *Don Quixote*, I see that there are only two characters: Don Quixote and Sancho Panza. At the beginning of Chapter 8, Quixote seems to be imagining that windmills are giants. He even says that the arms are two leagues in length. This is more than six miles, so I will infer that he is imagining the windmills as giants either because he has terrible eyesight, is deranged, or possibly both."

from Chapter 8

Of the good fortune which the valorous Don Quixote had in the terrifying and never-before-imagined adventure of the windmills, along with other events that deserve to be suitably recorded.

At this point they caught sight of thirty or forty windmills which were standing on the plain there, and no sooner had Don Quixote laid eyes upon them than he turned to his squire and said, "Fortune is guiding our affairs better than we could have wished; for you see there before you, friend Sancho Panza, some thirty or more lawless giants with whom I mean to do battle. I shall deprive them of their lives, and with the spoils from this encounter we shall begin to enrich ourselves; for this is righteous warfare, and it is a great service to God to remove so accursed a breed from the face of the earth."

"What giants?" said Sancho Panza.

"Those that you see there," replied his master, "those with the long arms, some of which are as much as two leagues in length."

"But look, your Grace, those are not giants but windmills, and what appear to be arms are their wings which, when whirled in the breeze, cause the millstone to go."

"It is plain to be seen," said Don Quixote, "that you have had little experience in this matter of adventures. If you are afraid, go off to one side and say your prayers while I am engaging them in fierce, unequal combat." Ⓐ

Saying this, he gave spurs to his steed Rocinante, without paying any heed to Sancho's warning that these were truly windmills and not giants that he was riding forth to attack. Nor even when he was close upon them did he perceive what they really were, but shouted at the top of his lungs, "Do not seek to flee, cowards and vile creatures that you are, for it is but a single knight with whom you have to deal!"

At that moment a little wind came up and the big wings began turning.

"Though you flourish as many arms as did the giant Briareus,"[1] said Don Quixote when he perceived this, "you still shall have to answer to me."

He thereupon commended himself with all his heart to his lady Dulcinea, beseeching her to succor him in this peril; and, being well covered with his shield and with his lance at rest, he bore down upon them at a full gallop and fell upon the first mill that stood in his way, giving a thrust at the wing, which was whirling at such a speed that his lance was broken into bits and both horse and horseman went rolling over the plain, very much battered indeed. Sancho upon his donkey came hurrying to his master's assistance as fast as he could, but when he reached the spot, the knight was unable to move, so great was the shock with which he and Rocinante had hit the ground. Ⓑ

"God help us!" exclaimed Sancho, "did I not tell your Grace to look well, that those were nothing but windmills, a fact which no one could fail to see unless he had other mills of the same sort in his head?"

"Be quiet, friend Sancho," said Don Quixote. "Such are the fortunes of war, which more than any other are subject to constant change. What is more, when I come to think of it, I am sure that this must be the work of that magician Frestón, the one who robbed me of my study and my books, and who has thus changed the giants into windmills in order to deprive me of the glory of overcoming them, so great is the enmity that he bears me; but in the end his evil arts shall not prevail against this trusty sword of mine."

"May God's will be done," was Sancho Panza's response. And with the aid of his squire the knight was once more mounted on Rocinante, who stood there with one shoulder half out of joint. And so, speaking of the adventure that had just befallen them, they

1. **Briareus:** in Greek mythology, a giant with a hundred arms who helped Zeus overthrow the Titans.

Ⓐ **Reading Focus** **Drawing Inferences About Character** What do Quixote's words here tell you about his character?

Ⓑ **Literary Focus** **Parody** How does Cervantes parody the knight's assault on the giants?

Vocabulary **vile** (vyl) *adj.:* evil, disgusting.
succor (SUHK uhr) *v.:* help in time of distress.
enmity (EHN muh tee) *n.:* hostility.

Advanced Learners

Enrichment Encourage students to read and discuss additional chapters of *Don Quixote*. They might also read Mark Twain's *A Connecticut Yankee in King Arthur's Court* (1889) and compare and contrast these parodies of romance literature written nearly three centuries apart.

✔ See **UA: Resources for Teaching Advanced Students** for strategies for teaching advanced learners.

Students with Disabilities

Have students compose two drawings of the windmills, one according to how they appear to Sancho, and another according to how they appear to Don Quixote. Have students compare their drawings with others and explain how they modified the windmills to make them look like giants.

✔ See **UA: Differentiating Instruction** for strategies for teaching students with disabilities.

Think About/Talk About

Comprehension

Ⓐ Reading Focus

Possible response: *Quixote does not care what Sancho says. He sees only his own overblown and incorrect vision of reality.*

Analysis

Ⓑ Literary Focus

Possible response: *Cervantes first has Quixote shout a challenge at the inanimate windmills. Then, he continues with the reference to Quixote's lady. When Quixote attacks the windmill, he is "defeated" in a most embarrassing manner and ends up rolling with his horse on the ground.*

Extend the Discussion

Summarizing Give a brief summary of the events described on this page. ***Possible response:*** *Don Quixote sights some windmills in the distance. Thinking they are giants, he sets up to attack him, despite the protests of Sancho Panza. When Don Quixote finally attacks the windmills, he is thrown off his horse and blames the evil workings of the magician Frestón for his defeat.*

Vocabulary: Own the Word

- **vile:** Tell students that the connotation of *vile* is "extremely unpleasant or repulsive," as opposed to just "unpleasant." For example, "The girl ignored the troll's unpleasant appearance but she could not stand the *vile* odor he was giving off." Ask students to create a pair or related statements that show how *vile* is stronger than *unpleasant*.
- **succor:** The word *succor* comes from the Latin *succurrere,* meaning "run to help." When you give *succor* to someone, you are giving them aid.
- **enmity:** Quixote claimed there was deep *enmity* between him and . . . ***Possible response:*** *the magician Frestón*

Model the Skill

- Provide students with copies of the Reading Skills Focus graphic organizer for *Don Quixote.* (See **Unit 3 Resources.**)
- Model the skill of **drawing inferences about character**. Explain that dialogue often provides clues about character. Read aloud the paragraph on p. 606 that begins with, "'Ah, that is the truth . . .'" Point out how Don Quixote shows his complete adherence to the code of knight-errant, even when the precepts clash with reality. Explain that from this statement, the reader can infer that Don Quixote's ideal of honor does not stem from personal experience, but from an obsession. He will do anything he can to adhere to the code, even when this seems senseless.

Words and Behaviors	Inference about Character
". . . if I do not speak of my sufferings, it is for the reason that it is not permitted knights-errant to complain of any wound whatsoever." (Don Quixote's words)	Don Quixote's adherence to the code of behavior of knights-errant is exaggerated and prevails over common sense.

Guided Practice: Apply

Read-Pair-Share Ask students to draw inferences about the character of Sancho Panza based on his words, actions, appearance, and thoughts on these pages.

continued along the Puerto Lápice highway; for there, Don Quixote said, they could not fail to find many and varied adventures, this being a much-traveled thoroughfare. The only thing was, the knight was exceedingly downcast over the loss of his lance.

"I remember," he said to his squire, "having read of a Spanish knight by the name of Diego Pérez de Vargas, who, having broken his sword in battle, tore from an oak a heavy bough or branch and with it did such feats of valor that day, and pounded so many Moors, that he came to be known as Machuca,[2] and he and his descendants from that day forth have been called Vargas y Machuca. I tell you this because I too, intend to provide myself with just such a bough as the one he wielded, and with it I propose to do such exploits that you shall deem yourself fortunate to have been found worthy to come with me and behold and witness things that are almost beyond belief."

"God's will be done," said Sancho. "I believe everything that your Grace says; but straighten yourself up in the saddle a little, for you seem to be slipping down on one side, owing, no doubt, to the shaking up that you received in your fall." **C**

"Ah, that is the truth," replied Don Quixote, "and if I do not speak of my sufferings, it is for the reason that it is not permitted knights-errant to complain of any wound whatsoever, even though their bowels may be dropping out."

"If that is the way it is," said Sancho, "I have nothing more to say; but, God knows, it would suit me better if your Grace did complain when something hurts him. I can assure you that I mean to do so, over the least little thing that ails me—that is, unless the same rule applies to squires as well."

Don Quixote laughed long and heartily over Sancho's simplicity, telling him that he might complain as much as he liked and where and when he liked, whether he had good cause or not; for he had read

2. **Machuca:** literally, "the pounder," the hero of an old ballad.

C **Reading Focus** **Drawing Inferences About Character**
What does Sancho's observation that Quixote is sliding off his horse reveal about Sancho?

TECHNOLOGY LINK

Windmill farm, Palm Springs, California.

From Windmills to Wind Turbines

The windmills that Don Quixote battled were wooden structures that used wind to produce energy. Windmills were common throughout Europe beginning in the twelfth century, but by the twentieth century, coal and oil were the dominant fuels, and many people had begun to look for alternative sources of energy that would create less pollution. Wind turbines are modern-day windmills used to generate electricity. They work the same way as traditional windmills: Wind strikes tilted blades, causing them to spin and rotate a central shaft. Unlike old wooden windmills, wind turbines are massive, often towering more than three hundred feet high.

Ask Yourself

Do you think Don Quixote would have done battle with a wind turbine? What other modern technology might he select? Why?

Cross-Curricular Connection

ART: The Allure of Arabesques

After converting to Islam, the Moors occupied Spain for more than seven hundred years from the eighth century to the fifteenth century. Moorish artisans made many important contributions to Spanish culture, particularly in the areas of art and architecture. Perhaps the best-known example is the Alhambra in Granada, Spain. The building is renowned for its use of arabesques: elaborate geometric designs shaped to create the impression of flowers, foliage, animals, and other images from nature.

Technology Link

Ask Yourself

Possible responses: *Don Quixote would have probably wanted to attack the wind turbines as well, but he probably would not have been knocked off by their blades, as wind turbines are much taller than windmills. Don Quixote would have probably attacked electric towers, or satellite dishes, which could be seen as the "giants" of our modern landscapes.*

nothing to the contrary in the ordinances[3] of chivalry. Sancho then called his master's attention to the fact that it was time to eat. The knight replied that he himself had no need of food at the moment, but his squire might eat whenever he chose. Having been granted this permission, Sancho seated himself as best he could upon his beast, and, taking out from his saddlebags the provisions that he had stored there, he rode along leisurely behind his master, munching his victuals[4] and taking a good, hearty swig now and then at the leather flask in a manner that might well have caused the biggest-bellied tavern-keeper of Málaga to envy him. Between drafts he gave not so much as a thought to any promise that his master might have made him, nor did he look upon it as any hardship, but rather as good sport, to go in quest of adventures however hazardous they might be.

The short of the matter is, they spent the night under some trees, from one of which Don Quixote tore off a withered bough to serve him as a lance, placing it in the lance head from which he had removed the broken one. He did not sleep all night long for thinking of his lady Dulcinea; for this was in accordance with what he had read in his books, of men of arms in the forest or desert places who kept a wakeful vigil,[5] sustained by the memory of their ladies fair. Not so with Sancho, whose stomach was full, and not with chicory water.[6] He fell into a dreamless slumber, and had not his master called him, he would not have been awakened either by the rays of the sun in his face or by the many birds who greeted the coming of the new day with their merry song.

Upon arising, he had another go at the flask, finding it somewhat more flaccid than it had been the night before, a circumstance which grieved his heart, for he could not see that they were on the way to remedying the deficiency within any very short space of time. Don Quixote did not wish any breakfast; for, as has been said, he was in the habit of nourishing himself on savorous memories. They then set out once more along the road to Puerto Lápice, and around three in the afternoon they came in sight of the pass that bears that name.

"There," said Don Quixote as his eyes fell upon it, "we may plunge our arms up to the elbow in what are known as adventures. But I must warn you that even though you see me in the greatest peril in the world, you are not to lay hand upon your sword to defend me, unless it be that those who attack me are rabble and men of low degree, in which case you may very well come to my aid; but if they be gentlemen, it is in no wise permitted by the laws of chivalry that you should assist me until you yourself shall have been dubbed a knight."

"Most certainly, sir," replied Sancho, "your Grace shall be very well obeyed in this; all the more so for the reason that I myself am of a peaceful disposition and not fond of meddling in the quarrels and feuds of others. However, when it comes to protecting my own person, I shall not take account of those laws of which you speak, seeing that all laws, human and divine, permit each one to defend himself whenever he is attacked."

"I am willing to grant you that," assented Don Quixote, "but in this matter of defending me against gentlemen you must restrain your natural impulses."

"I promise you I shall do so," said Sancho. "I will observe this precept as I would the Sabbath day. . . ." **D**

3. **ordinances:** authoritative commands.
4. **victuals:** provisions; food.
5. **vigil:** staying watchfully awake.
6. **chicory water:** inexpensive coffee substitute.

D **Literary Focus** **Parody** What is ironic about Sancho's promise to restrain his "natural impulses" if Don Quixote is attacked?

Vocabulary **flaccid** (FLAS ihd) *adj.:* limp; flabby.
disposition (dihs puh ZIHSH uhn) *n.:* natural qualities of personality.

Think About/Talk About

Comprehension

C **Reading Focus**

Possible response: *Sancho is firmly rooted in reality and in the present. He is not impressed with talk of past or future glories or adventures.*

Analysis

D **Literary Focus**

Possible response: *Don Quixote expects that Sancho's "natural impulses" might lead him to fight those who attack the knight. The reality is that Sancho would fight only if he himself is attacked. He willingly promises Quixote that he will not come to his aid.*

Extend the Discussion

Evaluating What is incongruous about the branch Don Quixote selects to replace the lance? ***Possible response:*** *Quixote selects a "withered branch" that is unlikely to be effective.*

Vocabulary: Own the Word

- **flaccid:** Ask students why Don Quixote was saddened at his *flaccid* flask. ***Possible response:*** *The flask's flaccidiness indicated there was hardly any left inside to drink.*
- **disposition:** Have students applaud to indicate how much they would want to be described as having an unpleasant *disposition.* ***Possible response:*** *No applause; students do not wish to be thought of as someone that others would not want to be around.*

California Standards, pp. 608–610

- **Reading Standard 3.1** Analyze characteristics of subgenres (e.g., satire, parody, allegory, pastoral) that are used in poetry, prose, plays, novels, short stories, essays, and other basic genres.
- **Reading Standard 3.3** Analyze the ways in which irony, tone, mood, the author's style, and the "sound" of language achieve specific rhetorical or aesthetic purposes or both.
- **Reading Standard 3.4** Analyze ways in which poets use imagery, personification, figures of speech, and sounds to evoke readers' emotions.
- **Grades 9–10 Review Reading Standard 1.1** Identify and use the literal and figurative meanings of words and understand word derivations.
- **Writing Standard 1.2** Use point of view, characterization, style (e.g., use of irony), and related elements for specific rhetorical and aesthetic purposes.
- **Writing Standard 2.1** Write fictional, autobiographical, or biographical narratives.
- **Writing Standard 2.2** Write responses to literature: **a.** Demonstrate a comprehensive understanding of the significant ideas in works or passages.
- **Writing Standard 2.3** Write reflective compositions: **a.** Explore the significance of personal experiences, events, conditions, or concerns by using rhetorical strategies (e.g., narration, description, exposition, persuasion).

Check for Understanding

Independent Practice

Reading Skills Focus

Possible responses:

1. *Quixote says an evil magician changed the giants into windmills.*
2. *He ignores the natural needs of eating and sleeping.*
3. *The absurd defense of the ideals of knighthood may serve to highlight how those ideals are unrealistic. This can be either a criticism of high ideals or a condemnation of a society that cannot inspire those ideals anymore.*
4. *Ask students to consider the exaggerations in the text and find which inferences explain those exaggerations.*

Literary Skills Focus

Possible responses:

5. *Calvin from "Calvin and Hobbes"; Doc Brown in "Back to the Future"; Walter Mitty in "The Secret Life of Walter Mitty." These characters have dreams and fantasies about how they would like their lives to be.*
6. *Exaggeration: Quixote says that the giants' arms can extend up to two leagues in length; Irony: Sancho says that he will obey Quixote's order to stay out of any fights. Incongruity: Quixote does not eat; Humorous imitation: Quixote read about a knight who used a stout oak as a weapon, but Quixote chooses a "withered branch."*
7. *Quixote is an idealist. Sancho is a realist. Quixote imagines that windmills are giants. Sancho tells him that they are windmills.*
8. *Cervantes did not believe in romanticizing war and heroism. He had a more pragmatic view of the world, one in which people responded to real events and people.*
9. *Sancho is grounded in reality. Quixote lives in fantasy based upon what he has read.*

Applying Your Skills

Reading Standard 3.1, 3.3, 3.4 (see pages A48–A50)
Writing Standard 1.2 (see pages A51–A52)

from Don Quixote

Literary Response and Analysis

Reading Skills Focus

Quick Check

1. After being knocked off his horse, how does Don Quixote explain the fact that the giants are, in fact, windmills?
2. What natural needs does Don Quixote ignore?

Read with a Purpose

3. What point is Cervantes making when he lets Quixote have delusions of knighthood?

Reading Skills: Drawing Inferences About Character

4. Review the examples and inferences in the chart you created. Then, add a column in which you summarize how the inference you made supports the humor and the genre of parody.

Words and Behaviors	Inference About Character	How It Fits the Parody
"'. . .it is a great service to God to remove so accursed a breed from the face of the earth.'" (Don Quixote's words)	Quixote believes he is a servant of God on a divine mission.	It seems funny that anyone given a divine mandate would fail so miserably all the time.
"Sancho upon his donkey . . ." (Sancho's actions)		

Literary Skills Focus

Literary Analysis

5. **Extend** The word *quixotic,* which means "a well-intentioned but impractical dreamer," comes from Don Quixote. What quixotic characters can you think of? What do they have in common?
6. **Analyze** In his parody, Cervantes uses the techniques of exaggeration, irony, incongruity, and humorous imitation. List one example of each technique used in this selection.
7. **Evaluate** An idealist sees the world as he or she thinks it should be. A realist sees the world as it is. Is Don Quixote an idealist or a realist? Which role does Sancho Panza play? Use examples from the text to support your answer.

Literary Skills: Parody

8. **Infer** Cervantes chose to parody previously idealized concepts such as chivalry and heroism. What does the focus of his parody tell you about his beliefs and philosophies?

Literary Skills Review: Foil

9. **Analyze** A **foil** is a character that is used as a contrast to another character. In what ways is Sancho Panza a foil to Don Quixote? Identify the behaviors that suggest they are opposites.

Writing Skills Focus

Think as a Reader/Writer

Use It in Your Writing Review the notes you took in your *Reader/Writer Notebook* about Cervantes's use of irony and incongruity. Then, write a few paragraphs, using these two devices in a convincing parody of a book, movie, or TV show.

What Do You Think Now

Why does Cervantes use a fictional character to poke fun at the outdated ideals of chivalry and medieval romance?

Universal Access

Struggling Writers

Some students may need additional scaffolding to complete the Writing Skills Focus activity. Suggest that students choose a famous literary work, movie, or show to parody, such as Shakespeare's works or *Lord of the Rings.* Remind students to focus on aspects of the work such as the worldview of the main characters, their appearances, and their actions.

What Do You Think Now?

Ask students to consider what Cervantes is saying about the ideals of chivalry and medieval romance through his fictional characters' words, actions, and appearances. Have them think about the effect these messages might have had on the people in Cervantes' time.

Grades 9–10 Review Reading Standard 1.1 (see pages A48–A50)

Vocabulary Development

✓ Vocabulary Check

Match each Vocabulary word with its synonym.

1. vile	**a.** temperament
2. succor	**b.** droopy
3. enmity	**c.** assist
4. flaccid	**d.** gross
5. disposition	**e.** hostility

Vocabulary Skills: Context Clues

One way to learn the meaning of a new word while reading is to search for context clues. A **context clue** is a word or phrase near an unfamiliar word that provides a hint to the meaning of the unfamiliar word. Clues might be (1) a clause or an adjective that seems related to the unknown word, (2) the subject or topic of the sentence or surrounding sentences, or (3) the object of the verb. Consider this excerpt from *Don Quixote:*

> He thereupon commended himself with all his heart to his lady Dulcinea, beseeching her to succor him in this peril. (page 605)

The context clues for the Vocabulary word *succor* can be found in the verb *beseeching* and the prepositional phrase *in this peril*. If Quixote is begging or praying for something in a situation of peril, then help or assistance is probably what he wants. Therefore, *succor* must have something to do with relief or assistance.

When searching for context clues, look for words you already know. Also consider the overall meaning of the sentence and the paragraph. These wider contexts can often give you general ideas about the word and point to its likely meaning.

Your Turn

Find each Vocabulary word in the selection. In a table like the one below, write the Vocabulary words and the context clues that hint at the meanings of the words. One word has been done for you.

Word	Context Clues
succor	"beseeching," "in this peril"

Language Coach

Homonyms Identify the homonyms for each word below.

1. affect	**4.** mane
2. stair	**5.** male
3. rein	**6.** slay

Academic Vocabulary

Talk About

How does Quixote <u>approach</u> his quest? How does he <u>convince</u> Sancho and those around him that he is a great warrior?

Universal Access: Vocabulary Development

EL English Learners

English for Academic Success Ask students to imagine they need to explain the meaning of the Vocabulary words to a younger student. Have them provide examples that a younger student could use as context clues to understand the word's meaning.

- Don Quixote has a fiery **disposition;** for instance, ______. [*he would throw himself into battle at the slightest provocation*]
- Most of us are not interested in eating such **vile** things as ______. [*spiders, cockroaches, and rotten fruit*]
- One way to **succor** the elderly is by a kindly gesture such as ______. [*holding the door open for them*]
- You can tell when a person feels **enmity** toward another person when he or she ______. [*speaks harshly to that person only*]
- Parts of your body might go **flaccid** if ______. [*left unexercised, such as your arm and stomach muscles*]

✔ See the **Academic and Selection Vocabulary Skill Builder** in **UA: Differentiating Instruction.**

Independent Practice

Vocabulary Development

Vocabulary Check

1. *d* **2.** *c*
3. *e* **4.** *b*
5. *a*

Your Turn

1. *vile: "cowards"*
2. *enmity: "the one who robbed me of my study and my books," "in order to deprive me of me of the glory of overcoming them," "his evil arts"*
3. *flaccid: "than it had the night before," "a circumstance which grieved his heart"*
4. *disposition: "I myself am of a peaceful," "and not fond of meddling in the quarrels and feuds of others"*

go.hrw.com **WordSharp: An Interactive Vocabulary Tutor,** more practice with academic language

English for Academic Success

Language Coach

Tell students that having some knowledge of common homonyms will help them write accurately and effectively. If they use homonyms like *their* and *there* or *your* and *you're* incorrectly, they may confuse their readers and fail to express themselves. [*1. effect; 2. stare; 3. rain, reign; 4. main; 5. mail; 6. sleigh*]

English for Academic Success

Academic Vocabulary

Possible response: *Quixote <u>approaches</u> his quest with vigor and enthusiasm. He <u>convinces</u> others that he is a great warrior by imitating the heroes of the medieval romances that he is obsessed with.*

Independent Practice

Grammar Link

Your Turn

1. *Don Quixote was published in the early seventeenth century.*
2. *The book describes the adventures of a delusional man named Don Quixote and his squire, Sancho.*
3. *At one point in the story, Quixote spots an army of giants, which he decides to vanquish from the earth.*

Choices: Evaluation Criteria

Review: Homework
Write a Song

- Students' lyrics are based on the excerpt from the novel.
- Students demonstrate a thorough understanding of the contradictions in Don Quixote's character.

Connect: Homework
Create Your Own Parody

- Students should use the elements of parody to form a modern social critique.
- Groups should perform their parody for their classmates and facilitate a discussion following their performance.

Extend: Homework
Continue the Story

- Students demonstrate a close reading and good understanding of the text.
- Students are able to recognize several uses of parody in the novel.
- Students include the major events and uses of irony or exaggeration in their summaries.

Applying Your Skills

Reading Standard 3.1 (see pages A48–A50)
Writing Standard 2.2a, 2.3a (see pages A51–A52)

from Don Quixote

Grammar Link

The Literary Present

Correct verb tense is a vital element of effective writing. When writing about events of the past, you write in the past tense. One exception to this rule is the **literary present,** a usage of present tense reserved for writing about events that take place in a literary work. Consider the following sentence:

> In the early seventeenth century, Cervantes published *Don Quixote,* a parody in which a middle-aged gentleman comes to believe that he is a noble knight in search of great adventure.

Because Cervantes published *Don Quixote* in the past, you write about that event in the past tense. However, when talking about what happens in the story, you use the literary present tense because the action is still occurring for readers. One exception occurs when you are writing about events that the characters describe in the past tense; in that case you use the past tense:

> *literary present tense*
> Quixote tells Sancho about the magician who robbed Quixote of his study and his books.
> *past tense*

Your Turn

Correct the tense in the following sentences, using the literary present when necessary.

1. *Don Quixote* is published in the early seventeenth century.
2. The book described the adventures of a delusional man named Don Quixote and his squire, Sancho.
3. At one point in the story, Quixote spotted an army of giants, which he decided to vanquish from the earth.

Writing Application Write a review or summary of this section of *Don Quixote,* and maintain the literary present tense.

CHOICES

As you respond to the Choices, use these **Academic Vocabulary** words as appropriate: approach, convince, dominate, enhance, participate.

REVIEW

Write a Song

In *Man of La Mancha,* Dale Wasserman's musical adaptation of *Don Quixote,* Quixote sings of his need to "dream the impossible dream." Review the excerpt from *Don Quixote,* and write some lyrics for your own song about this famous character who literally follows his dream.

CONNECT

Create Your Own Parody

TechFocus In a small group, work together to choose a popular song, movie, television show, or video game and create your own parody of it. Think carefully about what piece to choose and what elements of it you want to parody and why. Record your parody, or perform it live for your class. Then, ask the class to participate by discussing what social criticism, if any, they detected in your parody and whether or not the parody form allowed your group to make observations that would not be as easily accepted if said in a more direct way.

EXTEND

Continue the Story

Class Presentation Borrow a copy of Cervantes's *Don Quixote* from your school or local library. Read a few more chapters of the story or the entirety of Quixote's wild adventures. Summarize the chapters you read, and continue to take notes on Cervantes's use of parody. Present your summary of the continued adventures of Don Quixote and Sancho Panza to the class.

Universal Access: Grammar Link

EL English Learners

English for Academic Success To give students more practice with the literary present, have them fill in the blanks in the sentences below, following the rule of the literary present.

1. When Romeo _____ the mausoleum, he finds his lifeless lover, Juliet. [*enters*]
2. After the potion wears off, Juliet wakes up to find that Romeo _____ himself. [*has poisoned*]
3. Juliet, distraught over the loss of her lover, _____ her life as well. [*takes*]

✔ For more practice with the literary present, see **Warriner's Handbook, Grammar Notes,** and **Language Handbook Worksheets.**

COMPARING TEXTS
Wrap Up

World Literature: Satirical Novels

Writing Standard 2.2a–e (see pages A48–A50)

Writing Skills Focus

Write a Comparison-Contrast Essay

French writer Voltaire broadly criticized his contemporaries. Cervantes, one of the masters of Spanish literature, makes particular fun of the genre of medieval romances. Their works stand today as exemplars of the genre of satire. Using notes from your *Reader/Writer Notebook,* plan and write a comparison-contrast essay about these two examples of satire from *Candide* and from *Don Quixote.*

Review the elements of a comparison-contrast essay before you begin writing.

An Effective Comparison-Contrast Essay
• states the basis of the comparison and contrast in a thesis
• organizes ideas using the point-by-point method
• uses and cites text evidence to support each point of comparison and contrast
• contains few or no errors in spelling, punctuation, and usage

Prewriting

Begin a comparison-contrast essay with a strong basis of comparison. Then, look for differences that will reflect your close reading of the texts and provide additional points of discussion.

Gather Ideas Use a Venn diagram to record your notes about each selection. The major similarities will appear in the middle circle. Unique aspects of each selection will appear in the two outside circles, labeled "A" and "B." Categorize the differences into topics that form the basis of contrast.

Consider the following ideas as you review your notes:

- Compare and contrast the objects of each writer's satire.
- Compare and contrast the nature of the humor and tone in the selections.
- Compare and contrast the authors' styles.
- Compare and contrast the selections' themes.
- Compare and contrast the national perspective or interests revealed in each selection.

Develop a Thesis Statement Using your notes, develop a thesis statement that makes an assertion about both the similarities and differences in the two satires. Always begin with a basis of similarity (such as the use of exaggeration) and then focus on the differences in the two pieces.

Sample Thesis:

Although Cervantes and Voltaire are separated by a century, they both use exaggeration as a primary tool of their satire, creating works with very different tones and structures.

Drafting

Because you are using the **point-by-point** method of organization, begin with the strongest comparison linking the two selections. Develop it in your first body paragraph. Then your next body paragraphs will develop *either* additional similarities or differences. Discuss both selections in each paragraph. Your final body paragraph will focus on the differences between the two satires.

Text Evidence Use direct quotations from both selections to support each point. Punctuate the quotations correctly and interweave them into your own sentences.

Revising and Editing

Reread your draft to determine if you have fully supported your thesis with explanation and text evidence. Read again for grammatical and mechanics errors. Prepare a final copy that is error free and publish it.

What Do You Think Now?

How are Candide and Don Quixote affected by their own ideas of what order and civilization should be?

Independent Practice

What Do You Think Now?

Ask students to identify how each character's idea of order and civility differs from what they are expected to believe. Have them consider how each character defies the norms of their society and how this defiance affects them.

Assess

Unit 3 Resources, Selection Standards Check, p. 45

ThinkCentral Online Assessment, Selection Standards Check

Teacher One Stop™, editable Selection Standards Check

Reteach

ThinkCentral Online Remediation

Universal Access

Struggling Writers

Some students may need additional scaffolding to complete the Writing Skills Focus activity. As students complete their Venn diagram, remind them that in comparing and contrasting the two selections, they should have adequate text evidence to support each point of similarity or difference. Have them record as many direct quotations as possible to support each point so they can weave it into their directly or indirectly. Then, ask students to use their Venn diagram to construct an outline of their essay using the point-by-point method.

California Standards, p. 611

- **Writing Standard 2.2** Write responses to literature: **a.** Demonstrate a comprehensive understanding of the significant ideas in works or passages. **b.** Analyze the use of imagery, language, universal themes, and unique aspects of the text. **c.** Support important ideas and viewpoints through accurate and detailed references to the text and to other works. **d.** Demonstrate an understanding of the author's use of stylistic devices and an appreciation of the effects created. **e.** Identify and assess the impact of perceived ambiguities, nuances, and complexities within the text.

Chapter Objectives

- Students will understand the influence of neoclassical ideas on literature during the Age of Reason.
- Students will understand the characteristics of the era's popular literary genres, such as mock epics.
- Students will read and compare texts that address women's role in eighteenth-century society.

The Quotation

Ask students to comment on Pope's use of the word "art" in this quotation. ***Possible response:*** *Good writing takes study and practice; it does not happen spontaneously. "Art" refers to careful artistry or craft.*

Analyzing Visuals

Extension Activity In what way is the image related to the quote? ***Possible response:*** *The scene shows women engaging in musical performance, a kind of art, and surrounded by seemingly accomplished figures.*

CHAPTER **6**

Examined Lives

LITERARY SKILLS FOCUS

Form and Function in the Age of Reason

CONTENTS

"True ease in writing
comes from art, not
chance,
As those move easiest
who have learned to
dance." — **Alexander Pope**

The Sharp Family (1779–1781) by Johann Zoffany.
National Portrait Gallery, London.

Chapter 6

California Standards Overview

- **Reading Standard 2.1** Analyze both the features and the rhetorical devices of different types of public documents (e.g., policy statements, speeches, debates, platforms) and the way in which authors use those features and devices.
- **Reading Standard 2.2** Analyze the way in which clarity of meaning is affected by the patterns of organization, hierarchical structures, repetition of the main ideas, syntax, and word choice in the text.
- **Reading Standard 2.4** Make warranted and reasonable assertions about the author's arguments by using elements of the text to defend and clarify interpretations.
- **Reading Standard 2.5** Analyze an author's implicit and explicit philosophical assumptions and beliefs about a subject.
- **Reading Standard 3.1** Analyze characteristics of subgenres that are used in poetry, prose, plays, novels, short stories, essays, and other basic genres.
- **Reading Standard 3.2** Analyze the way in which the theme or meaning of a selection represents a view or comment on life, using textual evidence to support the claim.
- **Reading Standard 3.3** Analyze the ways in which irony, tone, mood, the author's style, and the "sound" of language achieve specific rhetorical or aesthetic purposes or both.
- **Reading Standard 3.4** Analyze ways in which poets use imagery, personification, figures of speech, and sounds to evoke readers' emotions.
- **Reading Standard 3.7** Analyze recognized works of world literature from a variety of authors: **a.** Contrast the major literary forms, techniques, and characteristics of the major literary periods (e.g., Homeric Greece, medieval, romantic, neoclassic, modern). **b.** Relate literary works and authors to the major themes and issues of their eras. **c.** Evaluate the philosophical, political, religious, ethical, and social influences of the historical period that shaped the characters, plots, and settings.
- **Reading Standard 3.8** Analyze the clarity and consistency of political assumptions in a selection of literary works or essays on a topic (e.g., suffrage, women's role in organized labor). (Political approach)
- **Reading Standard 3.9** Analyze the philosophical arguments presented in literary works to determine whether the authors' positions have contributed to the quality of each work and the credibility of the characters. (Philosophical approach)

Reading Standard 3.7a–c (see pages A48–A50)

Form and Function in the Age of Reason by Leila Christenbury

Influences on Form and Function in the Age of Reason

- Emphasis on reason, order, science, and philosophy
- Respect for classical forms
- Growth of the middle-class reading public
- Rise in the popularity of prose

The Age of Reason was characterized by the belief that rational thought could improve society. The conservative values of order, decorum, and clarity were of the utmost importance. Nothing during this time was what we would today call *natural*—neither dress, nor manners, nor poetry. Whether the topic was behavior (Alexander Pope), language (Samuel Johnson), or rights (Mary Wollstonecraft and Daniel Defoe), the writers of the eighteenth century relied on logic and structure to instruct their readers.

The Beauty of Order

Today when we think of great poetry, we often think of great feeling: the sonnets of Shakespeare, the private poems of Emily Dickinson, the works of Pablo Neruda or Robert Frost. These poems reveal the poets' innermost thoughts and emotions. Eighteenth-century poets, on the other hand, thought of poetry as having a public function, and they relied on well-defined poetic structures to share their ideas. If, for example, an important person died, a poet might celebrate the deceased in an **elegy,** a poem that mourns the loss of something or someone and often glorifies its subject.

At the opposite extreme, a poet might use satire to expose a certain behavior or person to public ridicule. Alexander Pope's *Rape of the Lock* uses classical epic format to mock the behaviors of the aristocracy. By presenting a frivolous subject in a form typically reserved for lofty characters and ideals, Pope made the structure of his poem a key factor in its satire.

Another poetic genre popular in the eighteenth century was the **ode,** a complex lyric poem on a serious subject. Poets used odes to express a public emotion, such as jubilation over a great victory, or to reflect on a single praiseworthy object or person in a more personal and meditative way.

Common to all of these variations of poetry were carefully constructed rhyme schemes and meter. Poems were never spontaneous and casual—just as people were never to appear in public except in fancy dress.

New Genres for a New Audience

The Age of Reason also produced genres that would appeal to the growing middle class. Newspapers such as the *Tatler* and the *Spectator* contained essays about politics, science, philosophy, literature, and, of course, gossip. Journalists, essayists, and novelists wrote in prose and treated their subjects realistically.

Although all genres emphasized reason, the literature of the eighteenth century is not without feeling. Sentimental dramas and the novels of this era often portray human beings as essentially noble and good, an optimistic view of humanity that pervades many of the period's literary forms.

Ask Yourself

1. How did the literature of the eighteenth century appeal to the intellects of its readers and writers?
2. How does eighteenth-century literature reflect the interests of different social groups?

Learn It Online
Explore the Age of Reason online with *PowerNotes*.
go.hrw.com H12-613 Go

Literary Skills Focus

Objectives

Students will
- evaluate the philosophical, political, religious, ethical, and social influences of a historical period
- understand and evaluate elements of literature from the Restoration and the eighteenth century

Unit 3 Resources, Literary Focus Skill Builder, p. 53

PowerNotes, interactive lesson presentation with activities

Teacher One Stop™, on-level lesson plan and all print resources

Direct Teach

The Beauty of Order

Have students read the Literary Skills Focus essay. Then, use the following question to discuss form and function in the Age of Reason.

Given their belief that rational thought could improve society, how did eighteenth-century writers view their social role?

Check for Understanding

Ask Yourself

Possible responses:

1. *Literature dealt with realistic subjects that appealed to the growing middle class.*
2. *Different genres appealed to the different classes. For example, writers wrote in prose to appeal to the middle class.*

Universal Access

EL English Learners/ Struggling Readers

English for Academic Success Help students to understand the essay by defining terms they may find difficult.

- ***rational***—based on reason; sensible; logical
- ***decorum***—adherence to standards of social behavior
- ***clarity***—clearness
- ***ridicule***—exposure to laughter or mockery
- ***optimistic***—characterized by a positive interpretation of events or by hope for the best outcome

California Standards, p. 613

- **Reading Standard 3.7** Analyze recognized works of world literature from a variety of authors: **a.** Contrast the major literary forms, techniques, and characteristics of the major literary periods (e.g., Homeric Greece, medieval, romantic, neoclassic, modern). **b.** Relate literary works and authors to the major themes and issues of their eras. **c.** Evaluate the philosophical, political, religious, ethical, and social influences of the historical period that shaped the characters, plots, and settings.

Learn It Online
For a multimedia version of the instruction found on this page, use the **PowerNotes** Literary Skills Focus presentation.
go.hrw.com H12-613 Go

Standards Focus

Objectives

Students will
- analyze the ways in which poets use literary devices
- analyze an author's implicit and explicit beliefs about a subject

Selection Introduction

Think About the Writer

Ask students how facing adversity can actually inspire and motivate a person to succeed. Have them also consider how facing life's struggles can give one a deeper perspective.

For Independent Reading

- *Candide,* Francois Voltaire
- *Cyrano de Bergerac,* Edmund Rostand

Motivate

What Do You Think?/QuickTalk

Ask students to consider how education has shaped their sense of civic responsibility and record their thoughts in their **Reader/Writer Notebooks.**

English for Academic Success

Academic Vocabulary

Look for opportunities to use the Academic Vocabulary words in this unit.

- **approach, *n.*:** a way of addressing something
- **convince, *v.*:** persuade
- **enhance, *v.*:** improve the quality of
- **participate, *v.*:** take part in

California Standards, pp. 614–619

- **Reading Standard 2.5** Analyze an author's implicit and explicit philosophical assumptions and beliefs about a subject.
- **Reading Standard 3.4** Analyze ways in which poets use imagery, personification, figures of speech, and sounds to evoke readers' emotions.

Preparing to Read

Heroic Couplets
from An Essay on Man
from The Rape of the Lock

What Do You Think? How can order and civilization affect human behavior?

QuickTalk

Pope believed that education from an early age is essential. Discuss with classmates how formal education can play a role in teaching people about society's expectations for orderly and civil behavior.

Alexander Pope, self-portrait, 1975.06. Bryn Mawr College Art Collection. Bryn Mawr, PA.

MEET THE WRITER

Alexander Pope
(1688–1744)

Alexander Pope, the most important poet of the eighteenth century, was a child prodigy who could speak in meter even before he could pronounce English properly.

This Long Disease

As a Roman Catholic in Protestant England, Pope was prohibited from attending a university. Fortunately, his father was a retired linen merchant who could afford to educate his son at home, an arrangement that suited Pope because of his delicate health. Early in life, Pope had contracted an illness that stunted his growth and disfigured his body. His servants laced him into a canvas brace so that he could sit upright. With the pains he continually suffered in his head, bones, and joints, it is no wonder Pope spoke of his life as "this long disease."

Success at a Young Age

In spite of his poor health, Pope led a remarkably productive life. At age twenty-three, he published *An Essay on Criticism,* a poem partially inspired by the Roman poet Horace's *Art of Poetry. The Rape of the Lock,* Pope's satiric classical epic, followed one year later. During his thirties, Pope translated into English two enormous Greek epics, Homer's *Iliad* and, with the help of two assistants, Homer's *Odyssey.* In these works, Pope was not limited by his classical models, but instead enhanced them by creating fresh and original works. For this reason, he is sometimes referred to as a neoclassical (that is, new classical) poet.

Pope's early successes inspired envy in lesser writers who then ridiculed him. To defend himself, Pope turned to satire. *The Dunciad* attacks dull writers and shows the forces of stupidity, ignorance, and folly in the world, while *Moral Essays* passes judgment on certain immoral men and women as well as on very rich people who lack common sense and good taste.

During his lifetime, Pope had a reputation for being cruel and ill-natured, but his many friends, including some of the best writers of the day, found him brilliant in conversation, affable, and generous.

Think About the Writer What do you think might have inspired Pope to be so productive despite his many difficulties?

Selection Readability	
Easily Accessible **Accessible** Challenging	These poems include historical context; accessible vocabulary; short excerpts and stanzas.

Heroic Couplets /
from An Essay on Man

Reading Standard 2.5, 3.4 (see pages A48–A50)

Literary Skills Focus

Antithesis Pope frequently uses antitheses. An **antithesis** (an TIHTH uh sihs) expresses contrasting ideas in a grammatically balanced statement: "Give me liberty, or give me death." ("Give me liberty, or kill me" fails as an antithesis because it is not parallel or balanced.) Similarly, Pope balances infinitive against infinitive and adjective against adjective in this line from "Heroic Couplets": "To err is human, to forgive, divine." By compressing elements of similarity and difference, antithesis makes a statement forceful and memorable.

Reading Skills Focus

Identifying the Writer's Stance As a writer, Pope intended to inspire and delight his readers. Thus, his poetry reflects his moral and social values as well as his brilliant ability to entertain. In the selections that follow, Pope uses the structure of heroic couplets (two rhyming lines of iambic pentameter) to concisely and explicitly express his **stance**—his opinion or position—on various topics. In some couplets, he uses antithesis to convey his stance in a more powerful way.

Into Action As you read these selections by Pope, **paraphrase** them, or restate them in your own words. Later, you will use your paraphrases to decipher Pope's stance on each of the topics he addresses.

Passage	Paraphrase
Couplet 1	Making music and writing poetry cannot be taught; these activities are divinely inspired.

Writing Skills Focus

Think as a Reader/Writer

Find It in Your Reading An **antithesis** uses parallel structure to balance contrasting ideas. For example, in couplet 6, "To err is human, to forgive, divine," Pope creates antithesis. As you read, record examples of antithesis in your *Reader/Writer Notebook*.

Language Coach

Antonyms Words with opposite meanings are called **antonyms.** Some antonym pairs are obvious, such as *good* and *bad.* Others are more subtle. In one couplet, Pope uses *art* and *chance* as antonyms. If in this comparison, art refers to "skill" and chance means "luck," then how are these meanings opposite? How are the words *human* and *divine* antonyms? Are the words *thought* and *passion* antonyms?

Reader/Writer Notebook

Use your **RWN** to complete the activities for these selections.

Learn It Online

Follow Pope across the Web with these links.

go.hrw.com H12-615 Go

Selection Resources

Unit 3 Resources, on-level practice and assessment, pp. 55, 59

Teacher One Stop™, on-level lesson plans and all print resources

Holt Audio Library

Holt Audio Library: Selections and Summaries in Spanish

UA: Differentiating Instruction, graphic organizer, pp. 137–138

UA: Supporting Instruction in Spanish, selection summary

ThinkCentral Online Assessment, Selection Standards Check

ThinkCentral Online Remediation

Preteach

English for Academic Success

Language Coach

After reading the **Language Coach,** have students work in pairs to answer the questions. ***Possible responses:*** Art, *or skill, refers to a person's natural ability, while* chance *refers to someone's good fortune.* Divine *means "of, from, or like God or a god," while* human *means "of, relating to, or characteristic of people."* Thought *requires a clear, logical processing of ideas, while* passion *is the absence of all thought and logic.*

Literary Skills Focus

As you read and discuss the selection with students, have them note contrasting ideas that Pope proposes.

Reading Skills Focus

Give students a copy of the Reading Skills Focus graphic organizer before they read. (See **Unit 3 Resources**.) Tell them to use their responses to answer questions on the Applying Your Skills page.

Writing Skills Focus

Have students record examples of antithesis in their **Reader/Writer Notebooks.** Students can use their notes to complete the Writing Skills Focus activity.

Learn It Online

The **Writers' Lives** feature of the Interactive Student Edition offers additional information about this author. Audio or video segments are provided for some authors.

go.hrw.com H12-615 Go

Teacher Preparation
Selection Summary
In these "Heroic Couplets" (and one triplet), Pope shares a variety of personal views and offers words of wisdom and counsel. Among these, Pope praises the artistry of music, advises moderation in accepting new ideas, and espouses quickness in offering praise as well as forgiveness.

Direct Teach

Think About/Talk About
Read with a Purpose Have students read the Read with a Purpose statement. Remind students that people of Pope's time believed that rational thought could improve society.

Analysis
A Literary Focus

Possible responses: *"A little learning" and "a dangerous thing" are parallel; each has an adjective and a noun. In the second line, "Drink deep" and "taste not" are parallel; both are commands consisting of an imperative verb followed by an adverb.*

Extend the Discussion
Comparing According to the first couplet, how are music and poetry similar? ***Possible response:*** *Good music and poetry can be created only by a master; these arts cannot be learned simply by reading a book.*

Antithesis In couplet 6, how does Pope use antithesis to link two different aspects of humanity? ***Possible response:*** *While human beings are capable of both frailty and compassion, compassion is a noble, "divine" trait. Pope creates parallel structure through the infinitives "to err" and "to forgive."*

COUPLETS

Heroic Couplets

by **Alexander Pope**

Read with a Purpose
Read to discover the author's views on subjects such as human nature, proper education, and good writing.

Build Background
Pope is the greatest master of the **heroic couplet,** two rhymed lines of iambic pentameter. (For variety, Pope occasionally introduces a triplet.) Though first used extensively by Chaucer, the heroic couplet derives its name from its appearances in Dryden's and Pope's translations of epic poems. Pope's couplets can stand alone, but they are so carefully arranged that they are more like links of a chain than separable units.

1 Music resembles poetry: in each
Are nameless graces° which no methods° teach,
And which a master hand alone can reach.
—*An Essay on Criticism,* lines 143–145

2 A little learning is a dangerous thing;
Drink deep, or taste not the Pierian° spring. (A)
—*An Essay on Criticism,* lines 215–216

3 Be not the first by whom the new are tried,
Nor yet the last to lay the old aside.
—*An Essay on Criticism,* lines 335–336

4 True ease in writing comes from art, not chance,
As those move easiest who have learned to dance.
—*An Essay on Criticism,* lines 362–363

5 Be thou the first true merit to befriend;
His praise is lost, who stays till all commend.
—*An Essay on Criticism,* lines 474–475

6 Good nature and good sense must ever join;
To err is human, to forgive, divine.
—*An Essay on Criticism,* lines 524–525

1. **nameless graces:** pleasing passages that cannot be explained; **methods:** instruction books for writing poetry.

2. **Pierian** (py IHR ee uhn): an allusion to the Muses, Greek goddesses of the arts and literature. The Muses were said to live in a district of Greece called Pieria.

(A) **Literary Focus** **Antithesis** What examples of parallel structure can you identify in this couplet? Describe the structure.

Universal Access

English Learners
English for Academic Success Help students to identify the subject, verb, and main clause in each couplet. Once they understand this core, ask them to decide how the poet has explained, qualified, or elaborated on it. Understanding the grammatical structure of the couplets will help students locate instances of parallelism.

✔ See the **English Language Skill Builder** in **UA: Differentiating Instruction.**

Struggling Readers
Benchmark Students Remind students that before they can identify the writer's beliefs, they must fully understand the author's message. Have students read couplet 3. You might say: "After I read these lines, I try to identify key words and phrases. I think the phrases 'Be not the first' and 'nor yet the last' and the words 'new' and 'old' are important to the meaning of the couplet. I can paraphrase these lines by saying 'Do not be the first person to accept new ideas; however, do not be the last to discard outdated ideas.'"

View Across Greenwich Park Toward London by Jean Rigaud (c. 1700–1757). Painted for the King Louis XV of France. Roy Miles Fine Paintings, London.

7 Hope springs eternal in the human breast:
Man never is, but always to be blest. **B**
—*An Essay on Man,* Epistle I, lines 95–96

8 'Tis education forms the common mind,
Just as the twig is bent, the tree's inclined.
—*Moral Essays,* Epistle I, lines 149–150

9 But when to mischief mortals bend their will,
How soon they find fit instruments of ill! **C**
—*The Rape of the Lock,* Canto III, lines 125–126

10 Satire's my weapon, but I'm too discreet
To run amuck, and tilt° at all I meet.
—*Imitations of Horace, Satire I,* Book II, lines 69–70

10. tilt: charge at or thrust a weapon toward an opponent.

B Literary Focus **Antithesis** What is the purpose of the comma in the second line of this couplet? How does this comma affect the antithesis?

C Reading Focus **Identifying the Writer's Stance** What does this couplet indicate about Pope's view of his fellow human beings?

Think About/Talk About

Comprehension

C Reading Focus

Possible response: *Pope cynically believes that when given the opportunity, people will not hesitate to do evil.*

Analysis

B Literary Focus

Possible response: *It indicates a pause and emphasizes the antithesis between actually being "blest" and hoping to be "blest."*

Extend the Discussion

Identifying Writer's Stance Based on couplet 8, what effect does Pope believe education has on the general public? ***Possible response:*** *Education forms the mind and directs its growth.*

Interpreting What relationship does the metaphor in couplet 8 illustrate? ***Possible response:*** *The metaphor of the twig and the tree probably means that the ideas people hold in their adulthood originate from their childhood education. Bending a twig, or an untrained mind, in a certain direction ensures that the tree, or educated mind, will follow.*

Advanced Learners

Enrichment Have students form pairs and choose two heroic couplets to analyze. Instruct partners to discuss the ideas expressed in the couplets. Do they agree with Pope's counsel? How do antithesis and parallel structure affect his tone? Have each pair share their thoughts with the class.

AAVE Students Who Use African American Vernacular English

English for Academic Success Read aloud couplet 8 on p. 617. Point out that in these lines, the poet uses informal, literary English, shortening the phrase *It is* into *'Tis.* Discuss with students why the author chooses to use informal constructions here, and why it is appropriate for the meter and structure of the couplet. As students read Pope's work, have them list other examples of informal English they notice in their **Reader/Writer Notebooks.**

PHILOSOPHICAL POEM

from An Essay on Man

by **Alexander Pope**

Read with a Purpose

Read to discover why Pope calls humanity the "glory, jest, and riddle of the world."

Build Background

Published when he was forty-five, *An Essay on Man* is Pope's long (1,304 lines) philosophical poem. Pope's lifetime of reading, in both English and foreign languages, greatly influenced its composition. The poem is concerned with "man," by which Pope means the whole human race, as well as the entire universe. Keep in mind that the ideas in the poem are not merely the private opinions of Pope and his friends but reflections that can be traced in the works of many authors, including Plato, Aristotle, St. Thomas Aquinas, Dante, Erasmus, Shakespeare, Bacon, and Milton.

Know then thyself,° presume not God to scan;°
The proper study of mankind is man.
Placed on this isthmus of a middle state,° **A**
A being darkly wise, and rudely great:
With too much knowledge for the skeptic° side,
With too much weakness for the Stoic's pride,°
He hangs between; in doubt to act, or rest;
In doubt to deem himself a god, or beast;
In doubt his mind or body to prefer;
Born but to die, and reasoning but to err;
Alike in ignorance, his reason such,
Whether he thinks too little, or too much:
Chaos of thought and passion, all confused;
Still° by himself abused, or disabused;°
Created half to rise, and half to fall; **B**
Great lord of all things, yet a prey to all;
Sole judge of truth, in endless error hurled:
The glory, jest, and riddle of the world!

1. Know then thyself: moral rule of Socrates and other ethical philosophers. **scan:** pry into; speculate about.
3. Placed . . . middle state: having the rational intellect of angels and the physical body of beasts.
5. skeptic: The ancient Skeptics doubted that humans can gain accurate knowledge of anything. They emphasized the limitations of human knowledge.
6. Stoic's pride: The ancient Stoics' ideal was a calm acceptance of life and an indifference to both pain and pleasure. Stoics are called proud because they refused to recognize human limitations.
14. still: always; continually. **disabused:** undeceived.

A **Reading Focus** **Identifying the Writer's Stance** What does Pope's choice of the word *isthmus* reveal about his thoughts on the place of humankind in the universe?

B **Literary Focus** **Antithesis** How is this line an example of antithesis? What does the antithesis reveal about humanity?

Analyzing Visuals

Connecting to the Text Eton College is an elite British high school founded by Henry VI and attended by many prominent people, including members of the royal family. In this photograph, boys from Eton are celebrating a school holiday. How might these boys exemplify Pope's line "The glory, jest, and riddle of the world"?

Teacher Preparation
Selection Summary

This excerpt from "An Essay on Man" is rich in antitheses. Pope explores his paradoxical view about humanity, which, he says, is "the glory, jest, and riddle of the world."

Direct Teach

Think About/Talk About

Read with a Purpose Ask students to note Pope's view of humanity's accomplishments, contradictions, and absurdities as they read.

Comprehension

A Reading Focus

Possible response: *Human beings are located on a middle ground between divine rationality and animal physicality.*

Analysis

B Literary Focus

Possible responses: *The poet repeats the words "half to . . ." before the contrasting verbs "rise" and "fall." This line reveals the opposition between the human mind, which helps people rise above their animal nature and physical passions, which can cause people to behave as beasts.*

Analyzing Visuals

Connecting to the Text: *The funny costumes the boys are wearing make them both a "jest" and a "riddle," since it is not clear why they are dressed this way. Some people might also consider them the "glory" of the world due to their social position.*

California Standards, p. 619

- **Reading Standard 2.5** Analyze an author's implicit and explicit philosophical assumptions and beliefs about a subject.
- **Reading Standard 3.3** Analyze the ways in which irony, tone, mood, the author's style, and the "sound" of language achieve specific rhetorical or aesthetic purposes or both.
- **Reading Standard 3.4** Analyze ways in which poets use imagery, personification, figures of speech, and sounds to evoke readers' emotions.
- **Writing Standard 1.4** Enhance meaning by employing rhetorical devices, including the extended use of parallelism, repetition, and analogy; the incorporation of visual aids (e.g., graphs, tables, pictures); and the issuance of a call for action.

Applying Your Skills

Reading Standard 2.5, 3.3, 3.4 (see pages A48–A50)
Writing Standard 1.4 (see pages A51–A52)

Heroic Couplets / *from* An Essay on Man

Literary Response and Analysis

Reading Skills Focus

Quick Check

1. To what does Pope compare an educated mind?
2. What is the "proper study of mankind"?
3. Who is "lord of all things, yet a prey to all"?

Read with a Purpose

4. After reading both selections, how do you think Pope sees human beings as the "glory" of this world? as its "jest"? as its "riddle"?

Reading Skills: Identifying the Writer's Stance

5. Add a column to your chart, explaining what Pope's ideas reveal about his beliefs and values.

Passage	Paraphrase	Writer's Stance
Couplet 1	Making music and writing poetry cannot be taught; these activities are divinely inspired.	Artistic inspiration comes from God.

Literary Skills Focus

Literary Analysis

6. **Extend** Think of some examples of how a little learning could be a dangerous thing (couplet 2).
7. **Interpret** How is satire a weapon? According to couplet 10, why does Pope show restraint in using satire?
8. **Infer** In *An Essay on Man,* Pope often says something flattering about humanity, only to follow it with something critical. Of what characteristics does he think we should be proud or ashamed?
9. **Compare** How does Pope's view of humanity compare with Hamlet's view in the following lines from *Hamlet,* Act II, Scene 2? How does it compare with your own view?

> What a piece of work is man! how noble in reason! how infinite in faculties! in form and moving how express and admirable! in action how like an angel! in apprehension how like a god! the beauty of the world, the paragon of animals!

Literary Skills: Antithesis

10. **Analyze** How is antithesis used in line 4 of the excerpt from *An Essay on Man*?
11. **Evaluate** How does Pope's use of antithesis help you understand his opinions about human nature?

Literary Skills Review: Tone

12. **Analyze** The attitude a writer takes toward his or her subject is called **tone.** Tone can usually be described with an adjective, such as *pessimistic* or *humorous.* Describe Pope's tone in the excerpt from *An Essay on Man*. Explain your answer, using evidence from the text.

Writing Skills Focus

Think as a Reader/Writer

Use It in Your Writing What are your beliefs about human nature, education, writing, giving praise, and other topics that Pope addresses? Use antithesis to write three statements that express your beliefs about some of these topics.

What Do You Think Now? Would Pope say that people are essentially civilized and ordered or essentially chaotic? Explain your answer.

Universal Access

Struggling Writers

Some students may need additional scaffolding to complete the Writing Skills Focus activity. Before they write their statements containing antithesis, have them work in pairs to analyze Pope's use of antithesis in his heroic couplets. Direct students to note how Pope often uses parallelism to present his contrasting ideas. After students review the examples of antithesis they noted in their **Reader/Writer Notebooks,** have them write a few sentences expressing their beliefs about education or human nature. Next, have students rewrite their sentences into statements expressing contrasting ideas that use parallel structure. Remind students that parallel structure repeats grammatical structures.

Check for Understanding

Independent Practice

Reading Skills Focus

Possible responses:

1. *a pruned tree*
2. *mankind itself*
3. *man*
4. *Man has the mental powers of a god, but is limited by base passions of the body like a beast. This contradiction makes him both the glory and jest of the world.*
5. *Have students explain what Pope's ideas reveal about his beliefs.*

Literary Skills Focus

Possible responses:

6. *Knowing a little about medicine but not enough to practice it safely can be dangerous if one attempts to practice it.*
7. *Satire is a weapon because it can be used to attack someone. Pope is too discreet to attack anyone with abandon.*
8. *Pope thinks we should be proud of qualities such as wisdom and judgment and ashamed of our weakness, doubt, and error.*
9. *Hamlet shares Pope's admiration for man's intellectual faculties, but does not lament the base passions of mankind.*
10. *"Darkly wise" and "rudely great" are grammatically and structurally parallel. Both consist of two-syllable adverbs preceding single-syllable adjectives. Each phrase also offers contrasts: We associate wisdom with light, not darkness, and greatness with refinement, not rudeness.*
11. *It gives emphasis to Pope's mixed feelings toward mankind.*
12. *Pope's tone is one of both of admiration and contempt.*

What Do You Think Now?

To help students respond to the question, have them consider the conditions that are conducive to an orderly society and the conditions that lead to confusion or chaos.

Reading Skills Focus

Objectives

Students will analyze the way in which irony achieves specific rhetorical or aesthetic purposes.

Unit 3 Resources, Reading Focus Skill Builder, p. 54

Teacher One Stop™, on-level lesson plan and all print resources

Direct Teach

Identifying Tone

This essay gives students practice in identifying the writer's tone in *The Rape of the Lock*. Have students read the feature and complete the Your Turn activity before reading the poem.

Check for Understanding

Your Turn

Possible response: *The Baron values fame and glory as revealed by the words, "triumph," "glorious," and "my honor, name and praise." The phrase "glorious prize" demonstrates Pope's view that the act is not brave but foolish and trivial. His tone is mocking and humorous.*

Learn It Online

For a multimedia version of the instruction found on this page, use the **PowerNotes** Reading Skills Focus presentation.

go.hrw.com H12-620 Go

Reading Skills Focus

Reading Standard 3.3 (see pages A48–A50)

from The Rape of the Lock

Identifying Tone by **Kylene Beers**

Tone can describe a person's voice, a piece of music, shades of color, or the tension in a muscle. In literature, **tone** reflects an author's attitude toward the subject, a character, or the reader. Authors do not always directly state what they think about what they write. Instead, they choose words and include details that imply their stance. These words and details contribute to the tone of a work of literature. Identifying tone can help you determine the author's purpose and lead you to the work's theme.

In *The Rape of the Lock,* Alexander Pope mocks the way aristocrats behave when they are "seeing and being seen." In the following passage, for example, Pope describes a group of wealthy, attractive young men and women as they meet at a fashionable court.

> In various talk th' instructive hours they
> passed,
> Who gave the ball, or paid the visit last;
> One speaks the glories of the British queen,
> And one describes a charming Indian screen;
> A third interprets motions, looks, and eyes;
> At every word a reputation dies.
> Snuff, or the fan, supply each pause of chat,
> With singing, laughing, ogling, and all that.

Notice the details Pope includes, and consider what they imply. The young people gossip about recent social events, flatter the queen, and anticipate each others' social mistakes, but what is their goal? Why are these behaviors and attitudes important to the young people? "At every word," Pope observes, "a reputation dies." Pope's wry language indicates that the young people vie for status and approval while hoping for the downfall of others. He renders their conversation superficial and their actions insignificant through his choice of the word *chat* and his use of the direct rhyme "and all that." Given the details he includes and the words he uses, what does Pope think about his characters? His tone indicates he finds them silly and more than a little phony. Pope's characters resemble today's celebrities who are "famous for being famous" rather than for anything they produce or do.

The Author and His Publisher (1784) by Thomas Rowlandson (1756–1827).
Yale Center for British Art, Paul Mellon Collection, U.S.

Your Turn

Read the following lines from *The Rape of the Lock,* and then discuss with a partner the tone of the Baron's victory speech. Which words reveal the Baron's values? Which words express Pope's views about the Baron's behavior? (In the third line, "nymphs" are lovely young women.) What is Pope's tone in this passage?

> "Let wreaths of triumph now my
> temples twine,"
> The victor cried, "the glorious prize is
> mine! . . .
> While nymphs take treats, or assigna-
> tions give,
> So long my honor, name, and praise
> shall live!"

Learn It Online

Learn how to identify tone through *PowerNotes*.

go.hrw.com H12-620 Go

California Standards, p. 620

- **Reading Standard 3.3** Analyze the ways in which irony, tone, mood, the author's style, and the "sound" of language achieve specific rhetorical or aesthetic purposes or both.

Reading Standard 3.1, 3.3 (see pages A48–A50)

from The Rape of the Lock

Literary Skills Focus

Mock Epic *The Rape of the Lock* is a **mock epic,** a poem that takes the form of an epic and treats a trivial subject in a lofty manner. Humor arises from the discrepancy between the insignificant subject (in this case, the snipping of a piece of hair) and the grandiose treatment. Pope combines the classic with the absurd by putting traditional devices found in serious epics into a tame, domestic context. For example, classical epics have deities who intervene in human affairs. Following these models, Pope creates "sylphs," tiny, airy spirits who try to prevent the assault on Belinda's curl.

Reading Skills Focus

Identifying Tone The attitude a writer takes toward the reader, a subject, or a character is called **tone.** Pope conveys a satirical tone through the mock epic form, contrasting lofty style with trivial subjects.

Into Action As you read, use a chart like the one below to record words and details that will help you identify Pope's tone.

Person or Event	Line Number(s)	Words and Details Pope Uses
Queen Anne	7–8	Pope describes the queen as taking "counsel," or advice, and "tea" as if they are equally important.

Writing Skills Focus

Think as a Reader/Writer

Find It in Your Reading Pope borrows the epic's convention of the **catalog,** a long list of objects or qualities. In an epic, a catalog details a warrior's weapons, qualities, and victories, or lists the characters' noble ancestry. Pope uses catalogs to lend a grandiose flair to his work, as when he describes how aristocrats pass their time. In your *Reader/Writer Notebook,* note Pope's catalogs and how they influence the poem's tone.

TechFocus As you read this selection, notice how Pope conveys his tone. How does he show that he is speaking satirically?

Vocabulary

reputation (rehp yoo TAY shuhn) *n.:* people's opinion of a person. *One young lady strives to maintain her reputation while ruining those of her rivals.*

stratagems (STRAT uh juhmz) *n. pl.:* clever plans to achieve a goal. *Belinda's stratagems help her win the card game.*

ambitious (am BIHSH uhs) *adj.:* aiming for a goal that is hard to reach. *The man who tries to win the affection of indifferent Belinda is ambitious indeed.*

radiant (RAY dee uhnt) *adj.:* shining with beams of light. *The many candles of Hampton Court projected a radiant glow on the fashionable crowd.*

consecrate (KAHN suh krayt) *v.:* make honorable and sacred. *A true gentleman would consecrate his affection for his lady by treating her well.*

Language Coach

Suffixes A suffix at the end of a word can help you identify the word's part of speech. The suffix *–ant* is found at the end of many adjectives, such as *radiant.* You can form a related verb by changing the suffix to *–ate.* What do you think the verb *radiate* means? What Vocabulary word shares the same suffix?

Learn It Online
Get to know the Vocabulary words online through Word Watch.
go.hrw.com H12-621 Go

Reader/Writer Notebook
Use your **RWN** to complete the activities for this selection.

California Standards, pp. 621–631

- **Reading Standard 3.1** Analyze characteristics of subgenres (e.g., satire, parody, allegory, pastoral) that are used in poetry, prose, plays, novels, short stories, essays, and other basic genres.
- **Reading Standard 3.3** Analyze the ways in which irony, tone, mood, the author's style, and the "sound" of language achieve specific rhetorical or aesthetic purposes or both.

Preteach

Introducing Vocabulary

- Review the Vocabulary words, definitions, and sentences.
- To reinforce the importance of the Vocabulary words, point out that the poem humorously contrasts the triviality of the act and the importance ascribed to it. In this account of a *radiant,* later *consecrated* lock of hair, Pope mocks the nobility's *ambitious* desires to advance their *reputations* through silly *stratagems.*

English for Academic Success

Language Coach

Have students think of other examples with adjectives that have the suffix *–ant.* [*brilliant, elegant, dormant, buoyant*] Then, have students work in pairs to answer the **Language Coach** questions. ***Possible responses:*** *The word* radiate *means "to emit light in the form of rays or waves." The Vocabulary word* consecrate *shares the same suffix.*

Literary Skills Focus

As students read and discuss the selection, have them point out details that characterize the writing as a mock epic.

Reading Skills Focus

Give students a copy of the Reading Skills Focus graphic organizer. (See **Unit 3 Resources.**) Tell them to use their responses to answer questions on the Applying Your Skills page.

Writing Skills Focus

Have students note Pope's use of catalogs and their effect on the poem's tone in their **Reader/Writer Notebooks.** Students can use their notes to complete the Writing Focus Skills activity.

Learn It Online
Send students to **Word Watch** for audio presentations, synonyms and antonyms, and brief histories of word origins.
go.hrw.com H12-621 Go

Teacher Preparation

Selection Plot Summary

By Canto III of *The Rape of the Lock,* the fair Belinda has joined friends at a gathering at Hampton Court. There, she and others of wealth and leisure, including the Baron, sip coffee, gossip, flirt, and play cards. The Baron schemes to shear a lock of Belinda's hair and does so despite the defensive efforts of the sylphs, or sprites. Using a volley of snuff and a hairpin, the outraged Belinda engages the Baron in battle. When the Baron shows no remorse, Belinda concedes her loss. Her consolation, the speaker suggests, is that her lock of hair will rise into heaven as a star, an absurd parody of a classical metamorphosis.

MOCK EPIC

from The Rape of the Lock

by **Alexander Pope**

Read with a Purpose

Read to experience Alexander Pope's amusing look at the battle of the sexes in eighteenth-century England.

Build Background

The title of Pope's comic masterpiece means "the violent theft of a lock of hair." The poem is based on a real incident in which a lock belonging to a rich and fashionable young lady named Arabella Fermor was stolen by an equally rich and fashionable young man named Robert, Lord Petre. When Robert snipped a curl of Arabella's hair, he caused a quarrel between the Fermor and Petre families. As it turned out, the feud subsided into laughter, thanks largely to Alexander Pope.

Pope's poem is divided into five sections called cantos. *Canto I begins like a proper epic, with a statement of the subject and an invocation to the Muse—a female deity who was supposed to inspire poets and other artists. Pope, however, clearly signals his comic intentions in the very first couplet:*

What dire offense from amorous causes springs,
 What mighty contests rise from trivial things,
 I sing—

In Canto II, Belinda and her friends take a boat up the river Thames to a party. All who see her admire the two beautiful curled locks that hang down her back. And despite the small army of sprites (spirits) assigned to protect Belinda's beautiful hair, the Baron resolves to possess these locks.

A Woman in Blue (Portrait of the Duchess of Beaufort) (1770) by Thomas Gainsborough. Hermitage, St. Petersburg, Russia.

Direct Teach

Think About/Talk About

Read with a Purpose Have students read the Read with a Purpose statement. Ask them to look for details that reveal Pope's perspective on members of the aristocracy, their preoccupation with marriage, and the socialization between the sexes.

Responses to Margin Questions

Lines 1–16 *Life at Hampton Court is full of scandal and gossip.*

Lines 21–22 *Judges and jury members get hungry around dinnertime, so they quickly finish up their work, signing papers that will result in hangings so they can rush home to eat on time. The couplet is witty because it expresses a sad truth about human selfishness and inhumanity in an elegant way.*

Lines 23–28 *Belinda "burns to encounter" knights; her ambition is to have young men fall in love with her and then to reject them.*

Lines 33–52 *Her companions cool coffee and guard her gown against spills. The Baron is also drinking coffee, and its "vapors" have inspired him to scheme about ways to get a lock of Belinda's hair.*

Universal Access

EL English Learners

English for Academic Success Explain to students that in this mock epic, Pope makes fun of the aristocracy, and he assumes the reader has a lot of background knowledge. For instance, "gave the ball" in line 12 refers to holding a social dance; "Indian screen" in line 14 denotes a fire screen made in India, often used to protect ladies from sparks; the "board" in line 33 is an archaic word for a "dining table"; the "nosegay" in line 69 is a corsage; and "peer" in line 75 means "nobleman." Have students work in pairs to find references they do not understand. Help students clarify any confusing passages.

from Canto III

Close by those meads, forever crowned with flowers,
Where Thames with pride surveys his rising towers,
There stands a structure° of majestic frame,
Which from the neighboring Hampton takes its name.
Here Britain's statesmen oft the fall foredoom
Of foreign tyrants, and of nymphs° at home;
Here thou, great Anna!° whom three realms obey,
Dost sometimes counsel take—and sometimes tea.
Hither the heroes and the nymphs resort,
To taste awhile the pleasures of a court;
In various talk th' instructive hours they passed,
Who gave the ball, or paid the visit last;
One speaks the glory of the British queen,
And one describes a charming Indian screen;
A third interprets motions, looks, and eyes;
At every word a reputation dies. Ⓐ
Snuff,° or the fan,° supply each pause of chat,
With singing, laughing, ogling, and all that.
Meanwhile, declining from the noon of day,
The sun obliquely shoots his burning ray;
The hungry judges soon the sentence sign,
And wretches hang that jurymen may dine. . . . Ⓑ
Belinda now, whom thirst of fame invites,
Burns to encounter two adventurous knights,
At omber° singly to decide their doom;
And swells her breast with conquests yet to come. . . .
The nymph exulting fills with shouts the sky;
The walls, the woods, and long canals reply.
Oh thoughtless mortals! ever blind to fate,
Too soon dejected and too soon elate.
Sudden, these honors shall be snatched away,
And cursed forever this victorious day.
For lo! the board with cups and spoons is crowned,
The berries° crackle, and the mill° turns round;
On shining altars of Japan° they raise

Ⓐ **Literary Focus** **Mock Epic** How is the epic form mocked in Canto III, lines 11–16?

Ⓑ **Reading Focus** **Identifying Tone** The central action of the poem is trivial. Lines 21–22, however, describe some real life-and-death situations. What tone does Pope use in these lines?

Vocabulary **reputation** (rehp yoo TAY shuhn) *n.:* people's opinion of a person.

3. structure: Hampton Court, a royal residence on the river Thames, upstream from London.

6. nymphs: young ladies.

7. Anna: Queen Anne (1665–1714), who ruled England, Ireland, and Scotland.

1–16. *In lines 1–8, notice how Pope juxtaposes, or places side by side, the grandiose and the trivial: At Hampton Court, statesmen discuss the fall of tyrants—and also of young ladies. Meanwhile, Queen Anne is sometimes served political counsel—and at other times, tea.*

? *What does line 16 tell you about life at the court?*

17. snuff: powdered tobacco product sniffed or rubbed on the teeth and gums. **fan:** standard equipment for a lady.

21–22. *These clever lines have been quoted for centuries.*

? *What do these two lines mean?*

25. omber: card game for three players, popular in the eighteenth century.

? **23–28.** *What is Belinda's ambition? How does Pope describe Belinda?*

33–52. *In this verse paragraph, Pope sets the scene for the grand offense. The rich are gathered in a sitting room at Hampton Court, drinking endless cups of coffee.*

? *What are Belinda's companions doing? What is the Baron doing?*

34. berries: coffee beans. **mill:** coffee grinder.

35. altars of Japan: small, lacquered tables.

Think About/Talk About

Comprehension

Ⓑ Reading Focus

Possible response: *Pope uses a serious tone in these lines, in which the sad truth about human selfishness and inhumanity is exposed.*

Analysis

Ⓐ Literary Focus

Possible response: *In lines 11–16, when describing the "various talk" of the characters, he mentions the conversational topic "the glory of the queen" as a topic alongside "who gave the ball," which trivializes the former topic. Pope ends these lines by characterizing the characters' conversation as malicious gossip when he writes, "At every word a reputation dies."*

Extend the Discussion

Antithesis Why is line 30 an example of antithesis? ***Possible response:*** *"Too soon dejected" and "too soon elate" are structurally parallel and show the paradoxical tendency of humankind to both despair and rejoice prematurely.*

Vocabulary: Own the Word

reputation: Ask students to name things that might improve a child's *reputation* in the eyes of his or her parents. ***Possible responses:*** *getting good grades in school; keeping his or her room clean; treating siblings with respect*

Struggling Readers

Benchmark Students Point out how the writer describes the card game in line 25 as if it were a major battle in an epic poem. What words and details render the card game a serious struggle? Ask students to define Pope's attitude toward the amusing pursuits of the rich.

✔ See **UA: Differentiating Instruction** for a graphic organizer to scaffold instruction for struggling readers.

Advanced Learners

Acceleration Explain to students that Pope uses certain literary devices to create his mock epic. Ask students the double meaning of the verb *take* in line 8. [*It means both to accept (advice) and to drink (tea).*] Explain that this figure of speech is called *zeugma* (ZOOG muh), which occurs when a verb has two subjects or objects, or an adjective modifies two nouns, yet the two contexts have different connotations. What is the effect of the zeugma here? [*By elevating the act of drinking tea to the level of talking to a royal counselor, Pope sets the comic tone of the mock epic.*]

Model the Skill

- Model how to analyze a **mock epic.** Explain to students that Pope, in order to mock the concerns of the aristocrats of eighteenth-century England, replaces elements of the traditional epic with less serious elements.
- Read aloud line 63 and lines 67–74. Explain that traditional epics featured Greek and Roman gods who played significant roles in aiding or deceiving humans. Line 63 in *The Rape of the Lock* shows sprites, rather than gods, coming to Belinda's aid.

Guided Practice: Apply

Read-Talk-Write Ask students to read lines 55–60. Have students form pairs to discuss what happens in these lines. Have students write down how Pope describes the "weapon" and how it illustrates the mock-epic genre.

Think About/Talk About

Extend the Discussion

Paraphrasing Why couldn't the sprites protect Belinda from the advancing Baron? ***Possible response:*** *Ariel, the chief sprite, discerns that Belinda loves the Baron, and the sprites are powerless to block true love.*

Responses to Margin Questions

Lines 55–62 *These lines describe how Clarissa arms the Baron (with scissors) as a lady would arm a knight.*

Lines 75–82 *Although a sylph is cut in two trying to protect the lock, the Baron succeeds in snipping a curl of Belinda's hair with scissors.*

Lines 83–88 *Belinda's shrieks are compared to those that might be heard when a husband or a lapdog dies or when an expensive piece of china breaks.*

Lines 89–100 *The Baron's attitude is amusing, for his deed is so trivial. Like the trendy activities he mentions, such as traveling in a coach with six horses and reading Atalantis, his fame will be short-lived.*

The silver lamp; the fiery spirits blaze:
From silver spouts the grateful liquors glide,
While China's earth° receives the smoking tide.° (C)
At once they gratify their scent and taste,
And frequent cups prolong the rich repast.
Straight hover round the fair her airy band;
Some, as she sipped, the fuming liquor fanned,
Some o'er her lap their careful plumes displayed,
Trembling, and conscious of the rich brocade.
Coffee (which makes the politician wise,
And see through all things with his half-shut eyes)
Sent up in vapors to the Baron's brain
New stratagems, the radiant lock to gain.
Ah, cease, rash youth! desist ere 'tis too late,
Fear the just gods, and think of Scylla's fate!°
Changed to a bird, and sent to flit in air,
She dearly pays for Nisus' injured hair!
    But when to mischief mortals bend their will,
How soon they find fit instruments of ill!
Just then, Clarissa drew with tempting grace
A two-edged weapon from her shining case:
So ladies in romance assist their knight,
Present the spear, and arm him for the fight.
He takes the gift with reverence, and extends
The little engine° on his fingers' ends;
This just behind Belinda's neck he spread,
As o'er the fragrant steams she bends her head.
Swift to the lock a thousand sprites repair,
A thousand wings, by turns, blow back the hair;
And thrice they twitched the diamond in her ear;
Thrice she looked back, and thrice the foe drew near.
Just in that instant, anxious Ariel° sought
The close recesses of the virgin's thought;
As on the nosegay in her breast reclined,
He watched th' ideas rising in her mind,
Sudden he viewed, in spite of all her art,
An earthly lover lurking at her heart.°
Amazed, confused, he found his power expired,
Resigned to fate, and with a sigh retired.
    The peer now spreads the glittering *forfex*° wide,
T' enclose the lock; now joins it, to divide.

38. China's earth: cups made of earthenware. **smoking tide:** coffee.

50. Scylla's fate: In Greek mythology, Scylla (SIHL uh) is turned into a seabird by the gods after she betrays her father, Nisus, by cutting off his purple lock of hair, on which his life and kingdom depend.

? **55–62.** *What action is described in these lines?*

60. engine: instrument.

63–74. *Having been armed by an accomplice, the Baron advances toward Belinda's back and then retreats three times in rapid sequence. This comical image mimics the rhythms of fencing.*

67. Ariel: chief of the heavenly sprites sent to protect Belinda.

72. earthly lover . . . heart: If in her heart Belinda wants the Baron to succeed, the sprites cannot protect her.

75. *forfex:* Latin for "scissors."

? **75–82.** *How is the theft of the lock accomplished?*

(C) **Literary Focus** **Mock Epic** In what ways is this treatment of coffee-making characteristic of a mock epic?

Vocabulary **stratagems** (STRAT uh juhmz) *n. pl.:* clever plans to achieve a goal.

Reaching Reluctant Readers

Present students with the following questions to establish connections between the poem and their own identities and experiences.

- How are wealthy people today like or unlike the wealthy courtiers in Pope's time?
- What modern recreational activities are as frivolous as the activities Pope's characters engage in?
- What trivial incident that could happen today would successfully satirize the concerns of the wealthy?
- When have you noticed people giving too much importance to trivial events?

Even then, before the fatal engine closed,
A wretched sylph too fondly interposed;
Fate urged the shears, and cut the sylph in twain,
(But airy substance soon unites again).
The meeting points the sacred hair dissever
From the fair head, forever, and forever!
 Then flashed the living lightning from her eyes,
And screams of horror rend th' affrighted skies.
Not louder shrieks to pitying Heaven are cast,
When husbands, or when lapdogs breathe their last;
Or when rich china vessels fallen from high,
In glittering dust, and painted fragments lie!
 "Let wreaths of triumph° now my temples twine,"
The victor cried, "the glorious prize is mine!
While fish in streams, or birds delight in air,
Or in a coach and six° the British fair,
As long as *Atalantis*° shall be read,
Or the small pillow grace a lady's bed,
While visits shall be paid on solemn days,
When numerous wax lights in bright order blaze,
While nymphs take treats, or assignations give,
So long my honor, name, and praise shall live!
What time would spare, from steel receives its date,°
And monuments, like men, submit to fate!" . . .

83–88. *Belinda screams in horror at the abduction of her lock.*
? *To what three kinds of shrieks is Belinda's shriek compared?*
89–100. *Like a victorious epic hero, the Baron sings of his mighty conquest, observing that while men and monuments shall pass away, his name shall live forever.*
? *Why is the Baron's attitude amusing? How long will the Baron's reputation really last—and how can you tell?*
89. wreaths of triumph: like the ones worn by athletic and military heroes in ancient times.
92. coach and six: coach with six horses.
93. *Atalantis:* *The New Atalantis* (1709), a fashionable novel by Mrs. Delarivière Manley, which thinly disguises some contemporary scandals.
99. date: destruction.

Think About/Talk About

Analysis

Ⓒ Literary Focus

Possible response: *Coffee-making, a mundane and leisurely activity, is treated as if it is a lofty and important activity.*

Extend the Discussion

Interpreting Using the gloss for line 50, how would you interpret lines 49–53? ***Possible response:*** *These lines warn the Baron: "Stop before it's too late." They remind the reader that Scylla in Greek mythology was changed into a bird because she cut her father's hair.*

Wit Why is the heroic couplet in lines 53–54 a good example of wit? ***Possible response:*** *It expresses a truth about human nature: that people have a tendency to make mischief and that it is all too easy a goal to achieve. This idea is expressed with economy and elegance.*

Vocabulary: Own the Word

stratagems: Ask students to explain what the Baron hoped to accomplish as a result of his *stratagems.* ***Possible response:*** *He hoped to devise a clever plan that would help him get a lock of Belinda's hair.*

MUSIC LINK

A View of the Fireworks and Illuminations at his Grace the Duke of Richmond's at Whitehall and on the River Thames (1749).

Water Music

In *The Rape of the Lock,* Belinda rides a "painted Vessel," a decorated barge, down the river, "While melting Musick steals upon the Sky." During Pope's time, noble families hired musicians to accompany their journeys along the Thames River. In 1717, German composer George Frideric Handel (1685–1759) composed his famous *Water Music* for a celebratory boat ride for the new king, George I. The debut was a hit with the king, who enjoyed the one-hour composition so much that he insisted it be played three times. In 2005, a London documentary team re-created the original performance, with musicians wearing authentic costumes and playing period instruments.

Ask Yourself

Do you think the aristocrats in Pope's poem would have appreciated Handel's music? Why or why not?

Universal Access

Students with Disabilities

Have students identify adjectives and actions that describe the characters of Belinda and the Baron. Ask them to consider how the portrayals of these characters support Pope's critical view of these characters.

✔ See **UA: Differentiating Instruction** for a graphic organizer to scaffold instruction for students with disabilities.

Music Link

Ask Yourself

Possible responses: *The aristocrats in Pope's poem would likely have appreciated Handel's music; the style of the music was well suited to royalty and celebratory occasions. The music would have suited Belinda's boat ride early in the poem perfectly.*

Model the Skill

- Model **identifying tone,** or inferring the writer's attitude toward people and events in the poem by analyzing details.
- Tell students that, in line 16, Belinda's weapon against the Baron is a handful of snuff, rather than a sword or axe as one would expect for a true battle. By having this comical assault serve as the turning point of the battle, Pope is trying to show the pointlessness and pettiness of most quarrels among the rich.

Guided Practice: Apply

Think-Pair-Share Have students form pairs to compare and contrast the battle scene Pope describes with a traditional battle scene in an epic poem. Ask students to compare and contrast the mood or atmosphere, tone, and overall effect of the scenes. After students have completed their work, invite volunteers to share their ideas with the class.

Think About/Talk About

Responses to Margin Questions

Lines 1–8 *Belinda and her friends shout at the Baron and begin an "attack." Pope describes these ridiculous actions as if Greek gods are waging war against each other.*

Lines 9–20 *In a true epic, the main characters would clash together in a fight to the death; in this mock battle, the weapons are snuff and a hairpin, and Belinda's victory takes the form of making the Baron sneeze.*

Lines 29–38 *Belinda cries for her lock to be replaced, but fate (or Heaven) determines that it is too precious for ordinary humans to keep.*

In Canto IV, Pope describes an incident that occurs in all proper epics: a descent into the underworld. Just as Virgil had Aeneas travel down to Hades, Pope has Umbriel, a "melancholy sprite," fly down to a dismal, imaginary place called the Cave of Spleen. (Spleen is the eighteenth-century term for depression; rich, idle people were particularly subject to spleen in Pope's day.) In the cave, Umbriel obtains a vial of "soft sobs, melting griefs, and flowing tears," as well as an immense bag full of "sighs, sobs, and passions," which somewhat resembles the bag of unfavorable winds in Homer's Odyssey, *given to Odysseus to keep tightly closed so his ship won't be blown off course. Umbriel then returns to the earth's surface and empties the contents of the bag and vial over Belinda and her friend, who is even angrier than Belinda. The canto ends with Belinda lamenting to the Baron:*

"O, hadst thou, cruel! been content to seize
Hairs less in sight, or any hairs but these!"

The others in Belinda's tea-party audience shed tears of pity, but the Baron ignores her pleas: "Fate and Jove had stopped the Baron's ears."

from Canto V

. . . "To arms, to arms!" the fierce virago° cries,
And swift as lightning to the combat flies.
All side in parties, and begin th' attack;
Fans clap, silks rustle, and tough whalebones° crack;
Heroes' and heroines' shouts confus'dly rise,
And bass and treble voices strike the skies. **D**
No common weapons in their hands are found,
Like gods they fight, nor dread a mortal wound. . . .°
 See, fierce Belinda on the Baron flies,
With more than usual lightning in her eyes:
Nor feared the chief th' unequal fight to try,
Who sought no more than on his foe to die.
But this bold lord with manly strength endued,
She with one finger and a thumb subdued:
Just where the breath of life his nostrils drew,
A charge of snuff the wily virgin threw;
The gnomes direct, to every atom just,
The pungent grains of titillating dust.
Sudden with starting tears each eye o'erflows,

1. virago: ferocious woman; here, Belinda's friend, who leads the attack on the Baron and his friends.
4. whalebones: Whalebones were used to shape and stiffen women's clothing.
8. Like gods . . . mortal wound: Like gods, who are immortal and do not fear physical wounds, these fighters do not fear wounds inflicted by words.

? **1–8.** *What is being described in these lines?*

9–20. *Belinda avenges herself by throwing snuff in the Baron's face to make him sneeze.*

? *How does this silly action reflect the mock epic genre?*

D **Literary Focus** **Mock Epic** How do the first six lines of Canto V parody a classical epic?

Universal Access

Struggling Readers

Benchmark Students Point out that lines 1–10 are made of a series of short sentences. Explain how the brevity of the sentences emphasizes the fast pace of the "battle," creating a tone that is brisk and energetic.

Activity Have students re-read the lines aloud with appropriate pausing and intonation to convey the excitement of the moment.

Advanced Learners

Acceleration Students may take special interest in the poem's allusions. Have them keep a list as they read. Then, using a good classical or mythological dictionary, students should explain how each allusion deepens the meaning or increases the satirical tone of the poem. Challenge students to think of alternative allusions from today's world that might enrich the poem's meaning.

Analyzing Visuals

Connecting to the Text The artist of this painting depicts a series of small interactions that are all important parts of a larger social scene. How do the movements described by Pope in *The Rape of the Lock* have a similar effect?

Sir Plume Demands the Restoration of the Lock (1854) by C. R. Leslie. Private Collection.

And the high dome re-echoes to his nose.
"Now meet thy fate," incensed Belinda cried,
And drew a deadly bodkin° from her side. . . . **E**
"Boast not my fall," he cried, "insulting foe!
Thou by some other shalt be laid as low.
Nor think, to die dejects my lofty mind:
All that I dread is leaving you behind!
Rather than so, ah, let me still survive,
And burn in Cupid's flames—but burn alive."
"Restore the lock!" she cries; and all around
"Restore the lock!" the vaulted roofs rebound.

22. bodkin: long, ornamental hairpin shaped like a dagger.

? **29–38.** *Paraphrase this verse paragraph. Why, according to the speaker, is the lock unable to be found?*

E **Literary Focus** **Mock Epic** What other form of revenge does Belinda threaten to take? How do her weapons compare to those used in a traditional epic?

Think About/Talk About

Analysis

D Literary Focus

Possible response: *Pope writes of this dispute as if it were a grand battle scene, a common element in classical epics.*

E Literary Focus

Possible responses: *She threatens to stick him with a hairpin. A hairpin is like a miniature version of the swords and daggers used in classical epics, thus adding to the comic effect. Her other weapon is snuff, which is also harmless compared to traditional weapons used in epic battles.*

Extend the Discussion

Mock Epic What scene from a classical epic does the Baron's speech on p. 627 parody? ***Possible response:*** *It parodies the typical speech of a brave warrior who has performed well in battle but suffered a mortal wound.*

Figurative Language What does the Baron mean by the symbolic metaphor in Canto V, lines 27–28, "let me still survive . . . but burn alive"? Explain in your own words. ***Possible response:*** *He is saying that he wants to live while burning with passionate love for Belinda ("Cupid's flames").*

Students with Disabilities

Have groups of students play the characters of Belinda, the Baron, Clarissa, Ariel, and Belinda's friend (the "virago" of Canto V, line 1). In a discussion of the poem's plot, have characters sum up what they have done and said so far and how they feel about what has happened. Encourage students to discuss comic aspects of their character that are characteristic of the mock epic genre.

Analyzing Visuals

Connecting to the Text: *In the poem, Pope describes the setting along with the general activities of the nobility. He then narrows his focus by describing the interactions between Belinda and the Baron, the nymphs and Belinda, etc.*

Think About/Talk About

Comprehension

F Reading Focus

Possible response: *It is so shallow and small that it can fit in a snuffbox.*

Analysis

G Literary Focus

Possible responses: *Belinda's old age and death; the Muse of poetry will make her and her lock of hair famous.*

Responses to Margin Questions

Lines 45–48 *It has become a comet.*

Lines 49–58 *At the end of Canto V, Belinda's lock rises into the sky as a new comet. According to Pope, Belinda is the true hero of the epic.*

Vocabulary: Own the Word

- **ambitious:** Tell students than an antonym for *ambitious* is *unmotivated.* For example: "The *ambitious* woman actively looked for a job, while the unmotivated man just sat on his couch."
- **radiant:** Ask students to make a list of things that can be described as *radiant.* [*a diamond ring*]
- **consecrate:** Remind students that *consecrate* means "to make something holy." How does this definition add a comic element in the Muse's decision to *consecrate* Belinda's lock of hair? [*People declare sacred relics or Bibles holy, not a lock of hair.*]

Not fierce Othello° in so loud a strain
Roared for the handkerchief that caused his pain.
But see how oft ambitious aims are crossed,
And chiefs contend till all the prize is lost!
The lock, obtained with guilt, and kept with pain,
In every place is sought, but sought in vain:
With such a prize no mortal must be blessed,
So Heaven decrees! with Heaven who can contest?
Some thought it mounted to the lunar sphere,
Since all things lost on earth are treasured there.
There heroes' wits are kept in ponderous vases,
And beaux'° in snuffboxes and tweezer cases. **F**
There broken vows and deathbed alms are found,
And lovers' hearts with ends of riband bound. . . .
But trust the Muse—she saw it upward rise,
Though marked by none but quick, poetic eyes: . . .
A sudden star, it shot through liquid air,
And drew behind a radiant trail of hair. . . .°
Then cease, bright nymph! to mourn thy ravished hair,
Which adds new glory to the shining sphere!
Not all the tresses that fair head can boast,
Shall draw such envy as the lock you lost.
For, after all the murders° of your eye,
When, after millions slain, yourself shall die;
When those fair suns shall set, as set they must,
And all those tresses shall be laid in dust,
This lock, the Muse shall consecrate to fame,
And midst the stars inscribe Belinda's name. **G**

31. Othello: Shakespeare's tragic hero Othello gave his wife a handkerchief, which his enemy stole and then used as false evidence of the wife's unfaithfulness.

42. beaux': fashionable gentlemen's.

? **45–48.** *What has become of the lock?*

48. trail of hair: The word *comet* derives from a Greek word for "long-haired."

53. murders: Just as Belinda's eyes are said to "eclipse the day" (Canto I, line 14), here they are said to murder the young men who admire her. Both compliments are ancient and overused in love poetry.

49–58. *Although the lock is gone forever, its very loss will ensure Belinda's lasting fame.* **?** *Who, according to the poet, is the true (though comic) hero?*

F Reading Focus **Identifying Tone** What does Pope seem to imply about the intelligence of beaux in Canto V, lines 41–42?

G Literary Focus **Mock Epic** What does Pope describe in Canto V, lines 51–58? What consolation does he offer?

Vocabulary **ambitious** (am BIHSH uhs) *adj.:* aiming for a goal that is hard to reach.
radiant (RAY dee uhnt) *adj.:* shining with beams of light.
consecrate (KAHN suh krayt) *v.:* make honorable and sacred.

California Standards, pp. 629–631

- **Reading Standard 3.1** Analyze characteristics of subgenres (e.g., satire, parody, allegory, pastoral) that are used in poetry, prose, plays, novels, short stories, essays, and other basic genres.
- **Reading Standard 3.3** Analyze the ways in which irony, tone, mood, the author's style, and the "sound" of language achieve specific rhetorical or aesthetic purposes or both.
- **Reading Standard 3.4** Analyze ways in which poets use imagery, personification, figures of speech, and sounds to evoke readers' emotions.
- **Grades 9–10 Review Reading Standard 1.1** Identify and use the literal and figurative meanings of words and understand word derivations.
- **Writing Standard 1.5** Use language in natural, fresh, and vivid ways to establish a specific tone.
- **Writing Standard 2.1** Write fictional, autobiographical, or biographical narratives: **a.** Narrate a sequence of events and communicate their significance to the audience. **e.** Make effective use of descriptions of appearance, images, shifting perspectives, and sensory details.
- **Writing Standard 2.6** Deliver multimedia presentations: **a.** Combine text, images, and sound and draw information from many sources (e.g., television broadcasts, videos, films, newspapers, magazines, CD-ROMs, the Internet, electronic media-generated images).
- **Listening and Speaking Standard 2.3** Deliver oral responses to literature: **a.** Demonstrate a comprehensive understanding of the significant ideas of literary works (e.g., make assertions about the text that are reasonable and supportable). **b.** Analyze the imagery, language, universal themes, and unique aspects of the text through the use of rhetorical strategies (e.g., narration, description, persuasion, exposition, a combination of those strategies). **c.** Support important ideas and viewpoints through accurate and detailed references to the text or to other works. **d.** Demonstrate an awareness of the author's use of stylistic devices and an appreciation of the effects created.

Applying Your Skills

Reading Standard 3.1, 3.3, 3.4 (see pages A48–A50)
Writing Standard 1.5 (see pages A51–A52)

from The Rape of the Lock

Literary Response and Analysis

Reading Skills Focus

Quick Check

1. How do the heroes of this mock epic differ from the conventional epic hero?
2. Why have "the heroes and the nymphs" gathered at Hampton Court?
3. What events serve as "epic battles"?

Read with a Purpose

4. Who and what is Pope mocking in this epic?

Reading Skills: Identifying Tone

5. Add a column labeled "Tone" to the right side of your chart. For each row, decide what Pope's choice of words and details suggests about his attitude toward the person or event that he describes. Write an adjective describing the tone and a short sentence explaining your choice. When you are finished, discuss with a partner the overall tone of the selection.

Person or Event	Line Number(s)	Words and Details Pope Uses	Tone
Queen Anne	7–8	Pope describes the queen as taking "counsel," or advice, and "tea" as if they are equally important.	Comic. By elevating the act of drinking to the level of talking to a royal counselor, Pope establishes a comic tone.

Literary Skills Focus

Literary Analysis

6. **Analyze** The worlds outside and inside the poem come together in Canto III (lines 7–8). What is the effect of the three words after the dash?
7. **Interpret** In Canto III, line 86, Pope **juxtaposes,** or places side by side, dying "husbands" and dying "lapdogs." What is the effect of this juxtaposition? Locate other surprising juxtapositions in the poem, and describe their effects.
8. **Extend** How does the poem apply to contemporary life? What passages could serve as satirical commentaries on people's behavior today?

Literary Skills: Mock Epic

9. **Analyze** Who, if anyone, is victorious at the end of the poem? How does the victor compare to the victor in a conventional epic? Cite lines from the poem to support your opinion.

Literary Skills Review: Epic Simile

10. **Analyze** A mock epic parodies the classic epic's style and conventions. Since Homer, the epic's hallmark has been the **epic simile,** or extended comparison between two unlike things. What things are compared in Canto III (lines 57–58 and 85–88) and Canto V (lines 31–32)?

Writing Skills Focus

Think as a Reader/Writer

Use It in Your Writing As you read, you noted how Pope uses catalogs to influence the poem's tone. In your *Reader/Writer Notebook,* write a short essay that incorporates a catalog. You might describe something common, such as a student's day, incorporating a list of activities. Include humorous and unexpected items to create a lighthearted tone, or scholarly items to convey a serious tone.

What Do You Think Now? What emotions provoke the breakdown in orderly behavior that leads to the fighting at Hampton Court?

Check for Understanding

Independent Practice

Reading Skills Focus

Possible responses:

1. *Unlike epic heroes, mock epic heroes do not fight bravely in dangerous battles. Instead, they spend their days trying to impress each other.*
2. *to have tea and socialize*
3. *In Canto III, an epic battle is represented by a game of cards. In Canto V, there is an epic battle (fought with snuff and a hairpin) between Belinda and the Baron.*
4. *The mock epic comments on the petty disputes that preoccupy the aristocracy of Pope's time.*
5. *Remind students that Pope satirizes the aristocracy. His purpose is reflected in the tone used by the speaker in the mock epic.*

Literary Skills Focus

Possible responses:

6. *They deflate the solemnity of royal councils.*
7. *The effect is humorous: because lapdogs are often the pets of women, Pope's comparison belittles husbands. Other examples are the British queen versus an Indian screen, and the heroes' wits versus the wits of the beaux.*
8. *Some people today gather to socialize and gossip.*
9. *The Baron gets the lock; Belinda wins fame. Both are compared to immortal gods who do not fear mortal wounds (Canto V, l. 8).*
10. *In Canto III, ll. 57–58, Pope compares Clarissa with medieval ladies preparing knights for battle. In lines 85–88, Belinda's cries are compared with cries evoked by serious matters such as death. In Canto V, ll. 31–32, Pope alludes to the handkerchief Othello gave to his wife, whose death is tragic compared to the death of the lock.*

Universal Access

Struggling Writers

Some students may need additional scaffolding to complete the Writing Skills Focus activity. Before they write their catalogs, have students begin the assignment by brainstorming a list of items that they use as part of their morning routine (toiletries, articles of clothing, eating utensils, etc.) Then, have them write a description of the process of getting ready for school. Ask them to strive for a light-hearted, humorous mock-epic tone.

What Do You Think Now?

Help students in answering the question by asking them to describe the feelings that led Baron to steal the lock and the emotions that gripped Belinda as a result. Ask students to consider how both characters violated the code of orderly behavior of Pope's time.

Independent Practice

Vocabulary Development

Vocabulary Check

1. *d* **2.** *b*
3. *e* **4.** *c*
5. *a*

Your Turn

Answers should include the Vocabulary words, etymologies, definitions, and related words from a dictionary used or accepted in classroom. For example:

Vocabulary word: reputation

Etymology: Latin *reputare,* "to consider"

Related Words: repute, reputed

Meaning: one's overall character as judged by others

Sample Sentence: The politician was determined to protect his *reputation* by trusting no one.

English for Academic Success

Language Coach

Possible responses:

1. *radiant*
2. *tolerate*
3. *dominant*
4. *stagnate*

English for Academic Success

Academic Vocabulary

Possible response: *The characterization of a mock epic might convince people of their own silliness. The epic would enhance their awareness of how trivial and shallow some of the activities they participate in are.*

Applying Your Skills

Grades 9–10 Review Reading Standard 1.1 (see pages A48–A50)

from The Rape of the Lock

Vocabulary Development

Vocabulary Check

Match the Vocabulary words with their definitions.

1. reputation **a.** make worthy of honor
2. stratagems **b.** clever plans
3. ambitious **c.** glowing
4. radiant **d.** people's opinion of a person
5. consecrate **e.** eager for great things

Vocabulary Skills: Etymology Maps

One important piece of information you find when you look up a word in the dictionary is its **etymology**—the word's origin and development over time. If you look up the word *etymology,* for example, you will learn that it comes from the Greek word *etymos,* meaning "true," and the Greek suffix *logos,* meaning "word." So, to know a word's etymology is to know its true meaning in the sense that you know its history—where it came from and how it came to its current usage.

An etymology map will help you organize information about a word's origin and development. It will also help you connect the word with ideas you already know so that you can remember it more easily. Look at this etymology map for *exulting,* a word Pope uses in his poem:

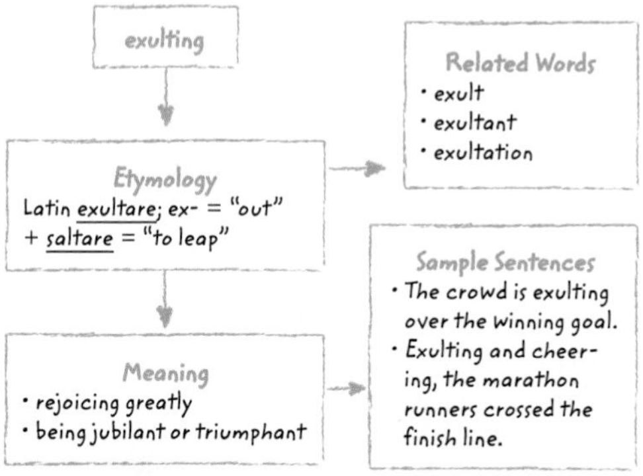

Your Turn

Use a dictionary to create an etymology map for each Vocabulary word. If you are ambitious, like the Baron, and want to know more about these words, consult the *Oxford English Dictionary* online or in a library. Compare your sample sentences with those of your classmates.

Language Coach

Suffixes Some adjectives are formed using the suffix *–ant.* Some verbs are formed using the suffix *–ate.* Choose the best word to complete each sentence. Consider whether the missing word should be an adjective or a verb. Use a dictionary to find the meanings of unfamiliar words.

1. The Baron was captivated by Belinda's (radiate, radiant) smile.
2. It seems that Belinda must (tolerant, tolerate) his advances.
3. Who do you think is the (dominant, dominate) fighter in their battle?
4. Their conflict would probably (stagnate, stagnant) if just one of them lost interest.

Academic Vocabulary

Talk About

In a small group, talk about how a mock epic might convince people that their behavior is silly or inappropriate by enhancing their self-awareness. Use the underlined Academic Vocabulary words as you participate in the discussion.

Universal Access: Vocabulary Development

EL English Learners

English for Academic Success Before completing the **Language Coach**, some students may need help in recognizing when to use an adjective and when to use a verb. Remind them that an adjective is a describing word that modifies a noun or a pronoun. Adjectives answer the questions *what kind, how many, which one,* and *how much.* Tell students that adjectives usually precede the words they modify. Then, explain that a verb is an action word that tells what the subject of a sentence is doing.

Pair students with a proficient English speaker and have them engage in an instructional conversation in which they work through the following exercises.

- The (hesitant, hesitate) young boy refused to raise his hand. [*hesitant*]
- The sounds of the music still (resonant, resonate) in my ears. [*resonate*]

✔ See the **Academic and Selection Vocabulary Skill Builder** in **UA: Differentiating Instruction.**

Reading Standard 3.3 (see pages A48–A50)
Writing Standard 2.1a, 2.1e, 2.6a (see pages A51–A52)
Listening and Speaking Standard 2.3a–d (see pages A53–A55)

Grammar Link

Sequence of Verb Tenses

When writing about events that occur at the same time, use verbs in the same tense. When writing about events that occur at different times, use verbs in different tenses to show the **sequence** of events.

I swim while Bill lifts weights. (The actions occur at the same time.)

Maria told Tim that she had mentioned the concert to John. (She mentioned the concert to John before she told Tim that she had mentioned it.)

Tense	Usage	Example
Past Perfect	happening before a specific time in the past	I had saved; she had saved
Past	happening in the past	I saved; he saved
Present Perfect	happening sometime before now; may be continuing now	I have saved; she has saved
Present	existing or happening now	I save; he saves
Future Perfect	happening before a specific time in the future	I will have saved; she will have saved
Future	happening in the future	I will save; he will save

Your Turn

Revise each sentence to correct the error in verb tense.

1. We appreciated Pope's saying that to err was human.
2. Would Pope have been cruel if he knew how his cruelty would affect his reputation?

Writing Application Look over a few paragraphs of an essay you have written. Circle any incorrect verb tenses and revise those sentences appropriately.

CHOICES

As you respond to the Choices activities, use these **Academic Vocabulary** words as appropriate: approach, convince, dominate, enhance, participate.

REVIEW

Illustrate the Scene

How might an illustration capture Pope's satirical tone? Choose a scene from the poem, along with lines to serve as a caption to incorporate into an illustration or place below it. Choose a medium, and use composition, line, space, color, or other artistic elements to convey Pope's tone through your illustration. Write a brief essay explaining your approach to expressing satire visually. What problems did you encounter, and how did you solve them?

CONNECT

Compose a Letter

Recall that Pope based his mock epic on a real incident: Robert, Lord Petre's snipping of a lock of Arabella Fermor's hair. Assume that Robert regretted his action. Write a letter from Robert to Arabella in which he sincerely tries to convince her that he is sorry for his behavior. Use a tone that conveys the formality and decorum associated with the social standing of the parties concerned. Then, rewrite the letter to give it a satirical tone.

EXTEND

Analyze and Compare Strategies

TechFocus Today, people sometimes have difficulty deciphering the tone of e-mail communications. Think of some examples, from your own experiences if possible, in which an e-mail's tone could be ambiguous. What strategies do people use in e-mails to convey their tones or their emotions about what they are writing? Compare these strategies with the ways Pope reveals his tone in *The Rape of the Lock*. Which way is more effective? Why? Share your conclusions with your class.

Universal Access: Grammar Link

English Learners

English for Academic Success To help students understand the present perfect tense of verbs, write these sentences on the board.

- *I **have** never **seen** that movie before.*
- *Yesterday, I **baked** a cake.*

Explain that the present perfect tense can not be used with specific expressions indicating time, such as *one day* or *last week*. But it can be used with unspecific expressions such as *never, once, before,* and *yet*.

Then, ask students if the following sentences are grammatically correct. If it is incorrect, ask them to replace the incorrect tense with the correct tense.

1. Last week, I have seen that movie. [*Last week, I saw that movie.*]
2. Two weeks ago, I had been to the store. [*Two weeks ago, I went to the store.*]
3. When I was a baby, I crawled on all fours. [*correct*]

✔ For more practice with sequence of verb tenses, see **Warriner's Handbook, GrammarNotes,** and **Language Handbook Worksheets.**

Independent Practice

Grammar Link

Your Turn

1. *We appreciate Pope's saying that to err is human.*
2. *Would Pope still have been cruel if he had known how his cruelty would affect his reputation?*

Choices: Evaluation Criteria

Review: Homework
Illustrate the Scene

- Students utilize artistic techniques and elements to convey Pope's tone.
- Essays explain how satire is incorporated into illustration.

Connect: Homework
Compose a Letter

- Letters are properly formatted.
- Students use a formal tone.

Extend: Homework
Analyze and Compare Strategies

- Students outline strategies for conveying certain tones through e-mail.
- Students compare these strategies with Pope's strategies in revealing tone in *The Rape of the Lock*.

Assess

Unit 3 Resources, Selection Standards Check, p. 62

go.hrw.com **ThinkCentral Online Assessment,** Selection Standards Check

Teacher One Stop™, editable Selection Standards Check

Reteach

To reteach **irony, tone, and author's style,** see **Reteaching Lessons,** pp. 1449O–1449P.

go.hrw.com **ThinkCentral Online Remediation**

Standards Focus

Objectives

Students will analyze the way in which clarity of meaning is affected by word choice in a text.

Selection Introduction

Think About the Writer

Before students answer, ask them to consider qualities Boswell and Johnson may have shared. Encourage students to use the information included in Johnson's biography to help them answer the question.

For Independent Reading

The Education of Robert Nifkin, Daniel Pinkwater

Motivate

What Do You Think?/QuickTalk

To help students answer the QuickTalk question, have them consider the benefits and drawbacks of having individuals determine the rules of language for society as a whole.

English for Academic Success

Academic Vocabulary

Look for opportunities to use the Academic Vocabulary words in this unit.

- **dominate, *v.*:** hold a commanding position
- **enhance, *v.*:** improve the quality of

California Standards, pp. 632–637

- **Reading Standard 2.2** Analyze the way in which clarity of meaning is affected by the patterns of organization, hierarchical structures, repetition of the main ideas, syntax, and word choice in the text.

Preparing to Read

from A Dictionary of the English Language

What Do You Think? How can order and civilization affect human behavior?

QuickTalk

Who, in your opinion, should determine a word's meaning and pronunciation? In a small group, discuss whether you think the rules of language should be maintained and changed by certain individuals or by society as a whole.

MEET THE WRITER

Samuel Johnson

(1709–1784)

An engaging speaker and a respected writer and critic, Samuel Johnson was so beloved that his century is often called the Age of Johnson.

Humble Beginnings

Johnson is famous primarily for three large and important projects: *A Dictionary of the English Language* (1755); an edition of Shakespeare with an important critical preface and useful notes (1765); and *The Lives of the English Poets* (1779–1781). His early life, however, did not seem to mark him for greatness. The son of an unsuccessful bookseller, he was small and sickly, and he lost his sight in one eye from an infection. As Johnson grew, however, his health improved and he developed a strong personality, although he retained the disfiguring scars of medical treatments and numerous personal tics that may have been symptoms of Tourette's syndrome. Anecdotes abound of his immense height, size, and strength—and of his sometimes odd behavior—but his most impressive feature was his intellect.

An English Institution

In 1737, Johnson moved to London, the city he came to admire above all others. In London, Johnson became the dominant literary figure of his day. He was considered an English institution not only because of his great circle of friends and forceful personality, but because of his numerous essays, poems, and magazine contributions. Johnson's literary output, even before he began his major projects, is impressive.

In 1763, Johnson met James Boswell, who would soon begin recording Johnson's conversations for posterity. Johnson remains a vivid figure because Boswell and many of Johnson's other contemporaries recorded their impressions of him.

Though one of the most learned men of his day, Johnson always insisted that knowledge was useless unless it helped people live in the real world.

Think About the Writer Which of Johnson's qualities do you think made him so interesting to Boswell and others?

Dr. Samuel Johnson (18th century) by Sir Joshua Reynolds (1723–1792). Private Collection.

Selection Readability	
Easily Accessible **Accessible** Challenging	accessible syntax; humorous content; familiar genre

Reading Standard 2.2 (see pages A48–A50)

Literary Skills Focus

Diction A writer's or speaker's choice of words is called **diction.** Speakers and writers use different types of words depending on the context—that is, their audience, subject, and purpose. Thus, diction can be formal, informal, colloquial, poetic, ornate, plain, and so on. For example, casual slang that would be suitable in a conversation with a friend would be unsuitable in a formal speech. Diction is an essential element of a writer's style and has a powerful effect on the tone of a piece of writing.

Through his diction in the *Dictionary of the English Language,* Johnson reveals his character and opinions. Some entries—"catsup. A kind of pickle, made from mushrooms"—are fairly straightforward and objective. They give us a direct description of the word. Other entries—"essay. A loose sally of the mind; an irregular indigested piece; not a regularly and orderly composition"—enhance the dictionary with Johnson's unique word choices and create memorable phrases. As you read, note the language and style of each dictionary entry, and analyze Johnson's diction in order to determine his opinion of the word.

Writing Skills Focus

Think as a Reader/Writer

Find It in Your Reading In *A Dictionary of the English Language,* Johnson often uses examples to clarify a word's meaning. Some examples involve synonyms; others replace the word with a phrase or an illustrative point; still others, as with the word *bedpresser,* employ examples of usage from famous authors such as Shakespeare. In your *Reader/Writer Notebook,* create a chart like the one below to keep track of the many kinds of examples Johnson uses.

Word	Example
to romp	A stool is the first weapon taken up in a general romping or skirmish. —Swift, Rules to Servants

Vocabulary

discourse (DIHS kawrs) *n.:* conversation or speech. *Johnson was much admired for his witty discourse and banter.*

sanguine (SANG gwihn) *adj.:* reddish in color; red-faced from effort. *The runner's face was sanguine from sprinting.*

servile (SUR vuhl) *adj.:* slavishly devoted. *The members of the court made servile bows whenever the king walked by them.*

countenances (KOWN tuh nuhns ehz) *v.:* extends approval to; favors. *Johnson countenances those who work vigorously, but he dislikes lazy people.*

eminence (EHM uh nuhns) *n.:* high rank or position. *Johnson was a man of eminence, beloved by many in the city of London.*

Language Coach

Word Origins The word *servile* comes from a Latin word meaning "slave." The word *eminence* comes from Latin words that mean "to stand out" and "to jut out." Explain how these roots relate to the current meanings of these words: *service, servant, disservice, eminent, preeminent.*

Learn It Online
Listen to this selection online.
go.hrw.com H12-633 Go

Reader/Writer Notebook
Use your **RWN** to complete the activities for this selection.

Selection Resources

Unit 3 Resources, on-level practice and assessment

Teacher One Stop™, on-level lesson plans and all print resources

Holt Audio Library

Holt Audio Library: Selections and Summaries in Spanish

UA: Differentiating Instruction, graphic organizer, p. 139

UA: Supporting Instruction in Spanish, selection summary

ThinkCentral Online Assessment, Selection Standards Check

ThinkCentral Online Remediation

Preteach

Introducing Vocabulary

Read aloud the Vocabulary words, definitions, and sample sentences. Then, use this activity to check students' understanding.

1. Explain how a **discourse** is different from a debate.
2. Name some events that might turn a person's face **sanguine.**
3. Identify a society from history that forced some people to be **servile** toward others.
4. Name acts that our society **countenances.**
5. Name a person of **eminence** that you admire.

English for Academic Success

Language Coach

After students answer the question, have them research the word origin of the other Vocabulary words.

Literary Skills Focus

As you read and discuss the selection with students, have them note how Johnson's diction helps reveal his opinion of each featured word.

Writing Skills Focus

As you read and discuss the selection with students, have them record examples that clarify a word's meaning in their **Reader/Writer Notebooks.**

Learn It Online
The online version of this selection includes audio support to engage all students and to help struggling readers with reading comprehension and vocabulary.
go.hrw.com H12-633 Go

Teacher Preparation

Selection Summary

The definitions are from *A Dictionary of the English Language,* the first comprehensive English dictionary, which was compiled over a nine-year period. Published in 1755, Johnson's dictionary defined thousands of words and included parts-of-speech designations, etymologies, variant meanings, and illustrative examples from professional writers. None of the entries given here is a complete entry.

Direct Teach

Think About/Talk About

Read with a Purpose Have students read the Read with a Purpose statement. Tell them to pay attention to definitions that reveal personal opinions, judgments, or personal references that would not be found in a modern dictionary.

DEFINITIONS

from

A Dictionary of the English Language

by **Samuel Johnson**

Read with a Purpose

Read to see how Johnson reveals his character and expresses his personality in his dictionary.

Build Background

Johnson's *Dictionary,* published in 1755, was the first comprehensive and authoritative dictionary in English. Johnson gathered information from many literary, religious, philosophical, scientific, and technical books, marking passages and underlining key words. Then, he had six copyists write out the marked passages on slips of paper, which were later pasted into eighty notebooks. Finally, using the passages, Johnson wrote definitions of the key words.

Johnson's *Dictionary* was the basis of all subsequent English dictionaries. The dictionary lives on today because it reflects its author's interesting character and sense of humor.

Natasha McEnroe, curator of the Museum at Dr. Samuel Johnson's House, holds up the revolutionary dictionary written by Johnson in the 17th century.

Universal Access

English Learners

English for Academic Success Have students identify the entries in Johnson's *Dictionary* that are familiar words in present-day English. Have them look up current meanings in a dictionary and compare and contrast them with Johnson's definitions. Model the activity by comparing Johnson's definition of the word *essay* with a modern definition.

✔ See the **English Language Skill Builder** in **UA: Differentiating Instruction.**

Struggling Readers

Remind students that Johnson's entries do not provide all the information that is found in modern dictionaries, such as the part of speech for each word. Have students supply the part of speech for words that are in current use and then check their accuracy in the dictionary. Students will notice that some words (for example, *essay* and *excise*) are attributed more than one part of speech.

✔ See **UA: Differentiating Instruction** for a graphic organizer to scaffold instruction for struggling readers.

alligator. The crocodile. This name is chiefly used for the crocodile of America, between which, and that of Africa, naturalists have laid down this difference, that one moves the upper, and the other the lower jaw; but this is now known to be chimerical,[1] the lower jaw being equally moved by both.

athletick. Strong of body; vigorous; lusty; robust.

> Science distinguishes a man of honor from one of those *athletick* brutes, whom undeservedly we call heroes.
>
> —Dryden. Ⓐ

autopsy. Ocular demonstration; seeing a thing oneself.

balderdash. Anything jumbled together without judgment; rude mixture; a confused discourse.

bedpresser. A heavy lazy fellow.

> This sanguine coward, this *bedpresser,* this horseback-breaker, this huge hill of flesh.
>
> —Shakespeare, *Henry IV,* Part 1.

catsup. A kind of pickle, made from mushrooms.

companion. A familiar term of contempt; a fellow.

> I scorn you, scurvy *companion!* What? you poor, base, rascally, cheating, lack-linen mate: Away, you moldy rogue, away.
>
> —Shakespeare, *Henry IV,* Part 2.

cough. A convulsion of the lungs, vellicated by some sharp serosity. It is pronounced *coff.*

dedication. A servile address to a patron.

dull. Not exhilarating; not delightful; as, to *make dictionaries is* dull *work.*

essay. A loose sally of the mind; an irregular indigested piece; not a regular and orderly composition.

excise. A hateful tax levied upon commodities, and adjudged not by the common judges of property, but wretches hired by those to whom excise is paid.

favorite. One chosen as a companion by his superior; a mean wretch whose whole business is by any means to please.

fillip. A jerk of the finger let go from the thumb.

frightfully. Disagreeably; not beautifully. A woman's word.

fun. (A low cant[2] word.) Sport; high merriment; frolicsome delight.

goose. A large waterfowl proverbially noted, I know not why, for foolishness.

gravy. The serous juice that runs from flesh not much dried by the fire.

> They usually boil and roast their meat until it falls almost off from the bones; but we love it half raw, with the blood trickling down from it, delicately terming it the *gravy,* which in truth looks more like an ichorous or raw bloody matter.
>
> —Harvey, *On Consumptions.*

to hiss. To utter a noise like that of a serpent and some other animals. It is remarkable, that this word cannot be pronounced without making the noise which it signifies.

immaterial. (1) Incorporeal; void of matter. (2) Unimportant; without weight; impertinent; without relation. This sense has crept into the conversation and writings of barbarians; but ought to be utterly rejected.

jogger. One who moves heavily and dully.

lexicographer. A writer of dictionaries; a harmless drudge, that busies himself in tracing the original, and detailing the signification of words. Ⓑ

lingo. Language; tongue; speech. A low cant word.

lunch, luncheon. As much food as one's hand can hold.

merrythought. A forked bone on the body of fowls; so called because boys and girls pull in play at the two sides, the longest part broken off betokening priority of marriage.

1. **chimerical** (kuh MEHR uh kuhl): fanciful.

2. **cant:** a word Johnson uses to describe language he perceives to be of base origins.

Ⓐ **Literary Focus Diction** How does Johnson's diction differ from Dryden's in the example provided for this word?

Ⓑ **Literary Focus Diction** Johnson satirizes many people and political groups in his witty definitions. Why might he refer to a maker of dictionaries as "a harmless drudge"? Whom does he satirize here?

Vocabulary **discourse** (DIHS kawrs) *n.:* conversation or speech.
sanguine (SANG gwihn) *adj.:* reddish in color; red-faced from effort.
servile (SUR vuhl) *adj.:* slavishly devoted.

Think About/Talk About

Analysis

Ⓐ Literary Focus

Possible response: *Johnson's definition has no negative connotation; whereas, Dryden's usage conveys contempt for athletic people, describing them as brutes.*

Ⓑ Literary Focus

Possible response: *Johnson is a lexicographer, or dictionary writer, so he is satirizing himself with this definition.*

Extend the Discussion

Comparing and Contrasting How does Johnson's definition of the word *companion* differ from the word's contemporary meaning? ***Possible response:*** *The word "companion" had a negative connotation in Johnson's time.*

Vocabulary: Own the Word

- **discourse:** Remind students that *discourse* means "a conversation or speech." Have students work in pairs to make a list of synonyms for the word *discourse.* ***Possible responses:*** *dialogue, conversation, discussion, communication*
- **sanguine:** Ask students to name a time when a person might have a *sanguine* face. ***Possible responses:*** *when he or she is embarrassed; after he or she has done a lot of exercise*
- **servile:** Someone who is willing to do whatever someone else wants can be described as *servile.* Synonyms are *fawning* and *groveling.* Have students put the word *servile* in the center of a web diagram and write examples of jobs in which a person must be *servile.* ***Possible responses:*** *personal assistant, roadie, unpaid intern*

Advanced Learners

Acceleration Remind students that Johnson's diction in the entries helps reveal his opinion of certain words and ideas. Draw students' attention to the entries for the words *excise* and *frightfully.* Have students analyze the definitions for these words to make inferences about Johnson and his opinions. Then, have students share their responses with the class. [*Students might note that the words* hateful and wretches *in the* excise *entry show that Johnson is strongly opposed to taxes. The phrase "a woman's word" in the* frightfully *entry shows that Johnson believes this a word that only women use.*]

Students with Disabilities

Students will gain a better understanding and appreciation of the selection by connecting the definitions to visual representations. Have students draw illustrations for three definitions in the selection. Under each illustration, have students write a caption explaining the illustration. Then, discuss the illustrations with the students.

Think About/Talk About

Analysis

C Literary Focus

Possible response: *Before giving the definition, Johnson labels it as a "cant" term, which indicates his disapproval. The supposition that the word means "savage" hints at his political bias.*

Vocabulary: Own the Word

- **countenances:** Tell students that *countenances* is the plural form of the verb *countenance,* and means "to tolerate, accept, or give approval to something." A teacher might not *countenance* the use of cell phones in school.
- **eminence:** The adjective form of the word *eminence* is *eminent.* The antonym of *eminent* is *unimportant*—something that is of little or no significance. Have students make a list of five *eminent* things and five unimportant things.

Monitor Students' Comprehension

Guide the class in answering these comprehension questions.

1. What is Johnson's attitude toward slang, which he calls "low" or "cant" words? [*He despises the use of such words.*]
2. Which words have a completely different meaning today? [*alligator, catsup, essay, jogger, mushroom, osprey, and whale*]
3. What words does Johnson use in his definition of the word *osprey* to indicate that the definition may not be scientifically accurate? [*He uses the words "of which it is reported" to preface a dubious claim about fishes' behavior toward ospreys.*]

mushroom. An upstart; a wretch risen from the dunghill; a director of a company.
network. Anything reticulated or decussated, at equal distances, with interstices between the intersections.
osprey. The sea-eagle, of which it is reported, that when he hovers in the air, all the fish in the water turn up their bellies, and lie still for him to seize which he pleases.
parody. A kind of writing, in which the words of an author or his thoughts are taken, and by a slight change adapted to some new purpose.
patron. One who countenances, supports, or protects. Commonly a wretch who supports with insolence, and is paid with flattery.
pension. An allowance made to anyone without an equivalent. In England it is generally understood to mean pay given to a state hireling for treason to his country.
to period. To put an end to. A bad[3] word.
rhinoceros. A vast beast in the East Indies armed with a horn in his front.
romance. A tale of wild adventures in war and love.
to romp. To play rudely, noisily, and boisterously.

A stool is the first weapon taken up in a general *romping,* or skirmish.

—Swift, *Rules to Servants.*

to sneeze. To emit wind audibly by the nose.
sonnet. A short poem consisting of fourteen lines, of which the rhymes are adjusted by a particular rule. It is not very suitable to the English language, and has not been used by any man of eminence since Milton.
stammel. Of this word I know not the meaning.
tittletattle. Idle talk; prattle; empty gabble.
torpedo. A fish which while alive, if touched even with a long stick, benumbs the hand that so touches it, but when dead is eaten safely.
tory. (A cant term, derived, I suppose, from an Irish word signifying a savage.) One who adheres to the ancient constitution of the state, and the apostolical hierarchy of the Church of England, opposed to a whig. C
unkindly. Unnatural; contrary to nature.
vivacious. Long-lived.
whale. The largest of fish.
whig. The name of a faction.
to worm. To deprive a dog of something, nobody knows what, under his tongue, which is said to prevent him, nobody knows why, from running mad.
zed. The name of the letter *z.*

3. **bad:** used here to mean "low" or "vulgar."

C Literary Focus Diction How does Johnson add his opinion to this entry, even before he defines the word?

Vocabulary **countenances** (KOWN tuh nuhns ehz) *v.:* extends approval to; favors.
eminence (EHM uh nuhns) *n.:* high rank or position.

Samuel Johnson's *Dictionary.* Dr. Johnson's House Trust, London.

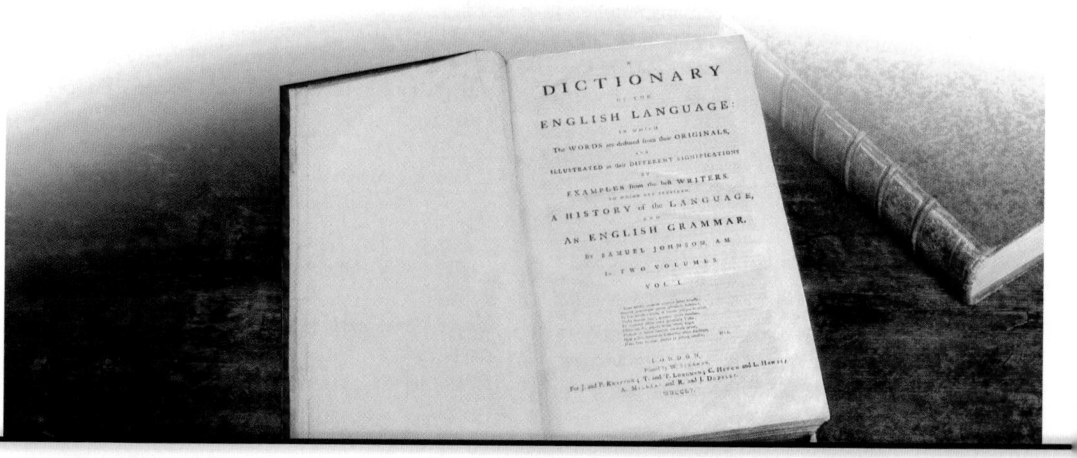

California Standards, p. 637

- **Reading Standard 2.2** Analyze the way in which clarity of meaning is affected by the patterns of organization, hierarchical structures, repetition of the main ideas, syntax, and word choice in the text.
- **Reading Standard 3.3** Analyze the ways in which irony, tone, mood, the author's style, and the "sound" of language achieve specific rhetorical or aesthetic purposes or both.
- **Writing Standard 2.2** Write responses to literature: **a.** Demonstrate a comprehensive understanding of the significant ideas in works or passages. **d.** Demonstrate an understanding of the author's use of stylistic devices and an appreciation of the effects created.

Applying Your Skills

Reading Standard 2.2, 3.3 (see pages A48–A50)
Writing Standard 2.2a, 2.2d (see pages A51–A52)

from A Dictionary of the English Language

Literary Response and Analysis

Reading Skills Focus

Quick Check

1. How does Johnson define *essay?* How does his definition differ from a modern definition?
2. Which word is listed without a definition? Why might Johnson have included this word?
3. Which definitions contain what we would regard as errors of fact?

Read with a Purpose

4. How does Johnson's voice in the *Dictionary* reveal his personality? Which definitions show the writer's sense of humor? Which show his political bias, religious preferences, and independence of mind?

Vocabulary Check

Match the Vocabulary words with their definitions.

5. discourse **a.** slavish
6. sanguine **b.** conversation
7. servile **c.** approves
8. countenances **d.** superiority
9. eminence **e.** reddish

Literary Skills Focus

Literary Analysis

10. **Compare and Contrast** Choose one word that Johnson defines in his *Dictionary.* Re-read Johnson's definition, and then read the definition of that word in a modern dictionary. How are the new and old entries alike and different?
11. **Draw Conclusions** What does Johnson think of patrons, or those who use their wealth to support artists and writers? Is a similar bias revealed in other entries? Which ones?
12. **Interpret** What is Johnson's attitude toward slang, which he calls "low" or "cant" words?
13. **Analyze** How do the dictionary entries reflect Johnson's insistence on thinking for himself?

Literary Skills: Diction

14. **Analyze** What effect does Johnson's diction create? How does his word choice help you learn about his political and social views?

Literary Skills Review: Style

15. **Analyze** Closely related to diction and syntax, **style** is the manner in which writers say what they wish to say. Describe Johnson's style. Is it consistent throughout the entries? Support your answer with examples from the text.

Writing Skills Focus

Think as a Reader/Writer

Use It in Your Writing The definitions in Johnson's *Dictionary* show us how words were used during his time. Look back at the chart you created of definitions and examples in Johnson's *Dictionary.* In your *Reader/Writer Notebook,* write your own one-page dictionary that includes words used frequently by your friends and family. Choose examples from your life that will help a reader to understand the meanings of the words you define.

What Do You Think Now? Johnson's *Dictionary* was the first comprehensive dictionary in English. How do you think this thorough and authoritative book affected the way people used language?

Universal Access

Struggling Writers

Some students may need additional scaffolding to complete the Writing Skills Focus activity. Before they write their definitions, ask students to think about ten everyday objects and have them define them orally to a partner. Then, ask students to use their discussions to write a definition for each object. Encourage students to write a sample sentence after each definition in which they use the words they chose to define.

What Do You Think Now?

Remind students of how the rules of language help people express themselves with clarity. Then, ask students to consider how people might have received a dictionary by an eminent thinker as Samuel Johnson and how they might have benefited by it.

Assess

Unit 3 Resources,
Selection Standards Check, p. 67

Check for Understanding

Independent Practice

Reading Skills Focus

Possible responses:

1. *He defines "essay" as a "loose sally of the mind." Today, an essay is a formal piece of writing.*
2. *"Stammel" is not defined. Perhaps Johnson included it because he found it was frequently used in books or in conversation.*
3. *Possible definitions include those for "alligator," "catsup," "essay," "jogger," "mushroom," "osprey," "sneeze," "torpedo," and "whale."*
4. *His voice reveals personality through the tone and diction. Humorous entries include those for "hiss," "lunch," and "goose." Political and religious references occur in the entries for "excise," "patron," and "pension."*

Vocabulary Check

5. *b* **6.** *e*
7. *a* **8.** *c*
9. *d*

Literary Skills Focus

Possible responses:

10. *In the selection, a "mushroom" is a type of person. In a modern dictionary, a "mushroom" is defined as a type of organism.*
11. *Johnson thinks patrons are people who use their wealth to gain false and unwarranted praise. A similar bias appears in the definitions of "pension" and "mushroom."*
12. *He considers people who use such words as inferior.*
13. *Many definitions reflect his personal opinion or experience.*
14. *Johnson's diction creates a sense of humor and informality. His opinions and political views are revealed through his diction in words such as "cant" and "excise."*
15. *Johnson's style is often humorous and opinionated. It is not consistent, however, because some entries are straightforward and formal.*

Standards Focus

Objectives

Students will make warranted and reasonable assertions about the author's arguments.

Selection Introduction

Think About the Writer

Ask students to think about the cultural characteristics unique to their community.

For Independent Reading

- *Something to Declare,* Julia Alvarez
- *Growing Up Asian American,* Maria Hong

Motivate

What Do You Think?/QuickTalk

Have students think and write about their own encounters with people from a different culture.

English for Academic Success

Academic Vocabulary

Look for opportunities to use the Academic Vocabulary words in this unit.

- **approach, *n.*:** a way of addressing something
- **convince, *v.*:** persuade; cause to believe
- **enhance, *v.*:** improve the quality of

INFORMATIONAL TEXT FOCUS

Preparing to Read

from The Meaning of Everything

What Do You Think? How can order and civilization affect human behavior?

QuickTalk

In a small group, share some examples of how language confusions and misunderstandings have caused comical or even serious situations that you or others have experienced.

Simon Winchester (2004)

MEET THE WRITER

Simon Winchester

(1944–)

Link to Today Simon Winchester's curiosity has taken him to countries around the world and deep into the history of people and language.

World Traveler

When British writer Simon Winchester was twenty-one years old, he finished a degree in geology at Oxford University and headed to Uganda to research copper. In his free time, he read a book about the first successful ascent of Mt. Everest and decided that he wanted to be a writer. Winchester now travels the world to learn about subjects for his writing, often to out-of-the-way places that might not have the comforts of hotels and regular modes of transportation. Winchester has worked as a journalist since 1967, writing articles, books, and film scripts on the many peoples, places, and languages he has encountered around the world.

The stress and demands of world travel do not discourage Winchester. He traveled over 100,000 miles during the three years he spent researching a book on the former British Empire. Another book resulted from the three months he spent in prison after he was incorrectly accused of being a spy. Despite such hardships, Winchester is delighted that interested readers make it possible for him to continue to travel and write.

The Lure of Language

Whenever Winchester travels, he observes the land and the people that inhabit it. He is fascinated by their stories, histories, and languages. He also appreciates the specificity of words—how each word means something unique—and believes that there are no true synonyms. With a geologist's scientific eye, he studies the history, use, and meaning of words. In his own detailed writing, he evokes a sense of place and time through painstakingly careful word choice—because only the *right* word will do.

Think About the Writer If Winchester traveled in your community, what might he observe about your culture and language? What stories might he choose to tell about your community?

California Standards, pp. 638–643

- **Reading Standard 2.4** Make warranted and reasonable assertions about the author's arguments by using elements of the text to defend and clarify interpretations.

Selection Readability	
Easily Accessible **Accessible** Challenging	accessible theme; familiar language

Selection Summary

In 2003, Winchester published a full-length history of the *Oxford English Dictionary* by Dr. Samuel Johnson. This excerpt explains how Johnson's dictionary differs from dictionaries of other languages, such as those in France and Italy. The OED describes a vital and fluid language spoken by both the educated and common classes.

Informational Text Focus

Critiquing an Author's Argument What makes an argument valid and compelling? An argument consists of claims, which must be explained thoroughly and supported by evidence in order to be convincing. When you read nonfiction, you critique an author's **argument** to judge its effectiveness.

In the selection that follows, Winchester argues that the English language is constantly evolving, and that Samuel Johnson understood the ever-changing nature of the language when he wrote his *Dictionary.* As a reader, it is your job to decide whether Winchester presents his argument clearly and supports his claims effectively.

Into Action As you read, use a flow chart like the one below to record each claim that Winchester makes in his argument. Beside each claim, list the evidence or examples that Winchester uses to support it. When you finish reading, you should have more than one flow chart.

Claim	Evidence/Examples 1	Evidence/Examples 2
Johnson's dictionary set the standard for English dictionaries that followed.	Johnson used a different method from the one other dictionary makers used.	Johnson didn't try to limit the meanings of words.

Writing Skills Focus

Preparing for Timed Writing As you read, notice how Winchester explains the contrast between descriptive and prescriptive dictionaries. Make a two-column chart in your *Reader/Writer Notebook,* and record ideas that help you understand these two approaches to defining words.

Descriptive	Prescriptive

Reader/Writer Notebook

Use your **RWN** to complete the activities for this selection.

Vocabulary

reiterate (ree IHT uh rayt) *v.:* repeat. *The author reiterates the main ideas.*

punctiliousness (puhngk TIHL ee uhs nuhs) *n.:* care for following rules and traditions exactly. *His careful speech and impeccable manners reflect his punctiliousness.*

prescribe (prih SKRYB) *v.:* limit by rules or laws; order. *Some grammar books prescribe English usage.*

copious (KOH pee uhs) *adj.:* plentiful; abundant. *Johnson compiled his dictionary from the copious notes that he and his assistants wrote about the English language.*

Language Coach

Prefixes A prefix is a word part that is added to the beginning of a word and changes its meaning. The prefix *re–* can mean "again." How is this meaning present in *reiterate?* The prefix *pre–* can mean "in advance or in preparation." How is this meaning present in *prescribe?* Explain how these prefixes affect the meanings of these words: *rearrange, prearrange, presume, resume.*

Learn It Online

Find an interactive flow chart online.

go.hrw.com H12-639 Go

Selection Resources

Unit 3 Resources, on-level practice and assessment, p. 70

Teacher One Stop™, on-level lesson plans and all print resources

Holt Audio Library

Holt Audio Library: Selections and Summaries in Spanish

UA: Differentiating Instruction, graphic organizer, p. 140

UA: Supporting Instruction in Spanish, selection summary

ThinkCentral Online Assessment, Selection Standards Check

ThinkCentral Online Remediation

Preteach

Introducing Vocabulary

Read aloud the Vocabulary words, definitions, and sample sentences. Then, use this activity to check students' understanding.

1. attract : lure :: repeat : _____. [*reiterate*]
2. _____ : bountiful :: common : trite. [*copious*]
3. codify : _____ :: destroy : raze [*prescribe*]
4. carelessness : _____ :: punctuality : tardiness. [*punctiliousness*]

English for Academic Success

Language Coach

Have students work in pairs to answer the questions. [*To* reiterate *something means to say something again. People* prescribe *things, such as laws, in order to prevent something that has not happened yet. If you* rearrange *something, you arrange it again. If you* prearrange *something, you make preparations for something before it has happened. If you* presume *something, you make a judgment before you have all the facts. When an activity* resumes, *it begins again.*]

Informational Text/ Writing Skills Focus

- Give students a copy of the Informational Text Focus graphic organizer before they read. Tell them to use their responses to answer the questions on the Applying Your Skills page.
- Have students record characteristics of descriptive and prescriptive dictionaries in their **Reader/Writer Notebooks.**

Learn It Online

If your students need help organizing a paper [or extra reading support for informational text], introduce them to **Interactive Graphic Organizers**—tools for generating and organizing ideas, comparing and contrasting, and other key skills.

go.hrw.com H12-639 Go

Link to Today

This selection explores the history and impact that the Oxford English Dictionary had on society during Dr. Samuel Johnson's time and the affect it has on the English language today.

Direct Teach

Think About/Talk About

Read with a Purpose Have students read the Read with a Purpose statement. Point out the word *prescribing* in the statement. Have students note the various times Winchester contrasts the word *prescriptive* with *descriptive* when discussing the inherent nature of the English language.

Analysis

A Informational Focus

Possible response: *Winchester's admiration of Johnson might make his argument slightly biased.*

Link to Today

This Link to Today explains how Samuel Johnson's *Dictionary* set the standard for all future English dictionaries.

Read with a Purpose

Read this selection to find out why Samuel Johnson's dictionary recorded English words as they were used instead of prescribing how they should be used.

Build Background

Dictionaries appear authoritative, so it is easy to think of them as filled with rules for language users to follow. However, most English dictionaries *describe* rather than *prescribe* language; they tell us how words are used rather than how they should be used. Samuel Johnson planned his *Dictionary* following a time when many authors despaired over the state of English. Many wanted a book that would set down rules for English and, in the words of Swift, "fix our language forever." Initially, Johnson agreed, but soon realized that English, by its nature, could not be fixed. His aim became not "to form, but to register" the language. The following excerpt discusses Johnson's descriptive *Dictionary* and its impact on English speakers everywhere.

HISTORY

from

The Meaning of Everything

by **Simon Winchester**

The magisterially[1] famous Dr Johnson created his great dictionary in 1755—in two volumes, in scores of editions, the book that all educated households possessed and took down whenever anyone asked simply for 'the dictionary,' set the standard for the following century, and some still think for all time, of just what an English dictionary should be. **A**

It is important to reiterate in this context that Johnson's work set standards for all future *English* dictionaries. For the way that English had developed, and the way that in the eighteenth century it was coming to be recognized at home, was profoundly different from the way that other languages were then being seen, and were being recognized and then collated and corralled into dictionaries elsewhere. The point is an obvious one: but it bears repeating, as it underlies—indeed, is vital in every way to—the making of the book that plays the central role in this story.

For English is not to be regarded in the same way as, say, French or Italian, and in one crucially important way. It is not a *fixed* language, the meaning of its words established, approved, and firmly set by some official committee charged with preserving its dignity and integrity. The French have had their Académie Française, a body made up of the much-feared Forty Immortals,

1. **magisterially:** with dignity and authority, perhaps so much as to be overbearing.

A Informational Focus **Critiquing an Author's Argument** What does Winchester's use of the phrase "magisterially famous" reveal about his opinion of Johnson? How might Winchester's opinion of Johnson affect his argument?

Vocabulary **reiterate** (ree IHT uh rayt) *v.:* repeat.

Universal Access

English Learners

To engage the students in a discussion about the modification of language and the adoption of new words, ask them to provide words from their own language that define modern objects such as computers, stereos, televisions, and mobile phones. Have students share the words with the class and discuss briefly about possible influences of different languages on the coinage of those words.

Struggling Readers

Strategic Students Draw a T-chart on the board. With students, categorize the differences between the evolution of English and the evolution of French or Italian. The column for English can include the words "descriptive" and "evolving." The column for French or Italian can include "controlled" and "linguistically pure." Then, ask students to give examples of words or phrases that are evolving and examples of words or phrases that are controlled.

which has done precisely this (and with an extreme punctiliousness and absolute want of humor) since 1634. The Italians have also had their Accademia della Crusca in Florence since 1582—since long before, in other words, there was even a nation called Italy. The task of both bodies was to preserve linguistic purity, to prevent the languages' ruin by permitting inelegant importations, and to guide the public on just how to write and speak. The two bodies were established, in short, to prescribe the use of the language. No such body has ever been set up in England, nor in any English-speaking country.[2] . . .

For English is a language that simply cannot be fixed, nor can its use ever be absolutely laid down. It changes constantly; it grows with an almost exponential joy. It evolves eternally; its words alter their senses and their meanings subtly, slowly, or speedily according to fashion and need. Dictionaries that record and catalogue the language thus cannot ever be *prescriptive*; they must always be entirely *descriptive,* telling of the language as it is, not as it should be. Samuel Johnson's majestic *Dictionary of the English Language,* published first in 1755 and remaining in print for well over the century following, is a classic of this kind. It is as full a record as Johnson and the six serving men who worked with him as amanuenses[3] for six years in cramped rooms south of Fleet Street could determine, of the entire assemblage of words that were employed by all who lived in the realm—the words used by the learned, the nobly born, the doctor, the dandy, and the divine and, most important of all, the words used by the common man of the street, the slum, the farm, and the field. . . . B

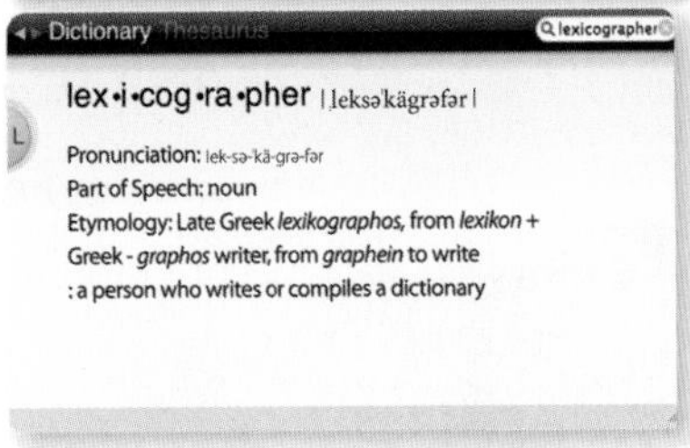

(top) Samuel Johnson's *Dictionary*, grammar page. Dr. Johnson's House Trust, London.

(bottom) An entry from an online dictionary.

2. Except South Africa, which has its own 'English Academy' based in Johannesburg, charged with promoting 'the effective use of English as a dynamic language'. The French and Italians would deny the use of the word 'dynamic', urging upon their respective peoples the need for linguistic stability and an abhorrence of change.
3. **amanuenses:** (uh man yoo EHN seez) people who copy notes or take dictation.

B Informational Focus Critiquing an Author's Argument Re-read the first two sentences in this paragraph. What examples can you think of to support Winchester's claims that English constantly changes, grows, and evolves? Might Winchester's opinion of Johnson affect his argument?

Vocabulary **punctiliousness** (puhngk TIHL ee uhs nuhs) *n.:* care for following rules and traditions exactly.
prescribe (prih SKRYB) *v.:* limit by rules or laws; order.

Think About/Talk About

Analysis

B Informational Focus

Possible responses: *Words such as* download *have evolved from our society's technological growth. Winchester views Johnson as an innovative man; therefore, he would be more likely to think that Johnson would create this publication with the understanding that it would evolve.*

Extend the Discussion

Finding Details What adjectives does Winchester choose that indicate his opinion about the English language and Johnson's contribution to it? ***Possible response:*** *Winchester writes that language grows with an "exponential joy" and that Johnson's dictionary is "majestic." These words indicate his admiration for the language and Johnson's contribution to it.*

Evaluating In what way does the scene of Johnson and the amanuenses on this page support Winchester's argument? ***Possible response:*** *The image of Johnson and his six amanuenses slaving away in a cramped room shows that the men sacrificed time and comfort for the benefit of all English speakers.*

Vocabulary: Own the Word

- **reiterate:** Winchester says it is important to *reiterate* that Johnson's work set the standard for all English dictionaries. What things might be important for a parent to *reiterate* to a child? [*to look both ways before crossing a street; to avoid speaking to strangers*]
- **punctiliousness:** Why might a teacher want a class to show *punctiliousness* in the classroom? [*to make sure students are adhering closely to the classroom rules*]
- **prescribe:** *Prescribe* means "to limit by rules or laws." What might a governor *prescribe* for the citizens of a state? [*laws for proper conduct; rules about respecting other people's property*]

Advanced Learners

Acceleration Ask students to imagine that there is a body of scholars policing the English language, such as France's Académie Francaise or Italy's Accademia della Crusca. Have them write a bulleted list of rules that this hypothetical English academy would impose. Have students discuss words that should be banned from American English. Then, have them write a brief paragraph about what impact on our language such policies would have.

Students with Disabilities

To help students understand the focus of the selection, ask students how they think new words are accepted into a dictionary. Explain that dictionaries are often reprinted to include new words when these words have become widespread or they define new objects of use (the word *surfing* now describes navigating the Internet). Have students brainstorm modern words that they think now appear in the dictionary, and help them verify their guesses.

Think About/Talk About

Analysis

Ⓒ Informational Focus

Possible responses: *Johnson's words lend validity to Winchester's argument. Johnson's reference to English as being "without order" and "without rules" supports Winchester's argument.*

Vocabulary: Own the Word

copious: Tell students that the word *copious* is derived from the Latin word *copiosus,* which means "plenty." Have students name something they would like to have *copious* amounts of. ***Possible responses:*** *candy; money; friends; food*

Monitor Students' Comprehension

Guide the class in answering these comprehension questions.

1. What was the influence of Johnson's dictionary according to Winchester? [*Johnson's dictionary set the standard for all subsequent English dictionaries.*]
2. What does the author mean by saying that "English is not a fixed language"? [*English does not follow a firm set of rules established by a committee.*]
3. Why does the author consider dictionaries descriptive? [*The role of dictionaries is that of recording the language as it is.*]

The approach that Johnson took was not to decide for himself what words meant, not (to reiterate the point) to *prescribe* how they should be used—but instead to let the printed record of centuries-worth of writing and literature illustrate how words had actually been used in the past, and tease from the record the variety of historic meanings, from the time each was invented and first introduced, and as their various senses shifted like silverfish over the succeeding centuries. 'When I took the first survey of my undertaking,' he wrote in his famous Preface,

I found our speech copious without order, and energetick without rules: wherever I turned my view, there was perplexity to be disentangled, and confusion to be regulated. Having therefore no assistance but from general grammar I applied myself to the perusal of our writers; and noting whatever might be used to ascertain or illustrate any word or phrase, accumulated in time the materials of a dictionary which, by degrees, I reduced to method. Ⓒ

This was a method which Johnson perhaps honored more in the breach than the observance. But it nonetheless set the pattern for all the best dictionaries for all time to come: no better means has ever been developed for producing as near as possible a complete record of a language.

Ⓒ **Informational Focus** **Critiquing an Author's Argument** Why do you think Winchester includes Johnson's own words? Which of Johnson's lines support Winchester's argument that English is constantly changing? How?

Vocabulary **copious** (KOH pee uhs) *adj.*: plentiful; abundant.

Simon Winchester, atop Mount Pinatubo, Pampanga Province, Luzon, Philippines, 2002.

California Standards, p. 643

- **Reading Standard 2.4** Make warranted and reasonable assertions about the author's arguments by using elements of the text to defend and clarify interpretations..
- **Writing Standard 1.3** Structure ideas and arguments in a sustained, persuasive, and sophisticated way and support them with precise and relevant examples.
- **Listening and Speaking Standard 2.3** Deliver oral responses to literature: **b.** Analyze the imagery, language, universal themes, and unique aspects of the text through the use of rhetorical strategies (e.g., narration, description, persuasion, exposition, a combination of those strategies). **c.** Support important ideas and viewpoints through accurate and detailed references to the text or to other works. **e.** Identify and assess the impact of perceived ambiguities, nuances, and complexities within the text.

INFORMATIONAL TEXT FOCUS

Applying Your Skills

from The Meaning of Everything

Reading Standard 2.4 (see pages A48–A50)
Listening and Speaking Standard 2.3b, 2.3c (see pages A53–A55)
Writing Standard 1.3 (see pages A51–A52)

Analyze Informational Texts

Informational Text Focus

Quick Check

1. Who are the Forty Immortals? What is their job?
2. Why does Winchester find English unique?
3. How did Johnson get the words and definitions that he included in his *Dictionary?*

Read with a Purpose

4. Why did Samuel Johnson make his dictionary descriptive instead of prescriptive?

Informational Skills: Critiquing an Author's Argument

5. Review your reading chart, and write a sentence that expresses Winchester's overall argument. Then, explain in a paragraph whether or not Winchester convincingly supports his argument with evidence and examples.

Claim	Evidence/ Examples 1	Evidence/ Examples 2
Johnson's dictionary set the standard for English dictionaries that followed.	Johnson used a different method from the one other dictionary makers used.	Johnson didn't try to limit the meanings of words.

Vocabulary Check

Match each Vocabulary word with its definition.

6. reiterate — a. care about following rules
7. punctiliousness — b. order
8. prescribe — c. abundant
9. copious — d. repeat

Text Analysis

10. **Compare and Contrast** Explain how a prescriptive definition of a word differs from a descriptive definition of a word.
11. **Analyze** Winchester uses the simile "shifted like silverfish" to describe English words and their meanings. Locate this simile in the selection, and explain its meaning.
12. **Extend** Why do you think English borrows so many words from other languages? How do words from other languages enhance English?
13. **Extend** Winchester says that English "simply cannot be fixed." What might happen if a committee tried to fix the meanings of English words? Would they succeed? Why or why not?

Listening and Speaking

14. **Analyze** With a partner, discuss your understanding of how language changes. How and when might new words come into common use in English? What effect do you think newspapers, television, radio, and the Internet have on language? Include examples from your own experiences.

Writing Skills Focus

Timed Writing As you read, you noted the differences between descriptive and prescriptive dictionaries. In an essay, briefly discuss the advantages and disadvantages of each way of defining words. Be sure to cite specific evidence in your response.

What Do You Think Now? How do descriptive dictionaries simultaneously impose order on language and reflect how language changes?

Check for Understanding

Independent Practice

Informational Text Focus

Possible responses:

1. *The Forty Immortals were the members of the Académie Francaise. They determined rules and usage of proper French.*
2. *Winchester finds English unique because it is constantly evolving.*
3. *Johnson selected the words and definitions based on common usage and literary references.*
4. *He probably wanted to defend his concept of proper English against the contamination of jargon.*
5. *Have students sift through the essay paragraph by paragraph, recording claims and evidence.*
6. *d*
7. *a*
8. *b*
9. *c*
10. *A prescriptive definition tells the reader what a word should mean and how it should be used. A descriptive definition tells what a word means in current usage.*
11. *The simile states that the silverfish travel mysteriously through water; they travel in large schools. Winchester means that words are abundant and travel quickly and mysteriously through time.*
12. *English does not follow a set of rules prescribed by a committee. In America, the societal melting pot may contribute to the inclusion of words from other languages. These words add to the diversity and evolution of the language.*
13. *Given the diversity of English, it would be impossible to retroactively impose such regulations.*
14. *Students reflect on the English that is accessible through the media, explaining which media use a more formal English, and which broadcast words and expressions that come from slang.*

Universal Access

Struggling Writers

Provide additional scaffolding to help students complete the Writing Skills Focus activity. Before writing their essay, have student pairs work together to come up with a definition for prescriptive and descriptive dictionaries. Students might note that prescriptive dictionaries impose strict rules on language usage; descriptive dictionaries tell the meaning of words as they are, not as they should be. Next, have them fill in a Venn diagram that outlines the benefits and disadvantages of each method. Have students use their diagrams to complete the essay.

What Do You Think Now?

Ask students to reflect on the differences between a prescriptive and a descriptive approach to language. Ask them to think how descriptive dictionaries might embrace both approaches.

Assess

Unit 3 Resources,
Selection Standards Check, p. 73

Standards Focus

Objectives

Students will
- analyze the characteristics of biographies
- analyze an author's point of view

Selection Introduction

Think About the Writer

Have students brainstorm a list of important people whom they admire and consider why writers would write biographies of these people.

For Independent Reading

The Autobiography of Mark Twain, Mark Twain

Motivate

What Do You Think?/QuickWrite

Use the QuickWrite to have students brainstorm a list of people in the past who led interesting lives. What about the person would make others want to read their biography?

English for Academic Success

Academic Vocabulary

Look for opportunities to use the Academic Vocabulary words in this unit.

- **approach, *n.*:** a way of addressing something
- **convince, *v.*:** cause to believe
- **dominate, *v.*:** hold a commanding position
- **enhance, *v.*:** improve the quality of
- **participate, *v.*:** take part in

California Standards, pp. 644–655

- **Reading Standard 3.1** Analyze characteristics of subgenres (e.g., satire, parody, allegory, pastoral) that are used in poetry, prose, plays, novels, short stories, essays, and other basic genres.
- **Reading Standard 3.2** Analyze the way in which the theme or meaning of a selection represents a view or comment on life, using textual evidence to support the claim.
- **Reading Standard 3.9** Analyze the philosophical arguments presented in literary works to determine whether the authors' positions have contributed to the quality of each work and the credibility of the characters. (Philosophical approach)

Preparing to Read

from The Life of Samuel Johnson

What Do You Think? How can order and civilization affect human behavior?

QuickWrite

If you were to write a biography, about whom would you write? Why? What would be the most interesting aspect of your biography?

(Background) *Perspective view of Covent Garden Flower Market.* Color engraving. Science Museum, London.

MEET THE WRITER

James Boswell

(1740–1795)

James Boswell admired Samuel Johnson's writing long before the two met. Based on their twenty-year friendship, Boswell authored what many people consider the world's greatest biography—*The Life of Samuel Johnson,* published in 1791. Boswell's methods for gathering information about his subject have influenced countless other biographers.

The Young Man from Scotland

Born in Scotland, Boswell was heir to a large fortune. His father, a stern judge who wanted Boswell to practice law, disapproved of Boswell's ambitions to travel, write, and meet great people. When Boswell was twenty-two years old, however, his father relented and allowed him to go to London. In 1763, Boswell met Johnson, who was then fifty-three and famous for his *Dictionary of the English Language.* Boswell returned to Scotland to practice law, but he maintained his friendship with Johnson and aspired to become Johnson's biographer—a task he completed nearly thirty years later. In the book's opening pages, Boswell explains, "I will venture to say that [Johnson] will be seen in this work more completely than any man who has ever yet lived."

A Biographer's Method

Early in their friendship, Johnson advised Boswell to "read diligently the great book of mankind." Boswell took this advice to heart. He trained his memory to recall exact details of an event, and he later wrote these observations down in private. Thus, over the years, Boswell kept a written record of his own and other people's behavior and conversation. To write Johnson's biography, begun four years after his friend's death, Boswell used as sources his own journals, Johnson's writings and letters, and information collected from Johnson's friends. Boswell's *Life* reveals more than Johnson's character; the biography also offers us a window into the literary world of London during the second half of the eighteenth century.

Think About the Writer If Boswell were looking for someone to write about today, whom might he choose? Why?

James Boswell (1765) by George Willison.
Scottish National Portrait Gallery, Edinburgh, Scotland.

Selection Readability	
Easily Accessible **Accessible** Challenging	accessible language; chronological order

Reading Standard 3.1, 3.2, 3.9 (see pages A48–A50)

Literary Skills Focus

Biography A **biography** is an account of a person's life written by another person. Biographers cannot tell every detail about a person's life—no book could contain that many pages—so they choose certain details to record about their subjects. As you read, consider why Boswell chose the details, conversations, and events he includes.

Literary Perspectives Apply the literary perspective described on page 647 as you read this selection.

Reading Skills Focus

Analyzing an Author's Point of View An author's **point of view** is the vantage point from which he or she tells a story. Boswell narrates from a **first-person point of view,** telling us only what he sees, hears, and experiences as a character in Johnson's life story. Boswell initially writes as an outsider; gradually, though, he moves into Johnson's circle of friends. This shift broadens his experiences and the range of details he can convey.

Into Action Use a chart like the one below to record the changes in Boswell's attitude as a narrator as his friendship with Johnson deepens and his vantage point changes.

Section Title	Boswell's Vantage Point
Boswell's First Meeting with Johnson, 1763	Boswell is a nervous guest, observing Johnson's circle from outside.

Writing Skills Focus

Think as a Reader/Writer

Find It in Your Reading In this biography, Boswell often includes **dialogue**—conversation between two or more people. In your *Reader/Writer Notebook,* record instances in which the dialogue reveals the characters' personalities, such as when Mr. Davies blurts that Boswell is from Scotland, although Boswell has asked him not to do so.

Reader/Writer Notebook

Use your **RWN** to complete the activities for this selection.

Vocabulary

reverence (REHV uhr uhns) *n.:* deep respect. *Boswell developed a reverence for Johnson's wisdom.*

apprehensive (ap rih HEHN sihv) *adj.:* feeling anxious, worried. *Boswell was apprehensive about making a good impression on Johnson.*

slovenly (SLUHV uhn lee) *adj.:* untidy. *Boswell was initially surprised by Johnson's slovenly apartment.*

whimsical (HWIHM zuh kuhl) *adj.:* fanciful. *Johnson took part in whimsical arguments simply because he enjoyed debate.*

singularities (sihng gyoo LAR uh teez) *n. pl.:* characteristics that make a person unique. *Johnson's personality, with its many singularities, charmed his friends.*

candor (KAN duhr) *n.:* honesty, openness. *Johnson believed candor was essential for successful communication.*

ingenuity (ihn juh NOO uh tee) *n.:* cleverness, inventiveness. *Boswell demonstrated great ingenuity by memorizing all the details he recorded about Johnson.*

Language Coach

Personal Definitions One way to remember the meaning of new words is to associate them with someone or something in your own life. For whom or what do you feel *reverence*? Give a specific answer that uses the word *reverence*. This association will help you remember the word's definition.

Learn It Online

Practice your vocabulary knowledge online with Word Watch.

go.hrw.com H12-645 Go

Selection Resources

Unit 3 Resources, on-level practice and assessment, p. 76

Teacher One Stop™, on-level lesson plans and all print resources

Holt Audio Library

Holt Audio Library: Selections and Summaries in Spanish

UA: Differentiating Instruction, graphic organizer, p. 141

UA: Supporting Instruction in Spanish, selection summary

ThinkCentral Online Assessment, Selection Standards Check

ThinkCentral Online Remediation

Preteach

Introducing Vocabulary

Read aloud the Vocabulary words, definitions, and sample sentences. Then, use this activity to check students' understanding.

1. Explain the qualities of a person for whom you feel **reverence.**
2. Describe a situation that makes you **apprehensive.**
3. Explain how a **slovenly** person would dress.
4. What kind of person would have **whimsical** thoughts?
5. List two or three **singularities** about your personality.
6. Explain why some people appreciate **candor** of speech.
7. Give an example of a profession that requires **ingenuity.**

English for Academic Success

Language Coach

Ask other questions to help students connect the words to their lives, such as "Talk about a time you showed *ingenuity.*"

Literary Skills Focus

As you read and discuss the selection with students, have them identify the characteristics of biography.

Reading Skills Focus

Give students a copy of the Reading Skills Focus graphic organizer before they read. (See **Unit 3 Resources.**) Tell them to use their responses to answer the questions on the Applying Your Skills page.

Writing Skills Focus

Have students record instances of dialogue that reveals the characters' personalities in their **Reader/Writer Notebooks.**

Learn It Online

Send students to **Word Watch** for audio pronunciations, synonyms and antonyms, and brief histories of word origins.

go.hrw.com H12-645 Go

Teacher Preparation
Selection Summary
These excerpts from *The Life of Samuel Johnson* are written by his younger friend and admirer James Boswell. They cover James Boswell's first meeting with Johnson, his first visit to Johnson's home, and a recollection of Johnson's personal quirks as well as his love of arguing a point.

Direct Teach

Think About/Talk About
Read with a Purpose Have students read the Read with a Purpose statement. Ask students as they read to note the awe and reverence that Boswell displays for Johnson. Ask students to consider how Boswell's feelings about the subject of his biography might influence his writing.

BIOGRAPHY

from The Life of Samuel Johnson

by **James Boswell**

Read with a Purpose
Read this selection to discover Johnson's wit and intellect and to understand Boswell's growing admiration for his mentor and friend.

Build Background
Throughout the biography we often see Boswell provoking Johnson to speak out on a topic. Boswell also manipulates the conversation for dramatic effect, in much the same way a playwright manages the dialogue of his or her characters. This amazing level of detail, drawn from the large number of conversations Boswell reports, distinguishes *The Life of Samuel Johnson* from other early biographies.

Statue of Samuel Johnson.
(Background) Perspective view of Covent Garden Flower Market (19th century).
Science Museum, London.

Universal Access

EL English Learners
To familiarize the students with different kinds of authors' points of view, explain that the first-person point of view of the selection is evident by the use of the personal pronoun *I*. Explain that another point of view is the third-person point of view, which refers to characters by using personal pronouns such as *she, he,* and *they.*

Activity Help students rewrite this sentence, which begins at the bottom of p. 647, so that it uses the third-person point of view: "Mr. Davies mentioned my name, and respectfully introduced me to him." [*Mr. Davies mentioned Boswell's name, and respectfully introduced him to Johnson.*]

Boswell's First Meeting with Johnson, 1763

This is to me a memorable year; for in it I had the happiness to obtain the acquaintance of that extraordinary man whose memoirs I am now writing; an acquaintance which I shall ever esteem as one of the most fortunate circumstances in my life. Though then but two-and-twenty, I had for several years read his works with delight and instruction, and had the highest reverence for their author, which had grown up in my fancy into a kind of mysterious veneration, by figuring to myself a state of solemn elevated abstraction, in which I supposed him to live in the immense metropolis of London. . . . Mr. Thomas Davies the actor, who then kept a bookseller's shop in Russel Street, Covent Garden, told me that Johnson was very much his friend, and came frequently to his house, where he more than once invited me to meet him; but by some unlucky accident or other he was prevented from coming to us. . . .

At last, on Monday the 16th of May, when I was sitting in Mr. Davies's back parlor, after having drunk tea with him and Mrs. Davies, Johnson unexpectedly came into the shop; and Mr. Davies having perceived him through the glass door in the room in which we were sitting, advancing toward us—he announced his awful[1] approach to me, somewhat in the manner of an actor in the part of Horatio, when he addresses Hamlet on the appearance of his father's ghost, "Look, my Lord, it comes." I found that I had a very perfect idea of Johnson's figure, from the portrait of him painted by Sir Joshua Reynolds soon after he had published his *Dictionary,* in the attitude of sitting in his easy chair in deep meditation, which was the first picture his friend did for him, which Sir Joshua very kindly presented to me, and from which an engraving has been made for this work. Mr. Davies mentioned my name, and respectfully introduced me to him. I was much agitated; and recollecting his prejudice against the Scotch, of which I had heard much, I said to Davies, "Don't tell where I come from."—"From Scotland," cried Davies roguishly. "Mr. Johnson (said I), I do indeed come from Scotland, but I cannot help it." I am willing to flatter myself that I meant this as light pleasantry to soothe and conciliate him, and not as an humiliating abasement at the expense of my country. But however that might be, this speech was somewhat unlucky; for with that quickness of wit for which he was so remarkable, he seized the expression "come from Scotland," which I used in the sense of being of that country, and, as if I had said that I had come away from it, or left it, retorted, "That, Sir, I find, is what a very great many of your countrymen cannot help." This stroke stunned

1. **awful:** used here to mean producing awe; now, the more common term is "awesome."

Literary Perspectives

Analyzing Biographical Information Knowing biographical information about a writer may help you understand and evaluate the writer's work. How did James Boswell's background prepare him to become Samuel Johnson's biographer, and how does his perspective shape the biography? What does he reveal about himself in his biography of Johnson? As a young man, Boswell admired Johnson's intellect and wit and aspired to lead the kind of life that Johnson enjoyed. Boswell wished to befriend Johnson not only because he admired the great writer, but also because Johnson could introduce him to the prominent intellectuals, artists, and politicians in London. Consider, then, how Boswell's admiration for and friendship with Johnson, as well as Boswell's interest in London's intellectual society, affect the content and tone of his biography of Johnson.

As you read, be sure to notice the questions in the text, which will guide you in using this perspective.

Vocabulary **reverence** (REHV uhr uhns) *n.:* deep respect.

Think About/Talk About

Extend the Discussion

Rereading What does Boswell mean when he says he flattered himself about his intentions to apologize for his country of origin? ***Possible response:*** *Boswell's awe of Johnson is more powerful than his pride in his heritage, and this embarrasses him. He flatters himself that he apologizes for being Scottish simply to smooth over the meeting.*

Characterization What does the reader learn about Mr. Davies's character when he blurts out Boswell's country of origin? ***Possible response:*** *We learn that he is playful and perhaps brutally honest. He does not pay deference to Boswell's fear of being disliked because of Boswell's nationality.*

Vocabulary: Own the Word

reverence: Tell students that the adjective form of *reverence* is *reverent,* or "a feeling of awe for a person, thing, or idea." The verb form is *revere,* which means "to show awe." Ask students to name a scientist, doctor, inventor, or politician they *revere.*

Literary Perspectives

Before students read the selection, have them read the **Literary Perspectives** about Analyzing Biographical Information. Have students focus on the first visit that James Boswell pays to Johnson and the acquaintances he can hope to make in that place. Ask them to transcribe names and situations and list the possible advantages that Boswell might gain.

Remind students to use the notes and questions at the bottom of the page to help them use the perspective.

Model the Skill

- Provide students with copies of the Reading Skills Focus graphic organizer for *The Life of Samuel Johnson.* (See **Unit 3 Resources**.)
- Tell students to pay special attention to the way Boswell changes his attitude towards Johnson as their acquaintance deepens. When Boswell first met Johnson, he was nervous and excited. On this first visit, Boswell does not seem nervous anymore; he is curious and then surprised. He reveals the uncouth appearance of Johnson, and he does not spare details in the description. The reverence for Johnson seems to have diminished. Add the conclusions about Boswell's vantage point in the graphic organizer.

Section's Title	Boswell's Vantage Point
Boswell's First Visit to Johnson	Boswell is surprised by the poor state of Johnson's appearance.

Guided Practice: Apply

Read-Think-Write As students fill in their graphic organizers, ask them to consider the changes in Boswell's attitude and point of view. Have them write their conclusion in a short paragraph.

me a good deal; and when we had sat down, I felt myself not a little embarrassed, and apprehensive of what might come next. He then addressed himself to Davies. "What do you think of Garrick?[2] He has refused me an order for the play for Miss Williams, because he knows the house will be full, and that an order would be worth three shillings." Eager to take any opening to get into conversation with him, I ventured to say, "O, Sir, I cannot think Mr. Garrick would grudge such a trifle to you." "Sir (said he, with a stern look), I have known David Garrick longer than you have done: and I know no right you have to talk to me on the subject." Perhaps I deserved this check; for it was rather presumptuous in me, an entire stranger, to express any doubt of the justice of his animadversion[3] upon his old acquaintance and pupil. I now felt myself much mortified, and began to think that the hope which I had long indulged of obtaining his acquaintance was blasted. And, in truth, had not my ardor been uncommonly strong, and my resolution uncommonly persevering, so rough a reception might have deterred[4] me forever from making any further attempts. Fortunately, however, I remained upon the field not wholly discomfited. . . . **A**

I was highly pleased with the extraordinary vigor of his conversation, and regretted that I was drawn away from it by an engagement at another place. I had, for a part of the evening, been left alone with him, and had ventured to make an observation now and then, which he received very civilly; so that I was satisfied that though there was a roughness in his manner, there was no ill nature in his disposition. Davies followed me to the door, and when I complained to him a little of the hard blows which the great man had given me, he kindly took upon him to console me by saying, "Don't be uneasy. I can see he likes you very well." **B**

Boswell's First Visit to Johnson

A few days afterward I called on Davies, and asked him if he thought I might take the liberty of waiting on Mr. Johnson at his Chambers in the Temple.[5] He said I certainly might, and that Mr. Johnson would take it as a compliment. So upon Tuesday the 24th of May, . . . I boldly repaired to Johnson. His Chambers were on the first floor of No. 1, Inner-Temple-lane, and I entered them with an impression given me by the Reverend Dr. Blair,[6] of Edinburgh, who had been introduced to him not long before, and described his having "found the Giant in his den," an expression, which, when I came to be pretty well acquainted with Johnson, I repeated to him, and he was diverted at this picturesque account of himself. . . .

He received me very courteously; but, it must be confessed, that his apartment, and furniture, and morning dress, were sufficiently uncouth. His brown suit of clothes looked very rusty; he had on a little old shriveled unpowdered wig, which was too small for his head; his shirtneck and knees of his breeches were loose; his black worsted stockings ill drawn up; and he had a pair of unbuckled shoes by way of slippers. But all these slovenly particularities were forgotten the moment that he began to talk. Some gentlemen, whom I do not recollect, were sitting with him; and when they went away, I also rose; but he said to me, "Nay, don't go." "Sir (said I), I am afraid that I intrude

2. **Garrick:** the English actor David Garrick (1717–1779), a former pupil of Johnson's.
3. **animadversion** (an uh mad VUR zhuhn): critical comment.
4. **deterred:** prevented.
5. **Temple:** area in London where lawyers and other professional people lived and worked.
6. **Blair:** Hugh Blair (1718–1800), a Presbyterian clergyman and writer.

A **Literary Perspectives** **Analyzing Biographical Information** What is Boswell's hope for himself during this first interview with Johnson? What do his words and actions suggest about his ambition?

B **Reading Focus** **Analyzing an Author's Point of View** What point of view has Boswell chosen? How does Boswell's point of view affect his portrayal of Samuel Johnson?

Vocabulary **apprehensive** (ap rih HEHN sihv) *adj.:* feeling anxious, worried.
slovenly (SLUHV uhn lee) *adj.:* untidy.

Universal Access

Struggling Readers

To help students read *The Life of Samuel Johnson,* model the reading skill of identifying the author's point of view. You might say: "While I read the selection, I try to find clues that tell me about the author's point of view. I think about elements that might influence his opinion, his feelings as he writes, and how he considers people and events around him." Encourage students as they read to ask themselves: "Where is the author in this scene? What are his feelings? How do his feelings influence his point of view?"

Advanced Learners

Enrichment Have students compare the style and tone of Boswell's biography of Johnson with any other biography they have read. Encourage students to notice how the choice of language and of details reveal the biographer's attitude toward the subject and in turn affects the reader's response to the subject.

James Boswell and Samuel Johnson at the Mitre Tavern in London (19th century).
The Granger Collection, NY.

upon you. It is benevolent to allow me to sit and hear you." He seemed pleased with this compliment, which I sincerely paid him, and answered, "Sir, I am obliged to any man who visits me." . . . C

Boswell Quizzes Johnson

I know not how so whimsical a thought came into my mind, but I asked, "If, Sir, you were shut up in a castle, and a newborn child with you, what would you do?" Johnson. "Why, Sir, I should not much like my company." Boswell. "But would you take the trouble of rearing it?" He seemed, as may well be supposed, unwilling to pursue the subject: but upon my persevering in my question, replied, "Why yes, Sir, I would; but I must have all conveniences. If I had no garden,

C **Literary Focus** **Biography** Identify some of the details that Boswell uses in his description of Johnson in this paragraph. How do these details affect your perception of Johnson?

Vocabulary **whimsical** (HWIHM zuh kuhl) *adj.:* fanciful.

Think About/Talk About

Comprehension

B Reading Focus

Possible response: *Boswell has chosen the first-person point of view, making his portrayal of Johnson more personal and subjective.*

Analysis

A Literary Perspectives

Possible responses: *Boswell wants to ingratiate himself to Johnson. He speaks of Garrick as if he knows the actor well in the hopes that Johnson would involve Boswell in their conversation.*

C Literary Focus

Possible responses: *Johnson's wig is too small, his shoes are not properly fastened, and his shirt and pants are worn loosely. It seems to be a non sequitur that such a great thinker would appear so disheveled.*

Vocabulary: Own the Word

- **apprehensive:** Ask students: "Have you ever felt *apprehensive* about something? Explain what you were *apprehensive* about and how your actions showed your *apprehension* (noun form)."
- **slovenly:** Tell students that synonyms for the word *slovenly* are *disheveled* and *unkempt.* Ask students: "How would you react if a person with a *slovenly* appearance approached you on the street?"
- **whimsical:** Remind students that *whimsical* means "slightly odd," "old-fashioned," or "playful, especially in an endearing way." Ask students to name things they would describe as *whimsical.*

Students with Disabilities

Ask students to look over the subheadings included in the selection and to skim the selection itself, noting key words and phases. Have them predict what information each section of the selection will provide and record questions in their reading notes that they expect will be answered in the biography.

✔ See **UA: Differentiating Instruction** for a graphic organizer to scaffold instruction for students with disabilities.

Model the Skill

- Review the concept of a **biography:** an account of a person's life written by another person. Biographers cannot tell every detail about a person's life, so they choose the most important details to record about their subjects.
- Tell students that by looking at the details that Boswell includes, readers can consider his motivation for writing a biography about Johnson.
- On p. 651, Boswell includes a long description of rather odd mannerisms that Johnson displays, including holding his head to one side and shaking it, making strange sounds with his mouth, and blowing out his breath. Explain that Boswell probably wanted readers to know that, although Johnson was considered by many to be a great thinker, he still displayed behaviors that many people would consider to be eccentric.

Guided Practice: Apply

Think-Pair-Share Have students form pairs to discuss the role and responsibilities of a biographer. Ask students to consider how personal attitudes, personal ideals, or personal gain can influence a biographer's objectivity.

I would make a shed on the roof, and take it there for fresh air. I should feed it, and wash it much, and with warm water to please it, not with cold water to give it pain." BOSWELL. "But, Sir, does not heat relax?" JOHNSON. "Sir, you are not to imagine the water is to be very hot. I would not *coddle*[7] the child. No, Sir, the hardy method of treating children does no good. I'll take you five children from London, who shall cuff[8] five Highland children. Sir, a man bred in London will carry a burden, or run, or wrestle, as well as a man brought up in the hardiest manner in the country." BOSWELL. "Good living, I suppose, makes the Londoners strong." JOHNSON. "Why, Sir, I don't know that it does. Our chairmen[9] from Ireland, who are as strong men as any, have been brought up upon potatoes. Quantity makes up for quality." BOSWELL. "Would you teach this child that I have furnished you with, anything?" JOHNSON. "No, I should not be apt to teach it." BOSWELL. "Would not you have a pleasure in teaching it?" JOHNSON. "No, Sir, I should *not* have a pleasure in teaching it." BOSWELL. "Have you not a pleasure in teaching men? *There* I have you. You have the same pleasure in teaching men, that I should have in teaching children." JOHNSON. "Why, something about that." . . . **D**

Johnson's Eccentricities

. . . Talking to himself was, indeed, one of his singularities ever since I knew him. I was certain that he was frequently uttering pious ejaculations; for fragments of the Lord's Prayer have been distinctly overheard. His friend Mr. Thomas Davies, of whom

7. **coddle:** cook in hot water. Johnson is having fun with the two distinct meanings of the word, the other being "treat tenderly."
8. **cuff:** win a fight or scuffle with.
9. **chairmen:** here, porters who transported people through the London streets in sedan chairs (covered seats).

D **Literary Focus** **Biography** What motivates Boswell to ask the "whimsical" question during this visit to Johnson?

Vocabulary **singularities** (sihng gyoo LAR uh teez) *n. pl.:* characteristics that make a person unique.

Analyzing Visuals

Connecting to the Text How does this painting reflect the atmosphere of conversation that Johnson and Boswell seem to enjoy? What can you infer about the characters in this scene?

Literary Perspectives

To help students answer the **Literary Perspectives** question on p. 651, point out that Samuel Johnson was an eminent intellectual of his time and had many prominent friends and acquaintances. While Boswell spent time with Johnson to gather information for the biography, Johnson introduced Boswell to many of these scholarly individuals.

Cross-Curricular Connection

LITERATURE: The First of Its Kind

Boswell's biography of Johnson was the first of its kind. Published in 1791, *The Life of Samuel Johnson* was recognized for its amazing wealth of details and its record of verbatim conversation between Johnson, Boswell, and others. The portrait of Johnson is also a portrait of the intellectual landscape of late eighteenth-century England, which Johnson dominated during his lifetime.

An Early London Coffeehouse (c. 1705).
The British Museum, London.

Churchill[10] says, "That Davies hath a very pretty wife," when Dr. Johnson muttered "lead us not into temptation," used with waggish and gallant humor to whisper [to] Mrs. Davies, "You, my dear, are the cause of this."

He had another particularity, of which none of his friends ever ventured to ask an explanation. It appeared to me some superstitious habit, which he had contracted early, and from which he had never called upon his reason to disentangle him. This was his anxious care to go out or in at a door or passage by a certain number of steps from a certain point, or at least so as that either his right or his left foot (I am not certain which) should constantly make the first actual movement when he came close to the door or passage. Thus I conjecture: For I have, upon innumerable occasions, observed him suddenly stop, and then seem to count his steps with a deep earnestness; and when he had neglected or gone wrong in this sort of magical movement, I have seen him go back again, put himself in a proper posture to begin the ceremony, and, having gone through it, break from his abstraction, walk briskly on, and join his companion. E

That the most minute singularities which belonged to him, and made very observable parts of his appearance and manner, may not be omitted, it is requisite to mention, that while talking or even musing as he sat in his chair, he commonly held his head to one side toward his right shoulder, and shook it in a tremulous manner, moving his body backward and forward, and rubbing his left knee in the same direction, with the palm of his hand. In the intervals of articulating he made various sounds with his mouth, sometimes as if ruminating, or what is called chewing the cud, sometimes giving a half whistle, sometimes making his tongue play backward from the roof of

---

10. **Churchill:** Charles Churchill (1731–1764), writer of satirical and comic poems.
11. **Isle of Skye:** largest of the Inner Hebrides, a group of islands off the west coast of Scotland.
12. **Leicesterfields** (LEHS tuhr feeldz): square in London.

E Literary Perspectives **Analyzing Biographical Information** With what sort of men does Boswell come into contact through his friendship with Johnson? How does his knowledge of these men affect the authority of his biography?

Think About/Talk About

Analysis

D Literary Focus

***Possible response:** Boswell admits he does not know why he asked the "whimsical" question. However, the question reveals Johnson's values in terms of responsibility.*

E Literary Perspectives

***Possible responses:** Boswell becomes acquainted with men in Johnson's circle, many of whom were great thinkers of their day. Boswell's knowledge of these men enhances his degree of authority.*

Extend the Discussion

Identifying Cause and Effect Why would Johnson sometimes enter a door twice? ***Possible response:** Johnson's obsessive nature led him to walk through a door by taking a definite number of steps. If he miscalculated the steps, then he would walk back and start again.*

Vocabulary: Own the Word

singularities: Remind students that *singularities* are traits that make a person stand out from others. *Singularities* is related to the adjective, *singular* meaning "one of a kind." Ask students to name their own *singularities.*

Developing Oral Fluency

Paired Activity Ask students to consider the section under the heading "Boswell Quizzes Johnson." Tell students to view that dialogue as part of a play. Divide students into pairs, and ask them to take either Johnson's or Boswell's role. Ask them to read the section and give expression to what they read by taking into account what they learned about the personalities of both characters. [*Boswell is excited and inquisitive; Johnson is grouchy and reluctant.*]

✔ See the **Oral Language Skill Builder** in **UA: Differentiating Instruction.**

Analyzing Visuals

***Connecting to the Text:** The painting depicts a group of people engaged in pleasant conversation in a warm, comfortable room of a house—an ideal setting for literary debates, which both Johnson and Boswell enjoyed. The characters who are sitting down talking or standing near the painting seem to be men of importance because they are formally dressed and are attended by servants.*

Think About/Talk About

Comprehension

F Reading Focus

Possible responses: *He is attempting to provide a realistic and accurate depiction of Johnson. He wants to make it clear that he is not ridiculing Johnson at all.*

Analysis

G Literary Focus

Possible responses: *Johnson enjoys taking the contrary position in an argument. This reveals Johnson's love for debate and his desire to show off his cleverness.*

Vocabulary: Own the Word

- **candor:** Ask students: "Why might you be afraid to show *candor* to a friend? ***Possible response:*** *A person might be afraid to show candor if being honest might hurt a friend's feelings.*
- **ingenuity:** According to Boswell, how does Johnson show his *ingenuity*? ***Possible response:*** *He shows his cleverness by coming up with witty statements to make when debating others.*

Monitor Students' Comprehension

Guide the class in answering the comprehension question: Where does Boswell first meet Johnson? [*They meet by chance at Mr. Davies's, an actor and friend of both Boswell and Johnson.*]

his mouth, as if clucking like a hen, and sometimes protruding it against his upper gums in front, as if pronouncing quickly under his breath, *too, too, too:* all this accompanied sometimes with a thoughtful look, but more frequently with a smile. Generally when he had concluded a period, in the course of a dispute, by which time he was a good deal exhausted by violence and vociferation, he used to blow out his breath like a whale. This I supposed was a relief to his lungs; and seemed in him to be a contemptuous mode of expression, as if he had made the arguments of his opponent fly like chaff before the wind.

I am fully aware how very obvious an occasion I here give for the sneering jocularity of such as have no relish of an exact likeness; which to render complete, he who draws it must not disdain the slightest strokes. But if witlings[13] should be inclined to attack this account, let them have the candor to quote what I have offered in my defense. . . . F

Johnson's Love of Argument

. . . I mentioned a new gaming club,[14] of which Mr. Beauclerk[15] had given me an account, where the members played to a desperate extent. JOHNSON. "Depend upon it, Sir, this is mere talk. *Who* is ruined by gaming? You will not find six instances in an age. There is a strange rout made about deep play: Whereas you have many more people ruined by adventurous trade,[16] and yet we do not hear such an outcry against it." THRALE. "There may be few people absolutely ruined by deep play; but very many are much hurt in their circumstances by it." JOHNSON. "Yes, Sir, and so are very many by other kinds of expense." I had heard him talk once before in the same manner; and at Oxford he said, "he wished he had learnt to play at cards." The truth, however, is, that he loved to display his ingenuity in argument; and therefore would sometimes in conversation maintain opinions which he was sensible were wrong, but in supporting which, his reasoning and wit would be most conspicuous. He would begin thus: "Why, Sir, as to the good or evil of card playing—" "Now (said Garrick), he is thinking which side he shall take." He appeared to have a pleasure in contradiction, especially when any opinion whatever was delivered with an air of confidence; so that there was hardly any topic, if not one of the great truths of religion and morality, that he might not have been incited to argue, either for or against. . . . G

13. **witlings:** people who think they are witty.
14. **gaming club:** gambling club.
15. **Beauclerk:** Topham Beauclerk (1739–1780), a fashionable gentleman descended from King Charles II.
16. **trade:** business.

F Reading Focus Analyzing an Author's Point of View What reasons does Boswell give to justify including a discussion of Johnson's odd personal habits? Why might he feel the need to explain his motives?

G Literary Focus Biography According to Boswell, what does Johnson enjoy most about argument? What does this information tell you about Johnson's personality?

Vocabulary **candor** (KAN duhr) *n.:* honesty, openness.
ingenuity (ihn juh NOO uh tee) *n.:* cleverness, inventiveness.

California Standards, pp. 653–655

- **Reading Standard 2.2** Analyze the way in which clarity of meaning is affected by the patterns of organization, hierarchical structures, repetition of the main ideas, syntax, and word choice in the text.
- **Reading Standard 3.1** Analyze characteristics of subgenres (e.g., satire, parody, allegory, pastoral) that are used in poetry, prose, plays, novels, short stories, essays, and other basic genres.
- **Reading Standard 3.2** Analyze the way in which the theme or meaning of a selection represents a view or comment on life, using textual evidence to support the claim.
- **Reading Standard 3.9** Analyze the philosophical arguments presented in literary works to determine whether the authors' positions have contributed to the quality of each work and the credibility of the characters. (Philosophical approach)
- **Grades 9–10 Review Reading Standard 1.1** Identify and use the literal and figurative meanings of words and understand word derivations.
- **Writing Standard 2.1** Write fictional, autobiographical, or biographical narratives: **a.** Narrate a sequence of events and communicate their significance to the audience. **c.** Describe with concrete sensory details the sights, sounds, and smells of a scene and the specific actions, movements, gestures, and feelings of the characters; use interior monologue to depict the characters' feelings. **e.** Make effective use of descriptions of appearance, images, shifting perspectives, and sensory details.
- **Listening and Speaking Standard 2.2** Deliver oral reports on historical investigations: **a.** Use exposition, narration, description, persuasion, or some combination of those to support the thesis. **b.** Analyze several historical records of a single event, examining critical relationships between elements of the research topic. **c.** Explain the perceived reason or reasons for the similarities and differences by using information derived from primary and secondary sources to support or enhance the presentation.

Applying Your Skills

Reading Standard 2.2, 3.1, 3.2, 3.9 (see pages A48–A50)
Writing Standard 2.1a, 2.1c, 2.1e (see pages A51–A52)

from The Life of Samuel Johnson

Literary Response and Analysis

Reading Skills Focus

Quick Check

1. In the first paragraph, how does Boswell convey Johnson's significance to Boswell's own life?
2. What peculiar mannerisms did Johnson exhibit when he talked?
3. Why, according to Boswell, did Johnson sometimes express opinions that he did not believe?

Read with a Purpose

4. Cite specific details from the biography that reflect Johnson's wit and intellect. Where can you find examples of Boswell's growing admiration for his mentor and friend?

Reading Skills: Analyzing an Author's Point of View

5. Review the chart that you made as you read. In a paragraph, explain how Boswell's attitude as a narrator changes as his relationship with Johnson changes. Do the changes in Boswell's attitude make him more credible as an authority on Johnson? Support your opinion with examples from your chart.

Literary Skills Focus

Literary Analysis

6. **Analyze** Cite specific details from the biography that reflect Samuel Johnson's independent attitudes.
7. **Extend** Do you think Johnson would have been more or less interesting had his behavior been more conventional? Why is eccentric behavior important to society? How is eccentricity regarded in our society today?
8. **Make Judgments** What was Johnson's greatest strength and greatest fault as a person?
9. **Interpret** Why does it require several encounters before Boswell befriends Johnson? Why doesn't Boswell consider their first meeting a success?
10. **Literary Perspectives** How did Boswell benefit from his friendship with Johnson?

Literary Skills: Biography

11. **Analyze** In the biography, Boswell often mentions himself—his own feelings, impressions, and conclusions about Johnson. Do you think these references contribute to Boswell's work, or should he have maintained a more detached and objective view of his subject? Explain.

Literary Skills Review: Diction

12. **Analyze** A writer or speaker's choice of words is called **diction**. In the biography, Boswell often quotes Johnson's exact words. Read Johnson's words, and write a sentence about his diction.

Writing Skills Focus

Think as a Reader/Writer

Use It in Your Writing Imagine you were able to talk for an hour with someone you admire. In your *Reader/Writer Notebook,* write a one-page excerpt of this imaginary dialogue. Be certain to communicate your subject's personality through the dialogue, just as Boswell's dialogues reveal Johnson's character.

What Do You Think Now Based on what you read, which elements of Johnson's life and thinking were orderly? Which were not? How do you think these elements contributed to Johnson's fame?

Universal Access

Struggling Writers

Some students may need additional scaffolding to complete the Writing Skills Focus activity. Before they write their essay, have students choose a person they admire from the list they brainstormed before reading. Have them write three to four questions they would ask this person. Encourage students to use the questions and answers as the basis for the dialogue.

What Do You Think Now?

Ask students to consider strengths and weaknesses in Johnson's personality as they conclude Boswell's account. Which details show his ingenuity and politeness? Which reveal his carelessness?

Check for Understanding

Independent Practice

Reading Skills Focus

Possible responses:

1. *Boswell states that he has studied Johnson's work for years.*
2. *physical tics*
3. *He enjoyed contradicting others.*
4. *Johnson's barb to Boswell about the Scottish indicates his wit. Boswell appreciates Johnson's willingness to include him in social discussions.*
5. *Make sure students glean details from each section of the text. Have students include one sentence drawn from each example.*

Literary Skills Focus

Possible responses:

6. *Johnson's appearance indicates an independence from social mores. His love of argument indicates an independent spirit.*
7. *Johnson would have been less interesting were he less eccentric. Because society constantly challenges norms we take for granted, eccentricity is important to society. Our society values conformity in some areas and applauds eccentricity in others.*
8. *His strength was his inquisitive mind. His greatest fault may have been his prejudiced feelings about those from other nations.*
9. *Johnson's harsh demeanor gives Boswell the impression that they are not friends and leads him to believe that their first meeting is a failure.*
10. *He made acquaintances with the most influential people of his time.*
11. *Readers learn more about Johnson's personality because they see him in relation to Boswell. On the other hand, a more objective portrayal might give a clearer picture of other aspects of Johnson's life.*
12. *Johnson's diction reveals his humor and wit.*

Independent Practice
Vocabulary Development
Vocabulary Check
1. *b* **2.** *e*
3. *d* **4.** *f*
5. *a* **6.** *g*
7. *c*

Your Turn

Sample response:
whimsical

How to pronounce it: HWIHM zih kuhl

Part of speech: adjective

What it means: unpredictable, often in an amusing way; quirky

Words I associate it with: whim *(an impulse),* whimsy *(playful, fanciful)*

Synonyms: unusual, quirky, unpredictable

Antonyms: matter-of-fact, realistic, sensible

Sample sentence: I made a whimsical decision about my summer trip, and now I wish I'd thought about it more.

English for Academic Success
Language Coach
Remind students how the Vocabulary words are significant to the selection. (Boswell feels *reverence* for Johnson. Boswell is *apprehensive* about meeting Johnson.) Explain that linking difficult words to their everyday lives can be an effective tool to broaden their vocabulary. After they complete the **Language Coach** activity, invite students to create a short story that includes all the Vocabulary words and read it to the class.

English for Academic Success
Academic Vocabulary
Possible response: *Johnson initially dominates the conversation by appearing argumentative. Boswell is able to participate once he learns that Johnson merely enjoys arguing and does not dislike him.*

Applying Your Skills

Grades 9–10 Review Reading Standard 1.1 (see pages A48–A50)

from The Life of Samuel Johnson

Vocabulary Development

Vocabulary Check
Match each Vocabulary word to its antonym.

1. reverence	**a.** commonalities
2. slovenly	**b.** disdain
3. apprehensive	**c.** deceit
4. whimsical	**d.** carefree
5. singularities	**e.** tidy
6. ingenuity	**f.** matter-of-fact
7. candor	**g.** dullness

Vocabulary Skills: Create Definitions
One way to remember a new word is to teach it to another person. You can do this by creating a definition of the new word. A definition includes everything a reader needs to know in order to use the word correctly while speaking or writing. Here is an example of a definition using a word from the selection:

abasement

How to pronounce it: uh BAYS muhnt

Part of speech: noun

What it means: a lowering in rank, importance, or esteem

Words I associate it with: basement (the lowest room in a house), base (not noble; unworthy)

Synonyms: belittlement, humiliation

Antonyms: advancement, elevation, promotion

Sample sentence: I don't want my friends to feel abasement, so I try not to make a big deal out of embarrassing situations.

Before creating your own definition of a word, look up the word in a dictionary to ensure you understand its meaning. Then, fill out the items listed on the note card above. To help yourself remember the new word, use everyday language that makes you comfortable.

Keep your note cards in a file for future reference. You can use them to review words on your own or to study with a partner.

Your Turn
Create your own definition for each of the Vocabulary words. Use the format you have just studied to create a complete and helpful definition.

Language Coach
Personal Definitions Linking words with people and things in your life will help you remember their definitions. Answer each question, being sure to use the vocabulary word in your answer.

1. What might happen if you do one of your chores in a *slovenly* way?
2. Whom do you know that is *apprehensive* about tests?
3. What book, movie, or poem would you call *whimsical*?
4. Whose *singularities* set him or her apart from other people?
5. Whom do you know that speaks with *candor*?
6. Whose *ingenuity* helped you to solve a problem?

Academic Vocabulary
Talk About
How does Johnson initially dominate conversations with Boswell? How does Boswell learn to participate in these conversations?

Universal Access: Vocabulary Development

English Learners
English for Academic Success Before students complete the **Language Coach** activity, have students take out the definition cards they created in the Your Turn activity. Encourage students to review the definitions of each Vocabulary word to make sure they have a strong grasp of the word's meaning. Ask students to discuss the word meanings with a partner to reinforce their understanding. Tell students that being comfortable with the actual definitions will make it easier for them to create personal definitions.

✔ See the **Academic and Selection Vocabulary Skill Builder** in **UA: Differentiating Instruction.**

Writing Standard 2.1a, 2.1c, 2.1e (see pages A51–A52) **Listening and Speaking Standard** 2.2a–c (see pages A53–A55)

Grammar Link

Irregular Verbs

Unlike a regular verb, an irregular verb forms its past and past participle in some way other than by adding *-d* or *-ed* to its base form. Look at the examples below featuring the irregular verb *write.*

Past: We *wrote* an essay about English literature.
Past participle: We have *written* many essays about English literature.

The chart below contains some common irregular verbs and their past and past participle forms.

Base Form	Past	Past Participle
do	did	[have *or* had] done
leave	left	[have *or* had] left
teach	taught	[have *or* had] taught
come	came	[have *or* had] come
shake	shook	[have *or* had] shaken
read	read	[have *or* had] read
eat	ate	[have *or* had] eaten

Your Turn

Complete each of the following sentences, using the correct past or past participle form of the italicized verb.

1. *write* Boswell ____ a memoir about Samuel Johnson, a man for whom he had great respect.
2. *leave* Mr. and Mrs. Davies ____ Boswell and Johnson alone to talk, which Boswell very much enjoyed.
3. *come* Johnson ____ to Mr. Davies' shop while Boswell was having tea in the parlor.

Writing Application Choose a piece of your own writing that includes an irregular verb, and then change the form of the verb. How does the irregular verb change?

CHOICES

As you respond to the Choices, use these **Academic Vocabulary** words as appropriate: approach, convince, dominate, enhance, participate.

REVIEW

Use Historical Perspective

Partner Activity The Age of Johnson is also called the Age of Reason. During this time, the scientific method came into full use, and writers, scientists, and philosophers valued clear, logical thought. With a partner, research the meaning of *empiricism* and what qualifies as *empirical evidence.* Then, discuss how Johnson modeled the empirical approach. Note also the instances in Boswell's biography in which Johnson fell short of clear, logical thought, and suggest why you think he might have done so.

CONNECT

Make a Documentary

TechFocus With a small group, create a documentary scene based on Boswell's *Life.* Using the text as a script, rehearse and film one scene from the biography. To determine how to act, use Boswell's comments about his and Johnson's moods. Then, organize a "Johnson Documentary Film Festival" so you can watch various groups' documentary scenes.

EXTEND

Write a Letter from the Good Doctor

Although Boswell's biography of Johnson is often considered the best biography in the English language, Johnson himself never had a chance to read it. Imagine that Johnson could read Boswell's biography. Write a letter to Boswell from Johnson's point of view. In your letter, explain Johnson's reaction to the biography. Which parts did he like, which did he dislike, and what reasons does he give for his opinions?

Universal Access: Grammar Link

English Learners

English for Academic Success Some students may have trouble with irregular verbs. Use this activity to reinforce the standard English usage of irregular verbs.

Show students how to find the past and past participle parts of irregular verbs in a dictionary. Then, have students use a dictionary to find the past tense and participle forms of the following irregular verbs.

1. sink [*sank, sunk*]
2. drive [*drove, driven*]
3. sing [*sang, sung*]

✔ For more practice with irregular verbs, see **Warriner's Handbook, GrammarNotes,** and **Language Handbook Worksheets.**

Independent Practice

Grammar Link

Your Turn

1. *Boswell wrote a memoir about Samuel Johnson, a man for whom he had great respect.*
2. *Mr. and Mrs. Davies left Boswell and Johnson alone to talk, which Boswell very much enjoyed.*
3. *Samuel Johnson had come to Mr. Davies's shop while Boswell was having tea in the parlor.*

Choices: Evaluation Criteria

Review: Homework
Use Historical Perspective

- Discussion demonstrates the understanding of the concept of empiricism.
- Discussion reveals examples of illogical or inconsequential reasoning in the selection.

Connect: Homework
Make a Documentary

Documentary shows thorough analysis of Boswell's and Johnson's characters.

Extend: Homework
Write a Letter from the Good Doctor

Letter is written in the style of Johnson's speech.

Assess

Unit 3 Resources, Selection Standards Check, p. 79

ThinkCentral Online Assessment, Selection Standards Check

Teacher One Stop™, editable Selection Standards Check

Review

ThinkCentral Online Remediation

Standards Focus

Objectives

Students will
- understand characteristics of elegy
- analyze the way in which clarity in meaning is affected by word choice in a text

Selection Introduction

Think About the Writer

Tell students to consider both Gray's personality and the historic era in which he lived. Also, ask students why a person of any era would be interested in country life and nature.

For Independent Reading

Novemberland: Selected Poems, 1956–1993, Gunter Grass

Motivate

What Do You Think?/QuickWrite

Use the QuickWrite to have students speculate what school or home would be like without any rules. Ask students to write their thoughts on the importance of rules in everyday life and in society.

English for Academic Success

Academic Vocabulary

Look for opportunities to use the Academic Vocabulary words in this unit.

- **dominate, *v.*:** hold a commanding position
- **enhance, *v.*:** improve the quality of
- **participate, *v.*:** take part in

California Standards, pp. 656–664

- **Reading Standard 2.2** Analyze the way in which clarity of meaning is affected by the patterns of organization, hierarchical structures, repetition of the main ideas, syntax, and word choice in the text.
- **Reading Standard 3.1** Analyze characteristics of subgenres (e.g., satire, parody, allegory, pastoral) that are used in poetry, prose, plays, novels, short stories, essays, and other basic genres.

Preparing to Read

Elegy Written in a Country Churchyard

What Do You Think? How can order and civilization affect human behavior?

QuickWrite

Rules often help maintain an orderly society. Think of the rules you must follow in school or at home. How do these rules affect your everyday life in particular and society in general? Record your thoughts in your *Reader/Writer Notebook.*

Thomas Gray by John Giles Eccardt. National Portrait Gallery, London.

MEET THE WRITER

Thomas Gray

(1716–1771)

Thomas Gray was considered England's premier lyric poet by his contemporaries. Even Samuel Johnson, who found much of Gray's poetry dull, recognized the universal appeal of Gray's famous "Elegy Written in a Country Churchyard." Johnson wrote, "The Churchyard abounds with images which find a mirror in every mind, and with sentiments to which every bosom returns an echo."

A Quiet Life

Painfully shy, Gray led a quiet life as a scholar at Cambridge University, reading literature in a variety of languages, studying assorted subjects, painting landscapes, and playing the harpsichord. Gray led such a secluded life that he did not participate in many activities considered customary for late eighteenth-century men. For example, he never rode a horse—a primary mode of transportation at that time. Furthermore, unlike all other professors at Cambridge, Gray never gave lectures.

The great crisis of Gray's life came when his close friend Richard West died of tuberculosis. Gray sought consolation in writing poetry. Reluctant to publish his work, he carefully and fastidiously revised and rewrote his verses. It took him nine years to complete "Elegy," which was published in 1751.

Gestures Toward Romanticism

Although his verse has ties to the neoclassical tradition that tended to dominate eighteenth-century literature, Gray is sometimes designated as a forerunner of Romantic poetry, and his "Elegy" combines elements from several literary traditions. Like the Romantic poets, Gray turns to subjects of country life and nature. His poems express sympathy with common humanity, and he uses the first-person point of view.

Although it is important never to assume that the speaker of a poem is the same person as the writer, it is not unwise to assume that parts of Gray's poem are autobiographical. Gray is buried alongside his mother in the cemetery immortalized in his "Elegy."

Think About the Writer Why do you think the subjects of country life and nature appealed to Thomas Gray?

Selection Readability	
Easily Accessible Accessible **Challenging**	historical context; complex narrative poem; unfamiliar vocabulary

Reading Standard 2.2, 3.1 (see pages A48–A50)

Literary Skills Focus

Elegy An **elegy** is a poem that mourns the death of a person or laments something lost. A type of **lyric,** an elegy may lament the passing of life and beauty or may meditate on the nature of death. An elegy usually uses formal language and structure and possesses a solemn or even melancholy **tone.** As you read, keep in mind that English poetry has a strong elegiac tradition—from the poems of the Anglo-Saxons, to the works of Ben Jonson, to the more modern poetry of A. E. Housman and Dylan Thomas. Although Gray was working within this long-standing poetic tradition when he wrote his "Elegy Written in a Country Churchyard," he still managed, in large part through his vivid **imagery** and word choice, to create a unique poem celebrated for its beauty.

Reading Skills Focus

Analyzing Word Choice and Word Order A poet creates the tone of a poem through his or her **word choice** and **word order.** For example, the tone of an elegy is usually solemn and melancholy. In his "Elegy," Gray chose words for their sounds, meanings, and **connotations**—the feelings and emotions associated with the word—to create images that recall quietness, solitude, and death. Gray's word order reflects his **meter** (iambic pentameter) and his **rhyme scheme** *(abab).*

Into Action As you read, use a chart like the one below to record your observations about word choice and word order in each stanza.

Stanza	Word Choice	Word Order
first	The connotations of words such as curfew and parting imply limits and ends.	word order in third line is inverted to fit abab rhyme scheme

Writing Skills Focus

Think as a Reader/Writer

Find It in Your Reading In "Elegy," Gray **personifies,** or gives human qualities to, abstract ideas and elements of the natural world, such as ambition and grandeur. As you read, record in your *Reader/Writer Notebook* other things that Gray personifies. How does this personification enhance the poem?

Reader/Writer Notebook

Use your **RWN** to complete the activities for this selection.

Vocabulary

annals (AN uhlz) *n. pl.:* records, organized by year, that tell someone's or something's history. *The speaker knows that the annals of the poor would contain information about farming.*

impute (ihm PYOOT) *v.:* attribute to someone or something, usually negatively. *Impute the poor's failure to succeed to society, not to the poor.*

sequestered (sih KWEHS tuhrd) *v.* used as *adj.:* set apart; isolated. *The sequestered graves were at the cemetery's far end.*

uncouth (uhn KOOTH) *adj.:* unsophisticated; awkward. *These forgettable gravestones are carved with uncouth rhymes that use simplistic language.*

tribute (TRIHB yoot) *n.:* something done to show respect. *This plain gravestone offers a moving tribute to the person buried here.*

Language Coach

Word Origins The noun *annals* comes from the Latin word for "year," as do other common English words such as *annual, biannual, semi-annual, annuity, anniversary,* and *Anno Domini,* usually abbreviated A.D. What does *annual* mean? What does it mean in relation to books? to plants? What do the other italicized words mean?

Learn It Online

Listen to this elegy through the online audio.

go.hrw.com H12-657 Go

Selection Resources

Unit 3 Resources, on-level practice and assessment, p. 82

Teacher One Stop™, on-level lesson plans and all print resources

Holt Audio Library

Holt Audio Library: Selections and Summaries in Spanish

UA: Differentiating Instruction, graphic organizer, p. 142

UA: Supporting Instruction in Spanish, selection summary

ThinkCentral Online Assessment, Selection Standards Check

ThinkCentral Online Remediation

Preteach

Introducing Vocabulary

- Review the Vocabulary words, definitions, and sentences with students.
- To reinforce the significance of the Vocabulary words, tell students that these words support the formal, somber tone of the elegy partly because, except for *uncouth,* they all have Latin origins. For example, *annals* comes from the Latin word *annus* meaning *year,* and it is also the root for *annual.*

English for Academic Success

Language Coach

Tell students that they can use the Latin root to help them decipher the meanings of unfamiliar words. [*An annual book has a new version every year, such as the phone book. Flowers that are annuals must be replaced every year.*]

Literary Skills Focus

As you read and discuss the poem with students, have them note characteristics of the elegy with which they are familiar from previous reading (especially Anglo-Saxon poetry).

Reading Skills Focus

Give students a copy of the Reading Skills Focus graphic organizer before they read. (See **Unit 3 Resources.**) Tell them to use their notes to answer the questions on the Applying Your Skills page.

Writing Skills Focus

Have students record examples of personification in their **Reader/Writer Notebooks.** Students can use their notes to complete the Writing Skills Focus activity.

Learn It Online

The online version of this poem includes audio support to engage all students and to help struggling readers with reading comprehension and vocabulary.

go.hrw.com H12–657 Go

Teacher Preparation
Selection Summary
In "Elegy Written in a Country Churchyard," the speaker is musing on the obscure lives of country people. By contrasting images of nature with those of pomp and power, the speaker expresses the central theme of the poem: Rich and poor, famous and humble share a common end—death and the grave.

Direct Teach
Think About/Talk About
Read with a Purpose Before students read the selection, ask them to discuss settings or landscapes that evoke a contemplative mood.

Comprehension
B Reading Focus
Possible responses: *Line 14 could read, "Where the turf heaves in many a mold'ring heap." The poet probably gave prominence to the word "heaves" to fit the rhyme scheme* abab.

Analysis
A Literary Focus
Possible response: *The image of the day ending and turning to dark night conveys elegiac melancholy, loneliness, and a sense of ending. The bell "tolls the knell" as it would to announce a death.*

POEM

Elegy Written in a Country Churchyard

by **Thomas Gray**

Read with a Purpose
Read to discover Gray's observations about life and death.

Build Background
Gray's "Elegy" combines elements from several literary traditions. First, it can be considered a **pastoral** elegy, in that its setting is a beautiful outdoor landscape that features idealized rural people. Second, the poem borrows from the **Gothic,** a literary mode that uses wild, mysterious, or natural elements (such as the "moping owl" and the graveyard) to help create atmosphere. Third, Gray follows the convention of other writers of the time by including yet another element, **generalizations** about life and death.

The curfew tolls the knell of parting day,
The lowing herd wind slowly o'er the lea,°
The plowman homeward plods his weary way,
And leaves the world to darkness, and to me. A

Now fades the glimmering landscape on the sight,
And all the air a solemn stillness holds;
Save where the beetle wheels his droning flight,
And drowsy tinklings lull the distant folds.

Save that from yonder ivy-mantled tower
The moping owl does to the moon complain
Of such, as wand'ring near her secret bower,
Molest her ancient solitary reign.

Beneath those rugged elms, that yew tree's shade,
Where heaves the turf in many a mold'ring heap,
Each in his narrow cell forever laid,
The rude° forefathers of the hamlet sleep. B

2. **lea:** meadow.

16. **rude:** uneducated; unpolished.

A Literary Focus **Elegy** Which images in this stanza convey emotions characteristic of an elegy?

B Reading Focus **Understanding Word Choice and Word Order** What words are inverted in this stanza? What is the effect of inverting these words?

Universal Access

EL English Learners
English for Academic Success The combination of inverted sentence structure, archaic vocabulary, and elliptical construction in the poem makes it a challenge for students. Let students work in small groups, and assign each group a few stanzas to paraphrase and interpret. Remind students to use context clues, questioning strategies, and reference material.

✔ See the **English Language Skill Builder** in **UA: Differentiating Instruction.**

Struggling Readers
Assist students in analyzing word choice and word order. Have students read lines 5–8 silently. Ask students to think about the implications and connotations of certain words. For example, *stillness* in line 6 can be associated with lifelessness, and the words *drowsy* and *lull* imply sleep. Tell students that in line 6, the verb *holds* follows *stillness* to preserve the meter in which every other syllable is stressed.

✔ See **UA: Differentiating Instruction** for a graphic organizer to scaffold instruction for struggling readers.

The breezy call of incense-breathing morn,
The swallow twitt'ring from the straw-built shed,°
The cock's shrill clarion, or the echoing horn,°
No more shall rouse them from their lowly bed.

For them no more the blazing hearth shall burn,
Or busy housewife ply her evening care:
No children run to lisp their sire's return,
Or climb his knees the envied kiss to share.

Oft did the harvest to their sickle yield,
Their furrow oft the stubborn glebe° has broke;
How jocund did they drive their team afield!
How bowed the woods beneath their sturdy stroke! **C**

18. shed: nest.
19. horn: hunting horn.

26. glebe: soil.

C Reading Focus **Understanding Word Choice and Word Order** Think about the connotations of the words *yield* and *broke*. What tone is created by ending these lines with these words?

Churchyard and chapel, South Devon, England.

Think About/Talk About

Comprehension

C Reading Focus

Possible responses: *The word "yield" suggests surrender and acceptance, while "broke" suggests a discontinuity. The mood created is one of painful acceptance.*

Extend the Discussion

Drawing Conclusions Who are the men mourned by the speaker? ***Possible response:*** *The men are simple, common laborers. The speaker represents them as having strength and hard-working vigor.*

Interpreting What does the speaker imply about death by calling the grave a "cell"? ***Possible response:*** *Death is a grim prison rather than a release from the burdens of earthly life.*

Advanced Learners

Enrichment Tell students to find images and information about the churchyard at Stoke Poges in Buckinghamshire, England, the setting for Gray's "Elegy" and place where he was buried. Tell students to present their findings to the class to add visual context to the reading of the poem.

Students with Disabilities

Explain to students that the elegy is not a narrative poem. It does not relate to a series of events; instead the elegy presents a series of images that convey a sense of sorrow and the message that all things must pass. Encourage students to work with partners to paraphrase each stanza after they read it. Students can sketch the images to enhance their understanding as they re-read the poem.

✔ See **UA: Differentiating Instruction** for a graphic organizer to scaffold instruction for students with disabilities.

Model the Skill

- Provide students with copies of the Reading Skills Focus graphic organizer for "Elegy Written in a Country Churchyard." (See **Unit 3 Resources.**)
- Tell students that to analyze the **word choice** and **word order** of the poem, they must remember that *word choice* refers to the poet's choice of words with specific connotations, whereas *word order* is the way words are arranged to create rhyme and meter.
- Read aloud lines 45–48 in stanza 12. You might say: "In these lines, the subject of the sentence, 'some heart,' appears only in the second line of the stanza. The conventional phrasing would be, 'Perhaps some heart, once pregnant with celestial fire, is laid in this neglected spot, as are hands that might have swayed the rod of empire or that might have waked the living lyre of ecstasy.'"

Stanza	Word Choice
twelfth	Phrases such as "celestial fire," "the rod of empire," and living lyre" suggest triumphs.

Word Order
Lines 45-48 are inverted to fit the rhyme scheme abab.

Guided Practice: Apply

Think-Pair-Share Have students locate instances of melancholy mood created through word choice. Ask students to discuss their choices and fill in the Reading Skills Focus graphic organizer.

Let not Ambition mock their useful toil,
Their homely joys and destiny obscure;
Nor Grandeur hear with a disdainful smile,
The short and simple annals of the poor.

The boast of heraldry,° the pomp of power,
And all that beauty, all that wealth e'er gave,
Awaits alike th' inevitable hour.
The paths of glory lead but to the grave.

Nor you, ye proud, impute to these the fault,
If Mem'ry o'er their tomb no trophies raise,
Where through the long-drawn aisle and fretted vault°
The pealing anthem swells the note of praise.

Can storied urn° or animated bust
Back to its mansion call the fleeting breath?
Can Honor's voice provoke° the silent dust,
Or Flatt'ry soothe the dull cold ear of Death?

Perhaps in this neglected spot is laid
Some heart once pregnant with celestial fire,
Hands that the rod of empire might have swayed,
Or waked to ecstasy the living lyre.

But Knowledge to their eyes her ample page
Rich with the spoils of time did ne'er unroll;
Chill Penury° repressed their noble rage,°
And froze the genial current° of the soul.

Full many a gem of purest ray serene,
The dark unfathomed caves of ocean bear:
Full many a flower is born to blush unseen,
And waste its sweetness on the desert air.

Some village Hampden° that with dauntless breast
The little tyrant of his fields withstood;
Some mute inglorious Milton here may rest,
Some Cromwell° guiltless of his country's blood.

33. boast of heraldry: pride in one's ancestry. Heraldry is the study of family coats of arms.

39. fretted vault: elaborately decorated church ceiling.

41. storied urn: an urn with an inscription on it.

43. provoke: evoke; call forth.

51. Penury: poverty. **rage:** emotion; feeling.

52. genial current: warm impulses.

57. village Hampden: an obscure person who, with opportunity, might have been famous like John Hampden (1594–1643), an English statesman who defied the king over unjust taxation shortly before the English Civil Wars.

60. Cromwell: Lord Protector Oliver Cromwell, who ruled England from 1653 to 1658.

Vocabulary **annals** (AN uhlz) *n. pl.:* records, organized by year, that tell someone's or something's history.
impute (ihm PYOOT) *v.:* attribute to someone or something, usually negatively.

Cross-Curricular Connection

LITERATURE: Heraldry and Coats of Arms

Small-Group Activity In line 33, Gray uses "the boast of heraldry" to sum up the pride in family history that has been important to the British aristocracy and that has left its mark on American life as well. Ask students to research the history of coats of arms and to illustrate and explain some of the symbols associated with them. Encourage students also to research the heraldry of their family names and share their results with the class.

Universal Access

AAVE Students Who Use African American Vernacular English

English for Academic Success Read aloud line 38 in the third stanza on p. 660. Explain to students that in poetry, it is common for writers to delete the pronunciation of certain sounds to maintain a casual tone or create a certain rhythm, such as *memory, never,* and *flattery,* which may become *mem'ry, ne'er,* and *flatt'ry,* respectively. Point out that these words reflect natural speech patterns. Point out that this contrasts with the patterns used in formal English.

CULTURE LINK

Real-Life Stories

Although Gray's elegy commemorates the lives of ordinary people buried in a country churchyard, the poem's speaker can only speculate about the particulars of their lives. While they lived, their humble circumstances prevented them from leaving a permanent record of their stories. Today, many people wish to honor the dignity—and to preserve the stories—of individual lives. The StoryCorps Project provides one means to this end.

StoryCorps enables people to preserve their stories through free broadcast-quality audio recordings. Since 2003, thousands of people have recorded interviews. At the end of each session, contributors get a CD of their interview, which also becomes part of the StoryCorps Archive, housed in the Library of Congress. The project's goal is to create an oral history of American life. (For more information, visit www.storycorps.net.)

The StoryCorps StoryBooth in Grand Central Station in New York City.

Ask Yourself

What might we learn about the eighteenth century if people then had left behind recorded interviews?

Th' applause of list'ning senates to command,
The threats of pain and ruin to despise,
To scatter plenty o'er a smiling land,
And read their hist'ry in a nation's eyes

Their lot forbade: nor circumscribed alone
Their growing virtues, but their crimes confined;
Forbade to wade through slaughter to a throne,
And shut the gates of mercy on mankind,

The struggling pangs of conscious° truth to hide,
To quench the blushes of ingenuous° shame,
Or heap the shrine of Luxury and Pride
With incense, kindled at the Muse's flame.°

Far from the madding° crowd's ignoble strife,
Their sober wishes never learned to stray;
Along the cool sequestered vale of life
They kept the noiseless tenor° of their way.

69. conscious: having an awareness; aware of oneself as a thinking being.
70. ingenuous: naively innocent.

72. incense . . . flame: tributes paid to them by poets.
73. madding: frenzied.

76. tenor: course.

Vocabulary **sequestered** (sih KWEHS tuhrd) *v.* used as *adj.:* set apart ; isolated.

Developing Oral Fluency

Paired Activity Once they understand the form of the elegiac stanza, have students practice reading certain stanzas aloud. Have students form pairs and take turns reading to each other, accenting alternating syllables as they read. Remind them to use punctuation and meaning to decide when to pause rather than simply stopping mechanically at the end of every line. Point out that rhyming words are not always the last word of each sentence or thought.

✔ See **UA: Differentiating Instruction** for practice passages for developing fluency.

Culture Link

Ask Yourself

Possible response: *From recordings of interviews with people who lived in the eighteenth century, we might have learned something about their personal lives, hardships and struggles, how they conducted their daily lives in and out of their households, and the differences between the lives of ordinary people and less ordinary people.*

Think About/Talk About

Extend the Discussion

Finding Details What does the speaker mourn in lines 45–56? ***Possible response:*** *He mourns what people might have done if circumstances had been different—for example, if they had not been born into poverty. He mourns potential that is unfulfilled because of fate and destiny.*

Speculating In lines 57–61, the three lines beginning with "some" unify the description of rural people that begins in line 46. Why does the speaker use the word "some" instead of "one"? ***Possible response:*** *"Some" denotes one among many and emphasizes the great number of such people. This is a subtle way in which the poet generalizes.*

Vocabulary: Own the Word

- **annals:** Ask students to name what things might be included in *annals* of their childhood. ***Possible responses:*** *report cards, birth certificates, photographs, awards*
- **impute:** Remind students that *impute* means "to attribute something negative to someone or something." To help students personally connect to the word, ask the following question: "How would you react if a teacher *imputed* a friend's bad behavior to you?"
- **sequestered:** Point out to students that synonyms for *sequestered* include *isolate, quarantine,* and *segregate.* Ask students why juries are *sequestered.* ***Possible response:*** *to keep the jury from being influenced by outside sources*

Guided Practice: Apply

Think as a Reader/Writer

Find It in Your Reading Point out to students the example of personification in lines 117–120.

Use It in Your Writing Tell students to write a two-line epitaph for a great personality of the past that contains at least one example of personification.

Think About/Talk About

Literary Connection

Bring students' attention to lines 81–84. Let students know that to "supply the place" means "to be a substitute" and that "teach . . . to die" means "teach a proper moral attitude about dying."

Yet ev'n these bones from insult to protect
Some frail memorial° still erected nigh,
With uncouth rhymes and shapeless sculpture decked,
Implores the passing tribute of a sigh. **D**

Their name, their years, spelt by th' unlettered muse,°
The place of fame and elegy supply:
And many a holy text around she strews,
That teach the rustic moralist to die.

For who to dumb Forgetfulness a prey,
This pleasing anxious being e'er resigned,
Left the warm precincts of the cheerful day,
Nor cast one longing ling'ring look behind?

On some fond breast the parting soul relies,
Some pious drops° the closing eye requires;
Ev'n from the tomb the voice of Nature cries,
Ev'n in our ashes live their wonted fires.

For thee,° who mindful of th' unhonored dead
Dost in these lines their artless tale relate;
If chance, by lonely Contemplation led,
Some kindred spirit shall inquire thy fate,

Haply° some hoary-headed swain° may say,
"Oft have we seen him at the peep of dawn
Brushing with hasty steps the dews away
To meet the sun upon the upland lawn.

"There at the foot of yonder nodding beech
That wreathes its old fantastic roots so high,
His listless length at noontide would he stretch,
And pore upon the brook that babbles by.

"Hard° by yon wood, now smiling as in scorn,
Mutt'ring his wayward fancies he would rove,
Now drooping, woeful wan, like one forlorn,
Or crazed with care, or crossed in hopeless love.

78. frail memorial: modest tombstone, in contrast to the elaborate tombs inside the church.
81. unlettered muse: humble engraver of the tombstone.

90. drops: mourners' tears.

93. thee: Gray himself.

97. haply: perhaps. **hoary-headed swain:** white-haired countryman.

105. hard: close.

D **Literary Focus** **Elegy** What words and images in this stanza are elegiac?

Vocabulary **uncouth** (uhn KOOTH) *adj.:* unsophisticated; awkward.
tribute (TRIHB yoot) *n.:* something done to show respect.

Universal Access

EL English Learners

English for Academic Success Students may have trouble with the archaic language. Point out that many words are no longer used but represent a way of speaking and writing in eighteenth-century England. Provide definitions for these words:

- **nigh** (line 78)—near, approaching
- **strews** (line 83)—scatters
- **wonted** (line 92)—habitual, usual
- **dost** (line 94)—do or does
- **rove** (line 106)—wander

Advanced Learners

Enrichment Encourage students to compare and contrast Gray's "Elegy Written in a Country Churchyard" with Milton's elegy "Lycidas." Tell them that both poets were moved to write by the loss of a young friend and that both employ conventional pastoral elements. Ask students to pay particular attention to the word choice, imagery, and metrical patterns of each poem.

"One morn I missed him on the customed hill,
Along the heath, and near his fav'rite tree;
Another came; nor yet beside the rill,°
Nor up the lawn, nor at the wood was he.

"The next with dirges due in sad array
Slow through the churchway path we saw him borne.
Approach and read (for thou canst read)° the lay,
Graved on the stone beneath yon aged thorn."° **E**

The Epitaph

Here rests his head upon the lap of Earth
A youth to Fortune and to Fame unknown:
Fair Science frowned not on his humble birth,°
And Melancholy marked him for her own.

Large was his bounty, and his soul sincere,
Heaven did a recompense as largely send:
He gave to Mis'ry all he had, a tear:
He gained from Heaven ('twas all he wished) a friend.

No farther seek his merits to disclose,
Or draw his frailties from their dread abode,
(There they alike in trembling Hope repose)
The bosom of his Father and his God.

111. rill: brook.

115. thou canst read: The speaker apparently cannot read.
116. thorn: hawthorn bush.

119. fair . . . birth: He was educated—*science* meant learning in general—despite his modest beginnings.

E **Literary Focus** **Elegy** What images in this stanza evoke a somber mood?

St. Mary's Churchyard, Rostheme, England.

California Standards, p. 664

- **Reading Standard 2.2** Analyze the way in which clarity of meaning is affected by the patterns of organization, hierarchical structures, repetition of the main ideas, syntax, and word choice in the text.
- **Reading Standard 3.1** Analyze characteristics of subgenres (e.g., satire, parody, allegory, pastoral) that are used in poetry, prose, plays, novels, short stories, essays, and other basic genres.
- **Reading Standard 3.4** Analyze ways in which poets use imagery, personification, figures of speech, and sounds to evoke readers' emotions.
- **Writing Standard 2.1** Write fictional, autobiographical, or biographical narratives: **e.** Make effective use of descriptions of appearance, images, shifting perspectives, and sensory details.

Think About/Talk About

Analysis

D Literary Focus

Possible response: *The image of a memorial that inevitably causes a passerby to sigh contributes to the elegy.*

E Literary Focus

Possible response: *The images of a funeral procession and an engraved headstone add to the solemnity of the elegy.*

Extend the Discussion

Monitoring Your Reading How do you know that in line 93 Gray refers to himself? What clues point to his self-reference? ***Possible response:*** *He defines "thee" as the person who is thinking of the unsung dead and who is writing the lines of poetry.*

Personification What is the effect of giving Earth a lap, Science a frown (or smile), and Melancholy the ability to mark in lines 117–120? ***Possible response:*** *These characteristics make the things depicted seem more like people, so that they evoke the reader's sympathy. They seem to be in a close relationship with the young poet.*

Vocabulary: Own the Word

- **uncouth:** Help students understand the meaning of the word *uncouth* by connecting it to a familiar character in literature. Tell students that in Shakespeare's *Macbeth,* the Porter behaves in an *uncouth* manner when he makes a drunken display outside the castle gates.
- **tribute:** Ask students: "Have you ever paid *tribute* to a person you admired? Explain how you paid *tribute* to this person."

Check for Understanding

Independent Practice

Reading Skills Focus

Possible responses:

1. *People may be obscure and unnoticed in life just as they are forgotten in death.*
2. *Responses will vary. Students should identify specific instances of word choice and word order that evoke sorrow.*

Vocabulary Check

3. *c* 4. *e*
5. *b* 6. *a*
7. *d*

Literary Skills Focus

Possible responses:

8. *The poem's sad tone and insistence on death's finality are common responses to death.*
9. *The hidden gem and unseen flower might symbolize wonderful qualities that go unnoticed.*
10. *He warns Ambition and Grandeur not to look down upon ordinary people.*
11. *They are engraved with names and dates of birth and death, and sometimes with phrases of scripture or wisdom.*
12. *The rhyme and meter provides a solemn serenity with their plodding or lulling regularity.*
13. *Line 36 emphasizes the elegiac view that all human struggle leads inevitably to death.*
14. *Yes; readers might assume that Gray revealed parts of himself in the poem, especially in the epitaph.*
15. *The poet personifies Memory to emphasize its neglect of the dead.*

Assess

Unit 3 Resources,
Selection Standards Check, p. 85

Applying Your Skills

Reading Standard 2.2, 3.1, 3.4 (see pages A48–A50)
Writing Standard 2.1e (see pages A51–A52)

Elegy Written in a Country Churchyard

Literary Response and Analysis

Reading Skills Focus

Read with a Purpose

1. How are Gray's views of life and death related? Cite one example.

Reading Skills: Analyzing Word Choice and Word Order

2. As you read, you analyzed word choice and word order within each stanza. Now, review your charts, and pick three stanzas that you analyzed. Write a paragraph explaining how the word choices and word order in the three stanzas affect the poem's tone.

Vocabulary Check

Match each Vocabulary word with its definition.

3. annals	**a.** unsophisticated
4. impute	**b.** secluded
5. sequestered	**c.** historical records
6. uncouth	**d.** payment, praise
7. tribute	**e.** attribute

Literary Skills Focus

Literary Analysis

8. **Evaluate** What ideas in the poem relate to ideas and feelings people have today?
9. **Make Judgments** In lines 53–56, what might a "gem of purest ray serene" and the "flower . . . born to blush unseen" symbolize?
10. **Interpret** The poet personifies Ambition and Grandeur in lines 29 and 31. What does he warn them not to do?
11. **Infer** According to lines 77–92, what evidence on the gravestones shows that humble, ordinary people also wish to be remembered?
12. **Analyze** How do the poem's rhyme scheme and meter enhance its meaning?

Literary Skills: Elegy

13. **Interpret** How does the famous line "The paths of glory lead but to the grave" (line 36) reflect the characteristics of an elegy?
14. **Extend** Many readers of the "Elegy" have assumed that Gray himself is the poet whose epitaph is given in the final lines. Is this assumption necessary to understanding the poem? Why might a reader like to make this assumption?

Literary Skills Review: Figures of Speech

15. **Analyze** A **figure of speech** is a word or phrase that describes one thing in terms of a dissimilar thing. Work with a partner to find and explain a figure of speech in Gray's poem.

Writing Skills Focus

Think as a Reader/Writer

Use It in Your Writing As you read, you noted Gray's use of personification. Now, write your own ten-line poem in which you personify an abstract idea, such as love or death, that is central to your poem's theme.

What Do You Think Now?

When dealing with death, why might people find comfort through established customs and traditions?

Universal Access

Struggling Writers

Some students may need additional scaffolding to complete the Writing Skills Focus activity. Before they write their poem, have students choose an abstract idea such as love, death, sadness, or joy. Then, have them think about a living thing that they could compare the abstract idea to. Give students an idea of possible comparisons they can make. For example, students might compare the intensity of love to the bright, intense light of the sun. Give students an opportunity to brainstorm ideas with a partner before they write their poems.

What Do You Think Now?

Ask students to consider the poem in terms of the traditions surrounding death. Have them consider the funeral traditions they are familiar with and ask themselves how these customs help mourners deal with death.

COMPARING TEXTS

Views on Women's Rights

Painting on the Terrace by Jules Frederic Ballavoine (1855–1901). Private Collection.

The women's rights movement, an ongoing series of political movements aimed at attaining educational, social, and political equality for women, arose primarily in England and the United States. Its roots lay both in humanistic thought and in the Industrial Revolution of the eighteenth and nineteenth centuries.

According to the dictates of both theology and law, married women of the eighteenth century could not own property, run a business, or control their own lives or those of their children. Social critics (male and female) began to contrast this state of affairs with the ideal of freedom that inspired the American and French Revolutions. The readings in this Comparing Texts section present some of the earliest shots fired in the battle for women's rights.

CONTENTS

Standards Focus

Objectives

Students will
- analyze an author's tone
- understand rhetorical devices
- note patterns of organization and word choice

English for Academic Success

Academic Vocabulary

Look for opportunities to use the Academic Vocabulary words in this unit.

- **approach, *n.*:** a way of addressing something
- **convince, *v.*:** persuade; cause to believe
- **dominate, *v.*:** hold a commanding position
- **enhance, *v.*:** improve the quality of
- **participate, *v.*:** take part in

Analyzing Visuals

Extension Activity Ask students to make inferences about the role of women in the eighteenth century based on the painting. ***Possible response:*** *The painting depicts four elegant women engaged in various intellectual activities: They are painting, discussing art, and reading. Their occupations may seem futile and disconnected from the real center of power.*

Selection Introduction

Think About the Writers

Before students answer the question, have them consider the privileges and rights women have today compared with the rights they had—or did not have—during the period in which these selections were written.

For Independent Reading

- *The Seneca Falls Inheritance,* Miriam Monfredo
- *Restless Spirit: The Life and Work of Dorothea Lange,* Elizabeth Partridge

Motivate

What Do You Think?/QuickWrite

Have students evaluate the current state of women's rights in education, employment, property ownership, marriage, and divorce. What areas, in their opinion, need a slight or dramatic change? Have students record their thoughts in their **Reader/ Writer Notebooks.**

Preparing to Read

MARY WOLLSTONECRAFT

from A Vindication of the Rights of Woman

DANIEL DEFOE

from The Education of Women

MARY, LADY CHUDLEIGH

To the Ladies

What Do You Think? How can order and civilization affect human behavior?

QuickWrite

Supporters of women's rights believe that men and women are equal as human beings and so should have equal respect and treatment in society. What rights do women in this country have now that they did not have in the past? In what areas are men and women still not treated equally? Write a brief paragraph responding to these questions.

MEET THE WRITERS

Mary Wollstonecraft

(1759–1797)

Mary Wollstonecraft demanded "JUSTICE for one half of the human race"—that is, women. She stands as the English pioneer of the women's movement. Inspired by the slogan of the French Revolution, "liberty, equality, fraternity," Wollstonecraft published her most famous work, *A Vindication of the Rights of Woman,* in 1792. This document is a passionate criticism of the social and economic institutions that promoted women's inequality. Wollstonecraft's daughter, Mary Shelley, penned the novel *Frankenstein* (1818) and is perhaps more well-known than Wollstonecraft.

Daniel Defoe

(1660–1731)

Daniel Defoe was at various times a businessman and a spy, but he was always a man who wrote—more than five hundred works in many forms and on many subjects, from choosing a wife to manufacturing glass. During Defoe's lifetime, his political writings led to notoriety, arrests, public punishment, and even jail time. It is a great irony of literary history that the prolific Defoe is now primarily remembered as the author of only one book, his novel about a survivor—a shipwrecked sailor named Robinson Crusoe.

Mary, Lady Chudleigh

(1656–1710)

The poems and essays of Mary, Lady Chudleigh address the concerns of women of her time and explore a philosophy of how to live a peaceful life. She adamantly opposed the idea that wives should submit to the will of their husbands, and she expressed this view in many of her works.

Think About the Writers How would these writers feel about the state of women's rights today?

California Standards, pp. 666–681

- **Reading Standard 2.1** Analyze both the features and the rhetorical devices of different types of public documents (e.g., policy statements, speeches, debates, platforms) and the way in which authors use those features and devices.
- **Reading Standard 3.3** Analyze the ways in which irony, tone, mood, the author's style, and the "sound" of language achieve specific rhetorical or aesthetic purposes or both.
- **Reading Standard 3.8** Analyze the clarity and consistency of political assumptions in a selection of literary works or essays on a topic (e.g., suffrage, women's role in organized labor) (Political approach).

Selection Readability	
Easily Accessible **Accessible** Challenging	These selections include familiar theme; accessible syntax; familiar vocabulary.

Reading Standard 2.1, 3.3, 3.8 (see pages A48–A50)

Literary Skills Focus

Tone The attitude a writer adopts toward the reader or a topic is **tone.** One way that writers control tone is through the use of words with specific **connotations**—associations and emotions that have become attached to a word. As you read, pay attention to words with strong connotations, and note the tone these words convey.

Literary Perspectives Apply the literary perspective described on page 669 as you read the excerpt from *A Vindication of the Rights of Woman*.

Reading Skills Focus

Analyzing Rhetorical Devices **Rhetorical devices** are methods writers or speakers use to make their language more effective. One device is the **rhetorical question**, asked to make a point the author assumes the audience will agree with. **Argument by analogy** reveals a parallel between two situations. **Historical allusion** is a reference to a person, place, or event from history that relates to the topic. **Repetition** emphasizes an author's point. **Appeals to authority** support an author's argument.

Into Action As you read, use a chart like the one below to record examples of the rhetorical devices each author uses and how each device supports his or her main point.

Device	Example	How It Supports the Main Point
rhetorical question	"Where are the masculine women?" (Vindication)	makes the point that equality does not make women into men

Writing Skills Focus

Think as a Reader/Writer

Find It In Your Reading The **analogies** in these works add power to the writers' arguments. As you read, record such analogies in your *Reader/Writer Notebook.*

Reader/Writer Notebook

Use your **RWN** to complete the activities for these selections.

Vocabulary

fastidious (fas TIHD ee uhs) *adj.:* picky; overly fussy. *The author says that men look at women with fastidious eyes.*

specious (SPEE shuhs) *adj.:* showy but false. *She says that men have fooled women with specious tributes to womanhood.*

cursory (KUR suhr ee) *adj.:* hasty; superficial. *The introduction contains a cursory summary of the author's arguments.*

propensity (pruh PEHN suh tee) *n.:* natural inclination. *The author believes that women have developed a propensity to assert their power in subtle ways.*

manifest (MAN uh fehst) *adj.:* evident; obvious. *Defoe claims it is manifest that the human soul separates civilized people from barbarians.*

vie (vy) *v.:* compete. *According to Defoe, men fear that educated women would vie with men to achieve great things.*

Language Coach

Antonyms Adjectives give specific descriptions that can apply to people, places, or things. One way to learn a new adjective is to think of a word that has an opposite meaning. A man who is fastidious in his habits is the opposite of careless. What is an adjective that means the opposite of *specious*? Can you name adjectives that are antonyms for *cursory* and *manifest*?

Learn It Online

Jump into this discussion through an online video introduction.

go.hrw.com H12-667 Go

Comparing Texts Resources

Unit 3 Resources, on-level practice and assessment, p. 88

PowerNotes, interactive lesson presentation with activities

Teacher One Stop™, on-level lesson plans and all print resources

Holt Audio Library

Holt Audio Library: Selections and Summaries in Spanish

UA: Holt Interactive Reader, p. 179

UA: Differentiating Instruction, modified lesson plans and leveled assessment, p. 143

UA: Supporting Instruction in Spanish, selection summary

UA: Resources for Teaching Advanced Students, lesson plans, p. 121

ThinkCentral Online Assessment, Selection Standards Check

ThinkCentral Online Remediation

Preteach

Introducing Vocabulary

Read aloud the Vocabulary words and sample sentences. Then, use this activity to check students' understanding.

1. List things that a **fastidious** person might do during dinner.
2. Explain how you would react to a **specious** argument.
3. Name problems that can arise from a **cursory** inspection.
4. Describe how someone with a **propensity** to kindness behaves.
5. Describe how people can make their happiness **manifest.**
6. List a few instances in which people would **vie** for power.

English for Academic Success

Language Coach

Show students how to use a thesaurus to find antonyms. ***Possible responses:*** *specious, genuine; cursory, thorough; manifest, obscure*

Literary Skills Focus

As you read and discuss the selection with students, have them note words with strong connotations.

Reading Skills Focus

Give students a copy of the Reading Skills Focus graphic organizer before they read. (See **Unit 3 Resources.**) Tell them to use their responses to answer the questions on the Applying Your Skills page.

Writing Skills Focus

Have students record examples of analogies in their **Reader/Writer Notebooks.** Students can use their notes to complete the Writing Skills Focus activity.

Learn It Online

The **PowerNotes** presentation for this lesson includes a short video that introduces the selections. The video is also available on the online version of this page.

go.hrw.com H12-667 Go

Teacher Preparation

Selection Summary

In the introduction to *A Vindication of the Rights of Woman,* Wollstonecraft focuses on women as wives and mothers and on educational equality, in keeping with the political realities of her time. She first posits the essay's main idea: Denying women an education impairs their "usefulness" as well as their happiness. She then sketches the essay's organization, noting that she will consider women as human beings first, females second, and that she will differentiate between the situations of upper-class and middle-class women. She also summarizes her arguments: conventional notions of femininity rob women of integrity and dignity; strength of character is women's greatest need (education can provide it); people fear women's gaining "too much courage or fortitude," but women's relative physical weakness makes that unlikely; and if men are "chaste and modest," women will be also.

Direct Teach

Think About/Talk About

Read with a Purpose Have students read the Read with a Purpose statement. Have students note Wollstonecraft's motivation and reasons for advocating women's rights.

Marriage à la Mode: The Marriage Settlement (c. 1743), by William Hogarth.
National Gallery, London.

PLATFORM

from A Vindication of the Rights of Woman

by **Mary Wollstonecraft**

Read with a Purpose

Read to discover how the author justifies her arguments in favor of women's rights.

Build Background

In much of the world today, the same educational opportunities are available to both men and women. Women have the right to vote, and they may study for and pursue virtually any career they wish. These opportunities, often taken for granted, were not always available to women. In England during the Restoration, the educated woman was the exception to the rule, and women were not allowed to vote. Keep these facts in mind as you read this excerpt from this famous essay.

Note that Wollstonecraft's use of the word *vindication* means "justification."

Real Issues, Real Experts

Holt author ***Sara Kajder*** *offers strategies for teaching Views on Women's Rights.*

I want students to think about how they can put these texts in dialogue with the historical periods they know. I ask students to work in small groups to develop presentations that amplify their understanding of these texts, given a close look at a similarly compelling period of history. I ask students to take advantage of twitter (www.twitter.com)—an online tool that is part blog, part IM tool, and part social networking site. Students are typically spread out around the school; some in the media center, some in the classroom. Through *twitter,* we provide students with a tool for concise writing (140 characters) within the group that is meant to synthesize and question a collective dialogue about their research findings. Students have access to one another's "tweets," creating a community and setting the bar in terms of audience as each post needs to make a meaningful contribution. Where some see twitter as a formative assessment tool, I think the power is in making students' thinking transparent.

Introduction

After considering the historic page, and viewing the living world with anxious solicitude,[1] the most melancholy emotions of sorrowful indignation have depressed my spirits, and I have sighed when obliged to confess, that either nature has made a great difference between man and man, or that the civilization which has hitherto taken place in the world has been very partial.[2] I have turned over various books written on the subject of education, and patiently observed the conduct of parents and the management of schools; but what has been the result?—a profound conviction that the neglected education of my fellow-creatures is the grand source of the misery I deplore; and that women, in particular, are rendered weak and wretched by a variety of concurring causes, originating from one hasty conclusion. The conduct and manners of women, in fact, evidently prove that their minds are not in a healthy state; for, like the flowers which are planted in too rich a soil, strength and usefulness are sacrificed to beauty; and the flaunting leaves, after having pleased a fastidious eye, fade, disregarded on the stalk, long before the season when they ought to have arrived at maturity. —One cause of this barren blooming I attribute to a false system of education, gathered from the books written on this subject by men who, considering females rather as women than human creatures, have been more anxious to make them alluring mistresses than affectionate wives and rational mothers; and the understanding of the sex has been so bubbled[3] by this specious homage, that the civilized women of the present century, with a few exceptions, are only anxious to inspire love, when they ought to cherish a nobler ambition, and by their abilities and virtues exact[4] respect. **A** **B**

In a treatise, therefore, on female rights and manners, the works which have been particularly written for their improvement must not be overlooked; especially when it is asserted, in direct terms, that the minds of women are enfeebled by false refinement; that the books of instruction, written by men of genius, have had the same tendency as more frivolous productions; and that, in the true style of Mahometanism,[5] they are treated as a kind of subor-

1. **solicitude:** care; concern.
2. **partial:** biased.
3. **bubbled:** be deluded with or distracted by flimsy evidence.
4. **exact:** demand; require.
5. **Mahometanism:** Islam, the religion of Muslims. Europeans mistakenly thought that the Koran teaches that women have no souls. In actuality, the Koran teaches that women are to be treated as equals to men.

Literary Perspectives

Analyzing Political Context Literary texts reflect social beliefs and practices and are influenced by the author's worldview, derived from his or her political perspective, gender, or social class. As you read this selection, consider the factors that shaped Mary Wollstonecraft's worldview. Wollstonecraft—as a woman in eighteenth-century England—was not allowed to attend college or to vote. Her father's violence toward her mother had left Wollstonecraft disillusioned about marriage. Nineteen and self-educated, Wollstonecraft left home to work in some of the few occupations legally available to single women. As a young woman during the American and French Revolutions, she was influenced by radical political thinkers such as Thomas Paine and inspired by the French slogan "liberty, equality, fraternity."

As you read, be sure to notice questions in the text, which will guide you in using this perspective.

A **Literary Perspectives** **Analyzing Political Context** In the first sentence, Mary Wollstonecraft invokes both "the historic page" and "the living world." How does this first sentence help establish a political context for the text?

B **Reading Focus** **Analyzing Rhetorical Devices** What analogy does Wollstonecraft use in the lines starting with "The conduct and manners of women" and ending with "maturity"? What point does Wollstonecraft make?

Vocabulary **fastidious** (fas TIHD ee uhs) *adj.:* picky; overly fussy.
specious (SPEE shuhs) *adj.:* showy but false.

Literary Perspectives

Before students read the selection, have them read the **Literary Perspectives** about Analyzing Political Context. Have students make a chart in which they list statements about the situation of women in the eighteenth century and today. Then, ask them to make inferences about the political and social changes that contributed to the present condition of women.

Remind students to use the notes and questions at the bottom of the page to help them use the perspective.

Think About/Talk About

Comprehension

B Reading Focus

Possible response: *Wollstonecraft uses the analogy of a flower to describe how women who are taught only to please men are like flowers whose soil is too rich: showy but unhealthy.*

Analysis

A Literary Perspectives

Possible response: *This sentence shows that the author is both well educated and sensitive to the plight of people. This places her somewhat outside of the "state of her fellow-creatures" that she seeks to describe here.*

Extend the Discussion

Summarizing What argument does Wollstonecraft set up in the first paragraph? ***Possible response:*** *She sets up the argument that eighteenth-century women are denied a proper education.*

Drawing Conclusions In eighteenth-century English, "the sex" meant "women." What does this term say about women? ***Possible response:*** *It was commonly believed that the supposed characteristics of their gender prevailed over their qualities as human beings.*

Vocabulary: Own the Word

- **fastidious:** Demonstrate the body language of a person who is *fastidious* about his or her appearance. Then, ask one or two students to describe the actions of a *fastidious* eater.
- **specious:** Ask students the following question: "Would you expect a lawyer who gave a *specious* argument in court to win the trial? Explain your answer."

Think About/Talk About

Build Background: Women's Rights

Tell students that French contemporaries of Wollstonecraft struggled for women's rights during the French Revolution. In 1791, a year before Wollstonecraft's *A Vindication of the Rights of Woman,* Olympe de Gouges published the *Declaration of the Rights of Woman.* Gouges was guillotined in 1793.

Extend the Discussion

Finding Details What issue does the author say she does not intend to "agitate"? ***Possible response:*** *She says she does not intend to agitate the issue of women's equality or inferiority.*

Social Studies Link

Ask Yourself

Possible response: *If Wollstonecraft were alive today, she would most likely be concerned with the lack of education and work for women in several parts of the world. She would also be concerned about the unequal status and pay of women in the workplace and the often unrealistic portrayals of women in the media.*
In her own time, she opposed the typical portrayal of women as "the weaker sex."

dinate beings, and not as a part of the human species, when improvable[6] reason is allowed to be the dignified distinction which raises men above the brute creation, and puts a natural scepter[7] in a feeble hand.

Yet, because I am a woman, I would not lead my readers to suppose that I mean violently to agitate the contested question respecting the equality or inferiority of the sex; but as the subject lies in my way, and I cannot pass it over without subjecting the main tendency of my reasoning to misconstruction,[8] I shall stop a moment to deliver, in a few words, my opinion.—In the government of the physical world it is observable that the female in point of strength is, in general, inferior to the male. This is the law of nature; and it does not appear to be suspended or abrogated[9] in favor of woman. A degree of physical superiority cannot, therefore, be denied—and it is a noble prerogative![10] But not content with this natural pre-eminence, men endeavor to sink us still lower, merely to render us alluring objects for a moment; and women, intoxicated by the adoration which men, under the influence of their senses, pay them, do not seek to obtain a durable interest in their hearts, or to become the friends of the fellow creatures who find amusement in their society. **C**

I am aware of an obvious inference:—from every quarter have I heard exclamations against masculine women; but where are they to be found? If by this appellation[11] men mean to inveigh[12] against their ardour in hunting, shooting, and gaming, I shall most cordially join in the cry; but if it be against the imitation of manly virtues, or, more properly speaking, the attainment of those talents and virtues, the exercise of which ennobles the human character, and which raise females in the scale of animal being, when they are comprehensively termed mankind;—all those who view them with a philosophic eye must, I should think, wish with me, that they may every day grow more and more masculine. **D**

This discussion naturally divides the subject. I shall first consider women in the grand light of human creatures, who, in common with men, are placed on this earth to unfold their faculties; and afterwards I shall more particularly point out their peculiar designation.

I wish also to steer clear of an error which many respectable writers have fallen into; for the instruction which has hitherto been addressed to women, has rather been applicable to *ladies,* if the little indirect advice, that is scattered through Sandford and Merton,[13] be excepted; but, addressing my sex in a firmer tone, I pay particular attention to those in the middle class, because they appear to be in the most natural state. Perhaps the seeds of false refinement, immorality, and vanity, have ever been shed by the great. Weak, artificial beings, raised above the common wants and affections of their race, in a premature unnatural manner, undermine the very foundation of virtue, and spread corruption through the whole mass of society! As a class of mankind they have the strongest claim to pity; the education of the rich tends to render them vain and helpless, and the unfolding mind is not strengthened by the practice of those duties which dignify the human character.—They only live to amuse themselves, and by the same law which in nature invariably produces certain effects, they soon only afford barren amusement. **E**

6. **improvable:** capable of being improved.
7. **scepter** (SEHP tuhr): symbol of authority.
8. **misconstruction:** misunderstanding.
9. **abrogated:** abolished; repeated.
10. **prerogative:** privilege.
11. **appellation:** name.
12. **inveigh:** complain loudly.
13. **Sandford and Merton:** reference to *The History of Sandford and Merton,* a children's book. A character in the book often cites the moral superiority of a poor boy over a rich one.

C Literary Focus Tone What is the tone of Wollstonecraft's insistence that she does not want to stir up controversy about gender equality?

D Reading Focus Analyzing Rhetorical Devices Here, Wollstonecraft poses the rhetorical question *Where are the masculine women?* What is her point?

E Literary Focus Tone In earlier English writings, *ladies* meant "upper-class women." How would you describe Wollstonecraft's attitude toward these women? What connotative words help establish this tone?

Universal Access

English Learners

English for Academic Success Assure students that many modern readers struggle with the complex, periodic sentences and elaborate diction of eighteenth-century writers. Encourage students to break down difficult sentences and to use the footnotes for help with unfamiliar words.

✔ See **UA: Differentiating Instruction** for strategies for teaching English learners.

Struggling Readers

Model the skill of understanding rhetorical devices. You might say: "In the last paragraph on p. 670, Wollstonecraft refers to the women in the middle class as 'weak, artificial beings,' whose education leaves them helpless. I notice also on p. 671, she deplores the 'epithets of weakness' and 'weak elegancy of mind' that men assign to women. Thus the repetition of *weak* serves as a rhetorical device in these paragraphs."

✔ See **UA: Differentiating Instruction** for strategies for teaching struggling readers.

SOCIAL STUDIES LINK

Women's Rights Today

Since Mary Wollstonecraft wrote her plea for women's equality, opportunities for women, including access to education, have improved. Colleges in many countries admit women. In fact, in the United States, more women than men attend college. Nevertheless, in some regions of the world, women's access to education remains as restricted as it was to English women in Wollstonecraft's time. Globally, 90 million girls of school age do not receive a primary education. Some are prevented by poverty, others by traditional beliefs. Of all children who do not attend school, two-thirds are girls. However, through financial support and strategic counseling, grass-roots organizations are providing educational opportunities to girls who have been denied them.

Other crucial issues remain to be solved, including attaining constitutional equality for women in all nations and ending violence against women. Today, many organizations continue to promote Wollstonecraft's ideals for women.

Ask Yourself

If Wollstonecraft were alive today, what issues do you think would concern her most? Why?

But as I purpose[14] taking a separate view of the different ranks of society, and of the moral character of women in each, this hint is, for the present, sufficient; and I have only alluded to the subject, because it appears to me to be the very essence of an introduction to give a cursory account of the contents of the work it introduces.

My own sex, I hope, will excuse me, if I treat them like rational creatures, instead of flattering their *fascinating* graces, and viewing them as if they were in a state of perpetual childhood, unable to stand alone. I earnestly wish to point out in what true dignity and human happiness consists—I wish to persuade women to endeavor to acquire strength, both of mind and body, and to convince them that the soft phrases, susceptibility of heart, delicacy of sentiment, and refinement of taste, are almost synonymous with epithets[15] of weakness, and that those beings who are only the objects of pity and that kind of love, which has been termed its sister, will soon become objects of contempt. **F**

Dismissing then those pretty feminine phrases, which the men condescendingly use to soften our slavish dependence, and despising that weak elegancy of mind, exquisite sensibility, and sweet docility of manners, supposed to be the sexual characteristics of the weaker vessel, I wish to shew[16] that elegance is inferior to virtue, that the first object of laudable[17] ambition is to obtain a character as a human being, regardless of

14. **purpose:** intend.

15. **epithets** (EHP uh thehts): names.
16. **shew:** archaic spelling of *show.*
17. **laudable:** praiseworthy.

F **Literary Focus** **Tone** These characteristics of women are examples of the "fascinating graces" that the author mentions in the first sentence of the paragraph. What is her attitude toward these graces?

Vocabulary **cursory** (KUR suhr ee) *adj.:* hasty; superficial.

Think About/Talk About

Comprehension

D Reading Focus

Possible response: *She is implying that women should develop strength of character, presumably a masculine trait.*

Analysis

C Literary Focus

Possible response: *Her tone is satirical. The irony is that in the previous paragraph, she has begun to attack the issue of equality, and she continues her attack after denying that she intends to do so.*

E Literary Focus

Possible response: *She has a negative attitude toward upper-class women, calling them "weak" and "artificial."*

F Literary Focus

Possible response: *She reveals that these "graces" are really weaknesses.*

Extend the Discussion

Analyzing Rhetorical Devices In paragraph 2 of p. 671, Wollstonecraft writes, "My own sex, I hope, will forgive me, if I treat them as rational creatures." How does her use of irony function as a rhetorical device here? ***Possible response:*** *Wollstonecraft is being ironic by asking forgiveness for treating women as rational creatures. In this instance, she is using irony to point out the absurdity of treating adult women as helpless children, as is the case when their education is neglected.*

Vocabulary: Own the Word

cursory: Ask students to complete the following sentence to demonstrate their knowledge of the Vocabulary word: "Because the witness had given the thief only a *cursory* glance, . . ." ***Possible response:*** *the witness could not provide a detailed description of the thief's appearance.*

Advanced Learners

Enrichment Before students read the selection, have them discuss in detail the different rhetorical devices presented on p. 667. Ask students to make predictions about how each rhetorical device will be used in the selections based on what they know about the content of the selections.

✔ See **UA: Resources for Teaching Advanced Students** for strategies for teaching advanced learners.

Students with Disabilities

Provide students with a copy of the selection from the **Holt Interactive Reader.** As students read the selection, have them pause after each paragraph to analyze the author's use of language. Encourage them to ask themselves: How is the author trying to get her point across? What devices does she use? Give students five minutes to underline examples of the author's use of rhetorical devices. After students finish reading the entire introduction, have them share lines from the text that they underlined and explain why they found these passages effective.

Model the Skill

- Provide students with copies of the Reading Skills Focus graphic organizer for *A Vindication of the Rights of Woman.* (See **Unit 3 Resources.**)
- Tell students that in order to understand **rhetorical devices,** they need to remember that the author uses such techniques to convince readers to agree with a particular point of view.
- Read the first paragraph of p. 673 aloud. Point out that the author compares women to children, since women's highest accomplishments are as trivial as children's pastimes. This is an example of analogy that serves to support the author's idea and present it more vividly to the reader.

Device	Example
Analogy	. . . they dress, they paint, they nickname God's creatures.

How It Supports the Main Point
Women are only expected to spend their time on, and apply their intellect to, matters of no consequence

Guided Practice: Apply

QuickWrite Have students create two or three rhetorical questions that highlight problems with the condition of women in the world today.

Mr. B. Finds Pamela Writing, by Joseph Highmore. Illustration for *Pamela* (1740), by Samuel Richardson.
Victoria & Albert Museum, London.

Analyzing Visuals

Connecting to the Text How do the postures of the man and the woman help express their attitudes and contribute to the overall tone of the painting? In what way is the painting's tone similar to or different from Wollstonecraft's tone in *A Vindication of the Rights of Woman?*

the distinction of sex; and that secondary views should be brought to this simple touchstone.[18] **G**

This is a rough sketch of my plan; and should I express my conviction with the energetic emotions that I feel whenever I think of the subject, the dictates of experience and reflection will be felt by some of my readers. Animated by this important object, I shall disdain to cull[19] my phrases or polish my style;—I aim at being useful, and sincerity will render me unaffected; for, wishing rather to persuade by the force of my arguments, than dazzle by the elegance of my language, I shall not waste my time in rounding periods, or in fabricating the turgid bombast[20] of artificial feelings, which, coming from the head, never reach the heart.—I shall be employed about things, not words!—and, anxious to render my sex more respectable members of society, I shall try to avoid that flowery diction which has slided from essays into novels, and from novels into familiar letters and conversation.

These pretty superlatives,[21] dropping glibly from the tongue, vitiate[22] the taste, and create a kind of sickly delicacy that turns away from simple unadorned truth; and a deluge of false sentiments and overstretched feelings, stifling the natural emotions of the heart, render the domestic pleasures insipid,[23] that ought to sweeten the exercise of those severe duties, which educate a rational and immortal being for a nobler field of action. **H**

18. **touchstone:** criterion; originally a stone used for testing the quality of gold and silver alloys by noting the color of the streak produced by rubbing the metals upon it.
19. **cull:** sort out.
20. **turgid bombast:** pompous rant or utterance.
21. **superlatives:** exaggerations.
22. **vitiate:** impair; weaken; spoil.
23. **insipid:** dull; flat.

G **Literary Perspectives** **Analyzing Political Context** In the preceding paragraphs, Wollstonecraft presents the aims of her argument. What does she hope to accomplish? In what ways is this argument a political one?

H **Reading Focus** **Analyzing Rhetorical Devices** Wollstonecraft mentions her intentions concerning her writing style a number of times. Why do you think she does this?

Literary Perspectives

To help students answer the **Literary Perspectives** questions on this page, give students practice in identifying political assumptions. Remind students that an assumption is an underlying idea that a speaker or writer accepts as needing no proof. Tell students that from the following statement "You'd better not do that because it is against the law," they can assume that disobeying the law is undesirable. As students analyze Wollstonecraft's arguments, encourage them to use this technique to read into her ideas.

Analyzing Visuals

Connecting to the Text: *The painting focuses on a woman in the midst of writing, who seems to have been caught by surprise by the man's entrance. From his advancing gesture and focused expression, one might conclude that he is trying to woo her. Wollstonecraft's essay challenges men to view women not just as beautiful creatures—the view held by the man in the painting—but also as beings possessing intelligence, like the woman intent on her writing.*

The education of women has, of late, been more attended to than formerly; yet they are still reckoned a frivolous sex, and ridiculed or pitied by the writers who endeavor by satire or instruction to improve them. It is acknowledged that they spend many of the first years of their lives in acquiring a smattering of accomplishments; meanwhile strength of body and mind are sacrificed to libertine[24] notions of beauty, to the desire of establishing themselves,—the only way women can rise in the world,—by marriage. And this desire making mere animals of them, when they marry they act as such children may be expected to act:—they dress; they paint, and nickname God's creatures. —Surely these weak beings are only fit for a seraglio![25] —Can they be expected to govern a family with judgment, or take care of the poor babes whom they bring into the world? Ⓘ

If then it can be fairly deduced from the present conduct of the sex, from the prevalent fondness for pleasure which takes place of ambition and those nobler passions that open and enlarge the soul; that the instruction which women have hitherto received has only tended, with the constitution of civil society, to render them insignificant objects of desire—mere propagators[26] of fools!—if it can be proved that in aiming to accomplish them, without cultivating their understandings, they are taken out of their sphere of duties, and made ridiculous and useless when the short-lived bloom of beauty is over,* I presume that *rational* men will excuse me for endeavoring to persuade them to become more masculine and respectable. Ⓙ

Indeed the word masculine is only a bugbear:[27] there is little reason to fear that women will acquire too much courage or fortitude; for their apparent inferiority with respect to bodily strength, must render them, in some degree, dependent on men in the various relations of life; but why should it be increased by prejudices that give a sex to virtue, and confound simple truths with sensual reveries?[28]

Women are, in fact, so much degraded by mistaken notions of female excellence, that I do not mean to add a paradox when I assert, that this artificial weakness produces a propensity to tyrannize, and gives birth to cunning, the natural opponent of strength, which leads them to play off those contemptible infantine airs that undermine esteem even whilst they excite desire. Let men become more chaste and modest, and if women do not grow wiser in the same ratio, it will be clear that they have weaker understandings. It seems scarcely necessary to say, that I now speak of the sex in general. Many individuals have more sense than their male relatives; and, as nothing preponderates[29] where there is a constant struggle for equilibrium, without it has naturally more gravity, some women govern their husbands without degrading themselves, because intellect will always govern. Ⓚ

*A lively writer, I cannot recollect his name, asks what business women turned of forty have to do in the world?

24. **libertine:** sensual.
25. **seraglio** (suh RAL yoh): a place in a Middle Eastern house where wives live; a harem.
26. **propagators:** breeders.
27. **bugbear:** anything causing needless fear.
28. **reveries:** musings.
29. **preponderates:** predominates.

Ⓘ **Reading Focus** **Analyzing Rhetorical Devices** What rhetorical device concludes this paragraph? What point does this device make?

Ⓙ **Literary Perspectives** **Analyzing Political Context** What social distinctions between men and women can be drawn from Wollstonecraft's discussion?

Ⓚ **Literary Focus** **Tone** What paradox does Wollstonecraft discuss in the final paragraph? What words reveal her attitude toward this paradox?

Vocabulary **propensity** (pruh PEHN suh tee) *n.:* natural inclination.

Think About/Talk About

Comprehension

Ⓗ Reading Focus

Possible response: *Wollstonecraft wants her ideas, not her skill in writing, to be central in this essay.*

Ⓘ Reading Focus

Possible response: *This paragraph ends with a rhetorical question to point out that better education will improve women's ability to run their households and raise their children.*

Analysis

Ⓖ Literary Perspectives

Possible responses: *The argument is that women should develop strength of body and mind through education. This argument is political because it challenges women's place in eighteenth-century English society.*

Ⓙ Literary Perspectives

Possible response: *Men are "useful" because of their intellect, while women are only "useful" as objects of desire.*

Ⓚ Literary Focus

Possible response: *Women's powerlessness makes them tyrannize others and put on "contemptible infantine airs" to get their way.*

Vocabulary: Own the Word

propensity: A *propensity* is a tendency to develop a particular behavior. Synonyms are *inclination* and *susceptibility.* Ask: "If you have a *propensity* for lying, how would people react to you?" [*They would not believe you.*]

Monitor Students' Comprehension

To check students' understanding, ask them what the author understands *masculine* to mean and what implicit assumptions underlie her use of the word. [*She understands "masculine" to describe "those talents and virtues, the exercise of which ennobles the human character." Her implicit assumption is that most men have these talents and virtues.*]

Word-Attack Skills Mini-Lesson

English for Academic Success Display this sentence from the essay: "One cause of this barren blooming I attribute to a false system of education." Ask students what part of speech *attribute* is and how it is pronounced. [*verb; uh TREEB yoot*]

Then, display this sentence: "False refinement is hardly a desirable attribute." Ask students what part of speech *attribute* is in this sentence and how it is pronounced. [*noun; AHT tree byoot*]

Explain that many words are pronounced differently depending on their part of speech.

Activity Ask students to determine the part of speech of each underlined word and then to pronounce it correctly.

1. How should girls conduct themselves? [*v.; kuhn DUHKT*]
2. The rules of conduct have changed. [*n.; KON duhkt*]
3. Indignation is precedent to change. [*adj.; prih SEE duhnt*]
4. Women's suffrage set a precedent. [*n.; PREHS uh duhnt*]
5. Watch as the dog proceeds to eat. [*v.; pro SEEDZ*]
6. He donated the proceeds to charity. [*n.; PRO seedz*]

Teacher Preparation
Selection Summary
In *The Education of Women,* written in the early 1700s, Defoe advocates educating women to make them better wives. He argues that denying them education is unfair and irrational; he suggests that they learn music, dance, speaking skills, history, and modern languages; and he assures readers that this education will not cause women to "encroach" on men's domains.

Direct Teach

Think About/Talk About
Read with a Purpose Have students read the Read with a Purpose statement. Point out that the word "controversial" indicates that there is disagreement over the issue of education for women. Ask students to note points of controversy in Defoe's essay on the education of women.

Extend the Discussion
Finding the Main Idea What is Defoe's central claim? ***Possible response:*** *Defoe's central claim is that women should receive an education.*

ESSAY

from

The Education of Women

by **Daniel Defoe**

Read with a Purpose
Read to find out why Defoe supported the controversial issue of education for women.

Build Background
Ironically, Defoe himself did not receive the standard education for young gentlemen of his era. His parents were Dissenters—Protestants who disapproved of the Church of England—so he was barred from attending the universities in Oxford and Cambridge. Instead, he studied law, history, economics, geography, and natural science at an alternative academy. When he was about twenty, he set himself up as a merchant, trading in haberdashery (men's hats, shirts, ties, and so on), wool, real estate, and at one point civet "cats" (cat-like animals that resemble a mongoose). By the time he married, at age twenty-four, he was already writing and publishing. "The Education of Women" is one of his numerous pamphlets on religious and political controversies. Some of his contemporaries apparently considered him a nuisance: Jonathan Swift wrote in 1708, "there is no enduring him," and Joseph Addison in 1713 called him "a false, shuffling, prevaricating rascal—unqualified to give his testimony in a Court of Justice."

I have often thought of it as one of the most barbarous customs in the world, considering us as a civilized and a Christian country, that we deny the advantages of learning to women. We reproach the sex every day with folly and impertinence; while I am confident, had they the advantages of education equal to us, they would be guilty of less than ourselves.

One would wonder, indeed, how it should happen that women are conversible[1] at all; since they are only beholden to natural parts, for all their knowledge. Their youth is spent to teach them to stitch and sew or make baubles. They are taught to read, indeed, and perhaps to write their names, or so; and that is the height of a woman's education. And I would but ask any who slight the sex for their understanding, what is a man (a gentleman, I mean) good for, that is taught no more? I need not give instances, or examine the character of a gentleman, with a good estate, or a good family, and with tolerable parts; and examine what figure he makes for want of education.

The soul is placed in the body like a rough diamond; and must be polished, or the luster of it will never appear. And 'tis manifest, that as the rational soul distinguishes us from brutes; so education carries on the distinction, and makes some less brutish than others. This is too evident to need any demonstration. But why then should women be denied the benefit of instruction? If knowledge and understanding had been useless additions to the sex, GOD Almighty would never have given them capacities; for he made

1. **conversible:** able to interact socially.

Vocabulary **manifest** (MAN uh fehst) *adj.:* evident; obvious.

Universal Access

English Learners
English for Academic Success To help students who are struggling with eighteenth-century diction, explain that in Defoe's time, *gentleman* meant "man of the upper class," *estate* meant "social standing," *parts* meant "character traits," *figure* meant "impression," and *for want of* meant "without."

✔ See the **English Language Skill Builder** in **UA: Differentiating Instruction.**

Struggling Readers
Point out the string of questions in the first paragraph on p. 675. You might say: "In the sentence that begins 'I would ask such . . . ' Defoe is using the rhetorical questions as support for his argument. The first question reads, 'What can they see in ignorance, that they should think it a necessary ornament to a woman?' The logical answer is that there is no reason ignorance would be a necessary or desirable trait in a woman. Defoe is trying to say that keeping women ignorant is of no benefit to anyone. This point supports his argument."

A Dame's School (1845), by Thomas Webster (1800–1886).
Tate Gallery, London.

nothing needless. Besides, I would ask such, What they can see in ignorance, that they should think it a necessary ornament to a woman? or how much worse is a wise woman than a fool? or what has the woman done to forfeit the privilege of being taught? Does she plague us with her pride and impertinence? Why did we not let her learn, that she might have had more wit? Shall we upbraid[2] women with folly, when 'tis only the error of this inhuman custom, that hindered them from being made wiser? Ⓐ Ⓑ

The capacities of women are supposed to be greater, and their senses quicker than those of the men; and what they might be capable of being bred to, is plain from some instances of female wit, which this age is not without. Which upbraids us with Injustice, and looks as if we denied women the advantages of education, for fear they should vie with the men in their improvements. . . .

[They] should be taught all sorts of breeding suitable both to their genius and quality. And in particular, Music and Dancing; which it would be cruelty to bar the sex of, because they are their darlings. But besides this, they should be taught languages, as particularly French and Italian: and I would venture the injury[3] of

2. **upbraid:** criticize.

3. **venture the injury:** take the risk.

Ⓐ **Literary Focus** **Tone** What are the connotations of the words *useless, needless, ignorance, plague, folly,* and *inhuman*? How do they contribute to the tone of Defoe's argument?

Ⓑ **Reading Focus** **Analyzing Rhetorical Devices** What analogy does Defoe use in this paragraph? What impact does the analogy make on his main idea?

Vocabulary **vie** (vy) *v.:* compete.

Advanced Learners

Enrichment Suggest to students that Defoe's "The Education of Women" may have been one of the "books of instruction, written by men of genius" that Mary Wollstonecraft refers to in her *A Vindication of the Rights of Woman.* Ask students, as they read Defoe's essay, to look for material justifying Wollstonecraft's assertions that these writers regard women as "a kind of subordinate species" and that "[Women] are still reckoned a frivolous sex, and ridiculed or pitied by the writers who endeavor by satire or instruction to improve them."

Students with Disabilities

Before students read "The Education of Women," have them listen to the selection in audio format in **The Holt Audio Library.** Then, have students write down words, sentences, and ideas that they consider especially relevant.

✔ See **UA: Differentiating Instruction** for strategies for teaching students with disabilities.

Think About/Talk About

Comprehension

Ⓑ Reading Focus

Possible responses: *"To polish" is to a diamond as "to educate" is to a soul. This analogy supports his argument that education can only improve a woman.*

Analysis

Ⓐ Literary Focus

Possible responses: *These words all have negative connotations. Defoe is using them to show that even the educated (men) are capable of ignorance.*

Extend the Discussion

Monitoring Reading What is the "inhuman custom" Defoe refers to in the first paragraph? ***Possible response:*** *Defoe says that neglecting the education of women is an "inhuman custom."*

Synthesizing How does the second paragraph show a point of agreement between Defoe and Wollstonecraft on the causes of the insufficient education of women? ***Possible response:*** *Defoe and Wollstonecraft agree that men deny adequate education to women out of fear that educated women will compete with them.*

Vocabulary: Own the Word

- **manifest:** Remind students that *manifest* means "evident or obvious." Ask students to explain the idea that Defoe describes as *manifest* in the selection. ***Possible response:*** *Defoe states that it is evident that education helps make people more civilized than those who are uneducated.*
- **vie:** Ask students: "Have you ever had to *vie* for attention from someone? Explain when you had to *vie* for someone's attention and why."

Think About/Talk About

Comprehension

D Reading Focus

Possible responses: *In the last paragraph, Defoe uses an illustrative anecdote. It is effective because it proves that some women share Defoe's opinions.*

Analysis

C Literary Focus

Possible response: *In this passage, Defoe uses a humorous tone to appeal to his predominantly male audience. His humor may have helped to defuse the touchy issue of women's rights to education.*

Extend the Discussion

Synthesizing In the last paragraph on p. 676, Defoe writes about a woman who has "an extraordinary shape and face." Why might Mary Wollstonecraft have objected to Defoe's description of this woman? ***Possible response:*** *Wollstonecraft might object to Defoe's praise of the woman's "extraordinary shape and face" as an example of the misguided standards applied to women, in which their physical attributes were deemed more important than their intellectual attributes.*

Monitor Students' Comprehension

Guide students in answering these comprehension questions.

1. What kind of education did women receive, according to the author? [*They were taught to read and do some functional writing.*]
2. Which two subjects in particular does the author suggest for women? [*music and dancing*]
3. In the author's opinion, what is the main difference between men and women? [*They differ in their levels of education.*]

giving a woman more tongues than one. They should, as a particular study, be taught all the graces of speech, and all the necessary air of conversation; which our common education is so defective in, that I need not expose it. They should be brought to read books, and especially history; and so to read as to make them understand the world, and be able to know and judge of things when they hear of them. **C**

To such whose genius would lead them to it, I would deny no sort of learning; but the chief thing, in general, is to cultivate the understandings of the sex, that they may be capable of all sorts of conversation; that their parts and judgments being improved, they may be as profitable in their conversation as they are pleasant.

Women, in my observation, have little or no difference in them, but as they are or are not distinguished by education. Tempers, indeed, may in some degree influence them, but the main distinguishing part is their Breeding. . . .

The great distinguishing difference, which is seen in the world between men and women, is in their education; and this is manifested by comparing it with the difference between one man or woman, and another.

And herein it is that I take upon me to make such a bold assertion, That all the world are mistaken in their practice about women. For I cannot think that GOD Almighty ever made them so delicate, so glorious creatures; and furnished them with such charms, so agreeable and so delightful to mankind; with souls capable of the same accomplishments with men: and all, to be only Stewards of our Houses, Cooks, and Slaves.

Not that I am for exalting the female government in the least: but, in short, *I would have men take women for companions, and educate them to be fit for it.* A woman of sense and breeding will scorn as much to encroach upon the prerogative of man, as a man of sense will scorn to oppress the weakness of the woman. But if the women's souls were refined and improved by teaching, that word would be lost. To say, the *weakness* of the sex, as to judgment, would be nonsense; for ignorance and folly would be no more to be found among women than men. **D**

I remember a passage, which I heard from a very fine woman. She had wit and capacity enough, an extraordinary shape and face, and a great fortune: but had been cloistered up all her time; and for fear of being stolen, had not had the liberty of being taught the common necessary knowledge of women's affairs. And when she came to converse in the world, her natural wit made her so sensible of the want of education, that she gave this short reflection on herself: "I am ashamed to talk with my very maids," says she, "for I don't know when they do right or wrong. I had more need go to school, than be married." . . .

'Tis a thing will be more easily granted than remedied. . . .

C Literary Focus Tone When Defoe plays on stereotypes of women as sharp-tongued and overly talkative and says that he will "venture the injury" (take the risk) of "giving a women more tongues than one," what is his tone?

D Reading Focus Analyzing Rhetorical Devices What rhetorical device does Defoe use in this paragraph? How effective is this device?

California Standards, pp. 678–681

- **Reading Standard 2.1** Analyze both the features and the rhetorical devices of different types of public documents (e.g., policy statements, speeches, debates, platforms) and the way in which authors use those features and devices.
- **Reading Standard 3.1** Analyze characteristics of subgenres (e.g., satire, parody, allegory, pastoral) that are used in poetry, prose, plays, novels, short stories, essays, and other basic genres.
- **Reading Standard 3.3** Analyze the ways in which irony, tone, mood, the author's style, and the "sound" of language achieve specific rhetorical or aesthetic purposes or both.
- **Reading Standard 3.8** Analyze the clarity and consistency of political assumptions in a selection of literary works or essays on a topic (e.g., suffrage, women's role in organized labor) (Political approach).
- **Grades 9–10 Review Reading Standard 1.1** Identify and use the literal and figurative meanings of words and understand word derivations.
- **Writing Standard 1.1** Demonstrate an understanding of the elements of discourse (e.g., purpose, speaker, audience, form) when completing narrative, expository, persuasive, or descriptive writing assignments.
- **Writing Standard 1.3** Structure ideas and arguments in a sustained, persuasive, and sophisticated way and support them with precise and relevant examples.

POEM

To the Ladies

by **Mary, Lady Chudleigh**

Read with a Purpose
Read to find out why the author compares a wife's position to that of a servant.

Build Background
"To the Ladies" is Chudleigh's most anthologized poem; it appeared in print in 1703 and was so popular that it has been found copied onto the flyleaves of other books. Lady Chudleigh's marriage may have been somewhat unrewarding, which perhaps contributed to the bitter tone of this poem.

Wife and Servant are the same,
But only differ in the Name:
For when that fatal Knot is ty'd,
Which nothing, nothing can divide:
When she the word *obey* has said,
And Man by Law supreme has made,
Then all that's kind is laid aside,
And nothing left but State° and Pride:
Fierce as an Eastern Prince he grows,
And all his innate Rigor shows:
Then but to look, to laugh, or speak,
Will the Nuptial Contract break.
Like Mutes she Signs alone must make,
And never any Freedom take:
But still be govern'd by a Nod,
And fear her Husband as her God:
Him still must serve, him still obey,
And nothing act, and nothing say,
But what her haughty Lord thinks fit,
Who with the Pow'r, has all the Wit. (A)
Then shun, oh! shun that wretched State,
And all the fawning Flatt'rers hate:
Value your selves, and Men despise,
You must be proud, if you'll be wise. (B)

8. State: ostentation; pretentiousness.

The Betrothal (1774), by Jacobus Buys (1724–1801). Oil on canvas. Tatton Park, Cheshire, England.

(A) **Reading Focus** **Analyzing Rhetorical Devices** In line 9, the speaker begins an analogy, extending it through line 19. To what does she compare a husband?

(B) **Literary Focus** **Tone** The use of hyperbole is one mark of a satirical tone. Where is the hyperbole in lines 13–19? What is the speaker satirizing in these lines?

Teacher Preparation
Selection Summary
In "To the Ladies," Mary, Lady Chudleigh argues that since a wife's position is little better than a servant's, women should avoid marriage and instead develop personal pride.

Think About/Talk About
Read with a Purpose Have students read the Read with a Purpose statement. Ask students to look for the solution to this problem in the poem.

Comprehension
(A) Reading Focus
Possible responses: *She compares him to an eastern prince who has absolute power over his wife.*

Analysis
(B) Literary Focus
Possible responses: *The phrase "fear her Husband as her God" is hyperbolic, satirizing the condition of the wife as subordinate to her husband.*

Extend the Discussion
Comparing and Contrasting What political issue is raised in lines 1–8? How does it differ from the issues raised by Wollstonecraft and Defoe?
Possible response: *This poem addresses women's rights in marriage rather than their rights to education.*

- **Writing Standard 2.2** Write responses to literature: **a.** Demonstrate a comprehensive understanding of the significant ideas in works or passages. **b.** Analyze the use of imagery, language, universal themes, and unique aspects of the text. **c.** Support important ideas and viewpoints through accurate and detailed references to the text and to other works. **d.** Demonstrate an understanding of the author's use of stylistic devices and an appreciation of the effects created. **e.** Identify and assess the impact of perceived ambiguities, nuances, and complexities within the text.
- **Writing Standard 2.6** Deliver multimedia presentations: **a.** Combine text, images, and sound and draw information from many sources (e.g., television broadcasts, videos, films, newspapers, magazines, CD-ROMs, the Internet, electronic media-generated images). **b.** Select an appropriate medium for each element of the presentation. **c.** Use the selected media skillfully, editing appropriately and monitoring for quality.
- **Listening and Speaking Standard 2.2** Deliver oral reports on historical investigations: **a.** Use exposition, narration, description, persuasion, or some combination of those to support the thesis. **b.** Analyze several historical records of a single event, examining critical relationships between elements of the research topic. **c.** Explain the perceived reason or reasons for the similarities and differences by using information derived from primary and secondary sources to support or enhance the presentation. **d.** Include information on all relevant perspectives and consider the validity and reliability of sources.

Check for Understanding

Independent Practice

Reading Skills Focus

Possible responses:

1. *They are considered inferior because they have less education.*
2. *Women's capacities are greater than those of men. Men fear that women will become powerful.*
3. *Women should value themselves.*
4. *All three use anecdotes, analogies, and restatement. Wollstonecraft and Defoe use counterargument and rhetorical questions. Each argues against the political marginalization of women.*
5. *Students' paragraphs should identify at least one rhetorical device from the text and analyze its effect on the tone and the argument.*

Literary Skills Focus

Possible responses:

6. *Both authors argue that an education will help women become better wives and mothers, but Wollstonecraft does not seek to limit the subjects in which women should be educated as Defoe does.*
7. *Readers might resent the equation of wives with servants. The poem reveals that wives cannot divorce.*
8. *Viewing her argument through a political lens helps me understand the inequality of women in the eighteenth century. The fact that women are now educated in many parts of the world shows that their power has increased.*
9. *Wollstonecraft's tone is satirical ["My own sex, I hope, will forgive me, if I treat them like rational creatures . . ."]. Defoe is occasionally humorous ["I would venture the injury of giving a woman more tongues than one"]. Chudleigh is satirical, using hyperbole ["fear her Husband as her God"].*
10. *She attacks the idea that educating women makes them masculine, arguing that "masculine" qualities are "respectable" qualities and should apply to both men and women.*

Applying Your Skills

Reading Standard 2.1, 3.1, 3.3, 3.8 (see pages A48–A50)
Writing Standard 2.2a, 2.2c (see pages A51–A52)

from **A Vindication of the Rights of Woman /**
from **The Education of Women / To the Ladies**

Literary Response and Analysis

Reading Skills Focus

Quick Check

1. According to Wollstonecraft, why are women considered inferior to men?
2. What does Defoe say about the "capacities of women"? Why does he say that men are afraid of educating women?
3. According to Chudleigh, what should women learn to value?

Read with a Purpose

4. What strategies do Wollstonecraft, Defoe, and Lady Chudleigh use to justify their arguments? Why does each advocate women's rights?

Reading Skills: Analyzing Rhetorical Devices

5. Review your chart of rhetorical devices. Does each author seem to favor one rhetorical device over other devices? Choose one of the selections that uses a particular rhetorical device more than once. Explain in a paragraph how the use of that device affects the author's argument and the overall tone of the piece.

Literary Skills Focus

Literary Analysis

6. **Compare** What arguments are advanced by Wollstonecraft and Defoe for granting women "the advantages of learning"? What arguments are advanced only by one writer or the other?
7. **Interpret** Why might readers in the eighteenth century have found the opening line of Lady Chudleigh's poem shocking? What details of the poem support the meaning of this line?
8. **Literary Perspectives** Wollstonecraft was a strong advocate of women's rights. How does viewing this text through a political lens enhance your understanding of the historical context as well as help you understand the focus of her argument?

Literary Skills: Tone

9. **Evaluate** What is the overall tone of each selection? What particular words, phrases, and passages contribute to each selection's tone?

Literary Skills Review: Satire

10. **Infer** A **satire** mocks the failings and flaws of people or social institutions in an attempt to bring about a change. In *Vindication,* Wollstonecraft satirizes the idea that certain intellectual qualities can be strictly masculine or feminine. How does she satirize the notion that educating women will make them masculine?

Writing Skills Focus

Think as a Reader/Writer

Use It in Your Writing Look back at the analogies you identified while reading. Using at least two original analogies, write a paragraph in your *Reader/Writer Notebook* explaining your views about one of the selections or about the topic of gender equality.

What Do You Think Now? How did social rules and order affect the lives of women in eighteenth-century Britain? How did these writers respond to those rules and social order?

Universal Access

Struggling Writers

Some students may need additional scaffolding to complete the Writing Skills Focus activity. Students may have difficulty creating analogies based on the selections. Ask them to write a paragraph discussing the selection whose ideas they most agree with. Encourage students to use a simile or analogy in their writing that explains why they relate to that particular selection.

What Do You Think Now?

Have students consider women's roles in eighteenth-century Britain. Then let them think about what social rules the writers of these selections wanted to change.

Grades 9–10 Review Reading Standard 1.1 (see pages A48–A50)

Vocabulary Development

Vocabulary Check

Match each Vocabulary word with its synonym.

1. fastidious — a. apparent
2. specious — b. superficial
3. cursory — c. particular
4. propensity — d. compete
5. manifest — e. fake
6. vie — f. inclination

Vocabulary Skills: Using a Dictionary

Scholarly documents such as Wollstonecraft's *A Vindication of the Rights of Woman* often contain difficult, specialized, or abstract vocabulary. If you find yourself puzzled by a word, look the word up in a dictionary. A dictionary can provide information about the word's meaning, part of speech, and etymology, or history.

In *Vindication,* for example, Wollstonecraft writes, "If by this appellation men mean to inveigh against their ardour. . . ." The chart below gives information about *appellation* that you may find in a dictionary.

Word: *appellation*	
Meaning	name or title
Part of speech	noun
Etymology	Latin ("a naming")

Your Turn

Use a dictionary to look up the following italicized words from the text. Using the chart as an example, fill out a similar chart for each word.

1. "After considering the historic page, and viewing the living world with anxious *solicitude* . . ."
2. ". . . and it does not appear to be suspended or *abrogated* in favor of woman."
3. "If by this appellation men mean to *inveigh* against their ardour [*ardor*] . . ."

Language Coach

Antonyms Words with opposite meanings are antonyms. Identifying antonyms can help you remember the meanings of new words. Replace each Vocabulary word in italics with one of the following antonyms: *thorough, relaxed, obscure, valid.* Read the new sentence aloud and explain how the meaning changes with the new word in place.

1. Men can be just as *fastidious* as women when it comes to their appearance.
2. She insists that the arguments for the new law are utterly *specious.*
3. A *cursory* review of the essay reveals several shifts in tone.
4. The writer's ideas are *manifest* to her readers.

Academic Vocabulary

Talk About

With a partner, discuss how educating girls and women affects individuals and societies. How can it enhance lives and lead people to participate more fully in life? Who might oppose education for girls and women? Why? How might you convince someone to support education for girls and women?

Independent Practice
Vocabulary Development
Vocabulary Check

1. *c* **2.** *e*
3. *b* **4.** *f*
5. *a* **6.** *d*

Your Turn

Possible responses:

1. ***solicitude***—*care, concern; noun; Latin ("anxious")*

2. ***abrogated***—*abolished; verb; Latin ("from/away" + "ask")*

3. ***inveigh***—*to protest strongly; verb; Latin ("to attack")*

ardor—*vigor; noun; Latin ("heat")*

English for Academic Success
Language Coach

Have students discuss whether using the antonym changes the meaning of the entire sentence to its opposite meaning or not. [*1. relaxed; 2. valid; 3. thorough; 4. obscure*]

English for Academic Success
Academic Vocabulary

Possible response: *Educating women can enhance people's lives by bringing a new outlook on issues of common interest. Educated women can effectively participate in the political and social life and offer their contribution and insight.*

Universal Access: Vocabulary Development

English Learners

English for Academic Success Help students gain meaning from the Vocabulary words. Pair students with a proficient English speaker, and have them work together to answer the following questions.

- What is the opposite of a *fastidious* person? [*a slob*]
- Why would you reject a *specious* argument? [*It has fallacies.*]
- What is the opposite of a *cursory* investigation? [*a thorough investigation*]
- What is the opposite of a *manifest* answer? [*an unclear answer*]
- If you have a *propensity* for shopping, do you enjoy shopping or abhor it? [*enjoy it*]
- If you *vie* for a championship, do you compete for it or pay for it? [*compete for it*]

✔ See the **Academic and Selection Vocabulary Skill Builder** in **UA: Differentiating Instruction.**

Independent Practice

Grammar Link

Your Turn

1. *were; past*
2. *not subjunctive*
3. *be sold; present*

Choices: Evaluation Criteria

Review: Homework
Create a Visual

- Sign reflects understanding of the political issue in question in the Wollstonecraft, Defoe, or Chudleigh selection.
- Sign uses imagery to reflect a political stance.

Connect: Timed Writing 40-50 Minutes

- Essay argues that Wollstonecraft's essay is or is not relevant to modern times.
- Students support their response with evidence from the text and their own lives.

Extend: Homework
Research the Women's Movement

- Presentation represents grasp of key people and events in the women's movement.
- Group uses a variety of research strategies and sources.

Applying Your Skills

from **A Vindication of the Rights of Woman /** *from* **The Education of Women / To the Ladies**

Writing Standard 2.2a, 2.2c–e, 2.6a–c (see pages A51–A52)
Listening and Speaking Standard 2.2a–d (see pages A53–A55)

Grammar Link

Subjunctive Mood

You use the **subjunctive mood** when you want to express a suggestion, a necessity, a condition contrary to fact, or a wish. The **present subjunctive** expresses a necessity or suggestion. The present subjunctive form of a verb is the same as the base form of the verb, such as *be* or *have*. As you can see in the examples below, the present subjunctive often occurs in subordinate clauses beginning with *that*.

The author suggested that women **be given** a chance to achieve equality in society.

Her husband recommended that the conversation **be postponed** until the next morning.

The **past subjunctive** expresses a condition contrary to fact or expresses a wish. The past subjunctive form is *were*. Note that the past subjunctive form is used in clauses beginning with *if, as if*, or *as though*.

If I **were** you, I'd be more careful.

I wish she **were** at the beach with us.

Your Turn

Read each sentence. If the sentence is written in the subjunctive mood, write down the subjunctive phrase and identify it as present or past subjunctive.

1. If the author's style were any more inflammatory, the book would be too hot to touch.
2. The men were at work all day, making money and interacting with their peers.
3. The author requested that her book be sold in stores where women shop.

Writing Application Write a paragraph in which you use the subjunctive mood to express a wish.

CHOICES

As you respond to the Choices, use these **Academic Vocabulary** words as appropriate: approach, convince, dominate, enhance, participate.

REVIEW

Create a Visual

Today, social activists participate in protests to convince others of their views. Many carry signs and pictures to communicate their messages to passersby. Review the works by Wollstonecraft, Defoe, and Chudleigh, and create a sign that communicates the message of one of the authors. Present your work to the class, explaining the imagery in your visual and how it relates to the selection you chose.

CONNECT

Evaluate for Relevance

Timed Writing In an expository essay, analyze the relevance of Wollstonecraft's essay for our time. Do her observations about the role of women hold true today, or are her arguments limited to the social realities of the eighteenth century? Which, if any, of her observations about men and women remain valid in the twenty-first century? Use textual details and real-life examples to support your response.

EXTEND

Research the Women's Movement

Group Activity Form a group and have each member research different aspects of the fight for women's rights in the twentieth century. Search reference sources, view documentaries, or conduct interviews with women who lived through eras important to the women's movement, such as the 1960s, 1970s, and 1980s. Who are leaders in the movement for women's rights? What does the women's movement have in common with the civil rights movement? Assemble a multimedia presentation to share your findings with the class.

Universal Access: Grammar Link

Struggling Readers

Provide students with a list of verbs that often take the subjunctive mood: *ask, command, demand, desire, determine, insist, move, order, pray, prefer, recommend, regret, request, require, suggest, and wish.* Ask students to write a short paragraph that uses at least three of these verbs in the subjunctive mood.

✔ For more practice with the subjunctive mood, see **Warriner's Handbook, GrammarNotes,** and **Language Handbook Worksheets.**

Writing Standard 1.1, 1.3, 2.2a–e (see pages A51–A52)

Views on Women's Rights

Writing a Comparison-Contrast Essay

Establish Similarities The selections *A Vindication of the Rights of Woman,* "The Education of Women," and "To the Ladies" have many similarities, and yet each is unique. Where do the authors' viewpoints on women's rights intersect? Do they use similar techniques?

Identify Differences Think about these questions and the suggestions below as you choose an approach to comparing and contrasting these selections.

Here are some specific topic ideas for your comparison-contrast essay:

- How is Chudleigh's poem different from the two essays, in content as well as in structure? What do the essays express that the poem does not?
- Compare and contrast the overall effectiveness of the selections. Which of the three selections is the most successful in making its point? Why?
- Compare and contrast the enduring relevance of the selections. Which of the three selections is most relevant for today's audiences? Why?

Create a Trifold Chart Create a chart to organize your thoughts. Write the title of one selection at the top of each column. As you analyze the theme, context, historical and modern relevance, and language use of each selection, record your notes in the appropriate column. Then, review your notes, looking for at least one major similarity. Begin your comparison-contrast essay with a basis of similarity beyond the obvious fact that all three address women's issues. Look closely for more insight. Use examples from the selections to support your arguments.

Create a Thesis Statement Using your notes, develop a thesis statement for your essay that makes an assertion about the similarities and differences in the three selections.

Organize your Essay The most important element of organization in a comparison-contrast essay is to begin with your basis of similarity, and then move to differences. Conclude with differences to stress that each selection is unique. Use a point-by-point organizational method by discussing each selection in each body paragraph.

Provide Text Evidence The body paragraphs focus on an element of similarity or difference and use sample quotations from each selection to prove the idea asserted in the paragraph. Be sure to follow each quotation with elaboration and explanation, linking the quotation to the main point of the essay.

Think About Today Since the topic of women's rights is still discussed today, one way to conclude is by relating the selections to current issues. If you choose that approach, think about the What Do You Think Now question that follows the chart below.

An effective comparison-contrast essay
• clearly states what is being compared and contrasted
• conveys a main idea through a thesis statement
• is organized logically and effectively
• cites text passages to support ideas
• contains few or no errors in spelling, punctuation, and grammar

What Do You Think Now?

Do you think it would be worth the risk of ridicule, punishment, or even imprisonment to speak out against an inequality today? Explain.

Universal Access

Struggling Writers

Some students may need additional scaffolding to complete the Writing Skills Focus activity. Students may have difficulty comparing and contrasting the content of multiple selections. Invite students to write an essay that compares Wollstonecraft's and Defoe's essays. Ask students to point out the arguments set forth by both authors and how the viewpoints of both authors are similar. Remind students to include evidence from the selections to support their points.

Independent Practice

What Do You Think Now?

Spark a discussion on political and social issues involving women that need attention today. Then discuss effective strategies for bringing attention to these issues.

Assess

Unit 3 Resources, Selection Standards Check, p. 91

ThinkCentral Online Assessment, Selection Standards Check

Teacher One Stop™, editable Selection Standards Check

Reteach

To reteach **irony, tone, and author's style,** see **Reteaching Lessons,** pp. 1449O–1449P.

ThinkCentral Online Remediation

Standards Focus

Objectives

Students will

- learn prewriting, drafting, and revising techniques for writing a persuasive essay
- learn how to proofread and publish their work

Preteach

Write with a Purpose Read aloud the essentials of a good persuasive essay to guide students' understanding of this type of writing. Also, refer students to the scoring guide on p. 690 for more information on persuasive essays that they can use throughout the workshop.

Direct Teach

Model the Skill

Think as a Reader/Writer Use the professional model on this page and others in the unit to provide examples of the elements of a good persuasive essay. Point out how the model tells readers exactly what the author wants to accomplish and why.

Think About the Model

Possible responses:

1. *The comparison shows that it is possible to accomplish the goal he wants to achieve.*
2. *The personification of Burma and reference to "her courage, sacrifice, and vision" creates a very powerful appeal.*

Writing Workshop

Persuasive Essay

Write with a Purpose

Write a persuasive essay supporting your position on an issue that is important to you. Your **purpose** for writing is to persuade your **audience**—your teacher and classmates or others who are affected by this issue.

Think as a Reader/Writer In this unit, you have read many works with persuasive elements. Before you write your own **persuasive essay,** take a few minutes to read this excerpt from Desmond Tutu's "Easy Praise, Empty Words." Tutu addresses human rights violations by the military government of the Southeast Asian country of Burma, also known as Myanmar. Among these violations is the house arrest of 1991 Nobel Peace Prize winner Aung San Suu Kyi.

> I make a direct call here to our friends on the UNSC [United Nations Security Council], many of whom fought hard against apartheid in South Africa, to help us now to support the people of Burma. As happened with the apartheid regime in South Africa, the people of Burma have unequivocally rejected their illegitimate rulers; and the legitimate representatives of Burma's people have urged the world to support them. I call upon my brothers and sisters on the UNSC to pass a resolution that binds Burma's regime into an irreversible contract—one that commits it to a transition to democratic government and ensures the release, not only of Aung San Suu Kyi, but of all those who have endured the darkness of a Burmese prison for the sake of freedom.
>
> If we commit ourselves wholeheartedly to this end, Burma will one day have a leader whose commitment to her people is unwavering, and whose integrity and vision have already been proven by her courage, sacrifice and vision. Just as Nelson Mandela no longer belongs only to South Africans, I believe that in the future Aung San Suu Kyi will be a shining light for Asia and the world.
>
> History has shown us that neither systems, nor governments, nor dictators are eternal, but the spirit of freedom is. Freedom then is our dangerous message, our potent weapon. We must ensure that it rings loud in the dark hallways of the dictators in Rangoon. Easy praise, empty words.

← **Tutu states his purpose clearly by urging action to help Burma.**

← **He compares Aung San Suu Kyi to another great leader, Nelson Mandela.**

← **Tutu restates his call to action and echoes the title.**

A Good Persuasive Essay

- addresses an issue important to you and others
- demonstrates evidence and reasoning to support your position
- addresses counterarguments opposing your position
- convinces readers to agree with your opinion, take a stand, or take action

See page 690 for a complete scoring guide.

Reader/Writer Notebook

Use your **RWN** to complete the activities for this workshop.

Think About the Professional Model

With a partner, discuss the following questions about the model.

1. What effect does the comparison of the situation in Burma with that in South Africa have on Tutu's argument?
2. What language appeals to your emotions most powerfully?

California Standards, pp. 682–689

- **Writing Standard 1.1** Demonstrate an understanding of the elements of discourse (e.g., purpose, speaker, audience, form) when completing narrative, expository, persuasive, or descriptive writing assignments.
- **Writing Standard 1.3** Structure ideas and arguments in a sustained, persuasive, and sophisticated way and support them with precise and relevant examples.
- **Writing Standard 1.4** Enhance meaning by employing rhetorical devices, including the extended use of parallelism, repetition, and analogy; the incorporation of visual aids (e.g., graphs, tables, pictures); and the issuance of a call for action.
- **Writing Standard 1.5** Use language in a natural, fresh, and vivid way to establish a specific tone.
- **Writing Standard 1.9** Revise text to highlight the individual voice, improve sentence variety and style, and enhance subtlety of meaning and tone in ways that are consistent with the purpose, audience and genre.

Writing Workshop Resources

UA: Holt Interactive Writer and Speaker, practice and assessment, p. 65

UA: Differentiating Instruction, modified lesson plans, p. 150

WritingNotes, interactive lesson presentations with activities

GrammarNotes, interactive lesson presentations with activities

Writing and Research in a Digital Age, interactive lesson presentations with activities

Writing Standard 1.1, 1.3, 1.4, 1.5, 1.9 (see pages A51–A52)
Language Conventions Standard 1.1, 1.2, 1.3 (see page A53)

Prewriting

Choose an Issue

In your essay, you will discuss an **issue,** a topic about which reasonable people can disagree. Is there an **occasion,** or real-life reason, that gives you a reason to write? Look around you at the places you go regularly. Is there something in your school or community that you would like to see accomplished or changed? List several potential issues, and then evaluate each one. Your final choice should be an issue that

- you feel strongly about, though not so strongly that your feelings interfere with your ability to argue reasonably
- has both positive and negative aspects, enabling you not only to argue your own opinion, but effectively respond to **opposing arguments**
- you can discuss using convincing evidence to support your opinion

Identify Your Thesis

Once you have an issue, write a sentence that defines your **perspective,** or **position,** on that issue. This will be your **thesis statement,** sometimes called a **position statement** or **opinion statement.** In persuasive writing, your thesis will include what you believe about the issue and how you propose to address it. Here's how the writer of the student model that begins on page 687 created his thesis statement, which identifies his opinion.

Topic: drug and alcohol abuse
Perspective: mentoring of various kinds can help
Thesis statement: We can combat the United States addiction problem by building relationships that teach kids the negative effects of drugs and alcohol.

Think About Purpose and Audience

Since your **purpose** for writing is to convince others that your perspective has merit, you will need to consider the knowledge and beliefs of your audience. In order to succeed in persuading your **audience,** you'll need to tailor your arguments to their needs. Use these questions to analyze your audience members:

1. **What are their ages, interests, education levels, and values?** Use this information to determine what reasons, evidence, and language your readers will find most persuasive.
2. **What do they already know about the issue?** If your readers are not familiar with your issue, you'll need to add background information to your essay.
3. **Where do they stand on the issue?** Readers who strongly disagree with your position will require much more convincing than those who share your views or who are undecided. Be prepared to address any objections they have to your ideas.

Idea Starters

- Talk to friends and classmates about issues that concern them.
- Talk to your family about issues in your community.
- Read local and national newspapers for current issues.
- Watch local and national news programs.
- Attend meetings of your school's student council, your school district's board of education, or your local city council.

Your Turn

Get Started Making notes in your **RWN,** choose an **issue.** Then draft a **thesis statement** that shows your position. Finally, make notes about your **audience** and their needs.

Learn It Online
To see how one writer completed this assignment, see the model persuasive essay online.
go.hrw.com H12-683 Go

Teacher One Stop™, on-level lesson plans and all print resources
Holt Six Traits for Writing, rubrics, prompts, and sample papers
Language and Sentence Skills Practice,
UA: Developmental Language and Sentence Practice
Language Handbook Worksheets, p.119
Formal Assessment, Midyear Summative Test
ThinkCentral Online Assessment, Writing Workshop Test
ThinkCentral Online Remediation
Holt Online Essay Scoring

Guided Practice: Apply

Choose an Issue

- Suggest that students break into groups to brainstorm issues and points of concern together.
- Have students create a chart with a row for each possible issue and columns for the following questions: Is the issue important to me? Is it an issue about which reasonable people might disagree? Can I support my point with evidence? Students should choose an issue that meets each of these criteria.

Think About Purpose and Audience

- Have students identify and list audiences who will read their persuasive essays.
- After students have identified potential audiences, ask them to identify their writing purpose and how it would change if the audience changed.

Your Turn

Get Started Give students a few minutes of silence to think before they begin brainstorming. Tell them to jot down notes about what they want their readers to do or gain after reading the essay.

Learn It Online
Interactive Writer's Models on the Interactive Student Edition provide annotated sample essays along with writing tips and strategies.
go.hrw.com H12-683 Go

Guided Practice: Apply

Support Your Position

- Explain to students that the primary purpose of a persuasive essay is to convince a reader to believe or act on the writer's position. To fulfill this purpose, the students must provide the reader with compelling reasons to do so.
- Inform students that using several different types of appeals will help persuade a diverse audience.

Gather Solid Evidence

- Explain to students that they need to present the readers with solid evidence that answers the question "Why should the reader agree with you?"
- Point out that the graphic organizer on this page illustrates how to organize evidence and explanations for the students' arguments.

Your Turn

Organize Your Support Have students complete the **Your Turn** as independent practice. Students can use graphic organizers to organize the ideas they gain from brainstorming. Encourage students to create several graphic organizers for different ideas and then assess which arguments are the strongest and most salient.

Writing Tip

If the connection between a reason and its supporting evidence is not self-evident, **elaborate** upon the evidence, showing how it connects to the reason.

Support Your Position

A tightly built argument depends on effective **support.** In your essay, include solid **reasons** why your readers should believe or act as you suggest in your thesis statement. Reasons may include appeals to logic, emotion, or ethics.

- **Logical appeals** engage your readers' ability to think clearly. Logical appeals should be the foundation of your essay.
- **Emotional appeals** stir readers' feelings and personalize the issue for your audience.
- **Ethical appeals** establish you as a fair and knowledgeable speaker and call upon your readers' sense of right and wrong.

Gather Solid Evidence

In order to persuade your audience, you must prove to them that your reasons are valid. You can do this by using relevant **evidence**—precise and relevant facts, examples, expert opinions, analogies, case studies, and anecdotes.

Types of Evidence	
Facts	**information** that can be proven true
Examples	**specific** instances of an idea or situation
Expert opinions	**quotations** or paraphrases by respected and knowledgeable individuals or institutions
Analogies	**comparisons** showing the similarities between two otherwise unrelated concepts
Case studies	**examples** from scientific studies
Anecdotes	**brief,** personal stories that illustrate a point

Use a graphic organizer like the one below to plan each supporting paragraph in your essay.

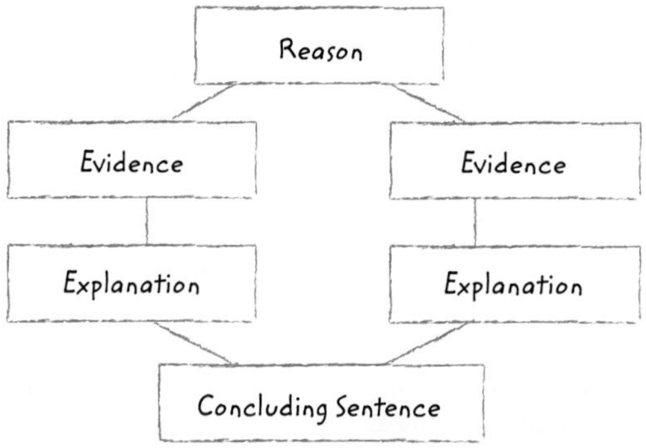

Your Turn

Organize Your Support Making notes in your **RWN,** use the **evidence chart** and the **graphic organizer** on this page to gather and organize **support** for your thesis. Share your organizer with a peer. Think about the feedback he or she provides, and consider adding, deleting, or reorganizing evidence. Remember to keep your **purpose** and **audience** in mind.

Persuasive Essay Writing Prompts

Students can choose their own persuasive essay idea or use one of the following prompts to write a persuasive essay.

History Choose a culture or area of history that you have not studied and would like to understand better. Write a persuasive essay presenting the case for studying it in school.

Physical Education Write a persuasive essay explaining why your school should add a sports team it does not currently have. Be sure to explain why the sport would benefit the school more than other sports do.

Social Studies Choose a current events topic you feel passionate about, such as a political conflict, an environmental concern, or a public health issue. Present a case for why other students should be concerned about this issue as well.

Drafting

Follow the Writer's Framework

Use your **graphic organizer** and the **Writer's Framework** on the right to help you write the first draft of your essay.

Framework for a Persuasive Essay
Introduction
• Tell how the issue affects readers.
• Give background information.
• Include a clear thesis statement.
Body
• Support your position with reasons and precise and relevent evidence.
• Use rhetorical devices.
• Organize evidence by strength.
Conclusion
• Restate your position and summarize your reasons.
• Call readers to action.

Add Rhetorical Devices

Rhetorical devices can make your writing more colorful and convincing.

- A **rhetorical question** is a question that gets readers to think about the issue—it is not meant to be answered, because the answer is obvious. For example, "Do you care about America's future?"
- **Argument by analogy** compares two situations in order to make a point. For example, Desmond Tutu compares Aung San Suu Kyi to Nelson Mandela and the situation in Burma to apartheid in South Africa.
- **Parallelism** supports important ideas by repeating words, phrases, or sentences that have the same grammatical structure or that restate a similar idea. Parallel words or word groups are often joined by **correlative conjunctions** *(both . . . and; either . . . or; neither . . . nor; not only . . . but also; whether . . . or).*

Grammar Link Using Correlative Conjunctions

One rhetorical strategy employed by Desmond Tutu in his speech is **parallelism,** including the use of the **correlative conjunctions** *neither . . . nor:*

> History has shown us that **neither** systems, **nor** governments, **nor** dictators are eternal, but the spirit of freedom is.

Two other pairs of correlative conjunctions help writers show relationships between ideas: *either . . . or* and *both . . . and*. The relationship of the ideas determines which word pair works better.

In the example above, the correlative conjunctions appear in a series and are separated by commas. When using correlative conjunctions, remember that the subject closest to the verb determines if the verb is singular or plural. A plural subject requires a plural verb.

Writing Tip

Most persuasive essays are arranged by **order of importance.** To capture your audience's attention immediately, begin your essay with your strongest reason; or, to make a strong final impression, end with your strongest reason.

Your Turn

Write Your Draft Use your **graphic organizer** and the **Writer's Framework** to write a **draft** of your persuasive essay. As you write, think about these questions:

- Which is your strongest piece of evidence?
- Would it be more effective to begin or end with your strongest piece of evidence?
- What rhetorical devices can you employ?
- Where can you use correlative conjunctions as a rhetorical strategy?

Guided Practice: Apply

Follow the Writer's Framework

Ask students to refer to their graphic organizers and decide which topic has the strongest reasons and evidence. Students should use the strongest information as the framework for their writing.

Add Rhetorical Devices

Have students note examples of rhetorical devices Tutu used and think about how to use them in their own writing. Have them consider the following questions: What rhetorical question could strengthen this argument? What ideas could be strengthened or clarified with analogies? What ideas should be expressed through parallelism?

Grammar Link

For practice, have students write three sentences related to their topics using correlative conjunctions.

Warriner's Handbook, Sixth Course, pp. 26, 476

Your Turn

Write Your Draft Ask students to complete the **Your Turn** as independent practice. Remind students to use their graphic organizer as they begin writing. Suggest that students use every other line as they write their drafts so they can more easily revise drafts later.

Real Issues, Real Experts

Holt author ***Carol Jago*** *offers strategies for writing a persuasive essay.*

Every teacher has had the experience of sitting down with a struggling student, trying to help him choose a topic, only to end up supplying one that is unsatisfactory to both student and teacher. Part of the problem is that teenagers are afraid of any subject that might seem "uncool." They are also reluctant to expose too much of themselves. Consequently, students often end up writing on dull, safe subjects.

One approach I have used to help my students find livelier topics for persuasive essays has been to start with the newspaper. Give students a copy of a newspaper, and ask them to scan the headlines for news stories that pique their interest. Don't limit students to stories from the front page. The sports, entertainment, fashion, and business pages can also provide food for thought and controversy.

After about twenty minutes, ask students to turn and talk to a partner about one idea they have for a topic. With their heads full of ideas, they can now begin the steps in the Writing Workshop for developing a persuasive essay.

Model the Skill

- Using a student draft on a transparency, model how to use the questions, tips, and revision techniques suggested in the chart. You might use a student's persuasive essay or a persuasive essay of your own creation to evaluate and revise using the steps in the chart.
- Ask volunteers to demonstrate using each of the steps on their own persuasive essays.

Peer Review

Allow students to choose their own peer review partners. Suggest that they seek out partners who know a lot about their topics and have a strong opinion about the issue that will be discussed in the essay.

Holt Six Traits for Writing, rubrics, prompts, and sample pages

Peer Review

Working with a peer, review your draft. Answer each question in the chart at the right to evaluate how your drafts can be improved. Then use the tips and revision techniques to revise your draft.

Evaluating and Revising

Now that you have written a draft of your persuasive essay, it is time to polish it by reading and evaluating. Check your use of rhetorical devices and precise and relevant evidence to make your essay as convincing as possible. The chart below will help you evaluate your draft and think of ways to revise it.

Persuasive Essay: Guidelines for Content and Organization

Evaluation Question	Tip	Revision Technique
1. Does the introduction grab readers' attention? Does it include necessary background information?	**Put brackets** around any sentence or sentences that are intended to draw reader interest. **Put a check mark** by any background information.	**Add** a question, anecdote, quotation, or provocative statement that will capture readers' interest. **Add** background facts the reader would need to understand the issue. **Elaborate** on background.
2. Does the introduction contain a clear thesis statement, or opinion statement?	**Circle** the thesis statement, or opinion statement.	**Add** a statement that expresses a clear position on the issue.
3. Does the essay include reasons and precise and relevant evidence to support the opinion?	**Underline** the reasons in the essay. **Double underline** sentences used as evidence for each reason.	**Add** reasons or **elaborate** on reasons already given. **Add** evidence (facts and statistics, examples, expert opinions, analogies, case studies, or anecdotes) that supports them.
4. Is there a mixture of logical, emotional, and ethical appeals?	**Put the letters *L*** by logical appeals, ***EM*** by emotional appeals, and ***ETH*** by ethical appeals. If your support uses only one kind of appeal, revise.	**Add** vivid language that addresses any of the appeals you have omitted.
5. Do rhetorical devices help shape the support for the opinion?	**Put a star** by any rhetorical questions, arguments by analogy, or use of parallelism.	**Add** rhetorical devices, such as rhetorical questions, argument by analogy, or parallelism.
6. Does the conclusion restate the writer's position? Does the conclusion include a call to action?	**Circle** the restatement of the position. **Highlight** the call to action.	**Add** a statement that restates your position. **Add** a call to action.

Real Issues, Real Experts

Holt Professional Learning for Language Arts

To watch videos on teaching **revision, grammar,** and **on-demand writing skills** featuring Linda Rief, Amy Benjamin, and Leila Christenbury, go to this page in **ThinkCentral, Teacher Access.**

Universal Access

EL English Learners

English for Academic Success Help students understand how to awaken the reader's interest by giving them examples of some attention-grabbing devices.

Statistic—"Thirty-one percent of adult Americans feel that human beings are responsible for global warming."

Quotation—According to Peter Patel, Ph.D., "Global warming is a problem that cannot be simply ignored and passed down to future generations."

Rhetorical question—"How are you doing your part to stop global warming?"

Read this student's draft with comments on its structure and suggestions for how it could be made even stronger.

Student Draft

The Plague upon the Land

by Stephen Lain, McCallum High School

According to Nora D. Volkow, the director of the National Institute on Drug Abuse, addiction affects nine percent of the United States population. This epidemic must be addressed where it begins—with our young people. The effects are too widespread and too many people are susceptible to the black hole of drug and alcohol addiction for us to ignore the problem. We can combat America's addiction problem by building relationships that teach kids the negative effects of drugs and alcohol.

← Stephen introduces his **issue** with a **statistic** and then states his **position.**

One way to create and nurture these relationships is through a mentoring program. Children who lack relationships with positive adult role models are more at risk to become drug and alcohol users. When kids connect with a responsible, caring mentor who engages them in productive and fun activities, they experience an alternative to drug use. A mentor can warn them about the power of peer pressure. Many kids who have avoided drinking and drugs will eventually try it. "It's just one sip; it can't hurt." But many times, that one sip will lead to one more, and then one more. A mentor can steer kids away from drugs, alcohol, and peer pressure in the drug culture.

← He offers one way to approach and solve this problem.

MINI-LESSON **How to Grab Your Reader's Attention**

You will not interest your audience in your issue if your introduction lacks appeal. To grab your reader's attention, add an interesting or startling fact, statistic, quotation, or anecdote, or ask a rhetorical question. Stephen found additional statistics that he wanted to use to emphasize the problem and draw readers into his essay.

Stephen's Draft of Paragraph 1

. . . This epidemic must be addressed where it begins—with our young people. The effects are too widespread and too many people are susceptible to the black hole of drug and alcohol addiction for us to ignore the problem.

Stephen's Revision of Paragraph 1

. . . This epidemic must be addressed where it begins—with our young people. The effects are too widespread and too many people are susceptible to the black hole of drug and alcohol addiction for us to ignore the problem. According to the national PTA, every day approximately 4,700 American youth under the age of eighteen try marijuana for the first time. This equals the enrollment in six average-sized high schools.

Your Turn

Grab Your Reader's Attention
Re-read the introduction of your draft to see if it grabs the audience's attention. Ask yourself the following questions:

- Do I give a clear idea of the extent of the problem?
- Could I be more specific?
- What strategy did I use to get the reader's attention?

Guided Practice: Apply

Student Draft

Explain that the Student Draft on this page is the first half of a persuasive essay written by the student. Model reading the draft and the annotations in blue, and explain that the yellow highlighting illustrates the student's language choices. Explain that a mini-lesson follows with helpful information about ways to improve this draft as well as their own.

Mini-Lesson

How to Grab Your Reader's Attention

- Explain that the student writer has revised his opening by using a surprising statistic.
- Remind students that evidence needs to be attention-grabbing but also appropriate for their argument.

Your Turn

Grab Your Reader's Attention As students complete the **Your Turn,** tell them to find two places in their drafts where eye-catching details could be added. The details may be used to support any part of their argument. Remind students to use the Grammar Link on p. 685 to help them punctuate their essays correctly.

Struggling Writers

Benchmark Students Help students develop an introductory sentence that captures their audience's attention by having them write down three interesting facts, statistics, or quotations about their subject. Have students present their bits of information to five peers and ask them which one they find the most intriguing. Have students consider their potential audience's opinion when choosing what information to include in their introductory sentence.

Students with Disabilities

If possible, allow students to use software to develop a visual presentation to convey their points. Instead of writing a full essay, they can give a presentation with bulleted information and explain it to the class.

✔ See **UA: Differentiating Instruction** for strategies for teaching students with disabilities.

Guided Practice: Apply

Student Draft

- Explain that the Student Draft is continued and completed on this page. Again, the draft is annotated and highlighted for the students.
- Read the draft and annotations aloud, and discuss. Ask students to point out examples of writing techniques that make the student's essay persuasive.

Mini-Lesson

How to Add Emotional Appeal to a Conclusion

- Tell students to make sure their persuasive essays end with an emotional appeal. Explain that by making the reader feel saddened, concerned, guilty, or angry, they might compel the reader to act on the issue.
- Then, explain to students that an emotional appeal should include a call to action that suggests how readers should act on the issue. Have students consider specific actions they would like their audience to take and incorporate them into their essay.

Your Turn

Add Emotional Appeal to Your Conclusion As students work to complete the **Your Turn,** have them think about what call to action they should add to their drafts and how it should be phrased for maximum effect. Remind students to make sure the call to action directly relates to the subject of their essays.

Student Draft *continues*

Stephen **develops** the role of parents and guardians in the fight against drug abuse and **cites an authoritative source as part of his supporting information.** →

Another way to combat drug use is to make a concerted effort in each household to teach kids that drugs and alcohol can ruin your life. The American Academy of Pediatrics states that parents or guardians are the most important influence in a teen's decisions about drug use. Children can be taught at an early age that drug use will lead to a life of destruction. Caring adults can teach children the facts: Alcohol abuse will lead to liver failure and ultimately death, and drugs such as crack cocaine can decimate your body and mind. The government can create standardized teaching tools to address the dangers of addiction, but the most important tool is the parents' or guardians' interest, communication, and role as a model for their children. Communication in homes may be the best weapon we have to fight drug abuse in kids.

He uses **parallel structure** at the end to emphasize his points. However, his **call to action** is vague, giving no specific actions readers can take on the issue. →

We can take action against this epidemic of drug abuse and addiction. We can urge the community to teach schools, churches, clubs, and families how to approach the subject of drug and alcohol abuse. We can create meaningful relationships with children through effective mentoring programs.

MINI-LESSON How to Add Emotional Appeal to a Conclusion

A good conclusion to a persuasive essay should stir the readers' emotions and prompt them to act on the issue. Stephen's conclusion lacks a strong emotional appeal, which he could make by adding a stirring, specific call to action and effective, moving language.

Stephen's Draft of the Conclusion

We can take action against this epidemic of drug abuse and addiction. We can urge the community to teach schools, churches, clubs, and families how to approach the subject of drugs and alcohol abuse. We can create meaningful relationships with children though effective mentoring programs.

Stephen's Revision of Conclusion

We can take action against this epidemic of drug abuse and addiction. We can urge the community to teach schools, churches, clubs, and families how to approach the subject of drugs and alcohol abuse. We can create meaningful relationships with children though effective mentoring programs. ^*As a society, we can attack this invader in our land if we work together to educate and mentor our young people. If you are a student, mentor younger children. If you are a teacher, ask about the opportunities in your school or community. If you are a parent or guardian, take action now. Our country's children are suffering from this plague upon our land.*

Your Turn

Add Emotional Appeal to Your Conclusion Re-read your draft's conclusion to assess whether it has maximum impact. Ask yourself these questions:

- Does my conclusion stir emotions in the reader?
- Is my call to action clear, inspiring readers to take specific action?

Universal Access

EL English Learners

Suggest the following sentence starters to students as they develop their emotional appeal and call to action.

- It is not too late to make a change . . .
- I cannot do it alone . . .
- We have a responsibility . . .
- If we commit ourselves . . .
- Now is the time . . .

AAVE Students Who Use African American Vernacular English

English for Academic Success Point out the revised last paragraph of the student model. Tell students that in this paragraph the author uses the plural form of the words *schools, churches, clubs, and families.* Tell students that in informal English they might be tempted to use the singular form of a noun when the plural form is actually required. If students are unsure whether to use the singular or plural form of a noun, remind students

Proofreading and Publishing

Proofread

Do not undermine your authority with mistakes in grammar, usage, or mechanics. Follow these tips to **proofread,** or **edit,** your essay. Read it aloud to catch missing words or awkward constructions. Refer to a grammar, usage, and mechanics handbook to ensure you have avoided common errors, such as forgetting to include a comma after an **introductory phrase** or **clause.**

Grammar Link Using Commas After Introductory Elements

Introductory phrases and clauses create transitions that help writers lead their readers through their arguments and supporting ideas. They also enliven writing by adding variety to sentence beginnings. When you use introductory phrases and clauses, be sure to separate them from the main clause of the sentence with a comma. Stephen correctly uses commas after introductory elements in these examples from the student model.

When kids connect with a responsible, caring mentor who engages them in productive and fun activities, they experience an alternative to drug use. [introductory clause]

But many times, that one sip will lead to one more, and then one more. [introductory phrase]

Reference Note For more on **phrases** and **clauses,** see the Language Handbook.

Publishing

To persuade readers, you first have to reach them. Here are some ways you can share your essay with a wider audience.

- Submit your essay to the school or local newspaper.
- Submit your essay to a Web site that focuses on your issue.
- Present your essay in a meeting of your school's student council, your school district's board of education, or your local city council.
- Conduct a panel discussion about this issue.
- Submit your essay to specialized periodicals, including newsletters and online magazines.

Reflect on the Process Thinking about how you researched and wrote your persuasive essay will help you with your future writing. In your **RWN,** write short response to the following questions:

1. What sources were most helpful in learning about your issue?
2. What evidence or rhetorical device do you feel contributed most to your essay's persuasive power, and why?

Proofreading Tip

If you write your essay on a computer, use all the tools available to you, such as grammar and spell-checkers. However, do not expect these tools to take the place of close, personal proofreading and peer review. You will often catch mistakes that your computer does not; for example, incorrect usage of *there, their,* and *they're* or *its* and *it's.*

Writing Tip

Ask yourself the following questions to identify introductory phrases and clauses.

- Does the phrase or clause come before the sentence's subject?
- Do the words in the phrase or clause work together as an adverb to tell when, where, or how often?

Your Turn

Proofread and Publish As you proofread your draft, circle any introductory phrases and clauses you have used. Check to make sure each one is followed by a comma. Read your paper one more time to make finishing touches, and then publish it.

Guided Practice: Apply

Proofreading

Integrating with Grammar, Usage, and Mechanics If students make errors in using commas after introductory elements as they are proofreading, send them to the Punctuation chapters in **Warriner's Handbook.**

Grammar Link

- Tell students to read their final draft and take note of how they have used commas in their persuasive essays.
- If students come across an introductory phrase in their essays, tell them to insert a comma after the phrase.

Publishing

Brainstorm with students additional ways to publish their persuasive essays.

Reflect on the Process

Have students reflect on their writing process as well as their final product. Challenge them to reflect metacognitively about how they can improve and apply what they have learned.

Your Turn

Proofread and Publish Have students highlight or underline the revisions and submit their drafts with their final persuasive essays so that you can check to make sure they are following the guidelines for content and organization on p. 686.

to ask themselves the following question: Am I referring to one [noun] or more than one [noun]? Tell students that the answer to this question will help them know which form to use. Have students read over their draft to look for any incorrect noun forms.

Advanced Learners

Acceleration Challenge students to create a short action plan to address readers who have been persuaded by their argument. Students should provide specific steps that address how the reader should answer the students' call to action.

Students with Disabilities

Have students design and illustrate a series of picket signs or propaganda posters that use emotional appeal to convey the same point that their call to action conveys. Have students present the artwork to the class and explain how the messages on the signs apply to their essays. Students should express why they chose certain words and what emotions they were attempting to evoke with their language.

Guided Practice

Scoring Guide

- Tell students that the best way to understand scoring guides is to use them to score actual writing.
- Have students use the scoring guide to evaluate the final copy of the persuasive essays they wrote in the Writing Workshop. Ask students to score their essays and then write a brief paragraph using the language of the scoring guide to explain the reasons for the scores.

Holt Six Traits for Writing, rubrics, prompts, and sample papers

Assess

UA: Holt Interactive Writer and Speaker, Persuasive Essay analytical scales and rubrics, p. 65

ThinkCentral Online Assessment, Writing Workshop Test

Teacher One Stop™, editable Writing Workshop Test

Reteach

ThinkCentral Online Remediation

Scoring Guide

Use the scoring guide below to evaluate your persuasive essay from the Writing Workshop or your response to the on-demand prompt on the next page.

	Thesis	Organization and Focus	Sentence Structure and Vocabulary	Language Conventions
4	• provides a *meaningful* thesis that is responsive to the writing task.	• *thoroughly* supports the thesis and main ideas with *specific* details and examples. • demonstrates a *clear* sense of audience. • demonstrates a consistent tone and focus, and illustrates a *purposeful* control of organization.	• provides a *variety* of sentence types and uses *precise, descriptive* language.	• contains *few, if any, errors* in the conventions of the English language. (Errors are generally first-draft in nature.)
	A Persuasive Composition: • states and maintains a position, *authoritatively* defends that position with precise and relevant evidence, and *convincingly* addresses the reader's concerns, biases, and expectations.			
3	• provides a thesis that is responsive to the writing task.	• supports the thesis and main ideas with details and examples. • demonstrates a *general* sense of audience. • demonstrates a consistent tone and focus; and illustrates a control of organization.	• provides a *variety* of sentence types and uses *some descriptive* language.	• may contain *some errors* in the conventions of the English language. (Errors do **not** interfere with the reader's understanding of the essay.)
	A Persuasive Composition: • states and maintains a position, *generally* defends that position with precise and relevant evidence, and addresses the reader's concerns, biases, and expectations.			
2	• provides a thesis or main idea that is related to the writing task.	• supports the thesis or main idea(s) with *limited* details and/or examples. • demonstrates *little* or **no** sense of audience. • demonstrates an *inconsistent* tone and focus; and illustrates *little, if any* control of organization.	• provides *few, if any,* types of sentence types, and basic, *predictable* language.	• may contain *several errors* in the conventions of the English language. (Errors **may** interfere with the reader's understanding of the essay.)
	A Persuasive Composition: • defends a position with *little* evidence and *may* address the reader's concerns, biases, and expectations.			
1	• *may* provide a *weak* thesis or main idea that is related to the writing task.	• *fails* to support the thesis or main ideas with details and/or examples. • may demonstrate ***no*** sense of audience. • demonstrates a *lack of* tone and focus; and illustrates ***no*** control of organization.	• may provide ***no*** sentence variety and uses *limited* vocabulary.	• may contain *serious errors* in the conventions of the English language. (Errors interfere with the reader's understanding of the essay.)
	A Persuasive Composition: • fails to defend a position with any evidence and *fails* to address the reader's concerns, biases, and expectations.			

California Standards, pp. 690–691

- **Writing Standard 1.1** Demonstrate an understanding of the elements of discourse (e.g. purpose, speaker, audience, form) when completing narrative, expository, persuasive or descriptive writing assignments.
- **Writing Standard 1.3** Structure ideas and arguments in a sustained, persuasive, and sophisticated way and support them with precise and relevant examples.
- **Writing Standard 1.4** Enhance meaning by employing rhetorical devices, including the extended use of parallelism, repetition, and analogy; the incorporation of visual aids (e.g., graphs, tables, pictures); and the issuance of a call for action.
- **Writing Standard 1.5** Use language in a natural, fresh, and vivid way to establish a specific tone.
- **Writing Standard 1.9** Revise text to highlight the individual voice, improve sentence variety and style, and enhance subtlety of meaning and tone in ways that are consistent with the purpose, audience, and genre.

Persuasive Essay Writing Prompts

Students can use the writing prompt in the Student Edition or one of the following prompts.

- Suggest that students write a persuasive essay to get tourists to visit their town. They should include things that are interesting about their town and suggestions about ways to get there and things to do or see.
- Suggest to students that they write a persuasive essay to convince their school to change a policy. Students may want to argue for permission to leave campus during lunch or to carry cell phones.

Preparing for Timed Writing

Persuasive Essay

Writing Standard 1.1, 1.3, 1.4, 1.5, 1.9 (see pages A51–A52)
Language Conventions Standard 1.1, 1.2, 1.3 (see page A53)

When responding to a prompt, use what you have learned from reading, writing your persuasive essay, and studying the scoring guide on page 690. Use the steps below to develop a response to the following prompt.

Writing Prompt

Imagine that your school board is thinking of implementing a graduation requirement mandating that students do part-time volunteer work. Write a persuasive essay to the school board convincing readers to support or oppose the requirement.

Study the Prompt

Read the prompt carefully. Then read it again, underlining the words that tell the type of writing, the topic, and the purpose.

Type of writing: *persuasive essay*
Topic: *a graduation requirement mandating that students do part-time volunteer work*
Purpose: *convincing readers to support or oppose the requirement*
Audience: *the school board*
Tip: Spend about five minutes studying the prompt.

Plan Your Response

Think about the **reasons** for each side of the **argument.** Make a list of pros and cons for the volunteering requirement. Then decide which side of the debate to **support.** Narrow your reasons down to your top three, and use the organizer below to help you gather support. List your reasons in the first column. In the second column, list at least two pieces of **evidence** (specific facts, statistics, anecdotes, examples) for each reason.

Reasons	Specific Evidence

Now draft a one-sentence **thesis statement** that states your position on the topic and lists your three main reasons. **Tip:** Spend about ten minutes planning your response.

Respond to the Prompt

Begin drafting your essay. You may want to start by simply stating your **thesis,** your position on the issue. As you write, keep the following points in mind:

- In the introduction, grab your readers' attention and state your position, considering what will convince your audience.
- In each body paragraph, give one reason for your position, with valid and specific evidence to support that reason. You can use examples from your experience or someone else's experience. Specific names, dates, and places add convincing detail to your argument.
- Conclude your essay with a statement of strong conviction that will appeal to your audience.

Tip: Spend about twenty minutes writing your persuasive essay.

Improve Your Response

Revising Review your response, and compare it to the prompt. Does your response state your position on the graduation requirement? Does it give evidence to support your position? Does it appeal to your audience? Is there anything you can add to your paper to make your arguments more convincing?

Proofreading Now find and correct any errors in grammar, usage, and mechanics. Vary your sentence structure. Pay attention to the words on the page to make sure they are grammatically correct and accurately convey your meaning. Be certain that your paper and any edits are neatly written and legible.

Checking Your Final Copy Before you turn in your paper, examine it once more to make sure that you have done your best work. **Tip:** Save five or ten minutes to improve your paper.

Standards Focus

Objectives

Students will learn the elements of writing a persuasive essay.

Direct Teach

Study the Prompt

Before students begin writing, encourage them to answer the following questions:

1. What is my time limit?
2. What are the key skills assessed in the scoring guide?
3. Who is my audience?
4. What is my purpose?

Plan Your Response

Remind students that the persuasive essay scoring guide emphasizes the focus on a consistent, clear, and reasonable position. Tell students that they should ask themselves these questions to evaluate their writing as they work on their drafts: Is my position consistent? Have I clearly stated my position? Are my ideas reasonable?

Improve Your Response

Point out that the scoring guide also emphasizes effective organization. Remind students to focus on organizing the main ideas of their argument and transitioning smoothly from one point to the next.

Assess

Use the scoring guide on p. 690 to assess students' persuasive essays.

Universal Access

English Learners

English for Academic Success Introduce students to the following words before they begin their writing exercise.

- **prompt**—a suggestion or reminder
- **implementing**—putting into action
- **support**—to approve
- **oppose**—to be against something
- **mandating**—creating an order to do something

Struggling Writers

Help students develop their position on the issue addressed in the writing prompt by having them write down the pros and cons of mandatory volunteering. Tell students to assess which side they feel more strongly about and write their essays from that position. If students have strong feelings on both sides of the issue, suggest they choose the position that will appeal to the adult readers who will evaluate their essay.

Standards Focus

Objectives

Students will deliver a persuasive speech.

Preteach

Speak with a Purpose Ask students to think about the differences between spoken language and written language and the challenges one might face when translating one to the other.

- Ask students to compare and contrast spoken language and written language.
- Brainstorm with students persuasive techniques that can be used when speaking to enhance the content of a speech.

Direct Teach

Model the Skill

Adapt Your Essay

Remind students to consider their audience when choosing which persuasive techniques to use in their speech. Suggest to them that anecdotes and rhetorical questions may have a stronger impact on a younger audience than historical allusions.

Guided Practice: Apply

For each part of their speeches, ask students to decide which rhetorical devices to use to help them connect to their audience. Have them share their ideas with a partner.

Presenting and Analyzing Speeches

Speak with a Purpose

Adapt your persuasive essay for a persuasive speech. Then, present it to an audience.

Think as a Reader/Writer Effective persuasive speeches incorporate the same techniques that are used to write persuasive essays. Presenting your position for listeners, rather than readers, however, can offer you another advantage—you can use your voice as well as your body language to make your point. In this workshop you will learn how to use the techniques of persuasion in a speech.

Adapt Your Essay

A persuasive speech consists of the same introduction, body, and conclusion as your written essay. However, you might need to make alterations to each of these parts of your essay so they will be better suited for a speech.

- The **introduction** to an effective persuasive speech is dramatic. Consider using a thought-provoking literary quotation, a touching anecdote that illustrates an aspect of the issue with which you are dealing, or a reference to an authority on the subject of your speech. Then, state your distinct perspective on the issue in a strong but simple opinion statement.
- The **body** of a persuasive speech supports the opinion statement and must consist of solid reasoning. To fit within your time limits, choose only the most effective reasons from your written essay, based on your audience. For example, an audience of classmates might respond favorably to reasons that appeal to their emotions. An audience of city council members might best respond to reasons that appeal to logic or ethics.
- The **conclusion** to an effective speech should be memorable. First, summarize the main points and restate your opinion. Finally, call the audience to action, using specific language.

As you adapt your essay, decide which of the following four basic types of persuasive speech you want to present. This decision will determine the wording of your opinion statement, which presents your distinct perspective.

1. A **proposition of fact** speech argues that a thesis can be seen as true or false.
2. A **proposition of policy** speech attempts to get the audience to support a particular plan of action, by offering a series of steps to follow.
3. A **proposition of problem** speech tries to persuade an audience that a specific problem exists and is serious enough to warrant action.
4. A **proposition of value** speech argues the relative merit of a person, place, or thing. You cannot prove a proposition of value, but you can provide evidence to support your belief.

Reader/Writer Notebook

Use your **RWN** to complete the activities in this workshop.

California Standards, pp. 692–693

- **Listening and Speaking Standard 1.4** Use rhetorical questions, parallel structure, concrete images, figurative language, characterization, irony, and dialogue to achieve clarity, force, and aesthetic effect.
- **Listening and Speaking Standard 1.5** Distinguish between and use various forms of classical and contemporary logical arguments, including: **a.** Inductive and deductive reasoning **b.** Syllogisms and analogies
- **Listening and Speaking Standard 1.6** Use logical, ethical, and emotional appeals that enhance a specific tone and purpose.
- **Listening and Speaking Standard 1.7** Use appropriate rehearsal strategies to pay attention to performance details, achieve command of the text, and create skillful artistic staging.
- **Listening and Speaking Standard 1.9** Use research and analysis to justify strategies for gesture, movement, and vocalization, including dialect, pronunciation, and enunciation.

Resources

UA: Holt Interactive Writer and Speaker, practice and assessment, p. 129

UA: Differentiating Instruction, modified lesson plans, p. 152

Teacher One Stop™, on-level lesson plans and all print resources

Listening and Speaking Standard 1.4, 1.5, 1.6, 1.7, 1.9 (see pages A53–A55)

Present Your Speech

Because your persuasive speech is on an issue about which you care deeply, consider delivering it as a formal speech. Write your speech out completely, and practice it until you have it memorized. On your written speech, note the pitch and volume that you intend to use at various points in the speech. Do the same thing for gestures, pauses, and eye contact. Also, do not forget to adopt a serious tone while presenting your appeals by avoiding slang, colloquialisms, and contractions.

Notes for Good Sense

If your speech includes facts, expert opinions, or statistics, it is important that you convey them accurately. It is helpful to have these items in writing in case you forget them while giving your speech. Write all facts, quotations, and statistics carefully on note cards, and number your cards in the order that they arise in your speech. Move each card to the back of the pile as you cover it, so the next card is ready for you exactly when you might need it. You do not want to lose time fumbling in your pile for the right quotation.

Practice Makes Perfect

Practice your speech for family or friends or in front of a mirror. You can also get a good idea of what is working and what needs work in your presentation if you record yourself practicing on camera. Pay special attention to the sound of your voice and the movements of your body. Are all of your words audible? Are you speaking at a normal rate? When you deliver your speech, stand in a natural, relaxed position, and use subtle but appropriate hand gestures to highlight points and ideas. Remember to look around the room at your audience and use your voice to emphasize specific points in the speech. As you practice, use the checklists below to evaluate your verbal and nonverbal techniques.

Voice

Audible volume	
Normal rate	
Varied pitch to emphasize important points	

Body

Natural, relaxed standing position	
Subtle and appropriate hand gestures	
Varied eye contact	

A Good Oral Presentation

- opens with a strong, powerful introduction that captures your audience's attention
- includes specific, valid reasons and evidence
- moves at a reasonable pace—not so slow as to bore the audience or so fast as to lose listeners
- relates well to the audience
- shows the time and care that went into planning and rehearsing the speech

Speaking Tip

If you falter while speaking, do not draw attention to it in a distracting way, which can cause your audience to forget your last point. If you suddenly forget what you wanted to say, pause and take a deep breath. Look at the written copy of your speech for guidance. It is okay to backtrack a little or even to skip ahead to keep yourself from rambling. When you look back up at your audience, smile confidently and resume speaking.

Learn It Online

Pictures, music, and animation can make your argument more compelling. See how on MediaScope.

go.hrw.com H12-693 Go

Model the Skill

Notes for Good Sense

Model for students how to create note cards to use during their speech. Remind students that they do not need to record their entire speech on the note cards. Instead, they should write down important facts and statistics that they do not want to forget to mention. Show students an example of a completed note card with a bulleted list of facts and figures.

Guided Practice: Apply

Give students an opportunity to create their own note cards. After students have completed their cards, encourage them to use the cards to practice delivering their speech.

Teaching Tip

Practice Makes Perfect Have students work with a partner to evaluate their speeches' content. Have them work for 20 minutes to revise their outlines to edit redundancies and unclear passages. Then, have students work with a partner to practice their delivery. Listeners should use a table to record comments about clarity, gestures, pauses, and rhetorical devices. Students will use the feedback to improve their presentations.

English for Academic Success

Have students read over their speeches and spell out any contractions they find to avoid giving their essay a casual tone.

Assess

UA: Holt Interactive Writer and Speaker, Persuasive Essay Evaluation Guide

Learn It Online

If students need help adding multimedia features to their projects, send them to the **MediaScope** mini-site, where students can work through an interactive tutorial on creating multimedia.

go.hrw.com H12–693 Go

Universal Access

EL English Learners

Pair English learners with advanced learners to discuss the analogies that they would like to use in their speeches. Advanced learners should give advice about which analogies would have the strongest impact on the audience.

Struggling Learners

Once students have written their speeches, have them highlight the words they wish to emphasize and insert red slashes at points in which they think they should pause. Students should then practice and memorize their speeches using these annotations.

Standards Focus

Objectives

Students will compare and contrast works from different literary periods.

Literary Skills Review

Review

If necessary, use the following questions to guide students in their reading before they answer questions at the end of the review.

Main Idea

Which topic do these two poems share? ***Possible response:*** *Both poems are about unreciprocated love.*

Mood

How does the mood of Behn's poem differ from the mood in Baudelaire's poem? ***Possible response:*** *The mood in Behn's poem is disappointed, bitter, defeated, and heartbroken. Baudelaire's poem expresses pleasure in the pursuit of a disdainful woman.*

Test-Taking Tip

Remind students to read all the answer choices carefully before attempting to choose the correct one, even if they feel sure they know the correct answer. If after reading all the answer choices they feel in doubt about the answer, suggest they move on to the next question and come back to the difficult question later.

California Standards, pp. 694–695

- **Reading Standard 3.7** Analyze recognized works of world literature from a variety of authors: **a.** Contrast the major literary forms, techniques, and characteristics of the major literary periods (e.g., Homeric Greece, medieval, romantic, neoclassic, modern).

STANDARDS REVIEW

Literary Skills Review

Comparing Literature **Directions:** Read the poems below, and answer the questions that follow.

The following poems provide two accounts of unrequited love—a topic chosen by poets throughout the centuries. Aphra Behn's (1640–1689) "Love Arm'd" offers a rare glimpse into the experiences of a female speaker. Charles Baudelaire's (1821–1867) "'I love you as I love . . .'" shows how even suffering can be pleasurable if one is truly in love.

Love Arm'd

by **Aphra Behn**

Love in Fantastique Triumph satt,
Whilst Bleeding Hearts a round him flow'd,
For whom Fresh paines he did Create,
And strange Tyranick power he show'd
From thy Bright Eyes he took his fire,
Which round about, in sport he hurl'd;
But 'twas from mine, he took desire,
Enough to undo the Amorous World.

From me he took his sighs and tears,
From thee his Pride and Crueltie;
From me his Languishments and Feares,
And every Killing Dart from thee;
Thus thou and I, the God have arm'd,
And sett him up a Deity;
But my poor Heart alone is harm'd,
Whilst thine the Victor is, and free.

"I love you as I love . . ."

by **Charles Baudelaire**
translated by **James McGowan**

I love you as I love the night's high vault
O silent one, o sorrow's lachrymal,°
And love you more because you flee from me,
And temptress of my nights, ironically
You seem to hoard the space, to take to you
What separates my arms from heaven's blue.

I climb to the assault, attack the source,
A choir of wormlets pressing towards a
corpse,
And cherish your unbending cruelty,
This iciness so beautiful to me.

2. **lachrymal:** a type of vase common to ancient Roman tombs, once thought to be meant for the tears of mourners.

Resources for Skills and Standards Review

Unit 3 Resources, Unit Standards Mastery, Unit Vocabulary Review, p. 97

UA: Differentiating Instruction, below-level Chapter Standards Mastery

Teacher One Stop™, editable Chapter Standards Mastery

Focus on Standards with CAHSEE Support

Preparing for the SAT and ACT

ThinkCentral Online Assessment, Chapter Standards Mastery

ThinkCentral Online Remediation

Holt Online Essay Scoring

Reading Standard 3.7a (see pages A48–A50)

1. In "Love Arm'd," what literary device does Aphra Behn use to illustrate love's power over humans?
   - **A** onomatopoeia
   - **B** simile
   - **C** synecdoche
   - **D** personification

2. In "Love Arm'd," which phrase illustrates that love has won and the speaker has lost?
   - **A** "And sett him up a Deity"
   - **B** "For whom Fresh paines he did Create"
   - **C** "Love in Fantastique Triumph satt"
   - **D** "From me he took his sighs and tears"

3. In the first stanza in "'I love you as I love...'," what does the speaker mean by the phrase "And love you more because you flee from me"?
   - **A** He both loves and hates his beloved.
   - **B** He is attracted by his beloved's coldness.
   - **C** His beloved loves heaven just as he does.
   - **D** His beloved is silent.

4. In "'I love you as I love ...'" which of the following illustrates that the speaker's love does not return his affections?
   - **A** "You seem to hoard the space"
   - **B** "night's high vault"
   - **C** "temptress of my nights"
   - **D** "O silent one"

5. Which poem illustrates the disappointment and failure of love?
   - **A** "I love you as I love ..."
   - **B** "Love Arm'd"
   - **C** both poems
   - **D** neither poem

6. In which poem is the speaker mourning a lost love?
   - **A** "'I love you as I love ...'"
   - **B** "Love Arm'd"
   - **C** both poems
   - **D** neither poem

7. What words best describe the tone of both poems?
   - **A** romantic and amorous
   - **B** sorrowful and lamenting
   - **C** peaceful and calm
   - **D** warmhearted and sentimental

Timed Writing

8. These poems both concern the experience of unrequited love—a love that is not returned. Write a brief essay comparing and contrasting the emotional effect of unrequited love on the speaker of each poem. Do the speakers feel the same way about their situations? How can you tell? Cite examples from the poems to support your answer.

Assess

Answers and Explanations

1. ***D*** *The poet uses the words* him, he *and* his *when referring to love. Onomatopoeia (A), simile (B), and synecdoche (C) are not used.*
2. ***C*** *This phrase uses the word* tri-umph, *which means "victory." The other phrases (A, B, D) do not use language specifically connected with victory.*
3. ***B*** *The coldness of the beloved makes the speaker love her all the more intensely. The phrase does not refer to mixed feelings (A), love of heaven (C), or silence (D).*
4. ***D*** *Compared to the other phrases (A, B, C), the phrase "O silent one" most clearly illustrates the beloved woman's unresponsiveness.*
5. ***C*** *In both poems, the speaker's love is not returned.*
6. ***D*** *"Love Arm'd" talks about the speaker's defeat but does not state whether the speaker has lost her love or is suffering from unrequited love. The speaker of "I love you as I love..." still pursues his love. Neither poem clearly alludes to a lost love.*
7. ***B*** *Both poems have a sad, mourn-ful tone; they are not romantic (A), peaceful (C), or warm-hearted (D).*

Timed Writing

8. *The speaker of the first poem is defeated; whereas, the speaker of the second poem is attracted to his love's silence and "iciness." Baudelaire thrives on the rejection more than Behn. Students should cite examples from the poems.*

Word-Attack Skills Mini-Lesson

English for Academic Success

Review Use the activities below to check students' grasp of the word-attack skills taught in this unit.

Activity Have students identify the syllable that is given the greatest stress in each underlined word.

1. She worked to <u>perfect</u> her backhand. [*second syllable*]
   Now her form is <u>perfect</u>. [*first syllable*]
2. Persistence is a valuable <u>attribute</u>. [*first syllable*]
   We <u>attribute</u> success to determination. [*second syllable*]
3. Sometimes it's necessary to <u>combat</u> discouragement. [*second syllable*]
   This sort of mental <u>combat</u> pays off. [*first syllable*]

Reteach

go.hrw.com **ThinkCentral Online Remediation**

Vocabulary Skills Review

Assess

Answers and Explanations

1. *D* Flaccid *is a synonym of* flabby.
2. *A* Specious *means "misleading," which is an antonym for* genuine.
3. *B* *Someone who is fastidious is also picky. Similarly, someone who is freed is also liberated.*
4. *C* *A tribute is meant to be complimentary, but an insult is not.* Conflict *is also the opposite of* accord. *A, B, and D are synonyms.*
5. *A* Impertinence *means "lack of respect." B, C, and D are synonyms.*
6. *D* Vie *is synonymous with* struggle. *Modify means to alter.*
7. *A* *Something that is sequestered is hidden, just as someone who is scrupulous is careful with details.*
8. *B* *To have a discourse is to communicate, which is an antonym for* silence. *Similarly,* solicitude *and* negligence *are antonyms.*
9. *C* *To have eminence is to be respected. Similarly, to scorn something is to feel hatred.*

Academic Vocabulary

10. *C* Dominate *and* prevail *are synonyms, as are* provoke *and* annoy.
11. *A* Enhance *and* improve *are synonyms, as are* console *and* comfort.

California Standards, p. 696

- **Reading Standard 1.3** Discern the meaning of analogies encountered, analyzing specific comparisons as well as relationships and inferences.

STANDARDS REVIEW

Vocabulary Skills Review

Reading Standard 1.3 (see pages A48–A50)

Analogies **Directions:** For each item, choose the lettered pair of words that expresses a relationship that is most similar to the relationship between the pair of capitalized words.

1. FLACCID : FLABBY ::
A timid : outspoken
B restful : restless
C tardy : punctual
D empty : vacant

2. SPECIOUS : GENUINE ::
A interested : bored
B limber : flexible
C aggressive : hostile
D flavorful : tasty

3. FASTIDIOUS : PICKY ::
A eager : indifferent
B freed : liberated
C calm : distressed
D thankful : ungrateful

4. TRIBUTE : INSULT ::
A mansion : castle
B liability : debt
C conflict : accord
D validation : support

5. IMPERTINENCE : RESPECT ::
A suppression : release
B slander : slur
C infection : illness
D mercy : compassion

6. VIE : STRUGGLE ::
A congratulate : commiserate
B release : snare
C avoid : pursue
D modify : alter

7. SEQUESTERED : HIDDEN ::
A scrupulous : careful
B miserly : generous
C serious : funny
D hopeless : optimistic

8. DISCOURSE : SILENCE ::
A fidelity : loyalty
B solicitude : negligence
C crimes : misdeeds
D truth : certainty

9. EMINENCE : DISTINCTION ::
A anticipation : despair
B sentiment : logic
C hatred : scorn
D neutrality : bias

Academic Vocabulary

10. DOMINATE : PREVAIL ::
A repel : attract
B hinder : facilitate
C provoke : annoy
D loathe : tolerate

11. ENHANCE : IMPROVE ::
A console : comfort
B recede : advance
C ignite : extinguish
D separate : combine

Vocabulary Review

Use this activity to assess whether students have retained the unit Vocabulary words. Ask students to choose the word from the box that fits the context of each sentence.

deplore	cursory	sequestered
apprehension	ingenuity	

1. I did not have time to think thoroughly about the question so I gave a ______ answer. [*cursory*]
2. I love spinach, but I ______ the taste of Brussels sprouts. [*deplore*]
3. Jason's prize-winning science project is so clever; it shows real ______. [*ingenuity*]
4. In order to keep the jury from hearing people's opinions about the defendant, they had to be ______. [*sequestered*]
5. I feel a lot of ______ about the algebra test because I did not study enough. [*apprehension*]

Writing Skills Review

Writing Standard 1.9 (see pages A51–A52)

Persuasive Essay **Directions:** The following passage is a rough draft. It may contain errors in grammar, punctuation, sentence structure, and organization. Read the passage below, and answer the questions that follow.

Rough Draft

(1) Jonathan Swift's "A Modest Proposal" employs many persuasive techniques to offer various solutions to the poverty problem in Ireland. (2) Although Swift uses logical and ethical persuasion to influence his audience, his most effective persuasive technique is his appeal to emotion. (3) He offers evidence to show how many poor people live in Ireland, plucking the heart-strings of his readers by describing how desperately the poor mothers have to live. (4) Swift then gains readers' trust by seeming to be open to others' opinions: "I am not so violently bent upon my own opinion, as to reject any offer, proposed by wise men, which shall be found equally innocent, cheap, easy, and effectual." (5) This seems like an ethical appeal, but his words—innocent, cheap, easy, and effectual—when referring to the wholesale slaughter of helpless babies, stir a powerful emotional response. (6) They are repulsive. (7) Swift also evokes an emotional reaction when he says that "A young healthy child well nursed is at a year old a most delicious, nourishing, and wholesome food, whether stewed, roasted, baked, or boiled." (8) The graphic image of a roasted infant helps the reader to conclude that Swift cannot seriously mean for the English to eat Irish babies. (9) His verbal irony makes the reader recoil in horror—quite an emotional reaction! (10) Everyone should be required to read "A Modest Proposal" before graduating.

1. The writer's main purpose in writing this essay is to convince readers
   - **A** that reading Swift's essay should be required
   - **B** that Swift's essay would not be effective without its emotional appeals
   - **C** that Swift was a genius at using verbal irony
   - **D** that Swift's most effective persuasive technique is his appeal to emotion

2. What is the BEST way to condense and combine the underlined sentences labeled 5 and 6?
   - **A** This seems like an ethical appeal, but his words stir a powerful emotional response: repulsion.
   - **B** This repulsion seems like an ethical appeal, but his words stir a powerful emotional response.
   - **C** This seems like an ethical appeal, but the repulsive words he uses stir a powerful emotional response.
   - **D** The repulsive words he uses stir a powerful emotional response, which makes this seem like an ethical appeal.

3. What evidence could the writer add to support the idea in sentence 3?
   - **A** a lengthy description of how the poor live
   - **B** an example of a reader who was emotionally moved by Swift's essay
   - **C** a quote of the evidence that Swift provides
   - **D** a specific number of people living in Ireland

4. Which persuasive technique does the writer of the essay use most in the passage?
   - **A** logical persuasion
   - **B** emotional persuasion
   - **C** ethical persuasion
   - **D** none of the above

5. Which sentence should be deleted because it does not support the essay's main idea?
   - **A** sentence 2
   - **B** sentence 6
   - **C** sentence 9
   - **D** sentence 10

Application
Persuasive Essay

Have students use what they have learned in this workshop to write a persuasive essay about a writer in this unit. Suggest to students that they look up some examples of persuasive essays that they can use as models. Encourage students to use evidence to support their opinion.

Extension Homework
Analyzing Arguments

Tell students that persuasive essays express the writer's opinion, or position, in the beginning, and then build an argument with evidence throughout the essay. For homework, have students read an editorial article in a local or national newspaper. Ask students to analyze the article and write a one-page summary explaining the main idea, supporting points, and types of persuasion used by the writer.

Writing Skills Review

Assess

Answers and Explanations

1. ***D*** *In paragraph 2, the writer states "Although . . . his most persuasive technique is his appeal to emotion." This is his main idea. A, B, and C are supporting points.*
2. ***D*** *This sentence best combines both sentences while keeping the author's original meaning intact. The other sentences (A, B, and C) are either awkwardly constructed or change the meaning of the original sentences.*
3. ***C*** *Since this essay is about Swift's writing, a quote from Swift would be the most appropriate support.*
4. ***A*** *The writer uses logic to prove his point; he refers only to the emotional and ethical persuasion of Swift to support his point.*
5. ***D*** *Unlike the other sentences, suggesting that students be required to read the essay does not support the essay's main idea—that Swift uses appeals to emotion effectively.*

Reteach

go.hrw.com **ThinkCentral Online Remediation**

California Standards, p. 697

- **Writing Standard 1.9** Revise text to highlight the individual voice, improve sentence variety and style, and enhance subtlety of meaning and tone in ways that are consistent with the purpose, audience, and genre.

Read On

If students enjoyed the themes and topics explored in this unit, you might recommend these titles for independent reading.

Assessment Options

The following projects can help you evaluate and assess your students' outside work. Videotapes or audiotapes of completed projects may be included in students' portfolios.

Notes for a Novel

Have students who read *Joseph Andrews* and *Shamela* develop an outline for a novel that tells the story of an imaginary encounter between Joseph and Shamela. Students should keep in mind both characters' traits and the novels' satirical intent.

Present a Monologue

Students who read the biography of *Isaac Newton* prepare and present a monologue in which Newton responds to the biographer.

Read On

For Independent Reading

DRAMA

The Misanthrope *and* Tartuffe

The French playwright Molière had a remarkable genius for exposing and satirizing the ills of society. In Richard Wilbur's translation of *Tartuffe* and *The Misanthrope,* you will meet two men whom Molière considered representative of his age: one a roguish hypocrite who charms everyone he meets and the other an eccentric recluse who shuns hypocrisy at a great cost to himself. Molière's comedies of manners, so relevant when they were written, have not lost their potency and humor today.

FICTION

Pamela

Samuel Richardson's early modern novel gives voice to a young servant who resists the improper advances of her employer. Among eighteenth-century Londoners, the book became a controversial best-seller both praised for its morality and vilified for its scandalous subject matter. Richardson intended for it to instruct and entertain. Through its examination of virtue and impropriety among the social classes, it remains a study in the abuse of power and an amusing artifact of eighteenth-century life.

FICTION

Shamela *and* Joseph Andrews

Henry Fielding wrote his short epistolary novel, *Shamela,* as a hilarious parody and satire of Samuel Richardson's famous novel *Pamela.* Richardson tells how the exceptionally virtuous Pamela Andrews deftly avoids the clutches of one Squire B., but in *Shamela* Fielding turns the tables. In his hands, Squire B. becomes the naive Squire Booby, who is tricked by the con artist Shamela. In *Joseph Andrews,* Fielding invented the English novel as we readers know and love it today—with an intrusive, witty narrator commenting on the zany exploits of young Joseph and his dotty friend Parson Adams.

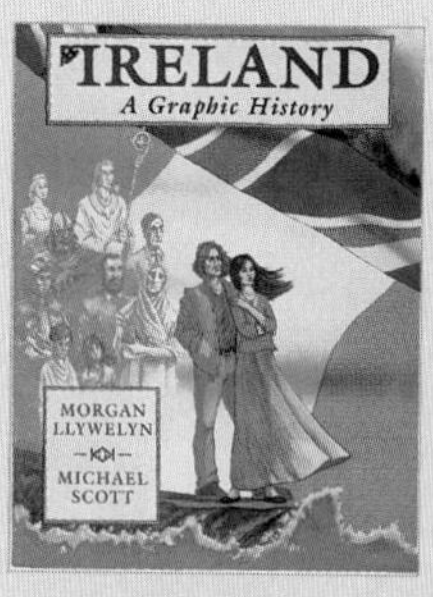

FICTION

Ireland: A Graphic History

Author Morgan Llywelyn and illustrator Michael Scott skillfully employ the graphic novel format to capture the beauty and violence intrinsic to Ireland's history. The panels and textual introductions provide a visual time line that begins by describing Belfast and goes on to trace the emergence of Viking settlements, the disastrous effects of the potato Famine, and the religious and political antagonism of the Troubles. Vivid depictions of Irish figures throughout the ages reveal the complex forces that shaped the development of this powerful island.

Word Counts and Readabilities of Read on Books

Fiction	Estimated Word Counts	Readability
The Misanthrope and *Tartuffe*	25,400	Accessible
Pamela	224,183	Challenging
Joseph Andrews and *Shamela*	144,216	Accessible
Ireland: A Graphic History	Graphic	Accessible

FICTION AND NONFICTION

Satire: From Horace to Yesterday's Comic Strips

Satire and its sidekick irony have been ridiculing human foibles for thousands of years. The jury is still deciding just how effectively satire influences people to change their ways, but no one doubts satire's ability to make us laugh and cry simultaneously. James Scott has compiled various genres that satirize people from Roman times to the present. He also includes questions with each selection to guide readers in understanding the point of the satire.

NONFICTION

English Society in the 18th Century

Tired of reading about the pampered life of English royalty at Buckingham Palace? Want to know what life was like for everybody else, what "public" schools (which were private) taught, what people ate and why it was fashionable to be fat, how people dressed and why cosmetics could literally kill you, where people worked and why the Industrial Revolution changed everything? Then you should read Roy Porter's witty account of the joys and horrors of English life in the eighteenth century and how the English persevered no matter what the odds.

NONFICTION

The Barbary Plague: The Black Death in Victorian San Francisco

In this captivating medical mystery, *Wall Street Journal* science reporter Marilyn Chase tells the story of Dr. Rupert Blue, the scientist charged with combating the bubonic plague in San Francisco. To rid the metropolis of the illness permanently, Blue must convince the government and the public of the disease's true source (fleas) while simultaneously dispelling various ethnic and racial stereotypes.

NONFICTION

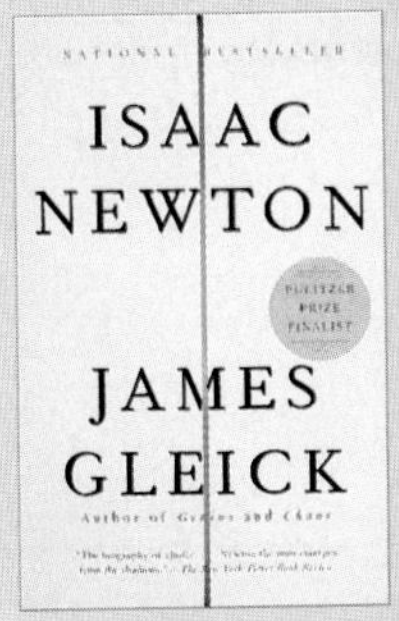

Isaac Newton

Alexander Pope summarized Isaac Newton's achievement in this witty couplet: "Nature and nature's laws lay hid in night; / God said, Let Newton be! And all was light." Newton, probably the most famous scientist who ever lived, formulated the laws of motion and explained the force of gravity. In this brief biography, James Gleick tells about Newton's lonely childhood and how Newton found solace in books and began to develop his scientific theories. Gleick also clearly explains the significance of Newton's discoveries.

Learn It Online
Found out more at *NovelWise*.
go.hrw.com H12-699 Go

Nonfiction	Estimated Word Counts	Readability
Satire: From Horace to Yesterday's Comic Strips	33,421	Accessible
English Society in the Eighteenth Century	128,235	Accessible
The Barbary Plague: The Black Death in Victorian San Francisco	67,290	Accessible
Isaac Newton	87,978	Easily Accessible

Assessment Options

Prepare a Lecture

After students have finished reading *Satire: From Horace to Yesterday's Comic Strips,* have them prepare a lecture on satire in the media, in poetry, in fiction, or in essays. Have students summarize the main points and cite specific examples.

Write a Journal Entry

Students who read *The Barbary Plague: The Black Death in Victorian San Francisco* should write a journal entry from the point of view of Dr. Rupert Blue. Journal entries should incorporate details from Chase's work.

Learn It Online
The **NovelWise** mini-site includes instruction on choosing, reading, and analyzing novels; it also contains a catalogue of book summaries, study guides, teaching guides, and PowerPoint presentations.
go.hrw.com H12–699 Go

The Romantic Period 1798–1832

Chapter 7

Features highlighted in **yellow** constitute a suggested minimum course of study.

Selection or Feature	For Independent Reading	Grade-Level Standards
The Romantic Period 1798–1832 **Link to Today:** *from* **A Reason for Hope** by Jane Goodall (Accessible, Lexile 1100)		
Literary Skills Focus: Themes of Romantic Poetry by Leila Christenbury		**Reading Standard 3.7:** Relate works to themes and issues of period.
Analyzing Visuals: Connecting to Romanticism		**Reading Standard 3.7:** Relate works to themes and issues of period.
• **To a Mouse** (Challenging, Lexile N/A) • **To a Louse** (Challenging, Lexile N/A) by Robert Burns	• **Of Mice and Men** by John Steinbeck • **The Road Not Taken** by Robert Frost	**Reading Standard 2.2:** Clarify meaning through structure, repetition, syntax, and word choice. **Reading Standard 3.3:** Analyze effects of irony, tone, mood, and style.
• **The Tyger** (Accessible, Lexile N/A) • **The Lamb** (Accessible, Lexile N/A) • **The Chimney Sweeper** *from* **Songs of Innocence** (Accessible, Lexile N/A) • **The Chimney Sweeper** *from* **Songs of Experience** (Accessible, Lexile N/A) • **A Poison Tree** (Accessible, Lexile N/A) by William Blake	• **Life Doesn't Frighten Me** by Maya Angelou • **The Personal History of David Copperfield** by Charles Dickens	**Reading Standard 2.2:** Clarify meaning through structure, repetition, syntax, and word choice. **Reading Standard 3.2:** Theme **Reading Standard 3.3:** Analyze effects of irony, tone, mood, and style. **Grades 9–10** **Review Reading Standard 3.7:** Literary devices **Grades 9–10 Review Reading Standard 1.2:** Denotative and connotative meanings
Reading Skills Focus: Recognizing Patterns of Organization by Kylene Beers		**Reading Standard 2.2:** Clarify meaning through structure, repetition, syntax, and word choice.
• **Lines Composed a Few Miles Above Tintern Abbey** (Accessible, Lexile N/A) • *from* **Ode: Intimations of Immortality** (Accessible, Lexile N/A) • **Composed upon Westminster Bridge** (Accessible, Lexile N/A) • **The World Is Too Much with Us** (Accessible, Lexile N/A) by William Wordsworth	• **The Land of Bliss** by Cathy Song • **Coming into the Country** by John McPhee	**Reading Standard 2.2:** Clarify meaning through structure, repetition, syntax, and word choice. **Reading Standard 3.3:** Analyze effects of irony, tone, mood, and style. **Reading Standard 3.4:** Analyze figures of speech. **Reading Standard 3.9:** Analyze philosophical arguments.
• **Kubla Khan** (Challenging, Lexile N/A) • **The Rime of the Ancient Mariner** (Accessible, Lexile N/A) by Samuel Taylor Coleridge	• **Gorillas in the Mist** by Dian Fossey	**Reading Standard 3.1:** Analyze subgenres. **Reading Standard 3.3:** Analyze effects of irony, tone, mood, and style. **Reading Standard 3.4:** Analyze figures of speech. **Reading Standard 3.9:** Analyze philosophical arguments.
Link to Today: *from* **Saving Creatures Great and Small** by Timothy Foote (Challenging, Lexile 1270)		**Reading Standard 2.2:** Clarify meaning through structure, repetition, syntax, and word choice.

Daily and Weekly Support

- **Reader/Writer Notebook**
- **Reading and Writing Transparencies**
- **Family Involvement Activities in Spanish**
- **Language Handbook Worksheets**
- **Holt Virtual File Cabinet for Language Arts**

Assessment Resources

- **Unit 4 Resources**, Chapter 7 Diagnostic Test; Selection Standards Checks, Chapter 7 Standards Mastery
- **Universal Access: Differentiating Instruction**, leveled assessment
- **English-Language Conventions Progress-Monitoring Tests**, Chapters 11–12
- **ThinkCentral Online Assessment**

Print Resources for Universal Access

Unit 4 • Chapter 7

	On-Level Learners	English Learners	Struggling Readers	Students Who Use African American Vernacular English	Advanced Learners	Students with Disabilities
Unit 4 Resources practice and assessment for selections and features in Chapter 7	✔				✔	
Universal Access: Holt Interactive Reader interactive readings for The Tyger, The Lamb, Lines Composed a Few Miles Above Tintern Abbey, Kubla Khan, The Rime of the Ancient Mariner		✔	✔	✔		✔
Universal Access: Differentiating Instruction modified lesson plans for The Tyger, The Lamb, Lines Composed a Few Miles Above Tintern Abbey, Kubla Khan, The Rime of the Ancient Mariner		✔	✔	✔		✔
Universal Access: Resources for Teaching Advanced Students lesson plans for The Tyger, The Lamb, Lines Composed a Few Miles Above Tintern Abbey, Kubla Khan, The Rime of the Ancient Mariner					✔	

Features highlighted in **yellow** constitute a suggested minimum course of study.

Chapter 8

Selection or Feature	For Independent Reading	Grade-Level Standards
Literary Skills Focus: **Forms of Romantic Poetry** by Leila Christenbury		**Reading Standard 3.1:** Analyze subgenres
• **She Walks in Beauty** (Accessible, Lexile N/A) • *from* **Childe Harold's Pilgrimage, Canto IV** (Accessible, Lexile N/A) by George Gordon, Lord Byron	• **The Complete Poems** by John Keats • **Wuthering Heights** by Emily Brontë	**Reading Standard 3.4:** Analyze figures of speech
Reading Skills Focus: **Comparing and Contrasting** by Kylene Beers		**Reading Standard 2.2:** Clarify meaning through structure, repetition, syntax, and word choice.
• **Ozymandias** (Accessible, Lexile N/A) • **Ode to the West Wind** (Accessible, Lexile N/A) • **To a Skylark** (Accessible, Lexile N/A) by Percy Bysshe Shelley	• **Blood on the Forehead: What I Know About Writing** by M. E. Kerr • **Frankstein** by Mar	**Reading Standard 2.2:** Clarify meaning through structure, repetition, syntax, and word choice. **Reading Standard 3.1:** Analyze subgenres. **Reading Standard 2.4:** Analyze an author's arguments. **Grades 9–10 Review Reading Standard 3.7:** Meaning of literary devices **Grades 9–10 Review Reading Standard 3.11:** Evaluate the aesthetic qualities of style.
Link to Today: **To a Mosquito** by W. S. Merwin (Easily Accessible, Lexile N/A)	• **Selected Poems of Pablo Neruda** by Pablo Neruda • **Silent Spring** by Rachel Carson	**Reading Standard 3.3:** Analyze effects of irony, tone, mood, and style.
• **On First Looking into Chapman's Homer** (Challenging, Lexile N/A) • **When I Have Fears** (Challenging, Lexile N/A) • **Ode to a Nightingale** (Challenging, Lexile N/A) • **Ode on a Grecian Urn** by John Keats (Challenging, Lexile N/A) • **Keats's Last Letter** (Challenging, Lexile 1090) by John Keats	• **The Discovery of Poetry** by Frances Mayes	**Reading Standard 2.2:** Clarify meaning through structure, repetition, syntax, and word choice. **Reading Standard 3.1:** Analyze subgenres. **Reading Standard 3.4:** Analyze figures of speech. **Grades 9–10 Review Reading Standard 2.5:** Analyze primary or secondary sources. **Grades 9–10 Review Reading Standard 3.9:** Analyze philosophical arguments.
Comparing Texts: Poetry Across Cultures • **Tanka** by Tanka Poets (Accessible, Lexile N/A) • **Haiku** by Haiku Poets (Accessible, Lexile N/A) • **Jade Flower Palace** by Tu Fu (Accessible, Lexile N/A) • **Night Thoughts Afloat** by Tu Fu (Accessible, Lexile N/A) • **Quiet Night Thoughts** by Li Po (Accessible, Lexile N/A) • **Question and Answer Among the Mountains** by Li Po (Accessible, Lexile N/A) • **Letter to His Small Children** by Li Po (Accessible, Lexile N/A)	• **Voices: Poetry and Art from Around the World** by Barbara Brenner • **Essential Haiku: Versions of Basho, Buson, and Issa** by Robert Hass	**Reading Standard 2.2:** Clarify meaning through structure, repetition, syntax, and word choice. **Reading Standard 3.3:** Analyze effects of irony, tone, mood, and style. **Reading Standard 3.4:** Analyze figures of speech. **Writing Standard 2.4:** Write historical investigation reports.

Daily and Weekly Support

- **Reader/Writer Notebook**
- **Reading and Writing Transparencies**
- **Family Involvement Activities in Spanish**
- **Language Handbook Worksheets**
- **Holt Virtual File Cabinet for Language Arts**

Assessment Resources

- **Unit 4 Resources**, Chapter 8 Diagnostic Test; Selection Standards Checks, Chapter 8 Standards Mastery
- **Universal Access: Differentiating Instruction**, leveled assessment
- **Formal Assessment**, Progress Monitoring Test 3
- **English-Language Conventions Progress-Monitoring Tests**, Chapter 13
- go.hrw.com **ThinkCentral Online Assessment**

Mastering the Skills

Selection or Feature	Grade-Level Standards
Writing Workshop: Reflective Composition	**Writing Standard 1.1:** Understand elements of discourse. **Writing Standard 1.5:** Establish tone. **Writing Standard 1.9:** Revise text . **Writing Standard 2.3:** Write reflective compositions.
Preparing for Timed Writing	**Writing Standard 2.3:** Write reflective compositions.
Listening and Speaking Workshop: Present a Reflective Composition	**Listening and Speaking Standard 2.1:** Deliver reflective presentations. **Listening and Speaking Standard 2.3:** Deliver oral responses to literature. **Grades 9–10 Review Listening and Speaking Standard 1.9:** Analyze audience; Verbal and nonverbal techniques.
Standards Review Literary Skills Review Vocabulary Skills Review Writing Skills Review	**Reading Standard 3.7:** Contrast literary forms. **Grades 9–10 Review Reading Standard 1.1:** Literal and figurative meanings of words **Writing Standard 2.3:** Write reflective compositions.

Print Resources for Universal Access

Unit 4 • Chapter 8

	On-Level Learners	English Learners	Struggling Readers	Students Who Use African American Vernacular English	Advanced Learners	Students with Disabilities
Unit 4 Resources practice and assessment for selections and features in Chapter 8	✔				✔	
Universal Access: Holt Interactive Reader Interactive readings for Ozymandias, Ode on a Grecian Urn		✔	✔	✔		✔
Universal Access: Differentiating Instruction modified lesson plans for Ozymandias, Ode on a Grecian Urn		✔	✔	✔		✔
Universal Access: Resources for Teaching Advanced Students lesson plans for Ozymandias, Ode on a Grecian Urn					✔	

Print Resources for Universal Access

All Chapters

	On-Level Learners	English Learners	Struggling Readers/Writers	Students Who Use African American Vernacular English	Advanced Learners	Students with Disabilities
Universal Access: Supporting Instruction in Spanish translations of selection summaries and key terms		✔				
Universal Access: Holt Interactive Writer and Speaker practice and assessment	✔	✔	✔	✔	✔	✔
Language and Sentence Skills Practice for Warriner's Handbook Chapters 11–13	✔				✔	
Universal Access: Developmental Language and Sentence Skills Practice for Warriner's Handbook Chapters 11–13		✔	✔	✔		✔

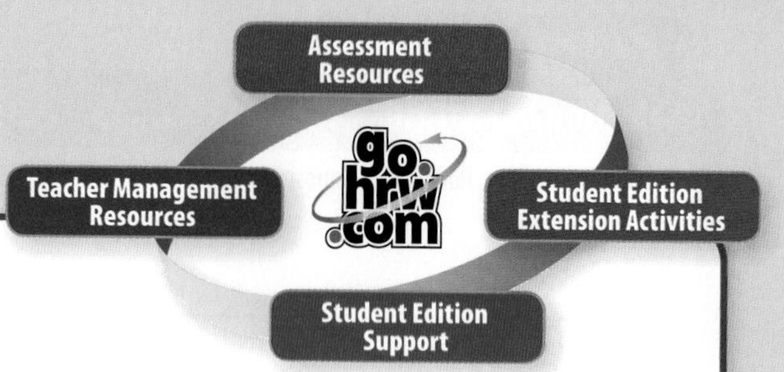

Technology Resources

Find all of Holt's technology resources at go.hrw.com. Technology resources are also listed at point of use in the Teacher's Edition wrap. Below are our featured components for Unit 4.

Teacher Management Resources

- ThinkCentral, Teacher Access
- **Teacher One Stop™**
- Holt Professional Learning for Language Arts

Spotlight on Teacher One Stop™

The **Teacher One Stop™** contains all of the print resources that you will need when using *Holt Literature and Language Arts.*

- Use the lesson plans for the selections in this unit, such as *The Rime of the Ancient Mariner* and "Ozymandias" to meet the needs of different student groups.

Student Edition Support

- PowerNotes
- ThinkCentral, Student Access
- **Student One Stop™**
- Interactive Reading Workshops
- Interactive Graphic Organizers
- Writers' Lives
- Holt Audio Library
- Holt Audio Library: Selections and Summaries in Spanish

Spotlight on Student One Stop™

The **Student One Stop™** contains an electronic version of all the important student resources in *Holt Literature and Language Arts.*

- Advise students without an Internet connection that they can access the text and audio for the poems in this unit by Burns, Blake, Wordsworth, Coleridge, Lord Byron, Shelley, and Keats with the **Student One Stop™**.

Student Edition Extension Activities

- **Digital Storytelling Mini-Site**
- NovelWise Mini-Site
- MediaScope Mini-Site
- WordSharp: An Interactive Vocabulary Tutor
- GrammarNotes
- WritingNotes
- Writing and Research in a Digital Age
- Literature Links

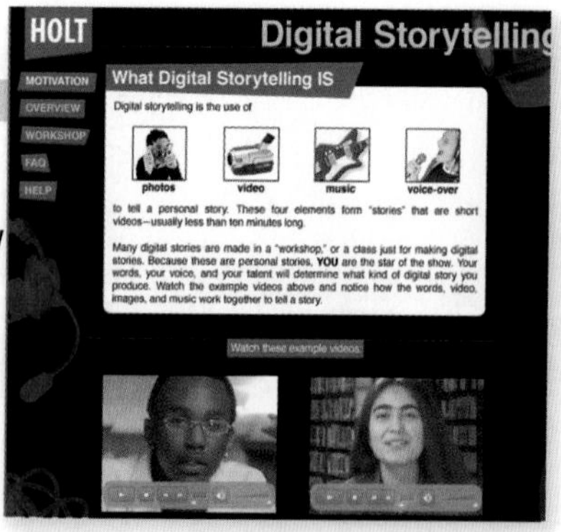

Spotlight on Digital Storytelling Mini-Site

This site will walk students through the step-by-step process of creating digital stories—personal narratives recorded aloud, and enhanced by video, pictures, music, and artifacts.

Universal Access: Advanced students in particular may appreciate an opportunity to work in new media.

Supported Strand: Writing

Assessment Resources

- **ThinkCentral Online Assessment**
- Holt Online Essay Scoring
- ThinkCentral Online Remediation

Spotlight on ThinkCentral Online Assessment

With online essay scoring, students can practice writing responses to essay prompts—and our system automatically scores them. Students will receive immediate feedback on their essays.

Real Issues, Real Experts

The wrap for these selections includes specific ideas and strategies from *Holt Literature and Language Arts* authors.

From the Authors

For "Lines Composed a Few Miles Above Tintern Abbey" p. 748

To help today's teens slow down enough to enjoy this poem, have them begin by writing about a place they've visited as a teen and as a youngster. Ask them to describe how their experiences there have changed. After finishing the poem, students should compare Wordsworths changing feelings about his own surroundings to their feelings they noted in their own writing.

Kylene Beers

For "Ozymandias" p. 820

Have students write a sonnet to help them appreciate how poetry tells stories with force and economy. After students read, have them rewrite in prose form the story told in the poem. Your students will discover many layers in "Ozymandias." Part of its lasting appeal is its commentary on what does and does not endure. Generations of readers have considered the ephemeral nature of the works of humankind, the fleeting power of rulers, and the enduring nature of literary art.

Deborah Appleman

Teacher to Teacher

Preteach To begin our study of Romanticism, I select a few poems for the class to analyze. As we examine these pieces together, we create a class list of literary elements (technical, figurative, and thematic) that we have observed in the poems, in an attempt to build our own definition of *Romanticism*. The students then compare the class's observations with the textbook's academic definition of the period.

Direct Teach In small groups, students research and present on the life of a poet, his literary style, and how his work reflects Romanticism.

Assess I evaluate the presentations. Group members also grade each other on participation and effort.

Chondra Winger
Elk Grove, California

Holt Professional Learning

Visit ThinkCentral, Teacher Access to link to Holt's Professional Learning site for English/Language Arts teachers. This site features:

- **Videos that share the insights of *Holt Literature and Language Arts* program authors and consultants and demonstrate proven classroom strategies with master teachers**
- **Study guides for publications by our authors and consultants**
- **Informative articles and useful Web links**
- **Help in planning your department's professional learning sessions**
- **A handbook for new teachers**

Re-engaging the Disengaged Student
with Alfred Tatum

VIDEO PRODUCTS

Strategies for Helping Struggling Readers
with Kylene Beers

Effective Vocabulary Instruction
with Carol Jago and Kylene Beers

Developing Critical Thinking about Literature
with Carol Jago and Deborah Appleman

Teaching Students to Revise, Not Recopy
with Linda Rief

Teaching English Learners
with Robin Scarcella

Using Literature Circles
with Harvey Daniels

Teaching On-Demand Writing Skills
with Leila Christenbury

Managing the Heterogeneous Classroom
with Leila Christenbury and Patrick Schwarz

Teaching Narrative and Expository Texts
with Judith Irvin and Deborah Appleman

Becoming a Tech-Savvy Teacher
with Sara Kajder

Re-engaging the Disengaged Student
with Alfred Tatum

Teaching Grammar in Context
with Amy Benjamin

UNIT 4

Unit Objectives

- Students will be introduced to the predominant themes of the Romantic period by examining imagination in the work of William Blake, the primacy of nature in the poetry of Wordsworth and Coleridge, and the ideas of beauty, power, and truth in the verse of Byron, Shelley, and Keats.
- Students will study the formal elements of the poetic forms favored by the Romantics: sonnets, odes, meditative poems, and ballads.
- Students will compare the treatment of the theme of nature in Romantic poetry with its treatment in Chinese and Japanese poetry.
- At the end of the unit, students will write and present a reflective composition.

Analyzing Visuals

Use the online textbook to project this image for viewing. Tell students that **Henry Pether** (1828–1865) was known mostly for painting moonlight scenes by the Thames River.

Extension Activity Ask students to consider how the scene depicted in the painting incorporates both truth and beauty. ***Possible response:*** *The soft moonlight delicately illuminating the figures and houses by the river gives this scene a romantic quality, while the peaceful, meditative mood encourages the viewer to consider the simplicity of life's meaning and truths.*

Unit Resources

On Course: Mapping Instruction
Unit 4 Resources
Warriner's Handbook
- Chapter 11, A Glossary of Usage
- Chapter 12, Capitalization
- Chapter 13, Punctuation

Teacher One Stop™
Formal Assessment, Progress Monitoring Test
English-Language Conventions Progress-Monitoring Tests
ThinkCentral Online Assessment
Holt Virtual File Cabinet for Language Arts, grammar, reading, and vocabulary resources
Holt Pronunciation Resources
- Phoneme Sounds and Spellings
- Support for Speakers of African American Vernacular English

ThinkCentral Online Remediation

A *Full Moon on the River at Brentford* by Henry Pether (1828–1865). Beaton Brown Fine Paintings, London.

UNIT 4

The Romantic Period 1798–1832

CHAPTER 7
Truth and Imagination

CHAPTER 8
The Quest for Beauty

"The divine arts of imagination: imagination, the real & eternal world of which this vegetable universe is but a faint shadow."

—**William Blake**

What Do You Think? How can we use imagination to discover truth?

Learn It Online
Learn more about the Romantics online.
go.hrw.com H12-701 Go

The Quotation

- Tell students that William Blake (1757–1827) was a visionary poet and artist now recognized as one of the most important English poets.
- Explain that Blake slightly preceded the Romantics chronologically but rejected the neoclassical focus on reason. Blake emphasized imagination and believed in the possibility of achieving progress by balancing seemingly contradictory ideas. Blake thought that the act of using one's imagination led to wisdom and insight, and he created his own prophetic mythology to explain his ideas.

Routines for California Classrooms

For ideas on classroom practices and approaches to grouping, see the discussion of routines on pages T34–T37 of this Teacher's Edition.

What Do You Think?

How can we use imagination to discover truth?

- Have students discuss what life might be like without imagination. Ask students to consider how the use of imagination results in new ideas and inventions.
- Ask students to think about times when imagination can be a distraction or obstruction to revelation or creativity.

Learn It Online
You can introduce some of the topics in this unit using brief videos about the literature of this period.
go.hrw.com H12-701 Go

Real Issues, Real Experts: Professional Learning

Spotlight on . . .
Thinking Critically About Literature

To help students appreciate Romantic literature, consider the suggestions you'll find in these videos:

Developing Critical Thinking About Literature, with **Carol Jago** and **Deborah Appleman,** provides an overview of several approaches to student responses to literature: written responses, discussions, close reading, and the use of literary perspectives.

In Re-engaging the Disengaged Student, Holt author **Alfred Tatum** explores ways to make literature come alive for students by making it relevant to their lives.

Each video is accompanied by printable articles, planning materials, Web links, and a training guide for supervisors. For these resources and more, visit **Holt Professional Learning** by going to this page in **ThinkCentral, Teacher Access.**

Direct Teach

Teach the Time Line

Give students five to ten minutes to study the time line. Then, ask the following questions:

- Which nations sought expansion or empire in the early nineteenth century? ***Possible response:*** *the United States, the Zulu nation, and France*
- What three significant scientific advances contributing to industrialization took place in Britain between 1804 and 1825? ***Possible response:*** *The steam engine was first used to drive a locomotive, Michael Faraday published research that led to the first electric motor, and George Stephenson invented the railroad locomotive.*
- Based on events in the World Events time line, what did France and Spain have in common? ***Possible response:*** *Both countries were faced with violent political and social upheavals, such as the French Revolution and the rebellion against Spanish rule in South America.*

The Romantic Period 1798–1832

This time line represents a snapshot of British literary events, British political and social events, and world events from 1789 to 1832. During this tumultuous period, the Industrial Revolution transformed Britain, the French Revolution galvanized France, and Romantic literature dominated Europe.

BRITISH LITERARY EVENTS

1789

1789 William Blake publishes *Songs of Innocence*

Mary Godwin, née Wollstonecraft by John Opie. Oil on canvas. Inv. 1237. National Portrait Gallery, London.

1792 Mary Wollstonecraft, in *A Vindication of the Rights of Woman,* critiques female educational restrictions

1800 Maria Edgeworth's *Castle Rackrent,* the first historical novel in English, satirizes absentee landowners in Ireland

1805

1807 Charles and Mary Lamb publish *Tales from Shakespeare*

1812 Charles Dickens, author of *A Christmas Carol,* is born

1813 Jane Austen publishes *Pride and Prejudice*

Charles Dickens (1830) by Janet Roos. Dickens House Museum, London.

BRITISH POLITICAL AND SOCIAL EVENTS

1789

1793 France declares war on England

1801 Act of Union creates United Kingdom of Great Britain and Ireland

1803 John Dalton develops modern atomic theory

1804 The steam engine is first used to drive a locomotive

Richard Trevithick's locomotive (1804). The Granger Collection, N.Y.

1805

1811 English artisans called Luddites, fearing that industrialism threatens their livelihoods, riot and destroy textile machines

1811 Charles Bell publishes *New Idea of Anatomy of the Brain,* which explores the connection between the brain and nervous system

WORLD EVENTS

1789

1789 U.S. Congress approves its Constitution

1789 French Revolution begins with the storming of the Bastille

Storming of the Bastille, July 14, 1789 by Charles Thevenin. Musée de la Ville de Paris, Musée Carnavalet, Paris, France.

1803 United States purchases Louisiana Territory from France

1805

1805–1815 Napoleonic Wars lead to France's conquest of most of Europe

1808 Johann Wolfgang von Goethe publishes Part 1 of *Faust*

1810 Simón Bolivar begins series of South American rebellions against Spain

Universal Access

English Learners/ Struggling Readers

English for Academic Success Read aloud each section of the time line and clarify the following words and phrases:

- **British Literature:** *critiques, restrictions, satirizes, absentee*
- **British Political and Social:** *textile, industrialism, nervous system, emancipation, naturalist, abolished*
- **World History:** *storming, conquest, composing, Symphony, verse, independence*

Advanced Learners

Acceleration Draw students' attention to the English artisans who called themselves Luddites. After a man named Ned Ludd accidentally broke some equipment at a factory, workers formed a guerilla army, destroying equipment at the factory and claiming General Ned Ludd had ordered them to do so. The workers also re-

California Standards, pp. 702–703

- **Reading Standard 3.7** Analyze recognized works of world literature from a variety of authors. **c.** Evaluate the philosophical, political, religious, ethical, and social influences of the historical period that shaped the characters, plots, and settings.

Reading Standard 3.7c (see pages A48–A50)

Your Turn

Review the time line with a partner. What historical events might have driven Romantic writers to turn away from the eighteenth-century emphasis on reason and instead embrace naturalness and imagination? Explain.

1815 — 1822 — 1832

1818 Mary Shelley, daughter of Mary Wollstonecraft, publishes *Frankenstein* >

1819 Sir Walter Scott publishes *Ivanhoe*

1819 John Keats writes his greatest poems between January and September

Cover of *Frankenstein* by Mary Shelley, late 19th century.

1824 Percy Bysshe Shelley's complete works are published after his death

1824 George Gordon, Lord Byron dies in Greece

1815 — 1822 — 1832

1815 Napoleon surrenders to the British at Waterloo

1820 George III, mentally unstable since 1810, dies

1821 Michael Faraday publishes research that leads to the first electric motor

Stephenson's "North Star" steam engine, 1837.

1825 George Stephenson invents the railroad locomotive

1829 Catholic Emancipation Act allows British Roman Catholics to hold public office

1831 Charles Darwin serves as naturalist on HMS *Beagle* during an expedition along the coast of South America

1833 Slavery is abolished in the British Empire >

Slaves planting cane cuttings, from *Ten Views in the Island of Antigua* (1823) by William Clark. Color engraving. The British Library, London.

1815 — 1822 — 1832

1816 Shaka becomes king and expands the Zulu nation

1817 Beethoven begins composing his Ninth Symphony

1821 Sequoyah develops a Cherokee system of writing

Zulu Kraal near Umlazi Natal, plate 27 from *The Kafirs Illustrated* (1849) by George French Angas. Color lithograph. Stapleton Collection, U.K.

1822 Liberia is founded as a home for former U.S. slaves

1823 Alexander Pushkin begins his novel in verse, *Eugene Onegin*

1829 Ottoman Empire recognizes Greek independence

quested reasonable wages, better working conditions, and quality control. They aimed to destroy property and never hurt people. Because of their disciplined attacks, many factory owners complied with their demands. Discuss whether the Luddites' actions can and should be justified.

Students with Disabilities

Tell students that the three time lines show events from the years 1789–1832. Explain that students can compare events on the three time lines by reading the page vertically. Model how to connect an event on the British literature time line to contemporary events in British and world history. For example, you might say: "Around 1800, William Blake published his *Songs of Innocence* and France declared war on England. At about that same time, the U.S. Congress approved its Constitution and the French Revolution was beginning."

Check for Understanding

Your Turn

Tell students that they should compare the World Events to the Literary Events and think about what kind of impact the former might have had on the latter.

Explore the Time Line

The following activity offers options for students to explore the literary, political, social, and world events presented on the time line.

Enrichment Point out to students that the time line is divided into three parts: literary, political and social, and world events.

- Divide the class into small groups. Have each group choose either the French Revolution or the Napoleonic Wars to learn how each influenced literature.
- Have each group research its assigned topic, focusing on these questions: In what ways did the conflict between France and England influence literature? What is the relationship between a society's government and the literature its writers produce?
- As students research their topic, remind them to relate their research to the unit question: How can we use imagination to discover truth?
- Have groups present their findings to the class. Remind students to discuss how works of imagination might reflect the truth.

Standards Focus

Objectives

Students will
- evaluate the philosophical, political, religious, ethical, and social influences of a historical period
- identify and understand elements of text structures

Preteach

Key Concepts

Use the Key Concepts to preview the unit introduction. Each key concept is addressed in a separate section of the essay that relates the concept to both the history and the literature of the times.

Set a Purpose for Reading

- Ask students to identify one piece of information from each key concept about which they want to learn more.
- Have students jot down any concepts, images, or phrases that come to mind when they think of Britain in the late eighteenth century. Suggest that students pay close attention to the impact of historical events and social conditions on British literature.
- Tell students to record each section's main ideas and important details in their **Reader/Writer Notebooks.**

California Standards, pp. 704–709

- **Reading Standard 2.2** Analyze the way in which clarity of meaning is affected by the patterns of organization, hierarchical structure, repetition of the main ideas, syntax, and word choice in the text.
- **Reading Standard 3.7** Analyze recognized works of world literature from a variety of authors. **b.** Relate the literary works and authors to the major themes and issues of their eras. **c.** Evaluate the philosophical, political, religious, ethical, and social influences of the historical period that shaped the characters, plots, and settings.

The Romantic Period

1798–1832

Beginning in the late eighteenth century, great political, economic, and social changes rocked English society. The neoclassical faith in reason and its reverence for order and tradition, which had dominated English thought and literature for more than a century, seemed inadequate in the face of these profound upheavals. People needed new ways of thinking, feeling, and responding to change.

KEY CONCEPTS

Revolution Spreads

History of the Times An age of revolution began in America in 1776 and then swept across western Europe, releasing political, economic, and social forces that produced some of the most radical changes ever experienced in human life. The violence of the French Revolution shocked Europe and spread fear that other monarchies would also fall.

Literature of the Times Idealistic British writers who embraced the French Revolution rebelled against eighteenth-century rationalism. Rejecting restraint and refinement, they created a literature based on imagination.

Conservatives Clamp Down

History of the Times After the French Revolution, the English people suffered from repressive government policies enacted by conservatives who feared political change. When England and its allies defeated Napoleon in 1815, many early supporters of the French Revolution felt that it was the defeat of one tyrant by another.

Literature of the Times Six poets led the Romantic movement: William Blake, William Wordsworth, Samuel Taylor Coleridge, Lord Byron, Percy Bysshe Shelley, and John Keats. Their works are marked by imagination, idealism, and emotion, as well as an interest in nature, simplicity, and the past.

Industrialization Finds a Foothold

History of the Times England led the Industrial Revolution and replaced much human labor with machinery. The business class adopted the policy of laissez-faire economics, which allowed owners to operate factories without government interference. The result was devastating exploitation of the working poor.

Literature of the Times Gothic literature had an unmistakable appeal during the Romantic era. With its eerie, supernatural style, this type of literature reflects the renewed interest in mysticism during the Romantic period.

Resources

Unit 4 Resources, on-level instruction, Historical Introduction Study Guide, p. 1

UA: Holt Interactive Reader, Key Concepts and Academic Vocabulary, p. 197

PowerNotes, interactive lesson presentations with activities

Teacher One Stop™, on-level lesson plans and all print resources

Universal Access

EL English Learners/ Struggling Readers

To help students understand the information presented in the unit introduction, review the definitions of the following words:
- **monarchy**—a state ruled or headed by a monarch who usually inherits the authority
- **rationalism**—reliance on reason as the best guide for belief and action
- **idealism**—the philosophical theory that abstract ideals and are as important as reality

Reading Standard 2.2, 3.7b, 3.7c (see pages A48–A50)

UNIT 4 INTRODUCTION

KEY CONCEPT

Revolution Spreads

History of the Times

The end of the eighteenth century was marked by revolution and violence. With its defeat in the American Revolution, England suffered a great economic blow and lost prestige and confidence as its thirteen American Colonies established their independence. It was the more radical revolution in France, which started with the storming of the Bastille prison on July 14, 1789, that had far more ominous effects. For the ruling classes in England, the French Revolution came to represent their worst fears: the overthrow of an anointed king by a democratic mob. To English conservatives, the French Revolution meant the triumph of radical principles, and they feared that the revolutionary fever would spread across the Channel.

Nevertheless, many British liberals supported the Revolution's purported ideals of "liberty, fraternity, and equality" until escalating violence and terror, such as the September 1792 massacre of hundreds of the nobility and clergy in France, disillusioned them.

In 1793, France and England declared war on each other. In the midst of the blood and turmoil, control of the French government again changed hands. Napoleon Bonaparte, an officer in the French army, emerged as dictator and then, in 1804, as emperor of France. In the end, Napoleon became just as ruthless as the executed king himself had been.

Literature of the Times

In 1798, two young, idealistic British poets, Samuel Taylor Coleridge and William Wordsworth, published *Lyrical Ballads, with a Few Other Poems.* Among the "few other poems" was Coleridge's long narrative, *The Rime of the Ancient Mariner* (see page 776) and a last-minute addition, Wordsworth's "Lines Composed a Few Miles Above Tintern Abbey" (see page 748).Both of these works are now among the most important poems in English literature.

Thus began in England what is now called the Romantic period. The Romantics turned to nature, to the past, or to a dream world that they felt was more genuine than the ugly, turbulent age in which they lived.

Comprehension Check

How did conservatives and democratic idealists respond differently to the French Revolution? Why?

Fast Facts

Political and Social Highlights

- The American and French Revolutions in the late 1700s deeply affect England. Conservative economic and political measures and a lengthy war against Napoleon strengthen the power of the rich.
- The growing industrialization of Britain leads to burgeoning urban populations and a rise in the number of poor workers.

Literary Highlights

- Romanticism arises as a response to social and economic changes caused by the Industrial Revolution.
- Wordsworth and Coleridge publish *Lyrical Ballads* in 1798.
- Keats, Byron, and Shelley write their greatest poems in the early nineteenth century.

Learn It Online
Find out more about this historical period online.
go.hrw.com H12-705 Go

(Opposite) James Watt's steam engine at an English coal mine in the 1790s. Contemporary painting by an unknown artist.
The Granger Collection, N.Y.

- **mysticism**—a belief in realities that exist beyond perception

Advanced Learners

Acceleration Have students discuss in small groups how novels today have supernatural elements and styles. Ask students to compare how imaginative literature appealed to eighteenth-century British society with how supernatural writings appeal to readers today.

Students with Disabilities

Have students work together in mixed-ability groups to take notes on the essay. Encourage groups to create a table, outline, or other organizational tool using the Key Concept titles and subheads within the essay. Students should pause at the end of each paragraph and summarize it in one or two sentences in their notes.

Direct Teach

Think About/Talk About

Motivate Tell students that during the Romantic period, the chaos of constant revolutions led authors and thinkers to use their imaginations to withdraw from the turmoil around them. Ask students to discuss ways that political and social conditions can influence all types of literature.

History of the Times

Tell students that the French Revolution was a major event for all of Europe, not just France itself. The ideals of the French Revolution transformed France from a monarchy to a republic and led the way to the process of democratization that eventually characterized many European nations and the United States.

Literature of the Times

Point out that Romantic writers created literature aimed at escapism from the harsh realities of everyday life. Authors such as Coleridge and Wordsworth hoped that their writing would encourage imagination in society.

Comprehension Check

Possible responses: *Conservatives were afraid that the "revolutionary fever" and subsequent "radical principles" would spread to Britain. Democratic idealists were excited about the change to a new form of government.*

Learn It Online
For a multimedia introduction to the key concepts covered in this unit, use the **PowerNotes** Unit 4 presentation.
go.hrw.com H12-705 Go

Think About/Talk About

History of the Times

Once Britain defeated Napoleon's navy at the battle of Trafalgar, Britain controlled the seas. Lacking freedom of the seas, Napoleon tried to lead the French into Russia, with disastrous results.

Literature of the Times

With the shift from rationalism to emotion, art and literature moved from the Age of Reason to the Romantic period. When emotions became its subject, art was intense, sincere, and passionate.

Analyzing Visuals

Connecting to the Text: *The artist seems to be parodying Napoleon and France's defeat. Napoleon is depicted in the middle with his crown flying off his head and hands lifted up in an act of surrender. He is unarmed and helpless before the British soldier on the left and the Prussian soldier on the right.*

KEY CONCEPT

Conservatives Clamp Down

History of the Times

The bewildering changes in western Europe made conservatives in England more rigid than ever. England instituted severe and repressive measures, outlawing collective bargaining and holding suspected spies or agitators in prison without a trial. After a brief peace from 1802 to 1803, England began a long war against Napoleon. English guns first defeated Napoleon's navy at the Battle of Trafalgar and with the help of allies finally sent Napoleon's army packing at Waterloo, Belgium.

Although the conservatives in England felt they had saved their country from a tyrant and from chaos, the early supporters of the Revolution felt betrayed. For them, Waterloo was simply the defeat of one tyrant by another.

Literature of the Times

The Romantic poets of the early nineteenth century were deeply aware of their revolutionary times and dedicated to bringing about change. They harbored no illusions about their very limited political power, but they believed in the force of literature. Frustrated by England's resistance to political and social change that they thought was certain to improve conditions, the Romantic poets turned from the formal, public verse of the eighteenth-century Augustans to a more private, spontaneous lyric poetry. These lyrics expressed the Romantics' belief that imagination,

Analyzing Visuals

Connecting to the Text The bright dress and playful postures of the figures suggest a comic overtone, despite their overtly violent movements. Who or what might the artist be parodying in this picture?

The Battle of Waterloo, 18th June 1815, published by Ackermann (1815–1820). Color engraving by the English School (19th century). Bibliothèque Nationale, Paris, France.

Cross-Curricular Connection

HISTORY: Napoleon's Reforms

Although conservatives in England categorized Napoleon as a tyrant, he did make some improvements in French life. He restored order, boosted the economy, weeded out corruption, and established a public school system. He also created a code, a set of laws for civil order. Under this code, called the Napoleonic Code, all male citizens were considered equal. Any form of primogeniture, inherited nobility, or class perquisite was eliminated.

Small-Group Activity Have students form groups of four to five people and discuss how the social change generated by Napoleon's reforms might have affected the literature of the Romantic period. If time permits, have students conduct additional research on the Napoleonic Code.

HSS Analysis Skills: HI 1

UNIT 4 INTRODUCTION

Link to Today

Long Live the Romantic Comedy

Picnic scene from *Sense and Sensibility* (1995). Kate Winslet, Gemma Jones, Emilie Francois, and Emma Thompson.

Jane Austen is one of the most beloved of all British authors. Her subject matter, ordinary people in everyday life, is hailed by many scholars as a direct influence on the modern novel. During Austen's life she saw four of her novels published within four years of each other; two were published after her death. The titles of Austen's novels, *Sense and Sensibility* (1811), *Pride and Prejudice* (1813), *Mansfield Park* (1814), *Emma* (1815), *Northanger Abbey* (1803), and *Persuasion* (1817), may be more recognizable to you as the titles of box-office hits and celebrated mini-series. Her best-known works have been made into movies, of which the most famous and funny, *Emma* and *Pride and Prejudice*, have been adapted several times for film and television—even as teen comedies and musicals.

Ask Yourself

Why might people continue to find humor and value in two-hundred-year-old novels?

rather than mere reason, was the best response to the forces of change.

Much of the literature of the Romantic period—as represented by *Lyrical Ballads*—is Romantic poetry. The Romantics thought of poets as extraordinary people, necessary to humanity and society. A poet has "a greater knowledge of human nature and a more comprehensive soul, than are supposed to be common among mankind," Wordsworth said. His compatriots agreed. Blake referred to poets as teachers, Keats called them "physicians," and Shelley saw them as "unacknowledged legislators of the world." The poet, wrote Coleridge, "brings the whole soul of man into activity" by employing "that synthetic and magical power . . . the imagination."

Although poetry dominated the literary scene, the novel also continued to thrive during the Romantic period. Key novelists included Jane Austen, Maria Edgeworth, and Sir Walter Scott. A leading author of great reputation, Austen wrote with humor and irony about English country life. Her works include *Pride and Prejudice, Sense and Sensibility,* and *Emma.*

Comprehension Check

What new values and responses to change did the Romantic poets offer?

Primary Source

Wordsworth and the Poet's Purpose

Responding to the changing cultural climate brought on by increasing political unrest, industrialization, and urbanization, Wordsworth described the conditions that called for a new poetic agenda. In the famous Preface to *Lyrical Ballads*, he wrote: "For a multitude of causes, unknown to former times, are now acting with a combined force to blunt the discriminating powers of the mind, and, unfitting it for all voluntary exertion, to reduce it to a state of almost savage torpor. The most effective of these causes are the great national events which are daily taking place, and the increasing accumulation of men in cities . . . "

Think About/Talk About

Link to Today
Long Live the Romantic Comedy

This feature describes the enduring popularity of British author Jane Austen and her works, still relevant nearly two centuries after her death.

1. Ask these questions to help students build background. What are the characteristics of a romantic comedy? How might a romantic comedy set in the early 1800s differ from a modern-day romantic comedy?
2. After students read the selection, ask them to speculate about why Austen's novels continue to be so popular.
3. Finally, ask students to respond to the **Ask Yourself** question. Use students' responses to spark a class discussion.
4. Encourage interested students to do further research on Jane Austen's influence on the modern novel.

Comprehension Check

Possible response: *The Romantic poets valued imagination over reason. By writing private, intimate lyric poetry, they put the focus on beauty, on the emotions of the heart, and the longing of the soul.*

Think About/Talk About

History of the Times

The historian Christopher Harvie writes that factory towns were squalid, "smoked and stank," and "were expensive both in terms of rent and of human life. . . . If housing was bad, sanitation was worse."

Literature of the Times

Continental Europe and America also experienced a rise in the popularity of Gothic literature. For example, American author Edgar Allan Poe wrote short stories such as "The Fall of the House of Usher" and "Ligeia"; Nathaniel Hawthorne, also American, wrote "The Minister's Black Veil." German author E.T.A. Hoffman wrote a collection of Gothic stories in *Tales of Hoffman.*

Link to Today

Urban Amusements

This feature describes the diverse activities available for London urbanites during the late 1800s.

1. Ask students to think of popular modern recreational activities, such as watching movies, that may be analogous to those of the early nineteenth century.
2. After students have read the feature, have them discuss how entertainment forms have changed or remained the same.
3. Have students respond to the **Ask Yourself** question. Interested students may research the history of the Burlington Arcade.

KEY CONCEPT

Industrialization Finds a Foothold

History of the Times

View of Sheffield, England, showing the city's many factories and steelworks. English engraving, 1879. The Granger Collection, NY

England was the first nation in the world to experience the effects of the Industrial Revolution. Previously, goods had been made by hand, at home. Now, production switched to factories, where machines worked many times faster than human beings could. Since factories were in cities, the urban populations increased, creating desperate living conditions that would appall us today.

In addition, the communal land once shared by small farmers was taken over by individual owners. Some of these owners transformed the fields into vast private parks, while others divided the land into privately held fields. As a result, large numbers of landless people migrated to cities in search of work or relied on the charity of the time: the poorhouse and begging.

The economic philosophy that propelled much of this misery was a policy called **laissez faire,** "let (people) do (as they please)." According to this policy, the new economic forces should be allowed to operate freely without government interference. Laissez faire enabled the rich to grow richer and caused the poor people to suffer even more. The system had its most tragic effects on those who were helpless, especially children. Small children of poor families were often used as beasts of burden. In the coal pits, for example, very small children were harnessed to carts for dragging coal, just as if they had been small donkeys.

Literature of the Times

Wars, revolutions, industrialization, and economic upheaval made the British feel adrift and frightened. One way of responding to this sense of unease was to explore the dark side of life in literature and art. For that reason, literature of the Romantic period is filled with examples of the eerie and supernatural. The Romantics' taste for terror grew from a sensibility called Gothic that set stories in gloomy medieval castles.

The Gothic was one way in which people of the age expressed a sense of helplessness about forces beyond their control. Gothic literature uses devices such as ghosts, the supernatural, death, violence, and decay to terrorize readers and allow them to purge their fears and worries within the safety of fantasy. Mary Shelley's *Frankenstein,* a pivotal Gothic novel, highlights the era's anxiety over the powers of science and technology.

The Gothic style also extended to art. A melancholy painting or a desolate landscape was thought to enhance spiritual awareness. Ann Radcliffe (1764–1823), one of the best-known Gothic novelists, describes this ideal awareness in *The Mysteries of Udolpho* (1794). In twilight gloom, a character finds "that delicious melancholy which no person, who had felt it once, would resign for the gayest pleasures. They awaken our best and purest feelings; disposing us to benevolence, pity, and friendship."

Academic Vocabulary

Talking and Writing About Literature

English for Academic Success Write the following questions on the board. Tell students these are the kinds of questions they will encounter on standardized tests. Discuss the meanings of the words. Then, have students use the historical introduction to answer the questions.

Comprehension Check
How did Gothic literature provide readers and writers in the Romantic period with a new way to deal with the political and social upheavals around them?

Link to Today

Urban Amusements

Many people today associate cities with a great variety of entertainment—from restaurants and shopping to zoos and amusement parks, as well as movies, music, and theater. Although the liberal philosopher Josiah Tucker called London under Kings George I, II, and III "no better than a wen," or wart, London was a veritable playground for those who could afford it. Ballooning was popular. Puppet shows, waxwork museums, and music halls attracted large audiences. One of the most frequented type of entertainment was boxing. (Lord Byron himself was taught to box by Gentleman Jackson, one of the leading fighters of the day.) Most families, whether aristocratic or common, had their portraits done. The upper class shopped at the new shopping arcades—the eighteenth-century version of malls—especially the Burlington Arcade in Piccadilly. In short, life in London during this time was as full of exciting diversions as city life is today.

Ask Yourself
How do the types of entertainment available in cities today compare to those available during the Romantic period?

The London Eye and County Hall on the bank of the River Thames, London.

Wrap Up

Talk About . . .
With a group, compare the poet's role in the Romantic period and in today's society. Try to use each Academic Vocabulary word **listed below** at least once in your discussion.

Write About . . .
Percy Bysshe Shelley wrote that the "great instrument of moral good is the imagination." Do you agree or disagree? Why?

Academic Vocabulary for Unit 4

Talking and Writing About Literature

Academic Vocabulary is the language you use to write and talk about literature. Use these words to discuss the literature you read in this unit. These words are underlined throughout the unit.

device (dih VYS) *n.:* something made for a particular purpose. *Imagery is a predominant literary device in Romantic poetry.*

differentiate (dihf uh REHN shee ayt) *v.:* distinguish; identify differences. *It is not difficult to differentiate between the styles of Romantic and Restoration poetry.*

function (FUHNGK shuhn) *n.:* the action for which a person or thing is specially fitted; purpose. *The Romantics believed the function of poets was to enlighten and lift up the masses.*

inherent (ihn HIHR uhnt) *adj.:* existing in something as a fixed, essential quality. *Many people now feel that exploitation is inherent in laissez-faire economics.*

technique (tehk NEEK) *n.:* method; way of using skills. *Evoking the powerful, emotionally rejuvenating effect of nature was a popular Romantic technique.*

Your Turn
In your *Reader/Writer Notebook*, compose a brief description of Romantic writing, using each of the Academic Vocabulary words.

UNIT 4 INTRODUCTION

Think About/Talk About

Comprehension Check
Possible response: *Readers and writers of Gothic literature could use its darker features, such as ghosts and death, to represent the fears they experienced in their lives.*

Check for Understanding

Talk About . . .
Ask students to comment briefly on the political and social scenarios of the modern era. Ask them to think about how literature, music, visual arts, and cinematography deal with modern social issues. Is art a way to escape reality or to improve it?

Write About . . .
Remind students that for the Romantics, imagination was the opposite of reason. Students who agree with the statement may respond that imagination is great because it is limitless, while those who disagree may claim that imagination lacks practicality.

PowerNotes, Academic Vocabulary lesson and activities

- As stated in the essay, what **devices** in Gothic literature were used to evoke a sense of helplessness and fear? ***Possible response:*** *Gothic literature featured supernatural elements such as ghosts and horrific elements such as violence, death, and decay.*
- How did Gothic works such as Mary Shelley's "Frankenstein" **differentiate** themselves from other works of the Romantic period? ***Possible response:*** *Gothic authors used dark devices such as ghosts and spirits to express the era's anxieties about forces that were beyond their control.*
- What might be some examples of "desperate living conditions" that were **inherent** in the era's urban areas? ***Possible response:*** *These conditions included overcrowding, disease, brutal child labor, and widespread poverty.*

Standards Focus

Objectives

Students will evaluate the philosophical, political, religious, ethical, and social influences of a historical period.

Link to Today

This article connects Goodall's unconventional path toward philosophical and spiritual enlightenment to the changing views on emotion, imagination, and reason characteristic of the literary period explored in Unit 4.

Unit 4 Resources, Historical Introduction Skill Builder, p. 1

UA: Differentiating Instruction, graphic organizer, p. 163

Teacher One Stop™, lesson plan and all print resources

Direct Teach

Think About/Talk About

Read with a Purpose Direct students to the Read with a Purpose statement. Point out the key words "natural world" and "heightened awareness." Tell students as they read to note the effects nature has on the author's state of mind.

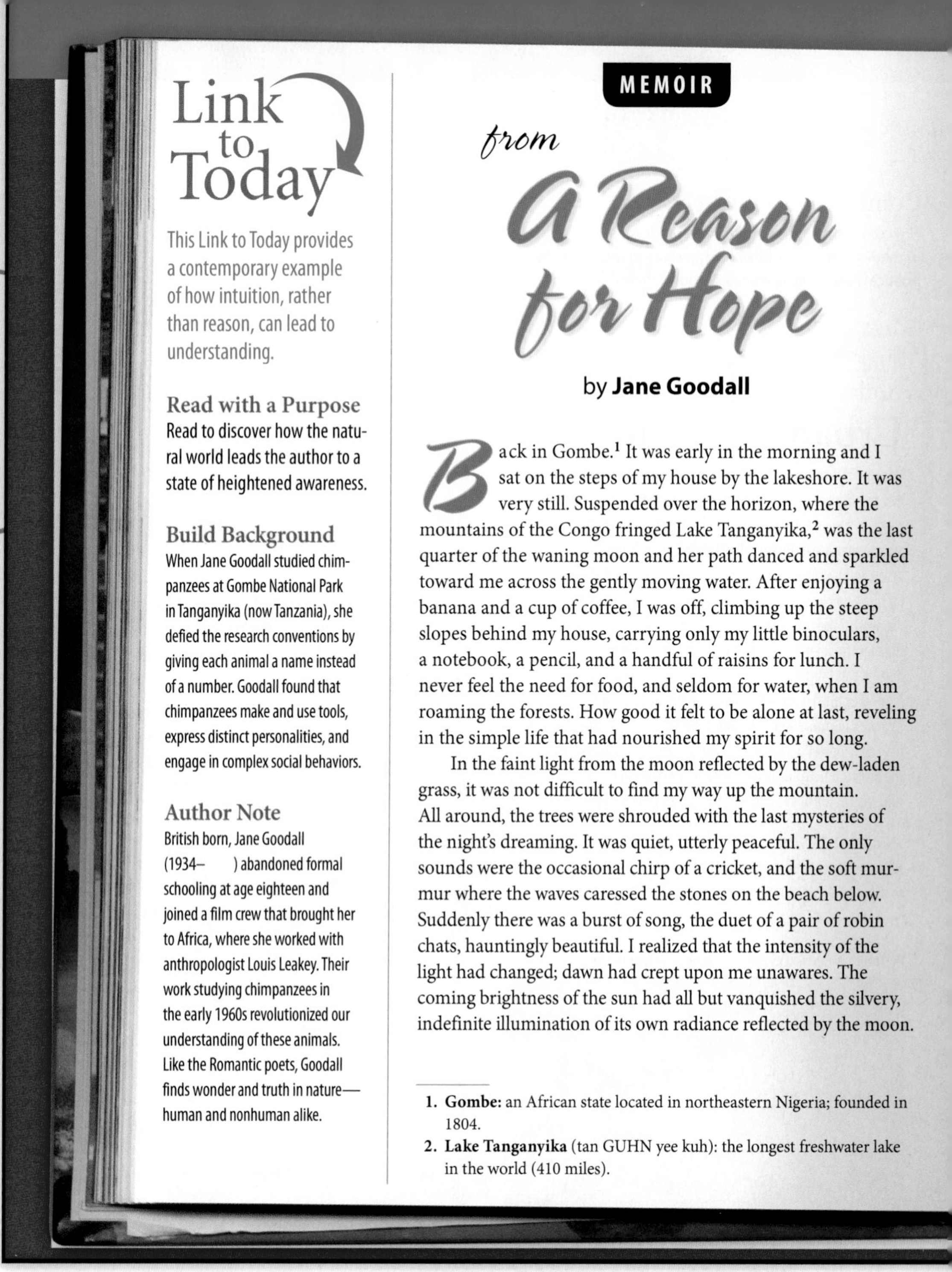

Link to Today

This Link to Today provides a contemporary example of how intuition, rather than reason, can lead to understanding.

Read with a Purpose

Read to discover how the natural world leads the author to a state of heightened awareness.

Build Background

When Jane Goodall studied chimpanzees at Gombe National Park in Tanganyika (now Tanzania), she defied the research conventions by giving each animal a name instead of a number. Goodall found that chimpanzees make and use tools, express distinct personalities, and engage in complex social behaviors.

Author Note

British born, Jane Goodall (1934–) abandoned formal schooling at age eighteen and joined a film crew that brought her to Africa, where she worked with anthropologist Louis Leakey. Their work studying chimpanzees in the early 1960s revolutionized our understanding of these animals. Like the Romantic poets, Goodall finds wonder and truth in nature—human and nonhuman alike.

MEMOIR

from **A Reason for Hope**

by **Jane Goodall**

Back in Gombe.[1] It was early in the morning and I sat on the steps of my house by the lakeshore. It was very still. Suspended over the horizon, where the mountains of the Congo fringed Lake Tanganyika,[2] was the last quarter of the waning moon and her path danced and sparkled toward me across the gently moving water. After enjoying a banana and a cup of coffee, I was off, climbing up the steep slopes behind my house, carrying only my little binoculars, a notebook, a pencil, and a handful of raisins for lunch. I never feel the need for food, and seldom for water, when I am roaming the forests. How good it felt to be alone at last, reveling in the simple life that had nourished my spirit for so long.

In the faint light from the moon reflected by the dew-laden grass, it was not difficult to find my way up the mountain. All around, the trees were shrouded with the last mysteries of the night's dreaming. It was quiet, utterly peaceful. The only sounds were the occasional chirp of a cricket, and the soft murmur where the waves caressed the stones on the beach below. Suddenly there was a burst of song, the duet of a pair of robin chats, hauntingly beautiful. I realized that the intensity of the light had changed; dawn had crept upon me unawares. The coming brightness of the sun had all but vanquished the silvery, indefinite illumination of its own radiance reflected by the moon.

1. **Gombe:** an African state located in northeastern Nigeria; founded in 1804.
2. **Lake Tanganyika** (tan GUHN yee kuh): the longest freshwater lake in the world (410 miles).

Selection Readability	
Easily Accessible **Accessible** Challenging	accessible vocabulary; familiar syntax; accessible theme

Selection Summary

Jane Goodall wrote this memoir about her return visit to Gombe, a natural environment where she studied the native chimpanzees. While reflecting on her surroundings, Goodall experienced a feeling of oneness with the natural world, which she describes as a heightened awareness of sounds, smells, and sights that she had never experienced before.

Analyzing Visuals

Connecting to the Text How does the Romantic depiction of a solitary figure facing the ocean compare to the experience Jane Goodall narrates in this excerpt from *A Reason for Hope*?

Left: *The Wanderer Above the Sea of Fog* (1818) by Caspar David Friedrich. Oil on canvas.
Hamburg Kunsthalle, Germany.
Below: Researcher Jane Goodall, on a peak overlooking Gombe, scans the forest through binoculars searching for chimpanzees.
The Jane Goodall Institute

Think About/Talk About

Extend the Discussion

Finding Details What types of observations does Goodall make about her surroundings as the sun starts to rise in the second paragraph? ***Possible response:*** *Goodall observes the quiet peace of the crickets chirping, the soft sound of the waves, the chatterings of a pair of robins, and the brightness of the sunrise.*

Interpreting What examples from the author's memoir show how her life was "simple" in Gombe? ***Possible response:*** *Her life is uncomplicated and not burdened with materialistic needs. She carries only a few items and needs very little to nourish her spirit.*

Analyzing Visuals

Caspar David Friedrich (1774–1840) is now considered the greatest German Romantic painter for his paintings of vast lonely landscapes depicting the sublime in nature, but he attained only modest fame during his lifetime.

Connecting to the Text: *Like the solitary figure in the Friedrich painting, Goodall faces nature and turns her back to the viewer or civilization. Both figures are dwarfed by the grandeur of nature but raised to a more intense plane of experience.*

Universal Access

EL English Learners

English for Academic Success Have students read the Link to Today blurb. Point out that the word *intuition* comes from a Latin root word that means "a looking at" or "consideration." To learn by intuition is to perceive a truth or fact directly without reasoning. Ask students as they read to consider what truths the writer perceives through her senses.

Struggling Readers

Have students record character traits about the writer, Jane Goodall, as they read. Tell students to draw a web diagram. Ask them to read the major details and decide what the details reveal about the writer. For example, the last sentence of the first paragraph reveals that the writer feels most at home when in nature, without distractions and complications. Students might write on one line in their diagram: "loves the simplicity of nature."

Think About/Talk About

Extend the Discussion

Comparing and Contrasting On p. 712, how does the memoir contrast the natural world with civilization? ***Possible response:*** *The author believes that the serenity of the forest dwarfs, yet enhances, human emotion, while civilization encourages selfishness and greed. Unlike people, the chimpanzees are undemanding and do not pity her.*

Evaluating Why do you think Goodall chooses to name the chimpanzees? ***Possible responses:*** *Goodall seems to view the chimpanzees as peers of humans, and therefore worthy of human names. This view is also exemplified in the way she portrays the behavior of the young chimpanzees. Her descriptions of their rest and play are similar to descriptions of a human child.*

Five minutes later I heard the rustlings of leaves overhead. I looked up and saw the branches moving against the lightening sky. The chimps had awakened. It was Fifi and her offspring, Freud, Frodo, and little Fanni. I followed when they moved off up the slope. Fanni riding on her mother's back like a diminutive[3] jockey. Presently they climbed into a tall fig tree and began to feed. I heard the occasional soft thuds as skins and seeds of figs fell to the ground.

For several hours we moved leisurely from one food tree to the next, gradually climbing higher and higher. On an open grassy ridge the chimps climbed into a massive mbula tree,[4] where Fifi, replete[5] from the morning's feasting, made a large comfortable nest high above me. She dozed through a midday siesta, little Fanni asleep in her arms, Frodo and Freud playing nearby. How healing it was to be back at Gombe again, and by myself with the chimpanzees and their forest. I had left the busy, materialistic world so full of greed and selfishness and, for a little while, could feel myself, as in the early days, a part of nature. I felt very much in tune with the chimpanzees, for I was spending time with them not to observe, but simply because I needed their company, undemanding and free of pity. From where I sat I could look out over the Kasakela Valley. Just below me to the west was the Peak. A surge of memories flooded through me: from that vantage point I had learned so much in the early days, sitting and watching while, gradually, the chimpanzees had lost their fear of the strange white ape who had invaded their world. I recaptured some of my long-ago feelings as I sat there, reflecting. The old excitement of discovery, of seeing things quite unknown to Western eyes. And the serenity[6] that had come from living, day after day, as a part of the natural world. A world that dwarfs yet somehow enhances human emotions.

As I reflected on these things I had been only partly conscious of the approach of a storm. Suddenly, I realized that it was no longer growling in the distance but was right above. The sky was dark, almost black, and the rain clouds had obliterated[7] the higher peaks. With the growing darkness came the stillness, the hush, that so often precedes a tropical downpour. Only the rumbling of the thunder, moving closer and closer, broke this stillness; the thunder and the rustling movements of the chimpanzees. All at once came a blinding flash of lightning, followed, a split second later, by an incredibly loud clap of thunder, that seemed almost to shake the solid

3. **diminutive:** small; tiny.
4. **mbula tree:** a medium-sized gnarled tree whose fruit, a plum-sized, custardlike apple, is a staple of the Gombe chimps' diet.
5. **replete:** stuffed with food and drink.
6. **serenity:** a feeling of peace or calm.
7. **obliterated:** completely blotted out.

Cross-Curricular Connection

SCIENCE: Chimpanzees

Chimpanzees inhabit the rain forests and savannas of Africa that are located near the equator. Adult chimpanzees can grow to be anywhere between three and five feet tall and weigh about 70 to 130 pounds. A chimpanzee's day begins at daybreak and is typically spent gallivanting through the trees and forest floor, then stopping for a midday rest. Late afternoons are spent searching for food. The standard diet for a chimpanzee consists of a large variety of different fruits, leaves, flowers, seeds, and insects.

Like humans, chimpanzees are able to walk upright, but they typically travel on all fours. They are talented swingers and can move with precision from branch to branch, but they usually cover long distances on the ground. After ending an active day, chimpanzees retreat to treetop nests made with leaves and branches for a night of rest.

Dr. Jane Goodall, touched by Jou Jou.

rock before it rumbled on, bouncing from peak to peak. Then the dark and heavy clouds let loose such torrential rain that sky and earth seemed joined by moving water. I sat under a palm whose fronds, for a while, provided some shelter. Fifi sat hunched over, protecting her infant; Frodo pressed close against them in the nest; Freud sat with rounded back on a nearby branch. As the rain poured endlessly down, my palm fronds no longer provided shelter and I got wetter and wetter. I began to feel first chilly and then, as a cold wind sprang up, freezing; soon, turned in on myself, I lost all track of time. I and the chimpanzees formed a unit of silent, patient, and uncomplaining endurance.

It must have been an hour or more before the rain began to ease as the heart of the storm swept away to the south. At four-thirty the chimps climbed down, and we moved off through the soaked, dripping vegetation, back down the mountainside. Presently we arrived on a grassy ridge overlooking the lake. A pale, watery sun had appeared and its light caught the raindrops so that the world seemed hung with diamonds, sparkling on every leaf, every blade of grass. I crouched low to avoid destroying a jeweled spider's web that stretched, exquisite and fragile, across the trail.

I heard sounds of greeting as Fifi and her family joined Melissa and hers. They all climbed into a low tree to feed on fresh young leaves. I moved to a place where I could stand and watch as they enjoyed their last meal of the day. Down below, the lake was still dark and angry with white flecks where the waves broke, and rain clouds remained black in the south. To the north the sky was clear with only wisps of gray clouds still lingering. The scene was breathtaking in its beauty. In the soft sunlight, the chimpanzees' black coats were shot with coppery brown, the branches

Think About/Talk About

Extend the Discussion

Rereading What strong contrasting images does Goodall describe in the last paragraph on p. 713? ***Possible response:*** *Goodall creates a strong image of contrasting colors when describing the chimpanzees' coppery brown coats against the dark ebony of the branches with brilliantly green leaves.*

Symbolism The descriptive imagery in the second paragraph compares the rain to diamonds. How does this symbolize the way Goodall values the natural world? ***Possible response:*** *Diamonds are very valuable in the materialistic world, but in the forest, the same value can be found in a simple act of nature.*

Universal Access

Advanced Learners

Enrichment Have students select a memoir from the school or public library to read independently. Instruct them to write a summary of the writer and his or her life. Remind students to include quotations and excerpts from the memoir that they think are significant. Have them present their work to the class. Students may find memoirs on people in the following categories:

- political or military leaders
- artists, musicians, writers
- scientists
- historians or journalists
- athletes

Students with Disabilities

Obtain photos of Gombe National Park from the Web and have students compare the contents of the photos with Goodall's descriptions. Ask students to point out specific phrases and descriptions in the text that seem to correspond well to the photos and explain why.

Think About/Talk About

Extend the Discussion

Finding Details How did Goodall emerge from her state of heightened awareness? What was her first reaction? ***Possible responses:*** *The sounds of the chimpanzees' "pant-hoots" awakened Goodall and brought her back to reality. Her initial response was to stay put and try to write a description of the feeling she just experienced.*

Imagery According to the first and second paragraphs of p. 714, how did a "heightened awareness" make the author feel? How did it affect her senses? ***Possible responses:*** *Goodall felt that her self was absent. Her senses were heightened, so she was aware of more sounds, sights, and smells than she would have noticed ordinarily.*

on which they sat were wet and dark as ebony, the young leaves a pale but brilliant green. And behind was the dramatic backcloth of the indigo sky where lightning flickered and distant thunder growled and rumbled.

Lost in awe at the beauty around me, I must have slipped into a state of heightened awareness. It is hard—impossible, really—to put into words the moment of truth that suddenly came upon me then. Even the mystics are unable to describe their brief flashes of spiritual ecstasy. It seemed to me, as I struggled afterward to recall the experience, that *self* was utterly absent: I and the chimpanzees, the earth and trees and air, seemed to merge, to become one with the spirit power of life itself. The air was filled with a feathered symphony, the evensong of birds. I heard new frequencies in their music and also in the singing insects' voices—notes so high and sweet I was amazed. Never had I been so intensely aware of the shape, the color of the individual leaves, the varied patterns of the veins that made each one unique. Scents were clear as well, easily identifiable: fermenting, overripe fruit; waterlogged earth; cold, wet bark; the damp odor of chimpanzee hair and, yes, my own too. And the aromatic scent of young, crushed leaves was almost overpowering. I sensed a new presence, then saw a bushbuck,[8] quietly browsing upwind, his spiraled horns gleaming and his chestnut coat dark with rain.

Suddenly a distant chorus of pant-hoots[9] elicited a reply from Fifi. As though wakening from some vivid dream I was back in the everyday world, cold, yet intensely alive. When the chimpanzees left, I stayed in that place—it seemed a most sacred place—scribbling some notes, trying to describe what, so briefly, I had experienced. I had not been visited by the angels or other heavenly beings that characterize the visions of the great mystics or the saints, yet for all that I believe it truly was a mystical experience.

Time passed. Eventually I wandered back along the forest trail and scrambled down behind my house to the beach. The sun was a huge red orb just vanishing behind the Congo hills and I sat on the beach watching the ever-changing sunset as it painted the sky red and gold and dark purple. The surface of the lake, calm after the storm, glinted with gold and violet and red ripples below the flaming sky.

Later, as I sat by my little fire, cooking my dinner of beans, tomatoes, and an egg, I was still lost in the wonder of my experience. Yes, I thought, there are many windows through which we humans, searching for meaning, can look out into the world around us. There are those carved out by

8. **bushbuck:** a reddish brown, white-striped African antelope.
9. **pant-hoots:** panting and hooting sounds chimpanzees make to communicate.

Reaching Reluctant Readers

Help students visualize what Goodall saw, heard, and felt in Gombe. First, have students close their eyes and imagine they are in Goodall's shoes. Read aloud the first full paragraph on p. 714 slowly. Have students share which descriptions were most prominent in their imagined experience in Gombe and why. Ask students how the observations made in this paragraph would differ if Goodall was a camouflaged soldier engaging in guerilla warfare. What sights, sounds, and smells would be heightened for the soldier?

Western science, their panes polished by a succession of brilliant minds. Through them we can see ever farther, ever more clearly, into areas which until recently were beyond human knowledge. Through such a scientific window I had been taught to observe the chimpanzees. For more than twenty-five years I had sought, through careful recording and critical analysis, to piece together their complex social behavior, to understand the workings of their minds. And this had not only helped us to better understand their place in nature but also helped us to understand a little better some aspects of our own human behavior, our own place in the natural world.

Yet there are other windows through which we humans can look out into the world around us, windows through which the mystics and the holy men of the East, and the founders of the great world religions, have gazed as they searched for the meaning and purpose of our life on earth, not only in the wondrous beauty of the world, but also in its darkness and ugliness. And those Masters contemplated the truths that they saw, not with their minds only but with their hearts and souls too. From those revelations came the spiritual essence of the great scriptures, the holy books, and the most beautiful mystic poems and writings. That afternoon, it had been as though an unseen hand had drawn back a curtain and, for the briefest moment, I had seen through such a window. In a flash of "outsight" I had known timelessness and quiet ecstasy, sensed a truth of which mainstream science is merely a small fraction. And I knew that the revelation would be with me for the rest of my life, imperfectly remembered yet always within. A source of strength on which I could draw when life seemed harsh or cruel or desperate.

Ask Yourself

1. **Read with a Purpose** Goodall says, "Lost in awe at the beauty around me, I must have slipped into a state of heightened awareness." What does Goodall mean by "a state of heightened awareness," and how did her experience in nature lead her to such a state?
2. How does Goodall's use of details affect your understanding of the experiences she relates here? Explain.
3. Goodall describes two types of "windows" through which humans can search for meaning. Explain these two types of windows. Through which window do you think most people look? Through which window do you look? Why?
4. Consider the mystical experience Goodall describes. Think about a time when something in the natural world, perhaps a dazzling sunset or a powerful storm, led you to a new understanding. Describe your experience, and explain how attention to the natural world can help us see the world in a new way.

UNIT 4 INTRODUCTION

Think About/Talk About

Extend the Discussion

Finding the Main Idea According to the final paragraph of the essay, what are the benefits of looking out of "windows" other than the scientific window? ***Possible response:*** *Looking out of other "windows" is one way people find meaning in life; these other windows can lead to spiritual revelations and artistic achievements.*

Recognizing Philosophical Assumptions Which assumptions does Goodall make about achieving a heightened sense of awareness? Think about the Romantic ideas of emotion, contemplation, and solitude. ***Possible response:*** *Goodall assumes that intellectual awareness can be increased through intense emotion and sensation. Like the Romantics, she does not believe that intellect and emotion compete with or negate each other. Her view integrates different aspects of the psyche that in many philosophies would be considered contradictory.*

Ask Yourself

Possible responses:

1. *Her senses became sharper and heightened in sensitivity. Her experiences being alone in the natural world led her to hear, see, and smell nature and thus to feel united with it.*
2. *Goodall's details allow readers to create a mental picture of the setting. This helps them to understand Goodall's experience fully.*
3. *There are scientific windows, which are looked through using reason, and spiritual windows, which a person looks through using the heart and spirit. Some may look through scientific windows because they can see clear facts. Others, guided by their intuition, may look through spiritual windows.*
4. *Responses should include a description of the natural event or scene and the kind of understanding the student gained through the experience.*

Chapter Objectives

- Students will learn about the themes of Romantic poetry by reading works by Robert Burns, William Blake, Simon Winchester, William Wordsworth, and Samuel Taylor Coleridge.
- Students will identify and interpret the Romantic poets' use of various stylistic and literary devices such as alliteration, symbolism, personification, and allusion.

The Quotation

Tell students that the literary skills focus for Chapter 7 is Romantic poetry. The Romantics celebrated the imagination, which they viewed as an important source of insight. Point out that Wordsworth uses the superlative (*clearest, most exalted*) to convey his view of imagination. Ask students what they think he means by the phrase "reason in her most exalted mood." ***Possible response:*** *Wordsworth suggests that imagination is reason at its best and thus is the most important mental faculty.*

Analyzing Visuals

Extension Activity What mood does this painting evoke? How does it reflect the Romantic belief in the supremacy of imagination? ***Possible responses:*** *The soft colors and blurry outlines create a dreamy mood. The misty landscape seems otherworldly and disconnected from everyday reality.*

CHAPTER **7**

Truth and Imagination

LITERARY SKILLS FOCUS
Themes of Romantic Poetry

CONTENTS

"This spiritual love acts not, nor can exist
Without Imagination, which in truth,
Is but another name for absolute power
And clearest insight, amplitude of mind,
And reason in her most exalted mood."

— **William Wordsworth**

Chapter 7

California Standards Overview

- **Reading Standard 2.2** Analyze the way in which clarity of meaning is affected by the patterns of organization, hierarchical structures, repetition of the main idea, syntax, and word choice in the text.
- **Reading Standard 3.1** Analyze characteristics of subgenres (e.g., satire, parody, allegory, pastoral) that are used in poetry, prose, plays, novels, short stories, essays, and other basic genres.
- **Reading Standard 3.2** Analyze the way in which the theme or meaning of a selection represents a view or comment on life, using textual evidence to support the claim.
- **Reading Standard 3.3** Analyze the way in which irony, tone, mood, the author's style, and the "sound" of language achieve specific rhetorical or aesthetic purposes or both.
- **Reading Standard 3.4** Analyze ways in which poets use imagery, personification, figures of speech, and sounds to evoke readers' emotions.
- **Reading Standard 3.7** Analyze recognized works of world literature from a variety of authors. **b.** Relate the literary works and authors to the major themes and issues of their eras.
- **Reading Standard 3.9** Analyze the philosophical arguments presented in literary works to determine whether the authors' positions have contributed to the quality of each work and the credibility of the characters. (Philosophical approach)
- **Grades 9–10 Review Reading Standard 3.7** Recognize and understand the significance of various literary devices, including figurative language, imagery, allegory, and symbolism, and explain their appeal.

LITERARY RESPONSE AND ANALYSIS

Literary Skills Focus

Reading Standard 3.7b (see pages A48–A50)

Themes of Romantic Poetry by Leila Christenbury

Influences on Romantic Poetry

- Spread of democratic ideals through the American and French Revolutions and the disillusionment created by the failure of the French Revolution
- Reactions against the harsh living and working conditions created for poor people in urban areas by the Industrial Revolution and laissez-faire economics
- Fascination with nature and country life, which seemed a blissful retreat compared to the squalor of city slums

A New Focus in Poetry

Inviting readers to feel power and passion, the poetry of the Romantic period looks at the world with new eyes and tries to capture the magic of personal experience. The poets of the Restoration wrote in an age when order had just been restored to a society that badly needed it, and, accordingly, the Augustans celebrated order, hierarchy, and enlightened rule. The Romantics, on the other hand, lived in a society desperately in need of social change, even revolution. They rebelled by writing about personal feelings, supporting individual rights, and using common, everyday language.

The word *romantic* comes from the term *romance,* one of the most popular medieval genres. Romantic writers consciously used the elements of romance in an attempt to transcend the refinements of neoclassical literature and explore more psychological and mysterious aspects of human experience.

Romantic poets are distinguished by three main characteristics:

- They turned away from the eighteenth century emphasis on reason and artifice and instead embraced imagination and naturalness.
- They wrote poetry that spoke of personal experiences and emotions, often in simple, unadorned language.
- They saw nature as transformative; they were fascinated by the ways nature and the human mind "mirrored" each other's creative properties.

Romantic themes still resonate with readers today. As you read the poems in this chapter, record the themes that you find meaningful.

Imagination: The Inspired Guide

The beginning of the Romantic movement in poetry is often dated to the 1798 publication of *Lyrical Ballads,* by William Wordsworth and Samuel Taylor Coleridge. Because many of these poems deal with nature, the Romantics are often mistakenly seen merely as nature poets. The Romantics should instead be considered "mind poets," for they sought a deeper understanding of the bond between human beings and the world of the senses.

Their search led them to a third, more mysterious element linking the mind to nature. In "Lines Composed a Few Miles Above Tintern Abbey," Wordsworth describes this link as "something far more deeply interfused." This "something" is a sort of creative inertia, a power that makes things happen. The Romantics identified this power as the imagination, a faculty they believed was superior to human reasoning. For that reason, Romantic poems usually present imaginative experiences as especially powerful or moving.

Learn It Online

Learn more about the themes of Romantic poetry through *PowerNotes* online.

go.hrw.com H12-717 Go

(opposite) *Dudley, Worcester* by Joseph Mallord William Turner. Watercolor on paper. Lady Lever Art Gallery, National Museums Liverpool.

Literary Skills Focus

Objectives

Students will understand the themes of Romantic poetry.

Unit 4 Resources, Literary Focus Skill Builder, p. 5

PowerNotes, interactive lesson presentation with activities

Teacher One Stop™, on-level lesson plan and all print resources

Direct Teach

A New Focus in Poetry

Have students read the Literary Skills Focus. Then, use the following questions to stimulate discussion of Romantic poets' views of political events, reason, and imagination.

- The Romantic movement emerged soon after the American and French revolutions. Why do you think Romantic poets were inspired by these political events? Why were they disillusioned by the outcome of the French Revolution?
- The Romantics praised imagination as a mental faculty distinct from reason. Why do you think they turned away from reason to embrace imagination?

Learn It Online

For a multimedia version of the instruction found on this page, use the **PowerNotes** Literary Skills Focus presentation.

go.hrw.com H12-717 Go

California Standards, pp. 717–718

- **Reading Standard 3.7** Analyze recognized works of world literature from a variety of authors. **b.** Relate the literary works and authors to the major themes and issues of their eras.

Universal Access

English Learners/ Struggling Readers

English for Academic Success Make sure students understand that the meaning of the word *Romantic* in this essay is different from its common contemporary meaning. Explain that in contemporary culture, the term *romantic* often refers to people falling in love. Point out that here, *Romantic* refers to an artistic movement. Romantic writers and artists valued emotion and imagination above reason and explored the relationship between human beings and the natural world.

Nature: The Wise Teacher

At times, the Romantics have been viewed mistakenly as mere nature poets, in part because of the enormous popularity of some of Wordsworth's lyrics. For example, most people know or recognize these lines:

I wandered lonely as a cloud
That floats on high o'er vales and hills,
When all at one I saw a crowd,
A host of golden daffodils . . .

Because of this poem, Wordsworth was often mockingly (and sometimes seriously) called the "daffodil poet." However, Wordsworth never wrote simply about nature; he wrote about nature and its effect on the human mind.

Check for Understanding

Ask Yourself

Possible responses:

1. *Romantic poets found inspiration in nature, in political rebellion, in rustic life, and in personal feelings.*
2. *In nature, the Romantics found a positive model of change; it showed them that change could be a force for renewal and growth. Nature also provided them with a calming place of refuge from the tumultuous social changes of their era.*

LITERARY RESPONSE AND ANALYSIS

Literary Skills Focus

While each of the six major Romantic poets had his own view of imagination, all believed that the imagination could be stimulated by nature and the mind. The poets had a strong sense of nature's mysterious forces, which inspire writers—as they do in Shelley's "Ode to the West Wind" (see page 825)—and hint at the causes of the great changes taking place in the world.

Nature: The Wise Teacher

If imagination is the Romantic poet's guide to seeking truth, nature is the teacher who can deliver the lesson. Romantic poets considered themselves special people who were, as Wordsworth wrote, "endowed with a more lively sensibility . . . a greater knowledge of human nature, and a more comprehensive soul, than are supposed to be common among mankind." Identifying themselves as bards, Romantics felt responsible for helping other people see the world in all its beauty and tenderness, as well as reflecting on the sadder subjects of human experience. They were, according to John Keats, to "pour out a balm upon the world."

For the Romantic poets, nature was a balm to soothe the relentless hounding of an industrialized world. The poets had a strong sense of nature's mysterious, transformative properties. A poet translated into words what he or she sensed from waves beating against the coastline, mountains shrouded in clouds, or silent groves, so that readers might perceive the power of natural forces to shape thought and feeling.

This inclination toward natural images and themes is one reason that the Gothic tradition in literature also thrived during this period. Novels such as Mary Shelley's *Frankenstein* drew attention to the mysterious side of nature and the power of the imagination through their eerie settings, supernatural events, and questions about the human ability to manipulate nature.

Experience: The Worthy Subject

Because they looked to nature for inspiration, Romantic poets favored idealized rural settings. The city, with its oppressive, crowded streets, held little appeal. However, the people who crowded those city streets were a source of fascination for some Romantic poets, who celebrated all types of human experience. The Romantic period was, historically, a time of growing awareness of the rights of individuals—including the right to healthful living conditions, the right to relief from political or economic oppression, and the right to self-expression.

Across Europe and in the former American Colonies, democracy grew stronger, and oppressive governments grew weaker. At the same time, economic oppression was on the rise as industrial factories drew workers away from small farms and family-run businesses. Burgeoning **laissez-faire** policies allowed businesses to function freely and with little restriction. As a result, workers, including young children, labored for long hours under dangerous conditions because no governmental regulations existed to protect them. It was of little consequence to employers when workers injured themselves and couldn't work, for there were always desperate people ready to replace them.

Some Romantic poets dreamed that poetry could improve these horrific conditions by offering an example of model behavior. Wordsworth wrote in *The Prelude:*

What we have loved,
Others will love, and we will teach them how;
Instruct them how the mind of man becomes
A thousand times more beautiful than the earth
On which he dwells. . . .

With the ability to cultivate the sensibilities of mankind, the poet thus becomes necessary to human beings and society.

Ask Yourself

1. Where did Romantic poets look for inspiration? Why?
2. Why do you think Romantic poets wrote about nature during a time of change?

Universal Access

Advanced Learners

Acceleration Provide students with print or online resources about the French philosopher Jean-Jacques Rousseau (1712–1778). Explain that Rousseau greatly influenced the development of Romantic thought, and one of his most enduring ideas was the concept of the *noble savage*—a person untainted by the corruption inherent in civilization. In small groups, ask students to discuss reasons why artists and thinkers of the late eighteenth and early nineteenth century might have viewed civilization as corrupting.

Students with Disabilities

Provide students with printouts or art books showing paintings from the Romantic period by painters such as Caspar David Friedrich, Camille Corot, J.M.W. Turner, Eugène Delacroix, and William Blake. Ask students to discuss elements of Romanticism they can trace in the paintings.

Analyzing Visuals

Reading Standard 3.7b (see pages A48–A50)

Connecting to Romanticism

Themes of Romantic poetry in the eighteenth and nineteenth centuries include the imagination, the inspiration of nature, and the questioning of tradition. This modern painting by Norman Adams shares some of those themes.

Guidelines

Use these guidelines to consider how this modern painting reflects some of the themes of Romantic poetry.

- Romantic poetry often focuses on the power of the imagination. In what way does this painting reflect a similar focus?
- How can nature be seen as an inspiration in this painting?
- In what ways does this painting question tradition?

Rainbow Painting (I) (1966) by Norman Adams (1927–2005). Oil on canvas. Tate, London. Presented by the Trustees of the Chantrey Bequest, 1969.

1. Why do you think the artist chose this color for the background? What might the background represent?
2. What might the shape of the rainbow express about the artist's view of nature?
3. How does this painting represent a nontraditional view of nature?

Your Turn Analyze Romantic Themes

Look through this book, and choose an image from any historical period. Discuss with a partner what themes the image has in common with themes of Romantic poetry.

Standards Focus

Objectives

Students will look for themes of Romantic poetry in a painting.

Analyzing Visuals Transparencies, Unit 4

Teacher One Stop™, lesson plan and all print resources

Direct Teach

Connect to the Literary Skill

Tell students that Romantic painters, not unlike Romantic poets, explored the mysterious aspects of nature.

Work with students to answer the guided questions.

Possible responses:

1. *The color red might symbolize life, while the darker colors at the bottom could represent death.*
2. *The circular shape of the rainbow suggests nature's cycles of life and death.*
3. *The painting goes against traditional views because of its abstract representation of nature.*

Check for Understanding

Your Turn

Alternative Listening and Speaking Assignment

Have students find a modern painting online and point out characteristics which give it a Romantic quality.

California Standards, p. 719

- **Reading Standard 3.7** Analyze recognized works of world literature from a variety of authors. **b.** Relate the literary works and authors to the major themes and issues of their eras.

Universal Access

Students with Disabilities

Have students illustrate their own nontraditional, abstract view of nature. Suggest that they use a dominant image in their illustration, such as a tree, the sky, or the moon. Tell them to use creative colors and blurry lines rather than clearly defined lines to evoke the imagination of the viewer. After students have finished, have other students find Romantic characteristics in their classmates' illustrations.

Standards Focus

Objectives

Students will

- understand dialect
- paraphrase for comprehension

Selection Introduction

Think About the Writer

Have students discuss whether their favorite films and stories feature ordinary people or individuals who are in some way extraordinary.

For Independent Reading

- *Of Mice and Men*, John Steinbeck
- "The Road Not Taken," Robert Frost

Motivate

What Do You Think?/QuickTalk

Use the QuickTalk to have students explore how and why writers use animals to explore human experience.

English for Academic Success

Academic Vocabulary

Look for opportunities to use the Academic Vocabulary words in this unit.

- **function, *n.*:** the action for which a person or thing is specially fitted; purpose
- **technique, *n.*:** method, way of using skills

California Standards, pp. 720–727

- **Reading Standard 2.2** Analyze the way in which clarity of meaning is affected by the patterns of organization, hierarchical structures, repetition of the main idea, syntax, and word choice in the text.
- **Reading Standard 3.3** Analyze the way in which irony, tone, mood, the author's style, and the "sound" of language achieve specific rhetorical or aesthetic purposes or both.

Preparing to Read

To a Mouse
To a Louse

What Do You Think? How can we use imagination to discover truth?

QuickTalk

What fables, songs, stories, and poems do you know in which humans learn a wise lesson from animals? With a partner, list these stories and share what you recall about each story's lesson.

MEET THE WRITER

Robert Burns
(1759–1796)

Hardworking farmer Robert Burns gained literary fame as a poet of the ordinary people. Hailed as the national poet of Scotland, Burns used the people's own way of speaking to celebrate their lives.

The Humble Plowman

Despite long hours of toil on his family's farm, Burns found time to study, often propping a book up on the table to read during meals. His father encouraged him in his studies, and his mother taught him old Scottish songs and stories, many of which he later turned into poems.

An acquaintance noted that Burns liked to pass himself off as an "illiterate ploughman who wrote from pure inspiration," when, in fact, he could write perfectly well in standard formal English. In his writing, Burns employed heavy Scottish dialect as well as combinations of folk idioms and literary language. His talent with dialects allowed him to assume the persona of the humble plowman while achieving great feats.

Symbol of Scottish Literature

Burns was catapulted to fame with the 1786 publication of *Poems, Chiefly in the Scottish Dialect*. The immediate popularity of this collection—the first edition sold out in a month—took Burns from his rural town of Ayrshire in southwestern Scotland to urban Edinburgh, where he became a celebrity.

After his first collection was published, Burns wrote relatively few new poems and instead collected, adapted, and wrote more than three hundred songs, including "Auld Lang Syne." He helped preserve Scotland's poetic heritage and established his reputation as an accomplished lyricist. Only ten years after the success of the 1786 *Poems*, Burns died of heart disease. His reputation continued to grow, however, and by the early nineteenth century, he was well on the way to becoming the single most important poet of Scottish literature.

Think About the Writer Burns wrote about everyday people doing everyday things. What do you think attracted him to these topics?

Robert Burns (1759–1796) by Alexander Nasmyth (1758–1840). Scottish National Portrait Gallery, Edinburgh, Scotland.

Selection Readability	
Easily Accessible Accessible **Challenging**	These selections include poetic language; use of dialect.

Reading Standard 2.2, 3.3 (see pages A48–A50)

Literary Skills Focus

Dialect When you watch a movie or television show, or listen to a radio broadcast, you may notice differences in the way people from various places speak. What you hear when you note the unique speech of people from New York, London, Dallas, or Chicago is **dialect,** speech that is characteristic of a particular region or group of people. Dialects of a language may have a distinct vocabulary, pronunciation system, and grammar. Writers who use dialect are often praised for their ability to capture the true expressions of everyday people. For his celebration of Scottish dialects, Robert Burns earned the love and respect of other Scots.

Reading Skills Focus

Paraphrasing When you **paraphrase** text, you restate its meaning in your own words. Paraphrasing is an important step in mastering new knowledge and information. Paraphrasing can be a particularly helpful technique when you read something written in an unfamiliar dialect.

Into Action As you read each stanza of the poems, ask yourself, "How might I express the same idea?" Use a chart like the one below to paraphrase each poem, stanza by stanza.

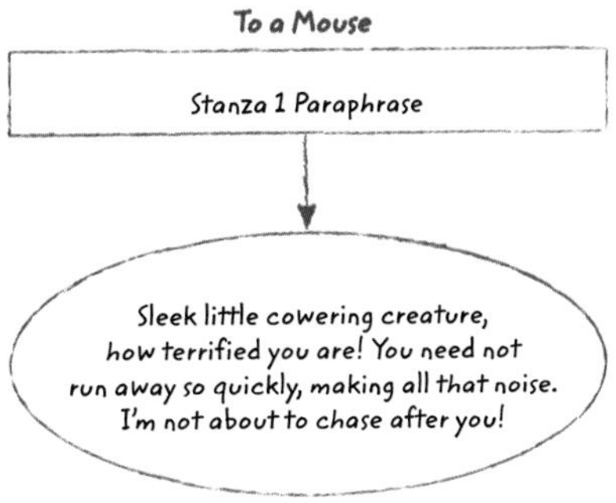

Writing Skills Focus

Think as a Reader/Writer

Find It in Your Reading Burns uses **apostrophe,** a device in which a speaker directly addresses an absent person or thing as if it could respond. Record uses of apostrophe in your *Reader/Writer Notebook.*

Reader/Writer Notebook

Use your **RWN** to complete the activities for these selections.

Language Coach

Homonyms Words that sound alike but have different spellings and meanings are called **homonyms.** The adjective *wee,* which means "small," should not be confused with the pronoun *we.* Can you explain the different meanings of these homonyms?

bare, bear
forward, foreword
poor, pour
airs, heirs

Read on to find out which word in each group Burns uses in one of the two poems.

Learn It Online

Listen to the dialect in these poems through the audio versions online.

go.hrw.com H12-721 Go

Preteach

English for Academic Success

Language Coach

After students read the **Language Coach,** have them brainstorm a list of English homonyms that people commonly mix up when writing. [*accept/except, affect/effect, allusion/illusion, principle/principal*]

Literary Skills Focus

As students read and discuss the poem, have them note instances of dialectal language and syntax.

Reading Skills Focus

Give students a copy of the Reading Skills Focus graphic organizer before they read. (See **Unit 4 Resources.**) Tell them to use their responses to answer the questions on the Applying Your Skills page.

Writing Skills Focus

As they read, have students record examples of apostrophe in their **Reader Writer Notebooks.** Students can use their notes to complete the Writing Skills Focus activity.

Selection Resources

Unit 4 Resources, on-level practice and assessment, p. 7

Teacher One Stop™, on-level lesson plans and all print resources

Holt Audio Library

Holt Audio Library: Selections and Summaries in Spanish

UA: Differentiating Instruction, graphic organizer, p. 164

UA: Supporting Instruction in Spanish, selection summary

ThinkCentral Online Assessment, Selection Standards Check

ThinkCentral Online Remediation

Learn It Online

The online version of this poem includes audio support to engage all students and to help struggling readers with reading comprehension and vocabulary.

go.hrw.com H12-721 Go

Teacher Preparation

Selection Summary

The speaker, a farmer who has turned up a mouse's nest with his plow, pities the creature and sympathizes with its humble ways and desperate situation. He compares his own lot in life with that of the mouse and considers the mouse more fortunate, because the mouse worries only about the present, while the farmer regrets the past and fears the future.

Direct Teach

Think About/Talk About

Read with a Purpose Have students read the Read with a Purpose statement. Ask them to predict what the speaker will feel after realizing he has accidentally harmed a living creature.

Comprehension

B Reading Focus

Possible responses: *"I am sorry human power has upset the balance of nature and caused in you a mistaken fear of me—a fellow creature of the world and fellow mortal." Human power interferes with natural order and can harm other creatures.*

Analysis

A Literary Focus

Possible responses: *It is a small and timid animal.* Sleeket *sounds like* sleek, *and* cowran *sounds like* cowering, *which means "shrinking in fear."*

Extend the Discussion

Evaluating How do lines 7–8 display a typical Romantic concern?

Possible response: *The speaker worries that humanity and nature are at odds, as humanity has disturbed or is destroying the balance of nature.*

POEM

To a Mouse

by **Robert Burns**

Read with a Purpose

Read to discover the speaker's feelings about accidentally destroying another living creature's home.

Build Background

Burns was a man of tremendous physical strength, as well as of great intellect, as this quotation by Allan Cunningham suggests: "I saw him one evening match himself with a number of masons; and out of five-and-twenty practised hands, the most vigorous young men in the parish, there was only one that could lift the same weight as Burns." Despite his own physical prowess, Burns understood and sympathized with the vulnerabilities of the smallest creatures. In this poem, the speaker addresses a mouse whose nest he has uncovered with his plow.

On Turning Her Up in Her Nest, with the Plow, November, 1785.

Wee, sleeket,° cowran, tim'rous beastie, **A**
O, what a panic's in thy breastie!
Thou need na start awa sae hasty,
Wi' bickering brattle!°
I wad be laith° to rin an' chase thee,
Wi' murd'ring pattle!°

I'm truly sorry man's dominion
Has broken Nature's social union,
An' justifies that ill opinion,
Which makes thee startle
At me, thy poor, earth-born companion,
An' fellow mortal! **B**

I doubt na, whyles,° but thou may thieve;
What then? poor beastie, thou maun° live!
A daimen-icker in a thrave°
'S a sma request:
I'll get a blessin wi' the lave,°
An' never miss 't!

1\. **sleeket:** sleek.
4\. **bickering brattle:** rattling sounds.
5\. **laith:** loath; unwilling.
6\. **pattle:** plow staff.
13\. **whyles:** sometimes.
14\. **maun:** must.
15\. **daimen-icker in a thrave:** occasional ear of grain out of a bundle.
17\. **lave:** remainder.

A Literary Focus Dialect What kind of creature is described in the first line? Which words used in this description sound like words we use today?

B Reading Focus Paraphrasing Paraphrase lines 7–12. What conflict exists between "man's dominion" and "Nature's social union"?

Universal Access

EL English Learners

English for Academic Success Help students understand the dialect used by Burns by providing them with the following additional glosses: *tim'rous* (timorous, fearful); *panic's* (panic is); *breastie* (breast); *na* (not); *sae* (so); *wad* (would); *rin* (run); *an'* (and); *wi'* (with); *'s a sma* (is a small); *housie* (house); *win's* (winds); *naething* (nothing); *ane* (one); *o'* (of); *baith* (both); *monie* (many); a' (all); *cauld* (cold); *e'e* (eye).

Struggling Readers

Strategic Students Assist students in paraphrasing the first stanza by having them fill in the blanks for the following incomplete paraphrase:

Oh small, __________ creature, how __________ you are! You don't have to __________, making __________ sounds! I would never __________ with a __________.

Thy wee-bit housie, too, in ruin!
It's silly wa's° the win's are strewin!
An' naething, now, to big° a new ane,
O' foggage° green!
An' bleak December's winds ensuin,
Baith snell° an' keen!

Thou saw the fields laid bare an' wast,
An' weary winter comin fast,
An' cozie here, beneath the blast,
Thou thought to dwell,
Till crash! the cruel coulter° past
Out thro' thy cell.

That wee-bit heap o' leaves an' stibble, **C**
Has cost thee monie a weary nibble!
Now thou's turn'd out, for a' thy trouble,
But° house or hald,°
To thole° the winter's sleety dribble,
An' cranreuch° cauld!

But Mousie, thou art no thy-lane,°
In proving foresight may be vain:
The best laid schemes o' mice an' men
Gang aft agley,°
An' lea'e us nought but grief an' pain,
For promis'd joy!

Still, thou art blest, compar'd wi' me!
The present only toucheth thee:
But och! I backward cast my e'e,
On prospects drear!
An' forward, tho' I canna see,
I guess an' fear! **D**

20. silly wa's: feeble walls.
21. big: build.
22. foggage: moss.
24. snell: bitter.
29. coulter: plow blade.
34. but: without. **hald:** land.
35. thole: endure.
36. cranreuch: frost.
37. no thy-lane: not alone.
40. gang aft agley: often go amiss.

Dormouse (1996) by James Lynch. Tempera on panel. The Maas Gallery, London, U.K.

C Literary Focus Dialect What is the effect of the repetition of *wee* and *wee-bit* in lines 1, 19, and 31?

D Reading Focus Paraphrasing First, put lines 45–48 into normal word order. Then, restate them in your own words. How are these lines a fitting conclusion to the poem?

Think About/Talk About

Comprehension

D Reading Focus

Possible response: *In normal word order, "backward" would come after "cast my e'e." The lines can be paraphrased as "Oh! I look back to sad events of the past and then I look at the future, although I don't know it, and worry about what may happen." The speaker's reflection on his past and future serves as an appropriate ending by contrasting his state with the mouse's preoccupation with the present.*

Analysis

C Literary Focus

Possible response: *The repeated use of* wee *emphasizes the smallness of the mouse.* Wee *also connotes something that is endearingly cute and tiny; therefore, this word colors the readers' perceptions of the speaker and his relationship with the mouse.*

Extend the Discussion

Comparing and Contrasting How would the poem be different if the Scottish dialect were replaced with modern English words? ***Possible responses:*** *It would be easier to read. The poem would lose some of its colloquial flavor and individuality. The reader would be less likely to want to read the poem aloud or hear it read. It would lose its lilt.*

Interpreting "The best laid schemes o' mice an' men / Gang aft agley" (lines 39–40) has become a common saying. How does the pairing of mice and men reinforce the meaning of these lines? ***Possible response:*** *It emphasizes the relative smallness of human beings and their desires in the broader scheme of the world. By equating mice and men, the line also emphasizes that, whether creatures are small or large, their plans are likely to go astray.*

Advanced Learners

Acceleration Remind students that Burns differs from most eighteenth-century poets in his use of dialect. Ask them to brainstorm a brief list of dialects used in drama, songs, films, and fiction today. Then, have them discuss how they feel about the use of dialect to convey realism.

Students with Disabilities

Have students listen to the poem in audio format in **Holt Audio Library.** Pause after every stanza or two and paraphrase for students the content of the poem. Ask students if they can recognize words from the Scottish dialect used by Burns. Finally, have them discuss for five to ten minutes the reason Burns wrote a poem in his own dialect instead of using standard English.

Teacher Preparation

Selection Summary

The speaker of "To a Louse" is an admirer of Jenny, the woman seated in front of him at church. Outraged by the sight of a louse (singular form of lice) on her bonnet, he thinks of places the louse would be better suited, such as on the skin of a homeless man or a poor boy. The speaker silently wishes Jenny will not shake her head, dispersing the louse. At the end of the poem, the speaker realizes that it would be a good thing if we could all see ourselves the way others do; we would be more humble and less foolish if we did.

Direct Teach

Think About/Talk About

Read with a Purpose Have students read the Read with a Purpose statement. Ask students to notice evidence in the poem that shows the speaker's appreciation for the louse.

Comprehension

B Reading Focus

Possible response: *The speaker wants the louse to move to a beggar's head "where combs will never dare disturb your large population."*

Analysis

A Literary Focus

Possible responses: *Words in Scottish dialect in this stanza include* blastit, wonner, saunt, fit, sae, *and* gae. *The words in dialect create a familiar, folksy tone.*

POEM

To a Louse

by **Robert Burns**

Read with a Purpose
Read to discover what the speaker appreciates about a creature that most people view with disgust.

Build Background
In "To a Louse," the speaker addresses a louse that is crawling across a lady's expensive bonnet. The speaker initially seems to be filled with indignation at the sight of the pest, but by the end of the poem, his true feelings are revealed.

On Seeing One on a Lady's Bonnet at Church.

Ha! wh'are ye gaun, ye crowlin' ferlie!°
Your impudence protects you sairly:°
I canna say but ye strunt° rarely,
    Owre gauze and lace;
Tho' faith! I fear ye dine but sparely
    On sic a place.

Ye ugly, creepin', blastit wonner,°
Detested, shunn'd by saunt an' sinner!
How dare ye set your fit° upon her,
    Sae fine a lady?
Gae somewhere else, and seek your dinner
    On some poor body. A

Swith, in some beggar's haffet squattle;°
There ye may creep, and sprawl, and sprattle°
Wi' ither kindred jumping cattle,
    In shoals and nations;
Where horn nor bane° ne'er dare unsettle
    Your thick plantations. B

1. **crowlin' ferlie:** crawling wonder.
2. **sairly:** greatly; sorely.
3. **strunt:** strut.
7. **blastit wonner:** blasted wonder.
9. **fit:** foot.
13. **Swith . . . squattle:** Off! Sprawl in some beggar's temple.
14. **sprattle:** scramble; struggle.
17. **horn nor bane** (bone): materials used to make combs.

A **Literary Focus** **Dialect** What words in this stanza are examples of Burns's Scottish dialect? What tone, or attitude toward his subject, does he create with these words?

B **Reading Focus** **Paraphrasing** Paraphrase lines 17 and 18. Where does the speaker want the louse to go?

Universal Access

Struggling Readers
As students read the poem, explain that the speaker conveys tone, or his attitude toward a subject, through his word choice. Point out that in the first stanza, the speaker calls the subject "ugly," "blasted," and "shunned" by all. Line 9 starts out with the speaker challenging the subject's right to be on the fine lady ("How dare ye"). In line 11, the speaker gives the subject a command, conveying his contempt for the subject.

Developing Oral Fluency

Whole-Class Activity Have students read "To a Mouse" and "To a Louse" aloud. Although they may find the dialect and syntax difficult, ask them to read as naturally as they can. After they have finished, discuss how it would feel to talk like this all the time.

✔ See the **Oral Language Skill Builder** in **UA: Differentiating Instruction.**

Analyzing Visuals

Connecting to the Text Notice how carefully the women are dressed for church. Why might a louse cause particular disgust in this setting? What might a louse's presence indicate about the women's efforts to look dignified?

The Chapel of the Château de Versailles (1917–1919) by Edouard Vuillard (1868–1940). Wallpaper mounted on canvas.
Musée d'Orsay, Paris, France. Artists Rights Society (ARS), NY/ADAGP, Paris..

Now haud ye there,° ye're out o' sight,
Below the fatt'rels,° snug an' tight;
Na, faith ye yet! ye'll no be right
　　Till ye've got on it,
The very tapmost tow'ring height
　　O' Miss's bonnet.

My sooth! right bauld° ye set your nose out,
As plump and gray as onie grozet;°
O for some rank mercurial rozet,°
　　Or fell red smeddum!°
I'd gie you sic a hearty doze o't,
　　Wad dress your droddum!° **C**

19. haud ye there: stay where you are.
20. fatt'rels: ribbon ends.
25. bauld: bold.
26. onie grozet: any gooseberry.
27. rozet: rosin, a substance derived from the resin given off by pine trees and used to make soap, varnish, and other products.
28. fell red smeddum: deadly red powder.
30. wad dress your droddum: would put an end to you.

C **Literary Focus** **Dialect** In this stanza, the speaker threatens the louse. How does the speaker's word choice make the tone comical rather than threatening?

Universal Access

Advanced Learners

Acceleration Have students work in small groups to compose a short response from the perspective of the louse that is addressed in this poem. Challenge them to use the Scottish dialect Burns uses. After students have finished, have one person from each group present their poem to the class.

Students with Disabilities

Have students communicate their understanding of the poem verbally by responding to the following questions:

- What is the setting of the poem?
- Why is the speaker upset?
- What does the speaker threaten to do?

✔ See **UA: Differentiating Instruction** for a graphic organizer to scaffold instruction for students with disabilities.

Think About/Talk About

Analysis

C Literary Focus

Possible response: *The speaker's colorful language makes the tone comical.*

? Extend the Discussion

Summarizing How can lines 19–30 be summarized? ***Possible response:*** *The louse disappears under the ribbon ends and seems to be heading toward the top of the bonnet. Then, the louse reappears and enrages the speaker even more.*

Tone What is the speaker's tone in "To a Louse"? How does it differ from the speaker's tone in "To a Mouse"? ***Possible responses:*** *The speaker's tone is one of outrage that changes to humility. The speaker in "To a Mouse" has a sad and regretful tone.*

Analyzing Visuals

Connecting to the Text: *A louse would cause disgust in a church because in this setting people are usually expected to display their best conduct and dress. The louse's presence indicates that the women's efforts to look respectful were poor.*

Think About/Talk About

Comprehension

D Reading Focus

Possible responses: *"Jenny, do not shake your head and let your hair fly; you do not know how fast the louse can move." The speaker stops scolding the louse for its social pretensions and starts worrying about Jenny's dignity, fearful that people are laughing at her because of the louse. He advises Jenny not to toss her head so that the louse will not be noticeable.*

Extend the Discussion

Recognizing Rhetorical Devices

How does the addressee of Burns's apostrophe change over the course of the poem? ***Possible response:*** *At first, the speaker scolds the louse for crawling on Jenny's bonnet, but then the focus shifts. The speaker worriedly realizes that Jenny's own place in the pecking order is far from secure. Finally, the speaker broadens the focus to include his readers, suggesting that most of us are foolishly vain and we would better understand our true place in the world if we could see ourselves as others see us.*

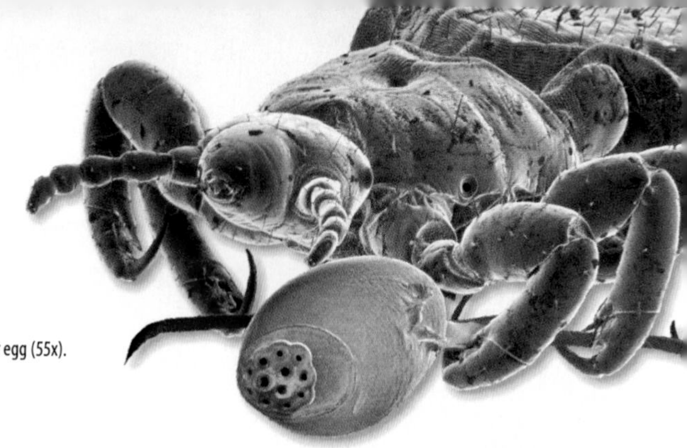

Head louse (*Pediculus humanus capitis*) with hair egg (55x).

I wad na been surpris'd to spy
You on an auld wife's flannen toy;°
Or aiblins° some bit duddie° boy,
On's wyliecoat;°
But Miss's fine Lunardi!° fie,
How daur ye do't?

O Jenny, dinna toss your head,
An' set your beauties a' abread!°
Ye little ken what cursèd speed
The blastie's makin'! D
Thae winks and finger-ends,° I dread,
Are notice takin'!

O wad some Pow'r the giftie gie us
To see oursels as others see us!
It wad frae mony a blunder free us,
And foolish notion:
What airs in dress an' gait wad leae us,
And ev'n devotion!°

32. flannen toy: flannel head-dress.
33. aiblins: perhaps.
bit duddie: small ragged.
34. wyliecoat: undershirt.
35. Lunardi: a kind of bonnet, probably with winglike ribbons, named for a balloonist of the day.
38. abread: abroad.

41. thae winks and finger-ends: those people winking and pointing.

47–48. airs in . . . devotion: false piety.

D Reading Focus Paraphrase Paraphrase lines 37–40. How has the speaker's attitude changed from what we've seen in previous stanzas? Why does he advise Jenny "dinna toss your head"?

California Standards p. 727

- **Reading Standard 2.2** Analyze the way in which clarity of meaning is affected by the patterns of organization, hierarchical structures, repetition of the main idea, syntax, and word choice in the text.
- **Reading Standard 3.3** Analyze the way in which irony, tone, mood, the author's style, and the "sound" of language achieve specific rhetorical or aesthetic purposes or both.
- **Reading Standard 3.4** Analyze ways in which poets use imagery, personification, figures of speech, and sounds to evoke readers' emotions.
- **Writing Standard 2.1** Write fictional, autobiographical, or biographical narratives: **a.** Narrate a sequence of events and communicate their significance to the audience.

Applying Your Skills

Reading Standard 2.2, 3.3, 3.4 (see pages A48–A50)
Writing Standard 2.1a (see pages A51–A52)

To a Mouse / To a Louse

Literary Response and Analysis

Reading Skills Focus

Quick Check

1. How does the speaker in "To a Mouse" feel about overturning the mouse's winter nest?
2. Why is the speaker in "To a Louse" surprised to see the louse on "sae fine a lady"?
3. Which of the louse's characteristics does the speaker mock? Which of the mouse's characteristics does the speaker praise?

Read with a Purpose

4. In "To a Mouse" and "To a Louse," the speaker addresses two creatures that most people notice with disgust or alarm. Why and how does he come to appreciate these creatures?

Reading Skills: Paraphrasing

5. Now that you have finished reading and paraphrasing the poems, re-read your paraphrases to decide what lesson each small creature conveys to the poems' speakers. Briefly explain these lessons in a paragraph, citing information from your charts to support your opinion.

Literary Skills Focus

Literary Analysis

6. **Evaluate** What lines from "To a Mouse" indicate the speaker's understanding of the relationship between mice and farmers?
7. **Interpret** What comparison between himself and the mouse does the speaker make in the last two stanzas of "To a Mouse"?
8. **Analyze** How would you describe Burns's tone in the beginning of "To a Louse"?
9. **Make Judgments** According to Burns, why would the louse's presence on a "flannen toy" (line 32) or a "bit duddie boy" (line 33) be more appropriate?
10. **Evaluate** What is Burns's underlying **theme,** or insight into life, in "To a Louse"? Is his main focus the louse or the lady? Explain.

Literary Skills: Dialect

11. **Analyze** How does Burns use dialect in these poems to convey strong emotions and to create memorable images?

Literary Skills Review: Speaker

12. **Make Judgments** The **speaker** is the imaginary voice assumed by the author of a poem. What does the speaker's response to plowing over a mouse's nest reveal about him?

Writing Skills Focus

Think as a Reader/Writer

Use It in Your Writing Choose one of the stories you listed during the QuickTalk activity. In your *Reader/Writer Notebook,* write the story, using apostrophe. Use everyday language just as Burns does to communicate important events and observations.

What Do You Think Now? How does Burns use his imagination to learn about life from even the smallest creatures?

Check for Understanding

Independent Practice

Reading Skills Focus

Possible responses:

1. *He feels sad and apologetic.*
2. *Lice are usually a sign of poverty and lack of hygiene.*
3. *The speaker of "To a Louse" mocks the insect's foolish boldness. The speaker of "To a Mouse" praises the creature's hard work.*
4. *The speaker appreciates the creatures because he learns something about his own condition.*
5. *A successful paragraph will utilize information the student has recorded in the graphic organizer.*

Literary Skills Focus

Possible responses:

6. *The speaker understands that farmers view mice as pests because they steal grain; however, he views the theft as justifiable.*
7. *Although the mouse feels panic at the loss of its home, it stays focused on the present, while humans contend with the past.*
8. *The tone is enraged and offended.*
9. *The unattractive, creeping (line 7) and crawling nature (line 1) of the louse makes its presence more fitting on a ragged boy.*
10. *The theme is that we would all be more humble if we could see ourselves as others do. The speaker's focus is on the louse.*
11. *In "To a Mouse," the speaker's use of diminutives expresses his sympathy. In "To a Louse," the speaker's rough language emphasizes his outrage . The language makes the images memorable.*
12. *It reveals his compassion, humility, and respect for all creatures.*

What Do You Think Now?

To help students respond to the question, ask them what they think the speaker of "To a Mouse" (or the speaker of "To a Louse") learns as a result of his encounter with another creature.

Universal Access

Struggling Writers

Some students may need additional scaffolding to complete the Writing Skills Focus activity. After students have chosen a story idea, have them construct a web diagram on the characteristics of each animal, including both positive and negative traits. Tell students to refer to their diagram as they write their story. Remind them to use ordinary language while making important observations.

Assess

Unit 4 Resources,
Selection Standards Check, p. 9

go.hrw.com **ThinkCentral Online Assessment,**
Selection Standards Check

Teacher One Stop™,
editable Selection Standards Check

Standards Focus

Objectives

Students will
- understand symbols
- use context clues

Selection Introduction

Think About the Writer

Ask students how an author's experiences might affect his or her perceptions. How would they expect poetry written by a blind person to compare with poetry written by a visual artist?

For Independent Reading

- "Life Doesn't Frighten Me," Maya Angelou
- *The Personal History of David Copperfield,* Charles Dickens

Motivate

What Do You Think?/QuickWrite

Tell students to write about suffering they have observed, such as a tragic accident. Then, have them discuss how people feel when they see injustice or misfortune.

English for Academic Success

Academic Vocabulary

Look for opportunities to use the Academic Vocabulary words in this unit.

- **function, *n.*:** the action for which a person or thing is specially fitted
- **inherent, *adj.*:** existing in something as a fixed, essential quality
- **technique, *n.*:** method, way of using skills

California Standards, pp. 728–736

- **Reading Standard 2.2** Analyze the way in which clarity of meaning is affected by the patterns of organization, hierarchical structures, repetition of the main idea, syntax, and word choice in the text.
- **Grades 9–10 Review Reading Standard 3.7** Recognize and understand the significance of various literary devices, including figurative language, imagery, allegory, and symbolism, and explain their appeal.

Preparing to Read

The Tyger

The Lamb

The Chimney Sweeper *from* Songs of Innocence

The Chimney Sweeper *from* Songs of Experience

A Poison Tree

What Do You Think? How can we use imagination to discover truth?

QuickWrite

What are some problems or issues you observe in today's society that really trouble you? Make quick notes about them in your *Reader/Writer Notebook.*

MEET THE WRITER

William Blake

(1757–1827)

Known today as much for his unique artwork as for his poetry, William Blake lived in poverty and never sought fame.

An Accomplished Artist

Compared to Coleridge, Shelley, and Keats, Blake did not live a particularly "romantic" or "poetic" life. By many accounts, he was happily married to the same woman for much of his life, never traveled, and lived outside London for only three years (1800–1803). At age ten, Blake began his artistic training when his father, a London shopkeeper, sent him to one of the best drawing schools. Apprenticed to an engraver when he was fourteen, Blake worked steadily at his craft as an engraver and an artist throughout his long life.

During his lifetime, Blake's work received little attention, and a great deal of his poetry was never published. Often when his work was noticed, readers and viewers concluded that it (and therefore Blake) was weird, confused, or insane. What we know of Blake from his vibrant and energetic poetry and artwork is that he was a great artist in the fullest sense.

"The Author of His Own Book"

The history of Blake the poet cannot be separated from that of Blake the visual artist. Not only did he provide illustrations for most of his poems, but he also printed much of his poetry himself, using engraving techniques he had created. One biographer writes that "the poet and his wife did everything in making the book [*Songs of Innocence* (1789)]—writing, designing, printing, engraving—everything except manufacturing the paper; the very ink, or color rather, they did make. Never before surely was a man so literally the author of his own book."

Much of what Blake wrote in addition to his poetry is cryptic and benefits from his illuminating art. However, one characteristic of the man himself clearly shines through even his most enigmatic writing: the optimism sustained by his continuous joy in the "one continued vision" of his art.

Think About the Writer How do you think Blake's background in the visual arts might have helped him see things with a unique perspective?

William Blake (1807) by Thomas Phillips. Oil on canvas. The Granger Collection, NY.

Selection Readability	
Easily Accessible **Accessible** Challenging	These poems include accessible subject matter; accessible vocabulary.

INTRODUCTION TO BLAKE'S POEMS

Innocence to Experience

William Blake first published *Songs of Innocence* in 1789. In 1794, that collection and *Songs of Experience* were issued together in one volume, whose title page promised a demonstration of "the two Contrary States of the Human Soul."

Analyzing Visuals

Viewing and Interpreting What do the details surrounding the portrait of Blake suggest about the role of the poet?

Stained glass window of William Blake, St. Mary's Church, Battersea, London

Innocence and Experience

Blake conceived the first of these states, "Innocence," as a state of genuine love and naive trust toward all humankind, accompanied by unquestioned belief in Christian doctrine. Though a firm believer in Christianity, Blake thought that its doctrines were being used by the English Church and other institutions as a form of social control to encourage among the people passive obedience and acceptance of oppression, poverty, and inequality. Recognition of this social agenda marks what Blake called the state of "Experience," a profound disillusionment with human nature and society. One entering the state of "Experience" sees cruelty and hypocrisy only too clearly but is unable to imagine a way out. In his later works, Blake expressed a third, higher state of consciousness that he called "Organized Innocence." In this state, one's sense of the divinity of humanity coexists with oppression and injustice, though one continues to recognize and actively oppose both of them.

Reading Blake

When you are reading *Songs of Innocence* and, to a lesser extent, *Songs of Experience*, it is important to remember that Blake did not intend them as simple expressions of religious faith. The poems are demonstrations of viewpoints that are necessarily limited or distorted by each narrator's or speaker's state of consciousness.

Think About/Talk About

Build Background: Blake's "Illuminated Painting"

Today, William Blake is known as much for his art as for his poetry. Using a technique he invented called "illuminated painting" (revealed to him, he claimed, by his dead brother in a vision), Blake engraved the text and illustrations of his books himself. He first printed each page in monochrome from an engraved plate of both text and illustration, produced by a type of relief etching. Then, with the help of his wife, he handcolored the prints with watercolor. Most of Blake's works were laboriously published in this way, ensuring that only a limited audience saw them during the artist's lifetime. Single-minded and unworldly, Blake did not seek fame; he and his wife lived in poverty and obscurity for much of their lives, aided by the generosity and dedication of a handful of friends, patrons, and collectors.

Analyzing Visuals

Connecting to the Text: *Stained glass is mostly used for religious themes, so the medium itself celebrates Blake's belief in the Christian doctrine. The poet's portrait is enclosed in a shrine and is placed above a stylized figure of a man reminiscent of Leonardo Da Vinci's study of man. This detail points to Blake's interest in human nature.*

Selection Resources

Unit 4 Resources, on-level practice and assessment, pp. 12, 13

PowerNotes, interactive lesson presentations with activities

Teacher One Stop™, on-level lesson plans and all print resources

Holt Audio Library

Holt Audio Library: Selections and Summaries in Spanish

UA: Holt Interactive Reader, pp. 201, 203

UA: Differentiating Instruction, modified lesson plans and leveled assessment, p. 165

UA: Supporting Instruction in Spanish, selection summary

UA: Resources for Teaching Advanced Students, lesson plans, p. 138

Analyzing Visuals Transparencies, p. 28

ThinkCentral Online Assessment, Selection Standards Check

ThinkCentral Online Remediation

Preteach

Introducing Vocabulary

To reinforce the importance of the Vocabulary words, tell students that Blake uses these words to portray awesome power. God has the power to *frame* life. He can *aspire* to create such wonders as the tiger. The *sinews* of the tiger's heart is evidence of the *dread* strength of his maker. As creator, God has the authority to *bid* his creatures to obey Him.

English for Academic Success

Language Coach

***Possible response*:** Bid *can also mean "to offer a price," "to invite," or "an attempt to reach some goal."* Have students find other meanings for *sinew*.

Literary Skills Focus

Tell students to note the figurative meaning of the tiger and the lamb.

Reading Skills Focus

Give students copies of the Reading Skills Focus graphic organizer. (**Unit 4 Resources.**) Tell them to use their responses to answer the questions on the Applying Your Skills page.

Writing Skills Focus

Have students record the speakers' rhetorical questions in their **Reader/Writer Notebooks**. Students can use their notes to complete the Writing Skills Focus activity.

Learn It Online

The **PowerNotes** presentation for this lesson includes a short video that introduces the poems. The video is also available on the online version of this page.

go.hrw.com H12-730 Go

Preparing to Read

Reading Standard 2.2 **Grades 9–10 Review Reading Standard** 3.7 (see pages A48–A50)

The Tyger / The Lamb

Literary Skills Focus

Symbol A **symbol** is something that stands for both itself and something more than itself. In literature, symbols have a literal meaning, as well as a figurative, or metaphorical, meaning, which involves feelings and experiences. As you read, look for clues to help you understand what the tiger and the lamb symbolize.

Reading Skills Focus

Using Context Clues Sometimes you can determine the meaning of an unfamiliar word by looking for **clues** in the **context,** or the surrounding words. When poets use words symbolically, context clues can help reveal the words' shades of meaning. As you read, use context clues to uncover the meanings of Blake's symbols.

Into Action Use a concept map to locate context clues to help you understand symbols. The map below is for "The Tyger." Create your own map for "The Lamb."

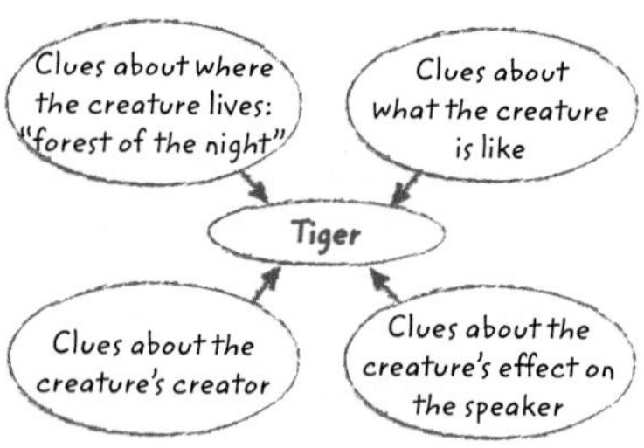

Writing Skills Focus

Think as a Reader/Writer

Find It in Your Reading The speaker in "The Lamb" asks, "Little Lamb, who made thee?" As you read, record the speakers' rhetorical questions.

TechFocus As you read, think about what modern objects in the material world could symbolize the same things as Blake's tiger and lamb.

Reader/Writer Notebook

Use your **RWN** to complete the activities for these selections.

Vocabulary

frame (fraym) *v.:* shape. *Blake's love and awe of nature frame his works of art.*

aspire (uh SPYR) *v.:* reach upward to a goal. *His illustrated poems aspire to an understanding of human nature*

sinews (SIHN yooz) *n. pl.:* powerful, tough connective tissues. *Can you see the strong sinews of the tiger in Blake's illustration?*

dread (drehd) *adj.:* inspiring fear and awe. *The dread face of the tiger terrifies some viewers.*

bid (bihd) *v.:* demanded; asked. *The boy in Blake's painting of the lamb bid the gentle creature to eat from his hand.*

Language Coach

Multiple-Meaning Words Many common words have more than one meaning. *Frame* can be a noun that names an underlying structure, the border around a painting, or the part of a pair of eyeglasses that holds the lenses. It can also be a verb that means "shape," "mount a picture in a frame," or "make an innocent person appear guilty." Clues in a sentence will help you figure out which meaning is being used. *Bid* can be a verb that means "command." What other meanings can this word have?

Learn It Online

Meet "The Tyger" and "The Lamb" through the introductory videos online.

go.hrw.com H12-730 Go

Universal Access

English Learners

Students might have trouble understanding the pronoun references in the poem. Help students paraphrase the poem, clarifying when the speaker is addressing the tiger and when he is asking questions about the tiger's creator. Have them create a table in which they list the characteristics of the tiger and that of its creator and then make inferences about the identity of each.

✔ See **UA: Differentiating Instruction** for strategies for teaching English learners.

Struggling Readers

Strategic Students Model using context clues in to understand what the tiger symbolizes. Read aloud lines 1–4. You might say: "I want to know what meanings the poet associates with the tiger. The first line reveals that the creature burns 'bright.' The tiger seems to represent some kind of power, so I'll note this in my graphic organizer. Line 2 reveals where the tiger is found: in the forests at night. Lines 3 and 4 suggest that some kind of immortal being created this beast. Its 'fearful symmetry' suggests a perfect beauty that fascinates the speaker."

POEM

The Tyger

from Songs of Experience

by **William Blake**

Read with a Purpose

Read to discover what the tiger reveals about the source and the nature of evil.

Build Background

Blake saw the entire material world as a set of signs or symbols representing religious or mystical realities. Any one of Blake's symbols—the "tyger," for instance—has such a rich array of meanings that we can never expect to understand fully what such a symbol meant to him. It is possible the tiger represents a strong revolutionary energy that can enlighten and transform society: a positive but volatile force Blake believed was operating in the French Revolution. Regardless, the poem's speaker cannot comprehend such a startling energy and can only wonder whether it is demonic or godlike.

Tyger! Tyger! burning bright
In the forests of the night,
What immortal hand or eye
Could frame thy fearful symmetry? **A**

In what distant deeps or skies
Burnt the fire of thine eyes?
On what wings dare he aspire?
What the hand dare seize the fire?

And what shoulder, and what art,
Could twist the sinews of thy heart?
And when thy heart began to beat,
What dread hand? and what dread feet?

What the hammer? what the chain?
In what furnace was thy brain?
What the anvil? what dread grasp
Dare its deadly terrors clasp?

When the stars threw down their spears,°
And watered heaven with their tears,
Did he smile his work to see?
Did he who made the Lamb make thee? **B**

Tyger! Tyger! burning bright
In the forests of the night,
What immortal hand or eye,
Dare frame thy fearful symmetry?

17. **stars . . . spears:** reference to the angels who fell with Satan and threw down their spears after losing the war in heaven.

A Reading Focus **Using Context Clues** Notice that Blake does not use the normal spelling of the word *tiger.* What clues can you find that hint at the tiger's extraordinary nature?

B Literary Focus **Symbol** Think about the qualities associated with a lamb. What might the speaker be implying by this question?

Vocabulary **frame** (fraym) *v.:* shape.
aspire (uh SPYR) *v.:* reach upward to a goal.
sinews (SIHN yooz) *n. pl.:* powerful, tough connective tissues.
dread (drehd) *adj.:* inspiring fear and awe.

Advanced Learners

Acceleration Tell students that Blake's biographer Peter Ackroyd has suggested that the tiger in Blake's illustration (p. 732) has a silly grin because it is amused at the critics who have produced "such a bewildering confusion of explanations" of this poem. Invite students to find two of these explanations and to discuss how they support or contradict one another.

✔ See **UA: Differentiating Instruction** for strategies for teaching advanced learners.

Students with Disabilities

Before students read the selection, help them understand symbols by reminding them that the American flag is a symbol of the United States. Spend five minutes brainstorming other symbols such as the bald eagle and the Statue of Liberty. Finally, have students list adjectives and phrases that describe the character of the two animals and help them make inferences about possible ideas that the animals may symbolize. [*The tiger may represent strength and aggressiveness; the lamb can represent innocence and defenselessness.*]

Teacher Preparation

Selection Summary

In a well-known apostrophe, the speaker in "The Tyger" asks the tiger what and how an immortal being, divine or demonic, could have created such a powerful and fearsome creature. Those questions remain unanswered.

Direct Teach

Think About/Talk About

Read with a Purpose As students read the poem, have them look for instances in which the tiger is described as an evil force.

Comprehension

A Reading Focus

Possible response: *In lines 5–6, the tiger's eyes are described as burning in "distant deeps or skies." In the rest of the poem, the speaker wonders what powerful and supernatural creature could have created such a remarkable animal.*

Analysis

B Literary Focus

Possible response: *"Did the lamb's creator create you as well?" Blake implies that the lamb, the symbol of Christ or simply of innocence, came from God; he wonders whether a creature as "fearful" and mysterious as the tiger could have the same source.*

Vocabulary: Own the Word

- **frame:** Have students answer the question asked in lines 3–4 using the word *frame.* ***Possible response:*** *God framed the tiger's symmetry.*
- **aspire:** Ask students what professional fields they *aspire* to enter.
- **sinews:** Have students construct a semantic web for the word *sinews* and add related attributes to the web.
- **dread:** Remind students that the word *dread* means "inspiring fear or awe." Ask students to exemplify a *dread* thing, such as a wildfire.

Teacher Preparation

Selection Summary

In "The Lamb," as in "The Tyger," the speaker asks who made the subject of the poem, but this time answers the question: Christ the Redeemer made the lamb. The speaker identifies himself as a child, linking his own innocence and that of the lamb to the innocence and purity of Christ.

Direct Teach

Think About/Talk About

Read with a Purpose Have students read the Read with a Purpose statement. Ask them to look for instances in which the lamb described in the poem displays purity and innocence.

Analyzing Visuals

Connecting to the Text: *Illustrations can be employed as an aesthetic background, but here they are definitely used as creative tools that complement and enhance the poem's themes. The illustration that accompanies "The Lamb," for example, represents a young shepherd with a herd of sheep. This reminds the reader of the Christian imagery of God as shepherd of souls and the lamb as a child of God. The illustration for "The Tyger" lacks human element and suggests a deeper connection with the human soul and its most secret passions.*

Above: *Songs of Innocence and of Experience: The Tyger* (ca. 1825) by William Blake. Relief etching printed in orange-brown ink and hand-colored with watercolor and gold. The Metropolitan Museum of Art, NY, Rogers Fund, 1917, 17.10.42.

Right: *Songs of Innocence and Experience Plate 7: The Lamb* (c. 1789–94) by William Blake. Relief etching finished in pen and watercolor. Fitzwilliam Museum, University of Cambridge, U.K.

Analyzing Visuals

Connecting to the Text Blake designed much of his artwork to accompany specific poems. What do you think is the function of an illustration? Is it merely background that aesthetically enhances writing, or does it play a larger role in the textual experience of reading a poem?

California Standards, pp. 734–736

- **Reading Standard 2.2** Analyze the way in which clarity of meaning is affected by the patterns of organization, hierarchical structures, repetition of the main idea, syntax, and word choice in the text.
- **Reading Standard 3.4** Analyze ways in which poets use imagery, personification, figures of speech, and sounds to evoke readers' emotions.
- **Grades 9–10 Review Reading Standard 1.2** Distinguish between the denotative and connotative meanings of words and interpret the connotative power of words.
- **Grades 9–10 Review Reading Standard 3.7** Recognize and understand the significance of various literary devices, including figurative language, imagery, allegory, and symbolism, and explain their appeal.
- **Writing Standard 2.2** Write responses to literature. **a.** Demonstrate a comprehensive understanding of the significant ideas in works or passages.
- **Literary and Speaking Standard 2.3** Deliver oral responses to literature: **d.** Demonstrate an awareness of the author's use of stylistic devices and an appreciation of the effects created.

Universal Access

Struggling Readers

Provide students with examples of Blake's engraving (you can use Blake's engravings for Dante's *Divine Comedy*), and ask students to mimic the artist's style to create an illustration for either "The Tyger" or "The Lamb." Challenge students to include their own symbols in their illustrations. Display students' illustrations in the classroom to reinforce the ideals of the Romantic period as you work through the rest of the chapter.

✔ Invite students to read the selection in interactive format in **UA: Holt Interactive Reader.**

POEM

The Lamb

from Songs of Innocence

by **William Blake**

Read with a Purpose

Read the poem to discover what the lamb reveals about innocence and purity.

Build Background

William Blake's poetry and art reflect his fascination with the Bible and his struggle to find answers to questions that profoundly disturbed him: What is the source of evil in the world? Why does God allow the innocent to suffer? Is evil inherent or can it be transformed or transcended?

One of the *Songs of Innocence,* this poem has often been read as a statement of Christian faith. However, we know that Blake's other writings show Christ not as the "meek" and "mild" lamb (the conventional symbolic rendering of Christ) with which this innocent speaker identifies but as an active fighter against injustice. The speaker's viewpoint is thus an incomplete representation of Blake's beliefs and just one aspect of Blake's worldview.

Little Lamb, who made thee?
Dost thou know who made thee?
Gave thee life, and bid thee feed
By the stream and o'er the mead,°
Gave thee clothing of delight,
Softest clothing, wooly, bright;
Gave thee such a tender voice,
Making all the vales° rejoice?
Little Lamb, who made thee?
Dost thou know who made thee?

Little Lamb, I'll tell thee,
Little Lamb, I'll tell thee:
He° is called by thy name,
For He calls himself a Lamb.
He is meek, and he is mild; Ⓐ
He became a little child.
I a child, and thou a lamb,
We are called by his name.
Little Lamb, God bless thee!
Little Lamb, God bless thee! Ⓑ

4. mead: meadow.
8. vales: valleys.
13. He: Christ.

Ⓐ **Reading Focus** **Using Context Clues** The word *He* is defined in the footnotes. What context clues in the poem help you confirm the definition given?

Ⓑ **Literary Focus** **Symbol** Where in the second stanza does Blake make explicit the Christian symbolism of his poem?

Vocabulary **bid** (bihd) *v.:* demanded; asked.

Cross-Curricular Connection

RELIGION: The Lamb as a Religious Symbol

The lamb is an important symbol in the Judeo-Christian tradition. The Bible compares humans to sheep watched over by God. The lamb also represents sacrifice. The Passover holiday commemorates the freeing of the Israelites (Exodus 12) from Egypt after God sent an angel to slay the firstborn sons of the Egyptians. The Israelites marked their doors with the blood of a lamb to signal the angel to "pass over" their homes. A sacrificial animal in many Middle Eastern religious rites, the lamb was adopted by early Christians as a symbol of Jesus' sacrifice, which redeems humanity. John 1:29 identifies Jesus as "the lamb of God"; in Revelation 14:1, the Redeemer is a triumphant lamb on Judgment Day.

Think About/Talk About

Comprehension

Ⓐ Reading Focus

Possible responses: *The speaker is answering his question ("Dost thou know who made thee?"), so* He *must refer to the creator of the lamb, that is, God. In lines 13–15,* He *is capitalized, following the Christian convention of capitalizing pronouns that refer to God.*

Analysis

Ⓑ Literary Focus

Possible response: *The symbolism is especially evident in lines 13–14, when the speaker notes that the creator of the lamb, God, "calls himself a Lamb."*

Extend the Discussion

Rereading What does the creator do for his creation in the first stanza of the poem? ***Possible response:*** *He gives the lamb life, food, clothing, and a gentle voice.*

Speculating Point out that Christ called himself a lamb because, like the Passover lamb slain to save the people of Israel, he sacrificed himself for the people. Ask students what they think this might imply about the fate of the young speaker of the poem. ***Possible response:*** *He may sacrifice himself for the good of others.*

Vocabulary: Own the Word

bid: Ask students these questions, "How much would you *bid* for an original painting by Van Gogh? Who might *bid* you to help them and how? How would you *bid* someone to come to your party? How do the meanings of *bid* differ in the preceding questions?"

Check for Understanding

Independent Practice

Reading Skills Focus

Possible responses:

1. *The speaker asks the tiger who its creator was; It is implied that the creator is either God or the devil.*
2. *The speaker says he is a child. One can infer that the speaker is naive.*
3. *If God created both the lamb and tiger, good and evil are essential elements of the human condition.*
4. *Have students support their explanations with clues from the text.*

Literary Skills Focus

Possible responses:

5. *The change suggests that creation is a dangerous act.*
6. *The speaker wonders in lines 4–8 whether God created the tiger. The imagery in lines 9–10 of twisting the animal's heart could suggest a demonic creator. The tools and furnace suggest a human creator.*
7. *the image of the tiger "burning bright"; "deadly terrors"*
8. *The speaker answers, naming God.*
9. *He gives the lamb life, food, clothing, and a gentle voice.*
10. *The speaker in "The Lamb" is an innocent child who accepts simple answers; the speaker in "The Tyger" is an adult with an awareness of the world's complexity.*
11. *There is something both magnificent and frightening about the tiger.*
12. *In "The Lamb," the lamb functions literally as a soft, wooly animal. The speaker's imaginative reflections about the lamb make it function as a symbol as well.*
13. *The repetition of a stanza ("The Tyger") or of an apostrophe ("The Lamb") creates a rhythmic cadence that resembles a song. Since both poems invoke God, implicitly or explicitly, the repetitions might want to mimic the rhythm of a religious chant.*

Applying Your Skills

Reading Standard 2.2, 3.4; **Grades 9–10 Review**
Reading Standard 3.7 (see pages A48–A50)
Writing Standard 2.2a (see pages A51–A52)

The Tyger / The Lamb

Literary Response and Analysis

Reading Skills Focus

Quick Check

1. What question does the speaker of "The Tyger" ask repeatedly? What answer is implied?
2. What are you told directly about the speaker of "The Lamb?" What inferences can you draw from this information?

Read with a Purpose

3. What do the tiger and the lamb tell us about the nature of good and evil?

Reading Skills: Using Context Clues

4. Review the concept maps in which you recorded context clues that help reveal the symbolic meaning of the tiger and the lamb. Write one paragraph in which you explain the symbolic meaning of the tiger, and another in which you explain the symbolic meaning of the lamb. Support your explanations with information from your concept maps.

Literary Skills Focus

Literary Analysis

5. **Interpret** The last stanza of "The Tyger" is almost identical to the first. What is the significance of the one word changed in the last stanza?
6. **Evaluate** Where in "The Tyger" does the speaker wonder if the tiger may have been created by God? What imagery tells us that the speaker also suspects that the tiger could be a demonic creation? List the images that suggest a human creator—like a blacksmith or a goldsmith.
7. **Draw Conclusions** What imagery suggests that the tiger could be a force of enlightenment? of revolutionary violence?
8. **Compare and Contrast** How does the second stanza of "The Lamb" respond to the questions asked in the first stanza?
9. **Analyze** What does the creator do for his creation in the first stanza of "The Lamb"?
10. **Evaluate** What differentiates the voice of the speaker in "The Tyger" from the voice of the speaker in "The Lamb"?

Literary Skills: Symbol

11. **Analyze** How does "The Tyger" represent people's attraction toward and repulsion from evil?
12. **Infer** In what ways is the lamb both a literal object and a symbol in "The Lamb"?

Literary Skills Review: Refrain

13. **Interpret** A **refrain** is a repeated word, phrase, line, or group of lines. Why might Blake use refrains as a technique in his poems? How do they affect each poem's meaning?

Writing Skills Focus

Think as a Reader/Writer

Use It in Your Writing In your *Reader/Writer Notebook,* write a paragraph in which you address a central question of "The Tyger": "Did he who made the Lamb make thee?" Include at least three thought-provoking rhetorical questions in your paragraph.

What Do You Think Now In a small group, discuss Blake's imaginative writing and if it is an effective way of exploring truth. How do symbols and images help us understand ideas?

Universal Access

Struggling Writers

Students may need additional scaffolding to complete the Writing Skills Focus activity. Have students re-read "The Tyger" and identify characteristics of the tiger about which the speaker wonders and questions. Why is the speaker so captivated by the tiger? Have students address these characteristics in their rhetorical questions.

What Do You Think Now?

To help students answer the question, have them consider Blake's use of symbolism and imagery in the two poems, their overall effect, and their relevance to exploring or discovering truth.

Grades 9–10 Review Reading Standard 1.2 (see pages A48–A50)

Vocabulary Development

Vocabulary Check

Match the Vocabulary words with their definitions.

1. frame	**a.** inspiring fear
2. aspire	**b.** connective tissues
3. sinews	**c.** strive for
4. dread	**d.** demand
5. bid	**e.** form

Vocabulary Skills: Denotation and Connotation

To comprehend a word fully, you must first understand its **denotation,** the literal meaning or dictionary definition. You must then also know a word's **connotations,** all the emotional ideas and feelings that people may ascribe to the word. For example, if you say to a friend, "Come on—have a heart!" you are not asking that friend to have an organ that pumps blood (its denotative meaning). Rather, you are asking your friend to be kind, to help you, and to show sympathy for you; you're using the word *heart* figuratively, based on its connotations of friendship, love, and kindness. Because connotations often elicit certain specific emotions, they can have powerful effects on a listener or reader. In poetry, structure often limits a poet's word choice. Every word must be denotatively and connotatively precise to convey a particular image and feeling.

Your Turn

Create a word map like the one on the right for each Vocabulary word. In the center, write the word and its denotative meaning. In the other ovals, list any connotative associations that you have for each word. Then, discuss in small groups how understanding both the denotations and connotations of these words helps you interpret Blake's poems.

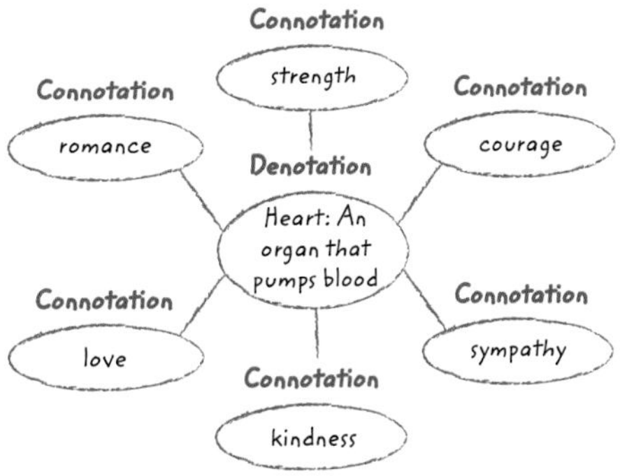

Language Coach

Multiple-Meaning Words When words have more than one meaning, context clues help you decide which meaning is being used. Choose the correct meaning of *frame* in these sentences.

1. The reproduction of Blake's poem is *framed* in antique wood.
2. Our reaction is *framed* by both the words and the illustration.
3. What was his *frame* of mind when he composed it?
4. A thief who stole a rare book tried to get away with it by *framing* the librarian.

Academic Vocabulary

Write About

What techniques does Blake use to differentiate between good and evil in "The Tyger" and "The Lamb"?

Learn It Online

Explore connotations online.

go.hrw.com H12-735 Go

Independent Practice

Vocabulary Development

Vocabulary Check

1. *e* **2.** *c*

3. *b* **4.** *a*

5. *d*

Your Turn

Possible responses:

1. *frame: order, clarity, simplicity*
2. *aspire: dream, ideal, faith*
3. *sinews: strength, agility, flexibility*
4. *dread: darkness, fear, awe*
5. *bid: submissiveness; compassion; kindness*

English for Academic Success

Language Coach

Tell students to substitute each meaning of *frame* into the sentence before choosing the correct definition. [*1. put in a frame; 2. constructed an idea; 3. state; 4. cause somebody to appear guilty*]

English for Academic Success

Academic Vocabulary

Possible response: *To differentiate between good and evil, Blake uses the technique of symbolism (the Lamb of God, or Christ) and repetition ("What dread hand? . . . and dread feet?" in line 12 of The Tyger). He also uses imagery ("the fire of thine eyes").*

Universal Access: Vocabulary Development

EL English Learners

English for Academic Success Have students work in pairs to create a word map for the two subjects of Blake's poems "The Tyger" and "The Lamb." Ask them to add descriptive words found in Blake's poems and, using a pen or pencil of a different color, their own descriptive words. For example, students might list such adjectives from "The Tyger" as *immortal, shining, nocturnal, deadly,* and *flawless,* while their own list might include *fierce, quiet,* and *bold.* When students have completed their assignment, discuss together the words and phrases they added to their word map. If there is time, have students rewrite the words in random order on a piece of paper to create a free-verse poem.

✔ See the **Academic and Selection Vocabulary Skill Builder** in **UA: Differentiating Instruction.**

Learn It Online

WordSharp: An Interactive Vocabulary Tutor provides additional support for vocabulary development. Multimedia tutorials show students how to apply vocabulary skills to unfamiliar words—and how to make those words their own.

go.hrw.com H12-735 Go

Independent Practice

Grammar Link

Your Turn

1. *were*
2. *gave*
3. *correct*

Choices: Evaluation Criteria

Review: Homework

Identify Sound Effects

- Students should demonstrate an understanding of alliteration and be able to identify examples in the poem.
- Students should articulate to a classmate how alliteration affects the meaning of the poem.

Connect: Homework

Create a Digital Collage

- Students' images should have a clear link to the poem.
- Students should be able to describe how their images visually express the ideas they read about in the poem.

Extend: Homework

Discuss the Work of Contemporary Visionaries

- Students should give specific examples of modern artists or works.
- Students should offer support for the opinions that they express.

Assess

Unit 4 Resources, Selection Standards Check, p. 16

go.hrw.com **ThinkCentral Online Assessment,** Selection Standards Check

Teacher One Stop™, editable Selection Standards Check

Reteach

go.hrw.com **ThinkCentral Online Remediation**

Applying Your Skills

Reading Standard 3.4; **Grades 9–10 Review Reading Standard** 3.7 (see pages A48–A50)
Listening and Speaking Standard 2.3d (see pages A53–A55)

The Tyger / The Lamb

Grammar Link

Verb-Tense Consistency

Verbs express actions or states of being, and a verb's **tense** indicates when that action or state of being occurs. Verb tenses that vary incorrectly can be confusing and awkward:

> It is not clear when William Blake writes "The Lamb," but he composed "The Tyger" in 1793.

To correct this sentence, make the verbs all past tense:

> It is not clear when William Blake **wrote** "The Lamb," but he **composed** "The Tyger" in 1793.

Different tenses can describe events at different times:

> These poems **make** me imagine what Blake **experienced** during his life.

Writing about literature can make verb-tense consistency challenging. In general, use the **literary present tense** to discuss a literary work's subject matter:

> The speaker of the poem **expressed** ideas that Blake believed in deeply. (incorrect)
> The speaker of the poem **expresses** ideas that Blake believed in deeply. (correct)

Your Turn

Correct unnecessary verb-tense changes in the following sentences. Write *correct* if the tenses are consistent.

1. Both poems are included in collections Blake wrote in the late eighteenth century.
2. Blake illustrated the books and gives them the titles *Songs of Innocence* and *Songs of Experience.*
3. The poems Blake included are about love or life.

Writing Application Write a paragraph in which you describe from your current perspective something that happened to you in the past. Be sure to include past- and present-tense verbs and avoid unnecessary tense changes.

CHOICES

As you respond to the Choices activities, use these **Academic Vocabulary** words as appropriate: differentiate, inherent, device, technique, function.

REVIEW

Identify Sound Effects

Review the definition of *alliteration* in the Handbook of Literary and Historical Terms. Then, read "The Tyger" aloud, listening for sound effects, especially alliteration. Make a list of the consonants that Blake chooses to repeat often. With a partner, describe the sounds of these consonants, and decide what effect each sound creates for the listener.

CONNECT

Create a Digital Collage

TechFocus What objects could function as symbols similar to Blake's tiger and lamb? Create a digital collage—a collection of pictures, short video clips, and sounds—for "The Tyger" or "The Lamb" that represent the same symbolic meaning. Present your digital collage to your class, and explain the meaning that each image, video, or sound represents for you.

EXTEND

Discuss the Work of Contemporary Visionaries

Many people in Blake's day dismissed his poetry because of its unorthodox style and Blake's own eccentricities. With a partner, talk about artists or writers today whose unusual work and personalities generate controversy, and discuss whether or not you think their work will stand the test of time.

Universal Access: Grammar Link

EL English Learners

English for Academic Success Some students may need help understanding when to use the simple past tense and when to use the past perfect tense. To illustrate the use of different tenses to describe actions that took place at different times in the past, write the following sentences on the board

- *By the time Blake was twenty-seven, he had published his first work of poetry.*

Explain that the first verb in the sentence (*was*) is in the simple past, but the second verb (*had published*) is in the past perfect because it refers to an action Blake performed before the action referred to earlier.

✔ For more practice with verb-tense consistency, see **Warriner's Handbook, GrammarNotes,** and **Language Handbook Worksheets.**

Reading Standard 2.2, 3.3 (see pages A48–A50)

The Chimney Sweeper *from* Songs of Innocence
The Chimney Sweeper *from* Songs of Experience

Literary Skills Focus

Parallelism When words, phrases, or sentences are arranged in balanced grammatical structures, they are said to be **parallel.** Poets, dramatists, preachers, and speechwriters are likely to use parallelism because the repetition it introduces enhances the rhythmic and emotional effect of their lines and makes them easier to remember. Blake's use of parallelism contributes to the childlike simplicity on the surface of his poems.

Reading Skills Focus

Drawing Conclusions About Meaning A **conclusion** is a judgment or opinion inferred from clues in a text. By analyzing details and literary devices within a poem, you can draw conclusions about its meaning. Then, draw conclusions about the purpose of the parallelism.

Into Action Use a Venn diagram like the one below to identify parallelism within these poems. In each oval, write down words, phrases, or grammatical structures that are part of a parallel structure.

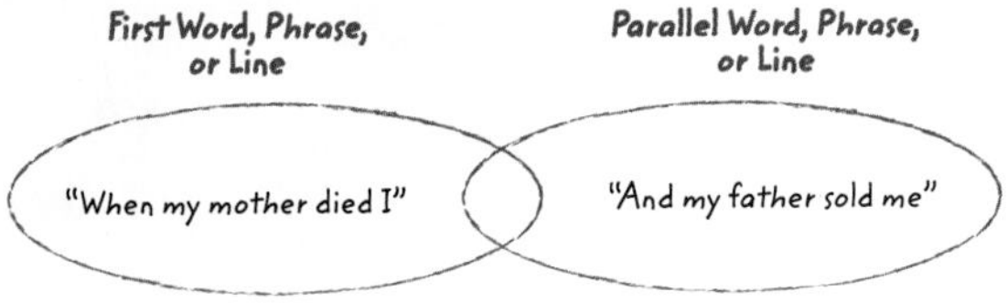

Writing Skills Focus

Think as a Reader/Writer

Find It in Your Reading Blake uses symbolism to create layers of meaning in his poems. As you read, take notes in your *Reader/Writer Notebook* about particular images that you think might be symbols.

Language Coach

Definitions The noun *woe* (woh) means "grief" or "deep sadness." The origin of the word relates to the way it sounds. Words that sound similar to *woe* are exclamations of sorrow in many languages, including Latin, Greek, German, Welsh, and Armenian. What does the common saying "woe is me!" mean?

Learn It Online
Use Word Watch online to develop your word knowledge.
go.hrw.com H12-737 Go

Reader/Writer Notebook
Use your **RWN** to complete the activities for these selections.

Preteach

English for Academic Success
Language Coach

Have students read the **Language Coach.** Ask students what English words sound similar to *woe* and how they may or may not be related. [*"Woe is me!" means "that is unfortunate for me."*]

Literary Skills Focus

As you read and discuss the poems with students, tell them to look for instances of parallelism.

Reading Skills Focus

Give students copies of the Reading Skills Focus graphic organizer. (See **Unit 4 Resources.**) Tell them to use their responses to answer the questions on the Applying Your Skills page.

Writing Skills Focus

Have students record examples of symbolism in their **Reader/Writer Notebooks.** Students can use their notes to complete the Writing Skills Focus activity.

Selection Resources

Unit 4 Resources, on-level practice, p. 19
Teacher One Stop™, on-level lesson plans
Holt Audio Library
Holt Audio Library: Selections and Summaries in Spanish
UA: Differentiating Instruction, graphic organizer, p. 168
UA: Supporting Instruction in Spanish, selection summary
ThinkCentral Online Assessment, Selection Standards Check

California Standards, p. 737

- **Reading Standard 2.2** Analyze the way in which clarity of meaning is affected by the patterns of organization, hierarchical structures, repetition of the main idea, syntax, and word choice in the text.
- **Reading Standard 3.3** Analyze the way in which irony, tone, mood, the author's style, and the "sound" of language achieve specific rhetorical or aesthetic purposes or both.

Learn It Online
Send students to **Word Watch** for audio pronunciations, synonyms and antonyms, and brief histories of word origins.
go.hrw.com H12–737 Go

Teacher Preparation
Selection Summary

In the first poem titled "The Chimney Sweeper" from *Songs of Innocence,* the speaker is a young boy whose father sold him to work as a chimney sweeper. The boy innocently tries to cheer himself and a fellow chimney sweeper, Tom Dacre. Tom has a dream in which an angel appears and reveals God to be a loving father who will reward the children with endless joy in heaven if they do their duty on earth. Despite their desperate plight, the speaker and Tom profess their trust in God.

Direct Teach

Think About/Talk About

Read with a Purpose Have students read the Read with a Purpose statement. Ask them to focus on the dreams of the child chimney sweeper.

POEM

The Chimney Sweeper
from Songs of Innocence

by **William Blake**

Read with a Purpose

Read to discover the dreams of a child chimney sweeper.

Build Background

In this poem from *Songs of Innocence,* and in its companion poem from *Songs of Experience,* Blake speaks for the poor children of his day who were forced to do backbreaking labor. In Blake's London, buildings were heated by coal- or wood-burning fireplaces, and every building had at least one chimney that required regular cleaning. Poor children were often used to do this hazardous work because they could fit into the narrow chimney passages. Desperate for money, some poor parents sold their children to "masters" who managed—and often mistreated—crews of young sweepers. In this poem from *Songs of Innocence,* the speaker is a child who tries to cheer himself and his fellow chimney sweeper, Tom Dacre, with the thought that they will one day have endless joy in heaven.

Universal Access

EL English Learners

English for Academic Success Model analyzing parallelism. Transcribe line 4 on the board, and underline the phrases "I sweep" and "I sleep." Explain that these two phrases consist of a first-person subject pronoun and a verb in the simple present, and that they also follow the same inverted word order (they follow an adverbial phrase). You might want to add abbreviations above each word or part of the sentence to clarify the grammatical structure of the line.

Struggling Readers

Benchmark Students Ask students to focus on one stanza at a time to look for instances of parallelism. Have them look for parallelism both on the same line and across lines. To give students additional help, bring their attention to the fourth stanza and ask them to find one example of parallelism within a line ("And wash in a river, and shine in the Sun") and one example of parallelism across lines (the word *and* at the beginning of lines 13 and 14).

When my mother died I was very young,
And my father sold me while yet my tongue
Could scarcely cry "'weep! 'weep! 'weep! 'weep!"°
So your chimneys I sweep, and in soot I sleep. **A**

There's little Tom Dacre, who cried when his head,
That curled like a lamb's back, was shaved: so I said
"Hush, Tom! never mind it, for when your head's bare
You know that the soot cannot spoil your white hair."

And so he was quiet, and that very night,
As Tom was a-sleeping, he had such a sight!—
That thousands of sweepers, Dick, Joe, Ned, and Jack,
Were all of them locked up in coffins of black.

And by came an Angel who had a bright key,
And he opened the coffins and set them all free;
Then down a green plain leaping, laughing, they run,
And wash in a river, and shine in the Sun.

Then naked and white, all their bags left behind,
They rise upon clouds and sport in the wind;
And the Angel told Tom, if he'd be a good boy,
He'd have God for his father, and never want° joy.

And so Tom awoke; and we rose in the dark,
And got with our bags and our brushes to work.
Though the morning was cold, Tom was happy and warm; **B**
So if all do their duty they need not fear harm.

3. "'weep . . . 'weep!": the child's attempt at the chimney sweepers' cry of "Sweep! Sweep!"

20. want: lack.

A **Literary Focus** **Parallelism** What repeated constructions can you find in the first stanza? What effect do they create?

B **Reading Focus** **Drawing Conclusions About Meaning** What thought keeps Tom "happy and warm," though the weather is cold and his work is hard?

(Opposite) Chimney sweeper on the roof in winter.

Two merry chimney sweeps of St. Moritz, Switzerland.

Think About/Talk About

Comprehension

B Reading Focus

Possible response: *He is kept "happy and warm" by thoughts of heaven and thoughts of his dream about life after death.*

Analysis

A Literary Focus

Possible responses: *The poem begins with parallel lines about the speaker's parents: "my mother died" and "my father sold me." There is a parallel between the statements beginning with "so" in line 4 and line 6. The clauses beginning with "so," as well as the frequent use of "and," suggest the rhythmic, singsong quality of a children's song, reinforcing the characterization of the speaker and heightening the contrast with his adult circumstances.*

Extend the Discussion

Summarizing What happens in Tom's dream in lines 11–20? ***Possible response:*** *Tom dreams about thousands of chimney sweepers who die and go to heaven, where they are finally free from soot and the struggles of their work.*

Interpreting How does Blake use white and black to suggest innocence and experience? ***Possible response:*** *Blake uses white to represent the purity, faith, and innocence of childhood (Tom's hair, the naked bodies of the little sweepers washed clean in the river, the snow), which is covered up and destroyed by the black soot of experience ("coffins of black," "we rose in the dark").*

Advanced Learners

Acceleration Have students consider the purpose of parallel structure and the social theme of the poem. Ask them to discuss how parallelism enhances Blake's denunciation of child labor.

Students with Disabilities

Have students listen to "The Chimney Sweeper" in audio format in the **Holt Audio Library.** Have them discuss whether they think the poem has a songlike quality and why. Help students recognize examples of rhyme, repetition, and simple parallelism in the poem.

✔ See **UA: Differentiating Instruction** for a graphic organizer to scaffold instruction for students with disabilities.

Teacher Preparation

Selection Summary

In the second "The Chimney Sweeper" from *Songs of Experience,* another young chimney sweeper weeps while his parents are at church. The system of church and government, he says, rationalizes his misery and creates a heaven for the ruling classes out of the misery of the poor.

Direct Teach

Think About/Talk About

Read with a Purpose Have students consider the various causes of the protagonist's struggle.

Comprehension

Ⓐ Reading Focus

Possible response: *He is very young, lonely, and forced to work in the harshest weather.*

Ⓒ Reading Focus

Possible response: *He blames his parents, but he also blames the government and organized religion for condoning his exploitation.*

Analysis

Ⓑ Literary Focus

Possible responses: *Both line 5 and line 9 use "because" to start adverb clauses. The repetition causes the reader to sympathize with the child, who tries to be good and keeps being rewarded with more suffering; the parallelism draws attention to the irony in the cause-and-effect relationship.*

Extend the Discussion

Irony How does the speaker convey irony in lines 5–8? ***Possible response:*** *Clothing and teaching a child are usually understood as acts of nurture; here the parents' actions bring their child harm.*

POEM

The Chimney Sweeper

from Songs of Experience

by **William Blake**

Read with a Purpose

Read to discover whom the child holds responsible for his fate.

Build Background

Blake was said to be confused or insane, not only because he saw visions but also because of the way some of his poems cry out violently against social problems around him. No one should go hungry, he said, in a land as green and wealthy as England. Like Blake, and unlike the sweeper in *Songs of Innocence,* this sweeper does not accept oppression and poverty. He recognizes that the people who pray for him (his parents) are the same ones who sold him into a life of hard labor. The first three lines are spoken by an adult who comes upon the pitiful child and asks him about his parents' whereabouts. The rest of the poem is the child's bitter answer to that sad question.

A little black thing among the snow Ⓐ
Crying "'weep, 'weep," in notes of woe!
"Where are thy father and mother? say?"
"They are both gone up to the church to pray.

"Because I was happy upon the heath,
And smil'd among the winter's snow;
They clothed me in the clothes of death,
And taught me to sing the notes of woe. Ⓑ

"And because I am happy, and dance and sing,
They think they have done me no injury,
And are gone to praise God and his Priest and King,
Who make up a heaven of our misery." Ⓒ

Chimney Sweep's trade sign (19th century) Cheltenham Art Gallery & Museums, Gloucestershire, U.K.

Ⓐ Reading Focus Drawing Conclusions About Meaning What details about the child does Blake give in the poem's first line? What conclusion can you draw about this child's life from these details?

Ⓑ Literary Focus Parallelism What constructions in this stanza are parallel? What does the parallelism accomplish?

Ⓒ Reading Focus Drawing Conclusions About Meaning Whom does the chimney sweeper blame for his misery?

California Standards, p. 741

- **Reading Standard 2.2** Analyze the way in which clarity of meaning is affected by the patterns of organization, hierarchical structures, repetition of the main idea, syntax, and word choice in the text.
- **Reading Standard 3.3** Analyze the way in which irony, tone, mood, the author's style, and the "sound" of language achieve specific rhetorical or aesthetic purposes or both.
- **Writing Standard 1.1** Demonstrate an understanding of the elements of discourse (e.g., purpose, speaker, audience, form) when completing narrative, expository, persuasive, or descriptive writing assignments.

Applying Your Skills

Reading Standard 2.2, 3.3 (see pages A48–A50)
Writing Standard 1.1 (see pages A51–A52)

The Chimney Sweeper *from* Songs of Innocence
The Chimney Sweeper *from* Songs of Experience

Literary Response and Analysis

Reading Skills Focus

Quick Check

1. In the first poem, how does the angel reassure Tom Dacre in his dream?
2. How does Tom Dacre's dream contrast with the actual conditions of his daily life?
3. In the second poem, how does the young chimney sweeper answer the adult's question? What do you think his "clothes of death" are?
4. Why don't the parents of the chimney sweeper in *Songs of Experience* see the harm they have done to their child?

Read with a Purpose

5. What contributes to the distinctly different attitudes expressed in the poems?

Reading Skills: Drawing Conclusions About Meaning

6. Review the Venn diagrams you worked on as you read. In the overlapping section of each diagram, draw a conclusion about the purpose each example of parallelism serves. After you have completed each diagram, review the overlapping sections to see what your conclusions can tell you about the overall meaning of each poem as a whole.

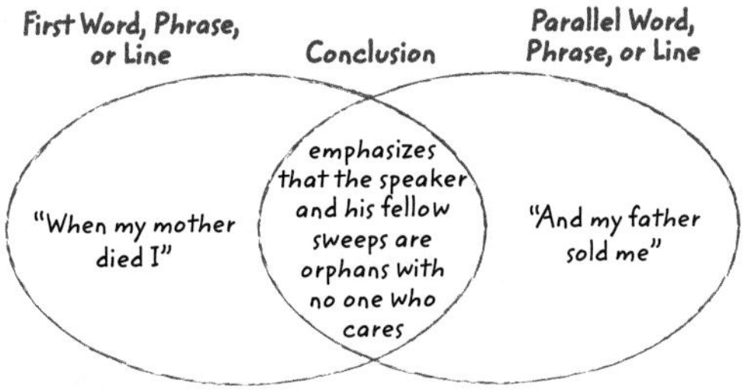

Literary Skills Focus

Literary Analysis

7. **Interpret** In the first poem, what might the "coffins of black" symbolize besides death?
8. **Evaluate** In each poem, what is the emotional effect of the child's mispronunciation of the chimney sweeper's cry?
9. **Extend** Do people today sometimes take the attitude expressed by the speaker of the first poem: If you are good, if you do your duty, you need not fear harm? Expand on your response.

Literary Skills: Parallelism

10. **Analyze** How does Blake's use of parallelism in both poems enhance their emotional effect?

Literary Skills Review: Dramatic Irony

11. **Infer** When readers understand or know something that a speaker in a literary work does not, **dramatic irony** occurs. What examples of dramatic irony can you find the first poem?

Writing Skills Focus

Think as a Reader/Writer

Use It in Your Writing Write a short essay describing a modern-day injustice or exploitative form of employment. Include at least one symbol in your essay, and use parallelism to enhance the emotional impact of your description.

What Do You Think Now? How does Blake use his imagination to disclose the truth about child chimney sweepers to his readers?

Universal Access

Struggling Writers

Some students may need additional scaffolding to complete the Writing Skills Focus activity. Before students write their essays, have them research modern-day injustices, like modern slavery in Africa and Asia. Then, have students write on one of the injustices and brainstorm objects that might symbolize death, hell, or oppression. Remind students to use parallelism for emphasis and emotional impact.

What Do You Think Now?

Point out that the speaker of each poem is not an adult but a child. Note that Blake's use of the children's point of view gives his depiction of the lives of child chimney sweepers both emotional impact and authenticity.

Assess

Unit 4 Resources,
Selection Standards Check, p. 21

Check for Understanding

Independent Practice

Reading Skills Focus

Possible responses:

1. *The angel tells Tom that when he dies he'll "have God for his father" and always be happy.*
2. *In his dream he is free to run and play in the sun, but in his waking life he spends his days working.*
3. *He explains that his parents have betrayed him. The "clothes of death" are clothes covered in soot from working on chimneys.*
4. *They accept justifications for child labor offered by their government.*
5. *The first poem ends optimistically, promising happiness in heaven. The second poem ends by affirming the harm done to exploited children and by reproaching those who rationalize children's misery.*
6. *Have students consider how the conclusions contribute to the overall meaning of each poem.*

Literary Skills Focus

Possible responses:

7. *They might symbolize the dark lives of the children or the death of innocence and childhood.*
8. *The child's mispronunciation is apt since it evokes the tears of children condemned to harsh labor.*
9. *Many people believe that if they work hard, they will be rewarded.*
10. *Blake's parallelism creates a singsong effect that reminds the reader of children's songs. The poems acquire a tone of innocence that only emphasizes the dramatic conditions of children in Blake's time.*
11. *A mature reader knows what the speaker does not—that all will most likely not turn out well.*

Preteach

English for Academic Success

Language Coach

Show students how to use a dictionary to find the pronunciation of unfamiliar words. [*The* w *in* wring *is silent. The vowel sound in* woe *is the same as* foe. *The vowel sound in* feign *is the same as* veiled.]

Literary Skills Focus

As you read the selection with students, have them discuss both the subject and the theme of the poem. Give students a copy of the graphic organizer before they read (See **Unit 4 Resources.**) Tell them to use their responses to answer the questions on the Applying Your Skills page.

Writing Skills Focus

Have students record examples of repetition in their **Reader/Writer Notebooks.** Students can use their notes to complete the Writing Skills Focus activity.

Learn It Online

The online version of this poem includes audio support to engage all students and to help struggling readers with reading comprehension and vocabulary.

go.hrw.com H12-742 Go

Preparing to Read

Reading Standard 3.2 (see pages A48–A50)

A Poison Tree

Literary Skills Focus

Theme The **theme** of a work of literature is its central idea or main insight about human nature or human life. The theme of a work is not the same as its **subject,** or topic, but is the writer's point of view on the subject. In the case of "A Poison Tree," Blake's subject is anger, and his theme is his insight into the function of anger. In poetry the theme is rarely stated directly. More often, it is implied by all the details, images, and symbols of the poem and must be deciphered by the reader.

Into Action In the first column of a chart like the one below, write down the subject of the poem. In the second column, record details, images, and symbols that strike you as important.

Subject of the Poem	Details, Images, and Symbols
This poem is about . . .	The speaker waters his wrath as if it is a tree.

Language Coach

Pronunciation Reading poetry aloud can help you understand its meaning, but it is important to pronounce words correctly. Remember that some English words include silent letters, such as the *w* in *wrath* (meaning "anger"). Vowel combinations can have unpredictable pronunciations. Read these words aloud:

foe (foh): enemy

veiled (vayld): covered; hid

How do the following words follow similar pronunciation patterns: *wring, woe, feign?*

Writing Skills Focus

Think as a Reader/Writer

Find It in Your Reading As you read "A Poison Tree," take note of how Blake uses **repetition.** In stanza 1, for example, the speaker repeats the word *I* four times, and begins each of the four lines with either *I was* or *I told.* This repetition contributes to the idea of growing, obsessive anger. While reading, record examples of Blake's use of repetition in your *Reader/Writer Notebook.* Think about how the repetition affects both the theme and the mood of the poem.

Reader/Writer Notebook

Use your **RWN** to complete the activities for this selection.

Learn It Online

Listen to this poem online.

go.hrw.com H12-742 Go

Selection Resources

Unit 4 Resources, on-level practice, p. 24

Teacher One Stop™, on-level lesson plans

Holt Audio Library

Holt Audio Library: Selections and Summaries in Spanish

UA: Differentiating Instruction, graphic organizer, p. 168

UA: Supporting Instruction in Spanish, selection summary

ThinkCentral Online Assessment, Selection Standards Check

California Standards, pp. 742–744

- **Reading Standard 3.2** Analyze the way in which the theme or meaning of a selection represents a view or comment on life, using textual evidence to support the claim.

POEM

A Poison Tree

from Songs of Innocence

by **William Blake**

Read with a Purpose

Read to discover two outcomes of anger.

Build Background

This poem presents another of the "contrary states of human nature" that so intrigued Blake and appeared throughout his *Songs of Innocence* and *Songs of Experience.* Like the speaker in "The Tyger," the speaker in "A Poison Tree" is intrigued by the nature of evil.

During his informal education, Blake was immersed in the biblical stories of good and evil, violence and forgiveness. In this poem, he describes an urge toward anger that many people confront at some time in their lives.

I was angry with my friend:
I told my wrath, my wrath did end.
I was angry with my foe:
I told it not, my wrath did grow. (A)

And I watered it in fears,
Night and morning with my tears;
And I sunned it with smiles,
And with soft deceitful wiles.°

And it grew both day and night,
Till it bore an apple bright;
And my foe beheld it shine,
And he knew that it was mine,

And into my garden stole
When the night had veiled the pole: (B)
In the morning glad I see
My foe outstretchd beneath the tree.

8. **wiles:** cunning tricks.

(A) **Literary Focus** **Theme** How would you restate the poem's comment on the effects of anger?

(B) **Literary Focus** **Theme** What do the speaker and the foe have in common? How does what they share relate to the poem's theme?

Teacher Preparation

Selection Summary

The speaker relates how he hides his anger from an enemy and secretly cultivates it. The anger grows into a tree that bears a poisonous apple, which the speaker's foe steals and eats. The foe dies, and the speaker is glad; he, too, has been poisoned by his secret anger.

Direct Teach

Think About/Talk About

Read with a Purpose Discuss with students the various ways people can express anger. As they read the poem, ask them to look for instances in which the speaker describes the outcomes of anger.

Analysis

(A) Literary Focus

Possible response: *If anger is honestly expressed, it dissipates. If anger is repressed, it poisons.*

(B) Literary Focus

Possible responses: *Both the speaker and the foe are being poisoned by the speaker's anger. This relates to the poem's theme that repressed anger poisons what it touches.*

Extend the Discussion

Determining Author's Purpose

Blake portrays the apple as "bright" in line 10. Why is it important that the apple is appealing and enticing? ***Possible response:*** *Temptation tends to dress things in appealing packages. This echoes the Biblical story of Eve and the apple. It is true that things that are wrong or dangerous often look attractive and harmless.*

California Standards, p. 744

- **Reading Standard 3.2** Analyze the way in which the theme or meaning of a selection represents a view or comment on life, using textual evidence to support the claim.
- **Grades 9–10 Review Reading Standard 3.7** Recognize and understand the significance of various literary devices, including figurative language, imagery, allegory, and symbolism, and explain their appeal.
- **Writing Standard 2.1** Write fictional, autobiographical, or biographical narratives. **e.** Make effective use of descriptions of appearance, images, shifting perspectives, and sensory details.

Universal Access

Struggling Readers

Strategic Students Tell students that by identifying details, images, and symbols in the poem, they can better understand the poem's theme and the speaker's information about the subject. Point out that the speaker's "wrath" in line 4 continues to grow throughout the second stanza. Direct students to lines 5 and 7, where the speaker waters and suns his "wrath," which students should recognize as a growing poison tree. Have students note how the poem ends and what the speaker might be trying to communicate about anger that is hidden yet continually growing.

Check for Understanding

Independent Practice

Reading Skills Focus

Possible responses:

1. *One approach is to express anger, which the speaker does with a friend. The other is to repress anger, as he does with his foe. One approach is healthy; the other is unhealthy or poisonous.*
2. *The speaker's wrath against his foe increases because he represses it.*
3. *The speaker's foe eats the poisoned apple and dies. He is a victim of his own greed and dishonesty as well as the speaker's anger.*
4. *The causes of the different outcomes of anger are the ways in which the speaker deals with his anger.*

Literary Skills Focus

Possible responses:

5. *The imagery of the poison tree describes repressed anger.*
6. *The speaker is a victim of his own anger. He is evil in that he takes pleasure in hurting his enemy, but good in that he has the capacity to evaluate his actions with honesty.*
7. *The speaker feeds it with fears, tears, and deceit.*
8. *Blake alludes to the Tree of Knowledge whose fruit God forbade Adam and Eve to eat.*
9. *The simplicity of the poem underscores Blake's points about anger. Small children often act vengefully, as the speaker does.*
10. *If students do not understand the theme, focus them on what main idea the symbol leads them to.*
11. *The garden may stand for the mind and the tree is repressed anger. The fruit is the action that the speaker takes. This fruit ends up killing the speaker's foe because it is vengeful.*

Applying Your Skills

Reading Standard 3.2; **Grades 9–10 Review Reading Standard** 3.7 (see pages A48–A50)
Writing Standard 2.1e (see pages A51–A52)

A Poison Tree

Literary Response and Analysis

Reading Skills Focus

Quick Check

1. What two ways of handling anger are mentioned in the poem? In what ways do these two approaches differ?
2. Why does the speaker's wrath against his foe increase?
3. What happens to the speaker's foe in the last stanza? Of whom or what is he a victim?

Read with a Purpose

4. What causes the two different outcomes of anger?

Literary Skills Focus

Literary Analysis

5. **Analyze** The poem differentiates between ways of handling anger. What imagery describes the second way?
6. **Make Judgments** How is the speaker of the poem a victim? Do you see the speaker as good or evil, or both? Give examples from the poem.
7. **Interpret** How does Blake compare the speaker's anger to a tree?
8. **Analyze** What allusion is Blake making when in the third stanza he refers to the forbidden fruit?
9. **Evaluate** Blake's use of parallelism and simple diction gives "A Poison Tree" an air of straightforward, even childlike, simplicity. Do you think this tone supports or diminishes the points being made about anger and its consequences? Explain.

Literary Skills: Theme

10. **Draw Conclusions** Look at the chart you made showing the poem's subject, details, images, and symbols. What do they tell you about the poem's theme? Add a third column to your chart, in which you write a brief sentence stating the theme of the poem.

Subject of the Poem	*Details, Images, and Symbols*	*Theme*
This poem is about . . .	*The speaker waters his wrath as if it is a tree.*	*The poem's theme is . . .*

Literary Skills Review: Symbol

11. **Analyze** A **symbol** is a person, place, thing, or event that stands for both itself and something beyond itself. What might the garden, tree, and apple symbolize in "A Poison Tree"? As you answer, remember that Blake relied on biblical allusion in much of his art.

Writing Skills Focus

Think as a Reader/Writer

Use It in Your Writing Review your notes about repetition in Blake's poem. Now, write two paragraphs about an emotion—whether anger, fear, frustration, joy, or a different emotion—that has the potential to keep growing. Use repetition to convey the theme and mood of your description.

What Do You Think Now? How does Blake's imaginative description of anger help you understand this powerful emotion?

Universal Access

Struggling Writers

Some students may need additional scaffolding to complete the Writing Skills Focus activity. Review with students the instances of repetition in "A Poison Tree." Point out the repetition of "I was angry," "my wrath," and "I __ed it." Encourage students to emphasize the mood and theme of their paragraph by using repeated grammatical constructions and phrases throughout their paragraph.

What Do You Think Now?

Ask students to consider how would they describe anger and compare their descriptions with the representation that Blake gives of this feeling in "A Poison Tree."

Assess

Unit 4 Resources,
Selection Standards Check, p. 24

Reading Skills Focus

Reading Standard 2.2 (see pages A48–A50)

Lines Composed a Few Miles Above Tintern Abbey

Recognizing Patterns of Organization by Kylene Beers

From writing both academic and personal essays, you know that logical organization is essential to clear writing. Like essayists, poets use **patterns of organization** as they compose their verse. As the backbone of a well-constructed poem, the organizational structure supports the poem's meaning. Recognizing and understanding the structure help us comprehend and enjoy a poem.

The most common pattern of organization in poetry is the **stanza,** a group of consecutive lines that form a single unit. The stanzaic organizational pattern is usually repeated throughout the poem. The **rhyme scheme,** the pattern of rhymed lines, and **meter,** the generally regular pattern of stressed and unstressed syllables, are also repeated within the poem. These predictable organizational patterns help the poet communicate his or her ideas, as well as enable the reader to more easily understand the message of the poem.

Romantic poet William Blake uses a four-line stanza in "The Tyger." The *aabb* rhyme scheme, the use of lines that usually end on a stressed syllable, and the **trochaic meter** (a pattern of alternating stressed and unstressed syllables) are repeated throughout the six stanzas. Read this four-line stanza aloud to hear the repeated rhyme scheme and meter.

> Tyger! Tyger! burning bright
> In the forests of the night,
> What immortal hand or eye
> Could frame thy fearful symmetry?

Poets often use other recurring organizational features as Blake does with the rhetorical question in each stanza of "The Tyger."

William Wordsworth organizes his poem "Lines Composed a Few Miles Above Tintern Abbey" into stanzas of **blank verse,** or unrhymed **iambic pentameter** (see page 747). Another organizational pattern used by Wordsworth and other Romantic poets is the **sonnet.** William Wordsworth uses the fourteen-line structure of the **Petrarchan sonnet** to make observations or pose problems in the **octave,** the first eight lines, and then to respond to them or pose a solution in the **sestet,** the last six lines.

Notice how Wordsworth applies this organization in "The World Is Too Much with Us" (page 764). After asserting "the world is too much with us," the speaker uses the octave's remaining lines to list the ways humans have disregarded nature's bounty, concluding "we are out of tune" (line 8). In the sonnet's sestet, the speaker then states that he'd rather be "a Pagan suckled in a creed outworn" (line 10). The predictable organization helps you recognize the shift from problem to solution, increasing your comprehension and appreciation of the poem.

Your Turn

Read the following lines from Wordsworth's sonnet, "Composed upon Westminster Bridge" (page 762) to see the organizational pattern of the **Petrarchan sonnet.** Wordsworth begins by admiring the sleeping city of London in "the beauty of the morning." He continues:

> Open unto the fields, and to the sky;
> All bright and glittering in the smokeless air.
> Never did sun more beautifully steep
> In his first splendor, valley, rock, or hill.
> (lines 7–10)

How does Wordsworth use the structure of the sonnet and its shift marked between lines 8 and 9 to help communicate the poem's meaning?

Reading Skills Focus

Objectives

Students will identify and understand patterns of organization.

Unit 4 Resources, Reading Focus Skill Builder, p. 27

Teacher One Stop™, lesson plan and all print resources

Direct Teach

Recognizing Patterns of Organization

This feature gives students practice in identifying patterns of text organization in a poem. Have students read the feature and complete the Your Turn activity before reading the poem.

Check for Understanding

Your Turn

Possible response:

Lines 7–8 conclude the poem's octave and offer a still image for the reader to contemplate. Lines 9–10 begin the poem's sestet and provide the quiet action of the sun breaking over the peaceful scene that was created in the octave.

California Standards, p. 745

- **Reading Standard 2.2** Analyze the way in which clarity of meaning is affected by the patterns of organization, hierarchical structures, repetition of the main ideas, syntax, and word choice in the text.

Universal Access

English Learners/ Struggling Readers

Students may struggle with the concept of meter. Provide kinesthetic and rhythmic support by reading the lines from "The Tyger" aloud with students, clapping with the meter and over-accentuating it. Write the lines on the board, and after reading them aloud, mark the stressed syllables with accent marks. After the passage is marked, read it again with students, clapping to accentuate the stressed syllables.

Standards Focus

Objectives

Students will
- understand blank verse
- identify patterns of organization

Selection Introduction

Think About the Writer

Review with students the difficulties in Wordsworth's life. Ask them to empathize with his experiences of being orphaned and disillusioned by war.

For Independent Reading

- *The Land of Bliss,* Cathy Song
- *Coming into the Country,* John McPhee

Motivate

What Do You Think?/QuickWrite

Ask students to reflect on experiences of early childhood. Have them explore how small children use their imaginations and connect their imaginative play with nature.

English for Academic Success

Academic Vocabulary

Look for opportunities to use the Academic Vocabulary words in this unit.

- **differentiate, *v.*:** distinguish
- **function, *n.*:** purpose
- **inherent, *adj.*:** existing in something as a fixed, essential quality
- **technique, *n.*:** method

California Standards, pp. 745–756

(For a full text of the standards, see pp. 000–000.

- **Reading Standard 2.2** Clarify meaning through structure, repetition, syntax, and word choice.
- **Reading Standard 3.3** Analyze effects of irony, tone, mood, and style.
- **Reading Standard 3.9** Analyze the philosophical arguments.

Preparing to Read

Lines Composed a Few Miles Above Tintern Abbey

from Ode: Intimations of Immortality

Composed upon Westminster Bridge

The World Is Too Much with Us

What Do You Think? How can we use imagination to discover truth?

QuickWrite

In your *Reader/Writer Notebook,* write about your favorite experience with nature and how it affected your imagination.

MEET THE WRITER

William Wordsworth

(1770–1850)

A lover of all natural forms, William Wordsworth believed that nature helped him "see into the life of things."

Finding His Calling

After his mother's death, Wordsworth was sent to attend school at Hawkhead in England's beautiful Lake District. His experiences in this setting fostered his love for nature and his belief in its inherent beneficent properties. During a walking tour of France and the Alps in 1790, Wordsworth was seized by the early idealism of the French Revolution. He returned to France in 1791 after completing his degree at Cambridge. As an educated man with no title, wealth, or head for business, Wordsworth had little interest in the few careers open to him, most notably, that of the Church. Thus began a decade of painful growth, as he searched for and eventually found his vocation as a poet.

The Power of Friendship

After Wordsworth returned from France in 1792, war broke out between France and England. Wordsworth was sickened by the war and gradually became disillusioned about his hopes for political and social change. In late 1793, he embarked on a walking tour of Europe, which, combined with his waning aspirations to perfect society, drove him to poetry.

In 1795, Wordsworth met poet Samuel Taylor Coleridge, and both men quickly became powerful galvanizing forces on each other's work. By June 1797, Wordsworth had produced a good deal of new poetry, none yet published, including a play and some stark narratives. *Lyrical Ballads* (1798) was the culmination of Wordsworth and Coleridge's friendship and mutual influence. The collection became one of the most important works of the Romantic era. In the Preface to *Lyrical Ballads,* Wordsworth wrote that poetry is the "spontaneous overflow of powerful feelings"; but he added that poems of value are produced only by one who has "thought long and deeply." The marriage of feeling and thought, as Coleridge recognized, made Wordsworth "the best poet of the age."

Think About the Writer What might have led Wordsworth to believe that both thought and feelings are necessary for good poetry?

William Wordsworth (1842) by Benjamin Robert Haydon. Oil on canvas. National Portrait Gallery, London; (Background) Tintern Abbey.

Selection Readability	
Easily Accessible **Accessible** Challenging	These poems include blank verse; pastoral imagery; accessible language.

Reading Standard 2.2, 3.3, 3.9 (see pages A48–A50).

Literary Skills Focus

Blank Verse With the exception of free verse, **blank verse** (unrhymed iambic pentameter) is the poetic form that sounds most like natural speech. In blank verse, each line of poetry contains five **iambs,** units of meter consisting of an unstressed syllable followed by a stressed syllable. A poet may vary this pattern slightly to draw attention to an idea or image in the text. As you read, think about how the flowing blank verse of "Tintern Abbey" contributes to its conversational tone.

Literary Perspectives Apply the literary perspective described on page 749 as you read this poem.

Reading Skills Focus

Analyzing Patterns of Organization Poets use various techniques to organize their verse. Common **organizational patterns** in poetry include the **stanza,** a group of consecutive lines that form a unit; **meter,** a generally regular pattern of stressed and unstressed syllables; and **rhyme.** In this poem, Wordsworth uses blank verse and stanzas to organize his ideas.

Into Action Look for punctuation and indentions that signal the end of one stanza and the beginning of another. Make notes in a chart like the one below on how Wordsworth uses stanzas to organize his ideas.

Stanza	Organization
1	description of landscape features; imagery of cottage grounds, pastoral farms, wreaths of smoke
2	
3	

Writing Skills Focus

Think as a Reader/Writer

Find It in Your Reading As you read "Tintern Abbey," note how Wordsworth uses long, flowing sentences that often start and stop in the middle of lines. Consider how his speaker uses first person and seems to address a listener. In your *Reader/Writer Notebook,* write how these techniques impart a conversational **tone,** as if the speaker is talking while walking.

Reader/Writer Notebook

Use your **RWN** to complete the activities for this selection.

Vocabulary

pastoral (PAS tuhr uhl) *adj.:* of simple or peaceful rural life. *The visit to the Wye Valley offered pastoral views of cottages and farms.*

sublime (suh BLYM) *adj.:* awe-inspiring due to majesty or nobility. *He saw a sublime vision when he journeyed to the beautiful Wye Valley.*

corporeal (kawr PAWR ee uhl) *adj.:* of the body. *Although our corporeal existence will someday end, Wordsworth believed that we will continue to exist in spirit.*

recompense (REHK uhm pehns) *n.:* payment or compensation in return for something lost. *The wisdom of experience is ample recompense for the loss of the pleasures of youth.*

impels (ihm PEHLZ) *v.:* forces; causes to move. *While visiting the Wye Valley, the speaker feels a presence that impels all things.*

zeal (zeel) *n.:* eager enthusiasm. *They will remember with zeal the happy experience that they shared together.*

Language Coach

Suffixes The suffix *–al* is often found at the end of adjectives. It can mean "of" or "relating to." Something that is *pastoral* relates to country life. Something that is *corporeal* relates to the body. To what do you think something that is *nocturnal* relates?

Learn It Online

Get to know Wordsworth through the Writers' Lives site online.

go.hrw.com H12-747 Go

Selection Resources

Unit 4 Resources, on-level practice and assessment, p. 27

PowerNotes, interactive lesson presentations with activities

Teacher One Stop™, on-level lesson plans and all print resources

Holt Audio Library

Holt Audio Library: Selections and Summaries in Spanish

UA: Holt Interactive Reader, p. 205

UA: Differentiating Instruction, modified lesson plans and leveled assessment, p. 169

UA: Supporting Instruction in Spanish, selection summary

UA: Resources for Teaching Advanced Students, lesson plans, p. 141

Analyzing Visuals Transparencies, p. 31

ThinkCentral Online Assessment, Selection Standards Check

ThinkCentral Online Remediation

Preteach

Introducing Vocabulary

- Review the Vocabulary words, definitions, and sentences with students.
- To reinforce the importance of the Vocabulary words, tell students that these words, in addition to providing key meaning to the poem, allow the author to create the meter of blank verse, or unrhymed iambic pentameter.

English for Academic Success

Language Coach

After students read the **Language Coach,** have them give additional examples of adjectives ending with the suffix *–al* along with their meanings.

Literary Skills Focus

As you read and discuss the poem with students, have them note the way each blank verse mimics natural speech.

Reading Skills Focus

Give students a copy of the Reading Skills Focus graphic organizer before they read (See **Unit 4 Resources.**) Tell them to use their responses to answer the questions on the Applying Your Skills page.

Writing Skills Focus

Have students record examples of conversational tone in their **Reader/Writer Notebooks.** Students can use their notes to complete the Writing Skills Focus activity.

Learn It Online

The **Writers' Lives** feature of the Interactive Student Edition offers additional information about this author. Audio or video segments are provided for some authors.

go.hrw.com H12-747 Go

Teacher Preparation

Selection Summary

"Lines Composed a Few Miles Above Tintern Abbey" is a meditation on what nature means to the speaker. He describes the physical beauty of a valley, and he asserts that the mere memory of this landscape has given him solace. Next, he explains how the passionate relationship he had with nature in his youth has given way to a more spiritual appreciation, a sense of the sublime presence that connects all things, including the human mind. Finally, the speaker addresses his sister. He tells her that seeing the landscape through her youthful eyes makes it even more precious to him. He hopes she will take comfort from his memory when he is dead and recall the pleasure he had in seeing the valley with her.

Direct Teach

Think About/Talk About

Read with a Purpose Have students read the Read with a Purpose statement. Discuss with students the contrasts between urban and rural lifestyles.

Analysis

A Literary Focus

Possible response: *At times there are two unstressed syllables in a row, such as "with the" in the first line. This enhances the conversational tone of the poem.*

Responses to Margin Questions

Lines 1–22 *He hears the murmuring of the water. He sees cliffs, the sky, a sycamore, cottages, orchards, groves, copses, hedgerows, farms, and smoke.*

Lines 23–41 *They have restored his tranquility, made him a kinder person, and lightened the weight of the world.*

Line 49 *An indentation and a split line are used to show where one stanza ends and another begins. The speaker addresses the river directly in line 56. He is back in the present.*

POEM

Lines Composed a Few Miles Above Tintern Abbey

On Revisiting the Banks of the Wye During a Tour. July 13, 1798

by **William Wordsworth**

Read with a Purpose

Read to discover the benefits a city dweller finds in returning to nature.

Build Background

"Tintern Abbey" is one of the most important lyric works in English literature. A major step in Wordsworth's writing and a definitive statement of Romantic ideals, it has inspired and guided many poets. Wordsworth wrote this landmark poem with astonishing ease during a 1798 walking tour in Wales. Soon after leaving the Wye River Valley, he composed "Tintern Abbey" in his head as he walked, finishing it, he claims, as he "was entering Bristol in the evening after a ramble of four or five days." Only then did he write it down, changing nothing.

"Tintern Abbey" demonstrates one of the most important lessons Wordsworth had learned from Coleridge: the use of a flowing blank verse and the easy maneuvering of the meditative poem.

Five years have past; five summers, with the length
Of five long winters! and again I hear **A**
These waters, rolling from their mountain springs
With a soft inland murmur.—Once again
Do I behold these steep and lofty cliffs,
That on a wild secluded scene impress
Thoughts of more deep seclusion; and connect
The landscape with the quiet of the sky.
The day is come when I again repose
Here, under this dark sycamore, and view
These plots of cottage ground, these orchard tufts,
Which at this season, with their unripe fruits,
Are clad in one green hue, and lose themselves
'Mid groves and copses.° Once again I see
These hedgerows,° hardly hedgerows, little lines

1–22. *The speaker describes a beloved place in nature to which he has returned after five years.*

? *Look for the verbs* hear, behold, view, *and* see. *What does the speaker hear? What does he see?*

14. copses: areas densely covered with shrubs and small trees.

15. hedgerows: rows of bushes, shrubs, and small trees that serve as fences.

A Literary Focus **Blank Verse** Wordsworth varies the meter of his iambic pentameter at the start of the poem. How does the meter of the first two lines vary from traditional iambic pentameter, in which an unstressed syllable is immediately followed by a stressed syllable? Why do you think Wordsworth begins the poem this way?

Universal Access

EL English Learners

Help students paraphrase the most difficult passages. You might say: "When I read a sentence or clause from the poem and don't understand its meaning, I can rewrite it in my head and figure out what Wordsworth is saying. For example, *Once again / Do I behold these steep and lofty cliffs, / That on a wild secluded scene impress / Thoughts of more deep seclusion* can be reworked like this: *After all this time I'm seeing these steep, high cliffs again. The solitude of this scene makes me want to be alone for a long time.*"

Struggling Readers

Benchmark Students Lines 23–36 are challenging because of their negative constructions: *have not been, unremembered, no slight or trivial influence, nameless, unremembered, Nor*. Help students untangle this language by modeling "positive" rephrasing: "if something has not been like *a landscape to a blind man's eye*, it must have been seen."

✔ Invite students to read the poem in interactive format in **UA: Holt Interactive Reader.**

Of sportive wood run wild: these pastoral farms,
Green to the very door; and wreaths of smoke
Sent up, in silence, from among the trees!
With some uncertain notice, as might seem
Of vagrant dwellers in the houseless woods,
Or of some Hermit's cave, where by his fire
The Hermit sits alone.

These beauteous forms, **B**
Through a long absence, have not been to me
As is a landscape to a blind man's eye:
But oft, in lonely rooms, and 'mid the din
Of towns and cities, I have owed to them
In hours of weariness, sensations sweet,
Felt in the blood, and felt along the heart;
And passing even into my purer mind,
With tranquil restoration:—feelings too
Of unremembered pleasure: such, perhaps,
As have no slight or trivial influence
On that best portion of a good man's life,
His little, nameless, unremembered acts
Of kindness and of love. Nor less, I trust,
To them I may have owed another gift,
Of aspect more sublime; that blessed mood,
In which the burden of the mystery,
In which the heavy and the weary weight
Of all this unintelligible world,
Is lightened:—that serene and blessed mood,
In which the affections° gently lead us on,—
Until, the breath of this corporeal frame
And even the motion of our human blood
Almost suspended, we are laid asleep
In body, and become a living soul:
While with an eye made quiet by the power
Of harmony, and the deep power of joy,
We see into the life of things.

Tintern Abbey.

? **23–41.** *According to the speaker, how have memories of this beloved landscape affected him?*

42. affections: feelings.

? **49.** *What visual clue signals that a new stanza is beginning here? How does the speaker's focus or emphasis change in the new stanza?*

B Reading Focus **Analyzing Patterns of Organization** Why does Wordsworth begin the second stanza in the middle of line 22?

Vocabulary **pastoral** (PAS tuhr uhl) *adj.:* of simple or peaceful rural life.
sublime (suh BLYM) *adj.:* awe inspiring due to nobility.
corporeal (kawr PAWR ee uhl) *adj.:* of the body.

Literary Perspectives

Analyzing Philosophical Context Philosophical context refers to an author's underlying assumptions regarding larger questions about life and its meaning. An author's philosophy influences his or her writing in various ways, such as the form in which the text is written and the overarching themes or messages the text conveys. In this poem, the speaker retreats to nature to escape the trials of urban life. While reflecting on the landscape, he considers how he has changed since his boyhood.

As you read, be sure to notice the questions in the text, which will guide you in using this perspective.

Think About/Talk About

Comprehension

B Reading Focus

Possible response: *By ending one stanza with the image of the hermit alone, and beginning the next with a mention of "beauteous forms," Wordsworth creates contrasting images. This is how he uses form to affect meaning in the stanza.*

Extend the Discussion

Rearranging Syntax How could the first sentence of the poem be reorganized to read like a sentence of prose? ***Possible response:*** *It has been five years of summers and winters since I have heard the rolling waters of these mountain springs.*

Evaluating How is the setting significant in lines 23–59? ***Possible response:*** *The setting comes alive in the memory of the speaker in moments of weariness and comforts him.*

Vocabulary: Own the Word

- **pastoral:** Ask students to describe what they picture when they think of a *pastoral* setting. ***Possible responses:*** *vast acres of farmland, grassy hills, sheep, streams*
- **sublime:** Something *sublime* is awe-inspiring. An antonym is *lowly* or *unattractive*. Use both words in a sentence: The *sublime* view of the mountain valley easily made the streets of our neighborhood seem unattractive.
- **corporeal:** Tell students that the Latin root for *corporeal* is *corpus*, which means "body." In line 43, "this corporeal frame" refers to… ***Possible response:*** *the physical body*

Literary Perspectives

Before students read the selection, have them read the **Literary Perspectives** about Analyzing Philosophical Context.

Remind students about the etymology of the word *philosophy* (from Greek, "love of knowledge"). Give examples of philosophical dilemmas that philosophers have tried to answer since ancient times, such as "What is the meaning of life? Is life preordained by fate or do we make free choices? How much does our perception of reality correspond to the truth?" As students read the selection, ask them to write down the underlying philosophical questions in Wordsworth's poem.

Remind students to use the notes and questions at the bottom of the page to help them use the perspective.

Model the Skill

- Tell students that when a poet organizes a poem, he or she creates an **organizational pattern** that complements the content of the work.
- Point out that the stanza that comprises lines 49–57 is much shorter than other stanzas. In blank verse, **stanzas** do not have to be of a fixed length (as they do in other verse forms). Also point out that the first line of the next stanza is not a continuation of the last line of the previous stanza (as it is for every other stanza transition). Explain that the stanza contains a passionate apostrophe to nature and its comforting role in memory.

Guided Practice: Apply

Think-Pair-Share Group students in pairs, and have them discuss how the stanza breaks in the poem complement the content of the stanzas.

Think About/Talk About

Responses to Margin Questions

Lines 65–85 *He loved nature with a passionate physical intensity.*

Lines 93–102 *The presence is a spirit that connects all living things.*

                                        If this
Be but a vain belief, yet, oh! how oft—
In darkness and amid the many shapes
Of joyless daylight; when the fretful stir
Unprofitable, and the fever of the world,
Have hung upon the beatings of my heart—
How oft, in spirit, have I turned to thee,
O sylvan° Wye! thou wanderer through the woods,
How often has my spirit turned to thee! **C**
   And now, with gleams of half-extinguished thought,
With many recognitions dim and faint,
And somewhat of a sad perplexity,
The picture of the mind° revives again:

56. sylvan: associated with the forest or woodlands.

61. picture of the mind: primarily the picture in the mind, but also the picture the individual mind has of itself.

C Reading Focus **Analyzing Patterns of Organization** In meditative lyrical poetry, stanzas do not have to be fixed in length. Why do you think Wordsworth made this stanza shorter than the others? How does the speaker's focus or emphasis change in this stanza?

Analyzing Visuals

Connecting to the Text What can you infer about Wordsworth's ideas of nature from this image? How might the elements of this environment represent "all in all" to him? What does it represent to you?

Tintern Abbey in the Wye Valley.

Analyzing Visuals

Connecting to the Text: *The image represents a serene and beautiful valley landscape. This can remind the reader of Wordsworth's appreciation of nature and his longing for an pure experience of nature that one can only have as a child. The presence of a church and a herd create the image of a harmonious nature.*

Real Issues, Real Experts

*Holt author **Kylene Beers** offers strategies for teaching "Lines Composed a Few Miles Above Tintern Abbey."*

To slow students down enough to enjoy this poem, begin by having students write briefly about a place they have visited as both a teen and a youngster—like a shopping mall, theater, or grandparent's house. Ask students to describe how their experiences in that place changed as they have grown older. To move into the poem, read aloud lines 1–22 to students. Next, re-read this one section and ask students to underline at least five lines (or portions of lines) they enjoyed. Then, ask students to read aloud

While here I stand, not only with the sense
Of present pleasure, but with pleasing thoughts
That in this moment there is life and food
For future years. And so I dare to hope,
Though changed, no doubt, from what I was when first
I came among these hills; when like a roe°
I bounded o'er the mountains, by the sides
Of the deep rivers, and the lonely streams,
Wherever nature led: more like a man
Flying from something that he dreads, than one
Who sought the thing he loved. For nature then
(The coarser pleasures of my boyish days,
And their glad animal movements all gone by)
To me was all in all.—I cannot paint
What then I was. The sounding cataract°
Haunted me like a passion: the tall rock,
The mountain, and the deep and gloomy wood,
Their colors and their forms, were then to me
An appetite; a feeling and a love,
That had no need of a remoter charm,°
By thought supplied, nor any interest
Unborrowed from the eye.—That time is past,
And all its aching joys are now no more,
And all its dizzy raptures. Not for this
Faint° I, nor mourn nor murmur; other gifts
Have followed; for such loss, I would believe,
Abundant recompense. For I have learned
To look on nature, not as in the hour
Of thoughtless youth; but hearing oftentimes
The still, sad music of humanity,
Nor harsh nor grating, though of ample power
To chasten and subdue. And I have felt
A presence that disturbs me with the joy
Of elevated thoughts; a sense sublime
Of something far more deeply interfused,
Whose dwelling is the light of setting suns,
And the round ocean and the living air,
And the blue sky, and in the mind of man:
A motion and a spirit, that impels
All thinking things, all objects of all thought,
And rolls through all things. Therefore am I still
A lover of the meadows and the woods,

67. roe: deer.

65–85. *With a hint of nostalgia, the speaker remembers the exhilarating times he spent in nature as a youth.*

? *How would you describe the speaker's relationship to nature when he was a boy?*

76. cataract: waterfall.

81. remoter charm: appeal other than the scene itself.

86. faint: become weak; lose heart.

? **93–102.** *Re-read these lines. In your own words, what is the "presence" (line 94) that the speaker describes?*

Vocabulary **recompense** (REHK uhm pehns) *n.:* payment or compensation in return for something lost.
impels (ihm PEHLZ) *v.:* forces; causes to move.

Think About/Talk About

Comprehension

C Reading Focus

Possible responses: *This stanza is specifically about the Wye Valley, and the speaker addresses the valley directly. The short stanza draws attention to this direct address.*

Extend the Discussion

Comparing and Contrasting How has the speaker's attitude changed in lines 83–91? ***Possible response:*** *Rapture has been replaced by mystical understanding.*

Determining Author's Purpose On p. 751, the speaker contrasts his views of nature as a youth with his views of nature as a mature adult. What is Wordsworth's purpose in having the speaker present this contrast? ***Possible response:*** *Wordsworth is showing the different relationships people have with nature at different points in their lives. He illustrates the calmer, more contemplative relationship one has with nature as one matures.*

Vocabulary: Own the Word

- **recompense:** Ask students, "Have you ever *recompensed* someone for some wrong or injury? Explain whom and when, and how you *recompensed* the person.
- **impels:** What, according to the poet, *impels* his thoughts? ***Possible response:*** *a motion and a spirit*

the lines they marked. As students share their lines, one at a time in no particular order, a found poem emerges. Finally, put students in pairs and have them continue reading the poem. Some pairs may choose to read silently, and others may choose to read aloud. Have students complete a T-chart as they read that lists on one side Wordsworth's feelings about nature when he was young and on the other his feelings now that he is older.

Universal Access

Students with Disabilities

Group students into pairs. Present each pair with a prepared Venn diagram on a sheet of paper. The left circle of the Venn diagram should be titled "Young," and the right circle should be titled "Mature." Have students study p. 751 and record the speaker's differing experiences with nature. In the central circle, students should record the ways in which the speaker views nature in the same way as a youth and as a mature adult.

Guided Practice: Apply

Think as a Reader/Writer

Find It in Your Reading Call students' attention to the sentence beginning with the word "Therefore" in line 102. Ask students to identify the line on which this sentence ends [*line 111*]. Remind students that by using long sentences across many lines of verse, Wordsworth mimics natural speech in his poetry.

Use It in Your Writing Give students a topic on which to write, such as pollution in rural or urban areas. Challenge students to write one sentence that spans at least three full lines of notebook paper. Then, ask students to think about the stressed and unstressed syllables in their sentence. If they were to turn their sentence into a poem of five to seven lines, where would they break the sentence and why?

Think About/Talk About

Responses to Margin Questions

Lines 111–115 *The speaker addresses his sister, Dorothy.*

Lines 116–134 *They do not rhyme; they are addressed to another person; one line often runs in to the next line.*

Lines 121–159 *The prayer is for Dorothy. The lines can be paraphrased as follows: "When your passion matures, as mine has, and you face hardships, take comfort from memories of this place; when I'm dead, remember me—how I loved this place more because we shared it."*

And mountains; and of all that we behold
From this green earth; of all the mighty world
Of eye, and ear, —both what they half create,
And what perceive; well pleased to recognize
In nature and the language of the sense
The anchor of my purest thoughts, the nurse,
The guide, the guardian of my heart, and soul
Of all my moral being. **D**
Nor perchance,
If I were not thus taught, should I the more
Suffer my genial spirits° to decay:
For thou art with me here upon the banks
Of this fair river; thou my dearest Friend,°
My dear, dear Friend; and in thy voice I catch
The language of my former heart, and read
My former pleasures in the shooting lights
Of thy wild eyes. Oh! yet a little while
May I behold in thee what I was once,
My dear, dear Sister! and this prayer I make,
Knowing that Nature never did betray
The heart that loved her; 'tis her privilege, **E**
Through all the years of this our life, to lead
From joy to joy: for she can so inform
The mind that is within us, so impress
With quietness and beauty, and so feed
With lofty thoughts, that neither evil tongues,
Rash judgments, nor the sneers of selfish men,
Nor greetings where no kindness is, nor all
The dreary intercourse° of daily life,
Shall e'er prevail against us, or disturb
Our cheerful faith, that all which we behold
Is full of blessings. Therefore let the moon **F**
Shine on thee in thy solitary walk;
And let the misty mountain winds be free
To blow against thee: and, in after years,
When these wild ecstasies shall be matured
Into a sober pleasure; when thy mind

? **111–115.** *What shift takes place in this final stanza?*

113. suffer my genial spirits: allow my creative powers.

115. my dearest Friend: Wordsworth's sister, Dorothy.

? **116–134.** *What makes these lines conversational?*

? **121–159.** *What prayer does the speaker make in these concluding lines? For whom is the prayer? Paraphrase the speaker's thoughts.*

131. intercourse: dealings; social contacts.

D **Literary Perspectives** **Philosophical Context** In lines 93–111, the speaker finds new meanings in his surroundings. What types of philosophical, spiritual, or religious meaning do you see in his words?

E **Literary Perspectives** **Philosophical Context** What might the speaker mean by "Nature never did betray / The heart that loved her" (lines 122–123)?

F **Literary Focus** **Blank Verse** Read lines 116–134 aloud, and note the rhythm of the words. How would you describe the speaker's tone here?

Universal Access

AAVE Students Who Use African American Vernacular English

English for Academic Success Read aloud lines 112–113. Point out that the phrase "If I were" uses the subjunctive mood in the past tense. Remind students that the subjunctive mood is used to express a condition that is doubtful or not factual. Tell students that when the verb *be* is used in the past subjunctive, *were* is used for all persons: *If I were taught, if he were taught,* instead of *if I was taught.* Have students create two statements in the subjunctive mood.

Reaching Reluctant Readers

Discuss with students the idea of a natural place in which people can express their true essence. Ask students to consider their own experience and tell about a place that they think stirs great emotions in them. It can be a place they visited or a place they would like to visit one day. Students can freewrite notes about the place to rearrange them in a poem of their own.

SOCIAL STUDIES **LINK**

The Wye Valley

The River Wye viewed west from Monsal Head and set in limestone dales, Bridge Peak District.

Some critics have faulted Wordsworth for painting an idyllic picture of the Wye Valley and effectively glossing over its poverty. Kenneth R. Johnson in *The Hidden Wordsworth* explains that the smoke Wordsworth saw rising through the trees was a product of the area's iron industry, which burned trees to produce charcoal for the forges. Wordsworth's suggestion that smoke "might seem" to come from "vagrant dwellers in the houseless woods" touches with extreme delicacy on a fact known to everyone who visited the abbey: that vagabonds made their living by begging from tourists. Today, the British government has designated the Wye Valley a Site of Special Scientific Interest, and the region is vigilantly protected from pollution.

Ask Yourself

Why might Wordsworth have omitted descriptions of poverty from his poem? Should knowledge about the iron industry in the Wye Valley and the beggars at the abbey change the way the poem is understood and enjoyed? Explain.

Shall be a mansion for all lovely forms,
Thy memory be as a dwelling place
For all sweet sounds and harmonies; oh! then,
If solitude, or fear, or pain, or grief,
Should be thy portion, with what healing thoughts
Of tender joy wilt thou remember me,
And these my exhortations! Nor, perchance—
If I should be where I no more can hear
Thy voice, nor catch from thy wild eyes these gleams
Of past existence—wilt thou then forget
That on the banks of this delightful stream
We stood together; and that I, so long
A worshipper of Nature, hither came
Unwearied in that service: rather say
With warmer love—oh! with far deeper zeal
Of holier love. Nor wilt thou then forget,
That after many wanderings, many years
Of absence, these steep woods and lofty cliffs,
And this green pastoral landscape, were to me
More dear, both for themselves and for thy sake!

Vocabulary **zeal** (zeel) *n.:* eager enthusiasm.

Think About/Talk About

Analysis

D Literary Perspectives

Possible response: *"Sense sublime," "deeply interfused," and "a spirit that impels all thinking things" all provide clues to Wordsworth's view of nature. These lines convey a spiritual calmness when experiencing nature. It is in spiritual calmness that one can best contemplate philosophical truths.*

E Literary Perspectives

Possible response: *Nature will not disappoint a creature that appreciates and honors her.*

F Literary Focus

Possible response: *Wordsworth varies the meter; it is not strictly iambic pentameter. There are extra unstressed syllables that create a more conversational tone.*

Social Studies Link

Ask Yourself

Possible response: *The poem deals with universal and philosophical issues such as the relationship between humans and nature and the way people's perceptions change with maturity. If Wordsworth had included descriptions of the poverty that affected the Wye Valley, the poem would have had a polemic tone that would have interfered with Wordsworth's philosophical speculation.*

Vocabulary: Own the Word

zeal: Write the word *zeal* in a center circle on the board along with its definition, "enthusiasm." Draw "spider legs" and elicit related attributes of the word from students. ***Possible responses:*** *fervor, spirit, zest, bustle, diligence, eagerness, earnestness, ardor, willingness, passion, hunger, devotion, vigor*

California Standards, pp. 754–756

- **Reading Standard 2.2** Analyze the way in which clarity of meaning is affected by the patterns of organization, hierarchical structures, repetition of the main ideas, syntax, and word choice in the text.
- **Reading Standard 3.2** Analyze the way in which the theme or meaning of a selection represents a view or comment on life, using textual evidence to support the claim.
- **Reading Standard 3.3** Analyze ways in which irony, tone, mood, the author's style, and the "sound" of language achieve specific rhetorical or aesthetic purposes or both.
- **Reading Standard 3.9** Analyze the philosophical arguments presented in literary works to determine whether the authors' positions have contributed to the quality of each work and the credibility of the characters. (Philosophical approach)
- **Grades 9–10 Review Reading Standard 1.1** Identify and use the literal and figurative meanings of words and understand word derivations.
- **Writing Standard 1.5** Use language in natural, fresh, and vivid ways to establish a specific tone.
- **Writing Standard 2.1** Write fictional, autobiographical, or biographical narrative. **b.** Locate scenes and incidents in specific places.
- **Writing Standard 2.3** Write reflective compositions. **a.** Explore the significance of personal experiences, events, conditions, or concerns by using rhetorical strategies (e.g., narration, description, exposition, persuasion).
- **Listening and Speaking Standard 2.3** Deliver oral responses to literature. **a.** Demonstrate a comprehensive understanding of the significant ideas of literary works.

Check for Understanding

Independent Practice

Reading Skills Focus

Possible responses:

1. *He has lost his youthful passionate response to nature.*
2. *He sees a passionate, spontaneous joy in nature in her eyes.*
3. *He remembers the beauty and spiritual gifts that nature offers. He relives his experiences through his memories and through sharing the experience with his sister.*
4. *Have students focus on the content and tone of each stanza to determine the poem's pattern of organization.*

Literary Skills Focus

Possible responses:

5. *He has received maturity and a deeper understanding of nature.*
6. *He has lost his innocence and perhaps felt despair.*
7. *Nature can heal and teach by guiding someone toward a quiet place of meditation and strength.*
8. *His sister offers him a look back at his youthful relationship with nature.*
9. *The speaker realizes that nature means even more to him now than before because he has a deeper appreciation of its spiritual significance and because he has shared the experience with Dorothy. Students' responses will vary.*
10. *In lines 100–105, Wordsworth states that nature has the power to lead humans toward their truth.*
11. *Lines 30–34 and lines 114–119 are especially conversational. Wordsworth varies the number of unstressed syllables to enhance the conversational quality of the poem.*
12. *Structure, word choice, imagery, and meter contribute to the theme of nature's profound impact on humanity.*

Applying Your Skills

Reading Standard 2.2, 3.2, 3.3, 3.9 (see pages A48–A50)
Writing Standard 1.5 (see pages A51–A52)

Lines Composed a Few Miles Above Tintern Abbey

Literary Response and Analysis

Reading Skills Focus

Quick Check

1. What has the speaker lost since he first "came among these hills" (line 67)?
2. What does the speaker see in his sister that makes him more aware of what he "was once" (lines 120–121)?

Read with a Purpose

3. What benefits does the speaker derive from returning to nature? How does he come to recognize these benefits?

Reading Skills: Analyzing Patterns of Organization

4. Review your chart. How does Wordsworth use the stanzas to organize his ideas? How does the structure of the stanzas contribute to the conversational quality of the poem?

Literary Skills Focus

Literary Analysis

5. **Interpret** What "gifts" (line 86) and "abundant recompense" (line 88) does the speaker believe he has received for his "loss" (line 87)?
6. **Draw Conclusions** What does the speaker mean when he says, in line 91, that he has heard "the still, sad music of humanity"?
7. **Evaluate** In lines 109–111, the speaker calls nature "the nurse, / The guide, the guardian of my heart, and soul / Of all my moral being." How can nature heal and teach?
8. **Analyze** What role does the speaker's sister play in the poem? How does the speaker regard her involvement?
9. **Extend** Summarize and comment on the speaker's conclusion (beginning with line 102). Have you had to face losing part of your past? How did you handle the loss?
10. **Literary Perspectives** As you read, you noted Wordsworth's philosophy about nature. What assumptions about nature does he express in this poem? Support your answer with examples.

Literary Skills: Blank Verse

11. **Analyze** Find two examples from the poem that sound especially conversational in tone. How does Wordsworth's use of blank verse enhance the conversational quality of the poem?

Literary Skills Review: Theme

12. **Evaluate** The central idea or insight about human experience revealed in a work of literature is called **theme.** What is this poem's theme? What do the text's structure, word choice, or imagery reveal about the theme?

Writing Skills Focus

Think as a Reader/Writer

Use It in Your Writing In "Tintern Abbey," Wordsworth writes a deeply personal meditation in a form he and Coleridge called the "conversation poem." As you read, you noted some techniques Wordsworth uses to create a conversational tone. Using a similar conversational tone, write a poem or a brief reflective composition about a subject of your choice.

What Do You Think Now? How can experiences with nature help us think creatively about "the dreary intercourse of daily life"?

Universal Access

Struggling Writers

Provide additional scaffolding for students to complete the Writing Skills Focus activity. Review the techniques Wordsworth used to create a conversational tone. Remind them that Wordsworth varied the rhythm in lines 30–34 and in lines 114–119. Have students write a poem on a nature using the pattern of alternating stressed and unstressed syllables. Then, have them go back and add an additional unstressed syllable in two lines to create a conversational tone.

What Do You Think Now?

Brainstorm with students the ways in which nature rejuvenates them in their daily lives. Then, discuss how those experiences help them think creatively about mundane aspects of their daily routines.

Grades 9–10 Review Reading Standard 1.1 (see pages A48–A50)

Vocabulary Development

Vocabulary Check

Match the Vocabulary words with their definitions.

1. corporeal	a. forces
2. zeal	b. enthusiasm
3. impels	c. bodily
4. recompense	d. compensation
5. pastoral	e. majestic
6. sublime	f. peaceful

Vocabulary Skills: Etymology

Knowledge of **etymology,** or word origins, can be an excellent tool for understanding meaning, usage, and related words. The chart below shows the etymology of the Vocabulary words from "Tintern Abbey."

English Word	Word Origin	Original Meaning
corporeal	Latin *corporeus*	belonging to the body
impels	Latin *impellere*	*in–*, on + *pellere,* to push
pastoral	Latin *pastoralis* < *pastor*	shepherd
recompense	Latin *recompensare*	*re–*, back + *compensare,* to balance out
sublime	Latin *sublimus*	uplifted; high; lofty
zeal	Latin *zelus* < Greek *zēlos*	ardor; jealousy

Your Turn

Match the Vocabulary words with words that have similar origins. Then, write sentences that explain the similarities and differences between the two words in each pair. Consult the chart to the left and a dictionary for help.

1. corporeal	a. pastor
2. zeal	b. pension
3. impels	c. corpse
4. recompense	d. sublimation
5. pastoral	e. compel
6. sublime	f. zealot

Language Coach

Suffixes The suffix *–al,* which can mean "of" or "relating to," is often found at the end of adjectives. The suffix can be added to words that stand alone as nouns *(convention, conventional)* or to roots that cannot stand alone *(corporeal).* Tell the meaning of each word in italics. Then, answer the questions.

1. How might *corporeal* beauty be both an advantage and a disadvantage?
2. Do poets give too much emphasis to *spiritual* concerns?
3. Does Wordsworth seem to agree with *conventional* ideas of youth and old age?
4. How can a poem produce two responses, one *emotional* and the other intellectual?

Academic Vocabulary

Write About

How does Wordsworth differentiate childhood from adulthood? Why does he say childhood functions as a state of heightened awareness?

Universal Access: Vocabulary Development

EL English Learners

English for Academic Success Have students find the etymology of each Academic Vocabulary word and organize their information in the vocabulary chart as shown on p. 755. Have them verbalize the relationship between the word origins to the original meanings. For example, one might say, "The word *inherent* comes from the Latin *inhaerére,* which means 'to stick.' Similarly, *inherent* refers to a quality existing or sticking onto something, or someone, permanently."

Struggling Readers

Reinforce students' understanding of the Academic Vocabulary words by discussing the meanings of related words. Have them use each word in a sentence.

- **differentiation**—the process of making something different
- **functional**—designed to be useful
- **inherently**—basically
- **technical**—of or derived from a method

Independent Practice

Vocabulary Development

Vocabulary Check

1. *c* **2.** *b*
3. *a* **4.** *d*
5. *f* **6.** *e*

Your Turn

Possible responses:

1. c; *both refer to the body, but a* corpse *refers to a dead body.*
2. f; Zealot, *a noun, refers to a person who shows zeal.*
3. e; *both words deal with a forward drive or urge, but* compel *connotes a stronger force.*
4. b; *a* pension *is a specific kind of compensation.*
5. a; pastoral *implies the rustic scene, while a pastor is a religious "shepherd."*
6. d; sublimation *is the noun form of sublime.*

English for Academic Success

Language Coach

Possible responses:

1. *"of the body"; Corporeal beauty is admired and appreciated, but not lasting.*
2. *"of the spirit"; No, spiritual concerns are emphasized when necessary.*
3. *"relating to convention"; Yes. Youth reflects passion and unawareness; old age reflects maturity*
4. *"of emotion"; poetry can evoke our emotions and also pose questions for us to ponder*

English for Academic Success

Academic Vocabulary

Possible response: *Wordsworth associates childhood with a fervent and spontaneous response to the sights of nature that diminishes with age. Childhood functions as a period of heightened awareness with strong impressions on the senses.*

Independent Practice

Grammar Link

Your Turn

1. *The speaker responds to a landscape he has visited before, a spot above the Wye River.*
2. *The beautiful woodland place stirs deep memories.*
3. *We are studying the works of Wordsworth, the Romantic poet.*

Choices: Evaluation Criteria

Review: Homework
Determine Style
Students compare and contrast lines of earlier poems with lines of "Tintern Abbey," referring to rhyme, meter, imagery, and poetic devices.

Connect: Timed Writing 40–50 Minutes
Students compare and contrast their experience of the place in the present with their experience of the place in the past.

Extend: Homework
Listen to Music
- Students demonstrate understanding of how the music captures the mood of the symphony's title.
- Students write from Wordsworth's philosophical perspective.

Assess

Unit 4 Resources, Selection Standards Check, p. 30

ThinkCentral Online Assessment, Selection Standards Check

Teacher One Stop™, editable Selection Standards Check

Reteach

To reteach **patterns of organization,** see **Reteaching Lessons,** pp. 1449D–1449E.

ThinkCentral Online Remediation

Applying Your Skills

Lines Composed a Few Miles Above Tintern Abbey

Grammar Link

Appositives

An **appositive** is a noun or pronoun placed beside another noun or pronoun to identify or describe it. An appositive with modifiers is an **appositive phrase.**

> William Wordsworth, **poet,** found his calling during the 1790s.
> His poems, **some of the most influential of his time,** are still read today.

A **nonessential** or **nonrestrictive appositive** is not essential to a sentence's meaning. These appositives are set off by commas to show that they interrupt sentences that would still be clear without them.

> He collaborated with Samuel Taylor Coleridge.
> He collaborated with Samuel Taylor Coleridge, **another founder of English Romanticism.**

An **essential** or **restrictive appositive,** which is not set off by commas, makes the noun or pronoun it describes more specific. Without the appositive, the sentence loses essential information or meaning.

> The collection appeared in 1798.
> The collection ***Lyrical Ballads*** appeared in 1798.

Your Turn

Rewrite the sentences by adding the italicized words as appositives. Use commas for nonessential appositives.

1. The speaker responds to a landscape he has visited before. *(a spot on the Wye River)*
2. The place stirs deep memories. *(a beautiful woodland)*
3. We are studying the works of the romantic poet. *(William Wordsworth)*

Writing Application Write a paragraph about a friend who has had a great positive influence on you. Use appositive phrases appropriately in your description.

CHOICES

As you respond to the Choices, use these **Academic Vocabulary** words as appropriate: differentiate, inherent, device, technique, function.

REVIEW
Determine the Style of the Poem
The style of Romantic literature differentiates it from many earlier literary works. From what you have read of British literature, do you think "Tintern Abbey" closely resembles the poetry that preceded it, or is it innovative, representing an overt break in tradition? In a small group, hold a panel discussion, with students debating both sides of the issue.

CONNECT
Share an Experience
Timed Writing Write a short essay in which you describe a place that evokes strong memories or holds emotional meaning for you. Describe the place with specific details, and explain why the location has special significance for you.

EXTEND
Listen to Music
The preeminent German composer Ludwig van Beethoven (1770–1827) was a leading musical figure in the transition between the Classical and Romantic periods. His Symphony No. 6 in F, the *Pastoral Symphony,* is one of the great program works in music history. An ode to nature, the cheerful, melodic first movement is labeled "The Awakening of Joyful Feelings upon Arrival in the Country." Listen to this movement, and discuss how it captures the mood of the title. Then, compose a journal entry, similar to what Wordsworth might have written, commenting on Beethoven's musical homage to nature and nature's inherent effect on the human mind and emotions.

Universal Access: Grammar Link

English Learners
English for Academic Success To give students more practice with appositives, have them write several sentences describing their favorite character in a book or film. Then, have them read over their sentences and combine them so that their sentences contain essential and nonessential appositives. As students revise their sentences, have them work with a partner to discuss whether their appositives are essential or nonessential.

✔ For more practice with appositives, see **Warriner's Handbook, GrammarNotes,** and **Language Handbook Worksheets.**

Reading Standard 3.4 (see pages A48–A50)

from Ode: Intimations of Immortality from Recollections of Early Childhood

Literary Skills Focus

Meter and Rhyme A poem's regular pattern of stressed and unstressed syllables is called its **meter.** Finding the meter, which creates the poem's rhythm, requires identifying patterns of stressed and unstressed syllables. **Rhyme** is the repetition of accented vowel sounds and all sounds following them in words close together in a poem; the most common type of rhyme, **end rhyme,** occurs at the ends of lines. **Rhyme scheme** describes a poem's overall pattern of rhyme. In "Ode," Wordsworth uses a variable meter of iambic lines of different lengths and a variable rhyme scheme.

Reading Skills Focus

Annotating a Poem When you **annotate** a poem, you add explanatory notes—definitions, interpretations, explanations, questions, or even personal reflections—to help you analyze and feel engaged by the text.

Into Action Annotate Wordsworth's "Ode" line by line in your *Reader/Writer Notebook.* Following the example below, indicate each type of note you make and be sure to include notes on meter and rhyme.

Stanza 1	Annotations
lines 1–4	**interpretation:** rhyme scheme = abab
line 2	**explanation:** paraphrase = beauty found in common sights
lines 4–5	**definition:** "apparelled" = clothed; "celestial," "glory" suggest heaven
line 6	**reflection:** "It is not now as it hath been" = change of opinion. What happened? "Yore" brings contrast between past and present.

Writing Skills Focus

Think as a Reader/Writer

Find It in Your Reading The use of language to evoke a concrete sensation of a person, thing, place, or experience is called **imagery.** As you read, take notes in your *Reader/Writer Notebook* on the words and phrases Wordsworth uses to create images that represent inherent changes that come with adulthood.

Vocabulary

piety (PY uh tee) *n.:* devotion to religion. *Wordsworth believed that children show piety through their simple acts of innocence and kindness.*

celestial (suh LEHS chuhl) *adj.:* heavenly. *According to Wordsworth, the soul is a celestial creation and therefore capable of becoming close to God.*

Language Coach

Word Origins *Piety* comes from a Latin word meaning "kind; dutiful." The adjective *pious,* which comes from the same Latin root, refers to religious devotion. What do you think *impiety* and *impious* mean?

Learn It Online
Practice your Vocabulary knowledge online with Word Watch.
go.hrw.com H12-757 Go

Reader/Writer Notebook
Use your **RWN** to complete the activities for this selection.

Preteach

Introducing Vocabulary

- Review the Vocabulary words, definitions, and sentences with students.
- To reinforce the importance of the Vocabulary words, tell students that both these words relate to the magical perspective of childhood.

English for Academic Success

Language Coach

Have students read the **Language Coach.** Tell students that the prefix *im–* is a variation of the prefix *in–* and often appears in front of words starting with *m* or *p*, like in *immature* and *imperfect*, turning a word meaning into its opposite.

Literary Skills Focus

As you read and discuss the selection with students, have them note when the meter or rhyme scheme changes.

Reading Skills Focus

Give students a copy of the Reading Skills Focus graphic organizer before they read. (See **Unit 4 Resources.**) Tell them to use their responses to answer the questions on the Applying Your Skills page.

Writing Skills Focus

Have students note in their **Reader/Writer Notebooks** language that evokes images and use their notes to complete the Writing Skills Focus activity.

Selection Resources

Unit 4 Resources, on-level practice, p. 33
Teacher One Stop™, on-level lesson plans
Holt Audio Library
Holt Audio Library: Selections and Summaries in Spanish
UA: Differentiating Instruction, graphic organizer, p. 172
UA: Supporting Instruction in Spanish, selection summary
ThinkCentral Online Assessment, Selection Standards Check

California Standards, pp. 757–760

- **Reading Standard 3.4** Analyze ways in which poets use imagery, personification, figures of speech, and "sounds" to evoke readers' emotions.

Learn It Online
Send students to **Word Watch** for audio pronunciations, synonyms and antonyms, and brief histories of word origins.
go.hrw.com H12-757 Go

Teacher Preparation

Selection Summary

After saying the child is father of the man, the speaker recalls the light and glory of childhood. In the first two stanzas of "Ode: Intimations of Immortality," his mood is elegiac, but it grows more philosophical in the fifth stanza, where he equates birth with a sleep in which we almost forget our heavenly origins, although we are "trailing clouds of glory." As the child ages, it fades "into the light of common day."

Direct Teach

Think About/Talk About

Read with a Purpose Before they read, have a few students share with the class a difficult situation in which they felt they responded as an adult rather than as a young person. How did the experience change the way they saw themselves?

Comprehension

A Reading Focus

Possible response: *Students should write down the references to see how the references to light are woven throughout the selection.*

Extend the Discussion

Determining Author's Purpose

Why might the writer have included the epigraph in the poem? ***Possible response:*** *Perhaps he included the epigraph to present his philosophical view to the reader before going on with his poem.*

ODE

from Ode

Intimations of Immortality from Recollections of Early Childhood

by **William Wordsworth**

Read with a Purpose

Read to discover the changes that occur within the human soul during the process of growing up.

Build Background

An **ode** is a complex, generally long lyric poem on a serious subject. The **epigraph,** or opening quotation, of Wordsworth's ode was taken from "My Heart Leaps Up," one of his best-loved poems. "Ode: Intimations of Immortality" is more than two hundred lines long; only three of the eleven stanzas are reprinted here. According to Wordsworth, two years passed between the writing of the first four stanzas and the remaining seven. In the poem, Wordsworth recalls the innocent joy of childhood, takes pleasure in the beauty of nature, and reflects on the rewards that come with maturity.

The Child is Father of the Man;
And I could wish my days to be
Bound each to each by natural piety.

1

There was a time when meadow, grove, and stream,
The earth, and every common sight,
To me did seem
Apparelled in celestial light, **A**
The glory and the freshness of a dream.
It is not now as it hath been of yore;—
Turn wheresoe'er I may,
By night or day,
The things which I have seen I now can see no more.

Master Hare, Francis George Hare (1788–1789) by Sir Joshua Reynolds (1723–1792). Louvre, Paris, France.

A Reading Focus **Annotating a Poem** Line 4 includes the first of several references to light, the sun, or the reflection of light. As you record these references, note how light imagery is woven throughout the poem.

Vocabulary **piety** (PY uh tee) *n.:* devotion to religion.
celestial (suh LEHS chuhl) *adj.:* heavenly.

Universal Access

English Learners

Some students might struggle to understand rhyme because of challenges with pronunciation. Explain that rhyming is an exact match of sounds. Review with them the different kinds of rhyme in this excerpt: end rhyme, internal rhyme, and feminine rhyme. End rhyme occurs when the words at the end of each line rhyme. Internal rhyme is when two rhyming words appear in the same line. Feminine rhyme is when two-syllable words rhyme.

Struggling Readers

Strategic Students Model annotating a poem for students. To help them recognize rhyme scheme, read the first stanza aloud to them, accentuating the last word in each line. Then, read only the last words of each line, stopping after each pair to allow students to recognize the rhyme. Under the column "Stanza 1," tell students they should write "ll. 1–9," and next to it, under "Annotations," students should write "interpretation: rhyme scheme = *ababacddc.*"

2

The Rainbow comes and goes,
And lovely is the Rose,
The Moon doth with delight
Look round her when the heavens are bare,
Waters on a starry night
Are beautiful and fair;
The sunshine is a glorious birth;
But yet I know, where'er I go, Ⓑ
That there hath passed away a glory from the earth.

. . . .

5

Our birth is but a sleep and a forgetting:
The Soul that rises with us, our life's Star,°
Hath had elsewhere its setting, Ⓒ
And cometh from afar:
Not in entire forgetfulness,
And not in utter nakedness,
But trailing clouds of glory do we come
From God, who is our home:
Heaven lies about us in our infancy!
Shades of the prison-house begin to close
Upon the growing Boy,
But He beholds the light, and whence it flows,
He sees it in his joy;
The Youth, who daily farther from the east
Must travel, still is Nature's Priest,
And by the vision splendid
Is on his way attended;
At length the Man perceives it die away,
And fade into the light of common day.

Master Bunbury (1780 or 1781) by Sir Joshua Reynolds (1723–1792). Oil on canvas.
The Philadelphia Museum of Art, Pennsylvania, The John Howard McFadden Collection, 1928.

---

20. **our life's Star:** the sun, a metaphor for the soul.

Ⓑ **Literary Focus** **Meter and Rhyme** How do the internal rhyme (rhyme within a line) and the repetition of the word *I* reinforce the attitude expressed by the speaker?

Ⓒ **Literary Focus** **Meter and Rhyme** In line 21, Wordsworth uses a two-syllable (or feminine) rhyme for the first time. What is the effect of this shift in rhyme?

California Standards, p. 760

- **Reading Standard 3.4** Analyze ways in which poets use imagery, personification, figures of speech, and sound to evoke readers' emotions.
- **Writing Standard 2.3** Write reflective compositions. **a.** Explore the significance of personal experiences, events, conditions, or concerns by using rhetorical strategies (e.g., narration, description, exposition, persuasion).

Think About/Talk About

Analysis

Ⓑ Literary Focus

Possible response: *The internal rhyme and repetition of the pronoun* I *create a childlike, singsong feeling in this line.*

Ⓒ Literary Focus

Possible responses: *The feminine rhyme softens the language of the poem. It also offers more complexity, which reinforces the meaning in this stanza.*

Extend the Discussion

Making Predictions Based on what you have read so far, what can you predict about the meter and rhyme of the last six stanzas of the poem? ***Possible response:*** *Since the poem progresses from discussing childhood to discussing adulthood, and since the stanzas here depict an increasing level of sophistication, it is reasonable to predict that the meter and rhyme will increase in complexity in the last six stanzas.*

Vocabulary: Own the Word

- **piety:** Tell students the root word for *piety* is *pietās,* which is Latin for "dutiful conduct." Ask students to name situations that especially call for *piety*.
- **celestial:** A *celestial* place is a waterfall. A *celestial* color is shimmery blue. Watching the sun rising over the ocean is a *celestial* scene.

Check for Understanding

Independent Practice

Reading Skills Focus

Possible responses:

1. *A child views the world as if everything is bathed in starlight.*
2. *Images of the sun, "life's Star," (line 20) are used to describe the soul.*
3. *The soul forgets past experiences when it is born in a new body.*
4. *Students should consider how variations in rhyme and meter affect the poem's meaning.*

Vocabulary Check

5. *I would look in the sky.*
6. *religious figures*

Literary Skills Focus

Possible responses:

7. *Childhood can teach adults to respond to life in original ways.*
8. *The speaker is expressing his loss of the magical reverence of a child's perspective. The image suggests holiness, purity, or eternity.*
9. *He regrets that nature is no longer as magical for him as it was.*
10. *The sun is a metaphor for the soul. The sun is powerful and lasts beyond mortal lifetimes.*
11. *The hardships of adult life close in around the boy like a prison.*
12. *Stanza 1—*ababacddc*; stanza 2—*aabcbcdeed*; stanza 3—*ababccddefefdgghhii*. Wordsworth uses several couplets in lines 32–37. Wordsworth uses couplets, alternating end rhymes, and internal rhyme to link ideas.*
13. *The speaker uses images of light to describe the superior state of the child who understands nature. As the child grows old, the light dims and the child can only remember the light thanks to an acquired understanding of life.*

Applying Your Skills

Reading Standard 3.4 (see pages A48–A50)
Writing Standard 2.3a (see pages A51–A52)

from **Ode: Intimations of Immortality from Recollections of Early Childhood**

Literary Response and Analysis

Reading Skills Focus

Quick Check

1. According to the speaker, how does a child view the world?
2. What images describe the human soul?
3. Why does the speaker call birth a "forgetting"?

Reading Skills: Annotating a Poem

4. Circle your annotations about meter and rhyme. Where do variations occur in the meter or rhyme scheme? What do these variations reveal about the poem's meaning? Refer to your annotations and to lines from the poem to explain your response. See the example below.

> Unlike earlier stanzas, stanza 5 ends in a heroic couplet (two lines of rhymed iambic pentameter). This tidy ending seems to put the final stamp on the permanent loss of childlike innocence experienced in adulthood.

Vocabulary Check

Check your understanding of the Vocabulary words by answering the following questions:

5. Where would you look to locate a **celestial** object?
6. Whom or what do you associate with **piety**?

Literary Skills Focus

Literary Analysis

7. **Analyze** The **epigraph,** or opening quotation, presents a **paradox,** an apparent contradiction. What can our childhood experiences teach us when we are adults?
8. **Interpret** In stanza 1, the speaker describes something he has lost. What is the speaker describing? What does the image "apparelled in celestial light" (line 4) make you visualize?
9. **Interpret** According to stanza 2, how does the speaker feel now when he looks at nature?
10. **Evaluate** How is the sun used in the **extended metaphor,** or comparison, in stanza 5?
11. **Extend** Give some examples of what you think the poet means by the "prison-house" that closes in "upon the growing Boy" in lines 28–29.

Literary Skills: Meter and Rhyme

12. **Analyze** Identify the rhyme scheme of the stanzas. Where does Wordsworth use several couplets? How does he use rhyme to link ideas?

Literary Skills Review: Imagery

13. **Analyze** Language that appeals to the senses, **imagery,** evokes a picture or concrete sensation of a person, place, thing, or experience. How are images of light and vision used to develop the poem's theme?

Writing Skills Focus

Think as a Reader/Writer

Use It in Your Writing What memories do you have of childhood? Choose a meaningful memory, and describe it in a reflective paragraph. Use imagery to capture the feeling of childhood as you remember it.

What Do You Think Now? How can we find truth by looking at the world through the imagination of a child?

Universal Access

Struggling Writers

Some students may need additional scaffolding to complete the Writing Skills Focus activity. Have them freewrite for ten minutes what they saw, heard, and felt during their memorable experience. Then, have them read stanza 2 and point out Wordsworth's use of personification of nature. Encourage students to use personification in their paragraphs as they write.

What Do You Think Now?

As students consider the question, ask them to think about the differences between a child's understanding of "truth" as compared to the "truth" of adults.

Assess

Unit 4 Resources, Selection Standards Check, p. 35

Preparing to Read

Reading Standard 3.4 (see pages A48–A50)

Composed upon Westminster Bridge

Literary Skills Focus

Personification Wordsworth breathes life into his sonnet by using **personification,** a type of metaphor in which a nonhuman thing is talked about as if it were human. Inanimate objects often strike us with the seeming humanity of their sounds and movements. To a poet or anyone with imagination, the stars may look as if they are winking at people on Earth, or the wind blowing in the trees may sound as if it is whispering. As you read "Composed upon Westminster Bridge," look for instances in which Wordsworth personifies the city, the sun, the river, and even the houses of London.

Writing Skills Focus

Think as a Reader/Writer

Find It in Your Reading In "Composed upon Westminster Bridge," Wordsworth describes a view of London in the early morning by using vivid adjectives, such as *glittering* and *smokeless,* to explain how the speaker feels and what he sees. As you read, record in your *Reader/Writer Notebook* some of the adjectives that the poet uses. What is the function of these adjectives? What impressions do they create?

Adjectives	Nouns or Pronouns Adjectives Describe	Effects
silent, bare	morning	stillness and quiet

Vocabulary

majesty (MAJ uh stee) *n.:* grandeur. *Wordsworth believes that the sight of Westminster Bridge in the morning is one of pure majesty.*

splendor (SPLEHN duhr) *n.:* great brightness; brilliant light. *The rising sun bathed the city in splendor.*

Language Coach

Related Words You can find related adjectives by adding certain suffixes to nouns. Add the suffix *–ic* to the noun *majesty,* for example, to form the adjective *majestic.* Add the suffix *–id* to the root of *splendor* to form the adjective *splendid.* What do *majestic* and *splendid* mean? Can you think of other adjectives that have these endings?

Learn It Online
Explore Wordsworth's world through these Internet links.
go.hrw.com H12-761 Go

Reader/Writer Notebook
Use your **RWN** to complete the activities for this selection.

Preteach

Introducing Vocabulary

- Review the Vocabulary words, definitions, and sentences with students.
- To reinforce the importance of the Vocabulary words, tell students that the poem celebrates the *majesty* of Westminster Bridge, appearing to the speaker in the *splendor* of the sun.

English for Academic Success

Language Coach

Point out to students that when the suffixes *–ic* and *–id* are added to the two Vocabulary words, the suffixes replace the words' *y* and *or* endings, respectively. ***Possible response:*** Majestic *means "grand."* Splendid *means "brilliant" or "excellent." Other adjectives with the endings* –ic *and* –id *are* pathetic, poetic, candid, *and* sordid.

Literary Skills Focus

As you read and discuss the poem with students, have them note the ways Wordsworth attributes human qualities to nonhuman things.

Writing Skills Focus

Have students record adjectives in their **Reader/Writer Notebooks.** Students can use their notes to complete the Writing Skills Focus activity.

Selection Resources

Unit 4 Resources, on-level practice, p. 39
Teacher One Stop™, on-level lesson plans
Holt Audio Library
Holt Audio Library: Selections and Summaries in Spanish
UA: Differentiating Instruction, graphic organizer, p. 172
UA: Supporting Instruction in Spanish, selection summary
ThinkCentral Online Assessment, Selection Standards Check

California Standards, pp. 761–765

- **Reading Standard 3.4** Analyze ways in which poets use imagery, personification, figures of speech, and sounds to evoke readers' emotions.

Learn It Online
The enhanced author biography offers more information on the life of the author as well as Holt's interactive resources pertaining to the author.
go.hrw.com H12-761 Go

Teacher Preparation
Selection Summary
"Composed upon Westminster Bridge" praises the quiet, shimmering beauty of London in the early-morning light. In the octave the speaker personifies the city, describing it as wearing the beauty of morning "like a garment." In the sestet the sun, the river, and the houses are also personified. The last line presents the paradoxical picture of a powerful city at rest.

Direct Teach
Think About/Talk About
Read with a Purpose Ask students if they have a different perception of a place at different times of the day. For example, how do students respond to being in an car very early in the morning, or in the school building at nighttime?

Analysis
A Literary Focus

Possible response: *The city "wears" morning like a "garment," and the "houses seem asleep."*

Extend the Discussion
Paradox What paradox, or seeming contradiction, can the reader find in the poem's last line? ***Possible response:*** *A heart cannot be both alive and still.*

Vocabulary: Own the Word
- **majesty:** Ask students what the poet meant when he pointed to London's *majesty.* ***Possible responses:*** *The silent beauty of the morning, the sleeping towers, domes, theaters, and temples against the background of a sunrise.*
- **splendor:** Remind students that when an object or event is described as exhibiting *splendor,* it is one of vast richness, brilliance, and beauty. Ask students to name events or objects that exhibit *splendor.* ***Possible responses:*** *a rainbow, a sunrise, gold*

SONNET

Composed upon Westminster Bridge

September 3, 1802

by **William Wordsworth**

Read with a Purpose
Read to find out how the speaker feels upon viewing the city of London at daybreak.

Build Background
Published in 1807, this sonnet shows that Wordsworth, even as an ardent lover of nature, could be moved by the majesty of a sleeping city (in this case, London) as well as by mountains and waterfalls. This London, seen from a distance, is clearly a different London from the one of Blake's chimney sweepers (see pages 739–740) and the one known as the "great wen [wart]" that shocked many of Wordsworth's contemporaries with its filth and poverty. Here, London's filth and poverty are disguised and transformed by the poet's imagination.

Earth has not anything to show more fair:
Dull would he be of soul who could pass by
A sight so touching in its majesty:
This City now doth, like a garment, wear
The beauty of the morning; silent, bare,
Ships, towers, domes, theaters, and temples lie
Open unto the fields, and to the sky;
All bright and glittering in the smokeless air.
Never did sun more beautifully steep
In his first splendor, valley, rock, or hill;
Ne'er saw I, never felt, a calm so deep!
The river glideth at his own sweet will:
Dear God! the very houses seem asleep;
And all that mighty heart is lying still! **A**

Westminster Bridge, London.

A Literary Focus **Personification** What details in the poem personify the city?

Vocabulary **majesty** (MAJ uh stee) *n.:* grandeur.
splendor (SPLEHN duhr) *n.:* great brightness; brilliant light.

Universal Access

EL English Learners
English for Academic Success Make sure students understand that *fair,* as used in line 1, means "beautiful" (not "impartial" or "just"). Also, help them with the syntax and diction of line 2. Offer this paraphrase: "The person who could pass by [without noticing the scene] must be slow to perceive [beauty]."

Advanced Learners
Acceleration Ask students to contrast the view of London that Wordsworth presents in this poem with the more realistic picture of a city of industry in the early nineteenth century.

Preparing to Read

Reading Standard 3.4 (see pages A48–A50)

The World Is Too Much with Us

Literary Skills Focus

Allusion An **allusion** is a reference to a statement, person, place, event, or thing that is known from literature, history, religion, mythology, politics, science, or popular culture. Writers often use allusions to give deeper meaning to their work. In Wordsworth's "The World Is Too Much with Us," the speaker alludes to Proteus and Triton, two sea gods from Greek mythology. By making reference to these gods, Wordsworth underscores an earlier idea in the poem. Look for this connection as you read.

Writing Skills Focus

Think as a Reader/Writer

Find It in Your Reading As you read "The World Is Too Much with Us," notice how Wordsworth uses adjectives to describe humans' relationship to the material world. Pay special attention to his use of participles (adjectives formed from verbs). Create a chart in your *Reader/Writer Notebook* to record some of the poem's adjectives and their effect in the poem.

Adjectives	Nouns or Pronouns Adjectives Describe	Effects
getting, spending	we	portrays man as wasteful and careless

Vocabulary

sordid (SAWR dihd) *adj.:* foul; filthy. *Sacrificing our integrity for material things is a sordid aspect of modern life.*

pagan (PAY guhn) *n.:* person who believes in many gods or no god. *Those who worshiped the gods of ancient Greece were called pagans.*

creed (kreed) *n.:* essential points of religious belief. *His creed requires that he show respect for all creatures.*

forlorn (fawr LAWRN) *adj.:* hopeless; wretched. *He felt forlorn when he witnessed the excessive spending and waste of the modern world.*

Language Coach

Connotations The ideas or feelings associated with words are their **connotations.** Some words have strong negative or judgmental connotations. *Sordid* has a similar meaning to *dirty,* but much more negative, moralistic connotations. The word *pagan,* which means someone who believes in many or no gods, is often assigned negative connotations. When you read the word in Wordsworth's poem, consider whether or not the speaker uses the word negatively.

Reader/Writer **Notebook**

Use your **RWN** to complete the activities for this selection.

Preteach

Introducing Vocabulary

- Review the Vocabulary words, definitions, and sentences with students.
- To reinforce the importance of the Vocabulary words, tell students that these words relate to the religious motif in the poem.

English for Academic Success

Language Coach

Have students read the **Language Coach.** Ask students to research other synonyms of the word *dirty* and to discuss the connotations of each.

Literary Skills Focus

As you read and discuss the selection with students, have them consider how the two allusions to Greek mythology are tied to the concept of religion.

Writing Skills Focus

Have students record verbal adjectives and their effect in their **Reader/Writer Notebooks.** Students can use their notes to complete the Writing Skills Focus activity.

Selection Resources

Unit 4 Resources, on-level practice, p. 40

Teacher One Stop™, on-level lesson plans

Holt Audio Library

Holt Audio Library: Selections and Summaries in Spanish

UA: Differentiating Instruction, graphic organizer, p. 172

UA: Supporting Instruction in Spanish, selection summary

ThinkCentral Online Assessment, Selection Standards Check go.hrw.com

California Standards, pp. 763–765

- **Reading Standard 3.4** Analyze ways in which poets use imagery, personification, figures of speech, and sounds to evoke readers' emotions.

Teacher Preparation

Selection Summary

"The World is Too Much with Us" laments our tendency to get caught up in material considerations ("the world") at the expense of the soul, or deeper self. In the octave—the first eight lines—and the first half of line 9, the speaker's tone is one of restrained disapproval as he states his theme: "We are out of tune" with nature. In the middle of line 9, the tone suddenly changes (as signaled by the exclamation "Great God!"), and the speaker passionately proclaims that he would rather be a pagan than remain cut off from nature and life's true meaning.

Direct Teach

Think About/Talk About

Read with a Purpose Before students respond to the question, have them reflect on what it means to give one's heart away.

Analysis

A Literary Focus

Possible responses: *The allusions refer to Greek mythology and underscore Wordsworth's reference to paganism. The allusions are powerful and may create trepidation in the reader.*

Vocabulary: Own the Word

- **sordid:** The sewer is a *sordid* place. A story's villain is often known for *sordid* behavior.
- **pagan:** A *pagan* is a believer in many or no gods. A synonym is *heathen.* Use each to fill in the blank in the sentence: They tried to convert the ________ with little success.
- **creed:** Tell students the root word for *creed* is *crēdō,* which is Latin for "believe." Someone who is reciting a *creed* is reciting a formal statement of what they believe.
- **forlorn:** Demonstrate to students having a *forlorn* look on one's face. Ask one or two students to demonstrate.

SONNET

The World Is Too Much with Us

by **William Wordsworth**

Read with a Purpose

Read to discover what has caused us to give "our hearts away."

Build Background

Wordsworth wrote the final draft of this sonnet in 1804, at a time when he realized that his imaginative powers were beginning to fail. Although he continued to compose new works and to edit *The Prelude,* a long poem published after his death, he knew he was no longer responding to nature with the youthful passion that had inspired his earlier poems. This sonnet counterattacks ferocious criticism that Wordsworth was receiving from conservative reviewers who thought the poet was conspiring against society, brooding needlessly over problems "instead of contemplating the wonders and pleasures which civilization has created for mankind."

The world is too much with us; late and soon,
Getting and spending, we lay waste our powers:
Little we see in Nature that is ours;
We have given our hearts away, a sordid boon!°
This Sea that bares her bosom to the moon;
The winds that will be howling at all hours,
And are up-gathered now like sleeping flowers;
For this, for everything, we are out of tune;
It moves us not.—Great God! I'd rather be
A Pagan suckled in a creed outworn;
So might I, standing on this pleasant lea,°
Have glimpses that would make me less forlorn;
Have sight of Proteus° rising from the sea;
Or hear old Triton° blow his wreathèd horn. **A**

4. **sordid boon:** foul gift. That is, the act of giving our hearts away is shameful.

11. **lea:** meadow.

13. **Proteus** (PROH tee uhs): in Greek mythology, a sea god who can change shape at will.

14. **Triton** (TRY tuhn): in Greek mythology, a sea god who controls the waves by blowing a conch shell.

A Literary Focus Allusion What is Wordsworth's purpose in alluding to mythology in the final two lines? What emotions do these allusions evoke?

Vocabulary **sordid** (SAWR dihd) adj.: foul; filthy.
pagan (PAY guhn) *n.:* person who believes in many gods or no god.
creed (kreed) *n.:* essential points of religious belief.
forlorn (fawr LAWRN) *adj.:* hopeless; wretched.

California Standards, p. 765

- **Reading Standard 3.2** Analyze the way in which the theme or meaning of a selection represents a view or comment on life, using textual evidence to support the claim.
- **Reading Standard 3.4** Analyze ways in which poets use imagery, personification, figures of speech, and sounds to evoke readers' emotions.
- **Writing Standard 2.1** Write fictional, autobiographical, or biographical narratives: **e.** Make effective use of descriptions of appearance, images, shifting perspectives, and sensory details.

Applying Your Skills

Reading Standard 3.2, 3.4 (see pages A48–A50)
Writing Standard 2.1e (see pages A51–A52)

Composed upon Westminster Bridge
The World Is Too Much with Us

Literary Response and Analysis

Reading Skills Focus

Quick Check

1. In "Composed upon Westminster Bridge," what details and features of the city does the speaker mention?
2. How does the speaker of "The World Is Too Much with Us" feel about "getting and spending"?

Read with a Purpose

3. Compare the mood of the speaker in "Composed upon Westminster Bridge" with that of the speaker in "The World Is Too Much with Us." Would you describe their outlooks as pessimistic or optimistic, realistic or idealistic? Explain.

Vocabulary Check

Match the Vocabulary words with their definitions.

4. creed — **a.** foul
5. forlorn — **b.** hopeless
6. pagan — **c.** brilliant light
7. sordid — **d.** set of beliefs
8. splendor — **e.** grandeur
9. majesty — **f.** believer in many gods or no god

Literary Skills Focus

Literary Analysis

10. **Analyze** What qualities of the scene in the first poem seem to move the speaker most deeply?
11. **Extend** How do the themes and images of "Composed upon Westminster Bridge" classify Wordsworth as a typical Romantic poet?
12. **Interpret** Why do you think the speaker in "The World Is Too Much with Us" would "rather be / A Pagan" (lines 9–10)?
13. **Evaluate** How are the ideas about materialism and progress in "The World Is Too Much with Us" relevant to today's world?

Literary Skills: Personification / Allusion

14. **Analyze** What details personify the sun in "Composed upon Westminster Bridge"? How does the image in lines 9–10 help us visualize the movement of the light?
15. **Analyze** What examples of **allusion** did you note while reading "The World is Too Much with Us"? How do these allusions affect the theme?

Literary Skills Review: Theme

16. **Analyze** The **theme** of a literary work is the main idea or central insight into human nature. Identify and compare the themes of the two sonnets. Does Wordsworth state these themes directly, or are they implied?

Writing Skills Focus

Think as a Reader/Writer

Use It in Your Writing Review your notes about Wordsworth's use of adjectives in "Composed upon Westminster Bridge" and "The World Is Too Much with Us." Write a descriptive paragraph about something in nature, building on one of Wordsworth's themes or addressing a theme of your own. As you write, choose adjectives to convey the images and effects you want.

What Do You Think Now

What parts of our world limit or hinder the imagination? What parts of our world nurture or inspire the imagination? Explain.

Universal Access

Struggling Writers
Some students may need additional scaffolding to complete the Writing Skills Focus activity. Tell them to write about one of Wordsworth's themes. Before students write, have them re-read the relevant sonnet and note the images, descriptions, and techniques used by Wordsworth. Invite students to imitate Wordsworth's use of imagery and to convey the theme.

What Do You Think Now?

Before answering the question, have students use a T-chart to jot down and discuss what aspects of their reality hinder their imagination and what aspects of their reality augment their imagination.

Assess

Unit 4 Resources,
Selection Standards Check, p. 40

Check for Understanding

Independent Practice

Reading Skills Focus

Possible responses:

1. *The speaker mentions the city's skyline, the "smokeless air," the river, the houses, and the silence.*
2. *The speaker thinks that too much attention is placed on "getting and spending."*
3. *The mood of "Westminster Bridge" is celebratory and optimistic in praising the London landmark. The mood of "The World Is Too Much with Us" is reproachful and pessimistic about the fate of the human soul.*

Vocabulary Check

4. *d* **5.** *b* **6.** *f*
7. *a* **8.** *c* **9.** *e*

Literary Skills Focus

Possible responses:

10. *The quiet of the city in conjunction with its power move the speaker.*
11. *Romantic elements include its simple language, a sense of awe, an awareness of a presence that unifies all things (as the sunlight seems to "steep" the city), and a turning away from the ugliness of the industrial world.*
12. *The speaker believes that pagans recognize the divine in nature.*
13. *People today are even more materialistic and estranged from nature than in Wordsworth's time.*
14. *The verb* steep *personifies the sun, which rises slowly above each valley and hill.*
15. *Wordsworth alludes to Greek mythology in lines 13–14; this underscores his comments about paganism.*
16. *The theme is the rejection of materialism for spiritual truth. This differs from the theme of "Westminster Bridge," which is to appreciate the way nature intersects with the city. The themes are implied in both sonnets.*

Standards Focus

Objectives

Students will
- analyze alliteration
- interpret imagery
- analyze the characteristics of a literary ballad

Selection Introduction

Think About the Writer

Ask students to consider how a personal experience can affect one's writing. Have them discuss how they might use their own experiences in their writing if they were authors.

For Independent Reading

Gorillas in the Mist, Dian Fossey

Motivate

What Do You Think?/QuickWrite

Remind students that since imagination is the opposite of reason, their utopian visions can appeal to the senses rather than logic.

English for Academic Success

Academic Vocabulary

Look for opportunities to use the Academic Vocabulary words in this unit.

- **device, *n.*:** something made for a particular purpose
- **differentiate, *v.*:** distinguish
- **function, *n.*:** the action for which a person or thing is specially fitted
- **inherent, *adj.*:** existing in something as a fixed, essential quality
- **technique, *n.*:** method

California Standards, pp. 766–773

- **Reading Standard 3.4** Analyze ways in which poets use imagery, personification, figures of speech, and sound to evoke readers' emotions.

Preparing to Read

Kubla Khan

The Rime of the Ancient Mariner

What Do You Think? How can we use imagination to discover truth?

QuickWrite

In "Kubla Khan," Coleridge presents his vision of an earthly paradise. Imagine your own version of the perfect place. What would it look like? In your *Reader/Writer Notebook,* write a paragraph describing this fantastic place.

MEET THE WRITER

Samuel Taylor Coleridge

(1772–1834)

Samuel Taylor Coleridge produced some of the most memorable poems and literary criticism of the Romantic era.

A Great Friendship

As a child, Coleridge was an avid reader and immersed himself in imaginative literature such as *The Arabian Nights' Entertainments.* He impressed classmates with his extraordinary memory and powerful, persuasive expression of ideas. While a student at Cambridge during the French Revolution, Coleridge was intrigued by discussions about the nature of society and troubled by the violence that had derailed the idealism of the Revolution. He left Cambridge without a degree and instead committed himself to creating a utopian colony in America. The experiment never materialized, but Coleridge continued to deliver radical lectures and married a member of the utopian movement. In 1796, with one book of poetry published but no career prospects, he moved to a village in Somerset, England.

In the countryside, Coleridge and the poet William Wordsworth formed a strong friendship, which greatly influenced the development of Coleridge's poetic techniques and style. The two years that followed, before Coleridge had even reached the age of thirty, were among the most prolific of his career. In 1798, Coleridge and Wordsworth published *Lyrical Ballads,* considered the seminal work of the English Romantic era.

The Troubled Artist

Much of Coleridge's later life was marked by pain and despair. His marriage collapsed, his friendship with Wordsworth ended, and his health deteriorated. Despite his suffering, Coleridge continued writing, mostly philosophy and literary criticism, until his death in London in 1834.

Think About the Writer How do you think Coleridge's troubles might have strengthened his imagination?

The Great Khan Releases his Angle Against a Doe by Boucicaut Master (1390–1430). Ms Fr 2810 f.31 v. Bibliothèque Nationale, Paris, France.
Samuel Taylor Coleridge (1795) by Peter Vandyke. Oil on canvas. National Portrait Gallery, London.

Selection Readability	
Easily Accessible Accessible **Challenging**	These poems include: unfamiliar setting; challenging imagery; unfamiliar subject matter.

Reading Standard 3.4 (see pages A48–A50)

Literary Skills Focus

Alliteration The repetition of consonant sounds in words that are close to one another is called **alliteration.** Alliteration can give a musical quality to a poem, emphasize a line or an idea, or help establish **rhythm**. Coleridge uses alliteration throughout "Kubla Khan" to help create the poem's enchanted mood. Alliteration can also suggest movement, as in line 25: "Five miles meandering with a mazy motion." The repeated /m/ sound in the line evokes the serpentine flow of the river. As you read the poem, look and listen for other examples of alliteration.

Reading Skills Focus

Interpreting Imagery Language that appeals to the senses is called **imagery.** While most imagery is visual, appealing to the sense of sight, imagery can also appeal to hearing, touch, taste, or smell. Study the language Coleridge uses to create and enhance his imagery in "Kubla Khan."

Into Action Record at least five striking images in your *Reader/Writer Notebook.* Underline examples of alliteration used in the images.

	Imagery in "Kubla Khan"
1	"Where Alph, the sacred river ran / Through caverns measureless to man"
2	

Writing Skills Focus

Think as a Reader/Writer

Find It in Your Reading As you read, note the ways Coleridge uses language, including alliteration and descriptive words, to create a dreamlike effect in the poem. In your *Reader/Writer Notebook,* record examples that you find especially effective.

TechFocus As you read "Kubla Khan," notice how Coleridge uses words to create imagery. Consider the ways in which modern artists use similar techniques.

Vocabulary

girdled (GUR duhld) *v.:* enclosed or circled around. *The fertile garden was girdled by walls and towers.*

sinuous (SIHN yoo uhs) *adj.:* winding; twisting. *Sinuous streams ran like snakes through Kubla Khan's gardens.*

turmoil (TUR moyl) *n.:* state of agitation or commotion. *The water churning over the rocks in the valley was in constant turmoil.*

meandering (mee AN duhr ihng) *v.* used as *adj.:* wandering with no clear direction. *Coleridge describes a sacred river meandering through a mystical forest.*

Language Coach

Verb Forms When you learn a new verb, be sure to learn its base form as well as forms that end with *–s, –ed,* and *–ing.* For example, *girdled* is a past-tense verb that means "encircled." Notice how the verb is used in these phrases:

- Towers *girdle* the garden.
- A moat *girdles* the castle.
- Armed soldiers were *girdling* our camp.

What verb forms are related to *meandering*? How can you use each form in a sentence?

Learn It Online
Find out more about Coleridge on the Writers' Lives site.

go.hrw.com H12-767 Go

Reader/Writer Notebook
Use your **RWN** to complete the activities for this selection.

Selection Resources

Unit 4 Resources, on-level practice and assessment, pp. 46, 52

PowerNotes, interactive lesson presentations with activities

Teacher One Stop™, on-level lesson plans and all print resources

Holt Audio Library

Holt Audio Library: Selections and Summaries in Spanish

UA: Holt Interactive Reader, pp. 215, 221

UA: Differentiating Instruction, modified lesson plans and leveled assessment, p. 173

UA: Supporting Instruction in Spanish, selection summary

UA: Resources for Teaching Advanced Students, lesson plans, pp. 144, 148

ThinkCentral Online Assessment, Selection Standards Check

ThinkCentral Online Remediation

Preteach

Introducing Vocabulary

Use this activity to check students' understanding of the Vocabulary words.

1. What geographic barriers **girdle** city parks, neighborhoods, and nature preserves?
2. What images in nature are **sinuous**?
3. How do people respond to public **turmoil**?
4. When and where are people likely to **meander**?

English for Academic Success

Language Coach

Remind students that the *–s* ending of verbs is used with singular nouns. For example: A wire fence *girdles* (not *girdle*) their backyard. ***Possible responses:*** *meanders, meander; The sheep meandered beyond the meadow. The boy meanders through the woods.*

Literary Skills Focus

As you read and discuss the selection with students, have students note examples of alliteration.

Reading Skills Focus

Give students a copy of the Reading Skills Focus graphic organizer before they read. (See **Unit 4 Resources.**) Tell them to use their responses to answer the questions on the Applying Your Skills page.

Writing Skills Focus

Have students record language that creates illusory effects in their **Reader/Writer Notebooks.** Students can use their notes to complete the Writing Skills Focus activity.

Learn It Online
The **Writers' Lives** feature of the Interactive Student Edition offers additional information about this author. Audio or video segments are provided for some authors.

go.hrw.com H12–767 Go

Teacher Preparation

Selection Summary

In "Kubla Khan," Coleridge sets forth a fantastic vision. His speaker states that Kubla Khan has built a majestic pleasure dome in Xanadu, with gardens, forests, and winding streams. Deep in a chasm, a fountain bursts forth, sending the sacred river Alph into a motionless ocean. Amid the noise of the river, Kubla hears voices prophesying war. The speaker then describes a vision of an Abyssinian (Ethiopian) woman. He claims that if he could recapture her music, he could rebuild the pleasure dome at Xanadu, which might arouse fear and awe in the people.

Direct Teach

Think About/Talk About

Read with a Purpose Have students read the Read with a Purpose statement. Ask students how they visualize paradise.

Comprehension

B Reading Focus

Possible response: *The garden sounds lush and idyllic. The sacred river and caverns that cannot be measured make Xanadu sound fantastical. "Incense-bearing trees" also make the scene seem otherworldly.*

Analysis

A Literary Focus

Possible response: *The repeated* m *sound in* measureless *and* man *provides a reverberant hum. The z and s sounds at the end of* caverns *and* measureless *also slow the language down.*

POEM

Kubla Khan

by **Samuel Taylor Coleridge**

Read with a Purpose

Read to find out about Kubla Khan's attempt to build a paradise on earth.

Build Background

Kubla Khan (c. 1216–1294), the grandson of Genghis Khan, was the Mongol conqueror of China. Coleridge's poem about this thirteenth-century warrior resembles a meditative ode in its lyrical tone and manner.

Coleridge claimed to have envisioned "Kubla Khan" during an opium-induced reverie after he had read a provocative passage in an old travel book. Upon waking from his dream, Coleridge began composing the poem but was interrupted by a visitor. After his visitor left an hour later, Coleridge could recall a mere fragment of his dream-poem.

In Xanadu did Kubla Khan
A stately pleasure-dome decree:
Where Alph,° the sacred river, ran
Through caverns measureless to man
    Down to a sunless sea. **A**
So twice five miles of fertile ground
With walls and towers were girdled round:
And there were gardens bright with sinuous rills,°
Where blossomed many an incense-bearing tree;
And here were forests ancient as the hills,
Enfolding sunny spots of greenery. **B**

But oh! that deep romantic chasm which slanted
Down the green hill athwart a cedarn cover!°
A savage place! as holy and enchanted
As e'er beneath a waning moon was haunted
By woman wailing for her demon-lover!
And from this chasm, with ceaseless turmoil seething,

3. **Alph:** probably a reference to the Greek river Alpheus, which flows into the Ionian Sea and whose waters are fabled to rise up again in Sicily.

8. **rills:** streams.

13. **athwart a cedarn cover:** crossing diagonally under a covering growth of cedar trees.

A Literary Focus **Alliteration** What examples of alliteration can you find in the first five lines? What is the effect of the alliteration?

B Reading Focus **Interpreting Imagery** What images in the stanza evoke a sense of a fantastic, otherworldly place? Explain your answer.

Vocabulary **girdled** (GUR duhld) *v.:* enclosed or circled around.
sinuous (SIHN yoo uhs) *adj.:* winding; twisting.
turmoil (TUR moyl) *n.:* state of agitation or commotion.

Universal Access

English Learners

English for Academic Success Point out the use of the suffix *–less* in the word *measureless* in line 4. Explain that the suffix *–less* means "without." Offer a simple example: Today is a sunless day. As they read, help students identify and define words ending in *–less* in the poem: *measureless, sunless, ceaseless, lifeless.* Ask what images these words convey.

✔ See **UA: Differentiating Instruction** for strategies for teaching English learners.

Struggling Readers

Have students keep a running list of striking images they notice as they read. Invite students to read "Kubla Khan" in interactive format in **UA: Holt Interactive Reader** and to use the sidenotes as aids to understanding the selection. The interactive version provides additional instruction, practice, and assessment of the skills taught in the Student Edition.

As if this earth in fast thick pants were breathing,
A mighty fountain momently° was forced:
Amid whose swift half-intermitted burst
Huge fragments vaulted like rebounding hail,
Or chaffy grain beneath the thresher's flail:°
And 'mid these dancing rocks at once and ever
It flung up momently the sacred river.
Five miles meandering with a mazy° motion
Through wood and dale the sacred river ran,
Then reached the caverns measureless to man,
And sank in tumult to a lifeless ocean:
And 'mid this tumult Kubla heard from far
Ancestral voices prophesying war!
The shadow of the dome of pleasure
Floated midway on the waves;
Where was heard the mingled measure°
From the fountain and the caves.
It was a miracle of rare device,
A sunny pleasure-dome with caves of ice! **C**

19. momently: at each moment.

22. thresher's flail: heavy, whiplike tool used to beat grain to separate the kernels from their chaff, or husks.

25. mazy: like a maze; having many turns.

33. measure: rhythmic sound.

C Reading Focus Interpreting Imagery What do you think of when you imagine caves of ice? Why do you think Coleridge included this image in his poem?

Vocabulary meandering (mee AN duhr ihng) *v.* used as *adj.*: wandering with no clear direction.

HISTORY LINK

The Great Khan

In his fantasy poem, Coleridge describes Kubla Khan's magnificent pleasure-dome in the mystical city of Xanadu. The existence of the real Kubla Khan was far less fanciful; the grandson of the formidable Mongol conqueror, Genghis Khan, Kubla consolidated the Mongols' hold over China by defeating the Chinese Sung dynasty in 1279. The word *khan,* attached to the names of both father and son, comes from the Mongolian word *ruler.*

As the first Great Khan of the Yuan dynasty, Kubla undertook many projects, such as expanding road networks, maintaining granaries, and rebuilding the Grand Canal, a trade route still present in China. The name *Xanadu* comes from Coleridge's imagination, but the city may have been based on Shang-du in Inner Mongolia, where Kubla was elected khan in 1260.

Kublai Khan (1216–1294), founder of the Mongol dynasty. Chinese silk album leaf, Yüan dynasty.
The Granger Collection, N.Y.

Ask Yourself

How might the poem "Kubla Khan" have influenced the image and perceptions of Eastern culture in the West?

Think About/Talk About

Comprehension

C Reading Focus

Possible responses: *I think of dark, cold, blue underground caverns when I think of caves of ice. Perhaps Coleridge included the image to show extreme contrasts, the same reason he included a lifeless ocean and the sounds of war. His vision includes every possibility, of light and dark.*

History Link

Ask Yourself

Possible response: *Coleridge's "Kubla Khan" might have sparked his contemporaries' interest in the historical figure of Kubla Khan and his empire. Readers might have been inspired to learn more about China and Mongolia. The poem might also have led Western readers to believe that the Far East was exotic and exciting, filled with lush natural wonders and gorgeous palaces.*

Vocabulary: Own the Word

- **girdled:** Have students contribute related concepts and attributes to the semantic web for *girdled.* ***Possible responses:*** *encircled, encompassed, surrounded*
- **sinuous:** Tell students the root word for *sinuous* is *sinus,* Latin for "curve, bend." A *sinuous* road has many curves and turns. Have students describe where they might find a *sinuous* path.
- **turmoil:** Tell students that the word *turmoil* connotes serious confusion. You might say, "Her cold manner made me confused, but her complete avoidance of me over the next few weeks left me in a state of *turmoil.*"
- **meandering:** Tell students that *meandering* originates from Maiandros, a river in Phrygia that was noted for its winding course. Ask students to describe a time when they had the opportunity to take a *meandering* path.

Advanced Learners

Acceleration The concept of a pleasure dome captivated English society in Coleridge's time. Pleasure halls such as Vauxhall Pleasure Gardens and Ranelagh Gardens were at the center of London social life. There, visitors enjoyed gardens, grottoes, concerts, and tea. Tell students to research one of these pleasure domes and to compare it with Coleridge's Xanadu.

✔ See **UA: Resources for Teaching Advanced Students** for strategies for teaching advanced learners.

Students with Disabilities

Offer these students an opportunity to describe orally what their own personal Xanadu might look like or contain. Pair students of limited writing ability with other students who can put their ideas down on paper.

✔ See **UA: Differentiating Instruction** for strategies for teaching students with disabilities.

Think About/Talk About

Analysis

D Literary Focus

Possible responses: *The* d *and* s *sounds are repeated frequently. The sibilance—the* s *sound—creates the effect of hushed whispering. The* d *sound is also soft, not harsh. These sounds give the lines a restful, dreamlike quality.*

Extend the Discussion

Interpreting What does the speaker long to do? What effect would this have? ***Possible responses:*** *He longs to "build that dome in air" (with music). He would be regarded with fear and awe.*

Analyzing Visuals

Connecting to the Text: *The guard's informal clothing, inattentive posture, and lowly expressions suggest that guarding the palace of Kubla Khan is not a position that promotes pride. The palace may be a place that is not beloved by those around it.*

A damsel with a dulcimer°
In a vision once I saw:
It was an Abyssinian° maid,
And on her dulcimer she played,
Singing of Mount Abora.°
Could I revive within me
Her symphony and song,
To such a deep delight 'twould win me,
That with music loud and long, **D**
I would build that dome in air,
That sunny dome! those caves of ice!
And all who heard should see them there,
And all should cry, Beware! Beware!
His flashing eyes, his floating hair!
Weave a circle round him thrice,
And close your eyes with holy dread,
For he on honeydew hath fed,
And drunk the milk of Paradise.

37. dulcimer: musical instrument with strings that are struck with small hammers.
39. Abyssinian: Ethiopian. Ethiopia is in northeastern Africa.
41. Mount Abora: likely a reference to John Milton's (1608–1674) *Paradise Lost,* in which Mount Amara in Ethiopia is depicted as a mythical earthly paradise.

D Literary Focus Alliteration Identify the examples of alliteration used in lines 37–45. How do they affect the rhythm of the poem?

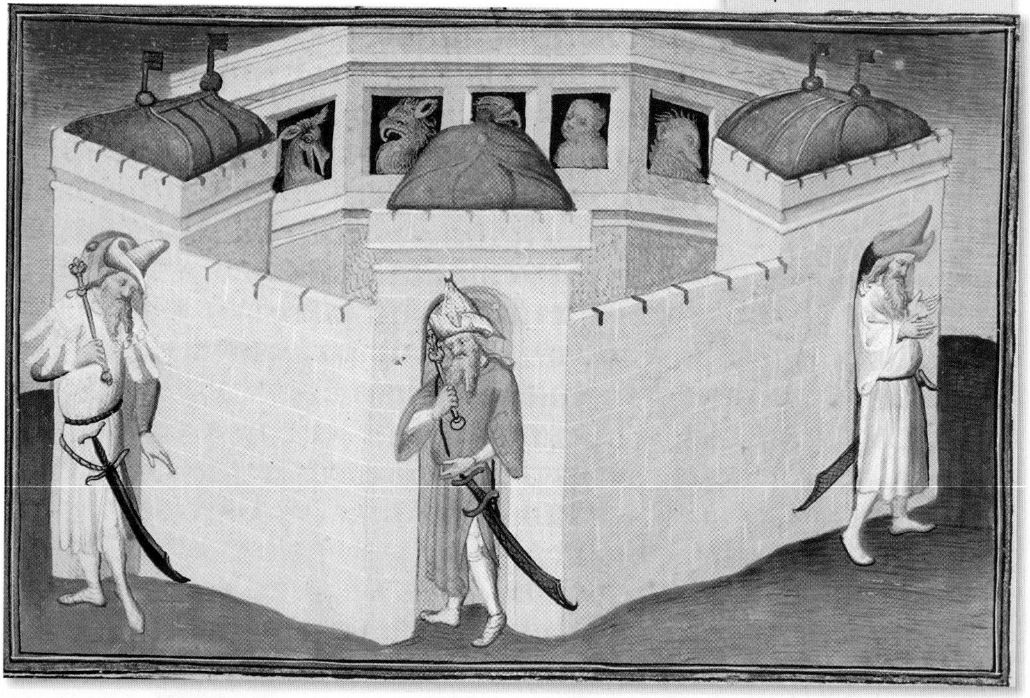

Kublai Khan's Palace, Peking (14th century). Miniature from the *Livres des Merveilles.* Manuscrits occidentaux-Français 2810, fol 37. Bibliothèque Nationale de France, Paris.

Analyzing Visuals

Connecting to the Text Note how each guard is paired with a tower. What do the guards' posture, clothing, and expressions suggest about the palace of Kubla Khan?

California Standards, pp. 771–773

- **Reading Standard 3.4** Analyze ways in which poets use imagery, personification, figures of speech, and sound to evoke readers' emotions.
- **Grades 9–10 Review Reading Standard 1.1** Identify and use the literal and figurative meanings of words and understand word derivations.
- **Grades 9–10 Review Reading Standard 2.5** Extend ideas presented in primary or secondary sources through original analysis, evaluation, and elaboration.
- **Grades 9–10 Review Reading Standard 3.7** Recognize and understand the significance of various literary devices, including figurative language, imagery, allegory, and symbolism, and explain their appeal.
- **Writing Standard 2.1** Write fictional, autobiographical, or biographical narratives: **e.** Make effective use of description of appearance, images, shifting perspectives, and sensory details.
- **Listening and Speaking Standard 2.4** Deliver multimedia presentations: **a.** Combine text, images, and sound incorporating information from a wide range of media, including films, newspapers, magazines, CD-ROMs, online information, television, videos, and electronic media-generated images.

Applying Your Skills

Reading Standard 3.4; Grades 9–10 Review
Reading Standard 3.7 (see pages A48–A50)
Writing Standard 2.1e (see pages A51–A52)

Kubla Khan

Literary Response and Analysis

Reading Skills Focus

Quick Check

1. In the first stanza, what images show that Xanadu is an extraordinary place?
2. What images shatter the depiction of Xanadu as peaceful and serene?
3. Why does the speaker yearn to re-create the damsel's symphony and song within himself?

Read with a Purpose

4. How does Kubla Khan build his paradise?

Reading Skills: Interpreting Imagery

5. As you read, you recorded images and noted alliteration. Add a column to comment on the effect of the image on the poem as a whole.

	Imagery in "Kubla Khan"	Effect
1	"Where Alph, the sacred river ran / Through caverns measureless to man"	Emphasizes the enormity of the place
2		

Literary Skills Focus

Literary Analysis

6. **Compare and Contrast** What does the imagery in lines 14–16 convey? Contrast this impression with that conveyed in lines 1–13. What phrases does Coleridge use to differentiate between the two places?
7. **Evaluate** Many ancient cultures revered poets as seers who had a special relationship with the gods. How might the last stanza allude to this belief?
8. **Extend** How could this poem itself be about the act of creating a poem?
9. **Make Judgments** In your opinion, does this poem celebrate the imagination or caution against its indulgence? Support your answer with evidence from the poem.

Literary Skills: Alliteration

10. **Analyze** Identify examples of alliteration, and explain their effects in the poem.

Literary Skills Review: Symbol

11. **Analyze** A **symbol** is a person, place, thing, or event that stands both for itself and for something beyond itself. What might the "dome in air" that the speaker wants to create symbolize?

Writing Skills Focus

Think as a Reader/Writer

Use It in Your Writing Review your QuickWrite describing a perfect place and your notes about how Coleridge creates a dreamlike effect. Then, write a short poem describing your vision of paradise. Use descriptive words, alliteration, and rhyme to emphasize ideas and create a musical, dreamlike effect.

What Do You Think Now? How does Coleridge's imagination reveal deeper truths?

Universal Access

Struggling Writers

Some students may need additional scaffolding to complete the Writing Skills Focus activity. Before students write, encourage students to read over the examples of alliteration in the poem. Then, have them read over their QuickWrite and revise some of their phrases to incorporate alliteration. Next, have students rewrite their sentences into a poem, spreading one sentence over two or three lines. After students have finished, ask them to go back over their poem and revise the lines to make the ends rhyme.

What Do You Think Now?

As students consider the question, remind them to look back on the poem and consider the tone and attitude of the speaker towards Xanadu.

Check for Understanding

Independent Practice

Reading Skills Focus

Possible responses:

1. *The images of the huge caverns, "sunless sea," and exotic gardens show that Xanadu is an extraordinary place.*
2. *In line 30, voices warn of war.*
3. *She represents the imaginative power it would take to recreate the pleasure dome. The speaker wants to harness that same creative force.*
4. *He decrees it, meaning he orders that it be built. In a sense, he wills it into existence.*
5. *Responses will vary. Students' concept maps should include specific examples of imagery and notes about its effect on the reader.*

Literary Skills Focus

Possible responses:

6. *The phrases "savage place," "woman wailing," and "ceaseless turmoil" convey a wild and dark mood in lines 14–16. In lines 1–13, phrases such as "gardens bright" convey a tranquil and enchanted mood.*
7. *The speaker describes how he would be celebrated and revered if he recreated the pleasure dome in his capacity as a poet "with music loud and long."*
8. *The poem is about creation; writing poetry is an inspired creative act often written to arouse emotional responses from people.*
9. *The poem celebrates the "miracle" of man's imagination, but suggests to "Beware!" of overindulging in pleasurable worlds.*
10. *Alliteration is used to create a mood. Much of the alliteration in the poem, such as the phrase "meandering with a mazy motion" in line 25 and the words "symphony and song" in line 43, is melodious and flowing.*
11. *The "dome in air" could symbolize heaven or the speaker's ideals.*

Independent Practice
Vocabulary Development
Vocabulary Check
1. *d*
2. *c*
3. *b*
4. *a*

Your Turn
sinuous [*"gardens bright with . . . rills" (streams)*]

turmoil [*"from this chasm"; "ceaseless . . . seething"*]

meandering [*"mazy motion . . . through wood and dale"*]

English for Academic Success
Language Coach
1. *b*
2. *c*
3. *d*
4. *a*

English for Academic Success
Academic Vocabulary
Possible response: *Literary techniques that promote repetitious sounds, such as assonance and alliteration, inherently add to the imagery of a poem. The alliterative line, "the babbling brook burst forth with beauty," helps the reader hear the sound of the water and feel the strong impact of its beauty. Lines that include assonance, such as "the wolf's loud howl lasted for hours," helps readers hear the sound of the wolf and imagine the extent of its howl.*

Applying Your Skills
Kubla Khan

Grades 9–10 Review Reading Standard 1.1 (see pages A48–A50)

Vocabulary Development

Vocabulary Check
Match each Vocabulary word with its definition.

1. girdled — a. wandering
2. sinuous — b. great disturbance
3. turmoil — c. having many bends or turns
4. meandering — d. enclosed or circled around

Vocabulary Skills: Context Clues
A word's **context**—the words and sentences that surround it—often gives clues to the word's meaning. Searching for context clues is an effective way to understand unfamiliar words as you read. When searching for context clues, start by identifying words you know. Also, consider the overall meaning of the sentence and the paragraph. Understanding the overall meaning will often allow you to make logical guesses about an unknown word.

One type of context clue is an example that illustrates a word's meaning. Consider this excerpt from the selection:

> Huge fragments *vaulted* like rebounding hail
> Or chaffy grain beneath the thresher's flail:

The phrase *like rebounding hail* contains a context clue for the word *vaulted.* If you know that rebounding hail is hail that bounces off the ground, you can infer from that clue that *vault* relates to jumping.

Another type of context clue is a word or phrase that describes the unknown word. Look for words and phrases that you do understand to see if they provide hints about the meaning of the unknown word.

Your Turn
Find each Vocabulary word in the selection. Using a table like the one that follows, write the context clues that could help you determine the meaning of the Vocabulary word if you did not already know its definition. Then, explain how context clues help determine the word's meaning.

Word	Context Clues
girdled	"with walls and towers"; "round"
sinuous	
turmoil	
meandering	

Language Coach
Verb Forms When you learn a new verb, you should also try to learn its related forms. For example, *meander,* the base form of *meandering,* means "to wander with no clear direction." Choose the correct form of *meander* to complete each sentence.

a. meander **c.** meandered
b. meanders **d.** meandering

1. The ancient river _____ before it empties into the sea.
2. The caravan _____ for weeks before it arrived in Xanadu.
3. A commanding voice urges the men to stop _____ and return to camp.
4. The buzzing insects _____ through the garden.

Academic Vocabulary
Talk About
With a partner, discuss how certain poetic techniques are more effective than others in conveying mood, theme, or imagery. Do certain devices inherently lend themselves to specific literary functions?

Universal Access: Vocabulary Development

EL English Learners
English for Academic Success Give students additional practice with the related forms of a verb. Tell them to supply the related verb forms for the following words taken from the poem. Then, have them create sentences using two of the related verb forms.

1. seething [*seethe, seethes, seethed*]
2. forced [*force, forces, forcing*]
3. flung [*fling, flinging, flings*]
4. sank [*sink, sinks, sinking*]
5. prophesying [*prophesy, prophesies, prophesied*]
6. mingled [*mingles, mingle, mingling*]
7. flashing [*flash, flashes, flashed*]
8. revived [*revive, revives, reviving*]

✔ See the **Academic and Selection Vocabulary Skill Builder** in **UA: Differentiating Instruction.**

Reading Standard 3.4; Grades 9–10 Review Reading Standard 2.5 (see pages A48–A50)
Listening and Speaking Standard 2.4a (see pages A53–A55)

Grammar Link

Prepositional Phrases

A **preposition** shows the relationship of a noun or pronoun, called the **object of the preposition,** to another word in the sentence. A **prepositional phrase** consists of a preposition, its object, and any words that modify the object. Prepositional phrases may be adjectival or adverbial.

Adjectival phrases modify nouns or pronouns, telling *what kind* or *which one.*

Samuel Taylor Coleridge was an important poet **of the English Romantic movement.**

Adverbial phrases modify verbs, adjectives, or adverbs, telling *how, when, where, why,* or *to what extent.*

He collaborated **with William Wordsworth.** Their work was beautiful **in a radical new way** that would change English poetry.

Your Turn

Identify the adjectival and adverbial prepositional phrases and the words they modify in the following sentences.

1. "Kubla Khan" is full of mysterious images. It brings readers on a journey, which leads to a sacred river.
2. The poem describes gardens glistening with streams and caves of ice.
3. Coleridge delivers a feverish rush of images.
4. The idea of the pleasure-dome fascinated readers of English Romanticism.

Writing Application Scan an essay you have already written, and underline all the prepositional phrases. Circle the object of the preposition, and note in the margin whether the phrase is adverbial or adjectival.

CHOICES

As you respond to the Choices, use these **Academic Vocabulary** words as appropriate: differentiate, inherent, device, technique, function.

REVIEW

Bring the Dream to Life

TechFocus In a small group, create a music video of "Kubla Khan." First, transform the poem into a song or dramatic reading, paying attention to musical effects created by alliteration. Then, choose or create visual images to accompany the poem's imagery. Your images need not literally represent the descriptions in "Kubla Khan" but should convey the same effect and mood. Share your video with your class.

CONNECT

Reflect on Dreams

Think about some of your past dreams, and take a few notes describing the functions of dreams. Are they logical or illogical? Do they tell coherent stories, or do they consist mostly of images and fragments of stories? Review your ideas with a partner. Then, discuss how your thoughts on the inherent nature of dreams compare to the dreamlike flow of "Kubla Khan." Does the poem read like a dream? Cite examples from the poem to support your answer.

EXTEND

Examine the Author's Life

With a partner, use the school library or the Internet to research the life of Samuel Taylor Coleridge. Try to draw connections between biographical events and the poem "Kubla Khan." Think about possible inspirations for the poem and what meaning the images may have held for Coleridge. Present your findings to the class, and ask your peers to comment on how Coleridge's life may have affected his work.

Learn It Online
Learn more about context clues online with *WordSharp.*

go.hrw.com H12-773 Go

Universal Access: Grammar Link

English Learners

English for Academic Success Encourage students to identify prepositions and prepositional phrases in everyday speech before they begin to search for them in Coleridge's work. Explain to students that prepositional phrases often tell about where something is in relation to another thing. Explain that in the sentence "The dog is on the porch," the word "on" is a preposition and the phrase "on the porch" is a prepositional phrase that helps readers understand where the dog is. Once students have mastered this concept, have them apply it to more difficult prepositional phrases, such as those in Coleridge's work.

✔ For more practice with prepositional phrases, see **Warriner's Handbook, GrammarNotes,** and **Language Handbook Worksheets.**

Independent Practice

Grammar Link

Your Turn

1. *of mysterious images and music; on a journey; to a sacred river*
2. *with streams; of ice*
3. *of images*
4. *of the pleasure-dome; of English Romanticism*

Choices: Evaluation Criteria

Review: Homework
Bring the Dream to Life
Students' chosen images should reflect the imagery and tone of the poem.

Connect: Homework
Reflect on Dreams

- Discussions should stay clearly connected to the poem.
- Notes should be written in comparison-and-contrast format, either point by point or block.

Extend: Homework
Examine the Author's Life
Presentations should focus on details about Coleridge's life that are relevant to understanding "Kubla Khan."

Assess

Unit 4 Resources, Selection Standards Check, p. 49

go.hrw.com **ThinkCentral Online Assessment,** Selection Standards Check

Teacher One Stop™, editable Selection Standards Check

Reteach

To reteach **poetic devices** such as alliteration, see **Reteaching Lessons,** pp. 1449Q–1449R.

go.hrw.com **ThinkCentral Online Remediation**

Preteach

Introducing Vocabulary

- Review the Vocabulary words, definitions, and sentences with students.
- To reinforce the importance of the Vocabulary words, tell students that the poem tells the *dismal* story of a Mariner whose ship was caught in a *tyrannous* storm and following his act of cruelty, was left with a *ghastly* crew.

English for Academic Success

Language Coach

Ask students to think of possible contexts for the other Vocabulary words and share them with the class. Remind them to think of appropriate settings, people, or events.

Literary Skills Focus

Ask students to think about how contemporary songs are similar to or different from literary ballads.

Reading Skills Focus

Give students a copy of the Reading Skills Focus graphic organizer before they read. (See **Unit 4 Resources.**) Tell them to use their responses to answer the questions on the Applying Your Skills page.

Writing Skills Focus

Have students record sensory images in their **Reader/Writer Notebooks.** Students can use their notes to complete the Writing Skills Focus activity.

Preparing to Read

Reading Standard 3.1, 3.3, 3.9 (see pages A48–A50)

The Rime of the Ancient Mariner

Literary Skills Focus

Literary Ballad A **ballad** is a song or poem that tells a story. Coleridge's **literary ballad** imitates the traditional **folk ballad** in content and form, blending real events with supernatural events and using simple language, repetition, and strong patterns of rhythm and rhyme. Coleridge varies the meter and rhyme scheme. He also uses internal rhyme, rhyming words within one line, and assonance, the repetition of vowel sounds in words close together.

Literary Perspectives Apply the literary perspective described on page 776 as you read this narrative poem.

Reading Skills Focus

Understanding Archaic Words To make his ballad seem authentic, Coleridge uses many **archaic,** or out-of-date, words. The meanings of many of these words appear in the page margins. Context clues can also suggest meanings, as in "The glorious Sun *uprist.*" Here, the prefix *up–* and your knowledge about the sun might lead you to guess that *uprist* means "rose."

Into Action Use a flowchart like the one below to record some of the archaic words and their meanings. List the archaic word in the first oval, its meaning in the next oval, and a modern replacement in the third.

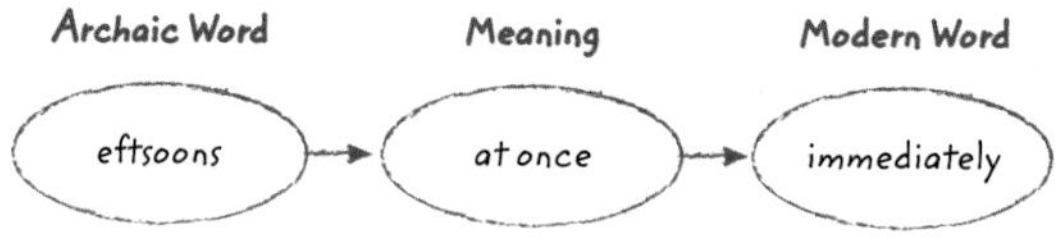

Writing Skills Focus

Think as a Reader/Writer

Find It in Your Reading Coleridge creates strong sensory **imagery** in his ballad. The line "It cracked and growled, and roared and howled" describes the sounds made by the ice. In your *Reader/Writer Notebook,* record examples of vivid sensory images from the ballad.

Vocabulary

tyrannous (TIHR uh nuhs) *adj.:* harsh; oppressive. *The tyrannous storm wreaked havoc with the Mariner's ship.*

dismal (DIHZ muhl) *adj.:* gloomy. *The light from the cliffs cast a dismal glow on the crew.*

ghastly (GAST lee) *adj.:* dreadful; ghostly. *The Mariner's crew mates looked at him with ghastly eyes.*

abated (uh BAYT ihd) *v.:* lessened. *The ship would slow down once the Mariner's trance abated.*

wrenched (rehncht) *v.:* anguished; grief-stricken. *The Mariner's expression was wrenched with the agony of his memories.*

Language Coach

Definitions and Context One way to remember word definitions is to think about possible contexts in which you might use a word. You probably would not use the adjective *dismal,* which means "gloomy," to describe someone's room unless you wanted to insult him or her. When might it be appropriate to use the word *dismal*? What kinds of settings, people, or events might it describe?

Reader/Writer Notebook

Use your **RWN** to complete the activities for this selection.

Learn It Online

Plunge into this poem with an online video introduction.

go.hrw.com H12-774 Go

California Standards, pp. 774–801

- **Reading Standard 3.1** Analyze characteristics of subgenres (e.g., satire, parody, allegory, pastoral) that are used in poetry, prose, plays, novels, short stories, essays, and other basic genres.
- **Reading Standard 3.3** Analyze the ways in which irony, tone, mood, the author's style, and the "sound" of language achieve specific rhetorical or aesthetic purposes or both.
- **Reading Standard 3.9** Analyze the philosophical arguments presented in literary works to determine whether the authors' positions have contributed to the quality of each work and the credibility of the characters. (Philosophical approach)

Selection Readability	
Easily Accessible **Accessible** Challenging	literary ballad; archaic words

NARRATIVE POEM

The Rime of the Ancient Mariner

by **Samuel Taylor Coleridge**

View of a Harbour (1815–1816) by Caspar David Friedrich. Schloss Sanssouci, Potsdam, Germany.

Read with a Purpose

Read to find out how the ancient Mariner's actions caused a terrible tragedy.

Build Background

Coleridge wrote *The Rime of the Ancient Mariner* as part of the collaboration with Wordsworth that culminated in the publication of *Lyrical Ballads*. Some of the poems in this volume were intended to present ordinary people and mundane events in fresh and interesting ways. Other poems, such as *The Rime of the Ancient Mariner,* were to present supernatural characters and events in a manner that would induce the reader to "procure for these shadows of imagination that willing suspension of disbelief for the moment, which constitutes poetic faith."

The poem does not explain the killing of the albatross; the results of the act, rather than the act itself, are what is important.

Teacher Preparation

Selection Plot Summary

The Rime of the Ancient Mariner explores the psychology of guilt and the expiation of sins against nature. Apparently set in the medieval era, the poem features the Ancient Mariner and the Wedding Guest to whom he tells his tale. The Mariner recounts his ship's initially auspicious voyage toward the South Pole. During the voyage, he commits a senseless crime—killing an albatross the sailors regard as a good omen—and thus enrages the Polar Spirit, who visits suffering and punishment upon the vessel. Two specters, Death and Life-in-Death, play dice for the crew, all of whom die except for the Mariner. Cursed by the albatross, the Mariner is nearly driven mad by isolation and guilt. The curse begins to abate only after he blesses a passing group of beautiful water snakes and falls asleep. When he awakens in a trance, the ship is being sailed by the crew's reanimated corpses, which are controlled by a troop of angels. His guilt expiated, the Mariner magically arrives back at his native land, but as the harbor Pilot comes to meet the ship, it sinks in a violent whirlpool. After rowing the pilot's boat to shore, the Mariner confesses his sin to a holy hermit. His penance is to wander the earth for the rest of his life, recounting his tale to strangers.

Direct Teach

Think About/Talk About

Read with a Purpose Have students read the Read with a Purpose statement. Ask them to consider the causal relationship between the Mariner's actions and the resulting tragedy.

Universal Access

EL English Learners

Explain that in most cases, Coleridge's marginal notes sum up the action. (One notable exception occurs in the description of the Polar Spirit.) Encourage students to read the marginal notes and expand upon them, adding more details. Have them record their versions in their **Reader/Writer Notebooks.**

✔ See **UA: Differentiating Instruction** for strategies for teaching English learners.

Struggling Readers

Strategic Students Model the skill of dealing with archaic words by saying: "If, as I am reading, I notice a word I do not know or a word that seems out of place, I use the context to try to figure out the meaning. If that does not work, I look to see whether the word is glossed in the margin; if it is, it may be an archaic word or a word being used in an archaic sense." Encourage students as they read to ask themselves: "Is this word archaic? Is it a word being used in an archaic sense?"

Learn It Online

The **PowerNotes** presentation for this lesson includes a short video that introduces the selection. The video is also available on the online version of this page.

go.hrw.com H12-775 Go

Model the Skill

- Review reading **archaic words.** Explain that archaic words and sentence structure give a literary ballad an authentic antique flavor. Ask students if they can name words and phrases that are archaic and tell when they are used. ***Possible response:*** *The words* thee *and* thou *are archaic forms of* you *that are used in poetry; these words may also be used in movies and books with a medieval setting.*
- Tell students that in this selection Coleridge uses **archaic words** whose spelling and pronunciation are often similar to their contemporary equivalents. Read aloud the "Argument" at the beginning of the selection. Explain that this introduction provides background and sets the tone of the poem. Next, read the first stanza and note the use of the words *stoppeth* and *stopp'st.* Point out that these words are archaic forms of the verb *stop.*

Guided Practice: Apply

Think-Pair-Share Have students form pairs and work together to find other archaic words on this page and identify their modern equivalents. Students may need to use a dictionary for this exercise. After students determine the meaning of the archaic words, have them paraphrase the lines in which the words appear.

Argument

How a Ship having passed the Line was driven by storms to the cold Country toward the South Pole; and how from thence she made her course to the tropical Latitude of the Great Pacific Ocean; and of the strange things that befell; and in what manner the Ancient Mariner came back to his own Country.

Part I

An ancient Mariner meeteth three Gallants bidden to a wedding feast, and detaineth one.

It is an ancient Mariner,
And he stoppeth one of three.
"By thy long gray beard and glittering eye,
Now wherefore stopp'st thou me?

The Bridegroom's doors are opened wide,
And I am next of kin;
The guests are met, the feast is set:
May'st hear the merry din." **(A)**

He holds him with his skinny hand,
"There was a ship," quoth he.
"Hold off! unhand me, gray-beard loon!"
Eftsoons° his hand dropt he.

12. eftsoons: archaic word meaning "at once."

The Wedding Guest is spellbound by the eye of the old seafaring man, and constrained to hear his tale.

He holds him with his glittering eye—
The Wedding Guest stood still,
And listens like a three years' child:
The Mariner hath his will. **(B)**

The Wedding Guest sat on a stone:
He cannot choose but hear;
And thus spake on that ancient man,
The bright-eyed Mariner.

23. kirk: church.

The Mariner tells how the ship sailed southward with a good wind and fair weather, till it reached the Line.

"The ship was cheered, the harbor cleared,
Merrily did we drop
Below the kirk,° below the hill,
Below the lighthouse top.

The Sun came up upon the left,
Out of the sea came he!
And he shone bright, and on the right
Went down into the sea.

(A) Literary Focus **Literary Ballad** How does Coleridge use setting and character to establish background?

(B) Literary Focus **Literary Ballad** Literary ballads often focus on particular characters. What do you learn about the Mariner from his words, appearance, and actions in lines 9–16?

Literary Perspectives

Analyzing Credibility in Literature Literature often asks us to believe in things that are not real, and there are times when we are especially aware that a story does not ring true. When a story is neither fable nor fairy tale, we expect the characters and the plot to be believable or credible. Strange events and even stranger characters play a major role in *The Rime of the Ancient Mariner.* As you read, you may find yourself questioning the credibility of the Mariner's fantastic narrative, given the fact that all the objects and events described in the story are seen only through his eyes and that his frame of mind appears to be constantly shifting.

As you read, be sure to notice the questions in the text, which will guide you in using this perspective.

Literary Perspectives

Before students read the selection, have them read the **Literary Perspectives** about Analyzing Credibility in Literature.

Ask students if they have ever been told a story that seemed unbelievable, even though the speaker insisted that it was true. What was it about the story that made it so far-fetched? What did the speaker have to do to gain credibility?

Remind students to use the notes and questions at the bottom of the page to help them use the perspective.

Higher and higher every day,
Till over the mast at noon°—"
The Wedding Guest here beat his breast,
For he heard the loud bassoon.

The bride hath paced into the hall,
Red as a rose is she;
Nodding their heads before her goes
The merry minstrelsy.°

The Wedding Guest he beat his breast,
Yet he cannot choose but hear;
And thus spake on that ancient man,
The bright-eyed Mariner. **C**

"And now the STORM-BLAST came, and he
Was tyrannous and strong:
He struck with his o'ertaking wings,
And chased us south along.

With sloping masts and dipping prow,
As who° pursued with yell and blow
Still° treads the shadow of his foe,
And forward bends his head,
The ship drove fast, loud roared the blast,
And southward aye° we fled.

And now there came both mist and snow,
And it grew wondrous cold:
And ice, mast-high, came floating by,
As green as emerald.

And through the drifts° the snowy cliffs°
Did send a dismal sheen:
Nor shapes of men nor beasts we ken°— **D**
The ice was all between.

30. over . . . noon: The ship has reached the equator, here called the Line.

The Wedding Guest heareth the bridal music; but the Mariner continueth his tale.

36. minstrelsy: group of musicians.

The ship driven by a storm toward the South Pole.

46. who: one.
47. still: archaic word meaning "always."

50. aye: archaic word meaning "continually."

The land of ice, and of fearful sounds where no living thing was to be seen.
55. drifts: windblown snow and fog. **cliffs:** icebergs.
57. ken: archaic word meaning "saw."

C Literary Focus **Literary Ballad** What is the effect of the repetition in lines 20 and 40?

D Reading Focus **Understanding Archaic Words** Look at the definition of the archaic word *ken*. Did the sailors see animals and people on this stretch of their journey? Explain.

Vocabulary **tyrannous** (TIHR uh nuhs) *adj.:* harsh; oppressive.
dismal (DIHZ muhl) *adj.:* gloomy.

Universal Access

Struggling Readers

Have students look through the poem before they read it. They should note that it is divided into seven parts. Tell students to make a chart with columns for the settings, the characters, the plot events, and the themes of each of the seven parts. Have them fill in the chart as they read as a way of clarifying the events of the plot and their meaning.

✔ Invite students to read the selection in interactive format in **UA: Holt Interactive Reader**.

Advanced Learners

Acceleration Reinforce students' understanding of the meter and rhyme patterns in a ballad by having them write their own four-line stanza modeled after the stanzas in this poem. Tell them that the first and third lines should have four stressed syllables, and the second and fourth lines should have three stressed syllables. Have students use the rhyme pattern *abab* or *abcb* in their stanza. Tell students to write on a topic of their choice.

Think About/Talk About

Comprehension

D Reading Focus

Possible response: *No, they did not see animals or people; the word* nor *means "no," so they saw ("ken") neither men nor animals.*

Analysis

A Literary Focus

Possible response: *The first two stanzas set the scene and introduce the characters, the Mariner and the Wedding Guest; the wedding feast may or may not be the main setting.*

B Literary Focus

Possible response: *The Mariner is skinny and gray-haired; he seems obsessed with telling his tale; he detains a stranger with his "glittering eye"; he seems to have power over the guest.*

C Literary Focus

Possible response: *It reminds us that this is a ballad, a song form in which repetition is often used.*

Vocabulary: Own the Word

- **tyrannous:** Remind students that *tyrannous* is often used to describe harsh governments or leaders. Have students brainstorm examples of *tyrannous* people, laws, or rules. ***Possible responses:*** *Adolf Hitler, Joseph Stalin, Pol Pot*
- **dismal:** Draw a semantic web on the chalkboard, with *dismal* written in the center circle. Have students think of other words that relate to the word *dismal* and record them in the web. ***Possible responses:*** *depressing, gruesome, hopeless, sorrowful, desolate*

Think About/Talk About

Literary Connection

In the last stanza of Part I, the Wedding Guest says, "God save thee ancient Mariner!" heralding the religious symbolism in the decisive act of killing the bird. The killing of an innocent could symbolize the sacrifice of a martyr or a more general religious idea of a lack of reverence for nature.

Build Background: Coleridge's Sources

Coleridge apparently based many of his images of the ice and snow on the descriptions in travel books about the Antarctic. Details of the ship's route may have come from the reports of sailors who traveled through the Strait of Magellan.

The albatross lands on the ship.

At length did cross an Albatross, Through the fog it came.

The ice was here, the ice was there,
The ice was all around:
It cracked and growled, and roared and howled,
Like noises in a swound!°

At length did cross an Albatross,
Through the fog it came;
As if it had been a Christian soul,
We hailed it in God's name.

It ate the food it ne'er had eat,
And round and round it flew.
The ice did split with a thunder fit;
The helmsman steered us through!

And a good south wind sprung up behind;
The Albatross did follow,
And every day, for food or play,
Came to the mariner's hello!

In mist or cloud, on mast or shroud,°
It perched for vespers° nine;
Whiles all the night, through fog-smoke white,
Glimmered the white Moonshine."

62. swound: swoon.

Till a great seabird, called the Albatross, came through the snow fog, and was received with great joy and hospitality.

And lo! the Albatross proveth a bird of good omen, and followeth the ship as it returned northward through fog and floating ice.

75. shroud: support rope that stretches from the top of the mast to the side of the ship.
76. vespers: evenings; also, evening prayers.

Reaching Reluctant Readers

Use lines 71–96 to engage students in a discussion of what it means to be part of a group that is striving for success. Have them discuss times when they took part in a group effort that succeeded or failed, such as participation in a sport. How did their own actions affect the outcome? Have they ever done something unexpected that affected the group as a whole? How did other members of the group treat them, based on their actions?

Help students draw connections between their experience and that of the Ancient Mariner. Point out that the crew is making a group effort to reach the South Pole—a goal that may be thwarted by the Ancient Mariner's impulsive action. Point out that he kills the albatross for reasons he himself does not understand, and the other members of the crew are quick to blame him for the disappearance of the wind. Have students discuss whether the crew's anger is justified and comment on how they might react in a similar situation. Ask students to identify the emotions the Ancient Mariner and the crew are likely to feel in this situation.

"God save thee, ancient Mariner!
From the fiends, that plague thee thus!—
Why look'st thou so?"—With my crossbow
I shot the ALBATROSS.

The ancient Mariner inhospitably killeth the pious bird of good omen.

Part II

The Sun now rose upon the right:
Out of the sea came he,
Still hid in mist, and on the left
Went down into the sea.

And the good south wind still blew behind,
But no sweet bird did follow,
Nor any day for food or play
Came to the mariner's hello!

And I had done a hellish thing,
And it would work 'em woe:
For all averred,° I had killed the bird
That made the breeze to blow.
Ah wretch! said they, the bird to slay,
That made the breeze to blow!

His shipmates cry out against the ancient Mariner, for killing the bird of good luck.

93. averred: asserted; claimed.

Nor dim nor red, like God's own head,
The glorious Sun uprist:
Then all averred, I had killed the bird
That brought the fog and mist.
'Twas right, said they, such birds to slay,
That bring the fog and mist. E

But when the fog cleared off, they justify the same, and thus make themselves accomplices in the crime.

The fair breeze blew, the white foam flew,
The furrow° followed free;
We were the first that ever burst
Into that silent sea.

The fair breeze continues; the ship enters the Pacific Ocean, and sails northward, even till it reaches the Line.

104. furrow: ship's wake.

Down dropt the breeze, the sails dropt down,
'Twas sad as sad could be;
And we did speak only to break
The silence of the sea!

The ship hath been suddenly becalmed.

E **Literary Focus** **Literary Ballad** Find three examples of internal rhyme in lines 91–102. How do these rhymes affect the meaning of the lines?

Think About/Talk About

Analysis

E Literary Focus

Possible response: averred/bird; they/slay; red/head. *The internal rhyme focuses attention on the issue the sailors are debating: Was it right to kill the albatross?*

Extend the Discussion

Finding Details How did the crew first react when the Mariner killed the albatross? Why did they change their opinion in lines 93–102? ***Possible responses:*** *At first, they were upset that he killed the bird because they believed the bird was good luck, but they changed their minds when the fog dissipated, because they thought the killing had caused the sun to return.*

Onomatopoeia Onomatopoeia is language that sounds like the thing it describes. What is the effect of the onomatopoeia in lines 59–62? ***Possible response:*** *Words like* cracked *convey the actual sound of the ice breaking, while the words* growled, roared, *and* howled *evoke the sound of a fierce wind. These words also give animal qualities to the wind, contributing to the reader's sense of nature as a powerful entity.*

Universal Access

EL English Learners

English for Academic Success Help students recognize instances of internal rhyme in the poem. Point out that they should look for words within a line that rhyme with the last word in the line. For example, in line 101, the last word is *slay.* The word in the line that rhymes with *slay* is *they.* Have students find two more examples of internal rhyme in lines 103–106.

✔ See **UA: Differentiating Instruction** for strategies for teaching English learners.

Students with Disabilities

Ask students to work with a partner and orally summarize the events in lines 63–110 from the arrival of the albatross to the immediate consequences of its murder. Guide students in their oral summaries by having them consider the following questions: How did the sailor greet the albatross? What were the albatross's activities and role on the ship? How did the crew react to the killing of the albatross at first and then later? What happened to the ship?

Model the Skill

- Review the characteristics of a **literary ballad.** Tell students that although ballads often use a very regular, almost singsong meter, reading lines as if they were speech helps prevent the meter from becoming monotonous.
- Read lines 149–161 aloud. Point out the regularity of the meter in these stanzas, which consist of alternating lines of four stresses and three stresses. Read the lines more than once if necessary to emphasize their regularity. Then, read lines 162–166. Point out that the exclamation point after "Gramercy!" breaks the rhythm by forcing the reader to pause in the middle of the line. Likewise, in the phrase "all at once" the final word is emphasized, causing the reader to pause at the moment when the sailors draw in their breath in wonder.

Guided Practice: Apply

Read-Talk-Write Have students form pairs and work together to record other instances where Coleridge subtly varies the rhythm. Encourage students to read stanzas aloud, listening for changes in volume or inflection indicated by the lines' punctuation or language.

Literary Connection

Lines 127–130 allude to Act I, Scene 3 of *Macbeth.* In this scene, three witches pronounce a curse on a sailor, sending storms to batter his ship, then declare in unison:

"The weird sisters, hand in hand, Posters of the sea and land, Thus do go about, about."

This Shakespearean allusion helps build an ominous, foreboding mood.

All in a hot and copper sky,
The bloody Sun, at noon,
Right up above the mast did stand,
No bigger than the Moon.

Day after day, day after day,
We stuck, nor breath nor motion;
As idle as a painted ship
Upon a painted ocean. **F**

Water, water, everywhere,
And all the boards did shrink;
Water, water, everywhere,
Nor any drop to drink.

The very deep did rot: O Christ!
That ever this should be!
Yea, slimy things did crawl with legs
Upon the slimy sea.

About, about, in reel and rout°
The death-fires° danced at night;
The water, like a witch's oils,
Burnt green, and blue and white.

And some in dreams assured were
Of the Spirit that plagued us so;
Nine fathom deep he had followed us
From the land of mist and snow. **G**

And every tongue, through utter drought,
Was withered at the root;
We could not speak, no more than if
We had been choked with soot.

Ah! welladay!° what evil looks
Had I from old and young!
Instead of the cross, the Albatross
About my neck was hung.

Water, water everywhere, Nor any drop to drink.

And the Albatross begins to be avenged.

A Spirit had followed them; one of the invisible inhabitants of this planet, neither departed souls nor angels; concerning whom the learned Jew, Josephus, and the Platonic Constantinopolitan, Michael Psellus, may be consulted. They are very numerous, and there is no climate or element without one or more.

127. reel and rout: violent, whirling movement.

128. death-fires: firelike, luminous glow that is said to be seen over dead bodies.

The shipmates, in their sore distress, would fain throw the whole guilt on the ancient Mariner: in sign whereof they hang the dead seabird round his neck.

139. welladay: archaic word meaning "alas," an exclamation of sorrow.

F **Literary Focus** **Literary Ballad** How does Coleridge's use of repetition reinforce the meaning of the stanza?

G **Literary Focus** **Literary Ballad** What do this passage and its annotation reveal about the cause of the sailors' plight?

Cross-Curricular Connection

SCIENCE: Explaining the Strange

Explain that many of the strange phenomena the Mariner recounts have scientific explanations. The "death-fires" in line 128 may be Saint Elmo's fire, an electrical discharge that sometimes appears on ships' masts during storms; some sailors regard it as a good omen. The oily, iridescent appearance of the water is probably caused by plankton, microscopic plant and animal life that float in massive drifts in ocean currents. Some plankton is bioluminescent and glows white and green in the dark. The slimy creatures mentioned in lines 125–126 may be polychaetes, a type of sea worm that has appendages resembling legs.

Individual Activity Have students research one of these phenomena in depth and present their findings to the class.

Part III

There passed a weary time. Each throat
Was parched, and glazed each eye.
A weary time! a weary time!
How glazed each weary eye,
When looking westward, I beheld
A something in the sky.

The ancient Mariner beholdeth a sign in the element afar off.

At first it seemed a little speck,
And then it seemed a mist;
It moved and moved, and took at last
A certain shape, I wist.° **H**

152. wist: archaic word meaning "knew."

A speck, a mist, a shape, I wist!
And still it neared and neared:
As if it dodged a water sprite,
It plunged and tacked and veered.°

156. tacked and veered: turned toward and then away from the wind.

With throats unslaked,° with black lips baked,
We could not laugh nor wail;
Through utter drought all dumb we stood!
I bit my arm, I sucked the blood,
And cried, A sail! a sail!

At its nearer approach, it seemeth him to be a ship; and at a dear ransom, he freeth his speech from the bonds of thirst.

157. unslaked: unrelieved of thirst.

With throats unslaked, with black lips baked,
Agape° they heard me call:
Gramercy!° they for joy did grin,
And all at once their breath drew in,
As they were drinking all. **I**

163. agape: with mouths wide open in wonder or fear.

A flash of joy;

164. gramercy: from Middle French *grand merci,* an exclamation of great thanks.

See! see! (I cried) she tacks no more!
Hither to work us weal;°
Without a breeze, without a tide,
She steadies with upright keel!

And horror follows. For can it be a ship that comes onward without wind or tide?

168. work us weal: do us good.

H **Reading Focus** **Understanding Archaic Words** What makes *welladay* (line 139) and *wist* (line 152) more fitting word choices for the ballad than *alas* and *knew?*

I **Reading Focus** **Understanding Archaic Words** Coleridge uses the word *gramercy* to give the poem an archaic quality. What other devices does he use to lend an archaic feel to lines 164–166?

Think About/Talk About

Comprehension

H Reading Focus

Possible response: *Welladay is a rhythmic word, which works with the meter and contributes to the songlike structure of the ballad. The archaic word wist rhymes with mist and reminds the reader that the ballad takes place in the distant past.*

I Reading Focus

Possible response: *He inverts the word order: "for joy did grin" instead of "grinned for joy"; "their breath drew in" instead of "drew in their breath"; "were drinking all" instead of "were all drinking."*

Analysis

F Literary Focus

Possible response: *The repetition emphasizes the hopeless monotony of the days the crew spent drifting at sea. The repetition of "day after day" and "painted" suggests the helpless, trapped feeling the sailors experience when the ship is becalmed.*

G Literary Focus

Possible response: *It reveals that something supernatural is pursuing and plaguing the ship.*

Universal Access

Struggling Readers

Have students work in groups of five to act out the events described in lines 115–161 in pantomime. Emphasize that students should not speak; instead, they should use their movements, gestures, and facial expressions to convey the sailors' distress and the Ancient Mariner's sense of guilt. Point out that students can vary their actions to change the mood of a scene. For example, when the crew hangs the albatross around the Ancient Mariner's neck, they may act angry and menacing or coldly judgmental.

Think About/Talk About

Literary Connection

Part III presents allegorical figures: Death and a female companion, Life-in-Death, play dice to determine the fate of the Mariner and his companions. While the allegory of Death can be found in literature of various periods, its appearance would probably be most notable in medieval works such as "The Pardoner's Tale" from Chaucer's *The Canterbury Tales*. Instances of death appearing as a seductive woman can be found in Petrarch and in representations of the Fates, Furies, and Harpies.

Build Background: The Flying Dutchman

The Rime of the Ancient Mariner recalls the legend of the Flying Dutchman, a story from the European maritime tradition. In this story, a spectral ship is doomed to wander forever because of the captain's rash pledge to sail around the Cape of Good Hope in a storm. As retribution for gambling his salvation, Vanderdecken, the captain, must sail that course for eternity.

The western wave was all aflame.
The day was well nigh done!
Almost upon the western wave
Rested the broad bright Sun;
When that strange shape drove suddenly
Betwixt us and the Sun.

And straight the Sun was flecked with bars,
(Heaven's Mother send us grace!)
As if through a dungeon grate he peered
With broad and burning face.

It seemeth him but the skeleton of a ship.

Alas! (thought I, and my heart beat loud)
How fast she nears and nears!
Are those *her* sails that glance in the Sun,
Like restless gossameres?°

And its ribs are seen as bars on the face of the setting Sun.

Are those *her* ribs through which the Sun
Did peer, as through a grate?
And is that Woman all her crew?
Is that a DEATH? and are there two?
Is DEATH that woman's mate?

184. gossameres: filmy cobwebs.

The Specter Woman and her Deathmate, and no other onboard the skeleton ship.

Her lips were red, *her* looks were free,
Her locks were yellow as gold:
Her skin was as white as leprosy,
The Nightmare LIFE-IN-DEATH was she,
Who thicks man's blood with cold. J

Like vessel, like crew!

The naked hulk alongside came,
And the twain were casting dice;
"The game is done! I've won! I've won!"
Quoth she, and whistles thrice.

Death and Life-in-Death have diced for the ship's crew, and she (the latter) winneth the ancient Mariner.

The Sun's rim dips; the stars rush out:
At one stride comes the dark;
With far-heard whisper, o'er the sea,
Off shot the specter bark.°

No twilight within the courts of the Sun.

202. specter bark: ghost ship.

J Literary Focus **Literary Ballad** Literary ballads often contain powerful imagery. In your own words, describe the image depicted in lines 185–194.

(right) The Death Ship nears.

Cross-Curricular Connection

SOCIAL STUDIES: Games of Dice

One of the most popular games of chance during the reigns of George II and George III involved dice. People have played with dice-like objects since the dawn of civilization. The earliest such objects were probably made from sheep's anklebones. The Greek historian Herodotus maintains that the Lydians invented dice during a famine in the reign of King Atys, but dice are mentioned in the *Rig Veda* (the ancient collection of hymns revered by Hindus). Dice have also been found in Egyptian tombs built before 2000 B.C. In ancient Greece, dice, or *astragaloi,* were associated with the fickleness of Fate.

Whole-Class Activity Ask students why a game of dice would be an appropriate way for Death and Life-in-Death to decide the Mariner's punishment for his misdeed.

Analyzing Visuals

Connecting to the Text How does this image portray the struggle between life and death onboard the ship?

Think About/Talk About

Analysis

J Literary Focus

Possible response: *The Mariner can see the setting sun through the boat because it has no crossbeams, only ribs, like a prison grate. On the ship stand two figures—Death and Life-in-Death, a ghostly woman with red lips, blond hair, and unnaturally white skin.*

Extend the Discussion

Summarizing In a few sentences, describe the events that take place in lines 171–201. ***Possible response:*** *As the sun is setting, a strange shape appears to block the sailors' view. Soon the Ancient Mariner realizes it is an approaching ship captained by two fearsome creatures: a ghastly-looking woman (Life-in-Death) and her mate, Death. They are playing a game of dice, which the woman wins. Immediately after she declares victory, the sun disappears below the horizon, leaving the sailors in darkness.*

Interpreting Across cultures, weather, season, and time of day have held similar symbolic meanings repeated through the ages. What natural symbolism occurs in lines 199–200? What supernatural, spiritual meaning does it hold here? ***Possible response:*** *The coming of darkness symbolizes the approach of Death.*

Analyzing Visuals

Connecting to the Text: *The men aboard the ship have distressed and anguished expressions as they look out to sea. The dark shades of color used to portray the figures cause the people aboard the ship to appear like ghosts. The overall mood is one of tension and unrest.*

Developing Oral Fluency

The poetry in this chapter is ideal for honing speaking and reading ability.

Ask students to list criteria for an oral presentation (volume, pronunciation, inflection, pacing, pitch, eye contact, facial expression, and body language). Next, model a short poetry reading several times, each time performing poorly on one or more criteria. Have students critique your performance.

Paired Activity Tell students to choose a passage of five to ten lines to memorize. Have them practice with an assigned partner, each evaluating the other according to the criteria they have chosen. Allow time for each performance. For every speaker, have two student evaluators provide written comments. Review comments before passing them on.

✔ See the **Oral Language Skill Builder** in **UA: Differentiating Instruction.**

Guided Practice: Apply

Think as a Reader/Writer

Find It in Your Reading Tell students that some **archaic words** in this poem, such as *clomb,* are no longer used today. Other words, such as *ghastly,* may sound old-fashioned and unfamiliar but are still acceptable to use, even though they are not used frequently. Point out other examples of words that are used infrequently but are not actually archaic, such as *nether* and *lank,* and have students look up their meaning.

Use It in Your Writing Have students write a few lines of dialogue that include words from three different categories: archaic words that have fallen out of use, words that are used infrequently but are not considered archaic, and words that are commonly used in everyday speech. Have students read their dialogue aloud and identify archaic words and those that are merely old-fashioned.

We listened and looked sideways up!
Fear at my heart, as at a cup,
My lifeblood seemed to sip!
The stars were dim, and thick the night,
The steersman's face by his lamp gleamed white;
From the sails the dew did drip—
Till clomb° above the eastern bar
The hornèd° Moon, with one bright star
Within the nether tip.°

At the rising of the Moon,

209. clomb: archaic form of "climbed."
210. hornèd: crescent.
210–211. star . . . tip: A star dogging, or following, the moon is believed by sailors to be an evil omen.

One after one, by the star-dogged Moon,
Too quick for groan or sigh,
Each turned his face with a ghastly pang,
And cursed me with his eye.

One after another,

Four times fifty living men,
(And I heard nor sigh nor groan)
With heavy thump, a lifeless lump,
They dropped down one by one.

His shipmates drop down dead.

The souls did from their bodies fly,—
They fled to bliss or woe!
And every soul, it passed me by,
Like the whizz of my crossbow!

But Life-in-Death begins her work on the ancient Mariner.

Part IV

"I fear thee, ancient Mariner!
I fear thy skinny hand!
And thou art long, and lank, and brown,
As is the ribbed sea sand.

The Wedding Guest feareth that a Spirit is talking to him;

I fear thee and thy glittering eye,
And thy skinny hand, so brown."—
Fear not, fear not, thou Wedding Guest!
This body dropt not down.

Alone, alone, all, all alone,
Alone on a wide wide sea!
And never a saint took pity on
My soul in agony.

But the ancient Mariner assureth him of his bodily life, and proceedeth to relate his horrible penance.

Vocabulary **ghastly** (GAST lee) *adj.:* dreadful; ghostly.

Universal Access

Struggling Readers

Some students may have difficulty understanding Coleridge's use of inverted word order. Point out that inverted word order contributes to the poem's archaic feel and allows Coleridge to maintain a regular rhythm and rhyme scheme—essential components of a ballad.

Next, read aloud the first stanza of Part IV. Model how to break it down into sentences and identify the subject and verb in each sentence. Then, paraphrase the last two lines, using modern language and conventional word order: "You are as long, and lank, and brown, as the ribbed sea sand is." Have students form small groups, and assign each group a four-line stanza to paraphrase. Have groups share their paraphrase with the rest of the class.

The many men, so beautiful!
And they all dead did lie:
And a thousand thousand slimy things
Lived on; and so did I.

He despiseth the creatures of the calm,

I looked upon the rotting sea,
And drew my eyes away;
I looked upon the rotting deck,
And there the dead men lay.

And envieth that they should live, and so many lie dead.

I looked to heaven, and tried to pray;
But or° ever a prayer had gusht,
A wicked whisper came, and made
My heart as dry as dust.

245. or: before.

I closed my lids, and kept them close,
And the balls like pulses beat;
For the sky and the sea, and the sea and the sky
Lay like a load on my weary eye,
And the dead were at my feet.

But the curse liveth for him in the eye of the dead men.

The cold sweat melted from their limbs,
Nor rot nor reek did they:
The look with which they looked on me
Had never passed away. (K)

An orphan's curse would drag to hell
A spirit from on high;
But oh! more horrible than that
Is the curse in a dead man's eye!
Seven days, seven nights, I saw that curse,
And yet I could not die.

In his loneliness and fixedness he yearneth toward the journeying Moon, and the stars that still sojourn, yet still move onward; and everywhere the blue sky belongs to them, and is their appointed rest, and their native country and their own natural homes, which they enter unannounced, as lords that are certainly expected and yet there is a silent joy at their arrival.

The moving Moon went up the sky,
And nowhere did abide:
Softly she was going up,
And a star or two beside—

(K) **Literary Focus** **Literary Ballad** How do supernatural and realistic elements work together in this stanza?

Think About/Talk About

Analysis

(K) Literary Focus

Possible response: *The bodies should have begun to decompose, yet the men seem to be sweating, and they continue gazing at him with eyes full of hatred.*

Extend the Discussion

Determining Author's Purpose The first stanza of Part IV reminds the reader that the Mariner is recounting his tale to a listener, the Wedding Guest. How does the Wedding Guest react as he listens to the Mariner's story? Why does Coleridge frame the narrative within a tale told to an audience appearing in the poem? ***Possible responses:*** *The Wedding Guest stands in for the reader of the poem. His reactions could be the reader's reactions. At first, the Mariner annoys him, but he becomes more and more engrossed in the tale of the Mariner's troubles. Coleridge may have wanted the Wedding Guest, and, therefore, the reader to feel the Mariner's passion and apply what he has learned from the Mariner to his own life.*

Vocabulary: Own the Word

ghastly: Demonstrate the difference in connotation between *ghastly* and a less pronounced adjective such as *terrible* or *frightening* by using a comparative sentence, for example: "The monster looked scary in the movie, but in real life it was just *ghastly*!" Have students compose their own comparative sentence.

Advanced Learners

Acceleration Point out that Coleridge uses a wide variety of poetic devices that contribute to the musicality of the ballad. If necessary, clarify for students the meaning of the terms *alliteration, assonance, onomatopoeia, repetition,* and *internal rhyme.* Have students form groups and have each group analyze one or two stanzas in Part IV in terms of which sound devices Coleridge uses and what effect these have on the reader.

Students with Disabilities

Point out that one of the most powerful literary devices Coleridge uses is also one of the simplest: repetition. Draw students' attention to lines 224–225 in Part IV, and point out that the repetition of the words *I fear* conveys the Wedding Guest's anxiety more effectively than using the phrase just once. As students read, help them identify other instances of repeated words and phrases and discuss what emotions or visual images the repetition conveys.

Think About/Talk About

Literary Connection

Coleridge's contemporary William Wordsworth, himself a noted Romantic poet, influenced the creation of *The Rime of the Ancient Mariner.* These are William Wordsworth's reminiscences on his contribution to this ballad: "Much the greatest part of the story was Mr. Coleridge's invention, but certain parts I suggested; for example, some crime was to be committed which should bring upon the Old Navigator, as Coleridge afterwards delighted to call him, the spectral prosecution, as a consequence of that crime and his own wanderings. . . . 'Suppose,' said I, 'you represent him as having killed one of these [albatrosses] on entering the South Sea, and that the tutelary spirits of these regions take upon them to avenge the crime.' . . . I also suggested the navigation of the ship by the dead men, but do not recollect that I had anything more to do with the scheme of the poem."

Her beams bemocked the sultry main,°
Like April hoarfrost° spread;
But where the ship's huge shadow lay,
The charmèd water burnt alway°
A still and awful red.

Beyond the shadow of the ship,
I watched the water snakes:
They moved in tracks of shining white,
And when they reared, the elfish light
Fell off in hoary° flakes.

Within the shadow of the ship
I watched their rich attire:
Blue, glossy green, and velvet black,
They coiled and swam; and every track
Was a flash of golden fire.

O happy, living things! no tongue
Their beauty might declare:
A spring of love gushed from my heart,
And I blessed them unaware:
Sure my kind saint took pity on me,
And I blessed them unaware.

The selfsame moment I could pray;
And from my neck so free
The Albatross fell off, and sank
Like lead into the sea. **L**

Part V

Oh sleep! it is a gentle thing,
Beloved from pole to pole!
To Mary Queen the praise be given!
She sent the gentle sleep from Heaven,
That slid into my soul.

The silly° buckets on the deck,
That had so long remained,
I dreamt that they were filled with dew;
And when I awoke, it rained.

267. main: archaic word meaning "open sea."
268. hoarfrost: frost.
270. alway: archaic form of "always."

By the light of the Moon he beholdeth God's creatures of the great calm.

276. hoary: white or gray.

Their beauty and their happiness.

He blesseth them in his heart.

The spell begins to break.

297. silly: simple; plain.

By grace of the holy Mother, the ancient Mariner is refreshed with rain.

L Reading Focus Understanding Archaic Words The word *selfsame* is rarely used today. It comes from the Middle English spelling *selue same* and is derived from the Old German *selbsama.* What do you think *selfsame* means? How is this word like the word *lifeblood*?

Universal Access

Struggling Readers

Strategic Students Model identifying the meter and rhyme scheme of the stanzas. Remind students that most of the stanzas in *The Rime of the Ancient Mariner* consist of four lines following the rhyme scheme *abcb* and have alternating lines of four stresses and three stresses. Tell students, "five of the seven stanzas on p. 786 are longer than the usual four-line stanza. In lines 267–271, the second line rhymes with the fifth line, (*spread/red*) and the third rhymes with the fourth line (*lay/always*). Lines 268 and 271 contain three stressed syllables, while the other lines in the stanza have four stressed syllables." Have students analyze the

GEOGRAPHY LINK

The frigid waters of the Southern Ocean meet the warmer ocean waters from the north.

Native to the Northern Hemisphere, reindeer have lived on South Georgia Island near Antarctica since Norwegian sailors left some there in the early 1900s.

Antarctic Convergence

Isolated and brutally cold, Antarctica and its surrounding islands feature a climate inhospitable to humans and most mammals, with the exception of marine life such as seals, whales, dolphins, and porpoises. With an absence of indigenous land mammals and an abundance of food, Antarctica is a haven for forty-five bird species, including albatrosses and, of course, penguins. Climatic conditions also help advance the proliferation of bird species. The Antarctic Circumpolar Current, driven by some of the most powerful winds on the planet, circles the continent of Antarctica and some of its surrounding islands. By allowing a complex exchange of water, heat, gases, salinity, and nutrients with the other oceans, the Circumpolar Current has a profound effect on the Earth's climate. In a twenty- to thirty-mile ribbon along the Southern Ocean's outer edge, the frigid waters of the current meet the fifty-degree waters of the Atlantic, Pacific, and Indian Oceans, causing a phenomenon known as the Antarctic Convergence. The convergence creates strange weather patterns and a hospitable environment for a surge of sea organisms that will feed fish, birds, and marine mammals.

Ask Yourself

Does learning about Antarctic geography and biology change your view of the events in the poem? What parts of the poem do you view differently? How does this knowledge affect your opinion of the Mariner's credibility? Explain.

My lips were wet, my throat was cold,
My garments all were dank;
Sure I had drunken in my dreams,
And still my body drank.

I moved, and could not feel my limbs:
I was so light—almost
I thought that I had died in sleep,
And was a blessèd ghost.

And soon I heard a roaring wind:
It did not come anear;
But with its sound it shook the sails,
That were so thin and sere.° (M)

He heareth sounds and seeth strange sights and commotions in the sky and the element.

312. sere: archaic word meaning "worn."

(M) **Reading Focus** **Understanding Archaic Words** What archaic word besides *sere* appears in this stanza? Use the word's prefix to think of another archaic word that has the opposite meaning.

meter and rhyme scheme of the next three stanzas.

✔ See **UA: Differentiating Instruction** for strategies for teaching struggling readers.

Advanced Learners

Enrichment Part IV includes references to red waters (which may suggest red tides), water snakes, and possibly the Aurora Australis, or Southern Lights. Explain that red tides are discolorations of the sea caused by red dinoflagellates, which kill fish and other organisms by releasing poison. Then, suggest that students find out where and why red tides occur. You might also tell them that water snakes are found in both fresh and salt water. Suggest that students do research on how far out in the ocean water snakes can live. Students might also be interested in investigating what causes the Aurora Australis and whether it is visible from the probable latitude of the Mariner's ship. Invite students to choose and research one or more of these topics and to share their findings with the class.

Think About/Talk About

Comprehension

(L) Reading Focus

Possible response: *Like* lifeblood, *selfsame has been replaced by a shorter, modern form. People use* blood, *not* lifeblood, *in everyday speech, and they use* same, *not* selfsame.

(M) Reading Focus

Possible responses: Anear *is an archaic word. The prefix* a– *(still used in its antonym,* afar*) often appears in archaic written English.*

Extend the Discussion

Literary Ballad Explain how the first stanza on p. 786 demonstrates a blend of the realistic and the fantastical. ***Possible response:*** *Beams of light from the moon fall on the sea to form a frostlike pattern on the water's surface—an image of the natural world that recalls Wordsworth. Yet the huge shadow cast by the cursed ship on the water is an unearthly red.*

Geography Link

Ask Yourself

Possible response: *Learning facts about the geography and biology of the setting helps explain some of the unusual events and fantastic imagery in the poem. Although the poem does include supernatural events, it's clear that some occurrences, such as the colors and "death-fires" in the water, could really have happened in nature. Knowing this makes the Ancient Mariner's tale more plausible and credible, even though he himself has a supernatural explanation for the events.*

Think About/Talk About

Extend the Discussion

Summarizing Describe the events that occur in lines 313–340. ***Possible response:*** *Suddenly the sky is filled with the lights of the aurora, which resembled colorful flags. A storm begins, with lightning, and heavy rains. The Mariner can hear the wind in the distance, but it has not yet reached the ship; nevertheless, the ship begins to move again. The dead crewmen appear to be coming back to life; they do not speak, but they groan, rise up, and begin working the ropes of the ship.*

Interpreting What is the literal and symbolic importance of the sudden rainstorm? ***Possible responses:*** *The rainstorm is important to the Ancient Mariner's physical survival. For weeks he has been adrift at sea with no water, and his shipmates have perished from thirst. The rainstorm is also symbolically significant. It occurs shortly after the Mariner blesses the water snakes and begins to pray again. The rainstorm may represent absolution or forgiveness "raining" down on him from above.*

The upper air burst into life!
And a hundred fire flags sheen,
To and fro they were hurried about!
And to and fro, and in and out,
The wan stars danced between.°

And the coming wind did roar more loud,
And the sails did sigh like sedge;°
And the rain poured down from one black cloud;
The Moon was at its edge.

The thick black cloud was cleft,° and still
The Moon was at its side:
Like waters shot from some high crag,
The lightning fell with never a jag,
A river steep and wide.

The loud wind never reached the ship,
Yet now the ship moved on!
Beneath the lightning and the Moon
The dead men gave a groan.

They groaned, they stirred, they all uprose,
Nor spake, nor moved their eyes;
It had been strange, even in a dream,
To have seen those dead men rise. (N)

The helmsman steered, the ship moved on;
Yet never a breeze up-blew;
The mariners all 'gan work the ropes,
Where they were wont° to do;
They raised their limbs like lifeless tools—
We were a ghastly crew.

The body of my brother's son
Stood by me, knee to knee:
The body and I pulled at one rope,
But he said nought to me.

313–317. The upper . . . danced between: apparently a description of the shifting lights of an aurora, which sometimes resemble waving, luminous folds of fabric.

319. sedge: reedy plants.

322. cleft: split.

The bodies of the ship's crew are inspired, and the ship moves on;

338. wont: accustomed.

(N) **Literary Focus** **Literary Ballad** Describe the supernatural element that appears in lines 327–334.

Universal Access

English Learners

English for Academic Success To help students understand the language of the selection, point out that Coleridge frequently uses shortened forms of modern English words. Explain that the missing letters are represented by an apostrophe, just like the missing letters in contractions such as *don't* and *can't.* Point out examples of shortened archaic forms on this page, such as *'gan* for *began* in line 337 and *'twas* for *it was* in lines 347 and 363.

Struggling Readers

Help students understand the archaic language of the selection by drawing their attention to verbs whose spelling and pronunciation are fairly similar to that of their modern equivalents, For example, the verb *spake* in line 332 is an archaic form of *spoke,* and the participle *blest* in line 349 is an archaic form of *blessed.* As students continue reading, have them note other examples of archaic verbs (especially past-tense forms) that resemble modern English verbs.

"I fear thee, ancient Mariner!"
Be calm, thou Wedding Guest!
'Twas not those souls that fled in pain,
Which to their corses° came again,
But a troop of spirits blest: (O)

For when it dawned—they dropt their arms,
And clustered round the mast;
Sweet sounds rose slowly through their mouths,
And from their bodies passed.

Around, around, flew each sweet sound,
Then darted to the Sun;
Slowly the sounds came back again,
Now mixed, now one by one.

Sometimes a-dropping from the sky
I heard the skylark sing;
Sometimes all little birds that are,
How they seemed to fill the sea and air
With their sweet jargoning!°

And now 'twas like all instruments,
Now like a lonely flute;
And now it is an angel's song,
That makes the heavens be mute.

It ceased; yet still the sails made on
A pleasant noise till noon,
A noise like of a hidden brook
In the leafy month of June,
That to the sleeping woods all night
Singeth a quiet tune. (P)

Till noon we quietly sailed on,
Yet never a breeze did breathe:
Slowly and smoothly went the ship,
Moved onward from beneath.

But not by the souls of the men, nor by demons of earth or middle air, but by a blessed troop of angelic spirits, sent down by the invocation of the guardian saint.

348. corses: archaic form of "corpses."

362. jargoning: archaic word meaning "twittering."

The dead men gave a groan.

(O) **Literary Perspectives** **Credibility in Literature** Why does the Wedding Guest tell the ancient Mariner that he fears him? What might he believe about the Mariner and his tale?

(P) **Literary Focus** **Literary Ballad** How does the imagery in this stanza communicate the tone of this part of the poem?

Think About/Talk About

Analysis

(N) Literary Focus

Possible response: *The dead sailors appear to be coming back to life.*

(O) Literary Perspectives

Possible responses: *The guest fears the Ancient Mariner because he thinks the Mariner himself might be a spirit or a dead man who has returned to life.*

(P) Literary Focus

Possible response: *The imagery is drawn from nature. The celestial song is compared to a brook singing in the summer woods. The images create a serene tone, suggesting that the Mariner has reconciled with nature.*

Extend the Discussion

Rearranging Syntax How would you rearrange and paraphrase the first three lines of the last stanza on p. 789 to create a normal word order? ***Possible response:*** *We sailed quietly on until noon. Although no breeze ever blew, the ship moved slowly and smoothly, pushed on from beneath the water.*

Advanced Learners

Acceleration Draw students' attention to archaic verbs such as *blest* and *singeth* and archaic contractions such as *'twas.* Guide students to understand the grammatical rules underlying these forms. For instance, past-tense verbs often end in *t* or *'d;* present-tense verbs may end in *–est* or *–eth;* and contractions may combine two words while using an apostrophe to indicate missing letters at the beginning of the first word (*'twas*). Ask students to summarize lines 293–376 using archaic language.

Literary Perspectives

To help students answer the **Literary Perspectives** question on this page, have students consider what the ancient Mariner has told the Wedding Guest in lines 330–344. Ask students whether the Wedding Guest seems to believe or express doubts about the Mariner's tale.

Think About/Talk About

Literary Connection

Tell students that Gustave Doré, the illustrator for *The Rime of the Ancient Mariner,* was one of the most famous nineteenth century illustrators. Beyond his work for Coleridge, Doré also created illustrations for *Don Quixote, The Divine Comedy* (particularly Dante's *Inferno*), and Edgar Allen Poe's "The Raven." In the library or on the Internet, have students look up these illustrations and compare and contrast them with the ones featured in this selection.

Under the keel nine fathom deep,
From the land of mist and snow,
The spirit slid: and it was he
That made the ship to go.
The sails at noon left off their tune,
And the ship stood still also.

The lonesome Spirit from the South Pole carries on the ship as far as the Line, in obedience to the angelic troop, but still requireth vengeance.

The Sun, right up above the mast,
Had fixed her° to the ocean:
But in a minute she 'gan stir,
With a short uneasy motion—
Backwards and forwards half her length
With a short uneasy motion.

384. fixed her: seemed to hold the ship motionless.

Then like a pawing horse let go,
She made a sudden bound:
It flung the blood into my head,
And I fell down in a swound. Q

How long in that same fit I lay,
I have not to declare;
But ere my living life returned,
I heard and in my soul discerned
Two voices in the air.

The Polar Spirit's fellow demons, the invisible inhabitants of the element, take part in his wrong; and two of them relate, one to the other, that penance long and heavy for the ancient Mariner hath been accorded to the Polar Spirit, who returneth southward.

"Is it he?" quoth one, "Is this the man?
By him who died on cross,
With his cruel bow he laid full low
The harmless Albatross.

The spirit who bideth by himself
In the land of mist and snow,
He loved the bird that loved the man
Who shot him with his bow."

The other was a softer voice,
As soft as honeydew:
Quoth he, "The man hath penance done,
And penance more will do." R

Q **Reading Focus** **Understanding Archaic Words** See line 62 for a definition of *swound.* Why might Coleridge have chosen to use this word instead of a more modern word?

R **Literary Focus** **Literary Ballad** What storytelling elements appear in lines 398–409?

(right) I fell down in a swound.

Reaching Reluctant Readers

Help students visualize the events in this section of the text by linking the text to the illustration that appears on p. 791. Place the section in context by reminding students that the ship has begun moving again through supernatural means, as there is no breeze. Briefly discuss the other unusual natural phenomena that occur in this section: The sun moves back and forth, then "[flings] the blood into [the Mariner's] head," causing him to faint. Explain that the illustration on p. 791 depicts the unconscious Ancient Mariner. After students read, have them describe how they picture other elements of the scene, such as the spirits who discuss the Mariner's sin as he lies in a trance.

Think About/Talk About

Comprehension

Q Reading Focus

Possible response: Swound *means "swoon or faint." Coleridge deliberately uses an archaic word to add a medieval flavor; the word also fits the ballad's rhyme scheme.*

Analysis

R Literary Focus

Possible response: *Coleridge uses dialogue to move the action of the story along. The two spirits summarize the Ancient Mariner's sin, allude to the penance he has already done, and state ominously that he will do more penance; this builds suspense, as the reader wonders what other difficulties the Ancient Mariner will undergo.*

Extend the Discussion

Literary Ballad According to the Mariner, how is the ship moving? In what way does his explanation reflect the traditional characteristics of literary ballads? ***Possible response:*** *A spirit is moving the ship from below (the keel). The blending of real and supernatural story elements is typical of folk and literary ballads.*

Universal Access

Students with Disabilities

Point out that the illustration on p. 791 portrays the events described in lines 391–392: "It flung the blood into my head, and I fell down in a swoon." Ask students to comment on how this illustration is like or unlike what they visualize when they read these lines. Have students choose another brief quotation (two or three lines) from this page and create an illustration for it. Students should label their illustrations with the chosen quotation.

Analyzing Visuals

Connecting to the Text: *One might infer from the Mariner's unconscious position that he is losing the battle. The ship is portrayed in an angled viewpoint as if in the midst of a short motion, while the Mariner is hanging on to the ropes with both hands to avoid being thrown off the ship.*

Think About/Talk About

Literary Connection

Direct students to line 468, where the ship crosses the bar. Tell students that in literature, crossing the bar into the harbor suggests a calm resolution, while crossing the bar into the sea suggests an encounter with the rough waters of sea and life. In Alfred, Lord Tennyson's "Crossing the Bar," the sandbar represents a transition between life and death, and the speaker in the poem accepts death with dignity.

Extend the Discussion

Monitoring Your Reading In what ways is the dialogue in Part VI potentially confusing to a reader? What strategies could you use to ensure that you understand this section of the text? ***Possible responses:*** *This section is somewhat confusing because at first it is not clear who the voices are. I could go back and re-read the end of Part V to determine whether these are the same voices the Ancient Mariner heard after he fainted. I could also check the notes in the margins to see whether they say anything about who is speaking in this part of the poem.*

Evaluating Re-read lines 410–429. Why do you think Coleridge chose to begin this section with dialogue featuring questions and answers? What effect does this have on the reader? ***Possible responses:*** *The questions the Second Voice answers are questions the reader may have. The dialogue is helpful because it explains what is happening to make the ship move. The final two lines of dialogue also build suspense about the Mariner's fate by suggesting that the ship's motion may slow down again.*

Part VI

FIRST VOICE

"But tell me, tell me! speak again,
Thy soft response renewing—
What makes that ship drive on so fast?
What is the ocean doing?"

SECOND VOICE

"Still as a slave before his lord,
The ocean hath no blast;°
His great bright eye most silently
Up to the Moon is cast—

If he may know which way to go;
For she guides him smooth or grim.
See, brother, see! how graciously
She looketh down on him."

FIRST VOICE

"But why drives on that ship so fast,
Without or wave or wind?"°

SECOND VOICE

"The air is cut away before,
And closes from behind.

Fly, brother, fly! more high, more high!
Or we shall be belated:
For slow and slow that ship will go,
When the Mariner's trance is abated."

I woke, and we were sailing on
As in a gentle weather:
'Twas night, calm night, the Moon was high;
The dead men stood together.

All stood together on the deck,
For a charnel dungeon° fitter:
All fixed on me their stony eyes,
That in the Moon did glitter.

415. blast: wind.

The Mariner hath been cast into a trance; for the angelic power causeth the vessel to drive northward faster than human life could endure.

423. without . . . wind: with neither wave nor wind.

The supernatural motion is retarded; the Mariner awakes, and his penance begins anew.

435. charnel dungeon: burial vault.

Vocabulary **abated** (uh BAYT ihd) *v.:* lessened.

Universal Access

Struggling Readers

Explain to students that lines 446–451 are an extended simile. Instruct them to read closely so they can understand the sequence of events.

Group Activity In groups, have students discuss this stanza. Instruct each group to discuss and prepare to answer the following questions: What is this stanza about? To what is the Mariner drawing the comparison? What makes the Mariner feel this way? Why? Have groups select a spokesperson to share their ideas with the class.

The pang, the curse, with which they died,
Had never passed away:
I could not draw my eyes from theirs,
Nor turn them up to pray.

And now this spell was snapt: once more
I viewed the ocean green,
And looked far forth, yet little saw
Of what had else° been seen— Ⓢ

The curse is finally expiated [removed, after penance is done].

445. had else: would otherwise have.

Like one, that on a lonesome road
Doth walk in fear and dread,
And having once turned round walks on,
And turns no more his head;
Because he knows, a frightful fiend
Doth close behind him tread.

But soon there breathed a wind on me,
Nor sound nor motion made:
Its path was not upon the sea,
In ripple or in shade.

It raised my hair, it fanned my cheek
Like a meadow gale of spring—
It mingled strangely with my fears,
Yet it felt like a welcoming.

Swiftly, swiftly flew the ship,
Yet she sailed softly too:
Sweetly, sweetly blew the breeze—
On me alone it blew.

Oh! dream of joy! is this indeed
The lighthouse top I see?
Is this the hill? is this the kirk?
Is this mine own countree? Ⓣ

And the ancient Mariner beholdeth his native country.

We drifted o'er the harbor bar,
And I with sobs did pray—
O let me be awake, my God!
Or let me sleep alway.

Ⓢ **Literary Perspectives** **Credibility in Literature** How did the Mariner describe the sea in line 240? How does he see it now? Why?

Ⓣ **Reading Focus** **Understanding Archaic Words** How would you rewrite the archaic words in this stanza to avoid archaic usage and spelling?

Cross-Curricular Connection

LITERATURE: Voyages in Classical Epics

Explain that literary ballads sometimes allude to the characters, plots, and settings of other works of literature. In Parts V and VI, the magical movement of the ship during the Mariner's trance recalls Odysseus's homeward journey in Homer's *Odyssey* (Book 13), in which the gods put Odysseus in a trance and then speed his ship home. Point out that this allusion may suggest a similarity between the two characters. It also suggests that this is an archetypal journey, both physical and spiritual, and gives the poem a classical flavor. Finally, it establishes the poem as a literary—rather than a folk—ballad.

Think About/Talk About

Comprehension

Ⓣ Reading Focus

Possible response: *The archaic spelling of* countree *can be changed to* country, *and the archaic usage* mine *can be changed to* my.

Analysis

Ⓢ Literary Perspectives

Possible responses: *He views the sea as green and living, as opposed to seeing it as "rot," (line 240) like death. Just as the expiation of sin is a rebirth for the Mariner, the sea is transformed from death to life. Also, the color green is often associated with nature and with living things, especially plant life. The Mariner probably sees the ocean as green and living because he has reconnected with the natural world.*

Extend the Discussion

Making Predictions Based on lines 464–467, do you think the Ancient Mariner will find his way back to his native country? Why or why not? ***Possible responses:*** *No, I think he may just be imagining that he sees his home; yes, the spirits seem to have decided that he has suffered enough, so I think they will allow him to return to his homeland.*

Literary Ballad What literary devices does Coleridge use in lines 460–463? What feelings do these devices convey? ***Possible response:*** *The alliteration of the* s *sound and the assonance in the words* sweetly, breeze, *and* me *mimic the soft wind and create a sense of harmony and joy.*

Vocabulary: Own the Word

abated: Tell students the antonym of *abated* is *increased* or *intensified.* Have students use both words in a sentence: The anger of the gods *abated* only after the people offered worthy sacrifices.

Think About/Talk About

Build Background: Seraphim

Point out that according to Christian theology, the seraphs Coleridge describes in lines 490–499 are one class of angels; other classes include cherubim and archangels. The seraphs' angelic nature is indicated by the fact that they appear as beings of light; this light may be what draws the rescuers toward the Mariner's ship. Explain that the word *angel* comes from the Greek word *angelos,* meaning "messenger." Ask students to discuss what message, if any, the appearance of the seraphs communicates to the Ancient Mariner.

The harbor bay was clear as glass,
So smoothly it was strewn!°
And on the bay the moonlight lay,
And the shadow of the Moon.

The rock shone bright, the kirk no less,
That stands above the rock:
The moonlight steeped in silentness
The steady weathercock.°

And the bay was white with silent light,
Till rising from the same,
Full many shapes, that shadows were,
In crimson colors came.

A little distance from the prow
Those crimson shadows were:
I turned my eyes upon the deck—
Oh, Christ! what saw I there!

Each corse lay flat, lifeless and flat,
And, by the holy rood!°
A man all light, a seraph° man,
On every corse there stood.

This seraph band, each waved his hand:
It was a heavenly sight!
They stood as signals to the land,
Each one a lovely light; (U)

This seraph band, each waved his hand,
No voice did they impart—
No voice; but oh! the silence sank
Like music on my heart.

But soon I heard the dash of oars,
I heard the Pilot's cheer;
My head was turned perforce away
And I saw a boat appear.

473. strewn: stretched out; calmed.

479. weathercock: rooster-shaped weather vane.

The angelic spirits leave the dead bodies,

And appear in their own forms of light.

489. rood: crucifix.
490. seraph: angel of the highest rank.

(U) **Literary Focus** **Literary Ballad** What characteristic elements of a literary ballad occur in this stanza?

Universal Access

Students Who Use African American Vernacular English

English for Academic Success Direct students to line 503. Read the line aloud, putting an emphasis on the word *saw.* Remind students not to substitute the past participle form (*seen*) for the past tense (*saw*). Tell them that the past participle form should be used with the verb *have.* For example: *I have seen the boat.* Not *I seen the boat.* Have students write the following sentences in the past tense: Two ships sink [*sank*] during the battle. I see [*have seen*] their wreckage in the water.

Advanced Learners

Acceleration Have students hold a mock trial for the Mariner upon his return to shore. Students should form two groups; one group will hold him accountable for the deaths of his crewmates, while the other group will contend that he is a victim, unjustly condemned for an act that is not even legally considered a crime. Both the prosecution and the defense teams should

The Pilot and the Pilot's boy,
I heard them coming fast:
Dear Lord in Heaven! it was a joy
The dead men could not blast.

I saw a third—I heard his voice:
It is the Hermit good!
He singeth loud his godly hymns
That he makes in the wood.
He'll shrieve° my soul, he'll wash away
The Albatross's blood.

Part VII

This Hermit good lives in that wood
Which slopes down to the sea.
How loudly his sweet voice he rears!
He loves to talk with marineres
That come from a far countree. Ⓥ

He kneels at morn, and noon, and eve—
He hath a cushion plump:
It is the moss that wholly hides
The rotted old oak stump.

The skiff boat° neared: I heard them talk,
"Why, this is strange, I trow!°
Where are those lights so many and fair,
That signal made but now?"

"Strange, by my faith!" the Hermit said—
"And they answered not our cheer!
The planks looked warped! and see those sails,
How thin they are and sere!
I never saw aught° like to them,
Unless perchance it were

The skiff boat neared: I heard them talk, "Why, this is strange, I trow!"

512. shrieve: archaic word meaning "release from guilt after hearing confession."

The Hermit of the Wood,

523. skiff boat: rowboat.
524. trow: archaic word meaning "believe."

Approacheth the ship with wonder.

531. aught: anything.

Ⓥ **Literary Focus** **Literary Ballad** What examples of alliteration and internal rhyme can you find in this stanza? How do these sound devices affect the mood of the poem?

Think About/Talk About

Analysis

Ⓤ Literary Focus

Possible response: *This stanza contains internal rhyme and end rhyme, alliteration, assonance, and supernatural characters.*

Ⓥ Literary Focus

Possible responses: *The internal rhyme in* good/wood *lends a childlike tone to this line. By linking* slopes/sea *and* come/countree *through alliteration, Coleridge emphasizes the movement from the sea to the country. Both of these devices reinforce the uplifting theme of redemption through nature.*

Extend the Discussion

Summarizing Briefly summarize the events that occur at the end of Part VI. ***Possible response:*** *The ship approaches the Mariner's home country. He sees crimson shadows and, turning toward the deck, sees his dead crewmates once again lying lifeless, with an angel standing on each corpse. Next he hears the Pilot and the Pilot's boy approaching and hears the voice of the Hermit.*

Symbolism In lines 508–513, Coleridge shifts focus to the Hermit. Based on his description, what do you think he represents? ***Possible response:*** *The Hermit represents everything the Mariner should be—pious, wholesome, joyful, respectful, and in harmony with nature.*

gather textual evidence and formulate logical arguments to strengthen their case. Depending on the class time available, students may also bolster their arguments with visual aids or appear as witnesses. After both teams have presented their arguments, have the class serve as the jury and decide upon a verdict.

✔ See **UA: Resources for Teaching Advanced Students** for strategies for teaching advanced learners.

Students with Disabilities

Have students write a few sentences describing how the Ancient Mariner has changed over the course of the events described in the poem. Guide students in this activity by asking them these questions: What character traits promoted the Ancient Mariner to kill the albatross at the beginning of the poem? What events cause him to change? What words would you use to describe his character now?

Think About/Talk About

Extend the Discussion

Rearranging Syntax Briefly restate lines 550–555 using conventional word order. ***Possible response:*** *The lines can be restated as follows: "Stunned by that loud and dreadful sound that smote the sky and ocean, my body lay afloat like one that had been drowned for seven days. But swift as dreams, I found myself within the Pilot's boat."*

Imagery In lines 533–537, the hermit uses natural imagery to describe his impression of the ship. What season is he describing? Why? ***Possible responses:*** *He describes winter, the season when things die. This is apt because the ship was the site of so much death.*

Brown skeletons of leaves that lag°
My forest brook along;
When the ivy tod° is heavy with snow,
And the owlet whoops to the wolf below,
That eats the she-wolf's young."

"Dear Lord! it hath a fiendish look—
(The Pilot made reply)
I am afeared"—"Push on, push on!"
Said the Hermit cheerily.

The boat came closer to the ship,
But I nor spake nor stirred;
The boat came close beneath the ship,
And straight° a sound was heard.

Under the water it rumbled on,
Still louder and more dread:
It reached the ship, it split the bay;
The ship went down like lead.

Stunned by that loud and dreadful sound,
Which sky and ocean smote,°
Like one that hath been seven days drowned
My body lay afloat;
But swift as dreams, myself I found
Within the Pilot's boat.

Upon the whirl, where sank the ship,
The boat spun round and round;
And all was still, save that the hill
Was telling of the sound.

I moved my lips—the Pilot shrieked
And fell down in a fit;
The holy Hermit raised his eyes,
And prayed where he did sit.

I took the oars: the Pilot's boy,
Who now doth crazy go,
Laughed loud and long, and all the while
His eyes went to and fro.
"Ha! ha!" quoth he, "full plain I see,
The Devil knows how to row."

533. lag: drift; move more slowly than the current.

535. ivy tod: clump of ivy.

545. straight: straightaway; at once.

The ship suddenly sinketh.

The ancient Mariner is saved in the Pilot's boat.

551. smote: struck.

It reached the ship, it split the bay; The ship went down like lead.

Universal Access

English Learners

English for Academic Success Parts V and VII introduce a series of new characters. Three people in a rowboat—the Pilot, the Pilot's boy, and a hermit—approach the Mariner's ship in response to the seraphs' lights. Explain that the term *Pilot* refers to someone who steers a ship in and out of a harbor. The Pilot's boy is his assistant. A hermit is a person who lives in seclusion, sometimes—as in this case—for religious reasons. Ask students to read one character's dialogue aloud. Point out that the Pilot's dialogue starts "Dear Lord! It hath a fiendish look" and ends mid-sentence in line 540 with "I am afeared." Here, the Hermit responds "Push on, push on!" Discuss the dialogue with students to help them understand the sequence of events and the various reactions of the new characters.

And now, all in my own countree,
I stood on the firm land!
The Hermit stepped forth from the boat,
And scarcely he could stand.

"O shrieve me, shrieve me, holy man!"
The Hermit crossed° his brow.
"Say quick," quoth he, "I bid thee say—
What manner of man art thou?" (W)

Forthwith° this frame of mine was wrenched
With a woeful agony,
Which forced me to begin my tale;
And then it left me free. (X)

Since then, at an uncertain hour,
That agony returns:
And till my ghastly tale is told,
This heart within me burns.

I pass, like night, from land to land;
I have strange power of speech;
That moment that his face I see,
I know the man that must hear me:
To him my tale I teach.

What loud uproar bursts from that door!
The wedding guests are there:
But in the garden bower the bride
And bridemaids singing are:
And hark the little vesper bell,
Which biddeth me to prayer!

The ancient Mariner earnestly entreateth the Hermit to shrieve him; and the penance of life falls on him.

575. crossed: made the sign of the cross.

578. forthwith: at once.

And ever and anon throughout his future life an agony constraineth him to travel from land to land;

(W) **Reading Focus** **Understanding Archaic Words** Use a dictionary to find the meanings of *shrift* and *shrieve.* What does the Mariner request in line 574?

(X) **Literary Focus** **Literary Ballad** Like many works of fiction, a literary ballad usually has a climax. Where does the climax occur, and what is it?

Vocabulary **wrenched** (rehncht) *v.:* anguished; grief-stricken.

Think About/Talk About

Comprehension

(W) Reading Focus

Possible response: *Shrift is a remission of sin. Shrieve means "to free from guilt." The Mariner is seeking absolution for his sin. Absolution generally follows confession and precedes penance.*

Analysis

(X) Literary Focus

Possible response: *The climax occurs when the Mariner begs the Hermit for forgiveness and the reader wonders what his fate will be.*

Extend the Discussion

Making Judgments Why do you think Coleridge has made the Ancient Mariner's fate to wander about, periodically gripped by the urge to retell his tale? Do you think the Mariner's fate is fair? Why or why not? ***Possible responses:*** *Coleridge has the Mariner wandering forever so that the Mariner can prevent others in whom he sees himself from acting without thinking and causing harm to others. Yes, it is fair because he should never forget that killing the albatross was a sin; no, it is not fair because he has suffered enough for his sin.*

Vocabulary: Own the Word

wrenched: Demonstrate the difference in connotation between *wrenched* and *saddened* with a comparative sentence. For example: "Sarah was saddened when her goldfish died, but when her cat passed away she was *wrenched.*" Have students compose their own comparative sentence.

Advanced Learners

Acceleration Point out that the reaction of the Pilot's boy to the Mariner reinforces the moral themes of the poem. Since the Pilot has fainted in terror, the Mariner takes up the oars and starts rowing. Seeing this, the Pilot's boy laughs hysterically and exclaims, "I see the Devil knows how to row." Ask students to reflect on this striking image and to write a short paragraph examining why the Pilot's boy would see the Mariner as the Devil. They should think about how the Mariner would appear after being dehydrated and starved for months at sea.

Students with Disabilities

Some students may have difficulty following the characters and the sequence of events. Before students read this section, introduce the characters and summarize the action in lines 500–569. Mention that as the ship nears a harbor, three people in a rowboat arrive to investigate the source of the lights. Although they are terrified, they row toward the ghost ship. The Mariner's ship suddenly sinks in a whirlpool, leaving him floating on the water to be rescued. The Mariner, fearing he would be swept under, knew he had to row fast and hard.

Think About/Talk About

Analysis

Y Literary Perspectives

Possible response: *He might exaggerate in order to make people listen to his tale, or his solitude may have made him imagine things.*

Z Literary Focus

Possible responses: *Nature exacts its own revenge for crimes committed against it; it is essential to love all creatures.*

Monitor Students' Comprehension

Guide the class in answering these comprehension questions.

1. Why is the Mariner forced to walk the earth, repeating his tale? [*He killed an albatross, and this is his penance.*]
2. What happened to the rest of his crew? [*They died of thirst when the boat was adrift at sea during a drought.*]
3. What is the reaction of the Wedding Guest to the Ancient Mariner's strange tale? [*He is frightened by the tale and by the Ancient Mariner's appearance and intensity. After the tale is finished, the dazed Wedding Guest does not end up going to the wedding.*]

O Wedding Guest! this soul hath been
Alone on a wide wide sea:
So lonely 'twas, that God himself
Scarce seemed there to be. Y

O sweeter than the marriage feast,
'Tis sweeter far to me,
To walk together to the kirk
With a goodly company!—

To walk together to the kirk,
And all together pray,
While each to his great Father bends,
Old men, and babes, and loving friends
And youths and maidens gay!

Farewell, farewell! but this I tell
To thee, thou Wedding Guest!
He prayeth well, who loveth well
Both man and bird and beast. Z

He prayeth best, who loveth best
All things both great and small;
For the dear God who loveth us,
He made and loveth all.

The Mariner, whose eye is bright,
Whose beard with age is hoar,
Is gone: and now the Wedding Guest
Turned from the bridegroom's door.

He went like one that hath been stunned,
And is of sense forlorn:°
A sadder and a wiser man,
He rose the morrow morn.

Alone on a wide wide sea.

And to teach, by his own example, love and reverence to all things that God made and loveth.

623. forlorn: deprived.

Y Literary Perspectives **Credibility in Literature** The Mariner mentions his loneliness at sea. How might his loneliness affect his credibility as a narrator?

Z Literary Focus **Literary Ballad** According to lines 610–617, what is the moral message or theme of the ballad?

California Standards, pp. 799–801

- **Reading Standard 1.3** Discern the meaning of analogies encountered, analyzing specific comparisons as well as relationships and inferences.
- **Reading Standard 3.1** Analyze characteristics of subgenres (e.g., satire, parody, allegory, pastoral) that are used in poetry, prose, plays, novels, short stories, essays, and other basic genres.
- **Reading Standard 3.3** Analyze the ways in which irony, tone, mood, the author's style, and the "sound" of language achieve specific rhetorical or aesthetic purposes or both.
- **Reading Standard 3.9** Analyze the philosophical arguments presented in literary works to determine whether the authors' positions have contributed to the quality of each work and the credibility of the characters. (Philosophical approach)
- **Grades 9–10 Review Reading Standard 2.3** Generate relevant questions about readings on issues that can be researched.
- **Writing Standard 1.2** Use point of view, characterization, style (e.g., use of irony), and related elements for specific rhetorical and aesthetic purposes.
- **Listening and Speaking Standard 2.3** Deliver oral responses to literature. **a.** Support important ideas and viewpoints through accurate and detailed references to the text or to other works.

Applying Your Skills

Reading Standard 3.1, 3.3, 3.9 (see pages A48–A50)
Writing Standard 1.2 (see pages A51–A52)

The Rime of the Ancient Mariner

Literary Response and Analysis

Reading Skills Focus

Quick Check

1. In Part II, what are the consequences of the Mariner's killing the albatross?
2. In Part IV, why is the Mariner unable to pray? What happens to change this situation?
3. At the end of the ballad, how does the Mariner describe his current life?

Read with a Purpose

4. What is the Mariner's tragic role? What one thing would he do differently? Explain.

Reading Skills: Understanding Archaic Words

5. Review the poem's archaic words and their meanings. For each word, add an additional circle to your chart and explain why Coleridge may have used the word instead of a modern term. Think about how the words work as sound devices and fit into the ballad's rhyme scheme.

Literary Skills Focus

Literary Analysis

6. **Evaluate** Coleridge once said that he would have preferred to write *The Rime of the Ancient Mariner* as a work of "pure imagination." He believed that the poem had "too much" of a moral and that the moral was stated too openly. Do you agree or disagree? Explain.
7. **Make Judgments** How is death represented in the poem? What do the actions of the spirits and the bodies of the crew suggest about Coleridge's view of the supernatural?
8. **Evaluate** Coleridge added the italicized sidenotes almost twenty years after he first published the poem. Do you think reading them alters the meaning of the poem? Explain.
9. **Literary Perspectives** You analyzed the credibility of the supernatural events and of the Mariner. How did this perspective affect your interpretation of the story?

Literary Skills: Literary Ballad

10. **Analyze** For the most part, this poem's form is the regular ballad stanza. Occasionally, however, Coleridge varies the meter and the stanza length. Explain how one of the irregular stanzas differs from a regular one. What effects do these changes have on the poem?

Literary Skills Review: Allegory

11. **Draw Conclusions** An **allegory** is a narrative in which characters, settings, or events symbolize people, places, or occurrences. What might be this ballad's allegorical meaning? Consider the Mariner, the wedding, the ship, and the albatross.

Writing Skills Focus

Think as a Reader/Writer

Use It in Your Writing Review your notes about Coleridge's use of vivid figurative language and memorable sound devices. Write a paragraph or a brief poem on a subject of your choice. Include at least one example of figurative language (simile, metaphor, or personification) and one example of a sound device (alliteration, assonance, or internal rhyme).

What Do You Think Now? How did Coleridge use his imagination to create a fantastic story? How does his story reveal truths about life or human nature?

Check for Understanding

Independent Practice

Reading Skills Focus

Possible responses:

1. *The breeze stops blowing, and the ship drifts at sea as the sailors endure days of drought.*
2. *A "wicked whisper" turns his heart as dry as dust. When he blesses the sea snakes, he is able to pray again.*
3. *He is destined to travel from land to land, telling his tale as penance.*
4. *The Mariner's impulsive killing of the albatross led to the deaths of all of his crewmates. He would probably undo this act.*
5. *Students should give plausible reasons for Coleridge's diction.*

Literary Skills Focus

Possible responses:

6. *Some may agree that the moral is unsuited to the tale; others may say that if the poem were a work of "pure imagination," reading it would be frustrating.*
7. *Death is represented by a seductive woman. The actions of the crew's bodies and spirits suggest Coleridge's belief in supernatural elements and in life after death.*
8. *No. The notes clarify details but do not change the poem's meaning.*
9. *The credibility of the Mariner's tale determines whether readers take its moral seriously. A reader who believed the story would probably take to heart its message.*
10. *Irregular stanzas keep the rhythm from becoming monotonous and draw the reader's attention to key events in the poem.*
11. *It could be viewed as a religious allegory in which the Mariner, like Adam, kills the albatross (eats the forbidden fruit), provoking heaven's wrath. The ship is like his soul that is denied wind (breath) and water (spiritual dryness). After the Mariner repents, he achieves salvation, is allowed to rejoin his world, and is sent to teach other men his lesson.*

Universal Access

Struggling Writers

Some students may need additional scaffolding to complete the Writing Skills Focus activity. Review the use of each sound device in the poem before students write. Direct students to these examples: simile (ll. 222–223); metaphor (190–194); personification (ll. 59–62); alliteration (l. 103); assonance (l. 199); internal rhyme (l. 99).

What Do You Think Now?

Have students make a list of all of the fantastical elements in the story. Which ones are common themes or elements in fantasy? Ask them to recall the moral of the story when responding to the second part of the question.

Independent Practice
Vocabulary Development
Vocabulary Check
1. *d* **2.** *a*
3. *e* **4.** *b*
5. *c*

Your Turn
1. *dismal*
2. *tyrannous*
3. *abated*
4. *wrenched*
5. *ghastly*

English for Academic Success
Language Coach
Ask students to explain why the words *ghastly* and *tyrannous* do not have neutral connotations. ***Possible responses:***
1. *Dismal writing is dull or poorly written. The word would be inappropriate for certain objects, such as a computer.*
2. *The news report might mention a storm abating.*
3. *Poem; people are more likely to use "twist" or "turn" in daily conversation instead of "wrenched."*

English for Academic Success
Academic Vocabulary
Possible response: *People might want to believe that certain things are inherently luckier than others because superstition gives them the illusion of control over chance. Superstition functions as a device to interpret fate.*

Applying Your Skills

Reading Standard 1.3 (see pages A48–A50)

The Rime of the Ancient Mariner

Vocabulary Development

Vocabulary Check
Match each Vocabulary word with its synonym.

1. tyrannous	**a.** bleak
2. dismal	**b.** weakened
3. ghastly	**c.** tormented
4. abated	**d.** ruthless
5. wrenched	**e.** grisly

Vocabulary Skills: Analogies
In literature, an **analogy** is a comparison designed to show a similarity or similarities between two things. In word analogies, the relationship between one pair of words is similar to the relationship between another pair of words. Consider this example:

ENGINE : CAR :: horse : carriage

To read this analogy, you say, "engine is to car as horse is to carriage." How are the paired items similarly related? An engine provides power for the car to move; similarly, a horse pulls a carriage to move it. Once you understand the relationship, you can read the analogy: "An engine is used to make a car go just as a horse is used to make a carriage go." The following chart shows other common relationships in analogies.

Relationship	Example	Analysis
Use	battery: flashlight	A battery is used to power a flashlight.
Type	puma : cat	A puma is a type of cat.
Cause/Effect	water : wet	Water causes something to be wet.
Synonyms	strange : unusual	*Strange* is synonymous with *unusual*.
Place	library: book	A library is a place where you would find a book.
Description	mean: bully	The adjective *mean* describes a bully.

Your Turn
Select the Vocabulary word that best completes each analogy.
1. JOYFUL : GLAD :: ________ : gloomy
2. LEARNED : SCHOLAR :: ________ : dictator
3. GATHERED : COLLECTED :: ________ : lessened
4. BUOYED : HOPE :: ________ : agony
5. LOVELY : BEAUTY :: ________ : horror

Language Coach
Definitions and Context Some neutral words fit naturally in many different contexts. Words like *object, place,* and *emotion* are useful in almost any situation. Other words, like *dismal,* are more specific. Thinking about how you might use these words can help you remember their definitions as you answer these questions:
1. When might you want to call a piece of writing *dismal*? When would this word be inappropriate?
2. How might the word *abated* be used on a nightly news report?
3. Do you think the word *wrenched* is more likely to appear in a poem or in daily conversation? Why?

Academic Vocabulary
Write About
The Mariner differentiates himself early in his story because of his disregard for the albatross, which the crew believes functions as a good luck charm. Write a few paragraphs in which you discuss why you think people like to believe that certain animals or objects, such as clovers, horseshoes, or pennies, are inherently luckier than others.

Universal Access: Vocabulary Development

EL English Learners
English for Academic Success Have students work with a partner and determine the relationships in the following analogies. Have them record the relationship and a short sentence describing it. Then, have students come up with their own analogies that demonstrate each relationship in the chart on p. 800.
- oppressive : tyrant
  [*Description; A tyrant can be described as oppressive.*]
- prompt : tardy
  [*Antonyms;* Prompt *is an antonym of* tardy.]
- thermometer : temperature
  [*Use; A thermometer is used to measure one's temperature.*]
- sport : ice hockey
  [*Type; Ice hockey is a type of sport.*]

✔ See the **Academic and Selection Vocabulary Skill Builder** in **UA: Differentiating Instruction.**

Grades 9–10 Review Reading Standard 2.3 (see pages A48–A50)
Listening and Speaking Standard 2.3a (see pages A53–A55)

Grammar Link

Infinitive Phrases

An **infinitive** is a verb form that can be used as a noun, an adjective, or an adverb. Most infinitives begin with *to.*

The effect of Samuel Taylor Coleridge's poetry is **to amaze.** (noun)
The albatross is a bird **to protect.** (adjective)
The poem has scenes that are hard **to imagine.** (adverb)

To is left out of some infinitives.

Careful reading can help you **(to) understand.**

An **infinitive phrase** is an infinitive and its modifiers or complements. Infinitive phrases act as nouns, adjectives, or adverbs.

To read this poem is a strange experience. (noun) These are the stanzas **to memorize for homework.** (adjective) Coleridge seems determined **to startle readers with bizarre images.** (adverb)

Do not confuse infinitive and prepositional phrases. *To* can also act as a preposition, and infinitive phrases can include prepositional phrases as modifiers.

Your Turn

Underline infinitive phrases in the following sentences, and identify each as a noun, an adjective, or an adverb.

1. A wedding guest happens to meet the Mariner.
2. The Mariner chooses to kill an albatross.
3. The sailors tie the albatross around the Mariner's neck to put the curse on his head.
4. He has many trials to face before he can be free.

Writing Application In a piece of your own writing, circle the word *to* every time it appears. State whether it is part of an infinitive or a prepositional phrase, or neither.

CHOICES

As you respond to the Choices, use these **Academic Vocabulary** words as appropriate: differentiate, inherent, device, technique, function.

REVIEW

Summarize the Poem

Re-read Part I of the ballad, and summarize it in a short paragraph. What important events occur in this part? What characters are introduced? Next, write a summary of Part II. Continue until you have a complete summary of the poem. Share your summary with a partner, and discuss whether your individual summaries are accurate and clear. How might you combine both summaries to create a better one?

CONNECT

Research Critical Comments

The supernatural events and narrative techniques of *The Rime of the Ancient Mariner* have attracted much critical attention, for the imagery lends itself to many interpretations. Use the Internet or library to research different critics' responses to the literary ballad. Summarize your findings in two or three paragraphs. Then, write a paragraph describing which critic you find most convincing and why.

EXTEND

Design a Video Game

TechFocus Create a concept for a five-level video game based on the ballad. For each level, describe a dilemma that must be solved before players can advance to the next level. Name the video game, create titles for each level, and provide a brief overview of the rules.

Independent Practice

Grammar Link

Your Turn

1. *to meet the Mariner: adverb*
2. *to kill an albatross: adverb*
3. *to put the curse on his head: adverb*
4. *to face: adjective*

Choices: Evaluation Criteria

Review: Homework
Summarize the Poem

- Students' summaries include only major events and characters.
- Students summarize events in their own words as much as possible.

Connect: Homework
Research Critical Comments

- Students consult a variety of sources.
- Students clearly state an opinion and support it with reasons and evidence.

Extend: Homework
Design a Video Game

- Students' games include problems that are connected to the plot of the ballad.
- Students provide clear directions for playing the game.

Assess

Unit 4 Resources, Selection Standards Check, p. 55

go.hrw.com **ThinkCentral Online Assessment,** Selection Standards Check

Teacher One Stop™, editable Selection Standards Check

Reteach

go.hrw.com **ThinkCentral Online Remediation**

Universal Access: Grammar Link

EL English Learners

English for Academic Success To help students distinguish between prepositional phrases and infinitive phrases, have them determine whether each sentence below is an infinitive phrase or a prepositional phrase. Remind students that *to* plus a noun will be a prepositional phrase and that *to* plus a verb will be an infinitive phrase.

1. Tom's mother sent Tom to the store for groceries. [*prepositional*]
2. We arrived at the stadium several hours early to get good seats. [*infinitive*]
3. We finally settled on a house to live in. [*infinitive*]
4. She never made it to the meeting. [*prepositional*]

✔ For more practice with infinitive phrases, see **Warriner's Handbook, GrammarNotes,** and **Language Handbook Worksheets.**

Standards Focus

Objectives
Students will analyze main idea and supporting details.

Motivate

What Do You Think?/QuickWrite
Have students write for five minutes, referencing opinions about personal experiences with animals.

Preteach

Introducing Vocabulary
1. Give synonyms for **relentlessly** and **conviction.**
2. List things considered **miniscule.**
3. How do runners lose **momentum?**
4. Give an antonym of **spontaneous.**

English for Academic Success

Language Coach
Have students look up the Latin root for *spontaneous* and relate the root to the word meaning. [spontāneus, *(of one's own accord), a spontaneous action is not forced or planned*]

Informational Text/ Writing Skills Focus
- Give students a copy of the graphic organizer before they read.
- Have students record ideas on how Coleridge's poem affect their reading of this scientific study in their **Reader/Writer Notebooks.**

California Standards, pp. 802–807
- **Reading Standard 2.2** Analyze the way in which clarity of meaning is affected by the patterns of organization, hierarchical structures, repetition of the main ideas, syntax, and word choice in the text.

INFORMATIONAL TEXT FOCUS
Preparing to Read

Reading Standard 2.2 (see pages A48–A50)

Saving Creatures Great and Small

What Do You Think How can we use imagination to discover truth?

QuickWrite
Can animals, like the albatross, teach us lessons about life? Write a paragraph in your *Reader/Writer Notebook* explaining how an animal has taught you a lesson about life.

Informational Text Focus
Analyzing Details and Main Idea When you read an informational text for the first time, there are many clues you can use to determine the main idea. Examining the title, the tone, and the publication in which the text appears can be helpful, and details also reveal many of the key ideas.

Into Action As you read, use a chart like the one below to record details that strike you as important. In the left-hand column, enter details from the article's discussion of Coleridge's tale. In the right-hand column, enter details from the article's discussion of scientists' study of the albatross.

Coleridge Details	Scientific Details
written more than 200 years ago	spend half their lives flying over the ocean

Writing Skills Focus
Preparing for **Timed Writing** As you read this article, consider why an author who wishes to convey scientific information about the albatross would devote his first three paragraphs to a Romantic poet's "goofy" creation. How does the discussion of Coleridge affect what you learn about scientific study of the albatross? Record your ideas in your *Reader/Writer Notebook.*

Reader/Writer Notebook
Use your **RWN** to complete the activities for this selection.

Vocabulary
relentlessly (rih LEHNT lihs lee) *adv.:* in an unyielding way; in a pitiless manner. *He imagines the Mariner relentlessly repeating the same story.*

spontaneous (spahn TAY nee uhs) *adj.:* caused by natural impulse; not forced. *The biologist's work is a spontaneous response to the plight of the albatross.*

minuscule (mih NUHS kyool) *adj.:* extremely small. *On a map, Midway Island is minuscule.*

momentum (moh MEHN tuhm) *n.:* force with which an object moves. *An albatross gains momentum by tacking much as a sailor does.*

conviction (kuhn VIHK shuhn) *n.:* firm belief or certainty. *The scientists trying to protect the albatross have a sincere conviction about the value of their work.*

Language Coach
Word Origins The adjective *minuscule* comes from the Latin word that means "less." You might recognize this root in the word *minus*. How does the idea of "less" relate to the meaning of the word *minuscule*? How does the same Latin root affect the meaning of the word *minimum*? The word *conviction* shares a Latin root with the word *convince*. How do you think these two words are related? Use a dictionary to find out more about their origins.

Selection Readability	
Easily Accessible Accessible **Challenging**	unfamiliar setting; higher-level vocabulary; sophisticated language

Selection Summary
On the Pacific island of Midway, biologists work to preserve the albatross by studying their habits. These huge birds mate for life, breed yearly, take turns sitting on one egg, and spend months at sea before returning to land to breed. Foote brings his conservationist argument full circle by ending with a Coleridge quotation about loving "all things both great and small."

Link to Today

This Link to Today provides a contemporary look at efforts to preserve the albatross species in the North Pacific Ocean.

Read with a Purpose

Read to learn how the author, a magazine editor, learns to appreciate the albatross as more than just a symbol in Coleridge's poem.

Build Background

Midway Atoll (also known as Midway Island) is an island in the North Pacific Ocean that is almost exactly "midway" between the United States and Asia. Classified as an unincorporated territory of the United States, Midway is home to thousands of species of seabirds, including the albatross, or "gooney bird." Although the albatross in Coleridge's poem was near Antarctica, the twenty different species of albatross in either the Northern or Southern Hemisphere share many of the same characteristics. Among the largest flying birds on earth, five of their species are considered endangered. Today, more than 400,000 albatross pairs nest at the National Wildlife Refuge on Midway Atoll.

MAGAZINE ARTICLE

Saving Creatures Great and Small

Timothy Foote, *Smithsonian* Magazine, September 2001

When I landed on Midway to do a story, I knew almost nothing about the life of the albatross. Lord of the air? Sure. Great flier? Yes. And, of course, it's really bad news if you kill one and have it hung round your neck! That last notion, I owed—like most people—not to the world of biology but to a work of Romantic literature: Samuel Taylor Coleridge's "The Rime of the Ancient Mariner," a goofy but absolutely astounding creation, written more than 200 years ago. The Ancient Mariner, who "stoppeth one of three," is still one of the most famous and most quoted poems in English.

The Mariner Shoots the Albatross (1877) by Gustave Doré. Collection Kharbine-Tapabor, Paris.

Nearly everyone vaguely remembers how it goes, and at least a few familiar lines. Just say aloud "It is an Ancient mariner, and he stoppeth one of three," and here comes the mariner himself, a dreadful sight, buttonholing guests late for a wedding, relentlessly telling his amazing story. How his ship sailed south and south until, with crossbow in hand, he shot an albatross that followed it, only to have the bird tied round his neck by his superstitious shipmates.

Soon natural and supernatural powers, displeased by his cruel act, begin to punish him, the crew, the ship itself, tormenting them with spectacular icebergs and huge storms followed by a deadly calm, when the helpless vessel lies for days "as idle as a painted ship upon a painted ocean." And, of course, unimaginable thirst: "Water, water everywhere, nor any drop to drink."

Vocabulary **relentlessly** (rih LEHNT lihs lee) *adv.:* in an unyielding way; in a pitiless manner.

Link to Today

Like *The Rime of the Ancient Mariner,* the scientists in this article appreciate the beauty and mystique of the albatross and spend their lives dedicated to serving the species.

Direct Teach

Think About/Talk About

Read with a Purpose Have students read the Read with a Purpose statement. Ask them to write down any impressions they gained about the albatross from Coleridge's ballad.

Extend the Discussion

Finding Details What does the writer know about the albatross upon his arrival to the Midway Atoll? ***Possible response:*** *almost nothing; that it is a great flyer; that it is bad to kill one and have it hung around your neck*

Allusion On this page, the writer alludes to *The Rime of the Ancient Mariner.* Why does he make this allusion? What tone does it set regarding the author's attitude toward the albatross? ***Possible responses:*** *The poem is world famous and most quoted—this fame and respect he has for it is transferred to the albatross. The writer makes this allusion to convey a tone of respect for the albatross.*

Vocabulary: Own the Word

relentlessly: Remind students that the definition of *relentlessly* connotes performing an action unyieldingly or without pity. Demonstrate the difference between something done often and something done *relentlessly* in a sentence, for example: "Coach Smith was always strict, but this year he has been yelling at the team *relentlessly.*"

Selection Resources

Unit 4 Resources, on-level practice and assessment, p. 58

Teacher One Stop™, on-level lesson plans and all print resources

Holt Audio Library: Selections and Summaries in Spanish

UA: Differentiating Instruction, graphic organizer, p. 176

UA: Supporting Instruction in Spanish, selection summary

Analyzing Visuals Transparencies, p. 34

ThinkCentral Online Assessment, Selection Standards Check

ThinkCentral Online Remediation

Model the Skill

- Tell students that when they need to find the **main idea** of the selection, they should consider which sentence would best summarize the selection.
- Model finding the main idea of the second paragraph of p. 804. You might say: "In this paragraph, we learned that the author was tempted to mention Coleridge's famous poem to some marine biologists and that he later begins to realize that he can draw some parallels between the poem and the work of the biologists." Provide students with this summary of the paragraph: "As he interviews the biologists, the author finds a parallel between their work and Coleridge's poem." Explain that this sentence retells all of the important details in the paragraph.

Guided Practice: Apply

Read-Talk-Write As they read the selection, have students discuss the important details of each paragraph. Then, have them write a sentence that represents the main idea of each paragraph.

Literary Connection

James Herriot, in *All Creatures Great and Small,* details his real-life experiences as a veterinarian in Yorkshire, England.

After all sorts of horrors, all hands die—except the mariner, left alone, alone, a worse fate perhaps in store. But at the last moment the damned mariner is saved when, even though *in extremis,*[1] he experiences a brief moment of spontaneous joy and, indeed, reverence, at the beauty of some "water-snakes," creatures not usually associated with much charm. **A**

On Midway, hip deep in fledgling albatross and busy asking dumb questions of the biologists and their helpers, I was not tempted to mention "The Ancient Mariner." They would just roll their eyes, I figured. Coleridge can seem as crazy as a hoot owl, and the poem is anything but scientific. Nevertheless, before leaving Midway, I came to think there is a revealing parallel between the words of the poet and the work of the island's committed field scientists.

We know a great deal more about biology and the world's creatures than was the case even a few

1. ***in extremis:*** Latin phrase meaning "in extreme circumstances."

A Informational Focus **Analyzing Details and Main Idea**
Why does the author include this clue about sea snakes?

Vocabulary **spontaneous** (spahn TAY nee uhs) *adj.:* caused by natural impulse; not forced.

Universal Access: Vocabulary

English Learners/ Struggling Readers

English for Academic Success Some students may have difficulty with the unfamiliar vocabulary found in this article. Have students review the following words to help them build a better understanding of the text.

- **astounding**—to be surprisingly impressive, or great. *The bird made an astounding turn in the air.*
- **superstitious**—The belief that supernatural, or nonscientific, forces have an effect on actions or events. *The superstitious girl*

Opposite: A pair of gray-headed albatrosses; a gray-headed albatross and chick.
Left: Bicyclist passing nesting Laysan Albatrosses (*Diomedia immutabilis*).
Below: Black-browed Albatross nesting colony (*Thalassarche melanophris*), Saunders Island, Falklands.
Bottom: Egg of a Waved Albatross (*Diomedea irrorata*), on Española Island, one of the Galapagos Islands.

Think About/Talk About

Comprehension

A Informational Focus

Possible response: *The author includes this clue to remind readers that the mariner blessed an ugly, seemingly insignificant creature. This supports the author's title that all creatures need to be saved and appreciated.*

Extend the Discussion

Making Inferences Why would the scientists "roll their eyes" at the mention of the poem? ***Possible response:*** *The writer says he has been asking dumb questions already; the poem is probably mentioned often to the scientists since it is famous, but it does not reveal the true nature of the albatross.*

Parallelism Why does the writer believe there is a "revealing parallel" between the words of Coleridge and the work of the scientists? What do you think this connection is? ***Possible response:*** *Coleridge developed a reverence and respect for the albatross from the curse; scientists also develop this feeling through study.*

Vocabulary: Own the Word

spontaneous: Ask students to share an example of a *spontaneous* decision they have made or a *spontaneous* event that they have witnessed. ***Possible responses:*** *going on a road trip with friends, a neighbor offering help with something*

carried a rabbit's foot for good luck during the test.

- **fledgling**—a young bird that has just developed feathers. *The biologist was surrounded by fledglings.*
- **labyrinth**—(figurative) a confusing arrangement. *The scientific study was a labyrinth of information that was difficult for students to understand.*
- **lingering**—lasting for a long time. *The lingering rain seemed to continue throughout the week.*

Then, ask students to write sentences using all the above words in context.

Compare and Contrast

Ask students to compare Foote's appreciation for the albatross with that of the Mariner in *The Rime of the Ancient Mariner*.

- **Similarities** Both feel the animal deserves respect. Both have committed their life to teaching others the importance of the albatross.
- **Differences** The Mariner views the albatross as a creature with mystical powers. The scientists view it as an important part of the ecosystem. The Mariner spreads a tale of superstition; the scientists share factual studies.

Think About/Talk About

Comprehension

B Informational Focus

Possible response: *The more you learn about a creature, the more able you are to help it.*

C Informational Focus

Possible response: *This shows that the albatross is an animal of mystery and that telemetric devices are needed to give scientists information that they cannot gain from observation.*

D Informational Focus

Possible response: *They support the need for reverence and love for all creatures and the need to study them in order to maintain our diverse ecosystem.*

Vocabulary: Own the Word

- **minuscule:** Highlight the extreme connotations of the word *miniscule* with other words meaning "small" by using it in a comparative sentence.
- **momentum:** Have students brainstorm various objects and the forces that give them *momentum.* ***Possible responses:*** *car engines, gravity*
- **conviction:** Many scientists defend their *conviction* that life exists on other planets because …

Monitor Students' Comprehension

Guide the class in answering these comprehension questions.

1. According to the writer, what do most people, not involved in the world of biology, think of when a reference is made to an albatross? [*Coleridge's* The Rime of the Ancient Mariner]
2. According to the writer, what does the scientist think of Coleridge and his work? [*Coleridge seems crazy, and his poem is not scientific.*]
3. How do albatrosses display their courtship? [*through ritual movements or dances that involve mutual bowing and nibbling*]

years back. Almost every week we hear that science has turned a new corner in the labyrinth of DNA. But when it comes to the study of wild creatures, especially ones like the albatross that spend half their lives flying over miles of ocean, we still rely on measuring, keeping track and slowly collecting data until it points to a specific, and maybe useful, conclusion. The main difference between then and now is that now a major aim of the work is to preserve the creatures under observation. The more you know about their habits, food and biology, the better you may be able to help them when the pinch of declining numbers comes to the shove of extinction. **B**

Today elaborate and precise descriptions abound of albatross life. Their courtship is famous, involving a stately gavotte[2] of ritual movements that include a series of mutual bowings and nibblings. Albatross couples mate for life, though some studies have noted an occasional "divorce." Once paired off, they breed pretty much every year, each year returning to the same nest site, within 20 yards or so of where the male was hatched. Sadly, they only get to dance their courtship dance once, the first time they meet. After that it's just domesticity. (Back home, when I mentioned this to a group of friends, one of the wives said, "Why am I not surprised?")

The resulting egg—only one a year—weighs nine ounces. Parents alternate sitting on it for sometimes as long as three weeks at a stretch without relief, while the absent mate forages hundreds, even thousands of miles at sea for food. Both talk to the egg while it's incubating, with three sounds, Eh-Eh-Eh, and other varying syllables, presumably so the chick will know them after hatching.

2. **gavotte:** a French folk dance.

It is only lately, with the help of minuscule new telemetric[3] devices attached to these birds, that we are beginning to have a clue about how and where they spend their months at sea. **C**

Albatross seem to be almost as dependent on wind as sailboats, which is why northern species stay in the Northern Hemisphere, and southern species keep to the Southern. Basically they are soarers and gliders, not flappers. The absence of strong sea breezes at the Equator keeps them from crossing the line. Like sailboats, they cannot sail into the wind; they have to tack. To do this they soar downwind to pick up both speed and height, then turn, using the acquired height and lingering momentum to let them glide down to the sea's surface more or less in the direction of the wind. Thus they may spend years at sea before returning to mate and rear their young on land—in our case on Midway.

The young biologists on Midway, like those who passionately advocate at-all-costs preservation of all endangered species, are driven by a conviction as absolute as that of any religion. Midway folk seem to me to be close in spirit to the mariner's act of faith, as, briefly stirred by the coiled beauty of the sea snakes, he blesses them "unaware." They might even accept one of Coleridge's last lines: "He prayeth best who loveth best all things both great and small." **D**

3. **telemetric:** related to the science and technology of automatic measurement and transmission of data by wire, radio, or other means from remote sources.

B Informational Focus **Analyzing Details and Main Idea** Based on the details in this paragraph, what do you think the main idea of the text is?

C Informational Focus **Analyzing Details and Main Idea** How does this sentence relate to the author's point about the nature of the albatross?

D Informational Focus **Analyzing Details and Main Idea** How do the quotations from Coleridge's poem support the main idea?

Vocabulary **minuscule** (mih NUHS kyool) *adj.:* extremely small.
momentum (moh MEHN tuhm) *n.:* force with which an object moves.
conviction (kuhn VIHK shuhn) *n.:* firm belief or certainty.

California Standards, p. 807

- **Reading Standard 2.2** Analyze the way in which clarity of meaning is affected by the patterns of organization, hierarchical structures, repetition of the main ideas, syntax, and word choice in the text.
- **Writing Standard 2.2** Write responses to literature: **c.** Support important ideas and viewpoints through accurate and detailed references to the text and to other works.
- **Listening and Speaking Standard 1.7** Use appropriate rehearsal strategies to pay attention to performance details, achieve command of the text, and create skillful artistic staging.

Reading Standard 2.2 (see pages A48–A50)
Writing Standard 2.2c (see pages A51–A52)
Listening and Speaking Standard 1.7 (see pages A53–A55)

Saving Creatures Great and Small

Analyze Informational Texts

Informational Text Focus

Quick Check

1. Why is the author reluctant to mention Coleridge's poem to the scientists on Midway?
2. How do researchers collect scientific data about albatrosses?
3. Why do albatrosses often spend years at sea before returning to land to mate?

Read with a Purpose

4. In the author's view, how does the albatross change from a symbol in Coleridge's poem to a creature worth saving?

Informational Skills: Analyzing Details and Main Idea

5. Look back at the chart you used to record two categories of details. For the "Coleridge" column, write a single sentence stating the idea these details support. Do the same for the "Scientific" column. Then, write a single sentence for the most important idea in the entire article.

Coleridge Details	Scientific Details
written more than 200 years ago	spend half their lives flying over the ocean

Vocabulary Check

Match the Vocabulary words with their definitions.

6. relentlessly	**a.** small
7. spontaneous	**b.** certainty
8. minuscule	**c.** inflexibly
9. momentum	**d.** unplanned
10. conviction	**e.** force

Text Analysis

11. Interpret What does the author mean by "They might even accept one of Coleridge's last lines: 'He prayeth best who loveth best all things both great and small'"?

12. Infer What characteristics of albatross life does the author seem to admire most?

13. Extend What other lines from *The Rime of the Ancient Mariner* might apply to the scientists on Midway?

Listening and Speaking

14. Interpret Foote quotes directly from *The Rime of the Ancient Mariner* throughout his article. With a partner, read this article aloud, dividing it into two sections: the narrative parts from Foote's point of view and the direct quotations from Coleridge's poem. Each reader should have a distinct voice for interpreting the lines. Rehearse before you share your interpretive reading with the class.

Writing Skills Focus

Timed Writing Briefly explain how the article's closing quotation contributes to the author's main idea. Support your response with specific evidence from the article.

What Do You Think Now? How can details about the beauty and spirit of the albatross teach us a lesson about life?

Universal Access

Struggling Writers

Some students may need additional scaffolding to complete the Writing Skills Focus activity. Before students answer the question, instruct them to go through the article and highlight details that support the main idea of the article. Then, have them read the closing quotation and consider how it supports the main idea.

What Do You Think Now?

To help students answer the question, ask them to consider what the albatross represents in Coleridge's *The Rime of the Ancient Mariner* and the information about this bird in "Saving Creatures Great and Small."

Assess

Unit 4 Resources,
Selection Standards Check, p. 58

Check for Understanding

Independent Practice

Informational Text Focus

Possible responses:

1. *It is not scientific, and it is probably the only reference that many non-scientists have about the albatross.*
2. *They use observation, measurement, and telemetric devices.*
3. *They must wait for winds on which to glide back because they are not "flappers." Since they cannot fly against wind, they must tack against crosswinds like a sailboat.*
4. *The importance and beauty of the albatross becomes much more real to him through scientific observation about its behavior.*
5. *Ask students to write sentences that support Coleridge's details and the scientific details. Then, have them summarize the main idea of the article in a single sentence.*

Vocabulary Check

6. *c* **7.** *d*
8. *a* **9.** *e*
10. *b*

11. *The scientists might agree because they show love for the albatross through tireless studies.*
12. *The author seems to admire the albatross's mating ritual, its life at sea in search of food, including its method of tacking like a sailboat, and the way it communicates with its young.*
13. *"Through the fog it came; As if it had a Christian soul, We hailed it in God's name." The scientist may view the albatross as an angelic creature worthy of admiration.*
14. *Remind students to read the lines as they interpret them. Ask students what overall effect dividing the parts in the article between two voices has on the listener.*

Chapter Objectives

- Students will learn about the forms and formal elements of Romantic poetry by reading poems by George Gordon, Lord Byron; Percy Bysshe Shelley; and John Keats.
- Students will compare British Romantic poetry with texts from the Golden Age of Chinese poetry and with Japanese haiku and tanka.

The Quotation

Tell students that the author of the quotation, Mary Shelley, was the creator of *Frankenstein* and the wife of Percy Bysshe Shelley. The quotation describes Shelley's imagination as the true creator, with herself as its passive instrument. Ask students to comment on how Romantic writers might have used their imagination in their writing. ***Possible response:*** *Samuel Taylor Coleridge imagined a wild, fantastical fate for the title character of* The Rime of the Ancient Mariner; *Mary Shelley invented an enduring horror story in* Frankenstein.

Analyzing Visuals

Extension Activity Look closely at the image on this page. In what way is the image related to the quote? ***Possible response:*** *The image shows people examining various paintings with interest, including both portraits and landscapes. It demonstrates the power that an artist's imaginative work can have over the person who experiences it.*

CHAPTER 8

The Quest for Beauty

LITERARY SKILLS FOCUS

Forms of Romantic Poetry

CONTENTS

"My imagination, unbidden, possessed and guided me, gifting the successive images that arose in my mind with a vividness far beyond the usual bound of reverie."

—Introduction to *Frankenstein* by Mary Shelley

Chapter 8

California Standards Overview

- **Reading Standard 2.2** Analyze the way in which clarity of meaning is affected by the patterns of organization, hierarchical structures, repetition of the main ideas, syntax, and word choice in the text.
- **Reading Standard 2.4** Make warranted and reasonable assertions about the author's arguments by using elements of the text to defend and clarify interpretations.
- **Reading Standard 3.1** Analyze characteristics of subgenres (e.g., satire, parody, allegory, pastoral) that are used in poetry, prose, plays, novels, short stories, essays, and other basic genres.
- **Reading Standard 3.3** Analyze the ways in which irony, tone, mood, the author's style, and the "sound" of language achieve specific rhetorical or aesthetic purposes or both.
- **Reading Standard 3.4** Analyze ways in which poets use imagery, personification, figures of speech, and sounds to evoke readers' emotions.
- **Reading Standard 3.9** Analyze the philosophical arguments presented in literary works to determine whether the authors' positions have contributed to the quality of each work and the credibility of the characters (Philosophical approach).
- **Grades 9–10 Review Reading Standard 3.7** Recognize and understand the significance of various literary devices, including figurative language, imagery, allegory, and symbolism, and explain their appeal.
- **Grades 9–10 Review Reading Standard 3.11** Evaluate the aesthetic qualities of style, including the impact of diction and figurative language on tone, mood, and theme, using the terminology of literary criticism. (Aesthetic approach).

Reading Standard 3.1 (see pages A48–A50)

Forms of Romantic Poetry by Leila Christenbury

Characteristics of Romantic Poetry

- Expresses the emotions and concerns of an individual as well as of society
- Varies the structure of traditional forms to suit a poem's purpose
- Focuses on a poet's personal connection to nature

Function over Form

The Romantic poets used their art to capture individual and emotional experience. William Wordsworth defined poetry not as form (meter or rhyme or rhythm) but as "emotion recollected in tranquility." That kind of focus was startlingly different from what had been—for the order-loving eighteenth-century poets—a strictly defined literary genre. Poetry, for the Romantics, was a playground of feelings: emotional and inventive, and not necessarily written in a traditional format. Function came first for Romantic poets, who felt free to use or to abandon the forms in which poetry had previously been written. Although the Romantic poets frequently used traditional forms, such as the ode and the sonnet, they also experimented with forms, creating natural rhythms and using simple, unadorned language. In "Tintern Abbey," for example, Wordsworth used for the first time a less formal "conversational" blank verse that sounds like the flowing rhythm of natural speech.

Romantic Forms

The **ode** was a poetic form favored by the Romantics, including William Wordsworth, Percy Bysshe Shelley, and John Keats. A long, complex poem (usually a meditation on a serious topic), the ode provided the Romantics with a form suited to their introspective, philosophical subject matter. Like many Romantic odes, Percy Bysshe Shelley's "Ode to the West Wind" looks both outward and inward. It exalts an aspect of nature, the powerful yet invisible wind, and contemplates the movement of unseen forces in the poet's own mind and life. However, the stanzas of "Ode to the West Wind" are unusual because they are each a variation on the **sonnet** form, a fourteen-line lyric form in iambic pentameter.

The sonnet's popularity was strong during the Renaissance after Thomas Wyatt introduced the form to England but had waned during the Restoration. Wordsworth reestablished its popularity during the Romantic period, and he and Keats were its masters.

Another Renaissance form used by Romantic poets, such as George Gordon, Lord Byron, is the nine-line **Spenserian stanza,** invented by the Renaissance poet Edmund Spenser.

The Interior of the British Institution Gallery (1829), by John Scarlett Davis. Oil on canvas. Yale Center for British Art, Paul Mellon Collection, U.S.

Disappointed Love (1821), by Francis Danby (1793–1861). Oil on panel. Victoria & Albert Museum, London.

Ask Yourself

1. What was more important to Romantic poets, form or function? Why?
2. What topics did Romantic poets pursue? Why?

Learn It Online
Explore Romantic poetry with *PowerNotes* online.
go.hrw.com H12-809 Go

Literary Skills Focus

Objectives

Students will analyze the role of traditional poetic forms and devices in Romantic poetry.

Unit 4 Resources, Literary Focus Skill Builder, p. 68

PowerNotes, interactive lesson presentation with activities

Teacher One Stop™, on-level lesson plan and all print resources

Direct Teach

Function over Form

Have students read the Literary Skills Focus essay. Then, use the following question to discuss poetic form. The Romantics emphasized content—the feelings they sought to express—and downplayed the importance of form in poetry. How is their work different from the poetry of the Age of Reason?

Check for Understanding

Ask Yourself

Possible responses:

1. *Function. For the Romantics, the object of poetry was to express emotion and imaginative ideas. Form grew out of this requirement.*
2. *They explored emotions, nature, social ideas, and the role of the imagination.*

Learn It Online
For a multimedia version of the instruction found on this page, use the **PowerNotes** Literary Skills Focus presentation.
go.hrw.com H12-809 Go

California Standards, p. 809

- **Reading Standard 3.1** Analyze characteristics of subgenres (e.g., satire, parody, allegory, pastoral) that are used in poetry, prose, plays, novels, short stories, essays, and other basic genres.

Universal Access

Struggling Readers

Point out that the author uses *form* in two ways: to refer to aspects of poetic language such as rhyme and rhythm, and to refer to traditional types of poems with well-defined structures, such as the sonnet, which has fourteen lines. Remind students that meter is the rhythmical pattern of stressed syllables in a line of poetry. Blank verse consists of lines of poetry that do not rhyme but have a regular rhythm (the same meter). A stanza is a group of lines within a larger poem.

Standards Focus

Objectives

Students will analyze the way in which the poet uses similes to evoke readers' emotions.

Selection Introduction

Think About the Writer

Ask students to consider how Byron's associations with other famous literary figures, as well as his extensive travels, affected the subject matter of his poetry and its sophisticated tone.

For Independent Reading

- *The Complete Poems,* John Keats
- *Wuthering Heights,** Emily Bronte

HRW LIBRARY *This title is available in the HRW library.

Motivate

What Do You Think?/QuickTalk

Brainstorm with students about what makes a person or a place beautiful. Record their ideas on the board.

English for Academic Success

Academic Vocabulary

Look for opportunities to use the Academic Vocabulary words in this unit.

- **device, *n.*:** something made for a particular purpose
- **function, *n.*:** purpose
- **technique, *n.*:** method, way of using skills

California Standards, pp. 810–816

- **Reading Standard 3.4** Analyze ways in which poets use imagery, personification, figures of speech, and sounds to evoke readers' emotions.

Preparing to Read

She Walks in Beauty

from Childe Harold's Pilgrimage, Canto IV

What Do You Think? How can we use imagination to discover truth?

QuickTalk

Who is the most beautiful person you know? Is the beauty physical or emotional? In your *Reader/Writer Notebook,* write about this person, describing his or her beauty.

MEET THE WRITER

George Gordon, Lord Byron

(1788–1824)

In his Romantic poetry, Lord Byron fused aristocratic living, wild pursuits, a sensitive outlook, and precise language.

Sudden Wealth and Fame

Were it not for a twist of fate, George Gordon, Lord Byron might have grown up confined by the harsh Calvinism of Scotland. When his cousin died in battle in 1794, six-year-old George became first in line to be the sixth Baron Byron of Rochdale; four years later, he assumed the title.

Byron's rise in literary circles came no less abruptly. In 1812, the midpoint of the Romantic period, he became a celebrity when the first two cantos of his poem *Childe Harold's Pilgrimage* were published. The poem is based on Byron's travels to Europe and Asia Minor. Byron later said, "I awoke one morning and found myself famous." Four years later, he left for the Continent, never to return to Great Britain.

The Neoclassical Romantic

When Byron left England in 1816, he made contact with Percy Shelley and his wife, Mary, in Switzerland, and Byron's writing life began in earnest. He then moved to Italy, and despite the tales of debauchery that surrounded his time in Venice, there is little doubt Byron worked hard at his writing. His wildness and aristocratic ease often obscured a period of great literary productivity.

As a poet, Byron was not a Romantic in style, for he admired the techniques of neoclassical writers who wrote with wit and precision. Throughout the nineteenth century, however, he was considered the incarnation of the "Romantic" sensibility. His premature death only reinforced this image. Byron sailed to Greece in July 1823 to support the Greek nationalists in their struggle for independence from Turkey. In a marshy Greek town called Missolonghi, he came down with fevers that took his life only a few months after his thirty-sixth birthday.

Think About the Writer How did Byron's early fame and wealth affect his lifestyle and writing? Explain.

Byron, Sixth Baron (detail) by Richard Westall (1765–1836). Private Collection.

Selection Readability	
Easily Accessible **Accessible** Challenging	These poems include simile, rhyme, accessible vocabulary; accessible content.

Reading Standard 3.4 (see pages A48–A50)

Literary Skills Focus

Simile A **simile** is a figure of speech that makes an imaginative comparison between two seemingly unlike things by using a connective word such as *like, as, than,* or *resembles.*

Some examples of similes are "He is as helpful as a doorknob on a bathtub," "She plays the flute better than the Pied Piper," and "They are like two peas in a pod." Writers often use similes to encourage readers to think about something in a fresh, new way. In "She Walks in Beauty," Byron compares a beautiful woman to the night. Identify the line in which Byron makes this comparison; then, note how he develops the comparison throughout the poem.

Writing Skills Focus

Think as a Reader/Writer

Find It in Your Reading In this short poem, Byron creates **rhythm** by using **repetition** to form pairs of phrases such as "How pure, how dear." In a chart like the one below, list pairs you find as you read the poem. Record some notes about how the pairs function in the poem.

Line Numbers	Paired Phrases
line 12	"How pure, how dear . . ."

Vocabulary

gaudy (GAW dee) *adj.:* overly bright or colorful. *During Byron's day, a woman in mourning avoided gaudy clothing and wore mostly black.*

impaired (ihm PAIRD) *v.:* marred; weakened. *The woman's dark clothing had not impaired her beauty.*

serenely (suh REEN lee) *adv.:* calmly; peacefully. *She moves serenely through the crowd and does not show her grief.*

Language Coach

Verbs Used as Adjectives Some verbs that end in *–ed* can be used as adjectives. Remember that adjectives describe a noun or pronoun. In this poem, Byron describes a woman's grace as *impaired.* The verb *impair* means "to weaken"; therefore, grace that is impaired is weakened. The poet also describes her eyes as *mellowed.* What does this verb mean? How can you tell that it is used as an adjective?

Learn It Online
Learn more about Byron and his world through these Internet links.
go.hrw.com H12-811 Go

Reader/Writer Notebook
Use your **RWN** to complete the activities for this selection.

Selection Resources

Unit 4 Resources, on-level practice and assessment, pp. 70, 71

Teacher One Stop™, on-level lesson plans and all print resources

Holt Audio Library

Holt Audio Library: Selections and Summaries in Spanish

UA: Differentiating Instruction, graphic organizer, p. 183

UA: Supporting Instruction in Spanish, selection summary

ThinkCentral Online Assessment, Selection Standards Check

ThinkCentral Online Remediation

Preteach

Introducing Vocabulary

To reinforce the importance of the Vocabulary words, tell students that Byron uses these words to express the particular kind of beauty he celebrates in this poem. Nighttime has an appeal different from the *gaudy* charm of daylight. People may express inner calm by conducting themselves *serenely.* Ugly clothing can do little to *impair* the appearance of a true beauty.

English for Academic Success

Language Coach

Give students other examples of verbs that can be used as adjectives. [*impressed, pleased, used*] Then, have students choose one of these verbs and write two sentences—one using the verb as a verb and the other using the verb as an adjective. Ask volunteers to share their sentences.

Literary Skills Focus

As you read and discuss the selection with students, have them note Byron's use of simile to convey the specific qualities of the woman's beauty.

Writing Skills Focus

Have students record pairs of phrases marked by repetition in their **Reader/Writer Notebooks**. Students can use their notes to complete the Writing Skills Focus activity.

Learn It Online
The Quest for Truth and Beauty video is a brief, fast-paced introduction to the Romantic period and the characteristics of Romantic poetry.
go.hrw.com H12-811 Go

Teacher Preparation
Selection Summary
The speaker describes a beautiful woman he sees at a ball. In her physical aspect, she somehow combines the best properties of both bright and dark, and in her demeanor, she projects sweetness, purity, innocence, and calm.

Direct Teach

Think About/Talk About
Read with a Purpose Have students read the Read with a Purpose statement. Ask them to pay attention to the speaker's tone and the way he describes the woman's beautiful features.

Analysis
A Literary Focus

Possible responses: *A woman's beauty and a starry night are being compared. Her particular type of beauty calls to mind the contrasts of bright and dark in the subtle beauty of the night.*

Vocabulary: Own the Word
- **gaudy:** Something that is overly bright or colorful can be described as *gaudy*. Synonyms are *showy* and *flashy*. Have students put the word *gaudy* in the center of a word web and write examples of things that could be *gaudy*. ***Possible responses:*** *a clown's costume, costume jewelry, Christmas decorations, makeup*
- **impaired:** Tell students that *impaired* is the past tense form of the verb *impair,* which means "to lessen the quality, strength, or effectiveness of something." Ask students to list things that might *impair* a student's ability to do well on a test. ***Possible responses:*** *lack of sleep, failure to study*
- **serenely:** Ask students to name things that should be done *serenely*. ***Possible responses:*** *reading a good book, taking a nap, walking on the beach*

POEM

She Walks in Beauty

by **George Gordon, Lord Byron**

Read with a Purpose
Read to discover the impression a beautiful woman makes on the speaker.

Build Background
"She Walks in Beauty," one of Byron's most famous poems, was supposedly inspired by Lady Wilmot Horton, a beautiful woman whom Byron saw at a ball, perhaps in the spring of 1814. Lady Horton was in mourning and, in the fashion of the times, was wearing a black dress decorated with glittering spangles.

She walks in beauty, like the night
  Of cloudless climes° and starry skies;
And all that's best of dark and bright
  Meet in her aspect° and her eyes:
Thus mellowed to that tender light
  Which heaven to gaudy day denies. **A**

One shade the more, one ray the less,
  Had half impaired the nameless grace
Which waves in every raven tress,
  Or softly lightens o'er her face;
Where thoughts serenely sweet express
  How pure, how dear their dwelling place.

And on that cheek, and o'er that brow,
  So soft, so calm, yet eloquent,
The smiles that win, the tints that glow,
  But tell of days in goodness spent,
A mind at peace with all below,
  A heart whose love is innocent!

2. climes: atmospheres; climates.
4. aspect: face; look.

A Literary Focus **Simile** What is being compared in this poem? Why would these two things be linked?

Vocabulary **gaudy** (GAW dee) *adj.:* overly bright or colorful.
impaired (ihm PAIRD) *v.:* marred; weakened.
serenely (suh REEN lee) *adv.:* calmly; peacefully.

Miranda (1878) by Sir Frank Dicksee.
The Maas Gallery, London.

Universal Access

EL English Learners
To help students understand the simile, arrange them in small mixed-ability groups to revisit this question: "What makes someone or something beautiful?" Have students share their ideas and develop a list of adjectives and phrases to describe beauty. Next, have students identify characteristics of the night that are depicted as beautiful in the poem.

✔ See the **English Language Skill Builder** in **UA: Differentiating Instruction.**

Struggling Readers
Strategic Students As students read, have them use a three-column chart to explore Byron's use of simile. In the first two columns, students can list the characteristics of the two things being compared in the extended simile. In the last column, students should include their interpretation of the simile. Students may work in small groups to formulate their interpretation.

✔ See **UA: Differentiating Instruction** for a graphic organizer to scaffold instruction for struggling readers.

Preparing to Read

Reading Standard 3.3, 3.4 (see pages A48–A50)

from Childe Harold's Pilgrimage, Canto IV

Literary Skills Focus

Apostrophe In a figure of speech called **apostrophe,** a speaker directly addresses an absent or dead person, an abstract quality, or something nonhuman as if it were present and capable of responding. Apostrophe was a popular poetic device used by the Romantics. In this poem, Byron apostrophizes the ocean.

Reading Skills Focus

Understanding Rhyme and Rhythm In *Childe Harold's Pilgrimage,* Byron uses the **Spenserian stanza,** invented by the Renaissance poet Edmund Spenser. Byron, Shelley, and Keats all employed this challenging verse form, which uses only three different end rhymes in each nine-line stanza. The rhyme scheme is *ababbcbcc.* The first eight lines of each stanza are written in **iambic pentameter,** and the ninth line adds a poetic foot, or beat, to create an **alexandrine,** a line of **iambic hexameter.** The alexandrine often summarizes a stanza or concludes it with a image.

Into Action Record each stanza's subject and how the alexandrine concludes it. Add a star if the alexandrine incorporates apostrophe.

Subject of Stanza	How Alexandrine Concludes Stanza
Stanza 1: The speaker tells of his love and enjoyment of nature.	Alexandrine explains nature's impact on speaker

Writing Skills Focus

Think as a Reader/Writer

Find It in Your Writing In this poem, as in "She Walks in Beauty," Byron uses parallel sets of words and phrases. Sometimes he uses a series of words with a similar sound, such as "unknelled, uncoffined, and unknown." In your *Reader/Writer Notebook,* record parallel words and phrases. Note the effect this **parallelism** has on the sound of the poem.

Vocabulary

rapture (RAP chuhr) *n.:* bliss; profound joy. *As he wanders, Childe Harold seeks rapture in nature.*

intrudes (ihn TROODZ) *v.:* pushes in; interrupts. *When a crowd intrudes on his thoughts, he travels to a secluded place.*

mingle (MIHNG guhl) *v.:* mix. *He has no wish to mingle with people on the city's noisy streets.*

protracted (proh TRAK tihd) *v.* used as *adj.:* drawn out over time. *He craves solitary, protracted visits with nature.*

linger (LIHNG guhr) *v.:* stay a long while. *Upon approaching a beautiful and remote landscape, he will linger for many hours before resuming his journey.*

Language Coach

Connotations Poets choose words for both their **denotations** (dictionary definitions) and their **connotations** (the meanings associated with them). *Rapture* means "profound joy" but also has religious and spiritual connotations. Why might Byron have written about "rapture on the lonely shore" rather than "deep joy on the lonely shore"?

Reader/Writer **Notebook**

Use your **RWN** to complete the activities for this selection.

Learn It Online

Listen to this poem online.

go.hrw.com H12-813 Go

California Standards, pp. 813–816

- **Reading Standard 3.3** Analyze the ways in which irony, tone, mood, the author's style, and the "sound" of language achieve specific rhetorical or aesthetic purposes or both.
- **Reading Standard 3.4** Analyze ways in which poets use imagery, personification, figures of speech, and sounds to evoke readers' emotions.

Preteach

Introducing Vocabulary

- Review with students the Vocabulary words, definitions, and sample sentences.
- To reinforce the importance of the Vocabulary words, tell students that Byron uses these words to express the speaker's emotions as he contemplates the ocean. He is in a state of *rapture.* He feels at one with nature as he *mingles* with the universe in a *protracted* state of dreamy contemplation. Reluctant to end his encounter with the ocean, he wishes to *linger* there.

English for Academic Success

Language Coach

Have students work in pairs to write two sample sentences for each of the Vocabulary words. Encourage students to write paired sentences that illustrate different connotations of the same word.

Literary Skills Focus

As you read and discuss the selection with students, point out Byron's use of apostrophe and the effects he creates with this device.

Reading Skills Focus

Give students a copy of the Reading Skills Focus graphic organizer before they read. (See **Unit 4 Resources.**) Tell them to use their responses to answer the questions on the Applying Your Skills page.

Writing Skills Focus

Have students record pairs of parallel words and phrases in their **Reader/Writer Notebooks.** Tell them they can use their notes to complete the Writing Skills Focus activity.

Learn It Online

The online version of this selection includes audio support to engage all students and to help struggling readers with reading comprehension and vocabulary.

go.hrw.com H12-813 Go

Teacher Preparation
Selection Summary
The speaker of "Childe Harold's Pilgrimage, Canto IV" expresses his love for nature, especially for the ocean. He notes that his poetic abilities are declining, but he hopes that his readers will remember something of what he wrote.

Direct Teach

Think About/Talk About
Read with a Purpose Have students read the Read with a Purpose statement. Ask them to notice the images of the ocean and how Childe Harold feels about this manifestation of nature's power.

Comprehension
A Reading Focus

Possible response: *The complex form could reflect the seriousness of Byron's subject and the complexity of his feelings. The shift from a ten-syllable line to a twelve-syllable line allows the poet to shift to a more reflective, pensive tone at the end of each stanza.*

NARRATIVE POEM

from Childe Harold's Pilgrimage, Canto IV

by **George Gordon, Lord Byron**

Read with a Purpose
Read to discover what Childe Harold learns about nature and himself.

Build Background
In medieval times, *childe* probably meant "a young noble awaiting knighthood." Byron uses it as a title, like *Lord* or *Sir*, for a youth of "gentle" birth. *Childe Harold's Pilgrimage* is a long, thinly disguised autobiographical poem about Byron's own journeys.

In this excerpt from the final canto, the speaker addresses the ocean. The last two stanzas present Byron's personal conclusion to the whole poem. At this point, Byron has ceased trying to separate himself from the figure of Childe Harold.

1

There is a pleasure in the pathless woods,
There is a rapture on the lonely shore,
There is society, where none intrudes,
By the deep sea, and music in its roar:
I love not man the less, but Nature more,
From these our interviews, in which I steal°
From all I may be, or have been before,
To mingle with the Universe, and feel
What I can ne'er express, yet cannot all conceal. **A**

2

Roll on, thou deep and dark blue Ocean—roll!
Ten thousand fleets sweep over thee in vain;
Man marks the earth with ruin—his control
Stops with the shore; upon the watery plain
The wrecks are all thy deed, nor doth remain

6. **steal:** remove myself.

A Reading Focus **Understanding Rhyme and Rhythm** In what way does the intricate form of the Spenserian stanzas fit the poem's subject?

Vocabulary **rapture** (RAP chuhr) *n.:* bliss; profound joy.
intrudes (ihn TROODZ) *v.:* pushes in; interrupts.
mingle (MIHNG guhl) *v.:* mix.

Developing Oral Fluency

Whole-Class Activity After students have read the excerpt from the poem silently a few times, have them take turns reading each of the stanzas aloud. Encourage them to express aloud the different emotions that are appropriate to each stanza. For example, the first stanza is reverent in its appreciation of the deep, solitary power of nature. The powerful, booming second stanza seems to echo the crashing waves and ends with a frightening image of a human being's smallness. The third has a lively physical energy and a current of nostalgia, as the speaker fondly thinks back to his boyhood days of frolicking in the ocean. The final two stanzas shift the scene from the shore to the poet's room, and so the tone also shifts. The speaker is now saying goodbye, withdrawing from his work, and sinking into silence.

✔ See the **Oral Language Skill Builder** in **UA: Differentiating Instruction.**

A shadow of man's ravage, save his own,
When, for a moment, like a drop of rain,
He sinks into thy depths with bubbling groan,
Without a grave, unknelled,° uncoffined, and unknown.

3

And I have loved thee, Ocean! and my joy
Of youthful sports was on thy breast to be
Borne, like thy bubbles, onward: From a boy
I wantoned° with thy breakers—they to me
Were a delight; and if the freshening° sea
Made them a terror—'twas a pleasing fear,
For I was as it were a child of thee,
And trusted to thy billows far and near,
And laid my hand upon thy mane—as I do here. **B**

4

My task is done, my song hath ceased, my theme
Has died into an echo; it is fit
The spell should break of this protracted dream.
The torch shall be extinguished which hath lit
My midnight lamp—and what is writ, is writ;
Would it were worthier! but I am not now
That which I have been—and my visions flit
Less palpably° before me—and the glow
Which in my spirit dwelt is fluttering, faint, and low.

5

Farewell! a word that must be, and hath been—
A sound which makes us linger;—yet—farewell!
Ye! who have traced the Pilgrim to the scene
Which is his last, if in your memories dwell
A thought which once was his, if on ye swell
A single recollection, not in vain
He wore his sandal shoon and scallop shell;°
Farewell! with *him* alone may rest the pain,
If such there were—with *you*, the moral of his strain.° **C**

18. unknelled (uhn NEHLD): without the traditional ringing of a church bell to announce his death.

22. wantoned: frolicked; played happily.
23. freshening: becoming rough as the wind comes up.

35. palpably: clearly.

43. sandal shoon . . . shell: *Shoon* is archaic for "shoes." Sandals and a scallop shell worn on a hat were traditional emblems of pilgrims. The scallop shell is a symbol of Saint James, whose shrine in Spain was a great attraction to pilgrims.
45. strain: passage of poetry or song.

B Literary Focus **Apostrophe** How does Childe Harold profess his love as he addresses the ocean in this apostrophe?

C Literary Focus **Apostrophe** What is the tone of the speaker's address to the reader? Why might he make such an emphatic farewell?

Vocabulary **protracted** (proh TRAK tihd) *v.* used as *adj.:* drawn out over time.
linger (LIHNG guhr) *v.:* stay a long while.

California Standards, p. 816

- **Reading Standard 3.3** Analyze the ways in which irony, tone, mood, the author's style, and the "sound" of language achieve specific rhetorical or aesthetic purposes or both.
- **Reading Standard 3.4** Analyze ways in which poets use imagery, personification, figures of speech, and sounds to evoke readers' emotions.
- **Writing Standard 1.4** Enhance meaning by employing rhetorical devices, including the extended use of parallelism, repetition, and analogy; the incorporation of visual aids (e.g., graphs, tables, pictures); and the issuance of a call for action.

Think About/Talk About

Analysis

B Literary Focus

Possible responses: *In line 25, he compares his relationship to the ocean with the relationship between child and parent. In line 27, he compares his affection for the ocean with a person's desire to stroke a beloved and trusted horse.*

C Literary Focus

Possible responses: *The tone is sorrowful and wistful. The speaker makes this wholehearted farewell to emphasize his true appreciation for nature.*

Extend the Discussion

Apostrophe In line 10, the speaker addresses the ocean as if it could respond. What effect does this apostrophe create? ***Possible response:*** *Though the stanza expresses the idea that human affairs are insignificant, the apostrophe implies that the speaker has a mystical connection with this powerful natural force.*

Vocabulary: Own the Word

- **rapture:** Remind students that *rapture* is a profound—not slight—joy. Ask students: "What event or experience would cause or has caused you to feel *rapture*?"
- **intrudes:** Remind students that *intrudes* can mean "interrupts." Ask students to complete the sentence: "My little brother *intrudes* on my phone conversations when he . . ."
- **mingle:** Ask students to list additional ways in which the narrator could "mingle with the Universe." [*climb to a mountain top, gaze at the stars*]
- **protracted:** In the adjective form, *protracted* means "drawn out over time;" the antonym is *abbreviated.* Use both words in a sentence: The baseball team won an abbreviated game due to a *protracted* downpour.
- **linger:** Ask students, "Why might you *linger* after someone has said goodbye? What would *lingering* look like?"

Check for Understanding

Independent Practice

Reading Skills Focus

Possible responses:

1. *The speaker is amazed by the lady's beauty, which inspires his admiration.*
2. *The speaker reveals his understanding of nature and himself by characterizing nature as a living force. In stanza 1, for instance, he finds "society" (l. 3) and "music" (l. 4) in nature, and describes his interactions with the ocean as "interviews" (l. 6). The apostrophe also attributes life to the ocean.*
3. *A successful response will address how each alexandrine serves to emphasize the themes of the stanza.*

Vocabulary Check

4. *f* **5.** *g* **6.** *c* **7.** *a*
8. *h* **9.** *d* **10.** *e* **11.** *b*

Literary Skills Focus

Possible responses:

12. *The balance of opposites appears in "One shade the more, one ray the less." Her "raven tress" is black but "lightens oe'r her face."*
13. *"And laid my hand upon thy mane" (l. 27). The comparison makes the relationship seem companionable, although the speaker acknowledges the sea's greater power.*
14. *He compares her beauty to a starry night. The simile evokes awe.*
15. *Urging the sea to "Roll on" depicts the sea's action. The repeated word echoes the ocean's roar.*
16. *"Cloudless climes," "starry skies," "day denies," and "serenely sweet" are all examples of alliteration, which adds emphasis.*

What Do You Think Now?

To help students answer this question, remind them that the speakers use figurative language (such as simile, metaphor, and apostrophe) to describe their subjects.

Applying Your Skills

Reading Standard 3.3, 3.4 (see pages A48–A50)
Writing Standard 1.4 (see pages A51–A52)

She Walks in Beauty
from Childe Harold's Pilgrimage, Canto IV

Literary Response and Analysis

Reading Skills Focus

Read with a Purpose

1. In "She Walks in Beauty," how does the woman's beauty affect the speaker?
2. In *Childe Harold's Pilgrimage,* how does the speaker reveal what he's learned about nature and himself?

Reading Skills: Understanding Rhyme and Rhythm

3. In your chart for *Childe Harold's Pilgrimage*, explain how each alexandrine helps you understand its stanza. Describe how each apostrophe affects its stanza's conclusion.

Subject of Stanza	How Alexandrine Concludes Stanza	How Alexandrine Helps Reader to Understand Stanza
Stanza 1: The speaker tells of his love and enjoyment of nature.	Alexandrine explains nature's impact on speaker	The speaker cannot fully describe his deep feelings about nature.

Vocabulary Check

Match each Vocabulary word to its definition.

4. serenely	**a.** breaks in; encroaches
5. gaudy	**b.** extreme joy
6. impaired	**c.** damaged
7. intrudes	**d.** move among; join in
8. linger	**e.** lasting for a while
9. mingle	**f.** calmly
10. protracted	**g.** loud in color or style
11. rapture	**h.** hang around

Literary Skills Focus

Literary Analysis

12. **Compare** The words "dark and bright" in line 3 of "She Walks in Beauty" suggest a balance of opposites. How is this idea developed in the poem?
13. **Analyze** In stanza 3 of *Childe Harold's Pilgrimage,* what metaphor compares the sea to a horse? What is the effect of this comparison?

Literary Skills: Simile / Apostrophe

14. **Analyze** Explain the simile in the first stanza of "She Walks in Beauty" and the emotions it evokes.
15. **Interpret** How does the use of apostrophe in line 10 of *Childe Harold's Pilgrimage* add to the description?

Literary Skills Review: Alliteration

16. **Analyze** The repetition of consonant sounds in words that are close to one another is **alliteration.** In each poem, identify an example of alliteration, and analyze its effect.

Writing Skills Focus

Think as a Reader/Writer

Use It in Your Writing Write a brief description of something you find beautiful or moving. Include at least three pairs or sets of parallel words and phrases to add rhythm and impact to your description.

What Do You Think Now? How do the speakers in both poems identify and describe true beauty? Explain.

Universal Access

Struggling Writers

Some students may need additional scaffolding to complete the Writing Skills Focus activity. After students have identified a subject, have them make a list of descriptive words and phrases about the subject. Encourage students to use their lists to help them as they write their description. Have students write some parallel phrases separately and incorporate them into their description. If students struggle to add parallel words and phrases to their paragraphs, tell them to use George Gordon, Lord Byron's poems as a model.

Assess

Unit 4 Resources, Selection Standards Check, p. 70

go.hrw.com **ThinkCentral Online Assessment,** Selection Standards Check

Teacher One Stop™, editable Selection Standards Check

Reading Standard 2.2 (see pages A48–A50)

Comparing and Contrasting by **Kylene Beers**

The act of comparing and contrasting helps us to see more, and to see more clearly. Holding two poems side by side and looking for similarities and differences often reveals features that escaped you when you read the poems separately. Comparing and contrasting requires us to re-read and gives us a deeper understanding of the writer's message.

To **compare and contrast,** you must establish a basis for comparison by asking how the two elements are similar. Two ideas, objects, people, or events should be similar in some way or exist in similar circumstances before you can compare them.

For example, the poems, "Ode to the West Wind" by Percy Bysshe Shelley and "Ode to a Nightingale" by John Keats, share attributes that we can compare: Both were written during the Romantic period, address an element of nature, and use the characteristics and structure of an ode. With the basis of comparison established, we may discover additional similarities and also consider differences.

While poems and other pieces of literature can be compared and contrasted, we can also apply the process within a single piece. Shelley's poem "Ozymandias" provides an opportunity to do just that.

The poem's speaker recounts a memorable experience retold by a "traveler from an antique land" who has seen the ruins of the statue of King Ozymandias. He describes the "trunkless legs of stone" and "shattered visage" of the once glorious statue. He establishes the basis for comparison and contrast: the statue as originally crafted by the sculptor's hand and as it now appears to the traveler untold years later. The traveler reads the inscription that the sculptor wrought:

"My name is Ozymandias, king of kings,
Look on my works, ye Mighty, and despair!"

The contrast between the haughty king whose "sneer of cold command" was once wrought in stone and that now exists only as a "colossal wreck" creates the image Shelley uses to communicate the ironic theme in the poem. Regardless of the power and might of a man and the monuments and tributes people create to honor him, only nature is as lasting and "boundless," as represented by the desert surrounding the ruins. Shelley's use of comparison and contrast creates a powerful image that expresses an unforgettable observation about nature, life, and death.

Your Turn

Read lines 11–14 from stanza 2 and lines 31–34 from stanza 4 of Keats's "Ode on a Grecian Urn."

2

Heard melodies are sweet, but those unheard
Are sweeter; therefore, ye soft pipes, play on;
Not to the sensual ear, but, more endeared,
Pipe to the spirit ditties of no tone:

4

Who are these coming to the sacrifice?
To what green altar, O mysterious priest,
Lead'st thou that heifer lowing at the skies,
And all her silken flanks with garlands dressed?

How do the first four lines of stanza 2 compare and contrast with the first four lines of stanza 4? What hints do these similarities and differences give you about the poem's theme? Later, when you read the complete poem, check to see if you were right.

Reading Skills Focus

Objectives

Students will learn how comparing and contrasting helps to understand a writer's message.

Unit 4 Resources, Reading Focus Skill Builder, p. 69

Teacher One Stop™, lesson plan and all print resources

Direct Teach

Comparing and Contrasting

This feature gives students practice comparing and contrasting elements within a poem. Have students read the feature and complete the Your Turn activity before reading "Ozymandias."

Check for Understanding

Your Turn

Have students work in pairs to find similarities and differences between the two stanzas. [*Both include sensory details and mystical overtones; however, stanza 2 makes statements while stanza 4 has a more uncertain tone. The similarities and differences hint at the beauty and spirituality in nature.*]

California Standards, p. 817

- **Reading Standard 2.2** Analyze the way in which clarity of meaning is affected by the patterns of organization, hierarchical structures, repetition of the main ideas, syntax, and word choice in the text.

Universal Access

English Learners/ Struggling Readers

To help students understand how to establish a basis for comparing details within a text, explain that they must find a parallel or underlying similarity between two or more elements. Note possible bases for comparison: a repeated element (such as two stanzas ending with a question mark), a shared role (such as two people or things a speaker addresses), or a common focus (such as two views of the same thing).

Standards Focus

Objectives

Students will
- understand irony
- compare and contrast

Selection Introduction

Think About the Writer

Ask students how Shelley's travels might influence his imagination.

For Independent Reading

- *Blood on the Forehead: What I Know About Writing,* M. E. Kerr
- *Frankenstein,** Mary Shelley

HRW LIBRARY *This title is available in the HRW library.

Motivate

What Do You Think?/QuickTalk

Tell students to write for five minutes about a natural phenomenon or human creation. Have them discuss the ideas that such sights evoke.

English for Academic Success

Academic Vocabulary

Look for opportunities to use the Academic Vocabulary words.
- **device, *n.*:** something made for a particular purpose.
- **differentiate, *v.*:** distinguish
- **function, *n.*:** the action for which a person or thing is specially fitted
- **inherent, *adj.*:** existing in something as a fixed, essential quality
- **technique, *n.*:** method

California Standards, pp. 818–823

- **Reading Standard 2.2** Analyze the way in which clarity of meaning is affected by the patterns of organization, hierarchical structures, repetition of the main ideas, syntax, and word choice in the text.
- **Reading Standard 3.3** Analyze the ways in which irony, tone, mood, the author's style, and the "sound" of language achieve specific rhetorical or aesthetic purposes or both.
- **Grades 9–10 Review Reading Standard 3.11** Evaluate the aesthetic qualities of style, including the impact of diction and figurative language on tone, mood, and theme, using the terminology of literary criticism. (Aesthetic approach).

Preparing to Read

Ozymandias
Ode to the West Wind
To a Skylark

What Do You Think? How can we use imagination to discover truth?

QuickTalk

What sights (natural or human-made) prompt you to think imaginatively about life? In your *Reader/Writer Notebook,* list at least three such sights, and describe the kinds of imaginative thoughts each sight generates in you.

MEET THE WRITER

Percy Bysshe Shelley
(1792–1822)

Percy Bysshe Shelley lived a turbulent life, but he believed deeply that human thought and expression had the inherent power to change life for the better.

Dramatic Life

At nineteen, estranged from his family, Shelley embarked on a career of courting the unconventional. To "rescue" her from a tyrannical father, he eloped with sixteen-year-old Harriet Westbrook, a classmate of his sisters. Three years later he abandoned Harriet and ran away with seventeen-year-old Mary Godwin, the daughter of two of the most important radical thinkers of the 1790s, Mary Wollstonecraft and William Godwin. Percy's alliance with Mary also involved responsibility for Mary's fifteen-year-old stepsister, Jane Clairmont, who soon changed her name to Claire and accompanied Shelley and Mary to Europe. Claire's brief affair with Byron brought Shelley and Byron together in 1816 in Switzerland in one of the age's most important literary relationships.

Shortly after the Shelleys' return to England, Harriet, only twenty-one, drowned herself in a pond in Hyde Park. Shelley could now wed Mary but was denied custody of his two children with Harriet.

Dramatic Death

Shelley and Mary fled their debts and notoriety in England and returned to the Continent. The next four years were Shelley's most productive, during which he wrote one inspired work after another.

In 1822, when he was not yet thirty, Shelley and a companion, Edward Williams, drowned when their sailboat, the *Ariel,* sank in a storm off the northwestern coast of Italy. Almost two weeks later, Shelley's body washed ashore, a copy of Sophocles' writing in one pocket and a copy of Keats's writing in the other. The body was burned in a pyre on the beach while friends (including Byron) stood by. Shelley's ashes were buried in the Protestant cemetery in Rome.

Think About the Writer What do Shelley's travels and relationships suggest about his imagination?

Percy Bysshe Shelley (1845) by Joseph Severn. Oil on canvas. Keats-Shelley Memorial House, Rome, Italy.

Selection Readability	
Easily Accessible **Accessible** Challenging	These poems include accessible theme, accessible vocabulary.

Reading Standard 2.2, 3.3; **Grades 9–10 Review**
Reading Standard 3.11 (see pages A48–A50)

Literary Skills Focus

Irony A discrepancy between expectation and reality is called **irony.** This poem turns on a kind of irony called **situational irony,** which is created when the opposite of an expected event or outcome occurs. Although "Ozymandias" is a short poem, several characters appear in its lines. Think about which characters expect one thing to happen, only to have something else occur. How might this ironic outcome relate to Shelley's poem in particular, and with works of art in general?

Literary Perspectives Apply the literary perspective described on page 820 as you read this sonnet.

Reading Skills Focus

Comparing and Contrasting To **compare** is to see how things are alike; to **contrast** is to see how they are different. Both skills define our world, helping us differentiate and categorize things around us. Irony requires us to compare and contrast, because we must compare what is expected with what really happens and note any differences.

Into Action As you read "Ozymandias," use the details in the poem to create a compare-and-contrast chart like the one below. Focus on what has changed since the statue was first completed.

Now	Then
The statue is in pieces.	The statue was whole and towered over everyone.
The statue is impressive even though it is in pieces.	The statue was impressive in its original form.

Vocabulary

antique (an TEEK) *adj.:* ancient. *The antique and decaying ruins fascinated the traveler.*

sneer (snihr) *n.:* proud, unkind facial expression. *The king's sneer caused his servants to tremble with fear.*

passions (PASH uhnz) *n. pl.:* strong emotions. *What passions led the king to command the creation of this statue?*

colossal (kuh LAHS uhl) *adj.:* magnificently huge. *Did he hope that the colossal work would endure forever?*

boundless (BOWND lihs) *adj.:* limitless. *The boundless reach of time eventually conquers mere stone.*

Language Coach

Pronunciation Read aloud the words *passions, colossal,* and *boundless.* What do you notice about the sounds the double *s* makes? Can you think of other words in which a double *s* makes the same sound as in *passions*? What general rule can you determine about when to use each pronunciation?

Writing Skills Focus

Think as a Reader/Writer

Find It in Your Reading In "Ozymandias," Shelley chooses his words carefully to create vivid **images** and a particular **tone,** as well as a particular **rhythm** and **rhyme** pattern. In your *Reader/Writer Notebook,* note the effects of some of Shelley's word choices.

Reader/Writer Notebook

Use your **RWN** to complete the activities for this selection.

Learn It Online

Get to know this poem through the video introduction online.

go.hrw.com H12-819 Go

Selection Resources

Unit 4 Resources, on-level practice and assessment, pp. 77, 83, 89

PowerNotes, interactive lesson presentation with activities

Teacher One Stop™, on-level lesson plans and all print resources

Holt Audio Library

Holt Audio Library: Selections and Summaries in Spanish

UA: Holt Interactive Reader, p. 255

UA: Differentiating Instruction, modified lesson plans and leveled assessment, pp. 184, 187

UA: Resources for Teaching Advanced Students, lesson plans, p. 151

UA: Supporting Instruction in Spanish, selection summary

ThinkCentral Online Assessment, Selection Standards Check

ThinkCentral Online Remediation

Preteach

Introducing Vocabulary

- Review the Vocabulary words, definitions, and sample sentences with students.
- To reinforce the importance of the Vocabulary words, tell students that Shelley uses them to describe the feelings, or *passions*, that a broken monument evokes. The face of the *antique* statue wears a *sneer*. The broken pieces of the statue are *colossal*, standing alone in the *boundless* desert.

English for Academic Success

Language Coach

After students complete the **Language Coach** activity, have them compare the sounds of the double *s* in the words *profession, helplessness,* and *dismissal.*

Literary Skills Focus

Have students note the ironic contrast between the statue's ruined condition and the boastful words on the pedestal.

Reading Skills Focus

Give students a copy of the Reading Skills Focus graphic organizer before they read. (See **Unit 4 Resources.**) Tell them to use their responses to answer the questions on the Applying Your Skills page.

Writing Skills Focus

Have pairs of students record effects of word choice on imagery, tone, rhythm, and rhyme in their **Reader/Writer Notebooks**. Students can use their notes for the Writing Skills Focus activity.

Learn It Online

The **PowerNotes** presentation for this lesson includes a short video that introduces the selection. The video is also available on the online version of this page.

go.hrw.com H12-819 Go

Teacher Preparation

Selection Summary

The speaker quotes a traveler who came upon the ruins of a monument to Ozymandias, a pharaoh of ancient Egypt. Amid the statue's ruins, the ruler's boastful inscription becomes an ironic comment on the vanity of human ambition. The desert sand and wind will destroy even the statue itself, erasing the artist's own bid for immortality and that of the pharaoh.

Direct Teach

Think About/Talk About

Read with a Purpose Ask students to contrast the king's inscribed words with the state of the statue itself.

Comprehension

Ⓐ Reading Focus

Possible response: *"Passions" and "lifeless" suggest the sculptor was a keen observer of his subject's emotions.*

Analysis

Ⓑ Literary Focus

Possible response: *The barren desert reinforces the idea that the king's works have vanished.*

Ⓒ Literary Perspectives

Possible response: *The poet uses assonance ("trunkless legs of stone") and alliteration ("cold command") to evoke images of the dusty remnants.*

Vocabulary: Own the Word

- **antique:** Ask students what they might see in an *antique* land.
- **sneer:** Have students finish the following thought: An arrogant veteran athlete might form a *sneer* (noun form) if he were . . ."
- **passions:** Have students list examples of *passions* a person may feel.
- **colossal:** Create a semantic web with *colossal* in the center. Have students add synonyms to the web.
- **boundless:** Ask students to list things that are or seem *boundless.*

SONNET

OZYMANDIAS

by **Percy Bysshe Shelley**

Read with a Purpose

Read to discover what became of a mighty king's legacy.

Build Background

One of Shelley's few sonnets, "Ozymandias" was written as part of a friendly and informal poetry competition in 1817. The poetic topic was Egypt, inspired by extraordinary Egyptian fragments that had recently been displayed at the British Museum in London. Some of these fragments were from the empire of Ramses II (c. 1290–1224 B.C.), who built monuments all over Egypt. Ozymandias is the Greek name for Ramses II.

The greatest colonnaded hall ever constructed, the Great Hall at Karnak was so huge that one hundred men could stand on the capital of each column.

Statue of Ramses II at Karnak, Luxor, Egypt.

I met a traveler from an antique land
Who said: Two vast and trunkless legs° of stone
Stand in the desert . . . Near them, on the sand,
Half sunk, a shattered visage° lies, whose frown,
And wrinkled lip, and sneer of cold command,
Tell that its sculptor well those passions read
Which yet survive, stamped on these lifeless things, Ⓐ
The hand that mocked them, and the heart° that fed;
And on the pedestal these words appear:
"My name is Ozymandias, king of kings,
Look on my works, ye Mighty, and despair!"
Nothing beside remains. Round the decay Ⓑ
Of that colossal wreck, boundless and bare
The lone and level sands stretch far away. Ⓒ

2. **trunkless legs:** the legs without the rest of the body.
4. **visage:** face; look.
8. **hand . . . heart:** the hand of the sculptor, who scorned the passions to which Ozymandias gave himself wholeheartedly.

Literary Perspectives

Analyzing Style Style is the way writers say what they wish to say. Even if writers express similar ideas, each writer has a unique manner of expressing those ideas. To analyze Shelley's style in "Ozymandias," pay close attention to how he uses language: Is the diction formal or casual? plain spoken or poetic? Is the tone serious, comic, or ironic? Does he use figures of speech, such as similes or metaphors?

As you read, be sure to notice the questions in the text, which will guide you in using this perspective.

Ⓐ **Reading Focus** **Comparing and Contrasting** Choose a word from line 6 and a word from line 7 that show contrasting details in the traveler's description of the statue. What does this contrast suggest about the sculptor?

Ⓑ **Literary Focus** **Irony** How does the setting described in lines 12–14 add to the irony of this inscription?

Ⓒ **Literary Perspectives** **Analyzing Style** As you read this poem, what images appear in your mind? What literary techniques does the poet use to help create those images?

Vocabulary **antique** (an TEEK) *adj.:* ancient.
sneer (snihr) *n.:* proud, unkind facial expression.
passions (PASH uhnz) *n. pl.:* strong emotions.
colossal (kuh LAHS uhl) *adj.:* magnificently huge.
boundless (BOWND lihs) *adj.:* limitless.

Real Issues, Real Experts

Holt author ***Deborah Appleman*** *offers tips for using "Ozymandias" to teach the relationship between form and meaning.*

Ask students to try their own hand at writing a sonnet, and then have them consider how the constraints of this form actually contribute to the power of the poem. Shelley does not merely describe a decaying statue; he constructs a dramatic situation in which two strangers meditate on art, humanity, and history. Ask students to rewrite, in prose form, the story that is told in this famous poem.

Literary Perspectives

Before students read the poem, have them read the **Literary Perspectives** about Analyzing Style.

The unconventional sentence structure of Shelley's style may pose a challenge for students. Explain that the clause "Which yet survive" refers to the passions of the pharaoh—passions that have lasted longer than the sculptor's mortal hands.

Remind students to use the notes and questions at the bottom of the page to help them use the perspective.

Applying Your Skills

Reading Standard 2.2, 3.1, 3.3; Grades 9–10 Review
Reading Standard 3.11 (see pages A48–A50)
Writing Standard 2.1a. 2.1c, 2.1e (see pages A51–A52)

Ozymandias

Literary Response and Analysis

Reading Skills Focus

Quick Check

1. According to the poem, what was the sculptor's attitude toward the subject of his artwork?
2. If we assume his statue represents him well, what kind of king was Ozymandias?
3. Who should "despair" in this poem? Why?

Read with a Purpose

4. Would Ozymandias be surprised at what happened to his statue? What message does the statue's fate send to readers of the poem?

Reading Skills: Comparing and Contrasting

5. Circle the contrasts you noted in the chart, and underline the comparisons. Then, write a few sentences explaining how the comparisons and contrasts work together to help deliver the poem's message.

Now	Then
The statue is in pieces.	The statue was whole and towered over everyone.
The statue is impressive even though it is in pieces.	The statue was impressive in its original form.

Literary Skills Focus

Literary Analysis

6. **Summarize** Even in the brief space of a sonnet, Shelley suggests a number of narrative frames. How many speakers do you hear in this poem? Summarize what each one says.
7. **Interpret** What is the poem's message about pride?
8. **Literary Perspectives** This poem is a sonnet, one of the most timeless, constrained, and formal types of poetry. How does Shelley's choice of the sonnet form enhance the overall effect of the poem? What does it suggest about his style?

Literary Skills: Irony

9. **Analyze** What did Ozymandias expect people to see when they looked at his "works"? What do they actually see?

Literary Skills Review: Sonnet

10. **Analyze** A **sonnet** is a fourteen-line lyric poem, usually written in iambic pentameter, that has one of several rhyme schemes. Many sonnets have a **turn,** a pivotal point in the sonnet at which a question is answered, a solution is proposed, or a comment is offered. Where is the turn in "Ozymandias"? What is the function of the lines that follow the turn?

Writing Skills Focus

Think as a Reader/Writer

Use It in Your Writing Now that you have read the poem and considered Shelley's word choices, focus on word choice in your own writing. In your *Reader/Writer Notebook,* write a descriptive or narrative paragraph about a scene or event that is vivid in your memory. Consider how the words you choose affect the way your writing sounds, the tone it conveys, and the images it creates for your readers.

What Do You Think Now? Imagine that you are standing in front of the ruins of Ozymandias's statue. What could you learn about immortality, pride, and memory from the condition of the fallen monument?

Universal Access

Struggling Writers

Some students may need additional scaffolding to complete the Writing Skills Focus activity. Ask students to think of a place that they can vividly describe and words that express their attitude toward the place. Have students brainstorm and record descriptive words first as prewriting. Ask students to determine what tone the descriptions suggest. Then, have them write a descriptive paragraph incorporating these words.

What Do You Think Now?

Tell students to think about the motives of the king who commissioned the statue and ordered the inscription on the pedestal. How do those motives contrast with the ruined statue?

Check for Understanding

Independent Practice

Reading Skills Focus

Possible responses:

1. *The sculptor understood the ruler's pride and perhaps disliked him as he sculpted the ruler's "sneer of cold command."*
2. *He was contemptuous and concerned that he be remembered.*
3. *According to the inscription, the mighty should despair about ever equaling the king's achievements. However, the poem implies that the most powerful should despair at the knowledge that human life and achievement is fleeting.*
4. *He would be surprised at not achieving fame and immortality through his works as he expected. The statue's fate reminds readers of the transience of glory.*
5. *Students' charts should note the irony produced by the contrasts.*

Literary Skills Focus

Possible responses:

6. *Speakers include the original "I" who narrates the poem, the traveler who tells him about finding the statue, and Ozymandias himself telling the Mighty to despair.*
7. *Pride is futile; even art is destroyed by time.*
8. *Shelley's choice of a traditional form suits the somberness in its theme.*
9. *He expected them to see mighty works, but people see only the ruins created by time and the elements.*
10. *The turn comes after line 8, when the traveler recalls the inscription on the statue that states the king's hope to be remembered. The lines following the turn establish an ironic contrast between the king's effort to ensure immortality and the ruins that are all that remain of that effort.*

Independent Practice
Vocabulary Development
Vocabulary Check

1. *d* **2.** *c*
3. *e* **4.** *b*
5. *a*

Your Turn

Sample response:
new word: *antique*
meaning: *belonging to earlier times*
part of speech: *adjective*
related words: *antiquely, antiqueness*
sample sentence: *She preferred antique furniture to modern furniture.*
source of info: *Merriam-Webster online*

English for Academic Success
Language Coach
Possible responses:

/s/ sound: *lesson, hassle, impassable, trunkless, possessing;*
/sh/ sound: *recession, missionary, pressure*

The double s is usually pronounced as /s/, but when it is followed by "ion" or "ure," it is pronounced as /sh/.

English for Academic Success
Academic Vocabulary
Possible response: *One way human beings can differentiate themselves is by leaving behind enduring words or works that inspire or encourage others.*

Applying Your Skills

Ozymandias

Vocabulary Development

Vocabulary Check

Match the Vocabulary words with their definitions.

1. antique	**a.** infinite
2. sneer	**b.** enormously grand
3. passions	**c.** unpleasant expression
4. colossal	**d.** old
5. boundless	**e.** strong emotions

Vocabulary Skills: Using Print and Online Sources

When you encounter an unfamiliar word, you can use print and online sources to learn about a word's meaning, use, and history. A dictionary is a good resource for finding help with words you do not know. Even if you are not sure how a word is spelled, you can usually find it in a dictionary by starting with your best guesses at its spelling. In a dictionary, you will learn the word's meaning, correct spelling, history, and related words. You can find print and online dictionaries in a library.

You can also use other online sources to study words. Several online dictionaries are free. Word lists for specific content areas are often found on specialized Web sites. If you need to differentiate the terms *ROM* and *RAM*, for example, you might check a site that explains computer terms. No matter what source you use, you can keep track of what you learn by creating vocabulary cards like this one:

new word	pedestal
meaning	support or foot of a column; base of an upright structure
part of speech	noun
related words	words with –ped– ("foot"), such as pedal
sample sentence	A strong pedestal will support a large statue.
source of info	Merriam–Webster online

Your Turn

Use five print and online sources to create vocabulary cards for the Vocabulary words. Follow the model of the vocabulary card for *pedestal.*

Language Coach

Pronunciation The double *s* in *colossal* and *boundless* is pronounced /s/. The double *s* in *passions* is pronounced /sh/. Sort the following words into a chart, and then complete the pronunciation rule below: *recession, lesson, missionary, hassle, impassable, trunkless, pressure, possessing.*

/s/ sound	/sh/ sound

The double *s* is usually pronounced as ________, but when it is followed by ________ or ________, it is pronounced as ________.

Academic Vocabulary

Write About

How can we differentiate ourselves in a meaningful, positive way? When we die, what can we leave behind to show that our passage through life mattered? Record some thoughts about whether—and how—human beings can create something through words and work that will outlive them.

California Standards, pp. 821–823

- **Reading Standard 2.2** Analyze the way in which clarity of meaning is affected by the patterns of organization, hierarchical structures, repetition of the main ideas, syntax, and word choice in the text.
- **Reading Standard 3.1** Analyze characteristics of subgenres (e.g., satire, parody, allegory, pastoral) that are used in poetry, prose, plays, novels, short stories, essays, and other basic genres.
- **Reading Standard 3.3** Analyze the ways in which irony, tone, mood, the author's style, and the "sound" of language achieve specific rhetorical or aesthetic purposes or both.
- **Grades 9–10 Review Reading Standard 3.11** Evaluate the aesthetic qualities of style, including the impact of diction and figurative language on tone, mood, and theme, using the terminology of literary criticism. (Aesthetic approach).
- **Writing Standard 2.1** Write fictional, autobiographical, or biographical narratives: **a.** Narrate a sequence of events and communicate their significance to the audience. **c.** Describe with concrete sensory details the sights, sounds, and smells of a scene and the specific actions, movements, gestures, and feelings of the characters; use interior monologue to depict the characters' feelings. **e.** Make effective use of descriptions of appearance, images, shifting perspectives, and sensory details.
- **Writing Standard 2.2** Write responses to literature: **a.** Demonstrate a comprehensive understanding of the significant ideas in works or passages. **c.** Support important ideas and viewpoints through accurate and detailed references to the text and to other works.
- **Writing Standard 2.6** Deliver multimedia presentations: **a.** Combine text, images, and sound and draw information from many sources (e.g., television broadcasts, videos, films, newspapers, magazines, CD-ROMs, the Internet, electronic media-generated images). **b.** Select an appropriate medium for each element of the presentation.

Writing Standard 2.2a, 2.2c, 2.6a, 2.6b (see pages A51–A52)

Grammar Link

Sentence Structure

Sentences are made up of **clauses,** or groups of words that contain both a subject and a verb. The kind and number of clauses in a sentence determine **sentence structure.** A **simple** sentence has one independent clause and no subordinate clauses.

Percy Bysshe Shelley was a student at Oxford.

A **compound** sentence has two or more independent clauses but no subordinate clauses.

Shelley was born in England, but he died in Italy.

A **complex** sentence contains one independent clause and one or more subordinate clauses.

Although sailors encountered Shelley's boat in a storm, Shelley refused their offer to go on board.

A **compound-complex** sentence contains two or more independent clauses and one or more subordinate clauses.

Shelley died before he was thirty, but his poems endure.

Your Turn

Identify the following sentences as simple, compound, complex, or compound-complex.

1. Shelley wrote relatively few sonnets, and "Ozymandias" is one of his best.
2. It describes the ruins of a statue that once stood in a far-off desert.
3. Although the words on the pedestal are proud, the king's mighty works have crumbled, and the barren desert surrounds them.

Writing Application Combine and revise sentences to vary the sentence structure in some paragraphs you have written in your *Reader/Writer Notebook.*

CHOICES

As you respond to the Choices, use these **Academic Vocabulary** words as appropriate: differentiate, inherent, device, technique, function.

REVIEW

Write an Inscription

The inscription on Ozymandias's statue seems ironic, given the once massive, awe-inspiring monument now lies in ruins. Write an inscription that is more in keeping with the statue's ruined condition.

CONNECT

Assess the Message

Timed Writing In a brief essay, compare and contrast the message of "Ozymandias" with the message of Keats's "Ode on a Grecian Urn" or Shakespeare's Sonnet 18. Citing examples, explain what each poem says about the lasting power of art.

EXTEND

Document the Past and the Future

TechFocus With a small group, create a digital presentation of images of famous ruins from different cultures. Also, include modern buildings or other objects that you think will survive into the future. What will these objects tell future people about the world today?

Temple of Inscriptions, Palenque, Mexico.

Learn It Online

Visit the MediaScope mini-site online for tips on how to create a great digital presentation.

go.hrw.com H12-823 Go

Universal Access: Grammar Link

English Learners

English for Academic Success Explain that an independent clause can stand on its own (as a simple sentence), while a subordinate clause cannot—it must be attached to another clause. Point out that subordinate clauses begin with subordinating conjunctions (words like *when, after, before,* and *although*) or relative pronouns (words like *which, that,* and *who*). Have students compose a paragraph on a topic of their choice using at least one compound, one complex, and one compound-complex sentence.

✔ For more practice with sentence structure, see **Warriner's Handbook, GrammarNotes,** and **Language Handbook Worksheets.**

Independent Practice

Grammar Link

Your Turn

1. *compound*
2. *simple*
3. *compound-complex*

Choices: Evaluation Criteria

Review: Homework
Write an Inscription

Inscriptions should be concise (5–10 lines) and addressed to the viewer of the statue.

Connect: Timed Writing 40–50 minutes

Essays should identify at least two similarities and two differences.

Extend: Homework
Documenting the Past and the Future

Presentations should identify the name and location of the ruins pictured in the images.

Assess

Unit 4 Resources, Selection Standards Check, p. 80

ThinkCentral Online Assessment, Selection Standards Check

Teacher One Stop™, editable Selection Standards Check

Reteach

To reteach **irony,** see **Reteaching Lessons,** pp. 1449O–1449P.

ThinkCentral Online Remediation

Learn It Online

For additional support analyzing media, students can go to the **MediaScope** site to analyze other types of media, such as a Web page, a TV news story, a political TV ad, and a print advertisement.

go.hrw.com H12-823 Go

Preteach

Introducing Vocabulary

- Review the Vocabulary words, definitions, and sample sentences with students.
- To reinforce the importance of the Vocabulary words, tell students that Shelley uses them to describe the wind's power. It drives *multitudes* of *withered* leaves through the air and makes the autumn *foliage* tremble. The wind's gusts sweep storm clouds to the *zenith* of the sky, producing a *tumult.*

English for Academic Success

Language Coach

Model for students how to break the example words into their smaller parts. For example, the word *multicolor* can be broken down into its prefix *multi–* and its base word *color.* Using this information, students can figure out that *multicolor* means "many colors." ***Possible responses***: *many cultures, many colors, many sides, many languages, many nations.*

Literary Skills Focus

As you read and discuss Shelley's ode, have students note its rhyme pattern and serious tone.

Writing Skills Focus

Have students note where sentences begin and end in Shelley's poem. Tell them to consider the effect produced by his long sentences, and have them record their reactions in their **Reader/Writer Notebooks**. Students can use their notes for the Writing Skills Focus activity.

Learn It Online

The **Writers' Lives** feature of the Interactive Student Edition offers additional information about this author. Audio or video segments are provided for some authors.

go.hrw.com H12-824 Go

Preparing to Read

Reading Standard 3.1 (see pages A48–A50)

Ode to the West Wind

Literary Skills Focus

Ode The **ode,** a complex, usually long, lyric poem written in dignified language about a serious subject, was a favorite poetic form among the Romantics. In ancient Greece and Rome, odes were written to be read in public on ceremonial occasions. In modern literature, odes tend to be more private, informal, and reflective. Like many Romantic odes, Shelley's "Ode to the West Wind" looks both outward and inward. It pays tribute to an aspect of nature—the powerful yet invisible wind—and connects the movement of the unseen wind with the power of the poet's imagination.

Shelley's ode consists of five sonnets written in a special **rhyme scheme,** or pattern, called **terza rima** (meaning "third rhyme"). This rhyme scheme uses interlocking three-line stanzas that rhyme in the pattern *aba bcb cdc ded.* The stanzas are described as interlocking because each three-line group picks up the rhyme of the second line in the previous group. In the Shakespearean manner, Shelley ends each sonnet with a rhymed **couplet:** *ee.* As you read, consider how this challenging rhyme scheme adds to the ode's elegant tone.

Writing Skills Focus

Think as a Reader/Writer

Find It in Your Reading As you read each stanza, use a chart like the one below to write down your thoughts on how Shelley's varied sentence lengths and structures affect the flow, rhythm, pacing, and meaning.

Stanza	Observations About Sentence Structure	Effect on Flow, Rhythm, Pacing, Meaning
I	one long sentence with multiple phrases and dependent clauses, some with inverted word order; main verb, an imperative, comes at the end and is repeated twice	provides a long, rolling list of the west wind's attributes and actions; varied length of phrases and clauses varies pace, sounds natural, despite lack of full-stop structure; establishes the wind as "destroyer and preserver," contrasted with Spring wind
II		
III		

Reader/Writer Notebook

Use your **RWN** to complete the activities for this selection.

Vocabulary

multitudes (MUHL tuh toodz) *n. pl.:* crowds; great numbers. *Multitudes of readers have experienced the powerful wind that blows through Shelley's ode.*

zenith (ZEE nihth) *n.:* highest point. *The cloud's zenith creates a mystical design against the sky.*

foliage (FOH lihj) *n.:* leafy plants. *Autumn winds strip the fall foliage from trees.*

tumult (TOO muhlt) *n.:* great noise; agitation. *The storms of autumn bring a tumult of thunder.*

withered (WIHTH uhrd) *v.* used as *adj.:* dried up. *As winter approaches, plants become withered and die in the colder winds.*

Language Coach

Word Origins The word *multitudes* comes from the Latin word meaning "many." The prefix *multi–* shares the same origin. Explain how this origin affects the meanings of these words: *multicultural, multicolor, multifaceted, multilingual, multinational.*

Learn It Online

Learn more about Shelley at the Writers' Lives site online.

go.hrw.com H12-824 Go

California Standards, pp. 824–828

- **Reading Standard 3.1** Analyze characteristics of subgenres (e.g., satire, parody, allegory, pastoral) that are used in poetry, prose, plays, novels, short stories, essays, and other basic genres.

ODE

Ode to the West Wind

by Percy Bysshe Shelley

Read with a Purpose
Read to discover the insight the speaker gains from experiencing the wind's power.

Build Background
Written in late October 1819, this major lyric was inspired by an oncoming storm near Florence, Italy, where Shelley was living at the time. The poem marks a temporary note of exaltation in Shelley's creative life after a period of intense grief over the death of his three-year-old son, William. The ode expresses Shelley's sense of purpose as a public poet and contains his personal thoughts about that role. To experience the poem's passionate and musical language, read the ode aloud.

I

O wild West Wind, thou breath of Autumn's being,
Thou, from whose unseen presence the leaves dead
Are driven, like ghosts from an enchanter fleeing,

Yellow, and black, and pale, and hectic° red,
Pestilence-stricken multitudes: O thou,
Who chariotest to their dark wintry bed

The winged seeds, where they lie cold and low,
Each like a corpse within its grave, until
Thine azure° sister of the Spring shall blow

Her clarion° o'er the dreaming earth, and fill
(Driving sweet buds like flocks to feed in air)
With living hues and odors plain and hill:

Wild Spirit, which art moving everywhere;
Destroyer and preserver; hear, O, hear! **A**

II

Thou on whose stream, 'mid the steep sky's commotion,
Loose clouds like earth's decaying leaves are shed,
Shook from the tangled boughs of Heaven and Ocean,

4. hectic: reference to the feverish flush caused by wasting diseases, such as tuberculosis.

9. azure: sky-blue.

10. clarion: type of trumpet.

A Literary Focus Ode The ode traditionally focuses on a significant subject. How do the two final lines of this section make the west wind seem especially important?

Vocabulary **multitudes** (MUHL tuh toodz) *n. pl.:* crowds; great numbers.

Universal Access

EL English Learners
English for Academic Success Be sure students understand that the entire poem is addressed to the west wind. In the early portions of the poem, Shelley uses extremely long sentences. To keep students from getting lost in these sentences, explain that the stanzas pile up images, emphasizing the wind's power. The actual unit of the sentence is less important than these images.

✔ See the **English Language Skill Builder** in **UA: Differentiating Instruction.**

Struggling Readers
Strategic Students Students may have trouble breaking down difficult text in Shelley's ode. Explain that the second stanza describes the wind's effect on clouds. Help students find Shelley's comparisons for the windswept cloud by telling them to look for the word *like*. For instance, in lines 16–17, the clouds are shaken from Heaven "*like* earth's decaying leaves are shed" from tree branches.

✔ See **UA: Differentiating Instruction** for a graphic organizer to scaffold instruction for struggling readers.

Teacher Preparation
Selection Summary
Shelley's "Ode to the West Wind" is an extended apostrophe to the powerful west wind. The speaker characterizes the wind as both "Destroyer and preserver" and ends by asking the wind to share its power with him so that his words might spark new life in the world.

Direct Teach

Think About/Talk About
Read with a Purpose Have students read the Read with a Purpose statement. Ask them to pay attention to the destructive and creative effects of the west wind on the leaves, the clouds, and the sea. Note that Shelley wishes to take on the wind's qualities for his own purposes.

Analysis
A Literary Focus
Possible response: *By calling the wind "Destroyer and preserver," the ode makes the wind seem like a life force or divinity.*

Extend the Discussion
Simile In stanza one, where does the poet use simile? ***Possible response:*** *He compares the leaves to ghosts (line 3), seeds to corpses (line 8), and buds to flocks (line 11).*

Vocabulary: Own the Word
multitudes: Ask students to name a place where they might encounter *multitudes* of people. ***Possible responses:*** *at a concert, at school, at the mall*

Model the Skill

- Remind students that an **ode** is a formal meditation on a serious subject. Tell students that the speaker directly addresses the west wind in an awe-stricken, formal tone throughout the ode.
- Model analyzing the poem for word choice and language that emphasize the power and importance of the west wind. You might say: "I notice that in lines 36–37, the speaker expresses reverence and wonder at how 'the Atlantic's level powers' separate to make way for the wind. In lines 40–41, the 'sapless foliage of the ocean' knows the voice of the wind and grows 'gray with fear,' trembling before it."

Guided Practice: Apply

Three-Minute Review Use Three-Minute Review to enhance active engagement. Have students point out and discuss in pairs other examples that illustrate the speaker's attitude toward the west wind. Have pairs share their findings with the rest of the class.

Build Background: The Origin of Poetry

In his famous essay "A Defense of Poetry," Shelley describes how poetry is inspired by a divine imaginative spirit: "Poetry is not like reasoning," he argues, "a power to be exerted according to the determination of will. A man cannot say, 'I will compose poetry,' . . . for the mind in creation is as a fading coal, which some invisible influence, like an inconstant wind, awakens to transitory brightness." Ask students to keep in mind as they read this poem Shelley's remarks about the "inconstant wind" that stirs the imagination.

Angels of rain and lightning: there are spread
On the blue surface of thine aery° surge,
Like the bright hair uplifted from the head

Of some fierce Maenad,° even from the dim verge
Of the horizon to the zenith's height,
The locks of the approaching storm. Thou dirge°

Of the dying year, to which this closing night
Will be the dome of a vast sepulcher,
Vaulted with all thy congregated might

Of vapors, from whose solid atmosphere
Black rain, and fire, and hail will burst: O, hear!

III

Thou who didst waken from his summer dreams
The blue Mediterranean, where he lay,
Lulled by the coil of his crystalline streams,

Beside a pumice° isle in Baiae's bay,°
And saw in sleep old palaces and towers
Quivering within the wave's intenser day,

All overgrown with azure moss and flowers
So sweet, the sense faints picturing them! Thou
For whose path the Atlantic's level powers

Cleave° themselves into chasms, while far below
The sea-blooms and the oozy woods which wear
The sapless foliage of the ocean, know

Thy voice, and suddenly grow gray with fear,
And tremble and despoil° themselves: O, hear!

IV

If I were a dead leaf thou mightest bear; **B**
If I were a swift cloud to fly with thee;
A wave to pant beneath thy power, and share

19. aery: archaic word meaning "airy"; unsubstantial; seen only in the mind.

21. Maenad (MEE nad): in Greek mythology, a woman who performs frenzied dances in the worship of Dionysus, the god of wine.

23. dirge: slow, solemn poem or song that expresses grief or mourning.

32. pumice: light, porous volcanic stone. **isle in Baiae's bay:** in the Bay of Naples, where pumice is found. These islands were once summer resorts for Roman nobility and, in Shelley's time, were notable for their ruins of ancient villas and monumental baths.

38. cleave: divide.

42. despoil: strip.

B **Literary Focus** **Ode** How do the references to the earlier parts of the poem in lines 43–45 affect your overall understanding of the poem?

Vocabulary **zenith** (ZEE nihth) *n.:* highest point.
foliage (FOH lihj) *n.:* leafy plants.

Universal Access

Advanced Learners

Acceleration Challenge students to write responses to these questions: How does the poem suggest the archetypal cycle of death and rebirth, both in the natural world and in the world of the poet? What do you think Shelley meant when he wrote, "Poets are the unacknowledged legislators of the world" in his essay "A Defense of Poetry"? What value might a poet's creativity have for the rest of the world?

✔ See **UA: Resources for Teaching Advanced Students** for strategies for teaching advanced learners.

Students with Disabilities

Provide students with photographs or other images to help them understand potentially unfamiliar vocabulary words in this poem, such as *commotion* (line 15), *crystalline* (line 31), *lyre* (line 57), and *incantation* (line 65).

The impulse of thy strength, only less free
Than thou, O uncontrollable! If even
I were as in my boyhood, and could be

The comrade of thy wanderings over Heaven,
As then, when to outstrip thy skiey° speed
Scarce seemed a vision; I would ne'er have striven

As thus with thee in prayer in my sore need.
Oh, lift me as a wave, a leaf, a cloud!
I fall upon the thorns of life! I bleed!

A heavy weight of hours has chained and bowed
One too like thee: tameless, and swift, and proud. Ⓒ

V

Make me thy lyre,° even as the forest is:
What if my leaves are falling like its own!
The tumult of thy mighty harmonies

Will take from both a deep, autumnal tone,
Sweet though in sadness. Be thou, Spirit fierce,
My spirit! Be thou me, impetuous° one!

Drive my dead thoughts over the universe
Like withered leaves to quicken a new birth!
And, by the incantation of this verse,

Scatter, as from an unextinguished hearth°
Ashes and sparks, my words among mankind! Ⓓ
Be through my lips to unawakened earth

The trumpet of a prophecy! O, Wind,
If Winter comes, can Spring be far behind?

50. skiey: like the sky; also, coming from the sky.

57. lyre: Aeolian (ee OH lee uhn) harp, a stringed instrument that emits sound when the wind blows across its strings.

62. impetuous: forceful; rushing.

66. unextinguished hearth: from Shelley's "A Defense of Poetry": "The mind in creation is as a fading coal, which some invisible influence, like an inconstant wind, awakens to transitory brightness."

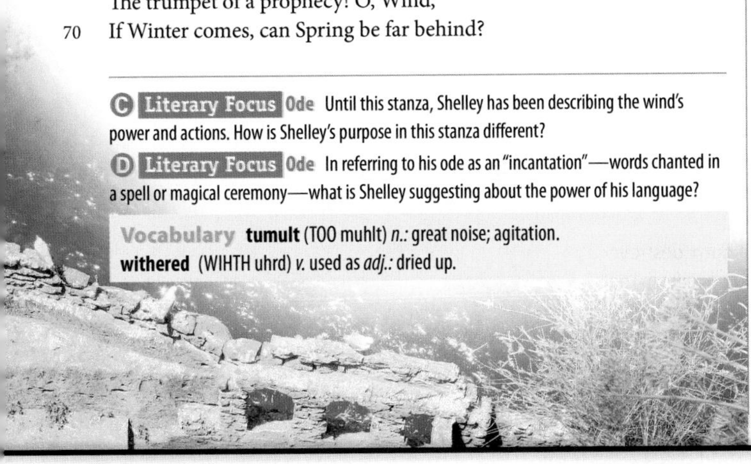

Ⓒ **Literary Focus** **Ode** Until this stanza, Shelley has been describing the wind's power and actions. How is Shelley's purpose in this stanza different?

Ⓓ **Literary Focus** **Ode** In referring to his ode as an "incantation"—words chanted in a spell or magical ceremony—what is Shelley suggesting about the power of his language?

Vocabulary **tumult** (TOO muhlt) *n.:* great noise; agitation.
withered (WIHTH uhrd) *v.* used as *adj.:* dried up.

Think About/Talk About

Analysis

Ⓑ Literary Focus

Possible response: *The references sum up the previous sections before moving on to something new.*

Ⓒ Literary Focus

Possible response: *In stanza three, the speaker shifts from describing the wind to focusing on his helplessness, longing for the wind to lift him.*

Ⓓ Literary Focus

Possible response: *He suggests that, like magic, language has a mysterious power to bring about concrete changes in the physical and social world.*

Extend the Discussion

Finding Details Which details in sections IV and V help convey the speaker's fatigue? ***Possible responses:*** *In section IV, he imagines himself as a "dead leaf," a passive object to be carried by the wind. He describes himself as weak and suffering ("I fall upon the thorns of life! I bleed!"). He expresses nostalgia for his lost "boyhood" and says that the passage of time has burdened him ("A heavy weight of hours has chained and bowed" him). In section V, he compares himself to a tree whose "leaves are falling," and says his thoughts are "dead."*

Vocabulary: Own the Word

- **zenith:** A *zenith* is a high point; the antonym is *nadir.* Use both words in a sentence. The *zenith* of last year was my graduation; the nadir was the loss of an old friend.
- **foliage:** Ask students to complete the following sentence: "The jungle *foliage* made the search difficult because . . ."
- **tumult:** Ask students to list things or events that could cause a *tumult.* [*a tornado, a landslide, a car accident*]
- **withered:** Ask students: "Have you ever seen something that was *withered*? Explain where, when, and how you saw it, and describe its appearance."

California Standards, p. 828

- **Reading Standard 3.1** Analyze characteristics of subgenres (e.g., satire, parody, allegory, pastoral) that are used in poetry, prose, plays, novels, short stories, essays, and other basic genres.
- **Reading Standard 3.4** Analyze ways in which poets use imagery, personification, figures of speech, and sounds to evoke readers' emotions.
- **Writing Standard 1.9** Revise text to highlight the individual voice, improve sentence variety and style, and enhance subtlety of meaning and tone in ways that are consistent with the purpose, audience, and genre.

Check for Understanding

Independent Practice

Reading Skills Focus

Possible responses:

1. *He sees himself as "tameless, swift and proud" (line 56) like the wind, and he longs to have the freedom and power of the wind.*
2. *He is less free and vigorous than he once was.*
3. *He asks the wind to lift him.*
4. *Destruction and decay may be harbingers of renewal and may be necessary for rebirth, just as winter is inevitably followed by springtime.*

Vocabulary Check

5. *zenith*
6. *withered*
7. *tumult*
8. *foliage*
9. *Multitudes*

Literary Skills Focus

Possible responses:

10. *The wind scatters leaves (lines 2–3) but also drops seeds (lines 6–7).*
11. *Instead of describing the wind's powerful effects, the speaker becomes reflective.*
12. *Lines 58–61 express how the forest feels in losing its leaves. As the wind blows through the barren forest, it creates harmonies "sweet though in sadness." Like the forest, the poet expresses knowledge gained from loss.*
13. *A smoldering hearth contains both dead ashes and fiery sparks. A poet's words are both "inert" and "inspiring." Shelley wants his inert words to inspire readers.*
14. *The powerful subject, dignified language, large-scale details, and serious meditation support the definition of the poem as an ode.*
15. *The image of blowing leaves and seeds evokes anxious activity; the shaken clouds evoke a sense of freedom from restraints, and the awakening of the sea creates a feeling of drowsy well-being.*

Applying Your Skills

Reading Standard 3.1, 3.4 (see pages A48–A50)
Writing Standard 1.9 (see pages A51–A52)

Ode to the West Wind

Literary Response and Analysis

Reading Skills Focus

Quick Check

1. Why does the speaker identify so intensely with the wind?
2. What does the speaker regret about his adult years, as compared to his boyhood?
3. What does the speaker request of the wind in Part IV?

Read with a Purpose

4. Review the poem's final sentence. Explain the insight Shelley captures in this famous line.

Vocabulary Check

Complete each sentence with a Vocabulary word.

foliage
multitudes
tumult
withered
zenith

5. At noon, the sun reaches the ____________ of its daily path.
6. She kept the ____________ bouquet as a reminder of the prom.
7. The skiers listened for the ____________ of an avalanche.
8. The dark green ____________ of the ivy stood out against the white walls.
9. ____________ of people stood in line to be first to see the new movie.

Literary Skills Focus

Literary Analysis

10. **Interpret** How can the wind be both "destroyer and preserver" (line 14)? Cite evidence from the text to support your ideas.
11. **Compare and Contrast** How do parts IV and V differ in tone and emphasis from the first three stanzas?
12. **Draw Conclusions** What lines of this ode suggest the grief of a parent who has just lost a child? What comfort does the parent find?
13. **Interpret** How do you explain the paradox, or seeming contradiction, that words are like "ashes and sparks" (line 67)?

Literary Skills: Ode

14. **Analyze** Explain how this poem fits the definition of an ode as a serious, complex meditation.

Literary Skills Review: Imagery

15. **Analyze** Language that appeals to the senses is **imagery.** What central image and emotion is evoked in each of the first three stanzas?

Writing Skills Focus

Think as a Reader/Writer

Use It in Your Writing Select a piece of your own writing, and analyze how its sentence lengths and structures affect its flow, pacing, rhythm, and meaning. Revise your sentences (combine, cut, use repetition and parallel structures) to improve your writing.

What Do You Think Now?

How can we discover truth from encounters with nature?

Universal Access

Struggling Writers

Some students may need additional scaffolding to complete the Writing Skills Focus activity. After students choose a piece of writing, have them use two different color pens or pencils to underline each sentence, alternating colors. Students can then determine the length of each sentence and the patterns of syntax used. Then, have students read their paper aloud to hear the rhythm. This close reading will help students identify awkward sentences that need to be revised.

What Do You Think Now?

Ask students to state what truth the speaker of "Ode to the West Wind" discovers. Have them reflect on personal experiences with nature.

Assess

Unit 4 Resources, Selection Standards Check, p. 81

Reading Standard 2.4; **Grades 9–10 Review Reading Standard** 3.7 (see pages A48–A50)

To a Skylark

Literary Skills Focus

Symbol A **symbol** is a person, place, thing, or event that stands both for itself and for something beyond itself. A symbol can operate on multiple levels. For example, in "To a Skylark," a speaker praises a bird for its beautiful song. At the same time, the skylark has another level of meaning for the speaker. Can you determine what the skylark symbolizes?

Reading Skills Focus

Drawing Inferences Readers **draw inferences** both from information stated directly and from hints or clues in the text. When you make intelligent guesses about a text based on the evidence or clues the writer has provided, you are drawing inferences. Inferences combine your own knowledge and experience with the information found in the text.

Into Action As you read, use a graphic organizer like the one below to record the evidence you use to draw inferences about the symbols Shelley uses in the poem.

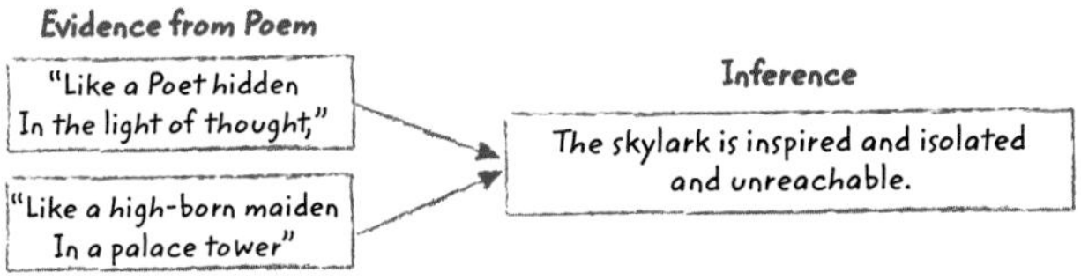

Writing Skills Focus

Think as a Reader/Writer

Find It in Your Reading As you read, take notes in your *Reader/Writer Notebook* on how Shelley uses figurative language to describe the skylark and evoke its **symbolism.** In the first line, for example, the speaker calls the skylark a "blithe Spirit," asserting it as a symbol, not as a bird.

Vocabulary

blithe (blyth) *adj.:* happy and cheerful. *The bird's blithe song cheered us.*

profuse (pruh FYOOS) *adj.:* very abundant. *The skylark's profuse melodies last throughout the evening.*

unpremeditated (uhn pree MEHD uh tay tihd) *adj.:* not planned in advance. *The listener admires the spontaneity of the bird's unpremeditated songs.*

languor (LANG guhr) *n.:* lack of interest or enthusiasm. *The man's languor disappeared when he heard the invigorating song.*

satiety (suh TY uh tee) *n.:* feeling of disgust or weariness caused by excess. *Love's excessive highs and lows may lead to satiety.*

Language Coach

Multiple Prefixes The adjective *unpremeditated* contains two prefixes: *un–*, which means "not," and *pre–*, which means "in advance." Both prefixes affect the meaning of the base word *meditated*, which means "planned." An *unpremeditated* action is one that is not planned in advance. Explain the meanings of these words with double prefixes: *unprepared, unreconstructed, nondisclosure.*

Learn It Online
Explore Shelley's work and his world further through these Internet links.
go.hrw.com H12-829 Go

Reader/Writer Notebook
Use your **RWN** to complete the activities for this selection.

California Standards, pp. 829–835

- **Reading Standard 2.4** Make warranted and reasonable assertions about the author's arguments by using elements of the text to defend and clarify interpretations.
- **Grades 9–10 Review Reading Standard 3.7** Recognize and understand the significance of various literary devices, including figurative language, imagery, allegory, and symbolism, and explain their appeal.

Preteach

Introducing Vocabulary

- Read the Vocabulary words, definitions, and sample sentences aloud.
- To reinforce the importance of the Vocabulary words, tell students that these words support the meanings the skylark holds for the speaker. The *blithe* bird pours forth *profuse* melodies of joyfulness, not *languor*.

English for Academic Success

Language Coach

Provide students with examples of words that use both prefixes *un–* and *pre–*. [*unprecedented, unpredictable*] Then, have them explain the meaning of each example.

Literary Skills Focus

As you read and discuss the selection with students, have them note the things to which Shelley compares the skylark. Have students consider what the skylark might symbolize in light of the comparisons.

Reading Skills Focus

Give students a copy of the Reading Skills Focus graphic organizer before they read. (See **Unit 4 Resources**.) Tell them to use their responses to answer the questions on the Applying Your Skills page.

Writing Skills Focus

Have students record details that evoke symbolism in their **Reader/Writer Notebooks**. Students can use their notes to complete the Writing Skills Focus activity.

Learn It Online
Literature Links directs students to prescreened Web sites offering more information related to a selection.
go.hrw.com H12–829 Go

Teacher Preparation

Selection Summary

In "To a Skylark," an extended apostrophe, the speaker addresses a skylark. The speaker first emphasizes the otherworldly quality of the bird and its song. He then compares the bird to an unknown poet, a lovelorn maiden, a glowworm, and a rosebud. The speaker next inquires about the source of the bird's joy and asks the skylark to teach him "half the gladness" so he can captivate readers with his poems in the same way the skylark captivates him with its song.

Direct Teach

Think About/Talk About

Read with a Purpose Have students read the Read with a Purpose statement. Point out that students should think about the goals of Romantic poets in general to understand what the speaker wants to learn from the skylark.

Comprehension

B Reading Focus

Possible response: *The speaker admires the skylark's ability to spontaneously create beautiful art and wishes that he could do the same.*

Analysis

A Literary Focus

Possible response: *The speaker is implying that the skylark is too beautiful to simply be a bird.*

ODE

To a Skylark

by **Percy Bysshe Shelley**

Read with a Purpose

Read to discover what the speaker wants to learn from the skylark.

Build Background

Shelley wrote "To a Skylark" in 1820 when he and his wife, Mary, were staying with friends near the Mediterranean coast of Italy. While on a walk, they heard the high-pitched musical song of the European skylark in flight. Mary later recalled, "It was on a beautiful summer evening, while wandering among the lanes whose myrtle hedges were the bowers of fireflies, that we heard the caroling of the skylark which inspired one of the most beautiful of his poems."

In this poem the speaker yearns to share in the skylark's joy and natural musicality.

Hail to thee, blithe Spirit!
  Bird thou never wert,
That from Heaven, or near it,
  Pourest thy full heart **A**
In profuse strains of unpremeditated art. **B**

Higher still and higher
  From the earth thou springest
Like a cloud of fire;
  The blue deep thou wingest,
And singing still dost soar, and soaring ever singest.

In the golden lightning
  Of the sunken sun,
O'er which clouds are bright'ning,
  Thou dost float and run;
Like an unbodied joy whose race is just begun.

A Literary Focus **Symbol** In these first few lines, why does the speaker say the skylark never was a bird?

B Reading Focus **Drawing Inferences** What does the speaker admire about the skylark? What does the speaker wish in regard to his own art?

Vocabulary **blithe** (blyth) *adj.:* happy and cheerful.
profuse (pruh FYOOS) *adj.:* very abundant.
unpremeditated (uhn pree MEHD uh tay tihd) *adj.:* not planned in advance.

Universal Access

EL English Learners

Because the joyful music of the skylark and of poetry itself is the theme of this work, help students realize that they can appreciate the message of the poem without having to understand every word. Before asking students to read the poem themselves, read it aloud or play a recording of it. Ask students to listen to its musical qualities—its cadence, rhythm, and rhymes.

✔ See the **English Language Skill Builder** in **UA: Differentiating Instruction.**

Struggling Readers

Benchmark Students Point out to students that Shelley uses several similes in the poem to assert that the bird is a symbol for something. Direct students' attention to lines 14–20. Tell students that in these lines Shelley uses a simile to compare the skylark to joyful emotions and a star. These comparisons reveal that the skylark is unexplainable and untouchable, but beautiful and joyful, too. As students read, have them note the similes that Shelley uses and analyze how they help establish the skylark as a symbol for a bigger idea.

The pale purple even°
  Melts around thy flight;
Like a star of Heaven,
  In the broad daylight
Thou art unseen, but yet I hear thy shrill delight,

Keen as are the arrows
  Of that silver sphere,°
Whose intense lamp narrows
  In the white dawn clear
Until we hardly see—we feel that it is there.

All the earth and air
  With thy voice is loud,
As, when night is bare,
  From one lonely cloud
The moon rains out her beams, and Heaven is overflowed.

What thou art we know not;
  What is most like thee?
From rainbow clouds there flow not
  Drops so bright to see
As from thy presence showers a rain of melody.

Like a Poet hidden
  In the light of thought,
Singing hymns unbidden,
  Till the world is wrought
To sympathy with hopes and fears it heeded not:

Like a high-born maiden
  In a palace-tower,
Soothing her love-laden
  Soul in secret hour
With music sweet as love, which overflows her bower:°

16. even: evening.

22. silver sphere: "a star of Heaven" (line 18).

45. bower: archaic word for a woman's bedroom.

Think About/Talk About

Extend the Discussion

Finding Details What does the speaker compare the skylark's music to in line 45? ***Possible response:*** *He compares it to a sweet, abundant love, which fills up a woman's bedroom to overflowing.*

Interpreting What is the speaker suggesting about himself as a poet? ***Possible response:*** *He is hinting that he feels ignored and unappreciated but hopes that someday the world will recognize him.*

Similes What does Shelley compare the skylark to in lines 14–20? What do these comparisons reveal about the bird? ***Possible responses:*** *Shelley compares the skylark to joyful emotions and a star. The skylark is cryptic and untouchable, but still beautiful and joyful.*

Vocabulary: Own the Word

- **blithe:** Ask students to applaud in order to indicate how much they would like to be described as *blithe* and why. ***Possible response:*** *Students applaud loudly because they want to be thought of as happy and cheerful.*
- **profuse:** Tell students that the root word for *profuse* is *prôfūsus* and means "to spread out." When something is *profuse,* it is ample and abundant. Ask students how a bird's song can be *profuse.*
- **unpremeditated:** Tell students that *unpremeditated* is a good example of the way prefixes change the meaning of a word. The base word *meditate* means "to think or plan." Add the prefix *pre–* and the word means "to plan ahead of time." Add *un–,* which means "not" and you have an adjective that means "not planned in advance." What is an example of an *unpremeditated* action? ***Possible response:*** *spontaneous applause or laughter*

Advanced Learners

Acceleration Challenge students to compare "To a Skylark" to others of Shelley's better-known works, such as "Ode to the West Wind" and "Ozymandias." Students should recognize that all three poems deal with the artist's sources of inspiration and the artist's role in society. Ask students to make inferences, based on their readings, about Shelley's ideas on inspiration.

Students with Disabilities

After students read the selection, help them paraphrase the parts that they found most difficult. Then, you can stimulate their appreciation of the poem by adopting the Save the Last Word for Me strategy. Provide students with an index card, and have them transcribe their favorite lines from the poem. On the back of the index card, have students write a sentence in which they explain their choice.

go.hrw.com *For more information about the Save the Last Word for Me strategy, see this page in* ***ThinkCentral, Teacher Access.***

Model the Skill

- Provide students with copies of the Reading Skills Focus graphic organizer for "To a Skylark." (See **Unit 4 Resources.**)
- Tell students that when **making an inference,** readers need to apply their own experience and general knowledge to the information from the selection.
- Model making inferences about the symbols the poet uses. Direct students to read lines 46–55: "The poem tells us the bird is like a glowworm and a rose. After filling in the boxes with these details, I might infer that the skylark's beauty is hidden from view."

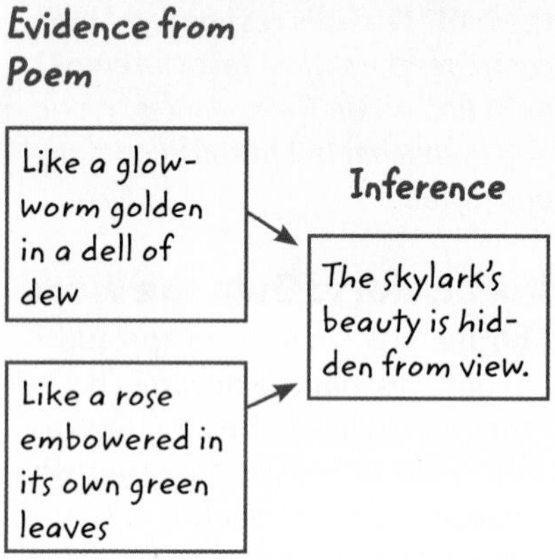

Guided Practice: Apply

Think-Pair-Share Group students into pairs to look over lines 61–70 and identify what the skylark symbolizes. Ask volunteers to share their discussions with the whole class.

Think as a Reader/Writer

Find It In Your Reading Point out that in lines 66–70, Shelley compares the skylark to a wedding song.

Use It in Your Writing Ask students to reword this comparison so that it refers to a contemporary celebration of a music genre.

Like a glow-worm golden
  In a dell° of dew,
Scattering unbeholden
  Its aereal hue
Among the flowers and grass, which screen it from the view!

Like a rose embowered°
  In its own green leaves,
By warm winds deflowered,
  Till the scent it gives
Makes faint with too much sweet those heavy-wingèd thieves:

Sound of vernal° showers
  On the twinkling grass,
Rain-awakened flowers,
  All that ever was
Joyous, and clear, and fresh, thy music doth surpass:

Teach us, Sprite° or Bird,
  What sweet thoughts are thine:
I have never heard
  Praise of love or wine
That panted forth a flood of rapture so divine.

Chorus Hymeneal,°
  Or triumphal chant,
Matched with thine would be all
  But an empty vaunt,°
A thing wherein we feel there is some hidden want.

What objects are the fountains
  Of thy happy strain?°
What fields, or waves, or mountains?
  What shapes of sky or plain?
What love of thine own kind? what ignorance of pain?

With thy clear keen joyance°
  Languor cannot be:
Shadow of annoyance
  Never came near thee:
Thou lovest—but ne'er knew love's sad satiety. **C**

47. dell: small valley.

51. embowered: enclosed in foliage.

56. vernal: occurring in the spring.

61. Sprite: spirit.

66. chorus Hymeneal: wedding song. *Hymeneal* is derived from Hymen, the Greek god of marriage.

69. vaunt: boast.

72. strain: melody.

76. joyance: rejoicing.

C Literary Focus Symbol What clues in this stanza point to the skylark's symbolism?

Vocabulary **languor** (LANG guhr) *n.:* lack of interest or enthusiasm.
satiety (suh TY uh tee) *n.:* feeling of disgust or weariness caused by excess.

Reaching Reluctant Readers

Tell students that the skylark's singing inspired Shelley's creative expression and response through poetry. Ask students to choose a feature of any kind of animal that they greatly admire and wish to imitate in some way. Tell them that their answers would depend on what they consider as praiseworthy, such as what talents or qualities they admire. For example, a runner might be inspired by the elegance of a cheetah's movements as it pursues its prey. Have students use a thesaurus or dictionary to brainstorm adjectives and phrases that describe the aspect or feature. Ask a few volunteers to share their descriptive phrases with the class.

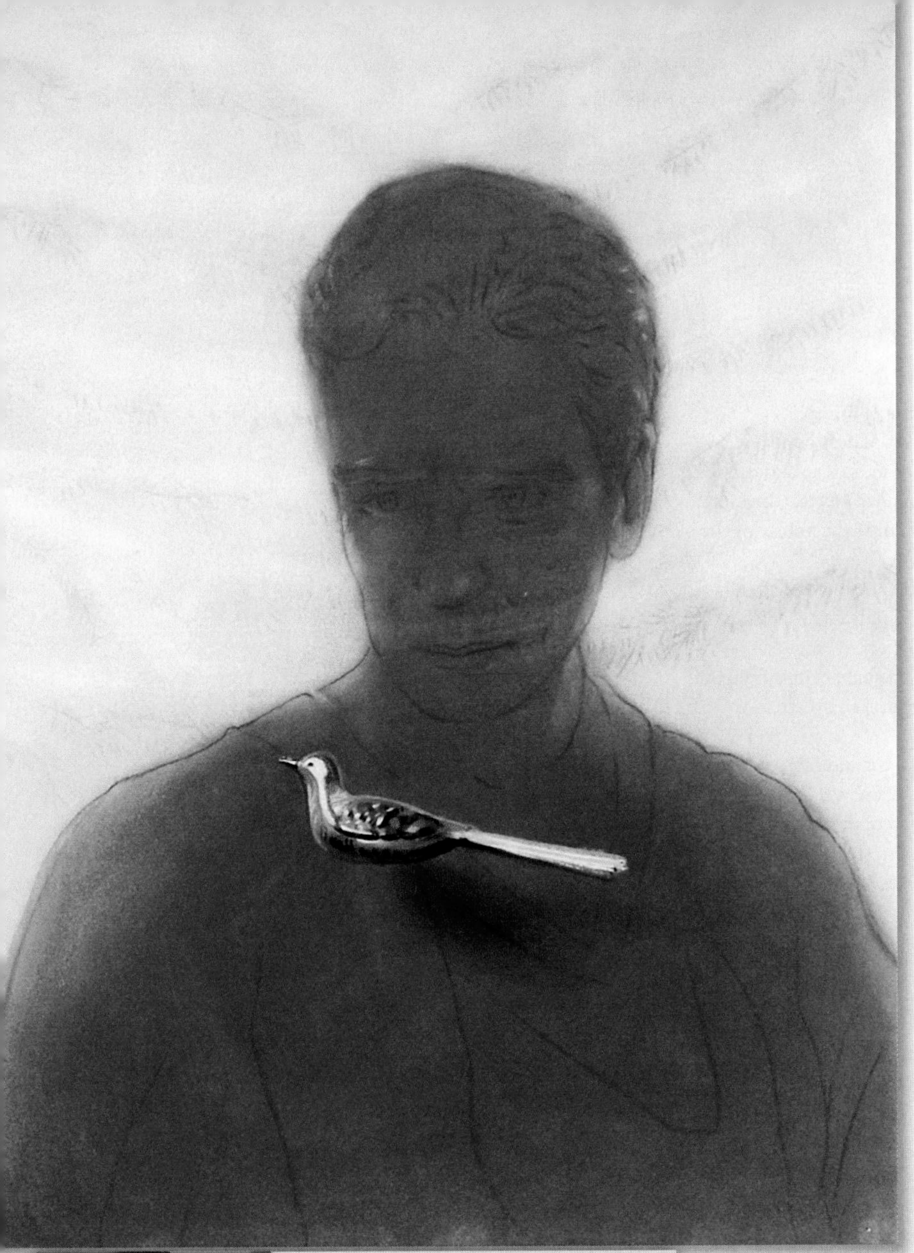

Analyzing Visuals

Connecting to the Text Study the illustration. To what areas are your eyes drawn? Why? How do the colors affect the mood? What effect do the image's realistic and unrealistic qualities have? How might the image connect with the ode's tone and symbolism?

Prospero's Magic Bird (2004) by David Saunders. Pastel on paper. Courtesy of the Fischbach Gallery, NY.

Think About/Talk About

See Student Edition p. 832 for the question that relates to the following answer.

Analysis

C Literary Focus

Possible response: *The poet marvels at the bird's "joyance" and absence of any "annoyance." The bird may represent joy and purity.*

Extend the Discussion

Paraphrasing Restate line 80 in your own words. ***Possible response:*** *You love joyfully and deeply, without experiencing its weariness and pain.*

Interpreting Why does the speaker want to learn the skylark's "sweet thoughts"? ***Possible responses:*** *He wants to experience the same joy as the skylark; he wants to be inspired to produce beautiful poems as the skylark is inspired to produce beautiful songs.*

Vocabulary: Own the Word

- **languor:** Demonstrate a person's posture and expression who expresses *languor* toward an activity. Ask one or two students to stand at their desks and demonstrate.
- **satiety:** Tell students that *satiated* is the adjective form of *satiety.* A person might become *satiated* after a large meal such as a Thanksgiving feast. (Show a picture of a turkey dinner.)

Developing Oral Fluency

Whole-Class Activity The short lines and short stanzas of the poem make it a good choice for reading aloud in class. Divide the class into three groups, and assign seven stanzas to each group. Groups might do a choral reading or a combination of choral and individual readings. Encourage students to emphasize the most vivid images by changing their pitch, pace, or volume. Remind students to pay attention to line breaks without inserting overly long pauses.

✔ See **UA: Differentiating Instruction** for practice passages for developing oral fluency.

Analyzing Visuals

Connecting to the Text: *The eyes of the viewer are drawn to the little bird and to the face of the man. The man is colored in blue, which suggest a melancholy mood. The man is only sketched, while the bird appears realistic and colorful. The sad and somber look cast by the man to the bird recalls Shelley's desire to enjoy the same happiness and creativity of the skylark.*

Think About/Talk About

Comprehension

D Reading Focus

Possible response: *The speaker might mean that his poetry would be beautiful and mysterious, just like the skylark's song.*

Extend the Discussion

Making Inferences How has the world come to listen, as the speaker desired? ***Possible response:*** *People are reading this poem, which reflects some of the pure and beautiful qualities of the skylark's song.*

Recognizing Philosophical Assumptions What is the speaker's philosophy on happiness? ***Possible response:*** *The speaker believes that people cannot know any joy without knowing sadness and suffering.*

Waking or asleep,
   Thou of death must deem
Things more true and deep
   Than we mortals dream,
Or how could thy notes flow in such a crystal stream?

We look before and after,
   And pine for what is not:
Our sincerest laughter
   With some pain is fraught;
Our sweetest songs are those that tell of saddest thought.

Yet if we could scorn
   Hate, and pride, and fear;
If we were things born
   Not to shed a tear,
I know not how thy joy we ever should come near.

Better than all measures
   Of delightful sound,
Better than all treasures
   That in books are found,
Thy skill to poet were, thou scorner of the ground!

Teach me half the gladness
      That thy brain must know,
Such harmonious madness
      From my lips would flow
The world should listen then—as I am listening now. **D**

D Reading Focus **Drawing inferences** What do you think the speaker means by "harmonious madness?

California Standards, p. 835

- **Reading Standard 2.4** Make warranted and reasonable assertions about the author's arguments by using elements of the text to defend and clarify interpretations.
- **Reading Standard 3.4** Analyze ways in which poets use imagery, personification, figures of speech, and sounds to evoke readers' emotions.
- **Grades 9–10 Review Reading Standard 3.7** Recognize and understand the significance of various literary devices, including figurative language, imagery, allegory, and symbolism, and explain their appeal.
- **Writing Standard 2.3** Write reflective compositions: **a.** Explore the significance of personal experiences, events, conditions, or concerns by using rhetorical strategies (e.g., narration, description, exposition, persuasion).

Applying Your Skills

Reading Standard 2.4, 3.4; **Grades 9–10 Review** Reading Standard 3.7 (see pages A48–A50)
Writing Standard 2.3a (see pages A51–A52)

To a Skylark

Literary Response and Analysis

Reading Skills Focus

Quick Check

1. What qualities does the speaker admire in the skylark?

Read with a Purpose

2. Who or what does the speaker think will be most affected by the skylark's lessons?

Reading Skills: Drawing Inferences

3. Use the inferences you drew from your reading to determine what the skylark symbolizes.

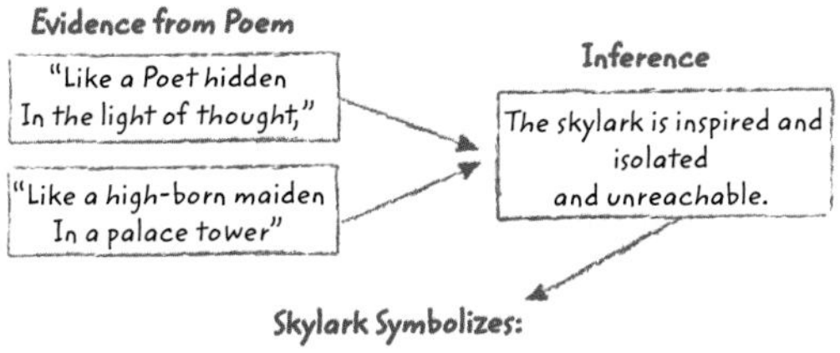

Vocabulary Check

Choose the synonym for each Vocabulary word.

4. blithe	**a.** abundant
5. languor	**b.** unplanned
6. profuse	**c.** cheerful
7. satiety	**d.** disinterest
8. unpremeditated	**e.** excess

Literary Skills Focus

Literary Analysis

9. **Interpret** Interpret these phrases: "unbodied joy" (line 15), "ignorance of pain" (line 75), and "scorner of the ground" (line 100).

10. **Analyze** A rhetorical question is asked for effect and not to elicit an answer. In lines 71–75, why does Shelley use rhetorical questions?

11. **Infer** What does "To a Skylark" reveal about the speaker's view of the life of an artist?

12. **Extend** Lines 86–90 are among the most frequently quoted in English poetry. Do the ideas expressed in these lines correspond with your own experiences? If so, explain how.

Literary Skills: Symbol

13. **Analyze** In what ways is the skylark an appropriate symbol for a Romantic poet to use?

Literary Skills Review: Simile

14. **Analyze** A **simile** is a figure of speech that compares two seemingly unlike things by using connective words such as *like, than,* or *as.* What do the similes in lines 36–55 compare, and what do they show about the skylark and the speaker?

Writing Skills Focus

Think as a Reader/Writer

Use It in Your Writing In a paragraph, use figurative language to describe a person, place, thing, or event that has had symbolic importance in your life.

What Do You Think Now? How can nature's smallest wonders inspire the imagination?

For **CHOICES** see page 841.

Universal Access

Struggling Writers

Some students may need additional scaffolding to complete the Writing Skills Focus activity. Remind students that a simile is a direct comparison of unlike things that uses the word *like* or *as,* and a metaphor is a direct comparison that does not use the word *like* or *as.* Write the following sentence frames on the board:
_______ is like _______; _______ is as _______ as _______; and _______ is _______. Encourage students to fill in the blanks to create similes and metaphors to use in their paragraphs.

Assess

Unit 4 Resources, Selection Standards Check, p. 87

ThinkCentral Online Assessment, Selection Standards Check

Teacher One Stop™, editable Selection Standards Check

Check for Understanding

Independent Practice

Reading Skills Focus

Possible responses:

1. *The speaker admires the way that the skylark can enjoy itself and inspire joy in the listener.*
2. *Poets would be most affected by the skylark's lessons.*
3. *Ask students to consider all the inferences they wrote and to think about what concept or condition would sum up their inferences.*

Vocabulary Check

4. *c* 5. *d*
6. *a* 7. *e*
8. *b*

Literary Skills Focus

Possible responses:

9. *The phrases reinforce the idea that the skylark is idealized, free, and untouched by the world.*
10. *He wants to indicate that the speaker is grasping for answers to his question of what inspires the skylark's joy.*
11. *The life of an artist is one of intense feeling flowing naturally into the creation of beautiful art.*
12. *Yes, because even wonderful experiences never last. No, because sorrow does not taint every happy experience we have.*
13. *The skylark's swift flight and sweet voice are a perfect representation of purity, joy, and beauty.*
14. *The speaker compares the skylark to an unappreciated poet, a maiden in a tower, an unseen glowworm, and a rose. The similes show that the speaker feels neglected and hopes to win attention through beautiful songs.*

What Do You Think Now?

Remind students about the symbolic meaning of the skylark in the poem. Then, ask them to think about an everyday object or place that they think can evoke vivid comparisons.

Standards Focus

Objectives

Students will
- understand diction
- analyze tone

Selection Introduction

Think About the Writer

Before students answer the question, have them review the characteristics of Romantic poetry.

For Independent Reading

- *Selected Poems of Pablo Neruda,* Pablo Neruda
- *Silent Spring,* Rachel Carson

Motivate

What Do You Think?/QuickTalk

Discuss the subtle and not-so-subtle differences in the meaning of a word in the English language and its meaning in another language. Have students write their responses in their **Reader/Writer Notebooks.**

English for Academic Success

Academic Vocabulary

Look for opportunities to use the Academic Vocabulary words in this unit.

- **device, *n.*:** something made for a particular purpose
- **function, *n.*:** the action for which a person or thing is specially fitted
- **technique, *n:*** method

California Standards, pp. 836–841

- **Reading Standard 3.3** Analyze the ways in which irony, tone, mood, the author's style, and the "sound" of language achieve specific rhetorical or aesthetic purposes or both.

Preparing to Read

To a Mosquito

What Do You Think? How can we use imagination to discover truth?

QuickTalk

Merwin's writing includes many volumes of translated works, including texts in Greek, Spanish, Sanskrit, Chinese, and Japanese. In your *Reader/Writer Notebook,* write a paragraph about how knowledge of other languages might help to stimulate someone's imagination.

Portrait of writer W. S. Merwin

MEET THE WRITER

W. S. Merwin

(1927–   )

Link to Today American poet Merwin is deeply concerned that humans are becoming alienated from their environment. Over five decades, Merwin's spare, deceptively simple poetry has urged readers to reconnect with the world.

Man of Many Travels

Pulitzer Prize WINNER

William Stanley Merwin was born in New York City in 1927. He grew up in New Jersey and Pennsylvania. The son of a Presbyterian minister, Merwin wrote hymns during his childhood. As a young man, he attended Princeton University, where he studied writing and Romance languages. After graduation he traveled to France, England, and Spain, earning his living first as a tutor and then as a translator of Latin, Spanish, and French poetry.

Poet and Translator

Merwin's first book of poetry, *A Mask for Janus* (1952), was selected by poet W. H. Auden for the Yale Series of Younger Poets Award. Merwin continued to travel, living in Boston, London, and New York, and then settling in Hawaii in 1976.

A prolific writer, Merwin has published over fifteen books of poetry and almost twenty books of translations, in addition to plays and prose works. His translations include *Sir Gawain and the Green Knight* and Dante's *Purgatorio.* Merwin has also been honored with numerous prizes. *The Carrier of Ladders,* published in 1970, was awarded the Pulitzer Prize for Poetry. Most recently, his *Migration: Selected Poems 1951–2001,* was awarded the National Book Award for Poetry and was selected as one of *The New York Times* 100 Notable Books of the Year.

Although his early poetry was somewhat formal, his writing has evolved into a style that is more personal and freer in form. Merwin has used his poetry to explore the natural world, one of his greatest passions. Today, he continues to write and works to promote the preservation of the environment.

Think About the Writer What qualities does Merwin share with the Romantic poets?

Selection Readability	
Easily Accessible Accessible Challenging	familiar language; accessible vocabulary; short stanzas

Selection Summary

In this six-stanza, free verse ode, the speaker explores the relationship between a common mosquito and a human. The first, second, and fourth stanzas describe the insect's sound and appearance. The third, fifth, and sixth stanzas describe its connection to the speaker and to all human beings. By the end of the poem, the insect is highly personified.

Reading Standard 3.3 (see pages A48–A50)

Literary Skills Focus

Diction A writer's choice of words is called **diction.** A writer might describe a character as "clever" instead of "smart," or "bewitching" instead of "attractive." Writers use different types of words depending on the audience they are addressing, the subject they are discussing, and the effect they are trying to produce. As you read "To a Mosquito," consider why Merwin chooses certain words and not others.

Reading Skills Focus

Analyzing Tone A writer's attitude toward the subject or audience is called **tone.** Romantic odes usually have a serious tone. In contrast, Merwin's light tone in "To a Mosquito" takes liberties with the traditional ode.

Into Action Read the poem aloud, and listen to its words and rhythms. In the first column of a chart like the one below, record the **diction,** or word choice, that strikes you as important. In the second column, explain how each word or phrase contributes to the poem's tone.

Diction	Tone
"me me me . . . me . . . be"	simple rhymes, like rhymes in a children's book, light in tone
"and rash though it may be"	rhythm sounds like a nursery rhyme, light in tone

Writing Skills Focus

Think as a Reader/Writer

Find It in Your Reading Record words and phrases that the author uses to describe the mosquito. For example, in line 6, the speaker says that the mosquito "[sings] out," rather than "buzzes." Use your *Reader/Writer Notebook* to record interesting descriptions of the mosquito.

TechFocus This poem is written in a casual style—without capitalization or punctuation. As you read, think about the style and tone the mosquito might use if it replied in a poem of its own.

Language Coach

Multiple-Meaning Words Writers can play with words that have more than one meaning. Merwin uses the phrase "rash though it may be" to describe a mosquito's singing out loud. In this phrase, *rash* means "hasty or impetuous." However, in his poem dedicated to a mosquito, Merwin is also clearly playing with the second meaning of *rash*: "an itchy outbreak on the skin." In a single word, the poet captures a surprising range of meaning. With a partner, discuss the various meanings of the word *blood* in this poem.

Reader/Writer Notebook

Use your **RWN** to complete the activities for this selection.

Learn It Online

Listen to this poem online.

go.hrw.com H12-837 Go

Selection Resources

Unit 4 Resources, on-level practice and assessment, p. 95

Teacher One Stop™, on-level lesson plans and all print resources

Holt Audio Library

Holt Audio Library: Selections and Summaries in Spanish

UA: Differentiating Instruction, graphic organizer, p. 188

UA: Supporting Instruction in Spanish, selection summary

ThinkCentral Online Assessment, Selection Standards Check

ThinkCentral Online Remediation

Preteach

English for Academic Success

Language Coach

Before they read the selection, have students brainstorm different meanings of the word *blood.* [*red vital fluid, heritage, temperament*]

Literary Skills Focus

As you read and discuss the selection, have students consider why Merwin chooses certain words and not others.

Reading Skills Focus

Give students a copy of the Reading Skills Focus graphic organizer before they read. (See **Unit 4 Resources.**) Tell them to use their responses to answer the questions on the Applying Your Skills page.

Writing Skills Focus

Have students record interesting words and phrases describing the mosquito in their **Reader/Writer Notebooks.** Students can use their notes to complete the Writing Skills Focus activity.

Learn It Online

The online version of this selection includes audio support to engage all students and to help struggling readers with reading comprehension and vocabulary.

go.hrw.com H12-837 Go

Link to Today

Like Shelley's "To a Skylark," Merwin's "To a Mosquito" uses apostrophe to imagine a direct dialogue with a nonhuman creature.

Direct Teach

Think About/Talk About

Read with a Purpose Have students read the Read with a Purpose statement. Have students focus on the words *you* and *me* as they read to help them discern the relationship between the speaker and the mosquito.

Comprehension

A Reading Focus

Possible response: *The narrator is speaking in the voice of the mosquito when he says these words. Before this statement he has repeated "me" many times. This repetition and rhyming with the word "be" on line 5 gives the phrase a childlike and light tone rather than a gloomy one.*

Analysis

B Literary Focus

Possible response: *The words* wings, fine, light, glinting, water, *and* death *convey a serious, lyric tone characteristic of Romantic poetry.*

ODE

Link to Today

This Link to Today gives new life to an old poetic form.

Read with a Purpose

Read to discover what relationship exists between the speaker and the mosquito.

Build Background

In Shelley's "To a Skylark," the speaker seeks to learn the mystery of the skylark's joyful song. In the following poem, contemporary poet W. S. Merwin ponders a different mystery: the intimate connection that exists between the human and the mosquito. Both poems employ **apostrophe,** a figure of speech in which the writer directly addresses an absent or dead person, an abstract quality, or something nonhuman as if it were present and capable of responding.

Colored scanning electron micrograph (SEM) of the head of a female yellow fever mosquito, *Aedes aegypti*.

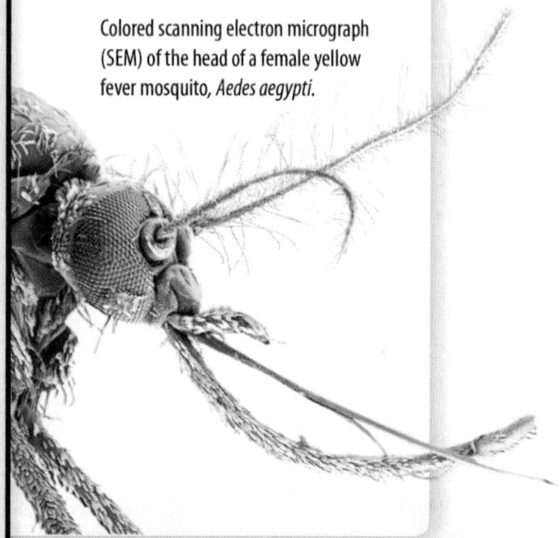

TO A MOSQUITO

by **W. S. Merwin**

Listen to you
me me me
nothing but *me*
even without a voice
and rash though it may be

to sing out anyway
here I am this is me
out for your blood **A**

do you mean to tell me
we are some kind of kin
blood relatives
your many offspring
something to me
by blood presumably
but with the gift of flight

on wings as fine
as light glinting across water
and with the deaths they carry **B**

you need not tell me
that you are here
because of me
you follow me everywhere
by my breath you find me

A Reading Focus **Analyzing Tone** What prevents the phrase "out for your blood" from making the poem's tone gloomy?

B Literary Focus **Diction** Which words in this three-line stanza give the poem a brief Romantic tone, and why?

Universal Access

Struggling Readers

To help students analyze tone, read aloud the fourth stanza. You might say: "In these lines, the speaker says the mosquito does not need to announce its presence because it is always around. While the speaker finds the insect's constant pestering annoying, the speaker does not seem angry at the insect. He repeats the words "you" and "me" to keep the tone from becoming belligerent. The childlike rhythm and the short lines also help create a light tone. The speaker tolerates the mosquito, much like an adult might tolerate a nagging child."

Advanced Learners

Acceleration Divide students into small groups. Assign one stanza to each group, and ask them to change the diction of the lines so that the language becomes formal and elegant. Tell students to use archaic words like *thou, thy, thee,* and *thine*. When students have finished, have them read their rewritten stanzas to the class. Ask students how the overall effect of the poem changed with different diction.

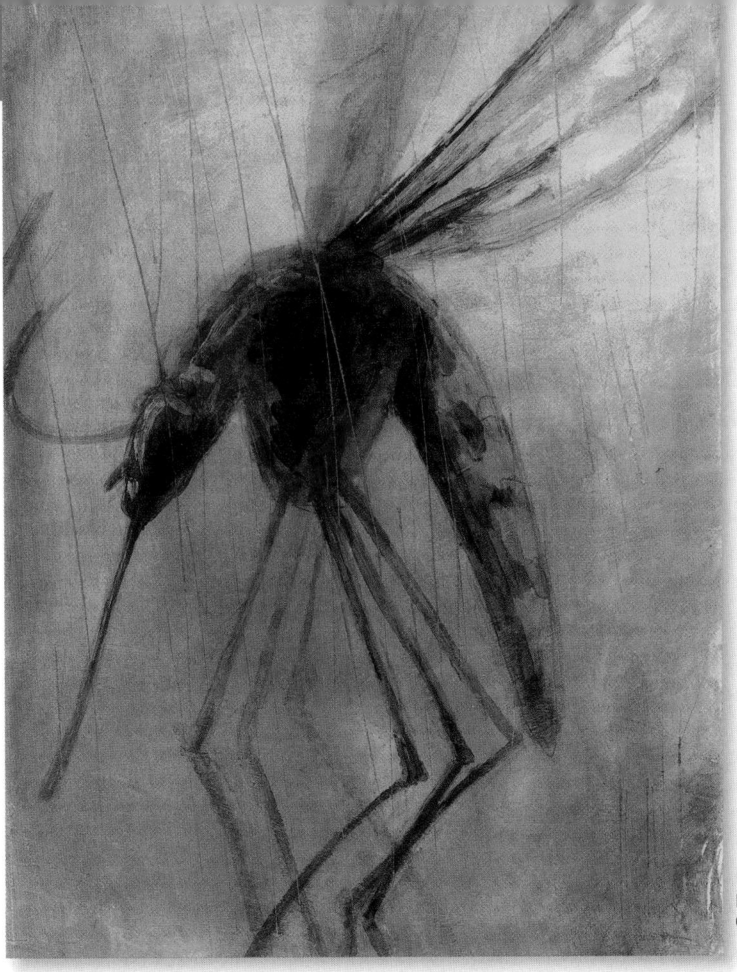

West Nile Delivery System (2007) by Jeff Faerber. Acrylic and varnish on board. Courtesy of the artist.

by the life of my body **C**
you hunger to be close to me
whatever I am doing

though we do not take
each other personally
you recognize me
I make the world right for you
it is as though you
believe I owe you something

C **Reading Focus** **Analyzing Tone** How many words can you find that echo the opening sounds of *me* and *be?* How do these words contribute to the poet's tone?

Think About/Talk About

Comprehension

C Reading Focus

Possible responses: *Other words that rhyme with* me *and* be *are* presumably, carry, body, *and* personally. *These words contribute to the light tone by continuing the overall rhyme with the sounds of* me *and* be.

Extend the Discussion

Paraphrasing Ask students to write in their own words what the following lines mean: *You need not tell me / that you are here / because of me / you follow me everywhere.* ***Possible response:*** *I know that you are always near me. You follow me everywhere because you need me.*

Interpreting In line 30 of the poem the narrator states: *I make the world right for you. . . .* What does this mean? ***Possible response:*** *He means that the human provides his blood to the mosquito and allows the mosquito to continue living and taking blood from more humans.*

California Standards, pp. 840–841

- **Reading Standard 3.3** Analyze the ways in which irony, tone, mood, the author's style, and the "sound" of language achieve specific rhetorical or aesthetic purposes or both.
- **Reading Standard 3.4** Analyze ways in which poets use imagery, personification, figures of speech, and sounds to evoke readers' emotions.
- **Writing Standard 1.2** Use point of view, characterization, style (e.g., use of irony), and related elements for specific rhetorical and aesthetic purposes.
- **Writing Standard 2.6** Deliver multimedia presentations: **a.** Combine text, images, and sound and draw information from many sources (e.g., television broadcasts, videos, films, newspapers, magazines, CD-ROMs, the Internet, electronic media-generated images).
- **Listening and Speaking Standard 2.1** Deliver reflective presentations: **a.** Explore the significance of personal experiences, events, conditions, or concerns, using appropriate rhetorical strategies (e.g., narration, description, exposition, persuasion). **b.** Draw comparisons between the specific incident and broader themes that illustrate the speaker's beliefs or generalizations about life.
- **Listening and Speaking Standard 2.3** Deliver oral responses to literature: **a.** Demonstrate a comprehensive understanding of the significant ideas of literary works (e.g., make assertions about the text that are reasonable and supportable). **d.** Demonstrate an awareness of the author's use of stylistic devices and an appreciation of the effects created.

Check for Understanding

Independent Practice

Reading Skills Focus

Possible responses:

1. *The speaker feels that he cannot get away from the very self-centered and annoying mosquito.*
2. *The mosquito can be totally focused on itself and does not have to worry about anything other than its own needs. It is like a child.*
3. *The mosquito follows the speaker everywhere so that it can drink the speaker's blood and survive.*
4. *The speaker tolerates the mosquito as an adult might tolerate a child who is constantly pestering him.*
5. *Give students several examples of words that can describe tone, and have them select the appropriate word.*

Literary Skills Focus

Possible responses:

6. *Lines 16–18 are written in a serious, Romantic tone. These lines change the tone for that section from a playful tone to a serious one.*
7. *It reminds the reader of the mosquito's buzzing sound.*
8. *Shelley's tone in "To a Skylark" is reverential and celebratory. Merwin's tone instead is annoyed and ironic.*
9. *The lack of punctuation emphazises the repetitions and mimics the swift movement of the insect.*
10. *Shelley's diction in "To a Skylark" creates a very serious and reverential tone in his poem. Merwin uses simpler words and simple rhyme to create a lighter tone.*
11. *The /m/ and /b/ sounds imitate the buzzing of the mosquito. In contrast to the speaker of "To a Skylark," who listens to the music of a bird, the speaker of "To a Mosquito" cheerfully listens to the annoying buzz of an insect.*

Applying Your Skills

Reading Standard 3.3, 3.4 (see pages A48–A50)
Writing Standard 1.2 (see pages A51–A52)

To a Mosquito

Literary Response and Analysis

Reading Skills Focus

Quick Check

1. How does the speaker feel about the mosquito?
2. What gift does the mosquito have that the speaker envies?
3. Why does the mosquito follow the speaker everywhere?

Read with a Purpose

4. What kind of relationship do you see between the speaker and the mosquito? Explain.

Reading Skills: Analyzing Tone

5. You have charted the connection between the poem's diction and its tone. Share your chart with a partner, and with your partner decide on a single word that you think best describes the poem's tone. Share your word with the class.

Diction	Tone
"me me me . . . me . . . be"	simple rhymes, like rhymes in a children's book, light in tone
"and rash though it may be"	rhythm sounds like a nursery rhyme, light in tone

Word that describes poem's tone: ____________

Literary Skills Focus

Literary Analysis

6. **Analyze** What effect is created in lines 16–18? How do these lines change or add to the poem's tone? Explain.
7. **Interpret** What is the function of the repetition of the word *me?*
8. **Contrast** How does Merwin's tone in "To a Mosquito" differ from Shelley's tone in "To a Skylark"?
9. **Analyze** Consider the poem's lack of punctuation and how the poem is broken into lines and stanzas. Why might Merwin have chosen to write the poem this way? What effects do these qualities create?

Literary Skills: Diction

10. **Contrast** What important differences do you see between Merwin's diction here and Shelley's diction in "To a Skylark"?

Literary Skills Review: Alliteration

11. **Analyze** The repetition of similar consonant sounds close together is **alliteration.** Why do you think Merwin repeats /m/ sounds and /b/ sounds so frequently?

Writing Skills Focus

Think as a Reader/Writer

Use It in Your Writing In your *Reader/Writer Notebook*, write a short paragraph describing an animal of your choice. Use descriptive adjectives and verbs that characterize the animal's movements, sounds, and most interesting qualities.

What Do You Think Now? How can unpleasant or annoying people, animals, or experiences serve to stimulate the imagination?

Universal Access

Struggling Writers

Some students may need additional scaffolding to complete the Writing Skills Focus activity. Have students brainstorm animals to discuss. Ask them to choose an animal and use the prewriting device of clustering to generate ideas. Have them write a few sentences from words in their clustering activity. Then, encourage students to incorporate these sentences into a short paragraph about the animal.

What Do You Think Now?

Encourage students to reflect upon character traits that are generally considered annoying. Ask them how imagination can help people bear with annoying situations.

Writing Standard 2.6a (see pages A51–A52)
Listening and Speaking Standard 2.1a, 2.1b, 2.3a, 2.3d (see pages A53–A55)

CHOICES

As you respond to the Choices, use these **Academic Vocabulary** words as appropriate: device, differentiate, function, inherent, technique.

REVIEW

Compare and Contrast Two Poems

Timed Writing Write an essay in which you compare and contrast "To a Skylark" and "To a Mosquito." Analyze the ways the authors use diction, figures of speech, and sound devices. How do the poems differ in tone and theme? Use quotations from both poems to develop your essay.

Write a Dialogue About Animals

Partner Activity If the speakers of these poems could converse about the connection between humans and animals, what would they say to each other? With a partner, write a dialogue between the two speakers in which they discuss what humans receive from animals. Write the dialogue in the form of a script, and present it to your class.

CONNECT

Write a Poem to an Animal

Write your own poem to an animal. Use a unique angle or technique to describe your animal, and elaborate on it in your poem. Just as Shelley and Merwin have done, use apostrophe, addressing the animal directly within the first line of the poem. Share your poem with the class by reading it aloud.

Compose a Message

TechFocus "To a Mosquito" is written in a light, informal style. How might the mosquito reply to the speaker? Create an oral response from the mosquito to the speaker in the form of a poem or speech. Then, record your response and enhance it with sound effects to help reveal the mosquito's point of view. Share your message with your class.

EXTEND

Research Mysteries of the Animal Kingdom

Presentation In the two poems, each speaker reflects upon a mystery of an animal—the beautiful song of the soaring skylark or the minor but persistent pestering of the mosquito. What other mysteries exist in the animal kingdom? Research some other animal mysteries that interest you, and prepare a ten-minute presentation about them. Include visuals.

Discuss the Role of the Artist

Group Discussion Shelley was concerned with the role of the artist in society. Hold a group discussion on the role of the artist in the modern world. Consider some of the topics addressed in "To a Skylark," such as these: From where do artists receive inspiration? How are artists regarded by others? How do they keep going when their works go unrecognized by others? You might want to expand your discussion by focusing also on musicians and their role in our society.

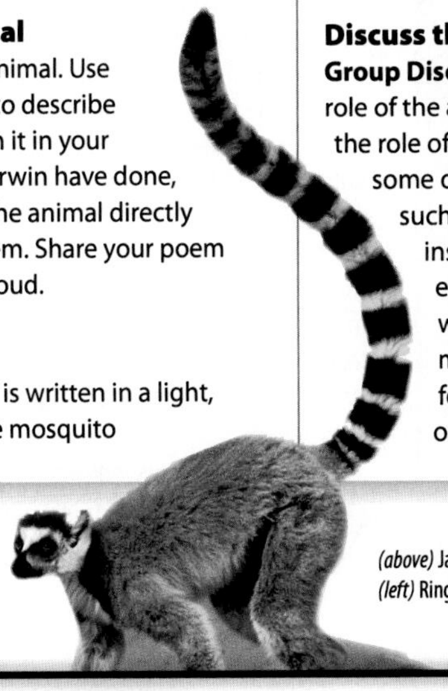

(above) Jackson's chameleon.
(left) Ring-tailed lemur. Madagascar.

Independent Practice

Choices: Evaluation Criteria

Review: Timed Writing 40–50 Minutes
Students explain, using quotes, how poems differ in tone and theme.

Review: Homework
Write a Dialogue about Animals
Students use dialogue form and write in the voice of the speaker.

Connect: Homework
Write a Poem to an Animal
- Poem addresses an animal directly at least once.
- Students describe the animal using a literary technique.

Connect: Homework
Compose a Message
- Students write from a mosquito's point of view.
- Students include sound effects.

Extend: Homework
Research Mysteries of the Animal Kingdom
Presentation is clear, reflects substantial research, and includes visuals.

Extend: Discuss the Role of the Artist
Students discuss topics from "To a Skylark" in relation to contemporary artists.

Assess

Unit 4 Resources, Selection Standards Check, pp. 92, 96

go.hrw.com **ThinkCentral Online Assessment,** Selection Standards Check

Teacher One Stop™, editable Selection Standards Check

Reteach

To reteach **tone,** see **Reteaching Lessons,** pp. 1449O–1449P.

go.hrw.com **ThinkCentral Online Remediation**

Standards Focus

Objectives

Students will

- understand the sonnet form
- identify the use of inverted syntax

Selection Introduction

Think About the Writer

To help students answer this question, tell them that it has been said that the way to immortality is to leave something behind that will endure, such as a work of art or literature.

For Independent Reading

*The Discovery of Poetry,** Frances Mayes

HRW LIBRARY *This title is available in the HRW library.

Motivate

What Do You Think?/QuickTalk

Ask students to share where they would go and what they would see, hear, and do in their creatively imagined adventure.

English for Academic Success

Academic Vocabulary

Look for opportunities to use the Academic Vocabulary words in this unit.

- **device, *n.:*** something made for a particular purpose
- **differentiate, *v.:*** distinguish; identify differences
- **function, *n.:*** the action for which a person or thing is specially fitted; purpose
- **technique, *n.:*** method; way of using skills

Preparing to Read

On First Looking into Chapman's Homer
When I Have Fears
Ode to a Nightingale
Ode on a Grecian Urn
Keats's Last Letter

What Do You Think? How can we use imagination to discover truth?

QuickTalk

If your imagination could take you on an adventure, what would that adventure be? Compare adventures with other students.

A portrait miniature of John Keats (c. 1818) by Joseph Severn. Ivory. No. 0713. Fitzwilliam Museum, University of Cambridge, UK.

842

MEET THE WRITER

John Keats
(1795–1821)

An unpropitious upbringing made it surprising that Keats became a poet at all; it is a greater wonder that when he died at twenty-five he had become one of England's major poets.

A Troubled Beginning

Keats's brief life was plagued with troubles, and he lacked the advantages most poets need to get started. His father, who ran a London stable, died when Keats was eight, and his mother died when he was fourteen. In 1811, Keats's guardian took him out of a school he loved and apprenticed him to a surgeon, a job that was then a step above that of a barber.

In 1816, Keats chose to become a poet rather than a surgeon, but harsh reviews of his first book of poetry (1817) stung him and made him doubt his commitment. By the autumn of 1818, Keats had assumed another burden: the care of his brother Tom, who was dying of tuberculosis, a disease that would soon claim Keats himself.

A Glorious Achievement

After Tom's death, Keats had a little more than two years to make what he could of his determination to lead "a literary life." Great passages and poems of near-perfect technique poured from him in that miraculous time. Meanwhile, Keats had fallen in love with a woman named Fanny Brawne, but they would never marry. When he began to cough up blood, his experience nursing Tom made the truth obvious: "That drop of blood is my death warrant." Believing his only chance for survival was to live in a warmer climate, Keats made the journey to Rome in late 1820 and settled in a house near the Spanish Steps. There, in February 1821, after weeks of suffering, Keats died.

The stark sadness of Keats's own life heightens our awareness of the qualities of his poems. Rich in sensuous detail, his poems are not subdued and depressed, but rather are exciting in their representation of intense emotional experiences. Instead of being heavy with resignation, they are rich in courageous hope for what the imagination can seize and enjoy in life.

Think About the Writer Keats requested that his epitaph be "Here lies one whose name was writ in water." What does this reveal about how Keats felt about his life work?

California Standards, pp. 842–846

- **Reading Standard 2.2** Analyze the way in which clarity of meaning is affected by the patterns of organization, hierarchical structures, repetition of the main ideas, syntax, and word choice in the text.
- **Reading Standard 3.1** Analyze characteristics of subgenres (e.g., satire, parody, allegory, pastoral) that are used in poetry, prose, plays, novels, short stories, essays, and other basic genres.

Selection Readability	
Easily Accessible Accessible **Challenging**	These selections include unfamiliar form, inverted syntax, unfamiliar vocabulary.

On First Looking into Chapman's Homer / When I Have Fears

Reading Standard 2.2, 3.1 (see pages A48–A50)

Literary Skills Focus

Sonnet Most poets who enjoy the challenge of structure love to attempt the **sonnet** form. Sonnets, which have fourteen lines and strict rhyme schemes, are usually classified as Petrarchan (Italian) or Shakespearean (English). The **Petrarchan sonnet** is divided into two parts, an octave (eight lines) and a sestet (six lines). The octave usually presents a problem, poses a question, or expresses an idea that the sestet then resolves, answers, or drives home. The **Shakespearean sonnet** has three quatrains (four lines each) and a concluding **couplet** (a pair of rhymed lines). The three quatrains usually express related ideas or examples, while the couplet summarizes the conclusion or message. Keats wrote "On First Looking into Chapman's Homer" in the Italian, or Petrarchan, form. "When I Have Fears," however, uses the Shakespearean form.

Reading Skills Focus

Understanding Inverted Syntax Keats often inverts the **syntax,** or word order, of his sentences to meet the demands of meter and rhyme. The usual word order in English sentences is subject-verb-complement.

Into Action Write down sentences in "On First Looking into Chapman's Homer" that do not follow standard word order. Circle the subjects, and underline the verbs. If the parts of a verb are split, as in the example below, draw an arrow from the first part of the verb to the second.

Line	Inverted Syntax
1	"Much have I traveled"

Writing Skills Focus

Think as a Reader/Writer

Find It In Your Reading Much of the beauty of Keats's poems comes from their rich figurative language. Keats uses **similes** (comparisons of two unlike things, using words such as *like* and *as*) and **metaphors** (direct comparisons between unlike things, without the use of specific words of comparison). In your *Reader/Writer Notebook*, record details about the extended similes in lines 9–10 and 11–12 of "On First Looking into Chapman's Homer."

Reader/Writer Notebook

Use your **RWN** to complete the activities for these selections.

Vocabulary

realms (rehlmz) *n. pl.:* kingdoms. *Keats compares reading classical poetry to traveling in realms of gold.*

gleaned (gleend) *v.:* gathered little by little or gradually. *The speaker of "When I Have Fears" says his pen gleaned words from his brain.*

teeming (TEEM ihng) *v.* used as *adj.:* full of; alive with; fruitful. *The speaker refers to his teeming brain.*

Language Coach

Related Words Learning the base form of verbs can help you expand your vocabulary. The base form of *teeming* is *teem,* which means "to be full of." Other related forms of this verb are *teemed* and *teems*. What do you think those verbs mean? What is the base form of *gleaned*? What are some other forms of this verb?

Learn It Online

Listen to these poems online.

go.hrw.com H12-843 Go

Selection Resources

Unit 4 Resources, on-level practice and assessment, pp. 98, 104, 110, 116

PowerNotes, interactive lesson presentations with activities

Teacher One Stop™, on-level lesson plans and all print resources

Holt Audio Library

Holt Audio Library: Selections and Summaries in Spanish

UA: Holt Interactive Reader, p. 261

UA: Differentiating Instruction, modified lesson plans and leveled assessment, pp. 189, 190

UA: Resources for Teaching Advanced Students, p. 154

UA: Supporting Instruction in Spanish, selection summary

ThinkCentral Online Assessment, Selection Standards Check

ThinkCentral Online Remediation

Preteach

Introducing Vocabulary

- Review the Vocabulary words, definitions, and sentences with students.
- To reinforce the importance of the Vocabulary words, explain that these words help Keats create metaphors. Keats will compare reading to traveling in *realms* of gold in "On First Looking into Chapman's Homer." He then compares writing to harvesting by saying his pen *gleaned* thoughts from his *teeming* head in "When I Have Fears."

English for Academic Success

Language Coach

Remind students that related words have similar meanings, but usually differ in part of speech. ***Possible responses:*** Teemed *and* teems *mean the same as* teeming *but are in different tenses. The base form of* gleaned *is* glean. *Other forms of* glean *are* gleaning, gleaner, *and* gleanable.

Literary Skills Focus

As you read and discuss the selection with students, have them identify structural differences between "On First Looking into Chapman's Homer" and "When I Have Fears."

Reading Skills Focus

Give students a copy of the Reading Skills Focus graphic organizer before they read. (See **Unit 4 Resources.**) Tell them to use their responses to answer the questions on the Applying Your Skills page.

Writing Skills Focus

Have students record instances of Keats's use of simile and metaphor in their **Reader/Writer Notebooks**.

Learn It Online

The online version of this selection includes audio support to engage all students and to help struggling readers with reading comprehension and vocabulary.

go.hrw.com H12-843 Go

Teacher Preparation

Selection Summary

In "On First Looking into Chapman's Homer," the speaker recalls how a reading of Homer's *Iliad* in translation ignited his sympathetic imagination. He perceived the poetry so intensely that the moment matched the excitement explorers feel when gazing upon a planet or an ocean they have never seen before.

Direct Teach

Think About/Talk About

Read with a Purpose Have students read the Read with a Purpose statement. Point out the key word *exploration*. Ask students to look for ways Keats creates his extended metaphor, comparing reading to exploration and discovery.

Comprehension

A Reading Focus

Possible responses: *"I have traveled much in the realms of gold and seen many goodly states and kingdoms; I have been around many western islands, which poets hold to Apollo in fealty." This standard construction destroys the rhyme and meter of the sonnet, making the same words read more like prose than poetry.*

Analysis

B Literary Focus

Possible responses: *The octave presents the idea of the reader as explorer. The subsequent sestet drives home the idea of reading as exploration by describing the speaker's feeling of discovery found in analyzing Homer's* Iliad.

SONNET

On First Looking into Chapman's Homer

by **John Keats**

Read with a Purpose

Read to discover how reading great literature can be an exciting exploration.

Build Background

Keats wrote "On First Looking into Chapman's Homer" in 1816, just before his twenty-first birthday. The poem was inspired by an evening Keats spent with his favorite teacher, Charles Cowden Clarke. The two had stayed up all night reading a translation of Homer's *Iliad* by George Chapman, a contemporary of Shakespeare. At dawn, Keats went home and by ten that morning sent Clarke this sonnet.

Trojan Horse and Greek soldiers (640 B.C.). Relief from an earthenware amphora from Mykonos. Archaeological Museum, Mykonos, Greece.

Much have I traveled in the realms of gold,
 And many goodly states and kingdoms seen;
 Round many western islands have I been
Which bards in fealty to Apollo° hold. **A**
Oft of one wide expanse had I been told
 That deep-browed Homer ruled as his demesne;°
 Yet did I never breathe its pure serene°
Till I heard Chapman speak out loud and bold:
Then felt I like some watcher of the skies
 When a new planet swims into his ken;°
Or like stout Cortez° when with eagle eyes
 He stared at the Pacific—and all his men
Looked at each other with a wild surmise—
 Silent, upon a peak in Darien. **B**

4. bards in fealty to Apollo: poets in loyal service (as feudal tenants to their lord) to Apollo, the Greek god of poetry.
6. demesne (dih MEEN): domain.
7. serene: archaic word meaning "clear air."
10. ken: range of vision.
11. Cortez: sixteenth-century Spanish explorer who conquered Mexico. *Stout* means "brave, strong." Keats made a now-famous mistake in this line: It was Balboa (not Cortez) who was the first European to see the eastern shore of the Pacific Ocean from the heights of Darien, in Panama.

A **Reading Focus** **Understanding Inverted Syntax** How can you reword the first four lines to reflect standard word order? How does this change affect the sound of the poem?

B **Literary Focus** **Sonnet** What idea is presented in the octave? How does the sestet drive home the speaker's point?

Vocabulary **realms** (rehlmz) *n. pl.:* kingdoms.

Universal Access

Struggling Readers

Benchmark Students Model the skill of reading inverted syntax. Read line 3 aloud, then explain that the author inverted syntax in order to preserve rhyme and meter. Then, rearrange the sentence in standard syntax: "I have been around many islands." As students read Keats, ask them to rewrite sentences in a subject-verb-complement order.

Students with Disabilities

Pair students with more advanced students to help them paraphrase the poem. Students should receive help in figuring out the meaning of difficult words and reordering the syntax. Have students write their paraphrases on a piece of paper and make one or two inferences about the causes of the emotional state of the speaker.

✔ See **UA: Differentiating Instruction** for a graphic organizer to scaffold instruction for students with disabilities.

SONNET

When I Have Fears

by **John Keats**

Read with a Purpose

As you read, think about the two things the speaker fears.

Build Background

Keats's first Shakespearean sonnet, "When I Have Fears," was written in early 1818—a year filled with disappointment in work and love and the beginning of the poet's ill health. The sonnet hauntingly anticipates Keats's death in 1821 at the age of twenty-five.

Melancholy (1894–1895) (detail) by Edvard Munch (1863–1944). Billedgaleri (Picture Gallery), Bergen, Norway/The Munch-Ellingsen Group/Artist Rights Society (ARS), NY.

When I have fears that I may cease to be
  Before my pen has gleaned my teeming brain,
Before high-pilèd books, in charact'ry,°
  Hold like rich garners the full-ripened grain;
When I behold, upon the night's starred face,
  Huge cloudy symbols of a high romance,
And think that I may never live to trace
  Their shadows, with the magic hand of chance;
And when I feel, fair creature of an hour,
  That I shall never look upon thee more, (A)
Never have relish in the fairy° power
  Of unreflecting love!—then on the shore
Of the wide world I stand alone, and think
Till Love and Fame to nothingness do sink. (B)

3. **charact'ry:** characters of the alphabet.

11. **fairy:** supernatural; unearthly.

(A) **Reading Focus** **Understanding Inverted Syntax** In standard English, modifiers are placed close to the words they modify. How would you reverse the words in this line so that the adverb *more* is close to the word it modifies? What effect does this change have on the poem?

(B) **Literary Focus** **Sonnet** What ideas are presented in the quatrains? How does the couplet summarize the speaker's point?

Vocabulary **gleaned** (gleend) *v.:* gathered little by little or slowly.
teeming (TEEM ihng) *v.* used as *adj.:* full of; alive with; fruitful.

Teacher Preparation

Selection Summary

In "When I Have Fears," the speaker worries that an early death may prevent him from fulfilling his earthly promise and separate him from his beloved. These dreary thoughts cause him to question the ultimate importance of fame and love.

Direct Teach

Think About/Talk About

Read with a Purpose Have students recall what they know about Keats's life (p. 842). As they read, ask them to consider in what ways this poem might be called prophetic.

Comprehension

(A) Reading Focus

Possible responses: *"I shall look upon thee never more" changes the meaning of the line so that the emphasis is on* never *instead of on* look.

Analysis

(B) Literary Focus

Possible responses: *In the quatrains, the speaker describes his three fears. First, he will die before his artistic work is complete; second, he will not be able to live out his romantic ideals of life; and third, he will never again see his beloved. In the final couplet, the speaker questions the value of fame and love, the two things of which he fears he will be deprived.*

Vocabulary: Own the Word

- **realms:** Have students complete the following sentence: I would identify governments as *realms* if they . . .
- **gleaned:** When you *gleaned,* you gathered something slowly. Have students make a list of things people could *glean* or have *gleaned.*
- **teeming:** A *teeming* (adj.) place is Times Square on New Year's Eve. A *teeming* season is spring. Many gardens are *teeming* with flowers.

California Standards, p. 846

- **Reading Standard 2.2** Analyze the way in which clarity of meaning is affected by the patterns of organization, hierarchical structures, repetition of the main ideas, syntax, and word choice in the text.
- **Reading Standard 3.1** Analyze characteristics of subgenres (e.g., satire, parody, allegory, pastoral) that are used in poetry, prose, plays, novels, short stories, essays, and other basic genres.
- **Reading Standard 3.3** Analyze the ways in which irony, tone, mood, the author's style, and the "sound" of language achieve specific rhetorical or aesthetic purposes or both.
- **Writing Standard 1.2** Use point of view, characterization, style (e.g., use of irony), and related elements for specific rhetorical and aesthetic purposes.

Check for Understanding

Independent Practice

Reading Skills Focus

Possible responses:

1. *reading Homer's* Iliad *in translation*
2. *The speaker fears that he will be separated from his beloved.*
3. *The speaker is addressing his beloved directly in line 10.*
4. *"On First Looking into Chapman's Homer" is a testament to Keats's belief in the power of literature. "When I Have Fears" reveals Keats's desire to write great works as well and his fear that he will die before fulfilling his ambitions.*
5. *Students' rewrites should reflect knowledge of standard syntax.*

Vocabulary Check

6. *A realm is a kingdom.*
7. *To glean is to collect it bit by bit.*
8. *Something teeming is full of life.*

Literary Skills Focus

Possible responses:

9. *The lines produce images of harvest and the night sky. The last lines create feelings of emptiness.*
10. *Keats has done much vicarious "traveling" through his extensive reading, which may have included some translation of Homer.*
11. *Cortez is just as good a symbol of discovery as Balboa, but the meter would change with the addition of the extra syllable, besides affecting the sound of the line.*
12. *In the octave, the speaker sums up his feelings of reading other books. The sestet describes reading Chapman's translation. The first three quatrains of "When I Have Fears" explain the speaker's fears of an early death. The couplet questions the value of his earthly desires of fame and love.*
13. *The speaker begins with an anxious, melancholy, and somewhat regretful tone. By the end, the tone is more calm and resigned.*

Applying Your Skills

Reading Standard 2.2, 3.1, 3.3 (see pages A48–A50)
Writing Standard 1.2 (see pages A51–A52)

On First Looking into Chapman's Homer / When I Have Fears

Literary Response and Analysis

Reading Skills Focus

Quick Check

1. What experience is the basis of the poem "On First Looking into Chapman's Homer"?
2. What does the speaker fear in the poem?
3. Whom does the speaker in "When I Have Fears" address? What line tells you this?

Read with a Purpose

4. How does "On First Looking into Chapman's Homer" add to your understanding of Keats's fears in "When I Have Fears"?

Reading Skills: Understanding Inverted Syntax

5. Rewrite lines with inverted syntax from "On First Looking" so that they conform to standard English word order. How does standard word order affect the rhyme and meter?

Vocabulary Check

Explain your answer to each of the following questions about the Vocabulary words.

6. Is a **realm** a kingdom or a river?
7. If you **glean** something, do you collect it bit by bit or scoop it up in a heap?
8. If something is **teeming,** is it full of life or dead?

Literary Skills Focus

Literary Analysis

9. **Analyze** What do the images in "When I Have Fears" make you visualize? What feeling is created by the image in the final two lines?
10. **Analyze** Keats's only foreign travel was the trip to Italy he made when he was dying. What then does Keats mean in "On First Looking into Chapman's Homer" when he says he has traveled and has seen many states, kingdoms, and islands?
11. **Extend** Does the mistake at the end of "On First Looking" affect the poem's power or quality? Would substituting *Balboa* work? Explain.

Literary Skills: Sonnet

12. **Interpret** How would you sum up the octave and sestet of "On First Looking into Chapman's Homer"? How would you sum up the three quatrains and couplet in "When I Have Fears"?

Literary Skills Review: Tone

13. **Analyze** The writer's attitude toward the reader or subject is called **tone.** Describe the tone in "When I Have Fears." Does it change? Explain.

Writing Skills Focus

Think as a Reader/Writer

Use It in Your Writing In your *Reader/Writer Notebook,* write a brief poem using similes and metaphors to describe a powerful experience. You could write an extended simile, like the two that conclude "On First Looking into Chapman's Homer."

What Do You Think Now? Keats and other Romantic poets saw imagination as a creative power that made things happen. How important do you think imagination is in the world today?

Universal Access

Struggling Writers

Some students may need additional scaffolding to complete the Writing Skills Focus activity. To help students write a simile that describes their experience, have them use Keats's simile at the end of "On First Looking into Chapman's Homer" as a model. Write the following sentence frame on the board:

"Then I felt like ______ / When ______."

Ask students to fill in the blanks to create a simile that describes their adventure. Have students incorporate the simile into their poem.

What Do You Think Now?

Ask students to discuss the place of incarnations of imagination in the literature, art, music, and theater of today's world.

Assess

Unit 4 Resources, Selection Standards Check, p. 96

go.hrw.com **ThinkCentral Online Assessment,** Selection Standards Check

Reading Standard 2.2, 3.4, 3.9 (see pages A48–A50)

Ode to a Nightingale

Literary Skills Focus

Synesthesia When writers use **synesthesia,** they describe one sense experience (such as smell) in terms of another sense (such as touch). For example, in "Ode to a Nightingale" the speaker remarks that he "cannot see… what soft incense hangs upon the boughs" (lines 41–42). Incense, usually perceived through smell, is here described as both something that might be soft to the touch and something that might be seen. By inviting us to use our senses in unexpected ways, Keats brings a startling new dimension to reality.

Literary Perspectives Apply the literary perspective described on page 849 as you read this poem.

Reading Skills Focus

Reading Closely To understand complex poems and their use of sophisticated techniques like synesthesia, you have to **read closely.** Techniques for effective close reading of poetry include adjusting your reading rate, pausing to reflect on the exact meaning of words, re-reading lines that puzzle you, and letting your imagination visualize what the poet is saying.

Into Action As you read, keep a list of questions you have and the reading strategies you can use to answer them. Your list might look like this:

Questions	Reading Strategies
Stanza 1: What does the speaker mean by "Lethewards"?	I need to use the sidenotes to understand words and allusions.

Writing Skills Focus

Think as a Reader/Writer

Find It In Your Reading In many instances in the poem, Keats **personifies** the natural world, that is to say, he gives human properties to nature. For example, when he calls the moon a queen and seats her on a throne, he is personifying the moon, as moons can't literally be crowned queen nor can they sit on thrones. Note in your *Reader/Writer Notebook* where Keats speaks of the natural world as if it has human attributes.

Vocabulary

melodious (muh LOH dee uhs) *adj.:* producing a sweet sound; tuneful. *Keats describes the plot of land where the nightingale sings as melodious.*

perplexes (pehr PLEHKS uhz) *v.:* confuses. *The nightingale fascinates and perplexes Keats, because his brain cannot understand the bird's song.*

murmurous (MUR muhr uhs) *adj.:* making consistent soft, low sounds. *The speaker enters a murmurous place where flies gather on summer evenings.*

Language Coach

Word Sounds and Word Meanings Some words sound like their meanings. (The use of a word whose sound imitates or suggests its meaning is called **onomatopoeia.**) If you read that rushing water *gurgles,* for example, you should be able to hear the sound of water in that verb. Say these Vocabulary words aloud: *melodious* and *murmurous.* Do the sounds of these words suggest what they mean?

Learn It Online
Take your study of Keats farther with these project ideas online.
go.hrw.com H12-847 Go

Reader/Writer Notebook
Use your **RWN** to complete the activities for this selection.

Preteach

Introducing Vocabulary

- Review the Vocabulary words, definitions, and sentences with students.
- To reinforce the importance of the Vocabulary words, explain how one or more words appeal to the senses. Ask students to describe a *melodious* sound, then have them imitate the sound of *murmurous* surroundings.

English for Academic Success

Language Coach

After students finish the **Language Coach** exercise, ask them how the sounds of the following words hint at their meanings: *cacophony, blabbermouth, ratchet.*

Literary Skills Focus

As you read and discuss the selection with students, have students note instances of synesthesia and the senses it describes.

Reading Skills Focus

Give students a copy of the Reading Skills Focus graphic organizer before they read. (See **Unit 4 Resources**.) Tell them to use their responses to answer the questions on the Applying Your Skills page.

Writing Skills Focus

Have students record instances where Keats personifies the natural world in their **Reader/Writer Notebooks**. Students can use their notes to complete the Writing Skills Focus activity.

California Standards, pp. 847–851

- **Reading Standard 2.2** Analyze the way in which clarity of meaning is affected by the patterns of organization, hierarchical structures, repetition of the main ideas, syntax, and word choice in the text.
- **Reading Standard 3.4** Analyze ways in which poets use imagery, personification, figures of speech, and sounds to evoke readers' emotions.
- **Reading Standard 3.9** Analyze the philosophical arguments presented in literary works to determine whether the authors' positions have contributed to the quality of each work and the credibility of the characters (Philosophical approach).

Learn It Online
MediaScope can help guide students through the process of creating a multimedia presentation—from choosing a subject and planning through publishing their finished project.
go.hrw.com H12-847 Go

Teacher Preparation

Selection Summary

The speaker in "Ode to a Nightingale" becomes intoxicated by the nightingale's song and the changes it evokes. He wishes for poetic inspiration and for the freedom to fly away from the suffering that time and change inflict on people. As the last notes of the bird's song fade, the speaker returns to ordinary consciousness, wondering if his experience was only a dream.

Direct Teach

Think About/Talk About

Read with a Purpose Have students read the Read with a Purpose statement. Ask students to consider how the speaker feels about the nightingale and its song.

Comprehension

Ⓐ Reading Focus

Possible response: *I feel sad, drowsy, and numb, as if I had just drunk some poison or drug that made me forget.*

Analysis

Ⓑ Literary Focus

Possible response: *These lines appeal to sight ("beechen green," "shadows") and sound ("melodious," "singest of summer in full-throated ease").*

Ⓒ Literary Focus

Possible response: *"Tasting of Flora and the country green" uses the sense of taste to describe sight, sound, and movement.*

ODE

Ode to a Nightingale

by **John Keats**

Read with a Purpose

As you read, think about what the speaker is saying to the nightingale.

Build Background

When Keats was twenty-three, he spent a few months at the Hampstead home of his friend Charles Brown. Keats's brother Tom had died a few months earlier. Brown remembers the scene:

> In the spring of 1819 a nightingale had built her nest near my house. Keats felt a tranquil and continual joy in her song, and one morning he took his chair from the breakfast table to the grass plot under a plum tree, where he sat for two or three hours. When he came into the house, I perceived he had some scraps of paper in his hand, and these he was quietly thrusting behind the books. On inquiry, I found those scraps, four or five in number, contained his poetic feeling on the song of our nightingale.

There are no nightingales in North America. Their unearthly, sad, sweet song can only be heard in the British Isles, in central and western Europe, and in Africa during the winter.

1

My heart aches, and a drowsy numbness pains
    My sense, as though of hemlock° I had drunk,
Or emptied some dull opiate to the drains°
    One minute past, and Lethewards° had sunk: Ⓐ
'Tis not through envy of thy happy lot,
    But being too happy in thine happiness—
        That thou, light-wingèd Dryad° of the trees,
            In some melodious plot
    Of beechen° green, and shadows numberless,
        Singest of summer in full-throated ease. Ⓑ

2

O, for a draft of vintage!° that hath been
    Cooled a long age in the deep-delvèd earth,
Tasting of Flora° and the country green,
    Dance, and Provençal° song, and sunburnt mirth! Ⓒ
O for a beaker full of the warm South,
    Full of the true, the blushful Hippocrene,°

2. **hemlock:** poison.
3. **drains:** dregs, particles that settle in the bottom of a cup.
4. **Lethewards** (LEE thee wuhrdz): toward Lethe. In Greek and Roman mythology, Lethe is the river of forgetfulness that flows through the underworld.
7. **Dryad** (DRY ad): in Greek mythology, nature goddess associated with trees.
9. **beechen:** archaic word meaning "pertaining to beech trees."
11. **vintage:** wine.
13. **Flora:** the Roman goddess of flowers.
14. **Provençal** (proh vuhn SAHL): from Provence, a region in southern France known in the Middle Ages for its troubadours who sang love songs.
16. **blushful Hippocrene** (HIHP uh kreen): wine, which he would drink for inspiration. In Greek mythology, Hippocrene is the Muses' fountain, whose waters inspire the poets who drink from it.

Ⓐ **Reading Focus** **Reading Closely** Stop and rephrase in your own words what is happening in this stanza.

Ⓑ **Literary Focus** **Synesthesia** To what senses does the image in lines 8–10 appeal?

Ⓒ **Literary Focus** **Synesthesia** What images using synesthesia do you find in lines 13–14?

Vocabulary **melodious** (muh LOH dee uhs) *adj.:* producing a sweet sound; tuneful.

Universal Access

Struggling Readers

Help students understand synesthesia by having them generate connections between the five senses. Ask students to think about the color blue and ask them to brainstorm sensations of sound, taste, smell, and touch that the color evokes in them. [*the smell of fresh bread, the sound of bells ringing, the sight of a cloud, a mildly sweet taste, and the texture of velvet.*] Repeat the exercise by asking about how odors, tastes, sights, and textures connect to other senses.

AAVE Students Who Use African American Vernacular English

English for Academic Success Students may eliminate *r* in pronouncing consonant clusters, such as *thr* and *br.* Direct them to l.10, p. 848: "Singest of summer in full-throated ease." Model the standard English pronunciation of *throated*. In pairs, have students practice pronouncing the following: *throw, through, brought.*

✔ For additional instruction, see **Holt Pronunciation Resources** and **ThinkCentral, Teacher Access.**

With beaded bubbles winking at the brim,
And purple-stainèd mouth;
That I might drink, and leave the world unseen,
And with thee fade away into the forest dim:

3

Fade far away, dissolve, and quite forget
What thou among the leaves hast never known,
The weariness, the fever, and the fret
Here, where men sit and hear each other groan;
Where palsy° shakes a few, sad, last gray hairs,
Where youth grows pale, and specter-thin, and dies;
Where but to think is to be full of sorrow
And leaden-eyed despairs
Where Beauty cannot keep her lustrous eyes,
Or new Love pine at them beyond tomorrow. **D**

4

Away! away! for I will fly to thee,
Not charioted by Bacchus and his pards,°
But on the viewless wings of Poesy,°
Though the dull brain perplexes and retards:
Already with thee! tender is the night,
And haply the Queen-Moon is on her throne,
Clustered around by all her starry Fays;°
But here there is no light,
Save what from heaven is with the breezes blown
Through verdurous° glooms and winding mossy ways. **E**

5

I cannot see what flowers are at my feet,
Nor what soft incense hangs upon the boughs,
But, in embalmèd° darkness, guess each sweet
Wherewith the seasonable month endows
The grass, the thicket, and the fruit tree wild;
White hawthorn, and the pastoral eglantine;°
Fast fading violets covered up in leaves;
And mid-May's eldest child,
The coming° musk rose, full of dewy wine,
The murmurous haunt of flies on summer eves.

25. palsy: disease of the nervous system that causes partial paralysis and involuntary shaking.

32. not . . . pards: not by getting drunk. Bacchus, the Roman god of wine, had a chariot pulled by leopards, shortened here to "pards."
33. on . . . Poesy: on the invisible wings of poetry; that is, by using his poetic imagination.
37. Fays: fairies.
40. verdurous (VUR juhr uhs): full of green foliage.
43. embalmèd: perfumed.
46. eglantine (EHG luhn tyn): kind of rose.
49. coming: soon to bloom.

D Literary Perspectives **Analyzing Philosophical Context**
What is the speaker's philosophical view of the actual world in which he lives?

E Literary Focus **Synesthesia** Why is the image of "light" being "blown" an example of synesthesia?

Vocabulary **perplexes** (pehr PLEHKS uhz) *v.:* confuses.
murmurous (MUR muhr uhs) *adj.:* making consistent soft, low sounds.

Literary Perspectives

Analyzing Philosophical Context Philosophy is a conscious search for truth. The philosophical context of a work refers to the writer's assumptions about life and its meaning. In this poem, the speaker searches for meaning while he listens to the sublime, almost overwhelming beauty of a nightingale's song. The poem consists of a series of propositions, each containing its own rejection, as to how the speaker might leave the world of suffering and fade away with the bird. He considers wine, poetry, and even death as ways to respond to the beauty of the bird's song. However, at the end of the poem the speaker is drawn back to his "sole self," not knowing if he has had a vision or if he has merely been asleep.

As you read, notice the questions in the text, which will guide you in using this perspective.

Literary Perspectives

Before students read the poetry, have them read the **Literary Perspectives** about Analyzing Philosophical Context.

Have students split up into small groups and discuss possible answers to the following questions: How does Keats seem to want to deal with life's problems? What does the poet seem to believe about the powers and capabilities of the imagination? What does he seem to say about the capabilities of the "dull brain" (line 34)? Make sure the groups comprise students from all populations.

To help students answer the **Literary Perspectives** question on this page, have students re-read the third stanza. Tell students that in this stanza the speaker explains that he wants to escape the sickness, aging, and death that is all a part of life. Explain to students that in lines 25-26, Keats describes the effects of tuberculosis, a leading cause of death in nineteenth-century Europe and the United States. A victim of the disease himself, Keats may be thinking of his brother Tom, who died from tuberculosis several months before this poem was written. Have students use this information to figure out the speaker's philosophical view of the world.

Think About/Talk About

Analysis

D Literary Perspectives

Possible response: *He thinks the actual world is full of suffering. The speaker wishes he could leave his reality, which suggests that he sees the actual world as constraining.*

E Literary Focus

Possible response: *Light is intangible, but to describe it as being "blown" is to assume that it has a density. This image uses the sense of touch to describe something that can only be seen.*

Extend the Discussion

Comparing and Contrasting In stanza 4, how are the images of the moon and the stars different from the images of the earthly world below? **Possible response:** *The moon is imaginatively depicted as an enthroned queen surrounded by fairy stars; the earthly realm, however, is described as dark, gloomy, twisting, leafy, and mossy.*

Tone How does the tone change in lines 31–33? **Possible response:** *The tone becomes less melancholy and more hopeful, as the speaker announces that poetry will help him escape his pain.*

Vocabulary: Own the Word

- **melodious:** *Melodious* means "producing a sweet sound"; its antonym is *raucous.* Use both words in a sentence: Although my accompanying voice sounded somewhat raucous, the singer's was *melodious.*
- **perplexes:** Ask students: "What *perplexes* readers when they study a difficult poem?" **Possible responses:** *unusual sentence structure; complex figurative language*
- **murmurous:** Ask students to list other things that might create *murmurous* noises. **Possible responses:** *distant voices, the wind, the strikes of a distant clock bell*

Think About/Talk About

Comprehension

G Reading Focus

Possible response: *To bring me back from you to myself. Goodbye, my imagination cannot delude me.*

Analysis

F Literary Perspectives

Possible response: *The nightingale's song changes the speaker's perspective on death. If he chose death, he would never again hear the nightingale's song.*

Extend the Discussion

Mood What is the mood in lines 51–56? ***Possible response:*** *morose, dispirited, passive*

Symbolism In stanza 7, where does the speaker imagine the nightingale has been heard? What does the bird come to symbolize for the speaker? ***Possible responses:*** *The speaker thinks the bird was heard in "ancient days." The bird's song comes to symbolize immortality or enduring beauty. It is a bridge between the temporary world of man and the eternal world. Though man is mortal, the nightingale's song gives man a taste of the eternal.*

6

Darkling° I listen; and, for many a time
I have been half in love with easeful Death,
Called him soft names in many a musèd rhyme,
To take into the air my quiet breath;
Now more than ever seems it rich to die,
To cease upon the midnight with no pain,
While thou art pouring forth thy soul abroad
In such an ecstasy!
Still wouldst thou sing, and I have ears in vain—
To thy high requiem° become a sod.° **F**

7

Thou wast not born for death, immortal Bird!
No hungry generations tread thee down;
The voice I hear this passing night was heard
In ancient days by emperor and clown:
Perhaps the self-same song that found a path
Through the sad heart of Ruth,° when, sick for home,
She stood in tears amid the alien corn;
The same that oft-times hath
Charmed magic casements,° opening on the foam
Of perilous seas, in fairy lands forlorn.

8

Forlorn! the very word is like a bell
To toll me back from thee to my sole self!
Adieu! the fancy° cannot cheat so well
As she is famed to do, deceiving elf. **G**
Adieu! adieu! thy plaintive° anthem fades
Past the near meadows, over the still stream,
Up the hillside; and now 'tis buried deep
In the next valley glades:
Was it a vision, or a waking dream?
Fled is that music:—Do I wake or sleep?

51. darkling: archaic word meaning "in the dark."

60. requiem (REHK wee uhm): mass or song for the dead.
sod: piece of topsoil held together by matted roots.

66. Ruth: in the Bible, a young widow who left her own people because of famine in their land to travel with her mother-in-law to a strange country. There she gathered grain (corn) for survival.
69. casements: windows. Images of open windows intrigued Keats.
73. fancy: imagination.

75. plaintive: sad; mournful.

Lacquer box decorated with a nightingale on the branch of a gingko tree (1870–1880). Musée des Arts Asiatiques-Guimet, Paris, France.

F Literary Perspectives **Analyzing Philosophical Context** How does the song of the bird affect the way the speaker feels about death?

G Reading Focus **Reading Closely** Pause in your reading, and put what the speaker says to the bird in lines 72–73 in your own words.

California Standards, p. 851

- **Reading Standard 2.2** Analyze the way in which clarity of meaning is affected by the patterns of organization, hierarchical structures, repetition of the main ideas, syntax, and word choice in the text.
- **Reading Standard 3.4** Analyze ways in which poets use imagery, personification, figures of speech, and sounds to evoke readers' emotions.
- **Reading Standard 3.9** Analyze the philosophical arguments presented in literary works to determine whether the authors' positions have contributed to the quality of each work and the credibility of the characters (Philosophical approach).
- **Writing Standard 1.2** Use point of view, characterization, style (e.g., use of irony), and related elements for specific rhetorical and aesthetic purposes.
- **Writing Standard 2.3** Write reflective compositions:
  a. Explore the significance of personal experiences, events, conditions, or concerns by using rhetorical strategies (e.g., narration, description, exposition, persuasion).

A shadow of man's ravage, save his own,
When, for a moment, like a drop of rain,
He sinks into thy depths with bubbling groan,
Without a grave, unknelled,° uncoffined, and unknown.

3

And I have loved thee, Ocean! and my joy
Of youthful sports was on thy breast to be
Borne, like thy bubbles, onward: From a boy
I wantoned° with thy breakers—they to me
Were a delight; and if the freshening° sea
Made them a terror—'twas a pleasing fear,
For I was as it were a child of thee,
And trusted to thy billows far and near,
And laid my hand upon thy mane—as I do here. **B**

4

My task is done, my song hath ceased, my theme
Has died into an echo; it is fit
The spell should break of this protracted dream.
The torch shall be extinguished which hath lit
My midnight lamp—and what is writ, is writ;
Would it were worthier! but I am not now
That which I have been—and my visions flit
Less palpably° before me—and the glow
Which in my spirit dwelt is fluttering, faint, and low.

5

Farewell! a word that must be, and hath been—
A sound which makes us linger;—yet—farewell!
Ye! who have traced the Pilgrim to the scene
Which is his last, if in your memories dwell
A thought which once was his, if on ye swell
A single recollection, not in vain
He wore his sandal shoon and scallop shell;°
Farewell! with *him* alone may rest the pain,
If such there were—with *you*, the moral of his strain.° **C**

18. unknelled (uhn NEHLD): without the traditional ringing of a church bell to announce his death.

22. wantoned: frolicked; played happily.
23. freshening: becoming rough as the wind comes up.

35. palpably: clearly.

43. sandal shoon . . . shell: *Shoon* is archaic for "shoes." Sandals and a scallop shell worn on a hat were traditional emblems of pilgrims. The scallop shell is a symbol of Saint James, whose shrine in Spain was a great attraction to pilgrims.
45. strain: passage of poetry or song.

B Literary Focus Apostrophe How does Childe Harold profess his love as he addresses the ocean in this apostrophe?

C Literary Focus Apostrophe What is the tone of the speaker's address to the reader? Why might he make such an emphatic farewell?

Vocabulary **protracted** (proh TRAK tihd) *v.* used as *adj.*: drawn out over time.
linger (LIHNG guhr) *v.*: stay a long while.

Think About/Talk About

Analysis

B Literary Focus

Possible responses: *In line 25, he compares his relationship to the ocean with the relationship between child and parent. In line 27, he compares his affection for the ocean with a person's desire to stroke a beloved and trusted horse.*

C Literary Focus

Possible responses: *The tone is sorrowful and wistful. The speaker makes this wholehearted farewell to emphasize his true appreciation for nature.*

Extend the Discussion

Apostrophe In line 10, the speaker addresses the ocean as if it could respond. What effect does this apostrophe create? ***Possible response:*** *Though the stanza expresses the idea that human affairs are insignificant, the apostrophe implies that the speaker has a mystical connection with this powerful natural force.*

Vocabulary: Own the Word

- **rapture:** Remind students that *rapture* is a profound—not slight—joy. Ask students: "What event or experience would cause or has caused you to feel *rapture*?"
- **intrudes:** Remind students that *intrudes* can mean "interrupts." Ask students to complete the sentence: "My little brother *intrudes* on my phone conversations when he . . ."
- **mingle:** Ask students to list additional ways in which the narrator could "mingle with the Universe." [*climb to a mountain top, gaze at the stars*]
- **protracted:** In the adjective form, *protracted* means "drawn out over time;" the antonym is *abbreviated.* Use both words in a sentence: The baseball team won an abbreviated game due to a *protracted* downpour.
- **linger:** Ask students, "Why might you *linger* after someone has said goodbye? What would *lingering* look like?"

California Standards, p. 816

- **Reading Standard 3.3** Analyze the ways in which irony, tone, mood, the author's style, and the "sound" of language achieve specific rhetorical or aesthetic purposes or both.
- **Reading Standard 3.4** Analyze ways in which poets use imagery, personification, figures of speech, and sounds to evoke readers' emotions.
- **Writing Standard 1.4** Enhance meaning by employing rhetorical devices, including the extended use of parallelism, repetition, and analogy; the incorporation of visual aids (e.g., graphs, tables, pictures); and the issuance of a call for action.

Check for Understanding

Independent Practice

Reading Skills Focus

Possible responses:

1. *The speaker is amazed by the lady's beauty, which inspires his admiration.*
2. *The speaker reveals his understanding of nature and himself by characterizing nature as a living force. In stanza 1, for instance, he finds "society" (l. 3) and "music" (l. 4) in nature, and describes his interactions with the ocean as "interviews" (l. 6). The apostrophe also attributes life to the ocean.*
3. *A successful response will address how each alexandrine serves to emphasize the themes of the stanza.*

Vocabulary Check

4. *f* **5.** *g* **6.** *c* **7.** *a*
8. *h* **9.** *d* **10.** *e* **11.** *b*

Literary Skills Focus

Possible responses:

12. *The balance of opposites appears in "One shade the more, one ray the less." Her "raven tress" is black but "lightens oe'r her face."*
13. *"And laid my hand upon thy mane" (l. 27). The comparison makes the relationship seem companionable, although the speaker acknowledges the sea's greater power.*
14. *He compares her beauty to a starry night. The simile evokes awe.*
15. *Urging the sea to "Roll on" depicts the sea's action. The repeated word echoes the ocean's roar.*
16. *"Cloudless climes," "starry skies," "day denies," and "serenely sweet" are all examples of alliteration, which adds emphasis.*

What Do You Think Now?

To help students answer this question, remind them that the speakers use figurative language (such as simile, metaphor, and apostrophe) to describe their subjects.

Applying Your Skills

Reading Standard 3.3, 3.4 (see pages A48–A50)
Writing Standard 1.4 (see pages A51–A52)

She Walks in Beauty
***from* Childe Harold's Pilgrimage, Canto IV**

Literary Response and Analysis

Reading Skills Focus

Read with a Purpose

1. In "She Walks in Beauty," how does the woman's beauty affect the speaker?
2. In *Childe Harold's Pilgrimage,* how does the speaker reveal what he's learned about nature and himself?

Reading Skills: Understanding Rhyme and Rhythm

3. In your chart for *Childe Harold's Pilgrimage,* explain how each alexandrine helps you understand its stanza. Describe how each apostrophe affects its stanza's conclusion.

Subject of Stanza	How Alexandrine Concludes Stanza	How Alexandrine Helps Reader to Understand Stanza
Stanza 1: The speaker tells of his love and enjoyment of nature.	Alexandrine explains nature's impact on speaker	The speaker cannot fully describe his deep feelings about nature.

Vocabulary Check

Match each Vocabulary word to its definition.

4. serenely	**a.** breaks in; encroaches
5. gaudy	**b.** extreme joy
6. impaired	**c.** damaged
7. intrudes	**d.** move among; join in
8. linger	**e.** lasting for a while
9. mingle	**f.** calmly
10. protracted	**g.** loud in color or style
11. rapture	**h.** hang around

Literary Skills Focus

Literary Analysis

12. **Compare** The words "dark and bright" in line 3 of "She Walks in Beauty" suggest a balance of opposites. How is this idea developed in the poem?
13. **Analyze** In stanza 3 of *Childe Harold's Pilgrimage,* what metaphor compares the sea to a horse? What is the effect of this comparison?

Literary Skills: Simile / Apostrophe

14. **Analyze** Explain the simile in the first stanza of "She Walks in Beauty" and the emotions it evokes.
15. **Interpret** How does the use of apostrophe in line 10 of *Childe Harold's Pilgrimage* add to the description?

Literary Skills Review: Alliteration

16. **Analyze** The repetition of consonant sounds in words that are close to one another is **alliteration.** In each poem, identify an example of alliteration, and analyze its effect.

Writing Skills Focus

Think as a Reader/Writer

Use It in Your Writing Write a brief description of something you find beautiful or moving. Include at least three pairs or sets of parallel words and phrases to add rhythm and impact to your description.

What Do You Think Now? How do the speakers in both poems identify and describe true beauty? Explain.

Universal Access

Struggling Writers

Some students may need additional scaffolding to complete the Writing Skills Focus activity. After students have identified a subject, have them make a list of descriptive words and phrases about the subject. Encourage students to use their lists to help them as they write their description. Have students write some parallel phrases separately and incorporate them into their description. If students struggle to add parallel words and phrases to their paragraphs, tell them to use George Gordon, Lord Byron's poems as a model.

Assess

Unit 4 Resources, Selection Standards Check, p. 70

ThinkCentral Online Assessment, Selection Standards Check

Teacher One Stop™, editable Selection Standards Check

Model the Skill

- Model the skill of **visualizing images.** Read stanza 4 aloud, recording visual details on the board. You might construct a list that includes the words *mysterious priest, heifer, silken flanks, garlands,* and *peaceful citadel.*
- Brainstorm visual interpretations of these images. Tell students that the phrase *mysterious priest* might make them think of a hooded priest wearing a dark cloak. Then, ask a volunteer to draw a cloaked priest whose distinct facial features are hidden under his hood.

Guided Practice: Apply

Think-Pair-Share Ask students to draw a visual interpretation of stanza 5. As they read, have them keep track of visual images. When they have completed their drawings, have students present their work to a neighbor, describing the images in the poem that inspired their artwork.

Art Link

Ask Yourself

Possible response: *I imagine the scenes on the urn that Keats describes feature red figures—the maidens, gods/men, heifer, priest, crowd—and black details—pipes, timbrels, altar.*

2

Heard melodies are sweet, but those unheard
Are sweeter; therefore, ye soft pipes, play on;
Not to the sensual ear, but, more endeared,
Pipe to the spirit ditties° of no tone:
Fair youth, beneath the trees, thou canst not leave
Thy song, nor ever can those trees be bare;
Bold Lover, never, never canst thou kiss,
Though winning near the goal—yet, do not grieve;
She cannot fade, though thou hast not thy bliss,
Forever wilt thou love, and she be fair!

14. ditties: short, simple songs.

Vocabulary **sensual** (SEHN shoo uhl) *adj.:* having to do with the five senses.

ART LINK

Ancient Greek Vase Painting

(top) Warrior (470–460 B.C.) by the Sabouroff Painter. Red-figure cup. Classical period. The Louvre, Paris, France.

(bottom) Armed warrior (6th century B.C.) by the Psiax Painter. Attic black-figure plate, INV:F2099. Antikensammlung, Staatliche Museen zu Berlin, Germany.

Although at one time a specific urn was thought to be the focus of this poem, critics now believe that Keats was inspired by the engravings of multiple urns and by the entire ancient Greek art collection at the British Museum in London. At the museum, he would also have seen the celebrated collection of marble sculptures recently taken from the Parthenon in Athens and brought to London by Lord Elgin.

In ancient Greece, fine pottery was often decorated with figures from mythology. Black-figure and red-figure were the two techniques used most extensively in these decorations. In black-figure pottery, the earliest form, the figures are black and details are carved in red. In red-figure pottery, the later form, the figures are red and the details are painted in black.

Black figures were drawn on the vase with a liquid form of clay called *slip,* which turned black when the clay was hardened by fire. To add detail to the design, a potter cut lines into the slip. The red showing through was simply the surface of the clay itself. Then, in about 530 B.C., a potter experimented with reversing the approach. A brush dipped in glaze was used to create red figures on the black vase. In time, the brush won over the knife, and red-figure pottery became more popular.

Ask Yourself

How do you envision the urn that Keats describes?

Universal Access

Advanced Learners

Acceleration Group students into pairs. Ask each pair to paraphrase the following quotation, taken from a letter from John Keats to a friend. Then, ask the pairs to determine how the quotation could shed light on the meaning of Keats's poem. "I am certain of nothing but of the holiness of the Heart's affections and of the truth of imagination. What the imagination seizes as Beauty must be truth—whether it existed before or not—for I have the same idea of all our passions as of love: they are all in their sublimity creative of essential beauty."

Students with Disabilities

Help students understand "Ode on a Grecian Urn" by guiding them in isolating the main idea in each stanza. As you complete each stanza, ask students to stop and write one sentence on a separate piece of paper, describing the most important things that are happening in the stanza.

✔ See **UA: Differentiating Instruction** for strategies for teaching students with disabilities.

ODE

Ode on a Grecian Urn

by **John Keats**

Read with a Purpose

Read to discover what the speaker learns from meditating on the figures on a Greek vase.

Build Background

Many antique Greek vases show gods, goddesses, heroes, and mortals entangled in adventures. Traditionally, urns have been used as containers or for burial. The urn Keats describes is painted around with a series of mythological scenes, but no one knows exactly which urn Keats had in mind when he wrote this ode. It is probably an imaginative combination of several vases he had seen in engravings and in the British Museum. Keats addresses the vase itself in the first stanza.

Greek red-figured hydria (c. 420–400 B.C.) by Vaspainter Meidias. British Museum, London.

1

Thou still unravished° bride of quietness,
 Thou foster child of silence and slow time,
Sylvan° historian, who canst thus express
 A flowery tale more sweetly than our rhyme: **A**
What leaf-fringed legend haunts about thy shape
 Of deities or mortals, or of both,
  In Tempe or the dales of Arcady?°
 What men or gods are these? What maidens loath?
What mad pursuit? What struggle to escape?
 What pipes and timbrels?° What wild ecstasy? **B**

1. unravished: pure; untouched.

3. sylvan: of the forest. (The urn is decorated with a rural scene.)

7. Tempe (TEHM pee) . . . **Arcady** (AHR kuh dee): valleys in ancient Greece; ideal types of rural beauty.

10. timbrels: tambourines.

A Literary Focus **Metaphor** What is the urn compared to in lines 1–4?

B Reading Focus **Visualizing Imagery** Describe the scene you visualize when you read lines 5–10.

Vocabulary **deities** (DEE uh teez) *n. pl.:* gods and goddesses.
loath (lohth) *adj.:* unwilling or reluctant.

Universal Access

English Learners

English for Academic Success Point out that when speaking directly to the urn, the speaker uses the archaic forms *thou* and *thy* to mean "you" and "your." *Ye* also means "you" (plural).

✔ See the **English Language Skill Builder** in **UA: Differentiating Instruction.**

Struggling Readers

Model the reading skill of visualizing imagery. You might say: "In lines 5–10, I read of a 'leaf-fringed legend' and 'Arcady.' I know that Arcadia is a Greek region that Greek, Roman, and Renaissance poetry celebrated as a blissful place where shepherds live in harmony with nature and compose beautiful verse. I can convert those images in a pastoral setting, where men or gods chase maidens while musicians play."

Teacher Preparation

Selection Summary

The speaker of "Ode on a Grecian Urn" addresses an antique Greek vase on which two scenes are painted. In the first scene, gods or men pursue maidens while musicians play. The second scene depicts a crowd leading a cow to a ritual sacrifice. The solemn mood here contrasts with the feverish excitement of the first scene.

Direct Teach

Think About/Talk About

Read with a Purpose Have students read the Read with a Purpose statement. Ask students to discuss the relationship between art and reality. Ask students: "How can works of art be said to speak to us across generations?"

Comprehension

B Reading Focus

Possible response: *In a pastoral setting, men or gods chase maidens while musicians play.*

Analysis

A Literary Focus

Possible response: *an innocent bride, a child, and a historian*

Extend the Discussion

Metaphor What do the metaphors in the first three lines tell you about the urn? ***Possible response:*** *The urn is undamaged by time, has been long protected, and preserves history.*

Vocabulary: Own the Word

- **deities:** Have students complete the following sentence: "The English teacher taught mythological *deities* such as . . ."
- **loath:** Tell students the root for *loath* is *lāth,* which is Old English and means "hateful" or "hostile." When you are *loath,* you are hostile toward an action and unwilling to do it. Have students make a list of things they are *loath* to do at home.

Preteach

Introducing Vocabulary

To reinforce the importance of the Vocabulary words, explain that these words help the poet create visual imagery. The urn in the poem shows *deities* pursuing maidens who are *loath* to be caught by them. It depicts musicians who are playing not to the *sensual* ear, but to the imagination.

English for Academic Success

Language Coach

Show that an antonym provides meaning in a sentence by offering the opposite meaning of the Voacbulary word. The context of the sentence is strengthened by the contrasting words. For example: The boy was *loath* to eat the vegetables on his plate, but the vegetarian was *eager* to eat them. ***Possible responses:*** *antonyms of* loath *are* eager, willing; *antonyms of* sensual *are* rational, spiritual

Literary Skills Focus

As you read and discuss the selection, have students find examples of metaphors. Students can record their observations in their **Reader/Writer Notebooks**.

Reading Skills Focus

Give students a copy of the Reading Skills Focus graphic organizer before they read. (See **Unit 4 Resources.**)

Writing Skills Focus

Have students record instances of repetition in their **Reader/Writer Notebooks**. Students can use their notes to complete the Writing Skills Focus activity.

Learn It Online

The **PowerNotes** presentation for this lesson includes a short video that introduces the selection. The video is also available on the online version of this page.

go.hrw.com H12-852 Go

Reading Standard 3.4 (see pages A48–A50)

Literary Skills Focus

Metaphor In the figure of speech known as **metaphor,** two seemingly unlike things are compared without using a connective word such as *like* or *as*. At the beginning of "Ode on a Grecian Urn," Keats uses three metaphors to describe the urn. For example, in line 1, he refers to the urn as "Thou still unravished bride of quietness." By comparing the urn to a virgin bride, the poet implies that the urn has remained untouched throughout the ages, quietly awaiting contact with the human world. As you read, look for other metaphors that describe the urn.

Reading Skills Focus

Visualizing Imagery Poets use **imagery,** language that appeals to the senses, to bring their subject matter to life. Most images are visual, but images can also appeal to the senses of hearing, smell, taste, and touch.

Into Action As you read "Ode on a Grecian Urn," stop after stanzas 1–3 and again after stanza 4 to write a few sentences describing how you visualize the urn's decorations. Make rough sketches of those images.

Stanza	What I Visualize
First Stanza: An urn is decorated with a rural scene showing men and gods pursuing maidens and musicians playing pipes and tambourines.	

Writing Skills Focus

Think as a Reader/Writer

Find It in Your Reading As you read "Ode on a Grecian Urn," record in your *Reader/Writer Notebook* the words Keats repeats and the effects of that repetition.

Reader/Writer Notebook

Use your **RWN** to complete the activities for this selection.

Vocabulary

deities (DEE uh teez) *n. pl.:* gods and goddesses. *Keats wonders what story of deities or mortals is represented on the vase.*

loath (lohth) *adj.:* unwilling or reluctant. *Keats imagines that the maidens on the vase are loath to be caught by the men and gods who pursue them.*

sensual (SEHN shoo uhl) *adj.:* having to do with the five senses. *Keats says that the musicians on the vase play not for the sensual ear but for the imagination.*

Language Coach

Antonyms You can learn some word meanings by thinking about opposites. When he looks at a Greek vase, Keats wonders if the figures are "deities or mortals." This phrase suggests the two words are **antonyms,** or opposites. *Deities* are gods and goddesses. You can then derive that *mortals* are humans. Deities live forever, but mortals will eventually die. Can you think of antonyms for the words *loath* or *sensual*?

Learn It Online

Meet this poem through the video introduction online.

go.hrw.com H12-852 Go

California Standards, pp. 852–858

- **Reading Standard 3.4** Analyze ways in which poets use imagery, personification, figures of speech, and sounds to evoke readers' emotions.

Reading Standard 2.2, 3.4, 3.9 (see pages A48–A50)
Writing Standard 1.2, 2.3a (see pages A51–A52)

Ode to a Nightingale

Literary Response and Analysis

Reading Skills Focus

Quick Check

1. What misfortunes does the speaker want to escape in the third stanza? What means of escape are considered in the fourth stanza?
2. What thoughts of death does the speaker have in stanza 6? How does he resolve these temptations?

Read with a Purpose

3. This poem is directly addressed to the nightingale. Summarize what the speaker is saying.

Reading Skills: Reading Closely

4. What reading strategies did you find most helpful for reading this poem closely?

Vocabulary Check

Check your knowledge of the Vocabulary words by answering the questions below.

5. Would you describe a symphony as **melodious** or **murmurous**?
6. Would you describe the sound of two people speaking in low tones as **melodious** or **murmurous**?
7. If something **perplexes** you, how will you feel about it?

Literary Skills Focus

Literary Analysis

8. **Analyze** How is the speaker's mood different at the poem's beginning than at its end?
9. **Identify** What differentiates the experience of the nightingale from that of the speaker?
10. **Make Judgments** Why does the speaker want to capture the nightingale's "ease"? Why is he "too happy in [its] happiness" (stanza 1)?
11. **Literary Perspectives** In the last stanza, the speaker points to the limits of fancy, or imagination, to fool him into forgetting himself when he is melancholy. What does this say about his belief about sadness and the power of imagination?

Literary Skills: Synesthesia

12. **Analyze** Review the uses of **synesthesia** in the poem (lines 8–10, 13–14, 28, 38–39, 41–43). What sensory experiences does each describe? What feeling or mood does the device help create?

Literary Skills Review: Allusions

13. **Analyze** A reference to someone or something from history, literature, religion, mythology, politics, sports, science, or pop culture is **allusion.** What allusions does Keats make to mythology and the Bible? What is the effect of the allusions?

Writing Skills Focus

Think as a Reader/Writer

Use It in Your Writing In a paragraph in your *Reader/Writer Notebook*, describe something abstract (perhaps fame or friendship) or something from nature (perhaps an animal or a hurricane). Address your subject directly, and personify it by giving it human feelings, thoughts, and actions.

What Do You Think Now? What does Keats discover about life, death, and the force of the imagination in "Ode to a Nightingale"?

Check for Understanding

Independent Practice

Reading Skills Focus

Possible responses:

1. *He wishes to escape the human suffering of illness and death. In stanza 4, he considers imagination and poetry as means of escape.*
2. *The speaker is enamored of death, but the bird's song reminds him that he would miss beauty.*
3. *The speaker wishes he could fly away with the nightingale and escape from suffering and pain. He admires the bird's freedom.*
4. *Students should include at least three strategies.*

Vocabulary Check

5. *melodious*
6. *murmurous*
7. *confused*

Literary Skills Focus

Possible responses:

8. *His mood in the end is less exalted because, as he returns to his "sole self," he realizes that he will never achieve the nightingale's ease. Or, the speaker's mood becomes more exalted because he sees poetry as a means to enduring beauty.*
9. *The speaker is subject to time, disease, and death; the nightingale lives in the eternal realm.*
10. *He wants to "ease" his own troubles. He is "too happy" because of the bird's beautiful song.*
11. *Though imagination is an effective temporary escape, man must return to his melancholy state.*
12. *Students should list instances of synesthesia in the poem and point out how synesthesia enhances the reader's ability to empathize with the content of the poem.*
13. *Allusions to mythology (lines 4, 7, 13, 16, 32) and biblical allusions (line 66) suggest that the bird transcends time and place, symbolizing eternity.*

Universal Access

Struggling Writers

Some students may need additional scaffolding to complete the Writing Skills Focus activity. Have students choose an animal and address it directly in a short paragraph. Remind students to describe it as if it could think, feel, and act like a human being. Before students begin their paragraphs, have them write a list of questions that they would like to ask the animal if they had the opportunity. Then, have students think about how the animal might answer the questions. Encourage students to use these thoughts as they write their paragraphs.

What Do You Think Now?

Have them consider the images Keats presents in "Ode to a Nightingale." Which images seem most powerful? What do these images seem to symbolize?

Assess

Unit 4 Resources, Selection Standards Check, p. 102

go.hrw.com **ThinkCentral Online Assessment,** Selection Standards Check

3

Ah, happy, happy boughs! that cannot shed
  Your leaves, nor ever bid the Spring adieu;
And, happy melodist, unwearied,
  Forever piping songs forever new;
More happy love! more happy, happy love!
  Forever warm and still to be enjoyed,
    Forever panting, and forever young;
All breathing human passion far above,
  That leaves a heart high-sorrowful and cloyed,°
    A burning forehead, and a parching tongue.

4

Who are these coming to the sacrifice?
  To what green altar, O mysterious priest,
Lead'st thou that heifer lowing° at the skies,
  And all her silken flanks° with garlands dressed?
What little town by river or seashore,
  Or mountain-built with peaceful citadel,°
    Is emptied of this folk, this pious morn?
And, little town, thy streets forevermore
  Will silent be; and not a soul to tell
    Why thou art desolate, can e'er return. **C**

5

O Attic° shape! Fair attitude!° with brede°
  Of marble men and maidens overwrought,°
With forest branches and the trodden weed;
  Thou, silent form, dost tease us out of thought
As doth eternity: Cold Pastoral!°
  When old age shall this generation waste,
    Thou shalt remain, in midst of other woe
  Than ours, a friend to man, to whom thou say'st,
"Beauty is truth, truth beauty,"—that is all
  Ye know on earth, and all ye need to know.

C Reading Focus **Visualizing Imagery** Describe the scene you visualize when you read stanza 4.

29. cloyed (kloyd): wearied with excess.

33. lowing: mooing.

34. flanks: sides between the ribs and the hips.

36. citadel (SIHT uh duhl): fortress.

41. Attic: Athenian; classically elegant. **attitude:** posture. **brede:** interwoven design.

42. overwrought: decorated to excess; also, in reference to the men and maidens, overexcited.

45. Pastoral: artwork depicting idealized rural life.

Think About/Talk About

Comprehension

C Reading Focus

Possible response: *In the scene, a mysterious priest leads a decorated, bellowing cow to an altar for sacrifice. So many people take part in the procession that Keats imagines their town empty of inhabitants during the somber event.*

Extend the Discussion

Theme How does "Ode on a Grecian Urn" express both the positive and negative sides of the search for beauty? ***Possible responses:*** *The quest is positive—the contemplation of ideal beauty gives us an experience of the eternal or timeless. The quest is negative—the very same contemplation reminds us of the transience of our own existence.*

Vocabulary: Own the Word

sensual: A *sensual* place is a greenhouse or crowded amusement park. Imagery conveys *sensual* information. Have students give examples of *sensual* pleasures found in nature. [*the smell of flowers, the sound of birds chirping, watching the sunrise, feeling a cool breeze on a hot day, tasting a fruit*]

California Standards, pp. 856–858

- **Reading Standard 3.4** Analyze ways in which poets use imagery, personification, figures of speech, and sounds to evoke readers' emotions.
- **Reading Standard 3.7** Analyze recognized works of world literature from a variety of authors: **c.** Evaluate the philosophical, political, religious, ethical, and social influences of the historical period that shaped the characters, plots, and settings.
- **Writing Standard 1.4** Enhance meaning by employing rhetorical devices, including the extended use of parallelism, repetition, and analogy; the incorporation of visual aids (e.g., graphs, tables, pictures); and the issuance of a call for action.
- **Writing Standard 2.3** Write reflective compositions: **a.** Explore the significance of personal experiences, events, conditions, or concerns by using rhetorical strategies (e.g., narration, description, exposition, persuasion). **b.** Draw comparisons between specific incidents and broader themes that illustrate the writer's important beliefs or generalizations about life. **c.** Maintain a balance in describing individual incidents and relate those incidents to more general and abstract ideas.
- **Listening and Speaking Standard 1.4** Use rhetorical questions, parallel structure, concrete images, figurative language, characterization, irony, and dialogue to achieve clarity, force, and aesthetic effect.
- **Listening and Speaking Standard 2.3** Deliver oral responses to literature: **a.** Demonstrate a comprehensive understanding of the significant ideas of literary works (e.g., make assertions about the text that are reasonable and supportable). **d.** Demonstrate an awareness of the author's use of stylistic devices and an appreciation of the effects created.

Check for Understanding

Independent Practice

Reading Skills Focus

Possible responses:

1. *Though love and beauty fade, they will be forever preserved in art.*
2. *The urn will still exist, reminding people that beauty is the only truth.*
3. *The speaker has learned that while life is temporary, it can be preserved through art. Art is eternal.*
4. *Ask students to see if their image descriptions include all the major details.*

Literary Skills Focus

Possible responses:

5. *Imagination can sometimes create something more exciting than a real experience. This is a typically Romantic idea.*
6. *The words are "happy" and "forever." The selection of these particular words shows the speaker's enthusiasm for everlasting art; it is an ironic comment on stasis and unfulfilled passion.*
7. *They describe the consequences of excessive passion.*
8. *It would be a state of mind beyond the material world of time and place.*
9. *Bride—the urn is undamaged by time; child—the urn has long been protected; historian—the urn preserves history. The elaborate metaphors open the ode with a reverential tone, leading to the poet's wonder at the scenes on the urn.*
10. *The setting reveals a blissful, lively mood in the first scene and a solemn, tranquil one in the second scene.*

Applying Your Skills

Reading Standard 3.4, 3.7c (see pages A48–A50)
Writing Standard 1.4 (see pages A51–A52)

Ode on a Grecian Urn

Literary Response and Analysis

Reading Skills Focus

Quick Check

1. In stanzas 2 and 3, what does the speaker say to the people and even to the trees depicted on the urn?
2. What will happen to the urn when the speaker and his generation are dead? What message does the urn continue to offer?

Read with a Purpose

3. By the end of "Ode on a Grecian Urn," what has the speaker learned about the nature of life and art?

Reading Skills: Visualizing Imagery

4. Review the chart you made with sketches showing how you visualized the imagery in the ode. Put a star next to those images you found most powerful. Compare your chart with a partner's. What details can you add to your chart?

Literary Skills Focus

Literary Analysis

5. **Draw Inferences** Why do you think "unheard" melodies (lines 11–14) are "sweeter" to the speaker? Do you agree with this typically Romantic idea? Explain your response to this famous line.
6. **Analyze** What two words does the speaker repeat in stanza 3? What significance do you see in the selection of those particular words?
7. **Interpret** How do you interpret lines 28–30?
8. **Draw Conclusions** If the urn could "tease us out of thought" (line 44), what state would we be in? In what sense would this state be superior to thought?

Literary Skills: Metaphor

9. **Analyze** Discuss your understanding of the three **metaphors** used to describe the urn in lines 2–4. To what are they comparing the urn? What do the metaphors tell you about the urn?

Literary Skills Review: Setting

10. **Analyze** The time and location of an action is its **setting.** In this poem, setting is handled in an unusual way. Although the speaker might be in a museum viewing the urn, that museum setting is never mentioned. Instead, we enter the setting depicted on the urn. How would you describe the mood established by the setting the speaker sees on the urn?

Writing Skills Focus

Think as a Reader/Writer

Use It in Your Writing In your *Reader/Writer Notebook,* write a paragraph describing a place. Use repetition to emphasize important details of the place and help create tone, mood, and rhythm.

What Do You Think Now?

In what ways has the imagination brought this vase to life for the speaker?

Universal Access

Struggling Writers

Students might need additional scaffolding to complete this task. Have them choose a place to write about and think about the atmosphere or mood of the place. Then, ask them to write a few sentences of the place describing why they associate a certain mood to the place. Suggest that students repeat certain words or phrases to reinforce this mood in their descriptive paragraphs. Encourage students to review their notes in their **Reader/Writer Notebooks** about the use and effects of repetition in the poem.

What Do You Think Now?

To help students answer this question, ask them to describe how Keats uses imagery and metaphor to describe what he sees in his mind as he studies the vase.

Vocabulary Development

Vocabulary Check

Check your mastery of the Vocabulary words by answering the following questions:

1. Which word is a synonym for the word ***deities:*** *gods* or *mortals?*
2. Which word is the opposite of the word ***loath:*** *willing* or *reluctant?*
3. How is the word *intellectual* opposite in meaning to the word ***sensual?***

Vocabulary Skills: Figurative Language

Figurative language, such as **similes, metaphors,** and **personification,** is usually visual. Figurative language creates pictures in our minds by helping us associate one thing with another, different thing.

Similes are explicit comparisons using a connective word such as *like, as, than,* or *resembles.* **Metaphors** are comparisons that are made directly, without using connective words. **Personification** is a metaphor in which a nonhuman or nonliving thing is described as if it has human or lifelike qualities.

Figure of Speech	Example
simile	"Thou, silent form, dost tease us out of thought / As doth eternity . . ." (uses *As*)
metaphor	"Thou foster child of silence and slow time" (directly compares urn to foster child; also a personification)
personification	"Ah, happy, happy boughs!" (gives human quality of happiness to boughs)

Your Turn

Rewrite these sentences with the indicated figure of speech.

1. The urn is an unravished bride. (simile)
2. My heart is sorrowful. (metaphor)
3. The heifer lows at the skies. (personification)

Language Coach

Antonyms Words with opposite meanings are called **antonyms.** Some words, such as *winning* and *losing*, are obvious antonyms. Other antonyms may not be immediately apparent. For example, the word *pious* means "devout; religious"; its obvious antonym is *impious*. Other antonyms include *irreverent, profane,* and *blasphemous*. Choose the antonym for each Vocabulary word below, and explain your choice.

1. deities
   a. angels b. humans c. fools
2. loath
   a. eager b. hated c. uncertain
3. sensual
   a. physical b. concrete c. intellectual

Academic Vocabulary

Talk About

Recall that **apostrophe** is a figure of speech in which a speaker directly addresses an absent or dead person, an abstract quality, or something nonhuman as if it were present and capable of responding. With a partner, discuss the advantages and limitations of this technique. How does this technique function, and what are its effects?

Learn It Online
Learn more about the Vocabulary words online.
go.hrw.com H12-857 Go

Independent Practice

Vocabulary Development

Vocabulary Check

1. *gods*
2. *willing*
3. *"Intellectual" means having to do with the mind; "sensual" means having to do with the senses.*

WordSharp: An Interactive Vocabulary Tutor

Your Turn

1. *The urn is like an unravished bride.*
2. *My heart is a widower.*
3. *The heifer pleads with the skies.*

English for Academic Success

Language Coach

1. *b*
2. *a*
3. *c*

English for Academic Success

Academic Vocabulary

Possible response: *Using the technique of apostrophe in a literary work allows the speaker to express his or her thoughts and emotions without restraint, which brings the inanimate object to life for the reader.*

Universal Access: Vocabulary Development

English Learners

English for Academic Success Some students may need additional practice recognizing different types of figurative language. Review the definitions of the three types of figurative language discussed in the Vocabulary Skills activity—simile, metaphor, and personification. Then, pair students and have them engage in an instructional conversation in which they determine what type of figurative language is being used in the following examples. Encourage students to look for key words that provide clues to the type of figurative language being used.

- The leaves are like emeralds shimmering in the sunlight. [*simile*]
- The branches waved to me as I walked by. [*personification*]
- The trees are soldiers shielding me from the sun. [*metaphor*]

✔ See the **Academic and Selection Vocabulary Skill Builder** in **UA: Differentiating Instruction.**

Learn It Online

WordSharp: An Interactive Vocabulary tutor provides additional support for vocabulary development. Multimedia tutorials show students how to apply vocabulary skills to unfamiliar words—and how to make those words their own.

go.hrw.com H12–857 Go

Independent Practice

Grammar Link

Your Turn

1. *Keats says, "Beauty is truth, truth beauty."*
2. *He believes that the people on the vase are immortal and forever young.*
3. *"What is the main idea in 'Ode on a Grecian Urn'?" asked the teacher.*

Choices: Evaluation Criteria

Review: Homework
Talk with Keats

- Dialogue exhibits understanding of Keats's work and attention to biographical information in this section.
- Questions refer to Keats's use of devices and techniques.

Connect: Homework
Address an Artwork

- Essay includes an explanation, questions, summary, and an opinion.
- Student identifies a message revealed through a work of art.

Extend: Timed Writing 40–50 Minutes

- Students use evidence from poem to support viewpoint.
- Students present argument in a logical and coherent manner.

Assess

Unit 4 Resources, Selection Standards Check, p. 113

go.hrw.com **ThinkCentral Online Assessment,** Selection Standards Check

Teacher One Stop™, editable Selection Standards Check

Reteach

go.hrw.com **ThinkCentral Online Remediation**

Applying Your Skills

Writing Standard 2.3a–c (see pages A51–A52)
Listening and Speaking Standard 1.4, 2.3a, 2.3d (see pages A53–A55)

Ode on a Grecian Urn

Grammar Link

Direct and Indirect Quotations

When you report a person's exact words, you use a **direct quotation.** In written language, quotation marks are used to enclose direct quotations. When a direct quotation is a question, notice that the question mark is put inside the quotation marks.

"What men or gods are these?" asks the speaker.

At the end of a quotation, periods are placed inside closing quotation marks. Semicolons and colons are placed outside the quotation marks.

He said, "The figures on the urn are forever frozen."

He said "good work"; then he left the room.

Single quotation marks enclose a quotation within another quotation:

"Let's read 'Ode on a Grecian Urn,'" he said.

An **indirect quotation** is a rewording of a person's actual words. Indirect quotations are not placed within quotation marks or set off with punctuation.

Keats believed that unheard melodies are sweeter.

Your Turn

Rewrite the following sentences as directed.

1. Keats says in line 49 that beauty is found in truth. (Change to a direct quotation.)
2. He believes the people on the vase are "Forever panting, and forever young." (Change to an indirect quotation.)
3. "What is the main idea in "Ode on a Grecian Urn," asked the teacher. (Correct the punctuation.)

Writing Application Add direct quotations to a piece of your own writing about literature. Use passages from the literary source itself.

CHOICES

As you respond to the Choices, use these **Academic Vocabulary** words as appropriate: device, differentiate, function, inherent, technique.

REVIEW

Talk with Keats

Partner Activity Imagine that you will be talking to John Keats about "Ode on a Grecian Urn." With a partner, select at least three passages to discuss with Keats. Decide who will play the role of Keats and who will act as the questioner. Review the poem, and write out your dialogue. Include questions about Keats's devices and techniques. Present your dialogue to your class.

CONNECT

Address an Artwork

Select a work of art reproduced in this book, and, as Keats does in "Ode on a Grecian Urn," directly address it. In an essay, tell what is happening in the work, ask it questions, sum up the message you think it reveals, and tell what you think and feel about it.

EXTEND

Evaluate Two Meanings

Timed Writing Keats's poem "Ode on a Grecian Urn" presents insight into the historical period that produced the urn as well as Keats's views on art and beauty. In an expository essay, explain the historical and philosophical insight the poem provides. Use evidence from the poem to support your analysis.

Universal Access: Grammar Link

Tell students that when changing direct speech into indirect speech, they should check that their tenses are changed or unchanged accordingly.

- June: "I love history." / June said that she loves history.
- Tom: "I am quitting my job next week." / Tom told me that he is quitting his job next week.
- Rachel: "Don't go into that room, Mabel!" / Rachel warned Mabel not to go into the room.

✔ For more practice with direct and indirect quotations, see **Warriner's Handbook, GrammarNotes,** and **Language Handbook Worksheets.**

Grades 9–10 Review Reading Standard 2.5 (see pages A48–A50)

Keats's Last Letter

Informational Text Focus

Analyzing Primary Sources A **primary source** is information that has been written or recorded by someone with firsthand knowledge of a topic. Primary sources include letters, autobiographies, historical documents, and eyewitness interviews. **Secondary sources** consist of information derived from, or about, primary sources or other secondary sources. Examples of secondary sources include encyclopedias, documentary films, biographies, history books, and interviews with historians. A scholar's biography about Keats is a secondary source, while Keats's letters are a primary source about Keats because they reveal his own thoughts and feelings. This last letter reflects Keats's attitude toward life and poetry as he faced imminent death.

Into Action As you read this letter, record details that tell you how Keats feels, what he thinks, and what he has been doing. Note why this information might provide valuable insights about Keats.

Information Keats reveals about his feelings, thoughts, and actions	Why this information might be valuable to a reader or researcher learning about Keats
"at my worst, . . . [I] summoned up more puns, . . . in one week than in any year of my life"	Even though Keats felt so ill, he continued to explore language. This may show Keats's commitment to the literary life, his extraordinary talent and gift with language, and his writing as a way to ease his suffering.

Writing Skills Focus

Preparing for Timed Writing Keats lived and wrote at a time when people generally wrote more formally than they do today. As you read, record in your *Reader/Writer Notebook* examples of Keats's rather formal style, which he uses even though he is writing a deeply personal letter to a close friend.

Vocabulary

habitual (huh BIHCH oo uhl) *adj.:* regular; steady. *At the time of this letter, Keats experienced habitual feelings of sadness.*

posthumous (PAHS choo muhs) *adj.:* happening after death. *Keats, though he was alive, felt he was living a posthumous existence.*

predominant (prih DAHM uh nuhnt) *adj.:* prevailing. *Keats feels that the predominant theme of his life is that he misses people and opportunities.*

Language Coach

Root Words Within some words are common root words. For example, *habitual* contains the root word *habit,* which means "something done often or repeatedly, often without awareness." How is the meaning of this root related to the meaning of *habitual*? Identify the root word in *predominated.* Tell how its meaning relates to *predominated* and *predominant.*

Learn It Online
Learn more about the life of Keats at the Writers' Lives site online.
go.hrw.com H12-859 Go

Reader/Writer Notebook
Use your **RWN** to complete the activities for this selection.

Preteach

Introducing Vocabulary

Read the Vocabulary words, definitions, and sample sentences aloud. Then, use this activity to check students' understanding.

1. List a few **habitual** actions that you perform in the morning.
2. Explain why someone might be awarded a **posthumous** honorary degree.
3. Describe a **predominant** theme in Romantic poetry.

English for Academic Success

Language Coach

Ask students to guess the meaning of *humous* if they know that *post–* means "after." [humous *comes from the Latin* humus, *meaning "ground, earth"*]

Informational Text Focus

- Give students a copy of the Informational Text Focus graphic organizer before they read. (See **Unit 4 Resources**.)
- As you read and discuss the selection with students, have them note details about Keats's commitment to poetry. Tell them to use their responses to answer the questions on the Applying Your Skills page.

Writing Skills Focus

Have students record Keats's use of formal language in their **Reader/Writer Notebooks**. Students can use their notes to complete the Writing Skills Focus activity.

California Standards, pp. 859–862

- **Grades 9–10 Review Reading Standard 2.5** Extend ideas presented in primary or secondary sources through original analysis, evaluation, and elaboration.

Learn It Online
The Writers' Lives feature of the Interactive Student Edition offers additional information about this author. Audio or video segments are provided for some authors.
go.hrw.com H12–859 Go

Teacher Preparation

Selection Summary

Keats, knowing he has tuberculosis, writes a letter to his good friend Charles Brown. In "Keats's Last Letter," he discusses his health and his regrets, including his lack of communication with his friends and his inability to continue with his poetry and to see his lover.

Direct Teach

Think About/Talk About

Read with a Purpose Have students read the Read with a Purpose statement. Point out that Keats knows he is dying, and ask how he might be feeling as he writes this letter.

Analyzing Visuals

Connecting to the Text: *The painting evokes a contemplative and quiet, yet serious mood, similar to that of the letter. The soft lines and contrasting colors of the dark room and the bright view outside produce a sense of gloominess.*

LETTER

Keats's Last Letter

by **John Keats**

Analyzing Visuals

Connecting to the Text Consider the colors, the contrast between light and dark, and the lines in this painting of Keats. What mood or feeling does the painting evoke? Compare the mood of the painting to that of Keats's letter.

Read with a Purpose

Read to discover Keats's state of mind as he says good-bye to a dear friend.

Build Background

Keats knew that he was very ill with tuberculosis, the disease that had killed his mother and brother. His doctors said that his only hope would be to leave the cold and damp of London and move to a warmer, drier climate. Keats made plans to embark on the long and difficult journey from London to Rome. Unable to travel alone, he had hoped that his good friend Charles Brown might go with him. However, Brown learned of the plan too late and just missed saying goodbye to Keats, who sailed for Italy on September 17, 1820, accompanied by another friend, the artist Joseph Severn. Once in Italy, Keats remained in contact with Brown through letters. This letter to Brown was the last written by Keats before he died on February 23, 1821.

The "her" Keats refers to so sadly in the letter is probably Fanny Brawne, the girl in England he loved and would never be able to marry. In fact, in an earlier letter, Keats had asked Charles Brown to befriend Fanny when he was dead. Also referred to in the letter is George, Keats's brother, who had immigrated to America in 1818.

John Keats (1821) by Joseph Severn. Oil on canvas.
The Granger Collection, NY.

Universal Access

Struggling Readers

As students read Keats's letter, guide them in noticing the pairs of contradictory words, images, and ideas; for example, he is so weak he cannot bear the sight of a friend's handwriting, yet he is able to go riding and to create puns. Have students list these contradictions in a two-column chart. Then, ask students to discuss what the pairs suggest about the author's state of mind.

✔ See **UA: Differentiating Instruction** for a graphic organizer to scaffold instruction for struggling readers.

Advanced Learners

Enrichment Have students find out more about the people mentioned in Keats's letter and the types of relationships he had with them. These people include Charles Brown, Dr. Clark, John Hamilton Reynolds, Joseph Severn, William Haslam, George Keats, and Fanny Keats (John Keats's sister). Have students share their information with the class.

Rome, 30 November 1820

My dear Brown,

'Tis the most difficult thing in the world to me to write a letter. My stomach continues so bad, that I feel it worse on opening any book, yet I am much better than I was in quarantine. Then I am afraid to encounter the pro-ing and con-ing of anything interesting to me in England. I have an habitual feeling of my real life having passed, and that I am leading a post-humous existence. God knows how it would have been—but it appears to me—however, I will not speak of that subject. I must have been at Bedhampton nearly at the time you were writing to me from Chichester—how unfortunate—and to pass on the river too! There was my star predominant! I cannot answer anything in your letter, which followed me from Naples to Rome, because I am afraid to look it over again. I am so weak (in mind) that I cannot bear the sight of any handwriting of a friend I love so much as I do you. Yet I ride the little horse, and, at my worst, even in quarantine, summoned up more puns, in a sort of desperation, in one week than in any year of my life. There is one thought enough to kill me; I have been well, healthy, alert, etc., walking with her, and now—the knowledge of contrast, feeling for light and shade, all that information (primitive sense) necessary for a poem, are great enemies to the recovery of the stomach. There, you rogue, I put you to the torture; but you must bring your philosophy to bear, as I do mine, really, or how should I be able to live? Dr. Clark is very attentive to me; he says, there is very little the matter with my lungs, but my stomach, he says, is very bad. I am well disappointed in hearing good news from George, for it runs in my head we shall all die young. I have not written to Reynolds yet, which he must think very neglectful; being anxious to send him a good account of my health, I have delayed it from week to week. If I recover, I will do all in my power to correct the mistakes made during sickness; and if I should not, all my faults shall be forgiven. Severn is very well, though he leads so dull a life with me. Remember me to all friends, and tell Haslam I should not have left London without taking leave of him, but from being so low in body and mind. Write to George as soon you receive this, and tell him how I am, as far as you can guess; and also a note to my sister—who walks about my imagination like a ghost—she is so like Tom. I can scarcely bid you goodbye, even in a letter. I always made an awkward bow. (A)

God bless you!
John Keats

(A) **Informational Focus** **Analyzing Primary Sources** Though this was his last letter, Keats lived for a few more months before dying. What does he say in the letter about his ability to write poetry?

Vocabulary **habitual** (huh BIHCH oo uhl) *adj.:* regular; steady.
posthumous (PAHS choo muhs) *adj.:* happening after death.
predominant (prih DAHM uh nuhnt) *adj.:* prevailing.

Think About/Talk About

Analysis

(A) Informational Focus

Possible response: *Keats says that the strong emotion he feels while writing poetry exacerbates his stomach illness.*

Extend the Discussion

Drawing Conclusions Why does Keats continue to make puns and go riding although he feels increasingly sick? ***Possible response:*** *He wants to keep busy, alert, and productive for as long as possible.*

Evaluating What does Keats's mentioning of Reynolds and Haslam reveal about his character? ***Possible response:*** *He feels bad about not writing to Reynolds yet, even though he has a good excuse for not doing so. He seems to be the kind of friend who tries to be as considerate as possible, even in his illness.*

Vocabulary: Own the Word

- **habitual:** Tell students that when we think of habits or behaviors that are repeated, we say these actions are *habitual.* What are some *habitual* behaviors you have? ***Possible responses:*** *biting my nails, twisting my chair, chewing gum*
- **posthumous:** Ask students the following question: "Why might you be more interested in *posthumous* publications?"
- **predominant:** Create a semantic web with *predominant* in the center. Then draw spider legs from the center circle as students add related concepts to the semantic web. ***Possible responses:*** *influential, superior, power, authority*

California Standards, p. 862

- **Grades 9–10 Review Reading Standard 2.5** Extend ideas presented in primary or secondary sources through original analysis, evaluation, and elaboration.
- **Writing Standard 2.2** Write responses to literature: **c.** Support important ideas and viewpoints through accurate and detailed references to the text and to other works. **d.** Demonstrate an understanding of the author's use of stylistic devices and an appreciation of the effects created.
- **Listening and Speaking Standard 1.4** Use rhetorical questions, parallel structure, concrete images, figurative language, characterization, irony, and dialogue to achieve clarity, force, and aesthetic effect.

Check for Understanding

Independent Practice

Informational Text Focus

Possible responses:

1. *Keats is unable to answer because it is too sad for him to see the handwriting of a friend he might never see again.*
2. *The doctor thinks that Keats's worst health problem is his stomach. This is inappropriate because we know Keats had tuberculosis, a disease that attacks the lungs.*
3. *He has difficulty saying goodbye.*
4. *Keats seems very melancholy and disappointed that he will never see his lover and friends or write poetry again. The fact of his pain in writing or even looking at a letter and his focus on death when he writes, "we shall all die young" tacitly suggest his distress.*
5. *Students should support their responses with evidence from the text.*
6. *The feeling is always present.*
7. *He feels ill.*
8. *His fate has always been to miss out on joys.*
9. *Keats was no longer able to write poetry because his illness prevented him from making observations. All that which was "necessary for a poem" were "great enemies" to his recovery.*
10. *bad stomach, but feels better than he was in quarantine; weak mind, yet writes more puns in one week than in his life—these reveal the author's mental confusion and instability*
11. *Simile; Keats's description of his sister evokes an image of her walking around "like a ghost."*
12. *I would write about how much my close friend has meant to me and express gratefulness. I would not dwell on the things that I cannot enjoy, unlike Keats.*

INFORMATIONAL TEXT FOCUS

Applying Your Skills

Grades 9–10 Review Reading Standard 2.5 (see pages A48–A50)
Listening and Speaking Standard 1.4 (see pages A53–A55)
Writing Standard 2.2c, 2.2d (see pages A51–A52)

Keats's Last Letter

Analyze Informational Texts

Informational Text Focus

Quick Check

1. Why is Keats unable to answer the questions from Brown's letter?
2. According to his doctor, what is Keats's most serious health problem? What is ironic, or inappropriate, about this diagnosis?
3. What does Keats mean when he says at the end, "I always made an awkward bow"?

Read with a Purpose

4. What is John Keats's state of mind as he writes this last letter to a friend? What details from the letter suggest what he is really thinking and feeling, in addition to what he writes explicitly?

Informational Skills: Analyzing Primary Sources

5. Review the chart you kept as you read this letter. Based on evidence in the letter, tell how Keats's illness affected his ability to write poetry—and letters to friends.

Vocabulary Check

Be sure you can explain your answers to these questions about the Vocabulary words.

6. Keats says he has a **habitual** feeling that his real life has passed. Does this statement suggest that the feeling is fleeting or that it is always present?
7. When Keats says he feels he is leading a **posthumous** existence, does he feel healthy or ill?
8. Keats says that passing his friend on the river without knowing it showed his star **predominant.** Does this mean that Keats feels his fate, or star, has always been to miss out on joys, or that he feels his fate is ever changing?

Text Analysis

9. **Interpret** Keats writes ". . . the knowledge of contrast, feeling for light and shade, all that information (primitive sense) necessary for a poem, are great enemies to the recovery of the stomach." What do you think he means by this statement? Support your answer with details from the text.
10. **Analyze** Notice the pairs of contradictory words, images, and ideas in Keats's letter. Write down some of these pairs, and explain what they reveal about the author's state of mind.
11. **Evaluate** What figure of speech does Keats use to describe his sister? What effect does he create by using these particular words?

Listening and Speaking

12. **Extend** Imagine that you are writing a letter to a close friend you may not see for many years. What things would you want to mention? What feelings would you express? Write down a few things you would include in your letter, and discuss your list with a partner. Are your concerns similar to the ones Keats expresses in his letter?

Writing Skills Focus

Timed Writing Review the notes you made in your *Reader/Writer Notebook* about Keats's formal style. Write a brief paragraph in which you contrast his style with the way a young person today would write to a close friend. Cite examples from Keats's letter.

What Do You Think Now? How has imagination now become a torment to Keats?

Universal Access

Struggling Writers

Students may need additional scaffolding to complete the Writing Skills Focus activity. Write the following examples of Keats's formal language on the board: "'Tis the most difficult thing in the world to me to write a letter," "Remember me to all friends," and "I have an habitual feeling of my real life having passed." Have students work with a partner to discuss how a person today might rewrite Keats's lines. Then, have students use what they have discussed to write a paragraph comparing Keats's style to the style of a contemporary person writing to a close friend.

What Do You Think Now?

Ask students to consider how imagination serves to exacerbate the torments of Keats's mind and body. Have students support their responses with evidence from the text.

Assess

Unit 4 Resources, Selection Standards Check, p. 114

COMPARING TEXTS: WORLD LITERATURE

Japanese and Chinese Poetry

Cormorant fisherman on bamboo raft, Li River, Yangshuo.

You have just read a number of British poems from the Romantic period. In this World Literature section, you will read Japanese tanka and haiku, which, like Romantic poetry, use images of nature. Unlike much Romantic poetry, these Japanese forms are concise and rigidly structured. You will also read poetry from two of China's master poets, Tu Fu and Li Po, who found great inspiration in nature. Most of these Japanese and Chinese poems were written hundreds of years before the Romantic period.

CONTENTS

Standards Focus

Objectives

Students will
- understand the use of imagery
- understand the way mood achieves specific rhetorical or aesthetic purposes
- use text structure to understand meaning

English for Academic Success

Academic Vocabulary

Look for opportunities to use the Academic Vocabulary words in this unit.

- **device, *n.*:** something made for a particular purpose
- **differentiate, *v.*:** distinguish; identify differences
- **function, *n.*:** the action for which a person or thing is specially fitted; purpose
- **inherent, *adj.*:** existing in something as a fixed, essential quality
- **technique, *n.*:** method; way of using skills

Analyzing Visuals

Extension Activity Have students look at the photograph on p. 863. Ask, "What emotions or ideas does this painting bring to mind? In other words, how would you describe the mood of this photograph?" ***Possible response:*** *The mood is calm and serene. The water is still, and the lighting is pale yellow and pink, which suggests that it is set at sunset.*

INTRODUCTION TO
Japanese and Chinese Poetry

Japanese Poetry

The **tanka** and the **haiku** are two of the most beloved forms of Japanese poetry. Both are very old, tanka dating from the eighth century A.D. and haiku from the thirteenth and fourteenth centuries. Both forms demand the compression of ideas and images into the space of a few words.

Japanese red-scroll garden.

The earliest-known tanka appear in a collection of poems called the *Manyoshu,* or *Collection of Ten Thousand Leaves.* **Tanka,** meaning "short songs," are brief and lyrical. Like other **lyric** poems, each tanka expresses a private emotion or thought, often on the theme of change, solitude, or love. The traditional tanka consists of exactly thirty-one syllables divided among five lines. Three of the poem's lines have seven syllables, and the other two have five. Lovers composed and exchanged tanka as expressions of affection. Aristocrats also played a game in which one person would invent the first three lines of a tanka and another person would finish it.

The Art of Haiku

Eventually, tanka inspired an even more condensed poetic form—the haiku. A **haiku** is a brief, unrhymed, three-line poem. The first and last lines each have five syllables, and the middle line has seven.

Examples of short verses similar to haiku have been found in thirteenth- and fourteenth-century Japanese literature. However, the art of haiku was not perfected until the seventeenth century, when the greatest of the classical haiku poets, Matsuo Bashō, lived. When English authors such as John Milton were composing epic, intricate poems, Bashō and his pupils were writing strikingly pure, compressed verses only a few words long. In the centuries since Bashō, the haiku form has been adopted by poets all over the world.

Unlike many Western poets, the classical haiku masters do not present similes, metaphors, or other figures of speech. Rather, haiku poets exhibit simple, unadorned images, and the reader must make an imaginative leap to understand the connection between the images.

Words Left Unsaid

With their precision, simple beauty, and economy of words, tanka and haiku embody an important principle of Japanese art and culture: What is not said is often as important as what is said. Understandably, this principle creates challenges for translators of both haiku and tanka. Form must sometimes be sacrificed, for the main work of translating any poem is to preserve its essence, the transcendent quality that stretches across distance and time to connect an author and a reader. This essence of Japanese poetry is summarized by Ki Tsurayuki, one of the editors of the great tenth-century tanka anthology, *Kokinshu,* in his preface to the collection:

> When we hear the notes of the nightingale among the blossoms, when we hear the frog in the water, we know that every living being is capable of song. Poetry, without effort, can move heaven and earth, can touch the gods and spirits. . . . [I]t turns the hearts of man and woman to each other and it soothes the soul of the fierce warrior.

Written over a thousand years ago, his comments still hold true for much of Japanese verse.

Chinese Poetry

Chinese civilization as a distinct and continuous society has existed for more than three thousand years, longer than any other culture in the world. The art of

Direct Teach

Think About/Talk About

Japanese Poetry

- Ask students what they know about tanka and haiku from earlier grades. Ask if they have questions about those forms, and suggest that they look for answers to those questions in the essay.
- Ask students to look for an answer to a question that you pose, such as "How does imagery in tanka and haiku differ from imagery in Western poetry?"

The Art of Haiku

- A traditional haiku consists of two images, one suggesting timelessness and the other one suggesting change, usually divided by a *kireji,* or "cutting word." Even if they do not translate the *kireji,* translators usually try to convey the tension or revelation produced by the word.
- American poets who have experimented with the haiku form include Ezra Pound, Amy Lowell, William Carlos Williams, Richard Wright, and Gary Snyder.

Universal Access

EL English Learners

Invite students to share traditional poems and songs from their own culture or heritage. Students may choose to recite the works aloud or to write them down. Point out that the poems in this selection reflect certain values of the cultures that produced them. Ask students to reflect on the cultural values reflected in the poems they choose.

Struggling Readers

Remind students that the information presented in this introduction will help them understand the poems they are about to read. Help students retain crucial information by creating an outline. Point out that the section headings, bolded words, and paragraph breaks give clues about the information students will want to remember.

writing developed in China between 2000 and 1000 B.C., and with it came the birth of a literary tradition that dwarfs all others. More than half the books ever written have been written in Chinese.

Harmony and Balance

Chinese poetry is characterized by **lyricism,** the intensely personal expression of the speaker's thoughts and feelings. Profoundly influenced by **Confucianism, Taoism,** and **Buddhism** (see pages 331–344), Chinese poets contemplate nature and search for harmony between inner and outer forces or worlds. At its essence Chinese poetry explores passing feelings and impressions and the interplay of opposites. It sees life as a process of continual change in which opposing forces balance one another. Thus, Chinese poets muse about the changing seasons and phases of the moon, and they create vivid pictures of scenes from nature, often recalled in solitude, with imagery that is spare and lean. This minimalist, or simplified, approach engages the reader with evocative word associations and layers of meaning. So rich are these associations that Chinese poetry has inspired poetic movements in other cultures, such as the imagist movement of twentieth-century England and the United States.

The Golden Age

Chinese lyrical poetry achieved its golden age during the T'ang dynasty (618–907). Although other arts also flourished during the T'ang period, poetry was perceived as the glory of this age, and the poet Tu Fu (see page 874) is considered one of the greatest of all Chinese poets. His early poetry celebrates nature's beauty and bemoans time's passage, while his later work incorporates social criticism and compassion for those who suffer.

Rivaling Tu Fu as China's greatest poet is his contemporary, Li Po. If Tu Fu represents the classical spirit of Chinese literature, then Li Po represents its creative spirit. He is the more Romantic poet, both in his views of life and in his poetry. He often celebrates the joys of drinking wine and writes about friendship, solitude, the passage of time, and the glory of nature. His hallmark is brilliant freshness of expression.

Grandfather teaching calligraphy with water brush on sidewalk in Beijing.

The poems of Li Po and Tu Fu resemble the English Romantic poetry written nearly one thousand years later. These poems focus on nature, they use the lyric form, and they employ simple images and language. The voice of Chinese poetry, however, is quieter than the voice of a Shelley or Wordsworth. As the translator Burton Watson observes, "The Chinese poem is the voice of the poet not self-consciously addressing posterity or the world at large, but speaking quietly to a few close friends, or perhaps simply musing to himself."

Paper, writing brush, ink slab.

Time Line

- c. 1500–1122 B.C. — Art of writing develops in China during the Shang dynasty
- 500s — Teachings of Laotzu give rise to Taoism in China
- 551–479 — Confucius teaches ethical principles known as Confucianism, recorded in his Analects
- A.D. 701–770 — Li Po and Tu Fu live
- 794–1185 — Tanka thrives during Heian period
- 1644–1738 — Matsuo Bashō and Uejima Onitsura live
- 1715–1826 — Taniguchi Buson and Kobayashi Issa live

Think About/Talk About

Harmony and Balance

- During the reign of Emperor Wu Ti (140–87 B.C.) of the Han Dynasty, Confucians were given charge of the education that trained officials for government service. Here is a Confucian teaching: "Learning without thought is labor lost; thought without learning is perilous."
- Invite students to suggest contemporary examples of this teaching. ***Possible responses:*** *"Learning without thought"—memorizing baseball statistics without understanding the game. "Thought without learning"—coming up with an idea for a cleaning product without knowing that the chemicals explode when mixed together.*

Advanced Learners

Acceleration Challenge students to write one tanka and one haiku that conform as closely as possible to the descriptions on this page. Encourage students to share their poems aloud or to illustrate them to display in the classroom.

Students with Disabilities

Help students retain key concepts by designating an area of the board for "Poetry Across Culture: Key Concepts." In this area, keep a running list of Academic Vocabulary words, Vocabulary words, and key concepts from the Reading Skills Focus and Literary Skills Focus featured in this Comparing Texts section.

Selection Introduction

Think About the Writers

Remind students that tanka poets use words sparingly. Ask students how they would describe someone who leaves much unsaid.

For Independent Reading

- *Voices: Poetry and Art from Around the World,* Barbara Brenner
- *Haiku en'kin,* Shuuton Kato
- *Essential Haiku: Versions of Bashō, Buson, and Issa,* Robert Hass

Motivate

What Do You Think?/QuickWrite

Invite students to share places and events they remember imagining as children. Ask students to compare their imaginary places with the places as they really are. Have them reflect on the power of imagination in their **Reader/Writer Notebooks**.

Preparing to Read

Japanese Poetry

What Do You Think? How can we use imagination to discover truth?

QuickWrite

In your *Reader/Writer Notebook,* compose a paragraph about a memorable journey you took, perhaps to a faraway city or to a nearby neighborhood. How did you imagine your destination before you arrived ? How accurate was your imagination in predicting the details about this place?

Playing karuta on New Year's Day in Kyoto, Japan.

MEET THE WRITER

Tanka Poets

Tanka of the ancient Japanese masters are so familiar that the poems are the basis of a "poem-card" game played in Japan at the New Year. Ironically, little is known about the poets whose words have become so ingrained in Japanese culture.

Princess Nukada (seventh century)

Princess Nukada was a favorite at the court of two emperors and the most accomplished female poet of her time. The only clues we have to her character are her poems, which are delicate and passionate. Some of them, including the one reproduced here, were written for her older sister, Princess Kagami.

Oshikochi Mitsune (late ninth century)

Oshikochi Mitsune was one of the greatest poets of the early Heian era and one of the editors of the *Kokinshu,* a collection of verse. Some of his verses appear in that anthology. Many of his poems are melancholy, but they are never sentimental.

Ki Tsurayuki (884–946)

Another editor of the *Kokinshu,* Ki Tsurayuki was a high court official as well as an accomplished writer and calligrapher. He also wrote a travel diary that interwove poetry with prose. Ki Tsurayuki differentiated himself by writing in Japanese at a time when most cultured Japanese men wrote prose in Chinese. To avoid ridicule, he published the diary under a woman's name.

Ono Komachi (mid-tenth century)

Celebrated for her beauty and the emotional power of her verse, Ono Komachi is perhaps the most revered of the poets whose tanka appeared in the *Kokinshu.*

Saigyo (1118–1190)

Among the most accomplished twelfth-century tanka poets was Saigyo, who abandoned his position as a royal bodyguard at the age of twenty-three to become a priest. His tanka were written during the years he spent wandering through the Japanese countryside.

Think About the Writers What characteristics do the poets who wrote Tanka have in common?

California Standards, pp. 866–871

- **Reading Standard 2.2** Analyze the way in which clarity of meaning is affected by the patterns of organization, hierarchical structures, repetition of the main ideas, syntax, and word choice in the text.
- **Reading Standard 3.4** Analyze ways in which poets use imagery, personification, figures of speech, and sounds to evoke readers' emotions.

Selection Readability	
Easily Accessible **Accessible** Challenging	These poems include accessible language, accessible imagery.

MEET THE WRITER

Haiku Poets

Like the tanka poets, these haiku masters came from different backgrounds and led very different lives. They are united, however, by the striking emotion and philosophical impact of their fine verse.

Matsuo Bashō (1644–1694)

The son of a samurai, Matsuo Bashō spent his youth in the service of a local lord. He began writing verses when he was nine and soon showed remarkable promise. Before he was thirty, he had won acclaim as a poet and had started his own poetry school.

Two major influences on Bashō's poetry were his devotion to Zen Buddhism and his travels. In 1684, at the age of forty, Bashō set out on the first of his many journeys through Japan. A lone traveler, Bashō endured great discomforts and loneliness. Some of his best haiku were composed on these lonely journeys.

Uejima Onitsura (1660–1738)

One of Bashō's greatest admirers was Uejima Onitsura. Like Bashō, Onitsura came from a samurai background and began writing poetry at an early age. Though Onitsura admired Bashō, he did not imitate Bashō's style. His poems are more joyful and exuberant, and somewhat less philosophical than the verse of Bashō.

Taniguchi Buson (1715–1783)

Taniguchi Buson, a younger contemporary of Onitsura, soon established his own poetic style. His haiku are generally regarded as second only to those of Bashō. Buson was an accomplished painter, and his poems reflect his fascination with light and color.

Kobayashi Issa (1762–1826)

Kobayashi Issa is one of the most beloved of Japan's haiku masters. His life was extraordinarily sad. His mother died when he was an infant, and his relations with his stepmother were so poor that his father sent him away from home to study when he was only fourteen. His first wife bore him five children, but all of them died in infancy. Eventually his wife succumbed to illness. Possibly because of these many sorrows, Issa's verses are taut with intense emotion.

Think About the Writers How might the writers' life experiences have affected their haiku?

(background) Geothermal pool, Chinoike Jigoku (Blood Pool Hell) Beppu, Japan. *(below)* Seated statue of Bashō (1644–1694), by Ran-Koo. Wood. Edo Period (1603–1868). Musée Historique des Tissus, Lyon, France.

Think About the Writers

Remind students that poets often use their art to express their innermost thoughts and experiences. Have students discuss what methods they use to express their own thoughts and feelings about their lives.

Preteach

Introducing Vocabulary

- Review the Vocabulary words, definitions, and sentences with students.
- To reinforce the importance of the Vocabulary words, tell students that the poets use these words to create imagery. Remind students that in tanka and haiku, what is left unsaid is as important as what is actually said in the poem. These poems use images to convey more meaning with fewer words. Ask students to consider the images these Vocabulary words convey.

English for Academic Success

Language Coach

After students complete the **Language Coach** exercise, help them brainstorm other homonym pairs. [*presents/presence, rain/reign, bridal/bridle*]

Literary Skills Focus

As you read and discuss the selection with students, have them note examples of imagery and how imagery contributes to the meaning of the poem.

Reading Skills Focus

Give students a copy of the Reading Skills Focus graphic organizer before they read. (See **Unit 4 Resources.**)

Writing Skills Focus

Have students note the senses that are invoked by the images in the poem in their **Reader/Writer Notebooks**. Students can use their notes to complete the Writing Skills Focus activity.

Learn It Online

The online version of this selection includes audio support to engage all students and to help struggling readers with reading comprehension and vocabulary.

go.hrw.com H12-868 Go

Preparing to Read

Reading Standard 2.2, 3.4 (see pages A48–A50)

Literary Skills Focus

Imagery Language that appeals to the senses (sight, hearing, touch, smell, and taste) is known as **imagery.** The Japanese tanka and haiku writers relied on imagery, often from nature, to suggest subtly and indirectly moods and themes. You, as the reader, must connect the images to the emotions they imply. Thus, the image of a fallen cherry blossom may suggest the brevity of love or even of life itself, and the image of the full moon may prompt philosophical musings about change and eternity. As you read, consider how imagery contributes to each poem's meaning.

Reading Skills Focus

Using Text Structures to Understand Meaning In Japanese, **tanka** and **haiku** adhere to a strict structure of line lengths and syllable counts. Although some structural elements are lost in translation, these poems retain the elegant simplicity of the originals. The poems express complex ideas and powerful emotions such as yearning and loneliness in just a few short lines. Some poems develop an image across several lines; some use just a single word. As you read, examine the structure of each image for clues to help you infer the poem's meaning.

Into Action Use a chart like the one below to record each poem's imagery. Write down how each image is presented and structured.

Image	Structure
In the tree-shade of the summer mountain I stood.	Image developed over three lines.

Writing Skills Focus

Think as a Reader/Writer

Find It in Your Reading In your *Reader/Writer Notebook,* record the words used by the poets to create **images** and to note which senses are invoked.

Vocabulary

reed (reed) *n.:* kind of tall grass with a hollow, jointed stalk that grows in wet places. *The speaker's body feels as fragile as a reed.*

gourd (gawrd) *n.:* vegetable with a hard rind that can be dried, hollowed out, and used as a bowl. *When the speaker has no rice to pour in his gourd, he can put a flower in its place.*

thatched (thacht) *v.:* covered with straw, leaves, or similar materials. *A vine in bloom has thatched the hut's roof.*

Language Coach

Homonyms Words that have the same pronunciation but different spellings and meanings are called **homonyms.** You will *read* the word *reed* in one of the poems. A tanka poem by Komachi describes a body like a *reed*, which refers to a tall grass. You will find one of each of these homonym pairs in the poems: *weighted/waited, mind/mined, gourd/gored, know/no.* Can you explain the difference between the words in each pair?

Reader/Writer Notebook

Use your **RWN** to complete the activities for these selections.

Learn It Online

Listen to these tanka and haiku online.

go.hrw.com H12-868 Go

Comparing Texts Resources

Unit 4 Resources, on-level practice and assessment, p. 121

Teacher One Stop™, on-level lesson plans and all print resources

Holt Audio Library

Holt Audio Library: Selections and Summaries in Spanish

UA: Differentiating Instruction, graphic organizer, p. 193

UA: Supporting Instruction in Spanish, selection summary

ThinkCentral Online Assessment, Selection Standards Check

ThinkCentral Online Remediation

POEMS

Tanka

translated by **Geoffrey Bownas** and **Anthony Thwaite**

Read with a Purpose

Read to discover how poets use images of nature to convey ideas.

Build Background

These poems were written by five different writers in five different centuries. Some features of the tanka form are lost in translation from Japanese to English; for example, only one of the poems retains the traditional thirty-one syllables required in tanka. Furthermore, the overall sounds of the poems differ from the sounds of the originals. The poems do, however, stay true to tanka's unrhymed style. The poems also make use of **assonance,** the repetition of vowel sounds in nearby words.

Moon over the five-story pagoda of Sensoji temple at night in Asakusa, Tokyo, Japan.

I waited and I
Yearned for you.
My blind
Stirred at the touch
Of the autumn breeze.
—Princess Nukada

The end of my journey
Was still far off,
But in the tree-shade
Of the summer mountain
I stood, my mind floating. **A**
—Oshikochi Mitsune

Now, I cannot tell
What my old friend is thinking:
But the petals of the plum
In this place I used to know
Keep their old fragrance. **B**
—Ki Tsurayuki

How helpless my heart!
Were the stream to tempt,
My body, like a reed
Severed at the roots,
Would drift along, I think.
—Ono Komachi

Every single thing
Changes and is changing
Always in this world.
Yet with the same light
The moon goes on shining. **C**
—Priest Saigyo

A **Reading Focus** **Using Text Structures to Understand Meaning** Tanka poems are traditionally unrhymed. What structural devices help readers understand the poem's meaning?

B **Literary Focus** **Imagery** What does the smell of the plum blossoms suggest about friendship?

C **Literary Focus** **Imagery** What does the image of the moon suggest about the relationship between change and permanence?

Vocabulary **reed** (reed) *n.:* kind of tall grass with a hollow, jointed stalk that grows in wet places.

Universal Access

Struggling Readers

The vocabulary and syntax of these poems are accessible enough for students to understand the poem's literal meaning easily. To help students familiarize themselves with the concept of imagery, ask them to focus on juxtaposed images in the poems. Students can create Venn diagrams to record the images in each poem and what feelings or ideas the images have in common.

Advanced Learners

Acceleration Explain to students that figurative language, such as similes, is rarely found in tanka poetry. Point out that a rare example of simile can be found in the tanka by Ono Komachi. Have students locate the simile used in the poem and analyze the feeling that it suggests. [*helplessness; dislocation*] Then, have students discuss why Komachi chose to use this simile in the poem instead of some other image. Encourage students to analyze the simile's importance to the meaning of the tanka.

Teacher Preparation

Selection Summary

Each of these tanka presents a moment—when the speaker is waiting for a lover, stopping during a journey, wondering what a friend is thinking, feeling adrift—and an image that captures that moment.

Direct Teach

Think About/Talk About

Read with a Purpose Have students read the Read with a Purpose statement. Ask them what themes they are familiar with from Japanese art they have seen or books they have read.

Comprehension

A Reading Focus

Possible response: *Images are developed throughout the length of the poem or juxtaposed with another image to indicate a connection between two ideas.*

Analysis

B Literary Focus

Possible response: *The imagery suggests that the essence of friendship remains even as old friends change over time.*

C Literary Focus

Possible response: *The image suggests that just as the moon changes phases but remains the same, change and permanence can coexist.*

Vocabulary: Own the Word

reed: Have students complete the following sentence: "The pursued fugitive cut a *reed* at the marsh because . . ."

Teacher Preparation

Selection Summary

Each of these haiku presents an image or juxtaposes two images: a crow on a withered branch, a village where bells do not ring at dusk, a time for putting flowers in rice bowls, a celebration of cherry blossoms, a woman reading in the moonlight by a pear tree in bloom, a hut covered in vines.

Direct Teach

Think About/Talk About

Read with a Purpose After students read the Read with a Purpose statement, ask them to consider an event or experience to which they attach strong emotion (the event may be from their own lives or one traditionally considered to be emotionally charged).

Comprehension

A Reading Focus

Possible response: *The diminishing length of the lines of this haiku can be compared to a day that slowly fades into an autumn sunset.*

Analysis

B Literary Focus

Possible response: *The cherries are so important that they command the awe of even the smallest, inanimate elements.*

C Literary Focus

Possible response: *The speaker's home is at one with nature.*

Vocabulary: Own the Word

- **gourd:** Ask students, "Have you ever seen a *gourd*? Explain where and when you saw it, and describe its appearance." Bring a *gourd* to class for students to see.
- **thatched:** Tell students that a *thatcher* (noun form of *thatched*) is someone who covers a roof with *thatch*. Show students a picture of a *thatched* roof.

POEMS

Haiku

The haiku by Bashō, Buson, and Issa are translated by Harold G. Henderson. The haiku by Onitsura is translated by Peter Beilenson and Harry Behn.

Read with a Purpose

Read to discover how one or two simple images can suggest complex emotions or ideas.

Build Background

The first three haiku you will read are by the greatest haiku master, the seventeenth-century poet Bashō. In all three poems, Bashō finds inherent beauty in seemingly ordinary objects or events. This practice is inspired by the Buddhist belief that anyone, through contemplation, can find great significance in even the humblest of things. Like tanka, haiku focus on only one or two images.

On a withered branch
A crow has settled—
autumn nightfall. **A**
—Matsuo Bashō

A village where they ring
no bells!—Oh, what *do* they do
at dusk in spring?
—Matsuo Bashō

No rice?—In that hour
we put into the gourd
a maiden-flower.
—Matsuo Bashō

Even stones in streams
of mountain water compose
songs to wild cherries. **B**
—Uejima Onitsura

Blossoms on the pear;
and a woman in the moonlight
reads a letter there. . . .
—Taniguchi Buson

A morning-glory vine
all blossoming has thatched
this hut of mine. **C**
—Kobayashi Issa

A Reading Focus **Using Text Structures to Understand Meaning** How does the visual representation of the three-line poem affect your understanding of it?

B Literary Focus **Imagery** What does the image of stones tell you about the beauty or importance of the wild cherries?

C Literary Focus **Imagery** What does the blossoming vine on the roof suggest about the speaker's feelings for his home?

Vocabulary **gourd** (gawrd) *n.:* vegetable with a hard rind that can be dried, hollowed out, and used as a bowl.
thatched (thacht) *v.:* covered with straw, leaves, or similar materials.

California Standards, p. 871

- **Reading Standard 2.2** Analyze the way in which clarity of meaning is affected by the patterns of organization, hierarchical structures, repetition of the main ideas, syntax, and word choice in the text.
- **Reading Standard 3.4** Analyze ways in which poets use imagery, personification, figures of speech, and sounds to evoke readers' emotions.
- **Grades 9–10 Review Reading Standard 3.7** Recognize and understand the significance of various literary devices, including figurative language, imagery, allegory, and symbolism, and explain their appeal.
- **Writing Standard 2.2** Write responses to literature: **b.** Analyze the use of imagery, language, universal themes, and unique aspects of the text. **d.** Demonstrate an understanding of the author's use of stylistic devices and an appreciation of the effects created.

Reading Standard 2.2, 3.4; **Grades 9–10 Review** Reading Standard 3.7 (see pages A48–A50)
Writing Standard 2.2b, 2.2d (see pages A51–A52)

Tanka / Haiku

Literary Response and Analysis

Reading Skills Focus

Quick Check

1. How does Saigyo use an image from nature in his tanka to contrast his thoughts on the changing world?
2. What generalization can you make about the themes of tanka poetry?
3. What images does Buson use in his haiku? What emotions do they evoke?

Read with a Purpose

4. What varied images are used to express themes common to both tanka and haiku?

Reading Skills: Using Text Structures to Understand Meaning

5. Review your charts for the poems, and connect the two boxes in each chart to a third box. How does each image and each poem's structure contribute to the meaning?

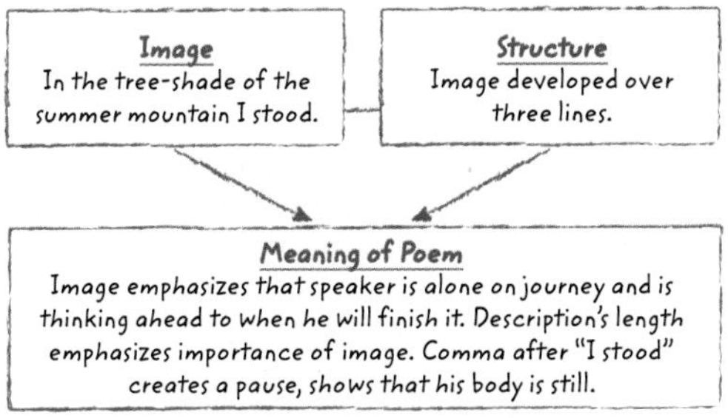

Vocabulary Check

Match each Vocabulary word with its synonym.

6. reed	**a.** vessel
7. gourd	**b.** covered
8. thatched	**c.** stalk

Literary Skills Focus

Literary Analysis

9. **Compare and Contrast** How do the emotions evoked in the first two tanka compare?
10. **Analyze** Find examples of an unexpected relationship between two things in Bashō's haiku.
11. **Extend** How do the six haiku translations depart from strict haiku form?

Literary Skills: Imagery

12. **Make Judgments** Which tanka most strongly suggests loneliness or quiet reflection? What images does the poet use to convey this mood?
13. **Analyze** Seasonal images are common in haiku. What seasonal images do you find in these haiku? What emotions do the images convey?

Literary Skills Review: Symbolism

14. **Analyze** A **symbol** is a person, place, animal, thing, or event that stands for itself and for something more than itself. What might each of the two contrasted things in Issa's haiku symbolize?

Writing Skills Focus

Think as a Reader/Writer

Use It in Your Writing Write a tanka or haiku with images that appeal to at least two different senses.

What Do You Think Now?

What feelings and actions can nature inspire?

Universal Access

Struggling Writers

Students may need additional scaffolding for this activity. Before students compose a haiku or tanka, ask them to look through magazines for pictures to help them choose an image. As they write, remind students to describe how the image invokes at least two of their senses.

Assess

Unit 4 Resources, Selection Standards Check, p. 119

ThinkCentral Online Assessment, Selection Standards Check

Teacher One Stop™, editable Selection Standards Check

Check for Understanding

Independent Practice

Reading Skills Focus

Possible responses:

1. *The moon goes through phases, yet remains the same.*
2. *permanence and change coexist; love creates yearning and even anguish; people are closely connected to nature and can be transformed and soothed by its beauty*
3. *The image of a woman reading in the moonlight near pear blossoms suggests tranquility.*
4. *The tree shade, plum fragrance, reed, and moon suggest permanence and change, love that is yearning, and the effects of nature's beauty on people.*
5. *Students should connect image and structure to meaning.*

Vocabulary Check

6. *c* **7.** *a* **8.** *b*

Literary Skills Focus

Possible responses:

9. *One is an anxious longing, and one is a daydreamer's longing.*
10. *a crow on a withered branch and autumn nightfall*
11. *All except Onitsura's depart from the pattern of seventeen syllables. All include rhymes except the first Bashō and the Onitsura haiku.*
12. *Mitsune's haiku evokes quiet reflection with the "mind floating."*
13. *The autumn image—a withered branch—evokes a mood of sadness. The spring images evoke a mood of hope.*
14. *The hut might symbolize the everyday world, which is transformed by the beauty of nature, symbolized by the vine.*

What Do You Think Now?

Have students think about how they feel when they are surrounded by nature. Students might note that they feel reflective and contemplative when they spend time outdoors.

Selection Introduction
Think About the Writers
To help students answer the question, ask them to consider the poets' family and educational backgrounds, occupations, and the political and social setting of their times. Students might note that both Tu Fu and Li Po were born into good families and spent most of their lives wandering around the country. Tu Fu did not experience the fame that Li Po experienced during his lifetime. Tu Fu's life was filled with hardships and trouble, while Li Po lived a charmed life.

For Independent Reading
- *A Book of Luminous Things*, Czeslaw Milosz
- *Opened Ground: Selected Poems, 1966–1996*, Seamus Heaney

Motivate
What Do You Think?/QuickWrite
Ask students to consider the lifestyle of a wandering poet or writer. For what particular needs might the wanderer use his or her imagination? What risks and dangers would he face in encountering new places and people? How does solitude inspire the imagination? Have students record their thoughts in a paragraph in their **Reader/Writer Notebooks**.

Preparing to Read

Chinese Poetry

What Do You Think? How can we use imagination to discover truth?

QuickWrite
Imagine you are a wandering writer, like the Chinese poets described on this page. In your *Reader/Writer Notebook,* write a paragraph about how you think a life of wandering might inspire your imagination.

Ceramic sculpture on roof of Kwan Tai Temple, Tai O, Lantau Island.

MEET THE WRITERS

Tu Fu
(712–770)

Tu Fu was born into a noble family of scholar-officials. His family connections and modest wealth would have assured him a life of relative comfort had not a violent rebellion in 755 ended the T'ang dynasty's days of glory. After the rebellion, Tu Fu was often on the road, searching for a way to make a living. Toward the end of his life, Tu Fu lived in hardship and poor health. He died in 770, on a houseboat near Hangzhou.

The uncertain course of Tu Fu's life is reflected in his poetry, which is often marked by bitterness and melancholy. In his youth, he wrote mainly about the beauty of nature and his own sorrows. As he grew older, however, Tu Fu's poems turned to more humanitarian themes. He became sensitive to people's sufferings and was the first Chinese poet to write at length about social concerns.

Although Tu Fu was not well known as a poet during his own lifetime, he wrote in an elegant style that influenced Chinese poets for centuries after his death.

Li Po
(701–762)

A well-educated youth from a good family, Li Po chose to forgo the test for imperial service taken by many young men of the upper classes. Young Li Po instead served as a wandering knight, a sword-wielding avenger of wrongs against women and children. At the age of twenty-five, he became a vagabond who wandered for most of his remaining days.

Li Po's travels in China spread his fame as a poet. Even the emperor admired him. In fact, Li Po abandoned his nomadic life for a time to serve the emperor as an imperial court poet. Li Po's traditional lyric poetry is characterized by its sense of playfulness, fantasy, and grace. The death of Li Po was sudden; an appropriately romantic legend asserts he drowned one night as he leaned from his boat to embrace the watery reflection of the moon.

Think About the Writers What aspects of these poets' lives were different, and which were similar?

Selection Readability	
Easily Accessible **Accessible** Challenging	These poems include accessible language, short lines, accessible themes.

California Standards, pp. 872–876
- **Reading Standard 2.2** Analyze the way in which clarity of meaning is affected by the patterns of organization.
- **Reading Standard 3.3** Analyze the ways in which irony, tone, mood, the author's style, and the "sound" of language achieve specific rhetorical or aesthetic purposes or both, hierarchical structures, repetition of the main ideas, syntax, and word choice in the text.

Reading Standard 2.2, 3.3 (see pages A48–A50)

Literary Skills Focus

Mood The overall feeling or atmosphere in a work of literature is called **mood.** A poem's mood might be cheerful or gloomy, defiant or accepting. Writers establish mood by using descriptive details and language, which evoke particular images or feelings. In traditional Chinese poetry of Tu Fu's time, a single mood usually characterized each poem. Tu Fu broke new ground by shifting the mood within a single poem.

Reading Skills Focus

Using Text Structures to Understand Meaning Although some of their structural elements are lost in translation, Tu Fu's writings retain their original essence. "Jade Flower Palace" and "Night Thoughts Afloat" express complex ideas and powerful emotions within precisely and elegantly structured text. To create particular moods in each of his poems, Tu Fu uses different structural techniques, one of which is the variation of the length of complete sentences. In these sentences, he asks questions, makes declarations, states facts, and interjects his personal views. What can you infer about a poem's meaning based on its structure and how its mood is created and developed?

Into Action As you read, use a chart like the one below to record the mood or moods of each poem. For each mood, write down examples of the poem's structure that help to create that mood.

"Jade Flower Palace":

Mood	Structure
Desolate	Short sentences create concrete images of desolation: "The stream swirls. The wind moans in / The pines. Gray rats scurry over / Broken tiles."

Writing Skills Focus

Think as a Reader/Writer

Find It In Your Reading A writer creates **mood** through a careful choice of words and phrasing. In your *Reader/Writer Notebook,* note the language that is most effective in creating the moods in Tu Fu's poems.

Vocabulary

scurry (SKUR ee) *v.:* run away quickly. *The rats scurry across the ruins of the ancient palace.*

courtiers (KAWR tee uhrz) *n.:* palace attendants. *When the ruler leaves the palace, his courtiers follow him.*

pathos (PAY thahs) *n.:* feeling of sadness or melancholy often brought on by a work of art. *The poet is moved to pathos when he tries to describe the passing of time.*

Language Coach

Word Origins The noun *pathos* comes from the Greek word meaning "suffering, feeling, emotion." The same Greek root is found in many related words, including *sympathy, empathy, apathy, pathology,* and *pathetic.* Try to guess the meaning of each word. Use a dictionary to find their meanings.

Learn It Online

Learn more about Tu Fu at the Writers' Lives site online.

go.hrw.com H12-873 Go

Comparing Texts Resources

Unit 4 Resources, on-level practice and assessment, p. 127

Teacher One Stop™, on-level lesson plans and all print resources

Holt Audio Library

Holt Audio Library: Selections and Summaries in Spanish

UA: Differentiating Instruction, graphic organizer, p. 193

UA: Supporting Instruction in Spanish, selection summary

ThinkCentral Online Assessment, Selection Standards Check

ThinkCentral Online Remediation

Preteach

Introducing Vocabulary

- Review the Vocabulary words, definitions, and sentences with students.
- To reinforce the importance of the Vocabulary words, tell students that a poet's word choice helps to establish the mood of a poem. Ask students whether the word *scurry* evokes a different feeling than the word *run*. Then ask students to describe the mood conveyed by the words *courtiers* and *pathos*.

English for Academic Success

Language Coach

Ask students what root word can be found in *courtiers* [*court*]. Have them look up the origin of *courtiers* in a dictionary and relate its origin to its meaning.

Literary Skills Focus

As you read and discuss the selection with students, have them note where a shift in mood occurs in Tu Fu's poems.

Reading Skills Focus

Give students a copy of the Reading Skills Focus graphic organizer before they read. (See **Unit 4 Resources.**) Tell them to use their responses to answer the questions on the Applying Your Skills page.

Writing Skills Focus

Have students use their **Reader/Writer Notebooks** to record words and phrases that are effective in creating the moods in Tu Fu's poetry. Students can use their notes to complete the Writing Skills Focus activity.

Learn It Online

The **Writers' Lives** feature of the Interactive Student Edition offers additional information about this author.

go.hrw.com H12-873 Go

Teacher Preparation

Selection Summary

In "Jade Flower Palace," the speaker describes the ruins of an old palace. The building is alive with memories and hints of past glory. The speaker wants to write a poem but is overcome by sad thoughts of the transience of all things.

Direct Teach

Think About/Talk About

Read with a Purpose Have students read the Read with a Purpose statement. Ask students to discuss how a setting like an old palace or an empty stadium might convey a certain mood. Discuss the emotions and images that come to mind when students think of places from their own experience.

Analysis

A Literary Focus

Possible responses: *The mood is melancholy and desolate. The phrases "wind moans," "rats scurry," and "broken tiles" contribute to this mood.*

B Literary Focus

Possible responses: *The mood is somber and sad; it suggests the speaker has close ties to the palace.*

Extend the Discussion

Summarizing What is happening in the last five lines of this poem? ***Possible response:*** *The speaker is sitting on the palace grounds trying to write a poem, but he is so overcome by emotion that he cannot continue.*

Tone What is the speaker's attitude toward the subject? ***Possible response:*** *Overcome by the ravages of time and the impermanence of all human endeavor, he becomes serious and unsettled.*

POEM

Jade Flower Palace

by **Tu Fu**

translated by **Kenneth Rexroth**

Read with a Purpose
Read to discover how hauntingly beautiful palace ruins inspire the speaker to contemplate life.

Build Background
Perhaps the most respected of all the ancient Chinese poets, Tu Fu focused on the affairs of the world and the hardships of his people. Of his goal as a poet, Tu Fu once said, "If my words aren't startling, death itself has no rest." As you read the poem, notice the vivid images and the concrete details that are hallmarks of Tu Fu's poetry.

The stream swirls. The wind moans in
The pines. Gray rats scurry over
Broken tiles. What prince, long ago, **A**
Built this palace, standing in
Ruins beside the cliffs? There are
Green ghost fires in the black rooms.
The shattered pavements are all
Washed away. Ten thousand organ
Pipes whistle and roar. The storm
Scatters the red autumn leaves.
His dancing girls are yellow dust.
Their painted cheeks have crumbled
Away. His gold chariots
And courtiers are gone. Only
A stone horse is left of his
Glory. I sit on the grass and
Start a poem, but the pathos of
It overcomes me. The future
Slips imperceptibly away.
Who can say what the years will bring? **B**

Painting and calligraphy from a Chinese album illustrating stories of Taoist immortals. ADD Ms. 22689, f16.
The British Library, London.

A **Literary Focus** **Mood** How would you describe the mood created by the setting? What images communicate this mood?

B **Literary Focus** **Mood** What mood do the final lines create? What does this mood suggest about the relationship between the palace and the speaker?

Vocabulary **scurry** (SKUR ee) *v.:* run away quickly.
courtiers (KAWR tee uhrz) *n.:* palace attendants.
pathos (PAY thahs) *n.:* feeling of sadness or melancholy often brought on by a work of art.

Universal Access

Struggling Readers

Model how to understand meaning through mood and structure. Read aloud the first four lines of "Night Thoughts Afloat." You might say: "The 'bent grasses,' 'gentle wind,' and the man being 'alone' all help to create a calm, quiet mood. I notice that each line contains a single image, reinforcing the stillness and calmness." Ask a volunteer to read lines 9–12 aloud, and have students comment on how the structure helps to create mood.

Advanced Learners

Acceleration Challenge students to write a poem in the style of Tu Fu. Have them begin by describing a setting in detail and then move to philosophical observations about life, the world, themselves. As they write, remind them to pay attention to imagery and to the way the physical world is a reflection of the world of our inner thoughts.

POEM

Night Thoughts Afloat

by **Tu Fu**

translated by **Arthur Cooper**

Li River cormorant fisherman with lantern on his bamboo raft at night, near Yangshuo.

Read with a Purpose

Read to discover the speaker's inner thoughts as he watches the night sky.

Build Background

Tu Fu wrote this poem while spending the final years of his life on a houseboat. As you read, think about how this setting could evoke conflicting emotions—a sense of peace and an awareness of failure.

By bent grasses
in a gentle wind
Under straight mast
I'm alone tonight,

And the stars hang
above the broad plain
But moon's afloat
in this Great River: **A**

Oh, where's my name
among the poets?
Official rank?
"Retired for ill health."

Drifting, drifting,
what am I more than
A single gull
between sky and earth? **B**

A Reading Focus **Using Text Structures to Understand Meaning** Notice the opposition between the first and third lines in each of the first two stanzas. How does this structure contribute to the poem's meaning?

B Literary Focus **Mood** What mood does the image of the single gull suggest?

California Standards, p. 876

- **Reading Standard 2.2** Analyze the way in which clarity of meaning is affected by the patterns of organization, hierarchical structures, repetition of the main ideas, syntax, and word choice in the text.
- **Reading Standard 3.3** Analyze the ways in which irony, tone, mood, the author's style, and the "sound" of language achieve specific rhetorical or aesthetic purposes or both.
- **Reading Standard 3.7** Analyze recognized works of world literature from a variety of authors: **c.** Evaluate the philosophical, political, religious, ethical, and social influences of the historical period that shaped the characters, plots, and settings.
- **Writing Standard 2.2** Write responses to literature: **b.** Analyze the use of imagery, language, universal themes, and unique aspects of the text. **d.** Demonstrate an understanding of the author's use of stylistic devices and an appreciation of the effects created.

Teacher Preparation

Selection Summary

In "Night Thoughts Afloat," the poet begins by painting a scene of the view from a boat on quiet water. However, he ends by mocking his own lack of achievement.

Direct Teach

Think About/Talk About

Read with a Purpose Have students read the Read with a Purpose statement. Ask students why a night sky is a common image in poetry. What mood does this image convey?

Comprehension

A Reading Focus

Possible response: *The opposition between the first and third lines in the two stanzas suggests conflict, which is present in the speaker's emotions.*

Analysis

B Literary Focus

Possible response: *The image of the gull suggests loneliness and insignificance.*

Vocabulary: Own the Word

- **scurry:** Ask students: "Have you ever seen a bug or animal *scurry*? Explain what animal you saw *scurrying* and tell where and when you saw it *scurry*." Ask for a volunteer to demonstrate *scurrying*.
- **courtiers:** Ask students, "Why might people become *courtiers*?"
- **pathos:** Ask students to name some images they have seen in real life or on television that evoked *pathos* in them. ***Possible responses:*** *a wounded soldier, a starving child, an abused animal, victims of a natural disaster*

Check for Understanding

Independent Practice

Reading Skills Focus

Possible responses:

1. *The palace is swiftly decaying just as the future "slips imperceptibly away" (line 19).*
2. *The night sky offers an image of solitude and contemplation.*
3. *Tell students to consider what idea the poet is trying to communicate through the structure and mood of each poem.*

Vocabulary Check

4. *b* **5.** *c* **6.** *a*

Literary Skills Focus

Possible responses:

7. *The present reveals a crumbled past. The present and future share a similar fate.*
8. *Tu Fu compares himself to a gull hanging between sky and earth, which suggests he is caught between two larger forces.*
9. *The first poem creates a gentle, melancholy mood. When the poet says he is overcome by pathos, the mood changes to a paralyzing fear. In the second poem, the quiet mood of the first two stanzas shifts to a despairing one.*
10. *In "Jade Flower Palace," "swirls" creates a feeling of excitement, "moans" produces a mournful tone, and "shattered" creates a sense of futility.*
11. *The first poem is set on a windy day at the ruins of a palace, suggesting destructive forces and mournfulness. The second describes an unknown man on boat at night, drifting alone.*

What Do You Think Now?

To help students answer this question, ask them to summarize the philosophical point of each poem in a single sentence. For example, for "Jade Flower Palace," a student might write, "Even the grandest palaces fall to ruin: Nothing is permanent."

Applying Your Skills

Reading Standard 2.2, 3.3, 3.7c (see pages A48–A50)
Writing Standard 2.2b, 2.2d (see pages A51–A52)

Jade Flower Palace / Night Thoughts Afloat

Literary Response and Analysis

Reading Skills Focus

Read with a Purpose

1. How does the speaker connect the ruins to the future in "Jade Flower Palace"?
2. In "Night Thoughts Afloat," why is it important that the speaker contemplates a night sky rather than a day sky?

Reading Skills: Using Text Structures to Understand Meaning

3. Connect the boxes in each chart to a third box. How do the moods contribute to each poem's meaning? How do the imagery and poem structures contribute to each poem's meaning?

"Jade Flower Palace":

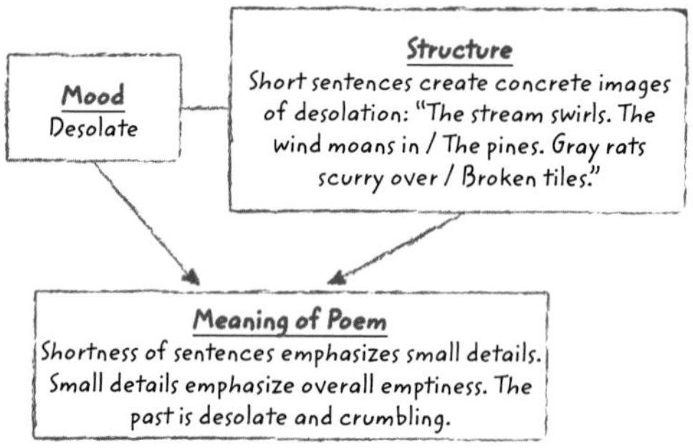

Vocabulary Check

Match the Vocabulary words with their antonyms.

4. scurry	**a.** joy
5. courtiers	**b.** plod
6. pathos	**c.** princes

Literary Skills Focus

Literary Analysis

7. **Interpret** What does Tu Fu say about the past, present, and future in "Jade Flower Palace"?
8. **Analyze** To what does the speaker compare himself in "Night Thoughts"? What emotions does he express through the comparison?

Literary Skills: Mood

9. **Make Judgments** Find at least one mood shift in each poem. How do these shifts affect your reading?
10. **Analyze** Explain how the verbs and verbs used as adjectives contribute to the poem's mood.

Literary Skills Review: Setting

11. **Analyze** The time and location in which a piece of literature takes place is its **setting.** What differentiates the settings in these poems? How do the settings contribute to each poem's meaning?

Writing Skills Focus

Think as a Reader/Writer

Use It in Your Writing Decide on a mood that you want to convey in an original poem. Use imagery and structure to communicate this mood in your poem. Share the poem with other students. Ask them to identify the mood you have created.

What Do You Think Now? What truths do you find in these poems? Explain.

Universal Access

Struggling Writers

Give students additional scaffolding to complete the Writing Skills Focus. Have students review their notes on imagery in their **Reader/Writer Notebooks.** Then, have students choose a specific mood that their poem will convey, and ask them to brainstorm examples of imagery to include in their poem. Remind students that imagery appeals to sight, sound, touch, taste, and smell.

Assess

Unit 4 Resources, Selection Standards Check, p. 125

go. hrw .com **ThinkCentral Online Assessment,** Selection Standards Check

Teacher One Stop™, editable Selection Standards Check

Reading Standard 2.2, 3.4 (see pages A48–A50)

Quiet Night Thoughts / Question and Answer Among the Mountains / Letter to His Two Small Children

Literary Skills Focus

Imagery To evoke readers' emotions, writers use **imagery,** language that appeals to the senses of sight, hearing, touch, smell, and taste. For example, a writer might describe an ocean as a "crashing gray tide" to build fear or as "rippling blue waves" to suggest tranquility. Instead of directly stating an emotion, Li Po's poems allow the reader to experience the emotional effect of the images.

Reading Skills Focus

Using Text Structures to Understand Meaning Although some elements are lost in translation, Li Po's writings retain the elegant simplicity of the originals. "Quiet Night Thoughts" and "Question and Answer" express complex ideas and powerful emotions, such as freedom and homesickness, in just a few short lines. The longer "Letter" uses its precise structure to evoke thoughts and feelings. The poems may develop an image across several lines or in just a single word. Examine each image's structure. What meanings can you infer from how imagery is developed?

Into Action Use a chart like the one below to record the imagery of each poem. Write down how the image is presented and structured.

"Quiet Night Thoughts":

Image	Structure
bright moonlight	Image is developed across 4 lines.

Writing Skills Focus

Think as a Reader/Writer

Find It in Your Reading In your *Reader/Writer Notebook,* record the words Li Po uses to create his **images,** and note the senses they evoke.

TechFocus As you read these poems, think about the images that come into your mind. How could you share these images with others?

Language Coach

Specific Nouns Poets often use precise nouns to create sharp, specific images. Li Po describes the *sprays* of a tree. A spray, in this context, is a branch of a plant, including its leaves and flowers. The noun suggests the delicate, natural shapes found within the tree. Later, the tree's height is described as being even with the *eaves*, the part of the roof that extends beyond the wall that supports it. How does this exact noun help you create a specific image in your mind?

Learn It Online

Learn more about Chinese literature and history online.

go.hrw.com H12-877 Go

Preteach

English for Academic Success

Language Coach

After students read the **Language Coach,** have them answer the question. [*Describing the height of a tree as level with the eaves provides a reference point for the tree's height and brings up an image of the tree juxtaposed with a rooftop.*]

Literary Skills Focus

As you read and discuss the selection with students, have them note the emotional effect of the images.

Reading Skills Focus

Give students a copy of the Reading Skills Focus graphic organizer before they read. (See **Unit 4 Resources.**) Tell them to use their responses to answer the questions on the Applying Your Skills page.

Writing Skills Focus

Have students note the senses that are invoked by the images in the poem and the words Li Po uses to create those images in their **Reader/Writer Notebooks**. Students can use their notes to complete the Writing Skills Focus activity.

Comparing Texts Resources

Unit 4 Resources, on-level practice and assessment, p. 133

Teacher One Stop™, on-level lesson plans and all print resources

Holt Audio Library

Holt Audio Library: Selections and Summaries in Spanish

UA: Differentiating Instruction, graphic organizer, p. 193

UA: Supporting Instruction in Spanish, selection summary

California Standards, pp. 877–880

- **Reading Standard 2.2** Analyze the way in which clarity of meaning is affected by the patterns of organization, hierarchical structures, repetition of the main ideas, syntax, and word choice in the text.
- **Reading Standard 3.4** Analyze ways in which poets use imagery, personification, figures of speech, and sounds to evoke readers' emotions.

Learn It Online

You can introduce some of the topics in this unit using brief videos about the literature of this period.

go.hrw.com H12-877 Go

Teacher Preparation

Selection Summaries

In powerful, deceptively simple language, the speaker in "Quiet Night Thoughts" meditates on what he sees from his bed: a patch of moonlight as white as snow. As he drifts off to sleep, he imagines he is home, implicitly connecting himself with the moonlight.

"Question and Answer" can be read as Li Po's defense of his wandering life, as the speaker answers a companion with a smile, while reflecting on the freedom of his heart.

Direct Teach

Think About/Talk About

Read with a Purpose After students read the Read with a Purpose statement, ask them to discuss the feelings that the images of moonlight or mountains call to mind.

Comprehension

B Reading Focus

Possible response: *"Home" in line 8 and "moon" in line 6 function as parallel entities. Thus, just as the moonlight is far away from its source, the speaker is far away from his home.*

Analysis

A Literary Focus

Possible response: *The first four lines create a feeling of peace and quiet.*

C Literary Focus

Possible response: *Like the peach blossom, the speaker has no roots or ties to anyone.*

Extend the Discussion

Monitoring Your Reading Why does the speaker in "Question and Answer Among the Mountains" choose to live alone? ***Possible response:*** *He has the freedom to live with a carefree heart.*

POEM

Read with a Purpose

In "Quiet Night Thoughts," read to discover what the speaker recalls while looking at moonlight. In "Question and Answer Among the Mountains," read to discover why the speaker has chosen to live alone in the mountains.

Build Background

Like most of his contemporaries, Li Po wrote in a wide variety of poetic forms. Yet, according to Chinese critics, Li Po's best poems consisted of four lines with five to seven words per line. "Quiet Night Thoughts" is considered a masterpiece of this form. (The English translation here has eight lines in order to accommodate the rhythms of English verse.) A lifelong observer of nature, Li Po was renowned for creating vivid images of China's best-known mountains and streams, often recalled in a mood of solitude. The following three poems, though different in form, all resonate with images of nature and the thoughts and emotions of the solitary poet.

Quiet Night Thoughts

by **Li Po**

translated by **Arthur Cooper**

Before my bed
there is bright moonlight
So that it seems
like frost on the ground: **A**

Lifting my head
I watch the bright moon,
Lowering my head
I dream that I'm home. **B**

Question and Answer Among the Mountains

by **Li Po**

translated by **Robert Kotewall** and **Norman L. Smith**

You ask me why I dwell in the green mountain;
I smile and make no reply for my heart is free of care.
As the peach-blossom flows down stream and is gone into
the unknown,
I have a world apart that is not among men. **C**

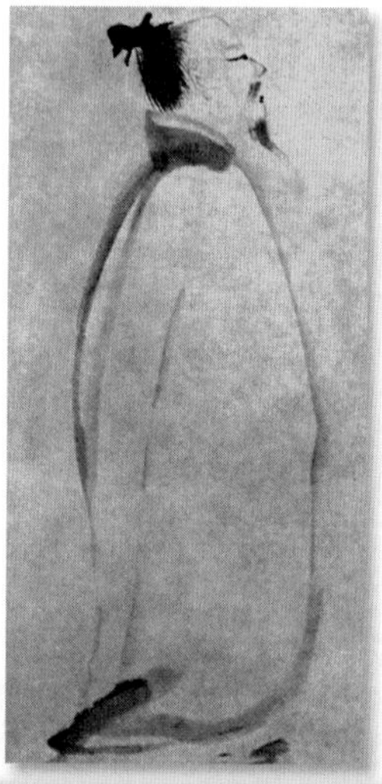

Li Po Chanting in Stroll, by Liang Kai. The Granger Collection, NY.

A Literary Focus **Imagery** What feeling is created by the image in the first four lines?

B Reading Focus **Using Text Structures to Understand Meaning** How does the structure of the poem help emphasize the speaker's distance from his home?

C Literary Focus **Imagery** How does the speaker use the image of the peach blossom to tell us something about himself?

Developing Oral Fluency

Small-Group Activity Divide the class into groups of six students. Have each group prepare a reading of "Letter to His Two Small Children." Groups might do a choral reading or a combination of choral and individual readings. One approach would be to have the whole group read the first two lines and have each member read a stanza. Make sure that students pause at line breaks and that their voices fall naturally when semicolons signal the end of clauses. Also, encourage students to find ways to bring out the translation's alliteration and rhymes within lines, such as "Oh to sow" and "Do the Spring things."

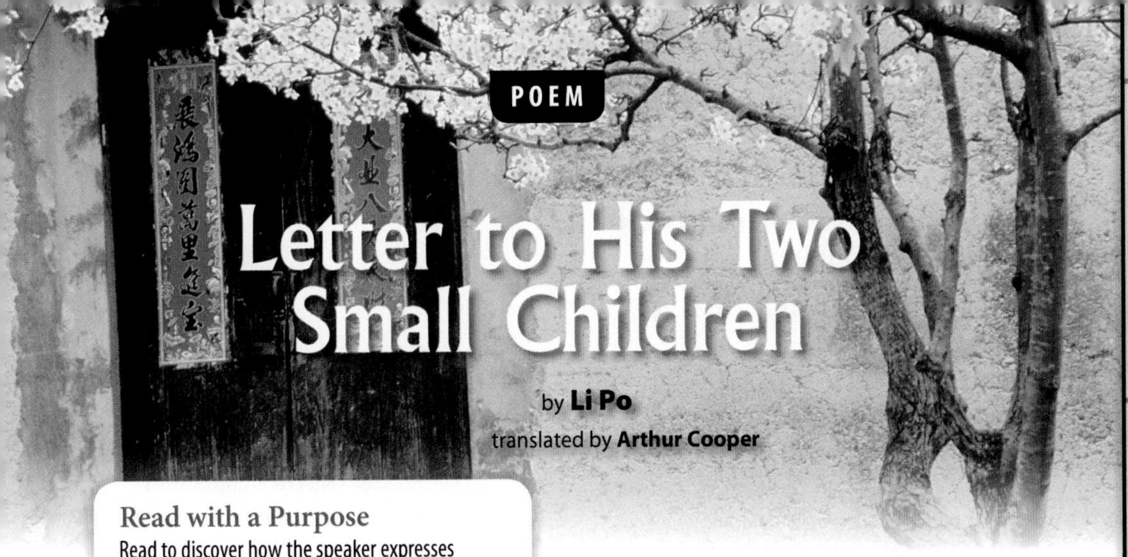

POEM

Letter to His Two Small Children

by **Li Po**

translated by **Arthur Cooper**

A local residence of Xidi Village, Shexian County, Anhui province, China.

Read with a Purpose

Read to discover how the speaker expresses his feelings for his children through images of nature.

Here in Wu° Land mulberry leaves are green,
Silkworms in Wu have now had three sleeps: **A**

My family, left in Eastern Lu,
Oh, to sow now Turtle-shaded fields,
Do the Spring things I can never join,
Sailing Yangtze° always on my own—

Let the South Wind blow you back my heart,
Fly and land it in the Tavern court
Where, to the East, there are sprays and leaves
Of one peach tree, sweeping the blue mist;

This is the tree I myself put in
When I left you, nearly three years past;
A peach tree now, level with the eaves,
And I sailing cannot yet turn home!

Pretty daughter, P'ing-yang is your name,
Breaking blossom, there beside my tree,
Breaking blossom, you cannot see me
And your tears flow like the running stream;

And little son, Po-ch'in you are called,
Your big sister's shoulder you must reach
When you come there underneath my peach,
Oh, to pat and pet you too, my child! **B**

I dreamt like this till my wits went wild,
By such yearning daily burned within;
So tore some silk, wrote this distant pang
From me to you living at Wen Yang. . .

1. **Wu:** river in central China.

6. **Yangtze:** the longest river in China, flowing from Tibet to the East China Sea.

A **Literary Focus** **Imagery** What does the speaker mean when he says, "Silkworms in Wu have now had three sleeps"? What is the effect of expressing the passage of time with this image?

B **Literary Focus** **Imagery** What does the poet associate with the image of the peach tree?

Teacher Preparation

Selection Summary

"Letter to His Two Small Children" is a beautiful, yearning evocation of the speaker's children who are far away. The speaker expresses his homesickness in delicate images, imagining his heart is in the peach tree near the home he left three years before.

Direct Teach

Think About/Talk About

Read with a Purpose Ask students to discuss the feelings that the images of nature suggest.

Analysis

A Literary Focus

Possible response: *Three years have passed. The speaker links time to natural cycles of birth and death, with an emphasis on death in "sleeps"; the silkworms' sleep creates an image a child might respond to.*

B Literary Focus

Possible response: *He associates the peach tree with home and the changes that happen there.*

Extend the Discussion

Alliteration What is the effect of the repetition of "breaking blossom" (ll. 16–17)? ***Possible response:*** *It emphasizes the identification of the speaker's daughter, P'ing-yang, with the peach blossoms breaking open in springtime. It also hints at his daughter "breaking" into womanhood.*

California Standards, pp. 880–881

- **Reading Standard 2.2** Analyze the way in which clarity of meaning is affected by the patterns of organization, hierarchical structures, repetition of the main ideas, syntax, and word choice in the text.
- **Reading Standard 3.4** Analyze ways in which poets use imagery, personification, figures of speech, and sounds to evoke readers' emotions.
- **Writing Standard 2.2** Write responses to literature: **a.** Demonstrate a comprehensive understanding of the significant ideas in works or passages. **b.** Analyze the use of imagery, language, universal themes, and unique aspects of the text. **c.** Support important ideas and viewpoints through accurate and detailed references to the text and to other works. **d.** Demonstrate an understanding of the author's use of stylistic devices and an appreciation of the effects created. **e.** Identify and assess the impact of perceived ambiguities, nuances, and complexities within the text.
- **Writing Standard 2.4** Write historical investigation reports: **a.** Use exposition, narration, description, argumentation, or some combination of rhetorical strategies to support the main proposition. Explain the perceived reason or reasons for the similarities and differences in historical records with information derived from primary and secondary sources to support or enhance the presentation.
- **Writing Standard 2.6** Deliver multimedia presentations: **a.** Combine text, images, and sound and draw information from many sources (e.g., television broadcasts, videos, films, newspapers, magazines, CD-ROMs, the Internet, electronic media-generated images). **b.** Select an appropriate medium for each element of the presentation.

Check for Understanding

Independent Practice

Reading Skills Focus

Possible responses:

1. *The mood is peaceful and reflective.*
2. *Why does the speaker prefer a solitary life in the mountains?*
3. *He has been away at sea for three years and longs to see them.*
4. *The moon makes him think of his home far away.*
5. *He is joyous at the freedom of living alone.*
6. *He regrets that he misses seeing them grow up.*
7. *Have students analyze the imagery and structure and suggest their own interpretations.*

Literary Skills Focus

Possible responses:

8. *The moon and its cold light, and the speaker's movements and actions convey a pensive or wistful mood.*
9. *The poet answering with silence seems to be a contradiction. However, it can also be regarded as a perfectly good answer since it proclaims his freedom from doing things he does not want to do.*
10. *Li Po uses a peach tree and the South Wind to emphasize solitude. Evoked emotions include loneliness, pride, sadness, yearning, and regret.*
11. *They are effective because the images are easy to visualize and the vivid images create a strong emotional response.*
12. *The contemplation of the moon's brightness is contrasted with his dreams of being home.*

Applying Your Skills

Reading Standard 2.2, 3.4 (see pages A48–A50)
Writing Standard 2.2b, 2.2d (see pages A51–A52)

Quiet Night Thoughts / Question and Answer Among the Mountains / Letter to His Two Small Children

Literary Response and Analysis

Reading Skills Focus

Quick Check

1. What is the mood of "Quiet Night Thoughts"?
2. What is the question in "Question and Answer"?
3. In "Letter to His Two Small Children," why does the speaker write to his children?

Read with a Purpose

4. In "Quiet Night Thoughts," what emotional effect does the moon have on the speaker?
5. In "Question and Answer," how does the speaker feel about living alone?
6. What feelings for his children does the speaker of "Letter" reveal in his use of nature imagery?

Reading Skills: Using Text Structures to Understand Meaning

7. Connect the two boxes in each chart to a third box. How does each image contribute to each poem's meaning? How does the structure of the image contribute to the meaning of the poem?

"Quiet Night Thoughts":

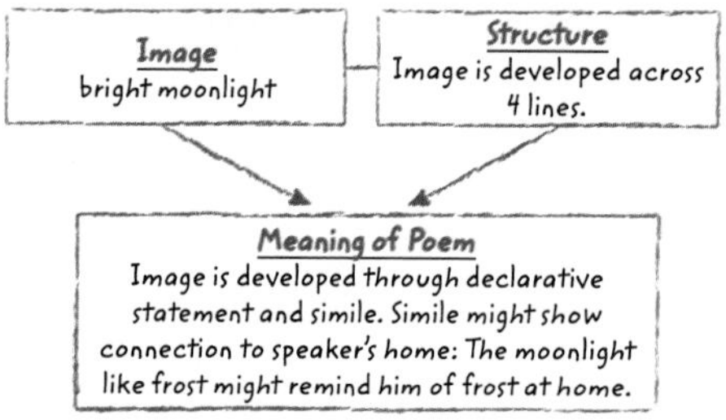

Literary Skills Focus

Literary Analysis

8. **Analyze** How does the poet use imagery to convey the mood of "Quiet Night Thoughts"?
9. **Interpret** In "Question and Answer," the speaker answers a question by not answering it. Explain this **paradox,** or seeming contradiction.
10. **Analyze** How does Li Po use images to emphasize solitude? What emotions does he evoke?

Literary Skills: Imagery

11. **Analyze** Do the speakers effectively express their feelings by using nature images? Explain.

Literary Skills Review: Parallelism

12. **Draw Conclusions** The repetition of words, phrases, or sentences that have the same grammatical structure or that restate a similar idea is **parallelism.** Explain the effect of this technique in the last four lines of "Quiet Night Thoughts."

Writing Skills Focus

Think as a Reader/Writer

Use It in Your Writing Review the examples of Li Po's imagery in your *Reader/Writer Notebook.* Use imagery as you write a poem about solitude.

What Do You Think Now? Why do simple nature images express feelings of solitude?

Universal Access

Struggling Writers

Some students may need additional scaffolding to complete the Writing Skills Focus activity. Before students begin writing their poems, have them brainstorm a list of images or ideas that they associate with solitude or with being alone. Give students an example to get them started. For example, you might say that you associate an untouched field covered with snow with solitude. After students have completed their lists, encourage them to incorporate the images they have brainstormed into their poems about solitude.

What Do You Think?

To help students answer this question, ask them to make a list of natural images that evoke ideas of solitude. As they record these images in their **Reader/Writer Notebooks**, have students ask themselves why they think these images came to mind.

Writing Standard 2.2a–e, 2.4a, 2.6a, 2.6b (see pages A51–A52)

Japanese and Chinese Poetry

Writing Skills Focus

Write a Comparison-Contrast Essay

In what ways is British Romantic poetry similar to and different from Japanese and Chinese poetry? Re-read the selections to clarify your ideas. Then, write an essay in which you compare and contrast the selections. Here are more specific topic ideas for your comparison-contrast essay:

- Compare and contrast the poets' use of imagery. What ideas and emotions does Romantic poetry evoke? How do these images, ideas, and emotions compare to those addressed by Japanese and Chinese poets?
- Compare and contrast the forms and structures of the poems. What differentiates the Romantic forms from those of the Japanese and Chinese? How do the poetic structures compare across cultures?
- Choose one of the Japanese or Chinese poems and a Romantic poem with a similar meaning or purpose. Compare and contrast the content, imagery, and structures of the two poems. Is one poem more effective in delivering its meaning or conveying its purpose? Explain your opinion with support from the texts.

Use examples from the selections to support your arguments. Weave your arguments together using transitional words, and remember to include a strong concluding statement.

What Do You Think Now? Do poets' imaginations help them interact with the world or escape it? Explain.

CHOICES

As you respond to the Choices, use these **Academic Vocabulary** words as appropriate: device, differentiate, function, inherent, technique.

REVIEW

Create a Visual

Choose an image from a Japanese or Chinese poem in the unit and a related image from a British Romantic poem in the unit. Create a collage, painting, or drawing of each image. Present your visuals to the class, explaining the connections between them.

CONNECT

Illustrate the Poems

TechFocus Choose two or three poems that you feel have powerful imagery, and create a Web page for each. The Web pages should contain the texts of the poems as well as images and sounds that illustrate the poems' imagery and meanings. You may also read the poems aloud and place audio or video recordings of your performance on the Web pages. Then, share your Web pages with your class.

EXTEND

Compare Poets' Lives Across Cultures

With a partner, use the school library or the Internet to research more about the lives of Tu Fu or Li Po and a British Romantic poet. How are their lives similar? What differentiates them? Present your findings to the class. Offer your peers the opportunity to comment on the cross-cultural similarities and differences between the poets you chose.

Learn It Online
Explore Chinese poetry further through these Internet links.
go.hrw.com H12-881 Go

Independent Practice

Choices: Evaluation Criteria

Review: Homework
Create a Visual
Students explain how their visual interpretations relate to each image.

Connect: Homework
Illustrate the Poems
Web page uses texts, images and sounds to illustrate imagery and meaning.

Extend: Homework
Compare Poets' Lives Across Cultures
Students include similarities and differences between the lives of the two poets.

Assess

Unit 4 Resources, Selection Standards Check, pp. 130, 134

ThinkCentral Online Assessment, Selection Standards Check

Teacher One Stop™, editable Selection Standards Check

Reteach

ThinkCentral Online Remediation

Universal Access

Struggling Writers

Have students write a short comparison-contrast essay on the use of imagery in a Romantic poem and a Japanese or Chinese poem. Instruct students to draw a Venn diagram with one side detailing the images and emotions of one poem, and the other side detailing those of the other poem. Remind students to use examples from the poems in their essay to support their points.

What Do You Think Now?

To help students answer this question, ask them to refer to specific examples in the poems to observe the way in which Tu Fu and Li Po applied their imaginations. What evidence is there, if any, that the poets' imagination serve as an escape to another world? What evidence shows that their imagination helped them to express their circumstances?

Learn It Online
Literature Links direct students to pre-screened Web sites offering more information related to a selection.
go.hrw.com H12-881 Go

Standards Focus

Objectives

Students will
- learn prewriting, drafting, and revising techniques for writing a reflective composition
- learn how to proofread and publish their work

Preteach

Write with a Purpose Read aloud the essentials of a good reflective composition to guide students' understanding of this type of writing. Also, refer them to the scoring guide (p. 890) for more information on reflective compositions.

Direct Teach

Model the Skill

Think as a Reader/Writer Use the professional model on this page and others in the unit to provide examples of the elements of a good reflective composition. Point out how the Goodall model reflects on the meaning of her experience.

Think About the Model

Possible responses:

1. *Goodall uses positive words like "peaceful" and "radiance" to show how she feels about the scene.*
2. *Goodall reflects that being back in Gombe gave her a chance to get away from materialistic concerns and find peace.*

Writing Workshop

Reflective Composition

Write with a Purpose

Write a reflective composition about a significant personal experience. Include the broader meaning of the experience. Your **purpose** for writing is to inspire and connect with your readers. Your **audience** is probably classmates, your teacher, and others who will appreciate the significance of the experience.

A Good Reflective Composition

- relates a personal experience and its broader significance
- draws comparisons between specific incidents in the experience and broader themes
- maintains a balance between the personal incident and its relationship to general and abstract ideas
- uses rhetorical devices for aesthetic purposes

See page 890 for a complete scoring guide.

Think as a Reader/Writer

Before you write your own **reflective composition,** read the following excerpt from "A Reason to Hope" by Jane Goodall, which can be found in its entirety beginning on page 710. Observe how she describes her experience and reflects on its importance.

In the faint light from the moon reflected by the dew-laden grass, it was not difficult to find my way up the mountain. All around, the trees were shrouded with the last mysteries of the night's dreaming. It was quiet, utterly peaceful. The only sounds were the occasional chirp of a cricket, and the soft murmur where the waves caressed the stones on the beach below. Suddenly there was a burst of song, the duet of a pair of robin chats, hauntingly beautiful. I realized that the intensity of the light had changed; dawn had crept upon me unawares. . . . ← Goodall introduces the scene of the experience.

Five minutes later I heard the rustlings of leaves overhead. I looked up and saw the branches moving against the lightening sky. The chimps had awakened. It was Fifi and her offspring, Freud, Frodo, and little Fanni. I followed when they moved off up the slope. Fanni riding on her mother's back like a diminutive jockey. Presently they climbed into a tall fig tree and began to feed. I heard the occasional soft thuds as skins and seeds of figs fell to the ground. ← The chimps are introduced.

For several hours we moved leisurely from one food tree to the next, gradually climbing higher and higher. On an open grassy ridge the chimps climbed into a massive mbula tree, where Fifi . . . made a large comfortable nest high above me. She dozed through a midday siesta, little Fanni asleep in her arms, Frodo and Freud playing nearby. How healing it was to be back in Gombe again, and by myself with the chimpanzees and their forest. I had left the busy, materialistic world so full of greed and selfishness and, for a little while, could feel myself, as in the early days, a part of nature. ← Goodall begins to reflect on the meaning of the experience.

Reader/Writer Notebook

Use your **RWN** to complete the activities for this workshop.

Think About the Professional Model

1. How do Goodall's descriptions convey what she feels about the scene?
2. Summarize the reflective comments Goodall makes about the experience.

California Standards, pp. 882–890

- **Writing Standard 1.1** Demonstrate an understanding of the elements of discourse (e.g., purpose, speaker, audience, form) when completing narrative, expository, persuasive, or descriptive writing assignments.
- **Writing Standard 1.5** Use language in a natural, fresh, and vivid way to establish a specific tone.
- **Writing Standard 1.9** Revise text to highlight the individual voice, improve sentence variety and style, and enhance subtlety of meaning and tone in ways that are consistent with the purpose, audience and genre.
- **Writing Standard 2.3** Write reflective compositions: **a.** Explore the significance of personal experiences, events, conditions or concerns by using rhetorical strategies (e.g., narration, description, exposition , persuasion). **b.** Draw comparisons between specific incidents and broader themes that illustrate the writer's important beliefs or generalizations about life. **c.** Maintain a balance in describing individual incidents and relate those incidents to more general and abstract ideas.

Writing Workshop Resources

UA: Holt Interactive Writer and Speaker, practice and assessment, p. 78

UA: Differentiating Instruction, modified lesson plans, p. 199

WritingNotes, interactive lesson presentations with activities

GrammarNotes, interactive lesson presentations with activities

Writing and Research in a Digital Age, interactive lesson presentations with activities

Writing Standard 1.1, 1.5, 1.9, 2.3a–c (see pages A51–A52)
Written and Oral Language Conventions Standard 1.1, 1.2, 1.3 (see page A53)

Prewriting

Choose an Experience

What experiences in your life have taught you the most important lessons? The experience could be something unusual, like a trip or a competition. Or it could be something you do every day, like visiting a friend's house. What matters most is that the experience means something to you. A trip might teach you about how other people live; a day with a friend might teach you about happiness.

If you cannot think of a significant experience, look through old yearbooks, photos, diaries, or journals. Also, try reading some published reflective pieces, such as poems, autobiographies and memoirs, and essays.

Gather and Record Details

To gather the details that will bring your experience and its meaning to life, list the individual events that were an integral part of your experience. The following suggestions may help you recall the events:

- Visualize the entire experience, picturing each event from beginning to end.
- Ask others who shared the experience with you to recall details.
- If you have mementos from the experience—photographs, letters, journal or diary entries—use them to help jog your memory.

Under each event in your list, record specific details about each event to help you create images in the minds of readers.

Types of Details	
Narrative details	• relate **actions, thoughts,** and **feelings** of people involved • include **dialogue** (what you or others said) • include **interior monologue** (your unspoken thoughts)
Descriptive details	• describe how **people** and **objects** look • describe the **setting** of the experience

Reflect on the Meaning

Reflective compositions go beyond describing your personal observations and perceptions to examining **abstract ideas**—love, patience, courage, honor. When you have chosen the experience, think about these questions to help you develop your reflections and think about the **significance** of the moment:

- What did you feel at the time of the experience?
- How do you feel about it now?
- How has the experience changed the way you think and act?
- What insight about life in general did you gain from the experience?

Idea Starters

- an achievement
- a disappointment
- an experience with nature
- a friendship
- a journey
- a job

Writing Tip

Both narratives and descriptions include **concrete sensory details** that appeal to the five senses: sight, sound, taste, smell, and touch.

Your Turn

Get Started Making notes in your **RWN,** choose an **experience** and reflect on its **meaning** for you. Then, note **details** that will help you convey the experience and its meaning to your audience.

Learn It Online
To see how one writer completed this assignment, see the model reflective essay online.
go.hrw.com H12-883 Go

Teacher One Stop™, on-level lesson plans and all print resources
Holt Six Traits for Writing, rubrics, prompts, and sample papers
Language and Sentence Skills Practice
UA: Developmental Language and Sentence Practice
Language Handbook Worksheets, p. 113
Formal Assessment, Progress Monitoring Test 3
ThinkCentral Online Assessment, Writing Workshop Test
ThinkCentral Online Remediation
Holt Online Essay Scoring

Guided Practice: Apply

Choose an Experience

- Suggest that students freewrite to help them think of a topic. They should use one of the following prompts: "It all changed when . . . ," "I'll never forget when . . . ," or "I surprised myself when. . . ."
- Have students highlight details from their freewriting that show the importance of the experience and then list other details that they feel are important to include.

Gather and Record Details

- Suggest that students sketch a visual representation of the experience to help them remember details.
- Remind students that their descriptions should address more than one sense. What did they see, hear, smell, taste, and feel during the experience? Which of these details stand out most to them?

Your Turn

Get Started Have students ask themselves, "What does this experience mean to me?" Give them a few minutes to brainstorm before writing out their answers. Then, students should review their responses and highlight important details.

Learn It Online
Interactive Writer's Models on the Interactive Student Edition provide annotated sample essays along with writing tips and strategies.
go.hrw.com H12–883 Go

Guided Practice: Apply

Think about Purpose and Audience

Remind students that they can engage their audiences by including specific sensory details that will help the reader imagine what it would be like to share their experience. Whatever they choose to write, they should keep their purpose and audience in mind as they develop their stories.

Organize Your Reflective Composition

- Suggest that students record each detail they remember on an index card and then arrange the index cards in chronological order. Then, have students insert cards with flashback or flash-forward experiences in the appropriate spots. Students may also choose to type their details on a computer and cut and paste the information in a chronological order.
- Explain how the experience related in the reflective composition action plan is organized in chronological order.

Your Turn

Organize Your Ideas Have students complete the **Your Turn** in pairs. After students have completed their reflective composition action plan, have them review the plan and remove any events or details that stray from the central experience.

Think About Purpose and Audience

Your **purpose** is to explore the connection between a personal experience and what it says about your life and, beyond that, what it says about the meaning of being human. You also share your experience with your **audience,** who will most likely be your classmates and teacher. As you think about your experience, consider what your audience needs to know to fully understand its significance to you and its broader meaning about life.

Organize Your Reflective Composition

Once you have gathered details, it is time to organize your essay. You will organize the events in **chronological order,** the order in which they happened. You could possibly vary this order by using **flashbacks** and **flash-forwards**—jumps forward or backward in time—for effect. Take note of details you will include and when you'll include them. Once you have finished retelling your experience, you will conclude by **reflecting** on its importance to you and its broader significance.

Create an Action Plan

Your **reflective composition action plan** begins with a statement of your experience. Think about what happened and how it unfolded. Then, organize your essay by planning the introduction, body, and conclusion. What scene best begins the essay? What events will you show that lead up to the experience? How will you state the experience's significance? Here is one writer's reflective essay action plan. Use the model to help you create your own plan.

Action Plan

Experience: picking up trash after the game, leaders not showing up

Introduction:
—the night after the "powder puff" game, picking up trash
—details: the sight and smell of the trash
—describe my disappointment when people didn't show up
—hint about the significance: leadership

Body:
—describe the meeting with other members of the leadership team
—tell my reaction to their "excuses"

Conclusion:
—discuss my reflections on the event; how I learned that what was important was my contribution, not what others did
—explain the idea that work should be its own reward

Your Turn

Organize Your Ideas Now that you have chosen an experience and gathered details, write a **reflective composition action plan.** Share your plan with a partner, and ask for feedback.

Reflective Composition Writing Prompts

Students can choose their own reflective composition idea or use one of the following prompts to write a reflective composition.

Physical Education Think about a sport or activity that tested your physical and mental limits. Explain what you learned about yourself and others through this experience.

Social Studies Write a reflective composition about a trip you took to a foreign country, and elaborate on what you learned from interacting with people from a different culture.

Workplace Challenge yourself to write a reflective composition that explains an experience at a job that taught you something. If you have not had a job, you may write about an experience that helped you realize what kind of job you may want in the future.

Drafting

Draft Your Reflective Essay

Now use your prewriting notes, including your reflective composition action plan, and the **Writer's Framework** to the right to draft your composition.

Use Language Effectively

Use the following types of descriptive language in natural, fresh, and vivid ways to establish a specific tone:

- Use **precise verbs:** Note the difference between *walking, ambling, strolling, sauntering,* and *hiking.* Each word has a slightly different meaning. Choose verbs that precisely describe actions in your experience.
- Use **figurative language** to help your reader imagine what you are describing. Think about both physical resemblances and more abstract relationships to build effective comparisons and descriptions.
- Use **adverbs and adverb phrases** to help readers follow the progression of events in your essay.

Framework for a Reflective Composition

Introduction
- Engage readers' attention.
- Provide necessary background information.

Body
- Use narrative and descriptive details to relate events.
- Organize events chronologically.

Conclusion
- Bring narrative to an end.
- Reflect on the experience: explicitly reveal its significance.
- Identify the insight into life the experience gave you.

Grammar Link Using Adverbs and Adverb Phrases

A reflective composition often progresses over time and changes settings as the writer leads the reader to the main experience. **Adverbs and adverb phrases** help the reader follow the progression from place to place and over time. These modifiers locate action in time and space by answering the questions *where* and *when*. In the model on page 882, note how Goodall uses adverbs and adverb phrases (usually prepositional phrases used as adverbs) as she marks her progress on the mountain in Gombe.

All around, the trees were shrouded . . .

Suddenly there was a burst of song . . .

Five minutes later I heard the rustlings of leaves overhead.

For several hours we moved . . .

On an open grassy ridge the chimps climbed . . .

Your Turn

Write Your Draft Following your **reflective composition action plan** and the **Writer's Framework,** write a draft of your essay. Also think about how you will use **adverbs** and **adverb phrases** as transitions to help your readers follow the progression of your experience.

Guided Practice: Apply

Draft Your Reflective Essay

Ask students to refer to their reflective composition action plan to begin writing about their experiences.

Use Language Effectively

Have students note examples of effective language Goodall used and think about how to use language effectively in their own writing. Have them consider the following questions: What precise verbs can show exactly what I mean? What vivid details can I include? Where can I add figurative language?

Grammar Link

For practice, have students add adverb phrases to the following sentences.

1. The girl waited for the bus.
2. I found myself alone in the room.
3. This was not the result I expected.

Warriner's Handbook, Sixth Course, pp. 338–340

Your Turn

Write Your Draft Ask students to complete the **Your Turn** as independent practice. Remind students to use their graphic organizers as they begin writing. Suggest that students use every other line as they write their drafts so they can more easily revise drafts later.

Universal Access

English Learners

Allow students to freewrite in their native languages first. Students can then switch to English when writing their reflective composition action plan.

Advanced Learners

Enrichment Challenge students to freewrite a short reflective composition from the point of view of someone else involved in their chosen experience. Have them ask themselves, "What was the experience like for that person, and what did he or she learn?" Have students incorporate some of the sensory detail from this activity into their draft.

Students with Disabilities

Give students sentence starters to help them develop an idea for the composition. In addition to using the sentence starters listed on p. 883, suggest that they begin sentences with "This experience changed me because . . . ," "What I learned was . . . ," or "I never expected that I would. . . ."

Model the Skill
Using a student draft on a transparency, model how to use the questions, tips, and revision techniques suggested in the chart. You might use a student's reflective composition or a reflective composition of your own creation to evaluate and revise using the steps in the chart.

Guided Practice: Apply
Ask volunteers to demonstrate using each of the steps in their own compositions.

Peer Review
Remind students to pay close attention to what they read in each other's drafts. After they finish reading, they should be able to look up from the paper and summarize what they have learned from their partner's experience.

Holt Six Traits for Writing, rubrics, prompts, and sample papers

Peer Review
With a partner, review your draft by answering each question in the chart to the right. Begin by reading the evaluation questions in the left-hand column, studying the tips in the center column, and then revising your composition as needed using the revision techniques in the right-hand column. Encourage your partner to note any details that are missing or need more explanation.

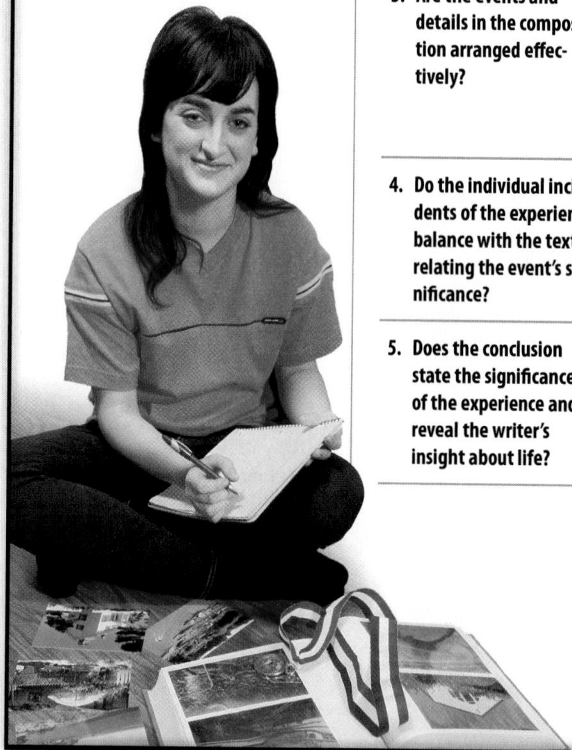

Evaluating and Revising
To ensure your reflective composition reflects your experience with accuracy and flair, use the chart below to evaluate and revise your essay's content and organization. As you revise, pay attention to your **audience** and **purpose.**

Reflective Essay: Guidelines for Content and Organization

Evaluation Question	Tip	Revision Technique
1. Does the introduction provide necessary background information and engage the reader's attention?	**Bracket** sentences that provide background information. **Circle** the engaging opening.	**Add** background information. **Add** an engaging opener or revise existing sentences to make them more gripping.
2. Does the essay's body use narrative and descriptive details to relate each event in fresh and vivid ways?	**Put a check mark** next to each narrative or descriptive passage.	**Add** details or elaborate on events to make them clear or revise description to make it fresh and clear.
3. Are the events and details in the composition arranged effectively?	**Number** events according to chronological order. If the numbers are not in sequence (unless you have purposely added a flashback or flash-forward), revise.	**Reorder** events to reflect chronological order. **Add** transitions, such as adverbs and adverb phrases, to improve the coherence of the narrative.
4. Do the individual incidents of the experience balance with the text relating the event's significance?	**Highlight** in one color the words relating the experience, and in another color, the words commenting on its broader significance.	To achieve balance, **add** effective language either to describe the incident or to explain its significance.
5. Does the conclusion state the significance of the experience and reveal the writer's insight about life?	**Highlight** the experience's significance. **Put a wavy line under** sentences that reveal the writer's insight about life.	**Add** one or more sentences that explicitly state the experience's significance and your insight about life.

Real Issues, Real Experts
Holt Professional Learning for Language Arts
To watch videos on teaching **revision, grammar,** and **on-demand writing skills** featuring Linda Rief, Amy Benjamin, and Leila Christenbury, go to this page in **ThinkCentral, Teacher Access.**

Universal Access
EL English Learners
Ask students to read their introduction aloud to you, then offer responses that begin in the following ways: "It seems like this experience is about . . . ," "It sounds as if you felt . . . ," "The important details I noticed were . . ." Guide students to recognize when they give irrelevant information and when their tone misleads the reader about how they felt. Then, have students suggest ways in which their introductions could be rewritten.

Read this student's draft with comments on its structure and suggestions for how it could be made even stronger.

Student Draft

On Commitment

by Steffi Yutan, Elk Grove High School

I glanced at my watch: 11:32 P.M. I looked around the stadium and saw only five members of the leadership team after the "powder puff" game.

Everyone had been there to watch, play, or cheer, but over half did not stay to clean up after the game. Sighing, I picked up my pace, encouraging those few around me.

The following Monday, we discussed the disappearance of half of our leadership team after the Friday night game. Our advisor, whom I have grown to respect more than most adults in my life, let us handle the situation on our own. I sat quietly—listening to several girls who barely held back tears as they explained how hurt and abandoned they felt. I nodded in agreement, but I was more angry than hurt. I wanted to scream at my peers for being selfish, for being irresponsible, for letting me down—for letting the team down. However, I knew no amount of yelling, kicking, or screaming would get through to them. They were long gone, rolling their eyes, staring blankly into space. Instead of apologies, they made excuses. "My ride was leaving," or just "I forgot." I wondered, "How can they be so self-centered?"

← In the introduction, Steffi hints at a **conflict** that is an important part of her **experience.**

← Steffi recounts an event that leads to her realization of the **significance of her experience.**

← Steffi uses **description, dialogue,** and **interior monologue** to describe the other characters' reactions to contrast her own.

MINI-LESSON **How to Add Details to an Introduction**

Creating a vivid scene with concrete sensory details is a good way to begin a reflective composition. Since the scene after the game is a catalyst for Steffi's reflection, She decided to revise it by adding details that clearly illustrate the problem and her reaction. These details create an emotional reaction in her readers.

Steffi's Revision of Paragraph 1

I sighed deeply, bent over stiffly to pick up another dripping plastic bottle from the bleachers, and dropped it with sticky fingers into my smelly, bulging garbage bag. Yawning, ^I glanced at my watch: 11:32 P.M. I looked around the stadium and saw only five members of the leadership team ^picking up trash after the "powder puff" game.

Everyone had been there to watch, play, or cheer, but over half did not stay to clean up after the game. Sighing, I picked up my pace, encouraging those around me^; only ninety-nine bottles to go.

Your Turn

Add Details to Your Introduction Read your draft and then ask,

- Do I use **descriptive language** to show, rather than just tell, what happened?
- What **concrete, sensory details** can I add to allow my readers to imagine the scene?

Guided Practice: Apply

Student Draft

Explain that the Student Draft on this page is the first half of a composition written by the student whose reflective composition action plan appears on p. 884. Model reading the draft and the annotations in blue, and explain that the yellow highlighting illustrates the student's language choices. Explain that a mini-lesson follows with helpful information about ways to improve this draft as well as their own.

Mini-Lesson

How to Add Details to an Introduction

- Explain that the student writer has revised her introduction by using concrete and sensory details to grab the reader's attention.
- Remind students to use vivid imagery in their writing to ensure that the reader can easily picture what they are writing about.

Your Turn

Add Details to Your Introduction

As students complete the **Your Turn,** tell them to find two places in their drafts where concrete details could be added. The details may be used to make any part of their experience clearer. Remind students to use the **Grammar Link** on p. 885 to help them add adverb phrases to their writing.

Struggling Writers

Benchmark Students When students have trouble visualizing a particular scene from their experience, suggest that they describe it to a partner aloud. Partners can write down any sensory details mentioned in the description. Students should use the partner's notes when writing the introduction.

Advanced Learners

Acceleration Ask students to write a letter addressed to the person they were prior to the experience described in the composition. What would they like to tell their earlier selves? Are there things they would tell themselves to do differently or to appreciate more? Suggest students use some of the insight from these answers to these questions in the introduction.

Students with Disabilities

Have students look for print or online images that represent the opening scene of their experience. Have them study these images and write down details that remind them of their experience. Encourage students to incorporate these details into their introductions.

Guided Practice: Apply

Student Draft

- Explain that the Student Draft is continued and completed on this page. Again, the draft is annotated and highlighted for students.
- Read the draft and annotations aloud and discuss. Refer students to the model on p. 887. Ask students to comment on the student's success with the writing assignment.

Mini-Lesson

How to Add Broad Generalizations About Life

- Tell students to make sure their compositions explain what they learned from the experience described. Explain that by including personal reflection, they let readers know why the experience was important to them.
- Encourage students to write out the answers to the questions posed in this lesson. Have students consider incorporating these answers into their concluding paragraphs.

Your Turn

Add Generalizations As students work to complete the **Your Turn,** have them think about where they can add reflective comments so readers understand the composition's significance throughout their reading. Their reflection should make it clear why each part of the experience is important enough to be included in the composition.

Student Draft *continues*

Steffi explains **when** and **how** she identified the real source of the problem. →

I realized then that we had different levels of ability, dedication, and expectations. Not once had we discussed the commitment our team required for the laborious work of leadership. Our team did not fall apart the night of the "powder puff" game, but months before. It is the same every year. We begin excited and optimistic, proud to be campus leaders, but slowly apathy invades, leaving behind shells of good leaders tasks left undone and only a select few to pick up the slack.

She uses **figurative language** to address apathy and its result. →

The **chronological organization** moves to the present year, setting up her most reflective insight. →

This year, as vice president of the leadership team, I led a discussion on individual expectations, dedication, and commitment. The conversation has made a world of difference. Although the occasional lack of passion or poor attitudes of my peers still frustrates me, their varying degrees of commitment cannot keep me from the job that I love.

In her **conclusion,** Steffi uses an image of the trash to lead to her final **reflection.** →

I now find myself looking forward to picking up plastic bottles after this year's "powder puff" game. But this time, with my whole team there, I know it will be worth the effort. Now I understand that real leadership is about helping others discover their own commitment.

MINI-LESSON **How to Add Broad Generalizations About Life**

A good reflective composition relates the personal experience to broader themes and generalizations about life. As Steffi re-read her draft, she decided that she wanted to add more reflective explanation to the fifth paragraph to balance the incident with reflective comments about its meaning to her. Reflective comments answer the questions *What does this experience mean to me? What have I learned from the experience? What does this experience illustrate about life in general?*

Steffi's Revision of Paragraph 5

This year, as vice president of the leadership team, I led a discussion on individual expectations, dedication, and commitment. The dialogue has made a world of difference. Although the occasional lack of passion or poor attitudes of my peers frustrate me, their varying degrees of commitment cannot keep me from the job that I love. ^Being the first person on campus and the last to leave invigorates me. No matter how many hours I put in or how little acknowledgment I receive, the work is always worthwhile because I know that I am contributing something important—to myself more than anything.

Your Turn

Add Generalizations Re-read your draft to determine if there are **additional reflective comments** that you can make about any part of your experience and its broader significance. Ask yourself, "What does this experience mean to me? What does this experience illustrate about life in general?"

Universal Access

EL English Learners

Encourage students to use the following sentence starters when reflecting on their experiences.

- Before I thought . . . ; now I have learned . . .
- Next time I'm faced with this situation I will . . .
- This experience has taught me . . .
- Although it was challenging . . .

✔ See **UA: Differentiating Instruction** for strategies for teaching English learners.

AAVE Students Who Use African American Vernacular English

English for Academic Success Point out the first two paragraphs of the student model on p. 888. Tell students that there are two negative statements, "Our team did not fall apart" and "their varying degrees of commitment cannot keep me from the job that I love." In informal English, these statements may be written, "Our team did not never fall apart" and "cannot keep me from not attending the job that I love."

Proofreading and Publishing

Proofread

Now that you have evaluated and revised your reflective composition, it is time to polish and present it. Edit your composition to correct any misspellings, capitalization and punctuation errors, and problems in sentence structure.

Form proofreading teams of four, and swap papers with another team. Each person on the team can focus on a different type of error: spelling, capitalization, punctuation, and sentence structure.

Commas can be particularly challenging in your proofreading. Read carefully, applying comma rules in your writing.

Grammar Link Punctuating Words, Phrases, and Clauses in a Series

Writers often present examples or descriptions in series of three or more elements. In your own writing, be sure to use commas to separate the items in a series, including words, phrases, and clauses.

Steffi often uses items in a series. As she proofread her final draft, she found places where she had omitted commas.

> We begin excited and optimistic, but slowly apathy invades, leaving behind shells of leaders^, tasks left undone^, and only a select few to pick up the slack.

Publishing

Your reflective composition tells a story only you can tell. Now it is time to share the story with others. Here are ways to get your composition to an audience.

- Give an oral presentation of your reflection to classmates or family members. Consider using audiovisual materials (such as presentation software) to enhance your presentation. For more on **presenting a reflection,** see page 892.
- Work with your classmates to arrange your compositions by themes (for example, friendship, family, courage, sacrifice). Then, shelve this collection in your school library as a class archive for future graduating classes and for your own class to look back on at class reunions.

Reflect on the Process Thinking about how you wrote your reflective composition will help you with other writing you will do in the future. In your **RWN,** write a short response to these questions:

1. What was the most challenging part of writing a reflective composition? Explain.
2. Would you use an action plan to help organize your ideas when writing other kinds of essays? Why or why not?

Proofreading Tip

If you have time, set aside your paper for a day and return to it with a fresh perspective. You may catch errors that you would otherwise miss. If you are uncertain whether you've included sentence fragments, ask a classmate for help.

Writing Tip

When the last two items in a series are joined by *and, or,* or *nor,* your teacher may prefer that you omit the comma before the conjunction, as long as the comma is not needed to make the meaning of the sentence clear.

Submission Ideas

- school newspaper
- community newspaper
- online magazine
- your personal Web page
- class or school Web page

Your Turn

Proofread and Publish As you are proofreading, read carefully to identify where your composition needs commas to separate items in a series. Proofread your entire paper for accuracy in spelling, punctuation, and usage. Then, print out a final copy, and publish it.

Guided Practice: Apply

Proofreading

Integrating with Grammar, Usage, and Mechanics If students make errors in using adverbs and adverb phrases or punctuating words, phrases, and clauses in a series as they are proofreading, send them to the Punctuation chapters in **Warriner's Handbook.**

Grammar Link

- Tell students to circle any words in a series in their compositions.
- Have students use the Grammar Link as a guide to punctuate their series.

Publishing

Brainstorm with students about additional ways to publish their reflective compositions.

Reflect on the Process

Have students reflect on their writing process as well as their final product. Challenge them to reflect metacognitively about how they can improve and apply what they have learned.

Your Turn

Proofread and Publish Have students highlight or underline the revisions and submit their drafts with their final reflective compositions so that you can check to make sure they are following the revision guidelines on p. 886.

Remind students that in formal English, only one negative word is used to signal a negation. The use of two negative words would result in a double negative, which is used in informal English but should be avoided in formal English. Have students read over their draft to look for any instances of double negatives.

✔ For additional instruction strategies, see **ThinkCentral, Teacher Access.**

Students with Disabilities

Allow students to reflect on their experiences as though they are writing in a personal journal or blog. Tell students they can freewrite their entries, but they should be sure to include their thoughts and feelings about their topics and what they feel they have gained from their experiences. Students should then incorporate their reflections into their compositions.

✔ See **UA: Differentiating Instruction** for strategies for teaching students with disabilities.

Guided Practice: Apply

Scoring Guide

- Tell students that the best way to understand scoring guides is to use them to score actual writing.
- Have students use the scoring guide to evaluate the final copy of the reflective compositions they wrote in the Writing Workshop. Ask students to score their compositions and then write a brief paragraph using the language of the scoring guide to explain the reasons for the score.

Holt Six Traits for Writing, rubrics, prompts, and sample papers

Assess

UA: Holt Interactive Writer and Speaker, reflective composition analytical scales and rubrics, p. 78

ThinkCentral Online Assessment, Writing Workshop Test

Teacher One Stop™, editable Writing Workshop Test

Reteach

ThinkCentral Online Remediation

California Standards, pp. 890–891

- **Writing Standard 1.1** Literal and figurative meanings.
- **Writing Standard 1.5** Using language to establish tone.
- **Writing Standard 1.9** Revise text.
- **Writing Standard 2.3** Write reflective compositions.

Scoring Guide

Use the scoring guide below to evaluate your reflective composition from the Writing Workshop or your response to the on-demand prompt on page 891.

	Reflective Composition	Organization and Focus	Sentence Structure and Vocabulary	Conventions
4	• develops a *meaningful* reflective narrative that is responsive to the writing task.	• *thoroughly* develops the reflective narrative with *specific* details and examples. • demonstrates a *clear* sense of audience. • demonstrates a consistent tone and focus, and illustrates a *purposeful* control of organization.	• provides a *variety* of sentence types and uses *precise, descriptive* language.	• contains *few, if any, errors* in the conventions of the English language. (Errors are generally first-draft in nature.)
3	• develops a reflective narrative that is responsive to the writing task.	• develops the reflective narrative with details and examples. • demonstrates a *general* sense of audience. • demonstrates a consistent tone and focus; and illustrates a control of organization.	• provides a *variety of* sentence types and uses *some descriptive* language.	• may contain *some errors* in the conventions of the English language. (Errors do **not** interfere with the reader's understanding of the essay.)
2	• develops a reflective narrative that is related to the writing task.	• develops the reflective narrative with *limited* details and/or examples. • demonstrates *little* or **no** sense of audience. • demonstrates an *inconsistent* tone and focus; and illustrates *little, if any* control of organization.	• provides *few, if any,* types of sentence types, and basic, *predictable* language.	• may contain *several errors* in the conventions of the English language. (Errors **may** interfere with the reader's understanding of the essay.)
1	• *may* develop a *weak* reflective narrative that is related to the writing task.	• *fails* to develop the reflective narrative with details and/or examples. • may demonstrate ***no*** sense of audience. • demonstrates a *lack of* tone and focus; and illustrates ***no*** control of organization.	• may provide ***no*** sentence variety and uses *limited* vocabulary.	• may contain *serious errors* in the conventions of the English language. (Errors interfere with the reader's understanding of the essay.)

Reflective Composition Writing Prompts

Students can use the writing prompt in the Student Edition or one of the following prompts.

- Ask students to write a reflective composition about a decision they have made that has had a significant impact on their lives.
- Suggest to students that they write about an unpleasant experience that they were afterwards glad to have had.
- Suggest that students write a reflective composition about a person they have met who has changed the way they look at the world.

Preparing for Timed Writing

Reflective Composition

Writing Standard 1.1, 1.5, 1.9, 2.3a–c (see pages A51–A52)

When responding to a prompt asking you to reflect on your experiences, use what you have learned from reading, writing your reflective composition, and studying the scoring guide on page 890. Use the steps below to develop a response to the following prompt.

Writing Prompt
Often an unexpected experience not only surprises us but teaches us a valuable lesson. Write a reflective composition about an unexpected experience that taught you something important.

Study the Prompt

Begin by reading the prompt carefully. Circle or underline key words: *unexpected experience, surprises, teaches, valuable lesson, important.* Think carefully about what makes something valuable or important. **Tip:** Spend about three minutes studying the prompt.

Plan Your Response

Make a list of unexpected life experiences that you remember well. Why was the experience unexpected? Why was it valuable? Once you have selected an experience, follow these steps to plan your response:

1. Write down what the experience was.
2. Describe the setting of the experience.
3. List at least two things that happened leading up to the experience.
4. List the other people who were involved.
5. Next to each event and person, note important narrative and descriptive details.
6. Beneath the details, describe your reactions to each event and person.
7. Summarize your feelings about the experience and tell what lesson you learned.
8. Comment on generalizations about life related to the experience.

Once you have written down these essential elements, plan your composition in an outline like the one at the top of the next column.

Introduction:
- Background information

Body:
- First event of experience
- Second event of experience, and so on

Conclusion:
- Reflection on experience
- Statement of what you learned and its broader meaning or theme about life

Tip: Spend about ten minutes planning your response.

Respond to the Prompt

Use your notes and your plan to begin writing your composition. Begin your reflective composition by creating a scene that leads to the important experience. You can use description or dialogue to provide readers the background information they may need to understand the narrative events of your experience. **Tip:** Spend about twenty minutes writing your reflective compositions.

Improve Your Response

Revising Return to the key aspects of the prompt. Does your composition detail an important experience? Have you explained what you learned and how you were the affected? Have you included statements about its broader themes? If not, add these elements.

Proofreading Edit your response to correct errors in grammar, spelling, punctuation, and capitalization. Be sure that your edits are neat and the paper is legible.

Checking Your Final Copy Before you turn in your response, read it one more time to catch any errors you may have missed. Readers will have an easier time sharing in your experience if they do not have to plow through errors to read it. **Tip:** Save five or ten minutes to improve your response.

Universal Access

English Learners

English for Academic Success Introduce students to the following words before they begin writing.

- **prompt**—a suggestion or reminder
- **unexpected**—not likely to happen
- **reflective**—relating to deep thought
- **essential**—very important

✔ See **UA: Differentiating Instruction** for strategies for teaching English learners.

Struggling Writers

Ask students to review their work and pay attention to the reflections they add. Is it clear why they have these reflections at particular points in the experience? What additional explanation might they provide?

✔ See **UA: Differentiating Instruction** for strategies for teaching struggling writers.

Standards Focus

Objectives

Students will learn the elements of writing a reflective composition.

Direct Teach

Study the Prompt

Before students begin writing, encourage them to answer the following questions:

1. What is my time limit?
2. What are the key skills assessed in the scoring guide?
3. Who is my audience?
4. What is my purpose?

Plan Your Response

Remind students that the reflective composition scoring guide emphasizes the focus on one experience or series of related experiences. Tell students that they should ask themselves these questions to evaluate their writing as they work on their drafts: Is all the information relevant to the composition? Should anything be connected better to the rest of the composition? Should anything be eliminated?

Improve Your Response

Point out that the scoring guide also emphasizes a creative and reflective approach. Remind students to focus on including details that make their work different from that of any other writer.

Assess

Use the scoring guide on p. 890 to assess students' reflective compositions.

Standards Focus

Objectives

Students will

- deliver reflective presentations
- rehearse oral messages
- use effective verbal and nonverbal delivery techniques

Preteach

Speak with a Purpose Ask students to think about a time when they spoke to someone in order to communicate an important feeling or idea. Have students share the following details with a partner:

- What was the situation?
- How did the listener respond?
- Did you communicate your feeling or idea effectively?

Direct Teach

Model the Skill

Adapt Your Reflective Composition

Provide students with examples of visuals they could use in their own presentations to help them show, rather than tell. For example, students may want to display time lines if there are many different incidents that make up their experiences.

Guided Practice: Apply

For each part of their speeches, ask students what type of visual they could incorporate to help their audience better understand their speech.

Listening & Speaking Workshop

Presenting a Reflective Composition

Speak with a Purpose
Adapt your reflective composition for an oral presentation, and then share it with your class.

Think as a Reader/Writer When you wrote your reflective composition, you shared a significant experience in your life and told your readers how the experience affected you and what insight into life you gained from it. In this workshop, you will adapt your reflective composition for an oral presentation, which will allow you to use your voice and body language to bring the totality of the experience to life for your listeners.

Adapt Your Reflective Composition

Keep It Moving

While the techniques used in delivering an oral presentation are different to some extent from those used in writing a composition, both activities share the same purpose: to narrate an experience and to connect your insight from that experience to life in general. Here are some suggestions for adapting your composition for an oral presentation.

- **Stage your presentation.** An important part of any presentation is **dialogue** that involves narration and characters. In your oral presentation, imitate the voices of the people involved in your experience. You can also act out your **movements, facial expressions,** and **gestures** and those of other people involved in your experience. Avoid overacting and exaggerated imitations, both of which can have a negative effect on your listeners. Also, consider using **visuals** and **sound effects** to heighten the effect of your presentation, but do not overdo it. Be sure that your experience remains the center of attention.
- **Explain yourself.** You can be subtle in writing, but in your oral presentation you must provide your audience with broad hints about the significance or effect of your experience. Plan to balance those hints with the narrative and details that describe each event. At the conclusion of your presentation, make sure your explicit statements about the significance or effect of the experience and the more general insight into life that you gained are clear enough for a listening audience.
- **Use effective language.** Effective language in a reflective presentation is clear, forceful, and **aesthetic,** that is to say, artistic and tasteful. Choose **concrete images** to narrate events and to describe places. Use rhetorical questions, parallelism, figurative language, and other **rhetorical devices** to enhance the effectiveness of your language. When used appropriately, **irony** is especially effective in oral presentations because it can be communicated through your tone of voice as well as through your words.

Reader/Writer Notebook
Use your **RWN** to complete the activities for this workshop.

California Standards, pp. 892–893

- **Listening and Speaking Standard 2.1** Deliver reflective presentations: **a.** Explore the significance of personal experiences, events, conditions, or concerns, using appropriate rhetorical strategies (e.g., narration, description, exposition, persuasion). **b.** Draw comparisons between the specific incident and broader themes that illustrate the speaker's beliefs or generalizations about life. **c.** Maintain a balance between describing the incident and relating it to more general, abstract ideas.
- **Listening and Speaking Standard 2.3** Deliver oral responses to literature: **a.** Demonstrate a comprehensive understanding of the significant ideas of literary works (e.g., make assertions about the text that are reasonable and supportable). **b.** Analyze the imagery, language, universal themes, and unique aspects of the text through the use of rhetorical strategies (e.g., narration, description, persuasion, exposition, a combination of those strategies). **c.** Support important ideas and viewpoints through accurate and detailed references to the text or to other works. **d.** Demonstrate an awareness of the author's use of stylistic devices and an appreciation of the effects created.
- **Grades 9–10 Review Listening and Speaking Standard 1.9** Analyze the occasion and the interests of the audience and choose effective verbal and nonverbal techniques (e.g., voice, gestures, eye contact) for presentations.

Universal Access

EL English Learners

Give students extra time to practice their enunciation and pronunciation. After students read through their speech several times, have students pair up. Instruct them to provide a copy of their speech to their partner. Then, have them perform their speech for their partner. Listeners should underline the words that the speaker mispronounces or does not enunciate. Students should continue to practice their speeches, paying careful attention to the words their partners have underlined.

Listening and Speaking Standard 2.1a–c, 2.3a–d; **Grades 9–10 Review Listening and Speaking Standard** 1.9 (see pages A53–A55)

Deliver Your Reflective Composition

Speak Extemporaneously

Reading a speech word for word usually sounds stiff and unnatural. Plan to present your reflection **extemporaneously** by following these steps:

1. Outline the main points that you want to cover in your presentation.
2. Highlight any quotations or passages in your essay that you want to deliver word for word.
3. Prepare notecards with key words and phrases for your outline, as well as the text of passages you want to deliver word for word.
4. Check the order of your cards to avoid surprises.

A Good Oral Presentation

- shares the details and significance of a single experience
- organizes ideas clearly for listeners
- re-creates the experience with dialogue, imagery, and rhetorical devices
- uses effective verbal and nonverbal speaking techniques

Use Verbal and Nonverbal Techniques

Sometimes the way you say something means as much as what you say. An oral presentation gives you the opportunity to use both verbal and nonverbal techniques to engage your audience. Here are some techniques to consider.

Delivery Techniques

Verbal Techniques	Nonverbal Techniques
Language: Use **standard American English** so everyone will understand your presentation, but with dialogue use **informal expressions** to capture the uniqueness of the people involved.	**Eye Contact:** Give individuals in your listening audience the impression that you are speaking directly to them by making eye contact with as many of them as you can.
Tone: Change the tone of your voice to reflect the nature of the events you are narrating. Humorous events require a light tone. Somber events require a serious tone.	**Gestures:** Use natural and unforced gestures. Be aware that overly dramatic gestures can detract from your presentation.
Volume: Vary the volume of your voice to fit the mood you want to create, but speak loudly enough to be heard.	**Facial Expressions:** Use facial expressions to convey your feelings and to characterize people involved in your experience.

Speaking Tip

Take notes after each practice session to guide your improvement.

Keep Practicing

Rehearsal will help you avoid nervousness and enable you to present your reflections effectively. These resources can be useful in practicing your presentation:

- Practice in front of a mirror.
- Enlist friends and family to see you rehearse and give feedback.
- Videotape yourself practicing and watch for trouble spots.

Learn It Online
Add music and pictures to your reflective essay.
go.hrw.com H12-893 Go

Model the Skill

Use Verbal and Nonverbal Techniques

If students struggle with using the correct tone of voice to convey an idea, explain that they use tone to convey ideas in everyday conversations. Take part in a conversation with a volunteer about a serious topic and then about a humorous topic. Have students note the change in the tone of your voice.

Guided Practice: Apply

Have students go through their speech to find which parts are more formal and should therefore be rendered through a serious tone, and which might be humorous or emotional and feature informal expressions and a more personal tone.

Teaching Tip

Keep Practicing To reteach the concept of rehearsal, have students practice their speech with a partner, who should note strengths and weaknesses of the presentation, evaluating its clarity, language, tone, and volume. Suggest students use a chart to evaluate these components.

English for Academic Success

Remind students that they should use standard American English in their presentation. They should use informal English only when a character is speaking.

Assess

UA: Holt Interactive Writer and Speaker, Reflective Composition Evaluation Guide

Learn It Online
If students need help adding multimedia features to their projects, send them to the **MediaScope** mini-site, where students can work through an interactive tutorial on creating multimedia.
go.hrw.com H12-893 Go

Struggling Learners

Some students may not yet be ready to present their speeches in front of their classmates. Require each student to attempt to deliver their speech in front of the entire class, but if it is clear that a student's performance is affected by anxiety or embarrassment, give the option to deliver their speech in front of only you and a small group of students that the struggling learner selects.

Resources

UA: Holt Interactive Writer and Speaker, practice and assessment, p. 134

UA: Differentiating Instruction, modified lesson plans, 201

Teacher One Stop™, on-level lesson plans and all print resources

Standards Focus

Objectives

Students will compare and contrast works from different literary periods.

Literary Skills Review

Review

If necessary, use the following questions to guide students in their reading before they answer the questions at the end of the review.

Tone

What is the tone of the two poems? ***Possible response:*** *The tone is critical and resigned. The speakers look at the two cities as hopelessly marked by poverty and social isolation.*

Imagery

Which of the five senses is mostly addressed in each of the poems? ***Possible responses:*** *"London" appeals mostly to the auditory sense, as the speaker describes the sighs, cries, and blasting curses of the people around him. "The Virgins" appeals mostly to sight, as the speaker describes colors and lights of Frederiksted.*

Test-Taking Tip

Explain to students that to answer multiple-choice questions about tone, they must analyze word choice.

California Standards, pp. 894–895

- **Reading Standard 3.7** Analyze recognized works of world literature from a variety of authors: **a.** Contrast the major literary forms, techniques, and characteristics of the major literary periods (e.g., Homeric Greece, medieval, romantic, neoclassic, modern).

STANDARDS REVIEW

Literary Skills Review

Comparing Literature **Directions:** Read the poems below, and answer the questions that follow.

The following two poems describe cities that the poets perceive as on the verge of social ruin. William Blake's "London" depicts the poor living conditions of England in the early nineteenth century. Derek Walcott's "The Virgins" describes Frederiksted, one of the oldest port cities on the U.S. Virgin Island of St. Croix. Frederiksted is now a free port where tourists can purchase goods without paying customs duties. Its economy, once based on sugar cane, is now dependent on tourism.

London

by **William Blake**

I wander through each chartered° street,
Near where the chartered Thames does flow,
And mark° in every face I meet
Marks of weakness, marks of woe.

In every cry of every man,
In every infant's cry of fear,
In every voice, in every ban,°
The mind-forged manacles I hear.

How the chimney sweeper's cry
Every blackning church appalls,°
And the hapless soldier's sigh
Runs in blood down palace walls.

But most through midnight streets I hear
How the youthful harlot's curse°
Blasts the newborn infant's tear
And blights with plagues the marriage hearse.

1. **chartered:** controlled by law.
3. **mark:** notice.
7. **ban:** legal prohibition, public condemnation, or curse; also, a marriage announcement (spelled *banns*).
10. **appalls:** causes to lose color; also, dismays, terrifies.
14. **harlot's curse:** curse upon the harlot or prostitute by a hypocritical society that pushed women into prostitution and then condemned them for it; also the curse the harlot utters in return.

The Virgins

by **Derek Walcott**

Down the dead streets of sun-stoned
  Frederiksted,
the first free port to die for tourism,
strolling at funeral pace, I am reminded
of life not lost to the American dream;
but my small-islander's simplicities
can't better our new empire's civilized
exchange of cameras, watches, perfumes,
  brandies
for the good life, so cheaply underpriced
that only the crime rate is on the rise
in streets blighted with sun, stone arches
and plazas blown dry by the hysteria
of rumor. A condominium drowns
in vacancy; its bargains are dusted,
but only a jeweled housefly drones
over the bargains. The roulettes spin
rustily to the wind—the vigorous trade
that every morning would begin afresh
by revving up green water round the pierhead
heading for where the banks of silver thresh.

Resources for Skills and Standards Review

Unit 4 Resources, Unit Standards Mastery, Unit Vocabulary Review, pp. 135, 138

UA: Differentiating Instruction, below-level Chapter Standards Mastery

Teacher One Stop™, editable Chapter Standards Mastery

Focus on Standards with CAHSEE Support

Preparing for the SAT and ACT

ThinkCentral Online Assessment, Chapter Standards Mastery

ThinkCentral Online Remediation

Holt Online Essay Scoring

Reading Standard 3.7a (see pages A48–A50)

1. In the first stanza of "London," the speaker is
- **A** describing how he loves London.
- **B** greeting fellow citizens of London.
- **C** noticing other people's unhappiness.
- **D** looking at the Thames.

2. Which of the following is an image of oppression and restriction used in "London"?
- **A** "the chartered Thames"
- **B** "the hapless soldier's sigh"
- **C** "the mind-forged manacles"
- **D** all of the above

3. In lines 11–12 of "London," the speaker suggests that
- **A** the sighing soldier is haunted by memories of violence.
- **B** all soldiers are poorly trained for battle.
- **C** patriotism is worth the loss of lives.
- **D** soldiers are rebelling.

4. In lines 1–4 of "The Virgins," the speaker implies that
- **A** he believes in the American dream.
- **B** he is pleased by what tourism has done for his city.
- **C** he doesn't remember what life was like before his city became a "new empire."
- **D** he thinks the American dream can be destructive.

5. Which of the following literary devices does Walcott use in "The Virgins"?
- **A** onomatopoeia
- **B** allusion
- **C** apostrophe
- **D** alliteration

6. What do such images as "plazas blown dry" and "the roulettes spin rustily" suggest about the setting Walcott is describing?
- **A** The streets are not kept clean.
- **B** The tourists are not in the mood for gambling.
- **C** Ruin is overcoming the city.
- **D** The city is suffering from a drought.

7. Like the speaker in "London," the speaker in "The Virgins" sees the living conditions of his city as being
- **A** recently improved.
- **B** easily fixed.
- **C** virtually beyond hope.
- **D** a source of hope for everyone.

8. Unlike Blake, Walcott focuses more on which aspect of his city's plight?
- **A** commercial activities
- **B** people's hypocrisy
- **C** unfair treatment of women
- **D** disease and poverty

Timed Writing

9. Briefly contrast the imagery in the two poems. Support your response with specific evidence.

Word-Attack Skills Mini-Lesson

Review Use the activities below to check the student's understanding of the word-attack skills taught in this unit.

Activity Display these pairs of words. The first word will reappear in the second word. Have students underline the syllable said with the greatest stress in each word. Have them consult a dictionary to check their work. Answers are underlined.

1. moment — momentous
2. position — deposition
3. super — superlative
4. magnet — magnetic

Activity The same word appears in each pair of sentences below. Have students tell in which sentence the word is pronounced with a long *a* in the final syllable. Answers are checked.

1. Please duplicate this document. ✔
   Keep the duplicate in the files.
2. This newspaper is part of a syndicate.
   They will syndicate the new comic strip. ✔
3. The new strip will alternate with another one. ✔
   The two will appear on alternate days.

Assess

Answers and Explanations

1. C *The speaker looks at his fellow citizens and at the Thames, but he focuses specifically on the unhappiness "in every face."*

2. D *The words* chartered, hapless *and* mind-forged *suggest that all these images represent various forms of psychic oppression.*

3. A *The soldier's sigh cannot literally "run in blood down palace walls," but the image connotes the violence that affects him emotionally.*

4. D *The fact that the port died "for tourism" tells us that the speaker is not pleased with its effect. He remembers "life not lost to the American dream" and shows its destructive side.*

5. D *The author describes sounds, but the words used do not create an onomatopoetic effect by imitating the sounds of those objects.* Down/dead, first/free, life/lost *and* small-islander's/simplicities *all exemplify instances of alliteration.*

6. C *The author is being figurative in line 11 ("blown dry") and is not referring to a drought. Numerous references to words associated with death provide context clues that tell us that the city is in ruin.*

7. C *The speakers are not focused on solutions, but rather the bleakness of pervasive problems and misery.*

8. A *Walcott focuses specifically on how tourism and trade regulations affected a city.*

Timed Writing

9. *Blake uses figurative images such as "mind-forged manacles" and "runs in blood down palace walls"; whereas, Walcott lists the objects of trade and tourism ruining the city.*

Reteach

go.hrw.com **ThinkCentral Online Remediation**

Vocabulary Skills Review

Assess

Answers and Explanations

1. ***B*** *The word* twisting *shows that the river curves through the valley.*
2. ***D*** *The word* greenery *indicates leaves.*
3. ***A*** *"With a cry" shows that the toddler forcefully took something from his playmate.*
4. ***C*** Gloomy *fits more with a hopeless situation.*
5. ***D*** *"Hearing the radio" provides the context clue that the definition must relate to auditory perception.*
6. ***A*** *The phrase "under his control" implies oppression.*
7. ***D*** Hopeless *describes one who has little chance of meeting an urgent need.*

Academic Vocabulary

8. ***C*** *Knowing how one concept differs with another clears up confusion.*
9. ***D*** *"Not stated directly" suggests the word* implicit.

Reteach

go.hrw.com **ThinkCentral Online Remediation**

California Standards, p. 896

- **Grades 9–10 Review Reading Standard**
  1.1 Identify and use the literal and figurative meanings of words and understand word derivations.

STANDARDS REVIEW

Vocabulary Skills Review

Grades 9–10 Review Reading Standard 1.1 (see pages A48–A50)

Context Clues **Directions:** Use the clues in each sentence to help you select the definition of the italicized word.

1. The twisting of the River Wye cut a beautifully *sinuous* path through the valley. *Sinuous* means
A filthy.
B curving; winding.
C pure; untouched.
D dried up.

2. The nightingale, hidden in the *foliage,* was just a beautiful voice among the greenery. *Foliage* means
A valley.
B brilliant light.
C highest point.
D leaves.

3. With a cry, the toddler *wrenched* the toy from his playmate's firm grip. *Wrenched* means
A pulled or twisted violently.
B lessened.
C encircled; surrounded.
D commanded.

4. When the Mariner's boat was stuck with no prospect of escape, the future looked *dismal. Dismal* means
A outrageous.
B hopeful.
C gloomy.
D heavenly.

5. With the *tumult* of eight puppies in one room, I could not hear the radio. *Tumult* means
A scent.
B anxiety.
C distress.
D great noise.

6. The *tyrannous* rule of the dictator struck fear in the hearts of those under his control. *Tyrannous* means
A oppressive.
B ghostly.
C foul.
D anxious.

7. Looking at the vast desert ahead, he experienced a *forlorn* feeling as he realized he had no water. *Forlorn* means
A lonely; lost.
B wild; untamed.
C unkind; callous.
D hopeless; desperate.

Academic Vocabulary

Directions: Use the clues in each passage to help you select the definition of the italicized word.

8. Good writers *differentiate* clearly between ideas so that readers do not confuse one concept with another. *Differentiate* means
A disagree; argue against.
B explain similarities.
C distinguish.
D alternate.

9. The value of emotions is an *inherent* principle of Romantic poetry. It is not always stated directly, but if you read between the lines, you will find it. *Inherent* means
A present at birth.
B irrational.
C unexpected.
D built in; implicit.

Vocabulary Review

Use this activity to assess whether students have retained the unit Vocabulary words. Ask students to choose the word from the box that fits the context of each sentence.

blithe	corporeal	intrudes
piety	turmoil	

1. Her interests were more _____ than spiritual, which explains her desire to earn a high income. [*corporeal*]

2. Susan could tell by Angela's _____ response that Angela hadn't given much thought to her plans for the evening. [*blithe*]

3. When the principal came into the classroom to check on the substitute teacher, he discovered the class was in _____. [*turmoil*]

4. The lifestyle of those who enter the monastery is one of _____. [*piety*]

5. Her mother dislikes the way your friend _____ at dinner hour. [*intrudes*]

Writing Skills Review

Writing Standard 2.3a–c (see pages A51–A52)

Write a Reflective Composition

Directions: The following passage is a rough draft. It may contain errors in grammar, punctuation, sentence structure, and organization. Read the passage below, and answer the questions that follow.

Rough Draft

(1) "There is something about fire that makes it beautiful and frightening at the same time," I thought to myself as I watched the flames engulf my home on that fateful August night. (2) Looking back, I ponder at what a peculiar thought that was to have at a time when all my worldly possessions were in the process of being destroyed. (3) I guess a person's mind does strange things when faced with traumatic events. (4) Even as I heard the sounds of firefighters shouting to each other, water spraying out of the large hose, and the gasps of curious neighbors as they arrived on the scene, my eyes were focused on the vibrant colors of red, yellow, and orange as I watched the flames dance in the night sky. (5) My trance was broken by my father, the strength of our family, as he walked up to me and put his large hand on my shoulder. (6) He squeezed firmly, <u>wanting to say something</u>, I imagine, but found no words to express his range of emotions. (7) I knew what he was trying to say but couldn't, and I replied, "It will be O.K., Dad. I love you, too." (8) "We're all here, we're all O.K.," I thought to myself, "and possessions can be replaced."

1. Reflective compositions examine abstract ideas through the description of personal experiences. What abstract idea is explored by this author?
   - **A** patience
   - **B** gratitude
   - **C** hopelessness
   - **D** acceptance

2. What skill might the writer have used to help remember and gather the details before writing this reflective composition?
   - **A** The writer might have visualized the events of the experience.
   - **B** The writer might have asked a family member to help recall events from the experience.
   - **C** The writer might have used photos or journal entries to help remember the events.
   - **D** All of the above

3. Which sentence best helps the reader understand the writer's father's thoughts and feelings?
   - **A** sentence 6
   - **B** sentence 4
   - **C** sentence 1
   - **D** sentence 8

4. Which two sentences include the inner dialogue of the writer?
   - **A** sentence 2 and sentence 4
   - **B** sentence 7 and sentence 8
   - **C** sentence 1 and sentence 8
   - **D** sentence 1 and sentence 3

5. Which of the following would be the MOST precise way to state the underlined words in the sentences labeled 6?
   - **A** wanting to yell something
   - **B** wishing to say something cheerfully
   - **C** wanting to say something else
   - **D** wanting to say something comforting

6. Which sentence contains an appositive?
   - **A** sentence 6
   - **B** sentence 4
   - **C** sentence 1
   - **D** sentence 5

Writing Skills Review

Assess

Answers and Explanations

1. **D** *The writer does not seem to react as negatively as others would; his attitude is one of quiet acceptance.*
2. **D** *All three of these strategies are effective when reconstructing memories.*
3. **A** *Sentence 6 states that the father "found no words to express his range of emotion," which relates directly to his thoughts and feelings.*
4. **C** *Both sentences 1 and 8 use the words "thought to myself," which provides the context clue that the dialogue is internal. Sentence 3 is not written as dialogue.*
5. **D** *The boy's father most likely wanted to say something comforting but could not think of any words appropriate for the situation. The other choices (A, B, C) are not the most precise way to rephrase the underlined words.*
6. **D** *"The strength of our family" is the appositive, and describes "my father." Sentence 4 uses commas in a series. Sentence 1 uses commas in dialogue. Sentence 6 does not rename a noun or noun phrase.*

Reteach

go.hrw.com **ThinkCentral Online Remediation**

Application Homework

Reflective Composition

Have students use what they have learned in this workshop to write a reflective composition. Students should focus on a pivotal experience they or someone else experienced. Remind students that a reflective composition touches on a larger human experience, such as the speaker's awareness of what is replaceable, as described in the selection.

Extension

Creating Poetry from Prose

Have students pull out their favorite lines and images from their reflective compositions. Then ask them to arrange the words to create an original "found" poem. Poems can be displayed in the classroom with students' permission.

California Standards, p. 897

- **Writing Standard 2.3** Write reflective compositions: **a.** Explore the significance of personal experiences, events, conditions, or concerns by using rhetorical strategies (e.g., narration, description, exposition, persuasion). **b.** Draw comparisons between specific incidents and broader themes that illustrate the writer's important beliefs or generalizations about life. **c.** Maintain a balance in describing individual incidents and relate those incidents to more general and abstract ideas.

Read On

If students enjoyed the themes and topics explored in this unit, you might recommend these titles for independent reading.

Assessment Options

The following projects can help you evaluate and assess your students' outside work. Videotapes or audiotapes of completed projects may be included in students' portfolios.

Write a Script

Ask students to choose their favorite scene from *Frankenstein* and write out a script. Students may need to exclude some details in the book. Remind students to include stage directions and monologues if necessary.

Contrast Women's Roles in Society

Have students compare the roles of women in society. Students can use *Pride and Prejudice* to examine the roles of women in that era with the roles of women in contemporary society. Students can give an oral presentation to the class to discuss their findings.

Read On

For Independent Reading

FICTION

Frankenstein

Mary Shelley said of her novel *Frankenstein* that she wanted to write a story that "would speak to the mysterious fears of our nature and awaken thrilling horror." She succeeded, writing an early science fiction novel as well as a vivid version of the Romantic mythology of the self. The wonder of Shelley's method of character development lies in the manner in which a monster, Frankenstein, simultaneously evokes our fear and our pity. As readers, we are called upon to question what we consider to be "human" and "natural."

FICTION

Pride and Prejudice

Originally published in 1813, Jane Austen's novel *Pride and Prejudice* is about five husband-hunting sisters in nineteenth-century England and the delicate tangles of love and courtship in which they ensnare themselves. What struck people then, and still strikes us now, is Austen's ability to make mundane people and events interesting and meaningful. The superficially trivial content is deceptive; it masks a deeper irony that exposes the manners and customs of the period.

FICTION

Hornblower and the *Hotspur*

Set during the Napoleonic Wars, C. S. Forester's exciting Hornblower novels are almost impossible to put down. Quick-thinking naval officer Horatio Hornblower and his crew sail from one battle to the next, each time facing a different enemy ship and adjusting to different weather conditions. Although one wrong choice can spell disaster, Hornblower must make life-or-death decisions with split-second timing. Despite his marvelous heroics, Hornblower is no superman. He often suffers from horrible seasickness and—even worse—self-doubt.

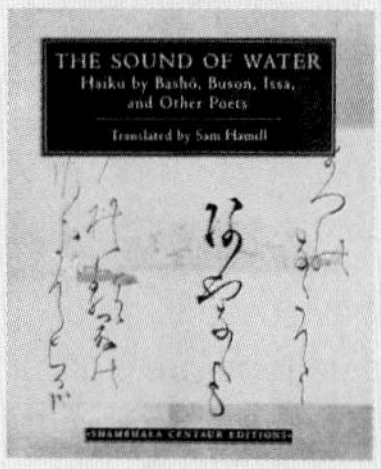

POETRY

The Sound of Water: Haiku by Bashō, Buson, Issa, and Other Poets

This pocket-sized, travel-friendly book reflects the magic of haiku: striking images, fervent emotion, and revelatory awareness in the tiniest of packages. In this masterful collection, renowned translator and poet Sam Hamill has gathered more than two hundred haiku spanning three hundred years. With their sparse yet powerful phrasing, the poems in this anthology are sure to delight and inspire new and old haiku aficionados.

Word Counts and Readabilities of Read On Books

Fiction	Estimated Word Counts	Readability
Frankenstein	87,000	Accessible
Pride and Prejudice	133,200	Accessible
Hornblower and the Hotspur	108,570	Accessible
The Sound of Water: Haiku by Bashō, Buson, Issa, and Other Poets	2,637	Easily Accessible

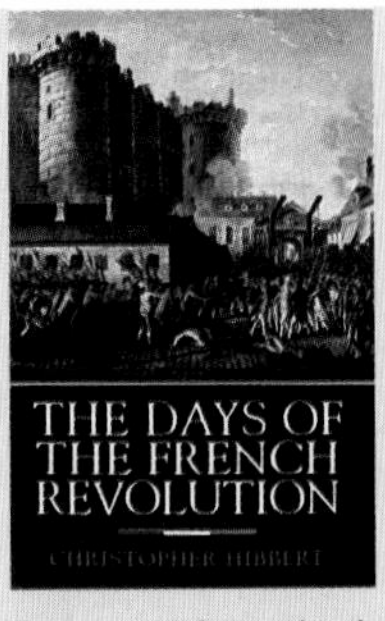

NONFICTION

The Days of the French Revolution

Christopher Hibbert's historical narrative brings all of the drama, turmoil, and bloodshed of the Reign of Terror to life. In this book, you will meet the principal players of the French Revolution—everyone from Robespierre to Marie Antoinette to Napoleon—and see their stories cast in new light, though not at the expense of truth. Swiftly plotted and gripping from start to finish, Hibbert's historical narrative reads like a good novel.

NONFICTION

The Grasmere and Alfoxden Journals

These journals reveal that Dorothy Wordsworth was as perceptive an observer of nature as was her famous brother, William. She records her responses to the natural beauty of the Lake District (the flowers, lakes, landscapes, and animals) that she sees on her daily walks as well as her reflections on the human misery (the beggars, ragged children, blind and infirm farmers, and poverty-stricken families) she encounters that stand in contrast to the region's beauty. She also informs readers of her brother's writing habits and of the visits from fellow poet Samuel Taylor Coleridge.

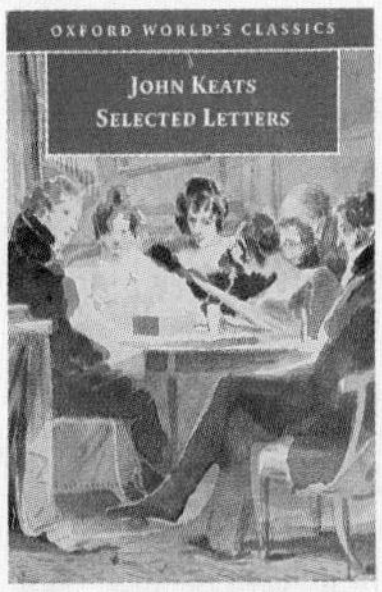

NONFICTION

John Keats: Selected Letters

Although John Keats died at the tragically young age of twenty-five, he left a wealth of correspondence that provides us with insight into his thoughts on a variety of topics, both spiritual and mundane. This particular collection of letters reflects the imagination and genius of the brilliant young poet. Keats candidly records many of the daily events of his life, along with, according to editor Robert Gittings, "some of the most profound comments on art, philosophy, and the human condition that any single person has produced."

NONFICTION

Prince of Pleasure

Saul David's biography of Prince George, the future king of England and the son of George III, is a lively account of a man who was highly intelligent, articulate, literate, and a great patron of art and music. Nevertheless, George—accompanied by a menagerie of notorious members of Parliament, courtesans, fops, rakes, gamblers, and other hangers-on—led a life of unrestrained indulgence. Ever at the forefront of both fashion and scandal, this prince of pleasure is thoroughly fascinating.

Learn It Online
Go online to explore other novels, and find tips for choosing, reading, and studying books.
go.hrw.com H12-899 Go

Nonfiction	Estimated Word Counts	Readability
The Days of the French Revolution	107,700	Challenging
The Grasmere and Alfoxden Journals	57,500	Accessible
John Keats: Selected Letters	193,800	Accessible
Prince of Pleasure	147,096	Challenging

Assessment Options

Reader's Theatre

Students can pull excerpts from *John Keats: Selected Letters* and bring the dialogue to life by presenting the excerpts aloud, as internal or paired dialogue. Students can present their Reader's Theatre to the class.

Make a Collage

Have students choose their favorite haiku from *The Sound of Water* and assemble magazine cutouts, photos, and drawings to make a collage based on the images and feelings of the haiku. Students' collages can be displayed in the classroom.

Movie Preview

Students who enjoyed reading either *The Days of the French Revolution* or *Prince of Pleasure* can choose their favorite scenes and quotes to create storyboards depicting a preview of the film version of either work. On the back of each storyboard, instruct students to write a brief paragraph briefly explaining the context and background of each scene. Ask volunteers to present their storyboards and have the audience give feedback on whether or not they would want to see the movie in person.

A Visitation from the Past

After reading *Hornblower and the* Hotspur or *The Grasmere and Alfoxden Journals*, students can prepare an oral presentation in which they dress in the character of Hornblower or Dorothy Wordsworth. Have students introduce themselves (in character) to the class and give a brief speech in which they reveal what they have learned from their life experiences.

Learn It Online
The **NovelWise** mini-site includes instruction on choosing, reading, and analyzing novels; it also contains a catalogue of book summaries, study guides, teaching guides, and PowerPoint presentations.
go.hrw.com H12-899 Go

The Victorian Period 1832–1901

Features highlighted in **yellow** constitute a suggested minimum course of study.

Chapter 9

Selection or Feature	For Independent Reading	Grade-Level Standards
The Victorian Period 1832–1901 **Link to Today: The Night-Soil Men** *from* **The Ghost Map** by Steven B. Johnson (Accessible, Lexile 1280)		
Literary Skills Focus: Figurative Language by Leila Christenbury		**Reading Standard 3.4:** Analyze figures of speech.
• **The Lady of Shalott** (Accessible, Lexile N/A) • **Ulysses** (Accessible, Lexile N/A) • *from* **In Memoriam A.H.H.** (Accessible, Lexile N/A) • **Crossing the Bar** (Accessible, Lexile N/A) by Alfred, Lord Tennyson	• **Road to Camlann: The Death of King Arthur** by Rosemary Sutcliff • **The Tempest** by William Shakespeare	**Reading Standard 2.4:** Analyze an author's arguments. **Reading Standard 3.2:** Theme **Reading Standard 3.3:** Analyze effects of irony, tone, mood, and style. **Reading Standard 3.4:** Analyze figures of speech. **Reading Standard 3.9:** Analyze philosophical arguments.
Reading Skills Focus: Drawing Inferences *from* **Textual Clues** by Kylene Beers		**Reading Standard 2.4:** Analyze an author's arguments.
• **My Last Duchess** (Challenging, Lexile N/A) • **Porphyria's Lover** (Challenging, Lexile N/A) by Robert Browning	**Rebecca** by Daphne Du Maurier • **The Taming of the Shrew** by William Shakespeare	**Reading Standard 2.4:** Analyze an author's arguments. **Reading Standard 3.1:** Analyze subgenres. **Grades 9–10** **Review Reading Standard 3.11:** Evaluate the aesthetic qualities of style.
• **Sonnet 43** by Elizabeth Barrett Browning (Accessible, Lexile N/A)	**Romeo and Juliet** by William Shakespeare	**Reading Standard 2.2:** Clarify meaning through structure, repetition, syntax, and word choice. **Reading Standard 3.1:** Analyze subgenres.
• **Pied Beauty** by Gerard Manley Hopkins (Accessible, Lexile N/A)	**A Joyful Noise: Poems for Two Voices** by Paul Fleischman	**Reading Standard 2.4:** Analyze an author's arguments. **Reading Standard 3.3:** Analyze effects of irony, tone, mood, and style.

Daily and Weekly Support

- **Reader/Writer Notebook**
- **Reading and Writing Transparencies**
- **Family Involvement Activities in Spanish**
- **Language Handbook Worksheets**
- **Holt Virtual File Cabinet for Language Arts**

Assessment Resources

- **Unit 5 Resources**, Chapter 9 Diagnostic Test; Selection Standards Checks, Chapter 9 Standards Mastery
- **Universal Access: Differentiating Instruction**, leveled assessment
- **English-Conventions Progress-Monitoring Tests**, Chapters14
- **ThinkCentral Online Assessment**

Print Resources for Universal Access

Unit 5 • Chapter 9

	On-Level Learners	English Learners	Struggling Readers	Students Who Use African American Vernacular English	Advanced Learners	Students with Disabilities
Unit 5 Resources practice and assessment for selections and features in Chapter 9	✔				✔	
Universal Access: Holt Interactive Reader interactive reading for The Lady of Shalott, My Last Duchess, and Sonnet 43		✔	✔	✔		✔
Universal Access: Differentiating Instruction modified lesson plans and leveled assessment for The Lady of Shalott, My Last Duchess, and Sonnet 43		✔	✔	✔		✔
Universal Access: Resources for Teaching Advanced Students lesson plans for The Lady of Shalott, My Last Duchess, and Sonnet 43					✔	

Features highlighted in **yellow** constitute a suggested minimum course of study.

Chapter 10

Selection or Feature	For Independent Reading	Grade-Level Standards
The Paradox of Progress **Literary Skills Focus: Realism** by Leila Christenbury		**Reading Standard 3.7:** Evaluate the historical period.
Analyzing Visuals: Connecting to Realism		**Reading Standard 3.7:** Evaluate the historical period.
Dover Beach by Matthew Arnold (Accessibleg, Lexile N/A)	**Fahrenheit 451** by Ray Bradbury	**Reading Standard 3.3:** Analyze effects of irony, tone, mood, and style. **Reading Standard 3.7:** Evaluate the historical period. **Grades 9–10 Review Reading Standard 3.12:** Analyze the way literature is related to themes of its historical period.
Reading Skills Focus: Making Generalizations by Kylene Beers		**Reading Standard 2.4:** Analyze an author's arguments.
• **The Darkling Thrush** by Thomas Hardy (Challenging, Lexile N/A) • **Ah, Are You Digging on My Grave?** (Challenging, Lexile N/A)	**Jude the Obscure** by Thomas Hardy	**Reading Standard 2.4:** Analyze an author's arguments. **Reading Standard 3.4:** Analyze figures of speech.
• **To an Athlete Dying Young** by A. E. Housman (Accessible, Lexile N/A) • **When I Was One-and-Twenty** (Accessible, Lexile N/A)	**A Tale of Two Cities** by Charles Dickens	**Reading Standard 2.2:** Clarify meaning through structure, repetition, syntax, and word choice. **Reading Standard 3.2:** Theme **Reading Standard 3.4:** Analyze figures of speech.
Link to Today: When Elements Go Extreme by Jason La Canfora (Accessible, Lexile 1410)		**Reading Standard 2.2:** Clarify meaning through structure, repetition, syntax, and word choice.
The Mark of the Beast by Rudyard Kipling (Accessible, Lexile 950)	• **Anthills of the Savannah** by Chinua Achebe • **Rumors of Rain** by Andre P. Brink	**Grades 9–10 Review Reading Standard 3.3:** Internal and external conflicts.
Comparing Texts: World Literature **Realism and the Short Story** • **How Much Land Does a Man Need?** by Leo Tolstoy (Accessible, Lexile 910)	• **Anna Karenina** by Leo Tolstoy • **Readings in World Literature,** anthology	**Reading Standard 2.2:** Clarify meaning through structure, repetition, syntax, and word choice. **Reading Standard 2.4:** Analyze an author's arguments.
• **The Bet** by Anton Chekhov (Accessible, Lexile 1050)	• **The Count of Monte Cristo** by Alexandre Dumas	**Reading Standard 3.1:** Analyze subgenres. **Reading Standard 3.2:** Theme
• **The Jewels** by Guy de Maupassant (Accessible, Lexile 1010)	• **Madame Bovary*** by Gustave Flaubert	**Reading Standard 3.3:** Analyze effects of irony, tone, mood, and style. **Reading Standard 3.9:** Analyze philosophical arguments.

**This book was published for an adult readership and thus contains mature content. Before handing the text to a child, educators and parents should read the book and know the child. (Recommended Literature: Kindergarten Through Grade Twelve)*

Daily and Weekly Support

- **Reader/Writer Notebook**
- **Reading and Writing Transparencies**
- **Family Involvement Activities in Spanish**
- **Language Handbook Worksheets**
- **Holt Virtual File Cabinet for Language Arts**

Assessment Resources

- **Unit 5 Resources**, Chapter 10 Diagnostic Test; Selection Standards Checks, Chapter 10 Standards Mastery
- **Universal Access: Differentiating Instruction**, leveled assessment
- **English-Language Conventions Progress-Monitoring Tests**, Chapters 15–16
- **ThinkCentral Online Assessment**

Mastering the Skills

Selection or Feature	Grade-Level Standards
Writing Workshop: Fictional Narrative	**Writing Standard 1.2:** Use point of view, characterization, and style . **Writing Standard 2.1:** Write narratives. **Writing Standard 1.9:** Revise text.
Preparing for Timed Writing	**Writing Standard 2.1:** Write narratives.
Listening and Speaking Workshop: Present a Story	**Listening and Speaking Standard 2.1:** Deliver reflective presentations . **Listening and Speaking Standard 1.8:** Use effective and interesting language. **Grades 9–10 Review Listening and Speaking Standard 1.9:** Analyze audience; Verbal and nonverbal techniques.
Standards Review: Literary Skills Review Vocabulary Skills Review Writing Skills Review	**Reading Standard 3.7:** Contrast literary forms. **Reading Standard 1.3:** Analogies **Writing Standard 2.1:** Write narratives.

Print Resources for Universal Access

Unit 5 • Chapter 10

	On-Level Learners	English Learners	Struggling Readers	Students Who Use African American Vernacular English	Advanced Learners	Students with Disabilities
Unit 5 Resources practice and assessment for selections and features in Chapter 10	✔				✔	
Universal Access: Holt Interactive Reader interactive reading for Dover Beach		✔	✔	✔		✔
Universal Access: Differentiating Instruction modified lesson plans and leveled assessment for Dover Beach		✔	✔	✔		✔
Universal Access: Resources for Teaching Advanced Students lesson plans for Dover Beach					✔	

Print Resources for Universal Access

All Chapters

	On-Level Learners	English Learners	Struggling Readers/Writers	Students Who Use African American Vernacular English	Advanced Learners	Students with Disabilities
Universal Access: Supporting Instruction in Spanish translations of selection summaries and key terms		✔	✔			
Universal Access: Holt Interactive Writer and Speaker practice and assessment	✔	✔	✔	✔	✔	✔
Language and Sentence Skills Practice for Warriner's Handbook Chapters 14–16	✔				✔	
Universal Access: Developmental Language and Sentence Skills Practice for Warriner's Handbook Chapters 14–16		✔	✔	✔		✔

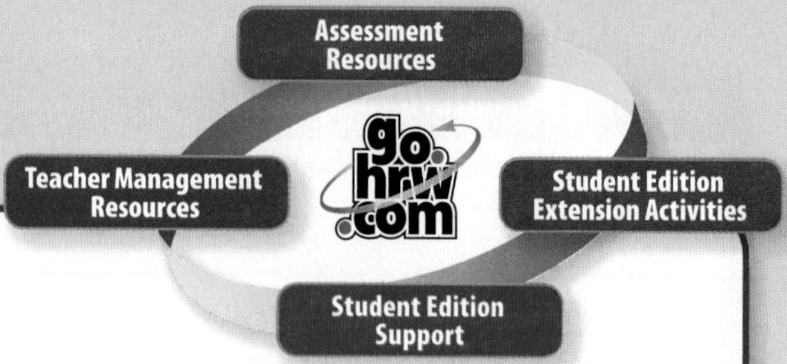

Technology Resources

Find all of Holt's technology resources at go.hrw.com. Technology resources are also listed at point of use in the Teacher's Edition wrap. Below are our featured components for Unit 5.

Teacher Management Resources

ThinkCentral, Teacher Access
Teacher One Stop™
Holt Professional Learning for Language Arts

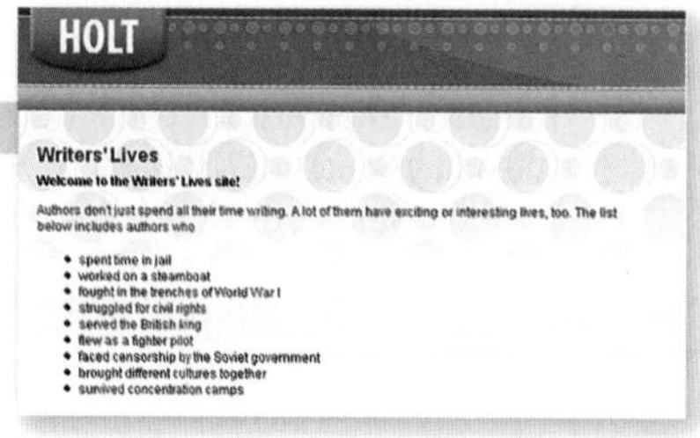

Spotlight on ThinkCentral, Teacher Access

All of the unit's resources are available on the online Teacher's Edition. Online suggestions:

- Use the point-of-use links to the Writers' Lives site to increase your students' knowledge of the lives of Alfred, Lord Tennyson, Anton Chekhov, Leo Tolstoy, Guy de Maupassant, and others.

Student Edition Support

PowerNotes
ThinkCentral, Student Access
Student One Stop™
Interactive Reading Workshops
Interactive Graphic Organizers
Writers' Lives
Holt Audio Library
Holt Audio Library: Selections and Summaries in Spanish

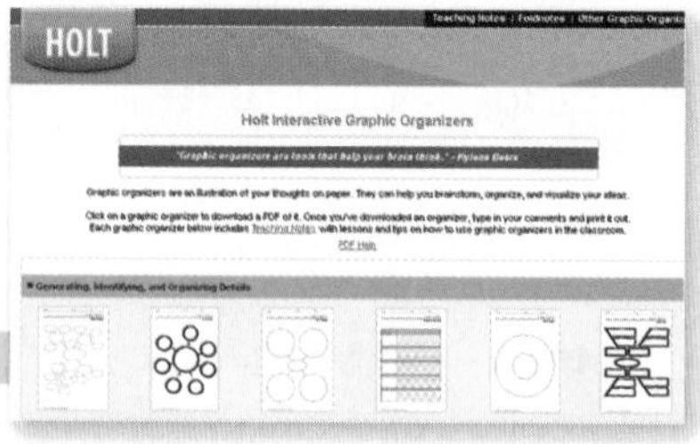

Spotlight on Graphic Organizers

As students read the selections in this unit, direct them to the Interactive Graphic Organizers Mini-site to find many different kinds of graphic organizers to help them as they read—and as they write the short story in this unit's Writing Workshop.

Student Edition Extension Activities

Digital Storytelling Mini-Site
NovelWise Mini-Site
MediaScope Mini-Site
WordSharp: An Interactive Vocabulary Tutor
GrammarNotes
WritingNotes
Writing and Research in a Digital Age
Literature Links

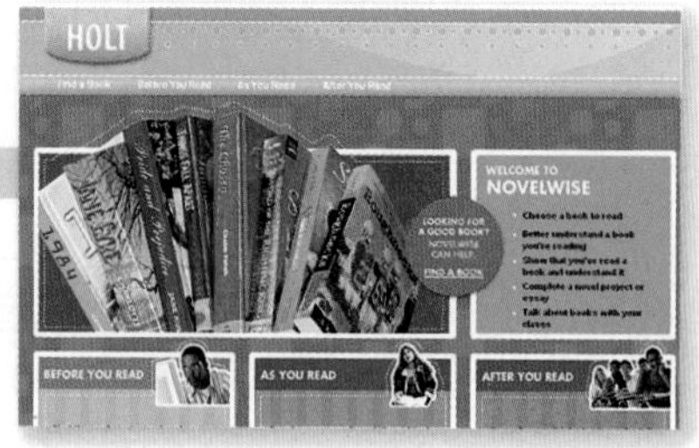

Spotlight on NovelWise Mini-Site

This site offers teaching and study guides for many novels, including Victorian works such as Thomas Hardy's *The Return of the Native*, Charles Dickens's *Great Expectations*, and Charlotte Brontë's *Jane Eyre*.

Differentiating Instruction: Advanced students may appreciate the opportunity to explore longer works.

Supported Strands: Reading, Literature, Writing

Assessment Resources

ThinkCentral Online Assessment
Holt Online Essay Scoring
ThinkCentral Online Remediation

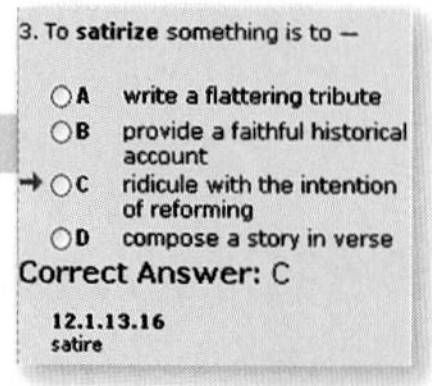
3. To **satirize** something is to —

A write a flattering tribute
B provide a faithful historical account
→ C ridicule with the intention of reforming
D compose a story in verse

Correct Answer: C

12.1.13.16
satire

Spotlight on ThinkCentral Online Assessment

Check your students' knowledge of the skills covered in this unit. Each test item is correlated to a specific skill.

Real Issues, Real Experts

The wrap for these selections includes specific ideas and strategies from *Holt Literature and Language Arts* authors.

From the Authors

For "My Last Duchess," p. 942 and "Porphyria's Lover," p. 947

First, I have students skim to notice the absence of stanza breaks. We speculate reasons for this. We note that the ends of lines in "Porphyria's Lover" all have some sort of punctuation, while this isn't true of "My Last Duchess." We discuss what this tells us we need to do while reading the poem. Then, I pair students to read the poems silently and ask them to write a summary together. Students read the poems aloud to each other and rewrite one poem from the deceased woman's point of view in the same monologue style.

Kylene Beers

For "Dover Beach," p. 964

Offering photographic vistas of the actual Dover Beach helps readers visualize the setting. This poem reflects on the confounding mixture of nature's joy and the sorrow that defines the modern human condition. I ask students to consider the "story behind the poem:" Who is the speaker? To whom is he addressing his words?

Deborah Appleman

Teacher to Teacher

Preteach To teach the Writing and Listening and Speaking Workshops, I begin with a list of thirty events and details loosely related to each other. For example: *The dog ran away, The doghouse is red, Tim bought a leash.* I then have the students choose fifteen events and details in groups of two or three and write a short narrative based on causation and chronology. Students share with the class.

Direct Teach I have one team of students post the events of their narrative in chronological order on the board and write the details corresponding to each event. We then discuss which elements are pertinent to the plot, which are useful in creating suspense, and which are use superfluous.

Assess I provide an established short story that I modified by inserting numerous useless details and irrelevant events. I have the students take a black marker and omit the unnecessary sentences.

Sigfried Abuel
Costa Meca, California

Holt Professional Learning

Managing the Heterogeneous Classroom
with Leila Christenbury and Patrick Schwarz

Visit ThinkCentral, Teacher Access to link to Holt's Professional Learning site for English/Language Arts teachers. This site features:

- **Videos that share the insights of *Holt Literature and Language Arts* program authors and consultants and demonstrate proven classroom strategies with master teachers**
- **Study guides for publications by our authors and consultants**
- **Informative articles and useful Web links**
- **Help in planning your department's professional learning sessions**
- **A handbook for new teachers**

VIDEO PRODUCTS

Strategies for Helping Struggling Readers
with Kylene Beers

Effective Vocabulary Instruction
with Carol Jago and Kylene Beers

Developing Critical Thinking about Literature
with Carol Jago and Deborah Appleman

Teaching Students to Revise, Not Recopy
with Linda Rief

Teaching English Learners
with Robin Scarcella

Using Literature Circles
with Harvey Daniels

Teaching On-Demand Writing Skills
with Leila Christenbury

Managing the Heterogeneous Classroom
with Leila Christenbury and Patrick Schwarz

Teaching Narrative and Expository Texts
with Judith Irvin and Deborah Appleman

Becoming a Tech-Savvy Teacher
with Sara Kajder

Re-engaging the Disengaged Student
with Alfred Tatum

Teaching Grammar in Context
with Amy Benjamin

UNIT 5

Unit Objectives

- Students will read a selection of poems by Alfred, Lord Tennyson, and will analyze the poet's use of sound devices, theme, tone, and metaphor.
- Students will read two dramatic monologues by Robert Browning and a sonnet by Elizabeth Barrett Browning and explore the characteristics of these literary forms.
- Students will read a poem by Gerard Manley Hopkins and explore his versification.
- Students will analyze poems by Matthew Arnold, Thomas Hardy, and A. E. Housman and a short story by Rudyard Kipling.
- Students will explore realism through literary works by Leo Tolstoy, Anton Chekhov, and Guy de Maupassant.
- At the end of the unit, students will write and present a short story.

Analyzing Visuals

The illustration shows the interior of the Crystal Palace, erected in Hyde Park in London to house the Great Exhibition of 1851. The exhibition displayed the latest technology of the Industrial Revolution.

Extension Activity Think about how technology affects your everyday life. What items would you display in a modern World's Fair exhibition? ***Possible response:*** *Personal computers, cell phones, and other ubiquitous modern devices.*

Unit Resources

On Course: Mapping Instruction

Unit 5 Resources

Warriner's Handbook
- Chapter 14, Punctuation
- Chapter 15, Spelling
- Chapter 16, Correcting Common Errors

Teacher One Stop™

Formal Assessment, Progress Monitoring Test 3

English-Language Conventions Progress-Monitoring Tests

ThinkCentral Online Assessment

Holt Virtual File Cabinet for Language Arts, grammar, reading, and vocabulary resources

Holt Pronunciation Resources,
- Phoneme Sounds and Spellings
- Support for Speakers of African American Vernacular English

ThinkCentral Online Remediation

The Transept of The Great Exhibition of 1851 by Joseph Nash (1808–1878). Watercolor and bodycolor. Inv.:73-1898. Victoria and Albert Museum, London.

UNIT 5

The Victorian Period

1832–1901

"For each age is a dream that is dying, / Or one that is coming to birth."

—**Arthur O'Shaughnessy**

What Do You Think? How can appearance be different from reality?

Learn It Online
Find out more about this historical period online.
go.hrw.com H12-901 Go

The Quotation

- Explain to students that Arthur O'Shaughnessy is a London-born poet who lived during the Victorian era.
- O'Shaughnessy expresses how one "age" does not necessarily end abruptly when another starts. There are periods of transition, when old "dreams" finally die and are replaced by dreams that are just coming to life. Each generation finds and defines itself in this cycle of change.

Routines for California Classrooms

For ideas on classroom practices and approaches to grouping, see the discussion of routines on pages T34–T37 of this Teacher's Edition.

What Do You Think?

How can appearance be different from reality?

- Ask students about times when it might be difficult to tell appearance and reality apart.
- Have students write for 3–5 minutes in their **Reader/Writer Notebooks** about a situation in which appearance and reality were profoundly different. Have students reflect on the order to "do as I do, not just as I say."
- Refer students to the time line on the next page to fuel their thinking about events such as the Opium Wars in which appearance and reality may be in conflict.

Learn It Online
You can introduce some of the topics in this unit using brief videos about the literature of this period.
go.hrw.com H12–901 Go

Real Issues, Real Experts: Professional Learning

Spotlight on . . .
Motivation and Vocabulary Videos
To raise students' interest and involvement in selections by writers such as Tennyson and Kipling, consider the suggestions you'll find in these videos:

In *Using Literature Circles,* Holt author **Harvey Daniels** provides a structure and philosophy for implementing student-directed book groups.

Managing the Heterogeneous Classroom, with **Leila Christenbury** and **Patrick Schwarz,** provides tips for classroom management, flexible grouping, and inclusion of students with special needs.

Each video is accompanied by printable articles, planning materials, Web links, and a training guide for supervisors. For these resources and more, visit **Holt Professional Learning** by going to this page in **ThinkCentral, Teacher Access.**

Direct Teach

Teach the Time Line

Give students five to ten minutes to study the time line. Then, ask the following questions:

- Which entries show a difference between the rights of men and the rights of women? ***Possible response:*** *The entries for the First Reform Bill (1832) and Second Reform Bill (1867), compared with the entry about Emmeline Pankhurst and women's suffrage (1889), show the continuing inequality of men and women.*
- What do the historical events of 1845 and 1847 suggest about the lives of the poor? ***Possible response:*** *Child labor and long hours in the factory were common for the poor. There was no social network to save millions of Irish people from dying during the Potato Famine.*
- What is the significance of the birth of Mohandas K. Gandhi to the British Empire? ***Possible response:*** *In the following century, Gandhi led India to its freedom from British rule, thus striking a blow to the Empire that had expanded so rapidly during Victorian times.*

The Victorian Period 1832–1901

This time line represents a snapshot of British literary events, British political and social events, and world events that took place primarily during Queen Victoria's reign from 1837 to 1901. During this period, Great Britain expanded as an industrial nation and as an empire, but beneath the successes were many social and moral problems.

Alice with the Duchess by John Tenniel. From Lewis Carroll's *Alice in Wonderland*. Color lithograph.

BRITISH LITERARY EVENTS

1832

1837–1838 Charles Dickens publishes installments of *Oliver Twist*, a novel revealing the exploitation of poor children in Victorian England

1847 Emily Brontë publishes *Wuthering Heights*; her sister Charlotte Brontë publishes *Jane Eyre*, a novel about a young woman coming of age

1848 Poet Dante Gabriel Rossetti and others form the Pre-Raphaelite Brotherhood, a group of artists who reject the ugliness of modern life

1850

1857 Mary Ann Evans publishes stories, using her pen name George Eliot

1865 Charles Darwin publishes his controversial scientific study *On the Origin of Species by Means of Natural Selection*

1867 Lewis Carroll publishes *Alice in Wonderland* ^

1867 Matthew Arnold publishes "Dover Beach," a poem that mourns a world without faith

BRITISH POLITICAL AND SOCIAL EVENTS

1832

1832 The First Reform Bill extends voting rights to men who own property worth ten pounds or more in annual rent

1842 Great Britain wins First Opium War, forcing China to open ports to trade in opium from British-controlled India; Hong Kong yielded to Britain

1845 Potato famine begins in Ireland; close to one million die of starvation and disease; massive emigration begins

1847 Ten Hours Act limits the number of hours women and children can work in factories

1850

1854 Florence Nightingale nurses soldiers in the Crimea

1858 Change in laws allow Lionel de Rothschild to become first Jewish member of Parliament

1867 Second Reform Bill gives the vote to most male industrial workers

1869 Suez Canal opens, allowing two-way navigation between Europe and Asia ⌄

The Inauguration Procession of the Suez Canal (1865) by Édouard Riou. Bibliotheque des Arts Decoratifs, Paris.

WORLD EVENTS

1832

1836 Mexican army defeats Texans at the Alamo

1848 Women's rights convention held in Seneca Falls, New York >

Elizabeth Cady Stanton addressing the first Women's Rights Convention. The Granger Collection, N.Y.

1850

1861 U.S. Civil War begins

1867 Last Japanese shogun resigns; power returns to emperor; old feudal system abolished in 1871; severe social problems result

1869 Mohandas K. Gandhi is born in India; he later leads India to independence and inspires civil rights worldwide

1869 Leo Tolstoy completes his novel *War and Peace* in Russia

California Standards, pp. 902–903

- **Reading Standard 3.7** Analyze recognized works of world literature from a variety of authors: **c.** Evaluate the philosophical, political, religious, ethical, and social influences of the historical period that shaped the characters, plots, and settings.

Universal Access

English Learners/ Struggling Readers

English for Academic Success Read through each section of the time line with students and clarify the following words and phrases that may impede their understanding:

- **British Literary Events:** *exploitation, coming of age, pen name, controversial, pessimistic, colonial, teeming*
- **British Political and Social Events:** *opium, yielded emigration, Parliament, navigation, suffrage, absorption*
- **World Events:** *shogun, feudal, agitating*

Advanced Learners

Acceleration As you discuss the time line, try to connect the descriptions of the literary works with what was occuring politically and socially. Why, for instance, would Charles Dickens be writing about the exploitation

Reading Standard 3.7c (see pages A48–A50)

Your Turn

Which details in the time line suggest the major social and moral concerns that dominated Britain during this time?

1870 **1890** **1901**

1878 Thomas Hardy publishes *The Return of the Native,* a pessimistic novel about thwarted desire

1887 Arthur Conan Doyle introduces Sherlock Holmes in *A Study in Scarlet*

Sherlock Holmes (1901). The Stapleton Collection, London.

1895 Oscar Wilde's satiric comedy *The Importance of Being Earnest* is staged, mocking an idle social class that has outlived its time

1901 Rudyard Kipling publishes *Kim,* a novel that presents a picture of English colonial life in the teeming world of India

Oscar Wilde.

1870 **1890** **1901**

1879 Zulu War against British in South Africa begins; Zulu nation eventually defeated

1889 Emmeline Parkhurst forms women's suffrage organization

Pankhurst is arrested outside Buckingham Palace. The Granger Collection, N.Y.

1899 Second Boer War begins, leading to absorption of two African republics into British Empire

1901 Queen Victoria dies

Queen Victoria, c. 1890.

1870 **1890** **1901**

1880 Dostoyevsky publishes novels *Crime and Punishment* and *The Brothers Karamazov* in Russia

1885 Mark Twain publishes novel *Adventures of Huckleberry Finn* in the U.S.

1885 Indian National Congress is formed; begins agitating for Indian self-rule

1893 Henry Ford builds his first car in Detroit, Michigan

1898 After the sinking of the battleship *Maine,* the U.S. declares war on Spain

1901 The first Nobel Prize is awarded

Henry Ford (1853–1947) photographed with his first automobile in 1896. The Granger Collection, N.Y.

of children? How did the Brontë sisters and George Eliot address the specific difficulties faced by women of the era? [*Responses will likely mention that many children faced poverty and child labor; women had limited freedoms and were often economically dependent on men.*]

Group Activity Then, challenge students to work in small groups to discuss briefly the importance of the social and political events on the time line. Have students share their ideas with the rest of the class.

Students with Disabilities

Tell students that the time line shows events during the reign of the British Queen Victoria, who gave her name to the period. Explain that students can compare events by reading the page vertically. Model connecting an event on the time line of British literature to contemporary events in British and world history. You might say: "India was a British colony through much of the nineteenth century and began agitating for independence in 1885. By the end of the century, British novelist Rudyard Kipling was writing about English colonists in India."

Check for Understanding

Your Turn

Have students refer to the time line and talk with a partner about the social problems preoccupying the writers of this period. Have them link these problems to the notion of appearance and reality discussed in the What Do You Think question. Then, have partners share their opinions with the rest of the class.

Explore the Time Line

The following activity offers options for students to explore the literary, political, social, and world events presented on the time line.

Enrichment Explain to students that coping with change is an important challenge for the individual within society, especially when the changes are massive and global.

- Divide the class into three groups. Assign each group one aspect of change to research: the role of women, the growth of empire, and the rise of the middle class.
- As students research their topic, remind them to relate their research to the unit question: How can appearance be different from reality?
- Have groups orally report their findings to the class.

Standards Focus

Objectives

Students will

- evaluate the philosophical, political, religious, ethical, and social influences of a historical period
- read to increase the culture of others and common elements across cultures
- understand elements of text structures

Preteach

Key Concepts

Use the Key Concepts to preview the unit introduction. Each key concept is addressed in a separate section of the essay that relates the concept to both the history and the literature of the times.

Set a Purpose for Reading

- Ask students to identify one piece of information from each key concept that particularly interests them.
- Have students write down any concepts, images, or phrases that come to mind when they think of Victorian England. Suggest that students look for information related to these concepts as they read.
- Tell students to record each section's main ideas in their **Reader/ Writer Notebooks.**

California Standards, pp. 904–909

- **Reading Standard 2.2** Analyze the way in which clarity of meaning is affected by the patterns of organization, hierarchical structures, repetition of the main ideas, syntax, and word choice in the text.
- **Reading Standard 3.7** Analyze recognized works of world literature from a variety of authors: **b.** Relate literary works and authors to the major themes and issues of their eras. **c.** Evaluate the philosophical, political, religious, ethical, and social influences of the historical period that shaped the characters, plots, and settings.

The Victorian Period

1832–1901

The Victorian period was a time of vast social, political, and economic progress; It was also a time of great suffering among the urban poor who lived in filthy tenements in the industrial cities. The self-confidence as well as the problems and anxieties of the age are revealed in the works of the great Victorian writers. Social commentary became a trend, and the novel rose in prominence.

KEY CONCEPTS

Riots and Reforms

History of the Times The Reform Bill of 1832 answered some of the demands of the rising middle classes. When widespread unemployment and soaring bread prices gave way to a severe depression, riots broke out. The repeal of the tax that had forced bread prices up helped save England from revolution.

Literature of the Times The enormously popular novels of Charles Dickens exposed the suffering of poor people and helped move the nation toward reform.

Progress Brings Prosperity

History of the Times A spirit of optimism lifted England in the middle of the century. Free trade with Europe brought prosperity to some, while a series of factory acts improved the lives of the working class. New legislation made education free and mandatory for every child.

Literature of the Times Thomas Babington Macaulay, a representative writer of this period, based his optimism on the belief that history, technology, free enterprise, and God were working toward the betterment of human beings.

Decorum and Doubt

History of the Times Middle-class society held to strict codes of decorum and morality. Many believed that life would be improved if it were more refined and better policed. Despite the optimism of the age, some people mocked the codes of decorum and questioned the view that material comforts satisfied human needs.

Literature of the Times Matthew Arnold's poem "Dover Beach" gave voice to the doubts and anxieties of the late Victorian period.

Resources

Unit 5 Resources, on-level instruction, Historical Introduction Study Guide, p. 1

UA: Holt Interactive Reader, Key Concepts and Academic Vocabulary, p. 269

PowerNotes, interactive lesson presentations with activities go.hrw.com

Teacher One Stop™, on-level lesson plans and all print resources

Universal Access

EL English Learners

English for Academic Success To help students understand the information presented in the unit introduction, review the definitions of the following words and phrases with students:

- **depression**—a period of economic downturn
- **tenements**—buildings like apartment houses that house many people in small quarters with poor sanitation and ventilation
- **codes of decorum**—spoken and unspoken rules of behavior that are often directed at keeping up appearances

Reading Standard 2.2, 3.7b, 3.7c (see pages A48–A50)

UNIT 5 INTRODUCTION

KEY CONCEPT

Riots and Reforms

History of the Times

The first decade of Victoria's reign was troubled. Although the Reform Bill of 1832 appeased the middle classes by giving the vote to more landowning men, the growth of industry led to serious social problems. In 1837, the year Victoria became queen, the country entered a severe depression that by 1842 had put 1.5 million unemployed workers on some form of poverty relief. This period became known as the Hungry Forties.

Government commissions learned of children mangled when they fell asleep at machines at the end of a twelve-hour working day. They discovered young girls and boys hauling sledges of coal through narrow mine tunnels and working shifts so long that in winter they saw the sun only on Sundays.

In Ireland a potato famine (1845–1849) killed perhaps a million and forced another two million to emigrate. Some went to England, where they lived in crowded slums that had two toilets for 250 people. The cities became filthy and disorderly as the population swelled.

Massive political rallies were held in the 1840s to protest policies that kept the price of bread high and deprived most working men (and all women) of the vote. Finally, Parliament repealed the tax that had forced bread prices up. In 1867, the Second Reform Act gave the right to vote to most working-class men. A series of factory acts limited child labor by reducing the workday to ten hours.

Literature of the Times

The novels of Charles Dickens, the most important figure in Victorian literature, attacked the excesses of Victorian affluence. They also attacked the neglect and exploitation of decent people. Children in his novels endure terrible suffering, including abuse from adults.

Other early Victorian writers who contributed to social reforms include John Ruskin and William Thackeray. Ruskin, a leading art and social critic, wrote on the problems of smog. Thackeray, who wrote *Vanity Fair,* commented on social pretense.

Comprehension Check

What social problems in the Victorian era resulted from material progress?

Fast Facts

Political and Social Highlights

- Industrialization leads to the growth of slums.
- Tax reform lowers bread prices and helps prevent revolution.
- A series of reform bills eventually gives greater power to the middle class by extending the vote to more men.

Literary Highlights

- Charles Dickens uses humor in his novels to attack moral and social injustices.
- Matthew Arnold's "Dover Beach" voices doubts in the age of progress.

The General Post Office at One Minute to Six by George Elgar Hicks (1824–1914). The Museum of London, U.K.

Learn It Online
Learn more about this historical period online.
go.hrw.com H12-905 Go

Direct Teach

Think About/Talk About

Motivate Ask students to consider the significance of the Victorian Period being named after Queen Victoria, who reigned from 1837 to 1901. Ask students to think about how the policies of a monarch and Parliament can affect the social culture and literature of the time. What might the topics and themes of literary works from the Victorian period tell us about each writer's feelings about the government?

History of the Times

- Inform students that industrialization changed how people lived and worked. Cities and the middle class expanded. The need for labor brought women and children off the farm and into factories.
- Point out that the difficulties faced by the working classes led to long-term social changes, including political reforms and mass immigration.

Comprehension Check

Possible response: *Social problems that resulted from material progress included exploitation of children and unsanitary living conditions.*

Struggling Readers

Help students to better understand the historical introduction by building background about the rise of industrialization and urbanization. Explain that during the eighteenth and nineteenth centuries, technology had advanced and industry had expanded. Many people moved from rural areas to cities that became overcrowded and unhygienic as a result of the influx of workers. Dependent on factory jobs for their survival, laborers had little choice but to endure the grim working and living conditions.

Advanced Learners

Acceleration Explain that the rise of the middle class during Victorian times makes that era resemble our own more closely than previous eras did. Women's suffrage, voting rights, child welfare laws, and acts of civil disobedience characterize both periods. Ask groups of students to examine the dominant issues of both Victorian and contemporary times and comment on how the seeds of modern society were sown during Queen Victoria's long reign.

Learn It Online
For a multimedia introduction to the key concepts covered in this unit, use the **PowerNotes** Unit 5 presentation.
go.hrw.com H12–905 Go

Think About/Talk About

History of the Times

Women as high-profile reformers were the exception, not the rule, in Victorian times. Writing about the role of women in Victorian England, Richard Altick in *Victorian People and Ideas* states, "Upper- and middle-class women were sedulously set apart from the world of commerce and, generally, of intellect. This represented a marked reversal of attitude and custom. In the eighteenth century, there had been plenty of middle-class businesswomen engaged in a variety of occupations." In the Victorian period, however, society imposed a stricter separation between home and business.

Analyzing Visuals

Extension Activity Explain that the map represents the territories that were part of the British Empire in the Victorian era. What role did the territories play in Great Britain's economy? ***Possible responses:*** *The map shows how, during the Victorian era, the British Empire extended over many countries around the world. This means that the British Empire could count on high levels of tax revenue from the colonies and on a great variety of goods coming from five continents.*

KEY CONCEPT

Progress Brings Prosperity

History of the Times

Though the Industrial Revolution created problems, it also steadily created new roads, new towns, new goods, new wealth, and new jobs for tens of thousands of people climbing up the levels of the middle class.

A new spirit of optimism lifted the nation during the middle years of the century. Reason and courage, most Victorians believed, could overcome the problems that had festered in the 1840s. In no other period of English culture before (and maybe since) were new ideas discussed and debated so vigorously by such a large segment of society. The Victorians were also voracious readers: They read not only the massive novels of Charles Dickens, William Thackeray, George Eliot, and Charlotte Brontë but also lengthy essays and religious tracts.

On the domestic front, the nation was stable and peaceful. On the world stage, Great Britain was expanding its empire, moving beyond its control of India and Ireland to China and Africa. By the beginning of the twentieth century, Great Britain's power extended to 200 million people beyond its borders.

During this era, England made great strides in improving social and political conditions. Reformers made their mark. Florence Nightingale's work in improving sanitation and nursing in hospitals during the Crimean War resulted in better medical care throughout the world. Social worker Octavia Hill worked on housing reform and conservation, and Josephine Butler campaigned for better treatment of women and girls.

In addition, education improved dramatically. With new legislation, education became free and required for every child. In 1870, Great Britain passed a law establishing state-supported schools. Schooling became mandatory in 1880, and in 1891 it was guaranteed to be free. As a result of better schooling, literacy increased, and the reading public expanded.

The BRITISH EMPIRE
circa 1901

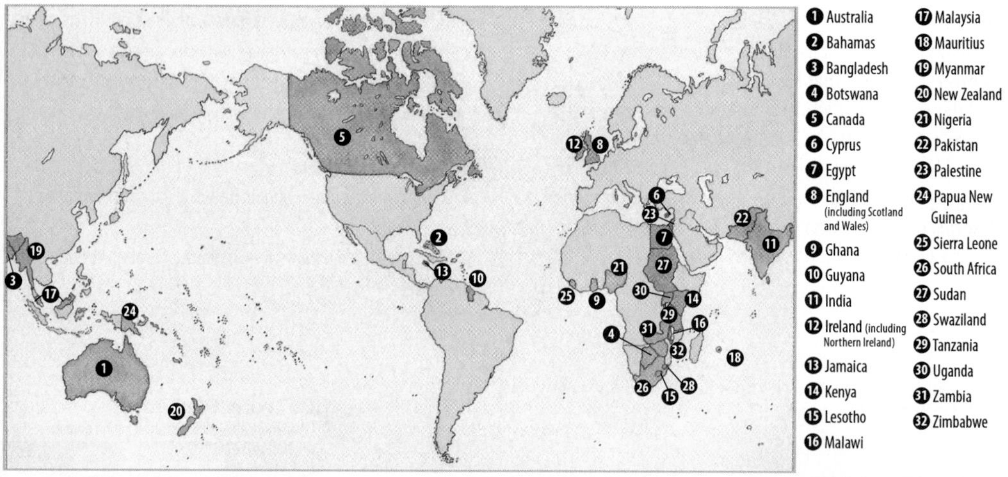

Cross-Curricular Connection

CIVICS: Progress toward Democracy

The push for greater democracy was embodied in the Chartist movement, which took its name from the People's Charter of 1838, the petition in which its demands were first presented to Parliament. Among the Chartists' demands were salaries for members of Parliament, use of the secret ballot, and repeal of property requirements for serving in Parliament. Eventually, almost all the Chartists' demands were met. In addition, most adult males in Britain gained the right to vote by 1884.

Progress was robust in science as well. Scientists came to understand the earth, its creatures, and its natural laws. Geologists worked out the history written in rocks and fossils. Darwin used his observations in the Galápagos Islands to explain the origin of species. Major advances were made in chemistry, physics, and medicine.

The showcase of the age was an enormous structure of glass and steel known as the Crystal Palace. The "palace" was designed to show, through the wonders of modern science and industry, England's confidence in its present and future accomplishments. (The Crystal Palace was destroyed by fire in 1936.)

Literature of the Times

The most eloquent spokesman for Victorian progress and optimism was Thomas Babington Macaulay. Macaulay believed that history, technology, free enterprise, and God were all working in harmony toward the betterment of human beings. Macaulay admired cleanliness and order. He wanted London streets free of garbage, drained, paved, lighted at night, and patrolled by a sober police force. He described the progress Victorian London had made in cleaning up its streets:

> We should greatly err if we were to suppose that any of the streets and squares then bore the same aspect as at present. . . . If the most fashionable parts of the capital could be placed before us, such as they then were, we should be disgusted by their squalid appearance, and poisoned by their noisome atmosphere. In Covent Garden a filthy and noisy market was held close to the dwellings of the great. Fruit women screamed, carters fought, cabbage stalks and rotten apples accumulated in heaps at the thresholds of the Countess of Berkshire and of the Bishop of Durham.
>
> —from *A History of England* by Thomas Babington Macaulay

Comprehension Check

What specific advances in social welfare, political rights, education, and science were made in the Victorian age?

Link to Today

Victorian Inventions

The Victorian period was a time of innovation in science and technology. In fact, Victorians believed in the power of invention—that humans could solve problems in their environment by using their intellects. Many staples of life today were Victorian inventions.

antiseptic—In 1867, Joseph Lister developed antiseptic techniques for treating wounds.

bicycle—Kirkpatrick Macmillan invented the bicycle in 1869.

chloroform—James Simpson in 1848 discovered chloroform, an effective anesthetic.

fingerprinting—Sir Francis Galton in 1872 established the method of fingerprinting for identification in forensics.

Kelvin temperature scale—William Thomson (Lord Kelvin) developed this scale in 1848.

modern photography—In 1835, William Henry Fox Talbot developed modern photography by using light-sensitive paper and short exposure times.

postage stamp—Roland Hill developed the idea of a uniform postal charge, and in 1840 the first stamp was produced.

subway—In 1863, London opened the world's first subway system, the Metropolitan.

The Cyclist by Giuseppe Wulz. (1868–1918)
Museo di Storia della Fotografia Fratelli Alinari, Florence

Ask Yourself

What inventions have been made in the past fifty years? Do those inventions help solve problems in our environments?

Primary Source

Macaulay: Proof of Progress

In 1830, Macaulay wrote in the *Edinburgh Review*, "History is full of the signs of this natural progress of society. We see in almost every part of the annals of mankind how the industry of individuals, struggling up against wars, taxes, famines, conflagrations, mischievous prohibitions, and more mischievous protections, creates faster than governments can squander, and repairs whatever invaders can destroy. We see the wealth of nations increasing, and all the arts of life approaching nearer and nearer to perfection, in spite of the grossest corruption and the wildest profusion on the part of rulers."

Think About/Talk About

Link to Today

Victorian Inventions

This feature includes information about the achievement made in the areas of science and technology during the Victorian Period.

1. Ask these questions to help students build background: "How would the invention of antiseptic and chloroform change the way doctors treat patients? How would fingerprinting and photography improve the way people and events were documented?"
2. After students have read the feature, ask them to speculate about which Victorian invention is most significant in today's culture.
3. Finally, ask students to read the **Ask Yourself** question. Have students create a time line that displays inventions developed in the last fifty years. Ask students to choose five inventions that they feel revolutionized how we live.
4. Encourage students to choose one Victorian invention and research how it directly affected the lives of those living in the Victorian era.

Comprehension Check

Possible response: *Improvements were made in sanitation and nursing, and better treatment for women was advocated. New wealth and new jobs were created. Education became free and mandatory. Major advances were made in chemistry, physics, medicine, geology, and biology.*

Think About/Talk About

History of the Times

- Victorian women had far fewer social and legal freedoms than women have today. Men who believed in equal rights for women were the exception, not the rule. When the economist John Stuart Mill married in 1851, he signed a document giving up his legal rights to his wife's "person, property, and freedom of action." In fact, it was not until 1882 that the Married Women's Property Act finally allowed married women to keep their own money.
- Victorian attitudes toward gender roles and sexuality were reflected in the popular culture of the era. Censorship was common. Perhaps the most famous literary censor of all times was Thomas Bowdler, who is best known for changing hundreds of words and even cutting entire scenes from Shakespeare's plays. Bowdler's *Family Shakespeare* (1818) was embraced by Victorian readers. Bowdler's efforts have been immortalized in the verb *bowdlerize.* The word, which means "cut or modify a work," suggests prudery and violation of textual integrity.

KEY CONCEPT

Decorum and Doubt

History of the Times

The Apple of their Eye by James Waite (1832–1920).

Many Victorians thought of themselves as progressing morally and intellectually, as well as materially. In fact, the powerful, mainly middle-class obsession with gentility or decorum has made prudery almost a synonym for Victorianism. Book publishers and magazine editors deleted or altered words and episodes that might, in the phrase of the day, bring "a blush to the cheek" of a young person.

Sex, birth, and death were softened in art and popular fiction by sentimental conventions, made into tender courtships, joyous motherhoods, and deathbed scenes in which old people were saints and babies were angels. In the real world, people were arrested for distributing information about sexually transmitted diseases. Victorian society regarded seduced or adulterous women (but not their male partners) as "fallen" and pushed them to the margins of society.

Victorian decorum also supported powerful ideas about authority. Many Victorians were uneasy about giving strong authority to a central government. In Victorian private lives, however, the autocratic father of middle-class households is a vivid figure in both fact (Elizabeth Barrett Browning's father, for example, forbade all of his children to marry) and fiction.

Women were subject to male authority. Middle-class women especially were expected to marry and make their homes a comfortable refuge for their husbands from the male domains of business, politics, and the professions. Women who did not marry had few occupations open to them. Working-class women could find jobs as servants in prosperous households, while unmarried middle-class women could be governesses or teachers.

The excesses, cruelties, and hypocrisies of all these repressions were obvious to many Victorians. However, the codes and barriers of decorum changed slowly because they were part of the ideology of progress. Prudery and social order were intended to control the immorality and sexual excesses that the Victorians associated with the violent political revolutions of the eighteenth century.

Despite the confidence of the age, there were voices asking questions and raising doubts. Speaking for many of their contemporaries, and speaking to others whom they thought shallow and complacent, Victorian writers asked whether material comfort fully satisfied human needs and wishes. They questioned the cost of exploiting the earth and human beings. They protested or mocked Victorian codes of decorum and authority.

Academic Vocabulary

Talking and Writing About Literature

English for Academic Success Write the following questions on the board. Tell students these are the kinds of questions they will encounter on standardized tests. Discuss the meaning of the words and then have students use the historical introduction to answer the questions.

UNIT 5 INTRODUCTION

Literature of the Times

The dominant note of much mid-Victorian writing is struck by Matthew Arnold in his poem "Dover Beach." "The Sea of Faith," Arnold writes, has ebbed. There is no certainty in the world, and the dwindling of religious faith has brought about a crisis of consciousness. By the end of the century, this skepticism had become pervasive in the works of Thomas Hardy, A. E. Housman, and others. The heroes and heroines of earlier writers, such as Dickens and Eliot, find happiness in nurturing marriages and in small communities of family and friends. But there are few such marriages and communities in the fiction and poetry of Hardy and Housman. These late-Victorian writers tell of lovers and friends betrayed by unfaithfulness, war, and other troubles that we humans add to the natural trials of mortal life. Matthew Arnold responds with sadness characteristic of the century's end. His famous poem "Dover Beach" mourns the world's retreat from faith.

Comprehension Check

According to some later writers, what realities lay beneath the surface optimism and proprieties of Victorian life?

Love, Innocence. Valentine Card, c. 1870. Color lithograph on paper.

Wrap Up

Talk About . . .

The Victorians admired material progress, but some thought progress was made at the expense of human values. With a partner, discuss how such questions are relevant today. Try to use each Academic Vocabulary word **listed below** at least once in your discussion.

Write About . . .

The Victorians disagreed on the amount of authority that should be given to the government. What responsibility should government have for social welfare; for care of the environment; and for censorship of books and television?

Academic Vocabulary for Unit 5

Talking and Writing About Literature

Academic Vocabulary is the language you use to write and talk about literature. Use these words to discuss the literature you read in this unit. These words are underlined throughout the unit.

benefit (BEHN uh fiht) *n.:* anything that is for the good of a person or thing. *How did progress in science benefit the Victorians?*

respond (rih SPAHND) *v.:* react. *Some Victorians responded critically to industrial progress.*

statistics (stuh TIHS tihks) *n. pl.:* numerical facts. *Statistics show that Victorians had a much shorter life expectancy than we do.*

publish (PUHB lihsh) v.: print and issue for the public. *Most of Gerard Manley Hopkins's poems were published after his death.*

complex (kuhm PLEHKS) *adj.:* hard to understand; complicated. *The factors causing the famine are complex.*

Your Turn

Copy the words into your *Reader/Writer Notebook.* Try to use these words as you answer questions about the literature in the unit that follows.

Think About/Talk About

Literature of the Times

One of the most prominent victims of Victorian censorship was the writer Thomas Hardy. Magazine editors constantly rejected parts or suggested alterations to his writing, mainly to eliminate any mention of sex. Hardy stubbornly resisted these efforts to change his work.

Comprehension Check

Possible response: *The underside of Victorian life might include the repression of women and sexuality, the abuse of parental authority, the harshness of child labor, hypocrisy, and cruelty.*

Check for Understanding

Talk About . . .

Students might mention that material progress is still valued highly in today's society and is sometimes put above social compassion.

Write About . . .

Students might mention, for instance, that the government should avoid taking an extreme role in censoring printed matter and media.

PowerNotes, Academic Vocabulary lesson and activities

go.hrw.com **WordSharp: An Interactive Vocabulary Tutor,** more practice with academic language

- What was one **benefit** England enjoyed as a result of the Industrial Revolution? ***Possible response:*** *The Industrial revolution brought new wealth and new jobs to thousands of people.*
- How would Victorians **respond** to the charge that Victorianism was a synonym for prudery? ***Possible response:*** *If they were in the middle class, they would agree.*
- What kind of writing did Charles Dickens **publish**? ***Possible response:*** *Charles Dickens is best known as the author of many novels.*
- What kind of **statistics** might a Florence Nightingale keep about her work? ***Possible response:*** *She might record information about sanitation and patient care to show the value of her work.*

Standards Focus

Objectives

Students will evaluate the philosophical, political, religious, ethical, and social influences of a historical period.

Link to Today

This excerpt from *The Ghost Map* explores how the Victorian era dealt with the waste products of their society. It explores the concept of appearances and reality, which is central to the literature discussed in Unit 5.

Unit 5 Resources, Historical Introduction Skill Builder, p. 1

UA: Differentiating Instruction, graphic organizer, p. 214

Teacher One Stop™, lesson plan and all print resources

Direct Teach

Think About/Talk About

Read with a Purpose Direct students to the Read with a Purpose statement. Point out to students that they should be looking not just for the dirty jobs that toshers and other scavengers did but also for reasons that those jobs were essential. Have them compare Victorian methods of waste disposal with contemporary methods.

Link to Today

This Link to Today provides a look at how the people of Victorian London dealt with waste.

Read with a Purpose

Read to see how the dirty jobs of London were essential to its operation.

Build Background

In 1854, London was struck with a cholera epidemic. Dr. John Snow argued that cholera was spread via contaminated food or water. Snow plotted the locations of cholera deaths on a map and was able to isolate a water pump on Broad Street as the source of the contamination. He convinced authorities to remove the handle of the pump, effectively containing the epidemic and demonstrating that cholera was a waterborne disease. This excerpt provides a snapshot of life in London during the cholera epidemic—before the invention of safe water sewers or a public health system.

Author Note

Steven B. Johnson (1968–) is the author of *Everything Bad Is Good for You, Mind Wide Open,* and *Emergence.* Johnson's writing has appeared in *The New Yorker, Harper's, The Guardian, The New York Times,* and *The Wall Street Journal.*

HISTORY

The Night-Soil Men

from The Ghost Map

by **Steven B. Johnson**

It is August 1854, and London is a city of scavengers. Just the names alone read like some kind of exotic zoological catalogue: bone-pickers, rag-gatherers, pure-finders, dredgermen, mud-larks, sewer-hunters, dustmen, night-soil men, bunters, toshers, shoremen. These were the London underclasses, at least a hundred thousand strong. So immense were their numbers that had the scavengers broken off and formed their own city, it would have been the fifth-largest in all of England. But the diversity and precision of their routines were more remarkable than their sheer number. Early risers strolling along the Thames would see the toshers wading through the muck of low tide, dressed almost comically in flowing velveteen coats, their oversized pockets filled with stray bits of copper recovered from the water's edge. The toshers walked with a lantern strapped to their chest to help them see in the predawn gloom, and carried an eight-foot-long pole that they used to test the ground in front of them, and to pull themselves out when they stumbled into a quagmire. The pole and the eerie glow of the lantern through the robes gave them the look of ragged wizards, scouring the foul river's edge for magic coins. Beside them fluttered the mud-larks, often children, dressed in tatters and content to scavenge all the waste that the toshers rejected as below their standards: lumps of coal, old wood, scraps of rope.

Above the river, in the streets of the city, the pure-finders eked out a living by collecting dog crap (colloquially called "pure") while the bone-pickers foraged for carcasses of any stripe. Below ground, in the cramped but growing network of tunnels beneath London's streets, the sewer-hunters slogged through the flowing waste of the metropolis. Every few months, an unusually dense pocket of methane gas would be ignited by one of their kerosene lamps and the hapless soul would be

Selection Readability	
Easily Accessible **Accessible** Challenging	familiar syntax; accessible theme

Selection Summary

The night-soil men are among the underclass of London. They are the scavengers who pick up the odd piece of coal, the carcasses of dead animals, dog feces, and other waste products of the thriving metropolis. This underground world, at the margin of society, mirrors the class and status distinctions of the world above as they provide a service that is the most vital of social operations.

incinerated twenty feet below ground, in a river of raw sewage.

The scavengers, in other words, lived in a world of excrement and death. Dickens began his last great novel, *Our Mutual Friend*, with a father-daughter team of toshers stumbling across a corpse floating in the Thames, whose coins they solemnly pocket. "What world does a dead man belong to?" the father asks rhetorically, when chided by a fellow tosher for stealing from a corpse. 'Tother world. What world does money belong to? This world." Dickens' unspoken point is that the two worlds, the dead and the living, have begun to coexist in these marginal spaces. The bustling commerce of the great city has conjured up its opposite, a ghost class that somehow mimics the status markers and value calculations of the material world.

Consider the haunting precision of the bone-pickers' daily routine, as captured in Henry Mayhew's pioneering 1844 work, *London Labour and the London Poor*: "It usually takes the bone-picker from seven to nine hours to go over his rounds, during which time he travels from 20 to 30 miles with a quarter to

Bottom: An old man fashions a shovel from a scrap piece of metal in a dilapidated yard (1900s). Museum of London, U.K.
Below: A man crushes chalk into tires used to build a house made of recycled tires, cans, bottles, carpet, wood, glass, and other objects.

Think About/Talk About

Extend the Discussion

Monitoring Reading What kinds of tasks did the underclasses of London perform? ***Possible response:*** *They scavenged for rags, scrap metals, bits of coal, and other stray items that people discarded.*

Speculating How might upper- or middle-class members of London society view night-soil men? ***Possible response:*** *They might think of them as dirty, uneducated rag pickers who were beneath them both socially and economically.*

Universal Access

English Learners/ Struggling Readers

English for Academic Success Before students read the selection, introduce the following words.

- **scavenger**—someone who gathers discarded material. *The scavengers found pounds of metal in the trash.*
- **zoological**—pertaining to the study of animals. *The word "zoo" is a shortened form of "zoological garden."*
- **tatters**—torn or ragged clothing. *The prisoner's clothing was in tatters after many years in jail.*
- **metropolis**—a large, busy city. *The travelers saw the tall buildings of the metropolis.*
- **hapless**—unlucky, unfortunate. *The hapless runner sprained an angle on a patch of ice.*
- **marginal**—situated at the borders, edges, or fringes. *These workers made a marginal living collecting trash.*

Then, challenge students to write a paragraph that uses at least three of these words.

Think About/Talk About

Literary Connection

R. C. Churchill remarks that the common feature of Dickens's novels of the late 1840s and 1850s is "a criticism of Victorian society, which, like that of the workhouse chapters of *Oliver Twist,* goes deep enough to be a universal criticism of human nature."

Extend the Discussion

Speculating How often might someone from the "ghost class" encounter one from the "living"? ***Possible response:*** *People walking in the city at night might see them. They are "ghosts" because they are ignored by the "living" but are physically present and performing important jobs.*

a half hundredweight[1] on his back. In the summer he usually reaches home about eleven of the day, and in the winter about one or two. On his return home he proceeds to sort the contents of his bag. He separates the rags from the bones, and these again from the old metal (if he be lucky enough to have found any). He divides the rags into various lots, according as they are white or colored; and if he have picked up any pieces of canvas or sacking, he makes these also into a separate parcel. When he has finished the sorting he takes his several lots to the ragshop or the marine-store dealer, and realizes upon them whatever they may be worth." . . .

The homeless continue to haunt today's postindustrial cities, but they rarely display the professional clarity of the bone-picker's impromptu trade, for two primary reasons. First, minimum wages and government assistance are now substantial enough that it no longer makes economic sense to eke out a living as a scavenger. (Where wages remain depressed, scavenging remains a vital occupation; witness the *pependadores* of Mexico City.) The bone collector's trade has also declined because most modern cities possess elaborate systems for managing the waste generated by their inhabitants. (In fact, the closest American equivalent to the Victorian scavengers—the aluminum-can collectors you sometimes see hovering outside supermarkets—rely on precisely those waste-management systems for their paycheck.) But

1. **hundredweight:** unit of measurement equal to 112 pounds; thus, a quarter to a half hundred weight is 28 to 56 pounds.

Below: Victorian rag pickers.
Right: Clothes being sorted and recycled at the Salvation Army Trading Company, Wellingborough, Northamptonshire, England, U.K.

Cross-Curricular Connection

SOCIAL STUDIES: Child Labor Laws
Have students work in groups to develop a brief report on child labor laws in Great Britain and the United States in the Victorian era. For example, the Education Act of 1880 made education compulsory in Great Britain only for children between the ages of five and ten. By 1901, the minimum working age had been raised to twelve, and children up to age fourteen could work only half a day. In the United States, it was not until 1938 that federal law dictated when children were allowed to work.

HSS Analysis Skills: HI 1

London in 1854 was a Victorian metropolis trying to make do with an Elizabethan public infrastructure. The city was vast even by today's standards, with two and a half million people crammed inside a thirty-mile circumference. But most of the techniques for managing that kind of population density that we now take for granted—recycling centers, public-health departments, safe sewage removal—hadn't been invented yet.

And so the city itself improvised a response—an unplanned, organic response, to be sure, but at the same time a response that was precisely contoured to the community's waste-removal needs. As the garbage and excrement grew, an underground market for refuse developed, with hooks into established trades. Specialists emerged, each dutifully carting goods to the appropriate site in the official market: the bone collectors selling their goods to the bone-boilers, the pure-finders selling their dog crap to tanners, who used the "pure" to rid their leather goods of the lime they had soaked in for weeks to remove animal hair. (A process widely considered to be, as one tanner put it, "the most disagreeable in the whole range of manufacture.")

We're naturally inclined to consider these scavengers tragic figures, and to fulminate against a system that allowed so many thousands to eke out a living by foraging through human waste. In many ways, this is the correct response. (It was, to be sure, the response of the great crusaders of the age, among them Dickens and Mayhew.) But such social outrage should be accompanied by a measure of wonder and respect: without any central planner coordinating their actions, without any education at all, this itinerant underclass managed to conjure up an entire system for processing and sorting the waste generated by two million people. The great contribution usually ascribed to Mayhew's *London Labour* is simply his willingness to see and record the details of these impoverished lives. But just as valuable was the insight that came out of that bookkeeping, once he had run the numbers: far from being unproductive vagabonds, Mayhew discovered, these people were actually performing an essential function for their community. "The removal of the refuse of a large town," he wrote, "is, perhaps, one of the most important of social operations." And the scavengers of Victorian London weren't just getting rid of that refuse—they were recycling it.

Ask Yourself

1. **Read with a Purpose** How does Johnson regard the dirty jobs of the scavengers and their role in Victorian London?
2. Why were there so many different types of scavengers in Victorian London? Why were such specific jobs necessary?
3. Why does the author state that the job of the bone-picker could not exist in today's cities?
4. Why do you suppose the bone-picker in the excerpt from Henry Mayhew's book gets home later in the day during winter?
5. What systems could a city put in place to prevent scavengers from interacting with harmful waste?

Think About/Talk About

Extend the Discussion

Summarizing The paragraph on p. 913 that begins "And so the city itself . . ." explains how the scavenger system developed. Why did it form? How did it become organized? ***Possible response:*** *The system developed to meet the city's waste-removal needs. Although improvised and unofficial, it organized itself as specialists emerged.*

Making Judgments Re-read the final paragraph. According to the author, what is the most remarkable and praiseworthy aspect of the scavenger system? Explain why you agree or disagree. ***Possible response:*** *The author is amazed that so complex a system was put into place without central planning by people who had no training. He also marvels at this early and spontaneous form of recycling. Students familiar with grassroots organizations may express less amazement.*

Ask Yourself

Possible responses:

1. *Johnson regards the scavengers' jobs as demeaning but necessary. For many, there was no other way to earn an income. For the city, there was no other way to get rid of the mountains of waste that its inhabitants generated.*
2. *The diversity of tasks that scavengers undertook reflected the different kinds of wastes produced by the community. Specific market sites existed for the corresponding jobs.*
3. *The author states that the bone collector's trade has declined because most modern cities possess elaborate systems for managing the waste produced by their population.*
4. *It may be harder to carry heavy burdens in the bad weather, and it may take longer to collect enough to produce an income.*
5. *Cities could pass laws regulating the collection of harmful waste and levy fines and severe penalties for purchasing potentially harmful waste from scavengers.*

Chapter Objectives

- Students will learn about the use of figurative language in the Victorian era by reading the poems of Alfred, Lord Tennyson, Robert Browning, Elizabeth Barrett Browning, and Gerard Manley Hopkins.
- Students will analyze sound devices in poems.

The Quotation

Tell students that the Literary Skills Focus for this chapter is figurative language. Ask students to consider Samuel Butler's statement about life and love. Then, ask them to consider why these ideas are so often the subject of poetry. ***Possible response:*** *Protecting love and life are the two greatest human drives. However, the pursuit of love and the meaning of life are difficult to discuss concretely. Writers often turn to figurative language to make sense of love and life.*

Analyzing Visuals

The Last Day in the Old Home (1862) shows a family on their final day in their house, which must be sold because of the father's gambling.

Extension Activity Why might Victorian poets have enjoyed writing about the scene in the painting? ***Possible response:*** *The family has contrasting emotions—the men seem carefree and the women appear apprehensive. Victorian poets would have used their writing to make sense of the family's emotions.*

CHAPTER 9

Love and Loss

LITERARY SKILLS FOCUS

Figurative Language

The Last Day in the Old Home (1862) by Robert Braithwaite Martineau (1826–1869). Tate Gallery, London.

CONTENTS

> "To live is like to love—all reason is against it, and all healthy instinct for it."
>
> —**Samuel Butler**

Chapter 9

California Standards Overview

- **Reading Standard 2.2** Analyze the way in which clarity of meaning is affected by the patterns of organization, hierarchical structures, repetition of the main ideas, syntax, and word choice in the text.
- **Reading Standard 2.4** Make warranted and reasonable assertions about the author's arguments by using elements of the text to defend and clarify interpretations.
- **Reading Standard 3.1** Analyze characteristics of subgenres (e.g., satire, parody, allegory, pastoral) that are used in poetry, prose, plays, novels, short stories, essays, and other basic genres.
- **Reading Standard 3.2** Analyze the way in which the theme or meaning of a selection represents a view or comment on life, using textual evidence to support the claim.
- **Reading Standard 3.3** Analyze the ways in which irony, tone, mood, the author's style, and the "sound" of language achieve specific rhetorical or aesthetic purposes or both.
- **Reading Standard 3.4** Analyze ways in which poets use imagery, personification, figures of speech, and sounds to evoke readers' emotions.
- **Reading Standard 3.9** Analyze the philosophical arguments presented in literary works to determine whether the authors' positions have contributed to the quality of each work and the credibility of the characters. (Philosophical approach)
- **Grades 9–10 Review Reading Standard 3.11** Evaluate the aesthetic qualities of style, including the impact of diction and figurative language on tone, mood, and theme, using the terminology of literary criticism. (Aesthetic approach)

Reading Standard 3.4 (see pages A48–A50)

Figurative Language by Leila Christenbury

Characteristics of Figurative Language

- Describes one thing in terms of another, dissimilar thing and is not meant to be understood literally
- Attempts to make abstract ideas concrete, such as love, life, death, and loss
- Unifies a poet's message
- Expresses universal ideas in fresh, new ways

The poets in this chapter are masters of figurative language. Their writing transforms ordinary words and phrases into memorable impressions that capture an experience uniquely yet universally. It is no accident that poets use figurative language extensively in the highly compressed genre of poetry. Through metaphors, similes, personification and other figures of speech, poets can fully express ideas about death, loss, life, and love in language that is unique and memorable.

Alfred, Lord Tennyson uses figurative language to explore his complex feelings about death and loss in an elegy written to honor his friend Arthur Henry Hallam. In the poem *In Memoriam A.H.H.*, Tennyson personifies Nature as a feminine power who wields life and death without remorse. Nature says, "I bring to life, I bring to death" (Lyric 56, line 6). By **personifying** Nature, giving it human qualities and the ability to speak, Tennyson uses a figure of speech to depict the unexpected and seemingly capricious will that results in the death of a young man.

Tennyson uses personification throughout *In Memoriam*. The forest becomes comforting: "and the trees / Laid their dark arms about the field." Tennyson also uses a metaphor in Lyric 95, lines 21–24 to express regret that Hallam died so young:

A hunger seized my heart; I read
  Of that glad year which once had been,
  In those fallen leaves which kept their green,
The noble letters of the dead.

In another memorable poem, "Crossing the Bar," Tennyson effectively uses an extended metaphor of death as one last voyage: "When I put out to sea" (line 4). The metaphor is developed with references to the sea journey that will occur "when I embark" (line 12). An **extended metaphor** uses multiple and consistent images to discuss a less familiar subject in terms of one that is more familiar to the reader. A nautical term even represents God: "I hope to see my Pilot face to face" (line 15). Tennyson's use of figurative language creates a coherent, concrete expression of the abstractions of death and heaven.

Paolo and Francesca (c. 1887) by Charles Edward Halle.

Ask Yourself

1. How does figurative language help a reader more fully understand the complex questions and circumstances explored in poetry?
2. What is the relationship between the relatively brief length of many poems and the use of figurative language?

Learn It Online
Learn about figurative language with *PowerNotes*.
go.hrw.com H12-915 Go

Literary Skills Focus

Objectives
Students will understand the uses of figurative language.

Unit 5 Resources, Literary Focus Skill Builder, p. 5

PowerNotes, interactive lesson presentations with activities

Teacher One Stop™, on-level lesson plan and all print resources

Direct Teach

Figurative Language

- Have students read the Literary Skills Focus essay. Then, use the following question to discuss figurative language.
- Many of the abstract concepts in Victorian poetry deal with the universal experience: life, love, loss, and death. Why is it appropriate to use figurative language for this subject matter? Why would a poet want to make these ideas more concrete?

Check for Understanding

Ask Yourself

Possible responses:

1. *A reader can better visualize a concrete experience than an abstract idea.*
2. *Figurative language provides a kind of shorthand, an abbreviated way to communicate a complicated idea.*

California Standards, p. 915

- **Reading Standard 3.4** Analyze ways in which poets use imagery, personification, figures of speech, and sounds to evoke readers' emotions.

Universal Access

English Learners/Struggling Readers

English for Academic Success Ensure students' understanding of the terms *abstract* and *concrete.* Explain that abstract refers to an intangible concept, like *love, idea,* and *justice.* These concepts can be embodied by concrete objects like a wedding, an invention, and a court of law. Ask students to determine whether the words below represent an abstract concept or a concrete object.

- pride [*abstract*]
- friendship [*abstract*]
- funeral [*concrete*]
- sorrow [*abstract*]
- nature [*abstract*]
- forest [*concrete*]

Learn It Online
For a multimedia version of the instruction found on this page, use the **PowerNotes** Literary Skills Focus presentation.
go.hrw.com H12-915 Go

Standards Focus

Objectives

Students will

- understand and analyze sound devices in poetry
- analyze contrasting images

Selection Introduction

Think About the Writer

Ask students what qualities draw fans to celebrities. Why do people pay attention to famous actors, athletes, writers, and musicians?

For Independent Reading

- *Road to Camlann: The Death of King Arthur,* Rosemary Sutcliff
- *The Tempest,* William Shakespeare

Motivate

What Do You Think?/QuickTalk

Ask students to share the plots of books, films, and video games set in the Middle Ages and make inferences about their appeal.

English for Academic Success

Academic Vocabulary

Look for opportunities to use the Academic Vocabulary words.

- **benefit, *n.*:** anything that is for the good of a person or thing
- **complex, *adj.*:** hard to understand
- **publish, *v.*:** print for the public
- **respond, *v.*:** react
- **statistics, *n.*:** numerical facts

California Standards, pp. 916–925

- **Reading Standard 3.4** Analyze ways in which poets use imagery, personification, figures of speech, and sounds to evoke readers' emotions.

Preparing to Read

The Lady of Shalott
Ulysses
from In Memoriam A.H.H.
Crossing the Bar

What Do You Think? How can appearance be different from reality?

QuickTalk

Discuss why you think people remain enchanted with stories of castles, knights, quests, dragons, and ancient times.

MEET THE WRITER

Alfred, Lord Tennyson
(1809–1892)

Alfred, Lord Tennyson attained a celebrity status in England similar to what top athletes, actors, and musicians experience in our country today.

Following the Romantics

When Alfred Tennyson learned that Lord Byron had died, he went to the woods and carved on a piece of sandstone, "Byron is dead." Tennyson was fourteen years old. He felt sure that he would be a poet, and he was already practicing the dramatic gestures of the Romantic poets he admired.

Tennyson's father encouraged Alfred's interest in poetry. At Cambridge University, Tennyson's friends believed that he was destined to become the greatest poet of their generation. In 1831, lack of funds forced Tennyson to leave Cambridge. In 1832, he published his first significant book of poems, which some reviewers mocked for its melancholy themes. The next year Tennyson was devastated by the death of his closest friend, Arthur Henry Hallam. Tennyson became engaged in 1836, but the marriage was postponed because of his uncertain financial prospects.

The Melancholy Poet

During this difficult period, when both his physical and mental health suffered, Tennyson apparently never considered any career but poetry. Critics responded favorably to his two-volume *Poems* (1842), and in 1845 the government granted him an annual pension of two hundred pounds. In 1850, he published *In Memoriam,* an elegy to Hallam, was named poet laureate, and finally married.

Over the next forty years, Tennyson published nearly a dozen volumes of poetry. He became Alfred, Lord Tennyson in 1884. His poems spoke of the fragility and sadness of life, but he also believed eventually all losses would be made whole.

Think About the Writer As poet laureate, Tennyson was extremely popular. What attracted Victorian readers so deeply to Tennyson's poetry?

Alfred Tennyson, 1st Baron Tennyson (c. 1840) by Samuel Laurence. Oil on canvas. National Portrait Gallery, London.

Selection Readability	
Easily Accessible **Accessible** Challenging	These poems include unfamiliar syntax and figurative language.

Reading Standard 3.4 (see pages A48–A50)

Literary Skills Focus

Sound Devices in Poetry Poets use a range of **sound devices** to create musical effects in their poems. In "The Lady of Shalott," Tennyson uses **meter,** or rhythm, and sound repetitions such as **rhyme, alliteration,** and **assonance** to create a musical current that carries the reader through the landscape of the poem. The hypnotic force of these rhythms and repetitions also contributes to the poem's dreamy, otherworldly mood.

Reading Skills Focus

Identifying Contrasting Images Poets sometimes use **contrasting images** to give their poems a subtle sense of tension. "The Lady of Shallot" is brimming with such images: the flat, flowing river and the upright, unchanging tower; the bustling lives of the villagers and the solitary life of the Lady; the weary whisper of the reaper and the robust song of Sir Lancelot. As you read the poem, note such oppositions in setting, actions, or imagery—and pay attention to how they affect the mood.

Into Action As you read, use a chart like the one below to record oppositions. Write down at least one opposition from each part of the poem. Then, label the opposition as setting, action, or imagery.

	Opposition	Setting, Action, or Imagery?
Part I	the barges sliding by; the Lady standing motionless in the tower window	action
Part II	the red cloaks of the passing villagers; the clear blue of the mirror	

Writing Skills Focus

Think as a Reader/Writer

Find It in Your Reading The musical **sounds** of "The Lady of Shalott" contrast with the poem's unsettling, haunting **images.** As you read, record in your *Reader/Writer Notebook* examples of such sounds and images.

TechFocus As you read, imagine "The Lady of Shalott" as a silent film. Keeping the poem's contrasting images in mind, think about kinds of music that might accompany each scene or the film as a whole.

Vocabulary

surly (SUR lee) *adj.:* rude or unfriendly. *The Lady of Shalott watches surly peasants traveling along the highway toward Camelot.*

brazen (BRAY zuhn) *adj.:* made of brass. *Sir Lancelot is clad in brazen armor.*

burnished (BUR nihsht) *v.* used as *adj.:* made bright and smooth. *The knights of Camelot wear burnished helmets.*

waning (WAYN ihng) *v.:* fading gradually. *The Lady weaves as the light is waning at nightfall.*

countenance (KOWN tuh nuhns) *n.:* facial appearance. *The Lady's blank countenance suggests that she is in a trance.*

Language Coach

Multiple-Meaning Words The word *brazen* can also mean "bold." How might this second meaning relate to a knight? Write two sentences about a medieval knight, using a different sense of the word *brazen* in each.

Learn It Online
Prepare to read this poem with the video introduction online.
go.hrw.com H12-917 Go

Reader/Writer Notebook
Use your **RWN** to complete the activities for this selection.

Selection Resources

Unit 5 Resources, on-level practice and assessment, p. 7

PowerNotes, interactive lesson presentations with activities

Teacher One Stop™, on-level lesson plans and all print resources

Holt Audio Library

Holt Audio Library: Selections and Summaries in Spanish

UA: Holt Interactive Reader, p. 273

UA: Differentiating Instruction, modified lesson plans and leveled assessment, p. 215

UA: Supporting Instruction in Spanish, selection summary

UA: Resources for Teaching Advanced Students, lesson plans, p. 167

ThinkCentral Online Assessment, Selection Standards Check

ThinkCentral Online Remediation

Preteach

Introducing Vocabulary

- Review the Vocabulary words, definitions, and sentences with students.
- To reinforce the importance of the Vocabulary words, explain that these words are used to create an image, or a sensory picture, for the reader. We can visualize a *surly* person wearing a dark *countenance,* a *brazen* and *burnished* doorway as glinting with light, and a *waning* smile as fading over time like the phases of the moon.

English for Academic Success

Language Coach

Ask students to think about how a medieval knight's actions might be considered *brazen* and what type of *brazen* armor they might wear.

Literary Skills Focus

As you read and discuss the poem with students, have them note the author's use of sound devices such as assonance, alliteration, and rhyme scheme.

Reading Skills Focus

Give students a copy of the Reading Skills Focus graphic organizer before they read. (See **Unit 5 Resources.**) Tell them to use their responses to answer the questions on the Applying Your Skills page.

Writing Skills Focus

Have students record contrasting sounds and images in their **Reader/Writer Notebooks.** Students can use their notes to complete the Writing Skills Focus activity.

Learn It Online
The **PowerNotes** presentation for this lesson includes a short video that introduces the poem. The video is also available on the online version of this page.
go.hrw.com H12-917 Go

Teacher Preparation

Selection Plot Summary

The Lady of Shalott is afflicted with a curse; she must sit alone in her tower and never look upon nearby Camelot. To pass the time, she concentrates on the tapestry she is weaving and watches life in Camelot through her crystal mirror. She is distracted from her weaving by the sound of Sir Lancelot's singing. She leaves her loom and looks toward Camelot, where-upon the mirror cracks and activates her curse. She then goes down the river, writes her name on the prow of a boat, and floats toward Camelot, singing. By the time she reaches the first house, she is dead. People gather around to see her, while Lancelot utters a prayer.

Direct Teach

Think About/Talk About

Read with a Purpose Have students read the Read with a Purpose statement. Point out the word *curse*. As students read, ask them to look for figurative language that calls to mind a curse.

Comprehension

Ⓐ Reading Focus

Possible response: *An island is set off from the land and the flow of human activity. The majesty of "many-towered Camelot" in the distance contrasts with the rural setting.*

Extend the Discussion

Finding Details What details about the landscape of the island of Shalott are given in the second stanza? ***Possible response:*** *The island has a city with four gray walls and four gray towers that overlook a field of flowers.*

Speculating What do you notice about the rhyme scheme so far? Why might this kind of rhyme pattern be appropriate for the subject matter in this poem? ***Possible response:*** *The rhyme makes the poem sound musical, almost sing-song. It seems appropriate because the poem is about the mythical land of Camelot, and the rhyme makes it sound almost like a fairy tale.*

NARRATIVE POEM

The Lady of Shalott

by **Alfred, Lord Tennyson**

Read with a Purpose

Read the poem to discover how a curse affects the life of the Lady of Shalott.

Build Background

Tennyson wrote "The Lady of Shalott" in 1832 and then extensively revised it in 1842. He once commented, "I met the story first in some Italian novelle: but the web, mirror, island, etc., were my own." The symbol of Arthur's Camelot—an orderly, patriarchal kingdom in which beautiful, enchanted women languish—appealed to Tennyson and to the Victorian imagination in general. Tennyson would return to this setting in such works as "Lancelot and Elaine" and the *Idylls of the King*, a series of twelve connected poems telling the story of King Arthur and the Knights of the Round Table.

Part I

On either side the river lie
Long fields of barley and of rye,
That clothe the wold° and meet the sky;
And through the field the road runs by
    To many-towered Camelot;°
And up and down the people go,
Gazing where the lilies blow°
Round an island there below,
    The island of Shalott. Ⓐ

Willows whiten,° aspens quiver,
Little breezes dusk and shiver
Through the wave that runs forever
By the island in the river
    Flowing down to Camelot.
Four gray walls, and four gray towers,
Overlook a space of flowers,
And the silent isle imbowers°
    The Lady of Shalott.

By the margin, willow-veiled,
Slide the heavy barges trailed
By slow horses; and unhailed
The shallop° flitteth silken-sailed
    Skimming down to Camelot:
But who hath seen her wave her hand?
Or at the casement seen her stand?
Or is she known in all the land,
    The Lady of Shalott?

Only reapers, reaping early
In among the bearded barley,

3. **wold:** rolling plain.
5. **Camelot:** legendary city, site of King Arthur's court and Round Table.
7. **blow:** blossom.
10. **whiten:** show the white undersides of their leaves when blown by the wind.
17. **imbowers:** shelters with trees, gardens, and flowers.
22. **shallop:** small, open boat.

Ⓐ **Reading Focus** **Identifying Contrasting Images** What contrasting images do you find in the first stanza?

Universal Access

EL English Learners

English for Academic Success Remind students that alliteration occurs when the same letter or sound repeats at the beginning of words that are close together. Point out the phrase "road runs" in line 4 and "willows whiten" in line 10. Have students read to find more instances of alliteration. Tell them to look for words that start with the same letter and that are close together.

✔ See **UA: Differentiating Instruction** for strategies for teaching English learners.

Struggling Readers

Strategic Students Model identifying contrasting images in a poem. Tell students that they should look for opposing settings, actions, or imagery. You might say: "As I read lines 1–4, I visualize fields of barley and rye lying on both sides of a river. Then I notice that lines 5–6 mention the "many-towered Camelot" where the people are going about their business. Thus I notice a contrast in the pastoral scene in the first few lines and the towers and people of Camelot." Have students think about other contrasting setting images as they read.

Hear a song that echoes cheerly°
From the river winding clearly,
Down to towered Camelot;
And by the moon the reaper weary,
Piling sheaves in uplands airy,
Listening, whispers "'Tis the fairy
Lady of Shalott." B

30. **cheerly:** archaic for "cheerily."

Analyzing Visuals

Connecting to the Text As you read "The Lady of Shalott," look for the scene that this painting illustrates. How do the painting's details, including the expression on the Lady of Shalott's face, reflect the **mood,** or atmosphere, of the poem?

The Lady of Shalott (1888) by John William Waterhouse (1849–1917). Tate Gallery, London.

B **Literary Focus** **Sound Devices** What sound devices are used to create a musical effect in this stanza?

Think About/Talk About

Analysis

B Literary Focus

Possible response: *Alliteration in phrases such as "bearded barley," assonance in "Listening, whispers 'Tis…," and end rhymes all help to create a musical effect.*

Extend the Discussion

Monitoring Your Reading What has the speaker told us so far about the Lady of Shalott? ***Possible response:*** *She lives on a tiny island off Camelot. No one has seen her, but her song is known to all.*

Interpreting Why do you think the author refers to the Lady of Shalott as "the fairy lady"? ***Possible response:*** *Because like a fairy she is delicate, fair, and a mystery to many.*

Analyzing Visuals

Connecting to the Text: *In this painting,* ***John Williams Waterhouse*** *(1849–1917) illustrates lines 127–140 of "The Lady of Shalott" with an almost literal faithfulness. "Robed in snowy white," the Lady loosens the chain and sets out for Camelot. She expresses anticipation in her face, which reflects the dramatic mood of the poem.*

Advanced Learners

Acceleration Challenge students to write a ballad about a mythical character from a movie, a book, a comic book, or their own imagination. Encourage them to mirror the sound patterns in "The Lady of Shalott."

✔ See **UA: Resources for Teaching Advanced Students** for strategies for teaching advanced learners.

Students with Disabilities

Have students sketch a rough map of the setting of the poem, showing the river and the island, the barley and rye fields, the rolling hills, the highway, and the towers of Camelot. Then, have students re-read the poem aloud with a partner, pointing to the various locations on their map as they read.

✔ Invite students to read the poem in interactive format in **UA: Holt Interactive Reader.**

Model the Skill

- Provide students with copies of the Reading Skills Focus graphic organizer (See **Unit 5 Resources**) and use the following information to model how to identify **contrasting images.**
- Remind students that they can look for oppositions in the setting (the way the speaker describes a scene), in action (the behavior of one or more characters), or in imagery (the figurative language the author uses).
- Draw students' attention to the first two stanzas in Part II. Point out that in lines 36–44, the speaker is telling us about the Lady's solitary existence, living alone on Shalott and weaving constantly. Lines 46–54 depict the action on the highway, where the market girls and damsels are walking to Camelot.

	Opposition	Setting, Action, or Imagery?
Part II	Lady weaving alone, solitary life in contrast to the busy life of villagers along the highway	Action

Guided Practice: Apply

Think-Pair-Share Use Think-Pair-Share to promote collaborative thinking prior to responses in class discussion. Have students work with a partner and discuss various places they have lived or visited and the differences between an active city and a quiet town. Then, as a class, have students discuss what might attract a person living in a subdued town to a big city. Ask students to draw a connection to the Lady's attraction to Camelot.

Part II

There she weaves by night and day
A magic web with colors gay.
She has heard a whisper say,
A curse is on her if she stay
    To look down to Camelot.
She knows not what the curse may be,
And so she weaveth steadily,
And little other care hath she,
    The Lady of Shalott.

And moving through a mirror clear°
That hangs before her all the year,
Shadows of the world appear.
There she sees the highway near
    Winding down to Camelot;
There the river eddy whirls,
And there the surly village churls,°
And the red cloaks of market girls,
    Pass onward from Shalott.

Sometimes a troop of damsels glad,
An abbot on an ambling pad,°
Sometimes a curly shepherd lad,
Or long-haired page in crimson clad,
    Goes by to towered Camelot;
And sometimes through the mirror blue
The knights come riding two and two:
She hath no loyal knight and true,
    The Lady of Shalott.

But in her web she still delights
To weave the mirror's magic sights,
For often through the silent nights
A funeral, with plumes and lights
    And music, went to Camelot;
Or when the moon was overhead,
Came two young lovers lately wed: **C**
"I am half sick of shadows," said
    The Lady of Shalott.

Part III

A bowshot from her bower eaves,
He rode between the barley sheaves,
The sun came dazzling through the leaves,
And flamed upon the brazen greaves°
    Of bold Sir Lancelot.
A red-cross knight° forever kneeled
To a lady in his shield,
That sparkled on the yellow field,
    Beside remote Shalott. **D**

The gemmy° bridle glittered free,
Like to some branch of stars we see
Hung in the golden Galaxy.°
The bridle bells rang merrily
    As he rode down to Camelot;
And from his blazoned baldric° slung
A mighty silver bugle hung,
And as he rode his armor rung,
    Beside remote Shalott.

All in the blue unclouded weather
Thick-jeweled shone the saddle leather,
The helmet and the helmet feather
Burned like one burning flame together,

46. mirror clear: Weavers worked on the back of the tapestry so that they could easily knot their yarns. To see the front of their designs, weavers looked in a mirror that reflected the front of the tapestry.
52. churls: peasants; country folk.
56. pad: easy-gaited horse.
76. greaves: armor for the lower legs.
78. red-cross knight: The red cross is the emblem of Saint George, England's patron saint.
82. gemmy: set with jewels.
84. galaxy: Milky Way.
87. blazoned baldric: richly decorated sash worn across the chest diagonally.

C Reading Focus Identifying Contrasting Images What contrasting images appear in lines 55–70?

D Literary Focus Sound Devices Read this stanza aloud. What sound devices are used? What is the overall effect of this jumble of sounds?

Vocabulary **surly** (SUR lee) *adj.*: rude or unfriendly.
brazen (BRAY zuhn) *adj.*: made of brass.

Universal Access

Students with Disabilities

Ensure that students understand the plot of "The Lady of Shalott" by having them create a time line. Explain that the poem tells the Lady's story in chronological order, so students can trace the development of the poem over time. Students can complete this activity on their own, in pairs, or collaborate on a time line for the whole class.

AAVE Students Who Use African American Vernacular English

English for Academic Success Remind students that in formal English, the article *a* is used before words that start with consonants and the article *an* comes before words that start with a vowel. Read aloud the examples on p. 920: "a whisper" in line 39, "a mirror" in line 46, "an abbot," and "an ambling pad" in line 56. Have students share a sentence describing themselves using *a* or *an*. For example: *I am an entertaining person*, not *I am a entertaining person.*

CULTURE LINK

Camelot

According to legend, Camelot was the capital city of King Arthur's realm. Arthur and his chivalrous knights would set off for their many heroic battles from Camelot, and to Camelot they would make their triumphant return. Within the castle at Camelot, the king and his knights—some versions of the legend give the number as sixteen hundred—would gather at the Round Table to make important decisions in a democratic fashion.

Though fictional, the idea of Camelot and the Round Table is so attractive and powerful that it has survived the centuries. The term *Camelot* is now used to refer to a time, a place, or a situation that seems in many ways perfect or ideal and that is governed by a strong leader and a fair, well-defined set of rules. In the 1960s, for example, the presidency of the young, charismatic John F. Kennedy was often referred to as Camelot. Both this well-loved president and the idealistic mood of that decade helped make smash hits out of the Broadway musical *Camelot* and the 1967 film of the same name.

Top: *Camelot*, Richard Harris, 1967.
Bottom: President John F. Kennedy and the First Lady at his inaugural parade.

Ask Yourself

Sir Lancelot, the most noble knight of the Round Table, ultimately contributes to the fall of Camelot. Think about the character of Lancelot in "The Lady of Shalott." What details make him seem ideal? What details make him seem less than ideal?

As he rode down to Camelot;
As often through the purple night,
Below the starry clusters bright,
Some bearded meteor, trailing light,
Moves over still Shalott.

His broad clear brow in sunlight glowed;
On burnished hooves his war horse trode;
From underneath his helmet flowed
His coal-black curls as on he rode,
As he rode down to Camelot.
From the bank and from the river
He flashed into the crystal mirror,
"Tirra lirra," by the river
Sang Sir Lancelot. **E**

She left the web, she left the loom,
She made three paces through the room,
She saw the waterlily bloom,
She saw the helmet and the plume,
She looked down to Camelot.
Out flew the web and floated wide;

E Reading Focus Identifying Contrasting Images How do the appearance and actions of Sir Lancelot contrast with those of the Lady?

Vocabulary burnished (BUR nihsht) *v.* used as *adj.*: made bright and smooth.

Reaching Reluctant Readers

To engage uninterested students, have them work in small groups and compose several verses of rap about the Lady of Shalott and Sir Lancelot as they are described in the poem. Suggest that students borrow a few lines from the poem and combine them with their own, using the rhyme scheme *aaaa* or *abbba*. Encourage students to add in a few lines of their own perceptions of the character and emotions of the knight and the lady.

Culture Link

Ask Yourself

Possible response: *Tennyson describes Lancelot as the picture of perfection; detailing the sun "dazzling" his armor (lines 75–85) and his "broad clear brow" (line 100) Lancelot's bridle is compared to a branch of stars, (lines 83–84), and he is trailed by a meteor (line 98). However, even with all of these dazzling qualities, Lancelot never realizes his effect on the Lady of Shalott.*

Think About/Talk About

Comprehension

C Reading Focus

Possible response: *The bustling world outside contrasts with the Lady's isolated life; the funeral is contrasted with the wedding; the shadows themselves are contrasts of light and dark.*

E Reading Focus

Possible response: *The sun flames on Lancelot's "brazen greaves"; his shield "sparkles"; his bridle glitters like a "branch of stars." By contrast, the Lady lives in a world of darkness and shadows: even her castle is gray. The contrast is between life and a pale reflection of life.*

Analysis

D Literary Focus

Possible response: *There is a heavy use of alliteration in this stanza, first with the repetition of the* b *sound in* bowshot/bower/barley/brazen; *then assonance with the* z *sound repeated in* dazzling/brazen. *These features make this stanza stand out, signaling a crucial point in the poem.*

Extend the Discussion

Interpreting What role does the mirror play in the Lady's life?
Possible response: *It enables her to catch glimpses of the outside world; she needs the mirror for her work.*

Vocabulary: Own the Word

- **surly:** Have a student give an example of *surly* behavior and compare *surly* behavior with polite behavior.
- **brazen:** Ask students for suggestions of objects that are *brazen.* ***Possible responses:*** *a brass trumpet, a statue.* Use an analogy to help clarify the word by comparing the relationship between *brass* and *brazen* to that of *wood* and *wooden.*
- **burnished:** Have students suggest various objects that they believe are *burnished* in appearance. ***Possible responses:*** *a copper nameplate, golden jewelry*

The mirror cracked from side to side;
"The curse is come upon me," cried
The Lady of Shalott.

Part IV

In the stormy east wind straining,
The pale yellow woods were waning,
The broad stream in his banks complaining,
Heavily the low sky raining
Over towered Camelot;
Down she came and found a boat
Beneath a willow left afloat,
And round about the prow° she wrote
The Lady of Shalott.

And down the river's dim expanse
Like some bold seër° in a trance,
Seeing all his own mischance—
With a glassy countenance
Did she look to Camelot.
And at the closing of the day
She loosed the chain, and down she lay;
The broad stream bore her far away,
The Lady of Shalott.

Lying, robed in snowy white
That loosely flew to left and right— **F**
The leaves upon her falling light—
Through the noises of the night
She floated down to Camelot;
And as the boat head wound along
The willowy hills and fields among,
They heard her singing her last song,
The Lady of Shalott.

Heard a carol, mournful, holy,
Chanted loudly, chanted lowly,
Till her blood was frozen slowly,
And her eyes were darkened wholly,
Turned to towered Camelot. **G**
For ere she reached upon the tide
The first house by the waterside,
Singing in her song she died,
The Lady of Shalott.

Under tower and balcony,
By garden wall and gallery,
A gleaming shape she floated by,
Dead-pale between the houses high,
Silent into Camelot.
Out upon the wharfs they came,
Knight and burgher,° lord and dame,
And round the prow they read her name,
The Lady of Shalott.

Who is this? and what is here?
And in the lighted palace near
Died the sound of royal cheer;
And they crossed themselves for fear,
All the knights at Camelot:
But Lancelot mused a little space;
He said, "She has a lovely face;
God in his mercy lend her grace,
The Lady of Shalott." **H**

---

125. prow: front part of a boat.
128. seër: prophet.
160. burgher: townsperson.

F **Reading Focus** **Identifying Contrasting Images** How does the Lady's clothing differ from Sir Lancelot's? What might this contrast symbolize?

G **Literary Focus** **Sound Devices** How do the sounds in these lines reflect what is happening at this point in the poem?

H **Literary Focus** **Sound Devices** What musical sound effects are used in the last two stanzas?

Vocabulary **waning** (WAYN ihng) *v.:* fading gradually.
countenance (KOWN tuh nuhns) *n.:* facial appearance.

Think About/Talk About

Comprehension

F Reading Focus

Possible response: *Lancelot is clothed in glittering armor while the Lady is dressed in a flowing white gown. White might symbolize the Lady's innocence in contrast with Lancelot's heavy armor.*

Analysis

G Literary Focus

Possible response: *Lines 145 and 146 are broken up by commas, causing readers to pause. This causes a choppy effect, making these lines sound chilling.*

H Literary Focus

Possible response: *Alliteration is used in* gallery *and* garden, houses *and* high; *consonance is used in repeated* l *sounds and blends; assonance is used in* high *and* silent *as well as* round *and* prow; *the continued regular meter, with its repeated rhymes, carries the reader to the end of the poem.*

Extend the Discussion

Recognizing Rhetorical Devices A pathetic fallacy occurs when a writer assigns emotions and moods to a force of nature. How does the first stanza in part four qualify as a pathetic fallacy? ***Possible response:*** *The disquietude of the wind and the river reflect the Lady's doom (or nature's protest against it); the sky seems to be mourning her fate.*

Vocabulary: Own the Word

- **waning:** Since *waning* means to grow less in intensity, ask students for examples of things that could be described as *waning*. ***Possible responses:*** *the moon, ocean waves, sunset, lights.*
- **countenance:** Have a student volunteer make a facial expression in front of the class. Have the other students guess what emotion the student is representing using the word *countenance* (for example, "John has an angry *countenance*.")

California Standards, pp. 923–925

- **Reading Standard 3.3** Analyze the ways in which irony, tone, mood, the author's style, and the "sound" of language achieve specific rhetorical or aesthetic purposes or both.
- **Reading Standard 3.4** Analyze ways in which poets use imagery, personification, figures of speech, and sounds to evoke readers' emotions.
- **Grades 9–10 Review Reading Standard 1.2.** Distinguish between the denotative and connotative meanings of words and interpret the connotative power of words.
- **Writing Standard 2.3** Write reflective compositions: **a.** Explore the significance of personal experiences, events, conditions, or concerns by using rhetorical strategies (e.g., narration, description, exposition, persuasion).
- **Listening and Speaking Standard 2.3** Deliver oral responses to literature: **a.** Demonstrate a comprehensive understanding of the significant ideas of literary works (e.g., make assertions about the text that are reasonable and supportable). **b.** Analyze the imagery, language, universal themes, and unique aspects of the text through the use of rhetorical strategies (e.g., narration, description, persuasion, exposition, a combination of those strategies). **c.** Support important ideas and viewpoints through accurate and detailed references to the text or to other works.
- **Listening and Speaking Standard 2.4** Deliver multimedia presentations: **a.** Combine text, images, and sound by incorporating information from a wide range of media, including films, newspapers, magazines, CD-ROMs, online information, television, videos, and electronic media-generated images. **b.** Select an appropriate medium for each element of the presentation. **c.** Use the selected media skillfully, editing appropriately and monitoring for quality.

Applying Your Skills

Reading Standard 3.3, 3.4 (see pages A48–A50)
Writing Standard 2.3a (see pages A51–A52)

The Lady of Shalott

Literary Response and Analysis

Reading Skills Focus

Quick Check

1. Describe where the Lady lives in relation to Camelot.
2. How can the Lady of Shalott avoid the curse?
3. After she hears Lancelot sing, what does the Lady do? What happens as a result?

Read with a Purpose

4. How does the Lady's life inside the tower differ from the life of others outside the tower?

Reading Skills: Identifying Contrasting Images

5. As you read, you recorded the poem's contrasts. Add a column to your chart, and tell what Tennyson achieves through each contrast. What central idea might the poet be trying to express?

	Opposition	Setting, Action, or Imagery?	Poet's Purpose?
Part I	the barges sliding by; the Lady standing motionless in the tower window	action	
Part II	red cloaks of the passing villagers; the clear blue of the mirror		

Literary Skills Focus

Literary Analysis

6. **Analyze** Explain how lines 66–72 could **foreshadow,** or hint at, Lancelot's arrival and the Lady's actions in the second half of the poem.
7. **Summarize** Summarize the plot of this poem. What moment marks the climax?
8. **Interpret** What role does the mirror play in the Lady's life? What might the mirror symbolize?
9. **Hypothesize** Why do you think Tennyson chose not to explain the curse in more detail?

Literary Skills: Sound Devices

10. **Analyze** Locate in the poem examples of rhyme, alliteration, and assonance. How do these sound devices help bring the poem's various contrasts to life?

Literary Skills Review: Meter and Rhyme Scheme

11. **Analyze** A pattern of stressed (´) and unstressed (˘) syllables in a poem is called **meter.** The pattern of rhymed lines in a poem (for example, *abab*) is called **rhyme scheme.** Scan the poem for its meter and rhyme scheme. How do these elements contribute to the poem's mood?

Writing Skills Focus

Think as a Reader/Writer

Use It in Your Writing Review the examples of sounds and images you listed in your *Reader/Writer Notebook*. In a paragraph, rewrite the soothing sounds with more representative descriptions of their images. What words don't sound like their ideas?

What Do You Think Now? How can a reflection in a mirror differ from reality?

Check for Understanding

Independent Practice

Reading Skills Focus

Possible responses:

1. *The Lady lives on an island in a river upstream from Camelot.*
2. *She must never "look down on Camelot."*
3. *She leaves her room and looks out the window. The mirror breaks and the curse descends upon her.*
4. *She lives alone with only her weaving to stay busy. In contrast, the people of Camelot are always scurrying about their business.*
5. *Have students think about what the poet might be trying to say about the allure of reality.*

Literary Skills Focus

Possible responses:

6. *Lines 66–72 contrast a funeral with a wedding, setting the contrast of life and death as a theme.*
7. *Threatened with a curse if she looks on Camelot, the Lady spends her time weaving. One day, she hears Lancelot singing. The climax occurs when she looks at him and at Camelot, activating the curse. She finds a boat and then, singing, drifts toward Camelot as she dies.*
8. *The Lady experiences everything through mirror reflections, which symbolizes how the Lady is only experiencing a reflection of life.*
9. *Perhaps Tennyson thought by not detailing the curse, it would add to the intriguing, unsettling mood.*
10. *The poem is written mostly in iambic tetrameter. The rhyme scheme is aaabcccb. The poem's lilt comes from alliteration ("Willows whiten" line 10), and assonance ("listening, whispers," line 35). These sound devices help create the contrasting moods—bustling life in Camelot and its dull reflection in the tower.*
11. *The singsong rhyme scheme in the beginning brings a light mood to the poem. The choppy meter at the end brings out the dramatic mood of the Lady's death.*

Universal Access

Struggling Writers

Provide additional scaffolding by asking students to create a T chart that lists sounds in one column and images/ideas in the other column. For example, soothing *l* sounds are found in line 147. The image in the line is that the Lady is dying because her blood flow is stopping. Point out that the sounds in line 147 do not represent the creepy image of death. Have students find other places where the sounds contrast with the images and ideas described. Then, have them rewrite one of the soothing sounds to better represent the idea or image.

What Do You Think Now?

To help students answer this question, discuss the mirror as a symbol. Ask students to share images of mirrors and reflections they recall from fairy tales and other stories.

Independent Practice

Vocabulary Development

Vocabulary Check

1. *c* 2. *e*
3. *b* 4. *d*
5. *a*

Your Turn

Sample response:

Word: *surly*

Feelings/associations: *gruff, mean, unpleasant*

Less powerful word: *unfriendly*

Good choice? Why? *Yes.* Surly *is a stronger word for describing someone's hostility and rudeness, while* unfriendly *is weaker and not as poignant.*

go.hrw.com **WordSharp: An Interactive Vocabulary Tutor,** more practice with academic language

English for Academic Success

Language Coach

Explain that students can select the correct definition of a word by looking at the sentence surrounding it.

Possible responses:

1. *The clues in the sentence show that the word* dusk *is a verb in this context. Definition* b, *"the time of day right after the sun goes down," will not work because it is a definition for a noun. Therefore,* dusk *must mean "to make dark or shadowy."*
2. *Definition* b *fits the context of the sentence, which does not mention anything about a page or a book.*

English for Academic Success

Academic Vocabulary

Possible responses: *Responses will vary. Students will quote a published work that tells about an ideal place and describe the place in detail.*

Applying Your Skills

Grades 9–10 Review Reading Standard 1.2. (see pages A48–A50)

The Lady of Shalott

Vocabulary Development

Vocabulary Check

Match the Vocabulary words with their definitions.

1. surly	a. facial appearance
2. brazen	b. made bright and smooth
3. burnished	c. rude or unfriendly
4. waning	d. fading gradually
5. countenance	e. made of brass

Vocabulary Skills: Connotations

Imagine the perfect pair of sunglasses. Are they a subdued color, such as black or brown, or are they a flashy gold or silver? Are the frames slim and streamlined, or big and round? Even though all sunglasses serve the same purpose, they express different aspects of the wearer's personality.

Words work the same way. Although two words might have the same meaning, they each carry their own connotations. **Connotations** are the feelings and associations attached to a word. For example, would you rather be described as *nerdy* or *bright*? If you answered *bright*, you probably are not alone. For most people, the word *bright* carries positive connotations, while the word *nerdy* carries negative ones.

The following chart contains some words from "The Lady of Shalott," the feelings and associations that go with each word, and a less powerful word the poet chose not to use.

Word	Feelings or Associations	Less Powerful Word
gazing (line 7)	dreamy, unhurried	looking
imbowers (line 17)	romantic; evokes images of the Garden of Eden	shelters
casement (line 25)	romantic, airy, antiquated	window

Your Turn

Using a table like the one below, write out the Vocabulary words from "The Lady of Shalott," the feelings or associations that go with each, and a less powerful synonym. Then, explain whether you think Tennyson made a good word choice and why.

Word	Feelings or Associations	Less Powerful Word	Good Choice? Why?

Language Coach

Multiple-Meaning Words Many words have more than one meaning, for example, the word *lie.* This word can mean "to recline or stretch out," but it can also mean "to say something that is not true."

Below are sentences from "The Lady of Shalott." Consider the meanings for the italicized word, and decide which meaning the poet intended.

1. "Little breezes *dusk* and shiver through the wave that runs forever."
   a. To make dark or shadowy
   b. The time of day right after the sun goes down
2. "By the *margin,* willow-veiled, slide the heavy barges."
   a. A blank space around the edge of a page
   b. The outer edge of something

Academic Vocabulary

Write About

Movies have been made, poems have been written, and books have been published about ideal places. In a short paragraph, describe a movie or piece of writing about an ideal place. Try to use the underlined Academic Vocabulary in your response.

Universal Access: Vocabulary Development

EL English Learners

English for Academic Success Give students additional practice with connotations. Have students read each sentence below, tell whether the underlined word has a positive, neutral, or negative connotation, and then substitute a more powerful word for the underlined word.

example: We were surprised to see that nothing had changed in the past few years. [*neutral connotation; amazed*]

1. The sound of happy voices echoed across the meadow. [*positive connotation; ecstatic*]
2. Samantha sadly waved farewell at everyone before leaving. [*negative connotation; tearfully*]
3. The unfriendly stranger ran off without even apologizing to the old man. [*negative connotation; hostile*]
4. When Tom showed off his good grade to his mother, she smiled. [*positive connotation; beamed*]
5. The group all thought the scary roller coaster ride was fun. [*positive connotation; exhilarating*]

Listening and Speaking Standard 2.3a–c, 2.4a–c (see pages A53–A55)

Grammar Link

Adjective or Adverb?

Both adjectives and adverbs modify, or describe, other words. However, sometimes they can look suspiciously similar: *clear* and *clearly*, for example, or *merry* and *merrily*. How can you tell which is which?

An **adjective** modifies a noun or a pronoun. It tells *what kind, which one, how many,* or *how much*. An **adverb** modifies a verb, an adjective, or another adverb. It tells *where, when, how,* or *to what extent*. Often, but not always, an adverb ends in *–ly*. Study this sentence from "The Lady of Shallot."

> The *bridle* bells rang *merrily*
> As he rode down to Camelot.

The first italicized word is an adjective. It modifies the noun *bells* by telling *what kind* of bells they are. The second italicized word is an adverb. It modifies the verb *rang* by telling how the bells rang.

Your Turn

Tell whether ieach italicized word is an adjective or an adverb. Then, identify the word it modifies and explain how it modifies that word.

1. *Long* fields of barley lie on either side of the river.
2. In a *gray* tower on an island lives a solitary Lady.
3. The Lady weaves *steadily* both night and day.
4. Villagers pass *onward* toward Shalott.
5. The Lady sees in her mirror a *red-cross* knight.
6. The knight's armor glints *brightly* in the sun.

Writing Application Choose a paragraph you have already written and underline the adjectives, circle the adverbs, or put a question mark next to the word if you are not sure.

CHOICES

As you respond to the Choices, use these **Academic Vocabulary** words as appropriate: benefit, respond, publish, statistics, complex.

REVIEW

Talk About Opposites and Theme

In "The Lady of Shalott," Tennyson explores the tension between numerous opposites—for example, life and death, shadows and realities, solitude and society. Choose one of these pairs of opposites, and jot down details or images in the poem that seem related to the pair you chose. What central idea about the opposites do you think Tennyson is trying to communicate through these details? Present your evidence and your conclusion in the form of a short speech.

CONNECT

Investigate the Tragedy

Group Activity What was the Lady thinking? Why did she do it? Do some investigative reporting to answer these questions. Have three classmates play the roles of a reaper, Sir Lancelot, and a townsperson. Before an audience, conduct "live" interviews with each character and obtain as much newsworthy information about the Lady as you can. Then, in a concluding report, speculate about why and how the Lady died. Offer observations, too, about crime statistics and how the Lady's death is affecting the community.

EXTEND

Make a Silent Movie

TechFocus Review your notes about the kinds of background music that would work well in a silent-movie version of "The Lady of Shalott." Next, work with three or four classmates to film a scene from the poem, silent-movie style. Experiment with different background music options, and analyze the effects of each. After finalizing your soundtrack, play the movie and its accompanying music for your class.

Universal Access: Grammar Link

EL English Learners

English for Academic Success Assign students partners, pairing English learners with native speakers when possible. Ask each student to think of an object he or she finds important, and to describe the object to his or her partner. Remind students to use adjectives to describe the object's size, color, weight, shape, and other features. The partner should write down the adjectives used to describe the object. Then, have the first student describe a daily routine (getting ready for school, packing a lunch) using as many adverbs as possible, while the second student records all adverbs used. For example, a student might mention that they *slowly* roll off their bed, *sleepily* brush their teeth, *hurriedly* rummage through their closets looking for something to wear, eat breakfast *hastily*, and then *frantically* run to catch the bus. Have students switch roles so that the teller becomes the recorder.

✔ For more practice with adjectives and adverbs, see **Warriner's Handbook, GrammarNotes, and Language Handbook Worksheets.**

Independent Practice

Grammar Link

Your Turn

1. *adjective; modifies "fields"*
2. *adjective; modifies "tower"*
3. *adverb; modifies "weaves"*
4. *adverb; modifies "pass"*
5. *adjective; modifies "knight"*
6. *adverb; modifies "glints"*

Choices: Evaluation Criteria

Review: Homework
Talk About Opposites and Theme
Student synthesizes observations about oppositions to create meaning.

Connect: Homework
Investigate the Tragedy
Student draws details of the plot from the text.

Extend: Homework
Make a Silent Movie
Student choose background music that works well with the movie.

Assess

Unit 5 Resources, Selection Standards Check, p. 10

go.hrw.com **ThinkCentral Online Assessment,** Selection Standards Check

Teacher One Stop™, editable Selection Standards Check

Reteach

go.hrw.com **ThinkCentral Online Remediation**

Preteach

Introducing Vocabulary

- Review the Vocabulary words, definitions, and sentences.
- To reinforce the importance of the Vocabulary words, explain that these words all relate to the subject of old age. Aging Ulysses is *vexed* by the thought of *hoarding* his remaining years instead of using them to see more of the world. He is comforted, though, that he can leave his kingdom to his *discerning* son, who will likely rule with *prudence,* while his father tends to his *abiding* thirst for adventure.

English for Academic Success

Language Coach

After students read the **Language Coach,** point out that phrases like *rather than, instead of,* or *not* might signal an antonym pair.

Literary Skills Focus

As you read and discuss the poem with students, have them look for patterns or ideas that recur throughout the poem. Explain that these recurring ideas will help them determine the theme.

Reading Skills Focus

Give students a copy of the Reading Skills Focus graphic organizer before they read. (See **Unit 5 Resources.**) Tell them to use their responses to answer the questions on the Applying Your Skills page.

Writing Skills Focus

Have students record lines that express the theme of the poem in their **Reader/Writer Notebooks.** Students can use their notes to complete the Writing Skills Focus activity.

Learn It Online

The online version of this poem includes audio support to engage all students and to help struggling readers with reading comprehension and vocabulary.

go.hrw.com H12-926 Go

Preparing to Read

Reading Standard 2.4, 3.2, 3.9 (see pages A48–A50)

Ulysses

Literary Skills Focus

Theme In works of literature, most writers attempt to convey a central idea or insight about a subject. This idea is called the **theme** of a work. A subject and a theme are not the same. A **subject** can be summed up in a word or two—*love* or *change,* for example. A theme, however, is a complete idea that can be stated as a sentence: *True love is an illusion,* or *Change is painful but leads to growth.* In "Ulysses," Tennyson's subject is old age. As you read, ask yourself what the theme might be.

Literary Perspectives Apply the literary perspective described on page 927 as you read this poem.

Reading Skills Focus

Summarizing Teasing out a poem's theme is often easier if you summarize sections of the poem as you read. When you **summarize,** you use your own words to create a shortened version of a text. A summary usually includes the most important ideas in that text or section of text, along with one or two key details.

Into Action As you read, use a chart like this one to summarize each of the following sections of "Ulysses": lines 1–17, lines 18–32, lines 33–43, lines 44–56, and lines 57–70.

"Ulysses"	Summary
lines 1–17	Ulysses is tired of life at home. He fondly recalls the years of his youth, during which he sailed to distant lands and fought in wars.
lines 18–32	Ulysses' experiences have left him wanting more. He feels that . . . .

Writing Skills Focus

Think as a Reader/Writer

Find It in Your Reading In your *Reader/Writer Notebook,* record lines that express the **theme** of the poem. Broad statements like "I will drink / Life to the lees" contain strong clues to the poem's theme.

Vocabulary

hoard (hawrd) *v.:* save or store, often in secret. *Ulysses longs to spend rather than hoard his remaining years.*

vexed (vehkst) *v.:* troubled or disturbed. *Strong winds vexed the surface of the sea.*

discerning (dih SURN ihng) *v.* used as *adj.:* displaying good judgment; perceptive. *Ulysses knows his discerning son will not be blind to the people's needs.*

prudence (PROO duhns) *n.:* cautious management. *Ulysses hopes his son will use prudence rather than carelessness in his role as king.*

abides (uh BYDZ) *v.:* endures. *Ulysses has lost strength, but his adventurous spirit abides.*

Language Coach

Antonyms If you see an unfamiliar word, look at other words in the sentence. Do any of them seem to be **antonyms,** or opposites, of the unknown word? If so, they might provide a clue to the word's meaning. Examples of antonyms are *simple/difficult* and *begin/finish.* Find an antonym for one of the Vocabulary words in the sample sentences given above.

Reader/Writer Notebook

Use your **RWN** to complete the activities for this selection.

Learn It Online

Listen to this poem online.

go.hrw.com H12-926 Go

California Standards, pp. 926–930

- **Reading Standard 2.4** Make warranted and reasonable assertions about the author's arguments by using elements of the text to defend and clarify interpretations.
- **Reading Standard 3.2** Analyze the way in which the theme or meaning of a selection represents a view or comment on life, using textual evidence to support the claim.
- **Reading Standard 3.9** Analyze the philosophical arguments presented in literary works to determine whether the authors' positions have contributed to the quality of each work and the credibility of the characters. (Philosophical approach).

Selection Resources

Unit 5 Resources, on-level practice and assessment, p. 13

Teacher One Stop™, on-level lesson plans and all print resources

Holt Audio Library

Holt Audio Library: Selections and Summaries in Spanish

POEM

Ulysses

by **Alfred, Lord Tennyson**

Read with a Purpose

Read to discover what this "idle king" longs to do.

Build Background

Ulysses (Odysseus in Greek) is one of the Greek leaders who fought in the ten-year-long Trojan war. Homer's epic poem the *Odyssey* tells of Ulysses' equally long journey home from Troy to Ithaca. In Tennyson's poem, Ulysses, now an old king, is at home with his wife and son, Telemachus (tuh LEHM uh kuhs). After an exciting life of both marvels and horrors, the old king might finally rest, but a final journey tempts him.

It little profits that an idle king,
By this still hearth, among these barren crags,
Matched with an aged wife, I mete and dole°
Unequal laws unto a savage race,
That hoard, and sleep, and feed, and know not me. **A**
I cannot rest from travel; I will drink
Life to the lees.° All times I have enjoyed
Greatly, have suffered greatly, both with those
That loved me, and alone; on shore, and when
Through scudding drifts the rainy Hyades°
Vexed the dim sea. I am become a name;
For always roaming with a hungry heart
Much have I seen and known,—cities of men
And manners, climates, councils, governments,
Myself not least, but honored of them all,—
And drunk delight of battle with my peers,
Far on the ringing plains of windy Troy.
I am a part of all that I have met;
Yet all experience is an arch wherethrough

3. **mete and dole:** measure and give out.

7. **lees:** dregs or sediment.

10. **Hyades** (HY uh deez): stars that were thought to indicate rainy weather.

A Reading Focus **Summarizing** How would you summarize Ulysses' complaint in the first five lines?

Vocabulary **hoard** (hawrd) *v.:* save or store, often in secret.
vexed (vehkst) *v.:* troubled or disturbed.

Literary Perspectives

Analyzing Biographical Information Use biographical information to consider how events in Tennyson's own life may have helped shape "Ulysses." About the poem, Tennyson himself said: "'Ulysses' was written soon after Arthur Hallam's death, and gave my feeling about the need of going forward, and braving the struggle of life perhaps more simply than anything in *In Memoriam*." (*In Memoriam* is Tennyson's famous elegy to his beloved friend.) As you read the poem, watch for words spoken by Ulysses that echo those of Tennyson.

As you read, be sure to notice the questions in the text, which will guide you in using this perspective.

Teacher Preparation

Selection Summary

In this poem, the mythical king Ulysses, now in his old age, recalls his past adventures and longs for the excitement of his younger days. He rejects the security of a settled life, preferring to keep testing the limits and expanding the boundaries of his experience.

Direct Teach

Think About/Talk About

Read with a Purpose Have students read the Read with a Purpose statement. Point out that the king is described as *idle,* but there is something he longs to do. Ask students to speculate as to why the king is idle.

Comprehension

A Reading Focus

Possible response: *Ulysses is tired of life at home, where all he does is spend time with his wife and attempt to govern his unruly people.*

Extend the Discussion

Theme What basic theme is expressed in line 18? ***Possible response:*** *Ulysses' experiences have developed and expanded his sense of self. He identifies with the entire world.*

Vocabulary: Own the Word

- **hoard:** Contrast the word *hoard* with a weaker verb, such as *collect.* Emphasize that while both words relate to the acquisition of objects, the word *hoard* connotes doing so in secret for the purpose of storing up on an object. For example: "Mary took an extra pencil just in case her first one broke, but Franny *hoarded* a whole box."
- **vexed:** Ask students to recall a time when someone or something has *vexed* them—a homework problem, a baby sibling, etc.—and how they felt in the situation.

UA: Differentiating Instruction, graphic organizer, p. 218
UA: Supporting Instruction in Spanish, selection summary
ThinkCentral Online Assessment, Selection Standards Check go.hrw.com
ThinkCentral Online Remediation go.hrw.com

Literary Perspectives

Before students read the selection, have them read the **Literary Perspectives** about Analyzing Biographical Information. An option to help all students read the text might be to focus on Ulysses as an autobiographical work. Students can consider the character of Ulysses as a symbol for the struggles in Tennyson's own life and evaluate the character's effectiveness as such a symbol.

Remind students to use the notes and questions at the bottom of the page to help them use the perspective.

Model the Skill

- Review the concept of **theme.** For example, you might emphasize the distinction between **subject** and **theme** by explaining that the **subject** of the National Anthem can be expressed in one word, "America," but its theme must be expressed as a complete idea, "The United States, symbolized here by its flag, will always stand strong in the face of adversity."
- Tell students that they can identify the theme of a work by first identifying the subject and then asking what the speaker is about to say about the subject. In this case, the speaker, Ulysses, is talking about old age and death.
- Show students that to identify the theme, they can look for places where the speaker makes a statement about the subject: old age and death. Draw their attention to lines 31–32, and point out Ulysses' wish to *follow knowledge . . . / Beyond the utmost bound . . .* You might say: "These lines hint at the theme by addressing the subject (old age) and tells me that the speaker, even in old age, longs to explore and learn as much as possible about the world." Encourage students to record this detail in their **Reader/Writer Notebooks**.

Guided Practice: Apply

Turn-and-Talk Have students work with a partner and discuss the theme that is stated in the final five lines of the poem. Ask them to consider how this applies to the overall theme of the poem.

Gleams that untraveled world whose margin fades
Forever and forever when I move.
How dull it is to pause, to make an end,
To rust unburnished, not to shine in use! **B**
As though to breathe were life! Life piled on life
Were all too little, and of one to me
Little remains; but every hour is saved
From that eternal silence, something more,
A bringer of new things; and vile it were
For some three suns to store and hoard myself,
And this gray spirit yearning in desire
To follow knowledge like a sinking star,
Beyond the utmost bound of human thought.
    This is my son, mine own Telemachus,
To whom I leave the scepter and the isle,°—
Well-loved of me, discerning to fulfill
This labor, by slow prudence to make mild
A rugged people, and through soft degrees

Analyzing Visuals

Connecting to the Text In Greek mythology, Polyphemus was a famous Cyclops and the son of Poseidon, the god of the sea. Where is Polyphemus in this painting? What does this representation of Polyphemus tell you about Ulysses, who manages to defeat Polyphemus in Homer's epic poem the *Odyssey?*

Ulysses Deriding Polyphemus by J. M. W. Turner (1775–1851). Oil on canvas. The National Gallery, London.

34. isle: Ithaca, Ulysses' island kingdom off the west coast of Greece.

B **Literary Focus** **Theme** How does Ulysses think life should be lived?

Vocabulary **discerning** (dih SURN ihng) *v.* used as *adj.:* displaying good judgment; perceptive.
prudence (PROO duhns) *adj.:* cautious management.

Universal Access

Struggling Readers

Ask students to stop after lines 5, 17, 32, 43, and 57 and summarize what they have read. Be sure they understand how Ulysses feels at each point about his present and past experiences. Have students connect his feelings about the past and present to the theme of the poem. Tell them to complete this sentence: "the poem's central message is. . ."

Analyzing Visuals

Connecting to the Text: *Polyphemus is on the upper left, on the crag, hurling a rock at the Greeks. He merges into the landscape, as if he were a natural force himself. The representation of Polyphemus tells us that Ulysses will courageously face and conquer even enemies as strong as forces of nature.*

Subdue them to the useful and the good.
Most blameless is he, centered in the sphere
Of common duties, decent not to fail
In offices of tenderness, and pay
Meet° adoration to my household gods,
When I am gone. He works his work, I mine. **C**
There lies the port; the vessel puffs her sail;
There gloom the dark, broad seas. My mariners,
Souls that have toiled, and wrought, and thought with me,—
That ever with a frolic welcome took
The thunder and the sunshine, and opposed
Free hearts, free foreheads,—you and I are old;
Old age hath yet his honor and his toil.
Death closes all; but something ere the end,
Some work of noble note, may yet be done,
Not unbecoming men that strove with Gods. **D**
The lights begin to twinkle from the rocks;
The long day wanes; the slow moon climbs; the deep
Moans round with many voices. Come, my friends,
'Tis not too late to seek a newer world.
Push off, and sitting well in order smite
The sounding furrows;° for my purpose holds
To sail beyond the sunset, and the baths
Of all the western stars, until I die. **E**
It may be that the gulfs will wash us down;
It may be we shall touch the Happy Isles,°
And see the great Achilles,° whom we knew.
Though much is taken, much abides; and though
We are not now that strength which in old days
Moved earth and heaven, that which we are, we are,—
One equal temper of heroic hearts,
Made weak by time and fate, but strong in will
To strive, to seek, to find, and not to yield.

42. meet: proper.

Ulysses and his son Telemachus. Mosaic, 1st century CE.
Kunsthistorisches Museum, Vienna, Austria.

58–59. smite . . . furrows: row against the waves.

63. Happy Isles: in Greek **mythology, Elysium** (ih LIHZ ee uhm), where dead heroes lived for eternity.
64. Achilles (uh KIHL eez): Greek warrior and leader in the Trojan War.

C Reading Focus **Summarizing** What will Telemachus's job be when Ulysses is gone? Summarize this verse paragraph.

D Literary Focus **Theme** What does Ulysses believe about old age?

E Literary Perspectives **Analyzing Biographical Information** How do lines 58–61 echo Tennyson's own words about life and death?

Vocabulary **abides** (uh BYDZ) *v.:* endures.

Think About/Talk About

Comprehension

C Reading Focus

Possible response: *Telemachus will become king. In this paragraph, Ulysses is describing how Telemachus will rule, with "slow prudence," remaining careful "not to fail" in accordance with what is expected of him.*

Analysis

B Literary Focus

Possible response: *Ulysses feels that life is precious and should not be wasted. We should not "rust" by doing nothing, but "shine in use" by always achieving.*

D Literary Focus

Possible response: *There is honor in old age; even toward the end of life, "noble work" may be done.*

E Literary Perspectives

Possible response: *Tennyson talks about "the need of going forward and braving the struggle." Here, Ulysses expresses a similar idea saying that it is never too late to "push off" into new worlds. In other words, he will continue "going forward" until his death.*

Vocabulary: Own the Word

- **discerning:** Ask students to think of careers in which it would be important to be *discerning.* ***Possible responses:*** *a counselor, judge*
- **prudence:** Have students give examples from their own lives of decisions that they have made with *prudence* or with a lack of *prudence.*
- **abides:** Examine the way in which the word *abide* is used in the poem, pointing out how its meaning differs from the typical use of *abide* (i.e. abide by a decision.) Discuss what Ulysses may be referring to in the line "though much is taken, much *abides*"—what has been taken, and what endures?

California Standards, p. 930

- **Reading Standard 2.4** Make warranted and reasonable assertions about the author's arguments by using elements of the text to defend and clarify interpretations.
- **Reading Standard 3.2** Analyze the way in which the theme or meaning of a selection represents a view or comment on life, using textual evidence to support the claim.
- **Reading Standard 3.4** Analyze ways in which poets use imagery, personification, figures of speech, and sounds to evoke readers' emotions.
- **Reading Standard 3.9** Analyze the philosophical arguments presented in literary works to determine whether the authors' positions have contributed to the quality of each work and the credibility of the characters. (Philosophical approach).
- **Writing Standard 2.2** Write responses to literature: **a.** Demonstrate a comprehensive understanding of the significant ideas in works or passages. **b.** Analyze the use of imagery, language, universal themes, and unique aspects of the text. **c.** Support important ideas and viewpoints through accurate and detailed references to the text and to other works.

Check for Understanding

Independent Practice

Reading Skills Focus

Possible responses:

1. *Aging Ulysses is reflecting on his life and feeling unproductive.*
2. *He knows his son will be a fair and careful ruler.*
3. *He addresses his loyal sailors, commanding them to continue their noble work until the end.*
4. *His purpose is to finish his work.*
5. *Students should select words and phrases that reflect the theme.*

Vocabulary Check

6. *d* 7. *c*
8. *e* 9. *b*
10. *a*

Literary Skills Focus

Possible responses:

11. *Ulysses' present life is unsatisfying compared with his spectacular, heroic past. He values adventure over security.*
12. *He describes experience as an arch through which he sees a boundless world to be explored.*
13. *In line 3 he calls his wife aged, suggesting she is unattractive. He loves his son but seems to find him dull.*
14. *Ulysses is strong willed and curious, or restless and selfish.*
15. *His feelings of loss are apparent in lines 69–70, where he says he is "made weak by time and fate, but strong in will," thus expressing the resolve to press on.*
16. *Life without adventure is wasted; even in old age, one must continue to push on and live life.*
17. *In line 55, the "slow moon climbs" and in line 56, the sea "moans round with many voices." Ulysses expresses the desire to "sail beyond the sunset . . . (line 60)" To Ulysses, nature is a companion he would like to spend the rest of his life with.*

Applying Your Skills

Reading Standard 2.4, 3.2, 3.4, 3.9 (see pages A48–A50)
Writing Standard 2.2a–c (see pages A51–A52)

Ulysses

Literary Response and Analysis

Reading Skills Focus

Quick Check

1. Describe Ulysses' current situation as he portrays it in lines 1–11 of the poem.
2. Why is Ulysses comforted by his son's presence?
3. What other individuals does Ulysses address?

Read with a Purpose

4. What does Ulysses claim is his purpose?

Reading Skills: Summarizing

5. While reading, you summarized five different sections of the poem. Review these summaries. In a new column, choose a few words and phrases from your summaries that seem most strongly related to the poem's central meaning.

"Ulysses"	Summary	Key Words and Phrases
lines 1–17		

Vocabulary Check

Match the Vocabulary words with their definitions.

6. hoard	a. endures
7. vexed	b. cautious management
8. discerning	c. disturbed
9. prudence	d. stockpile
10. abides	e. perceptive

Literary Skills Focus

Literary Analysis

11. **Compare and Contrast** How does Ulysses contrast his past and present lives? What conclusions can you draw about his values?
12. **Interpret** What does Ulysses mean by his metaphor describing "all experience"?
13. **Infer** What do Ulysses' references to his wife and son reveal about his feelings toward them?
14. **Evaluate** What do you think of Ulysses' decision to "sail beyond the sunset"?
15. **Literary Perspectives** Tennyson's close friend Arthur Hallam died at the young age of twenty-two, and Tennyson wrote "Ulysses" shortly thereafter. How are Tennyson's feelings of loss represented in the poem?

Literary Skills: Theme

16. **Evaluate** In your view, what is the theme of "Ulysses"? Before stating the poem's theme, you may want to review the last column of your summary chart, as well the notes you made in your *Reader/Writer Notebook.*

Literary Skills Review: Imagery

17. **Analyze** Poets often use **imagery,** or language that appeals to the senses. Find three images in the last verse paragraph of "Ulysses" that describe elements of nature. What do these images tell you about the old king's attitude toward nature?

Writing Skills Focus

Think as a Reader/Writer

Use It in Your Writing Review the grand statements made by Ulysses that you recorded in your *Reader/Writer Notebook.* Choose one with which you disagree, and write your own opposing declaration. Use this declaration in a short poem addressed to Ulysses.

What Do You Think Now What does Ulysses say about the appearance and reality of old age?

Universal Access

Struggling Writers

Some students may need scaffolding to complete the Writing Skills Focus activity. Ask students to begin by writing down three or four main points that support their opposing declaration. Then, have students transition each point into a line of poetry by adding meter or a rhyme scheme.

What Do You Think Now?

To help students answer the question, have students consider how Telemachus might view his father versus how Ulysses views himself.

Assess

Unit 5 Resources,
Selection Standards Check, p. 16

ThinkCentral Online Assessment,
Selection Standards Check

Reading Standard 3.3 (see pages A48–A50) .

from In Memoriam A.H.H.

Literary Skills Focus

Tone The **tone** of a literary work is the author's attitude toward the subject. For example, the tone of a work might be reverent, sarcastic, exultant, or somber. *In Memoriam* (Latin for "in memory of") is an elegy, or a poem that mourns the death of someone important. As you might guess, the tone of such a poem is not light or playful. As you read, compare the tone at the beginning of the elegy with the tone of the later verses. As Tennyson processes his grief, his attitude toward death and loss changes.

Reading Skills Focus

Analyzing an Author's Style An **author's style** is the manner in which he or she expresses ideas. Style results from how a poet selects and uses certain tools, including words, images, sounds, rhythms, and **syntax,** or sentence structure. Look closely at what kinds of words Tennyson chooses and how he arranges them into phrases and sentences. Even as the tone of the poem shifts, what stylistic elements stay the same?

Into Action As you read, use a chart like this one to record words and phrases, images, and sound patterns that you find "uniquely Tennyson."

Words and Phrases	Images	Sounds
"dust and chaff" (55, l. 18)	"Nature, red in tooth and claw" (56, l. 15)	Alliteration: "falter where I firmly trod" (55, l. 13)

Writing Skills Focus

Think as a Reader/Writer

Find It in Your Reading If you have ever lost something or someone you loved, you know that mourning often begins with the question "Why?" As you read Lyrics 55 and 56 of *In Memoriam,* record in your *Reader/Writer Notebook* some of the **rhetorical questions** Tennyson poses.

TechFocus As you read this elegy, think about modern ways that people remember their loved ones.

Vocabulary

derives (dih RYVZ) *v.:* comes from a certain source. *The poet's feeling of despair derives from his grief.*

discord (DIHS kawrd) *n.:* conflict. *There is often discord between our desires and reality.*

redress (rih DREHS) *n.:* compensation or payment for a loss. *Tennyson seeks redress for the loss of his close friend.*

diffusive (dih FYOO sihv) *adj.:* spread out; not concentrated in one place. *The poet senses the diffusive presence of his friend's spirit.*

Language Coach

Roots The Latin word *cor* means "heart." Words built on *cor* include *accord,* which means "agreement or harmony," and *cordial,* meaning "warm and friendly." Which Vocabulary word on the list above is related to these words?

Reader/Writer Notebook

Use your **RWN** to complete the activities for this selection.

Learn It Online
Learn more about the events that shaped Tennyson at the Writers' Lives site online.

go.hrw.com H12-931 Go

Selection Resources

Unit 5 Resources, on-level practice, p. 19
Teacher One Stop™, on-level lesson plans
Holt Audio Library
Holt Audio Library: Selections and Summaries in Spanish
UA: Differentiating Instruction, graphic organizer, p. 218
UA: Supporting Instruction in Spanish, selection summary
ThinkCentral Online Assessment, Selection Standards Check

California Standards, pp. 931–940

- **Reading Standard 3.3** Analyze the ways in which irony, tone, mood, the author's style, and the "sound" of language achieve specific rhetorical or aesthetic purposes or both.

Preteach

Introducing Vocabulary

- Review the Vocabulary words, definitions, and sentences with students.
- To reinforce the importance of the Vocabulary words, explain that the narrator's choice of words *derives* from a feeling of *discord* with nature. The narrator is looking for *redress* for the loss of his close friend. The narrator eventually develops an appreciation for the *diffusive* power of nature.

English for Academic Success

Language Coach

Have students think of other words containing *cor*: [*corresponds, correlate*] Explain that *dis–* is a Latin prefix that means "away" or "apart." *Discord* literally means "apart from the heart."

Literary Skills Focus

As you read the selection with students, have them note when the poem's tone changes.

Reading Skills Focus

Give students a copy of the Reading Skills Focus graphic organizer before they read. (See **Unit 5 Resources**.) Tell them to use their responses to answer the questions on the Applying Your Skills page.

Writing Skills Focus

Have students record rhetorical questions in their **Reader/Writer Notebooks**. Students can use their notes to complete the Writing Skills Focus activity.

Learn It Online
The **Writers' Lives** feature of the Interactive Student Edition offers additional information about this author. Audio or video segments are provided for some authors.

go.hrw.com H12-931 Go

Teacher Preparation
Selection Summary
Printed here are four lyrics of Tennyson's elegy for his close friend Arthur Henry Hallam. In Lyric 55, the speaker wonders if belief in God is contradicted by the study of Nature. In Lyric 56, Nature claims power over life and expresses indifference to human ideals and hope. In Lyric 95, the speaker reads a letter written long ago by his friend. In Lyric 130, the speaker finds consolation and joy in a newfound sense of unity of God and Nature.

Direct Teach

Think About/Talk About
Read with a Purpose Have students read the Read with a Purpose statement. Point out that in this poem Tennyson grieves for the loss of a friend and struggles with his own beliefs about life after death. Ask students to note how his attitude toward life after death changes during the poem.

Comprehension
A Reading Focus

Possible response: *The speaker is saying that his faith is weak as he tries to grasp something concrete that will allow him to believe in God. The length and complexity of this sentence reflect how far he must stretch to reach anything solid.*

Extend the Discussion
Speculating Why does the speaker grasp only *dust* and *chaff* (that which is discarded when the grain is winnowed) in line 18 of Lyric 55?

Possible response: *He has little faith, and he does not find anything more sustaining.*

POEM

from In Memoriam A.H.H.

by **Alfred, Lord Tennyson**

Read with a Purpose
Read to discover what Tennyson ultimately believes about life after death.

Build Background
In Memoriam is Tennyson's elegy for Arthur Henry Hallam, his closest friend at Cambridge and his sister's fiancé. In the 131 separate lyrics of this elegy, written over seventeen years, Tennyson asks and gradually answers profound questions about life and death, religion and science, and the immortality of the soul. Tennyson considered *In Memoriam* so intensely personal that he did not plan to publish it; however, in 1850 he did finally publish what is often considered his masterpiece.

55

The wish, that of the living whole
No life may fail beyond the grave,
Derives it not from what we have
The likest God within the soul?

Are God and Nature then at strife,
That Nature lends such evil dreams?
So careful of the type° she seems,
So careless of the single life,

That I, considering everywhere
Her secret meaning in her deeds,
And finding that of fifty seeds
She often brings but one to bear,

I falter where I firmly trod,
And falling with my weight of cares
Upon the great world's altar stairs
That slope through darkness up to God,

I stretch lame hands of faith, and grope,
And gather dust and chaff, and call
To what I feel is Lord of all,
And faintly trust the larger hope.° **A**

7. type: species.

20. larger hope: Tennyson explains this phrase in his Memoirs: "that the whole human race would through, perhaps, ages of suffering, be at length purified and saved."

A Reading Focus **Analyzing an Author's Style** Paraphrase lines 17–20. How does the length and complexity of this single sentence reflect the idea it expresses?

Vocabulary **derives** (dih RYVZ) *v.:* comes from a certain source.

Universal Access

EL English Learners
English for Academic Success The frequent use of pronouns and relative pronouns might give English learners difficulty in understanding the poem. As you read the selection with students, ask them to identify the antecedent of each pronoun (*she, I, who, he*) as they read.

✔ See the **English Language Skill Builder** in UA: **Differentiating Instruction.**

Struggling Readers
Benchmark Students Explain that while all four lyrics are about the death of Tennyson's friend, each expresses a different view or mood. Have students read each lyric separately, paraphrase it in writing, and characterize its mood. Make sure that students understand that the speaker, like all who have endured a great loss, is grieving and trying to find meaning in his experience.

Clytie (c.1890) by Frederick Leighton (1830–1896). Oil on canvas.
Fitzwilliam Museum, University of Cambridge, U.K.

56

"So careful of the type?" but no.
  From scarpèd° cliff and quarried stone
  She° cries, "A thousand types are gone;
I care for nothing, all shall go.

"Thou makest thine appeal to me:
  I bring to life, I bring to death;
  The spirit does but mean the breath:
I know no more." And he, shall he, **B**

Man, her last work, who seemed so fair,
  Such splendid purpose in his eyes,
  Who rolled the psalm to wintry skies,
Who built him fanes° of fruitless prayer,

Who trusted God was love indeed
  And love Creation's final law—
  Though Nature, red in tooth and claw°
With ravine, shrieked against his creed—

Who loved, who suffered countless ills,
  Who battled for the True, the Just,
  Be blown about the desert dust,
Or sealed within the iron hills?°

2. scarpèd: eroded to a steep slope.
3. She: Nature.

12. fanes: temples.

15. red . . . claw: The phrase refers to the view of all life as a ruthless struggle for survival.

20. sealed . . . hills: preserved like fossils in rock.

B Reading Focus **Analyzing an Author's Style** What words, phrases, and sounds are echoed in this verse?

Think About/Talk About

Comprehension

B Reading Focus

Possible response: *The words* I, type, *and* he *are repeated in these stanzas. In line 6 of Lyric 56, both phrases begin with "I bring." The "I," nature, responds to humanity as an anonymous type, one species among many.*

Extend the Discussion

Finding Details How does the narrator describe man? ***Possible response:*** *He describes man as nature's last work, a beautiful specimen devoted to praising higher powers.*

Rhyme This poem is written in iambic tetrameter and follows a rhyme scheme of *abba*. How do the poem's short lines and stanzas and the rhyme scheme affect you as a reader? ***Possible response:*** *The short lines and stanzas make the poem move quickly and casually, creating an intimate tone, but the regular rhyme emphasizes the serious formality of the poem.*

Vocabulary: Own the Word

derives: Have students use the word *derive* to create sentences about themselves. ***Possible responses:*** *My work ethic derives from my desire to do well in school. My happiness is derived from looking forward to the weekend.*

Advanced Learners

Acceleration After students have read this excerpt, ask pairs to engage in a silent dialogue about the speaker's feelings about nature. Have students, in character, converse on paper by passing a sheet of paper back and forth. One member of the pair can assume the identity of the speaker, while the other assumes the identity of nature. Note that at the beginning of the poem, the speaker is completely grief stricken and feels that nature is cold and cruel. By the end, he seems to have come to terms with his grief and has different feelings toward nature.

Students with Disabilities

Tennyson's images can be vague, and the ideas in his poetry may be difficult for some students to decipher. Nevertheless, students can appreciate how the mood of the speaker changes as does the tone of the poem. Ask students to notice words that describe the various changes in tone from grief to a joyful sense of trust. For instance, the words *strife, evil, cares,* and *darkness* in the first lyric evoke doubt and conflict; whereas the words *sun, fair love,* and *rejoice* in the last lyric convey optimism and happiness.

Model the Skill

- Point out to students that this poem, in memory of Tennyson's friend, begins with a mournful and pessimistic **tone**. However, as the poet works through his thoughts and feelings, he gradually comes to a more hopeful conclusion.
- Read aloud line 25 of Lyric 56: "O life as futile, then, as frail!" Explain that this line conveys hopelessness and despair as the speaker longs for his lost friend.
- Then, read the final four lines of the poem aloud. Point out that the tone has now changed to one of hope and contentment, as the speaker feels that time and death will not break his spiritual bond with his friend.

Guided Practice: Apply

Three-Minute Review Use a Three-Minute Review to enhance active engagement and long term retention of information. After reading, group students in pairs to review the poem and look for words or phrases that create different **tones**. Have them complete a chart listing on the left the words Tennyson uses and on the right the **tone** these words create. After pairs complete their work, ask volunteers to share their charts with the whole class.

No more? A monster then, a dream,
A discord. Dragons of the prime,
That tare° each other in their slime,
Were mellow music matched with him.

O life as futile, then, as frail!
O for thy° voice to soothe and bless!
What hope of answer, or redress? **C**
Behind the veil, behind the veil.°

23. tare: archaic for "tore."

26. thy: Hallam's.

28. veil: veil of death.

95

By night we lingered on the lawn,
For underfoot the herb was dry;
And genial warmth; and o'er the sky
The silvery haze of summer drawn; **D**

And calm that let the tapers° burn
Unwavering: Not a cricket chirred;
The brook alone far off was heard,
and on the board the fluttering urn.°

And bats went round in fragrant skies,
And wheeled or lit the filmy shapes°
That haunt the dusk, with ermine capes
And woolly breasts and beaded eyes; **E**

While now we sang old songs that pealed
From knoll to knoll, where, couched at ease,
The white kine° glimmered, and the trees
Laid their dark arms about the field.

But when those others, one by one,
Withdrew themselves from me and night,
And in the house light after light
Went out, and I was all alone,

5. tapers: candles.

8. fluttering urn: teapot or coffee urn heated by a candle.

10. filmy shapes: moths.

15. kine: archaic word meaning "cattle."

C **Literary Focus** **Tone** How do the exclamation points and question mark help convey a certain tone?

D **Literary Focus** **Tone** How do the images in this verse help signal a shift in tone?

E **Reading Focus** **Analyzing an Author's Style** Find seven repetitions of the word *and* in the first three stanzas of this lyric. How does this repetition help create a certain mood?

Vocabulary **discord** (DIHS kawrd) *n.:* conflict.
redress (rih DREHS) *n.:* compensation or payment for a loss.

Universal Access

Struggling Readers

Strategic Students Model the skill of analyzing an author's style. Read aloud lines 25–28. You might say: "After reading this stanza, I notice the repeating phrase 'behind the veil' in line 28. Instead of referring to his former companion as 'gone' or 'under the earth,' he chooses to write 'behind the veil,' which makes the boundary between life and death seem more transparent. I'll note this phrase in my graphic organizer in the Words and Phrases column."

Cross-Curricular Connection

SOCIAL STUDIES: Science vs. Faith

In Victorian times, expanding knowledge of science began to challenge traditional religious views. When the speaker finds God and nature "at strife" (line 5 of Lyric 55), he is embodying not just his own conflict but a prevailing conflict of his times. Many writers and intellectuals of the day took an interest in the subject and engaged in amateur investigations of natural history. Tennyson himself belonged to the Royal Society, an academy of science, and he associated with many scientists of his day.

A hunger seized my heart; I read
Of that glad year which once had been,
In those fallen leaves which kept their green,
The noble letters of the dead.

And strangely on the silence broke
The silent-speaking words, and strange
Was love's dumb cry defying change
To test his worth; and strangely spoke

The faith, the vigor, bold to dwell
On doubts that drive the coward back,
And keen through wordy snares to track
Suggestion to her inmost cell.

So word by word, and line by line,
The dead man touched me from the past,
And all at once it seemed at last
The living soul° was flashed on mine,

And mine in this was wound, and whirled
About empyreal° heights of thought,
And came on that which is, and caught
The deep pulsations of the world,

Aeonian° music measuring out
The steps of Time—the shocks of Chance—
The blows of Death. At length my trance
Was canceled, stricken through with doubt.

Vague words! but ah, how hard to frame
In matter-molded forms of speech,
Or even for intellect to reach
Through memory that which I became; **F**

Till now the doubtful dusk revealed
The knolls once more where, couched at ease,
The white kine glimmered, and the trees
Laid their dark arms about the field;

And sucked from out the distant gloom
A breeze began to tremble o'er
The large leaves of the sycamore,
And fluctuate all the still perfume,

36. the living soul: Originally, the phrase read "his living soul." Tennyson said he changed it because he wanted the soul to be not Hallam's but the soul of "the Deity, maybe."
38. empyreal (ehm PIHR ee uhl): heavenly.
41. aeonian (ee OH nee uhn): eternal.

F **Literary Focus** **Tone** How does the poet express his attitude here?

Think About/Talk About

Comprehension

E Reading Focus

Possible response: *Repeating the word* and *emphasizes the flood of pleasant memories that overtakes the speaker as he remembers his friend. Listing the numerous joys as a series shows how fully he experienced happiness on that occasion.*

Analysis

C Literary Focus

Possible response: *The exclamation points and question marks convey the speaker's despair.*

D Literary Focus

Possible response: *The phrases "genial warmth" and "silvery haze of summer drawn" describe a pleasant pastoral scene. The warm and happy tone of these stanzas distinguishes them from the previous stanzas, which sound hopeless and despairing.*

F Literary Focus

Possible response: *He is awestruck by his experience and cannot fully comprehend it or put it into words.*

Extend the Discussion

Interpreting In lines 21–22 of Lyric 56, what is Tennyson suggesting by bringing up the violence of dragons? ***Possible response:*** *The dragons fighting each other are mellow in comparison to a God who will let humans simply die and turn to dust.*

Vocabulary: Own the Word

- **discord:** Draw a semantic web of *discord* on the board and ask students to add related concepts to the web. ***Possible responses:*** *conflict, disagreement, disharmony*
- **redress:** Examine how Tennyson uses the word *redress* in his poem. What has been lost? Can it be compensated for? ***Possible response:*** *His friend, Hallam, is no more. There is no compensation.*

Universal Access

EL English Learners

English for Academic Success Point out the use of the word *laid* in line 52. Tell students that *laid* is the past tense of the verb *lay,* meaning "to place" and can be confused with the verb *lie,* meaning "to recline." The past tense of *lie* is *lay: I lay down on the sofa after a long day.* Have students compose sentences using the present and past tense of the verbs *lie* and *lay.*

Think About/Talk About

Comprehension

Ⓖ Reading Focus

Possible response: *He uses alliteration in the words "freshlier," "full-foliaged," "folded," "flung," and "fro." Energetic verbs like "gathering" and "rocked," as well as the rhyme in "swung" and "flung," embody movement and vitality. The fertile images of the "full-foliaged elms" and the "heavy-folded rose" create a sense of hope and renewal.*

Analysis

Ⓗ Literary Focus

Possible response: *They are archaic words and make the tone more formal.*

Extend the Discussion

Figurative Language How does Tennyson combine imagery and symbolism in lines 61–64 of Lyric 95 to create a sense of renewal? ***Possible response:*** *He uses the image of the dawn breaking into day. He relies upon classical symbols of life and death: the East (place of the rising sun and therefore of life) and the West (place of the setting sun and therefore of death). The image conveys a sense of hope.*

Vocabulary: Own the Word

diffusive: Show students how the word *diffusive* is derived from the roots *dis* (apart) and *fundere* (to pour). Have students draw a link between the word *diffusive* and the idea of pouring out. Relate it to other words such *effusive* (pouring forth emotion), *refuse* (to pour back), or *infused* (to pour something into).

And gathering freshlier overhead
    Rocked the full-foliaged elms, and swung
    The heavy-folded rose, and flung
The lilies to and fro, and said, Ⓖ

"The dawn, the dawn," and died away;
    And East and West, without a breath,
    Mixed their dim lights, like life and death,
To broaden into boundless day.

130

Thy° voice is on the rolling air;
    I hear thee where the waters run;
    Thou standest in the rising sun,
And in the setting thou art fair.

What art thou then? I cannot guess;
    But though I seem in star and flower
    To feel thee some diffusive power,
I do not therefore love thee less.

My love involves the love before;
    My love is vaster passion now;
    Though mixed with God and Nature thou,
I seem to love thee more and more.

Far off thou art, but ever nigh;
    I have thee still, and I rejoice;
    I prosper, circled with thy voice;
I shall not lose thee though I die. Ⓗ

1. **thy:** Hallam's.

Ⓖ **Reading Focus** **Analyzing an Author's Style** What poetic devices does Tennyson use in this stanza?

Ⓗ **Literary Focus** **Tone** How do words like *art, thee,* and *thy* help the poet establish a certain tone in this lyric?

Vocabulary **diffusive** (dih FYOO sihv) *adj.:* spread out; not concentrated in one place.

Autumn Morning by John Atkinson Grimshaw (1836–1893). Oil on canvas.
Mallett Gallery, London.

Universal Access

Advanced Learners

Acceleration Explain that Tennyson's reaction to the death of his friend was not considered excessive at the time. Victorians took the matter of death and grieving very seriously. Have students research Victorian attitudes toward death and grieving. They may wish to consult *The Victorian Celebration of Death* by James Curl (Sutton Publishing, 2001). Give students these questions to guide their research: How did the Victorians use art forms such as poetry, song, and sculpture to express their grief? What traditions or rituals did the Victorians follow after the death of a loved one?

Reading Standard 3.4 (see pages A48–A50)

Crossing the Bar

Literary Skills Focus

Metaphor A **metaphor** is a comparison between two seemingly unlike things: for example, *Life is a journey.* By using metaphors, poets can make abstract ideas more concrete and understandable.

A metaphor does not use a connective word such as *like* or *as*. Instead, the comparison is either directly stated (*You are my sunshine*) or implied (*The rays of your love warm my life*). Note that in the implied metaphor, you must use the clues *rays* and *warm* to guess that your love is being compared to sunshine.

An **extended metaphor** is a comparison that is extended or developed over the course of several lines or verses, or even throughout an entire poem. "Crossing the Bar" is an example of the latter. In it, Tennyson uses a common experience—setting out to sea—as a metaphor for a profound and mysterious human experience.

Into Action Once you identify both halves of the comparison Tennyson makes, use a chart like the one below to record images in the poem and the ideas they may represent.

Image	Idea
"sound and foam"	the distractions of life

Writing Skills Focus

Think as a Reader/Writer

Find It in Your Reading Rather than ask questions, Tennyson forcefully declares his statements. As you read the poem, keep track of the verbs that Tennyson uses in these statements by writing them down in your *Reader/Writer Notebook*.

Language Coach

Multiple-Meaning Words The word *bar* has several meanings in the English language. In this poem, *bar* refers to a sandbar, or a long underwater ridge of sand near a shore. Use a dictionary to discover at least three other meanings for the word *bar*. Do any of these other meanings seem relevant to the poem?

Reader/Writer Notebook

Use your **RWN** to complete the activities for this selection.

Learn It Online

Check out Tennyson in the twenty-first century with these Internet links.

go.hrw.com H12-937 Go

Preteach

English for Academic Success

Language Coach

Tell students that *bar* can be a verb meaning "to shut off" or "close." It can also be a noun meaning "a broad line," as of light or color, or a law court or system of courts. Have students think of two other words that have multiple meanings.

Literary Skills Focus

As you read and discuss the selection with students, have them note examples of extended metaphor in the poem.

Writing Skills Focus

As the students read, have them record verbs used by Tennyson to declare his statements in their **Reader/Writer Notebooks**. Students can use their notes to complete the Writing Skills Focus activity.

Selection Resources

- **Unit 5 Resources,** on-level practice, p. 20
- **Teacher One Stop™,** on-level lesson plans
- **Holt Audio Library**
- **Holt Audio Library: Selections and Summaries in Spanish**
- **UA: Differentiating Instruction,** graphic organizer, p. 218
- **UA: Supporting Instruction in Spanish,** selection summary
- **ThinkCentral Online Assessment,** Selection Standards Check

California Standards, pp. 937–940

- **Reading Standard 3.4** Analyze ways in which poets use imagery, personification, figures of speech, and sounds to evoke readers' emotions.

Learn It Online

The enhanced author biography offers more information on the life of the author as well as Holt's interactive resources pertaining to the author.

go.hrw.com H12-937 Go

Teacher Preparation
Selection Summary
In "Crossing the Bar," a poem of farewell, the speaker represents the passage from life to death as a gentle, inevitable pull of the tide. He requests no "sadness of farewell" from those left behind and expresses the hope of seeing his "Pilot" when he reaches his destination.

Direct Teach

Think About/Talk About
Read with a Purpose Have students read the Read with a Purpose statement. Ask students to speculate what "crossing the bar" might metaphorically represent.

Analysis
Ⓐ Literary Focus

Possible response: *The sea represents God, the universe, or simply the mystery of whatever comes before and after death.*

Ⓑ Literary Focus

Possible response: *The Pilot is God, or whatever spiritual force creates human beings and calls them back after they die.*

Extend the Discussion
Making Generalizations How would you characterize the speaker's attitude toward death? ***Possible response:*** *The speaker is awed by the mysteries of death and the afterlife but determined to meet both with dignity; he is at peace with the natural cycle of life and death.*

POEM

Crossing the Bar

by **Alfred, Lord Tennyson**

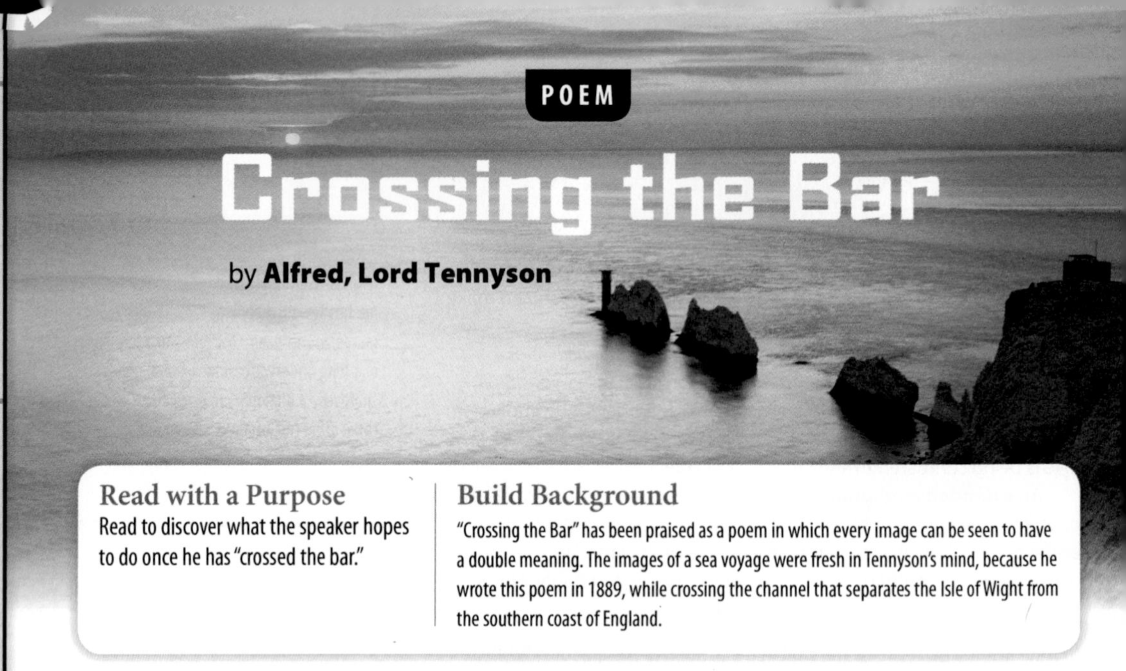

Sunset over the Needles Lighthouse and rocks, Alum Bay, Freshwater Bay, Isle of Wight, England.

Read with a Purpose
Read to discover what the speaker hopes to do once he has "crossed the bar."

Build Background
"Crossing the Bar" has been praised as a poem in which every image can be seen to have a double meaning. The images of a sea voyage were fresh in Tennyson's mind, because he wrote this poem in 1889, while crossing the channel that separates the Isle of Wight from the southern coast of England.

Sunset and evening star,
    And one clear call for me!
And may there be no moaning of the bar,
    When I put out to sea,

But such a tide as moving seems asleep,
    Too full for sound and foam,
When that° which drew from out the boundless deep Ⓐ
    Turns again home.

Twilight and evening bell,
    And after that the dark!
And may there be no sadness of farewell,
    When I embark;

For though from out our bourne° of Time and Place
    The flood may bear me far,
I hope to see my Pilot face to face Ⓑ
    When I have crossed the bar.

7. that: the soul.
13. bourne (bawrn): archaic word meaning "boundary."

13. bourne (bawrn): archaic word meaning "boundary."

Ⓐ **Literary Focus** **Metaphor** Metaphorically speaking, what is the "boundless deep" of the sea?

Ⓑ **Literary Focus** **Metaphor** To whom or what is Tennyson implicitly comparing the pilot of a ship?

California Standards, pp. 939–940
- **Reading Standard 3.3** Analyze the ways in which irony, tone, mood, the author's style, and the "sound" of language achieve specific rhetorical or aesthetic purposes or both.
- **Reading Standard 3.4** Analyze ways in which poets use imagery, personification, figures of speech, and sounds to evoke readers' emotions.
- **Grades 9–10 Review Reading Standard 3.7** Recognize and understand the significance of various literary devices, including figurative language, imagery, allegory, and symbolism, and explain their appeal.
- **Writing Standard 1.3** Structure ideas and arguments in a sustained, persuasive, and sophisticated way and support them with precise and relevant examples.
- **Writing Standard 2.2** Write responses to literature: **c.** Support important ideas and viewpoints through accurate and detailed references to the text and to other works. **d.** Demonstrate an understanding of the author's use of stylistic devices and an appreciation of the effects created.
- **Writing Standard 2.6** Deliver multimedia presentations: **c.** Use the selected media skillfully, editing appropriately and monitoring for quality.
- **Listening and Speaking Standard 2.2** Deliver oral reports on historical investigations: **a.** Use exposition, narration, description, persuasion, or some combination of those to support the thesis. **b.** Analyze several historical records of a single event, examining critical relationships between elements of the research topic. **c.** Explain the perceived reason or reasons for the similarities and differences by using information derived from primary and secondary sources to support or enhance the presentation.

Applying Your Skills

Reading Standard 3.3, 3.4 (see pages A48–A50)
Writing Standard 1.3, 2.2d (see pages A51–A52)

from In Memoriam A.H.H. / Crossing the Bar

Literary Response and Analysis

Reading Skills Focus

Quick Check

1. In Lyric 55 of *In Memoriam*, what complaint does the speaker voice against Nature?
2. The speaker of "Crossing the Bar" is a mariner, or sailor. What is the mariner about to do?

Read with a Purpose

3. What do these two poems reveal about Tennyson's views of life after death?

Reading Skills: Analyzing an Author's Style

4. Review the words and phrases you recorded in your chart for In *Memoriam*. Then, write a sentence or two in which you make some generalizations about Tennyson's style. Which elements of his style seem most dominant?

Vocabulary Check

Complete each sentence with a Vocabulary word:

derives discord redress diffusive

5. *In Memoriam* addresses the confusion and ______ that can follow the death of a loved one.
6. The speaker complains that after such a loss, adequate ______ seems impossible.
7. The speaker discovers that true joy ______ from a deep connection to nature.
8. He realizes that in nature, he can sense the ______ presences of his friend's immortal soul.

Literary Skills Focus

Literary Analysis

9. **Compare and Contrast** Compare the aspects of Nature described in Lyrics 55 and 56 with those in Lyric 130. What difference is there?
10. **Analyze** Lyric 95 moves from a local scene to "empyreal heights of thought" (line 38) and back. How is this movement related to the speaker's **mood** in Lyrics 55 and 56, as well as in Lyric 130?
11. **Interpret** Paraphrase each of the speaker's wishes and hopes, and explain what they show about the speaker's feelings.

Literary Skills: Tone / Metaphor

12. **Evaluate** How would you characterize the poet's **tone** in Lyrics 55 and 56 of *In Memoriam?* How does this tone change in Lyrics 95 and 130?
13. **Analyze** In "Crossing the Bar," Tennyson uses the experience of a sailor embarking on a long voyage as a **metaphor** for death. Use details from the poem to explain how the metaphor is extended.

Literary Skills Review: Rhyme

14. **Compare and Contrast** The pattern of rhymed lines in a poem is called its **rhyme scheme.** How do the different rhyme schemes of the two poems contribute to the poems' moods?

Writing Skills Focus

Think as a Reader/Writer

Use It in Your Writing Review the notes you took on Tennyson's use of questions and direct statements. Pose your own question, and use at least three of Tennyson's verbs as you try to answer the question.

What Do You Think Now How can we view death as a beginning instead of an ending?

Universal Access

Struggling Writers

Some students may need additional scaffolding to complete the Writing Skills Focus activity. Ask them first to create one list of questions in the poem and another list of Tennyson's verbs. After reviewing both lists, have students generate their own question about death and use at least three verbs from their list to answer the question in one declarative statement.

What Do You Think Now?

Remind students that both poems express a view that death can be a beginning rather than an ending. Ask students to write down their own ideas of how death can be a beginning.

Check for Understanding

Independent Practice

Reading Skills Focus

Possible responses:

1. *The speaker finds no evidence of life after death in Nature.*
2. *He is about to set out to sea.*
3. *He sees the afterlife as a final resting place for souls to be with God.*
4. *Students should base their comments on Tennyson's use of images, phrases, and sounds.*

Vocabulary Check

5. *discord* 6. *redress*
7. *derives* 8. *diffusive*

Literary Skills Focus

Possible responses:

9. *Lyrics 55 and 56 present nature in conflict with God and with mankind. In Lyric 130, the speaker is at peace with nature and with the reality of death.*
10. *Lyrics 55 and 56 express the speaker's despair, and Lyric 130 expresses faith in life and death. In this change of heart, as well as that of Lyric 95, the speaker returns to the original scene, but with a new perspective.*
11. *The speaker of "In Memoriam A.H.H." rails against death but hopes to hold on to his friend's memory. The speaker of "Crossing the Bar" compares death to a gentle tide and hopes to meet his "Pilot," showing his acceptance of death and his belief in an afterlife.*
12. *His anguished tone becomes calmer and more accepting.*
13. *He extends it through the imagery of a gently pulling tide, a bell calling for someone, and a Pilot waiting to welcome the speaker.*
14. *The* abba *rhyme scheme of the first poem lends itself to the extended sentences that express the speaker's confusion in "In Memoriam." The* abab *rhyme scheme of the second poem is more like that of a hymn and conveys the speaker's calmness.*

Independent Practice

Choices: Evaluation Criteria

Review: Homework
Identify Tone of Voice

Students' readings use different tones appropriately.

Review: Homework
Picture This Word Picture

Students' visual representations address both the literal and figurative meanings in the poem.

Connect: Homework
Analyze Modern Elegies

- Students point out advantages and disadvantages in online or modern memorials and Tennyson's poem.
- Students compare the modern memorials to Tennyson's version.

Connect: Timed Writing 40–50 Minutes

Students' opinions are supported by textual evidence.

Extend: Homework
Research Victorian Grief

Students demonstrate thorough research of Victorian attitudes toward death.

Extend: Homework
Research Victorian Science

- Students' writings show a connection between science and Tennyson's poems.
- Students write in the voice of a Victorian scientist.

Applying Your Skills

from In Memoriam A.H.H. / Crossing the Bar

Reading Standard 3.3; **Grades 9–10 Review Reading Standard** 3.7 (see pages A48–A50)
Writing Standard 1.3, 2.2c, 2.6c (see pages A51–A52)
Listening and Speaking Standard 2.2a–c (see pages A53–A55)

CHOICES

As you respond to the Choices, use these **Academic Vocabulary** words as appropriate: benefit, respond, publish, statistics, complex.

REVIEW

Identify Tone of Voice

Literary tone is closely linked with tone of voice. In a conversation, you can identify a person's tone by considering the topic and by listening to the rhythms and pitches of the voice. You might decide that the speaker's tone is sullen, earnest, or pleading. With a partner, take turns reading aloud "Crossing the Bar" or a lyric from *In Memoriam.* Use a different tone of voice each time. Then discuss which tone seems more consistent with Tennyson's and why.

Picture This Word Picture

A metaphor is a kind of word picture: It helps a reader envision an everyday object or idea in a fresh, surprising way. If it is a powerful metaphor, the image lingers in the reader's mind and haunts it long after the book is closed. The extended metaphor in Tennyson's "Crossing the Bar" is this kind of metaphor. Though the poem is short, the image it presents is clear, simple, and strong. Using the medium of your choice, create a visual representation of the metaphor. As you plan your rendering, consider what details you might use to suggest both the literal and the figurative meanings present in the poem.

CONNECT

Analyze Modern Elegies

TechFocus How do modern people create memorials for their loved ones? Compile a list of different types of online or modern memorials, and compare and contrast them to Tennyson's poem. What advantages are there in a poetic elegy? What benefits does technology provide? Do modern memorials also address the questions of life and death that Tennyson did? Share your findings with your class.

Argue About Life and Death

Timed Writing The speaker's attitude toward death in "Crossing the Bar" can be described as noble, courageous, accepting, reverent, complex—and unusual. Was the mariner able to live up to his lofty ideas about death when it came time for him to "cross"? Write an expository essay analyzing the views on death and the use of language in "Crossing the Bar." Be sure to cite passages from the text to support your response.

EXTEND

Research Victorian Grief

Tennyson's response to the death of his friend was not considered excessive at the time. Victorians took the matter of death and grieving very seriously. With a partner, research Victorian attitudes toward death and grieving. In addition to your own questions, use these questions to guide your research:

- What traditions did the Victorians follow after the death of a relative?
- How did the Victorians use art forms such as poetry, song, and sculpture to express their grief?

A Victorian mourning card (1896).

Research Victorian Science

Choose a natural phenomenon in the poem—such as the evening star or ocean tides—and research how it was perceived or explained by Victorian scientists. Do your findings shed additional light on Tennyson's poem? Posing as a Victorian scientist and fan of Tennyson, present your findings to the class.

Assess

Unit 5 Resources,
Selection Standards Check, p. 22

ThinkCentral Online Assessment,
Selection Standards Check

Teacher One Stop™,
editable Selection Standards Check

Reteach

ThinkCentral Online Remediation

Reading Skills Focus

Reading Standard 2.4 (see pages A48–A50)

My Last Duchess / Porphyria's Lover

Drawing Inferences from Textual Clues by Kylene Beers

To understand complex poetry, you need to be a bit of a detective. Like a skilled crime-scene investigator, good readers draw inferences from clues in the poem and their own experience. You will find clues in the author's use of language, character description, and events. Putting all of the clues together will help you unravel the poem's mysteries.

The poet supplies the textual clues in the poem, and you provide the background information or internal clues from your experience. Together, this information becomes an inference—a connection between mind and text. An active reader is always making inferences and then reading further to confirm or adjust his or her inferences as information is revealed. The clues reveal the mysteries of reading poetry.

In Robert Browning's dramatic monologue "My Last Duchess," the reader has the opportunity to practice inference skills. The first character introduced is the poem's speaker, the Duke. The reader can immediately begin to infer aspects of the Duke's personality from his words (textual clues).

> But to myself they turned (since none puts by
> The curtain I have drawn for you, but I)
> And seemed as they would ask me, if they
> durst. (lines 9–11)

The Duke's words remind us of people we have known who were arrogant ("if they durst") and controlling ("none . . . but I"). The words and our experience (internal clues) combine so that we can infer that the Duke is a domineering and haughty man who sought to control the Duchess as well as everyone else. As you continue to read, this inference may be confirmed and expanded, or you may adjust the inference about the Duke.

The Duke continues to speak in lines 31–34:

> She thanked men—good! but thanked
> Somehow—I know not how—as if she
> ranked
> My gift of a nine-hundred-years-old name
> With anybody's gift.

These lines confirm the first inference that the Duke is an arrogant, egotistical man who expects subservience and obedience from his wife. While the Duke criticizes his late wife, his words actually confirm and expand our inference about him.

Your Turn

Re-read lines 31–34. Focus this time on making inferences about the Duchess. Combine your background experience with people (internal clues) and the words describing the Duchess (textual clues) to make an inference about her. What kind of person can we infer her to be, based on the text and our experience?

Read lines 43–45 to add clues to your inference about the Duchess.

> Oh, sir she smiled, no doubt,
> Whene'er I passed her; but who passed
> without
> Much the same smile?

How does this additional information confirm or adjust your inferences about the Duke and his last Duchess?

Reading Skills Focus

Objectives

Students will draw inferences from textual clues.

Unit 5 Resources, Reading Focus Skill Builder, p. 6

PowerNotes, interactive lesson presentations with activities

Teacher One Stop™, on-level lesson plan and all print resources

Direct Teach

Drawing Inferences from Textual Clues

This feature gives students practice in drawing inferences from textual clues in "My Last Duchess," a poem that has many details in its dramatic dialogue. Have students read the feature and complete the Your Turn activity before reading the poem.

Check for Understanding

Your Turn

Ask students to infer a trait about the duchess based on lines 31–34. [*Answers may include ingratitude, indifference, shallowness, or insincerity.*] Once they have started the process of making an inference, ask them to read lines 43–45 and confirm or adjust their initial conclusions about the duchess. [*Students may confirm their inference that the duchess is insincere or conclude that she is genuinely friendly.*]

California Standards, p. 941

- **Reading Standard 2.4** Make warranted and reasonable assertions about the author's arguments by using elements of the text to defend and clarify interpretations.

Universal Access

English Learners

English for Academic Success To help students understand the Reading Skills Focus, review the meanings of the following words:

- **unravel**—clear up, solve. *After new evidence was uncovered, the lawyer could finally unravel the complicated case.*
- **domineering**—overbearing, overpowering. *Whenever they argued, he always lost to his domineering wife.*
- **egotistical**—wrapped up in oneself. *His egotistical nature was not helpful for job interviews.*

Standards Focus

Objectives

Students will

- understand dramatic monologue
- make reasonable assertions about the author's argument

Selection Introduction

Think About the Writer

Ask students to think about the Brownings' courtship in letters, their bold elopement, and subsequent marriage. Students could reflect on the view of love embodied in Robert Browning's actions and poems.

For Independent Reading

- *Rebecca*, Daphne Du Maurier
- *The Taming of the Shrew*, William Shakespeare

Motivate

What Do You Think?/QuickWrite

Have students write in their **Reader/ Writer Notebooks** about a time when they misjudged someone else's attitude or intention.

English for Academic Success

Academic Vocabulary

Look for opportunities to use the Academic Vocabulary words in this unit.

- **complex, *adj.*:** hard to understand
- **publish, *v.*:** print and issue for the public
- **respond, *v.*:** react

California Standards, pp. 942–951

- **Reading Standard 2.4** Make warranted and reasonable assertions about the author's arguments by using elements of the text to defend and clarify interpretations.
- **Reading Standard 3.1** Analyze characteristics of subgenres (e.g., satire, parody, allegory, pastoral) that are used in poetry, prose, plays, novels, short stories, essays, and other basic genres.
- **Grades 9–10 Review Reading Standard 3.11** Evaluate the aesthetic qualities of style, including the impact of diction and figurative language on tone, mood, and theme, using the terminology of literary criticism. (Aesthetic approach).

Preparing to Read

My Last Duchess
Porphyria's Lover

What Do You Think? How can appearance be different from reality?

QuickWrite

What does true love look like? Can you tell it when you see it? Write a quick description of how people appear when they are in love, and then think about how the appearance of love can mask real motives that have little to do with love.

MEET THE WRITER

Robert Browning
(1812–1889)

Robert Browning pioneered psychological portraiture in poetry by digging into fascinating and macabre characters to discover their motives.

Ambitions and Education

Robert Browning aspired to dazzle the world with his range and variety as a poet. His education allowed him to indulge his wide-ranging interests in music, art, the history of medicine, drama, literature, entomology, and other widely varying topics. Browning was mainly educated at home by tutors and by his wide reading in his banker-father's extensive library. As a teenager, Browning was brilliant, undisciplined, and determined to be a poet like his idol, Percy Bysshe Shelley. After a term at the University of London, he published (at his family's expense) several poems and plays, but not until he began writing the short dramatic monologues of the 1840s—poems like "My Last Duchess"—did he find his proper form.

A Marriage of True Minds

In 1845, Browning wrote to Elizabeth Barrett, already an established poet: "I do . . . love these books with all my heart—and I love you too." Four months after the two poets began their correspondence, they met and fell in love. They secretly married in 1846, and a week later they eloped to Italy. Mr. Barrett, who forbade his daughter to marry, estranged himself from his famous daughter for the rest of her life.

Browning's happy marriage confirmed his belief that only by acting boldly can one wrest what is good from an imperfect world. He lived in Italy until Elizabeth's death in 1861, when he returned to England with their son. During the 1860s, his fame began to grow. Readers understood that by asking them to figure out and judge wicked men like the Duke in "My Last Duchess," Browning was really challenging them to discover when love nourished and why it kills. Browning believed that human beings must act by a moral standard and that those who act bravely will be rewarded.

Think About the Writer How did Browning's ideas about love in his own life work their way into his poetry?

Robert Browning (1858) by Michele Gordigiani. Oil on canvas. National Portrait Gallery, London.

Selection Readability	
Easily Accessible Accessible **Challenging**	These poems include unfamiliar setting; historical context; serious subject matter; complex syntax; abstract symbolism.

Reading Standard 2.4, 3.1; **Grades 9–10 Review**
Reading Standard 3.11 (see pages A48–A50)

Literary Skills Focus

Dramatic Monologue "My Last Duchess" and "Porphyria's Lover" are two of Browning's earliest and most popular **dramatic monologues,** poems in which a speaker who is not the poet addresses a listener who does not speak. Instead of telling us directly what the speakers and the other characters are like, Browning allows the speakers to reveal themselves, the other characters, and the situation by dropping indirect clues that we must piece together.

Literary Perspectives Apply the literary perspective described on page 944 as you read these poems.

Reading Skills Focus

Drawing Inferences from Textual Clues Reading one of Browning's dramatic monologues is like having a curtain pulled slowly aside to reveal a portrait of the speaker. By putting what you "see"—clues from the text—together with what you already know about human behavior, you can **draw inferences,** or logical conclusions, about each speaker's motives and character traits.

Into Action As you read each poem, use a chart to record the speaker and each character he introduces. Then, write down details from the poem that give clues to each person's character and to the situation.

Character	Clues About the Character	Clues About the Situation
Duke	No one draws aside the curtain except him.	He is showing someone a portrait of his late wife.
Duchess	She is no longer the Duchess.	

Writing Skills Focus

Think as a Reader/Writer

Find It in Your Reading Browning heightens the tension in "My Last Duchess" with **rhetorical questions,** or questions that the listener is not meant to answer. Record these questions in your *Reader/Writer Notebook.*

TechFocus As you read these poems, think about how you would present them as a podcast.

Vocabulary

officious (uh FIHSH uhs) *adj.:* eager to give unwanted help. *The Duke remembers his wife's kind response to officious young men.*

munificence (myoo NIHF uh suhns) *n.:* generosity. *The Duke views munificence as a form of weakness.*

pretense (prih TEHNS) *n.:* weakly supported claim. *The Duke's pretense that his wife was foolish goes unchallenged.*

object (AHB jihkt) *n.:* goal or purpose. *What was the Duke's true object in showing the portrait?*

displaced (dihs PLAYST) *v.* used as *adj.:* moved from its usual location. *Porphyria's displaced hair gives the speaker an evil idea.*

Language Coach

Multiple-Meaning Words The word *last* has several meanings in English. In the title "My Last Duchess," *last* means "previous" (as in "last night" or "last week") rather than "final." What does this use of the word *last* imply about the Duke and his wife or wives?

Learn It Online
Meet "My Last Duchess" through the video introduction online.
go.hrw.com H12-943 Go

Reader/Writer Notebook
Use your **RWN** to complete the activities for these selections.

Selection Resources

Unit 5 Resources, on-level practice and assessment, p. 25

PowerNotes, interactive lesson presentations with activities

Teacher One Stop™, on-level lesson plans and all print resources

Holt Audio Library

Holt Audio Library: Selections and Summaries in Spanish

UA: Holt Interactive Reader, p. 283

UA: Differentiating Instruction, modified lesson plans and leveled assessment, p. 219

UA: Supporting Instruction in Spanish, selection summary

UA: Resources for Teaching Advanced Students, lesson plans, p. 170

ThinkCentral Online Assessment, Selection Standards Check

ThinkCentral Online Remediation

Preteach

Introducing Vocabulary

- Review the Vocabulary words, definitions, and sentences with students.
- Tell students that the *object* of these words is to clarify the Duke's dramatic monologue. The Duke informs his guest that his deceased wife's frequent kindness toward *officious* men was *displaced.* Although the Duke makes a *pretense* of graciousness in his manner toward his guest, he has already shown his true lack of *munificence* in calling for the death of his wife, the last Duchess.

English for Academic Success

Language Coach

Tell students that the Duke uses the word *last* because he expects to find another Duchess to replace the previous one. The word also implied that the speaker might have killed other wives, too.

Literary Skills Focus

As you read and discuss the poem, have students note what the monologues reveal about the speakers, characters, and the situation.

Reading Skills Focus

Give students a copy of the Reading Skills Focus graphic organizer before they read. (See **Unit 5 Resources.**) Tell them to use their responses to answer the questions on the Applying Your Skills page.

Writing Skills Focus

Tell students to record any rhetorical questions asked in their **Reader/Writer Notebooks.**

Learn It Online
The **PowerNotes** presentation for this lesson includes a short video that introduces the poem. The video is also available on the online version of this page.
go.hrw.com H12-943 Go

Teacher Preparation

Selection Summary

In this dramatic monologue, a duke invites a guest to examine a painting of his "last" duchess. The listener learns that the powerful duke was jealous of the attention his young wife bestowed on others, and so he "gave commands" to have the duchess put to death. At the end of the poem, the reader discovers that the silent listener is representing a count whose daughter the duke is negotiating to marry.

Direct Teach

Think About/Talk About

Read with a Purpose Have students read the Read with a Purpose statement. Ask students to consider whether the Duke's disapproval of his wife was justified.

Analysis

A Literary Focus

Possible response: *The reader understands that this is to be a monologue because the speaker asks a question, but he does not allow the listener to answer.*

Build Background: The Brownings

After their elopement, Robert and Elizabeth Browning lived in the Casa Guidi in Florence, Italy. Named the "Casa Guidi" by Elizabeth, the suite of eight rooms in the fifteenth-century Palazzo Guidi remained the Brownings' home for fourteen years and the place where they wrote many of their most famous poems.

Responses to Margin Questions

Lines 1–13 *The speaker is showing the guest a portrait of his last wife. The speaker remarks that, like all strangers who see the portrait, the guest seems to be wondering why the Duchess wears a passionate expression.*

Lines 13–21 *Frà Pandolf's compliments made her blush.*

POEM

My Last Duchess

by **Robert Browning**

Read with a Purpose

Read to discover why the "last" Duchess is no longer the Duke's wife.

Build Background

Browning identified his speaker as Alfonso II d'Este (1533–1597), the fifth and last Duke of Ferrara, a powerful Italian nobleman of the Renaissance. The Duke's three marriages were all political alliances. His first wife, Lucrezia de' Medici, the fourteen-year-old daughter of the Duke of Florence, died two years into the marriage—possibly from poisoning. In the poem the Duke is negotiating to marry the daughter of a Count.

That's my last Duchess painted on the wall,
Looking as if she were alive. I call
That piece a wonder, now; Frà Pandolf's° hands
Worked busily a day, and there she stands.
Will 't please you sit and look at her? I said
"Frà Pandolf" by design, for never read
Strangers like you that pictured countenance,
The depth and passion of its earnest glance,
But to myself they turned (since none puts by
The curtain I have drawn for you, but I)
And seemed as they would ask me, if they durst,
How such a glance came there; so, not the first
Are you to turn and ask thus. Sir, 'twas not **A**
Her husband's presence only, called that spot
Of joy into the Duchess' cheek; perhaps
Frà Pandolf chanced to say, "Her mantle° laps
Over my lady's wrist too much," or, "Paint
Must never hope to reproduce the faint
Half flush that dies along her throat." Such stuff
Was courtesy, she thought, and cause enough
For calling up that spot of joy. She had
A heart—how shall I say?—too soon made glad,

? **1–13.** *Paraphrase these opening lines. What are the speaker and his guest doing? What does the guest ask the speaker?*

3. Frà Pandolf's: reference to Brother Pandolf, a fictitious painter and monk.

? **13–21.** What does the speaker think brought the "spot of joy" (line 21) to his wife's face?

16. mantle: cloak.

A **Literary Focus** **Dramatic Monologue** What clues in lines 1–13 suggest that the poem is going to be a monologue rather than a conversation?

Literary Perspectives

Analyzing Style You can use this perspective to identify elements of these two poems that make them dramatic monologues—for example, a speaker and a silent listener—and to evaluate how well Browning executes the form. You can also use this perspective to identify and analyze other formal elements of the poems, such as meter, rhyme scheme, word choice, and imagery, that contribute to Browning's style. How do these elements affect the poems' overall tone and meaning?

As you read, be sure to notice the questions in the text, which will guide you in using this perspective.

Literary Perspectives

Before students read the selection, have them read the **Literary Perspectives** about Analyzing Style. Ask students if they have ever "talked the ear off" of someone. Use their responses to discuss dramatic monologues. Have students make a list of reasons why the speaker of the poem may not allow a response. Ask students to discuss if the poem would be more or less effective if it were a dialogue between two characters.

Remind students to use the notes and questions at the bottom of the page to help them use the perspective.

Universal Access

Struggling Readers

To help students read "My Last Duchess," model the reading skill of drawing inferences from textual clues. You might say: "When you read that the Duke refers to his wife as his 'last' Duchess, you can infer that for some reason she is no longer the Duchess." Encourage students to pay attention to detail in the poem that offer clues to the Duchess' fate.

Analyzing Visuals

Connecting to the Text How does this image convey "the depth and passion of its earnest glance?" How does the woman in the painting compare with the "last" Duchess in the poem?

The Veiled Woman, or La Donna Velata (c. 1516) by Raphael (Raffaello Sanzio of Urbino) (1483–1520). Palazzo Pitti, Florence, Italy.

Real Issues, Real Experts

*Holt author **Kylene Beers** offers strategies for teaching "My Last Duchess" and "Porphyria's Lover."*

Point out that "My Last Duchess" and "Porphyria's Lover" do not include stanza breaks. Most sentences in "My Last Duchess" lack punctuation at the end of the line. The reader must read the whole monologue without pause through the end of the lines to the next line, in imitation of the uninterrupted speech of the Duke himself. However, "Porphyria's Lover" does include punctuation at the end of most lines, making the reader pause before continuing. The speaker in "Porphyria's Lover" delivers his monologue deliberately and slowly, building suspense.

Have students work in pairs, first reading the poems alone and then writing a summary together. The pairs should share their summaries with the class and rewrite a dramatic monologue of one of the poems from the point of view of the deceased woman. In writing their version of the poem, students should think about the details in the poems, as well as the role of women during the Victorian period.

Think About/Talk About

Extend the Discussion

Making Inferences In line 22, the Duke comments that his last wife had a heart "too soon made glad." What might he be saying about the Duchess? ***Possible response:*** *The Duchess was too frivolous and easily charmed by others.*

Dramatic Monologue Why might the Duke be so eager to discuss the painting of his "last" wife with visitors? ***Possible response:*** *The Duke may wish to brag about the beauty and charm of his former wife to curious visitors who often ask him about her.*

Analyzing Visuals

Connecting to the Text: *The woman seems to look directly at the viewer, conveying depth and passion through her steady, purposeful gaze. The woman in the painting, like the last Duchess, is blushing and seems pleased.*

Think About/Talk About

Comprehension

Ⓒ Reading Focus

Possible response: *The speaker considers it beneath him to have to teach his wife to be less attentive to other men.*

Ⓓ Reading Focus

Possible response: *The Duke said he "gave commands" and "all smiles stopped together," which suggests that he gave an order to have her killed.*

Analysis

Ⓑ Literary Perspectives

Possible response: *The rhyming words "fool" and "mule" have negative connotations, implying stupidity; perhaps the Duke thought his wife unintelligent.*

Response to Margin Question

Lines 21–34 *The Duke complains that the Duchess did not seem to value her husband's attentions more than the attentions of other men. He is suggesting that she was unfaithful.*

Vocabulary: Own the Word

- **officious:** Have students give examples from their everyday lives of people who are overly *officious,* providing help when it is not solicited.
- **munificence:** Demonstrate the difference in connotation between generosity and *munificence.* You might say: "Giving away old outgrown clothing is certainly generous, but to give away your brand new designer sneakers is sheer *munificence.*"
- **pretense:** Ask students, "Have you ever excused yourself from a meal on a *pretense?*" Explain when and what the *pretense* was.
- **object:** What was the Duke's *object,* according to lines 52 and 53? ***Possible response:*** *to wed the Count's daughter*

Too easily impressed; she liked whate'er
She looked on, and her looks went everywhere.
Sir, 'twas all one! My favor° at her breast,
The dropping of the daylight in the West,
The bough of cherries some officious fool
Broke in the orchard for her, the white mule Ⓑ
She rode with round the terrace—all and each
Would draw from her alike the approving speech,
Or blush, at least. She thanked men—good! but thanked
Somehow—I know not how—as if she ranked
My gift of a nine-hundred-years-old name
With anybody's gift. Who'd stoop to blame
This sort of trifling? Even had you skill
In speech—(which I have not)—to make your will
Quite clear to such an one, and say, "Just this
Or that in you disgusts me; here you miss,
Or there exceed the mark"—and if she let
Herself be lessoned so, nor plainly set
Her wits to yours, forsooth,° and made excuse,
—E'en then would be some stooping; and I choose
Never to stoop. Oh sir, she smiled, no doubt, Ⓒ
Whene'er I passed her; but who passed without
Much the same smile? This grew; I gave commands;
Then all smiles stopped together. There she stands
As if alive. Will 't please you rise? We'll meet Ⓓ
The company below, then. I repeat,
The Count your master's known munificence
Is ample warrant° that no just pretense
Of mine for dowry will be disallowed;
Though his fair daughter's self, as I avowed
At starting, is my object. Nay, we'll go
Together down, sir. Notice Neptune,° though,
Taming a seahorse, thought a rarity,
Which Claus of Innsbruck° cast in bronze for me!

25. favor: gift; token of love.

? 21–34. *What complaints does the speaker make against the Duchess's character in these lines? What most bothers him?*

41. forsooth: archaic for "in truth."

50. warrant: guarantee.

54. Neptune: in Roman mythology, god of the sea.

56. Claus of Innsbruck: imaginary sculptor.

Ⓑ Literary Perspectives Analyzing Style What are the rhyming words in this couplet (lines 27–28)? What does this word choice imply about the speaker's attitude toward his wife?

Ⓒ Reading Focus Drawing Inferences from Textual Clues What inferences can you draw about the Duke from these lines?

Ⓓ Reading Focus Drawing Inferences from Textual Clues What do you suspect happened to the Duchess? On what clues do you base this guess?

Vocabulary **officious** (uh FIHSH uhs) *adj.:* eager to give unwanted help.
munificence (myoo NIHF uh suhns) *n.:* generosity.
pretense (prih TEHNS) *n.:* weakly supported claim.
object (AHB jihkt) *n.:* goal or purpose.

Universal Access

Advanced Learners

Acceleration Challenge students to research the political philosopher Niccolò Machiavelli (1469–1527), author of a famous treatise on statecraft titled *The Prince.* Machiavelli believed that in politics, ethical considerations are secondary to effectiveness. Ask students to relate the views of Browning's Duke to Machiavelli's philosophy in a short essay.

Literary Perspectives

Guide students in answering the **Literary Perspectives** question on this page. Ask students to consider the connotation of a *fool.* Contrast the meaning of this word with alternative word choices, such as *secret admirer* or *gentleman.*

POEM

Porphyria's Lover

by **Robert Browning**

Read with a Purpose
Read to discover the mental state of Porphyria's lover.

Build Background
Like the American writer Edgar Allan Poe, Browning had a taste for morbid psychology; he once accused his wife, Elizabeth Barrett Browning, of lacking "a scientific interest in evil." In "Porphyria's Lover," he pursues that interest, exploring the complexity of human motivation.

The rain set early in tonight,
The sullen wind was soon awake,
It tore the elm tops down for spite,
And did its worst to vex the lake:
I listened with heart fit to break.
When glided in Porphyria; straight
She shut the cold out and the storm,
And kneeled and made the cheerless grate
Blaze up, and all the cottage warm;
Which done, she rose, and from her form
Withdrew the dripping cloak and shawl,
And laid her soiled gloves by, untied
Her hat and let the damp hair fall,
And, last, she sat down by my side
And called me. When no voice replied,
She put my arm about her waist,
And made her smooth white shoulder bare,
And all her yellow hair displaced,
And, stooping, made my cheek lie there,
And spread, o'er all, her yellow hair,
Murmuring how she loved me—she
Too weak, for all her heart's endeavor,
To set its struggling passion free
From pride, and vainer ties dissever,°
And give herself to me forever. **A**
But passion sometimes would prevail,
Nor could tonight's gay feast restrain
A sudden thought of one so pale
For love of her, and all in vain:
So, she was come through wind and rain.
Be sure I looked up at her eyes
Happy and proud; at last I knew
Porphyria worshipped me: Surprise **B**
Made my heart swell, and still it grew
While I debated what to do.
That moment she was mine, mine, fair,
Perfectly pure and good: I found
A thing to do, and all her hair
In one long yellow string I wound
Three times her little throat around,
And strangled her. No pain felt she;
I am quite sure she felt no pain.
As a shut bud that holds a bee,
I warily oped° her lids; again
Laughed the blue eyes without a stain.

24. dissever: separate.
44. oped: archaic for "opened."

Vocabulary **displaced** (dihs PLAYST) *v.* used as *adj.:* moved from its usual location.

A **Reading Focus** **Drawing Inferences from Textual Clues** What appears to be the main obstacle to this relationship?

B **Literary Focus** **Dramatic Monologue** What does the speaker reveal about himself and his perceptions in lines 26–33?

Universal Access

Struggling Readers
Tell students to pay close attention to Browning's punctuation in lines 6–7 and elsewhere in the poem because phrases or sentences often continue on to the next line. Tell students that in couplets, each pair of lines is a distinct meaning unit. Suggest that reading the poem aloud may help them more readily identify such sentences.

Advanced Learners
Enrichment After students have read the poem, have them work in small groups. Ask them to discuss the personal qualities of Porphyria and her lover—her sensuousness, his almost clinical detachment from the act of killing her. Then, ask students to contrast the two characters with the Duke and his "Last" Duchess in "My Last Duchess." Ask students which character they sympathize with the most and why.

Teacher Preparation
Selection Summary
This dramatic monologue opens with a description of the setting—a violently windy and rainy night. The speaker waits for Porphyria. He describes her entrance and her loving embrace. Although she worships him, he believes that she is too weak to commit to him totally, so he strangles her with her own hair, imagining that she welcomes her own death as a release from unwanted bonds. At the end of the poem, the speaker notices that God has not reacted to his awful deed.

Direct Teach

Think About/Talk About
Read with a Purpose Have students read the Read with a Purpose statement. Point out the key word "strangled" (line 41) and the key phrase "And thus we sit together now" (line 58) to determine what occurs and when the action takes place.

Comprehension
A Reading Focus
Possible response: *Porphyria seems to be reluctant or unable to commit fully to the speaker; she seems to have other bonds or ties that she cannot or will not break.*

Analysis
B Literary Focus
Possible response: *He realizes that Porphyria "worshipped" him at that moment. This realization seems to come almost as a surprise to him.*

Vocabulary: Own the Word
displaced: Ask students to give examples of *displaced* persons in history or in the present. ***Possible response:*** *Native Americans in colonial times*

Think About/Talk About

Analysis

Ⓒ Literary Focus

Possible response: *The lines suggest that the speaker wants to hold on to this moment of perfect love. He feels she is glad to be dead.*

Ⓓ Literary Perspectives

Possible response: *The meter of the poem is very regular, with lines often flowing into other lines, creating a feeling of unruffled, detached smoothness.*

Extend the Discussion

Irony In what way is the speaker's behavior after he strangles Porphyria the very opposite of love? ***Possible response:*** *The speaker feels close to Porphyria only after she is dead.*

Analyzing Visuals

Connecting to the Text: *This image represents how the speaker longs to have Porphyria's love, just like her "yellow hair," stay wrapped around him forever.*

Analyzing Visuals

Connecting to the Text How might this image represent the speaker's feelings about Porphyria?

Mannshode I Kvinnehar (Man's Head in Woman's Hair) (1896) by Edvard Munch (1863–1944).
The Museum of Modern Art, N.Y. / The Munch-Ellingsen Group / Artists Rights Society (ARS), N.Y.

And I untightened next the tress
About her neck; her cheek once more
Blushed bright beneath my burning kiss:
I propped her head up as before,
Only, this time my shoulder bore
Her head, which droops upon it still;
The smiling rosy little head,
So glad it has its utmost will,
That all it scorned at once is fled,
And I, its love, am gained instead! Ⓒ
Porphyria's love: She guessed not how
Her darling one wish would be heard.
And thus we sit together now,
And all night long we have not stirred,
And yet God has not said a word! Ⓓ

Ⓒ **Literary Focus** **Dramatic Monologue** What do lines 46–55 suggest about the speaker?

Ⓓ **Literary Perspectives** **Analyzing Style** Is the meter of this poem regular or irregular? How does the meter contribute to the poem's cold, detached tone?

California Standards, pp. 949–951

- **Reading Standard 2.4** Make warranted and reasonable assertions about the author's arguments by using elements of the text to defend and clarify interpretations.
- **Reading Standard 3.1** Analyze characteristics of subgenres (e.g., satire, parody, allegory, pastoral) that are used in poetry, prose, plays, novels, short stories, essays, and other basic genres.
- **Reading Standard 3.3** Analyze the ways in which irony, tone, mood, the author's style, and the "sound" of language achieve specific rhetorical or aesthetic purposes or both.
- **Grades 9–10 Review Reading Standard 1.1** Identify and use the literarl and figurative meanings of words and understand word derivations.
- **Grades 9–10 Review Reading Standard 3.11** Evaluate the aesthetic qualities of style, including the impact of diction and figurative language on tone, mood, and theme, using the terminology of literary criticism. (Aesthetic approach).
- **Writing Standard 1.4** Enhance meaning by employing rhetorical devices, including the extended use of parallelism, repetition, and analogy; the incorporation of visual aids (e.g., graphs, tables, pictures); and the issuance of a call for action.
- **Writing Standard 2.2** Write responses to literature: **d.** Demonstrate an understanding of the author's use of stylistic devices and an appreciation of the effects created.
- **Listening and Speaking Standard 1.7** Use appropriate rehearsal strategies to pay attention to performance details, achieve command of the text, and create skillful artistic staging.
- **Listening and Speaking Standard 1.9** Use research and analysis to justify strategies for gesture, movement, and vocalization, including dialect, pronunciation, and enunciation.
- **Listening and Speaking Standard 2.4** Deliver multimedia presentations: **a.** Combine text, images, and sound by incorporating information from a wide range of media, including films, newspapers, magazines, CD-ROMs, online information, television, videos, and electronic media-generated images. **b.** Select an appropriate medium for each element of the presentation.

Applying Your Skills

Reading Standard 2.4, 3.1, 3.3; **Grades 9–10 Review** Reading Standard 3.11 (see pages A48–A50)
Writing Standard 1.4, 2.2d (see pages A51–A52)

My Last Duchess / Porphyria's Lover

Literary Response and Analysis

Reading Skills Focus

Read with a Purpose

1. In "My Last Duchess," how does the Duke's version of the demise of the last Duchess differ from your interpretation of the events? Why?
2. At the end of "Porphyria's Lover," how does understanding when the monologue occurs change your understanding of the events?

Reading Skills: Drawing Inferences from Textual Clues

3. Now that you have read the poems, review the textual clues you recorded in your charts. Add another column to your chart, and record at least two inferences about each character in it.

Character	Character Clues	Situation Clues	Inferences
Duke	No one draws aside the curtain except him.	He is showing someone a portrait of his late wife.	1. 2.

Literary Skills Focus

Literary Analysis

4. **Infer** Assume that the Count's emissary in "My Last Duchess" is an insightful person. What impression is the Duke unintentionally making?
5. **Analyze** Read the last sentence of "My Last Duchess." Is it an effective conclusion? What might the speaker intend to convey with such a comment?
6. **Evaluate** What leads the speaker in "Porphyria's Lover" to assert that Porphyria "felt no pain"? What do you think of this claim?
7. **Extend** "Porphyria's Lover" was originally published with another monologue under the title *Madhouse Cells.* How does knowing the collection's title affect your interpretation of the poem?
8. **Literary Perspectives** Choose either rhyme, meter, or word choice, and explain how Browning's use of this formal element contributes to the **mood,** or feel, of each poem. Use specific examples from the poems to support your claims.

Literary Skills: Dramatic Monologue

9. **Analyze** In a dramatic monologue, the reader sees things only through the perspective of the speaker. Summarize each speaker's attitude toward his former lover. Why might you question their assessments?

Literary Skills Review: Irony

10. **Analyze** A discrepancy between what is said and what is really meant, or between what appears to be true and what is really true, is irony. What irony can you find in "My Last Duchess" and "Porphyria's Lover"?

Writing Skills Focus

Think as a Reader/Writer

Use It in Your Writing Review the rhetorical questions you recorded in your *Reader/Writer Notebook* as you read "My Last Duchess." Choose one of them, and use it as a starting point for your own dramatic monologue in response to the Duke.

What Do You Think Now? Which speaker more successfully hides reality from us? Explain.

Universal Access

Struggling Writers

Some students may need additional scaffolding to complete the Writing Skills Focus activity. Have students brainstorm characteristics of the Duchess before writing from her point of view. For example, students might perceive the Duchess as arrogant and flirtatious, or timid and loyal. Encourage students to create a web diagram. Then, have them address the question in line 35 or the one in line 45. Remind students to reveal the character of the Duchess through her words.

What Do You Think Now?

To help students answer this question, have them compare how readers discover that the Duchess and Porphyria were killed. The narrator of "My Last Duchess" simply states, "I gave commands; / Then all smiles stopped together," whereas the narrator of "Porphyria's Lover" specifically states that he strangled her. Have them point to other evidence that supports their position.

Check for Understanding

Independent Practice

Reading Skills Focus

Possible responses:

1. *The Duke admits no guilt, but readers know otherwise.*
2. *Understanding that the speaker is currently sitting beside Porphyria's corpse adds to the morbid mood of the poem.*
3. *Have students make two inferences about each character and add them to their Reading Skills Focus graphic organizer.*

Literary Skills Focus

Possible responses:

4. *The Duke suggests that the life of the next duchess may also be at risk.*
5. *The last line develops the tactful but uncaring character of the Duke, making this a good conclusion.*
6. *The speaker is trying to justify his actions by claiming that he did not cause her any additional pain by killing her.*
7. *The speaker's actions are less surprising if the readers already associate him with a madhouse.*
8. *The couplets in "My Last Duchess" add to the formal tone employed by the Duke. In "Porphyria's Lover," the alternating rhyme followed by couplets give the poem a scattered feeling, which accentuates the madness of the speaker.*
9. *The speaker in "Porphyria's Lover" loves Porphyria deeply and killed her because he thought it was in her best interest. The Duke is indifferent about his last Duchess and had her killed because it was in his best interest. Their assessments are to be questioned because both men attempt to justify their actions.*
10. *The irony lies in the conflict between the actual deaths of each woman and the way the speakers present those deaths.*

Independent Practice
Vocabulary Development

Vocabulary Check

1. *b* **2.** *a*
3. *c* **4.** *e*
5. *d*

Your Turn

Word: *object*

Meanings: something material that can be perceived by the senses; to oppose something firmly with words or arguments; Word Origin: Latin objicere, *"to throw in the way"*

Word: *stoop*

Meaning 1: a habitual or temporary forward bend of the back and shoulders; Word Origin: from Middle English stoupen.

Meaning 2: a platform or entrance stairway to a house' Word Origin: from Dutch stoep, *"step in a stair"*

Word: *fair*

Meaning 1: pleasing to the eye; Word Origin: from Old English faeger, *"beautiful"*

Meaning 2: a gathering of buyers and sellers at a place; an exhibition; Word Origin: from Latin fēria, *"holiday"*

go.hrw.com **WordSharp: Interactive Vocabulary Tutor,** more practice with academic language

English for Academic Success
Language Coach

Give students other examples of idioms from Porphyria's Lover—"Surprise made my heart swell," "my burning kiss." The kiss does not literally burn, nor does the speaker's heart literally swell up. Burning here means "passionate," and a "swelling heart" refers to emotional intensity.

English for Academic Success
Academic Vocabulary

Possible responses: *Responses will vary. Students should discuss the importance of communication, mutual understanding, trust, and what they consider a "romantic" relationship. Students should also include modern-day examples in their* *response.*

Grades 9–10 Review Reading Standard 1.1 (see pages A48–A50)

My Last Duchess / Porphyria's Lover

Vocabulary Development

Vocabulary Check

Match each Vocabulary word with its meaning.

1. officious	**a.** generosity
2. munificence	**b.** eager to give unwanted help
3. pretense	**c.** weak claim
4. object	**d.** moved
5. displaced	**e.** goal or purpose

Vocabulary Skills: Multiple-Meaning Words

Many words have, over time, accumulated more than one meaning. Consider Browning's usage of the word *favor* in line 25 of "My Last Duchess." Browning uses the word *favor* in a sense that was common from the medieval period through the Victorian age—to refer to a small token of romantic love. Today, when we refer to a trinket given or received at a party—a "party favor"—we are invoking this meaning of the word. If we say, "You favor your father," we are using the word in a very different sense—to resemble someone in appearance. All of these definitions of *favor* are related, however, in that they share the same origin: They all come from a Latin word meaning "to regard with goodwill."

	Meanings:	**Word Origin:**
favor	• a small gift of love • to resemble someone	Latin favere meaning "regard with goodwill"

Your Turn

Using a dictionary, find two meanings for each of the following words: *object, stoop, fair.* If both the meanings share the same origin, create for that word a chart like the one for *favor.* If they have different origins, create a chart like the following.

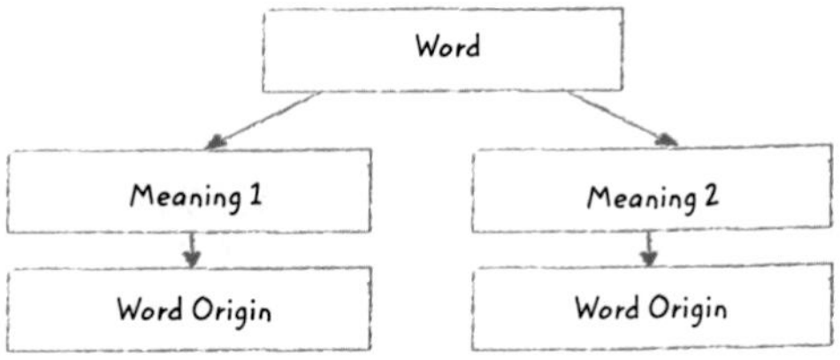

Language Coach

Idioms An **idiom** is a frequently used expression that is not meant to be taken literally. For example, the Duke says that in some of her behaviors, the Duchess *missed the mark.* This does not mean that she was literally trying to hit a target and missed. It means that her words or actions were in some way not appropriate. To help you remember the meanings of these expressions, try making a simple sketch for each that suggests both their literal and nonliteral meanings.

Academic Vocabulary

Talk About

In a small group, discuss the complex aspects of romantic relationships revealed in the two monologues by Browning. Do these situations exist today? Specify modern-day examples in your response.

Universal Access: Vocabulary Development

EL English Learners

English for Academic Success To give students more practice with idioms, have them discuss the literal and nonliteral meanings of the following idioms with a partner. Then, have them use each of the idioms in a sentence.

1. a gray area [*something that can not be clearly defined*]
2. give someone credit [*recognize someone for doing something well*]
3. scratch the surface [*not getting the core information, just a part*]
4. cold shoulder [*treating someone coldly*]
5. out of the blue [*unexpected*]
6. by the book [*according to the rules*]
7. give someone the slip [*hide from someone*]
8. tough cookie [*a stubborn person*]

Reading Standard 2.4, 3.1 (see pages A48–A50)
Listening and Speaking Standard 1.7, 1.9, 2.4a, 2.4b (see pages A53–A55)

Grammar Link

Using Participles to Combine Sentences

A **participle** is a verb form that can be used as an adjective, or modifier. For example, in the phrase *falling star,* the participle *falling* modifies the noun *star.* A **participial phrase** is made up of a participle and all of its own modifiers and complements. Consider the opening sentence from "My Last Duchess":

> That's my last Duchess painted on the wall,
> **Looking as if she were alive.**

In this sentence, the participial phrase *looking as if she were alive* modifies the noun *Duchess.* Participial phrases like this one are often used to combine two sentences. For example, Browning might have expressed the same idea in this way:

> That's my last Duchess painted on the wall.
> She looks as if she were alive.

In your view, which version is more effective? Why?

Your Turn

Use a participle or a participial phrase to combine each pair of sentences.

1. The Duke drew the curtain aside. He smiled at his guest.
2. The Duke turned to leave. He pointed out a bronze sculpture of Neptune.
3. Porphyria knelt. She lit a fire in the hearth.
4. Porphyria unwrapped her shawl. She sat down next to her lover.
5. She looked in his eyes. She drew her last breath.

Writing Application Choose a composition or essay you have already written, and look for short or choppy sentences that can be combined by using participles. Rewrite a few of these sentences. How does the use of participles affect the sound and flow of your writing?

CHOICES

As you respond to the Choices, use these **Academic Vocabulary** words as appropriate: benefit, respond, publish, statistics, complex.

REVIEW

Perform a Dramatic Reading

Group Activity Because a dramatic monologue is a kind of poetic speech, it begs to be read aloud. Work with a partner to prepare two dramatic readings of either of Browning's poems, each one conveying a different interpretation of the Duke's tone. (For example, the Duke's words may sound sinister if read one way, but regretful or mournful if read another way.) Use facial expressions, gestures, and tone of voice to create two distinct impressions. Perform your dramatic readings for the class.

CONNECT

Conduct an Interview

Choose either the Duke or Porphyria's lover, and work with a partner to conduct a TV interview with that character. During the course of the interview, the speaker should be questioned about his relationship to either the Duchess or Porphyria and his role in her disappearance. Prepare some questions that can be answered by quoting directly from the poem. After rehearsing your interview, present it to the class or publish a transcript of it in your school paper.

EXTEND

Capture the Story Digitally

TechFocus Choose one of these poems, and record it as a podcast. As you read, pay attention to the tone of voice you use to bring the dramatic monologues alive. How can you use your voice to illustrate the tone and mood of the poem, as well as to reveal the character of the speaker? Share your finished podcast with your class.

Learn It Online
Explore Multiple Meaning words online.
go.hrw.com H12-951 Go

Universal Access: Grammar Link

Struggling Learners

English for Academic Success Some students may have difficulty with using participles to combine sentences. Use this lesson to reinforce the standard English use of participial phrases as modifiers. Remind students that the main clause expresses the most important idea and that the participial phrase expresses the idea of lesser importance. Participial phrases may be placed at the beginning or the end of the sentence or between the subject and the predicate. Encourage students to experiment with the placement of these phrases until they find the one that works best.

✔ For more practice with participles, see **Warriner's Handbook, GrammarNotes,** and **Language Handbook Worksheets.**

Independent Practice

Grammar Link

Your Turn

1. *Smiling at his guest, the Duke drew the curtain aside.*
2. *Turning to leave, the Duke pointed out a bronze sculpture of Neptune.*
3. *Kneeling, Porphyria lit a fire..*
4. *Unwrapping her shawl, Porphyria sat down next to her lover.*
5. *Looking in his eyes, she drew her last breath.*

Choices: Evaluation Criteria

Review: Homework
Perform a Dramatic Reading
Students effectively interpret the speaker's words.

Connect: Homework
Conduct an Interview
Students question the speaker based on details in the text.

Extend: Homework
Capture the Story Digitally
Slideshow accurately illustrates students' vision of how the story is told.

Assess

Unit 5 Resources, Selection Standards Check, p. 29

go.hrw.com **ThinkCentral Online Assessment,** Selection Standards Check

Teacher One Stop™

Reteach

go.hrw.com **ThinkCentral Online Remediation**

Learn It Online
WordSharp: An Interactive Vocabulary Tutor provides additional support for vocabulary development. Multimedia tutorials show students how to apply vocabulary skills to unfamiliar words—and how to make those words their own.
go.hrw.com H12-951 Go

Standards Focus

Objectives

Students will
- analyze the Petrarchan sonnet form
- paraphrase a text to clarify meaning

Selection Introduction

Think About the Writer

Ask students to consider the kind of effects that Elizabeth Barrett Browning's physical limitations and her relationship with her father had on her poetry. Ask students to also think about how her father may have appeared to community members versus what he was really like, and how that may have affected Elizabeth Barrett Browning.

Motivate

What Do You Think?/QuickWrite

Ask students to think of examples in real life, literature, or film where love powerfully brought about some kind of change. Have students write about the kind of effects love can have on people in their **Reader/Writer Notebooks.**

For Independent Reading

Romeo and Juliet, William Shakespeare

English for Academic Success

Academic Vocabulary

Look for opportunities to use the Academic Vocabulary words in this unit.

- **publish, *v.*:** print and issue for the public

Preparing to Read

Sonnet 43

What Do You Think? How can appearance be different from reality?

QuickWrite

What kind of love do you think is most powerful—romantic love, love between friends, love of family, or some other kind of love? Record your thoughts in your *Reader/Writer Notebook.*

Elizabeth Barrett Browning (1858) by Michele Gordigiani. Oil on canvas. National Portrait Gallery, London.

MEET THE WRITER

Elizabeth Barrett Browning

(1806–1861)

Elizabeth Barrett Browning was one of the most famous poets of her day—more successful during her lifetime than her husband, Robert Browning.

A Renaissance Woman

Barrett Browning is remembered today for her *Sonnets from the Portuguese,* of which "How Do I Love Thee?" is the best known. During her lifetime, Barrett Browning was well known as a daring, versatile poet who frequently wrote on intellectual, religious, and political matters. When she was young, she studied Greek, Latin, French, Italian, history, and philosophy—an uncommon education for a woman in nineteenth-century England. She published long narratives, a novel in verse, translations of Greek plays, and poems that dealt with the abolition of slavery, the exploitation of children in factories, religious belief, and Italian nationalism.

Through Suffering to Freedom

Through the first half of her busy literary career, Elizabeth Barrett was a semi-invalid. Her illnesses have been variously diagnosed: She may have had a lung problem dating from childhood, as well as an injured spine from a fall she took as a teenager. It is certain, however, that her ailments were intensified by the sometime bullying protectiveness of her father and by the drugs routinely prescribed in those days for a "nervous collapse."

In 1845, she met Robert Browning. During their secret courtship, Barrett wrote forty-four sonnets tracing the development of her love for him. The next year they married secretly and eloped to the Continent. Her father never forgave her for the marriage (he had forbidden all his children to marry), nor did he ever see her again. Barrett Browning flourished in Italy and bore a son when she was forty-three years old: her own "young Florentine" with "brave blue English eyes."

Think About the Writer How do you think childhood experiences contribute to a person's development?

California Standards, pp. 952–955

- **Reading Standard 2.2** Analyze the way in which clarity of meaning is affected by the patterns of organization, hierarchical structures, repetition of the main ideas, syntax, and word choice in the text.
- **Reading Standard 3.1** Analyze characteristics of subgenres (e.g., satire, parody, allegory, pastoral) that are used in poetry, prose, plays, novels, short stories, essays, and other basic genres.

Selection Readability	
Easily Accessible **Accessible** Challenging	accessible theme; accessible vocabulary

Reading Standard 2.2, 3.1 (see pages A48–A50)

Literary Skills Focus

Petrarchan Sonnet All forty-four poems in *Sonnets from the Portuguese* are written in the form of the **Petrarchan sonnet.** This kind of sonnet, also called Italian, is organized into a group of eight lines (an octave) followed by a sestet (six lines). Each line is in **iambic pentameter** and rhymes *abbaabba cdcdcd.* Petrarchan sonnets often have a break in thought, or **turn,** between the octave and the sestet. Sonnet 43, however, lacks this feature and is instead broken into short units of thought.

Reading Skills Focus

Paraphrasing The key to understanding what you read is being able to express it in your own words. When you **paraphrase** a sentence or passage, you not only replace the original words with your own but also use new grammar and sentence structure.

Into Action As you read, create a chart like the one below to practice paraphrasing. First, list each of the ways of loving that the speaker identifies. Then, paraphrase that statement in your own language, using your own sentence structure.

Original Sentence	Paraphrase
"I love thee to the depth and breadth and height / My soul can reach, when feeling out of sight / For the ends of Being and ideal Grace."	My love for you extends as far as my spirit can seek out the very reason for existence.

Writing Skills Focus

Think as a Reader/Writer

Find It in Your Reading As you read, note how the writer begins the poem by asking a question and then uses **repetition** as she tries to answer it. In your *Reader/Writer Notebook,* identify where the repetition occurs and make notes about how it enhances the poem's rhythm as well as its theme.

Language Coach

Synonyms Barrett Browning uses language that would have been considered old-fashioned at the time (for example, *thee* instead of *you*) to make her work sound more serious and poetic. As you paraphrase the poem, think of modern or simpler word choices that have the same meaning. These words may literally mean the same thing as Barrett Browning's, but how do they change the tone of the poem?

Reader/Writer Notebook

Use your **RWN** to complete the activities for this selection.

Learn It Online

Listen to this famous sonnet online.

go.hrw.com H12-953 Go

Selection Resources

Unit 5 Resources, on-level practice and assessment, p. 32

PowerNotes, interactive lesson presentation with activities

Teacher One Stop™, on-level lesson plans and all print resources

Holt Audio Library

Holt Audio Library: Selections and Summaries in Spanish

Holt Interactive Reader, p. 289

UA: Differentiating Instruction, modified lesson plans and leveled assessment, p. 223

UA: Supporting Instruction in Spanish, selection summary

UA: Resources for Teaching Advanced Students, lesson plans, p. 173

ThinkCentral Online Assessment

ThinkCentral Online Remediation

Preteach

English for Academic Success

Language Coach

Have students read the poem aloud once as is and again using simpler words. ***Possible response:*** *Replacing* thee *in the poem with* you *makes the poet sound less mature and not as elegant.*

Literary Skills Focus

As you read and discuss the poem with students, have them notice how Elizabeth Barrett Browning does not include the customary turn in this Petrarchan sonnet. Instead she divides her thoughts into separate units. Point out that each unit describing how she loves begins with the phrase "I love thee. . . ."

Reading Skills Focus

Give students a copy of the Reading Skills Focus graphic organizer before they read. (See **Unit 5 Resources**.) Tell them to use their responses to answer the questions on the Applying Your Skills page.

Writing Skills Focus

Have students record examples of repetition and its effect on the rhythm and theme in their **Reader/Writer Notebooks**. Students can use their notes to complete the Writing Skills Focus activity.

Learn It Online

The online version of this poem includes audio support to engage all students and to help struggling readers with reading comprehension and vocabulary.

go.hrw.com H12-953 Go

Teacher Preparation
Selection Summary

This Petrarchan sonnet asks the question "How do I love thee?" and answers with several paradoxical descriptions of the way the speaker feels about her beloved. The speaker's love is divine and everyday, childlike and mature. It will exist through life and persist after death.

Direct Teach

Think About/Talk About

Read with a Purpose Tell students to think about the ways in which Elizabeth Barrett Browning's descriptions may be considered descriptions of "mature love."

Comprehension

A Reading Focus

Possible response: *"In how many ways do I love you? Let me list them. I love you to the full dimensions my soul can extend when contemplating the mysteries of existence and divine love." Paraphrasing helps the reader understand what the writer is trying to explain about the extent of her love for her beloved.*

Analysis

B Literary Focus

Possible response: *The poem contains eight units of thought.*

POEM

Sonnet 43

by **Elizabeth Barrett Browning**

Read with a Purpose

Read to discover the many aspects of mature love.

Build Background

Elizabeth Barrett Browning wrote her sonnets before her marriage but did not show them to her husband until two years later. Reluctant to publish the poems because they were so personal, she deliberately gave them a title that suggested that they were translated into English from an original Portuguese source.

Love Among the Ruins by Sir Edward Burne-Jones (1833–1898). Oil on canvas. Wightwick Manor, Staffordshire, U.K.

How do I love thee? Let me count the ways.
I love thee to the depth and breadth and height
My soul can reach, when feeling out of sight
For the ends of Being and ideal Grace. **A**
I love thee to the level of everyday's
Most quiet need, by sun and candlelight.
I love thee freely, as men strive for Right;
I love thee purely, as they turn from Praise. **B**
I love thee with the passion put to use
In my old griefs, and with my childhood's faith.
I love thee with a love I seemed to lose
With my lost saints°—I love thee with the breath,
Smiles, tears, of all my life!—and, if God choose,
I shall but love thee better after death.

12. lost saints: childhood faith.

A Reading Focus **Paraphrasing** Put the first four lines into your own words. How does your paraphrase help you understand the poem's theme?

B Literary Focus **Petrarchan Sonnet** In a regular Petrarchan sonnet, a turn of thought would occur here. Instead of having one major division, how many units of thought does the poem contain?

Universal Access

EL English Learners

English for Academic Success The sonnet form often takes up an abstract concept as its subject. In this sonnet, the speaker names the many ways she loves in specific terms, but some students may have difficulty following abstract descriptions. Explain that the words *Being, Grace, Right,* and *Praise* are capitalized because they are proper nouns referring correspondingly to standard concepts of existence, divine love, justice, and flattery.

California Standards, p. 955

- **Reading Standard 2.2** Analyze the way in which clarity of meaning is affected by the patterns of organization, hierarchical structures, repetition of the main ideas, syntax, and word choice in the text.
- **Reading Standard 3.1** Analyze characteristics of subgenres (e.g., satire, parody, allegory, pastoral) that are used in poetry, prose, plays, novels, short stories, essays, and other basic genres.
- **Writing Standard 1.4** Enhance meaning by employing rhetorical devices, including the extended use of parallelism, repetition, and analogy; the incorporation of visual aids (e.g., graphs, tables, pictures); and the issuance of a call for action.

Applying Your Skills

Reading Standard 2.2, 3.1 (see pages A48–A50)
Writing Standard 1.4 (see pages A51–A52)

Sonnet 43

Literary Response and Analysis

Reading Skills Focus

Quick Check

1. How many distinct ways does the speaker say that she loves her beloved?
2. In lines 2–6, what are the two contrasting levels of love that the poet expresses?
3. In lines 9–14, what are the three stages of life that the speaker contrasts?

Read with a Purpose

4. How would you define *mature love* based on the features identified by the speaker of the poem?

Reading Skills: Paraphrasing

5. As you read the poem, you paraphrased each statement in your own words. Re-read each sentence, both the original and your paraphrase, and rate how easy it is to understand by writing a number from 5 (most difficult to understand) to 1 (easiest to understand) next to it. If any of your paraphrases received less than a 5, rewrite them so that they are easier to understand and are expressed as much as possible in your own voice.

Original Sentence	Paraphrase
"I love thee to the depth and breadth and height / My soul can reach, when feeling out of sight / For the ends of Being and ideal Grace." Rating: 5	My love for you extends as far as my spirit can seek out the very reason for existence. Rating: 2

Literary Skills Focus

Literary Analysis

6. **Infer** What do you think the poem expresses about the speaker's religious faith?
7. **Analyze** How are the pauses in the last three lines different in rhythm from those in the rest of the poem? What is the emotional effect of this change in rhythm?
8. **Evaluate** In your opinion, has Barrett Browning described all of the important emotional aspects of love? Explain your response.

Literary Skills: Petrarchan Sonnet

9. **Compare and Contrast** How would Sonnet 43 have been different if Barrett Browning had written it as a Shakespearean sonnet (see page 390)?

Literary Skills Review: Diction

10. **Analyze** A writer or speaker's choice of words is called **diction.** What examples of concrete and abstract words can you find in the poem?

Writing Skills Focus

Think as a Reader/Writer

Use It in Your Writing In your *Reader/Writer Notebook,* write a poem or a short speech that begins with a question. (If you choose to write a poem, you do not have to use meter and rhyme.) Then, use repetition as you try to answer your question in a variety of different ways.

What Do You Think Now? What else is love about besides creating happiness?

Check for Understanding

Independent Practice

Reading Skills Focus

Possible responses:

1. *eight ways*
2. *She contrasts everyday, ordinary love with spiritual love.*
3. *The three stages are childhood, her whole (adult) life, and death (afterlife).*
4. *Responses will vary. Students should point out how the speaker views mature love as a feeling that invests all of our soul, intellect, and experience.*
5. *Have students see if their paraphrases successfully express the same ideas with simpler words and phrasing.*

Literary Skills Focus

Possible responses:

6. *The poem suggests that Elizabeth Barrett Browning's beliefs have matured beyond the innocent faith of childhood to an adult faith that accepts doubt and the possibility of sorrow.*
7. *The dashes create a choppy rhythm in the final lines, contrasting with the more measured declarations of the previous lines. Students may think that the new rhythm suggests an upwelling of emotion in response to possible challenges to love's smooth course.*
8. *Students may suggest that similar values and interests or physical attraction are also important parts of love.*
9. *Some students may feel that the poem would be disrupted by division into quatrains and a couplet. Others may feel that the division would make the poet's ideas easier to grasp.*
10. *Concrete words include "sun," "candlelight," and "tears." Abstract words include "love," "soul," and "faith." These words suggest both the spiritual and commonplace emotions of love.*

Universal Access

Struggling Writers

Some students may need additional scaffolding to complete the Writing Skills Focus activity. Display sample questions on the board for students to choose from. Students might write a poem or speech on an abstract concept, such as love, beauty, freedom, or peace. Remind students to use a repeating phrase in their answers.

What Do You Think Now?

Ask students to think of reasons, other than happiness, for which people want to love or be loved. Ask whether love brings only positive feelings and consequences.

Assess

Unit 5 Resources,
Selection Standards Check, p. 33

ThinkCentral Online Assessment,
Selection Standards Check

Standards Focus

Objectives

Students will
- understand alliteration and assonance and their effects
- draw conclusions about meaning

Selection Introduction

Think About the Writer

Tell students to take note of different ways Hopkins went against convention and the negative reactions he sometimes received. Discuss the benefits he might have gained by pushing the artistic and spiritual boundaries of his community and the difficulties his unconventionality might have caused.

For Independent Reading

A Joyful Noise: Poems for Two Voices, Paul Fleischman

Motivate

What Do You Think?/QuickWrite

Ask students to brainstorm strange, everyday things in their own environment. Have them write their ideas down in their **Reader/Writer Notebooks**. Tell them to think about how life would be different without these things.

California Standards, pp. 956–959

- **Reading Standard 2.4** Make warranted and reasonable assertions about the author's arguments by using elements of the text to defend and clarify interpretations.
- **Reading Standard 3.3** Analyze the ways in which irony, tone, mood, the author's style, and the "sound" of language achieve specific rhetorical or aesthetic purposes or both.

Preparing to Read

Pied Beauty

What Do You Think? How can appearance be different from reality?

QuickWrite

Hopkins commented that his poetry "errs on the side of oddness" by rejoicing in strange, surprising aspects of creation. What meaning do you find in small, everyday things?

Gerard Manley Hopkins (1844–1889).

MEET THE WRITER

Gerard Manley Hopkins

(1844–1889)

Throughout his short life, Gerard Manley Hopkins combined learning, service, and religious conviction with a desire to push the established bounds of poetry.

A Journey of Faith

The eldest son of highly educated parents devoted to the Church of England, Hopkins attended Highgate, a London boarding school, where he won a poetry prize and later a scholarship to study classics at Oxford. Hopkins intended to enter the Anglican ministry, but after much soul-searching, he converted to Roman Catholicism in 1866—a shocking thing to do at the time.

In 1868, Hopkins joined the Jesuits, a Roman Catholic order dedicated to teaching, and burned almost all his poetry. For seven years he wrote no poetry until, in 1875, he was asked to write an ode to five Franciscan nuns who had drowned at sea. He sent "The Wreck of the *Deutschland*" to a Jesuit periodical. The poem's form was so eccentric that the editors "dared not print it."

Poetic Innovation

Hopkins composed a small but very powerful body of poetry that he sent to his friends with explanations of his ideas for using native English vocabulary. Hopkins's poems are characterized by assonance, alliteration, internal rhyme, and what he called **sprung rhythm,** which imitates the sound of natural speech. Unlike conventional metrics, sprung rhythm does not employ only one kind of metrical unit (for example, the alternation of unstressed and stressed syllables in iambic pentameter). Despite his metrical and linguistic creativity, Hopkins shared with the Romantics a focus on nature, the transcendent, and personal struggle.

Think About the Writer What challenges do you think Hopkins faced in going against convention in both his spiritual and artistic lives? Discuss.

Selection Readability	
Easily Accessible **Accessible** Challenging	familiar context; accessible theme; short poem

Reading Standard 2.4, 3.3 (see pages A48–A50)

Literary Skills Focus

Alliteration and Assonance In much of his poetry, Hopkins uses two sound devices: **alliteration,** the repetition of consonant sounds, and **assonance,** the repetition of vowel sounds. Like tongue-twisters, Hopkins's poetry can be challenging to read aloud as a result. In "Pied Beauty," the repeated sounds also serve a thematic purpose. Like the creatures' colorful spots, the sounds create points of connection between otherwise unlike things—"Fresh-firecoal chestnut-falls" and "finches' wings," for example, are united by the *f* sound they share. Try reading the poem aloud, and consider the emotions these sounds conjure as you read.

Reading Skills Focus

Drawing Conclusions About Meaning When you read carefully, you **draw conclusions** from a text based on the evidence before you. In poetry as challenging as "Pied Beauty," you may need to re-read a line several times and draw **inferences** about words or phrases you don't understand by studying their context.

Into Action As you read, use a Venn diagram like the one below to draw conclusions about each image that Hopkins presents in lines 2–5. In the left-hand circle, record something for which the speaker is thankful. On the right, record something with which it is compared or juxtaposed. Keep in mind that some of these comparisons are made directly as **similes** but others are not.

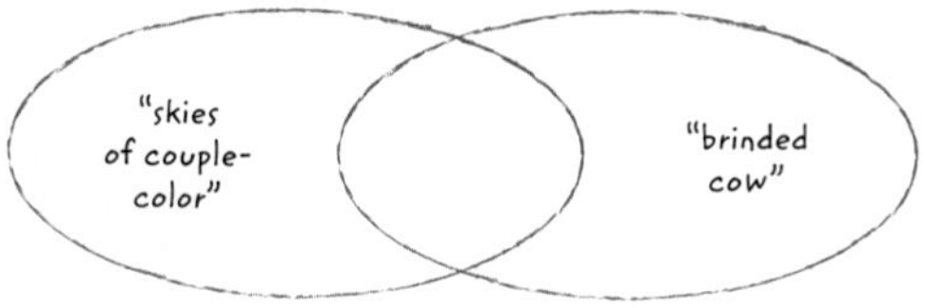

Writing Skills Focus

Think as a Reader/Writer

Find It in Your Reading In your *Reader/Writer Notebook,* identify examples of how Hopkins uses **assonance** and **alliteration**. Record each example according to the consonant or vowel that is repeated, for example "*G:* 'Glory be to God.'"

Language Coach

Word Definitions Hopkins uses several words that are either archaic (that is, no longer in use) or that he invented himself. Make a list of unfamiliar words, and use context clues, definitions provided with the poem, and a dictionary to discover their meanings.

Reader/Writer Notebook

Use your **RWN** to complete the activities for this selection.

Learn It Online

Learn more about Hopkins with these Internet links.

go.hrw.com H12-957 Go

Preteach

English for Academic Success

Language Coach

Inform students that in addition to archaic and invented words, Hopkins puts words in unfamiliar combinations such as "Fresh-firecoal chestnut-falls." Have students add unusual word combinations to their list of unfamiliar words.

Literary Skills Focus

As you read and discuss the poem with students, have them notice the function of alliteration and assonance in the poem. Discuss if the examples they have noted mimic a sound or convey a specific feeling or tone.

Reading Skills Focus

Give students a copy of the Reading Skills Focus graphic organizer before they read. (See **Unit 5 Resources**.) Tell them to use their responses to answer the questions on the Applying Your Skills page.

Writing Skills Focus

Have students record examples of assonance and alliteration in their **Reader/Writer Notebooks**. Students can use their notes to complete the Writing Skills Focus activity.

Selection Resources

- **Unit 5 Resources,** on-level practice and assessment, p. 36
- **Teacher One Stop™,** on-level lesson plans and all print resources
- **Holt Audio Library**
- **Holt Audio Library: Selections and Summaries in Spanish**
- **UA: Differentiating Instruction,** graphic organizer p. 226
- **UA: Supporting Instruction in Spanish,** selection summary
- **ThinkCentral Online Assessment,** Selection Standards Check
- **ThinkCentral Online Remediation**

Learn It Online

The enhanced author biography offers more information on the life of the author as well as Holt's interactive resources pertaining to the author.

go.hrw.com H12-957 Go

Teacher Preparation
Selection Summary

In this verbally innovative poem, the speaker praises God for the wonder of creation in all its motley beauty. He enumerates various aspects of nature, society, and sensation and attributes their source to God's eternal beauty.

Direct Teach

Think About/Talk About

Read with a Purpose Tell students to read the Read with a Purpose statement. Point out the images of diversity in the poem. Discuss what these diverse elements and their juxtaposition say about God's greatness.

Comprehension

B Reading Focus

Possible response: *The list of opposites accentuates the idea of contrast that the poet sees in creation.*

Analysis

A Literary Focus

Possible response: *The alliteration and assonance link unlike things through sound. A "rose" does not generally call to mind "moles," but through juxtaposition and assonance these two things combine in a new definition of beauty. In their verbal energy, these sounds also convey the flashing movements of the trout.*

POEM

Pied Beauty

by **Gerard Manley Hopkins**

Read with a Purpose

Read to discover how the speaker uses nature's diversity to praise God.

Build Background

"Pied Beauty" is a song of praise to God for all things that are pied—that is, covered with different-colored spots. Hopkins composed the poem in 1877, shortly before he was ordained a Roman Catholic priest. Before then, he had kept a "seven-year silence" by refusing to write poetry. He did, however, keep journals that provided material for much of his later verse. For example, on an 1872 vacation to the Isle of Man, Hopkins described the hillsides as "plotted and painted" with square fields, the origin of the poem's phrase "plotted and pieced."

Glory be to God for dappled things—
For skies of couple-color as a brinded° cow;
For rose-moles all in stipple° upon trout that swim; **A**
Fresh-firecoal chestnut-falls;° finches' wings;
Landscape plotted and pieced°—fold, fallow, and plow;
And áll trádes, their gear and tackle and trim.
All things counter, original, spare, strange;
Whatever is fickle, freckled (who knows how?)
With swift, slow; sweet, sour; adazzle, dim; **B**
He fathers-forth° whose beauty is past change:
Praise him.

2. brinded: archaic for "brindled"; having a light brown or gray coat streaked with a darker color.
3. stipple: random dots or spots.
4. chestnut-falls: chestnuts falling from a tree.
5. pieced: parceled into fields.
10. fathers-forth: creates.

A Literary Focus **Alliteration and Assonance** In this line, what effect is created by the alliteration of *s, t,* and *z* sounds and the assonance of *o* (*rose moles*) and short *i* (*stipple/swim*)?

B Reading Focus **Drawing Conclusions About Meaning** What image of creation is conveyed by listing these three pairs of opposites?

California Standards, p. 959

- **Reading Standard 2.4** Make warranted and reasonable assertions about the author's arguments by using elements of the text to defend and clarify interpretations.
- **Reading Standard 3.1** Analyze characteristics of subgenres (e.g., satire, parody, allegory, pastoral) that are used in poetry, prose, plays, novels, short stories, essays, and other basic genres.
- **Reading Standard 3.3** Analyze the ways in which irony, tone, mood, the author's style, and the "sound" of language achieve specific rhetorical or aesthetic purposes or both
- **Writing Standard 1.2** Use point of view, characterization, style (e.g., use of irony), and related elements for specific rhetorical and aesthetic purposes.
- **Writing Standard 2.3** Write reflective compositions: **a.** Explore the significance of personal experiences, events, conditions, or concerns by using rhetorical strategies (e.g., narration, description, exposition, persuasion).

Universal Access

English Learners

English for Academic Success Tell students that Hopkins meant for this poem to be a mouthful, with its surprising, unfamiliar words and twisting syntax. Like many of Hopkins's other poems, "Pied Beauty" is not supposed to flow easily; rather, it is meant to make the reader pause and focus on individual images and sounds. Go over the more difficult archaic vocabulary, and help students see each vivid picture painted by the poet. Then, read the poem aloud to let students hear the wealth of sounds he brings together.

Applying Your Skills

Reading Standard 2.4, 3.1, 3.3 (see pages A48–A50)
Writing Standard 1.2, 2.3a (see pages A51–A52)

Pied Beauty

Literary Response and Analysis

Reading Skills Focus

Quick Check

1. What specific examples of "pied beauty" does the poet mention in lines 2–6?
2. What do you think the poet means by saying "all things counter" (line 7)?
3. In line 10, what contrast does the poet make between the beauty of the physical world and that of God the creator?

Read with a Purpose

4. How does Hopkins's poem create a visual image or landscape in praise of God?

Reading Skills: Drawing Conclusions About Meaning

5. You created a Venn diagram to record each comparison that Hopkins makes between a thing in nature and something else. Now you can complete your understanding of how these two seemingly different things relate. Determine the meanings of any unfamiliar words. Then, in the space where the two circles overlap, write the feature that both things share.

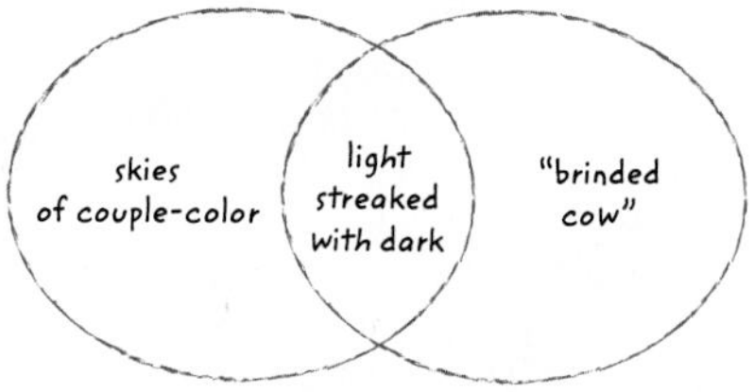

Literary Skills Focus

Literary Analysis

6. **Interpret** Most of the poem is concerned with animals and other aspects of nature. In what line does Hopkins indirectly mention people?
7. **Make Judgments** Is the poet's praise for that which is varied and changing typical of literature written in praise of a person or of God? Explain.

Literary Skills: Alliteration and Assonance

8. **Compare and Contrast** How does the use of alliteration and assonance in "Pied Beauty" compare with that in *Sir Gawain and the Green Knight* (page 195)? Do you notice any similarities in the meter of both poems?

Literary Skills Review: Metaphysical Poetry

9. **Extend** A type of poetry is known for its startling imagery, philosophical and spiritual content, verbal wit, and irregular meter is called **metaphysical poetry**. What aspects of "Pied Beauty" could qualify it for this definition?

Writing Skills Focus

Think as a Reader/Writer

Use It in Your Writing In your *Reader/Writer Notebook,* write a paragraph or poem in praise of a thing, not a person, whose beauty should be celebrated. Use alliteration or assonance to link images and ideas.

What Do You Think Now? How can unusual language help reveal hidden beauty?

Check for Understanding

Independent Practice

Reading Skills Focus

Possible responses:

1. *He mentions a multicolored sky, rose-colored spots on a trout, roasted chestnuts, finches' wings, and a patchwork landscape.*
2. *"Counter" could mean something in opposition. The speaker suggests that all things have an opposite.*
3. *The beauty of the world is varied, surprising, and transitory—changeable, in other words. God's beauty is eternal and unchanging.*
4. *He uses vivid imagery to paint a picture of the variety of God's creation. "Couple-color," "brinded cow," and "rose-mole" portray nature's multicolored palette. Shape and line are delineated by words like "plotted," "pieced," "fold," and "plow."*
5. *The shared features should elaborate on the meaning of the words in the diagrams and further the students' understanding of the poem.*

Literary Skills Focus

Possible responses:

6. *In line 6, he mentions people indirectly through their various "trades" and the tools and "gear" they use in their work.*
7. *Some students may believe that poems praising something often honor its symmetrical or eternal qualities. Others may point to exceptions, like Shakespeare's Sonnet 130.*
8. *Both poems use irregular meter, alliteration, and assonance, but for different purposes. Hopkins juxtaposes words and sounds to convey a religious idea, whereas these elements serve a more narrative function in "Sir Gawain and the Green Knight."*
9. *This poem also includes startling imagery and uses clever techniques to convey meaning and tone about a spiritual theme.*

Universal Access

Struggling Writers

Some students may need additional scaffolding to complete the Writing Skills Focus activity. After students review instances of alliteration and assonance in "Pied Beauty," instruct them to brainstorm adjectives that describe the beauty of a creature or place. Have students use the adjectives to help them write a poem celebrating its beauty. Then, ask students to review the poem and look for places to add alliteration or assonance.

What Do You Think Now?

Ask students to reflect on which aspects of a creature or object can be glorified through strange and unusual language.

Assess

Unit 5 Resources, Selection Standards Check, p. 37

ThinkCentral Online Assessment, Selection Standards Check

Chapter Objectives

- Students will learn about realism by reading poems by Matthew Arnold, Thomas Hardy, and A. E. Housman, and short stories by Rudyard Kipling, Leo Tolstoy, Anton Chekhov, and Guy de Maupassant.
- Students will connect realism to political, social, ethical, and philosophical ideas.

The Quotation

Tell students that a paradox involves the coexistence of conditions that seem contradictory. Note that the quote expresses a paradox that could apply to the merits and missteps of scientific and social progress in the nineteenth century. Which positive changes might contemporary idealists have hoped for, and which changes might they have regretted? ***Possible response:*** *Many people expected technological advances to improve people's lives, but the rapid transformation of farmers into factory workers undermined traditional beliefs.*

Analyzing Visuals

Extension Activity The selections in this chapter address issues of progress and change. What details in the image on p. 960 reflect the spirit of Oscar Wilde's statement? ***Possible response:*** *The locomotive serves as a symbol of progress. At the same time, the painting depicts the dusty smoke from coal fires spewing from smokestacks and filling the blue sky. This is the darker side of progress.*

CHAPTER **10**

The Paradox of Progress

LITERARY SKILLS FOCUS

Realism

CONTENTS

"In this world there are only two tragedies. One is not getting what one wants, and the other is getting it."

–**Oscar Wilde**

Chapter 10

California Standards Overview

- **Reading Standard 2.2** Analyze the way in which clarity of meaning is affected by the patterns of organization, hierarchical structures, repetition of the main ideas, syntax, and word choice in the text.
- **Reading Standard 2.4** Make warranted and reasonable assertions about the author's arguments by using elements of the text to defend and clarify interpretations.
- **Reading Standard 3.1** Analyze characteristics of subgenres (e.g., satire, parody, allegory, pastoral) that are used in poetry, prose, plays, novels, short stories, essays, and other basic genres.
- **Reading Standard 3.2** Analyze the way in which the theme or meaning of a selection represents a view or comment on life, using textual evidence to support the claim.
- **Reading Standard 3.3** Analyze the ways in which irony, tone, mood, the author's style, and the "sound" of language achieve specific rhetorical or aesthetic purposes or both.
- **Reading Standard 3.4** Analyze ways in which poets use imagery, personification, figures of speech, and sounds to evoke readers' emotions.
- **Reading Standard 3.7** Analyze recognized works of world literature from a variety of authors: **a.** Contrast the major literary forms, techniques, and characteristics of the major literary periods (e.g., Homeric Greece, medieval, romantic, neoclassic, modern). **b.** Relate literary works and authors to the major themes and issues of their eras. **c.** Evaluate the philosophical, political, religious, ethical, and social influences of the historical period that shaped the characters, plots, and settings.
- **Reading Standard 3.9** Analyze the philosophical arguments presented in literary works to determine whether the authors' positions have contributed to the quality of each work and the credibility of the characters. (Philosophical approach)
- **Grades 9–10 Review Reading Standard 3.3** Analyze interactions between main and subordinate characters in a literary text (e.g., internal and external conflicts, motivations, relationships, influences) and explain the way those interactions affect the plot.
- **Grades 9–10 Review Reading Standard 3.12** Analyze the way in which a work of literature is related to the themes and issues of its historical period.

LITERARY RESPONSE AND ANALYSIS

Literary Skills Focus

Reading Standard 3.7a–c (see pages A48–A50)

Realism by Leila Christenbury

Influences on Realism

- Transition from a farming society to an industrialized nation
- Rejection of the Romantic idealism that had previously dominated literature
- Emergence of scientific objectivity as a goal in writing
- Enthusiasm of writers across the globe for the themes of realism

The Switch to Industrialization

As England moved from an agrarian society to a world force and an industrial power, its material progress and prosperity also meant change. People left the security of small villages for the urban centers where they worked in manufacturing. Industries and cities dominated, new ways of living caused upheaval, and traditional beliefs and customs were questioned. The writers in this chapter felt these changes keenly and described them using factual detail and direct language, often in the context of the lives of everyday people. Look for the sense of stoic pessimism in this literature, and in particular, consider the last few lines of "Dover Beach." They are some of the most famous—and chilling—in English poetry and signal a belief that the world had entered a new era of unprecedented change.

A Reaction to Romanticism

Realism was an attempt to produce an accurate portrayal of real life without filtering it through personal feelings or Romantic idealism. Noting that liberal reforms and the revolutions of the nineteenth century had failed to bring about an era of justice, realist writers rejected the century's earlier Romantic emotionalism, seeing it as an ineffective tool for reforming—or even describing—industrial society.

Realism concerned itself with more than just the details of daily life, however. It also sought to explain why ordinary people behave the way they do. Realist novelists often relied on the emerging sciences of human and animal behavior—biology, psychology, and sociology—as well as on their own insights and observations. Realists could be divided into several different camps: Some emphasized social reform, others stressed scientific objectivity, and still others leaned toward social satire.

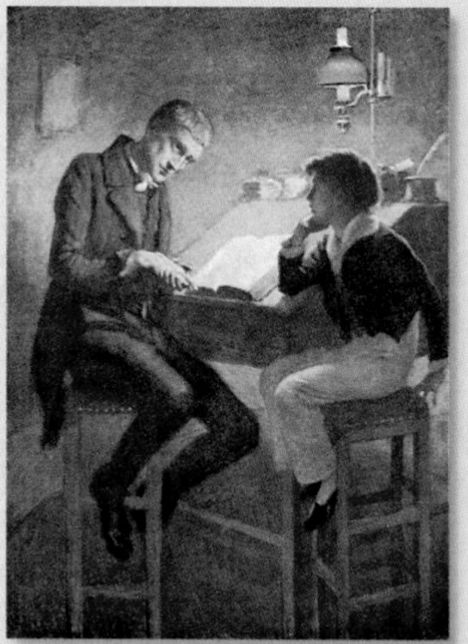

Uriah Heep and David Copperfield. Illustration by Harold Copping for *Character Sketches from Dickens*, compiled by B. W. Matz (1924).

The values of realism, such as social satire and an unflinching factual observation of ordinary people's lives, still exert a powerful influence on literature and thought.

France: Scientific Objectivity

French realists, led by novelist Gustave Flaubert, tried to make a science of their art by eliminating all sentimentality. They aimed simply to mirror life, without judgment or distortion. Nevertheless, a novel like Flaubert's *Madame Bovary* is admired today not so much for its objectivity as for its perfect prose and its satire of the middle class.

The Louth-London Royal Mail Traveling by Train from Petersborough East in December 1845, by James Pollard. Oil on canvas.
Yale Center for British Art, Paul Mellon Collection.

Literary Skills Focus

Objectives

Students will

- evaluate and analyze the influences of a historical period on a literary genre
- understand realism

Unit 5 Resources, Literary Focus Skill Builder, p. 45

PowerNotes, interactive lesson presentation with activities

Teacher One Stop™, on-level lesson plan and all print resources

Direct Teach

Realism

Have students read the Literary Skills Focus essay. Then, use the following question to discuss the aims and values of realist writers.

Realist writers rejected the emotionalism and idealism associated with Romanticism. Instead, they sought to portray the daily lives of ordinary people accurately and without sentimentality. Like the Romantics, realist writers sometimes aimed to expose social injustice and call for reform. What makes realism a good literary genre for writers interested in social commentary?

California Standards, pp. 961–962

- **Reading Standard 3.7:** Analyze recognized works of world literature from a variety of authors: **a.** Contrast the major literary forms, techniques, and characteristics of the major literary periods (e.g., Homeric Greece, medieval, romantic, neoclassic, modern). **b.** Relate literary works and authors to the major themes and issues of their eras. **c.** Evaluate the philosophical, political, religious, ethical, and social influences of the historical period that shaped the characters, plots, and settings.

Check for Understanding

Independent Practice

Ask Yourself

Possible responses:

1. *They felt that the sentimentality of the Romantics was not an effective means to describe or reform their society.*
2. *The failures of reform movements influenced the rise of realism by making writers turn away from emotionalism and idealism and strive instead for a sober representation of reality. In addition, efforts to bring about social justice prompted writers to draw inspiration from social sciences, which seemed to offer ways to explain the human condition.*
3. *Dickens chose to show children's suffering to encourage his readers to acknowledge and protest against cruelty and injustice. Such portrayals counteracted the idea that the poor deserved their fate.*
4. *Realism's emphasis on candid portrayals of the lives of ordinary people inspired writers all over the world. The fundamental philosophical and social questions realism addressed could be understood regardless of specific national concerns.*

Learn It Online

For a multimedia version of the instruction found on this page, use the **PowerNotes** Literary Skills Focus presentation.

go.hrw.com H12-962 Go

LITERARY RESPONSE AND ANALYSIS

Literary Skills Focus

Naturalism, a radical offshoot of realism, arose in the 1870s. Led by Emile Zola, naturalist writers considered free will an illusion and often portrayed their characters as helpless victims of heredity, fate, and circumstance. These writers tried to abolish the boundary between scientist and artist. Relying heavily on the growing scientific disciplines of psychology and sociology, they tried to dissect human behavior with as much objectivity as a scientist would dissect a frog or a cadaver. For naturalists, human life seemed a grim, losing battle against forces beyond the individual's control. The most talented naturalists, however, could not stay within the narrow ideology of their school. Guy de Maupassant (see page 1032), for example, is sometimes called a naturalist, but his work is sharpened by irony and by a gift for choosing the right details to illuminate.

Dickens: A Master at Work

In Victorian England, no one embodied realist principles more than Charles Dickens. A master storyteller, Dickens was able to combine calls for social reform with biting satire and comedy. The son of a debt-ridden clerk, Dickens lived out one of the favorite myths of the age. Through his own enormous talents and energy, he rose from poverty to become a wealthy and famous man. His success was made possible by increasing affluence and literacy, which gave him a large reading public, and by improved printing and distribution technology.

The conventional happy endings of Dickens's novels satisfied his readers', and probably his own, conviction that things usually work out well for decent people, but many of Dickens's most memorable scenes show decent people neglected, abused, and exploited. Children, especially, endure terrible suffering. The hungry Oliver Twist begs for more gruel in the workhouse; Tiny Tim in *A Christmas Carol* cheerfully hobbles toward his possible early death; and young David Copperfield is abused by his stepfather, the cold, dark Mr. Murdstone.

Russia: Ultimate Questions

Realistic Russian novels began with those of Ivan Turgenev, whose ornate, lyrical prose brimmed with sympathy and warmth. Later Russian novelists, including Leo Tolstoy (see page 1008) and Fyodor Dostoevsky, wrote epic, sprawling novels filled with violence, love, and family crises, and populated with characters from a wide cross-section of society. The novels of these writers helped foster a powerful movement that called for the liberation of the serfs (peasants) and, later, the entire society. Yet the primary aim of Russian realists was not social reform, but a desire to answer the ultimate questions of human life. In different ways, Tolstoy and Dostoevsky repeatedly asked, "How should people live?" and "What are good and evil?"

Unlike these two giants, the playwright and short-story writer Anton Chekhov (see page 1022) worked on a much smaller scale. Chekhov found his subjects and themes in the common illusions and daily sufferings of unremarkable people. Like Tolstoy and Dostoevsky, however, Chekhov dealt with the meanings of life and death. His stories and plays are about people's attempts—usually frustrated—to find meaning and purpose in their lives.

Ask Yourself

1. Why did realists try to shed the sentimental ideas of Romantic idealism?
2. How did the struggle for social justice influence the rise of realism?
3. Why did Dickens choose to show children suffering?
4. What universal aspects of realism inspired writers around the world?

Learn It Online

Explore realism through *PowerNotes* online.

go.hrw.com H12-962 Go

Universal Access

EL English Learners

English for Academic Success Students may be unfamiliar with some of the vocabulary in the essay. Explain that *agrarian* means agricultural or farming-related. Note that *material*, in this context, is an adjective referring to physical (as opposed to spiritual) well-being; *prosperity* means economic well-being; an *upheaval* is a violent disruption; and *stoic* means unaffected by joy or suffering.

Advanced Learners

Enrichment Emile Zola, Gustave Flaubert, and Ivan Turgenev are giants of realism whose works are not included among these selections. Recommend the novels of these authors in translation: Zola's *The Fortune of the Rougons*, Flaubert's *Madame Bovary,* and Turgenev's *Fathers and Sons*.

Reading Standard 3.7a, 3.7c (see pages A48–A50)

Connecting to Realism

As the rise of industry and science created a new, urban way of life, many writers and visual artists turned to realism, a movement that stressed the observation of the lives of ordinary people. The photograph on this page shows a scene from everyday life, without idealization or sentimentalism.

Guidelines

Use these guidelines to consider how this photograph reflects realism.

- How does the photograph's **setting** relate to concerns of realist writers?
- Realist writers used factual details to describe characters and situations. What details in the photograph help you understand the boy's daily life?
- How effective would this photograph have been for social reform? Explain.

1. What do you notice about the boy's clothing? What does this detail tell you about him?
2. Why do you think the photographer chose to show so much of the machine instead of focusing more on the boy?
3. What do you see on the floor? What can you infer from this evidence about working conditions?

Young boy working in a Lancashire cotton mill, c. 1880s.

Your Turn Analyze Realism

Choose another image in this chapter, and write a short paragraph explaining how it conveys the themes and values of the realist movement.

California Standards, p. 963

- **Reading Standard 3.7** Analyze recognized works of world literature from a variety of authors: **a.** Contrast the major literary forms, techniques, and characteristics of the major literary periods (e.g., Homeric Greece, medieval, romantic, neoclassic, modern). **c.** Evaluate the philosophical, political, religious, ethical, and social influences of the historical period that shaped the characters, plots, and settings.

Standards Focus

Objectives

Students will

- analyze elements of literature from the Victorian period
- understand realism

Analyzing Visuals Transparencies, Unit 5

Teacher One Stop™, lesson plan and all print resources

Direct Teach

Connect to the Literary Skill

Tell students that photography can be considered the ideal medium for realism, as it shows more easily all the details of reality.

Work with students to answer the guided questions.

Possible responses:

1. *The boy has no safety gear on, making him vulnerable to injury.*
2. *This point of view emphasizes the frailty of the young boy.*
3. *Cotton dust and sharp fragments lie next to his bare feet on the floor. The conditions seem hazardous.*

Check for Understanding

Your Turn

Alternative Listening and Speaking Assignment

Have students find and present to the class a photograph that represents a historical era in a way that reflects realist values.

Standards Focus

Objectives

Students will
- understand mood
- visualize setting

Selection Introduction

Think About the Writer

Ask students to think about personalities or groups that are raising awareness about certain problematic issues of our time (pollution, poverty, world politics, diseases, etc.).

For Independent Reading

Fahrenheit 451, Ray Bradbury

Motivate

What Do You Think?/QuickWrite

Have students make a list of the people, places, and things they value and explain why they value them. Ask students to discuss how they would feel about losing one of them.

English for Academic Success

Academic Vocabulary

Look for opportunities to use the Academic Vocabulary words in this unit.

- **benefit, *n.*:** anything that is for the good of a person or thing
- **complex, *adj.*:** complicated
- **publish, *v.*:** print and issue for the public
- **respond, *v.*:** react

Preparing to Read

Dover Beach

What Do You Think? How can appearance be different from reality?

QuickWrite

To what do people cling in times of crisis? In your *Reader/Writer Notebook*, write a short list of people, places, or things you value and depend on the most when times are tough.

MEET THE WRITER

Matthew Arnold

(1822–1888)

Unlike the other major Victorian poets, Matthew Arnold is as famous today for his essays of literary and social criticism as he is for his poetry.

An Uneven Start

In his youth Matthew Arnold had difficulty living up to the expectations of his famous father, Dr. Thomas Arnold, a leading thinker of the Victorian era and headmaster of Rugby School. Although his performance at his father's school was inconsistent, Arnold nevertheless won a scholarship to Oxford University in 1841. His performance at Oxford was a failure by Rugby standards, and he graduated without knowing what he wanted to do.

Arnold won prizes for his poetry at both Rugby and Oxford. In 1849, he published his first book of poetry, *The Strayed Reveller,* to mixed reviews. Two more volumes of poetry followed in 1852 and 1853; as a result, he was elected an Oxford professor of poetry in 1857.

Success Beyond Poetry

After his marriage in 1851, Arnold became a government inspector of schools for poor children, a job he held for thirty-five years. It became increasingly difficult for him to write poetry, and he told a friend, "My pen, it seems to me, is even stiffer and more cramped than my feelings."

After 1860, Arnold almost completely stopped writing poetry and began a separate career as a critic. His travels had given him firsthand knowledge of social problems, and he became an energetic essayist and lecturer on literary, political, social, and religious questions. In his essays, Arnold warns that without the steadying influence of culture, the nineteenth century's technological and political changes would create a grossly materialistic society. Throughout his life, Arnold knew both the excitement of trying to change the values of his age and the loneliness of not being comfortable in his own time.

Think About the Writer In what way has Arnold's warning about the influence of technology and political change come true? Explain.

Matthew Arnold (1880) by George Frederic Watts. Oil on canvas. National Portrait Gallery, London.

California Standards, pp. 964–970

- **Reading Standard 3.1** Analyze characteristics of subgenres (e.g., satire, parody, allegory, pastoral) that are used in poetry, prose, plays, novels, short stories, essays, and other basic genres.
- **Reading Standard 3.3** Analyze the ways in which irony, tone, mood, the author's style, and the "sound" of language achieve specific rhetorical or aesthetic purposes or both.
- **Reading Standard 3.7c** Evaluate the philosophical, political, religious, ethical, and social influences of the historical period that shaped the characters, plots, and settings.
- **Grades 9–10 Review Reading Standard 3.12** Analyze the way in which a work of literature is related to the themes and issues of its historical period.
- **Writing Standard 2.3a** Explore the significance of personal experiences, events, conditions, or concerns by using rhetorical strategies (e.g., narration, description, exposition, persuasion).

Selection Readability	
Easily Accessible **Accessible** Challenging	familiar vocabulary; accessible syntax

Reading Standard 3.3, 3.7c; **Grades 9–10 Review**
Reading Standard 3.12 (see pages A48–A50)

Literary Skills Focus

Mood Arnold creates a mood that shifts at certain points in the poem like the ebb and flow of the tide he describes. **Mood** is the feeling, or emotional **atmosphere,** in a work created by the writer's choice of descriptive details, images, and sounds.

Literary Perspectives Apply the literary perspective described on page 966 as you read this poem.

Reading Skills Focus

Visualizing Setting Writers like Arnold pack their writing with visual details to help you picture a particular place at a particular time. As you read, focus on descriptive words that give you a sense of the **setting**, the time and place of the events in the literary work. You may find it useful to pause every few lines and summarize the specific details of the setting. While details are often visual, the writer may appeal to other senses by indicating how the place sounds, smells, feels, or even tastes.

Into Action To visualize the setting of "Dover Beach," make an idea map like the one below. In the center circle, write the name of the place Arnold describes. Then, write each element of the setting outside the center, circle it, and draw a line connecting it to the center circle.

Writing Skills Focus

Think as a Reader/Writer

Find It in Your Reading In your *Reader/Writer Notebook,* record words that you think help Arnold create a particular **mood**. Some of these words, such as *calm* (line 1), may be adjectives, but others, such as *Gleams* (line 4) or *roar* (line 9) , may be verbs or nouns.

Vocabulary

blanched (blancht) *v.* used as *adj.:* made white or pale. *The pale light of the moon creates a blanched scene.*

tremulous (TREHM yuh luhs) *adj.:* quivering; wavering. *The tremulous waves beat back and forth.*

cadence (KAY duhns) *n.:* the beat of a repetitive motion; a sound that rises and falls. *The sea, which at first seemed calm, beats on the shore with a steady cadence.*

turbid (TUR bihd) *adj.:* cloudy; confused. *In the turbid waves, Sophocles sees a metaphor for human suffering.*

melancholy (MEHL uhn kahl ee) *adj.:* sad or causing sadness. *The loss of faith leaves the speaker feeling melancholy.*

certitude (SUR tuh tood) *n.:* a feeling of sureness. *Changes in values and ideas leave the speaker without certitude.*

Language Coach

Latin and French Roots The word *blanched* comes from the French word *blanc,* meaning "white." Although English belongs to the same language family as German, Dutch, Norwegian, Danish, and Swedish, over time many words from Latin and French have come into the English language. Knowing the original meanings of some of these root words can help you understand English words that include them. Since both French and Spanish developed from Latin, knowing related Spanish words can also help you understand these roots.

Learn It Online
Meet this poem with an introductory video online.
go.hrw.com H12-965 Go

Reader/Writer Notebook
Use your **RWN** to complete the activities for this selection.

Selection Resources

- **Unit 5 Resources,** on-level practice and assessment, p. 47
- **PowerNotes,** interactive lesson presentations with activities
- **Teacher One Stop™,** on-level lesson plans and all print resources
- **Holt Audio Library**
- **Holt Audio Library: Selections and Summaries in Spanish**
- **UA: Holt Interactive Reader,** p. 295
- **UA: Differentiating Instruction,** modified lesson plans and leveled assessment, p. 233
- **UA: Supporting Instruction in Spanish,** selection summary
- **UA: Resources for Teaching Advanced Students,** lesson plans, p. 176
- **Analyzing Visuals Transparencies,** p. 37
- **ThinkCentral Online Assessment,** Selection Standards Check
- **ThinkCentral Online Remediation**

Preteach

Introducing Vocabulary

- Review with students the Vocabulary words, definitions, and sample sentences.
- To reinforce the importance of the Vocabulary words, tell students that Arnold uses them to describe Dover Beach and the feelings it inspires in him. The cliffs at the shore are *blanched*, and the *tremulous* action of the waves produces a steady *cadence*.

English for Academic Success

Language Coach

Tell students that the word *turbid* comes from the Latin root *turbidus,* meaning "confused." *Turbid* also has a related word in Spanish—*turbio.* Have students explain how having this information about a word's origin can help them figure out the meaning of the word. Then, ask them to work with a partner to research the etymology of another Vocabulary word.

Literary Skills Focus

As you read and discuss the poem with students, have them note points in the poem where the mood shifts.

Reading Skills Focus

Give students a copy of the Reading Skills Focus graphic organizer before they read. (See **Unit 5 Resources.**) Tell them to use their responses to answer the questions on the Applying Your Skills page.

Writing Skills Focus

Have students record in their **Reader/Writer Notebooks** words Arnold uses to create a mood. Students can use their notes to complete the Writing Skills Focus activity.

Learn It Online
The **PowerNotes** presentation for this lesson includes a short video that introduces the poem. The video is also available on the online version of this page.
go.hrw.com H12-965 Go

Teacher Preparation

Selection Summary

The speaker in "Dover Beach" is looking out at Dover Beach on the English coast on a moonlit night. He calls his beloved to the window to breathe the sweet night air. He hears the endless roar of the waves, a sound that suggests eternal sadness. The speaker remarks that the ancient Greek dramatist Sophocles heard the same sound long ago, and it also reminded him of the ebb and flow of human misery. According to the speaker, the Sea of Faith, once full like the tide, is now retreating. He cries out to his beloved, imploring that they be true to one another. The world seems beautiful and fresh but is actually full of cruelty, uncertainty, and pointless conflict. Love is the only consolation.

Direct Teach

Think About/Talk About

Read with a Purpose Have students read the Read with a Purpose statement. Note that an analogy is a comparison and that the poem's setting is a beach. Ask students to consider how the image of waves against the shore might be used as a symbol of a condition of social crisis.

Comprehension

Ⓑ Reading Focus

Possible responses: *The "grating roar" and the sea flinging pebbles add a note of uneasiness.*

Analysis

Ⓐ Literary Focus

Possible responses: *The sturdy cliffs above the calm sea convey stability and serenity. The light effects add to the mood by creating an impression of beauty and clarity.*

POEM

Dover Beach

by **Matthew Arnold**

Read with a Purpose

Read to understand the analogy Arnold makes between the physical setting that he describes and the crises of his time.

Build Background

Arnold wrote during a complex time, much like our own, when scientific discoveries threatened to undermine traditional beliefs. Political upheavals were also eroding social stability: In 1848, just three years before Arnold began writing this poem, several European countries were rocked by rebellions. Arnold believed that art should unify a culture, a function traditionally served by religion.

The sea is calm tonight.
The tide is full, the moon lies fair
Upon the straits°—on the French coast the light
Gleams and is gone; the cliffs of England stand,
Glimmering and vast, out in the tranquil bay. Ⓐ
Come to the window, sweet is the night air!
Only, from the long line of spray
Where the sea meets the moon-blanched land,
Listen! you hear the grating roar
Of pebbles which the waves draw back, and fling,
At their return, up the high strand,°
Begin, and cease, and then again begin,
With tremulous cadence slow, and bring Ⓑ
The eternal note of sadness in.

Sophocles° long ago
Heard it on the Aegean,° and it brought
Into his mind the turbid ebb and flow
Of human misery; we
Find also in the sound a thought,
Hearing it by this distant northern sea.

3. straits: Strait of Dover, a body of water separating southeastern England and northwestern France.

11. strand: shore.
15. Sophocles (SAHF uh kleez) (c. 496–406 B.C.): writer of tragedies in ancient Greece.
16. Aegean (ee JEE uhn): sea between Greece and Turkey.

Ⓐ **Literary Focus** **Mood** What feelings are conveyed by the image of the sturdy cliffs standing above the calm sea?

Ⓑ **Reading Focus** **Visualizing Details** What sounds and sights does Arnold draw attention to in lines 9–13?

Vocabulary **blanched** (blancht) *v.* used as *adj.:* made white or pale.
tremulous (TREHM yuh luhs) *adj.:* quivering; wavering.
cadence (KAY duhns) *n.:* the beat of a repetitive motion; a sound that rises and falls.
turbid (TUR bihd) *adj.:* cloudy; confused.

Literary Perspectives

Analyzing Historical Context Understanding the social climate of the mid-nineteenth century can help you appreciate the mood of alienation and uncertainty in "Dover Beach." Arnold began writing the poem in 1851, three years after revolutions in France, central Europe, the Italian peninsula, Poland, and Brazil. He did not publish the poem, however, for sixteen years. In the meantime, Charles Darwin explained his theory of evolution in *On the Origin of Species by Means of Natural Selection*, published in 1859.

As you read, be sure to notice the questions in the text, which will guide you in using this perspective.

Real Issues, Real Experts

Holt author ***Deborah Appleman*** *offers strategies for teaching about the enduring qualities of poetry.*

If you want to convince your students of the enduring qualities of poetry, teach "Dover Beach." Its timeless beauty and relevance make the case for poetry. This poem is quintessentially Victorian, offering a melancholy meditation on what has been as well as what is to come. Arnold's work in general and this poem in particular offer a reflection of the confounding mixture of nature's joy and the sorrow that defines the modern human condition.

This is an apt opportunity for an interdisciplinary lesson, in which either you or your history colleagues could offer students some useful background information on the long-ago skirmishes to which the poem alludes. It might also be helpful to provide a geographical context as well. While Arnold masterfully evokes the seascape, one of the best English teachers I know swears by the power of offering photographic vistas of the actual Dover Beach to help readers visualize the setting.

The Sea of Faith
Was once, too, at the full, and round earth's shore
Lay like the folds of a bright girdle° furled.
But now I only hear
Its melancholy, long, withdrawing roar,
Retreating, to the breath
Of the night wind, down the vast edges drear
And naked shingles° of the world. **C**

Ah, love, let us be true
To one another! for the world, which seems
To lie before us like a land of dreams,
So various, so beautiful, so new,
Hath really neither joy, nor love, nor light,
Nor certitude, nor peace, nor help for pain;
And we are here as on a darkling° plain
Swept with confused alarms of struggle and flight,
Where ignorant armies clash by night.

23. girdle: belt.

28. shingles: here, beaches covered with pebbles.

35. darkling: growing gloomy or dark.

C Literary Perspectives **Analyzing Historical Context** How does Arnold contrast the religious outlook of an earlier time with that of his own?

Vocabulary **melancholy** (MEHL uhn kahl ee) *adj.:* sad or causing sadness.
certitude (SUR tuh tood) *n.:* a feeling of sureness.

Pegwell Bay, Kent—A Recollection of October 5, 1858 by William Dyce (1806–1864).
Tate Gallery, London.

It is also useful to emphasize the romantic and lyric frame of the poem. I ask students to consider the "story behind the poem." Who is the speaker? To whom is he addressing his words? You might even consider having students write out a brief dramatic scene that sets the characters and context.

Finally, invite your students to ruminate on the last stanza, writing about its relevance and resonance to the twenty-first century.

Literary Perspectives

Before students read the poem, have them read the **Literary Perspectives** about Analyzing Historical Context. Emphasize that the revolutions in France, central Europe, the Italian peninsula, Poland, and Brazil, and the publication of Darwin's theories of evolution are emblematic of widespread change. Ask students to discuss the positive and negative implications of these developments. How did they support the ideals of progress? What were the fears that Arnold and others might have had about these developments? In hindsight, were these fears founded?

Think About/Talk About

Analysis

C Literary Perspectives

Possible response: *He contrasts an earlier period's robust religious faith and the protection that faith provided to his own time's loss of religious faith and feeling of naked vulnerability.*

Extend the Discussion

Finding Details What does Arnold find lacking in his world? ***Possible response:*** *According to Arnold, the world lacks joy, love, light, certainty, peace, and healing.*

Vocabulary: Own the Word

- **blanched:** Arnold describes the land as "moon-*blanched.*" Ask students how else something might be figuratively or literally *blanched*.
- **tremulous:** Link the word *tremulous* to *tremble*. Explain that just as "to tremble" means to shake, *tremulous* connotes "shaking or quivering."
- **cadence:** Ask students to brainstorm different *cadences* that they hear frequently, such as the beat of a popular song or the sound of the school bell.
- **turbid:** Draw a semantic web on the board, with *turbid* written in the center circle. Have students brainstorm objects or ideas related to the word *turbid* and record them in the web. ***Possible responses:*** *foggy, opaque*
- **melancholy:** Ask students to recall a time when they have felt *melancholy* or consoled someone else who was feeling *melancholy.*
- **certitude:** Relate the word *certitude* to a familiar word, such as *certain.* You might say: "When you feel *certain* of something, you are sure of it. If you have *certitude,* you have a feeling of sureness."

Check for Understanding

Independent Practice

Reading Skills Focus

Possible responses:

1. *He is in a room overlooking the sea in Dover, England. He is addressing a loved one.*
2. *Human suffering comes and goes for no clear reason.*
3. *The "folds" suggest plenitude, the "girdle" security.*
4. *He draws an analogy between the sea and the beliefs that he fears are disappearing from the world.*
5. *Students should add sensory details to describe the setting.*

Literary Skills Focus

Possible responses:

6. *The "Sea of Faith" once surrounded the world like the folds of a bright belt that supported the earth.*
7. *His faith has weakened.*
8. *He urges that he and his love be true to each other, as life is difficult, painful, and uncertain.*
9. *Contrasting images—a calm sea and pebbles flung wildly—add a sense of conflict to the poem's meaning.*
10. *Arnold began the poem a few years after several European countries and Brazil were rocked by political revolutions. The last three lines might refer to these events.*
11. *"Only" disturbs the peaceful mood. "Listen!" breaks the mood.*
12. *They create a reflective mood.*
13. *The speaker's mood changes from thoughtful to melancholy.*
14. *It is like an elegy in that it expresses sadness about a loss. Unlike most elegies, "Dover Beach" does not mourn the death of an individual.*

What Do You Think Now?

Ask students to compare the way Arnold describes the physical setting of the sea and the "Sea of Faith" for which it serves as a metaphor.

Applying Your Skills

Reading Standard 3.1, 3.3, 3.7c; **Grades 9–10**
Review Reading Standard 3.12 (see pages A48–A50)
Writing Standard 2.3a (see pages A51–A52)

Dover Beach

Literary Response and Analysis

Reading Skills Focus

Quick Check

1. From where is the speaker viewing the scene (line 6)? To whom do you think he is speaking?
2. How would you paraphrase "the turbid ebb and flow / Of human misery" (lines 17–18)?
3. How does the image of "the folds of a bright girdle furled" convey a sense of safety and certainty?

Read with a Purpose

4. What analogy does Arnold make between the physical setting that he describes and the crises of his time?

Reading Skills: Visualizing Setting

5. Look back at the idea map that you drew as you read the poem. In each circle that describes an element of the setting, add words that describe it in greater detail.

Literary Skills Focus

Literary Analysis

6. **Interpret** Explain the image of the "Sea of Faith" in lines 21–23.
7. **Infer** What do you think has happened to the speaker's faith, according to lines 24–28?
8. **Summarize** What does the speaker urge in the last stanza, and why?
9. **Compare and Contrast** What contrasting images can you find in the poem? How do these contrasts contribute to the poem's meaning?
10. **Literary Perspectives** You considered how Arnold responded to the scientific and political developments of his time. How does reading the poem in the context of the mid-nineteenth century affect the way you interpret it?

Literary Skills: Mood

11. **Interpret** How do the words *Only* (line 7) and *Listen* (line 9) affect the mood of the opening?
12. **Analyze** Notice that Arnold often places commas in the middle of lines. How do these pauses contribute to the poem's mood?
13. **Draw Conclusions** Is the poem's mood the same throughout, or does it change? Support your answer with details from the text.

Literary Skills Review: Elegy

14. **Extend** An **elegy** is poem that mourns the death of a person or laments something lost. A type of lyric, an elegy is usually formal in language and structure and solemn or even melancholy in tone. In what ways is "Dover Beach" like an elegy? How is it different?

Writing Skills Focus

Think as a Reader/Writer

Use It in Your Writing Review your response to the QuickWrite, and write a short essay about the particular person, place, or thing to which you turn in difficult times. Determine what kind of mood you want to set. How can you represent the anxiety of encountering difficulties and the relief of finding support?

What Do You Think Now? How does Arnold see appearance as different from reality?

Universal Access

Struggling Writers

To complete the Writing Skills Focus activity, provide additional scaffolding for students by having them create T-charts about the person, place, or thing to which they turn during difficult times. On the left side, have them list at least two traits or qualities that describe the subject of their essay. For example, their subject might be "compassionate." On the right side, have them list an example or action that could identify this trait, such as "always puts others first in times of trouble."

Remind students to use the chart as they write about a turbulent experience they have had and explain how their particular person, place, or thing helped them survive.

Trait	Example
compassionate	always puts others first in times of trouble

Vocabulary Development

Vocabulary Check

Match the Vocabulary words with their definitions.

1. turbid	**a.** made white or pale
2. melancholy	**b.** cloudy; confused
3. cadence	**c.** quivering; wavering
4. blanched	**d.** a feeling of sureness
5. tremulous	**e.** sad or causing sadness
6. certitude	**f.** the beat of a repetitive motion; a sound that rises and falls

Vocabulary Skills: Figurative Language

If poets used language only in its most literal sense, there would not be much to poetry! Writers generate extra meaning by using words in surprising ways.

Figurative language involves bringing together seemingly unlike things, often to express a subtle or abstract meaning. Common figurative uses of language include **metaphor** and **personification**.

The dominant metaphor in "Dover Beach," for example, is the "Sea of Faith." Matthew Arnold joins the concrete noun *sea* to a very abstract one, *faith*, to conjure up the image of a time when religious belief was like an all-encompassing ocean that surrounded the world. That figurative use of language paves the way for others: If faith was once (figuratively) a sea, it now has withdrawn from the world like the withdrawing tide. The following graphic organizer charts one figurative use of language from the poem.

Example	Literal Meaning	Figurative Meaning
"the grating roar / Of pebbles which the waves draw back, and fling" (lines 9-10)	People usually fling objects.	The waves are personified as if they intended to fling the pebbles.

Your Turn

For each of the following uses of figurative language, complete a graphic organizer like the one on this page. Identify both the literal meaning of the boldface expression and its figurative use.

1. "[The waves] Begin, and cease, and then again begin, / With tremulous cadence slow, and bring / The eternal **note** of sadness in" (lines 12–15)
2. "the turbid **ebb and flow** / Of human misery" (lines 17–18)
3. "And we are here as on a **darkling plain**" (line 35)

Language Coach

Latin and French Roots Below are two Latin roots, along with related words in Spanish. Choose the Vocabulary word that is derived from each root.

Latin *certus*, "sure," related to Spanish *cierto*

Latin *cadere*, "fall," related to Spanish *cadencia*

Use a dictionary to help you find meanings for other words with Latin and French roots. You will find this information in the **etymology,** or word history, which is usually enclosed in brackets.

Academic Vocabulary

Talk About

With a partner, discuss a complex issue that causes anxiety for our time. How might we respond to the problem in a way that could benefit society?

Independent Practice
Vocabulary Development
Vocabulary Check

1. *b* **2.** *e*
3. *f* **4.** *a*
5. *c* **6.** *d*

Your Turn

1. *A note is a musical tone; figuratively, a note can mean a sign of emotion.*
2. *The phrase "ebb and flow" usually refers to the daily movement of ocean tides; figuratively, "ebb and flow" can refer to the decline and increase of intangible things like faith or love.*
3. *A "darkling plain" is a flat expanse of land at night; figuratively, a "darkling plain" might refer to a situation of confusion.*

go.hrw.com **WordSharp: An Interactive Vocabulary Tutor**

English for Academic Success
Language Coach

Possible responses: *Latin* certus—certitude; *Latin* cadere—cadence

English for Academic Success
Academic Vocabulary

Possible response: *Responses will vary. Students might discuss violence in schools, global warming, poverty, immigration, etc. Students' responses should include solutions that clearly promote peace and benefit society in some way.*

Universal Access: Vocabulary Development

English Learners

English for Academic Success Students may have difficulty distinguishing between the literal and figurative meaning of words. Write the following example on the board: "Get your head in the game," the coach *barked* at the team. Have students explain the literal meaning of the word *barked* [*to make the loud sound of a dog or a fox*]. Tell them that the writer does not mean that the coach *barked* like a dog. Instead, the writer is using figurative language to show that the coach yelled loudly. Pair students with a proficient English speaker and have them work through the following examples to identify both the literal and figurative meanings of the italicized words.

- The truck's *song* was heard throughout the neighborhood.
- The brilliant colors on the wall made the room come *alive*.
- Mark did not give the report because he got *cold feet.*

✔ See the **Academic and Selection Vocabulary Skill Builder** in **UA: Differentiating Instruction.**

Independent Practice

Grammar Link

Your Turn

1. *The world has changed, so the speaker is in doubt.*
2. *Because faith is not as strong, he turns to love.*
3. *Although the speaker offers this hope, he still sees the world as a dark place, and the poem ends on a melancholy note.*

Choices: Evaluation Criteria

Review Homework
Track the Mood of a Poem

- Students' graphs should indicate hope in the first six lines, doubt in the second half of the first stanza, and hope again in lines 29–30.
- Students may assess the hopefulness in the last stanza differently.

Connect: Timed Writing 45–50 minutes

Students should clearly differentiate their summaries of events or developments from their personal reactions to these events.

Extend Homework
Write a Poetic Sequel

- Students' poems should clearly relate to the details and themes in "Dover Beach."
- Poems should describe a setting to evoke a mood.

Assess

Unit 5 Resources, Selection Standards Check, p. 50

ThinkCentral Online Assessment, Selection Standards Check

Teacher One Stop™, editable Selection Standards Check

Reteach

ThinkCentral Online Remediation

Applying Your Skills

Reading Standard 3.3 (see pages A48–A50)
Writing Standard 2.3a–c (see pages A51–A52)

Dover Beach

Grammar Link

Sentence Structure

As you have already learned, there are four types of sentence structures: A **simple sentence** contains one independent clause and no subordinate clauses (Matthew Arnold was a poet and critic.); a **compound sentence** contains more than one independent clause and no subordinate clauses (Matthew Arnold was a poet, and he also was a critic.); a **complex sentence** contains one independent clause and at least one subordinate clause (After he almost completely stopped writing poetry, he began a career as a critic.); and a **compound-complex sentence** contains more than one independent clause and at least one subordinate clause (When he was about forty, he began a career as a critic, but he still wrote some poetry.)

Notice that the **coordinating conjunctions** *and* and *but* are used above to join independent clauses to form compound sentences. Other compound conjunctions include *or, yet, nor, for,* and *so.*

The **subordinating conjunctions** *after* and *when* are used above in the subordinate clauses of complex and compound-complex sentences. Other common subordinating conjunctions are *as, before, since, until, while, because, although,* and *if.*

Your Turn

Combine the following sentences as directed.

1. The world has changed. The speaker is in doubt. (*compound*)
2. Faith is not as strong. He turns to love. (*complex*)
3. The speaker offers this hope. He still sees the world as a dark place. The poem ends on a melancholy note. (*compound-complex*)

Writing Application Choose a piece of your own writing, and revise it to add a variety of sentence structures.

CHOICES

As you respond to the Choices, use these **Academic Vocabulary** words as appropriate: benefit, complex, publish, respond, statistics.

REVIEW

Track the Mood of a Poem

The mood of "Dover Beach" pivots between contentment and anxiety, hope and despair. Re-read the poem, and identify places where the mood shifts between these extremes. Rank each section on a scale of 1 to 5, where 1 equals "very doubtful" and 5 equals "very hopeful." Then, represent the shifting emotions of the poem visually as a graph by plotting the changing values according to the lines that express each mood.

CONNECT

Examine Current Events

Timed Writing Arnold wrote his poem in response to the scientific and political developments of his day. Think of an event or development in the world that causes you to feel concerned or worried and another event or development that gives you hope. Write an essay explaining the event or development and your reaction to it. Be sure to use specific details in your response.

EXTEND

Write a Poetic Sequel

The speaker of "Dover Beach" presents his thoughts to his beloved as she stands by him looking out the window at the ocean scene. Write a poem that expresses her answer to him. She may agree with the speaker and share his pessimistic mood. For an example of a response to a previously written poem, compare "The Passionate Shepherd to His Love" (page 278) and "The Nymph's Reply to the Shepherd" (page 279).

Universal Access: Grammar Link

EL English Learners

English for Academic Success Students may have difficulty distinguishing a compound sentence from a run-on sentence. Explain that a compound sentence has two or more independent clauses joined either by a semicolon or by a comma and a coordinating conjunction (*and, but, or, nor, for, yet,* and *so*). A run-on sentence consists of two or more independent clauses that are merged into a single sentence without the appropriate joining elements. Note that a comma alone does not properly join two independent clauses (this type of run-on sentence is sometimes called a comma splice).

✔ For more practice with sentence structure, see **Warriner's Handbook, GrammarNotes,** and **Language Handbook Worksheets.**

Reading Skills Focus

Reading Standard 2.4 (see pages A48–A50)

The Darkling Thrush / Ah, Are You Digging on My Grave?

Making Generalizations by **Kylene Beers**

When you generalize, you extend the meaning of one situation to other situations or express something in general terms on the basis of specifics. For instance, after reading about several specific battles in a war, you could generalize that the cost of war, both in human terms and in economic terms, is always high.

Making generalizations from the experiences we have each day is a natural process. If the road you take to school on Monday and Tuesday is congested with traffic, making you late, you will probably conclude that it often will be congested on weekdays and that you should take another route or leave home earlier to get to school on time.

When we make generalizations about literature, we use much the same process. Instead of using clues from our environment, we use evidence from the text—language and structure—and background knowledge to help us draw conclusions about the author's purpose and theme. We combine this information with our own experience to support generalizations we then make to relate literature to universal themes and our own lives.

We can use Thomas Hardy's poem "The Darkling Thrush" to practice making generalizations.

The speaker in the poem describes winter with dismal, ghost-like images:

> When Frost was specter-gray,
> And Winter's dregs make desolate
> The weakening eye of the day

The poet compares the barren, frozen landscape to the "Century's corpse" and uses language that extends the metaphor: "crypt" and "death-lament." The poem's speaker then makes his own generalization from the clues to make this conclusion:

> And every spirit upon earth
> Seemed fervorless as I.

Knowing that Hardy wrote the poem on December 31, 1900, the last day of the nineteenth century, allows us to observe that the poem implies a general depression among the people as they face a new century. The tone in the first half of the poem is as desolate as the landscape.

Structure also helps us make generalizations about purpose and theme. The second half of the poem shifts from winter to focus on "an aged thrush" that provides a "full-hearted evensong."

Your Turn

Read the last stanza of "The Darkling Thrush" to practice making generalizations about the purpose and theme.

> So little cause for carolings
> Of such ecstatic sound
> Was written on terrestrial things
> Afar or nigh around,
> That I could think there trembled through
> His happy good-night air
> Some blessed Hope, whereof he knew
> And I was unaware.

One caveat: We risk making invalid generalizations if we use faulty reasoning or inadequate information. Be sure to use sufficient and relevant information in your generalizations and to note exceptions.

1. How does the language in this last stanza differ from that of the first two stanzas? What images suggest a change in Hardy's tone?
2. How does the structure and language help us generalize about the way the poem's speaker and others will actually greet the new century?

Reading Skills Focus

Objectives

Students will make generalizations.

Unit 5 Resources, Reading Focus Skill Builder, p. 46

Teacher One Stop™, lesson plan and all print resources

Direct Teach

Making Generalizations

This feature gives students practice in making generalizations while they read Thomas Hardy's poem "The Darkling Thrush." Have students read the feature and complete the Your Turn activity before reading the entire poem.

Check for Understanding

Your Turn

Possible responses:

1. *Words such as "ecstatic," "happy," and "blessed," as well as auditory images like "ecstatic sound" and "happy good-night air," suggest a shift to a mood of joy and hope.*
2. *In lines 15–16, the speaker says that "every spirit on earth / Seemed fervorless as I," but the last stanza ends on a note of hope, so readers can generalize that the speaker and others will greet the new century with optimism.*

California Standards, p. 971

- **Reading Standard 2.4** Make warranted and reasonable assertions about the author's arguments by using elements of the text to defend and clarify interpretations.

Universal Access

English Learners

English for Academic Success Help students understand the unfamiliar words that Hardy uses by providing the following definitions:

- **dregs**—the least desirable parts of something
- **desolate**—gloomy; barren; joyless
- **fervorless**—without intensity or passion
- **ecstatic**—filled with intense happiness
- **terrestrial**—of or belonging to the earth
- **nigh**—near [archaic]

Standards Focus

Objectives

Students will
- identify the speaker of a text
- make generalizations

Selection Introduction

Think About the Writer

To help students answer the question, ask them to consider the themes of Hardy's novels and the skills and personality usually associated with the author's careers.

For Independent Reading

Jude the Obscure, Thomas Hardy

Motivate

What Do You Think?/QuickWrite

Discuss how mood can color people's perspective. Have students record their responses in their **Reader/Writer Notebooks.**

English for Academic Success

Academic Vocabulary

Look for opportunities to use the Academic Vocabulary words in this unit.

- **complex,** ***adj.:*** hard to understand; complicated
- **publish,** ***v.:*** print and issue for the public
- **respond,** ***v.:*** react

California Standards, pp. 972–979

- **Reading Standard 2.4** Make warranted and reasonable assertions about the author's arguments by using elements of the text to defend and clarify interpretations.
- **Reading Standard 3.4** Analyze ways in which poets use imagery, personification, figures of speech, and sounds to evoke readers' emotions.

Preparing to Read

The Darkling Thrush

Ah, Are You Digging on My Grave?

What Do You Think?

How can appearance be different from reality?

QuickWrite

How can events change your mood? What might make you feel more optimistic or pessimistic about a situation? In your *Reader/Writer Notebook*, record a few memories about times when your mood changed unexpectedly. What caused each change?

MEET THE WRITER

Thomas Hardy

(1840–1928)

One of Victorian Britain's principal novelists, Hardy began and ended his literary career as a poet.

From Village to City and Back Again

Thomas Hardy was born in a small village in Dorsetshire, an area in southwestern England, which was the setting (under the ancient name of Wessex) of many of his novels and poems. He attended the village school until he was sixteen, when he was apprenticed to an architect.

In 1862, Hardy began working as an architect in London, writing poems and stories in his free time. He tried without success to publish his poems, but by the time he returned to Dorset in 1867, he had started to publish fiction. After the publication of his fourth novel, *Far from the Madding Crowd* (1874), Hardy was able to stop working as an architect and devote himself entirely to writing.

A Dark Vision of the World

The plots and themes of Hardy's fourteen novels express his belief in a world governed by chance and natural laws that are indifferent to what humans want and deserve. In some novels, the entire course of a character's life is determined by coincidence. People make matters worse by adding the misery of war, the cruelty of ingratitude and neglect, and the irrationality of laws and customs that frustrate talent and desire.

The bleakness, pessimism, and irony of Hardy's novels disturbed many readers. After *Tess of the D'Urbervilles* received unfavorable reviews in 1892, and *Jude the Obscure* was denounced in 1895, Hardy turned away from writing novels.

Hardy published *Wessex Poems* in 1898, when he was in his late fifties. The tone and style of his poems reveal a late-Victorian mood of somberness, with language that has an informal directness. He frequently uses archaic words or homely diction as a reaction against the elaborate language of some late-Victorian verse. Hardy's verse, though deceptively simple, resounds with the voice of twentieth-century poetry.

Think About the Writer Why might it seem ironic that Hardy said he believed that humans can change for the better?

Thomas Hardy by Reginald Grenville Eves (1876–1941). Oil on canvas. Towner Art Gallery, Eastbourne, UK.

Selection Readability	
Easily Accessible Accessible **Challenging**	These poems include unfamiliar vocabulary; challenging syntax.

Reading Standard 2.4, 3.4 (see pages A48–A50)

Literary Skills Focus

Speaker You might think of every poem as talking to readers with its own unique voice. The **speaker** is the imaginary voice assumed by the author of a poem. In many poems, the speaker is close to the author, reflecting his or her personality and thoughts. You should not, however, assume that the speaker of the poem is the same as the author. Poets may shift the persona for each poem they write. The speaker of one poem might be a passionate lover; another speaker may be an isolated loner.

Reading Skills Focus

Making Generalizations From textual clues, we can make **generalizations**, or broad assertions. The more evidence we have, the more accurate our generalization is likely to be. Limited evidence often leads to weak generalizations. For example, if you read three lines from Hardy and determine that he is a pessimist, you have generalized too quickly and with too little evidence. If you read two poems and determine that Hardy sometimes uses elements of nature to represent various moods, you have made a generalization from a larger amount of evidence. You must then prove the accuracy of your generalization by returning to the texts.

Into Action As you read the poems, take notes on the following topics.

Topic	Ah, Are You Digging . . .	The Darkling Thrush
Death		
Winter		

Writing Skills Focus

Think as a Reader/Writer

Find It in Your Reading Hardy chooses adjectives to create vivid images. As you read these poems, make a list in your *Reader/Writer Notebook* of adjectives that effectively create vivid mental images.

TechFocus As you read the poems, think about how the speaker of each poem might identify himself or herself on a social networking Web site.

Vocabulary

desolate (DEHS uh liht) *adj.:* uninhabited; barren; dreary. *The desolate landscape includes just one frail tree and nothing else.*

ecstatic (ehk STAT ihk) *adj.:* extremely joyful; showing great pleasure. *Seeing even one ray of sunshine would make me ecstatic on this gloomy, rainy day.*

prodding (PRAHD ihng) *v.:* poking; jabbing. *Someone is prodding in the dirt, looking for something lost there.*

fidelity (fuh DEHL uh tee) *n.:* loyalty; faithfulness. *Dogs show their fidelity by protecting and guarding their owners.*

Language Coach

Double Letters The verb *prod* has one syllable, a short vowel sound, and ends with a single consonant. When you add *-ing* to this verb, you double the *d* and spell the verb *prodding.* What other verbs can you think of that follow this double-letter rule?

Reader/Writer Notebook

Use your **RWN** to complete the activities for these selections.

Learn It Online
Listen to these poems online.
go.hrw.com H12-973 Go

Selection Resources

Unit 5 Resources, on-level practice and assessment, p. 53

Teacher One Stop™, on-level lesson plans and all print resources

Holt Audio Library

Holt Audio Library: Selections and Summaries in Spanish

UA: Differentiating Instruction, graphic organizer, p. 236

UA: Supporting Instruction in Spanish, selection summary

ThinkCentral Online Assessment, Selection Standards Check

ThinkCentral Online Remediation

Preteach

Introducing Vocabulary

- Review the Vocabulary words, definitions, and sentences with students.
- Tell students that Hardy uses these words to evoke vivid feelings. The speaker of "The Darkling Thrush" finds his setting *desolate* until he hears the *ecstatic* song of a thrush. The speaker of "Ah, Are You Digging on My Grave?" conveys her annoyance when she asks if it is her enemy *prodding* her grave. On learning that it is her dog, she mistakenly attributes his actions to *fidelity.*

English for Academic Success

Language Coach

Have students think of an example for each short vowel sound. Encourage volunteers to share their responses with the class. ***Possible responses:*** *napping, betting, sitting, mopping, running*

Literary Skills Focus

As you read and discuss the poems with students, have them look for clues about the characteristics of the poems' respective speakers.

Reading Skills Focus

Give students copies of the Reading Skills Focus graphic organizer before they read. (See **Unit 5 Resources.**) Tell them to use their responses to answer the questions on the Applying Your Skills page.

Writing Skills Focus

Have students record in their **Reader/Writer Notebooks** the vivid adjectives that Hardy uses. Students can use their notes to complete the Writing Skills Focus activity.

Learn It Online
The online version of this poem includes audio support to engage all students and to help struggling readers with reading comprehension and vocabulary.
go.hrw.com H12–973 Go

Teacher Preparation

Selection Summary

"The Darkling Thrush" is set in a desolate winter landscape. The speaker hears the joyful song of an old, frail thrush—a hearty sound in stark contrast to the barren earth. The speaker is deeply moved by the bird's song, which seems to express a hope that the speaker himself does not possess.

Direct Teach

Think About/Talk About

Read with a Purpose Have students read the Read with a Purpose statement. Point out that the poem's title provides a clue about the sign that will produce a change of mood. Ask students to predict how the thrush will bring about this change.

POEM

The Darkling Thrush

by **Thomas Hardy**

Read with a Purpose

Read to discover how a small sign can lead to a surprising change of mood.

Build Background

"The Darkling Thrush" was written on December 31, 1900, the last day of the nineteenth century. As night falls, the speaker in the poem hears a thrush (a bird) singing joyfully. His thrush, like the century, is worn out and diminished—but still singing.

Universal Access

English Learners

English for Academic Success Students may be unfamiliar with some of the vocabulary in the poem. Review the Vocabulary words introduced on p. 973, and provide explanations of other unfamiliar words in this poem. For example, explain that a *specter* is a ghost and a *crypt* is a burial chamber. Point out that a *lyre* is an ancient Greek instrument. *Evensong* means evening prayer, and *blast,* in this context, refers to a gust of wind.

Struggling Readers

Benchmark Students Model how to make generalizations about the text. You might say: "In the last stanza, the author suggests that although the speaker would like to admire the old thrush for singing so bravely, there is 'little cause for carolings' (l. 25). This indicates to me that the speaker has only a faint sense of hope for the future of humanity. He does not understand why the bird sings because there is so little to sing about." As students read, have them look for clues that

I leant upon a coppice° gate
  When Frost was specter-gray,
And Winter's dregs made desolate
  The weakening eye of day.
The tangled bine-stems° scored the sky
  Like strings of broken lyres,
And all mankind that haunted nigh
  Had sought their household fires. **A**

The land's sharp features seemed to be
  The Century's corpse outleant,°
His crypt the cloudy canopy,
  The wind his death-lament.
The ancient pulse of germ° and birth
  Was shrunken hard and dry,
And every spirit upon earth
  Seemed fervorless as I. **B**

At once a voice arose among
  The bleak twigs overhead
In a fullhearted evensong
  Of joy illimited;
An aged thrush, frail, gaunt, and small,
  In blast-beruffled plume,
Had chosen thus to fling his soul
  Upon the growing gloom.

So little cause for carolings
  Of such ecstatic sound
Was written on terrestrial things
  Afar or nigh around,
That I could think there trembled through
  His happy good-night air
Some blessed Hope, whereof he knew
  And I was unaware.

1. coppice: thicket of small trees or shrubs.

5. bine-stems: climbing plants.

10. outleant: leaning out. Here, the word refers to leaning out of the crypt.

13. germ: seed or bud.

A **Literary Focus** **Speaker** What image do you have of the speaker after reading the first stanza?

B **Reading Focus** **Making Generalizations** What generalization can you make about why the speaker lacks energy?

Vocabulary **desolate** (DEHS uh liht) *adj.:* uninhabited; barren; dreary.
ecstatic (ehk STAT ihk) *adj.:* extremely joyful; showing great pleasure.

Think About/Talk About

Comprehension

B Reading Focus

Possible response: *The speaker's allusions to weakness and preoccupation with images of death suggest he may lack energy because he is old.*

Analysis

A Literary Focus

Possible responses: *He is weary (leans on a gate), pessimistic (finds the day "desolate"), and alone (others are at their "household fires").*

Extend the Discussion

Finding Details What sensory details in the first two stanzas help convey the dreariness of the setting? ***Possible responses:*** *Daylight is weak and fading; the wind is blowing, and the land is hard and dry.*

Recognizing Philosophical Assumptions What kind of philosophical assumptions does the speaker of "The Darkling Thrush" bring to his interpretation of nature's signs? ***Possible responses:*** *He admits that he "could think" that the bird has some reason for hope, but his bleak uncertainty leaves readers with the idea that no matter what the bird knows, he himself is unaware of any reason to hope.*

Vocabulary: Own the Word

- **desolate:** Draw a semantic web on the board with *desolate* written in the center circle. Have students brainstorm objects or ideas related to the word *desolate* and record them in the web. ***Possible responses:*** *lonely, empty, abandoned*
- **ecstatic:** Ask students to recall an example from their own lives of a time when they felt *ecstatic.*

support and contradict the generalization that there is only a faint sense of hope for the future of humanity.

Advanced Learners

Enrichment Much is made by critics of the fact that Hardy wrote "The Darkling Thrush" on the last day of the nineteenth century. Have students find a poem written during the last year of the twentieth century (2000) and compare the two poems. Do students notice any common threads? Have them read aloud the modern-day poems and share their observations.

Developing Oral Fluency

Invite students to prepare and perform part or all of "The Darkling Thrush" as a dramatic reading. Encourage students to try to capture not only Hardy's poetic rhythm and imagery but also what they imagine to be the speaker's mental condition. Students should make creative use of the pitch, tone, and volume of their voices and gestures.

✔ See **UA: Differentiating Instruction** for practice passages for developing oral fluency.

Teacher Preparation

Selection Summary

The first speaker, a dead woman, hears someone digging on her grave and asks who it is. She guesses that it may be her beloved, her family, or her worst enemy. The digger answers no to all three guesses. The woman learns that the digger is her dog, who is merely burying a bone, not visiting her.

Direct Teach

Think About/Talk About

Read with a Purpose Point out that the poem's title provides a clue to the identity of the speaker. Ask students to predict who the "you" in the title refers to.

Comprehension

B Reading Focus

Possible response: *According to the speaker, our feelings for people tend to fade after they die, and we become indifferent to them.*

Analysis

A Literary Focus

Possible response: *She is dead and buried, and she cannot see the person to whom she is talking. She hopes people miss her.*

C Literary Focus

Possible responses: *The speaker of the final stanza is the dead woman's former dog. She might respond to the dog's words with anger and disappointment.*

POEM

Ah, Are You Digging on My Grave?

by **Thomas Hardy**

Read with a Purpose

Read to discover the identity of an unusual speaker—and the surprising answer to her mysterious question.

Build Background

"Ah, Are You Digging on My Grave?" is written in the form of a dialogue. The poem's speaker has only limited information about her situation—and she therefore receives some very unexpected answers to her repeated questions.

"Ah, are you digging on my grave,
My loved one?—planting rue?"° **A**
—"No: Yesterday he went to wed
One of the brightest wealth has bred.
'It cannot hurt her now,' he said,
'That I should not be true.'"

"Then who is digging on my grave?
My nearest dearest kin?"
—"Ah, no: They sit and think, 'What use!
What good will planting flowers produce?
No tendance of her mound can loose
Her spirit from Death's gin.'"°

"But some one digs upon my grave?
My enemy?—prodding sly?"
—"Nay: When she heard you had passed the Gate
That shuts on all flesh soon or late,
She thought you no more worth her hate,
And cares not where you lie." **B**

"Then, who is digging on my grave?
Say—since I have not guessed!"
—"O it is I, my mistress dear,
Your little dog, who still lives near,
And much I hope my movements here
Have not disturbed your rest?"

"Ah, yes! *You* dig upon my grave . . .
Why flashed it not on me
That one true heart was left behind!
What feeling do we ever find
To equal among human kind
A dog's fidelity!"

"Mistress, I dug upon your grave
To bury a bone, in case
I should be hungry near this spot
When passing on my daily trot.
I am sorry, but I quite forgot
It was your resting place." **C**

2. rue: yellow-flowered herb associated with grief.
12. gin: trap.

A Literary Focus **Speaker** Who is the speaker, and what is her situation?

B Reading Focus **Making Generalizations** What can you generalize from this stanza about how we feel about people after they die?

C Literary Focus **Speaker** Who speaks in the poem's final lines? How might the speaker of the poem respond to these lines?

Vocabulary **prodding** (PRAHD ihng) *v.:* poking; jabbing. **fidelity** (fuh DEHL uh tee) *n.:* loyalty; faithfulness.

Universal Access

Struggling Readers

This poem includes two speakers, along with the reported speech of others. Review with students the use of quotation marks. The first two stanzas of the poem make use of single quotation marks within double quotation marks. Be sure that students understand that such punctuation indicates one speaker is repeating the exact words of another. It may help students to rewrite the poem in the form of a dialogue with the words of each speaker following his or her name.

Advanced Learners

Enrichment Have students read some of the poems of American poet Edgar Lee Masters from his *Spoon River Anthology* and compare his characters to Hardy's. What, for example, might Masters's Lucinda Matlock say to Hardy's speaker in this poem?

Analyzing Visuals

Connecting to the Text Does this image illustrate "a dog's fidelity" toward humans, or something else? Explain.

Give a Dog a Bone (1888) by William Henry Hamilton Trood (1860–1899). Private Collection.

Think About/Talk About

Extend the Discussion

Summarizing Summarize the questions the speaker of the poem asks and the replies she receives. ***Possible response:*** *She asks whether the following people are digging on her grave: her lover, her family, and her enemy. Her dog replies that her lover has married someone else, her family neglects her grave, and her enemy is indifferent to her now that she is dead. Finally, her dog reveals his identity. The speaker is touched at the dog's loyalty but is then informed that he only wanted to bury a bone.*

Vocabulary: Own the Word

- **prodding:** Remind students that *prodding* has the connotation of poking someone very hard. You might say, for example, "She did not wake up when I tapped her—I practically had to *prod* her in the side to get her to open her eyes."
- **fidelity:** Ask students to give an example from their own lives when they have proven their *fidelity* to someone or something—a friend, an ideal, an opinion—or when someone has proven their *fidelity* to them.

Analyzing Visuals

Connecting to the Text: *The dog in the image guards a bone in front of him. He keeps his back to the viewer and turns his head slightly to see who might be eyeing his treasure. This painting portrays "a dog's fidelity" as ironically as does Hardy's poem on the same subject.*

California Standards, pp. 978–979

- **Reading Standard 2.4** Make warranted and reasonable assertions about the author's arguments by using elements of the text to defend and clarify interpretations.
- **Reading Standard 3.3** Analyze the ways in which irony, tone, mood, the author's style, and the "sound" of language achieve specific rhetorical or aesthetic purposes or both.
- **Reading Standard 3.4** Analyze ways in which poets use imagery, personification, figures of speech, and sounds to evoke readers' emotions.
- **Grades 9–10 Review Reading Standard 1.1** Identify and use the literal and figurative meanings of words and understand word derivations.
- **Writing Standard 2.2** Write responses to literature: **a.** Demonstrate a comprehensive understanding of the significant ideas in works or passages. **b.** Analyze the use of imagery, language, universal themes, and unique aspects of the text. **c.** Support important ideas and viewpoints through accurate and detailed references to the text and to other works. **d.** Demonstrate an understanding of the author's use of stylistic devices and an appreciation of the effects created.
- **Writing Standard 2.6** Deliver multimedia presentations: **a.** Combine text, images, and sound and draw information from many sources (e.g., television broadcasts, videos, films, newspapers, magazines, CD-ROMs, the Internet, electronic media-generated images).

Applying Your Skills

Reading Standard 2.4, 3.3, 3.4 (see pages A48–A50)
Writing Standard 2.2a, 2.2b (see pages A51–A52)

The Darkling Thrush /
Ah, Are You Digging on My Grave?

Literary Response and Analysis

Reading Skills Focus

Quick Check

1. At what time of day and year does "The Darkling Thrush" take place?
2. What noise disturbs the speaker's train of thought, and how does he respond to it?
3. The speaker of "Ah, Are You Digging on My Grave?" suspects three people of disturbing her peace. Who are they?

Read with a Purpose

4. How does the speaker of each poem receive a surprise? What change does each surprise create?

Reading Skills: Making Generalizations

5. Review the notes you made while reading the two poems. Think about the broad generalizations you can make about Thomas Hardy's poetry. Write two statements that make valid generalizations that can be supported with the evidence in your notes. Choose two of the following sentence stems to help you write the statements. Be prepared to support your generalizations with evidence from the poems.

Hardy asserts that ______________________________
______________________________.

Hardy demonstrates that ______________________________
______________________________.

Hardy is optimistic/pessimistic (choose one)
because ______________________________
______________________________.

Literary Skills Focus

Literary Analysis

6. **Draw Conclusions** Does the speaker's **mood,** or emotion, change significantly in the course of "The Darkling Thrush"? If so, how?
7. **Interpret** What do you think is the significance of the word *darkling* in the title? Do you think the thrush's song seems hopeful or hopeless?
8. **Analyze** How does the character of the dog combine animal traits with human qualities?

Literary Skills: Speaker

9. **Compare and Contrast** How are the speakers of these two poems different? Which speaker do you associate more closely with Hardy? Why?

Literary Skills Review: Tone

10. **Analyze** How would you describe the **tone,** or attitude toward the subject, of each poem? How do you think Hardy feels about sentimental attitudes toward nature and death?

Writing Skills Focus

Think as a Reader/Writer

Use It in Your Writing In your *Reader/Writer Notebook,* write a brief description of a person, place, or thing that you think creates a strong emotion or mood. Follow Hardy's model, and use precise, vivid adjectives to sharpen your description.

What Do You Think Now? Which speaker grows more pessimistic as the poem continues? Which speaker's mood improves? Why?

Check for Understanding

Independent Practice

Reading Skills Focus

Possible responses:

1. *It takes place on a winter evening on the last day of the year.*
2. *A bird's joyful song disturbs his thoughts; he finds it out of place.*
3. *She suspects her beloved, her closest relatives, and her greatest enemy.*
4. *One speaker, surprised by the cheerful song of a thrush in a gloomy landscape, is given the possibility of hope. The other speaker is surprised to see who is visiting her grave and why.*
5. *Students' generalizations should be consistent with the tone of the poems and be supported with details.*

Literary Skills Focus

Possible responses:

6. *Most students will sense some hope in the speaker at the poem's end; others may feel that his hopeless mood remains.*
7. *Darkling means "in the dark"; the word suggests emotional gloom as well as physical darkness.*
8. *Animal traits include routine surveillance of territory and burying of bones. Human traits include speaking, apologizing for having disturbed the grave, and preparing for the future.*
9. *The speaker of "The Darkling Thrush" is more skeptical and thus seems more closely associated with Hardy than the more naïve speaker of "Ah, Are You Digging on My Grave?"*
10. *"The Darkling Thrush" conveys gloom mingled with faint hope; in expressing doubt about the bird's reason for singing, Hardy mocks sentimental attitudes toward nature. The tone of "Ah, Are You Digging on My Grave" is wry, ironic, and bitter; Hardy seems to be mocking sentimental ideas toward death and grieving.*

Universal Access

Struggling Writers

To help students write descriptively, tell them to start by making a list of three important qualities of the person, place, or thing they are describing. Have students elaborate on each quality by jotting down some related adjectives or verbs. Have them use their list of key terms to write a description of the person, place, or thing. Tell them to include at least one sentence about each of the three qualities.

What Do You Think Now?

To help students answer this question, have them compare the beginning and ending of each poem. Point out that the first stanza of "The Darkling Thrush" includes the words *dregs, desolate, broken,* and *haunted,* while the last stanza includes the words *ecstatic, happy, blessed,* and *hope.*

Grades 9–10 Review Reading Standard 1.1 (see pages A48–A50)
Writing Standard 2.2a–d, 2.6a (see pages A51–A52)

Vocabulary Development

Vocabulary Check

Complete each item. Use the boldface Vocabulary word in your response.

1. List three reasons for **prodding** the ground.
2. Describe a **desolate** setting for a movie.
3. Identify one sign of a pet's **fidelity** to its owner.
4. Describe what makes you feel **ecstatic**.

Vocabulary Skills: Synonyms

Synonyms are words with the same or similar meanings. If you replace a word in a sentence and the meaning of the sentence does not change significantly, the words are synonyms:

Original: Show your **fidelity** to our team by coming to the game on Saturday.
Replacements: Show your **trust** to our team by coming to the game on Saturday. Show your **loyalty** to our team by coming to the game on Saturday.

The word *trust* changes the meaning of the sentence, so *fidelity* and *trust* are not synonyms. The word *loyalty* does not greatly change the meaning of the sentence, so *fidelity* and *loyalty* are synonyms.

Your Turn

Write sentences to test whether or not each pair of words are synonyms. Explain your answers.

1. desolate; deserted
2. desolate; shadowy
3. ecstatic; energetic
4. ecstatic; thrilled

Language Coach

Double Letters Recall that when you add *-ing* to the verb *prod*, you double the *d* and spell *prodding*. What other verbs in "Ah, Are You Digging on My Grave?" follow this pattern?

CHOICES

As you respond to the Choices, use these **Academic Vocabulary** words as appropriate: benefit, complex, publish, respond, statistics.

REVIEW

Retell What Happens

Review the key events in each poem by writing a short summary of what happens. For each poem, create a chart to record the basic information to include in your retellings. In one column include the language of the poem, and then write your own retelling in a second column.

CONNECT

Create a Social Networking Page

TechFocus Choose one of these poems and create a page as if on a social networking site for the poem's speaker. Use clues in the poem to identify the speaker's character and possible interests. Based on the poem, what kind of person is the speaker? How would he or she want to be presented to the world? Share your completed page with your class.

EXTEND

Draft a Response

Timed Writing The speaker in "The Darkling Thrush" seems to feel little hope that the problems of the world can be solved. Do you agree or disagree? Are there problems in today's society that you think are so complex and overwhelming that they will never go away? Write an essay in which you respond to Hardy's position.

Learn It Online
Develop your vocabulary with Word Watch online.
go.hrw.com H12-979 Go

Independent Practice

Choices: Evaluation Criteria

Review: Homework
Retell What Happens
Summaries include the most important events of each poem.

Connect: Homework
Create a Social Networking Page
Make sure the page describes speaker's character and his or her possible interests based on clues in the poem.

Extend: Timed Writing 45–50 minutes
Students' essays cite evidence to support their views.

Assess

Unit 5 Resources, Selection Standards Check, p. 56

ThinkCentral Online Assessment, Selection Standards Check

Teacher One Stop™, editable Selection Standards Check

Reteach

ThinkCentral Online Remediation

Vocabulary Development

Vocabulary Check

1. *Prodding the ground can be a way to look for worms, buried treasure, or bones.*
2. *A land made barren by fire would be a* desolate *landscape.*
3. *A dog shows fidelity by protecting its owner.*
4. *Getting a perfect score on a test makes me feel ecstatic.*

Your Turn

1. *Synonyms;* Desolate *means* deserted.
2. Shadowy *has to do with darkness;* desolate *denotes hopelessness.*
3. Energetic *means active, not* thrilled.
4. *Synonyms;* Ecstatic *means* thrilled.

English for Academic Success

Language Coach

Possible response: *digging*

Learn It Online
Send students to **Word Watch** for audio pronunciations, synonyms and antonyms, and brief histories of word origins.
go.hrw.com H12-979 Go

Standards Focus

Objectives

Students will
- analyze couplets
- connect form and meaning
- understand theme

Selection Introduction

Think About the Writer

Discuss how Housman's scholarly background might have shaped his approach to poetry.

Motivate

What Do You Think?/QuickWrite

Have students think about representations of love and death in movies or novels. Then, have them consider stories they read in which love or death is personified.

For Independent Reading

A Tale of Two Cities, Charles Dickens

English for Academic Success

Academic Vocabulary

Look for opportunities to use the Academic Vocabulary words in this unit.

- **publish, *v.*:** print and issue for the public
- **respond, *v.*:** react
- **statistics, *n.*:** numerical facts

California Standards, pp. 980–987

- **Reading Standard 2.2** Analyze the way in which clarity of meaning is affected by the patterns of organization, hierarchical structures, repetition of the main ideas, syntax, and word choice in the text.
- **Reading Standard 3.4** Analyze ways in which poets use imagery, personification, figures of speech, and sounds to evoke readers' emotions.

Preparing to Read

To an Athlete Dying Young

When I Was One-and-Twenty

What Do You Think? How can appearance be different from reality?

QuickWrite

What are some of the familiar ideas that people have about love and death? Brainstorm a list of images and ideas people commonly associate with each topic. Which of these ideas do you think are sometimes—or always—false?

Alfred Edward Housman, English scholar and poet, aged eighteen.

MEET THE WRITER

A. E. Housman

(1859–1936)

A. E. Housman said that he was careful not to think of poetry while he was shaving, for "if a line of poetry strays into my memory, my skin bristles so that the razor ceases to act."

Finding Poetry in Self-Control

For Alfred Edward Housman, poetry was all feeling. He said the source of his poetry was "the pit of the stomach," but his poetry is more restrained than this comment suggests. His poems evoke a narrow range of subdued feelings that are controlled by simple, tight verse forms and clear language and syntax.

During his lifetime, Housman published only two books of poetry. His first collection, *A Shropshire Lad* (1896), became popular because its graceful recollection of youthful pleasures and their transience fit a late-century mood of disillusionment that had "much good, but much less good than ill." In "Terence, This Is Stupid Stuff," Housman acknowledged that his poems could be dismissed as self-indulgent whining. The test of poetry, he believed, is not what is said but how it is said. In the refined elegance of his poems, he expressed his pessimistic vision of a cold, empty world.

Overcoming Early Failure

Born in Worcestershire in western England, Housman was close to his mother, who died on his twelfth birthday. His father, a lawyer, allowed his practice to dwindle away. At sixteen, Housman won a scholarship to Oxford, where he studied classical literature. He attended classes irregularly, though, preferring to study on his own, and failed his final examination.

In 1882, Housman took a job as a clerk in the patent office, but remained determined to prove himself as a classical scholar. For the next ten years, he set for himself a rigorous program and published several papers on Greek and Latin literature. In 1892, he won an appointment as professor of Latin at London University. He stayed until 1911, when he moved to Cambridge University. He spent the rest of his life as a formal and rather aloof teacher and authority in classical scholarship.

Think About the Writer How might Housman's careers as a clerk and a scholar have influenced his poetry?

Selection Readability	
Easily Accessible **Accessible** Challenging	These poems include chronological order; accessible vocabulary; accessible theme; short stanzas.

Reading Standard 2.2, 3.4 (see pages A48–A50)

Literary Skills Focus

Couplet "To an Athlete Dying Young" is written entirely in couplets. A **couplet** is a pair of lines, one after another, that rhyme. The lines in a couplet usually share the same meter as well. In Housman's poem, each couplet is joined with another to form a four-line stanza. The strong rhythm created by this pattern fits the poem's somber subject matter—death—and mimics the slow, mournful tempo of a funeral procession.

Reading Skills Focus

Analyzing the Relationship of Form and Meaning The form of a poem is the way it is structured. Most poems arrange ideas in lines and stanzas, and many poems use meter. In "To an Athlete Dying Young," Housman's form is two-line couplets paired in four-line stanzas. Each line has four stresses. Thinking about form as you read will help you understand the **meaning** the writer wants to communicate through poetry. Ask yourself, "Why did the poet choose this form rather than another? How does this form support the meaning of the poem?"

Into Action Use a chart like the one below to paraphrase each stanza as you read. Paying attention to the meaning of each stanza will help you understand how the poet structures ideas.

Stanza	Paraphrase
1	When you won the race, we carried you through town, celebrating your victory.
2	Today we're once again carrying you on our shoulders, but it's a much quieter occasion.
3	

Writing Skills Focus

Think as a Reader/Writer

Find It in Your Reading Housman was a master of **understatement**. He expressed deep emotions, but never exaggerated or embellished them. In his careful language, the world of the dead becomes simply "a stiller town." As you read, record in your *Reader/Writer Notebook* other examples of understatement that express strong feelings.

Reader/Writer Notebook

Use your **RWN** to complete the activities for this selection.

Vocabulary

withers (WIHTH uhrz) *v.:* fades; dries up. *After it blooms, the rose soon withers and dies.*

renown (rih NOWN) *n.:* fame; celebrity. *He was an athlete of such great renown that everyone referred to him by his first name alone.*

Language Coach

Pronunciation Remember that poets choose words for both their meaning and their sound. Take time to learn how to pronounce unfamiliar words—it will help you hear what the poet wants you to hear. Notice that *renown* rhymes with *town,* not *own.* How does knowing how to pronounce *renown* help you appreciate "To an Athlete Dying Young"?

Learn It Online

Take your study of this poem further with these project suggestions online.

go.hrw.com H12-981 Go

Selection Resources

Unit 5 Resources, on-level practice and assessment, pp. 59–60

Teacher One Stop™, on-level lesson plans and all print resources

Holt Audio Library

Holt Audio Library: Selections and Summaries in Spanish

UA: Differentiating Instruction, graphic organizer p. 237

UA: Supporting Instruction in Spanish, selection summary

ThinkCentral Online Assessment, Selection Standards Check

ThinkCentral Online Remediation

Preteach

Introducing Vocabulary

- Review the Vocabulary words, definitions, and sentences with students.
- Tell students that the Vocabulary words are used to describe an athlete whose *renown* endures because he died young. Unlike other athletes' fame, his does not *wither* away.

English for Academic Success

Language Coach

Encourage students to examine the couplet containing a "half rhyme" (ll. 5–6, *come* and *home*). Inform students they should still use proper pronunciation for both words.

Literary Skills Focus

As you read and discuss the poem with students, have them note the form of each line and think about how it relates to the meaning of the poem.

Reading Skills Focus

Give students a copy of the Reading Skills Focus graphic organizer. (See **Unit 5 Resources.**) Have students use their notes to answer the questions on the Applying Your Skills page.

Writing Skills Focus

Have students record examples of understatement in their **Reader/Writer Notebooks** and use their notes to complete the Writing Skills Focus activity.

Learn It Online

MediaScope can help guide students through the process of creating a multimedia presentation—from choosing a subject and planning to publishing their finished project.

go.hrw.com H12-981 Go

Teacher Preparation

Selection Summary

In "To an Athlete Dying Young," the speaker addresses a young athlete who once received the town's adulation and was carried aloft in victory. Now the young man's body is held high in a funeral procession. The speaker claims that the athlete is lucky to have died young, as he will never see his records surpassed or his name forgotten. Instead he will amaze the "strengthless" dead with his unfading youth and glory.

Direct Teach

Think About/Talk About

Read with a Purpose Have students read the Read with a Purpose statement. Have students note any positive views of death they find in the poem.

Comprehension

B Reading Focus

Possible response: *The speaker suggests the athlete is clever to die before his fame and glory fade.*

Analysis

A Literary Focus

Possible responses: *The first couplet is iambic, alternating between unstressed and stressed syllables. Not all, but most, of the couplets share this rhythm.*

C Literary Focus

Possible response: *The phrase "fleet foot" puts two stressed syllables together for emphasis.*

Extend the Discussion

Metaphor Line 5 refers to "the road all runners come." What does the road represent? Why is this metaphor effective? ***Possible response:*** *The "road all runners come" represents death. This metaphor is effective because the young man was known for being a great runner, but the "road" of his life ultimately ends in death, just as it does for everyone else.*

POEM

To an Athlete Dying Young

by **A. E. Housman**

Read with a Purpose

Read to discover how one speaker views dying young.

Build Background

"To an Athlete Dying Young" appeared in 1896 in the first edition of *A Shropshire Lad*, a volume Housman himself paid to have published. The poet scarcely made a profit from this book of sixty-three verses, which often tell stories in the voice of a young soldier or farm boy. However, Housman lived to see his poems become enormously popular during the Boer War. Soldiers fighting in South Africa identified with the homesick lad from Shropshire and heard in his voice the echo of their own melancholy.

The time you won your town the race
We chaired you through the marketplace; **A**
Man and boy stood cheering by,
And home we brought you shoulder-high.

Today, the road all runners come,
Shoulder-high we bring you home,
And set you at your threshold down,
Townsman of a stiller town.

Smart lad, to slip betimes° away
From fields where glory does not stay
And early though the laurel° grows
It withers quicker than the rose. **B**

Eyes the shady night has shut
Cannot see the record cut,
And silence sounds no worse than cheers
After earth has stopped the ears:

Now you will not swell the rout
Of lads that wore their honors out,
Runners whom renown outran
And the name died before the man.

So set, before its echoes fade,
The fleet foot on the sill of shade, **C**
And hold to the low lintel° up
The still-defended challenge cup.

And round that early-laureled head
Will flock to gaze the strengthless dead,
And find unwithered on its curls
The garland briefer than a girl's.

9. betimes: archaic for "early."
11. laurel: classical symbol of victory. Victorious Greek and Roman athletes were crowned with laurel wreaths.
23. lintel: top of a door frame.

A Literary Focus Couplet Describe the rhythm of the poem's first couplet. Do the other couplets follow the same rhythm?

B Reading Focus Analyzing Form and Meaning What idea does the speaker introduce in the third stanza?

C Literary Focus Couplet How does the rhythm of line 22 differ from that of line 21? What effect does the poet create with this variation?

Vocabulary **withers** (WIHTH uhrz) *v.:* fades; dries up.
renown (rih NOWN) *n.:* fame; celebrity.

Universal Access

EL English Learners

English for Academic Success Point out to students that line 2 includes a noun that is converted into a verb: *chaired*. Inform students that, like other English verbs that stem from a noun, such as *faxed, e-mailed,* or *videotaped,* the word *chaired* is used to explain an action (verb) performed with a *chair* (noun).

✔ See the **English Language Skill Builder** in **UA: Differentiating Instruction.**

Struggling Readers

Benchmark Students Draw students' attention to the first stanza of the poem. Point out the lines "We chaired you though the market place" (line 2) and "And home we brought you shoulder-high" (line 4). Ask students to discuss why Housman expressed his ideas in this form instead of "We carried you on a chair through the marketplace" and "We brought you home at the height of our shoulders." Have students read the stanzas with these altered lines and write down two ways they change the form of the poem.

Analyzing Visuals

Connecting to the Text How does this image reflect the glory to which the poem's speaker refers?

Alem Techale of Ethiopia (far right) wins the World Youth title in the 1500 meter race in 2003. Techale collapsed and died during a routine training run in 2005, when she was 18.

Think About/Talk About

Extend the Discussion

Comparing and Contrasting What details emphasize the contrast between the young athlete who has died and his living peers? ***Possible responses:*** *Unlike his living peers, the dead young athlete is now indifferent to breaking records or hearing a crowd cheering him; also, his glory will never fade away because unlike them, he died while still in his prime.*

Speculating In line 26, the speaker refers to the "strengthless dead" who will gaze admiringly at the young athlete. What makes the dead "strengthless"? ***Possible response:*** *They died after their glory had faded and their strength was sapped by age.*

Vocabulary: Own the Word

- **withers:** In the poem, the author uses the image of a garland that *withers* to parallel the withering of the athlete's renown. Have students brainstorm other things that can *wither,* either literally or figuratively.
- **renown:** Ask students to name people from their own lives who have experienced some degree of *renown.* ***Possible responses:*** *a friend who was quoted in the news; the star of the school play*

Analyzing Visuals

Connecting to the Text: *In the poem, Housman describes an athlete who experiences victory and then dies at a young age. The photograph shows runner Alem Techale who won the World Youth title and died shortly thereafter. Like the athlete in the poem, Techale will never see her records surpassed or her name forgotten.*

Advanced Learners

Acceleration Point out to students that Housman uses diction and imagery that evoke a classical past—for example, archaic words like *betimes* and the reference to the laurels worn by the victorious athlete. Ask students to think about why Housman chose words and references that make the poem seem antiquated. Have students work in groups of three to four and discuss how contemporary society views legends who died at their height of greatness and legends who continue to live among us.

Students with Disabilities

The poem's somewhat archaic diction and sentence structure may be difficult for some readers, but the simple, touching subject—an athlete who has died young—is likely to appeal to them. Listening to a volunteer read the poem aloud will help their comprehension. Have students work in pairs to paraphrase what the speaker is saying to the dead athlete in each stanza.

✔ See **UA: Differentiating Instruction** for a graphic organizer to scaffold instruction for students with disabilities.

Preteach

Introducing Vocabulary

- Review the Vocabulary words, definitions, and sentences with students.
- Tell students that the Vocabulary words are used to describe how a young man's efforts to show his *fancy* for another person turned out to be in *vain*.

English for Academic Success

Language Coach

Give students other examples of words that are often preceded by the preposition *in*, such as *in spite of, in accordance with,* and *in lieu of.*

Literary Skills Focus

As you read and discuss the poem with students, have them note details in the poem that might relate to the theme.

Writing Skills Focus

Tell students to note the characters' words that reveal their personality in their **Reader/Writer Notebooks.** Students can use their notes to complete the Writing Skills Focus activity.

Learn It Online

Literature Links direct students to pre-screened Web sites offering more information related to a selection.

go.hrw.com H12-984 Go

Preparing to Read

Reading Standard 3.2 (see pages A48–A50)

When I Was One-and-Twenty

Literary Skills Focus

Theme The **theme** of a poem is its central idea or insight about human experience. Most themes are implied rather than directly stated, so you need to piece together clues in order to understand the writer's message. Many themes give an insight or perspective on a topic, such as death, friendship, or family. However, keep in mind that a theme is not the same as a topic, which is simply a subject that can usually be expressed in a word or two. A theme is an idea or perspective about the topic.

Into Action You can use a chart like the one below to organize your thoughts about a poem's topics and themes. Here are examples of topics and their related themes.

Topic	Theme
death	It is better to die young than to face the miseries of aging.
education	You can learn more by doing something than by reading about it.

In the poem "When I was One-and-Twenty," Housman presents a theme about the topic of love. As you read the poem, take notes about what the speaker experiences and learns about love. Then write a statement of the poem's theme about love.

Writing Skills Focus

Think as a Reader/Writer

Find It in Your Reading There are two **characters** in this poem: a wise man and the speaker. Notice how Housman uses the characters' words to reflect their personalities. Record examples that show how each character's words bring his personality to life.

TechFocus As you read this poem, think about how you might use technology to show that the theme of the poem is still relevant today. Think about fonts you might choose for the words or an illustration you could create to help new readers connect with the poem.

Vocabulary

fancy (FAN see) *n.:* a liking for something or someone. *The young couple took a fancy to one another at first sight.*

vain (vayn) *adj.:* of no use; producing no good result. *He made a vain attempt to warn the young man, but he would not listen.*

Language Coach

In Vain The word *vain* is often preceded by the preposition *in,* as in this sentence: "He gave his heart in vain because she did not return his love." Something that is done *in vain* is done unsuccessfully or without effect. When might a student have studied for a test in vain? Name three other actions that might be done in vain.

Reader/Writer Notebook

Use your **RWN** to complete the activities for this selection.

Learn It Online

Explore more of Housman's poetry—and the inspirations behind it—with these Internet links.

go.hrw.com H12-984 Go

California Standards, pp. 984–987

- **Reading Standard 3.2** Analyze the way in which the theme or meaning of a selection represents a view or comment on life, using textual evidence to support the claim.

POEM

When I Was One-and-Twenty

by **A. E. Housman**

Read with a Purpose

Read to discover how one year changes the speaker's view of life and love.

Build Background

Like "To an Athlete Dying Young," the poem "When I Was One-and-Twenty" is from *A Shropshire Lad.* Housman described the Shropshire lad as "an imaginary figure, with something of my own temper and view of life." This brief lyric is a good example of Housman's ability to compress much meaning into a few lines. The poem clearly shows Housman's characteristic directness, melodic beauty, simplicity of form, and meticulous expression of emotion.

When I was one-and-twenty
  I heard a wise man say,
"Give crowns and pounds and guineas°
  But not your heart away;
Give pearls away and rubies
  But keep your fancy free."
But I was one-and-twenty,
  No use to talk to me.

When I was one-and-twenty
  I heard him say again,
"The heart out of the bosom
  Was never given in vain;
'Tis paid with sighs a plenty
  And sold for endless rue."° (A)
And I am two-and-twenty,
  And oh, 'tis true, 'tis true.

3. crowns and pounds and guineas: units of money in Great Britain.
14. rue: sorrow; regret.

(A) **Literary Focus** **Theme** What idea about love does the wise man express in his advice?

Vocabulary **fancy** (FAN see) *n.:* a liking for something or someone.
vain (vayn) *adj.:* of no use; producing no good result.

Teacher Preparation

Selection Summary

In "When I Was One-and-Twenty," the twenty-two-year-old speaker recalls that when he was twenty-one, a wise man warned him to not give himself over to love. The speaker was headstrong and did not take the advice. Now he is suffering the pain of a failed love affair and believes that the wise man was right.

Direct Teach

Think About/Talk About

Read with a Purpose Have students read the Read with a Purpose statement. Have students note the clue in the text that tells them that a year has passed.

Analysis

(A) Literary Focus

Possible response: *The wise man warns him against falling in love, because love brings pain, sorrow, and regret.*

Extend the Discussion

Interpreting By the end of the poem, when the speaker is twenty-two, what do you think has happened? ***Possible response:*** *The speaker has, in the preceding year, fallen in love and experienced the pain and regret of which the older, wiser man warned him.*

Vocabulary: Own the Word

- **fancy:** Ask students to name someone or something that they *fancy.* Have them explain what they have done to pursue this person or thing.
- **vain:** Ask students to recall a time in their lives when they pursued a task in *vain.* Then, ask them to recount something that they did that was not in *vain.*

California Standards, pp. 986–987

- **Reading Standard 1.3** Discern the meaning of analogies encountered, analyzing specific comparisons as well as relationships and inferences.
- **Reading Standard 2.2** Analyze the way in which clarity of meaning is affected by the patterns of organization, hierarchical structures, repetition of the main ideas, syntax, and word choice in the text.
- **Reading Standard 3.2** Analyze the way in which the theme or meaning of a selection represents a view or comment on life, using textual evidence to support the claim.
- **Reading Standard 3.4** Analyze ways in which poets use imagery, personification, figures of speech, and sounds to evoke readers' emotions.
- **Writing Standard 2.2** Write responses to literature: **a.** Demonstrate a comprehensive understanding of the significant ideas in works or passages. **b.** Analyze the use of imagery, language, universal themes, and unique aspects of the text. **c.** Support important ideas and viewpoints through accurate and detailed references to the text and to other works. **d.** Demonstrate an understanding of the author's use of stylistic devices and an appreciation of the effects created.
- **Writing Standard 2.3** Write reflective compositions: **a.** Explore the significance of personal experiences, events, conditions, or concerns by using rhetorical strategies (e.g., narration, description, exposition, persuasion).
- **Writing Standard 2.6** Deliver multimedia presentations: **c.** Use the selected media skillfully, editing appropriately and monitoring for quality.

Check for Understanding

Independent Practice

Reading Skills Focus

Possible responses:

1. *The speaker in both poems presents the view that life and love will eventually come to a disappointing end; therefore, it is better to die at the height of one's glory or never fall in love than to risk pain or failure.*
2. *Students should identify the dominant image or idea in each stanza and analyze its meaning.*

Literary Skills Focus

Possible responses:

3. *In both stanzas, the athlete is being carried down a street at shoulder height. In the first stanza, fans are cheering him, and in the next stanza he is in a coffin, carried by pallbearers.*
4. *The last two stanzas evoke the image of people still admiring the dead athlete's trophies and gazing upon him as he lies in his coffin.*
5. *The repetition of "'Tis true" emphasizes the speaker's attitude, making him sound dramatic and self-important. Repetition is also found in lines 1 and 9 as well as in lines 2 and 10.*
6. *Students should offer opinions about whether or not love is worth the risk of possible pain.*
7. *Every couplet ends in exact rhyme, except for lines 5–6, which end with half rhyme: come, home.*
8. *It is foolish to give your love away because doing so will ultimately bring pain and regret.*
9. *Alliteration appears in the poem in lines such as "The fleet foot on the sill of shade" (line 22). Assonance appears in lines such as "And hold to the low lintel up" (line 23).*

Applying Your Skills

Reading Standard 2.2, 3.2, 3.4 (see pages A48–A50)
Writing Standard 2.3a (see pages A51–A52)

To an Athlete Dying Young / When I Was One-and-Twenty

Literary Response and Analysis

Reading Skills Focus

Read with a Purpose

1. How does the speaker in each poem present a view that you might not expect?

Reading Skills: Analyzing the Relationship of Form and Meaning

2. Review the chart you made for "To an Athlete Dying Young," and add a column to note and analyze the meaning of each stanza. Identify each central image or idea. These key ideas will help you understand how Housman arranges his poem to convey his ideas.

Stanza	Paraphrase	Meaning/Analysis
1	When you won the race, we carried you through town, celebrating your victory.	Image of the athlete in the past, at the height of his glory.
2	Today we're once again carrying you on our shoulders, but it's a much quieter occasion.	Image of the athlete, now dead, being carried to his grave. Parallel shows contrast.
3		

Literary Skills Focus

Literary Analysis

3. **Compare and Contrast** What parallel events are described in the first and second stanzas of "To an Athlete Dying Young"?
4. **Draw Conclusions** What scene do you imagine when you read the last two stanzas of "To an Athlete Dying Young"?
5. **Identify** What is the effect of Housman's use of repetition in the last line of "When I was One-and-Twenty"? What other kinds of repetition do you find in the poem?
6. **Evaluate** How would you respond to the wise man's advice in "When I was One-and-Twenty"?

Literary Skills: Couplet / Theme

7. **Interpret** Poets can use **exact** rhyme *(tune/moon)* or **half rhyme** *(moon/man),* also called approximate rhyme. Look at the end rhymes in "To an Athlete Dying Young." What pattern of rhyming sounds do you hear?
8. **Analyze** What do you think is the theme, or message, of "When I Was One-and-Twenty"?

Literary Skills Review: Alliteration and Assonance

9. **Evaluate** Housman creates verbal music by using **alliteration,** the repetition of consonant sounds, and **assonance,** the repetition of vowel sounds. Where do you hear these sound patterns in "To an Athlete Dying Young"?

Writing Skills Focus

Think as a Reader/Writer

Use It in Your Writing Apply Housman's uses of understatement and of characterization as you write your own description of a dramatic event you experienced or witnessed.

What Do You Think Now How do these poems present unconventional ideas about the reality of death and love?

Universal Access

Struggling Writers

Students may need additional scaffolding to complete the Writing Skills Focus activity. Have them think about a dramatic event they have experienced or witnessed. Encourage students to make a list of words and phrases that describe their experiences. Remind students that in the poems, Housman used understatement, which is a form of description that does not exaggerate or embellish. Have students review their lists and revise their words and phrases to include understatement. Ask students to incorporate the information from their lists in their paragraphs.

What Do You Think Now?

Have students discuss conventional attitudes toward death and love. Then, have them review the poet's attitudes toward death and toward love and identify how these attitudes depart from conventional views.

Reading Standard 1.3 (see pages A48–A50)
Writing Standard 2.2a–d, 2.6c (see pages A51–A52)

Vocabulary Development

Vocabulary Check

Match each Vocabulary word to its antonym.

1. fancy	a. obscurity
2. withers	b. successful
3. renown	c. dislike
4. vain	d. thrives

Vocabulary Skills: Analogies

An **analogy** shows a comparison between two pairs of words. Analogies are shown in this form:

SONNET : POEM :: tragedy : drama

Here is one way to read this analogy: "*Sonnet* is related to *poem* in the same way that *tragedy* is related to *drama*." In this analogy, a sonnet is a type of poem, and a tragedy is a type of drama.

Your Turn

Complete each analogy with a word from the box.

ages anxious courage weakness

1. VAIN : INEFFECTIVE :: nervous : ________.
2. CELEBRITY : RENOWN :: hero : ________.
3. FLOWER : WITHERS :: person : ________.
4. FANCY : HATRED :: power : ________.

Language Coach

Pronunciation How does knowing how to pronounce words such as *renown* in poems affect your understanding of a poem's rhythm, rhyme, assonance, and alliteration?

CHOICES

As you respond to the Choices, use these **Academic Vocabulary** words as appropriate: benefit, complex, respond, publish, statistics.

REVIEW

Build a Topic Web

Reflect on how these poems explore the topics of love and death. Complete a web like the one below for each poem by adding details from each poem to support each category. Include your own responses to the form and theme.

CONNECT

Film Interviews

TechFocus In a small group, film a series of interviews with the speaker of "When I Was One-and-Twenty" at age twenty-one, twenty-two, and an older age. Members of your group can act as the speaker or as friends describing him at various stages of his life. In each interview, encourage the speaker to explain his point of view on life and love.

EXTEND

Write an Essay

Timed Writing Housman's poetry was popular with young soldiers fighting in the Boer War. In an expository essay, analyze the characteristics of Housman's poetry that might have appealed to young people in his time and those that would appeal to young people in our time. Use text evidence to support your analysis.

Learn It Online
Learn more with Word Watch online.
go.hrw.com H12-987 Go

Universal Access: Vocabulary Development

English Learners

English for Academic Success Students may need additional practice with the concept of analogies. Remind them that in an analogy, the relationship of a word pair on one side must equal the relationship of the word pair on the other side. Tell students that determining the relationship between the first pair of words will help them better be able to complete the analogy. Pair students with a proficient English speaker; then, have them engage in an instructional conversation in which they work through the following examples, completing the analogy with an appropriate word.

- MERCHANT : CUSTOMER :: doctor : _____ [*patient*]
- DIVERSE : ALIKE :: anonymous : _____ [*identified*]
- CONSUME : EAT :: destroy : _____ [*damage*]

✔ See the **Academic and Selection Vocabulary Skill Builder** in **UA: Differentiating Instruction.**

Independent Practice

Vocabulary Development

Vocabulary Check

1. *c* **2.** *d* **3.** *a* **4.** *b*

Your Turn

1. *anxious* **2.** *courage*
3. *ages* **4.** *weakness*

English for Academic Success

Language Coach

Possible response: *Knowing the correct pronunciation of words helps one to recognize rhythm, rhyme, and instances of assonance or alliteration.*

Choices: Evaluation Criteria

Review: Homework
Build a Topic Web
Students include own observations about the form and theme.

Connect: Homework
Film Interviews
Interviews show how speaker changes as he ages.

Extend: Timed Writing 40–50 Minutes
Essays include evidence from text.

Assess

Unit 5 Resources, Selection Standards Check, p. 63

ThinkCentral Online Assessment, Selection Standards Check

Teacher One Stop™, editable Selection Standards Check

Reteach

ThinkCentral Online Remediation

Learn It Online
Send students to **Word Watch** for audio pronunciations, synonyms and antonyms, and brief histories of word origins.
go.hrw.com H12–987 Go

Standards Focus

Objectives

Students will analyze causes and effects.

Motivate

What Do You Think?/QuickWrite

Have students write their assumptions about a varsity football team practicing in extremely hot weather. Ask students to explain how and why they came to these assumptions.

Preteach

Introducing Vocabulary

Guide students through this exercise.

1. Name a beverage you use to **replenish** your body.
2. Describe **oppressive** heat.
3. List three **precautions** a person takes before driving a car.
4. Name one reason someone might take a **supplement.**
5. Describe an action you took, **rendering** a problem solved.

Informational Text/ Writing Skills Focus

- Give students a copy of the Informational Text Focus graphic organizer before they read.
- Have students record statistics the writer presents in their **Reader/ Writer Notebooks.**

California Standards, pp. 988–991

- **Reading Standard 2.2** Analyze the way in which clarity of meaning is affected by the patterns of organization, hierarchical structures, repetition of the main ideas, syntax, and word choice in the text.

INFORMATIONAL TEXT FOCUS

Preparing to Read

Reading Standard 2.2 (see pages A48–A50)

Link to Today **When Elements Go Extreme**

What Do You Think How can appearance be different from reality?

QuickWrite

Suppose you see a varsity football team practicing on a hot and humid day. What assumptions might you make about the players? Which of your assumptions are mostly likely to be true? Which ones are probably unfounded?

Informational Text Focus

Analyzing Cause and Effect Many informational texts follow a cause-and-effect organization. The writer describes one event that leads to another. The first event is the cause of the second, which is its effect. The order can also be reversed: The writer first tells you what happened (effect) and then explains why (cause).

Into Action Use cause-and-effect charts as you read to understand the reasons behind key events and their impact on other events.

- If you want to know why an event was important, or how it influenced other events, write it in the Cause box. Then try to identify the effect of the event as you read.
- If you want to understand why something happened; write the event in the Effect box. Then, look for the cause as you read.

Causes		Effects
The football player became dehydrated.	→	He cramped up on the field and was unable to move.

Writing Skills Focus

Preparing for Timed Writing Statistics are numerical data. Like many journalists, this writer uses statistics to support his statements. As you read, make a list in your *Reader/Writer Notebook* of the statistics the writer presents and note why he includes each piece of information.

Vocabulary

rendering (REHN duh rihng) *v.* used as *adj.:* causing to be or become; making. *The heat was extreme, rendering the team helpless.*

replenish (rih PLEHN ihsh) *v.:* to fill again; to renew. *When you exercise, it is important to replenish the water in your body.*

oppressive (uh PREHS ihv) *adj.:* hard to bear. *The football game was canceled because the oppressive heat made play dangerous.*

precautions (prih KAW shuhnz) *n.:* care taken in advance; safeguards. *Stretching your muscles after you exercise is one of the precautions you can take to avoid injuries.*

supplement (SUHP luh muhnt) *n.:* something added to make complete or to enrich. *It is always wise to check with a doctor before you begin to take a dietary supplement.*

Language Coach

Prefixes Sometimes prefixes attach to word parts that are not words by themselves. The prefix *re–* means "again" and *replenish* means "fill again," but *plenish* on its own is not a word. Find words with the prefix *re–* in the selection. What do they mean? Can their parts stand alone?

Reader/Writer Notebook

Use your **RWN** to complete the activities for this selection.

Selection Readability	
Easily Accessible **Accessible** Challenging	familiar subject matter; accessible vocabulary

Selection Summary

"When Elements Go Extreme" describes the medical risks athletes face when playing or practicing in extremely hot weather. It provides statistics about the number of fatalities that have occurred among athletes due to heatstroke and discusses measures coaches have taken to prevent heatstroke.

Link to Today

This Link to Today looks at how hot weather can affect even the strongest athletes.

Read with a Purpose

Read this article to learn how athletes can keep playing safely when the temperature rises.

Build Background

Heatstroke is a sudden, uncontrolled increase in body temperature. It can occur when people are exposed to high temperature and humidity for several hours. A person suffering from heatstroke may feel dizzy, weak, nauseated, restless, or confused. If not treated promptly, heatstroke can lead to collapse and coma. Keeping track of outdoor temperature is one key to preventing heatstroke, but it is also important to consider the impact of the humidity. When humidity is high, the air feels hotter and the threat of heat-related illnesses such as heatstroke is greater. That is why many experts refer to the heat index (HI), which takes into account both air temperature and relative humidity. It measures how hot the air feels. An HI above 105°F is considered threatening.

NEWSPAPER ARTICLE

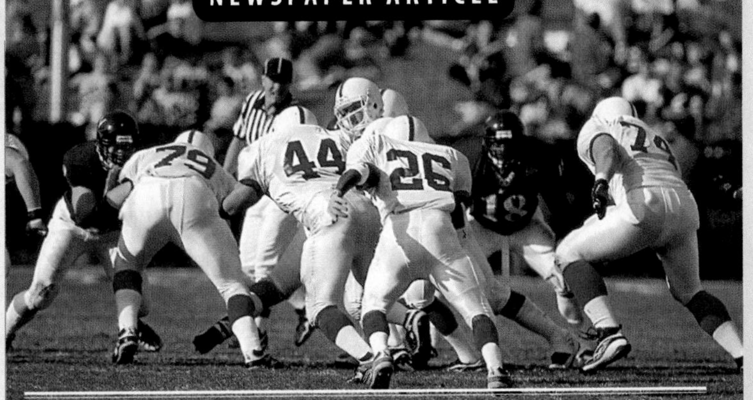

When Elements Go Extreme

by **Jason La Canfora**

Washington Post, Wednesday, August 2, 2006

Sometime during the Washington Redskins' first training camp practice in the summer of 2006, fullback Mike Sellers felt his lower body lock up. The cramps leveled him, rendering him suddenly unable to move. After being carted off the field, three intravenous treatments were required to replenish his system.

Sellers estimates he drank about a gallon of water that day, but even that was insufficient to fully hydrate him in the oppressive heat and humidity that is testing the will of Redskins players, coaches and fans. (A)

The next day Sellers was able to return for practices at Redskins Park, where the heat index reached 108 degrees, but the team's medical staff—not to mention his teammates—was watching him closely. Keeping players healthy and cool is serious business for trainers and coaches, and players are reminded frequently about the need to drink water and report any signs of discomfort, such as rapid breathing or weakness.

(A) **Informational Focus** **Causes and Effects** What cause does the second paragraph identify for the effects described in the first paragraph? Explain.

Vocabulary **rendering** (REHN duh rihng) *v.* used as *adj.:* causing to be or become; making.
replenish (rih PLEHN ihsh) *v.:* to fill again; to renew.
oppressive (uh PREHS ihv) *adj.:* hard to bear.

Selection Resources

Unit 5 Resources, on-level practice and assessment, p. 66

Teacher One Stop™, on-level lesson plans and all print resources

Holt Audio Library: Selections and Summaries in Spanish

UA: Differentiating Instruction, graphic organizer, p. 238

UA: Supporting Instruction in Spanish, selection summary

ThinkCentral Online Assessment, Selection Standards Check

ThinkCentral Online Remediation

Link to Today

Like Housman's poem, this article emphasizes that, despite the appearance of strength, athletes can be extremely vulnerable.

Direct Teach

Think About/Talk About

Read with a Purpose Have students read the Read with a Purpose statement. Then, direct their attention to the word *safely.* Ask students to look for examples of how an athlete's safety is taken into consideration throughout the article.

Comprehension

(A) Informational Focus

Possible response: *The extreme heat and humid conditions dehydrated the fullback, causing severe muscle cramps that left him immobile.*

Extend the Discussion

Speculating Why would Sellers's coaches and teammates continue to "watch him closely" after he was approved to return to practice? ***Possible response:*** *He might still be suffering from symptoms of dehydration. It was extremely hot, which could cause dehydration to occur again.*

Vocabulary: Own the Word

- **rendering:** According to the text, cramps leveled Mike Sellers, *rendering* him immobile. Ask students to think of other things that might *render* someone immobile. What might *render* someone unable to work?
- **replenish:** Ask students to give examples of how they *replenish* their energy after a long day at school or work. ***Possible responses:*** *taking a nap; eating a snack; watching TV*
- **oppressive:** Ask students to brainstorm rules or laws that they consider *oppressive,* either in their own experience or in the governments of other nations.

Think About/Talk About

Comprehension

B Informational Focus

Possible response: *Korey Stringer collapsed from heatstroke.*

C Informational Focus

Possible response: *Korey Stringer's weight, combined with the effects of strenuous exercise, the supplement ephedrine, and extreme heat and humidity all led to Stringer's condition.*

Extend the Discussion

Making Judgments Why do you think it is important for athletes to stay out of direct sunlight and eat regularly throughout the day? ***Possible response:*** *Staying out of the sun will help them to avoid becoming overheated and dehydrated. Eating throughout the day will fuel their bodies and prepare them for an active day.*

Vocabulary: Own the Word

- **precautions:** Suggest a hypothetically dangerous activity or undertaking, such as, performing an operation. Have students make a list of *precautions* that one ought to take in that situation, using the word *precaution* in their answers.
- **supplement:** In the text, the word *supplement* refers to athletic performance enhancers. Have students list other types of *supplements,* for example: "Having an internship can be a helpful *supplement* to the learning experience."

In 2001, Minnesota Vikings offensive lineman Korey Stringer collapsed and died during training camp in Mankato, Minn., from complications of heatstroke. His collapse, which received intense media attention, came on a day when the heat index reached 109, and it reinforced the importance of safeguarding against dehydration and heatstroke for NFL teams. B

Although the number of deaths from heatstroke in professional, college, high school and youth football is not high, according to the University of North Carolina's National Center for Catastrophic Sport Injury Research, it says there is "no excuse for any number of heatstroke deaths since they are all preventable with the proper precautions."

The center reports that 26 football players—20 high school, 4 college, and 2 professional—have died from heat stroke over the last 10 years. Around the time of Mike Sellers's collapse, a 15-year-old high school player in suburban Atlanta died from heat stroke after collapsing one day earlier following an off-season workout.

Size can play a role, too. Korey Stringer's weight at the time of his death was 336 pounds, and, according to the Vikings' report on his death, the now-banned diet supplement ephedrine was found in his system. C

"I think it's always a concern for us," Redskins Coach Joe Gibbs said of the severe heat and humidity. "The reality is, you always start in the heat and you just do the best job you can. We're going to try to start as late [in the day] as you can and start as early as you can, and give them a rest in the middle of the day....

"But having said that, it's one of my biggest concerns and one of our concerns always, because you've got big guys there in the heat trying to be competitive and it's something you really have to watch."

Baltimore Ravens players cooling off on sidelines with water spray during training camp at McDaniel College.

"We've got a plan of weighing them in [before practice] and weighing them out, and we monitor their body weights and make sure they recover," said Bubba Tyer, the team's director of sports medicine. "And if they don't recover, we either pull them out of practice the next day or monitor them closely during practice. You see us working out there, and it's a job to work. We're icing them down and watering them down, and they get water every chance they can get."

After most practices, large tubs of freezing water are coveted spots for players, helping them quickly lower their body temperature. "The guys like it," Tyer said of the icy baths. "It's a mess of a deal, but it seems to work. It cools them off a little bit fairly quickly."

Salt tablets are available, if necessary, and "common sense" practices are best applied to all athletes training in these conditions, whether amateur or professional, Tyer said. He urges Redskins players to find a cool spot after practice, drink plenty of water and, after a brief rest, to begin moving around again to prevent cramping. It is also essential that they eat throughout the day and stay out of direct sunlight when possible, he said.

B **Informational Focus** Causes and Effects What was the cause of Korey Stringer's collapse?

C **Informational Focus** Causes and Effects How did multiple causes lead to Korey Stringer's condition?

Vocabulary **precautions** (prih KAW shuhnz) *n.:* care taken in advance; safeguards.

supplement (SUHP luh muhnt) *n.:* something added to make complete or to enrich.

California Standards, p. 991

- **Reading Standard 2.2** Analyze the way in which clarity of meaning is affected by the patterns of organization, hierarchical structures, repetition of the main ideas, syntax, and word choice in the text.
- **Writing Standard 2.2** Write responses to literature: **a.** Demonstrate a comprehensive understanding of the significant ideas in works or passages. **c.** Support important ideas and viewpoints through accurate and detailed references to the text and to other works. **d.** Demonstrate an understanding of the author's use of stylistic devices and an appreciation of the effects created.
- **Grades 9–10 Review Listening and Speaking Standard 2.3** Apply appropriate interviewing techniques: **a.** Prepare and ask relevant questions. **b.** Make notes of responses. **c.** Use language that conveys maturity, sensitivity, and respect. **d.** Respond correctly and effectively to questions. **e.** Demonstrate knowledge of the subject or organization. **f.** Compile and report responses. **g.** Evaluate the effectiveness of the interview.

Universal Access

EL English Learners

English for Academic Success Have students list scientific terms found in the article, such as *dehydration* or *intravenous,* that may be unfamiliar to them. Students may work in pairs to find the definition of these words in the dictionary. Then, have partners explain the causes and treatment of heatstroke to the class, incorporating scientific terms.

✔ See the **English Language Skill Builder** in **UA: Differentiating Instruction.**

INFORMATIONAL TEXT FOCUS

Applying Your Skills

Reading Standard 2.2 (see pages A48–A50)
Grades 9–10 Review Listening and Speaking Standard 2.3a–g (see pages A53–A55)
Writing Standard 2.2a, 2.2c, 2.2d (see pages A51–A52)

When Elements Go Extreme

Analyze Informational Texts

Informational Text Focus

Quick Check

1. How did Korey Stringer die? What factors contributed to his death?

2. How does Bubba Tyer help players avoid cramping after a practice?

Read with a Purpose

3. How can a coach help keep players safe when temperature and humidity rise to threatening levels?

Informational Skills: Analyzing Cause and Effect

4. As you review the cause-and-effect charts you made while reading, think again about why things happened. Many causes have more than one effect; many effects have more than one cause. Add boxes to your charts as needed to show multiple causes or effects. This chart shows two effects of one cause.

Causes	Effects
The football player became dehydrated.	He cramped up on the field and was unable to move.
	He received fluid intravenously.

Vocabulary Check

Match each Vocabulary word with its definition.

5. precautions	**a.** almost unbearable
6. supplements	**b.** causing to become
7. rendering	**c.** safeguards
8. replenish	**d.** additions
9. oppressive	**e.** renew

Text Analysis

10. Interpret Why do sports medicine experts at the University of North Carolina say that heatstroke deaths are "all preventable"?

11. Infer Why is it important to know the heat index, rather than just the temperature?

12. Apply What items would you put on a checklist to evaluate a team's preparations for extreme heat conditions? Explain.

Listening and Speaking

13. Analyze Using information from this article, conduct an interview with a classmate about the dangers of heatstroke and how to avoid them. Work with a partner to plan the questions. Decide who will be the interviewer and who will be the expert. When you present your interview, ask your audience to listen for inaccurate or incomplete answers.

Writing Skills Focus

Timed Writing Write a paragraph about how statistics in this article contribute to your understanding of heatstroke. Be sure to cite specific evidence to support your response.

What Do You Think Now? Does this article support or challenge the assumptions you make about athletes in general, and about football players in particular?

Check for Understanding

Independent Practice

Informational Text Focus

Possible responses:

1. *Korey Stringer's death was due to complications from heatstroke. A combination of hot-weather exercise, ephedrine, and weight led to his dehydration and heatstroke.*

2. *Tyer tells them to move around again after a brief rest.*

3. *A coach can monitor the players' water intake constantly and schedule practice early in the morning or later in the afternoon, when the weather is slightly cooler.*

4. *Students should add boxes to their charts that show multiple causes and effects.*

5. *c*

6. *d*

7. *b*

8. *e*

9. *a*

10. *They are all preventable with the proper precautions.*

11. *The heat index reflects the amount of humidity in the air and the temperature. Extreme humidity can affect dehydration as well.*

12. *The checklist would mention water, blood pressure gauges, ice, and food.*

13. *A successful presentation will include interview questions relevant to heatstroke, accurate information, and complete answers to the interview questions.*

What Do You Think Now?

Have students list assumptions they had about athletes in general before reading the article. Ask them to share if any of these assumptions were proven true or false based on information in the article.

Universal Access

Struggling Writers

Some students may struggle to explain statistics in their own words. To help students understand the statistics they may find in their research, tell them to look for these crucial pieces of information: *who, what, when, how,* and *why.* Remind students to cite a few statistics they find in the text to support their explanations of how statistics contributed to their understanding of heatstroke.

Assess

Unit 5 Resources, Selection Standards Check, p. 69

go.hrw.com **ThinkCentral Online Assessment,** Selection Standards Check

Teacher One Stop™, editable Selection Standards Check

Standards Focus

Objectives

Students will
- analyze internal conflict and external conflict
- identify conflicts and resolutions

Selection Introduction

Think About the Writer

Remind students that Kipling supported the British Empire and the influence of British culture on Britain's colonies.

For Independent Reading

- *Anthills of the Savannah,* Chinua Achebe
- *Rumors of Rain,* Andre Philippus Brink

Motivate

What Do You Think?/QuickWrite

Have students consider how a difference in perception can lead to a difference in opinion. Ask them to record their thoughts in their **Reader/Writer Notebooks.**

English for Academic Success

Academic Vocabulary

Look for opportunities to use the Academic Vocabulary words in this unit.

- **benefit,** ***n.:*** anything that is for the good of a person or thing
- **complex,** ***adj.:*** hard to understand; complicated
- **publish,** ***v.:*** print and issue for the public
- **respond,** ***v.:*** react

California Standards, pp. 992–1006

- **Grades 9–10 Review Reading Standard 3.3** Analyze interactions between main and subordinate characters in a literary text (e.g., internal and external conflicts, motivations, relationships, influences) and explain the way those interactions affect the plot.

Preparing to Read

The Mark of the Beast

What Do You Think? How can appearance be different from reality?

QuickWrite

Think about a time when you and a friend had different explanations for why something occurred. What caused the differences in opinion? Record your ideas in a paragraph.

Joseph Rudyard Kipling (1899) by Sir Philip Burne-Jones. Oil on canvas. National Portrait Gallery, London.

MEET THE WRITER

Rudyard Kipling

(1865–1936)

Nobel Prize WINNER

Rudyard Kipling's popularity and public influence during his lifetime can be attributed in part to his endorsement of the British Empire. However, his ideas about "empire" are controversial today.

Unhappy Youth and Early Success

Joseph Rudyard Kipling was born in Bombay, India, where his father was a professor at the University of Bombay. When Kipling was six years old, he and his sister were sent home to England for their education. Left in the care of foster parents, they lived in a type of boarding house, which Kipling would later refer to as "the house of desolation."

At seventeen, Kipling returned to India to work as a journalist. He quickly became popular for his stories, sketches, and poems that were published in newspapers and then collected in cheap editions sold at Indian railroad stations. His books were distributed in England as well, preparing the way for his return to England as a writer in 1889. By the end of Queen Victoria's reign, Kipling had become the most popular British poet since Tennyson and the most popular prose writer since Dickens. He was awarded the Nobel Prize in Literature in 1907.

Cultural Conflicts

Kipling's views about the British Empire were complex. He was fascinated by the conflicts between European civilization and ancient cultures. This conflict is the theme of many of his Indian works, beginning with *Plain Tales from the Hills* (1888) and continuing in *Kim* (1901), his novel about an Irish orphan submerged in the mystery of India. Kipling did not always see European culture as superior (though he nearly always presented it as such), and he knew that empires do fall. He urged readers not to trust in guns to justify their dominion over large parts of the earth. The purpose of the British Empire, he argued, was not to make the imperial nation rich, but rather to extend British efficiency, decency, and comfort throughout the world. Today, however, many readers view his argument as a rationalization of the often brutal practices of British imperialism.

Think About the Writer What might Kipling have to say about the cultural conflicts in the world today?

Selection Readability	
Easily Accessible **Accessible** Challenging	simple sentence structure; familiar vocabulary; accessible theme

Grades 9–10 Review Reading Standard 3.3 (see page A48–A50)

Literary Skills Focus

Conflict A **conflict** is a struggle or clash between opposing characters, forces, or emotions. When a conflict is **external,** a character or group struggles against an outside force, such as another character or group or a force of nature. When a conflict is **internal,** a struggle takes place within a character between opposing beliefs, responsibilities, desires, or emotions. As you read this story, be sure to note the conflict suggested by the proverb at the beginning of the story, and consider its thematic significance.

Reading Skills Focus

Identifying Conflicts and Resolutions Stories are often built on a series of conflicts. To identify all the conflicts in a story, look for cause-and-effect relationships. Think about how one conflict leads to another conflict, and consider how external and internal conflicts are interrelated. Note, too, that the resolution of one conflict may lead to the resolution of another, but sometimes all the conflicts in a story are not resolved.

Into Action As you read, fill in a three-column chart. Write down the two sides of the conflict, and indicate whether each conflict is external or internal. Then, record how the conflict is—or is not—resolved.

Conflict	External or Internal?	Resolution
Providence and Church of England vs. gods and devils of Asia	external	

Writing Skills Focus

Think as a Reader/Writer

Find It in Your Reading Like many horror stories, "The Mark of the Beast" starts normally enough, with three British civil servants drinking too much at a New Year's Eve party, but events gradually escalate to a horrible climax. As you read, record in your *Reader/Writer Notebook* the techniques Kipling uses to create **suspense** in the story.

TechFocus As you read, think about the similarities and differences between this story and horror movies you have seen. Consider the techniques Kipling and the filmmakers use to tell their stories.

Reader/Writer Notebook

Use your **RWN** to complete the activities for this selection.

Vocabulary

genial (JEEN yuhl) *adj.:* friendly. *The genial men celebrated New Year's Eve together.*

distraught (dihs TRAWT) *adj.:* extremely agitated. *The beast was distraught as it struggled to free itself from its bonds.*

redress (REE drehs) *n.:* payment or action that serves to remedy an injustice or injury. *By offering redress, Strickland tries to right a wrong committed by his friend.*

delusion (dih LOO zhuhn) *n.:* false belief. *The narrator tries to distinguish between truth and delusion.*

dispassionately (dihs PASH uh niht lee) *adv.:* without emotion; impartially. *Strickland spoke dispassionately to the doctor who was in a state of shock.*

Language Coach

Synonyms Words that have similar—but not necessarily the same—meanings are **synonyms**. They may have different shades of meaning or be used in different contexts. For example, note the difference between *genial* and *amiable,* two words that mean "friendly." *Amiable* indicates that a person is good-natured and likable, while *genial* suggests that a person is cheerful and sociable.

Learn It Online

Learn more about Kipling and his world through these Internet links.

go.hrw.com H12-993 Go

Selection Resources

Unit 5 Resources, on-level practice and assessment, p. 71

Teacher One Stop™, on-level lesson plans and all print resources

Holt Audio Library

Holt Audio Library: Selections and Summaries in Spanish

UA: Differentiating Instruction, graphic organizer p. 239

UA: Supporting Instruction in Spanish, selection summary

ThinkCentral Online Assessment, Selection Standards Check

ThinkCentral Online Remediation

Preteach

Introducing Vocabulary

Use this activity to check students' understanding.

1. If you feel **genial** toward someone, is he or she a friend?
2. Identify something that makes you feel **distraught.**
3. In what kind of situation would you expect **redress?**
4. What might cause someone to have a **delusion?**
5. How does a person who speaks **dispassionately** sound?

English for Academic Success

Language Coach

Discuss other pairs of synonyms with different connotations, such as *funny/witty, talented/skilled,* and *happy/joyful.*

Literary Skills Focus

As you read the selection with students, have them note the conflicts and how they relate to the theme.

Reading Skills Focus

Give students a copy of the Reading Skills Focus graphic organizer before they read. (See **Unit 5 Resources.**) Students can use their responses to answer the questions on the Applying Your Skills page.

Writing Skills Focus

Tell students to note in their **Reader/Writer Notebooks** Kipling's techniques for creating suspense.

Learn It Online

The enhanced author biography offers more information on the life of the author as well as Holt's interactive resources pertaining to the author.

go.hrw.com H12-993 Go

Teacher Preparation
Selection Plot Summary

In "The Mark of the Beast," the narrator tells a story about an eerie adventure in colonial India that he shared with two other English civil service officers, Fleete and Strickland. The three are returning from a party when Fleete, who is drunk, enters a temple and grinds his cigar into a statue of the Hindu god Hanuman. After this act of desecration, a leper named the Silver Man touches Fleete's chest. A priest ominously suggests that the god will take his revenge. The next day, a black mark appears on Fleete's chest, and he starts to behave like a wolf, craving raw meat, frightening horses, howling, and snarling. Fleete degenerates quickly into a wild beast, forcing his friends to tie him up. A doctor cannot help, and the two friends decide the Silver Man must be responsible. They capture the leper to force him to remove the curse. Fleete returns to normal with no memory of his condition. The narrator wonders if anyone will believe the story.

Direct Teach

Think About/Talk About

Read with a Purpose Draw students' attention to the phrase "nature of evil." Have students discuss the characteristics of something evil and predict what might happen in the story.

Analysis

A Literary Focus

Possible responses: *Fleete appears to have no respect for the Indian language or culture. This kind of attitude could result in conflicts with Indians.*

SHORT STORY

THE MARK OF THE BEAST

by **Rudyard Kipling**

Read with a Purpose

Read this story to explore the meaning of its title and the nature of evil.

Build Background

This story is set in colonial India during the late nineteenth century. As a member of the British ruling class, Kipling witnessed the conflicts that inevitably occur when two cultures are brought into contact by force. Although the battle lines between imperial Britain and colonial India seem clearly drawn in this story, the identity of the victor (if there is one) is less obvious.

The title of the story is an **allusion**, or reference, to the final book of the New Testament, the Book of Revelation. According to chapter 13, great evil will take over the world at some point in the future. A many-headed monster called "The Beast" will rule, and the beast's followers will be branded with its mark.

"Your Gods and my Gods—do you or I know which are the stronger?"

—*Indian Proverb*

East of Suez, some hold, the direct control of Providence ceases; Man being there handed over to the power of the Gods and Devils of Asia, and the Church of England Providence only exercising an occasional and modified supervision in the case of Englishmen.

This theory accounts for some of the more unnecessary horrors of life in India; it may be stretched to explain my story.

My friend Strickland of the Police, who knows as much of natives of India as is good for any man, can bear witness to the facts of the case. Dumoise, our doctor, also saw what Strickland and I saw. The inference which he drew from the evidence was entirely incorrect. He is dead now; he died in a rather curious manner, which has been elsewhere described.

When Fleete came to India he owned a little money and some land in the Himalayas, near a place called Dharmsala. Both properties had been left him by an uncle, and he came out to finance them. He was a big, heavy, genial, and inoffensive man. His knowledge of natives was, of course, limited, and he complained of the difficulties of the language. **A**

He rode in from his place in the hills to spend New Year in the station, and he stayed with Strickland. On New Year's Eve there was a big dinner at the club, and the night was excusably wet.[1] When men foregather from the uttermost ends of the Empire they have a right to be riotous. The Frontier had sent down a contingent o' Catch-'em-Alive-O's[2] who had not seen twenty white faces for a year, and were used to ride fifteen miles to dinner at the

1. **the night was excusably wet:** In other words, the men drank a lot.
2. **Catch-'em-Alive-O's:** men who were forced into service as soldiers.

A Literary Focus Conflict What might Fleete's lack of knowledge concerning the Indian people and his complaints about their language suggest about his attitude toward the Indian culture? What kinds of conflicts might result from this attitude?

Vocabulary **genial** (JEEN yuhl) *adj.:* friendly.

Universal Access

English Learners

English for Academic Success To help students understand the internal and external conflicts that occur in this story, introduce students to the following words that may be unfamiliar to them.

- **solemnly**—acting without cheer, quiet. *The crowd sat solemnly as they waited for the service to begin.*
- **paroxysm**—a violent expression of emotion. *The angry dog burst into a paroxysm of barking.*
- **degradation**—the process of being treated in a way that is disrespectful or humiliating. *The degradation of the statue angered the people in the village.*
- **vengeance**—punishment or revenge for an injury or wrongdoing. *They sought vengeance because of his disrespect.*
- **palliative**—relieving pain without curing the problem. *The man's life could not be saved, but he was given palliative treatment to make him more comfortable.*

next Fort at the risk of a Khyberee[3] bullet where their drinks should lie. They profited by their new security, for they tried to play pool with a curled-up hedgehog found in the garden, and one of them carried the marker round the room in his teeth. Half a dozen planters had come in from the south and were talking "horse" to the Biggest Liar in Asia, who was trying to cap all their stories at once. Everybody was there, and there was a general closing up of ranks and taking stock of our losses in dead or disabled that had fallen during the past year. It was a very wet night, and I remember that we sang "Auld Lang Syne" with our feet in the Polo Championship Cup, and our heads among the stars, and swore that we were all dear friends. Then some of us went away and annexed Burma, and some tried to open up the Sudan and were opened up by Fuzzies[4] in that cruel scrub outside Suakim,[5] and some found stars and medals, and some were married, which was bad, and some did other things which were worse, and the others of us stayed in our chains and strove to make money on insufficient experiences.

Analyzing Visuals

Connecting to the Text The narrator of the story describes Hanuman as "a leading divinity worthy of respect." How does this statue convey a sense of respect and reference?

Hanuman statue at Durgiana Temple, Amritsar, Punjab, India.

Fleete began the night with sherry and bitters, drank champagne steadily up to dessert, then raw, rasping Capri with all the strength of whiskey, took benedictine with his coffee, four or five whiskeys and sodas to improve his pool strokes, beer and bones[6] at half-past two, winding up with old brandy. Consequently, when he came out, at half-past three in the morning, into fourteen degrees of frost, he was very angry with his horse for coughing, and tried to leapfrog into the saddle. The horse broke away and went to his stables; so Strickland and I formed a Guard of Dishonor to take Fleete home.

Our road lay through the bazaar, close to a little temple of Hanuman, the Monkey-god, who is a leading divinity worthy of respect. All gods have good points, just as have all priests. Personally, I attach much importance to Hanuman, and am kind to his people—the great gray apes of the hills. One never knows when one may want a friend.

There was a light in the temple, and as we passed we could hear voices of men chanting hymns. In a native temple the priests rise at all hours of the night to do honor to their god. Before we would stop him, Fleete dashed up the steps, patted two priests on the back, and was gravely grinding the ashes of his cigar butt in to the forehead of the red stone image of Hanuman. Strickland tried to drag him out, but he sat down and said solemnly:

---

3. **Khyberee:** reference to the people of Khyber, a region now part of Pakistan and Afghanistan.
4. **Fuzzies:** Sudanese natives. British soldiers gave them this name because of their long, frizzy hair. In the poem "Fuzzy-Wuzzy" (1890), Kipling calls the Sudanese soldier "a first-class fightin' man."
5. **Suakim:** Suakin, Sudan; city on the Red Sea.
6. **bones:** dice.

Think About/Talk About

Extend the Discussion

Finding Details How does the narrator justify the Englishman's "riotous" behavior? ***Possible response:*** *He states that when men gather from the "uttermost ends of the empire," they have the "right" to be rowdy and disorderly.*

Making Judgments What impression of the narrator do you get from the passage that describes the night of carousing at the station? ***Possible response:*** *He seems like a genial Englishman who is cynical about the pros and cons of serving the Empire abroad. He is condescending toward the native people, as shown by his insulting reference to the "Fuzzies."*

Analyzing Visuals

Connecting to the Text: *The facial expression on the statue conveys seriousness, and its praying hands seem to command quietness and respect. The importance of the statue is evident in the bright wreath of flowers decorating it.*

Vocabulary: Own the Word

genial: Make a chart on the board comparing the word *genial* with one of its antonyms, "hostile." Have student volunteers give examples of how a person in either category might behave.

Struggling Readers

Benchmark Students Before they read, have students review the concept of conflict and resolution. Discuss the title of the story and the opening epigraph, explaining that the story's title is an allusion to the book of Revelation in the Bible. Ask students what they expect the conflict and the atmosphere of the story will be.

✔ See **UA: Differentiating Instruction** for a graphic organizer to scaffold instruction for struggling readers.

Advanced Learners

Acceleration Before they read, have students read and discuss the Indian proverb at the beginning of the story. Ask students to make general predictions about the story and its examination of cultural conflict based on Kipling's inclusion of this proverb. Ask students to discuss with the class examples of historical conflicts that occurred because of a difference in religious beliefs.

Model the Skill

- Review the concepts of **conflict** and **suspense.** Explain that suspense creates a feeling of anxiety or uncertainty about what is going to happen.
- Re-read paragraph 6 on this page, beginning with "Strickland was very angry . . ."
- Explain to students that, although the incident is over, and the Englishmen have left unharmed, the conflict has not been resolved. Point out to students how the writer uses suspense to hint that the conflict is not over by including the priest's statement, "Hanuman is not done with him," which is an example of the literary technique of foreshadowing.

Guided Practice: Apply

Jigsaw with Experts Use Jigsaw with Experts to facilitate a collaborative approach to reading especially lengthy assignments. Have students review a section of the story to find words, thoughts, actions, and details that build suspense and hint that the conflict is not over. Have students meet and discuss their thoughts with other students who were assigned the same section. Finally, lead a discussion with the whole class about the entire story.

"Shee that? Mark of the B—beasht! *I* made it. Ishn't it fine?" **B**

In half a minute the temple was alive and noisy, and Strickland, who knew what came of polluting gods, said that things might occur. He, by virtue of his official position, long residence in the country, and weakness for going among the natives, was known to the priests and he felt unhappy. Fleete sat on the ground and refused to move. He said that "good old Hanuman" made a very soft pillow.

Then, without any warning, a Silver Man came out of a recess behind the image of the god. He was perfectly naked in that bitter, bitter cold, and his body shone like frosted silver, for he was what the Bible calls "a leper as white as snow." Also he had no face, because he was a leper of some years' standing, and his disease was heavy upon him. We two stooped to haul Fleete up, and the temple was filling and filling with folk who seemed to spring from the earth, when the Silver Man ran in under our arms, making a noise exactly like the mewing of an otter, caught Fleete round the body and dropped his head on Fleete's breast before we could wrench him away. Then he retired to a corner and sat mewing while the crowd blocked all the doors.

The priests were very angry until the Silver Man touched Fleete. That nuzzling seemed to sober them.

At the end of a few minutes' silence one of the priests came to Strickland and said, in perfect English, "Take your friend away. He has done with Hanuman but Hanuman has not done with him." The crowd gave room and we carried Fleete into the road. **C**

Strickland was very angry. He said that we might all three have been knifed, and that Fleete should thank his stars that he had escaped without injury.

Fleete thanked no one. He said that he wanted to go to bed. He was gorgeously drunk.

We moved on, Strickland silent and wrathful, until Fleete was taken with violent shivering fits and sweating. He said that the smells of the bazaar were overpowering, and he wondered why slaughterhouses were permitted so near English residences. "Can't you smell the blood?" said Fleete.

We put him to bed at last, just as the dawn was breaking, and Strickland invited me to have another whiskey and soda. While we were drinking he talked of the trouble in the temple, and admitted that it baffled him completely. Strickland hates being mystified by natives, because his business in life is to overmatch them with their own weapons. He has not yet succeeded in doing this, but in fifteen or twenty years he will have made some small progress.

"They should have mauled us," he said, "instead of mewing at us. I wonder what they meant. I don't like it one little bit."

I said that the Managing Committee of the temple would in all probability bring a criminal action against us for insulting their religion. There was a section of the Indian Penal Code which exactly met Fleete's offense. Strickland said he only hoped and prayed that they would do this. Before I left I looked into Fleete's room, and saw him lying on his right side, scratching his left breast. Then I went to bed cold, depressed, and unhappy, at seven o'clock in the morning.

At one o'clock I rode over to Strickland's house to inquire after Fleete's head. I imagined that it would be a sore one. Fleete was breakfasting and seemed unwell. His temper was gone, for he was abusing the cook for not supplying him with an underdone chop. A man who can eat raw meat after a wet night is a curiosity. I told Fleete this and he laughed.

"You breed queer mosquitoes in these parts," he said. "I've been bitten to pieces, but only in one place."

"Let's have a look at the bite," said Strickland. "It may have gone down since this morning."

While the chops were being cooked, Fleete opened his shirt and showed us, just over his left breast, a mark, the perfect double of the black rosettes—the five or six irregular blotches arranged in a circle—on a leopard's hide. Strickland looked and said, "It was only pink this morning. It's grown black now."

Fleete ran to a glass.

"By Jove!" he said, "this is nasty. What is it?"

We could not answer. Here the chops came in, all red and juicy, and Fleete bolted three in a most offensive manner. He ate on his right grinders only, and threw his head over his right shoulder as he snapped

B **Reading Focus** **Identifying Conflicts and Resolutions**
What conflict is set in motion here?

C **Reading Focus** **Identifying Conflicts and Resolutions**
What conflict might the priest's statement foreshadow?

Cross-Curricular Connection

SCIENCE: Medicine for Leprosy

In the past, people with leprosy, a disease that corrodes human flesh, were forced to live in isolation from others for fear of contagion. Scientists today know that leprosy is only mildly contagious and can be treated, although a permanent cure has yet to be developed. In Kipling's day, however, the fear of leprosy was intense and almost universal. In one particular type of leprosy, the mucous membranes of the eyes, nose, and throat become infected, and the voice may change dramatically. In addition, appendages such as the nose, fingers, and toes may become brittle and break off.

Individual Activity Ask students to research information about the recent developments in the treatment of leprosy.

HSS Analysis Skills: HI 1

the meat. When he had finished, it struck him that he had been behaving strangely, for he said apologetically, "I don't think I ever felt so hungry in my life. I've bolted like an ostrich."

After breakfast Strickland said to me, "Don't go. Stay here, and stay for the night."

Seeing that my house was not three miles from Strickland's, this request was absurd. But Strickland insisted, and was going to say something, when Fleete interrupted him by declaring in a shamefaced way that he felt hungry again. Strickland sent a man to my house to fetch over my bedding and a horse, and we three went down to Strickland's stables to pass the hours until it was time to go out for a ride. The man who has a weakness for horses never wearies of inspecting them; and when two men are killing time in this way they gather knowledge and lies the one from the other.

There were five horses in the stables, and I shall never forget the scene as we tried to look them over. They seemed to have gone mad. They reared and screamed and nearly tore up their pickets;[7] they sweated and shivered and lathered and were distraught with fear. Strickland's horses used to know him as well as his dogs; which made the matter more curious. We left the stable for fear of the brutes throwing themselves in their panic. Then Strickland turned back and called me. The horses were still frightened, but they let us "gentle" and make much of them, and put their heads in our bosoms.

"They aren't afraid of *us,*" said Strickland. "D'you know, I'd give three months' pay if *Outrage* here could talk."

But *Outrage* was dumb, and could only cuddle up to his master and blow out his nostrils, as is the custom of horses when they wish to explain things but can't. Fleete came up when we were in the stalls, and as soon as the horses saw him, their fright broke out afresh. It was all that we could do to escape from the place unkicked. Strickland said, "They don't seem to love you, Fleete."

7. **pickets:** hitching posts.

Vocabulary **distraught** (dihs TRAWT) *adj.:* extremely agitated.

The interior of the Lakshmana Temple was built during the 11th and 12th centuries. Khajuraho, Madhya Pradesh, India.

Think About/Talk About

Comprehension

B Reading Focus
Possible response: *Fleete publicly defaces the statue of the Indian god Hanuman, angering the Indians in the temple.*

C Reading Focus
Possible response: *The priest's statement indicates that Hanuman will respond to Fleete's insult in the future.*

Extend the Discussion

Finding Details What is it about Fleete's eating habits that the narrator and Strickland find "curious"? ***Possible responses:*** *He quickly devours meat that is almost rare; his table manners are animal-like, and he is perpetually hungry.*

Symbolism Is the skin condition described on p. 996 the "mark of the beast"? What do you think it represents? ***Possible responses:*** *It is probably the mark mentioned in the title. It may represent the animal kingdom, which Fleete offended when he defiled the temple of Hanuman. It may signify that Fleete himself is or has become a kind of beast.*

Vocabulary: Own the Word

distraught: Ask students to recall a time when they were *distraught* about something or when they were in the position of consoling someone who was *distraught.*

Universal Access

Struggling Readers

Benchmark Students Remind students that suspense creates a feeling of anxiety or uncertainty in the reader about what is going to happen. Explain that suspense helps build the conflict in a story. Have students read aloud the paragraph beginning, "There were five horses" on p. 997. Ask them to pay attention to the list of compound verbs used in several sentences to describe the actions of the horses. Ask about the cumulative effect of that list. Point out that Kipling piles on one verb after another, connecting them with the word *and,* thus creating an impression of increasing panic among the animals; finally the horses and the paragraph wind down together with the word *gentle.* Ask students to explain how this paragraph contributes to the conflict of the story. Then, have students discuss what the paragraph reveals about the character of Fleete.

Think About/Talk About

Build Background: The Age of Empire

European powers once controlled much of Asia and Africa during the late nineteenth and early twentieth centuries. They were motivated mainly by economic reasons: there were lucrative markets for the raw materials of these countries such as rubber, oil, and cotton. Great Britain often justified the often-difficult relationships with overseas colonies as being a small price to pay for access to these valuable raw materials. Now, in the aftermath of colonialism, these formerly occupied countries sometimes struggle to integrate the legacy of colonialism into their new identities as independent nations.

Extend the Discussion

Making Inferences What might be inferred from the horses' behavior? ***Possible response:*** *They are clearly disturbed by Fleete and may be sensing a disturbance in the natural order that the humans sense only dimly.*

Making Judgments How does Strickland's remark about possibly hurting the priest affect your impression of him? ***Possible responses:*** *Strickland now becomes a potential source of violence; he seems to lack insight.*

"Nonsense," said Fleete; "my mare will follow me like a dog." He went to her; she was in a loose box;[8] but as he slipped the bars she plunged, knocked him down, and broke away into the garden. I laughed, but Strickland was not amused. He took his moustache in both fists and pulled at it till it nearly came out. Fleete, instead of going off to chase his property, yawned, saying that he felt sleepy. He went to the house to lie down, which was a foolish way of spending New Year's Day.

Blue-eyed horse.

Strickland sat with me in the stables and asked if I had noticed anything peculiar in Fleete's manner. I said that he ate his food like a beast; but that this might have been the result of living alone in the hills out of the reach of society as refined and elevating as ours for instance. Strickland was not amused. I do not think that he listened to me, for his next sentence referred to the mark on Fleete's breast, and I said that it might have been caused by blister flies, or that it was possibly a birthmark newly born and now visible for the first time. We both agreed that it was unpleasant to look at, and Strickland found occasion to say that I was a fool.

"I can't tell you what I think now," said he, "because you would call me a madman; but you must stay with me for the next few days, if you can. I want you to watch Fleete, but don't tell me what you think till I have made up my mind." **D**

8. **loose box:** stall in which the horse is free to move about.

D **Literary Focus** **Conflict** What explanation can you offer for Strickland's internal conflict concerning the possible cause of the mark on Fleete's chest? To what larger conflict and theme might his internal conflict point?

"But I am dining out tonight," I said.

"So am I," said Strickland, "and so is Fleete. At least if he doesn't change his mind."

We walked about the garden smoking, but saying nothing—because we were friends, and talking spoils good tobacco—till our pipes were out. Then we went to wake up Fleete. He was wide awake and fidgeting about his room.

"I say, I want some more chops," he said. "Can I get them?"

We laughed and said, "Go and change. The ponies will be round in a minute."

All right," said Fleete. "I'll go when I get the chops—underdone ones, mind."

He seemed to be quite in earnest. It was four o'clock, and we had had breakfast at one; still, for a long time, he demanded those underdone chops. Then he changed into riding clothes and went out into the veranda. His pony—the mare had not been caught—would not let him come near. All three horses were unmanageable—mad with fear—and finally Fleete said that he would stay at home and get something to eat. Strickland and I rode out wondering. As we passed the Temple of Hanuman the Silver Man came out and mewed at us.

"He is not one of the regular priests of the temple," said Strickland. "I think I should peculiarly like to lay my hands on him."

There was no spring in our gallop on the racecourse that evening. The horses were stale, and moved as though they had been ridden out.

"The fright after breakfast has been too much for them," said Strickland.

That was the only remark he made through the remainder of the ride. Once or twice, I think, he swore

Word-Attack Skills Mini-Lesson

English for Academic Success *Y* is the only letter in the alphabet that can be both a consonant or a vowel. As a consonant, its sound is /y/, as in *year* and *yawned.* As a vowel occurring at the end of a word, it can stand for /ē/ or /ī/. Using the words *only, theory, necessary, my, story, any, entirely, by, heavy, excusably,* and *twenty,* help students recognize that final *y* most often stands for /ē/. It stands for /ī/ only when it is the principle vowel in a word. Use these selection words to explore the sounds of medial *y.*

hydrophobia	strychnine
physically	asylum
paroxysm	hysteria

Help students recognize that when *y* occurs between two consonants, it can stand for /i/ or /ī/. Have them note the two words in which medial *y* stands for /ī/. [*hydrophobia, asylum*]

to himself; but that did not count.

We came back in the dark at seven o'clock, and saw that there was no lights in the bungalow. "Careless ruffians my servants are!" said Strickland.

My horse reared at something on the carriage drive, and Fleete stood up under its nose.

"What are you doing, groveling about the garden?" said Strickland.

But both horses bolted and nearly threw us. We dismounted by the stables and returned to Fleete, who was on his hands and knees under the orange bushes.

"What the devil's wrong with you?" said Strickland.

"Nothing, nothing in the world," said Fleete, speaking very quickly and thickly. "I've been gardening—botanizing, you know. The smell of the earth is delightful. I think I'm going for a walk—a long walk—all night."

Then I saw that there was something excessively out of order somewhere, and I said to Strickland, "I am not dining out." E

"Bless you!" said Strickland. "Here, Fleete, get up. You'll catch fever there. Come in to dinner and let's have the lamps lit. We'll dine at home."

Fleete stood up unwillingly, and said, "No lamps—no lamps. It's much nicer here. Let's dine outside and have some more chops—lots of 'em and underdone—bloody ones with gristle."

Now a December evening in Northern India is bitterly cold, and Fleete's suggestion was that of a maniac.

"Come in," said Strickland sternly. "Come in at once."

Fleete came, and when the lamps were brought, we saw that he was literally plastered with dirt from head to foot. He must have been rolling in the garden. He shrank from the light and went to his room. His eyes were horrible to look at. There was a green light behind them, not in them, if you understand, and the man's lower lip hung down.

Strickland said, "There is going to be trouble—big trouble—tonight. Don't you change your riding things."

We waited and waited for Fleete's reappearance, and ordered dinner in the meantime. We could hear him moving about his own room, but there was no light there. Presently from the room came the long-drawn howl of a wolf.

People write and talk lightly of blood running cold and hair standing up, and things of that kind. Both sensations are too horrible to be trifled with. My heart stopped as though a knife had been driven through it, and Strickland turned as white as the tablecloth.

The howl was repeated, and was answered by another howl far across the fields.

That set the gilded roof on the horror. Strickland dashed into Fleete's room. I followed, and we saw Fleete getting out of the window. He made beast noises in the back of his throat. He could not answer us when we shouted at him. He spat.

I don't quite remember what followed, but I think that Strickland must have stunned him with the long bootjack,[9] or else I should never have been able to sit on his chest. Fleete could not speak, he could only snarl, and his snarls were those of a wolf, not of a man. The human spirit must have been giving way all day and have died out with the twilight. We were dealing with a beast that had once been Fleete. F

The affair was beyond any human and rational experience. I tried to say "hydrophobia,"[10] but the word wouldn't come, because I knew that I was lying.

We bound this beast with leather thongs of the punkah[11] rope, and tied its thumbs and big toes together, and gagged it with a shoehorn, which makes a very efficient gag if you know how to arrange it. Then we carried it into the dining room, and sent a man to Dumoise, the doctor, telling him to come over at

9. **bootjack:** device for pulling off boots, often made of cast iron.
10. **hydrophobia:** rabies. One of the effects of rabies is an inability to swallow water.
11. **punkah:** swinging fan suspended from the ceiling. It is operated by pulling an attached cord or rope.

E **Literary Focus** **Conflict** What does the narrator's use of the phrase "out of order"—instead of a word such as *wrong*—suggest about the nature of the conflicts and their effects in the story?

F **Reading Focus** **Identifying Conflicts and Resolutions** Explain the internal conflict described in this passage. How is it resolved?

Think About/Talk About

Comprehension

F Reading Focus

Possible response: *The narrator is coming to terms with the idea that Fleete is being transformed into something not human. He tries to explain it as rabies but stops because he knows it is not true. His conflict is between what he believes to be possible and what he observes to be true.*

Analysis

D Literary Focus

Possible responses: *Strickland suspects a supernatural cause for the mark but is hesitant to say so for fear he will sound like a madman. His internal conflict points to the external conflict between Fleete and the god Hanuman, which represents the clash between Indian and British culture.*

E Literary Focus

Possible response: *The narrator recognizes that Fleete's behavior is not following the British culture's interpretation of order. This behavior is a result of Fleete not following the Indian culture's interpretation of order, which involves respecting Hindu gods.*

Extend the Discussion

Style What exaggerated expressions does the narrator use in the paragraph starting with "People write and talk . . ."? What is the effect of these expressions? ***Possible responses:*** *The reference to his "blood running cold," and his heart stopping "as though a knife had been driven through it," and turning "as white as a tablecloth" are all exaggerations. The hyperbolic expressions add to the disturbing atmosphere of the story, increasing suspense.*

Activity Have students group these words according to the sound of medial *y*.

Encourage them to draw conclusions about when *y* stands for /i/ [*s*] and /ī/. [*l*].

cryptogram [*s*]	hyperbole [*l*]
hypertension [*l*]	paralysis [*s*]
dysentery [*s*]	analyst [*s*]

Students may conclude that /i/ is the more common sound, but particularly after *h,* medial *y* stands for /ī/.

Developing Oral Fluency

Small Group Activity Have students form groups of three to conduct an oral reading of the text on pp. 998–999. Have groups choose individuals to read the lines of the narrator, Strickland, and Fleete. Remind students to think about each character's state of mind at this point in the story and the emotions each character is feeling. Students should convey these emotions in the tone of their voice when reading the lines. After each group is finished reading, ask group members to discuss ways to improve their oral interpretation of the text and re-read sections they found difficult.

Guided Practice: Apply

Think as a Reader/Writer

Find It in Your Reading Point out to students that on pp. 999–1000, Kipling builds suspense in this story as the narrator and Strickland continue to hear the sounds of mewing encircling the house. Kipling leaves his characters and his readers questioning whether the sound is coming from a cat or the Silver Man.

Use It in Your Writing Have students write a short paragraph describing an eerie sound or sight. Have students build suspense by leading the reader to question whether the cause of the phenomenon is a natural force or a supernatural force.

Think About/Talk About

Literary Connection

In classical literature and mythology, the "mark of the beast," imposed upon those who defy the gods or defile their sacred places, is a theme with a long history. In ancient Greek mythology, Actaeon, a hunter, accidentally saw the virgin goddess Artemis bathing; as punishment, he was transformed into a stag and torn apart by his own hounds. Similarly, King Pentheus offended the god Dionysus by refusing to allow the god to be worshipped. As punishment, Pentheus was torn apart by maenads (frenzied women) who perceived him to be an animal. These tales remind people that denying or defiling the divine is an "inhuman" act—the act of an animal.

once. After we had dispatched the messenger and were drawing breath, Strickland said, "It's no good. This isn't any doctor's work." I, also, knew that he spoke the truth.

The beast's head was free, and it threw it about from side to side. Anyone entering the room would have believed that we were curing a wolf's pelt. That was the most loathsome accessory of all.

Strickland sat with his chin in the heel of his fist, watching the beast as it wriggled on the ground, but saying nothing. The shirt had been torn open in the scuffle and showed the black rosette mark on the left breast. It stood out like a blister.

In the silence of the watching we heard something without mewing like a she-otter. We both rose to our feet, and, I answer for myself, not Strickland, felt sick—actually and physically sick. We told each other, as did the men in *Pinafore,*[12] that it was the cat.

Dumoise arrived, and I never saw a little man so unprofessionally shocked. He said that it was a heart-rending case of hydrophobia, and that nothing could be done. At least any palliative measures would only prolong the agony. The beast was foaming at the mouth. Fleete, as we told Dumoise, had been bitten by dogs once or twice. Any man who keeps half a dozen terriers must expect a nip now and again. Dumoise could offer no help. He could only certify that Fleete was dying of hydrophobia. The beast was then howling, for it had managed to spit out the shoehorn. Dumoise said that he would be ready to certify to the cause of death, and that the end was certain. He was a good little man, and he offered to remain with us; but Strickland refused the kindness. He did not wish to poison Dumoise's New Year. He would only ask him not to give the real cause of Fleete's death to the public.

So Dumoise left, deeply agitated; and as soon as the noise of the cart wheels had died away, Strickland told me, in a whisper, his suspicions. They were so wildly improbable that he dared not say them out aloud; and I, who entertained all Strickland's beliefs, was so ashamed of owning to them that I pretended to disbelieve.

"Even if the Silver Man had bewitched Fleete for polluting the image of Hanuman, the punishment could not have fallen so quickly." **G**

As I was whispering this the cry outside the house rose again, and the beast fell into a fresh paroxysm of struggling till we were afraid that the thongs that held it would give way.

"Watch!" said Strickland. "If this happens six times I shall take the law into my own hands. I order you to help me."

He went into his room and came out in a few minutes with the barrels of an old shotgun, a piece of fishing line, some thick cord, and his heavy wooden bedstead. I reported that the convulsions had followed the cry by two seconds in each case, and the beast seemed perceptibly weaker.

Strickland muttered, "But he can't take away the life! He can't take away the life!"

I said, though I knew that I was arguing against myself, "It may be a cat. It must be a cat. If the Silver Man is responsible, why does he dare to come here?"

Strickland arranged the wood on the hearth, put the gun barrels into the glow of the fire, spread the twine on the table, and broke a walking stick in two. There was one yard of fishing line, gut lapped with wire, such as is used for *mahseer*[13] fishing, and he tied the two ends together in a loop.

Then he said, "How can we catch him? He must be taken alive and unhurt."

I said that we must trust in Providence, and go out softly with polo sticks into the shrubbery at the front of the house. The man or animal that made the cry was evidently moving round the house as regularly as a night watchman. We could wait in the bushes till he came by and knock him over. **H**

12. **Pinafore:** *H.M.S. Pinafore* (1878), a comic operetta by W. S. Gilbert and Arthur Sullivan. Lovers in the play attempt to elope. When they are discovered, the cast sings, "Why, what was that? . . . It was—it was the cat!"

13. ***mahseer*** (MAH suhr): large Indian freshwater fish of the carp family.

G **Reading Focus** **Identifying Conflicts and Resolutions** Explain the narrator's internal conflict. How is his conflict the result of external conflicts in the story?

H **Literary Focus** **Conflict** To what force is the narrator referring when he says they must "trust in Providence"? What does this statement suggest about his attitude toward the conflicts in the story?

Cross-Curricular Connection

LITERATURE: Transformation Stories

Many cultures have legends, folk tales, and myths about beings that change form from human to animal—or the other way around. Encourage students to share any stories they know that address this subject and invite students to draw conclusions about the stories' themes. Have students compare the messages of these stories with that of "The Mark of the Beast."

CULTURE LINK

Hanuman

The Hindu deity Hanuman, an offspring of the wind god and a nymph, is usually portrayed as a red-faced monkey who stands erect like a human. Hanuman appears in the Indian epics the *Ramayana* and the *Mahabharata* as a brave and loyal aid to the hero-god Rama. Hanuman is regarded as a helpful guardian spirit, and his loyalty to Rama is considered the perfect model of *bhakti*, or human devotion to a god. Also called Mahavira, "The Great Hero," Hanuman is seen as a sympathetic helper of humans. One of the most common species of Indian monkeys is named after him and is considered sacred. Hanuman is worshipped to this day in temples devoted to him throughout India. He is often portrayed holding a mace, a symbol of strength and protection.

Ask Yourself

Of all the Hindu gods, why is it significant that Fleete is disrespectful to Hanuman in "The Mark of the Beast"?

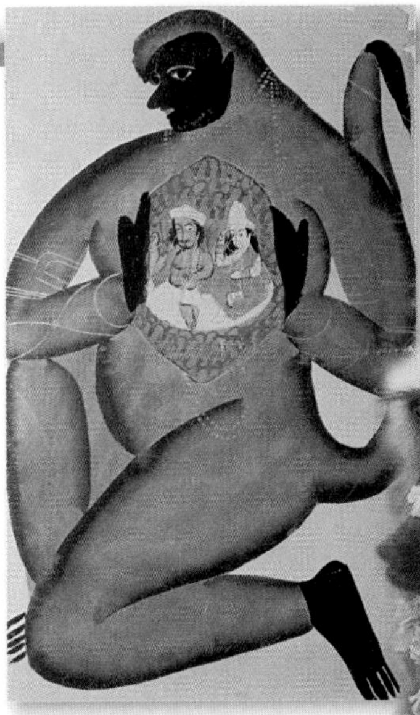

(above) *Hanuman Revealing Rama and Sita Enshrined in his Heart* (1880) by a member of the Patua caste, Bengal School. Watercolor on paper. Victoria & Albert Museum, London.

Strickland accepted this suggestion, and we slipped out from a bathroom window into the front veranda and then across the carriage drive into the bushes.

In the moonlight we could see the leper coming round the corner of the house. He was perfectly naked, and from time to time he mewed and stopped to dance with his shadow. It was an unattractive sight, and thinking of poor Fleete, brought to such degradation by so foul a creature, I put away all my doubts and resolved to help Strickland from the heated gun barrels to the loop of twine—from the loins to the head and back again—with all tortures that might be needful.

The leper halted in the front porch for a moment and we jumped out on him with the sticks. He was wonderfully strong, and we were afraid that he might escape or be fatally injured before we caught him. We had an idea that lepers were frail creatures, but this proved to be incorrect. Strickland knocked his legs from under him and I put my foot on his neck. He mewed hideously, and even through my riding boots I could feel that his flesh was not the flesh of a clean man.

He struck at us with his hand- and feet-stumps. We looped the lash of a dog-whip round him under the armpits, and dragged him backward into the hall and so into the dining room where the beast lay. There we tied him with trunk straps. He made no attempt to escape, but mewed.

When we confronted him with the beast the scene was beyond description. The beast doubled backward into a bow as though he had been poisoned with strychnine, and moaned in the most pitiable fashion. Several other things happened also, but they cannot be put down here.

"I think I was right," said Strickland. "Now we will ask him to cure this case."

But the leper only mewed. Strickland wrapped a towel round his hand and took the gun barrels out of the fire. I put the half of the broken walking stick through the loop of fishing line and buckled the leper comfortably to Strickland's bedstead. I understood

Culture Link

Ask Yourself

Possible response: *It is significant because Hanuman is regarded as the model of human respect for a god. For that reason, Fleete's disrespect for Hanuman signifies additional violation of Hindu culture.*

Think About/Talk About

Comprehension

G Reading Focus

Possible responses: *His internal conflict is based on the fact that the doctor could not determine a medical cause of Fleete's transformation. Other possible causes are hard for the narrator to believe because they are "wildly improbable." This is a result of the external conflict between Eastern and Western beliefs about the causes of illness.*

Analysis

H Literary Focus

Possible responses: *He is referring to the Judeo-Christian god. He has faith that his God is in control and can aid them, despite the curse placed on Fleete by a Hindu god. This suggests that he assumes that in any conflict between Hindus and Christians, Christianity will prevail.*

Extend the Discussion

Drawing Conclusions Why did the narrator pretend not to believe Strickland when he confessed his suspicions? ***Possible response:*** *The suspicions seemed so improbable that he was ashamed to admit he believed them himself.*

Speculating What is the effect of the reference to the comic operetta *H.M.S. Pinafore*? ***Possible response:*** *The reference to something comic relieves the tension a little. It suggests that he may be trying to reassure himself with humor and with references to something familiar and entertaining.*

Model the Skill

- Provide students with copies of the Reading Skills Focus graphic organizer for "The Mark of the Beast." (See **Unit 5 Resources.**)
- Tell students that when identifying the **conflict** in a story they should look for cause-and-effect relationships. Identifying these relationships can also help them to identify the **resolution** of a conflict.
- Point out to students that as a result of the torture inflicted on the Silver Man, the conflict between Hanuman and Fleete is resolved and Fleete becomes human again.
- Ask students to note this resolution to this external conflict in their Reading Skills Focus graphic organizers.

Conflict	External or Internal?	Resolution
Fleete vs. Hanuman and the Silver Man	External	The narrator and Strickland torture the Silver Man and make him remove the evil spirit.

Guided Practice: Apply

Think-Pair-Share Ask students to consider whether all of the external conflicts in the story are resolved. Ask students to work in pairs and discuss any external conflicts introduced in the story that will persist after it ends.

then how men and women and little children can endure to see a witch burnt alive; for the beast was moaning on the floor, and though the Silver Man had no face, you could see horrible feelings passing through the slab that took its place, exactly as waves of heat play across red-hot iron—gun barrels, for instance.

Strickland shaded his eyes with his hands for a moment and we got to work. This part is not to be printed.

The dawn was beginning to break when the leper spoke. His mewings had not been satisfactory up to that point. The beast had fainted from exhaustion and the house was very still. We unstrapped the leper and told him to take away the evil spirit. He crawled to the beast and laid his hand upon the left breast. That was all. Then he fell face down and whined, drawing in his breath as he did so.

We watched the face of the beast, and saw the soul of Fleete coming back into the eyes. Then a sweat broke out on the forehead and the eyes—they were human eyes—closed. We waited for an hour, but Fleete still slept. We carried him to his room and bade the leper go, giving him the bedstead, and the sheet on the bedstead to cover his nakedness, the gloves and the towels with which we had touched him, and the whip that had been hooked round his body. He put the sheet about him and went out into the early morning without speaking or mewing. **I**

Strickland wiped his face and sat down. A night gong, far away in the city, made seven o'clock.

"Exactly four-and-twenty hours!" said Strickland. "And I've done enough to ensure my dismissal from the service, besides permanent quarters in a lunatic asylum. Do you believe that we are awake?"

The red-hot gun barrel had fallen on the floor and was singeing the carpet. The smell was entirely real. **J**

That morning at eleven we two together went to wake up Fleete. We looked and saw that the black leopard rosette on his chest had disappeared. He was very drowsy and tired, but as soon as he saw us, he said, "Oh! Confound you fellows. Happy New Year to you. Never mix your liquors. I'm nearly dead."

"Thanks for your kindness, but you're over time," said Strickland. "Today is the morning of the second. You've slept the clock round with a vengeance."

The door opened, and little Dumoise put his head in. He had come on foot, and fancied that we were laying out Fleete.

"I've brought a nurse," said Dumoise. "I suppose that she can come in for . . . what is necessary."

"By all means," said Fleete cheerily, sitting up in bed. "Bring on your nurses."

Dumoise was dumb. Strickland led him out and explained that there must have been a mistake in the diagnosis. Dumoise remained dumb and left the house hastily. He considered that his professional reputation had been injured, and was inclined to make a personal matter of the recovery. Strickland went out too. When he came back, he said that he had been to call on the Temple of Hanuman to offer redress for the pollution of the god, and had been solemnly assured that no white man had ever touched the idol, and that he was an incarnation of all the virtues laboring under a delusion. "What do you think?" said Strickland.

I said, "'There are more things . . .'"[14]

14. **"There are more things":** reference to William Shakespeare's *Hamlet,* Act I, Scene 5, lines 166–167: "There are more things in heaven and earth, Horatio, than are dreamt of in your philosophy."

I Reading Focus Identifying Conflicts and Resolutions Which phrase or phrases in this passage indicate that at least some of the conflicts in the story have been resolved?

J Literary Focus Conflict The narrator does not respond when Strickland asks, "Do you believe that we are awake?" However, the narrator does tell the reader that the smell of the burned carpet is "entirely real." If the narrator were to answer Strickland's question, what does this detail suggest he might say?

Vocabulary **redress** (REE drehs) *n.:* payment or action that serves to remedy an injustice or injury.
delusion (dih LOO zhuhn) *n.:* false belief.

Universal Access

AAVE Students Who Use African American Vernacular English

English for Academic Success Read aloud the seventh full paragraph on p. 1002. Write the clause, "they were human eyes" on the board and underline *were.* Explain to students that *were* is a past tense form of the verb *to be.* Point out that in formal English, when the subject of the verb is plural, *were* is used. When the subject of the verb is singular, *was* is used. In pairs, have students create two examples of the use of *was* and *were* according to the conventions of formal English.

✔ For additional instruction and strategies, see **ThinkCentral, Teacher Access.**

But Strickland hates that quotation. He says that I have worn it threadbare.

One other curious thing happened which frightened me as much as anything in all the night's work. When Fleete was dressed he came into the dining room and sniffed. He had a quaint trick of moving his nose when he sniffed. "Horrid doggy smell, here," said he. "You should really keep those terriers of yours in better order. Try sulfur, Strick."

But Strickland did not answer. He caught hold of the back of a chair, and, without warning, went into an amazing fit of hysterics. It is terrible to see a strong man overtaken with hysteria. Then it struck me that we had fought for Fleete's soul with the Silver Man in that room, and had disgraced ourselves as Englishmen forever, and I laughed and gasped and gurgled just as shamefully as Strickland, while Fleete thought that we had both gone mad. We never told him what we had done. (K)

Some years later, when Strickland had married and was a churchgoing member of society for his wife's sake, we reviewed the incident dispassionately, and Strickland suggested that I should put it before the public.

I cannot myself see that this step is likely to clear up the mystery; because, in the first place, no one will believe a rather unpleasant story, and, in the second, it is well known to every right-minded man that the gods of the heathen are stone and brass, and any attempt to deal with them otherwise is justly condemned.

A Hindu ascetic traditionally regarded as having magical powers.

WE HAD FOUGHT FOR FLEETE'S SOUL WITH THE SILVER MAN IN THAT ROOM, AND HAD DISGRACED OURSELVES FOREVER.

(K) **Literary Focus** **Conflict** How have Strickland and the narrator "disgraced" themselves "as Englishmen forever" as a result of the conflicts in the story?

Vocabulary **dispassionately** (dihs PASH uh niht lee) *adv.:* without emotion; impartially.

Think About/Talk About

Comprehension

(I) Reading Focus

Possible response: *The words "We watched the face of the beast, and saw the soul of Fleete coming back into the eyes," indicate that the mystery of the cause of Fleete's problem has been solved, and the leper has capitulated.*

Analysis

(J) Literary Focus

Possible response: *The narrator would probably answer that they were awake, it was not a dream, and it was entirely real.*

(K) Literary Focus

Possible response: *They violated the boundaries of common decency by torturing another man, and they solved a problem by negotiating with a "heathen" god instead of using logic.*

Vocabulary: Own the Word

- **redress:** Ask students to craft an example of an appropriate *redress* for various small offenses, such as talking in class.
- **delusion:** What does it mean that Strickland is "laboring under a *delusion?*" Have students brainstorm examples from history of people laboring under a *delusion.* ***Possible response:*** *searching for the fountain of youth*

Monitor Students' Comprehension

Guide students in answering these comprehension questions.

1. What crime does Fleete commit against the Hindu people? [*He defiles a temple of Hanuman by putting his cigar out on the statue's forehead.*]
2. What details does the narrator omit? [*He does not give information about how he and Strickland torture the Silver Man.*]
3. How does the narrator feel about the "Eastern Gods" at the end of the story? [*He has greater respect for their power.*]

California Standards, pp. 1004–1006

- **Grades 9–10 Review Reading Standard 1.2** Distinguish between the denotative and connotative meanings of words and interpret the connotative power of words.
- **Grades 9–10 Review Reading Standard 3.3** Analyze interactions between main and subordinate characters in a literary text (e.g., internal and external conflicts, motivations, relationships, influences) and explain the way those interactions affect the plot.
- **Grades 9–10 Review Reading Standard 3.9** Explain how voice, persona, and the choice of a narrator affect characterization and the tone, plot, and credibility of a text.
- **Writing Standard 2.1** Write fictional, autobiographical, or biographical narratives: **a.** Narrate a sequence of events and communicate their significance to the audience. **b.** Locate scenes and incidents in specific places. **c.** Describe with concrete sensory details the sights, sounds, and smells of a scene and the specific actions, movements, gestures, and feelings of the characters; use interior monologue to depict the characters' feelings. **d.** Pace the presentation of actions to accommodate temporal, spatial, and dramatic mood changes.
- **Writing Standard 2.6** Deliver multimedia presentations: **a.** Combine text, images, and sound and draw information from many sources (e.g., television broadcasts, videos, films, newspapers, magazines, CD-ROMs, the Internet, electronic media-generated images). **b.** Select an appropriate medium for each element of the presentation. **c.** Use the selected media skillfully, editing appropriately and monitoring for quality. **d.** Test the audience's response and revise the presentation accordingly.

Check for Understanding

Independent Practice

Reading Skills Focus

Possible responses:

1. *The priests realize Hanuman will avenge himself on Fleete.*
2. *He craves barely cooked meat, eats like an animal, scares the horses, rolls in the dirt, and wants to walk all night.*
3. *Fleete's friends captured and presumably tortured him until he removed the evil spirit.*
4. *Chapter 13 of the book of Revelations reads, in part, "And the beast that I saw was like a leopard." The blisters on Fleete's chest were shaped like a leopard's spots. His insensitivity toward sacred Hindu images marks him as beast-like, even evil.*
5. *Students' charts should address the cultural misunderstandings involved in the conflicts.*

Literary Skills Focus

Possible responses:

6. *The story shows that the British did not really try to understand Indian culture.*
7. *There is no clear victor in this situation. Although the Englishmen succeeded in removing the evil spirit from Fleete, they had to disgrace themselves in the process.*
8. *This proverb implies that no one can decide who wins in the clash between cultures.*
9. *Fleete learns nothing because he does not remember the incident. Strickland and the narrator learn that they are capable of horrific acts and that no one wins in a struggle between cultures.*
10. *He is thoughtful and candid about his emotions but vague about his actions. The narrator's reluctance to divulge unpleasant details implies that he is ashamed of his actions. All of these details lead the reader to trust the narrator and believe his story.*

Applying Your Skills

Grades 9–10 Review Reading Standard 3.3, 3.9 (see page A48–A50)
Writing Standard 2.1a–d (see page A51–A52)

The Mark of the Beast

Literary Response and Analysis

Reading Skills Focus

Quick Check

1. After Fleete's act of disrespect, why do the priests allow the men to leave the temple, seemingly unharmed?
2. What clues reveal that Fleete is becoming something nonhuman?
3. Why does the Silver Man remove the evil spirit from Fleete?

Read with a Purpose

4. The title of the story is an allusion to the Book of Revelation in the Bible. Find other places in the story where Kipling alludes to the Book of Revelation. What do these allusions suggest about Fleete's character and actions? Although the Silver Man bewitches Fleete, in what way is Fleete's wolflike behavior symbolic of the beast—or the evil—inherent in him?

Reading Skills: Identifying Conflicts and Resolutions

5. Review the chart you filled in as you read. Then, add a fourth column to the chart, and use a check mark to indicate which conflicts in the story result from cultural misunderstandings.

Conflict	External or Internal?	Resolution	Cultural Misunderstandings (√)
Providence and Church of England vs. gods and devils of Asia	external		

Literary Skills Focus

Literary Analysis

6. **Evaluate** What does this story suggest were the issues that marked the British presence in India?
7. **Analyze** Do you think there is a clear victor in the story? Why or why not?
8. **Interpret** Re-read the Indian proverb at the beginning of the story. How does the proverb relate to the story's theme?

Literary Skills: Conflict

9. **Infer** Do Fleete, Strickland, and the narrator learn anything from the internal and external conflicts they undergo? Support your response with evidence from the story.

Literary Skills Review: Narrative Voice

10. **Make Judgments** A writer's **narrative voice** is created by tone, diction, and distinctive use of language. Describe the narrator's voice in this story. What does his voice suggest about his character, and how does it affect the telling of the tale?

Writing Skills Focus

Think as a Reader/Writer

Use It in Your Writing Write a scene for a story in which a conflict leads to a terrible result. Use suspense to create a gripping scene and capture your reader's attention.

What Do You Think Now In the end, why does the narrator consider the events in the story to be a "mystery"? To support your answer, consider his actions, statements, and tone.

Universal Access

Struggling Writers

Have students begin by identifying a character, something that the character desires, and an obstacle to the character's desire. Then, have students use their ideas to create a graphic organizer that charts the cause-and-effect relationships that will occur in their story. Have students mark, on their charts, examples of plot events that develop the conflict.

What Do You Think Now?

To help students answer the question, have them think about how the narrator and Strickland feel about the incident years later. Tell them to re-read the conclusion for clues to the narrator's feelings.

Grades 9–10 Review Reading Standard 1.2 (see page A48–A50)

Vocabulary Development

Vocabulary Check

Write the Vocabulary word that best completes the meaning of each sentence: **genial, distraught, redress, delusion, dispassionately.**

1. Presenting both sides of the issue, the journalist wrote ________ about the case.
2. The lost child was frightened and ________.
3. A tour guide should be ________.
4. The victims sought for the crime.
5. The king's ________ that he was all powerful caused him to underestimate his enemies.

Vocabulary Skills: Connotations

To determine which word to use in a passage, writers consider a word's shades of meaning as well as its **connotations,** the emotions and associations evoked by a word. Consider, for example, why Kipling might have chosen to use the word *dispassionately* instead of *objectively* in the following passage from "The Mark of the Beast":

> Some years later,... we reviewed the incident dispassionately, and Strickland suggested that I should put it before the public.

Both *dispassionately* and *objectively* mean "in a manner free of bias; impartially." However, "emotionlessly" and "passionlessly" are also part of the **denotation** (the dictionary definition) of *dispassionately.* While *objectively* is a neutral word, *dispassionately* often connotes an emotional coldness. Kipling might have chosen to use *dispassionately* to create a contrast with the intense, complex emotions Strickland and the narrator experienced during their struggles years ago.

Keep in mind that although a word's denotation is objective, its connotations are subjective. A word might evoke different emotions and associations for each reader.

Your Turn

To enhance your understanding of connotations, answer the following questions:

1. The narrator comments, "We were dealing with a **beast** that had once been Fleete." What does the word *beast* suggest that *animal* does not?
2. The narrator says, "Though the Silver Man had no face, you could see horrible feelings passing through the **slab** that took its place." What images and associations does *slab* call to mind?

Language Coach

Synonyms You can find synonyms of a word in a thesaurus, but you should use a dictionary to check the precise definition of each synonym. Often a dictionary will include examples that show the contexts in which a word is used. Sometimes a dictionary entry will also include a list of synonyms and an explanation of their shades of meaning.

For each of the following words, *distraught, redress,* and *delusion,* list two synonyms, and explain the different shades of meaning of each word and its synonyms. Use a thesaurus and a dictionary to complete this activity.

Academic Vocabulary

Talk About

In a small group, discuss the benefits of learning about other cultures and the risks of responding disrespectfully to cultural differences.

Learn It Online

Learn more about connotations with *WordSharp.*

go.hrw.com H12-1005 Go

Independent Practice

Vocabulary Development

Vocabulary Check

1. *dispassionately*
2. *distraught*
3. *genial*
4. *redress*
5. *delusion*

go.hrw.com **WordSharp: An Interactive Vocabulary Tutor**

Your Turn

1. Beast *connotes something monstrous or fiendish, while* animal *can be applied to all wildlife.*
2. Slab *conjures up images of something flattened and lifeless.*

English for Academic Success

Language Coach

Possible responses:

distraught: anxious *is a more restless worrying;* concerned *is being troubled but not necessarily showing it*

redress: vengeance *is a harmful type of redress;* relief *can refer to freedom from any kind of pain or wrong*

delusion: deception *is a deliberate act of misleading or deluding;* hallucination *usually results from a physical or mental problem*

English for Academic Success

Academic Vocabulary

Possible response: *Students might mention that learning about other cultures benefits people because it increases the chances of responding to others with understanding.*

Universal Access: Vocabulary Development

English Learners

English for Academic Success While students may understand the meaning of a word, they may need additional practice in determining a word's connotations. Pair students with a proficient English speaker; then, have them engage in an instructional conversation in which they work through the following pairs of words, deciding on the difference in connotation for each word.

- *berate* and *scold*
- *thin* and *emaciated*
- *gaudy* and *colorful*
- *teasing* and *mocking*

✔ See the **Academic and Selection Vocabulary Skill Builder** in **UA: Differentiating Instruction.**

Learn It Online

WordSharp: An Interactive Vocabulary Tutor provides additional support for vocabulary development. Multimedia tutorials show students how to apply vocabulary skills to unfamiliar words—and how to make those words their own.

go.hrw.com H12–1005 Go

Independent Practice

Grammar Link

Your Turn

1. *Grinding cigar ashes into the image of Hanuman is an insult to the god.*
2. *After Fleete is bewitched by the leper, his presence provokes fear in the horses.*
3. *When their friend Fleete is transformed into a beast, the narrator and Strickland have to take action.*

Choices: Evaluation Criteria

Review: Homework
Create a Horror Movie
Students invent a scene that reflects the conventions of the horror genre.

Connect: Homework
Evaluate the Story
Students' essays clearly state an opinion.

Extend: Homework
Write a Story
- Students' stories include a well-developed conflict.
- Students incorporate details about Dumoise accurately.

Assess

Unit 5 Resources, Selection Standards Check, p. 91

go.hrw.com ThinkCentral Online Assessment, Selection Standards Check

Teacher One Stop™, editable Selection Standards Check

Reteach

go.hrw.com ThinkCentral Online Remediation

Applying Your Skills

Writing Standard 2.1a–d, 2.6a–d (see page A51–A52)

The Mark of the Beast

Grammar Link

Dangling Modifiers

What would you think if you came across the following sentence in your reading?

> Fascinated by British and Indian cultural conflicts, some of Kipling's stories are set in India.

Would you wonder *who* was fascinated by the conflicts? This sentence is confusing because it contains a **dangling modifier**—a word, phrase, or clause that does not sensibly, or reasonably, modify any word or group of words in a sentence. There are three ways to correct dangling modifiers:

- Add the word that the modifier describes or qualifies, and reword the sentence as necessary:

  > Fascinated by British and Indian cultural conflicts, Kipling set some of his stories in India.

- Add words to the modifier to make its meaning clear:

  > Since Kipling was fascinated by British and Indian cultural conflicts, some of his stories are set in India.

- Reword the entire sentence:

  > Kipling was fascinated by British and Indian cultural conflicts, so he set some of his stories in India.

Your Turn

Rewrite to correct the dangling modifiers.

1. Grinding cigar ashes into the image of Hanuman, it insults the god.
2. Bewitched by the leper, Fleete's presence provokes fear in the horses.
3. Transformed into a beast, the narrator and Strickland have to take action.

Writing Application Correct a dangling modifier in a paragraph you have already written.

CHOICES

As you respond to the Choices, use these **Academic Vocabulary** words as appropriate: benefit, complex, publish, respond, statistics.

Movie poster for *The Island of Dr Moreau* (1977), based on a novel by H. G. Wells.

REVIEW

Create a Horror Movie

TechFocus Think about the techniques Kipling uses to create a sense of horror in this story. Then, in a small group, create a short video adaptation of a scene from "The Mark of the Beast." Carefully consider what techniques you will use to horrify your audience and how these techniques differ from or are the same as Kipling's.

CONNECT

Evaluate the Story

Critics have called "The Mark of the Beast" "nasty," "poisonous," and even "sadistic." What is your evaluation of the story? Do you think it is a well-told, suspenseful horror story? Is it a complex, insightful examination of British imperialism? Write an essay expressing your views of the work. Be sure to support your points with evidence from the text.

EXTEND

Write a Story

In the beginning of "The Mark of the Beast," the narrator says that Dumoise "died in a rather curious manner." Write your own story telling how and why Dumoise died. Use a first-person narrator, and consider how your choice of narrator will affect the telling of your tale. Make sure the details in your story are consistent with what you know about Dumoise.

Universal Access: Grammar Link

EL English Learners

English for Academic Success To help students understand the confusion created by dangling modifiers, write the following example on the board:

Bringing the chicken to the table, the delicious aroma of roasted garlic filled the air.

Explain that this example is confusing because a reader would wonder who brought the chicken to the table. Point out that no matter what method students use to correct the sentence, it is important first to identify to whom or what the modifier refers.

Have students work with a partner to correct the dangling modifiers in the following examples:

- To win the contest, your help will be needed. [*If I am to win the contest, your help will be needed.*]
- Before moving to the coast, Idaho had been his home. [*Before Paul moved to the coast, Idaho had been his home.*]

✔ For more practice with dangling modifiers, see **Warriner's Handbook, GrammarNotes,** and **Language Handbook Worksheets.**

COMPARING TEXTS: WORLD LITERATURE

Realism and the Short Story

The Stone Breakers (1849) by Gustave Courbet (1819–1877). Oil on canvas.
Galerie Neue Meister, Dresden, Germany/ © Staatliche Kunstammlungen, Dresden.

You have just read "The Mark of the Beast" by Rudyard Kipling. In this Comparing Texts: World Literature section, you will read three short stories from other countries that exemplify the style known as realism.

CONTENTS

Standards Focus

Objectives

Students will

- read stories from various cultures that exemplify realism
- understand theme and allegory
- understand situational and dramatic irony
- make predictions and draw inferences

English for Academic Success

Academic Vocabulary

Look for opportunities to use the Academic Vocabulary words in this unit.

- **benefit, *n.*:** something that promotes well-being
- **complex, *adj.*:** complicated
- **publish, *v.*:** to print a book or journal to make it generally known
- **respond, *v.*:** to reply or react
- **statistics, *n.*:** numerical data

Analyzing Visuals

Extension Activity Ask students to make inferences about the men in the painting based on their appearance. Then, ask them how this painting exemplifies realism. ***Possible response:*** *The men appear to be hard at work breaking stones. The painting conveys the principles of realism because its representation of the men is highly detailed and because it depicts members of the working class.*

Selection Introduction

Think About the Writer

Tell students that, in the last thirty years of his life, Count Tolstoy, the former aristocrat, dressed in peasant clothing, became a vegetarian, worked in the fields alongside his former serfs, and refused royalties on his published writings. He championed the poor and fostered the principles of community and social justice. His ideas inspired later pacifist reformers such as Mohandas Gandhi and Martin Luther King, Jr.

For Independent Reading

- *Anna Karenina,* Leo Tolstoy
- *Readings in World Literature**

HRW LIBRARY *This title is available from the HRW library.

Motivate

What Do You Think?/QuickWrite

Work with students to help them identify things that are true necessities and not simply goods that someone craves. Then, have students write their responses to the question in their **Reader/Writer Notebooks.**

Preparing to Read

How Much Land Does a Man Need?

What Do You Think How can appearance be different from reality?

QuickWrite

Take a few notes in your *Reader/Writer Notebook* on the difference between "wants" and "needs." Do most people want more than they need?

Leo Tolstoy dresses as a peasant.

MEET THE WRITER

Leo Tolstoy

(1828–1910)

The death of Count Leo Nikolayevich Tolstoy was front-page news in England and America. At the age of eighty-two, the great writer had run away from his family, seeking a place where he could lead a simple, hermit's life. He became ill in a remote train station and died of pneumonia in the stationmaster's office.

An Aristocratic Beginning

Tolstoy was born to wealthy aristocratic parents who died before Tolstoy was nine. He and his siblings were raised by his aunts on the family estate. At nineteen, Tolstoy split his inheritance with his brothers and became the master of his family's estate and its three hundred serfs. Within three years, he had gambled away about one fourth of his inheritance. Looking for adventure, he joined the Russian army and fought bravely during the Crimean War. Tolstoy's contemplative nature and serious moral outlook emerged in response to the suffering that he witnessed during the war.

In 1859, Tolstoy opened a school on his estate for his serfs' children. Soon after, he married Sonya Andreyevna Bers, who, in addition to bearing thirteen children, laboriously recopied her husband's manuscripts. She also took over the management of his estate, which freed Tolstoy to write his greatest works, *War and Peace* (1869) and *Anna Karenina* (1877).

A Spiritual Conversion

After years of moral questioning, Tolstoy underwent a shattering spiritual conversion. Convinced that the purpose of life was to do good works, he began to emulate Russia's Christian peasants. He renounced private ownership, the Orthodox Church, and the czarist government. Although Tolstoy repudiated his early works for their focus on aristocracy, his reputation today rests primarily on those early novels: *War and Peace*, a monumental telling of the lives of five aristocratic families during the Napoleonic Wars, and *Anna Karenina*, the tragic story of a woman who gives up her husband and child for what she thinks is true love.

Think About the Writer How would you describe the two distinct parts of Tolstoy's life?

California Standards, pp. 1008–1021

- **Reading Standard 3.1** Analyze characteristics of subgenres (e.g., satire, parody, allegory, pastoral) that are used in poetry, prose, novels, short stories, essays, and other basic genres.
- **Reading Standard 3.2** Analyze the way in which the theme or meaning of a selection represents a view or comment on life, using textual evidence to support the claim.

Selection Readability	
Easily Accessible **Accessible** Challenging	familiar syntax; simple dialogue; accessible theme

Reading Standard 3.1, 3.2 (see pages A48–A50)

Literary Skills Focus

Allegory Tolstoy's story "How Much Land Does a Man Need?" is an **allegory,** a story that operates on both literal and symbolic levels. The characters, settings, and events of an allegory can therefore be understood both for what they are (the literal meaning) and for the abstract principles they represent (the symbolic meaning). Characters in allegories often stand for virtues and vices—pride, for example, or innocence, or greed. As you read this story, try to determine what the various elements (such as Pahom, the Devil, and the land itself) symbolize.

Reading Skills Focus

Identifying Theme A **theme** is the central idea or insight revealed in a work of literature. Writers rarely state the theme of a story explicitly; instead, they reveal the theme by letting us see characters in action. By the end of a story, the characters have often discovered something about themselves, and, we, the readers, also participate in this discovery. That discovery about human life is the story's theme.

Into Action There are several ways to identify theme. You can ask yourself what the main character has discovered at the story's conclusion, or look for key passages that seem especially important. You can also check the story's title, which sometimes gives a clue to its theme. As you read this story, use a chart like the one below to record key details that might point to the theme.

Clues to Theme	
The peasant sister says "Gain and pain are brothers twain."	→ This statement seems to relate to the story's title.

Writing Skills Focus

Find It in Your Reading The characters, events, and settings of an **allegory** stand for abstract things or ideas. For example, a character might stand for temptation or a setting might represent despair or happiness. In your *Reader/Writer Notebook,* write down your ideas about how this story could be made into a modern allegory by updating the characters, events, setting, and title.

Vocabulary

piqued (peekt) *v.* used as *adj.:* provoked; resentful. *The peasant woman was piqued when her older, wealthier sister boasted of the benefits of town life.*

disparaged (dihs PAR ihjd) *v.:* belittled; spoke negatively of. *The peasant woman disparaged her sister's prosperous life.*

aggrieved (uh GREEVD) *v.* used as *adj.:* offended. *Pahom felt aggrieved when the Judges acquitted Simon of any wrongdoing.*

arable (AIR uh buhl) *adj.:* fit to be farmed or cultivated. *Much of Pahom's new land was arable.*

haggled (HAG uhld) *v.:* argued about a price. *Pahom haggled with the peasant to get a lower price on the land.*

prostrate (PRAHS trayt) *adj.:* lying flat. *In his dream, Pahom saw himself lying prostrate on the ground.*

Reader/Writer Notebook

Use your **RWN** to complete the activities for this selection.

Learn It Online

Learn more about Tolstoy on the Writers' Lives site.

go.hrw.com H12-1009 Go

Preteach

Introducing Vocabulary

Use this activity to check students' understanding of the Vocabulary words.

1. Name two driving behaviors that can make other drivers **piqued.**
2. How do you feel when someone has **disparaged** your accomplishments?
3. Do you feel **aggrieved** when someone else takes credit for a good deed you did?
4. What is the main purpose of **arable** land?
5. In what situation might a buyer **haggle?**
6. Where is someone likely to be **prostrate?**

Literary Skills Focus

As you read and discuss the selection with students, have them note details of plot, setting, and characterization that contribute to the allegory.

Reading Skills Focus

Give students a copy of the Reading Skills Focus graphic organizer before they read. (See **Unit 5 Resources.)** Tell them to use their responses to answer the questions on the Applying Your Skills page.

Writing Skills Focus

Have students take note of elements in the story that could be updated to form a modern allegory in their **Reader/Writer Notebooks.**

Learn It Online

The **Writers' Lives** feature of the Interactive Student Edition offers additional information about this author.

go.hrw.com H12-1009 Go

Comparing Texts Resources

Unit 5 Resources, on-level practice and assessment, p. 77

Teacher One Stop™, on-level lesson plans and all print resources

Holt Audio Library

Holt Audio Library: Selections and Summaries in Spanish

UA: Differentiating Instruction, graphic organizer, p. 240

UA: Supporting Instruction in Spanish, selection summary

Analyzing Visuals Transparencies, p. 40

ThinkCentral Online Assessment, Selection Standards Check

ThinkCentral Online Remediation

Teacher Preparation
Selection Plot Summary
Pahom, a Russian peasant, boasts to himself that if he just had enough land, he would not even fear the Devil. Overhearing this, the Devil plots to exploit Pahom's greed. After buying land locally, Pahom goes to the region of the Bashkirs with all his savings to buy even more land. The Bashkirs agree to sell him as much land as he can pace off in a day as long as he returns to his starting point before sunset. He walks a great distance and encircles a great expanse of land. However, in his wild rush to get back before nightfall, he dies, ending up with only six feet of land for his grave.

Direct Teach

Think About/Talk About
Read with a Purpose Have students read the Read with a Purpose statement. Point out the phrase "greed consumes him." Ask students to predict how greed might affect the peasants described in the background information about the story.

SHORT STORY

How Much Land Does a Man Need?

by **Leo Tolstoy**

translated by **Louise** and **Aylmer Maude**

Read with a Purpose
Read to discover how a man's greed consumes him.

Build Background
Until Czar Alexander II ordered their emancipation in 1861, Russian peasants, called *serfs,* were the virtual slaves of landowners and aristocrats. Serfs could be bought or sold, and were not allowed to own property. When Tolstoy wrote this story in 1886, serfs had already experienced twenty-five years of freedom. While no one (and certainly not Tolstoy the reformer) wished to see them thrown back into bondage, Tolstoy questions in this parable whether the peasants' progress had brought changes they would come to regret.

Universal Access

English Learners
English for Academic Success Have students note the proverb "Loss and gain are brothers twain." Inform them that "twain" is an archaic word for "two" or "twin." Then, ask students to discuss the proverb's meaning and predict what bearing it might have on the theme of the story. Invite students to think of other English proverbs, or proverbs in their native language, that have a similar theme or message.

Struggling Readers
To help students read "How Much Land Does a Man Need?" model the reading skill of identifying theme. You might say: "Suppose you read that the main character in this story wants more land. That's a conflict, so look for the outcome. If he gets land and ends up happy, the theme might involve the benefits of ambition. If he is unhappy, the theme might involve the perils of greed." Urge students as they read to ask themselves, "What lesson might the resolution of the conflict reveal?"

A Settler's Family (c. 1907–1915) by Sergei Mikhailovich Prokudin-Gorskii.

An elder sister came to visit her younger sister in the country. The elder was married to a tradesman in town, the younger to a peasant in the village. As the sisters sat over their tea talking, the elder began to boast of the advantages of town life: saying how comfortably they lived there, how well they dressed, what fine clothes her children wore, what good things they ate and drank, and how she went to the theater, promenades, and entertainments.

The younger sister was piqued, and in turn disparaged the life of a tradesman, and stood up for that of a peasant.

"I would not change my way of life for yours," said she. "We may live roughly, but at least we are free from anxiety. You live in better style than we do, but though you often earn more than you need, you are very likely to lose all you have. You know the proverb, 'Loss and gain are brothers twain.' It often happens that people who are wealthy one day are begging their bread the next. Our way is safer. Though a peasant's life is not a fat one, it is a long one. We shall never grow rich, but we shall always have enough to eat." **A**

The elder sister said sneeringly:

"Enough? Yes, if you like to share with the pigs and the calves! What do you know of elegance or manners! However much your goodman may slave, you will die as you are living—on a dung heap—and your children the same."

"Well, what of that?" replied the younger. "Of course our work is rough and coarse. But, on the other hand, it is sure, and we need not bow to anyone. But you, in your towns, are surrounded by temptations; today all may be right, but tomorrow the Evil One may tempt your husband with cards, wine, or women, and all will go to ruin. Don't such things happen often enough?" **B**

A Reading Focus **Identifying Theme** The appearance of proverbs in a story is usually important. How would you state the proverb in this paragraph in your own words?

B Literary Focus **Allegory** The two sisters are described as complete opposites. Which sister might stand for boastfulness? Which sister might stand for acceptance of her lot in life?

Vocabulary **piqued** (peekt) *v.* used as *adj.:* provoked; resentful.
disparaged (dihs PAR ihjd) *v.:* belittled; spoke negatively of.

Think About/Talk About

Comprehension

A Reading Focus

Possible responses: *Loss and gain go together. A gain in one area often means a loss in another area; good fortune can quickly turn to bad.*

Analysis

B Literary Focus

Possible response: *The elder sister, who comes from town, could stand for boastfulness. The younger sister could stand for acceptance because she accepts her way of life in the country.*

Extend the Discussion

Making Predictions Using the title of the story and the sisters' statements about city values and country values, what can you predict about the rest of the story? ***Possible response:*** *The story will be about the consequences of striving for what you want and the possible benefits of striving only for what you need.*

Determining Author's Purpose In the last paragraph on this page, how does Tolstoy suggest that the story will be an allegory? ***Possible response:*** *Allegories often have characters that stand for specific abstract qualities. Here, the Evil One is the tempter.*

Vocabulary: Own the Word

- **piqued:** Ask students to recall a time when they were *piqued* or saw someone become *piqued.* What had provoked them?
- **disparaged:** Ask students to think of examples of people or ideas that are frequently *disparaged* by society. Did they deserve this treatment?

Advanced Learners

Enrichment Deepen students' analysis by pointing out Tolstoy's mastery of dramatic irony, the art of providing indirect clues to let readers know more than the character. For example, Pahom is certain that his neighbor Simon has felled his trees, but the judges' responses and the lack of evidence show readers that Pahom's "certainty" is actually a growing irrationality. Ask students to stay alert for more examples of indirect clues that create dramatic irony. Have students use these clues as they identify the theme of the parable.

Students with Disabilities

Students may have some difficulty understanding the settings and characters that Tolstoy describes in the selection. Tell students that easy-to-read reference books can provide students with drawings and photographs to help them understand Tolstoy's settings and characters. One such reference is Edward Crankshaw's *Tolstoy: The Making of a Novelist.* Encourage students to use these references to help them understand the themes and ideas presented in the story.

Model the Skill

- Provide students with copies of the Reading Skills Focus graphic organizer for "How Much Land Does a Man Need?" (See **Unit 5 Resources.**)
- Tell students that one way to attempt to identify a **theme** is to look for a connection between key passages and the title of the story.
- Model adding key details that relate to **theme** to the graphic organizer. For example, you might say, "On p. 1012, Pahom makes the bold statement that he would not fear the Devil if he had plenty of land. Pahom's desire for 'plenty of land' relates to the question posed in the title of the story. I will note this clue about theme in the chart."

Clues to Theme		
Pahom says, "If I had plenty of land, I would fear the Devil himself!"	→	This statement seems to relate to the story's title.

Guided Practice: Apply

Three-Minute Review Use Three-Minute Review to enhance comprehension. Have students think about what Pahom considers "plenty of land" at this point in the story. Ask students to work with a partner and discuss how Pahom's concept of "plenty of land" might change throughout the story and how this relates to the theme. Have pairs share their reviews with the class.

Pahom, the master of the house, was lying on the top of the stove[1] and he listened to the women's chatter.

"It is perfectly true," thought he. "Busy as we are from childhood tilling mother earth, we peasants have no time to let any nonsense settle in our heads. Our only trouble is that we haven't land enough. If I had plenty of land, I shouldn't fear the Devil himself!"

The women finished their tea, chatted a while about dress, and then cleared away the tea things and lay down to sleep.

But the Devil had been sitting behind the stove, and had heard all that was said. He was pleased that the peasant's wife had led her husband into boasting, and that he had said that if he had plenty of land he would not fear the Devil himself.

"All right," thought the Devil. "We will have a tussle. I'll give you land enough; and by means of that land I will get you into my power." **C**

Close to the village there lived a lady, a small landowner who had an estate of about three hundred acres. She had always lived on good terms with the peasants until she engaged as her steward an old soldier, who took to burdening the people with fines. However careful Pahom tried to be, it happened again and again that now a horse of his got among the lady's oats, now a cow strayed into her garden, now his calves found their way into her meadows—and he always had to pay a fine.

Pahom paid up, but grumbled and, going home in a temper, was rough with his family. All through that summer, Pahom had much trouble because of this steward, and he was even glad when winter came and the cattle had to be stabled. Though he grudged the fodder when they could no longer graze on the pastureland, at least he was free from anxiety about them.

In the winter the news got about that the lady was going to sell her land and that the keeper of the inn on the high road was bargaining for it. When the peasants heard this they were very much alarmed.

"Well," thought they, "if the innkeeper gets the land, he will worry us with fines worse than the lady's steward. We all depend on that estate."

So the peasants went on behalf of their Commune,[2] and asked the lady not to sell the land to the innkeeper, offering her a better price for it themselves. The lady agreed to let them have it. Then the peasants tried to arrange for the Commune to buy the whole estate, so that it might be held by them all in common. They met twice to discuss it, but could not settle the matter; the Evil One sowed discord among them and they could not agree. So they decided to buy the land individually, each according to his means; and the lady agreed to this plan as she had to the other. **D**

Presently Pahom heard that a neighbor of his was buying fifty acres, and that the lady had consented to accept one half in cash and to wait a year for the other half. Pahom felt envious.

"Look at that," thought he, "the land is all being sold, and I shall get none of it." So he spoke to his wife.

"Other people are buying," said he, "and we must also buy twenty acres or so. Life is becoming impossible. That steward is simply crushing us with his fines."

So they put their heads together and considered how they could manage to buy it. They had one hundred rubles[3] laid by. They sold a colt and one half of their bees, hired out one of their sons as a laborer, and took his wages in advance; borrowed the rest from a brother-in-law, and so scraped together half the purchase money.

Having done this, Pahom chose out a farm of forty acres, some of it wooded, and went to the lady to bargain for it. They came to an agreement, and he shook hands with her upon it and paid her a deposit in advance. Then they went to town and signed the deeds, he paying half the price down, and undertaking to pay the remainder within two years.

So now Pahom had land of his own. He borrowed seed, and sowed it on the land he had bought. The harvest was a good one, and within a year he had man-

1. **lying… stove:** In Russian houses, large stoves made of brick or tile radiated heat to warm a room. Rich people would not lie on top of their stoves.

2. **Commune:** village council.
3. **rubles:** units of money in Russia.

C **Reading Focus** **Identifying Theme** What plan does the Devil form to entrap and control Pahom?

D **Literary Focus** **Allegory** How does the Evil One influence the outcome of the discussion?

Developing Oral Fluency

Individual Activity Invite students to choose a favorite passage of two or three paragraphs from the selection. Ask students to practice reading the passages until they can do so fluently. Also, have them prepare a short introduction to the piece that provides some background and tells why they find the writing moving or the ideas important. Then, have students give their introductions and read their selections aloud to the class.

✔ See the **Oral Language Skill Builder** in **UA: Differentiating Instruction.**

aged to pay off his debts both to the lady and to his brother-in-law. So he became a landowner, plowing and sowing his own land, making hay on his own land, cutting his own trees, and feeding his cattle on his own pasture. When he went out to plow his fields, or to look at his growing corn,[4] or at his grass meadows, his heart would fill with joy. The grass that grew and the flowers that bloomed there seemed to him unlike any that grew elsewhere. Formerly, when he had passed by that land, it had appeared the same as any other land, but now it seemed quite different.

So Pahom was well contented, and everything would have been right if the neighboring peasants would only not have trespassed on his cornfields and meadows. He appealed to them most civilly, but they still went on: Now the Communal herdsmen would let the village cows stray into his meadows, then horses from the night pasture would get among his corn. Pahom turned them out again and again, and forgave their owners, and for a long time he forbore to prosecute anyone. But at last he lost patience and complained to the District Court. He knew it was the peasants' want of land, and no evil intent on their part, that caused the trouble, but he thought:

"I cannot go on overlooking it or they will destroy all I have. They must be taught a lesson." **E**

So he had them up, gave them one lesson, and then another, and two or three of the peasants were fined. After a time Pahom's neighbors began to bear him a grudge for this, and would now and then let their cattle on to his land on purpose. One peasant even got into Pahom's wood at night and cut down five young lime trees[5] for their bark. Pahom passing through the wood one day noticed something white. He came nearer and saw the stripped trunks lying on the ground, and close by stood the stumps where the trees had been. Pahom was furious.

"If he had only cut one here and there it would have been bad enough," thought Pahom, "but the rascal has actually cut down a whole clump. If I could only find out who did this, I would pay him out."

He racked his brain as to who it could be. Finally he decided: "It must be Simon—no one else could have done it." So he went to Simon's homestead to have a look round, but he found nothing, and only had an angry scene. However, he now felt more certain than ever that Simon had done it, and he lodged a complaint. Simon was summoned. The case was tried, and retried, and at the end of it all Simon was acquitted, there being no evidence against him. Pahom felt still more aggrieved, and let his anger loose upon the Elder and the Judges.

"You let thieves grease your palms," said he. "If you were honest folk yourselves you would not let a thief go free."

So Pahom quarreled with the Judges and with his neighbors. Threats to burn his building began to be uttered. So though Pahom had more land, his place in the Commune was much worse than before. **F**

About this time a rumor got about that many people were moving to new parts.

"There's no need for me to leave my land," thought Pahom. "But some of the others might leave our village and then there would be more room for us. I would take over their land myself and make my estate a bit bigger. I could then live more at ease. As it is, I am still too cramped to be comfortable." **G**

One day Pahom was sitting at home when a peasant, passing through the village, happened to call in. He was allowed to stay the night, and supper was given him. Pahom had a talk with this peasant and asked him where he came from. The stranger answered that he came from beyond the Volga,[6] where he had been working. One word led to another, and the man went on to say that many people were settling in those parts. He told how some people from his village had settled there. They had joined the Commune, and had had

4. **corn:** any plants producing grain, such as wheat or oats.
5. **lime trees:** linden trees.
6. **Volga:** river in western Russia flowing into the Caspian Sea.

E Reading Focus **Identifying Theme** How does Pahom become like the landowner he once resented?

F Reading Focus **Identifying Theme** How does land ownership ultimately harm Pahom's standing in the Commune?

G Reading Focus **Identifying Theme** Relate Pahom's statement to the story's title. How much land does Pahom think he needs?

Vocabulary **aggrieved** (uh GREEVD) *v.* used as *adj.*: offended.

Think About/Talk About

Comprehension

C Reading Focus

Possible response: *The Devil plans to give Pahom "enough land" to make him feel dissatisfied and strive for more.*

E Reading Focus

Possible response: *He fines the peasants for trespassing on his land in order to teach them a lesson. Just like the steward, he puts the condition of the land above compassion for others.*

F Reading Focus

Possible response: *Pahom attacks and insults many members of the Commune because he thinks they threaten his land.*

G Reading Focus

Possible response: *Pahom states that the land he has is not enough. He needs more than his forty acres.*

Analysis

D Literary Focus

Possible response: *The Evil One creates conflict and disagreement among the many peasants attempting to buy the land.*

Vocabulary: Own the Word

aggrieved: Ask students to recall a time when they or someone else they knew felt *aggrieved* about something. How did they react?

Cross-Curricular Connection

ECONOMICS: Land Ownership

In Russia in the late 1800s, aristocrats still held much of the land in private ownership. Some land, however, was owned communally by groups of peasants. In 1861, Czar Alexander II had issued the Edict of Emancipation, effectively freeing over twenty million serfs (about a third of the Russian population). Groups of these serfs, who came to be called "state peasants," were allotted land and given forty-nine years to pay for it.

HSS Analysis Skills: HI 1

Model the Skill

- Review the concept of **allegory.** Remind students that the elements in an **allegory** can be interpreted on both a literal and a symbolic level.
- Tell students that characters in an allegory often stand for virtues and vices.
- Read aloud Pahom's thoughts in the second paragraph on p. 1014. Point out how Pahom's feelings about his land have changed.

Guided Practice: Apply

Turn-and-Talk Have students work with a partner and read the paragraph that begins at the bottom of p. 1014 and continues onto p. 1015. Ask pairs to compare the way Pahom describes his land when he first owns it to the way he describes it now. What does Pahom's continuous need for more land symbolize? ***Possible response:*** *His growing desire for more land symbolizes his increasing greed.*

Think About/Talk About

Extend the Discussion

Finding Details Pahom is not the only one in the Commune who desires more land. How does the yearning for more land affect those working on communal land? ***Possible response:*** *The land was good so everyone wanted more, causing many fights among the communal farmers.*

Making Judgments Does the reader remain sympathetic with Pahom's quest for more land? Why or why not? ***Possible response:*** *Tolstoy makes it harder to be sympathetic because Pahom's greed for more land becomes more predictable and intense. The Evil One is clearly winning.*

twenty-five acres per man granted them. The land was so good, he said, that the rye sown on it grew as high as a horse, and so thick that five cuts of a sickle made a sheaf. One peasant, he said, had brought nothing with him but his bare hands, and now he had six horses and two cows of his own.

Pahom's heart kindled with desire. He thought:

"Why should I suffer in this narrow hole, if one can live so well elsewhere? I will sell my land and my homestead here, and with the money I will start afresh over there and get everything new. In this crowded place one is always having trouble. But I must first go and find out all about it myself." **H**

Toward summer he got ready and started. He went down the Volga on a steamer to Samara,[7] then walked another three hundred miles on foot, and at last reached the place. It was just as the stranger had said. The peasants had plenty of land: Every man had twenty-five acres of Communal land given him for his use, and anyone who had money could buy, besides, at a ruble an acre as much good freehold land as he wanted.

Having found out all he wished to know, Pahom returned home as autumn came on, and began selling off his belongings. He sold his land at a profit, sold his homestead and all his cattle, and withdrew from membership in the Commune. He only waited till the spring, and then started with his family for the new settlement.

As soon as Pahom and his family reached their new abode, he applied for admission into the Commune of a large village. He stood treat to the Elders[8] and obtained the necessary documents. Five shares of Communal land were given him for his own and his sons' use: that is to say—125 acres (not all together, but in different fields) besides the use of the Communal pasture. Pahom put up the buildings he needed, and bought cattle. Of the Communal land alone he had three times as much as at his former home, and the land was good corn land. He was ten times better off than he had been. He had plenty of arable land and pasturage, and could keep as many head of cattle as he liked. **I**

At first, in the bustle of building and settling down, Pahom was pleased with it all, but when he got used to it he began to think that even here he had not enough land. The first year, he sowed wheat on his share of the Communal land and had a good crop. He wanted to go on sowing wheat, but had not enough

Analyzing Visuals

Connecting to the Text Does this painting represent Pahom's ideas about land? Is farming romanticized in the painting? Explain.

7. **Samara:** city on the Volga River in southwestern Russia.
8. **stood treat to the Elders:** provided the Elders with a meal.

H **Reading Focus** **Identifying Theme** How have Pahom's desires changed?

I **Literary Focus** **Allegory** Events in allegories often occur in patterns. Notice how Pahom has acquired more and more land. If he follows the pattern of his past actions, what can we predict will happen next?

Vocabulary **arable** (AIR uh buhl) *adj.:* fit to be farmed or cultivated.

Cross-Curricular Connection

GEOGRAPHY: Russia's Rivers

Stretching 2,290 miles from the Valdai Hills between Moscow and St. Petersburg in the north and to the Caspian Sea in the south, the Volga River is Russia's most important and longest river. The Volga makes a hairpin turn—the Samara Bend—where it joins the Samara River. At this junction lies the city of Samara. In the mid-nineteenth century, Samara became an important center for milling flour and trading grains. In recent decades, it has become one of Russia's most important producers of agricultural and automotive equipment.

Harvest Time (1887) by Grigory Myasoyedov. The State Russian Museum.

Communal land for the purpose, and what he had already used was not available; for in those parts wheat is only sown on virgin soil or on fallow land. It is sown for one or two years, and then the land lies fallow till it is again overgrown with prairie grass. There were many who wanted such land and there was not enough for all; so that people quarreled about it. Those who were better off wanted it for growing wheat, and those who were poor wanted it to let to dealers, so that they might raise money to pay their taxes. Pahom wanted to sow more wheat, so he rented land from a dealer for a year. He sowed much wheat and had a fine crop, but the land was too far from the village—the wheat had to be carted more than ten miles. After a time Pahom noticed that some peasant dealers were living on separate farms and were growing wealthy; and he thought: "If I were to buy some freehold land and have a homestead on it, it would be a different thing altogether. Then it would all be nice and compact."

The question of buying freehold land recurred to him again and again.

He went on in the same way for three years, renting land and sowing wheat. The seasons turned out well and the crops were good, so that he began to lay money by. He might have gone on living contentedly, but he grew tired of having to rent other people's land every year, and having to scramble for it. Wherever there was good land to be had, the peasants would rush for it and it was taken up at once, so that unless you were sharp about it you got none. It happened in the third year that he and a dealer together rented a piece of pastureland from some peasants; and they had already plowed it up, when there was some dispute and the peasants went to law about it, and things fell out so that the labor was all lost.

"If it were my own land," thought Pahom, "I should be independent, and there would not be all this unpleasantness." **J**

J **Reading Focus** **Identifying Theme** What does Pahom want even though he "might have gone on living contentedly"?

Analyzing Visuals

Connecting to the Text: *The land looks plentiful and has no obvious owner, and the scene depicted is peaceful and idyllic. Instead of suggesting dissatisfaction and discontentment, the elements of the painting suggest that land can be enjoyed by anyone, regardless of who owns it.*

Think About/Talk About

Comprehension

H Reading Focus

Possible response: *Pahom wants to "start fresh" with untouched land on a new commune.*

J Reading Focus

Possible response: *He wants to acquire more land and to own it independently.*

Analysis

I Literary Focus

Possible response: *If Pahom continues in his current pattern, he will become greedy again. Eventually, he will decide his current one hundred and twenty-five acres are not enough, and again he will want more land.*

Extend the Discussion

Making Predictions Events in parables and allegories often recur in patterns. Re-read the passage that describes Pahom's farm on the Communal land and notice how well-off he is now. If he follows the pattern he has set so far, what will happen next? ***Possible responses:*** *His contentment will fade; he will want more land and expect it to bring him happiness; he will get more land and his contentment will fade again.*

Theme After Pahom finishes building and settling down, he again begins to feel that his land is not enough. What message do you think Tolstoy is trying to deliver by repeating this narrative pattern? ***Possible response:*** *When you spend your life being led by your desires, you will never be content no matter how much you have.*

Vocabulary: Own the Word

arable: Draw a semantic web on the board with *arable* written in the center circle. Ask students to suggest words or phrases that relate to *arable* and record them in the web. ***Possible responses:*** *fertile, harvest*

Guided Practice: Apply

Think as a Reader/Writer

Find It in Your Reading Point out that the tradesman tells Pahom that all he must do to get thirteen hundred acres of land is to make friends with the chiefs. This arrangement might symbolize a deal with the Devil.

Use It in Your Writing Tell students to rewrite Pahom's conversation with the tradesman, using updated details that would make the scene seem modern. Remind students to include some sort of an arrangement symbolizing the main character entering into a deal with the Devil.

Think About/Talk About

Build Background: The Sharing of Tea

In this story, discussions are held and business is transacted over tea. While not carrying the spiritual associations of the Japanese tea ceremony, the sharing of tea is a traditional social ritual in Russian culture.

Extend the Discussion

Finding Details When Pahom reaches the place where the Bashkirs live, what observations does he make about the Bashkir people? ***Possible responses:*** *They do not farm their land, and they let their cattle roam free. The men only drink, eat, and play music all day and do not think of working.*

Questioning to Monitor Reading
What questions might you ask about the dealer's statements about the Bashkirs in the fifth paragraph? ***Possible responses:*** *Are the Bashkirs really "as simple as sheep"? Is there a catch to their low land prices? Does the dealer have an ulterior motive? Might he be the Devil in another form?*

So Pahom began looking out for land which he could buy; and he came across a peasant who had bought thirteen hundred acres, but having got into difficulties was willing to sell again cheap. Pahom bargained and haggled with him, and at last they settled the price at 1,500 rubles, part in cash and part to be paid later. They had all but clinched the matter when a passing dealer happened to stop at Pahom's one day to get a feed for his horses. He drank tea with Pahom and they had a talk. The dealer said that he was just returning from the land of the Bashkirs,[9] far away, where he had bought thirteen thousand acres of land, all for 1,000 rubles. Pahom questioned him further, and the tradesman said:

"All one need do is to make friends with the chiefs. I gave away about one hundred rubles' worth of silk robes and carpets, besides a case of tea, and I gave wine to those who would drink it; and I got the land for less than a penny an acre." And he showed Pahom the title deeds, saying:

"The land lies near a river, and the whole prairie is virgin soil."

Pahom plied him with questions, and the tradesman said:

"There is more land there than you could cover if you walked a year, and it all belongs to the Bashkirs. They are as simple as sheep, and land can be got almost for nothing."

"There now," thought Pahom, "with my one thousand rubles, why should I get only thirteen hundred acres, and saddle myself with a debt besides? If I take it out there, I can get more than ten times as much for the money." **K**

Pahom inquired how to get to the place, and as soon as the tradesman had left him, he prepared to go there himself. He left his wife to look after the homestead, and started on his journey taking his man with him. They stopped at a town on their way and bought a case of tea, some wine, and other presents, as the tradesman had advised. On and on they went until they had gone more than three hundred miles, and on the seventh day they came to a place where the Bashkirs had pitched their tents. It was all just as the tradesman had said. The people lived on the steppes, by a river, in felt-covered tents. They neither tilled the ground, nor ate bread. Their cattle and horses grazed in herds on the steppe. The colts were tethered behind the tents, and the mares were driven to them twice a day. The mares were milked, and from the milk kumiss[10] was made. It was the women who prepared kumiss, and they also made cheese. As far as the men were concerned, drinking kumiss and tea, eating mutton, and playing on their pipes was all they cared about. They were all stout and merry, and all the summer long they never thought of doing any work. They were quite ignorant, and knew no Russian, but were good natured enough.

As soon as they saw Pahom, they came out of their tents and gathered round their visitor. An interpreter was found, and Pahom told them he had come about some land. The Bashkirs seemed very glad; they took Pahom and led him into one of the best tents, where they made him sit on some down cushions placed on a carpet, while they sat round him. They gave him some tea and kumiss, and had a sheep killed, and gave him mutton to eat. Pahom took presents out of his cart and distributed them among the Bashkirs, and divided the tea amongst them. The Bashkirs were delighted. They talked a great deal among themselves, and then told the interpreter to translate.

"They wish to tell you," said the interpreter, "that they like you, and that it is our custom to do all we can to please a guest and to repay him for his gifts. You have given us presents, now tell us which of the things we possess please you best, that we may present them to you."

"What pleases me best here," answered Pahom, "is your land. Our land is crowded and the soil is exhausted; but you have plenty of land and it is good land. I never saw the like of it."

9. **Bashkirs:** Turkish-speaking peoples who live on the Russian steppes, or plains.

10. **kumiss:** fermented drink made from mare's milk.

K **Reading Focus** **Identifying Theme** Why is Pahom tempted to go to the Bashkirs?

Vocabulary **haggled** (HAG uhld) *v.:* argued about a price.

Universal Access

EL English Learners

English for Academic Success Have students pay special attention to the unfamiliar words and places mentioned on this page. Since not all unfamiliar words have footnotes, write the following words and definitions on the board before students read this section.

- **steppe**—*a large area of flat land*
- **mares**—*female horses*
- **mutton**—*sheep meat*
- **spade**—*a tool with a large blade for digging*

Struggling Readers

Benchmark Students The tradesman described the Bashkir people as "simple as sheep," and the narrator later refers to them as "quite ignorant." Have students form small groups and discuss if the Bashkirs are truly foolish or if Pahom is underestimating their intellect. Then, direct students' attention to the paragraph that begins, "The interpreter translated . . ." Pahom interprets the Bashkirs' laughter as indicating pleasure with his gifts and happiness about his interest in their land. Ask groups to consider another interpretation of this laugh-

The interpreter translated. The Bashkirs talked among themselves for a while. Pahom could not understand what they were saying, but saw that they were much amused and that they shouted and laughed. Then they were silent and looked at Pahom while the interpreter said:

"They wish me to tell you that in return for your presents they will gladly give you as much land as you want. You have only to point it out with your hand and it is yours."

The Bashkirs talked again for a while and began to dispute. Pahom asked what they were disputing about, and the interpreter told him that some of them thought they ought to ask their chief about the land and not act in his absence, while others thought there was no need to wait for his return.

While the Bashkirs were disputing, a man in a large fox-fur cap appeared on the scene. They all became silent and rose to their feet. The interpreter said, "This is our chief himself." **L**

Pahom immediately fetched the best dressing gown and five pounds of tea, and offered these to the chief. The chief accepted them, and seated himself in the place of honor. The Bashkirs at once began telling him something. The chief listened for a while, then made a sign with his head for them to be silent, and addressing himself to Pahom, said in Russian:

"Well, let it be so. Choose whatever piece of land you like; we have plenty of it."

"How can I take as much as I like?" thought Pahom. "I must get a deed to make it secure, or else they may say, 'It is yours,' and afterward may take it away again."

"Thank you for your kind words," he said aloud. "You have much land, and I only want a little. But I should like to be sure which bit is mine. Could it not be measured and made over to me? Life and death are in God's hands. You good people give it to me, but your children might wish to take it away again." **M**

"You are quite right," said the chief. "We will make it over to you."

"I heard that a dealer had been here," continued Pahom, "and that you gave him a little land, too, and signed title deeds to that effect. I should like to have it done in the same way."

The chief understood.

"Yes," replied he, "that can be done quite easily. We have a scribe, and we will go to town with you and have the deed properly sealed."

"And what will be the price?" asked Pahom.

"Our price is always the same: one thousand rubles a day."

Pahom did not understand.

"A day? What measure is that? How many acres would that be?"

"We do not know how to reckon it out," said the chief. "We sell it by the day. As much as you can go round on your feet in a day is yours, and the price is one thousand rubles a day."

Pahom was surprised.

"But in a day you can get round a large tract of land," he said.

The chief laughed.

"It will all be yours!" said he. "But there is one condition: If you don't return on the same day to the spot whence you started, your money is lost." **N**

"But how am I to mark the way that I have gone?"

"Why, we shall go to any spot you like, and stay there. You must start from that spot and make your round, taking a spade with you. Wherever you think necessary, make a mark. At every turning, dig a hole and pile up the turf; then afterward we will go round with a plow from hole to hole. You may make as large a circuit as you please, but before the sun sets you must return to the place you started from. All the land you cover will be yours."

Pahom was delighted. It was decided to start early next morning. They talked a while, and after drink-

---

L **Literary Focus** **Allegory** Foxes are known for their cleverness. Who do you suspect the chief might be?

M **Reading Focus** **Identifying Theme** When proverbs and wise sayings appear in a story, they often point to the theme. Why might Pahom's statement, "Life and death are in God's hands," be important in this story?

N **Literary Focus** **Allegory** In many traditional folk stories, bargains are made with the Devil. What bargain is struck with the chief?

ter. Have them consider whether Pahom could be the ignorant person in this situation. Invite groups to share their thoughts with the class and use their responses to start a class discussion on the true nature of the Bashkir people and what they symbolize in this story.

✔ See **UA: Differentiating Instruction** for a graphic organizer to scaffold instruction for struggling readers.

Think About/Talk About

Comprehension

K Reading Focus

Possible response: *He is tempted by the idea of getting far more land for the same price.*

M Reading Focus

Possible response: *Pahom uses this proverb as a way to justify protecting his interests. Ironically, Pahom underestimates God despite his fatalistic words. He does not think about the fact that everything God has given him can also be taken away.*

Analysis

L Literary Focus

Possible response: *The Chief could be the Evil One, or an agent of the Devil, because the Devil is also known for being clever.*

N Literary Focus

Possible response: *The bargain struck with the chief requires that Pahom return to his starting point by the end of the same day he sets out, or his money will be lost.*

Vocabulary: Own the Word

haggled: Demonstrate the meaning of *haggled* by acting it out. Ask a student to suggest a price for some object and then *haggle* with him or her. Have students practice *haggling* with one another.

Model the Skill

- Remind students that characters in an allegory usually symbolize a particular aspect of morality.
- Have students read the third full paragraph on p. 1018 that describes Pahom's dream. Inform students that in this scene, Pahom is warned that the chief, the dealer, and the peasant from Volga were all pawns of the Devil.

Guided Practice: Apply

Read-Talk-Write Have students think about what Pahom's life would be like if he had realized that these men and their temptations were sent by the Devil. Have students discuss with a partner the point at which Pahom should have resisted temptation and simply been content with the amount of land he owned. Ask students to write a brief summary of their discussion.

Think About/Talk About

Literary Connection

The Bashkir chief's words on p. 1019 parallel the words of the Devil in the Bible, who, as a temptation, took Jesus up the high mountain and offered him the kingdoms of the world. From here on in the story, the element of suspense will intensify as Pahom, in his greed, tries to outpace the sun.

Extend the Discussion

Determining Author's Purpose

How do you think Tolstoy wants readers to interpret the bargain that Pahom makes with the chief? ***Possible response:*** *Some students may decide that the bargain he strikes with the Bashkir chief is too good to be true. His greed blinds him to any possible outcome except the one he desires.*

ing some more kumiss and eating some more mutton, they had tea again, and then the night came on. They gave Pahom a featherbed to sleep on, and the Bashkirs dispersed for the night, promising to assemble the next morning at daybreak and ride out before sunrise to the appointed spot.

Pahom lay on the featherbed, but could not sleep. He kept thinking about the land.

"What a large tract I will mark off!" thought he. "I can easily do thirty-five miles in a day. The days are long now, and within a circuit of thirty-five miles what a lot of land there will be! I will sell the poorer land, or let it to peasants, but I'll pick out the best and farm it. I will buy two ox teams, and hire two more laborers. About a hundred and fifty acres shall be plow land, and I will pasture cattle on the rest."

Pahom lay awake all night, and dozed off only just before dawn. Hardly were his eyes closed when he had a dream. He thought he was lying in that same tent and heard somebody chuckling outside. He wondered who it could be, and rose and went out, and he saw the Bashkir chief sitting in front of the tent holding his sides and rolling about with laughter. Going nearer to the chief, Pahom asked: "What are you laughing at?" But he saw that it was no longer the chief, but the dealer who had recently stopped at his house and had told him about the land. Just as Pahom was going to ask, "Have you been here long?" he saw that it was not the dealer, but the peasant who had come up from the Volga, long ago, to Pahom's old home. Then he saw that it was not the peasant either, but the Devil himself with hoofs and horns, sitting there and chuckling, and before him lay a man barefoot, prostrate on the ground, with only trousers and a shirt on. And Pahom dreamt that he looked more attentively to see what sort of a man it was that was lying there, and he saw that the man was dead, and that it was himself! He awoke horror-struck. **O**

"What things one does dream," thought he.

Looking round he saw through the open door that the dawn was breaking.

"It's time to wake them up," thought he. "We ought to be starting."

He got up, roused his man (who was sleeping in his cart), bade him harness, and went to call the Bashkirs.

"It's time to go to the steppe to measure the land," he said.

The Bashkirs rose and assembled, and the chief came too. Then they began drinking kumiss again, and offered Pahom some tea, but he would not wait.

"If we are to go, let us go. It is high time," said he.

The Bashkirs got ready and they all started: some mounted on horses, and some in carts. Pahom drove in his own small cart with his servant and took a spade with him. When they reached the steppe, the morning red was beginning to kindle. They ascended a hillock

Man in the Field by Vladimir Yegorovich Makovsky (1846–1920).

O **Reading Focus** **Identifying Theme** Dreams are often used in literature to foretell the future. What lesson is found in Pahom's dream?

Vocabulary **prostrate** (PRAHS trayt) *adj.:* lying flat.

Cross-Curricular Connection

MATHEMATICS: Land Measurement

Pahom wants his land properly measured and deeded to him. Remind students that land measurement involves principles of plane geometry.

Activity Pahom estimates that he can walk thirty-five miles in a day. Ask students to calculate whether Pahom would get more land if his thirty-five mile circuit were in the shape of a square, a rectangle fifteen miles long by two and one-half miles wide, or a circle. [*Square—Each side is 8.75 mi. (35÷4) the area is about 76.6 square miles or 49,000 acres. (1 acre = 1/640 sq. mi.) Rectangle—Area is 37.5 sq. mi (15 x 2.5) or 24,000 acres. Circle—Radius is 5.57 mi. (35 ÷ 2π); area is about 97.5 sq. mi. or 62,400 acres.*]

(called by the Bashkirs a *shikhan*) and dismounting from their carts and their horses, gathered in one spot. The chief came up to Pahom and stretching out his arm toward the plain: **P**

"See," said he, "all this, as far as your eye can reach, is ours. You may have any part of it you like."

Pahom's eyes glistened: It was all virgin soil, as flat as the palm of your hand, as black as the seed of a poppy, and in the hollows different kinds of grasses grew breast high.

The chief took off his fox-fur cap, placed it on the ground, and said:

"This will be the mark. Start from here, and return here again. All the land you go round shall be yours."

Pahom took out his money and put it on the cap. Then he took off his outer coat, remaining in his sleeveless undercoat. He unfastened his girdle and tied it tight below his stomach, put a little bag of bread into the breast of his coat, and tying a flask of water to his girdle, he drew up the tops of his boots, took the spade from his man, and stood ready to start. He considered for some moments which way he had better go—it was tempting everywhere.

"No matter," he concluded, "I will go toward the rising sun."

He turned his face to the east, stretched himself, and waited for the sun to appear above the rim.

"I must lose no time," he thought, "and it is easier walking while it is still cool."

The sun's rays had hardly flashed above the horizon, before Pahom, carrying the spade over his shoulder, went down into the steppe.

Pahom started walking neither slowly nor quickly. After having gone a thousand yards he stopped, dug a hole, and placed pieces of turf one on another to make it more visible. Then he went on; and now that he had walked off his stiffness he quickened his pace. After a while he dug another hole.

Pahom looked back. The hillock could be distinctly seen in the sunlight, with the people on it, and the glittering tires of the cart wheels. At a rough guess Pahom concluded that he had walked three miles. It was growing warmer; he took off his undercoat, flung it across his shoulder, and went on again. It had grown quite warm now; he looked at the sun, it was time to think of breakfast.

"The first shift is done, but there are four in a day, and it is too soon yet to turn. But I will just take off my boots," said he to himself.

He sat down, took off his boots, stuck them into his girdle, and went on. It was easy walking now.

"I will go on for another three miles," thought he, "and then turn to the left. This spot is so fine, that it would be a pity to lose it. The further one goes, the better the land seems."

He went straight on for a while, and when he looked round, the hillock was scarcely visible and the people on it looked like black ants, and he could just see something glistening there in the sun.

"Ah," thought Pahom, "I have gone far enough in this direction, it is time to turn. Besides I am in a regular sweat, and very thirsty."

He stopped, dug a large hole, and heaped up pieces of turf. Next he untied his flask, had a drink, and then turned sharply to the left. He went on and on; the grass was high, and it was very hot.

Pahom began to grow tired: He looked at the sun and saw that it was noon.

"Well," he thought, "I must have a rest."

He sat down, and ate some bread and drank some water; but he did not lie down, thinking that if he did he might fall asleep. After sitting a little while, he went on again. At first he walked easily: The food had strengthened him; but it had become terribly hot and he felt sleepy, still he went on, thinking: "An hour to suffer, a lifetime to live."

He went a long way in this direction also, and was about to turn to the left again, when he perceived a damp hollow: "It would be a pity to leave that out," he thought. "Flax would do well there." So he went on past the hollow, and dug a hole on the other side of it before he turned the corner. Pahom looked toward the hillock. The heat made the air hazy: It seemed to be quivering, and through the haze the people on the hillock could scarcely be seen. **Q**

P **Literary Focus** **Allegory** How have the Bashkir chief, the dealer, and the peasant all furthered the Devil's plan?

Q **Reading Focus** **Identifying Theme** How does greed drive Pahom?

Universal Access

Advanced Learners

Enrichment After students finish reading the parable, lead them in discussing how it reflects Victorian views of the paradox of progress. The discussion might touch on the following points:

- As Pahom progresses financially, he puts himself in increasing danger of ruin.
- As Pahom progresses up the economic ladder he regresses socially, making more and more enemies.
- As Pahom progresses materially, he increasingly loses sight of the moral implications of his actions.
- As Pahom seeks to increase his holdings, his outlook becomes more narrow, confined, and obsessive.

Think About/Talk About

Comprehension

Q Reading Focus

Possible response: *Evil can be found behind tempting opportunities, and greed can lead a person to a tragic demise.*

Q Reading Focus

Possible response: *Pahom himself says, "It would be a pity to leave that out." There is so much land for the taking that his greed makes him overly ambitious.*

Analysis

P Literary Focus

Possible response: *The Bashkir chief, the dealer, and the peasant have all tempted Pahom and furthered the Devil's plan by enticing him with the idea of more land.*

Extend the Discussion

Making Predictions Knowing what you know about Pahom's dream and his extensive marking off of land, what do you think will happen to him at the end of the story? ***Possible response:*** *Pahom's dream hints that he will die. Judging from the amount of effort he expends to choose his land, his death seems likely.*

Interpreting How does Pahom react when the Devil appears in his dream? Why does Pahom miss the message conveyed in the dream? ***Possible response:*** *Pahom is alarmed but not concerned. His obsession with acquiring more land leads him to dismiss the warning.*

Vocabulary: Own the Word

prostrate: Draw a chart comparing the words *prostrate* and its antonym, *erect*. Have students list the connotations of each word and record their answers in the chart.

Think About/Talk About

Comprehension

R Reading Focus

Possible response: *When Pahom says, "I have grasped too much and ruined the whole affair," it shows that he may have finally understood his folly.*

S Reading Focus

Possible response: *Pahom remembers his dream and realizes his greed may lead to his death. He finally has "plenty of land" but wonders if God will let him live on it.*

Analysis

T Literary Focus

Possible response: *The chief is laughing at Pahom's foolishness. The Devil has clearly answered the question, "How much land does a man need?" He needs six feet to bury his body.*

Monitor Students' Comprehension

Guide the class in answering these comprehension questions.

1. What does Pahom claim is the only thing that troubles a peasant? [*Peasants do not have enough land.*]
2. Why does Pahom leave his first plot of land? [*He feels it is too cramped to be comfortable, and he has continuous disputes with fellow Commune members.*]
3. What deal do the Bashkirs offer Pahom? [*For one thousand rubles, he may have as much land as he can walk around in a day.*]

"Ah!" thought Pahom, "I have made the sides too long; I must make this one shorter." And he went along the third side, stepping faster. He looked at the sun: It was nearly halfway to the horizon, and he had not yet done two miles of the third side of the square. He was still ten miles from the goal.

"No," he thought, "though it will make my land lopsided, I must hurry back in a straight line now. I might go too far, and as it is I have a great deal of land."

So Pahom hurriedly dug a hole, and turned straight toward the hillock.

Pahom went straight toward the hillock, but he now walked with difficulty. He was done up with the heat, his bare feet were cut and bruised, and his legs began to fail. He longed to rest, but it was impossible if he meant to get back before sunset. The sun waits for no man, and it was sinking lower and lower.

"Oh dear," he thought, "if only I have not blundered trying for too much! What if I am too late?"

He looked toward the hillock and at the sun. He was still far from his goal, and the sun was already near the rim.

Pahom walked on and on; it was very hard walking but he went quicker and quicker. He pressed on, but was still far from the place. He began running, threw away his coat, his boots, his flask, and his cap, and kept only the spade which he used as a support.

"What shall I do," he thought again. "I have grasped too much and ruined the whole affair. I can't get there before the sun sets." **R**

And this fear made him still more breathless. Pahom went on running, his soaking shirt and trousers stuck to him, and his mouth was parched. His breast was working like a blacksmith's bellows, his heart was beating like a hammer, and his legs were giving way as if they did not belong to him. Pahom was seized with terror lest he should die of the strain.

Though afraid of death, he could not stop. "After having run all that way they will call me a fool if I stop now," thought he. And he ran on and on, and drew near and heard the Bashkirs yelling and shouting to him, and their cries inflamed his heart still more. He gathered his last strength and ran on.

The sun was close to the rim, and cloaked in mist looked large, and red as blood. Now, yes now, it was about to set! The sun was quite low, but he was also quite near his aim. Pahom could already see the people on the hillock waving their arms to hurry him up. He could see the fox-fur cap on the ground and the money on it, and the chief sitting on the ground holding his sides. And Pahom remembered his dream. **S**

"There is plenty of land," thought he, "but will God let me live on it? I have lost my life, I have lost my life! I shall never reach that spot!"

Pahom looked at the sun, which had reached the earth: One side of it had already disappeared. With all his remaining strength he rushed on, bending his body forward so that his legs could hardly follow fast enough to keep him from falling. Just as he reached the hillock it suddenly grew dark. He looked up—the sun had already set! He gave a cry: "All my labor has been in vain," thought he, and was about to stop, but he heard the Bashkirs still shouting, and remembered that though to him, from below, the sun seemed to have set, they on the hillock could still see it. He took a long breath and ran up the hillock. It was still light there. He reached the top and saw the cap. Before it sat the chief laughing and holding his sides. Again Pahom remembered his dream, and he uttered a cry: His legs gave way beneath him, he fell forward and reached the cap with his hands. **T**

"Ah, that's a fine fellow!" exclaimed the chief. "He has gained much land!"

Pahom's servant came running up and tried to raise him, but he saw that blood was flowing from his mouth. Pahom was dead!

The Bashkirs clicked their tongues to show their pity.

His servant picked up the spade and dug a grave long enough for Pahom to lie in, and buried him in it. Six feet from his head to his heels was all he needed.

R Reading Focus **Identifying Theme** What words in this paragraph might be significant in summarizing what is happening to Pahom?

S Reading Focus **Identifying Theme** What thought here might be a key to the story's theme?

T Literary Focus **Allegory** Why might the chief be holding his sides?

California Standards, p. 1021

- **Reading Standard 3.1** Analyze characteristics of subgenres (e.g., satire, parody, allegory, pastoral) that are used in poetry, prose, plays, novels, short stories, essays, and other basic genres.
- **Reading Standard 3.2** Analyze the way in which the theme or meaning of a selection represents a view or comment on life, using textual evidence to support the claim.
- **Reading Standard 3.3** Analyze the ways in which irony, tone, mood, the author's style, and the "sound" of language achieve specific rhetorical or aesthetic purposes or both.
- **Writing Standard 1.2** Use point of view, characterization, style (e.g., use of irony), and related elements for specific rhetorical and aesthetic purposes.
- **Writing Standard 2.1** Write fictional, autobiographical, or biographical narratives: **a.** Narrate a sequence of events and communicate their significance to the audience.

Applying Your Skills

Reading Standard 3.1, 3.2, 3.3 (see pages A48–A50)
Writing Standard 1.2, 2.1a (see pages A51–A52)

How Much Land Does a Man Need?

Literary Response and Analysis

Reading Skills Focus

Quick Check

1. What happens when Pahom buys more land?
2. How does the Devil triumph over Pahom?

Read with a Purpose

3. What does the story reveal about how we come to confuse what we want with what we need?

Reading Skills: Identifying Theme

4. Review the chart you filled out. Put an asterisk beside details that most strongly support a theme. Then, write at least one sentence summarizing what Pahom discovers.

Clues to Theme	
The peasant sister says "Gain and pain are brothers twain."	This statement seems to relate to the story title.
Theme:	

Vocabulary Check

Be sure you can justify your answers to these questions about the Vocabulary words.

5. If you are **piqued**, are you happy or irritated?
6. Would you feel honored or upset after being **disparaged**?
7. If you are **aggrieved**, do you feel wronged or flattered?
8. Would **arable** land be fertile or unproductive?
9. When two people **haggled** about something, would you say they argued or agreed?
10. Pahom found himself **prostrate**. Was he flat on the ground or sitting on the ground?

Literary Skills Focus

Literary Analysis

11. **Analyze** Think about the discussion between the sisters at the story's beginning. How does their conversation foreshadow Pahom's end?
12. **Draw Conclusions** Based on the story's events, how do you think Tolstoy views ambition?
13. **Extend** Consider the contrast between what Pahom wants and "all he needs." How could Tolstoy's parable about materialism apply today?

Literary Skills: Allegory

14. **Summarize** Outline this story as an allegory. Follow this format: The story is about ______. The devil stands for ______, while Pahom stands for ______. Pahom's attempt to get as much land as he could cover in a day represents ______. The land itself stands for ______.

Literary Skills Review: Tone

15. **Interpret** A writer's **tone** is the attitude he or she takes toward the subject matter or the audience. How would you describe Tolstoy's tone?

Writing Skills Focus

Think as a Reader/Writer

Use It in Your Writing You wrote in your *Reader/Writer Notebook* how this story could be set in today's world. Now, use your notes to write your own brief allegory about materialism today.

What Do You Think Now? What did Pahom think he was winning as he gained more and more land?

Universal Access

Struggling Writers

Some students may have difficulty writing a modern allegory. Invite students to start writing by thinking about materialism in today's society. Then, have students write down notes about several objects or characters that could symbolize materialism and the features that make the objects or characters representative of the vice.

Assess

Unit 5 Resources, Selection Standards Check, p. 80

go.hrw.com **ThinkCentral Online Assessment,** Selection Standards Check

Teacher One Stop™, editable Selection Standards Check

Check for Understanding

Independent Practice

Reading Skills Focus

Possible responses:

1. *He starts to want even more land.*
2. *The Devil exploits Pahom's greed. Pahom's greed eventually leads to his death.*
3. *If we live for our wants, we will not have enough, but if we live for our needs, we will have enough.*
4. *Students should refer to details in the story and summarize Pahom's discovery in one or two sentences.*

Vocabulary Check

5. *irritated* 6. *upset*
7. *wronged* 8. *fertile*
9. *argued* 10. *flat*

Literary Skills Focus

Possible responses:

11. *Pahom's wife mentions, "Loss and gain are brothers twain," foreshadowing the eventual loss of his gains.*
12. *According to Tolstoy's parable, unchecked ambition and greed destroy people. Pahom's death proves the harm of striving too much for material gain.*
13. *Current scandals show that people still behave foolishly or unethically in pursuit of wealth.*
14. *The story is about greed. The devil stands for temptation, while Pahom stands for human weakness. Pahom's attempt to get as much land as he could in one day represents covetousness. The land itself stands for material desires.*
15. *Tolstoy is critical of Pahom but not bitterly satiric. A tacit amusement at Pahom's predicament softens the condemnation of his weakness.*

What Do You Think Now?

To help students answer the question, have them look at Pahom's progress from the Evil One's perspective. Have students consider how the Evil One felt as Pahom's desire for land grew.

Selection Introduction

Think About the Writer

To help students think about the question, tell them to consider the daily work of a doctor. Chekhov's writing delves into the motivations behind people's actions and asks them to confront deep truths about themselves. Chekhov, the doctor, examined the body; might Chekhov, the writer, have similarly examined the mind?

For Independent Reading

The Count of Monte Cristo, Alexandre Dumas

Motivate

What Do You Think?/QuickTalk

Have students think about powerful experiences that have affected their own lives or the lives of people they know. These experiences could have come suddenly, such as a major insight into a personal problem, or over time, as the result of hard work and dedication.

Preparing to Read

The Bet

What Do You Think? How can appearance be different from reality?

QuickTalk

What sorts of powerful experiences can totally change the way someone thinks about life? With a partner, talk about some possibilities. Record your ideas in your *Reader/Writer Notebook.*

Anton Pavlovich Chekhov (1898) by Osip Emmanuilovich Braz (1873–1936). Tretyakov Gallery, Moscow, Russia.

MEET THE WRITER

Anton Chekhov

(1860–1904)

Shortly before his death, Chekhov joked that people would read his work for only seven more years. A century later, his brilliant short stories and plays show no signs of being forgotten.

A Doctor and Writer

Anton Pavlovich Chekhov was born in the seaport town of Taganrog in the south of Russia. When he was sixteen, his father went bankrupt and fled with the rest of the family to Moscow to avoid a prison sentence. Left behind as a "hostage" to his father's creditors, Chekhov tutored the creditor's son at a cheap rate, finished school, and went to Moscow to study medicine on a scholarship. To support himself and his family, who were living in a slum, Chekhov wrote comic stories to sell to periodicals. Comic stories soon gave way to more serious pieces, in which, as Chekhov said, questions were asked but not answered.

Studying medicine greatly benefited the young writer. As a doctor, Chekhov became acquainted with hundreds of ordinary people. He continued to write while practicing medicine and gave up his full-time practice only when it took too much time away from his writing.

Humanity, Reason, and Generosity

It was not until the last years of his brief life that Chekhov achieved some affluence. He moved his parents and sister to a large country estate, where he organized famine relief, fought cholera epidemics, and treated poor patients free of charge. Although the theme of many of his works is alienation, Chekhov's real-life activities demonstrate that humanity, reason, and generosity were among his highest values.

His finest stories were all written in the 1890s, and his four great plays, *The Sea Gull* (1896), *Uncle Vanya* (1897), *Three Sisters* (1901), and *The Cherry Orchard* (1904), were written while he was fatally ill with tuberculosis. In 1901 he married the actress who played the lead role in *The Sea Gull,* but the couple spent their honeymoon in a sanitarium. Three years later Chekhov died at the age of forty-four, still at the height of his creativity.

Think About the Writer How did Chekhov's experiences as a doctor affect his writing?

California Standards, pp. 1022–1031

- **Reading Standard 2.2** Analyze the way in which clarity of meaning is affected by the patterns of organization, hierarchical structures, repetition of the main ideas, syntax, and word choice in the text.
- **Reading Standard 3.2** Analyze the way in which the theme or meaning of a selection represents a view or comment on life, using textual evidence to support the claim.
- **Reading Standard 3.9** Analyze the philosophical arguments presented in literary works to determine whether the authors' positions have contributed to the quality of each work and the credibility of the characters. (Philosophical approach)

Selection Readability	
Easily Accessible **Accessible** Challenging	familiar setting; simple dialogue; accessible vocabulary

Literary Skills Focus

Theme The truth or insight about human life revealed in a story is its **theme.** For example, the theme of a story about growing up might be that disillusionment is inherently part of the maturation process. To identify theme, the reader must consider all of a story's elements, and then infer the truths or insights the story reveals. The theme is often illuminated at the end of the story in the main character's discovery about life. Identifying themes requires a tolerance for ambiguity, especially in open-ended stories like "The Bet," which raises more questions than it answers.

Literary Perspectives Apply the Literary Perspective described on page 1024 as you read this story.

Reading Skills Focus

Making Predictions A **prediction** is a special kind of **inference,** or educated guess, about what will happen next. Some predictions turn out to be inaccurate, and modifying them is an essential—and enjoyable—part of active reading. Because Chekhov begins this story with a debate about capital punishment, you might predict that the story will explore that subject. As you read, see if you have made a correct prediction, or if Chekhov has surprised you by focusing instead on some larger issue.

Into Action As you read, make predictions based on clues that suggest or foreshadow what will happen to the characters later in the story. Use a chart like the one below to record the clues and your predictions.

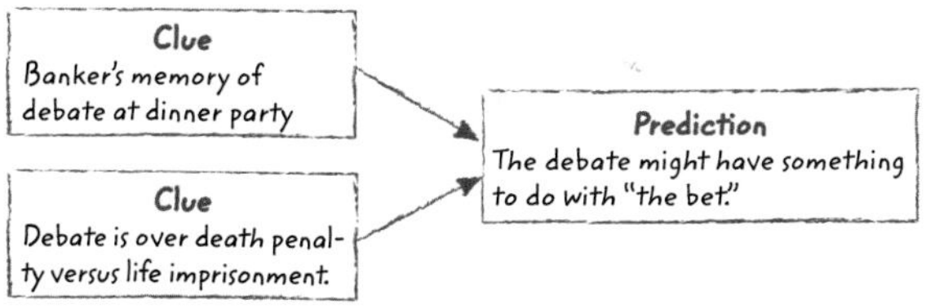

Writing Skills Focus

Think as a Reader/Writer

Find It in Your Reading This story spans fifteen years, from the time of the bet's inception to its conclusion. As you read, record in your *Reader/Writer Notebook* how Chekhov marks the passage of time in years, hours, and minutes.

Reader/Writer Notebook

Use your **RWN** to complete the activities for this selection.

Vocabulary

frivolous (FRIHV uh luhs) *adj.:* light-minded; lacking seriousness. *The frivolous banker made a large bet without thinking.*

compulsory (kuhm PUHL suhr ee) *adj.:* required; enforced. *The banker argues that voluntary confinement is more unbearable than compulsory imprisonment.*

caprice (kuh PREES) *n.:* sudden notion or desire. *The banker realizes that the bet was the result of unwise caprice.*

zealously (ZEHL uhs lee) *adv.:* fervently; devotedly. *The prisoner spends his time zealously studying books and languages.*

indiscriminately (ihn dihs KRIHM uh niht lee) *adv.:* without making careful distinctions; randomly. *The lawyer reads indiscriminately, diving into any book he can get.*

ethereal (ih THIHR ee uhl) *adj.:* light and delicate; unearthly. *After reading the poems, the lawyer was visited by ethereal visions.*

renounce (rih NOWNS) *v.:* formally give up; reject. *The lawyer decides to renounce his claim to the money.*

Language Coach

Roots Knowing a word's root can help you figure out the meanings of related words. For example, the Vocabulary word *indiscriminately* comes from the Latin root *discrīmināre,* which means "to separate." Now that you know this word's root, can you figure out the definitions of the words *discriminate* and *discrimination?*

Learn It Online

Explore the vocabulary words inside and out through Word Watch online.

go.hrw.com H12-1023 Go

Comparing Texts Resources

Unit 5 Resources, on-level practice and assessment, p. 83

Teacher One Stop™, on-level lesson plans and all print resources

Holt Audio Library

Holt Audio Library: Selections and Summaries in Spanish

UA: Differentiating Instruction, graphic organizer, p. 240

UA: Supporting Instruction in Spanish, selection summary

ThinkCentral Online Assessment, Selection Standards Check

ThinkCentral Online Remediation

Preteach

Introducing Vocabulary

Use this activity to check students' understanding of the Vocabulary words.

1. Tell about a time when you acted out of **caprice,** shopped **indiscriminately,** and bought something **frivolous.**
2. Should all speed limits be **compulsory** and **zealously** monitored?
3. Should clothing designers **renounce** the use of **ethereal** fabrics in favor of materials that will hold up longer?

English for Academic Success

Language Coach

Possible response: *The verb* discriminate *means "to make distinctions between things," that is, to separate one thing from another.* Discrimination *is the act of discriminating.*

Literary Skills Focus

Have students consider what truth about human life is revealed in the story.

Reading Skills Focus

Give students a copy of the Reading Skills Focus graphic organizer. (See **Unit 5 Resources.**) Tell them to use their responses to answer the questions on the Applying Your Skills page.

Writing Skills Focus

Have students take note of Chekhov's use of time in their **Reader/Writer Notebooks.** Students can use their notes to complete the Writing Skills Focus activity.

Learn It Online

Send students to **Word Watch** for audio pronunciations, synonyms and antonyms, and brief histories of word origins.

go.hrw.com H12-1023 Go

Teacher Preparation

Selection Plot Summary

During an argument about the humaneness of capital punishment versus life imprisonment, a banker impulsively bets a young lawyer (who claims he would choose life imprisonment) two million dollars to stay in solitary confinement for five years. The lawyer agrees and raises the stakes to fifteen years. For nearly fifteen years, the young man has remained in solitary confinement, but the banker, now no longer rich, realizes that paying the debt will bankrupt him. On the eve of the lawyer's release, the banker goes to kill him, but instead finds him asleep and emaciated, with a note in front of him renouncing the bet.

Direct Teach

Think About/Talk About

Read with a Purpose Have students read the Read with a Purpose statement. Point out that this bet is considered "unusual." Have students predict what they think the bet will entail and what risks will be involved.

Comprehension

A Reading Focus

Possible response: *The story appears to be a debate about the merits of capital punishment versus life imprisonment.*

SHORT STORY

The Bet

by **Anton Chekhov**

translated by **Constance Garnett**

Read with a Purpose
Read to discover the stakes and the surprising outcome of an unusual bet.

Build Background
Would you give up all human company for years to win an amazing fortune? A character in this famous Russian story bets that he can do it, and his voluntary solitude raises serious questions for him and for readers.

1

It was a dark autumn night. The old banker was walking up and down his study and remembering how, fifteen years before, he had given a party one autumn evening. There had been many clever men there, and there had been interesting conversations. Among other things, they had talked of capital punishment. The majority of the guests, among whom were many journalists and intellectual men, disapproved of the death penalty. They considered that form of punishment out of date, immoral, and unsuitable for Christian states. In the opinion of some of them, the death penalty ought to be replaced everywhere by imprisonment for life.

"I don't agree with you," said their host, the banker. "I have not tried either the death penalty or imprisonment for life, but if one may judge a priori,[1] the death penalty is more moral and more humane than imprisonment for life. Capital punishment kills a man at once, but lifelong imprisonment kills him slowly. Which executioner is the more humane, he who kills you in a few minutes or he who drags the life out of you in the course of many years?" **A**

"Both are equally immoral," observed one of the guests, "for they both have the same object—to take away life. The state is not God. It has not the right to take away what it cannot restore when it wants to."

Among the guests was a young lawyer, a young man of five-and-twenty. When he was asked his opinion, he said: "The death sentence and the life sentence are equally immoral, but if I had to choose between the death penalty and imprisonment for life, I would

1. **a priori:** Latin for "from the first." Here, a generalization based on theory not experience.

A Reading Focus **Making Predictions** Based on these first paragraphs, what do you think will be the main subject of the story?

Literary Perspectives

Analyzing Credibility in Literature Literature often asks us to believe in things that do not seem possible, and there are times when we are especially aware that a story does not ring true. A situation in a story, such as an improbable bet, might ask us to question our own beliefs, but if it causes us to question the credibility of the story or storyteller, we often lose interest and trust in the story. Samuel Taylor Coleridge coined the phrase "suspension of disbelief" to describe "dramatic truth," or the truth that operates within the work of art. As a reader, your willingness to accept the "truth" of the story hinges on the fact that you can temporarily suspend your judgment of what is possible in order to enjoy the story. However, you should still take note when you find inconsistencies within the story, or if you believe that the story is not playing by its own rules.

As you read, be sure to notice the questions in the text, which will guide you in using this perspective.

Literary Perspectives

Before students read the selection, have them read the **Literary Perspectives** about Analyzing Credibility in Literature. Then, tell students that D.H. Lawrence famously suggested to never trust the artists, but to trust the story, warning readers to read skeptically. Ask students to think about an improbable story in literature or film that encouraged them to trust the artist and suspend their disbelief. What aspects of the story made them accept the narrative despite its fantastic elements?

Remind students to use questions at the bottom of the page to help them use the perspective.

certainly choose the second. To live anyhow is better than not at all."

A lively discussion arose. The banker, who was younger and more nervous in those days, was suddenly carried away by excitement; he struck the table with his fist and shouted at the young man: "It's not true! I'll bet you two million you wouldn't stay in solitary confinement for five years."

"If you mean that in earnest," said the young man, "I'll take the bet, but I would stay not five, but fifteen years."

"Fifteen? Done!" cried the banker. "Gentlemen, I stake two million!"

"Agreed! You stake your millions and I stake my freedom!" said the young man.

And this wild, senseless bet was carried out! The banker, spoiled and frivolous, with millions beyond his reckoning, was delighted at the bet. At supper he made fun of the young man and said: "Think better of it, young man, while there is still time. To me two million is a trifle, but you are losing three or four of the best years of your life. I say three or four, because you won't stay longer. Don't forget either, you unhappy man, that voluntary confinement is a great deal harder to bear than compulsory. The thought that you have the right to step out in liberty at any moment will poison your whole existence in prison. I am sorry for you."

And now the banker, walking to and fro, remembered all this and asked himself: "What was the object of that bet? What is the good of that man's losing fifteen years of his life and my throwing away two million? Can it prove that the death penalty is better or worse than imprisonment for life? No, no. It was all nonsensical and meaningless. On my part it was the caprice of a pampered man, and on his part simple greed for money. . . ." **B**

Then he remembered what followed that evening. It was decided that the young man should spend the years of his captivity under the strictest supervision in one of the lodges in the banker's garden. It was agreed that for fifteen years he should not be free to cross the threshold of the lodge, to see human beings, to hear the human voice, or to receive letters and newspapers. He was allowed to have a musical instrument and books and was allowed to write letters, to drink wine, and to smoke. By the terms of the agreement, the only relations he could have with the outer world were by a little window made purposely for that object. He might have anything he wanted—books, music, wine, and so on—in any quantity he desired, by writing an order, but could receive them only through the window. The agreement provided for every detail and every trifle that would make his imprisonment strictly

The Painter Konstantin Alekseevich Korovin (1891) by Valentin Serov (1865–1939). Tretyakov Gallery, Moscow, Russia.

B Reading Focus **Making Predictions** How has the banker's view of the bet changed in fifteen years? What do you predict he will do next?

Vocabulary **frivolous** (FRIHV uh luhs) *adj.:* light-minded; lacking seriousness.
compulsory (kuhm PUHL suhr ee) *adj.:* required; enforced.
caprice (kuh PREES) *n.:* sudden notion or desire.

Think About/Talk About

Comprehension

B Reading Focus

Possible responses: *The banker, fifteen years later, views the bet as "nonsensical and meaningless" and characterizes it in terms of caprice and greed. He may want to find a way to get himself out of the bet.*

Extend the Discussion

Finding Sequence of Events Where and when does the story begin? Where and when does the story's flashback take place? ***Possible responses:*** *The story begins in the home of the banker, on the night before the deadline that would allow the lawyer to regain his freedom. The story then presents a flashback to a dinner party that took place in the banker's home fifteen years ago.*

Vocabulary: Own the Word

- **frivolous:** Ask students to name books, television shows, or magazines that they consider *frivolous.* What differentiates these from more serious works?
- **compulsory:** Ask students to think of tasks that are *compulsory.* Have them use the word *compulsory* in sentences, for example: "Going to college is voluntary, but attending school until age 16 is *compulsory.*"
- **caprice:** Remind students that *caprice* refers to a very sudden desire. Use the word in the following sentence: "While she had planned to adopt a pet for some time, her sudden decision to purchase an iguana was pure *caprice.*"

Universal Access

EL English Learners

English for Academic Success Have students pay attention to context clues in the first five paragraphs to help them understand the meanings of *capital punishment* and *confinement.* Clues about *capital punishment* include "death penalty," "kills a man at once," "kills you in a few minutes," and "death sentence." Clues about the meaning of *confinement* include "life sentence" and "imprisonment for life." Remind students to pay attention to context clues when they encounter unfamiliar words and phrases.

Struggling Readers

Strategic Students To help students read "The Bet," model the reading skill of making predictions. You might say: "Suppose you read that an older character challenges a younger one to a bet. You predict that the younger one will win because he seems more determined. But the younger character changes before the bet ends, making him less likely to win, and so you alter your prediction." Encourage students as they read to ask themselves, "As the story unfolds, how might each successive change affect my predictions for the story's outcome?"

Model the Skill

- Discuss how the **theme,** or a truth about life that a story reveals, unfolds in the words and deeds of the characters.
- Tell students that one **theme** in "The Bet" is how imprisonment affects a person's quality of life.
- Read aloud the first two full paragraphs on p. 1026 and model the thought process you used to discover **theme.** For instance, you might say: "I see how the prisoner changes; his loneliness and depression have become anger and tears. He experiences mental anguish. Chekhov is illustrating the theme that people cannot be happy when they have no contact with others."

Guided Practice: Apply

QuickWrite Use a QuickWrite to help students connect personally with issues presented in the selection. Using the selection as a starting point, have students write about whether voluntary confinement would be more difficult to endure than involuntary confinement. Have students frame their responses into an analysis of universal truths that transcend cultures and national boundaries.

solitary, and bound the young man to stay there *exactly* fifteen years, beginning from twelve o'clock of November 14, 1870, and ending at twelve o'clock of November 14, 1885. The slightest attempt on his part to break the conditions, if only two minutes before the end, released the banker from the obligation to pay him two million.

For the first year of his confinement, as far as one could judge from his brief notes, the prisoner suffered severely from loneliness and depression. The sounds of the piano could be heard continually day and night from his lodge. He refused wine and tobacco. Wine, he wrote, excites the desires, and desires are the worst foes of the prisoner; and besides, nothing could be more dreary than drinking good wine and seeing no one. And tobacco spoiled the air of his room. In the first year the books he sent for were principally of a light character—novels with a complicated love plot, sensational and fantastic stories, and so on. **C**

In the second year the piano was silent in the lodge, and the prisoner asked only for the classics. In the fifth year music was audible again, and the prisoner asked for wine. Those who watched him through the window said that all that year he spent doing nothing but eating and drinking and lying on his bed, frequently yawning and talking angrily to himself. He did not read books. Sometimes at night he would sit down to write; he would spend hours writing and in the morning tear up all that he had written. More than once he could be heard crying.

In the second half of the sixth year the prisoner began zealously studying languages, philosophy, and history. He threw himself eagerly into these studies—so much so that the banker had enough to do to get him the books he ordered. In the course of four years, some six hundred volumes were procured at his request. It was during this period that the banker received the following letter from his prisoner: **D**

"My dear Jailer, I write you these lines in six languages. Show them to people who know the languages. Let them read them. If they find not one mistake, I implore you to fire a shot in the garden. That shot will show me that my efforts have not been thrown away. The geniuses of all ages and of all lands speak different languages, but the same flame burns in them all. Oh, if you only knew what unearthly happiness my soul feels now from being able to understand them!" The prisoner's desire was fulfilled. The banker ordered two shots to be fired in the garden.

Then, after the tenth year, the prisoner sat immovably at the table and read nothing but the Gospels. It seemed strange to the banker that a man who in four years had mastered six hundred learned volumes should waste nearly a year over one thin book easy of comprehension. Theology[2] and histories of religion followed the Gospels.

In the last two years of his confinement, the prisoner read an immense quantity of books quite indiscriminately. At one time he was busy with the natural sciences; then he would ask for Byron or Shakespeare. There were notes in which he demanded at the same time books on chemistry, and a manual of medicine, and a novel, and some treatise on philosophy or theology. His reading suggested a man swimming in the sea among the wreckage of his ship and trying to save his life by greedily clutching first at one spar[3] and then at another.

2

The old banker remembered all this and thought: "Tomorrow at twelve o'clock he will regain his freedom. By our arrangement I ought to pay him two million. If I do pay him, it is all over with me: I shall be utterly ruined."

Fifteen years before, his millions had been beyond his reckoning; now he was afraid to ask himself which

2. **theology:** study of religious teachings concerning God and God's relation to the world.
3. **spar:** pole that supports or extends a ship's sail.

C **Literary Perspectives** **Analyzing Credibility in Literature** What makes the story seem believable so far?

D **Literary Focus** **Theme** Based on this description of the prisoner's activities, what can you infer about the story's theme?

Vocabulary **zealously** (ZEHL uhs lee) *adv.*: fervently; devotedly.
indiscriminately (ihn dihs KRIHM uh niht lee) *adv.*: without making careful distinctions; randomly.

Universal Access

Struggling Readers

The reader, like the banker, receives clues about the lawyer's state of mind during his years of confinement and interprets these signs. To the banker, the short notes and the sound of the piano mean that the lawyer is lonely. Tell students to think about the lawyer's state of mind in his subsequent years of confinement and what his behavior at each phase might mean.

✔ See **UA: Differentiating Instruction** for a graphic organizer to scaffold instruction for struggling readers.

Advanced Learners

Acceleration To guide students toward deeper philosophical analysis, present the following brief anecdote: Olga, Chekhov's wife, once asked him in a letter, "What is the meaning of life?" Chekhov replied, "It is like asking what a carrot is. A carrot is a carrot and nothing more is known." Invite students to analyze "The Bet" to determine whether it reinforces or contradicts Chekhov's idea.

were greater, his debts or his assets. Desperate gambling on the Stock Exchange, wild speculation, and the excitability which he could not get over even in advancing years had by degrees led to the decline of his fortune, and the proud, fearless, self-confident millionaire had become a banker of middling rank, trembling at every rise and fall in his investments. "Cursed bet!" muttered the old man, clutching his head in despair. "Why didn't the man die? He is only forty now. He will take my last penny from me, he will marry, will enjoy life, will gamble on the Exchange, while I shall look at him with envy like a beggar and hear from him every day the same sentence: 'I am indebted to you for the happiness of my life; let me help you!' No, it is too much! The one means of being saved from bankruptcy and disgrace is the death of that man!" **E**

It struck three o'clock. The banker listened; everyone was asleep in the house, and nothing could be heard outside but the rustling of the chilled trees. Trying to make no noise, he took from a fireproof safe the key of the door which had not been opened for fifteen years, put on his overcoat, and went out of the house.

It was dark and cold in the garden. Rain was falling. A damp, cutting wind was racing about the garden, howling and giving the trees no rest. The banker strained his eyes but could see neither the earth nor the white statues, nor the lodge, nor the trees. Going to the spot where the lodge stood, he twice called the watchman. No answer followed. Evidently the watchman had sought shelter from the weather and was now asleep somewhere either in the kitchen or in the greenhouse.

"If I had the pluck to carry out my intention," thought the old man, "suspicion would fall first upon the watchman."

He felt in the darkness for the steps and the door and went into the entry of the lodge. Then he groped his way into a little passage and lighted a match. There was not a soul there. There was a bedstead with no bedding on it, and in the corner there was a dark cast-iron stove. The seals on the door leading to the prisoner's rooms were intact.

Analyzing Visuals

Connecting to the Text Note how the books and documents are tightly bound. How is this image a metaphor for the bet?

Still Life with Book Sheets and Pictures (1783) by Russian School. Oil on canvas. Tretyakov Gallery, Moscow, Russia.

E **Reading Focus** **Making Predictions** What new problem arises in this passage? What could happen next?

Think About/Talk About

Comprehension

E Reading Focus

Possible response: *The banker's financial situation has changed and paying the prisoner two million will ruin him. In an ironic reversal, the banker imagines the young man giving him money. The banker's thoughts turn to murder. He could possibly attempt to kill the prisoner.*

Analysis

C Literary Perspectives

Possible responses: *The story seems believable in that only one year has passed since the undertaking of the bet. On p. 1025, the terms of the confinement are outlined in detail, and the young man follows the terms, also adding to the story's plausibility.*

D Literary Focus

Possible response: *The theme of the story may be isolation and what a person does in the absence of human contact. People may try to distract themselves, write, study, cry, or simply feel extremely bored.*

Extend the Discussion

Synthesizing How does the banker's mental state help develop the theme of the story? ***Possible response:*** *Even though the banker has his freedom, he may lose all of the joys in his life if he has to give up his money. In this sense, the lawyer will metaphorically take the banker's life.*

Vocabulary: Own the Word

- **zealously:** Ask students to recall a time when they became *zealously* interested in something—a movie star, a hobby, an article from the news—and to describe how they pursued their interest.
- **indiscriminately:** In the text, the prisoner reads *indiscriminately.* What does this mean? How might one read with purpose? What are the advantages or disadvantages of both approaches?

Students with Disabilities

Help students understand the sequence of events during the lawyer's period of captivity. All of these can be found in the flashback that traces the changes he undergoes from year one through year fifteen. Have students identify the phrases indicating time that appear at the beginning of the paragraphs. If necessary, have them organize the events on a time line.

✔ See **UA: Differentiating Instruction** for a graphic organizer to scaffold instruction for students with disabilities.

Analyzing Visuals

Connecting to the Text: *The image is reminiscent of the hundreds of books read by the prisoner. Hanging on the wall, the pages are useless, just like a life of self-inflicted confinement and solitary philosophical speculation.*

Think About/Talk About

Literary Connection

After dashing off nearly three hundred mediocre but crowd-pleasing pieces for humor magazines, Chekhov was somewhat surprised when critics began taking him seriously. He then began to experiment with longer and more carefully revised stories, dramas, and novels. His humanitarian values motivated him to seek prison reforms, and his one nonfiction book, *Sakhalin Island* (1892), describes life at a remote Siberian prison.

Extend the Discussion

Drawing Conclusions The banker assumes that the lawyer is dreaming of money. What does the banker's assumption show about his own values and perceptiveness? ***Possible response:*** *He values money above all and assumes that the lawyer does too. He is too shallow to grasp that the lawyer's outer changes suggest inner changes.*

Making Judgments What ambiguity do you see in the lawyer's position? ***Possible response:*** *He boasts of the knowledge and wisdom he gained from books but then says he finds them worthless.*

Analyzing Visuals

Connecting to the Text: *For both the banker and the lawyer, the open window could symbolize a changed vision or perception of the world. After years of experiencing life through books, the lawyer has re-entered the real world that he now despises. The banker, after reading the lawyer's letter, has a "window" of insight and feels contempt for himself. The lawyer probably opened the window when he escaped, breaking their contract.*

When the match went out, the old man, trembling with emotion, peeped through the little window. A candle was burning dimly in the prisoner's room. He was sitting at the table. Nothing could be seen but his back, the hair on his head, and his hands. Open books were lying on the table, on the two easy chairs, and on the carpet near the table.

Five minutes passed and the prisoner did not once stir. Fifteen years' imprisonment had taught him to sit still. The banker tapped at the window with his finger, and the prisoner made no movement whatever in response. Then the banker cautiously broke the seals off the door and put the key in the keyhole. The rusty lock gave a grating sound and the door creaked. The banker expected to hear at once footsteps and a cry of astonishment, but three minutes passed and it was as quiet as ever in the room. He made up his mind to go in. (F)

At the table a man unlike ordinary people was sitting motionless. He was a skeleton with the skin drawn tight over his bones, with long curls like a woman's, and a shaggy beard. His face was yellow with an earthy tint in it, his cheeks were hollow, his back long and narrow, and the hand on which his shaggy head was propped was so thin and delicate that it was dreadful to look at it. His hair was already streaked with silver, and seeing his emaciated, aged-looking face, no one would have believed that he was only forty. He was asleep. . . . In front of his bowed head there lay on the table a sheet of paper, on which there was something written in fine handwriting.

"Poor creature!" thought the banker, "he is asleep and most likely dreaming of the millions. And I have only to take this half-dead man, throw him on the bed, stifle him a little with the pillow, and the most conscientious expert would find no sign of a violent death. But let us first read what he has written here. . . ."

The banker took the page from the table and read as follows:

"Tomorrow at twelve o'clock I regain my freedom and the right to associate with other men, but before I leave this room and see the sunshine, I think it necessary to say a few words to you. With a clear conscience I tell you, as before God, who beholds me, that I despise freedom and life and health and all that in your books is called the good things of the world.

"For fifteen years I have been intently studying earthly life. It is true I have not seen the earth or men, but in your books I have drunk fragrant wine, I have sung songs, I have hunted stags and wild boars in the forests, I have loved women. . . . Beauties as ethereal as clouds, created by the magic of your poets and geniuses, have visited me at night and have whispered in my ears wonderful tales that have set my brain in a whirl. In your books I have climbed to the peaks of Elburz and Mont Blanc,[4] and from there I have seen the sun rise and have watched it at evening flood the sky, the ocean, and the mountaintops with gold and crimson. I have watched from there the lightning flashing over my head and cleaving the storm clouds. I have seen green forests, fields, rivers, lakes, towns. I have heard the singing of the sirens,[5] and the strains of the shepherds' pipes; I have touched the wings of comely devils who flew down to converse with me of God. . . . In your books I have flung myself into the bottomless pit, performed miracles, slain, burned towns, preached new religions, conquered whole kingdoms. . . .

"Your books have given me wisdom. All that the unresting thought of man has created in the ages is compressed into a small compass in my brain. I know that I am wiser than all of you.

"And I despise your books, I despise wisdom and the blessings of this world. It is all worthless, fleeting, illusory, and deceptive, like a mirage. You may be proud, wise, and fine, but death will wipe you off the face of the earth as though you were no more than mice burrowing under the floor, and your posterity,

4. **Elburz and Mont Blanc:** Elburz is a mountain range in northern Iran; Mont Blanc, in France, is the highest mountain in the Alps.
5. **sirens:** in Greek mythology, partly human female creatures who lived on an island and lured sailors to their death with their beautiful singing.

(F) **Literary Perspectives** **Analyzing Credibility in Literature** Does the banker's hesitation seem believable here? Why or why not?

Vocabulary **ethereal** (ih THIHR ee uhl) *adj.:* light and delicate; unearthly.

Universal Access

AAVE Students Who Use African American Vernacular English

Students may form sentences in the simple past with the past participle. For instance, they may say "I seen" instead of "I saw." Explain that in formal English the past participle is used in the past perfect tenses. Read aloud the paragraph that begins "For fifteen years" to demonstrate the use of the past participle as it appears in the past perfect tense.

Literary Perspectives

To help students answer the **Literary Perspectives** question, remind them of the banker's reason for visiting the prisoner—the banker wants to kill him. Then, have students think about how someone who is grappling with a moral dilemma might react. Students might note that anyone with a conscience would not be eager to commit murder and would hesitate before taking such a vicious action. Have students look for other clues on p. 1028 that help make the banker's actions believable.

your history, your immortal geniuses will burn or freeze together with the earthly globe.

"You have lost your reason and taken the wrong path. You have taken lies for truth and hideousness for beauty. You would marvel if, owing to strange events of some sort, frogs and lizards suddenly grew on apple and orange trees instead of fruit or if roses began to smell like a sweating horse; so I marvel at you who exchange heaven for earth. I don't want to understand you.

"To prove to you in action how I despise all that you live by, I renounce the two million of which I once dreamed as of paradise and which now I despise. To deprive myself of the right to the money, I shall go out from here five minutes before the time fixed and so break the compact. . . ." **G**

When the banker had read this, he laid the page on the table, kissed the strange man on the head, and went out of the lodge, weeping. At no other time, even when he had lost heavily on the Stock Exchange, had he felt so great a contempt for himself. When he got home, he lay on his bed, but his tears and emotion kept him for hours from sleeping.

Next morning the watchmen ran in with pale faces and told him they had seen the man who lived in the lodge climb out of the window into the garden, go to the gate, and disappear. The banker went at once with the servants to the lodge and made sure of the flight of his prisoner. To avoid arousing unnecessary talk, he took from the table the writing in which the millions were renounced and, when he got home, locked it up in the fireproof safe. **H**

Analyzing Visuals

Connecting to the Text What might this open window symbolize to both the banker and the lawyer? Who do you think opened the window? Why?

The Veranda at Liselund (1916) by Peter Ilsted (Danish, 1861–1933). Oil on canvas. Courtesy of Adelson Galleries, New York.

G Literary Focus Theme In one sense, the lawyer spends his years of imprisonment searching for the meaning of life. What do you think he discovers by the story's end?

H Reading Focus Making Predictions Do the banker's actions at the end of the story surprise you? What ending to the story did you predict?

Vocabulary **renounce** (rih NOWNS) *v.:* formally give up; reject.

Think About/Talk About

Comprehension

H Reading Focus

Possible responses: *The banker's action at the end would be surprising if his character were truly materialistic and unscrupulous. But from the beginning, Chekhov suggests the complexity and ambiguity of both characters. He sets up the ironic twist by which the lawyer's discovery leads to the banker's revelation about himself.*

Analysis

F Literary Perspectives

Possible response: *Students may say that the banker's hesitation is believable because he is "trembling with emotion" about his prospective deed.*

G Literary Focus

Possible responses: *He discovers that the achievements of humanity and its "immortal genius" are ultimately meaningless because they cannot keep a person from death.*

Vocabulary: Own the Word

- **ethereal:** On the chalkboard, create a chart comparing the word *ethereal* with an antonym such as *tangible.* Ask students to list ideas or objects that are related to each word.
- **renounce:** In the text, the prisoner decides to *renounce* wealth on moral grounds. Ask the students a hypothetical question—if they had to *renounce* something for one day, what would it be and why?

California Standards, pp. 1030–1031

- **Reading Standard 2.2** Analyze the way in which clarity of meaning is affected by the patterns of organization, hierarchical structures, repetition of the main ideas, syntax, and word choice in the text.
- **Reading Standard 3.2** Analyze the way in which the theme or meaning of a selection represents a view or comment on life, using textual evidence to support the claim.
- **Reading Standard 3.9** Analyze the philosophical arguments presented in literary works to determine whether the authors' positions have contributed to the quality of each work and the credibility of the characters. (Philosophical approach)
- **Grades 9–10 Review Reading Standard 1.1** Identify and use the literal and figurative meanings of words and understand word derivations.
- **Grades 9–10 Review Reading Standard 3.3** Analyze interactions between main and subordinate characters in a literary text (e.g., internal and external conflicts, motivation.
- **Writing Standard 2.1** Write fictional, autobiographical, or biographical narratives: **a.** Narrate a sequence of events and communicate their significance to the audience. **d.** Pace the presentation of actions to accommodate temporal, spatial, and dramatic mood changes.
- **Writing Standard 2.3** Write reflective compositions: **a.** Explore the significance of personal experiences, events, conditions, or concerns by using rhetorical strategies (e.g., narration, description, exposition, persuasion). **b.** Draw comparisons between specific incidents and broader themes that illustrate the writer's important beliefs or generalizations about life.
- **Listening and Speaking Standard 2.2** Deliver oral reports on historical investigations: **a.** Use exposition, narration, description, persuasion, or some combination of those to support the thesis.
- **Listening and Speaking Standard 2.3** Deliver oral responses to literature: **a.** Demonstrate a comprehensive understanding of the significant ideas of literary works (e.g., make assertions about the text that are reasonable and supportable). **c.** Support important ideas and viewpoints through accurate and detailed references to the text or to other works.

Check for Understanding

Independent Practice

Reading Skills Focus

Possible responses:

1. *to prove that life imprisonment is worse than the death penalty*
2. *The banker is no longer well-off.*
3. *to kill the lawyer and avoid paying the debt*
4. *The lawyer deliberately breaks the terms of the bet because he no longer wants the money.*
5. *The banker wins because he no longer has to pay. Or, the lawyer wins because he has gained new insight into life. Ultimately, neither profits, so neither wins.*
6. *Predictions should be based on details from the text, regardless of whether they are right or wrong.*

Literary Skills Focus

Possible responses:

7. *He feels a great contempt for himself. Chekhov may be showing the importance of self-knowledge over material wealth.*
8. *His health worsens; he becomes alienated; he gains knowledge from reading and realizes the emptiness of earthly pursuits.*
9. *Imprisonment gave him time to reflect but limited his access to the world. His view might have been more moderate otherwise.*
10. *The banker's actions are more credible because they revolve around his wealth and desire to prove a point. If the lawyer had failed to uphold his end of the bet, the story would have been more plausible but less interesting.*
11. *Freedom does not ensure happiness; earthly possessions and pursuits mean nothing; a capricious, self-indulgent man gains little.*
12. *The lawyer's initial motivation was most likely pride, in addition to greed. If he were motivated solely by greed, he would not have increased the term of the sentence without any guarantee of winning extra money.*

Applying Your Skills

Reading Standard 2.2, 3.2, 3.9; **Grades 9–10 Review Reading Standard** 3.3 (see pages A48–A50) **Writing Standard** 2.1a, 2.1d (see pages A51–A52)

The Bet

Literary Response and Analysis

Reading Skills Focus

Quick Check

1. Why do the lawyer and the banker make a bet?
2. At the end of the fifteen years, how has the banker's situation changed?
3. Why does the banker go to the lodge on the last night of the lawyer's imprisonment?
4. What decision does the lawyer announce in a letter? Why does he make this decision?

Read with a Purpose

5. Who wins the bet—the banker, the lawyer, or neither character? Explain your answer.

Reading Skills: Making Predictions

6. Now that you have finished reading, add a box next to your "Prediction" box. In this box, tell whether your prediction was right or wrong; if it was wrong, tell what actually happened.

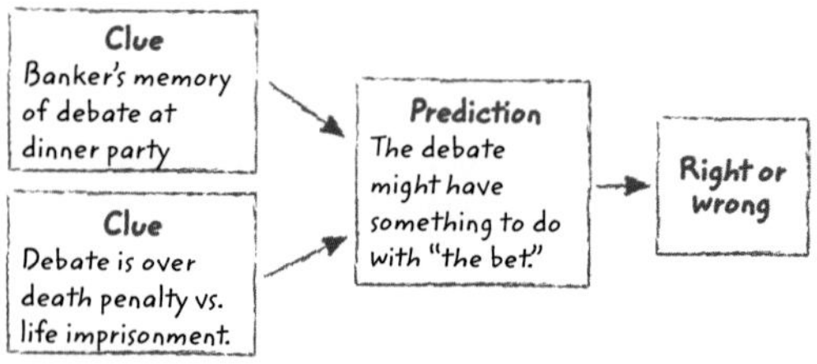

Literary Skills Focus

Literary Analysis

7. **Interpret** In retrospect, the banker views his bet as "the caprice of a pampered man." How does he feel about himself at the end of the fifteen years? What does this reveal about Chekhov's view about what is important in life?
8. **Analyze** Like a psychiatrist, Chekhov meticulously describes the effects of the lawyer's solitary exile. How does isolation affect the prisoner at different stages over the fifteen-year period?
9. **Evaluate** Do you think the lawyer would have had such a dismal view of the world had he not been imprisoned? Explain your answer.
10. **Literary Perspectives** Whose actions did you find more credible: the banker's or the lawyer's? How would you change the story to make it more believable?

Literary Skills: Theme

11. **Interpret** State in a full sentence what you think is the story's main theme—the insight it provides about human experience. Do you think this story has more than one theme? Explain.

Literary Skills Review: Motivation

12. **Make Judgments** The reason or reasons behind a character's behavior are called **motivation.** The banker believes that "greed for money" was the lawyer's motivation for betting. Do you agree? Cite textual evidence that supports your position.

Writing Skills Focus

Think as a Reader/Writer

Use It in Your Writing Chekhov indicates the passage of time with words and phrases. Using similar phrases, write a story of your own that involve events that take place over a large period of time.

What Do You Think Now What did you expect the lawyer to learn about himself and life after fifteen years in solitude? Did the reality surprise you? Explain your responses.

Universal Access

Struggling Writers

Some students may struggle to add time transitions to their writing. Inform students that transitions do not have to begin with a specific time such as, "At one o'clock P.M. . . ." Have students write a few lines about any subject of their choice, beginning the first paragraph with the phrase, "As the sun began to set on the third day. . ."

What Do You Think Now?

To help students answer the question, have them refer to the predictions they made in the beginning of the story. Have students compare their previous predictions with a partner's. Then have pairs share their responses to the question with the rest of the class.

Grades 9–10 Review Reading Standard 1.1 (see pages A48–A50)
Writing Standard 2.3a, 2.3b (see pages A51–A52)
Listening and Speaking Standard 2.2a, 2.3a, 2.3c (see pages A53–A55)

Vocabulary Development

Vocabulary Check

Answer the questions about the Vocabulary words.

1. Is the lawyer **frivolous**? Explain.
2. Is attending college **compulsory**?
3. Why does the banker consider the bet a **caprice**?
4. What does it mean that the prisoner **zealously** studied books and languages in prison?
5. In the last two years, the lawyer read **indiscriminately.** What sorts of books did he read?
6. If the prisoner's visions were **ethereal,** were they delicate or nightmarish?
7. The lawyer **renounced** the money. Does that mean he claimed it, or that he rejected it?

Vocabulary Skills: Synonyms

A synonym for a word should be of the same part of speech. *Compulsory* and *obligation,* for example, (which both refer to something mandatory) are not synonyms since they are different parts of speech. The proper synonym for *compulsory (adj.)* is *obligatory (adj.)*

Your Turn

Match each Vocabulary word with its synonym.

1. frivolous	a. whim
2. caprice	b. reject
3. zealously	c. enthusiastically
4. renounce	d. silly

Language Coach

The Greek word *zēlos* means "enthusiasm for a cause." For which Vocabulary word is *zēlos* a root? What are the related noun forms for this word?

CHOICES

As you respond to the Choices, use these **Academic Vocabulary** words as appropriate: benefit, complex, publish, respond, statistics.

REVIEW

Conduct a Panel Discussion

Group Activity In this story, the lawyer's letter to his "jailer" is specific about the lawyer's philosophy of life. In a small group, read the letter and hold a round-table discussion of the lawyer's views. Choose a leader who will make sure that all who speak offer reasons and examples to support their views. At the close of the discussion, prepare a summary of the group's responses to the lawyer's philosophy.

CONNECT

Write About Solitary Confinement

Timed Writing Imagine yourself in the lawyer's place. How would solitary confinement affect you? The rules of your confinement include no human contact, no exit, no television, no access to technology. You may ask for books, musical instruments, and exercise equipment. Write a brief essay in which you tell how you might spend one year alone.

EXTEND

Debate an Issue

The question of capital punishment versus solitary confinement is a complex issue that is still debated today. Form two teams to debate the issue discussed at the party at the start of the story, one to support solitary confinement as punishment and one to support capital punishment. Find evidence to support your position.

Learn It Online
Explore Chekhov's world through these Internet links.
go.hrw.com H12-1031 Go

Independent Practice

Vocabulary Development

Vocabulary Check

1. *Yes, he agreed to be imprisoned.*
2. *No, one can choose to go to college.*
3. *He made the bet impulsively.*
4. *He studied the books fervently.*
5. *He read books of all subjects.*
6. *His visions were delicate.*
7. *He rejected it.*

Your Turn

1. *d* 2. *a* 3. *c* 4. *b*

English for Academic Success

Language Coach

Possible response: Zêlos *is a root for* zealously. *A related noun form is* zeal.

Choices: Evaluation Criteria

Review: Homework
Conduct a Panel Discussion
Views should be supported.

Connect: Timed Writing
40–50 minutes
Essays offer and explain activities.

Extend: Homework
Debate an Issue
Arguments are clearly developed.

Assess

Unit 5 Resources, Selection Standards Check, p. 86

ThinkCentral Online Assessment, Selection Standards Check

Reteach

ThinkCentral Online Remediation

Learn It Online
Literature Links direct students to pre-screened Web sites offering more information related to a selection.
go.hrw.com H12-1031 Go

Universal Access: Vocabulary Development

Struggling Readers

Benchmark Students Help students demonstrate their knowledge of the meanings of the Vocabulary words. Divide students into pairs and have them complete each sentence below. After students have completed each sentence, have them share their sentences with the class.

- Because the leader made major decisions by *caprice* alone . . .
- The girl had an *ethereal* appearance because . . .
- Although Mary *renounced* John's proposal . . .
- The boy ate *indiscriminately,* which made the chef feel . . .
- It was *compulsory* that we attend the meeting, so . . .
- We knew Juan was a *frivolous* person, so we were not surprised when . . .
- The club's members *zealously* guarded . . .

✔ See the **Academic and Selection Vocabulary Skill Builder** in **UA: Differentiating Instruction.**

Selection Introduction

Think About the Writer

Ask students to think about why a privileged writer like Maupassant would choose to write stories about middle-class and lower-income characters. Then, ask students to discuss whether a writer can create more "realistic" stories about these types of characters than about wealthy characters.

For Independent Reading

- *Madame Bovary,* Gustave Flaubert
- *A Doll's House,* Henrik Ibsen

Motivate

What Do You Think?/QuickWrite

In their **Reader/Writer Notebooks,** have students write about a time their first impression about a person turned out to be wrong and how their actions or view changed after discovering the truth about the person.

California Standards, pp. 1032–1041

- **Reading Standard 2.4** Make warranted and reasonable assertions about the author's arguments by using elements of the text to defend and clarify interpretations.
- **Reading Standard 3.3** Analyze the ways in which irony, tone, mood, the author's style, and the "sound" of language achieve specific rhetorical or aesthetic purposes or both.

Preparing to Read

The Jewels

What Do You Think? How can appearance be different from reality?

QuickWrite

In your *Reader/Writer Notebook,* write a paragraph about a time when you had a false impression of someone or something. What was it like to discover the truth?

Engraved portrait of Guy de Maupassant, an illustration from *Le Monde Illustre* (1894).

MEET THE WRITER

Guy de Maupassant
(1850–1893)

Maupassant's terse, realistic stories have informed generations of American writers, from Edgar Allan Poe to Stephen King.

An Interest in Realism

Guy de Maupassant came from a wealthy family in rural Normandy. His parents separated when he was young, and Maupassant was raised by his mother, a daring woman who once raised eyebrows because she wore her skirts above her ankles. Among his mother's friends was the great realist novelist Gustave Flaubert (1821–1880), who, along with Maupassant's mother, encouraged him to write from an early age.

As a young man, Maupassant served in the army and studied law. He then took a civil service job in Paris, where he reconnected with Flaubert, who, now aging and lonely, became a mentor to the young man. Every week, leading realist writers, such as Émile Zola (1840–1902) and Russian novelist Ivan Turgenev (1818–1883), met at Flaubert's house to discuss literature. At that time, Maupassant was writing poems, historical dramas, and horror stories, but under the influence of his new friends, he turned to realistic fiction.

Later Maupassant joined a group of younger realists, or naturalists, who met at Zola's house. They were less interested in style and more intent on analyzing social conditions.

Darkly Ironic

By the time he was in his thirties, Maupassant had become one of France's best-known artists and enjoyed the rare benefit of being able to support himself independently as a writer. In 1883 alone, he turned out two novels and seventy short stories. Those darkly ironic stories boast a knowledge of life both in rural Normandy and in seedy and fashionable Paris, and their characters are often victims of their own greed or vanity.

Few of Maupassant's friends suspected that the strong young writer was in constant pain and nearly blind from overwork and syphilis. At the end of 1891, Maupassant suffered a complete mental breakdown, from which he never recovered. He died in an asylum before his forty-third birthday.

Think About the Writer Where did Maupassant get the material for his stories?

Selection Readability	
Easily Accessible **Accessible** Challenging	background information; familiar syntax; chronological order; accessible theme

Reading Standard 2.4, 3.3 (see pages A48–A50)

Literary Skills Focus

Irony The discrepancy between appearances and reality is known as **irony.** There are three basic types of irony. In **verbal irony,** a person says something but means something very different, as when, for example, someone remarks in the middle of a hurricane, "Nice day we're having." In **situational irony,** what actually happens is different from what you would expect to happen. When it rains on the weather forecasters' picnic or when the police officer's son robs the bank, we perceive situational irony. In **dramatic irony,** a character believes something to be true, while the reader knows better. A character might think he is safe in his house, but the reader knows that a robber is approaching the back window. As you read "The Jewels," look for examples of situational and dramatic irony.

Reading Skills Focus

Drawing Inferences An **inference** is an educated guess. As you read "The Jewels," pay close attention to what is *not* said as well as to what *is* said. Stay alert, for Maupassant often drops crucial clues in the space of one or two words. Sometimes you have to draw inferences about a character, an event, or even just about the significance of a brief remark.

Into Action Use a graphic organizer like the one below to record details and then draw inferences based on those details.

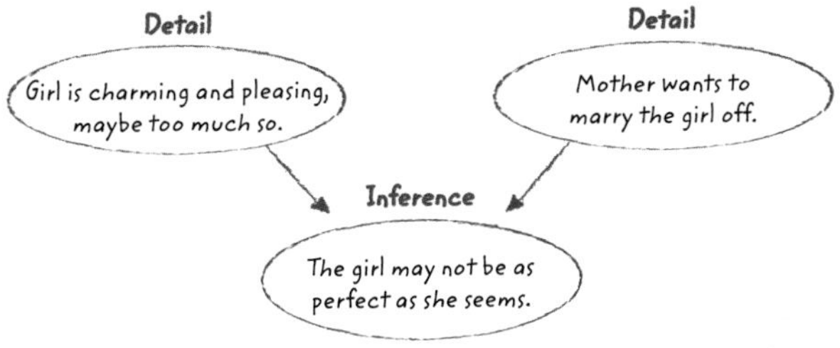

Writing Skills Focus

Think as a Reader/Writer

Find It in Your Reading The **dialogue** in this story is written mostly in short sentences that realistically convey information about the characters and their situation. In your *Reader/Writer Notebook,* write down two or three sentences you consider realistic. Give reasons for your choices.

Reader/Writer Notebook

Use your **RWN** to complete the activities for this selection.

Vocabulary

unpretentious (uhn prih TEHN shuhs) *adj.:* modest. *Madame Lantin's dresses were simple and unpretentious.*

assuage (uh SWAYJ) *v.:* ease; calm. *Lantin was so grief-stricken that even a great expanse of time could not assuage his sorrow.*

incurred (ihn KUHRD) *v.:* brought upon oneself. *Monsieur Lantin incurred a number of debts that thrust him into a bad financial situation.*

surreptitiously (suhr uhp TIHSH uhs lee) *adv.:* in a secret or sneaky manner. *The jewelers looked at Lantin surreptitiously to hide their amusement.*

contemptuous (kuhn TEHMP choo uhs) *adj.:* scornful. *He gave the carriages contemptuous looks because the rich would no longer look down on him.*

Language Coach

Prefixes and Suffixes Word parts added to the beginning of words to change their meaning are called **prefixes;** word parts added to the ends of words to change their meaning or part of speech are called **suffixes.** Find two Vocabulary words with prefixes. Find a word with a suffix that changes the word's tense. Find another word with a suffix that changes the word's part of speech.

Learn It Online

Learn more about Maupassant's life and work at the Writers' Lives site.

go.hrw.com H12-1033 Go

Comparing Texts Resources

Unit 5 Resources, on-level practice and assessment, p. 89

Teacher One Stop™, on-level lesson plans and all print resources

Holt Audio Library

Holt Audio Library: Selections and Summaries in Spanish

UA: Differentiating Instruction, graphic organizer, p. 240

UA: Supporting Instruction in Spanish, selection summary

Analyzing Visuals Transparencies, p. 43

ThinkCentral Online Assessment, Selection Standards Check

ThinkCentral Online Remediation

Preteach

Introducing Vocabulary

Use this activity to check students' understanding.

1. Which word describes how a thief moves? [*surreptitiously*]
2. Which word shows the action that water has on thirst? [*assuage*]
3. Which word describes a used compact car with no extras? [*unpretentious*]
4. Which word describes the feeling a haughty king would have toward others? [*contemptuous*]
5. Identify which word best fits in the sentence: *The man borrowed money and _____ a debt.* [*incurred*]

English for Academic Success

Language Coach

Possible responses: *Prefixed words: unpretentious; incurred; Suffixed word: contemptuous*

Literary Skills Focus

As students read the story, have them identify moments in which either they were surprised or Monsieur Lantin was surprised. Use these passages to illustrate the concepts of irony.

Reading Skills Focus

Give students a copy of the Reading Skills Focus graphic organizer before they read. Tell them to use their responses to answer the questions on the Applying Your Skills page.

Writing Skills Focus

Tell students to write down in their **Reader/Writer Notebooks** any details from the story that they find realistic. Students can use these details to complete the Writing Skills Focus activity.

Learn It Online

The **Writers' Lives** feature of the Interactive Student Edition offers additional information about this author. Audio or video segments are provided for some authors.

go.hrw.com H12-1033 Go

Teacher Preparation
Selection Plot Summary

In "The Jewels," Monsieur Lantin, a middle-class government worker, adores his wife and complains only that she likes the theater too much and collects gaudy costume jewelry. Her death after a few years leaves him inconsolable and unable to make ends meet. Lantin tries to sell his wife's costume jewelry only to discover that the jewelry is real. Devastated, he realizes that the jewels were gifts from wealthy lovers. Selling all the jewelry, he quits his job and marries a woman who remains faithful but makes him miserable.

Direct Teach

Think About/Talk About

Read with a Purpose Have students read the Read with a Purpose statement. Ask them to notice in the text any early clues as to the real value of the jewelry.

Comprehension

A Reading Focus

Possible response: *Maupassant uses the word* seem *twice and the phrase "gave the impression" once. These are clues that the girl's appearance is in contrast to her true nature.*

Extend the Discussion

Characterization What do you learn about the girl from the account of her background? Does this description give you a sense of her character? ***Possible responses:*** *The girl is middle class but poor. She is beautiful, charming, and "decent," and she seems ideal and angelic. The description is brief, sketchy, and subjective; we do not yet see her in action.*

SHORT STORY

The Jewels

by **Guy de Maupassant**

translated by **Roger Colet**

Read with a Purpose

Read to discover how a woman's jewelry collection is not what it seems to be.

Build Background

Guy de Maupassant, like his fellow realists, rejected the Romantic notion that the world was essentially good. Instead, Maupassant's stories reveal surprising and sometimes shocking truths about people's inner lives. Maupassant's characters are not members of the upper classes and nobility; they are ordinary people, such as peasants, minor government officials, even prostitutes.

You may notice that Maupassant uses only a few sentences to describe major events and characters. This terse style is partly attributed to the fact that many of his stories were originally published in newspapers, which restricted the length of his material.

Monsieur Lantin had met the girl at a party given one evening by his office superior and love had caught him in its net.

She was the daughter of a country tax collector who had died a few years before. She had come to Paris then with her mother, who struck up acquaintance with a few middle-class families in her district in the hope of marrying her off. They were poor and decent, quiet and gentle. The girl seemed the perfect example of the virtuous woman to whom every sensible young man dreams of entrusting his life. Her simple beauty had a modest, angelic charm and the imperceptible smile which always hovered about her lips seemed to be a reflection of her heart.

Everybody sang her praises and people who knew her never tired of saying: "Happy the man who marries her. Nobody could find a better wife." **A**

Monsieur Lantin, who was then a senior clerk at the Ministry of the Interior with a salary of three thousand five hundred francs[1] a year, proposed to her and married her.

He was incredibly happy with her. She ran his household so skillfully and economically that they gave the impression of living in luxury. She lavished attention on her husband, spoiling and coddling him,

1. **francs:** In the late nineteenth century, a franc was worth about twenty cents in American currency.

A **Reading Focus** **Drawing Inferences** How many times does Maupassant use a form of the word *seem* in his description of the girl? What inference can you make based on the use of this word?

The Eiffel Tower stands overlooking the promenades and fairgrounds of the Paris Exposition (1889).

Universal Access

English Learners

Maupassant describes Monsieur Lantin as a "senior clerk at the Ministry of the Interior" and grants him a salary that sounds substantial if the reader does not know its value. This ambiguity could be confusing for some students. Be sure students understand that a clerk is essentially a secretary or an administrative assistant. Monsieur Lantin is not an official; he is a relatively low-level employee in a government office.

Struggling Readers

Many details in this story hint at a double meaning or suggest irony. For example, the praise Lantin's wife elicits from others, "Happy the man who marries her. Nobody could find a better wife," could be interpreted, or even intended, ironically. Have students find instances of other such details in the story. While the language of irony may be simple, its significance often is not. Ask students to discuss various interpretations of the examples of irony they find in the text.

and the charm of her person was so great that six years after their first meeting he loved her even more than in the early days.

He found fault with only two of her tastes: her love for the theater and her passion for imitation jewelry.

Her friends (she knew the wives of a few petty officials) often obtained a box at the theater for her for popular plays, and even for first nights; and she dragged her husband along willy-nilly to these entertainments, which he found terribly tiring after a day's work at the office. He therefore begged her to go to the theater with some lady of her acquaintance who would bring her home afterwards. It was a long time before she gave in, as she thought that this arrangement was not quite respectable. But finally, just to please him, she agreed, and he was terribly grateful to her.

Now this love for the theater soon aroused in her a desire to adorn her person. True, her dresses remained very simple, always in good taste, but unpretentious; and her gentle grace, her irresistible, humble, smiling charm seemed to be enhanced by the simplicity of her gowns. But she took to wearing two big rhinestone earrings which sparkled like diamonds, and she also wore necklaces of fake pearls, bracelets of imitation gold, and combs set with colored glass cut to look like real stones.

Her husband, who was rather shocked by this love of show, often used to say: "My dear, when a woman can't afford to buy real jewels, she ought to appear adorned with her beauty and grace alone: those are still the rarest of gems."

But she would smile sweetly and reply: "I can't help it. I like imitation jewelry. It's my only vice.

Vocabulary **unpretentious** (uhn prih TEHN shuhs) *adj.:* modest.

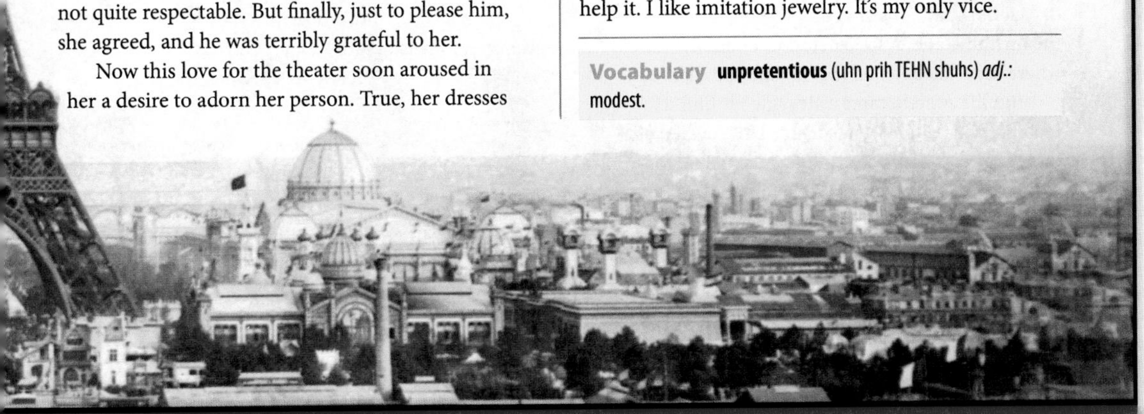

Think About/Talk About

Extend the Discussion

Drawing Conclusions Lantin begs his wife to find a "lady of her acquaintance" for her visits to the theater, which she does, reluctantly. Why is Lantin grateful to her for this? ***Possible response:*** *He is tired from a long day at the office, and he is bored by the theater. He is grateful to be excused from her evening entertainment.*

Interpreting When Lantin's wife says, "I like imitation jewelry. It's my only vice," how is this statement ironic? ***Possible response:*** *After reading the full story, we can recognize this line as an example of irony because Lantin's wife is wearing real jewelry, not imitation jewelry, and because her vice is adultery, not vanity.*

Vocabulary: Own the Word

unpretentious: On the chalkboard, create a chart comparing the word *unpretentious* with an antonym such as *extravagant*. Ask students to describe different objects in each category.

Advanced Learners

Acceleration Maupassant's stories are famed for their use of irony. Ask students to read another story by Maupassant involving jewelry called, "The Necklace." In both stories, a surprise ending changes the way readers think about the details in the story. Students can compare the ironic elements in the language and narrative of both stories and reflect on the symbolism of jewelry. They can then present their analyses to the class to start a general discussion about these ideas.

Students with Disabilities

Have students make two columns in a notebook, one labeled "Appearance" and one labeled "Reality." Then have students find details in the story that give them clues about what is reality or appearance and place them in the appropriate column.

✔ See **UA: Differentiating Instruction** for a graphic organizer to scaffold instruction for struggling readers.

Model the Skill

- Model for students how to **make inferences** about a character or situation.
- Read aloud the last one and a half paragraphs on p. 1037. Point out that Monsieur Lantin demonstrates his concern about his wife's love of imitation jewelry by gently suggesting an alternative. His words and tone reveal that he does not want to upset her, but that he does believe his wife is going too far. He also thinks his wife is beautiful enough without jewelry. This shows that he is completely smitten by his wife.

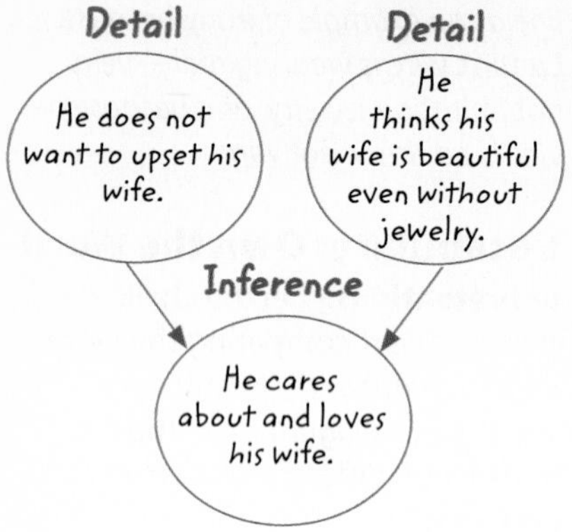

Guided Practice: Apply

Read-Talk-Write Ask students to read the paragraph starting with "Her friends . . ." on p. 1037 and to work in pairs to write realistic dialogue that could take the place of the interaction between Lantin and his wife.

Think About/Talk About

Build Background: Critiquing the Middle Class

Tell students that Maupassant's artfully chosen details create individual characters who also represent distinct social types. The couple in this story are members of the French *bourgeoisie*, or middle class, which expanded greatly during the nineteenth century. Lacking the vast wealth of the aristocracy, the bourgeoisie relied on hard work and on advances made possible by political and technological change.

I know you're right, but people can't change their natures. I would have loved to own some real jewels."

Then she would run the pearl necklaces through her fingers and make the cut-glass gems flash in the light, saying: "Look! Aren't they beautifully made? Anyone would swear they were real."

He would smile and say: "You have the taste of a gypsy."

Sometimes, in the evening, when they were sitting together by the fireside, she would place on the tea table the leather box in which she kept her "trash," as Monsieur Lantin called it. Then she would start examining these imitation jewels with passionate attention, as if she were enjoying some deep and secret pleasure; and she would insist on hanging a necklace around her husband's neck, laughing uproariously and crying: "How funny you look!" And then she would throw herself into his arms and kiss him passionately. **B**

One night in winter when she had been to the opera, she came home shivering with cold. The next morning she had a cough, and a week later she died of pneumonia.

Lantin very nearly followed her to the grave. His despair was so terrible that his hair turned white within a month. He wept from morning to night, his heart ravaged by unbearable grief, haunted by the memory, the smile, the voice, the every charm of his dead wife.

Time did nothing to assuage his grief. Often during office hours, when his colleagues came along to chat about the topics of the day, his cheeks would suddenly puff out, his nose wrinkle up, his eyes fill with tears, and with a terrible grimace he would burst out sobbing.

He had left his wife's room untouched, and every day would shut himself in it and think about her. All the furniture and even her clothes remained exactly where they had been on the day she had died.

But life soon became a struggle for him. His income, which in his wife's hands had covered all their expenses, was now no longer sufficient for him on his own; and he wondered in amazement how she had managed to provide him with excellent wines and rare delicacies which he could no longer afford on his modest salary. **C**

He incurred a few debts and ran after money in the way people do when they are reduced to desperate shifts. Finally, one morning, finding himself without a sou[2] a whole week before the end of the month, he decided to sell something; and immediately the idea occurred to him of disposing of his wife's "trash." He still harbored a sort of secret grudge against those false gems which had irritated him in the past, and indeed the sight of them every day somewhat spoiled the memory of his beloved.

He rummaged for a long time among the heap of gaudy trinkets she had left behind, for she had stubbornly gone on buying jewelry until the last days of her life, bringing home a new piece almost every evening. At last he decided on the large necklace which she had seemed to like best, and which, he thought, might well be worth six or seven francs, for it was beautifully made for a piece of paste.[3]

He put it in his pocket and set off for his Ministry, following the boulevards and looking for a jeweler's shop which inspired confidence.

At last he spotted one and went in, feeling a little ashamed of exposing his poverty in this way, and of trying to sell such a worthless article.

"Monsieur," he said to the jeweler, "I would like to know what you think this piece is worth."

The man took the necklace, examined it, turned it over, weighed it, inspected it with a magnifying glass, called his assistant, made a few remarks to him in an undertone, placed the necklace on the counter and looked at it from a distance to gauge the effect.

Monsieur Lantin, embarrassed by all this ritual, was opening his mouth to say: "Oh, I know perfectly well that it isn't worth anything," when the jeweler

2. **sou:** French coin worth about two cents in American currency in the late nineteenth century.
3. **paste:** kind of glass used to make fake gems.

B **Reading Focus** **Drawing Inferences** What inference can you make about the wife from her words and actions?

C **Reading Focus** **Drawing Inferences** What do you think might account for Madame Lantin's amazing ability to stretch her husband's salary?

Vocabulary **assuage** (uh SWAYJ) *v.:* ease; calm.
incurred (ihn KUHRD) *v.:* brought upon oneself.

Cross-Curricular Connection

SOCIOLOGY: Marks of Affluence

The Industrial Revolution made possible mass-production techniques that encouraged a proliferation of imitation jewelry—paste gems made of glass and settings made of fake gold, cut steel, and ceramics. Whereas before 1830, French aristocrats wore jewels that reflected their social status, by Maupassant's era the middle class could purchase fakes that only experts could distinguish from the real thing.

Whole-Class Activity Encourage the class to discuss the popularity of imitation designer styles in today's clothing and jewelry. How might this trend reflect modern socioeconomic developments?

said: "Monsieur, this necklace is worth between twelve and fifteen thousand francs; but I couldn't buy it unless you told me where it came from." **D**

The widower opened his eyes wide and stood there gaping, unable to understand what the jeweler had said. Finally he stammered: "What was that you said?... Are you sure?"

The other misunderstood his astonishment and said curtly: "You can go somewhere else and see if they'll offer you more. In my opinion it's worth fifteen thousand at the most. Come back and see me if you can't find a better price."

Completely dumbfounded, Monsieur Lantin took back his necklace and left the shop, in obedience to a vague desire to be alone and to think.

Once outside, however, he felt an impulse to laugh, and he thought: "The fool! Oh, the fool! But what if I'd taken him at his word? There's a jeweler who can't tell real diamonds from paste!"

And he went into another jeweler's shop at the beginning of the Rue de la Paix. As soon as he saw the necklace, the jeweler exclaimed: "Why, I know that necklace well: it was bought here."

Monsieur Lantin asked in amazement: "How much is it worth?"

"Monsieur, I sold it for twenty-five thousand. I am prepared to buy it back for eighteen thousand once you have told me, in accordance with the legal requirements, how you came to be in possession of it." **E**

This time Monsieur Lantin was dumbfounded. He sat down and said: "But... but... examine it carefully, Monsieur. Until now I thought it was paste."

"Will you give me your name, Monsieur?" said the jeweler.

"Certainly. My name's Lantin. I'm an official at the Ministry of the Interior, and I live at No. 16, Rue des Martyrs."

The jeweler opened his books, looked for the entry, and said: "Yes, this necklace was sent to Madame Lantin's address, No. 16, Rue des Martyrs, on the 20th of July 1876."

The two men looked into each other's eyes, the clerk speechless with astonishment, the jeweler scenting a thief. Finally the latter said: "Will you leave the necklace with me for twenty-four hours? I'll give you a receipt."

"Why, certainly," stammered Monsieur Lantin. And he went out folding the piece of paper, which he put in his pocket.

Then he crossed the street, walked up it again, noticed that he was going the wrong way, went back as far as the Tuileries, crossed the Seine, realized that he had gone wrong again, and returned to the Champs-Élysées,[4] his mind a complete blank. He tried to think it out, to understand. His wife couldn't have afforded to buy something so valuable—that was certain. But in that case it was a present! A present! But a present from whom? And why was it given her?

He halted in his tracks and remained standing in the middle of the avenue. A horrible doubt crossed his mind. Her? But in that case all the other jewels were presents, too! The earth seemed to be trembling under his feet and a tree in front of him to be falling; he threw up his arms and fell to the ground unconscious. **F**

He came to his senses in a chemist's shop into which the passersby had carried him. He took a cab home and shut himself up.

He wept bitterly until nightfall, biting on a handkerchief so as not to cry out. Then he went to bed worn out with grief and fatigue and slept like a log.

A ray of sunlight awoke him and he slowly got up to go to his Ministry. It was hard to think of working after such a series of shocks. It occurred to him that he could ask to be excused and he wrote a letter to his superior. Then he remembered that he had to go back to the jeweler's and he blushed with shame. He spent a long time thinking it over, but decided that he could not leave the necklace with that man. So he dressed and went out. **G**

4. **Champs-Élysées:** elegant boulevard in Paris.

D **Reading Focus** **Drawing Inferences** Why do you suppose the jeweler wants to know the origin of the necklace?

E **Literary Focus** **Irony** What is ironic or unexpected about Lantin's discovery of the true value of the jewelry?

F **Reading Focus** **Drawing Inferences** What can you infer about the manner in which Madame Lantin came to possess the jewels?

G **Reading Focus** **Drawing Inferences** Why is Lantin feeling shameful?

Think About/Talk About

Comprehension

B Reading Focus

Possible response: *She seems excessively and strangely pleased by her "imitation jewels" and gets a "deep and secret pleasure" from them. Her sudden amused affection toward her husband seems puzzling and could be mocking.*

C Reading Focus

Possible response: *She may have been getting money from an outside source, or she may have been running up debts.*

D Reading Focus

Possible response: *Monsieur Lantin does not know the true value of the jewels, so the jeweler suspects they might be stolen.*

F Reading Focus

Possible response: *Lantin's wife probably had a lover, or several lovers, who lavished her with expensive jewelry.*

G Reading Focus

Possible response: *Lantin feels that the jeweler has realized that Lantin's wife was unfaithful.*

Analysis

E Literary Focus

Possible response: *Assuming the jewels were fakes, Lantin expected the jewelry to be worth much less.*

Vocabulary: Own the Word

- **assuage:** Ask students to recall a time when they were required to *assuage* someone's fear or when their own fears were *assuaged.*
- **incurred:** Ask students to recall a time when they or someone they know *incurred* something (anger, annoyance, debt).

Developing Oral Fluency

Small-Group Activity Have students form small groups of three. Ask students to divide up the roles of Monsieur Lantin, the jeweler at Rue de la Paix, and the narrator. Instruct them to practice reading aloud the narration and dialogue between the jeweler and Monsieur Lantin, taking care to express appropriate emotions such as surprise and suspicion through the intonation and pitch of their voices. As groups present their readings, ask other students in the class to give feedback about which parts were dramatized well and which parts could use some improvement.

Universal Access

AAVE Students Who Use African American Vernacular English

English for Academic Success Some students may transpose adjacent consonants. Explain that in formal English, consonant sounds need to be pronounced in the order in which they appear. Remind students to say "Monsieur Lantin *asked*" instead of "Monsieur Lantin *aksed*." Have one student read column one of p. 1037 aloud while the other listens and provides feedback.

Guided Practice: Apply

Think as a Reader/Writer

Find It in Your Reading Point out that in the first five paragraphs of the story, Maupassant reveals many facts about the characters' family histories, their careers, and their wealth or lack of wealth.

Use It in Your Writing Have students write a paragraph about a real or imaginary character. The paragraph should reveal a great deal of information about the character's financial and family background.

Think About/Talk About

Extend the Discussion

Finding Details In the last five paragraphs of the story, Lantin lies twice about his "inheritance," the value going up one hundred thousand francs each time. Why? ***Possible response:*** *Perhaps he hopes that the richer he feels, the less his wife's betrayal will hurt him.*

Speculating Lantin muses on how lucky rich people are, and then he says, "Oh, if only I were rich!" Do you think that, once he has sold the jewelry and become rich, he will feel lucky? ***Possible response:*** *He is probably too bitter about his first wife and too miserable with his second wife to feel lucky.*

Analyzing Visuals

Connecting to the Text: *The jewels are very ornate and gaudy. Whether they are real or not, they appear ostentatious and overly elaborate. They suggest that their owner is someone who intensely values luxury and material finery; he or she may also be someone who likes to attract other people's attention and admiration.*

Jolie Madame (Pretty Woman) (1973) by Audrey Flack. National Gallery of Australia.

Analyzing Visuals

Connecting to the Text How do these objects suggest a person who, like Madame Lantin, enjoys the theater? How might they be something other than what they appear to be?

It was a fine day and the city seemed to be smiling under the clear blue sky. People were strolling about the streets with their hands in their pockets.

Watching them, Lantin said to himself: "How lucky rich people are! With money you can forget even the deepest of sorrows. You can go where you like, travel, enjoy yourself. Oh, if only I were rich!"

He began to feel hungry, for he had eaten nothing for two days, but his pocket was empty. Then he remembered the necklace. Eighteen thousand francs! Eighteen thousand francs! That was a tidy sum, and no mistake!

When he reached the Rue de la Paix he started walking up and down the pavement opposite the jeweler's shop. Eighteen thousand francs! A score of times he almost went in, but every time shame held him back.

He was hungry, though, very hungry, and he had no money at all. He quickly made up his mind, ran across the street so as not to have any time to think, and rushed into the shop.

As soon as he saw him the jeweler came forward and offered him a chair with smiling politeness. His assistants came into the shop, too, and glanced surreptitiously at Lantin with laughter in their eyes and on their lips.

Vocabulary **surreptitiously** (suhr uhp TIHSH uhs lee) *adv.:* in a secret or sneaky manner.

Universal Access

English Learners

English for Academic Success Although Maupassant does not use complicated vocabulary, a few words may be unfamiliar to students. Clarify that *a tidy sum* in this context means a "fairly large" sum; *a score of times* means "twenty" times; *unmoved* means "emotionally unaffected," and *coyness* means "artful shyness or sly hesitance." The phrase *to play leapfrog* means "to jump over."

Advanced Learners

Enrichment Point out that "The Jewels" is set in a specific place and time: Paris in the 1870s. Ask students to research political and social conditions in Paris during the late 1800s. They might explore the level of industrialization, the cost of living, working conditions, workers' rights and benefits, women's rights, and the stratified social class structure. Students' findings can provide insights into the Lantins' circumstances and actions in "The Jewels."

"I have made inquiries, Monsieur," said the jeweler, "and if you still wish to sell the necklace, I am prepared to pay you the price I offered you."

"Why, certainly," stammered the clerk.

The jeweler took eighteen large bank notes out of a drawer, counted them and handed them to Lantin, who signed a little receipt and with a trembling hand put the money in his pocket.

Then, as he was about to leave the shop, he turned towards the jeweler, who was still smiling, and lowering his eyes said: "I have… I have some other jewels which have come to me from… from the same legacy. Would you care to buy them from me, too?"

The jeweler bowed.

"Certainly, Monsieur."

One of the assistants went out, unable to contain his laughter; another blew his nose loudly. **H**

Lantin, red faced and solemn, remained unmoved.

"I will bring them to you," he said.

And he took a cab to go and fetch the jewels.

When he returned to the shop an hour later he still had had nothing to eat. The jeweler and his assistants began examining the jewels one by one, estimating the value of each piece. Almost all of them had been bought at that shop.

Lantin now began arguing about the valuations, lost his temper, insisted on seeing the sales registers, and spoke more and more loudly as the sum increased.

The large diamond earrings were worth twenty thousand francs, the bracelets thirty-five thousand, the brooches, rings, and lockets sixteen thousand, a set of emeralds and sapphires fourteen thousand, and a solitaire pendant on a gold chain forty thousand—making a total sum of one hundred and ninety-six thousand francs.

The jeweler remarked jokingly: "These obviously belonged to a lady who invested all her savings in jewelry."

Lantin replied seriously: "It's as good a way as any of investing one's money."

And he went off after arranging with the jeweler to have a second expert valuation the next day.

Out in the street he looked at the Vendôme column[5] and felt tempted to climb up it as if it were a greasy pole. He felt light enough to play leapfrog with the statue of the Emperor perched up there in the sky. **I**

He went to Voisin's for lunch and ordered wine with his meal at twenty francs a bottle.

Then he took a cab and went for a drive in the Bois.[6] He looked at the other carriages with a slightly contemptuous air, longing to call out to the passersby: "I'm a rich man, too! I'm worth two hundred thousand francs!" **J**

Suddenly he remembered his Ministry. He drove there at once, strode into his superior's office, and said: "Monsieur, I have come to resign my post. I have just been left three hundred thousand francs."

He shook hands with his former colleagues and told them some of his plans for the future; then he went off to dine at the Café Anglais.

Finding himself next to a distinguished-looking gentleman, he was unable to refrain from informing him, with a certain coyness, that he had just inherited four hundred thousand francs.

For the first time in his life he was not bored at the theater, and he spent the night with some prostitutes.

Six months later he married again. His second wife was a very virtuous woman, but extremely bad-tempered. She made him very unhappy. **K**

5. **Vendôme column:** monument in Paris honoring Napoleon.
6. **Bois:** Bois de Bologne, a park in Paris.

H Reading Focus **Drawing Inferences** What do you infer is the reason the clerks are laughing at Lantin?

I Reading Focus **Drawing Inferences** Lantin and the jeweler both know that Madame Lantin did not save her money to invest in jewelry. Why does Lantin maintain this pretense?

J Literary Focus **Irony** How does Lantin change as he becomes wealthy? What is ironic about the way he feels now?

K Literary Focus **Irony** What is ironic about the description of Lantin's second wife? (Would you expect a virtuous woman to make him unhappy?)

Vocabulary **contemptuous** (kuhn TEHMP choo uhs) *adj.:* scornful.

Think About/Talk About

Comprehension

H Reading Focus

Possible response: *The clerks laugh because Lantin makes it obvious that his wife has been unfaithful not once, but many times.*

I Reading Focus

Possible response: *He maintains the pretense in order to save face; if he does not maintain the pretense, he will have admitted to having an unfaithful wife.*

Analysis

J Literary Focus

Possible response: *He spends money extravagantly, but he does not seem happy about it.*

K Literary Focus

Possible response: *It is ironic that in his second marriage Lantin gets what he wants—a faithful wife, yet he is miserable.*

Vocabulary: Own the Word

- **surreptitiously:** Ask students: "How would you expect someone who was acting *surreptitiously* to behave?" ***Possible responses:*** *sneaky; secretly; furtively; as if he or she was afraid of being caught*
- **contemptuous:** Why did Lantin look at the passersby with a *contemptuous* air? ***Possible response:*** *He wanted to make himself feel superior by looking down on others.*

Monitor Students' Comprehension

Guide the class in answering these comprehension questions.

1. When the story opens, what is Monsieur Lantin's job? [*He is a government clerk.*]
2. What happens a week after Lantin's wife returns from the opera with a cough? [*She dies of pneumonia.*]
3. How does Lantin try to pay his debts? [*He tries to sell his wife's "trash" necklace.*]

California Standards, pp. 1040–1041

- **Reading Standard 2.4** Make warranted and reasonable assertions about the author's arguments by using elements of the text to defend and clarify interpretations.
- **Reading Standard 3.3** Analyze the ways in which irony, tone, mood, the author's style, and the "sound" of language achieve specific rhetorical or aesthetic purposes or both.
- **Grades 9-10 Review Reading Standard 3.7** Recognize and understand the significance of various literary devices, including figurative language, imagery, allegory, and symbolism, and explain their appeal.
- **Writing Standard 1.3** Structure ideas and arguments in a sustained, persuasive, and sophisticated way and support them with precise and relevant examples.
- **Writing Standard 1.9** Revise text to highlight the individual voice, improve sentence variety and style, and enhance subtlety of meaning and tone in ways that are consistent with the purpose, audience, and genre.
- **Writing Standard 2.1** Write fictional, autobiographical, or biographical narratives: **a.** Narrate a sequence of events and communicate their significance to the audience.
- **Writing Standard 2.2** Write responses to literature: **a.** Demonstrate a comprehensive understanding of the significant ideas in works or passages. **c.** Support important ideas and viewpoints through accurate and detailed references to the text and to other works. **e.** Identify and assess the impact of perceived ambiguities, nuances, and complexities within the text.

Check for Understanding

Independent Practice

Reading Skills Focus

Possible responses:

1. *They are quite fond of each other. Lantin's wife makes Lantin's salary stretch to cover little luxuries.*
2. *He cannot figure out how to make ends meet, as his wife had done.*
3. *She seems devoted and virtuous; in reality, she was quite unfaithful.*
4. *Students should detail from their charts the progression from detail to inference. Discuss inferences that turned out to be incorrect.*

Vocabulary Check

5. *b* 6. *c*
7. *d* 8. *e*
9. *a*

Literary Skills Focus

Possible responses:

10. *He is embarrassed to profit from his wife's adultery and ashamed that people will know he is a cuckold.*
11. *Maupassant examines middle-class attempts to climb the social hierarchy by living or pretending to live like the privileged class.*
12. *Maupassant seems to suggest that living a virtuous life does not necessarily lead to happiness.*
13. *Lantin now enjoys the theater. He no longer seems to care about his own virtue and carouses with prostitutes. He marries a virtuous woman but ends up unhappy.*
14. *Ironically, although the jewels are real, they symbolize the falseness and betrayal of Lantin's wife.*

Applying Your Skills

Reading Standard 2.4, 3.3; **Grades 9–10 Review**
Reading Standard 3.7 (see pages A48–A50)
Writing Standard 2.1a (see pages A51–A52)

The Jewels

Literary Response and Analysis

Reading Skills Focus

Quick Check

1. Describe the Lantins' married life, including how they feel about each other and their economic circumstances.
2. How does the death of his wife affect Monsieur Lantin's standard of living?

Read with a Purpose

3. What kind of person does Madame Lantin seem to be? What is she really?

Reading Skills: Drawing Inferences

4. Look back at the inferences you drew while reading the story. Add a circle above each "Inference" circle in your chart. In this circle, revise any inferences that turned out to be incorrect.

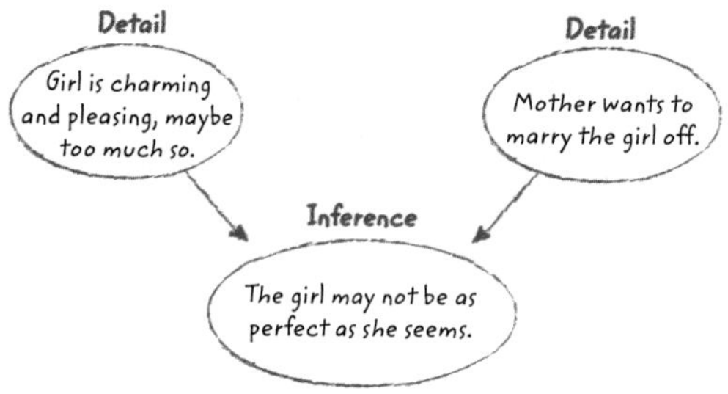

Vocabulary Check

Match each Vocabulary word with its synonym.

5. unpretentious	a. disapproving
6. assuage	b. humble
7. incurred	c. soothe
8. surreptitiously	d. invited
9. contemptuous	e. secretly

Literary Skills Focus

Literary Analysis

10. **Interpret** Why do you think Lantin hesitates to accept the eighteen thousand francs?
11. **Extend** Maupassant used fiction to examine social issues. With what particular problem does "The Jewels" deal?
12. **Draw Conclusions** What does Maupassant suggest about the connection between virtue and happiness?

Literary Skills: Irony

13. **Analyze** Re-read the last two paragraphs of the story. What is ironic about how Lantin changes after he sells the jewels?

Literary Skills Review: Symbol

14. **Evaluate** A **symbol** is a person, place, or thing that has meaning in itself and also stands for something else. What do the jewels symbolize in this story?

Writing Skills Focus

Think as a Reader/Writer

Use It in Your Writing Using the realistic dialogue from "The Jewels" as a model, write at least six lines of realistic dialogue on your own.

What Do You Think Now? Why might Lantin find it preferable to assume the jewels are fake? What does his decision later to sell the jewels suggest about his values?

Universal Access

Struggling Writers

Students may need additional scaffolding to complete the Writing Skills Focus activity. Have students analyze Maupassant's use of dialogue in "The Jewels." Tell students that the dialogue in the selection is realistic because it sounds like conversations that people engage in every day. Encourage students to recall a conversation that they have had with a friend, family member, or acquaintance. Have students write an excerpt from this conversation. Tell students to try to write what was actually said during the conversation to make the dialogue as realistic as possible.

What Do You Think Now?

Have students consider which feelings moved Lantin to action in different moments of the story.

COMPARING TEXTS
Wrap Up

Writing Standard 1.3, 1.9, 2.2a, 2.2c, 2.2e (see pages A51–A52)

World Literature: Realism and the Short Story

Writing Skills Focus

Write a Comparison-Contrast Essay

In what ways are these three short stories similar and different? Consider how these works exhibit some of the characteristics of realism: the use of characters from ordinary life; an unflinching look at how changes in society affect ordinary people; an examination of the motivations of human behavior; a realistic—even ironic—view of human life. Re-read the selections to determine specific points of similarity and difference.

Prewriting

Consider the following topics or develop your own:

- Compare and contrast the desires of and lessons learned by the main characters in the stories.
- Compare the use of irony in the stories.
- Compare and contrast the writers' views of life.
- Compare and contrast the ways the stories contrast appearances with reality.
- Compare and contrast themes.

Review the Elements of the Writing Form Once you have chosen a topic, review the elements of what makes a successful comparison-contrast essay before you begin.

An effective comparison-contrast essay

- states the basis of the comparison-contrast in a thesis
- organizes ideas, using the point-by-point method
- uses and cites text evidence to support each point of comparison and contrast
- contains few or no errors in spelling, punctuation, and usage

Gather Ideas Create a three-column chart like the one on the right to record your thoughts about each story. Look for patterns of similarities and differences.

"How Much Land . . . ?"	"The Bet"	"The Jewels"
Pahom and devil—owning land debt free	lawyer and banker bet	clerk marries beautiful but poor woman
greed; could not stop	two million	discovers jewelry was real; she was not
irony: greed leads to death	irony: renounces and disappears	irony: wife deceived husband

Develop a Thesis Statement Using your notes and observations, develop a thesis that makes an assertion about the similarities and differences in the selections. Use a basis of similarity (such as ironic conclusions), and then focus on the differences in the three selections. Sample thesis:

The ironic endings of the three stories emphasize their realism, but the main characters have very different motives for their actions.

Drafting

Because you are using the point-by-point method of organization, begin with the strongest comparison linking the three stories. Develop it in your first body paragraph. Then, depending on your analysis, your next body paragraphs will develop either additional similarities or differences. Your final body paragraph will focus on the differences.

Revising and Editing

Re-read your draft to determine if you have fully supported your thesis with explanation and text evidence. Then read for grammatical, mechanics, and usage errors. Prepare a final copy that is error-free. Publish.

What Do You Think Now? How does reality interfere with our expectations of how life should be?

Universal Access

Struggling Writers

Students may need additional scaffolding to complete the Writing Skills Focus activity. These stories develop many complex themes that may pose difficulties for some students. To simplify the activity, have students write a comparison-contrast essay examining the obvious theme of wealth in the three selections. They can start by noting that the main characters all undergo a change in financial status.

Independent Practice

What Do You Think Now?

To help students answer this question, have students identify some instances in which a person or a situation turned out to be the opposite of what he, she, or it seemed to be. Then have students discuss how that surprising knowledge affected them.

Assess

Unit 5 Resources, Selection Standards Check, pp. 80, 86, 92

ThinkCentral Online Assessment, Selection Standards Check

Teacher One Stop™, editable Selection Standards Check

Reteach

To reteach **theme,** see **Reteaching Lessons,** pp. 1449M–1449N.

ThinkCentral Online Remediation

Standards Focus

Objectives

Students will

- learn prewriting, drafting, and revising techniques for writing a fictional narrative
- proofread and publish their work

Preteach

Write with a Purpose Read aloud the essentials of a good fictional narrative to guide students' understanding of this type of writing. Also, refer students to the scoring guide on p. 1050 for more information on fictional narratives that they can use throughout the workshop.

Direct Teach

Model the Skill

Think as a Reader/Writer Use the professional model on this page and others in the unit to provide examples of the elements of a good fictional narrative. Point out how the Desai model uses dialogue and other details to describe the characters instead of using explicit descriptions.

Think About the Model

Possible responses:

1. *The narrative is set somewhere with a warm climate. This is clear because the author describes the intense effects of the heat.*
2. *The characters want to play outdoors, but their mother will not allow them because it is too hot.*

Writing Workshop

Fictional Narrative

Write with a Purpose

Write a fictional narrative with a plot, setting, and characters of your creation. Your **purpose** for writing is to entertain readers and communicate the significance of the events. Because your **audience** includes your teacher and classmates, make sure your narrative avoids content that is inappropriate for a school setting.

A Good Fictional Narrative

- Narrates a sequence of events and communicates their significance to the audience
- Locates scenes and incidents in specific places
- Describes with sensory details the scene and specific actions and feelings of characters
- Uses interior monologue to depict characters' feelings
- Paces the presentation of actions to accommodate mood changes
- Uses descriptions, images, perspectives and sensory details effectively

See page 1050 for complete scoring guide.

Reader/Writer Notebook

Use your **RWN** to complete the activities for this workshop.

Think as a Reader/Writer

In this workshop, you will share your insight, imagination, and experience in a **fictional narrative.** Before you begin writing, take a few minutes to read the following excerpt from "Games at Twilight" by Anita Desai (page 1416).

It was still too hot to play outdoors. They had had their tea, they had been washed and had their hair brushed, and after the long day of confinement in the house that was not cool but at least a protection from the sun, the children strained to get out. Their faces were red and bloated with the effort, but their mother would not open the door, everything was still curtained and shuttered in a way that stifled the children, made them feel that their lungs were stuffed with cotton wool and their noses with dust and if they didn't burst out into the light and see the sun and feel the air, they would choke.

← Desai introduces the **characters** and begins to describe the **setting.**

"Please, ma, please," they begged. "We'll play on the veranda and porch—we won't go a step out of the porch."

← **Dialogue** adds to the plot and characterization.

"You will, I know you will, and then—"

"No—we won't, we won't," they wailed so horrendously that she actually let down the bolt of the front door so that they burst out like seeds from a crackling, overripe pod into the veranda, with such wild, maniacal yells that she retreated to her bath and the shower of talcum powder and the fresh sari that were to help her face the summer evening.

← She uses the words *horrendously* and *maniacal* to set the story's **mood.**

They faced the afternoon. It was too hot. Too bright. The white walls of the veranda glared stridently in the sun. The bougainvillea hung about it, purple and magenta, in livid balloons. The garden outside was like a tray made of beaten brass, flattened out on the red gravel and the stony soil in all shade of metal—aluminum, tin, copper, and brass.

← She helps readers visualize the **scene** through **figurative language** and **descriptive details.**

Think About the Professional Model

With a partner, discuss the following questions about the model:

1. Where is the narrative set? What sensory details tell you about the setting?
2. What problem do the characters in the excerpt face?

California Standards, pp. 1042–1050

- **Writing Standard 1.2** Use point of view, characterization, style (e.g., use of irony) and related elements for specific rhetorical and aesthetic purposes.
- **Writing Standard 1.9** Revise text to highlight the individual voice, improve sentence variety and style, and enhance subtlety of meaning and tone in ways that are consistent with the purpose, audience, and genre.
- **Writing Standard 2.1** Write fictional, autobiographical, or biographical narratives: **a.** Narrate a sequence of events and communicate their significance to the audience. **b.** Locate scenes and incidents in specific places. **c.** Describe with concrete sensory detail the specific actions, movements, gestures, and feelings of characters; use interior monologue to depict the characters' feelings. **d.** Pace the presentation of actions to accommodate temporal, spatial, and dramatic mood changes. **e.** Make effective use of description of appearance, images, shifting perspectives, and sensory details.

Writing Workshop Resources

UA: Holt Interactive Writer and Speaker, practice and assessment, p. 91

UA: Differentiating Instruction, modified lesson plans, p. 245

Writing Notes, interactive lesson presentations with activities

GrammarNotes, interactive lesson presentations with activities

Writing and Research in a Digital Age, interactive lesson presentations with activities

Writing Standard 1.2, 1.9, 2.1a–e (see pages A51–A52)
Language Conventions Standard 1.1, 1.2, 1.3 (see page A53)

Prewriting

Imagine a Story

Begin creating your fictional narrative by imagining a sequence of events that occur in scenes in specific places. Use the following questions to guide your brainstorming:

- Who are the **characters**? What do they look and act like? What are their feelings about the events as they unfold?
- Where and when do the **incidents** and **scenes** occur?
- What is the **conflict** that advances the action of the plot?
- What is **significant** about this sequence of events?

Identify Your Characters

Your narrative's characters become believable as you describe their actions, movements, gestures, and feelings, in addition to their appearance, with specific, sensory details. The **motivation,** or reasons *why* the characters act, is critical. Depending on the point of view you use for the fictional narrative, you can reveal characters' motivations through the narrator, dialogue, or interior monologue. In the student model that follows, "Buttons," the limited-omniscient narrator allows us to know why Mary wants a new coat so desperately:

And every year she pulled out the same faded red jacket, worn thin from years of hand-me-downing and cold . . . , wishing immensely that it were a new tweed blazer or the handsome peacoat. . . .

These insights help the author lead the audience to fully understand the **significance** of the narrative events.

Define Your Conflict

There are two main types of conflict: **internal** and **external.** Use the flowchart below to decide what kind of conflict will drive your narrative.

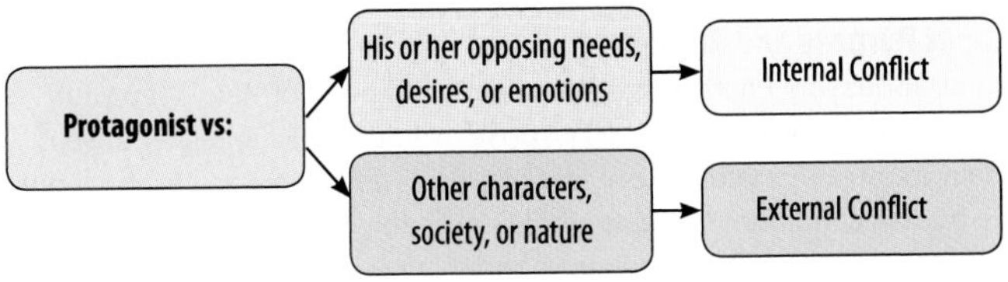

In the excerpt from "Games at Twilight," one external conflict is the children's desires versus their mother's wishes. Complex stories usually have more than one conflict, plus a mixture of internal and external conflicts.

Idea Starters

- Base characters on people you know. Be sure to change their names and some other details.
- Choose a setting based on places you have visited, read about, or seen on TV or in movies.
- Get plot ideas from real-life incidents (your own, those of people you know, or ones you have heard about).

Your Turn

Get Started Taking notes in your **RWN,** answer the questions on this page to determine the basic elements of your story. Then, analyze your characters and define your narrative's conflict.

Learn It Online

To see how one writer completed this assignment, see the model short story online.

go.hrw.com H12-1043 Go

Teacher One Stop™, on-level lesson plans and all print resources

Holt Six Traits for Writing, rubrics, prompts, and sample papers

Language and Sentence Skills Practice,

UA: Developmental Language and Sentence Practice

Language Handbook Worksheets, p. 113

Formal Assessment, Progress Monitoring Test 4

ThinkCentral Online Assessment, Writing Workshop Test

ThinkCentral Online Remediation

Holt Online Essay Scoring

Guided Practice: Apply

Imagine a Story

- Have students sit and write whatever comes into their heads for five minutes without worrying about grammar or structure.
- Give students a choice of writing prompts to help them get started. Possibilities include "It all started when . . ."; "I'll never forget the time . . . ," and "They couldn't believe the way. . . ."

Identify Your Characters

Have students create an individual profile for each character in their narratives. Have students include several characteristics—names, ages, appearances, and motivations—as well as defining physical features or gestures. Students may also choose to draw a picture of each character to include in the character's profile.

Your Turn

Get Started Give students a few minutes of silence to think before they begin brainstorming. Tell them to give themselves plenty of space to answer each bulleted question. If they think of an answer to one question while they are working on another, encourage them to move on to the question they feel more comfortable with.

Learn It Online

Interactive Writer's Models on the Interactive Student Edition provide annotated sample essays along with writing tips and strategies.

go.hrw.com H12-1043 Go

Guided Practice: Apply

Plot Your Narrative

- Inform students that unlike the sprawling plot of a novel, the plot of their narratives will have to be compressed into a few pages. Suggest that students include only events that are significant to the progression of their plots.
- Encourage students to be as specific as possible when developing their plot plans.

Choose a Point of View

- Inform students that an omniscient narrator's point of view can relate a story from shifting perspectives; that is, the narrator can tell how two or more characters perceive the same events.
- Suggest that students write a few sentences about one event in their narratives from three different points of view. Students should then compare each writing sample and decide which point of view works best for their narratives.

Your Turn

Plan Your Narrative Have students complete the **Your Turn**, first working alone and then comparing plot plans with a partner. Encourage students to create several plot plans for different ideas and then assess which ideas will make the most interesting stories.

Writing Tips

- All the events in your narrative should help move the plot forward. Events not closely related to the plot may confuse readers and cause them to lose interest.
- Your narrative's plot should generate **suspense**—a feeling of uncertainty and curiosity about what will happen next.

Plot Your Narrative

Unfold the narrative events in your story chronologically, or in time order. A classic plot structure begins with the **exposition,** which introduces the characters and conflict; moves through **complications,** which arise as characters attempt to resolve the conflict; builds toward the **climax,** the moment when the conflict's outcome is imminent; and ends with the **resolution,** or **denouement,** when the problems are resolved and the narrative ends. To outline your plot, write a **plot plan** like this one, created by the writer of the student model (pages 1047–1048).

Plot Plan

Exposition	Mary attends a school in which new clothes are a status symbol. She is snubbed each year by her classmates because she is too poor to afford a new coat.
Complications	Mary sews buttons on her old coat to make it look new and fashionable. She imagines the next day at school.
Climax	Mary wears her coat to school expecting that her classmates will admire it.
Resolution/ Denouement	Frustrated and angry because of her classmates' rejection, Mary breaks down, screaming, and tears the buttons off her coat.

Choose a Point of View

Now you must choose the point of view from which your story's **narrator** will tell the story. Use the following chart to choose a point of view:

Omniscient Narrator	all-knowing and outside the action; can tell readers the thoughts and feelings of all the characters; uses third-person pronouns, such as *he, she,* and *they.*
First-Person Narrator	witness of or participant in the story; can tell only what he or she knows, thinks, or feels; uses first-person pronouns such as *I* and *we.*
Third-Person-Limited Narrator	outside of the action, but not all knowing; focuses on the thoughts and feelings of one character; uses third-person pronouns, such as *he, she,* and *they.*

Think About Purpose and Audience

As you think about your characters, setting, plot, and point of view, keep your **purpose** and **audience** in mind. Your **purpose** in writing a fictional narrative is to entertain your readers with a story that expresses a **theme**—an insight about life or the human condition. Your **audience** is probably your classmates and your teacher or other individuals who enjoy a good story.

- Will they care about your characters and the conflict they face?
- Will they identify with the events of the plot?
- Will the resolution give them insight into the significance of the events?

Your Turn

Plan Your Narrative Use the chart on this page to make a **plot plan** of your narrative. Share your chart with a peer, and consider the feedback he or she provides. Revise your plot as needed, keeping in mind your **purpose** and **audience.**

Fictional Narrative Writing Prompts

Students can choose their own fictional narrative idea or use one of the following prompts to write a fictional narrative.

World Languages Write a narrative about someone making a transition to a new country and the obstacles he or she encounters while learning a new language and customs.

History Write a fictional narrative that takes place in a historical period that you have studied. Show how the events of the time period affect the main character.

Physical Education Create a narrative about a fictional character who has to overcome a physical disability in order to succeed in a sport.

Drafting

Draft Your Fictional Narrative

Use your prewriting notes, **plot plan,** and the **Writer's Framework** to the right to begin writing your fictional narrative.

Framework for Fictional Narrative

Beginning
- Describe setting.
- Introduce characters and establish point of view.
- Set the plot in motion with the conflict.

Middle
- Develop characters through actions, dialogue, description, and sensory details.
- Introduce complications.

End
- Build suspense or plot intensity to the climax.
- Resolve the conflict.
- Reveal the final outcome.
- Make the significance clear to readers.

Use Dialogue

Your characters should speak, using realistic dialogue, for two purposes:

- to advance the action of the plot
- to reveal characters' personalities, motivations, and feelings

Start a new paragraph every time the speaker changes, and use quotation marks to enclose each speaker's words.

Create Mood

Your narrative's **mood,** or **atmosphere,** is the overall emotion it creates, such as peaceful, festive, ominous, or playful. Mood is created through your choice of words and details. For instance, in the following sentence from the student model, the words *faded, worn thin,* and *coffin* create a sad, bleak mood:

And every year she pulled out the same faded red jacket, worn thin from years of hand-me-downing and cold, from its cardboard coffin . . . .

Dialogue can help set the mood, by using the natural rhythm of spoken language, including the use of **contractions.**

Grammar Link Using Contractions with Dialogue

While **contractions** are not usually acceptable in formal writing, such as a research paper, you can use contractions in fictional narratives to help with characterization and mood. If you are wondering whether to use a contraction, ask yourself whether the separated words sound stilted. If they do, replace them with a contraction. Look at these examples from "Games at Twilight" (page 1042):

> "Please, ma, please," they begged. "We'll play on the veranda and porch—we won't go a step out of the porch."
>
> "You will, I know you will, and then—"
>
> "No—we won't, we won't," they wailed. . . . "

The author, Desai, uses the contraction *we'll* instead of *we will* and *won't* instead of *will not* in order to replicate authentic speech for the dialogue and create an informal mood in her story.

Writing Tip

To make the people, places, and things in your story come alive for the reader, use **sensory details** that appeal to sight, hearing, smell, touch, and taste as well as **figurative language,** such as simile and metaphor.

Your Turn

Write Your Draft Use your **plot plan** and the **Writer's Framework** to write a draft of your fictional narrative. As you write, ask yourself,

- Where can I use **dialogue** to enhance my narrative?
- Will **contractions** make the dialogue more realistic?
- What **mood** do I want to convey in my narrative?

Guided Practice: Apply

Use Dialogue

Have students note examples of the way Desai used dialogue and think about how to use it in their own writing. Have them consider the following questions: What do I want readers to know about my characters? How do I need to advance the plot? How can I use dialogue to create settings? Remind students that dialogue in short writings can decrease the need for long descriptions. Good dialogue helps the reader infer information about the characters and the action.

Create Mood

Remind students that words with similar denotations can have very different connotations. Suggest that students always consider the connotation of their words and replace any words that have connotations that conflict with the mood of the narrative.

Grammar Link

For practice, have students underline places where contractions could be used and write in the contractions if they believe they are appropriate.

1. I do not want to leave yet. [*do not; don't*]
2. I bet she is. [*she is; contraction is not appropriate*]
3. He will help you with that. [*He will; He'll*]

Warriner's Handbook, Sixth Course, p. 378

Your Turn

Write Your Draft Ask students to complete the **Your Turn** as independent practice. Remind students to use their plot plan as they begin writing. Suggest that students use every other line as they write their drafts so they can more easily revise the drafts later. If they are using a computer, explain to students how to use double spacing.

Universal Access

EL English Learners

English for Academic Success Help students understand how to develop a plot by giving them simple definitions of the elements in a plot structure.

- **exposition**—introduction of background information
- **complications**—events that have bad results
- **climax**—the most exciting or important part of a story
- **resolution**—the event that solves the story's conflict
- **denouement**—the point in which parts of a plot come together and matters are made clear

AAVE Students Who Use African American Vernacular English

English for Academic Success Some students may struggle to pronounce end consonants in contractions. Tell students that when speaking in a setting that requires formal English, it is important to enunciate the *t* sound on the end of a contraction. Model pronouncing *won't* and *doesn't*. Then, have partners practice saying the following consonants aloud, with one partner speaking while the other listens for the *t* sound: *can't, don't, hasn't, musn't.*

Model the Skill

- Using a student draft on a transparency, model how to use the questions, tips, and revision techniques suggested in the chart. You might use a student's fictional narrative or a fictional narrative of your own creation to evaluate and revise using the steps in the chart.
- Ask volunteers to explain how they used each of the steps in the chart in their own fictional narratives.

Peer Review

If possible, allow students to find a quiet place to meet with their partners; you might send some of them to work in the hallway to reduce the noise level in the room and make it easier for them to concentrate on each other's papers.

Holt Six Traits for Writing, rubrics, prompts, and sample papers

Peer Review

Ask a peer to read your fictional narrative, evaluating it by using the chart to the right. Then, ask the following questions to find out how well you communicated your ideas:

- Did the characters seem real?
- Did you care about the conflict?
- Was the resolution satisfying?

Use peer feedback to improve your narrative.

Evaluating and Revising

Evaluating and revising your draft are essential steps in producing a fictional narrative. Examine your characterization, descriptions, and plot to make your narrative the best it can be. The chart below will help you evaluate and revise your draft. With a partner, begin on the left side of the chart, and work through each revision question, tip, and suggestion.

Fictional Narrative: Guidelines for Content and Organization

Evaluation Question	Tip	Revision Technique
1. Do the first few paragraphs introduce the setting, characters, and conflict?	**Circle** facts about characters. **Bracket** information about the conflict. **Underline** facts about the setting.	**Add** descriptions of characters or setting or a hint about the conflict.
2. Does the narrative maintain a consistent point of view?	**Highlight** all pronouns referring to characters and make sure they are in the same person.	**Replace** pronouns as needed for consistency.
3. Do all the events move the plot forward?	**Number** each event. In the margin, write a corresponding note explaining how the event relates to the plot.	**Cut** events that are not essential to the plot.
4. Is dialogue used appropriately to advance the story's plot and to reveal character?	**Put a star** beside any dialogue.	**Add** dialogue that reveals character or forwards the plot. **Replace** unnecessary dialogue with a paraphrase.
5. Does the narrative create a consistent mood?	**Circle** words and details that create mood.	**Add** language and details that evoke the mood you are trying to achieve.
6. Does the resolution clearly reveal the significance of the events?	**Underline** the sentences that comment on or reveal the significance.	**Add** sentences that comment on the significance of events.

Real Issues, Real Experts

Holt Professional Learning for Language Arts

To watch videos on teaching **revision, grammar,** and **on-demand writing skills** featuring Linda Rief, Amy Benjamin, and Leila Christenbury, go to this page in **ThinkCentral, Teacher Access.**

Universal Access

Struggling Writers

Strategic Students Give students examples of how interior monologue can be used with various points of view.

Omniscient narrator: As Claire prepared to jump from the plane, she thought, "I can't believe I'm doing this." Meanwhile, Max reluctantly watched from the ground and figured, "She's not going to go through with it."

First-person narrator: I heard the skydive instructor begin counting down from five, and I thought to myself, "There's no going back now."

Read this student's draft; note the comments on its structure and suggestions for how it could be made even stronger.

Student Draft

Buttons

by Tawnee Cunningham, Kane Area Senior High School

It was getting colder; everyone had new coats. Coats appeared with shiny buttons, gleaming like pebbles in a stream, wool thick and as soft as a cloud. Everyone but her. It was like that every year. The others in her class wore new sweaters and mittens, some the latest hat or skirt, showing off what they could afford and flaunting what she couldn't. And every year she pulled out the same faded red jacket, worn thin from years of hand-me-downing and cold, from its cardboard coffin, wishing immensely that it were a new tweed blazer or the handsome peacoat she'd seen in the window of a department store uptown. And every year she endured the snubbing and repulsed looks of her peers, ignoring the stares at the frayed edges and the too-short sleeves.

← Tawnee introduces the **protagonist** and **conflict.**

← She uses vivid **sensory details** to describe the shabby coat.

This year would be no different. The style of choice this fall was fancy buttons, at the seams, on the lapels; anywhere one could sew a button. Walking past the variety store, she suddenly had an idea. Into the little shop she went, searching her pockets for loose change. The bell over the door rang with happy thoughts of acceptance and contentment.

← The main character finds a possible solution to her problem.

MINI-LESSON **How to Add Interior Monologue**

One way to help readers understand characters' motivation is to use **interior monologue**—characters' unspoken internal flow of thoughts and feelings. In her draft, Tawnee doesn't tell what the girl is thinking when she goes into the variety store. The addition of interior monologue makes her motivation clearer. The revision allows the reader to "hear" her thoughts.

Tawnee's Revision of Paragraph 2

This year would be no different. The style of choice this fall was fancy buttons, at the seams, on the lapels; anywhere one could sew a button. Walking past the variety store, she suddenly had an idea. ^"Buttons cost little. What can it hurt? Just a few additions to my coat could save me from another season of torture."

Into the little shop she went, searching her pockets for loose change. The bell over the door rang with happy thoughts of acceptance and contentment.

Your Turn

Add Interior Monologue Reread your draft to find places where you could clarify characters' motivations by adding interior monologue. Ask yourself:

- Is it clear why the characters do what they do?
- Can readers tell what the characters think and feel about the events of the plot?

Third-person limited narrator: Claire couldn't stop telling herself, "This is amazing!" after she pulled open her parachute. As she got closer to the ground, she could see the shocked look on Max's face.

✔ See **UA: Differentiating Instruction** for strategies for teaching struggling writers.

Students with Disabilities

Help students understand the difference between dialogue and interior monologue by showing them a section of a comic strip or graphic novel that has both dialogue bubbles and thought bubbles. Inform students that thought bubbles, like interior monologue, give information that only the reader and the character generating the thought know.

Guided Practice: Apply

Student Draft

Explain that the Student Draft on this page is the first half of a fictional narrative written by the student whose plot plan appeared on p. 1044. Model reading the draft and the annotations in blue, and explain that the yellow highlighting illustrates the student's language choices. Explain that a mini-lesson follows with helpful information about ways to improve this draft as well as their own.

Mini-Lesson

How to Add Interior Monologue

- Explain that the student writer has revised her story by adding interior monologue to show what the main character is thinking.
- Remind students to use interior monologue in their narratives to show what the events of the narrative make the main character think and feel.

Your Turn

Add Interior Monologue As students complete the **Your Turn,** tell them to find two places in their drafts where interior monologue could be added. The monologue may show why the characters do what they do or just show how events make them feel. Remind students to use the **Grammar Link** on p. 1045 to help them decide when and how to add contractions.

Guided Practice: Apply

Student Draft

- Explain that the Student Draft is continued and completed on this page. Again, the draft is annotated and highlighted for the students.
- Read the draft and annotations aloud and discuss. Refer students to the plot plan on p. 1044. Ask students to comment on the student's success with applying the plot plan to the narrative "Buttons."

Mini-Lesson

How to Clarify Transitions

- Tell students to make sure their fictional narratives contain transitional phrases, as professional stories usually do. Explain that by including transitions, they help changes in setting or points of view make better sense to the reader.
- Point out that adding a transitional phrase can help get readers into the appropriate mood for a new scene.

Your Turn

Clarify Transitions As students work to complete the **Your Turn**, have them think about where they need transitional phrases and what phrases they should add. The transitions might be a few words labeling a new setting or a few sentences giving suitable imagery.

Student Draft *continues*

Tawnee details the **character's thoughts** as she replaces the old buttons. →

Finally at home, she brought out the little cedar box she kept her needlework in. Carefully, she removed the tarnished buttons from their thread bindings. In each place, she attached a new one, blue and twisted in a little centipede pattern. As she sewed, she heard the compliments she would receive the next day. They would greet her as she removed her jacket, begging to know where she'd gotten such a beautiful coat. She would just smile modestly and shrug, she imagined, and accept their invitations to sit with them during lunch. That night, she could barely sleep for the excitement of it all.

She moves the conflict toward its resolution. →

She set off to the school, her head held high. The others crowded around the door, talking and gossiping, conversations whispered behind hands in expensive leather gloves. No one noticed her. It didn't matter, she knew they would.

The **denouement**, or **resolution**, is achieved. →

She uses **figurative language** to emphasize the loss of the buttons. →

But there were no shared lunches—only sarcasm and disdain. Mary Green started screaming and would not stop. When her parents finally came for her, they asked why her coat was ripped and torn. The answer lay on the sidewalk, splayed about like dropped pennies, the buttons she'd sewed the night before, glinting in the sun like round, azure tears.

MINI-LESSON How to Clarify Transitions

Tawnee's draft does not always provide sufficient **transitions**—words, phrases, and sentences that provide a smooth flow from one idea to the next. Her readers can get lost when Tawnee abruptly changes setting. Between paragraphs 3 and 4, she decided to add some transitional information to indicate that the events of paragraph 4 occur the next day. She also adds some imagery that shows the change in setting and allows the reader insight into the character's thinking.

Tawnee's Draft of Paragraphs 3 and 4

That night, she could barely sleep for the excitement of it all.
She set off to the school, her head held high.

Tawnee's Revision of Paragraph 4

That night, she could barely sleep for the excitement of it all.
She set off to the school, her head held high.

The next morning, the ground sparkled with a layer of white frost, making the flowers shiver in protest. It was a perfect time to debut her new jacket.

Your Turn

Clarify Transitions Look through your draft for places where transitions would be useful. Pay close attention to transitions between paragraphs, and make sure the reader can tell

- *where* the action is happening
- *when* the action is happening
- and *what* the characters think and feel about the actions

Universal Access

English Learners

English for Academic Success Remind students that transitions help writers organize their writing chronologically and help readers understand the chain of events in a story. Provide students with a list of transitional words and phrases. Examples might include *finally, then, after that, later,* and *next.* Tell students to use these words to link the events in their story and to ensure that the reader knows the order in which they happened.

Struggling Writers

Give students examples of transitional phrases that help explain a change in time or setting in a narrative.

- Now that the sun had set . . .
- As her alarm clock blared to awaken her, . . .
- Across town, the local news station was buzzing about the report.
- Over the next few months, the cold, crisp air blew in and covered the green pastures with a bed of snow.

Proofreading and Publishing

Proofread

Errors can distract readers from your story and ruin its effect. Follow these tips to **proofread,** or **edit,** your fictional narrative:

- Consult a style manual to answer questions of grammar, usage, and mechanics. Review the section on punctuating dialogue.
- Start proofreading at the end of your narrative and work your way back to the beginning, checking the spelling of each word.
- Look at each sentence to make sure that it contains a subject and a verb and that it expresses a single, complete thought. If a sentence contains two or more complete thoughts running together with only a comma between them, then you have a **comma splice,** which should be corrected.

Grammar Link Avoiding Comma Splices

In her draft, Tawnee includes a **comma splice**—a run-on sentence in which only a comma separates two independent clauses. One quick fix for a comma splice is to replace the comma with a semicolon.

Tawnee's Revision

It didn't matter; she knew they would.

You can also correct comma splices by adding a coordinating conjunction (such as *and, but, for, nor, or, so,* and *yet*) after the comma or by turning each independent clause into a separate sentence.

Publishing

You've worked hard to write an interesting, insightful fictional narrative. Try these ideas for sharing your piece with an audience outside your classroom:

- Submit your fictional narrative to a print or online literary magazine.
- Host a fiction reading at which you and your peers can read your work out loud to an audience.
- Use desktop publishing software to improve your narrative's **presentation**—how it actually looks on the page. Print, then bind it in a folder, and give it to a friend or family member as a gift.

Reflect on the Process Thinking about the process of writing your fictional narrative will help you with your future writing. Write a short response to each of these questions in your **RWN:**

1. What prewriting technique helped you the most?
2. What is the strongest part of your fictional narrative? Why?

Proofreading Tip

Use your intuition when proofreading. When something in your draft seems wrong, stop and examine it carefully before you move on. If you cannot find the problem, ask your teacher or a peer to help.

Writing Tip

To find comma splices, highlight every comma in your draft. For each one found, ask these questions:

- Does the comma come between two independent clauses that could stand on their own as separate sentences?
- If so, is the comma followed by a coordinating conjunction, such as *and* or *but?*

Your Turn

Proofread and Publish As you proofread your draft, check carefully for **comma splices** and other sentence flaws. After correcting any errors, publish your narrative.

Guided Practice: Apply

Proofreading

Integrating with Grammar, Usage, and Mechanics If students make errors using contractions and commas as they are proofreading, send them to the Punctuation chapters in **Warriner's Handbook.**

Grammar Link

- Tell students to circle all the commas in their fictional narratives.
- If students come across a comma splice in their narratives, tell them to separate the two independent clauses with a semicolon or a period.

Publishing

Brainstorm with students additional ways to publish their fictional narratives.

Reflect on the Process

Have students reflect on their writing process as well as their final product. Challenge them to reflect metacognitively about how they can improve and apply what they have learned.

Your Turn

Proofread and Publish Have students highlight or underline the revisions and submit their drafts with their final fictional narratives so that they can check they are following the revision guidelines on p. 1046.

Advanced Learners

Acceleration Challenge students to create a transition that can answer the *where, when,* and *what* questions from the **Your Turn** in as few sentences as possible. Encourage students to combine some of this information so their transitions are smooth and not broken-up bits of information.

Students with Disabilities

Have students write transitions directly into their outlines using a different color ink or pencil from the original outline. They should ask themselves if each transition relates to the paragraph before it as well as the paragraph after it.

✔ See **UA: Differentiating Instruction** for strategies for teaching students with disabilities.

Guided Practice

Scoring Guide

- Tell students that the best way to understand scoring guides is to use them to score actual writing.
- Have students use the scoring guide to evaluate the final copy of the fictional narratives they wrote in the Writing Workshop. Ask students to score their narratives, then write a brief paragraph using the language of the scoring guide to explain the reasons for their score.

Holt Six Traits for Writing, rubrics, prompts, and sample papers

Assess

UA: Holt Interactive Writer and Speaker, Fictional Narrative analytical scales and rubrics, p. 91

ThinkCentral Online Assessment, Writing Workshop Test

Teacher One Stop™, editable Writing Workshop Test

Reteach

ThinkCentral Online Remediation

Scoring Guide

Use the scoring guide below to evaluate your fictional narrative from the Writing Workshop or your response to the on-demand prompt on the next page.

	Fictional Narrative	Organization and Focus	Sentence Structure and Vocabulary	Language Conventions
4	• develops a *meaningful* story that is responsive to the writing task.	• *thoroughly* develops both the story and its characters with *specific* details and examples. • demonstrates a *clear* sense of audience. • demonstrates a *consistent* tone and focus, and illustrates a *purposeful* control of pacing and organization.	• provides a *variety of* sentence types and uses *precise, descriptive* language.	• contains *few, if any, errors* in the conventions of the English language. (Errors are generally first-draft in nature.)
3	• develops a story that is responsive to the writing task.	• develops the story and its characters with details and examples. • demonstrates a *general* sense of audience. • demonstrates a consistent tone and focus; and illustrates a control of pacing and organization.	• provides a *variety of* sentence types and uses *some descriptive* language.	• may contain *some errors* in the conventions of the English language. (Errors do *not* interfere with the reader's understanding of the essay.)
2	• develops a story that is related to the writing task.	• develops the story and its characters with *limited* details and/or examples. • demonstrates *little* or *no* sense of audience. • demonstrates an inconsistent tone and focus; and illustrates *little, if any* control of packing and organization.	• provides *few, if any,* types of sentence types, and basic, predictable language.	• may contain *several errors* in the conventions of the English language. (Errors *may* interfere with the reader's understanding of the essay.)
1	• *may* develop a *weak* story that is related to the writing task.	• *fails* to develop the story or its characters with details and/or examples. • may demonstrate *no* sense of audience. • demonstrates a *lack* of tone and focus; and illustrates *no* control of pacing or organization.	• may provide *no* sentence variety and uses limited vocabulary.	• may contain *serious errors* in the conventions of the English language. (Errors interfere with the reader's understanding of the essay.)

California Standards, pp. 1050–1051

- **Writing Standard 1.2** Use point of view, characterization, style (e.g., use of irony), and related elements for specific rhetorical and aesthetic purposes.
- **Writing Standard 1.9** Revise text to highlight the individual voice, improve sentence variety and style, and enhance subtlety of meaning and tone in ways that are consistent with the purpose, audience, and genre.
- **Writing Standard 2.1** Write fictional, autobiographical, or biographical narratives: **a.** Narrate a sequence of events and communicate their significance to the audience. **b.** Locate scenes and incidents in specific places. **c.** Describe with concrete sensory detail the specific actions, movements, gestures, and feelings of characters; use interior monologue to depict the characters' feelings. **d.** Pace the presentation of actions to accommodate temporal, spatial, and dramatic mood changes. **e.** Make effective use of description of appearance, images, shifting perspectives, and sensory details.

Fictional Narrative Writing Prompts

Students can use the writing prompt in the Student Edition or one of the following prompts.

- Ask students to write a fictional narrative about an event that requires a character to show courage.
- Suggest to students that they write about a character who gets something he or she has always wanted and discovers that it is not what he or she expected.
- Suggest that students write a story about a character who experiences something he or she has dreaded.

Preparing for Timed Writing

Fictional Narrative

Writing Standard 1.2, 1.9, 2.1a–e (see pages A51–A52)

When responding to a prompt, use what you have learned from reading, writing your fictional narrative, and studying the scoring guide on page 1050. Use the steps below to develop a response to the following prompt:

Writing Prompt
Write a fictional narrative about a time when freedom was won or lost. In your story, create a setting, conflict, and events that illustrate the gain or loss of freedom.

Study the Prompt
Begin by reading the prompt carefully. Read it a second time, circling or underlining words that identify important information: *time, freedom, won, lost, setting, conflict,* and *events.*

Because this task requires a narrative structure, you must create characters to respond to the **conflict** (for freedom) in a distinct setting (time and place). You must decide what kind of freedom your characters will win or lose and how that happens. **Tip:** Spend about five minutes studying the prompt.

Plan Your Response
Ask yourself questions about the imaginary situation suggested by the prompt to help you create the **literary elements** that will go into your story.

- What kind of freedom is at stake in your story? personal, physical freedom? freedom of the spirit? intellectual freedom?
- What is the **setting**? Where and when will the struggle for freedom occur?
- What will the **major characters** be like?
- What **minor characters** will be in the narrative?
- What **point of view** will your narrative use?
- How will the **plot** unfold? What will the **complications** be that move the narrative action forward?
- How will the **conflict** in your narrative be resolved? Will freedom be won or lost?

Answer these questions carefully but quickly, and make some notes. **Tip:** Spend about ten minutes planning your response.

Respond to the Prompt
Start writing, even if you are unsure about how to begin. The most important thing is to get your ideas on paper. One way to begin is to create a **dialogue** between your main character and others that will reveal the setting and conflict. As you write, remember the following points:

- Use **descriptive details** to allow your reader to "see" the characters and their experience. Be as specific as you can when you describe the characters and what happens.
- Include **narrative details** to illustrate the conflict and lead to its resolution.
- Communicate the **significance of the events**. One way to do that is through dialogue or interior monologue.
- Make the **resolution** clear.

Tip: Spend about twenty minutes writing your fictional narrative.

Improve Your Response
Revising Go back to the key aspects of the prompt. Does your response include characters, a setting, a conflict, complications, and a resolution? Have you used dialogue or description to make the characters and action clear? Does your narrative have a beginning, middle, and end? Have you communicated the significance of the events?

Proofreading Take a few minutes to proofread to correct errors in grammar, spelling, punctuation, and capitalization. Make sure that all your edits are neat, and check that your paper is legible.

Checking Your Final Copy Before you turn in your narrative, read it one more time to catch any errors you may have missed. You will be glad you took one more look to present your best writing. **Tip:** Save five or ten minutes to improve your response.

Universal Access

English Learners
English for Academic Success Introduce students to the following words before they begin their writing exercise.

- **prompt**—a suggestion or reminder
- **distinct**—recognizably different
- **aspect**—a particular part or feature of something
- **consistent**—unchanging

Struggling Writers
Ask students to review their work and pay attention to the transitions between scenes. Is it clear when characters move from one place to another? Does the story establish an appropriate mood for each scene? Have students add transitions where necessary.

Standards Focus

Objectives
Students will learn the elements of writing a fictional narrative.

Direct Teach

Study the Prompt
Before students begin writing, encourage them to answer the following questions:

1. What is my time limit?
2. What are the key skills assessed in the scoring guide?
3. Who is my audience?
4. What is my purpose?

Plan Your Response
Remind students that the fictional narrative scoring guide emphasizes a focus on a consistent and unified event or series of events. Tell students that they should ask themselves these questions to evaluate their writing as they work on their drafts: Have I focused on one plot? Is it clear how everything in this narrative relates to that plot?

Improve Your Response
Point out that the scoring guide also emphasizes effective narrative sequence. Remind students to focus on organizing the story in chronological order or another order that makes sense, as well as on transitioning smoothly from one scene to the next.

Assess

Use the scoring guide on p. 1050 to assess students' fictional narratives.

Standards Focus

Objectives

Students will

- organize and present oral interpretations of short stories
- demonstrate effective verbal and nonverbal techniques

Preteach

Speak with a Purpose Ask students to think about a time when they were told a good story. Have them answer the following questions:

- What was it about the story that sparked your interest?
- Could you relate to the topic?
- Did the speaker's delivery of the story contribute to your interest?

Direct Teach

Model the Skill

Adapt Your Short Story

Model for students how to make a connection between their listeners and the story. You might suggest that students mention a common experience that relates to the subject of the story. For example, "When I was younger, I couldn't get enough of the outdoors."

Guided Practice: Apply

For each part of their narratives, ask students to find ways to make connections to their audience. Have them share their ideas with a partner.

California Standards, pp. 1052–1053

- **Listening and Speaking Standard 1.8** Use effective and interesting language, including: **a.** Informal expressions for effect **b.** Standard American English for clarity.
- **Listening and Speaking Standard 2.1** Deliver reflective presentations: **a.** Explore the significance of personal experiences, events, conditions, or concerns, using appropriate rhetorical strategies (e.g., narration, description, exposition, persuasion).
- **Grades 9–10 Review Listening and Speaking Standard 1.9** Analyze the occasion and the interests of the audience and choose effective verbal and nonverbal techniques (e.g., voice, gestures, eye contact) for presentations.

Listening & Speaking Workshop

Presenting a Story

Speak with a Purpose

Adapt your short story into an oral presentation. Practice telling your story, and then present it to your class.

Think as a Reader/Writer The processes of speaking and listening are similar to those of writing and reading. Speakers, like writers, attempt to express ideas in a clear, engaging manner. Listeners, like readers, aim to absorb and understand the ideas being expressed.

Storytelling is an ancient art form, but it also takes place every day, all around us. In fact, you probably tell stories all the time. At the dinner table, you might tell your family an amusing anecdote about something that happened at school; or in line for concert tickets, you might swap "concert stories" with your friends. Now, you can share a short story of your own by adapting it as an oral presentation.

Adapt Your Short Story

Consider Your Listeners

A reader has the luxury of setting his or her own pace, re-reading for clarity or enjoyment, or pausing to answer the phone, fix a snack, or take a catnap. A listener, on the other hand, has only one chance to register what is being said. As you adapt your story for an oral presentation, consider doing the following:

- **Keep It Simple and Vivid** On paper, an extended metaphor comparing your dog to Beowulf may have worked. In an oral presentation, though, it might confuse—or exasperate—your listeners. Read through your story, marking images that are simple, strong, and vivid for use in your presentation. Cut those that are abstract or complicated, or that require elaborate background knowledge.
- **Streamline Your Organization** Remember that listeners do not have the benefit of seeing a paragraph break on a page, or of flipping back and forth to see what happened when. To help listeners follow the progression of events, add verbal cues such as transitional words and phrases, or brief references to earlier key events. Also consider limiting your use of flashback and foreshadowing, which can wreak chronological havoc in a listener's mind.
- **Spell Out the Main Idea** In literature, an implicit theme can contribute to a work's artisitic quality and depth of meaning. In an oral presentation, however, you may need to guide your listeners toward your main point in language that is somewhat direct. Consider having your main character reflect aloud on a lesson learned, or take an action that clearly shows how he or she has changed.

Reader/Writer Notebook

Use your **RWN** to complete the activities for this workshop.

Resources

UA: Holt Interactive Writer and Speaker, practice and assessment, p. 138

UA: Differentiating Instruction, modified lesson plans, p. 247

Teacher One Stop™, on-level lesson plans and all print resources

Listening and Speaking Standard 1.8a, 1.8b, 2.1a; **Grades 9–10 Review Listening and Speaking Standard** 1.9 (see pages A53–A55)

Deliver Your Short Story

Use Effective Language

When presenting a short story orally, you probably will not read it word-for-word. Instead, you may choose words and craft sentences somewhat spontaneously. To make sure you use appropriate, effective language, keep the following in mind:

- Standard American English should be used for clarity in the bulk of your narrative.
- Informal language may be used occasionally, for effect.
- Technical language may be used for specificity, but only when no other kind of language will do.

Polish Your Performance

After you have adapted your story for listeners and decided what kinds of language to use, apply the tips in this checklist to craft and practice your performance.

Tip for Polishing Your Performance	Done?
Read your story aloud until you are very familiar with it. If you trip over certain words or phrases, practice them in isolation, or change them altogether.	
Practice adjusting your voice. Use a different pitch for each character; vary your rate to match the story's action; and change your tone of voice to convey mood.	
Use gestures and facial expressions to add interest. Practice using movements that are expressive, but not distracting.	

To Note or Not to Note?

Make a set of notecards and put them in order. Then, practice both with and without them. If they increase your comfort and confidence, use them during your presentation. If you find them difficult to handle, set them aside and trust your own storytelling instincts.

Use Nonverbal Techniques

Facial expressions and gestures add meaning to your oral narrative. Use gestures to emphasize high points of conflict or humor. Keep in mind that your eyes convey emotion—involve your listeners by making frequent eye contact with them. Be sure to tailor your gestures and tone to your audience. For instance, exaggerated facial expressions might be appropriate for small children, but not for your classmates.

A Good Oral Presentation

- uses vivid images that the listener can easily understand
- organizes events so they are easy to follow
- uses appropriate words and sentences
- uses effective nonverbal techniques

Speaking Tip

You may have heard that looking above the heads of your listeners is an effective public speaking technique. It is not—especially in a small space such as a classroom. Try looking at your listeners instead. Friendly eye contact will connect you to your audience in a personal way and will keep your listeners involved in the story. Avoid extended or intense eye contact, which can make a listener uncomfortable.

Universal Access

Struggling Learners

Some students may not feel comfortable giving an oral presentation of a short story that includes transitions between text and dialogue. Have students practice their presentations in groups of 3–4 people. Ask students to concentrate on creating subtle differences in the pitch and sound of their voice for each character in the story. Remind students that the changes do not have to be dramatic, but should be consistent and should contrast with the voice they use as the narrator, or speaker.

Advanced Learners

Enrichment Challenge students to create a brief summary of their short story that is similar to what might be found on the back cover of a book or DVD. Students should use language that will spark readers' interest in their story. Their summaries should have a clear main idea or theme and should refer to images related to important events in the story. Ask students to share their summaries with the class while practicing good performance techniques.

Model the Skill

To Note or Not to Note?

Model for students how to use notecards to help them give a presentation. Give an impromptu speech to the class and hold a set of notecards as you give the speech. Demonstrate for students how to shuffle through the cards as you speak and to maintain eye contact with the audience.

Guided Practice: Apply

Have students try different forms of notes. Some students may prefer notecards; others might create an outline or story map. Some students may find they can tell a story effectively while referring only occasionally to notes. Encourage students to find a method that works well for them.

Teaching Tip

After students practice delivering their speech, have them self-assess their performance on a scale of 1–5 in the areas of speech rate, eye contact, use of nonverbal techniques, and overall comfort. Instruct students to keep practicing until they see improvement in their performance.

English for Academic Success

Remind students to use formal English when delivering their speech. They should use informal English, such as slang, only when a character is speaking.

Assess

UA: Holt Interactive Writer and Speaker, Fictional Narrative Evaluation Guide

Standards Focus

Objectives

Students will compare and contrast works from different literary periods.

Literary Skills Review

Review

Guided Practice

If necessary, use the following questions to guide students in their reading before they answer the questions at the end of the review.

Mood

How does the first stanza in "The Sleeper of the Valley" contrast with the first stanza in "Drummer Hodge"? ***Possible response:*** *Rimbaud's first stanza is cheerful, whereas Hardy's is bleak.*

Tone

How are the images conveyed by the final stanzas of each poem similar? ***Possible response:*** *Both poems end with the image of a dead soldier who has become part of the landscape, emphasizing death's inevitability.*

Test-Taking Tip

Advise students to read all of the questions first and quickly answer those they are sure of. Then, have them go back to the puzzling questions and rephrase them in their own words.

California Standards, pp. 1054–1055

- **Reading Standard 3.7** Analyze recognized works of world literature from a variety of authors: **a.** Contrast the major literary forms, techniques, and characteristics of the major literary periods (e.g., Homeric Greece, medieval, romantic, neo-classic, modern).

Literary Skills Review

Comparing Literature **Directions:** Read the poems below, and answer the questions that follow.

The following two nineteenth-century poems are examples of two different literary traditions. Thomas Hardy (1840–1928), an English novelist who became a poet late in life, was a realist and pessimist. Arthur Rimbaud (1854–1891) was a young French symbolist—one of a group of poets who reacted against the idealism of Romanticism and sought to express their ironic view of the world, using rhythmical language and sometimes shocking imagery. "Drummer Hodge" is set in South Africa during the Boer War (1899–1902) in which the British defeated the Boers, South Africans of Dutch descent. Hardy uses some words from Afrikaans, the language spoken by the Boers. "The Sleeper of the Valley" is set in an unspecified time and place.

Drummer Hodge

by **Thomas Hardy**

1

They throw in Drummer Hodge, to rest
Uncoffined—just as found:
His landmark is a kopje°-crest
That breaks the veldt° around;
And foreign constellations west°
Each night above his mound.

2

Young Hodge the Drummer never knew—
Fresh from his Wessex home—
The meaning of the broad Karoo,°
The Bush,° the dusty loam,
And why uprose to nightly view
Strange stars amid the gloam.

3

Yet portion of that unknown plain
Will Hodge forever be;
His homely Northern breast and brain
Grow to some Southern tree,
And strange-eyed constellations reign
His stars eternally.

3. **kopje** (KAHP ee): (Afrikaans) small hill.
4. **veldt** (vehlt): (Afrikaans) prairie.
5. **west:** move westward.
9. **Karoo** (kuh ROO): (Hottentot) dry plain.
10. **Bush:** uncleared, outlying area.

The Sleeper of the Valley

by **Arthur Rimbaud**
translated by **Ludwig Lewisohn**

There's a green hollow where a river sings
Silvering the torn grass in its glittering flight,
And where the sun from the proud mountain flings
Fire—and the little valley brims with light.

A soldier young, with open mouth, bare head,
Sleeps with his neck in the dewy watercress,
Under the sky and on the grass his bed,
Pale in the deep green and the light's excess.

He sleeps amid the iris and his smile
Is like a sick child's slumbering for a while.
Nature, in thy warm lap his chilled limbs hide!

The perfume does not thrill him from his rest.
He sleeps in sunshine, hand upon his breast,
Tranquil—with two red holes in his right side.

Resources for Skills and Standards Review

Unit 5 Resources, Unit Standards Mastery, Unit Vocabulary Review, p. 98

UA: Differentiating Instruction, below-level Unit Standards Mastery

Teacher One Stop™, editable Unit Standards Mastery

Focus on Standards with CAHSEE Support

Preparing for the SAT and ACT

ThinkCentral Online Assessment, Unit Standards Mastery

ThinkCentral Online Remediation

Holt Online Essay Scoring

Reading Standard 3.7a (see pages A48–A50)

1. Hardy uses the word *throw* (line 1) to describe the manner in which Drummer Hodge is buried. What does this word suggest about the feelings of those burying him?
   A relief
   B contentment
   C indifference
   D grief

2. According to "Drummer Hodge," what will happen to Hodge in the future?
   A He will be given a formal burial.
   B He will go to heaven.
   C He will become a permanent part of the landscape.
   D He will be remembered.

3. What word *best* describes the landscape in which the soldier lies in "The Sleeper of the Valley"?
   A tropical
   B pastoral
   C urban
   D arid

4. In "The Sleeper of the Valley," the contrast between the beautiful language and imagery and the reality of the soldier's death is an example of
   A irony.
   B symbolism.
   C alliteration.
   D Romanticism.

5. Which statement about both poems is *incorrect?*
   A Both are patriotic.
   B Both are rhymed.
   C Both use irony.
   D Both use imagery.

6. In "The Sleeper of the Valley," what detail *most* strongly suggests that the soldier is dead before we read the last line?
   A The grass is torn.
   B His limbs are chilled.
   C His head is bare.
   D His mouth is open.

7. In both "Drummer Hodge" and "The Sleeper of the Valley," there is evidence that
   A a dead soldier is deeply mourned.
   B people are glad that a soldier is dead.
   C some people are saddened by a soldier's death and some people are happy about it.
   D a particular soldier's death can go unnoticed.

Timed Writing

8. Write a brief essay about the theme of "Drummer Hodge" and "The Sleeper of the Valley." Be sure to support your response with specific evidence from the poems.

Assess

Answers and Explanations

1. ***C*** *Persons experiencing "relief" (A) "contentment" (B) or "grief" (D) would not be able to "throw" a coffinless body into a grave.*
2. ***C*** *It is clear that Hodge is buried without ceremony (A); it does not state that he will be remembered (D) or go to heaven (B).*
3. ***B*** *There is not enough detail to suggest that it is tropical (A). No details suggest that the setting is urban (C) or arid (D).*
4. ***A*** *An unexpected contrast is ironic (A). It is not an example of symbolism (B) or alliteration (C), nor does it reflect Romantic ideals (D).*
5. ***A*** *Both use rhyme (B) and imagery (D), and they present the irony of death's occurring in a beautiful setting (C).*
6. ***B*** *Chilled limbs (B) are usually associated with death.*
7. ***D*** *In both poems, there is a total absence of human response.*

Timed Writing

8. *The theme of both poems is the effect of death. The two soldiers have died violently in war, yet they rest peacefully after death. Their bodies become one with the land that they fought for. There are no parades or salutes for their sacrifice.*

Reteach

ThinkCentral Online Remediation

Word-Attack Skills Mini-Lesson

Review Use the activities below to check student's grasp of the word-attack skills taught in this collection.

Activity Have students identify the two words in each set that rhyme. Answers are in bold.

1. malice	**valise**	**police**
2. barrage	**carriage**	**marriage**
3. **chemise**	demise	**caprice**
4. **decoupage**	encourage	**entourage**
5. message	**massage**	**dressage**
6. **steerage**	mirage	**peerage**
7. **ménage**	manage	**fuselage**

Activity Have students identify the word in each set in which *t* stands for /ch/. Answers are in bold.

1. cultivate	**culture**	coloratura
2. pastoral	pastorale	**pasturage**
3. **conjecture**	contusion	contumacy
4. punditry	**punctual**	punctilious
5. overturn	overtly	**overture**
6. matutinal	**maturation**	matinee
7. creation	creativity	**creatural**
8. opportunity	**fortunate**	attuned

Vocabulary Skills Review

Assess

Answers and Explanations

1. *D "Empty" and "complete," like the given words, are opposites.*
2. *A "Anger" and "contentment," like the given words, are opposites.*
3. *B "Charity" and "giving," like the given words, are a noun and an adjective related in meaning.*
4. *C "Generous" and "giving" are adjectives and synonyms.*
5. *C Like the given words, "wild" and "domesticated" are opposites.*
6. *A "Pulchritude" and "gorgeous" are a noun and an adjective with related meanings.*
7. *B "Harsh" and "bitter" are adjectives with similar meanings, like the given words.*
8. *D A hermit is solitary, while a dictator is oppressive.*

Academic Vocabulary

9. *D "Retain" and "lose," like the given words, are verbs with opposite meaning.*
10. *B "Tense" and "anxious" are adjectives with opposite meaning.*

Reteach

go.hrw.com ThinkCentral Online Remediation

California Standards, p. 1056

- **Reading Standard 1.3** Discern the meaning of analogies encountered, analyzing specific comparisons as well as relationships and inferences.

STANDARDS REVIEW

Vocabulary Skills Review

Reading Standard 1.3 (see pages A48–A50)

Analogies **Directions:** For each item, choose the lettered pair of words that expresses a relationship that is most similar to the relationship between the pair of capitalized words.

1. MELANCHOLY : CHEERFUL ::
A restless : fitful
B punctual : prompt
C report : interpretation
D empty : complete

2. CERTITUDE : DOUBT ::
A anger : contentment
B belief : faithful
C obstinate : hostile
D palate : flavorful

3. FIDELITY : UNWAVERING ::
A vile : venomous
B charity : giving
C repudiate : confirmation
D elementary : perplexing

4. OPPRESSIVE : OVERBEARING ::
A hateful: demanding
B libel : lawsuit
C generous : giving
D comedy : funny

5. DISTRAUGHT : CALM ::
A mourner : joyful
B vessel : ocean
C wild : domesticated
D fortitude : strength

6. DELUSION : UNCONVINCING ::
A pulchritude : gorgeous
B mountain : altitude
C illness : physician
D soil : seedling

7. GENIAL : PERSONABLE ::
A secretive : public
B harsh : bitter
C dime : coin
D allow : permit

8. OPPRESSIVE : DICTATOR ::
A anticipatory : despair
B obnoxious : hostess
C hatred : dislike
D solitary : hermit

Academic Vocabulary

9. RESPOND : IGNORE ::
A energetic : animated
B prevent : avert
C puncture : pierce
D retain : lose

10. COMPLEX : INTRICATE ::
A frantic : indifferent
B tense : anxious
C calm : distressed
D languid : invigorating

Vocabulary Review

Use this activity to assess whether students have retained the unit Vocabulary. Ask students fill in the blanks below with a boxed Vocabulary word.

redress	hoard	dispassionately
vexed	displaced	

1. The teacher was very _____ that the class did not complete the assignment. [*vexed*]
2. The judge ordered the defendant to pay $500 to _____ the grievances of the plaintiff. [*redress*]
3. In the fall, squirrels _____ nuts in their nests to use during the winter months. [*hoard*]
4. The committee member _____ voted in the election, as he did not have a favorite candidate. [*dispassionately*]
5. Because of the remodeling in the school many students were _____ and had to use lockers on the other side of the building. [*displaced*]

STANDARDS REVIEW

Writing Skills Review

Writing Standard 2.1a–e (see pages A51–A52)

Editing a Short Story **Directions:** The following passage is a rough draft. It may contain errors in grammar, punctuation, sentence structure, and organization. Read the passage, and answer the questions that follow.

Rough Draft

(1) Maya glanced again at the grimy scrap of notebook paper: *twenty-four, thirty-six, twenty-four.* (2) She stuffed the paper into her pocket and began to spin the lock's dial. (3) With a downward tug, the lock opened. She was in! (4) "Excuse me," came a deep voice from behind. (5) *Oh, no,* Maya thought. (6) With a weary sigh, she turned around and began to explain to the vice principal that her sister was home sick and needed her math book.

1. To help establish a suspenseful tone, how could the writer change sentence 2?

A She stuffed the paper into her pocket, carefully adjusted her headband, and began to spin the lock's dial.

B She crumpled the paper, tossed it carelessly aside, and began to spin the lock's dial.

C She folded the paper, stuck it in her backpack, and began to spin the lock's dial.

D She stuffed the paper into her pocket, glanced up and down the corridor, and began to spin the lock's dial.

2. Which verb could replace the word *opened* in sentence 3 to improve the precision of the writing?

A clicked

B disconnected

C disengaged

D snapped

3. Which of the following would be the BEST way to condense the sentence labeled 6?

A Sighing wearily, she turned to explain to the vice principal that her sister was home sick and needed her math book.

B She sighed wearily and turned around and began to explain that her sister was home sick and needed her math book.

C With a weary sigh, she turned to explain to the vice principal that her sister, who was home sick, needed her math book.

D Sighing wearily, she turned around and explained to the vice principal that her sister, who was home sick, needed her math book.

4. To heighten the story's conflict, which of the following could the writer add after sentence 5?

A I should clean out my locker before I start losing things.

B After two detentions this month, he'll never believe me.

C If I close the locker quietly, maybe he won't notice me.

D Even though I'm breaking a rule, I have a good reason for it.

5. To create irony in the story, which of the following could the writer add after sentence 6?

A "There's no need to explain, Maya," Mr. Harvey said. "I just wanted to let you know that Tara will need her history book, too."

B "You'll have to explain later, Maya," Mr. Harvey said. "I'm late for an important meeting."

C "There's no need to explain, Maya," Mr. Harvey said. "Just shut the locker and come with me to the front office."

D "You'll have to explain later, Maya," Mr. Harvey said. "I'm looking forward to hearing what your excuse will be this time."

Writing Skills Review

Assess

Answers and Explanations

1. D *Looking up and down the corridor creates suspense. The other options just take up time.*

2. C *The precise action of the lock is becoming detached, or disengaged. The other options do not reveal a precise action.*

3. A *This option best condenses sentence 6 in the paragraph and excludes unnecessary phrases, such as "began to" and "with a." The other choices (B, C, D) are either awkwardly constructed or do not condense the ideas in the sentence.*

4. B *"He'll never believe me" shows a clear conflict between Maya and the vice principal. (A) does not show a relationship to the story, and (C) and (D) do not clearly show the conflict.*

5. A *This option is ironic because Maya thinks she is getting in trouble, but Mr. Harvey just wants to give her some helpful information. In (C) and (D) it appears that Maya will get in trouble, and in (B) it seems Maya will have to face punishment at a later time.*

Reteach

go.hrw.com **ThinkCentral Online Remediation**

Application

Short Story (Homework)

Have students use what they have learned in the writing workshop to write a one-page short story describing their typical school day. Ask students to describe more than simple actions like coming and going from class, but think about small details in their day such as who they see or typical rituals. Encourage students to use precise language and include information that will slow down the story and give background information to the reader.

Extension

Reporting Observations

Have students go to a public area like a park or mall and report about the people around them. Ask students to choose one person or group of people to observe for five minutes and take detailed notes about their actions. Then, have students write 5–10 sentences describing their subject's behavior. Ask students to use detailed information about the setting and vivid imagery to make even simple actions suspenseful or exciting. Ask students to share their writing with the class.

California Standards, p. 1057

- **Writing Standard 2.1** Write fictional, autobiographical, or biographical narratives: **a.** Narrate a sequence of events and communicate their significance to the audience. **b.** Locate scenes and incidents in specific places. **c.** Describe with concrete sensory details the sights, sounds, and smells of a scene and the specific actions, movements, gestures, and feelings of the characters; use interior monologue to depict the characters' feelings. **d.** Pace the presentation of actions to accommodate temporal, spatial, and dramatic mood changes. **e.** Make effective use of descriptions of appearance, images, shifting perspectives, and sensory details.

Read On
If students enjoyed the themes and topics explored in this unit, you might recommend these titles for independent reading.

A Note on Web Sites
Web sites and online materials change continually and without notice. Holt cannot ensure the accuracy and appropriateness of these materials. Students, teachers, and guardians should assume responsibility for checking all online materials. The sites described on these Read On pages are well established and have been developed for—and in some cases, by—students.

Assessment Options
The following projects can help you evaluate and assess your students' outside work. Videotapes or audiotapes of completed projects may be included in students' portfolios.

Create a Satire
Drawing inspiration from Oscar Wilde's drama, ask students to create a character that satirizes the values of today's society. Have students consider how the character would look, his or her lifestyle, and behavior in public. Challenge students to create dialogue between their character and a member of society that could possibly become a short story or play.

Read On
For Independent Reading

FICTION
Jane Eyre
Meet Jane Eyre, an independent young woman who defies Victorian England's superficial expectations. In this gothic romance, author Charlotte Brontë tells the story of a governess who captures the heart of her employer, Mr. Rochester, despite her plain appearance. Battling a series of secrets and obstacles, Jane Eyre eventually finds the happiness she seeks through her steadfast intelligence, strong will, and moral integrity.

FICTION
David Copperfield
Charles Dickens's favorite and most autobiographical novel contains some of his most memorable characters, including the optimistic Mr. Micawber; the devoted Clara Pegotty; the brutal Mr. Creakle, headmaster of Salem House School; and of course, one of the creepiest of all Dickens's villains, the unctuous, hypocritical Uriah Heep. Told in the first person, the novel depicts David's up-and-down relationships with numerous characters and his gradual realization that his calling is to be a novelist.

FICTION
Silas Marner
Silas Marner is a recluse and miser whose gold is stolen, but then symbolically replaced by a golden-haired child who crawls into his cottage on a freezing winter night. Marner raises the little girl with the mysterious origins, and his life is changed for the better. George Eliot shows her readers that even a small English village holds enough secrets about crimes, misunderstandings, and forbidden relationships to fill a novel.

DRAMA
The Importance of Being Earnest
In his famous play *The Importance of Being Earnest,* Oscar Wilde—no friend of the British class system— satirizes the British obsession with respectability. Jack Worthing, a respectable man in his community, creates a double life and imaginary identity as a way to escape the social pressures of money and success. The result is a witty play that presents Wilde's alternative philosophy at every turn: "The truth is rarely pure and never simple."

Word Counts and Readabilities of Read On Books

Fiction	Estimated Word Counts	Readability
Jane Eyre	185,686	Accessible
David Copperfield	17,774	Accessible
The Importance of Being Earnest	36,200	Accessible
Silas Marner	71,347	Challenging

NONFICTION

What Jane Austen Ate and Charles Dickens Knew

Welcome to nineteenth-century England! In this entertaining book, Daniel Pool gives new life to the daily routines of the Victorian period, covering the era's nitty-gritty details (How did they keep clean?) and formal etiquette (How did one address a duke?). Find out what the Victorians ate, what they wore, how they traveled, and whom they married.

NONFICTION

Dared & Done: The Marriage of Elizabeth Barrett and Robert Browning

Julia Markus shows how the courtship and marriage of the Victorian poets Elizabeth Barrett and Robert Browning were the equivalent of an A-list celebrity romance and marriage today, except that this marriage succeeded. After Robert read Elizabeth's poetry, he fell in love with her, confessing his admiration in an ardent letter that she answered. When they met four months later, he loved her even more—but how could Elizabeth defy her tyrannical father to marry Robert?

NONFICTION

Queen Victoria

Victoria reigned longer than any other British monarch (1837–1901), and as the embodiment of the Victorian Age, believed that she was capable of boundless improvement, a belief instilled in her by her devoted husband, Albert. In this brief book, Elizabeth Longford describes, with anecdotes and carefully researched facts, Victoria's life before her marriage to Albert, their happy, productive years together, her decades of mourning and seclusion, and her gradual return to public life after Albert's death.

WEB SITE

The Victorian Web

The wide-ranging site www.victorianweb.org includes articles on everything from political and social history to theosophy and railways. In addition to the full text of many Victorian poems, stories, plays, and reviews, the Victorian Web features paintings, sculpture, drawings, photographs, and other Victorian art. A section on what Victorians wore includes images of hairstyles, footwear, hats, coats, dresses, and children's clothing.

Learn It Online
Explore more novels with *NovelWise*.
go.hrw.com H12-1059 Go

Nonfiction	Estimated Word Counts	Readability
What Jane Austen Ate and Charles Dickens Knew	110,400	Easily Accessible
Dared and Done: The Letters of Robert Browning and Elizabeth Barrett	160,060	Challenging
Queen Victoria	32,922	Accessible
The Victorian Web	Web site	Accessible

Assessment Options

Advertise a Miniseries

- Ask individual students to imagine that Charles Dickens's *David Copperfield* is being produced as a television miniseries.
- Have them decide how many episodes would be needed; then, have them write a summary of each segment for a television program guide and the copy for a television or newspaper advertisement promoting the series.
- A group of student writers and artists can also work together to plan a comprehensive advertising campaign for the series and then present their plans to the class.

Compare and Contrast

- Use the book *What Jane Austen Ate and Charles Dickens Knew* as a way to compare and contrast life in the Victorian period and modern times.
- Have students write a short story that involves them swapping places in time with either Jane Austen or Charles Dickens. Ask students to include details about how they would react to the conditions of the Victorian period and how Austen or Dickens would respond to the advancements of modern life.

Learn It Online
The **NovelWise** mini-site includes instruction on choosing, reading, and analyzing novels; it also contains a catalogue of book summaries, study guides, teaching guides, and PowerPoint presentations.
go.hrw.com H12–1059 Go

The Modern World: 1900 to the Present

Features highlighted in **yellow** constitute a suggested minimum course of study.

Chapter 11

Selection or Feature	For Independent Reading	Grade-Level Standards
The Modern World: 1900 to the Present: **Link to Today: Spacecraft Voyager 1 Has Boldly Gone** by Alice Oswald (Accessible, Lexile N/A)		
Literary Skills Focus: War Literature by Leila Christenbury		**Reading Standard 3.7:** Analyze world literature.
• **Dulce et Decorum Est** by Wilfred Owen (Accessible, Lexile N/A) • **The Soldier** by Rupert Brooke (Accessible, Lexile N/A)	• **Sonny's War** by Valerie Hobbs • **A Farewell to Arms** by Ernest Hemingway	**Reading Standard 2.2:** Clarify meaning through structure, repetition, syntax, and word choice. **Reading Standard 3.4:** Analyze figures of speech.
• **The Rear-Guard** (Accessible, Lexile N/A) • **A Soldier's Declaration** (Accessible, Lexile 1400) by Siegfried Sassoon	• **Dawn** by Elie Wiesel	**Reading Standard 2.2:** Clarify meaning through structure, repetition, syntax, and word choice. **Reading Standard 3.3:** Analyze effects of irony, tone, mood, and style. **Reading Standard 2.6:** Critique arguments.
Link to Today: Under Heavy Fire in Iraq by Richard Norton-Taylor (Accessible, Lexile 1310)		**Reading Standard 2.2:** Clarify meaning through structure, repetition, syntax, and word choice.
On the Bottom *from* Survival in Auschwitz by Primo Levi (Accessible, Lexile 980)	• **Maus: A Survivor's Tale** by Art Spiegelman • **In My Hands, Memories of a Holocaust Rescuer** by Irene Gut Opdyke	**Reading Standard 3.1:** Analyze subgenres. **Reading Standard 3.7:** Analyze world literature. **Grades 9 10 Review Reading Standard 3.12:** Analyze the way in which literature is related to themes of its historical period.
Never Shall I Forget by Elie Wiesel (Accessible, Lexile N/A)	• **Thura's Diary: My Life in Wartime Iraq** by Thura Al-Windawi • **Safe Area Gorazde: The War in Eastern Bosnia 1992–1995** by Joe Sacco	**Reading Standard 2.5:** Analyze an author's beliefs. **Reading Standard 3.4:** Analyze figures of speech.
Reading Skills Focus: Identifying and Critiquing an Author's Argument by Kylene Beers		**Reading Standard 2.6:** Critique arguments.
Blood, Sweat, and Tears by Winston Churchill (Accessible, Lexile 1170)	• **Profiles in Courage** by John F. Kennedy • **Nobel acceptance speech** by William Faulkner • **Nobel Lectures in Literature, (1991–1995)** by Sture Allen (ed.)	**Reading Standard 2.6:** Critique arguments. **Reading Standard 3.3:** Analyze effects of irony, tone, mood, and style.
The Demon Lover by Elizabeth Bowen (Accessible, Lexile 1000)	• **Restless, A Ghost's Story** by Rich Wallace • **The Grave** by James Heneghan	**Reading Standard 2.2:** Clarify meaning through structure, repetition, syntax, and word choice. **Grades 9–10 Review Reading Standard 3.6:** Analyze development of time and sequence.
The Destructors by Graham Greene (Accessible, Lexile 790)	• **Daises in the Junkyard** by Michael Enright	**Reading Standard 3.7c:** Evaluate the historical period. **Grades 9–10 Review Reading Standard 3.4:** Determine characters' traits.
Shooting an Elephant by George Orwell (Accessible, Lexile 1060)	• **The Orwell Reader** by George Orwell • **A Brave New World** by Aldous Huxley	**Reading Standard 2.5:** Analyze an author's beliefs. **Reading Standard 3.3:** Analyze effects of irony, tone, mood, and style.

Selection or Feature *continued*	For Independent Reading	Grade-Level Standards
• **"I Believe in a British Empire"** by Joseph Chamberlain (Challenging, Lexile 1360) • **"The Noble Mansions of Free India"** by Jawaharlal Nehru (Challenging, Lexile 1230)	• **Nehru: The Invention of India** by Shashi Tharoor • **Gifts** by Ursula K. Le Guin	**Reading Standard 2.5:** Analyze an author's beliefs.
Comparing Texts: **Author Study: Virginia Woolf** • *from* **A Room of One's Own** (Accessible, Lexile 1270) • *from* **Jacob's Room** (Accessible, Lexile 810) • **A Haunted House** (Accessible, Lexile 560) • *from* **The Letters of Virginia Woolf** (Accessible, Lexile 980)	• **Margaret Bourke-White: Her Pictures Were Her Life** by Susan Goldman Rubin • **How Reading Changed My Life** by Anna Quindlen	**Reading Standard 2.5:** Analyze an author's beliefs. **Reading Standard 3.1:** Analyze subgenres. **Reading Standard 3.3:** Analyze effects of irony, tone, mood, and style.

Daily and Weekly Support

- **Reader/Writer Notebook**
- **Reading and Writing Transparencies**
- **Family Involvement Activities in Spanish**
- **Language Handbook Worksheets**
- **Holt Virtual File Cabinet for Language Arts**

Assessment Resources

- **Unit 6 Resources**, Chapter 11 Diagnostic Test; Selection Standards Checks, Chapter 11 Standards Mastery
- **Universal Access: Differentiating Instruction**, leveled assessment
- **Formal Assessment**, Progress Monitoring Test 4
- **English-Language Conventions Progress Monitoring Tests**, Chapters 17–18
- go.hrw.com **ThinkCentral Online Assessment**

Features highlighted in **yellow** constitute a suggested minimum course of study.

Chapter 12

Selection or Feature	For Independent Reading	Grade-Level Standards
Modern and Contemporary Poetry: Literary Skills Focus: **Themes of Modern and Contemporary Poetry** by Leila Christenbury		**Reading Standard 3.1:** Analyze subgenres. **Reading Standard 3.2:** Theme
The Hollow Men by T. S. Eliot (Accessible, Lexile N/A)	• **All the King's Men** by Robert Penn Warren • **Collected Poem, 1909–1962** by T. S. Eliot	**Reading Standard 2.5:** Analyze an author's beliefs. **Reading Standard 3.4:** Analyze figures of speech. **Reading Standard 3.9:** Analyze philosophical arguments.
Comparing Texts: **Author Study** **William Butler Yeats** • **The Second Coming** (Accessible, Lexile N/A) • **The Lake Isle of Innisfree** (Accessible, Lexile N/A) • **The Wild Swans at Coole** (Accessible, Lexile N/A) • **Sailing to Byzantium** (Accessible, Lexile N/A) • *from* **The Autobiography of William Butler Yeats** (Accessible, Lexile 1200)	• **Poet's Choice: Poems for Everyday Life** by Robert Haas • **Quilting the Black-Eyed Pea: Poems and Not Quite Poems** by Nikki Giovanni	**Reading Standard 2.5:** Analyze philosophical beliefs. **Reading Standard 3.2:** Theme **Reading Standard 3.3:** Analyze effects of irony, tone, mood, and style. **Reading Standard 3.4:** Analyze figures of speech. **Grades 9–10 Review Reading Standard 3.7:** Recognize and understand literary devices.
Musée des Beaux Arts by W. H. Auden (Accessible, Lexile N/A)	• **Mythology** by Edith Hamilton	**Reading Standard 3.2:** Theme **Reading Standard 3.3:** Analyze effects of irony, tone, mood, and style.

Selection or Feature *continued*	For Independent Reading	Grade-Level Standards
Reading Skills Focus: **Analyzing Details** by Kylene Beers		**Reading Standard 3.3:** Analyze effects of irony, tone, mood, and style
• **Fern Hill** (Accessible, Lexile N/A) • **Do Not Go Gentle into That Good Night** by Dylan Thomas (Accessible, Lexile N/A)	• **Eden** by Stanislaw Lem • **The Accident** by Elie Wiesel	**Reading Standard 3.1:** Analyze subgenres **Reading Standard 3.3:** Analyze effects of irony, tone, mood, and style **Reading Standard 3.9:** Analyze philosophical arguments
Not Waving but Drowning by Stevie Smith (Accessible, Lexile N/A)	• **King Lear** by William Shakespeare	**Reading Standard 3.3:** Analyze effects of irony, tone, mood, and style
Lot's Wife by Anna Akhmatova (Accessible, Lexile N/A)	• **Paradise of the Blind** by Thu Huong Duong	**Reading Standard 3.2:** Theme
• **Lot's Wife** (Accessible, Lexile N/A) • *from* **Nobel Lecture: The Poet and the World** (Accessible, Lexile 1180) by Wislawa Szymborska	• **The Little World of Don Camillo** by Giovanni Guareschi • **Love that Dog** by Sharon Creech	**Reading Standard 2.5:** Analyze an author's beliefs **Reading Standard 3.4:** Analyze figures of speech
Fear by Gabriela Mistral (Accessible, Lexile N/A)	• **The Member of the Wedding** by Carson McCullers • **Daughter of the Sea** by Berlie Doherty	**Reading Standard 3.3:** Analyze effects of irony, tone, mood, and style
• **Sonnet 79/Soneto 79** by Pablo Neruda (Accessible, Lexile N/A)	• **Tomorrowland: Ten Stories About the Future** by Michael Cart	**Reading Standard 3.4:** Analyze figures of speech
The Explosion by Philip Larkin (Accessible, Lexile N/A)	• **Into Thin Air: A Personal Account of the Mt. Everest Disaster** by Jon Krakauer	**Reading Standard 3.4:** Analyze imagery **Grades 9–10 Review Reading Standard 3.8:** Interpret and evaluate the impact of ambiguities in a text
Link to Today: **Trapped Australian Miners Rescued** by Duncan Campbell and Alex Kumi (Accessible, Lexile 1370)		**Reading Standard 2.4:** Analyze an author's argument
The Horses by Ted Hughes (Accessible, Lexile N/A)	• **Chosen by a Horse** by Susan Richards	**Reading Standard 3.3:** Analyze effects of irony, tone, mood, and style
Digging by Seamus Heaney (Accessible, Lexile N/A)	• **The Distant Land of My Father** by Bo Caldwell	**Reading Standard 2.2:** Clarify meaning through structure, repetition, syntax, and word choice **Reading Standard 3.4:** Analyze imagery
Mushrooms by Margaret Atwood (Accessible, Lexile N/A)	• **Oranges** by John McPhee	**Reading Standard 3.2:** Theme **Reading Standard 3.4:** Analyze imagery
Atlantis—A Lost Sonnet by Eavan Boland (Accessible, Lexile N/A)	• **The Temple of the Golden Pavilion*** by Yukio Mishima	**Reading Standard 2.4:** Analyze an author's argument **Reading Standard 3.1:** Analyze subgenres

**This book was published for an adult readership and thus contains mature content. Before handing the text to a child, educators and parents should read the book and know the child. (Recommended Literature: Kindergarten Through Grade Twelve)*

Daily and Weekly Support

- **Reader/Writer Notebook**
- **Reading and Writing Transparencies**
- **Family Involvement Activities in Spanish**
- **Language Handbook Worksheets**
- **Holt Virtual File Cabinet for Language Arts**

Assessment Resources

- **Unit 6 Resources**, Chapter 12 Diagnostic Test; Selection Standards Checks, Chapter 12 Standards Mastery
- **Universal Access: Differentiating Instruction**, leveled assessment
- **English-Language Conventions Progress-Monitoring Tests**, Chapters 18–19
- **ThinkCentral Online Assessment**

Features highlighted in **yellow** constitute a suggested minimum course of study.

Chapter 13

Selection or Feature	For Independent Reading	Grade-Level Standards
Expectation and Reality: **Literary Skills Focus:** Irony by Leila Christenbury		**Reading Standard 3.3:** Analyze effects of irony, tone, mood, and style.
Analyzing Visuals: Analyzing a Sculpture		**Reading Standard 3.3:** Analyze effects of irony, tone, mood, and style.
Reading Skills Focus: Identifying Cause and Effect by Kylene Beers		**Reading Standard 2.2:** Clarify meaning through structure, repetition, syntax, and word choice.
The Doll's House by Katherine Mansfield (Accessible, Lexile 760)	• **Complete Shorter Fiction of Virginia Woolf** by Virginia Woolf	**Reading Standard 2.2:** Clarify meaning through structure, repetition, syntax, and word choice. **Grades 9–10 Review Reading Standard 3.9:** Explain how voice affects characterization and the tone, plot, and credibility of a text.
The Rocking-Horse Winner by D. H. Lawrence (Accessible, Lexile 700)	• **Pale Horse, Pale Rider** by Katherine Anne Porter	**Grades 9–10 Review Reading Standard 3.3:** Analyze interactions between main and subordinate characters. **Grades 9–10 Review Reading Standard 3.4:** Determine characters' traits. **Grades 9–10 Review Reading Standard 3.6:** Analyze development of time and sequence using foreshadowing.
Araby by James Joyce (Accessible, Lexile 930)	• **The Dictionary of Imaginary Places** by Alberto Manguel	**Reading Standard 3.3:** Analyze effects of irony, tone, mood, and style. **Grades 9–10 Review Reading Standard 3.3:** Analyze interactions between main and subordinate characters.
The Book of Sand by Jorge Luis Borges (Accessible, Lexile 730)	• **Changing Planes** by Ursula K. Le Guin • **The Little Prince** by Antoine de Saint Exupery	**Reading Standard 2.4:** Make reasonable assertions about an argument. **Reading Standard 3.4:** Analyze figures of speech.
Come and Go by Samuel Beckett (Easily Accessible, Lexile N/A)	• **The Bald Soprano and Other Plays** by Eugene Ionesco	**Reading Standard 3.1:** Analyze subgenres. **Reading Standard 3.2:** Theme
That's All by Harold Pinter (Challenging, Lexile N/A)	• **In the Penal Colony** by Franz Kafka	**Reading Standard 2.2:** Clarify meaning through structure, repetition, syntax, and word choice. **Grades 9–10 Review Reading Standard 3.10:** Identify and describe the function of dialogue.

Selection or Feature *continued*	For Independent Reading	Grade-Level Standards
No Witchcraft for Sale by Doris Lessing (Accessible, Lexile 1020)	• **Waiting for the Mahatma** by R. K. Narayan	**Reading Standard 3.2:** Theme **Reading Standard 3.7c:** Evaluate the historical period.
Once upon a Time by Nadine Gordimer (Easily Accessible, Lexile 1390)	• **Kaffir Boy: The True Story of a Black Youth's Coming of Age in Apartheid South Africa*** by Mark Mathabane • **Waiting for the Barbarians** by J. M. Coetzee	**Reading Standard 2.2:** Clarify meaning through structure, repetition, syntax, and word choice. **Grades 9–10** **Review Reading Standard 3.7:** Recognize and understand literary devices.
Marriage Is a Private Affair by Chinua Achebe (Easily Accessible, Lexile 830)	• **The Bride Price** by Buchi Emecheta • **Ties That Bind, Ties That Break: A Novel** by Lensey Namioka	**Reading Standard 3.3:** Analyze effects of irony, tone, mood, and style. **Reading Standard 3.7c:** Evaluate the historical period.
Telephone Conversation by Wole Soyinka (Accessible, Lexile N/A)	• **The Song of Solomon*** by Toni Morrison • **Mama Day*** by Gloria Naylor	**Reading Standard 2.5:** Analyze an author's beliefs. **Reading Standard 3.1:** Analyze subgenres.
Comparing Texts **Postcolonial Literature** • *from* **Omeros** by Derek Walcott (Challenging, Lexile N/A) • **B. Wordsworth** by V. S. Naipaul (Accessible, Lexile 700) • *from* **Sir Vidia's Shadow** by Paul Theroux (Accessible, Lexile 780) • **Games at Twilight** by Anita Desai (Accessible, Lexile 1180)	• **The Odyssey** by Homer • **Dreaming in Color, Living in Black and White: Our Own Stories of Growing Up Black in America** by Laurel Holliday (ed.) • **Travels with My Aunt** by Graham Greene • **In the Light of India** by Octavio Paz	**Reading Standard 2.5:** Analyze an author's beliefs. **Reading Standard 3.2:** Theme **Reading Standard 3.3:** Analyze effects of irony, tone, mood, and style. **Reading Standard 3.6:** Analyze archetypes. **Reading Standard 3.7:** Analyze recognized works of literature. **Grades 9–10** **Review Reading Standard 3.7:** Recognize and understand literary devices.

**This book was published for an adult readership and thus contains mature content. Before handing the text to a child, educators and parents should read the book and know the child. (Recommended Literature: Kindergarten Through Grade Twelve)*

Daily and Weekly Support

- **Reader/Writer Notebook**
- **Reading and Writing Transparencies**
- **Family Involvement Activities in Spanish**
- **Language Handbook Worksheets**
- **Holt Virtual File Cabinet for Language Arts**

Assessment Resources

- **Unit 6 Resources**, Chapter 13 Diagnostic Test; Selection Standards Checks, Chapter 13 Standards Mastery
- **Universal Access: Differentiating Instruction**, leveled assessment
- **Formal Assessment**, End-of-Year Summative Test
- **English-Language Conventions Progress-Monitoring Tests**, Chapter 19
- go.hrw.com **ThinkCentral Online Assessment**

Mastering the Skills

Selection or Feature	Grade-Level Standards
Writing Workshop: Biographical Narrative	**Writing Standard 1.1:** Demonstrate an understanding of discourse. **Writing Standard 1.9:** Revise text. **Writing Standard 2.1:** Write biographical narratives.
Preparing for Timed Writing	**Writing Standard 1.1:** Demonstrate an understanding of discourse.
Media Workshop: Analyzing and Using Media	**Writing Standard 2.6:** Deliver multimedia presentations.
Standards Review: Literary Skills Review Vocabulary Skills Review Writing Skills Review	**Reading Standard 3.7:** Compare works of literature. **Grades 9–10** **Review Reading Standard 1.1:** Identify the literal and figurative meanings of words.

Print Resources for Universal Access

		On-Level Learners	English Learners	Struggling Readers	Students Who Use African American Vernacular English	Advanced Learners	Students with Disabilities
Unit 6• Collections 11–13	**Unit 6 Resources** practice, and assessment for selections and features in Chapters 11–13	✔				✔	
	Universal Access: Holt Interactive Reader interactive readings for Minimum-Course-of-Study Selections		✔	✔	✔		✔
	Universal Access: Differentiating Instruction modified lesson plans and leveled assessment for Minimum-Course-of-Study Selections		✔	✔	✔		✔
	Universal Access: Resources for Teaching Advanced Students lesson plans for Minimum-Course-of-Study Selections					✔	
All Chapters	**Universal Access: Supporting Instruction in Spanish** translations of selection summaries and key terms		✔				
	Universal Access: Holt Interactive Writer and Speaker practice and assessment	✔	✔	✔	✔	✔	✔
	Language and Sentence Skills Practice for Warriner's Handbook Chapters 17–19	✔				✔	
	Universal Access: Developmental Language and Sentence Skills Practice for Warriner's Handbook Chapters 17–19		✔	✔	✔		✔

Assessment Resources
Teacher Management Resources
go.hrw.com
Student Edition Extension Activities
Student Edition Support

Technology Resources

Find all of Holt's technology resources at go.hrw.com. Technology resources are also listed at point of use in the Teacher's Edition wrap. Below are our featured components for Unit 6.

Teacher Management Resources

ThinkCentral, Teacher Access
Teacher One Stop™
Holt Professional Learning for Language Arts

Spotlight on Teacher One Stop™

The Teacher One Stop™ contains all of the print resources that you will need when using *Holt Literature and Language Arts*. Online suggestions:

- Use the *ExamView Assessment Suite* to access editable banks of questions; create customized tests for your classes.

Student Edition Support

PowerNotes
Holt Audio Library: Selections and Summaries in Spanish
ThinkCentral, Student Access
Student One-Stop™
Interactive Reading Workshops
Interactive Graphic Organizers
Writer's Lives
Holt Audio Library

Spotlight on Holt Audio Library: Selections and Summaries in Spanish

Students whose first language is Spanish can listen to Spanish translations or Spanish summaries of selections to scaffold their English language development before reading the selections in English.

Student Edition Extension Activities

Digital Storytelling Mini-Site
NovelWise Mini-Site
MediaScope Mini-Site
WordSharp: An Interactive Vocabulary Tutor
GrammarNotes
WritingNotes
Writing and Research in a Digital Age
Literature Links

Spotlight on Digital Storytelling Mini-Site

This site will walk students through the step-by-step process of creating digital stories—personal narratives recorded aloud, and enhanced by video, pictures, music, and artifacts.

Universal Access: Advanced students in particular may appreciate an opportunity to work in new media.

Supported Strand: Writing

Assessment Resources

ThinkCentral Online Assessment
Holt Online Essay Scoring
ThinkCentral Online Remediation

Spotlight on Holt Online Essay Scoring

With online essay scoring, students can practice writing responses to essay prompts—and our system automatically scores them. Students will receive immediate feedback on their essays.

Real Issues, Real Experts

The wrap for these selections includes specific ideas and strategies from *Holt Literature and Language Arts* authors.

From the Authors

For "A Room of One's Own," p. 1162

I use online resources to access digital copies of original Virginia Woolfe journal entries. Students engage differently when we're examining an original draft as opposed to an edition devoid of corrections and stains.

Sara Kajder

For Author Study: Yeats, p. 1197

In "Lake Isle" and "The Wild Swans," students can explore the theme of how life changes affect our view of nature. In "Second Coming" and "Byzantium," students will need guidance to note Yeats's observations on modern life. The autobiographical piece can be examined for its commentary on Yeats himself.

Leila Christenbury

For Biographical Narrative, p. 1429

To help students learn to write biographical narratives and explore the fleeting nature of fame, I ask them to write a narrative about someone who has risen to fame and soon after has fallen into oblivion. This assignment helps give students the tools necessary to meet the demands of California's writing standards.

Carol Jargo

Teacher to Teacher

Preteach Based on the principle that we learn best by teaching others, I introduce a new literary era with an assignment. Each student designs and teaches a lesson plan for a text from the unit.

Direct Teach After we read the unit, I explain the four basic parts of an effective lesson plan (*Goal of the Lesson, Materials Needed for the Activity, Steps to be Taken,* and *Assessment of Student Learning*). Then, the class collaboratively researches the literature of the unit. After students research, they write original lesson plans. Finally, each student teaches his or her lesson to the class and administers the assessment.

Assess I use a scoring rubric based on the assignment requirements. Each section of the lesson plan is worth one hundred points. I assess their work based on the design and delivery of the lesson plan.

Lisa Davidson
San Francisco, California

Holt Professional Learning

Developing Critical Thinking about Literature
with Carol Jago and Deborah Appleman

Visit ThinkCentral, Teacher Access to link to Holt's Professional Learning site for English/Language Arts teachers. This site features:

- **Videos that share the insights of *Holt Literature and Language Arts* program authors and consultants and demonstrate proven classroom strategies with master teachers**
- **Study guides for publications by our authors and consultants**
- **Informative articles and useful Web links**
- **Help in planning your department's professional learning sessions**
- **A handbook for new teachers**

VIDEO PRODUCTS

Strategies for Helping Struggling Readers
with Kylene Beers

Effective Vocabulary Instruction
with Carol Jago and Kylene Beers

Developing Critical Thinking about Literature
with Carol Jago and Deborah Appleman

Teaching Students to Revise, Not Recopy
with Linda Rief

Teaching English Learners
with Robin Scarcella

Using Literature Circles
with Harvey Daniels

Teaching On-Demand Writing Skills
with Leila Christenbury

Managing the Heterogeneous Classroom
with Leila Christenbury and Patrick Schwarz

Teaching Narrative and Expository Texts
with Judith Irvin and Deborah Appleman

Becoming a Tech-Savvy Teacher
with Sara Kajder

Re-engaging the Disengaged Student
with Alfred Tatum

Teaching Grammar in Context
with Amy Benjamin

UNIT 6

Unit Objectives

- Students are introduced to poetry, fiction, and nonfiction that explores a world at war in the first half of the twentieth century and will read works by writers who exemplify the period, such as Primo Levi, Elie Wiesel, Winston Churchill, George Orwell, and Virginia Woolf.
- Students will read and analyze poems by William Butler Yeats, T. S. Eliot, W. H. Auden, Dylan Thomas, Philip Larkin, Ted Hughes, Seamus Heaney, Margaret Atwood, and other modern and contemporary voices.
- Students will read short stories by noted twentieth-century writers from many different cultures whose work explores the theme of how expectations relate to reality.
- At the end of the unit, students will write and present an analysis of a work of nonfiction.

Analyzing Visuals

Use the online textbook to project this image for viewing. Explain to students that this is a photograph of two landmarks in London, England.

Extension Activity Ask students to share their thoughts about how the photograph exemplifies a transforming world. ***Possible responses:*** *The photograph juxtaposes two landmarks from two different eras. In the background, we can see the Tower Bridge, which was built in 1894. In the foreground we can see the GLA City Hall, which was completed in 2002. The image thus highlights the transformation that the city of London is undergoing: the past still appears in the distance while the new is conquering its own position.*

Unit Resources

On Course: Mapping Instruction

Unit 6 Resources

Warriner's Handbook

- Chapters 17–19, Improving Sentences

Teacher One Stop™

Formal Assessment, End-of-Year Summative Test

English-Language Conventions Progress-Monitoring Tests

ThinkCentral Online Assessment

Holt Virtual File Cabinet for Language Arts, grammar, reading, and vocabulary resources

Holt Pronunciation Resources

- Phoneme Sounds and Spellings
- Support for Speakers of African American Vernacular English

ThinkCentral Online Remediation

Tower Bridge and GLA City Hall. London, England, U.K.

UNIT 6

The Modern World

1900 to the Present

"Life spends itself in the act of transformation, dissolving, bit by bit, the world as it appeared."

—Rainer Maria Rilke

What Do You Think? How does experience shape our view of the world?

Learn It Online
What's this historical period all about? Watch a short video introduction online.

go.hrw.com H12-1061 Go

The Quotation

- Explain to students that Austro-German poet Rainer Marie Rilke (1875–1926) wrote these lines, from the fourth of his *Duino Elegies*, during the winter of 1912, when he was a houseguest at Duino Castle, near Trieste, Italy.
- Discuss transformations that students may be familiar with—from one time period to another, from one set of political or social beliefs, certainties, or assumptions to another set—and how those transformations affect our understanding of the world. Encourage students to draw upon personal and vicarious experiences to address the issue of change.

Routines for California Classrooms

For ideas on classroom practices and approaches to grouping, see the discussion of routines on pages T34–T37 of this Teacher's Edition.

What Do You Think?

How does experience shape our view of the world?

- Have students make connections between the unit question, their own experiences, and the experiences of others to decide upon a topic to write about. Ask students how they tell appearance and reality apart and what clues they look for to make the distinction.
- Have students write for a few minutes about a situation in which personal experiences—their own or another's—profoundly affected their perception of what is most important or meaningful in life.

Real Issues, Real Experts: Professional Learning

Spotlight on . . .
Understanding Modern Literature

To help students understand and appreciate modern literature, consider the suggestions you'll find in these videos:

Developing Critical Thinking About Literature, featuring Holt authors **Carol Jago** and **Deborah Appleman**, provides an overview of several approaches to student responses to literature: written responses, whole-class discussion, close reading, and the use of literary perspectives.

In ***Teaching English Learners,*** **Robin Scarcella,** an expert on working with English learners, discusses levels of language acquisition from beginning to advanced, with a focus on academic English.

Each video is accompanied by printable articles, planning materials, Web links, and a training guide for supervisors. For these resources and more, visit **Holt Professional Learning** by going to this page in **ThinkCentral, Teacher Access.**

Learn It Online
You can introduce some of the topics in this unit using brief videos about the literature of this period.

go.hrw.com H12-1061 Go

Direct Teach

Teach the Time Line

Give students five to ten minutes to study the time line. Then, ask the following questions:

- Which entries show Britain at the height of its political power? When does that power start to wane? ***Possible responses:*** *The entries up to and including World War II (which ended in 1945) show Britain at its most powerful. Thereafter, its empire begins to collapse.*
- The two World Wars contributed to people's sense that the world was changing very rapidly—and not for the better. What other political changes or historical events during this time period probably exacerbated this feeling? ***Possible responses:*** *The British executed leaders of the Easter Rebellion in Ireland in 1916; Germany and Russia were ruled by brutal totalitarian governments during the 1930s.*
- The Great Depression started in 1929 in the United States and lasted through most of the 1930s. What effect did the Great Depression appear to have on literature? Why? ***Possible responses:*** *The time line mentions no important literature written during the period of the Great Depression. Maybe people wanted to escape from serious concerns by seeking lighter forms of entertainment.*

California Standards, pp. 1062–1063

- **Reading Standard 3.7** Analyze recognized works of world literature from a variety of authors: **c.** Evaluate the philosophical, political, religious, ethical, and social influences of the historical period that shaped the characters, plots, and settings.

The Modern World
1900 to the Present

This time line represents a snapshot of British literary events, British political and social events, and world events from 1900 to the present. During this period, two world wars, economic depression, the creation of new nations from old colonial holdings, and revolutionary developments in technology changed the world significantly.

Peggy Ashcroft in *A Passage to India* (1984).

BRITISH LITERARY EVENTS

1900

1902 Joseph Conrad publishes *Heart of Darkness*

1904 W. B. Yeats and Lady Gregory found Dublin's Abbey Theatre to produce plays by and about the Irish

1913 G. B. Shaw's *Pygmalion* is first produced; D. H. Lawrence publishes *Sons and Lovers* ›

1916 James Joyce publishes *A Portrait of the Artist as a Young Man*

1920

1922 Joyce publishes *Ulysses;* T. S. Eliot publishes *The Waste Land*

1924 E. M. Forster publishes *A Passage to India* ^

1927 Virginia Woolf publishes *To the Lighthouse*

Sons and Lovers (1960), with Wendy Hiller, Dean Stockwell, and Trevor Howard.

BRITISH POLITICAL AND SOCIAL EVENTS

1900

1901 Queen Victoria dies and is succeeded by her son Edward VII

1910 Britain loses South Africa

1914 England declares war on Germany on August 4, under a treaty to protect Belgium

1916 Easter Rebellion fails in Dublin; uprising's leaders are executed by British

1918 World War I ends; voting rights are extended to British women over age thirty

1920

1922 Britain divides Ireland by treaty, with six northern counties remaining part of United Kingdom; civil war begins in Ireland

1939 After Germany invades Poland, Britain declares war on Germany ›

Proclamation of War by British. Mr. W. T. Boston, Saltbearer and acting town crier.

WORLD EVENTS

1900

1910 Union of South Africa is formed; racial segregation becomes governing rule

1914 World War I begins with the assassination of Austrian Archduke Franz Ferdinand

1915 Czech writer Franz Kafka publishes *The Metamorphosis*

1917 United States enters World War I; Russian Revolution begins

1918 World War I ends with nearly ten million casualties

1920

1929 United States stock market crashes, triggering a worldwide depression

1933 Adolf Hitler appointed chancellor of Germany; Germans build first concentration camp at Dachau

1934–1938 Stalinist purges in Russia force over ten million people into labor camps

1939 Germany invades Poland; World War II begins ›

Recruitment poster from World War II (1939). Color lithography.

Universal Access

English Learners/ Struggling Readers

English for Academic Success Read through each section of the time line with students and clarify the following words and phrases that may impede their understanding.

- **British Literary Events:** *satire, totalitarianism, absurdist*
- **British Political and Social Events:** *succeeded, uprising, executed, hiatus, revolutionizes*
- **World Events:** *segregation, governing rule, metamorphosis, casualties, triggering, concentration camp, fleet*

Use a map to help students understand the important place names, such as the Suez Canal and the location of South Africa, India, Ireland, Germany, Japan, Russia, Poland, Nigeria, Palestine, Saigon, and Iraq.

Reading Standard 3.7c (see pages A48–A50)

Your Turn

Review the time line, and discuss this question with a partner: What historical events might have prompted twentieth-century writers to reject forms and subjects of the past?

1940 — **1960** — **2010**

1945 George Orwell's satire on totalitarianism, *Animal Farm,* is published

1947 W. H. Auden publishes his long poem *The Age of Anxiety*

1953 Samuel Beckett's ground-breaking play *Waiting for Godot* is first produced in Paris ❯

Johnny Murphy and Barry McGovern in *Waiting for Godot.*

1960 Harold Pinter's absurdist play *The Caretaker* is first produced

1966 Tom Stoppard's absurdist, humorous play *Rosencrantz and Guilderstern Are Dead* is staged ❯

1998 Ted Hughes publishes *Birthday Letters,* poems about his relationship with his former wife, Sylvia Plath

2005 Zadie Smith publishes *On Beauty*

Nicholas Rowe and James Wallace in *Rosencrantz and Guildenstern Are Dead.*

1940 — **1960** — **2010**

1940 Battle of Britain; Royal Air Force prevents German invasion

1945 Germany surrenders; World War II ends

1948 London hosts the first Summer Olympics after the games' twelve-year hiatus

1949 Twenty-six counties in Ireland achieve full status as an independent republic; Britain retains control of six counties in the north

1960 Britain loses Nigeria

1960s British singing group The Beatles revolutionizes popular music ❯

2003 Britain joins the United States in war against Iraq

2005 Terrorists attack London's public transportation system

The Beatles at Abbey Road studios for *Our World* TV broadcast (1967).

1940 — **1960** — **2010**

1941 Japan bombs United States fleet at Pearl Harbor; United States declares war on Japan, Germany, and Italy

1945 Germany surrenders; United States drops atom bombs over Hiroshima and Nagasaki, ending the war with Japan

1947 Mohandas Gandhi is assassinated in India; State of Israel is created

1948 UN partitions Palestine; Arab-Israeli war results

1961 Berlin wall is built to separate East and West Germany

1975 Fall of Saigon marks end of Vietnam War

1991 Soviet Union is dissolved

2001 Terrorists hijack planes and destroy the World Trade Towers in New York and part of the Pentagon in Washington, D.C.

2003 United States and Britain go to war with Iraq

2007 Doris Lessing wins the Nobel Prize in Literature

Check for Understanding

Your Turn

Have students talk with a partner about what they know from reading texts or from viewing documentaries about life on the home front during World War I, World War II, or the Cold War. Next, have partners work to use that information to explain why twentieth-century writers rejected the literary forms and subjects of the past. After partners discuss this topic together, have them share their opinions with the class.

Explore the Time Line

Enrichment The following activity offers options for students to explore the literary, political, social, and world events presented on the time line.

- Explain to students that transformation in response to world changes is an important challenge for the writer.
- Divide the class into three groups. Assign each group one agent of transformation to research: the end of colonialism, the atomic bomb, and the rise and fall of totalitarian states.
- Have each group research its assigned topic, focusing on identifying and analyzing its causes and effects.
- As students research their topic, remind them to relate their research to the unit question: How does experience shape our view of the world?
- Have groups orally report their findings to the class.

Advanced Learners

Acceleration As you discuss the time line, compare the war years of 1914–1918 and 1939–1945. During which of these time periods were many major works of literature produced? Discuss how war affected the themes and approaches of the literature that was produced. [*Responses should focus on the horrors of the Holocaust and the dropping of the atomic bomb as indicators of the harshness of World War II, and the rise of absurdist literature and George Orwell's writings as responses to World War II.*]

Students with Disabilities

Tell students that the time lines show events from 1900 to 2010. Explain that students can compare events on the time lines by reading the page vertically. Model connecting an event on the time line of British literature to contemporary events in British and world history. You might say: "In 1916, two years after Great Britain declared war on Germany, Irish writer James Joyce published *A Portrait of the Artist as a Young Man.* That same year, the Easter Rebellion failed in Dublin, where Joyce lived. One year later, in 1917, the United States entered World War I."

Standards Focus

Objectives

Students will

- evaluate and analyze elements of literature from the modern world
- increase knowledge of the culture of others and the common elements across cultures

Preteach

Key Concepts

Use the Key Concepts to preview the unit introduction. Each key concept is addressed in a separate section of the essay that relates the concept to both the history and the literature of the times.

Set a Purpose for Reading

- Ask students to identify one piece of information from each key concept that they want to learn more about.
- Have students jot down any concepts, images, or phrases that come to mind when they think of the modern world from 1900 to the present. Suggest that students look for information related to these concepts as they read.
- Tell students to record each section's main ideas and important details in their notes.

California Standards, pp. 1064–1069

- **Reading Standard 2.2** Analyze the way in which clarity of meaning is affected by the patterns of organization, hierarchical structures, repetition of the main ideas, syntax, and word choice in the text.
- **Reading Standard 3.7** Analyze recognized works of world literature from a variety of authors: **b.** Relate literary works and authors to the major themes and issues of their eras. **c.** Evaluate the philosophical, political, religious, ethical, and social influences of the historical period that shaped the characters, plots, and settings.

The Modern World 1900 to the Present

"The center cannot hold," wrote poet William Butler Yeats, and indeed, in the early twentieth century, the prosperity and stability of the Victorian era dissolved into chaos and conflict. Two world wars and a major economic depression eroded Great Britain's political and economic power and brought a slow death to the once-mighty empire.

KEY CONCEPTS

World War I: The Great War

History of the Times In early twentieth-century Europe, rising nationalism, competition for colonies, and growing military capabilities helped create an environment ripe for conflict. By its terrible end in 1918, World War I had cost Britain not only 750,000 lives but also its confidence and optimism.

Literature of the Times Writers experimented with form and content. Literature reflected the disillusionment and cynicism people felt after the war.

World War II and Its Aftermath

History of the Times Poverty caused by an economic slump in the 1930s spawned dictatorships in Germany, Italy, and Russia. The German dictator Hitler invaded Poland in 1939, igniting World War II. The horrors of this war, particularly nuclear devastation and the Nazi concentration camps, changed the world forever.

Literature of the Times Much of the literature written after World War II has been a blistering response to war and the limits set on freedom.

Identity and Diversity

History of the Times After World War II, most of Britain's remaining colonies declared independence. Many nations in Europe and Latin America were politically redefined. Formerly marginalized groups, such as women and ethnic minorities, began demanding self-determination. None of these changes were achieved without conflict.

Literature of the Times Globalization is the word in literature and in economics. World writers as well as writers from Britain's former colonies explore the political, racial, and gender issues of the time in a bitingly honest fashion.

Mature students in computer class at adult education center, Camden, London.

Resources

Unit 6 Resources, on-level instruction, Historical Introduction Study Guide, p. 1

UA: Holt Interactive Reader, Key Concepts and Academic Vocabulary, p. 302

PowerNotes, interactive lesson presentations with activities go.hrw.com

Teacher One Stop™, on-level lesson plans and all print resources

Universal Access

EL English Learners/ Struggling Readers

To help students understand the information presented in the unit introduction, have them create a graphic organizer, such as a tree diagram or a word web, to record what they learn. Students can use the subheads, the names of writers, or historical events to help them organize the information they gather. After they read, ask students whether this strategy helped them process information.

Reading Standard 2.2, 3.7b, 3.7c (see pages A48–A50)

KEY CONCEPT

World War I: The Great War

History of the Times

When Germany invaded Belgium in 1914, Europe was plunged into World War I, the so-called Great War. Victorian writer Rudyard Kipling was right in celebrating the British character as essentially patriotic, for when Britain then declared war on Germany, young men rushed to enlist. Six months later, many of the same young men lay slaughtered in the rain-soaked, vermin-infested trenches of France. Over the course of four years, a generation of young Englishmen was fed to the insatiable furnace of the war.

With the armistice in 1918, a new cynicism arose. The old values of national honor and glory had endorsed a devastating war. Pessimism about the state and the individual's relation to society emerged from feelings of disillusionment. In response to the "romantic nonsense" of the past, and, in particular, to the propaganda machine that had led the nation into war, a new realism began to pervade literary thought.

Literature of the Times

The carnage of war transformed poetry. Poets, including those who had served on the Western Front, now questioned or even mocked the values that had sent so many young men to their deaths.

Novelists focused on introspection. The century's most influential writer was the Irishman James Joyce, whose 1922 novel *Ulysses* appeared to a storm of controversy. In a revolutionary manner, Joyce drew on myth and symbol, Freudian explorations of sexuality, and new conceptions of time and the workings of human consciousness. Literary critics called this experimentation with form and content **modernism.**

Comprehension Check

How did the war change the way people thought about themselves and society?

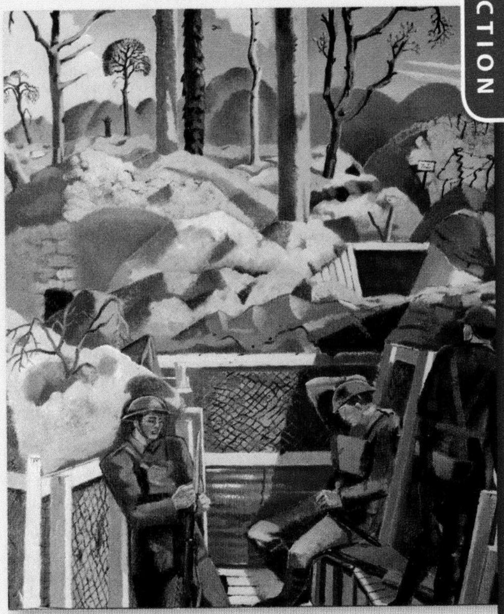

Spring on the Trenches, Ridge Wood (1917) by Paul Nash.

Fast Facts

Political and Social Highlights

- World War I, the Great Depression, and World War II alter Great Britain's position as a world power and dramatically change its society.
- After World War II, most of Great Britain's colonies gain independence.

Literary Highlights

- Joseph Conrad, James Joyce, Virginia Woolf, and D. H. Lawrence experiment with the form and content of the novel.
- Writers from former British colonies and other countries explore the effects of cultural domination, racism, sexism, and war.

Direct Teach

Think About/Talk About

Motivate Tell students that the common epithets for World War I—the "Great War" and the "War to End All Wars"—give clues to its extensive and devastating effect on lives. Start a class discussion about how writers and others must have adapted themselves and their art to that change.

History of the Times

- Tell students that trench warfare, massive artillery barrages, and machine-gun fire characterized the battles of World War I.
- Explain that in modern warfare, the carnage of battle became more salient than its glory. Shell shock, as a synonym for "battle fatigue," entered the language during the war years.

Literature of the Times

Discuss how James Joyce explored previously taboo topics and themes in his work, using literary techniques very different from those of the Victorian Age. Point out that, along with novelist Virginia Woolf and poets Ezra Pound and T.S. Eliot, Joyce influenced the development of the modernist style.

Comprehension Check

Possible responses: *The war replaced glory with disillusionment and pessimism. After the war, people wanted to break out of the old constraints that once governed behavior.*

Advanced Learners

Acceleration Encourage students to use a stream-of-consciousness writing style to record their responses to the Key Concepts essay on p. 1065. This style, which is very much like the prewriting technique called freewriting, allows writers to express their thoughts and feelings without worrying about narrative sequence or logical structure. Have students share their diary entries with a partner and then have partners present a summary to the class.

Students with Disabilities

Have students organize the information from the Key Concepts essay in a T-chart. Ask them to label the left column "Before the War" and the right column "After the War." Tell them to list characteristics of British society, politics, and literature before World War I in one column and after the war in another column. After students have finished, have them summarize the impact of World War I on Great Britain in one sentence using the information in the chart.

Think About/Talk About

History of the Times

- Tell students that the first half of the twentieth century was a time of great economic, political, and social upheaval. The 1917 Russian Revolution, which ended czarist rule, effectively took Russia out of World War I. Continued unrest led to the rise of the Communist Party rule, which persisted until 1991.
- The Treaty of Versailles placed so many burdens on a defeated Germany that Germany turned to a führer and the new Nazi party to restore the country's broken pride.
- The Roaring Twenties, with their flappers and freedom, a response to the horrors of World War I, ended abruptly with the stock market crash of 1929 and the Great Depression. This worldwide phenomenon especially affected the United States and Europe.
- The 1930s ended in warfare as Nazi Germany invaded Poland in 1939. After the fall of France in 1940, Great Britain fought on alone until the United States joined the war in late 1941 after the bombing of Pearl Harbor. This war was fought, in part, in British skies when German bombers attacked British cities during the Battle of Britain.

KEY CONCEPT

World War II and Its Aftermath

History of the Times

World War I, which had been called a war to end all wars, ironically led to another war, even more savage than the first. The League of Nations, the idealistic dream of U.S. President Woodrow Wilson, had no sooner been created than it was abandoned by a newly isolationist U.S. government. A worldwide economic depression that began in 1929 fostered the rise of dictators in Germany, Italy, and Russia.

In Italy and Germany the form of totalitarianism that developed was **fascism,** a type of government that is rigidly nationalistic and that relies on the rule of a single dictator whose power is absolute and backed by force. Benito Mussolini, who came to power in Italy in 1922, asserted control through brutality and manipulation. Adolf Hitler and the Nazi party capitalized on Germany's economic woes to convince many Germans that their problems were caused by Jews, Communists, and immigrants.

Russia's totalitarian government, based on the political theories of the economist Karl Marx, was Communist. Its founder, Vladimir Ilyich Lenin, had sought in the 1920s to create a society without a class system, one in which the state would distribute the country's wealth equally among the people. In reality, however, the new government became as repressive as the rule of the Russian czars. After Lenin's death in 1924, Joseph Stalin assumed power. In 1941, he became premier and continued to rule with an iron fist. Under Stalin's rule as many as fifteen million men and women were sent to the gulag, or system of forced-labor and detention camps.

By 1939, the Nazis were sweeping through Europe with their motorized army and superior air force. Hitler's plan for the systematic destruction of the Jews and other minorities, scapegoats on whom he blamed Germany's economic woes, resulted in the deaths of millions of innocent men, women, and children—including the six million Jews who were murdered in the Holocaust.

Only twenty years after the "war to end all wars," Europe had again plunged into a bloody, brutal conflict. In 1940, Germany occupied France and then prepared to invade Britain by launching devastating air attacks against London and other cities. Prime Minister Winston Churchill declared: "We shall go on to the end." The British did persevere, but only after the Soviet Union and the United States entered the war did Germany's defeat become inevitable.

For Japan, which had allied itself with Germany and Italy, the war ended in a new horror. On August 6, 1945, the entire city of Hiroshima was wiped out by a single atomic bomb dropped from an American plane. When the Japanese emperor still did not surrender, on August 9, a second atom bomb was dropped on Nagasaki.

While recovering from the war and rebuilding its own shattered economy, Great Britain was unable to retain control of its many colonies. Most, including India, the "jewel in the crown," became independent nations.

Literature of the Times

Much world literature in the twentieth century has been a direct and bitter response to war and limits on human freedom. In *All Quiet on the Western Front* (1928), the German writer Erich Maria Remarque describes the horrors of World War I with such vehemence that the novel was banned in Germany.

Even this harrowing war novel paled in comparison to the haunting personal testaments to suffering endured during the Holocaust, such as those of the Italian writer Primo Levi (see page 1092) and the Romanian writer Elie Wiesel (see page 1102), both interned in Nazi concentration camps. Writers in the former Soviet Union—such as Aleksandr Solzhenitsyn and Anna Akhmatova (see page 1242)—made an art of defying governmental attempts to regulate their writing.

Cross-Curricular Connection

HISTORY: World War II, 1939–1945

Although the Second World War cost fewer British lives than did the first, the Nazis posed more of a threat to Great Britain than had the Kaiser. With the British army driven from Europe in 1940 and British cities and ships under relentless Nazi air and submarine attack, Prime Minister Neville Chamberlain was considering a negotiated peace with Hitler. Winston Churchill, elected prime minister in 1940, was determined to continue fighting despite the bleak odds. British success that year in the Battle of Britain blunted German air power sufficiently to force Hitler to call off Operation Sea Lion, his planned invasion of Great Britain.

Germany's invasion of the Soviet Union in June 1941 took the immediate pressure off the British, and the United States' entry into the war allied Great Britain with the world's most powerful economy. Although German submarines exacted a huge toll on British shipping, the Anglo-American alliance provided the strength to achieve victory.

HSS Analysis Skills: HI 4

(*above*) Crowds gather in Piccadilly Circus, London, to celebrate V-E Day (May 8, 1945). (*right*) People dancing in the streets of London during celebrations of V-E Day.

British dramatists responded to the fragmentation of the times by experimenting with form and subject matter. Samuel Beckett even went so far as to undermine the very idea of logical coherence in *Waiting for Godot* (1953), called the most significant play of the twentieth century. The plays of the prolific Tom Stoppard combine extensive comic wordplay with serious questions about philosophical issues. His prize-winning trilogy *Coast of Utopia* (2002) deals with the origins of modern radicalism in Russia.

Much of the work written since World War II is categorized as **postmodern** by literary critics and historians. Directly or indirectly, this body of writing is concerned with women's rights, multiculturalism, and the ever-present question of identity in postmodern society.

Comprehension Check

How did the rise of totalitarianism lead to the violence and oppression that characterize the modern world?

Primary Source

Churchill on the Fall of France

In June 1940, with the Nazis overrunning France, Prime Minister Winston Churchill (1874–1965) broadcast the following statement: "The news from France is very bad, and I grieve for the gallant French people who have fallen into this terrible misfortune. Nothing will alter our feelings toward them or our faith that the genius of France will rise again. What has happened in France makes no difference to our actions and purpose. We have become the sole champions now in arms to defend the world cause. We shall do our best to be worthy of this high honour. We shall defend our island home, and with the British Empire we shall fight on unconquerable until the curse of Hitler is lifted from the brows of mankind."

Think About/Talk About

Literature of the Times

- Just as the war poets Wilfred Owen, Rupert Brooke, and Siegfried Sassoon and the German writer Erich Maria Remarque responded to the horrors of World War I, writers such as Primo Levi and Elie Wiesel responded to the horrors of World War II. In what was then the Soviet Union, underground publications, collectively called samizdat, or "self-publishing," kept literature and dissent alive following Stalin's death in 1953.
- The writings of playwrights such as Samuel Beckett, Harold Pinter, and Eugène Ionesco have been called the Theater of the Absurd, which experimented with both form and content. In Beckett's famous play *Waiting for Godot,* the main character, Godot, never arrives. Two tramps, the supporting characters, have no certainty who Godot is or whether Godot will ever come, but still they wait. On stage, they sit beneath a tree and never move.

Comprehension Check

Possible response: *Totalitarian governments in Italy, Germany, and the former Soviet Union often relied on repression and violence, thus making violence more commonplace.*

Think About/Talk About

History of the Times

- When Australia, Canada, and South Africa separated from the British Empire, they formed the self-governing British Commonwealth, which still had ties to Great Britain. South Africa left the Commonwealth in 1961 but rejoined in 1994.
- Germany and France, the two other major colonial powers of Europe, lost their colonies because of the war or to local independence movements, as in the case of French Indochina, now Vietnam. Many German colonies in Africa became British protectorates, but by 1970 most British colonies in East Africa and West Africa had become independent nations. Among the last holdouts was Kenya, where many Europeans and Asians had settled. Kenya became independent in 1963.

Comprehension Check

Possible response: *"Identity" may refer to the sense of identities that many newly independent countries in Asia and Africa and older countries in Latin America felt as their independence and local literatures bloomed. "Diversity" may refer to the differences that still separate Israelis and Palestinians and many in the Muslim world from the nations in the West.*

KEY CONCEPT

Identity and Diversity

History of the Times

Prior to World War II, countries such as Australia, Canada, and South Africa had already separated from the British Empire. The end of World War II sealed the empire's fate, and in the late 1940s and 1950s, most of Britain's remaining colonies declared independence.

As a result of the decline of Western imperial powers after World War II, dozens of independent states emerged in Africa and Asia, and many older nations in Europe and Latin America were politically redefined. These nations and others began to assert their own identities and reclaim territories. For example, India declared independence from Britain in 1946, and Nigeria did the same in 1960.

In 1947, the State of Israel was created to provide a homeland for the millions of Jews who had become refugees during World War II. The creation and subsequent population of Israel displaced hundreds of thousands of Palestinians from their homes, and the fighting over territory in that area continues today.

In 1989, the Berlin Wall that separated Communist East Germany from West Germany was torn down. Five years later, Nelson Mandela was elected president in the first South African election open to all races.

Despite momentous demonstrations of independence and progress, injustice, war, and genocide persist. A new worldwide threat has presented itself in the form of international terrorism, manifested in the 2001 devastating attacks on the World Trade Towers in New York City and on the Pentagon in Washington, D.C. Our human effort to understand one another has never been more challenging or more essential.

Literature of the Times

Innovations in technology and transportation have linked people in ways our ancestors couldn't have imagined. Ideas travel as fast as electronic channels can carry them, and one writer may influence another living continents away.

Current world literature frequently focuses on political and social problems. Literally hundreds of writers from former British colonies explore issues of personal identity and the effects of cultural domination and racism. Literary critics call the works of these writers **postcolonial literature.** These writers have seen their local cultures uprooted by colonialism or foreign influence, and they have had to ask themselves continually whether they are to celebrate their native traditions, imitate foreign models, or create new modes of expression.

Comprehension Check

To what does the title "Identity and Diversity" refer?

March outside British fort wall by Troops Out, calling for the removal of British troops from Northern Ireland.

Academic Vocabulary

Talking and Writing About Literature

English for Academic Success Write the following questions on the board. Tell students these are the kinds of questions they will encounter on standardized tests. Discuss the meaning of the words and then have students use the historical introduction to answer the questions.

- Is war the **inevitable** outcome of a major dispute, or can nations **adapt** and find peaceful solutions? ***Possible response:*** *Wars do not have to occur repeatedly. Germany, for instance, has tamed its militaristic heritage.*
- Was there **considerably** more artistic experimentation during Victorian times or during the modern era? ***Possible response:*** *There has been much more artistic experimentation during the modern era than before.*
- From the **perspective** of Britain's war poets, must one **exhibit** only courage in the face of death? ***Possible response:*** *The war poets allowed themselves to express fear as well as courage.*

UNIT 6 INTRODUCTION

Link to Today

The Second Sex

Political concerns in postwar world literature are not the sole domain of nations and cultures; women's voices are some of the strongest to emerge in the postwar world. Many feminist writers work to expose women's lack of power in a world controlled by men. In the influential feminist work *The Second Sex* (1949), French writer Simone de Beauvoir analyzes women's secondary status in society and denounces the male middle class for perceiving women as objects; she demands an end to the "slavery of half of humanity." The Nigerian feminist Buchi Emecheta has informed numerous women writers from various African countries and uses motherhood (but not marriage) as a symbol for artistic creativity in her fiction. In *The Handmaid's Tale* (1985), the Canadian writer Margaret Atwood presents a grim cautionary tale that warns readers of a possible future world in which a puritanical dictatorship seeks to repress and control women.

Ask Yourself

What issues or concerns do feminist writers address today?

British technical aid worker teaching dress-making to woman in Malawi.

Wrap Up

Talk About . . .

What is the value in reading works of literature from other cultures? Explain. Try to use each Academic Vocabulary Word **listed below** at least once in your discussion.

Write About . . .

Does art continue to challenge norms, or does it reflect a new social stability? Answer this question in a brief essay, considering not only literature but also other modern technological forms of communication.

Academic Vocabulary for Unit 6

Talking and Writing About Literature

Academic Vocabulary is the language you use to write and talk about literature. These words will be underlined throughout the unit.

perspective (puhr SPEHK tihv) *n.:* particular way of looking at something. *Many poets changed their perspective on World War I when they saw the terrible suffering it caused.*

inevitable (ihn EHV uh tuh buhl) *adj.:* unavoidable. *When the United States and the Soviet Union entered World War II, Germany's defeat became inevitable.*

considerably (kuhn SIHD uhr uh blee) *adv.:* by a large amount. *Great Britain became considerably weaker after World War II.*

adapt (uh DAPT) *v.:* adjust for a new purpose. *Russia's totalitarian government adapted Karl Marx's theories to create a new society.*

exhibit (ehg ZIHB iht) *v.:* show, demonstrate. *Former British colonies still exhibit the effects of cultural domination.*

Your Turn

Copy the words from the Academic Vocabulary list into your *Reader/Writer Notebook.* Make a point of trying to use these words as you discuss the selections in the chapters that follow.

- What issues do the former British colonies **inevitably** face in **adapting** to their new independent state? ***Possible response:*** *These colonies struggle with their cultural identity and do not know whether to adopt foreign models or continue their native traditions.*
- How did feminist writers challenge society's **perspective** on the role of women in society? ***Possible response:*** *Some deplored women's secondary status in society and others depicted the role of women creatively in their writing.*

Think About/Talk About

Link to Today
The Second Sex

This feature is about feminist literature in developed and developing nations.

1. What was the catalyst for the growth of feminist literature?
2. After students have read the feature, ask them to speculate about the response Simone de Beauvoir's books received.
3. Finally, ask students to respond to the **Ask Yourself** question. Use students' responses to spark class discussion.
4. Encourage interested students to conduct research on feminist literature in the Middle East.

Check for Understanding

Talk About . . .

Have students discuss what different cultures, including cultures very different from one's own, can learn from another's perspective.

Write About . . .

Have students discuss which contemporary forms of art and media—such as performance art, stand-up comedy, podcasts, Web sites, and blogs—exhibit extreme perspectives and challenge cultural norms, and which forms seem settled or even complacent. Remind writers to give specific examples.

Standards Focus

Objectives

Students will evaluate and analyze the philosophical, political, religious, ethical, and social influences of a historical period.

Link to Today

This contemporary poem celebrates space exploration, which gives humanity new pathways to explore. It develops the themes of transformation and change, which are central to the literature discussed in Unit 6.

Unit 6 Resources, Historical Introduction Skill Builder, p. 1

UA: Differentiating Instruction, graphic organizer, p. 260

Teacher One Stop™, lesson plan and all print resources

Direct Teach

Think About/Talk About

Read with a Purpose Direct students to the Read with a Purpose statement. Point out to students that they should be looking for images that treat the spacecraft as a mechanical device and images that treat it as an explorer. Ask students to record their own feelings and attitudes toward space exploration in their **Reader/Writer Notebooks.**

Link to Today

This Link to Today celebrates the wonder of space exploration.

Read with a Purpose

Read this poem to see how the speaker describes the journey of *Voyager 1* into the outer reaches of space.

Build Background

Two unpiloted spacecrafts, *Voyager 1* and *Voyager 2*, were launched in 1977 to explore outer space and send scientific information back to NASA. *Voyager 1* has traveled farther from Earth than any object made by humans; in 2006, its distance from the Earth was 100 times that of the sun. Guided by a ten-person flight team at NASA, *Voyager 1* is traveling about one million miles per day at the outer edge of our solar system, approaching interstellar space, which is filled with material from the explosions of stars.

Author Note

Alice Oswald (1966–) has worked as a gardener, and her love of the natural world permeates her poetry. It took her three years to complete her poem *Dart,* which describes the long journey of the Dart River as it flows into the sea. The speakers in *Dart* include the voices of the many people who work and live along the river, along with those of animals, plants, and insects. Oswald won the T. S. Eliot Prize for poetry in 2003. She lives in England with her family.

SONNET

Spacecraft Voyager 1 Has Boldly Gone

by **Alice Oswald**

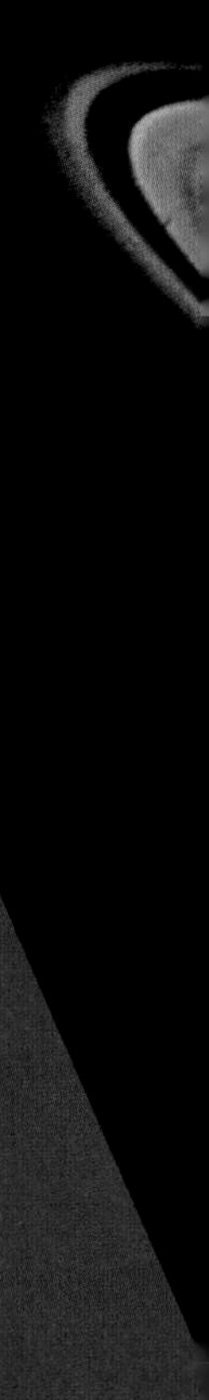

Spacecraft Voyager 1 has boldly gone
into Deep Silence carrying a gold-plated disc inscribed with
whale-song
it has bleeped back a last infra-red fragment of language
and floated way way up over the jagged edge
of this almost endless bright and blowy enclosure of weather
to sink through a new texture as tenuous as the soft upward
pressure of an elevator
and go on and on falling up steep flights of blackness with
increasing swiftness
beyond the Crystalline Cloud of the Dead beyond Plato° beyond
Copernicus°
O meticulous swivel cameras still registering events
among those homeless spaces gathering in that silence
that hasn't yet had time to speak in that increasing sphere
of tiny runaway stars notched in the year
now you can look closely at massless light
that is said to travel freely but is probably in full flight

8. **Plato:** ancient Greek philosopher (c. 428 B.C.– c. 348 B.C.); the ancient Greeks constructed the first "model" of the solar system based on mathematical theories.
Copernicus: Polish astronomer (1473–1543) who proposed a controversial idea that the sun was at the center of the universe, and the planets, including Earth, rotated around it.

Bright rings of Saturn and its northern hemisphere defined by bright features.

Selection Readability	
Easily Accessible **Accessible** Challenging	chronological order; accessible theme

Selection Summary

The poem celebrates the more than thirty-year journey of the spacecraft *Voyager I* into deep space. Oswald describes the initial launch through Earth's "enclosure of weather" and Voyager's flight "up steep flights of blackness" past the end of the solar system, all the while sending visual images back to Earth.

Ask Yourself

1. **Read with a Purpose** What imagery and vivid verbs does the poet use to describe the journey of the *Voyager*. How do her references to everyday objects help you imagine the journey?
2. The poem's first line refers to the popular science-fiction series *Star Trek*, which tells the story of a spacecraft whose mission is "to boldly go where no one has gone before." What does this allusion tell you about the journey of *Voyager 1*?
3. In what way might pictures and other data sent back from *Voyager 1* help the "Deep Silence" "speak" to people today? What "messages" might it send us?
4. To Plato and Copernicus (mentioned in line 8), the solar system was a mystery yet to be unraveled. In what way does *Voyager 1* go "beyond" them? What mysteries related to science would you like to see explained in your lifetime?

Universal Access

EL English Learners/ Struggling Readers

English for Academic Success Before students read the poem, introduce the following words.

- **tenuous**—thin in form or consistency. *The prisoner's self-serving statement has a tenuous connection to the truth.*
- **meticulous**—taking or showing extreme care about minute details. *The hand-drawn map showed the cartographer's meticulous attention to detail.*
- **massless**—without mass or weight. *The photons in sunlight are massless.*

Then, challenge students to write a sentence that uses at least two of these words.

Think About/Talk About

Extend the Discussion

Finding Details Have students look for details in the poem that refer to the physical parts of the spacecraft. ***Possible responses:*** *Students may mention the gold-plated disk, the bleep of the signal back to Earth, and the swivel camera.*

Recognizing Rhetorical Devices In addition to the allusion to the television show *Star Trek*, the writer makes allusions to two historical figures, Plato and Copernicus. Have students discuss why Oswald made those references. ***Possible response:*** *Oswald refers to thinkers of the past who increased humanity's knowledge of the known universe, just as* Voyager 1 *is doing.*

Ask Yourself

Possible responses:

1. *She uses the imagery of floating and climbing to help readers visualize the flight. Images such as the comparison of the acceleration of the spacecraft to the feeling of an elevator ride, along with vivid verbs like "bleeped," "sink," and "registering," help readers "see" the journey.*
2. *The reference tries to capture the excitement about space exploration that imbued* Star Trek *episodes. The familiar reference helps the poet appeal to the popular imagination.*
3. *The pictures and other data from "Deep Silence" will become the "voice" through which the edge of the universe will "speak" to us. It will give messages about what is out there.*
4. *The* Voyager I *spacecraft goes "beyond" Plato and Copernicus metaphorically, because they probably could not have conceived of a vessel that could explore space, Their conceptions of the universe were limited and inaccurate. In my lifetime, I hope that scientists will make more discoveries about whether life exists on other planets.*

Chapter Objectives

- Students will learn about the effect of wartime experiences on writers and their writing.
- Students will connect their own experiences with the experiences of the war poets.

The Quotation

Tell students that the Literary Skills Focus of Chapter 11 is war literature, which expresses the glory and horror of war. Have students comment on the quotation from writer Doris Lessing (1919–). Have them address how humanity is "twisted and warped by war" and, from the evidence of wars that followed World War I, why "we seem to forget it."
Possible responses: *War changes the perceptions of all who have gone off to fight. We tend to forget the horrors of war, to forget its harm; instead, we tend to use it for political ends or economical gains.*

Analyzing Visuals

Extension Activity What details in the image support Lessing's statement that we are "made by war, twisted and warped by war"?
Possible responses: *Everything in the image is twisted and broken. The human heads are bound in chains; staircases lead nowhere; human bodies are twisted. Destruction is everywhere.*

CHAPTER **11**

The World at War

LITERARY SKILLS FOCUS
War Literature

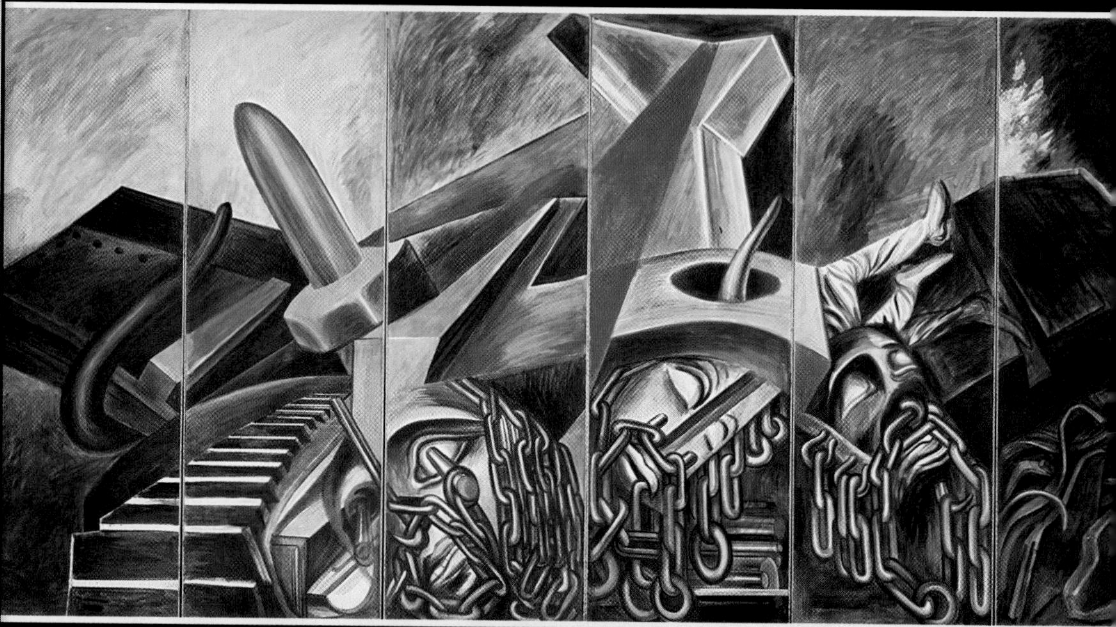

Dive Bomber and Tank (1940) by Jose Clement Orozco (1883–1949).
The Museum of Modern Art, N.Y. /Artists Rights Society (ARS), N.Y.

CONTENTS

"We are all of us made by war, twisted and warped by war, but we seem to forget it."

—Doris Lessing

Chapter 11

California Standards Overview

- **Reading Standard 2.2** Analyze the way in which clarity of meaning is affected by the patterns of organization, hierarchical structures, repetition of the main ideas, syntax, and word choice in the text.
- **Reading Standard 2.5** Analyze an author's implicit and explicit philosophical assumptions and beliefs about a subject.
- **Reading Standard 2.6** Critique the power, validity, and truthfulness of arguments set forth in public documents; their appeal to both friendly and hostile audiences; and the extent to which the arguments anticipate and address reader concerns and counterclaims (e.g., appeal to reason, to authority, to pathos and emotion).
- **Reading Standard 3.1** Analyze characteristics of subgenres (e.g., satire, parody, allegory, pastoral) that are used in poetry, prose, plays, novels, short stories, essays, and other basic genres.
- **Reading Standard 3.3** Analyze the ways in which irony, tone, mood, the author's style, and the "sound" of language achieve specific rhetorical or aesthetic purposes or both.
- **Reading Standard 3.4** Analyze ways in which poets use imagery, personification, figures of speech, and sounds to evoke readers' emotions.
- **Reading Standard 3.7** Analyze recognized works of world literature from a variety of authors: **b.** Relate literary works and authors to the major themes and issues of their eras. **c.** Evaluate the philosophical, political, religious, ethical, and social influences of the historical period that shaped the characters, plots, and settings.
- **Reading Standard 3.8** Analyze the clarity and consistency of political assumptions in a selection of literary works or essays on a topic (e.g., suffrage, women's role in organized labor) (Political approach).

Reading Standard 3.7b, 3.7c (see pages A48–A50)

War Literature by Leila Christenbury

Features of War Literature

- Poems that express the glory and horror of battle
- Memoirs that recount the experiences of soldiers and concentration camp victims
- Short stories that depict the lives of ordinary citizens affected by war
- Elegies that mourn the loss of loved ones, fellow soldiers, and civilians
- Speeches that evoke national pride and encourage citizens to keep their faith in the war cause

War from All Perspectives

As battles raged during two world wars, writers captured the horror of battle, the unfathomable suffering endured in prisoner-of-war and concentration camps, and the sacrifice, the fear, and the losses felt by civilians. The authors of the literature in this chapter were eyewitnesses to two world wars. All of them suffered terribly in war, and one, Wilfred Owen, died on the battlefield.

The poems of the World War I soldiers reflect the mood of Britain. As the war progressed, taking 750,000 British lives and leaving the soldiers who returned haunted with memories of trench warfare, the poems' themes shifted from the early idealism and patriotic glory of Rupert Brooke to the dejection and horror of Wilfred Owen and Siegfried Sassoon.

Survivors Reflect

World War II brought further horror. As British civilians lost loved ones overseas and Londoners suffered nightly bombings, Prime Minister Winston Churchill made impassioned speeches over the radio, urging fortitude and patience. The war, which did not distinguish between soldiers and civilians, took more than forty million lives. The era's literature is as vast as its suffering, encompassing the perspectives of soldiers, civilians, and prisoners alike. Desperate to recount their experiences and find meaning in the war, writers crafted **memoirs** and **elegies** to express the loss and grief occasioned by the twentieth century's costliest and deadliest war. Experiences in the Nazi concentration camps prompted the graphic true accounts of writers such as Primo Levi, Victor Frankl, and Elie Wiesel.

Analyzing Visuals

Connecting to the Text How do the colors and lines in these sketches convey the atmosphere of war?

Illustration from *All Quiet on the Western Front* (1929) by Erich Maria Remarque.

Ask Yourself

1. What can you learn about war from these civilian and soldier writers?
2. What value is there in writing and reading war literature?

Learn It Online
Explore war literature with *PowerNotes* online.
go.hrw.com H12-1073 Go

Literary Skills Focus

Objectives
Students will understand characteristics of war literature.

Unit 6 Resources, Literary Focus Skill Builder, p. 5

PowerNotes, interactive lesson presentation with activities

Teacher One Stop™, on-level lesson plan and all print resources

Direct Teach

War from All Perspectives

Use the following question to discuss war and the human experience: When soldiers enlisting for World War I were motivated by "idealism and patriotic glory," what do you think they expected to experience?

Check for Understanding

Ask Yourself

Possible responses:

1. *We can experience war vicariously by understanding how it changed wartime writers' lives.*
2. *Reading and writing war literature helps readers to think more deeply about this harsh human experience.*

California Standards, p. 1073

- **Reading Standard 3.7** Analyze recognized works of world literature from a variety of authors: **b.** Relate literary works and authors to the major themes and issues of their eras. **c.** Evaluate the philosophical, political, religious, ethical, and social influences of the historical period that shaped the characters, plots, and settings.

Analyzing Visuals

Connecting to the Text: *The roughly sketched lines and chaotic blend of colors convey the disorder and darkness that render people and objects indistinguishable on the battlefield.*

Learn It Online
For a multimedia version of the instruction found on this page, use the **PowerNotes** Literary Skills Focus presentation.
go.hrw.com H12-1073 Go

Standards Focus

Objectives

Students will
- analyze figures of speech
- analyze poetic structure
- use context clues

Selection Introduction

Think About the Writers

Ask students how a person's perspective on war might be affected by the experience of going to war. Point out that both Owen and Brooke volunteered to fight. Brooke died in 1915. Owen died in action in 1918, one week before peace was declared. Then, ask students to predict how the two poets' perspectives on war might differ.

For Independent Reading

- *Sonny's War,* Valerie Hobbs
- *A Farewell to Arms,* Ernest Hemingway

Motivate

What Do You Think?/QuickTalk

Have students list activities involved in military service that make going to war like embarking on an adventure. Then, ask them to list ways that military service differs from adventure.

English for Academic Success

Academic Vocabulary

Look for opportunities to use the Academic Vocabulary words in this unit.

- **considerably,** ***adv.:*** by a large amount
- **perspective,** ***n.:*** a particular way of looking at something

Preparing to Read

WILFRED OWEN

Dulce et Decorum Est

RUPERT BROOKE

The Soldier

What Do You Think? How does experience shape our view of the world?

QuickTalk

Discuss in a small group why young men and women might view going to war as an adventure. Do you agree with this view?

Wilfred Owen (1916). The Granger Collection, NY.

Rupert Brooke (1910) portrait by Sherril Schell.

MEET THE WRITERS

Wilfred Owen

(1893–1918)

Wilfred Owen is one of the most poignant figures in modern literature. To learn his craft, he immersed himself in the history of English poetry and studied the French modernist poets, but these literary influences were to become secondary to the devastating impact of a war Owen witnessed firsthand.

World War I broke out when Owen was twenty-one. He joined the British army, and the course of his life was determined. His progress in poetry was made not in the halls of an ancient university or in country retreats but in the muddy purgatory of trench warfare and the twilight existence of military hospitals. His gift for lyricism was bitterly tempered by "the pity of war, the pity war distilled." In November 1918, and a mere seven days before the war ended, Owen was listed among those killed in action.

Rupert Brooke

(1887–1915)

Handsome and charismatic, Rupert Brooke was England's golden poet. After distinguishing himself as an athlete and scholar in private school, he studied at Cambridge and in Germany, and traveled through Italy, Canada, the United States, and the South Seas. His popular early poems celebrated love and nature.

When World War I broke out, Brooke received a commission in the Royal Navy. The war sonnets he wrote during a lull in fighting in 1914 enjoyed considerable and immediate popularity. Although the poems were later criticized for being overly sentimental and overlooking the devastating effects of war, Brooke's works captured the hope and patriotism of a country that believed in the war efforts. His death from blood poisoning early in the war was mourned by all of England, including Winston Churchill, who called him one of "England's noblest sons."

Think About the Writers Owen served in the war considerably longer than Brooke. What different views of the war do you think their poems might reflect? Why?

California Standards, pp. 1074–1079

- **Reading Standard 2.2** Analyze the way in which clarity of meaning is affected by the patterns of organization, hierarchical structures, repetition of the main ideas, syntax, and word choice in the text.
- **Reading Standard 3.4** Analyze ways in which poets use imagery, personification, figures of speech, and sounds to evoke readers' emotions.

Selection Readability	
Easily Accessible **Accessible** Challenging	These poems include familiar language; familiar context.

Reading Standard 2.2, 3.4 (see pages A48–A50)

Literary Skills Focus

Figures of Speech A **figure of speech** is a word or phrase that describes one thing in terms of another. Among the most common figures of speech are **similes, metaphors,** and **symbols.** An **oxymoron** (plural: *oxymora*) is a figure of speech that combines opposite or contradictory ideas. The phrase *sweet sorrow*, used to describe the feeling of being happy and sad at the same time, is an example of an oxymoron.

Reading Skills Focus

Using Context Clues When you read poetry, you may encounter an unfamiliar word or a familiar word used in a new way (such as a figure of speech). You can use **context clues,** or the words, ideas, and information around the unfamiliar word, to help you guess the word's meaning. The poems in this chapter refer to World War I trench warfare; therefore, if you read that the men slept underground in dark and muddy trenches, you could use context clues to guess that a trench is a hole in the ground. If you read that the men dropped into "hellish battle holes," you could use context clues to guess that this figure of speech refers to trenches.

Into Action In a chart like the one below, write unfamiliar words you find in the poem. Then, write any context clues that might help you determine the words' meanings. These clues might include other words in the poem or an explanation of the general context, or what is happening.

Unfamiliar Word	Context Clues
flound'ring	The men are stumbling to put on their gas masks.

Writing Skills Focus

Think as a Reader/Writer

Find It in Your Reading Owen uses startling **figures of speech** to convey war's horror. Note the **simile** he uses to describe the injured man: "his hanging face, like a devil's sick of sin." In your *Reader/Writer Notebook,* note other figures of speech from the poem.

Reader/Writer Notebook

Use your **RWN** to complete the activities for this selection.

Vocabulary

writhing (RY thihng) *v.* used as *adj.:* twisting and turning, as in pain. *The soldier, writhing in agony, had suffered a bullet wound.*

vile (vyl) *adj.:* disgusting. *The vile, oozing sores on the man's leg made his friends turn away in horror.*

ardent (AHR duhnt) *adj.:* eager; enthusiastic. *The soldiers were ardent for victory over their enemies.*

Language Coach

Word Origins The word *writhing* comes from an Old English word meaning "to twist, wind about." Other modern English words from this root include *wreath, wreathe,* and *wry*. Using the knowledge of the root's meaning, explain the meaning of these phrases: "a wry face," "wry humor," "things gone awry."

Learn It Online

Learn more with these Internet links.

go.hrw.com H12-1075 Go

Selection Resources

Unit 6 Resources, on-level practice and assessment, p. 7

Teacher One Stop™, on-level lesson plans and all print resources

Holt Audio Library

Holt Audio Library: Selections and Summaries in Spanish

UA: Differentiating Instruction, graphic organizer, p. 261

UA: Supporting Instruction in Spanish, selection summary

ThinkCentral Online Assessment, Selection Standards Check

ThinkCentral Online Remediation

Preteach

Introducing Vocabulary

- Read the Vocabulary words and sample sentences aloud. Use the activity below to check students' understanding.
- To reinforce the importance of the Vocabulary words, tell students that Owen uses them to evoke the experience of war. When soldiers are wounded, their bodies can be seen *writhing* with pain. Bullets can create repulsive, *vile* wounds. People generally show more *ardent* support for war before combat has begun than they do after a military conflict has persisted.

English for Academic Success

Language Coach

Ask students to relate the words *wreath* and *wreathe* to the meaning of the root word. [*"wry face" describes a contorted facial expression; "wry humor" refers to bitter humor; "things gone awry" means things have taken an unexpected turn*]

Literary Skills Focus

As you read and discuss the poem with students, have them note contradictory ideas.

Reading Skills Focus

Give students a copy of the Reading Skills Focus graphic organizer before they read. (See **Unit 6 Resources.**) Tell them to use their responses to answer the questions on the Applying Your Skills page.

Writing Skills Focus

Have students record in their **Reader/Writer Notebooks** figures of speech Owen uses to convey the experience of war. Students can use their notes to complete the Writing Skills Focus activity.

Learn It Online

Literature Links direct students to pre-screened Web sites offering more information related to a selection.

go.hrw.com H12-1075 Go

Teacher Preparation
Selection Summary
The speaker in "Dulce et Decorum Est" is marching with a group of battle-weary soldiers when a poison-gas shell explodes nearby. The soldiers scramble to don their gas masks, but one falls, and the others watch helplessly while the fumes choke him to death. The speaker says that, in all his dreams, he still sees the man dying. Then, he directly addresses the reader, asserting that if "you" could see that too, you would not teach children the vicious lie that it is sweet and honorable to die for one's country.

POEM

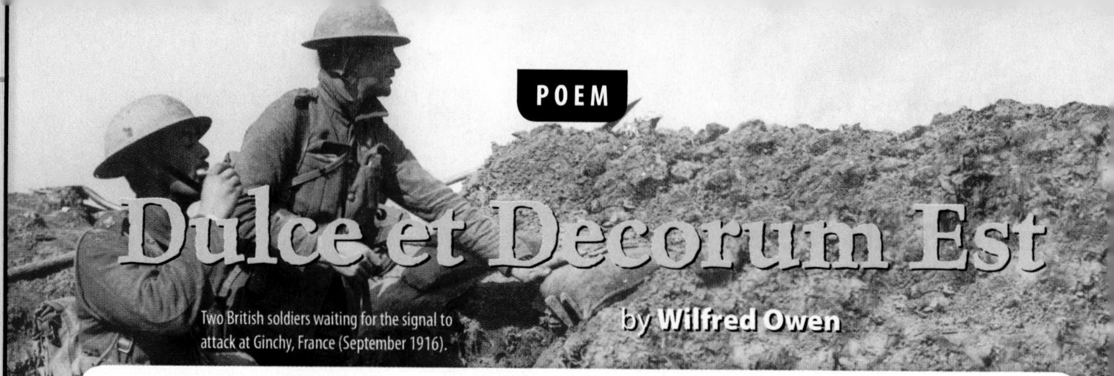

Two British soldiers waiting for the signal to attack at Ginchy, France (September 1916).

Dulce et Decorum Est

by **Wilfred Owen**

Read with a Purpose
Read this poem to discover how the poet conveys the horrors of war.

Build Background
This poem's title comes from the Latin statement *Dulce et decorum est pro patria mori*, which means "It is sweet and honorable to die for one's country." The statement has been used for centuries as a morale builder—and as a gravestone inscription—for soldiers.

After poison gas became a battlefield weapon during World War I, every soldier in the trenches had a gas mask. This poem describes the horrible consequences of failing to put on the mask in time.

Bent double, like old beggars under sacks,
Knock-kneed, coughing like hags, we cursed through sludge,
Till on the haunting flares we turned our backs
And toward our distant rest began to trudge.
Men marched asleep. Many had lost their boots
But limped on, blood-shod. All went lame; all blind;
Drunk with fatigue; deaf even to the hoots
Of tired, outstripped Five-Nines° that dropped behind.

Gas! GAS! Quick, boys!—An ecstasy of fumbling,
Fitting the clumsy helmets just in time;
But someone still was yelling out and stumbling
And flound'ring like a man in fire or lime° . . .
Dim, through the misty panes and thick green light,
As under a green sea, I saw him drowning. **A** **B**

In all my dreams, before my helpless sight,
He plunges at me, guttering, choking, drowning.

If in some smothering dreams you too could pace
Behind the wagon that we flung him in,
And watch the white eyes writhing in his face,
His hanging face, like a devil's sick of sin;
If you could hear, at every jolt, the blood
Come gargling from the froth-corrupted lungs,
Obscene as cancer, bitter as the cud
Of vile, incurable sores on innocent tongues,—
My friend, you would not tell with such high zest
To children ardent for some desperate glory,
The old Lie: *Dulce et decorum est*
Pro patria mori

8. Five-Nines: 5.9-caliber gas shells.
12. lime: powder produced from heat on limestone. It can cause severe skin irritations.

A **Literary Focus** **Figures of Speech** What oxymoron appears in this stanza?

B **Reading Focus** **Using Context Clues** Use context clues to figure out what the speaker means by "misty panes." What words or details help you guess the meaning?

Vocabulary **writhing** (RY thihng) *v.* used as *adj.:* twisting and turning, as in pain.
vile (vyl) *adj.:* disgusting.
ardent (AHR duhnt) *adj.:* eager; enthusiastic.

Direct Teach

Think About/Talk About
Read with a Purpose Have students read the Read with a Purpose statement. Ask them to predict what kinds of language the poet will use to convey the horrors of war.

Comprehension
B Reading Focus
Possible responses: *The "misty panes" are the gas mask's panes of plastic the wearer looks through; they are misty from clouds of poison gas. The words "Gas! GAS!" (l. 9) and "Fitting the clumsy helmets just in time" suggest the speaker is referring to gas masks.*

Analysis
A Literary Focus
Possible response: *"An ecstasy of fumbling" (lines 8–9) is an oxymoron.*

Vocabulary: Own the Word
- **writhing:** Draw a word web of the word *writhing*. Have students suggest words related to *writhing* and record them in the web.
- **vile:** *Vile* is derived from the Latin root *vilis,* meaning "worthless, base." Ask students to relate the root to the meaning of *vile.*
- **ardent:** In the poem, Owen describes children who are *ardent* for glory. Ask students what they are *ardent* for—or what they have an *ardent* interest in now.

Universal Access

EL English Learners
English for Academic Success To assist students in guessing the meaning of unfamiliar words using context clues, suggest they visualize the other words. For example, in lines 11–12, they might visualize a person yelling, stumbling as he walks, and "flound'ring like a man in fire . . ." How else might students visualize a victim hit by a gas shell? Besides screaming and stumbling, his body might be jerking since he would have trouble breathing.

Struggling Readers
Strategic Students Model for students how to use context clues to decipher the meaning of an unfamiliar word. Read the first three lines of the poem out loud. You might say: "I do not know what *knock-kneed* in line 2 means, so I look at the words and phrases before *knock-kneed.* Lines 1 and 2 mention the soldiers bent over and cursing through sludge. I make a guess that *knock-kneed* describes a kind of condition where the soldier has difficulty walking normally."

Reading Standard 3.3 (see pages A48–A50)

The Soldier

Literary Skills Focus

Poetic Structure The way a poem is constructed—its number of lines, rhyme scheme, and rhythm—is its **poetic structure**. Sonnets have similar poetic structures. They have fourteen lines, have one of several rhyme schemes, and are usually written with a meter called iambic pentameter. **Iambic pentameter** is a line of verse with five iambs. An **iamb** is a unit of measure consisting of an unstressed syllable followed by a stressed syllable. There are two major types of sonnets, each with a slightly different poetic structure. As you read "The Soldier," note how Brooke uses elements from both types.

The **Petrarchan sonnet** is divided into two parts: an eight-line octave with the rhyme scheme *abbaabba* and a six-line **sestet** with the rhyme scheme *cdecde* or *cdcdcd.* The octave usually presents a problem, poses a question, or expresses an idea, which the sestet then resolves, answers, or drives home. The transition from octave to sestet is known as the **turn.**

The **Shakespearean sonnet** has three four-line units, or **quatrains,** followed by a concluding two-line unit, or **couplet.** The three quatrains often express related ideas or examples, while the couplet sums up the message expressed in the quatrains. The turn usually occurs during the transition from the third quatrain to the couplet. The rhyme scheme of the Shakespearean sonnet is *abab cdcd efef gg.*

Writing Skills Focus

Think as a Reader/Writer

Find It in Your Reading Poets often use sounds in their poems to emphasize message and tone. Brooke uses **alliteration,** the repetition of consonant sounds in words that are close to each other, to enhance the positive tone of his poem. In your *Reader/Writer Notebook,* use a chart like the one below to record examples of alliteration and the specific effects they create.

Example	Effect
"Her sights and sounds; dreams happy as her day"	The gliding sounds of /s/ and /z/ create a light tone.

Vocabulary

concealed (kuhn SEELD) *v.:* hidden. *The soldier's body will be concealed under the cold, hard ground.*

eternal (ih TUR nuhl) *adj.:* forever; everlasting. *The soldiers hoped the monument would be an eternal reminder of their comrades' sacrifice.*

Language Coach

Proper Nouns and Proper Adjectives
Nouns are words that name a person, place, thing, or idea: *woman, city, desk, hope.* Proper nouns are capitalized and name a specific person, place, thing, or idea: *Rupert Brooke, England, Romanticism.* Adjectives describe nouns. Proper adjectives are formed from proper nouns, and they, too, are capitalized: *English* soldiers, *Georgian* poets.

Tell whether the boldface words are proper nouns or proper adjectives.

1. The **German** troops marched across **Europe.**
2. Soldiers from **New Zealand** and **Australia** joined the **British** war effort.
3. **Woodrow Wilson** was the **American** president during the war.

Learn It Online
Explore the Vocabulary words online with Word Watch.
go.hrw.com H12-1077 Go

Reader/Writer Notebook
Use your **RWN** to complete the activities for this selection.

Preteach

Introducing Vocabulary

- Review with students the Vocabulary words, definitions, and sample sentences.
- To reinforce the importance of the Vocabulary words, tell students that these words describe Brooke's contemplations on dying in war. He faces the fact that he may die, *concealed* in the ground, yet existing in some form in the *eternal* mind.

English for Academic Success

Language Coach

Tell students that a proper adjective, like any other adjective, is followed by a noun. Have students write a sentence containing a proper adjective and a proper noun.

Literary Skills Focus

As you read and discuss the poem with students, have them note lines that are structured in the pattern of a Petrarchan sonnet and lines structured in the pattern of a Shakespearean sonnet.

Writing Skills Focus

Have students record in their **Reader/Writer Notebooks** examples of alliteration in the poem and their effects. Students can use their notes to complete the Writing Skills Focus activity.

California Standards, pp. 1077–1079

- **Reading Standard 3.3** Analyze the ways in which irony, tone, mood, the author's style, and the "sound" of language achieve specific rhetorical or aesthetic purposes or both.

Learn It Online
Send students to **Word Watch** for audio pronunciations, synonyms and antonyms, and brief histories of word origins.
go.hrw.com H12-1077 Go

Teacher Preparation

Selection Summary

Brooke's sonnet, "The Soldier," is a contemplation of death. In the first eight lines—the octave—the speaker asks that if he should die in a foreign land, his loved ones think of his body as a piece of England. The final six lines—the sestet—mark a turn away from the physical aspect of the speaker's death to the spiritual. The speaker believes that his spirit will enter heaven, a kind of idealized dream of England.

Direct Teach

Think About/Talk About

Read with a Purpose Have students read the Read with a Purpose statement. Ask them to consider the poet's word choice and tone to infer his attitude toward dying for his country.

Analysis

Ⓐ Literary Focus

Possible response: *The Biblical idea of "dust to dust" is presented through the image.*

Ⓑ Literary Focus

Possible response: *The poet expands on the idea of "dust" by focusing the sestet on the spiritual aspect of dying.*

Vocabulary: Own the Word

- **concealed:** Tell students that an antonym of *concealed* is reveal. Have students use both words in a sentence: We *concealed* the cookies in our mouths, but the empty cookie jar revealed they had been eaten.
- **eternal:** On the board, make a chart comparing *eternal* with an antonym such as *temporal.* Have students compare the words and make lists of ideas, objects, or images that would fall under each category.

SONNET

THE SOLDIER

by **Rupert Brooke**

Read with a Purpose

Read this poem to discover how the speaker feels about dying for his country.

Build Background

When war broke out, Brooke enlisted in the navy and served briefly in Belgium. His war sonnets express idealistic patriotism. Had Brooke lived to witness the horrors of trench warfare, he might have developed a more cynical and disillusioned attitude about war; however, he died of blood poisoning en route to the Dardanelles with the British Mediterranean Expeditionary Force. He was buried on the island of Skyros in the Aegean Sea, a "corner of a foreign field that is forever England."

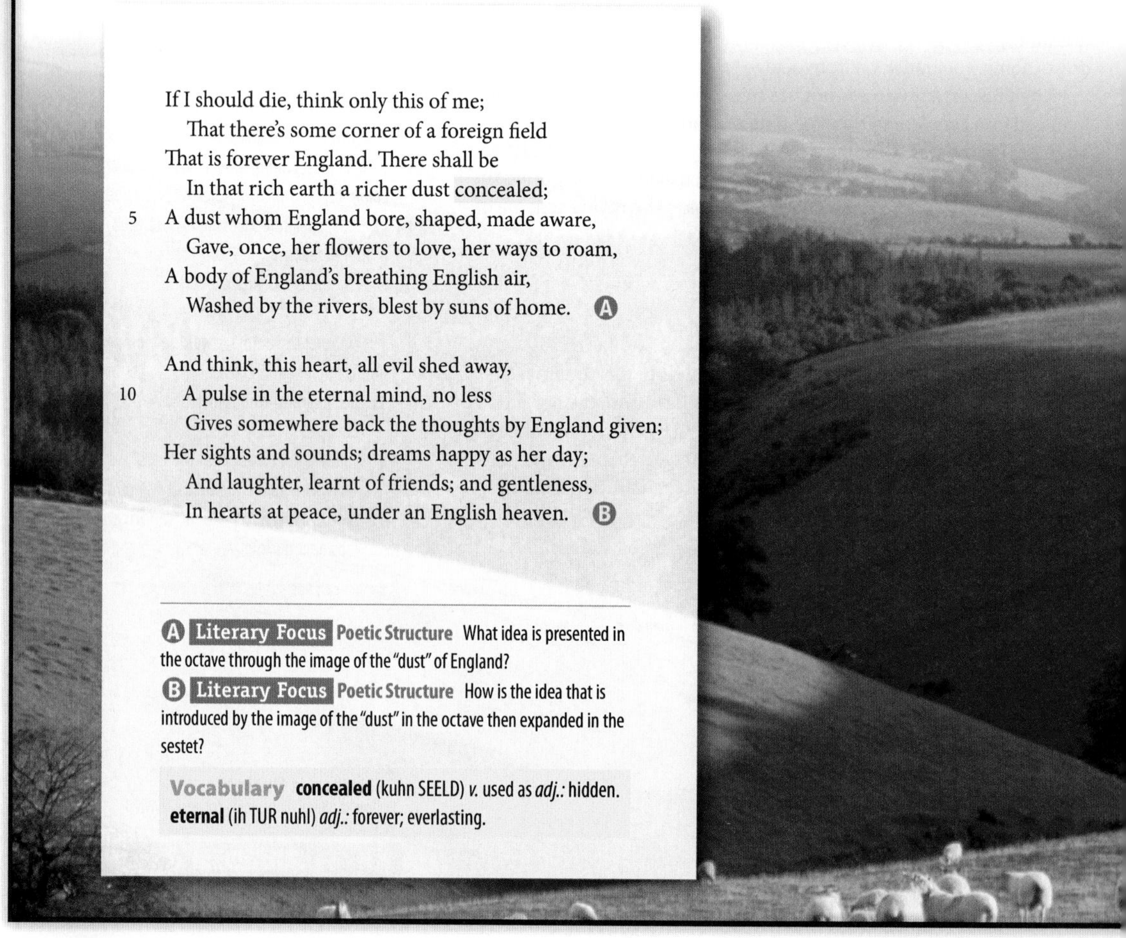

If I should die, think only this of me;
 That there's some corner of a foreign field
That is forever England. There shall be
 In that rich earth a richer dust concealed;
A dust whom England bore, shaped, made aware,
 Gave, once, her flowers to love, her ways to roam,
A body of England's breathing English air,
 Washed by the rivers, blest by suns of home. Ⓐ

And think, this heart, all evil shed away,
 A pulse in the eternal mind, no less
 Gives somewhere back the thoughts by England given;
Her sights and sounds; dreams happy as her day;
 And laughter, learnt of friends; and gentleness,
 In hearts at peace, under an English heaven. Ⓑ

Ⓐ **Literary Focus** **Poetic Structure** What idea is presented in the octave through the image of the "dust" of England?

Ⓑ **Literary Focus** **Poetic Structure** How is the idea that is introduced by the image of the "dust" in the octave then expanded in the sestet?

Vocabulary **concealed** (kuhn SEELD) *v.* used as *adj.:* hidden.
eternal (ih TUR nuhl) *adj.:* forever; everlasting.

California Standards, p. 1079

- **Reading Standard 2.2** Analyze the way in which clarity of meaning is affected by the patterns of organization, hierarchical structures, repetition of the main ideas, syntax, and word choice in the text.
- **Reading Standard 3.2** Analyze the way in which the theme or meaning of a selection represents a view or comment on life, using textual evidence to support the claim.
- **Reading Standard 3.3** Analyze the ways in which irony, tone, mood, the author's style, and the "sound" of language achieve specific rhetorical or aesthetic purposes or both.
- **Reading Standard 3.4** Analyze ways in which poets use imagery, personification, figures of speech, and sounds to evoke readers' emotions.
- **Writing Standard 2.3** Write reflective compositions: **a.** Explore the significance of personal experiences, events, conditions, or concerns by using rhetorical strategies (e.g., narration, description, exposition, persuasion).

Applying Your Skills

Reading Standard 2.2, 3.2, 3.3, 3.4 (see pages A48–A50)
Writing Standard 2.3a (see pages A51–A52)

Dulce et Decorum Est / The Soldier

Literary Response and Analysis

Reading Skills Focus

Read with a Purpose

1. In each poem, how does the speaker feel about the war and the cause for which he might die?

Reading Skills: Using Context Clues

2. Complete your chart for "Dulce et Decorum Est" by writing what you think each word or phrase means. Then compare your chart with a partner's, and discuss how context clues helped you guess meaning.

Unfamiliar Word	Context Clues	Meaning
flound'ring (floundering)	The men are stumbling to put on their gas masks.	making uncontrolled movements; nearly falling

Vocabulary Check

Match each Vocabulary word with its definition.

3. concealed — a. everlasting
4. writhing — b. hidden
5. vile — c. eager
6. ardent — d. disgusting
7. eternal — e. twisting about in pain

Literary Skills Focus

Literary Analysis

8. **Analyze** Who is the "you" addressed in the final stanza of "Dulce et Decorum Est"? What is the effect of Owen's ending the poem in this way?
9. **Interpret** How is the idea of immortality linked with the idea of patriotism in "The Soldier"?
10. **Contrast** How would you describe the difference in tone between the two poems?

Literary Skills: Figures of Speech / Poetic Structure

11. **Analyze** What oxymoron can you find in the last stanza of "Dulce et Decorum Est"? What emotions or insights does it evoke?
12. **Interpret** Explain the similes in lines 23–24 of "Dulce et Decorum Est." How do they relate to the other ideas expressed in the poem?
13. **Extend** How does "The Soldier" combine elements of both the Petrarchan and Shakespearean sonnet forms?
14. **Analyze** How does the structure of "The Soldier" contribute to the message? What ideas about death are expressed in each part of the poem?

Literary Skills Review: Theme

15. **Interpret** The central idea or insight about human experience revealed in a work is called the **theme.** Write a sentence telling the theme of each of these two poems.

Writing Skills Focus

Think as a Reader/Writer

Use It in Your Writing Review the notes you took about figurative language in "Dulce et Decorum Est" and about alliteration in "The Soldier." Then, write a personal poem that uses figurative language and alliteration to convey your ideas about war.

What Do You Think Now? How do the two poets' ideas about war differ? How might their experiences have affected their perceptions of war?

Universal Access

Struggling Writers

Some students may need additional scaffolding to complete the Writing Skills Focus activity. Before writing their poem, ask students what image comes to mind when they think about war and have them describe the image using a simile or metaphor. After they have described several images in a few sentences, have them use their sentences to write a poem. As they write, encourage them to incorporate alliteration in a few places.

What Do You Think Now?

Ask students to consider the main idea expressed by the poets in their poems. Have them think about how these ideas reflect these poets' different experiences of war.

Assess

Unit 6 Resources,
Selection Standards Check, p. 10

Check for Understanding

Independent Practice

Reading Skills Focus

Possible responses:

1. *The speaker in "Dulce" is cynical about war. The speaker in "The Soldier" is attached to England and believes in the cause.*
2. *Have students guess the meaning of the words and phrases based on their notes on context clues.*

Vocabulary Check

3. *b* 4. *e*
5. *d* 6. *c*
7. *a*

Literary Skills Focus

Possible responses:

8. *The "you" refers to advocates of simplistic patriotism and intensifies the condemnation of war.*
9. *A part of England will reside wherever he is laid to rest.*
10. *The tone in Owen's poem is agonized. Brooke's tone is content.*
11. *"Desperate glory" evokes the enthusiasm of enlisting in the military to die in patriotic sacrifice.*
12. *The similes compare the soldier's dying to something "obscene" like cancer. They relate to the other ideas by suggesting that war, a hideous disease, corrupts the innocent, and it is not sweet to die for one's country.*
13. *The poem begins by following a Shakespearean sonnet rhyme scheme. The second stanza follows the six-line sestet structure of the Petrarchan sonnet. The turn reflects elements of both sonnet types.*
14. *The first part focuses on the physical aspect of death: a part of England rests in foreign ground. The second part discusses the spiritual aspect of death giving way to eternal life.*
15. *"Dulce" reveals that war is anything but sweet and honorable. "The Soldier" revolves around noble and patriotic sacrifice.*

Standards Focus

Objectives

Students will
- understand imagery
- learn to visualize details
- analyze political statements

Selection Introduction

Think About the Writer

Have students think about how writing poetry, keeping diaries, or doing other creative activities have helped many people come to terms with personal difficulties.

For Independent Reading

Dawn, Elie Wiesel

Motivate

What Do You Think?/QuickWrite

Have students think about Wilfred Owen's poem "Dulce et Decorum Est" as they reflect upon the situations that soldiers experience in battle. What is the best and the worst that soldiers could find in themselves? What unique troubles do they face in war? Ask students to record their responses in their **Reader/Writer Notebooks**.

English for Academic Success

Academic Vocabulary

Look for opportunities to use the Academic Vocabulary words in this unit.

- **exhibit, *v.*:** show, demonstrate
- **perspective, *n.*:** a particular way of looking at something

Preparing to Read

The Rear-Guard

A Soldier's Declaration

What Do You Think? How does experience shape our view of the world?

QuickWrite

Why might the experience of war make people react to situations in ways they would not have thought possible? In your *Reader/Writer Notebook,* write a brief response to this question.

Novelist Siegfried Sassoon in military uniform (1915), England.

MEET THE WRITER

Siegfried Sassoon

(1886–1967)

World War I veteran Siegfried Sassoon's graphic and vivid poems exposed the brutal effects of the war.

From Idealism to Horror

Siegfried Sassoon had an upbringing of great privilege, his family having made its fortune in India. Like many other upper-class British men, he signed up for the war with the intention of having a great adventure, which he thought would be much like the exciting fox hunts of his youth. During Sassoon's convalescence from a riding accident that delayed his deployment, his brother was killed in battle. Despite his grief, Sassoon's initial poems during this period reflect an idealistic perspective.

However, Sassoon's own battles in the trenches shattered this idealism. Known as "Mad Jack" for his extraordinary bravery on the war front, Sassoon was awarded the Military Cross for his courage. Nevertheless, he became a pacifist and an ardent voice against the war. (For years, he was rumored to have hurled his Military Cross into the Mersey River in protest, but the Cross was discovered in his son's attic in 2007.) While he was hospitalized for shell-shock in 1917, he met and influenced the soldier and poet Wilfred Owen.

Driven by Memories

Sassoon was haunted by memories of the war. His poems caused an uproar with some readers for their graphic depiction of battle, while other readers accused him of being unpatriotic. Nevertheless, his poetry books sold well and boosted his reputation as a passionate voice for his generation. His later novels and autobiographies memorialize his fellow soldiers, exhibit the atrocities of war, and reveal his own inner wounds.

During World War II, Sassoon opened his home to British and American soldiers and war refugees. He continued to write and was awarded a Queen's Gold Medal. Much of his later work reflects his views on religion (he converted from Judaism to Catholicism in 1957), but he is best remembered for the great war poems of his youth.

Think About the Writer How might writing about the war have helped Sassoon heal from the tragedy of his experiences?

California Standards, pp. 1080–1083

- **Reading Standard 2.2** Analyze the way in which clarity of meaning is affected by the patterns of organization, hierarchical structures, repetition of the main ideas, syntax, and word choice in the text.
- **Reading Standard 3.3** Analyze the ways in which irony, tone, mood, the author's style, and the "sound" of language achieve specific rhetorical or aesthetic purposes or both.

Selection Readability	
Easily Accessible **Accessible** Challenging	These selections include accessible vocabulary; accessible theme.

Reading Standard 2.2, 3.3 (see pages A48–A50)

Literary Skills Focus

Imagery Language that appeals to the senses is called **imagery.** Most images appeal to the sense of sight, but imagery can also appeal to the senses of hearing, touch, taste, or smell. While imagery is featured in all types of writing, it is especially important in poetry.

Reading Skills Focus

Visualizing Details You will have a fuller, more enjoyable experience of poetry and prose if you visualize details as you read. **Visualizing details** means picturing them in your mind: using your imagination and the information you read to "see" what you are reading. You might use the following techniques to help you visualize a poem:

- Read a few lines, and then stop and consider the images the lines evoke.
- Describe the images to a peer.
- Draw a picture of what you have read.

Into Action In a chart like the one below, note the details you visualize as you read. First, write the line numbers; then, write what you visualize.

Line Numbers	What I Visualize
1–3	I visualized a man underground, making his way tentatively through the darkness with his flashlight. He sniffs, smells something terrible, and wrinkles up his nose in disgust.

Language Coach

Prefix *un–* When added to an adjective or a participle, the prefix *un–* means the absence of a quality. For example, the adjective *unwholesome* means that the quality of wholesomeness is missing. When added to a verb or a participle, *un–* means the reversal, or "undoing," of an action. For example, *unloading* in the last line represents the reversal of the action of loading a gun. What other word with the prefix *un–* can you find in the poem? What part of speech is it, and how does the prefix *un–* contribute to its meaning?

Writing Skills Focus

Think as a Reader/Writer

Find It in Your Reading The images and words writers choose convey a **tone,** or attitude toward their subject. Note how the words and **images** in the following lines help create a bitter, tormented tone: "Dawn's ghost that filtered down a shafted stair / To the dazed, muttering creatures underground." As you read the poem, record in your *Reader/Writer Notebook* words and images that help Sassoon create a bitter tone.

TechFocus "The Rear-Guard" presents a soldier's perspective. Imagine a movie camera panning the area and then zooming in to reveal the setting. What do you see in each shot?

Reader/Writer Notebook
Use your **RWN** to complete the activities for this selection.

Learn It Online
Find graphic organizers online to help you organize your thoughts as you read.
go.hrw.com H12-1081 Go

Selection Resources

Unit 6 Resources, on-level practice and assessment, p. 13

Teacher One Stop™, on-level lesson plans and all print resources

Holt Audio Library

Holt Audio Library: Selections and Summaries in Spanish

UA: Differentiating Instruction, graphic organizer, p. 261

UA: Supporting Instruction in Spanish, selection summary

ThinkCentral Online Assessment, Selection Standards Check

ThinkCentral Online Remediation

Preteach

English for Academic Success

Language Coach

After reading the **Language Coach,** have students brainstorm other words containing the prefix *un–*. Then, have students answer the questions. Students might note that the words *unanswering* (line 14) and *unloading* (line 25) both contain the prefix *un–*. Point out that the prefix in *underground* is *under–*, not *un–*.

Literary Skills Focus

As you read and discuss the selection with students, have them record examples of sensory words.

Reading Skills Focus

Give students a copy of the Reading Skills Focus graphic organizer before they read. (See **Unit 6 Resources.**) Tell them to use their responses to answer the questions on the Applying Your Skills page.

Writing Skills Focus

As students read, have them compile a list of words and images that help create the bitter tone of the poem in their **Reader/Writer Notebooks.** Students may use their notes to complete the Writing Skills Focus activity.

Learn It Online
If your students need extra reading support for informational texts, introduce them to **Interactive Graphic Organizers**—tools for generating and organizing ideas, comparing and contrasting, and other key skills.
go.hrw.com H12-1081 Go

Teacher Preparation

Selection Summary

During the grim trench warfare of World War I, a weary British officer in "The Rear-Guard" prowls a tunnel fifty feet below the ground while a battle rages overhead. He trips over a soldier and becomes abusive when the soldier does not respond to his demand for directions. Then the officer realizes that the soldier has been dead for days. He continues moving until he finds a stairway lit by a shaft of dawn's light and makes his way above ground.

Direct Teach

Think About/Talk About

Read with a Purpose Have students read the Read with a Purpose statement. Discuss how trench warfare might have affected the humanity of the participants.

Comprehension

A Reading Focus

Possible response: *The image is of a man walking on pieces of glass ("mirror smashed') in a dark tunnel ("fifty feet below"), with the only light coming from his flashlight and shells exploding overhead. He trips and finds a "half-hidden" body slumped at his feet.*

Analysis

B Literary Focus

Possible response: *Line 22 ("The boom of shells in muffled sound") appeals to the sense of hearing. He hears shells exploding above the tunnel.*

Extend the Discussion

Irony What is ironic about the officer's "unloading hell behind him step by step"? ***Possible response:*** *He is going back into the above-ground hell of the battlefield.*

POEM

The Rear-Guard

by **Siegfried Sassoon**

Read with a Purpose
Read to understand one soldier's horrifying experience in the trenches.

Build Background
During World War I, soldiers sometimes lived for years in interconnected underground caverns infested by rats and only occasionally illuminated by dim shafts of natural light.

(Hindenburg Line,° April 1917.)
Groping along the tunnel, step by step,
He winked his prying torch° with patching glare
From side to side, and sniffed the unwholesome air.

Tins, boxes, bottles, shapes too vague to know,
A mirror smashed, the mattress from a bed;
And he, exploring fifty feet below
The rosy gloom of battle overhead.

Tripping, he grabbed the wall; saw someone lie
Humped at his feet, half-hidden by a rug,
And stooped to give the sleeper's arm a tug. **A**
"I'm looking for headquarters." No reply.
"God blast your neck!" (For days he'd had no sleep.)

"Get up and guide me through this stinking place."
Savage, he kicked a soft, unanswering heap,
And flashed his beam across the livid face
Terribly glaring up, whose eyes yet wore
Agony dying hard ten days before;
And fists of fingers clutched a blackening wound.

Alone he staggered on until he found
Dawn's ghost that filtered down a shafted stair
To the dazed, muttering creatures underground
Who hear the boom of shells in muffled sound.
At last, with sweat of horror in his hair,
He climbed through darkness to the twilight air,
Unloading hell behind him step by step. **B**

Hindenburg Line: German defensive barricade running across northern France. It was made of massive barbed-wire entanglements and deep trenches.
2. torch: flashlight.

Fusilier returning from trenches during World War I (c. 1915).

A Reading Focus **Visualizing Details** What images come to mind as you read lines 5–10? What words or phrases help you visualize?
B Literary Focus **Imagery** What line in the poem appeals to the sense of hearing?

Universal Access

Students with Disabilities

Guide students in identifying imagery that appeals to the senses of hearing, touch, taste, or smell. Instruct them to create a chart with four columns, labeling each column with one of the senses, other than sight. Model filling in the chart. Tell students that when the soldier gropes his way along the tunnel (line 1), they might visualize him feeling along the sides with every step. Tell them to record this detail under the "touch" column. Ask students to find other imagery that appeals to the senses in the poem and to record these instances in their chart..

California Standards, p. 1083

- **Reading Standard 2.2** Analyze the way in which clarity of meaning is affected by the patterns of organization, hierarchical structures, repetition of the main ideas, syntax, and word choice in the text.
- **Reading Standard 3.3** Analyze the ways in which irony, tone, mood, the author's style, and the "sound" of language achieve specific rhetorical or aesthetic purposes or both.
- **Writing Standard 2.3** Write reflective compositions:
  c. Maintain a balance in describing individual incidents and relate those incidents to more general and abstract ideas.

Applying Your Skills

Reading Standard 2.2, 3.3 (see pages A48–A50)
Writing Standard 2.3c (see pages A51–A52)

The Rear-Guard

Literary Response and Analysis

Reading Skills Focus

Quick Check

1. Why might the poet describe the battle as a "rosy gloom"?
2. What details does the poet include to show that men live in this underground "hell"?

Read with a Purpose

3. What information about life in the trenches did you learn by reading this poem?

Reading Skills: Visualizing Details

4. Review your chart about visualizing details. Then, write a sentence or two describing the types of imagery Sassoon uses in the poem.

Line Numbers	What I Visualize
1–3	I visualized a man underground. He is carrying a flashlight and trying to make his way through the darkness. He sniffs, smells something terrible, and wrinkles up his nose in disgust.

Literary Skills Focus

Literary Analysis

5. **Analyze** What reason does the speaker give for how he treats the man on the ground? What else in the poem might explain the speaker's reaction?
6. **Interpret** Who are the "dazed, muttering creatures"? How does this description, along with the speaker's description of himself and the dead man, emphasize war's dehumanizing effect?
7. **Evaluate** The speaker does not describe how he feels upon realizing the man he has kicked is dead. Does this omission add to or detract from the power of the poem? Explain your response.
8. **Extend** Many readers in England, even the leaders of the pacifist movement, were shocked by the graphic violence in Sassoon's poems. Do you think a poem such as this would have hurt or helped the pacifist cause? Explain.

Literary Skills: Imagery

9. **Evaluate** How does the poet use imagery to convey the atrocity of war? In your opinion, which image is most compelling? Why?

Literary Skills Review: Enjambment

10. **Analyze** A **run-on line,** or **enjambment,** is a line of poetry that does not stop at the end of the line but instead continues on to the next line. Poets carefully choose where they will end lines, not only for rhythm, rhyme, and meter, but also to effect meaning. Look at lines 14–17 to see how Sassoon uses enjambment to slowly reveal the state of the man lying on the ground. How does this measured revelation affect the reader?

Writing Skills Focus

Think as a Reader/Writer

Use It in Your Writing Review your notes on the words and details Sassoon uses to convey tone. Write a short poem or paragraph about a recent news event. Decide what tone you will convey, and carefully choose words and details to help you convey it.

What Do You Think Now? Given what you have learned about the trenches, do the speaker's actions in this poem make sense to you? Why or why not?

For CHOICES see page 1087.

Universal Access

Struggling Writers

Some students may need additional scaffolding to complete the Writing Skills Focus activity. Review Sassoon's use of words and phrases such as "sweat of horror" and "unloading hell behind him" to convey his opinion on the horrors of war. Provide students with copies of a recent news article. After students have finished reading and forming an opinion on the issue addressed, have them brainstorm words and details that will convey their desired tone before writing their paragraph or poem.

What Do You Think Now?

Have students imagine being in the speaker's place. How would their actions be similar or different from the speaker's?

Check for Understanding

Independent Practice

Reading Skills Focus

Possible responses:

1. *The words may refer to bombs or shells exploding in the distance and lighting up the horizon.*
2. *He names many "daily life" items—tins, boxes, bottles, a mirror, a mattress, and a blanket.*
3. *The smells, sounds, and sight of death all around help convey the experience of life in the trenches.*
4. *Have students write detailed descriptions of the sights, smells, sounds, and actions in the poem.*

Literary Skills Focus

Possible responses:

5. *The speaker is looking for headquarters. His exhaustion might explain his angry reaction.*
6. *The "dazed, muttering creatures" are other soldiers down in the tunnel. Normal peacetime behaviors are totally missing, which shows how the soldiers have become dehumanized.*
7. *It adds to the impact of the poem because it shows how common death is in those circumstances.*
8. *Governments often suppress the grim details of what happens at the front. The details in this poem would upset many people and probably help the pacifist cause.*
9. *Choices of image will vary, but images such as "sweat of horror in his hair," "unloading hell behind him step by step" and details describing the dead soldier's body are images that many students will find compelling.*
10. *In lines 14–17, the enjambment forces the reader to absorb the details of the description without the pauses created by end punctuation. This use of punctuation builds the reader's sense of suspense, allowing the reader to identify more fully with the soldier who is looking at a corpse.*

Preteach

English for Academic Success

Language Coach

Possible response: Aggression *means "an offensive attack," while* defense *means "resistance against attack."* Liberation, *"the act of freeing," is opposite in meaning to* conquest, *"the act of vanquishing." The pairs of words bring into sharp focus how Sassoon thinks the purpose of the war has changed.*

Informational Text Focus

Give students a copy of the Informational Text Focus graphic organizer before they read. (See **Unit 6 Resources.**) Tell them to use their responses to answer the questions on the Applying Your Skills page.

Writing Skills Focus

Have students record Sassoon's loaded language in their **Reader/Writer Notebooks.** Tell them that these words are sometimes called "fighting words" because they are meant to provoke a response. Students can use their notes to complete the Writing Skills Focus activity.

Learn It Online

For additional support analyzing media, students can go to the **MediaScope** site to analyze other types of media, such as a Web page, a TV news story, a political TV ad, and a print advertisement.

go.hrw.com H12-1084 Go

INFORMATIONAL TEXT FOCUS

Preparing to Read

Reading Standard 2.6 (see pages A48–A50)

Informational Text Focus

Analyzing Political Statements Like other forms of persuasion, a political statement is intended to convince the audience to agree with the author's point of view and to take a certain course of action. A political statement includes

- an explicit statement of the writer or speaker's core belief
- details, facts, and/or opinions that support or elaborate on the central statement of belief
- appeals to the reader's emotions, logic, or ethics (sense of right and wrong)

Into Action As you read "A Soldier's Declaration," use a graphic organizer like the one below to record Sassoon's central statement of belief. Then, record details and ideas that support his argument.

Sassoon believes ______.	
Support: As a soldier, Sassoon knows what battle is like.	
Support:	
Support:	
Support:	

Writing Skills Focus

Preparing for **Timed Writing** Persuasive writers often use **loaded language**—words or phrases intended to evoke a strong reaction in their readers. For example, rather than saying that soldiers are dying, Sassoon says they "are being sacrificed." Note the powerful effect of the word *sacrificed*. As you read, look for other examples of loaded language, and record them in your *Reader/Writer Notebook*.

TechFocus This declaration was read in front of the House of Parliament, the English government. As you read, imagine how you might present it as a podcast.

Language Coach

Antonyms An **antonym** is a word with an opposite, or nearly opposite, meaning to another word. In the second line of his statement, Sassoon uses two pairs of antonyms: *defense* : *aggression* and *liberation* : *conquest*. Look up these words in a dictionary, and state how they are opposites, or antonyms. How does the use of antonyms help Sassoon strengthen his argument?

Reader/Writer Notebook

Use your **RWN** to complete the activities for this selection.

Learn It Online

Examine modern forms of persuasion at the MediaScope mini-site online.

go.hrw.com H12-1084 Go

California Standards, pp. 1084–1087

- **Reading Standard 2.6** Critique the power, validity, and truthfulness of arguments set forth in public documents; their appeal to both friendly and hostile audiences; and the extent to which the arguments anticipate and address reader concerns and counterclaims (e.g., appeal to reason, to authority, to pathos and emotion).

Selection Resources

Unit 6 Resources, on-level practice, p. 14

Teacher One Stop™, on-level lesson plans

Holt Audio Library

Holt Audio Library: Selections and Summaries in Spanish

UA: Differentiating Instruction, graphic organizer, p. 261

UA: Supporting Instruction in Spanish, selection summary

ThinkCentral Online Assessment, Selection Standards Check

go.hrw.com

POLITICAL STATEMENT

A Soldier's Declaration

by **Siegfried Sassoon**

Read with a Purpose

Read this declaration to learn how a soldier expressed his opposition to the First World War.

Build Background

After Siegfried Sassoon's first tour of duty, he befriended the philosopher and pacifist Bertrand Russell and became vehemently opposed to the war. He wrote "A Soldier's Declaration" on June 15, 1917, and it was read before the House of Commons and published in a London newspaper in July. Sassoon refused to return to battle, hoping his protest would further publicize his cause and help end the war. A friend, worried that Sassoon would be court-martialed and jailed, convinced Sassoon's commanding officers that the poet was suffering from trauma induced by the war. Sassoon was hospitalized and later volunteered to rejoin his fellow soldiers in battle.

I am making this statement as an act of willful defiance of military authority, because I believe the war is being deliberately prolonged by those who have the power to end it. **A**

I am a soldier, convinced that I am acting on behalf of soldiers. I believe that this war, upon which I entered as a war of defense and liberation, has now become a war of aggression and conquest. I believe that the purposes for which I and my fellow soldiers entered upon this war should have been so clearly stated as to have made it impossible to change them, and that, had this been done, the objects which actuated us[1] would now be attainable by negotiation.

I have seen and endured the suffering of the troops, and I can no longer be a party to prolong these sufferings for ends which I believe to be evil and unjust. **B**

I am not protesting against the conduct of the war, but against the political errors and insincerities for which the fighting men are being sacrificed.

On behalf of those who are suffering now I make this protest against the deception which is being practiced on them; also I believe that I may help to destroy the callous complacence with which the majority of those at home regard the continuance of agonies which they do not share, and which they have not sufficient imagination to realize.

Siegfried L. Sassoon, July 1917

1. **actuated us:** made us act.

A British soldier on duty at barbed-wire gate in France during World War I.

A **Informational Focus** **Analyzing Political Statements** What is Sassoon's main idea?

B **Informational Focus** **Analyzing Political Statements** Does this statement appeal primarily to reader's logic, emotion, or ethics (sense of right and wrong)? Explain.

Teacher Preparation

Selection Summary

The writer of "A Soldier's Declaration" believes that the war is being deliberately prolonged. He says its focus has changed from defense to conquest. He is upset that the objectives for the war were never clearly stated, because they could have been achieved by negotiation. The troop's suffering motivates him to protest against political errors for which soldiers are sacrificed. He wants people at home to act.

Direct Teach

Think About/Talk About

Read with a Purpose Have students read the Read with a Purpose statement. Discuss Sassoon's state of mind when he wrote his declaration.

Analysis

A Informational Focus

Possible response: *He believes "the war is being deliberately prolonged by those who have the power to end it."*

B Informational Focus

Possible response: *Words like "evil" and "unjust" appeal to the reader's ethics and convey Sassoon's moral outrage.*

Extend the Discussion

Recognizing Rhetorical Devices

Why does Sassoon protest "On behalf of those who are suffering now"? To what is he appealing? ***Possible response:*** *He implies that the actions of those back home could end the suffering (emotional appeal) and that this course of action is right (ethical appeal).*

California Standards, pp. 1086–1087

- **Reading Standard 2.6** Critique the power, validity, and truthfulness of arguments set forth in public documents; their appeal to both friendly and hostile audiences; and the extent to which the arguments anticipate and address reader concerns and counterclaims (e.g., appeal to reason, to authority, to pathos and emotion).
- **Writing Standard 2.2** Write responses to literature: **d.** Demonstrate an understanding of the author's use of stylistic devices and an appreciation of the effects created.
- **Writing Standard 2.3** Write reflective compositions: **b.** Draw comparisons between specific incidents and broader themes that illustrate the writer's important beliefs or generalizations about life.
- **Writing Standard 2.6** Deliver multimedia presentations: **b.** Select an appropriate medium for each element of the presentation. **c.** Use the selected media skillfully, editing appropriately and monitoring for quality.
- **Listening and Speaking Standard 1.6** Use logical, ethical, and emotional appeals that enhance a specific tone and purpose.
- **Listening and Speaking Standard 1.11** Critique a speaker's diction and syntax in relation to the purpose of an oral communication and the impact the words may have on the audience.
- **Listening and Speaking Standard 2.5** Recite poems, selections from speeches, or dramatic soliloquies with attention to performance details to achieve clarity, force, and aesthetic effect and to demonstrate an understanding of the

Check for Understanding

Independent Practice

Informational Text Focus

Possible responses:

1. *A war of "defense and liberation" is fought to protect the nation and free its allies. A war of "aggression and conquest" is fought to acquire territory.*
2. *He generalizes that they are unaware of war's agonies.*
3. *The alternative he proposes is a negotiated peace, which is out of the question now because the aims of the war have changed.*
4. *Remind students that appeals to logic use reason and facts, appeals to emotion use details or charged language to elicit an emotional response, and appeals to ethics call for moral judgments.*
5. *Sassoon adopts a superior tone in his appeal, implying that he knows more than government officials do. He is an officer and a member of the upper class and writes from that perspective.*
6. *Sassoon does not want to blame soldiers for the government's mistakes.*
7. *It is always dangerous to attack the very people you want to persuade. However, his appeal is ethical. The people at home may bridle against the accusation that they are callous but agree that they have been wrongly complacent.*
8. *Responses will vary. Soldiers like Sassoon who can personally testify to the brutality of war and the sacrifice of the fighting men should at least be heard. There should only be a few, health-related cases where soldiers are permitted to refuse to serve.*
9. *Students present clear points in their discussion and demonstrate their understanding of the themes in Sassoon's work.*

INFORMATIONAL TEXT FOCUS

Applying Your Skills

Reading Standard 2.6 (see pages A48–A50)
Listening and Speaking Standard 2.5 (see pages A53–A55)
Writing Standard 2.2d (see pages A51–A52)

A Soldier's Declaration

Analyze Informational Texts

Informational Text Focus

Quick Check

1. What do you think is the difference between a war of "defense and liberation" and a war of "aggression and conquest"?
2. What generalization about the people in England does Sassoon make in his final paragraph?

Read with a Purpose

3. Sassoon suggests that there could have been an alternative to continuing the war. What is this alternative, and what has prevented it, according to Sassoon?

Informational Skills: Analyzing Political Statements

4. Review each supporting item you recorded in your chart. Then, determine whether each appeals to logic, emotion, or ethics. (Some may appeal to more than one.) Then, choose the most persuasive part of this political statement, and discuss it with a small group of your peers.

Sassoon believes ______	Logic, emotion, or ethics
Support: As a soldier, Sassoon knows what battle is like.	fact; appeals to logic
Support:	
Support:	
Support:	

Text Analysis

5. **Analyze** What is Sassoon's **tone,** or attitude toward his subject, in this political statement? What might account for this tone?
6. **Infer** In the third paragraph, Sassoon makes a distinction between the conduct of the war and its political errors and insincerities. Why might he have been careful to make this distinction?
7. **Evaluate** Sassoon harshly criticizes those "at home." Do you think this is an effective persuasive technique? Why or why not?
8. **Make Judgments** Under what circumstances, if any, should soldiers be allowed to speak out against a war? Should they ever be permitted to refuse to serve? Explain your response.

Listening and Speaking

9. **Extend** With a partner, stage a debate in which one of you takes the part of Sassoon (against the war) and the other expresses the opposite view (for the war). Support your side as persuasively as possible. Ask another classmate to judge who is the winner of the debate.

Writing Skills Focus

Timed Writing In a brief essay, discuss Sassoon's use of loaded language in "A Soldier's Declaration." Be sure to cite specific evidence to support your response.

What Do You Think Now?

How might Sassoon's experiences of war have influenced his perspective about his country and its politics?

Universal Access

Struggling Writers

Some students may need additional scaffolding to complete the Writing Skills Focus activity. Have students review Sassoon's "fighting words" they recorded in their **Reader/Writer Notebooks** and discuss their effectiveness in evoking a reaction. Have students write a brief outline before writing their essay that reflects the discussion. Tell students to include their evaluation of Sassoon's use of loaded language in their essay's concluding paragraph.

What Do You Think Now?

Ask students to consider what kind of positive or negative wartime experiences may turn Sassoon toward or against the policies that sent him and his comrades to the trenches.

Writing Standard 2.3b, 2.6b, 2.6c (see pages A48–A50)
Listening and Speaking Standard 1.6, 1.11 (see pages A53–A55)

CHOICES

As you respond to the Choices, use these **Academic Vocabulary** words as appropriate: adapt, considerably, exhibit, inevitable, perspective.

REVIEW

Use Imagery to Describe a Scene

Group Activity Most of the imagery Sassoon includes in "The Rear-Guard" appeals to the sense of sight. In a small group, use your imagination and the details in the poem to describe the smells, feelings, and sounds a soldier might experience as he makes his way through the trenches. Choose a representative to present your description to the class.

Make a Podcast of a Political Statement

TechFocus Imagine that Sassoon asked you to read his declaration aloud to the English government. On a copy of the declaration, underline or highlight the words or phrases you will emphasize. Mark when you will pause, when you will make eye contact with your audience, and what gestures you will use for effect. Ask classmates to prepare responses as members of Parliament. Then, make a podcast of your statement and the responses.

CONNECT

Create Storyboards

TechFocus Imagine you are a movie director planning to shoot the scene Sassoon conveys in "The Rear-Guard." Re-read the poem, and create storyboards, brief sketches that plan the main shots for each part of a scene. Tell how you will zoom and pan the scene with a camera to slowly reveal the fate of the man on the ground. In a short paragraph, explain the scene's action and setting.

Write a Letter to the Editor

Timed Writing In "A Soldier's Declaration," Sassoon says that people at home do not have "sufficient imagination" to realize the suffering of soldiers in World War I. Do you think that today's mass media has strengthened peoples' ability to understand the realities of war? Write your response in a brief essay. Be sure to include details to support your thesis.

EXTEND

Design a World War I Memorial

Throughout history, artists and architects have designed memorials to celebrate and honor those who served in battle. Use details from "The Rear-Guard" and the other World War I poems you have read in this chapter as a springboard to design a World War I memorial to be exhibited in the center of your hometown. You might do research online for ideas about how other wars have been memorialized. Share your designs with the class, and explain why you included each element.

Presentation on War Memories

Ask your family and friends if they remember someone who served in World War I or who was alive during that time. Request that they tell any memories this person shared about life during that war. You might also bring in old letters from this time, provided they are not too personal. Use your notes on these memories, along with letters, photographs, or magazine clippings, to create a class multimedia exhibit called "War Memories."

Statue of a World War I British soldier. Winchester, U.K.

Independent Practice

Choices: Evaluation Criteria

Review: Homework
Use Imagery to Describe a Scene
Students use sensory words that appeal to hearing, touch, and smell to describe moving through a trench.

Review: Homework
Make a Podcast of a Political Statement
Students read Sassoon's declaration with proper emphasis, make eye contact, and add gestures for effect.

Connect: Homework
Create Storyboards
Text includes information about action, setting, and descriptive technical data for the shoot.

Connect: Timed Writing 40–50 Minutes
Students clearly state the main idea and make direct references to Sassoon's declaration.

Extend: Homework
Design a World War I Memorial
War memorial plans reflect the war literature in this chapter.

Extend: Homework
Presentation on War Memories
The multimedia presentation is centered on the recollections and supported by letters, photos, or clippings.

Assess

Unit 6 Resources, Selection Standards Check, p. 15

ThinkCentral Online Assessment, Selection Standards Check

Teacher One Stop™, editable Selection Standards Check

Reteach

ThinkCentral Online Remediation

Standards Focus

Objectives

Students will analyze the sequence of events.

Motivate

What Do You Think?/QuickWrite

Have students list situations, personality traits, and values that lead people to perform acts of bravery. Then, ask them to write about the emotions people feel after doing something unusually brave.

Preteach

Introducing Vocabulary

Read aloud the Vocabulary words and sample sentences. Then, use this activity to check students' understanding.

1. skirmishes : _____ :: barricade : barrier [*engagements*]
2. incapacitated : able-bodied :: _____ : harmless [*noxious*]
3. _____ : wary :: calm : anxious [*oblivious*]

Informational Text/ Writing Skills Focus

- Give students the Informational Text Focus graphic organizer before they read. (See **Unit 6 Resources.**) Tell them to use their responses to answer the questions on the Applying Your Skills page.
- Have students record salient details in their **Reader/Writer Notebooks.** Students can use their notes to complete the Writing Skills Focus activity.

Learn It Online

Send students to **Word Watch** for audio pronunciations, synonyms and antonyms, and brief histories of word origins.

go.hrw.com H12-1088 Go

INFORMATIONAL TEXT FOCUS

Preparing to Read

Reading Standard 2.2 (see pages A48–A50)

Link to Today

Under Heavy Fire in Iraq

What Do You Think

How does experience shape our view of the world?

QuickWrite

What makes people perform extraordinary acts of bravery? How might they react to the experience afterward? Record some notes in your *Reader/Writer Notebook.*

Informational Text Focus

Analyzing Sequence of Events To get your attention, journalists often start with the most critical part of a story. They do not necessarily tell everything that happened in the order in which it occurred. As a result, when you read news stories, you must **analyze the sequence of events,** or determine what happened when. As you read "Under Heavy Fire in Iraq," make a chart to organize information about the three main events Norton-Taylor describes. Then, determine the sequence of events by noting their relationship to one another.

Main Events:	When It Occurred	Key Events of Main Event
Beharry wins Victoria Cross	March 2005, after events in Iraq	

Writing Skills Focus

Preparing for **Timed Writing** The details the speaker uses to tell what happened, or the **narrative information,** play an important role in this article. Use your *Reader/Writer Notebook* to record details that especially impress you.

Vocabulary

engagements (ehn GAYJ muhnts) *n.:* military battles. *The newspaper reported three engagements between the two forces.*

incapacitated (ihn kuh PAS uh tayt ihd) *v.:* disabled; deprived of power. *The bomb blast incapacitated the commander.*

noxious (NAHK shuhs) *adj.:* very harmful, often poisonous. *The noxious gas left the soldiers violently ill and unable to move.*

oblivious (uh BLIHV ee uhs) *adj.:* unaware or paying no attention. *The brave soldier seemed oblivious to danger.*

Language Coach

Multiple-Meaning Words You can use context to help you define multiple-meaning words. Find two meanings for the multiple-meaning words listed below; then, use context clues to help you determine the meaning of each word as it is used in the selection.

citation turret hatch
mine lodged brass

Reader/Writer Notebook

Use your **RWN** to complete the activities for this selection.

Learn It Online

Get to know these Vocabulary words online with Word Watch.

go.hrw.com H12-1088 Go

California Standards, pp. 1088–1091

- **Reading Standard 2.2** Analyze the way in which clarity of meaning is affected by the patterns of organization, hierarchical structures, repetition of the main ideas, syntax, and word choice in the text.

Selection Readability	
Easily Accessible **Accessible** Challenging	familiar situations; familiar syntax; accessible language

Selection Summary

This 2005 news report, published in the British newspaper *The Guardian,* celebrates Grenada-born Johnson Beharry, the first soldier awarded the Victoria Cross since 1969. Private Beharry displayed dramatic heroism during two separate ambushes in Iraq.

Link to Today

This link to today shows the timelessness of courage under fire.

Read with a Purpose
Read to see how one soldier's bravery earned him England's highest military honor.

Build Background
In March 2003, the United States and Great Britain declared war on Iraq. Baghdad and other critical sites were bombed; 300,000 U.S. and British coalition troops entered Iraq; and, by April, Baghdad was controlled by the coalition. The operation was considered a success, but almost immediately, resistance forces in Iraq (insurgents from Iraq and other Middle Eastern countries) began attacking British and American soldiers. By 2007, more than 64,000 Iraqi civilians, 149 British soldiers, and nearly 3,500 U.S. soldiers had been killed in the war.

NEWSPAPER ARTICLE

Under Heavy Fire in Iraq

The Guardian

Friday, March 18, 2005

A young soldier has been awarded the Victoria Cross, the highest military honor, for bravery under fire in some of the fiercest, and largely unreported, engagements between British forces and insurgents in south-eastern Iraq.

Private Johnson Beharry, 25, is the first soldier to receive the VC since the Falklands war in 1982[1] and the first living recipient since 1969, when two Australians were given the award for action in Vietnam.

The citation[2] describes his "great heroism" in two separate encounters in the town of Amara, north of Basra. In the first, the Warrior armored vehicle he was driving was hit by multiple rocket-propelled grenades (RPGs).

His company, the citation says, had been ordered to extract a foot patrol pinned down by small arms and heavy machine-gun fire and an attack by an improvised explosive device and RPGs. (A)

As they passed a roundabout[3] on their way to the pinned-down patrol, his platoon noticed that the road ahead was empty of civilians and traffic, an indicator of a potential ambush. The platoon commander ordered the vehicle to halt so that he could assess the situation. The vehicle was then hit by RPGs.

The citation continues: "As a result of this ferocious initial volley of fire, both the platoon commander and the vehicle's gunner were incapacitated by concussion and other wounds, and a number of the soldiers in the rear of the vehicle were also wounded."

1. **Falklands war:** brief war between England and Argentina over control of the Falkland Islands, located in the South Atlantic Ocean.
2. **citation:** honorable mention of a soldier in war.
3. **roundabout:** British term for a traffic circle.

(A) **Informational Focus** **Analyzing Sequence of Events** How does the writer use a shift in tense to show that the order occurred before the armored vehicle was hit?

Vocabulary **engagements** (ehn GAYJ muhnts) *n.:* military battles.
incapacitated (ihn kuh PAS uh tayt ihd) *v.:* disabled; deprived of power.

Private Johnson Beharry (25) at Buckingham Palace in London after receiving the Victoria Cross from Queen Elizabeth (April 27, 2005).

Link to Today
Like the writings of Wilfred Owen, Rupert Brooke, and Siegfried Sassoon, this article explores what soldiers experience in combat.

Direct Teach

Think About/Talk About

Read with a Purpose Have students read the Read with a Purpose statement. Ask them to speculate about what sort of act of bravery the soldier performed to earn the prestigious military award.

Comprehension

(A) Informational Focus
Possible response: *The writer uses the past perfect tense ("had been ordered") to show that the order occurred before the vehicle was hit.*

Extend the Discussion

Making Inferences What can you infer from the writer's comment that the absence of civilians and traffic is an indicator of a potential ambush?
Possible response: *Civilians may become aware that an ambush is under way before attackers' targets—soldiers—become aware.*

Vocabulary: Own the Word

- **engagements:** Ask students to complete the following statement. Because of several *engagements* with the enemy, the squadron . . .
- **incapacitated:** Have you ever been *incapacitated* (adjective form) in a situation? Explain where, when, and why you were *incapacitated.*

Selection Resources

Unit 6 Resources, on-level practice and assessment, p. 18

Teacher One Stop™, on-level lesson plans and all print resources

Holt Audio Library: Selections and Summaries in Spanish

UA: Differentiating Instruction, graphic organizer, p. 262

UA: Supporting Instruction in Spanish, selection summary

ThinkCentral Online Assessment, Selection Standards Check go.hrw.com

Think About/Talk About

Comprehension

B Informational Focus

Possible responses: *The commander and gunner were incapacitated by the initial volley of fire. Beharry's actions were particularly brave because at the time he performed them, he was unable to communicate with his incapacitated commander and with other vehicles. This means he did not simply follow orders but acted on his own initiative, risking his life in the process.*

C Informational Focus

Possible response: *The first event occurred in late May.*

D Informational Focus

Possible response: *Beharry received his award on Thursday, March 17, 2005.*

Vocabulary: Own the Word

- **noxious:** *Noxious* smoke filled the vehicle he was driving. How does his exposure to the smoke make Private Beharry more heroic? ***Possible response:*** *Poisonous smoke would have incapacitated an ordinary soldier or human being.*
- **oblivious:** Ask: "Have you ever been *oblivious* to someone's words or actions? Explain the reasons for your being *oblivious.*"

Monitor Students' Comprehension

Guide the class in answering these comprehension questions.

1. Why was Private Beharry awarded the Victoria Cross? [*He was awarded this honor for his bravery under fire during engagements between British forces and insurgents in Iraq.*]
2. What was Beharry doing when the insurgents attacked? [*He was driving a Warrior armored vehicle.*]
3. How does Beharry explain his bravery? [*He says he was doing his job and thinking of his fellow soldiers.*]

Private Beharry had no means of communication with the turret crew or any of the other Warriors around him. He did not know if his commander or crew were still alive or how serious their injuries were.

"On his own initiative, he closed his driver's hatch and moved forward through the ambush position to try to establish some form of communications, halting just short of a barricade across the road."

The Warrior was hit again by the RPGs. It caught fire and filled with thick, noxious smoke. **B**

Private Beharry, continues the citation, "assessed that his best course of action to save the lives of his crew was to push through, out of the ambush. He drove his Warrior directly through the barricade, not knowing if there were mines or improvised explosive devices placed there to destroy his vehicle. By doing this he was able to lead the remaining five Warriors behind him towards safety."

Another RPG hit the Warrior. "The flames and force of the blast passed directly over him, down the driver's tunnel, further wounding the semi-conscious gunner in the turret."

Private Beharry was "forced to drive the vehicle along the rest of the ambushed route, some 1,500 meters, with his hatch opened up and his head exposed to enemy fire, all the time with no communications with any other vehicle."

A 7.62mm bullet penetrated his helmet and remained lodged on its inner surface.

Private Beharry then climbed on to the turret of the burning vehicle and, "seemingly oblivious to the incoming enemy small arms fire, manhandled his wounded platoon commander out of the turret, off the vehicle and to the safety of a nearby Warrior."

Remounting his burning vehicle for the third time, he drove it through "a complex chicane and into the security of the defended perimeter of the outpost, thus denying it to the enemy." Once inside, he collapsed from physical and mental exhaustion.

A few weeks later, on June 11, another Warrior convoy he was leading was ambushed. A grenade detonated six inches from his head. **C**

"With the blood from his head injury obscuring his vision, Beharry managed to continue to control his vehicle and forcefully reversed the Warrior out of the ambush," says the citation. He then collapsed, unconscious.

The Grenada-born[4] private was paraded by the top brass yesterday among his comrades in the 1st Battalion, the Princess of Wales's Royal Regiment, and other recipients of high military honors. **D**

"I was just doing my job. I was just thinking of the guys in the vehicle and the guys behind me," he said.

He was asked what was going through his mind at the time. "An RPG," Private Beharry promptly replied.

He was not afraid at the time, only afterward. Asked why he had left Grenada, he said he wanted "a change of life."

Asked if he would be Britain's first black general, he quickly replied, "No."

His wife, Lynthia, said that after he had been injured he was told he had only a 50-50 chance of surviving. She said her husband would return to Iraq "if he has to."

Private Beharry's award was described by Gary Sheffield, a leading historian of the modern British army, as "a classic in the VC mold—he was rescuing colleagues."

—Richard Norton-Taylor is the security affairs editor for The Guardian. *He is also a playwright.*

4. **Grenada-born:** Grenada is an island in the Caribbean Sea.

B Informational Focus **Analyzing Sequence of Events** When do the commander and gunner become incapacitated? How does the sequence of events make Beharry's behavior particularly brave?

C Informational Focus **Analyzing Sequence of Events** What does this paragraph tell you about when the first event occurred?

D Informational Focus **Analyzing Sequence of Events** Read the date of the article. On what date did Beharry receive his award?

Vocabulary **noxious** (NAHK shuhs) *adj.:* very harmful, often poisonous.
oblivious (uh BLIHV ee uhs) *adj.:* unaware or paying no attention.

California Standards, p. 1091

- **Reading Standard 2.2** Analyze the way in which clarity of meaning is affected by the patterns of organization, hierarchical structures, repetition of the main ideas, syntax, and word choice in the text.
- **Writing Standard 2.2** Write responses to literature: **b.** Analyze the use of imagery, language, universal themes, and unique aspects of the text.
- **Listening and Speaking Standard 2.4** Deliver multimedia presentations: **a.** Combine text, images, and sound by incorporating information from a wide range of media, including films, newspapers, magazines, CD-ROMs, online information, television, videos, and electronic media-generated images.

Universal Access

Advanced Learners

Enrichment Have students research other heroic accounts in the past decade and compare the actions of the soldiers in these accounts. Have them address different aspects of each situation as they compare the accounts in terms of the level of danger, risk, and injury involved. Ask them to compare these accounts to Private Beharry's as well. Tell students to summarize their findings in a brief oral presentation.

Reading Standard 2.2 (see pages A48–A50)
Listening and Speaking Standard 2.4a (see pages A53–A55)
Writing Standard 2.2b (see pages A51–A52)

Under Heavy Fire in Iraq

Analyze Informational Texts

Informational Text Focus

Quick Check

1. What did Beharry do to earn the Victoria Cross?
2. Beharry had to make decisions without help from his commanding officer or his colleagues. What choices did he make? What do these choices suggest about his abilities as a soldier?

Read with a Purpose

3. How does Beharry's experience compare to that of the three World War I poets? What do all wars have in common? How does modern warfare differ from warfare during World War I?

Informational Skills: Analyzing Sequence of Events

4. Review the chart, and notice the amount of time between the first and second event. When was Beharry's Warrior hit in each case? What did Beharry do afterward? How does analyzing the sequence of events help you better understand Beharry's actions as a soldier?

Text Analysis

9. **Analyze** Why did the writer include the details in the second paragraph? What do they suggest about the importance of Beharry's award?
10. **Infer** How does Beharry respond to the question about what was going through his mind at the time of the engagement? What does his response reveal about his personality?
11. **Interpret** What does the inclusion of the historian's quotation at the end of the article suggest about the writer's perspective, or point of view?
12. **Make Judgments** What was Beharry's bravest act? Cite evidence from the selection.

Listening and Speaking

13. **Extend** In a small group, plan a TV broadcast of this story. Write a script of a news anchor introducing the story and a field reporter interviewing Beharry, his commanding officer, and the historian Gary Sheffield. Include details from the article. Assign each group member a role. Present, and if possible, videotape your broadcast.

Vocabulary Check

Match the Vocabulary words to their definitions.

5. engagements	a. unaware
6. incapacitated	b. deprived of power or disabled
7. noxious	c. military battles
8. oblivious	d. very dangerous or poisonous

Writing Skills Focus

Timed Writing Briefly discuss the effect of the details included in this article. Be sure to cite evidence from the article to support your response.

What Do You Think Now? Beharry notes that he was not scared at the time, only afterward. Why do you think this was the case? How might his experiences have affected his view of the world?

Check for Understanding

Independent Practice

Informational Text Focus

Possible responses:

1. *He acted bravely under fire, rescuing fellow soldiers.*
2. *He chose to keep going through the barricade. His choices show he has the courage to risk his life and act on his own initiative. He has the qualities of a leader.*
3. *Like Sassoon, Beharry showed great courage and spirit as a soldier. Unlike Owen, he did not die in combat. All wars seem to instill in soldiers a sense of camaraderie, but modern warfare requires a stronger camaraderie since it is fought differently than WWI.*
4. *In the first event, the Warrior was hit after it came to a halt. A few weeks passed between the two events. The second time, another Warrior was hit during an ambush. In each incident, Beharry acted with great bravery after his vehicle was hit. Analyzing the sequence of events helps understand the dangers and risks Beharry was under.*
5. *c*
6. *b*
7. *d*
8. *a*
9. *These details show what a rare and impressive honor it is to be awarded the Victoria Cross.*
10. *Beharry's uncomplicated response to the question illustrates his straightforward personality.*
11. *The quotation suggests that the writer is interested in the military as a cultural institution.*
12. *With the first ambush, Beharry acted fearlessly to help save the lives of fellow soldiers; in the second attack, he acted bravely again, this time under injury.*
13. *Presentations should be based on facts and opinions in the article.*

Universal Access

Struggling Writers

Provide additional scaffolding for students. Ask students to review the list of details they recorded in their **Reader/Writer Notebooks.** Next to or below each detail, have them record how the details added to their understanding of the events in the article. When students have finished noting the effects of each detail, have them summarize in a paragraph the effect of the details.

What Do You Think Now?

Have students consider how they or others they know respond to stressful situations. Point out that people may be energized or paralyzed by pressure. Do they expect Beharry's war experiences to have made him braver or more cautious?

Assess

Unit 6 Resources,
Selection Standards Check, p. 21

Standards Focus

Objectives

Students will

- analyze the characteristics of a memoir
- evaluate historical context

Selection Introduction

Think About the Writer

Have students consider how various people might describe a terrible crime or accident. Ask them what sort of details they would expect a painter to focus on, as opposed to a doctor. Then, ask them if they think Levi's scientific background influenced his approach to describing his experiences at Auschwitz.

For Independent Reading

- *Maus: A Survivor's Tale,* Art Spiegelman
- *In My Hands, Memories of a Holocaust Rescuer,* Irene Gut Opdyke

Motivate

What Do You Think?/QuickWrite

Ask students why people read and write memoirs. Then, have them write for five minutes in their **Reader/Writer Notebooks** about why survivors of tragic events might want to share their stories.

English for Academic Success

Academic Vocabulary

Look for opportunities to use the Academic Vocabulary words in this unit.

- **adapt, *v.*:** adjust for a new purpose
- **exhibit, *v.*:** show, demonstrate
- **inevitable, *adj.*:** unavoidable
- **perspective, *n.*:** a particular way of looking at something

Preparing to Read

On the Bottom *from* Survival in Auschwitz

What Do You Think? How does experience shape our view of the world?

QuickWrite

Why do you think Primo Levi and others felt they had to write about their experiences in Nazi concentration camps? Why is it essential that the atrocities of the Holocaust be remembered generation after generation? Write down your thoughts in your *Reader/Writer Notebook.*

Primo Levi (1919-1987)

MEET THE WRITER

Primo Levi

(1919–1987)

Primo Levi recorded his horrible experiences "not to weep and wail, but to be a witness, to give readers material for judgment."

The Camps

Primo Levi was studying chemistry at the University of Turin in Italy when World War II erupted in Europe. After the German army occupied northern Italy, Levi, a Jew, joined a resistance group and was soon arrested by Italian Fascists. Levi thought that he would wait out the war in a detention center, but when the Germans took over his detention camp, all Jews were immediately deported. In February 1944, Levi and 649 others were sent to Auschwitz (now called Auschwitz-Birkenau Nazi German Concentration and Death Camp). He was one of only twenty-three of the group who survived until the camp was liberated less than a year later.

After liberation, Levi returned to Italy and resumed work as a chemist. Soon he began writing, chronicling his experiences in the death camp and his journey back to Italy in his first books, *Survival in Auschwitz* (1947) and *The Reawakening* (1963).

Lessons of the Holocaust

Levi did not confine his writing to Holocaust experiences. He also published poems, essays, short stories, novels, and memoirs; he even dabbled in science fiction. Levi's last book, *The Drowned and the Saved* (1986), is a meditation on the meaning of the Nazi barbarity. To the critic Alexander Stille, who considered Levi's work "ultimately hopeful," this last book seemed to reflect a pessimistic perspective, causing the critic to speculate that "by the end of his life, Levi had become increasingly convinced that the lessons of the Holocaust were destined to be lost as it took a place among the routine atrocities of history."

On April 11, 1987, Levi fell to his death down the stairwell of his apartment. Some believe that the fall was an accident; others believe that Levi took his own life. Did Levi ultimately lose faith in humanity? That question may never be answered.

Think About the Writer How might Levi's science career have influenced his decision to set aside emotions and write as "a witness" to Nazi atrocities?

California Standards, pp. 1092–1101

- **Reading Standard 3.1** Analyze characteristics of subgenres (e.g., satire, parody, allegory, pastoral) that are used in poetry, prose, plays, novels, short stories, essays, and other basic genres.
- **Reading Standard 3.7** Analyze recognized works of world literature from a variety of authors: **c.** Evaluate the philosophical, political, religious, ethical, and social influences of the historical period that shaped the characters, plots, and settings.
- **Grades 9–10 Review Reading Standard 3.12** Analyze the way in which a work of literature is related to the themes and issues of its historical period.

Selection Readability	
Easily Accessible **Accessible** Challenging	familiar language; simple sentence structure; accessible theme

Reading Standard 3.1, 3.7c; **Grades 9–10 Review**
Reading Standard 3.12 (see pages A48–A50)

Literary Skills Focus

Memoir A **memoir** records the memories of its author. In this sense, a memoir is a type of autobiography, or writing about the self. Unlike an **autobiography,** a memoir usually focuses on a particular time period in the writer's life, often one of historical prominence. Primo Levi's memoir describes his experience in Auschwitz, a concentration camp constructed in Poland by the Nazis. The excerpt you will read focuses on Levi's arrival at the camp in 1944, when he was twenty-four years old.

Literary Perspectives Apply the literary perspective described on page 1095 as you read this memoir.

Reading Skills Focus

Evaluating Historical Context Memoirs are usually shaped by their **historical context,** that is, by the political, ethical, and social influences that characterize a particular time and place.

Into Action As you read this excerpt, think about what you know about its historical context. In a chart like the one below, note details that you think are particularly powerful. In the second column, note what each detail tells you about the Holocaust.

Historical Details	What It Tells Me
The door the prisoners go through says "Arbeit Macht Frei," meaning "work makes you free."	Shows the psychological cruelty of the Nazis, since no matter how hard the prisoners worked, they would never be free. In fact, most would die. Sign held out cruel and false hope.

Writing Skills Focus

Think as a Reader/Writer

Find It in Your Reading Although Primo Levi writes about something that happened in the past, he primarily uses the present tense. As you read, note how his use of the present tense brings an immediacy to the writing. In your *Reader/Writer Notebook,* record three instances where Levi's use of present tense draws you into the narrative.

Vocabulary

taciturn (TAS uh turn) *adj.:* not talkative. *The taciturn soldier spoke little to the men and did not answer their questions.*

disconcerted (dihs kuhn SUR tihd) *v.* used as *adj.:* confused. *The unwillingness of the camp soldiers to tell what would happen next left the men feeling disconcerted.*

livid (LIHV ihd) *adj.:* pale; grayish. *The men's livid faces reflected their fright.*

sordid (SAWR dihd) *adj.:* filthy; foul. *The sordid conditions of the camp promoted the spread of disease.*

demolition (dehm uh LIHSH uhn) *n.:* destruction. *The demolition of the men's identity began when they lost their possessions.*

affinity (uh FIHN uh tee) *n.:* kinship; bond. *Their isolation and despair left the men feeling no affinity with one another.*

Language Coach

The Sounds of *C* The letter *c* in English can have a soft or a hard sound. The soft sound of /s/ is seen in words such as *center* and *cyst,* while the hard sound of /k/ occurs in words like *count* and *crib.* The general rule for pronouncing *c* is as follows: The letter *c* is sounded as /s/ when it occurs before the letters *e, i,* or *y*. Otherwise, it is sounded as /k/. Find a Vocabulary word with only one *c,* which is sounded as /s/. Find another Vocabulary word with two *c*'s, one sounded as /k/ and the other sounded as /s/.

Learn It Online
Watch the video introduction online to learn more about the experiences that inspired this memoir.

go.hrw.com H12-1093 Go

Reader/Writer Notebook
Use your **RWN** to complete the activities for this selection.

Selection Resources

Unit 6 Resources, on-level practice and assessment, p. 24

PowerNotes, interactive lesson presentations with activities

Teacher One Stop™, on-level lesson plans and all print resources

Holt Audio Library

Holt Audio Library: Selections and Summaries in Spanish

UA: Holt Interactive Reader, p. 307

UA: Differentiating Instruction, modified lesson plans and leveled assessment, p. 263

UA: Supporting Instruction in Spanish, selection summary

UA: Resources for Teaching Advanced Students, lesson plans, p. 190

ThinkCentral Online Assessment

ThinkCentral Online Remediation

Preteach

Introducing Vocabulary

Use this activity to check students' understanding of the Vocabulary words.

1. Why would a **taciturn** friend be uncomfortable at a party?
2. List three things that would make living conditions **sordid**.
3. Draw a picture of a **disconcerted** face.
4. Describe why you have an **affinity** with a friend.
5. Tell why a **livid** face might be unattractive.
6. Explain one way the **demolition** of the rainforest hurts the environment.

English for Academic Success

Language Coach

Give students other examples of words containing the letter *c*, sounded as /c/ or /k/, such as *conceited, civilian, coalesce,* and *cylinder.*

Literary Skills Focus

Have students note details that describe both one individual's experience and the historical conditions affecting millions.

Reading Skills Focus

Give students a copy of the Reading Skills Focus graphic organizer before they read. (See **Unit 6 Resources.**) Tell them to use their responses to answer the questions on the Applying Your Skills page.

Writing Skills Focus

Have students record in their **Reader/Writer Notebooks** instances of the present tense in the narrative and use their notes to complete the Writing Skills Focus activity.

Learn It Online
The **PowerNotes** presentation for this lesson includes a short video that introduces the memoir. The video is also available on the online version of this page.

go.hrw.com H12-1093 Go

Teacher Preparation

Selection Summary

Levi recalls his arrival at Buna, a work camp that is part of the Auschwitz complex. Levi and the other men among the new arrivals, tired and thirsty, are told to remove and bundle their clothes. They are shaved and then locked in a shower room. During the night, a fellow prisoner, the camp's dentist, visits them secretly; he tells them where they are and what kind of life they can expect at Buna. The showers finally go on; the prisoners bathe quickly and then are hustled off to dress. Afterward, Levi and the other prisoners are shocked at their phantom-like appearance. The excerpt concludes with Levi's reflections about having had everything taken from him—and about gaining a new understanding of the term *extermination camp* and the expression *to lie on the bottom*.

Direct Teach

Think About/Talk About

Read with a Purpose Have students read the Read with a Purpose statement. Point out that the quotation marks around "the bottom" indicate that it is a figurative expression. Note that hitting the bottom implies sinking to the farthest possible point. Have students predict what circumstances will lead the speaker to believe he has hit the bottom, how he will feel there, and what behavior he will observe.

Comprehension

A Reading Focus

Possible response: *At Buna, the work is done by prisoners, who have little hope and no guarantee of attaining freedom.*

MEMOIR

On the Bottom

from Survival in Auschwitz

by **Primo Levi** translated by **Stuart Woolf**

Read with a Purpose

Read to learn how humans feel and what they might do when they believe they have hit "the bottom."

Build Background

Beginning in the 1930s, Nazi Germany started to remove Jews and other so-called "undesirables"—homosexuals, Roma, Poles, political dissidents, members of various religious groups, and the disabled—to concentration camps. By 1942, the greatest mass murder in the history of humanity had begun; by the time it ended, in 1945, perhaps eleven million human beings had been starved, tortured, and murdered. Six million of the victims were Jews. The excerpt from Primo Levi's memoir that you are about to read begins early in 1944 after Levi and 649 other Jews were packed into twelve cattle cars, with no food or water or toilets. Eleven days later the cattle cars arrived at Auschwitz, a notorious camp in German-occupied Poland.

Levi's group was quickly divided into those who were able-bodied and those who were not. In Levi's convoy, ninety-six men and twenty-nine women were selected to work in the labor camps of Auschwitz. All the others were murdered. As this excerpt begins, the prisoners have been taken by a lorry, or truck, to a room inside the camp.

The journey did not last more than twenty minutes. Then the lorry stopped, and we saw a large door, and above it a sign, brightly illuminated (its memory still strikes me in my dreams): *Arbeit Macht Frei,*[1] work gives freedom. **A**

We climb down, they make us enter an enormous empty room that is poorly heated. We have a terrible thirst. The weak gurgle of water in the radiators makes us ferocious; we have had nothing to drink for four days. But there is also a tap—and above it a card which says that it is forbidden to drink as the water is dirty. Nonsense. It seems obvious that the card is a joke, "they" know that we are dying of thirst and they put us in a room, and there is a tap, and *Wassertrinken Verboten.*[2] I drink and I incite my companions to do likewise, but I have to spit it out, the water is tepid and sweetish, with the smell of a swamp.

This is hell. Today, in our times, hell must be like this. A huge, empty room: we are tired, standing on our feet, with a tap which drips while we cannot drink the water, and we wait for something which will certainly be terrible, and nothing happens and nothing continues to happen. What can one think about? One cannot think any more; it is like being already dead. Someone sits down on the ground. The time passes drop by drop.

We are not dead. The door is opened and an SS[3] man enters, smoking. He looks at us slowly and asks, *"Wer kann Deutsch?"*[4] One of us whom I have never seen, named Flesch, moves forward; he will be our

1. ***Arbeit Macht Frei*** (AHR byt mahkht fry).
2. ***Wassertrinken Verboten*** (VAHS ehr TRIHNK ehn fehr BOH tehn): German for "Drinking water is forbidden."
3. **SS:** abbreviation for *Schutzstaffel* ("elite guard"), the Nazi units in charge of the extermination camps during World War II.
4. ***Wer kann Deutsch?*** (vehr kahn doych): German for "Who knows German?"

A Reading Focus **Evaluating Historical Context** Given what you know about the fate of most prisoners, how is the sign ironic?

Universal Access

English Learners

English for Academic Success Help students better grasp the details of the selection by providing the following definitions:

- **lorry**—a large truck designed to carry heavy loads
- **illuminated**—lit up
- **radiator**—series of pipes used as a heating device
- **incite**—urge
- **tepid**—lukewarm
- **robust**—strong and healthy

Struggling Readers

Benchmark Students As is true of memoirs in general, this selection blends factual detail and personal commentary. To help students distinguish historical observation from personal commentary, suggest that they keep a list of key facts from the account and, wherever appropriate, note a related personal comment from Levi.

✔ See **UA: Differentiating Instruction** for strategies for teaching struggling readers.

Auschwitz (1948) by Heinrich Ehmsen (1886–1964). Oil on plywood.
Horst Ehmsen, Vienna/Nationalgalerie, Staatliche Museen zu Berlin, Germany..

interpreter. The SS man makes a long, calm speech; the interpreter translates. We have to form rows of five, with intervals of two yards between man and man; then we have to undress and make a bundle of the clothes in a special manner, the woolen garments on one side, all the rest on the other; we must take off our shoes but pay great attention that they are not stolen.

Stolen by whom? Why should our shoes be stolen? And what about our documents, the few things we have in our pockets, our watches? We all look at the interpreter, and the interpreter asks the German, and the German smokes and looks him through and through as if he were transparent, as if no one had spoken.

I had never seen old men naked. Mr. Bergmann wore a truss[5] and asked the interpreter if he should take it off, and the interpreter hesitated. But the German understood and spoke seriously to the interpreter pointing to someone. We saw the interpreter swallow and then he said: "The officer says, take off the truss, and you will be given that of Mr. Coen." One could see the words coming bitterly out of Flesch's mouth; this was the German manner of laughing. **B**

Now another German comes and tells us to put the shoes in a certain corner, and we put them there, because now it is all over and we feel outside this world and the only thing is to obey. Someone comes with a broom and sweeps away all the shoes, outside the door in a heap. He is crazy, he is mixing them all together, ninety-six pairs, they will be all unmatched. The outside door opens; a freezing wind enters and we are naked and cover ourselves up with our arms. The wind blows and slams the door; the German reopens it and stands watching with interest how we writhe to hide from the wind, one behind the other. Then he leaves and closes it. **C**

Now the second act begins. Four men with razors, soapbrushes, and clippers burst in; they have

5. **truss:** belt with a pad, worn to support a hernia, a rupture of the intestine through the abdominal wall.

Literary Perspectives

Analyzing Historical Context At the time Levi wrote his memoir, just after World War II ended, the full horror of the concentration camps set up by Nazi Germany and its collaborators was not yet known to the world. As Allied forces marched across Europe into Germany and Poland in 1944, they liberated Auschwitz and other camps. For the first time, outsiders bore witness to the atrocities perpetuated in the camps. While the stories told by these liberators and the photographs they took communicated unspeakable horror to the rest of the world, it was the first-person accounts told by the victims themselves that provided the more vivid and detailed testament.

As you read, be sure to notice the questions in the text, which will guide you in using this perspective.

B Literary Focus **Memoir** What personal details make this more than a strictly historical account?

C Reading Focus **Evaluating Historical Context** How do the Nazis' actions in this paragraph reflect their belief that their victims are less than human?

Think About/Talk About

Comprehension

C Reading Focus

Possible response: *The German watches the prisoners' discomfort with mild interest, as if they were animals in some kind of experiment.*

Analysis

B Literary Focus

Possible response: *Levi notes that he had never seen old men naked. He remarks that the translator appears to speak bitterly.*

Extend the Discussion

Making Generalizations When Levi declares, "hell must be like this," what is he implying to be generally true of hellish situations? ***Possible response:*** *They are situations that deny people's desperate needs and impress a feeling of doom on the people involved; time would pass slowly.*

Recognizing Rhetorical Devices The first full paragraph on p. 1095 begins with a series of unanswered questions. What does this series of questions convey? ***Possible response***: *It conveys the prisoners' anxiety and uncertainty about what is going to happen to them.*

Literary Perspectives

Before students read the selection, have them read **Literary Perspectives** about Analyzing Historical Context.

Ask students to think about how a description of Auschwitz made by a member of the Allied forces might differ from a prisoner's description. How might each person describe the conditions, mood, and people differently? As they read, have students note details that could be described only by a person living in the prison.

Remind students to use the notes and questions at the bottom of the page to help them use the perspective.

Model the Skill

- Tell students that when they evaluate the **historical context** of a work, they should think about what they know about the political, social, and ethical circumstances that helped to shape the work.
- Provide students with copies of the Reading Skills Focus graphic organizer. (See **Unit 6 Resources.**)
- To model evaluating historical context, begin by pointing out that one of the historical details presented in the memoir is that new prisoners at the work camp had their clothes taken away and hair shaved until they were barely recognizable. Tell students to note that fact in the appropriate column.
- Inform students that this detail tells the reader something about the Holocaust. Have students note in their organizer that it shows the dehumanizing side of the Nazi's treatment of the prisoners.

Guided Practice: Apply

Turn-and-Talk Have students work with a partner and discuss their knowledge of the historical events surrounding the Holocaust prior to their reading this selection. Then, have students share any new information or insight they have gained from this selection.

trousers and jackets with stripes, with a number sewn on the front; perhaps they are the same sort as those others of this evening (this evening or yesterday evening?), but these are robust and flourishing. We ask many questions but they catch hold of us and in a moment we find ourselves shaved and sheared. What comic faces we have without hair! The four speak a language which does not seem of this world. It is certainly not German, for I understand a little German.

Finally another door is opened: here we are, locked in, naked, sheared and standing, with our feet in water—it is a shower room. We are alone. Slowly the astonishment dissolves, and we speak, and everyone asks questions and no one answers. If we are naked in a shower room, it means that we will have a shower. If we have a shower it is because they are not going to kill us yet. But why then do they keep us standing, and give us nothing to drink, while nobody explains anything, and we have no shoes or clothes, but we are all naked with our feet in the water, and we have been traveling five days and cannot even sit down.

And our women?

Mr. Levi asks me if I think that our women are like us at this moment, and where they are, and if we will be able to see them again. I say yes, because he is married and has a daughter; certainly we will see them again. But by now my belief is that all this is a game to mock and sneer at us. Clearly they will kill us, whoever thinks he is going to live is mad, it means that he has swallowed the bait, but I have not; I have understood that it will soon all be over, perhaps in this same room, when they get bored of seeing us naked, dancing from foot to foot and trying every now and again to sit down on the floor. But there are two inches of cold water and we cannot sit down. **D**

We walk up and down without sense, and we talk, everybody talks to everybody else, we make a great noise. The door opens, and a German enters; it is the officer of before. He speaks briefly, the interpreter translates. "The officer says you must be quiet, because this is not a rabbinical[6] school." One sees the words which are not his, the bad words, twist his mouth as they come out, as if he was spitting out a foul taste. We beg him to ask what we are waiting for, how long we will stay here, about our women, everything; but he says no, that he does not want to ask. This Flesch, who is most unwilling to translate into Italian the hard, cold German phrases and refuses to turn into German our questions because he knows that it is useless, is a German Jew of about fifty, who has a large scar on his face from a wound received fighting the Italians on the Piave.[7] He is a closed, taciturn man, for whom I feel an instinctive respect as I feel that he has begun to suffer before us.

The German goes and we remain silent, although we are a little ashamed of our silence. It is still night and we wonder if the day will ever come. The door opens again, and someone else dressed in stripes comes in. He is different from the others, older, with glasses, a more civilized face, and much less robust. He speaks to us in Italian.

By now we are tired of being amazed. We seem to be watching some mad play, one of those plays in which the witches, the Holy Spirit, and the devil appear. He speaks Italian badly, with a strong foreign accent. He makes a long speech, is very polite, and tries to reply to all our questions.

We are at Monowitz, near Auschwitz, in Upper Silesia,[8] a region inhabited by both Poles and Germans. This camp is a workcamp, in German one says *Arbeitslager*,[9] all the prisoners (there are about ten thousand) work in a factory which produces a type of rubber called Buna, so that the camp itself is called Buna.

6. **rabbinical** (ruh BIHN uh kuhl): of or relating to rabbis, teachers of Jewish law.

7. **Italians on the Piave:** During World War I, Austria and Germany defeated 600,000 Italian troops in the Battle of Caporetto; the Italian forces were pushed back to the Piave River near Venice.

8. **Upper Silesia:** region including parts of southwestern Poland, eastern Germany, and the northern Czech Republic. After World War I, Germany and Poland divided northern Silesia; southern Silesia fell under the rule of Czechoslovakia.

9. ***Arbeitslager*** (AHR byts LAHG ehr).

D **Literary Focus** **Memoir** What personal details in this paragraph can help readers understand the horror of the camps?

Vocabulary **taciturn** (TAS uh turn) *adj.:* not talkative.

Word-Attack Skills Mini-Lesson

English for Academic Success Direct attention to the selection word *disconcerted* (p. 1098). Help students recognize that the base word is the verb *concert.* Compare the pronunciation of *concert* when used as a verb (kuhn SUHRT) and as a noun (KAHN surht). Point out that *concert* can function as more than one part of speech and that it has a different pronunciation depending on its role in a sentence.

Activity The following words can function as different parts of speech. Have volunteers compose sentences that illustrate the words' different uses.

1. **articulate:** adjective and verb [*adjective (ar TIHK yoo liht); verb (ar TIHK yoo layt)*]
2. **abuse:** noun and verb [*noun (uh BYOOS); verb (uh BYOOZ)*]
3. **object:** noun and verb [*noun (AHB jehkt); verb (uhb JEHKT*]

1935 . . . 1940 (20th century) by Russian school. Color lithograph.

Analyzing Visuals

Connecting to the Text Levi describes how the prisoners were transformed into phantoms after arriving at Auschwitz. How does this image capture this idea?

We will be given shoes and clothes—no, not our own—other shoes, other clothes, like his. We are naked now because we are waiting for the shower and disinfection, which will take place immediately after the reveille,[10] because one cannot enter the camp without being disinfected. **E**

Certainly there will be work to do; everyone must work here. But there is work and work: he, for example, acts as a doctor. He is a Hungarian doctor who studied in Italy and he is the dentist of the Lager.[11] He has been in the Lager for four and a half years (not in this one: Buna has only been open for a year and a half), but we can see that he is still quite well, not very thin. Why is he in the Lager? Is he Jewish like us? "No," he says simply, "I am a criminal."

We ask him many questions. He laughs, replies to some and not to others, and it is clear that he avoids certain subjects. He does not speak of the women: he says they are well, that we will see them again soon, but he does not say how or where. Instead he tells us other things, strange and crazy things, perhaps he too is playing with us. Perhaps he is mad—one goes mad in the Lager. He says that every Sunday there are concerts and football matches. He says that whoever boxes well can become cook. He says that whoever works well receives prize coupons with which to buy tobacco and soap. He says that the water is really not drinkable, and that instead a coffee substitute is distributed every day, but generally nobody drinks it as the soup itself is sufficiently watery to quench thirst. We beg him to find us something to drink, but he says he cannot, that

10. **reveille** (REHV uh lee): early-morning bugle call to waken military troops.
11. **Lager:** short for *Arbeitslager.*

E Reading Focus Evaluating Historical Context Today, thousands of shoes of the murdered prisoners are exhibited at Auschwitz. How might knowing about this exhibit affect a reader's reaction to this portion of the memoir?

4. **initiate:** noun and verb [noun (*ihn IHSH ee iht*); *verb (ihn IHSH ee ayt)*]
5. **reject:** noun and verb [*noun (REE jehkt); verb (ree JEHKT)*]
6. **alternate:** verb and noun [*verb (AWL tuhr nayt); noun (AWL tuhr niht)*]
7. **congregate:** verb and adjective [*verb (KAHN greh gayt); adjective (KAHN greh giht)*]

Analyzing Visuals

Connecting to the Text: *The sea of pale, emotionless faces with barely perceptible figures that blend in with the background portray the prisoners in a spooky light, rendering them as phantom-like beings.*

Think About/Talk About

Comprehension

E Reading Focus

Possible response: *Knowing about the exhibit of shoes at Auschwitz, a reader might think about all the people who, before being murdered, were told to undress and were falsely promised that they would receive other clothes and shoes.*

Analysis

D Literary Focus

Possible response: *Levi alludes to the added anxiety of a prisoner who has a wife and daughter from whom he is separated; he worries about what is happening to them and whether he will see them again.*

Extend the Discussion

Finding Details What "strange and crazy things" does the Hungarian dentist tell the prisoners about life in Auschwitz? ***Possible response:*** *He tells them there will be concerts, football matches, and prizes that will win them tobacco and soap.*

Characterization Think about what Flesch, the translator, does and does not do and what Levi says about him. Do you agree that Flesch is someone who deserves respect? Why or why not? ***Possible responses:*** *Yes, because Levi says that Flesch obviously does not want to translate the SS officer's crude jokes, and although Flesch suffered and fought for his country in World War I, he, too, is a prisoner here. No, Flesch could do more to help the new arrivals, yet he refuses.*

Vocabulary: Own the Word

taciturn: Ask students to applaud in order to indicate how much they would like to be described as *taciturn* and why. ***Possible response:*** *Students do not applaud and explain that they do not want to be thought of as quiet.*

Think About/Talk About

Analysis

F Literary Focus

Possible responses: *Levi does not want to be toyed with; he prefers the truth to reassuring illusions and false hope. The man may be lying not to be deceitful but to cheer the prisoners up.*

G Literary Focus

Possible response: *Levi notes that he and the other men avoided looking at each other. They know that another's appearance is a physical reflection of their own despondent state.*

H Literary Focus

Possible response: *It is the moment that Levi realizes he has hit "the bottom." He comes to the conclusion that a man cannot be more hopeless, empty, or dehumanized than he is at this moment.*

I Literary Perspectives

Possible response: *Knowing how brutally the Nazis treated prisoners and how few of the people imprisoned in concentration camps survived, readers can appreciate that Levi truly had "to lie on the bottom."*

Vocabulary: Own the Word

- **disconcerted:** The antonym of *disconcerted* is *calm*. Use both in a sentence. The news of the attack left me *disconcerted,* but the leader's address helped me become calm.
- **livid:** Ask students to complete the following sentence: The woman's face turned *livid* when . . .
- **sordid:** Create a semantic web with *sordid* in its center. Ask students for attributes and examples. ***Possible responses:*** *vile, squalor, foul*
- **demolition:** Ask students to list additional reasons for the *demolition* of a person's identity, as Primo did. ***Possible responses:*** *loss of health, loss of sanity*
- **affinity:** Ask: "When might you feel an *affinity* toward other people?"

he has come to see us secretly, against SS orders, as we still have to be disinfected, and that he must leave at once; he has come because he has a liking for Italians, and because, he says, he "has a little heart." We ask him if there are other Italians in the camp and he says there are some, a few, he does not know how many; and he at once changes the subject. Meanwhile a bell rang and he immediately hurried off and left us stunned and disconcerted. Some feel refreshed but I do not. I still think that even this dentist, this incomprehensible person, wanted to amuse himself at our expense, and I do not want to believe a word of what he said. **F**

At the sound of the bell, we can hear the still dark camp waking up. Unexpectedly the water gushes out boiling from the showers—five minutes of bliss; but immediately after, four men (perhaps they are the barbers) burst in yelling and shoving and drive us out, wet and steaming, into the adjoining room which is freezing; here other shouting people throw at us unrecognizable rags and thrust into our hands a pair of broken-down boots with wooden soles; we have no time to understand and we already find ourselves in the open, in the blue and icy snow of dawn, barefoot and naked, with all our clothing in our hands, with a hundred yards to run to the next hut. There we are finally allowed to get dressed.

When we finish, everyone remains in his own corner and we do not dare lift our eyes to look at one another. There is nowhere to look in a mirror, but our appearance stands in front of us, reflected in a hundred livid faces, in a hundred miserable and sordid puppets. We are transformed into the phantoms glimpsed yesterday evening.[12] **G**

12. **We are transformed . . . evening:** Levi is referring to the inmates at Auschwitz whom he and the other new prisoners witnessed briefly upon arriving at the camp on the previous evening.

Then for the first time we became aware that our language lacks words to express this offense, the demolition of a man. In a moment, with almost prophetic intuition, the reality was revealed to us: we had reached the bottom. It is not possible to sink lower than this; no human condition is more miserable than this, nor could it conceivably be so. Nothing belongs to us any more; they have taken away our clothes, our shoes, even our hair; if we speak, they will not listen to us, and if they listen, they will not understand. They will even take away our name: and if we want to keep it, we will have to find ourselves the strength to do so, to manage somehow so that behind the name something of us, of us as we were, still remains. **H**

We know that we will have difficulty in being understood, and this is as it should be. But consider what value, what meaning is enclosed even in the smallest of our daily habits, in the hundred possessions which even the poorest beggar owns: a handkerchief, an old letter, the photo of a cherished person. These things are part of us, almost like limbs of our body; nor is it conceivable that we can be deprived of them in our world, for we immediately find others to substitute the old ones, other objects which are ours in their personification and evocation of our memories.

Imagine now a man who is deprived of everyone he loves, and at the same time of his house, his habits, his clothes, in short, of everything he possesses: he will be a hollow man, reduced to suffering and needs, forgetful of dignity and restraint, for he who loses all often easily loses himself. He will be a man whose life or death can be lightly decided with no sense of human affinity, in the most fortunate of cases, on the basis of a pure judgment of utility. It is in this way that one can understand the double sense of the term "extermination camp," and it is now clear what we seek to express with the phrase: "to lie on the bottom." **I**

F Literary Focus **Memoir** Why do you think Levi is so cynical? Do you think the man is lying to be deceitful or for another reason? Explain.

G Literary Focus **Memoir** What details make this passage more than an impersonal recounting of historical events?

H Literary Focus **Memoir** In this passage, Levi leaves the narrative to offer extended commentary. From his perspective, how is this moment more than just the completion of the entry process?

I Literary Perspectives **Analyzing Historical Context** What knowledge helps you understand Levi's concluding sentence?

Vocabulary **disconcerted** (dihs kuhn SUR tihd) *v.* used as *adj.:* confused.
livid (LIHV ihd) *adj.:* pale; grayish.
sordid (SAWR dihd) *adj.:* filthy; foul.
demolition (dehm uh LIHSH uhn) *n.:* destruction.
affinity (uh FIHN uh tee) *n.:* kinship; bond.

California Standards, pp. 1099–1101

- **Reading Standard 3.1** Analyze characteristics of subgenres (e.g., satire, parody, allegory, pastoral) that are used in poetry, prose, plays, novels, short stories, essays, and other basic genres.
- **Reading Standard 3.7** Analyze recognized works of world literature from a variety of authors: **c.** Evaluate the philosophical, political, religious, ethical, and social influences of the historical period that shaped the characters, plots, and settings.
- **Grades 9–10 Review Reading Standard 1.1** Identify and use the literal and figurative meanings of words and understand word derivations.
- **Grades 9–10 Review Reading Standard 3.12** Analyze the way in which a work of literature is related to the themes and issues of its historical period.
- **Writing Standard 2.2** Write responses to literature: **a.** Demonstrate a comprehensive understanding of the significant ideas in works or passages.
- **Writing Standard 2.3** Write reflective compositions: **a.** Explore the significance of personal experiences, events, conditions, or concerns by using rhetorical strategies (e.g., narration, description, exposition, persuasion).
- **Listening and Speaking Standard 1.6** Use logical, ethical, and emotional appeals that enhance a specific tone and purpose.

Applying Your Skills

Reading Standard 3.1, 3.7c; **Grades 9–10 Review** Reading Standard 3.12 (see pages A48–A50)
Writing Standard 2.3a (see pages A51–A52)

On the Bottom *from* Survival in Auschwitz

Literary Response and Analysis

Reading Skills Focus

Quick Check

1. When Levi arrives in Auschwitz, what factors lead him to conclude that it is "hell"?
2. Describe how the prisoners are "dehumanized."

Read with a Purpose

3. What details in the memoir reveal what people will do when they "hit bottom"? How were some people able to survive the inhuman treatment that Levi and others endured?

Reading Skills: Evaluating Historical Context

4. As you read, you noted details about the political, ethical, and social background of the Holocaust. Now, in a new column, explain how these details deepened your reading experience.

Historical Detail	What It Tells Me	How Knowing Detail Enriches My Reading
The door prisoners go through says "Arbeit Macht Frei," meaning "work makes you free."	Shows the psychological cruelty of the Nazis, since no matter how hard prisoners worked, they never would be free. In fact, most would die. Sign held out cruel and false hope.	

Literary Skills Focus

Literary Analysis

5. **Interpret** Explain Levi's reference to the double meaning of the term "extermination camp."
6. **Analyze** Why does Levi use the phrase "second act" to describe what happens to the men after they undress?
7. **Interpret** What does it mean to be "hollow"? Why does Levi conclude that it is easy to decide if a "hollow" man lives or dies?
8. **Extend** Levi says that the Nazis' offense was the "demolition of a man." At what other times in history has one group of people "demolished" other people and tried to rob them of their humanity?
9. **Literary Perspectives** How does knowing the Holocaust's massive scale of suffering and death affect your understanding of this memoir?

Literary Skills: Memoir

10. **Contrast** How is Levi's memoir different from a newspaper article about the camps?

Literary Skills Review: Setting

11. **Analyze** The time and place of a story is its **setting.** What sensory details—sight, smell, hearing, touch, and taste—help you imagine this setting?

Writing Skills Focus

Think as a Reader/Writer

Use It in Your Writing As you read this memoir, you took notes on Levi's use of the present tense. Now, write a brief personal memoir in which you use the present tense to help your reader feel as if he or she is sharing your experience. Try to write about an incident that is set in some specific historical context.

What Do You Think Now How would Levi's experiences in Auschwitz account for his view of the world?

Universal Access

Struggling Writers

Guide students in completing the Writing Skills Focus activity by providing additional scaffolding. After students have brainstormed a few memorable events in their life, have them choose the one that is set in a historical context, if possible. Then, ask them to construct an outline to help them organize the sequence of events in their memoir. Remind students to use as many sensory details as possible as if they are reliving the experience, and to write in the present tense.

What Do You Think Now?

To help students answer the question, ask them to point out key words and phrases in the reading that show Levi's attitude toward his experience in the camp.

Check for Understanding

Independent Practice

Reading Skills Focus

Possible responses:

1. *The men are thirsty and given no water; they are exhausted but are forced to stand and wait.*
2. *They are forced to undress, have their heads shaved, and stand in the cold without water, food, or information about their fate.*
3. *Levi suggests that, when people "hit bottom," they lose their sense of human dignity. To survive, some people may have held on to their faith, or to the hope of uniting with their families.*
4. *Ask students to explain how knowing details enhanced their reading experience.*

Literary Skills Focus

Possible response:

5. *It is designed not only to destroy lives but also their identities.*
6. *Levi finds the situation so horrendous that he likens it to being in—or watching—a play. He may also sense that his captors are "watching" the prisoners as if watching actors in a play.*
7. *A "hollow" man is a person who has lost everything, including his identity. It might be easy for a captor to view such a person as less than human and, as a result, to casually decide the person's fate.*
8. *For centuries, Europeans and their descendants in North America, Latin America, and the Caribbean robbed Africans of their humanity by enslaving them.*
9. *It makes Levi's survival seem all the more extraordinary.*
10. *Levi's memoir offers insight into the psychological nightmare they experienced. It shows the prisoners as people, not simply victims.*
11. *The illuminated sign above the camp door, the water that smells like a swamp, the "freezing wind," and the "icy snow of dawn" all help to visualize the setting.*

Independent Practice
Vocabulary Development
Vocabulary Check
1. *a person who is not talkative*
2. *confused*
3. *pale*
4. *a filthy tenement*
5. *destroy it*
6. *close to him or her*

Your Turn
1. *livid*
2. *taciturn*
3. *affinity*
4. *demolition*
5. *sordid*
6. *disconcerted*

English for Academic Success
Language Coach
Possible responses:

In *scant*, *c* is sounded like /k/,
In *scent*, *sc* is sounded like /s/,
In *since*, *c* is sounded like /s/,
In *sequence*, *c* is sounded like /s/,
In *tacit*, *c* is sounded like /s/,
In *tactical*, each *c* is sounded like /k/,
In *census*, *c* is sounded like /s/,
In *soccer*, *cc* is sounded like /k/,
In *muscle*, *sc* is sounded like /s/.
If the general rule were followed, *soccer* and *muscle* would be pronounced incorrectly, with the *cc* sounding like /s/ and *sc* sounding like /k/.

English for Academic Success
Academic Vocabulary
Possible response: *Responses will vary. In their paragraphs, students should explain the difficulties and losses experienced and show how people adapted to the challenging situation and exhibited extraordinary abilities.*

Applying Your Skills

Grades 9–10 Review Reading Standard 1.1 (see pages A48–A50)

On the Bottom *from* Survival in Auschwitz

Vocabulary Development

Vocabulary Check

Be sure you can justify your answer to each of the following questions about the Vocabulary words.

1. Which person could be described as **taciturn**—a person who speaks a great deal or a person who is not talkative?
2. If someone is **disconcerted,** would he or she feel confused or satisfied?
3. If a face is described as **livid,** is it pale or rosy red?
4. Which setting would be described as **sordid:** a filthy tenement or a tidy farmhouse?
5. If you are going to cause the **demolition** of a building, are you going to start building it or destroy it?
6. If you have **affinity** with someone, do you feel close to him or her or do you feel envious?

Vocabulary Skills: Synonyms and Antonyms

Synonyms are words with the same or nearly the same meaning: *Sad* and *sorrowful* are both adjectives that mean "unhappy." **Antonyms** are words with opposite meanings: *Happy* and *miserable* are adjectives which have opposite meanings.

Although synonyms have more or less the same meaning, many synonyms do not share exact meanings. When you are selecting a synonym or antonym for your writing, you should refer to a good dictionary to be certain that you have chosen the most precise word. For example, *robust* and *healthy* are synonyms that mean about the same thing; however, *healthy* usually implies simply the absence of disease, while *robust* is used to describe someone who is strong and energetic.

Your Turn

Use each Vocabulary word to complete the exercise.

taciturn	sordid	livid
disconcerted	demolition	affinity

1. _____ is a synonym for *pale.*
2. _____ is an antonym for *chatty.*
3. _____ is a synonym for *connection.*
4. _____ is an antonym for *construction.*
5. _____ is an antonym for *clean.*
6. _____ is an synonym for *confuse.*

Language Coach

The Sounds of *C* The letter *c* can be sounded like /k/ or like /s/. The general rule governing the pronunciation of words with the letter *c* is this: The letter *c* is sounded like /s/ when it comes before the letters *e*, *i*, and *y*. At other times *c* is sounded like the /k/ sound.

Sound out each of these words: *scant, scent, since, tacit, tactical, census.* How is the letter *c* sounded?

There are some exceptions to the rule. How is the letter *c* pronounced in the words *soccer* and *muscle?* How would the words be pronounced if the general rule were followed?

Academic Vocabulary

Write About

Throughout history people have exhibited the ability to adapt to difficult conditions and withstand extraordinary loss. Write a paragraph about a survival experience that you have heard or read about.

Universal Access: Vocabulary Development

Struggling Readers

Have students work in pairs to find synonyms for the Academic Vocabulary words *adapt, considerably, exhibit, inevitable,* and *perspective.* Then, have them compare the slight difference in meaning between each word and its synonym(s). Tell students to organize their information in a chart such as the following:

✔ See the **Academic and Selection Vocabulary Skill Builder** in **UA: Differentiating Instruction.**

Word & Meaning	Synonym	Difference in meaning
adapt—adjust for a new purpose	modify	The word modify means "to change something slightly," while adapt refers to a change for a specific purpose

Writing Standard 2.2a (see pages A51–A52)
Listening and Speaking Standard 1.6 (see pages A53–A55)

Grammar Link

Punctuating for Clarity: Semicolons, Colons, Dashes

The purpose of punctuation is clarity; a misplaced mark of punctuation can cause confusion. Levi, or his translator, uses several kinds of punctuation to show relationships among ideas within a sentence.

A **semicolon** connects independent clauses that are closely related in thought and are not joined by a coordinating conjunction (such as *and, but, nor*):

> One cannot think any more; it is like being already dead.

A **colon** joins two independent clauses when the second clause explains the idea of the first clause:

> Just then, with almost prophetic intuition, the reality was revealed to us: we had reached the bottom.

A **dash** sets off an abrupt break in thought or is used to mean *namely, in other words,* or *that is* before an explanation. Dashes are sharp and dramatic breaks into the main thought of a sentence.

> We will be given shoes and clothes—no, not our own—other shoes, other clothes, like his.

Your Turn

Punctuate the paragraph below with colons, semicolons, and dashes.

> The physical abuse the concentration camp prisoners endured was terrible however, Levi also describes a horrible sort of emotional abuse a stripping away of identity. The prisoners by losing their material possessions and acquiring new uniforms became property themselves.

Writing Application Revise a piece of your writing in your *Reader/Writer Notebook* to include semicolons, colons, and dashes.

CHOICES

As you respond to the Choices, use these **Academic Vocabulary** words as appropriate: adapt, considerably, exhibit, inevitable, perspective.

REVIEW

Compare and Contrast Accounts

Visit an online Holocaust exhibit to watch an interview with a Holocaust survivor, or with an Allied soldier who participated in the liberation of one of the camps. Then, compare and contrast this account with Levi's. What is similar or different about the level of detail and the tone of the accounts? Is the emotional impact of watching an interview greater than the impact of reading a printed document?

CONNECT

Hold a Group Discussion

Group Activity Have you ever seen a bumper sticker that says, "Think globally, but act locally"? This statement suggests that people can help solve the world's problems by improving life in their own communities. This memoir's events reflect an extreme and tragic result of categorizing people into "us" and "them." In a group, brainstorm ideas about how to bring unity to your school and community.

EXTEND

Write About the Power of Words

Timed Writing Like many Holocaust survivors, Levi felt the need to serve as a "witness" and tell his story so that such events would never be repeated. Are such events inevitable, or do you think memoirs such as Levi's can prevent something similar from happening again? In a brief essay, explain your thoughts, citing specific examples from Levi's text.

Universal Access: Grammar Link

English Learners

English for Academic Success Point out to students that semicolons connect closely related independent clauses. Give students additional practice with semicolons by having them write sentences that express a cause-and-effect relationship. Write the following examples on the board:

After the first race I trained harder and more frequently; at the starting line of the second race, I knew I could win.

The prisoners were given black coffee and stale bread twice a day; when one week had gone by, the prisoners looked famished and malnourished.

✔ For more practice wtih semicolons, colons, and dashes, see **Warriner's Handbook, GrammarNotes,** and **Language Handbook Worksheets.**

Independent Practice

Grammar Link

Your Turn

Possible response: *The physical abuse—the concentration camp prisoners endured—was terrible; however, Levi also describes a horrible sort of emotional abuse: a stripping away of identity. The prisoners, by losing their material possessions and acquiring new uniforms, became property themselves.*

Choices: Evaluation Criteria

Review: Homework
Compare and Contrast Accounts

Students' essays should note both similarities and differences between Levi's account and the account of the survivor or soldier.

Connect: Homework
Hold a Group Discussion

Groups should come up with specific ways to promote unity in the school or community or both.

Extend: Timed Writing 45–50 Minutes

- Students' essays should state a clear opinion as to whether memoirs can affect the course of history.
- Students should support their opinions with details from Levi's memoir.

Assess

Unit 6 Resources, Selection Standards Check, p. 27

go.hrw.com **ThinkCentral Online Assessment,** Selection Standards Check

Teacher One Stop™, editable Selection Standards Check

Reteach

go.hrw.com **ThinkCentral Online Remediation**

Standards Focus

Objectives

Students will
- understand repetition
- draw inferences about an author's beliefs

Selection Introduction

Think About the Writer

Have students think about how time can help a person heal and gain insight after a traumatic event. Ask students how time affected Wiesel's ability to write about his experiences during the Holocaust.

For Independent Reading

- *Thura's Diary: My Life in Wartime Iraq,* Thura Al-Windawi
- *Safe Area Gorazde: The War in Eastern Bosnia 1992–1995,* Joe Sacco

Motivate

What Do You Think?/QuickWrite

Use the QuickWrite to have students think about how concentration camp survivors view the world. Ask them to consider how their values would change if they were to undergo such an experience. Students can record their thoughts in their **Reader/Writer Notebooks**.

English for Academic Success

Academic Vocabulary

Look for opportunities to use the Academic Vocabulary words in this unit.

- **considerably, *adv.*:** by a large amount

Preparing to Read

Never Shall I Forget

What Do You Think? How does experience shape our view of the world?

QuickWrite

How would imprisonment in a camp like Auschwitz forever affect the way a survivor would view the world? Write a brief response to this question in your *Reader/Writer Notebook.*

Writer Elie Wiesel (1984)

MEET THE WRITER

Elie Wiesel

(1928–   )

Nobel Prize WINNER

Elie Wiesel survived the Holocaust to write his story: to try to convey the unspeakable so that the world would not forget the horror he and millions of others had experienced. As he explained, "We [survivors] believe that if we survived, we must do something with our lives. The first task is to tell the tale."

Nightmare Youth

Wiesel was fifteen years old when he and all other Jews in his Romanian village were deported to concentration camps in German-occupied Poland in 1944. A serious student of Judaism, Wiesel had thought that he would spend his life in his small village, working at the family store and devoting his life to religious study. Instead, he and his father were taken to Auschwitz (now called Auschwitz-Birkenau Nazi German Concentration and Death Camp) and then to camps at Buna, Gleiwitz, and Buchenwald, where his father died. Wiesel's mother and younger sister were both victims of the gas chambers. Against considerable odds, Wiesel and his two older sisters survived.

A Voice for the Lost

After the war, Wiesel lived in a French orphanage and then studied philosophy and literature at the Sorbonne, in Paris, and worked as a journalist. In 1955, after breaking a self-imposed vow never to write about the Holocaust, Wiesel poured his memories into a nine-hundred-page volume, soon condensed and republished as *Night.* Wiesel has said that his works have in common "their commitment to memory." He is torn between silence and a need to communicate. "You can speak," he says, "but how can you, when the full story is beyond language?"

Wiesel now lives in the United States, where he has served as the Chairman of the President's Commission on the Holocaust and where he was awarded the Congressional Medal of Achievement. In 1986, Wiesel won the Nobel Peace Prize. He continues to write and to advocate for the remembrance of the Holocaust and for the end of racism, hatred, and genocide.

Think About the Writer What reasons might Wiesel have had for not wanting to write about the Holocaust? What might have changed his mind?

California Standards, pp. 1102–1106

- **Reading Standard 2.5** Analyze an author's implicit and explicit philosophical assumptions and beliefs about a subject.
- **Reading Standard 3.4** Analyze ways in which poets use imagery, personification, figures of speech, and sounds to evoke readers' emotions.

Selection Readability	
Easily Accessible **Accessible** Challenging	familiar language; accessible theme; selection provides background information

Reading Standard 2.5, 3.4 (see pages A48–A50).

Literary Skills Focus

Repetition Writers, especially poets, use **repetition** for many reasons: to emphasize important ideas, to create an emotional impact, and to add rhythm to the writing. In "Never Shall I Forget," Wiesel uses repetition for all of those reasons, but his most dramatic use of repetition is a refrain that emphasizes his main idea—"Never shall I forget." Read the poem aloud to experience the emotional effect of the repetition.

Reading Skills Focus

Drawing Inferences About an Author's Beliefs As you read some texts, you find yourself drawing **inferences,** or educated guesses, about the writer's beliefs or views of the world. When you discuss inferences you draw about a writer, be sure you can cite passages from the text to support your inferences. You might be surprised that different readers of the same text draw different inferences.

Into Action As you read "Never Shall I Forget," note key words and passages.

Key Words and Passages
Repeated 7 times "Never shall I forget"

Writing Skills Focus

Think as a Reader/Writer

Find It in Your Reading The repetition of words, phrases, or sentences that have the same grammatical structure or that state a similar idea is called **parallelism.** Like other forms of repetition, parallelism can add emphasis and create rhythm in a text. Note how Wiesel uses parallelism by beginning each sentence with the same statement, "Never shall I forget . . ." In your *Reader/Writer Notebook*, note another use of parallel structure in the poem.

Vocabulary

nocturnal (nahk TUR nuhl) *adj.:* occurring at night. *The terror of daily camp life was not relieved by the nocturnal silence.*

condemned (kuhn DEHMD) *v.:* doomed. *He was condemned to live with the horrible memories of the camps.*

Language Coach

Silent Letters Many words in English have silent letters, that is, one or more letters that are not pronounced. The word *condemned,* above, for example, is sounded /kuhn DEHMD/. The second *n* is silent. Here are two more words with silent *n*'s: *solemn, column.* Respond to the following items.

1. Here are words with silent *w*'s. How is each word pronounced? *who, two, answer*
2. Here are three words with silent *g*'s. How is each word pronounced? *might, sign, gnat*
3. What is the silent letter in each of these words? *know, island, business*
4. A common silent letter in English words is the final *e*. Find three words in the poem that end with a silent *e*.

Learn It Online
Listen to this powerful poem online.
go.hrw.com H12-1103 Go

Reader/Writer Notebook
Use your **RWN** to complete the activities for this selection.

Preteach

Introducing Vocabulary

- Review the Vocabulary words, definitions, and sentences with students.
- To reinforce the importance of the Vocabulary words, tell students that these words help to tell a story of a young boy who is *condemned* to a life in a concentration camp. The speaker recalls his *nocturnal* thoughts and memories of his traumatizing experience.

English for Academic Success

Language Coach

Tell students that the first letter in the letter combinations *mn, gn, ps* and *kn* are often not pronounced. ***Possible responses:*** *1. (hwoo), (too), (AHN suhr) 2. (myt), (syhn), (nat) 3. The letters* k, s *and* i *are silent. 4. life, smoke, whose*

Literary Skills Focus

As you read and discuss the poem with students, have them note the emotional effect of repetition in the poem.

Reading Skills Focus

Give students a copy of the Reading Skills Focus graphic organizer before they read. (See **Unit 6 Resources**.) Tell them to use their responses to answer the questions on the Applying Your Skills page.

Writing Skills Focus

Have students record uses of parallelism in their **Reader/Writer Notebooks**. Students can use their notes to complete the Writing Skills Focus activity.

Learn It Online
The online version of this poem includes audio support to engage all students and to help struggling readers with reading comprehension and vocabulary.
go.hrw.com H12-1103 Go

Selection Resources

Unit 6 Resources, on-level practice and assessment, p. 30

Teacher One Stop™, on-level lesson plans and all print resources

Holt Audio Library

Holt Audio Library: Selections and Summaries in Spanish

UA: Differentiating Instruction, graphic organizer, p. 263

UA: Supporting Instruction in Spanish, selection summary

ThinkCentral Online Assessment, Selection Standards Check

ThinkCentral Online Remediation

Teacher Preparation

Selection Summary

Using the refrain "Never shall I forget," Wiesel presents a series of images related to the Holocaust. He remembers how the "night" of his soul began with his arrival at a concentration camp and how children died there; he recalls the flames and nighttime silence that he associates with the place. Most of all, he always will remember—even if he lives forever—how the concentration camp destroyed his dreams, his religious faith, and his very desire to live.

Direct Teach

Think About/Talk About

Read with a Purpose Have students read the Read with a Purpose statement. Point out that the statement asks students to determine what Elie Wiesel will "never forget." Have students note images and events that stand out in Wiesel's memory. Ask students to point out descriptive details the author uses to characterize these recollections.

Comprehension

Ⓐ Reading Focus

Possible response: *His life is an extension of the first night in the camp and is forever haunted by the horrific sights and sounds he experienced.*

Analysis

Ⓑ Literary Focus

Possible response: *By repeating the title of the poem, he emphasizes the seriousness of the evils he witnessed and his firm resolve to commit these to memory.*

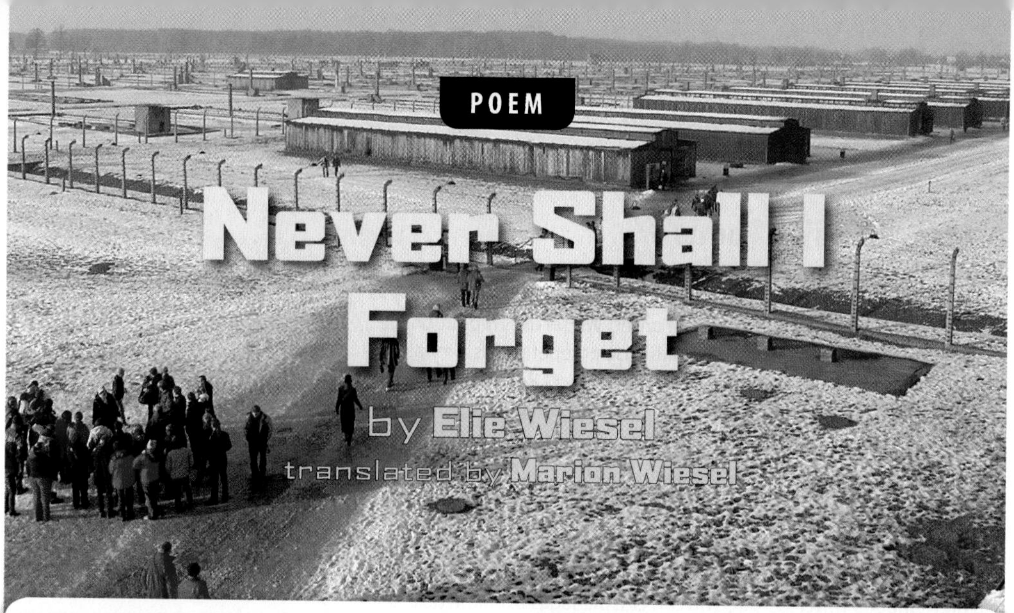

POEM

Never Shall I Forget

by Elie Wiesel

translated by Marion Wiesel

Read with a Purpose

Read to learn what this survivor will never forget.

Build Background

While working as a young journalist in the 1950s, Wiesel interviewed a French novelist named François Mauriac, who urged Wiesel to tell his story. Wiesel's first autobiographical work, *Night,* tells the story of a teenaged boy who survives the concentration camps and is haunted by questions of how God could have allowed so many of his people to be murdered. The following excerpt from *Night,* "Never Shall I Forget," originally appeared as a prose passage in the condensed version of the book.

Never shall I forget that night, the first night in the camp, that turned
my life into one long night seven times sealed. Ⓐ
Never shall I forget that smoke.
Never shall I forget the small faces of the children whose
bodies I saw transformed into smoke under a silent sky.
Never shall I forget those flames that consumed my faith
forever.
Never shall I forget the nocturnal silence that deprived me
for all eternity of the desire to live.
Never shall I forget those moments that murdered my God
and my soul and turned my dreams to ashes.
Never shall I forget those things, even were I condemned to
live as long as God Himself.
Never. Ⓑ

Visitors at the Auschwitz-Birkenau Nazi Concentration and Death Camp, Poland.

Ⓐ **Reading Focus** **Reading Focus Drawing Inferences** What can you infer about Wiesel's beliefs about his own life?

Ⓑ **Literary Focus** **Repetition** What does Wiesel emphasize by repeating the poem's title as a kind of refrain?

Vocabulary **nocturnal** (nahk TUR nuhl) *adj.:* occurring at night.
condemned (kuhn DEHMD) *v.:* doomed.

Universal Access

Struggling Readers

Explain to students that much of Wiesel's work is autobiographical, or written about his own life and experiences. Point out that the prefix *auto–* comes from a Greek root word that means *self* or same.

Tell students that as they read the poem, they should look for details that give insight into Wiesel's own life and beliefs. For example, students might note that witnessing the horror at the concentration camp caused Wiesel to lose faith in God and his personal hopes and dreams.

Advanced Learners

Enrichment Ask students to write their own autobiographical poem modeled after the format of Wiesel's poem. Have them choose a memorable experience to relate, along with a refrain that summarizes and unifies their poems. Encourage students to use figurative language and other poetic techniques to enhance their writing.

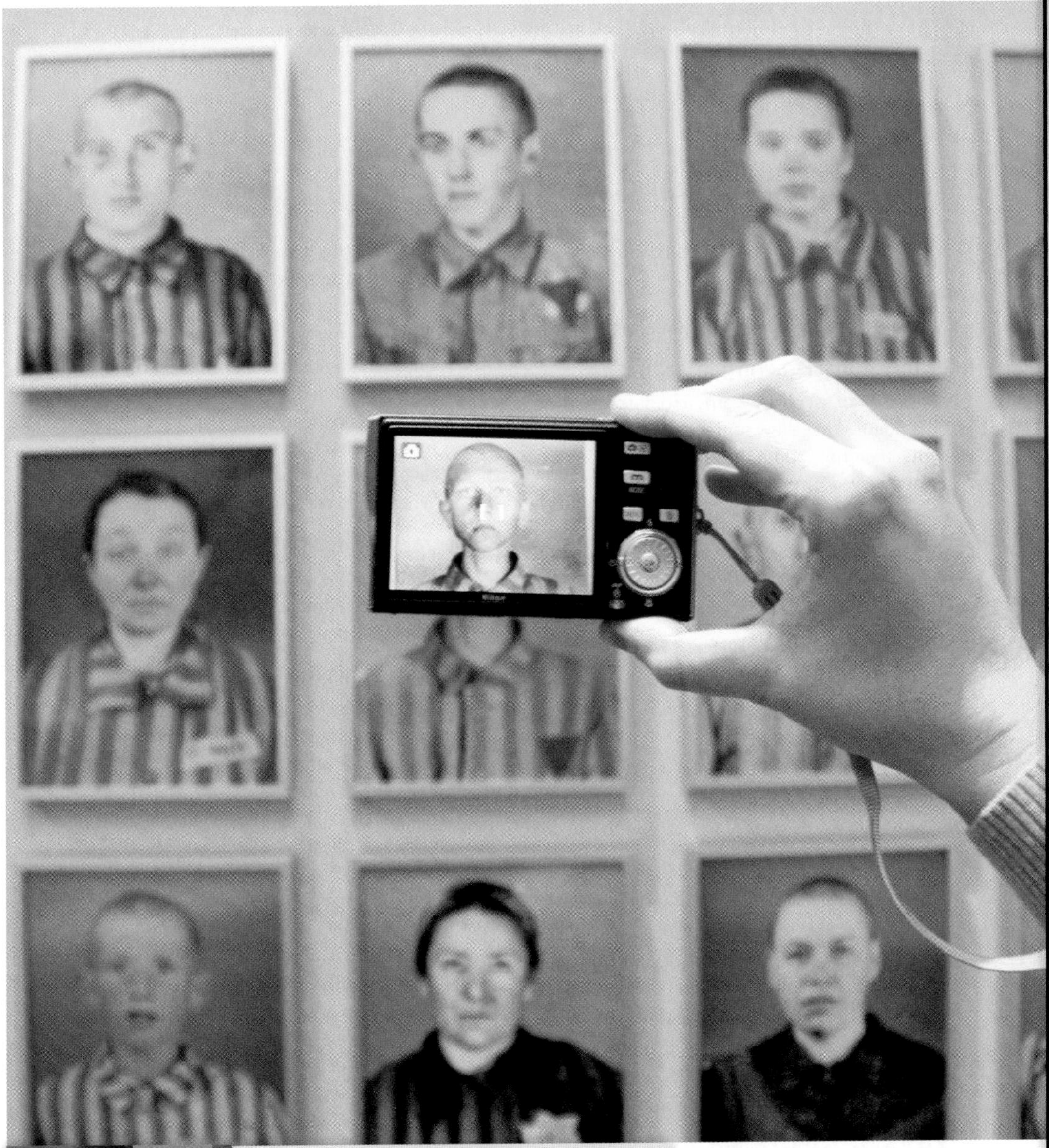

Analyzing Visuals

Connecting to the Text What is significant about a visitor selecting just one person's picture out of group of people's pictures to photograph? How does this image convey the message of the refrain "Never shall I forget"?

Photos of victims of the Nazi Holocaust. Deutsches Historisches Museum, Berlin (2006).

California Standards, p. 1106

- **Reading Standard 2.5** Analyze an author's implicit and explicit philosophical assumptions and beliefs about a subject.
- **Reading Standard 3.4** Analyze ways in which poets use imagery, personification, figures of speech, and sounds to evoke readers' emotions.
- **Writing Standard 2.3** Write reflective compositions: **a.** Explore the significance of personal experiences, events, conditions, or concerns by using rhetorical strategies (e.g., narration, description, exposition, persuasion).

Think About/Talk About

Extend the Discussion

Finding Details According to the speaker's description, what happens to children at the concentration camp? ***Possible response:*** *Many of them are burned and turned into smoke while the world says nothing.*

Determining Author's Purpose In the second stanza, why does Wiesel refer to the blue sky immediately after describing the murders of the children? ***Possible response:*** *He uses this juxtaposition to show how the cruelty and injustice of the Nazis caused him to lose his faith and innocence.*

Analyzing Visuals

Connecting to the Text: *The visitor zooms in on one person's picture out of a group of people's pictures, just as Elie Wiesel zooms in on the details of that one night, out of all the nights in the camp. By zooming in on one individual, the image helps convey the message of the refrain. The image suggests that although there are several photographs hanging on the wall, each individual life is important and must be remembered.*

Vocabulary: Own the Word

- **nocturnal:** *Nocturnal* means "nighttime"; its antonym is *diurnal.* Use both words in a sentence: The noise from the animals' *nocturnal* activity disturbed my sleep; as a result, my diurnal activities required greater effort.
- **condemned:** Ask students to finish the following thought: The Caspian Tiger was *condemned* to extinction because . . . ***Possible responses:*** *There were not enough resources to support its survival. The dinosaurs proved formidable predators.*

Check for Understanding

Independent Practice

Reading Skills Focus

Possible responses:

1. *Wiesel will never forget seeing innocent children burned to death; feeling the heavy, eerie silence; and suffering a loss of faith in God and humanity.*
2. *Ask students to make inferences about what Wiesel valued and what values he might have rejected.*

Vocabulary Check

3. *c* **4.** *b*

Literary Skills Focus

Possible response:

5. *Wiesel uses night as a metaphor for darkness, pain, and suffering. Because of the horror of his memories, his life will be a "night" devoid of happiness and peace.*
6. *Given his firsthand knowledge of the atrocities committed by other humans, Wiesel feels that life is a punishment or condemnation, not a gift. He is deeply disenchanted with humanity.*
7. *Wiesel says that his life is "seven times cursed and seven times sealed." This allusion suggests that Wiesel believes he has experienced evil and suffering on an epic, larger-than-life scale.*
8. *By frequently repeating the mantra "never shall I forget," Wiesel proves his commitment to remembrance.*
9. *Wiesel uses personification when he describes the "nocturnal silence" that has the power to deprive him of his will to live, and "those moments" that murder his faith.*

What Do You Think Now?

To help students answer the question, have them think about why the loss of a loved one, or any other significant loss, prompts a person to question his or her faith.

Applying Your Skills

Reading Standard 2.5, 3.4 (see pages A48–A50)
Writing Standard 2.3a (see pages A51–A52)

Never Shall I Forget

Literary Response and Analysis

Reading Skills Focus

Read with a Purpose

1. Cite all the things Wiesel will never forget.

Reading Skills: Drawing Inferences

2. Review your list of key words and passages from the poem. Write a few sentences explaining your inferences about the author's beliefs and worldview.

Key Words and Passages
Repeated 7 times "Never shall I forget"
What I Infer About Writer's Beliefs and Worldview

Vocabulary Check

Choose the correct letter to complete these statements about Vocabulary words.

3. The **nocturnal** silence described by Wiesel is experienced (a) in the morning, (b) in the afternoon, (c) at night.
4. Choose the more likely context for *condemned*: (a) She was **condemned** to spend time with friends; (b) Her illness **condemned** her to spend hours in agony.

Literary Skills Focus

Literary Analysis

5. **Interpret** What do you think Wiesel means when he says his life has been turned "into one long night"?
6. **Analyze** Why does Wiesel use the word *condemned* to describe living forever? What does this suggest about his state of mind?
7. **Interpret** *Seven* is symbolic in the Jewish and Christian traditions. For example, God rested on the seventh day of creation; there are seven branches on the menorah and seven blessings for a Jewish wedding. In the Christian tradition, seven sealed books foretell the end of the world. Where does Wiesel use *seven* in this poem? Why?

Literary Skills: Repetition

8. **Evaluate** Wiesel has said that his works' focus is "their commitment to memory." How does repetition in the poem emphasize this commitment?

Literary Skills Review: Personification

9. **Analyze** Talking about a nonhuman or nonliving thing or quality as if it were human or had life is **personification.** What words suggest that Wiesel sees "nocturnal silence" and "those moments" as if they were living things that acted willfully to destroy his hope and his faith?

Writing Skills Focus

Think as a Reader/Writer

Use It in Your Writing In your *Reader/Writer Notebook,* you noted examples of Wiesel's use of parallelism. Now, write a paragraph or poem about an important event in your life or in the life of someone else. Use parallelism to emphasize your tone or feelings.

What Do You Think Now? According to the poem, how has Wiesel's experience affected his faith?

Universal Access

Struggling Writers

Guide students in completing the Writing Skills Focus activity by providing additional scaffolding. Ask students to choose an event that had a significant impact on their perspective on life. Then, tell them to think of a phrase such as Wiesel's "never shall I forget" to convey the emotional impact of the event or their response to the event. Encourage students to use this phrase at the beginning of almost every line or sentence.

Assess

Unit 6 Resources, Selection Standards Check, p. 33

go.hrw.com **ThinkCentral Online Assessment,** Selection Standards Check

Teacher One Stop™, editable Selection Standards Check

Reading Skills Focus

Reading Standard 2.6 (see pages A48–A50)

Blood, Sweat, and Tears

Identifying and Critiquing an Author's Argument by **Kylene Beers**

When you read persuasive writing, you have two tasks: first, to identify the author's argument (What is he or she trying to convince you to believe?), and second, to critique, or evaluate, that argument (What kind of evidence does the author use?).

Authors of persuasive writing want to convince you that their ideas or positions are best. The writer of an advertisement, for example, wants you to buy the product; the author of a newspaper editorial wants you to agree with his or her opinion. Politicians and world leaders often use persuasion to try to gain the public's support for particular actions.

As England's prime minister during World War II, Winston Churchill had the inevitably difficult job of convincing English citizens that the war effort was worthwhile. He used powerful language to persuade them that they would not only be able to endure hardship but also achieve victory.

In a persuasive speech, an author usually directly states his or her arguments and may use repetition to alert listeners to important points. In Churchill's "Blood, Sweat, and Tears" speech, he states that he has "nothing to offer but blood, toil, tears, and sweat." These humble images of hard work and sacrifice support his argument urging all English people to join the fight. Churchill further asserts that his sacrifice and that of the English will "go forward together with our united strength." The language of effort and unity signals a major argument: Together we will be victorious.

Once you **identify the argument,** evaluate the evidence used to support it. Evidence can include **logical appeals** (reasons, facts, statistics, and other forms of evidence); **emotional appeals** (moving language and vivid descriptions that arouse strong feelings in readers); and **ethical appeals** (statements and examples that invoke commonly held moral standards and social values).

To critique this evidence, you must determine how well it supports the author's argument:

- Does the evidence directly pertain to the argument?
- Is the evidence convincing? Are there facts, expert opinions, or logical reasons to support the claims?
- Are the emotional appeals effective? Is the argument also supported by logical appeals, or does the author rely solely on emotions to convince the audience?
- Is the author unbiased, credible, and knowledgeable?
- If the argument is a solution to a problem, does the author provide evidence that the solution will work?

Your Turn

Read this excerpt from Churchill's speech. Identify his argument (the main idea), and critique it by applying the above criteria. Record your thoughts in a paragraph, using evidence from the text.

> We have before us an ordeal of the most grievous kind. We have before us many, many long months of struggle and of suffering. You ask, What is our policy? I will say: "It is to wage war, by sea, land and air, with all our might and with all the strength that God can give us: to wage war against a monstrous tyranny, never surpassed in the dark, lamentable catalogue of human crime. That is our policy." You ask, What is our aim? I can answer in one word: Victory—victory at all costs, victory in spite of all terror, victory however long and hard the road may be; for without victory there is no survival.

Learn It Online
Practice these skills with *PowerNotes* online.
go.hrw.com H12-1107 Go

Reading Skills Focus

Objectives

Students will practice identifying and critiquing an author's argument.

Unit 6 Resources, Reading Focus Skill Builder, p. 6

Teacher One Stop™, lesson plan and all print resources

Direct Teach

Identifying and Critiquing an Author's Argument

This feature gives students practice in analyzing and critiquing an author's argument while they read an excerpt from Winston Churchill's May 1940 speech to Parliament. Have students read the feature and complete the Your Turn activity before reading the entire speech.

Check for Understanding

Your Turn

Possible response: *Student responses will vary. Students should recognize Churchill's main idea—that the British should fight the Axis powers with as much strength and determination as they can muster. Churchill's reference to the "monstrous tyranny" they are fighting provides both a logical support for his argument and an emotional appeal to the listener.*

California Standards, p. 1107

- **Reading Standard 2.6** Critique the power, validity, and truthfulness of arguments set forth in public documents; their appeal to both friendly and hostile audiences; and the extent to which the arguments anticipate and address reader concerns and counterclaims (e.g., appeal to reason, to authority, to pathos and emotion).

Universal Access

Struggling Readers

Students may be better able to understand the three types of appeals if they can connect these appeals to their everyday experiences. Have students work in groups of three to brainstorm a short list of situations in which they might need to present an effective argument. For example, an argument justifying a later curfew or asking to be allowed to drive the family car. Have each group choose one situation and develop an appropriate logical, emotional, and ethical appeal that could be included in their argument. Encourage groups to share their ideas with the class.

Learn It Online
For a multimedia version of the instruction found on this page, use the **PowerNotes** Reading Skills Focus presentation.
go.hrw.com H12-1107 Go

Standards Focus

Objectives

Students will
- understand oratory
- identify and critique an author's argument

Selection Introduction

Think About the Writer

Ask students if they are surprised to learn that Churchill was a writer as well as a politician. Tell them to consider how politicians get elected and win support for their policies. Then, ask them if they think Churchill's language skills helped him become a successful leader, and if so, how.

For Independent Reading

- *Profiles in Courage,* John F. Kennedy
- *Nobel Lectures in Literature, 1991–1995,* Sture Allen, ed.

Motivate

What Do You Think?/QuickWrite

Ask students to name people they consider effective leaders. Then, have them write for five minutes in their **Reader/Writer Notebooks** about the qualities people look for in their political leaders, particularly in times of war or natural disaster.

English for Academic Success

Academic Vocabulary

Look for opportunities to use the Academic Vocabulary words in this unit.

- **adapt, *v.*:** adjust for a new purpose
- **considerably, *adv.*:** by a large amount
- **exhibit, *v.*:** show, demonstrate
- **perspective, *n.*:** a particular way of looking at something

Preparing to Read

Blood, Sweat, and Tears

What Do You Think? How does experience shape our view of the world?

QuickWrite

What qualities make a good leader? What qualities are especially critical for a national leader in times of war? Write your answers in a brief paragraph in your *Reader/Writer Notebook.*

Sir Winston Leonard Spencer Churchill (1943) by Robert Elliot. National Portrait Gallery, London.

MEET THE WRITER

Winston Churchill
(1874–1965)

Nobel Prize WINNER

Winston Churchill was a soldier, a statesman, a man of letters, and a Nobel laureate. As prime minister during the deadliest war of the century, he inspired Britain's soldiers and civilians.

Soldier and Writer

Churchill was the son of a British politician, Lord Randolph Churchill, and his American wife, Jennie Jerome. Of his schooling, Churchill said, "I got into my bones the essential structure of the ordinary British sentence—which is a noble thing." His father, however, lacked confidence in young Winston's academic abilities and insisted he prepare for a military career.

In 1895, Churchill volunteered to visit Cuba to observe Spain's war against Cuban rebels and to send dispatches to a British newspaper. On his return, he began his simultaneous careers as a politician and a writer.

They Owe Him Liberty

Churchill became prime minister in 1940. One of his great triumphs was persuading his War Cabinet to challenge Hitler rather than negotiate with him. An unparalleled orator, Churchill rallied the nation never to surrender, especially during the "blitz," when Germany bombed London for fifty-seven successive nights. Of the British pilots who fought the Germans night after night, Churchill said, "Never in the field of human conflict has so much been owed by so many to so few." Few comments on war are as poignant or memorable.

After leaving politics, Churchill published history books, including four volumes of the *History of the English Speaking People* and five volumes of the monumental *Second World War.* In 1953, Churchill was awarded the Nobel Prize for Literature. He is best known, however, for the enviable war leadership he exhibited, of which his daughter Mary said, "I owe you what every Englishman, woman and child does—Liberty itself." Churchill's ties to the United States remained close, and in 1963, President Kennedy awarded him honorary U.S. citizenship.

Think About the Writer How did Churchill's language skills help him in his political life, as well as in his literary life?

California Standards, pp. 1108–1115

- **Reading Standard 2.6** Critique the power, validity, and truthfulness of arguments set forth in public documents; their appeal to both friendly and hostile audiences; and the extent to which the arguments anticipate and address reader concerns and counterclaims (e.g., appeal to reason, to authority, to pathos and emotion).
- **Reading Standard 3.3** Apply the ways in which irony, tone, mood, the author's style, and the "sound" of language achieve specific rhetorical or aesthetic purposes or both.

Selection Readability	
Easily Accessible **Accessible** Challenging	familiar language; accessible theme

Literary Skills Focus

Oratory The art of public speech is **oratory.** Because listeners cannot return to an oral speech if they miss a point, orators often state their main ideas and then use **repetition** of words, phrases, and sentence structures to emphasize their key points. Repetition also creates **rhythm** in speaking. Note Churchill's stirring use of this oratorical device as you read.

Reading Skills Focus

Identifying and Critiquing an Author's Argument To persuade listeners or readers to agree with their arguments, orators and writers can use two types of appeals: **logical appeals,** directed to the listeners' intellect, and **emotional appeals,** directed to the listeners' feelings. Churchill begins his speech by listing the methodical, reasonable steps he took to form his government. He then arouses strong feelings in his audience by using emotionally charged words like *ordeal, struggle,* and *tyranny.*

Into Action Make a graphic organizer like the one below, and list words, phrases, and sentences that appeal to logic and emotions. Later, you will explain the purpose of the appeals and evaluate their effectiveness.

Logical Appeals	forming large Administration is "serious undertaking"
Emotional Appeals	

Writing Skills Focus

Think as a Reader/Writer

Find It in Your Reading In his speech, Churchill uses several rhetorical devices, including **parallelism,** the repetition of sentence structures and key words. Parallelism creates a kind of rhythm in speech which Churchill's listeners would have found moving and pleasing to hear. In your *Reader/Writer Notebook,* record some examples of parallelism in this speech.

TechFocus As you read, think about how modern technology could be used to enhance the logical and emotional appeals of this speech.

Reader/Writer Notebook
Use your **RWN** to complete the activities for this selection.

Vocabulary

rigor (RIHG uhr) *n.:* severity. *Churchill explained that the rigor of the situation called for speedy action.*

grievous (GREE vuhs) *adj.:* outrageous; horrible. *The grievous acts of German troops as they invaded their neighbors horrified British citizens.*

lamentable (luh MEHN tuh buhl) *adj.:* regrettable; unfortunate. *Sending young troops to war was lamentable but necessary.*

buoyancy (BOY uhn see) *n.:* lightness of spirit; cheerfulness. *Despite the hard task ahead of him, Churchill felt a sense of buoyancy about the future.*

Language Coach

Suffix *–ous* The suffix *–ous* is added to words or roots to make adjectives. The Vocabulary word *grievous,* for example, is formed by adding *–ous* to the verb *grieve.* (Note that the *e* is dropped from the end of the word when the suffix is added.) Identify one Vocabulary word to which the suffix *–ous* could be added to form an adjective.

Learn It Online
Explore the Vocabulary words with Word Watch.
go.hrw.com H12-1109 Go

Selection Resources

Unit 6 Resources, on-level practice and assessment, p. 36

PowerNotes, interactive lesson presentations with activities

Teacher One Stop™, on-level lesson plans and all print resources

Holt Audio Library

Holt Audio Library: Selections and Summaries in Spanish

UA: Holt Interactive Reader p. 317

UA: Differentiating Instruction, modified lesson plans and leveled assessment, p. 267

UA: Supporting Instruction in Spanish, selection summary

UA: Resources for Teaching Advanced Students, lesson plans, p. 192

ThinkCentral Online Assessment

ThinkCentral Online Remediation

Preteach

Introducing Vocabulary

To reinforce students' understanding of the Vocabulary words, have them complete the analogies below. Remind them that in word analogies, pairs of words may be synonyms or antonyms, or one word might express a characteristic of the other.

1. loyal : faithful :: _____ : regrettable [*lamentable*]
2. punishment : forgiveness :: _____ : flexibility [*rigor*]
3. wisdom : foolishness :: _____ : gloom [*buoyancy*]
4. remote : distant :: _____ : terrible [*grievous*]

English for Academic Success

Language Coach

After students read the **Language Coach,** have them change the following words into adjectives: *fury, caution, poison, anxiety, fame, grace.*

Literary Skills Focus

As you read and discuss the speech with students, have them note Churchill's use of repetition.

Reading Skills Focus

Give students a copy of the Reading Skills Focus graphic organizer before they read. (See **Unit 6 Resources.**) Tell them to use their responses to answer the questions on the Applying Your Skills page.

Writing Skills Focus

Have students record in their **Reader/Writer Notebooks** examples of parallelism. Students can use their notes to complete the Writing Skills Focus activity.

Learn It Online
Send students to **Word Watch** for audio pronunciations, synonyms and antonyms, and histories of word origins.
go.hrw.com H12-1109 Go

Teacher Preparation

Selection Summary

Churchill's immediate audience for his first speech, "Blood, Sweat, and Tears" as prime minister was the House of Commons, but he clearly had a much wider audience in mind—not only other Britons but also the rest of the world, foes as well as friends. He devotes his first two paragraphs to appeals based on reason, establishing his credibility by explaining what he has accomplished since being named prime minister the previous Friday and what he plans to do next. Then, making the transition to emotional appeals, he uses repetition, parallelism, and personal references to convey the urgency of the situation, to declare his devotion to the tasks before him, and to exhort his listeners to unite in the cause of victory.

Direct Teach

Think About/Talk About

Read with a Purpose Have students read the Read with a Purpose statement. Point out that the title of the speech alludes to the costs of sacrifice and struggle. Ask students to predict how this title will be connected with Churchill's effort in this speech to rally the British to meet the challenges of a difficult war.

Comprehension

B Reading Focus

Possible responses: *He cites "the extreme urgency and rigor of events." He uses simple language in stating this point, making an appeal to reason, not emotion.*

Analysis

A Literary Focus

Possible response: *The main idea is stated directly in the paragraph's third sentence: "I have completed the most important part of this task" (the formation of a coalition government).*

SPEECH

Blood, Sweat, and Tears

by **Winston Churchill**

Read with a Purpose

Read this speech to see how a new prime minister tries to persuade his citizens to prepare for a long and difficult war.

Build Background

In September 1939, Britain declared war on Germany after German troops invaded Poland. When Churchill gave this speech to Parliament in May 1940, the Germans had also marched into Holland and Belgium and were driving deep into France. Churchill knew the Battle of Britain was imminent. As newly elected prime minister, Churchill had just formed a coalition government of Labour and Liberals; he knew that he had to inspire the country with an unwavering belief in its ability to survive, triumph, and endure. Few who heard Churchill's radio speeches during the war ever forgot them.

On Friday evening last I received His Majesty's Commission[1] to form a new Administration. It was the evident wish and will of Parliament and the nation that this should be conceived on the broadest possible basis and that it should include all Parties, both those who supported the last Government and also the Parties of the Opposition. I have completed the most important part of this task. A War Cabinet has been formed of five Members, representing, with the Opposition Liberals,[2] the unity of the nation. The three Party Leaders have agreed to serve, either in the War Cabinet or in high executive office. The three Fighting Services have been filled. It was necessary that this should be done in one single day, on account of the extreme urgency and rigor of events. A number of other key positions were filled yesterday, and I am submitting a further list to His Majesty tonight. I hope to complete the appointment of the principal Ministers during tomorrow. The appointment of the other Ministers usually takes a little longer, but I trust that, when Parliament meets again, this part of my task will be complete in all respects. A B

1. **His Majesty's Commission:** The king at the time was George VI. After his or her party is elected, the prime minister is officially appointed by the monarch.
2. **Opposition Liberals:** Churchill was a member of the Conservative Party; those belonging to the Liberal Party were in the opposition.

A Literary Focus **Oratory** What main idea does Churchill express in this paragraph?

B Reading Focus **Identifying and Critiquing an Author's Argument** What argument does Churchill make to support the necessity of creating a War Cabinet quickly? Does this argument appeal to reason or emotion?

Vocabulary **rigor** (RIHG uhr) *n.:* severity.

Universal Access

EL English Learners

English for Academic Success Remind students that in a passive sentence, the object of an active sentence becomes the subject, and the past participle verb form is used. For example, instead of "I formed a War Cabinet," the fourth sentence in his speech says "A War Cabinet has been formed." In the second sentence, the subject receives the action of the verb, and the doer of the action is not mentioned.

✔ See **UA: Differentiating Instruction** for strategies for teaching English learners.

Struggling Readers

Benchmark Students Model for students identifying and critiquing an author's argument. Point out that to evaluate Churchill's claim in the first paragraph that he has "completed the most important part of [the] task" of forming a new government, a reader needs to identify the evidence he uses to support this claim. Have students paraphrase the remaining sentences in the first paragraph, listing each of the actions Churchill sets forth.

✔ Invite students to read the selection in interactive format in **UA: Holt Interactive Reader.**

I considered it in the public interest to suggest that the House should be summoned to meet today. Mr. Speaker agreed, and took the necessary steps, in accordance with the powers conferred upon him by the Resolution of the House. At the end of the proceedings today, the Adjournment of the House will be proposed until Tuesday, 21st May, with, of course, provision for earlier meeting if need be. The business to be considered during that week will be notified to Members at the earliest opportunity. I now invite the House, by the Resolution which stands in my name, to record its approval of the steps taken and to declare its confidence in the new Government.[3]

To form an Administration of this scale and complexity is a serious undertaking in itself, but it must be remembered that we are in the preliminary stage of one of the greatest battles in history, that we are in action at many points in Norway and in Holland, that we have to be prepared in the Mediterranean, that the air battle is continuous, and the many preparations have to be made here at home. In this crisis I hope I may be pardoned if I do not address the House at

3. **the new Government:** that is, the recently elected administration led by Churchill.

TECHNOLOGY LINK

Family in England listening to speech by Winston Churchill (1945).

Radio Broadcasts

Private English citizens would have heard Churchill's speech on the radio. Radio waves, like sound waves, fluctuate in the air, and operate on certain frequencies. The national government typically assigns each radio station a carrier frequency, which is silent until information is added to the carrier wave by the radio station's transmitter. When you tune a radio to the station's frequency, your radio amplifies the signal many times so that you can hear the transmission. Radio broadcasting emerged around 1920, and by World War II, the English people received much of their war news via broadcast programs. The radio was an equally powerful communication tool for the Axis as well as the Allied powers. German radio broadcasts became an important part of Adolf Hitler's proganda campaigns and were successful in convincing many German citizens that the Reich was justified in invading and occupying neighboring countries.

Ask Yourself

How did leaders on both sides of the conflict use the radio to affect the way people felt about the war?

Think About/Talk About

Extend the Discussion

Identifying Author's Argument
How does Churchill anticipate and address his listeners' concerns? ***Possible response:*** *He explains the actions he has taken thus far, lays out his plans for the coming days, assures his listeners that they will be kept informed, and requests their approval of his actions to date and of the government he has formed.*

Making Judgments Point out that the stature of public figures is shaped by the way they present themselves in public addresses. Ask students how they would characterize Churchill after reading his speech. ***Possible responses:*** *He is serious, candid, and decisive. He is hardworking and prepared to make sacrifices for the sake of his country. He takes personal responsibility for his actions but seeks to work with others for the common good.*

Technology Link

Ask Yourself ________
Possible response: *Leaders on both sides use radio to try to shape public opinion and to communicate information.*

Vocabulary: Own the Word

rigor: Ask students the following question: "When might you experience a situation characterized by *rigor*?" ***Possible responses:*** *a college entrance examination, an interview, a marathon, a final exam*

Advanced Learners

Acceleration Have students get into groups of three or four and prepare a TV news report addressing viewers in the 1940s. Suggest that two students act as anchors and one as the on-site journalist reporting from the site of Churchill's speech. Encourage students to be creative in introducing, summarizing, and quoting from Churchill's speech in their news presentation.

✔ See **UA: Resources for Teaching Advanced Students** for strategies for teaching advanced learners.

Students with Disabilities

Invite students to read "Blood, Sweat, and Tears" in interactive format in **UA: Holt Interactive Reader,** and to use the sidenotes as aids to understanding the selection. The interactive version provides additional instruction, practice, and assessment of the skills taught in the Student Edition.

✔ See **UA: Differentiating Instruction** for strategies for teaching students with disabilities.

Think About/Talk About

Analysis

C Literary Focus

Possible response: *Emotionally charged words such as* blood, toil, tears, *and* sweat *are used to persuade Churchill's listeners.*

D Literary Focus

Possible response: *He repeats the words* victory *and* survival.

Vocabulary: Own the Word

- **grievous:** The connotation for *grievous* is horror or outrage. What led Churchill to label the situation *grievous*? ***Possible responses:*** *war deaths, the imminent attack on Britain*
- **lamentable:** You might say: "To *lament* (verb) is to express deep regret over something. A situation that is *lamentable* involves this action." Ask students to share a *lamentable* situation they know.
- **buoyancy:** Tell students that just as a *buoy* (related noun) floats on water, a person feeling *buoyancy* tends to float with cheerfulness. Ask students how they might create *buoyancy* during a problem situation.

Winston Churchill inspecting ruins of the House of Commons (May 1941).

any length today. I hope that any of my friends and colleagues, or former colleagues, who are affected by the political reconstruction, will make all allowance for any lack of ceremony with which it has been necessary to act. I would say to the House, as I said to those who have joined this Government: "I have nothing to offer but blood, toil, tears, and sweat." **C**

We have before us an ordeal of the most grievous kind. We have before us many, many long months of struggle and of suffering. You ask, What is our policy? I will say: "It is to wage war, by sea, land and air, with all our might and with all the strength that God can give us: to wage war against a monstrous tyranny, never surpassed in the dark, lamentable catalogue of human crime. That is our policy." You ask, What is our aim? I can answer in one word: Victory—victory at all costs, victory in spite of all terror, victory however long and hard the road may be; for without victory there is no survival. Let that be realized; no survival for the British Empire; no survival for all that the British Empire has stood for; no survival for the urge and impulse of the ages, that mankind will move forward towards its goal. But I take up my task with buoyancy and hope. I feel sure that our cause will not be suffered to fail among men. At this time I feel entitled to claim the aid of all, and I say, "Come, then, let us go forward together with our united strength." **D**

C Literary Focus Oratory What powerful words does Churchill use to persuade his listeners to support him?

D Literary Focus Oratory What words or phrases does Churchill repeat to emphasize his goal?

Vocabulary **grievous** (GREE vuhs) *adj.:* outrageous; horrible.
lamentable (luh MEHN tuh buhl) *adj.:* regrettable; unfortunate.
buoyancy (BOY uhn see) *n.:* lightness of spirit; cheerfulness.

California Standards, pp. 1113–1115

- **Reading Standard 1.3** Discern the meaning of analogies encountered, analyzing specific comparisons as well as relationships and inferences.
- **Reading Standard 2.6** Critique the power, validity, and truthfulness of arguments set forth in public documents; their appeal to both friendly and hostile audiences; and the extent to which the arguments anticipate and address reader concerns and counterclaims (e.g., appeal to reason, to authority, to pathos and emotion).
- **Reading Standard 3.3** Analyze the ways in which irony, tone, mood, the author's style, and the "sound" of language achieve specific rhetorical or aesthetic purposes or both.
- **Grades 9–10 Review Reading Standard 3.7** Recognize and understand the significance of various literary devices, including figurative language, imagery, allegory, and symbolism, and explain their appeal.
- **Writing Standard 1.3** Structure ideas and arguments in a sustained, persuasive, and sophisticated way and support them with precise and relevant examples.
- **Writing Standard 1.4** Enhance meaning by employing rhetorical devices, including the extended use of parallelism, repetition, and analogy; the incorporation of visual aids (e.g., graphs, tables, pictures); and the issuance of a call for action.
- **Listening and Speaking Standard 1.6** Use logical, ethical, and emotional appeals that enhance a specific tone and purpose.
- **Listening and Speaking Standard 1.7** Use appropriate rehearsal strategies to pay attention to performance details, achieve command of the text, and create skillful artistic staging.
- **Listening and Speaking Standard 2.6** Deliver multimedia presentations: **a.** Combine text, images, and sound and draw information from many sources (e.g., television broadcasts, videos, films, newspapers, magazines, CD-ROMs, the Internet, electronic media-generated images).

Applying Your Skills

Reading Standard 2.6, 3.3 Grades 9–10 Review
Reading Standard 3.7 (see pages A48–A50)
Writing Standard 1.3, 1.4 (see pages A51–A52)

Blood, Sweat, and Tears

Literary Response and Analysis

Reading Skills Focus

Quick Check

1. Why was it important to Churchill to include members of the opposition party in his War Cabinet?
2. What did Churchill want approved?
3. How did Churchill apologize for "any lack of ceremony"?

Read with a Purpose

4. How successful would a leader be today if he or she used a similar speech to persuade citizens to prepare for a long and difficult war?

Reading Skills: Identifying and Critiquing an Author's Argument

5. Look back at the chart you created identifying the speech's logical and emotional appeals. At the bottom, summarize Churchill's purpose in making the appeals and evaluate the effectiveness of his arguments.

Literary Skills Focus

Literary Analysis

6. **Interpret** How would you interpret Churchill's statement, "I have nothing to offer but blood, toil, tears, and sweat"? How could the statement make the people feel that their leader would suffer with them and give up his life for them?
7. **Evaluate** The credibility of a public figure is often revealed in public addresses. How would you characterize Churchill after reading his speech? Does he convince you of his competence and command of the situation? Explain.
8. **Hypothesize** Churchill knew that German leaders would read his speech. What effect do you think he wanted it to have on his enemy?

Literary Skills: Oratory

9. **Make Judgments** How does Churchill use repetition and parallelism to emphasize his points in the last two paragraphs?
10. **Analyze** What call to action does Churchill include in his speech? He uses the word *united* in the call to action. What effect do you think that word would have on his listeners?

Literary Skills Review: Symbol

11. **Interpret** A **symbol** is something that stands both for itself and for something beyond itself. In his speech, Churchill refers to the "British Empire" and all it "has stood for." What do you think the British Empire symbolized to Churchill and his English audience? In contrast, how does Churchill characterize the enemy?

Writing Skills Focus

Think as a Reader/Writer

Use It in Your Writing As you read the speech, you noted examples of parallelism in your *Reader/Writer Notebook*. Now, choose a topic for a short persuasive speech of your own. Develop your argument with logical and emotional appeals. Try to use some examples of parallelism to give your speech a memorable and pleasing cadence, or rhythmic movement.

What Do You Think Now? What experiences might have shaped Churchill's view of the world? How do you think people like Churchill acquire the gift of speaking with eloquence?

Check for Understanding

Independent Practice

Reading Skills Focus

Possible responses:

1. *He feels it is important for all parties to be represented in government so that all will support it. He seeks a unified government to foster solidarity among the people.*
2. *He wanted approval for his new coalition government.*
3. *To apologize for his "lack of ceremony," he cites the urgency of the threat and the need to act quickly.*
4. *It would be effective today because an audience would still respond to logical and emotional appeals and to the timeless call for unity to fight against tyranny.*
5. *Ask students how Churchill did or did not achieve his purpose in making the appeals.*

Literary Skills Focus

Possible responses:

6. *He is being honest about the suffering ahead and is stressing his own readiness to sacrifice.*
7. *His decisive actions demonstrate competence; his ability to form a government shows credibility; his plans and his sense of urgency show command of the situation.*
8. *He might have been trying to convince them that Britain would never surrender.*
9. *He uses parallelism to keep his message simple. He repeats "victory" to emphasize his goal and "survival" to emphasize the extreme stakes of the struggle.*
10. *He ends his speech with a call to action, urging citizens to join him in the fight against the Axis powers: "Come, then, let us go forward together with our united strength." His call probably increased the country's unity by encouraging the hesitant ones to support him.*
11. *He refers to the empire as a symbol of British history, influence, and power. He characterizes the enemy as tyrannical.*

Universal Access

Struggling Writers

Some students may need additional scaffolding to complete the Writing Skills Focus activity. After students have chosen their topic, ask them to freewrite for five minutes on the topic. Tell them to read the freewrite to identify logical appeals or emotional appeals, underlining the logical appeals in blue and the emotional in red. Check each student's response for content. Tell students to add appeals so that the number of logical appeals equals the emotional appeals. Have students imitate one of Churchill's parallel statements to incorporate into their final draft.

What Do You Think Now?

To help students answer the question, remind them of Churchill's background. Tell them he was the son of a politician, had one British and one American parent, and served in the military; note also that he was a war correspondent as a young man and wrote books on history after leaving politics. Ask students which aspects of his background they think may have contributed to his ability to communicate.

Independent Practice
Vocabulary Development
Vocabulary Check
1. *a challenging one*
2. *a horrible one*
3. *regrettable*
4. *His outlook is hopeful.*

Your Turn
1. *grievous*
2. *lamentable*
3. *rigor*
4. *buoyancy*

English for Academic Success
Language Coach
Possible responses:
1. villainous *means "vicious"*
2. *cannot add –ous*
3. *cannot add –ous*
4. monstrous *means "horrible"*
5. victorious *means "triumphant"*

English for Academic Success
Academic Vocabulary
Possible response: *Responses will vary. Ask students to cite textual evidence that reveal the perspective of Churchill's audience and examples of language and delivery adapted to cater to this kind of audience.*

Applying Your Skills

Reading Standard 1.3 (see pages A48–A50)

Blood, Sweat, and Tears

Vocabulary Development

Vocabulary Check

Be sure you can justify your answer to each of the following Vocabulary questions.

1. If a class were known for its **rigor,** would it be an easy class or a challenging one?
2. If a wound is described as **grievous,** is it a minor wound or a horrible one?
3. Churchill says that Hitler's tyranny has never been surpassed in the **lamentable** catalogue of human crime. Does ***lamentable*** mean understandable or regrettable?
4. When he says he takes up his post with **buoyancy,** what is Churchill suggesting about his outlook for the future?

Vocabulary Skills: Solving Word Analogies

A **word analogy** compares two pairs of words. The relationship between the first pair of words is the same as that of the second pair. Common types of relationships expressed in word analogies are **synonyms, antonyms,** and **characteristic.**

CRY : WEEP :: laugh : chuckle

[*Cry* and *weep* are **synonyms,** or words with similar meanings, as are *laugh* and *chuckle.*]

SULLEN : CHEERY :: generous : stingy

[*Sullen* and *cheery* are **antonyms,** or words with opposite meanings, as are *generous* and *stingy.*]

COMEDIANS : FUNNY :: lions : fierce.

[*Funny* is a **characteristic** of *comedians,* just as *fierce* is a characteristic of *lions.*]

To complete a word analogy, it helps to "read" the relationship. The colon [:] stands for the phrase "is/are related to." The double colon between the pairs stands for the phrase "in the same way as." Thus, the previous analogies would be stated like this: *Cry* is related to *weep* in the same way *laugh* is related to *chuckle. Sullen* is related to *cheery* in the same way that *generous* is related to *stingy. Comedians* are related to *funny* in the same way that *lions* are related to *fierce.*

Your Turn

Complete each of the following analogies with one of the boldface words in the Vocabulary Check.

1. ARID : DRY :: ________ : horrible
2. BIRTH : JOYFUL :: death : ________
3. SILENCE : QUIET :: ________ : severity
4. WEALTH : POVERTY :: ________ : sadness

Language Coach

The Suffix *–ous* The suffix *–ous* means "full of," or "characterized by." To which of the following words from the selection can you add the suffix *–ous* to make adjectives? If necessary, use a dictionary for help. You will have to change the spelling of some words in order to add the suffix. What does each word mean when the suffix is added?

1. villain
2. horror
3. struggle
4. monster
5. victor

Academic Vocabulary

Talk About

Effective persuasive speeches and writing often require the speaker or writer to think from the perspective of his or her audience. In a small group, discuss how Churchill may have adapted his delivery and language to make a greater impact on his listeners.

Universal Access: Vocabulary Development

EL English Learners

English for Academic Success Spark an academic discussion with students using the Academic Vocabulary words in this unit. Display the following questions on the board, and have students work in groups to provide a verbal response for each question.

- From Churchill's *perspective,* why did the English have no choice but to wage war?
- How do we know Churchill was a man of *considerable* influence?
- How did Churchill *adapt* the government structure for this new challenge?
- What noble traits does Churchill *exhibit* through his words?
- What hardships would they *inevitably* face in the coming months, according to Churchill?

✔ See the **Academic and Selection Vocabulary Skill Builder** in **UA: Differentiating Instruction.**

Listening and Speaking Standard 1.6, 1.7, 2.6a (see pages A53–A55)

Grammar Link

Connecting Ideas

In a coherent composition, ideas are connected clearly, and every sentence and paragraph flows smoothly and sensibly to the next. One way to create coherence in a composition is by using clear transitional expressions.

Transitions show *how* ideas are connected. Often transitional words show chronological or spatial relationships (for example, *next, after, nearby, adjacent*). Transitions may also show relationships of cause and effect *(because, since, as a result)* or of contrast *(but, although, on the other hand)*. In the second sentence below, *consequently* shows a cause-and-effect relationship and makes a clear transition from one sentence to another.

> During the blitz, the Germans targeted London. *Consequently*, many Londoners moved to the countryside.

Your Turn

Add coherence to the sentences that follow by inserting effective transitions as directed.

1. Churchill had a lonely childhood that haunted him all his life. He always had a close relationship with his nanny. *[Indicate contrast.]*
2. Churchill inspired his country throughout the war. He is considered a great British leader. *[Indicate cause and effect.]*
3. Churchill had ambivalent feelings toward Europe after the war. He believed that there was a special relationship between Britain and the United States. *[Indicate contrast.]*
4. Winston Churchill was Colonial Secretary in 1921. He helped create the countries of Iraq and Jordan. *[Indicate chronology.]*

Writing Application Look over a piece of your writing. Circle any transitional expressions you used and add additional transitions to make your writing clearer.

CHOICES

As you respond to the Choices, use these **Academic Vocabulary** words as appropriate: perspective, considerably, adapt, exhibit, inevitable.

REVIEW

Compose Compelling Orations

Identify an issue you think is important. Write a short speech explaining why this topic matters considerably to you as well as why it should matter to others. Use emotional, ethical, and logical appeals and make notes in the margin about tone and delivery.

CONNECT

Design a Multimedia Version

TechFocus Design a multimedia version of "Blood, Sweat, and Tears," using modern technology such as music and video to enhance the logical and emotional appeals of Churchill's speech. Show your presentation to your class, and then discuss the effects that modern technology had on the viewers. How do you think your presentation would have affected Churchill's listeners?

EXTEND

Conduct Research

Churchill gave many impassioned speeches during the war. Use the Internet to find another of his speeches, and determine whether he uses logical appeals, emotional appeals, or both. What is his purpose in this speech? If possible, find an audio recording of the speech, and note how listening to his delivery affects your reaction to it. Two speeches to look for are usually known as "We shall fight on the beaches" (June 4, 1940) and "Their finest hour" (June 18, 1940), both delivered to the House of Commons.

Learn It Online
Learn how to create a great multimedia presentation at the MediaScope site.
go.hrw.com H12-1115 Go

Independent Practice

Grammar Link

Your Turn

1. ***Although*** *Churchill had a lonely childhood that haunted him all his life, he always . . .*
2. *. . . throughout the war.* ***As a result,*** *he is considered . . .*
3. *. . . after the war,* ***but*** *he believed . . .*
4. *. . . in 1921* ***when*** *he helped . . .*

Choices: Evaluation Criteria

Review: Homework
Compose Compelling Orations
Students use persuasive appeals to explain the importance of the issue.

Connect: Homework
Design a Multimedia Version
Students effectively apply modern technology to deliver the speech.

Extend: Homework
Conduct Research
Students' reports focus on the appeals used in a single speech.

Assess

Unit 6 Resources, Selection Standards Check, p. 39

ThinkCentral Online Assessment, Selection Standards Check

Teacher One Stop™, editable Selection Standards Check

Reteach

To reteach **analyzing arguments,** see **Reteaching Lessons,** pp. 1449F–1449H.

ThinkCentral Online Remediation

Learn It Online
For an in-depth look at media literacy, direct students to the **MediaScope** mini-site, which shows students how to create, analyze, and critique media.
go.hrw.com H12-1115 Go

Universal Access: Grammar Link

English Learners

English for Academic Success Tell students that other transition groups include the following:

- comparison/contrast: *in contrast, instead, likewise, on one hand, on the other hand, on the contrary, rather, similarly, yet, but, however, still, nevertheless*
- illustration: *for example, for instance, for one thing, to illustrate*
- summarizing: *in brief, in conclusion, on the whole, in short, in summary, to sum up, to summarize, finally*
- addition: *also, besides, furthermore, in addition, likewise, moreover*
- emphasis: *above all, chiefly, especially, particularly, singularly*

Have students look at a recent essay they have written and combine short sentences using some of the transitions listed above.

✔ For more practice with connecting ideas, see **Warriner's Handbook, GrammarNotes,** and **Language Handbook Worksheets.**

Standards Focus

Objectives

Students will
- understand flashback
- make and modify predictions

Selection Introduction

Think About the Writer

To help students answer the question, have them think about what they have learned or gained through the challenges or troubles they faced during their childhood.

For Independent Reading

- *Restless, A Ghost's Story,* Rich Wallace
- *The Grave,* James Heneghan

Motivate

What Do You Think?/QuickTalk

Have students consider the emotional distress civilians had to endure from the fear of invasion and the loss of loved ones. Ask them to imagine having to flee their homes because of the constant threat of air raids.

English for Academic Success

Academic Vocabulary

Look for opportunities to use the Academic Vocabulary words in this unit.

- **adapt,** ***v.:*** adjust for a new purpose
- **exhibit,** ***v.:*** show, demonstrate
- **perspective,** ***n.:*** a particular way of looking at something

Preparing to Read

The Demon Lover

What Do You Think? How does experience shape our view of the world?

QuickTalk

You've read about how the two World Wars affected soldiers and prisoners. In a small group, discuss the impact wars might have on civilians. What losses might they suffer?

Writer Elizabeth Bowen by Robin Adler.

MEET THE WRITER

Elizabeth Bowen

(1899–1973)

Much of Elizabeth Bowen's writing is concerned with the processes of growing up, of losing innocence, and of coming to terms with reality. Her main characters are often wealthy, well-mannered women (like herself); yet her novels also reveal a sense that life cannot be trusted, that existence is a struggle.

"No Trouble"

Elizabeth Bowen was born in Dublin and spent her early years in County Cork on her family's country estate. As Bowen later wrote, her family tried "to live as though living gave them no trouble." An only child, Bowen was looked after by a governess and taught to dance, wear gloves, and exhibit good manners. On her mother's orders she was not taught to read until she was seven. When her father was confined to a mental hospital, Elizabeth was not allowed to dwell on his condition. Her father recovered, but her mother contracted fatal cancer. Twelve-year-old Elizabeth was not allowed to attend her mother's funeral or to mourn her.

Literature and War

After attending a boarding school in England, Bowen moved to London to write stories. There she attended readings at the Poetry Bookshop, where she made the first of the literary friendships that were to become the fabric of her life.

In 1923, Bowen published her first collection of stories, *Encounters.* She married Alan Cameron, a teacher, and moved to Oxford, where she wrote industriously, producing story collections regularly and writing nearly a novel a year.

In 1935, the couple moved back to London, where Bowen became a notable hostess of the literary world. During World War II, with its nightly air raids on London, Bowen was a dedicated air-raid warden, but she went right on giving parties. She also wrote the stories published in *The Demon Lover* (1945), a collection she called a "diary" of her reactions to the war.

After the war, Cameron died of a heart attack. Predictably, Bowen became more active than ever. She died of lung cancer in 1973 and is buried in an Irish churchyard.

Think About the Writer How would pretending that life is no trouble affect a child?

California Standards, pp. 1116–1125

- **Reading Standard 2.2** Analyze the way in which clarity of meaning is affected by the patterns of organization, hierarchical structures, repetition of the main ideas, syntax, and word choice in the text.
- **Grades 9–10 Review Reading Standard 3.6** Analyze and trace an author's development of time and sequence, including the use of complex literary devices (e.g., foreshadowing, flashbacks).

Selection Readability	
Easily Accessible **Accessible** Challenging	simple sentence structure; familiar language; accessible vocabulary

Reading Standard 2.2; **Grades 9–10 Review**
Reading Standard 3.6 (see pages A48–A50)

Literary Skills Focus

Flashback A **flashback** is a scene in a narrative or dramatic work that interrupts the present action to tell what happened at an earlier time. "The Demon Lover" uses a flashback to provide important background information about the main character, Mrs. Drover. To recognize where the flashback begins, look for the sudden appearance of a verb in the past perfect tense (that is, preceded by the helping verb *had*).

Reading Skills Focus

Making and Modifying Predictions Making **predictions,** or educated guesses about what will happen in a story, will add to your understanding and enjoyment. As you read, you will often learn new information that will cause you to **modify your predictions.** In "The Demon Lover," the flashback will provide you with new information about Mrs. Drover and her life. Use this pattern of organization to help you modify your predictions.

Into Action Read the story up until the flashback, and then in a chart like the one below, predict what will happen next. Then, read the flashback, and modify your prediction. As you continue to read, add new information to the chart, and modify your predictions accordingly.

My prediction	A woman will meet a mysterious man.
Details in the flashback	
My modified prediction	
New information	
My modified prediction	

Writing Skills Focus

Think as a Reader/Writer

Find It in Your Reading The descriptive details writers use to create a setting also help establish a story's **mood,** or atmosphere. As you read Bowen's description of the empty house, record in your *Reader/Writer Notebook* details that create an unsettling mood.

TechFocus Imagine you are adapting this story for a television movie. Consider how you will stage the flashback.

Reader/Writer Notebook
Use your **RWN** to complete the activities for this selection.

Vocabulary

prosaic (proh ZAY ihk) *adj.:* ordinary; dull. *The woman's life story seemed prosaic until she revealed her secret from long ago.*

assent (uh SEHNT) *n.:* acceptance. *The woman had learned to view her rather ordinary life with a feeling of assent.*

intermittent (ihn tuhr MIHT uhnt) *adj.:* starting and stopping; periodic. *The rain was not constant but intermittent.*

precipitately (prih SIHP uh tiht lee) *adv.:* suddenly. *She turned precipitately to see what had caused the noise that startled her.*

emanated (EHM uh nayt ihd) *v.:* flowed; came forth. *The noise emanated from downstairs.*

impassively (ihm PAS ihv lee) *adv.:* calmly; indifferently. *She set aside her anxiety and impassively descended the stairs to see what had happened.*

Language Coach

Suffix *–ly* The suffix *–ly* is added to some adjectives (words that describe people, places, things, or ideas) to form adverbs (words that describe verbs, adjectives, or other adverbs). Which two Vocabulary words are adverbs that end in *–ly*? To which two Vocabulary words could you add *–ly* to form adverbs?

Learn It Online
Enhance your study of this story with these project ideas online.
go.hrw.com H12-1117 Go

Selection Resources

Unit 6 Resources, on-level practice and assessment, p. 42
Teacher One Stop™, on-level lesson plans and all print resources
Holt Audio Library
Holt Audio Library: Selections and Summaries in Spanish
UA: Differentiating Instruction, graphic organizer, p. 270
UA: Supporting Instruction in Spanish, selection summary
ThinkCentral Online Assessment, Selection Standards Check
ThinkCentral Online Remediation

Preteach

Introducing Vocabulary

Use this activity to check students' understanding of the Vocabulary words.

1. The woman showed her _____ for the gift with a small smile. [*assent*]
2. The sunlight _____ from the living room into the kitchen. [*emanated*]
3. The bus driver _____ hit his brakes when he saw the ball roll into the road. [*precipitately*]
4. The movie was _____ and bored the audience. [*prosaic*]
5. Surprisingly, the woman acted _____ during the alarming event. [*impassively*]
6. The _____ sound of the bells came every two to three hours. [*intermittent*]

English for Academic Success

Language Coach

Remind students that some adverbs, like *after* and *now,* do not end in *–ly.* ***Possible responses:*** *precipitately, impassively; prosaically, intermittently*

Literary Skills Focus

Have students note changes in verb tense in this story, indicating the beginning or end of a flashback.

Reading Skills Focus

Give students a copy of the Reading Skills Focus graphic organizer before they read. Tell them to use their responses to answer the questions on the Applying Your Skills page.

Writing Skills Focus

Have students record details that help create the mood in their **Reader/Writer Notebooks**. Students can use their notes to complete the Writing Skills Focus activity.

Learn It Online
The **MediaScope** mini-site provides hands-on resources for understanding, analyzing, creating, and critiquing media and multimedia.
go.hrw.com H12-1117 Go

Teacher Preparation

Selection Plot Summary

In "The Demon Lover," a married woman returns during World War II to her closed-up London house to collect some personal items. There, she discovers a recent letter from a soldier she promised to marry twenty-five years earlier. The man, who was reported lost in action during World War I, reminds her of the promise and claims that he is confident she will keep the appointment. In a flashback to 1916, the woman recalls their loveless affair and the man's intimidating ways. To escape the memory, she rushes from the house and catches a cab. When the driver turns to face her, she screams as she recognizes him as the dreaded fiancé. She beats on the closed windows as the car speeds away into the empty streets.

Direct Teach

Think About/Talk About

Read with a Purpose Have students read the Read with a Purpose statement. Point out the phrase "strange encounter." As students read, have them note any occurrences that may be viewed as strange.

Comprehension

A Reading Focus

Possible responses: *The setting is described as very eerie and unnatural. Mrs. Drover seems to be unaffected by her environment and unaware that a strange encounter will occur in the house. These details make me expect something unusual will happen to her.*

SHORT STORY

The Demon Lover

by **Elizabeth Bowen**

Read with a Purpose

Read this story to find out about one woman's strange encounter with her past.

Build Background

"The Demon Lover" takes place in London during World War II, when frequent German air raids drove many Londoners to leave the city. The story's title comes from a British ballad, in which a woman is lured away from her second husband and her children by her first husband, who has been missing at sea and has come into great wealth. She goes to sea with him—only to find that he has a demon's cloven foot. The demon lover then breaks the ship in half, sinking it, and sending the two of them to hell.

Toward the end of her day in London Mrs. Drover went round to her shut-up house to look for several things she wanted to take away. Some belonged to herself, some to her family, who were by now used to their country life. It was late August; it had been a steamy, showery day: At the moment the trees down the pavement glittered in an escape of humid yellow afternoon sun. Against the next batch of clouds, already piling up ink-dark, broken chimneys and parapets[1] stood out. In her once familiar street, as in any unused channel, an unfamiliar queerness had silted up; a cat wove itself in and out of railings, but no human eye watched Mrs. Drover's return. Shifting some parcels under her arm, she slowly forced round her latchkey in an unwilling lock, then gave the door, which had warped, a push with her knee. Dead air came out to meet her as she went in.

The staircase window having been boarded up, no light came down into the hall. But one door, she could just see, stood ajar, so she went quickly through into the room and unshuttered the big window in there. Now the prosaic woman, looking about her, was more perplexed than she knew by everything that she saw, by traces of her long former habit of life—the yellow smoke stain up the white marble mantelpiece, the ring left by a vase on the top of the escritoire;[2] the bruise in the wallpaper where, on the door being thrown open widely, the china handle had always hit the wall. The piano, having gone away to be stored, had left what looked like claw marks on its part of the parquet.[3] Though not much dust had seeped in, each object wore a film of another kind; and, the only ventilation being the chimney, the whole drawing room smelled of the cold hearth. Mrs. Drover put down her parcels on the escritoire and left the room to proceed upstairs; the things she wanted were in a bedroom chest. **A**

She had been anxious to see how the house was—the part-time caretaker she shared with some neighbors was away this week on his holiday, known to be not yet back. At the best of times he did not look

1. **parapets** (PAR uh pehts): low walls around rooftops.
2. **escritoire** (es krih TWAHR): writing table.
3. **parquet** (pahr KAY): wood floor made of boards arranged in geometric patterns.

A Reading Focus **Making and Modifying Predictions** Reread the title and first two paragraphs in the story. Think about the description of the setting and of Mrs. Drover. Then, predict what will happen to Mrs. Drover in this story.

Vocabulary **prosaic** (proh ZAY ihk) *adj.:* ordinary; dull.

Universal Access

English Learners

Help students verbally express their thoughts on the mood of a story. Read aloud starting from the sentence "In her once familiar street . . ." to the end of the paragraph. Ask students to express their thoughts on the atmosphere. Tell students to use the text to support their opinions. Suggest that students begin with "I sense a . . . mood when I read that . . . , because. . . ."

✔ See the **English Language Skill Builder** in **UA: Differentiating Instruction.**

Struggling Readers

Benchmark Students To help students create and modify their predictions, inform them that the tone of the story can give readers clues as to what might occur next. After students read a paragraph, have them indicate the tone of the paragraph and write down a few words or phrases that help establish the tone. Remind students to consider tone when making predictions.

✔ See **UA: Differentiating Instruction** for a graphic organizer to scaffold instruction for struggling readers.

in often, and she was never sure that she trusted him. There were some cracks in the structure, left by the last bombing, on which she was anxious to keep an eye. Not that one could do anything—

A shaft of refracted[4] daylight now lay across the hall. She stopped dead and stared at the hall table—on this lay a letter addressed to her.

She thought first—then the caretaker *must* be back. All the same, who, seeing the house shuttered, would have dropped a letter in at the box? It was not a circular, it was not a bill. And the post office redirected, to the address in the country, everything for her that came through the post. The caretaker (even if he *were* back) did not know she was due in London today—her call here had been planned to be a surprise—so his negligence in the manner of this letter, leaving it to wait in the dusk and the dust, annoyed her. Annoyed, she picked up the letter, which bore no stamp. But it cannot be important, or they would know . . . She took the letter rapidly upstairs with her, without a stop to look at the writing till she reached what had been her bedroom, where she let in light. The room looked over the garden and other gardens: The sun had gone in; as the clouds sharpened and lowered, the trees and rank lawns seemed already to smoke with dark. Her reluctance to look again at the letter came from the fact that she felt intruded upon—and by someone contemptuous of her ways. However, in the tenseness preceding the fall of rain she read it: It was a few lines.

> Dear Kathleen: You will not have forgotten that today is our anniversary, and the day we said. The years have gone by at once slowly and fast. In view of the fact that nothing has changed, I shall rely upon you to keep your promise. I was sorry to see you leave London, but was satisfied that you would be back in time. You may expect me, therefore, at the hour arranged. Until then . . .
> K. **B**

4. **refracted:** bent by its passage from one medium to another.

Martha (1925) by Georg Schrimpf (1889–1938). Oil on canvas.
Private Collection/Artists Rights Society (ARS), NY/VG Bild-Kunst, Bonn.

Mrs. Drover looked for the date: It was today's. She dropped the letter onto the bedsprings, then picked it up to see the writing again—her lips, beneath the remains of lipstick, beginning to go white. She felt so much the change in her own face that she went to the mirror, polished a clear patch in it, and looked at once urgently and stealthily in. She was confronted by a woman of forty-four, with eyes starting out under a hat brim that had been rather carelessly pulled down. She had not put on any more powder since she left the shop where she ate her solitary tea.[5] The pearls her husband had given her on their marriage hung loose round her now rather thinner throat, slipping in the V of the pink wool jumper her sister knitted last autumn as they sat round the fire. Mrs. Drover's most normal expression was one of controlled worry, but of assent.

5. **tea:** in Britain, a light late-afternoon meal, served with tea.

B Reading Focus Making and Modifying Predictions What is mysterious about the arrival of the letter? Modify your prediction about what will happen based on what you have learned so far.

Vocabulary **assent** (uh SEHNT) *n.:* acceptance.

Think About/Talk About

Comprehension

B Reading Focus

Possible responses: *The letter is inside the house despite the fact that the caretaker is away, and it does not appear to be delivered by the postal service. Readers could predict that the content of the letter will be disturbing and that it is probably from the "demon lover."*

Extend the Discussion

Making Inferences What does the change in Mrs. Drover's coloring suggest about the letter or its writer? ***Possible response:*** *It suggests that she recognizes the writer and is shocked or frightened by the contents of the letter.*

Tone How does the author use descriptive detail to set an ominous tone in the first two paragraphs? ***Possible response:*** *The mysterious letter is inside the house, the sky and lawns are darkening, and the woman is tense and fearful.*

Vocabulary: Own the Word

- **prosaic:** Tell students that the root word for *prosaic* is *prōsa,* which is Latin for "straightforward. Something or someone that is *prosaic* is easy to understand and may be considered as dull or ordinary. Ask students to describe an experience they found to be *prosaic.*
- **assent:** Role play a person who reacts to an unpleasant or unexpected change with *assent,* possibly with a "no problem" attitude. Ask one or two students to stand at their desks and do the same.

Advanced Learners

Acceleration Have students analyze the contents of the mysterious letter Mrs. Drover receives. Ask students to pretend that they are reading this letter with no prior knowledge of the events or people connected with it. Have students work with a partner to discuss how they would interpret the solitary letter. Then, start a class discussion on how the text leading up to the letter changes the tone of the letter.

Students with Disabilities

To emphasize that the story includes a long flashback to past events, you may want to create an audiotape of the story using two readers with distinctly different voices. One would read the present action of the story and the other, the flashback. Alert students to the fact that they will hear two readers when they listen to the tape; afterward, ask them to discuss why the tape was created in this way. Ask students to identify how the events presented in the flashback connect to present-day events in the story.

Model the Skill

- Review the concept of **flashback**. Explain that a change in the verb tense—from the present to the past tense, or from the past tense to the past perfect tense—indicates that a writer is referring to events that took place prior to the main events of the story.
- Tell students that a flashback might also be indicated by a change in setting or a reference to the passing of time.
- Read the third paragraph that begins "The young girl . . ." aloud. Then, point out the change in setting (a garden), the inclusion of verbs in the past perfect tense ("has not ever seen"), and the indication of time (August 1916).

Guided Practice: Apply

QuickWrite Use QuickWrite to help students connect personally with issues presented in the selection. Ask students to think about the benefits and detriments of including a flashback in a story. How does moving from the present action of a story to a past event engage the reader? What difficulties might a reader encounter when transitioning into a flashback? Students can record their responses in their **Reader/Writer Notebooks.**

Since the birth of the third of her little boys, attended by a quite serious illness, she had had an intermittent muscular flicker to the left of her mouth, but in spite of this she could always sustain a manner that was at once energetic and calm.

Turning from her own face as precipitately as she had gone to meet it, she went to the chest where the things were, unlocked it, threw up the lid, and knelt to search. But as rain began to come crashing down she could not keep from looking over her shoulder at the stripped bed on which the letter lay. Behind the blanket of rain the clock of the church that still stood struck six—with rapidly heightening apprehension she counted each of the slow strokes. "The hour arranged . . . My God," she said, "*what* hour? How should I . . . ? After twenty-five years . . . "

The young girl talking to the soldier in the garden had not ever completely seen his face. It was dark; they were saying goodbye under a tree. Now and then—for it felt, from not seeing him at this intense moment, as though she had never seen him at all—she verified his presence for these few moments longer by putting out a hand, which he each time pressed, without very much kindness, and painfully, on to one of the breast buttons of his uniform. That cut of the button on the palm of her hand was, principally, what she was to carry away. This was so near the end of a leave from France that she could only wish him already gone. It was August 1916. Being not kissed, being drawn away from and looked at intimidated Kathleen till she imagined spectral glitters in the place of his eyes. Turning away and looking back up the lawn she saw, through branches of trees, the drawing-room window alight: She caught a breath for the moment when she could go running back there into the safe arms of her mother and sister, and cry: "What shall I do, what shall I do? He has gone." C

Hearing her catch her breath, her fiancé said, without feeling: "Cold?"

"You're going away such a long way."

"Not so far as you think."

"I don't understand?"

"You don't have to," he said. "You will. You know what we said."

"But that was—suppose you—I mean, suppose."

"I shall be with you," he said, "sooner or later. You won't forget that. You need do nothing but wait."

Only a little more than a minute later she was free to run up the silent lawn. Looking in through the window at her mother and sister, who did not for the moment perceive her, she already felt that unnatural promise drive down between her and the rest of all humankind. No other way of having given herself could have made her feel so apart, lost and forsworn.[6] She could not have plighted a more sinister troth.[7]

Kathleen behaved well when, some months later, her fiancé was reported missing, presumed killed. Her family not only supported her but were able to praise her courage without stint[8] because they could not regret, as a husband for her, the man they knew

6. **forsworn** (fawr SWAWRN): having sworn falsely; perjured.
7. **plighted . . . troth:** made a more sinister promise of marriage.
8. **stint:** limitation.

C **Literary Focus** **Flashback** What are the signals that a flashback begins here?

Vocabulary **intermittent** (ihn tuhr MIHT uhnt) *adj.:* starting and stopping; periodic.
precipitately (prih SIHP uh tiht lee) *adv.:* suddenly.

Reaching Reluctant Readers

Tell students that a good horror story, ghost story, or suspenseful story uses specific techniques. Explain how mysterious circumstances make the reader want to read on to learn more. The author uses suspense to keep readers on the edge of their seats and good descriptive detail to help readers sympathize with the main character's situation.

Activity Have the class discuss different horror movies, suspenseful novels, and ghost stories that have kept them on the edge of their seats. Tell them to determine why they found these works successful. Next, break the class into small groups in which each student takes turns writing a section of a ghost story using the techniques discussed, such as descriptive detail, foreshadowing, and suspense. Have each group choose one student to read the group's work to the class. Encourage

Girl Reading a Letter in an Interior (1908) by Peter Vilhelm Ilsted (1861–1933).

almost nothing about. They hoped she would, in a year or two, console herself—and had it been only a question of consolation things might have gone much straighter ahead. But her trouble, behind just a little grief, was a complete dislocation from everything. She did not reject other lovers, for these failed to appear: For years she failed to attract men—and with the approach of her thirties she became natural enough to share her family's anxiousness on this score. She began to put herself out,[9] to wonder; and at thirty-two she was very greatly relieved to find herself being courted by William Drover. She married him, and the two of them settled down in this quiet, arboreal[10] part of Kensington: In this house the years piled up, her children were born, and they all lived till they were driven out by the bombs of the next war. Her movements as Mrs. Drover were circumscribed, and she dismissed any idea that they were still watched. **D**

As things were—dead or living the letter writer sent her only a threat. Unable, for some minutes, to go on kneeling with her back exposed to the empty room, Mrs. Drover rose from the chest to sit on an upright chair whose back was firmly against the wall. The desuetude[11] of her former bedroom, her married London home's whole air of being a cracked cup from which memory, with its reassuring power, had either evaporated or leaked away, made a crisis—and at just this crisis the letter writer had, knowledgeably, struck. The hollowness of the house this evening canceled years on years of voices, habits, and steps. Through the shut windows she only heard rain fall on the roofs around. To rally herself, she said she was in a mood—and for two or three seconds shutting her eyes, told herself that she had imagined the letter. But she opened them—there it lay on the bed. **E**

On the supernatural side of the letter's entrance she was not permitting her mind to dwell. Who, in London, knew she meant to call at the house today? Evidently, however, this had been known. The caretaker, *had* he come back, had had no cause to expect her: He would have taken the letter in his pocket, to forward it, at his own time, through the post. There was no other sign that the caretaker had been in—but, if not? Letters dropped in at doors of deserted houses do not fly or walk to tables in halls. They do not sit on the dust of empty tables with the air of certainty that they will be found. There is needed some human hand—but nobody but the caretaker had a key. Under circumstances she did not care to consider, a house can be entered without a key. It was possible that she was not alone now. She might be being waited for, downstairs. Waited for—until when? Until "the hour arranged." At least that was not six o'clock: Six has struck.

She rose from the chair and went over and locked the door. **F**

9. **put herself out:** vex or distress herself.
10. **arboreal** (ahr BAWR ee uhl): full of trees.
11. **desuetude** (DEHS wih tood): disuse.

D **Literary Focus** **Flashback** What information about Mrs. Drover's past do you learn in the flashback?

E **Literary Focus** **Flashback** How does this flashback end? What signal returns the story to the present?

F **Reading Focus** **Making and Modifying Predictions** What do you think will happen to Mrs. Drover? What new information helps you modify your prediction?

Think About/Talk About

Comprehension

F Reading Focus

Possible response: *Mrs. Drover may be confronted with something supernatural because of the letter's strange entrance.*

Analysis

C Literary Focus

Possible response: *The author uses a verb in the past perfect tense ("had not ever seen"), and the setting has changed.*

D Literary Focus

Possible response: *Before her unkind fiancé left for the war, Kathleen promised to marry him. The man was later reported missing. After many years, Kathleen married another man and had children.*

E Literary Focus

Possible response: *The author sums up Mrs. Drover's life right until the present moment of the war, after which the words "As things were" signal a return to the present.*

Extend the Discussion

Making Predictions In what fashion do you expect the fiancé to make his appearance at the "hour arranged"? ***Possible response:*** *Considering the mysterious arrival of the letter, I would expect the man to arrive in a similarly unexpected and unexplainable fashion.*

Vocabulary: Own the Word

- **intermittent:** Ask students to list things that are *intermittent.* ***Possible responses:*** *rainfall, stock market rallies, windshield wiping*
- **precipitately:** Ask students: "When might you react to something *precipitately?*" ***Possible responses:*** *during an emergency situation, out of fear*

students to enhance their story with sound effects. Tell students that their audience will be middle school students. Have students critique the stories on how or why they were successful. Were they suspenseful? How did they use descriptive details about the setting to create suspense? Did they include details that foreshadowed later events?

Universal Access

AAVE Students Who Use African American Vernacular English

English for Academic Success Read the sentence, "They hoped she would, in a year or two, console herself" (p. 1121). Students might be inclined to say "console her" instead of "console herself." Remind students that the reflexive pronoun is used when the object of the sentence is the same as the subject. Ask which sentence requires a reflexive pronoun: 1. The boy looked at him in the mirror. 2. Jamie told her mother a lie.

Model the Skill

- Provide students with copies of the Reading Skills Focus graphic organizer for "The Demon Lover." (See **Unit 6 Resources.**)
- Tell students that when creating or **modifying predictions**, they should look for details in the flashback that provide additional information about a character or occurrences that may change their predictions about future events.
- Model modifying predictions using the graphic organizer. For example, you might say, "From the letter that Mrs. Drover finds I predict that she is going to meet a man from her past. Details in the flashback inform me that the man is a former fiancé with a sinister past. I modify my prediction to state that Mrs. Drover will meet a former fiancé who is challenging her promise of marriage."

My prediction	Mrs. Drover will meet a man from her past.
Details in the flashback	The man is a former fiancé with a sinister past.
My modified prediction	The man will challenge her promise of marriage.

Guided Practice: Apply

Think-Pair-Share Tell students to read the first five paragraphs of p. 1123 and think about the details that may help them to form or modify predictions. Then, have students form pairs to discuss the details of this section. Instruct them to modify their predictions accordingly and then discuss their reasons with their partner.

Shepherd Returning from the War by Peter Brook. Oil on canvas. Leeds Museums and Galleries (City Art Gallery), UK.

Analyzing Visuals

Connecting to the Text How might this painting represent Mrs. Drover's feelings as she returns to her closed-up house?

The thing was, to get out. To fly? No, not that: She had to catch her train. As a woman whose utter dependability was the keystone of her family life she was not willing to return to the country, to her husband, her little boys, and her sister, without the objects she had come up to fetch. Resuming work at the chest she set about making up a number of parcels in a rapid, fumbling-decisive way. These, with her shopping parcels, would be too much to carry; these meant a taxi—at the thought of the taxi her heart went up and her normal breathing resumed. I will ring up the taxi now; the taxi cannot come too soon: I shall hear the taxi out there running its engine, till I walk calmly down to it through the hall. I'll ring up— But no: the telephone is cut off . . . She tugged at a knot she had tied wrong.

Word-Attack Skills Mini-Lesson

English for Academic Success Explain that over the centuries, English has borrowed words from other languages. As a result, the regular letter-sound relationships of English do not apply to all the words in the language. Remind students of the phonogram *–et*. Words with this phonogram are very common in English—for example, *get, let, met, net, pet, wet.* Point out that the phonogram *–et* appears in two words in the selection: *parapet* and *parquet*. Write the words on the chalkboard and explain that although both words have French origins, *parapet* has taken on a typically English pronunciation, whereas in *parquet*, *–et* retains the French sound (ay).

Activity Have students read the following sentences and identify the words in which *–et* stands for (ay).

1. From the garret, she watched them play croquet on the lawn.
2. Her gimlet eye spotted his white beret.
3. A bouquet from him graced the spinet.
4. They dined on filet of beef and claret.

The idea of flight . . . He was never kind to me, not really. I don't remember him kind at all. Mother said he never considered me. He was set on me, that was what it was—not love. Not love, not meaning a person well. What did he do, to make me promise like that? I can't remember— But she found that she could.

She remembered with such dreadful acuteness that the twenty-five years since then dissolved like smoke and she instinctively looked for the weal[12] left by the button on the palm of her hand. She remembered not only all that he said and did but the complete suspension of *her* existence during that August week. I was not myself—they all told me so at the time. She remembered—but with one white burning blank as where acid has dropped on a photograph: *Under no conditions* could she remember his face.

So, wherever he may be waiting, I shall not know him. You have no time to run from a face you do not expect.

The thing was to get to the taxi before any clock struck what could be the hour. She would slip down the street and round the side of the square to where the square gave on the main road. She would return in the taxi, safe, to her own door, and bring the solid driver into the house with her to pick up the parcels from room to room. The idea of the taxi driver made her decisive, bold: She unlocked her door, went to the top of the staircase, and listened down.

She heard nothing—but while she was hearing nothing the *passé*[13] air of the staircase was disturbed by a draft that traveled up to her face. It emanated from the basement: Down there a door or window was being opened by someone who chose this moment to leave the house. G

The rain had stopped; the pavements steamily shone as Mrs. Drover let herself out by inches from her own front door into the empty street. The unoccupied houses opposite continued to meet her look with their damaged stare. Making toward the thoroughfare and the taxi, she tried not to keep looking behind. Indeed, the silence was so intense—one of those creeks of London silence exaggerated this summer by the damage of war—that no tread could have gained on hers unheard. Where her street debouched[14] on the square where people went on living, she grew conscious of, and checked, her unnatural pace. Across the open end of the square two buses impassively passed each other: Women, a perambulator,[15] cyclists, a man wheeling a barrow signalized, once again, the ordinary flow of life. At the square's most populous corner should be—and was—the short taxi rank. This evening, only one taxi—but this, although it presented its blank rump, appeared already to be alertly waiting for her. Indeed, without looking round the driver started his engine as she panted up from behind and put her hand on the door. As she did so, the clock struck seven. The taxi faced the main road: To make the trip back to her house it would have to turn—she had settled back on the seat and the taxi had turned before she, surprised by its knowing movement, recollected that she had not "said where." She leaned forward to scratch at the glass panel that divided the driver's head from her own. H

The driver braked to what was almost a stop, turned round, and slid the glass panel back: The jolt of this flung Mrs. Drover forward till her face was almost into the glass. Through the aperture[16] driver and passenger, not six inches between them, remained for an eternity eye to eye. Mrs. Drover's mouth hung open for some seconds before she could issue her first scream. After that she continued to scream freely and to beat with her gloved hands on the glass all round as the taxi, accelerating without mercy, made off with her into the hinterland of deserted streets.

12. **weal** (weel): lump; welt.
13. ***passé*** (pah SAY): no longer fresh; rather old.
14. **debouched** (dee BOOSHT): came out; emerged.
15. **perambulator** (puhr AM byoo layt uhr): chiefly British for "baby carriage." The word is often shortened to *pram*.
16. **aperture:** opening.

G **Reading Focus** **Making and Modifying Predictions** What do these lines suggest might happen next? Why is Mrs. Drover afraid?

H **Reading Focus** **Making and Modifying Predictions** How do you think the ending will resolve the story's tension?

Vocabulary **emanated** (EHM uh nayt ihd) *v.:* flowed; came forth.
impassively (ihm PAS ihv lee) *adv.:* calmly; indifferently.

Think About/Talk About

Comprehension

G Reading Focus

Possible responses: *These lines suggest that the person who left the letter was in the house the whole time and is now leaving to go to "the spot." Mrs. Drover is afraid because she is being watched by the person who sent the threatening letter.*

H Reading Focus

Possible response: *The ending will resolve tension by revealing who the letter writer is and what intentions he has toward Mrs. Drover.*

Vocabulary: Own the Word

- **emanated:** Ask students to complete the following statement. A pleasant smell *emanated* from the kitchen when . . . .
- **impassively:** Role-play an *impassive* reaction to news or an event, such as the announcement of no school due to snowfall. Ask one or two students to demonstrate at their desks.

Analyzing Visuals

Connecting to the Text: *The striking contrast of light and dark colors along with the thick shadows cast on the walls contribute to an atmosphere of sadness. Mrs. Drover is about to leave her house in London and, most likely after receiving the letter, her peaceful married life.*

California Standards, pp. 1124–1125

- **Reading Standard 2.2** Analyze the way in which clarity of meaning is affected by the patterns of organization, hierarchical structures, repetition of the main ideas, syntax, and word choice in the text.
- **Grades 9–10 Review Reading Standard 1.1** Identify and use the literal and figurative meanings of words and understand word derivations.
- **Grades 9–10 Review Reading Standard 3.6** Analyze and trace an author's development of time and sequence, including the use of complex literary devices (e.g., foreshadowing, flashbacks).
- **Writing Standard 2.1** Write fictional, autobiographical, or biographical narratives: **c.** Describe with concrete sensory details the sights, sounds, and smells of a scene and the specific actions, movements, gestures, and feelings of the characters; use interior monologue to depict the characters' feelings.
- **Writing Standard 2.6** Deliver multimedia presentations.

Check for Understanding

Independent Practice

Reading Skills Focus

Possible responses:

1. *She describes the dead air, the filmy residue on everything, and the boarded-up windows. This establishes an ominous mood.*
2. *He was an unkind man, and the promise he made her agree to was unnatural.*
3. *She is tense and afraid, but she accepts it.*
4. *Ask students to include additional rows containing new information about what actually happened in the story.*

Literary Skills Focus

Possible responses:

5. *During wartime, people experience "complete dislocation from everything," even love. The theme suggests a sober, even pessimistic outlook about the effects of war.*
6. *She is generally anxious and sometimes "perplexed" (p. 1118); she normally wears an expression of "controlled worry" (p. 1119).*
7. *She builds suspense through Mrs. Drover's fear of the mysterious letter, the use of flashbacks, and the description of an ominous setting. The story is frightening because the reader is unsure of Mrs. Drover's fate.*
8. *It is effective, given her disorientation. Or, it is confusing because the reader does not see the connection between Mrs. Drover and the girl until well into the flashback.*
9. *The hallucination theory, which must cover the letter as well as the taxi, is supported by all the references to the damage and dislocation of the war.*
10. *The lover's injury to her hand, his coldness, and his final words, "sooner or later . . ." all foreshadow a disturbing reunion. The growing darkness and the clock chime foreshadow a sinister ending.*

Applying Your Skills

Reading Standard 2.2; **Grades 9–10 Review**
Reading Standard 3.6 (see pages A48–A50)
Writing Standard 2.1c (see pages A51–A52)

The Demon Lover

Literary Response and Analysis

Reading Skills Focus

Quick Check

1. How does Bowen convey that Mrs. Drover's house has been empty for some time? What mood does she establish with this description?
2. Why does Kathleen feel free when the soldier goes missing? Why is the betrothal "sinister"?

Read with a Purpose

3. How does Mrs. Drover react to this undesirable encounter with her past?

Reading Skills: Making and Modifying Predictions

4. Look back at the predictions you made while reading. Complete your chart by writing in what actually happened. Write a brief description of what new information helped you modify your predictions as you read, and how closely your predictions matched what actually happened.

Literary Skills Focus

Literary Analysis

5. **Analyze** During each war, Mrs. Drover experiences dislocation and confusion, and during each war, the demon lover is part of her life. What do these strands—the war, Mrs. Drover's inner turmoil, and the demon lover's appearances—tell you about the story's theme?
6. **Interpret** The use of an omniscient narrator allows Bowen to give readers information about Mrs. Drover's psychological makeup that Mrs. Drover herself is not consciously aware of. Identify several such passages in the text. How do you interpret Mrs. Drover's psychological state?
7. **Evaluate** How does Bowen create suspense in this story? Did you experience Mrs. Drover's fear, or do you think the story is too unrealistic to be frightening? Explain your response.

Literary Skills: Flashback

8. **Make Judgments** Do you think the abrupt shift into the past in the flashback is effective or merely confusing? Why?
9. **Interpret** Some readers believe Mrs. Drover's experience is a hallucination. Her powers of imagination have combined with the pressures of wartime to transform reality into a waking nightmare. What details in the flashback support this interpretation of the story?

Literary Skills Review: Foreshadowing

10. **Analyze** When writers use **foreshadowing,** they drop hints about what will happen later in the story. What details in the lovers' last meeting foreshadow a sinister, threatening reunion? What other details in the story foreshadow a scary ending to Mrs. Drover's day?

Writing Skills Focus

Think as a Reader/Writer

Use It in Your Writing Look back at the notes you took about the descriptive details Bowen uses to create an unsettling mood. Then, write a descriptive paragraph in which you use details and images to create a particular mood.

What Do You Think Now?

How do you think Mrs. Drover's life has been affected by the two wars? How might her perspective of the world have changed?

Universal Access

Struggling Writers

Some students may need additional scaffolding to complete the Writing Skills Focus activity. Have them read the sixth paragraph on p. 1123, and ask them to note various descriptive details that create an eerie and suspenseful mood as Mrs. Drover steps onto the London streets. Then, have students create a web diagram with the particular mood in the center circle. Ask them to brainstorm descriptive details and images and add them to the web. Have students use the diagram to guide them with their descriptive paragraph.

What Do You Think Now?

To help students answer this question, ask students to think about how war affects civilians and the sacrifices they must make in order to survive.

Grades 9–10 Review Reading Standard 1.1, 3.6 (see pages A48–A50)
Writing Standard 2.1, 2.6 (see pages A51–A52)

Vocabulary Development

Vocabulary Check

Match the Vocabulary words with their definitions.

1. emanated	**a.** indifferently
2. assent	**b.** ordinary, dull
3. prosaic	**c.** flowed, came forth
4. impassively	**d.** acceptance
5. intermittent	**e.** suddenly
6. precipitately	**f.** periodic

Vocabulary Skills: Etymology

English comprises words that originated in many different languages. By looking in the dictionary, you can learn a word's **etymology,** or origin. Look at this sample dictionary entry for the word ***prosaic:***

> **pro·sa·ic** *adj.* [LL *prosaicus,* fr. L *prosa* prose] 1. dull, unimaginative 2. ordinary

The information in brackets tells you the etymology—that the word came from the Late Latin word *prosaicus,* which came from the Latin word *prosa.* The dictionary will include a key to the abbreviations.

Your Turn

Use a dictionary to determine the etymology of *assent, intermittent, precipitately,* and *emanated.*

Language Coach

Suffix –*ly* Remember that the suffix –*ly* is added to some words to form adverbs, words that describe verbs, adjectives, or other adverbs. Find the adverb *impassively* in the story. Tell what word it describes. Then find two other –*ly* adverbs in the story and tell what words they describe.

CHOICES

As you respond to the Choices, use these **Academic Vocabulary** words as appropriate: perspective, considerably, adapt, exhibit, inevitable.

REVIEW

Create a Story Map

Use the following chart to create a story map for "The Demon Lover." Note when the flashback occurs.

Situation	
Characters	
Conflict	
Event	
Climax	
Resolution	

CONNECT

Plan a TV Flashback

TechFocus In a group, plan a TV adaptation of the flashback in this story. Use storyboards to explain how you will use camera angles, fades, lighting, setting and costumes, and other techniques to alert the audience to the flashback and then to return them to the present. In a class presentation, have a group member share your ideas for adapting the flashback.

EXTEND

Tell What Happens Next

Some readers believe that Mrs. Drover's experience is a figment of her imagination, while others consider the story to be an out-and-out ghost tale. Choose the interpretation you prefer, or develop one of your own, and write a paragraph telling what happens next in the story.

Learn It Online
Learn more about Bowen and her work through these Internet links.
go.hrw.com H12-1125 Go

Universal Access: Vocabulary Development

English Learners

English for Academic Success Students sometimes have difficulty understanding that the role of adverbs is to modify a verb, an adjective, or another adverb. Explain to students that adverbs answer the questions *Where? When? How? How often?* or *To what extent?* Read the following sentence aloud: *The dog barked noisily at the passing cars.* Ask students if there are any words in the sentence that answer the questions you mentioned earlier. [*noisily—how?*] Tell students that *noisily* is an adverb that modifies the verb *barked. Noisily* tells the reader *how* the dog *barked.* Pair English learners with a proficient English speaker; then, have them identify the adverbs and the words they modify in the sentences below.

- We did not read the text thoroughly before answering the questions. [*thoroughly; read*]
- The boy ran rapidly through the street. [*rapidly; ran*]

✔ See the **Academic and Selection Vocabulary Skill Builder** in **UA: Differentiating Instruction.**

Independent Practice

Vocabulary Development

Vocabulary Check

1. *c* **2.** *d* **3.** *b*
4. *a* **5.** *f* **6.** *e*

Your Turn

Possible responses: assent *(Latin* assentārī*),* intermittent *(Latin* intermittere*),* precipitately *(Latin* praecipitāre*),* emanated *(Latin* ēmānāre*)*

English for Academic Success

Language Coach

Impassively *(p. 1123) describes* passed. Rapidly *and* carelessly *(p. 1119) describe* took *and* pulled, *respectively.*

Choices: Evaluation Criteria

Review: Homework
Create a Story Map
Students demonstrate understanding of literary terms.

Connect: Homework
Plan a TV Flashback
Project utilizes various film techniques to portray flashback.

Extend: Homework
Tell What Happens Next
Students use details from the text to support their interpretation.

Assess

Unit 6 Resources, Selection Standards Check, p. 45

Reteach

ThinkCentral Online Remediation

Learn It Online
Literature Links direct students to pre-screened Web sites offering more information related to a selection.
go.hrw.com H12-1125 Go

Standards Focus

Objectives

Students will

- understand setting
- draw inferences about characters' motivations

Selection Introduction

Think About the Writer

How does a keen interest in other people help Greene uncover specific, subtle details about human nature and interaction? Why are such fine points essential to creating compelling characters?

For Independent Reading

Daisies in the Junkyard, Michael Enright

Motivate

What Do You Think?/QuickWrite

Use the QuickWrite to have students think about why most people work hard to form and maintain friendships, even if those relationships are sometimes difficult. Have students use their **Reader/Writer Notebooks** to record their thoughts.

English for Academic Success

Academic Vocabulary

Look for opportunities to use the Academic Vocabulary word in this unit.

- **exhibit,** ***v.:*** show, demonstrate

California Standards, pp. 1126–1139

- **Reading Standard 3.7c** Evaluate the philosophical, political, religious, ethical, and social influences of the historical period that shaped the characters, plots, and settings.
- **Grades 9–10 Review Reading Standard 3.4** Determine characters' traits by what the characters say about themselves in narration, dialogue, dramatic monologue, and soliloquy.

Preparing to Read

The Destructors

What Do You Think?

How does experience shape our view of the world?

QuickWrite

Why do you think some people are so influenced by peer pressure? Write a paragraph on this topic in your *Reader/Writer Notebook.*

Graham Greene at his home in Nice (May 1982).

MEET THE WRITER

Graham Greene

(1904–1991)

In his serious novels as well as in his light "entertainments" and thrillers, Graham Greene's intention was always to tell the truth, which he saw as the primary duty of the artist.

An Early Literary Triumph

Henry Graham Greene was born to a comfortable family in Hertfordshire, England. As he grew into adolescence, he became depressed and unhappy at school. After trying to run away, he was sent to London for psychoanalysis. He would later recall those six months in London as among the happiest of his life.

While he was still at school, a local newspaper published one of Greene's stories, and he recalled feeling a sense of true literary triumph "for the first and last time." The experience convinced him to become a professional writer. He attended Oxford University, where he wrote a novel and published a book of poems.

A Hungry Curiosity

In 1926, Greene became engaged to Vivien Dayrell-Browning and began to take instruction in her faith, Roman Catholicism. Formerly an atheist, he became convinced of "the probable existence of something we call God." Greene later exhibited his religious concerns in his fiction with the novels *Brighton Rock* (1938) and *The Power and the Glory* (1940), in which he explored good and evil and the workings of divine grace.

Greene worked as a journalist until his first novel, *The Man Within,* was published in 1929. Although his next books received little attention, Greene came into his own with the thriller *Stamboul Train* (1932; also published as *Orient Express*).

Greene wrote more than twenty novels, as well as works in a dozen other genres, including children's stories and screenplays. In his autobiography, he revealed his motive for writing fiction as "a desire to reduce the chaos of experience to some sort of order, and a hungry curiosity. We cannot love others, so the theologians teach, unless in some degree we can love ourselves, and curiosity too begins at home."

Think About the Writer How might a hungry curiosity and a strong desire for new experiences serve a writer?

Selection Readability	
Easily Accessible **Accessible** Challenging	accessible vocabulary; complex characterization

Literary Skills Focus

Setting The **setting** is the time and place of a story. The setting of this story reflects both political and social influences of the historical period: a drab corner of a city still reeling from war. As the story progresses, though, the setting becomes not just a backdrop, but rather a key plot element that helps to shape the characters. Greene's characteristic use of coarse **imagery** and language creates a seedy, drab world full of shabby violence and a pessimistic mood.

Reading Skills Focus

Drawing Inferences About Characters' Motivations Characters' words and actions, as well as the author's description of the characters, will help you **draw inferences about characters' motivations,** or their reasons for behaving the way they do. In "The Destructors," each of the four numbered sections gives you a bit more insight into T., the enigmatic main character. Greene slowly reveals more about the character's motivations as the story progresses.

Into Action On a spider map, note particular words and actions that you find most revealing about each of the following characters. When you have finished reading the story, you will use these clues to draw inferences about the characters' motivations.

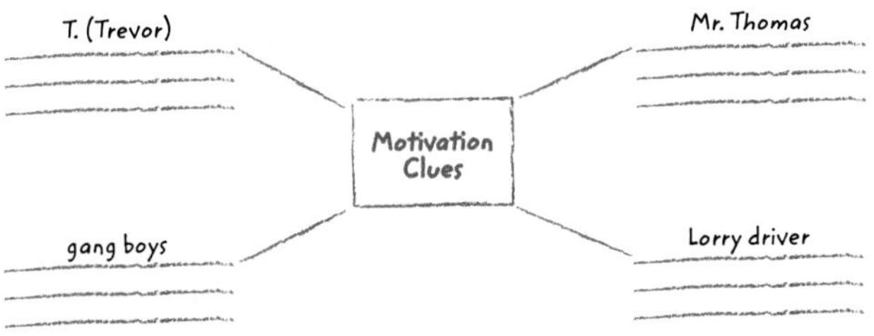

Writing Skills Focus

Think as a Reader/Writer

Find It in Your Reading As you read, note how Greene uses dialogue to tell you about the characters. What does the dialogue reveal about the important characters in the story? In your *Reader/Writer Notebook,* record lines of dialogue you think are key to understanding the characters.

Reader/Writer Notebook

Use your **RWN** to complete the activities for this selection.

Vocabulary

ignoble (ihg NOH buhl) *adj.:* shameful; degrading. *The parents felt much distress because of the boys' ignoble behavior.*

exploit (EHKS ployt) *n.:* daring act. *The boys' exploit was more cruel than brave.*

daunted (DAWNT ihd) *v.* used as *adj.:* intimidated. *The young boy, daunted by his confident older friends, lacked confidence.*

fickleness (FIHK uhl nuhs) *n.:* changeableness. *The young boy's fickleness annoyed the older boy.*

altruistic (al troo IHS tihk) *adj.:* unselfish. *It was unclear whether Mr. Thomas's gift was a bribe or an altruistic act.*

exhilaration (ehg zihl uh RAY shuhn) *n.:* excitement; high spirits. *Their actions caused them to feel exhilaration despite their fear.*

abstain (ab STAYN) *v.:* refrain. *Mike abstains from destroying the house.*

stealthy (STEHL thee) *adj.:* secret; sly. *The stealthy child climbed unseen over the fence.*

Language Coach

Heteronyms The word *exploit* is a **heteronym,** a word that is pronounced differently depending on its meaning and part of speech. How and when does the pronunciation of the following heteronyms change?

1. *converse* (noun meaning "the opposite"); *converse* (verb meaning "talk")
2. *contest* (noun meaning "competition"); *contest* (verb meaning "dispute")

Learn It Online

Explore the Vocabulary words further with Word Watch online.

go.hrw.com H12-1127 Go

Selection Resources

Unit 6 Resources, on-level practice and assessment, p. 48

Teacher One Stop™, on-level lesson plans and all print resources

Holt Audio Library

Holt Audio Library: Selections and Summaries in Spanish

UA: Differentiating Instruction, graphic organizer, p. 271

UA: Supporting Instruction in Spanish, selection summary

ThinkCentral Online Assessment, Selection Standards Check

ThinkCentral Online Remediation

Preteach

Introducing Vocabulary

Use this activity to check students' understanding of the Vocabulary.

1. Give some examples of **ignoble** behavior.
2. Explain why skydiving is a daring **exploit.**
3. Discuss why someone might be **daunted** by an 800-page novel.
4. Describe why the **fickleness** of a patron might annoy a waiter.
5. List **altruistic** things that a Peace Corps worker might do.
6. Name some amusement park rides that give people a sense of **exhilaration.**
7. Explain why a person might **abstain** from coffee.
8. List some animals that are known for being **stealthy.**

English for Academic Success

Language Coach

Have students list additional heteronyms such as *bow, close, conduct, refuse* and practice the different pronunciations of each.

Literary Skills Focus

Have students note specific images that Greene describes to make the setting seem depressing.

Reading Skills Focus

Give students a copy of the Reading Skills Focus graphic organizer before they read. Have them use their responses to answer the questions on the Applying Your Skills page.

Writing Skills Focus

Have students record examples of key dialogue in their **Reader/Writer Notebooks.**

Learn It Online

Send students to **Word Watch** for audio pronunciations, synonyms and antonyms, and brief histories of word origins.

go.hrw.com H12-1127 Go

Teacher Preparation

Selection Plot Summary

In "The Destructors," T. (Trevor) assumes the leadership of the Wormsley Common gang when he suggests the destruction of a historic house that survived the German blitz. While the house's owner, Mr. Thomas, is away, the gang demolishes the house's interior. When Mr. Thomas returns early, they lock him in his outhouse. During the night, the gang weakens the house's foundation and rigs a truck parked nearby so that, on the next morning, the unwitting driver pulls down the house as he drives away. When the driver releases Mr. Thomas from the outhouse, Mr. Thomas is devastated, but the driver laughs at the situation.

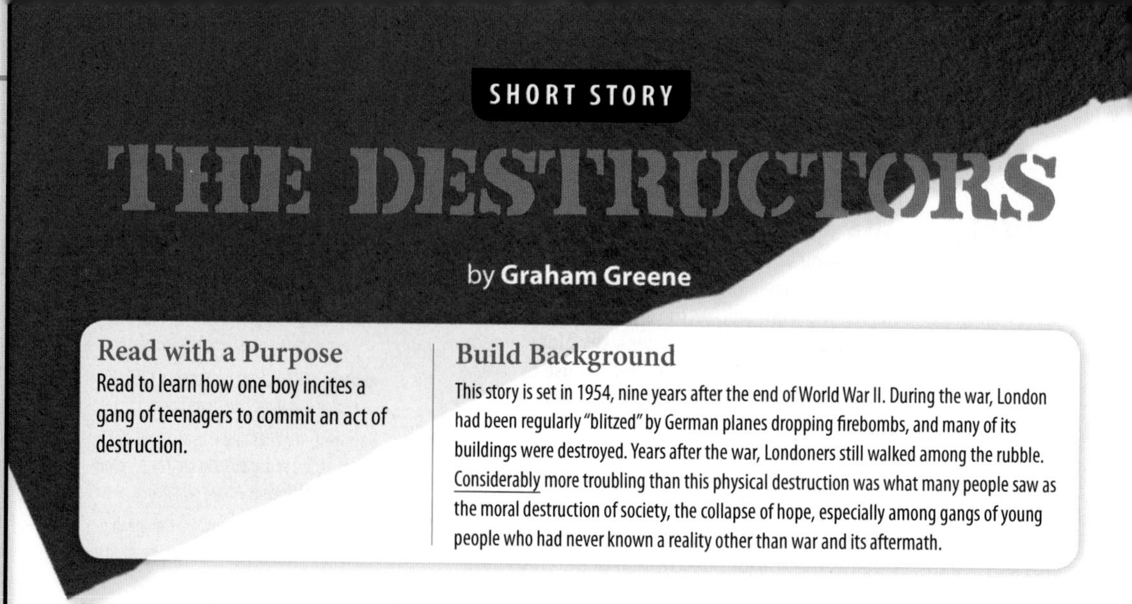

SHORT STORY

THE DESTRUCTORS

by **Graham Greene**

Read with a Purpose

Read to learn how one boy incites a gang of teenagers to commit an act of destruction.

Build Background

This story is set in 1954, nine years after the end of World War II. During the war, London had been regularly "blitzed" by German planes dropping firebombs, and many of its buildings were destroyed. Years after the war, Londoners still walked among the rubble. Considerably more troubling than this physical destruction was what many people saw as the moral destruction of society, the collapse of hope, especially among gangs of young people who had never known a reality other than war and its aftermath.

It was on the eve of August Bank Holiday that the latest recruit became the leader of the Wormsley Common gang. No one was surprised except Mike, but Mike at the age of nine was surprised by everything. "If you don't shut your mouth," somebody once said to him, "you'll get a frog down it." After that Mike had kept his teeth tightly clamped except when the surprise was too great. **A**

The new recruit had been with the gang since the beginning of the summer holidays, and there were possibilities about his brooding silence that all recognized. He never wasted a word even to tell his name until that was required of him by the rules. When he said "Trevor" it was a statement of fact, not as it would have been with the others a statement of shame or defiance. Nor did anyone laugh except Mike, who finding himself without support and meeting the dark gaze of the newcomer opened his mouth and was quiet again. There was every reason why T., as he was afterward referred to, should have been an object of mockery—there was his name (and they substituted the initial because otherwise they had no excuse not to laugh at it), the fact that his father, a former architect and present clerk, had "come down in the world" and that his mother considered herself better than the neighbors. What but an odd quality of danger, of the unpredictable, established him in the gang without any ignoble ceremony of initiation? **B**

The gang met every morning in an impromptu car-park, the site of the last bomb of the first blitz. The leader, who was known as Blackie, claimed to have heard it fall, and no one was precise enough in his dates to point out that he would have been one year old and fast asleep on the down platform of Wormsley Common Underground[1] Station. On one side of the car-park leaned the first occupied house, number 3, of the shattered Northwood Terrace—literally leaned, for it had suffered from the blast of the bomb and the side walls were supported on wooden struts. A smaller bomb and some incendiaries[2] had fallen beyond, so that the house stuck up like a jagged tooth and carried

1. **Underground:** British for "subway."
2. **incendiaries:** firebombs.

A **Literary Focus** **Setting** What are the time and place of this story?

B **Reading Focus** **Drawing Inferences About Characters' Motivations** What might be the cause of T.'s "brooding silence" and seeming unpredictability?

Vocabulary **ignoble** (ihg NOH buhl) *adj.:* shameful; degrading.

Soldiers look on at damage in Trafalgar Square caused by German bombs (1942).

Direct Teach

Think About/Talk About

Read with a Purpose Point out that the Read with a Purpose statement asks students to determine how T. is able to lead his gang to behave in a cruel manner. As you read the story, have students look for reasons why the boys fear T. enough to follow him.

Comprehension

B Reading Focus

Possible response: *T. comes from an unhappy, conflicted home, and his temperament reflects the atmosphere in which he has been raised.*

Analysis

A Literary Focus

Possible response: *The story is set in Wormsley Common on the eve of August Bank Holiday.*

Universal Access

EL English Learners

English for Academic Success Explain to students that this story uses many terms that are specific to the building trade. Have them look through the selection for unfamiliar words that relate to construction, such as *hacksaw, sledgehammer, chisel, plaster,* and *banister.* Then, have students define these terms and create drawings or find pictures of the items.

✔ See the **English Language Skill Builder** in **UA: Differentiating Instruction.**

Struggling Readers

Strategic Students Model analyzing the character of T. as he is introduced in the story. You might say: "In the beginning of the story, we learn that T. is characterized by a 'brooding silence' and that he did not speak in shame or defiance as most would expect of new gang recruits. From these details, we know that T. is different from the other boys. He seems confident, composed, yet mysterious. The last sentence of the second paragraph confirms that there is a dangerous quality about him."

on the further wall relics of its neighbor, a dado,[3] the remains of a fireplace. T., whose words were almost confined to voting "Yes" or "No" to the plan of operations proposed each day by Blackie, once startled the whole gang by saying broodingly, "Wren[4] built that house, father says." Ⓒ

"Who's Wren?"

"The man who built St. Paul's."[5]

"Who cares?" Blackie said. "It's only Old Misery's."

Old Misery—whose real name was Thomas—had once been a builder and decorator. He lived alone in the crippled house, doing for himself: Once a week you could see him coming back across the common with bread and vegetables, and once as the boys played in the car-park he put his head over the smashed wall of his garden and looked at them.

"Been to the loo,"[6] one of the boys said, for it was common knowledge that since the bombs fell something had gone wrong with the pipes of the house and Old Misery was too mean[7] to spend money on the property. He could do the redecorating himself at cost price, but he had never learned plumbing. The loo was a wooden shed at the bottom of the narrow garden with a star-shaped hole in the door: It had escaped the blast which had smashed the house next door and sucked out the window frames of number 3.

The next time the gang became aware of Mr. Thomas was more surprising. Blackie, Mike, and a thin

---

3. **dado:** wood paneling along the lower part of the walls of a room.
4. **Wren:** Sir Christopher Wren (1632–1723), a celebrated English architect.
5. **St. Paul's:** cathedral in London.
6. **loo:** British slang for "bathroom."
7. **mean:** stingy.

Ⓒ **Literary Focus** **Setting** How does the setting already seem fitting for the story's title?

Think About/Talk About

Analysis

Ⓒ Literary Focus

Possible response: *The setting consists of buildings destroyed by bombs, with one house hardly supporting itself.*

Extend the Discussion

Finding Details What descriptive details does Greene offer about T. to differentiate him from the other boys? ***Possible response:*** *T. comes from a higher social class. His father, a former architect, has "come down in the world," T.'s mother feels superior to other people in the neighborhood, and T.'s name, Trevor, seems pretentious to the other boys.*

Making Inferences What can you infer about the relationship between Old Misery and the gang? ***Possible responses:*** *The fact that the boys call him "Old Misery" suggests they see him as a gloomy man who keeps to himself; they do not seem to want to befriend him in any way. The old man may be suspicious or afraid of the gang's activities near his home.*

Vocabulary: Own the Word

ignoble: *Ignoble* means base; its antonym is *noble*. Use both words in a sentence: The reasons for war seemed noble; however, the resulting violence was *ignoble*.

Advanced Learners

Acceleration T. and Mr. Thomas share some similarities, including their initial, T., and the fact that they both understand the value and importance of architecture. What else unites these characters? Is one Old Misery and the other "young misery"? In each one's worldview, are there "only things"? Urge students to read with this focus and to jot down their ideas.

Students with Disabilities

Have students write down the name of each character mentioned in the story on separate note cards. As they read the story and learn more about each character, tell students to record quotations and descriptions from the text that reveal information about each character. For example, students might write the following about Old Misery: "lived alone in a crippled house," and "watchful of the boys." Ask students to refer to their note cards to help them complete their Reading Skills Focus graphic organizer.

Model the Skill

- Use the Reading Skills Focus graphic organizer to model **drawing inferences about characters' motivations.**
- Point out that an author's direct description often reveals a great deal about a character. When an author uses this type of description, it is easier to make inferences. For instance, Greene describes the gang's bewildered response at Mr. Thomas's friendly gesture by writing that they "were perturbed by this action and tried to explain it away," implying that the boys remain pessimistic toward adults' intentions. Tell students to note this textual reference in their charts.

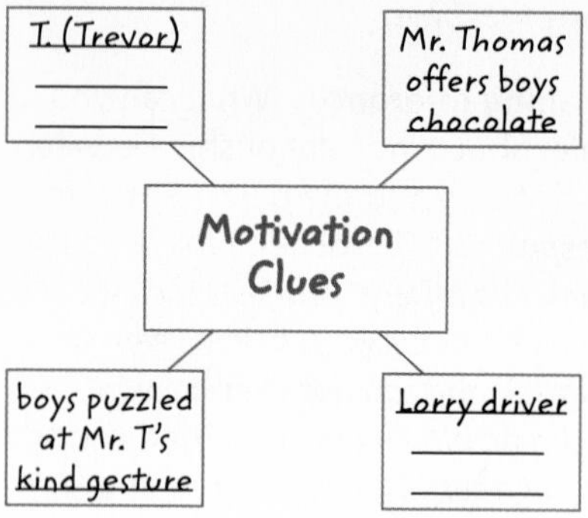

Guided Practice: Apply

Read-Talk-Write Pair students to read pp. 1130–1131, and have them look for another example of direct characterization.

Think About/Talk About

Build Background: Fleeing the Cities

Shortly after the war began in 1939, many young children were evacuated out of urban areas to the countryside. Some mothers went with their children, but more often, groups of children were sent off, each with a suitcase and gas mask, to stay with older couples in the countryside. Many of the evacuees had returned to London by the time the blitz started in 1940. They, and the others who had never been evacuated, spent many evenings sleeping in stations of the London Underground while bombs fell from the sky.

yellow boy, who for some reason was called by his surname[8] Summers, met him on the common coming back from the market. Mr. Thomas stopped them. He said glumly, "You belong to the lot that play in the car-park?"

Mike was about to answer when Blackie stopped him. As the leader he had responsibilities. "Suppose we are?" he said ambiguously.

"I got some chocolates," Mr. Thomas said. "Don't like 'em myself. Here you are. Not enough to go round, I don't suppose. There never is," he added with somber conviction. He handed over three packets of Smarties. **D**

The gang were puzzled and perturbed by this action and tried to explain it away. "Bet someone dropped them and he picked 'em up," somebody suggested.

"Pinched[9] 'em and then got in a bleeding funk," another thought aloud.

"It's a bribe," Summers said. "He wants us to stop bouncing balls on his wall."

"We'll show him we don't take bribes," Blackie said, and they sacrificed the whole morning to the game of bouncing that only Mike was young enough to enjoy. There was no sign from Mr. Thomas. **E**

Next day T. astonished them all. He was late at the rendezvous, and the voting for that day's exploit took place without him. At Blackie's suggestion the gang was to disperse in pairs, take buses at random, and see how many free rides could be snatched from unwary conductors (the operation was to be carried out in pairs to avoid cheating). They were drawing lots for their companions when T. arrived.

"Where you been, T.?" Blackie asked. "You can't vote now. You know the rules."

"I've been *there*," T. said. He looked at the ground, as though he had thoughts to hide.

"Where?"

"At Old Misery's." Mike's mouth opened and then hurriedly closed again with a click. He had remembered the frog.

"At Old Misery's?" Blackie said. There was nothing in the rules against it, but he had a sensation that T. was treading on dangerous ground. He asked hopefully, "Did you break in?"

"No. I rang the bell."

"And what did you say?"

"I said I wanted to see his house."

"What did he do?"

"He showed it me."

"Pinch anything?"

"No."

"What did you do it for then?"

The gang had gathered round: It was as though an impromptu court were about to form and to try some case of deviation. T. said, "It's a beautiful house," and still watching the ground, meeting no one's eyes, he licked his lips first one way, then the other.

"What do you mean, a beautiful house?" Blackie asked with scorn.

"It's got a staircase two hundred years old like a corkscrew. Nothing holds it up."

"What do you mean, nothing holds it up. Does it float?"

"It's to do with opposite forces, Old Misery said."

"What else?"

"There's paneling."

"Like in the Blue Boar?"

"Two hundred years old."

"Is Old Misery two hundred years old?"

Mike laughed suddenly and then was quiet again. The meeting was in a serious mood. For the first time since T. had strolled into the car-park on the first day of the holidays his position was in danger. It only needed a single use of his real name and the gang would be at his heels.

"What did you do it for?" Blackie asked. He was just, he had no jealousy, he was anxious to retain T. in the gang if he could. It was the word "beautiful" that

8. **surname:** last name.
9. **pinched:** British for "stole."

D **Reading Focus** **Drawing Inferences About Characters' Motivations** Why do you think Mr. Thomas gives the boys candy?

E **Reading Focus** **Drawing Inferences About Characters' Motivations** What do the boys think Mr. Thomas's motive is for offering them candy? What does this suggest about their attitude toward adults?

Vocabulary **exploit** (EHKS ployt) *n.:* daring act.

Cross-Curricular Connection

ARCHITECTURE: Sir Christopher Wren

Greene could have chosen any architect, but he chose Sir Christopher Wren. Why? Invite students to find out by researching Wren's career, influences, and philosophy. Form three mixed-ability groups, assign one of the three topics to each group, and have the groups report back to the whole class. Students will learn that Wren was a Renaissance man (who actually lived just after the Renaissance), gifted in mathematics and science as well as in architecture. For the purposes of this story, however, the key facts are that Wren was most notably and consistently a church architect. He was obsessed with the way the strong clarity of geometry could create beauty and focus the public's thoughts on God.

worried him—that belonged to a class world that you could still see parodied at the Wormsley Common Empire by a man wearing a top hat and a monocle,[10] with a haw-haw accent. He was tempted to say, "My dear Trevor, old chap," and unleash his hell hounds. "If you'd broken in," he said sadly—that indeed would have been an exploit worthy of the gang. **F**

"This was better," T. said. "I found out things." He continued to stare at his feet, not meeting anybody's eye, as though he were absorbed in some dream he was unwilling—or ashamed—to share.

"What things?"

"Old Misery's going to be away all tomorrow and Bank Holiday."

Blackie said with relief, "You mean we could break in?"

"And pinch things?" somebody asked.

Blackie said, "Nobody's going to pinch things. Breaking in—that's good enough, isn't it? We don't want any court stuff."

"I don't want to pinch anything," T. said. "I've got a better idea."

"What is it?"

T. raised his eyes, as gray and disturbed as the drab August day. "We'll pull it down," he said. "We'll destroy it."

Blackie gave a single hoot of laughter and then, like Mike, fell quiet, daunted by the serious implacable gaze. "What'd the police be doing all the time?" he said.

"They'd never know. We'd do it from inside. I've found a way in." He said with a sort of intensity, "We'd be like worms, don't you see, in an apple. When we came out again there'd be nothing there, no staircase, no panels, nothing but just walls, and then we'd make the walls fall down—somehow." **G**

"We'd go to jug,"[11] Blackie said.

"Who's to prove? And anyway we wouldn't have pinched anything." He added without the smallest flicker of glee, "There wouldn't be anything to pinch after we'd finished."

"I've never heard of going to prison for breaking things," Summers said.

"There wouldn't be time," Blackie said. "I've seen housebreakers at work."

"There are twelve of us," T. said. "We'd organize."

"None of us know how—"

"I know," T. said. He looked across at Blackie. "Have you got a better plan?"

"Today," Mike said tactlessly, "we're pinching free rides—"

"Free rides," T. said. "You can stand down, Blackie, if you'd rather. . . ."

"The gang's got to vote."

"Put it up then."

Blackie said uneasily, "It's proposed that tomorrow and Monday we destroy Old Misery's house."

"Here, here," said a fat boy called Joe.

"Who's in favor?"

T. said, "It's carried."

"How do we start?" Summers asked.

"He'll tell you," Blackie said. It was the end of his leadership. He went away to the back of the car-park and began to kick a stone, dribbling it this way and that. There was only one old Morris[12] in the park, for few cars were left there except lorries:[13] Without an attendant there was no safety. He took a flying kick at the car and scraped a little paint off the rear mudguard. Beyond, paying no more attention to him than to a stranger, the gang had gathered round T.; Blackie was dimly aware of the fickleness of favor. He thought of going home, of never returning, of letting them all discover the hollowness of T.'s leadership, but suppose after all what T. proposed was possible—nothing like it had ever been done before. The fame of the Wormsley

10. **monocle:** eyeglass for one eye.
11. **jug:** slang for "jail."
12. **Morris:** car made by the Morris firm, a British automaker.
13. **lorries:** British for "trucks."

F Reading Focus **Drawing Inferences About Characters' Motivations** What details in this paragraph convey the boys' distrust of the upper-class world? How might this distrust motivate them to treat T.?

G Reading Focus **Drawing Inferences About Characters' Motivations** What do you think has led T. to devise this destructive plan?

Vocabulary **daunted** (DAWNT ihd) *v.* used as *adj.:* intimidated.
fickleness (FIHK uhl nuhs) *n.:* changeableness.

Think About/Talk About

Comprehension

D Reading Focus

Possible response: *He is a lonely but kind man who hopes his gesture will endear him to the gang and help protect his property.*

E Reading Focus

Possible responses: *They guess that he found the candy somewhere, stole it, or is offering it as a bribe. The boys are suspicious and distrusting of adults.*

F Reading Focus

Possible response: *T.'s use of the word* beautiful *worries Blackie, who was tempted to mock T.*

G Reading Focus

Possible response: *T. may be trying to maintain his position as the gang's leader. His "disturbed" eyes suggest that he is beyond hope and conscience; seeing the house's beauty has inspired an urge to destroy what he cannot have. His desire to destroy an architectural masterpiece may also be a means of rebelling against his father.*

Vocabulary: Own the Word

- **exploit:** Ask students to list possible *exploits* for the gang, as Blackie does. ***Possible responses:*** *steal from a store, trespass on private property, graffiti public property*
- **daunted:** Have you ever been *daunted* by a situation? Explain when, where, and why you were *daunted.*
- **fickleness:** Ask students to list things that they might associate with *fickleness.* ***Possible responses:*** *health, wealth, personality, weather*

Universal Access

EL English Learners

English for Academic Success Review with students the difference between the possessive form of *it* and the contraction *it's*. Remind them that the word *its*, without any apostrophe, indicates possession; the contraction *it's* stands for the words *it is*. Have students point out where *it's* occurs twice on p. 1131. Then, have them compose two sentences, one with *its*, the possessive form, and another with *it's*.

AAVE Students Who Use African American Vernacular English

English for Academic Success Display the following:

- *When we came out again there'd be nothing there.*
- *When we came out again there be nothing there.*

Tell students that the second sentence is missing *will*. One can say *there would be nothing there*, but not *there be nothing there*. Remind students that the verb *will* is used with the verb *be* when expressing something that may happen in the future.

Think About/Talk About

Literary Connection

Tell students that Graham Greene's worldview is not wholly positive. Greene directly expressed his lack of faith in human nature, once remarking, "Goodness has only once found a perfect incarnation in a human body and never will again, but evil can always find a home there. Human nature is not black and white but black and gray."

Extend the Discussion

Determining the Author's Purpose How do T.'s actions make it apparent that Mike is a lesser member of the gang? ***Possible response:*** *T. singles Mike out for his first direct orders—obtaining nails and a hammer—because he knows that Mike will offer the least resistance. T. also makes it a point to tell Mike not to bring a "child's" saw.*

Symbolism Catholicism was an important force in Graham Greene's life. What element of the story's setting might possibly be construed as an allusion to Biblical legend? ***Possible response:*** *The garden in Old Misery's backyard could be symbolic of the Garden of Eden in the book of Genesis, the setting for the birth of evil and Adam and Eve's "original sin."*

PERHAPS AFTER ALL NOBODY HAD TURNED UP: THE PLAN HAD BEEN A WILD INVENTION: THEY HAD WOKEN WISER.

Common car-park gang would surely reach around London. There would be headlines in the papers. Even the grown-up gangs who ran the betting at the all-in wrestling and the barrow-boys[14] would hear with respect of how Old Misery's house had been destroyed. Driven by the pure, simple, and altruistic ambition of fame for the gang, Blackie came back to where T. stood in the shadow of Misery's wall. **H**

T. was giving his orders with decision: It was as though this plan had been with him all his life, pondered through the seasons, now in his fifteenth year crystallized with the pain of puberty. "You," he said to Mike, "bring some big nails, the biggest you can find, and a hammer. Anyone else who can better bring a hammer and a screwdriver. We'll need plenty of them. Chisels too. We can't have too many chisels. Can anybody bring a saw?"

"I can," Mike said.

"Not a child's saw," T. said. "A real saw."

Blackie realized he had raised his hand like any ordinary member of the gang.

"Right, you bring one, Blackie. But now there's a difficulty. We want a hacksaw."[15]

What's a hacksaw?" someone asked.

"You can get 'em at Woolworth's," Summers said.

The fat boy called Joe said gloomily, "I knew it would end in a collection."

"I'll get one myself," T. said. "I don't want your money. But I can't buy a sledgehammer."

Blackie said, "They are working on number fifteen. I know where they'll leave their stuff for Bank Holiday."

"Then that's all," T. said. "We meet here at nine sharp."

"I've got to go to church," Mike said.

"Come over the wall and whistle. We'll let you in."

2

On Sunday morning all were punctual except Blackie, even Mike. Mike had had a stroke of luck. His mother felt ill, his father was tired after Saturday night, and he was told to go to church alone with many warnings of what would happen if he strayed. Blackie had had difficulty in smuggling out the saw, and then in finding the sledgehammer at the back of number 15. He approached the house from a lane at the rear of the garden, for fear of the policeman's beat along the main road. The tired evergreens kept off a stormy sun: Another wet Bank Holiday was being prepared over the Atlantic, beginning in swirls of dust under the trees. Blackie climbed the wall into Misery's garden. **I**

There was no sign of anybody anywhere. The loo stood like a tomb in a neglected graveyard. The curtains were drawn. The house slept. Blackie lumbered nearer with the saw and the sledgehammer. Perhaps after all nobody had turned up: The plan had been a wild invention: They had woken wiser. But when he came close to the back door he could hear a confusion of sound, hardly louder than a hive in swarm: a clickety-clack, a bang bang bang, a scraping, a

14. **barrow-boys:** boys who sold fruit or vegetables from a barrow, or cart.
15. **hacksaw:** saw made for cutting metal.

H **Reading Focus** **Drawing Inferences About Characters' Motivations** Why does Blackie decide to support T.'s plan?

Vocabulary **altruistic** (al troo IHS tihk) *adj.:* unselfish.

I **Literary Focus** **Setting** What is the effect of the story's being set on Sunday and of the references to going to church?

Universal Access

EL English Learners

English for Academic Success Point out the word *shambles* ("a scene of ruin and disorder") in the paragraph that begins "It was nearly lunchtime . . ." on p. 1133. Point out that this word ends in *-s,* which shows it is a plural noun, but is used with a singular verb ("The kitchen was a shambles"). Have students compose a sentence using the expression "is/was a shambles" or "in a shambles."

Struggling Readers

Strategic Students Blackie, the gang's former leader, is a rather unwilling participant in T.'s scheme. During this portion of the reading, have students pay special attention to Greene's description of Blackie's arrival at the house on Sunday morning. Tell them to jot down textual evidence that suggests Blackie's reluctance to participate in the plan.

✔ See **UA: Differentiating Instruction** for a graphic organizer to scaffold instruction for struggling readers.

creaking, a sudden painful crack. He thought, It's true, and whistled.

They opened the back door to him and he came in. He had at once the impression of organization, very different from the old happy-go-lucky ways under his leadership. For a while he wandered up and down stairs looking for T. Nobody addressed him: He had a sense of great urgency, and already he could begin to see the plan. The interior of the house was being carefully demolished without touching the outer walls. Summers with hammer and chisel was ripping out the skirting-boards[16] in the ground floor dining room: He had already smashed the panels of the door. In the same room Joe was heaving up the parquet[17] blocks, exposing the soft wood floorboards over the cellar. Coils of wire came out of the damaged skirting and Mike sat happily on the floor, clipping the wires. **J**

On the curved stairs two of the gang were working hard with an inadequate child's saw on the banisters—when they saw Blackie's big saw they signaled for it wordlessly. When he next saw them a quarter of the banisters had been dropped into the hall. He found T. at last in the bathroom—he sat moodily in the least cared-for room in the house, listening to the sounds coming up from below.

"You've really done it," Blackie said with awe. "What's going to happen?"

"We've only just begun," T. said. He looked at the sledgehammer and gave his instructions. "You stay here and break the bath and the washbasin. Don't bother about the pipes. They come later."

Mike appeared at the door. "I've finished the wire, T.," he said.

"Good. You've just got to go wandering round now. The kitchen's in the basement. Smash all the china and glass and bottles you can lay hold of. Don't turn on the taps—we don't want a flood—yet. Then go into all the rooms and turn out drawers. If they are locked get one of the others to break them open. Tear up any papers you find and smash all the ornaments. Better take a carving knife with you from the kitchen. The bedroom's opposite here. Open the pillows and tear up the sheets. That's enough for the moment. And you, Blackie, when you've finished in here crack the plaster in the passage up with your sledgehammer."

"What are you going to do?" Blackie asked.

"I'm looking for something special," T. said. **K**

It was nearly lunchtime before Blackie had finished and went in search of T. Chaos had advanced. The kitchen was a shambles of broken glass and china. The dining room was stripped of parquet, the skirting was up, the door had been taken off its hinges, and the destroyers had moved up a floor. Streaks of light came in through the closed shutters where they worked with the seriousness of creators—and destruction after all is a form of creation. A kind of imagination had seen this house as it had now become.

Mike said, "I've got to go home for dinner."

"Who else?" T. asked, but all the others on one excuse or another had brought provisions with them.

They squatted in the ruins of the room and swapped unwanted sandwiches. Half an hour for lunch and they were at work again. By the time Mike returned, they were on the top floor, and by six the superficial damage was completed. The doors were all off, all the skirtings raised, the furniture pillaged and ripped and smashed—no one could have slept in the house except on a bed of broken plaster. T. gave his orders—eight o'clock next morning—and to escape notice they climbed singly over the garden wall, into the car-park. Only Blackie and T. were left; the light had nearly gone, and when they touched a switch, nothing worked—Mike had done his job thoroughly.

"Did you find anything special?" Blackie asked.

T. nodded. "Come over here," he said, "and look." Out of both pockets he drew bundles of pound notes. "Old Misery's savings," he said. "Mike ripped out the mattress, but he missed them."

"What are you going to do? Share them?"

"We aren't thieves," T. said. "Nobody's going to steal anything from this house. I kept these for you

16. **skirting-boards:** baseboards; boards placed along the base of the walls of a room.
17. **parquet** (PAR kay): fancy wood floor made of boards arranged in geometric patterns.

J Reading Focus **Drawing Inferences About Characters' Motivations** What do you think motivates the gang to put so much effort into the destruction of the house?

K Literary Focus **Setting** What is T.'s attitude toward the house he is destroying? What do his actions toward this element of the setting reveal about his thoughts and feelings?

Think About/Talk About

Comprehension

H Reading Focus

Possible response: *He rationalizes that because what T. is planning has never been done before and is on such a "monumental" scale, it will bring fame and respect to the gang.*

J Reading Focus

Possible responses: *They are eager to carry out T.'s plan, to earn his approval; they want to achieve the notoriety this act will bring them; destroying things gives them a thrill and, ironically, a sense of purpose.*

Analysis

I Literary Focus

Possible response: *The Sunday setting heightens the irony of the destruction because Sunday is the Christian Sabbath, or day of rest; it is the day Christians are often reminded in church sermons to do right and avoid evil.*

K Literary Focus

Possible responses: *T. is outwardly unemotional and sees the destruction of the house as a project to be organized and executed. He is methodically destroying for the sake of destroying.*

Vocabulary: Own the Word

altruistic: Tell students that the root word for altruistic is *alter*, which is Latin and means "other. An *altruistic* act would serve other people rather than the self. Ask students to list examples of *altruistic* acts.

Advanced Learners

Acceleration Have students consider other real-world situations that might encourage children to engage in senseless or destructive activities. How are hope and beauty minimized in these situations? Ask students to place themselves in the shoes of the leader of a non-profit organization dedicated to rebuilding a sense of purpose and community in the lives of young people. What kind of projects and programs would they develop? What kind of impact would their projects be aimed at achieving?

Students with Disabilities

After students read pp. 1132–1133, have them draw up a battle plan of what T. had in mind. Suggest that they draw an outline of the interior of the house and label the drawing based on details in the reading. When students have finished, have them compare each other's drawings and point out major details that stood out to all of them.

Model the Skill

Remind students that, throughout the selection, Graham Greene consistently describes the **setting** as a bleak, hopeless place in order to reinforce the dark nature of the boys' deed.

Guided Practice: Apply

Think-Pair-Share Have students read p. 1134 and individually jot down descriptive elements, images, or other references that convey the bleakness of the setting. Ask students to discuss their observations with a partner, then have pairs share their thoughts with the rest of the class.

Think as a Reader/Writer

Find It in Your Reading Point out that T. reacts with childish rage, stammering and protesting, when he finds out that his plan may be compromised.

Use It in Your Writing Tell students to write a short paragraph about a time when they experienced a feeling of disappointment that prompted them to react like a frustrated child. Have them describe the situation and include their reaction. Ask students to use specific details to convey the height of their distress.

and me—a celebration." He knelt down on the floor and counted them out—there were seventy in all. "We'll burn them," he said, "one by one," and taking it in turns they held a note upward and lit the top corner, so that the flame burnt slowly toward their fingers. The gray ash floated above them and fell on their heads like age. "I'd like to see Old Misery's face when we are through," T. said. **L**

"You hate him a lot?" Blackie asked.

"Of course I don't hate him," T. said. "There'd be no fun if I hated him." The last burning note illuminated his brooding face. "All this hate and love," he said, "it's soft, it's hooey. There's only things, Blackie," and he looked round the room crowded with the unfamiliar shadows of half things, broken things, former things. "I'll race you home, Blackie," he said. **M**

3

Next morning the serious destruction started. Two were missing—Mike and another boy, whose parents were off to Southend and Brighton in spite of the slow warm drops that had begun to fall and the rumble of thunder in the estuary like the first guns of the old blitz. "We've got to hurry," T. said.

Summers was restive.[18] "Haven't we done enough?" he said. "I've been given a bob for slot machines.[19] This is like work."

"We've hardly started," T. said. "Why, there's all the floors left, and the stairs. We haven't taken out a single window. You voted like the others. We are going to *destroy* this house. There won't be anything left when we've finished."

They began again on the first floor picking up the top floorboards next the outer wall, leaving the joists[20] exposed. Then they sawed through the joists and retreated into the hall, as what was left of the floor heeled and sank. They had learned with practice, and the second floor collapsed more easily. By the evening an odd exhilaration seized them as they looked down the great hollow of the house. They ran risks and made mistakes: When they thought of the windows it was too late to reach them. "Cor,"[21] Joe said, and dropped a penny down into the dry rubble-filled well. It cracked and span among the broken glass.

"Why did we start this?" Summers asked with astonishment; T. was already on the ground, digging at the rubble, clearing a space along the outer wall. "Turn on the taps," he said. "It's too dark for anyone to see now, and in the morning it won't matter." The water overtook them on the stairs and fell through the floorless rooms.

It was then they heard Mike's whistle at the back. "Something's wrong," Blackie said. They could hear his urgent breathing as they unlocked the door.

"The bogies?"[22] Summers asked.

"Old Misery," Mike said. "He's on his way." He put his head between his knees and retched. "Ran all the way," he said with pride.

"But why?" T. said. "He told me. . . ." He protested with the fury of the child he had never been, "It isn't fair."

"He was down at Southend," Mike said, "and he was on the train coming back. Said it was too cold and wet." He paused and gazed at the water. "My, you've had a storm here. Is the roof leaking?"

"How long will he be?"

"Five minutes. I gave Ma the slip and ran."

"We better clear," Summers said. "We've done enough, anyway."

"Oh, no, we haven't. Anybody could do this—" "This" was the shattered hollowed house with nothing left but the walls. Yet walls could be preserved. Façades[23] were valuable. They could build inside

18. **restive:** impatient; nervous.
19. **a bob for slot machines:** a shilling for vending machines.
20. **joists:** parallel beams that support a floor.
21. **cor:** British exclamation of strong surprise or irritation.
22. **bogies** (BOH gees): slang for "police."
23. **façades** (fuh SAHDZ): fronts of buildings.

L Reading Focus **Drawing Inferences About Characters' Motivations** Why do you think T. chooses Old Misery's money as "something special" he wants to destroy himself?

M Reading Focus **Drawing Inferences About Characters' Motivations** What do T.'s words reveal about his motivations?

Vocabulary **exhilaration** (ehg zihl uh RAY shuhn) *n.:* excitement; high spirits.

Reaching Reluctant Readers

Ask students to re-read Summers's quote in the second paragraph of the third section of text. How do his comments make it clear that he would rather not participate in the demolition of the house? Encourage students to compare their own life experiences to those detailed in the story: Have they ever done something that made them uncomfortable or nervous just to be part of a group? How does T., or any other leader for that matter, exploit the boys' desire to belong?

Analyzing Visuals

Connecting to the Text
Notice that the title of this painting is *Street Kids.* What do the figures in the painting have in common with the chracters in the story?

Street Kids (c. 1949–1951) by Joan Eardley (1921–1963).
Oil on canvas.
Scottish National Gallery of Modern Art, Edinburgh, U.K.

Think About/Talk About

See Student Edition p. 1134 for the questions that relate to the following answers.

Comprehension

L Reading Focus

Possible response: *Since T.'s family income has declined, burning Old Misery's money, rather than stealing it, may seem to T. the ultimate way to show that he finds no value in what the world finds meaningful.*

M Reading Focus

Possible response: *T. is completely detached—he neither hates nor loves; he destroys passionlessly; his tough words cover some terrible anger or shame relating to his family.*

Extend the Discussion

Characterization How does T. take advantage of his leadership role during the destruction of the house? ***Possible response:*** *He does not allow them to finish the task halfheartedly. When Summers wants to stop, for example, T. declares that they will "destroy" the house completely until nothing is left.*

Vocabulary: Own the Word

exhilaration: Role-play an expression or gesture that indicates your *exhilaration*. Ask one or two students to demonstrate at their desks.

Universal Access

Advanced Learners

Acceleration Ask students to write a physical character description of T., Blackie, Summers, Mike, and Old Misery, based on what the story reveals about each character. Tell students to include particular facial features, hair color, clothing, and physical build. Remind students that most of their description will be fictional, but should be realistic. Students who are artistically talented might opt to draw each character.

Analyzing Visuals

Connecting to the Text: *The three boys are sitting in close proximity, suggesting comradeship. The boys' relaxed body language implies that they are comfortable with each other, but makes them look idle and bored. The appearance and behavior of these street kids reminds the reader of the protagonists of this short story.*

Think About/Talk About

Extend the Discussion

Making Predictions How do you think T. feels at this point? What do you think T. will do to fix the situation? ***Possible responses:*** *T. is probably feeling nervous and desperate, as there appears a possibility for his plan to fail after all their hard work. T. might make some kind of excuse or lie to prevent Mr. Thomas from going into his house.*

Characterization What does Mr. Thomas's behavior and attitude in the loo suggest about his general outlook on life? ***Possible response:*** *After having survived the bombing only to face annihilation at the hands of a gang, Mr. Thomas feels defeated and world-weary. He puts his "head between his hands" and resigns himself to the fact that he will not be let out of captivity until the boys are ready to release him.*

again more beautifully than before. This could again be a home. He said angrily, "We've got to finish. Don't move. Let me think." **N**

"There's no time," a boy said.

"There's got to be a way," T. said. "We couldn't have got thus far . . ."

"We've done a lot," Blackie said.

"No. No, we haven't. Somebody watch the front."

"We can't do any more."

"He may come in at the back."

"Watch the back too." T. began to plead. "Just give me a minute and I'll fix it. I swear I'll fix it." But his authority had gone with his ambiguity. He was only one of the gang. "Please," he said.

"Please," Summers mimicked him, and then suddenly struck home with the fatal name. "Run along home, Trevor."

T. stood with his back to the rubble like a boxer knocked groggy against the ropes. He had no words as his dreams shook and slid. Then Blackie acted before the gang had time to laugh, pushing Summers backward. "I'll watch the front, T.," he said, and cautiously he opened the shutters of the hall. The gray wet common stretched ahead, and the lamps gleamed in the puddles. "Someone's coming, T. No, it's not him. What's your plan, T.?"

"Tell Mike to go out to the loo and hide close beside it. When he hears me whistle he's got to count ten and start to shout."

"Shout what?"

"Oh, 'Help,' anything."

"You hear, Mike," Blackie said. He was the leader again. He took a quick look between the shutters. "He's coming, T."

"Quick, Mike. The loo. Stay here, Blackie, all of you till I yell."

"Where are you going, T.?"

"Don't worry. I'll see to this. I said I would, didn't I?" **O**

Old Misery came limping off the common. He had mud on his shoes and he stopped to scrape them on the pavement's edge. He didn't want to soil his house, which stood jagged and dark between the bomb sites, saved so narrowly, as he believed, from destruction. Even the fanlight had been left unbroken by the bomb's blast. Somewhere somebody whistled. Old Misery looked sharply round. He didn't trust whistles. A child was shouting: It seemed to come from his own garden. Then a boy ran into the road from the car-park. "Mr. Thomas," he called, "Mr. Thomas."

"What is it?"

"I'm terribly sorry, Mr. Thomas. One of us got taken short, and we thought you wouldn't mind, and now he can't get out."

"What do you mean, boy?"

"He's got stuck in your loo."

"He'd no business—Haven't I seen you before?"

"You showed me your house."

"So I did. So I did. That doesn't give you the right to—"

"Do hurry, Mr. Thomas. He'll suffocate."

"Nonsense. He can't suffocate. Wait till I put my bag in."

"I'll carry your bag."

"Oh, no, you don't. I carry my own."

"This way, Mr. Thomas."

"I can't get in the garden that way. I've got to go through the house."

"But you *can* get in the garden this way, Mr. Thomas. We often do."

"You often do?" He followed the boy with a scandalized fascination. "When? What right . . ."

"Do you see . . . ? The wall's low."

"I'm not going to climb walls into my own garden. It's absurd." **P**

"This is how we do it. One foot here, one foot there, and over." The boy's face peered down, an arm shot out, and Mr. Thomas found his bag taken and deposited on the other side of the wall.

"Give me back my bag," Mr. Thomas said. From the loo a boy yelled and yelled. "I'll call the police."

N **Literary Focus** **Setting** What do you think the house represents to T.? Why is it important to him that it is utterly destroyed?

O **Reading Focus** **Drawing Inferences About Characters' Motivations** What do T.'s responses in this stressful situation reveal about his motivation?

P **Literary Focus** **Setting** What details of the setting are emphasized here? What is the significance of these details?

Cross-Curricular Connection

ARTS: Film Noir

The characters in "The Destructors" would fit perfectly in one of the violent movies known as film noir (French for "black film"). Springing from World War II's legacy of disillusionment and anxiety, these black-and-white movies of the 1940s and 1950s were filled with immoral and amoral tough guys, devious criminals, and treacherous gangs. Alienated from society, film noir characters were often not only destructive, but also self-destructive.

One of the earliest and most successful films in this genre was *Farewell, My Lovely,* a 1944 film based on a novel by Raymond Chandler. Other early noir classics include *The Killers* (1946) and *Out of the Past* (1947). In 1958, Orson Welles created one of the darkest examples of film noir, *Touch of Evil*. What links these movies is a mood of paranoia, corruption, and fatalism. More recent noir classics included *Mean Streets* (1973), *Taxi Driver* (1976), and *Blood Simple* (1984). *One False Move* (1992) and *L.A. Confidential* (1997) exemplify the genre at the end of the twentieth century.

"Your bag's all right, Mr. Thomas. Look. One foot there. On your right. Now just above. To your left." Mr. Thomas climbed over his own garden wall. "Here's your bag, Mr. Thomas."

"I'll have the wall built up," Mr. Thomas said. "I'll not have you boys coming over here, using my loo." He stumbled on the path, but the boy caught his elbow and supported him. "Thank you, thank you, my boy," he murmured automatically. Somebody shouted again through the dark. "I'm coming, I'm coming," Mr. Thomas called. He said to the boy beside him, "I'm not unreasonable. Been a boy myself. As long as things are done regular. I don't mind you playing round the place Saturday mornings. Sometimes I like company. Only it's got to be regular. One of you asks leave and I say Yes. Sometimes I'll say No. Won't feel like it. And you come in at the front door and out at the back. No garden walls." Q

"Do get him out, Mr. Thomas."

"He won't come to any harm in my loo," Mr. Thomas said, stumbling slowly down the garden. "Oh, my rheumatics,"[24] he said. "Always get 'em on Bank Holiday. I've got to go careful. There's loose stones here. Give me your hand. Do you know what my horoscope said yesterday? 'Abstain from any dealings in first half of week. Danger of serious crash.' That might be on this path," Mr. Thomas said. "They speak in parables and double meanings." He paused at the door of the loo. "What's the matter in there?" he called. There was no reply.

"Perhaps he's fainted," the boy said.

"Not in my loo. Here, you, come out," Mr. Thomas said, and giving a great jerk at the door he nearly fell on his back when it swung easily open. A hand first supported him and then pushed him hard. His head hit the opposite wall and he sat heavily down. His bag hit his feet. A hand whipped the key out of the lock and the door slammed. "Let me out," he called, and heard the key turn in the lock. "A serious crash," he thought, and felt dithery and confused and old.

24. **rheumatics:** type of severe arthritis.

A voice spoke to him softly through the star-shaped hole in the door. "Don't worry, Mr. Thomas," it said, "we won't hurt you, not if you stay quiet."

Mr. Thomas put his head between his hands and pondered. He had noticed that there was only one lorry in the car-park, and he felt certain that the driver would not come for it before the morning. Nobody could hear him from the road in front, and the lane at the back was seldom used. Anyone who passed there would be hurrying home and would not pause for what they would certainly take to be drunken cries. And if he did call "Help," who, on a lonely Bank Holiday evening, would have the courage to investigate? Mr. Thomas sat on the loo and pondered with the wisdom of age. R

After a while it seemed to him that there were sounds in the silence—they were faint and came from the direction of his house. He stood up and peered through the ventilation-hole—between the cracks in one of the shutters he saw a light, not the light of a lamp, but the wavering light that a candle might give. Then he thought he heard the sound of hammering and scraping and chipping. He thought of burglars—perhaps they had employed the boy as a scout, but why should burglars engage in what sounded more and more like a stealthy form of carpentry? Mr. Thomas let out an experimental yell, but nobody answered. The noise could not even have reached his enemies.

4

Mike had gone home to bed, but the rest stayed. The question of leadership no longer concerned the gang. With nails, chisels, screwdrivers, anything that was sharp and penetrating they moved around the inner walls worrying at the mortar between the bricks. They started too high, and it was Blackie who hit on the damp course[25] and realized the work could be halved if they weakened the joints immediately above. It was a

25. **damp course:** layer of waterproof material placed between two layers of brick in a house's foundation to keep moisture from rising up through the walls.

Q Reading Focus Drawing Inferences About Characters' Motivations What do these comments suggest about Mr. Thomas?

R Literary Focus Setting What message do you think is conveyed by the setting of this scene?

Vocabulary **abstain** (ab STAYN) *v.:* refrain.
stealthy (STEHL thee) *adj.:* secret; sly.

Developing Oral Fluency

Small-Group Activity Several scenes in the story consist primarily of dialogue, such as the conversation between T. and the gang after T. has seen Old Misery's house. Have students work in small groups to choose a scene and prepare a dramatic reading. Remind them to choose one member of the group to be the narrator who reads the lines that are not direct quotations.

✔ See the **Oral Language Skill Builder** in **UA: Differentiating Instruction.**

Think About/Talk About

Comprehension

Q Reading Focus

Possible responses: *He thinks quickly; he has qualities of leadership; he is single-minded and efficient.*

Q Reading Focus

Possible response: *Mr. Thomas prefers having set rules and boundaries in life. He believes in courtesy and respect when it comes to someone's privacy. However, he is basically kind and flexible. He does not mind sharing his property with the boys, provided they show the requisite degree of respect.*

Analysis

N Literary Focus

Possible responses: *The house, which has survived the terrors of war and preserved the achievements of another time period, represents meaning, beauty, and hope. Total destruction is T.'s way of asserting his own nihilistic philosophy that everything in life is worthless.*

P Literary Focus

Possible responses: *The garden and its low walls are emphasized. The vulnerability of the grounds suggests that Old Misery has inadequate defenses against the evil that T. is promoting.*

R Literary Focus

Possible response: *Locking Mr. Thomas in the loo, a dirty, humiliating place, further emphasizes the darkness of the overall plot: even when the boys are confronted face-to-face with their victim, they afford him no dignity.*

Vocabulary: Own the Word

- **abstain:** Ask students to complete the following statement: A person might *abstain* from eating sweets if . . .
- **stealthy:** Explain to students that *stealthy* comes from *steal.* A person who steals tends to be *stealthy* to avoid attention during the theft. Ask students to name other reasons for *stealthy* behavior.

Think About/Talk About

Comprehension

Ⓢ Reading Focus

Possible response: *The boys are primarily interested in doing psychological damage to Mr. Thomas. If they harm their victim, it may detract from the shock and horror they want him to experience.*

Analysis

Ⓣ Literary Focus

Possible response: *Because of the war—the destruction, death, the Holocaust, the atomic bomb—the sensibilities of people would never be the same. The world had become a different place physically, politically, psychologically, culturally, and spiritually.*

Monitor Students' Comprehension

Guide the class in answering these comprehension questions.

1. How does the setting of "The Destructors" reflect the overall theme and mood of the story? [*The dreary nature of the old home reflects the isolation and disenchantment that many people—including the gang—felt during the postwar era.*]
2. What motivates T. to destroy the home of an innocent old man? [*T., a jaded, unfeeling youth, is jealous that Old Misery still has something of value and meaning in his life and wishes to crush what is left of the old man's optimism.*]
3. Why do the other boys in the gang follow T.'s lead? [*They have never encountered a boy as cynical and sophisticated as T.*]

long, tiring, unamusing job, but at last it was finished. The gutted house stood there balanced on a few inches of mortar between the damp course and the bricks.

There remained the most dangerous task of all, out in the open at the edge of the bomb site. Summers was sent to watch the road for passers by, and Mr. Thomas, sitting on the loo, heard clearly now the sound of sawing. It no longer came from his house, and that a little reassured him. He felt less concerned. Perhaps the other noises too had no significance.

A voice spoke to him through the hole. "Mr. Thomas."

"Let me out," Mr. Thomas said sternly.

"Here's a blanket," the voice said, and a long gray sausage was worked through the hole and fell in swathes over Mr. Thomas's head.

"There's nothing personal," the voice said. "We want you to be comfortable tonight."

"Tonight," Mr. Thomas repeated incredulously.

"Catch," the voice said. "Penny buns—we've buttered them, and sausage-rolls. We don't want you to starve, Mr. Thomas." Ⓢ

Mr. Thomas pleaded desperately. "A joke's a joke, boy. Let me out and I won't say a thing. I've got rheumatics. I got to sleep comfortable."

"You wouldn't be comfortable, not in your house, you wouldn't. Not now."

"What do you mean, boy?" but the footsteps receded. There was only the silence of night: no sound of sawing. Mr. Thomas tried one more yell, but he was daunted and rebuked by the silence—a long way off an owl hooted and made away again on its muffled flight through the soundless world.

At seven next morning the driver came to fetch his lorry. He climbed into the seat and tried to start the engine. He was vaguely aware of a voice shouting, but it didn't concern him. At last the engine responded and he backed the lorry until it touched the great wooden shore[26] that supported Mr. Thomas's house.

HE GAVE A SOBBING CRY. "MY HOUSE," HE SAID. "WHERE'S MY HOUSE?"

That way he could drive right out and down the street without reversing. The lorry moved forward, was momentarily checked as though something were pulling it from behind, and then went on to the sound of a long rumbling crash. The driver was astonished to see bricks bouncing ahead of him, while stones hit the roof of his cab. He put on his brakes. When he climbed out the whole landscape had suddenly altered. There was no house beside the car-park, only a hill of rubble. He went round and examined the back of his car for damage, and found a rope tied there that was still twisted at the other end round part of a wooden strut. Ⓣ

The driver again became aware of somebody shouting. It came from the wooden erection which was the nearest thing to a house in that desolation of broken brick. The driver climbed the smashed wall and unlocked the door. Mr. Thomas came out of the loo. He was wearing a gray blanket to which flakes of pastry adhered. He gave a sobbing cry. "My house," he said. "Where's my house?"

"Search me," the driver said. His eye lit on the remains of a bath and what had once been a dresser and he began to laugh. There wasn't anything left anywhere.

"How dare you laugh," Mr. Thomas said. "It was my house. My house."

"I'm sorry," the driver said, making heroic efforts, but when he remembered the sudden check to his lorry, the crash of bricks falling, he became convulsed again. One moment the house had stood there with such dignity between the bomb sites like a man in a top hat, and then, bang, crash, there wasn't anything left—not anything. He said, "I'm sorry. I can't help it, Mr. Thomas. There's nothing personal, but you got to admit it's funny."

26. **shore:** beam.

Ⓢ **Reading Focus** **Drawing Inferences About Characters' Motivations** Why do you think the boys give Mr. Thomas a blanket and some buns?

Ⓣ **Literary Focus** **Setting** How might the phrase "the whole landscape had suddenly altered" describe many countries following World War II?

California Standards, p. 1139

- **Reading Standard 3.2** Analyze the way in which the theme or meaning of a selection represents a view or comment on life, using textual evidence to support the claim.
- **Reading Standard 3.7** Analyze recognized works of world literature from a variety of authors: **c.** Evaluate the philosophical, political, religious, ethical, and social influences of the historical period that shaped the characters, plots, and settings.
- **Grades 9–10 Review Reading Standard 3.4** Determine characters' traits by what the characters say about themselves in narration, dialogue, dramatic monologue, and soliloquy.
- **Writing Standard 2.1** Write fictional, autobiographical, or biographical narratives: **a.** Narrate a sequence of events and communicate their significance to the audience.

Applying Your Skills

Reading Standard 3.2, 3.7c Grades 9–10 Review
Reading Standard 3.4 (see pages A48–A50)
Writing Standard 2.1a (see pages A51–A52)

The Destructors

Literary Response and Analysis

Reading Skills Focus

Quick Check

1. The gang's hierarchy, or leadership structure, is important at the beginning of the story. Why do you think the gang is no longer concerned with who is the leader as they destroy the house?
2. How does the destruction of the house deviate from the gang's normal activities?

Read with a Purpose

3. How could tearing down Mr. Thomas's house be seen as an expression of T.'s feelings of loss?

Reading Skills: Drawing Inferences About Characters' Motivations

4. Using the clues you collected for your spider map, draw inferences about the motivations of T., the other gang members, Mr. Thomas, and the lorry driver.

Vocabulary Check

Match the Vocabulary words with their definitions.

5. altruistic	a. shameful
6. exploit	b. secret
7. abstain	c. daring act
8. daunted	d. intimidated
9. stealthy	e. unselfish
10. ignoble	f. changeableness
11. fickleness	g. high excitement
12. exhilaration	h. refrain

Literary Skills Focus

Literary Analysis

13. **Analyze** A gang is a social group with a shared set of values. What are this gang's values, and where do you think they come from?
14. **Interpret** How would you explain T.'s response when Blackie asks if he hates Mr. Thomas? In what sense does T.'s response reveal what might happen even to children in the aftermath of war?
15. **Extend** Images of emptiness and internal rot appear throughout the story. Identify these images and explain how they apply to the house, to Wormsley Common, and to the characters.

Literary Skills: Setting

16. **Evaluate** Describe the setting of the Wormsley Common carpark and its surroundings. How does it add to the story's emotional atmosphere?

Literary Skills Review: Theme

17. **Interpret** A story's **theme** is the general message that it conveys. Consider the comparison the lorry driver makes between the house and a "top hat." How does this relate to the theme?

Writing Skills Focus

Think as a Reader/Writer

Use It in Your Writing Using Greene's dialogue as a model, write a short conversation between two people that reveals important information about their personalities.

What Do You Think Now Why do you think the young boys in this story were so eager to belong to a group?

Universal Access

Struggling Writers

Some students may need additional scaffolding to complete the Writing Skills Focus activity. Before students write their dialogue, have them brainstorm situations that would spark a short dialogue. Then, have them write a short description of the two characters' personalities. Have them think about whether their characters will be talkative or more reserved, and what kind of language each character will use. Tell students to include a short description of the setting in the beginning of their dialogue.

What Do You Think Now?

Ask students to consider their life experiences. What groups or clubs have they belonged to thus far? Did it make them feel good to be part of a group? Why or why not?

Assess

Unit 6 Resources,
Selection Standards Check, p. 51

Check for Understanding

Independent Practice

Reading Skills Focus

Possible responses:

1. *Once they accept T.'s orders and go about their task, they become absorbed more in the work that they will produce as a team.*
2. *The gang's energy is focused on destroying the house.*
3. *T. has lost his capacity to care about life. He wants to deprive Mr. Thomas of the one thing he values: his home.*
4. *Have students make inferences about the reasons for their actions and words.*

Vocabulary Check

5. *e* 6. *c* 7. *h*
8. *d* 9. *b* 10. *a*
11. *f* 12. *g*

Literary Skills Focus

Possible responses:

13. *The gang values amusement, destruction, and their reputation. These values may arise from their inability to find purpose.*
14. *T. denies hating Mr. Thomas because it diminishes the joy of destroying. T.'s words suggest that the alienation from war can give rise to random crime and have negative psychological effects.*
15. *At one point, the boys are able to look down the "great hollow" of the house. The members of the gang are hollow in that they band together just to avoid loneliness and boredom. Wormsley Common is empty of purpose and damaged internally.*
16. *The area is lonely and desolate, heightening the mood of alienation.*
17. *The war has caused the social structure to collapse. Both upper and lower classes feel uneasy about the strangeness of the new world.*

Standards Focus

Objectives

Students will
- analyze irony, including verbal and situational irony
- determine the writer's purpose or intent

Selection Introduction

Think About the Writer

To help students answer the question, ask them to think about the values and concerns of the working class. Then, have them consider how these matters shape people's political views.

For Independent Reading

- *The Orwell Reader**, George Orwell
- *A Brave New World,* Aldous Huxley

HRW LIBRARY *This title is available in the HRW library.

Motivate

What Do You Think?/QuickWrite

Have students think about things that they, or their peers, have done as a result of peer pressure. Then, have the students use their **Reader/Writer Notebooks** to write about how peer pressure can sometimes overrule a person's better judgment.

English for Academic Success

Academic Vocabulary

Look for opportunities to use the Academic Vocabulary words in this unit.
- **exhibit,** ***v.:*** show, demonstrate
- **inevitable,** ***adv.:*** unavoidable
- **perspective,** ***n.:*** particular way of looking at something

Preparing to Read

Shooting an Elephant

What Do You Think? How does experience shape our view of the world?

QuickWrite

What compels people to act against their better judgment? How might outside pressures affect people's decision-making? Record some thoughts in your *Reader/Writer Notebook.*

George Orwell broadcasting over BBC, London (1943). The Granger Collection, NY.

MEET THE WRITER

George Orwell

(1903–1950)

George Orwell is famous for his novels that depict a frightening vision of a totalitarian future. He wrote, "Every line of serious work that I have written since 1936 has been written, directly or indirectly, *against* totalitarianism and *for* democratic socialism."

Child Writer

George Orwell was born Eric Blair in Bengal, India, where his British father was a member of the Indian civil service. A few years later, his family returned to England. A lonely child, Orwell spent much time making up stories and poems. He later wrote that from an early age he knew he was going to be a writer.

After graduating from Eton College, a prep school, Orwell joined the Indian Imperial Police, serving in Burma (now Myanmar) from 1922 to 1927, when he resigned to devote more time to writing. Returning to Europe, he took part-time, ill-paying jobs in France and England. His first book, *Down and Out in Paris and London* (1933), is based on those experiences. He based his next novel, *Burmese Days* (1934), on his life in Burma.

Fighter of Fascism

Writing under his own name as a journalist, Orwell used the pseudonym George Orwell for his books. After publishing three novels, he wrote about conditions among English industrial workers for the socialist Left Book Club. *The Road to Wigan Pier* (1937) is a moving portrait of the lives of the working class.

Deeply disturbed by the rise of fascism in the 1930s, Orwell fought against the Nationalists (fascists) in the Spanish Civil War and published a book based on these experiences—*Homage to Catalonia* (1938). His most famous novels, *Animal Farm* (1945) and *1984* (1949), exhibit his dedication to political freedom. *Animal Farm* is a political allegory that reveals the dangers of totalitarianism. And *1984* has given us an entire vocabulary for the excesses of totalitarian regimes, including the terms *newspeak* and *Big Brother.* In *1984,* Orwell stresses the connections between language, thought, and power and shows how corrupt language can promote political oppression.

Think About the Writer How might Orwell's own experiences working at low-paying jobs have affected his political views?

California Standards, pp. 1140–1149

- **Reading Standard 2.5** Analyze an author's implicit and explicit philosophical assumptions and beliefs about a subject.
- **Reading Standard 3.3** Analyze the ways in which irony, tone, mood, the author's style, and the "sound" of language achieve specific rhetorical or aesthetic purposes or both.

Selection Readability	
Easily Accessible **Accessible** Challenging	background information; simple sentence structure; familiar language

Reading Standard 2.5, 3.3 (see pages A48–A50)

Literary Skills Focus

Irony A discrepancy between expectation and reality or between appearance and reality is called **irony.** Irony is the dominant literary mode in the twentieth century. Orwell employs several strategies to create irony. He uses **verbal irony,** saying one thing and meaning something else (often just the opposite), and **situational irony,** in which something happens that is different from what is expected or appropriate.

Reading Skills Focus

Identifying the Author's Purpose The purpose of an **informal essay,** such as this one by Orwell, is often to express the personality and opinions of its author. In the essay's first sentence, Orwell admits that he was "hated by large numbers of people" in Burma because he represented British tyranny. This hatred controlled and at times even tyrannized Orwell himself. This ironic situation was not Orwell's alone; it was shared by most colonists. The ironies Orwell points out, as well as other details, can help you **identify the author's purpose.**

Into Action Make a chart like the one below. In one column, list details describing Orwell's personal dilemma in the essay, and in the second, list details describing the cultural dilemma presented by colonialism. Think about how these dilemmas relate to his purpose for writing.

Orwell's Personal Dilemma	Colonialism's Cultural Dilemma
He's "in charge" but feels pressured by the group.	

Writing Skills Focus

Think as a Reader/Writer

Find It in Your Reading When describing events from their past, writers often remark on their motivations at the time. In your *Reader/Writer Notebook,* note when Orwell shifts from storytelling to commenting on his own thoughts and actions. How does this technique help him reveal **situational irony?** What clarity about the situation does he have from the vantage point of the future?

TechFocus As you read, think about how Orwell shares his personal experience. What experience would you like to share in a digital story?

Reader/Writer Notebook

Use your **RWN** to complete the activities for this selection.

Vocabulary

perplexing (puhr PLEHK sihng) *v.* used as *adj.:* confusing. *Because he secretly supported the Burmese, Orwell found their hatred of him perplexing.*

wretched (REHCH ihd) *adj.:* miserable; deprived. *The convicts were wretched in their filthy prisons.*

supplant (suh PLANT) *v.:* replace; displace. *Young Orwell did not realize that one empire could just as easily supplant another.*

squalid (SKWAHL ihd) *adj.:* foul; dirty. *Many villagers lived in squalid conditions that caused disease and unhappiness.*

unendurable (uhn ehn DUR uh buhl) *adj.:* more than can be tolerated. *To be squashed by an elephant would be unendurable.*

innumerable (ih NOO muhr uh buhl) *adj.:* too many to count. *Orwell was overwhelmed by the innumerable crowd following him through the streets.*

pretext (PREE tehkst) *n.:* excuse. *The British used the law as a pretext for both subtle and overt forms of racism.*

Language Coach

Negative Prefixes Adding the prefixes *–in* and *–un* to the beginning of a word often produces a word with the opposite meaning. For example, *unendurable* means "not able to be tolerated or endured." What other Vocabulary word uses the prefix *–in* or *–un?* How does the prefix help you understand the meaning of the word?

Learn It Online
Learn more about Orwell at the Writers' Lives site.

go.hrw.com H12-1141 Go

Selection Resources

Unit 6 Resources, on-level practice and assessment, p. 54

Teacher One Stop™, on-level lesson plans and all print resources

Holt Audio Library

Holt Audio Library: Selections and Summaries in Spanish

UA: Differentiating Instruction, graphic organizer, p. 272

UA: Supporting Instruction in Spanish, selection summary

ThinkCentral Online Assessment, Selection Standards Check

ThinkCentral Online Remediation

Preteach

Introducing Vocabulary

Read aloud the Vocabulary words and sample sentences. Then, use this activity to check students' understanding.

1. Living conditions at the refugee camp are incredibly ______. [*squalid*]
2. I came up with some silly ______ for my lateness. [*pretext*]
3. Do you think that e-mail will ______ letter writing? [*supplant*]
4. I had the flu all week and felt ______. [*wretched*]
5. I do not understand what they were thinking. The whole situation is ______. [*perplexing*]
6. The political situation in that country has become ______ for many citizens. [*unendurable*]
7. The houses destroyed by the disaster were ______. [*innumerable*]

English for Academic Success

Language Coach

Have students write a sentence using a word with the prefix *–in* or *–un* in context.

Literary Skills Focus

As you read and discuss the selection with students, have them note the ways in which Orwell uses verbal and situational irony.

Reading Skills Focus

Give students a copy of the Reading Skills Focus graphic organizer before they read. (See **Unit 6 Resources.**)

Writing Skills Focus

Have students record Orwell's techniques for creating situational irony in their **Reader/Writer Notebooks.**

Learn It Online
The **Writers' Lives** feature of the Interactive Student Edition offers additional information about this author. Audio or video segments are provided for some authors.

go.hrw.com H12-1141 Go

Teacher Preparation
Selection Summary
Orwell recounts an experience he had while serving as a police officer of the British Empire in colonial Burma (now called Myanmar). One day, a frenzied elephant goes on a rampage in a bazaar, killing one person. By the time Orwell arrives on the scene to deal with the matter, a large crowd of Burmese has gathered to watch. Although he hates his job (which he calls doing "the dirty work of the Empire") and does not want to kill the elephant, Orwell feels pressured by the crowd and his position to take action; otherwise, he will risk looking foolish. He therefore shoots the animal repeatedly and awkwardly, causing the elephant a protracted and agonizing death.

Direct Teach

Think About/Talk About
Read with a Purpose Have students read the Read with a Purpose statement. Call students' attention to the phrase "overwhelming pressure to act against his conscience." As students read, have them look for the source of this pressure.

ESSAY

Shooting an Elephant

by **George Orwell**

Read with a Purpose
Read this essay to discover how a British police officer in a British colony deals with overwhelming pressure to act against his conscience.

Build Background
This essay is set in Burma, a southeast Asian country conquered by the British in the 1800s. As a British police officer in Burma in the 1920s, George Orwell did not just symbolize foreign rule—he was its agent. His awareness of being an enemy in another culture kindled enormous conflicts within him. Though given some self-rule in 1937, Burma did not become fully independent until 1948, after a harsh period of Japanese occupation during World War II. In 1989, the government changed the country's official name to the Union of Myanmar, the country's Burmese name since the 13th century.

A British soldier serving in India (1912).

Universal Access

English Learners
English for Academic Success In his essay, Orwell often uses words that were borrowed from other languages and given English pronunciations and spellings. Before students begin reading, call attention to the terms *raj, mahout, coolie,* and *sahib.* Point out that the footnotes give the pronunciation, derivation, and meaning of each word. Ask students to think about Orwell's purpose behind including these words.

Struggling Readers
To help students read "Shooting an Elephant," model the reading skill of identifying the author's purpose. Choose a paragraph from this page and ask, "What does Orwell talk about here? How does he feel about it?" Demonstrate how students can put together statements and highly connotative words to conclude that his purpose at this point is to recall the animosity that the Burmese felt toward the British and Orwell's dislike of his job. Have students read on to see if Orwell maintains that purpose as the essay continues.

In Moulmein, in Lower Burma, I was hated by large numbers of people—the only time in my life that I have been important enough for this to happen to me. I was subdivisional police officer of the town, and in an aimless, petty kind of way anti-European feeling was very bitter. No one had the guts to raise a riot, but if a European woman went through the bazaars alone somebody would probably spit betel juice over her dress. As a police officer I was an obvious target and was baited whenever it seemed safe to do so. When a nimble Burman tripped me up on the football field and the referee (another Burman) looked the other way, the crowd yelled with hideous laughter. This happened more than once. In the end the sneering yellow faces of young men that met me everywhere, the insults hooted after me when I was at a safe distance, got badly on my nerves. The young Buddhist priests were the worst of all. There were several thousands of them in the town and none of them seemed to have anything to do except stand on street corners and jeer at Europeans. **A**

All this was perplexing and upsetting. For at that time I had already made up my mind that imperialism was an evil thing and the sooner I chucked up my job and got out of it the better. Theoretically—and secretly, of course—I was all for the Burmese and all against their oppressors, the British. As for the job I was doing, I hated it more bitterly than I can perhaps make clear. In a job like that you see the dirty work of Empire at close quarters. The wretched prisoners huddling in the stinking cages of the lockups, the gray, cowed faces of the long-term convicts, the scarred buttocks of the men who had been flogged with bamboos—all these oppressed me with an intolerable sense of guilt. But I could get nothing into perspective. I was young and ill-educated and I had had to think out my problems in the utter silence that is imposed on every Englishman in the East. I did not even know that the British Empire is dying, still less did I know that it is a great deal better than the younger empires that are going to supplant it. All I knew was that I was stuck between my hatred of the empire I served and my rage against the evil-spirited little beasts who tried to make my job impossible. With one part of my mind I thought of the British Raj[1] as an unbreakable tyranny, as something clamped down, *in saecula saeculorum,*[2] upon the will of prostrate peoples; with another part I thought that the greatest joy in the world would be to drive a bayonet into a Buddhist priest's guts. Feelings like these are the normal by-products of imperialism; ask any Anglo-Indian official, if you can catch him off duty. **B**

One day something happened which in a roundabout way was enlightening. It was a tiny incident in itself, but it gave me a better glimpse than I had had before of the real nature of imperialism—the real motives for which despotic governments act. Early one morning the subinspector at a police station the other end of the town rang me up on the phone and said that an elephant was ravaging the bazaar. Would I please come and do something about it? I did not know what I could do, but I wanted to see what was happening and I got on to a pony and started out. I took my rifle, an old .44 Winchester and much too small to kill an elephant, but I thought the noise might be useful *in terrorem.*[3] Various Burmans stopped me on the way and told me about the elephant's doings. It was not, of course, a wild elephant, but a tame one which had gone "must."[4] It had been chained up, as tame elephants always are when their attack of "must" is due, but on the previous night it had broken its

1. **Raj** (rahj): rule over India. The word is derived from *rajya,* Hindi for "kingdom."
2. ***in saecula saeculorum*** (ihn SEE koo luh SEE koo LAWR uhm): Latin for "forever and ever" (literally, "into ages of ages").
3. ***in terrorem*** (ihn tehr AWR uhm): Latin for "for terror." In other words, the gun might serve to frighten the elephant.
4. **must:** state of frenzy in animals. The word comes from *mast,* Hindi for "intoxicated."

A **Literary Focus** **Irony** How is the first sentence of the essay an example of situational irony?

B **Literary Focus** **Irony** What is ironic about the statement that begins, "All I knew was that I was stuck . . ."?

Vocabulary **perplexing** (puhr PLEHK sihng) *v.* used as *adj.:* confusing.
wretched (REHCH ihd) *adj.:* miserable; deprived.
supplant (suh PLANT) *v.:* replace; displace.

Advanced Learners

Acceleration Suggest that students consider this essay from the point of view of one of the Burmese bystanders (for example, the elephant's owner) and analyze how the essay's main idea changes when events are viewed from a radically different point of view. Have students summarize the fourth paragraph on pp. 1143–1144 once from the narrator's point of view and again from the mahout's point of view. Ask students to compare and contrast the two summaries and consider how their differences reflect the author's purpose.

Students with Disabilities

Ask students to construct a character web to explore Orwell's personality traits and make inferences about his background from the first three paragraphs. For example, from the first sentence, one can infer that Orwell had never previously occupied a position that carried as much power and status as a foreign police officer of a town.

✔ See **UA: Differentiating Instruction** for a graphic organizer to scaffold instruction for students with disabilities.

Think About/Talk About

Analysis

A Literary Focus

Possible response: *The narrator feels important only because he is hated.*

B Literary Focus

Possible response: *Orwell hates the notion of empire, with its built-in assumptions of power and superiority; in the same breath, however, he expresses a resentful and condescending attitude toward "the evil-spirited little beasts" that he helps to oppress.*

Extend the Discussion

Monitoring Your Reading How does Orwell describe his emotional reactions to his situation? Why does he hate his job in the colonial government? ***Possible responses:*** *His reactions are "perplexing" and "upsetting." He does not like seeing "the dirty work of Empire at close quarters" and being forced to take part in it.*

Vocabulary: Own the Word

- **perplexing:** Draw a semantic web on the chalkboard with *perplexing* written in the center circle. Have students suggest words and concepts associated with *perplexing* and record them in the web. ***Possible responses:*** *confusing, befuddling, puzzling*
- **wretched:** Provide a personal context by asking students: "Why might you feel *wretched?*" ***Possible responses:*** *feeling unprepared for an exam, fight with a friend*
- **supplant:** Tell students that the root word for *supplant* is *supplantāre,* which is Latin for "to overthrow." When you *supplant* a ruler, you overthrow and replace him or her.

Model the Skill

- Provide students with copies of the Reading Skill Focus graphic organizer (See **Unit 6 Resources**.)
- Tell students that people often look back on their youthful actions with a new perspective—one that is almost impossible to have at the time one lives through a particular situation. Orwell uses this hindsight to expose the problems he sees with colonialism. This is his reason—or **purpose**—for writing.
- Model identifying the author's purpose. You might say: "On p. 1145, Orwell describes his realization that '[he] ought not to shoot [the elephant]' because it had ended its rampage. In the next paragraph, he describes the crowd of natives goading him on by their very presence and their expectations. He realizes that he will have to kill the elephant because the natives will laugh at him if walks away. By describing his experiences in Burma, Orwell exposes behaviors exhibited by many colonialists."

Orwell's Personal Dilemma	Colonialism's Cultural Dilemma
The elephant ended its rampage, but the narrator feels pressure from the crowd to shoot it.	The struggle between who is in charge, the Burmese or the British.

Guided Practice: Apply

Turn-and-Talk Have students re-read the two paragraphs beginning with "I had halted . . ." on p. 1145. After re-reading, ask students to discuss how Orwell must have felt after seeing the crowd and why he was conflicted.

chain and escaped. Its mahout,[5] the only person who could manage it when it was in that state, had set out in pursuit, but had taken the wrong direction and was now twelve hours' journey away, and in the morning the elephant had suddenly reappeared in the town. The Burmese population had no weapons and were quite helpless against it. It had already destroyed somebody's bamboo hut, killed a cow, and raided some fruit stalls and devoured the stock; also it had met the municipal rubbish van and, when the driver jumped out and took to his heels, had turned the van over and inflicted violences upon it. **C**

The Burmese subinspector and some Indian constables were waiting for me in the quarter where the elephant had been seen. It was a very poor quarter, a labyrinth of squalid bamboo huts, thatched with palm leaf, winding all over a steep hillside. I remember that it was a cloudy, stuffy morning at the beginning of the rains. We began questioning the people as to where the elephant had gone and, as usual, failed to get any definite information. That is invariably the case in the East; a story always sounds clear enough at a distance, but the nearer you get to the scene of events the vaguer it becomes. Some of the people said that the elephant had gone in one direction, some said that he had gone in another, some professed not even to have heard of any elephant. I had almost made up my mind that the whole story was a pack of lies, when we heard yells a little distance away. There was a loud, scandalized cry of "Go away, child! Go away this instant!" and an old woman with a switch in her hand came round the corner of the hut, violently shooing away a crowd of naked children. Some more women followed, clicking their tongues and exclaiming; evidently there was something that the children ought not to have seen. I rounded the hut and saw a man's dead body sprawling in the mud. He was an Indian, a black Dravidian coolie,[6] almost naked, and he could not have been dead many minutes. The people said that the elephant had come suddenly upon him round the corner of the hut, caught him with its trunk, put its foot on his back, and ground him into the earth. This was the rainy season and the ground was soft, and his face had scored a trench a foot deep and a couple of yards long. He was lying on his belly with arms crucified and head sharply twisted to one side. His face was coated with mud, the eyes wide open, the teeth bared and grinning with an expression of unendurable agony. (Never tell me, by the way, that the dead look peaceful. Most of the corpses I have seen looked devilish.) The friction of the great beast's foot had stripped the skin from his back as neatly as one skins a rabbit. As soon as I saw the dead man I sent an orderly to a friend's house nearby to borrow an elephant rifle. I had already sent back the pony, not wanting it to go mad with fright and throw me if it smelled the elephant. **D**

The orderly came back in a few minutes with a rifle and five cartridges, and meanwhile some Burmans had arrived and told us that the elephant was in the paddy fields below, only a few hundred yards away. As I started forward practically the whole population of the quarter flocked out of the houses and followed me. They had seen the rifle and were all shouting excitedly that I was going to shoot the elephant. They had not shown much interest in the elephant when he was merely ravaging their homes, but it was different now that he was going to be shot. It was a bit of fun to them, as it would be to an English crowd;

5. **mahout** (muh HOWT): elephant keeper. The word derives from *mahaut,* Hindi for "great in measure" and, thus, "important officer."

6. **Dravidian coolie:** *Dravidian* denotes any of several intermixed races living chiefly in southern India and northern Sri Lanka. A coolie is an unskilled laborer. The word is derived from *quli,* Hindi for "hired servant," and is considered offensive.

C **Reading Focus** **Identifying the Author's Purpose** What do you learn about the setting in this paragraph? What do you think is Orwell's purpose in describing this setting?

D **Reading Focus** **Identifying the Author's Purpose** How does Orwell's description of the dead man make you feel? What purpose might such a description serve?

Vocabulary **squalid** (SKWAHL ihd) *adj.:* foul; dirty.
unendurable (uhn ehn DUR uh buhl) *adj.:* more than can be tolerated.

Cross-Curricular Connection

Geography: Myanmar

Ask groups of students to do more research about the various natural resources in Myanmar. Suggest that they use the Geography Link to gather their thoughts and then use the Internet to find information and images that depict life in Myanmar today. They might want to talk about staple crops, protected wildlife, or Myanmar's position in the global community in terms of natural resources and industrial waste. Have students create a brief presentation with visuals and share their findings with the class.

Universal Access

Struggling Readers

Strategic Students To help students understand the situational irony of the narrator and the crowd on this page, ask them to consider what the narrator's position was and what privileges are normally associated with the position. Ask students how they would expect someone in his position to feel walking among the locals. Is it surprising for us to learn how self-conscious he is? Why or why not?

✔ See **UA: Differentiating Instruction** for a graphic organizer to scaffold instruction for struggling readers.

besides they wanted the meat. It made me vaguely uneasy. I had no intention of shooting the elephant—I had merely sent for the rifle to defend myself if necessary—and it is always unnerving to have a crowd following you. I marched down the hill, looking and feeling a fool, with the rifle over my shoulder and an ever-growing army of people jostling at my heels. At the bottom, when you got away from the huts, there was a metaled[7] road and beyond that a miry waste of paddy fields a thousand yards across, not yet plowed but soggy from the first rains and dotted with coarse grass. The elephant was standing eight yards from the road, his left side toward us. He took not the slightest notice of the crowd's approach. He was tearing up bunches of grass, beating them against his knees to clean them, and stuffing them into his mouth. E

I had halted on the road. As soon as I saw the elephant I knew with perfect certainty that I ought not to shoot him. It is a serious matter to shoot a working elephant—it is comparable to destroying a huge and costly piece of machinery—and obviously one ought not to do it if it can possibly be avoided. And at that distance, peacefully eating, the elephant looked no more dangerous than a cow. I thought then and I think now that his attack of "must" was already passing off; in which case he would merely wander harmlessly about until the mahout came back and caught him. Moreover, I did not in the least want to shoot him. I decided that I would watch him for a little while to make sure that he did not turn savage again, and then go home.

But at that moment I glanced round at the crowd that had followed me. It was an immense crowd, two thousand at the least and growing every minute. It blocked the road for a long distance on either side. I looked at the sea of yellow faces above the garish clothes—faces all happy and excited over this bit of fun, all certain that the elephant was going to be shot. They were watching me as they would watch a conjurer about to perform a trick. They did not like me, but with the magical rifle in my hands I was momen-

7. **metaled:** paved with cinders, stones, or the like.

E **Literary Focus** **Irony** What is the situational irony in the march of British police officer "down [a] hill, looking and feeling a fool"?

GEOGRAPHY LINK

Myanmar

Workers transplanting rice fields in Mandalay, Myanmar.

The British already had colonized India when they set their sights on Burma, first gaining control of the coastline and then moving inland. In addition to harvesting the valuable teak from Burma's forests, the British also planned to extract rubies and oil. While Burma did not, as the British had hoped, contain an easy trade route to China, the opening of the Suez Canal did create a demand for rice that led to the expansion of rice farming in the Irrawaddy delta.

Burma gained full independence in 1948, and in 1989, the government changed the country's name to Myanmar (the U.S., however, only recognizes the name Burma). Although the British exhausted the ruby mines, Myanmar is still the world's primary source of teak. Rice remains a key export while oil is extracted only for domestic consumption. The subtropical and tropical forests covering half the country are home to various birds and other wildlife like monkeys, leopards, tigers, and cobras. Elephants are plentiful and still used for labor, but the rhinoceros and the wild buffalo are protected species.

Ask Yourself

What details about Britain's interest in Burma's geography explain why the Burmese people resented the British?

Think About/Talk About

Comprehension

C Reading Focus

Possible responses: *At the time, Burma was poor and undeveloped. In Orwell's description, people live in bamboo huts; fruit is sold in open-air stalls. The Burmese are unarmed. Orwell's purpose in describing the setting is to show that the Burmese depend on their British overlords for protection, perhaps even for survival. This reality reinforces Orwell's conflicted feelings about colonialism.*

D Reading Focus

Possible response: *Orwell's description of the dead man is meant to evoke pity, sorrow, and fear. It also helps readers understand the pressure put on Orwell to take action.*

Analysis

E Literary Focus

Possible response: *The narrator, who is seen as a powerful official, is "feeling a fool." He finds the crowd's attention "unnerving."*

Extend the Discussion

Speculating How do you think the narrator will feel afterward if he shoots the elephant? ***Possible response:*** *He will probably have mixed feelings about it. He might feel relieved if his action keeps the crowd from taunting him, but at the same time he will probably regret shooting the elephant because he feels he should not do so.*

Students with Disabilities

Help students compare characters' motivations. Tell them to construct a Venn diagram. Have students list the narrator's thoughts about the elephant in the left circle, and the crowd's thoughts about the elephant in the right circle. Tell students to include similarities in each group's thinking in the center oval. After students have finished, have them make a prediction about what will happen to the elephant.

Geography Link

Ask Yourself

Possible response: *The British were primarily interested in Burma's natural resources and improving its methods of trade. The Burmese people may have felt resentment toward the British because maintaining the Burmese culture and way of life was not a priority of the British Empire. The people of Burma may have felt used and exploited by the British government.*

Vocabulary: Own the Word

- **squalid:** *Squalid* means "unsanitary"; the antonym is *clean*. Use both words in a sentence: Hercules diverted a river to sanitize *squalid* stables; within a day, they became clean.
- **unendurable:** Ask students to list situations in which they would feel *unendurable* pain. ***Possible responses:*** *injury from an accident, a tooth extraction, kidney stones*

Model the Skill

- Remind students that **irony** is based upon contrast—a contrast between expected words and situations and what actually is said or actually happens.
- Model completing a sentence in an unexpected way and then discuss the ironies in the resulting words and situations. Write the first half of the sentence on the board: *When I waved at the passing fire engine that afternoon,* _____. Then, you might say, "I never imagined that it would be putting out a fire at my house." You could add, "This is ironic because I did not expect such a thing to occur."

Guided Practice: Apply

Read-Talk-Write Have small groups of students re-read the last four paragraphs of the selection and find and discuss the ironies. Then have them write four or five sentences summarizing their discussion.

tarily worth watching. And suddenly I realized that I should have to shoot the elephant after all. The people expected it of me and I had got to do it; I could feel their two thousand wills pressing me forward, irresistibly. And it was at this moment, as I stood there with the rifle in my hands, that I first grasped the hollowness, the futility of the white man's dominion in the East. Here was I, the white man with his gun, standing in front of the unarmed native crowd—seemingly the leading actor of the piece; but in reality I was only an absurd puppet pushed to and fro by the will of those yellow faces behind. I perceived in this moment that when the white man turns tyrant it is his own freedom that he destroys. He becomes a sort of hollow, posing dummy, the conventionalized figure of a sahib.[8] For it is the condition of his rule that he shall spend his life in trying to impress the "natives," and so in every crisis he has got to do what the "natives" expect of him. He wears a mask, and his face grows to fit it. I had got to shoot the elephant. I had committed myself to doing it when I sent for the rifle. A sahib has got to act like a sahib; he has got to appear resolute, to know his own mind and do definite things. To come all that way, rifle in hand, with two thousand people marching at my heels, and then to trail feebly away, having done nothing—no, that was impossible. The crowd would laugh at me. And my whole life, every white man's life in the East, was one long struggle not to be laughed at. **F** **G**

But I did not want to shoot the elephant. I watched him beating his bunch of grass against his knees, with that preoccupied grandmotherly air that elephants have. It seemed to me that it would be murder to shoot him. At that age I was not squeamish about killing animals, but I had never shot an elephant and never wanted to. (Somehow it always seems worse to kill a *large* animal.) Besides, there was the beast's owner to be considered. Alive, the elephant was worth at least a hundred pounds; dead, he would only be worth the value of his tusks, five pounds, possibly. But I had got to act quickly. I turned to some experienced-looking Burmans who had been there when we arrived, and asked them how the elephant had been behaving. They all said the same thing: He took no notice of you if you left him alone, but he might charge if you went too close to him.

It was perfectly clear to me what I ought to do. I ought to walk up to within, say, twenty-five yards of the elephant and test his behavior. If he charged, I could shoot; if he took no notice of me, it would be safe to leave him until the mahout came back. But also I knew that I was going to do no such thing. I was a poor shot with a rifle and the ground was soft mud into which one would sink at every step. If the elephant charged and I missed him, I should have about as much chance as a toad under a steamroller. But even then I was not thinking particularly of my own skin, only of the watchful yellow faces behind. For at that moment, with the crowd watching me, I was not afraid in the ordinary sense, as I would have been if I had been alone. A white man mustn't be frightened in front of "natives"; and so, in general, he isn't frightened. The sole thought in my mind was that if anything went wrong those two thousand Burmans would see me pursued, caught, trampled on, and reduced to a grinning corpse like that Indian up the hill. And if that happened it was quite probable that some of them would laugh. That would never do. There was only one alternative. I shoved the cartridges into the magazine and lay down on the road to get a better aim. **H**

The crowd grew very still, and a deep, low, happy sigh, as of people who see the theater curtain go up at last, breathed from innumerable throats. They were

8. **sahib** (SAH ihb): master; sir. In colonial India the title was used as a sign of respect for a European gentleman.

F Reading Focus **Identifying the Author's Purpose** How is the comparison of the narrator to a puppet ironic? What does it reveal about the author's purpose?

G Literary Focus **Irony** What is ironic about the white man's "one long struggle" in the East?

H Reading Focus **Identifying the Author's Purpose** What comment about colonialism is Orwell making in this paragraph? How does this comment help reveal his purpose?

Vocabulary **innumerable** (ih NOO muhr uh buhl) *adj.:* too many to count.

Universal Access

Advanced Learners

Acceleration Orwell's essays and novels can be read as protests against economic and social injustices. In fact, a critic once wrote that Orwell "would not blow his nose without moralizing on conditions in the handkerchief industry."

Paired Activity Pair students to identify the political and social themes in this essay and to comment on the effectiveness of Orwell's rhetoric.

Cross-Curricular Connection

HISTORY: The Burmese Story

Group Activity To learn more about Burma and its relationship to the British Empire, have students complete the following tasks in small groups:

- Speculate about the feelings of the Burmese when their country was made a province of India, "the jewel in the crown" of the empire.
- Research the role of Burma in World War II.
- Find out about the human rights work of Aung San Suu Kyi, the 1991 Nobel Peace Prize winner.

going to have their bit of fun after all. The rifle was a beautiful German thing with cross-hair sights. I did not then know that in shooting an elephant one would shoot to cut an imaginary bar running from earhole to earhole. I ought, therefore, as the elephant was sideways on, to have aimed straight at his earhole; actually I aimed several inches in front of this, thinking the brain would be further forward. I

When I pulled the trigger I did not hear the bang or feel the kick—one never does when a shot goes home—but I heard the devilish roar of glee that went up from the crowd. In that instant, in too short a time, one would have thought, even for the bullet to get there, a mysterious, terrible change had come over the elephant. He neither stirred nor fell, but every line of his body had altered. He looked suddenly stricken, shrunken, immensely old, as though the frightful impact of the bullet had paralyzed him without knocking him down. At last, after what seemed a long time—it might have been five seconds, I dare say—he sagged flabbily to his knees. His mouth slobbered. An enormous senility seemed to have settled upon him. One could have imagined him thousands of years old. I fired again into the same spot. At the second shot he did not collapse but climbed with desperate slowness to his feet and stood weakly upright, with legs sagging and head drooping. I fired a third time. That was the shot that did for him. You could see the agony of it jolt his whole body and knock the last remnant of strength from his legs. But in falling he seemed for a moment to rise, for as his hind legs collapsed beneath him he seemed to tower upward like a huge rock toppling, his trunk reaching skyward like a tree. He trumpeted, for the first and only time. And then down he came, his belly toward me, with a crash that seemed to shake the ground even where I lay. J

I got up. The Burmans were already racing past me across the mud. It was obvious that the elephant would never rise again, but he was not dead. He was breathing very rhythmically with long rattling gasps, his great mound of a side painfully rising and falling. His mouth was wide open—I could see far down into caverns of pale pink throat. I waited a long time for him to die, but his breathing did not weaken. Finally I fired my two remaining shots into the spot where I thought his heart must be. The thick blood welled out of him like red velvet, but still he did not die. His body did not even jerk when the shots hit him, the tortured breathing continued without a pause. He was dying, very slowly and in great agony, but in some world remote from me where not even a bullet could damage him further. I felt that I had got to put an end to that dreadful noise. It seemed dreadful to see the great beast lying there, powerless to move and yet powerless to die, and not even to be able to finish him. I sent back for my small rifle and poured shot after shot into his heart and down his throat. They seemed to make no impression. The tortured gasps continued as steadily as the ticking of a clock.

In the end I could not stand it any longer and went away. I heard later that it took him half an hour to die. Burmans were bringing dahs[9] and baskets even before I left, and I was told they had stripped his body almost to the bones by the afternoon.

Afterward, of course, there were endless discussions about the shooting of the elephant. The owner was furious, but he was only an Indian and could do nothing. Besides, legally I had done the right thing, for a mad elephant has to be killed, like a mad dog, if its owner fails to control it. Among the Europeans opinion was divided. The older men said I was right, the younger men said it was a damn shame to shoot an elephant for killing a coolie, because an elephant was worth more than any damn Coringhee[10] coolie. And afterward I was very glad that the coolie had been killed; it put me legally in the right and it gave me a sufficient pretext for shooting the elephant. I often wondered whether any of the others grasped that I had done it solely to avoid looking a fool. K

---

9. **dahs** (dahz): large carving knives.
10. **Coringhee** (kawr IHNG ee): port in southeastern India.

I **Literary Focus** **Irony** What is ironic about this detail of Orwell's situation?

J **Reading Focus** **Identifying the Author's Purpose** How do these details help Orwell achieve his purpose?

K **Literary Focus** **Irony** Why is Orwell glad the man died? How does the ending further Orwell's point?

Vocabulary **pretext** (PREE tehkst) *n.:* excuse.

Think About/Talk About

Comprehension

F Reading Focus

Possible responses: *It shows that people who are perceived as leaders are actually followers. The author is showing that under imperialism, no one is free.*

H Reading Focus

Possible responses: *Orwell is saying that colonial imperialism forces a person to "wear a mask" that his face eventually grows to fit. He is revealing the irony of colonialism.*

J Reading Focus

Possible response: *The description of the elephant's death supports Orwell's negative feelings about colonialism.*

Analysis

G Literary Focus

Possible response: *The white "sahibs" believe themselves to be in control, but in reality, they are forced to behave in certain ways to maintain their positions of strength.*

I Literary Focus

Possible response: *The narrator is in charge of shooting the elephant and has been invested with much power by local people. However, he does not want to shoot the elephant and does not know how to shoot it competently.*

K Literary Focus

Possible responses: *The man's death gives Orwell a legal excuse for killing an animal, an action he took to avoid looking foolish. It reaffirms the selfish motives of the colonial power.*

Vocabulary: Own the Word

- **innumerable:** Point out to students that *innumerable* contains a root they are familiar with: *numerals* ("numbers"). Adding the prefix *in–* ("not") results in the meaning: "without numbers."
- **pretext:** The connotation for *pretext* is a false excuse. What does the narrator say that indicates his excuse to kill the elephant was false?

California Standards, pp. 1148–1149

- **Reading Standard 2.5** Analyze an author's implicit and explicit philosophical assumptions and beliefs about a subject.
- **Reading Standard 3.3** Analyze the ways in which irony, tone, mood, the author's style, and the "sound" of language achieve specific rhetorical or aesthetic purposes or both.
- **Grades 9–10 Review Reading Standard 1.2** Distinguish between the denotative and connotative meanings of words and interpret the connotative power of words.
- **Grades 9–10 Review Reading Standard 3.7** Recognize and understand the significance of various literary devices, including figurative language, imagery, allegory, and symbolism, and explain their appeal.
- **Writing Standard 1.3** Structure ideas and arguments in a sustained, persuasive, and sophisticated way and support them with precise and relevant examples.
- **Writing Standard 2.3** Write reflective compositions: **a.** Explore the significance of personal experiences, events, conditions, or concerns by using rhetorical strategies (e.g., narration, description, exposition, persuasion).
- **Writing Standard 2.6** Deliver multimedia presentations: **a.** Combine text, images, and sound and draw information from many sources (e.g., television broadcasts, videos, films, newspapers, magazines, CD-ROMs, the Internet, electronic media-generated images).

Check for Understanding

Independent Practice

Reading Skills Focus

Possible responses:

1. *Orwell feels he should approach the elephant to see if it is still dangerous, but the ground is swampy and he is afraid of the humiliation that might occur if he falls and is trampled. To resolve this conflict, he decides to shoot the elephant.*
2. *Clues include: "They . . . were all shouting excitedly that I was going to shoot the elephant"; "It made me . . . uneasy."*
3. *Orwell realizes that if he walks away without killing the elephant, he will be laughed at by the natives. He plays the role of an imperialist driven by fear.*
4. *Students should note that the narrator explains how he felt while he was caught up in the situation.*

Literary Skills Focus

Possible responses:

5. *Orwell does not believe that the British should rule the Burmese, but he is angry with individual Burmese who taunt him on the job. By referring to the Burmese as "little beasts," he implicates himself in the imperialist's perspective.*
6. *He would choose not to shoot the elephant because his reasons for acting are the same as those the Empire uses to justify its actions.*
7. *Orwell causes readers to sympathize with the animal.*
8. *Orwell has mixed feelings about imperialism and his role as its agent, yet he follows the rules. His actions suggest that colonialism is inherently contradictory.*
9. *Tyrants must act according to the expectations of those they oppress. This is ironic because tyrants should be in control, not controlled by the oppressed.*
10. *The elephant symbolizes what the Empire was doing to its Asian colonies—destroying their culture and their people.*

Applying Your Skills

Reading Standard 2.5, 3.3; **Grades 9–10 Review**
Reading Standard 3.7 (see pages A48–A50)
Writing Standard 2.3a (see pages A51–A52)

Shooting an Elephant

Literary Response and Analysis

Reading Skills Focus

Quick Check

1. What is Orwell's inner conflict, and how does he deal with it?
2. What clues in the essay suggest the outcome?

Read with a Purpose

3. Why does Orwell act against his better judgment? What role does imperialism play?

Reading Skills: Identifying the Author's Purpose

4. Add a column to the chart you made while reading. Explain the author's purpose for writing the essay. What opinions about himself and his situation compel him to write the essay?

Orwell's Personal Dilemma	Colonialism's Cultural Dilemma	Author's Purpose
He's "in charge" but feels pressured by the group.		

Literary Skills Focus

Literary Analysis

5. **Interpret** What is Orwell's attitude toward the Burmese? Do his thoughts and actions embody the perspective of an imperialist?
6. **Make Predictions** Based on Orwell's commentary, do you think he would make the same choice to shoot the elephant if he had the chance to repeat the day? Why or why not?
7. **Evaluate** Orwell describes at length the shooting and the death of the elephant. Is the gruesome detail necessary? How does it add to or detract from the essay?
8. **Extend** What does this essay reveal about Orwell's code of ethics or behavior as a young police officer in Burma? What does it reveal about the true nature of colonialism? Are these insights related? Explain.

Literary Skills: Irony

9. **Analyze** Explain the meaning of Orwell's insight that tyrants destroy their own freedom, as well as the freedom of the people they oppress. Why is this insight an example of situational irony?

Literary Skills Review: Symbol

10. **Analyze** The elephant is an important **symbol,** a person, place, thing, or idea that stands both for itself and for something beyond itself. What political idea or assumption might the elephant symbolize? In other words, what political idea confronted, confused, and inevitably weakened Orwell? With supporting details from the text, explain the elephant's symbolic importance.

Writing Skills Focus

Think as a Reader/Writer

Use It in Your Writing Using Orwell's essay as a guide, write a short narrative essay about when you or someone you know experienced inner conflict and had to make an important decision. Intersperse your narrative with commentary, looking back on the event from your current perspective. What do you see about the incident now that you couldn't see then?

What Do You Think Now? How does a fear of appearing foolish paralyze the British colonialists? Do you think this fear often causes people to make bad decisions? Why or why not?

Universal Access

Struggling Writers

Some students may struggle to write a narrative that includes inner conflict. Invite students to begin by writing down the details of a situation where they had to make an important decision. Have them list the possible choices in this decision and the pros and cons of each. Then, have students think about how they feel about the situation now as opposed to how they felt when they made the decision.

What Do You Think Now?

To help students answer this question, remind them that the British needed to maintain a constant show of strength in order to control the colony. Ask students if they have ever felt as if they needed to keep up a certain appearance—especially one that they may not agree with. It might be an "appearance" associated with belonging to a certain social group or behaving in a certain way in front of adults.

Reading Standard 3.3; Grades 9–10 Review Reading Standard 1.2 (see pages A48–A50)
Writing Standard 1.3, 2.3a, 2.6a

Vocabulary Development

Vocabulary Check

Match the Vocabulary words with their definitions.

1. supplant	a. confusing
2. pretext	b. foul or unclean
3. perplexing	c. too many to be counted
4. unendurable	d. miserable
5. squalid	e. more than one can tolerate
6. innumerable	f. replace
7. wretched	g. excuse

Vocabulary Skills: Connotations

Connotations are the ideas and feelings associated with a word that go beyond its dictionary definition. Authors carefully choose words with certain connotations that will evoke the intended response in their readers. Orwell may have chosen to use *peacefully,* as opposed to *calmly,* to describe the elephant's eating, because *peacefully* more strongly suggests the elephant is no longer dangerous.

Your Turn

Answer these questions about connotation.

1. When Orwell says that "the crowd yelled with hideous laughter," why is *hideous* an unusual word to use? What emotional response does the word evoke in you?
2. Orwell uses agony to describe both the death of the Indian and the death of the elephant. What does *agony* suggest that *intense pain* does not?

Language Coach

Negative Prefixes Add the prefix *–un* or *–in* to the following words to reverse the meanings. Use a dictionary if necessary.

1. breakable
2. variably
3. tolerable
4. healthy

CHOICES

As you respond to the Choices, use these **Academic Vocabulary** words as appropriate: adapt, considerably, exhibit, inevitable, perspective.

REVIEW

Discuss Irony

In a small group, discuss the passage in which the elephant comes into view. What is Orwell's first impression of the creature? What words does he use to describe the elephant? Then, discuss the irony in this situation. Given the elephant's demeanor, what is ironic about what ultimately happens to it?

CONNECT

Create a Blog

In addition to imperialism and its negative effects, Orwell's essay raises a number of important issues: racism and oppression, animal rights, societal pressures, and shame and its effects. Choose one of these issues, and write a short blog entry discussing your opinion. Use ideas from the essay, as well as from your own experience, to support your opinions.

EXTEND

Tell Your Own Story

TechFocus Choose an event from your life that has had a strong effect on you and create a digital story to share this event and its meaning to you with others. Include clips from home movies or scanned images, and choose music that suits the tone and message of the story. Finally, create a voice-over that uses tone to convey your message. Remember to include commentary that expresses your current perspective on the event.

Learn It Online

Learn the steps of making a digital story online at the Digital Storytelling site.

go.hrw.com H12-1149 Go

Universal Access: Vocabulary Development

English Learners

English for Academic Success Pair students with a proficient English speaker, and have them identify the following as true or false, and briefly explain their answer.

- It is a good idea to supplant unhealthy habits with healthy ones. [*T; supplant is a synonym for replace.*]
- A room that has been thoroughly cleaned would be described as squalid. [*F; a squalid room is filthy.*]
- A pretext can offered by someone who is honest. [*F; an honest person would avoid using an excuse.*]
- A perplexing story plot is easy to follow. [*F; perplexing means "confusing" so the plot would be difficult to follow.*]
- An unendurable lecture is fun to listen to. [*F; it would be painful to listen to.*]
- It is miserable to be around a wretched person. [*T; wretched is a synonym for miserable.*]
- Counting *innumerable* objects would be impossible. [*T; innumerable means "too many to count."*]

✔ See the **Academic and Selection Vocabulary Skill Builder** in **UA: Differentiating Instruction.**

Independent Practice

Vocabulary Development

Vocabulary Check

1. *f* 2. *g* 3. *a* 4. *e* 5. *b* 6. *c* 7. *d*

go.hrw.com **WordSharp: An Interactive Vocabulary Tutor**

Your Turn

1. *Describing laughter as "hideous" is unexpected. It creates a chilling response in the reader.*
2. *Agony implies a more intense feeling.*

English for Academic Success

Language Coach

1. *unbreakable*
2. *invariably*
3. *intolerable*
4. *unhealthy*

Choices: Evaluation Criteria

Review: Discuss Irony

Students show understanding of irony.

Connect: Homework
Create a Blog

Blog entries demonstrate students' views on an important issue.

Extend: Homework
Tell Your Own Story

Commentaries clearly express students' perspective.

Assess

Unit 6 Resources, Selection Standards Check, p. 57

Reteach

To reteach **irony**, see **Reteaching Lessons,** pp. 1449O–1449P.

Learn It Online

The **Digital Storytelling** mini-site shows students how to take a personal experience and craft it into a short film—complete with music, images, and special effects.

go.hrw.com H12-1149 Go

Standards Focus

Objectives

Students will recognize political statements.

Selection Introduction

Think About the Writers

To help students answer the question, ask them to think about what values and interests may have been prevalent in Britain and in India during the periods when these speeches were given.

For Independent Reading

- *The Conch Bearer: A Novel,* Chitra Banerjee Divakaruni
- *Gifts**, Ursula K. Le Guin

HRW LIBRARY *This title is available in the HRW library.

Motivate

What Do You Think?/QuickWrite

Have students take a few minutes to reflect on their thoughts and opinions about world politics. Then, have students choose one of their opinions and list the values, concerns, and experiences that have helped to form that political opinion.

English for Academic Success

Academic Vocabulary

Look for opportunities to use the Academic Vocabulary words in this unit.

- **exhibit, *v.:*** show, demonstrate
- **inevitable, *adj.,*** unavoidable
- **perspective, *n.,*** particular way of looking at something

INFORMATIONAL TEXT FOCUS

Preparing to Read

JOSEPH CHAMBERLAIN

"I Believe in a British Empire"

JAWAHARLAL NEHRU

"The Noble Mansion of Free India"

What Do You Think? How does experience shape our view of the world?

QuickWrite

Political opinions are shaped by many influences, including personal experience, family values, and individual interests. Briefly write about the influences that have shaped your political perspective.

Joseph Chamberlain (1896), by John Singer Sargent, oil on canvas. National Portrait Gallery, London.

Jawaharlal Nehru (1955).

MEET THE WRITERS

Joseph Chamberlain

(1836–1914)

The son of a wealthy shoe manufacturer in London, Joseph Chamberlain began working at age 16 and used his shrewd business sense to make his fortune and retire by age 38. He began his political life as a radical liberal, supporting social reform such as free education and improved housing for the poor. He split with the Liberal party over Irish Home Rule and joined other dissident Liberals, called Liberal Unionists. Chamberlain eventually abandoned his radical perspective and turned toward imperialism. In 1895, he joined the Conservative Cabinet. He believed the British Empire should be self-reliant, looking to its own colonies—and not to foreign allies—for economic and military reinforcement. However, the tariffs he supported were unpopular with the British, who feared rising prices, and the Conservatives lost the next election. Although Chamberlain was reelected to parliament, he suffered a debilitating stroke in 1906 that ended his political career.

Jawaharlal Nehru

(1889–1964)

The son of a well-known lawyer, Nehru was educated by English and Indian tutors in India and then attended Harrow and Cambridge and studied law in England. After Nehru returned to India, his interest in gaining India's freedom from Britain led him to the great Indian leader Mohandas Gandhi, who believed that India's freedom could be attained through nonviolent resistance. Nehru joined the Indian Congress Party and worked for Indian independence from Great Britain for twenty-eight years before he saw it become a reality, in 1947. In that year, Nehru was elected the first prime minister of the newly independent nation.

Think About the Writers How do these men's politics reflect the values and interests of their nations?

California Standards, pp. 1150–1158

- **Reading Standard 2.5** Analyze an author's implicit and explicit philosophical assumptions and beliefs about a subject.

Selection Readability	
Easily Accessible Accessible **Challenging**	These selections include historical content; complex syntax; sophisticated language.

Reading Standard 2.5 (see pages A48–A50)

Informational Text Focus

Recognizing Political Assumptions When politicians like Chamberlain and Nehru deliver speeches, they often make **political assumptions,** or unsupported statements they believe to be true. While these assumptions are not necessarily false, they may be generalizations or statements that are difficult to prove, or they may be statements the speaker assumes the audience believes to be true. Both Chamberlain and Nehru make political assumptions in their speeches; Nehru, for example, claims that prosperity for India will benefit all countries. This statement is an assumption because Nehru believes it to be true but does not support it with evidence. As you analyze political speeches, **recognizing political assumptions** will help you identify the speaker's perspective on a subject and show you how the speaker uses unsupported claims to convince his or her audience to support a point of view.

Into Action As you read each speech, fill in a chart like the one below. Note each speaker's point of view regarding colonialism, and then note the political assumptions the speaker makes.

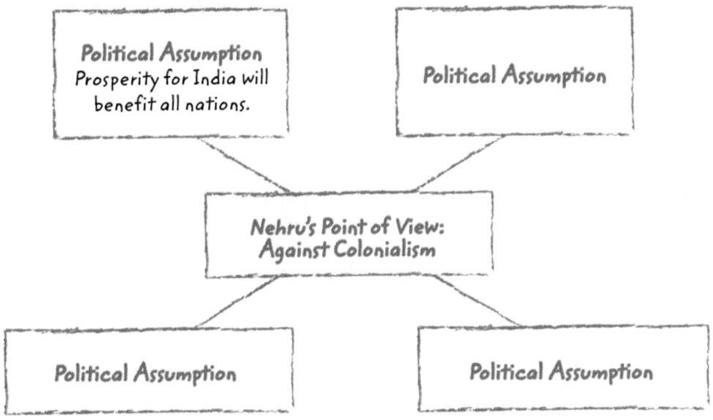

Writing Skills Focus

Preparing for **Timed Writing** Politicians and other persuasive writers and speakers use **loaded language**—words and phrases that have strong emotional overtones and that evoke strong emotional responses, either positive or negative. As you read the speeches by Chamberlain and Nehru, use your *Reader/Writer Notebook* to record examples of loaded language.

Reader/Writer Notebook

Use your **RWN** to complete the activities for these selections.

Vocabulary

"I Believe in a British Empire"

obtained (uhb TAYND) *v.:* got; acquired. *Britain obtained many colonies, some by force and others peacefully.*

apathy (AP uh thee) *n.:* lack of interest. *The speaker accused his opponents of apathy.*

cultivate (KUHL tuh vayt) *v.:* develop; promote. *To prevent war, it is important to cultivate understanding between countries.*

prosperity (prahs PEHR uh tee) *n.:* wealth or good fortune. *Chamberlain believed colonialism would ensure British prosperity.*

"The Noble Mansion of Free India"

pledge (plehj) *n.:* promise or vow. *Nehru's pledge was to help India retain its glory.*

endured (ehn DURD) *v.:* suffered, put up with. *He asserted that India had endured much hardship under British rule.*

incessant (ihn SEHS uhnt) *adj.:* constant; never ending. *Nehru claimed that India's good fortune would require incessant work.*

indivisible (ihn duh VIHZ uh buhl) *adj.:* unable to be separated. *India's fortunes are indivisible from the fortunes of the rest of the world.*

Language Coach

Latin Word Origins The Latin word *dūrāre* means "to last or harden." Words derived from *dūrāre* include *duration,* "a period of time that something lasts" and *durable,* meaning "tough enough to last." Which Vocabulary word is related to these words?

Learn It Online
Listen to these speeches online.
go.hrw.com H12-1151 Go

Selection Resources

Unit 6 Resources, on-level practice and assessment, pp. 60, 61

Teacher One Stop™, on-level lesson plans and all print resources

Holt Audio Library

Holt Audio Library: Selections and Summaries in Spanish

UA: Differentiating Instruction, graphic organizer, p. 272

UA: Supporting Instruction in Spanish, selection summary

ThinkCentral Online Assessment, Selection Standards Check

ThinkCentral Online Remediation

Preteach

Introducing Vocabulary

Use this activity to check students' understanding.

1. Name something you have **obtained** from a family member.
2. Why might high school students feel **apathy** toward political elections?
3. Name four crops that a farmer in Hawaii might **cultivate**.
4. List three ways to gain financial **prosperity**.
5. Name a **pledge** you have taken in the last year.
6. Suggest three ways a person might **endure** cold weather.
7. Explain what might be annoying about an **incessant** noise.
8. State what an **indivisible** nation values.

English for Academic Success

Language Coach

Give students examples of other words that originate with *durare,* such as *during* and *obdurate.*

Informational Text Focus

Give students a copy of the Informational Text Focus graphic organizer before they read. (See **Unit 6 Resources.**) Tell them to use their responses to answer the questions on the Applying Your Skills page.

Writing Skills Focus

Have students record in their **Reader/Writer Notebooks** examples of loaded words used by Chamberlain and Nehru.

Learn It Online
The online version of this selection includes audio support to engage all students and to help struggling readers with reading comprehension and vocabulary.
go.hrw.com H12-1151 Go

Teacher Preparation
Selection Summary
The two speeches in this feature present contrasting views of colonialism. "I Believe in a British Empire" is a speech from a British statesman of the early twentieth century who staunchly advocated colonialism.

Direct Teach

Think About/Talk About
Read with a Purpose Have students read the Read with a Purpose statement. Point out that Chamberlain expects his listeners to agree that colonialism is in England's best interests. Ask students whether they feel colonialism was in the best interest of those native to the colony.

Analysis
Ⓐ Informational Focus

Possible responses: *Chamberlain assumes that people are fighting for love of country rather than some other reason, such as personal gain or fear. His statement is a political assumption because it is unsupported.*

Extend the Discussion
Tone How does Chamberlain's phrase "our children beyond the sea" reveal what he expects from English emigrants living in the colonies?

Possible response: *He expects the people, or children, in the colonies to be loyal and defend their "mother country."*

SPEECH

"I Believe in a British Empire"

by **Joseph Chamberlain**

Read with a Purpose
Read this speech to learn how Chamberlain supports his view that colonialism is in England's best interest.

Build Background
This speech, delivered in 1903, in Birmingham, England, was part of a Conservative party tariff-reform campaign. Since many European countries viewed England as a bully for its aggression in the Boer War, Chamberlain believed England could not rely on European nations as allies. His speech exhibits tenets of both colonialism and isolationism, the belief that one's country should not have pacts and alliances with other nations. As he begins, Chamberlain refers to his political enemies, the Liberals who oppose tariff reform.

I cannot look forward without dread to handing over the security and existence of this great Empire to the hands of those who have made common cause with its enemies, who have charged their own countrymen with methods of barbarism,[1] and who apparently have been untouched by that pervading[2] sentiment which I found everywhere where the British flag floats, and which has done so much in recent years to draw us together. I should not require to go to South Africa in order to be convinced that this feeling has obtained deep hold on the minds and hearts of our children beyond the seas.[3] It has had a hard life of it, this feeling of Imperial patriotism. It was checked for a generation by the apathy and the indifference which were the characteristics of our former relations with our Colonies, but it was never extinguished. The embers were still alight, and when in the late war[4] this old country of ours showed that it was still possessed by the spirit of our ancestors, and that it was still prepared to count no sacrifice that was necessary in order to maintain the honor and the interests of the Empire, then you found a response from your children across the seas that astonished the whole world by a proof, an undeniable proof, of affection and regard. Ⓐ

1. **charged . . . barbarism:** Many British citizens were appalled by the brutal methods that were used to help win the Boer War.
2. **pervading:** spreading throughout.
3. **children beyond the seas:** the colonists—Canadians, Australians, New Zealanders, and even some black South Africans—who helped England fight and win the Boer War.
4. **the late war:** the Boer War (1899–1902) fought between Britain and the two Boer republics in South Africa. (Boers are South Africans of Dutch descent.)

Ⓐ Informational Focus **Recognizing Political Assumptions** What other reasons, besides "affection and regard," might colonies have had for fighting in the war? How is Chamberlain's statement an example of a political assumption?

Vocabulary **obtained** (uhb TAYND) *v.:* got; acquired. **apathy** (AP uh thee) *n.:* lack of interest.

Universal Access

Struggling Readers
Strategic Students Students may have difficulty identifying and understanding the impact of the loaded language used by Chamberlain. To help students understand the concept of loaded language, guide them though this activity.

1. Which word seems more powerful, *kingdom* or *country*? [*kingdom*]
2. Which word seems less severe, *battle* or *quarrel*? [*quarrel*]
3. Which phrase more strongly suggests the idea of people being cooperative, "standing shoulder-to-shoulder" or "standing next to each other"? [*standing shoulder-to-shoulder*]
4. Which phrase seems demeaning, "Little England" or "the state of England"? [*Little England*]

✔ See **UA: Differentiating Instruction** for a graphic organizer to scaffold instruction for struggling readers.

Is it to end there? Are we to sink back into the old policy of selfish isolation which went very far to dry and even to sap the loyalty of our colonial brethren? I do not think so. I think these larger issues touch the people of this country. I think they have awakened to the enormous importance of a creative time like the present, and of taking advantage of the opportunities offered in order to make permanent what has begun so well. Remember, we are a kingdom, an old country. We proceed here on settled lines. We have our quarrels and our disputes, and we pass legislation which may be good or bad; but we know that, whatever changes there may be, at all events the main stream will ultimately reach its appointed destination. That is the result of centuries of constitutional progress and freedom.

Politician Joseph Chamberlain holding loaves of bread at Bingley Hall.

But the Empire is not old. The Empire is new—the Empire is in its infancy. Now is the time when we can mold that Empire and when we and those who live with us can decide its future destinies. Just let us consider what that Empire is; I am not going tonight to speak of those hundreds of millions of our Indian and native fellow subjects for whom we have become responsible. I consider for the moment only our relations to that white British population that constitutes the majority in the great self-governing colonies of the Empire. Here in the United Kingdom there are some forty millions of us. Outside there are ten millions of men either directly descended from ancestors who left this country or more probably men who themselves in their youth left this country in order to find their fortunes in our possessions abroad. How long do you suppose that this proportion of population is going to endure? The development of those colonies has been delayed by many reasons—but mainly probably by a more material reason—by the fact that the United States of America has offered a greater attraction to British emigration.

But that has changed. The United States, with all their vast territory, are filling up; and even now we hear of tens of thousands of emigrants leaving the United States in order to take up the fresh and rich lands of our colony in Canada. It seems to me not at all an impossible assumption that before the end of this present century we may find our fellow subjects beyond the seas as numerous as we are at home. I want you to look forward. I want you to consider the infinite importance of this not only to yourselves but to your descendants. Now is the time when you can exert influence. Do you wish that if these ten millions become forty millions they shall still be closely, intimately, affectionately

Think About/Talk About

Extend the Discussion

Drawing Conclusions Between 1901 and 1910, nearly nine million people immigrated to the United States. Why did this fact upset Chamberlain? ***Possible response:*** *He felt that the British should emigrate to the colonies and build up the empire.*

Interpreting In paragraph 2, how does Chamberlain serve as an apologist for England—someone who justifies and defends a belief or policy? How can you tell that he assumes his listeners agree with him? ***Possible responses:*** *He makes a strong appeal to unity among his listeners as supporters of the Empire like himself. He uses words and phrases such as "brethren" and "we are a kingdom."*

Vocabulary: Own the Word

- **obtained:** Ask: "Have you ever *obtained* a desired thing or outcome with effort? Explain when, where, and how you *obtained* what you wanted."
- **apathy**: *Apathy* is indifference; the antonym is *interest*. Use both words in a sentence: During the presentation, my *apathy* changed to interest when the presenter displayed vivid visuals.

Advanced Learners

Acceleration As students read through Chamberlain's speech, they will find that he makes several assumptions. On p. 1153, Chamberlain states that "the United States of America has offered a greater attraction to British emigration. But that has changed. The United States . . . are filling up; and even now we hear tens of thousands of emigrants leaving in order to take up . . . lands of our colony in Canada." Have students research British emigration activity during 1903 and determine whether Chamberlain's assumptions were correct.

Students with Disabilities

To give students additional help with understanding political assumptions, have them practice differentiating between assumptions and facts. Ask students to point out which of the following are assumptions and why.

- A colony is subject to the colonizer.
- Colonialism always provides prosperity for the colonist.
- An empire has extensive rule over a number of territories and nations.
- Whoever rules an empire wields much power.

Think About/Talk About

Analysis

B Informational Focus

Possible responses: *He claims they should act now or a growing population of fellow subjects overseas will eventually cut off all ties from the empire. His tone assumes that his listeners would agree.*

C Informational Focus

Possible responses: *Chamberlain wants to promote a relationship that consists of deep, abiding loyalty. He assumes that such a relationship would make Great Britain more powerful, wealthier, and also stronger militarily.*

D Informational Focus

Possible responses: *He believes the colonies would come to the aid of England because they are part of the empire. He bases his assumption on the participation of colonial soldiers in the Boer War.*

E Informational Focus

Possible response: *Believing the rest of the world to be hostile toward and envious of England, Chamberlain also believes in maintaining the empire as the only way to be self-sufficient and to compete successfully with other nations.*

Vocabulary: Own the Word

- **cultivate:** Tell students that the root word for *cultivate* is *cultivare*, which is Latin for "to till." When you *cultivate* something, you till it— or promote growth— as though it were a crop. Ask students what else they could *cultivate*.
- **prosperity:** Ask students to complete the following idea: The business experienced *prosperity* because . . . . ***Possible response:*** *Its profits increased dramatically.*

united to you, or do you contemplate the possibility of their being separated, going off each in his own direction, under a separate flag? Think what it means to your power and influence as a country; think what it means to your position among the nations of the world; think what it means to your trade and commerce—I put that last. B C

What is the meaning of an Empire? What does it mean to us? We have had a little experience. We have had a war, a war in which the majority of our children abroad had no apparent direct interest. We had no hold over them of any kind, and yet at one time during this war, by the voluntary decision of these people, at least 50,000 Colonial soldiers were standing shoulder to shoulder with British troops, displaying a gallantry equal to their own and the keenest intelligence. It is something for a beginning, and if this country were in danger, I mean if we were, as our forefathers were, face to face some day—Heaven forfend[5]—with some great coalition of hostile nations, when we had with our backs to the wall to struggle for our very lives, it is my firm conviction there is nothing within the power of these self-governing colonies they would not do to come to our aid. I believe their whole resources in men and in money would be at the disposal of the Mother Country in such an event. That is something—something which it is wonderful to have achieved, and which it is worth almost any sacrifice to maintain. . . . D

I believe in a British Empire, in an Empire which, though it should be its first duty to cultivate friendship with all the nations of the world, should yet, even if alone, be self-sustaining and self-sufficient, able to maintain itself against the competition of all its rivals. And I do not believe in a Little England which shall be separated from all those to whom it would in the natural course look for support and affection, a Little England which would then be dependent absolutely on the mercy of those who envy its present prosperity, and who have shown they are ready to do all in their power to prevent its future union with the British races throughout the world. E

5. **forfend:** prevent.

B Informational Focus Recognizing Political Assumptions How does Chamberlain justify and defend colonialism? How can you tell he assumes his listeners agree with him?

C Informational Focus Recognizing Political Assumptions What kind of relationship between Great Britain and the colonies does Chamberlain want to promote? What does he assume will be the result of this kind of relationship?

D Informational Focus Recognizing Political Assumptions What does Chamberlain assume the colonies would do if England were in danger and why does he think they would they do it? On what basis does he make this assumption?

E Informational Focus Recognizing Political Assumptions Why does Chamberlain "believe in a British Empire"? What assumption does he appear to make about the rest of the world?

Vocabulary **cultivate** (KUHL tuh vayt) *v.:* develop; promote.
prosperity (prahs PEHR uh tee) *n.:* wealth or good fortune.

Cross-Curricular Connection

HISTORY: The Boer War

After Great Britain colonized southern Africa, resentment built between the Boers (the Dutch descendants) and British colonists. The tension culminated in the Boer withdrawal from the region, the Great Trek (1835–1837), as the Boers established settlements in Natal, Transvaal, and the Orange Free State. The scene was set for the Boer War (1899–1902) by the discovery of gold in the southern Transvaal. British prospectors flooded the region, engendering the resentment of the Boer farmers. Tensions built for several years, ultimately resulting in a British revolt in Johannesburg against the Boer government.

Wealthy Cecil Rhodes, premier of the Cape of Good Hope Colony, set off the revolt in hopes of uniting all of southern Africa under British rule. The first victories went to the Boers, who captured the British-held Natal and Cape Colony. Within four months, however, the

SPEECH

"The Noble Mansion of Free India"

by **Jawaharlal Nehru**

Read with a Purpose

Read to find out what Nehru believes the Indian government owes its people and the world and how it can fulfill this responsibility.

Build Background

Jawaharlal Nehru was renowned for his efforts to establish a democratic government in India. He also sought to raise the standard of living for Indians, even while opposing alliances with powerful nations and adopting a policy of nonaggression. Nehru gave the following speech on the eve of Indian independence from Great Britain (August 14, 1947) to the members of the Indian Parliament.

Long years ago we made a tryst[1] with destiny, and now the time comes when we shall redeem our pledge, not wholly or in full measure, but very substantially. At the stroke of the midnight hour, when the world sleeps, India will awake to life and freedom. A moment comes, which comes but rarely in history, when we step out from the old to the new, when an age ends, and when the soul of a nation, long suppressed, finds utterance. It

1. **tryst:** rendezvous.

Vocabulary **pledge** (plehj) *n.:* promise or vow.

Indian Prime Minister Jawaharlal Nehru with his entourage at an airport in India (c. 1960).

Teacher Preparation

Selection Summary

Diametrically opposing Chamberlain's view, the second speech comes from an Indian statesman celebrating the end of Britain's colonial era.

Direct Teach

Think About/Talk About

Read with a Purpose Have students read the Read with a Purpose statement. Point out the word "responsibility." Ask students to consider how a government is responsible for the safety and well-being of its people.

Extend the Discussion

Finding Details What words and phrases does Nehru use to personify India? ***Possible response:*** *He states that India will "awake" to life and freedom. Nehru also refers to "the soul of a nation" rising from a state of suppression.*

Speculating What message do you think Nehru is trying to present to his audience in the first two sentences of his speech? ***Possible response:*** *Nehru is trying to evoke positive emotions in his audience and convince them that an independent India will be a new beginning for the country and an opportunity for change.*

Vocabulary: Own the Word

pledge: Tell students that the root word for *pledge* is *plebium*, which is Latin for "security." When you make a *pledge* (noun form), you offer an assurance that you will fulfill a promise. Ask students to name *pledges* that people might make.

British gained the upper hand. Still, Boer guerilla fighters kept their cause alive for another year, halted only through the stringent efforts of the new British commander, Herbert Kitchener.

The Treaty of Vereeniging succeeded in bringing political unity and peace to South Africa, but the Boers remained socially and culturally apart from the British.

HSS Analysis Skills: HI 1

Universal Access

Advanced Learners

Acceleration After students read both "I Believe in the British Empire" and " The Noble Mansion of Free India," have students think about each speaker's perspective on colonialism. Have them compare and contrast the diction, structure, tone, style, and rhetorical devices used in each speech. Then, ask students to start a class discussion on which text makes a stronger case—Chamberlain's or Nehru's.

Think About/Talk About

Analysis

A Informational Focus

Possible response: *Colonialism caused India's decline, resulting in "ill fortune" and a loss or compromise of its identity.*

B Informational Focus

Possible responses: *"Service" refers to the government's responsibility to end poverty, ignorance, disease, and inequality of opportunity. Nehru believes the government is responsible for its people and assumes that it has the ability to end this suffering.*

C Reading Focus

Possible response: *Nehru recognizes that it is sometimes difficult for people to overcome petty differences and difficulties, but exhorts people to make the attempt in order to build a better world.*

Vocabulary: Own the Word

- **endured:** Ask students to make a list of possible obstacles India *endured* during their struggle for independence. ***Possible responses:*** *opposition from Britain, tension between religious factions in India, police brutality*
- **incessant:** Remind students to think about the prefix *in–* which means "not," with the word *cease,* which means "to stop." Ask students to complete the following idea: Because of the computer server's *incessant* loud whirling . . . .
- **indivisible:** Remind students to apply the prefix *in–* to the base word *divide,* which they are familiar with, to understand *indivisible.* Ask students to list things that are normally *indivisible.* ***Possible responses:*** *emotions, water, weather*

is fitting that at this solemn moment we take the pledge of dedication to the service of India and her people and to the still larger cause of humanity.

At the dawn of history India started on her unending quest, and trackless centuries are filled with her striving and the grandeur of her success and her failures. Through good and ill fortune alike she has never lost sight of that quest or forgotten the ideals which gave her strength. We end today a period of ill fortune and India discovers herself again. The achievement we celebrate today is but a step, an opening of opportunity, to the greater triumphs and achievements that await us. Are we brave enough and wise enough to grasp this opportunity and accept the challenge of the future? **A**

Freedom and power bring responsibility. The responsibility rests upon this Assembly,[2] a sovereign body representing the sovereign people of India. Before the birth of freedom we have endured all the pains of labor and our hearts are heavy with the memory of this sorrow. Some of those pains continue even now. Nevertheless, the past is over and it is the future that beckons to us now.

That future is not one of ease or resting but of incessant striving so that we may fulfill the pledges we have so often taken and the one we shall take today. The service of India means the service of the millions who suffer. It means the ending of poverty and ignorance and disease and inequality of opportunity. The ambition of the greatest man of our generation[3] has been to wipe every tear from every eye. That may be beyond us, but as long as there are tears and suffering, so long our work will not be over. **B**

And so we have to labor and to work, and work hard, to give reality to our dreams. Those dreams are for India, but they are also for the world, for all the nations and peoples are too closely knit together today for any one of them to imagine that it can live apart. Peace has been said to be indivisible; so is freedom, so is prosperity now, and so also is disaster in this One World that can no longer be split into isolated fragments.

To the people of India, whose representatives we are, we make an appeal to join us with faith and confidence in this great adventure. This is no time for petty and destructive criticism, no time for ill will or blaming others. We have to build the noble mansion of free India where all her children may dwell. **C**

2. **Assembly:** Indian Parliament.
3. **greatest . . . generation:** Mohandas Gandhi.

A Informational Focus **Recognizing Political Assumptions** According to Nehru, how did colonialism affect India?

B Informational Focus **Recognizing Political Assumptions** What does "service" mean to Nehru? What assumption does he make about the role of government?

C Informational Focus **Recognizing Political Assumptions** What assumptions does Nehru make about the relationships among nations and peoples?

Vocabulary **endured** (ehn DURD) *v.:* suffered, put up with.
incessant (ihn SEHS uhnt) *adj.:* constant; never ending.
indivisible (ihn duh VIHZ uh buhl) *adj.:* unable to be separated.

California Standards, pp. 1157–1158

- **Reading Standard 1.1** Trace the etymology of significant terms used in political science and history.
- **Reading Standard 2.5** Analyze an author's implicit and explicit philosophical assumptions and beliefs about a subject.
- **Writing Standard 2.2** Write responses to literature: **b.** Analyze the use of imagery, language, universal themes, and unique aspects of the text.
- **Listening and Speaking Standard 2.3** Deliver oral responses to literature: **c.** Support important ideas and viewpoints through accurate and detailed references to the text or to other works.

INFORMATIONAL TEXT FOCUS

Applying Your Skills

Reading Standard 2.5 (see pages A48–A50)
Listening and Speaking Standard 2.3c (see pages A53–A55)
Writing Standard 2.2b (see pages A51–A52)

"I Believe in a British Empire"
"The Noble Mansion of Free India"

Analyze Informational Texts

Informational Text Focus

Quick Check

1. In the opening sentence of his speech, how does Chamberlain establish his perspective on Britain's colonialism? Explain.
2. How does Nehru use a description of India's past to support his belief that "greater triumphs and achievements" are inevitable?

Read with a Purpose

3. Which speech is more convincing? Why?

Informational Skills: Recognizing Political Assumptions

4. Look over each chart you created as you read. Then, write a short discussion of **political assumptions** in the two speeches. What assumptions does each speaker make about the effects of colonialism? How would you describe each man's view of the role of government based on these assumptions?

Text Analysis

5. **Make Inferences** What kind of attitude toward British colonists does Chamberlain exhibit in the expression "our children beyond the seas?"
6. **Analyze** What group of people does Chamberlain consider when he says "The Empire"? How does he feel about the group he excludes?
7. **Evaluate** Identify some emotional appeals in Chamberlain's speech. Do you think these appeals add to or detract from his argument?
8. **Evaluate** Does Chamberlain believe one can be critical of the British Empire and still be patriotic? How can you tell?
9. **Analyze** What effect does Nehru create by personifying India? Explain.
10. **Interpret** How does the image of the "noble mansion" sum up Nehru's message?
11. **Analyze** How would you describe the tone of Nehru's speech? What historical context accounts for this tone?
12. **Extend** Which speaker's vision of the future of colonialism and the relationships among nations do you think is closer to being realized? Explain.

Listening and Speaking

13. **Extend** With a partner, examine the next to last paragraph in Nehru's speech. Discuss how peace, freedom, prosperity, and disaster might be described as indivisible in today's world.

Writing Skills Focus

Timed Writing In a brief essay, discuss Chamberlain and Nehru's use of loaded language in "I Believe in a British Empire" and "The Noble Mansion of Free India." Be sure to support your response with specific evidence from the speeches.

What Do You Think Now? What experiences, values, and interests shaped the politics of Chamberlain and Nehru?

Check for Understanding

Independent Practice

Informational Text Focus

Possible responses:

1. *He refers to "this great Empire" and accuses his liberal opponents of treason.*
2. *He says that India never lost sight of the quest to improve itself.*
3. *Chamberlain's because he made a strong argument; Nehru's because he connects with his audience.*
4. *Chamberlain assumes that colonialism is a benefit, while Nehru assumes it is destructive. Nehru believes that the role of government is to serve and protect its people; Chamberlain believes that a citizen's role is to support one's government—no matter what.*
5. *He is paternalistic and condescending; he thinks that Great Britain should rule the colonists as an adult would rule children.*
6. *He is referring to British white colonists. His attitude is patronizing ("for whom we have become responsible").*
7. *He appeals to pride and economic security. His emotional appeal helps to raise a feeling of patriotism in his audience.*
8. *No; he assails his political opponents who criticized Britain's war tactics.*
9. *He makes India seem more appealing; he states that India is "coming to life" as a nation.*
10. *It suggests India's continued grandeur, a spirit of cooperation, inclusion, and self-determination.*
11. *The tone is positive and uplifting, probably because of India's approaching independence.*
12. *Chamberlain's vision that colonialism is what is best for the English empire is extremely clear; Nehru delivers his vision by painting a picture of an independent and prosperous India.*
13. *Students explain how one nation's peace, freedom, prosperity, and disaster benefited another.*

Universal Access

Struggling Writers

Some students may need additional scaffolding to complete the Writing Skills Focus activity. Before students write their essays, have them create a T-chart outlining examples of loaded language from each speech in separate columns. Ask students to address in their essays why each speaker chose to use certain loaded words and what emotional response they hoped to evoke from listeners. Have them apply what they learned from the writer's technique in each speech to their own writing.

What Do You Think Now?

To help students answer this question, remind them that the two speeches represent a fundamental difference in political opinion that had a direct impact on the lives of millions of people. Point out that the interests, biases, and perspectives of the citizens of Great Britain and India may also have been at odds with one another. Ask students how the citizens of Great Britain and India may have influenced Chamberlain and Nehru.

Independent Practice
Vocabulary Development
Vocabulary Check

synonyms: *1, 2, 5, 6, 8*

antonyms: *3, 4, 7*

Your Turn

Sample responses:

coup d'etat: Fr. "stroke or blow of the state"; "the overthrow of a government by a small group"

detente: Fr. "loosening"; "the relaxation of tensions"

electorate: Latin "chooser"; "all the people in an area who are able to vote"

fascist: Latin "group"; "a political philosophy"

monarch: Latin "sole ruler"; "one person ruling over a kingdom"

English for Academic Success
Language Coach

Possible responses: Incessant: cessare *meaning "to delay"* (cease, cessation); Cultivate: colere *meaning "to till"* (culture, cult, bucolic)

English for Academic Success
Academic Vocabulary

Possible response: *Responses will vary. Students should discuss the characteristics of the major conflict, the differing perspectives of the groups involved, how others may have had to adapt their lives in some way as a result of the conflict, and the unavoidable short and long-term effects of the conflict.*

Assess

Unit 6 Resources, Selection Standards Check, p. 64

ThinkCentral Online Assessment, Selection Standards Check

Teacher One Stop™, editable Selection Standards Check

Applying Your Skills

Reading Standard 1.1 (see pages A48–A50)

"I Believe in a British Empire"
"The Noble Mansion of Free India"

Vocabulary Development

Vocabulary Check

Tell whether each Vocabulary word is paired with its synonym or an antonym.

1. **pledge**/promise
2. **indivisible**/inseparable
3. **obtained**/lost
4. **apathy**/interest
5. **incessant**/constant
6. **cultivate**/develop
7. **prosperity**/poverty
8. **endured**/suffered

Vocabulary Skills: The Etymology of Political Science and Historical Terms

New words and phrases are introduced into our vocabulary nearly every day. Many English political science and historical terms have been borrowed from other languages. Consider the following terms.

Term	Word Origin	Meaning
apartheid	Afrikaans, "the state of being separate," (Dutch *apart* "separate," from French *a part*, + Dutch *–heid*, "-hood")	official South African policy of strict racial segregation and discrimination (c. 1948–1991)
democracy	Greek *demokratia*, "rule by the people," (*demos*, "the people," + *kratein*, "to rule")	government in which all citizens take part and limit the power of rulers
imperialism	Latin *imperialis*, "empire," from *imperare*, "to command"	domination of a powerful nation over the political, economic, and cultural affairs of another nation or region

Your Turn

Use a dictionary to learn the history of the political science and historical terms listed below. Determine the language the word is borrowed from, its original meaning, and its current meaning.

Term	Word Origin	Meaning
coup d'état		
détente		
electorate		
fascist		
monarch		
parliament		
laissez-faire		
veto		

Language Coach

Latin Word Origins Find the Latin words from which the Vocabulary words *incessant* and *cultivate* originate. How does knowing each word's Latin origin help you understand the word's meaning? Find another word that comes from each Latin word and record its meaning.

Academic Vocabulary

Talk About

With a partner, discuss what you know about a significant conflict between groups in the world today. What characteristics does the conflict exhibit? What are the perspectives of the groups involved? How have people adapted to the problems created by the conflict? What are the inevitable effects of the conflict?

Universal Access: Vocabulary Development

English Learners

English for Academic Success While students may understand the meaning of a word, they may need additional practice in identifying whether a word is paired with its synonym or antonym. Pair students with a proficient English speaker; then, have them engage in an instructional conversation in which they work through the following pairs of words, deciding whether the word pairs are synonyms or antonyms. Tell students that at least one word in each pair is a former Vocabulary word from this chapter, so they should be familiar with its meaning.

- perplexing/bewildering [*synonyms*]
- taciturn/outgoing [*antonyms*]
- rigor/flexibility [*antonyms*]
- vile/loathsome [*synonyms*]

✔ See the **Academic and Selection Vocabulary Skill Builder** in **UA: Differentiating Instruction.**

What Do You Think?

How does experience shape our view of the world?

QuickWrite

What do you think contributes most to a person's success in life: opportunity, talent, confidence, or some other quality? Record your thoughts in your *Reader/Writer Notebook.*

CONTENTS

(Center) Garden at Virginia Woolf's country home of Monk's house. *(Bottom right)* Virginia Woolf with her niece Angelica Garnett (née Bell) in 1934.
The Granger Collection, NY.

Objectives

Students will

- understand and analyze the characteristics of an essay
- identify the author's beliefs revealed through the text

Motivate

What Do You Think?/QuickWrite

Have students think about factors that have contributed to the success of people they have heard of or know. Then, have them use their **Reader/Writer Notebooks** to write about which factor is most important in determining a person's success.

English for Academic Success

Academic Vocabulary

Look for opportunities to use the Academic Vocabulary words in this unit.

- **adapt,** ***v.:*** adjust for a new purpose
- **exhibit,** ***v.:*** show, demonstrate
- **inevitable,** ***adj.:*** unavoidable
- **perspective,** ***n.:*** particular way of looking at something

Analyzing Visuals

Extension Activity How is the setting in the picture conducive to Woolf's writing style? ***Possible response:*** *The beauty and peacefulness of her home serves as an ideal setting for Woolf to explore and express the inner thoughts of her characters.*

Selection Introduction
Meet the Writer

- Virginia Woolf was exposed to literature and the arts from an early age. Along with her sister, the painter Vanessa Bell, and her husband, writer Leonard Woolf, Virginia Woolf became an integral figure within the circle of London artists and intellectuals known as the Bloomsbury group. She began publishing her writing early in the twentieth century.
- Like her Irish contemporary James Joyce, Woolf is known for her innovative literary style. She was one of the pioneers of the "stream-of-consciousness" style, which sought to present characters' jumbled, impressionistic thoughts and feelings realistically. Woolf described her artistic goal as the creation of "some kind of whole made of shivering fragments."
- Woolf challenged literary as well as social conventions. Writing at a time when women's educational and vocational prospects were limited, Woolf sought to win greater respect for female artists. In her essay collection, *A Room of One's Own,* Woolf argued that women's unequal educational and economic opportunities had prevented them from fulfilling their artistic potential.
- Though she struggled throughout her life with depression and loss, Virginia Woolf was one of the twentieth century's most prolific authors. By the end of her career, her résumé included many novels and short stories as well as essays and other works of nonfiction.

MEET THE WRITER

Virginia Woolf
(1882–1941)

Despite describing herself as "a born melancholic," Virginia Woolf was bright, passionate, and quick-witted. She battled periods of paralyzing self-doubt and severe depression and anxiety to become one of the twentieth-century's most innovative writers, conveying unlike any writer before her "an ordinary mind on an ordinary day."

From Privilege to Tragedy to Bloomsbury

Virginia Woolf was born in Victorian London to the scholar and literary critic Sir Leslie Stephen and his artistic wife, Julia. In her youth, Woolf enjoyed all the advantages of a financially comfortable and intellectually challenging environment. Too frail to attend school regularly, she was privately tutored and given the luxury of access to her father's extensive library. Her father encouraged her to read only what she liked.

When her mother died in 1895, Woolf experienced her first episode of severe depression. A few years later she suffered a series of tragedies with the death of her half sister in 1902 and her father in 1904.

After her father's death, Virginia, her sister, Vanessa, and their two brothers moved to the area of London known as Bloomsbury. Soon they and their friends began to meet in what came to be called the Bloomsbury Group, an intellectual circle whose other prominent members included the writer E. M. Forster, the artist Duncan Grant, and the economist John Maynard Keynes. An informal gathering with the highest cultural standards, the Bloomsbury Group helped provide the right environment for Virginia Woolf's sensitive, experimental fiction. One member of the group was Leonard Woolf, a journalist and economist. Although Virginia had considered in her journals the possibility that she might never choose to marry, she and Leonard Woolf wed in 1912.

Creativity and Despair

Leonard Woolf provided Virginia with encouragement and stability during her bouts of depression and through her difficult writing process, which was similar with every book she composed. She began with an inspiration, wrote for often more than a year with intermittent bouts of productivity and paralyzing writer's block, and then, after extensive revisions, worked with Leonard to prepare her books for production. She would end the process exhausted and often mentally unstable, but would inevitably find during this time the inspiration for her next work.

A Woolf Time Line

1880 — 1890 — 1900

1882 Virginia Stephen is born to a wealthy family in London

1895 Woolf's mother, Julia Stephen, dies

1902 Woolf's half sister, Stella Duckworth, dies

1904 Woolf's father, Leslie Stephen, dies

1904–1905 Moves to London; meets the members of the Bloomsbury group

1905–1907 English instructor at Morley College, London; writes reviews and feature articles for the *Times Literary Supplement*

1906 Woolf's beloved brother, Toby, dies

Virginia and Adrian Stephen playing cricket (c. 1886).
Presented by Quentin and Anne Oliver Bell. Mortimer Rare Book Room, Smith College/Society of Authors, U.K.

Selection Readability	
Easily Accessible **Accessible** Challenging	familiar situations; familiar syntax; accessible language

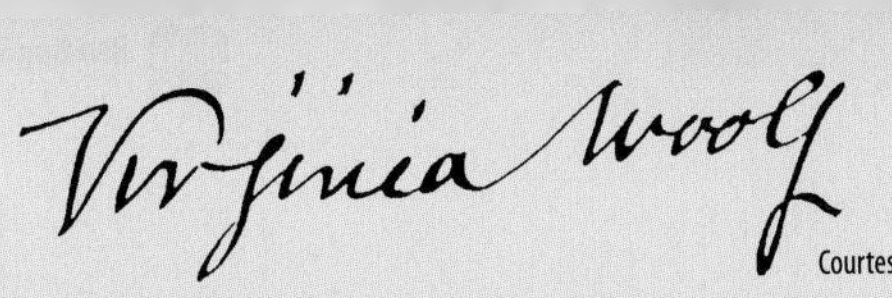

Courtesy Society of Authors, U.K.

Woolf had been writing since she was fourteen and reviewing books since her early twenties, but it was not until she was thirty-three that her first novel, *The Voyage Out,* was published. The subsequent publication of *Jacob's Room* (1922) and *Mrs. Dalloway* (1925) established her position as one of the foremost writers of her time. With these novels—and with her later novels *To the Lighthouse* (1927) and *The Waves* (1931)—Woolf pursued an experimental vision that emphasizes personal impressions over external events and focuses on the experience of life as it is being lived.

Like James Joyce, Woolf employs the technique of stream of consciousness, although her version is somewhat different. For example, while *Mrs. Dalloway,* like Joyce's *Ulysses,* seeks to cover the entire lifetime of a character in the chronicle of a single day, the former work does so mainly by linking characters' thoughts of mundane, domestic tasks to related, more emotionally dense moments. Woolf was a great admirer of Joyce's *A Portrait of the Artist as a Young Man,* but she considered *Ulysses* an "illiterate, underbred book." Still, she worried that "what I am doing is probably being better done by Mr. Joyce." The novelist E. M. Forster, in writing about *Mrs. Dalloway,* disagreed with her concern, noting that "to convey the actual process of thinking is a creative feat, and I know of no one except Virginia Woolf who has accomplished it."

Woolf also wrote a great many reviews and essays, in which she explored the work of female writers, often focusing on a particular author whom she felt had been neglected. In 1917, she and her husband established the Hogarth Press, which published many of the most important male and female writers of the day.

A Tragic End

Woolf's depression, for which no medication was available at that time, deepened with the German bombing raids over England in World War II. In March 1941, fearing she could not endure yet another bout of intense suffering, she wrote a note to Leonard expressing her love for him and then took her own life.

Think About the Writer How might Woolf's fragile health have fueled her desire to write about the thoughts and feelings of her characters instead of about their actions?

Key Elements of Woolf's Writing

- Stream of consciousness, which follows the thoughts and feelings of characters
- Emphasis on impressions and ideas rather than on plot and action
- Experimentation with new techniques, such as conveying everyday events in elevated style

Learn It Online
Find out more about Virginia Woolf online.
go.hrw.com H12-1161 Go

Virginia Woolf with her husband Leonard Woolf in Cassis, on the French Riviera in 1928.
The Granger Collection, N.Y.

1910

1912 Marries Leonard Woolf

1915 Publishes first novel, *The Voyage Out*

1917 Establishes the Hogarth Press with Leonard Woolf

1920

Nicole Kidman as Virginia Woolf in *The Hours* (2002).

1925 Publishes *Mrs. Dalloway* (novel)

1927 Publishes *To the Lighthouse* (novel)

1928 Delivers feminist lectures at Cambridge University

1929 Publishes *A Room of One's Own* (essays)

1930

1931 Publishes *The Waves* (novel)

1937 Julian Bell, Woolf's beloved nephew, is killed in the Spanish Civil War

1940

1941 Dies in Sussex, England

Selection Introduction

Think About the Writer

Tell students to think about Woolf's bouts of depression, as well as her poor health as a child. How might a person spend her day if she were unable to exert herself physically?

For Independent Reading

- *Margaret Bourke-White: Her Pictures Were Her Life,* Susan Goldman Rubin
- *How Reading Changed My Life,* Anna Quindlen

Learn It Online
The **Writers' Lives** feature of the Interactive Student Edition offers additional information about this author. Audio or video segments are provided for some authors.
go.hrw.com H12-1161 Go

Comparing Texts Resources

Unit 6 Resources, on-level practice and assessment, p. 67

PowerNotes, interactive lesson presentation with activities

Teacher One Stop™, on-level lesson plans and all print resources

Holt Audio Library

Holt Audio Library: Selections and Summaries in Spanish

UA: Holt Interactive Reader, p. 323

UA: Differentiating Instruction, modified lesson plans and leveled assessment, pp. 273, 276

UA: Supporting Instruction in Spanish, selection summary

Resources for Teaching Advanced Students, lesson plans, p. 196

ThinkCentral Online Assessment

ThinkCentral Online Remediation

Preteach

Introducing Vocabulary

Use this activity to check students' understanding.

1. What qualities would you expect from someone with a **servile** personality?
2. Give an instance in history where freedoms have been **suppressed**.
3. What conditions create a **propitious** environment for studying?
4. What other words might you use to describe a **prodigious** win?
5. For what transgression is Benedict Arnold **notorious**?
6. Name an obstacle you have overcome which seemed **formidable**.

English for Academic Success

Language Coach

Write these words on the board: *glamorous and victorious.* Then, use these words to show students that you can deduce the meanings of unfamiliar words by breaking them into their smaller parts.

Literary Skills Focus

As you read and discuss this informal essay with students, have them make note of features that reveal Woolf's beliefs toward the subject.

Reading Skills Focus

Give students a copy of the Reading Skills Focus graphic organizer before they read. (See **Unit 6 Resources.**) Tell them to use their responses to answer the questions on the Applying Your Skills page.

Writing Skills Focus

Have students record vivid details in their **Reader/Writer Notebooks** and use their notes to complete the Writing Focus activity.

Learn It Online

The **PowerNotes** presentation for this lesson includes a short video that introduces the essay. The video is also available on the online version of this page.

go.hrw.com H12-1162 Go

Preparing To Read

Reading Standard 2.5, 3.1, 3.8 (see pages A48–A50)

from A Room of One's Own

Literary Skills Focus

Essay An **essay** is a short piece of nonfiction writing that explores a particular topic. Formal essays are usually impersonal in tone and tend to be highly organized and full of facts. An **informal essay** is highly subjective, usually dominated by the author's own personal perspective and beliefs. Although informal essays can be casual in tone, they often reveal deeply held principles and touch upon controversial aspects of society.

Literary Perspectives Apply the literary perspective described on page 1163 as you read this essay.

Reading Skills Focus

Identifying the Author's Beliefs Note that at times Woolf states her beliefs directly, and at other times she only hints at them. To **identify the author's beliefs,** look for words and phrases such as *I think* and *I agree* that indicate an opinion. Also look for **loaded language,** language with strong emotional connotations, and for evidence that supports the author's beliefs.

Into Action Create a word web and identify four or five of Woolf's beliefs.

Writing Skills Focus

Think as a Reader/Writer

Find It in Your Reading To show the effects of sexual discrimination, Woolf imagines what would have happened had Shakespeare had a talented sister named Judith. In your *Reader/Writer Notebook,* note Woolf's use of vivid details to exhibit the effects of discrimination on Judith's life.

Vocabulary

servile (SUR vyl) *adj.:* like a slave; submissive. *Some people believed women should set aside their own wants and be servile.*

suppressed (suh PREHST) *v.* used as *adj.:* kept from being known. *She was a novelist and suppressed poet.*

propitious (pruh PIHSH uhs) *adj.:* favorable. *The most propitious place for a writer is a quiet room of one's own.*

prodigious (pruh DIHJ uhs) *adj.:* enormous. *Woolf was often exhausted by the prodigious energy writing required.*

notorious (noh TAWR ee uhs) *adj.:* widely but unfavorably known. *Some writers are notorious for turning in manuscripts late.*

formidable (FAWR muh duh buhl) *adj.:* hard to surmount. *Finding time to write was a formidable task for women with children.*

Language Coach

Suffixes The adjectival suffixes *–ous* and *–ious* mean "full of" or "characterized by" a particular quality. Note that in the Vocabulary word *notorious* the letter *i* before *–ous* is pronounced /ee/. However, in *propitious* and *prodigious* the *i* before *–ous* is not pronounced at all. Look at the syllabic spellings for these words. How are the *t* in *propitious* and the *g* in *prodigious* pronounced?

Learn It Online

Jump into this essay with the video introduction online.

go.hrw.com H12-1162 Go

Reader/Writer Notebook

Use your **RWN** to complete the activities for this selection.

California Standards, pp. 1162–1171

- **Reading Standard 2.5** Analyze an author's implicit and explicit philosophical assumptions and beliefs about a subject.
- **Reading Standard 3.1** Analyze characteristics of subgenres (e.g., satire, parody, allegory, pastoral) that are used in poetry, prose, plays, novels, short stories, essays, and other basic genres.
- **Reading Standard 3.8** Analyze the clarity and consistency of political assumptions in a selection of literary works or essays on a topic (e.g., suffrage, women's role in organized labor) (Political approach).

ESSAY

from

A Room of One's Own

by **Virginia Woolf**

Read with a Purpose

Read to discover what life might have been like for William Shakespeare's equally brilliant sister.

Build Background

A Room of One's Own is considered a pioneering work of feminist criticism. The aims of feminist criticism include exposing sexist attitudes in or toward literature, reinterpreting earlier works from a feminist perspective, uncovering neglected female writers, and analyzing how gender affects a writer's subjects, themes, and even style.

Here am I asking why women did not write poetry in the Elizabethan age, and I am not sure how they were educated; whether they were taught to write; whether they had sitting rooms to themselves; how many women had children before they were twenty-one; what, in short, they did from eight in the morning till eight at night. They had no money evidently; according to Professor Trevelyan[1] they were married whether they liked it or not before they were out of the nursery, at fifteen or sixteen very likely. It would have been extremely odd, even upon this showing, had one of them suddenly written the plays of Shakespeare, I concluded, and I thought of that old gentleman, who is dead now, but was a bishop, I think, who declared that it was impossible for any woman, past, present, or to come, to have the genius of Shakespeare. He wrote to the papers about it. He also told a lady who applied to him for information that cats do not as a matter of fact go to heaven, though they have, he added, souls of a sort. How much thinking those old gentlemen used to save one! How the borders of ignorance shrank at their approach! Cats do not go to heaven. Women cannot write the plays of Shakespeare. Ⓐ Ⓑ

1. **Professor Trevelyan:** G. M. Trevelyan, author of *The History of England* (1926).

Ⓐ **Literary Perspectives** **Analyzing Political Context** What information about the lives of women in the Elizabethan age do you learn here? Do you think the bishop's remark is sexist? Why or why not?

Ⓑ **Literary Focus** **Essay** How would you describe Woolf's tone in this paragraph? What does it suggest about her opinion of the bishop's remarks?

Literary Perspectives

Analyzing Political Context When we analyze political context from the perspective of gender, we examine patterns of thought, behavior, and power in relations between the sexes. Many pioneering women and men have worked diligently to point out how sexism, or inequality between the sexes, hurts both women and men. The struggle for equal rights for women has been long and often difficult. For example, women in England did not win the right to vote until 1918 (for women over 30) and 1928 (for women over 18), and it took marches, rallies, and thousands of women being jailed and protesting to achieve this victory. The essay you are about to read originated from two lectures Woolf delivered at women's colleges at Cambridge University in 1928.

As you read, be sure to notice the questions in the text, which will guide you in using this perspective.

Teacher Preparation

Selection Summary

In this informal essay, *A Room of One's Own,* Woolf imagines that Shakespeare had a sister, Judith, who was as talented as her famous brother. Because Judith was a woman, Woolf believes, she would not have been allowed to develop or express her genius. Had she done so, she would have been rejected by her family and her society. Woolf describes the difficulties that women faced in the sixteenth century—and by implication still faced during her lifetime in the twentieth century—in trying to succeed as a writer, artist, and creative public figure.

Direct Teach

Think About/Talk About

Read with a Purpose Before reading the selection, ask students to discuss possible reasons that there are few famous women writers from Shakespeare's time. According to Woolf, what are the conditions required for someone to create great art?

Analysis

Ⓐ Literary Perspectives

Possible responses: *Women had little money of their own and were usually married in their late teens. The bishop's remarks are sexist because they assume that women are fundamentally incapable of possessing the genius ascribed to Shakespeare.*

Ⓑ Literary Focus

Possible response: *Woolf's tone is sarcastic, indicating that she believes that the bishop is wrong.*

Literary Perspectives

Before students read the selection, have them read the **Literary Perspectives** about Analyzing Political Context.

Ask students to try using the political perspective from the point of view of gender to examine things in the media, government, or the corporate world. For instance, they could use this perspective to think about a film or apply it to observing the positions of people .in government and in businesses. Their analysis may be formal or may maintain the informal tone of Woolf's essay.

Remind students to use the notes and questions at the bottom of the page to help them use the perspective.

Universal Access

EL English Learners

English for Academic Success Help students familiarize themselves with potentially unfamiliar words in the essay:

- **heiress**—a woman who inherits great wealth
- **poached**—to trespass on someone's property to take game
- **escapade**—a wild, adventurous act
- **inglorious**—shameful
- **beguiling**—misleading

Model the Skill

- Provide students with a copy of the Reading Skills Focus graphic organizer. (See **Unit 6 Resources.**)
- Read aloud the paragraph that begins on the bottom of p. 1163. Point out that the phrase "I could not help thinking . . ." indicates that this paragraph will present the author's beliefs.
- Model **identifying the author's beliefs.** You might say something like: "Woolf states that the author might be right in his opinion that a woman could not have written the plays of Shakespeare. She suggests that, if Shakespeare had a sister as imaginative and talented as he was, she could have not have gotten an education because women's education was frowned upon at that time."

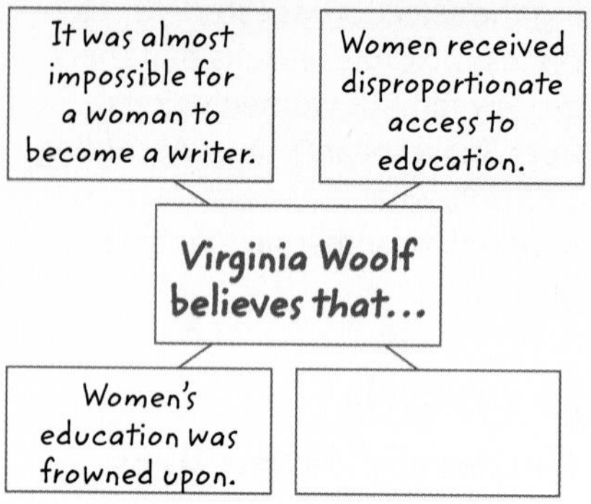

Guided Practice: Apply

Think-Pair-Share Group students into pairs to find clues revealing the author's beliefs. Point out the cultural factors affecting women that are described in the subsequent sentences, as well as the exclamation points in the previous paragraph.

Build Background: Virginia Woolf and the Education of Women

Although she was very well read, Virginia Woolf never had a formal education like her father and brothers, who attended Cambridge University. Woolf delivered an excerpt from *A Room of One's Own* as a speech at Cambridge's two women's colleges Newnham and Girton.

Be that as it may, I could not help thinking, as I looked at the works of Shakespeare on the shelf, that the bishop was right at least in this; it would have been impossible, completely and entirely, for any woman to have written the plays of Shakespeare in the age of Shakespeare. Let me imagine, since facts are so hard to come by, what would have happened had Shakespeare had a wonderfully gifted sister, called Judith, let us say. Shakespeare himself went, very probably—his mother was an heiress—to the grammar school, where he may have learnt Latin—Ovid, Virgil, and Horace—and the elements of grammar and logic. He was, it is well known, a wild boy who poached rabbits, perhaps shot a deer, and had, rather sooner than he should have done, to marry a woman in the neighborhood, who bore him a child rather quicker than was right. That escapade sent him to seek his fortune in London. He had, it seemed, a taste for the theater; he began by holding horses at the stage door. Very soon he got work in the theater, became a successful actor, and lived at the hub of the universe, meeting everybody, knowing everybody, practicing his art on the boards, exercising his wits in the streets, and even getting access to the palace of the queen. Meanwhile his extraordinarily gifted sister, let us suppose, remained at home. She was as adventurous, as imaginative, as agog to see the world as he was. But she was not sent to school. She had no chance of learning grammar and logic, let alone of reading Horace and Virgil. She picked up a book now and then, one of her brother's perhaps, and read a few pages. But then her parents came in and told her to mend the stockings or mind the stew and not moon about with books and papers. They would have spoken sharply but kindly, for they were substantial people who knew the conditions of life for a woman and loved their daughter—indeed, more likely than not she was the apple of her father's eye. Perhaps she scribbled some pages up in an apple loft on the sly, but was careful to hide them or set fire to them. Soon, however, before she was out of her teens, she was to be betrothed to the son of a neighboring wool stapler.[2] She cried out that marriage was hateful to her, and for that she was severely beaten by her father. Then he ceased to scold her. He begged her instead not to hurt him, not to shame him in this matter of her marriage. He would give her a chain of beads or a fine petticoat, he said; and there were tears in his eyes. How could she disobey him? How could she break his heart? The force of her own gift alone drove her to it. She made up a small parcel of her belongings, let herself down by a rope one summer's night, and took the road to London. She was not seventeen. The birds that sang in the hedge were not more musical than she was. She had the quickest fancy, a gift like her brother's, for the tune of words. Like him, she had a taste for the theater. She stood at the stage door; she wanted to act, she said. Men laughed in her face. The manager—a fat, loose-lipped man—guffawed. He bellowed something about poodles dancing and women acting—no woman, he said, could possibly be an actress. He hinted—you can imagine what. She could get no training in her craft. Could she even seek her dinner in a tavern or roam the streets at midnight? Yet her genius was for fiction and lusted to feed abundantly upon the lives of men and women and the study of their ways. At last—for she was very young, oddly like Shakespeare the poet in her face, with the same gray eyes and rounded brows—at last Nick Greene the actor-manager took pity on her; she found herself with child by that gentleman and so—who shall measure the heat and violence of the poet's heart when caught and tangled in a woman's body?—killed herself one winter's night and lies buried at some crossroads where the omnibuses now stop outside the Elephant and Castle.[3] **C**

That, more or less, is how the story would run, I think, if a woman in Shakespeare's day had had Shakespeare's genius. But for my part, I agree with

2. **wool stapler:** dealer in wool, a product sorted according to its fiber, or "staple."

3. **buried . . . Elephant and Castle:** Suicides, who were for years not permitted church burials, were commonly buried at a crossroads as a kind of punishment, perhaps to ensure that their souls would wander forever. The Elephant and Castle is a pub at a busy crossroads in south London.

C **Literary Focus** **Essay** What point, or main idea, is Woolf trying to prove by inventing Judith Shakespeare?

Real Issues, Real Experts

Holt author ***Sara Kajder*** *offers strategies for teaching "A Room of One's Own."*

As a student studying Virginia Woolf at the British Library in London, I enjoyed the ultimate author-study experience. I was situated in a context where the writer came alive, sitting in a chair in the Reading Room, paging through volumes of her diaries, journals, and drafts while speaking with renowned Woolf scholars about both her work and my ideas. While I know that I cannot provide my students with that kind of access, I can do two things to enrich my teaching and bring them as close to that as possible. I use online resources that present students with digital copies of original diary and journal entries. Students engage differently when we are examining a handwritten, original draft as opposed to an edited edition devoid of corrections and coffee stains. We start with the online collections at the British Library Web site and go from there.

Analyzing Visuals

Connecting to the Text Note the muted quality of the subject's face. Why might Vanessa Bell (Woolf's sister) have obscured the woman's features? How does this device contribute to the woman's identity?

Virginia Woolf in a Deck Chair by Vanessa Bell (1879–1961).

Analyzing Visuals

Connecting to the Text: *Vanessa Bell might have obscured the woman's facial features to depict the anonymity that characterized many women of her day. This device offers the woman no opportunity to express her individuality.*

Think About/Talk About

See Student Edition p. 1164 for the question that relates to the following answer.

Analysis

C Literary Focus

Possible response: *Social factors and imposed social norms, rather than a lack of genius, kept women from succeeding as writers in the sixteenth century.*

Extend the Discussion

Expressing an Opinion Do you agree with Woolf's argument about the likely fate of Shakespeare's sister? Why or why not? ***Possible responses:*** *Yes, any woman of genius would have faced similar obstacles and found no other way out. No, Woolf presents unproven hypotheses as facts, and a woman supposedly as clever as Judith Shakespeare would have found a way to write.*

Evaluating In the story of Shakespeare's sister, Woolf imagines a woman analogous to Shakespeare's sister experiencing a very different life than Shakespeare would have experienced. What elements does she use to dramatize the hypothetical story for the reader? How successful are these elements? ***Possible responses:*** *She invents an imaginative story with realistic details about Judith fleeing to London. She describes the faces of the men who laughed at her and her suicide, caused in part by her despair over an unwanted pregnancy. All of these realistic elements succeed in making the reader identify with Judith's situation.*

Model the Skill

- Review the characteristics of the **essay**. Point out that while Woolf's essay is informal, it presents an important perspective on a controversial issue and supports the main point with a variety of examples.
- Model how to determine the main point of an essay and follow the supporting arguments. You could begin by saying: "Woolf argues that genius exists among women, and that women should be allowed the necessary creative space and support that have always been available to men. She supports her argument by citing the examples of genius among women such as Emily Brontë and Jane Austen. To show what happens when that genius cannot flourish, she recounts the story of Shakespeare's hypothetical sister."

Guided Practice: Apply

Double-Entry Journal Use the Double-Entry Journal to increase comprehension of the material. Have students analyze the argument in the essay and find examples of evidence supporting Woolf's main point. Once they identify an example, have students explain in writing how it supports the main idea. Ask volunteers to share their analyses with the whole class.

Literary Connection

Brontë, a nineteenth century novelist and poet, wrote the famous novel *Wuthering Heights*. Robert Burns, an eighteenth-century poet famous for "Auld Lang Syne," was the son of a struggling tenant farmer.

the deceased bishop, if such he was—it is unthinkable that any woman in Shakespeare's day should have had Shakespeare's genius. For genius like Shakespeare's is not born among laboring, uneducated, servile people. It was not born in England among the Saxons and the Britons. It is not born today among the working classes. How, then, could it have been born among women whose work began, according to Professor Trevelyan, almost before they were out of the nursery, who were forced to it by their parents and held to it by all the power of law and custom? Yet genius of a sort must have existed among women as it must have existed among the working classes. Now and again an Emily Brontë or a Robert Burns blazes out and proves its presence. But certainly it never got itself onto paper. When, however, one reads of a witch being ducked, of a woman possessed by devils, of a wise woman selling herbs, or even of a very remarkable man who had a mother, then I think we are on the track of a lost novelist, a suppressed poet, of some mute and inglorious[4] Jane Austen, some Emily Brontë who dashed her brains out on the moor or mopped and mowed about the highways crazed with the torture that her gift had put her to. Indeed, I would venture to guess that Anon, who wrote so many poems without signing them, was often a woman. It was a woman Edward Fitzgerald,[5] I think, suggested who made the ballads and the folk songs, crooning them to her children, beguiling her spinning with them, or the length of the winter's night. D

4. **mute and inglorious:** allusion to line 59 of Thomas Gray's poem "Elegy Written in a Country Churchyard."
5. **Edward Fitzgerald** (1809–1883): English and poet.

D Literary Perspectives Analyzing Political Context How does what you have read about women's lives support the idea that "Anonymous" was likely a woman? What does Woolf mean by this statement?

Vocabulary **servile** (SUR vyl) *adj.:* like a slave; submissive.
suppressed (suh PREHST) *v.* used as *adj.:* kept from being known.

Drawing room at Charleston Farm, home to the Bloomsbury Group.

Universal Access

Struggling Readers

Benchmark Students Tell students that Woolf employs a conversational tone, dry humor and occasional sarcasm in this essay that may mislead readers about her real opinions. For example, we know Woolf quotes Pericles facetiously when she says, "the chief glory of a woman is not to be talked of" because Woolf immediately qualifies her statement: ". . . said Pericles, himself a much-talked-of man." Therefore, her next statement, "Anonymity runs in their blood," could not be an expression of Woolf's own belief.

Advanced Learners

Acceleration Encourage students to investigate two famous feminist documents that precede *A Room of One's Own:* Mary Wollstonecraft's *A Vindication of the Rights of Women* (1792) and John Stuart Mill's *The Subjection of Women* (1869). Have students compare the argument and tone of each selection and present their findings to the class.

✔ See **UA: Resources for Teaching Advanced Students** for strategies for teaching advanced learners.

This may be true or it may be false—who can say?—but what is true in it, so it seemed to me, reviewing the story of Shakespeare's sister as I had made it, is that any woman born with a great gift in the sixteenth century would certainly have gone crazed, shot herself, or ended her days in some lonely cottage outside the village, half witch, half wizard, feared and mocked at. For it needs little skill in psychology to be sure that a highly gifted girl who had tried to use her gift for poetry would have been so thwarted and hindered by other people, so tortured and pulled asunder by her own contrary instincts, that she must have lost her health and sanity to a certainty. No girl could have walked to London and stood at a stage door and forced her way into the presence of actor-managers without doing herself a violence and suffering an anguish which may have been irrational—for chastity may be a fetish invented by certain societies for unknown reasons—but were nonetheless inevitable. Chastity had then, it has even now, a religious importance in a woman's life, and has so wrapped itself round with nerves and instincts that to cut it free and bring it to the light of day demands courage of the rarest. To have lived a free life in London in the sixteenth century would have meant for a woman who was poet and playwright a nervous stress and dilemma which might well have killed her. Had she survived, whatever she had written would have been twisted and deformed, issuing from a strained and morbid imagination. And undoubtedly, I thought, looking at the shelf where there are no plays by women, her work would have gone unsigned. That refuge she would have sought certainly. It was the relic of the sense of chastity that dictated anonymity to women even so late as the nineteenth century. Currer Bell, George Eliot, George Sand,[6] all the victims of inner strife as their writings prove, sought ineffectively to veil themselves by using the name of a man. Thus they did homage to the convention, which if not implanted by the other sex was liberally encouraged by them (the chief glory of a woman is not to be talked of, said Pericles,[7] himself a much-talked-of man), that publicity in women is detestable. Anonymity runs in their blood. The desire to be veiled still possesses them. They are not even now as concerned about the health of their fame as men are, and, speaking generally, will pass a tombstone or a signpost without feeling an irresistible desire to cut their names on it, as Alf, Bert, or Chas. must do in obedience to their instinct, which murmurs if it sees a fine woman go by, or even a dog, *Ce chien est à moi.*[8] And, of course, it may not be a dog, I thought, remembering Parliament Square, the Sieges Allee,[9] and other avenues; it may be a piece of land or a man with curly black hair. It is one of the great advantages of being a woman that one can pass even a very fine negress without wishing to make an Englishwoman of her. **E** **F**

That woman, then, who was born with a gift of poetry in the sixteenth century, was an unhappy woman, a woman at strife against herself. All the conditions of her life, all her own instincts, were hostile to the state of mind which is needed to set free whatever is in the brain. But what is the state of mind that is most propitious to the act of creation, I asked. Can one come by any notion of the state that furthers and makes possible that strange activity? Here I opened the volume containing the Tragedies of Shakespeare. What was Shakespeare's state of mind, for instance, when he wrote *Lear* and *Antony and Cleopatra?* It was certainly the state of mind most favorable to poetry that there

6. **Currer Bell, George Eliot, George Sand:** male pseudonyms for the female writers Charlotte Brontë, Mary Ann Evans, and Amantine-Aurore-Lucile Dupin.

7. **Pericles** (c. 495–429 B.C.): Athenian legislator and general.

8. ***Ce chien est à moi*** (suh shee EHN ayt ah mwah): French for "This dog is mine."

9. **Sieges Allee:** busy thoroughfare in Berlin, German for "Avenue of Victory."

E Reading Focus **Identifying the Author's Beliefs** According to Woolf, what does the female writers' use of male pseudonyms at late as the nineteenth century prove?

F Literary Perspectives **Analyzing Political Context** What impulse does Woolf attribute to men but not to women? How might political context account for this difference?

Vocabulary **propitious** (pruh PIHSH uhs) *adj.:* favorable.

Literary Perspectives

Assist students with answering the **Literary Perspectives** question on this page by having them consider the political motives, ambitions, and situation of Britain at the time. Alternatively, ask students to consider the message in Joseph Chamberlain's speech, "I Believe in a British Empire" and its connection to Woolf's thoughts.

Think About/Talk About

Comprehension

E Reading Focus

Possible response: *The use of pseudonyms by women shows that even in the nineteenth century, they felt they needed to hide and give up a certain amount of publicity and fame for the sake of propriety.*

Analysis

D Literary Perspectives

Possible response: *Although there are few works ascribed to women writers, women always had the same potential and talent as men and have always produced some literature "anonymously."*

F Literary Perspectives

Possible responses: *According to Woolf, men instinctively aspire to conquer all that they see and remake the world in their own image. Women, on the other hand, do not. Even if they did possess this impulse, they have not had the opportunity to behave in the same way as men. Britain in the early twentieth century, like other European powers, was exercising its dominion over several overseas colonies, including those in Africa.*

Vocabulary: Own the Word

- **servile:** *Servile* and *servant* (noun form) are derivatives of *serve* (verb). Both servants and slaves submit to the will of superiors. Ask students for situations involving *servile* behavior.
- **suppressed:** Ask students: "How might you advise a *suppressed* writer about achieving publication of her work?"
- **propitious**: Ask students: "What might you identify as *propitious* indicators of good weather?"

Think About/Talk About

Comprehension

G Reading Focus

Possible response: *She cites the interruptions of everyday life (barking dogs, the interruptions of friends, the need to make a living, and the afflictions of poor health), as well as the indifference of the world at large, as evidence of the difficulty of writing a work of genius.*

H Reading Focus

Possible response: *Women faced both the material difficulties—the personal space and the independent income—and the immaterial difficulties of a hostile world.*

Extend the Discussion

Imagery What is the function of the "empty shelves" described in the last paragraph? ***Possible response:*** *The shelves symbolize all of the works of genius that could have been produced by creative women, had their ambition and talent not been stifled.*

Vocabulary: Own the Word

- **prodigious:** Act out eating a *prodigious* slice of pie. Ask one or two students to demonstrate the meaning at their seats.
- **notorious:** Tell students that *notorious* means "well known," but is used with a negative connotation. Ask students to name some *notorious* public figures past and present.
- **formidable:** Draw a semantic web on the board with *formidable* written in the center circle. Have students suggest words related to *formidable* and examples of *formidable* situations. Record them in the web.

Monitor Students' Comprehension

To check students' understanding of the selection, ask them for what purpose Woolf invents Judith Shakespeare. [*Her purpose is to show what she feels is the real reason that an Elizabethan woman could not have written plays of William Shakespeare's caliber.*]

has ever existed. But Shakespeare himself said nothing about it. We only know casually and by chance that he "never blotted a line." Nothing indeed was ever said by the artist himself about his state of mind until the eighteenth century perhaps. Rousseau[10] perhaps began it. At any rate, by the nineteenth century self-consciousness had developed so far that it was the habit for men of letters to describe their minds in confessions and autobiographies. Their lives also were written, and their letters were printed after their deaths. Thus, though we do not know what Shakespeare went through when he wrote *Lear,* we do know what Carlyle went through when he wrote *The French Revolution;* what Flaubert went through when he wrote *Madame Bovary;* what Keats was going through when he tried to write poetry against the coming of death and the indifference of the world.

And one gathers from this enormous modern literature of confession and self-analysis that to write a work of genius is almost always a feat of prodigious difficulty. Everything is against the likelihood that it will come from the writer's mind whole and entire. Generally material circumstances are against it. Dogs will bark; people will interrupt; money must be made; health will break down. Further, accentuating all these difficulties and making them harder to bear is the world's notorious indifference. It does not ask people to write poems and novels and histories; it does not need them. It does not care whether Flaubert finds the right word or whether Carlyle scrupulously verifies this or that fact. Naturally, it will not pay for what it does not want. And so the writer, Keats, Flaubert, Carlyle, suffers, especially in the creative years of youth, every form of distraction and discouragement. A curse, a cry of agony, rises from those books of analysis and confession. "Mighty poets in their misery dead"[11]—that is the burden of their song. If anything comes through in spite of all this, it is a miracle, and probably no book is born entire and uncrippled as it was conceived. G

But for women, I thought, looking at the empty shelves, these difficulties were infinitely more formidable. In the first place, to have a room of her own, let alone a quiet room or a soundproof room, was out of the question, unless her parents were exceptionally rich or very noble, even up to the beginning of the nineteenth century. Since her pin money,[12] which depended on the goodwill of her father, was only enough to keep her clothed, she was debarred from such alleviations[13] as came even to Keats or Tennyson or Carlyle, all poor men, from a walking tour, a little journey to France, from the separate lodging which, even if it were miserable enough, sheltered them from the claims and tyrannies of their families. Such material difficulties were formidable; but much worse were the immaterial. The indifference of the world which Keats and Flaubert and other men of genius have found so hard to bear was in her case not indifference but hostility. The world did not say to her as it said to them, Write if you choose; it makes no difference to me. The world said with a guffaw, Write? What's the good of your writing? H

10. **Rousseau:** Jean-Jacques Rousseau (1712–1778), French author whose candid, autobiographical *Confessions* began a vogue in literature for confessional accounts.

11. **"Mighty poets . . . dead":** line from William Wordsworth's poem "Resolution and Independence."

12. **pin money:** small allowance for personal expenses.

13. **alleviations:** things that lighten or relieve burdens or suffering or make it easier to bear.

G Reading Focus Identifying the Author's Beliefs What evidence does Woolf offer to prove that writing a work of genius is very difficult?

H Reading Focus Identifying the Author's Beliefs According to Woolf, what two difficulties faced by all writers are even more formidable for female writers?

Vocabulary **prodigious** (pruh DIHJ uhs) *adj.:* enormous.
notorious (noh TAWR ee uhs) *adj.:* widely but unfavorably known.
formidable (FAWR muh duh buhl) *adj.:* hard to surmount.

California Standards, pp. 1169–1171

- **Reading Standard 2.5** Analyze an author's implicit and explicit philosophical assumptions and beliefs about a subject.
- **Reading Standard 3.1** Analyze characteristics of subgenres (e.g., satire, parody, allegory, pastoral) that are used in poetry, prose, plays, novels, short stories, essays, and other basic genres.
- **Reading Standard 3.3** Analyze the ways in which irony, tone, mood, the author's style, and the "sound" of language achieve specific rhetorical or aesthetic purposes or both.
- **Reading Standard 3.8** Analyze the clarity and consistency of political assumptions in a selection of literary works or essays on a topic (e.g., suffrage, women's role in organized labor). (Political approach)
- **Grades 9–10 Review Reading Standard 1.1** Identify and use the literal and figurative meanings of words and understand word derivations.
- **Writing Standard 2.3** Write reflective compositions: **a.** Explore the significance of personal experiences, events, conditions, or concerns by using rhetorical strategies (e.g., narration, description, exposition, persuasion).
- **Listening and Speaking Standard 2.6** Deliver multimedia presentations: **a.** Combine text, images, and sound and draw information from many sources (e.g., television broadcasts, videos, films, newspapers, magazines, CD-ROMs, the Internet, electronic media-generated images).

Applying Your Skills

Reading Standard 2.5, 3.1, 3.3, 3.8 (see pages A48–A50)
Writing Standard 2.3a (see pages A51–A52)

from A Room of One's Own

Literary Response and Analysis

Reading Skills Focus

Quick Check

1. How would you summarize Woolf's response to the bishop's argument?
2. Why might marriage have been "hateful" to Judith Shakespeare? How does her father's reaction show how little he understands her?

Read with a Purpose

3. What might have happened to Judith if she had been allowed to develop her talents?

Reading Skills: Identifying the Author's Beliefs

4. Look over the chart you created, and place a check mark next to the belief that you think is most central to the essay. In a sentence or two, explain why this belief is the most important.

Literary Skills Focus

Literary Analysis

5. **Interpret** Woolf says of women "Anonymity runs in their blood." According to Woolf, why do women shy away from the limelight? Given what you know about women's history, does her explanation make sense to you? Why or why not?
6. **Infer** Woolf describes the writing process in great detail. What can you infer about her experience of writing from this description?
7. **Make Judgments** Does Woolf make any generalizations that you think are unsupported by historical or contemporary evidence? Explain your response and cite examples of political and historical events.
8. **Evaluate** Is Woolf's use of an invented biography convincing to you? Why or why not?
9. **Draw Conclusions** In this essay, Woolf expresses several beliefs—some quite strongly, others more subtly. In your opinion, which belief is most central to the theme of the essay?
10. **Literary Perspectives** Woolf's essay critiques gender roles in the early twentieth century. How relevant are her concerns to men and women today? Explain.

Literary Skills: Essay

11. **Analyze** What elements of this essay make it informal? Consider the subject matter, humor, the subjectivity of the writer, and the language.

Literary Skills Review: Tone

12. **Evaluate** How would you describe this essay's **tone,** the attitude a writer takes toward the subject? Does this tone serve Woolf's purpose? Support your ideas with textual examples.

Writing Skills Focus

Think as a Reader/Writer

Use It in Your Writing Return to a piece of persuasive writing you have composed on an important issue, or think of a new issue. Using vivid details, write an anecdote about a real or imagined person affected by the issue. Share your anecdote with a partner, and discuss whether it advances your argument.

What Do You Think Now? From this essay, what can you infer that Woolf values most in life? Explain.

Universal Access

Struggling Writers

Some students may need additional scaffolding to complete the Writing Skills Focus activity. First, provide students with topics to choose from. Topics might include abortion, cloning, affirmative action, or capital punishment. Ask students to express their stance on the issue in a short paragraph to organize their thoughts. Then have them write a short outline tracing ways in which the real or fictional character in their anecdote is affected by the issue. If time remains, have students share their anecdotes with a partner and provide each other with feedback.

What Do You Think Now?

To help students answer this question, remind them that this essay is an expression of Virginia Woolf's personal beliefs. Ask students to discuss why the issue of women in the arts is an important one for Woolf.

Check for Understanding

Independent Practice

Reading Skills Focus

Possible responses:

1. *Women could not have produced great works like Shakespeare's because of cultural oppression, not inability.*
2. *Women were expected to be the caretaker at the expense of their personal ambition. Her father's gifts show misunderstanding about Judith's resistance to typical women's roles.*
3. *She could have been as prolific and successful as Shakespeare.*
4. *Charts should accurately present the beliefs of the author as revealed through this selection.*

Literary Skills Focus

Possible responses:

5. *Women were taught to believe that it is not appropriate for them to draw attention to themselves. Yes, history shows women faced many struggles for equal rights.*
6. *Woolf herself has struggled with the creative process.*
7. *Most of Woolf's evidence is anecdotal and hypothetical, so it is not supported by historical fact.*
8. *Yes, it imagines what life might have been like for a woman writer in the sixteenth century; no, her example is not rooted in fact.*
9. *Women need the space and freedom—that men have enjoyed throughout history—to write.*
10. *Her argument is still relevant. Women have won acceptance in the arts, but there are still fields where they face difficulties.*
11. *Woolf's reliance on personal opinion and anecdote, along with her conversational, humorous tone, make this essay informal.*
12. *The contemptuous, ironic tone shows her distaste for the idea that women do not have the creative capacity of men. It is especially evident when she mentions the bishop's views.*

Independent Practice
Vocabulary Development
Vocabulary Check
1. *inefficient*
2. *submissive*
3. *difficult to beat*
4. *censored*
5. *a criminal*
6. *hold it as planned*

Your Turn
1. *A helpful person offers to assist others; a servile person sacrifices his own well-being to serve others.*
2. *Restrained can have positive connotations, like prudent or reserved; suppressed means that freedoms are limited.*
3. *Propitious deals with favorable conditions, but not necessarily fortune or luck.*
4. *If a task is formidable, it is very difficult and foreboding; if it is insurmountable, it is impossible.*
5. *Large is a common description of size; prodigious describes something that is extremely big, or gigantic.*

English for Academic Success
Language Coach
Possible responses: *spacious, grievous, nervous, mischievous, glamorous, capacious, famous, glorious, adventurous*

go.hrw.com **WordSharp: An Interactive Vocabulary Tutor**

English for Academic Success
Academic Vocabulary
Possible responses: *Students might say that the challenges faced by female writers are far from inevitable in a time in which equality between the sexes is not debatable anymore. Students can also point out that challenges are still present, and that many female writers refuse to adapt to gender stereotypes and social restriction by voicing their opinions with passion and intelligence.*

Applying Your Skills

Grades 9–10 Review Reading Standard 1.1 (see pages A48–A50)

from **A Room of One's Own**

Vocabulary Development

Vocabulary Check
Be sure you can justify your answers to the following Vocabulary questions.

1. Is a car that uses a **prodigious** amount of gasoline energy efficient or inefficient?
2. Are **servile** people submissive or combative?
3. If your opponent is **formidable,** do you consider that person easy or difficult to defeat?
4. Are the **suppressed** works of a writer widely published or censored?
5. Who is more likely to be called **notorious**—a criminal or notary public?
6. If the timing of an event is **propitious,** would it be better to postpone the event or hold it as planned?

Vocabulary Skills: Distinguishing Word Meanings
Distinguishing between the meanings of different words can be difficult. Words may have similar meanings with subtle or sometimes not-so-subtle differences. For example, consider the words *famous* and *notorious.* A person might be flattered to be called *famous,* or well known, but might not take so kindly to being called *notorious,* which also means "well known," but in an unfavorable or undesirable way. A woman who saves someone's life might become famous, while a woman who robs a string of banks would become notorious.

So how do you tell the difference? If you're uncertain, use a dictionary to help you distinguish meaning between words.

Your Turn
Answer each of the following questions. The boldface words are Vocabulary words.

1. What is the difference between ***servile*** and *helpful?*
2. What is the difference between ***suppressed*** and *restrained?*
3. What is the difference between ***propitious*** and *lucky?*
4. What is the difference between ***formidable*** and *insurmountable?*
5. What is the difference between ***prodigious*** and *large?*

Language Coach
Suffixes For each of these nouns, write a related adjective ending with the suffix *–ous* or *–ious.*

space	mischief	fame
grief	glamour	glory
nerve	capacity	adventure

If the adjective has an *i* before *–ous,* is the *i* pronounced? What consonant sounds in the adjectives are different from those in the nouns?

Academic Vocabulary
Talk About
Given Woolf's perspective, do you think the challenges faced by female writers are inevitable? Must women artists always adapt themselves to social restrictions? Discuss your thoughts with a partner.

Universal Access: Vocabulary Development

English Learners
English for Academic Success Give students additional practice with distinguishing word meanings. Have them read the following sentences and determine which sentence contains proper word choice.

1. The *humble* assistant bragged that he would get the promotion. [*incorrect*]
2. The *servile* assistant showered her boss daily with compliments. [*correct*]
3. He wanted to be *celebrated* someday for solving the toughest crimes. [*correct*]
4. He wanted to be *notorious* someday for solving the toughest crimes. [*incorrect*]
5. The rebellion was *suppressed* by the government. [*correct*]
6. Her *suppressed* frown was quite noticeable. [*incorrect*]

✔ See the **Academic and Selection Vocabulary Skill Builder** in **UA: Differentiating Instruction.**

Reading Standard 2.5 (see pages A48–A50)
Listening and Speaking Standard 2.6a (see pages A53–A55)

Grammar Link

Independent and Subordinate Clauses

A clause is a group of words made up of a verb and its subject. An **independent clause** expresses a complete thought and can act as a sentence; a **subordinate clause** expresses an incomplete thought and cannot stand alone. Subordinate clauses can be one of three types:

1. An **adjective clause** modifies a noun or a pronoun. It begins with a relative pronoun, such as *that, who, whom,* or *whose,* or a relative adverb, such as *where* or *when.*

   Virginia Woolf, **who wrote "Shakespeare's Sister,"** was a talented writer.

2. A **noun clause** performs the same function as a noun. Words used to introduce noun clauses include *how, that, what, who, whoever,* and *why.*

   The teacher will give extra credit to **whoever writes a paper on Virginia Woolf.**

3. An **adverb clause** modifies a verb, adjective, or adverb and tells where, how, when, why, or to what extent. Subordinating conjunctions like *as though* or *than* introduce adverb clauses.

   Woolf wrote **as if Judith Shakespeare actually existed.**

Your Turn

What type of clauses are the underlined words?

1. Despite periods of severe depression, Woolf continued to write.
2. Whatever you write should be edited carefully.
3. Writers must decide when to take a break.

Writing Application In your own piece of writing, find two independent clauses you can combine by making one clause subordinate.

CHOICES

As you respond to the Choices, use these **Academic Vocabulary** words as appropriate: perspective, considerably, adapt, exhibit, inevitable.

REVIEW

Determine Fact Versus Opinion

Sometimes it is difficult to distinguish fact from opinion. Remember that facts can be proven, while opinions express someone's thoughts and ideas on a topic and cannot necessarily be supported with hard evidence. Return to the essay, and discuss some of Woolf's statements. Which are facts? Which are opinions veiled as facts? Which are clearly opinions?

CONNECT

Start a Classroom Blog

TechFocus With a group of classmates, start a classroom blog about the issues raised in this selection. Discuss how life for women has changed since the time Woolf wrote her essay and what issues related to feminism affect your lives. Would American culture today encourage a woman with Shakespeare's genius? Why or why not? Ask your classmates and students in other classes for their perspectives.

EXTEND

Create a Multimedia Time Line

Learn more about the feminist movement and its leaders in the twentieth and twenty-first centuries. Form a group of five, and assign each member a period of time to research online. Find out who the important people were and what they achieved. Then, create a multimedia time line, using video, still images, and voice-overs. Share your time line with the rest of the class.

Universal Access: Grammar Link

English Learners

English for Academic Success To give students additional practice with noun clauses, have students turn the following noun clauses into complete sentences.

1. Whoever left this gift at my door __________. [*Whoever left this gift at my door must have had a reason.*]
2. __________ that she refused to go to school [*She was so intimidated by the school bully that she refused to go to school.*]
3. The thought of failing another class __________. [*The thought of failing another class did not seem to scare her.*]

✔ For more practice with independent and subordinate clauses, see **Warriner's Handbook, GrammarNotes,** and **Language Handbook Worksheets.**

Independent Practice

Grammar Link

Your Turn

1. *Independent clause*
2. *Subordinate clause; noun clause*
3. *Subordinate clause; adverb clause*

Choices: Evaluation Criteria

Review: Homework
Determine Fact Versus Opinion

- Students should be able to identify the evidence Woolf uses to support her claim.
- Students should be able to accurately differentiate between fact and opinion.

Connect: Homework
Start a Classroom Blog

- Blog should address issues of gender equality in Woolf's time and today.
- Students should be able to explain why genius is or is not encouraged in women today.

Extend: Homework
Create a Multimedia Time Line

- Students should use a variety of media to create the time line.
- Time lines should include the major events and key figures of the feminist movement in either the U.S. or Britain and explain their significance.

Assess

Unit 6 Resources, Selection Standards Check, p. 70

go.hrw.com **ThinkCentral Online Assessment,** Selection Standards Check

Teacher One Stop™, editable Selection Standards Check

Reteach

go.hrw.com **ThinkCentral Online Remediation**

Preteach

Introducing Vocabulary

Read aloud the Vocabulary words and sample sentences. Then, use this activity to check students' understanding.

1. How would you describe the difference between **bawling** and crying?
2. What is a **contemptuous** act?
3. How would you feel after dancing **feverishly** at a party?
4. How would a **defiant** person behave towards authority?
5. If you experienced **immobility** in your limbs, what would you be feeling?

English for Academic Success

Language Coach

After students read the **Language Coach,** have students come up with additional examples of words with the prefix *im–*. [*immoral, immoderate, imbalanced*]

Literary Skills Focus

As you read and discuss the selection with students, have them note elements of Woolf's style.

Reading Skills Focus

Give students a copy of the Reading Skills Focus graphic organizer before they read. (See **Unit 6 Resources.**) Tell them to use their responses to answer the questions on the Applying Your Skills page.

Writing Skills Focus

Have students record in their **Reader/Writer Notebooks** sensory details and use their notes to complete the Writing Skills Focus activity.

Learn It Online

Send students to **Word Watch** for audio pronunciations, synonyms and antonyms, and brief histories of word origins.

go.hrw.com H12-1172 Go

Preparing To Read

Reading Standard 3.3 (see pages A48–A50)

from Jacob's Room

Literary Skills Focus

Style The manner in which writers express what they want to say is **style.** With *Jacob's Room*, Woolf believed she had finally begun "to say something in my own voice." Instead of a traditional plot, Woolf provides glimpses of characters and impressionistic details of experience. As you read, note the following stylistic elements: compound phrases that link impressions; repetitions that draw unexpected connections; and a succession of images that conveys a sense of simultaneous experience.

Reading Skills Focus

Reading Closely Virginia Woolf's style in this excerpt requires close reading. When **reading closely,** you must pay attention to details and stop often to ensure you understand. You may have to re-read certain portions and monitor your comprehension by asking and answering questions.

Into Action Read the excerpt closely. Stop after each paragraph, and complete a chart like the one below. Re-read if necessary to find the answers.

Question	Paragraph 1	Paragraph 2	Paragraph 3 [etc.]
What is the scene?			
What vivid details does the narrator describe?	London lamps like "burning bayonets."		
Are there people in the scene? What are they doing?			

Writing Skills Focus

Think as a Reader/Writer

Find It in Your Reading Woolf uses sensory details: for example, "Sticks and leaves caught in the frozen grass." In your *Reader/Writer Notebook*, identify the words she uses to appeal to the senses of sight, sound, and touch. How do these details help you "see," "hear," and "feel" each scene?

Vocabulary

bawling (BAWL ihng) *v.* used as *adj.:* crying loudly. *Bawling women grieved as they walked.*

contemptuous (kuhn TEHMP choo uhs) *adj.:* showing dislike. *The men's eyes showed their contemptuous feelings for their ill-mannered neighbors.*

feverishly (FEE vuhr ihsh lee) *adv.:* in an agitated manner. *Readers turned the pages feverishly to find out what would happen next.*

defiant (dih FY uhnt) *adj.:* rebellious; disobedient. *The little boy was defiant, refusing to obey his mother.*

immobility (ihm oh BIHL uh tee) *n.:* lack of movement. *Immobility kept the old ladies' bodies stiff and sore.*

Language Coach

Prefixes When added to some words, the prefix *im–*, like the prefixes *un–*, *in–*, *il–*, and *dis–*, means "not." *Immobility* for example, means "no mobility." Use your knowledge of prefixes to tell the meanings of these words:

immature	impurity
impatience	impartial

Reader/Writer Notebook

Use your **RWN** to complete the activities for this selection.

Learn It Online

Discover more about the Vocabulary words online with Word Watch.

go.hrw.com H12-1172 Go

California Standards, pp. 1172–1176

- **Reading Standard 3.3** Analyze the ways in which irony, tone, mood, the author's style, and the "sound" of language achieve specific rhetorical or aesthetic purposes or both.

NOVEL

from

Jacob's Room

by **Virginia Woolf**

Read with a Purpose

Read to experience impressions and images that relate to one man on one day in London.

Build Background

Woolf's novel *Jacob's Room* is set in pre-World War I London and tells the story of a young man named Jacob Flanders, who eventually dies in the war. The name Flanders was inspired by the Flanders region of Belgium, the site of prolonged fighting in World War I. The character of Flanders was inspired by Woolf's brother Toby, who had died of typhoid fever in 1906.

The lamps of London uphold the dark as upon the points of burning bayonets. The yellow canopy[1] sinks and swells over the great four-poster. Passengers in the mail-coaches running into London in the eighteenth century looked through leafless branches and saw it flaring beneath them. The light burns behind yellow blinds and pink blinds, and above fanlights, and down in basement windows. The street market in Soho[2] is fierce with light. Raw meat, china mugs, and silk stockings blaze in it. Raw voices wrap themselves round the flaring gas-jets. Arms akimbo,[3] they stand on the pavement bawling—Messrs. Kettle and Wilkinson; their wives sit in the shop, furs wrapped round their necks, arms folded, eyes contemptuous. Such faces as one sees. The little man fingering the meat must have squatted before the fire in innumerable lodging-houses, and heard and seen and known so much that it seems to utter itself even volubly[4] from dark eyes, loose lips, as he fingers the meat silently, his face sad as a poet's, and never a song sung. Shawled women carry babies with purple eyelids; boys stand at street corners; girls look across the road—rude illustrations, pictures in a book whose pages we turn over and over as if we should at last find what we look for. Every face, every shop, bedroom window, public-house, and dark square is a picture feverishly turned—in search of what? It is the same with books. What do we seek through millions of pages? Still hopefully turning the pages—oh, here is Jacob's room. **A**

He sat at the table reading the *Globe*. The pinkish sheet was spread flat before him. He propped his face in his hand, so that the skin of his cheek was wrinkled in deep folds. Terribly severe he looked, set, and

1. **canopy:** covering.
2. **Soho:** area in West-Central London.
3. **akimbo:** bent or arched.
4. **volubly:** fluently, talkatively.

A **Literary Focus** **Style** Notice all the images of facial and body parts. What effect do these images create?

Vocabulary **bawling** (BAWL ihng) *v.* used as *adj.:* crying loudly.
contemptuous (kuhn TEHMP choo uhs) *adj.:* showing dislike.
feverishly (FEE vuhr ihsh lee) *adv.:* in an agitated manner.

Teacher Preparation
Selection Plot Summary

This selection from *Jacob's Room* offers a snapshot description of Woolf's main character, Jacob Flanders. In her characteristic modernist style, Woolf invites the reader on a bird's-eye view of London, finally settling on the windowsill of Jacob's room as he sits reading his evening paper.

Direct Teach

Think About/Talk About

Read with a Purpose Have students read the Read with a Purpose statement. Ask students to discuss ways that authors can convey the daily experiences of a particular character to readers.

Analysis

A Literary Focus

Possible response: *The images of facial and body parts create the effect of crowded streets in a town bustling with people. By the time the narrator settles on the description of Jacob, it is clear that he is just one man in a sea of people.*

Vocabulary: Own the Word

- **bawling:** Remind students that *bawling* is crying loudly. You might say: "The starved baby was *bawling* while the vexed mother was crying." Ask student to create a pair of related statements that show how *bawling* is louder than crying.
- **contemptuous:** To sneer may be a *contemptuous* facial expression. A person's hiss may be a *contemptuous* noise. Turning your back on someone may be a *contemptuous* gesture.
- **feverishly:** Demonstrate a person's actions and/or emotions while doing something *feverishly.* Ask one or two students to stand at their desks and demonstrate.

Universal Access

Students with Disabilities

Help students follow the narrative by providing them with a general outline. Tell them to refer to this outline to help them fill out their graphic organizer.

Part 1: London at night, a street market, people

Part 2: Jacob reading in his room

Part 3: outside sights and sounds

Part 4: Jacob going to bed

Remind students to look for specific details—how Woolf describes certain objects, sounds, and people's actions. Ask them what words or phrases help them to visualize the details vividly. Suggest that students illustrate before describing the details in their graphic organizer.

✔ See **UA: Differentiating Instruction** for a graphic organizer to scaffold instruction for students with disabilities.

Model the Skill

- Point out that Woolf intentionally uses unusual impressionistic detail and other stylistic techniques to achieve a specific literary effect.
- Read aloud the first paragraph of the selection. Create a list on the board of the elements of Woolf's **style** apparent in this paragraph. Your list might include the following: unique imagery (lampposts as bayonets); emphasis of color and light (yellow canopy, yellow blinds, pink blinds, dark eyes); and the juxtaposition of numerous images.
- In a sentence or two, describe the effect of these stylistic techniques. You might say: "This paragraph creates an image of London as a bustling city engaged in a battle between light and dark."

Guided Practice: Apply

Turn-and-Talk Have students continue to read the excerpt from *Jacob's Room*. At the conclusion of each paragraph, have students discuss Woolf's stylistic choices with a partner. Then, have each pair write a sentence that describes the effect of the stylistic elements they have identified.

Analyzing Visuals

Connecting to the Text: *The central figure stretches diagonally across most of the painting. He dominates and defines the space. However, the angular planes of the figure and the space around him are the same, showing that he is continuous with his environment and defined by it. Solo figures tend to blend in with their world as they react to its social and political influences as well as the physical environment.*

The Result (1924) by William McCance (1894–1940). Oil on canvas.
The Fleming Wyfold Art Foundation.

Analyzing Visuals

Connecting to the Text Note the proportions of the man reclining on the sofa. What might have motivated the artist to construct the central figure in such a manner? In what ways, if any, do solo figures like the man in the painting and Jacob in Woolf's novel become defined by their surroundings?

Universal Access

Struggling Readers

Strategic Students Model identifying sensory details in the selection. You might say something like, "As I read the first full paragraph on p. 1175, I visualize a snowy hill with clumps of grass at the top and dark bushes. I can almost feel the cold wind when I read 'the flurries of frozen particles' blown by the wind. I also hear a soft, *whish* sound as of a broom sweeping." Ask students to read the next few paragraphs and verbalize what they see, hear, and feel.

Advanced Learners

Enrichment Using the selection as a model, have students mimic the writer's style in providing impressionistic details of characters and experience in a short story about their neighborhood, nearby city or any other place they can describe vividly. Remind students to incorporate the stylistic elements of Woolf such as compound phrases, repetition, and series of images.

defiant. (What people go through in half an hour! But nothing could save him. These events are features of our landscape. A foreigner coming to London could scarcely miss seeing St. Paul's[5].) He judged life. These pinkish and greenish newspapers are thin sheets of gelatine pressed nightly over the brain and heart of the world. They take the impression of the whole. Jacob cast his eye over it. A strike, a murder, football, bodies found; vociferation[6] from all parts of England simultaneously. How miserable it is that the *Globe* newspaper offers nothing better to Jacob Flanders! When a child begins to read history one marvels, sorrowfully, to hear him spell out in his new voice the ancient words. . . . (B)

The snow, which had been falling all night, lay at three o'clock in the afternoon over the fields and the hill. Clumps of withered grass stood out upon the hill-top; the furze bushes were black, and now and then a black shiver crossed the snow as the wind drove flurries of frozen particles before it. The sound was that of a broom sweeping—sweeping. (C)

The stream crept along by the road unseen by any one. Sticks and leaves caught in the frozen grass. The sky was sullen grey and the trees of black iron. Uncompromising was the severity of the country. At four o'clock the snow was again falling. The day had gone out.

A window tinged yellow about two feet across alone combatted the white fields and the black trees. . . . At six o' clock a man's figure carrying a lantern crossed the field. . . . A raft of twig stayed upon a stone, suddenly detached itself, and floated towards the culvert.[7] . . . A load of snow slipped and fell from a fir branch. . . . Later there was a mournful cry. . . . A motor car came along the road shoving the dark before it. . . . The dark shut down behind it. . . . (D)

Spaces of complete immobility separated each of these movements. The land seemed to lie dead. . . . Then the old shepherd returned stiffly across the field. Stiffly and painfully the frozen earth was trodden under and gave beneath pressure like a treadmill. The worn voices of clocks repeated the fact of the hour all night long. (E)

Jacob, too, heard them, and raked out the fire. He rose. He stretched himself. He went to bed.

5. **St. Paul's:** London cathedral where many important British ceremonies, including royal weddings and birthday celebrations, are performed.
6. **vociferation:** shouting.
7. **culvert:** drain that carries water underground.

(B) **Reading Focus** **Reading Closely** What do you find out about Jacob in this paragraph? List some details you have learned about him.

(C) **Reading Focus** **Reading Closely** How does the scene shift between the second and third paragraphs? What is the narrator describing in this paragraph?

(D) **Literary Focus** **Style** What effect does Woolf create by using ellipses to end her sentences?

(E) **Literary Focus** **Style** How does Woolf show the impact of time on physical surroundings?

Vocabulary **defiant** (dih FY uhnt) *adj.:* rebellious; disobedient.
immobility (ihm oh BIHL uh tee) *n.:* lack of movement.

Think About/Talk About

Comprehension

(B) Reading Focus

Possible response: *Jacob is an earnest student of his surroundings; he studies the newspaper intently with a serious expression on his face.*

(C) Reading Focus

Possible response: *The second paragraph is set in Jacob's room, where Jacob is engaged in reading his newspaper. In the third paragraph, the scene shifts outside and describes the field over a stretch of time from three in the afternoon until the evening.*

Analysis

(D) Literary Focus

Possible response: *The ellipses allow Woolf to shift from scene to scene without breaking her rhythm. She uses these ellipses to separate one image from the next and to indicate the passage of time.*

(E) Literary Focus

Possible response: *Woolf points out the land as lying "dead," then describes the "frozen earth" giving way under the pressure of people and animals as time passes.*

Vocabulary: Own the Word

- **defiant:** Ask students to applaud to indicate how much they would like to be described as *defiant* and why.
- **immobility:** Remind students that *immobility* uses the prefix *im-* ("not") with the root word they already know, *mobile,* or "able to move". The resulting meaning is "not able to move."

Monitor Students' Comprehension

Check students' understanding by asking them to compare the description of the snowy landscape to that of London's. [*While London is described as crowded with flashes of color in the darkness, the landscape is described as immobile and dead.*]

California Standards, p. 1176

- **Reading Standard 3.3** Analyze the ways in which irony, tone, mood, the author's style, and the "sound" of language achieve specific rhetorical or aesthetic purposes or both.
- **Grades 9–10 Review Reading Standard 3.9** Explain how voice, persona, and the choice of a narrator affect characterization and the tone, plot, and credibility of a text.
- **Writing Standard 2.1** Write fictional, autobiographical, or biographical narratives: **b.** Locate scenes and incidents in specific places. **c.** Describe with concrete sensory details the sights, sounds, and smells of a scene and the specific actions, movements, gestures, and feelings of the characters; use interior monologue to depict the characters' feelings.

Check for Understanding

Independent Practice

Reading Skills Focus

Possible responses:

1. *The butcher's melancholy mood is shown by his dark eyes and his face as sad as a poet's although he has never "sung" verse.*
2. *He seems depressed by the news of strikes, murders, and other problems throughout England.*
3. *The excerpt is a study in contrasts: liveliness versus deadly quiet; a single face within a crowd.*
4. *Students' descriptions should demonstrate close reading and specify problem sections.*

Vocabulary Check

5. *c* **6.** *e*
7. *d* **8.** *b*
9. *a*

Literary Skills Focus

Possible responses:

10. *The world is bustling, but underneath, the noise is sad. Jacob's response is to shut out the world.*
11. *She compares it to looking through the pages of a book. Both involve searching through millions of pictures or pages.*
12. *Yes, newspapers reflect the experience of most people by reporting the news that has the greatest impact. No, newspapers only give a portion of the large-scale events.*
13. *The first paragraph repeats images of light and color, creating a rhythmic effect.*
14. *The narrator focuses on sights (the man with the lantern, a falling clump of snow, a twig raft) and sounds (a mournful cry, the rumble of the car motor). The effect is like a time-lapse camera surveying the landscape and zooming in on certain figures.*
15. *The narrator is omniscient. She seems to know everything that is going on and is not limited by the point of view of one character.*

Applying Your Skills

Reading Standard 3.3; **Grades 9–10 Review Reading Standard** 3.9 (see pages A48–A50)
Writing Standard 2.1b, 2.1c (see pages A51–A52)

from Jacob's Room

Literary Response and Analysis

Reading Skills Focus

Quick Check

1. What is the mood of the butcher in the first paragraph? What details indicate his feelings?
2. How does reading the newspaper seem to affect Jacob? Explain your response.

Read with a Purpose

3. How do the descriptions of London and Jacob's room help you understand the excerpt?

Reading Skills: Reading Closely

4. Look over the chart you completed. Then, write a brief description of the experience of reading this excerpt closely. What parts of the selection did you have to re-read? What questions did you have after reading each paragraph? Share your experiences with a partner.

Vocabulary Check

Match the Vocabulary words with their definitions.

5. bawling	**a.** lack of movement
6. contemptuous	**b.** rebellious
7. feverishly	**c.** crying loudly
8. defiant	**d.** anxiously
9. immobility	**e.** showing strong disrespect

Literary Skills Focus

Literary Analysis

10. **Interpret** Critics have argued that *Jacob's Room* is not ultimately about Jacob but rather about the world that creates him. How would you describe this world? How does it affect Jacob?
11. **Compare and Contrast** To what does the narrator compare the experience of looking for Jacob's room? How are the two experiences similar?
12. **Extend** Do you agree that newspapers "take the impression of the whole," that is, that they reflect the experiences of all people? Why or why not?

Literary Skills: Style

13. **Analyze** What repetitions can you find in the first paragraph? What effect do they create?
14. **Evaluate** Woolf's narrator surveys the countryside by skipping from image to image. On what details does Woolf focus, and how does she describe them? What is the effect of this style?

Literary Skills Review: Point of View

15. **Analyze** The vantage point from which an author tells a story, or point of view, is often classified as **first person** (the narrator is a character who uses the pronoun *I*); **third-person limited** (the narrator is external and tells the story from one character's perspective); or **omniscient** (the narrator is outside the story but knows everything that is going on). How would you describe the point of view in this excerpt?

Writing Skills Focus

Think as a Reader/Writer

Use It in Your Writing Using Woolf's descriptions as a model, describe a scene. Focus on certain details and choose words with sensory appeal to help your reader "see," "hear," and "feel" the scene.

What Do You Think Now Woolf wrote *Jacob's Room* after World War I. How might the war have affected her worldview and values? How might this explain the details included in the story?

Universal Access

Struggling Writers

Some students may need additional scaffolding to complete the Writing Skills Focus activity. First, have students brainstorm two or three scenes. They might choose a quiet night scene or a busy day scene. Then, have them create a chart that lists details for each sense in a separate column. Tell students as they write to choose the words that help the reader feel as if he or she were standing in the middle of the scene and seeing, hearing, or feeling the details in the scene.

What Do You Think Now?

To help students answer the question, remind them of the effects of the war on other writers. Point out that Woolf experienced the war indirectly but chose the subject of a young man reading reports of distressing news.

Reading Standard 3.3 (see pages A48–A50)

A Haunted House

Literary Skills Focus

Imagery Language that appeals to the senses is called **imagery.** Although most images are visual, imagery can also appeal to your sense of hearing, touch, taste, or smell. "A Haunted House" is alive with vivid imagery conveyed in unique ways. Note how Woolf appeals to the senses in her description of this scene, allowing the reader to see, hear, and feel what she describes: "The wind roars up the avenue. Trees stoop and bend this way and that. Moonbeams splash and spill widely in the rain."

Reading Skills Focus

Visualizing Setting Using story details to see a scene in your mind's eye is called **visualizing setting.** Try the following techniques to help you visualize the setting:

- Read a paragraph or two. Then, stop and visualize what you have read.
- Read aloud. Sometimes hearing the words helps to visualize the scene.
- Create a picture in your mind as you read. Add to or adjust your picture as you learn more details about the setting.

Into Action Using a chart like this one, briefly summarize the reading, and note what you visualize.

What I Read	What I Visualize
It is raining, and the wind is blowing hard and bending trees. Inside the light is still, and the ghostly couple open windows.	stormy dark night; trees bending in the wind; a soft light inside a peaceful house; windows opening and shutting gently

Writing Skills Focus

Think as a Reader/Writer

Find It in Your Reading Note how Woolf chooses words and phrases that create clear, vivid **imagery** and communicate the **connotation** (or emotional meaning) she intends. In your *Reader/Writer Notebook,* record similar instances, where words and phrases, such as *gently* and *the pulse of a heart,* have clear connotations and create a vivid picture.

Language Coach

Denotation / Connotation To express themselves precisely and create vivid imagery, writers rely not only on a word's **denotations,** or dictionary definitions, but also on its connotations. **Connotations,** the ideas and feelings a word evokes, can cause a description to take on a negative or positive tone. For example, describing something that does not cost much as *cheap* might imply that its quality is poor because *cheap* has more negative connotations. The word *inexpensive,* however, has more neutral connotations.

Reader/Writer **Notebook**

Use your **RWN** to complete the activities for this selection.

Learn It Online

Find graphic organizers online to help you as you read.

go.hrw.com H12-1177 Go

California Standards, pp. 1177–1180

- **Reading Standard 3.3** Analyze the ways in which irony, tone, mood, the author's style, and the "sound" of language achieve specific rhetorical or aesthetic purposes or both.

Preteach

English for Academic Success

Language Coach

Tell students that the word *safe* is repeated three times in a phrase that recurs throughout the piece. Explain that repetition emphasizes the meaning and shows that the house, like a living entity, has a "heart" and a "pulse" that beats "safe" from its core.

Literary Skills Focus

As you read and discuss the selection with students, have them note imagery that appeals to the senses.

Reading Skills Focus

Give students a copy of the Reading Skills Focus graphic organizer before they read. (See **Unit 6 Resources.**) Have them use their responses to answer the Applying Your Skills questions.

Writing Skills Focus

Have students record the connotations of imagery in their **Reader/Writer Notebooks** and use their notes to complete the Writing Skills Focus activity.

Learn It Online

If your students need extra reading support for literary texts, introduce them to **Interactive Graphic Organizers**—tools for generating and organizing ideas, comparing and contrasting, and other key skills.

go.hrw.com H12-1177 Go

Teacher Preparation

Selection Plot Summary

In *A Haunted House,* Woolf describes the visit of a "ghostly couple" to their former house in search of their "buried treasure." The narrator, who lives in the house, describes their visit in subjective, impressionistic detail.

Direct Teach

Think About/Talk About

Read with a Purpose Have students read the Read with a Purpose statement. Ask them, as they read, to think about what kind of "buried treasure" the couple was looking for.

Comprehension

A Reading Focus

Possible responses: *The setting is a house in the country, its rooms and garden. The mention of doors shutting, reading in a drawing room, reflections in the window panes, and sleeping at night all help the reader visualize the scene.*

Analysis

B Literary Focus

Possible response: *The window-panes reflecting the apples, roses, and leaves in the garden and the shadow of a thrush on the carpet provide a vivid daylight image of the drawing room. A wood pigeon's cooing breaks the silence of this scene.*

SHORT STORY

A Haunted House

by **Virginia Woolf**

Read with a Purpose
Read this story to find out what compels a ghostly couple to return to their home.

Build Background
A *Haunted House and Other Stories* was published by Leonard Woolf three years after Virginia's death. Like many of Woolf's stories, "A Haunted House" focuses on thoughts and impressions instead of on actions. In classic Woolf style, "A Haunted House" is delightfully unpredictable—a ghost story like no other.

Whatever hour you woke there was a door shutting. From room to room they went, hand in hand, lifting here, opening there, making sure—a ghostly couple.

"Here we left it," she said. And he added, "Oh, but here too!" "It's upstairs," she murmured, "And in the garden," he whispered. "Quietly," they said, "or we shall wake them."

But it wasn't that you woke us. Oh, no. "They're looking for it; they're drawing the curtain," one might say, and so read on a page or two. "Now they've found it," one would be certain, stopping the pencil on the margin. And then, tired of reading, one might rise and see for oneself, the house all empty, the doors standing open, only the wood pigeons bubbling with content and the hum of the threshing machine sounding from the farm. "What did I come in here for? What did I want to find?" My hands were empty. "Perhaps it's upstairs then?" The apples were in the loft. And so down again, the garden still as ever, only the book had slipped into the grass. **A**

But they found it in the drawing-room. Not that one could ever see them. The window-panes reflected apples, reflected roses; all the leaves were green in the glass. If they moved in the drawing-room, the apple only turned its yellow side. Yet, the moment after, if the door was opened, spread about the floor, hung upon the walls, pendant from ceiling—what? My hands were empty. The shadow of a thrush crossed the carpet; from the deepest wells of silence the wood pigeon drew its bubble of sound. "Safe, safe, safe," the pulse of the house beat softly. "The treasure buried; the room . . ." the pulse stopped short. Oh, was that the buried treasure? **B**

A moment later the light had faded. Out in the garden then? But the trees spun darkness for a wandering beam of sun. So fine, so rare, coolly sunk beneath the surface the beam I sought always burnt behind the glass. Death was the glass; death was between us; coming to the woman first, hundreds of years ago, leaving the house, sealing all the windows; the rooms were darkened. He left it, left her, went North, went East, saw the stars turned in the Southern sky; sought the house, found it dropped beneath the Downs. "Safe, safe, safe," the pulse of the house beat gladly, "The treasure yours."

The wind roars up the avenue. Trees stoop and bend this way and that. Moonbeams splash and spill wildly in the rain. But the beam of the lamp falls straight from the window. The candle burns stiff and still. Wandering through the house, opening the windows, whispering not to wake us, the ghostly couple seek their joy.

"Here we slept," she says. And he adds, "Kisses without number." "Waking in the morning—" "Silver between the trees—" "Upstairs—" "In the garden—"

A Reading Focus **Visualizing Setting** Describe the setting. What details help you visualize the scene?

B Literary Focus **Imagery** What imagery helps you see and hear this scene?

Universal Access

EL English Learners

English for Academic Success Although her language seems superficially simple, Woolf's style and descriptive imagery can be challenging. Break down difficult text with students and make sure they understand the images. For example, the phrase "the trees spun darkness for a wandering beam of sun" places the word *spun* in an unusual context. Explain that the phrase shows how sunlight hitting the shaking branches creates shadows that seem to spin.

Struggling Readers

Strategic Students Students may find it difficult to follow the change of speakers and the sequence of events. Have them select a paragraph and identify the speakers, their dialogue, and the events. For instance, in the third paragraph, the narrator says, "it wasn't you that woke us," addressing the ghosts. In the middle of writing she stops and notices, "They're looking for it . . ." At other times, "tired of reading," she looks for the ghosts around the house.

Home Sweet Home (1971) by Silvia Quandt (b. 1939).

Analyzing Visuals

Connecting to the Text Note how the house becomes "small" when framed by the flowers. How does Woolf use descriptions of nature to affect the reader's perspective of the haunted house?

"When summer came—" "In winter snowtime—" The doors go shutting far in the distance, gently knocking like the pulse of a heart. **C**

Nearer they come; cease at the doorway. The wind falls, the rain slides silver down the glass. Our eyes darken; we hear no steps beside us; we see no lady spread her ghostly cloak. His hands shield the lantern. "Look," he breathes. "Sound asleep. Love upon their lips." **D**

Stooping, holding their silver lamp above us, long they look and deeply. Long they pause. The wind drives straightly; the flame stoops slightly. Wild beams of moonlight cross both floor and wall, and, meeting, stain the faces bent; the faces pondering; the faces that search the sleepers and seek their hidden joy. **E**

"Safe, safe, safe," the heart of the house beats proudly. "Long years—" he sighs. "Again you found me." "Here," she murmurs, "sleeping; in the garden reading; laughing, rolling apples in the loft. Here we left our treasure—" Stooping, their light lifts the lids upon my eyes. "Safe! safe! safe!" the pulse of the house beats wildly. Waking, I cry "Oh, is this *your*—buried treasure? The light in the heart."

C Reading Focus Visualizing Setting Woolf gives just a few details here as the ghostly couple remember their days in the house. Are you able to visualize the setting based on so few words? Why or why not?

D Reading Focus Visualizing Setting What is the setting of this scene? What is happening?

E Literary Focus Imagery How does the image of the ghostly couple in this scene help you get to know them?

California Standards, p. 1180

- **Reading Standard 3.3** Analyze the ways in which irony, tone, mood, the author's style, and the "sound" of language achieve specific rhetorical or aesthetic purposes or both.
- **Reading Standard 3.4** Apply ways in which poets use imagery, personification, figures of speech, and sounds to evoke readers' emotions.
- **Writing Standard 2.1** Write fictional, autobiographical, or biographical narratives: **b.** Locate scenes and incidents in specific places.

Think About/Talk About

Comprehension

C Reading Focus

Possible responses: *Yes, one can visualize the setting because the house may have not have changed that much; no, one cannot visualize it because the reader does not know when the couple lived in the house.*

D Reading Focus

Possible response: *The living are in their bedroom sleeping, and the ghostly couple is peering at them in the moonlight.*

Analysis

E Literary Focus

Possible response: *In this scene, the faces of the ghostly couple are illuminated by the moonlight. The faces are "pondering" and investigating the hidden feelings of those sleeping.*

Analyzing Visuals

Connecting to the Text: *Woolf depicts nature's creatures and objects as peaceful, delicate, and full of life, causing the reader to perceive the haunted house as almost one with nature, and therefore harmless.*

Monitor Students' Comprehension

To check students' understanding of the selection, ask them to explain why, at the end of the story, the narrator asks, "Oh, is this *your*—buried treasure? The light in the heart." What is the "light in the heart," and why is *your* italicized? [*The "light in the heart" may be the vitality and emotion of the couple. The word "your" is italicized to indicate that the narrator questions to whom the "light" or "treasure" belongs. Both the living and the ghosts may think they own it.*]

Check for Understanding

Independent Practice

Reading Skills Focus

Possible responses:

1. *They were a very loving couple who recalled "kisses without number." Death came "to the woman first" and he left the house, traveled, and came back.*
2. *The narrator refers to it as "the light in the heart," and the ghostly couple finds it all over the house.*
3. *They want to keep the "buried treasure." The house beats "Safe, safe, safe" in response to their search for the buried treasure.*
4. *Students should note how their visualization of the setting helped them follow the movements and actions of the characters.*

Literary Skills Focus

Possible responses:

5. *The narrator describes the ghosts' activities on different occasions. She describes herself becoming aware of them at different times.*
6. *Her tone is casual. She cannot see them but notes changes in the room's shadows as they move around in the drawing room.*
7. *This story consists of a series of observations and descriptions culminating with an emotional realization.*
8. *Woolf explores the idea that the outer landscape reflects an inner one; intimacy and happiness are timeless qualities. The ghost story shows that the dead couple had the same sense of joy as the living.*
9. *In "The Rocking-Horse Winner", the repetition of "There must be more money" creates an anxious, ominous feeling. By contrast, "safe, safe, safe" is reassuring.*
10. *Woolf focuses on images of sunlight, moonlight, light from lamps, and the dancing shadows.*
11. *"Death was the glass" is a metaphor that defines death as transparent and reflective, playing on the idea of ghosts and shadows.*

Applying Your Skills

Reading Standard 3.3, 3.4 (see pages A48–A50)
Writing Standard 2.1b (see pages A51–A52)

A Haunted House

Literary Response and Analysis

Reading Skills Focus

Quick Check

1. What can you infer about the ghostly couple's experience when they lived in the house? Provide two details that support your response.
2. How does the narrator refer to the treasure the couple has come to find? Where do they find it?

Read with a Purpose

3. What do the ghostly couple plan to do with the "buried treasure"?

Reading Skills: Visualizing Setting

4. Add a third column to your chart noting how visualizing helped you understand the story.

What I Read	What I Visualize	How It Helped Me Understand
Paragraphs 1 and 2	ghostly couple in a house with many rooms, an upstairs, and a garden	

Literary Skills Focus

Literary Analysis

5. **Interpret** How does the narrator convey a sense that the ghostly couple's visits are ongoing?
6. **Evaluate** What details in the third paragraph show the narrator is not afraid of the couple? Describe the narrator's **tone,** or attitude.
7. **Analyze** Most stories follow the classic plot structure consisting of situation, conflict, main event, climax, and resolution. How does the structure of Woolf's story differ from this format?
8. **Evaluate** What message about life does Woolf express in this story? Why do you think she chose a "ghost story" to convey this message?
9. **Compare and Contrast** The house in this story repeats the phrase "safe, safe, safe." Read D. H. Lawrence's story "The Rocking Horse Winner" (on page 1309 of this book), another story in which a house seems to repeat a phrase. Compare the phrases that the two houses repeat. How does the repetition create very different feelings?

Literary Skills: Imagery

10. **Interpret** This story emphasizes the pleasure of lightness, both physical and emotional. How does the imagery reinforce this idea?

Literary Skills Review: Figures of Speech

11. **Analyze** A **figure of speech** is a word or phrase that describes one thing in terms of another, dissimilar thing. **Metaphors** ("the world is his oyster") make direct comparisons. **Similes** ("the world is like an oyster") use connecting words, such as *like* or *as,* to make comparisons. Find figures of speech in the story. What effects do they create?

Writing Skills Focus

Think as a Reader/Writer

Use It in Your Writing Using Woolf's techniques as a model, describe a setting with a strange, mysterious mood. Be sure to use key details and rich images.

What Do You Think Now

What things or experiences are important to the ghostly couple? Are these also important to the narrator? How do you know?

Universal Access

Struggling Writers

Some students may need additional scaffolding to complete the Writing Skills Focus activity. First, review Woolf's stylistic techniques with students. Point out her use of personification ("wind roars," "Trees stoop") in her descriptions of nature, and metaphor ("Death was the glass"). Ask students how they would depict images of nature to convey a mysterious mood. Remind them to add sensory details in their descriptions.

What Do You Think Now?

Tell students to think about the rooms the ghosts visit and what they say as they reminisce. Point out the parallels between the ghostly couple and the narrator.

Preparing to Read

Reading Standard 3.3 (see pages A48–A50)

from The Letters of Virginia Woolf

Literary Skills Focus

Diction A writer's or speaker's choice of words, **diction,** is an essential element of his or her style. Authors select words for their **denotations,** or dictionary meanings, and their **connotations,** or emotional associations, to convey their ideas precisely. Diction is also adapted to fit the writer's audience, subject, and purpose. Instead of stating that Murry's eyes gave the impression that he was unpleasantly eager to please her, Woolf wrote about his "oleaginous eyes," a concise, more evocative description.

Reading Skills Focus

Identifying Tone Paying close attention to a writer's choice of words and details is critical in **identifying tone,** or the writer's attitude toward a subject, a character, or the reader. For example, Woolf conveys a critical tone by describing the poet Byron as "tawdry and melodramatic."

Into Action In Woolf's letter, she uses different tones as she describes people and events in her life. Note each instance of tone in a chart like the one below. Tell what words express her tone, or attitude, about each.

Subject	Strachey's health	
Choice of Words	"distressed," "plagued"	
Tone	concerned, but also humorous	

Writing Skills Focus

Think as a Reader/Writer

Find It in Your Reading Writers utilize different elements of **syntax,** the arrangement of words in a sentence. They may play with word order or emphasize sentence parts to create rhythm (see the repetition of "He said" and "I said" in Woolf's description of her conversation with Murry). In your *Reader/Writer Notebook,* take notes on Woolf's syntax, including sentence length and construction, and how she creates rhythm.

Vocabulary

plagued (playgd) *v.:* afflicted. *Strachey was plagued with severe illnesses.*

sepulchral (suh PUHL kruhl) *adj.:* deep and gloomy. *Eliot's sepulchral voice boomed into the telephone.*

distorting (dihs TAWRT ihng) *v.* used as *adj.:* misshaping; deforming. *The distorting glass, broken in places, made the visitors look much taller and skinnier than they actually were.*

confounded (kahn FOWND ihd) *v.:* confused. *Virginia was confounded by Murry's behavior.*

hoarding (HAWR dihng) *v.:* storing; accumulating. *She was hoarding ideas to share with Strachey when she could finally meet him.*

coherently (koh HIHR uhnt lee) *adv.:* clearly and logically. *Writers use transitions to make sure their ideas are presented coherently.*

Language Coach

Literal and Figurative Meanings Some words have both a literal (original or exact) meaning and a figurative meaning. For example, *coherent* literally means "glued or stuck together," but over time, it has also come to have a figurative meaning as well: "logically connected." What is the relationship between the literal and figurative meanings of the words?

Learn It Online
Learn more about these Vocabulary words online.
go.hrw.com H12-1181 Go

Reader/Writer Notebook
Use your **RWN** to complete the activities for this selection.

California Standards, pp. 1181–1185

- **Reading Standard 3.3** Analyze the ways in which irony, tone, mood, the author's style, and the "sound" of language achieve specific rhetorical or aesthetic purposes or both.

Preteach

Introducing Vocabulary

Read aloud the Vocabulary words and sample sentences. Use the following activity to check students' understanding.

1. Why might it be difficult to speak **coherently** in front of a crowd?
2. How would a painting of a **distorting** nature make a viewer feel?
3. What might you be **hoarding** before a huge snowstorm?
4. Describe a situation that left you **confounded.**
5. What kind of mood does **sepulchral** music tend to produce?
6. How would a person **plagued** with a rash feel?

English for Academic Success

Language Coach

Tell students that *sepulchral* literally means "funeral" but also "deep and dismal."

Literary Skills Focus

As you read the selection with students, have them note Woolf's diction and the tone it produces.

Reading Skills Focus

Give students a copy of the **Reading Skills Focus** graphic organizer before they read. (See **Unit 6 Resources.**) Tell them to use their responses to answer the questions on the Applying Your Skills page.

Writing Skills Focus

Have students make notes on Woolf's syntax in their **Reader/Writer Notebooks** and use their notes to complete the Writing Skills Focus activity.

Learn It Online
Send students to **Word Watch** for audio pronunciations, synonyms and antonyms, and brief histories of word origins.

go.hrw.com H12-1181 Go

Teacher Preparation
Selection Summary
In this letter to her friend, Lytton Strachey, Woolf describes her move to London and her life among the literati and artists of her day.

Direct Teach

Think About/Talk About
Read with a Purpose Have students read the Read with a Purpose statement. Ask them to notice Woolf's response to life's annoyances.

Comprehension
A Reading Focus
Possible responses: *Woolf uses an affectionate tone. She seems to be praising him since she says she turns to his books always in "moments of crisis."*

Read with a Purpose
Read this letter to learn how Virginia Woolf handles "moments of crisis" in her daily life.

Build Background
Biographer Lytton Strachey was a close friend of Woolf's and a member of the Bloomsbury group. Woolf wrote this letter to him after moving from Brighton to London with her husband, Leonard. The letter reflects her literary life, full of references to writers and artists: poet T. S. Eliot, writers Lord Harold Nicolson and his wife Vita Sackville-West, writer John Middleton Murry (Katherine Mansfield's husband), art critic Clive Bell, who married Woolf's sister Vanessa ("Nessa"), and painter Dora Carrington.

Virginia Woolf; Giles Lytton Strachey (June 1923) by Lady Ottoline Morrell. Vintage snapshot print. National Portrait Gallery, London.

LETTER

from The Letters of Virginia Woolf

by **Virginia Woolf**

1454: TO LYTTON STRACHEY 52 Tavistock Square W.C.
March 21st 1924

Dearest Lytton,

I am greatly distressed to hear that you are still plagued by diseases of all kinds—just as I was snatching a few moments to read Books & Characters[1] too. Why do I always fly to your works when the electricians are in the hall, the gasmen in the basement, and the telephone ringing with Tom's [Eliot] sepulchral voice? It's a very queer fact, but in moments of crisis, I always turn to you but supply me with another book soon. I open at page 173, and say Oh but I know this by heart; and it will soon be the case with all the pages: and this is no exaggeration; and I daresay no particular praise either; only one of your peculiarities as an author. Another is to beget[2] Nicolsons. But the mixture is not appetizing to me, for all the praises of Clive and Desmond, who have drunk too many glasses of his [Harold Nicolson's] champagne to be trusted. But then Byron seems to me tawdry and melodramatic. And Claire and Trelawny[3] and so and so on—I conceive them like a cave at some Earl's Court Exhibition—a grotto[4] I mean lined with distorting mirrors and plastered with oyster shells. Do not trouble to unwind this metaphor. **A**

1. **Books and Characters:** *Books and Characters: French and English,* a book of literary criticism by Lytton Strachey, was published in 1922.
2. **beget:** produce (used figuratively).
3. **Claire and Trelawny:** Claire Clairmont, step-sister of novelist Mary Shelley, and Edward John Trelawny, friend of poets Byron and Shelley. Trelawny wrote a literary memoir of Byron and Shelley.
4. **grotto:** fake cave.

A Reading Focus **Identifying Tone** What tone does Woolf use when describing her experience of reading Strachey's book? Do you think she is praising him? Explain.

Vocabulary **plagued** (playgd) *v.:* afflicted.
sepulchral (suh PUHL kruhl) *adj.:* deep and gloomy.

Universal Access

Struggling Readers
Strategic Students Model identifying the tone of an author. Remind students that a writer chooses particular words to convey their tone or feelings about someone or something. Point out that when Woolf is describing her experience of reading Strachey's book, she uses the phrase "fly to your works," which reveals her willingness and desire to read his books at particular moments. She also admits that "in moments of crisis, I always turn to you but supply me with another book soon," which indicates she does not get enough of his books, and the reader can infer that Woolf respects and enjoys his works.

As students continue reading, tell them to pay attention to her words and actions that indicate a positive or negative tone.

✔ See **UA: Differentiating Instruction** for a graphic organizer to scaffold instruction for struggling readers.

I am jangled and splintered by the move, and only hook together words by the force of affection: Say one word, and I will come down, and talk in a gentle and soothing voice about—well, did you hear how I rushed into Murry's arms at the Nation dinner the other night? He forced himself upon me. He has rolling and oleaginous[5] eyes. I said we were enemies. He said we were in different camps. He said one must write with one's instincts. I said one must write with one's mind. He said Bloomsbury was a tangle of exquisite sensibilities. I said come and see me there. He said no. I said very well. He said I like you. I said come and see me then. He said no. So I got up and flounced out of the room, saying Not for ten years—Undoubtedly, he has been rolling in dung, and smells impure. **B** **C**

We live largely in the basement—The confusion is still confounded—busts of my mother standing upon rolls of carpet, chamber pots stuffed full of book binding tools, and my unfortunate books—oh never let the undertakers pack your books when you move—I haven't a single volume left whole. In compensation, Nessa and Duncan have painted me a room, where you must come instantly and sit and talk and talk and talk, and never have to catch a taxi, and so by degrees get delivered of that vast mass of communication which I assure you has been hoarding up within me, and so perhaps in you, these ten years. We will sit in the Square and let Dadie [Rylands] play tennis before us. This will be in the summer, with the leaves out, and exquisite ladies—but your taste doesn't lie that way.

I will write more coherently later.

Ask Carrington to let me hear how you are.

Yr.
V.W.

Giles Lytton Strachey; Virginia Woolf (June 1923) by Lady Ottoline Morrell. Vintage snapshot print. National Portrait Gallery, London.

5. **oleaginous:** oily; unpleasantly eager to please.

B Literary Focus Diction What images come to mind from Woolf's description of herself as "jangled and splintered"? To which senses do those words appeal? How does Woolf's word choice fit the tone and style of the letter?

C Reading Focus Identifying Tone What words or phrases help you identify Woolf's tone, or attitude, toward Murry?

Vocabulary **distorting** (dihs TAWRT ihng) *v.* used as *adj.:* misshaping; deforming.
confounded (kahn FOWND ihd) *v.:* confused.
hoarding (HAWR dihng) *v.:* storing; accumulating.
coherently (koh HIHR uhnt lee) *adv.:* clearly and logically.

Think About/Talk About

Comprehension

C Reading Focus

Possible response: *She describes Murry's eyes as "rolling and oleaginous" and adds that "he has been rolling in dung and smells impure."*

Analysis

B Literary Focus

Possible responses: *The words "jangled and splintered" evoke images of something rattling and disjointed. They appeal to the senses of sound and sight and fit with the fragmented and emotional tone of the letter.*

Vocabulary: Own the Word

- **plagued:** Ask: "Have you ever been *plagued* by a serious illness? Explain when and how you were *plagued* and how you recovered."
- **sepulchral:** Act out a *sepulchral* voice. Have one student or two demonstrate at their desks.
- **distorting:** Have students complete the following thought: The *distorting* mirror reflected an image of . . . ***Possible response:*** *the opposite wall as if it were far away*
- **confounded:** Ask students to list things that make them feel *confounded.* ***Possible responses:*** *rules, decisions by others, news events, crossword puzzles*
- **hoarding:** Have students complete the statement: After years of not seeing her friend, Woolf was *hoarding* . . . ***Possible response:*** *information about her life and possibly the lives of others*
- **coherently:** Tell students the Latin root for *coherently* is *cohaerére*, meaning "to stick together." Ask students to relate the Latin root meaning to the definition.

California Standards, pp. 1184–1185

- **Reading Standard 3.3** Analyze the ways in which irony, tone, mood, the author's style, and the "sound" of language achieve specific rhetorical or aesthetic purposes or both.
- **Writing Standard 1.3** Structure ideas and arguments in a sustained, persuasive, and sophisticated way and support them with precise and relevant examples.
- **Writing Standard 1.5** Use language in natural, fresh, and vivid ways to establish a specific tone.
- **Writing Standard 1.9** Revise text to highlight the individual voice, improve sentence variety and style, and enhance subtlety of meaning and tone in ways that are consistent with the purpose, audience, and genre.
- **Writing Standard 2.2** Write responses to literature: **a.** Demonstrate a comprehensive understanding of the significant ideas in works or passages. **b.** Analyze the use of imagery, language, universal themes, and unique aspects of the text. **c.** Support important ideas and viewpoints through accurate and detailed references to the text and to other works.
- **Writing Standard 2.3** Write reflective compositions: **a.** Explore the significance of personal experiences, events, conditions, or concerns by using rhetorical strategies (e.g., narration, description, exposition, persuasion).

Check for Understanding

Independent Practice

Reading Skills Focus

Possible responses:

1. *Woolf had just moved to London and was settling into her house.*
2. *Woolf had many interactions with other writers and discussed her theories of writing with them.*
3. *She turns to books, particularly Strachey's, and that calms her.*
4. *Students should explain how the particular word connotes a certain tone and leads the reader to make judgments about Woolf's beliefs.*

Vocabulary Check

5. *hoarding*
6. *coherently*
7. *distorting*
8. *plagued*
9. *confounded*
10. *sepulchral*

Literary Skills Focus

Possible responses:

11. *They are still close because she wants to talk to him at leisure.*
12. *Writing with "one's instincts" allows spontaneous and emotional expression. Writing with "one's mind" emphasizes ideas and intellect.*
13. *Reading is an integral part of Woolf's life, and she relates intimately to what she reads.*
14. *Woolf conveys how she deals with the stresses of life (electricians and gasmen, "the move") and shares her opinions of a writer or artist who drinks "too many glasses" or "smells impure."*
15. *A grotto is an artificial cave. She may have meant that they were artificial and that they distorted themselves or others into things they were not. She found their work false and contrived.*
16. *Woolf's style is mocking, familiar, and a little challenging. She makes casual references to famous people and criticizes literature freely. Her style in describing her feelings is a little hysterical and playfully dramatic.*

Applying Your Skills

Reading Standard 3.3 (see pages A48–A50)
Writing Standard 2.3a (see pages A51–A52)

from The Letters of Virginia Woolf

Literary Response and Analysis

Reading Skills Focus

Quick Check

1. What was occurring in Woolf's life at the time she wrote this letter? What details suggest why she feels so "jangled"?
2. What can you infer about Woolf's relationships with other writers from this letter?

Read with a Purpose

3. How does Woolf deal with life's "moments of crisis"? Are those solutions effective for her?

Reading Skills: Identifying Tone

4. Look back on the chart you created. What can you infer from Woolf's tone about her opinion of each subject?

Vocabulary Check

Fill in each blank with one of the Vocabulary words.

plagued, sepulchral, distorting, confounded, hoarding, coherently

5. The squirrel was ____ acorns for the winter.
6. Express your ideas ____.
7. The ____ mirrors twisted our reflections.
8. Woolf was ____ by depression and anxiety.
9. She was ____ by the writer's odd behavior.
10. The music's ____ tone subdued the audience.

Literary Skills Focus

Literary Analysis

11. **Infer** Woolf notes that it has been ten years since she has seen Strachey. Does her letter suggest the two of them are still close? Why or why not?
12. **Extend** Murry says, "one must write with one's instincts," and Woolf replies, "one must write with one's mind." What is the difference between these two methods of writing?
13. **Analyze** What role does reading play in Woolf's life?
14. **Interpret** What messages is Woolf conveying to Strachey about her life and opinions? Use information from the letter to support your response.

Literary Skills: Diction

15. **Analyze** What is the difference between a cave and a grotto? Why did Woolf make this distinction in describing Claire, Trelawny, and the other writers? What was she saying about their work?

Literary Skills Review: Style

16. **Evaluate** The way a writer says what he or she wishes to say is called **style.** Style includes diction, sentence structure, imagery, rhythm, and arrangement of ideas. Style can be casual or formal, plain or ornate, as well as comic, poetic, or forceful. Describe Woolf's style in the letter.

Writing Skills Focus

Think as a Reader/Writer

Use It in Your Writing Following Woolf's style, write a short letter telling about your day. In your letter, vary your syntax, use both long and short sentences to create interest, and employ repetition to create rhythm. Read your letter aloud to ensure it flows.

What Do You Think Now? After reading this letter, what people, things, and ideas can you infer are important to Woolf?

Universal Access

Struggling Writers

Guide students with additional scaffolding to complete the Writing Skills Focus activity. Suggest that students write about a problem they are facing. Encourage students to use dashes, colons, semicolons, and conjunctions to create long sentences, and also sprinkle short sentences in their letter. Remind them to keep a casual tone and employ repetition by starting a series of sentences the same way, (He said . . . , She said . . . , I said . . .).

What Do You Think Now?

To help students think about this question, ask them to note the various people, objects, and conversations Woolf mentions in her letter.

Writing Standard 1.3, 1.5, 1.9, 2.2a–c (see pages A51–A52)

Author Study: Virginia Woolf

Writing Skills Focus

Write a Comparison-Contrast Essay

Think about the four different selections you have read by Virginia Woolf. Choose at least two of the selections to compare and contrast. Remember to begin with a basis of comparison other than shared authorship. Re-read your notes from the four selections to determine commonalities. Once you have analyzed and compared the two selections, analyze them again to see differences.

Prewriting

Select a Topic Use your own ideas or one of the following topics in a comparison-contrast essay.

- the relationship between physical space and happiness
- the effect of the external world on the character
- descriptions of people's external worlds to hint at or reflect their inner experiences
- the freedom and restrictions of daily life

An effective comparison-contrast essay

- states what is being compared/contrasted
- conveys a main idea through a thesis statement
- has an effective and logical organization that includes similarities and differences
- cites and explains text passages to support ideas
- contains few or no errors in spelling, punctuation, and grammar

Gather Details Record your ideas in an H chart. In the center of the H, record the main similarity. At the top of the H, write the title of each selection you have chosen. Record your notes about each selection, and write a thesis statement that includes the similarities and the differences that you can support with text evidence.

A Room of One's Own		Letters
education of women/limited		writing to her friend
servile; marriage		interruptions
difficulties for a woman/genius	household interruptions, daily toil, work/life	moving
		turns to reading to escape
production	Both	reception

Thesis Statement
Although both "A Room of One's Own" and "Letters" by Virginia Woolf acknowledge the interruptions of daily life for women, the pieces differ greatly in their portrayal of the impact they have on women's lives.

Drafting

Since you are writing a comparison-contrast essay, use the point-by-point method. Include at least one body paragraph to develop the basis of similarity. Then, continue with similarities or discuss differences in the selections you have chosen to analyze.

Point-by-Point Method	Block Method
Topic Sentence/Paragraph: Selection 1 Selection 2	Topic Sentence/Paragraph: Selection 1 Selection 2

Revising and Editing

- Read your paper. Have you proven your thesis? Do you return to it in the closing paragraph?
- Add text evidence if it does not appear to support each point.
- Proofread your essay and correct any errors in spelling, mechanics and usage.

What Do You Think Now? How did Woolf's experiences affect her view of the world?

Independent Practice

What Do You Think Now?

To help students answer the question, ask them to think about how the selections, *A Room of One's Own,* and *A Haunted House*, reflect Woolf's own experiences as a female writer and war civilian.

Assess

Unit 6 Resources, Selection Standards Check, pp. 76, 80, 86

ThinkCentral Online Assessment, Selection Standards Check

Teacher One Stop™, editable Selection Standards Check

Reteach

ThinkCentral Online Remediation

Universal Access

Struggling Writers

Some students may need additional scaffolding to complete the Writing Skills Focus activity. First, have students fill out an H-chart after choosing two selections to compare and contrast. Then, have them construct an outline before drafting. Tell them to write their proposed thesis at the top of their outline. Have them write "Introduction" next to roman numeral "I," then either "Similarities" or "Differences" next to "II–IV," depending on how many body paragraphs they will have. Tell them to also include "Conclusion" next to the last roman numeral. Under each item, have them list at least two major details they will include in that section. Students should use their H-chart to fill out their outline. Remind them to include references to the text in their outline and essay.

Chapter Objectives

- Students will learn about the themes of modern and contemporary poetry by reading works by poets such as T. S. Eliot, William Butler Yeats, Gabriela Mistral, and Margaret Atwood.
- Students will draw inferences about poetry using evidence from the text and from their experiences.

The Quotation

Tell students that Chapter 12 focuses on the themes of modern and contemporary poetry, which include feelings of alienation and the hopes and fears associated with life and love. Ask students which poets, those of the modern age or the contemporary age, would be more likely to agree with Neruda's idea of the ultimate goal. ***Possible response:*** *The contemporary poets would have been more likely to agree with Neruda's idea that the purpose of life and of poetry is to share what we are with others.*

Analyzing Visuals

Extension Activity How does the image of the eye support Neruda's statement that we seek to convey what we are? ***Possible responses:*** *The eye could be the window of the soul and reveals what we are. It may also be a play on words—the eye, the organ for seeing, and "I," the self.*

CHAPTER 12

Modern and Contemporary Poetry

LITERARY SKILLS FOCUS

Themes of Modern and Contemporary Poetry

CONTENTS

"All paths lead to the same goal: to convey to others what we are."

—Pablo Neruda

Chapter 12

California Standards Overview

- **Reading Standard 2.2** Analyze the way in which clarity of meaning is affected by the patterns of organization, hierarchical structures, repetition of the main ideas, syntax, and word choice in the text.
- **Reading Standard 2.4** Make warranted and reasonable assertions about the author's arguments by using elements of the text to defend and clarify interpretations.
- **Reading Standard 2.5** Analyze an author's implicit and explicit philosophical assumptions and beliefs about a subject.
- **Reading Standard 3.1** Analyze characteristics of subgenres (e.g., satire, parody, allegory, pastoral) that are used in poetry, prose, plays, novels, short stories, essays, and other basic genres.
- **Reading Standard 3.2** Analyze the way in which the theme or meaning of a selection represents a view or comment on life, using textual evidence to support the claim.
- **Reading Standard 3.3** Analyze the ways in which irony, tone, mood, the author's style, and the "sound" of language achieve specific rhetorical or aesthetic purposes or both.
- **Reading Standard 3.4** Analyze ways in which poets use imagery, personification, figures of speech, and sounds to evoke readers' emotions.
- **Reading Standard 3.9** Analyze the philosophical arguments presented in literary works to determine whether the authors' positions have contributed to the quality of each work and the credibility of the characters. (Philosophical approach)
- **Grades 9–10 Review Reading Standard 3.7** Recognize and understand the significance of various literary devices, including figurative language, imagery, allegory, and symbolism, and explain their appeal.
- **Grades 9–10 Review Reading Standard 3.8** Interpret and evaluate the impact of ambiguities, subtleties, contradictions, ironies, and incongruities in a text.

LITERARY RESPONSE AND ANALYSIS

Literary Skills Focus

Reading Standard 3.1, 3.2 (see pages A48–A50)

Themes of Modern and Contemporary Poetry by Leila Christenbury

Characteristics of Themes in Modern and Contemporary Poetry

- Depict life as chaotic, dangerous, and uncontrollable
- Portray loss and death as universal experiences
- Value humanity and artistic expression as antidotes to despair

The Modern Age

A sense of increasing chaos, along with a feeling of alienation from nature and humanity, pervades the poetry of the modern age, an age ushered in by the turmoil of World War I. Modernist poets rejected traditional values and assumptions and the rules by which these were expressed.

This chapter opens with two significant poets of the modern era: the American expatriate T. S. Eliot, whose poem *The Wasteland* was the single most important poem published in England during this period, and William Butler Yeats, whose mature poetry ranks among the best twentieth-century poetry in English. With its note of despair, "The Hollow Men" by Eliot introduces this chapter. The writing of Yeats is highly inventive and filled with memorable imagery, vivid language, and references not only to nature but also to a private mythology that Yeats created and to which he occasionally refers. Yeats revisits the story of "The Second Coming" from the book of Revelation in the Bible and examines the threats of modern life, showing readers what we have to fear. Then, in "Sailing to Byzantium," his focus shifts to the importance of art and its redemptive value.

As World War II approached, W. H. Auden wrote his famous poem "Musée des Beaux Arts" about human suffering. He said of poetry, "In so far as poetry, or any of the arts, can be said to have an ulterior purpose, it is, by telling the truth, to disenchant and disintoxicate." This tradition continues throughout the contemporary age.

(Opposite) *Eye* (2000) by Howard Hodgkin (b. 1932). Hand-colored etching with carborundum. Alan Cristea Gallery, London.

The Contemporary Age

Following World War II, poets continued with modernist themes but moved away from elaborate symbolism and complex forms until, by the mid 1960s, the contemporary age had emerged. This chapter presents a variety of contemporary poets. Philip Larkin, influenced by the Victorian poet Thomas Hardy, shaped tough and unsentimental but intensely emotional poems from ordinary experience, as in his poem "The Explosion." In "Lot's Wife," Wislawa Szymborska, like the earlier poet Anna Akhmatova, explores a woman's separation from her homeland. The Irish poet Seamus Heaney gives voice to the experience and richness of his rural heritage through his poem "Digging." These and other examples of modern and contemporary poetry embrace universal ideas about hope, fear, and loss in life and love.

Ask Yourself

1. How does modern and contemporary poetry reflect the experiences of people in the modern age?
2. In your opinion, what value is there in poetry? Do you agree with Auden that the purpose of poetry should be "to disenchant?" Explain.

Learn It Online

Explore modern themes online with *PowerNotes.*

go.hrw.com H12-1187 Go

Literary Skills Focus

Objectives

Students will understand and analyze themes of modern and contemporary poetry.

Unit 6 Resources, Literary Focus Skill Builder, p. 94

PowerNotes, interactive lesson presentation with activities

Teacher One Stop™, on-level lesson plan and all print resources

Direct Teach

The Contemporary Age

Have students read the Literary Skills Focus essay. Then, use the following question to initiate a discussion on twentieth-century poetry: Both World War I and the Cold War influenced the themes addressed by modern and contemporary writers. How do events around the world affect the themes of today's popular culture?

Check for Understanding

Ask Yourself

Possible responses:

1. *The subject matter of modern and contemporary poetry reflects society's experiences and attitudes.*
2. *Poetry can make people think and consider new perspectives. If poetry disenchants readers, as Auden suggests, then it might force readers to think harder about the poet's opinions.*

California Standards, p. 1187

- **Reading Standard 3.1** Analyze characteristics of subgenres (e.g., satire, parody, allegory, pastoral) that are used in poetry, prose, plays, novels, short stories, essays, and other basic genres.
- **Reading Standard 3.2** Analyze the way in which the theme or meaning of a selection represents a view or comment on life, using textual evidence to support the claim.

Learn It Online

For a multimedia version of the instruction found on this page, use the **PowerNotes** Literary Skills Focus presentation.

go.hrw.com H12-1187 Go

Standards Focus

Objectives

Students will understand allusions and draw inferences.

Selection Introduction

Think About the Writer

Have students think about Eliot's beliefs about the importance of the poem versus the poet.

For Independent Reading

- *All the King's Men,** Robert Penn Warren
- *Collected Poems 1909–1962,* T. S. Elliot

HRW LIBRARY *This title is available in the HRW library.

Motivate

What Do You Think?/QuickWrite

Ask students to record reasons for the despairing or hopeful state of humanity in their **Reader/Writer Notebooks.**

English for Academic Success

Academic Vocabulary

Look for opportunities to use the Academic Vocabulary words in this unit.

- **considerably, *adv.*:** by a large amount
- **exhibit, *v.*:** show, demonstrate
- **inevitable, *adj.*:** unavoidable
- **perspective, *n.*:** a particular way of looking at something

California Standards, pp. 1188–1196

- **Reading Standard 2.5** Analyze an author's implicit and explicit philosophical assumptions and beliefs about a subject.
- **Reading Standard 3.4** Analyze ways in which poets use imagery, personification, figures of speech, and sounds to evoke readers' emotions.
- **Reading Standard 3.9** Analyze the philosophical arguments presented in literary works to determine whether the authors' positions have contributed to the quality of each work and the credibility of the characters. (Philosophical approach)

Preparing to Read

The Hollow Men

What Do You Think? How does experience shape our view of the world?

QuickWrite

"The Hollow Men" describes a world of godless despair without the promise of salvation. In your *Reader/Writer Notebook*, write your thoughts about the condition of humanity today.

Thomas Stearns Eliot in his first year at Harvard (1906).

MEET THE WRITER

T. S. Eliot

(1888–1965)

Nobel Prize WINNER

Unlike poets whose long, outstanding careers eventually turn them into cultural monuments, Thomas Stearns Eliot was a monument who later became known as a man.

Aristocratic Beginnings

Internationally famous, Eliot was the product of an aristocratic New England family that valued privacy. He saw the poet as an artisan whose work, all important, stood apart from its creator. Consequently, millions of readers knew T. S. Eliot less as a real personality than as a presence. He was remote, disciplined, and self-possessed, a man whose modest output was nevertheless the most celebrated and influential poetry written in English over a span of three decades.

T. S. Eliot was born in 1888 in St. Louis, Missouri, where his grandfather established Washington University. Despite this geographical displacement, the Eliots remained New Englanders. Eliot was educated at Harvard College, after which he attended graduate school at the Sorbonne in Paris, France. Like many young American writers of his generation, Eliot found life abroad so stimulating that he decided not to return home. Settling in London before World War I, he worked in a bank, married an Englishwoman, and became an editor and a publisher. Eliot made his expatriation complete by becoming a British citizen in 1927.

Influential Writing

Eliot had a vast influence as a poet. His techniques, along with those of his friend and fellow American expatriate, Ezra Pound, became the hallmarks of modern poetry. For over thirty years, Eliot's was the voice that expressed the dislocation and despair of the twentieth century. His world-weariness and his grave, restrained, and impersonal cadences—so much like the voices he heard in New England pulpits—were widely imitated and recognized. A Nobel Prize recipient, Eliot was so popular that 14,000 people once filled an arena to hear him speak.

Think About the Writer How do you think Eliot would view this discussion of his life as an introduction to reading his poetry?

Selection Readability	
Easily Accessible **Accessible** Challenging	simple sentence structure, accessible vocabulary

Reading Standard 2.5, 3.4, 3.9 (see pages A48–A50)

Literary Skills Focus

Allusion An **allusion** is a reference to a statement, person, place, event, or thing that is known from literature, history, or other subjects. "The Hollow Men" opens with two allusions. The line *"Mistah Kurtz—he dead,"* from Joseph Conrad's novel *Heart of Darkness,* refers to a character who is emotionally dead long before he is physically dead. This reference strikes a note of futility echoed throughout the entire poem. The second allusion, *A penny for the Old Guy,* refers to Guy Fawkes, the man chosen to light the fuse in the notorious Gunpowder Plot of 1605 (see Build Background on page 1190).

"The Hollow Men" exhibits many other allusions, especially to works by Shakespeare and Dante. As you read, think about the associations and emotions these allusions evoke.

Literary Perspectives Apply the literary perspective described on page 1190 as you read this poem.

Reading Skills Focus

Drawing Inferences Writers often expect readers to "read between the lines." Readers must use evidence from the text, along with their own prior knowledge and experience, to **draw inferences.**

Into Action As you read, draw inferences about the hollow men and analyze their character traits to show how effectively they represent Eliot's view of human history. Use a chart like the one below to note details about the hollow men and to record your inferences.

Evidence	Inference
"Headpiece filled with straw" (line 4)	If their heads are filled with straw, they can't think.

Writing Skills Focus

Think as a Reader/Writer

Find It in Your Reading The **allusions** to works and events set the **tone** in Eliot's poem. As you read the poem, note allusions in your *Reader/Writer Notebook* and think about how each affects the poem's tone.

Reader/Writer Notebook

Use your **RWN** to complete the activities for this selection.

Vocabulary

supplication (suhp luh KAY shuhn) *n.:* humble plea. *The priest prayed for his supplication to be heard.*

perpetual (purh PEHCH oo uhl) *adj.:* lasting forever. *He gloomily predicted perpetual suffering.*

conception (kuhn SEHP shuhn) *n.:* the originating of something. *The conception of the new book was an elaborate vision.*

potency (POH tuhn see) *n.:* strength; power. *The potency of the vitamins was tested.*

Language Coach

Noun Suffixes The words *supplication* and *conception* both end in the suffix *–ion,* meaning "the act of." The *-ion* suffix changes the verbs *supplicate* and *conceive* into nouns. What other nouns with this suffix can you find in the poem? From what verbs are these nouns formed?

Learn It Online

Prepare to read this poem through the video introduction online.

go.hrw.com H12-1189 Go

Selection Resources

Unit 6 Resources, on-level practice and assessment, p. 96

PowerNotes, interactive lesson presentations with activities

Teacher One Stop™, on-level lesson plans and all print resources

Holt Audio Library: Selections and Summaries in Spanish

UA: Holt Interactive Reader, p. 337

UA: Differentiating Instruction, modified lesson plans and leveled assessment, p. 283

UA: Supporting Instruction in Spanish, selection summary

UA: Resources for Teaching Advanced Students, lesson plans, p. 199

ThinkCentral Online Assessment, Selection Standards Check

ThinkCentral Online Remediation

Preteach

Introducing Vocabulary

- Review the Vocabulary words, definitions, and sentences with students.
- Tell students that Eliot uses these words to express his philosophy of humanity. He views humanity as hollow, dead men of weakening *potency* making *supplication* to "stone images," hoping to enter a *perpetual* state of bliss.

English for Academic Success

Language Coach

Point out the word *motion* used in line 12 of the poem. Work with students to figure out that *motion* is the noun form of *move.* Then, have students point out other nouns with the *–ion* suffix used in the poem. ***Possible responses:*** *"creation" from the verb "create"; "emotion" from the verb "emote"*

Literary Skills Focus

As you read and discuss the poem with students, have them note the emotions and associations evoked by the allusions.

Reading Skills Focus

Give students a copy of the Reading Skills Focus graphic organizer before they read. (See **Unit 6 Resources.**) Tell them to use their responses to answer the questions on the Applying Your Skills page.

Writing Skills Focus

Have students record allusions in their **Reader/Writer Notebooks.** Students can use their notes to complete the Writing Skills Focus activity.

Learn It Online

The **PowerNotes** presentation for this lesson includes a short video that introduces the poem. The video is also available on the online version of this page.

go.hrw.com H12-1189 Go

Teacher Preparation

Selection Summary

Part I of the "The Hollow Men" introduces and describes "the hollow men . . . stuffed men" and notes that those who have entered Paradise regard them as hollow, not violent. In Part II the speaker inhabits "death's dream kingdom," a realm of diverted gazes, empty voices, distance, and disguise. Part III extends the description of the "dead land," lamenting its stone-cold hardness, lack of intimacy, and futility of prayer. In Part IV, the inhabitants of this land, sightless and voiceless, gather to cross an archetypal river into absolute death. Part V presents in enigmatic and fragmented language the shadowy moment of death, which is, Eliot seems to say, the constant companion of the hollow man from birth, through life, and until the last, world-ending whimper.

Direct Teach

Think About/Talk About

Read with a Purpose Ask students think about what the repeated words reveal about the poet's view of humanity.

Comprehension

Ⓐ Reading Focus

Possible response: *The hollow men cannot think. Their "dried voices" like "rats' feet over broken glass" suggest the futility of their actions.*

Analysis

Ⓑ Literary Perspectives

Possible response: *He sees people as one-dimensional and purposeless.*

Responses to Margin Questions

Lines 11–12 *The paradoxes "shape without form," "shade without color," and "gesture without motion" suggest that the men are one-dimensional.*

Lines 37–38 *It might be death or damnation.*

Lines 39–44 *These lines describe a lifeless desert; the description reflects the barren interior of the hollow men.*

POEM

The Hollow Men

by **T. S. Eliot**

Read with a Purpose

Read to discover one view of humanity after World War I.

Build Background

The allusion to "the Old Guy" in the epigraph refers to the failed Gunpowder Plot of 1605. On November 5 of that year, a band of conspirators planned to kill King James I (and others) by placing barrels of gunpowder in the cellars of Parliament. A soldier named Guy Fawkes was supposed to light the fuse, but the plot failed, and Fawkes was arrested and sentenced to be hanged, drawn, and quartered. To commemorate this grisly event, huge bonfires are set all over England every year on November 5. When these fires are lit, straw-filled effigies of Fawkes that look like scarecrows—the "stuffed men" of the poem—go up in flames, lighting the skies. Children join in the fun by carrying a "guy" and becoming beggars who ask passersby to give them "a penny for the guy" so that they can buy fireworks.

Mistah Kurtz—he dead.
A penny for the Old Guy

I

We are the hollow men°
We are the stuffed men
Leaning together
Headpiece filled with straw. Alas!
Our dried voices, when
We whisper together
Are quiet and meaningless
As wind in dry grass
Or rats' feet over broken glass
In our dry cellar. Ⓐ

Shape without form, shade without color, Ⓑ
Paralyzed force, gesture without motion;

1. **hollow men:** allusion to Shakespeare's *Julius Caesar* (Act IV, Scene 2, lines 23–27): "hollow men ... sink in the trial" (fail when put to the test).

11–12. A **paradox** is an apparent contradiction that is actually true.

? *What paradoxes are listed in these lines? What do these paradoxes tell you about the hollow men?*

Ⓐ **Reading Focus** **Drawing Inferences** What inferences can you draw about the hollow men so far?

Ⓑ **Literary Perspectives** **Analyzing Philosophical Context** What does Eliot's description of "hollow" and "stuffed" men tell you about his outlook on humanity?

Literary Perspectives

Analyzing Philosophical Context Philosophical context refers to an author's underlying assumptions about larger questions of life and its meaning. To read literary works from this perspective, we must uncover and consider the philosophical arguments of the author. When T. S. Eliot wrote "The Hollow Men" in 1923, World War I had shaken the foundations of British society, and this once powerful nation was overcome by cynicism and hopelessness. Hundreds of thousands of people had died in combat, the British Empire and many of its traditions were disintegrating, and a new suspicion toward government had emerged. As you read, consider how these historical conditions may have influenced Eliot's philosophical approach to "modern man."

As you read, be sure to notice the questions in the text, which will guide you in using this perspective.

Literary Perspectives

Before students read the poem, have them read the **Literary Perspectives** about Analyzing Philosophical Context.

Remind students of the impact of World War I on Great Britain, focusing on the hundreds of thousands of lives lost in combat and the toppling of the old empire. Encourage students to consider how these historical conditions influenced Eliot's philosophical approach to "modern man."

Remind students to use the notes and questions at the bottom of the page to help them use the perspective.

Those who have crossed
With direct eyes, to death's other Kingdom°
Remember us—if at all—not as lost
Violent souls, but only
As the hollow men
The stuffed men. **C**

II

Eyes I dare not meet in dreams
In death's dream kingdom
These do not appear:
There, the eyes are
Sunlight on a broken column
There, is a tree swinging
And voices are
In the wind's singing
More distant and more solemn
Than a fading star.

Let me be no nearer
In death's dream kingdom
Let me also wear
Such deliberate disguises
Rat's coat, crowskin, crossed staves°
In a field
Behaving as the wind behaves
No nearer—

Not that final meeting
In the twilight kingdom

III

This is the dead land
This is cactus land
Here the stone images
Are raised, here they receive
The supplication of a dead man's hand
Under the twinkle of a fading star. **D**

13–14. Those … Kingdom: Those with "direct eyes" have crossed from the world of the hollow men into Paradise. The allusion is to Dante's *Paradiso.*

Analyzing Visuals

Connecting to the Text Consider the effect of the elongated proportions and rough surface of the sculpture. In what ways does the sculpture portray the hollow men described in Eliot's poem? How does it deviate?

L'Homme Qui Marche (1947) by Alberto Giacometti (1901–1966). Inv. Nr. GS 30. Kunsthaus, Zürich/Artists Rights Society (ARS), NY/ADAGP, Paris.

33. staves: rods or staffs. "crossed staves / In a field" form a scarecrow.

? **37–38.** *What might the "final meeting / In the twilight kingdom" be? How might this explain what the speaker is afraid of?*

39–44. *What kind of setting is described here? How is this setting appropriate to the nature of the hollow men?*

C Reading Focus **Drawing Inferences** What does it mean for the hollow men to be both "hollow" and "stuffed"?

D Literary Focus **Allusion** In line 44, the image of the star is an allusion to Dante, who used the star to symbolize God. Of what do "stone images" make you think? What might "prayers to broken stone" be?

Vocabulary **supplication** (suhp luh KAY shuhn) *n.:* humble plea.

Think About/Talk About

Comprehension

C Reading Focus

Possible response: *They are hollow in that they have no core or substance and are instead stuffed with dead matter. Their condition is paradoxical; they are full, but filled with worthless straw, so they might as well be empty.*

Analysis

D Literary Focus

Possible responses: *The phrase "stone images" alludes to the "graven images" of the Bible. "Prayers to broken stone" suggests both impotent pleas and impotent idols.*

Vocabulary: Own the Word

supplication: Ask students: "Under what circumstances might a person make a *supplication*? To whom might a *supplication* be directed?"

Analyzing Visuals

Connecting to the Text: *Alberto Giacometti (1901–1966) is best known for his thin, elongated figures that suggest a consciousness pared down to its bare essence—a visual metaphor of the postwar, anxiety-ridden world. The barrenness of the sculpture, especially the gauntness of the human figure, reflects the hollow men and bleak world described in Eliot's poem. Unlike the figures Eliot describes, however, Giacometti's figures are not formless.*

Universal Access

AAVE Students Who Use African American Vernacular English

English for Academic Success Some students may struggle with the pronunciation of the final consonant sound in ending blends. Read the following line aloud: "Remember us—if at all—not as lost / Violent souls." Explain to students that in informal English, the *st* ending blend may be voiced as /s/. In formal English, however, both consonant sounds in an ending blend are voiced: /st/. Have students practice voicing the consonant sounds in an end blend by repeating the following words from the poem as a class after you: *direct, distant, hand.*

✔ For additional instruction and strategies, see **Holt Pronunciation Resources** and **ThinkCentral Teacher Access.**

Model the Skill

- Tell students that **allusions** are usually subtle references to music, history, current events, other literature, or another subject area. Eliot's allusions are less subtle. He "borrows" complete lines, incorporating them into "The Hollow Men."
- To help students identify allusions, point out that many songs contain allusions. Ask them if any of their favorites contain allusions to other songs' titles or lyrics or mention famous people or current events.
- Model identifying the significance of an allusion. You might say: "By opening the poem with a line from *Heart of Darkness*, Eliot raises issues from that work. Even before he physically dies, Kurtz is emotionally dead; in fact, Marlowe describes him as 'hollow at the core.' All the colonialists in the novel are described as 'hollow men.' Kurtz has realized that evil is at the very heart of life, and his last chilling words are, 'The horror! The horror!'"

Guided Practice: Apply

Read-Talk-Write Have students re-read lines 13–21. Tell them that Beatrice, who represents the celestial in Dante's *Inferno*, is so holy that Dante cannot meet her gaze. Have partners discuss this allusion and then write a paragraph explaining what they think Eliot is trying to say.

Responses to Margin Questions

Lines 68–71 *The circular motion symbolizes a fruitless, repetitive existence. The prickly pear could be seen as threatening or foreboding.*

Lines 95–98 *A "whimper" is pathetic and hardly noticeable, supporting the idea that the hollow men's lives have no meaning. A "bang," on the other hand, might signify a victory or at least a dramatic defeat.*

Is it like this
In death's other kingdom
Waking alone
At the hour when we are
Trembling with tenderness
Lips that would kiss
Form prayers to broken stone.

IV

The eyes are not here
There are no eyes here
In this valley of dying stars
In this hollow valley
This broken jaw of our lost kingdoms

In this last of meeting places
We grope together
And avoid speech
Gathered on this beach of the tumid river°

Sightless, unless
The eyes reappear
As the perpetual star
Multifoliate rose°
Of death's twilight kingdom
The hope only
Of empty men.

V

Here we go round the prickly pear°
Prickly pear prickly pear
Here we go round the prickly pear
At five o'clock in the morning.

Between the idea
And the reality
Between the motion
And the act°
Falls the Shadow
For Thine is the Kingdom°

Vocabulary **perpetual** (purh PEHCH oo uhl) *adj.:* lasting forever.

60. tumid river: Hell's swollen river, the Acheron (AK uh rahn), in Dante's *Inferno*. The damned must cross this river to enter the land of the dead.

64. multifoliate rose: Dante describes Paradise as a rose of many leaves (*Paradiso*, Canto 32).

68. prickly pear: cactus.

68–71. These lines are a parody of a children's rhyme that begins, "Here we go 'round the mulberry bush." The mulberry bush was traditionally a symbol of fertility. To go around and around means to never reach a destination; it is a pointless action.

? *How would you interpret going around and around a prickly pear—a type of cactus?*

74–75. between ... act: reference to Shakespeare's *Julius Caesar*: "Between the acting of a dreadful thing / And the first motion, all the interim is / Like a phantasma or a hideous dream" (Act II, Scene 1, lines 63–65).

77. For ... Kingdom: closing lines of the Lord's Prayer: "For thine is the kingdom, and the power, and the glory, forever and ever."

Universal Access

EL English Learners

Have students listen to the audio recording, replaying it as many times as needed so that students form some idea of the poem's meaning before reading it on their own.

✔ See **UA: Differentiating Instruction** for strategies for teaching English learners.

Struggling Readers

Strategic Students To help students read "The Hollow Men," model the reading skill of analyzing the author's philosophical arguments. For instance, you might say: "The poem's title—'The Hollow Men'—gives you a clue about how Eliot views twentieth-century humanity: He believes that something essential is missing." Encourage students to ask themselves, "What is a hollow person lacking?"

✔ See **UA: Differentiating Instruction** for strategies for teaching struggling readers.

Between the conception
And the creation
Between the emotion
And the response
Falls the Shadow
Life is very long

Between the desire
And the spasm
Between the potency
And the existence
Between the essence
And the descent°
Falls the Shadow
For Thine is the Kingdom

For Thine is
Life is
For Thine is the

This is the way the world ends
This is the way the world ends
This is the way the world ends
Not with a bang but a whimper. E

88–89. between ... descent: The Greek philosopher Plato defined "the essence" as an unattainable ideal and "the descent" as its imperfect expression in material or physical reality.

95–98. These lines are a continuation of the children's singsong rhyme, parodying the original words, "This is the way we clap our hands."

? *What does it mean for the world to end with a "whimper" instead of a "bang"?*

E Literary Perspectives **Analyzing Philosophical Context** How would you describe the view of the future expressed in the final four lines of the poem?

Vocabulary **conception** (kuhn SEHP shuhn) *n.:* the originating of something.
potency (POH tuhn see) *n.:* strength; power.

City Square (La Place) (1948) by Alberto Giacometti. Bronze. The Museum of Modern Art, NY/Artists Rights Society (ARS), New York/ADAGP, Paris.

Think About/Talk About

Analysis

E Literary Perspectives

Possible response: *The view of the future is pessimistic, hopeless, and ultimately disappointing.*

Vocabulary: Own the Word

- **perpetual:** Write *perpetual* in a center circle on the board and provide a student-friendly definition ("unending"). Draw spider legs from the center circle as students add concepts and attributes. ***Possible responses:*** *eternal, permanent*
- **conception:** Here, the *conception* is the origin of something. Ask students how the *conception* of something differs from its creation. ***Possible response:*** *The conception is the idea and the creation is the thing itself.*
- **potency:** Tell students that the word *potency* comes from the Latin root *potens* which means "powerful." The *potency* of something is its power or force. What are some examples of things we describe as *potent* (adjective form)?

California Standards, pp. 1194–1196

- **Reading Standard 2.5** Analyze an author's implicit and explicit philosophical assumptions and beliefs about a subject.
- **Reading Standard 3.2** Analyze the way in which the theme or meaning of a selection represents a view or comment on life, using textual evidence to support the claim.
- **Reading Standard 3.4** Analyze ways in which poets use imagery, personification, figures of speech, and sounds to evoke readers' emotions.
- **Reading Standard 3.9** Analyze the philosophical arguments presented in literary works to determine whether the author's positions have contributed to the quality of each work and the credibility of the characters. (Philosophical approach).
- **Grades 9–10 Review Reading Standard 1.1** Identify and use the literal and figurative meanings of words and understand word derivations.
- **Writing Standard 2.2** Write responses to literature: **a.** Demonstrate a comprehensive understanding of the significant ideas in works or passages. **b.** Analyze the use of imagery, language, universal themes, and unique aspects of the text. **c.** Support important ideas and viewpoints through accurate and detailed references to the text and to other works.
- **Writing Standard 2.3** Write reflective compositions: **b.** Draw comparisons between specific incidents and broader themes that illustrate the writer's important beliefs or generalizations about life.
- **Listening and Speaking Standard 2.3** Deliver oral responses to literature: **a.** Demonstrate a comprehensive understanding of the significant ideas of literary works (e.g., make assertions about the text that are reasonable and supportable). **c.** Support important ideas and viewpoints through accurate and detailed references to the text or to other works.

Check for Understanding

Independent Practice

Reading Skills Focus

Possible responses:

1. *The hollow men lack water and blood—symbolically, vitality.*
2. *It locks people with a direct gaze, and the sounds are of disembodied voices obscured by the wind.*
3. *Eliot's view is pessimistic overall, but he offers a glimmer of hope.*
4. *Students should support their opinions about Eliot's view of history with evidence from the text.*

Literary Skills Focus

Possible responses:

5. *The comparison suggests that the hollow men, like Fawkes's effigy, lack substance and are bound to be incinerated or destroyed. Unlike the historical Fawkes, they also lack commitment and courage.*
6. *The imagery conveys a sense of bleakness, loneliness, and finality.*
7. *The hollow men hope for redemption; sight may symbolize faith or spiritual wholeness. The hollow men cannot regain their sight because they have lost faith.*
8. *The "Shadow" may represent doubt, death, or damnation. The speaker cannot complete the Lord's Prayer because he has no faith or because he is dying.*
9. *It is ironic because the hollow men lack self-knowledge.*
10. *The chant-like quality of the poem and the characterization of the "hollow men" support the idea, so verbally he builds a good argument. Factually, the poem does not mention any historical events.*
11. *By infusing this poem with ideas and themes from other works, Eliot enriches and clarifies the poem's meaning.*
12. *The allusion to a children's rhyme yields a chilling effect by suggesting that life is meaningless.*
13. *The cold, despairing tone supports the theme of humanity's loss of faith and sense of alienation.*

Applying Your Skills

Reading Standard 2.5, 3.2, 3.4, 3.9 (see pages A48–A50)
Writing Standard 2.3b (see pages A51–A52)

The Hollow Men

Literary Response and Analysis

Reading Skills Focus

Quick Check

1. Eliot refers to twentieth-century people as "hollow men." What is a hollow person lacking?
2. According to lines 20–28, what is "death's dream kingdom" like?

Read with a Purpose

3. What have you learned about Eliot's view of humanity after World War I?

Reading Skills: Drawing Inferences

4. As you read the poem, you recorded your inferences about the hollow men. Now, use your inferences to assess how well the hollow men represent Eliot's view of human history.

Literary Skills Focus

Literary Analysis

5. **Compare and Contrast** In Part I, the hollow men are compared with effigies of Guy Fawkes and contrasted with the historical Fawkes. What does this comparison and contrast tell you?
6. **Analyze** In Part III, what mood—or emotional effect—does the imagery convey?
7. **Analyze** In Part IV, what is the hope of the hollow men? What might regaining sight symbolize? Why do you think the hollow men are powerless to regain sight by themselves?
8. **Analyze** In Part V, what is "the Shadow" that intervenes between thought and action? Why can the speaker not complete the Lord's Prayer?
9. **Draw Conclusions** What is ironic about the hollow men's ability to describe vividly their particular character traits and deficiencies?
10. **Literary Perspectives** Do you think Eliot effectively demonstrates his argument that contemporary history is an "immense panorama of futility and anarchy"? Use evidence from the poem to support your answer.

Literary Skills: Allusion

11. **Analyze** How do Eliot's allusions to Dante's and Shakespeare's work affect your reading of the selection? What do the allusions add to the theme or meaning of the poem?
12. **Analyze** How does Eliot's allusion to a children's rhyme affect the mood of the poem?

Literary Skills Review: Theme

13. **Interpret** The **theme** is a work's main message or insight into life. How would you state the theme of this poem? How is this theme supported by the poem's **tone**—the author's attitude toward the subject or the reader?

Writing Skills Focus

Think as a Reader/Writer

Use It in Your Writing Now that you have seen Eliot's use of allusion, use an allusion in your own writing. Write a brief poem or reflective composition expressing your view of humanity today and include an allusion to reinforce your message.

What Do You Think Now? What in Eliot's experience might account for the bleak view of humanity expressed in this poem?

Universal Access

Struggling Writers

Students may need additional scaffolding to complete the Writing Skills Focus activity. Have students think about a line from Eliot's poem that they found particularly interesting or insightful. Ask students to discuss the line they have chosen with a partner and explain what they find interesting about it. Then, encourage students to write a poem about humanity using Eliot's line as an allusion to reinforce their message. Remind students to use what they discussed with their partners to help them write their poems.

What Do You Think Now?

Remind students of the devastation and upheaval caused by World War I. Ask them to consider how they would feel if everything they knew seemed to disappear before their very eyes. What sort of attitude would they have toward society in a similar situation?

Grades 9–10 Review Reading Standard 1.1 (see pages A48–A50)

Vocabulary Development

Vocabulary Check

Match each Vocabulary word with its definition.

1. supplication	**a.** strength
2. perpetual	**b.** origination
3. conception	**c.** humble plea
4. potency	**d.** lasting forever

Vocabulary Skills: Context Clues

Sometimes you can determine the meaning of an unfamiliar word by looking for clues in the **context**—the surrounding words. Some of the most useful types of context clues include **restatement, comparison, contrast**, and **synonym.** The chart that follows shows some kinds of context clues, as well as definitions and examples.

Type of Context Clue	Definition	Example
restatement	A difficult word is rephrased in more accessible language.	He showed *deference*, or great respect, to his professor.
comparison	Comparison shows the likeness between an unfamiliar word and familiar words surrounding it.	He was incredibly *reserved*, as if he wanted to prevent anyone from really knowing him.
synonym	A nearby word has a similar meaning to the unfamiliar word.	He had always been *cynical* and only became more and more jaded.

Your Turn

In your *Reader/Writer Notebook,* copy any unfamiliar words from the poem. Then look back over the poem to investigate the context clues provided for each of the words. Be sure to look beyond that same stanza in order to determine the words' meanings. Record the clues, and explain your thinking process in using them.

Language Coach

Noun Suffixes The suffix *–ion* means "the act of" and can change a word's part of speech to form a noun. When changing a word that ends in *–ceive*, change the *ive* to a *p* and add *–tion*. What is the noun form of the word *receive?* What is the verb form of the word *conception?*

Academic Vocabulary

Talk About

From your perspective, what conditions in today's world contribute to alienation and despair? How do people exhibit this alienation? How might they adapt to stressful conditions so that alienation does not become inevitable? Discuss these questions with a partner. Use the underlined Academic Vocabulary words in your discussion.

Learn It Online

Visit *WordSharp* for another look at context clues.

go.hrw.com H12-1195 Go

Independent Practice

Vocabulary Development

Vocabulary Check

1. *c*

2. *d*

3. *b*

4. *a*

Your Turn

Possible responses: *Students may note unfamiliar words and context clues such as the following: The "stone images" seem to be monuments, and the "hand raised in supplication" indicates an image of prayer. The "perpetual star" contrasts with the dying men in the "last" valley, indicating that* perpetual *may mean something permanent and lasting. The poem sets up an analogy: conception triggers creation as emotion triggers response. Potency is set up as something that comes before (or causes) existence.*

English for Academic Success

Language Coach

Possible responses: *reception; conceive*

English for Academic Success

Academic Vocabulary

Possible response: *Responses will vary. Students might want to discuss modern wars, global warming, and terrorism. They should explain how people around the world are adapting to the latest political scenarios and how their own perspective on each issue has changed.*

Universal Access: Vocabulary Development

English Learners

English for Academic Success As students complete the Vocabulary Development activity, they might have difficulty locating the context clues in the poem. Explain to students that sometimes a writer signals a context clue with certain words and phrases. For example, a writer might signal a restatement clue by using the words *or, which means,* or *meaning.* Encourage students to look for these signal words when trying to identify the context clues in the sentences.

Struggling Readers

Benchmark Students To give students more practice with context clues, have them write sentences in which they define each Vocabulary word using a type of context clue. Encourage students to use a different type of context clue in each sentence. Then, have students give their sentences to a partner and ask pairs to identify the context clues used in the sentences.

✔ See the **Academic and Selection Vocabulary Skill Builder** in **UA: Differentiating Instruction.**

Learn It Online

WordSharp: An Interactive Vocabulary Tutor provides additional support for vocabulary development. Multimedia tutorials show students how to apply vocabulary skills to unfamiliar words—and how to make those words their own.

go.hrw.com H12-1195 Go

Independent Practice

Grammar Link

Your Turn

1. *demonstrative adjective*: *this*
2. *demonstrative pronoun*: *Those*
3. *demonstrative adjective*: *this*
4. *demonstrative adjective*: *that*

Choices: Evaluation Criteria

Review: Timed Writing 40–50 minutes

The essay contains a clear thesis statement that describes the effect of the allusions on the theme.

Connect: Homework
Add Hypertext

- Students provide links to explanations, illustrations, and questions.
- Discussion addresses the effect of the hypertext.

Extend: Homework
Investigate Allusions

Students demonstrate understanding of the works to which Eliot alludes.

Assess

Unit 6 Resources, Selection Standards Check, p. 99

ThinkCentral Online Assessment, Selection Standards Check

Teacher One Stop™, editable Selection Standards Check

Reteach

ThinkCentral Online Remediation

Learn It Online
The enhanced author biography offers more information on the life of the author as well as Holt's interactive resources pertaining to the author.

go.hrw.com H12-1196 Go

Applying Your Skills

The Hollow Men

Grammar Link

Demonstrative Pronouns and Adjectives

The words *this, that, these,* and *those* are called **demonstrative pronouns** when they point out (or demonstrate) a noun or pronoun.

This is a poem about the futility of existence after World War I. (*This* replaces "The Hollow Men.")

That is the writer I was telling you about. (*That* replaces the name of the writer.)

These are my favorite poems by T. S. Eliot. (*These* replaces the titles of the poems.)

Those are the famous lines that end the poem. (*Those* replaces the line numbers or the words in the lines.)

This, that, these, and *those* are called **demonstrative adjectives** when they modify nouns or pronouns.

This poem is about the futility of existence after World War I.

These poems are my favorite ones by T. S. Eliot.

Your Turn

Identify each demonstrative adjective and demonstrative pronoun in the paragraph below.

You may research the allusions in this poem. Those from literature may be found in works by Dante, Shakespeare, and Conrad, but this reference is from history, and that one is from the Bible.

Writing Application Write your own paragraph using demonstrative adjectives and demonstrative pronouns.

CHOICES

As you respond to the Choices, use these **Academic Vocabulary** words as appropriate: adapt, considerably, exhibit, inevitable, perspective.

REVIEW

State the Theme

Timed Writing Write an essay about Eliot's use of allusions in "The Hollow Men." Be sure to discuss how the allusions contribute to the poem's theme. Include details that support your thesis, and conclude your essay with a summary of your argument.

CONNECT

Add Hypertext

TechFocus Create a hypertext version of "The Hollow Men" that provides links to explanations, illustrations, and questions regarding the poem's allusions. Compare the experiences of reading the poem with and without the hypertext. Do the links add considerably to the experience? In what ways do you think they detract from the reading?

EXTEND

Investigate Allusions

Choose one text that Eliot alludes to in his poem, such as *Julius Caesar, Inferno, Paradiso,* or the Bible. Investigate that work and then discuss with a partner how your experience with that work supports your reading of the poem itself. What understanding did you gain from investigating the allusions?

Learn It Online
Find out more about Eliot and his work through these Internet links.

go.hrw.com L12-1196 Go

Universal Access: Grammar Link

English Learners

English for Academic Success Students may have some difficulty telling the difference between demonstrative pronouns and demonstrative adjectives. Remind students that an adjective *modifies* a noun or pronoun and a pronoun *takes the place of* a noun or another pronoun. Provide the following example:

- ADJECTIVE—T.S. Eliot wrote **both** poems. [*Both* modifies the noun *poems.*]
- PRONOUN—T.S. Eliot wrote **both.** [*Both* takes the place of the noun *poems.*]

Then, ask students to identify the demonstrative adjective or pronoun in each of the following sentences.

1. Those people seem to resemble the hollow men Eliot discusses in his poem. [*Those, adj.*]
2. These are the elements hollow men lack. [*These, pronoun*]
3. Eliot believes those without faith are lost. [*those, pronoun*]

✔ For more practice with demonstrative pronouns and adjectives, see **Warriner's Handbook, Grammar-Notes,** and **Language Handbook Worksheets.**

COMPARING TEXTS: AUTHOR STUDY

William Butler Yeats

(right) William Butler Yeats.
(background) Ruins of a church at Cloncha, Inishowen Peninsula, County Donegal, Ireland.

What Do You Think? How does experience shape our view of the world?

QuickWrite

In your *Reader/Writer Notebook,* write down some of your most significant experiences and some goals you would like to achieve.

CONTENTS

Overview

This Author Study presents poetry by William Butler Yeats. The poems explore the mysticism and symbolism inherent to Yeats's poetry and provide examples of Yeats's concept of poetry as "heightened speech."

Standards Focus

Objectives

Students will

- understand, analyze, and compare themes, imagery, and poetic devices in various works by William Butler Yeats
- make connections between self and text
- write poems, descriptive essays, and comparison-contrast essays

Motivate

What Do You Think?/QuickWrite

Ask students to think about their goals and how those goals may influence the decisions they make in the present. Have students record their responses in their **Reader/Writer Notebooks.**

English for Academic Success

Academic Vocabulary

Look for opportunities to use the Academic Vocabulary words in this unit.

- **adapt,** ***v.:*** adjust for a new purpose
- **considerably,** ***adv.:*** by a large amount
- **exhibit,** ***v.:*** show, demonstrate
- **inevitable,** ***adj.:*** unavoidable
- **perspective,** ***n.:*** a particular way of looking at something

Selection Introduction

Think About the Writer

- William Butler Yeats, one of the greatest English-language poets of the twentieth century, was Irish by birth. His Anglo-Irish family was Protestant—a numerical minority in the predominantly Roman Catholic population, but the dominant social class in Ireland during that time. Yeats's background set him apart from Irish political reformers, such as the nationalist leader Charles Stewart Parnell and the Catholic leaders of the Easter Rebellion of 1916. At the same time, he felt alienated from Anglo-Protestant society, whose materialism Yeats strongly rejected. For many of his themes, Yeats returned to the myths of pre-Christian Ireland, as did other writers of the Celtic Revival.
- As a child, Yeats spent much of his time in Sligo with his grandparents; his affinity with the bucolic countryside was reflected in his works. His unrequited love for Maud Gonne also inspired much of his poetry. She eventually rejected him, and in 1917, Yeats married Georgie Hyde-Lees.
- With Lady Gregory, he established Dublin's Abbey Theatre in 1904 and had his plays performed there. In 1923, he was awarded the Nobel Prize in Literature. Active politically as well as poetically, Yeats also served as a senator of the Irish Free State from 1922 to 1928. Although he died in 1939, in Roquebrune, France, in 1948 his body, accompanied by a military honor guard, was moved back to Ireland for burial in Drumcliffe churchyard. His grave was inscribed with his own epitaph: "Cast a cold eye on life, on death. Horseman, pass by!"

MEET THE WRITER

Nobel Prize WINNER

William Butler Yeats

(1865–1939)

Generally regarded as the twentieth century's greatest poet writing in English, William Butler Yeats was born in a suburb of Dublin, Ireland. The son of a well-known portrait painter, Yeats spent much of his childhood with his grandparents in the Sligo countryside, where he studied Irish history and mythology, topics that would heavily influence his early writing. Yeats attended the Metropolitan School of Art in Dublin from 1884 to 1886, during which time he published some of his first poems in the *Dublin University Review.*

Art Nouveau

Yeats arrived on the literary scene during the revival of the Pre-Raphaelite movement of the mid-nineteenth century. Known as Art Nouveau, this revival emphasized the mysterious and the unfathomable, especially those recesses of the mind now known as the unconscious, which was just then being scrutinized by pioneering psychologists Sigmund Freud and Carl Jung. Particularly in poetry, the revival valued suggestion above statement, symbols above facts, and musical measures above common speech. It was within this atmosphere that the young Yeats established a reputation as a lyricist of great delicacy and as a versifier of old tales drawn from Irish folklore and mythology.

Celtic Pride

In a collection of his early poems, *The Wanderings of Oisin and Other Poems* (1889), Yeats was very much a romantic dreamer, evoking the mythic and heroic past of Ireland. Determined to make the Irish conscious of their heroic past, he was a major advocate of the Celtic Revival, a movement for Ireland's social, intellectual, and political independence from England. In some ways, Yeats saw himself as the prophet-priest of Ireland's national destiny. The Celtic Revival was partially successful, and he moved from the cultural to the political side of the movement. A part of the Anglo-Irish Protestant minority, Yeats participated in the politics of the civil war that followed the annexation of Northern Ireland. From 1922 to 1928, he served as a senator of the newly formed Irish Free State. In his poem "Easter, 1916," written two years before "The Second Coming," Yeats reflected on the unsuccessful revolt of the Irish Nationalists against the British government. He asserts, "Too long a sacrifice / Can make a stone of the heart." This sentiment applied to his personal life as well.

An Irish and an English Love

For years, Yeats had idolized and yearned for Maud Gonne, the beautiful Irish political activist who rejected him and instead chose another, more politically radical suitor. Upon later reflecting on his relationship with Gonne, Yeats pronounced it a "miserable love affair."

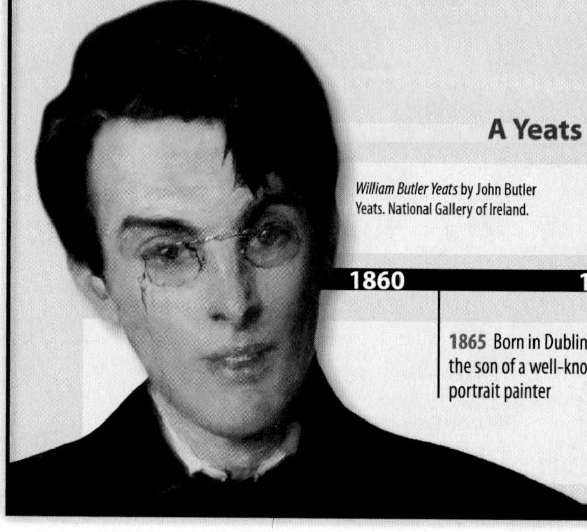

William Butler Yeats by John Butler Yeats. National Gallery of Ireland.

A Yeats Time Line

1860 — 1880 — 1900

1865 Born in Dublin, Ireland, the son of a well-known portrait painter

1884–1886 Attends the Metropolitan School of Art in Dublin

1889 Publishes *The Wanderings of Oisin and Other Poems*

1904 Helps to establish the Abbey Theatre

The room at Lissadell House, where Yeats wrote plays and poems, County Sligo, Ireland.

Selection Readability	
Easily Accessible **Accessible** Challenging	These selections include familiar syntax; concrete situations and imagery; accessible vocabulary.

Yeats finally accepted Gonne's rejection, and in 1917, at age fifty-two, he married Georgie Hyde-Lees, an Englishwoman with whom he eventually had two children. Hyde-Lees would remain his "delight and comfort" for the next twenty-two years.

Poet and Playwright

In 1914, Yeats set out to create a stark, chiseled, and eloquently resonant type of poetry. That same year, he published a volume of poetry aptly titled *Responsibilities.* Some critics have said Yeats carved out of English a language distinctly his own, one that was monumentally sparse and unadorned. This style ("cold and passionate as the dawn" in Yeats's words) confirms the basic definition of poetry as "heightened speech." W. H. Auden, a fellow poet, reflected that Yeats wrote "some of the most beautiful poetry" of the time. Yeats toured the United States, giving ritualized readings of the poems for which he was awarded the 1923 Nobel Prize in Literature.

In addition to being a poet, Yeats was a dramatist and helped his friend Lady Gregory establish Dublin's Abbey Theatre as a monument to Irish culture and high literary standards. When the Abbey Theatre opened its doors in 1904, the repertory boasted three plays, two of which were by William Butler Yeats. Yeats's interest in drama waned after a few years, and he soon gave up an active role in the management of the Abbey, but the institution went on to play a critical part in the development of modern drama. Some audiences may agree with Yeats himself, who felt that some of his most memorable poems are embedded, like gems, in the scripts of his plays.

During his life, Yeats profoundly affected the history of Ireland and the canon of poetry. Ten years after his 1939 death and burial in the south of France, his body was disinterred and sent back to Ireland. Like a primitive king, with full ceremony and military pomp, Yeats returned to Ireland on the deck of a battleship.

Think About the Writer How might Yeats's involvement with the movement for Irish independence from England have affected his writing?

Key Elements of Yeats's Writing

- Lyricism and mysticism predominate
- Irish heritage is celebrated
- Style provides an example of poetry as heightened speech
- Allusions to places and literature enliven and enrich poems

Learn It Online
Learn more about Yeats at the Writers' Lives site.
go.hrw.com H12-1199 Go

1910

1914 Publishes *Responsibilities,* a volume of poetry

1916 Writes "The Wild Swans at Coole," while in love with Maud Gonne

1917 Marries Georgie Hyde-Lees

1920

1921 Writes "The Second Coming"

1922–1928 Serves as a senator of the newly formed Irish Free State

1923 Awarded the Nobel Prize in Literature

1930

1939 Dies in the south of France

Yeats with his wife Georgie Hyde-Lees and their children, Anne and Michael.

Comparing Texts Resources

Unit 6 Resources, on-level practice and assessment, pp. 102, 108, 118

PowerNotes, interactive lesson presentations with activities

Teacher One Stop™, on-level lesson plans and all print resources

Holt Audio Library

Holt Audio Library: Selections and Summaries in Spanish

UA: Holt Interactive Reader, p. 345

UA: Differentiating Instruction, modified lesson plans and leveled assessment, pp. 286, 289

UA: Supporting Instruction in Spanish, selection summary

UA: Resources for Teaching Advanced Students, lesson plans, p. 202

ThinkCentral Online Assessment, Selection Standards Check

ThinkCentral Online Remediation

Selection Introduction

Think About the Writer

To help students think about the question, remind them that the topics of poems like "Easter 1916" and "The Second Coming" relate to the events of the Irish Independence movement. Point out that in 1922, Yeats became a senator in the government of the new Irish Free State. Students can reflect on the ideas of poetic inspiration, purpose, and prophecy in Yeats's work.

For Independent Reading

- *Poet's Choice: Poems for Everyday Life,* Robert Haas
- *Quilting the Black-Eyed Pea: Poems and Not Quite Poems,* Nikki Giovanni

Learn It Online
The **Writers' Lives** feature of the Interactive Student Edition offers additional information about this author. Audio or video segments are provided for some authors.
go.hrw.com H12-1199 Go

Preteach

Introducing Vocabulary

- Review the Vocabulary words, definitions, and sentences with students.
- Tell students that the words help the author develop the theme of the poem. Have students use the Vocabulary words and other images to help them discover the poem's message.

English for Academic Success

Language Coach

Tell students that an online dictionary or etymology site can help them identify words that contain the suffix *–archy*. ***Possible responses:*** *hierarchy, matriarchy, monarchy, oligarchy, patriarchy*

Literary Skills Focus

As you read and discuss the poem with students, have them think about how the Christian prophecy of the Second Coming relates to the theme of the poem.

Reading Skills Focus

Give students a copy of the Reading Skills Focus graphic organizer before they read. (See **Unit 6 Resources**.) Tell them to use their responses to answer the questions on the Applying Your Skills page.

Writing Skills Focus

As students read, have them compile a list of images that help to develop theme in their **Reader/Writer Notebooks**. Students can use their notes to complete the Writing Skills Focus activity.

Learn It Online

The **PowerNotes** presentation for this lesson includes a short video that introduces the poem. The video is also available on the online version of this page.

go.hrw.com H12-1200 Go

Preparing to Read

Reading Standard 3.2, 3.4 (see pages A48–A50)

The Second Coming

Literary Skills Focus

Theme The poem's title and many of its images allude to a Christian perspective of history, specifically, a prophecy from the Bible's Book of Revelation. (An **allusion** is a reference to something that is widely known from religion, literature, or politics.) The poem's **theme,** or central insight, relies upon this allusion and turns it inside out. Consider why Yeats refers to this Christian idea of a just, peaceful end of time, especially in the context of the chaos of World War I and the 1917 Russian Revolution. (Yeats wrote this poem in 1921.) What idea about the Second Coming, or the security of Christian hope, might Yeats be trying to express?

Reading Skills Focus

Visualizing Imagery Poets often exhibit theme, the work's central insight, through imagery. **Imagery** is language that appeals to the senses. Although most images are visual, imagery can also appeal to the senses of hearing, touch, taste, or smell. To visualize imagery, pay attention to the details the poet uses that create a picture in your mind.

Into Action To visualize the poem's central image, note elements of its description in an idea web. In the web's center, write the word "beast." In the surrounding ovals, describe images that relate to the beast.

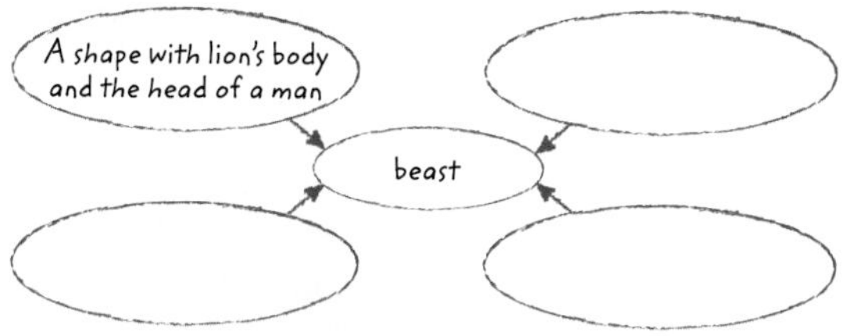

Writing Skills Focus

Think as a Reader/Writer

Find It in Your Reading In your *Reader/Writer Notebook*, record the images Yeats uses to convey theme.

TechFocus Consider what pictures or sounds the poem evokes in your mind. How do these different elements work with, or against, each other?

Reader/Writer Notebook

Use your **RWN** to complete the activities for this selection.

Vocabulary

anarchy (AN uhr kee) *n.:* disorder and confusion. *Anarchy prevailed during the Russian Revolution.*

conviction (kuhn VIHK shuhn) *n.:* firm belief. *She was firm in her conviction that Ireland should be independent.*

intensity (ihn TEHN suh tee) *n.:* great vigor. *He embraced the task with intensity.*

revelation (rehv uh LAY shuhn) *n.:* act of making known. *The people await a revelation that will confirm their hopes.*

vexed (vehkst) *v.:* troubled. *The peace seekers were vexed by the violence.*

Language Coach

Suffix *–archy* The suffix *–archy* means "rule, government." In the word *anarchy,* it is combined with the prefix *an–*, meaning "without," to form a word that means "without rule or government." With a partner, think of other words that include the suffix *–archy* to form words that refer to different types of rule or government.

Learn It Online

Get a different look at "The Second Coming" through the video introduction online.

go.hrw.com H12-1200 Go

California Standards, pp. 1200–1204

- **Reading Standard 3.1** Analyze characteristics of subgenres (e.g., satire, parody, allegory, pastoral) that are used in poetry, prose, plays, novels, short stories, essays, and other basic genres.
- **Reading Standard 3.2** Analyze the way in which the theme or meaning of a selection represents a view or comment on life, using textual evidence to support the claim.
- **Reading Standard 3.3** Analyze the ways in which irony, tone, mood, the author's style, and the "sound" of language achieve specific rhetorical or aesthetic purposes or both.
- **Reading Standard 3.4** Analyze ways in which poets use imagery, personification, figures of speech, and sounds to evoke readers' emotions.
- **Grades 9–10 Review Reading Standard 1.1** Identify and use the literal and figurative meanings of words and understand word derivations.
- **Writing Standard 2.3** Write reflective compositions: **b.** Draw comparisons between specific incidents and broader themes that illustrate the writer's important beliefs or generalizations about life.
- **Writing Standard 2.6** Deliver multimedia presentations: **a.** Combine text, images, and sound and draw information from many sources (e.g., television broadcasts, videos, films, newspapers, magazines, CD-ROMs, the Internet, electronic media-generated images). **b.** Select an appropriate medium for each element of the presentation. **c.** Use the selected media skillfully, editing appropriately and monitoring for quality.

POEM

The Second Coming

by **William Butler Yeats**

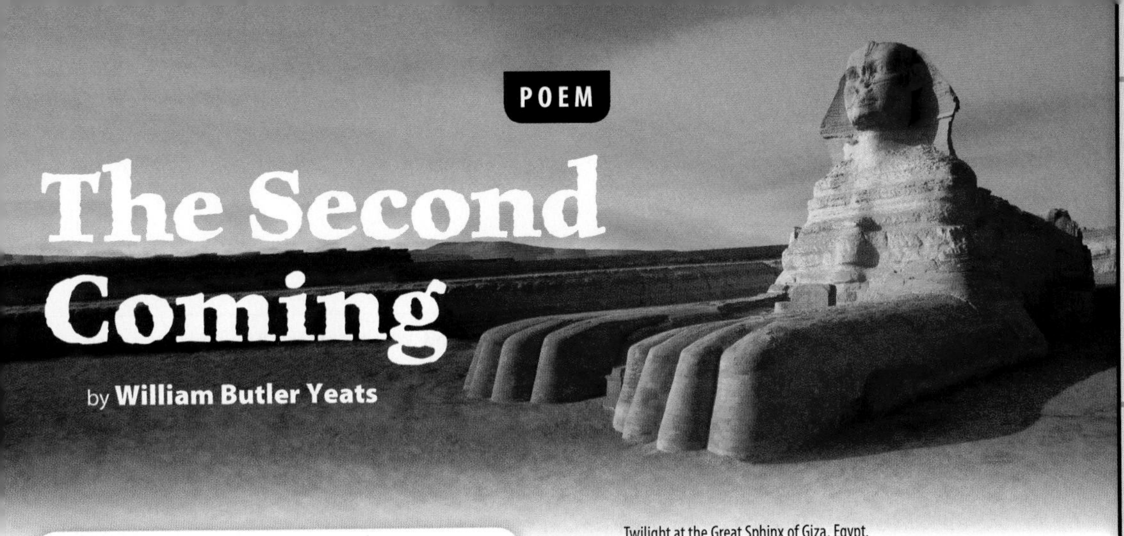

Twilight at the Great Sphinx of Giza, Egypt.

Read with a Purpose

Read to discover the speaker's dire predictions about the future.

Background

In Christianity, the Second Coming refers to the belief that Jesus will one day return to Earth and usher in an era of peace and justice. The "first coming" was the birth of Jesus in Bethlehem in Judea, just over two thousand years ago.

This poem addresses not only the Christian conception of the universe but also Yeats's cyclical view of history. Each cycle, known as a gyre (jyr), begins in a rational state and then gradually dissolves into chaos and irrationality.

Turning and turning in the widening gyre
The falcon cannot hear the falconer;
Things fall apart; the center cannot hold;
Mere anarchy is loosed upon the world,
The blood-dimmed tide is loosed, and everywhere
The ceremony of innocence is drowned;
The best lack all conviction, while the worst
Are full of passionate intensity. **A**

Surely some revelation is at hand;
Surely the Second Coming is at hand.
The Second Coming! Hardly are those words out
When a vast image out of Spiritus Mundi°
Troubles my sight: somewhere in sands of the
desert
A shape with lion body and the head of a man,
A gaze blank and pitiless as the sun,
Is moving its slow thighs, while all about it
Reel shadows of the indignant desert birds.
The darkness drops again; but now I know
That twenty centuries of stony sleep
Were vexed to nightmare by a rocking cradle
And what rough beast, its hour come round at
last,
Slouches towards Bethlehem to be born? **B**

12. Spiritus Mundi: Latin for "the world's soul or spirit"; for Yeats, the collective reservoir of human memory from which artists draw their images.

A Literary Focus **Theme** If the falcon and the falconer represent order, what does the breakdown in their relationship suggest about Yeats's attitude toward conditions in his times?

B Reading Focus **Visualizing Imagery** What details does Yeats use to help you visualize "the beast"?

Vocabulary **anarchy** (AN uhr kee) *n.:* disorder and confusion.
conviction (kuhn VIHK shuhn) *n.:* firm belief.
intensity (ihn TEHN suh tee) *n.:* great vigor.
revelation (rehv uh LAY shuhn) *n.:* act of making known.
vexed (vehkst) *v.:* troubled.

Real Issues, Real Experts

*Holt author **Leila Christenbury** offers strategies for teaching the poetry of William Butler Yeats.*

The four poems in this collection are best grouped into two pairs which reflect Yeats's thoughts on nature ("Lake Isle of Innisfree" and "The Wild Swans at Coole") and his commentary on contemporary life ("The Second Coming" and "Sailing to Byzantium"). The autobiographical piece can be considered separately or as a companion to all four poems.

In the first pair, students can look for the theme of how life changes affect our view of nature. What delights the speaker in "Innisfree," and what does he fear in "Wild Swans," published twenty-six years later?

In the second pair, students will need guidance about Yeats's observations regarding modern life and its dissatisfactions. Most students will intuitively appreciate the drama of Yeats's commentary and the music of his language, even if they do not understand every line. Pointing out famous phrases can help them appreciate Yeats's craft.

The autobiographical piece can be examined as a commentary on Yeats himself. It underscores the poet's sensitive nature as it revisits the themes of passing time and loss.

Teacher Preparation

Selection Summary

Although the title of "The Second Coming" alludes to the Christian belief in the Second Coming of Christ, the speaker ironically reverses our expectations. As the Second Coming is described in the poem, humanity will experience a ghastly new era of warfare and savagery.

Direct Teach

Think About/Talk About

Read with a Purpose Have students discuss why the speaker might have dire predictions for the future.

Comprehension

B Reading Focus

Possible response: *He describes the beast's sphinx-like body, blank gaze, and slow thighs.*

Analysis

A Literary Focus

Possible response: *Yeats believes a time of chaos is coming.*

Vocabulary: Own the Word

- **anarchy:** The word *anarchy* comes from two Greek roots, *an–* ("without") and *archos* ("leader"). What other words with the root *arch* relate to leaders?
- **conviction:** Ask students whether they hold any beliefs that they consider strong enough to be called *convictions.* Call on volunteers to identify a personal *conviction.*
- **intensity:** *Intensity* is power and its antonym is *moderation.* Use both words in a sentence: Although she practices her sport with *intensity,* she approaches most other aspects of her life with moderation.
- **revelation:** *Revelation* is based on the word *reveal* (verb form). When you experience a *revelation,* something that was not clear to you before is *revealed.*
- **vexed:** Ask a volunteer to act out the appearance of a person who is *vexed* (angry, irritated, upset).

Check for Understanding

Independent Practice

Reading Skills Focus

Possible responses:

1. *Yeats foresees a time of chaos and anarchy in which evil dominates.*
2. *Summaries will vary. Students may describe a sphinx-like creature, its gaze blank and pitiless, moving ponderously.*

Literary Skills Focus

Possible responses:

3. *"Center" suggests order or morality. "The center cannot hold" suggests the triumph of chaos.*
4. *The "blood-dimmed tide" may refer to warfare. "The ceremony of innocence" may refer to baptism.*
5. *He expresses dread of the future.*
6. *"Mere" is ironic when used with "anarchy"; "pitiless" connotes danger; "indignant" suggests that nature itself is outraged; "stony" suggests heartlessness; "slouches" suggests menacing contempt. In context, the words are very vivid.*
7. *The rhythm changes in line 5 as the imagery of chaos becomes more vivid before chaos takes over the poem. The poem's irregular meter reflects its theme of chaos.*
8. *The question requires readers to define the beast for themselves.*
9. *Responses will vary. Yeats presents a very negative vision of the future, with which students may or may not agree.*
10. *The lines illustrate that the center is not holding because a falcon is trained to return to its handler.*
11. *The "rough beast" is evil or anarchy. This relates to the theme that the world is falling apart and goodness will not prevail.*
12. *The Second Coming is ironic because instead of Christ's coming to bring peace and justice, a frightening beast appears in darkness. The irony is frightening because it suggests that the beast's destructiveness is as infinite as God's goodness.*

Applying Your Skills

Reading Standard 3.2, 3.3, 3.4 (see pages A48–A50)
Writing Standard 2.3b (see pages A51–A52)

The Second Coming

Literary Response and Analysis

Reading Skills Focus

Read with a Purpose

1. What do you think Yeats foresees for the future?

Reading Skills: Visualizing Imagery

2. While reading, you noted descriptions of one of the poem's central images, the beast, in an idea web. Now, write a summary of what you see when you visualize the image of the beast described in the poem. Note some of the specific words that make this imagery especially vivid.

Literary Skills Focus

Literary Analysis

3. **Interpret** What do you think the poet means by the word *center* in line 3? What condition does the phrase "the center cannot hold" describe?
4. **Make Judgments** To what might the "blood-dimmed tide" in line 5 refer? What could the "ceremony of innocence" in line 6 mean? Explain your interpretation.
5. **Analyze** If you had to name one dominant emotion expressed by the speaker, what would it be?
6. **Evaluate** Consider the poet's use of each of the following words: *mere* (line 4), *pitiless* (line 15), *indignant* (line 17), *stony* (line 19), and *slouches* (line 22). Think about the connotations of each word. What idea or emotion does each word help convey? How vivid or forceful do you find each word in its context?
7. **Analyze** Notice how the approximate rhyme of the first lines changes to unrhymed verse. Notice also the variation of the iambic pentameter. Where do the rhyme and rhythm change, and what is the effect? How does the poem's rhythm reflect the theme?
8. **Extend** Why might Yeats have ended the poem with a question? Explain.

Literary Skills: Theme

9. **Interpret** What message about the inevitable future does Yeats express in the poem? Do you agree with this message? Why or why not?
10. **Analyze** The first two lines of the poem present the image of a falconer who is unable to limit the flight of his released falcon. How does this image help convey one of the poem's central themes? (Remember that **theme** is the main message or insight of a literary work.) Consider the poem's historical context in your response.
11. **Make Judgments** How would you answer the poem's concluding question? How does your answer relate to the poem's theme?

Literary Skills Review: Irony

12. **Analyze** A discrepancy between what is expected and what happens is called **irony.** How does the idea of the Second Coming become **ironic** in the second stanza? How is this irony frightening?

Writing Skills Focus

Think as a Reader/Writer

Use It in Your Writing Identify a message that you would like to express to readers. Then, write a poem or a paragraph that uses vivid imagery to convey this theme. Share your writing with the class.

What Do You Think Now? What world events may have influenced Yeats to write this poem? Why?

Universal Access

Struggling Writers

Students may need additional scaffolding to complete the Writing Skills Focus activity. Before students write, brainstorm a list of possible messages or themes with students. Invite students to choose one of the themes from the list to write a poem or paragraph about. Give students five minutes to make a list of descriptive words or phrases that relate to their chosen theme. Then, have them use their lists as they write their poem or paragraph.

What Do You Think Now?

Point out the images of war and chaos, and remind students that Yeats wrote the poem in 1921, just after the end of World War I.

Grades 9–10 Review Reading Standard 1.1 (see pages A48–A50)

Vocabulary Development

Vocabulary Check

Match the Vocabulary words with their definitions.

1. anarchy
2. conviction
3. intensity
4. revelation
5. vexed

a. troubled
b. disorder
c. great vigor
d. act of making known
e. firm belief

Vocabulary Skills: Etymology

Etymology is the history of a word. In many dictionaries, a precise etymology is given for each word, taking its history back to its origin. By studying etymologies, you can familiarize yourself with certain roots and their meanings. Doing so will help you determine the meanings of related words. Look at the following dictionary entry:

> **anarchy** (AN uhr kee) *n.* [ML *anarchia* < Gr *anarchos,* having no ruler < *an–,* without + *archos* ruler] a state of disorder.

The information in brackets gives the history of the word. The dictionary should have a key in the front to help you decipher the abbreviations. In this case, the word is traced back through Middle Latin (ML) to Greek (Gr). Other common abbreviations include *G* for German, *OE* for Old English, *ME* for Middle English, *F* for French, and *L* for Latin. Always check the dictionary's key to make certain you are reading the etymology properly.

Your Turn

Use a dictionary to look up the etymologies of the Vocabulary words. Use a chart like the one on the right to record the information you find.

Word	Language of Origin	Original Word and Meaning
anarchy	Greek	*anarchos,* meaning "having no ruler"
conviction		
intensity		
revelation		
vexed		

Language Coach

Suffix *-archy* With a partner, look over the list of words with the suffix *-archy* that you identified. Use a dictionary to look up the meaning of each of the words. Based on their meanings, can you guess the meanings of the prefixes they include?

Academic Vocabulary

Talk About

Yeats possessed the ability to exhibit strong themes in both his poetic and his dramatic writing. With a partner, record reasons why Yeats might have been able to adapt to these considerably different forms.

Learn It Online
Develop your vocabulary online with Word Watch.
go.hrw.com H12-1203 Go

Universal Access: Vocabulary Development

English Learners

English for Academic Success Help students gain meaning from the Vocabulary words. Pair students with a proficient English speaker, and have them work together to answer the following questions.

- What would you expect to happen if you had a *revelation* about a problem? [*I would expect to find the answer to my problem.*]
- If you are *vexed* with your sister, are you happy with her or upset with her? [*upset with her*]
- If you have a *conviction* about a law, do you strongly believe in it or strongly oppose it? [*strongly believe in it*]
- If you enjoy *anarchy,* do you like chaos or abhor it? [*you like chaos*]
- If you look at something with *intensity,* do you glance at it or stare hard at it? [*stare hard at it*]

✔ See the **Academic and Selection Vocabulary Skill Builder** in **UA: Differentiating Instruction.**

Independent Practice

Vocabulary Development

Vocabulary Check

1. *b* **2.** *e*
3. *c* **4.** *d*
5. *a*

Your Turn

Possible responses:
conviction—from Latin. Convincere *means "to conquer."*
intensity—from Latin. Intendere *means "to stretch out."*
revelation—from Latin. Revelare *means "to reveal."*
vexed—from Latin. Vexare *means "to agitate."*

English for Academic Success

Language Coach

Possible responses:

hierarchy—*any system of persons or things ranked one above another; Greek* hierarchia *means "rule by the high priest."*

matriarchy—*rule by women;* matr– *means "mother."*

monarchy—*rule by one person, usually a king or queen;* mono– *means "one."*

oligarchy—*rule by a small number of people;* olig– *means "few."*

patriarchy—*rule by males;* patr– *means "father."*

English for Academic Success

Academic Vocabulary

Possible response: *Responses will vary. Students' notes should cite elements in Yeats's work that exhibit his capacity to adapt to considerably different forms of writing.*

Learn It Online
Send students to **Word Watch** for audio pronunciations, synonyms and antonyms, and brief histories of word origins.
go.hrw.com H12-1203 Go

Independent Practice

Grammar Link

Your Turn

1. *Yeats wrote "The Second Coming."*
2. *Critics consider Yeats one of the best poets of the twentieth-century.*
3. *Students in schools and universities study his work.*
4. *Critics appreciate his poetry and drama.*

Choices: Evaluation Criteria

Review: Homework
Analyze Allusion
- Students explain the history of the sphinx.
- Students explain why Yeats used the image in his poem.

Connect: Homework
Make a Digital Collage
- Digital collages include text, images, and sound.
- Collages convey an understanding of the theme.

Extend: Homework
Give a Poetic Answer
- Poems express the student's view of the future.
- Students use vivid language to express the theme of the poem.

Assess

Unit 6 Resources, Selection Standards Check, p. 105

ThinkCentral Online Assessment, Selection Standards Check

Teacher One Stop™, editable Selection Standards Check

Reteach

ThinkCentral Online Remediation

Applying Your Skills

Reading Standard 3.1, 3.2, 3.3 (see pages A48–A50)
Writing Standard 2.3b. 2.6a–c (see pages A51–A52)

The Second Coming

Grammar Link

Active and Passive Voice Verbs

A verb in the **active voice** expresses an action performed by its subject:

The student reads the poem.

[The subject, *student,* performs the action.]

A verb in the passive voice expresses an action performed on its subject:

The poem is read by the student.

[The subject, *poem,* is acted upon. Notice the passive voice is a verb phrase with a *be* verb (in this case, *is*) + the past participle (in this case, *read*).]

Active voice generally makes writing more powerful and precise than the passive voice does. However, sometimes writers use the passive voice for good reasons. For instance, Yeats uses the passive voice frequently in "The Second Coming" to suggest that the forces at work are beyond anyone's control.

Mere anarchy is loosed upon the world,
The blood-dimmed tide is loosed, and everywhere
The ceremony of innocence is drowned;

Your Turn

In the following sentences, change the passive voice to the active voice. Add subjects where necessary.

1. "The Second Coming" was written by Yeats.
2. Yeats is considered one of the best poets of the twentieth century.
3. His work is studied in schools and universities.
4. His poetry and drama are appreciated by critics.

Writing Application Scan an essay you have written for sentences in which you used passive voice. Change the cases of passive voice to active voice, and read those sentences aloud. Do they sound more powerful?

CHOICES

As you respond to the Choices, use these **Academic Vocabulary** words as appropriate: perspective, considerably, adapt, exhibit, inevitable.

Great Sphinx against the pyramid of Khafra, on the Giza Plateau at the west bank of the Nile River, near Cairo, Egypt.

REVIEW

Analyze Allusion

Remember, an **allusion** is a reference in a work to another work or historical event. In this selection, Yeats alludes to the Sphinx at Giza. Review the poem and research the Sphinx. Write an essay exploring why Yeats chose this allusion.

CONNECT

Make a Digital Collage

TechFocus Make a digital collage of text, visual images, and sounds to illustrate "The Second Coming." Try to convey the poem's theme in your collage. Then, exhibit the collage for your class.

EXTEND

Give a Poetic Answer

Write a poem responding to the question posed in the final lines of "The Second Coming." You might share Yeats's perspective, or you might express a more positive viewpoint. Use vivid imagery to express your theme.

Universal Access: Grammar Link

EL English Learners

English for Academic Success When students rephrase passive-voice sentences in the active voice, have them think about who is performing the action before they choose a subject for the reworded sentence. Sometimes a possible agent, introduced by the word *by,* is given in the sentence; other times, the sentence leaves the agent unstated. To reword sentence 2 in the active voice, have students ask, "*Who* considered Yeats one of the best poets of twentieth-century British literature?" The answer will be the subject of the new sentence. Have students use the following examples to practice rewording passive-voice sentences.

- His poems are loved by people everywhere. [*People everywhere love his poems.*]
- Collections of his work are sold in many bookstores. [*Many bookstores sell collections of his work.*]

✔ For more practice with active and passive voice verbs, see **Warriner's Handbook, GrammarNotes,** and **Language Handbook Worksheets.**

Preparing to Read

Reading Standard 3.2, 3.4 (see pages A48–A50)

The Lake Isle of Innisfree

Literary Skills Focus

Assonance and Alliteration **Assonance** is the repetition of vowel sounds in words that are close together; **alliteration** is the repetition of consonant sounds in words that are close together. Yeats's lyrical skills, especially his haunting use of assonance and alliteration, create poetry whose verbal music echoes in readers' memories. The lilting rhythms of the poem and the repetition of vowel and consonant sounds soothe and transport the reader. As you read, consider how these techniques affect the message and the emotional force of the poem.

Reading Skills Focus

Connecting Text to Experience When you connect what you read with your experiences, you will better understand the ideas and feelings the text conveys. In this poem, the speaker imagines a retreat on a beautiful island. When your life becomes stressful, do you imagine a place or a time in which you feel calm and free? Have you experienced such a retreat?

Into Action Create a chart to record connections between the text and your own experience. In the first column, write details from the text about the speaker's imagined trip to Innisfree. In the second column, write details from a real or imagined peaceful retreat you have experienced.

Text	My Experience
The speaker will go to a small cabin on Innisfree.	I have spent some weekends camping outdoors in beautiful woods.

Writing Skills Focus

Think as a Reader/Writer

Find It in Your Reading In addition to **alliteration** and **assonance,** Yeats uses inverts word order and uses repetition to create verbal music. In your *Reader/Writer Notebook,* record examples of these techniques in the poem.

Vocabulary

glade (glayd) *n.:* small open space in a forest. *The deer rested and nibbled grass in the glade.*

glimmer (GLIHM uhr) *n.:* faint, unsteady light. *He watched the glimmer of the stars in the night sky.*

Language Coach

Poetry Recitation Reading poetry aloud is sometimes difficult because the reader gets caught up in the rhythm of the poem and puts too much stress on the rhymes. Practice reading the sentences in the poem aloud. Try to read naturally and with fluency.

Reader/Writer Notebook

Use your **RWN** to complete the activities for this selection.

Learn It Online

Listen to the rhythms of this poem for yourself online.

go.hrw.com H12-1205 Go

California Standards, pp. 1205–1207

- **Reading Standard 3.2** Analyze the way in which the theme or meaning of a selection represents a view or comment on life, using textual evidence to support the claim.
- **Reading Standard 3.4** Analyze ways in which poets use imagery, personification, figures of speech, and sounds to evoke readers' emotions.

Preteach

Introducing Vocabulary

- Review the Vocabulary words, definitions, and sentences with students.
- Tell students that these words are used by the author to create alliteration and rhyme. Have students use the Vocabulary words to help them discover the poem's rhythm and repetition of sounds.

English for Academic Success

Language Coach

Explain that part of the power of some poems is a tension between the singsong rhythm created by the rhyme and meter and the natural spoken rhythm heard when the poem is read for meaning.

Literary Skills Focus

As you read and discuss the poem, have students note the effect of assonance and alliteration on the poem's message and emotional power.

Reading Skills Focus

Give students a copy of the Reading Skills Focus graphic organizer before they read. (See **Unit 6 Resources**.) Tell them to use their responses to answer the questions on the Applying Your Skills page.

Writing Skills Focus

Have students record examples of inversion and repetition in their **Reader/Writer Notebooks**. Students can use their notes to complete the Writing Skills Focus activity.

Learn It Online

The online version of this poem includes audio support to engage all students and to help struggling readers with reading comprehension and vocabulary.

go.hrw.com H12-1205 Go

Teacher Preparation

Selection Summary

In this decisive and dreamlike lyric, the speaker determines to leave his urban home and go to the lake island of Innisfree (a real island in County Sligo, Ireland). On that island, he will build a cabin and live in harmony with nature, looking forward to the peace and transcendent natural beauty of the island. Deep in his heart, he hears the sound of the lake water lapping along the shoreline.

Direct Teach

Think About/Talk About

Read with a Purpose Have students read the Read with a Purpose statement. Ask them to reflect on the qualities that make Innisfree so idyllic.

Comprehension

B Reading Focus

Possible response: *Students' answers should describe the peacefulness of a particular place or experience and explain why it is peaceful.*

Analysis

A Literary Focus

Possible response: *Examples include the alliteration of the* s, p, d, m, *and* n *sounds and the assonance in* slow *and* grow *and in* midnight, linnet, glimmer *and* wings.

Vocabulary: Own the Word

- **glade:** Tell students that in lines 3–4, the speaker imagines himself in a "bee-loud *glade*." Aside from bees, what other creatures might one expect to see in a *glade*? ***Possible responses:*** *squirrels, birds, rabbits, deer*
- **glimmer:** A twinkling star might be said to *glimmer*. Lights in the distance *glimmer*. A flickering candle can *glimmer* in a window.

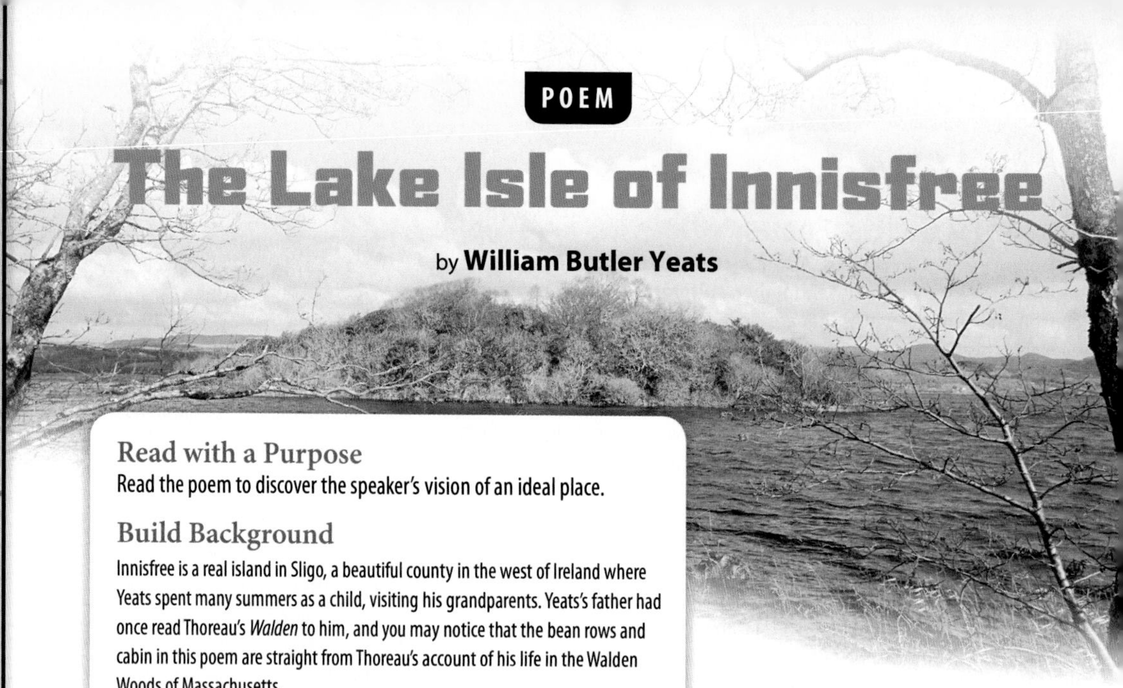

POEM

The Lake Isle of Innisfree

by **William Butler Yeats**

Read with a Purpose
Read the poem to discover the speaker's vision of an ideal place.

Build Background
Innisfree is a real island in Sligo, a beautiful county in the west of Ireland where Yeats spent many summers as a child, visiting his grandparents. Yeats's father had once read Thoreau's *Walden* to him, and you may notice that the bean rows and cabin in this poem are straight from Thoreau's account of his life in the Walden Woods of Massachusetts.

I will arise and go now, and go to Innisfree,
And a small cabin build there, of clay and wattles° made:
Nine bean-rows will I have there, a hive for the honey-bee,
And live alone in the bee-loud glade.

And I shall have some peace there, for peace comes dropping slow,
Dropping from the veils of the morning to where the cricket sings;
There midnight's all a glimmer, and noon a purple glow,
And evening full of the linnet's° wings. A

I will arise and go now, for always night and day
I hear lake water lapping with low sounds by the shore;
While I stand on the roadway, or on the pavements gray,
I hear it in the deep heart's core. B

2. wattles: interwoven twigs or branches.

8. linnet's: A linnet is a European songbird.

A Literary Focus **Assonance and Alliteration** What examples of alliteration and assonance create verbal music in lines 5–8?

B Reading Focus **Connecting Text to Experience** When have you felt peaceful at your "heart's core"? Do you associate the feeling with a particular place and time? Explain.

Vocabulary **glade** (glayd) *n.:* small open space in a forest.
glimmer (GLIHM uhr) *n.:* faint, unsteady light.

Universal Access

EL English Learners

English for Academic Success Explain that Yeats invents the word *bee-loud* to show that the glade is loud with bees buzzing. Similarly, the "evening full of linnet's wings" evokes the numerous birds flying around in the evening. Then tell them that "midnight's all a glimmer" portrays the shimmer of the moonlight. Likewise, "noon's all a purple glow" explains how the bright noon sun casts a purple light in the deep shade.

California Standards, p. 1207

- **Reading Standard 3.2** Analyze the way in which the theme or meaning of a selection represents a view or comment on life, using textual evidence to support the claim.
- **Reading Standard 3.3** Analyze the ways in which irony, tone, mood, the author's style, and the "sound" of language achieve specific rhetorical or aesthetic purposes or both.
- **Reading Standard 3.4** Analyze ways in which poets use imagery, personification, figures of speech, and sounds to evoke readers' emotions.

Reading Standard 3.2, 3.3, 3.4 (see pages A48–A50)
Writing Standard 2.1c (see pages A51–A52)

The Lake Isle of Innisfree

Literary Response and Analysis

Reading Skills Focus

Read with a Purpose

1. What attributes of Innisfree does the speaker find ideal?

Reading Skills: Connecting Text to Experience

2. Look over the chart you made as you read. Add to each entry the speaker's feelings and your own feelings from your experience. How does this exercise help you connect with the text?

Vocabulary Check

Fill in the blanks in the following sentence, using the Vocabulary words, ***glimmer*** and ***glade.***

3. That evening we spread our picnic blanket in the _____ and watched the _____ of the flitting fireflies .

Literary Skills Focus

Literary Analysis

4. **Classify** How would you classify the kind of life the speaker wants to lead on the island?
5. **Infer** To what does the speaker compare peace? Why might he have had a hard time finding peace in the city?
6. **Drawing Conclusions** What does the last stanza say about the speaker's relationship with nature?
7. **Make Judgments** The pronoun *I* appears seven times in this twelve-line poem. Why do you think the speaker so often inserts himself into the scene he describes? Does this presence make the poem more or less soothing to you? Explain.

Literary Skills: Assonance and Alliteration

8. **Compare and Contrast** What is Yeats's message about the future and its possibilities? How does this message compare to that of "The Second Coming"? Why do you think Yeats wrote poems with such different messages?
9. **Evaluate** What vowel sounds dominate the first stanza?
10. **Analyze** Explain how alliteration helps you experience the sights and sounds described in line 10.
11. **Extend** Read the poem aloud to a partner. Describe the total effect of the vowel sounds in the poem. How would the poem have been different if the poet had used more hard consonants, such as *k, d,* or *p*?

Literary Skills Review: Tone

12. **Analyze** The attitude a writer takes toward the reader, a subject, or a character is called **tone.** How would you describe the **tone** of the poem? Do you think it could be called a Romantic poem? Explain why or why not.

Writing Skills Focus

Think as a Reader/Writer

Use It in Your Writing Review your notes on Yeats's use of alliteration, assonance, inversion, and repetition. Then, write a poem or a paragraph about a special place, using these techniques to create verbal music. If you like, begin with the words "I will arise and go now. . . ."

What Do You Think Now? What role does daydreaming play in your life? Do you think the kind of daydreaming the speaker does in this poem is helpful? Why or why not?

■ **Writing Standard 2.1** Write fictional, autobiographical, or biographical narratives: **c.** Describe with concrete sensory details the sights, sounds, and smells of a scene and the specific actions, movements, gestures, and feelings of the characters; use interior monologue to depict the characters' feelings.

Universal Access

Struggling Writers

Students may need additional scaffolding to complete the Writing Skills Focus activity. Some students may struggle to use multiple sound devices in their poems. Invite students to employ only one sound device, such as alliteration, in their writing. Before students write their poems, have them brainstorm a list of adjectives that describe their special place. Encourage students to think of adjectives that have similar consonant sounds to help them use alliterative language in their writing.

Check for Understanding

Independent Practice

Reading Skills Focus

Possible responses:

1. *the gentle sounds of wildlife and water at the shore*
2. *Ask students how the exercise helped them connect to the text.*

Vocabulary Check

3. *glade; glimmer*

Literary Skills Focus

Possible responses:

4. *pastoral, idyllic, ideal*
5. *The speaker describes peace as dew that drops slowly from morning mist. In contrast, the city is busy with vehicles.*
6. *Nature is what gives the poet peace in his heart's core.*
7. *His intentions and emotions are highly personal. Many students will find the repetition of the long* I *sound soothing.*
8. *"Innisfree" presents the possibility of finding inner peace. Its theme is the opposite of the theme of "The Second Coming," which promises future turmoil. Yeats may have believed that cultivating inner serenity was a way to cope with external turmoil.*
9. *The dominant vowel sounds are long* i, *long* o, *long* e, *and long* a.
10. *The repeated* l *sound suggests the sound of the water.*
11. *The vowel sounds have a soothing effect. The hard sounds would create a harsh effect.*
12. *The tone is lyrical, nostalgic, and muted. The poem could be called Romantic in its focus on the peacefulness of the natural world.*

What Do You Think Now?

Students can think about when they daydream and what they daydream about. Their opinions about the function of daydreaming in this poem should be supported by the text.

Preteach

Introducing Vocabulary

- Review the Vocabulary words, definitions, and sentences with students.
- Tell students that these words are used by the author to describe the swans as a symbol. Have them use the Vocabulary words and other details to discover what the swans might represent.

English for Academic Success

Language Coach

Remind students that context clues can help them determine the meaning of a multiple-meaning word. Point out that in line 25, Yeats uses *still* as an adjective to describe the water. ***Possible response:*** *In lines 19 and 24,* still *means "up to this time." In line 25,* still *means "tranquil."*

Literary Skills Focus

Before you read and discuss the poem with students, have students discuss what images people might use to symbolize feelings such as anger, faithfulness, and deprivation.

Writing Skills Focus

Have students record details about the swans and their symbolic meaning in their **Reader/Writer Notebooks**. Students can use their notes to complete the Writing Skills Focus activity.

Learn It Online

Additional, high-interest information is available about the author and his life, including projects and activities.

go.hrw.com H12-1208 Go

Preparing to Read

The Wild Swans at Coole

Grades 9–10 Review Reading Standard 3.7 (see pages A48–A50)

Literary Skills Focus

Symbol A **symbol** is a figure of speech in which a person, place, thing, or event stands both for itself and for something beyond itself. A symbol can be understood literally (for what it is) and also figuratively (as representative of something beyond itself). If Yeats's swans are to be regarded as symbols, what do they represent? As you read this poem, keep in mind that symbols are open-ended: Their meanings are various and open to interpretation.

Into Action The symbolism of the swans works well in the context in which they appear; the passing of time is central to the poem's meaning. Using a graphic organizer like the one below, track the references and images of time. Copy the words and phrases that reference time or the passing of time. Record the line number as in the examples below. What do the images suggest about time? How does the context of passing time affect your reading of the poem and the symbolism of the swans?

Images of Time	Meaning
"autumn beauty" (1)	Autumn suggests passing of time, getting older.
"October twilight" (3)	October is late in the year, and twilight is late in the day. Both suggest time passing, including aging and approaching death.

Writing Skills Focus

Think as a Reader/Writer

Find It in Your Reading Look for the **symbolism** that Yeats uses in "The Wild Swans at Coole." Consider what you already know about Yeats's life. Also keep in mind that swans are migratory, returning annually to the same places, and monogamous (they mate for life). As you read, record in your *Reader/Writer Notebook* details about how Yeats describes the swans in each stanza, and brainstorm ideas about what the swans might represent, or symbolize. Do the swans symbolize the same thing in each stanza of the poem, or does what they represent vary?

Vocabulary

clamorous (KLAM uhr uhs) *adj.:* loud and noisy. *The clamorous cries of the birds broke the stillness.*

passion (PASH uhn) *n.:* strong emotion. *Disappointments had dampened the man's passion for life.*

Language Coach

Multiple-Meaning Words Some words have more than one meaning. For example, Yeats uses the word *still* to mean "motionless" or "tranquil" in line 4. *Still* can also be used as an adverb to mean "up to this or that time." To determine which meaning is intended, study the word's context. How is *still* used in lines 19, 24, and 25?

Reader/Writer Notebook

Use your **RWN** to complete the activities for this selection.

Learn It Online

Find projects and activities online to take your study of Yeats further.

go.hrw.com H12-1208 Go

California Standards, pp. 1208–1211

- **Grades 9–10 Review Reading Standard 3.7** Recognize and understand the significance of various literary devices, including figurative language, imagery, allegory, and symbolism, and explain their appeal.

POEM

The Wild Swans at Coole

by **William Butler Yeats**

Bewick's Swans over a Pearly Sea (1975) by Sir Peter Scott (1909–1989). Oil on canvas.

Read with a Purpose

Read to find out how the passage of time has affected the speaker's response to the familiar sight of the swans.

Build Background

Yeats's friend Lady Gregory lived on an estate known as Coole Park in Ireland's County Galway. When Yeats first visited there in 1897, he was in love with Maud Gonne, the political activist for Irish independence, who was more interested in politics than in Yeats. This poem, written in 1916, recalls Yeats's first view of the swans. Nineteen years later, he realizes, "All's changed."

The trees are in their autumn beauty,
The woodland paths are dry,
Under the October twilight the water
Mirrors a still sky;
Upon the brimming water among the stones
Are nine-and-fifty swans. (A)

The nineteenth autumn has come upon me
Since I first made my count;
I saw, before I had well finished,
All suddenly mount
And scatter wheeling in great broken rings
Upon their clamorous wings.

(A) **Literary Focus** **Symbol** What does autumn often symbolize? Think about the time of year and what happens in nature.

Vocabulary **clamorous** (KLAM uhr uhs) *adj.:* loud and noisy.

Universal Access

Struggling Readers

Strategic Students To help students understand the symbolism of the swans, ask them to analyze and paraphrase the fourth stanza (lines 19–24). Point out the phrases "lover by lover," "companionable streams," and "passion or conquest."

✔ See **UA: Differentiating Instruction** for a graphic organizer to scaffold instruction for struggling readers.

Advanced Learners

Acceleration Explain to students that starting in 1898, Yeats spent summers at Coole Park. In 1917, he bought and restored a Norman tower in the area called Thoor Ballylee. Having been rejected by Maud Gonne in 1899, he proposed to and was rejected by Maud Gonne's twenty-two-year-old daughter, Iseult, in 1917. That same year, he married George (Georgie) Hyde-Lees and wrote "Wild Swans at Coole." Interested students can research Yeats's life further to explore the biographical context of his poetry.

Teacher Preparation

Selection Summary

In autumn, the speaker walks down to the water, where he counts fifty-nine swans. He first counted them nineteen years ago. As he counts them again, they start to scatter clamorously into the air. Turning thoughtful, the speaker's "heart is sore" as he realizes how much has changed in those nineteen years. But the swans have not changed. They have not grown old. They still feel "passion or conquest." He wonders where they will go when one day they fly away for good.

Direct Teach

Think About/Talk About

Read with a Purpose Have students read the Read with a Purpose statement. Point out words and phrases that indicate how the speaker once felt as opposed to the way he feels now.

Analysis

(A) Literary Focus

Possible response: *Autumn is the time when nature prepares itself for winter and when trees and flowers begin to die. In poetry, autumn often symbolizes the approaching end of a person's life.*

Extend the Discussion

Symbolism What do the swans symbolize in the first stanza? ***Possible response:*** *The swans may symbolize permanence and beauty. They have been there for the speaker whenever he visits the lake.*

Vocabulary: Own the Word

clamorous: The wings of the swans are described as being *clamorous* because . . . ***Possible response:*** *There are so many flying at once, and they create a loud sound together.*

Think About/Talk About

Analysis

(B) Literary Focus

Possible responses: *The words* mysterious *and* beautiful *establish the swans' function as symbols. They symbolize fidelity, fulfillment, and eternal beauty.*

Extend the Discussion

Making Predictions Where does the speaker think the swans will go when he wakes to find them gone? ***Possible response:*** *He imagines them by a "lake's edge" or nesting among rushes. Although he cannot answer his own final question, he views their flight as signaling the end of his life.*

Vocabulary: Own the Word

passion: Remind students that the connotation of *passion* is a strong feeling. You might say, "I am fond of oranges, but I have *passion* for chocolate." Ask students to create their own statements to show how *passion* is stronger than fondness.

Analyzing Visuals

Connecting to the Text: *The swan in the image is so majestic and tranquil that an observer might walk "with a lighter tread" so as not to disturb the creature. The image gives the reader insight into why Yeats was so captivated by the birds.*

I have looked upon those brilliant creatures,
And now my heart is sore.
All's changed since I, hearing at twilight,
The first time on this shore,
The bell-beat of their wings above my head,
Trod with a lighter tread.

Unwearied still, lover by lover,
They paddle in the cold
Companionable streams or climb the air;
Their hearts have not grown old;
Passion or conquest, wander where they will,
Attend upon them still.

But now they drift on the still water,
Mysterious, beautiful;
Among what rushes will they build,
By what lake's edge or pool
Delight men's eyes when I awake some day
To find they have flown away? (B)

(B) Literary Focus **Symbol** In order to serve as a symbol, the swans must possess qualities that allow them to stand not only for themselves but also for something else. What words in lines 25–29 help establish the swans' status as symbols? What do you think the swans symbolize to the speaker?

Vocabulary **passion** (PASH uhn) *n.:* strong emotion.

Analyzing Visuals

Connecting to the Text What about the image might cause an observer to walk "with a lighter tread"?

Swan on River Wey, Sussex, England.

California Standards, p. 1211

- **Reading Standard 3.3** Analyze the ways in which irony, tone, mood, the author's style, and the "sound" of language achieve specific rhetorical or aesthetic purposes or both.
- **Grades 9–10 Review Reading Standard 3.7** Recognize and understand the significance of various literary devices, including figurative language, imagery, allegory, and symbolism, and explain their appeal.
- **Writing Standard 1.1** Demonstrate an understanding of the elements of discourse (e.g., purpose, speaker, audience, form) when completing narrative, expository, persuasive, or descriptive writing assignments.

Cross-Curricular Connection

MUSIC: Swan Song

Ask students to locate a recording or to invent a melody that captures the essence of the poem. Point out that the tone and mood of the poem change as it progresses, and then suggest that the music they choose or create should reflect these changes. Students may want to play their musical selections as they read the poem to the class. The class should discuss how well each student's music reflects the tone and mood of the poem.

Applying Your Skills

Reading Standard 3.3; Grades 9–10 Review
Reading Standard 3.7 (see pages A48–A50)
Writing Standard 1.1 (see pages A51–A52)

The Wild Swans at Coole

Literary Response and Analysis

Reading Skills Focus

Quick Check

1. How does the speaker feel as he gazes at the swans?
2. How did he feel nineteen years earlier when he heard the beating of their wings?
3. Why do you think the speaker's heart is "sore"?

Read with a Purpose

4. How has the speaker's response to the swans changed over time? How do you account for this change?

Vocabulary Check

Answer the questions about the Vocabulary words ***clamorous*** and ***passion.***

5. Which word or words would you associate with **passion**—*love, hatred, boredom?*
6. Which would be **clamorous** near a concession stand at the beach—gulls or crabs?

Literary Skills Focus

Literary Analysis

7. **Paraphrase** State in your own words the question the speaker asks in the last stanza.
8. **Interpret** The word *awake* in line 29 can be interpreted in different ways. Do you think that the speaker means it literally, as in *wake up in the morning,* or figuratively, as in *wake up from a daydream or illusion?* How might this word offer a clue about the theme of the poem?
9. **Extend** An **elegy** is a poem that mourns the death of a person or laments something that has been lost. Why might this poem be thought of as an elegy? How does the poem relate in theme, tone, and imagery to any of the other famous elegies in this book (pages 310, 982, and 1236)?

Literary Skills: Symbol

10. **Evaluate** What do you think is Yeats's message to readers in this poem about love and about the passage of time? Support your response with details from the poem.
11. **Make Judgments** What qualities of the swans do you think the speaker envies? Why? What might the swans symbolize to the speaker? Do the swans symbolize different things at different times in the speaker's life? Explain.

Literary Skills Review: Mood

12. **Analyze** The emotional atmosphere a poem evokes is called **mood.** How are the time of day and year in the poem appropriate to its **mood?**

Writing Skills Focus

Think as a Reader/Writer

Use It in Your Writing Review your notes on Yeats's use of symbolism. Choose a common object that has qualities that could be seen as symbolic (a door, for example, might symbolize opportunity). Then, write a poem or paragraph in your *Reader/Writer Notebook* using the object as a symbol for something beyond what its literal meaning indicates.

What Do You Think Now? Having read this poem, what are your thoughts on how the passage of time can change a person and his or her responses to familiar things?

Check for Understanding

Independent Practice

Reading Skills Focus

Possible responses:

1. *Looking at the swans makes him morose and aware of changes.*
2. *He was happier then.*
3. *He is saddened by the passage of time and the changes in his world.*
4. *His response is melancholy and wistful. His heart may have grown old.*

Vocabulary Check

5. *love; hatred*
6. *gulls*

Literary Skills Focus

Possible responses:

7. *Where will the swans build their nests when they leave here?*
8. *The word can have both meanings. There may come an actual day when the swans leave; the speaker may also* awake *to find that everything important to him no longer exists.*
9. *The speaker laments his growing old and is saddened by how much has changed in his world This poem uses pastoral imagery, like "Elegy Written in a Country Churchyard." The tone is doubtful, like parts of "In Memoriam: A.H.H." All take a mournful tone.*
10. *His message is that love changes and time passes, but the essential elements of life, symbolized by the swans, can still inspire him because "their hearts have not grown old."*
11. *He envies their mystery and enduring passion—qualities he may have lost. They symbolize timeless beauty or perfect love. Yes, his response to them has changed over time.*
12. *It is the evening of the day, the evening of the year, and the evening of the speaker's life. The time fits the somber, reflective mood of the poem.*

Universal Access

Struggling Writers

Students may need additional scaffolding to complete the Writing Skills Focus activity. Have students brainstorm ideas of symbols to use in their poems or paragraphs. Point out to students that some symbols are widely recognized: A lion can be a symbol of strength and power, and a dove can be a symbol of peace. After students have generated a list of symbols, have them choose one to focus on in their writing.

What Do You Think Now?

Have students reflect on the changes in their own lives or in the lives of their peers since beginning high school. Suggest that students choose one or two familiar activities, places, or objects they once prized but that no longer have the same appeal—and another that has become increasingly important to them. Have them answer the question with these changes in mind.

Preteach

Introducing Vocabulary

To reinforce the importance of the Vocabulary words, tell students that these words support the symbolism in the poem. In line 7, "caught in that *sensual* music" refers to those living for temporary things, while in line 24, the *artifice* of eternity refers to an ageless work of art.

English for Academic Success

Language Coach

After reading the **Language Coach,** write the word *sensual* in the center off the board. Then, create a web with the related words: *sense, sensuous, sensually, sensualist, sensitive.* Have students look these words up in the dictionary and write the definition in their own words next to the word. Repeat this activity for the word *artifice.*

Literary Skills Focus

As you read and discuss the selection with students, have them make a list of metaphors they find in the text and analyze the comparison made in each metaphor.

Reading Skills Focus

Give students a copy of the Reading Skills Focus graphic organizer before they read. (See **Unit 6 Resources**.) Tell them to use their responses to answer questions on the Applying Your Skills page.

Writing Skills Focus

Have students write down where they find instances of the use of extended metaphor in their **Reader/ Writer Notebooks**. Students can use their notes to complete the Writing Skills Focus activity.

Learn It Online

The enhanced author biography offers more information on the life of the author as well as Holt's interactive resources pertaining to the author.

go.hrw.com H12-1212 Go

Preparing to Read

Reading Standard 3.3, 3.4 (see pages A48–A50)

Sailing to Byzantium

Literary Skills Focus

Metaphor In a **metaphor,** two seemingly unlike things are compared without using a connective word, such as *like* or *as.* A metaphor talks of one thing as if it were another. Poets use metaphors to convey emotion and to suggest more than is possible with literal speech. For example, Yeats uses metaphors to speak about old age and art in the poem "Sailing to Byzantium." Look for other metaphors as you read.

Reading Skills Focus

Analyzing Style The unique manner in which writers use language to express their ideas is called **style.** An author's style is closely connected to **diction,** or word choice, and **syntax,** or sentence construction. A writer's style may be categorized as formal, casual, plain, elevated, abstract, concrete, or any of a number of other descriptive words. A writer's use of **figurative language,** such as metaphor, is also part of his or her style.

Into Action As you read, use a spider map like the one below to analyze Yeats's style. Consider different elements of style, including diction, syntax, and figurative language.

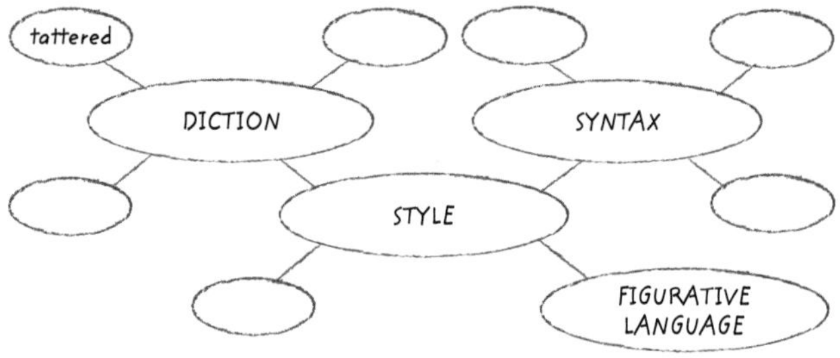

Writing Skills Focus

Think as a Reader/Writer

Find It in Your Reading Yeats uses several **extended metaphors,** or metaphors that are developed throughout the poem. As you read, note in your *Reader/Writer Notebook* to what Yeats compares created things, including art. How are they different from "any natural thing"?

Vocabulary

sensual (SEHN shoo uhl) *adj.:* appealing to bodily senses rather than to the mind. *He distrusts sensual pleasures of food and drink.*

artifice (AHR tuh fihs) *n.:* human skill or craft, as opposed to what is natural. *He admired the artifice of the ornate buildings.*

Language Coach

Word Families Explore the word family of each Vocabulary word. Word families include words that are related because they have the same base word. For example, the word *sense* is related to *sensual*, and *artificial* is related to *artifice*. What other words can you find for each word family?

Reader/Writer Notebook

Use your **RWN** to complete the activities for this selection.

Learn It Online

Explore Yeats and his work through these Internet links.

go.hrw.com H12-1212 Go

California Standards, pp. 1212–1215

- **Reading Standard 3.3** Analyze the ways in which irony, tone, mood, the author's style, and the "sound" of language achieve specific rhetorical or aesthetic purposes or both.
- **Reading Standard 3.4** Analyze ways in which poets use imagery, personification, figures of speech, and sounds to evoke readers' emotions.

POEM

Sailing to Byzantium

by **William Butler Yeats**

Teacher Preparation
Selection Summary

In the first stanza of "Sailing to Byzantium," the speaker—an old man—contemplates a country defined by the physical, not the spiritual. In the second stanza, the speaker, unnerved by the shriveling effect of age on his body, decides to take a journey to Byzantium, an ancient city known for its beautiful art. In the third stanza, the speaker expresses his wish to be made immortal by wise men. In the final stanza, he explains that he would prefer to take his immortal form in the shape of a golden bird.

Read with a Purpose

Read to see how the speaker views art, as opposed to the natural world.

Build Background

Byzantium was an important symbol to Yeats, because the art created there during the fifth and sixth centuries represents humanity in a highly stylized and artificial way. For Yeats, the artificiality of the work shows the perfect union of form and idea and the perfect expression of spirit in a physical form that, unlike the human body, will never decay.

I

That is no country for old men. The young
In one another's arms, birds in the trees
—Those dying generations—at their song,
The salmon-falls, the mackerel-crowded seas,
Fish, flesh, or fowl, commend all summer long
Whatever is begotten, born, and dies.
Caught in that sensual music all neglect
Monuments of unaging intellect. (A)

(A) **Literary Focus** **Metaphor** For what are "Monuments of unaging intellect" a metaphor?

Vocabulary **sensual** (SEHN shoo uhl) *adj.:* appealing to bodily senses rather than to the mind.

Blue Mosque and Hagia Sophia, Istanbul, Turkey. The first known name for Istanbul was Byzantium; later the city was called Constantinople, after the Roman emperor Constantine.

Direct Teach

Think About/Talk About

Read with a Purpose Have students read the Read with a Purpose and Build Background statements. Ask students to note what aspects of art make it seem "perfect" to Yeats.

Analysis

(A) Literary Focus

Possible response: *The image is a metaphor for the creations of the mind, which are permanent and do not age—unlike those "caught in that sensual music."*

Extend the Discussion

Comparing and Contrasting What two opposing sets of images does Yeats use in stanza 1? Why? ***Possible responses:*** *He contrasts the young, who are caught up in the "sensual music" of life but who will still die, with "the Monuments of unaging intellect" that they neglect. Yeats contrasts those who will age and die with the ageless.*

Vocabulary: Own the Word

sensual: The word *sensual* comes from *sense,* which means "to perceive by a sense or the senses" (noun and verb form). Just as you use your body to *sense* what happens around you, a *sensual* experience uses one or more of your *senses:* smell, taste, touch, feeling, hearing, or sight.

Universal Access

English Learners

English for Academic Success Explain to students that Yeats's diction makes reading his poetry a challenge. Point out that Yeats uses words that can be nouns or verbs. In this context, *neglect* (line 7) and *perne* (line 19) work as verbs, but *dress* (line 12) is used as a noun. Yeats also takes liberties with plural and singular forms; in line 11, *Soul* takes the plural verbs *clap* and *sing*.

✔ See the **English Language Skill Builder** in **UA: Differentiating Instruction.**

Struggling Readers

Students might be confused by the poem's lack of narrative structure. Have them work in small groups to discuss what the following lines reveal about the speaker: "That is no country for old men" (line 1); "An aged man is but a paltry thing" (line 9); "gather me / into the artifice of eternity" (lines 23–24), and "I shall never take my bodily form from any natural thing" (lines 25–26).

✔ See **UA: Differentiating Instruction** for a graphic organizer to scaffold instruction for struggling readers.

Think About/Talk About

Comprehension

Ⓒ Reading Focus

Possible response: *The language in this stanza is very formal, almost like the language of prayer, as the speaker calls upon the "sages standing in God's holy fire."*

Ⓓ Reading Focus

Possible responses: *The series of prepositional phrases and repeated words like* gold *serve to develop a stylized, symmetrical diction and syntax, almost as if the speaker has become the artifact he longs to be. The stylized diction and stanza contribute to a stiff and formal tone.*

Analysis

Ⓑ Literary Focus

Possible response: *He compares an aged man to a scarecrow, "A tattered coat upon a stick."*

Extend the Discussion

Visualizing In stanza 4, what form does the speaker want to take once he is "out of nature"? ***Possible response:*** *The images describe him as a gold and enamel bird that will "sit upon a golden bough" and sing about what is ageless, "of what is past, or passing, or to come."*

Making Judgments What internal evidence within the poem clearly shows that it was written during Yeats's final years? ***Possible response:*** *The scarecrow metaphor, the reference to "every tatter in mortal dress," the desire to become ageless, "out of nature," where he can sing his songs for the lords and ladies of his ideal world, Byzantium.*

Vocabulary: Own the Word

artifice: Tell students that in these lines the poet addresses the "*artifice* of eternity," a man-made idea or construct. What are some other examples of *artifice* from the world around us?

II

An aged man is but a paltry thing,
A tattered coat upon a stick, unless
Soul clap its hands and sing, and louder sing
For every tatter in its mortal dress,
Nor is there singing school but studying
Monuments of its own magnificence;
And therefore I have sailed the seas and come
To the holy city of Byzantium. Ⓑ

III

O sages standing in God's holy fire
As in the gold mosaic of a wall,°
Come from the holy fire, perne in a gyre,°
And be the singing-masters of my soul.
Consume my heart away; sick with desire
And fastened to a dying animal
It knows not what it is; and gather me
Into the artifice of eternity. Ⓒ

IV

Once out of nature I shall never take
My bodily form from any natural thing,
But such a form as Grecian goldsmiths make
Of hammered gold and gold enameling
To keep a drowsy Emperor awake;
Or set upon a golden bough to sing°
To lords and ladies of Byzantium
Of what is past, or passing, or to come. Ⓓ

17–18. sages ... wall: Wise men and saints are depicted in gold mosaic on the walls of Byzantine churches in Ravenna, Italy, and in Sicily.

19. perne in a gyre: a spool spinning in a spiraling motion. For Yeats, this is an image of historical cycles.

29–30. a drowsy Emperor ... sing: Yeats wrote, "I have read somewhere that in the Emperor's palace at Byzantium was a tree made of gold and silver, and artificial birds that sang."

Ⓑ Literary Focus Metaphor To what does the speaker compare an "aged man"?

Ⓒ Reading Focus Analyzing Style How would you describe the author's style in this stanza? For instance, is it formal or casual, simple or ornate, modern or antiquated, prosaic or poetic?

Ⓓ Reading Focus Analyzing Style What do you notice about the author's diction and syntax? How do they affect the tone of the poem?

Vocabulary artifice (AHR tuh fihs) *n.:* human skill or craft, as opposed to what is natural.

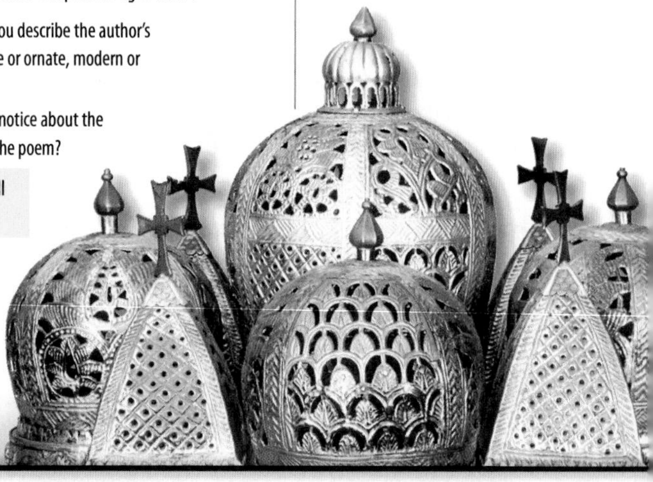

Incense burner in the form of a cupola (12th century). St. Mark's Basilica, Venice, Italy.

California Standards, p. 1215

- **Reading Standard 3.3** Analyze the ways in which irony, tone, mood, the author's style, and the "sound" of language achieve specific rhetorical or aesthetic purposes or both.
- **Reading Standard 3.4** Analyze ways in which poets use imagery, personification, figures of speech, and sounds to evoke readers' emotions.
- **Grades 9–10 Review Reading Standard 3.7** Recognize and understand the significance of various literary devices, including figurative language, imagery, allegory, and symbolism, and explain their appeal.
- **Writing Standard 2.3** Write reflective compositions: **a.** Explore the significance of personal experiences, events, conditions, or concerns by using rhetorical strategies (e.g., narration, description, exposition, persuasion).

Applying Your Skills

Reading Standard 3.3, 3.4; Grades 9–10 Review
Reading Standard 3.7 (see pages A48–A50)
Writing Standard 2.3a (see pages A51–A52)

Sailing to Byzantium

Literary Response and Analysis

Reading Skills Focus

Quick Check

1. What do the "Fish, flesh, or fowl" in line 5 represent?
2. Of what is the speaker afraid? What does he seek by sailing to Byzantium?
3. What might the soul that "clap[s] its hands, and sing[s]" represent?

Read with a Purpose

4. What does art represent to the speaker? How is it a way to rise above the human condition?

Reading Skills: Analyzing Style

5. While reading "Sailing to Byzantium," you used a spider map to help analyze the writer's style. Now that you have finished reading, review your spider map and determine how you would characterize Yeats's style in this poem.

Vocabulary Check

Use the Vocabulary words, ***sensual*** and ***artifice,*** to fill in the blanks in the following sentence.

6. The sculptor used eye-catching ______ and ______ materials, such as smooth, cool marble, to create fascinating statues.

Literary Skills Focus

Literary Analysis

7. **Contrast** How is the country in the first stanza contrasted to Byzantium?
8. **Interpret** What does Yeats mean by "Monuments of unaging intellect" in line 8?
9. **Infer** What form does the speaker choose as a reflection of his soul? What does his choice tell you of his feelings about old age and death?
10. **Extend** The **rhyme scheme** is the pattern of rhymed lines in a poem. It can be indicated with the letters of the alphabet, as in *abcb*. Each new rhyme is assigned a new letter. What is the rhyme scheme of each stanza of this poem? (Consider the use of slant, or imperfect, rhyme in your answer.) How does the rhyme scheme affect your understanding and enjoyment of the poem?

Literary Skills: Metaphor

11. **Analyze** Choose a metaphor from the poem, identify the things being compared, and explain how the comparison contributes to the poem's meaning.

Literary Skills Review: Symbol

12. **Analyze** A **symbol** is a person, place, thing, or event that stands both for itself and for something beyond itself. Byzantium is a symbol in this poem. What other symbols can you find? What does each symbol represent for Yeats?

Writing Skills Focus

Think as a Reader/Writer

Use It in Your Writing Now that you have studied how Yeats uses an extended metaphor, try using one in your own writing. Write a paragraph describing a place that you find magical. Use at least one extended metaphor in your description.

What Do You Think Now? How do you think Yeats's experience of aging might have shaped his views about art and his writing?

Universal Access

Struggling Writers

Students may need additional scaffolding to complete the Writing Skills Focus activity. Draw students' attention to stanza 3 of Yeats's poem. Explain to students that in this stanza, Yeats develops an extended metaphor that compares an aged man to a scarecrow. As students write their own poems, have them use this stanza as a model. For example, they might want to begin their poems by saying, "A ______ is but a ______ / A ______ upon a ______." Encourage students to use these lines as a frame to begin their extended metaphor.

What Do You Think Now?

Ask students to compare the theme of aging in this poem and in "The Wild Swans at Coole." Have them consider Yeats's feelings about growing old as revealed in these poems.

Check for Understanding

Independent Practice

Reading Skills Focus

Possible responses:

1. *They represent living creatures.*
2. *He is afraid of old age. Byzantium stands for timelessness and immortality.*
3. *The soul might represent someone with artistic creativity.*
4. *Art represents immortality. The artifacts that a poet creates live after him and give him immortality.*
5. *Students' maps should identify diction, syntax, metaphor, and uses of figurative language.*

Vocabulary Check

6. *artifice; sensual*

Literary Skills Focus

Possible responses:

7. *The country in the first stanza is the country of mortals.*
8. *They might refer to intellectual ideas, literature, art, or architecture.*
9. *He chooses the form of a finely crafted gold and enamel bird that will sing forever "of what is past, or passing, or to come." He fears and wishes to avoid old age and death.*
10. *The rhyme scheme is ottava rima (abababcc, efefefgg, etc.). The use of the traditional stanza form supports the theme of artifice and immortality.*
11. *The major metaphors are the scarecrow and the bird. The scarecrow metaphor compares the old man's weakening body to a scarecrow; the bird, in contrast, is an immortal singer whose words live on forever.*
12. *"Fish, flesh, or fowl" symbolize mortality. The "form as Grecian goldsmith's make" symbolizes immortal art. "Sensual music" could be corporeal vitality.*

Preteach

Introducing Vocabulary

Read aloud the Vocabulary words, definitions, and sample sentences. Then, use this activity to check students' understanding.

1. Has a person who experiences **disillusionment** retained or lost faith in his or her beliefs?
2. Are people who are speaking **vehemently** more likely to be arguing or praising each other?
3. Is an **incoherent** speaker unable to talk or likely to ramble while talking?

English for Academic Success

Language Coach

Have students brainstorm a list of words with the negating prefix *in–*. ***Possible responses:*** Inaccurate *and* inactive *start with* in–; dis– *is also a negating prefix, as in the word* disillusionment.

Literary Skills Focus

As you read and discuss the selection with students, have them make a list of evocative words from the selection and list their connotations.

Reading Skills Focus

Give students a copy of the Reading Skills Focus graphic organizer before they read. (See **Unit 6 Resources**.) Tell them to use their responses to answer the questions on the Applying Your Skills page.

Writing Skills Focus

Have students record adjectives that describe Gonne along with their connotations in their **Reader/Writer Notebooks**. Students can use their notes to complete the Writing Skills Focus activity.

Learn It Online
Send students to **Word Watch** for audio pronunciations, synonyms and antonyms, and brief histories of word origins.
go.hrw.com H12-1216 Go

Preparing to Read

Reading Standard 2.5, 3.3 (see pages A48–A50)

from The Autobiography of William Butler Yeats

Literary Skills Focus

Connotations All of the associations and emotions that have come to be attached to a word are its **connotations.** For example, the word *cheap* means "economical," but it also has the negative connotation of being poor in quality. *Inexpensive* can also mean "economical" but lacks the negative connotation. Writers choose words with specific connotations to express particular ideas and to elicit certain responses from readers.

Reading Skills Focus

Analyzing Author's Perspective The **author's perspective** is his or her viewpoint, or opinion, about the topic of the writing. The author shares his or her perspective by choosing precise words with just the right connotations and by including certain details. Sometimes authors state their perspective, but more often the reader must infer the author's perspective by analyzing word choice, connotations, and details.

Into Action Use a chart like the one below to record words, phrases, and details that convey the author's perspective. Note where these details appear in the text as in the example below.

Words, phrases, details	Perspective
"her great height" (p. 1217)	She is physically tall, but her height also serves as a metaphor. She looms large in the author's mind. She is a larger-than-life figure.

Writing Skills Focus

Think as a Reader/Writer

Find It in Your Reading Yeats includes many adjectives to describe Maud Gonne. For instance, he describes her as "wasted," and "gentle and indolent." As you read, record in your *Reader/Writer Notebook* the adjectives Yeats uses to describe Gonne, as well as their **connotations.**

Reader/Writer Notebook
Use your **RWN** to complete the activities for this selection.

Vocabulary

disillusionment (dihs ih LOO zhuhn muhnt) *n.:* being disenchanted, or freed from a false idea. *Disillusionment followed when she learned that her cause had been betrayed.*

vehemently (VEE uh muhnt lee) *adv.:* with strong feeling; passionately. *Yeats spoke vehemently in his proposal.*

incoherent (ihn koh HIHR uhnt) *adj.:* confused; rambling. *The incoherent outburst revealed the depth of her grief.*

Language Coach

Negating Prefixes Prefixes that reverse the meaning of a word are called **negating prefixes.** The prefix *in–* can work as a negating prefix, as in *incoherent,* which is the opposite of *coherent.* List two other words that start with the negating prefix *in–*. Can you identify another Vocabulary word that has a different negating prefix?

Learn It Online
Practice the Vocabulary words with Word Watch online.
go.hrw.com H12-1216 Go

California Standards, pp. 1216–1220

- **Reading Standard 2.5** Analyze an author's implicit and explicit philosophical assumptions and beliefs about a subject.
- **Reading Standard 3.3** Analyze the ways in which irony, tone, mood, the author's style, and the "sound" of language achieve specific rhetorical or aesthetic purposes or both.

AUTOBIOGRAPHY

from

The Autobiography of William Butler Yeats

by **William Butler Yeats**

Read with a Purpose

Read to discover the intensity of Yeats's feelings for Maud Gonne, with whom he was obsessed for decades.

Build Background

This selection is mainly about Yeats's relationship with Maud Gonne, a radical political activist who spent time in prison for fighting for her country's rights. Yeats spent most of his adulthood enamored with Gonne and proposed marriage to her twice.

A few months later I was again in Ireland and I heard that she was in Dublin. I called and waited for her at a little hotel in Nassau Street, which no longer exists, in a room overlooking the College Park. At the first sight of her as she came through the door, her great height seeming to fill it, I was overwhelmed with emotion, an intoxication of pity. She did not seem to have any beauty, her face was wasted, the form of the bones showing, and there was no life in her manner. As our talk became intimate, she hinted at some unhappiness, some disillusionment. The old hard resonance had

Vocabulary **disillusionment** (dihs ihh LOO zhehn muhnt) *n.:* being disenchanted; being freed from a false idea.

Analyzing Visuals

Connecting to the Text Note the figure's exaggerated proportions. Why might an artist or writer overemphasize certain features when depicting a subject or even himself or herself?

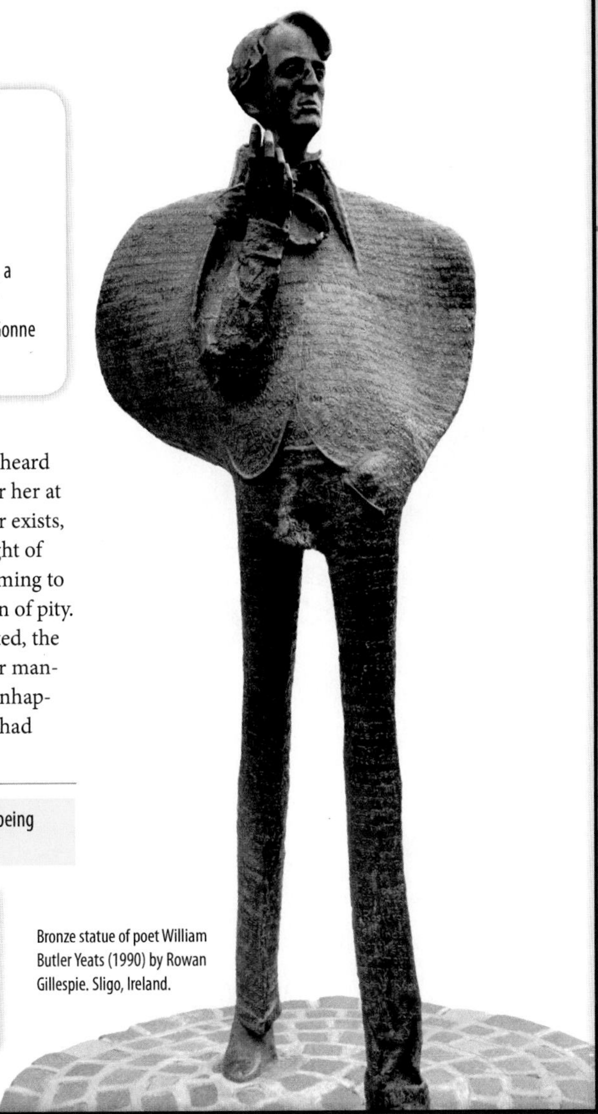

Bronze statue of poet William Butler Yeats (1990) by Rowan Gillespie. Sligo, Ireland.

Universal Access

English Learners

English for Academic Success Direct students' attention to the phrase "intoxication of pity." Explain how, until that phrase, the narrator seems overcome by a powerful, yet positive, emotion. The woman's "great height" and the narrator being "overwhelmed with emotion" lead the reader to conclude that the encounter is a positive one. Yet, the word *intoxication* has a negative connotation; in fact, it refers to something poisonous. This word shows how the narrator was overwhelmed by a mixture of very different and powerful emotions.

Analyzing Visuals

Connecting to the Text: *An artist or writer might overemphasize certain features to make a point or to endow those features with extra symbolic significance. This sculpture of Yeats exaggerates his chest, perhaps to show the strength of his emotions. His legs may be made into long stalks to indicate his great stature as a poet.*

Teacher Preparation

Selection Summary

Yeats hears that Maud Gonne is in Dublin and goes to meet her. She is different from how he remembers her, but he loves her still. They part, and a few days later Yeats receives a letter from her that brings him back to Dublin in the hope of marrying her. Maud turns down his proposal but wants to remain friends. Yeats tells Maud he has come to understand her and the good works and causes that give her no rest. Suddenly called away, she writes from France in great grief that her adopted child has died and tells him of the circumstances.

Direct Teach

Think About/Talk About

Read with a Purpose Have students read the Read with a Purpose statement. Students can think about the unrequited love for Maud Gonne that Yeats harbored during much of his adult life and how he might have felt hearing from her again.

Extend the Discussion

Determining Author's Purpose
What first impressions does Yeats give you of Maud Gonne? How is Yeats affected? ***Possible responses:*** *The first impression is of a woman who is not at all as she was. She is worn, tired, and empty. As soon as he sees her, he is deeply moved and full of pity.*

Vocabulary: Own the Word

disillusionment: Remind students that the connotation of *disillusionment* is serious disappointment. An *illusion*—a sense or impression—of something has been taken away or changed. To be *disillusioned* is to be let down.

Model the Skill

- Explain that **connotations** of a word are the associations and emotions connected to it that give it its full meaning.
- Explain that the connotations of the words Yeats uses to describe Maud Gonne help you understand his feelings for her.
- Read aloud the last sentence of the first paragraph. Model your thought process as you analyze connotations. For instance, you might say: "Yeats says that Maud Gonne needs protection and peace. *Protection* is a word that a father might use for a daughter. What kind of feelings does Maud Gonne inspire in Yeats?"

Guided Practice: Apply

Turn-and-Talk Have partners find and discuss other examples of words with strong connotations.

gone and she had become gentle and indolent. I was in love once more and no longer wished to fight against it. I no longer thought what kind of wife would this woman make, but of her need for protection and for peace. **A** **B**

Yet I left Dublin next day to stay somewhere in Orange Ulster with the brilliant student of my old Dublin school, Charles Johnston, and spent a week or ten days with him and his elder brother, making fire balloons.[1] We made the fire balloons of tissue paper and then chased them over the countryside, our chase becoming longer and longer as our skill in manufacture improved. I was not, it seems – not altogether – captive; but presently came from her a letter touching a little upon her sadness, and telling of a dream of some past life.[2] She and I had been brother and sister somewhere on the edge of the Arabian desert, and sold together into slavery. She had an impression of some long journey and of miles upon miles of the desert sand. I returned to Dublin at once, and that evening, but a few minutes after we had met, asked her to marry me. I remember a curious thing. I had come into the room with that purpose in my mind, and hardly looked at her or thought of her beauty. I sat there holding her hand and speaking vehemently. She did not take away her hand for a while. I ceased to speak, and presently as I sat in silence I felt her nearness to me and her beauty. At once I knew that my confidence had gone, and an instant later she drew her hand away. No, she could not marry – there were reasons – she would never marry; but in words that had no conventional ring she asked for my friendship. We spent the next day upon the cliff paths at Howth and dined at a little cottage near the Baily Lighthouse, where her old nurse lived, and I overheard the old nurse asking if we were engaged to be married. At the day's end I found I had spent ten shillings, which seemed to me a very great sum. **C**

1. **fire balloons:** small, unmanned hot-air balloons.

2. **a dream of some past life:** Yeats was a believer in reincarnation.

A **Literary Focus** **Connotations** What connotation does *intoxication* have in this paragraph? What does it add to Yeats's description of his feelings? What connotation does *wasted* have in this paragraph? What does it add to the description of Gonne?

B **Reading Focus** **Analyzing Author's Perspective** How does Yeats view being "in love once more"? What is his attitude toward Gonne?

C **Reading Focus** **Analyzing Author's Perspective** How does Yeats perceive Gonne as he enters the room? What does he think about?

Vocabulary **vehemently** (VEE uh muhnt lee) *adv.:* with strong feeling; passionately.

I returned to Dublin at once, and that evening, but a few minutes after we had met, asked her to marry me.

Maud Gonne (1865–1953)

Universal Access

Struggling Readers

Model for students the skill of analyzing an author's perspective. You might say: "Yeats expresses his fascination with Maud Gonne by describing her somewhat mercurial, or unpredictable, character. For example, in the first full paragraph on p. 1218, Yeats describes how Maud holds his hand and shows some tenderness toward him. However, in the next sentence he explains how she pulls her hand away and tells him she will never marry. It is precisely this unpredictability that keeps Yeats intrigued."

Students with Disabilities

Students may have difficulty picking up on the connotations of the words Yeats uses in the excerpt from his autobiography. Invite students to listen to the audio recording of the selection in the **Holt Audio Library.** Have students pay attention to the tone of voice of the reader to figure out which words have positive connotations and which have negative connotations. Encourage students to share their ideas with the class.

She had adopted a little child, she told me, some three years ago, and now this child had died.

Maud Gonne.
National Library of Ireland.

I saw her day after day. I read her my unfinished *The Countess Cathleen,*[3] and I noticed that she became moved at the passage, 'the joy of losing joy, of ceasing all resistance' –

[there is a kind of joy
In casting hope away, in losing joy,
In ceasing all resistance]

3. ***The Countess Cathleen:*** play by Yeats that was first produced in 1899.

and thought, she is burdened by a sense of responsibility for herself. I told her after meeting her in London I had come to understand the tale of a woman selling her soul to buy food for a starving people as a symbol of all souls who lose their peace, or their fineness, or any beauty of the spirit in political service, but chiefly of her soul that had seemed so incapable of rest. For the moment she had no political work nor plan of any, and we saw each other continually. Suddenly she was called back to France, and she told me in confidence that she had joined a secret political society and though she had come to look upon its members as self-seekers and adventurers she could not disobey this, the first definite summons it had sent to her. I stayed in Ireland, probably at Sligo with my uncle, George Pollexfen, finishing *The Countess Cathleen* that had become but the symbolical song of my pity. Then came a letter of wild sorrow. She had adopted a little child, she told me, some three years ago, and now this child had died. Mixed into her incoherent grief were accounts of the death bird that had pecked at the nursery window the day when it was taken ill, and how at sight of the bird she had brought doctor after doctor. D E

D Reading Focus Analyzing Author's Perspective What do you make of Yeats's comparison of Gonne to a woman who sells her soul to buy food for starving people? What does it reveal about his view of Gonne?

E Reading Focus Analyzing Author's Perspective What does Yeats's reference to his play as the "symbolical song of my pity" tell you about his perspective on his situation with Gonne?

Vocabulary **incoherent** (ihn koh HIHR uhnt) *adj.:* confused; rambling.

Think About/Talk About

Comprehension

B Reading Focus

Possible responses: *Yeats is still in love with her "and no longer wished to fight against it." He loves her and wants to protect her.*

C Reading Focus

Possible responses: *He hardly looks at her. Yeats is caught up in his desire to propose marriage. At that moment, he is more aware of his own thoughts than of her.*

D Reading Focus

Possible response: *Yeats understands that Gonne is not at peace and that the actions and events of her life have used up her "beauty of spirit."*

E Reading Focus

Possible response: *The words imply that Yeats's deepest feelings for Gonne involve pity for what she has become.*

Analysis

A Literary Focus

Possible responses: *The word "intoxication" connotes the absorption and sense of delirium in his feelings of pity. "Wasted" suggests not only her thinness but also the pointless expenditure of energy that caused it.*

Vocabulary: Own the Word

- **vehemently:** Ask students, "Have you ever had a reason to speak *vehemently?* Explain the context of the situation that had you speaking *vehemently.*"
- **incoherent:** Tell students that *incoherent* speech is jumbled and all over the place; antonyms are *clear* and *logical.* Use both words in a sentence: Known to be perfectly clear and logical in class, the professor was *incoherent* when he talked in his sleep.

California Standards, pp. 1220–1221

- **Reading Standard 2.5** Analyze an author's implicit and explicit philosophical assumptions and beliefs about a subject.
- **Reading Standard 3.1** Analyze characteristics of subgenres (e.g., satire, parody, allegory, pastoral) that are used in poetry, prose, plays, novels, short stories, essays, and other basic genres.
- **Reading Standard 3.3** Analyze the ways in which irony, tone, mood, the author's style, and the "sound" of language achieve specific rhetorical or aesthetic purposes or both.
- **Writing Standard 2.2** Write responses to literature: **a.** Demonstrate a comprehensive understanding of the significant ideas in works or passages. **b.** Analyze the use of imagery, language, universal themes, and unique aspects of the text. **c.** Support important ideas and viewpoints through accurate and detailed references to the text and to other works.
- **Writing Standard 2.3** Write reflective compositions: **a.** Explore the significance of personal experiences, events, conditions, or concerns by using rhetorical strategies (e.g., narration, description, exposition, persuasion).

Check for Understanding

Independent Practice

Reading Skills Focus

Possible responses:

1. *Yeats felt unrequited love for her for many years.*
2. *He was hoping that he could see her. Proposing marriage might have been on his mind.*
3. *He takes her rejection in silence. The implication is that this was not the first time she rejected him.*
4. *His relationship with her is one-sided. Gonne was his first love and the inspiration for many poems but never reciprocated that love.*
5. *Students' observations should cite the text to support their conclusions about Yeats's perspective.*

Vocabulary Check

6. *discovered cheating*
7. *excited*
8. *exhausted, upset, nervous*

Literary Skills Focus

Possible responses:

9. *The irony is that she will not marry him.*
10. *He feels passionate; he speaks "vehemently" to her in the hope he can convince her.*
11. *She is independent but also confused. She is involved with causes that have left her looking "wasted."*
12. *Three important words are as follows: "overwhelmed"—left powerless; "indolent"—lethargic; "protection"—what is given to someone helpless. The connotations show that Yeats felt controlled by his feelings.*
13. *Unrequited love makes a person even more in love with the love object, constantly hoping for a change of heart. Gonne sees the passage as describing her. Her adopted child is dead. Her political associates are adventurers. Her life in many ways is not working out for her.*

Applying Your Skills

Reading Standard 2.5, 3.1, 3.3 (see pages A48–A50)
Writing Standard 2.3a (see pages A51–A52)

from The Autobiography of William Butler Yeats

Literary Response and Analysis

Reading Skills Focus

Quick Check

1. Why is Yeats "overwhelmed with emotion" upon first seeing Maud Gonne?
2. Why do you think Yeats returns to Dublin after reading Maud Gonne's letter about her dream?
3. How does Yeats respond to Gonne's rejection?

Read with a Purpose

4. How would you describe Yeats's relationship with Maud Gonne?

Reading Skills: Analyzing Author's Perspective

5. Review the chart you filled in as you read. Based on the words, phrases, and details you noted and the perspectives they revealed, what is Yeats's perspective on his relationship with Maud Gonne? Add a row to the bottom of the chart, analyzing his overall perspective.

Vocabulary Check

Answer the questions about the Vocabulary words.

6. Are you more likely to feel **disillusionment** if your favorite athlete loses a game honestly or if you discover he or she has won by cheating?
7. Would a person who speaks **vehemently** be described as calm or excited?
8. Would you be more likely to be **incoherent** when you 're exhausted or well rested? calm or upset? confident or nervous?

Literary Skills Focus

Literary Analysis

9. **Analyze** What is ironic about Yeats's description of Gonne and his love for her?
10. **Infer** What is Yeats's state of mind when he asks Gonne to marry him? How do you know?
11. **Make Judgments** Based on what you've read, what do you think of Gonne's character? Explain.

Literary Skills: Connotations

12. **Analyze** Choose three words from the selection whose connotations are important to understanding Yeats's feelings about Maud Gonne. Explain how those connotations affect your understanding of the author's feelings.

Literary Skills Review: Paradox

13. **Analyze** An apparent contradiction that is actually true is called a **paradox.** What does Yeats mean by "there is a kind of joy / in casting hope away, in losing joy, / in ceasing all resistance" (page 1219)? Why do you think Gonne was moved by the passage?

Writing Skills Focus

Think as a Reader/Writer

Use It in Your Writing Review the adjectives you noted as you read. In a paragraph, describe a person who inspires you. Choose adjectives with powerful connotations to express your feelings.

What Do You Think Now?

How do you think Yeats's experience with unrequited love might have affected him as a writer?

Universal Access

Struggling Writers

Students may need additional scaffolding to complete the Writing Skills Focus activity. Have students create a list of adjectives that describe the person who inspires them. Encourage students to circle five adjectives from the list that best capture the spirit of the person. Remind students that they can often use a thesaurus to find words that are similar in meaning but have different connotations. Have students look up their circled words in a thesaurus to find adjectives with more appropriate connotations. Then, have students use the words they found in a paragraph.

What Do You Think Now?

To help students think about this question, ask them to reflect on the tone of poems like "Wild Swans at Coole" in light of the details of Yeats's life revealed in his autobiography.

Writing Standard 2.2a–c (see pages A51–A52)

Author Study: William Butler Yeats

Writing Skills Focus

Write a Comparison-Contrast Essay

Review the criteria for a good comparison-contrast essay before you begin.

An effective comparison-contrast essay
• states the basis of the comparison and contrast in a thesis
• organizes ideas using the point-by-point method
• uses and cites text evidence to support each point of comparison and contrast
• contains few or no errors in spelling, punctuation, and usage

Prewriting

William Butler Yeats expressed his personal pessimism and his concern for the world's future in a unique style that marks him as one of the twentieth century's foremost poets. Choose any two of his poems to compare and contrast. First, choose poems that have a strong basis of similarity, other than having the same author. As you study the poems, also look closely for ways in which they differ. Your analysis should include both similarities and differences.

Gather Details Use a T-chart like the one below to record notes about each poem. Read the poems closely, noting Yeats's use of language and theme.

The Second Coming	*Sailing to Byzantium*

Re-read your T-chart to discover at least one strong basis of similarity. Circle those notes in one color. Look again to determine if there is another strong similarity. Circle those notes in another color. If there is only one major similarity, proceed to the differences. Use another color to identify at least one significant difference. You will have color-coded your close reading of the poems to discover your analysis points. Consider the following ideas or your own for analyzing two of Yeats's poems:

- Compare and contrast Yeats's view of the future.
- Compare and contrast the use of allusion.
- Compare and contrast the use of irony.
- Compare the influence of Irish heritage.

Develop a Thesis Statement Using your notes, develop a thesis statement that makes an assertion about both the similarities and differences in the poems you select. Always begin with a basis of similarity (such as the use of allusions), and then focus on the differences in the two poems. Sample thesis:

Yeats uses religious and historical allusions to express a pessimism about both the past and the future.

Drafting

Because you are using the point-by-point method of organization, begin with the strongest comparison linking the two poems. Develop it in your first body paragraph. In your following body paragraphs, develop either additional similarities or differences. Discuss both poems in each paragraph. In your final body paragraph, focus on the differences between the two poems.

Text Evidence Use direct quotations from both poems to support each point. Punctuate the quotations as the author did, and interweave them into your own sentences.

Revising and Editing

Re-read your draft to determine if you have fully supported your thesis with explanation and text evidence. Correct any grammar and mechanics errors.

What Do You Think Now?

After reading poems that appeared throughout Yeats's life, how do you think his experiences affected his writing?

Independent Practice

What Do You Think Now?

Remind students of the themes of Yeats's poems and have them consider those poems in light of the autobiographical selection.

Assess

Unit 6 Resources, Selection Standards Check, pp. 112, 115, 121

go.hrw.com **ThinkCentral Online Assessment,** Selection Standards Check

Teacher One Stop™, editable Selection Standards Check

Reteach

go.hrw.com **ThinkCentral Online Remediation**

Universal Access

Struggling Writers

Students may need additional scaffolding to complete the Writing Skills Focus activity. Allusion and irony may be difficult aspects of poetry to analyze. To simplify the activity, have students write a comparison/contrast essay addressing the tone of two of the poems. For example, they could compare the melancholy tone of "Wild Swans at Coole" with the sense of contentment conveyed in "The Lake Isle of Innisfree." While both poems describe pastoral scenes, the emotional tone of the poems differs.

Standards Focus

Objectives

Students will
- understand diction
- identify theme

Selection Introduction

Think About the Writer
Ask students to think about the social and political events that occurred in Europe during the 1930s. Have students consider how these events created an atmosphere of anxiety.

For Independent Reading

Mythology, Edith Hamilton

Motivate

What Do You Think?/QuickWrite
Have students think about recent news stories that deal with some aspect of human suffering. Have them consider how they and their peers react to such stories. Are individuals and their sufferings important to us? If not, what is? Tell students to write their thoughts in their **Reader/Writer Notebooks.**

English for Academic Success

Academic Vocabulary
Look for opportunities to use the Academic Vocabulary words in this unit.

- **perspective,** ***n.:*** a particular way of looking at something

Preparing to Read

Musée des Beaux Arts

What Do You Think? How does experience shape our view of the world?

QuickWrite
To what extent do you think people today are indifferent to human suffering? Do you think our society values the individual, or are things such as progress or money or power deemed more important? Record your thoughts and conclusions in your *Reader/Writer Notebook.*

W. H. Auden by Jeffrey Morgan.

MEET THE WRITER

W. H. Auden
(1907–1973)

Wystan Hugh Auden named the times in which he lived the "Age of Anxiety," but as far as poetry was concerned, that same era could have been called the Age of Auden given the breadth and depth of his influence.

The Early Influences of Religion

Auden was born in York, a city in northern England. His father was a physician and his mother a nurse. In his adolescence, Auden discovered poetry, and he studied all its forms with an analytical eye. By the time Auden entered Oxford, he was as much a teacher as a student, and quickly surrounded himself with other young poets who accepted him as their leader.

Auden's sympathies during the 1930s were with the Left, and, like many young intellectuals of the time, he went to Spain during its Civil War to serve as an ambulance driver on the left-wing Republican side. However, he was disturbed by the Republicans' looting of Roman Catholic churches and left Spain without doing anything to help the Republican cause.

Back in England Auden saw economic stagnation and mass unemployment. At first his work was influenced by Freud and Marx, but gradually his poetry reflected a more religious perspective, as he found reality more ambiguous and troubling than he had imagined.

A Move to America

Auden shocked his British compatriots when, in 1939, as Hitler's divisions were about to march into Poland and ignite World War II, he decided to make his home in the United States. Auden had received an invitation to teach at the University of Michigan, and with the rise of fascism in Europe, he believed his chances of enjoying creative freedom were greatest in America. In 1946, he became a U.S. citizen.

Auden's immigration to the United States was at the time regarded as a defection, but when he moved back to England in the last year of his life, to seek safety and companionship in a university community, the British welcomed him back.

Think About the Writer Why do you think Auden called his times the "Age of Anxiety"?

California Standards, pp. 1222–1226

- **Reading Standard 3.2** Analyze the way in which the theme or meaning of a selection represents a view or comment on life, using textual evidence to support the claim.
- **Reading Standard 3.3** Analyze the ways in which irony, tone, mood, the author's style, and the "sound" of language achieve specific rhetorical or aesthetic purposes or both.

Selection Readability	
Easily Accessible **Accessible** Challenging	familiar language; accessible theme

Reading Standard 3.2, 3.3 (see pages A48–A50)

Literary Skills Focus

Diction In addition to the great masters of poetry and the music of British dance halls, the blues songs of America also influenced Auden. As you read this poem, note where he adopts **colloquial language,** the common language of daily life. Auden purposefully pairs this colloquial language alongside eloquent poetic language to create contrasting **diction,** or word choice. This diction works to surprise the reader, who may expect only lofty, dignified language in poetry, as well as creates an offhand tone that unnerves the reader by mirroring the randomness of the real world.

Reading Skills Focus

Identifying Theme A theme is a central idea or insight about human experience revealed in a work of literature. Writers do not usually state their themes directly but instead imply them through subtle diction and various literary devices. As a reader, you must piece together the significant details and determine what theme those details reveal. No two readers of the same work will state its theme in exactly the same way; indeed, sometimes, literature reveals more than one theme.

Into Action As you read, use an idea web to organize theme-related details in the poem that seem especially important, even puzzling.

Writing Skills Focus

Think as a Reader/Writer

Find It in Your Reading As you read the poem, note in your *Reader/Writer Notebook* the speaker's occasional use of colloquial, or informal, **diction** to describe what he sees. Does the informal language give you an especially vivid picture of the scene? Use examples from the text to explain your answer.

Reader/Writer Notebook

Use your **RWN** to complete the activities for this selection.

Vocabulary

reverently (REHV uhr uhnt lee) *adv.:* with reverence and respect. *Auden imagines the aged reverently waiting for a miraculous birth.*

martyrdom (MAHR tuhr duhm) *n.:* death of a martyr, someone who dies for his or her beliefs. *Auden refers to paintings of people who suffered martyrdom for their religion.*

leisurely (LEE zhuhr lee) *adv.:* without hurry; taking plenty of time. *As Icarus fell, the unhurried plowman continued to plow leisurely.*

forsaken (fawr SAY kuhn) *adj.:* forlorn; abandoned. *Auden imagines he hears the falling boy's forsaken cry.*

Language Coach

Adverbs and Adjectives Many adverbs (words that modify verbs, adjectives, or other adverbs) end in *–ly.* Adjectives (words that modify nouns or pronouns) do not often end in *–ly.* You can sometimes change an adverb to an adjective by deleting the *–ly.* Which Vocabulary word can you change to an adjective by removing the *–ly*? Is there a Vocabulary word that ends with *–ly* and that can be used as an adverb or an adjective?

Learn It Online

Find out more about Auden and his inspiration for this poem through these Internet links.

go.hrw.com H12-1223 Go

Selection Resources

Unit 6 Resources, on-level practice and assessment, p. 124

Teacher One Stop™, on-level lesson plans and all print resources

Holt Audio Library

Holt Audio Library: Selections and Summaries in Spanish

UA: Differentiating Instruction, graphic organizer, p. 290

UA: Supporting Instruction in Spanish, selection summary

ThinkCentral Online Assessment, Selection Standards Check

ThinkCentral Online Remediation

Preteach

Introducing Vocabulary

- Review the Vocabulary words, definitions, and sentences with students.
- Tell students that these words explain how Auden *reverently* analyzes a painting that depicts the suffering of the *forsaken* Greek legend Icarus. In his poem, Auden expresses the feeling that society often ignores the *martyrdom* of others. Instead people proceed to go *leisurely* about their day with no concern for things that do not directly affect them.

English for Academic Success

Language Coach

Have pairs work together to answer the questions. ***Possible responses:*** *Without* –ly, reverently *becomes the adjective* reverent. Leisurely *can be used as both an adjective ("a leisurely walk") and as an adverb ("walking leisurely").*

Literary Skills Focus

As you read and discuss the selection with students, have them note examples of Auden's colloquial language.

Reading Skills Focus

Give students a copy of the Reading Skills Focus graphic organizer before they read. (See **Unit 6 Resources**.) Tell them to use their responses to answer the questions on the Applying Your Skills page.

Writing Skills Focus

As they read, have students record their reactions to Auden's informal language in their **Reader/Writer Notebooks**. Students can use their notes to complete the Writing Skills Focus activity.

Learn It Online

The enhanced author biography offers more information on the life of the author as well as Holt's interactive resources pertaining to the author.

go.hrw.com H12-1223 Go

Teacher Preparation

Selection Summary

As he walks through the Musée de Beaux Arts, or Fine Arts Museum, in Brussels, Belgium, the speaker states that the Old Masters understood that even the most dramatic suffering is often met with indifference.

Direct Teach

Think About/Talk About

Read with a Purpose Have students read the Read with a Purpose statement. Have students look for examples of human suffering in the poem.

Comprehension

A Reading Focus

Possible response: *While one person suffers, others go about their business undisturbed.*

C Reading Focus

Possible responses: *The plowman keeps going about his daily business. Although sailors on the ship probably saw Icarus's fall, their ship calmly stays on course. These lines demonstrate the point that Auden makes in the first four lines, that most people are indifferent to others' sufferings.*

Analysis

B Literary Focus

Possible response: *The phrases "doggy life" and "scratches its innocent behind" are colloquial; lines 4 and 7 may seem "unpoetic."*

POEM

Musée des Beaux Arts

by **W. H. Auden**

Read with a Purpose

Read to discover what this speaker sees in the museum that makes him think about human suffering.

Build Background

The source and inspiration for this poem are found in Pieter Bruegel's famous sixteenth-century painting *The Fall of Icarus,* which depicts a dramatic moment in the Greek legend of the great craftsman Daedalus and his son Icarus. According to the legend, the two men were imprisoned on the island of Crete. Daedalus made wings of feathers and wax, and together he and his son used these wings to fly off the island. In his excitement, Icarus flew too high. The sun's heat melted the wax in his wings, causing him to plummet into the sea, where he drowned.

About suffering they were never wrong,
The Old Masters: ° how well they understood
Its human position; how it takes place
While someone else is eating or opening a window or just walking
    dully along; **A**
How, when the aged are reverently, passionately waiting
For the miraculous birth, there always must be
Children who did not specially want it to happen, skating
On a pond at the edge of the wood:
They never forgot
That even the dreadful martyrdom must run its course
Anyhow in a corner, some untidy spot
Where the dogs go on with their doggy life and the torturer's horse
Scratches its innocent behind on a tree. **B**

In Bruegel's *Icarus,* for instance: how everything turns away
Quite leisurely from the disaster; the plowman may
Have heard the splash, the forsaken cry,
But for him it was not an important failure; the sun shone
As it had to on the white legs disappearing into the green
Water; and the expensive delicate ship that must have seen
Something amazing, a boy falling out of the sky,
Had somewhere to get to and sailed calmly on. **C**

---

2. Old Masters: European painters of great skill who painted before 1800.

A **Reading Focus** **Identifying Theme** What is the ironic contrast in the first four lines?

B **Literary Focus** **Diction** What words in the first stanza seem colloquial or unpoetic to you?

C **Reading Focus** **Identifying Theme** What do the plowman and the ship do when Icarus falls into the sea and drowns? How do these actions relate to details in the first four lines?

Vocabulary **reverently** (REHV uhr uhnt lee) *adv.:* with reverence and respect.
martyrdom (MAHR tuhr duhm) *n.:* death of a martyr, someone who dies for his or her beliefs.
leisurely (LEE zhuhr lee) *adv.:* without hurry; taking plenty of time.
forsaken (fawr SAY kuhn) *adj.:* forlorn; abandoned.

Universal Access

EL English Learners

Have students compare two phrases from the poem to help them better understand and recognize colloquial language—lines 5 and 6: "reverently, passionately waiting / For the miraculous birth" and line 12: "Where the dogs go on with their doggy life." Have them discuss the words that sound colloquial to their ears.

✔ See the **English Language Skill Builder** in **UA: Differentiating Instruction.**

Struggling Readers

Have students work in groups to review the last stanza of the poem and compare the details in Auden's interpretation to the details in the painting on p. 1225. Ask students to point out evidence in the painting that supports Auden's analysis and also to look for details that might support an alternative interpretation. Have students share their thoughts with the class.

✔ See **UA: Differentiating Instruction** for a graphic organizer to scaffold instruction for struggling readers.

The Fall of Icarus (c. 1558) by Pieter Bruegel the Elder. Royal Museums of Fine Arts of Belgium.

ART LINK

Bruegel's *The Fall of Icarus*

According to one critic, Pieter Bruegel's painting *The Fall of Icarus* represents "the greatest conception of indifference" in the history of art. The indifference, whether it is that of the artist or a strategy of technique, lies in its unexpected focus. The painting's center of interest is not Icarus but a peasant plowing a field. The peasant is handsomely dressed—in medieval rather than ancient Greek costume—and the furrows he tills are richly realistic. In the lower right-hand corner, almost as an afterthought, Icarus is seen splashing into the water not far from a passing ship.

Ask Yourself

Study the painting, and find the figure of the boy falling into the sea. Has Auden expressed in words what Bruegel expressed with paint? Which expression of the theme, written or painted, do you find more compelling? Why?

California Standards, p. 1226

- **Reading Standard 3.2** Analyze the way in which the theme or meaning of a selection represents a view or comment on life, using textual evidence to support the claim.
- **Reading Standard 3.3** Analyze the ways in which irony, tone, mood, the author's style, and the "sound" of language achieve specific rhetorical or aesthetic purposes or both.
- **Writing Standard 2.3** Write reflective compositions: **a.** Explore the significance of personal experiences, events, conditions, or concerns by using rhetorical strategies (e.g., narration, description, exposition, persuasion).

Art Link

Ask Yourself

Possible response: *Icarus is represented in the bottom right corner of the painting. Students might address the theme of the futility of human ideals and hopes, or the beauty of simple, everyday living that continues undisturbed notwithstanding the efforts of great heroes.*

Think About/Talk About

Extend the Discussion

Allusions For readers trying to interpret this poem, how does it help to know that lines 5–10 probably refer to two other nearby paintings—a Nativity scene and the martyrdom of an unnamed saint? ***Possible response:*** *The allusions become clearer, giving the reader a better sense of the speaker's experience.*

Synthesizing Auden uses Bruegel's interpretation of the myth of Icarus as inspiration for his own poetic commentary on 1930s Europe, where traditional values were shaken by fascism. Is Auden's message limited to the pre-war period, or does it continue to have meaning today? Why? ***Possible responses:*** *Many students will see that the poem's theme is still relevant today because suffering in many war-torn countries is still ignored.*

Vocabulary: Own the Word

- **reverently:** Tell students that just as to *revere* (verb form) someone is to look up to that person, *reverence* (noun form) is admiration and esteem. Ask students to name ways that people behave *reverently.*
- **martyrdom:** Write the word *martyrdom* in a circle on the board along with its definition ("death for a cause"). Draw spider legs from the circle as students add concepts and attributes. ***Possible responses:*** *death, sacrifice*
- **leisurely:** Tell students that something done in a *leisurely* way is done slowly and in a laid-back manner. An antonym is *frantic.* Use both words in a sentence: The rush-hour drive to work was *frantic,* but the pace at work was quite *leisurely.*
- **forsaken:** Ask students to applaud to indicate the degree to which they would like to be described as having been *forsaken* and then explain their response. ***Possible response:*** *Students do not applaud because to be forsaken is to be abandoned.*

Check for Understanding

Independent Practice

Reading Skills Focus

Possible responses:

1. *The Old Masters realized that most people are indifferent to the suffering of others because they are immersed in their own concerns.*
2. *He uses what happened to Icarus in Bruegel's painting as an example. No one paid more than passing attention to Icarus's fall.*
3. *Auden may have seen parallels between Bruegel's insight and 1930s Europe, since fascism valued the state over the individual.*
4. *Have students highlight important details in the poem and then state the theme in their own words.*

Vocabulary Check

5. *b* **6.** *d*
7. *c* **8.** *a*

Literary Skills Focus

Possible responses:

9. *The paintings are probably a nativity scene and a depiction of a saint's martyrdom; the bystanders in both paintings are indifferent.*
10. *Words that serve as clues are "reverently," "miraculous birth," and "dreadful martyrdom."*
11. *The "failure" has no effect on anything that concerns the plowman.*
12. *Auden's interpretation is correct; the plowman in the painting shows no concern for Icarus.*
13. *Responses will vary depending on students' experiences.*
14. *The diction varies from serious to colloquial. Another contrasting pair of phrases is "reverently . . . waiting" in line 5 and "scratches its innocent behind on a tree" in line 13. This style reflects the jarring contrast between momentous events and everyday routine.*
15. *Auden's tone is generally earnest, but occasionally becomes casual and even crass.*

Applying Your Skills

Reading Standard 3.2, 3.3 (see pages A48–A50)
Writing Standard 2.3a (see pages A51–A52)

Musée des Beaux Arts

Literary Response and Analysis

Reading Skills Focus

Quick Check

1. According to lines 1–4, what did the Old Masters understand about suffering?
2. What example of his theory about the Old Masters does the speaker offer in lines 14–21?

Read with a Purpose

3. Why did this painting inspire the speaker?

Reading Skills: Identifying Theme

4. Remember that **theme** is the central idea or truth about life revealed in a text. In the idea web you created, highlight the details from the poem that you think are especially important. Then, in your own words, state the theme of the poem in the center circle of the web. Be sure to compare your thematic statements in class.

Vocabulary Check

Match each Vocabulary word with its definition.

5. reverently	**a.** abandoned
6. martyrdom	**b.** with respect
7. leisurely	**c.** without hurry
8. forsaken	**d.** death of someone on behalf of a cause

Literary Skills Focus

Literary Analysis

9. **Hypothesize** Lines 5–13 describe two other paintings, perhaps by Bruegel, perhaps by other Old Masters. Based on hints in these lines, what events do you think are portrayed in these two paintings? How do bystanders in the paintings respond to these events?
10. **Hypothesize** What details in lines 5–13 suggest that these other paintings to which the speaker refers might be religious in nature?
11. **Interpret** What is meant by line 17: "for [the plowman] it was not an important failure"?
12. **Evaluate** Re-read lines 14–21 of the poem. Has Auden correctly interpreted the meaning of Bruegel's painting? Use evidence from both the text and the painting to support your ideas.
13. **Make Judgments** Do you agree with Auden's view of how people respond to the suffering of others? Explain.

Literary Skills: Diction

14. **Compare and Contrast** What contrast in diction can you see between expressions such as "dreadful martyrdom" and "doggy life"? Find another example of contrasting diction and explain its effect.

Literary Skills Review: Tone

15. **Analyze** The attitude a writer takes toward a subject is called **tone.** What tone do you detect in Auden's poem? Is he sorrowful, bitter, sarcastic, cynical, humorous, or something else?

Writing Skills Focus

Think as a Reader/Writer

Use It in Your Writing As you read, you noted Auden's use of colloquial diction to describe what is happening in Bruegel's painting. Now, select one of the paintings in this book and write a poem about it. Use colloquial diction to describe the painting.

What Do You Think Now What experiences did Auden have that might explain his perspective on the way people respond to the suffering of others?

Universal Access

Struggling Writers

Students may need additional scaffolding to complete the Writing Skills Focus activity. Give students the option of working in pairs to examine a painting in the textbook. Then, have pairs brainstorm casual descriptive phrases that relate to the painting. Encourage students to make a list of these phrases and use them as they write their poems. Have students review Auden's use of colloquial diction before they begin to write.

What Do You Think Now?

To help students answer the question, remind them that Auden was an ambulance driver for the anti-fascist side during the Spanish Civil War (1936–1939).

Assess

Unit 6 Resources,
Selection Standards Check, p. 127

Reading Skills Focus

Fern Hill

Reading Standard 3.3 (see pages A48–A50)

Analyzing Details by Kylene Beers

Look through this book and identify a piece of artwork that appeals to you. Now consider what you liked about that piece of art. While you probably liked the image overall, you may have been drawn to particular details—the subtle (or bold) colors, the position or physical stance of an object, the expression on the subject's face. Details provide more meaning and more substance to what we see or read. When you read, you find details in the same way that you saw details in the art: You look carefully not at the whole, but at the parts.

Poets select details that express emotions or experiences in unique and memorable ways. Carefully chosen details form the basis of vivid images and figurative language. By analyzing details you can come to a richer understanding of a poem. Follow these steps to analyze details in a poem:

First, read and re-read a poem to identify the striking details. In Dylan Thomas's "Fern Hill," for example, the poem's speaker describes himself as "green and carefree," and then as "green and dying," creating a contrasting and contradictory image. Let us focus on Thomas's use of the word *green,* which he repeats throughout the poem to describe the setting and the speaker.

Next, consider what the details represent literally. The word *green* denotes a color and suggests youth, vigor, freshness, and inexperience. When *green* describes a natural setting, one imagines plants, as in the spring or summer.

Because poetry expresses meaning figuratively, you next should explore meaning beyond the literal level. A young person described as green may be full of hope and potential. If the landscape is green, then it is probably fertile and fruitful. Therefore, *green* in both cases can be read as promising new life.

Finally, consider how the detail fits together with the rest of the poem. *Green* suggests the promise of new life, yet it is ironically and paradoxically juxtaposed in the second-to-last line with the word *dying,* highlighting one of Thomas's persistent themes—the lurking presence of death in life, of the worm in the seed.

To analyze details from any poem, not only one of Thomas's, ask yourself these questions:

- What are the most striking or memorable details?
- Does the poet repeat any words or phrases?
- What do these words or images represent on a literal level? on a figurative level?
- How do they make me feel?
- Why does the poet choose these particular details?
- What is their overall meaning in the work?
- What meaning can I **infer** from these details?

Your Turn

Read the second stanza of "Fern Hill" printed below. Identify memorable details. Then use the analysis questions to help you interpret them. Write a constructed response analyzing the details you find most striking.

And as I was green and carefree, famous
among the barns
About the happy yard and singing as the farm
was home,
In the sun that is young once only,
Time let me play and be
Golden in the mercy of his means,
And green and golden I was huntsman and
herdsman, the calves
Sang to my horn, the foxes on the hills barked
clear and cold,
And the Sabbath rang slowly
In the pebbles of the holy streams.

Learn It Online
Learn how to analyze details the multimedia way through *PowerNotes* online.
go.hrw.com H12-1227 Go

Reading Skills Focus

Objectives

Students will analyze details in a poem.

Unit 6 Resources, Reading Focus Skill Builder, p. 95

Teacher One Stop™, lesson plan and all print resources

Direct Teach

Analyzing Details

This feature gives students practice in analyzing the details in "Fern Hill" so that students can come to a richer understanding of the poem. Have students read the feature and complete the Your Turn activity before reading the poem.

Check for Understanding

Your Turn

Ask students to compare their responses with another student. [*Students' choices of memorable details may include "green and carefree," "famous among the barns," "golden in the mercy of his means," "green and golden," and many other phrases. The repetition of the words "green" and "golden" is especially striking. Many of the most striking sensory details relate to sight or hearing.*]

California Standards, p. 1227

- **Reading Standard 3.3** Analyze the ways in which irony, tone, mood, the author's style, and the "sound" of language achieve specific rhetorical or aesthetic purposes or both.

Universal Access

Struggling Readers

Help students understand how details can provide information on both the literal and the figurative levels. Remind them that figurative language refers most often to similes, metaphors, and symbols. Poets rarely explain what the details in a poem mean; they leave it to readers to infer the theme—that is, to uncover it for themselves—as they read.

Learn It Online
For a multimedia version of the instruction on this page, use the **PowerNotes** Reading Skills Focus presentation.
go.hrw.com H12-1227 Go

Standards Focus

Objectives

Students will
- understand the characteristics of lyric poetry
- analyze details

Selection Introduction

Think About the Writer

To help students answer this question, have them think about the pitfalls of fame and admiration. Why might Thomas have struggled to adapt to life as a "found" poet?

For Independent Reading

- *Eden,* Stanislaw Lem
- *The Accident,* Elie Wiesel

Motivate

What Do You Think?/QuickWrite

Ask students to discuss reasons people tend to romanticize the past and view it as an easier and more enjoyable time than the present.

English for Academic Success

Academic Vocabulary

Look for opportunities to use the Academic Vocabulary words in this unit.

- **adapt, *v.*:** adjust for a new purpose
- **exhibit, *v.*:** show, demonstrate
- **inevitable, *adj.*:** unavoidable
- **perspective, *n.*:** a particular way of looking at something

California Standards, pp. 1228–1234

- **Reading Standard 3.1** Analyze characteristics of subgenres (e.g., satire, parody, allegory, pastoral) that are used in poetry, prose, plays, novels, short stories, essays, and other basic genres.
- **Reading Standard 3.3** Analyze the ways in which irony, tone, mood, the author's style, and the "sound" of language achieve specific rhetorical or aesthetic purposes or both.
- **Reading Standard 3.9** Analyze the philosophical arguments presented in literary works to determine whether the authors' positions have contributed to the quality of each work and the credibility of the characters.

Preparing to Read

Fern Hill

Do Not Go Gentle into That Good Night

What Do You Think? How does experience shape our view of the world?

QuickWrite

Childhood is often remembered as a time of carefree innocence. Take a few minutes to free-write about one happy childhood memory of your own in your *Reader/Writer Notebook.*

Dylan Thomas (c. 1937) by Augustus Edwin John. National Museum of Wales, Cardiff. © Courtesy of the Estate of Augustus John.

MEET THE WRITER

Dylan Thomas
(1914–1953)

Dylan Thomas was a prodigy, a supremely gifted youth who wrote some of his most famous works before he was twenty.

Early Success and Early Struggles

Born in Swansea, Wales, Dylan Thomas was largely self-educated, choosing the rough-and-tumble life of a newspaper reporter over the comparative serenity of a university education. His recognition by the leading poets and critics of Britain and the United States came early, and with it came international fame. Neither was enough to prevent him from living on the edge of poverty. The temporary solace he found in alcohol led to his early death.

Universally Celebrated

A man of magical presence with a transparent hunger for affection, Thomas charmed both his British and American contemporaries. When he first came to America in 1950, he was regarded as the most charismatic British visitor since Oscar Wilde in 1885, and those who attended Thomas's readings responded to his personal magnetism. They also heard something new in modern poetry, a kind of expression combining the oratorical *hywl,* or chanting eloquence, of the Welsh chapel service with the theatrical delivery of Victorian actors who thrilled audiences with recitations from Shakespeare and Marlowe.

His *Collected Poems,* published in 1952, established Thomas as a major twentieth-century poet. Nevertheless, Thomas found it increasingly difficult to concentrate sufficiently to write poetry. Consequently, he turned to other genres and produced two works that became familiar around the world: the play *Under Milk Wood* (1954) and the lyrical memoir *A Child's Christmas in Wales* (1955).

Celebrated by critics, sought after by American lecture agencies, and idolized almost like a rock star, Thomas died at the height of a fame he could neither accept nor enjoy. "Once I was lost and proud," he told a *New York Times* reporter, "now I'm found and humble. I prefer that other."

Think About the Writer What do you think Thomas meant by his statement (quoted in the last paragraph above) to the *New York Times* reporter?

Selection Readability	
Easily Accessible **Accessible** Challenging	These poems include familiar themes, language, and syntax.

Reading Standard 3.1, 3.3, 3.9 (see pages A48–A50)

Literary Skills Focus

Lyric Poetry Rather than telling a story, **lyric poetry** focuses on expressing emotions or thoughts. In the lyric poem "Fern Hill," Dylan Thomas uses a range of **sound effects** and **figures of speech** to convey vivid memories of a young boy's enchanted life in the Welsh countryside. Although the speaker's memories are colored by reflection and experience, the exuberance of his feelings, above all, claims our attention.

Literary Perspectives Apply the literary perspective described on page 1230 as you read this poem.

Reading Skills Focus

Analyzing Details The details that a writer includes in his or her work are carefully chosen to convey thoughts, feelings, and impressions. In poetry, many of the details are **sensory details,** or details that appeal to the senses of sight, sound, smell, taste, and touch. **Analyzing details** can help you better understand the emotions and thoughts conveyed by lyric poetry.

Into Action As you read, use a graphic organizer like the one below to record details that help you imagine the scene and share the speaker's feelings and experiences. You might group details according to the senses to which they appeal.

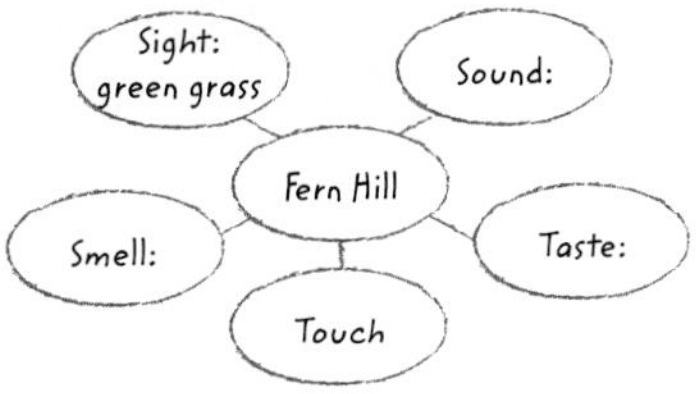

Writing Skills Focus

Think as a Reader/Writer

Find It in Your Reading As you read "Fern Hill," use your *Reader/Writer Notebook* to record the concrete nouns that Thomas includes in his poem. For instance, in the first stanza these nouns include *apple boughs, house, grass, eyes, wagons, prince, trees, leaves, daisies, barley, rivers,* and *light.* Consider how these details create mental pictures as you read.

Reader/Writer Notebook

Use your **RWN** to complete the activities for this selection.

Vocabulary

lilting (LIHLT ihng) *v.* used as *adj.:* singing or speaking with a gentle rhythm. *The child's lilting voice expressed his joy.*

carefree (KAIR free) *adj.:* without worry; happy. *The speaker in "Fern Hill" recalls the happy, carefree days he spent outdoors as a child.*

heedless (HEED lihs) *adj.:* careless. *He ran heedless through the fields, unmindful of any threats or dangers.*

tuneful (TOON fuhl) *adj.:* musical; melodious. *The tuneful song of the birds filled the sky.*

Language Coach

Antonyms Pairs of words that have opposite meanings are called **antonyms.** It is relatively easy to think of antonyms for certain words. For example, you might be able to quickly decide that *worried* is an antonym for *carefree* and that *careful* is an antonym for *heedless.* What about the words *lilting* and *tuneful?* Can you find appropriate antonyms for them? What words can you think of that have meanings nearly opposite to theirs?

Learn It Online

Discover this poem with the introductory video online.

go.hrw.com H12-1229 Go

Selection Resources

Unit 6 Resources, on-level practice and assessment, p. 130

PowerNotes, interactive lesson presentations with activities

Teacher One Stop™, on-level lesson plans and all print resources

Holt Audio Library

Holt Audio Library: Selections and Summaries in Spanish

UA: Holt Interactive Reader, p. 351

UA: Differentiating Instruction, modified lesson plans and leveled assessment, p. 291

UA: Supporting Instruction in Spanish, selection summary

UA: Resources for Teaching Advanced Students, lesson plans, p. 205

ThinkCentral Online Assessment, Selection Standards Check

ThinkCentral Online Remediation

Preteach

Introducing Vocabulary

- Review the Vocabulary words, definitions, and sentences with students.
- To reinforce the importance of the words, point out that *lilting* and *tuneful* both refer to pleasant sounds. You might describe a person's laugh as *lilting* but a bird's song as *tuneful.* Explain that to be *carefree* means to be happy or at ease, while to be *heedless* carries the connotation of ignoring facts.

English for Academic Success

Language Coach

Explain that an antonym creates a context by sharing some model sentences using both the Vocabulary word and its antonym. For example: The young child was *carefree* on the swings, but his parents felt *anxious* as they watched. ***Possible response:*** *Possible antonyms for* lilting *might be* deadpan *or* monotonous; *for* tuneful, discordant *or* cacophonous.

Literary Skills Focus

As you read and discuss the selection with students, have them note sound effects and figures of speech that display the feelings of the speaker.

Reading Skills Focus

Give students a copy of the Reading Skills Focus graphic organizer before they read. (See **Unit 6 Resources.**) Tell them to use their responses to answer the questions on the Applying Your Skills page.

Writing Skills Focus

Have students record concrete nouns in their **Reader/Writer Notebooks.** Students can use their notes to complete the Writing Skills Focus activity.

Learn It Online

The **PowerNotes** presentation for this lesson includes a short video that introduces the selection. The video is also available on the online version of this page.

go.hrw.com H12-1229 Go

Teacher Preparation

Selection Summary

The speaker recalls his idyllic childhood at Fern Hill, the Welsh farm where he spent his younger days in carefree, imaginative play. To him, Fern Hill was like the Garden of Eden, a place where he was the lord of nature, exuberant, independent, and unaware of the passage of time. He concludes by musing that he did not know then, as he does now, that time would take him from that magical place and reveal to him his mortality.

Direct Teach

Think About/Talk About

Read with a Purpose Have students read the Read with a Purpose statement. Point out the key word *carefree.* Ask students how the description of concrete things can express an author's exuberance.

Comprehension

A Reading Focus

Possible responses: *He is saying that the sky above the valley was filled with stars. The word* dingle *creates a sense of a magical place, and by reversing the expected word order, the poet crafts a more rhythmic, musical line.*

POEM

Fern Hill by Dylan Thomas

Read with a Purpose

Read to understand the speaker's feelings about his carefree childhood.

Build Background

As a child, Thomas spent his summers among relatives who worked on a farm that, in his poem, he refers to as Fern Hill. Set in an apple orchard, the farmhouse is constructed of the whitewashed stucco typical of Wales. Fern Hill looks down upon enormous tidal flats, an ever-changing seascape that provides a bountiful habitat for water birds.

Now as I was young and easy under the apple boughs
About the lilting house and happy as the grass was green,
The night above the dingle° starry,
Time let me hail and climb
Golden in the heydays of his eyes,
And honored among wagons I was prince of the apple towns
And once below a time I lordly had the trees and leaves
Trail with daisies and barley
Down the rivers of the windfall light. **A**

And as I was green and carefree, famous among the barns
About the happy yard and singing as the farm was home,
In the sun that is young once only,
Time let me play and be
Golden in the mercy of his means,
And green and golden I was huntsman and herdsman, the calves
Sang to my horn, the foxes on the hills barked clear and cold,
And the sabbath rang slowly
In the pebbles of the holy streams.

3. **dingle:** little wooded valley, nestled between steep hills.

Literary Perspectives

Analyzing Biographical Information Because authors typically explore topics about which they care deeply and know well, the literary works they create often reflect the events and circumstances of their own lives. Although readers must be careful to distinguish between the author of a poem and its speaker (the imaginary voice assumed by the author), knowing particular aspects of the author's life can provide insight into the author's work. Two key elements that enrich our understanding of "Fern Hill" are (1) the importance to Thomas of the Welsh countryside in which he grew up and (2) his inability to reconcile the adult world and its responsibilities with the idyllic world of his childhood.

As you read, be sure to notice the questions in the text, which will guide you in using this perspective.

A Reading Focus **Analyzing Details** To what is the speaker referring in the line "The night above the dingle starry"? What effect does the unusual word choice and word order create?

Vocabulary **lilting** (LIHLT ihng) *v.* used as *adj.:* singing or speaking with a gentle rhythm.
carefree (KAIR free) *adj.:* without worry; happy.

Literary Perspectives

Before students read the poem, have them read the **Literary Perspectives** about Analyzing Biographical Information.

To Thomas, Fern Hill was a sanctuary for peace and happiness. Have students think about a place that gives them that same sense of serenity—whether it is a favorite vacation spot or a room in the student's home. Have students write down five words or phrases that literally describe the favorite place and also figuratively describe how students feel when they are in it.

California Standards, pp. 1232–1234

- **Reading Standard 3.1** Analyze characteristics of subgenres (e.g., satire, parody, allegory, pastoral) that are used in poetry, prose, plays, novels, short stories, essays, and other basic genres.
- **Reading Standard 3.3** Analyze the ways in which irony, tone, mood, the author's style, and the "sound" of language achieve specific rhetorical or aesthetic purposes or both.
- **Reading Standard 3.4** Analyze ways in which poets use imagery, personification, figures of speech, and sounds to evoke readers' emotions.

All the sun long it was running, it was lovely, the hay
Fields high as the house, the tunes from the chimneys, it was air
  And playing, lovely and watery
    And fire green as grass.
  And nightly under the simple stars
As I rode to sleep the owls were bearing the farm away,
All the moon long I heard, blessed among stables, the nightjars°
  Flying with the ricks,° and the horses
    Flashing into the dark. (B)

And then to awake, and the farm, like a wanderer white
With the dew, come back, the cock on his shoulder: it was all
  Shining, it was Adam and maiden,
    The sky gathered again
  And the sun grew round that very day.
So it must have been after the birth of the simple light
In the first, spinning place, the spellbound horses walking warm
  Out of the whinnying green stable
    On to the fields of praise. (C)

And honored among foxes and pheasants by the gay house
Under the new made clouds and happy as the heart was long,
  In the sun born over and over,
    I ran my heedless ways,
  My wishes raced through the house high hay
And nothing I cared, at my sky blue trades, that time allows
In all his tuneful turning so few and such morning songs
  Before the children green and golden
    Follow him out of grace,

Nothing I cared, in the lamb white days, that time would take me
Up to the swallow thronged loft by the shadow of my hand,
  In the moon that is always rising,
    Nor that riding to sleep
  I should hear him fly with the high fields
And wake to the farm forever fled from the childless land.
Oh as I was young and easy in the mercy of his means,
    Time held me green and dying
  Though I sang in my chains like the sea. (D)

25. nightjars: common gray-brown nocturnal birds, named for their jarring cries.
26. ricks: haystacks.

Dylan Thomas's son, Colm (c. 1950–1951).

(B) **Literary Focus** **Lyric Poetry** What feelings do the images of earth, air, fire, and water in lines 19–22 evoke?

(C) **Literary Perspectives** **Analyzing Biographical Information** Thomas's childhood experiences inspired this poem. How are childhood impressions sometimes distorted?

(D) **Literary Perspectives** **Analyzing Biographical Information** Based on what you know of Thomas's life, why do you think he used the phrase "green and dying"? How do you interpret this phrase?

Vocabulary **heedless** (HEED lihs) *adj.:* careless.
tuneful (TOON fuhl) *adj.:* musical; melodious.

- **Reading Standard 3.9** Analyze the philosophical arguments in literary works to determine whether the authors' positions have contributed to the quality of each work and the credibility of the characters. (Philosophical approach)
- **Grades 9–10 Review Reading Standard 1.1** Identify and use the literal and figurative meanings of words and understand word derivations.
- **Writing Standard 2.3** Write reflective compositions: **a.** Explore the significance of personal experiences, events, conditions, or concerns by using rhetorical strategies (e.g., narration, description, exposition, persuasion).
- **Writing Standard 2.6** Deliver multimedia presentations: **a.** Combine text, images, and sound and draw information from many sources (e.g., television broadcasts, videos, films, newspapers, magazines, CD-ROMs, the Internet, electronic media-generated images). **b.** Select an appropriate medium for each element of the presentation. **c.** Use the selected media skillfully, editing appropriately and monitoring for quality.
- **Listening and Speaking Standard 1.6** Use logical, ethical, and emotional appeals that enhance a specific tone and purpose.

Think About/Talk About

Analysis

(B) Literary Focus

Possible response: *They evoke feelings of joy, freedom, and serenity.*

(C) Literary Perspectives

Possible response: *Childhood impressions are often distorted because the adult remembers only the most pleasant aspects of childhood.*

(D) Literary Perspectives

Possible responses: *"Green and dying" is a paradox, connoting life and renewal while describing death. The phrase might mean that even during the carefree days of childhood, time is passing, bringing us closer to death.*

Extend the Discussion

Interpreting What does the speaker mean in stanza 5 when he says that time allows a few careless days before leading children "out of grace"? ***Possible response:*** *The days of carefree childhood, when one is unaware of mortality, are brief compared with adulthood.*

Vocabulary: Own the Word

- **lilting:** Tell students an example of a *lilting* song might be a lullaby. A person who is in a good mood might whistle and *lilt* (verb form) as he or she walks down the street.
- **carefree:** Ask students the following questions: How might you spend a *carefree* weekend? Why might a child be described as *carefree*?
- **heedless:** Tell students that *heedless* means "reckless"; the antonym is *careful*. Use both words in a sentence: Avoid *heedless* mistakes by being careful and double-checking all of your work.
- **tuneful:** Demonstrate the definition of *tuneful* by holding a hand to your ear and smiling to indicate what you hear is pleasant. Ask one or two students to demonstrate how a person would respond to something *tuneful.*

Check for Understanding

Independent Practice

Reading Skills Focus

Possible responses:

1. *Like the speaker, many people feel most carefree during childhood.*
2. *He idealizes his childhood experiences, viewing this "golden" period in his life as a gift from time.*
3. *Students' summary sentences will probably focus on colors and on words denoting strong emotions.*

Literary Skills Focus

Possible responses:

4. *The speaker implies that childhood is free of the worries and concerns of the adult world. In line 10, the speaker states, "and as I was green and carefree."*
5. *The speaker's childhood, like life in the Garden of Eden, was innocent and filled with joy in nature. The boy's "awakening" into adulthood and mortality may be compared to Adam and Eve's fall.*
6. *As a child, the speaker was oblivious to how fleeting his carefree days actually were.*
7. *In lines 4 and 13, time is obliquely personified as an indulgent parent who allows the boy the freedom to be happy. In lines 42, 46, and 53, time is a guiding parental force, leading the child into adulthood and finally to death.*
8. *Perhaps Thomas regretted the judgmental connotation of "heedless." Students' opinions will vary.*
9. *This fact gives the reader more understanding as to why Fern Hill was such a retreat for Thomas.*
10. *There is no plot line in the poem and no linear telling of events. The focus is on imagery and emotion.*
11. *Alliteration is used in line 16 ("clear and cold"), line 20 ("high as the house"), lines 28–29 ("wanderer white/with"), and line 43 ("tuneful turning"). The effect is similar throughout the poem: the alliteration enhances the poem's musical quality.*

Applying Your Skills

Reading Standard 3.1, 3.3, 3.4, 3.9 (see pages A48–A50)
Writing Standard **2.3a** (see pages A51–A52)

Fern Hill

Literary Response and Analysis

Reading Skills Focus

Quick Check

1. In what ways is the experience described in the poem a universal childhood experience?

Read with a Purpose

2. How would you summarize the adult speaker's perspective on his childhood?

Reading Skills: Analyzing Details

3. Review the graphic organizer you filled in as you read. What feeling or impression do the details you noticed convey? Write a few sentences summarizing how the details contribute to the emotional impact of the poem.

Literary Skills Focus

Literary Analysis

4. **Infer** What does the poem imply about childhood innocence? On what details do you base your inference?
5. **Analyze** In line 30, the speaker refers to "Adam and maiden" from the Biblical story of Adam and Eve. In what specific ways was the speaker's childhood like the life Adam and Eve led in the Biblical garden of Eden? In what ways is the boy's "waking" in the last stanza like the "waking" of Adam and Eve as they left the garden?
6. **Interpret** In lines 42–45, the speaker says that as a child he ignored the fact that time allows few carefree days before leading children "out of grace." What does he mean?
7. **Analyze** Where is time personified in the poem? Describe the different types of intentions that time seems to have regarding the boy.
8. **Extend** Thomas once called the line *I ran my heedless ways* "bloody bad." Why do you think Thomas felt this way about a line most people accept and even admire? Do you agree with him?
9. **Literary Perspectives** Thomas wrote "Fern Hill" at the end of World War II. When Swansea was bombed, his parents retreated to their cottage near Fernhill, Wales, and Thomas visited them there. How does this knowledge affect your understanding of the poem's subject and mood?

Literary Skills: Lyric Poetry

10. **Evaluate** The focus of lyric poetry is on expressing emotions and thoughts rather than telling a story. How does "Fern Hill" fit this definition?

Literary Skills Review: Alliteration

11. **Analyze** Note Thomas's use of **alliteration,** the repetition of consonant sounds, as in line 15 of the poem: "And green and golden I was huntsman and herdsman." It helps produce the musical quality of a lyric poem. Where else does Thomas use alliteration? What is its effect?

Writing Skills Focus

Think as a Reader/Writer

Use It in Your Writing Using what you learned about the effect of concrete nouns, write a paragraph describing a childhood memory. Include many concrete nouns as details. For example, if you write about a beach memory, you might include concrete nouns such as *sand, shells, waves, crabs,* and *sun.*

What Do You Think Now?

How do our experiences in childhood affect us as adults?

Universal Access

Struggling Writers

Students may need additional scaffolding to complete the Writing Skills Focus activity. Remind students that a concrete noun names a person, place, or thing that can be perceived by one or more of the senses (sight, hearing, taste, touch, and smell). Tell students that *sneeze, book, The Statue of Liberty, pizza,* and *Abraham Lincoln* are all examples of concrete nouns. Have students begin writing by listing five to ten concrete nouns that relate to a childhood memory. Then, instruct students to include these nouns in their paragraph.

What Do You Think Now?

Brainstorm with students about different anecdotes they have heard from adults that reveal how their childhood experiences shaped the perceptions of the adults.

Grades 9–10 Review Reading Standard 1.1 (see pages A48–A50)

Vocabulary Development

Vocabulary Check

Match each Vocabulary word with its definition.

1. lilting — a. melodious
2. carefree — b. without worry
3. heedless — c. thoughtless
4. tuneful — d. singing with a gentle rhythm

Vocabulary Skills: Suffixes

A **suffix** is a word part added to the end of a word or root to create a new word.

A suffix can change a word's part of speech:

Suffix	added to	forms a(n)	Examples
–ness; –ity	adj.	noun	swiftness; timidity
–ly	adj.	adv.	thoroughly
–less; –ful	noun	adj.	heedless; tuneful
–ing	verb	verb, adj., or noun	bearing, lilting, turning

A suffix can change a word's meaning:

Suffix	Meaning	Example
–less	without	heedless: without heed or care
–ful	filled with, full of	tuneful: filled with tune or song

Adding a suffix may change the spelling of the root word:

- Most words that have two or more syllables and end in *–y* change the *y* to *i* before adding *–ness, –less, or –ly:*
  - *happy + –ness = happiness*
  - *merry + –ly = merrily*
  - *penny + –less = penniless*
- Words that end in a silent *e* will lose the *e* before a suffix that begins with a vowel:
  - *live + –ing = living*
  - *active + –ity = activity*
- Words that end in a silent *e* will usually keep the silent *e* before a suffix that begins with a consonant:
  - *tune + –ful = tuneful*
  - *care + –less = careless*
  - EXCEPTIONS: *true + –ly = truly; awe + –ful = awful*

Your Turn

Add appropriate suffixes to the following words, and make spelling changes as necessary.

1. coincide
2. grave
3. creepy
4. hope

Language Coach

Antonyms "Fern Hill" contains many adjectives that describe sensory details. List the poem's vivid adjectives, and write an antonym for each of the words. If you cannot find an antonym for a word, explain why it is difficult to find the word's opposite.

Academic Vocabulary

Write About

Thomas's childhood experiences are overtly exhibited in his poetry. Do the events of childhood inevitably influence the work of writers and poets? Write a short essay in which you argue whether or not it is possible to adopt a completely new perspective.

Independent Practice

Vocabulary Development

Vocabulary Check

1. *d* **2.** *b*
3. *c* **4.** *a*

Your Turn

Possible responses:

1. *–ing/coinciding*
2. *–ity/gravity*
3. *–ily/creepily*
4. *–fully/hopefully*

WordSharp: An Interactive Vocabulary Tutor (go.hrw.com)

English for Academic Success

Language Coach

Possible responses:

line 2: *lilting/monotonous*
line 18: *holy/evil*
line 21: *lovely/horrid*
line 34: *spellbound/disenchanted*
line 35: *whinnying/(antonym would be praising but horses do not praise)*
line 40: *heedless/attentive*

English for Academic Success

Academic Vocabulary

Possible response: *Students discuss the reasons childhood experiences might leave such an indelible mark on our future lives and how our perspective can be affected by them. Students should especially discuss whether this process is inevitable or not.*

Universal Access: Vocabulary Development

EL English Learners

English for Academic Success Use this activity to help students connect new vocabulary to prior knowledge. Have students write three words that use each of the following suffixes. Then, based on what they know about the words they associated with the affix, have them determine what the suffix means. Have students record the definitions of these affixes in their **Reader/Writer Notebooks.**

- *–less* [*restless, expressionless, emotionless; "without"*]
- *–ly* [*elegantly, excitedly, slowly; "how something is done" (adverb) or "what something is like" (adjective)*]
- *–able* [*culpable, excusable, bendable; "capable of"*]
- *–tion* or *–sion* [*instruction, direction, extension; "the act or process of"*]

✔ See the **Academic and Selection Vocabulary Skill Builder** in **UA: Differentiating Instruction.**

Independent Practice

Grammar Link

Your Turn

1. *The sleeping child dreamed about the farm.*
2. *Running through the field, the excited boy chased the birds.*
3. *The girl, exhausted from her play, curled up in her mother's lap and slept.*

Choices: Evaluation Criteria

Review: Homework
Illustrate the Details
Students visually represent the moods and images of the poem.

Connect: Make a Case
Students supply an argument for agreeing or disagreeing with Thomas's view of childhood.

Extend: Timed Writing 40–50 Minutes
Essay included details explaining why the place was a significant part of the student's childhood.

Assess

Unit 6 Resources, Selection Standards Check, p. 133

go.hrw.com **ThinkCentral Online Assessment,** Selection Standards Check

Teacher One Stop™, editable Selection Standards Check

Reteach

go.hrw.com **ThinkCentral Online Remediation**

Learn It Online
MediaScope can help guide students through the process of creating a multimedia presentation—from choosing a subject and planning through publishing their finished project.
go.hrw.com H12-1234 Go

Applying Your Skills

Fern Hill

Writing Standard 2.3a, 2.6a–c (see pages A51–A52) Listening and Speaking Standard 1.6 (see pages A53–A55)

Grammar Link

Participles and Participial Phrases

A **participle** is a verb form that is used as an adjective. A **participial phrase** consists of a participle and all the words related to the participle. Participles are classified as either **present participles** or **past participles.**

A **present participle** ends in *–ing.*

The child played along the **curving** stream.

Playing in the orchard, the speaker is carefree. [Participial phrase *playing in the orchard* modifies *speaker.*]

Most **past participles** end in *–d* or *–ed*, but some are irregular.

The **tormented** poet acted recklessly.

Appreciated by critics, "Fern Hill" is a timeless poem. [The participial phrase *appreciated by critics* modifies the noun phrase *"Fern Hill."*]

Written after World War II, the poem reflects Thomas's disillusionment. [The participial phrase *written after World War II* modifies *poem.*]

Your Turn

Underline each participle and participial phrase.

1. The sleeping child dreamed about the farm.
2. Running through the field, the excited boy chased the birds.
3. The girl, exhausted from her play, curled up in her mother's lap and slept.

Writing Application Circle all the participles in something you have written. Then, write in the margins whether they are past or present and what they modify.

CHOICES

As you respond to the Choices, use these **Academic Vocabulary** words as appropriate: adapt, considerably, exhibit, inevitable, perspective.

REVIEW
Illustrate the Details
Create a visual (or multimedia) representation of "Fern Hill," illustrating with color, light, and form the details that Thomas includes in his poem. You can choose any medium—water colors, collage, mosaic, oil paints, or even multimedia. When you have finished your work, share it with classmates, explaining how you chose to adapt the details from the poem to the different media.

CONNECT
Make a Case
Work with a small group of students to make a case for agreeing or disagreeing with Thomas's view of childhood and time. Then, debate your group's perspective with another group. Use support from the poem and your own experience to further your case.

EXTEND
Describe a Place
Timed Writing Write a short essay in which you describe a place where you spent significant time as a child. Be sure to use details in your description.

Learn It Online
Learn how to create an eye-popping multimedia presentation! Visit MediaScope online.
go.hrw.com H12-1234 Go

Universal Access: Grammar Link

English Learners

English for Academic Success Tell students that a common mistake with participial phrases is to have them modify the wrong noun or noun phrase. Write the following sentence on the board: *Displaying its playful nature, I laughed when my puppy scampered away with a sock in its mouth.*

Point out to students that in this sentence, the participial phrase "Displaying its playful nature" is set up so that it modifies the pronoun *I* instead of the noun *puppy.* The corrected sentence reads as follows: *Displaying its playful nature, my puppy scampered away with a sock in its mouth, leaving me laughing.*

Have students identify the participles and participial phrases in the following examples:

- Beloved by readers everywhere, Dylan Thomas is a master poet.
- The exhausted mother lost sight of her son.

✔ For more practice with participles and participial phrases, see **Warriner's Handbook, GrammarNotes,** and **Language Handbook Worksheets.**

Preparing to Read

Reading Standard 3.1 (see pages A48–A50)

Do Not Go Gentle into That Good Night

Literary Skills Focus

Elegy An **elegy** is a poem that mourns the death of someone or laments something lost. A type of **lyric,** an elegy is usually formal in language and structure, and solemn or melancholy in tone. The typical elegy mourns a death that has already occurred. This poem is a bit different. It is an elegy spoken to a dying man, urging him not to surrender but to meet death in a spirit of challenge. As he often did in his poetry, here Thomas gives his own twist to a familiar subject. The poem may invite charges of irreverence, but its lyrical solemnity, not its argument, is what echoes most in the reader's mind.

The particular form of this elegy is called a **villanelle,** a nineteen-line poem divided into five tercets (three-line stanzas), each with the **rhyme scheme** *aba,* and a final quatrain with the rhyme scheme *abaa.* Note that the first and third lines of the first tercet alternate as the last line of tercets 2 through 5, and are combined as a final couplet in the quatrain. Villanelles typically have only two end-rhyme sounds in the entire poem. As you read, notice how the repetition of the end-rhyme sounds, skillfully blended with the iambic pentameter, helps create somber, delicate music appropriate for this elegy.

Language Coach

Multiple-Meaning Words Some words have more than one definition. One way to determine a word's meaning is to look at the word's context. For example, the word *grave* can mean "a cemetery plot" or "serious." Which meaning does Thomas intend in line 13? Is it possible that the poet intends both meanings? Explain.

Writing Skills Focus

Think as a Reader/Writer

Find It in Your Reading In your *Reader/Writer Notebook*, create a graphic organizer like the one below. As you read the poem, record repeated words as well as strong, vivid, and even violent words and phrases. Some examples are provided to get you started. Record the line numbers as in the examples below.

Repetition	Strong, Vivid Words/Phrases
"Do not go gentle" (1, 6, 12, 18)	"Rage, rage," (3, 9)
"dying of the light" (3, 9, 15, 19)	"blaze like meteors" (14)

Reader/Writer Notebook

Use your **RWN** to complete the activities for this selection.

Selection Resources

Unit 6 Resources, on-level practice and assessment, p. 133

Teacher One Stop™, on-level lesson plans and all print resources

Holt Audio Library

Holt Audio Library: Selections and Summaries in Spanish

UA: Differentiating Instruction, graphic organizer, p. 294

UA: Supporting Instruction in Spanish, selection summary

ThinkCentral Online Assessment, Selection Standards Check

ThinkCentral Online Remediation

Preteach

English for Academic Success

Language Coach

Facilitate class discussion to answer the question in the **Language Coach.** Help students see that Thomas uses a play on words so that *grave* can mean both a *cemetery plot* and *serious.*

Literary Skills Focus

As you read and discuss the selection with students, have them note the musical effect of the meter and repetitive end-rhyme sounds.

Writing Skills Focus

Have students record repeated words and strong or violent words in their **Reader/Writer Notebooks.** Students can use their notes to complete the Writing Skills Focus activity.

California Standards, pp. 1235–1237

- **Reading Standard 3.1** Analyze characteristics of subgenres (e.g., satire, parody, allegory, pastoral) that are used in poetry, prose, plays, novels, short stories, essays, and other basic genres.

Teacher Preparation

Selection Summary

The speaker urges his father not to submit quietly to death, contending that people who are near death should struggle "against the dying of the light." He asserts that those with true wisdom rage against death, even though they know it is inevitable. He looks for a sign that his father will challenge death.

Direct Teach

Think About/Talk About

Read with a Purpose Have students read the Read with a Purpose statement. Ask students to consider Thomas's plea to his father as they read this poem. What does this plea reveal about the speaker's relationship with his father?

Analysis

A Literary Focus

Possible response: *The end rhymes and the use of strong words* such as burn, rave, *and* rage *establish a solemn tone that is maintained throughout the poem.*

Extend the Discussion

Making Inferences What four types of men does the speaker describe in stanzas 2–5? What do they all have in common? ***Possible response:*** *Wise men, good men, wild men, and grave men all find reason for sorrow or regret at the coming of death, and they all fight against it.*

California Standards, p. 1237

- **Reading Standard 3.1** Analyze characteristics of subgenres (e.g., satire, parody, allegory, pastoral) that are used in poetry, prose, plays, novels, short stories, essays, and other basic genres.
- **Reading Standard 3.4** Analyze ways in which poets use imagery, personification, figures of speech, and sounds to evoke readers' emotions.
- **Writing Standard 2.3** Write reflective compositions: **a.** Explore the significance of personal experiences, events, conditions, or concerns by using rhetorical strategies (e.g., narration, description, exposition, persuasion).

POEM

Do Not Go Gentle into That Good Night

by **Dylan Thomas**

Read with a Purpose

Read the poem to discover how a son advises his father to approach impending death.

Build Background

In this poem the use of *gentle* instead of the adverb *gently* may at first seem ungrammatical. However, when we read the line as "Do not go, gentle, into that good night," as Thomas insisted, we gain the additional meaning of all that is gentle, including the gentle man who was Thomas's father.

Do not go gentle into that good night,
Old age should burn and rave at close of day;
Rage, rage against the dying of the light. **A**

Though wise men at their end know dark is right,
Because their words had forked no lightning they
Do not go gentle into that good night.

Good men, the last wave by, crying how bright
Their frail deeds might have danced in a green bay,
Rage, rage against the dying of the light.

Wild men who caught and sang the sun in flight,
And learn, too late, they grieved it on its way,
Do not go gentle into that good night.

Grave men, near death, who see with blinding sight
Blind eyes could blaze like meteors and be gay,
Rage, rage against the dying of the light.

And you, my father, there on the sad height,
Curse, bless, me now with your fierce tears, I pray.
Do not go gentle into that good night.
Rage, rage against the dying of the light.

A Literary Focus Elegy How does the first tercet establish the solemn, intense mood of this elegy?

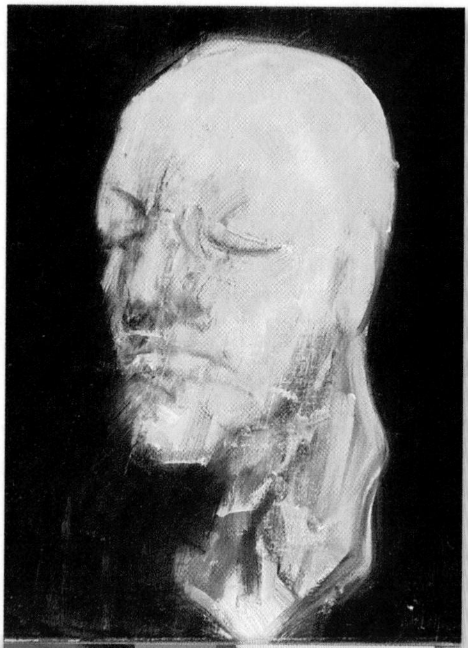

Analyzing Visuals

Connecting to the Text If the subject of the painting were facing death, what might his closed eyes suggest?

Study for Portrait V (after the life mask of William Blake) (1956) by Francis Bacon. Estate of Francis Bacon/Artists Rights Society (ARS), NY/DACS, London.

Analyzing Visuals

Connecting to the Text: *The closed eyes of the subject of the painting might indicate that he has accepted death and is not going to fight for life. He has chosen to "go gentle into the good night."*

Universal Access

EL English Learners

Attitudes about death vary from one culture to another. Explain that this poem is written by a young man who feels that death is something to be resisted. Encourage students to discuss different views of death and, if they wish, to discuss perspectives on death common in their home culture.

✔ See the **English Language Skill Builder** in **UA: Differentiating Instruction.**

Applying Your Skills

Reading Standard 3.1, 3.4 (see pages A48–A50)
Writing Standard 2.3a (see pages A51–A52)

Do Not Go Gentle into That Good Night

Literary Response and Analysis

Reading Skills Focus

Quick Check

1. What is the main point of this poem?
2. What does the speaker pray for at the end of the poem?
3. What is the "good night"? Explain the pun, or play on words, in this phrase.

Read with a Purpose

4. How does the speaker feel about facing death? How does he want his father to face it?

Literary Skills Focus

Literary Analysis

5. **Interpret** Given the speaker's feelings about the "good night," do you see anything contradictory in his use of the word *good?* Explain.
6. **Analyze** What does the speaker's prayer at the end indicate about the relationship between this father and son?
7. **Compare and Contrast** How do each of the types of people described in stanzas 2–5 respond to the "dying of the light"?
8. **Extend** Soon after this poem was finished, Thomas sent it to Princess Caetani in Rome, hoping she might publish it in her literary magazine. In an accompanying letter, he wrote: "The only person I can't show the little enclosed poem to is, of course, my father, who doesn't know he's dying." Given the fact that the poem became one of the most famous elegies of the century, do you think Thomas's reluctance was justified? Why or why not? What would you have done in his situation?
9. **Make Judgments** Note how Thomas features words that relate to images of light *(fire, lightning, sun, blaze, bright).* How does Thomas present a man's relationship to light in the poem? Does this relationship evolve or stay the same? Support your answer with details from the poem.

Literary Skills: Elegy

10. **Analyze** The elegy form goes back to the ancient Greeks and Romans, who used the term to refer to any serious meditation, including poems about love, war, and death. Today, *elegy* refers exclusively to poems of mourning. In what ways does Thomas's poem fit both definitions?

Literary Skills Review: Metaphor

11. **Interpret** A comparison of two seemingly unlike things is called a **metaphor.** When an author uses metaphor, he or she speaks of one thing as if it were another. Identify at least three metaphors for death or dying in this poem. How do they contribute to the elegiac tone of the poem?

Writing Skills Focus

Think as a Reader/Writer

Use It in Your Writing Re-read the language you recorded in your graphic organizer. What is Thomas's tone? Using your own repetitions and strong, vivid verbs, write a paragraph about the way you think people should face death.

What Do You Think Now? How has this poem influenced your perspective on death?

Check for Understanding

Independent Practice

Reading Skills Focus

Possible responses:

1. *Man should not welcome death, but rage against it.*
2. *He prays that his father will fight death and not let it take him.*
3. *The "good night" is death. It also creates a play on words, since death is often described as sleep, and "good night" is often spoken to someone who is going to sleep.*
4. *The speaker feels that wise men should challenge death. He wants his father to fight death.*

Literary Skills Focus

Possible responses:

5. *He does not welcome death; he sees it as a cause for sorrow and rage. It seems paradoxical that he would describe death as "good."*
6. *The son is asking the father to bequeath to him a love of life through a refusal to accept death. This request shows a loving relationship between father and son.*
7. *Wise men are angry because their counsels did not influence others; good men deplore the ineffectuality of their deeds; wild men learn that time is fleeting; grave men regret their failure to enjoy life.*
8. *Responses will vary. Some students will understand Thomas's reticence. Discuss the concept of self-censorship with students.*
9. *Thomas explains that man needs light, and he must do everything he can to stop the "dying of the light." The relationship evolves as it becomes inevitable that man and light will have to separate.*
10. *The poem is about mourning death and affirming life.*
11. *Metaphors include "that good night" (lines 1, 6, 12, 18), "the dying of the light" (lines 3, 9, 15, 19), "dark" (line 4), and "last wave by" (line 7). Each of these metaphors relates to the lamenting of the speaker.*

Universal Access

Struggling Writers

Students may need additional scaffolding to complete the Writing Skills Focus activity. Some students may struggle to think of strong, vivid verbs for their paragraphs. Have students work with a partner to brainstorm suitable verbs. Encourage students to use a thesaurus to choose more powerful verbs. Then, have students use the verbs from the lists in their paragraphs.

What Do You Think Now?

Lead a full-class discussion on attitudes toward death. For instance, you might ask why the villanelle is an appropriate vehicle for expressing thoughts on death.

Assess

Unit 6 Resources,
Selection Standards Check, p. 133

Standards Focus

Objectives

Students will
- understand irony
- analyze tone

Selection Introduction

Think About the Writer

To help students answer this question, ask them how common things can have elaborate meanings.

For Independent Reading

King Lear, William Shakespeare

Motivate

What Do You Think?/QuickWrite

Ask students to consider how having two different experiences with an issue can lead to miscommunication or a misunderstanding. Have students record their thoughts in their **Reader/Writer Notebooks.**

English for Academic Success

Academic Vocabulary

Look for opportunities to use the Academic Vocabulary words in this unit.

- **considerably,** ***adv.:*** by a large amount
- **exhibit,** ***v.:*** show, demonstrate
- **perspective,** ***n.:*** a particular way of looking at something

California Standards, pp. 1238–1241

- **Reading Standard 3.3** Analyze the ways in which irony, tone, mood, the author's style, and the "sound" of language achieve specific rhetorical or aesthetic purposes or both.

Preparing to Read

Not Waving but Drowning

What Do You Think? How does experience shape our view of the world?

QuickWrite

In your *Reader/Writer Notebook,* write about a time when you or another person misunderstood someone's words, gestures, or intentions. What were the consequences of the misunderstanding?

English poet and novelist, Stevie Smith (1954).

MEET THE WRITER

Stevie Smith

(1902–1971)

Florence Margaret Smith was nicknamed "Stevie" because she was short like the British jockey Steve Donoghue. Although all of her works reflect her offbeat outlook and writing style, it is in her poems that she fully displays her cleverness.

"Cheerfully Gruesome"

Smith was born in Yorkshire but was raised by her mother and aunt in Palmers Green, a suburb of London. Smith lived with her aunt for sixty-six years until "Auntie Lion" died in 1968 at the age of ninety-six. Smith herself died only three years later.

After finishing school, Smith worked as a secretary for a magazine publisher, a post she retained for thirty years. In her early thirties, Smith began to publish poetry and fiction. Her first publication, *Novel on Yellow Paper* (1936), is a playful monologue, which some critics have compared to the writing of Gertrude Stein. In 1937, Smith began to publish her poems. *A Good Time Was Had by All* revealed short, matter-of-fact verses and exhibited a childishly simple but biting tone that would become characteristic of her poems. Smith's poems often deal with death, loneliness, or despair, but she is not self-pitying. Her sometimes whimsical humor adds sparkle, allowing her to distance herself from her subject.

Smith summarized her style when she claimed that she was "straightforward, but not simple." The poet Robert Lowell described her poetic voice as "cheerfully gruesome," and the humorist Ogden Nash admired her "songs of deadly innocence."

Artist and Performer

Stevie Smith accompanied many of her poems with drawings that she called "doodles." She loved to perform her poetry, reading it on the radio and occasionally singing her verses. During the 1960s, interest in Smith's work increased considerably, in part because of these public readings. In 1969, she received the Queen's Gold Medal for Poetry. Since her death in 1971, she has been the subject of a play written by Hugh Whitemore called *Stevie,* later adapted as a film.

Think About the Writer What do you think Smith means when she says her writing is "straightforward, but not simple"?

Selection Readability	
Easily Accessible **Accessible** Challenging	familiar themes, language, and syntax

Reading Standard 3.3 (see pages A48–A50)

Literary Skills Focus

Irony The discrepancy between expectations and reality or between appearances and reality is called **irony**. **Verbal irony** occurs when a writer or speaker says one thing but really means something quite different—often the opposite of what he or she has said. **Situational irony** happens when a situation unfolds differently than expected, and **dramatic irony** occurs when the reader has important information that the characters in a work do not have. In "Not Waving but Drowning," Smith explores and develops the irony inherent in a tragic misunderstanding.

Reading Skills Focus

Analyzing Tone The attitude a writer takes toward the reader, a subject, or a character is called **tone.** Tone is conveyed through the writer's choice of words and details. In "Not Waving but Drowning," Smith provides details from three perspectives to create the poem's tone.

Into Action As you read "Not Waving but Drowning," use a chart like the one below to record the details and words that the poet uses to help convey tone.

Detail	Tone
"Poor chap, he always loved larking"	

Writing Skills Focus

Think as a Reader/Writer

Find It in Your Reading Writers use different points of view to give readers different ways of thinking about a situation. As you read, take notes in your *Reader/Writer Notebook* about how Smith shifts perspective in this poem, from the speaker ("Nobody heard him") to the drowned man ("I was much further out") to the friends on the beach ("It must have been too cold for him"). How does she indicate a shift? What is the effect of including three different perspectives in such a short poem? How does presenting each one help Smith create the irony and tone of the poem?

Language Coach

Commonly Misused Words The verbs *lay* and *lie* are often misused. Here is an explanation of their different forms and tenses:

Present	Past	Past Participle
lay	laid	[has] laid
lie	lay	[has] lain

Lay (meaning "put down" or "place") is a transitive verb, which takes an object: [verb] [object]

***Lay the book** on the table.*

Lie (meaning "recline") is an intransitive verb, which does not take an object:

***Lie** on the bed and rest.*

In this poem, is *lay* in the present tense, or is it the past tense of *lie?*

Reader/Writer Notebook

Use your **RWN** to complete the activities for this selection.

Learn It Online

Listen to this poem online.

go.hrw.com H12-1239 Go

Selection Resources

Unit 6 Resources, on-level practice and assessment, p. 136

Teacher One Stop™, on-level lesson plans and all print resources

Holt Audio Library

Holt Audio Library: Selections and Summaries in Spanish

UA: Differentiating Instruction, graphic organizer, p. 295

UA: Supporting Instruction in Spanish, selection summary

ThinkCentral Online Assessment, Selection Standards Check

ThinkCentral Online Remediation

Preteach

English for Academic Success

Language Coach

Have students supply the correct word in the following sentences.

1. After the race, she was very tired so she went home to ______ down a while. [*lie*]
2. ______ out all the flowers for the ceremony. [*Lay*]

Literary Skills Focus

As you read and discuss the poem with students, ask them to note examples of verbal and situational dramatic irony.

Reading Skills Focus

Give students a copy of the Reading Skills Focus graphic organizer before they read. (See **Unit 6 Resources**.) Tell them to use their responses to answer the questions on the Applying Your Skills page.

Writing Skills Focus

Have students record in their **Reader/Writer Notebooks** places in the selection where the perspective, or point of view, shifts. Students can use their notes to complete the Writing Skills Focus activity.

Learn It Online

The online version of this poem includes audio support to engage all students and to help struggling readers with reading comprehension and vocabulary.

go.hrw.com H12-1239 Go

Teacher Preparation

Selection Summary

A man drowns when his cries and gestures for help are misinterpreted as playful waving. Some people speculate that he died of a heart attack caused by the icy water. The man responds that he had always been "too cold" and "too far out" and distant from humanity.

Direct Teach

Think About/Talk About

Read with a Purpose Have students read the Read with a Purpose statement. Ask students to consider, as they read, the perspectives of the man and of the spectators.

Comprehension

B Reading Focus

Possible responses: *The tone of the last stanza is ironic. The speaker plays on the words "too cold" and "too far out" to make a statement not about the man in the water, but about his relationship to other people.*

Analysis

A Literary Focus

Possible response: *The people on the beach think the man was "larking" or playing in the water, but the reader knows he was calling for help.*

POEM

Not Waving but Drowning

by **Stevie Smith**

Read with a Purpose

Read this poem to see how a misunderstanding turns deadly.

Build Background

Stevie Smith said that "Not Waving but Drowning" was about "misunderstandings which may prove fatal." Smith has been called "one of the absolute originals of English literature" because her work defies classification. As you read the following poem, think about the specific ways in which it is unusual or offbeat.

Nobody heard him, the dead man,
But still he lay moaning:
I was much further out than you thought
And not waving but drowning.

Poor chap, he always loved larking°
And now he's dead
It must have been too cold for him his heart gave way,
They said. **A**

Oh, no no no, it was too cold always
(Still the dead one lay moaning)
I was much too far out all my life
And not waving but drowning. **B**

5. **larking:** playing; having a good time.

A **Literary Focus** **Irony** How is the reaction of the people on the beach an example of dramatic irony? What do you know that these people do not?

B **Reading Focus** **Analyzing Tone** What is the tone of the last stanza? What words does Smith use to convey this tone?

Universal Access

English Learners

English for Academic Success Detecting the detached tone of the poem may be difficult. Direct students' attention to line 5. Inform them that the word *chap* is an informal expression for "guy" or "young man." The speaker's impersonal reference to the dead man creates a detached tone in the poem. Ask students to look for other examples of words that contribute to the detached tone.

Struggling Readers

Benchmark Students Remind students that situational irony reveals a discrepancy between the appearance of the situation and the situation itself. You might ask: "What would you think if a playful person seemed to be waving while he was swimming? How would you have responded as an observer in this situation?"

✔ See **UA: Differentiating Instruction** for a graphic organizer to scaffold instruction for struggling readers.

California Standards, p. 1241

- **Reading Standard 2.2** Analyze the way in which clarity of meaning is affected by the patterns of organization, hierarchical structures, repetition of the main ideas, syntax, and word choice in the text.
- **Reading Standard 3.3** Analyze the ways in which irony, tone, mood, the author's style, and the "sound" of language achieve specific rhetorical or aesthetic purposes or both.
- **Writing Standard 2.1** Write fictional, autobiographical, or biographical narratives: **a.** Narrate a sequence of events and communicate their significance to the audience. **e.** Make effective use of descriptions of appearance, images, shifting perspectives, and sensory details.

Applying Your Skills

Reading Standard 2.2, 3.3 (see pages A48–A50)
Writing Standard 2.1a, 2.1e (see pages A51–A52)

Not Waving But Drowning

Literary Response and Analysis

Reading Skills Focus

Quick Check

1. Explain this poem's title. What, besides a swimming disaster, might Smith be describing?
2. What does the drowned man mean by "it was too cold always" (line 9) and "I was much too far out all my life" (line 11)?
3. What is unusual or offbeat about this poem? Use details to support your opinions.

Read with a Purpose

4. What causes the misunderstanding between the man and the people on the beach?

Reading Skills: Analyzing Tone

5. The tone of this poem has been described as pessimistic, yet also humorous. Highlight details in your chart that support either or both of these tones.

Details	Tone
"Poor chap, he always loved larking"	Spectator's words convey sympathy; that the spectators thought swimmer was playing when he was drowning is darkly humorous

Literary Skills Focus

Literary Analysis

6. **Interpret** The people on the beach refer to the drowned man's reaction to the cold. What might the "cold" associated with the drowned man's "heart" symbolize?
7. **Infer** What kind of person did the dead man appear to be? Look to the second stanza for the basis of your response.
8. **Extend** How could this poem be a summary of one's whole life? How could this poem summarize the human condition in general?
9. **Evaluate** Smith said that good writing had to be "sad, true, economical, and funny." Do you think her poem meets these criteria?

Literary Skills: Irony

10. **Evaluate** Name two instances of irony in the poem. Explain what makes them ironic, and tell whether they are examples of dramatic, verbal, or situational irony.

Literary Skills Review: Repetition

11. **Analyze** The **repetition** of lines and verses often occurs in poetry. In this poem, a variation of the couplet that ends the first stanza also ends the last stanza. What is the effect of this repetition? What is the author emphasizing?

Writing Skills Focus

Think as a Reader/Writer

Use It in Your Writing Look at your QuickWrite that describes a misunderstanding. Now, write a short description of the event from at least two points of view. Show how the different perspectives helped cause the misunderstanding.

What Do You Think Now?

How do the poem's three different speakers influence each view of the event that takes place?

Universal Access

Struggling Writers

Tell students that they should write one description from the perspective of the person who is misunderstood and another from the perspective of the person who misunderstands someone else. Before students begin writing, have them think about a time when they were misunderstood. Ask them, "How did you feel? What did you do?" Then, have students think about a time when they misunderstood someone else. Ask them, "What caused the misunderstanding? How did you feel?" Encourage students to use their answers to help them as they write.

What Do You Think Now?

Before students answer the What Do You Think Now question, have three students read the poem aloud, taking the voices of the narrator, the dead man, and the man's friend and adjusting their tone accordingly.

Assess

Unit 6 Resources,
Selection Standards Check, p. 139

Check for Understanding

Independent Practice

Reading Skills Focus

Possible responses:

1. *Students may say the title sums up the literal meaning of the poem. It may also suggest ways people fail to communicate their needs or are not heard.*
2. *He may mean that he was lonely; he lived out of the mainstream and felt removed from people.*
3. *The poem treats a serious subject with humor and irony by including the line "Poor chap, he always loved larking / and now he's dead."*
4. *The misunderstanding is caused by the separation the man experienced throughout his life and by the bystanders' casual assumption that he is playing.*
5. *Responses will vary. Students should highlight details that are pessimistic and humorous.*

Literary Skills Focus

Possible responses:

6. *The cold water symbolizes the coldness of the world. In both interpretations, the intensity of that coldness is too much for the man's heart to bear.*
7. *The man appeared to the outside world to be playful and happy.*
8. *This poem could summarize someone's whole life with the last two lines. In general, people may alienate themselves because they do not feel understood.*
9. *Responses will vary. Students may agree that the poem meets her criteria, but they may also point out the paradoxical requirements to be both sad and funny.*
10. *The first two lines exemplify situational irony, and the last stanza represents dramatic irony.*
11. *The repetition draws readers to the main focus of the poem and emphasizes the misunderstandings between society and those whom it alienates.*

Standards Focus

Objectives

Students will understand theme.

Selection Introduction

Think About the Writer

Inform students that socialist realism, the official literary philosophy in the Soviet Union in the 1930s, demanded that all art depict the struggle of the proletariat for a better life realistically—that is, from the Communist point of view.

For Independent Reading

Paradise of the Blind, Thu Huong Duong

Motivate

What Do You Think?/QuickWrite

Have students think about moving to a new home, another school, or any other place they would be reluctant to go. Ask students to write about what they would miss the most after leaving their old home or school in their **Reader/Writer Notebooks.**

English for Academic Success

Academic Vocabulary

Look for opportunities to use the Academic Vocabulary words in this unit.

- **exhibit,** ***v.:*** show, demonstrate
- **perspective,** ***n.:*** particular way of looking at something

California Standards, pp. 1242–1245

- **Reading Standard 3.2** Analyze the way in which the theme or meaning of a selection represents a view or comment on life, using textual evidence to support the claim.

Preparing to Read

Lot's Wife

What Do You Think? How does experience shape our view of the world?

QuickWrite

Think of a time when you were sorry to leave a place. What did you value about your experience in that place, and what did you miss after leaving? Record your thoughts in your *Reader/Writer Notebook.*

Anna Akhmatova (1889–1966).

MEET THE WRITER

Anna Akhmatova

(1889–1966)

In some countries, writers who express political views in their work run into problems with government authorities. Anna Akhmatova, however, was persecuted by the Soviet government because her writing did not exhibit political themes.

A Poet Suppressed

Akhmatova grew up just outside St. Petersburg in a suburb that for centuries had served as the summer palace of the czars, or emperors. Here she became part of the thriving artistic community of prerevolutionary St. Petersburg. With her husband, Nikolai Gumilev, she helped found acmeism, a literary movement that rejected the vagueness and ambiguity of symbolism and focused instead on clarity and precision.

Akhmatova's early successes ended abruptly with the 1917 Russian Revolution. In the years following the revolution, only "socially useful" art was tolerated. Akhmatova was viciously attacked and her poems suppressed because they were too personal. When Gumilev, her ex-husband by that time, was executed for allegedly plotting against the Soviet government, Akhmatova was deemed guilty by association. As punishment, she was not allowed to publish at all from 1922 to 1940.

Life in Stalinist Russia

During the years of Stalinist terror (1924–1953), Akhmatova lived in one room with only a bed, desk, and four books (Pushkin, Shakespeare, Dante, and the Bible). She memorized her poetry instead of writing it down, and although not published, her poems lived in the minds of her fellow Russians. After giving a reading during one of Stalin's wartime "thaws" (periods of fewer restrictions), she received a standing ovation from three thousand people in Moscow's largest auditorium. (The thaw ended when Stalin reportedly asked who had organized the standing ovation.) In 1946, she was expelled from the Union of Soviet Writers. Her own son was imprisoned until 1953, the year of Stalin's death. In her final years, Akhmatova was again recognized officially and allowed to travel to the West.

Think About the Writer What can you infer about Akhmatova from her refusal to write "socially useful" poems despite pressure from the government?

Selection Readability	
Easily Accessible **Accessible** Challenging	accessible theme; familiar syntax; accessible vocabulary

Reading Standard 3.2 (see pages A48–A50)

Literary Skills Focus

Theme The **theme** is the central idea or insight of a work of literature. The theme is different from the topic, or subject, of a poem. As you read the following poem, you might note that its subject is exile, but what does the poem express about exile? What theme does the poem convey? Remember that Akhmatova's poems were shaped by the political events of her time. As you read the poem, consider the following:

- Akhmatova was an artist suppressed by the Soviet government.
- Other artists in the Soviet Union were arrested and sent to prison camps, never to return.
- After her ex-husband's execution, Akhmatova made the difficult decision to stay in Russia rather than flee.

Into Action Use a graphic organizer like the one below to help you identify the theme of the poem.

Vocabulary

hulking (HUHLK ihng) *v.* used as *adj.:* big and clumsy. *The man's hulking figure filled the doorway.*

native (NAY tihv) *adj.:* belonging to a person because of birth. *She left her native city when she was a child.*

welded (WEHLD ihd) *v.:* joined; sealed. *The steel walls and doors of the safe are carefully welded to make the safe strong.*

Language Coach

Connotations Remember that words have **connotations,** or feelings or ideas, associated with them. What feelings or ideas come to you when you hear the word *hulking?* How does this word differ from the word *massive?* If necessary, use a dictionary or thesaurus to help you understand the different connotations of the words.

Writing Skills Focus

Think as a Reader/Writer

Find It in Your Reading Writers use many techniques to help them convey a message to their readers. As you read "Lot's Wife," note how Akhmatova uses a story from the Bible and then has the speaker comment on the story. In your *Reader/Writer Notebook,* record notes about the words and phrases that you think most effectively express the ideas of the story and the speaker's perspective.

Reader/Writer Notebook

Use your **RWN** to complete the activities for this selection.

Learn It Online

Learn more about Akhmatova and her world through these Internet links.

go.hrw.com H12-1243 Go

Selection Resources

Unit 6 Resources, on-level practice and assessment, p. 136

Teacher One Stop™, on-level lesson plans and all print resources

Holt Audio Library

Holt Audio Library: Selections and Summaries in Spanish

UA: Differentiating Instruction, graphic organizer, p. 296

UA: Supporting Instruction in Spanish, selection summary

ThinkCentral Online Assessment, Selection Standards Check

ThinkCentral Online Remediation

Preteach

Introducing Vocabulary

- Review the Vocabulary words, definitions, and sentences with students.
- To reinforce the importance of the Vocabulary words, tell students that these words deal with the subject of exile. The *hulking* angelic figure warned Lot and his family to abandon their *native* city and not look back, or their eyes would be *welded* shut forever.

English for Academic Success

Language Coach

Students may feel the word *hulking* has the connotation of being *overmuscled, ponderous,* and *clumsy.* Discuss whether these connotations are negative, neutral, or positive.

Literary Skills Focus

As you read and discuss the poem with students, have them look for clues that help them decide upon the theme. Discuss why Akhmatova might have chosen this particular Biblical story to retell.

Writing Skills Focus

As they read, have students record words and phrases that effectively express the poem's ideas and the speaker's point of view in their **Reader/Writer Notebooks.** Students can use their notes to complete the Writing Skills Focus activity.

Learn It Online

The enhanced author biography offers more information on the life of the author as well as Holt's interactive resources pertaining to the author.

go.hrw.com H12-1243 Go

Teacher Preparation
Selection Summary
In "Lot's Wife," the speaker describes Lot, the just man, who follows his angel guide out of Sodom. The speaker then focuses on Lot's wife, who hears a voice inside her crying that it is not too late to look back one last time on the city where she has loved her husband and given birth to her children. When she turns to look, she is transformed into a pillar of salt.

Direct Teach

Think About/Talk About
Read with a Purpose Have students read the Read with a Purpose statement. Have students look for words and phrases that reveal how Lot's wife feels about her native home.

Analysis
Ⓐ Literary Focus

Possible response: *It helps to develop the theme that the pain of exile may be too much for some people to bear.*

Ⓑ Literary Focus

Possible response: *The speaker will not forget her because the woman traded her life for a glimpse of the city.*

Vocabulary: Own the Word
- **hulking:** Write *hulking* in a center circle. Draw spider legs from the circle and have students add concepts and attributes associated with the word. ***Possible responses:*** *bulky, large, awkward, cumbersome*
- **native:** Remind students that *native* means "belonging to a person because of birth." Have students name characteristics of their *native* town or city.
- **welded:** Tell students that the word *welded* is most commonly used to describe how metal pieces are fused together. Point out that in the poem, the speaker uses the word to describe the woman's eyes. Ask students: Why were the woman's eyes *welded* shut? ***Possible response:*** *Her eyes were welded shut from pain.*

POEM

Lot's Wife

by **Anna Akhmatova**

translated by **Richard Wilbur**

Read with a Purpose
Read to discover how Lot's wife feels about her home.

Build Background
The poem is based on the Biblical incident recounted in Genesis 19. Angered by the wickedness of the city of Sodom, God sends angels to punish the inhabitants. Only one man, Lot, is looked upon favorably by God. Lot is told to flee Sodom with his family and to never look back. As Lot's family escapes, however, his wife disobeys the command and turns her head to gaze back upon the city. She is immediately turned into a pillar of salt.

The just man followed then his angel guide
Where he strode on the black highway, hulking and bright;
But a wild grief in his wife's bosom cried,
Look back, it is not too late for a last sight Ⓐ

Of the red towers of your native Sodom, the square
Where once you sang, the gardens you shall mourn,
And the tall house with empty windows where
You loved your husband and your babes were born.

She turned, and looking on the bitter view
Her eyes were welded shut by mortal pain;
Into transparent salt her body grew,
And her quick feet were rooted in the plain.

Who would waste tears upon her? Is she not
The least of our losses, this unhappy wife?
Yet in my heart she will not be forgot
Who, for a single glance, gave up her life. Ⓑ

Ⓐ **Literary Focus** **Theme** How does the "wild grief" that "cried" within the woman relate to the poem's theme?

Ⓑ **Literary Focus** **Theme** Why will the speaker never forget the woman?

Vocabulary **hulking** (HUHLK ihng) *v.* used as *adj.:* big and clumsy.
native (NAY tihv) *adj.:* belonging to a person because of birth.
welded (WEHLD ihd) *v.:* joined; sealed.

Head of Akhmatova (1916–1918) by Natan Altman. Museum Ludwig, Köln.

California Standards, p. 1245

- **Reading Standard 3.2** Analyze the way in which the theme or meaning of a selection represents a view or comment on life, using textual evidence to support the claim.
- **Reading Standard 3.4** Analyze ways in which poets use imagery, personification, figures of speech, and sounds to evoke readers' emotions.
- **Writing Standard 2.1** Write fictional, autobiographical, or biographical narratives: **a.** Narrate a sequence of events and communicate their significance to the audience. **b.** Locate scenes and incidents in specific places. **c.** Describe with concrete sensory details the sights, sounds, and smells of a scene and the specific actions, movements, gestures, and feelings of the characters; use interior monologue to depict the characters' feelings.

Reading Standard 3.2, 3.4 (see pages A48–A50)
Writing Standard 2.1a–c (see pages A51–A52)

Literary Response and Analysis

Reading Skills Focus

Quick Check

1. What makes Lot's wife care about Sodom, despite its evils?
2. What does the phrase "mortal pain" (line 10) suggest about how we should view the attitude of Lot's wife?
3. Why do you think the speaker is so affected by Lot's wife?

Read with a Purpose

4. How does Lot's wife feel about her home? What does "bitter view" (line 9) suggest about her feelings?

Vocabulary Check

Match each Vocabulary word with its definition.

5. hulking — a. belonging to a person because of birth
6. native — b. joined; sealed
7. welded — c. big and clumsy

Literary Skills Focus

Literary Analysis

8. **Interpret** In line 5, Akhmatova refers to the "red towers" and the "square" of Sodom. To what other square and city might she be referring?
9. **Analyze** How would you describe the tone of this poem? What words or phrases contribute to this tone?
10. **Make Judgments** Do you think that Lot's wife should be remembered and pitied? Explain.
11. **Infer** Re-read the biography of Akhmatova on page 1242. How might "Lot's Wife" have been shaped by the events of Akhmatova's life and the political situation in Russia at the time she wrote the poem?

Literary Skills: Theme

12. **Evaluate** How would you state the theme of "Lot's Wife"? What view of life does this theme reflect, and how is this view of life shaped by historical influences?

Literary Skills Review: Allusion

13. **Analyze** A reference within a literary work to another literary work or historical event is called an **allusion.** The entire poem is based on the allusion to the Biblical story of Sodom and Gomorrah. What similarities might Akhmatova have seen between Stalinist Russia and the city of Sodom? between herself and Lot's wife?

Writing Skills Focus

Think as a Reader/Writer

Use It in Your Writing Choose a message about life you want to convey and a familiar story you can use to express this message. Using "Lot's Wife" as a model, write a short poem that retells the story. Communicate your theme by carefully choosing words that express your ideas and by commenting on the story or on one of the characters at the end of your poem.

What Do You Think Now

How might you feel if you had to leave your homeland because life there had become intolerable? Would you regard your departure as desertion or as a wise investment in the future? Explain.

Check for Understanding

Independent Practice

Reading Skills Focus

Possible responses:

1. *The city is the place where she loved her husband and raised her family.*
2. *It suggests that her pain is extreme enough to kill her.*
3. *The speaker may identify with the pain that Lot's wife is feeling; it is possible that the speaker has also experienced the pain of exile.*
4. *The words "bitter view" suggest that the destruction of her city deeply affected her.*

Vocabulary Check

5. *c*
6. *a*
7. *b*

Literary Skills Focus

Possible responses:

8. *She might be referring to the Red Square in Moscow.*
9. *The tone is compassionate. The speaker asks rhetorically, "Who would waste tears upon her?" implying that the speaker would cry for Lot's wife.*
10. *Yes, she was forced to leave her dear home. No, she disobeyed and foolishly sacrificed her life.*
11. *The poet may be looking back wistfully to pre-Revolutionary times as a gesture of reminiscence; for Akhmatova, the past may have been preferable to the present.*
12. *The theme is that the homeland is precious. This view of life suggests that separation from one's roots—something many people experienced in Stalin's Soviet Union—is very painful.*
13. *Sodom is a place of wickedness; by extension, Russia may also be wicked because of what Communism has done to it. Akhmatova, like Lot's Wife, may mourn the loss of the place her homeland once was.*

Universal Access

Struggling Writers

Students may need additional scaffolding to complete the Writing Skills Focus activity. Help students select a familiar story. It can be one of Aesop's fables, a popular song, or some other popular story. Generate a list of possible stories on the board. Encourage students to select one story to which they most relate. Then, suggest that they identify with one of the characters, so that they can communicate their theme to the reader.

What Do You Think Now?

Discuss the two alternatives presented in the question: Is leaving your homeland desertion or a wise investment in the future? How could each alternative be true in some ways?

Assess

Unit 6 Resources, Selection Standards Check, p. 139

Standards Focus

Objectives

Students will identify characteristics of the speaker.

Selection Introduction

Think About the Writer

Draw students' attention to the fact that Wislawa Szymborska lived under two totalitarian regimes during her lifetime: Nazism and Communism. Ask students to consider how her experiences during times of political strife might have affected her view of happiness and sadness.

For Independent Reading

- *The Little World of Don Camillo,* Giovanni Guareschi
- *Love that Dog,* Sharon Creech

Motivate

What Do You Think?/QuickWrite

Have students think about a time when they had to cope with a problem that stemmed from a misunderstanding. Ask students to explain how they were able to solve the problem.

English for Academic Success

Academic Vocabulary

Look for opportunities to use the Academic Vocabulary word in this unit.

- **adapt,** ***v.:*** adjust for a new purpose

California Standards, pp. 1246–1250

- **Reading Standard 3.4** Analyze ways in which poets use imagery, personification, figures of speech, and sounds to evoke readers' emotions.

Preparing to Read

Lot's Wife

from Nobel Lecture: The Poet and the World

What Do You Think? How does experience shape our view of the world?

QuickWrite

Think about a time when someone misinterpreted your actions. In your *Reader/Writer Notebook,* write what happened and how you felt.

1996 Nobel Prize winner Wislawa Szymborska, Zakopane.

MEET THE WRITER

Wislawa Szymborska

(1923–   )

Nobel Prize WINNER

Wislawa Szymborska (vees WAH ah vah sheem BAWR skah) has said she aims to write "poems that are ambiguous, that are both happy and sad, like a coin with two sides." Her poetry appeals to young and old alike; one poem inspired a critically acclaimed film, and another became lyrics to a hit rock song.

War and Politics

Born in a small town in Poland, Szymborska began writing poems at the age of five. In 1931, her family moved to Krakow, where Szymborska has since spent much of her life. Of her family, she says, "We talked a lot about books. We read a lot." When she was sixteen, Germany's invasion of Poland ignited World War II. In Krakow, Germans executed the university staff, sent thousands to labor and death camps, and closed the schools. Although the Soviets liberated Poland in 1945, they went on to establish their own form of repression, Communism. Under the Communist policy of socialist realism, artists were expected to adapt their works to glorify the Communist system. After publication of her poems was blocked, Szymborska published two volumes that conformed to socialist realist requirements. By 1957, she had become disillusioned with Communism, and her later poetry has shunned overtly political themes, focusing instead on human relationships and details of everyday life.

World-Class Poet

Szymborska's ability to reveal simply and directly the unexpected in the ordinary has attracted a wide readership. One critic praised "the wit and clarity of Szymborska's turns of phrase. Under her pen, simple language becomes striking." Despite their often somber subjects, her poems allow, as another critic stated, "rays of light to penetrate [their] bleak landscapes." Preferring to live privately, Szymborska has never sought publicity and was not well known outside Poland until she won the Nobel Prize in Literature in 1996.

Think About the Writer What do you think about Szymborska's commitment to writing "ambiguous" poems?

Selection Readability	
Easily Accessible **Accessible** Challenging	These selections include accessible theme; familiar syntax; accessible vocabulary.

Reading Standard 3.4 (see pages A48–A50)

Lot's Wife

Literary Skills Focus

Speaker The **speaker** of a poem is the voice, or persona, assumed by the author of the poem. This voice is often not identified immediately or directly. Rather, the reader gradually comes to understand that a unique voice is speaking and that this speaker's characteristics must be interpreted as they are revealed. Although the speaker is often not the poet, the poet may use the speaker's voice to express his or her ideas about a subject or to interpret an event. As you read the poem, consider how Szymborska gives voice to the possible thoughts and motivations of the speaker of this poem.

Into Action Use a graphic organizer like the one below to help you understand the characteristics of the speaker in "Lot's Wife" and any other poem you read. Answer the prompts about characteristics, using short sentences or phrases from the poem. What motivates the speaker? What does he or she want? What does he or she regret?

	Names I Have	Things I Say Often	Relationships I Have	Actions I Take	Emotions I Feel
Speaker #1					
Speaker #2					

Language Coach

Using *Set* and *Sit* Sometimes speakers and writers use *set* and *sit* interchangeably, but the words have distinct meanings and uses. The verb *set* means "to put [something] in a place." *Set* generally takes a direct object. The verb *sit* means "to be seated in an upright position." *Sit* generally does not have a direct object. In the following sentences, choose the correct verb form in parentheses.

1. She (*set, sat*) down her pack while she tied her shoes.
2. After he fumbled the ball, he (*set, sat*) on the bench.
3. The city (*sits, sets*) on a hill by the sea.

Writing Skills Focus

Think as a Reader/Writer

Find It in Your Reading One way that writers, particularly poets, emphasize ideas is through **parallelism,** the repetition of words, phrases, and sentences that have the same grammatical structures. In "Lot's Wife," Szymborska uses parallelism to express and emphasize the motivations of the speaker: "I looked back for all the reasons given above. / I looked back involuntarily." In your *Reader/Writer Notebook,* take notes on the effect of this repetition. Note the different reasons the speaker gives for looking back and how the poet uses repetition to express the idea that there were many possible reasons for the speaker's actions. Then, read the poem aloud to note how the use of repetition adds rhythm to the poem. Be sure to record your impressions in your notebook.

Reader/Writer Notebook

Use your **RWN** to complete the activities for this selection.

Learn It Online

Listen to this poem's speaker for yourself online.

go.hrw.com H12-1247 Go

Selection Resources

Unit 6 Resources, on-level practice and assessment, p. 136

Teacher One Stop™, on-level lesson plans and all print resources

Holt Audio Library

Holt Audio Library: Selections and Summaries in Spanish

UA: Differentiating Instruction, graphic organizer, p. 296

UA: Supporting Instruction in Spanish, selection summary

ThinkCentral Online Assessment, Selection Standards Check

ThinkCentral Online Remediation

Preteach

English for Academic Success

Language Coach

Explain that in the first example, the direct object of *set* is *pack*. Ask students to write their own sentence using *set* or *sit* correctly.

Literary Skills Focus

As you read and discuss the poem with students, have them look for clues that help them decide who the speaker is and what tone or attitude the speaker has toward the subject. Discuss why Szymborska might have chosen this particular voice or persona.

Writing Skills Focus

Tell students that repetition creates an echo effect and helps to emphasize particular ideas. As they read, have students use their **Reader/Writer Notebooks** to record their reactions to Szymborska's use of repetition and their ideas about the effect of repetition on the poem's meaning. Students can use their notes to complete the Writing Skills Focus activity.

Learn It Online

The online version of this poem includes audio support to engage all students and to help struggling readers with reading comprehension and vocabulary.

go.hrw.com H12-1247 Go

Teacher Preparation

Selection Summary

"Lot's Wife" uses the first-person voice of a Biblical character. In it, Lot's wife describes the many reasons why she turned back toward the burning city of Sodom (and thereby turned into a pillar of salt, as the story goes). She is torn between fleeing and staying, between following her family and the shame she feels over the destruction of Sodom. At this moment, she is part of a community of fleeing animals and "mass panic," until she stumbles and bends to tie her sandal strap. When she looks back, she seals her fate, consciously choosing the city behind her over the path ahead.

Direct Teach

Think About/Talk About

Read with a Purpose Have students read the Read with a Purpose statement. Have students note the reasons Szymborska gives for why Lot's wife looked back.

Analysis

A Literary Focus

Possible response: *The speaker is Lot's wife, but she could also be any person whose motives for an action are in question.*

B Literary Focus

Possible response: *She misses her home and her former life. She feels shame and despair.*

Extend the Discussion

Monitoring Your Reading List some of the reasons the speaker gives in lines 1–24 for why she looked back. ***Possible response:*** *She missed her silver bowl; she was tired of staring at her husband's neck and stooped to tie her sandal strap, thinking he would not care if she died; she felt old and weary; she was looking for a place to set her bundle and foot; she was in despair.*

POEM

LOT'S WIFE

by **Wislawa Szymborska**

translated by **Stanislaw Baranczak** and **Clare Cavanagh**

Read with a Purpose
Read to discover how one poet interprets the experience of Lot's wife.

Build Background
The poem is based on Chapter 19 in the Bible's Book of Genesis, in which God destroys the city and inhabitants of Sodom but spares Lot, its one righteous man. God tells Lot and his family to flee and literally never look back. Lot's wife, however, turns back to look at Sodom and is turned into a pillar of salt.

They say I looked back out of curiosity. **A**
But I could have had other reasons.
I looked back mourning my silver bowl.
Carelessly, while tying my sandal strap.
So I wouldn't have to keep staring at the righteous nape
of my husband Lot's neck.
From the sudden conviction that if I dropped dead
he wouldn't so much as hesitate.
From the disobedience of the meek.
Checking for pursuers.
Struck by the silence, hoping God had changed his mind.
Our two daughters were already vanishing over the hilltop.
I felt age within me. Distance.
The futility of wandering. Torpor.
I looked back setting my bundle down.
I looked back not knowing where to set my foot.
Serpents appeared on my path,
spiders, field mice, baby vultures.
They were neither good nor evil now—every living thing
was simply creeping or hopping along in the mass panic.
I looked back in desolation.
In shame because we had stolen away.
Wanting to cry out, to go home. **B**
Or only when a sudden gust of wind

A **Literary Focus** **Speaker** Notice that the speaker refers to herself as *I*. Who is the speaker of this poem?

B **Literary Focus** **Speaker** How does the speaker feel about the home she is leaving?

Croat woman prepares to flee her village in Bosnia during Yugoslavian civil war.

Universal Access

Advanced Learners

Acceleration Have students read the story of Lot's wife in the Book of Genesis 19:1–17 to get first-hand knowledge of the Biblical text that inspired both Szymborska's and Akhmatova's poems. Discuss why this particular story would appeal to writers living in totalitarian states.

Struggling Readers

Benchmark Students Reinforce the concept of the speaker by discussing how the poem would be different if Lot himself—a man who never looked back—were the speaker. Include in the discussion how Lot might have felt knowing that his wife perished and he survived. Have students express their thoughts in a freewriting exercise or a short poem.

unbound my hair and lifted up my robe.
It seemed to me that they were watching from the walls of Sodom
and bursting into thunderous laughter again and again.
I looked back in anger.
To savor their terrible fate.
I looked back for all the reasons given above.
I looked back involuntarily.
It was only a rock that turned under foot, growling at me.
It was a sudden crack that stopped me in my tracks.
A hamster on its hind paws tottered on the edge.
It was then we both glanced back.
No, no. I ran on,
I crept, I flew upward
until darkness fell from the heavens
and with it scorching gravel and dead birds.
I couldn't breathe and spun around and around.
Anyone who saw me must have thought I was dancing. **C**
It's not inconceivable that my eyes were open.
It's possible I fell facing the city.

C Literary Focus **Speaker** What does the speaker imply by stating that anyone who witnessed her actions must have interpreted them as "dancing"?

Analyzing Visuals

Connecting to the Text What does the woman's facial expression suggest about the effects of even preparing for a long journey? With that in mind, why might have Lot's wife needed to take just one look back?

Think About/Talk About

Analysis

C Literary Focus

Possible response: *She implies that her death throes might, to a casual or distant observer, have looked like dancing.*

Extend the Discussion

Finding Details Why does the speaker feel as if the people of Sodom are laughing at her? ***Possible response:*** *She feels this way because her robe was lifted by the wind and because she is fleeing the city.*

Analyzing Visuals

Connecting to the Text: *The expression on the woman's face is troubled and weary. She seems to be slightly turned back, indicating that she is unsure about what she is leaving behind and apprehensive about where she is heading.*

California Standards, p. 1250

- **Reading Standard 3.4** Analyze ways in which poets use imagery, personification, figures of speech, and sounds to evoke readers' emotions.
- **Grades 9–10 Review Reading Standard 3.3** Analyze interactions between main and subordinate characters in a literary text (e.g., internal and external conflicts, motivations, relationships, influences) and explain the way those interactions affect the plot.
- **Writing Standard 1.4** Enhance meaning by employing rhetorical devices, including the extended use of parallelism, repetition, and analogy; the incorporation of visual aids (e.g., graphs, tables, pictures); and the issuance of a call for action.

Check for Understanding

Independent Practice

Reading Skills Focus

Possible responses:

1. *The phrase "my husband Lot's neck" (line 6) implies that the speaker is Lot's wife.*
2. *They were all fleeing from Sodom, so in a sense, there is no distinction between good and evil.*
3. *She strongly implies that looking back was a mere accident, while still keeping some ambiguity in the explanation.*

Literary Skills Focus

Possible responses:

4. *She may not share his convictions and is sick of his righteousness.*
5. *While both the Biblical story and the poem tell the same tale, they are from two different points of view. Szymborska does not mention a pillar of salt. She stresses Lot's wife's emotions, not the punishment she received.*
6. *The image serves to show that Lot's wife was not alone in her mistake.*
7. *By developing the ambiguity around Lot's wife's death, Szymborska changes Lot's wife from a flat character who stood for disobedience to a round character who is misunderstood.*
8. *As a successful female poet, Szymborska seems stronger and more self-aware than the speaker of the poem.*
9. *Usually first-person point of view reveals only what the speaker knows, but the speaker brings up ambiguities of what happened, giving an outsider's view of herself.*
10. *The conflict is between appearances and reality. Lot's wife may actually have felt all the conflicts that the speaker ascribes to her—desolation, shame, and curiosity—but none of those actually made her turn around.*

Applying Your Skills

Reading Standard 3.4; **Grades 9–10 Review Reading Standard** 3.3 (see pages A48–A50)
Writing Standard 1.4 (see pages A51–A52)

Lot's Wife

Literary Response and Analysis

Reading Skills Focus

Quick Check

1. What clues tell you who the first-person speaker of the poem is?
2. What does the speaker mean when she says that "every living thing" was "neither good nor evil now"? What has changed?

Read with a Purpose

3. How does Szymborska interpret the motivations and experience of Lot's wife's?

Literary Skills Focus

Literary Analysis

4. **Infer** In lines 5–6, what does Szymborska imply about Lot's wife's feelings toward Lot? Explain.
5. **Compare and Contrast** Compare and contrast the speaker's fate in the last lines of the poem with the Bible's account of the wife's fate: She "looked back . . . and . . . became a pillar of salt."
6. **Hypothesize** Why do you think Szymborska includes the image of the hamster in line 34?
7. **Evaluate** Often, characters in stories that convey a moral message are flat, built on a single dominant trait. Has Szymborska changed Lot's wife from a flat character into a round character—a character with depth and complexity? Explain.

Literary Skills: Speaker

8. **Analyze** The **speaker** of a poem is the voice, or persona, assumed by the author. From what you know about Szymborska, how does her actual persona seem to differ from that of the speaker? How, in any way, is she similar to the speaker?
9. **Hypothesize** In this poem, the speaker refers to herself as *I*. How does the use of first person affect the feelings the poem elicits? Review your graphic organizer to help you answer.

Literary Skills Review: Conflict

10. **Analyze** A struggle between opposing characters, forces, or emotions is called **conflict.** In **external conflict,** a character struggles against some outside force. An **internal conflict** is a struggle between opposing needs, desires, or emotions within a single character. Explain the conflicts Lot's wife experiences in the poem.

Writing Skills Focus

Think as a Reader/Writer

Use It in Your Writing Review how Szymborska uses repetition, including parallelism, to emphasize her ideas. Write your own five-line poem explaining a reason that someone did something. Begin each line with the same phrase to create a rhythm to the poem.

What Do You Think Now?

How did the experience of Lot's wife shape her worldview?

Universal Access

Struggling Writers

Some students may need additional scaffolding to complete the Writing Skills Focus activity. Have students refer to their response to the QuickWrite question. Tell them to explain their actions and behavior in a five-line poem. Remind them to begin each line with the same phrase to create repetition. Encourage them to add feeling to their poem.

What Do You Think Now?

Ask students how Lot's wife's experiences might have taught her about the importance of not judging actions or events from the outside.

Assess

Unit 6 Resources,
Selection Standards Check, p. 139

Reading Standard 2.5 (see pages A48–A50)

from Nobel Lecture: The Poet and the World

Informational Text Focus

Analyzing an Author's Beliefs To **analyze an author's beliefs,** you must consider the author's ideas and how he or she expresses them. What kinds of language does the author use? What problems does he or she describe? What characters or real people does the author esteem?

Into Action As you read Szymborska's Nobel lecture, think about TOPICAL questions (questions regarding Title, Opinion, Problem, Insight, Characters, Action, and Language) to help you analyze her beliefs. Using the chart below as a guide, record your answers.

Title	What connotations/associations does the title suggest? Does the title tell you the subject?	The subject will have to do with the relationship of poets to the world.
Opinion	What is the writer's attitude about the subject? What language does she use to indicate her opinion?	
Problem	What problem or issue is this writer exploring? What is the author's solution to the problem?	
Insight	What special insight does the author have on this subject? Why?	
Characters	Who are the important characters or people that have influenced the author's attitude?	
Action	What action will she take?	
Language	What language does the author use that is particularly striking? What images support her perspective?	

Writing Skills Focus

Preparing for Timed Writing Good writers present their beliefs coherently by logically moving from one idea to the next. As you read, record in your *Reader/Writer Notebook* Szymborska's main ideas and note how she moves from one idea to the next. For example, she presents examples of scientists who said "I don't know" and then begins the next paragraph by stating, "Poets, if they're genuine, must also keep repeating 'I don't know.'" In what other ways does she create coherence and unity in her writing?

Reader/Writer Notebook

Use your **RWN** to complete the activities for this selection.

Vocabulary

inspiration (ihn spuh RAY shuhn) *n.:* influence of thought and strong feelings on actions, especially good actions. *Inspiration for the project came to the artist in a dream.*

quell (kwehl) *v.:* bring under control by subduing. *The poet had to quell her fear of rejection before sending her poems to agents.*

fervor (FUR vuhr) *n.:* intense emotion. *She expressed her beliefs with a fervor her fellow poets had never before seen.*

lethal (LEE thuhl) *adj.:* deadly. *The snake had a lethal bite.*

impotence (IHM puh tuhns) *n.:* helplessness. *Though frustrated by her impotence, the writer continued to fight for equal rights.*

epithet (EHP uh theht) *n.:* descriptive expression. *He used the epithet "honest" to describe his friend Abe, as in "Honest Abe."*

deviate (DEE vee ayt) *v.:* turn aside from a way, norm, or truth. *Writers will lose their inspiration if they deviate from their desire to learn more about the world.*

Language Coach

Word Families Words that are related by the base or root are called **word families.** For example, *lethal* and *lethally* are part of the same word family. Can you name two words that are related to *inspiration?*

Learn It Online
Get to know the Vocabulary words through Word Watch online.

go.hrw.com H12-1251 Go

Selection Resources

Unit 6 Resources, on-level practice, p. 142
Teacher One Stop™, on-level lesson plans
Holt Audio Library
Holt Audio Library: Selections and Summaries in Spanish
UA: Differentiating Instruction, graphic organizer, p. 296
UA: Supporting Instruction in Spanish, selection summary
ThinkCentral Online Assessment, Selection Standards Check

California Standards, pp. 1251–1255

- **Reading Standard 2.5** Analyze an author's implicit and explicit philosophical assumptions and beliefs about a subject.

Preteach

Introducing Vocabulary

Read the Vocabulary words and sample sentences aloud. Then, use this activity to check students' understanding.

1. Use an **epithet** to describe the weather.
2. Describe a situation that gives you a feeling of **impotence**.
3. Name a recent event that you reacted to with **fervor**.
4. Name someone or something you regard as an **inspiration**.
5. Name an animal with a **lethal** bite.
6. Describe a way to **quell** an argument between two people.
7. Explain a way you **deviate** from a popular trend.

English for Academic Success

Language Coach

Students may answer the question with words such as *inspire, inspiring, inspirational,* and *inspirationally.* Ask them to list words that relate to the rest of the Vocabulary words.

Informational Text/Writing Skills Focus

- Give students a copy of the Informational Text Focus graphic organizer before they read. (See **Unit 6 Resources.**) Tell them to use their responses to answer the questions on the Applying Your Skills page.
- As they read, have students record the transitional expressions that Szymborska uses in their **Reader/Writer Notebooks.** Students can use their notes to complete the Writing Skills Focus activity.

Learn It Online
Send students to **Word Watch** for audio pronunciations, synonyms and antonyms, and brief histories of word origins.

go.hrw.com H12-1251 Go

Teacher Preparation

Selection Summary

"The Poet and the World" is an excerpt from a 1996 speech about inspiration, a motivation, according to Szymborska, that grows from a continuous attitude of "I don't know." The poet admits that most people work simply to get by, but she acknowledges that much of the world's best work and art comes from a posture of not knowing. Innovators such as Madame Curie and Isaac Newton are prime examples, as are genuine poets. The world is an astonishing place, Szymborska writes. In the language of poetry, nothing is ordinary or usual, and every human existence is part of a "measureless theater" to which we each have a reserved ticket for a "laughably short" time.

Direct Teach

Think About/Talk About

Read with a Purpose Have students read the Read with a Purpose statement. Ask students to note examples of contributions poets make to the world.

SPEECH

from Nobel Lecture: The Poet and the World December 7, 1996

by **Wislawa Szymborska**

translated by **Stanislaw Baranczak** and **Clare Cavanagh**

Read with a Purpose

Read to discover the role Szymborska believes poets play in the world.

Build Background

In 1895, Swedish intellect Alfred Nobel signed a will leaving most of his estate to establish prizes given in physics, chemistry, peace, physiology or medicine, and literature (an award for economics was established in 1968). Szymborska was awarded the Nobel Prize in Literature in 1996 "for poetry that with ironic precision allows the historical and biographical context to come to light in fragments of human reality." She gave this lecture after receiving the prize.

London's City Hall illuminated with Wislawa Szymborska's poetry (2006) by Jenny Holzer.

Universal Access

English Learners

English for Academic Success Inform students that the phrase "I don't know" is repeatedly used throughout the poem to support the theme of Szymborska's speech. Inform students that the phrase is used both literally as a quote and figuratively as a symbol for the act of questioning the extent of one's own knowledge. Ask students to share a time when they had an "I don't know" moment.

Struggling Readers

Model for students how to analyze an author's beliefs. Direct them to the Problem question in their Informational Text Focus graphic organizer. Tell students that the speaker reveals in the third paragraph that those who claim to "know" and are satisfied with what they know pose "a legal threat to society." Thus, the speaker brings up the issue of failing to pursue knowledge; when knowledge stops people from continually questioning, life becomes uninspiring and loveless.

Inspiration is not the exclusive privilege of poets or artists. There is, there has been, there will always be a certain group of people whom inspiration visits. It's made up of all those who've consciously chosen their calling and do their job with love and imagination. It may include doctors, teachers, gardeners—I could list a hundred more professions. Their work becomes one continuous adventure as long as they manage to keep discovering new challenges in it. Difficulties and setbacks never quell their curiosity. A swarm of new questions emerges from every problem that they solve. Whatever inspiration is, it's born from a continuous "I don't know." Ⓐ

There aren't many such people. Most of the earth's inhabitants work to get by. They work because they have to. They didn't pick this or that kind of job out of passion; the circumstances of their lives did the choosing for them. Loveless work, boring work, work valued only because others haven't got even that much—this is one of the harshest human miseries. And there's no sign that coming centuries will produce any changes for the better as far as this goes.

And so, though I deny poets their monopoly on inspiration, I still place them in a select group of Fortune's darlings. Ⓑ

At this point, though, certain doubts may arise in my audience. All sorts of torturers, dictators, fanatics, and demagogues[1] struggling for power with a few loudly shouted slogans also enjoy their jobs, and they, too, perform their duties with inventive fervor. Well, yes; but they "know," and whatever they know is enough for them once and for all. They don't want to find out about anything else, since that might diminish the force of their arguments. But any knowledge that doesn't lead to new questions quickly dies out: it fails to maintain the temperature required for sustaining life. In the most extreme cases, cases well known from ancient and modern history, it even poses a lethal threat to society. Ⓒ

This is why I value that little phrase "I don't know" so highly. It's small, but it flies on mighty wings. It expands our lives to include spaces within us as well as the outer expanses in which our tiny Earth hangs suspended. If Isaac Newton had never said to himself, "I don't know," the apples in his little orchard might have dropped to the ground like hailstones, and at best he would have stooped to pick them up and gobble them with gusto. Had my compatriot Marie Sklodowska-

1. **demagogues:** leaders who try to gain power by appealing to people's emotions.

Ⓐ **Informational Focus** **Analyzing an Author's Beliefs** What main idea or belief does Szymborska express in this paragraph? How does repetition help convey the main belief?

Ⓑ **Informational Focus** **Analyzing an Author's Beliefs** What is Szymborska's evaluation of poets?

Ⓒ **Informational Focus** **Analyzing an Author's Beliefs** What tone does Szymborska adopt toward "dictators, fanatics, and demagogues"? How does this tone reflect her beliefs?

Vocabulary **inspiration** (ihn spuh RAY shuhn) *n.:* influence of thought and strong feelings on actions, especially good actions.
quell (kwehl) *v.:* bring under control by subduing.
fervor (FUR vuhr) *n.:* intense emotion.
lethal (LEE thuhl) *adj.:* deadly.

Advanced Learners

Enrichment Have students find Harold Pinter's Nobel Lecture speech titled "Art, Truth, Politics." Ask students to read through the speech and look for details that express Pinter's view of a poet's role in the world. Remind them that the British poet Percy Bysshe Shelley claimed that poets are the unacknowledged legislators of the world. Have students compare and contrast the beliefs of Pinter and Szymborska based on their statements in their respective Nobel Lectures.

Students with Disabilities

Have students think about a time when admitting, "I don't know," led them to learn something new or gain a fresh perspective. Perhaps it was looking up the definition of an unfamiliar vocabulary word, asking a question in class, or consulting a friend for an opinion. Then, have students think of a time when they were reluctant to admit, "I don't know." What consequences did they face by not asking questions or seeking answers? Ask students if they agree with Szymborska that the phrase "I don't know" should be valued in our culture.

Think About/Talk About

Analysis

Ⓐ Informational Focus

Possible response: *Inspiration does not come only to artists, but to all those people who perform their jobs with curiosity and imagination. Their work becomes an adventure because they are always discovering new challenges. Their inspiration comes from their curiosity, from always saying, "I don't know."*

Ⓑ Informational Focus

Possible response: *Poets are within the select group of people who are inspired when they work.*

Ⓒ Informational Focus

Possible response: *She sees the limitations in the slogans and fervor of dictators, demagogues, and people like them. She puts them down because they lack curiosity and do not want to see any side of an issue but their own. This leads to their demise.*

Vocabulary: Own the Word

- **inspiration:** Tell students that the root word for *inspiration* is *inspirare,* which is Latin for "breathe into." The word was originally used to mean, "to impart or breathe an idea into someone." Ask students to describe things that give them *inspiration.*
- **quell:** Tell students that *quell* means "to suppress or defeat" and an antonym is *stimulate.* Have students use both words in a sentence. ***Possible response:*** *Reading can stimulate the imagination, but fatigue can very easily quell the urge to read.*
- **fervor:** Ask students: Why might you perform a task with *fervor*? How might you perform a task with *fervor*? Then, ask one student to demonstrate completing a task with *fervor.*
- **lethal:** Ask students to complete the sentence: According to the author, knowledge that does not lead to new questions is *lethal* to society because . . . ***Possible response:*** *it means that society will not continue its advance.*

Think About/Talk About

Analysis

D Informational Focus

Possible response: *Her belief is that astonishment is a state in its own right.*

E Informational Focus

Possible response: *Poets are among "Fortune's darlings" because, unlike most people, they work with passion and inventive fervor. Thus, the fortunate few will have explored all the "astonishing" things that exist in the world, for the benefit of those who cannot.*

Vocabulary: Own the Word

- **impotence:** Tell students that the roots for *impotence* come from Latin. The prefix *im–* is related to *in–*, which means "not," and *potens* which means 'potent' or powerful. *Impotence* is "powerlessness." Ask students to explain what might cause a poet to feel *impotence*.
- **epithet:** Explain that an *epithet* is a short description, a label, or a kind of nickname. Why does the author consider the word "astonishing" an epithet?" ***Possible response:*** *It acts as a short answer, but it does not really capture what is being said.*
- **deviate:** Tell students that *deviate* means "to depart from or differ from" and an antonym is to *stick to*. Use both words in a sentence: I usually stick to the basics at breakfast with cereal and juice, but today I decided to *deviate* and eat eggs.

Curie never said to herself, "I don't know," she probably would have wound up teaching chemistry at some private high school for young ladies from good families and ended her days performing this otherwise perfectly respectable job. But she kept on saying, "I don't know," and these words led her, not just once but twice, to Stockholm, where restless, questing spirits are occasionally rewarded with the Nobel Prize.

Poets, if they're genuine, must also keep repeating, "I don't know." Each poem marks an effort to answer this statement, but as soon as the final period hits the page, the poet begins to hesitate, starts to realize that this particular answer was pure makeshift, absolutely inadequate. So the poets keep on trying, and sooner or later the consecutive results of their self-dissatisfaction are clipped together with a giant paperclip by literary historians and called their "oeuvres."[2]...

The world—whatever we might think when we're terrified by its vastness and our own impotence or when we're embittered by its indifference to individual suffering, of people, animals, and perhaps even plants (for why are we so sure that plants feel no pain?); whatever we might think of its expanses pierced by the rays of stars surrounded by planets we've just begun to discover, planets already dead, still dead, we just don't know; whatever we might think of this measureless theater to which we've got reserved tickets, but tickets whose lifespan is laughably short, bounded as it is by two arbitrary dates; whatever else we might think of this world—it is astonishing.

But "astonishing" is an epithet concealing a logical trap. We're astonished, after all, by things that deviate from some well-known and universally acknowledged norm, from an obviousness to which we've grown accustomed. But the point is, there is no such obvious world. Our astonishment exists per se, and it isn't based on a comparison with something else. **D**

Granted, in daily speech, where we don't stop to consider every word, we all use phrases such as "the ordinary world," "ordinary life," "the ordinary course of events." But in the language of poetry, where every word is weighed, nothing is usual or normal. Not a single stone and not a single cloud above it. Not a single day and not a single night after it. And above all, not a single existence, not anyone's existence in this world.

It looks as though poets will always have their work cut out for them. **E**

2. **oeuvres** (UHR vruhz): the collected life works of artists.

D Informational Focus **Analyzing an Author's Beliefs** What belief about the world does Szymborska elaborate through the analysis of the word *astonishing*?

E Informational Focus **Analyzing an Author's Beliefs** How does this belief compare to her previous statement about poets being "Fortune's darlings"? Explain.

Vocabulary **impotence** (IHM puh tuhns) *n.:* helplessness.
epithet (EHP uh theht) *n:.* descriptive expression.
deviate (DEE vee ayt) *v.:* turn aside from a way, norm, or truth.

California Standards, p. 1255

- **Reading Standard 2.5** Analyze an author's implicit and explicit philosophical assumptions and beliefs about a subject.
- **Writing Standard 1.1** Demonstrate an understanding of the elements of discourse (e.g., purpose, speaker, audience, form) when completing narrative, expository, persuasive, or descriptive writing assignments.
- **Writing Standard 1.3** Structure ideas and arguments in a sustained, persuasive, and sophisticated way and support them with precise and relevant examples.
- **Writing Standard 2.2** Write responses to literature: **a.** Demonstrate a comprehensive understanding of the significant ideas in works or passages. **b.** Analyze the use of imagery, language, universal themes, and unique aspects of the text. **c.** Support important ideas and viewpoints through accurate and detailed references to the text and to other works.
- **Listening and Speaking Standard 2.1** Deliver reflective presentations: **a.** Explore the significance of personal experiences, events, conditions, or concerns, using appropriate rhetorical strategies (e.g., narration, description, exposition, persuasion).

Universal Access

AAVE Students Who Use African American Vernacular English

English for Academic Success Read aloud the following sentence from the speech "Our astonishment exists per se, and it isn't based on a comparison with something else." Point out the author's use of the contraction *isn't*. Tell students that in informal English, some might be tempted to use *ain't* instead of *isn't*. Explain to students that *ain't* is considered to be nonstandard English and should not be used in formal speech or writing. Have students practice forming negative statements using *isn't*.

INFORMATIONAL TEXT FOCUS

Applying Your Skills

Reading Standard 2.5 (see pages A48–A50)
Listening and Speaking Standard 2.1a (see pages A53–A55)
Writing Standard 1.1, 1.3, 2.2a–c (see pages A51–A52)

from Nobel Lecture: The Poet and the World

Analyze Informational Texts

Informational Text Focus

Quick Check

1. How are the people the poet describes in the first paragraph different from those she describes in the second? What does she say is "one of the harshest human miseries"?
2. What counterargument to her ideas does the poet raise in the fourth paragraph? Summarize her response to the counterargument.

Read with a Purpose

3. According to Szymborska, how does knowledge endure?

Informational Skills: Analyzing an Author's Beliefs

4. Add another column to your chart, and draw **inferences,** or educated guesses based on what you have read and what you already know, about the author's beliefs.

Vocabulary Check

Match each Vocabulary word with its definition.

5. inspiration	a. bring under control
6. quell	b. helplessness
7. fervor	c. descriptive expression
8. lethal	d. turn aside
9. impotence	e. deadly
10. epithet	f. intense emotion
11. deviate	g. motivation

Text Analysis

12. **Interpret** What does Szymborska mean by the phrase "Fortune's darlings" (page 1253)?
13. **Analyze** Szymborska reveals extraordinary truths while speaking of everyday things. Why might it be important for a poet to recognize "nothing is usual or normal" (page 1254)?
14. **Compare and Contrast** What can be the difference between people who say, "I don't know" and people who say, "I know"? Why can "knowing" be negative and, at times, even deadly, according to Szymborska?
15. **Make Judgments** Do you agree with Szymborska's opinion of the phrases "I don't know" and "I know"? What exceptions might you make?
16. **Analyze** Szymborska says the world is "astonishing" (page 1254). How might viewing the world in this way lead to inspiration? What everyday elements of the world do you find astonishing?

Listening and Speaking

17. **Extend** Research a question or subject that inspires you or stimulates your curiosity. Prepare an oral presentation for your classmates about your thoughts and discoveries. Your presentation may be a report, story, poem, or discussion.

Writing Skills Focus

Timed Writing Do you agree with Szymborska that work should be inspiring? In your *Reader/Writer Notebook,* write two short paragraphs that express your opinion. Use transitions to connect your ideas.

What Do You Think Now? How does Szymborska's experience as a poet affect how she sees the world?

Universal Access

Struggling Writers

Students may need additional scaffolding to complete the Writing Skills Focus activity. Some students may struggle to write paragraphs that express their opinion and includes transitions. Have students write down three main points that state why they agree or disagree with Szymborska. Ask students to write three or four sentences elaborating on those points. Then, have students weave their sentences into a paragraph and add word that help each main point flow smoothly to the next.

What Do You Think Now?

Inform students that as a poet, Szymborska very likely approaches the world with the passion and inventive fervor that she describes in the speech. Her insights into the character of Lot's wife demonstrate her curiosity and her approach. If she had never said to herself, "I don't know," she never would have wondered what was going on in Lot's wife's mind as she fled Sodom. Have students suggest other "I don't know" experiences Szymborska may have had in her life.

Check for Understanding

Independent Practice

Informational Text Focus

Possible responses:

1. *The first paragraph describes the artist; the second paragraph describes the average person. "One of the harshest human miseries" is boring, meaningless work.*
2. *The counterargument is that "all sorts of torturers, dictators, fanatics, and demagogues" also work with "inventive fervor." However, these people are not open to disagreement or opposition.*
3. *Knowledge endures because people continuously admit, "I don't know" and explore things beyond their usual frame of reference.*
4. *Have students make educated assumptions about the author's beliefs.*

Vocabulary Check

5. *g* **6.** *a*
7. *f* **8.** *e*
9. *b* **10.** *c*
11. *d*

Text Analysis

Possible responses:

12. *People lucky enough to lead creative lives are "Fortune's darlings."*
13. *"Usual" and "normal" are subjective terms, and to be truthful a poet must be objective.*
14. *People who "know" only accept things that confirm their beliefs. Those who "don't know" are open to all ideas. "Knowing" can be deadly because it thwarts the expansion of knowledge and acceptance of new ideas.*
15. *Students may value defending one's belief-driven position (political, religious, or scientific) against all opponents rather than being as open as Szymborska recommends.*
16. *If the world is "astonishing," then there is a constant source of inspiration for creative projects.*
17. *Presentations should reflect adequate and insightful research.*

Standards Focus

Objectives

Students will understand refrain.

Selection Introduction

Think About the Writer

Invite students to think about how the childhood of a person who was abandoned by a parent or guardian might differ from that of someone who grew up with both his or her parents or guardians.

For Independent Reading

- *The Member of the Wedding,* Carson McCullers
- *Daughter of the Sea,* Berlie Doherty

Motivate

What Do You Think?/QuickWrite

Have students try to put themselves in an adult family member's shoes as they think about their fears for themselves or for their children. Have them record their thoughts in their **Reader/Writer Notebooks.**

English for Academic Success

Academic Vocabulary

Look for opportunities to use the Academic Vocabulary word in this unit.

- **perspective,** ***n.:*** a particular way of looking at something

California Standards, pp. 1256–1259

- **Reading Standard 3.3** Analyze the ways in which irony, tone, mood, the author's style, and the "sound" of language achieve specific rhetorical or aesthetic purposes or both.

Preparing to Read

Fear

What Do You Think? How does experience shape our view of the world?

QuickWrite

What mixed emotions might parents have as a child grows up? What fears might they have for their children and themselves? In your *Reader/Writer Notebook,* write a paragraph explaining your thoughts.

Chilean poet and Nobel Prize winner Gabriela Mistral (1945).

MEET THE WRITER

Gabriela Mistral

(1889–1957)

Nobel Prize WINNER

In 1945, Gabriela Mistral became the first female poet and the first Latin American to win the Nobel Prize in Literature. She was of Spanish, Basque, and Indian heritage.

An Angel in the Wind

Mistral was born Lucilla Godoy Alcayaga in the village of Vicuna, Chile, high in the Andes Mountains. Her father, a schoolteacher and poet, abandoned the family when she was a small child. He left his daughter a garden, in which Mistral, as her mother remembers, sat and conversed with the birds and the trees. At the age of fifteen, Mistral began teaching school but continued to pursue a literary career and published poems under a variety of different names. In 1913, she settled on the pen name Gabriela Mistral. The first part of her pen name refers to the archangel Gabriel; the second part refers to the cold, dry *mistral,* a wind that blows across southern France.

Mistral wrote much of her early poetry in response to the suicide of a man she loved and to whom she had been engaged to marry. She received worldwide attention when Federico de Onis, a Spanish professor at Columbia University in New York "discovered" and published her poetry.

Poet and Activist

Mistral continued to write poetry while working as a principal and, later, as an international ambassador. In the 1920s, she helped reorganize the rural school systems of Mexico; and in the 1930s, she served as Chile's cultural representative to the League of Nations. After World War II, Mistral acted as the Chilean consul in Los Angeles and Italy. She was also a delegate to a United Nations subcommittee on women's rights. On her frequent trips back to Chile, Mistral was often greeted by thousands of schoolchildren singing her poems. When she received the Nobel Prize in Literature, she remarked, with a characteristically good-humored perspective, that she must have been voted in by women and children.

Think About the Writer How do you think the experiences of Mistral's childhood might have inspired her later works?

Selection Readability	
Easily Accessible **Accessible** Challenging	common theme; familiar syntax; accessible vocabulary

Reading Standard 3.3 (see pages A48–A50)

Literary Skills Focus

Refrain A **refrain** is a repeated word, phrase, line, or group of lines. Refrains are commonly used in poetry and sung to create **rhythm,** build suspense, and emphasize important words or ideas. Although they usually occur at the end of a stanza, refrains can appear elsewhere. As you read "Fear," note the location of the refrain and how often it is repeated. What effect does the refrain create?

Writing Skills Focus

Think as a Reader/Writer

Find It in Your Reading Poets use **refrains** and organizational structure to give their poems a songlike quality to help their readers "hear" and "feel" the rhythm and music of the poem. The cause-effect structure of Mistral's poem "Fear" supports the speaker's use of three scenarios where she loses her beloved child, the essence of every parent's fear. Each possibility grows more devastating than the one preceding it. In your *Reader/Writer Notebook,* use a graphic organizer like the below to record the cause of her fear: the transformation, the images that describe it, and the feared result of each imagined transformation. Note how the cause-effect structure is repeated in each stanza.

Stanza	Transformation	Images	Effect
1	a swallow	"fly far away . . . nest in the eaves"	could not comb her hair
2	a princess	"tiny golden slippers"	could never sleep by her side
3			

Reader/Writer Notebook

Use your **RWN** to complete the activities for this selection.

Language Coach

Connotations Good writers choose words with certain **connotations,** the emotions, ideas, and even specific images a word evokes. With a partner, discuss the thoughts, feelings, ideas, or images that come to mind when you read the following words. Think in particular of how this collection of words calls to mind fairy tales you have read.

swallow	straw bed
princess	glass slipper
queen	throne

Learn It Online

Hear this poem read aloud online.

go.hrw.com H12-1257 Go

Preteach

English for Academic Success

Language Coach

As students discuss the listed words, their associations will vary. Students may connect the words to the following fairy tales: *swallow*—Thumbelina; *straw bed*—Cinderella; *princess*—The Princess and the Pea; *glass slipper*—Cinderella; *queen*—The Snow Queen; *throne*—The Fisherman and His Wife.

Literary Skills Focus

As you read and discuss the poem with students, have them look for the refrain in each stanza and note its frequency and effect on the poem.

Writing Skills Focus

Give students a copy of the Writing Skills Focus graphic organizer. (See **Unit 6 Resources.**) As they read, have students record in their graphic organizer the images describing the speaker's fear and ask them to note the cause-effect structure throughout the poem. Students can use their notes to complete the Writing Skills Focus activity.

Learn It Online

The online version of this poem includes audio support to engage all students and to help struggling readers with reading comprehension and vocabulary.

go.hrw.com H12-1257 Go

Selection Resources

Unit 6 Resources, on-level practice and assessment, p. 147

Teacher One Stop™, on-level lesson plans and all print resources

Holt Audio Library

Holt Audio Library: Selections and Summaries in Spanish

UA: Differentiating Instruction, graphic organizer, p. 296

UA: Supporting Instruction in Spanish, selection summary

ThinkCentral Online Assessment, Selection Standards Check

ThinkCentral Online Remediation

Teacher Preparation
Selection Summary
The speaker does not want "them" to turn her daughter into a swallow, which would fly away. She does not want her daughter to become a princess because she would never sleep next to her mother again. Above all, she does not want her daughter to become a queen on a throne because her mother could never see her again.

Direct Teach

Think About/Talk About
Read with a Purpose Have students read the Read with a Purpose statement. Have students discuss the characteristics of a mother-daughter relationship.

Analysis
A Literary Focus

Possible response: *She repeats "I don't want them to turn / my little girl into a swallow." The repetition creates a songlike effect, making the poem sound like a sad lullaby.*

B Literary Focus

Possible response: *The refrain creates progression from "swallow" to "princess" to "queen," which suggests the process of growing up.*

California Standards, p. 1259
- **Reading Standard 3.2** Analyze the way in which the theme or meaning of a selection represents a view or comment on life, using textual evidence to support the claim.
- **Reading Standard 3.3** Analyze the ways in which irony, tone, mood, the author's style, and the "sound" of language achieve specific rhetorical or aesthetic purposes or both.
- **Writing Standard 2.3** Write reflective compositions: **a.** Explore the significance of personal experiences, events, conditions, or concerns by using rhetorical strategies (e.g., narration, description, exposition, persuasion).

POEM

Fear

by **Gabriela Mistral**

translated by **Doris Dana**

Read with a Purpose
Read to discover how a mother feels about her daughter growing up.

Build Background
When Mistral won the Nobel Prize in Literature, she was called "the poet of motherhood by adoption" because of her great love for and commitment to children. This love is reflected in much of her writing, as in the poem you are about to read.

I don't want them to turn
my little girl into a swallow.
She would fly far away into the sky
and never fly again to my straw bed,
or she would nest in the eaves
where I could not comb her hair.
I don't want them to turn
my little girl into a swallow. **A**

I don't want them to make
my little girl a princess.
In tiny golden slippers
how could she play on the meadow?
And when night came, no longer
would she sleep at my side.
I don't want them to make
my little girl a princess.

And even less do I want them
one day to make her queen.
They would put her on a throne
where I could not go to see her.
And when nighttime came
I could never rock her . . .
I don't want them to make
my little girl a queen! **B**

A **Literary Focus** **Refrain** What words does the speaker repeat? What is the effect of this repetition?

B **Literary Focus** **Refrain** What effect does the refrain have at the end of the poem? What thoughts or emotions does it elicit?

Märchenprinzessin mit Fächer (Fairy Tale Princess with Fan) (1912) by Alexej van Jawlensky. Museum Ludwig, Köln/Artists Rights Society (ARS), NY/VG, Bildkunst, Bonn.

Universal Access

EL English Learners
English for Academic Success Be sure that students recognize that "them," an unidentified group, has no antecedent in the poem. Help students see that by leaving the identity of "them" vague, the poem makes "them" seem less like actual people and more like some inevitable process or unstoppable force.

✔ See the **English Language Skill Builder** in **UA: Differentiating Instruction.**

Reading Standard 3.2, 3.3 (see pages A48–A50)
Writing Standard 2.3a (see pages A51–A52)

Fear

Literary Response and Analysis

Reading Skills Focus

Quick Check

1. What does the image of a "straw bed" suggest about the social and economic situation of the speaker? What else might the image suggest?
2. In the second stanza, the speaker evokes the image of "tiny golden slippers… on the meadow" as incongruous or out of place. In what other way would the slippers be incongruous in the situation?
3. Why do you think the speaker moves from the image of a bird to a princess to a queen in the poem?

Read with a Purpose

4. How do negatives words such as *don't, never,* and *not* emphasize the mother's feelings?

Literary Skills Focus

Literary Analysis

5. **Interpret** A swallow is a bird that migrates, usually nesting in widely separated summer and winter regions. Given this information, why do you think Mistral uses the specific image of a swallow rather than simply any bird?
6. **Infer** Why do you think the speaker fears that she could no longer see her own daughter if her daughter were made a queen? (In your answer, consider the connotations of the words *queen* and *throne.*)
7. **Analyze** What is ironic about a mother's fear that her daughter will become a "queen," that is, someone who lives a life untouched by common cares and daily concerns?
8. **Make Judgments** Why do you think this poem is titled "Fear"? Does the poem match your idea of what the topic of a poem with this title would be? Explain.
9. **Extend** We are not told who the *them* of the poem are. Who do you think they are? Would the emotional impact of the poem be increased or reduced if the speaker identified *them*? Explain your response.

Literary Skills: Refrain

10. **Analyze** Remember that a **refrain** is a repeated word, phrase, line, or group of lines. Identify the refrain in the poem. Explain how the refrain helps reveal the speaker's emotional state.

Literary Skills Review: Theme

11. **Interpret** The central idea or message of a literary work is referred to as **theme.** In one sentence, state the theme of the poem. What comment on life does this theme make?

Writing Skills Focus

Think as a Reader/Writer

Use It in Your Writing Using the images in Mistral's poem as a guide, write a brief essay describing something or someone you are afraid of losing. (If you prefer, write about someone else's fears.) Consider what words or phrases you can use to help your reader "see" the images in your essay. If you choose, use a refrain to add a musical quality to your essay.

What Do You Think Now?

What experiences might have shaped the mother's fears? What advice would you give to her?

Universal Access

Struggling Writers

Students may need additional scaffolding to complete the Writing Skills Focus activity. Help students think about the theme of personal loss—their own or someone else's. Have them think of one central image that could symbolize their fear associated with the loss. Then, have students list characteristics of the image that correspond with their fear. Ask students to include those characteristics in a short essay.

What Do You Think Now?

As a class, discuss the mother's fears and anxieties. Are her fears justified? Are her anxieties reasonable? Have students think about how a mother's own experiences during childhood might affect her relationship with her daughter.

Assess

Unit 6 Resources,
Selection Standards Check, p. 149

Check for Understanding

Independent Practice

Reading Skills Focus

Possible responses:

1. *It suggests the speaker is poor or lives in a rural setting. It could also suggest the simple, intimate bond between mother and child.*
2. *Gold slippers might be incongruous in a poor, rural community.*
3. *The images suggest the process of growing up.*
4. *The mother fears that changes in her daughter's life will create barriers between them.*

Literary Skills Focus

Possible responses:

5. *The swallow's long migratory journey would suggest a wide gap between mother and daughter.*
6. *The social gap between a poor mother and a royal daughter would be unbridgeable.*
7. *It is ironic that the mother is more concerned about what the loss will mean to her than what the success will mean to her daughter.*
8. *Rather than describing the fear, the poem represents the mother's attempt, probably futile, to keep her fears at bay.*
9. *The "them" in the poem might be the forces that cause a child to grow away from his or her parents. The emotional power of the poem would be reduced if the speaker identified "them," because a faceless enemy is more menacing than one who is identified.*
10. *The core of the refrain is "I don't want them to. . . ." The repetition creates the effect of an incantation, as if the speaker, unable to stop the separation process in any other way, is repeating a prayer to keep her child with her. It gives the poem a childlike tone.*
11. *The theme is that parents sometimes find it hard to accept a child's growing up. Family and the outside world exert competing forces.*

Standards Focus

Objectives

Students will understand metaphor.

Selection Introduction

Think About the Writer

Have students think about common themes in poetry to which most people can relate.

For Independent Reading

Tomorrowland: Ten Stories About the Future, Michael Cart

Motivate

What Do You Think?/QuickWrite

Before they write, have students think about the power of romantic love and familial love, including paternal, maternal, and fraternal love. Have them consider how each one shapes us in different ways. Tell them to record their thoughts in their **Reader/Writer Notebooks.**

English for Academic Success

Academic Vocabulary

Look for opportunities to use the Academic Vocabulary word in this unit.

- **perspective,** ***n.:*** a particular way of looking at something

California Standards, pp. 1260–1263

- **Reading Standard 3.4** Analyze ways in which poets use imagery, personification, figures of speech, and sounds to evoke readers' emotions.

Preparing to Read

Sonnet 79 / Soneto 79

What Do You Think? How does experience shape our view of the world?

QuickWrite

In what ways does love empower us? In your *Reader/Writer Notebook,* record notes on your responses to this question.

Nobel Prize winning poet Pablo Neruda (1971).

MEET THE WRITER

Pablo Neruda

(1904–1973)

Nobel Prize WINNER

"Poetry is like bread," Neruda said, "and it must be shared by everyone, the men of letters and the peasants, by everyone in our vast, incredible, extraordinary family of man."

Poetry Is a Gift

When the Chilean poet Pablo Neruda was a boy searching for "creaturely things" behind his house, he saw a child's hand poking through a hole in the fence, offering him a toy sheep made of real wool. Thrilled, Neruda raced home to return with his most treasured possession, a fragrant pine cone, which he dropped through the hole for the unseen friend. Neruda often related this incident. From his perspective, poetry was a gift to be shared with the world—a gift that always brought something in return.

Neruda became a poet when he was still a teenager in Temuco, a frontier town in southern Chile. Born Neftali Ricardo Reyes Basoalto, Neruda adopted his pen name to avoid upsetting his father, a railroad worker who frowned on his son's poetic ambitions. A bohemian in black clothing, Neruda was only twenty years old when he published a collection of love poems that eventually sold two million copies worldwide.

The Poet as Protester

Neruda's serious involvement with politics began when he was appointed to the diplomatic service. As consul in Spain, Neruda became close friends with the Spanish poet Federico García Lorca. When García Lorca was murdered by Fascist forces in the Spanish Civil War, Neruda joined the Communist Party and wrote letters attacking Chile's repressive government. In 1946, he was accused of treason and forced to flee his homeland. Neruda returned to Chile in 1952 and began writing *Elementary Odes* (1954), poems in praise of simple things from socks to onions. In 1959, returning to his earlier themes of love and nature, he wrote *One Hundred Love Poems* for his wife, Matilde Urrutia. Neruda won the Nobel Prize in Literature in 1971.

Think About the Writer If Neruda believed that poetry should "be shared by everyone," what would you predict would be the topics of his poems?

Selection Readability	
Easily Accessible **Accessible** Challenging	accessible theme; familiar syntax; accessible vocabulary

Reading Standard 3.4 (see pages A48–A50)

Literary Skills Focus

Metaphor Poets use **metaphors** to make imaginative comparisons between two basically unlike things. Because they can suggest much more than literal statements, metaphors are very useful in writing. Most metaphors are visual and convey strong emotion. For example, in the English translation of the first line of this sonnet, the speaker asks his love to "tie your heart to mine." The rope is a metaphor for love; both things tie two people together. In Spanish, the line reads "amarra tu corazón al mío." The verb *amarrar* in Spanish can specifically refer to mooring a boat to some safe harbor. Neruda could therefore be comparing his lover's heart to a boat that is moored or tied up safely alongside his heart. Note the visual picture that the metaphor creates in your mind and how the image makes you feel.

If you fail to understand a poet's metaphors, you have missed an important part of the poem. Sometimes metaphors are complex, and several interpretations are possible. When you encounter a complex metaphor, talk about it with a classmate. Discussing poetry and solving its puzzles are part of the pleasure of reading it.

Writing Skills Focus

Think as a Reader/Writer

Find It in Your Reading Poets use comparisons to help their readers see the world in new and imaginative ways. In a **simile,** the poet compares two unlike things using a specific word of comparison, such as *like* or *as.* In a **metaphor,** the poet directly identifies two unlike things without the use of *like* or *as.* In your *Reader/Writer Notebook,* use a chart like the one below to record the metaphors and similes you find in Neruda's poem. See if you can name the two things that are being compared. Then, briefly note how you think those things are similar.

Stanza	Simile/Metaphor	What is being compared?	How are they similar?

Reader/Writer Notebook

Use your **RWN** to complete the activities for this selection.

Vocabulary

punctual (PUHNGK choo uhl) *adj.:* prompt; on time. *The poet says that sleep is as punctual as a train.*

constancy (KAHN stuhn see) *n.:* faithfulness; loyalty. *The speaker tells of the constancy that he finds in his lover's heart.*

Language Coach

Synonyms Words with the same or nearly the same meanings are called **synonyms.** In the definitions above, the word *prompt* is a synonym for *punctual,* and the words *faithfulness* and *loyalty* are synonyms for *constancy.* When writers translate a poem from one language to another, they must be aware of the slight differences in meanings among synonyms. They must choose the word that best matches the word in the original language. Neruda's translator uses *punctual* and *constancy* for the Spanish words *puntualidad* and *tenacidad.* If you speak Spanish or have access to a Spanish-English dictionary, look up the Spanish words *puntualidad* and *tenacidad.* Do you think the translator used the best English synonyms in his translation?

Learn It Online

Learn more about Neruda online at the Writers' Lives site.

go.hrw.com H12-1261 Go

Selection Resources

Unit 6 Resources, on-level practice and assessment, p. 147

Teacher One Stop™, on-level lesson plans and all print resources

Holt Audio Library

Holt Audio Library: Selections and Summaries in Spanish

UA: Supporting Instruction in Spanish, selection summary

ThinkCentral Online Assessment, Selection Standards Check

ThinkCentral Online Remediation

Preteach

Introducing Vocabulary

- Review the Vocabulary words, definitions, and sentences with students.
- To reinforce the importance of the Vocabulary words, ask whether a *punctual* response to a loved one's distress is a sign of *constancy.*

English for Academic Success

Language Coach

Ask students to look up the definition of *faithfulness* and discuss differences in meaning between this word and the word *constancy.* [*Constancy implies an unchanging mind in any circumstance, while* faithfulness *is usually associated with staying true to people or promises.*]

Literary Skills Focus

As you read and discuss the poem with students, have them note any metaphors that they find unclear or confusing.

Writing Skills Focus

Give students a copy of the Writing Skills Focus graphic organizer before they read. (See **Unit 6 Resources.**) As they read, have students record the metaphors and similes that Neruda weaves into the fabric of the poem in their graphic organizer. Students can use their notes to complete the Writing Skills Focus activity.

Learn It Online

The **Writers' Lives** feature of the Interactive Student Edition offers additional information about this author. Audio or video segments are provided for some authors.

go.hrw.com H12-1261 Go

Teacher Preparation

Selection Summary

The speaker of "Sonnet 79" begins by asking his love to "tie" her heart to his. He goes on to evoke, by means of surreal images, the fearful mystery of night and sleep. He also suggests that love—specifically his love—can connect him "to a purer motion," a "constancy" that answers questions and unlocks doors.

Direct Teach

Think About/Talk About

Read with a Purpose Have students read the Read with a Purpose statement. Point out the word *accomplish*. Ask students to consider how love can be capable of accomplishing something.

Analysis

Ⓐ Literary Focus

Possible response: *"Night travel" may refer to where we go in our dreams or in our subconscious.*

Ⓑ Literary Focus

Possible response: *He compares her heartbeat, "the constancy that beats in [her] chest," to the beating of the wings of a swan underwater.*

Vocabulary: Own the Word

- **punctual:** Ask students to applaud to indicate the degree to which they would like to be described as *punctual*. ***Possible response:*** *Students applaud strongly and explain that they would want to be thought of as punctual or prompt and on time.*
- **constancy:** Tell students that *constant* is the adjective form of *constancy*. *Constant* means "steady or regular" and also "loyal and devoted." A *constant* friend is one who stays with you throughout all situations. Ask students to name animals that are known for their *constancy*.

SONNET

Read with a Purpose
Read this poem to discover what the speaker believes love can accomplish.

Build Background
Sonnet 79 comes from Neruda's book *One Hundred Love Poems.* The book is divided into four parts (morning, afternoon, evening, and night), each corresponding to a different stage in a person's life. As you read Sonnet 79, think about to which stage of life it refers.

Sonnet 79

by **Pablo Neruda**
translated by **Stephen Tapscott**

By night, Love, tie your heart to mine, and the two
together in their sleep will defeat the darkness
like a double drum in the forest, pounding
against the thick wall of wet leaves.

Night travel: black flame of sleep
that snips the threads of the earth's grapes,
punctual as a headlong train that would haul
shadows and cold rocks, endlessly. Ⓐ

Because of this, Love, tie me to a purer motion,
to the constancy that beats in your chest
with the wings of a swan underwater, Ⓑ

so that our sleep might answer all the sky's
starry questions with a single key,
with a single door the shadows had closed.

Soneto 79

De noche, amada, amarra tu corazón al mío
y que ellos en el sueño derroten las tinieblas
como un doble tambor combatiendo en el bosque
contra el espeso muro de las hojas mojadas.

Nocturna travesía, brasa negra del sueño
interceptando el hilo de las uvas terrestres
con la puntualidad de un tren descabellado
que sombra y piedras frías sin cesar arrastrara.

Por eso, amor, amárrame al movimiento puro,
a la tenacidad que en tu pecho golpea
con las alas de un cisne sumergido,

para que a las preguntas estrelladas del cielo
responda nuestro sueño con una sola llave,
con una sola puerta cerrada por la sombra.

Ⓐ **Literary Focus** **Metaphor** To what does the metaphor "Night travel" refer?

Ⓑ **Literary Focus** **Metaphor** What is being compared to the "wings of a swan"?

Vocabulary **punctual** (PUHNGK choo uhl) *adj.:* prompt; on time. **constancy** (KAHN stuhn see) *n.:* faithfulness; loyalty.

California Standards, p. 1263

- **Reading Standard 3.1** Analyze characteristics of subgenres (e.g., satire, parody, allegory, pastoral) that are used in poetry, prose, plays, novels, short stories, essays, and other basic genres.
- **Reading Standard 3.4** Analyze ways in which poets use imagery, personification, figures of speech, and sounds to evoke readers' emotions.
- **Writing Standard 1.4** Enhance meaning by employing rhetorical devices, including the extended use of parallelism, repetition, and analogy; the incorporation of visual aids (e.g., graphs, tables, pictures); and the issuance of a call for action.

Reading Standard 3.1, 3.4 (see pages A48–A50)
Writing Standard 1.4 (see pages A51–A52)

Sonnet 79 / Soneto 79

Literary Response and Analysis

Reading Skills Focus

Quick Check

1. In line 2, what does the speaker say he and his love will do together?
2. In lines 12–14, what does the speaker say their sleep will accomplish?

Read with a Purpose

3. How can love do things that seem impossible?

Vocabulary Check

Answer the following questions about each Vocabulary word.

4. Antonyms are words with opposite meanings. Which of the following words is an antonym for the word ***punctual?***
   - **a.** tidy
   - **b.** late
   - **c.** prompt
   - **d.** suitable
5. Which of the following words is an antonym for the word ***constancy?***
   - **a.** fickleness
   - **b.** steadiness
   - **c.** devotion
   - **d.** love

Literary Skills Focus

Literary Analysis

6. **Evaluate** Explain the extended simile in lines 2–4. How does this comparison make you feel?
7. **Make Judgments** What do you think are the "sky's / starry questions" in lines 12–13?
8. **Evaluate** Work with a classmate who speaks or reads Spanish, and evaluate the effectiveness and accuracy of the English translation. (For example, what do you think of the translation of "brasa negra" in line 5 as "black flame"?)
9. **Hypothesize** Why is the speaker so fearful of "the darkness"?
10. **Extend** What do you think of the idea that love completes people—that it unites them so that they can be one person? In what other poems in this book have you encountered this idea?

Literary Skills: Metaphor

11. **Analyze** On what comparison is the extended metaphor in line 5–8 based? What images does this metaphor call to mind?

Literary Skills Review: Petrarchan Sonnet

12. **Make Judgments** Although this sonnet follows the form of the **Petrarchan sonnet** (see page 267), it does not follow its traditional rhyme scheme. Neruda's nontraditional sonnet does, however, contain the abrupt turn of thought of the classic sonnet. Where do you think the change, or turn, occurs in Sonnet 79?

Writing Skills Focus

Think as a Reader/Writer

Use It in Your Writing Write a brief poem or paragraph in which you use at least two **metaphors** or **similes** to describe something the way Neruda describes love, sleep, and death—perhaps something like hope, joy, or fear. One way to begin is to identify the emotion directly with something concrete. For example, you might write, "Hope is…" or "Joy is…" Try to use metaphors or similes that create vivid images and express strong feelings.

What Do You Think Now? Do you agree with the speaker that "tying" your heart to another person can protect you and possibly conquer fears of death?

Check for Understanding

Independent Practice

Reading Skills Focus

Possible responses:

1. *Together, they will defeat the darkness.*
2. *Their sleep will unlock the mystery of all the "sky's starry questions."*
3. *The speaker believes that love completes people and makes them more powerful together than they are individually.*

Vocabulary Check

4. *b* **5.** *a*

Literary Skills Focus

Possible responses:

6. *The speaker compares two hearts beating together to a "double drum." The image conveys fear of the dark and the consolation of companionship.*
7. *"The sky's / starry questions" could be about the meaning and value of life, their love, uncertainties about the future, or other concerns.*
8. Brasa *literally means "ember." Translating it as "flame" creates the image of something powerful and destructive rather than something that may flare up or die out.*
9. *The "darkness" may symbolize death, the uncertainties of life, or the speaker's inner demons.*
10. *Students may recall similar themes in Shakespeare's sonnets. Their personal responses to the theme will differ.*
11. *Sleep is compared to a "black flame" and "a headlong train." The extended metaphor expresses how sleep (or one's subconscious) becomes more forceful and menacing. It calls to mind images of an accelerating train, shadows, cold rocks, a black flame.*
12. *The turn is at line 9, the first line of the sestet. The speaker's focus shifts from fear of the night to the comfort and security that love offers.*

Universal Access

Struggling Writers

Students may need additional scaffolding to complete the Writing Skills Focus activity. Invite students to work with a partner and brainstorm universal emotions to which they both can relate. Students may have an easier time generating similes than metaphors. Encourage pairs to think of two similes for these emotions and then have them incorporate the figurative language into their poems.

What Do You Think Now?

Students may agree or disagree with Neruda's beliefs about the power of love. During discussion, ask students to show a mature understanding of and regard for the feelings and beliefs of others.

Assess

Unit 6 Resources,
Selection Standards Check, p. 149

Standards Focus

Objectives

Students will
- analyze ways in which poets use imagery
- use prior knowledge

Selection Introduction

Think About the Writer

Have students think about something they could describe thoroughly even though they have never experienced it. Ask students to discuss the differences between a firsthand and secondhand description.

For Independent Reading

Into Thin Air: A Personal Account of the Mt. Everest Disaster, Jon Krakauer

Motivate

What Do You Think?/QuickWrite

As students write their descriptions in their **Reader/Writer Notebooks,** remind them to focus primarily on how people responded to news of the disaster. They can include people in the scene interviewed by the news media or people they were with when the news was announced.

English for Academic Success

Academic Vocabulary

Look for opportunities to use the Academic Vocabulary words in this unit.
- **considerably, *adv.*:** by a large amount
- **exhibit, *v.*:** show, demonstrate

Preparing to Read

The Explosion

What Do You Think? How does experience shape our view of the world?

QuickWrite

Think of a local, national, or international tragedy that has made the headlines. In your *Reader/Writer Notebook,* record a brief description of how people responded to the news of the disaster.

Philip Arthur Larkin (1974), by Fay Godwin. National Portrait Gallery, London.

MEET THE WRITER

Philip Larkin

(1922–1985)

Philip Larkin originally aspired to become a jazz drummer. After a few pivotal academic experiences, however, he gave up that ambition to pursue a literary career.

An Ordinary Life

Larkin describes his early life as middle class and ordinary. He was born in Coventry, England. His father was city treasurer, and his mother was a homemaker. Larkin was a good student, but during childhood did not exhibit any special talent for writing. As he approached the British equivalent of high school, he did read nearly a book a day. Then, he began writing. "I wrote ceaselessly," he said, "... now verse, which I sewed up into little books, now prose, a thousand words a night after homework."

An Unassuming Poet

Educated at Oxford, Larkin spent most of his life as librarian at the University of Hull. He maintained an uneasy and sometimes yearning bachelorhood, and he wrote of romantic love in terms of bittersweet comedy or outright farce. Although Larkin shared much of the disillusionment of his fellow postwar writers, he was considerably shyer about dealing with the issues they addressed with the same passionate or satiric tone.

This decision not to engage with wider social issues seemed more characteristic of Larkin's personality than indicative of a general absence of conviction. In their quiet way, his poems reflect the themes of contemporary experience. When grappling with these themes, Larkin keeps to an intimately human scale, in which the balance lies somewhere between disgust and disdain, and heartbreak and despairing humor.

Larkin was the most widely admired poet of the generation that succeeded Dylan Thomas. Unlike Thomas, Larkin scrupulously avoided public attention. He refused hundreds of invitations to read or lecture in the United States and Great Britain. He seemed content to cultivate his own talents without reference to the choruses of praise and delight that attended the publication of each of his few but flawless collections of poetry.

Think About the Writer Can someone write movingly about something he or she has not experienced? Explain.

California Standards, pp. 1264–1267
- **Reading Standard 3.4** Analyze ways in which poets use imagery, personification, figures of speech, and sounds to evoke readers' emotions.
- **Grades 9–10 Review Reading Standard 3.8** Interpret and evaluate the impact of ambiguities, subtleties, contradictions, ironies, and incongruities in a text.

Selection Readability	
Easily Accessible **Accessible** Challenging	accessible theme; familiar vocabulary

Reading Standard 3.4; Grades 9–10 Review
Reading Standard 3.8 (see pages A48–A50)

Literary Skills Focus

Imagery Language that evokes sensory impressions is known as **imagery.** Most imagery is visual, appealing to the sense of sight, but imagery can also appeal to the senses of hearing, touch, smell, and taste. In addition to creating sensory impressions, imagery can evoke emotion. The word *slagheap* in line 3, for example, helps you visualize the heap of debris at the pit mouth; the image also can create a sense of foreboding or even disgust. The words *freshened silence* in line 6 help you feel the fresh morning air and hear the silence; the image can also create a feeling of well-being. As you read the poem, let the imagery help you imagine this scene and understand the writer's feelings about what happened.

Reading Skills Focus

Using Prior Knowledge The information and experience you possess before you read a poem or literary work is your **prior knowledge.** For example, if you are familiar with coal mining, you might be able to picture the pithead, or opening of the coal mine, in this poem. Use whatever prior knowledge you have about the subject matter (mining) to help you interpret details that are unfamiliar, subtle, or ambiguous.

Into Action As you read, use a KWL (Know-Want-Learn) chart like the one below to record what you know, want to know, and have learned.

What I Know	What I Want to Know	What I Learned
This poem is about a coal-mine explosion. Coal mining is a dangerous job.	What happens to the miners?	

Writing Skills Focus

Think as a Reader/Writer

Find It in Your Reading Larkin wants us to imagine vividly the coal mine, the miners coming down the lane, the cows, the dimmed sun, and the men walking toward their wives after the disaster. In your *Reader/Writer Notebook,* record the precise **imagery** Larkin uses to help you imagine the scene leading up to the disaster, the explosion itself, and what the wives saw later.

Reader/Writer Notebook

Use your **RWN** to complete the activities for this selection.

Language Coach

Defining Unfamiliar Words Because many poets love diverse language, they sometimes use words you do not often read or hear in regular speech. To determine the meaning of some of these words, see if the word is built from a word you recognize. For example, Larkin describes the coal miners "shouldering off" the freshened silence. You know what shoulders are: What do you think "shouldering off" might mean? Check a dictionary to see if your guess is correct.

Learn It Online

Find an interactive KWL chart online.

go.hrw.com H12-1265 Go

Preteach

English for Academic Success

Language Coach

Students may respond to the question by stating that "shouldering off" means "to push with or as if with the shoulder." Have students look for other forms of diverse language.

Literary Skills Focus

As you read and discuss the poem with students, have them use the imagery to help them imagine the scene.

Reading Skills Focus

Give students a copy of the Reading Skills Focus graphic organizer before they read. (See **Unit 6 Resources.**) Tell them to use their responses to answer the questions on the Applying Your Skills page.

Writing Skills Focus

As they read, have students record in their **Reader/Writer Notebooks** three sets of images—from before, during, and after the explosion. Students can use their notes to complete the Writing Skills Focus activity.

Selection Resources

Unit 6 Resources, on-level practice and assessment, p. 152

Teacher One Stop™, on-level lesson plans and all print resources

Holt Audio Library

Holt Audio Library: Selections and Summaries in Spanish

UA: Differentiating Instruction, graphic organizer, p. 297

UA: Supporting Instruction in Spanish, selection summary

ThinkCentral Online Assessment, Selection Standards Check

ThinkCentral Online Remediation

Learn It Online

If your students need help organizing a paper, introduce them to **Interactive Graphic Organizers**—tools for generating and organizing ideas, comparing and contrasting, and other key skills.

go.hrw.com H12-1265 Go

Teacher Preparation

Selection Summary

The speaker describes the men walking toward the mine on the day of the explosion. Dressed in work gear, they walk through the morning silence and go through the gate into the mine. At noon, the ground shakes, and the sun briefly dims. A death announcement is seen. Then, for a second, the wives see the men of the explosion walking toward them.

Direct Teach

Think About/Talk About

Read with a Purpose Have students read the Read with a Purpose statement. Then, have them note the use of the word *emerging* and predict how a mine might be used as a metaphor in this poem.

Comprehension

B Reading Focus

Possible response: *Underground explosions are powerful and shake the ground. Dust raised by the blast might obscure the sun.*

Analysis

A Literary Focus

Possible response: *Readers can see the miners' boots, beards, and clothing and see them chase after rabbits and look for lark's eggs. Readers can hear their coughing, rough talk, nicknames, and laughter.*

POEM

THE EXPLOSION

by **Philip Larkin**

Read with a Purpose

Read this poem to find a vision of life emerging from death.

Build Background

Mining coal is a difficult and dangerous job. Underground mines are ventilated to prevent miners from inhaling noxious gases, but these gases are flammable. Despite efforts to take safety precautions, explosions inside the mines, like the one described in the following poem, do occur. The *pithead* mentioned in line 2 is the opening to the mine; a *slagheap* (line 3) is the mountain of coal dust and mineral waste produced in the mining process. Larkin, who wrote this poem many years ago, might be referring to one of the terrible disasters that took place in the coal mines in Wales. Those mines are now almost all closed.

Miner pauses in a tunnel before starting a shift in Britain's most modern iron ore mine. Irthlinborough, Northamptonshire.

On the day of the explosion
Shadows pointed towards the pithead:
In the sun the slagheap slept.

Down the lane came men in pitboots
Coughing oath-edged talk and pipe-smoke,
Shouldering off the freshened silence.

One chased after rabbits; lost them;
Came back with a nest of lark's eggs;
Showed them; lodged them in the grasses.

So they passed in beards and moleskins,°
Fathers, brothers, nicknames, laughter,
Through the tall gates standing open. **A**

At noon, there came a tremor; cows
Stopped chewing for a second; sun,
Scarfed as in a heat-haze, dimmed. **B**

The dead go on before us, they
Are sitting in God's house in comfort,
We shall see them face to face—

Plain as lettering in the chapels
It was said, and for a second
Wives saw men of the explosion

Larger than in life they managed—
Gold as on a coin, or walking
Somehow from the sun towards them,

One showing the eggs unbroken.

10. moleskins: trousers made of thick, durable cotton fabric.

A Literary Focus **Imagery** What images so far help you "see" and "hear" the miners as they head toward work?

B Reading Focus **Using Prior Knowledge** What do you know about underground explosions that would explain the tremor and the dimmed sun?

California Standards, p. 1267

- **Reading Standard 3.4** Analyze ways in which poets use imagery, personification, figures of speech, and sounds to evoke readers' emotions.
- **Grades 9–10 Review Reading Standard 3.7** Recognize and understand the significance of various literary devices, including figurative language, imagery, allegory, and symbolism, and explain their appeal.
- **Grades 9–10 Review Reading Standard 3.8** Interpret and evaluate the impact of ambiguities, subtleties, contradictions, ironies, and incongruities in a text.
- **Writing Standard 2.3** Write reflective compositions: **a.** Explore the significance of personal experiences, events, conditions, or concerns by using rhetorical strategies (e.g., narration, description, exposition, persuasion).

Universal Access

Struggling Readers

To help students visualize the poem, lead them to discover that the poem can be broken into three segments. The first segment describes the miners on their way to the pit. The second segment, starting on line 13, describes the explosion. The final segment, starting on line 16, describes the wives of the miners and what they see after the explosion. Explain that many chapels (what various dissenting Protestant denominations in Great Britain called their churches) are covered inside with memorial plaques honoring the dead.

Applying Your Skills

Reading Standard 3.4; Grades 9–10 Review Reading Standard 3.7, 3.8 (see pages A48–A50)
Writing Standard 2.3a (see pages A51–A52)

The Explosion

Literary Response and Analysis

Reading Skills Focus

Quick Check

1. What three events are described in this poem? What happened in the morning, at noon, and later in the chapels?

Read with a Purpose

2. What details in the poem indicate that the speaker sees life emerging from death? What do you think the "tall gates" (line 12) could be?

Reading Skills: Using Prior Knowledge

3. As you read the poem, you filled out a KWL chart. Now, complete the chart by filling in the "What I Learned" column.

What I Know	What I Want to Know	What I Learned
This poem is about a coal-mine explosion. Coal mining is a dangerous job.	What happens to the miners?	The miners die in the explosion.

Literary Skills Focus

Literary Analysis

4. **Interpret** What does the description in lines 4–12 tell you about the miners? Besides the pipe-smoke, what do you think might cause the coughing?
5. **Compare and Contrast** The first part of the poem is written in an almost singsong rhythm that sounds at times like a children's rhyme. Where does the rhythm change? How does the tone of the poem in the first four stanzas contrast with the tone of the last five?
6. **Infer** Who is most likely speaking the italicized words in lines 16–18? Where are these words being spoken (or sung), and why?

Literary Skills: Imagery

7. **Evaluate** Review the images in lines 13–15 that describe the moment of impact. How do these images of the cow and sun contrast with the explosion itself and with the deaths that resulted from it? What do the images suggest about nature's response to human tragedy?

Literary Skills Review: Symbol

8. **Analyze** A **symbol** is something that stands both for itself and for something beyond itself. What might the eggs in the poem symbolize? Consider when the man finds the eggs, as well as the image of the "eggs unbroken" at the end of the poem. What message do you think this symbol conveys?

Writing Skills Focus

Think as a Reader/Writer

Use It in Your Writing Write a short essay describing an accident or disaster that you read about or witnessed. Use imagery to help your reader imagine not only the sights at the scene but also the sounds and, possibly, the smells and tastes. (If you prefer, describe a happy event instead of an accident or disaster: You might describe a wedding or a personal triumph.) Try opening your essay with Larkin's words: "On the day of the..."

What Do You Think Now? How do you think the speaker of this poem is affected by the tragic events he describes? What clues help you make this inference?

Universal Access

Struggling Writers

Some students may need additional scaffolding to complete the Writing Skills Focus activity. Have students create a five-senses chart to help them generate a list of images to use in their essays. Tell students to draw a five-column chart with one of the five senses—sight, smell, taste, touch, hearing—written at the top of each column. Ask students to write one to two images in each column that describe the accident or disaster. Encourage students to incorporate these images into their essays.

What Do You Think Now?

Ask students to consider why Larkin wrote this poem. Did he write out of respect for the miners' camaraderie, in praise of their hard work, or out of sympathy for their families?

Assess

Unit 6 Resources,
Selection Standards Check, p. 153

Check for Understanding

Independent Practice

Reading Skills Focus

Possible responses:

1. *The three events are the miners walking to work, the explosion occurring underground, and the emergence of the dead miners into another life.*
2. *The speaker describes how the miners emerge "larger than in life" and gold-colored. The gates they pass through are the gates of the mine but may also be "the pearly gates" leading into heaven.*
3. *Students may focus on details of what happened to the miners or what the italicized words represent.*

Literary Skills Focus

Possible responses:

4. *The reader learns how the miners behave toward each other and how they walk to work concerned with life (chasing rabbits) rather than death. The miners may be coughing because miners often suffer from various coal-dust-related lung ailments.*
5. *The rhythm changes in stanza five. The tone changes from lighthearted to matter-of-fact and then becomes mystical.*
6. *Mourners could be speaking or singing the words, or they could be written on a chapel wall to commemorate the miners' deaths.*
7. *The explosion was just slightly noticed above ground. The cow briefly stopped chewing. The sun was dimmed but not blacked out. All of these images suggest that "life goes on."*
8. *The eggs initially stand for the fragility of life. The unbroken eggs symbolize the fact that although life on earth is over for the miners, they are not broken, and life will continue in heaven.*

Standards Focus

Objectives

Students will use graphics to understand text.

Motivate

What Do You Think?/QuickWrite

Before students write, discuss with them the conditions that a trapped person might face. Then, have students think about how they might react in the same situation.

Preteach

Introducing Vocabulary

Use this activity to check students' understanding.

1. Would an **encampment** of people set up permanent shelter in a location?
2. Why might **hydraulic** equipment be dangerous to operate?
3. Do runners wear **thermal** gear in the snow or in the sun?

Informational Text/ Writing Skills Focus

- Give students a copy of the Informational Text Focus graphic organizer before they read. (See **Unit 6 Resources.**) Tell them to use their responses to answer the questions on the Applying Your Skills page.
- Have students record their responses to the graphic organizer in their **Reader/Writer Notebooks**.

Learn It Online

Send students to **Word Watch** for audio pronunciations, synonyms and antonyms, and brief histories of word origins.

go.hrw.com H12-1268 Go

INFORMATIONAL TEXT FOCUS

Preparing to Read

Reading Standard 2.4 (see pages A48–A50)

Link to Today

Trapped Australian Miners Rescued

What Do You Think

How does experience shape our view of the world?

QuickWrite

How would you expect someone who was trapped in a mine for a week to react? Explain your thoughts in your *Reader/Writer Notebook.*

Informational Text Focus

Using Graphics to Understand Text Many informational texts include graphics to clarify the text. Visuals can present a great deal of information in limited space. Diagrams can help readers quickly visualize and understand complex topics. Labels focus attention on the most important visual details.

Into Action As you read the article, use the graphic on page 1270 to help you visualize the situation. Note specific elements in the diagram, and explain what new information each element contributes to your understanding.

Element	New Information
illustration of safety cage	the metal safety cage kept the miners from being crushed

Writing Skills Focus

Preparing for Timed Writing Some stories are newsworthy; others are not. What makes the story of these Australian miners news? Record your thoughts in your *Reader/Writer Notebook* as you read. Note details that you think would interest a large audience.

Vocabulary

thermal (THUR muhl) *adj.:* relating to heat. *The thermal imaging camera uses infrared technology to detect variations in heat.*

encampment (ehn KAMP muhnt) *n.:* gathering of people who have set up temporary shelter. *An encampment of rescuers and reporters formed during the two-week ordeal.*

hydraulic (hy DRAW lihk) *adj.:* operated by fluid that is under pressure. *Rescuers used powerful hydraulic equipment to split the rock that trapped the miners.*

Language Coach

Word Origins The Vocabulary word *hydraulic* comes from the Greek word for water, and the Vocabulary word *thermal* comes from the Greek word for heat. What might the English word *hydrothermal* mean? What are some other English words with one of these roots, and how does the meaning of the root relate to the meaning of the words?

Reader/Writer Notebook

Use your **RWN** to complete the activities for this selection.

Learn It Online

Develop your vocabulary knowledge with Word Watch online.

go.hrw.com H12-1268 Go

Selection Readability	
Easily Accessible **Accessible** Challenging	familiar vocabulary; simple sentence structure; accessible theme

Selection Summary

This news story describes a 2006 mining disaster in which one Tasmanian miner died and two others were rescued. Rescuers discovered that the men were alive with a thermal imaging camera. They ground through hard rock to provide a delivery tube for food and water. The two men were pulled from the mine, and the townspeople united in celebration.

NEWSPAPER ARTICLE

Trapped Australian Miners Rescued

by Duncan Campbell, Alex Kumi, and agencies

The Guardian, Tuesday, May 9, 2006

Link to Today

This Link to Today shows the timelessness of courage.

Read with a Purpose
Read to find out how two miners reacted to a drastic situation.

Build Background
Gold was first discovered in Tasmania (an island southeast of Australia), in 1852. The gold there is encased in solid rock. To extract the precious metal, miners dig underground shafts and tunnels. Like coal mining, hard rock is extremely dangerous for the miners because accidents can cause cave-ins.

Two Tasmanian gold miners trapped 3,000 feet underground for 14 days were rescued, ending a saga that had gripped Australia. The rescue of the pair, who had been feared dead, has been described as "an inspiring example of Australian mateship."[1]

Todd Russell, 34, and Brant Webb, 37, were trapped in a safety cage in the mine in Beaconsfield, Tasmania, after a 2.1 magnitude earthquake[2] caused a collapse of underground rocks and killed their colleague, 44-year-old Larry Knight. Initially, it was feared that the two men, both married and both with three children, had also perished, but investigators using a thermal imaging camera[3] five days after the collapse found them still alive, and the non-stop effort to bring the pair to safety began. (A)

The men were able to walk unaided from the mine's main lift shaft, despite their ordeal and cramped muscles. Hundreds of locals from the close-knit town of Beaconsfield, in the island state of Tasmania, gathered at the gates of the mine to welcome the men, who have become national heroes. Television cameras, photographers, and journalists shouting questions also greeted the men above ground, reflecting the enormous media encampment that had followed every twist of the rescue effort.

The miners received medical treatment before appearing in front of members of the public. They appeared to be in good health and smiled broadly,

Miners Todd Russell *(left)* and Brant Webb *(second from left)* emerge from mine at Beaconsfield, Australia.

1. **mateship:** Australian term for friendship and unconditional assistance, especially during hard times.
2. **magnitude earthquake:** The magnitude, or energy, of an earthquake is measured using the Richter scale; a 2.1 magnitude earthquake is small enough that it is usually not felt.
3. **thermal imaging camera:** camera that detects infrared radiation; warm objects, such as humans, are visible against cooler backgrounds, such as rock.

(A) **Informational Focus** **Using Graphics to Understand Text** After reading the first two paragraphs, what visual image do you have of the accident?

Vocabulary **thermal** (THUR muhl) *adj.:* relating to heat.
encampment (ehn KAMP muhnt) *n.:* gathering of people who have set up temporary shelter.

Link to Today

Like "The Explosion," this article explores the dangerous job of mining and the struggles and sacrifices the miners must endure.

Direct Teach

Think About/Talk About

Read with a Purpose Have students read the Read with a Purpose statement. Have them discuss the dangers that miners face on a daily basis and also during extraordinary circumstances.

Comprehension

(A) Informational Focus

Possible response: *The description helps the reader picture the two miners in a dire situation. The reader can visualize the miners surrounded by large rocks and darkness in the underground cage.*

Vocabulary: Own the Word

- **thermal:** Tell students that the root for *thermal* comes from the Greek word *therme,* which means "heat." Have students suggest other heat-related words with the same root. ***Possible responses:*** *thermos, thermometer, hypothermia*
- **encampment:** Tell students that *encampment* means "a gathering of people who have set up temporary shelter." Ask students to name places one might see an *encampment* of people. ***Possible responses:*** *People might camp out to see their favorite celebrity or to buy concert tickets.*

Selection Resources

Unit 6 Resources, on-level practice, p. 155
Teacher One Stop™, on-level lesson plans
Holt Audio Library: Selections and Summaries in Spanish
UA: Differentiating Instruction, graphic organizer, p. 298
UA: Supporting Instruction in Spanish, selection summary
ThinkCentral Online Assessment, Selection Standards Check
ThinkCentral Online Remediation

California Standards, pp. 1268–1271

- **Reading Standard 2.4** Make warranted and reasonable assertions about the author's arguments by using elements of the text to defend and clarify interpretations.

Think About/Talk About

Comprehension

B Informational Focus

Possible response: *Viewing the diagram should help students develop a more precise image of the men's situation, including the metal safety cage in which they were trapped and the location of the rescue team.*

C Informational Focus

Possible response: *The labels describe the step-by-step rescue process, providing exact details about the three main phases of the rescue.*

Vocabulary: Own the Word

hydraulic: Tell students that *hydraulic* means "operated by a fluid under pressure." Ask students to explain why rescuers might need to use *hydraulic* equipment. ***Possible responses:*** *It is extremely powerful and can break through difficult materials.*

Monitor Students' Comprehension

Guide the class in answering these comprehension questions.

1. How long did it take for rescuers to get the men out? [*nine days: the men spent 14 days underground, and the rescue began five days after the collapse.*]
2. How did Mr. Russell and Mr. Webb survive for the five days before rescuers discovered them? [*by sharing a cereal bar and licking water from the rocks*]
3. What metaphor does the union official use to describe the families' relief at the rescue? [*The union official states, "A giant rock of pressure has been taken off these families."*]

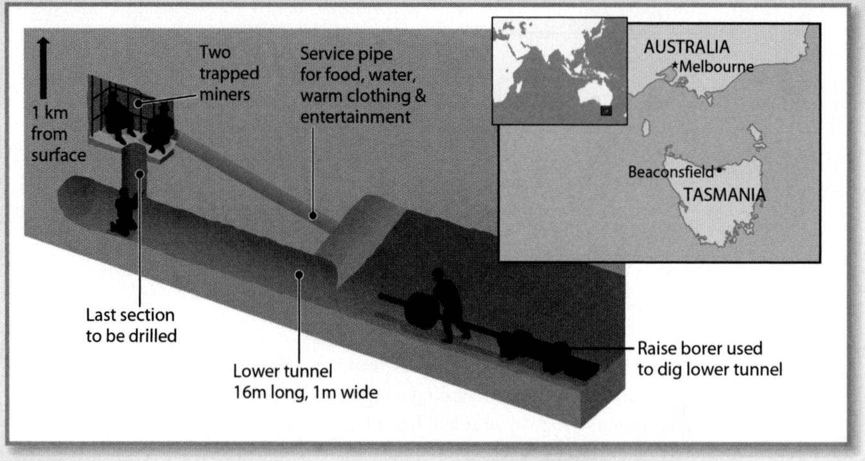

Graphic of the rescue. **B**

punching the air in jubilation and waving to well-wishers. "The great escape is over," union official Bill Shorten told Nine Network television after the men emerged. "A giant rock of pressure has been taken off these families." Mine manager Matthew Gill, who is a close friend of the pair, said the men were "incredible people," adding "I am amazed at their condition."

He said the rescue operation had involved keeping the miners horizontal for as long as possible in case they were injured. The men were then pulled to safety through a vertical tunnel.

The men had displayed an impressively laid-back attitude to their fate throughout their ordeal. They survived the first week on a cereal bar and by licking the water from the rocks and then were fed meals passed down to them through a 40-foot pipe. On a psychologist's advice, some of their favorite music was also sent through the pipe to keep up their spirits.

According to the local newspaper, they made an unsuccessful request for chips and gravy to be sent down, but doctors would only agree to chicken and cheese bread rolls with some tinned[4] fruit for dessert. Omelets and homemade soups were also dispatched through a device similar to a dumbwaiter. The trapped men also joked about asking for the classified-ads column from the local paper so that they could see what other jobs might be on offer.

The rescue team worked around the clock, using low-impact explosives, hydraulic rock splitters, hand-held drills, and diamond-tipped chainsaws. They faced enormous problems in trying to drill their way in zig-zag fashion through the rock without endangering the lives of the men as they tried to cut them a meter-wide escape tunnel in the 77-degree underground heat. The two men had to help their rescuers by spreading grout over loose rocks to prevent collapses around them as the final push was made in an area where gold had been discovered in 1877. **C**

As the rescuers appeared to be getting closer, excitement mounted. "The fat lady might not have sung but I can certainly hear her clearing her vocal cords," Mr. Shorten, national secretary of the Australian Workers Union, told the Associated Press shortly before the men emerged.

4. **tinned:** canned

B Informational Focus Using Graphics to Understand Text How does looking at the diagram contribute to your understanding of the men's situation?

C Informational Focus Using Graphics to Understand Text What details do the diagram labels add to the text description of the rescue effort?

Vocabulary **hydraulic** (hy DRAW lihk) *adj.:* operated by fluid that is under pressure.

California Standards, p. 1271

- **Reading Standard 2.4** Make warranted and reasonable assertions about the author's arguments by using elements of the text to defend and clarify interpretations.
- **Writing Standard 1.1** Demonstrate an understanding of the elements of discourse (e.g., purpose, speaker, audience, form) when completing narrative, expository, persuasive, or descriptive writing assignments.
- **Writing Standard 1.3** Structure ideas and arguments in a sustained, persuasive, and sophisticated way and support them with precise and relevant examples.
- **Writing Standard 2.2** Write responses to literature: **a.** Demonstrate a comprehensive understanding of the significant ideas in works or passages. **b.** Analyze the use of imagery, language, universal themes, and unique aspects of the text. **c.** Support important ideas and viewpoints through accurate and detailed references to the text and to other works. **d.** Demonstrate an understanding of the author's use of stylistic devices and an appreciation of the effects created.
- **Listening and Speaking Standard 2.4** Deliver multimedia presentations: **a.** Combine text, images, and sound by incorporating information from a wide range of media, including films, newspapers, magazines, CD-ROMs, online information, television, videos, and electronic media-generated images. **b.** Select an appropriate medium for each element of the presentation. **c.** Use the selected media skillfully, editing appropriately and monitoring for quality.

INFORMATIONAL TEXT FOCUS

Applying Your Skills

Trapped Australian Miners Rescued

Reading Standard 2.4 (see pages A48–A50)
Listening and Speaking Standard 2.4a–c (see pages A53–A55)
Writing Standard 1.1, 1.3, 2.2a–d (see pages A51–A52)

Analyze Informational Texts

Informational Text Focus

Quick Check

1. How did the miners become trapped?
2. What difficulties did the rescue team face?
3. What steps did the rescue team take to successfully free the trapped men?

Read with a Purpose

4. What attitude did the miners exhibit throughout their two weeks of confinement? Do you think their outlook was an important factor in their survival? Explain.

Informational Skills: Using Graphics to Understand Text

5. Look over the chart you created as you read. How does the diagram help you better understand the article? What additional information does the diagram provide? How does it use both words and graphics to clarify what happened?

Vocabulary Check

Answer the following questions about the Vocabulary words.

6. Is a photographer likely to use a **thermal** imaging camera to photograph an afternoon football game? Explain.
7. Which is a more likely scenario, an **encampment** of fans waiting to buy tickets for a popular music concert or an **encampment** of journalists waiting to report on a local softball game? Explain.
8. Might a **hydraulic** system use oil to operate? Explain.

Text Analysis

9. **Analyze** Why did the writer include details about the miners "punching the air" in the article? What tone does this phrase create?
10. **Interpret** A familiar proverb about opera says, "It ain't over till the fat lady sings." What does this proverb mean, and how does the representative of the Australian Workers Union apply its meaning to the miners' predicament?

Listening and Speaking

11. **Extend** Work with a small group to prepare a short news broadcast of the mining rescue. Write the story, and then assign team roles, including news anchors, director, and camera operator (if you have access to a video camera). Share your video broadcast with the rest of the class. If you cannot record your report, present the broadcast live.

Writing Skills Focus

Timed Writing The story of the Australian miners captured interest around the world. Why do you think this event received attention in news broadcasts far from Australia? Explain what features of the story attracted audience interest. Use details from the text and graphic to support your answer.

What Do You Think Now How do you think the two miners felt after their rescue? How might the experience have affected their perspective on the world and on their work?

Check for Understanding

Independent Practice

Informational Text Focus

Possible responses:

1. *They became trapped after an earthquake caused a collapse of underground rocks.*
2. *They had difficulties drilling through the rock without endangering the trapped men.*
3. *The rescuers dug a tunnel beneath the place where the men were trapped. Then, they dug upward until they reached the miners.*
4. *The miners reacted with courage, tenacity, and humor. Their attitude helped them remain positive and hopeful about their fate.*
5. *Student should mention details of the tunneling efforts and what the graphic adds and clarifies.*
6. *No, a thermal imaging camera is one that detects heat.*
7. *An encampment of fans is more likely because tickets for a popular music concert would be in high demand.*
8. *Yes, the system would probably have a lot of moving parts that require oil to operate.*
9. *The article begins with the successful rescue. It sets an upbeat tone that engages readers.*
10. *The proverb means that victory (or defeat) is not certain until the contest or situation has reached its completion. The proverb is fitting because it suggests that people should not give up hope until the miners are saved or their bodies are found.*
11. *Students dramatizing the news report may wish to assign roles to miners, family members, mine executives, and rescue crew members. They may wish to film close-ups of the graphic and the map in the article to add interest.*

Universal Access

Struggling Writers

Some students may struggle to identify why the story of the Australian miners captured the world's interest. Students may have an easier time explaining why they found the story interesting. Have students begin writing by listing three details from the story that they found compelling. Then, encourage them to tell a partner why they found these details interesting. Have students include these observations in their paragraph.

What Do You Think Now?

Have students consider how their thoughts or opinions about mining have changed after reading this article. What emotions might be similar to those experienced by the rescued miners?

Assess

Unit 6 Resources,
Selection Standards Check, p. 158

Standards Focus

Objectives

Students will understand poetic structure.

Selection Introduction

Think About the Writer

Ask students to make a list of characteristics that they believe a "survivor" is likely to possess. Then, ask them if they believe Ted Hughes possessed those characteristics.

For Independent Reading

*Chosen by a Horse,** Susan Richards

HRW LIBRARY *This title is available in the HRW library.

Motivate

What Do You Think?/QuickWrite

Have students describe a memorable encounter they had with an animal or plant. Have students write their responses in their **Reader/Writer Notebooks**.

English for Academic Success

Academic Vocabulary

Look for opportunities to use the Academic Vocabulary words in this unit.

- **considerably,** ***adv.:*** by a large amount
- **exhibit,** ***v.:*** show, demonstrate
- **perspective,** ***n.:*** a particular way of looking at something

Preparing to Read

The Horses

What Do You Think? How does experience shape our view of the world?

QuickWrite

Think about an encounter you have had in nature with an animal or plant. In your *Reader/Writer Notebook,* write about how the encounter affected you emotionally.

Ted Hughes, Yorkshire, England.

MEET THE WRITER

Ted Hughes

(1930–1998)

Ted Hughes often used violent nature imagery in his poetry to symbolize the human condition. Born in West Yorkshire, England, Hughes was influenced considerably by the landscape of his hometown surroundings.

A Private Life

Hughes served two years in the Royal Air Force before attending Cambridge University. In 1956, he married the American poet Sylvia Plath. Plath committed suicide in 1963 after the couple had separated. An intensely private person, Hughes was silent for decades about his relationship with Plath and the accusations that he was somehow responsible for her death. In 1998, he broke that silence with the publication of a collection of poems, *Birthday Letters.*

The Poet's Work

Hughes's recurring subjects are reflected in the titles of a number of his books: *The Hawk in the Rain* (1957), *Animal Poems* (1967), *Crow* (1970), *Cave Birds* (1975), and *Wolfwatching* (1989). The critic A. Alvarez called Hughes a "survivor-poet" because Hughes sees parallels between human beings and animals—both are creatures that will do anything to ensure survival. Although Hughes writes about nature, he has little in common with the Romantics, who saw in nature a reflection of divine providence and primeval innocence. In Hughes's poems, nature often represents the darkest impulses of the human heart; violence is not only an accepted fact of life but also a tendency that links all creatures on earth. Hughes sees humans as alienated from nature, with instincts that have been diminished by reason and civilization. To see the world from the perspective of an animal, in Hughes's thinking, is to recover a power that has been lost.

In 1984, Hughes was named Poet Laureate of the United Kingdom, a title he held until his death.

Think About the Writer How is the term "survivor-poet" appropriate for both Hughes's poetry and his personal life?

California Standards, pp. 1272–1277

- **Reading Standard 3.3** Analyze the ways in which irony, tone, mood, the author's style, and the "sound" of language achieve specific rhetorical or aesthetic purposes or both.

Selection Readability	
Easily Accessible **Accessible** Challenging	common theme; short stanzas; accessible vocabulary

Reading Standard 3.3 (see pages A48–A50)

Literary Skills Focus

Poetic Structure The literary techniques that a writer uses to organize and create a poem make up that poem's **poetic structure.** One unit of poetic structure is the **line,** traditionally a single thought expressed on one physical line of the poem. A group of consecutive lines that form a single unit make up a **stanza,** which is itself separated by blank lines. Two-line stanzas that rhyme are called **couplets.** Hughes, however, does not follow any of these traditional organizational patterns exactly. Sometimes a line in his poem breaks in midthought and sometimes in midstanza. Although most of the stanzas in "The Horses" contain two lines, one contains a single line. Finally, Hughes does not rhyme his couplets and instead uses assonance and alliteration to give his poem a musical sound.

Writing Skills Focus

Think as a Reader/Writer

Find It in Your Reading The line and stanza breaks in Hughes's poems are not random. As you read, ask yourself why Hughes breaks lines at certain points in the poem. Identify the effect of each break. Does it signal a change of thought? Does it emphasize some quality? Next to each break, write a short note about its effect. In your *Reader/Writer Notebook,* record your findings in a graphic organizer like the one below, making certain to use ellipsis points and quotation marks accurately.

Line #	Line	Effect of Line Break
1	"hour-before-dawn dark"	sets the scene; hyphens and alliteration emphasize time
2	"Evil air, a frost-making stillness"	reader must pause and be still
4	"A world cast in frost. . . . above the wood"	creates feeling of suspense and stillness

TechFocus As you read "The Horses," think about what other visual images, in addition to the ones Hughes evokes, might help elaborate on the **theme,** or message, of the poem. How might photographs, drawings, or even computer illustrations represent the poem's language?

Reader/Writer Notebook
Use your **RWN** to complete the activities for this selection.

Vocabulary

tortuous (TAWR choo uhs) *adj.:* characterized by twists and turns. *We drove slowly down the tortuous mountain road.*

moorline (MUR lyn) *n.:* edge of a heath or wasteland. *The horses were eating grass near the moorline.*

dregs (drehgz) *n. pl.:* sediment. *The dregs of the coffee clung to the bottom of the mug.*

erupted (ih RUHPT ihd) *v.:* burst forth. *My anger erupted at the injustice.*

Language Coach

Compound Nouns Compound nouns are nouns made up of more than one word; for example, *moor* + *line* = *moorline.* Compound nouns can be closed (*moorline*), open (*ice cream*), or hyphenated (*mother-in-law*). As you read the poem, look for compound nouns. Be careful not to mistake hyphenated adjectives for compound nouns.

Learn It Online
Listen to this poem online.
go.hrw.com H12-1273 Go

Selection Resources

Unit 6 Resources, on-level practice and assessment, p. 160

Teacher One Stop™, on-level lesson plans and all print resources

Holt Audio Library

Holt Audio Library: Selections and Summaries in Spanish

UA: Differentiating Instruction, graphic organizer, p. 299

UA: Supporting Instruction in Spanish, selection summary

ThinkCentral Online Assessment, Selection Standards Check

ThinkCentral Online Remediation

Preteach

Introducing Vocabulary

- Review the Vocabulary words, definitions, and sentences with students.
- To reinforce the importance of the Vocabulary words, tell students that Hughes does not employ a *tortuous* or complex poetic structure. His poems find meaning in even the *moorline* and *dregs* that exist in nature. Hughes's brilliant portrayals of the darkest aspects of nature *erupted* at a time when many other poets focused on nature's innocence.

English for Academic Success

Language Coach

As they read the poem, students may notice the compound nouns, *hindhooves* and *moor-ridge.* Ask students to use one of these words in a sentence.

Literary Skills Focus

As you read and discuss the poem with students, have them note elements of Hughes's nontraditional poetic structure.

Writing Skills Focus

Give students a copy of the Writing Skills Focus graphic organizer. (See **Unit 6 Resources.**) Have students record the effects of each line and stanza break in their graphic organizer. Students can use their notes to complete the Writing Skills Focus activity.

Learn It Online
The online version of this poem includes audio support to engage all students and to help struggling readers with reading comprehension and vocabulary.
go.hrw.com H12-1273 Go

Teacher Preparation
Selection Summary

The speaker in "The Horses" observes a group of wild horses while taking an early morning walk. In vivid, visual language, the speaker captures the sights and sounds of the horses and the dawn. The images are so vivid that the speaker expects to remember them later, when he is walking on crowded city streets.

Direct Teach

Think About/Talk About

Read with a Purpose Have students read the Read with a Purpose statement. Ask them to consider how an encounter with nature might affect someone.

Analysis

A Literary Focus

Possible responses: *Most of the stanzas are two lines. The line pairings are not rhyming couplets, and they do not have a regular rhythm.*

B Literary Focus

Possible response: *By setting line 15 alone, Hughes emphasizes the silence of the scene: "a grey silent world."*

Extend the Discussion

Setting When and where is the poem set? ***Possible response:*** *It takes place just before dawn, outside in a place where there are woods, a valley, and moors.*

Speculating Why do you think Hughes set the poem in paired lines? ***Possible response:*** *Hughes might have used the line pairings to give the poem, which is in free verse, some sort of visual organization.*

POEM

The Horses by Ted Hughes

Read with a Purpose Read to envision one man's encounter with nature.

I climbed through woods in the hour-before-dawn dark.
Evil air, a frost-making stillness,

Not a leaf, not a bird—
A world cast in frost. I came out above the wood

Where my breath left tortuous statues in the iron light.
But the valleys were draining the darkness

Till the moorline—blackening dregs of the brightening grey—
Halved the sky ahead. And I saw the horses: (A)

Huge in the dense grey—ten together—
Megalith°-still. They breathed, making no move,

With draped manes and tilted hind-hooves,
Making no sound.

I passed: not one snorted or jerked its head.
Grey silent fragments

Of a grey silent world. (B)

I listened in emptiness on the moor-ridge.
The curlew's° tear turned its edge on the silence.

10. megalith: huge stone, often used in the monuments constructed by ancient people.

17. curlew's: referring to a large brown shorebird.

A Literary Focus Poetic Structure What length are most of the stanzas within this poem? What do you notice about Hughes's stanzas?

B Literary Focus Poetic Structure Why do you think Hughes sets line 15 alone? What is the effect of this organization?

Vocabulary **tortuous** (TAWR choo uhs) *adj.:* characterized by twists and turns.
moorline (MUR lyn) *n.:* edge of a heath or wasteland.
dregs (drehgz) *n. pl.:* sediment.

Universal Access

EL English Learners

English for Academic Success Words such as *moorline, dregs, megalith, moor, curlew,* and *manes* may be unfamiliar to students. Also, hyphenated words such as *hour-before-dawn, hind-hooves, megalith-still,* and *moor-ridge* may be unfamiliar. Explain that Hughes does not provide many context clues to help readers. Remind students to use the glosses to define words and to use their knowledge of word parts to guess the meanings of unfamiliar words.

Advanced Learners

Enrichment Explain to students that in "The Horses," Hughes uses free verse—a form of poetry that has no regular meter or rhyme scheme. Poets who use free verse often rely on other poetic devices, such as alliteration, internal rhyme, onomatopoeia, and imagery, to make their poems memorable. Ask students to analyze Hughes's poem and to explain in a few sentences what poetic devices make the poem outstanding.

Slowly detail leafed from the darkness. Then the sun
Orange, red, red erupted

Silently, and splitting to its core tore and flung cloud,
Shook the gulf open, showed blue,

And the big planets hanging—.
I turned

Stumbling in the fever of a dream, down towards
The dark woods, from the kindling tops,

And came to the horses.
There, still they stood,
But now steaming and glistening under the flow of light, Ⓒ

Their draped stone manes, their tilted hind-hooves
Stirring under a thaw while all around them

The frost showed its fires. But still they made no sound.
Not one snorted or stamped,

Their hung heads patient as the horizons,
High over valleys, in the red levelling rays—

In din of the crowded streets, going among the years, the faces,
May I still meet my memory in so lonely a place

Between the streams and the red clouds, hearing curlews,
Hearing the horizons endure.

Ⓒ **Literary Focus** Poetic Structure How does the three-line stanza affect the overall rhythm of the poem? How does it support the themes of the poem?

Vocabulary **erupted** (ih RUHPT ihd) *v.:* burst forth.

Think About/Talk About

Analysis

Ⓒ Literary Focus

Possible responses: *The three-line stanza sets off the speaker's meeting with nature. It supports the theme by showing that humans are set apart from nature.*

Extend the Discussion

Imagery What visual images does Hughes use to describe the sunrise? What is the effect of the imagery on readers? ***Possible response:*** *He uses the colors orange, red, and blue to describe the sunrise; he also uses the image of the sun erupting from the darkness. The visual imagery helps readers form a picture in their minds; the poem becomes almost like a painting.*

Vocabulary: Own the Word

- **tortuous:** Write *tortuous* in a center circle on the board along with its definition: "twisting." Draw spider legs from the circle as students add concepts and attributes. ***Possible responses:*** *winding, not straight, snakelike*
- **moorline:** Tell students that the *moorline* is the place where the high ground meets the sky. Ask students: In the poem, what is happening to the *moorline* in the early dawn light? ***Possible response:*** *It is staying dark while the sky turns a lighter grey.*
- **dregs:** Remind students that the connotation of *dregs* is of the leftover bits, the residue, or remains of something. For example, you might say: "The last cup of coffee was not flavorful and rich but was just the *dregs* of the pot."
- **erupted:** Tell students that the word *erupted* can be used to describe an active volcano, a sudden loud chord in a song, or an angry person's temper. Ask students to what might cause a crowd's *eruption.*

California Standards, pp. 1276–1277

- **Reading Standard 3.3** Analyze the ways in which irony, tone, mood, the author's style, and the "sound" of language achieve specific rhetorical or aesthetic purposes or both.
- **Reading Standard 3.4** Analyze ways in which poets use imagery, personification, figures of speech, and sounds to evoke readers' emotions.
- **Writing Standard 2.2** Write responses to literature: **a.** Demonstrate a comprehensive understanding of the significant ideas in works or passages. **b.** Analyze the use of imagery, language, universal themes, and unique aspects of the text. **d.** Demonstrate an understanding of the author's use of stylistic devices and an appreciation of the effects created.
- **Writing Standard 2.6** Deliver multimedia presentations: **a.** Combine text, images, and sound and draw information from many sources (e.g., television broadcasts, videos, films, newspapers, magazines, CD-ROMs, the Internet, electronic media-generated images).
- **Listening and Speaking Standard 2.4** Deliver multimedia presentations: **a.** Combine text, images, and sound by incorporating information from a wide range of media, including films, newspapers, magazines, CD-ROMs, online information, television, videos, and electronic media-generated images.

Check for Understanding

Independent Practice

Reading Skills Focus

Possible responses:

1. *Hughes depicts a predawn winter landscape. The poet emphasizes the colors of the day—grey and black before dawn—and natural elements, such as the hooves and steamy breath of the horses.*
2. *The horses are motionless and silent. "Megalith-still" suggests giant ancient monuments. The horses are as ageless and still as stone sculptures.*
3. *The silence of the horses and the setting contrasts with the "din of crowded streets."*
4. *The encounter gives the speaker a new insight and appreciation for nature.*

Literary Skills Focus

Possible responses:

5. *The poet felt like a part of nature: both the narrator and the horses are silent and create steamy breath in the predawn frost. Or, the narrator is alienated; he only watches the horses.*
6. Red *appears twice in line 19. "Draped manes" and "tilted hind-hooves" are repeated in lines 11 and 28, giving the poem* a song-like quality. *Alliteration in line 33: "Their hung heads patient as the horizons" and in line 35:* may, meet, *and* memory *emphasizes his soft tone.*
7. *Students might mention their emotional reaction to observing salmon swimming upstream or a large animal being frightened by a much smaller one.*
8. *He hopes that the astounding stillness of nature will endure.*
9. *Some may feel the structure emphasizes humanity's disconnectedness from nature.*
10. *Hearing—"curlew's tear turned its edge on the silence." Touch—"a world cast in frost."*

Applying Your Skills

Reading Standard 3.3, 3.4 (see pages A48–A50)
Writing Standard 2.2a (see pages A51–A52)

The Horses

Literary Response and Analysis

Reading Skills Focus

Quick Check

1. What kind of landscape is evoked in "The Horses"? What aspects of the scene does the poet emphasize?
2. How are the horses described? What does "Megalith-still" (line 10) suggest?
3. Why do you think Hughes emphasizes the silence of the scene?

Read with a Purpose

4. What effect does the encounter with nature have on the speaker of the poem?

Literary Skills Focus

Literary Analysis

5. **Evaluate** Do you think "The Horses" expresses the poet's union with nature or his alienation from it? Explain.
6. **Interpret** Although Hughes does not use end rhyme, he achieves subtle musical effects by employing other devices. How does he use repetition, alliteration, and other techniques of sound? What are their effects?
7. **Extend** Hughes appears to say in the poem that the horses' stillness is ominous because they do not react the way we expect, or want them to, in the presence of a stranger. What contradictions or abnormalities have you witnessed in animals or other elements of nature (for example, the silence before a storm)? How did the experience make you feel?
8. **Analyze** Hughes ends the poem with the phrase "Hearing the horizons endure." What do you think he means by this line? Notice the incongruity of the descriptions with their subject, the horizons.

Literary Skills: Poetic Structure

9. **Make Judgments** How does Hughes's use of poetic structure contribute to the poem's meaning? Explain your answer by using examples from the poem.

Literary Skills Review: Imagery

10. **Analyze** Language that appeals to the senses is called **imagery.** Most images are visual, but imagery can also appeal to the senses of hearing, touch, taste, or smell. Identify an image from the poem that appeals to a sense other than sight.

Writing Skills Focus

Think as a Reader/Writer

Use It in Your Writing Now that you have seen how a master poet like Ted Hughes uses line and stanza breaks to create and reinforce meaning, write your own short poem about the natural world. Think carefully about your poem's structure, and make sure you have a reason for each of your line and stanza breaks.

What Do You Think Now How do you think an experience with nature such as that described in this poem might affect a person's view of the world?

Universal Access

Struggling Writers

Some students may need additional scaffolding to complete the Writing Skills Focus activity. Have students begin writing by making a list of words that describe how they feel about some aspect of the natural world. Instruct them to try to choose words that are descriptive and powerful—words that could evoke strong emotion in a reader. Using words from their list, students should write a few lines of poetry that describe their feelings about nature.

What Do You Think Now?

Ask students to think about whether Hughes would be likely to feel alienated or inspired by such an occurrence. Then, ask them how they think other people might be affected. How might one see the world differently after such a memorable experience?

Writing Standard 2.2a, 2.2b, 2.2d, 2.6a (see pages A51–A52)
Listening and Speaking Standard 2.4a (see pages A53–A55)

Vocabulary Development

Vocabulary Check

Respond to the following items.

1. Identify something that can be **tortuous.**
2. Tell where you might see a **moorline.**
3. Name one thing that has **dregs.**
4. Identify something that could have **erupted.**

Vocabulary Skills: Figurative Language

Figurative language is used to describe one thing in terms of another, dissimilar thing. The following are three common types of figurative language:
Simile: a figure of speech that makes a comparison between two seemingly unlike things by using a connective word such as *like* or *as.* ("My love is like a red, red rose.")
Metaphor: the same kind of comparison without a connective word. ("Your eyes are diamonds.")
Personification: a form of metaphor in which a nonhuman or nonliving thing is talked about as if it were human or had life. ("Death, be not proud.")

Your Turn

Label each of the following figures of speech as simile, metaphor, or personification.

1. The road was as **tortuous** as a slithering snake.
2. The gritty **dregs** swam happily in the coffee pot.
3. The children waited like frightened deer when their neighbor's anger **erupted.**

Language Coach

Compound Nouns Look at the list of compound nouns that you found in the poem. Divide each into its component words, and write a short explanation of how the meanings of the component words combine to form the compound noun.

CHOICES

As you respond to the Choices, use these **Academic Vocabulary** words as appropriate: perspective, considerably, adapt, exhibit, inevitable.

REVIEW

Write an Essay

Timed Writing In "The Horses," Hughes uses **free verse,** a form of poetry with no regular rhyme scheme or meter. Poets who use free verse often rely on other poetic devices, such as alliteration, internal rhyme, and imagery, to make their poems memorable. Analyze Hughes's use of poetic devices, and explain how they contribute to the poem's theme and mood.

CONNECT

Express Your Experience

Re-read the poem "The Horses," noting how the experience affected the speaker long after the event. Think of a lasting experience of your own, and record the reasons it made an impression. From your notes, construct a poem that expresses your experience. Include figurative language, meaningful stanza divisions, and sound techniques in your poem.

EXTEND

Create a Collage

TechFocus Illustrate Hughes's poem by making a collage. You might first copy the poem in your own handwriting and then draw or cut out magazine pictures. Consider using a computer graphics program to create your collage and type in the poem. Whichever medium you choose, be sure to capture not just the events but also the feelings of the poem. Exhibit your finished collage in your classroom.

Universal Access: Vocabulary Development

Struggling Readers

While students may understand literal language, they may have some difficulty understanding figurative language. Remind students that figurative language is used to describe one thing in terms of another. For example, in the poem "The Horses," the speaker says "hearing the horizons endure." Explain to students that Hughes animates the horizon, implying that a it is able to make sound, which is something that only a living thing can do. Review the types of figurative language with students. Then, have students write examples of each type of figurative language—simile, metaphor, and personification. Ask students to trade their examples with a partner and have their partners identify which type of figurative language is being used.

Independent Practice

Vocabulary Development

Vocabulary Check

1. *a maze*
2. *a forest preserve*
3. *a river bed*
4. *a volcano*

Your Turn

1. *simile*
2. *metaphor*
3. *personification*

English for Academic Success

Language Coach

Sample response: Moorline *is formed from the words* moor *and* line. *One might guess that a* moorline *refers to the line or edge of a moor, or a wasteland.*

Choices: Evaluation Criteria

Review: Timed Writing 40–50 Minutes
Essays should contain clear thesis statements expressing students' analyses of poetic devices.

Connect: Homework
Express Your Experience
Figurative language, sound techniques, and stanza divisions should express personal impressions.

Extend: Homework
Create a Collage
Images should express the meaning of the poem.

Assess

Unit 6 Resources, Selection Standards Check, p. 163

go.hrw.com **ThinkCentral Online Assessment,** Selection Standards Check

Teacher One Stop™, editable Selection Standards Check

Reteach

go.hrw.com **ThinkCentral Online Remediation**

Standards Focus

Objectives

Students will
- understand extended metaphor
- compare and contrast

Selection Introduction

Think About the Writer

To help students answer the question, ask them what—or who—comes to mind when they are asked to think about their childhoods.

For Independent Reading

*The Distant Land of My Father,** Bo Caldwell

HRW LIBRARY *This title is available in the HRW library.

Motivate

What Do You Think?/QuickWrite

Ask students to think about what characteristics they admire or respect in people who belong to an older generation, and what opportunities students have that previous generations did not. Have students write their thoughts in their **Reader/Writer Notebooks**.

English for Academic Success

Academic Vocabulary

Look for opportunities to use the Academic Vocabulary word in this unit.

- **considerably, *adv.*:** by a large amount

California Standards, pp. 1278–1283

- **Reading Standard 2.2** Analyze the way in which clarity of meaning is affected by the patterns of organization, hierarchical structures, repetition of the main ideas, syntax, and word choice in the text.
- **Reading Standard 3.4** Analyze ways in which poets use imagery, personification, figures of speech, and sounds to evoke readers' emotions.

Preparing to Read

Digging

What Do You Think? How does experience shape our view of the world?

QuickWrite

How do you relate to the older generations in your family or community? In your *Reader/Writer Notebook,* write a brief description of the way the older generations have influenced your view of the world.

Seamus Heaney relaxes in a London park (1995).

MEET THE WRITER

Seamus Heaney

(1939–   )

Nobel Prize WINNER

Seamus Heaney was born to Roman Catholic parents in largely Protestant Northern Ireland. His boyhood on a farm in County Derry profoundly contributed to his identity as a poet. He earned his education as a scholarship student at Queens University in Belfast, where, still in his midtwenties, he was appointed lecturer in English.

Roots in the Bogs

Instead of leading him away from his Irish roots, Heaney's studies—particularly those regarding the history and psychology of myth—forged for him a new way of seeing both the grandeur of his native landscape and its figures who, unknowingly, unite past with present. Heaney believes that through his writing, generations of his ancestors will find a voice.

Heaney's poetry was considerably influenced by archaeologist P. V. Glob's book *The Bog People,* which describes several corpses found in northern European bogs. Although deposited thousands of years ago, the corpses looked newly dead—a result of the bogs' high acid content. Some of the "bog people" appeared to have been ritually sacrificed, and others seem to have been murdered. The bog people suggested to Heaney "an idea of bog as the memory of the landscape, or as a landscape that remembered everything that happened in and to it." The images of the bog people also reminded him of the atrocities, past and present, in Irish political and religious struggles.

An Ancient Epic Versus a Bestseller

The American poet Robert Lowell regarded Heaney as "the best Irish poet since William Butler Yeats." In 1995, Heaney was awarded the Nobel Prize in Literature for his works "of lyrical beauty and ethical depth, which exalt everyday miracles and the living past." Four years later, Heaney's new translation of *Beowulf* accomplished what seemed to be impossible: The ancient epic overtook *Harry Potter and the Prisoner of Azkaban* for Britain's coveted Whitbread Book of the Year Award.

Think About the Writer How is Heaney's past reflected in the subject matter of his poetry?

Selection Readability	
Easily Accessible **Accessible** Challenging	accessible theme; familiar vocabulary

Reading Standard 2.2, 3.4 (see pages A48–A50)

Literary Skills Focus

Extended Metaphor In a **metaphor,** two seemingly unlike things are compared without the use of a connective word, such as *like* or *as.* Poets use metaphor to help us see the world imaginatively and to suggest more than is possible with literal speech. An **extended metaphor** is developed over a few lines or throughout an entire poem. For example, if you were planning to use an extended metaphor comparing friendship to a rose, you might think of these similarities:

- Both begin small and gradually grow larger.
- Both bring delight but sometimes also pain.
- Both can wither and die.

Until you read the last line, you may not realize "Digging" is built on an extended metaphor.

Reading Skills Focus

Comparing and Contrasting To see the similarities between two things is **comparing;** to see the differences is **contrasting.** To understand an extended metaphor, you must be able to analyze the comparison it makes.

Into Action In your *Reader/Writer Notebook,* create a Venn diagram like this one to compare and contrast the kinds of "digging" in the poem. Write the similarities in the space where the ovals overlap.

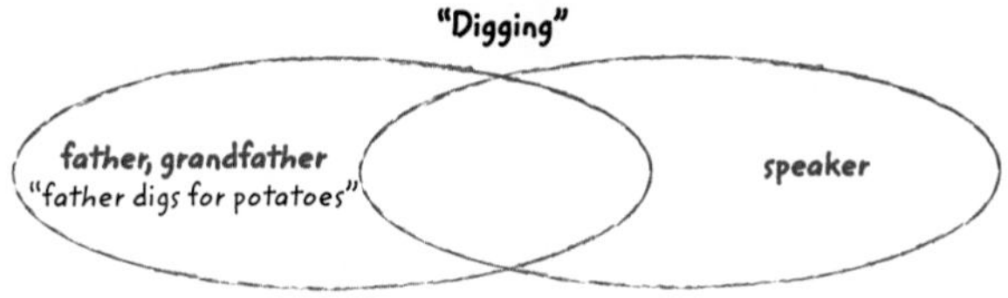

Writing Skills Focus

Think as a Reader/Writer

Find It in Your Reading The **imagery** in this poem helps us imagine the writer sitting at his desk; his father digging in the garden and in the potato fields; and his grandfather digging turf in the bog. In your *Reader/Writer Notebook,* record words that you think create especially vivid sensory images, not only of sight but also of sound, touch, and smell.

Reader/Writer Notebook

Use your **RWN** to complete the activities for this selection.

Vocabulary

coarse (kawrs) *adj.:* of low quality; rough. *The poet's father wore coarse boots.*

nestled (NEHS uhld) *v.:* snugly settled, as in a nest. *The old man's boot nestled in a mound of dirt.*

Language Coach

Multiple-Meaning Words Find where the following words are used in the poem, and put them in a list. Beside each word, indicate its part of speech as used in the poem (noun, verb, adjective, adverb). With a partner, discuss other meanings each word can have. How could the words be used as other parts of speech? Use a dictionary if necessary.

squat	ground
bends	handle

Learn It Online

Learn more about Heaney through these Internet links.

go.hrw.com H12-1279 Go

Selection Resources

Unit 6 Resources, on-level practice and assessment, p. 160

Teacher One Stop™, on-level lesson plans and all print resources

Holt Audio Library

Holt Audio Library: Selections and Summaries in Spanish

UA: Differentiating Instruction, graphic organizer, p. 299

UA: Supporting Instruction in Spanish, selection summary

ThinkCentral Online Assessment, Selection Standards Check

ThinkCentral Online Remediation

Preteach

Introducing Vocabulary

- Review the Vocabulary words, definitions, and sentences with students.
- To reinforce the importance of the Vocabulary words, tell students that these words develop the extended metaphors *nestled* in Heaney's poem. He depicts the act of digging as both *coarse* and profound.

English for Academic Success

Language Coach

Students may respond to the activity by suggesting these words: *squat, adj.*—could be used as a verb meaning "to sit on one's haunches;" *ground, n.*—could be used as a verb meaning "to mash into tiny fragments;" *bends, v.*—could also be used as a noun meaning "a type of illness;" *handle, v.*—could be used as a noun meaning "something to hold on to."

Literary Skills Focus

Have students note how Heaney extends a metaphor throughout the poem.

Reading Skills Focus

Give students a copy of the Reading Skills Focus graphic organizer before they read. (See **Unit 6 Resources.**) Tell them to use their responses to answer the questions on the Applying Your Skills page.

Writing Skills Focus

Have students record sensory details in their **Reader/Writer Notebooks** and use their notes to complete the Writing Skills Focus activity.

Learn It Online

The enhanced author biography offers more information on the life of the author as well as Holt's interactive resources pertaining to the author.

go.hrw.com H12-1279 Go

Teacher Preparation

Selection Summary

In "Digging," the speaker meditates on his father digging in his flower garden. The sight reminds him of his father digging potatoes twenty years earlier and of his grandfather, who could cut more peat in a day than any other farmer in the area. The speaker comments that he has no spade to dig as his father and grandfather did, but he will dig up meaning with his pen.

Man picking potatoes, Shea Head, Ireland.

Universal Access

EL English Learners

English for Academic Success Ask students to read the poem aloud and to pay special attention to the hard, rough sounds of words like *gravelly, lug, curt,* and *cuts.* Suggest to students that these sounds evoke the hard physical labor that Heaney describes. Have students write a sentence using one of these words and attempt to evoke the feeling of doing hard physical labor.

✔ See the **English Language Skill Builder** in **UA: Differentiating Instruction.**

Struggling Readers

Benchmark Students Students may benefit from a brief discussion on how the tools or technology used in people's work might play a major role in shaping identities and self-esteem. Ask students to name some objects associated with a particular line of work or profession (such as a fire engine, basketball, camera, telephone, or computer) and to tell how these objects (like Heaney's pen) can define a way of life, establish values, and confer meaning and satisfaction.

Digging Ⓐ by **Seamus Heaney**

Read with a Purpose
Read to find out why the poem is called "Digging."

Build Background
In the not-too-distant past, Irish farmers dug two things in particular: potatoes and turf, or peat. The peat was dug from bogs, the huge soggy areas of decaying vegetable matter that have produced for Ireland, especially in previous centuries, the material that is dried and burned in fires for cooking and heat.

Between my finger and my thumb
The squat pen rests; snug as a gun.

Under my window, a clean rasping sound
When the spade sinks into gravelly ground:
My father, digging. I look down

Till his straining rump among the flowerbeds
Bends low, comes up twenty years away
Stooping in rhythm through potato drills°
Where he was digging.

The coarse boot nestled on the lug,° the shaft
Against the inside knee was levered firmly.
He rooted out tall tops, buried the bright edge deep
To scatter new potatoes that we picked
Loving their cool hardness in our hands.

By God, the old man could handle a spade.
Just like his old man.

8. drills: furrows or rows of planted seeds.

10. lug: piece of the spade that projects out.

Ⓐ **Literary Focus** **Extended Metaphor** How is the title related to the metaphor that extends to the end of the poem?

Vocabulary **coarse** (kawrs) *adj.:* of low quality; rough.
nestled (NEHS uhld) *v.:* snugly settled, as in a nest.

Analyzing Visuals

Connecting to the Text How does the photograph on the opposite page echo the images Heaney conveys in stanza 3?

Direct Teach

Think About/Talk About

Read with a Purpose Have students read the Read with a Purpose statement. Ask them what things people might "dig" for. Ask them to think about what else "digging" might mean.

Analysis

Ⓐ Literary Focus

Possible response: *The title establishes the metaphor that extends to the end of the poem.*

Vocabulary: Own the Word

- **coarse:** Write *coarse* in a center circle on the board along with its definition: rough. Draw spider legs from the circle as students add concepts and attributes. ***Possible responses:*** *uneven, prickly, scratchy, not smooth*
- **nestled:** Give students the following examples: Sleepy children can be *nestled* in their parents' laps. Eggs might be carefully *nestled* in a basket. Delicate dishes could be *nestled* in a corner of a cabinet. Ask students to name some things that are *nestled* in the corner of their bedrooms.

Analyzing Visuals

Connecting to the Text: *The man in the photograph is stooping and seemingly straining as he digs through the "drills," or rows of planted seeds.*

Advanced Learners

Acceleration Explain that much of Heaney's poetry reflects his rural upbringing and the extended sectarian conflict in Northern Ireland. Heaney analyzes the internecine violence in unique terms, protesting the unwillingness of both sides to speak out freely. As the speaker in "Digging" asserts, Heaney feels that through his writing, generations of his rural ancestors will find a voice. Have students read more of Heaney's poetry and trace his analyses and commentary of human emotion and experience.

Students with Disabilities

To help students understand how a writer can "dig" into the human experience with a pen, ask students the following questions: What kind of emotions might a writer of inspirational literature dig into? What kind of feelings or reaction is a writer of science-fiction novels trying to "dig up"? What type of thoughts might an investigative reporter want to "dig up" in the minds of his or her readers?

✔ See **UA: Differentiating Instruction** for a graphic organizer to scaffold instruction for students with disabilities.

Think About/Talk About

Comprehension

Ⓑ Reading Focus

Possible responses: *He can dig into, or explore, his memory of the collective memory of his family or culture. He can dig into the minds and hearts of people, creating poems that illuminate human experience. Digging, unlike writing, requires physical labor and strength.*

Extend the Discussion

Making Inferences What does the speaker admire about his grandfather? ***Possible response:*** *He has a very strong work ethic. He takes a brief break to drink some milk and then gets right back to work.*

Social Studies Link

Ask Yourself

Possible response: *Although he does not share their talent for digging potatoes and peat, Heaney admires the farmers who have been in his family for generations. He feels united with them through blood, memory, and the soil.*

My grandfather cut more turf in a day
Than any other man on Toner's bog.
Once I carried him milk in a bottle
Corked sloppily with paper. He straightened up
To drink it, then fell to right away
Nicking and slicing neatly, heaving sods
Over his shoulder, going down and down
For the good turf. Digging.

The cold smell of potato mould, the squelch and slap
Of soggy peat, the curt° cuts of an edge
Through living roots awaken in my head.
But I've no spade to follow men like them.

Between my finger and my thumb
The squat pen rests.
I'll dig with it. Ⓑ

26. curt: here, short.

Ⓑ **Reading Focus** **Comparing and Contrasting** In what ways is writing like digging? In what ways is it different?

SOCIAL STUDIES LINK

Agriculture in Ireland

Most people in nineteenth-century Ireland subsisted on small family farms that grew potatoes, the main source of food for the impoverished Irish people suffering under British rule. From 1845 to 1849, Ireland experienced a colossal famine (called in Irish *An Gorta Mór,* "The Great Hunger") when a blight rendered much of the potato crop useless. One and a half million people died during the famine, and another million immigrated to America. Today, farming accounts for just 3 percent of Ireland's gross national product. Since Ireland has joined the European Union, potato production has declined—as have the small farms like the one Heaney describes.

Ask Yourself

How does Heaney feel about the farmers that had been in his family for generations?

California Standards, p. 1283

- **Reading Standard 2.2** Analyze the way in which clarity of meaning is affected by the patterns of organization, hierarchical structures, repetition of the main ideas, syntax, and word choice in the text.
- **Reading Standard 3.4** Analyze ways in which poets use imagery, personification, figures of speech, and sounds to evoke readers' emotions.
- **Writing Standard 2.1** Write fictional, autobiographical, or biographical narratives: **a.** Narrate a sequence of events and communicate their significance to the audience. **b.** Locate scenes and incidents in specific places. **c.** Describe with concrete sensory details the sights, sounds, and smells of a scene and the specific actions, movements, gestures, and feelings of the characters; use interior monologue to depict the characters' feelings. **e.** Make effective use of descriptions of appearance, images, shifting perspectives, and sensory details.

Applying Your Skills

Reading Standard 2.2, 3.4 (see pages A48–A50)
Writing Standard 2.1a–c, 2.1e (see pages A51–A52)

Digging

Literary Response and Analysis

Reading Skills Focus

Quick Check

1. What does the speaker see from his window?
2. What does he remember about his grandfather's digging?
3. With what does the speaker say he'll dig?

Read with a Purpose

4. What is the speaker's goal for his writing?

Reading Skills: Comparing and Contrasting

5. Complete your diagram comparing the kinds of digging mentioned in the poem. How is the speaker's digging similar to and different from the digging done by his father and grandfather?

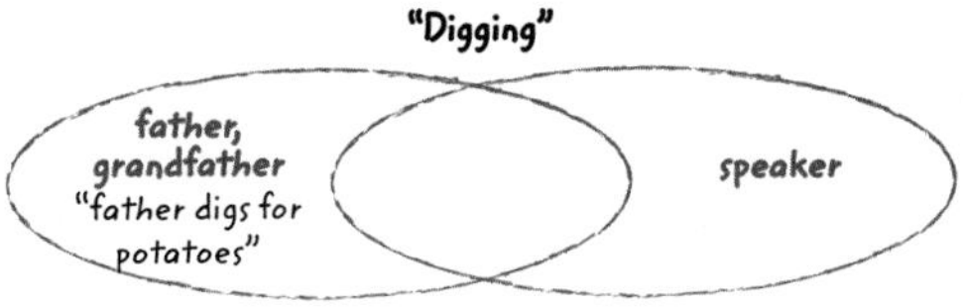

Vocabulary Check

Be sure you can justify your answers to these questions about the Vocabulary words.

6. Would you describe something that is fine and delicate as **coarse?**
7. If a baby is **nestled** in your arms, is the baby uncomfortable or snug?

Literary Skills Focus

Literary Analysis

8. **Analyze** To what things does the speaker compare his pen? What is significant about these comparisons?
9. **Infer** In lines 25–27, the spade cuts through the "living roots." How might digging, either the kind done by the speaker's father or that done by the speaker himself, be seen as violent?
10. **Analyze** Identify other images of violence or destruction in the poem. What might the poet be suggesting about the relationship between creation and destruction?

Literary Skills: Extended Metaphor

11. **Evaluate** Note the occurrences of the verb *dig* or *digging*, and examine the poem's extended metaphor. Why is the verb *digging* a good way to describe the work of a writer?

Literary Skills Review: Alliteration

12. **Analyze** The repetition of initial consonant sounds of words close together in a text is called **alliteration.** Identify and analyze the effect of three uses of alliteration in the poem.

Writing Skills Focus

Think as a Reader/Writer

Use It in Your Writing Review your notes about the images in "Digging." In your *Reader/Writer Notebook*, write a short essay in which you describe a person in a particular scene. Use words that will help your reader to imagine the sights, sounds, smells, tastes, and tactile feelings of the scene's details.

What Do You Think Now

How does the poet's family background affect his aims in writing?

For **CHOICES** see page 1289.

Universal Access

Struggling Writers

Some students may need additional scaffolding to complete the Writing Skills Focus activity. Invite students to begin writing by jotting down a few sentences describing someone they admire or respect. Remind them to describe the qualities that make this person admirable. Encourage students to incorporate their sentences into their essay about the person they admire.

What Do You Think Now?

To help students answer this question, ask them how their own backgrounds and/or the backgrounds of their families influence the decisions they make and the goals they set for themselves.

Assess

Unit 6 Resources, Selection Standards Check, p. 163

Check for Understanding

Independent Practice

Reading Skills Focus

Possible responses:

1. *The speaker sees his father stooping to dig with a spade.*
2. *He dug more peat in a day than any other farmer in the area.*
3. *He will dig with his pen.*
4. *He wants to create enduring written works through determination and precision.*
5. *Ask students to compare the tools and purposes of the speaker's digging and his father's and grandfather's digging.*

Vocabulary Check

6. *no* 7. *snug*

Literary Skills Focus

Possible responses:

8. *He compares it to a gun and a spade. The gun comparison suggests the power of writing. The spade comparison links the speaker's heritage to his writing.*
9. *Digging to cultivate the soil might be regarded as intruding the natural environment. "Digging" into people's experiences might be regarded as intrusive.*
10. *Violent images include "rooted out tall tops," "buried the bright edge deep" (line 12) and "nicking and slicing neatly" (line 22). He may be suggesting that creation too requires boldness, determination, and precision.*
11. *"Digging" is repeated in lines 5, 9, and 24, while "dig" is used in the last line. The speaker compares his work to that of his ancestors. Just as they dug the earth to produce food and fuel, he intends to dig into the human experience for spiritual and emotional sustenance.*
12. *In line 2 ("squat . . . snug") creates a rhythmical effect; line 4 ("spade sinks," "gravelly ground") and line 5 ("digging . . . down") suggest the repeated movements of digging.*

Standards Focus

Objectives

Students will
- analyze the way in which theme represents a view on life
- analyze imagery

Selection Introduction

Think About the Writer

To help students answer the question, ask them to think about how their surroundings influence them.

For Independent Reading

Oranges, John McPhee

Motivate

What Do You Think?/QuickWrite

As students describe the items on their lists, have them pretend that they have discovered something that no one has ever seen before (even if they have listed such items as trees or squirrels). Suggest that they use descriptive words that will effectively introduce their new discoveries to the world.

English for Academic Success

Academic Vocabulary

Look for opportunities to use the Academic Vocabulary word in this unit.

- **exhibit, *v.*:** show, demonstrate

Preparing to Read

Mushrooms

What Do You Think? How does experience shape our view of the world?

QuickWrite

How does interacting with nature shape how you think about the world? In your *Reader/Writer Notebook,* jot down a quick list of five things in nature that you know well. Think about how you would describe each item on your list to someone who has no experience with it.

Margaret Atwood (1939).

MEET THE WRITER

Margaret Atwood

(1939–)

The Man Booker Prize WINNER

Canadian novelist, poet, and critic Margaret Atwood applies a strict moral intelligence to her investigations of individual responsibility, social justice, and the natural world.

Choosing a Writer's Life

As a child, Margaret Atwood experienced both city and country life. Her family spent April to November living in the wilderness of Quebec and the remainder of the year in cities, including Ottawa and Toronto. Accordingly, Atwood's writings reflect insights into human society and a passionate love of nature.

Inspired by Edgar Allan Poe, Atwood began writing poetry in high school. At age sixteen, while walking home one day and drafting a poem in her head, she had a realization: Writing was "suddenly the only thing I wanted to do." Her subsequent dedication to the literary life has produced works ranging from poems and novels to book reviews and literary criticism.

A Sharp Look at Human Society

In 1972, Atwood published *Survival,* a landmark study of Canadian literature. The same year, her novel *Surfacing* reflected her growing interest in women's roles. Another novel, *The Penelopiad* (2005), retells the story of the *Odyssey* from the point of view of Penelope, Odysseus's wife.

Atwood's novels often focus on the relationship between the personal and the political. *The Handmaid's Tale* (1985), for example, is a nightmarish vision of a future dictatorship in which women are valued only for their ability to breed. In *The Blind Assassin* (2000), a Canadian family saga reflects shaping events in twentieth-century Canada, and *Oryx and Crake* (2003) explores the consequences of genetic manipulation.

Although Atwood is wary of how we use technology, she emphasizes that science is not the problem: "The driving force in the world today is the human heart—that is, human emotions.... Our tools have become very powerful. Hate, not bombs, destroys cities. Desire, not bricks, rebuilds them."

Think About the Writer How might growing up in both cities and remote wilderness have affected Atwood's views?

California Standards, pp. 1284–1289

- **Reading Standard 3.2** Analyze the way in which the theme or meaning of a selection represents a view or comment on life, using textual evidence to support the claim.
- **Reading Standard 3.4** Analyze ways in which poets use imagery, personification, figures of speech, and sounds to evoke readers' emotions.

Selection Readability	
Easily Accessible **Accessible** Challenging	accessible theme; familiar syntax; accessible vocabulary

Reading Standard 3.2, 3.4 (see pages A48–A50)

Literary Skills Focus

Theme The **theme** of a poem is the central insight it expresses about human experience. Theme is not the same as the subject, for while the subject is communicated directly, the theme is usually implied. The subject of "Mushrooms" is the growth of mushrooms, but Atwood uses this subject to comment on the broader relationship between experience and poetry. Writers develop theme through imagery, form, language, tone, and style.

Reading Skills Focus

Interpreting Imagery One tool poets use to convey theme is **imagery,** language that appeals to the five senses. Looking at a poem's images will help you understand the theme the writer wants to communicate. Many images appeal to the sense of sight, but Atwood also appeals to the senses of hearing, taste, and smell as she explores the mushrooms' growth.

Into Action As you read, list in a chart like this one the imagery in "Mushrooms." In the first column, record these images and the lines where you found them. In the next column, identify the senses to which the image appeals. Then, add your impressions about what the imagery suggests.

Imagery (lines)	Sense(s)	Impressions of Image
"tiny / bright red balloons / filling with water" (lines 6–8)	sight; touch	growing, expanding; whimsical, surprising
"a sound below sound" (line 9)	hearing	

Writing Skills Focus

Think as a Reader/Writer

Find It in Your Reading Atwood uses **figurative language,** primarily similes and metaphors, to compare the mushrooms with inanimate objects and natural elements. As you read, notice how the comparisons and vivid **images** combine to create sensory appeal. In your *Reader/Writer Notebook,* record two or three examples that you find most effective.

TechFocus In this poem, Atwood examines a biological subject from a poet's point of view. Notice that she refers to scientific details about the life cycle of mushrooms. What words would you type into a search engine to find out more about these references?

Reader/Writer Notebook

Use your **RWN** to complete the activities for this selection.

Vocabulary

embers (EHM buhrz) *n. pl.:* glowing remains of a fire. *We tried to put out the campfire, but the embers still burned dimly in the night.*

parallel (PAR uh lehl) *adv.:* in line with, but without meeting. *I watch the bird fly parallel to the ground, and it never touched down.*

underfoot (uhn duhr FUT) *adv.:* between the feet and the ground. *After the storm, the wet lawn felt spongy underfoot.*

decay (dih KAY) *n.:* wasting away; rotting; decline in quality. *Decay had already eaten away the edges of the old tree stump.*

Language Coach

Compound Words A compound word is one word formed by putting two or more words together. Which Vocabulary word is a compound word? In this poem, Atwood invents some of her own compound words. What compound words might you invent to describe your favorite place in nature?

Learn It Online

Practice your vocabulary knowledge with Word Watch online.

go.hrw.com H12-1285 Go

Selection Resources

Unit 6 Resources, on-level practice and assessment, p. 166

Teacher One Stop™, on-level lesson plans and all print resources

Holt Audio Library

Holt Audio Library: Selections and Summaries in Spanish

UA: Differentiating Instruction, graphic organizer, p. 299

UA: Supporting Instruction in Spanish, selection summary

ThinkCentral Online Assessment, Selection Standards Check

ThinkCentral Online Remediation

Preteach

Introducing Vocabulary

- Review the Vocabulary words, definitions, and sentences with students.
- Tell students that the Vocabulary words help the author develop the theme through imagery, language, and tone. Tell students to use these words and elements of the writer's style to help them discover the theme.

English for Academic Success

Language Coach

Students may notice that *underfoot* is a compound word. To help students come up with their own compound words, have them make a list of descriptive words that portray their favorite place. Then, have students experiment with creating compound words from the words on their list.

Literary Skills Focus

As you read and discuss the poem with students, have them note the way in which Atwood develops her theme.

Reading Skills Focus

Give students a copy of the Reading Skills Focus graphic organizer before they read. (See **Unit 6 Resources.**) Tell them to use their responses to answer the questions on the Applying Your Skills page.

Writing Skills Focus

Have students record 2–3 examples of figurative language in their **Reader/Writer Notebooks**. Students can use their notes to complete the Writing Skills Focus activity.

Learn It Online

Send students to **Word Watch** for audio pronunciations, synonyms and antonyms, and brief histories of word origins.

go.hrw.com H12-1285 Go

Teacher Preparation

Selection Summary

In section one of "Mushrooms," the speaker describes the outbreak of mushrooms after a damp night. In section two, she describes how mushrooms spread. The third section describes where and how mushrooms live. The final section reveals the speaker's attraction to mushrooms and the way in which she relates them to burgeoning creativity.

Direct Teach

Think About/Talk About

Read with a Purpose Have students read the Read with a Purpose statement. Remind students that poets often make comparisons to develop their themes. Ask them to define a "creative life."

Mushrooms

by **Margaret Atwood**

White Beech mushrooms.

Read with a Purpose

Read to discover how a writer connects collecting mushrooms with her own creative life.

Build Background

Mushrooms and other fungi are not plants—scientists classify them in a different kingdom of living things because they lack chlorophyll, the green material plants use to turn light energy into food. Instead, mushrooms obtain energy by absorbing nutrients from dead animal and plant materials. Mushrooms have two main parts. The first part, the threadlike, underground *mycelium,* absorbs food and can live for many years in soil or wood. The *fruiting body,* the second part, is typically what you see of a mushroom growing in the woods. It includes the stalk, cap, and gills. Often appearing after rainfall, the fruiting body usually lives only a few days. During its short lifetime, the mushroom reproduces by releasing spores from which new mycelia can grow.

Universal Access

EL English Learners

Students may have difficulty understanding the relationship between mushrooms and creative expression. Have students reread the Build Background note and brainstorm a list of words that describe mushrooms. Then, have students list thoughts and feelings that those words evoke. As they read the poem, have them note similar emotions.

✔ See the **English Language Skill Builder** in **UA: Differentiating Instruction.**

Struggling Readers

Students may have difficulty reading "Mushrooms" because it does not use traditional punctuation and capitalization. Have students read the poem in pairs. Tell them to experiment by pausing in different places. Once they decide what sounds best, have them insert commas, periods, dashes, or other punctuation marks. Have the pairs join small groups so that each pair can share their work.

i

In this moist season,
mist on the lake and thunder
afternoons in the distance

they ooze up through the earth
during the night,
like bubbles, like tiny
bright red balloons
filling with water;
a sound below sound, the thumbs of rubber
gloves turned softly inside out.

In the mornings, there is the leaf mold
starred with nipples,
with cool white fishgills,
leathery purple brains,
fist-sized suns dulled to the color of embers,
poisonous moons, pale yellow. **A**

ii

Where do they come from?

For each thunderstorm that travels
overhead there's another storm
that moves parallel in the ground.
Struck lightning is where they meet.

Underfoot there's a cloud of rootlets,
shed hairs or a bundle of loose threads
blown slowly through the midsoil.
These are their flowers, these fingers
reaching through darkness to the sky,
these eyeblinks
that burst and powder the air with spores.

iii

They feed in shade, on halfleaves
as they return to water,
on slowly melting logs,
deadwood. They glow
in the dark sometimes. They taste
of rotten meat or cloves
or cooking steak or bruised
lips or new snow. **B**

iv

It isn't only
for food I hunt them
but for the hunt and because
they smell of death and the waxy
skins of the newborn,
flesh into earth into flesh. **C**

Here is the handful
of shadow I have brought back to you:
this decay, this hope, this mouth-
ful of dirt, this poetry.

Fungus found in a West Sussex wood.

A **Reading Focus** **Interpreting Imagery** Why do you think that the poet compares mushrooms to both suns and moons?

B **Literary Focus** **Theme** What key idea about mushrooms and their place in the world is suggested by this list of images?

C **Reading Focus** **Interpreting Imagery** How would you describe this image in your own words?

Vocabulary **embers** (EHM buhrz) *n. pl.:* glowing remains of a fire.
parallel (PAR uh lehl) *adv.:* in line with, but without meeting.
underfoot (uhn duhr FUT) *adv.:* between the feet and the ground.
decay (dih KAY) *n.:* wasting away; rotting; decline in quality.

Think About/Talk About

Comprehension

A Reading Focus
Possible response: *She makes this comparison to create an image of contrasting forms and colors.*

C Reading Focus
Possible response: *The mushrooms smell old, but feel new; they represent life and death.*

Analysis

B Literary Focus
Possible responses: *They are both good and bad. They feed off of other organisms, and they feed other organisms.*

Vocabulary: Own the Word

- **embers:** Ask students the following questions: When might you see *embers*? What color are *embers*?
- **parallel:** Hold out your arms so that they are *parallel* to one another. Ask two students to walk in two separate *parallel* lines.
- **underfoot:** Remind students that *underfoot* is a compound word that combines the words *under* and *foot*. In autumn, you can hear fallen leaves crunch *underfoot*. Walking on a beach, you can feel the sand *underfoot*.
- **decay:** Stress the connection between *decay* and rot. Ask students to list things they associate with *decay*. ***Possible responses:*** *teeth, health, tree roots, fruit*

California Standards, p. 1288

- **Reading Standard 3.2** Analyze the way in which the theme or meaning of a selection represents a view or comment on life, using textual evidence to support the claim.
- **Reading Standard 3.4** Analyze ways in which poets use imagery, personification, figures of speech, and sounds to evoke readers' emotions.
- **Grades 9–10 Review Reading Standard 3.7** Recognize and understand the significance of various literary devices, including figurative language, imagery, allegory, and symbolism, and explain their appeal.

Check for Understanding

Independent Practice

Reading Skills Focus

Possible responses:

1. *She has brought back poetry.*
2. *Mushrooms are like creative thoughts that lie dormant and then burst forth with inspiration. Like mushrooms, creativity can feed off other organisms to create a unique form that is then passed on to others.*
3. *Have students add a column to their chart that connects images to reveal the theme of the poem.*

Vocabulary Check

Possible responses:

4. *The two parallel roads follow the same course.*
5. *The week-old bouquet of flowers shows signs of decay.*
6. *The soft moss is underfoot.*
7. *Only the fiery embers remain from last night's blaze.*

Literary Skills Focus

Possible responses:

8. *The consonant sound "b."*
9. *Assonance—"ooze" (line 4) and "afternoons" (line 3), "thumbs . . . rubber gloves" (lines 9–10). Alliteration—"moist . . . mist" (lines 1–2), "poisonous . . . pale" (line 16), and "flowers . . . fingers" (line 25). Repeated grammatical structures such as those found in lines 34–36 and lines 45–46 produce rhythm.*
10. *She refers to life, death, and rebirth.*
11. *This placement allows the reader to read the line as "mouthful of dirt" or "mouth full of dirt."*
12. *Decay, hope, and dirt are all part of the cycle of life and, figuratively speaking, the cycle of creativity. Poetry and mushrooms, like life, can be raw, dangerous, delicious, and beautiful.*
13. *The mushrooms most likely symbolize lines of poetry produced from the soil of creativity, inspiration, and experience.*

Applying Your Skills

Reading Standard 3.2, 3.4; **Grades 9–10 Review Reading Standard** 3.7 (see pages A48–A50)
Writing Standard 2.2b (see pages A51–A52)

Mushrooms

Literary Response and Analysis

Reading Skills Focus

Quick Check

1. In the final stanza, what does the speaker say she has brought back from her hunt?

Read with a Purpose

2. How is collecting mushrooms similar to writing poetry?

Reading Skills: Interpreting Imagery

3. Thinking about how a poem's images relate to each other is part of interpreting poetic imagery. In a new column of your chart, compare each image with other images in the poem. Using the connections you discover, write a statement of the poem's theme.

Vocabulary Check

Change each sentence so that the Vocabulary word is used logically.

4. The two roads run **parallel** until they meet at a crowded intersection.
5. The fresh bouquet of flowers shows signs of **decay.**
6. A stormy gray sky spreads **underfoot**.
7. Only the icy **embers** remain from last night's blaze.

Literary Skills Focus

Literary Analysis

8. **Identify** In lines 6–10, what repeated consonant suggests the sound of the fingers of rubber gloves turning inside out?
9. **Analyze** What uses of assonance and alliteration help create the poem's music? Where do repeated grammatical structures help create a rhythm?
10. **Interpret** To what does the speaker refer when she describes the cycle of "flesh into earth into flesh" in line 42?
11. **Analyze** Why might Atwood have chosen to break the word *mouthful* between lines 45 and 46? What is the effect of this break?

Literary Skills: Theme

12. **Draw Conclusions** Explain the poem's last four lines. How could mushrooms suggest decay, hope, a mouthful of dirt, and poetry? How do these lines contribute to the poem's theme?

Literary Skills Review: Symbol

13. **Interpret** A **symbol** is a person, place, thing, or event that stands both for itself and for something beyond itself. What might the mushrooms symbolize?

Writing Skills Focus

Think as a Reader/Writer

Use It in Your Writing Review Atwood's use of similes and metaphors. In your *Reader/Writer Notebook*, write a paragraph in which you use imagery and figurative language, including similes and metaphors, to compare an inanimate object, such as a car, to something animate or abstract, such as freedom.

What Do You Think Now? What is the speaker's attitude toward new experiences? If you adopted her attitude for a day, how might it change the way you experience the natural world?

Universal Access

EL Struggling Writers

Some students may need additional scaffolding to complete the Writing Skills Focus activity. Before students begin writing, have them think about what abstract concept comes to mind when thinking about the origin, appearance, and functions of their inanimate object. Then, have them write a few sentences developing this metaphor. Remind them to use vivid details that appeal to sight, sound, taste, smell, or touch.

What Do You Think Now?

To help students answer this question, remind them that the speaker likes mushrooms. Tell them that some varieties of mushrooms can be poisonous, and point out that the speaker even mentions this fact in the poem. Considering the potential danger of some mushrooms, ask students to explain whether a person who takes interest in mushrooms would be curious or cautious.

Writing Standard 2.2a–c, 2.6a–c (see pages A51–A52)
Listening and Speaking Standard 1.7, 1.9 (see pages A53–A55)

CHOICES

As you respond to the Choices, use these **Academic Vocabulary** words as appropriate: adapt, considerably, exhibit, inevitable, perspective.

REVIEW

Write a Comparison Essay

Timed Writing In "Digging," Heaney compares digging to writing. In a brief essay, compare another activity or occupation to writing. Use details to support your thesis.

Prepare a Summary Chart

Use a chart like the one below to summarize the main images and ideas of each part of "Mushrooms." Compare your chart with that of another student, noting which details you each included. Talk about which ideas you think are essential and which details can be left out of your summary.

Part	Summary
i	
ii	
iii	
iv	

CONNECT

Write an E-mail Recommendation

One joy of literature is sharing it with friends and relatives. Think about your experience reading "Digging." What friend or family member do you think would most enjoy this poem? Write an e-mail or letter in which you recommend that this person read the poem. You might want to quote a few memorable lines or include an analysis of the poem's theme.

Present a Radio Program

Create a poetry reading of "Digging" or "Mushrooms" (or both) that could be broadcast over the radio. Write material for a brief introduction that will prepare listeners for the poem. Practice reading the poem aloud, and create a reading script that notes where you will pause, how you will vary your pace, and which words you will emphasize. When you record your program, be sure to read slowly enough so that your listeners can follow your presentation.

EXTEND

Create a Field Guide

TechFocus Use Internet resources to learn more about mushrooms. Then, use presentation software to exhibit the information in the form of a digital field guide, including both illustrations and text. Although your guide will have a scientific and informative tone, try to also incorporate at least a hint of Atwood's poetic sense of wonder and mystery. You might consider including a line from her poem as a caption or heading.

Plan an Anthology

Create the table of contents for a poetry anthology that includes "Digging" and "Mushrooms." Choose a theme and title for your anthology, as well as a list of other poems you would include. You might combine poems by well-known authors with those written by yourself or classmates. Create a cover that gives readers an accurate impression of what they can expect to find inside.

California Standards, pp. 1288–1289

- **Writing Standard 2.2** Write responses to literature: **a.** Demonstrate a comprehensive understanding of the significant ideas in works or passages. **b.** Analyze the use of imagery, language, universal themes, and unique aspects of the text. **c.** Support important ideas and viewpoints through accurate and detailed references to the text and to other works.
- **Writing Standard 2.6** Deliver multimedia presentations: **a.** Combine text, images, and sound and draw information from many sources (e.g., television broadcasts, videos, films, newspapers, magazines, CD-ROMs, the Internet, electronic media-generated images). **b.** Select an appropriate medium for each element of the presentation. **c.** Use the selected media skillfully, editing appropriately and monitoring for quality.
- **Listening and Speaking Standard 1.7** Use appropriate rehearsal strategies to pay attention to performance details, achieve command of the text, and create skillful artistic staging.
- **Listening and Speaking Standard 1.9** Use research and analysis to justify strategies for gesture, movement, and vocalization, including dialect, pronunciation, and enunciation.

Independent Practice

Choices: Evaluation Criteria

Review: Timed Writing 40–50 Minutes
Students should show a clear comparison between an activity or occupation and writing.

Review: Homework
Prepare a Summary Chart
Charts should include essential details of each part of the poem.

Connect: Homework
Write an E-mail Recommendation
E-mails should include reasons why someone should read the poem.

Connect: Homework
Present a Radio Program
Readings should include pauses and vocal variation.

Extend: Homework
Create a Field Guide
Guides should reflect research and include images and text.

Extend: Homework
Plan an Anthology
The selected poems should be linked by a common theme.

Assess

Unit 6 Resources, Selection Standards Check, pp. 163, 170

go.hrw.com **ThinkCentral Online Assessment,** Selection Standards Check

Teacher One Stop™, editable Selection Standards Check

Reteach

go.hrw.com **ThinkCentral Online Remediation**

Standards Focus

Objectives

Students will
- understand the sonnet form
- draw inferences

Selection Introduction

Think About the Writer

To help students answer the question, remind them that many Americans pride themselves on their ethnicity or heritage. Ask students to think about their own connections to an ethnic group or heritage and what that connection means to them.

For Independent Reading

The Temple of the Golden Pavilion, Yuko Mishima

Motivate

What Do You Think?/QuickWrite

Have students record memories or experiences that are connected to their hometown in their **Reader/ Writer Notebooks.**

English for Academic Success

Academic Vocabulary

Look for opportunities to use the Academic Vocabulary word in this unit.

- **perspective, *n.*:** a particular way of looking at something

California Standards, pp. 1290–1293

- **Reading Standard 2.4** Make warranted and reasonable assertions about the author's arguments by using elements of the text to defend and clarify interpretations.
- **Reading Standard 3.1** Analyze characteristics of subgenres (e.g., satire, parody, allegory, pastoral) that are used in poetry, prose, plays, novels, short stories, essays, and other basic genres.

Preparing to Read

Atlantis—A Lost Sonnet

What Do You Think? How does experience shape our view of the world?

QuickWrite

What would you miss about your hometown or state if you had to move away? What people and things would you have the most trouble leaving? Record your response in your *Reader/Writer Notebook.*

Eavan Boland.

MEET THE WRITER

Eavan Boland (1944–)

Born in Dublin, Ireland, Eavan Boland was the youngest of five children. Her father was a diplomat, and her mother was a painter. When she was five, her family moved to London, and then six years later, to New York City. Returning to Ireland in her teens was difficult for Boland; she has described having to reacquaint herself with Ireland and feeling a lack of belonging—a theme that appears frequently in her poetry.

Feminist and Love Poet

Some critics call Boland a feminist writer because of her realistic look at the difficulty of obtaining and maintaining freedom as a married woman. In her verse, however, she finds balance between her love of domestic life and her feminist ideas.

"So much of European love poetry is court poetry, coming out of the glamorous traditions of the court. . . . There's little about the ordinariness of love," said Boland in an interview for *The New Yorker* magazine. In response to what she found lacking in love poetry, Boland has presented the "dailiness," as she calls it, of love and life. Although she titled her 2001 collection *Against Love Poetry,* Boland's poetry is a reaction not against love but against the portrayal of an idealized romantic love. In her poems, Boland examines from a realistic perspective the conflicts faced in life and love.

A Great Irish Poet

Early in her career Boland established herself as an important poet, but she did not receive formal recognition for several decades. After publishing several poetry collections and receiving many prizes, including the Poetry Book Society Choice award for *The Journey,* Boland became increasingly well known. By 1999, her poetry, along with that of Seamus Heaney and other great Irish poets, became a requirement for study at Irish high schools. Boland has taught at Trinity College and is currently a professor at Stanford University in California.

Think About the Writer Considering the isolation Boland felt from Ireland in her youth, how do you think she would respond to being named among the great Irish poets?

Selection Readability	
Easily Accessible **Accessible** Challenging	common theme; familiar syntax; accessible vocabulary

Reading Standard 2.4, 3.1 (see pages A48–A50)

Literary Skills Focus

Sonnet The traditional **sonnet** form includes fourteen lines. Depending on the type of sonnet, these lines are traditionally divided into an octave and a sestet (an eight-line and a six-line stanza in a Petrarchan sonnet) or into quatrains and a couplet (three four-line stanzas and one two-line stanza in a Shakespearean sonnet). Sonnets also traditionally have an intricate rhyme scheme and are often written in iambic pentameter.

Throughout literary history, poets have experimented with the sonnet, creating new versions by manipulating length, rhyme scheme, and meter. Boland's "Atlantis—A Lost Sonnet" is a variation on the sonnet form but does contain one important element common to most sonnets: the **turn,** in which the concluding lines either answer the question posed by the speaker or summarize the message found in the beginning lines.

Reading Skills Focus

Drawing Inferences Authors, especially poets, expect readers to **draw inferences,** or make educated guesses based on prior knowledge and clues from the text. As you read "Atlantis—A Lost Sonnet," read "between the lines" and use your own prior knowledge and experience to draw inferences about the poem's subject, speaker, and theme.

Into Action In your *Reader/Writer Notebook,* use a chart like the one below to record your inferences about the poem as you read.

Prior Experience	Clues	Inference
I miss the city I used to live in and the people I knew there.	The speaker talks about the everyday things she misses about the "old city."	

Writing Skills Focus

Think as a Reader/Writer

Find It in Your Reading As you read, notice Boland's descriptions of Atlantis and of the city that she has lost. In your *Reader/Writer Notebook,* record the details she uses to describe each place. How does she use these details to establish a general image of Atlantis and a more intimate image of her own lost city?

Reader/Writer Notebook

Use your **RWN** to complete the activities for this selection.

Vocabulary

convey (kuhn VAY) *v.:* communicate; express. *The speaker found it difficult to convey her sorrow about her loss.*

traditions (truh DIHSH uhnz) *n. pl.:* customs, values, or ideas handed down from generation to generation. *Family traditions can provide people with a sense of stability and continuity.*

Language Coach

Etymology The **etymology,** or origins of words, can help you understand more about their meaning. Use a dictionary to find the etymology of *convey* and *traditions.* From what ancient language did both words originate? Identify their original meanings, and tell how knowing this information helps you understand the current meaning of the words.

Learn It Online

Let the online audio version of this poem bring it alive for you.

go.hrw.com H12-1291 Go

Selection Resources

Unit 6 Resources, on-level practice and assessment, p. 167

Teacher One Stop™, on-level lesson plans and all print resources

Holt Audio Library

Holt Audio Library: Selections and Summaries in Spanish

UA: Differentiating Instruction, graphic organizer, p. 299

UA: Supporting Instruction in Spanish, selection summary

ThinkCentral Online Assessment, Selection Standards Check

ThinkCentral Online Remediation

Preteach

Introducing Vocabulary

- Review the Vocabulary words, definitions, and sentences with students.
- To reinforce the importance of the Vocabulary words, tell students that Boland uses these words as she varies established poetic *traditions* while *conveying* new ideas.

English for Academic Success

Language Coach

After students read the **Language Coach,** have them answer the question. ***Possible response:*** *Students will find that* convey *(from Latin* conviare*) means "to accompany;"* traditions *(from Latin* tradere*) means "to hand over." The etymology of the words should create a clearer understanding of the meaning.*

Literary Skills Focus

As you read and discuss the selection with students, have them note how this poem follows or doesn't follow the traditional sonnet form.

Reading Skills Focus

Give students a copy of the Reading Skills Focus graphic organizer before they read. (See **Unit 6 Resources.**) Tell them to use their responses to answer the questions on the Applying Your Skills page.

Writing Skills Focus

Have students record descriptive details in their **Reader/Writer Notebooks**. Students can use their notes to complete the Writing Skills Focus activity.

Learn It Online

The online version of this poem includes audio support to engage all students and to help struggling readers with reading comprehension and vocabulary.

go.hrw.com H12-1291 Go

Teacher Preparation

Selection Summary

The speaker begins by asking "How did it happen?" that the mythical continent of Atlantis sank beneath the sea. In the second stanza, the speaker compares the mythical city of Atlantis to a real city where she met someone and made a home. Both old cities are "gone forever," symbolic representations of sorrow and loss. Both have been named and seemingly drowned—but both are still the subjects of stories, longings, and sonnets.

Direct Teach

Think About/Talk About

Read with a Purpose Have students read the Read with a Purpose statement. Ask them if they have ever lost something important to them. Have them consider what they might compare their loss to.

Comprehension

Ⓑ Reading Focus

Possible response: *They want to bury their sorrow and their loss.*

Analysis

Ⓐ Literary Focus

Possible response: *She wonders how Atlantis simply disappeared.*

Vocabulary: Own the Word

- **convey:** Have you ever had to *convey* important news or information? Explain to whom, when, and why you *conveyed* that news or information. Then, ask students to explain the meaning of a *conveyor* belt.
- **traditions:** Ask students the following questions: What are some *traditions* that your family has? Why do certain practices become *traditions*?

SONNET

Atlantis—A Lost Sonnet

by **Eavan Boland**

Read with a Purpose

Read to discover how the speaker compares her loss to the loss of the legendary island of Atlantis.

Build Background

The story of the lost island of Atlantis originated about 335 B.C. with the Greek philosopher Plato. In his writings, he tells the story of an advanced society established in honor of the sea god Poseidon. Allegedly, the citizens became greedy and willful, so the island was destroyed by the sea. Many have debated whether or not such a civilization actually existed. Theories abound, but its origins and identity remain uncertain.

How on earth did it happen, I used to wonder
that a whole city—arches, pillars, colonnades,°
not to mention vehicles and animals—had all
one fine day gone under?

I mean, I said to myself, the world was small then.
Surely a great city must have been missed?
I miss our old city—

white pepper, white pudding,° you and I meeting
under fanlights and low skies to go home in it. Maybe
what really happened is Ⓐ

this: the old fable-makers searched hard for a word
to convey that what is gone is gone forever and
never found it. And so, in the best traditions of

where we come from, they gave their sorrow a name
and drowned it. Ⓑ

2. **colonnades:** series of columns supporting a roof.

8. **white pudding:** sausage made from pork and oatmeal that is part of a traditional Irish breakfast.

Underwater Roman ruins, Pamukkale, Costa del Egeo, Turkey.

Ⓐ **Literary Focus** **Sonnet** What ideas does Boland present in the beginning lines of the sonnet?

Ⓑ **Reading Focus** **Drawing Inferences** According to the speaker, why do the "fable-makers" want to drown Atlantis?

Vocabulary **convey** (kuhn VAY) *v.:* communicate; express.
traditions (truh DIHSH uhnz) *n. pl.:* customs, values, or ideas handed down from generation to generation.

California Standards, p. 1293

- **Reading Standard 2.4** Make warranted and reasonable assertions about the author's arguments by using elements of the text to defend and clarify interpretations.
- **Reading Standard 3.1** Analyze characteristics of subgenres (e.g., satire, parody, allegory, pastoral) that are used in poetry, prose, plays, novels, short stories, essays, and other basic genres.
- **Reading Standard 3.4** Analyze ways in which poets use imagery, personification, figures of speech, and sounds to evoke readers' emotions.
- **Writing Standard 1.5** Use language in natural, fresh, and vivid ways to establish a specific tone.

Applying Your Skills

Reading Standard 2.4, 3.1, 3.4 (see pages A48–A50)
Writing Standard 1.5 (see pages A51–A52)

Literary Response and Analysis

Reading Skills Focus

Quick Check

1. What does the speaker wonder about in the first two stanzas of the poem? What does she mean when she says that "the world was small then"?
2. What does the speaker compare to Atlantis? What emotions does she convey through this comparison?
3. How would you describe the speaker's relationship to loss? What seems to be her perspective?

Read with a Purpose

4. How does the speaker regard the story of the lost island of Atlantis? Explain your opinion.

Reading Skills: Drawing Inferences

5. Complete the chart you began while reading. Write down what you can infer from your prior experience and the clues in the poem.

Vocabulary Check

Answer these questions about the Vocabulary words.

6. What would you **convey** to someone who is celebrating a birthday?
7. What **traditions** does your family observe?

Literary Skills Focus

Literary Analysis

8. **Infer** Why do you think the poet includes references to the everyday, such as "vehicles and animals," "white pepper," and "fanlights and low skies"? Explain.
9. **Extend** What do you think compels people to want to "drown" sorrows or forget their losses?
10. **Analyze** How many lines does this sonnet have? Why do you think Boland uses this number of lines?
11. **Interpret** Why do you think Boland calls her poem "A Lost Sonnet"? How does this relate to the story of Atlantis?

Literary Skills: Sonnet

12. **Analyze** Most sonnets have a **turn,** or a shift in thought that summarizes or explains the ideas presented earlier in the poem or answers a question posed in the poem. At which point does the turn occur in Boland's poem? How does she summarize or explain the ideas that she introduces in the beginning lines?

Literary Skills Review: Allusion

13. **Evaluate** An **allusion** is a reference within a literary work to another literary work or historical event. Boland bases her entire poem on an allusion to the lost island of Atlantis. How does she interpret this object of allusion? How does the story influence her poetry?

Writing Skills Focus

Think as a Reader/Writer

Use It in Your Writing Think of three details about your hometown or state that would identify it to most readers. Then, write a short poem or a paragraph about how you would (or would not) miss your hometown if you left it. Choose details and use vivid language to help you establish the tone you want.

What Do You Think Now? How do you think the experience of loss has affected the speaker's view of the world?

Universal Access

EL Struggling Writers

Some students may need additional scaffolding to complete the Writing Skills Focus activity. Before students begin writing, have them list details about their hometown. Instruct them to choose three details from their list that best convey their feelings about the place. Then, encourage students to incorporate theses details in a poem about the potential loss of their hometown.

What Do You Think Now?

To help students answer this question, ask them if they believe Boland's worldview is positive or negative as a result of the loss of her homeland.

Assess

Unit 6 Resources, Selection Standards Check, p. 170

Check for Understanding

Independent Practice

Reading Skills Focus

Possible responses:

1. *She wonders how a city could disappear when the small population of the world was so closely connected.*
2. *She compares her loss—moving to a new city—to Atlantis. She conveys sadness, but also a willingness to remember what she has lost.*
3. *The speaker seems to have experienced loss, but she does not want to forget.*
4. *The speaker views Atlantis as a poem that has been lost to the world.*
5. *Students should call upon prior experience when writing down inferences.*

Vocabulary Check

6. *You might convey birthday wishes.*
7. *Birthdays, holidays, customs, etc.*

Literary Skills Focus

Possible responses:

8. *She lists the everyday things that she misses most about her home.*
9. *Memories are painful, so some people would rather forget them.*
10. *There are 15 lines. Boland may have used one more line than a traditional sonnet to symbolize traditions that have been lost.*
11. *Her "lost sonnet" expresses her feelings about what she has lost by leaving her home behind.*
12. *The turn occurs in lines 10–11 when she says, "Maybe what really happened is / this:" She explains that the fable-makers were unable to explain loss or give it a name, so instead they tried to forget—or drown—it.*
13. *She compares Atlantis to a sorrow that people try to forget. Instead, she says, Atlantis lives on forever in human imagination and wonder. She believes losses should not be forgotten.*

Chapter Objectives

- Students will learn how irony in literature is a response to modern life.
- Students will understand the importance of verbal, situational, and dramatic irony in a range of works by contemporary authors.

The Quotation

Tell students that the Literary Skills Focus of Chapter 13 is irony, which is the gap between what is expected or assumed and what really happens. Ask students how the fine art on p. 1294 supports the contention of Nigerian-born poet and novelist Ben Okri (1959–) that human imperfection is the most important component of storytelling. What kind of "unease" does the work of art suggest? ***Possible response:*** *The somewhat unnerving image hints at the imminent likelihood of danger or collapse.*

Analyzing Visuals

Extension Activity What details in the image support Okri's statement that "storytelling hints at fundamental human unease . . . [and] human imperfection"? ***Possible response:*** *The absence of people, the ordinariness of the background compared with the slanted foreground, and the odd assemblage of objects all hint at something dire happening.*

CHAPTER **13**

Expectation and Reality

LITERARY SKILLS FOCUS
Irony

The Evil Genius of a King (Paris, 1914–1915) by Giorgio de Chirico (1888–1978). Oil on canvas.
The Museum of Modern Art, NY/ARS,NY.

CONTENTS

"The fact of storytelling hints at a fundamental human unease, hints at human imperfection. Where there is perfection there is no story to tell."

—**Ben Okri**

Chapter 13

California Standards Overview

(For a full text of the standards, see pp. A48–A55.)

- **Reading Standard 2.2** Clarify meaning through structure, repetition, syntax, and word choice.
- **Reading Standard 2.4** Analyze an author's arguments.
- **Reading Standard 2.5** Analyze philosophical beliefs.
- **Reading Standard 3.1** Analyze subgenres.
- **Reading Standard 3.2** Theme.
- **Reading Standard 3.3** Analyze effects of irony, tone, mood, and style.
- **Reading Standard 3.4** Figurative language.
- **Reading Standard 3.7** Analyze world literature: **c.** Evaluate the historical period.
- **Reading Standard 3.8** Analyze political assumptions.
- **Reading Standard 3.9** Analyze philosophical arguments.
- **Grades 9–10 Review Reading Standard 3.3** Analyze interactions between characters.
- **Grades 9–10 Review Reading Standard 3.4** Determine characters' traits.
- **Grades 9–10 Review Reading Standard 3.6** Analyze time and sequence.
- **Grades 9–10 Review Reading Standard 3.7** Recognize literary devices.
- **Grades 9–10 Review Reading Standard 3.9** Understand voice, persona, and the choice of a narrator.
- **Grades 9–10 Review Reading Standard 3.10** Understand dramatic literature.

LITERARY RESPONSE AND ANALYSIS

Literary Skills Focus

Reading Standard 3.3 (see pages A48–A50)

Irony by Leila Christenbury

Types of Irony

- Verbal irony: The narrator or a character says one thing but means something different.
- Situational irony: The opposite of what is expected happens.
- Dramatic irony: The reader or audience knows something a character does not.

A Response to Modern Life

Saying one thing but meaning another is one way to define **irony,** a term that also refers to the gap between what is expected or assumed and what really happens. One critic has called a person's ability to detect irony "one of the surest tests of intelligence and sophistication." In the literature in this chapter, irony occurs in different forms and degrees; however, in almost all the pieces, the use of irony underscores serious and thought-provoking themes. The heartbreaking incongruity between what is desired and what is realized is characteristic of much of this literature.

The first half of the twentieth century was a time when much of what people assumed to be true about the world was called into question. Darwin's theory of evolution and Freud's ideas about the subconscious made people re-examine their own identities. Two horrific world wars and the Holocaust shook people's faith in God and human kindness. It is unsurprising that many people adopted an ironic perspective—irony had come to reflect their experience of reality. The dissonance resulting from the fact that life was not as they expected or dreamed it to be is reflected in the irony of that period's literature.

In D. H. Lawrence's "The Rocking-Horse Winner," for example, Paul's desire to win his mother's affection by making her rich is thwarted only when she desires, "more money!—more than ever!" In such instances of **situational irony,** the opposite of one's expectations becomes the reality.

Irony in the Atmosphere

Today, it can be difficult for us to recognize irony because its influence is so pervasive. Many people we hear or interact with every day use verbal irony. Everyone, from the morning DJs on our favorite radio stations, to our friends and families, to characters in our favorite TV shows and movies, says one thing and means another. The surface meaning of one statement likely has a different underlying meaning. Sarcasm, a heavy-handed manner of speaking meant to ridicule and mock, is an even stronger expression of **verbal irony.** As a part of the atmosphere of life in the twenty-first century, sarcasm is a synonym for what is cool, hip, and cynically detached.

Dramatic irony can be another way to make an individual look foolish because the reader or audience has information the character does not possess. The contrast in dramatic irony is not between what is stated and what is meant, but rather between what the character says or thinks and the true state of affairs. In all instances of irony, disparate information and intentions affect how we see characters, ourselves, and the world.

Ask Yourself

1. Could you go for a whole day without saying anything ironic? Why or why not?
2. Think of a favorite ironic line or moment from a book, TV show, or movie. What do you like about it?

Learn It Online
Learn about irony through *PowerNotes* online.
go.hrw.com H12-1295 Go

Literary Skills Focus

Objectives

Students will understand and analyze irony, including verbal and situational irony.

Unit 6 Resources, Literary Focus Skill Builder, p. 178

PowerNotes, interactive lesson presentation with activities

Teacher One Stop™, on-level lesson plan and all print resources

Direct Teach

Irony

Have students read the Literary Skills Focus. Then, use the following question to discuss irony: "How do people's hopes for themselves and their futures carry the potential for situational and dramatic irony?"

Check for Understanding

Ask Yourself

Possible responses:

1. *No; it would be difficult to go a whole day without saying something ironic since ironic statements are sometimes made subconsciously.*
2. *Students' examples will vary. If the irony is not obvious, have students justify their choices.*

Learn It Online
For a multimedia version of the instruction found on this page, use the **PowerNotes** Literary Skills Focus presentation.
go.hrw.com H12-1295 Go

California Standards, p. 1295

- **Reading Standard 3.3** Analyze the ways in which irony, tone, mood, the author's style, and the "sound" of language achieve specific rhetorical or aesthetic purposes or both.

Universal Access

Struggling Readers

To help students understand the differences between verbal, situational, and dramatic irony, provide a few examples from everyday experience or from familiar works of literature or pop culture. Next, have partners work together to generate additional examples of each type of irony. Examples can come from literature, media, or personal experience. Encourage partners to share their examples with the class.

Standards Focus

Objectives

Students will analyze irony in a sculpture by Tony Cragg.

Analyzing Visuals Transparencies, Unit 6

Teacher One Stop™, lesson plan and all print resources

Direct Teach

Connect to the Literary Skill

Tell students that irony can be visual as well as verbal. A sculptor, especially one who creates nonrepresentational forms, can present an ironic view of the world by depicting a contrast between expectation and reality.

Work with students to answer the guided questions.

Possible responses:

1. *It represents a human head changing from one form into another.*
2. *It suggests the ambiguity of the figure's response to its environment.*
3. *An unnatural human shape placed in a natural environment reaches an ironic effect.*

Check for Understanding

Your Turn

Alternative Listening and Speaking Assignment

Have students work with a partner to find another work of art in the textbook used as an illustration in Unit 6 that expresses an ironic point of view. Encourage students to analyze and discuss the artist's perspective.

Analyzing Visuals

Reading Standard 3.3 (see pages A48–A50)

Connecting to Irony

Irony, the contrast, or discrepancy, between expectation and reality, became one of the dominant literary modes in the twentieth century. Today, an ironic point of view continues to be expressed in literature as well as in the visual arts, as in, for example, this sculpture by Tony Cragg.

Guidelines

Use these guidelines to consider how this sculpture expresses irony:

- How does the sculpture show a contrast between expectation and reality?
- A re-examination of identity helped engender irony in the twentieth century. What does this sculpture suggest about identity?
- How might the sculpture's title, *Bent of Mind,* be considered ironic?

1. What might the overall shape of the sculpture represent?
2. Note that the faces are pointed away from each other. What does this positioning suggest?
3. Does the placement of this sculpture in an outdoor setting increase or decrease the ironic effect?

Bent of Mind by Tony Cragg. Cass Sculpture Foundation, U.K.

Your Turn Analyze Irony

Choose another image in this book, and write a short paragraph explaining how the image conveys a sense of irony.

Universal Access

Students with Disabilities

Help students express what they see when they view the photograph of Tony Cragg's sculpture *Bent of Mind*. Suggest that they consider the name of the sculpture as they think about the ideas the sculptor had in mind when he created the work. What message does the sculpture send about man's relationship to the environment?

California Standards, p. 1296

- **Reading Standard 3.3** Analyze the ways in which irony, tone, mood, the author's style, and the "sound" of language achieve specific rhetorical or aesthetic purposes or both.

Reading Standard 2.2 (see pages A48–A50)

Identifying Cause and Effect by Kylene Beers

"Why?" is the question so often on people's minds. We wonder why people behave as they do, why events turn out a certain way, why the world is the way it is. Whenever we ask why, we are trying to determine a cause, or a reason, for an effect we have witnessed or experienced: a friend's failure to speak, a team's thrilling victory, or a destructive storm.

We also ask, "Then what happened?," when we hear about an event and wonder what will happen as a result. If we find out that a popular baseball player is in a serious slump, for instance, we wonder about the effects. Will he be fired? Will he sit on the bench while a rookie takes his place? Will his team suffer losses?

As in life, literature is made up of an interlocking chain of **causes and effects.** Identifying this cause-and-effect sequence will help you understand a story's plot and characters' motivations. In stories such as "The Doll's House," you will be asked to infer causes and effects based on subtle clues.

When analyzing causes and effects, begin by identifying a circumstance that is the result of other factors (the effect). For example, in "The Doll's House" a major aspect of the plot is a clearly stated effect: "The Kelveys were shunned by everybody." The exclusion and unkind treatment of children is a scenario that causes the reader to ask "Why?" A careful reader asks questions to find the causes.

Read the following passage. Three causes, or reasons, for the ostracism of the Kelvey children are mentioned in the text. Write them in a chart like this one:

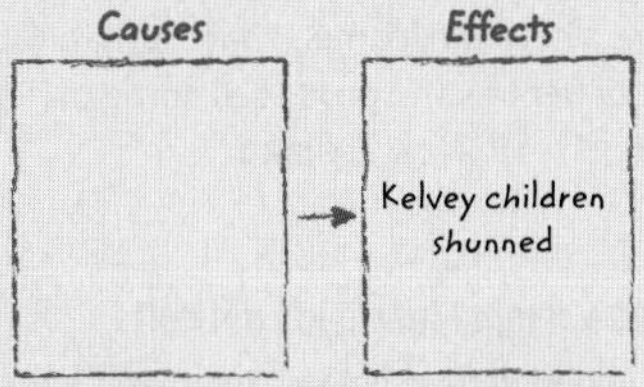

They [the Kelveys] were the daughters of a spry, hardworking little washerwoman, who went about from house to house by the day. This was awful enough. But where was Mr. Kelvey? Nobody knew for certain. But everybody said he was in prison. So they were the daughters of a washerwoman and a jailbird. . . . And they looked it! . . . The truth was they were dressed in "bits" given to her by the people for whom she worked.

Your Turn

Read the following passage from "The Doll's House." Create another chart reflecting the causes and effects.

"How dare you ask the little Kelveys into the courtyard?" said her cold, furious voice. "You know as well as I do, you're not allowed to talk to them. Run away, children, run away at once. And don't come back again," said Aunt Beryl. And she stepped into the yard and shooed them out as if they were chickens. . . .

. . . They did not need telling twice. Burning with shame, shrinking together, Lil huddling along like her mother, our Else dazed, somehow they crossed the big courtyard and squeezed through the white gate. . . .

The afternoon had been awful. A letter had come from Willie Brent, a terrifying, threatening letter, saying if she did not meet him that evening in Pulman's Bush, he'd come to the front door and ask the reason why! But now that she had frightened those little rats of Kelveys and given Kezia a good scolding, her heart felt lighter. That ghastly pressure was gone. She went back to the house humming.

Reading Skills Focus

Objectives

Students will analyze cause-and-effect organization.

Unit 6 Resources, Reading Focus Skill Builder, p. 179

Teacher One Stop™, lesson plan and all print resources

Direct Teach

Identifying Cause and Effect

This essay gives students practice in recognizing cause-and-effect relationships in "The Doll's House" by identifying the reasons the Kelvey children are shunned. Have students read the essay and complete the Your Turn activity before reading the story.

Check for Understanding

Your Turn

Possible responses:

Cause: *Aunt Beryl scolds Kezia and chases the Kelvey children away.*

Effects: *The Kelvey children run away, ashamed. Aunt Beryl no longer feels pressured from the terrifying letter Willie Brent had sent.*

California Standards, p. 1297

- **Reading Standard 2.2** Analyze the way in which clarity of meaning is affected by the patterns of organization, hierarchical structures, repetition of the main idea, syntax, and word choice in the text.

Universal Access

English Learners

To help students understand the reading skill discussed in the essay, remind them that certain words and phrases often indicate cause-and-effect relationships. These words and phrases are *so, as a result, therefore, consequently, because, since, then, thus,* etc. Ask students to write a few sentences using some of these words to better understand cause-and-effect relationships.

Standards Focus

Objectives

Students will understand narrative voice and its effects.

Selection Introduction

Think About the Writer

Have students think about the perspective a person who grew up feeling like an outsider would have about other people's lives.

For Independent Reading

*Complete Shorter Fiction of Virginia Woolf,** Virginia Woolf

HRW LIBRARY *This title is available in the HRW library.

Motivate

What Do You Think?/QuickTalk

Have students think about an act of bullying that they observed or experienced. Ask them to consider the feelings of the participants as well as any specific actions they recall.

English for Academic Success

Academic Vocabulary

Look for opportunities to use the Academic Vocabulary words in this unit.

- **adapt, *v.*:** adjust for a new purpose
- **considerably, *adv.*:** by a large amount
- **exhibit, *v.*:** show, demonstrate
- **perspective, *n.*:** a particular way of looking at something

California Standards, pp. 1298–1307

- **Reading Standard 2.2** Analyze the way in which clarity of meaning is affected by the patterns of organization, hierarchical structures, repetition of the main ideas, syntax, and word choice in the text.
- **Grades 9–10 Review Reading Standard 3.9** Explain how voice, persona, and the choice of a narrator affect characterization and the tone, plot, and credibility of a text.

Preparing to Read

The Doll's House

What Do You Think? How does experience shape our view of the world?

QuickTalk

Think of groups of people others might ridicule or tease. In your *Reader/Writer Notebook,* take notes on how the experience of bullying affects both the victims and the bullies.

Katherine Mansfield seated in a deck chair, France, 1916.
Alexander Turnbull Library, New Zealand.

MEET THE WRITER

Katherine Mansfield
(1888–1923)

When Katherine Mansfield began to write, short stories were expected to have strong plots and cleverly devised endings. Mansfield's stories were different. Some readers complained that nothing happened in them. Indeed, often very little happened externally in her stories, but a great deal occurred in the minds of her characters.

An Unhappy Childhood

Katherine Mansfield was born in New Zealand. A considerably unhappy child, she shared her mother's distaste for being "out here," oceans away from England, the source of their culture. At school she was moody and had few friends; one teacher described her as dumpy and unattractive. Although Mansfield had her father's talent for math and could memorize verse at sight, she was a careless scholar. When she was fifteen, her family enrolled her in Queen's College in London. Mansfield loved London and grieved when summoned home to New Zealand.

A New Life, an Early Death

When she was nineteen, Mansfield's family permitted her to return by herself to London. The child once regarded as homely had become a beauty, with porcelain skin and keen eyes. With almost no allowance from her father, Mansfield was painfully poor. (She called her father "the richest man in New Zealand, and the meanest.") Her first literary success came in 1910, when several of her stories were accepted by a journal. Around the same time, a man named John Middleton Murry accepted a story of hers for his literary magazine. The two began a long and stormy relationship.

When Mansfield's younger brother, Leslie, died in World War I, she was overcome with grief. From that point forward, she vowed to write about New Zealand as a "debt of love. . . . I shall tell everything, even of how the laundry basket squeaked."

At twenty-nine, Mansfield learned that she had tuberculosis. In the last year of her life, she produced some of her finest stories, many of them set in New Zealand.

Think About the Writer How might Mansfield's difficult childhood have helped her imagine the inner lives of other people?

Selection Readability	
Easily Accessible **Accessible** Challenging	accessible theme; simple sentence structure; familiar vocabulary

Reading Standard 2.2; **Grades 9–10 Review**
Reading Standard 3.9 (see pages A48–A50)

Literary Skills Focus

Narrative Voice The **narrator** is the **voice** that tells a story. The narrator can be a character in the story, in which case he or she speaks as *I*, or the narrator can be an external presence. The voice of the narrator may be ironic, sympathetic, humorous, critical, or distant. Mansfield excelled at creating distinct voices for her narrators. In almost all her stories, the narrator reveals interior moods by using evocative language. The narrator of "The Doll's House" penetrates the characters' minds so thoroughly that we feel as if we are participating with them in the action. In fact, you'll notice that the narrator's voice at times sounds like the voices of the children, and at other times, like the voices of the narrow-minded adults.

Reading Skills Focus

Identifying Cause and Effect Most plots are built around a series of causes and their effects. A **cause** is the reason that some action takes place. An **effect** is the result, or consequence, of some action or event. Most traditional plots are built on a cause-and-effect chain: One event causes another event, which causes another event, which causes another event. Multiple causes in a plot may be responsible for a single effect, or a single cause may have multiple effects.

Into Action As you read, use a graphic organizer like the one below to note the chain of causes and effects on which the story is constructed. Add circles and arrows for additional causes and effects as needed.

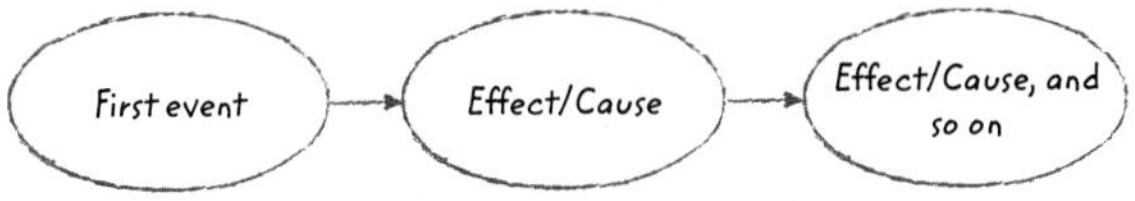

Writing Skills Focus

Think as a Reader/Writer

Find It in Your Reading The **narrative voice** we hear in this story sometimes sounds like the children thinking and sometimes sounds like the adults. In your *Reader/Writer Notebook*, note the details the narrator uses to make you feel as if you are hearing these characters' thoughts.

TechFocus As you read "The Doll's House," consider how you might record this story for a radio broadcast or a podcast.

Vocabulary

congealed (kuhn JEELD) *v.* used as *adj.:* thickened. *The congealed paint on the doll's house had formed into big lumps.*

conspicuous (kuhn SPIHK yoo uhs) *adj.:* attracting attention. *The Kelvey children were conspicuous in their poor clothes.*

flagged (flagd) *v.:* declined; lost strength or interest. *After a few days, interest in the doll's house flagged.*

clambered (KLAM buhrd) *v.:* climbed clumsily. *Kezia clambered back onto the gate to see the Kelveys as they passed.*

Language Coach

Idioms When learning a new language, you may encounter certain phrases that seem bizarre or don't make sense. Many of these phrases are **idioms,** expressions whose actual meaning differs from their literal meaning. If you say someone "bad-mouthed" you, for example, you are using an idiom. Here are some idioms from the story. Discuss with classmates what each italicized idiom means.

1. The children *burned to tell* everybody.
2. They just had time to *fall into line.*
3. *The line had to be drawn somewhere,* so the children would not talk to the Kelveys.
4. They walked past the Kelveys *with their heads in the air.*

Learn It Online
Find projects and activities online to take your reading of "The Doll's House" further.
go.hrw.com H12-1299 Go

Reader/Writer Notebook
Use your **RWN** to complete the activities for this selection.

Selection Resources

Unit 6 Resources, on-level practice and assessment, p. 180

Teacher One Stop™, on-level lesson plans and all print resources

Holt Audio Library

Holt Audio Library: Selections and Summaries in Spanish

UA: Differentiating Instruction, graphic organizer, p. 306

UA: Supporting Instruction in Spanish, selection summary

ThinkCentral Online Assessment, Selection Standards Check

ThinkCentral Online Remediation

Preteach

Introducing Vocabulary

Read aloud the Vocabulary words and sample sentences. Then, use this activity to check students' understanding.

1. Would **congealed** paint be hard or easy to stir?
2. Would you be **conspicuous** if you **clambered** up on a table?
3. If your interest in a topic has **flagged,** how much do you still care about it?

English for Academic Success

Language Coach

Ask students to list two or three examples of idioms they have used recently. ***Possible responses:* 1.** *were eager;* **2.** *do something similar;* **3.** *someone had to indicate that a particular action was not considered acceptable;* **4.** *in a haughty manner, ignoring them deliberately*

Literary Skills Focus

As you read and discuss the selection with students, have them pay special attention to the voice of the narrator.

Reading Skills Focus

Give students a copy of the Reading Skills Focus graphic organizer before they read. (See **Unit 6 Resources.**) Tell them to use their responses to answer the questions on the Applying Your Skills page.

Writing Skills Focus

As they read, have students record the important details they discover about the characters' personalities and motivations in their **Reader/Writer Notebooks.** Students can use their notes to complete the Writing Skills Focus activity.

Learn It Online
Additional, high-interest information about the story, including projects and activities, is available.
go.hrw.com H12-1299 Go

Teacher Preparation

Selection Plot Summary

In "The Doll's House," the Burnell sisters—Isabel, Lottie, and Kezia—are given a large doll's house, which delights them and dazzles their schoolmates. The wealthy Burnells live in a rural area of New Zealand where all the local children attend the same school, no matter what their social position. The Burnell children invite all their schoolmates to see the doll's house except for Else and Lil Kelvey, to whom they are forbidden to speak. At school, the Kelveys are mocked, shunned for their poverty, and taunted with the accusation that their absent father is in prison.

One day, the youngest Burnell, Kezia, sees Else and Lil passing by and invites them over to see the doll's house. They are surprised by fierce Aunt Beryl, who scolds Kezia and makes the Kelveys leave. Still, Else Kelvey is deeply moved by her glimpse of the prized doll's house with its beckoning little lamp.

Direct Teach

Think About/Talk About

Read with a Purpose Have students read the Read with a Purpose statement. Have them discuss how the theme of "childhood cruelty" could have universal application in any social grouping in which economic and social disparities exist.

SHORT STORY

The Doll's House

by **Katherine Mansfield**

Universal Access

English Learners

English for Academic Success Before students read the selection, introduce the following words and phrases.

- **knocker**—a hinged metal device used to knock on a door
- **frightfully**—very (Brit.)
- **set the fashion**—be the one who is imitated by others
- **slammed the doll's house to**— slammed the doll's house closed

Struggling Readers

Strategic Students To help students understanding cause-and-effect organization, suggest that they jot down short sentences to summarize all the events in the selection in chronological order (as they appear in the story). When they are finished reading, ask them to work in pairs to create a chain of causes and effects by using arrows. Help students formulate sentences orally such as "X happened as a result of Y" and "because of Y, X happened."

Read with a Purpose

Read to discover the causes and the effects of childhood cruelty.

Build Background

The story is set early in the twentieth century in a small village in New Zealand, which was at that time still a British colony. In the process of colonization, the British had brought England's rigid class system with them to their new home. Under this system, people's worth was automatically determined by their family background and by the amount of money they had. As you read, think about whether the situation in this story could still happen today, with children anywhere in the world.

(Left) *Two Girls with Blue Aprons* (1904–1905) by Edvard Munch (1863–1944).
Munch Museum, Oslo, Norway/ARS, NY.
(Below) View of dining room in a doll's house (c. 1735 –1740).

When dear old Mrs. Hay went back to town after staying with the Burnells, she sent the children a doll's house. It was so big that the carter[1] and Pat carried it into the courtyard, and there it stayed, propped up on two wooden boxes beside the feed-room door. No harm could come of it; it was summer. And perhaps the smell of paint would have gone off by the time it had to be taken in. For, really, the smell of paint coming from that doll's house ("Sweet of old Mrs. Hay, of course; most sweet and generous!")—but the smell of paint was quite enough to make anyone seriously ill, in Aunt Beryl's opinion. Even before the sacking was taken off. And when it was …

There stood the doll's house, a dark, oily, spinach green, picked out with bright yellow. Its two solid little chimneys, glued onto the roof, were painted red and white, and the door, gleaming with yellow varnish, was like a little slab of toffee. Four windows, real windows, were divided into panes by a broad streak of green. There was actually a tiny porch, too, painted yellow, with big lumps of congealed paint hanging along the edge.

But perfect, perfect little house! Who could possibly mind the smell? It was part of the joy, part of the newness.

"Open it quickly, someone!"

The hook at the side was stuck fast. Pat pried it open with his penknife, and the whole housefront swung back, and—there you were, gazing at one and the same moment into the drawing room and dining room, the kitchen and two bedrooms. That is the way for a house to open! Why don't all houses open like that? How much more exciting than peering through the slit of a door into a mean little hall with a hatstand and two umbrellas! That is—isn't it?—what you long to know about a house when you put your hand on the knocker. Perhaps it is the way God opens houses at dead of night when He is taking a quiet turn with an angel … **A**

1. **carter:** delivery person.

A Literary Focus **Narrative Voice** What details suggest that the narrator is entering into the minds of the children?

Vocabulary **congealed** (kuhn JEELD) *v. used as adj.:* thickened.

Think About/Talk About

Analysis

A Literary Focus

Possible response: *Most of the final paragraph on p. 1301 reads like an interior monologue. It shows the girls' instant approval ("That is the way for a house to open! Why don't all houses open like that?") as well as related thoughts that go through their minds as they explore the doll's house for the first time.*

Extend the Discussion

Making Generalizations What were your first impressions of the doll's house as it was just being unpacked? How does this impression change? ***Possible response:*** *The first impression is not positive. The house smells strongly of paint, the colors are a little odd, and lumps of congealed paint hang off the porch. Once opened, however, the doll's house becomes something special.*

Theme At what point does the reader become aware of the theme of privilege and wealth in this story? ***Possible response:*** *This theme is introduced when "dear old Mrs. Hay" sends the Burnell girls a large and expensive doll's house, not a gift that a poor child would be likely to get.*

Vocabulary: Own the Word

congealed: Give the following analogies: *Congealed* gravy is lumpy and thick. *Congealed* glue is sticky and thick but not yet dry. Ask students to explain why food might become *congealed.* ***Possible response:*** *when it is left to dry on a plate*

Advanced Learners

Enrichment Have students read other stories set in New Zealand or Australia, including works by the New Zealander Christina Stead or the Nobel Prize-winner Patrick White from Australia. Have students use their reading to deepen their understanding of the social and cultural conflicts that Mansfield explores. Discuss as a class examples of similar conflicts found in stories and films. Ask students why status is a perpetual theme in literature and media.

Students with Disabilities

Suggest that students jot down all references to rank, class, status, and hierarchy in the story. For example, it is important to Isabel that she be the first to tell about the doll's house. Have students work in small groups to discuss examples of similar behavior found in contemporary stories, films, or television shows. Then, ask students to discuss why status continues to be a universal theme in literature and media.

Model the Skill

- Tell students that understanding **narrative voice** will help them catch the subtle nuances that a writer builds into a story.
- On p. 1302, starting with the paragraph that begins "The Burnell children could hardly walk to school fast enough . . . ," read aloud to the end of the first column.
- Have students discuss whether the narrator is being ironic, sympathetic, humorous, mocking, critical, or distant in those lines.
- Lead off the discussion by describing what you notice about the narrator's voice. For instance, you might say: "I first notice that the Burnell girls *burned* to tell about the doll's house, and the narrator admits that the girls wish to *boast* about their new possession. The narrator shows sharp awareness of the girls' character flaws, describing Isabel as *bossy,* noting how the Burnell girls keep the others at a social distance, and making fun of Isabel's attempts to look 'very important and mysterious.'"

Guided Practice: Apply

Read-Talk-Write Have students review the Burnell children's reaction to the doll's house and their conversation on the way to school on p. 1302. Ask students to talk with a partner about what personality traits the narrator reveals about each of the Burnell girls in these paragraphs. Then, have students write a three- or four-sentence character description for each of the Burnell sisters in the voice of the narrator.

Think About/Talk About

Literary Connection

The "ring" of girls around Isabel, which the writer compares to a royal court, symbolizes the unbridgeable gap between the classes. Just as a British commoner would not approach the queen of England, so the Kelveys dare come only within earshot of the upper-class Burnells. This is another example of the story's focus on social stratification.

"O-oh!" The Burnell children sounded as though they were in despair. It was too marvelous; it was too much for them. They had never seen anything like it in their lives. All the rooms were papered. There were pictures on the walls, painted on the paper, with gold frames complete. Red carpet covered all the floors except the kitchen; red plush chairs in the drawing room, green in the dining room; tables, beds with real bedclothes, a cradle, a stove, a dresser with tiny plates, and one big jug. But what Kezia liked more than anything, what she liked frightfully, was the lamp. It stood in the middle of the dining-room table, an exquisite little amber lamp with a white globe. It was even filled all ready for lighting, though, of course, you couldn't light it. But there was something inside that looked like oil, and that moved when you shook it.

The father and mother dolls, who sprawled very stiff as though they had fainted in the drawing room, and their two little children asleep upstairs, were really too big for the doll's house. They didn't look as though they belonged. But the lamp was perfect. It seemed to smile at Kezia, to say, "I live here." The lamp was real.

The Burnell children could hardly walk to school fast enough the next morning. They burned to tell everybody, to describe, to—well—to boast about their doll's house before the school bell rang.

"I'm to tell," said Isabel, "because I'm the eldest. And you two can join in after. But I'm to tell first."

There was nothing to answer. Isabel was bossy, but she was always right, and Lottie and Kezia knew too well the powers that went with being eldest. They brushed through the thick buttercups at the road edge and said nothing.

"And I'm to choose who's to come and see it first. Mother said I might."

For it had been arranged that while the doll's house stood in the courtyard they might ask the girls at school, two at a time, to come and look. Not to stay to tea, of course, or to come traipsing[2] through the house. But just to stand quietly in the courtyard while Isabel pointed out the beauties, and Lottie and Kezia looked pleased . . .

2. **traipsing** (TRAYPS ihng): colloquial for "wandering" or tramping about.

But hurry as they might, by the time they had reached the tarred palings[3] of the boys' playground the bell had begun to jangle. They only just had time to whip off their hats and fall into line before the roll was called. Never mind. Isabel tried to make up for it by looking very important and mysterious and by whispering behind her hand to the girls near her, "Got something to tell you at playtime."

Playtime came and Isabel was surrounded. The girls of her class nearly fought to put their arms round her, to walk away with her, to beam flatteringly, to be her special friend. She held quite a court under the huge pine trees at the side of the playground. Nudging, giggling together, the little girls pressed up close. And the only two who stayed outside the ring were the two who were always outside, the little Kelveys. They knew better than to come anywhere near the Burnells. **B**

For the fact was, the school the Burnell children went to was not at all the kind of place their parents would have chosen if there had been any choice. But there was none. It was the only school for miles. And the consequence was all the children in the neighborhood, the Judge's little girls, the doctor's daughters, the storekeeper's children, the milkman's, were forced to mix together. Not to speak of there being an equal number of rude, rough little boys as well. But the line had to be drawn somewhere. It was drawn at the Kelveys. Many of the children, including the Burnells, were not allowed even to speak to them. They walked past the Kelveys with their heads in the air, and as they set the fashion in all matters of behavior, the Kelveys were shunned by everybody. Even the teacher had a special voice for them, and a special smile for the other children when Lil Kelvey came up to her desk with a bunch of dreadfully common-looking flowers.

They were the daughters of a spry, hardworking little washerwoman, who went about from house to house by the day. This was awful enough. But where was Mr. Kelvey? Nobody knew for certain. But everybody said he was in prison. So they were the daughters

3. **palings** (PAY lihngs): fence stakes.

B **Literary Focus** **Narrative Voice** Does the narrator want us to sympathize with the Burnells? How can you tell?

Universal Access

EL English Learners

English for Academic Success Review compound adjectives with students. Remind students that a compound adjective is formed when two or more adjectives are used to describe or modify the same noun. Point out that a hyphen is used to group the adjectives. Have students find two uses of compound adjectives on p. 1302. [*dining-room table, common-looking*] Ask them to come up with their own compound adjective modifying a noun.

Advanced Learners

Acceleration Have students think about the concept of a doll's house. Point out to students that an outsider can open up the wall of the house and observe the inner details of a home and the family who lives there. Ask students to imagine opening up the walls of the Burnell house and observing the family. Have students use the information that the narrator gives about the family to write a short paragraph describing what they might witness on an average day in the Burnell home.

of a washerwoman and a jailbird. Very nice company for other people's children! And they looked it. Why Mrs. Kelvey made them so conspicuous was hard to understand. The truth was they were dressed in "bits" given to her by the people for whom she worked. Lil, for instance, who was a stout, plain child, with big freckles, came to school in a dress made from a green art-serge[4] tablecloth of the Burnells, with red plush sleeves from the Logans' curtains. Her hat, perched on top of her high forehead, was a grown-up woman's hat, once the property of Miss Lecky, the postmistress. It was turned up at the back and trimmed with a large scarlet quill.[5] What a little guy[6] she looked! It was impossible not to laugh. And her little sister, our Else, wore a long white dress, rather like a nightgown, and a pair of little boy's boots. But whatever our Else wore she would have looked strange. She was a tiny wishbone of a child, with cropped hair and enormous solemn eyes—a little white owl. Nobody had ever seen her smile; she scarcely ever spoke. She went through life holding on to Lil, with a piece of Lil's skirt screwed up in her hand. Where Lil went our Else followed. In the playground, on the road going to and from school, there was Lil marching in front and our Else holding on behind. Only when she wanted anything, or when she was out of breath, our Else gave Lil a tug, a twitch, and Lil stopped and turned round. The Kelveys never failed to understand each other.

Now they hovered at the edge; you couldn't stop them listening. When the little girls turned round and sneered, Lil, as usual, gave her silly, shamefaced smile, but our Else only looked. **C**

And Isabel's voice, so very proud, went on telling. The carpet made a great sensation, but so did the beds with real bedclothes, and the stove with an oven door.

When she finished Kezia broke in. "You've forgotten the lamp, Isabel."

"Oh, yes," said Isabel, "and there's a teeny little lamp, all made of yellow glass, with a white globe that stands on the dining-room table. You couldn't tell it from a real one."

"The lamp's best of all," cried Kezia. She thought Isabel wasn't making half enough of the little lamp. But nobody paid any attention. Isabel was choosing the two who were to come back with them that afternoon and see it. She chose Emmie Cole and Lena Logan. But when the others knew they were all to have a chance, they couldn't be nice enough to Isabel. One by one they put their arms round Isabel's waist and walked her off. They had something to whisper to her, a secret. "Isabel's *my* friend."

Only the little Kelveys moved away forgotten; there was nothing more for them to hear. Days passed, and as more children saw the doll's house, the fame of it spread. It became the one subject, the rage. The one

4. **art-serge** (ahrt suhrj): type of woven wool fabric.
5. **quill:** feather.
6. **guy:** British for "odd-looking person."

C Literary Focus Narrative Voice Whose attitude toward the "little Kelveys" are we hearing in these paragraphs?

Vocabulary conspicuous (kuhn SPIHK yoo uhs) *adj.:* attracting attention.

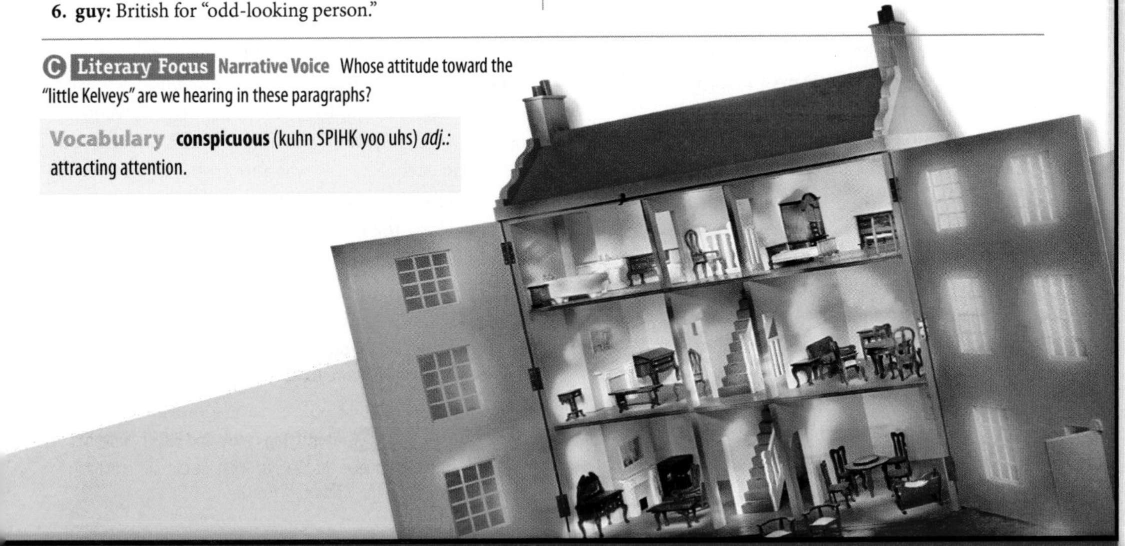

Students with Disabilities

Have students visualize the architectural details of the exterior and interior of the doll's house and draw diagrams of the contents to help other students picture the doll's house. Remind students to include important details mentioned in the text, such as the way the house opens, the furniture included, the doll family, and items that are of special importance to the girls. Have students label the important details and jot down phrases from the text that describe these details.

AAVE Students Who Use African American Vernacular English

English for Academic Success Page 1303 presents a particular challenge because of the frequent use of *'s* for contractions (*there's*) and for possessives (*people's children*). One such construction involves proper nouns that some students routinely follow with the verb *be* in informal English (*Isabel be my friend*). Point out that in formal English, this construction is pronounced with the *'s* and not *be* (*Isabel's my friend*). Ask students to construct three sentences accurately using the formal singular possessive with a proper name.

Think About/Talk About

Analysis

B Literary Focus

Possible response: *The narrator does not encourage the reader to feel sympathy for the Burnell girls. Rather, the narrator directs sympathy toward the Kelvey girls, who are always left out, in contrast to Isabel, who "held quite a court under the huge pine tree."*

C Literary Focus

Possible response: *These paragraphs about the Kelvey girls reflect the judgmental attitudes of the community—for example, in the sarcastic line, "Very nice company for other people's children!"*

Extend the Discussion

Identifying Cause and Effect What effect did the Burnells' refusal to speak to the Kelveys have on the other children? ***Possible response:*** *All the other children, even the teacher, shunned the Kelveys, for the Burnells were models to follow for the children in terms of behavior.*

Characterization Kezia and Isabel fuss about the lamp in the doll's house but totally exclude the little Kelveys and mock their clothing. What determination can you make about these characters based on this passage? ***Possible response:*** *They are very self-absorbed and spoiled.*

Vocabulary: Own the Word

conspicuous: Remind students that *conspicuous* means "obvious or noticeable." Ask students: What things might you find *conspicuous* about someone?" ***Possible responses:*** *a person's height, certain accessories such as bags and jewelry, flashy clothes*

Model the Skill

- Provide students with copies of the Reading Skills Focus graphic organizer for "The Doll's House." (See **Unit 6 Resources**.)
- Tell students when **identifying cause and effect**, they must look for reasons why an action takes place (causes) and the results or consequences of that action (effects). Point out that one effect might be the result of multiple causes, and an effect can become the cause of the next event in the chain.
- Model adding causes and effects to the graphic organizer. For example, you might say, "The social shunning of the Kelvey girls causes Kezia Burnell's sympathy for them, which in turn causes her to invite them into the courtyard to see the doll's house. This event results in the quiet happiness that Else Kelvey expresses at the end of the story, delighted that she saw the lamp in the doll's house."

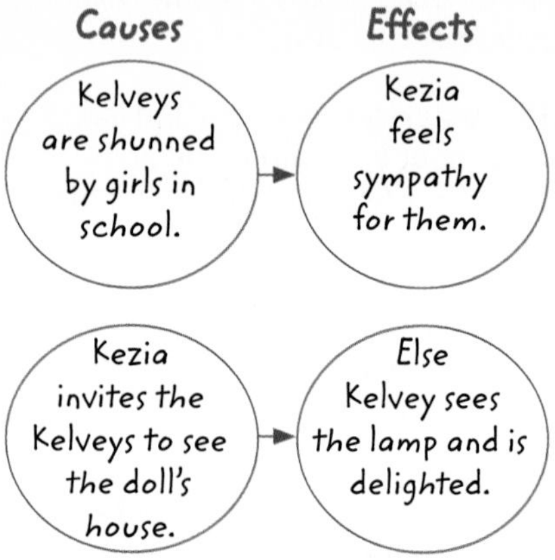

Guided Practice: Apply

Reciprocal Teaching Have students read the rest of pp. 1304–1305. Divide students in small groups and ask them to come up with 4–5 questions about causes and effects in the selection. Then, have groups exchange their set of questions and discuss the responses.

Burnells' doll's house? Oh, ain't it lovely!" "Haven't you seen it? Oh, I say!"

Even the dinner hour was given up to talking about it. The little girls sat under the pines eating their thick mutton sandwiches and big slabs of johnny cake spread with butter. While always, as near as they could get, sat the Kelveys, our Else holding on to Lil, listening too, while they chewed their jam sandwiches out of a newspaper soaked with large red blobs …

"Mother," said Kezia, "can't I ask the Kelveys just once?"

"Certainly not, Kezia."

"But why not?"

"Run away, Kezia; you know quite well why not."

At last everybody had seen it except them. On that day the subject rather flagged. It was the dinner hour. The children stood together under the pine trees, and suddenly, as they looked at the Kelveys eating out of their paper, always by themselves, always listening, they wanted to be horrid to them. Emmie Cole started the whisper.

"Lil Kelvey's going to be a servant when she grows up."

"O-oh, how awful!" said Isabel Burnell, and she made eyes at Emmie.

Emmie swallowed in a very meaning way and nodded to Isabel as she'd seen her mother do on those occasions.

"It's true—it's true—it's true," she said.

Then Lena Logan's little eyes snapped. "Shall I ask her?" she whispered.

"Bet you don't," said Jessie May.

"Pooh, I'm not frightened," said Lena. Suddenly she gave a little squeal and danced in front of the other girls. "Watch! Watch me! Watch me now!" said Lena. And sliding, gliding, dragging one foot, giggling behind her hand, Lena went over to the Kelveys.

Lil looked up from her dinner. She wrapped the rest quickly away. Our Else stopped chewing. What was coming now?

"Is it true you're going to be a servant when you grow up, Lil Kelvey?" shrilled Lena.

Dead silence. But instead of answering, Lil only gave her silly, shamefaced smile. She didn't seem to mind the question at all. What a sell[7] for Lena! The girls began to titter. **D**

Lena couldn't stand that. She put her hands on her hips; she shot forward. "Yah, yer father's in prison!" she hissed, spitefully.

A bedroom in "Mrs. Bryant's Pleasure," a doll's house (1860–1865). Bethnal Green Museum, London.

This was such a marvelous thing to have said that the little girls rushed away in a body, deeply, deeply excited, wild with joy. Someone found a long rope, and they began skipping. And never did they skip so high, run in and out so fast, or do such daring things as on that morning.

In the afternoon Pat called for the Burnell children with the buggy and they drove home. There were visitors. Isabel and Lottie, who liked visitors, went upstairs to change their pinafores.[8] But Kezia thieved out at the back. Nobody was about; she began to swing on the big white gates of the courtyard. Presently, looking along the road, she saw two little dots. They grew bigger, they were coming toward her. Now she

7. **sell:** slang for "trick."
8. **pinafores** (PIHN uh fawrz): sleeveless, apronlike garments that girls wore to keep their dresses clean.

Vocabulary **flagged** (flagd) *v.:* declined; lost strength or interest.

D **Reading Focus** **Identifying Cause and Effect** What has caused the girls to be cruel to the Kelveys? What are the effects of their cruelty?

Reaching Reluctant Readers

Some teenage male students might see little value in the doll's house and have difficulty identifying with the girls in the story. Discuss with these students what kind of story a contemporary author might tell to communicate the same general themes. Ask questions like the following: Who are the twenty-first-century equivalents of the Kelveys, the Burnells, Aunt Beryl, and other characters in the story? What might replace the doll's house as a symbol of privilege that is unattainable for most people?

Use these questions to spark a discussion of the core truths in Mansfield's story.

Developing Oral Fluency

Small-Group Activity Have students prepare a group reading of a scene from "The Doll's House." First, help them choose a scene and determine how many readers are needed. Then, have them prepare a script and provide each reader with a copy. Tell students to try out different ways of interpreting their characters' feelings and delivering their lines. Before the final reading, have students rehearse before a small group and ask for an evaluation of their performance.

✔ See the **Oral Language Skill Builder** in **UA: Differentiating Instruction.**

could see that one was in front and one close behind. Now she could see that they were the Kelveys. Kezia stopped swinging. She slipped off the gate as if she was going to run away. Then she hesitated. The Kelveys came nearer, and beside them walked their shadows, very long, stretching right across the road with their heads in the buttercups. Kezia clambered back on the gate; she had made up her mind; she swung out.

"Hullo," she said to the passing Kelveys.

They were so astounded that they stopped. Lil gave her silly smile. Our Else stared.

"You can come and see our doll's house if you want to," said Kezia, and she dragged one toe on the ground. But at that Lil turned red and shook her head quickly.

"Why not?" asked Kezia.

Lil gasped, then she said, "Your ma told our ma you wasn't to speak to us."

"Oh, well," said Kezia. She didn't know what to reply. "It doesn't matter. You can come and see our doll's house all the same. Come on. Nobody's looking."

But Lil shook her head still harder.

"Don't you want to?" asked Kezia.

Suddenly there was a twitch, a tug at Lil's skirt. She turned round. Our Else was looking at her with big, imploring eyes; she was frowning; she wanted to go. For a moment Lil looked at our Else very doubtfully. But then our Else twitched her skirt again. She started forward. Kezia led the way. Like two little stray cats they followed across the courtyard to where the doll's house stood.

"There it is," said Kezia.

There was a pause. Lil breathed loudly, almost snorted; our Else was still as a stone.

"I'll open it for you," said Kezia kindly. She undid the hook and they looked inside.

"There's the drawing room and the dining room, and that's the—"

"Kezia!"

Oh, what a start they gave!

"Kezia!"

It was Aunt Beryl's voice. They turned round. At the back door stood Aunt Beryl, staring as if she couldn't believe what she saw.

"How dare you ask the little Kelveys into the courtyard?" said her cold, furious voice. "You know as well as I do, you're not allowed to talk to them. Run away, children, run away at once. And don't come back again," said Aunt Beryl. And she stepped into the yard and shooed them out as if they were chickens.

"Off you go immediately!" she called, cold and proud.

They did not need telling twice. Burning with shame, shrinking together, Lil huddling along like her mother, our Else dazed, somehow they crossed the big courtyard and squeezed through the white gate.

"Wicked, disobedient little girl!" said Aunt Beryl bitterly to Kezia, and she slammed the doll's house to.

The afternoon had been awful. A letter had come from Willie Brent, a terrifying, threatening letter, saying if she did not meet him that evening in Pulman's Bush, he'd come to the front door and ask the reason why! But now that she had frightened those little rats of Kelveys and given Kezia a good scolding, her heart felt lighter. That ghastly pressure was gone. She went back to the house humming. **E**

When the Kelveys were well out of sight of Burnells', they sat down to rest on a big red drainpipe by the side of the road. Lil's cheeks were still burning; she took off the hat with the quill and held it on her knee. Dreamily they looked over the hay paddocks,[9] past the creek, to the group of wattles[10] where Logan's cows stood waiting to be milked. What were their thoughts?

Presently our Else nudged up close to her sister. But now she had forgotten the cross lady. She put out a finger and stroked her sister's quill; she smiled her rare smile.

"I seen the little lamp," she said, softly.

Then both were silent once more. **F**

---

9. **paddocks** (PAD uhks): enclosed pieces of land.
10. **wattles** (WAHT uhlz): here, acacia trees, used to make wattles, fences made of twisted twigs.

Vocabulary **clambered** (KLAM buhrd) *v.:* climbed clumsily.

E **Literary Focus** **Narrative Voice** Whose feelings are we hearing in this passage?

F **Reading Focus** **Identifying Cause and Effect** What is the ultimate cause of this return to silence?

Think About/Talk About

Comprehension

D Reading Focus

Possible responses: *The girls are anxious about their own social status and trying to impress each other. Their cruelty has multiple effects. Lena appears foolish because Lil does not respond to her initial taunts, which causes Lena to exclaim that Mr. Kelvey is in prison. The overall effect is to make the girls feel exuberant: "Never did they skip so high, run in and out so fast, or do such daring things. . . ."*

F Reading Focus

Possible response: *The silence is caused by satisfaction because Else Kelvey had a glimpse of perfection—the little lamp.*

Analysis

E Literary Focus

Possible response: *We are hearing Aunt Beryl's feelings. The narrator tells us very little about Aunt Beryl, leaving the significance of the disturbing letter a mystery.*

Vocabulary: Own the Word

- **flagged:** Tell students that *flagged* means "weakened" or "declined" and two antonyms are *rallied* or *perked up*. Have students use the two words in a sentence. ***Possible response:*** *Around mile ten the runner's energy flagged as he ran the marathon, but he perked up when his best friend joined him to finish the race.*
- **clambered:** Demonstrate what a bear might have looked like as it *clambered* out of its cave after a long winter. Ask a student or two to demonstrate how an animal or person might *clamber* along.

California Standards, pp. 1306–1307

- **Reading Standard 2.2** Analyze the way in which clarity of meaning is affected by the patterns of organization, hierarchical structures, repetition of the main ideas, syntax, and word choice in the text.
- **Reading Standard 3.3** Analyze the ways in which irony, tone, mood, the author's style, and the "sound" of language achieve specific rhetorical or aesthetic purposes or both.
- **Grades 9–10 Review Reading Standard 1.1** Identify and use the literal and figurative meanings of words and understand word derivations.
- **Grades 9–10 Review Reading Standard 3.9** Explain how voice, persona, and the choice of a narrator affect characterization and the tone, plot, and credibility of a text.
- **Writing Standard 1.2** Use point of view, characterization, style (e.g., use of irony), and related elements for specific rhetorical and aesthetic purposes.
- **Grades 9–10 Review Listening and Speaking Standard 2.1** Deliver narrative presentations. **a.** Narrate a sequence of events and communicate their significance to the audience.

Check for Understanding

Independent Practice

Reading Skills Focus

Possible responses:

1. *The Kelvey girls are poor and beneath the Burnells in social class rank.*
2. *The teacher looks down on them.*
3. *Lil and Else both understand how it feels to be mocked and left out.*
4. *The author might blame social stratification for the cruel treatment of the Kelveys.*
5. *Students should list effects under the appropriate column.*

Literary Skills Focus

Possible responses:

6. *Isabel wants to show off. Kezia may invite Lil and Else because she wants to share the lamp's "light" of warmth and belonging.*
7. *One theme is the desire for status, as gauged by the importance of possessions and the Burnells' power to impress others. The Burnells wish to use their family's status to lord it over others.*
8. *Many students will be offended by the cruelty.*
9. *The usually quiet Else tells readers her thoughts: "I seen the little lamp." The Kelvey girls seem to be daydreaming about the doll's house.*
10. *Many students will recognize the behavior in this story as commonplace. People of all ages are ostracized because of hardship and poverty.*
11. *If the narrator focused only on Lil and Else, readers would not know how the Burnells and the other girls reacted to the doll's house, how Beryl reacted to the mysterious letter, and how the teacher felt about the poorer children. The story would be one-dimensional.*
12. *To Kezia, the lamp may signify hospitality and belonging. Sharing the lamp signifies that Kezia is willing to open her home to the Kelveys.*

Applying Your Skills

Reading Standard 2.2, 3.3; **Grades 9–10 Review** Reading Standard 3.9 (see pages A48–A50)
Writing Standard 1.2 (see pages A51–A52)

The Doll's House

Literary Response and Analysis

Reading Skills Focus

Quick Check

1. Why aren't the Burnells allowed to speak to the Kelveys?
2. What is the teacher's attitude toward the Kelveys?
3. Why do you think the Kelveys understand each other so well?

Read with a Purpose

4. According to this story, what are the causes and effects of childhood cruelty?

Reading Skills: Identifying Cause and Effect

5. As you read the story, you charted its main events with a cause-and-effect map. Review the events that occurred after the arrival of the doll's house at the Burnells' home. Sort the effects into two lists—one of positive effects and one of negative effects.

Positive Effects	Negative Effects

Literary Skills Focus

Literary Analysis

6. **Compare and Contrast** Why does Isabel invite friends to see the doll's house? Why does Kezia invite Lil and Else to see it?
7. **Analyze** How would you state the story's theme? Use textual evidence for support.
8. **Make Judgments** How do you feel about the cruelty exhibited by Lil and Else's classmates?
9. **Interpret** At the end of the story, the narrator asks of Lil and Else, "What were their thoughts?" What do you believe they were thinking?
10. **Evaluate** Is this story realistic, that is, do events like this happen anywhere, anytime? Explain.

Literary Skills: Narrative Voice

11. **Analyze** Find details in the story that show that the narrator is able to enter into the feelings and minds of all the main characters. How would the story change if the narrator focused only on Lil and Else?

Literary Skills Review: Symbol

12. **Interpret** A **symbol** stands both for itself and for something beyond itself. Find details in the story that suggest that the doll's house might symbolize an imaginary world more perfect and more ordered than the one in which the girls live. How would this symbol make Kezia's desire to share that world with the Kelveys more significant?

Writing Skills Focus

Think as a Reader/Writer

Use It in Your Writing Review the details you noted that helped you enter the minds and feelings of the children in this story. Then, write one or two paragraphs about an incident in which one child is cruel to another. Write as an omniscient narrator, and use details that will help your readers feel as if they are sharing the thoughts and perspective of the children.

What Do You Think Now? How do you think their experience of rejection will shape the Kelveys' view of the world? What kinds of adults might the other children in the story grow up to be?

Universal Access

Struggling Writers

Guide students with additional scaffolding to complete the Writing Skills Focus activity. Remind them that an omniscient, or "all-knowing" narrator can move in and out of the thoughts of every character in a story. Have students freewrite for five minutes about a true or fictional incident involving childhood cruelty. Encourage them to include a few lines of dialogue as well as sentences that reveal the thoughts and emotions of each character involved.

What Do You Think Now?

To help students answer the question, have them think about the characteristics of a bully and those of a person who is continually harassed. How would those characteristics affect the person's perspective of the world as an adult?

Grades 9–10 Review Reading Standard 1.1 (see pages A48–A50)
Writing Standard 1.2 (see pages A51–A52)
Grades 9–10 Review Listening and Speaking Standard 2.1a (see pages A53–A55)

Vocabulary Development

Vocabulary Check

Match the Vocabulary words with their definitions.

1. congealed — a. lost momentum
2. conspicuous — b. climbed awkwardly
3. flagged — c. easy to spot
4. clambered — d. thickened

Vocabulary Skills: Context Clues

As you come across an unfamiliar word in your reading, use context clues to help determine its meaning.

"Even before the *sacking* was taken off."

To determine what *sacking* is, you can use these clues: (1) It is something that can cover a doll's house; (2) it can come off; (3) the word *sack* is in it.

Your Turn

Go back to the text and locate each of the Vocabulary words in the list below. On a separate sheet of paper, note any context clues that would help you define the word if it weren't defined at the bottom of the page.

congealed — flagged

conspicuous — clambered

Language Coach

Multiple Meanings If you encounter a familiar word that does not make sense in its context, the word may have more than one meaning. What do the italicized words mean in these sentences?

1. "How much more exciting than peering through the slit of a door into a *mean* little hall."
2. "They *burned* to tell everybody."
3. "They only just had time to ... fall into line before the *roll* was called."

CHOICES

As you respond to the Choices, use the **Academic Vocabulary** words as appropriate: perspective, considerably, adapt, exhibit, inevitable.

REVIEW

See Through Different Eyes

The narrator of "The Doll's House" has a strong voice that enters the thoughts of all the story's main characters. Choose a narrator with a more limited point of view, and, using the pronoun *I*, rewrite a scene from the story. Use that narrator's perspective and voice. You may choose a character in the story, or you can invent an outside narrator.

CONNECT

Record a Dramatic Reading

TechFocus Choose a section of "The Doll's House" to perform as a radio show or podcast. Before you begin, consider how your voice should sound as you read aloud different passages, and think about how you can adapt the story and bring to life a particular narrative voice in your pacing and tone. Play your recorded podcast for your class.

EXTEND

Analyze a Modern Schoolyard

Could the scenes in this story take place in a contemporary schoolyard? Would the snobbishness today be based on social class, as it is in this story, or might the cruelty have some other cause? Would the bullies and the victims be likely to behave the way they do in "The Doll's House"? Write a brief essay about bullies and childhood cruelty in today's times.

Learn It Online
Explore Katherine Mansfield and her world further through these Internet links.
go.hrw.com H12-1307 Go

Independent Practice

Choices: Evaluation Criteria

Review: Homework
See Through Different Eyes
- Students rewrite a scene from the story with a first-person narrator.
- Narrator's voice reflects the thoughts and feelings of the character.

Connect: Homework
Record a Dramatic Reading
- The completed reading gives clear evidence of planning.
- Students choose an appropriate pace and tone of voice.

Extend: Homework
Analyze a Modern Schoolyard
- Students update the story, giving it a contemporary setting.
- Students take a position about the causes of childhood cruelty.

Assess

Unit 6 Resources, Selection Standards Check, p. 183

ThinkCentral Online Assessment, Selection Standards Check

Teacher One Stop™, editable Selection Standards Check

Reteach

ThinkCentral Online Remediation

Vocabulary Development

Vocabulary Check

1. *d* **2.** *c* **3.** *a* **4.** *b*

Your Turn

1. *congealed—"big lumps . . . hanging around the edge"*
2. *conspicuous—any clues about what made their dress stand out*
3. *flagged—"At last everybody had seen it but them."*
4. *clambered—"back on the gate"*

English for Academic Success

Language Coach

Possible responses:

1. *very*
2. *very much wanted*
3. *list of class members*

Learn It Online
The enhanced author biography offers more information on the life of the author as well as Holt's interactive resources pertaining to the author.
go.hrw.com H12-1307 Go

Standards Focus

Objectives
Students will
- understand foreshadowing
- interpret character

Selection Introduction
Think About the Writer
Have students consider whether Lawrence's novels would stir up as much controversy today as it did when it was first published.

For Independent Reading
*Pale Horse, Pale Rider,** Katherine Anne Porter

HRW LIBRARY *This title is available in the HRW library.

Motivate
What Do You Think?/QuickWrite
Discuss how worries about money can often become intertwined with worries about maintaining a standard of living. Have students use their **Reader/Writer Notebooks** to note examples of how money can affect a person's standard of living.

English for Academic Success
Academic Vocabulary
Look for opportunities to use the Academic Vocabulary words in this unit.
- **considerably, *adv.*:** by a large amount
- **exhibit, *v.*:** show, demonstrate
- **perspective, *n.*:** a particular way of looking at something

California Standards, pp. 1308–1323
- **Grades 9–10 Review Reading Standard 3.3** Analyze interactions between main and subordinate characters in a literary text (e.g., in internal and external conflicts, motivations, relationships, influences) and explain the way these interactions affect the plot.
- **Grades 9–10 Review Reading Standard 3.4** Determine characters' traits by what the characters say about themselves in narration, dialogue, dramatic monologue, and soliloquy.
- **Grades 9–10 Review Reading Standard 3.6** Analyze and trace an author's development of time and sequence, including the use of complex literary devices (e.g., foreshadowing, flashbacks).

Preparing to Read

The Rocking-Horse Winner

What Do You Think? How does experience shape our view of the world?

QuickWrite
How is our experience of life affected by money—or the absence of it? Record your thoughts in your *Reader/Writer Notebook.*

D. H. Lawrence (ca. 1910–1925).

MEET THE WRITER

D. H. Lawrence
(1885–1930)

David Herbert Lawrence was the frailest child of a coal miner and his disappointed wife, whose ambition was to keep her sons out of the mines and her daughters from servitude. Lawrence fulfilled his mother's wishes and became a schoolmaster.

A Scandalous Start
In 1912, Lawrence left his teaching job. In preparation for a European tour, he visited his old French professor and fell in love with the professor's wife, Frieda, a German baroness and the mother of three children. Within weeks, Frieda had fled with Lawrence to Germany and then to Italy, where Lawrence finished *Sons and Lovers* (1913).

Reviews of the novel were cautiously favorable, but the moral controversy over Lawrence's work was intensifying: One critic found the novel's amorous parts "too graphic." Lawrence began to see industrialized England as corrosive and oppressive. He embraced a belief in "blood knowledge," in balancing the animal self with the intellect. From his perspective, England was overcivilized and prudish, and now he took aim at it.

Furious Censors
When a privately printed edition of *Women in Love* was published in 1920, one critic judged it "a loathsome study of sex depravity leading youth to unspeakable disaster." Despite the uproar, or maybe because of it, Lawrence's books began selling well. In 1928, Lawrence published *Lady Chatterley's Lover,* about a wealthy woman who becomes romantically involved with her husband's gamekeeper. The novel, which became one of the most notable books of the twentieth century, drew new waves of anger from the censors. U.S. customs officers seized copies as they arrived on the docks, and the novel was banned in Britain. As a result, all of Lawrence's work, including his poetry, became considerably more popular.

Lawrence died of tuberculosis at age forty-five. He is buried in Taos, New Mexico, where he and Frieda lived for a time to treat his lung disease.

Think About the Writer How would Lawrence's life have been different if he had been born a century later, in 1985?

Selection Readability	
Easily Accessible **Accessible** Challenging	familiar setting; simple dialogue; common theme; accessible language

Grades 9–10 Review Reading Standard 3.3, 3.4, 3.6 (see pages A48–A50)

Literary Skills Focus

Foreshadowing When writers use **foreshadowing,** they provide clues that hint at what might happen later in the story. Sometimes those clues are events that immediately arouse our curiosity and create suspense. Sometimes the clues are subtle—small details that we later recognize as clues pointing to something revealed at the story's conclusion. Part of the pleasure of reading stories is spotting those elements that foreshadow what is to come.

Reading Skills Focus

Interpreting Character Perhaps even more enjoyable than predicting what will happen next in a story is **interpreting character,** figuring out the general psychology of the people in the story. To start your analysis of character, you should pay close attention to what the characters say, what traits they exhibit, how they dress, and why they act the way they do. In some stories a character's needs or fears serve as clues.

Into Action As you read, use a chart like the one below to analyze the two main characters in "The Rocking-Horse Winner."

	The Mother	Paul
Key statements about character	"woman who was beautiful, who started with all the advantages"	Says of himself, "I'm a lucky person"
Character's actions		
Character's wants or needs		
Character's fears		

Writing Skills Focus

Think as a Reader/Writer

Find It in Your Reading Lawrence supplies precise descriptive details in the first paragraph, as we meet Paul's mother, a key character in the story. In your *Reader/Writer Notebook,* write down some of the details Lawrence supplies to give you a sense of what this woman is like.

Reader/Writer Notebook

Use your **RWN** to complete the activities for this selection.

Vocabulary

asserted (uh SURT ihd) *v.:* declared. *The child asserted that he was lucky.*

obscure (uhb SKYUR) *adj.:* little known. *The boy wanted to bet on an obscure horse named Daffodil.*

reiterated (ree IHT uh rayt ihd) *v.:* repeated. *The gardener reiterated that the boy was lucky.*

uncanny (uhn KAN ee) *adj.:* strange; eerie; weird. *The boy's blue eyes had an uncanny cold fire in them.*

iridescent (ihr ih DEHS uhnt) *adj.:* showing rainbowlike colors. *The cushions on the sofa were covered in iridescent fabrics.*

overwrought (oh vuhr RAWT) *adj.:* overly excited. *The mother noticed that the boy was overwrought about the race.*

remonstrated (rih MAHN strayt ihd) *v.:* protested. *The mother remonstrated that the boy was too big for a rocking horse.*

arrested (uh REHST ihd) *v.* used as *adj.:* checked; stopped in motion. *The rocking horse stood in an arrested prance in the boy's bedroom.*

Language Coach

Multiple Meanings Which Vocabulary words have other meanings that are different from the definitions provided?

Learn It Online

Get to know the Vocabulary words inside and out through Word Watch online.

go.hrw.com H12-1309 Go

Selection Resources

Unit 6 Resources, on-level practice and assessment, p. 186

Teacher One Stop™, on-level lesson plans and all print resources

Holt Audio Library

Holt Audio Library: Selections and Summaries in Spanish

UA: Differentiating Instruction, graphic organizer, p. 307

UA: Supporting Instruction in Spanish, selection summary

Analyzing Visuals Transparencies, p. 46

ThinkCentral Online Assessment, Selection Standards Check

ThinkCentral Online Remediation

Preteach

Introducing Vocabulary

Use this activity to check students' understanding of the Vocabulary words.

1. Name an **obscure** color in an **iridescent** box of crayons.
2. What situation might make you **overwrought**?
3. Describe a time you **asserted** a strong opinion in school.
4. State a phrase you have heard **reiterated.**
5. Describe an **uncanny** event.
6. Tell about a time you have **remonstrated** with someone.
7. Is a car whose motion is **arrested** accelerating or decelerating?

English for Academic Success

Language Coach

Students may notice that *obscure* can also mean "not clear" and *arrested* can also mean "taken into police custody." Have students use the alternative meanings in sentences.

Literary Skills Focus

As you read and discuss the selection with students, have them note clues that hint at what might happen later in the story.

Reading Skills Focus

Give students a copy of the Reading Skills Focus graphic organizer before they read. (See **Unit 6 Resources**.) Tell them to use their responses to answer the questions on the Applying Your Skills page.

Writing Skills Focus

As they read, have students record important details they discover about the mother in their **Reader/Writer Notebooks**.

Learn It Online

Send students to **Word Watch** for audio pronunciations, synonyms and antonyms, and brief histories of word origins.

go.hrw.com H12-1309 Go

Teacher Preparation

Selection Plot Summary

Paul, a young British boy, desperately wants to gain the love of his mother, who is distant and depressed. When he asks why their family always seems short of money, she tells him about the family's need for "luck." The confused but determined boy discovers that when he rides his rocking horse in a mad frenzy, he can foresee the winners of actual horse races. Paul uses these uncanny revelations to change the family's fortunes. Working with the gardener and Uncle Oscar, the boy makes a great deal of money and has it turned over to his mother through the family lawyer. He hopes that the money will finally stop the mysterious voices in the house from "whispering" for more money; however, the voices only "whisper" more madly. Finally, in order to predict the winner of the Derby, Paul makes a last frenzied rocking-horse ride. He successfully predicts the winner, after which he collapses. Critically ill, Paul is informed by the gardener that he has won over seventy thousand pounds. After asserting to his mother that he is lucky, the boy dies in the night, leaving his mother to contemplate what she has gained and what she has lost.

Direct Teach

Think About/Talk About

Read with a Purpose Have students read the Read with a Purpose statement. Have students discuss how the word *winner* can sometimes be a subjective term.

The Rocking-Horse Winner

by D. H. Lawrence

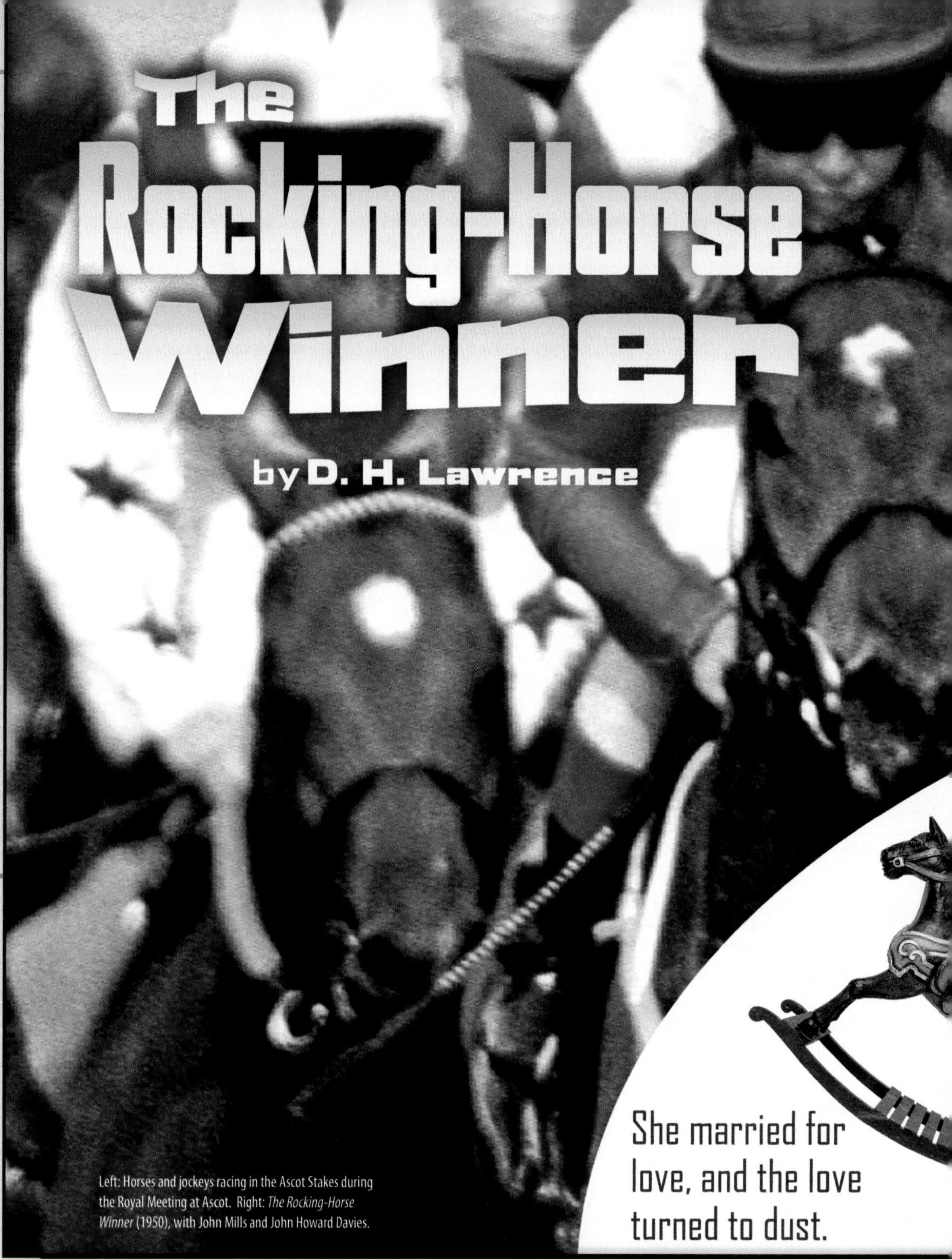

Left: Horses and jockeys racing in the Ascot Stakes during the Royal Meeting at Ascot. Right: *The Rocking-Horse Winner* (1950), with John Mills and John Howard Davies.

She married for love, and the love turned to dust.

Universal Access

EL English Learners

English for Academic Success To help students understand the story's subject matter, introduce the following words and phrases associated with horse racing.

- **Derby**—an annual horse race founded in 1780 by the twelfth Earl of Derby
- **put anything on**—place a bet, usually in the form of cash
- **a tip**—a prediction or a piece of expert information
- **reserve**—something set aside and not used

Struggling Readers

Strategic Students Model for students how to interpret character based on the first paragraph. You might start out by saying: "The first few sentences on p. 1311 tell me that the mother in this story started out with everything but ended up in a loveless marriage with children whom she did not love. Then, the next several sentences discuss the discrepancy between her behavior in public and her inner feelings. This characteristic must be important, so I will note this as a key statement of her character, 'Only she herself knew that at the center

Think About/Talk About

Comprehension

A Reading Focus

Possible response: *The paragraph explores the stresses and tensions in the mother's life. She has no luck, her marriage has turned sour, and she feels no love for her children, who sense her coldness. She overcompensates to make up for these feelings, and other people consider her an exemplary mother.*

Extend the Discussion

Irony What ironic contrasts do you see between the mother's thoughts and how she is perceived by others? ***Possible response:*** *The mother's demons are all internal. From the outside, she leads the perfect life for a woman of her time: She has beauty, "advantages," and a seemingly happy family. She sees herself as unable to love anyone but is perceived by outsiders as a model mother. Only her children know the truth about her: "They read it in each other's eyes."*

Read with a Purpose

Read to find out if the boy in the story is really a winner.

Build Background

Lawrence saw men and women as torn between the promptings of their instincts and the demanding voices of their upbringing and education. He believed that instincts were naturally better than a forced system of education and conformity. As you read "The Rocking-Horse Winner," which is told like a modern fable, notice which voices are most dominant in the house and what effects these voices have on the characters.

Lawrence also felt that people should surmount their fear and lust for money. He once said he would advise the young not to be wage slaves.

There was a woman who was beautiful, who started with all the advantages, yet she had no luck. She married for love, and the love turned to dust. She had bonny children, yet she felt they had been thrust upon her, and she could not love them. They looked at her coldly, as if they were finding fault with her. And hurriedly she felt she must cover up some fault in herself. Yet what it was that she must cover up she never knew. Nevertheless, when her children were present, she always felt the center of her heart go hard. This troubled her, and in her manner she was all the more gentle and anxious for her children, as if she loved them very much. Only she herself knew that at the center of her heart was a hard little place that could not feel love, no, not for anybody. Everybody else said of her: "She is such a good mother. She adores her children." Only she herself, and her children themselves, knew it was not so. They read it in each other's eyes. **A**

A Reading Focus **Interpreting Character** What does the first paragraph specifically state about the mother?

of her heart was a hard little place that could not feel love.'"

Advanced Learners

Acceleration Ask students to notice the way this story begins: "There was a woman who was beautiful. . . ." Note that such a beginning usually signals a fable, a fairy tale, or a satirical tale. As they read, ask students to think about which category best fits the story. Encourage students to decide on a category and to defend their decision with their classmates.

Students with Disabilities

Ask students to think about the meaning of the title. Then, have them note each time the rocking horse is mentioned in the text and ask themselves what it symbolizes. Remind students that a symbol carries another meaning besides its literal meaning.

✔ See **UA: Differentiating Instruction** for a graphic organizer to scaffold instruction for students with disabilities.

Model the Skill

- Tell students that when **interpreting character**, they must examine the character's words, personal traits, and the motivations.
- Read aloud the third and fourth paragraphs on p. 1312, beginning with "At last the mother said." Tell students to analyze the character of the mother. Have them take note of her actions, the key statements the narrator makes about her, her wants or needs, and her fears.
- Model adding this information to the graphic organizer. For example, you might say: "The first thing I notice is the key statement, *There must be more money.* I put this statement in the graphic organizer. As I read on, I notice that the mother continues to spend money frivolously and is unsuccessful in her ventures to make more money. After filling this information in on the next line of the graphic organizer, I discover that this information reveals that the mother's needs and wants are focused on acquiring more money. Her fears focus on losing money."

	The Mother
Key statement about character	"There must be more money."
Character's actions	She spends money frivolously.
Character's wants or needs	She wants to acquire more money.
Character's fears	She is afraid of losing money.

Guided Practice: Apply

Turn-and-Talk Invite students to work with a partner to include the information from this passage in their graphic organizers. Ask students to discuss other passages that might aid in interpreting the characters in this story.

There were a boy and two little girls. They lived in a pleasant house, with a garden, and they had discreet servants, and felt themselves superior to anyone in the neighborhood.

Although they lived in style, they felt always an anxiety in the house. There was never enough money. The mother had a small income,[1] and the father had a small income, but not nearly enough for the social position which they had to keep up. The father went into town to some office. But though he had good prospects, these prospects never materialized. There was always the grinding sense of the shortage of money, though the style was always kept up.

At last the mother said: "I will see if *I* can't make something." But she did not know where to begin. She racked her brains, and tried this thing and the other, but could not find anything successful. The failure made deep lines come into her face. Her children were growing up, they would have to go to school. There must be more money, there must be more money. The father, who was always very handsome and expensive in his tastes, seemed as if he never *would* be able to do anything worth doing. And the mother, who had a great belief in herself, did not succeed any better, and her tastes were just as expensive.

And so the house came to be haunted by the unspoken phrase: *There must be more money! There must be more money!* The children could hear it all the time, though nobody said it aloud. They heard it at Christmas, when the expensive and splendid toys filled the nursery. Behind the shining modern rocking horse, behind the smart doll's house, a voice would start whispering: "There *must* be more money! There *must* be more money!" And the children would stop playing, to listen for a moment. They would look into each other's eyes, to see if they had all heard. And each one saw in the eyes of the other two that they too had heard. "There *must* be more money! There *must* be more money!"

It came whispering from the springs of the still-swaying rocking horse, and even the horse, bending his wooden, champing head, heard it. The big doll, sitting so pink and smirking in her new pram,[2] could hear it quite plainly, and seemed to be smirking all the more self-consciously because of it. The foolish puppy, too, that took the place of the teddy bear, he was looking so extraordinarily foolish for no other reason but that he heard the secret whisper all over the house: "There *must* be more money!" **B**

Yet nobody ever said it aloud. The whisper was everywhere, and therefore no one spoke it. Just as no one ever says: "We are breathing!" in spite of the fact that breath is coming and going all the time.

"Mother," said the boy Paul one day, "why don't we keep a car of our own? Why do we always use uncle's, or else a taxi?"

"Because we're the poor members of the family," said the mother.

"But why *are* we, mother?"

"Well—I suppose," she said slowly and bitterly, "it's because your father has no luck."

The boy was silent for some time.

"Is luck money, mother?" he asked, rather timidly.

"No, Paul. Not quite. It's what causes you to have money."

"Oh!" said Paul vaguely. "I thought when Uncle Oscar said *filthy lucker,* it meant money."

"*Filthy lucre*[3] does mean money," said the mother. "But it's lucre, not luck."

"Oh!" said the boy. "Then what is luck, mother?"

"It's what causes you to have money. If you're lucky you have money. That's why it's better to be born lucky than rich. If you're rich, you may lose your money. But if you're lucky, you will always get more money."

"Oh! Will you? And is father not lucky?"

"Very unlucky, I should say," she said bitterly.

The boy watched her with unsure eyes.

"Why?" he asked.

"I don't know. Nobody ever knows why one person is lucky and another unlucky."

"Don't they? Nobody at all? Does *nobody* know?"

"Perhaps God. But He never tells."

"He ought to, then. And aren't you lucky either, mother?"

1. **income:** money from an inheritance or investments—not a salary.
2. **pram:** baby carriage, short for "perambulator."
3. **filthy lucre** (LOO kuhr): filthy money.

B **Literary Focus** **Foreshadowing** What could the whispering foreshadow? What do you think will happen next?

Cross-Curricular Connection

SOCIAL STUDIES: Hypnosis

Paul claims to receive his premonitions by entering a hypnotic trance when forcefully riding his rocking horse.

Activity To explore this claim, have students investigate hypnosis and report their findings to the class. Set up groups to research the following subjects:

- The history of hypnosis, including the forerunner of hypnotism, the work of Franz Anton Mesmer.
- Modern medical uses of hypnotism.
- Self-hypnotism, or the trace state.

Have students contrast this logical information and the fairy-tale qualities of this work to discuss whether Lawrence intended to make "The Rocking-Horse Winner" a fantasy or a realistic satire.

HSS Analysis Skills: CS 1

"I can't be, if I married an unlucky husband."

"But by yourself, aren't you?"

"I used to think I was, before I married. Now I think I am very unlucky indeed."

"Why?"

"Well—never mind! Perhaps I'm not really," she said.

The child looked at her to see if she meant it. But he saw, by the lines of her mouth, that she was only trying to hide something from him.

"Well, anyhow," he said stoutly,[4] "I'm a lucky person."

"Why?" said his mother, with a sudden laugh.

He stared at her. He didn't even know why he had said it.

"God told me," he asserted, brazening it out.[5]

"I hope He did, dear!" she said, again with a laugh, but rather bitter.

"He did, mother!"

"Excellent!" said the mother, using one of her husband's exclamations.

The boy saw she did not believe him; or rather, that she paid no attention to his assertion. This angered him somewhere, and made him want to compel her attention.

He went off by himself, vaguely, in a childish way, seeking for the clue to "luck." Absorbed, taking no heed of other people, he went about with a sort of stealth, seeking inwardly for luck. He wanted luck, he wanted it, he wanted it. When the two girls were playing dolls in the nursery, he would sit on his big rocking horse, charging madly into space, with a frenzy that made the little girls peer at him uneasily. Wildly the horse careered,[6] the waving dark hair of the boy tossed, his eyes had a strange glare in them. The little girls dared not speak to him.

When he had ridden to the end of his mad little journey, he climbed down and stood in front of his rocking horse, staring fixedly into its lowered face. Its red mouth was slightly open, its big eye was wide and glassy-bright.

"Now!" he would silently command the snorting steed. "Now, take me to where there is luck! Now take me!"

And he would slash the horse on the neck with the little whip he had asked Uncle Oscar for. He *knew* the horse could take him to where there was luck, if only he forced it. So he would mount again and start on his

4. **stoutly** (STOWT lee): bravely; boldly.
5. **brazening it out:** acting boldly and defiantly.

6. **careered:** rushed wildly.

Vocabulary **asserted** (uh SURT ihd) *v.:* declared.

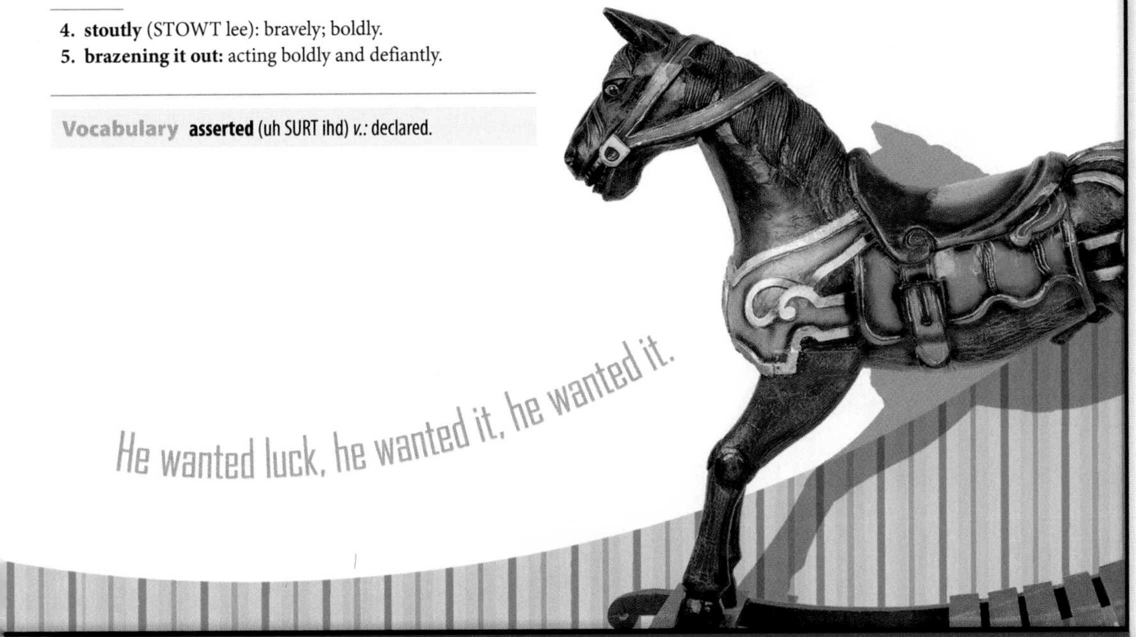

Universal Access

Struggling Readers

To help these students understand the characters in the story, have groups of students read aloud and record portions of the dialogue. Suggest that students read from p. 1312, starting with "'Mother,' said the boy Paul one day," to the end of the first column on the following page. Then, have students listen to the recording and note places where the characters display strong emotion such as confusion, concern, or excitement. Ask students to discuss each character's feelings toward the idea of "luck."

AAVE Students Who Use African American Vernacular English

English for Academic Success Read aloud the sentence "But he saw, by the lines of her mouth, that she was only trying to hide something from him." Some students might say *mouf* instead of *mouth*, and *somefing* instead of *something*. Emphasize that in standard English, the *th* sound in words should not be pronounced as *f*.

✔ For additional instruction, see **Holt Pronunciation Resources** and **ThinkCentral, Teacher Access.**

Think About/Talk About

Analysis

B Literary Focus

Possible responses: *The whispering could foreshadow some crisis caused by the lack of money. Students may think the family will soon run out of money or something will happen to the family as they pursue money.*

Extend the Discussion

Making Judgments The word *lucky* plays an important role in the story. When Paul asks, "Then what is luck, mother?" she explains that luck determines whether or not a person has money. Do you agree? Tell why or why not. ***Possible response:*** *Some students may argue that hard work and careful spending, in addition to luck, can affect the amount of money a person has, although these do not guarantee financial security.*

Speculating The sixth paragraph on p. 1313 states, "The child looked at her to see if she meant it. But he saw, by the lines of her mouth, that she was only trying to hide something from him." What might Paul's mother be trying to hide from him? ***Possible response:*** *She might be trying to hide her fear that she has brought about her own bad luck through her insecurity, her self-doubt, and her feeling that getting married and having children was a mistake.*

Vocabulary: Own the Word

asserted: Tell students that *asserted* is the past tense form of the verb *assert,* which means "to state or claim." An *assertion,* then, is a declaration. For example, you might say: "His *assertion* was that he was absent that day." Have students share a recent *assertion* they have made.

Model the Skill

- Tell students that words often have **multiple meanings** and that they must be sure to choose the meaning that best fits the context.
- Read aloud the paragraph at the bottom of column 1 on p. 1314 that begins "But Paul only gave a blue glare." Model for students how to determine the meaning of the word *blue*. For example, you might say: "What kind of a glare is a 'blue' glare? I know that *blue* often means the color blue, but that meaning does not make sense here. *Blue* can also mean 'dejected' or 'depressed,' as in the expression *feeling blue*. That definition is more appropriate for describing Paul."
- Follow the same procedure to discuss the phrase *in full tilt*, which means "at top speed." Note that here, the word *tilt* does not mean "slope over."

Guided Practice: Apply

Read-Talk-Write Have students read through the rest of the selection and look for other words with multiple meanings. Have students share their findings with the class. Then, ask students to choose a word and write a few sentences that display the word's multiple meanings.

furious ride, hoping at last to get there. He knew he could get there. **C**

"You'll break your horse, Paul!" said the nurse.

"He's always riding like that! I wish he'd leave off!" said his elder sister Joan.

But he only glared down on them in silence. Nurse gave him up. She could make nothing of him. Anyhow, he was growing beyond her.

One day his mother and his Uncle Oscar came in when he was on one of his furious rides. He did not speak to them.

"Hallo, you young jockey! Riding a winner?" said his uncle.

"Aren't you growing too big for a rocking horse? You're not a very little boy any longer, you know," said his mother.

But Paul only gave a blue glare from his big, rather close-set eyes. He would speak to nobody when he was in full tilt. His mother watched him with an anxious expression on her face.

C Reading Focus **Interpreting Character** What does Paul want?

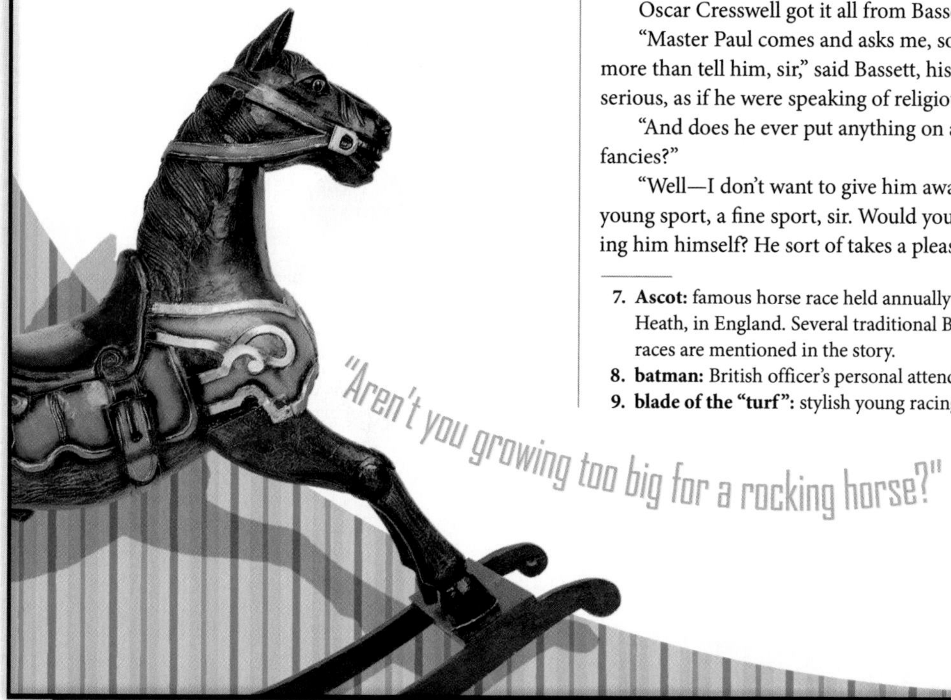

At last he suddenly stopped forcing his horse into the mechanical gallop and slid down.

"Well, I got there!" he announced fiercely, his blue eyes still flaring, and his sturdy long legs straddling apart.

"Where did you get to?" asked his mother.

"Where I wanted to go," he flared back at her.

"That's right, son!" said Uncle Oscar. "Don't you stop till you get there. What's the horse's name?"

"He doesn't have a name," said the boy.

"Gets on without all right?" asked the uncle.

"Well, he has different names. He was called Sansovino last week."

"Sansovino, eh? Won the Ascot.[7] How did you know this name?"

"He always talks about horse races with Bassett," said Joan.

The uncle was delighted to find that his small nephew was posted with all the racing news. Bassett, the young gardener, who had been wounded in the left foot in the war and had got his present job through Oscar Cresswell, whose batman[8] he had been, was a perfect blade of the "turf."[9] He lived in the racing events, and the small boy lived with him.

Oscar Cresswell got it all from Bassett.

"Master Paul comes and asks me, so I can't do more than tell him, sir," said Bassett, his face terribly serious, as if he were speaking of religious matters.

"And does he ever put anything on a horse he fancies?"

"Well—I don't want to give him away—he's a young sport, a fine sport, sir. Would you mind asking him himself? He sort of takes a pleasure in it, and

7. **Ascot:** famous horse race held annually at Ascot Heath, in England. Several traditional British races are mentioned in the story.
8. **batman:** British officer's personal attendant.
9. **blade of the "turf":** stylish young racing fan.

Universal Access

English Learners

English for Academic Success As students read, tell them to note that as Paul persists in his riding, Lawrence uses more and more exclamations in the story's dialogue. The result is an increasingly desperate tone.

Individual Activity Have students rewrite the following paragraph, adding exclamation points to achieve variety and emphasis. Then, have them compare the decisions they made as writers by having a few students read their paragraphs aloud.

She reached the top of the hill and looked down. The sidewalk stretched away, a concrete ribbon unfurling to the street below. Seeing it filled the child with both delight and dread. She started down, skates making their familiar low-level grating. Down and down. Trees and houses became a blur. Cars zipped by, indistinguishable in the speed of her racing. Vainly, she wondered where the bottom was.

✔ See the **English Language Skill Builder** in **UA: Differentiating Instruction.**

perhaps he'd feel I was giving him away, sir, if you don't mind."

Bassett was serious as a church.

The uncle went back to his nephew and took him off for a ride in the car.

"Say, Paul, old man, do you ever put anything on a horse?" the uncle asked.

The boy watched the handsome man closely.

"Why, do you think I oughtn't to?" he parried.

"Not a bit of it! I thought perhaps you might give me a tip for the Lincoln."

The car sped on into the country, going down to Uncle Oscar's place in Hampshire.

"Honor bright?" said the nephew.

"Honor bright, son!" said the uncle.

"Well, then, Daffodil."

"Daffodil! I doubt it, sonny. What about Mirza?"

"I only know the winner," said the boy. "That's Daffodil."

"Daffodil, eh?"

There was a pause. Daffodil was an obscure horse comparatively.

"Uncle!"

"Yes, son?"

"You won't let it go any further, will you? I promised Bassett."

"Bassett be damned, old man! What's he got to do with it?"

"We're partners. We've been partners from the first. Uncle, he lent me my first five shillings, which I lost. I promised him, honor bright, it was only between me and him; only you gave me that ten-shilling note I started winning with, so I thought you were lucky. You won't let it go any further, will you?"

The boy gazed at his uncle from those big, hot, blue eyes, set rather close together. The uncle stirred and laughed uneasily.

"Right you are, son! I'll keep your tip private. Daffodil, eh? How much are you putting on him?"

"All except twenty pounds," said the boy. "I keep that in reserve."

The uncle thought it a good joke.

"You keep twenty pounds in reserve, do you, you young romancer?[10] What are you betting, then?"

"I'm betting three hundred," said the boy gravely. "But it's between you and me, Uncle Oscar! Honor bright?"

The uncle burst into a roar of laughter.

"It's between you and me all right, you young Nat Gould,"[11] he said, laughing. "But where's your three hundred?"

"Bassett keeps it for me. We're partners."

"You are, are you! And what is Bassett putting on Daffodil?"

"He won't go quite as high as I do, I expect. Perhaps he'll go a hundred and fifty."

"What, pennies?" laughed the uncle.

"Pounds," said the child, with a surprised look at his uncle. "Bassett keeps a bigger reserve than I do."

Between wonder and amusement Uncle Oscar was silent. He pursued the matter no further, but he determined to take his nephew with him to the Lincoln races.

"Now, son," he said, "I'm putting twenty on Mirza, and I'll put five on for you on any horse you fancy. What's your pick?"

"Daffodil, uncle."

"No, not the fiver on Daffodil!"

"I should if it was my own fiver," said the child.

"Good! Good! Right you are! A fiver for me and a fiver for you on Daffodil."

The child had never been to a race meeting before, and his eyes were blue fire. He pursed his mouth tight and watched. A Frenchman just in front had put his money on Lancelot. Wild with excitement, he flayed his arms up and down, yelling *"Lancelot! Lancelot!"* in his French accent.

Daffodil came in first, Lancelot second, Mirza third. The child, flushed and with eyes blazing, was curiously serene. His uncle brought him four five-pound notes, four to one. **D**

10. **romancer:** imaginative storyteller.
11. **Nat Gould:** famous British authority on racing.

Vocabulary **obscure** (uhb SKYUR) *adj.:* little known.

D **Literary Focus** **Foreshadowing** What do you think the description of the child foreshadows here?

Cross-Curricular Connection

SOCIAL STUDIES: Horse Racing

Horse racing was a popular pastime in England many years before the discovery of the Americas. Today it is still looked upon as one of the country's chief pastimes, much as baseball is in the United States. British royalty usually has been keen on horse racing, which is referred to as the "sport of kings." It is no wonder, then, that Uncle Oscar delights in his nephew's interest in horse racing. It is an interest he would consider fitting for a gentleman. Notable races mentioned in the story include the Ascot, St. Leger at Doncaster, the Grand National, the Lincolnshire, and Derby Day at Epsom.

Think About/Talk About

Comprehension

C Reading Focus

Possible response: *Paul is looking for luck, his mother's love, and the means to get both.*

Analysis

D Literary Focus

Possible response: *The description foreshadows the child's great skill at predicting the outcomes of horse races. "Eyes blazing" foreshadows how Paul's compulsion to prove himself lucky in his mother's eyes becomes all-consuming.*

Extend the Discussion

Finding the Main Idea What arrangement does Paul have with Bassett, and why does Paul ask his uncle to "keep it between you and me"? ***Possible responses:*** *Paul and Bassett are partners, and each bets on the horse Paul designates, keeping only a certain amount of money in reserve. Paul wants to keep the secret of his betting from his parents. He seems to fear earning their disapproval and perhaps inheriting their "bad luck."*

Speculating Why do you think Uncle Oscar is reluctant to place a bet on Daffodil, the horse Paul has chosen? ***Possible response:*** *He may think his young nephew is simply playing games and guessing the winners. He has not seen proof of Paul's ability, and the idea that he can, with certainty, pick the winner of the race seems preposterous.*

Vocabulary: Own the Word

obscure: Explain that something *obscure* is not widely known, so a person might use this adjective to refer to a movie only a few people have seen. Ask students to name other things that can be described as *obscure* ***Possible responses:*** *books, facts*

Think About/Talk About

Literary Connection

Lawrence wrote this story for his friend Cynthia Asquith. Cynthia was born into the upper class of British society, the daughter of the eleventh Earl of Wemyss. She married a man with too little money and was always short of cash. Her sons found her to be a neglectful mother whose love was conditional, depending on their successes. Lawrence translated his impressions of the Asquith family into "The Rocking-Horse Winner."

Extend the Discussion

Comparing and Contrasting How do Uncle Oscar's attitudes toward Paul's betting tips differ from Bassett's? ***Possible response:*** *While Uncle Oscar is amused and skeptical, Bassett firmly believes in Paul's ability to predict the winners.*

Speculating Why do you think Bassett is so quick to attribute Paul's knowledge to the supernatural? ***Possible response:*** *Bassett has little education and cannot imagine any other source for Paul's knowledge. Gamblers are often superstitious, and Bassett believes that Paul is divinely inspired.*

"What am I to do with these?" he cried, waving them before the boy's eyes.

"I suppose we'll talk to Bassett," said the boy. "I expect I have fifteen hundred now; and twenty in reserve; and this twenty."

His uncle studied him for some moments.

"Look here, son!" he said. "You're not serious about Bassett and that fifteen hundred, are you?"

"Yes, I am. But it's between you and me, uncle. Honor bright?"

"Honor bright all right, son! But I must talk to Bassett."

"If you'd like to be a partner, uncle, with Bassett and me, we could all be partners. Only, you'd have to promise, honor bright, uncle, not to let it go beyond us three. Bassett and I are lucky, and you must be lucky, because it was your ten shillings I started winning with. . . ."

Uncle Oscar took both Bassett and Paul into Richmond Park for an afternoon, and there they talked.

"It's like this, you see, sir," Bassett said. "Master Paul would get me talking about racing events, spinning yarns, you know, sir. And he was always keen on knowing if I'd made or if I'd lost. It's about a year since, now, that I put five shillings on Blush of Dawn for him: And we lost. Then the luck turned, with that ten shillings he had from you: That we put on Singhalese. And since that time, it's been pretty steady, all things considering. What do you say, Master Paul?"

"We're all right when we're sure," said Paul. "It's when we're not quite sure that we go down."

"Oh, but we're careful then," said Bassett.

"But when are you *sure*?" smiled Uncle Oscar.

"It's Master Paul, sir," said Bassett in a secret, religious voice. "It's as if he had it from heaven. Like Daffodil, now, for the Lincoln. That was as sure as eggs." **E**

"Did you put anything on Daffodil?" asked Oscar Cresswell.

"Yes, sir. I made my bit."

"And my nephew?"

Bassett was obstinately silent, looking at Paul.

"I made twelve hundred, didn't I, Bassett? I told uncle I was putting three hundred on Daffodil."

"That's right," said Bassett, nodding.

"But where's the money?" asked the uncle.

"I keep it safe locked up, sir. Master Paul he can have it any minute he likes to ask for it."

"What, fifteen hundred pounds?"

"And twenty! And *forty,* that is, with the twenty he made on the course."

"It's amazing!" said the uncle.

"If Master Paul offers you to be partners, sir, I would, if I were you: if you'll excuse me," said Bassett.

Oscar Cresswell thought about it.

"I'll see the money," he said.

They drove home again, and sure enough, Bassett came round to the garden house with fifteen hundred pounds in notes. The twenty pounds reserve was left with Joe Glee, in the Turf Commission[12] deposit.

"You see, it's all right, uncle, when I'm *sure!* Then we go strong, for all we're worth. Don't we, Bassett?"

"We do that, Master Paul."

"And when are you sure?" said the uncle, laughing.

"Oh, well, sometimes I'm *absolutely* sure, like about Daffodil," said the boy; "and sometimes I have an idea; and sometimes I haven't even an idea, have I, Bassett? Then we're careful, because we mostly go down."

"You do, do you! And when you're sure, like about Daffodil, what makes you sure, sonny?"

"Oh, well, I don't know," said the boy uneasily. "I'm sure, you know, uncle; that's all."

"It's as if he had it from heaven, sir," Bassett reiterated.

"I should say so!" said the uncle.

But he became a partner. And when the Leger was coming on Paul was "sure" about Lively Spark, which

12. **Turf Commission:** committee of the Jockey Club, the chief governing body for horse racing. This committee operates a bank in which bettors can deposit money for future bets.

E **Literary Focus** **Foreshadowing** What might the words *secret* and *religious* foreshadow about the relationship between Bassett and the boy?

Vocabulary **reiterated** (ree IHT uh rayt ihd) *v.:* repeated.

Cross-Curricular Connection

RELIGION: Dervishes

In the middle ages, Muslim mystics who were members of one of the many Sufi brotherhoods achieved a trance state in their rituals through the repetition of a short prayer and wild whirling and dancing. Members of these brotherhoods were called *dervishes.* The descriptive term *whirling dervish* is a reference to this form of ritualistic behavior. In the United States, the Shakers also used whirling and dancing in their worship rituals for similar mystical purposes.

The Rocking-Horse Winner (1950), John Mills, John Howard Davies.

was a quite inconsiderable horse. The boy insisted on putting a thousand on the horse, Bassett went for five hundred, and Oscar Cresswell two hundred. Lively Spark came in first, and the betting had been ten to one against him. Paul had made ten thousand.

"You see," he said, "I was absolutely sure of him."

Even Oscar Cresswell had cleared two thousand.

"Look here, son," he said, "this sort of thing makes me nervous."

"It needn't, uncle! Perhaps I shan't be sure again for a long time."

"But what are you going to do with your money?" asked the uncle.

"Of course," said the boy, "I started it for mother. She said she had no luck, because father is unlucky, so I thought if *I* was lucky, it might stop whispering."

"What might stop whispering?"

"Our house. I *hate* our house for whispering."

"What does it whisper?"

"Why—why"—the boy fidgeted—"why, I don't know. But it's always short of money, you know, uncle."

"I know it, son, I know it."

"You know people send mother writs,[13] don't you, uncle?"

"I'm afraid I do," said the uncle.

"And then the house whispers, like people laughing at you behind your back. It's awful, that is! I thought if I was lucky——"

"You might stop it," added the uncle.

The boy watched him with big blue eyes, that had an uncanny cold fire in them, and he said never a word.

"Well, then!" said the uncle. "What are we doing?"

13. **writs:** legal papers; here, ones demanding payment.

Vocabulary **uncanny** (uhn KAN ee) *adj.:* strange; eerie; weird.

Reaching Reluctant Readers

After students have read the story, have them work in small groups. Have them discuss any parallel situations they know or have read about in which a child feels that he or she somehow has the responsibility to bring the family together again, or to save it from some problem for which the child has no actual responsibility. Ask students to compare this child's motivations and actions with Paul's. Did the child succeed in solving the problem? How did the child's actions affect the family?

Think About/Talk About

Analysis

E Literary Focus

Possible response: *The words could foreshadow the closeness between Paul and Bassett at the end of the story or the mystical nature of Paul's ability.*

Extend the Discussion

Drawing Conclusions Why is Paul uneasy about telling his uncle how he gets his racing tips? ***Possible responses:*** *Paul may be afraid that telling will bring bad luck; he may not completely trust his uncle; he may not "know" or be able to articulate what he does.*

Imagery Why do you think the author chose the image of the house "whispering"? Is the image effective? Explain. ***Possible responses:*** *Whispering is indirect. Nothing is ever said out loud, but money worries are the background noise of their lives. The image is effective because it creates the picture of a house "haunted" by the fear of impoverishment.*

Vocabulary: Own the Word

- **reiterated:** Ask students: "When might you have *reiterated* an answer? How would you *reiterate* an answer? Why might you *reiterate* it?"
- **uncanny:** Write *uncanny* in a center circle on the board and provide a definition: "weird." Draw spider legs from the center and have students add concepts and attributes. ***Possible responses:*** *creepy, mysterious, feeling, déjà vu*

Model the Skill

- Guide students to **understand foreshadowing** in the story. Explain that an author uses foreshadowing to help readers predict what will happen and to keep readers engaged.
- Read aloud the paragraph in column 1 that begins "Paul's mother had her birthday in November." As you read, share your thinking about where events are leading. For example, you might say: "The whispering is getting stronger. I know that Paul hopes to silence the whispers and please his mother by giving her money for her birthday, but I don't think she will be satisfied. I don't think she will ever be satisfied."

Guided Practice: Apply

Think-Pair-Share Have students think about how the whispers of the house foreshadow events to come. With a partner, have students review the passages where the whispers are mentioned. Have students determine what the whispers are foreshadowing at each point in the story. Then, as a class, discuss students' predictions about whether the whispers will ever stop or become louder.

Think About/Talk About

Extend the Discussion

Comparing and Contrasting How do the voices change? ***Possible response:*** *When Paul's mother has the full five thousand pounds, she needs even more. "The voices in the house suddenly [go] mad" and she goes on a spending spree.*

"I shouldn't like mother to know I was lucky," said the boy.

"Why not, son?"

"She'd stop me."

"I don't think she would."

"Oh!"—and the boy writhed in an odd way—"I *don't* want her to know, uncle." **F**

"All right, son! We'll manage it without her knowing."

They managed it very easily. Paul, at the other's suggestion, handed over five thousand pounds to his uncle, who deposited it with the family lawyer, who was then to inform Paul's mother that a relative had put five thousand pounds into his hands, which sum was to be paid out a thousand pounds at a time, on the mother's birthday, for the next five years.

"So she'll have a birthday present of a thousand pounds for five successive years," said Uncle Oscar. "I hope it won't make it all the harder for her later."

Paul's mother had her birthday in November. The house had been "whispering" worse than ever lately, and, even in spite of his luck, Paul could not bear up against it. He was very anxious to see the effect of the birthday letter, telling his mother about the thousand pounds.

When there were no visitors, Paul now took his meals with his parents, as he was beyond the nursery control. His mother went into town nearly every day. She had discovered that she had an odd knack of sketching furs and dress materials, so she worked secretly in the studio of a friend who was the chief "artist" for the leading drapers.[14] She drew the figures of ladies in furs and ladies in silk and sequins for the newspaper advertisements. This young woman artist earned several thousand pounds a year, but Paul's mother only made several hundreds, and she was again dissatisfied. She so wanted to be first in something, and she did not succeed, even in making sketches for drapery advertisements.

She was down to breakfast on the morning of her birthday. Paul watched her face as she read her letters. He knew the lawyer's letter. As his mother read it, her face hardened and became more expressionless. Then a cold, determined look came on her mouth. She hid the letter under the pile of others, and said not a word about it.

"Didn't you have anything nice in the post for your birthday, mother?" said Paul.

"Quite moderately nice," she said, her voice cold and absent. **G**

She went away to town without saying more.

But in the afternoon Uncle Oscar appeared. He said Paul's mother had had a long interview with the lawyer, asking if the whole five thousand could not be advanced at once, as she was in debt.

"What do you think, uncle?" said the boy.

"I leave it to you, son."

"Oh, let her have it, then! We can get some more with the other," said the boy.

"A bird in the hand is worth two in the bush, laddie!" said Uncle Oscar.

"But I'm sure to *know* for the Grand National; or the Lincolnshire; or else the Derby. I'm sure to know for *one* of them," said Paul.

So Uncle Oscar signed the agreement, and Paul's mother touched the whole five thousand. Then something very curious happened. The voices in the house suddenly went mad, like a chorus of frogs on a spring evening. There were certain new furnishings, and Paul had a tutor. He was *really* going to Eton,[15] his father's school, in the following autumn. There were flowers in the winter, and a blossoming of the luxury Paul's mother had been used to. And yet the voices in the house, behind the sprays of mimosa and almond blossom, and from under the piles of iridescent cushions, simply trilled and screamed in a sort of ecstasy: "There *must* be more money! Oh-h-h; there must be more money. Oh, now, now-w! Now-w-w—there *must* be

14. **drapers:** dealers in cloth.

15. **Eton:** Eton College, exclusive prep school, near London.

F **Literary Focus** **Foreshadowing** What could the description of the boy's eyes and the word *odd* foreshadow about Paul?

G **Reading Focus** **Interpreting Character** What words in this sentence tell you something about the mother's character?

Vocabulary **iridescent** (ihr ih DEHS uhnt) *adj.:* showing rainbowlike colors.

Universal Access

English Learners

Ask students to compare the relationship between Paul and his mother to the relationship between Paul and his uncle. What adjectives can be used to describe each relationship? Trusting or suspicious, intimate or distant, respectful or disrespectful, cold or warm? What motivates Paul to foster each relationship? Encourage students to find specific words, thoughts, and actions of characters in the story that reveal the nature of each relationship.

Struggling Readers

Benchmark Students Draw student's attention to the proverb, "A bird in the hand is worth two in the bush," recited by Uncle Oscar on p. 1318. Inform students that this statement implies that it is better to be satisfied with what you already have than to risk losing it all by attempting to pursue something that is better but not guaranteed. Ask students to think about how this proverb applies to the overall theme of the story.

✔ See **UA: Differentiating Instruction** for a graphic organizer to scaffold instruction for struggling readers.

more money!—more than ever! More than ever!"

It frightened Paul terribly. He studied away at his Latin and Greek with his tutor. But his intense hours were spent with Bassett. The Grand National had gone by: He had not "known," and had lost a hundred pounds. Summer was at hand. He was in agony for the Lincoln. But even for the Lincoln he didn't "know," and he lost fifty pounds. He became wild-eyed and strange, as if something were going to explode in him. H

"Let it alone, son! Don't you bother about it!" urged Uncle Oscar. But it was as if the boy couldn't really hear what his uncle was saying.

"I've got to know for the Derby! I've got to know for the Derby!" the child reiterated, his big blue eyes blazing with a sort of madness.

His mother noticed how overwrought he was.

"You'd better go to the seaside. Wouldn't you like to go now to the seaside, instead of waiting? I think you'd better," she said, looking down at him anxiously, her heart curiously heavy because of him.

But the child lifted his uncanny blue eyes.

"I couldn't possibly go before the Derby, mother!" he said. "I couldn't possibly!"

"Why not?" she said, her voice becoming heavy when she was opposed. "Why not? You can still go from the seaside to see the Derby with your Uncle Oscar, if that's what you wish. No need for you to wait here. Besides, I think you care too much about these races. It's a bad sign. My family has been a gambling family, and you won't know till you grow up how much damage it has done. But it has done damage. I shall have to send Bassett away, and ask Uncle Oscar not to talk racing to you, unless you promise to be reasonable about it: Go away to the seaside and forget it. You're all nerves!" I

"I'll do what you like, mother, so long as you don't send me away till after the Derby," the boy said.

"Send you away from where? Just from this house?"

"Yes," he said, gazing at her.

"Why, you curious child, what makes you care about this house so much, suddenly? I never knew you loved it."

He gazed at her without speaking. He had a secret within a secret, something he had not divulged, even to Bassett or to his Uncle Oscar.

But his mother, after standing undecided and a little bit sullen for some moments, said:

"Very well, then! Don't go to the seaside till after the Derby, if you don't wish it. But promise me you won't let your nerves go to pieces. Promise you won't think so much about horse racing and *events,* as you call them!"

"Oh no," said the boy casually, "I won't think much about them, mother. You needn't worry. I wouldn't worry, mother, if I were you."

"If you were me and I were you," said his mother, "I wonder what we *should* do!"

"But you know you needn't worry, mother, don't you?" the boy repeated.

"I should be awfully glad to know it," she said wearily.

"Oh, well, you *can,* you know. I mean, you *ought* to know you needn't worry," he insisted.

"Ought I? Then I'll see about it," she said.

Paul's secret of secrets was his wooden horse, that which had no name. Since he was emancipated from a nurse and a nursery-governess, he had had his rocking horse removed to his own bedroom at the top of the house.

"Surely you're too big for a rocking horse!" his mother had remonstrated.

"Well, you see, mother, till I can have a *real* horse, I like to have *some* sort of animal about," had been his quaint answer.

"Do you feel he keeps you company?" she laughed.

"Oh yes! He's very good, he always keeps me company, when I'm there," said Paul.

So the horse, rather shabby, stood in an arrested prance in the boy's bedroom.

The Derby was drawing near, and the boy grew

H Literary Focus Foreshadowing What details in these last two paragraphs seem to signal trouble?

I Literary Focus Foreshadowing What might the mother's remarks about gambling foreshadow?

Vocabulary **overwrought** (oh vuhr RAWT) *adj.:* overly excited.
remonstrated (rih MAHN strayt ihd) *v.:* protested.
arrested (uh REHST ihd) *v.* used as *adj.:* checked; stopped in motion.

Advanced Learners

Acceleration After students have finished reading the selection, discuss how imagination and reality become blurred in this story. Have students consider what in the story is imagined by Paul and what is "real" within the world of the story. Have students organize their thoughts in a two-column chart with one column representing Paul's imagination and the other column representing reality. Then, have students work with a partner and discuss any differences in perception.

Students with Disabilities

Tell students that the argument involving Paul and his mother on p. 1319 arises from a difference between what Paul wants and what his mother wants for him. Have students create a T-chart and list Paul's wants in the left column and what his mother wants for Paul in the right column. After finishing, have them orally summarize each column, giving a reason to explain each character's desires. ("Paul wants . . . because . . . ; however, his mother wants . . . because . . .").

Think About/Talk About

Comprehension

G Reading Focus

Possible response: *Her "cold and absent" voice shows she is unaware of Paul's intense need to please her.*

Analysis

F Literary Focus

Possible response: *The word "odd" suggests supernatural power or an intensity bordering on madness. This foreshadows a tragic event that may occur while Paul tries to predict the Derby winner.*

H Literary Focus

Possible response: *The voices now scream, "Oh-h-h; there must be more money," signifying Paul's mother's increasing needs. However, Paul does not "know" the winner, which means he may not be able to silence the voices.*

I Literary Focus

Possible response: *She does not know about his gambling. Her words suggest that Paul will eventually understand the "damage" that gambling can cause.*

Vocabulary: Own the Word

- **iridescent:** *Iridescent* clothes were popular during the 1970s. *Iridescent* ponds can be peaceful places to visit. An *iridescent* necklace might be made of diamonds and pearls.
- **overwrought:** Have students complete the following sentence: The mother in the story notices how *overwrought* her son is because . . .
- **remonstrated:** Tell students that to *remonstrate* is to argue against something or object to it. Ask students: "Why has the mother in the story *remonstrated* that the boy is too big for a rocking horse?"
- **arrested:** *Arrested* means "to stop," but it is commonly used in the context of people seized by legal authority. We say that they have been *arrested* for a crime. Discuss the similarities between the two meanings.

Model the Skill

- Use the Reading Skills Focus graphic organizer to model **interpreting character**.
- Have students focus on the mother and discuss what they learn about her on p. 1320. Read the first two paragraphs aloud, and explain what you notice about her behavior. For example, you might say: "I observe that Paul's mother is starting to worry about him. She has changed from the beginning of the story, when the narrator wrote, 'when her children were present, she always felt the center of her heart go hard.' In this instance, she feels a connection to her son and a sense of concern for his safety."

Guided Practice: Apply

Turn-and-Talk Have students discuss this section of the story with a classmate. Ask them to think about how Paul's mother's needs and fears are different at this point in the story than they were in the beginning. Instruct students to fill out their graphic organizers with their responses.

Think as a Reader/Writer

Find It in Your Reading After students read the narrator's descriptions of the mother's thoughts and feelings on p. 1320, point out to students that the narrator builds up tension and emotion by describing in short sentences and questions what the mother sees and hears at the bottom of p. 1320 before entering Paul's room.

Use It in Your Writing Have students write about a tense, suspenseful moment in which they describe the inner thoughts, questions, and feelings of a character, who is about to make an important discovery. Encourage them to use short sentences that gradually reveal more detail about what they will discover.

more and more tense. He hardly heard what was spoken to him, he was very frail, and his eyes were really uncanny. His mother had sudden strange seizures of uneasiness about him. Sometimes, for half an hour, she would feel a sudden anxiety about him that was almost anguish. She wanted to rush to him at once, and know he was safe.

Two nights before the Derby, she was at a big party in town, when one of her rushes of anxiety about her boy, her firstborn, gripped her heart till she could hardly speak. She fought with the feeling, might and main, for she believed in common sense. But it was too strong. She had to leave the dance and go downstairs to telephone to the country. The children's nursery-governess was terribly surprised and startled at being rung up in the night. **J**

"Are the children all right, Miss Wilmot?"

"Oh yes, they are quite all right."

"Master Paul? Is he all right?"

"He went to bed as right as a trivet.[16] Shall I run up and look at him?"

"No," said Paul's mother reluctantly. "No! Don't trouble. It's all right. Don't sit up. We shall be home fairly soon." She did not want her son's privacy intruded upon.

"Very good," said the governess.

It was about one o'clock when Paul's mother and father drove up to their house. All was still. Paul's mother went to her room and slipped off her white fur cloak. She had told her maid not to wait up for her. She heard her husband downstairs, mixing a whiskey and soda.

And then, because of the strange anxiety at her heart, she stole upstairs to her son's room. Noiselessly she went along the upper corridor. Was there a faint noise? What was it?

She stood, with arrested muscles, outside his door, listening. There was a strange, heavy, and yet not loud noise. Her heart stood still. It was a soundless noise, yet rushing and powerful. Something huge, in violent, hushed motion. What was it? What in God's name was it? She ought to know. She felt that she knew the noise. She knew what it was.

Yet she could not place it. She couldn't say what it was. And on and on it went, like a madness.

Softly, frozen with anxiety and fear, she turned the door handle.

The room was dark. Yet in the space near the window, she heard and saw something plunging to and fro. She gazed in fear and amazement.

Then suddenly she switched on the light, and saw her son, in his green pajamas, madly surging on the rocking horse. The blaze of light suddenly lit him up, as he urged the wooden horse, and lit her up, as she stood, blonde, in her dress of pale green and crystal, in the doorway.

"Paul!" she cried. "Whatever are you doing?"

"It's Malabar!" he screamed in a powerful, strange voice. "It's Malabar!"

His eyes blazed at her for one strange and senseless second, as he ceased urging his wooden horse. Then he fell with a crash to the ground, and she, all her tormented motherhood flooding upon her, rushed to gather him up.

But he was unconscious, and unconscious he remained, with some brain fever. He talked and tossed, and his mother sat stonily by his side. **K**

"Malabar! It's Malabar! Bassett, Bassett, I *know!* It's Malabar!"

So the child cried, trying to get up and urge the rocking horse that gave him his inspiration.

"What does he mean by Malabar?" asked the heart-frozen mother.

"I don't know," said the father stonily.

"What does he mean by Malabar?" she asked her brother Oscar.

"It's one of the horses running for the Derby," was the answer.

And, in spite of himself, Oscar Cresswell spoke to Bassett, and himself put a thousand on Malabar: at fourteen to one.

The third day of the illness was critical: They were waiting for a change. The boy, with his rather long,

16. **trivet:** short-legged stand used for placing hot dishes on a table.

J **Literary Focus** **Foreshadowing** What details in this paragraph and the previous one foreshadow trouble?

K **Reading Focus** **Interpreting Character** What word reveals something about the mother here?

Universal Access

Advanced Learners

Enrichment Have students read the following quotation from a letter that D. H. Lawrence wrote to an admirer in 1927: "If I were talking to the young, I should say only one thing to them: Don't you live just to make money, either for yourself or for anybody else. Don't look on yourself as a wage slave. Try to find out what life is, and live. Repudiate the money idea. . . . They must first overthrow in themselves the money-fear and money-lust. . ."

Small-Group Activity Have students discuss the excerpt's relevance to the story. Ask them to consider what message Lawrence is trying to send to young people and discuss Lawrence's outlook on life and money.

The Rocking-Horse Winner (1950), Valerie Hobson.

curly hair, was tossing ceaselessly on the pillow. He neither slept nor regained consciousness, and his eyes were like blue stones. His mother sat, feeling her heart had gone, turned actually into a stone.

In the evening, Oscar Cresswell did not come, but Bassett sent a message, saying could he come up for one moment, just one moment? Paul's mother was very angry at the intrusion, but on second thoughts she agreed. The boy was the same. Perhaps Bassett might bring him to consciousness.

The gardener, a shortish fellow with a little brown moustache and sharp little brown eyes, tiptoed into the room, touched his imaginary cap to Paul's mother, and stole to the bedside, staring with glittering, smallish eyes at the tossing, dying child.

"Master Paul!" he whispered. "Master Paul! Malabar came in first all right, a clean win. I did as you told me. You've made over seventy thousand pounds, you have; you've got over eighty thousand. Malabar came in all right, Master Paul."

"Malabar! Malabar! Did I say Malabar, mother? Did I say Malabar? Do you think I'm lucky, mother? I knew Malabar, didn't I? Over eighty thousand pounds! I call that lucky, don't you, mother? Over eighty thousand pounds! I knew, didn't I know I knew? Malabar came in all right. If I ride my horse till I'm sure, then I tell you, Bassett, you can go as high as you like. Did you go for all you were worth, Bassett?"

"I went a thousand on it, Master Paul."

"I never told you, mother, that if I can ride my horse, and *get there,* then I'm absolutely sure—oh, absolutely! Mother, did I ever tell you? I *am* lucky!"

"No, you never did," said his mother.

But the boy died in the night.

And even as he lay dead, his mother heard her brother's voice saying to her: "My God, Hester, you're eighty-odd thousand to the good, and a poor devil of a son to the bad. But, poor devil, poor devil, he's best gone out of a life where he rides his rocking horse to find a winner."

Think About/Talk About

Comprehension

K Reading Focus

Possible response: *Paul's mother cannot respond to his needs. She sits "stonily" by his bedside. The same word is used seven lines later to describe the father's behavior.*

Analysis

J Literary Focus

Possible response: *The details foreshadow something dire happening to Paul. He is "tense," unresponsive, "very frail," and "his eyes were really uncanny." His mother's "rushes of anxiety" add to the feeling of impending disaster.*

Extend the Discussion

Synthesizing What do you learn about Paul's basic motivation for making all the money that he has made? Does he die happy or not? ***Possible responses:*** *His motives have not changed: He wants to win his mother's love by proving to her that he is lucky. He proves his luck, but he does not witness her love.*

Monitor Students' Comprehension

Guide the class in answering these True-or-False comprehension questions.

1. Paul believes his family needs luck. [*T*]
2. As he rides his rocking horse, Paul is at ease. [*F*]
3. Uncle Oscar's attitude toward Paul's death is acceptance. [*T*]

California Standards, pp. 1322–1323

- **Reading Standard 3.3** Analyze the ways in which irony, tone, mood, the author's style, and the "sound" of language achieve specific rhetorical or aesthetic purposes or both.
- **Grades 9–10 Reading Review Standard 1.2** Distinguish between the denotative and connotative meanings of words and interpret the connotative power of words.
- **Grades 9–10 Reading Review Standard 3.3** Analyze interactions between main and subordinate characters in a literary text (e.g., in internal and external conflicts, motivations, relationships, influences) and explain the way these interactions affect the plot.
- **Grades 9–10 Reading Review Standard 3.4** Determine characters' traits by what the characters say about themselves in narration, dialogue, dramatic monologue, and soliloquy.
- **Grades 9–10 Reading Review Standard 3.6** Analyze and trace an author's development of time and sequence, including the use of complex literary devices (e.g., foreshadowing, flashbacks).
- **Writing Standard 2.1** Write fictional, autobiographical, or biographical narratives. **a.** Narrate a sequence of events and communicate their significance to the audience. **c.** Describe with concrete sensory details the sights, sounds, and smells of a scene and the specific actions, movements, gestures, and feelings of the characters; use interior monologue to depict the characters' feelings.
- **Writing Standard 2.2** Write responses to literature. **a.** Demonstrate a comprehensive understanding of the significant ideas in works or passages.

Check for Understanding

Independent Practice

Reading Skills Focus

Possible responses:

1. *The woman is unable to love her children; she feels flawed. She is not as rich as she hoped to be and is never satisfied with her life.*
2. *Paul thinks that luck and money are the same thing. He does not realize that people can be lucky in other ways and money can be earned from hard work.*
3. *Paul bets on horses and wins a great deal of money.*
4. *Responses will vary. Some students will consider Paul's frenzied death to be in vain because he does not win his mother's love.*
5. *Ask students to consider how the characters' actions, wants, and fears reflect their motivations.*

Literary Skills Focus

Possible responses:

6. *The voices represent his mother's materialism and the family's debts. The children perceive the voices because they are extra sensitive at that stage.*
7. *Paul wills himself into a psychic frenzy. He had "brain fever" (p. 1320), and his "eyes were like blue stones" (p. 1321).*
8. *It could stand for a child's desire for his mother's love. It could also stand for something inconsequential that can never become real.*
9. *Yes; he has encouraged Paul's gambling habit.*
10. *Yes; the desire for money is still prevalent.*
11. *The foreshadowing succeeds in constantly reminding readers that something bad will happen and Paul's successes come with consequences.*
12. *The atmosphere of the story reflects the tension in the house as well as Paul's vain hope to silence the whispers and win his mother's love. The foreshadowing creates a generally ominous atmosphere.*

Applying Your Skills

Reading Standard 3.3; **Grades 9–10 Reading Review Standard** 3.3, 3.4, 3.6 (see pages A48–A50)
Writing Standard 2.1c (see pages A51–A52)

The Rocking-Horse Winner

Literary Response and Analysis

Reading Skills Focus

Quick Check

1. How has the woman in the story been unlucky?
2. How is Paul confused about the word *luck?*
3. What does Paul do to ease his mother's anxiety over the family debts?

Read with a Purpose

4. Now that you have read the story, do you think Paul is a winner? Why or why not?

Reading Skills: Interpreting Character

5. Review the character chart you kept as you read. Now, add a row to the bottom called "Character's motivations for actions." In the space provided, analyze the motivations of the mother and Paul.

	The Mother	Paul
Key statements about character	"woman who was beautiful, who started with all the advantages"	Says of himself, "I'm a lucky person"
Character's actions		
Character's wants or needs		
Character's fears		
Character's motivations for actions		

Literary Skills Focus

Literary Analysis

6. **Hypothesize** How do you explain the ever louder voices in the house? Why do only Paul and his sister hear and react to the voices?
7. **Analyze** How would you explain what has really happened to Paul? What clues suggest that he has gone mad?
8. **Analyze** Think about the title of the story. What could the rocking horse symbolize?
9. **Interpret** Uncle Oscar says that Paul is best gone out of a life where he rides a rocking horse to find a winner. Do you think Uncle Oscar has been complicit in Paul's tragedy? Explain.
10. **Evaluate** Do you think Lawrence's fable is applicable to life today? Explain.

Literary Skills: Foreshadowing

11. **Evaluate** Review all the details that foreshadow Paul's tragic end. How does the foreshadowing in the story prepare you for the conclusion?

Literary Skills Review: Atmosphere

12. **Analyze** The mood or feeling created in a literary work is called **atmosphere.** How would you describe the atmosphere of this story?

Writing Skills Focus

Think as a Reader/Writer

Use It in Your Writing Review your notes about the ways the mother is characterized in the first paragraph of the story. Then, write a one-paragraph character description of your own. In your description, tell the reader precisely what your character sees or feels.

What Do You Think Now? How does an obsession with money affect each of these family members—especially Paul?

Universal Access

Struggling Writers

Ask students to construct a chart similar to their Reading Skills Focus graphic organizer detailing their character's actions, wants, and fears. Then, have them write a descriptive paragraph based on the chart.

What Do You Think Now?

When students answer this question, have them consider what each character hoped to gain by building wealth. Could their goals be met without acquiring money? Why or why not?

Grades 9–10 Reading Review Standard 1.2 (see pages A48–A50)
Writing Standard 2.1a, 2.1c, 2.2a (see pages A51–A52)

Vocabulary Development

Vocabulary Check

Be sure you can justify your answers to these questions about Vocabulary words.

1. ***Assert, reiterate,*** and ***remonstrate*** all describe the way people speak to one another. Which means "to declare"? Which means "to repeat"? Which means "to protest"?
2. The boy's eyes in the story are often described as "uncanny." If something is **uncanny,** is it likely to be a bit frightening or to be comforting?
3. Would an **obscure** book be popular or not well known?
4. How is an **iridescent** color different from a regular color?
5. Paul was often **overwrought.** Does this mean he was overexcited or depressed?

Vocabulary Skills: Connotations

Connotations are all the meanings, associations, or emotions that have come to be attached to a word. For example, Paul wonders about "filthy lucre," a negative expression that even suggests something debased. The effect would be different if Paul had said "money."

Your Turn

Which Vocabulary word in each of these pairs has a stronger connotation, that is, has more intensity?

said/asserted	uncanny/weird
overwrought/excited	objected/remonstrated

Language Coach

Multiple Meanings How many different meanings can each boldface word have?

She will **rack** her brains for the answer.
She wore a **smart** hat.
The **spring** in the rocking horse broke.

CHOICES

As you respond to the Choices, use the **Academic Vocabulary** words as appropriate: perspective, considerably, adapt, exhibit, inevitable.

REVIEW

Continue the Story

Now that you have analyzed the characters from "The Rocking-Horse Winner," you should have a good idea of how they might behave in another situation. Decide what you think would happen if the story were to continue. Write a follow-up scene that features at least one of the characters from the story.

Mother and Son (1990) by Vladimir Sherbakov (b. 1935). Oil on canvas.

CONNECT

Hypothesize About Motivation

Timed Writing Write a brief essay proposing possible explanations and motivations for the behavior of Paul's mother in "The Rocking-Horse Winner." Use examples from the story to support your analysis.

EXTEND

Write a Song

Review the story again, and brainstorm ideas for lyrics to a song about Master Paul. Decide on a perspective; then come up with a title for your song. Make a list of words, phrases, and images suggested by the title. After you write the lyrics of the song, revise them and then share the song with your class.

Learn It Online
Learn more about connotations with *WordSharp*.
go.hrw.com H12-1323 Go

Independent Practice

Choices: Evaluation Criteria

Review: Homework
Continue the Story

- Scene clearly indicates a continuation of Lawrence's story.
- Scene features at least one character from the original story.

Connect: Timed Writing 40–50 Minutes

- Students include more than one possible explanation.
- Students support their explanations with evidence from the story.

Extend: Homework
Write a Song

- Lyrics reflect an accurate understanding of Paul's character.
- Student's perspective remains consistent throughout song.

Assess

Unit 6 Resources, Selection Standards Check, p. 189

ThinkCentral Online Assessment, Selection Standards Check

Teacher One Stop™, editable Selection Standards Check

Reteach

ThinkCentral Online Remediation

Vocabulary Development

Vocabulary Check

1. *Assert—"declare"; reiterate—"repeat"; remonstrate—"protest"*
2. *frightening*
3. *not well known*
4. *It displays a rainbow-like play of colors.*
5. *overexcited*

Your Turn

Possible responses: *asserted, overwrought, uncanny, remonstrated*

WordSharp: An Interactive Vocabulary Tutor

English for Academic Success

Language Coach

1. Rack *can also be used as a noun meaning "a framework on which to hang things."*
2. Smart, *as an adjective, can mean "intelligent," and "clever," as well as "sophisticated."*
3. Spring, *as a verb, means "leap" or "issue forth." It is also a season.*

Learn It Online
WordSharp: An Interactive Vocabulary Tutor provides additional support for vocabulary development. Multimedia tutorials show students how to apply vocabulary skills to unfamiliar words—and how to make those words their own.
go.hrw.com H12-1323 Go

Standards Focus

Objectives

Students will
- understand epiphany
- compare and contrast aspects of a story

Selection Introduction

Think About the Writer

To help students answer the question, have them think of a time when a new experience or a new acquaintance gave them a new outlook about life. Ask whether their attitudes would have changed without the new experience.

For Independent Reading

*The Dictionary of Imaginary Places,** Alberto Manguel

HRW LIBRARY *This title is available in the HRW library.

Motivate

What Do You Think?/QuickTalk

Have students describe a time they were disappointed by something that they had really looked forward to. Ask them if they learned anything from the experience. Instruct students to write their thoughts in their **Reader/Writer Notebooks.**

English for Academic Success

Academic Vocabulary

Look for opportunities to use the Academic Vocabulary words in this unit.

- **considerably, *adv.*:** by a large amount
- **exhibit, *v.*:** show, demonstrate
- **perspective, *n.*:** a particular way of looking at something

Preparing to Read

Araby

What Do You Think? How does experience shape our view of the world?

QuickTalk

With a partner, discuss a trip or event that you greatly anticipated. Did the trip or event live up to your expectations? Why or why not? Record your thoughts in your *Reader/Writer Notebook.*

James Joyce (1934) by Jacques-Émile Blanche.
Courtesy The National Gallery of Ireland/Artists Rights Society (ARS), NY/ADAGP, Paris.

MEET THE WRITER

James Joyce
(1882–1941)

James Joyce's controversial novel *Ulysses* (1922) changed the face of modern fiction. Based on Homer's epic poem the *Odyssey, Ulysses* addresses issues of cultural identity, nationhood, history, and family in the modern world by chronicling the movements of two characters on one summer day in Dublin.

Early Struggles

Born in Rathgar, Ireland, a Dublin suburb, James Joyce was one of ten children in an impoverished family. Although he was educated in Roman Catholic schools, he had lost his faith by the time he entered University College, Dublin. After graduating, Joyce went to Paris, where he gave English lessons and wrote book reviews. In 1903, he returned home to be with his dying mother. The next year, he fell in love with a student named Nora Barnacle. When Joyce's debts mounted, he persuaded Nora to leave Ireland with him. The penniless couple settled first in the Italian city of Trieste, where their two children were born. Joyce's luck began to improve when the American poet Ezra Pound favorably reviewed Joyce's short-story collection *Dubliners* and persuaded a British magazine to serialize his novel *A Portrait of the Artist as a Young Man.*

Ulysses Brings Scandal and Fame

When Italy entered World War I, the Joyces left Trieste for Zurich. Gifts from anonymous patrons eased Joyce's financial troubles, but his physical problems increased considerably. Between 1917 and 1930, he had twenty-five operations for glaucoma and cataracts.

British publishers found *Ulysses* so scandalous that they refused to set it in type. In 1922, however, Sylvia Beach, the owner of a Paris bookstore, agreed to publish it. Despite many favorable reviews, the book was banned in Britain and the United States. In 1934, after a famous court case, *Ulysses* was published in America. A British edition soon followed, and Joyce's fame spread worldwide. He died at the age of fifty-eight.

Think About the Writer *Ulysses* describes the events of a single day in Dublin. How might living abroad have influenced Joyce to choose this topic?

California Standards, pp. 1324–1333

- **Reading Standard 3.3** Analyze the ways in which irony, tone, mood, the author's style, and the "sound" of language achieve specific rhetorical or aesthetic purposes or both.
- **Reading Standard 3.9** Analyze the philosophical arguments presented in literary works to determine whether the authors' positions have contributed to the quality of each work and the credibility of the characters. (Philosophical approach)
- **Grades 9–10 Review Reading Standard 3.3** Analyze interactions between main and subordinate characters in a literary text (e.g., internal and external conflicts, motivations, relationships, influences) and explain the way those interactions affect the plot.

Selection Readability	
Easily Accessible **Accessible** Challenging	accessible vocabulary; simple sentence structure; familiar syntax

Reading Standard 3.3, 3.9; Grades 9–10 Review
Reading Standard 3.3 (see pages A48–A50)

Literary Skills Focus

Epiphany Joyce called a moment of insight or a revelation experienced by one of his characters an **epiphany.** Before Joyce used the word in this manner, an *epiphany* referred solely to a religious experience, a moment during which a human being felt an intense connection with the divine or understood a spiritual truth. Since Joyce, an epiphany has come to refer to any moment of sudden insight or revelation experienced by a character in fiction. Although Joyce gave the word a modern, literary meaning, you will see that the main character's epiphany in "Araby" is described with religious language and imagery.

Literary Perspectives Apply the literary perspective described on page 1327 as you read this story.

Reading Skills Focus

Comparing and Contrasting In "Araby," the main character's vivid imagination sometimes causes him to misunderstand the realities of his life. His perspective on life noticeably contrasts with that of the people around him. Comparing his imaginings about the world with reality will help you understand his epiphany at the end of the story.

Into Action As you read the story, look for differences between the way the character imagines things to be and the way they really are. List these differences in a comparison-and-contrast chart like the one below.

Imagination	Reality
The word Araby fills him with an "Eastern enchantment."	

Writing Skills Focus

Think as a Reader/Writer

Find It in Your Reading James Joyce is a master of **imagery,** the use of words to create pictures of places and events. As you read, choose three places in the story that seem real to you. For each one, keep a list in your *Reader/Writer Notebook* of the words or phrases that are most effective in helping you form a mental image.

Vocabulary

imperturbable (ihm puhr TUR buh buhl) *adj.:* calm, impassive. *The man was imperturbable in the face of the boy's excitement.*

somber (SAHM buhr) *adj.:* gloomy. *The dark, dirty street on which he lived was somber.*

impinge (ihm PIHNJ) *v.:* strike; touch. *The dropped coins impinge upon the silence.*

annihilate (uh NY uh layt) *v.:* destroy; make nonexistent. *Failure can annihilate a person's hopes.*

monotonous (muh NAHT uh nuhs) *adj.:* unvarying. *The boy found his classwork monotonous.*

garrulous (GAR uh luhs) *adj.:* talkative. *The boy became impatient with the garrulous ladies as he tried to read his book in peace.*

improvised (IHM pruh vyzd) *v.* used as *adj.:* made for the occasion from whatever is handy. *The improvised tent covered the vendor's wares.*

pervades (puhr VAYDZ) *v.:* spreads throughout. *Gloom pervades the neighborhood.*

Language Coach

Homographs Words that are spelled the same but have different meanings are called **homographs.** For example, note how the word *blind* is used in this story. As you read, use a dictionary to find all the meanings of *blind* and other homographs you find.

Learn It Online
Discover more about Joyce's world online.
go.hrw.com H12-1325 Go

Reader/Writer Notebook
Use your **RWN** to complete the activities for this selection.

Selection Resources

Unit 6 Resources, on-level practice and assessment, p. 192

PowerNotes, interactive lesson presentations with activities

Teacher One Stop™, on-level lesson plans and all print resources

Holt Audio Library

Holt Audio Library: Selections and Summaries in Spanish

UA: Holt Interactive Reader, p. 359

UA: Differentiating Instruction, modified lesson plans and leveled assessment, p. 308

UA: Supporting Instruction in Spanish, selection summary

UA: Resources for Teaching Advanced Students, lesson plans, p. 208

ThinkCentral Online Assessment, Selection Standards Check

ThinkCentral Online Remediation

Preteach

Introducing Vocabulary

Use this activity to check students' understanding of the Vocabulary words.

1. An unhappy atmosphere _____ the room. [*pervades*]
2. Sandra's fear of spiders made her want to _____ them entirely. [*annihilate*]
3. The soldier's letters _____ lightly upon the possibility of death. [*impinge*]
4. The long speech was boring and _____. [*monotonous*]
5. When the actor forgot his lines, he _____. [*improvised*]
6. The _____ mood was cheered by the entrance of smiling toddlers. [*somber*]
7. The _____ boy talked through the entire movie. [*garrulous*]
8. She remained _____ throughout the long ordeal. [*imperturbable*]

English for Academic Success

Language Coach

Students may note that *blind* can also mean "a window covering" or "a dead-end street."

Literary Skills Focus

As you read and discuss the selection with students, have them watch for the narrator's epiphany.

Reading Skills Focus

Give students a copy of the Reading Skills Focus graphic organizer before they read.

Writing Skills Focus

Have students record examples of imagery in their **Reader/Writer Notebooks**.

Learn It Online
The **Writers' Lives** feature of the Interactive Student Edition offers additional information about this author. Audio or video segments are provided for some authors.
go.hrw.com H12-1325 Go

Teacher Preparation

Selection Plot Summary

The young narrator in "Araby" has a crush on a neighborhood girl. The girl tells him she longs to go to Araby, a visiting bazaar, but cannot. The narrator decides to go and bring her something from what he imagines will be a thrillingly romantic place. After a series of frustrations, he arrives late, as the bazaar is closing. Instead of fulfilling his dreams of exotic luxury, Araby is dreary. It features cheap trinkets and is staffed by ordinary workers. The narrator has a desultory conversation with a young vendor. He leaves feeling disillusioned and ashamed of his vain dream.

Direct Teach

Think About/Talk About

Read with a Purpose Have students read the Read with a Purpose statement. Ask them to note the main character's expectations of what Araby would be like and whether they were fulfilled.

Extend the Discussion

Personification In the first paragraph, Joyce describes the houses on the narrator's dead-end street, using diction that personifies them. What specific words give the house human qualities? ***Possible response:*** *Words and phrases like "conscious," "gazed," and "imperturbable faces" help to personify the houses.*

SHORT STORY

Araby

by **James Joyce**

Read with a Purpose

Read to discover what Araby is and what the main character finds there.

Build Background

On May 14, 1894, a five-day charity bazaar came to the city of Dublin. The bazaar was called *Araby,* a reference to Arabia, where bazaars, markets with long rows of stalls or shops, are common. For the children of Dublin, Arabia seemed a mysterious, exotic place, very different from the dreary streets of the city in which they lived.

The house in this story is based on one in which Joyce and his family actually lived. It stood on the same blind (dead-end) street as the Christian Brothers' School Joyce attended.

North Richmond Street, being blind, was a quiet street except at the hour when the Christian Brothers' School set the boys free. An uninhabited house of two stories stood at the blind end, detached from its neighbors in a square ground. The other houses of the street, conscious of decent lives within them, gazed at one another with brown imperturbable faces.

The former tenant of our house, a priest, had died in the back drawing-room. Air, musty from having been long enclosed, hung in all the rooms, and the waste room behind the kitchen was littered with old useless papers. Among these I found a few paper-covered books, the pages of which were curled and damp: *The Abbot,* by Walter Scott, *The Devout Communicant,* and *The Memoirs of Vidocq.*[1] I liked the last best because its leaves were yellow. The wild garden behind the house contained a

1. ***The Abbott . . . Vidocq*** (vee DUHK): respectively, a historical romance about Mary, Queen of Scots, by Sir Walter Scott; an 1813 religious manual written by a Franciscan friar; and the memoirs (though not actually written by François Vidocq) of a French criminal who later became a detective.

Vocabulary **imperturbable** (ihm puhr TUR buh buhl) *adj.:* calm; impassive.

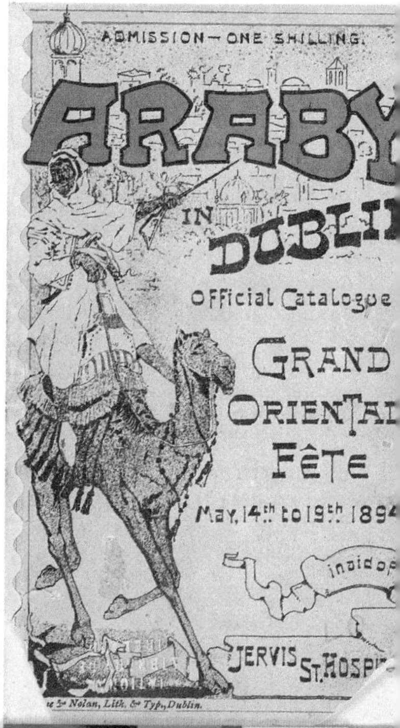

Analyzing Visuals

Connecting to the Text How might the characters in this story have reacted to this poster if they had seen it hanging in Dublin?

Araby poster, Dublin.
Courtesy of the National Library of Ireland.

Universal Access

Advanced Learners

Enrichment For Joyce, the Ireland of his time—its society, religion, and culture—was in a state of decay. The gap between Ireland's traditional ideals and present reality was the main source of Joyce's sense of irony. Ask students to learn more about Ireland—past and present. Have them consider how traditional Irish ideals of Joyce's time sync with Ireland's current state of reality.

✔ See **UA: Resources for Teaching Advanced Students** for strategies for teaching advanced learners.

Analyzing Visuals

Connecting to the Text: *The narrator and Mangan's sister would both have believed that the poster was an announcement for an authentic event that would be exotic, romantic, and adventurous.*

central apple-tree and a few straggling bushes under one of which I found the late tenant's rusty bicycle-pump. He had been a very charitable priest; in his will he had left all his money to institutions and the furniture of his house to his sister.

When the short days of winter came dusk fell before we had well eaten our dinners. When we met in the street the houses had grown somber. The space of sky above us was the color of ever-changing violet and toward it the lamps of the street lifted their feeble lanterns. The cold air stung us and we played till our bodies glowed. Our shouts echoed in the silent street. The career[2] of our play brought us through the dark muddy lanes behind the houses where we ran the gauntlet[3] of the rough tribes from the cottages, to the back doors of the dark dripping gardens where odors arose from the ashpits, to the dark odorous stables where a coachman smoothed and combed the horse or shook music from the buckled harness. When we returned to the street light from the kitchen windows had filled the areas. If my uncle was seen turning the corner we hid in the shadow until we had seen him safely housed. Or if Mangan's sister came out on the doorstep to call her brother in to his tea we watched her from our shadow peer up and down the street. We waited to see whether she would remain or go in and, if she remained, we left our shadow and walked up to Mangan's steps resignedly. She was waiting for us, her figure defined by the light from the half-opened door. Her brother always teased her before he obeyed and I stood by the railings looking at her. Her dress swung as she moved her body and the soft rope of her hair tossed from side to side.

2. **career:** course; path.
3. **gauntlet** (GAWNT liht): series of challenges. Derived from *gatlopp*, Swedish for "running down a lane," the term originally referred to a form of military punishment in which a wrongdoer had to run between two rows of soldiers who struck him as he passed.

A Reading Focus **Comparing and Contrasting** The word *yet* in the last sentence of this paragraph signals a contrast. What is being contrasted in this sentence?

Vocabulary **somber** (SAHM buhr) *adj.:* gloomy.

Every morning I lay on the floor in the front parlor watching her door. The blind was pulled down to within an inch of the sash so that I could not be seen. When she came out on the doorstep my heart leaped. I ran to the hall, seized my books, and followed her. I kept her brown figure always in my eye and, when we came near the point at which our ways diverged, I quickened my pace and passed her. This happened morning after morning. I had never spoken to her, except for a few casual words, and yet her name was like a summons to all my foolish blood. A

Her image accompanied me even in places the most hostile to romance. On Saturday evenings when my aunt went marketing I had to go to carry some of the parcels. We walked through the flaring streets, jostled by drunken men and bargaining women, amid the curses of laborers, the shrill litanies[4] of shop-boys who stood on guard by the barrels of pigs' cheeks, the nasal chanting of street-singers, who sang a *come-all-you* about O'Donovan Rossa,[5] or a ballad about the troubles in our native land. These noises converged

4. **litanies:** repeated sales cries. Literally, a litany is a prayer composed of a series of specific invocations and responses.
5. ***come-all-you* ...Rossa:** A come-all-you (kuhm AL yuh) is a type of Irish ballad that usually begins "Come all you [young lovers, rebels, Irishmen, and so on]." O'Donovan Rossa was Jeremiah O'Donovan (1831–1915) of County Cork. He was active in Ireland's struggle against British rule in the mid-nineteenth century.

Literary Perspectives

Analyzing Credibility in Literature You learn much of what you know about a story from its narrator. Some stories have an omniscient, or all-knowing, narrator who objectively reports "reality." Other stories, such as "Araby," attempt to depict a character's unique, imperfect way of seeing the world. In these stories, the writer often uses first-person point of view, in which the character "speaks" in the first person. It is up to the reader to decide when the character is reporting something real and when the character is imagining or misinterpreting events.

As you read, be sure to notice the questions in the text, which will guide you in using this perspective.

Think About/Talk About

Comprehension

A Reading Focus

Possible response: *The sentence contrasts reality and illusion. The reality is that the narrator hardly knows Mangan's sister; the illusion is the image of love and romance that he has conjured.*

Extend the Discussion

Finding Details Why is the speaker so intrigued by Mangan's sister? ***Possible response:*** *He is enchanted by her figure, which is defined by the light from the house. He enjoys watching her dress swing as she moves her body and tosses her long hair from side to side.*

Making Inferences What can you infer about how the speaker's attitude toward his uncle differs from his attitude toward Mangan's sister? ***Possible response:*** *His uncle is feared, because the speaker hides in the shadows from him. Mangan's sister is respected and admired, because the speaker anxiously awaits her presence.*

Vocabulary: Own the Word

- **imperturbable:** Tell students that *imperturbable* is based on the verb *perturb* which means "to bother." When you add on the prefix *im–* ("not") and the suffix *–able* ("capable of"), the word comes to mean "not capable of being disturbed." When might it be difficult for a person to be *imperturbable*?
- **somber:** Act out the behaviors and show the expression of someone in a *somber* situation (sigh heavily, look sad and serious). Ask students to think of some *somber* situation or occasion and show how a person might look and act.

Literary Perspectives

Before students read the selection, have them read the **Literary Perspectives** about Analyzing Credibility in Literature.

In "Araby," Joyce uses irony to establish the discrepancy between the narrator's romantic views and reality. The boy's love for Mangan's sister is obviously an overblown adolescent crush. He seeks some exotic gift from Araby, but this, too, becomes an ironic quest. Have students evaluate the narrator's credibility by deciding if the details provided refer to the reality or to the boy's romantic imaginings.

Remind students to use the notes and questions at the bottom of the page to help them use the perspective.

Model the Skill

- Provide students with copies of the Reading Skills Focus graphic organizer for "Araby." (See **Unit 6 Resources**.)
- Tell students that they should be looking for discrepancies between the character's perspective on things and the actual state of things. Tell them that noting the contrasts between his imaginative views of the world and reality will lead them to recognize and understand the epiphany that occurs toward the end of the story.
- Model **comparing and contrasting** the character's imagination to the reality around him. You might say: "At the top of p. 1328, the boy envisions himself carrying a chalice through a 'throng of foes,' when in reality he is carrying his aunt's bags and walking through a crowded and noisy street."

Imagination	Reality
The boy carries a chalice through a "throng of foes."	He is carrying his aunt's bags through a noisy street.

Guided Practice: Apply

Double-Entry Journal Use the Double-Entry Journal to enhance comprehension. Have students read the rest of p. 1328. Ask students to discuss with a partner the reason the boy relies so heavily on imagination. Have them record information in their Double-Entry Journal under the headings "Quotes from the Text" and "My Notes."

in a single sensation of life for me: I imagined that I bore my chalice[6] safely through a throng of foes. Her name sprang to my lips at moments in strange prayers and praises which I myself did not understand. My eyes were often full of tears (I could not tell why) and at times a flood from my heart seemed to pour itself out into my bosom. I thought little of the future. I did not know whether I would ever speak to her or not or, if I spoke to her, how I could tell her of my confused adoration. But my body was like a harp and her words and gestures were like fingers running upon the wires. **B**

One evening I went into the back drawing-room in which the priest had died. It was a dark rainy evening and there was no sound in the house. Through one of the broken panes I heard the rain impinge upon the earth, the fine incessant needles of water playing in the sodden beds. Some distant lamp or lighted window gleamed below me. I was thankful that I could see so little. All my senses seemed to desire to veil themselves and, feeling that I was about to slip from them, I pressed the palms of my hands together until they trembled, murmuring: *O love! O love!* many times.

At last she spoke to me. When she addressed the first words to me I was so confused that I did not know what to answer. She asked me was I going to *Araby.* I forget whether I answered yes or no. It would be a splendid bazaar, she said; she would love to go.

—And why can't you? I asked.

While she spoke she turned a silver bracelet round and round her wrist. She could not go, she said, because there would be a retreat that week in her convent.[7] Her brother and two other boys were fighting for their caps and I was alone at the railings. She held one of the spikes, bowing her head toward me. The light from the lamp opposite our door caught the white curve of her neck, lit up her hair that rested there and, falling, lit up the hand upon the railing. It fell over one side of her dress and caught the white border of a petticoat, just visible as she stood at ease.

—It's well for you,[8] she said.

—If I go, I said, I will bring you something.

What innumerable follies laid waste my waking and sleeping thoughts after that evening! I wished to annihilate the tedious intervening days. I chafed against the work of school. At night in my bedroom and by day in the classroom her image came between me and the page I strove to read. The syllables of the word *Araby* were called to me through the silence in which my soul luxuriated and cast an Eastern enchantment over me. I asked for leave to go to the bazaar on Saturday night. My aunt was surprised and hoped it was not some Freemason[9] affair. I answered few questions in class. I watched my master's face pass from amiability to sternness; he hoped I was not beginning to idle. I could not call my wandering thoughts together. I had hardly any patience with the serious work of life which, now that it stood between me and my desire, seemed to me child's play, ugly monotonous child's play. **C**

On Saturday morning I reminded my uncle that I wished to go to the bazaar in the evening. He was fussing at the hallstand, looking for the hat-brush, and answered me curtly:

6. **chalice** (CHAL ihs): cup; specifically, the cup used for Holy Communion wine. Joyce's use of the term evokes the image of a young man on a sacred mission.
7. **retreat... convent:** temporary withdrawal from worldly life by the students and teachers at the convent school, to devote time to prayer, meditation, and study.
8. **It's well for you:** "You're lucky" (usually said enviously).
9. **Freemason:** The Freemasons are a secret society whose practices were originally drawn from those of British medieval stonemasons' guilds. In Ireland its members were almost exclusively Protestant and were often hostile to Catholics. The aunt apparently associates the bazaar with the mysterious practices of Freemasonry.

B **Literary Perspectives** **Analyzing Credibility in Literature** How does the narrator's description contrast with what is actually going on around him? How can you tell?

C **Reading Focus** **Comparing and Contrasting** How do the narrator's thoughts distract him from reality? Which of his worlds, imaginary or real, do you think he prefers?

Vocabulary **impinge** (ihm PIHNJ) *v.:* strike; touch.
annihilate (uh NY uh layt) *v.:* destroy; make nonexistent.
monotonous (muh NAHT uh nuhs) *adj.:* unvarying.

Universal Access

EL English Learners

English for Academic Success Students may be confused by the word *bazaar,* the meaning of which varies from culture to culture. Explain that in this story the word is used to mean "traveling fair" or "carnival." Then, invite students to describe comparable events that take place in their own culture.

✔ See **UA: Differentiating Instruction** for strategies for teaching English learners.

Students with Disabilities

Read aloud or have a volunteer read aloud the first six paragraphs of the story. Then, ask students to summarize the events. Next, have them predict what will happen in the rest of the story. They should write down the answers to the following questions: Will the girl find out how the boy feels? If so, how will she react? What might the boy do to show his love? Will the girl fall in love with the boy? When they finish the story, have students compare their predictions with what actually happens.

—Yes, boy, I know.

As he was in the hall I could not go into the front parlor and lie at the window. I left the house in bad humor and walked slowly toward the school. The air was pitilessly raw and already my heart misgave me.

When I came home to dinner my uncle had not yet been home. Still it was early. I sat staring at the clock for some time and, when its ticking began to irritate me, I left the room. I mounted the staircase and gained the upper part of the house. The high cold empty gloomy rooms liberated me and I went from room to room singing. From the front window I saw my companions playing below in the street. Their cries reached me weakened and indistinct and, leaning my forehead against the cool glass, I looked over at the dark house where she lived. I may have stood there for an hour, seeing nothing but the brown-clad figure cast by my imagination, touched discreetly by the lamplight at the curved neck, at the hand upon the railings and at the border below the dress.

When I came downstairs again I found Mrs. Mercer sitting at the fire. She was an old garrulous woman, a pawnbroker's widow, who collected used stamps for some pious purpose. I had to endure the gossip of the tea-table. The meal was prolonged beyond an hour and still my uncle did not come. Mrs. Mercer stood up to go: She was sorry she couldn't wait any longer, but it was after eight o' clock and she did not like to be out late, as the night air was bad for her. When she had gone I began to walk up and down the room, clenching my fists. My aunt said:

—I'm afraid you may put off your bazaar for this night of Our Lord.

At nine o' clock I heard my uncle's latchkey in the halldoor. I heard him talking to himself and heard the hallstand rocking when it had received the weight of his overcoat. I could interpret these signs. When he was midway through his dinner I asked him to give me the money to go to the bazaar. He had forgotten.

St. Patrick's Day Close, Dublin by Walter Osborne.
Courtesy The National Gallery of Ireland.

—The people are in bed and after their first sleep now, he said.

I did not smile. My aunt said to him energetically:

—Can't you give him the money and let him go? You've kept him late enough as it is.

My uncle said he was very sorry he had forgotten. He said he believed in the old saying: *All work*

Vocabulary **garrulous** (GAR uh luhs) *adj.:* talkative.

Word-Attack Skills Mini-Lesson

English for Academic Success Use these pairs of words to review the effect of final *e* on the vowel sounds in words. Have students compare the sounds in these pairs of words.

sooth, soothe	stag, stage
tic, entice	ping, impinge

Help students make the following generalizations about the effect of final *e* on the preceding consonant sound.

- *Unvoiced "th," as in "sooth," becomes voiced "th," as in "soothe."*
- *Hard "c," as in "tic," becomes soft "c", as in "entice."*
- *Hard "g," as in "stag," becomes soft "g," as in "stage."*
- *Hard "g," as in "ping," becomes soft "g," as in "impinge."*

Activity Have students identify the two words in each of the following sentences that demonstrate the effect of final *e* on the preceding consonant sound.

1. The door hangs heavy on its hinges.
2. One day a strange visitor rang the bell.
3. Clothed in light, frothy garments, she opened the door.
4. She breathed in the chill air blowing in from the heath.

Think About/Talk About

Comprehension

C Reading Focus

Possible responses: *He is unable to concentrate in school. He prefers his dreams to reality.*

Analysis

B Literary Perspectives

Possible responses: *The narrator imagines himself on a mission while he accompanies his aunt through the crowded streets of Dublin. We know this is the case because he describes the atmosphere as well as his musings.*

Extend the Discussion

Characterization How would you characterize the aunt and the uncle and their relationship with the boy? ***Possible responses:*** *The aunt is religious and thoughtful; the uncle is self-absorbed and forgetful. They both seem to care for the boy but are somewhat distant from him; their understanding of him is superficial.*

Vocabulary: Own the Word

- **impinge:** Discuss with students how the connotation of *impinge* is of imposing or intruding. In the story, the rain *impinges* upon the earth. Ask students to name things that might *impinge* on a picnic.
- **annihilate:** Write *annihilate* in a center circle on the board and provide a definition: "destroy." Draw spider legs from the center and have students add concepts and attributes. [*obliterate, defeat, crush*]
- **monotonous:** Give the following examples: A *monotonous* song might be the ABC song, especially if a child sings it 25 times a day. A *monotonous* job might be to sharpen a thousand pencils. Have students describe a task they find *monotonous*.
- **garrulous:** Ask: "Have you ever known a *garrulous* person? Explain who that person was, how you knew he or she was *garrulous*, and what he or she talked about most."

Think About/Talk About

Comprehension

D Reading Focus

Possible response: *The reality is disappointing. The narrator expects to find something brightly lit and bustling. Instead, he finds a dark, silent, and gloomy hall.*

Analysis

E Literary Focus

Possible response: *He realizes that his hopes were unrealistic; he sees himself as vain and naïve for having had such high hopes.*

Extend the Discussion

Speculating What emotions overwhelm the boy? How do they differ from the emotions he expected to feel? ***Possible responses:*** *He feels humiliation, futility, and disillusionment. He expected to feel triumphant and valued.*

Vocabulary: Own the Word

- **improvised:** Tell students that just as *improv* (noun form) comedy is made up on the spot, off the cuff, anything *improvised* is made out of what is there in front of you. A plan can be *improvised* on the spot, an outfit can be *improvised* from what is in the closet.
- **pervades:** Ask students: "What kind of sound might *pervade* a room? Can you think of an idea that *pervades* your mind so much you cannot think of anything else?"

Monitor Students' Comprehension

Guide the class in answering these True-False questions.

1. The narrator goes to the fair to buy a present for his aunt. [*F*]
2. The word *Araby* suggests romance to the narrator. [*T*]
3. Araby turns out to be everything the narrator hoped it would be. [*F*]

and no play makes Jack a dull boy. He asked me where I was going and, when I had told him a second time he asked me did I know *The Arab's Farewell to his Steed.*[10] When I left the kitchen he was about to recite the opening lines of the piece to my aunt.

I held a florin[11] tightly in my hand as I strode down Buckingham Street toward the station. The sight of the streets thronged with buyers and glaring with gas recalled to me the purpose of my journey. I took my seat in a third-class carriage of a deserted train. After an intolerable delay the train moved out of the station slowly. It crept onward among ruinous houses and over the twinkling river. At Westland Row Station a crowd of people pressed to the carriage doors; but the porters moved them back, saying that it was a special train for the bazaar. I remained alone in the bare carriage. In a few minutes the train drew up beside an improvised wooden platform. I passed out on to the road and saw by the lighted dial of a clock that it was ten minutes to ten. In front of me was a large building which displayed the magical name.

I could not find any sixpenny entrance and, fearing that the bazaar would be closed, I passed in quickly through a turnstile, handing a shilling to a weary-looking man. I found myself in a big hall girdled at half its height by a gallery. Nearly all the stalls were closed and the greater part of the hall was in darkness. I recognized a silence like that which pervades a church after a service. I walked into the center of the bazaar timidly. A few people were gathered about the stalls which were still open. Before a curtain, over which the words *Café Chantant*[12] were written in colored lamps, two men were counting money on a salver.[13] I listened to the fall of the coins.

Remembering with difficulty why I had come I went over to one of the stalls and examined porcelain vases and flowered tea-sets. At the door of the stall a young lady was talking and laughing with two young gentlemen. I remarked their English accents and listened vaguely to their conversation.

—O, I never said such a thing!

—O, but you did!

—O, but I didn't!

—Didn't she say that?

—Yes. I heard her.

—O, there's a… fib!

Observing me the young lady came over and asked me did I wish to buy anything. The tone of her voice was not encouraging; she seemed to have spoken to me out of a sense of duty. I looked humbly at the great jars that stood like eastern guards at either side of the dark entrance to the stall and murmured:

—No, thank you.

The young lady changed the position of one of the vases and went back to the two young men. They began to talk of the same subject. Once or twice the young lady glanced at me over her shoulder.

I lingered before her stall, though I knew my stay was useless, to make my interest in her wares seem the more real. Then I turned away slowly and walked down the middle of the bazaar. I allowed the two pennies to fall against the sixpence in my pocket. I heard a voice call from one end of the gallery that the light was out. The upper part of the hall was now completely dark. **D**

Gazing up into the darkness I saw myself as a creature driven and derided by vanity; and my eyes burned with anguish and anger. **E**

10. ***The Arab's . . . Steed:*** popular sentimental poem by the English writer Caroline Norton (1808–1877).
11. **florin:** British coin at the time worth the equivalent of about fifty cents.
12. ***Café Chantant*** (ka FAY SHAHN tahn): The name refers to a coffeehouse with musical entertainment..
13. **salver** (SAL vuhr): serving tray.

Vocabulary **improvised** (IHM pruh vyzd) *v.* used as *adj.:* made for the occasion from whatever is handy.
pervades (puhr VAYDZ) *v.:* spreads throughout.

D Reading Focus **Comparing and Contrasting** How does the reality of the Araby bazaar differ from the what the boy imagined?

E Literary Focus **Epiphany** What does the boy realize about himself?

California Standards, pp. 1331–1333

- **Reading Standard 1.3** Discern the meaning of analogies encountered, analyzing specific comparisons as well as relationships and inferences.
- **Reading Standard 3.3** Analyze the ways in which irony, tone, mood, the author's style, and the "sound" of language achieve specific rhetorical or aesthetic purposes or both.
- **Reading Standard 3.9** Analyze the philosophical arguments presented in literary works to determine whether the authors' positions have contributed to the quality of each work and the credibility of the characters. (Philosophical approach)
- **Grades 9–10 Review Reading Standard 3.3** Analyze interactions between main and subordinate characters in a literary text (e.g., internal and external conflicts, motivations, relationships, influences) and explain the way those interactions affect the plot.
- **Writing Standard 2.1** Write fictional, autobiographical, or biographical narratives: **a.** Narrate a sequence of events and communicate their significance to the audience. **b.** Locate scenes and incidents in specific places.
- **Writing Standard 2.2** Write responses to literature: **d.** Demonstrate an understanding of the author's use of stylistic devices and an appreciation of the effects created.

Reading Standard 3.3, 3.9; Grades 9–10 Review Reading Standard 3.3 (see pages A48–A50)
Writing Standard 2.1b (see pages A51–A52)

Araby

Literary Response and Analysis

Reading Skills Focus

Quick Check

1. What clues does the story provide that the narrator is a man remembering his childhood from a mature perspective?
2. How often have the narrator and Mangan's sister spoken to each other?
3. What is the purpose of the narrator's quest—his journey to the bazaar?

Read with a Purpose

4. What did Araby turn out to be? What did the narrator find there?

Reading Skills: Comparing and Contrasting

5. Look back at your chart, in which you compared what the narrator imagines with what is real. How would you summarize the difference? Add a row to the bottom of the chart you made, and summarize the comparison.

Imagination	Reality
The word Araby fills him with an "Eastern enchantment."	He finds that the people who work there are ordinary.
Summary of comparison:	

Literary Skills Focus

Literary Analysis

6. **Draw Conclusions** What conclusions can you draw about the uncle? What kind of person is he, and what problems may he have?
7. **Make Judgments** In what ways are the lives of the characters narrow, or restricted?
8. **Infer** How does the narrator deal with intrusions of reality into his fantasy: at the market, for example? What do his reactions tell you about him?
9. **Extend** There are many religious references in this story—for example, a dead priest, a chalice, the narrator's prayer-like utterances, and the bazaar's churchly silence. How do these references inform your understanding of the narrator's state of mind and quest?
10. **Literary Perspectives** How would you evaluate the story's ending? Is the narrator's description of his feelings realistic or exaggerated? Explain.

Literary Skills: Epiphany

11. **Analyze** What epiphany has the narrator experienced by the end of the story? What details support your answer?

Literary Skills Review: Tone

12. **Interpret** How would you describe the writer's **tone,** or attitude toward the characters and what happens to them? Cite specific textual examples.

Writing Skills Focus

Think as a Reader/Writer

Use It in Your Writing Review your notes on Joyce's use of imagery to create places that seem real. Think of the most enchanting place you have ever been. Then, write a paragraph using imagery to describe it. Try to make your place seem real to the reader. Finally, share your description with a classmate.

What Do You Think Now? How does the narrator's experience of life in a dreary Dublin neighborhood shape his view of the world?

Universal Access

Struggling Writers

Some students may need additional scaffolding to complete the Writing Skills Focus activity. Review the description of the main character playing in the streets in winter and his visit to the market with his aunt on p. 1327. Then, have students brainstorm the colorful sights, sounds, and smells of a real or seemingly real place. Tell them to list their descriptive words and phrases in a three-column chart, with the columns "Sights," "Sounds," and "Smells." Have them refer to the chart while they compose their paragraph.

What Do You Think Now?

Remind students that Joyce himself left Dublin in search of opportunity. Ask students to think about where Joyce's narrator might look to find an escape from his everyday life.

Check for Understanding

Independent Practice

Reading Skills Focus

Possible responses:

1. *The complexity of the narrator's diction indicates he is older than the main character.*
2. *The narrator has spoken only a few words to Mangan's sister.*
3. *The purpose of it is to buy a gift at the bazaar for Mangan's sister.*
4. *Araby turns out to be a tacky enterprise run by ordinary English vendors. He finds an assortment of common knick-knacks.*
5. *Ask students how the narrator's imaginings are more or less attractive than the realities.*

Literary Skills Focus

Possible responses:

6. *The uncle is self-absorbed and forgetful. He might drink heavily.*
7. *Their lives are restricted by tedious routines; opportunities, in general, are limited, as is money.*
8. *At the market, the boy imagines that he bears his "chalice safely through a throng of foes." This suggests that the narrator is imaginative and romantic.*
9. *The religious references add a sense of depth and reverence to the narrator's feelings for Mangan's sister; they also suggest that the narrator is fanciful and perhaps even melodramatic.*
10. *Students may feel that the ending is realistic because it reveals how misplaced the boy's expectations have been or that it is overblown because it is melodramatic.*
11. *At the end of the story, the boy realizes that his romantic fantasies are illusions. His tears of "anguish and anger" show his frustration and disappointment.*
12. *The writer's tone is sympathetic, yet bleak. The writer depicts the narrator's youthful emotions vividly but seems to share the older narrator's cynicism.*

Independent Practice
Vocabulary Development
Vocabulary Check
1. *impinge* 2. *annihilate*
3. *pervades* 4. *monotonous*
5. *imperturbable* 6. *improvised*
7. *somber* 8. *garrulous*

Your Turn
1. *monotonous*
2. *garrulous*
3. *somber*
4. *imperturbable*
5. *improvised*
6. *pervades*

English for Academic Success
Language Coach
Possible response: *unseeing*

English for Academic Success
Academic Vocabulary
Possible response: *The point of view or perspective that Joyce exhibits is one of cynicism and disillusionment. The boy's romantic quest for love is overblown and later shattered by a realization of his vanity. The relationship between the boy's aunt and uncle demonstrates a kind of love that is not even remotely close to the boy's ideals of love.*

Applying Your Skills

Reading Standard 1.3 (see pages A48–A50)

Araby

Vocabulary Development

Vocabulary Check

Complete each of the following sentences with one of the Vocabulary words: **imperturbable, somber, impinge, annihilate, monotonous, garrulous, improvised, pervades.**

1. Do not let this unfortunate event _______ on your happiness.
2. Krista was determined to _______ the colony of ants living in her kitchen.
3. A bad odor _______ the garage where the puppy spent the night.
4. Keisha yawned; she found the speech dull and _______.
5. The other people at the horror movie screamed and covered their eyes, but Bruce was _______.
6. Raul used a tablecloth as a(n) _______ cape and pretended to fight a bull.
7. The doctor looked _______ when he told Megan she had broken both legs.
8. The _______ man at the bus stop would not stop talking to Marco.

Vocabulary Skills: Analogies

A **word analogy** is a formally written statement that compares two pairs of words. In a word analogy, the relationship between the first pair of words is the same as the relationship between the second pair of words. For example, *cool* and *chilly* have a synonymous relationship to each other, as do the words *mad* and *angry*. To express this relationship, you would write

COOL : CHILLY :: mad : angry

The colon (:) stands for the phrase *is related to*. The double colon (::) between the two pairs of words stands for the phrase *in the same way that*.

Here are two ways to read the analogy:

COOL is related to CHILLY in the same way that *mad* is related to *angry*.

COOL is to CHILLY as *mad* is to *angry*.

Two types of relationships frequently expressed in word analogies are **synonyms** and **antonyms.** The example used above (COOL : CHILLY :: mad : angry) expresses a synonymous relationship. The following word analogy expresses an antonymous, or opposite, relationship:

SOILED : CLEAN :: careless : careful

Your Turn

Work with a partner to complete each analogy below with a Vocabulary word.

imperturbable	somber	monotonous
garrulous	improvised	pervades

1. EXCITING : THRILLING :: _______ : tedious
2. BRIGHT : DULL :: _______ : uncommunicative
3. SPICY : BLAND :: _______ : festive
4. SMART : INTELLIGENT :: _______ : calm
5. RAMSHACKLE : STURDY :: _______ : rehearsed
6. FLOWS : RUNS :: _______ : permeates

Language Coach

Homographs There is yet another homograph for one of the words from the selection: *blind.* In addition to meaning "a window covering" or "unquestioning," what else can *blind* mean?

Academic Vocabulary

Write About

Write about the narrative perspective and point of view Joyce exhibits in this story.

Universal Access: Vocabulary Development

EL English Learners

English for Academic Success Provide students with additional practice with homographs. Have them find the different meanings along with their parts of speech for the following words:

- concert
- desert
- live
- minute
- present
- resume
- refuse
- wound
- produce
- dove

Then, have students choose one of the homographs and create sentences using each of the different meanings in their appropriate contexts.

✔ See the **Academic and Selection Vocabulary Skill Builder** in **UA: Differentiating Instruction.**

Writing Standard 2.1a, 2.1b, 2.2d (see pages A51–A52)

Grammar Link

Independent and Subordinate Clauses

James Joyce uses sophisticated sentences—grammatically complex constructions with more than one clause. A **clause** is a group of words that contains a verb and its subject and that is used as part of a sentence. There are two types of clauses.

An **independent** clause expresses a complete thought and can stand by itself as a sentence.

SUBJECT VERB
James Joyce wrote *Ulysses.*

A **subordinate clause** does not express a complete thought and cannot stand alone as a sentence.

SUBJECT VERB
after he moved to Zurich

To function grammatically, a subordinate clause must be combined with an independent clause:

James Joyce wrote *Ulysses* after he moved to Zurich.

Subordinate clauses can serve as adjectives, nouns, or adverbs in a sentence.

Your Turn

Circle the subordinate clause in each sentence below.

1. Joyce lived briefly in a former military fortification, where he began to write an autobiographical novel.
2. Sylvia Beach was an American who owned a bookstore in Paris.
3. Ezra Pound believed that Joyce's writing deserved to be published.

Writing Application Choose a piece of your own writing. Underline the independent and subordinate clauses. Be sure that you have varied your sentence patterns, and revise independent and subordinate clauses as necessary.

CHOICES

As you respond to the Choices, use the **Academic Vocabulary** words as appropriate: perspective, considerably, adapt, exhibit, inevitable.

REVIEW

Compare and Contrast Through Art

Write down everything you know from the story about the narrator's real world. Then, write down his expectations for Araby. Divide a large sheet of paper or poster board in half. On one half, create a visual representation of the narrator's real world. You may draw, paint, or create a collage. On the other half, create a visual representation of the narrator's idea of Araby. Exhibit your project for the class.

CONNECT

Write a Travel Brochure

From the narrator's perspective, Araby represents a place where his dreams will come true. Is there a place that you think would transform you if you could visit or live there? Research this exciting locale in your library or on the Internet. Then, write a travel brochure encouraging people to visit. Make it sound as alluring as possible.

EXTEND

Write a "Before and After" Essay

Timed Writing We all have experienced epiphanies, those moments when we suddenly understand things in a new way. Think of an epiphany you have experienced. Then, write a short personal essay describing you and your life before and after the epiphany. Choose an epiphany that is not too personal and that you feel comfortable sharing with your classmates.

Learn It Online
Discover Joyce's influence on the modern world through these Internet links.
go.hrw.com H12-1333 Go

Universal Access: Grammar Link

English Learners

English for Academic Success Use this lesson to reinforce the standard English use of independent and subordinate clauses. Have students underline the subordinate clause in each sentence below.

1. *Ulysses* is Joyce's most famous work although it was not published in the United States until 1934.
2. Sylvia Beach agreed to publish *Ulysses* when no one else would.
3. The poet Ezra Pound believed that "Araby" could be any town.
4. When the war began, Joyce moved to Switzerland.

✔ For more practice with independent and subordinate clauses, see **Warriner's Handbook, GrammarNotes,** and **Language Handbook Worksheets.**

Independent Practice

Grammar Link

Your Turn

1. *where he began to write an autobiographical novel*
2. *who owned a bookstore in Paris*
3. *that Joyce's writing deserved to be published*

Choices: Evaluation Criteria

Review: Homework
Compare and Contrast Through Art
Poster should illustrate both the real and the imaginary worlds described in the story.

Connect: Homework
Write a Travel Brochure
Brochure should use vivid descriptions of a place.

Extend: Timed Writing 40–50 Minutes
Essays should have a beginning, middle, and end. Body paragraphs should develop "before" and "after" events.

Assess

Unit 6 Resources, Selection Standards Check, p. 195

ThinkCentral Online Assessment, Selection Standards Check

Teacher One Stop™, editable Selection Standards Check

Reteach

ThinkCentral Online Remediation

Learn It Online
The enhanced author biography offers more information on the life of the author as well as Holt's interactive resources pertaining to the author.
go.hrw.com H12-1333 Go

Standards Focus

Objectives

Students will
- understand paradox
- make predictions as a strategy for comprehension

Selection Introduction

Think About the Writer

To help students answer the question, ask them to think about how new experiences might inspire the imagination.

For Independent Reading

- *Changing Planes,** Ursula K. Le Guin
- *The Little Prince,* Antoine de Saint-Exupery

HRW LIBRARY *This title is available in the HRW library.

Motivate

What Do You Think?/QuickWrite

Have students think about the people or things on which they depend, such as electricity or gasoline. Then, have students write their responses to the QuickWrite in their **Reader/Writer Notebooks**.

English for Academic Success

Academic Vocabulary

Look for opportunities to use the Academic Vocabulary words in this unit.
- **adapt, *v.*:** adjust for a new purpose
- **inevitable, *adj.*:** unavoidable
- **perspective, *n.*:** a particular way of looking at something

Preparing to Read

The Book of Sand

What Do You Think? How does experience shape our view of the world?

QuickWrite

In your *Reader/Writer Notebook,* write down a dependable reality of daily life, such as gravity. What would the world would be like if that reality shifted slightly—or simply no longer existed?

Jorge Luis Borges (1883).

MEET THE WRITER

Jorge Luis Borges

(1899–1986)

A native of Argentina, Jorge Luis Borges (BOHR hehs) announced at age six that he intended to become a writer. He began working at his chosen profession immediately. At age nine, he translated Oscar Wilde's fairy tale "The Happy Prince" into Spanish. Borges later credited his father with inspiring his writing career. He felt that his father had made him aware of poetry, specifically of the idea that words can be powerful and symbolic, and not just a means of everyday communication.

A Cosmopolitan Life

Borges learned English at an early age from his English-born grandmother and subsequently devoured his father's extensive library. He loved the horror stories of Edgar Allan Poe, the adventures of Robert Louis Stevenson, and the fairy tales in *The Thousand and One Nights*. Ironically, Borges first read the great Spanish classics *El Cid* and *Don Quixote* in English translations. Later, when he read *Don Quixote* in its original Spanish, he said it sounded like a bad translation!

The Borges family was traveling in Europe when World War I broke out. They took refuge in neutral Switzerland, where Borges attended school and adapted quickly to his new environment by learning three more languages: French, Latin, and German. After the war the family moved first to Italy, then to Spain, and finally back to Argentina.

Creating His Own World

Borges began his career as a poet, and he always considered himself a poet first and foremost. In the 1940s, however, Borges turned to experimental prose, writing stories about transparent tigers; wizards who conjure up visions in a bowl of ink; and encyclopedias that do not record events but cause them. The stories in *The Garden of Forking Paths* (1941) and *El Aleph* (1949) ignore plot and character and most of the usual elements of fiction. They instead blend fact and fantasy in a world of games and riddles, literary mystery, and philosophical inquiry.

Think About the Writer How might Borges's extensive travels have helped develop his imagination?

California Standards, pp. 1334–1341

- **Reading Standard 2.4** Make warranted and reasonable assertions about the author's arguments by using elements of the text to defend and clarify interpretations.
- **Reading Standard 3.4** Analyze the ways in which poets use imagery, personification, figures of speech, and sounds to evoke readers' emotions.

Selection Readability	
Easily Accessible **Accessible** Challenging	familiar syntax; simple dialogue; challenging theme; abstract ideas

Literary Skills Focus

Paradox Statements or situations that contain two seemingly contradictory truths are called **paradoxes.** In forcing us to conceive of reality in new and different ways, paradoxes challenge the limits of our intellect. Borges was a master of paradox, in part because he set his outrageous events in an everyday context. In the following story, Borges drops his paradox into the lap of a harmless book lover who discovers that loving a book and hating a book can be infinitely the same thing.

Reading Skills Focus

Making Predictions A **prediction** is a type of **inference,** a guess based on evidence. In a story that presents a mystery or a puzzle, we read carefully, looking for clues. We base our predictions on the characters and their situations as well as on our own experiences and knowledge about life. We typically make initial guesses early in a work and adjust them as the story unfolds to fit new events and information. Sometimes, despite our careful reading, what seems inevitable can turn out to be uncertain.

Into Action As you read "The Book of Sand," jot down any predictions you form. Later, you'll see if your predictions were true.

Predictions

The book will turn out to be fake. →

Writing Skills Focus

Think as a Reader/Writer

Find It In Your Reading The mood, or feeling, in a literary work is called its **atmosphere.** In "The Book of Sand," Borges's descriptions and language evoke an atmosphere of mystery and dread. As you read, write in your *Reader/Writer Notebook* the words and phrases that you think contribute to the story's atmosphere.

Reader/Writer Notebook

Use your **RWN** to complete the activities for this selection.

Vocabulary

pedantic (peh DAN tihk) *adj.:* showing an exaggerated concern for books, learning, and rules. *The old man adopted a pedantic tone with his visitor.*

discomfiture (dihs KUHM fih chuhr) *n.:* frustration; embarrassment. *His discomfiture was obvious from his faltering speech.*

caste (kast) *n.:* social class. *In India your caste is determined at birth.*

defiled (dih FYLD) *v.:* made unclean. *In turning the pages of the book with dirty hands, you defiled the pages.*

diabolic (dy uh BAHL ihk) *adj.:* of or having to do with evil or the devil. *Obsession can become diabolic if it causes people to lose their sanity.*

bibliophile (BIHB lee uh fyl) *n.:* one who loves books. *The old man was such a bibliophile that his apartment was filled with books.*

misanthropy (mih SAN thruh pee) *n.:* hatred for humankind. *Those who are afflicted with misanthropy often live solitary lives.*

artifice (AHRT uh fihs) *n.:* trickery; deception. *When he first saw the remarkable book, he thought there might be artifice involved.*

Language Coach

Foreign Words Words and phrases in italics are often foreign. The phrase *more geometrico* is Latin and pronounced "MOH ray gee oh MEHT rih coh." In Latin, an *e* at the end of a word is always pronounced.

Learn It Online

Discover more about Borges online.

go.hrw.com H12-1335 Go

Selection Resources

Unit 6 Resources, on-level practice and assessment, p. 198

Teacher One Stop™, on-level lesson plans and all print resources

Holt Audio Library

Holt Audio Library: Selections and Summaries in Spanish

UA: Differentiating Instruction, graphic organizer, p. 311

UA: Supporting Instruction in Spanish, selection summary

ThinkCentral Online Assessment, Selection Standards Check

ThinkCentral Online Remediation

Preteach

Introducing Vocabulary

Use this activity to check students' understanding of the Vocabulary words.

1. His _____ caused him to look down on everyone regardless of _____. [*misanthropy; caste*]
2. The scholar was a _____ who sometimes sounded _____ when discussing his books. [*bibliophile; pedantic*]
3. Her mind was haunted by the _____ and cunning schemes of the past; although now she is without any _____. [*diabolic; artifice*]
4. After he realized the beauty of his lawn had been _____, his _____ was obvious. [*defiled; discomfiture*]

English for Academic Success

Language Coach

Have students pronounce the Latin phrase, *pro tempore* (pro tehm POHR ay), meaning "for the time being."

Literary Skills Focus

As you read the selection, have students note its paradoxes.

Reading Skills Focus

Give students a copy of the Reading Skills Focus graphic organizer before they read. (See **Unit 6 Resources**.) Tell them to use their responses to answer the questions on the Applying Your Skills page.

Writing Skills Focus

Have students record details that create atmosphere in their **Reader/Writer Notebooks**. Students can use their notes to complete the Writing Skills Focus activity.

Learn It Online

The enhanced author biography offers more information on the life of the author as well as Holt's interactive resources pertaining to the author.

go.hrw.com H12-1335 Go

Teacher Preparation

Selection Plot Summary

The narrator of "The Book of Sand" recalls a visit from a tall stranger from abroad who sells Bibles. Since the narrator is a bibliophile who already possess several rare Bibles, he has no interest. But then the foreigner shows the narrator a sacred book acquired in northern India. As the narrator examines this volume, it looks more and more bizarre. For example, the pages are not numbered consecutively, and the book seems to have neither a beginning nor an end. Intrigued, the narrator trades his pensions and a rare Bible for the Book of Sand. After the peddler departs, the narrator hides the book, but he finds himself becoming obsessed with it, even to the point of insomnia. Feeling that the book is monstrous and has made him monstrous, he covertly deposits the volume on a shelf at the National Library.

SHORT STORY

The Book of Sand

by **Jorge Luis Borges** translated by **Andrew Hurley**

Read with a Purpose
Read to find out what the Book of Sand is and how it affects the narrator's life.

Build Background
Borges believed that reality consists not only of what we have actually seen and done, but also of what we have read and of what our reading has led us to imagine.

. . . thy rope of sands . . .
—George Herbert (1593–1633)

The line consists of an infinite number of points; the plane, of an infinite number of lines; the volume, of an infinite number of planes; the hypervolume, of an infinite number of volumes . . . No—this, *more geometrico,*[1] is decidedly not the best way to begin my tale. To say that the story is true is by now a convention of every fantastic tale; mine, nevertheless, is true. **A**

I live alone, in a fifth-floor apartment on Calle Belgrano.[2] One evening a few months ago, I heard a knock at my door. I opened it, and a stranger stepped in. He was a tall man, with blurred, vague features, or perhaps my nearsightedness made me see him that way. Everything about him spoke of honest poverty: he was dressed in gray, and carried a gray valise. I immediately sensed that he was a foreigner. At first I thought he was old; then I noticed that I had been misled by his sparse hair, which was blond, almost white, like the Scandinavians'. In the course of our conversation, which I doubt lasted more than an hour, I learned that he hailed from the Orkneys.[3]

1. ***more geometrico:*** in the geometrical manner.
2. **Calle Belgrano:** street in Buenos Aires.
3. **Orkneys:** group of islands off the northern coast of Scotland.

A Literary Focus **Paradox** If the opening sentences are not the best way to begin, why does the narrator begin with them anyway?

Head of a Man (Diego) (1964) by Alberto Giacometti.
Kunsthaus, Zurich, Switzerland/Artists Rights Society (ARS), NY/ADAGP, Paris.

Direct Teach

Think About/Talk About

Read with a Purpose Have students read the Read with a Purpose statement. Ask them if they have ever owned something that seemed to consume all or most of their time. Ask them how this possession interfered with normal daily activities such as school, homework, or social life.

Analysis

A Literary Focus

Possible response: *He wants to establish the paradox that this fantastic story is as "true" as the axioms of geometry, but he admits that offering mathematical proof may not verify the veracity of the events to others.*

Universal Access

English Learners

English for Academic Success The details pertaining to books may confuse some students. Explain that the *spine* refers to the back binding of the book. A *volume* is a copy of a book, and *clothbound* refers to a book covered in cloth rather than paper. The word *scripture* refers to religious writing. Ask students to make note of any other terms or phrases that may be unfamiliar to them.

✔ See the **English Language Skill Builder** in **UA: Differentiating Instruction.**

Struggling Readers

Tell students that writers will set the mood in a story through descriptions of people and settings. For example, a tragic story might establish a serious mood with grey skies, dark colors, and depressing characters. Point out that on p. 1336, this "fantastic tale" begins with a stranger of "blurred, vague features" in a grey outfit, setting a mysterious, almost ominous mood. Have students continue reading and look for other descriptions that contribute to this mysterious atmosphere.

I pointed the man to a chair. He took some time to begin talking. He gave off an air of melancholy, as I myself do now.

"I sell Bibles," he said at last.

"In this house," I replied, not without a somewhat stiff, pedantic note, "there are several English Bibles, including the first one, Wyclif's.[4] I also have Cipriano de Valera's,[5] Luther's[6] (which is, in literary terms, the worst of the lot), and a Latin copy of the Vulgate. As you see, it isn't exactly Bibles I might be needing."

After a brief silence he replied.

"It's not only Bibles I sell. I can show you a sacred book that might interest a man such as yourself. I came by it in northern India, in Bikaner."

He opened his valise and brought out the book. He laid it on the table. It was a clothbound octavo[7] volume that had clearly passed through many hands. I examined it; the unusual heft[8] of it surprised me. On the spine was printed *Holy Writ,* and then *Bombay.*

"Nineteenth century, I'd say," I observed.

"I don't know," was the reply. "Never did know."

I opened it at random. The characters were unfamiliar to me. The pages, which seemed worn and badly set, were printed in double columns, like a Bible. The text was cramped, and composed into versicles.[9]

4. **Wyclif's:** first English translation of the Bible. John Wycliffe (c. 1330–1384) took charge of the project and perhaps did some translating.
5. **Cipriano de Valera's:** Spanish translation of the Bible; Casiodoro de Reina (1520–1594) translated the Bible, and Cipriano de Valera (1531–1602) edited it.
6. **Luther's:** German translation of the Bible. Martin Luther (1483–1546) was the German priest who set in motion the Protestant Reformation.
7. **octavo:** book, the pages of which have been made from sheets of paper that have been folded eight times.
8. **heft:** heaviness.
9. **versicles:** little verses.

At the upper corner of each page were Arabic numerals. I was struck by an odd fact: the even-numbered page would carry the number 40,514, let us say, while the odd-numbered page that followed it would be 999. I turned the page; the next page bore an eight-digit number. It also bore a small illustration, like those one sees in dictionaries: an anchor drawn in pen and ink, as though by the unskilled hand of a child. **B**

It was at that point that the stranger spoke again.

"Look at it well. You will never see it again."

There was a threat in the words, but not in the voice.

I took note of the page, and then closed the book. Immediately I opened it again. In vain I searched for the figure of the anchor, page after page. To hide my discomfiture, I tried another tack.

"This is a version of Scripture in some Hindu language, isn't that right?"

"No," he replied.

Then he lowered his voice, as though entrusting me with a secret.

"I came across this book in a village on the plain, and I traded a few rupees[10] and a Bible for it. The man who owned it didn't know how to read. I suspect he saw the Book of Books as an amulet.[11] He was of the lowest caste; people could not so much as step on his shadow without being defiled. He told me his book was called the Book of Sand because neither sand nor this book has a beginning or an end."

He suggested I try to find the first page.

I took the cover in my left hand and opened the book, my thumb and forefinger almost touching. It was impossible: several pages always lay between the

10. **rupees:** basic monetary unit of many Asian countries, including India, Pakistan, and Nepal.
11. **amulet:** ornament often inscribed with a magical incantation or symbol to protect the wearer from evil.

Vocabulary **pedantic** (peh DAN tihk) *adj.:* showing an exaggerated concern for books, learning, and rules.
discomfiture (dihs KUHM fih chuhr) *n.:* frustration; embarrassment.
caste (kast) *n.:* social class.
defiled (dih FYLD) *v.:* made unclean.

B Reading Focus **Making Predictions** From the book's curious features, and from what you know of the narrator's character, what do you predict the narrator will do about the book?

Advanced Learners

Acceleration Scottish philosopher David Hume was a skeptic who believed that absolute knowledge of the world is impossible and that what human beings interpret as cause and effect is merely the mind's linking of ideas and impressions. Challenge students to find out more about Hume's philosophy and to discuss how it relates to the ideas of an endlessly shifting universe that Borges explores in "The Book of Sand."

Students with Disabilities

The abstract ideas in this selection may present challenges for students' comprehension. To help them visualize the "The Book of Sand," ask students to draw a picture of the book showing some of its characteristics. For instance, they could make a drawing of a book with the number 40,514 at the top of one page, the number 999 on the next page, and an eight-digit number like 10,000,000 on the following page. Point out the other characteristics of the book that could be readily illustrated, such as the unknown characters and the double columns.

Think About/Talk About

Comprehension

B Reading Focus

Possible responses: *The narrator will try to acquire the book to solve its mysterious puzzles; he will become obsessed with the book.*

Extend the Discussion

Symbolism What might the nonsequential numbers and the disappearing illustration symbolize? ***Possible responses:*** *The numbers may have an order but not the one the narrator expects. They might show that life cannot be predicted or that one would have to look deeply to find a predictable order. The disappearing illustration could symbolize the way a moment in time happens only once and cannot be repeated. For an orderly, pedantic person like the narrator, these features would be disturbing but also fascinating.*

Vocabulary: Own the Word

- **pedantic:** Tell students that the connotation of *pedantic* is that someone is a little stiff and tries to come across as clever. So you might say: "He was not academic, and he sounded *pedantic* when he bragged about doing crosswords."
- **discomfiture:** The character tries to hide his *discomfiture* by asking a different way. Ask students ways that people try to hide their *discomfiture* ("awkwardness"). ***Possible responses:*** *cover a blush, walk away, clear throat*
- **caste:** Write *caste* in a center circle on the board and provide a definition: "social class." Draw spider legs from the center as students add concepts and attributes. ***Possible responses:*** *social position, rank, background, place*
- **defiled:** Ask students to applaud to indicate whether they would like their reputation to be *defiled.* Ask students to explain their responses. ***Possible response:*** *Students do not applaud to show they want a clean, untainted reputation.*

Model the Skill

- Provide students with copies of the Reading Skills Focus graphic organizer. (See **Unit 6 Resources.**)
- Tell students that **making predictions** while reading will help them gain a better understanding of the literature by making them find and think about clues provided in the text.
- Model making predictions and adding them to the graphic organizer. You might say: "Suppose you read that the current owner of the Book of Sand appears melancholy, or sad, and calls the book "diabolic," or wicked. Knowing this, you might predict that if the narrator buys the book, it will somehow make him melancholy, too."

"If he buys the book, he will be melancholy."	➔	

Guided Practice: Apply

Turn-and-Talk Have students form pairs to look for clues that will help them make predictions. Tell them to start by paying attention to details that reveal the character of the narrator and the Bible salesman. Then, they can reflect on the particulars of the situation in which the characters find themselves. Finally, they can make predictions about what will happen in the story. Ask volunteers to share their predictions with the class.

cover and my hand. It was as though they grew from the very book.

"Now try to find the end."

I failed there as well. **C**

"This can't be," I stammered, my voice hardly recognizable as my own.

"It can't be, yet it *is*," the Bible peddler said, his voice little more than a whisper. "The number of pages in this book is literally infinite. No page is the first page; no page is the last. I don't know why they're numbered in this arbitrary way, but perhaps it's to give one to understand that the terms of an infinite series can be numbered any way whatever."

Then, as though thinking out loud, he went on.

"If space is infinite, we are anywhere, at any point in space. If time is infinite, we are at any point in time."

His musings irritated me.

"You," I said, "are a religious man, are you not?"

C **Literary Focus** **Paradox** What is paradoxical about the book as the narrator describes it?

MATHEMATICS LINK

Infinity

In common parlance, infinity is defined as something without end, but in mathematics, infinity has a more precise definition. Although philosophers, mathematicians, and scientists have written about the concepts of infinity for more than two thousand years, infinity wasn't well defined mathematically until the late nineteenth century, when Georg Cantor developed the theory behind finite and infinite sets. In mathematical terms, infinity is something that is equal to some of its parts. For example, consider how all whole numbers (1, 2, 3, 4, and so on) can be matched with all even whole numbers (2, 4, 6, 8, and so on), implying that the number of whole numbers is equal to the number of even whole numbers.

Furthermore, infinities come in two sizes, the infinitely large and the infinitely small. The science journalist Peter Tyson explains: "As Jonathan Swift wrote, 'So, naturalists observe, a flea / Has smaller fleas that on him prey / And these have smaller still to bite 'em / And so proceed ad infinitum.' We may not be able to conceive of Swift's infinitesimal fleas, because reason insists they don't exist, but we can imagine ever smaller numbers without much trouble. It's no hardship, for example, to grasp the notion of an infinity of numbers stretching between, say, the numerals 2 and 3. Take half of the 1 that separates them,... then half of that half, then half of that half, and so proceed ad infinitum.... [Yet here's] another of those confounding paradoxes: the numerals 2 and 3 are separated by both a finite number (1) and an infinity of numbers."

Ask Yourself:

How might the study of infinity apply to science as well as to mathematics?

Mathematics Link

Ask Yourself

Possible response: *The concept of infinity is found in astronomy: the universe extends infinitely and there are infinite celestial bodies that compose it. In mathematics, fractions often represent numbers with infinite decimals.*

"Yes, I'm Presbyterian. My conscience is clear. I am certain I didn't cheat that native when I gave him the Lord's Word in exchange for his diabolic book."

I assured him he had nothing to reproach[12] himself for, and asked whether he was just passing through the country. He replied that he planned to return to his own country within a few days. It was then that I learned he was a Scot, and that his home was in the Orkneys. I told him I had great personal fondness for Scotland because of my love for Stevenson and Hume.[13]

"And Robbie Burns,"[14] he corrected.

As we talked I continued to explore the infinite book.

"Had you intended to offer this curious specimen to the British Museum, then?" I asked with feigned indifference.

"No," he replied, "I am offering it to you," and he mentioned a great sum of money.

I told him, with perfect honesty, that such an amount of money was not within my ability to pay. But my mind was working; in a few moments I had devised my plan.

"I propose a trade," I said. "You purchased the volume with a few rupees and the Holy Scripture; I will offer you the full sum of my pension, which I have just received, and Wyclif's black-letter[15] Bible. It was left to me by my parents."

"A black-letter Wyclif!" he murmured.

I went to my bedroom and brought back the money and the book. With a bibliophile's zeal he turned the pages and studied the binding.

"Done," he said.

I was astonished that he did not haggle. Only later was I to realize that he had entered my house already determined to sell the book. He did not count the money, but merely put the bills into his pocket.

We chatted about India, the Orkneys, and the Norwegian jarls[16] that had once ruled those islands. Night was falling when the man left. I have never seen him since, nor do I know his name.

I thought of putting the Book of Sand in the space left by the Wyclif, but I chose at last to hide it behind some imperfect volumes of the *Thousand and One Nights*.

I went to bed but could not sleep. At three or four in the morning I turned on the light. I took out the impossible book and turned its pages. On one, I saw an engraving of a mask. There was a number in the corner of the page—I don't remember now what it was—raised to the ninth power.

I showed no one my treasure. To the joy of possession was added the fear that it would be stolen from me, and to that, the suspicion that it might not be truly infinite. Those two points of anxiety aggravated my already habitual misanthropy. I had but few friends left, and those, I stopped seeing. A prisoner of the Book, I hardly left my house. I examined the worn binding and the covers with a magnifying glass, and rejected the possibility of some artifice. I found that the small illustrations were spaced at two-thousand-page intervals. I began noting them down in an alphabetized notebook, which was very soon filled. They never repeated themselves. At night, during the rare intervals spared me by insomnia,[17] I dreamed of the book. **D**

Summer was drawing to a close, and I realized that the book was monstrous. It was cold consolation

12. **reproach:** criticize or censure.
13. **Stevenson and Hume:** Robert Louis Stevenson (1850–1894), Scottish author; David Hume (1711–1776), Scottish philosopher.
14. **Robbie Burns:** Robert Burns (1759–1796), Scottish poet.
15. **black-letter:** typeset used in early printed books.
16. **jarls:** Scandinavian nobles ranking directly below a king.
17. **insomnia:** inability to sleep.

Vocabulary **diabolic** (dy uh BAHL ihk) *adj.:* of or having to do with evil or the devil.
bibliophile (BIHB lee uh fyl) *n.:* one who loves books.
misanthropy (mih SAN thruh pee) *n.:* hatred for humankind.
artifice (AHRT uh fihs) *n.:* trickery; deception.

D Reading Focus **Making Predictions** Now that the narrator has acquired the book, what do you think will happen?

Think About/Talk About

Comprehension

D Reading Focus
Possible responses: *He will be tortured by the book's mysteries; he will go insane.*

Analysis

C Literary Focus
Possible response: *The book has a finite form, yet its apparent ability to "grow" new pages makes it infinite.*

Extend the Discussion

Finding Details What details in this passage reveal that the narrator is really very eager to acquire the Book of Sand? ***Possible response:*** *The phrases "feigned indifference" and "devised my plan" reveal the narrator's eagerness.*

Vocabulary: Own the Word

- **diabolic:** Tell students that the root for diabolic is *diabolos,* which is Greek for "devil." In Spanish, for example, the devil is called *El Diablo.* Have students describe a book or film character who plotted a *diabolic* plan.
- **bibliophile:** Tell students the word *bibliophile* is a combination of two Greek roots, *biblio,* meaning "relating to books," and *philos,* meaning "love." A *bibliophile* is a book lover. Ask: "Would you describe yourself as a *bibliophile?*"
- **misanthropy:** *Misanthropy* is "hatred for humanity"; its antonym is *philanthropy* or "love for humankind." Have students use both in a sentence: He stayed away from people, citing his *misanthropy,* but his wife was involved in all kinds of philanthropy projects.
- **artifice:** Have students complete the following sentence: The character rejects the possibility that there may be any *artifice* about the book because . . . ***Possible response:*** *The book is a treasure to him; he cannot stand the idea that there might be anything deceitful about it.*

Cross-Curricular Connection

LITERATURE: Bible Translations

Interested students might research one or more of the Bible translations mentioned here, or any other translation with which they are familiar, and report the findings to the rest of the class. Areas to explore could include the circumstances under which the translation was undertaken; the backgrounds of the translator(s); the intended audience; and the work's reception by the reading public, Bible scholars, and literary critics.

Universal Access

Advanced Learners

Enrichment After students finish reading the story, have them write a sequel featuring the Book of Sand. Tell them to write about a different character who comes across the same book and wrestles with keeping it or tossing it away. Their character might be a religious figure or a child. Tell students to establish the same, mysterious atmosphere in their sequel. Remind students to include dialogue and references to the concept of infinity.

Think About/Talk About

Extend the Discussion

Speculating The narrator says that he "tried" not to notice exactly where he left the book. What does this suggest about his future? ***Possible response:*** *The word "tried" suggests that he did not succeed; he may be drawn back to it over and over again, ad infinitum.*

Monitor Students' Comprehension

To check students' understanding of the story, ask them to recount all the main events of the story from beginning to end. [*In this story, a salesman shows the narrator what he claims to be a sacred book from India, called the Book of Sand. The pages of the book are oddly numbered; the book seems to have no beginning or end; the illustrations appear and disappear mysteriously. The narrator becomes obsessed with the book and cuts himself off from all human contact to focus on the book's mysteries. Finally, he hides the book in the library.*]

Analyzing Visuals

Connecting to the Text: *The book illustrates the concept of an infinite number of pages by showing pages folded within pages folded within pages. Although the book's physical dimensions are not large, the viewer senses that the pages could go on forever, becoming smaller and smaller.*

Open Book (1930) by Paul Klee.
Guggenheim Museum, New York/Artists Rights Society (ARS), New York/VG Bild-Kunst, Bonn.

Analyzing Visuals

Connecting to the Text How does this painting illustrate the idea of a book with an "infinite" number of pages without depicting the book as thick or heavy?

to think that I, who looked upon it with my eyes and fondled it with my ten flesh-and-bone fingers, was no less monstrous than the book. I felt it was a nightmare thing, an obscene thing, and that it defiled and corrupted reality.

I considered fire, but I feared that the burning of an infinite book might be similarly infinite, and suffocate the planet in smoke.

I remembered reading once that the best place to hide a leaf is in the forest. Before my retirement I had worked in the National Library, which contained nine hundred thousand books; I knew that to the right of the lobby a curving staircase descended into the shadows of the basement, where the maps and periodicals are kept. I took advantage of the librarians' distraction to hide the Book of Sand on one of the library's damp shelves; I tried not to notice how high up, or how far from the door.

I now feel a little better, but I refuse even to walk down the street the library's on.

California Standards, p. 1341

- **Reading Standard 2.4** Make warranted and reasonable assertions about the author's arguments by using elements of the text to defend and clarify interpretations.
- **Reading Standard 3.3** Analyze the ways in which irony, tone, mood, the author's style, and the "sound" of language achieve specific rhetorical or aesthetic purposes or both.
- **Reading Standard 3.4** Analyze the ways in which poets use imagery, personification, figures of speech, and sounds to evoke readers' emotions.
- **Writing Standard 2.1** Write fictional, autobiographical, or biographical narratives. **e.** Make effective use of descriptions of appearances, images, shifting perspectives, and sensory details.

Applying Your Skills

Reading Standard 2.4, 3.3, 3.4 (see pages A48–A50)
Writing Standard 2.1e (see pages A51–A52)

The Book of Sand

Literary Response and Analysis

Reading Skills Focus

Quick Check

1. What can you infer about the book from its outward appearance?
2. Why doesn't the stranger give the narrator his name?
3. Why does the narrator come to feel that the book is "monstrous"?

Read with a Purpose

4. What did the Book of Sand turn out to be?

Reading Skills: Making Predictions

5. As you read "The Book of Sand," you made predictions about the story. Identify which of your predictions were true and which ones you changed because they were inaccurate.

Vocabulary Check

Match the Vocabulary words with their definitions.

6. pedantic	a. evil
7. discomfiture	b. hatred of people
8. caste	c. trick
9. defiled	d. lover of books
10. diabolic	e. scholarly
11. bibliophile	f. dirtied
12. misanthropy	g. class
13. artifice	h. embarrassment

Literary Skills Focus

Literary Analysis

14. **Infer** Why do you think Borges gave his story the same title as the book in the story?
15. **Compare and Contrast** Write two brief descriptions of the main character, one at the beginning of the story and the other at the end. What accounts for the differences in his perspective and personality?
16. **Evaluate** What dependable realities does Borges question in this story?

Literary Skills: Paradox

17. **Analyze** The illustrations in "The Book of Sand" are both there and not there. How would you explain this paradox? Identify and explain another paradox in the story.

Literary Skills Review: Situational Irony

18. **Analyze** When what actually happens is the opposite of what is expected or appropriate, **situational irony** occurs. How is the narrator's fear that the book will be stolen ironic?

Writing Skills Focus

Think as a Reader/Writer

Use It in Your Writing Review your list of eerie words and phrases. In a paragraph, describe something scary or supernatural that you have witnessed or heard about. Try to create a spooky atmosphere in your description with carefully chosen words and phrases.

What Do You Think Now How did the narrator's experience with the Book of Sand affect his view of the world?

Universal Access

Struggling Writers

Some students may need additional scaffolding to complete the Writing Skills Focus activity. After students review their list of haunting words and phrases, have them create two web diagrams and write "Setting" in the center circle of one diagram and "People" in the center circle of the other diagram. Ask students to use the diagrams to brainstorm their own words and phrases describing the setting and people, and have them refer to their diagrams while they write their descriptive paragraph.

What Do You Think Now?

Ask students to think about a problem they could not solve. Then ask them how they felt after this experience. Did it affect the way they thought about people, society, or themselves?

Assess

Unit 6 Resources,
Selection Standards Check, p. 201

Check for Understanding

Independent Practice

Reading Skills Focus

Possible responses:

1. *It is old, and many people have owned it, probably because the book's owners try to get rid of it once they become obsessed with its secrets.*
2. *His name is not important. His only goal is to get rid of the book.*
3. *He thinks that his obsession with it has brought out the worst in him.*
4. *The book is infinity itself.*
5. *Students should evaluate the predictions they made in order to determine their accuracy.*

Vocabulary Check

6. *e* 7. *h*
8. *g* 9. *f*
10. *a* 11. *d*
12. *b* 13. *c*

Literary Skills Focus

Possible responses:

14. *Borges wanted to suggest that the texts share the qualities of mystery, paradox, and infinitude.*
15. *At first, the narrator seems self-assured, even smug. At the end, he has become a recluse, obsessed with the book even after it is gone. The book has altered his view of the universe.*
16. *Borges questions the concept of sequence (the page numbers) and the idea that objective reality is predictable (the illustrations). Students may say the story made them realize that they take certain realities for granted.*
17. *In addition to the paradox of the illustrations, the book appears to have no beginning and no end. The book may symbolize an infinitely shifting reality or the infinitely varied imagination.*
18. *It is ironic because he would have been better off had the book been stolen.*

Standards Focus

Objectives

Students will
- understand the theater of the absurd
- draw inferences

Selection Introduction

Think About the Writer

To help students answer the question, ask them to think about the connection between depression and meaninglessness.

For Independent Reading

The Bald Soprano and Other Plays, Eugene Ionesco

Motivate

What Do You Think?/QuickTalk

Ask students to make a list of things, people, and activities that are important to them. Next, ask some of them to explain to the class what makes each item on their lists valuable.

English for Academic Success

Academic Vocabulary

Look for opportunities to use the Academic Vocabulary words in this unit.

- **exhibit, *v.*:** show, demonstrate
- **perspective, *n.*:** a particular way of looking at something

California Standards, pp. 1342–1349

- **Reading Standard 3.1** Analyze characteristics of subgenres (e.g., satire, parody, allegory, pastoral) that are used in poetry, prose, plays, novels, short stories, essays, and other basic genres.
- **Reading Standard 3.2** Analyze the way in which the theme or meaning of a selection represents a view or comment on life, using textual evidence to support the claim.

Preparing to Read

Come and Go

What Do You Think? How does experience shape our view of the world?

QuickTalk

With a partner, discuss what you believe makes life meaningful.

Samuel Beckett (1906–1989).

MEET THE WRITER

Samuel Beckett

(1906–1989)

Nobel Prize WINNER

Although Samuel Beckett was born in Ireland, he lived most of his life in France and wrote in both French and English. His plays are prime examples of the theater of the absurd.

Struggling Against Darkness

Beckett attended Trinity College in Dublin, where he was good at sports but did poorly in his studies during his first two years. In his third year he began studying French. He excelled, graduated first in his class in modern languages, and was awarded a two-year post at the École normale supérieure in Paris. Beckett seemed to be headed for a career in the classroom.

In Paris, Beckett met fellow Irishman James Joyce and joined the circle of young Irishmen who helped Joyce, whose eyesight was poor. In 1930, Beckett published his first book.

By the time Beckett returned to Dublin, he realized that he did not want to teach. He found life in Ireland with his family confining. There he suffered his first depression, a condition that was to recur over several years as he struggled for success and the means to return to Paris. In 1937, he decided that living in poverty was better than staying in Ireland, and he returned to Paris, where he met his wife, a French pianist.

After France fell to Germany in World War II, Beckett put aside his writing to join the French Resistance. His group was infiltrated, and Beckett and his wife fled for their lives. In 1945, they returned to Paris, where Beckett received the *Croix de Guerre* and the *Médaille de la Résistance*.

Success at Last

Beckett always considered himself primarily a novelist. "I turned to writing plays to relieve myself of the awful depression the prose had led me into," he explained. It was his play *Waiting for Godot* that made him famous at the age of forty-seven. He received the Nobel Prize in Literature in 1969.

Think About the Writer How do you think Beckett's depression might have affected his outlook on life?

Selection Readability	
Easily Accessible Accessible Challenging	simple sentence structure; simple dialogue; familiar language; unfamiliar setting; challenging theme

Reading Standard 3.1, 3.2 (see pages A48–A50)

Literary Skills Focus

Theater of the Absurd The plays of a small group of playwrights working in the 1950s and early 1960s have come to be called the **theater of the absurd.** Although the plays are sometimes humorous, *absurd* in this context means "pointless." Absurdist playwrights believed that human life has no purpose, and their works illustrate this lack of purpose. The action of absurdist plays does not follow the familiar pattern of conflict, climax, and resolution, but circles back on itself to exhibit the futility of action. The point of an absurdist play's language is not to communicate the characters' thoughts and feelings, but to show that language is not adequate to communicate anything of value—or even that there is nothing of value to communicate.

Reading Skills Focus

Drawing Inferences An **inference** is an intelligent guess based on clues in the text. *Come and Go* gives the audience or reader little information with which to work: no setting, no exposition, only the tersest possible dialogue—some of which is whispered incomprehensibly between the characters. Beckett relies on his audience to infer the meaning of his play.

Into Action As you read, use a chart like the one below to note each inference you draw and the clues on which you based it.

Inference	Clues
The characters have met before.	Vi asks, "When did we three last meet?"

Writing Skills Focus

Think as a Reader/Writer

Find It in Your Reading Beckett's language is stripped down to the bare essentials. He uses few literary devices. However, he does use **repetition.** As you read, make note of instances of repetition in the play.

TechFocus Imagine that you write a theater-review Web page or blog. As you read, take notes about the play, and then formulate an opinion about it. Try to judge it on its own terms—that is, determine what effect the playwright intended to create, and decide whether he succeeded.

Reader/Writer Notebook
Use your **RWN** to complete the activities for this selection.

Vocabulary

undeterminable (uhn dih TUR muh nuh buhl) *adj.:* not able to be measured or decided. *The setting of the play is undeterminable.*

erect (ih REHKT) *adj.:* upright. *The actresses stand erect for their entrances and exits.*

appalled (uh PAWLD) *v.* used as *adj.:* dismayed. *Appalled at the play's bleak theme, many in the audience refused to applaud.*

resume (rih ZOOM) *v.:* begin again. *The play will resume after the intermission.*

successive (suhk SEHS ihv) *adj.:* following in consecutive order. *The players were so popular, they made their third successive bow.*

accommodate (uh KAHM uh dayt) *v.:* provide room for. *The theater could accommodate five hundred people.*

compatible (kuhm PAT uh buhl) *adj.:* able to exist or work together. *The two actors could not appear in the same play because their styles were not compatible.*

Language Coach

Prefixes *un–* and *in–* The prefixes *un–* and *in–* mean "not" or "the opposite of." *Un–* appears in the Vocabulary word *undeterminable.* To which Vocabulary word can you add the prefix *in–*? With the prefix, what does the word mean?

Learn It Online
Increase your vocabulary knowledge online with Word Watch.
go.hrw.com H12-1343 Go

Selection Resources

Unit 6 Resources, on-level practice and assessment, p. 204

Teacher One Stop™, on-level lesson plans and all print resources

Holt Audio Library

Holt Audio Library: Selections and Summaries in Spanish

UA: Differentiating Instruction, graphic organizer, p. 312

UA: Supporting Instruction in Spanish, selection summary

ThinkCentral Online Assessment, Selection Standards Check

ThinkCentral Online Remediation

Preteach

Introducing Vocabulary

Read aloud the Vocabulary words and sample sentences. Then, use this activity to check students' understanding.

1. The proud girl stood ______. [*erect*]
2. The students spoke in ______ order. [*successive*]
3. She and I are definitely not ______; in fact, I was ______ by her behavior. [*compatible; appalled*]
4. The hotel was unable to ______ the entire team. [*accommodate*]
5. The game will ______ after the half-time break, but when it will end is ______. [*resume; undeterminable*]

English for Academic Success

Language Coach

Ask students to think of other prefixes that mean "not" or "the opposite of." [*im–, anti–, contra–/counter–*]

Literary Skills Focus

As you read and discuss the play with students, have them notice characteristics of the theater of the absurd.

Reading Skills Focus

Give students a copy of the Reading Skills Focus graphic organizer before they read. (See **Unit 6 Resources.**) Tell them to use their responses to answer the questions on the Applying Your Skills page.

Writing Skills Focus

Have students record examples of repetition in their **Reader/Writer Notebooks.** Students can use their notes to complete the Writing Skills Focus activity.

Learn It Online
Send students to **Word Watch** for audio pronunciations, synonyms and antonyms, and brief histories of word origins.
go.hrw.com H12-1343 Go

Teacher Preparation

Selection Summary

There are three characters in "Come and Go," (Flo, Vi, and Ru) each dressed in a long faded coat of violet, red, or yellow and a wide-brim hat. As the play opens, they sit on a plain bench in soft light from above. Their dialogue is brief and simple. When one of them leaves, the others ask about her, then whisper something, and then react with an exclaimed "Oh!" One asks if the absent character knows what is happening. The answer is no. These three exchanges are separated by nostalgic reminiscences of a shared past. In the end, the three interlock hands. The script is followed by explicit directions about the action and set.

Direct Teach

Think About/Talk About

Read with a Purpose Have students read the Read with a Purpose statement. Remind students that the point of the theater of the absurd is not to communicate the characters' thoughts and feelings to the audience or reader.

▶ Extend the Discussion

Drawing Conclusions Why do you think the characters are sitting side-by-side? ***Possible response:*** *They are sitting the way they used to sit when they were young: "On the log. . . . Holding hands . . . that way. Dreaming of . . . love."*

DRAMA

Come *and* Go

by **Samuel Beckett**

Read with a Purpose Read to find out how the characters feel about their lives.

Come and Go by Samuel Beckett, director: Annie Ryan; image details.

Cast of Characters

FLO
VI
RU
(Age undeterminable)

Sitting center side by side stage right to left FLO, VI, *and* RU. *Very erect, facing front, hands clasped in laps.*

Silence.

VI: Ru.
RU: Yes.
VI: Flo.
FLO: Yes.
VI: When did we three last meet?
RU: Let us not speak.

Silence.

Exit VI *right.*

Silence.

FLO: Ru.
RU: Yes.
FLO: What do you think of Vi?
RU: I see little change. (FLO *moves to center seat, whispers in* RU*'s ear. Appalled.*)

Vocabulary **undeterminable** (uhn dih TUR muh nuh buhl) *adj.:* not able to be measured or decided.
erect (ih REHKT) *adj.:* upright.
appalled (uh PAWLD) *v.* used as *adj.:* dismayed.

Universal Access

EL English Learners

English for Academic Success Beckett intentionally uses very simple language in this play, but some idioms and phrases may be unfamiliar to non-native speakers. Explain that "find" in the phrase "How do you find Flo?" means "How does she seem to you?" The expressions "God grant not" and "God forbid" are different ways of saying "I hope not."

✔ See the **English Language Skill Builder** in **UA: Differentiating Instruction.**

Struggling Readers

Students may have difficulty making inferences with such limited information. Before reading, give students additional background about the play. Suggest that perhaps the three characters are old school friends who do not recognize (or who do not want to recognize) that they have aged. Faced with each other, they refuse to discuss the past (thereby acknowledging that time has passed), but do begin to notice signs of age in the others. As students read, see if they can identify the passage that reveals the story you have described.

Oh! (*They look at each other.* FLO *puts her finger to her lips.*) Does she not realize? Ⓐ

FLO: God grant not.

Enter VI. FLO and RU turn back front, resume pose. VI sits right. Silence. Ⓑ

FLO: Just sit together as we used to, in the playground at Miss Wade's.

RU: On the log.

Silence.

Exit FLO *left.*

Silence.

RU: Vi.

VI: Yes.

RU: How do you find Flo?

VI: She seems much the same. (RU *moves to center seat, whispers in* VI*'s ear. Appalled.*) Oh! (*They look at each other.* RU *puts her finger to her lips.*) Has she not been told? Ⓒ

RU: God forbid.

Enter FLO. RU *and* VI *turn back front, resume pose.* FLO *sits left.*

RU: Holding hands . . . that way. Ⓓ

FLO: Dreaming of . . . love.

Silence.

Exit RU right.

Silence.

VI: Flo.

FLO: Yes.

VI: How do you think Ru is looking?

FLO: One sees little in this light. (VI *moves center seat, whispers in* FLO*'s ear.*

Ⓐ **Reading Focus** **Drawing Inferences** What can you infer from this exchange and Flo's earlier question about Vi? Is your inference general or specific?

Ⓑ **Literary Focus** **Theater of the Absurd** How does the play so far differ from other plays you have read or seen?

Ⓒ **Reading Focus** **Drawing Inferences** Do these lines change or add to your inference about Vi? What can you infer about Flo?

Ⓓ **Literary Focus** **Theater of the Absurd** What earlier part of the conversation does this line continue? Why don't you think the playwright makes the connection clear?

Vocabulary **resume** (rih ZOOM) *v.:* begin again.

Advanced Learners

Enrichment Tell students that absurdist playwrights like Samuel Beckett agreed with the Existential philosopher Albert Camus that life has no purpose. Recommend to students other examples of the theater of the absurd that they might read if interested. Students might read works by playwrights including Eugene Ionesco, Jean Genet, Edward Albee, and Harold Pinter.

Students with Disabilities

The idea of the absurd may pose difficulties for students. Ask students to work in groups of three to pantomime the play. They should use gestures and expressions instead of words to express themselves. For instance, when Vi says "Ru", the student playing Vi can point to the student playing Ru. In this way, they will experience a sense of the absurdity in the play even if they do not fully comprehend its many nuances of dialogue.

Think About/Talk About

Comprehension

Ⓐ Reading Focus

Possible responses: *The women seem to be meeting for the first time in many years. Flo seems to notice something different about Vi. She tells Ru something—perhaps a rumor—that evokes the first emotional response in the play. My inference is general at first and then becomes more specific.*

Ⓒ Reading Focus

Possible response: *Ru tells Vi something about Flo that evokes the second show of emotion in the play. My guess is that Flo has changed in some way.*

Analysis

Ⓑ Literary Focus

Possible response: *There is nothing to explain the play's setting and very little to describe the characters' thoughts, feelings, and appearance.*

Ⓓ Literary Focus

Possible response: *These lines continue the conversation about sitting on a log in the playground. The author does not make the connection clear to emphasize the discontinuity.*

Vocabulary: Own the Word

- **undeterminable:** Tell students that the base word, *determine,* means "to decide or agree on something." Adding *un–* and *–able* to *determine* changes the word to mean "unable to be figured out." Have students name something that is *undeterminable.*
- **erect:** Explain that the word *erect* comes straight from the Latin word *erectus,* which means "upright." When a person is standing in an *erect* position, he or she is fully upright, with a strong, tall posture.
- **appalled:** Show the facial expression and gestures of someone who is *appalled* (cover your mouth, widen your eyes).
- **resume:** When might you have to *resume* playing a game? How might a person mark her spot so she can *resume* reading where she left off?

Model the Skill

- Tell students that the **theater of the absurd** focuses on the unsaid as much as what is said. Explain that in order to understand "Come and Go," they will need not only to read the lines of the play, but also to infer what is left unsaid.
- Model discussing theater of the absurd. You might say: "Flo says towards the end, 'One sees little in this light.' I think Flo only sees what she wants to see, despite the quantity of light."

Guided Practice: Apply

Think-Pair-Share Have students re-read the last page of dialogue. Tell them to select features that suggest something implied but not said outright. Ask them to work in pairs to discuss their observations. Then, have volunteers share their analyses with the class.

Build Background: Influences on the Theater of the Absurd

The theater of the absurd drew its theatrical influences from commedia dell'arte, vaudeville, acrobatics, and mime. Its philosophical and literary ideas developed alongside those of the Existentialists, Surrealists, Expressionists, and the absurdist works of Franz Kafka. As the movement began to decline in 1960s, its ideas and elements became integrated into the mainstream theater. Today, its influence can be found in the black humor and sense of pointlessness in films like *Dr. Strangelove*. In drama, Tom Stoppard's play *Rosenkrantz and Guildenstern Are Dead* invites obvious comparisons to Samuel Beckett's *Waiting for Godot*.

Appalled.) Oh! (*They look at each other.* VI *puts her finger to her lips.*) Does she not know? **E**

VI: Please God not.

Enter RU. VI *and* FLO *turn back front, resume pose.* RU *sits right. Silence.*

VI: May we not speak of the old days? *(Silence.)* Of what came after? *(Silence.)* Shall we hold hands in the old way?

After a moment they join hands as follows : VI*'s right hand with* RU*'s right hand.* VI*'s left hand with* FLO*'s left hand,* FLO*'s right hand with* RU*'s left hand,* VI*'s arms being above* RU*'s left arm and* FLO*'s right arm. The three pairs of clasped hands rest on the three laps.*

Silence.

FLO: I can feel the rings.

Silence. **F**

Notes

Successive *positions*

1	FLO	VI	RU
2	FLO		RU
		FLO	RU
3	VI	FLO	RU
4	VI		RU
	VI	RU	
5	VI	RU	FLO
6	VI		FLO
		VI	FLO
7	RU	VI	FLO

E **Reading Focus** **Drawing Inferences** Do these lines change or add to your inferences about Vi and Flo? What do you now understand about all three characters?

F **Literary Focus** **Theater of the Absurd** Why do you think the play ends with silence rather than with Vi's last line? What feeling do you have about the characters' lives and about life in general at the end of the play?

Vocabulary **successive** (suhk SEHS ihv) *adj.*: following in consecutive order.

Developing Oral Fluency

Paired Activity Read the first exchange of the selection aloud, modeling for students how to pace yourself as you read. Tell students that good readers maintain an even pace while reading aloud, but they can sometimes speed up or slow down, depending upon the content of the text. For example, if the dialogue conveys excitement, you might read more quickly. Have pairs of students take turns reading the exchanges. Tell them they should monitor their pacing as they read.

Universal Access

Struggling Readers

To help students understand the concept of the theater of the absurd, tell them that the point is for the absurdity of the situation to communicate the absurdity and meaninglessness of life. The repetition of dialogue and the uniformity of the characters prevent the play's audience from finding the kind of distinctions that create meaning. Students should examine the selection closely to find other "absurd" aspects.

Analyzing Visuals

Connecting to the Text What is the effect of the characters' holding hands here? How can FLO "feel the rings?"

Come and Go, directed by Annie Ryan, with Barbara Brennan, Susan Fitzgerald, and Bernadette McKenna. London, 2006.

Hands

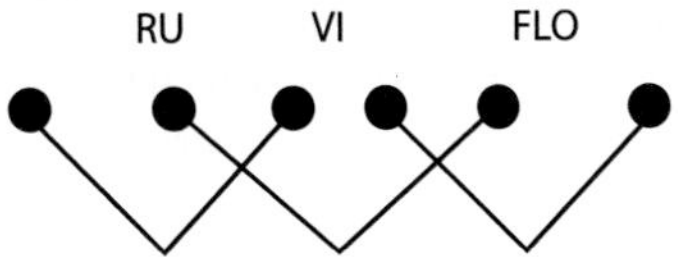

Lighting

Soft, from above only and concentrated on playing area. Rest of stage as dark as possible.

Costume

Full-length coats, buttoned high, dull violet (RU), dull red (VI), dull yellow (FLO). Drab nondescript hats with enough brim to shade faces. Apart from color differentiation three figures as alike as possible. Light shoes with rubber soles. Hands made up to be as visible as possible. No rings apparent.

Seat

Narrow bench-like seat, without back, just long enough to accommodate three figures almost touching. As little visible as possible. It should not be clear what they are sitting on.

Exits

The figures are not seen to go off stage. They should disappear a few steps from lit area. If dark not sufficient to allow this, recourse should be had to screens or drapes as little visible as possible. Exits and entrances slow, without sound of feet.

Ohs

Three very different sounds.

Voices

As low as compatible with audibility. Colorless except for three "ohs" and two lines following.

Vocabulary **accommodate** (uh KAHM uh dayt) *v.:* provide room for.
compatible (kuhm PAT uh buhl) *adj.:* able to exist or work together.

Think About/Talk About

Comprehension

E Reading Focus

Possible responses: *These lines add to the reader's inferences about Vi and Flo. All three women notice something about the others that they do not seem to see in themselves.*

Analysis

F Literary Focus

Possible responses: *The play ends in silence because nothing more can be said to elucidate the situation. The characters' lives are repetitious, and they themselves are interchangeable. Once we have seen the pattern of empty repetition, the silence is as meaningful or meaningless as dialogue.*

Analyzing Visuals

Connecting to the Text: *The characters' joined hands convey a sense of unity and strength. Flo is holding both friends' hands and can literally "feel the rings" on their fingers, and figuratively, she might also feel the bonds that unite them all.*

Vocabulary: Own the Word

- **successive:** *Successive* numbers are 5, 6, 7, and 8. *Successive* letters of the alphabet are A, B, and C. *Successive* ranks in the military are private, corporal, sergeant, and major.
- **accommodate:** Explain that just as a person making travel *accommodations* finds a place to stay, to *accommodate* means to "have room for" or "be big enough for." Ask students how many people their classroom *accommodates.*
- **compatible:** Point out that the prefix *com–* ("with," "together,") along with the root word *pati–* (Latin for "to undergo" or "suffer") and suffix *–ible* ("able to") results in the meaning, "able to suffer together."

California Standards, pp. 1348–1349

- **Reading Standard 3.1** Analyze characteristics of subgenres (e.g., satire, parody, allegory, pastoral) that are used in poetry, prose, plays, novels, short stories, essays, and other basic genres.
- **Reading Standard 3.2** Analyze the way in which the theme or meaning of a selection represents a view or comment on life, using textual evidence to support the claim.
- **Grades 9–10 Review Reading Standard 1.1** Identify and use the literal and figurative meanings of words and understand word derivations.
- **Grades 9–10 Review Reading Standard 3.1** Articulate the relationship between the expressed purposes and the characteristics of different forms of dramatic literature (e.g., comedy, tragedy, drama, dramatic monologue).
- **Grades 9–10 Review Reading Standard 3.10** Identify and describe the function of dialogue, scene designs, soliloquies, asides, and character foils in dramatic literature
- **Writing Standard 1.2** Use point of view, characterization, style (e.g., use of irony), and related elements for specific rhetorical and aesthetic purposes.
- **Writing Standard 2.2** Write responses to literature.
- **Writing Standard 2.3** Write reflective compositions: **b.** Draw comparisons between specific incidents and broader themes that illustrate the writer's important beliefs or generalizations about life.

Check for Understanding

Independent Practice

Reading Skills Focus

Possible responses:

1. *Miss Wade's was probably a school.*
2. *It has probably been a long time.*
3. *The women have grown older.*
4. *The women seem to have been friends in the past. They held hands on the playground. They seem to be friends now, but something has come between them—perhaps time or age.*
5. *Responses will vary. Students might consider that, given the tension of the scene, the longing for a distant past, and the unspoken secrets about the characters, the three women cannot feel good about their lives.*
6. *Ask students what message is conveyed through the play.*

Literary Skills Focus

Possible responses:

7. *The actors come and go from the stage. People and events come and go in life. Life is transient.*
8. *The characters seem to notice that the others have aged. They are probably whispering similar things to one another.*
9. *No, their dreams of love have not been fulfilled. They are obviously still searching for something.*
10. *The characters are similar in almost all respects. They are dressed in a similarly nondescript fashion. They wear hats to obscure their facial features.*
11. *Yes. By saying less, the playwright communicates the meaninglessness and absurdity of life.*
12. *The image of three older women sitting side-by-side and continually changing positions is absurd.*
13. *For the play to be staged in a way that fulfills his vision, Beckett describes every detail of the play. The stage directions reinforce the absurdity of the dialogue.*

Applying Your Skills

Reading Standard 3.1, 3.2; **Grades 9–10 Review**
Reading Standard 3.10 (see pages A48–A50)
Writing Standard 1.2 (see pages A51–A52)

Come and Go

Literary Response and Analysis

Reading Skills Focus

Quick Check

1. What do you think "Miss Wade's" was?
2. How long do you think it has been since the characters last met?
3. What has happened to the three women since "the old days"?
4. Are the women close friends? Explain.

Read with a Purpose

5. How do you think the characters feel about their lives? Why do you think so?

Reading Skills: Drawing Inferences

6. As you read the play, you used a graphic organizer to note the inferences you drew and the clues you used to draw them. Now, add a box below the column of inferences, and use it to write a sentence that you feel expresses the theme, or meaning, of the play.

Inference	Clues
Theme	

Literary Skills Focus

Literary Analysis

7. **Interpret** Why do you think Beckett titles his play *Come and Go*?
8. **Infer** What do you think the characters whisper to one another? Do they each whisper the same thing or something different?
9. **Draw Conclusions** Have the characters' dreams of love been fulfilled? Explain.
10. **Compare and Contrast** Do the characters differ from one another in any significant way? Give examples from the play to support your response.
11. **Make Judgments** Do you think that the phrase "less is more" applies to this play? Explain why or why not.

Literary Skills: Theater of the Absurd

12. **Evaluate** What features of the play contribute to a sense of absurdity, or pointlessness?

Literary Skills Review: Stage Directions

13. **Analyze** The playwright's instructions for staging the play—where the characters are on stage, what they wear, what they do, what the stage looks like, and so on—are called **stage directions.** Why do you think Beckett's stage directions are so specific? How do the stage directions reinforce the play's meaning? Give specific examples.

Writing Skills Focus

Think as a Reader/Writer

Use It in Your Writing Now it's your turn to write terse dialogue like Beckett's that includes some repetition. Start by writing a conversation between two people. Then, cross out everything that is not essential to its meaning. Include, however, the repetition of a key word or phrase. Finally, rewrite your stripped-down dialogue, and share it with a partner.

What Do You Think Now? How do you think the characters' experiences shape their views of life? Remember that you will have to infer most of their experiences and their current views.

Universal Access

Struggling Writers

Help students complete the Writing Skills Focus activity. Suggest that students repeat one or two questions and answers throughout the conversation. Students might include whispering between the two characters and insert ellipses to reinforce discontinuity.

What Do You Think Now?

To help students answer this question, remind them that Beckett has included only the barest information about the characters and that the brevity has as much meaning as the existing dialogue. Keeping in mind the playwright's attitude toward life, ask students how they think three middle-aged women might view their lives to communicate the absurdity of the situation.

Grades 9–10 Review Reading Standard 1.1, 3.1 (see pages A48–A50)
Writing Standard 2.2, 2.3b (see pages A51–A52)

Vocabulary Development

Vocabulary Check

undeterminable
erect
appalled
resume
successive
accommodate
compatible

Complete each sentence with one of the Vocabulary words.

1. Our team has won five ________ championships.
2. Jan was ________ when she saw that she had failed the class.
3. Dale's new software is not ________ with his old computer.
4. The players will ________ their computer game after the pizza arrives.
5. The music was so loud and distorted that the lyrics were ________.
6. In yoga, Kai learned to straighten his spine and stand ________.
7. A ramp is being added to the school's entrance to ________ wheelchairs.

Vocabulary Skills: Synonyms

Part of the skill of a good writer lies in choosing the right word among many with similar meanings. Words that have similar meanings are called synonyms.

Your Turn

Using a thesaurus, find at least one synonym for each of the Vocabulary words listed at the top of the page.

Language Coach

Prefixes *un–* and *in–* Which prefix can be affixed to these Vocabulary words and related words?

appalled **accommodating**

How does the prefix change each word's meaning?

CHOICES

As you respond to the Choices, use the **Academic Vocabulary** words as appropriate: adapt, considerably, exhibit, inevitable, perspective.

REVIEW

Write a Psychological Profile

Referring to the play and the information in Meet the Writer, draw inferences about Beckett as a person. What do you think he was like? Make inferences about how his struggle with depression affected his perspective on life and influenced his writing. Check your inferences by researching Beckett's life and work in your library or on the Internet. Then, write a short psychological profile of the playwright.

CONNECT

Create a Theater Review Web Page

TechFocus Design your own theater review Web page or blog. Then, look at your notes and opinions about *Come and Go.* Post a short review in which you judge the play on its own terms. Then, offer your classmates a chance to post their comments about your review and about the play.

EXTEND

Compare Plays from the Theater of the Absurd

Research the theater of the absurd, and choose a representative play to read on your own. Write a short paper comparing and contrasting this play with *Come and Go,* and share your findings with your classmates.

Poster advertising a production of Eugene Ionesco's *Rhinoceros.*

Learn It Online
Improve your vocabulary skills with *WordSharp.*
go.hrw.com H12-1349 Go

Independent Practice

Choices:
Evaluation Criteria

Review: Homework
Write a Psychological Profile
Inferences should be checked against research about Beckett.

Connect: Homework
Create a Theater Review Web Page
Reviews should evaluate play's merits or shortcomings.

Extend: Homework
Compare Plays from the Theater of the Absurd
Essays should compare and contrast the concept of the "absurd" in both plays.

Assess

Unit 6 Resources, Selection Standards Check, p. 207

go.hrw.com **ThinkCentral Online Assessment,** Selection Standards Check

Teacher One Stop™, editable Selection Standards Check

Reteach

go.hrw.com **ThinkCentral Online Remediation**

Vocabulary Development

Vocabulary Check

1. *successive*
2. *appalled*
3. *compatible*
4. *resume*
5. *undeterminable*
6. *erect*
7. *accommodate*

Your Turn

undeterminable/indefinite, erect/straight, appalled/shocked, resume/continue, successive/consecutive, accommodate/conform, compatible/suitable

English for Academic Success

Language Coach

Possible responses: *unappalled, unaccommodating; the prefix changes each word to its opposite*

Learn It Online
WordSharp: An Interactive Vocabulary Tutor provides additional support for vocabulary development. Multimedia tutorials show students how to apply vocabulary skills to unfamiliar words—and how to make those words their own.
go.hrw.com H12-1349 Go

Standards Focus

Objectives

Students will
- understand dialogue
- identify and understand patterns of organization

Selection Introduction

Think About the Writer

Have students think about how an actor's experiences in reading and delivering dialogue might help him write better dialogue.

For Independent Reading

In the Penal Colony, Franz Kafka

Motivate

What Do You Think?/QuickWrite

Have students think about how ordinary conversations between people can reveal complexities in relationships, past experiences, and personal characteristics. Have students use their **Reader/Writer Notebooks** to record their thoughts.

English for Academic Success

Academic Vocabulary

Look for opportunities to use the Academic Vocabulary words in this unit.

- **adapt, *v.*:** adjust for a new purpose

Preparing to Read

That's All

What Do You Think? How does experience shape our view of the world?

QuickTalk

Think of an everyday conversation that you often have with a parent, sibling, or friend. For example, perhaps you and a friend often discuss plans for the weekend. In your *Reader/Writer Notebook*, write a few lines of this conversation in dialogue form.

Harold Pinter (c. 1970).

MEET THE WRITER

Harold Pinter

(1930–)

Nobel Prize WINNER

Harold Pinter, an avowed disciple of Beckett and probably the most influential of the contemporary English playwrights, is on the fringe of absurdist theater. While Beckett's absurdist drama often deals with grotesque characters and bizarre settings, Pinter generally gives us more or less real settings and identifiable characters speaking everyday language. The whole, however, is stylized in a manner that is now called Pinteresque.

Actor, Playwright, and Director

Pinter was born in East London. He attended drama school briefly and later worked as an actor on television and the stage. His first play, *The Room,* appeared in 1957. In 1965, his play *The Homecoming* was produced by the Royal Shakespeare Company. In addition to writing for the stage, Pinter has written many screenplays. He has adapted his plays for radio and television and has directed productions of his own plays as well as those of others.

A Different Kind of Theater

Pinter presents a world in which reality is menacing, pregnant pauses (all carefully indicated by Pinter) are frightening, and banal speech is full of mystery. Also, unlike traditional plays, Pinter's plays do not probe the complex psychology of character. Instead, Pinter's characters are often without pasts—or they have contradictory pasts.

Pinter's recurrent themes are "time, memory, and the power of the past over the present." Many of his characters are haunted by some recollection, whether true or imaginary. The director Peter Hall has said that enigma is at the heart of Pinter's plays and that audiences must piece together the story in order to judge it.

Pinter, who has been politically active throughout his career, announced in 2005 that he would no longer write plays but would devote himself to politics and poetry. Later that year, Pinter won the Nobel Prize in Literature.

Think About the Writer How do you think Pinter's experience as an actor might have affected his playwriting?

California Standards, pp. 1350–1355

- **Reading Standard 2.2** Analyze the way in which clarity of meaning is affected by the patterns of organization, hierarchical structures, repetition of the main ideas, syntax, and word choice in the text.
- **Grades 9–10 Review Reading Standard 3.10** Identify and describe the function of dialogue, scene designs, soliloquies, asides, and character foils in dramatic literature.

Selection Readability	
Easily Accessible Accessible **Challenging**	complex character interactions; abstract ideas

Reading Standard 2.2; Grades 9–10 Review
Reading Standard 3.10 (see pages A48–A50)

Literary Skills Focus

Dialogue Writers use **dialogue**—a conversation between two or more characters— to advance the plot or pattern of the work; to present an interplay of ideas and personalities; and to reveal the background, occupation, or social level of the characters through tone and dialect.

You are already an expert at analyzing dialogue. Every day you analyze conversations for a wealth of spoken and unspoken information. Here are some questions you subconsciously consider:

- What can I infer about the speaker's background?
- How does the speaker feel about what he or she is saying?
- What does the speaker avoid saying?
- What do the speaker's silences and pauses imply?
- Is the speaker saying what he or she really thinks?

The play you are about to read focuses on both what is said and unsaid.

Language Coach

British Phrases This short play contains some British phrases that may be unfamiliar to you. Take a look at these two phrases:

put on the kettle: prepare tea for a visitor
come round: come over to visit

If you are uncertain of the meaning of any idiomatic phrases in the play, check with your teacher.

Reading Skills Focus

Understanding Patterns of Organization Pinter organizes his short play as a dialogue between two people. He primarily structures the dialogue around repetition and pauses.

Into Action As you read, use a chart to record patterns in the dialogue.

Patterns	Observations
How the sketch begins	In mid-conversation
How the conversation is balanced between speakers	
Repetition and how it varies	
Pattern of pauses and how the pattern shifts	

Writing Skills Focus

Think as a Reader/Writer

Find It in Your Reading Writers use words and phrases from everyday speech to make their dialogue sound more natural. Note in your *Reader/Writer Notebook* how the sentence structure, word choice, repetition, and pauses in the play mimic everyday speech (and how they vary from it) and what they reveal about the speakers.

Reader/Writer Notebook
Use your **RWN** to complete the activities for this selection.

Learn It Online
Listen to an audio performance of this play online.
go.hrw.com H12-1351 Go

Selection Resources

Unit 6 Resources, on-level practice and assessment, p. 210

Teacher One Stop™, on-level lesson plans and all print resources

Holt Audio Library

Holt Audio Library: Selections and Summaries in Spanish

UA: Differentiating Instruction, graphic organizer, p. 312

UA: Supporting Instruction in Spanish, selection summary

ThinkCentral Online Assessment, Selection Standards Check

ThinkCentral Online Remediation

Preteach

English for Academic Success

Language Coach

Have students list and define idioms frequently used in American English. Students might be familiar with the idioms such as "hold your horses," "make ends meet," or "spill the beans."

Literary Skills Focus

As you read and discuss the play with students, have them note how often both characters pause. Who pauses more often? Also, direct students to observe the length and nature of each woman's contributions to the conversation.

Reading Skills Focus

Give students a copy of the Reading Skills Focus graphic organizer before they read. (See **Unit 6 Resources.**) Tell them to use their responses to answer the questions on the Applying Your Skills page.

Writing Skills Focus

Have students record examples of everyday speech in their **Reader/Writer Notebooks**. Students can use their notes to complete the Writing Skills Focus activity.

Learn It Online
The online version of this play includes audio support to engage all students and to help struggling readers with reading comprehension and vocabulary.
go.hrw.com H12-1351 Go

Teacher Preparation
Selection Summary
This short play is a dialogue between two women, Mrs. A and Mrs. B. Mrs. A dominates the conversation with remarks about a third woman who does not appear in the play. Mrs. B listens amiably until the end of the play. The play is punctuated by many pauses, during which characters consider their comments.

Direct Teach

Think About/Talk About
Read with a Purpose Have students read the Read with a Purpose statement. Point out that the statement asks students to discover what really lurks under the veneer of a seemingly superficial conversation. Have students consider how the dialogue, with its lengthy, frequent pauses, reveals the motivations of Mrs. A, Mrs. B, and the unnamed character.

Build Background
"Pause" is used frequently in Pinter's plays. He believes that people communicate by their silence, that what is not said is often more important than what is said. Audiences can examine what the characters do not say and can try to ascertain why they do not say it.

Analyzing Visuals

Connecting to the Text How does this image reflect the ordinary nature of the dialogue in the play? How might the women respond to each other here?

Universal Access

English Learners
English for Academic Success Explain that when Mrs. A mentions that her unnamed friend moved "up there," she is indicating that her friend moved to a town located in the North. Explain that prepositions and colloquial phrases sometimes indicate geographic proximity. Ask students to list other such examples. They might indicate expressions such as "down there," "back East," or "over yonder."

Struggling Readers
Strategic Students The pauses and mundane nature of the dialogue may confuse students. Pair students with more proficient readers to practice reading dialogue aloud. Make sure readers pause for a few seconds when a long pause is indicated. Have the students take note of the type of mood that these long pauses create. Point out to students that the dialogue is supposed to sound like the kind of idle, meaningless conversation that people have on a regular basis.

DRAMA

That's All

by **Harold Pinter**

Read with a Purpose

Read to discover the emotion and meaning that lie beneath the surface of the mundane dialogue in this play.

Build Background

Pinter's dialogue is the hallmark of his art. He has taken everyday speech and stylized it to the point where it becomes a kind of poetry. His dialogue is filled with repetitions and pauses; it has been described as an evasion of communication. Pinter believes that people communicate by their silence—that what is not said is often more important than what is said. The following revue sketch titled *That's All* is one of five comedy sketches first presented on BBC Radio in 1964. This is the entire text.

Mrs. A. I always put the kettle on about that time.
Mrs. B. Yes. *(Pause.)*
Mrs. A. Then she comes round.
Mrs. B. Yes. *(Pause.)*
Mrs. A. Only on Thursdays.
Mrs. B. Yes. *(Pause.)*
Mrs. A. On Wednesdays I used to put it on. When she used to come round. Then she changed it to Thursdays.
Mrs. B. Oh yes.
Mrs. A. After she moved. When she used to live round the corner, then she always came in on Wednesdays, but then when she moved she used to come down to the butcher's on Thursdays. She couldn't find a butcher up there.
Mrs. B. No.
Mrs. A. Anyway, she decided she'd stick to her own butcher. Well, I thought, if she can't find a butcher, that's the best thing.
Mrs. B. Yes. *(Pause.)* (A)

(A) **Literary Focus** **Dialogue** In plays, characters are revealed through their words and actions. What have you learned about the characters of Mrs. A and Mrs. B based on their dialogue so far?

Opposite: Spectators at an archery match in the Forest of Arden (1950), Warwickshire, England.

Think About/Talk About

Analysis

(A) Literary Focus

Possible response: *Mrs. A is the dominant character. She talks a great deal and seems to know a lot about the third woman. Mrs. B seems quiet and agreeable because she almost always answers "yes" to Mrs. A.*

Extend the Discussion

Summarizing Briefly summarize the main points of the women's conversation on this page. ***Possible response:*** *Mrs. A talks to Mrs. B about when she puts the kettle on for tea. She has changed her habits because an unnamed acquaintance, who has moved, now comes by at a different time.*

Characterization What emotions of the two characters are revealed through the dialogue so far? ***Possible response:*** *Mrs. A seems to have a lot to say, thus she might be feeling tense or upset. In contrast, Mrs. B seems quite passive and hardly displays any emotion.*

Advanced Learners

Acceleration While some dramas open with a narrator explaining background details, this play offers no exposition. Ask students to write an opening monologue setting the stage for the play.

Students with Disabilities

Give students these details before they read: Mrs. A and Mrs. B are discussing a friend who used to live nearby; Mrs. A tends to dominate Mrs. B; Mrs. A may be hurt, as she hardly sees her old friend anymore.

Analyzing Visuals

Connecting to the Text: *There is nothing unusual or out of place in this black-and-white scene. The women in this image seem to share a close bond. Just as the play gives a brief glimpse into the daily lives of two women, the image shows a snapshot of an ordinary day in the lives of two women.*

Think About/Talk About

Comprehension

Ⓑ Reading Focus

Possible response: *The back-and-forth nature of the dialogue is fairly consistent with the patterns of mundane everyday conversation. Some dialogue in ordinary conversation, however, includes more interruptions and incomplete thoughts.*

Ⓒ Reading Focus

Possible responses: *The pauses indicate that each character is carefully considering her statements and most likely leaving out some thoughts or opinions. The pauses also suggest that there may be an underlying element of mistrust or caution between the two characters.*

Analysis

Ⓓ Literary Focus

Possible responses: *By the end of the dialogue, Mrs. B has detected a contradiction in Mrs. A's account of the third woman's habits and has sensed Mrs. A's overriding loneliness. Mrs. B cannot resist pointing out these discoveries and takes pleasure in her triumph.*

Mrs. A. So she started to come down on Thursdays. I didn't know she was coming down on Thursdays until one day I met her in the butcher.

Mrs. B. Oh yes.

Mrs. A. It wasn't my day for the butcher. I don't go to the butcher on Thursday.

Mrs. B. No, I know. *(Pause.)*

Mrs. A. I go on Friday.

Mrs. B. Yes. *(Pause.)*

Mrs. A. That's where I see you.

Mrs. B. Yes. *(Pause.)*

Mrs. A. You're always in there on Fridays.

Mrs. B. Oh yes. *(Pause.)*

Mrs. A. But I happened to go in for a bit of meat, it turned out to be a Thursday. I wasn't going in for my usual weekly on Friday. I just slipped in, the day before.

Mrs. B. Yes. Ⓑ

Mrs. A. That was the first time I found out she couldn't find a butcher up there, so she decided to come back here, once a week, to her own butcher.

Mrs. B. Yes.

Mrs. A. She came on Thursday so she'd be able to get meat for the weekend. Lasted her till Monday, then from Monday to Thursday they'd have fish. She can always buy cold meat, if they want a change.

Mrs. B. Oh yes. *(Pause.)* Ⓒ

Mrs. A. So I told her to come in when she came down after she'd been to the butcher's and I'd put a kettle on. So she did. *(Pause.)*

Mrs. B. Yes. *(Pause.)*

Mrs. A. It was funny because she always used to come in Wednesdays. *(Pause.)* Still, it made a break. *(Long pause.)*

Mrs. B. She doesn't come in no more, does she? *(Pause.)*

Mrs. A. She comes in. She doesn't come in so much, but she comes in. *(Pause.)*

Mrs. B. I thought she didn't come in. *(Pause.)* Ⓓ

Mrs. A. She comes in. *(Pause.)* She just doesn't come in so much. That's all.

Ⓑ **Reading Focus** **Understanding Patterns of Organization** This dialogue is very regular. Mrs. A speaks, and then Mrs. B responds briefly. How is this pattern the same as or different from the conversations you have every day?

Ⓒ **Reading Focus** **Understanding Patterns of Organization** How do the frequent pauses contribute to the conversation?

Ⓓ **Literary Focus** **Dialogue** Why do you think Mrs. B suddenly takes a more active role in the conversation? What is the meaning of her remark?

California Standards, p. 1355

- **Reading Standard 2.2** Analyze the way in which clarity of meaning is affected by the patterns of organization, hierarchical structures, repetition of the main ideas, syntax, and word choice in the text.
- **Grades 9–10 Review Reading Standard 3.10** Identify and describe the function of dialogue, scene designs, soliloquies, asides, and character foils in dramatic literature.
- **Writing Standard 2.2** Demonstrate an understanding of the author's use of stylistic devices and an appreciation of the effects created.

Applying Your Skills

Reading Standard 2.2; Grades 9–10 Review
Reading Standard 3.10 (see pages A48–A50)
Writing Standard 2.2 (see pages A51–A52)

That's All

Literary Response and Analysis

Reading Skills Focus

Quick Check

1. Summarize the conversation between Mrs. A and Mrs. B.
2. How do you picture Mrs. A and Mrs. B? Explain.

Read with a Purpose

3. What is the underlying meaning and emotion in the dialogue?

Reading Skills: Understanding Patterns of Organization

4. You used a chart to record patterns in the dialogue. Add a column, and explain the effect of the patterns.

Patterns	Observations	Effect
How sketch begins	In mid-conversation	It engages us to piece together what's missing.
How conversation is balanced between speakers		
Repetition and how it varies		
Pattern of pauses and how the pattern shifts		

Literary Skills Focus

Literary Analysis

5. **Compare and Contrast** How are the two characters distinguished from each other by what they say? Why are they identified by letters of the alphabet?
6. **Analyze** What do you learn about Mrs. A, Mrs. B, and the woman they discuss?
7. **Interpret** Why do you think Pinter chose "That's All" as the title of his play?
8. **Compare and Contrast** How is the dialogue in *That's All* like and unlike conversations that you hear every day? How is the dialogue like a poem?
9. **Interpret** *That's All* was first performed on the radio. Explain how a radio performance of the sketch would differ from a stage performance.
10. **Analyze** What might be Pinter's theme?

Literary Skills: Dialogue

11. **Analyze** The play begins with a special form of dialogue called **stichomythia**, wherein two speakers in a verbal duel alternate brief speeches of a single line. How does this form of dialogue help characterize Mrs. A?

Literary Skills Review: Exposition

12. **Analyze** In traditional drama, much of the first scene provides **exposition**—an introduction to the play's characters, setting, and major conflict. How does the lack of exposition in this play affect the audience?

Writing Skills Focus

Think as a Reader/Writer

Use It in Your Writing Look over your notes about sentence structure, word choice, repetition, and pauses in Pinter's dialogue. Using conversational patterns familiar to you, write a brief dialogue between two people discussing a third person. Try to shape all three characters through what is said and unsaid.

What Do You Think Now? What sort of life experiences do these women discuss? How do these experiences affect their worldview?

Universal Access

Struggling Writers

Remind students that thoughts and feelings can be conveyed by more than just words and pauses. Students can include the sound *ahem,* a throat clearing, to indicate that someone is uncomfortable, or they can use expressions like *uh* or *um* to imply confusion or uncertainty. Encourage students to think of other aspects of a natural conversation to include in their dialogue.

What Do You Think Now?

Before students answer the question, encourage them to consider why Mrs. A feels disappointed. Furthermore, why does Mrs. B feel a subtle sense of satisfaction at her friend's expense?

Assess

Unit 6 Resources,
Selection Standards Check, p. 211

Check for Understanding

Independent Practice

Reading Skills Focus

Possible responses:

1. *The conversation is about a third woman, who does not appear; her visits to the butcher; and her visiting for tea.*
2. *Both seem like older women who have time to be occupied with the mundane details in life.*
3. *Under the dialogue and pauses, Mrs. A seems unsatisfied and lonely.*
4. *Students should explain the effect of the patterns in dialogue.*

Literary Skills Focus

Possible responses:

5. *Mrs. A talks more than Mrs. B. Mrs. B usually responds "yes" or no." By giving them letters for names, the playwright may be suggesting that they are generic characters, people with no specific identity.*
6. *Both seem isolated and lonely. The third woman is more independent than they are.*
7. *Titles usually help audiences make sense of a play. Here, Pinter may be suggesting that there is no greater meaning to the play and that the mundane, pause-filled dialogue is all there is to the play and to life.*
8. *The play's dialogue illustrates how much meaning is hidden in everyday banter. Like a poem, it reveals a great deal using few words, pauses, and repetition.*
9. *A radio performance would rely on conveying meaning through pauses and inflection, while stage actors can communicate with gestures and facial expressions.*
10. *Pinter may be trying to comment on the insufficiency of ordinary communication.*
11. *The stichomythia shows Mrs. A as a lonely woman with a life turned into a meaningless routine.*
12. *It causes the reader to feel uncertain and uneasy.*

Standards Focus

Objectives

Students will
- understand theme
- identify historical context

Selection Introduction

Think About the Writer

Ask students how growing up in Africa might give Lessing special insight into the evils of racism and colonialism. Why might she be more deeply affected by these social issues than the average British citizen?

For Independent Reading

Waiting for the Mahatma, R. K. Narayan

Motivate

What Do You Think?/QuickWrite

Use the QuickWrite to have students discuss factors, such as religious or economic differences, that cause cultures or groups to clash today. Have students use their **Reader/Writer Notebooks** to record their thoughts.

English for Academic Success

Academic Vocabulary

Look for opportunities to use the Academic Vocabulary words in this unit.

- **inevitable,** ***adj.:*** unavoidable
- **perspective,** ***n.:*** a particular way of looking at something

Preparing to Read

No Witchcraft for Sale

What Do You Think? How does experience shape our view of the world?

QuickWrite

What clashes of cultures trouble the world today? With a partner, discuss the usual causes of these cases of cultural strife. Record your thoughts in your *Reader/Writer Notebook.*

Doris Lessing at the Edinburgh International Book Festival, Edinburgh, Scotland, UK (2001).

MEET THE WRITER

Doris Lessing

(1919–)

Nobel Prize WINNER

Doris Lessing was born in Persia (now Iran) to British parents who had fled England to escape what they saw as its narrowness and provincialism. When she was five, the family moved yet again, this time to a three-thousand-acre farm in Southern Rhodesia (now Zimbabwe). The farm employed some thirty to fifty black African laborers, who each earned the equivalent of about $1.50 a month and lived in mud huts with no sanitation.

Searching for Direction

In Africa, Lessing's mother was often ill and her father grew increasingly eccentric. A lonely child, Lessing educated herself by reading the classics of European and American fiction.

At fourteen, Lessing left school and went to work in Salisbury, the capital of Southern Rhodesia, first as a nursemaid and then as a stenographer and telephone operator. Salisbury had a white population of about ten thousand and a larger black population that Lessing discovered "didn't count." When her first marriage collapsed, she entered radical politics. At twenty-six, she married again, but that marriage also ended in divorce.

An Instrument of Change

"I can't remember a time when I didn't want to come to England," she recalled. In 1949, she left Africa for England with her two-year-old son and a manuscript of her first novel, *The Grass Is Singing* (1950). The book, which depicts the complex relationship between a white farmer's wife and her black servant, was one of the earliest novels about racial inequality in Africa. Lessing's most widely read and discussed book is *The Golden Notebook* (1962), an ambitious and complex work that explores politics, mental illness, and women's issues in modern life.

Lessing was awarded the Nobel Prize in Literature in 2007. Her work reflects her belief that she has the responsibility to be "an instrument of change." "It is not merely a question of preventing evil," she says "but of strengthening a vision of a good which may defeat the evil."

Think About the Writer How might Lessing's childhood in Africa have influenced her work?

California Standards, pp. 1356–1367

- **Reading Standard 3.2** Analyze the way in which the theme or meaning of a selection represents a view or comment on life, using textual evidence to support the claim.
- **Reading Standard 3.7** Analyze recognized works of world literature from a variety of authors: **c.** Evaluate the philosophical, political, religious, ethical, and social influences of the historical period that shaped the characters, plots, and settings.
- **Reading Standard 3.8** Analyze the clarity and consistency of political assumptions in a selection of literary works or essays on a topic (e.g., suffrage, women's role in organized labor). (Political approach)

Selection Readability	
Easily Accessible **Accessible** Challenging	short story; provides historical context; some difficult syntax

Reading Standard 3.2, 3.7c, 3.8 (see pages A48–A50)

Literary Skills Focus

Theme Most fiction can be categorized as one of two types: escape fiction or interpretive fiction. **Escape fiction** is pure entertainment; it gives us pleasure and helps us temporarily escape from the world. Theme is not a primary element in escape fiction. **Interpretive fiction,** on the other hand, is not meant to help us escape from the world but rather to help us understand it better. Even if it is fantasy, interpretive fiction gives us a different perspective on what it means to be human. This truth about life revealed in a story is called **theme.**

Lessing's story is an example of interpretive fiction. As you will see, a powerful theme does not have to come from a complex story. Lessing's tale is simple but has a forceful, provocative, and timely theme.

Literary Perspectives Apply the literary perspective described on page 1359 as you read this story.

Reading Skills Focus

Identifying Historical Context Regardless of whether a story is escape fiction or interpretive fiction, it has a **historical context.** (In fact, many readers choose fiction such as detective novels and romances because of their historical context.) Lessing's tale is set in Southern Rhodesia at a time when the British ruled that part of Africa. The servants in the story are black Africans; the Farquars are part of the British ruling class.

Into Action As you read, consider how the characters and their conflicts are products of a particular historical context. In your *Reader/Writer Notebook,* use an idea web like the one below to record details.

Writing Skills Focus

Think as a Reader/Writer

Find It in Your Reading Lessing presents her characters by using a few strong descriptive words: Mrs. Farquar felt "she had achieved a very great thing"; Teddy had "miraculous fair hair and Northern blue eyes." In your *Reader/Writer Notebook,* record some of the words Lessing uses to delineate her characters.

Reader/Writer Notebook

Use your **RWN** to complete the activities for this selection.

Vocabulary

reverently (REHV uhr uhnt lee) *adv.:* with great respect or awe, as for something sacred. *Gideon reverently held the child's lustrous curls.*

efficacy (EHF uh kuh see) *n.:* ability to produce a desired effect. *Mrs. Farquar had heard of the efficacy of native herbs.*

perfunctory (puhr FUHNGK tuhr ee) *adj.:* halfhearted; disinterested. *The scientist was somewhat perfunctory as he explained the benefits of the new drug.*

annulled (uh NUHLD) *v.:* erased; canceled. *The Farquars' anger annulled the guilt they felt toward Gideon.*

perversely (puhr VURS lee) *adv.:* disagreeably; contrarily. *Because the family did not understand Gideon's culture, they considered him to be perversely obstinate.*

Language Coach

Suffix –ly The suffix *–ly* is added to some adjectives to form adverbs, words that describe verbs, adjectives, or other adverbs. What two Vocabulary words are adverbs formed by adding *–ly* to an adjective? What verb does each adverb describe in the sample sentences above? How could you form an adverb out of the adjective *inevitable*?

Learn It Online

Jump into this story with the video introduction online.

go.hrw.com H12-1357 Go

Selection Resources

Unit 6 Resources, on-level practice and assessment, p. 214

PowerNotes, interactive lesson presentations with activities

Teacher One Stop™, on-level lesson plans and all print resources

Holt Audio Library

Holt Audio Library: Selections and Summaries in Spanish

UA: Holt Interactive Reader, p. 371

UA: Differentiating Instruction, modified lesson plans and leveled assessment, p. 313

UA: Supporting Instruction in Spanish, selection summary

UA: Resources for Teaching Advanced Students, lesson plans, p. 211

ThinkCentral Online Assessment, Selection Standards Check

ThinkCentral Online Remediation

Preteach

Introducing Vocabulary

Use this activity to check students' understanding.

1. Name some objects that one would handle **reverently**.
2. Share some remedies that are known for their **efficacy** at eliminating hiccups.
3. Compare a **perfunctory** handshake to an eager greeting.
4. List some documents or legal agreements that can be **annulled**.
5. Explain why a person might behave **perversely** if he or she is insulted.

English for Academic Success

Language Coach

Have students list adverbs that end in *–ly*. Point out that spelling changes, such as the addition of extra letters or syllables, can result when the suffix is added to a root word, such as *happily, uneasily,* and *enthusiastically*.

Literary Skills Focus

As you read and discuss the story with students, have them note the theme of the story. Point out how a strong theme can make an older selection relevant to current life.

Reading Skills Focus

Give students a copy of the Reading Skills Focus graphic organizer. They can use their responses on the Applying Your Skills page.

Writing Skills Focus

Have students record examples of descriptive words in their **Reader/Writer Notebooks**. Students can use their notes to complete the Writing Skills Focus activity.

Learn It Online

The **PowerNotes** presentation for this lesson includes a short video that introduces the selection. The video is also available on the online version of this page.

go.hrw.com H12-1357 Go

Teacher Preparation

Selection Plot Summary

The Farquars, a white couple living in South Africa during apartheid, finally have a child, named Teddy. Their cook, Gideon, lovingly nurtures the boy but knows there is an unbridgeable gap between the boy and himself because of their races. The friendship eventually cools when Teddy dismisses Gideon's son as "only a black boy." One day, a snake spits in Teddy's eyes. As the boy begins to go blind, Gideon uses a root to cure him. When a white scientist arrives to ask Gideon to share the ancient remedy, Gideon refuses to cooperate. The whites do not understand that Gideon's knowledge of herbal medicine is part of the inherited culture of his people and that the Farquars and the scientist are insulting him by expecting him to reveal it.

Direct Teach

Think About/Talk About

Read with a Purpose Have students read the Read with a Purpose statement. Point out that the political climate of a country can create a hierarchy of various races and cultural groups.

Build Background

Students will understand and appreciate the story better if they know the early colonial history of Rhodesia (now Zimbabwe). Explain that when British colonists arrived in the country they called Rhodesia (named for British financier Cecil Rhodes) in the late 1800s, they seized the country's most fertile, productive farmland for themselves. Africans were removed from their ancestral homelands to communal lands, where the soil was poor and raising crops was difficult. The displaced African farmers became a source of cheap labor in cities and mines. As a result, the white minority enjoyed a high standard of living while the black majority barely scraped by.

Read with a Purpose

As you read, think about how political realities affect human relationships.

Build Background

In her preface to *African Stories* (1964), the collection from which this story is taken, Lessing writes: "If people had been prepared to listen, two decades earlier, to the small, but shrill-enough, voices crying out for the world's attention, perhaps the present suffering in South Africa and Southern Rhodesia could have been prevented. Britain, who is responsible, became conscious of her responsibility too late; and now the tragedy must play itself out."

In 1980, after years of conflict, Southern Rhodesia emerged as the Republic of Zimbabwe under the leadership of a black African, Robert Mugabe.

This story, which is not about witchcraft at all, reads like a contemporary parable.

The Farquars had been childless for years when little Teddy was born; and they were touched by the pleasure of their servants, who brought presents of fowls and eggs and flowers to the homestead when they came to rejoice over the baby, exclaiming with delight over his downy golden head and his blue eyes. They congratulated Mrs. Farquar as if she had achieved a very great thing, and she felt that she had—her smile for the lingering, admiring natives was warm and grateful.

Later, when Teddy had his first haircut, Gideon the cook picked up the soft gold tufts from the ground, and held them reverently in his hand. Then he smiled at the little boy and said: "Little Yellow Head." That became the native name for the child. Gideon and Teddy were great friends from the first. When Gideon had finished his work, he would lift Teddy on his shoulders to the shade of a big tree, and play with him there, forming curious little toys from twigs and leaves and grass, or shaping animals from wetted soil. When Teddy learned to walk it was often Gideon who crouched before him, clucking encouragement, finally catching him when he fell, tossing him up in the air till they both became breathless with laughter. Mrs.

Vocabulary **reverently** (REHV uhr uhnt lee) *adv.:* with great respect or awe, as for something sacred.

Word-Attack Mini-Lesson

English for Academic Success Remind students that breaking a word into parts is a useful strategy when dealing with long words. With some words, you can separate prefixes and suffixes and then deal with the word part that remains. Demonstrate this using the word *protuberance* (p. 1360).

- Identify *pro–* and *–ance*.
- Recognize that the word part *tuber* requires a long vowel sound (TOO behr).
- Put the parts together to read the word (proh TOO behr uhns).

Activity Have students divide these words into word parts to make them easier to read.

1. perfunctory [*per funct ory*]
2. indestructible [*in de struct ible*]
3. neocolonialism [*neo colonial ism*]
4. subarachnoid [*sub arach noid*]
5. procrastinate [*pro cras tin ate*]

Farquar was fond of the old cook because of his love for her child.

There was no second baby; and one day Gideon said: "Ah, missus, missus, the Lord above sent this one; Little Yellow Head is the most good thing we have in our house." Because of that "we" Mrs. Farquar felt a warm impulse toward her cook; and at the end of the month she raised his wages. He had been with her now for several years; he was one of the few natives who had his wife and children in the compound and never wanted to go home to his kraal,[1] which was some hundreds of miles away. Sometimes a small piccanin[2] who had been born the same time as Teddy, could be seen peering from the edge of the bush, staring in awe at the little white boy with his miraculous fair hair and Northern blue eyes. The two little children would gaze at each other with a wide, interested gaze, and once Teddy put out his hand curiously to touch the black child's cheeks and hair. **A**

Gideon, who was watching, shook his head wonderingly, and said: "Ah, missus, these are both children, and one will grow up to be a baas,[3] and one will be a servant"; and Mrs. Farquar smiled and said sadly, "Yes, Gideon, I was thinking the same." She sighed. "It is God's will," said Gideon, who was a mission boy.[4] The Farquars were very religious people; and this shared feeling about God bound servant and masters even closer together.

Teddy was about six years old when he was given a scooter, and discovered the intoxications of speed. All day he would fly around the homestead, in and out of flowerbeds, scattering squawking chickens and irritated dogs, finishing with a wide dizzying arc into the kitchen door. There he would cry: "Gideon, look at me!" And Gideon would laugh and say: "Very clever, Little Yellow Head." Gideon's youngest son, who was now a herdsboy, came especially up from the compound to see the scooter. He was afraid to come near it, but Teddy showed off in front of him. "Piccanin," shouted Teddy, "get out of my way!" And he raced in circles around the black child until he was frightened, and fled back to the bush.

"Why did you frighten him?" asked Gideon, gravely reproachful.

Teddy said defiantly: "He's only a black boy," and laughed. Then, when Gideon turned away from him without speaking, his face fell. Very soon he slipped into the house and found an orange and brought it to Gideon, saying: "This is for you." He could not bring himself to say he was sorry; but he could not bear to lose Gideon's affection either. Gideon took the orange unwillingly and sighed. "Soon you will be going away to school, Little Yellow Head," he said wonderingly, "and then you will be grown up." He shook his head gently and said, "And that is how our lives go." He seemed to be putting a distance between himself and

1. **kraal** (krahl): South African village.
2. **piccanin** (PIHK uh nihn): black African child. Derived from *pequeno* (pay KAY noo), Portuguese for "small." The term is now considered offensive.
3. **baas** (bahs): Afrikaans for "master." Afrikaans, a language developed from seventeenth-century Dutch, is spoken in South Africa.
4. **mission boy:** one educated by Christian missionaries.

A **Reading Focus** **Identifying Historical Context** How do you think most servants' jobs affect their families?

Literary Perspectives

Analyzing Political Context Literary texts are often shaped by the author's particular worldview, which can be influenced by his or her political perspective, gender, or social class. In "No Witchcraft for Sale," Lessing sets the story of the two men's friendship against the backdrop of a rigid racial and economic hierarchy in Africa. The political, economic, and, indeed, gender inequalities present in the society inevitably contribute to the evolution of the relationship between Gideon and the Farquars. As you read, note how the divergent social and vocational expectations for Gideon and Teddy may influence their behavior toward each other. Is the role each of these characters assumes determined by the political context or by innate character traits that remain independent of societal pressures? If born into different circumstances, how might Gideon and Teddy have related to each other? Would their friendship have been more or less likely to exist at all?

As you read, be sure to notice the questions in the text, which will guide you in using this perspective.

Think About/Talk About

Comprehension

A Reading Focus

Possible response: *Many servants had to work and live far away from their families. A few servants were able to move their families to the "compounds" of white families.*

Extend the Discussion

Irony Given the context of this culture, what do you think is ironic about the "miraculous" appearance of Teddy's hair? ***Possible response:*** *The white child's hair is no more "miraculous" than the black child's. The only thing remarkable about Teddy's blond hair is that in this society it will confer power and prestige upon him as he matures (and will deny the same to the black boy).*

Evaluating Why are Mrs. Farquar's Christian sensibilities rather hypocritical? ***Possible response:*** *Mrs. Farquar's belief in Christianity does not affect or inform her life on a deep level. It does not prompt her to question her right to place herself on a plane above Gideon or her willingness to exploit a person of another race for her own convenience.*

Vocabulary: Own the Word

reverently: Remind students that *reverently* means "with great awe and respect." Ask students why Gideon treats Teddy's trimmed locks of hair so *reverently.* ***Possible response:*** *He is fond of Teddy and knows Teddy will be his master someday.*

Literary Perspectives

Before students read the selection, have them read the **Literary Perspectives** about Analyzing Political Context. To help students examine literature from the perspective of social power, invite groups of students to brainstorm a list of television shows or films that depict members of different social classes interacting. Have students discuss how different characters' social backgrounds affect their interactions with one another.

Remind students to use the notes and questions at the bottom of the page to help them use the perspective.

Universal Access

Struggling Readers

Model identifying the historical context in this selection. Remind students that the setting of the story is in a part of Africa that was under British rule. Ask students: "How do the conflicts in this story reflect the political situation?" Point out that on p. 1359, Gideon's close relationship to Teddy changes when Teddy frightens Gideon's son, saying he is "only a black boy." Tell students that Teddy's comment reflects his condescending attitude toward the boy and Africans in general. Have students record other observations about the historical context in their graphic organizers.

Model the Skill

- Review the definition of **theme** with students. Explain that some themes hold universal messages or truths about life and the human condition that apply to all cultures and time periods. Most stories have multiple themes.
- Tell students that one possible theme of this story might be *that social structures sometimes prevent human beings from communicating or interacting authentically.* During class discussion, encourage students to explain how the relationships between Mrs. Farquar and Gideon, as well as Teddy and Gideon, have already supported this premise.

Guided Practice: Apply

Think-Pair-Share Have students form pairs, and ask them to determine another theme in the story. Encourage students to discuss how this theme is conveyed, using specific textual evidence. Then, instruct students to explore how the theme makes the story relevant to contemporary life. After pairs have completed their work, ask volunteers to share with the whole class.

Teddy, not because of resentment, but in the way a person accepts something inevitable. The baby had lain in his arms and smiled up into his face: The tiny boy had swung from his shoulders and played with him by the hour. Now Gideon would not let his flesh touch the flesh of the white child. He was kind, but there was a grave formality in his voice that made Teddy pout and sulk away. Also, it made him into a man: With Gideon he was polite, and carried himself formally, and if he came into the kitchen to ask for something, it was in the way a white man uses toward a servant, expecting to be obeyed. (B)

But on the day that Teddy came staggering into the kitchen with his fists to his eyes, shrieking with pain, Gideon dropped the pot full of hot soup that he was holding, rushed to the child, and forced aside his fingers. "A snake!" he exclaimed. Teddy had been on his scooter, and had come to a rest with his foot on the side of a big tub of plants. A tree snake, hanging by its tail from the roof, had spat full into his eyes. Mrs. Farquar came running when she heard the commotion. "He'll go blind," she sobbed, holding Teddy close against her. "Gideon, he'll go blind!" Already the eyes, with perhaps half an hour's sight left in them, were swollen up to the size of fists: Teddy's small white face was distorted by great purple oozing protuberances.[5] Gideon said: "Wait a minute, missus, I'll get some medicine." He ran off into the bush.

Mrs. Farquar lifted the child into the house and bathed his eyes with permanganate.[6] She had scarcely heard Gideon's words; but when she saw that her remedies had no effect at all, and remembered how she had seen natives with no sight in their eyes, because of the spitting of a snake, she began to look for the return of her cook, remembering what she heard of the efficacy of native herbs. She stood by the window, holding the terrified, sobbing little boy in her arms, and peered helplessly into the bush. It was not more than a few minutes before she saw Gideon come bounding back, and in his hand he held a plant.

"Do not be afraid, missus," said Gideon, "this will cure Little Yellow Head's eyes." He stripped the leaves from the plant, leaving a small white fleshy root. Without even washing it, he put the root in his mouth, chewed it vigorously, and then held the spittle there while he took the child forcibly from Mrs. Farquar. He gripped Teddy down between his knees, and pressed the balls of his thumbs into the swollen eyes, so that the child screamed and Mrs. Farquar cried out in protest: "Gideon, Gideon!" But Gideon took no notice. He knelt over the writhing child, pushing back the puffy lids till chinks of eyeball showed, and then he spat hard, again and again, into first one eye, and then the other. He finally lifted Teddy gently into his mother's arms, and said: "His eyes will get better." But Mrs. Farquar was weeping with terror, and she could hardly thank him: It was impossible to believe that Teddy could keep his sight. In a couple of hours the swellings were gone: The eyes were inflamed and tender but Teddy could see. Mr. and Mrs. Farquar went to Gideon in the kitchen and thanked him over and over again. They felt helpless because of their gratitude: It seemed they could do nothing to express it. They gave Gideon presents for his wife and children, and a big increase in wages, but these things could not pay for Teddy's now completely cured eyes. Mrs. Farquar said: "Gideon, God chose you as an instrument for His goodness," and Gideon said: "Yes, missus, God is very good." (C)

Now, when such a thing happens on a farm, it cannot be long before everyone hears of it. Mr. and Mrs. Farquar told their neighbors and the story was discussed from one end of the district to the other. The bush is full of secrets. No one can live in Africa, or at least on the veld,[7] without learning very soon that there is an ancient wisdom of leaf and soil and season

5. **protuberances** (proh TOO buhr uhns ihz): swellings; bulges.
6. **permanganate** (puhr MANG guh nayt): dark purple chemical compound used as a disinfectant.
7. **veld:** in South Africa, open country with very few bushes or trees; grassland. *Veld,* also spelled *veldt,* is Afrikaans for "field."

(B) **Literary Focus** **Theme** This is a key moment in the story. What has happened here?

(C) **Reading Focus** **Identifying Historical Context** Why might the Farquars feel unable to express their gratitude to Gideon?

Vocabulary **efficacy** (EHF uh kuh see) *n.:* ability to produce a desired effect.

Universal Access

(EL) English Learners

English for Academic Success Direct students to the word *formality* in the sentence at the top of p. 1360: "He was kind, but there was a grave formality in his voice." Point out the root word *formal* in the word *formality* helps students guess its meaning ("a required procedure"). Tell students that the suffix *–ity* is used in abstract nouns and expresses a condition or state.

✔ See the **English Language Skill Builder** in **UA: Differentiating Instruction.**

Struggling Readers

Point out the vivid descriptions that help readers visualize Teddy's face after the snake attack: "Teddy's small white face was distorted by great purple oozing protuberances." Have students compose their own sentence describing something vividly using multiple adjectives to modify two or three nouns.

✔ Invite students to read the selection in interactive format in **UA: Holt Interactive Reader.**

Neverdie Mushwana, a South African "witch doctor," in front of his home with one of his snakes. Tzaneen, South Africa (1997).

Analyzing Visuals

Connecting to the Text In "No Witchcraft for Sale," knowledge of herbal medicine is a valued part of Gideon's inherited culture. How does this image relate to ideas about traditional medicine expressed in the story?

Think About/Talk About

See Student Edition p. 1360 for the questions that relate to the following answers.

Comprehension

C Reading Focus

Possible response: *The Farquars can show their gratitude only by giving Gideon money and token presents, acts that reinforce their superiority and Gideon's dependence.*

Analysis

B Literary Focus

Possible response: *Teddy's comment and his inability to apologize to Gideon show that he regards Gideon and his son as inferiors. From this point on, Gideon and Teddy's relationship will transform from an innocent, sincere friendship to an unequal dynamic typical of the social environment.*

Extend the Discussion

Comparing and Contrasting How does Mrs. Farquar's reaction to the snakebite crisis differ from Gideon's response? ***Possible response:*** *Mrs. Farquar, the "mistress" of the house, is hysterical and helpless, while Gideon, a servant, demonstrates a calm competence that ultimately saves Teddy from harm.*

Characterization What do Gideon's actions after the snakebite suggest about his true feelings for Teddy? ***Possible response:*** *Gideon still feels deep affection for Teddy in spite of the newfound formality of their relationship.*

Vocabulary: Own the Word

efficacy: *Efficacy* means "effectiveness" or "usefulness." Its antonym is therefore *inefficiency* or *uselessness.* Have students use both words in a sentence. ***Possible response:*** *I was impressed by the efficacy of the medicine on my headache; however, its uselessness on my cough was unfortunate.*

Advanced Learners

Acceleration Encourage pairs or groups of students to discuss the role of Christianity in colonial Africa. How did black Africans benefit from the work of Christian missions? Conversely, how did white Africans use Christianity to further their own agendas?

✔ See **UA: Resources for Teaching Advanced Students** for strategies for teaching advanced learners.

Analyzing Visuals

Connecting to the Text: *The healer's possession of a snake reinforces my assumption that herbal medicine involves unconventional healing methods and medicines. The healer's coat and car challenge the assumption that those who practice traditional medicine are disconnected from the modern world.*

Model the Skill

- Provide students with copies of the Reading Skills Focus graphic organizer. (See **Unit 6 Resources**.)
- Tell students that **identifying the historical context** and social backdrop of the story will help them understand the conflicts, relationships, and themes depicted. Gideon, for instance, has conflicting emotions regarding Teddy: He has played an almost paternal role in the boy's life, yet must eventually accept Teddy as a superior.
- Model adding a character and his or her corresponding details to the web. For instance, you might add Mrs. Farquar and say, "Mrs. Farquar is part of the ruling white class. In the historical context of this story, she is above Gideon and is responsible for his well-being." Explain that various conflicts arise from this dynamic:

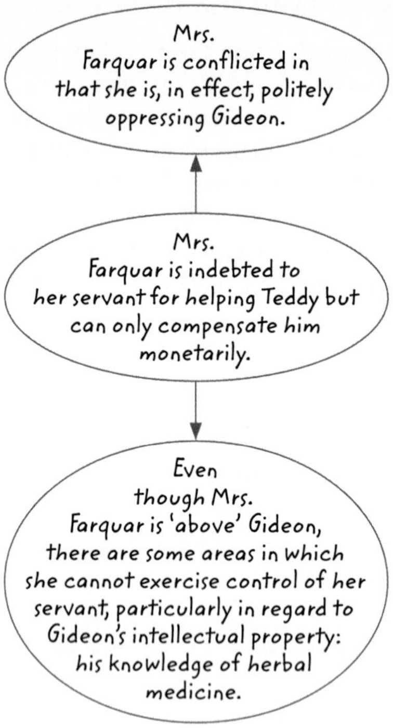

Guided Practice: Apply

Turn-and-Talk Ask students to work with a neighbor to complete an analysis for another character in the story. Then, ask volunteers to share their assessments with the entire class.

—and, too, perhaps most important of all, of the darker tracts of the human mind—which is the black man's heritage. Up and down the district people were telling anecdotes, reminding each other of things that had happened to them.

"But I saw it myself, I tell you. It was a puff-adder bite. The kaffir's[8] arm was swollen to the elbow, like a great shiny black bladder. He was groggy after a half a minute. He was dying. Then suddenly a kaffir walked out of the bush with his hands full of green stuff. He smeared something on the place, and next day my boy was back at work, and all you could see was two small punctures in the skin."

This was the kind of tale they told. And, as always, with a certain amount of exasperation, because while all of them knew that in the bush of Africa are waiting valuable drugs locked in bark, in simple-looking leaves, in roots, it was impossible to ever get the truth about them from the natives themselves. **D**

The story eventually reached town; and perhaps it was at a sundowner party,[9] or some such function, that a doctor, who happened to be there, challenged it. "Nonsense," he said. "These things get exaggerated in the telling. We are always checking up on this kind of story, and we draw a blank every time."

Anyway, one morning there arrived a strange car at the homestead, and out stepped one of the workers from the laboratory in town, with cases full of test tubes and chemicals.

Mr. and Mrs. Farquar were flustered and pleased and flattered. They asked the scientist to lunch, and they told the story all over again, for the hundredth time. Little Teddy was there too, his blue eyes sparkling with health, to prove the truth of it. The scientist explained how humanity might benefit if this new drug could be offered for sale; and the Farquars were even more pleased: They were kind, simple people, who liked to think of something good coming about because of them. But when the scientist began talking of the money that might result, their manner showed discomfort. Their feelings over the miracle (that was how they thought of it) were so strong and deep and religious, that it was distasteful to them to think of money. The scientist, seeing their faces, went back to his first point, which was the advancement of humanity. He was perhaps a trifle perfunctory: It was not the first time he had come salting the tail of a fabulous bush secret.[10]

Eventually, when the meal was over, the Farquars called Gideon into their living room and explained to him that this baas, here, was a Big Doctor from the Big City, and he had come all that way to see Gideon. At this Gideon seemed afraid; he did not understand; and Mrs. Farquar explained quickly that it was because of the wonderful thing he had done with Teddy's eyes that the Big Baas had come.

8. **kaffir's** (KAF uhrz): *Kaffir* is a contemptuous term for a black African, derived from *kāfir,* Arabic for "infidel."
9. **sundowner party:** British colloquial term for "cocktail party." The term derives from the colonials' custom of gathering for drinks at sunset.
10. **salting ... bush secret:** allusion to the ironic advice given to children about catching a bird by putting salt on its tail. In other words, the scientist knows his search may be futile.

D **Literary Focus** **Theme** What details here establish the separation between black Africans and white Africans?

Vocabulary **perfunctory** (puhr FUHNGK tuhr ee) *adj.:* half-hearted; disinterested.

Universal Access

AAVE Students Who Use African American Vernacular English

English for Academic Success Point out that students should distinguish between singular nouns and plural nouns in formal English. Students might say "we laughed at all his joke" instead of "we laughed at all his jokes." Call on a volunteer to read aloud the first several paragraphs on p. 1362. Remind the students to pronounce the *–s* sound in plural nouns such as *tracts, hands,* and *punctures.* Then, have the other students take turns reading p. 1362 to each other in pairs.

Cross-Curricular Connection

SCIENCE: Spitting Snakes

Paired Activity Partner students to research and share information about the species of snake that attacked Teddy. Students should learn whether the snake's venom could cause blindness and, if so, how. In addition, students may want to research information about various remedies for snakebites from snakes living in their vicinity as well as in Africa.

Gideon looked from Mrs. Farquar to Mr. Farquar, and then at the little boy, who was showing great importance because of the occasion. At last he said grudgingly: "The Big Baas want to know what medicine I used?" He spoke incredulously, as if he could not believe his old friends could so betray him. Mr. Farquar began explaining how a useful medicine could be made out of the root, and how it could be put on sale, and how thousands of people, black and white, up and down the continent of Africa, could be saved by the medicine when that spitting snake filled their eyes with poison. Gideon listened, his eyes bent on the ground, the skin of his forehead puckering in discomfort. When Mr. Farquar had finished he did not reply. The scientist, who all this time had been leaning back in a big chair, sipping his coffee and smiling with skeptical good humor, chipped in and explained all over again, in different words, about the making of drugs and the progress of science. Also, he offered Gideon a present. **E**

There was silence after this further explanation, and then Gideon remarked indifferently that he could not remember the root. His face was sullen and hostile, even when he looked at the Farquars, whom he usually treated like old friends. They were beginning to feel annoyed; and this feeling annulled the guilt that had been sprung into life by Gideon's accusing manner. They were beginning to feel that he was unreasonable. But it was at that moment that they all realized he would never give in. The magical drug would remain where it was, unknown and useless except for the tiny scattering of Africans who had the knowledge, natives who might be digging a ditch for the municipality in a ragged shirt and a pair of patched shorts, but who were still born to healing, hereditary healers, being the nephews or sons of the old witch doctors whose ugly masks and bits of bone and all the uncouth properties of magic were the outward signs of real power and wisdom. **F**

The Farquars might tread on that plant fifty times a day as they passed from house to garden, from cow kraal to mealie[11] field, but they would never know it.

But they went on persuading and arguing, with all the force of their exasperation; and Gideon continued to say that he could not remember, or that there was no such root, or that it was the wrong season of the year, or that it wasn't the root itself, but the spit from his mouth that had cured Teddy's eyes. He said all these things one after another, and seemed not to care they were contradictory. He was rude and stubborn. The Farquars could hardly recognize their gentle, lovable old servant in this ignorant, perversely obstinate African, standing there in front of them with lowered eyes, his hands twitching his cook's apron, repeating over and over whichever one of the stupid refusals that first entered his head. **G**

And suddenly he appeared to give in. He lifted his head, gave a long, blank angry look at the circle of whites, who seemed to him like a circle of yelping dogs pressing around him, and said: "I will show you the root."

They walked single file away from the homestead down a kaffir path. It was a blazing December afternoon, with the sky full of hot rain clouds. Everything was hot: The sun was like a bronze tray whirling overhead, there was a heat shimmer over the fields, the soil was scorching underfoot, the dusty wind blew gritty and thick and warm in their faces. It was a terrible day, fit only for reclining on a veranda with iced drinks, which is where they would normally have been at that hour.

From time to time, remembering that on the day of the snake it had taken ten minutes to find the root, someone asked: "Is it much further, Gideon?" And Gideon would answer over his shoulder, with

11. **mealie:** corn.

E Reading Focus Identifying Historical Context How does the white scientist treat Gideon?

F Literary Focus Theme How does the balance of power shift in this conversation?

G Literary Perspectives Analyzing Political Context Why has the power structure changed at this point in the story?

Vocabulary **annulled** (uh NUHLD) *v.:* erased; canceled.
perversely (puhr VURS lee) *adv.:* disagreeably; contrarily.

Universal Access

Students with Disabilities

Help students better understand the setting by encouraging them to conduct research on Rhodesia and which countries occupy its territory today. Direct them to use the Internet, books, or periodicals to find pictures or short articles that provide insight into the culture, location, climate, people, and topography of the country.

✓ See **UA: Differentiating Instruction** for strategies for teaching students with disabilities.

Literary Perspectives

Guide students in answering the **Literary Perspectives** question on this page. To help students analyze the political context in this situation, ask them who is in a position to give and who is in a position to receive at this point in the story, compared to before. Have them consider whether the giver or the receiver has more power and why.

Think About/Talk About

Comprehension

E Reading Focus

Possible response: *He condescends to Gideon because he cannot believe that a black Rhodesian could understand the intricacies of the pharmaceutical industry and the progress of science.*

Analysis

D Literary Focus

Possible response: *The Africans view the healing plants as simple, special treasures of their culture, but the whites view them as commodities that could be transformed into profitable, mass-marketed drugs.*

F Literary Focus

Possible response: *The power shifts from the white ruling class, represented by the scientist and the Farquars, to the servant class, exemplified by Gideon.*

G Literary Perspectives

Possible response: *Gideon is in power because he refuses to reveal his knowledge and drops his usual compliant manner to become defiant.*

Vocabulary: Own the Word

- **perfunctory:** *Perfunctory* has the connotation of being unenthusiastic. Ask students to explain why an audience might give *perfunctory* applause at a show.
- **annulled:** Tell students that *annulled* means "erased or cancelled." Have students explain what it means to have a marriage *annulled*. ***Possible response:*** *It means to end a marriage after a short time.*
- **perversely:** *Perversely* means "disagreeably." An antonym is *obediently*. Ask students: "In the story, why are the Farquars surprised by Gideon's *perversely* stubborn behavior?" ***Possible response:*** *He is normally obedient and calm.*

Think About/Talk About

Analysis

Ⓗ Literary Perspectives

Possible response: *To conform to social customs, Teddy and Gideon have limited their interactions to the polite banter typical of an amiable master and servant.*

Extend the Discussion

Synthesizing In Hebrew history, Gideon led his people to victory. Then he refused the crown of Israel, saying that only God was Israel's king. Why do you think Lessing named her character after this Hebrew hero? ***Possible response:*** *The Biblical Gideon refused the crown because he believed in a higher authority; Lessing's hero refuses gifts because he refuses to violate his heritage.*

Monitor Students' Comprehension

Guide the class in answering these comprehension questions.

1. What changed the relationship between Teddy and Gideon? [*Teddy demeaned Gideon's son.*]
2. How does Gideon help Teddy in a time of dire need? [*He uses herbs to save Teddy from blindness.*]
3. Why does Gideon refuse to share his remedy with the scientist? [*He is loyal to his heritage.*]

angry politeness: "I'm looking for the root, baas." And indeed, he would frequently bend sideways and trail his hand among the grasses with a gesture that was insulting in its perfunctoriness. He walked them through the bush along unknown paths for two hours, in that melting destroying heat, so that the sweat trickled coldly down them and their heads ached. They were all quite silent: the Farquars because they were angry, the scientist because he was being proved right again; there was no such plant. His was a tactful silence.

At last, six miles from the house, Gideon suddenly decided they had had enough; or perhaps his anger evaporated at that moment. He picked up, without an attempt at looking anything but casual, a handful of blue flowers from the grass, flowers that had been growing plentifully all down the paths they had come.

He handed them to the scientist without looking at him, and marched off by himself on the way home, leaving them to follow him if they chose.

When they got back to the house, the scientist went to the kitchen to thank Gideon: He was being very polite, even though there was an amused look in his eyes. Gideon was not there. Throwing the flowers casually into the back of his car, the eminent visitor departed on his way back to his laboratory.

Gideon was back in his kitchen in time to prepare dinner, but he was sulking. He spoke to Mr. Farquar like an unwilling servant. It was days before they liked each other again.

The Farquars made inquiries about the root from their laborers. Sometimes they were answered with distrustful stares. Sometimes the natives said: "We do not know. We have never heard of the root." One, the cattle boy, who had been with them a long time, and had grown to trust them a little, said: "Ask your boy in the kitchen. Now, there's a doctor for you. He's the son of a famous medicine man who used to be in these parts, and there's nothing he cannot cure." Then he added politely: "Of course, he's not as good as the white man's doctor, we know that, but he's good for us."

After some time, when the soreness had gone from between the Farquars and Gideon, they began to joke: "When are you going to show us the snake root, Gideon?" And he would laugh and shake his head, saying, a little uncomfortably: "But I did show you, missus, have you forgotten?"

Much later, Teddy, as a schoolboy, would come into the kitchen and say: "You old rascal, Gideon! Do you remember that time you tricked us all by making us walk miles all over the veld for nothing? It was so far my father had to carry me!"

And Gideon would double up with polite laughter. After much laughing, he would suddenly straighten himself up, wipe his old eyes, and look sadly at Teddy, who was grinning mischievously at him across the kitchen: "Ah, Little Yellow Head, how you have grown! Soon you will be grown up with a farm of your own. . . ." Ⓗ

Ⓗ Literary Perspectives **Analyzing Political Context** How is the relationship between Teddy and Gideon influenced by their social classes?

California Standards, pp. 1365–1367

- **Reading Standard 3.2** Analyze the way in which the theme or meaning of a selection represents a view or comment on life, using textual evidence to support the claim.
- **Reading Standard 3.7** Analyze recognized works of world literature from a variety of authors: **c.** Evaluate the philosophical, political, religious, ethical, and social influences of the historical period that shaped the characters, plots, and settings.
- **Reading Standard 3.8** Analyze the clarity and consistency of political assumptions in a selection of literary works or essays on a topic (e.g., suffrage, women's role in organized labor). (Political approach)
- **Grades 9–10 Review Reading Standard 1.1** Identify and use the literal and figurative meanings of words and understand word derivations.
- **Grades 9–10 Review Reading Standard 3.4** Determine characters' traits by what the characters say about themselves in narration, dialogue, dramatic monologue, and soliloquy.
- **Writing Standard 1.1** Identify and use the literal and figurative meanings of words and understand word derivations.
- **Writing Standard 1.2** Use point of view, characterization, style (e.g., use of irony), and related elements for specific rhetorical and aesthetic purposes.
- **Writing Standard 1.3** Structure ideas and arguments in a sustained, persuasive, and sophisticated way and support them with precise and relevant examples.
- **Writing Standard 2.1** Write fictional, autobiographical, or biographical narratives: **c.** Describe with concrete sensory details the sights, sounds, and smells of a scene and the specific actions, movements, gestures, and feelings of the characters; use interior monologue to depict the characters' feelings.
- **Writing Standard 2.3** Write reflective compositions: **a.** Explore the significance of personal experiences, events, conditions, or concerns by using rhetorical strategies (e.g., narration, description, exposition, persuasion).
- **Writing Standard 2.4** Write historical investigation reports: **a.** Use exposition, narration, description, argumentation, or some combination of rhetorical strategies to support the main proposition.

Applying Your Skills

Reading Standard 3.2, 3.7c, 3.8; Grades 9–10
Review Reading Standard 3.4 (see pages A48–A50)
Writing Standard 1.2 (see pages A51–A52)

No Witchcraft for Sale

Literary Response and Analysis

Reading Skills Focus

Quick Check

1. Describe the relationship between Gideon and Teddy at the start of the story. What incident causes a change in their relationship?
2. What happens when the scientist tries to get the plant's name from Gideon?

Read with a Purpose

3. How would you describe the relationship between the Farquars and Gideon? How is the relationship affected by the political climate?

Reading Skills: Identifying Historical Context

4. As you read, you took notes on historical context, characters, and conflicts. Now, make a general statement about ways that politics and social class can affect human relationships.

Literary Skills Focus

Literary Analysis

5. **Infer** Why do you think Gideon refuses to share his wisdom with the Farquars? Do you think his refusal is justified? Explain your response.
6. **Analyze** Re-read Gideon's comment at the end of the story. What does it reveal about his understanding of the relationship between white European and black African cultures?
7. **Interpret** In her preface to *African Stories,* Lessing reveals that she holds the British responsible for much of the suffering in Southern Rhodesia. Does she really feel the Farquars are people of goodwill, or is there some irony in her attitude? Support your answer with details from the story.
8. **Evaluate** Mrs. Farquar tells Gideon he is "an instrument for [God's] goodness." Do you think Gideon considers this statement to be a compliment? Why or why not?
9. **Literary Perspectives** The events Lessing narrates are definitely affected by their political context. However, could the basic conflict occur anywhere, at any time, in any culture? Explain.

Literary Skills: Theme

10. **Draw Conclusions** How would you state the theme of the story? Use evidence from the story to support your response.

Literary Skills Review: Characterization

11. **Analyze** The process by which a writer reveals the personality of a character, **characterization,** can be direct or indirect. What direct statements does Lessing provide to help us understand the character of Mrs. Farquar?
12. **Compare and Contrast** The writer subtly contrasts Teddy with Gideon's own little son. Find details that make you aware of the differences.

Writing Skills Focus

Think as a Reader/Writer

Use It in Your Writing In your *Reader/Writer Notebook,* you recorded words Lessing uses to describe her characters. Now, write a description of another character who might take part in a conflict similar to the one in the story. Use direct and indirect methods to make your character come alive.

What Do You Think Now Do Mrs. Farquar and Gideon "agree to disagree"? Do the characters in the story accept that a certain degree of social and cultural conflict is inevitable? Explain.

Universal Access

Struggling Writers

Some students may need additional scaffolding to complete the Writing Skills Focus activity. Remind students that *direct* characterization involves overtly revealing information about a character, while *indirect* characterization reveals what the character is like through his or her speech, thoughts, actions, and interactions with other characters. This difference can be explained as "telling" for direct and "showing" for indirect. Have students create a list of characteristics and traits describing their character. Tell them to use both characterizations in their paragraph.

What Do You Think Now?

Encourage students to consider the different background and motivations of the two characters. Ask them to consider why Mrs. Farquar and Gideon would prefer to "agree to disagree" than maintain a relationship of conflict.

Check for Understanding

Independent Practice

Reading Skills Focus

Possible responses:

1. *They are close at first; a change occurs when Teddy says of Gideon's son, "He's only a black boy."*
2. *Gideon refuses to provide the men with his ancestral remedy.*
3. *The Farquars are generally kind but would never consider a servant an equal.*
4. *Have students make a general statement about the effects of politics and social class on natural interactions between people.*

Literary Skills Focus

Possible responses:

5. *He believes that the plant is only for those "born to healing." Some may feel his viewpoint is justified and reflects pride and dignity; others may find his refusal selfish.*
6. *Gideon's final comment shows his understanding that the colonialists have control of the land.*
7. *Some may argue the author finds the Farquars reprehensible. Others may feel that Lessing sees the Farquars as pawns of a larger social structure. Lessing may have been sarcastic when she wrote "It is God's will" regarding the master-servant dynamic of the boys.*
8. *Yes, he is pleased to be used by God. No, Mrs. Farquar seems to view everything as an instrument for [God's] goodness.*
9. *Students should recognize that this type of conflict could arise in any hierarchical society.*
10. *Politics and social class create a powerful barrier between people that inhibits natural interactions.*
11. *She "felt a warm impulse toward her cook"; "Mr. and Mrs. Farquar were flustered and pleased and flattered."*
12. *Gideon's son was afraid to come near the scooter, but Teddy "showed off in front of him."*

Independent Practice
Vocabulary Development
Vocabulary Check
1. *b* **2.** *a*
3. *a* **4.** *b*
5. *a*

Your Turn
Possible responses:
1. *with great love and affection*
2. *using it to restore*
3. *barely saying "hello" and "goodbye"*

go.hrw.com **WordSharp: An Interactive Vocabulary Tutor**

English for Academic Success
Language Coach
Possible responses:
1. helplessly *modifies* peered
2. vigorously *modifies* chewed
3. forcibly *modifies* took

English for Academic Success
Academic Vocabulary
Possible response: *Responses will vary. Have students support their viewpoints on the cause of the changes in Gideon's behavior with evidence from the text.*

Applying Your Skills

Grades 9–10 Review Reading Standard 1.1 (see pages A48–A50)

No Witchcraft for Sale

Vocabulary Development

Vocabulary Check

Be sure you can justify your answer to each question below about the Vocabulary words.

1. Which word is the opposite of **reverently?** (a) respectively (b) mockingly
2. What word means the same as **efficacy?** (a) effectiveness (b) ineffectiveness
3. Which word describes someone who is **perfunctory?** (a) indifferent (b) enthusiastic
4. If something is **annulled,** is it (a) verified or (b) canceled?
5. If you say someone is acting **perversely,** do you mean that the person is acting (a) in a contrary way or (b) in an eager way?

Vocabulary Skills: Context Clues

Context refers to the words and sentences that surround a particular word. Sometimes the context of an unfamiliar word can give you a clue to the word's meaning. There are several types of context clues:

1. **Restatement clues:** The meaning of the unfamiliar word is restated somewhere in its context.

   The mother's *fortitude*—her *courage and perseverance*—saw her through the ordeal.

2. **Contrast clues:** The unfamiliar word is contrasted with a familiar word.

   One explorer's *fortitude* contrasted with the other's *weakness.*

3. **Example clues:** An example of the word is found in its context.

   Men like Gideon had to show *fortitude* to survive; for example, they had to exhibit *courage in the face of racism.*

Your Turn

What context clues might help you guess the meanings of the boldface Vocabulary words?

1. With great love and affection, Gideon **reverently** held the little boy's curls.
2. Gideon proved the **efficacy** of the root he found by using it to restore Teddy's sight.
3. They had a **perfunctory** conversation, barely saying "hello" and "goodbye."

Language Coach

Suffix *-ly* Remember that the suffix *-ly* is added to some words to create adverbs. Read the following sentences that include adverbs from the story. Name the adverb, and tell what word in the sentence it modifies, or describes.

1. She peered helplessly into the bush.
2. He chewed the root vigorously.
3. He took the child forcibly from his mother.

Academic Vocabulary

Write About

From Gideon's perspective, the change in his relationship to Teddy is inevitable, and he seems to adapt automatically to a different role as Teddy grows older. In a short essay, analyze whether the behavior Gideon exhibits toward Teddy alters because of the Farquars' or society's expectations.

Universal Access: Vocabulary Development

Struggling Readers

Review the three types of context clues introduced on p. 1366. Then, have students create sentences using the Vocabulary words from the selection. Tell them to insert clues that provide information about the meaning of the word. Encourage students to use restatement, contrast, and example clues in their sentences. Then, pair students and have them read each other's sentences and determine whether sufficient context clues are provided for them to guess the meaning of the Vocabulary word.

✔ See the **Academic and Selection Vocabulary Builder** in **UA: Differentiating Instruction.**

Writing Standard 1.1, 1.3, 2.1c, 2.3a, 2.4a (see pages A51–A52)

Grammar Link

Effective Sentences: Parallelism

When you use **parallelism** within sentences, you use the same grammatical form to express two or more equally important ideas. Always use the same form to

- coordinate ideas

  Correct: The servant's duties included cooking and growing plants. *Incorrect:* The servant's duties included to cook and growing plants.

- compare and contrast ideas

  Correct: She was better at ordering her servants than at cleaning the house herself. *Incorrect:* She was better at ordering her servants than to clean the house herself.

- link ideas with correlative conjunctions (*both ... and, either ... or, neither ... nor, not only ... but also*)

  Correct: The scooter was neither new nor cheap. *Incorrect:* The scooter was neither new and it wasn't cheap.

Your Turn

Use parallelism to rewrite the following sentences.

1. Gideon was not only a kind man but also he was good at healing.
2. Teddy liked to ride his scooter and frightening Gideon's little boy.
3. Teddy loved Gideon for saving his life and because he gave the boy a lot of attention.
4. Gideon ignored the doctor, marching into the house and who demanded the herbs.

Writing Application Scan a piece of your writing, and underline any instances of parallelism. Check to see if you have used parallelism correctly to coordinate ideas, compare and contrast ideas, or link ideas with correlative conjunctions.

CHOICES

As you respond to the Choices, use these **Academic Vocabulary** words as appropriate: perspective, considerably, adapt, exhibit, inevitable.

REVIEW

Use Another Point of View

"No Witchcraft for Sale" is told by an **omniscient narrator,** a narrator who is outside the story and knows everything that is going on in the story. Rewrite a scene from the story from a first-person perspective (using the pronoun *I*), perhaps from the point of view of Mrs. Farquar or Gideon. You might even choose to let the scientist or doctor tell the story, or you might have Teddy tell the story years after the incident happened.

CONNECT

Make a Policy Recommendation

Timed Writing Think of an inequity that exists in today's society. What can be done to correct it? Write a brief essay in which you suggest one way to make our society more just. Define what you see as the problem, tell why it merits attention, and propose your solution.

EXTEND

Research Colonialism in Africa

What do you know about colonialism and its lingering effects? Choose a sub-Saharan African country other than Liberia. Use library or Internet resources to learn about the country's colonial history and its effects. Write a short report to share with your class.

Learn It Online
Explore context clues with *WordSharp*.
go.hrw.com H12-1367 Go

Independent Practice

Grammar Link

Your Turn

1. *Gideon was not only kind but also good at healing.*
2. *Teddy liked to ride his scooter and frighten the little boy.*
3. *Teddy loved Gideon not only because Gideon saved his life but also because Gideon gave him a lot of attention.*
4. *Gideon refused the request of the doctor, who marched into the house and demanded herbs.*

Choices: Evaluation Criteria

Review: Homework
Use Another Point of View

Scenes are consistent with the characterization, themes, and plot depicted in the original story.

Connect: Timed Writing 40–50 Minutes

Students clearly identify a problem, explain why that problem is significant, and propose a solution.

Extend: Homework
Research Colonialism in Africa

Reports demonstrate adequate research of a country's colonial history and its effects.

Assess

Unit 6 Resources,
Selection Standards Check, p. 217

Reteach

ThinkCentral Online Remediation

Learn It Online
WordSharp: An Interactive Vocabulary Tutor provides additional support for vocabulary development. Multimedia tutorials show students how to apply vocabulary skills to unfamiliar words—and how to make those words their own.
go.hrw.com H12-1367 Go

Universal Access: Grammar Link

Struggling Writers

To help students understand the use of correlative conjunctions, write the following sentences on the board:

- Carlos is either studying with Jeff or practicing football.
- Sarah is not only popular but also friendly.

Explain that both sentences use pairs of conjunctions (*either . . . or; not only . . . but also*) to link ideas. For this reason, the words that follow each part of the conjunction are grammatically parallel. In the first sentence, the words *either* and *or* are both followed by gerunds. In the second sentence, the words *not only* and *but also* are both followed by adjectives.

✔ For more practice with parallelism, see **Warriner's Handbook, GrammarNotes,** and **Language Handbook Worksheets.**

Standards Focus

Objectives

Students will
- understand the use of symbols
- evaluate language structures

Selection Introduction

Think About the Writer

Ask students if they have ever disagreed with U.S. policies, attitudes, or military actions, and, if so, whether they think their dissent makes them less patriotic.

For Independent Reading

- *Kaffir Boy: The True Story of a Black Youth's Coming of Age in Apartheid South Africa,* Mark Mathabane
- *Waiting for the Barbarians,* J. M. Coetzee

Motivate

What Do You Think?/QuickWrite

Ask students to think about how and why people isolate themselves. Can one do so without the aid of physical barriers? Have students use their **Reader/Writer Notebooks** to record their thoughts.

English for Academic Success

Academic Vocabulary

Look for opportunities to use the Academic Vocabulary words in this unit.

- **considerably,** ***adv.:*** by a large amount

California Standards, pp. 1368–1375

- **Reading Standard 2.2** Analyze the way in which clarity of meaning is affected by the patterns of organization, hierarchical structures, repetition of the main ideas, syntax, and word choice in the text.
- **Grades 9–10 Review Reading Standard 3.7** Recognize and understand the significance of various literary devices, including figurative language, imagery, allegory, and symbolism, and explain their appeal.

Preparing to Read

Once upon a Time

What Do You Think? How does experience shape our view of the world?

QuickWrite

People use all sorts of devices to "wall themselves off," or to keep themselves away from others. In your *Reader/Writer Notebook,* make a list of these "walls" or ways in which people separate themselves.

Nadine Gordimer, New York (1991).

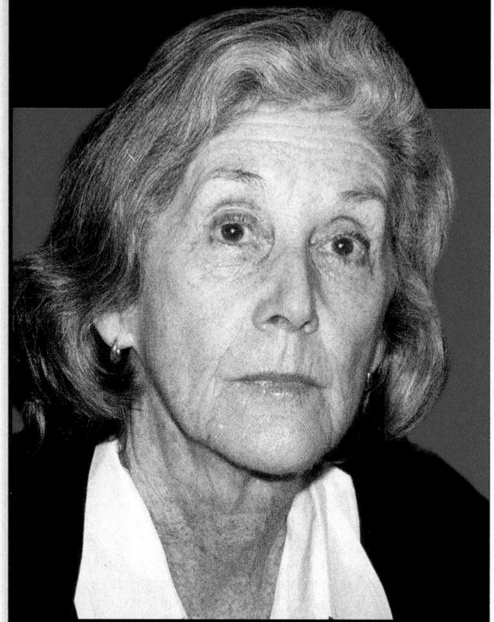

MEET THE WRITER

Nadine Gordimer

(1923–)

Nobel Prize Winner

Nadine Gordimer, the daughter of a Lithuanian father and an English mother, grew up in a small mining town about thirty miles from Johannesburg, South Africa. Like most colonials, her family adopted European conventions and values. Gordimer spent most of her childhood reading because she found middle-class colonial society extremely dull. This society, and its injustices, later served as the inspiration for much of her writing, which explores the devastating effects of racism.

A Strong New Voice

Gordimer began writing at the age of nine during a period in which she was removed from school because of sickness. When her short story collection *The Soft Voice of the Serpent* appeared in 1952, critics hailed Gordimer as a strong new voice who drew fresh, authentic perceptions of African life. Among her best-known novels is *July's People* (1981), in which the white people in South Africa become servants of the black Africans. In 1991, she won the Nobel Prize in Literature.

A Society out of Joint

One critic has called Gordimer "one of the very few links between white and black in South Africa. . . ." Although much of Gordimer's writing concerns the troubles of her nation, she does not see herself as a political writer. "Here I live in a society which is fundamentally out of joint. One can't but be politically concerned," she has said. Nevertheless, she disclaims a political agenda: "I don't understand politics except in terms of what politics does to influence lives. What interests me is the infinite variety of effects apartheid has on men and women."

When apartheid was in effect, Gordimer's writing irked the government of South Africa considerably, and three of her novels were subsequently banned. Nevertheless, she has always considered herself "an intensely loyal South African. I care deeply for my country."

Think About the Writer How do you think Gordimer could still love her country if it forced people to live under laws she considered unjust and destructive?

Selection Readability	
Easily Accessible **Accessible** Challenging	simple sentence structure; chronological order; accessible theme; familiar genre

Reading Standard 2.2; Grades 9–10 Review
Reading Standard 3.7 (see pages A48–A50)

Literary Skills Focus

Symbols A **symbol** is something that stands both for itself and for something beyond itself. Established symbols—sometimes known as public symbols—include the flags that stand for various states or nations, the dove that represents peace, and the bald eagle that stands for the United States. Writers and artists often create their own personal, unique symbols, the meanings of which are revealed in the course of a poem, story, or novel. As you read this story, note how Gordimer uses symbolism to dramatize the chilling effect of racial prejudice and inequality.

Reading Skills Focus

Identifying Language Structures When a story begins "Once upon a time ...," you assume you are about to hear a fairy tale because you recognize the characteristic **language structure.** In "Once upon a Time," Gordimer uses several language structures from the literature of fairy tales, and because she repeats these phrases and sentences, her story "sounds" like a fairy tale. Her insistent repetition of these language structures also adds to the story's dramatic momentum, for we soon realize this is no fairy tale.

Into Action As you read Gordimer's story, record in a chart like the one below language structures that remind you of fairy tales. You may wish to begin with the title and move chronologically through the story.

Typical Fairy-Tale Phrases and Sentences
1. Title of story is "Once upon a time"
2.
3.
4.

Writing Skills Focus

Think as a Reader/Writer

Find It in Your Reading In addition to containing repeated language structures, fairy tales feature stock character types and plot events. As you read, record in your *Reader/Writer Notebook* details in the story that are reminiscent of fairy tales. Concentrate on character types and events.

Reader/Writer Notebook
Use your **RWN** to complete the activities for this selection.

Vocabulary

apertures (AP uhr churz) *n.:* openings. *The woman was listening so intensely that she felt as if the apertures of her ears were widening.*

distend (dihs TEHND) *v.:* expand; swell. *Having eaten both a large breakfast and lunch, the worker felt his stomach distend.*

itinerant (y TIHN uhr uhnt) *adj.:* migratory. *Itinerant workers came to the suburb looking for employment.*

audaciously (aw DAY shuhs lee) *adv.:* boldly. *Some intruders audaciously drank the whiskey in the cabinets of the houses they robbed.*

aesthetics (ehs THEHT ihks) *n.:* principles of beauty. *The writer ridiculed the homeowners by saying they tried to combine the aesthetics of prison architecture with Spanish villa style.*

serrated (SEHR ay tihd) *v.* used as *adj.:* marked along the edge with jagged, sawlike notches. *Serrated blades of steel were placed all along the metal coil in order to tear apart any intruder who tried to climb over it.*

Language Coach

Accented Syllables In the pronunciation guide to the Vocabulary words, the accented syllable is printed in capital letters. Practice pronouncing each of the Vocabulary words, paying special attention to the syllable that is accented. Which two Vocabulary words are not accented on the second syllable?

Learn It Online
There is more to words than just definitions. Get the whole story with Word Watch online.
go.hrw.com H12-1369 Go

Selection Resources

Unit 6 Resources, on-level practice and assessment, p. 220

Teacher One Stop™, on-level lesson plans and all print resources

Holt Audio Library

Holt Audio Library: Selections and Summaries in Spanish

UA: Differentiating Instruction, graphic organizer, p. 316

UA: Supporting Instruction in Spanish, selection summary

Analyzing Visuals Transparencies, p. 49

ThinkCentral Online Assessment, Selection Standards Check

ThinkCentral Online Remediation

Preteach

Introducing Vocabulary

Read aloud the Vocabulary words and sample sentences. Then, use this activity to check students' understanding.

1. Explain why all cameras have **apertures**.
2. Tell what happens to something when it **distends**.
3. Explain why many farms hire **itinerant** workers.
4. Name a celebrity who is known for behaving **audaciously**.
5. List one occupation that requires someone to appreciate **aesthetics**.
6. Explain why a good bread knife must be **serrated**.

English for Academic Success

Language Coach

After students practice saying the Vocabulary words, model for students the correct pronunciation of these related words: *overture, extend, itinerary, loquacious, athletics, corrugated.*

Literary Skills Focus

During reading, direct students to jot down symbols that develop the theme of racial inequality.

Reading Skills Focus

Give students a copy of the Reading Skills Focus graphic organizer before they read. (See **Unit 6 Resources**.)

Writing Skills Focus

Have students record examples of fairy-tale language structures, character types, and plot events in their **Reader/Writer Notebooks**. Students can use their notes to complete the Writing Skills Focus activity.

Learn It Online
Send students to **Word Watch** for audio pronunciations, synonyms and antonyms, and brief histories of word origins.
go.hrw.com H12-1369 Go

Teacher Preparation

Selection Plot Summary

In "Once Upon a Time," the writer is awakened one night and makes up a bitter parody of a fairy tale to lull herself back to sleep. In the story, a wealthy white couple and their son seem to be living a "happily ever after" kind of life. They live in a society torn by racial strife, however. For protection, the couple invests in a series of increasingly elaborate security devices. Finally, in desperate fear, the wealthy couple installs a coil of serrated metal atop the walls surrounding their home and yard. One day their young son climbs into the tunnel of blades and is ensnared in its deadly grip. He is hacked out of the "razor teeth" and carried into the house, his fate unresolved at the story's end.

Direct Teach

Think About/Talk About

Read with a Purpose Have students read the Read with a Purpose statement. Point out that the statement asks students to determine if this story is intended for children or adults. As students read the story, have them look for disturbing imagery or events that would not be suitable for children.

SHORT STORY

ONCE UPON A TIME

by **Nadine Gordimer**

Read with a Purpose

Read to find out whether this fairy tale is written for children or for adults.

Build Background

Until the 1990s, South Africa under white rule enforced a policy called apartheid (ah PAHRT hayt), the legal separation of races. Black South Africans and other people who were not white experienced brutal political and economic discrimination.

Most black South Africans were forced to live in remote areas or all-black "townships" bordering white cities. The only black people who could live in white cities were those with employment, a practice that in effect split up families. To enter cities, black and other nonwhite South Africans were required to show "passbooks" that identified them by name, residency, and race.

In 1993, after decades of riots and rebellions that left thousands of black people dead and most of their leaders jailed, the white government—under both internal and international pressure—repealed the apartheid laws. One year later, the first all-race election swept the black South African leader Nelson Mandela, a former political prisoner, into office as president. "Once upon a Time" is set during the era when apartheid was still law.

Someone has written to ask me to contribute to an anthology of stories for children. I reply that I don't write children's stories; and he writes back that at a recent congress/book fair/seminar a certain novelist said every writer ought to write at least one story for children. I think of sending a postcard saying I don't accept that I "ought" to write anything.

And then last night I woke up—or rather was wakened without knowing what had roused me.

A voice in the echo chamber of the subconscious?

A sound.

A creaking of the kind made by the weight carried by one foot after another along a wooden floor. I listened. I felt the apertures of my ears distend with concentration. Again: the creaking. I was waiting for it; waiting to hear if it indicated that feet were moving from room to room, coming up the passage—to my door. I have no burglar bars, no gun under the pillow,

Vocabulary **apertures** (AP uhr churz) *n.:* openings.
distend (dihs TEHND) *v.:* expand; swell.

Universal Access

English Learners

English for Academic Success Some of the terms describing mining may be unfamiliar to some students. Explain that *buckling* means bending or collapsing. *Undermined ground* refers to ground that has been excavated but also weakened by the digging underneath. In mining, the *face* designates the front of an area being excavated.

✔ See the **English Language Skill Builder** in **UA: Differentiating Instruction.**

Struggling Readers

Strategic Students Model identifying language structures in this story. Tell students that they should note repeated phrases and sentences that remind them of fairy tales. Point out on p. 1371 the story starts with the structure, "In a . . . , there was a . . . . who . . . . ." Then the structure "They had . . ." repeats. Tell students that since these structures are commonly used to begin fairy tales, they should note these phrases in their graphic organizer.

but I have the same fears as people who do take these precautions, and my windowpanes are thin as rime,[1] could shatter like a wineglass. A woman was murdered (how do they put it) in broad daylight in a house two blocks away, last year, and the fierce dogs who guarded an old widower and his collection of antique clocks were strangled before he was knifed by a casual laborer he had dismissed without pay.

I was staring at the door, making it out in my mind rather than seeing it, in the dark. I lay quite still—a victim already—but the arrhythmia[2] of my heart was fleeing, knocking this way and that against its body-cage. How finely tuned the senses are, just out of rest, sleep! I could never listen intently as that in the distractions of the day; I was reading every faintest sound, identifying and classifying its possible threat.

But I learned that I was to be neither threatened nor spared. There was no human weight pressing on the boards, the creaking was a buckling, an epicenter[3] of stress. I was in it. The house that surrounds me while I sleep is built on undermined ground; far beneath my bed, the floor, the house's foundations, the stopes[4] and passages of gold mines have hollowed the rock, and when some face trembles, detaches, and falls, three thousand feet below, the whole house shifts slightly, bringing uneasy strain to the balance and counterbalance of brick, cement, wood, and glass that hold it as a structure around me. The misbeats of my heart tailed off like the last muffled flourishes on one of the wooden xylophones made by the Chopi and Tsonga[5] migrant miners who might have been down there, under me in the earth at that moment. The stope where the fall was could have been disused, dripping water from its ruptured veins; or men might now be interred there in the most profound of tombs. **A**

I couldn't find a position in which my mind would let go of my body—release me to sleep again. So I began to tell myself a story; a bedtime story.

In a house, in a suburb, in a city, there were a man and his wife who loved each other very much and were living happily ever after. They had a little boy, and they loved him very much. They had a cat and a dog that the little boy loved very much. They had a car and a caravan trailer for holidays, and a swimming pool which was fenced so that the little boy and

1. **rime:** tiny ice crystals that can form on grass and leaves.
2. **arrhythmia** (uh RIHTH mee uh): irregular beating.
3. **epicenter:** central point.

4. **stopes:** excavations.
5. **Chopi** (CHOH pee) **and Tsonga** (TSAHNG gah): Bantu-speaking peoples of Mozambique in southeastern Africa. *Tsonga* is often spelled *Thonga.*

A Literary Focus Symbols What might be symbolic about a house that rests on shaky ground?

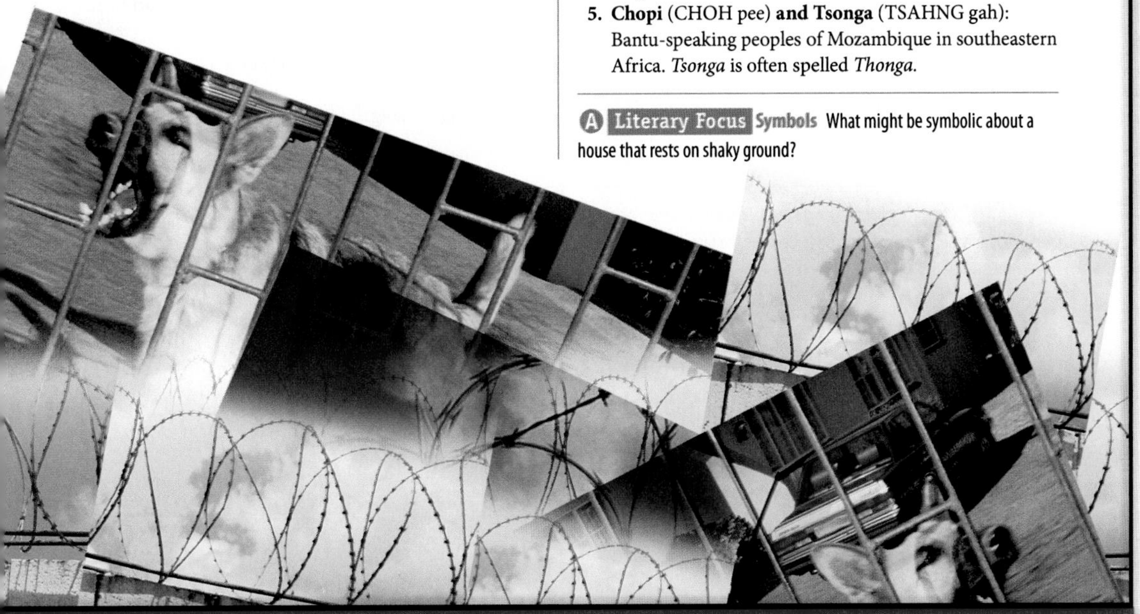

Advanced Learners

Acceleration Challenge students to analyze Gordimer's diction, specifically the denotation and connotation of key words and phrases in this story. Students can begin their analysis with the following questions.

- Each time the word *housemaid* appears in the story, the adjective *trusted* modifies it. Why? What are the implications of this word choice?
- The family's cat is usually referred to as the "pet cat." What is Gordimer's reason for using the adjective *pet*?

Students and Disabilities

Explain to students that the author wishes to establish an unsettling mood from the onset of the story by employing language and images typically associated with fear. As students read, encourage them to record words, images, or symbols that suggest apprehension.

✔ See **UA: Differentiating Instruction** for a graphic organizer to scaffold instruction for students with disabilities.

Think About/Talk About

Analysis

A Literary Focus

Possible response: *The house is in danger of crashing down, mirroring the unsound foundations of a society built on racial injustice. The search for gold (the cause of the weakened ground beneath the house) has undermined a basic human need: domestic security.*

Extend the Discussion

Drawing Conclusions What are the writer's beliefs concerning the kind of works that writers produce? ***Possible response:*** *Gordimer believes that a writer is never bound to certain standards and expectations; writers should be able to write freely in whatever form they choose, not forced.*

Determining Author's Purpose Why does the author choose to open the story with an account of herself lying alone and helpless at night? ***Possible response:*** *The opening sets an immediate tone of vulnerability by describing a universal fear: the threat of being ambushed or attacked by an intruder in the dark of night.*

Vocabulary: Own the Word

- **apertures:** Remind students that the word *apertures* means "openings." Ask students to explain what Gordimer meant when she said the *apertures* of her ears were widening. ***Possible responses:*** *She meant that she was listening intently to each little sound that she heard.*
- **distend:** Write *distend* in a center circle on the board and provide a definition: "swell." Draw spider legs from the center and ask students to add concepts and attributes. ***Possible responses:*** *inflate, expand, open up*

Model the Skill

- Remind students that a **symbol** stands for itself and for something beyond itself. Explain that interpreting a symbol requires thinking about it within the context of a story; the same element may have different meanings in different works.
- Model interpreting a symbol in the context of this story. You might say: "The burglar bars that the family attaches to their doors and windows symbolize their fear of intrusion but also demonstrate their imprisonment within their own system. We know this because the family now sees 'the trees and sky through bars.'"

Guided Practice: Apply

Turn-and-Talk Have students work in small groups to find symbols and interpret them by examining the text closely for clues. Ask volunteers to share their interpretations with the class.

his playmates would not fall in and drown. They had a housemaid who was absolutely trustworthy and an itinerant gardener who was highly recommended by the neighbors. For when they began to live happily ever after they were warned, by that wise old witch, the husband's mother, not to take on anyone off the street. They were inscribed[6] in a medical benefit society, their pet dog was licensed, they were insured against fire, flood damage, and theft, and subscribed to the local Neighborhood Watch, which supplied them with a plaque for their gates lettered YOU HAVE BEEN WARNED over the silhouette of a would-be intruder. He was masked; it could not be said if he was black or white, and therefore proved the property owner was no racist. **B**

It was not possible to insure the house, the swimming pool, or the car against riot damage. There were riots, but these were outside the city, where people of another color were quartered. These people were not allowed into the suburb except as reliable housemaids and gardeners, so there was nothing to fear, the husband told the wife. Yet she was afraid that some day such people might come up the street and tear off the plaque YOU HAVE BEEN WARNED and open the gates and stream in .... Nonsense, my dear, said the husband, there are police and soldiers and tear gas and guns to keep them away. But to please her—for he loved her very much and buses were being burned, cars stoned, and schoolchildren shot by the police in those quarters out of sight and hearing of the suburb—he had electronically controlled gates fitted. Anyone who pulled off the sign YOU HAVE BEEN WARNED and tried to open the gates would have to announce his intentions by pressing a button and speaking into a receiver relayed to the house. The little boy was fascinated by the device and used it as a walkie-talkie in cops and robbers play with his small friends.

The riots were suppressed, but there were many burglaries in the suburb and somebody's trusted housemaid was tied up and shut in a cupboard by thieves while she was in charge of her employers' house. The trusted housemaid of the man and wife and little boy was so upset by this misfortune befalling a friend left, as she herself often was, with responsibility for the possessions of the man and his wife and the little boy that she implored her employers to have burglar bars attached to the doors and windows of the house, and an alarm system installed. The wife said, She is right, let us take heed of her advice. So from every window and door in the house where they were living happily ever after they now saw the trees and sky through bars, and when the little boy's pet cat tried to climb in by the fanlight[7] to keep him company in his little bed at night, as it customarily had done, it set off the alarm keening[8] through the house.

The alarm was often answered—it seemed—by other burglar alarms, in other houses, that had been

6. **inscribed:** enrolled.

7. **fanlight:** semicircular window over a door or a larger window.

8. **keening:** wailing.

B **Reading Focus** **Identifying Language Structures** What fairy-tale language does Gordimer use to describe the family's situation?

Vocabulary **itinerant** (y TIHN uhr uhnt) *adj.:* migratory.

Universal Access

Students with Disabilities

Have students retell this story in a mini picture book. Tell them to use language structures that are found in fairy tales, and encourage them to include their own minor details, adding more fairy-tale effects to the story. Remind students to base their drawings and sentences on the descriptions in the story.

Developing Oral Fluency

Individual Activity Invite interested students to prepare a dramatic reading of the fairy tale in "Once Upon a Time." Allow students sufficient time to practice reading the story and to practice using appropriate body language and vocal pitch and volume to capture the story's irony and theme. You may wish to record student performances for further analysis or sharing.

✔ See the **Oral Language Skill Builder** in **UA: Differentiating Instruction.**

triggered by pet cats or nibbling mice. The alarms called to one another across the gardens in shrills and bleats and wails that everyone soon became accustomed to, so that the din roused the inhabitants of the suburb no more than the croak of frogs and musical grating of cicadas'[9] legs. Under cover of the electronic harpies'[10] discourse intruders sawed the iron bars and broke into homes, taking away hi-fi equipment, television sets, cassette players, cameras and radios, jewelry and clothing, and sometimes were hungry enough to devour everything in the refrigerator or paused audaciously to drink the whiskey in the cabinets or patio bars. Insurance companies paid no compensation for single malt, a loss made keener by the property owner's knowledge that the thieves wouldn't even have been able to appreciate what it was they were drinking.

Then the time came when many of the people who were not trusted housemaids and gardeners hung about the suburb because they were unemployed. Some importuned for a job: weeding or painting a roof; anything, *baas*,[11] madam. But the man and his wife remembered the warning about taking on anyone off the street. Some drank liquor and fouled the street with discarded bottles. Some begged, waiting for the man or his wife to drive the car out of the electronically operated gates. They sat about with their feet in the gutters, under the jacaranda[12] trees that made a green tunnel of the street—for it was a beautiful suburb, spoiled only by their presence—and sometimes they fell asleep lying right before the gates in the midday sun. The wife could never see anyone go hungry. She sent the trusted housemaid out with bread and tea, but the trusted housemaid said these were loafers and *tsotsis*,[13] who would come and tie her up and shut her in a cupboard. The husband said, She's right. Take heed of her advice. You only encourage them with your bread and tea. They are looking for their chance. ... And he brought the little boy's tricycle from the garden into the house every night, because if the house was surely secure, once locked and with the alarm set, someone might still be able to climb over the wall or the electronically closed gates into the garden.

You are right, said the wife, then the wall should be higher. And the wise old witch, the husband's mother, paid for the extra bricks as her Christmas present to her son and his wife—the little boy got a Space Man outfit and a book of fairy tales.

But every week there were more reports of intrusion: in broad daylight and the dead of night, in the early hours of the morning, and even in the lovely summer twilight—a certain family was at dinner while the bedrooms were being ransacked upstairs. The man and his wife, talking of the latest armed robbery in the suburb, were distracted by the sight of the little boy's pet cat effortlessly arriving over the seven-foot wall, descending first with a rapid bracing of extended fore-paws down on the sheer vertical surface, and then a graceful launch, landing with swishing tail within the property. The whitewashed wall was marked with the

9. **cicadas'** (suh KAY duhz): Cicadas are large insects that make a shrill sound.
10. **harpies':** Harpies are hideous monsters from Greek mythology that have the head and trunk of a woman and the tail, legs, and talons of a bird. In some myths they are guardians of a treasure.
11. ***baas*** (bahs): Afrikaans for "master." Afrikaans, a language developed from seventeenth-century Dutch, is spoken in South Africa.
12. **jacaranda** (jak uh RAN duh): tropical tree with large clusters of blue or lavender flowers.
13. ***tsotsis*** (TSAHT sihs): colloquial expression for "flashily dressed street thugs."

Vocabulary **audaciously** (aw DAY shuhs lee) *adv.:* boldly.

Universal Access

Advanced Learners

Enrichment The author tells this story from the perspective of a white family, but other characters doubtless see the same things quite differently. Divide the class into small groups to retell the story from the point of view of the loafers, the housemaid, and the gardener. To understand the characters' perspectives, students should extrapolate from the text but also use their imagination.

Cross-Curricular Connection

HISTORY: South Africa

Under apartheid, the Population Registration Act of 1950 classified people as Bantu (black Africans of all nationalities), Colored (mixed race), and white. The reference to riots may be to the 1976 riot in Soweto (an overcrowded Johannesburg suburb), where black Africans were forced to live apart from whites.

Think About/Talk About

Comprehension

B Reading Focus

Possible responses: *Some examples include "in a house, in a suburb, in a city, there was a man and his wife"; "living happily ever after"; "wise old witch"; and "YOU HAVE BEEN WARNED."*

Extend the Discussion

Finding Details What are the two kinds of "people of another color" mentioned in the story? ***Possible response:*** *There are the trustworthy and "reliable housemaids and gardeners" allowed to work in the suburbs and the unwanted loafers or "tsotsis" who hang around looking for work.*

Interpreting In what ways is the house in this story an ironic parody of a fairy tale's "enchanted castle"? ***Possible response:*** *The house is more like a fortress or jail than a fairy-tale castle, and the adults inside live in fear. Even everyday acts such as letting in the cat at night have "alarming" effects.*

Vocabulary: Own the Word

- **itinerant:** Remind students that *itinerant* means "traveling from place to place." Have students explain what it would be like to be an *itinerant* salesperson. ***Possible responses:*** *lonely, unpredictable, exciting*
- **audaciously:** Ask students: "Have you ever acted *audaciously* and done something you never thought you would? Explain what you did, the reason why you acted so *audaciously,* and when this all occurred."

Think About/Talk About

Comprehension

Ⓒ Reading Focus

Possible response: *Dragons sometimes symbolize death and destruction. In their quest for security, the husband and wife may be courting death.*

Extend the Discussion

Making Judgments Do you think that the violent ending is necessary to make the author's point? Why or why not? ***Possible responses:*** *Yes, it drives home the story's cruel irony: The "protective devices" can harm the things they are supposed to protect. No, the ending is out of character with the rest of the fairy-tale structure of the story.*

Vocabulary: Own the Word

- **aesthetics:** Just as an *aesthete* is a person who appreciates beauty, especially in the arts, *aesthetics* is an idea of what is artistic, the study of beauty, or the way something looks. Have students describe *aesthetics* they would like to see in their bedroom.
- **serrated:** Remind students that *serrated* means "marked along the edge with jagged notches." Ask students to give examples of objects that are *serrated.* ***Possible responses:*** *knives, saws, barbed wire*

Monitor Students' Comprehension

Guide the class in answering these comprehension questions.

1. What does the author fear when she hears sounds in the night? [*She fears an intrusion.*]
2. Why does the family install gates? [*They install the gates as protection from violence.*]
3. How is the boy injured at the end of the story? [*He is cut by the jagged wire.*]

cat's comings and goings; and on the street side of the wall there were larger red-earth smudges that could have been made by the kind of broken running shoes, seen on the feet of unemployed loiterers, that had no innocent destination.

When the man and wife and little boy took the pet dog for its walk round the neighborhood streets they no longer paused to admire this show of roses or that perfect lawn; these were hidden behind an array of different varieties of security fences, walls, and devices. The man, wife, little boy, and dog passed a remarkable choice: There was the low-cost option of pieces of broken glass embedded in cement along the top of walls, there were iron grilles ending in lance points, there were attempts at reconciling the aesthetics of prison architecture with the Spanish Villa style (spikes painted pink) and with the plastic urns of neoclassical façades (twelve-inch pikes finned like zigzags of lightning and painted pure white). Some walls had a small board affixed, giving the name and telephone number of the firm responsible for the installation of the devices. While the little boy and the pet dog raced ahead, the husband and wife found themselves comparing the possible effectiveness of each style against its appearance; and after several weeks when they paused before this barricade or that without needing to speak, both came out with the conclusion that only one was worth considering. It was the ugliest but the most honest in its suggestion of the pure concentration-camp style, no frills, all evident efficacy. Placed the length of walls, it consisted of a continuous coil of stiff and shining metal serrated into jagged blades, so that there would be no way of climbing over it and no way through its tunnel without getting entangled in its fangs. There would be no way out, only a struggle getting bloodier and bloodier, a deeper and sharper hooking and tearing of flesh. The wife shuddered to look at it. You're right, said the husband, anyone would think twice…

And they took heed of the advice on a small board fixed to the wall: Consult DRAGON'S TEETH The People For Total Security. Ⓒ

Next day a gang of workmen came and stretched the razor-bladed coils all round the walls of the house where the husband and wife and little boy and pet dog and cat were living happily ever after. The sunlight flashed and slashed, off the serrations, the cornice of razor thorns encircled the home, shining. The husband said, Never mind. It will weather. The wife said, You're wrong. They guarantee it's rustproof. And she waited until the little boy had run off to play before she said, I hope the cat will take heed…. The husband said, Don't worry, my dear, cats always look before they leap. And it was true that from that day on the cat slept in the little boy's bed and kept to the garden, never risking a try at breaching security.

One evening, the mother read the little boy to sleep with a fairy story from the book the wise old witch had given him at Christmas. Next day he pretended to be the Prince who braves the terrible thicket of thorns to enter the palace and kiss the Sleeping Beauty back to life: He dragged a ladder to the wall, the shining coiled tunnel was just wide enough for his little body to creep in, and with the first fixing of its razor teeth in his knees and hands and head he screamed and struggled deeper into its tangle. The trusted housemaid and the itinerant gardener, whose "day" it was, came running, the first to see and to scream with him, and the itinerant gardener tore his hands trying to get at the little boy. Then the man and his wife burst wildly into the garden and for some reason (the cat, probably) the alarm set up wailing against the screams while the bleeding mass of the little boy was hacked out of the security coil with saws, wire cutters, choppers, and they carried it—the man, the wife, the hysterical trusted housemaid, and the weeping gardener—into the house.

Ⓒ **Reading Focus** **Identifying Language Structures** How does the "Dragon's Teeth" advertisement link the story to older fairy tales?

Vocabulary **aesthetics** (ehs THEHT ihks) *n.:* principles of beauty.
serrated (SEHR ay tihd) *v.:* used as *adj.:* marked along the edge with jagged, sawlike notches.

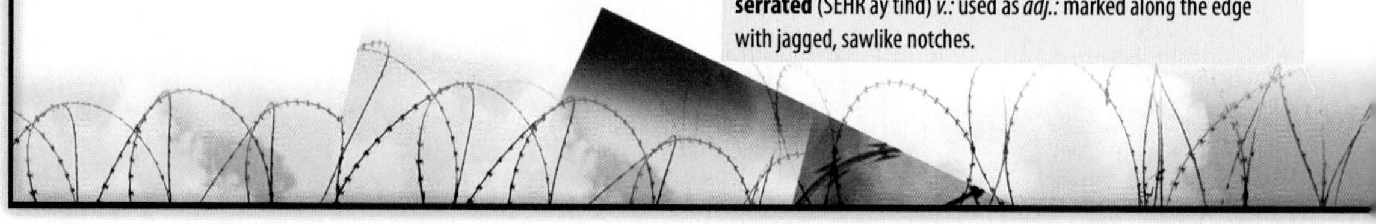

California Standards, p. 1375

- **Reading Standard 2.2** Analyze the way in which clarity of meaning is affected by the patterns of organization, hierarchical structures, repetition of the main ideas, syntax, and word choice in the text.
- **Reading Standard 3.3** Analyze the ways in which irony, tone, mood, the author's style, and the "sound" of language achieve specific rhetorical or aesthetic purposes or both.
- **Grades 9–10 Review Reading Standard 3.7** Recognize and understand the significance of various literary devices, including figurative language, imagery, allegory, and symbolism, and explain their appeal.
- **Writing Standard 2.1** Write fictional, autobiographical, or biographical narratives: **c.** Describe with concrete sensory details the sights, sounds, and smells of a scene and the specific actions, movements, gestures, and feelings of the characters; use interior monologue to depict the characters' feelings.

Applying Your Skills

Reading Standard 2.2, 3.3; **Grades 9–10 Review**
Reading Standard 3.7 (see pages A48–A50)
Writing Standard 2.1c (see pages A50–A51)

Once upon a Time

Literary Response and Analysis

Reading Skills Focus

Quick Check

1. What four measures do the husband and wife take to protect themselves?

Read with a Purpose

2. Is the intended audience for this story children or adults? What do you think Gordimer's purpose was in telling this "bedtime story"?

Reading Skills: Identifying Language Structures

3. As you read, you noted the fairy-tale elements of the story. Review your chart, and tell how the fairy-tale style affected your response to the story. What did you think about the way the style contrasted with the violence in the story?

Vocabulary Check

Answer these questions about Vocabulary words.

4. Is an **aperture** an opening or a closing?
5. If your eyes **distend,** do they swell or contract?
6. Is an **itinerant** person someone who stays at home or wanders around?
7. If you speak **audaciously,** are you shy or bold?
8. If you are studying **aesthetics,** are you studying ideas of beauty or theories of revolution?
9. If a knife is **serrated,** is it smooth or jagged?

Literary Skills Focus

Literary Analysis

10. **Analyze** Fairy tales often contain moral lessons. What is the moral of "Once upon a Time"?

11. **Make Judgments** Are the couple innocent homeowners who are only trying to feel secure, or are they the cause of the tragedy? Explain.

Literary Skills: Symbols

12. **Interpret** How can the security systems in the story—especially the wall—be seen as symbols? Be sure to consider the double meaning of the plaque "YOU HAVE BEEN WARNED."

Literary Skills Review: Situational Irony

13. **Analyze** When what happens is the opposite of what we expect will happen, **situational irony** occurs. What is this story's central irony? What did the parents hope to accomplish with their security systems? What actually happened?

Writing Skills Focus

Think as a Reader/Writer

Use It in Your Writing Review your notes about character types and events related to fairy tales, as well as your Into Action chart. Think of a social issue (perhaps one involving a clash of cultures) on which you could base a fairy tale with a moral lesson. Write such a fairy tale, using the appropriate character types, events, and language.

What Do You Think Now? What experiences have given this couple their fearful view of the world? Based on their experience, what might be the world-view of the story's black African characters?

Check for Understanding

Independent Practice

Reading Skills Focus

Possible responses:

1. *They protect themselves by hiring help with good references, putting bars on their windows, installing an alarm and gate, and putting razor wire on top of the high wall that surrounds their house.*
2. *Gordimer tells this story to adults and mature children to prompt them to examine the evils of racism.*
3. *Students' responses will vary. Students may feel that the contrast heightened the irony and made Gordimer's message more powerful or that it was too disturbing or contrived to be effective.*

Vocabulary Check

4. *opening* 5. *swell*
6. *wanders* 7. *bold*
8. *beauty* 9. *jagged*

Literary Skills Focus

Possible responses:

10. *Unlike most fairy tales, which are not concerned with social equality, this fairy tale seeks to teach the reader that security cannot exist in a society that is based on inequality.*
11. *They can be seen as part of the problem because they accept the racism of their society. They also can be seen as victims of a racist society that they did not create.*
12. *The wall and the security system symbolize racism and fear. The warning posted on the wall is ironic because the warning applies to the couple inside the barriers as well as those outside them.*
13. *The wall, which was supposed to protect the family, ends up harming it. The razor wire injures the couple's young son.*

Universal Access

Struggling Writers

Some students may need additional scaffolding to complete this task. First, provide students with a list of social issues to choose from, such as racial or gender inequality, illegal immigration, or poverty. Have students brainstorm possible character types and events reminiscent of fairy tales that they could use in their story. Then, have them express the moral lesson of their story in a sentence. As students write, tell them to refer to the language structure chart they composed earlier so that they can incorporate similar structures in their story.

What Do You Think Now?

Encourage students to consider the riots and government injustice that black South Africans experienced on a routine basis. Ask them to speculate on how such experiences would have created a climate of fear.

Assess

Unit 6 Resources,
Selection Standards Check, p. 223

Standards Focus

Objectives

Students will

- analyze irony, including verbal and situational irony
- identify and understand cultural characteristics of a text

Selection Introduction

Think About the Writer

Ask students to compare Achebe's belief about the purpose of art to other perspectives people have about art's purpose.

For Independent Reading

- *The Bride Price*, Buchi Emecheta
- *Ties That Bind, Ties That Break: A Novel*, Lensey Namioka

Motivate

What Do You Think?/QuickTalk

Have partners brainstorm social customs that have been challenged in the United States in the past centuries. Were they justified? Why or why not?

English for Academic Success

Academic Vocabulary

Look for opportunities to use the Academic Vocabulary words in this unit.

- **exhibit, *v.*:** show, demonstrate
- **perspective, *n.*:** particular way of looking at something

California Standards, pp. 1376–1383

- **Reading Standard 3.3** Analyze the ways in which irony, tone, mood, the author's style, and the "sound" of language achieve specific rhetorical or aesthetic purposes or both.
- **Reading Standard 3.7** Analyze recognized works of world literature from a variety of authors: **c.** Evaluate the philosophical, political, religious, ethical, and social influences of the historical period that shaped the characters, plots, and settings.

Preparing to Read

Marriage Is a Private Affair

What Do You Think? How does experience shape our view of the world?

QuickTalk

With a partner, discuss this question: "When, if ever, is it justifiable to challenge the customs of your society?" In your *Reader/Writer Notebook,* take notes on both your and your partner's thoughts.

Chinua Achebe, Germany (2002).

MEET THE WRITER

Chinua Achebe

(1930–)

Nigerian writer Chinua Achebe (CHIHN wah ah CHAY bay) planned to study medicine, but literature and his country's nationalist movement changed his plans.

Redefining Africa

Achebe was born in the eastern Nigerian town of Ogidi, where his father, a Christian convert, taught at the mission school. As a student, Achebe realized the destructive effects of colonialism and dedicated himself to redefining Africa and telling the true story of Africans. According to Achebe, the European idea that "Africa was the Primordial Void, was sheer humbug .... Africa had a history, a religion, a civilization." Achebe chose to write in English, which he had begun to learn at the age of eight, in order to reach a wide audience.

Stories for a Human Purpose

Achebe's novels, beginning with the celebrated *Things Fall Apart* (1958), focus on how dramatically Nigeria changed in the twentieth century. The novels trace the evolution of life in Nigeria—sometimes presented as a fictionalized nation—from the arrival of early English missionaries, through the years of colonial rule, to the post-independence era rife with corruption and political turmoil. Although Achebe believes that "Africa's meeting with Europe must be accounted a terrible disaster in this matter of human understanding and respect," he does not idealize his African characters. He instead holds them responsible for their private decisions and for solving the problems that threaten their nation's future.

During Nigeria's civil war in the late 1960s, Achebe worked for the cause of the secessionist Biafrans. Since that time he has taught and encouraged promising young writers. He believes that at the heart of the African oral tradition is the perspective that art is and always was at the service of humans. "Our ancestors created their myths," he has said, "and told their stories for a human purpose." Through his fiction, nonfiction, and poetry, he has been a catalyst for an entire generation of African writers.

Think About the Writer What do you think of Achebe's belief about the purpose of art?

Selection Readability	
Easily Accessible **Accessible** Challenging	familiar syntax; simple dialogue; familiar language; accessible theme; familiar genre

Reading Standard 3.3, 3.7c (see pages A48–A50)

Literary Skills Focus

Verbal Irony When a writer or speaker says one thing but means something else (usually the opposite of what is stated), **verbal irony** occurs. For example, if you tell a friend that you "just love being kept waiting in the rain," you are probably using verbal irony. A classic literary example of verbal irony occurs in Jonathan Swift's essay "A Modest Proposal" (page 580), in which Swift suggests that the Irish solve their social problems by selling their babies to their English landlords as food. Verbal irony is often used to point out the lunacy of an idea. Instead of saying to a friend, "You shouldn't cheat," you might make the idea ridiculous by stating, "Sure, go ahead and cheat on the test. Then you will feel really proud of yourself."

Reading Skills Focus

Identifying Cultural Characteristics Reading is the least expensive way to travel. Without leaving your room, you can spend time in any country in the world, among people of widely differing cultures. When you read, just as when you travel, you encounter attitudes and behaviors different from your own.

Into Action As you read Achebe's story, make a cluster chart like the one below to identify what the story reveals about Nigerian culture. Add as many ovals as you need around the central idea.

Writing Skills Focus

Think as a Reader/Writer

Find It in Your Reading Good writers show rather than tell; they let us draw conclusions about a character by exhibiting the character in action and by letting us hear what the character says. For example, instead of telling us directly, "Joe was a good person," the writer will show Joe in action as he does something positive for someone else or says something that demonstrates his virtues. In your *Reader/Writer Notebook,* note instances where Achebe reveals a character's traits by letting us hear the person's words and by showing the person in action.

Reader/Writer Notebook

Use your **RWN** to complete the activities for this selection.

Vocabulary

cosmopolitan (kahz muh PAHL uh tuhn) *adj.:* worldly; sophisticated. *The old Ibo customs about marriage seemed outdated in the cosmopolitan atmosphere of the city.*

rash (rash) *adj.:* foolhardy. *The father thought his son's sudden decision to marry was rash.*

commiserate (kuh MIHZ uh rayt) *v.:* feel sorrow or pity for; sympathize. *The old men came to commiserate with the father about his son's marriage plans.*

persevered (pur suh VIHRD) *v.:* persisted despite difficulty or opposition. *The old man persevered in putting his son out of his mind.*

perfunctorily (puhr FUHNGK tuhr uh lee) *adv.:* mechanically; carelessly. *The father read the letter perfunctorily.*

Language Coach

Multiple-Meaning Words Some words have more than one meaning and can be used as different parts of speech. For example, *rash* means "foolhardy" when it is used as an adjective; when it is used as a noun, it means "a red, itchy skin condition." Find the following words in the story. Use context clues to define each word and to identify its part of speech as it is used in the sentence. What other meanings can each word have?

leave	sound	engaged
spent	object	sentence
account	steel	broke

Learn It Online

Learn more about Achebe's life online at the Writers' Lives site.

go.hrw.com H12-1377 Go

Selection Resources

Unit 6 Resources, on-level practice and assessment, p. 226

Teacher One Stop™, on-level lesson plans and all print resources

Holt Audio Library

Holt Audio Library: Selections and Summaries in Spanish

UA: Differentiating Instruction, graphic organizer p. 316

UA: Supporting Instruction in Spanish, selection summary

Analyzing Visuals Transparencies, p. 52

ThinkCentral Online Assessment, Selection Standards Check

ThinkCentral Online Remediation

Preteach

Introducing Vocabulary

Read aloud the Vocabulary words, definitions, and sample sentences. Then, use this activity to check students' understanding.

1. People from all over the world make New York a very ______ city. [*cosmopolitan*]
2. The athlete ______ and finally reached his goals. [*persevered*]
3. Think carefully, and do not make a ______ decision. [*rash*]
4. Not interested in the subject, the politician ______ delivered the speech. [*perfunctorily*]
5. Those eliminated from the beauty competition tearfully gathered to ______. [*commiserate*]

English for Academic Success

Language Coach

Point out the multiple meanings of each word. For instance, a *sound* can be heard; the word may also describe something solid or valid.

Literary Skills Focus

As students read and discuss the selection, have them note examples of verbal irony.

Reading Skills Focus

Give students a copy of the Reading Skills Focus graphic organizer. (See **Unit 6 Resources.**) Tell them to use their responses to answer the questions on the Applying Your Skills page.

Writing Skills Focus

Have students record instances revealing character traits in their **Reader/Writer Notebooks.** Students can use their notes to complete the Writing Skills Focus activity.

Learn It Online

The **Writers' Lives** feature of the Interactive Student Edition offers additional information about this author. Audio or video segments are provided for some authors.

go.hrw.com H12-1377 Go

Teacher Preparation
Selection Plot Summary

A young Ibo man named Nnaemeka returns from the city of Lagos in Nigeria to the countryside where he was born to tell his father that he plans to marry Nene, a young woman whom he has met in the city. Okeke, his father, refuses to accept the marriage because Nene is not an Ibo. In fact, as tradition dictates, Nnaemeka's father has chosen an Ibo wife for him. Nnaemeka, however, is determined to marry the woman he loves, so he returns to Nene in the city. Equally adamant, Okeke returns the wedding picture that his son later sends, but he cuts Nene out of it. No reconciliation seems possible. Years later, however, Nene writes to Okeke that her two sons dearly want to meet their grandfather. At last the old man regrets the barriers that he has placed between himself and his son's family, and he resolves to make up for lost time.

Direct Teach

Think About/Talk About

Read with a Purpose Have students read the Read with a Purpose and the Build Background statements. Have them discuss how marriage is not a totally private affair, even in this country, because family, friends, neighbors, and even co-workers become involved. Discuss the advantages and disadvantages of marrying a person from a different background.

SHORT STORY

Marriage Is a Private Affair

by **Chinua Achebe**

Read with a Purpose

Read to find out if marriage really is a private affair.

Build Background

The West African nation of Nigeria has more than 250 ethnic groups, which often speak different languages and frequently differ in religion, customs, and traditions. Both the Ibo and the Ibibio people live in southeastern Nigeria but traditionally did not intermarry. In Achebe's story, a young Ibo man and a young Ibibio woman have moved from their native regions to Lagos, a large, modern city in southwestern Nigeria. Like the young man in the story, Achebe is Ibo.

"Have you written to your dad yet?" asked Nene[1] one afternoon as she sat with Nnaemeka[2] in her room at 16 Kasanga Street, Lagos.[3]

"No. I've been thinking about it. I think it's better to tell him when I get home on leave!"

"But why? Your leave is such a long way off yet—six whole weeks. He should be let into our happiness now."

Nnaemeka was silent for a while, and then began very slowly as if he groped for his words: "I wish I were sure it would be happiness to him."

"Of course it must," replied Nene, a little surprised. "Why shouldn't it?"

"You have lived in Lagos all your life, and you know very little about people in remote parts of the country."

"That's what you always say. But I don't believe anybody will be so unlike other people that they will be unhappy when their sons are engaged to marry."

"Yes. They are most unhappy if the engagement is not arranged by them. In our case it's worse—you are not even an Ibo."[4]

This was said so seriously and so bluntly that Nene could not find speech immediately. In the cosmopolitan atmosphere of the city it had always seemed to her something of a joke that a person's tribe could determine whom he married.

At last she said, "You don't really mean that he will object to your marrying me simply on that account? I had always thought you Ibos were kindly disposed to other people."

"So we are. But when it comes to marriage, well, it's not quite so simple. And this," he added, "is not

1. **Nene** (NAY nay).
2. **Nnaemeka** (ihn naw ay MAY kuh).
3. **Lagos** (LAY gahs): former capital of Nigeria.
4. **Ibo** (EE boh): member of an African ethnic group living chiefly in southeastern Nigeria.

Vocabulary **cosmopolitan** (kahz muh PAHL uh tuhn) *adj.:* worldly; sophisticated.

Universal Access

English Learners

English for Academic Success The language of this story is simple, but a few idioms may be puzzling for nonnative speakers. Explain that *let into our happiness* means "informed of our happiness." Similarly, to *grope* for words means "to search for them." In the phrase "peculiar to the Ibos," the word *peculiar* means "restricted to" or "particular to."

✔ See the **English Language Skill Builder** in **UA: Differentiating Instruction.**

Struggling Readers

Model for students identifying what the story tells them about Nigerian culture. You might say: "When Nnaemeka expresses his uncertainty about how pleased his father will be about their engagement, he seems slightly afraid of his father's reaction. In Nigerian culture, the father's approval of marriage and perhaps other important decisions in their child's life seem to carry much weight. I will make a note of this in my chart." Tell students to look for other characteristics of Nigerian culture that are revealed as they continue reading.

(Facing page, masks): Ibo Wood mask, Nigeria.
The British Museum, London.
(Above painting): Couple with Leaves (1979), by Laura James, acrylic on canvas.

Analyzing Visuals

Connecting to the Text How does the artist use colors, angles, and patterns in this painting to convey that the subjects are a loving couple?

Advanced Learners

Acceleration Explain to students that Achebe has centered his writing on the African oral tradition—that "art is, and always was, at the service of man. Our ancestors created their myths and told their stories for a human purpose," he explains. As a result, Achebe believes that "any good story, any good novel, should have a message, should have a purpose." Have students predict what this purpose might be and, after they read, reach a group consensus about it.

Students with Disabilities

To monitor students' comprehension closely, have them form questions as they read the selection. For example, after reading p. 1378, students might write, "How will Nnaemeka's father react to his son's engagement to a non-Ibo woman? How close is Nnaemeka to his father? How will other people in Nnaemeka's village react to his engagement? Will they call off the marriage if Nnaemeka's parents refuse to acknowledge their union?" After students finish reading, have them review their list of questions and answer as many as possible.

Think About/Talk About

Extend the Discussion

Making Generalizations What major conflicts does Achebe introduce on the first page of the story? What are the parameters of these conflicts? ***Possible responses:*** *The conflicts are between "cosmopolitan" city people and rural people, between traditional and modern ways of doing things, between two different ethnic groups, between Western and African ways, and between parent and child. Nene's parents are out of the picture. The personal conflicts are all between Nnaemeka and his father.*

Interpreting How do you respond to Nene's statement "I don't believe anybody will be so unlike other people that they will be unhappy when their sons are engaged to marry"? What cliché does it seem to embody? ***Possible responses:*** *Her statement essentially means "love conquers all." The story implicitly poses the question "Will it?"*

Analyzing Visuals

Connecting to the Text: *The brown and golden tones, along with the soft patterns of the leaves and the flowers on the woman's dress, create a mood of gentleness and warmth. This mood is enhanced by the soft angles and the curved lines of the subjects' faces.*

Vocabulary: Own the Word

cosmopolitan: Tell students that the root for *cosmopolitan* is from the Greek *kosmopolites,* which is a combination of *kosmos,* meaning "world," and *polites,* meaning "citizen." Ask students to explain what it means to have a *cosmopolitan* outlook. ***Possible response:*** *It means to have an open mind about things.*

Model the Skill

- Tell students that **identifying the cultural characteristics** of a text will help them catch the subtle nuances that a writer builds into a story.
- Have students read aloud the letter from Nnaemeka's father. Model adding an entry about cultural characteristics to the Reading Skills Focus graphic organizer.
- Lead the discussion by indicating that you notice the father, Okeke, has certain values. For instance, you might say: "I first notice how Okeke simply accepts the marriage as a given and expects to choose a wife for his son. He looks for an Ibo woman who is moral, with the appropriate upbringing, and a woman trained to be a wife. There is no talk of love or of what Nnaemeka wants. I will write that *arranged marriages were a tradition* in an oval and draw an arrow connecting it to the center oval."

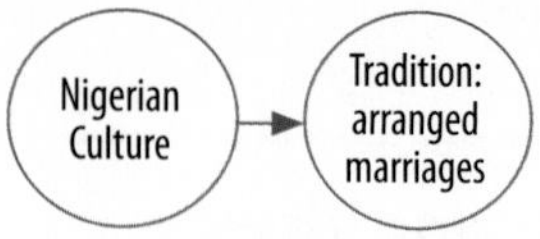

Guided Practice: Apply

Read-Talk-Write Have students read the rest of pp. 1380–1381 and discuss their own observations about Nigerian culture before adding it to their graphic organizers.

peculiar to the Ibos. If your father were alive and lived in the heart of Ibibio-land[5] he would be exactly like my father." **A**

"I don't know. But anyway, as your father is so fond of you, I'm sure he will forgive you soon enough. Come on then, be a good boy and send him a nice lovely letter ... "

"It would not be wise to break the news to him by writing. A letter will bring it upon him with a shock. I'm quite sure about that."

"All right, honey, suit yourself. You know your father."

As Nnaemeka walked home that evening he turned over in his mind different ways of overcoming his father's opposition, especially now that he had gone and found a girl for him. He had thought of showing his letter to Nene but decided on second thoughts not to, at least for the moment. He read it again when he got home and couldn't help smiling to himself. He remembered Ugoye[6] quite well, an Amazon[7] of a girl who used to beat up all the boys, himself included, on the way to the stream, a complete dunce at school.

I have found a girl who will suit you admirably—Ugoye Nweke,[8] the eldest daughter of our neighbor, Jacob Nweke. She has a proper Christian upbringing. When she stopped schooling some years ago her father (a man of sound judgment) sent her to live in the house of a pastor where she has received all the training a wife could need. Her Sunday school teacher has told me that she reads her Bible very fluently. I hope we shall begin negotiations when you come home in December.

On the second evening of his return from Lagos, Nnaemeka sat with his father under a cassia tree. This was the old man's retreat where he went to read his Bible when the parching December sun had set and a fresh, reviving wind blew on the leaves.

"Father," began Nnaemeka suddenly, "I have come to ask for forgiveness."

"Forgiveness? For what, my son?" he asked in amazement.

"It's about this marriage question."

"Which marriage question?"

"I can't—we must—I mean it is impossible for me to marry Nweke's daughter."

"Impossible? Why?" asked his father.

"I don't love her."

"Nobody said you did. Why should you?" he asked. **B**

"Marriage today is different…"

"Look here, my son," interrupted his father, "nothing is different. What one looks for in a wife are a good character and a Christian background."

Nnaemeka saw there was no hope along the present line of argument.

"Moreover," he said, "I am engaged to marry another girl who has all of Ugoye's good qualities, and who…"

His father did not believe his ears. "What did you say?" he asked slowly and disconcertingly.

"She is a good Christian," his son went on, "and a teacher in a girls' school in Lagos."

"Teacher, did you say? If you consider that a qualification for a good wife I should like to point out to you, Emeka, that no Christian woman should teach. St. Paul in his letter to the Corinthians[9] says that women should keep silence." He rose slowly from his seat and paced forward and backward. This was his pet subject, and he condemned vehemently those church leaders who encouraged women to teach in their schools. After he had spent his emotion on a long homily he at last came back to his son's engagement, in a seemingly milder tone. **C**

5. **Ibibio-land** (ihb uh BEE oh land): area of southeastern Nigeria that is the traditional homeland of the Ibibio, another African ethnic group.
6. **Ugoye** (oo GOH yay).
7. **Amazon:** tall, strong, aggressive woman. The Amazons were a group of warrior women in Greek mythology.
8. **Nweke** (ihn WAY kay).
9. **St. Paul . . . Corinthians:** reference to a passage in the Bible (1 Corinthians 14:34).

A **Literary Focus** **Verbal Irony** Given what you have read so far, what is ironic about the story's title?

B **Reading Focus** **Identifying Cultural Characteristics** What does this conversation suggest about traditional Ibo marriages?

C **Reading Focus** **Identifying Cultural Characteristics** What is the traditional Ibo definition of a good wife?

Universal Access

EL English Learners

English for Academic Success Point out that the word *engagement* has multiple meanings besides "a betrothal." For instance, the word can also mean "an appointment," "an obligation," "a period of employment," "to participate," or "a conflict." The verb forms of the word are *engage, engaging,* and *engaged.* Have students tell which meaning of *engagement* is used in the following sentences:

1. Last night's grueling *engagement* left the troops fatigued and hungry. [*conflict*]
2. The students were *engaged* in a heated class debate. [*participate*]
3. His schedule for the day was packed with social and business *engagements.* [*appointment*]

"Whose daughter is she, anyway?"

"She is Nene Atang."

"What!" All the mildness was gone again. "Did you say Neneataga, what does that mean?"

"Nene Atang from Calabar.[10] She is the only girl I can marry." This was a very rash reply and Nnaemeka expected the storm to burst. But it did not. His father merely walked away into his room. This was most unexpected and perplexed Nnaemeka. His father's silence was infinitely more menacing than a flood of threatening speech. That night the old man did not eat.

When he sent for Nnaemeka a day later he applied all possible ways of dissuasion. But the young man's heart was hardened, and his father eventually gave him up as lost.

Iknega Headdress, X65.7994. Fowler Museum at UCLA.

"I owe it to you, my son, as a duty to show you what is right and what is wrong. Whoever put this idea into your head might as well have cut your throat. It is Satan's work." He waved his son away.

"You will change your mind, Father, when you know Nene."

"I shall never see her," was the reply. From that night the father scarcely spoke to his son. He did not, however, cease hoping that he would realize how serious was the danger he was heading for. Day and night he put him in his prayers. **D**

Nnaemeka, for his own part, was very deeply affected by his father's grief. But he kept hoping that it would pass away. If it had occurred to him that never in the history of his people had a man married a woman who spoke a different tongue, he might have been less optimistic. "It has never been heard," was the verdict of an old man speaking a few weeks later. In that short sentence he spoke for all of his people. This man had come with others to commiserate with Okeke[11] when news went round about his son's behavior. By that time the son had gone back to Lagos.

"It has never been heard," said the old man again with a sad shake of his head.

"What did Our Lord say?" asked another gentleman. "Sons shall rise against their Fathers; it is there in the Holy Book."

"It is the beginning of the end," said another.

The discussion thus tending to become theological, Madubogwu, a highly practical man, brought it down once more to the ordinary level.

"Have you thought of consulting a native doctor about your son?" he asked Nnaemeka's father.

"He isn't sick," was the reply.

"What is he then? The boy's mind is diseased and only a good herbalist can bring him back to his right senses. The medicine he requires is *Amalile,* the same that women apply with success to recapture their husbands' straying affection."

"Madubogwu is right," said another gentleman. "This thing calls for medicine." **E**

"I shall not call in a native doctor." Nnaemeka's father was known to be obstinately ahead of his more superstitious neighbors in these matters. "I will not be another Mrs. Ochuba. If my son wants to kill himself let him do it with his own hands. It is not for me to help him."

"But it was her fault," said Madubogwu. "She ought to have gone to an honest herbalist. She was a clever woman, nevertheless."

10. **Calabar:** seaport city in southeastern Nigeria.

11. **Okeke** (oh KAY kay).

D **Reading Focus** **Identifying Cultural Characteristics** What do you infer about the importance of tradition from the father's reaction?

E **Reading Focus** **Identifying Cultural Characteristics** What do the reactions of the father's friends suggest about Ibo culture?

Vocabulary **rash** (rash) *adj.:* foolhardy.
commiserate (kuh MIHZ uh rayt) *v.:* feel sorrow or pity for; sympathize.

Think About/Talk About

Comprehension

B Reading Focus

Possible response: *The conversation indicates that traditional Ibo marriages are not based on love. Love is meant to grow after the marriage occurs.*

C Reading Focus

Possible response: *The father presents the traditional definition when he says, "What one looks for in a wife are a good character and a Christian background." He also feels that silence is a valuable trait in a woman.*

D Reading Focus

Possible response: *For the father, maintaining tradition is essential. Defying tradition is the work of the devil.*

E Reading Focus

Possible response: *The suggestions of Okeke's friends show that traditional Ibo culture values herbal medicine and "native" doctors, as well as traditional Christian doctrine.*

Analysis

A Literary Focus

Possible response: *The irony is that Nnaemeka's marriage is the opposite of private. His father sees himself as very involved.*

Vocabulary: Own the Word

- **rash:** Ask students to applaud to indicate the degree to which they would like to be thought of as *rash* or making a *rash* decision. ***Possible response:*** *Students do not applaud or applaud little to indicate they are not foolish.*
- **commiserate:** To *commiserate* with someone means "to truly identify with his or her pain." Why did people come to *commiserate* with Okeke in the story? ***Possible response:*** *They felt sorry for him because of his son's rude behavior.*

Developing Oral Fluency

Small-Group Activity Divide the class into small groups. Have each group practice reading aloud with fluency by doing a dramatic reading of the passage that begins "On the second evening of his return from Lagos" and continues to the end of the page. In preparation, discuss each character's emotional state and assumptions. Have students look for clues that indicate how the text should be read. Have groups present their dramatizations to the class.

✔ See **UA: Differentiating Instruction** for practice passages for developing oral fluency.

Universal Access

Students with Disabilities

Have students choose an important statement in the text and then make a sketch or a digital photograph to illustrate it. Tell students not to worry about accuracy of costuming or setting. Instead, have them concentrate on facial expressions and poses that capture the essential meaning of the statement. Have them use the statement as a caption for their art.

✔ See **UA: Differentiating Instruction** for a graphic organizer to scaffold instruction for students with disabilities.

Think About/Talk About

Extend the Discussion

Irony Re-read the paragraph in the left column that begins, "The prejudice against Nnaemeka's marriage was not confined to his little village." How does this paragraph clarify the verbal irony of the story's title? ***Possible response:*** *Nnaemeka's marriage is hardly private. Even in Lagos, the big city, Ibo women initially treat Nene as an outsider. It takes her many years to gain some respect.*

Evaluating How is Nene's letter to Okeke a breakthrough? How does it contribute to the development of the plot? ***Possible responses:*** *The letter introduces a new element—grandchildren—which, culturally, has meaning to Okeke. However, his stubbornness has cut him off from them. In the next-to-last paragraph, the change in the weather mirrors his internal conflict.*

Vocabulary: Own the Word

- **persevered:** Write *persevered* in a center circle on the board and provide a definition: "stuck with." Draw spider legs from the center and ask students to add concepts and attributes ***Possible responses:*** *continued, kept at it, persisted*
- **perfunctorily:** Ask students for examples of some actions they perform *perfunctorily.* ***Possible responses:*** *tying shoes, zipping clothes, chewing gum*

Monitor Students' Comprehension

Guide the class in answering these comprehension questions.

1. What is Nnaemeka's attitude toward his father throughout the story? [*He thinks his father is a good man who will someday change his mind.*]
2. For years, what is the only way father and son communicate? [*by letter*]
3. What begins to make Okeke more open to Nnaemeka's marriage? [*his grandchildren*]

"She was a wicked murderess," said Jonathan, who rarely argued with his neighbors because, he often said, they were incapable of reasoning. "The medicine was prepared for her husband, it was his name they called in its preparation, and I am sure it would have been perfectly beneficial to him. It was wicked to put it into the herbalist's food, and say you were only trying it out."

Six months later, Nnaemeka was showing his young wife a short letter from his father:

It amazes me that you could be so unfeeling as to send me your wedding picture. I would have sent it back. But on further thought I decided just to cut off your wife and send it back to you because I have nothing to do with her. How I wish that I had nothing to do with you either.

When Nene read through this letter and looked at the mutilated picture her eyes filled with tears, and she began to sob.

"Don't cry, my darling," said her husband. "He is essentially good-natured and will one day look more kindly on our marriage." But years passed and that one day did not come.

For eight years, Okeke would have nothing to do with his son, Nnaemeka. Only three times (when Nnaemeka asked to come home and spend his leave) did he write to him.

"I can't have you in my house," he replied on one occasion. "It can be of no interest to me where or how you spend your leave—or your life, for that matter."

The prejudice against Nnaemeka's marriage was not confined to his little village. In Lagos, especially among his people who worked there, it showed itself in a different way. Their women, when they met at their village meeting, were not hostile to Nene. Rather, they paid her such excessive deference as to make her feel she was not one of them. But as time went on, Nene gradually broke through some of this prejudice and even began to make friends among them. Slowly and grudgingly they began to admit that she kept her home much better than most of them.

The story eventually got to the little village in the heart of the Ibo country that Nnaemeka and his young wife were a most happy couple. But his father was one of the few people in the village who knew nothing about this. He always displayed so much temper whenever his son's name was mentioned that everyone avoided it in his presence. By a tremendous effort of will he had succeeded in pushing his son to the back of his mind. The strain had nearly killed him but he had persevered, and won.

Then one day he received a letter from Nene, and in spite of himself he began to glance through it perfunctorily until all of a sudden the expression on his face changed and he began to read more carefully.

. . . Our two sons, from the day they learnt that they have a grandfather, have insisted on being taken to him. I find it impossible to tell them that you will not see them. I implore you to allow Nnaemeka to bring them home for a short time during his leave next month. I shall remain here in Lagos . . .

The old man at once felt the resolution he had built up over so many years falling in. He was telling himself that he must not give in. He tried to steel his heart against all emotional appeals. It was a reenactment of that other struggle. He leaned against a window and looked out. The sky was overcast with heavy black clouds and a high wind began to blow, filling the air with dust and dry leaves. It was one of those rare occasions when even Nature takes a hand in a human fight. Very soon it began to rain, the first rain in the year. It came down in large sharp drops and was accompanied by the lightning and thunder which mark a change of season. Okeke was trying hard not to think of his two grandsons. But he knew he was now fighting a losing battle. He tried to hum a favorite hymn but the pattering of large raindrops on the roof broke up the tune. His mind immediately returned to the children. How could he shut his door against them? By a curious mental process he imagined them standing, sad and forsaken, under the harsh angry weather—shut out from his house.

That night he hardly slept, from remorse—and a vague fear that he might die without making it up to them.

Vocabulary **persevered** (pur suh VIHRD) *v.:* persisted despite difficulty or opposition.
perfunctorily (puhr FUHNGK tuhr uh lee) *adv.:* mechanically; carelessly.

California Standards, p. 1383

- **Reading Standard 3.3** Analyze the ways in which irony, tone, mood, the author's style, and the "sound" of language achieve specific rhetorical or aesthetic purposes or both.
- **Reading Standard 3.7** Analyze recognized works of world literature from a variety of authors: **c.** Evaluate the philosophical, political, religious, ethical, and social influences of the historical period that shaped the characters, plots, and settings.
- **Grades 9–10 Review Reading Standard 3.6** Analyze and trace an author's development of time and sequence, including the use of complex literary devices (e.g., foreshadowing, flashbacks).
- **Writing Standard 2.1** Write fictional, autobiographical, or biographical narratives: **c.** Describe with concrete sensory details the sights, sounds, and smells of a scene and the specific actions, movements, gestures, and feelings of the characters; use interior monologue to depict the characters' feelings.

Applying Your Skills

Reading Standard 3.3, 3.7c; **Grades 9–10 Review** Reading Standard 3.6 (see pages A48–A50)
Writing Standard 2.1c (see pages A51–A52)

Marriage Is a Private Affair

Literary Response and Analysis

Reading Skills Focus

Quick Check

1. What is the source of the conflict in this story?
2. What details suggest the amount of time that passes between the time of the marriage and the story's end? During that time, how does Okeke act toward his son?
3. What finally resolves the conflict between father and son and daughter-in-law?

Read with a Purpose

4. How does Nnaemeka's decision to marry affect his family in the short run and in the long run?

Reading Skills: Identifying Cultural Characteristics

5. As you read the story, you noted details that revealed something about Nigerian culture. Would you describe that culture—as it is embodied in the old men of the father' village—as conservative, liberal, or both? What details suggest that the culture will change in the future?

Vocabulary Check

Be ready to justify your answers to these questions.

6. Lagos is described as **cosmopolitan.** Does this mean the city is worldly or primitive?
7. If Nnaemeka gives a **rash** reply, is he being cautious or foolhardy?
8. The old men came to **commiserate** with Okeke. Were they comforting him or scolding him?
9. If the father **persevered** in trying to forget his son, did he persist or give up?
10. The father read his daughter-in-law's letter **perfunctorily.** Did he read it carelessly or carefully?

Literary Skills Focus

Literary Analysis

11. **Analyze** In his depiction of the conflict between Nnaemeka and his father, does Achebe seem to favor strongly one side or the other? Explain.
12. **Interpret** What might the rain at the end of the story symbolize? Find a detail in the next-to-last paragraph that suggests this symbolism.
13. **Analyze** What do you think is the story's theme?
14. **Extend** How might Achebe's story relate to conflicts that exist today within a multicultural society such as the United States?

Literary Skills: Verbal Irony

15. **Interpret** The story's title is an example of **verbal irony**—it says something different from what it means. In what other ways could the title apply to the resolution at the end of the story?

Literary Skills Review: Plot

16. **Summarize** Write a summary of the **plot** of the story, detailing the exposition, conflict, complicating events, climax, and resolution.

Writing Skills Focus

Think as a Reader/Writer

Use It in Your Writing Write a paragraph describing a fictional character from your own culture who is in the midst of a conflict. Like Achebe, use words and actions to *show* rather than tell about the character.

What Do You Think Now? How are the views of the three main characters in the story influenced by their experiences?

Universal Access

Struggling Writers

Some students may need additional scaffolding to complete the Writing Skills Focus activity. Model prewriting for this exercise. You might say: "First, I need to think of a conflict that arises from cultural differences. I might choose to write about a girl who wants to pursue a career before thinking about marriage, while her parents disagree and keep pressuring her to marry. I will describe my characters' thoughts and actions that reveal the emotional tension in the house and also include dialogue to reveal the personalities and attitudes of each character."

What Do You Think Now?

To answer the question, students should think about what the characters have experienced, whether they live in the city or the country, and how "traditional" or "modern" their views are.

Assess

Unit 6 Resources, p. 229

Check for Understanding

Independent Practice

Reading Skills Focus

Possible responses:

1. *The conflict is generational and also cultural—between "city" ways and "traditional" ways.*
2. *The story says that Okeke would have nothing to do with his son for eight years after the marriage.*
3. *Nene's letter makes Okeke relent in order to see his grandchildren.*
4. *In the short term, his decision to marry causes a rift with his father and alienates others in his village. In the long run, however, his wife's letter softens his father's heart.*
5. *Students may note that the old men's culture is traditional. Okeke shares many of their attitudes but does not agree with them about native doctors. His willingness to see his grandchildren signals a change in traditional beliefs.*

Vocabulary Check

6. *worldly*
7. *foolhardy*
8. *comforting*
9. *persist*
10. *carelessly*

Literary Skills Focus

Possible responses:

11. *Achebe favors Nnaemeka because he acts from love, not adherence to tradition.*
12. *The rain may symbolize the storminess of Okeke's thoughts. The "lightning and thunder" marked "a change of season."*
13. *the importance of valuing family ties above social customs*
14. *People who have grown up in the U. S. might have values that differ from those of family members raised in other cultures.*
15. *Okeke will probably accept marriage as a private affair because of his grandchildren.*
16. *Students' responses should summarize the plot chronologically from the exposition through the climax and resolution.*

Standards Focus

Objectives

Students will
- analyze the characteristics of satire
- analyze an author's perspective

Selection Introduction

Think About the Writer

Tell students to think about contemporary comedians who deal with issues of racism and sexism. Discuss how humor can present a problem from a different perspective.

For Independent Reading

- *The Song of Solomon,* Toni Morrison
- *Mama Day,* Gloria Naylor

Motivate

What Do You Think?/QuickWrite

Ask students to go beyond the facts to consider how witnessing the incident of racial discrimination or hearing about it affected them intellectually and emotionally.

English for Academic Success

Academic Vocabulary

Look for opportunities to use the Academic Vocabulary words in this unit.

- **perspective,** ***n.:*** a particular way of looking at something

California Standards, pp. 1384–1388

- **Reading Standard 2.5** Analyze an author's implicit and explicit philosophical assumptions and beliefs about a subject.
- **Reading Standard 3.1** Analyze characteristics of subgenres (e.g., satire, parody, allegory, pastoral) that are used in poetry, prose, plays, novels, short stories, essays, and other basic genres.

Preparing to Read

Telephone Conversation

What Do You Think? How does experience shape our view of the world?

QuickWrite

In your *Reader/Writer Notebook,* write briefly about an incident of racial discrimination you have heard about or witnessed.

Wole Soyinka, Cambridge, Massachusetts (1995).

MEET THE WRITER

Wole Soyinka

(1934–)

Nobel Prize WINNER

A voice of modern Africa, Wole Soyinka became the first African to win the Nobel Prize in Literature. Soyinka's favorite African deity is Ogun, god of both war and creative fire—a fitting muse for a multi-talented writer and performer whose plays, songs, novels, and poetry combine political activism, universal themes, and African traditions.

A Child of Two Worlds

Born Akinwande Oluwole Soyinka in a village in western Nigeria, Soyinka was the son of the principal of a Christian school and a teacher. His parents both supported European-style education, but his father also retained strong ties to his heritage as a member of the Yoruba people. As Soyinka grew up, he struggled with but respected both traditions; his 1981 autobiography, *Aké: The Years of Childhood,* relates his perspective on this dual heritage.

After attending University College at Ibadan, Nigeria, Soyinka studied English literature in England at the University of Leeds. In the late 1950s, he wrote plays and poetry in London for theater and radio. During this period of African nationalism and pressure for independence, Soyinka treated themes of racism, injustice, tyranny, and corruption all with satiric wit. Soyinka was also concerned with the collision of ancient traditions with modern realities, and he peppered his plays with vivid Yoruba masquerade rituals.

Suffering for Liberty

Soyinka experienced brutal despotism firsthand during Nigeria's civil war of the late 1960s, when he was imprisoned for two years for the so-called crime of meeting with secessionist leaders such as the writer Chinua Achebe. He describes these experiences in *The Man Dies: Prison Notes,* published in 1972. Today, Soyinka continues to record and dramatize, with passion and humor, the struggle and spirit of modern-day Africa.

Think About the Writer What do you think of Soyinka's use of humor to fight oppression? Do you think this approach can be effective? Explain.

Selection Readability	
Easily Accessible **Accessible** Challenging	conversational tone; humorous; accessible theme; short poem; complex syntax; sophisticated language

Reading Standard 2.5, 3.1 (see pages A48–A50)

Literary Skills Focus

Satire Writing that ridicules the foolish or even destructive actions of humans with the intention of bringing about awareness and reform is called **satire.** In satire, writers exaggerate or skew the human attitude or action that they are targeting. By making the action or attitude appear foolish, or even preposterous, satirists hope to inspire people to recognize it and make changes. In the following poem, Wole Soyinka uses satire to reveal the absurdity of racial discrimination.

Reading Skills Focus

Analyzing Author's Perspective When you read satire, it is especially important that you have a clear notion of the writer's perspective. **Perspective** refers to a way of looking at the world, including assumptions, attitudes, biases, and insecurities. When you analyze a writer's perspective, you must remember that the person who speaks in a poem or story is not necessarily the author.

Into Action As you read, use an organizer like the one below to take notes on the perspectives of the poem's two characters, the speaker and the landlady he is addressing. Remember that perspective encompasses assumptions and attitudes, including biases and insecurities.

Speaker's Perspective	*Landlady's Perspective*
1. Does not want to waste his time talking to a landlady who will not rent a place to him because he is African	
2.	

Writing Skills Focus

Think as a Reader/Writer

Find It in Your Reading The thrust of this poem comes from a dialogue between two characters who have different perspectives: One character is in a phone booth, and the other is in her home. The dialogue is both funny and sad. As you read, make a list of the characteristics of this dialogue you find interesting or most effective. Note also the way the writer describes the voice of the woman to whom he is speaking and his surroundings in the phone booth.

Reader/Writer Notebook

Use your **RWN** to complete the activities for this selection.

Vocabulary

revelation (rehv uh LAY shuhn) *n.:* something revealed. *It was a revelation to him that he might be rejected on the basis of his skin color.*

clinical (KLIHN uh kuhl) *adj.:* objective; without emotion. *The landlady took a hard, clinical look at the prospective tenant.*

impersonality (ihm pur suh NAL uh tee) *n.:* lack of human connection. *The landlady's impersonality in dealing with her prospective tenant was chilling.*

conceding (kuhn SEED ihng) *v.:* admitting as true. *The landlady was finally conceding that she did not know what West African sepia was.*

Language Coach

Word Families When you encounter an unfamiliar word, look closely to see if there is a familiar word embedded in it. For example, the word *reveal* is embedded in the word *revelation* (spelled slightly differently). This knowledge might help you guess that *revelation* means "something revealed." What words are embedded in *impersonality, clinical,* and *conceding?*

Learn It Online
Get to know the Vocabulary words online.
go.hrw.com H12-1385 Go

Selection Resources

Unit 6 Resources, on-level practice and assessment, p. 232

Teacher One Stop™, on-level lesson plans and all print resources

Holt Audio Library

Holt Audio Library: Selections and Summaries in Spanish

UA: Differentiating Instruction, graphic organizer p. 317

UA: Supporting Instruction in Spanish, selection summary

ThinkCentral Online Assessment, Selection Standards Check

ThinkCentral Online Remediation

Preteach

Introducing Vocabulary

Read aloud the Vocabulary words, definitions, and sample sentences. Then, use this activity to check students' understanding.

1. Can something you have known for a long time still be a **revelation**?
2. Is a **clinical** statement wildly emotional?
3. Does **impersonality** imply coldness?
4. When you are **conceding** a point, are you winning the argument?

English for Academic Success

Language Coach

Model for students how to complete the exercise. For example, point out that the word *impersonality* contains the word *impersonal,* which means the opposite of *personal.* Therefore, showing *impersonality* most likely means "lacking human warmth."

Literary Skills Focus

As you read and discuss the poem with students, have them note examples of satire.

Reading Skills Focus

Give students a copy of the Reading Skills Focus graphic organizer before they read. (See **Unit 6 Resources.**) Tell them to use their responses to answer the questions on the Applying Your Skills page.

Writing Skills Focus

As they read, have students use their **Reader/Writer Notebooks** to record their insights about the perspectives of the two characters. Students can use their notes to complete the Writing Skills Focus activity.

Learn It Online
Send students to **Word Watch** for audio pronunciations, synonyms and antonyms, and brief histories of word origins.
go.hrw.com H12-1385 Go

Teacher Preparation

Selection Summary

The black speaker of "Telephone Conversation" is having a telephone conversation with a white landlady about renting an apartment. To save himself a wasted trip if the woman is racist, the speaker tells her that he is an African. She hesitates and then asks whether he is dark-skinned or light-skinned. Stunned, the speaker gives absurd details about his "color" in a flood of shame and fury that ends in a well-placed insult.

Direct Teach

Think About/Talk About

Read with a Purpose Have students read the Read with a Purpose statement. Point out phrases in the poem that help the reader visualize the two people.

Comprehension

A Reading Focus

Possible response: *The writer seems shocked by the woman's ignorance and prejudice and identifies with the shock and anger of the speaker.*

Extend the Discussion

Irony What is ironic about the speaker's use of the word *self-confession* in line 4? Why did she ask how dark his skin color was? ***Possible responses:*** *For the landlady, having the wrong skin color seems to be a crime. Her question implies that light-skinned Africans are acceptable because he could pass for being white.*

Interpreting How does the landlady's question about the speaker's skin color undercut the description of her in lines 6–9? ***Possible response:*** *She initially seems elegant and well bred, but her words undercut that impression.*

POEM

Telephone Conversation

by **Wole Soyinka**

Read with a Purpose

As you read, try to hear the two people who are having this telephone conversation. How do you picture them?

Build Background

The speaker in Soyinka's poem is talking from one of the red public telephone booths that were especially common in London years ago. Such phones had two buttons, A and B; pressing A put one through to the recipient of the call. The speaker is a well-educated black African; the woman with whom he is conversing is a white British woman who has property to rent.

When Soyinka was a college student in London in the late 1950s, millions of people from former British colonies were flooding into England in search of educational opportunities and employment. This poem records one of Soyinka's own experiences with racial discrimination during that time.

The price seemed reasonable, location
Indifferent. The landlady swore she lived
Off premises. Nothing remained
But self-confession. "Madam," I warned,
"I hate a wasted journey—I am African."
Silence. Silenced transmission of
Pressurized good-breeding. Voice, when it came,
Lipstick coated, long gold-rolled
Cigarette-holder pipped. Caught I was, foully.

"HOW DARK?"... I had not misheard... "ARE YOU LIGHT
OR VERY DARK?" Button B. Button A. Stench
Of rancid breath of public hide-and-speak.
Red booth. Red pillar-box.° Red double-tiered
Omnibus° squelching tar. It *was* real! Shamed
By ill-mannered silence, surrender
Pushed dumbfoundment to beg simplification.
Considerate she was, varying the emphasis— **A**

13. pillar-box: British for "mailbox," red like the phone booth.
13–14. double-tiered omnibus: bus with two decks, or tiers.

A Reading Focus **Analyzing Author's Perspective** Judging from what you have read so far, how would you say the writer feels about these two conversationalists?

Vocabulary **revelation** (rehv uh LAY shuhn) *n.:* something revealed.
clinical (KLIHN uh kuhl) *adj.:* objective; without emotion.

Universal Access

English Learners / Struggling Readers

English for Academic Success The satire in this poem relies heavily on Soyinka's diction and phrasing. Point out examples such as "pressurized good-breeding" and "public hide-and-speak." Explain that the word *pressurized* evokes the idea of something forced but also of tension. This suggests that the landlady's "good breeding" may be tense and forced. Discuss some of the other phrases in the poem.

Advanced Learners

Enrichment Soyinka's poem effectively uses dramatic dialogue to highlight the absurdity of racial prejudice. Discuss an incident illustrating civil rights issues. Ask students to write their own dialogue poem based on characters involved in the event. For instance, a poem could represent the dialogue between Rosa Parks and the people who told her to move to the back of the bus.

The Man (2001), by Francks Deceus, mixed media on canvas.

Analyzing Visuals

Connecting to the Text Examine the spatial placement of the subject and the apartment building and consider its meaning. How is this literal and metaphorical distance similar to the separation of the characters in "Telephone Conversation"?

"ARE YOU DARK? OR VERY LIGHT?" Revelation came.
"You mean—like plain or milk chocolate?"
Her assent was clinical, crushing in its light
Impersonality. Rapidly, wavelength adjusted,
I chose. "West African sepia"—and as an afterthought,
"Down in my passport." Silence for spectroscopic
Flight of fancy,° till truthfulness clanged her accent
Hard on the mouthpiece. "WHAT'S THAT?" conceding,
"DON'T KNOW WHAT THAT IS." "Like brunette." **B**

"THAT'S DARK, ISN'T IT?" "Not altogether.
Facially, I am brunette, but madam, you should see
The rest of me. Palm of my hand, soles of my feet
Are a peroxide blonde. Friction, caused—
Foolishly, madam—by sitting down, has turned
My bottom raven black—One moment madam!"—sensing
Her receiver rearing on the thunderclap
About my ears—"Madam," I pleaded, "wouldn't you rather
See for yourself?"

23–24. spectroscopic (spehk truh skahp ihk) **flight of fancy:** wide range, or spectrum, of ideas.

B Literary Focus Satire How does the speaker mock the woman in this exchange?

Vocabulary **impersonality** (ihm pur suh NAL uh tee) *n.:* lack of human connection.
conceding (kuhn SEED ihng) *v.:* admitting as true.

Think About/Talk About

Analysis

B Literary Focus

Possible response: *The speaker gives an elaborate, fanciful reply that the landlady cannot understand. He describes his skin color in a term used to describe artists' paint, "sepia," but modifies it by adding "West African."*

Vocabulary: Own the Word

- **revelation:** Act out the face and gestures of someone who has a *revelation* or insight (the *aha* face and response like a slap to the forehead). Ask students to demonstrate the action of someone who has had a *revelation.*
- **clinical:** Have students complete the following sentence: The speaker in the poem calls the landlady *clinical* in her response to him because she is . . . ***Possible response:*** *trying to sound uninvolved and objective rather than biased*
- **impersonality:** *Impersonality* is the noun form of *impersonal* (adj.), the opposite of *personal* (adj.). Ask students why they might write an *impersonal* letter. ***Possible responses:*** *when they do not care about the recipient; when they want to sound cold and distant*
- **conceding:** In the poem, the landlady is *conceding* that she does not know what something means by admitting it. Ask students to list other uses of *conceding.* ***Possible responses:*** *conceding defeat, conceding a point in an argument*

California Standards, p. 1388

- **Reading Standard 2.5** Analyze an author's implicit and explicit philosophical assumptions and beliefs about a subject.
- **Reading Standard 3.1** Analyze characteristics of subgenres (e.g., satire, parody, allegory, pastoral) that are used in poetry, prose, plays, novels, short stories, essays, and other basic genres.
- **Reading Standard 3.4** Analyze ways in which poets use imagery, personification, figures of speech, and sounds to evoke readers' emotions.
- **Writing Standard 2.3** Write reflective compositions: **a.** Explore the significance of personal experiences, events, conditions, or concerns by using rhetorical strategies (e.g., narration, description, exposition, persuasion).

Analyzing Visuals

Connecting to the Text: *The man in this image stands on the far right, while the apartment building is situated on the far left, seemingly inaccessible to the man. The noticeable distance between these subjects reflects the distance created between the man in the poem and the landlady solely on account of his skin color.*

Check for Understanding

Independent Practice

Reading Skills Focus

Possible responses:

1. *1: The black speaker telephones a white landlady about renting an apartment. To avoid a wasted trip, the speaker tells her he is African. 2: She asks whether he is dark or light-skinned. 3: She continues to ask about his skin tone. The choice of words in his reply goes over her head. 4: The speaker clarifies by giving absurd details about his "color" and she hangs up.*
2. *Each sees the other as a representative of his or her race rather than as an individual. Each assumes that racial differences will determine how they interact.*
3. *Students should add a third column analyzing the author's perspective in the poem.*

Vocabulary Check

4. *clear*
5. *objective and without emotion*
6. *showed a lack of human connection*
7. *admitting something*

Literary Skills Focus

Possible responses:

8. *The irony is that she lacks good breeding, and she is anything but "considerate" of his feelings.*
9. *The put-down is the result of rage and frustration. It may make her feel that her prejudice is justified.*
10. *The theme is that racial prejudice is absurd.*
11. *Soyinka satirizes the landlady and everyone like her. He wants to see an end to racial discrimination.*
12. *Satire can raise consciousness about a problem. By itself, it cannot correct the problem.*
13. *He mentions milk chocolate, sepia, brunette, peroxide blonde, and raven black. The use of precise colors highlights how absurd racial discrimination is.*

Applying Your Skills

Reading Standard 2.5, 3.1, 3.4 (see pages A48–A50)
Writing Standard 2.3a (see pages A51–A52)

Telephone Conversation

Literary Response and Analysis

Reading Skills Focus

Quick Check

1. Paraphrase (restate in your own words) what happens in each stanza of this poem.

Read with a Purpose

2. What does each person on either end of the telephone conversation "see" about the other person? What do the landlady and prospective tenant assume about each other?

Reading Skills: Analyzing Author's Perspective

3. Add a third column to your perspectives chart in which you describe the *author's* perspective in this poem. Do you think the author shares either the African man's or the landlady's perspective? Why do you think so?

Vocabulary Check

Be ready to justify your responses to the questions about Vocabulary words.

4. When the writer says "**revelation** *came*," does he mean that something became clear to him or that something became obscure to him?
5. When the writer describes the landlady's agreement as **clinical,** does he mean she was emotional or that she was objective and without emotion?
6. When the writer says the landlady's agreement is crushing in its **impersonality,** does he mean she agreed in a very warm and human way or she showed a lack of human connection?
7. When the landlady is described as **conceding,** is she admitting something, or is she refusing to change her mind?

Literary Skills Focus

Literary Analysis

8. **Analyze** What is ironic about the speaker's reference to the landlady's "good-breeding"? What is ironic about his calling her "considerate"?
9. **Evaluate** What do you think of the speaker's final question? How will it affect the landlady?
10. **Analyze** What is the **theme,** or truth about life, revealed in this poem?

Literary Skills: Satire

11. **Interpret** Who or what is the target of Soyinka's satire in this poem? What change in society does this satirist want to see occur?
12. **Evaluate** How effective do you think the methods of this satire will be in inspiring change?

Literary Skills Review: Imagery

13. **Analyze** Language that appeals to the senses is **imagery.** What colors does Soyinka use to help us visualize skin color? What is communicated by using precise colors to describe skin tones?

Writing Skills Focus

Think as a Reader/Writer

Use It in Your Writing Re-read your notes about this poem's use of dialogue. In a poem or prose passage, write about a difficult personal encounter you have read about or experienced. Use dialogue to make the description more vivid.

What Do You Think Now? What people and events might have shaped the landlady's view of the world?

Universal Access

Struggling Writers

Some students may need additional scaffolding to complete the Writing Skills Focus activity. Have students brainstorm on their own a conversation or encounter that involved some kind of absurd discrimination. Tell them to complete a T-chart that lists the thoughts and emotions of the two sides involved. Then, have them write their poem or prose passage, and remind them to include dialogue that mimics Soyinka's style.

What Do You Think Now?

To understand the landlady's view of the world, students could consider the causes of racial prejudice, such as ignorance or upbringing.

Assess

Unit 6 Resources,
Selection Standards Check, p. 235

COMPARING TEXTS

Postcolonial Literature

Captain Justin Bootah of the Lifeguards from India addresses a Queen's Guard at Trooping the Color.

When European colonies gained their independence, they also began to assert their own literary voices. Brilliant postcolonial writers such as Derek Walcott, V. S. Naipaul, and Anita Desai began to express the experiences of their peoples and countries, while others like American writer Paul Theroux have documented the postcolonial aftermath in the course of traveling and living abroad. Shaped by a dual heritage, that of the European colonizer and that of the original culture, such writers have struggled to forge their own identities. As you read the following selections, notice how the form and content of Walcott's, Naipaul's, and Desai's texts are influenced by the colonial experience.

CONTENTS

Standards Focus

Objectives

Students will
- understand and compare works by Walcott, Naipaul, Theroux, and Desai
- understand setting
- make inferences about theme
- analyze details
- write comparison-contrast essays using appropriate organization

English for Academic Success

Academic Vocabulary

Look for opportunities to use the Academic Vocabulary words in this unit.

- **adapt, *v.*:** adjust for a new purpose
- **considerably, *adv.*:** by a large amount
- **exhibit, *v.*:** show, demonstrate
- **inevitable, *adj.*:** unavoidable
- **perspective, *n.*:** a particular way of looking at something

Analyzing Visuals

Extension Activity Ask students to study the photograph. Lead a discussion with students, allowing them to access their prior knowledge by asking what they already know about the officers in the photograph.

Selection Introduction

Think About the Writer

Discuss with students the idea of Walcott's "schizophrenic boyhood" and the complexities of being biracial in modern and contemporary societies. Ask students how Walcott's process of writing may have helped heal his schizophrenic feelings. What issues cause us to feel schizophrenic in our society?

For Independent Reading

The Odyssey, Homer

Motivate

What Do You Think?/QuickWrite

Have students think about both famous and obscure people whom they would like to acknowledge for their noble and respectable actions. Have students explain their choices in their **Reader/Writer Notebooks.**

Preparing to Read

from Omeros

What Do You Think? How does experience shape our view of the world?

QuickWrite

Think about someone you know or have heard of whose good deeds you might celebrate in a poem. What did this person do to impress you? Write a few sentences about this person in your *Reader/Writer Notebook.*

Derek Walcott, St. Malo, France (1993).

MEET THE WRITER

Derek Walcott

(1930–)

Nobel Prize WINNER

Derek Walcott was born on the Caribbean island of St. Lucia, then under British rule. Walcott lost his father at a very young age. His mother, a schoolteacher, encouraged Walcott's love of reading and provided him with a thorough background in the Western classics.

Caught Between Two Worlds

With black and white grandparents on both sides of his family, Walcott grew up with a biracial heritage that often presented difficulties for him. His inability to identify completely with either black or white people was only one reason for what he called his "schizophrenic boyhood." As a lover of Western literature and his island home, Walcott lived "two lives: the interior life of poetry and the outward life of action and dialect."

Another cause of Walcott's ambivalent perspective was his knowledge of Britain's role in slavery and the oppression of his people. This awareness coexisted with Walcott's love of British poetry. As he grew older, Walcott also began to feel uncomfortable with the strict Catholic culture of St. Lucia. He fled to Kingston, Jamaica, where he earned a degree at the University of the West Indies, and quickly joined the thriving arts community. In 1957, he received a Rockefeller Foundation grant to study theater arts in New York City. Though Walcott disliked living in New York, it was later to be the site of production for his award-winning play, *Dream on Monkey Mountain.*

Classical Poet with a New Subject

During the 1960s, Walcott began to focus on writing poetry. Much of Walcott's form is derived from the British poetry he loves. He writes in a rich, expressive style and makes liberal use of classical allusions. Much of his subject matter, however, comes from the Caribbean islands.

In 1992, the quincentennial of Columbus's landing in the Caribbean, Walcott was awarded the Nobel Prize in Literature. The Swedish Academy stated, "In him, West Indian culture has found its great poet."

Think About the Writer How do you think writing helped Derek Walcott forge an identity for himself?

California Standards, pp. 1390–1395

- **Reading Standard 3.1** Analyze characteristics of subgenres (e.g., satire, parody, allegory, pastoral) that are used in poetry, prose, plays, novels, short stories, essays, and other basic genres.
- **Reading Standard 3.6** Analyze the way in which authors through the centuries have used archetypes drawn from myth and tradition in literature, film, political speeches, and religious writings (e.g., how the archetypes of banishment from an ideal world may be used to interpret Shakespeare's tragedy *Macbeth*).
- **Reading Standard 3.7** Analyze recognized works of world literature from a variety of authors: **c.** Evaluate the philosophical, political, religious, ethical, and social influences of the historical period that shaped the characters, plots, and settings.

Selection Readability	
Easily Accessible Accessible **Challenging**	difficult vocabulary; epic poem; unfamiliar setting

Reading Standard 3.1, 3.6, 3.7c (see pages A48–A50)

Literary Skills Focus

Contemporary Epic An **epic** is a long narrative poem that tells the story of a larger-than-life hero who embodies the values of a particular society. Originally an oral tradition, epics were memorized and recited so they could be passed from one generation to the next. Those that were written down, such as *Gilgamesh,* the *Iliad,* and the *Odyssey,* became some of the earliest works of literature. Early epics tend to be about archetypes like kings or fierce warriors who fight battles or make dangerous journeys to unknown lands. Later epics, such as Milton's *Paradise Lost,* reflect the preoccupations of their times. **Contemporary epics** often focus on ordinary protagonists or even antiheroes (characters obviously lacking any heroic qualities) while retaining elements of the epic form, such as the long narrative.

Reading Skills Focus

Using Background Knowledge To understand and enjoy a contemporary epic, such as *Omeros,* you need some **background knowledge.** First, you must understand the epic form, including its use of grandiose language and long narratives. Second, you must recognize allusions to earlier epics or other works of literature. Finally, you should know, or be able to infer, something of the culture the epic represents.

Into Action As you read, use a chart like the one below to record notes on the epic's form and allusions, as well as the culture it represents.

Epic Form	Allusions	Culture
Grandiose language: Walcott uses grandiose language and epic style to describe everyday things, such as the hero's shoes.		

Writing Skills Focus

Think as a Reader/Writer

Find It in Your Reading Like most epic writers, Walcott uses language that combines specific, realistic detail with **figurative language** in the form of simile or metaphor. Make two columns on a sheet of paper. Label one "Realistic Detail" and the other "Figurative Language." As you read, note examples of each in the correct column.

Reader/Writer Notebook

Use your **RWN** to complete the activities for this selection.

Vocabulary

ascended (uh SEHND ihd) *v.:* went up. *The gull ascended from the beach.*

idyll (YD uhl) *n.:* short work of prose or poetry about an idealized country scene. *The poet composed an idyll about the beaches of the Caribbean.*

goblet (GAHB liht) *n.:* drinking vessel, often ornate. *The guest of honor was presented with a goblet of wine.*

epilogue (EHP uh lawg) *n.:* short section at the end of a literary work that often tells what happened after the end of the story. *In the epilogue, the audience discovered that the hero later became a dentist.*

Language Coach

Roots The word *epilogue* contains the root *logos,* meaning "speech," "word," or "reason." Use your knowledge of affixes and roots to write definitions for the following words, and tell how their meanings relate to the root *logos: prologue, illogical,* and *dialogue.*

Learn It Online

Get the scoop on the author's life and work online.

go.hrw.com H12-1391 Go

Comparing Texts Resources

Unit 6 Resources, on-level practice and assessment, p. 238

Teacher One Stop™, on-level lesson plans and all print resources

Holt Audio Library

Holt Audio Library: Selections and Summaries in Spanish

UA: Differentiating Instruction, graphic organizer p. 321

UA: Supporting Instruction in Spanish, selection summary

ThinkCentral Online Assessment, Selection Standards Check

ThinkCentral Online Remediation

Preteach

Introducing Vocabulary

Read aloud the Vocabulary words and sample sentences. Then, use this activity to check students' understanding.

1. Why do some things that have **ascended** from the ground eventually descend?
2. Is an **idyll** composed in writing or in music?
3. What might you find in a **goblet**?
4. Where would you find the **epilogue** in a book?

English for Academic Success

Language Coach

Have students read the **Language Coach.** Remind students that the prefix *pro–* means "before," *il–* means "the opposite of," and *di–* means "two." Ask students which meaning of the root *logos* is used in the words *prologue, illogical,* and *dialogue.*

Literary Skills Focus

As students read and discuss the poem, have them note which details seem typical of an epic and which seem contemporary.

Reading Skills Focus

Give students a copy of the Reading Skills Focus graphic organizer before they read. (See **Unit 6 Resources.**) Tell them to use their responses to answer the questions on the Applying Your Skills page.

Writing Skills Focus

As students read, have them record in their **Reader/Writer Notebooks** examples of realistic detail and figurative language. Students can use their notes to complete the Writing Skills Focus activity.

Learn It Online

The enhanced author biography offers more information on the life of the author as well as Holt's interactive resources pertaining to the author.

go.hrw.com H12-1391 Go

Teacher Preparation
Selection Plot Summary

Walcott borrows the setting, characterization, and theme for his epic poem, *Omeros,* from Homer's *Iliad*. In *Omeros*, Achille, Hector, and Helen appear in a story of Caribbean fishermen on the island of St. Lucia. The epic as a whole addresses the theme of colonial tension. In this brief excerpt, the speaker uses an extended metaphor to illustrate the fragile life of the fishermen and the fate of Hector.

Direct Teach

Think About/Talk About

Read with a Purpose Have students read the Read with a Purpose statement. Ask them to make notes of words and images that denote Achille's character.

Comprehension

A Reading Focus

Possible response: *It repeats words from the opening of the Iliad: "sing/sang," "Achille/Achilles," and "son." The mood is also similar.*

Analysis

B Literary Focus

Possible response: *Contemporary details include references to an elevator, a passport, and a waiter.*

Extend the Discussion

Interpreting Why does the author include in parentheses the comment about Achille never reading this epic? ***Possible response:*** *This comment helps make Achille seem separate from the process of composing the contemporary epic and makes him seem timeless.*

EPIC POEM

from Omeros

by **Derek Walcott**

Read with a Purpose

Read to find out how the speaker remembers Achille and his journey.

Build Background

The title of this poem, *Omeros,* is the modern Greek word for *Homer,* the poet who is thought to have written the *Iliad* and the *Odyssey.* The *Iliad's* main character is Achilles, a hero of the Trojan War. In the *Odyssey,* the main character, Odysseus, has many adventures traveling home from the Trojan War. The main character of Walcott's epic is a fisherman named Achille, who journeys with a friend to the West African coast from which their ancestors came. The opening of *Omeros* even echoes some of the language from the beginning of the *Iliad:*

> *Sing, O goddess, the anger of Achilles son of Peleus, that brought countless ills upon the Achaeans. Many a brave soul did it send hurrying down to Hades, and many a hero did it yield a prey to dogs and vultures.*

I sang of quiet Achille, Afolabe's son, **A**
who never ascended in an elevator,
who had no passport, since the horizon needs none,

never begged nor borrowed, was nobody's waiter, **B**
whose end, when it comes, will be a death by water
(which is not for this book, which will remain unknown

and unread by him). I sang the only slaughter
that brought him delight, and that from necessity—
of fish, sang the channels of his back in the sun.

A Reading Focus **Using Background Knowledge** How does this line echo language from the *Iliad?*

B Literary Focus **Contemporary Epic** What details does the poet include that make it clear this is a contemporary epic?

Vocabulary **ascended** (uh SEHND ihd) *v.:* went up.

Universal Access

English Learners

English for Academic Success Give students practice with the Academic Vocabulary words in this unit. Have them use the following prompts to form questions:

- **perspective** Have students form a question that addresses the narrator's view on a character or issue.
- **adapt** Have students form a question about the differences between contemporary and traditional epics.
- **exhibit** Have students form a question addressing the poem's mood.

Struggling Readers

In pairs or small groups, have students re-read the excerpt. Ask each group to assign a note taker, and have that individual write "Background Knowledge" at the top of a piece of paper. Then, have the group dictate to the note taker all the words and phrases that are familiar to them from their study of epics. Students should brainstorm and share their background knowledge with one another as they compose their list.

Omeros book cover by Derek Walcott.
Courtesy of Rhona Pilgrim.

Analyzing Visuals

Connecting to the Text Consider the somewhat hazy and indistinct presentation of the boaters in this painting by Derek Walcott. What might he be suggesting about their journey? Do you think this painting represents *Omeros?* Why or why not?

I sang our wide country, the Caribbean Sea.
Who hated shoes, whose soles were as cracked as a stone,
who was gentle with ropes, who had one suit alone,

whom no man dared insult and who insulted no one,
whose grin was a white breaker cresting,° but whose frown
was a growing thunderhead, whose fist of iron (C)

14. a white breaker cresting: a foam-topped wave reaching its highest point.

(C) **Literary Focus** **Contemporary Epic** What do you learn here about this epic's hero, Achille?

Think About/Talk About

Analysis

(C) Literary Focus

Possible response: *We learn that he has a great deal of integrity, since he speaks ill of no one and no one dares speak ill of him. His smile is as glorious as his frown is dreadful. We understand from this description that he has heroic, almost superhuman qualities.*

Extend the Discussion

Making Predictions Based on the information on pp. 1390–1391 and your background knowledge, what do you expect is going to happen to Achille? What clues help you to predict how he will handle challenges? ***Possible responses:*** *We know that epics are full of action and suspense, so we can expect something to complicate Achille's life. We can tell from the speaker's description that he has the strength of character to meet any challenge.*

Analyzing Visuals

Connecting to the Text: *He might be suggesting that the boaters are going nowhere or that their journey will never end. The painting depicts locals sailing near a small island, similar to the setting of the poem.*

Vocabulary: Own the Word

ascended: *Ascended* means "rose"; its antonym is *descended.* Have students use both words in a sentence. ***Possible response:*** *He ascended the stairs to brush his teeth and go to bed, but he forgot a glass of water from the kitchen so he descended again.*

Advanced Learners

Enrichment Inform students that during the early nineteenth century, St. Lucia was often referred to as "the Helen of the West." Have students research the role of England and France in the occupancy of St. Lucia during this time. Then, have students apply their knowledge of the *Iliad* to explain in a discussion the logic behind the comparison.

Students with Disabilities

Point out to students that in *Omeros*, Walcott draws analogies between characters in the *Iliad* and ordinary people in St. Lucia. Review the characteristics of the people in this poem and their counterparts in the *Iliad*. Then, ask students to compare one character with a person from their neighborhood or town. Have students give two reasons why the comparison is appropriate.

✔ See **UA: Differentiating Instruction** for a graphic organizer to scaffold instruction for students with disabilities.

Think About/Talk About

Comprehension

D Reading Focus

Possible response: *The speaker is dying at sea, imagining how Hector died in Homer's story. Because he is thinking of Hector, he is figuratively traveling with him at this moment.*

Extend the Discussion

Paraphrasing How could the four sentences in lines 21–24 be rewritten in contemporary English? ***Possible response:*** *They could be rewritten as follows: "There is so much I still have to write about. My coffin is open. I am wrapped up in a sail made from a flour sack. Dirt is being shoveled into my open coffin."*

Interpreting Why did Walcott create a metaphoric relationship between the canoe and the coffin? ***Possible response***: *For the characters in the epic, a death at sea was a very real possibility. The metaphor also represents the journey to the afterlife.*

Vocabulary: Own the Word

- **idyll:** Tell students that an *idyll* idealizes simple pastoral or rural scenes. Ask students, "Why might a person compose an *idyll*? What might an *idyll* be about? Who might compose an *idyll*?"
- **goblet:** Ask students the following questions: Which is more likely to be served in a *goblet,* wine or root beer? [*wine*] Who is more likely to drink from a *goblet,* a cowboy or a king? [*king*]
- **epilogue:** *Epilogue* comes from the Latin word *epilogus* or the Greek *epilogos,* meaning "conclusion of a speech." In an *epilogue,* the author wraps up the story. Ask students how the *epilogue* of their life stories might read.

would do me a greater honour if it held on
to my casket's oarlocks° than mine lifting his own
when both anchors are lowered in the one island,

but now the idyll dies, the goblet is broken,
and rainwater trickles down the brown cheek of a jar
from the clay of Choiseul.° So much left unspoken

by my chirping nib!° And my earth-door lies ajar.
I lie wrapped in a flour-sack sail. The clods thud
on my rope-lowered canoe. Rasping shovels scrape

a dry rain of dirt on its hold, but turn your head
when the sea-almond rattles or the rust-leaved grape
from the shells of my unpharaonic° pyramid

towards paper shredded by the wind and scattered
like white gulls that separate their names from the foam
and nod to a fisherman with his khaki dog

that skitters from the wave-crash, then frown at his form
for one swift second. In its earth-trough, my pirogue°
with its brass-handled oarlocks is sailing. Not from

but with them, with Hector,° with Maud in the rhythm **D**
of her beds trowelled over, with a swirling log
lifting its mossed head from the swell; let the deep hymn

of the Caribbean continue my epilogue;
may waves remove their shawls as my mourners walk home
to their rusted villages, good shoes in one hand,

passing a boy who walked through the ignorant foam,
and saw a sail going out or else coming in,
and watched asterisks of rain puckering the sand.

17. oarlocks: metal hoops in a ship or boat that hold the oars in place.

21. Choiseul: one of the western Solomon Islands.

22. nib: tip of a fountain pen.

27. unpharaonic: not like or fitting for a pharaoh.

32. pirogue: type of canoe made of a hollowed-out tree trunk.

34. Hector: the most important warrior of the Trojan army in the *Iliad.* In the ancient epic, he is killed by Achilles.

D Reading Focus **Using Background Knowledge** Read the sidenote that explains the character of Hector. In what sense is the speaker of the poem "traveling" with Hector?

Vocabulary **idyll** (YD uhl) *n.:* short work of prose or poetry about an idealized country scene.
goblet (GAHB liht) *n.:* drinking vessel, often ornate.
epilogue (EHP uh lawg) *n.:* short section at the end of a literary work that often tells what happened after the end of the story.

California Standards, p. 1395

- **Reading Standard 3.1** Analyze characteristics of subgenres (e.g., satire, parody, allegory, pastoral) that are used in poetry, prose, plays, novels, short stories, essays, and other basic genres.
- **Reading Standard 3.3** Analyze the ways in which irony, tone, mood, the author's style, and the "sound" of language achieve specific rhetorical or aesthetic purposes or both.
- **Reading Standard 3.6** Analyze the way in which authors through the centuries have used archetypes drawn from myth and tradition in literature, film, political speeches, and religious writings (e.g., how the archetypes of banishment from an ideal world may be used to interpret Shakespeare's tragedy *Macbeth*).
- **Reading Standard 3.7** Analyze recognized works of world literature from a variety of authors: **c.** Evaluate the philosophical, political, religious, ethical, and social influences of the historical period that shaped the characters, plots, and settings.
- **Writing Standard 2.3** Write reflective compositions: **a.** Explore the significance of personal experiences, events, conditions, or concerns by using rhetorical strategies (e.g., narration, description, exposition, persuasion).

Applying Your Skills

Reading Standard 3.1 3.3, 3.6 3.7c (see pages A48–A50)
Writing Standard 2.3a (see pages A51–A52)

from Omeros

Literary Response and Analysis

Reading Skills Focus

Quick Check

1. How would you describe Achille? What kind of person does he seem to be? Give details to support your description. (Consider what Achille kills and why.)
2. Where is the speaker of this poem? What has happened to him?
3. Why does the speaker ask the "deep hymn / of the Caribbean" to continue his epilogue?

Read with a Purpose

4. What is the speaker's opinion of Achille and his actions?

Reading Skills: Using Background Knowledge

5. Review the chart you made as you read. Now, create a Venn diagram. Label one circle "Epic Form and Allusions," and in it write what the poem owes to ancient Western literature. Label the other circle "Culture," and in it write how the poem represents Caribbean culture. In the intersecting space, describe how the Caribbean subject matter and the classical form combine.

Vocabulary Check

Match the Vocabulary words with their definitions.

6. ascended	**a.** drinking vessel
7. idyll	**b.** went up
8. goblet	**c.** final part of a story or poem
9. epilogue	**d.** pastoral poem or story

Literary Skills Focus

Literary Analysis

10. **Analyze** To what does the poet compare the coffin in line 27? Why do you think he chose this metaphor?
11. **Compare and Contrast** How is Achille similar to and different from traditional epic heroes? Consider that most heroes have adventures, often during war.
12. **Make Judgments** How does the speaker feel about the setting? How can you tell?

Literary Skills: Contemporary Epic

13. **Interpret** Do you think the epic form enriches the meaning of this poem? Why or why not?

Literary Skills Review: Diction

14. **Analyze** What diction, or word choice, does the poet use that does not seem to belong to the world in which the poem is set?

Writing Skills Focus

Think as a Reader/Writer

Use It in Your Writing As you read the excerpt, you noted Walcott's use of realistic detail and figurative language. Now, recall your QuickWrite. What person did you name whose deeds you might want to celebrate? Write a short poem praising this person. Use both specific, realistic detail and figurative language. Your poem does not have to rhyme.

What Do You Think Now? How is Walcott's experience living in the Caribbean reflected in the poem?

Check for Understanding

Independent Practice

Reading Skills Focus

Possible responses:

1. *Achille is a person with few material possessions (lines 11–12) and with great personal power (lines 13–15).*
2. *The speaker of the poem is in his boat, which is metaphorically a coffin. He is dying in a storm at sea.*
3. *He asks this because he is going to die, so he will not be able to retell the story.*
4. *The speaker is in awe of Achille, saying he would rather Achille hold his coffin than hold Achille's coffin himself (lines 16–17).*
5. *Remind students to use their background knowledge of the Caribbean to complete the Venn diagram.*

Vocabulary Check

6. *b* **7.** *d*
8. *a* **9.** *c*

Literary Skills Focus

Possible responses:

10. *He compares his coffin with a pyramid, accentuating his humble heritage and demise.*
11. *Achille has the qualities of a hero, but he is fishing for food, not fighting a war. This is Walcott's comment on the realities of colonial oppression.*
12. *The character feels deeply familiar with the setting but nevertheless in awe of it. The images of waves crashing (line 31) and the log swirling (line 35) convey the power of the sea.*
13. *Students' responses will vary depending on their appreciation of the epic form.*
14. *Words that don't seem to fit the setting include "elevator" (line 2), "passport" (line 3), and "asterisks" (line 42).*

Universal Access

Struggling Writers

Have students create a T-chart in order to brainstorm characteristics about their subject. Students can use the chart to classify each characteristic as "realistic" or "figurative." Then, have students write two or three stanzas about the person whom they admire.

What Do You Think Now?

Review with students the references to setting in this excerpt from *Omeros*. Discuss how these details reflect Walcott's experience living in the Caribbean.

Assess

Unit 6 Resources,
Selection Standards Check, p. 241

Selection Introduction

Think About the Writer

Introducing students to the following quote from V. S. Naipaul: "I began to write, I'm afraid, for no other reason than I thought it would be nice to be a writer. . . . One assumed it was all very interesting, writing these fabulous things, without pausing to consider what went before—and during—the writing of the fabulous things. . . . In fact writing is just a sort of disease, a sickness, it's a form of incompleteness, it's a form of anguish, it's despair." Ask students how this quote supports the notion that Naipaul's life as an outsider caused him to be disconnected from his own writing.

For Independent Reading

Dreaming in Color, Living in Black and White: Our Own Stories of Growing Up Black in America, Laurel Holliday, ed.

Motivate

What Do You Think?/QuickWrite

Before students write in their **Reader/Writer Notebooks**, have them work as a class to brainstorm adjectives about poets. Discuss any stereotypes or assumptions that are unearthed through this brainstorming session.

California Standards, pp. 1396–1405

- **Reading Standard 3.2** Analyze the way in which the theme or meaning of a selection represents a view or comment on life, using textual evidence to support the claim.
- **Reading Standard 3.7** Analyze recognized works of world literature from a variety of authors: **c.** Evaluate the philosophical, political, religious, ethical, and social influences of the historical period that shaped the characters, plots, and settings.

Preparing to Read

B. Wordsworth

What Do You Think? How does experience shape our view of the world?

QuickWrite

In your *Reader/Writer Notebook,* write out four or five qualities you associate with poets. As you read, see how your image of poets corresponds with that of the poet in the story.

V. S. Naipaul, Edinburgh, Scotland (2001).

MEET THE WRITER

V. S. Naipaul

(1932–)

Nobel Prize WINNER

Naipaul's works have been acclaimed for their bitter yet compassionate insights into the human struggle for identity and survival.

Escape from the Island

When V. S. (Vidiadhar Surajprasad) Naipaul was born, his homeland, the Caribbean island of Trinidad, was still under British colonial rule. His family had immigrated to Trinidad in the nineteenth century to work as indentured servants on the sugar plantations. With their Asian background and Hindu religion, the Naipauls felt like members of a transplanted society. As a result, from his earliest days, Naipaul felt a degree of rootlessness. He also found it difficult to adapt to life on the small island, a world that at times seemed a sort of prison.

Fortunately, Naipaul was an outstanding student. Scholastic honors won him a place at Trinidad's Queen's Royal College and gave him a chance to leave the island. Later, he was granted a scholarship to England's Oxford University, where he was one of only a few dark-skinned students at a university famous for educating England's privileged white upper classes.

When Naipaul left Oxford, he had no desire to return to Trinidad. He began working part time for the British Broadcasting Corporation (BBC) and tried his hand at writing fiction about the island life he had fled. His first short stories, which later became *Miguel Street,* went unnoticed until he was able to publish two novels set in Trinidad.

A Place in the Limelight

Naipaul's first masterpiece, *A House for Mr. Biswas,* concerns a poor Trinidadian's desperate quest for a house of his own. The book, which some critics have compared to the works of Charles Dickens, established Naipaul as a major novelist throughout the literary world.

Naipaul has won numerous awards, including the Nobel Prize in Literature. His search for roots has led him to travel back to the West Indies and then to Africa, the Middle East, and India as he pursues the meaning of his own mixed heritage.

Think About the Writer How do you think Naipaul's sense of being an outsider might affect his life and his writing?

Selection Readability	
Easily Accessible **Accessible** Challenging	simple sentence structure; simple dialogue; familiar language

Reading Standard 3.2, 3.7c (see pages A48–A50)

Literary Skills Focus

Setting The time and place of a story is known as its **setting.** The setting of this story is the back streets of Port-of-Spain, capital of Trinidad, where Naipaul lived as a child. Naipaul uses imagery and dialogue, as well as factual details, to enliven the setting. Several of the story's details, such as beggars asking for pennies, suggest it takes place during the Great Depression in the 1930s, the years of Naipaul's own childhood. As you will see, the main characters of "B. Wordsworth," a young boy and an old, self-proclaimed poet, seem to be set apart from their harsh surroundings. At arm's length from the story's other, more desperate characters, the pair are determined to find and appreciate spots of beauty in an otherwise violent—or at best indifferent—world.

Reading Skills Focus

Drawing Inferences About Theme Few stories explicitly state their **theme,** or central idea or insight about human experience. The reader is expected to **infer** the theme from clues in the text. Every element of a story—its plot; the thoughts, feelings, and actions of its characters; its language; and its setting—work together to express a theme.

Into Action As you read, ask yourself how each element of the story reflects the theme. Write your notes in an organizer like the one below.

Plot	Characterization	Language	Setting
	B. Wordsworth describes himself as a poet.		

Writing Skills Focus

Think as a Reader/Writer

Find It in Your Reading In this story, Naipaul uses **dialect,** or a variant form, of English. In your *Reader/Writer Notebook,* record the lines of dialect and list ways it differs from standard English. How might the story change if these lines were in standard English? What would the story lose or gain?

TechFocus Imagine that you are in charge of adapting this story to the big screen. Take notes describing the characters and the setting, and decide how you would convey them on film.

Reader/Writer Notebook

Use your **RWN** to complete the activities for this selection.

Vocabulary

botanical (buh TAN uh kuhl) *adj.:* of plants or plant life; relating to the science of botany. *The old man had a great deal of botanical knowledge about trees and flowers.*

rite (ryt) *n.:* formal ceremony. *A rite was held to remember those who died in the war.*

patronize (PAY truh nyz) *v.:* be a customer of. *The man and the boy considered carefully which shop to patronize.*

distill (dihs TIHL) *v.:* draw out the essence of. *The old man was able to distill all his wisdom into a few words.*

keenly (KEEN lee) *adv.:* strongly and clearly. *The boy felt the poet's pain so keenly that he was overcome with sadness.*

Language Coach

Multiple-Meaning Words The Vocabulary word *patronize* has more than one meaning. In addition to the definition provided above, *patronize* can mean "look down on or be condescending toward" or "support an art or cause." Use context clues to help you tell which meaning is used in each sentence:

1. Their friends *patronize* the ballet by buying tickets for each performance.
2. The young poets *patronize* the local bookstore.
3. The women *patronize* the teenager by pretending to like her poetry.

Learn It Online

Hear a professional actor read this story online.

go.hrw.com H12-1397 Go

Comparing Texts Resources

Unit 6 Resources, on-level practice and assessment, p. 244

Teacher One Stop™, on-level lesson plans and all print resources

Holt Audio Library

Holt Audio Library: Selections and Summaries in Spanish

UA: Differentiating Instruction, graphic organizer p. 321

UA: Supporting Instruction in Spanish, selection summary

ThinkCentral Online Assessment, Selection Standards Check

ThinkCentral Online Remediation

Preteach

Introducing Vocabulary

- Read aloud the Vocabulary words and sample sentences. Then, use this activity to check students' understanding.
- Have students add the Vocabulary word that fits each blank in the following paragraph.

During the day, I like to ______ [*patronize*] that outdoor café and to enjoy the beautiful ______ [*botanical*] gardens nearby. As a nightly ______ [*rite*], I return to the scene to stargaze. What knowledge I ______ [*distill*] from these nights at the café! I am ______ [*keenly*] aware of the insights I receive from the experience.

English for Academic Success

Language Coach

Ask students to explain how the context clues in each sentence help them understand which meaning of the word is used.

Literary Skills Focus

As you read and discuss the selection with students, have them note details about setting in the imagery and dialogue.

Reading Skills Focus

Give students a copy of the Reading Skills Focus graphic organizer before they read. (See **Unit 6 Resources**.) Tell them to use their responses to answer the questions on the Applying Your Skills page.

Writing Skills Focus

Have students record examples of dialect in their **Reader/Writer Notebooks**. Students can use their notes to complete the Writing Skills Focus activity.

Learn It Online

The online version of this story includes audio support to engage all students and to help struggling readers with comprehension and vocabulary.

go.hrw.com H12-1397 Go

Teacher Preparation

Selection Plot Summary

A small, neatly dressed stranger asks to come inside a boy's yard to watch bees. He tells the boy he is "Black" [B.] Wordsworth, a poet who shares "White" Wordsworth's heart; however, he has never sold a poem. The man insists that the boy is also a poet, and the two become friends. B. Wordsworth encourages the boy to approach even mundane events with reverent delight. He tells him a story of two poets who married and lived happily until the girl poet and her unborn baby died in childbirth. He claims to be writing "the greatest poem in the world" at the rate of one line per month, but he reveals only one line: "The past is deep." One day the boy finds his friend lying ill in his spare, one-room hut. B. Wordsworth tells the boy that he invented the story about the two poets and asks him never to return. A year later the boy finds the hut and lush garden replaced by a modern, concrete building.

Direct Teach

Think About/Talk About

Read with a Purpose Have students read the Read with a Purpose statement. Then, have students review the list of adjectives they created in the QuickWrite. Ask students to look for those attributes in the character of B. Wordsworth.

Analysis

A Literary Focus

Possible response: *Details that help readers visualize the setting include gru-gru palm trees, an Indian in his dhoti, rice in a tin cup, the old woman smoking a pipe, and a blind man being led by a boy.*

SHORT STORY

B. WORDSWORTH

by **V. S. Naipaul**

Papiamento (1987), by Julio Larraz, oil on canvas. Marlborough Gallery, New York.

Read with a Purpose

Read to discover what makes B. Wordsworth a poet.

Build Background

The poet in this story is a black Trinidadian who calls himself B. [Black] Wordsworth, "brother" to William Wordsworth. Recall that English poet William Wordsworth introduced a new theory of poetry that glorified everyday things and everyday language.

Three beggars called punctually every day at the hospitable houses in Miguel Street. At about ten an Indian came in his dhoti[1] and white jacket, and we poured a tin of rice into the sack he carried on his back. At twelve an old woman smoking a clay pipe came and she got a cent. At two a blind man led by a boy called for his penny. **A**

Sometimes we had a rogue.[2] One day a man called and said he was hungry. We gave him a meal. He asked for a cigarette and wouldn't go until we had lit it for him. That man never came again.

The strangest caller came one afternoon at about four o'clock. I had come back from school and was in my home clothes. The man said to me, "Sonny, may I come inside your yard?"

He was a small man and he was tidily dressed. He wore a hat, a white shirt, and black trousers.

I asked, "What you want?"

He said, "I want to watch your bees."

We had four small gru-gru palm trees[3] and they were full of uninvited bees.

1. **dhoti** (DOH tee): loincloth worn by many Hindu men.
2. **rogue** (rohg): archaic for "wandering beggar."
3. **gru-gru** (GROO groo) **palm trees:** spiny-trunked West Indian palms.

A Literary Focus **Setting** What details help you visualize the scene on Miguel Street?

Universal Access

Struggling Readers

This story is a series of episodes tied together through the two main characters. As students read, urge them to notice how the relationship between the characters deepens and to consider what each character is giving to the other. Whenever the students reach a new episode with a new setting, have them draw a square on a sheet of paper and write down the location of the setting and the characters within it. They can use this as a visual aid to study the deepening relationship between B. Wordsworth and the boy.

Advanced Learners

Acceleration As students read the story, ask them to consider the validity of the title character's declaration that he and William Wordsworth "share one heart." In what ways is this true? In what ways are the two men very different? Have students refer to specific Wordsworth poems when formulating their opinions. They can discuss their findings with the class.

I ran up the steps and shouted, "Ma, it have a man outside here. He say he want to watch the bees."

My mother came out, looked at the man, and asked in an unfriendly way, "What you want?"

The man said, "I want to watch your bees."

His English was so good, it didn't sound natural, and I could see my mother was worried.

She said to me, "Stay here and watch him while he watch the bees."

The man said, "Thank you, Madam. You have done a good deed today."

He spoke very slowly and very correctly as though every word was costing him money.

We watched the bees, this man and I, for about an hour, squatting near the palm trees.

The man said, "I like watching bees. Sonny, do you like watching bees?"

I said, "I ain't have the time."

Think About/Talk About

Extend the Discussion

Making Predictions Based on the interactions among B. Wordsworth, the boy, and the mother, how do you think their relationship will evolve? ***Possible response:*** *The mother seems suspicious of B. Wordsworth, so tension might develop between the two. The boy is intrigued by B. Wordsworth's deliberate nature, so the boy might develop a fascination with the poet.*

Speculating Why might B. Wordsworth find it important to study the bees in the boy's yard? ***Possible responses:*** *Watching the bees would provide stimulation for the senses of sight, sound, and possibly smell, which would appeal to a poet. B. Wordsworth may also want an opportunity to connect with the boy; he may be watching the bees to fulfill that purpose.*

Students with Disabilities

Discuss with students how poets tend to rely on their senses to communicate their experiences. Ask students to write down the five senses in a column: *sight, sound, touch, taste,* and *smell.* Tell them they are to go on a "scavenger hunt" to find an example of how B. Wordsworth uses each of these senses in the story.

✔ See **UA: Differentiating Instruction** for a graphic organizer to scaffold instruction for students with disabilities.

Cross-Curricular Connection

GEOGRAPHY: Trinidad

Have students review the story to find examples of descriptive details about the setting, such as the abundance of gru-gru palm trees or the juicy mangos. Then, have students deepen their understanding of Naipaul's choice of details by researching information about the natural history of the two islands of Trinidad and Tobago. Possible focal points for research include the islands' geologic origins, characteristic flora and fauna, and climate. Have students share their findings with the class.

Think About/Talk About

Extend the Discussion

Drawing Conclusions Given the boy's reference to his mother beating him, what can you conclude about cultural views of parental discipline in Port of Spain at that time? ***Possible response:*** *The boy seems to accept the fact that his mother beats him, so it must be commonplace for parents to discipline their children in this way.*

Determining Author's Purpose Why do you think Naipaul included the detail about the constellation of Orion the Hunter? ***Possible response:*** *The constellation could be a metaphor for the larger world awaiting the boy through the art of observation and the world of poetry.*

He shook his head sadly. He said, "That's what I do, I just watch. I can watch ants for days. Have you ever watched ants? And scorpions, and centipedes, and *congorees*[4]—have you watched those?"

I shook my head.

I said, "What you does do, mister?"

He got up and said, "I am a poet."

I said, "A good poet?"

He said, "The greatest in the world."

"What your name, mister?"

"B. Wordsworth."

"B for Bill?"

"Black. Black Wordsworth. White Wordsworth was my brother. We share one heart. I can watch a small flower like the morning glory and cry."

I said, "Why you does cry?"

"Why, boy? Why? You will know when you grow up. You're a poet, too, you know. And when you're a poet you can cry for everything."

I couldn't laugh.

He said, "You like your mother?"

"When she not beating me."

He pulled out a printed sheet from his hip pocket and said, "On this paper is the greatest poem about mothers and I'm going to sell it to you at a bargain price. For four cents."

I went inside and I said, "Ma, you want to buy a poetry for four cents?"

My mother said, "Tell that blasted man to haul his tail away from my yard, you hear."

I said to B. Wordsworth, "My mother say she ain't have four cents."

B. Wordsworth said, "It is the poet's tragedy."

And he put the paper back in his pocket. He didn't seem to mind.

I said, "Is a funny way to go round selling poetry like that. Only calypsonians[5] do that sort of thing. A lot of people does buy?"

He said, "No one has yet bought a single copy."

"But why you does keep on going round, then?"

He said, "In this way I watch many things, and I always hope to meet poets."

I said, "You really think I is a poet?"

"You're as good as me," he said. **B**

And when B. Wordsworth left, I prayed I would see him again.

About a week later, coming back from school one afternoon, I met him at the corner of Miguel Street.

He said, "I have been waiting for you for a long time."

I said, "You sell any poetry yet?"

He shook his head.

He said, "In my yard I have the best mango tree in Port-of-Spain.[6] And now the mangoes are ripe and red and very sweet and juicy. I have waited here for you to tell you this and to invite you to come and eat some of my mangoes." **C**

He lived in Alberto Street in a one-roomed hut placed right in the center of the lot. The yard seemed all green. There was the big mango tree. There was a coconut tree and there was a plum tree. The place looked wild, as though it wasn't in the city at all. You couldn't see all the big concrete houses in the street. **D**

He was right. The mangoes were sweet and juicy. I ate about six, and the yellow mango juice ran down my

4. ***congorees*** (KAHNG guh reez): conger eels; long, scaleless eels found in the warm waters of the West Indies.

5. **calypsonians** (kuh lihp SOH nee uhnz): West Indian folk musicians who traditionally perform satirical, syncopated songs that are improvised, or composed on the spot. *Calypso* possibly comes from *kaiso,* a Trinidadian dialect word meaning "town crier."

6. **Port-of-Spain:** seaport on the island of Trinidad; capital of Trinidad and Tobago.

B **Reading Focus** **Making Inferences About Theme** What do you think B. Wordsworth means when he says that the boy is a poet? What might being a poet have to do with the theme of the story?

C **Literary Focus** **Setting** How does the tropical setting of Trinidad help form B. Wordsworth's ideas about life?

D **Literary Focus** **Setting** What can you infer about B. Wordsworth's values from this description of his home?

Word-Attack Skills Mini-Lesson

English for Academic Success Explain that George Bernard Shaw once observed that English spelling is so irregular that *fish* could be spelled *ghoti—gh* for /f/, as *cough*; or *o* for /i/, as in *women*; *ti* for /sh/, as in *action*.

The Hindu word *dhoti* (DOH tee), which appears in this selection, is very similar in spelling to *ghoti* and contains two common but irregular letter-sound correspondences: silent *h* and *i* for long *e*. Silent *h* has been dealt with in an earlier mini-lesson. Explore with students words in which *i* stands for /ee/.

Activity Have students study the words that follow and identify those in which *i* stands for /ee/. Then, ask students to develop some general rules about when *i* stands for /ee/.

<u>maniac</u>	maniacal	biology
<u>craniology</u>	facial	fictitious
<u>ambient</u>	resilient	alliance
<u>dalliance</u>	<u>perennial</u>	<u>vegetarian</u>
vegetation	<u>melodious</u>	<u>oriel</u>

Students might conclude that *i* usually stands for /ee/ when it precedes another vowel in a syllable other than arms to my elbows and down my mouth to my chin and my shirt was stained.

My mother said when I got home, "Where you was? You think you is a man now and could go all over the place? Go cut a whip for me."

She beat me rather badly, and I ran out of the house swearing that I would never come back. I went to B. Wordsworth's house. I was so angry, my nose was bleeding.

B. Wordsworth said, "Stop crying, and we will go for a walk."

I stopped crying, but I was breathing short. We went for a walk. We walked down St. Clair Avenue to the Savannah[7] and we walked to the racecourse.

B. Wordsworth said, "Now, let us lie on the grass and look up at the sky, and I want you to think how far those stars are from us."

I did as he told me, and I saw what he meant. I felt like nothing, and at the same time I had never felt so big and great in all my life. I forgot all my anger and all my tears and all the blows.

When I said I was better, he began telling me the names of the stars, and I particularly remembered the constellation of Orion the Hunter,[8] though I don't really know why. I can spot Orion even today, but I have forgotten the rest.

Then a light was flashed into our faces, and we saw a policeman. We got up from the grass.

The policeman said, "What you doing here?"

B. Wordsworth said, "I have been asking myself the same question for forty years."

7. **Savannah** (suh VAN uh): two-hundred-acre park in the center of Port-of-Spain. The racecourse is located there.
8. **Orion** (aw RY uhn) **the Hunter:** constellation named for a hunter in Greek and Roman mythology whom Diana—the goddess of the moon and of hunting—loves but accidentally kills.

We became friends, B. Wordsworth and I. He told me, "You must never tell anybody about me and about the mango tree and the coconut tree and the plum tree. You must keep that a secret. If you tell anybody, I will know, because I am a poet."

I gave him my word and I kept it.

I liked his little room. It had no more furniture than George's front room,[9] but it looked cleaner and healthier. But it also looked lonely.

One day I asked him. "Mister Wordsworth, why you does keep all this bush in your yard? Ain't it does make the place damp?"

He said, "Listen, and I will tell you a story. Once upon a time a boy and girl met each other and they fell in love. They loved each other so much they got married. They were both poets. He loved words. She loved grass and flowers and trees. They lived happily in a single room, and then one day, the girl poet said to the boy poet, 'We are going to have another poet in the family.' But this poet was never born, because the girl died, and the young poet died with her, inside her. And the girl's husband was very sad, and he said he would never touch a thing in the girl's garden. And so the garden remained, and grew high and wild." **E**

I looked at B. Wordsworth, and as he told me this lovely story, he seemed to grow older. I understood his story.

We went for long walks together. We went to the Botanical Gardens and the Rock Gardens. We climbed Chancellor Hill in the late afternoon and watched the darkness fall on Port-of-Spain, and watched the lights go on in the city and on the ships in the harbor.

He did everything as though he were doing it for the first time in his life. He did everything as though he were doing some church rite. **F**

9. **George's front room:** George is a character in another story in Naipaul's book *Miguel Street.*

E Reading Focus **Making Inferences About Theme** What does B. Wordsworth's story tell you about his definition of a poet? What can you guess about the theme from his story and his definition of a poet?

F Reading Focus **Making Inferences About Theme** What do B. Wordsworth's attitudes suggest about how a poet should approach everyday life?

Vocabulary **botanical** (buh TAN uh kuhl) *adj.:* of plants or plant life; relating to the science of botany.
rite (ryt) *n.:* formal ceremony.

Think About/Talk About

Comprehension

B Reading Focus

Possible responses: *B. Wordsworth might feel that every human is potentially a poet, which would relate to the theme. He might also recognize something singular in the boy that speaks to B. Wordsworth's poetic nature.*

E Reading Focus

Possible responses: *B. Wordsworth reveals that he contemplates nature for years or even decades and finds meaning in even the smallest details. This indicates a patience and reverence that is central to his definition of a poet. It also develops the theme of the story: that everything has a voice and purpose.*

F Reading Focus

Possible response: *B. Wordsworth's attention to detail and powers of observation suggest that poets must have the time and temperament to study their environment with reverence.*

Analysis

C Literary Focus

Possible response: *B. Wordsworth appreciates the beauty of the island's insects, flowers, and fruits and takes the time to enjoy them.*

D Literary Focus

Possible response: *His home reflects his love of nature in its wild state.*

Vocabulary: Own the Word

- **botanical:** Ask students for examples of what the characters would have seen at the *Botanical* Gardens. ***Possible responses:*** *plants, flowers, shrubs, grasses*
- **rite:** Write *rite* in a center circle on the board and provide a definition: "ceremony." Draw spider legs from the center as students add concepts and attributes. ***Possible responses:*** *ritual, sacrament, custom*

the first syllable. Exceptions are as follows:

- when *i* follows *c* or *t* and has the effect of making those letters have the sound /sh/—*facial, fictitious, vegetation*
- when *i* follows *l* or *n* and has the sound /yuh/—*resilient, spaniel*
- in words with suffixes in which *l* replaces *y* pronounced /y/ in the base word—*ally, alliance*
- in words where there is an unusual stress shift when a suffix is added—*maniac, maniacal*

Universal Access

EL English Learners

English for Academic Success Read aloud the sentence on p. 1401: "It had no more furniture than George's front room, but it looked cleaner and healthier." Remind students that the comparative compares two things. It can be formed by adding *–er* at the end of a short adjective or by inserting *more* before a long adjective. Tell students that they should never use both. For instance: "His room was *more cleaner* than mine" should be "His room was *cleaner* than mine."

Model the Skill

- Provide students with a copy of the Reading Skills Focus graphic organizer for "B. Wordsworth." (See **Unit 6 Resources.**)
- Tell students that when making an inference about **theme,** they must evaluate setting, character, and language.
- Model completing a line from the graphic organizer. You might say: "At this point in the plot, B. Wordsworth takes the boy to patronize a café. Write under 'Plot,' 'B. Wordsworth takes the boy to a café.' This indicates B. Wordsworth's pleasure in celebration. Write this under 'Character.' The language of B. Wordsworth is precise and studied, while the boy's language is a street dialect. Write this under 'Language.' The setting is at a café in Trinidad. Write this information under 'Setting.'"

Plot	Characterization
B. Wordsworth takes the boy to a café.	B. Wordsworth enjoys celebrations.
Language	**Setting**
precise and studied	Café in Trinidad

Guided Practice: Apply

Think-Pair-Share Have students think about the relevance of these details to the story's theme. Have students work with a partner to discuss the importance of taking time to celebrate small details and moments. Have pairs find a small detail they both appreciate and share it with the class.

The Trial (1986), by Julio Larraz, oil on canvas. Marlborough Gallery, New York.

Analyzing Visuals

Connecting to the Text Note that the subject's face is blurred but his wedding ring is quite visible. How do artists and writers emphasize or downplay certain traits to construct a subject's or character's identity? What distinguishing characteristics does Naipaul give to B. Wordsworth?

He would say to me, "Now, how about having some ice cream?"

And when I said, yes, he would grow very serious and say, "Now, which café shall we patronize?" As though it were a very important thing. He would think for some time about it, and finally say, "I think I will go and negotiate the purchase with that shop."

The world became a most exciting place. One day, when I was in his yard, he said to me, "I have a great secret which I am now going to tell you."

I said, "It really secret?"

"At the moment, yes."

I looked at him, and he looked at me. He said, "This is just between you and me, remember. I am writing a poem."

"Oh." I was disappointed.

He said, "But this is a different sort of poem. This is the greatest poem in the world."

I whistled.

He said, "I have been working on it for more than five years now. I will finish it in about twenty-two years from now, that is, if I keep on writing at the present rate."

"You does write a lot, then?"

He said, "Not any more. I just write one line a month. But I make sure it is a good line."

I asked, "What was last month's good line?"

He looked up at the sky, and said, *"The past is deep."*

I said, "It is a beautiful line."

B. Wordsworth said, "I hope to distill the experiences of a whole month into that single line of poetry.

Vocabulary **patronize** (PAY truh nyz) *v.:* be a customer of.
distill (dihs TIHL) *v.:* draw out the essence of.

Cross-Curricular Connection

HISTORY: Before Independence

V. S. Naipaul writes, "The society I came from was colonial, and was originally a slave society, to which, later, people like myself, from Asia, went." Ask students to research the political and social history of Trinidad, including the effects of British rule. For example, Naipaul reports, "When I was a child in Trinidad . . . there were eight or perhaps twelve free places in the secondary schools. Twelve free places in an island that had a population of over half a million. What an attitude to human beings."

Analyzing Visuals

The works of **Julio Larraz** (1944–), a Cuban artist, often suggest multiple interpretations, requiring the viewer to participate in creating meaning.

Connecting to the Text: *Soft colors and blurry lines are often used to downplay certain features or characteristics. Sharply contrasting colors and crisp outlines, on the other hand, can emphasize particular details. Naipaul emphasizes B. Wordsworth's poetic attachment to nature and his childlike spirit.*

So, in twenty-two years, I shall have written a poem that will sing to all humanity."

I was filled with wonder.

Our walks continued. We walked along the sea wall at Docksite one day, and I said, "Mr. Wordsworth, if I drop this pin in the water, you think it will float?"

He said, "This is a strange world. Drop your pin, and let us see what will happen."

The pin sank.

I said, "How is the poem this month?"

But he never told me any other line. He merely said, "Oh, it comes, you know. It comes."

Or we would sit on the sea wall and watch the liners come into the harbor.

But of the greatest poem in the world I heard no more.

I felt he was growing older.

"How you does live, Mr. Wordsworth?" I asked him one day.

He said, "You mean how I get money?"

When I nodded, he laughed in a crooked way.

He said, "I sing calypsos in the calypso season."

"And that last you the rest of the year?"

"It is enough."

"But you will be the richest man in the world when you write the greatest poem?"

He didn't reply.

One day when I went to see him in his little house, I found him lying on his little bed. He looked so old and so weak, that I found myself wanting to cry.

He said, "The poem is not going well."

He wasn't looking at me. He was looking through the window at the coconut tree, and he was speaking as though I wasn't there. He said, "When I was twenty I felt the power within myself." Then, almost in front of my eyes, I could see his face growing older and more tired. He said, "But that—that was a long time ago."

And then—I felt it so keenly, it was as though I had been slapped by my mother. I could see it clearly on his face. It was there for everyone to see. Death on the shrinking face.

He looked at me, and saw my tears and sat up.

He said, "Come." I went and sat on his knees.

He looked into my eyes, and he said, "Oh, you can see it, too. I always knew you had the poet's eye." **G**

He didn't even look sad, and that made me burst out crying loudly.

He pulled me to his thin chest, and said, "Do you want me to tell you a funny story?" and he smiled encouragingly at me.

But I couldn't reply.

He said, "When I have finished this story, I want you to promise that you will go away and never come back to see me. Do you promise?"

I nodded.

He said, "Good. Well, listen. That story I told you about the boy poet and the girl poet, do you remember that? That wasn't true. It was something I just made up. All this talk about poetry and the greatest poem in the world, that wasn't true, either. Isn't that the funniest thing you have heard?"

But his voice broke.

I left the house, and ran home crying, like a poet, for everything I saw.

I walked along Alberto Street a year later, but I could find no sign of the poet's house. It hadn't vanished, just like that. It had been pulled down, and a big, two-storied building had taken its place. The mango tree and the plum tree and the coconut tree had all been cut down, and there was brick and concrete everywhere. **H**

It was just as though B. Wordsworth had never existed.

G Reading Focus **Making Inferences About Theme** What does B. Wordsworth mean when he says that the boy possesses "the poet's eye"?

H Literary Focus **Setting** What do these changes in the setting signify?

Vocabulary **keenly** (KEEN lee) *adv.:* strongly and clearly.

Think About/Talk About

Comprehension

G Reading Focus

Possible response: *He means that the boy sees things as a poet would or that the boy has the perception and sensibility of a poet.*

Analysis

H Literary Focus

Possible responses: *The changes could signify the encroachment of modern urban life on nature; the tendency of modern life to stifle poetic ideas; or the idea that poetry has no lasting effect on modern life.*

Vocabulary: Own the Word

- **patronize:** Tell students that just as a *patron* of a restaurant is a supporter or client; to *patronize* a place is to support it by being a paying customer. Ask students to name some places they *patronize.*
- **distill:** Ask students to explain why B. Wordsworth wants to *distill* a month into a line of poetry. ***Possible response:*** *to condense the experience and extract the most possible meaning from it*
- **keenly:** Ask students: "Have you ever felt something so *keenly* that you could not forget that feeling? Explain what it was that you felt so *keenly,* why the feeling was so intense, and how you look back on the experience now."

Monitor Students' Comprehension

Guide the class in answering these comprehension questions:

1. Why does B. Wordsworth want to enter the boy's yard? [*to observe the bees in the tree*]
2. How would the boy describe B. Wordsworth's home? [*a simple hut with lush fruit trees*]
3. What does B. Wordsworth reveal to the boy to be untrue? [*that the girl poet and the baby died*]

California Standards, pp. 1404–1405

- **Reading Standard 3.2** Analyze the way in which the theme or meaning of a selection represents a view or comment on life, using textual evidence to support the claim.
- **Reading Standard 3.7** Analyze recognized works of world literature from a variety of authors: **c.** Evaluate the philosophical, political, religious, ethical, and social influences of the historical period that shaped the characters, plots, and settings.
- **Grades 9–10 Review Reading Standard 1.1** Identify and use the literal and figurative meanings of words and understand word derivations.
- **Grades 9–10 Review Reading Standard 3.4** Determine characters' traits by what the characters say about themselves in narration, dialogue, dramatic monologue, and soliloquy.
- **Writing Standard 2.1** Write fictional, autobiographical, or biographical narratives: **c.** Describe with concrete sensory details the sights, sounds, and smells of a scene and the specific actions, movements, gestures, and feelings of the characters; use interior monologue to depict the characters' feelings.
- **Listening and Speaking Standards 1.10** Evaluate when to use different kinds of effects (e.g., visual, music, sound, graphics) to create effective productions.

Check for Understanding

Independent Practice

Reading Skills Focus

Possible responses:

1. *He means they are connected and "share the same heart."*
2. *He felt like "nothing" and at the same time felt powerful.*
3. *The boy greatly admires B. Wordsworth and cares deeply for him. B. Wordsworth taught the boy to see beauty in nature.*
4. *Review with students their initial thoughts about what defines a poet.*
5. *Students' sentences should include references to what makes someone a poet.*

Literary Skills Focus

Possible responses:

6. *He is questioning the purpose of life. Many poets seek to understand the purpose of life.*
7. *If the story is true, he denies it because he wants the boy to accept mystery. If the story is not true, he tells it to inspire the boy's imagination.*
8. *He may have felt that the end of his life was near and found it difficult to appreciate living things.*
9. *Naipaul might want to show how a love of beauty softens and improves one's perspective.*
10. *The inspiration of natural beauty and the frustrations of poverty and colonialism all play a part in Naipaul's becoming a writer. Naipaul believes that poets play a crucial role in affirming nature's beauty and the potential of human beings.*
11. *Students may recollect the lushness of B. Wordsworth's yard, the palm trees humming with the bees, and the starry sky, including the constellation Orion.*
12. *Students' responses will vary. Students should support their responses with specific examples of characterization from the text.*

Applying Your Skills

Reading Standard 3.2, 3.7c; **Grades 9–10 Review**
Reading Standard 3.4 (see pages A48–A50)
Writing Standard 2.1c (see pages A51–A52)

B. Wordsworth

Literary Response and Analysis

Reading Skills Focus

Quick Check

1. What does B. Wordsworth mean when he says that White Wordsworth was his "brother"?
2. What did the boy find comforting about looking at the stars?
3. How does the boy feel about B. Wordsworth? What does the boy learn from him?

Read with a Purpose

4. Now that you have read the story, do you agree that B. Wordsworth is a poet? If not, why not? If so, what do you think makes him a poet?

Reading Skills: Drawing Inferences About Theme

5. Review the notes you made on plot, characterization, language, and setting in your chart. Think about how these elements work together, and write a sentence expressing the story's **theme,** or central idea or insight about life. Look back at your chart to make sure each element supports your interpretation of the theme.

Literary Skills Focus

Literary Analysis

6. **Analyze** Consider what B. Wordsworth says to the policeman who asks, "What you doing here?" How is B. Wordsworth's reply significant? (Is his response what poets also seek to know?)
7. **Make Judgments** Do you think B. Wordsworth's tragic story about the boy poet and the girl poet is true? If not, why did he tell it in the first place?
8. **Draw Conclusions** Why do you think B. Wordsworth stopped writing his poem?
9. **Compare and Contrast** Consider the contrast between the mother's no-nonsense ways and the poetic vision of B. Wordsworth. What might Naipaul want to express about the nature of poetry and the role of the poet in society?
10. **Hypothesize** If we think of the story's narrator as the author's recollection of himself at that age, what does the story suggest about the influences (historical, political, cultural) that made Naipaul a writer? What does it suggest about his view of the poet's position and role in society?

Literary Skills: Setting

11. **Evaluate** What parts of the setting are most vivid in your mind? If you were going to illustrate the story, on what images would you focus?

Literary Skills Review: Characterization

12. **Analyze** Writers develop their characters through dialogue, description, expression of their feelings and actions, and other characters' reactions. Which of these methods of **characterization** made the boy most real for you? What made B. Wordsworth most real for you?

Writing Skills Focus

Think as a Reader/Writer

Use It in Your Writing Re-read the lines of dialect you wrote in your *Reader/Writer Notebook.* Now, write a brief character sketch of an imaginary person. Use dialogue that gives your character a particular way of talking to reveal his or her background.

What Do You Think Now? What experiences do you think might have shaped B. Wordsworth's unique view of the world?

Universal Access

Struggling Writers

Some students may need additional scaffolding to complete the Writing Skills Focus activity. Remind students that the complexity of a character's language can reveal his or her age; dialect can reveal a character's location or place in time. Have students consider these points when writing their sketch.

What Do You Think Now?

Review with students the setting of "B. Wordsworth," particularly the level of poverty described.

Grades 9–10 Review Reading Standard 1.1 (see pages A48–A50)
Writing Standard 2.1c (see pages A51–A52)
Listening and Speaking Standard 1.10 (see pages A53–A55)

Vocabulary Development

Vocabulary Check

Match the Vocabulary words with their definitions.

1. botanical	a. concentrate
2. rite	b. strongly and clearly
3. patronize	c. ceremony
4. distill	d. of plants
5. keenly	e. buy from

Vocabulary Skills: Idioms

An **idiom** is a phrase whose meaning cannot be determined by the literal meanings of its individual words:

I met someone who told me she was a famous violinist, but she was just pulling my leg.

To *pull someone's leg,* for example, means "to tease or play a joke on someone," not to literally pull their leg.

The actress was a seasoned performer, but she still got butterflies in her stomach at performances.

To *have butterflies in your stomach* does not mean your stomach is filled with insects but that you feel nervous.

Your Turn

Read each sentence below, and identify the idioms.

1. His mother had a hard time making ends meet.
2. When the boy came home late, his mother was fit to be tied and punished him severely.
3. B. Wordsworth said the story was funny, but his voice was breaking as he told it.

Language Coach

Multiple-Meaning Words Write two definitions for each of the following words from the selection: *watch, flower, fell, present, last, broke.*

CHOICES

As you respond to the Choices, use these **Academic Vocabulary** words as appropriate: perspective, considerably, adapt, exhibit, inevitable.

REVIEW

Videotape a Scene

TechFocus In small groups, use the notes you made as you read to create and videotape one scene from the story. Have actors use their voices, body language, and costumes to develop the characters. Be creative about setting: You might videotape your scene in a garden, for example, and use mangoes to convey the idea that you are in B. Wordsworth's garden. Exhibit your final product to the class.

CONNECT

Write a Journal Entry

In the story, B. Wordsworth finds poetry in the intense appreciation of life. Write a journal entry about an experience that you appreciated intensely. Use sensory details to try to re-create the moment.

EXTEND

Research Calypsos

B. Wordsworth claims to make his living singing calypsos. Use library or Internet resources to find out more about calypsos. What are they typically about? What is their structure? Then, write a calypso of your own and share it with a small group of classmates.

Learn It Online

Use the Digital Storytelling site to help you develop a script and videotape your scene!

go.hrw.com H12-1405 Go

Vocabulary Check

1. *d* 2. *c*
3. *e* 4. *a*
5. *b*

Your Turn

1. *making ends meet*
2. *fit to be tied*
3. *his voice was breaking*

English for Academic Success

Language Coach

Possible responses:

watch—*to guard; a small timepiece*

flower—*a plant; to blossom*

fell—*caused to fall; destructive*

present—*a gift; current*

last—*the most recent; final*

broke—*penetrated; reduced to fragments*

Independent Practice

Choices: Evaluation Criteria

Review: Homework
Videotape a Scene

- Students should use their bodies, voices, language, and costumes to develop characterization.
- Settings should be creative and include details from the text.

Connect: Homework
Write a Journal Entry

- Students should include sensory details in their writing.
- Entries should express a deep appreciation for the subject.

Extend: Homework
Research Calypsos

- Students should include information from a reputable source on calypso singing.
- Students should apply what they have discovered during their research to their writing.

Assess

Unit 6 Resources, Selection Standards Check, p. 247

ThinkCentral Online Assessment, Selection Standards Check

Teacher One Stop™, editable Selection Standards Check

Reteach

ThinkCentral Online Remediation

Learn It Online

The **Digital Storytelling** mini-site shows students how to take a personal experience and craft it into a short film—complete with music, images, and special effects.

go.hrw.com H12-1405 Go

Selection Introduction

Think About the Writer

Ask students to consider what the United States has in common with postcolonial nations such as those discussed in the works by Derek Walcott and V. S. Naipaul. Then, have students think about how the political, economic, and social problems of these nations might concern an American writer.

For Independent Reading

Travels with My Aunt, Graham Greene

Motivate

What Do You Think?/QuickWrite

Discuss with students the idea of mentorship. What makes mentor-student relationships successful? What makes them fail? Then, have students write a few sentences in their **Reader/Writer Notebooks** about a mentor in their lives.

Preparing to Read

from Sir Vidia's Shadow

What Do You Think? How does experience shape our view of the world?

QuickWrite

In your *Reader/Writer Notebook,* record a few thoughts about someone you consider to be a mentor and how that person has helped you.

Paul Theroux, Clapham, London (1989).

MEET THE WRITER

Paul Theroux

(1941–)

Described as "the quintessential explorer with a talent for noticing the odd, compelling detail," Paul Theroux is one of America's most skilled travel writers.

A World Traveler

Theroux was born in Medford, Massachusetts, into a large, working-class family. As a child, he was a voracious reader, but only after taking a creative writing class in college did he consider becoming a writer. After graduation, Theroux joined the Peace Corps and was sent to teach English in Malawi, southern Africa. After becoming connected with a political group the government distrusted, Theroux was deported. Nevertheless, he soon returned to Africa and settled in Uganda, where he met V. S. Naipaul, already an acclaimed novelist. Naipaul became Theroux's mentor, and the two writers struck up a friendship that would last for thirty years. Theroux's first novel, *Waldo,* was published while he was living in Uganda.

An Ironic Wit

From Uganda, Theroux moved to Singapore and then to London, where he began writing full time. In 1975, he published *The Great Railway Bazaar,* a bestselling travel book about his four-month train trip across Europe and Asia. Though set in many countries, all of Theroux's novels exhibit ironic wit and an acerbic perspective. According to Nadine Gordimer, "Paul Theroux is without peer as the merciless obituarist of colonialism. He knows his way matchlessly about the milieu where no one was ever at home. . . . Theroux novels are neither apologia nor accusation; wit is his rare medium, and that lays bare both."

Since 1967, Theroux has published more than forty-seven works of travel writing, novels, short story collections, and criticism. His work has won or been nominated for several awards, and four of his novels have been made into films. Theroux says that his main goal is to amuse his readers. "My fear is that I'll be boring. You never actually run out of ideas, but you might run out of ideas that are intelligent, amusing, original."

Think About the Writer What might the American writer Theroux have in common with postcolonial writers?

California Standards, pp. 1406–1413

- **Reading Standard 2.5** Analyze an author's implicit and explicit philosophical assumptions and beliefs about a subject.
- **Reading Standard 3.3** Analyze the ways in which irony, tone, mood, the author's style, and the "sound" of language achieve specific rhetorical or aesthetic purposes or both.

Selection Readability	
Easily Accessible **Accessible** Challenging	familiar vocabulary; accessible syntax; common theme

Applying Your Skills

Reading Standard 2.5, 3.3 (see pages A48–A50)
Writing Standard 2.3a (see pages A51–A52)

from Sir Vidia's Shadow

Literary Response and Analysis

Reading Skills Focus

Quick Check

1. Why is the author in London? How does he feel when he first arrives there?
2. Why did Sir Vidia not begin publishing his work in Trinidad?

Read with a Purpose

3. Who is Sir Vidia? What kind of "shadow" does the author believe Sir Vidia casts on him?

Reading Skills: Analyzing Author's Purpose

4. Add a row labeled "Summary" to the bottom of the organizer you made while reading. In the second column, summarize what the excerpt reveals about the author. In the third column, summarize what it reveals about Sir Vidia. Use this information to infer the author's purpose.

Vocabulary Check

Match the Vocabulary words with their definitions.

5. ritualistic	a. driven by impulse
6. compulsive	b. rejected
7. connoisseur	c. try to please
8. presumptuous	d. ceremonial
9. rebuffed	e. tasteful person
10. ingratiate	f. forward

Literary Skills Focus

Literary Analysis

11. **Analyze** What feelings does the author express about the festival? Is his attitude consistent throughout the excerpt? Explain your answer.
12. **Interpret** What do you think Sir Vidia meant when he called the life of a writer "terrible"?
13. **Evaluate** Are Sir Vidia's actions and possible motivations described in an objective way? Give examples to support your opinion.
14. **Make Judgments** At the end of the excerpt, the author states that he did not mind Sir Vidia's uncooperative behavior. How true do you think that statement is? Explain your answer.

Literary Skills: Tone

15. **Analyze** Describe the tone the author takes toward Sir Vidia. Explain whether it changes throughout the excerpt or remains consistent.

Literary Skills Review: Point of View

16. **Analyze** The perspective from which a story is told is **point of view.** From what point of view are these events told? How does the point of view affect your perception of the events?

Writing Skills Focus

Think as a Reader/Writer

Use It in Your Writing Review your list of realistic details from the excerpt. Write a paragraph about an event you have experienced. Use realistic details to help your readers visualize the event.

What Do You Think Now Theroux and Naipaul's friendship ended before Theroux wrote this account. How do you think this fact affected Theroux's perception of the events?

Universal Access

Struggling Writers

Students may need additional scaffolding to complete the Writing Skills Focus activity. Encourage students to write about a memorable event of no more than a few hours' duration, such as a first date or a rock concert. Before students begin writing, have them brainstorm a list of sensory details they remember, organized in categories (sights, sounds, etc.).

What Do You Think Now?

Ask students how they feel when they run into a person who used to be their friend. Discuss the feelings they have and the tone that develops during such chance meetings.

Assess

Unit 6 Resources,
Selection Standards Check, p. 253

Check for Understanding

Independent Practice

Reading Skills Focus

Possible responses:

1. *He is in London to catch a train to Hay-on-Wye. He is excited to take his ritual tour through the city.*
2. *Trinidad was not industrial.*
3. *Sir Vidia is V. S. Naipaul. Theroux once felt as if he was in the shadow of his mentor and that his writing was less known and acclaimed than Naipaul's.*
4. *Students' summaries should be supported by textual evidence.*

Vocabulary Check

5. *d* 6. *a*
7. *e* 8. *f*
9. *b* 10. *c*

Literary Skills Focus

Possible responses:

11. *Theroux's excitement about the festival diminishes because of Sir Vidia's attitude. We can tell he is excited at first because he quickly drops off his bag to go. The tension on the stage causes his interest to wane.*
12. *From what we know about Naipaul, writing for him was emotionally painful.*
13. *The details are told from a subjective point of view—Theroux's. He may try to be fair, but he is biased.*
14. *While he claims no longer to care what Sir Vidia thinks, if he were honest with himself, Theroux would probably realize that he feels sadness over the ending of an important relationship that spanned three decades.*
15. *At first Theroux's tone is hopeful, but after the two meet at Hay-on-Wye he becomes wary. Once they are on the stage, his tone becomes frustrated and even disdainful.*
16. *The story is told in first person, from Theroux's point of view. Readers are not privy to Naipaul's version of events and cannot hear his thoughts on this situation.*

Selection Introduction

Think About the Writer

To help students answer the question, have them think about the roles of women in different cultures and how those roles affect a woman's perspective on the world.

For Independent Reading

*In Light of India,** Octavio Paz

HRW LIBRARY *This title is available in the HRW library.

Motivate

What Do You Think?/QuickWrite

Encourage students to describe games like hide-and-seek or sports activities, not video games. Have students use their **Reader/Writer Notebooks** to explain details such as the rules and purpose of the game as well as strategies for winning.

English for Academic Success

Academic Vocabulary

Look for opportunities to use the Academic Vocabulary words in this unit.

- **adapt, *v.*:** adjust for a new purpose
- **considerably, adv.:** by a large amount
- **exhibit, *v.*:** show, demonstrate
- **inevitable, *adj.*:** unavoidable
- **perspective, *n.*:** particular way of looking at something

California Standards, pp. 1414–1424

- **Reading Standard 3.3** Analyze the ways in which irony, tone, mood, the author's style, and the "sound" of language achieve specific rhetorical or aesthetic purposes or both.
- **Grades 9–10 Review Reading Standard 3.7** Recognize and understand the significance of various literary devices, including figurative language, imagery, allegory, and symbolism, and explain their appeal.

Preparing to Read

Games at Twilight

What Do You Think? How does experience shape our view of the world?

QuickWrite

In your *Reader/Writer Notebook,* describe briefly a childhood game you frequently played and what you learned from playing it.

MEET THE WRITER

Anita Desai

(1937–)

Anita Desai has been described as "such a consummate artist that she [is able to suggest], beyond the confines of the plot and the machinations of her characters, the immensities that lie beyond them—the immensities of India."

Early Instincts

Born in Musoorie, India, Desai claims to have been writing "as instinctively as I breathe" since age seven. Her father was Bengali, and her mother was German, so Desai grew up hearing Hindi, English, and German spoken at home. English, however, was the language in which Desai learned to read and write. Desai was educated at the University of Delhi and began publishing her writing in 1963.

Reaching for Truth

Desai's novels often focus on the emotional and spiritual lives of wives, older women, or sisters who take responsibility for others but are unable to create satisfactory lives for themselves. Her novels include *Cry, the Peacock* (1963), *In Custody* (1984), *Baumgartner's Bombay* (1988), *Journey to Ithaca* (1995), *Fasting, Feasting* (1999), and *The Zigzag Way* (2004).

Desai's fiction also explores the trials of contemporary Indian characters as they struggle to adapt to cultural and social change. She sees her work as an attempt to discover "the truth that is nine-tenths of the iceberg that lies submerged beneath the one-tenth visible portion we call Reality." To evoke this "truth," Desai uses vivid, sensual language and intense imagery. Because of her sensuous style and use of rich imagery and symbolism, Desai has been referred to as an "imagist-novelist."

Desai has taught at Mount Holyoke and Smith Colleges and at the Massachusetts Institute of Technology. Her daughter Kiran Desai is the prize-winning author of the novel *The Inheritance of Loss.*

Think About the Writer How do you think Desai's cultural heritage might have affected her writing? Why might she have chosen to focus her writing on the experiences of women?

Kiran Desai and Anita Desai. Venice, Italy (2006).

Selection Readability	
Easily Accessible **Accessible** Challenging	accessible theme; familiar vocabulary

Reading Standard 3.3; **Grades 9–10 Review**
Reading Standard 3.7 (see pages A48–A50)

Literary Skills Focus

Imagery Fiction writers use **imagery,** language that appeals to the five senses, to help readers envision a given scene. Desai does not use simple imagery but rather drenches us in the smells, textures, sounds, and colors of a summer afternoon in India. From the bursting open of a door to the crushed silence of a defeated child, Desai enables us to experience the world through the eyes and ears of her characters.

Reading Skills Focus

Analyzing Details Although one detail may not have much meaning in itself, many details together give depth and meaning to a story. Without details, a scene can be unsatisfying to read. For example, the scene *The children played a game* requires more detail: You want to know who the children were, when and where they played, what happened, and how they felt about it.

Into Action As you read, use a chart like the one below to record details that help you imagine the scene and learn about the characters.

Details / Imagery	What I Learn About the Characters and the Scene
"everything was curtained and shuttered in a way that stifled the children"	

Writing Skills Focus

Think as a Reader/Writer

Find It in Your Reading To make her fiction seem more real, Desai uses strong, active verbs. For example, the verb *to lie* tells you only the position of a person's body; the verb *to sprawl* tells you not just that the person is lying down but that he or she is lying unselfconsciously, with legs and arms flung out. As you read, note the strong, active verbs that fire your imagination.

TechFocus This story is about a group of Indian children playing games. As you read, take notes for a Web page about children's games around the world.

Reader/Writer Notebook

Use your **RWN** to complete the activities for this selection.

Vocabulary

maniacal (muh NY uh kuhl) *adj.:* crazed; wildly enthusiastic. *The boy's maniacal laughter revealed his enjoyment of the game.*

stridently (STRY duhnt lee) *adv.:* harshly; sharply. *The boy yelled stridently at the disobedient dog.*

superciliously (soo puhr SIHL ee uhs lee) *adv.:* disdainfully; scornfully. *The girl superciliously rejected her sister's request to play.*

temerity (tuh MEHR uh tee) *n.:* reckless boldness. *The girl had the temerity to stand on her bike seat while going downhill.*

intoxicating (ihn TAHK suh kay tihng) *v.* used as *adj.:* causing wild excitement, often beyond the point of self-control. *The child found hide-and-seek intoxicating.*

dogged (DAWG ihd) *adj.:* stubbornly persistent. *The boy was dogged in his determination to win the game.*

lugubrious (loo GOO bree uhs) *adj.:* solemn or mournful, especially in an excessive way. *The children made a lugubrious sound when they were forced to come in for the night.*

ignominy (IHG nuh mihn ee) *n.:* shame; disgrace. *He could hardly stand the ignominy of having lost the game.*

Language Coach

Word Families Word families group words that share the same root. Notice that *maniacal* contains the root *maniac.* What words share roots with the Vocabulary words?

Learn It Online

Learn more online about Desai's life and work.

go.hrw.com H12-1415 Go

Preteach

Introducing Vocabulary

Use this activity to check students' understanding.

1. The older runners made a _____ effort to finish the race. [*dogged*]
2. Eyebrows raised, he glanced _____ at his opponent. [*superciliously*]
3. The song was not merely sad, but _____. [*lugubrious*]
4. The fans reacted to the victory with _____ glee. [*maniacal*]
5. The victors had the _____ feeling of winning. [*intoxicating*]
6. The _____ of their defeat plunged the team into gloom. [*ignominy*]
7. The spectators objected _____ to the referee's call. [*stridently*]
8. Mary had the _____ to challenge the coach's orders. [*temerity*]

English for Academic Success

Language Coach

Remind students that roots can be found by detaching the suffix or prefix. ***Possible responses:*** *strident, supercilious, intoxicate*

Literary Skills Focus

Have students note images that appeal to the senses of touch, taste, and smell as well as sight and sound.

Reading Skills Focus

Give students a copy of the graphic organizer before they read. (See **Unit 6 Resources.**) Tell them to use their responses to answer the questions in the Applying Your Skills page.

Writing Skills Focus

As they read, have students record the strong active verbs used in the story in their **Reader/Writer Notebooks.**

Learn It Online

The enhanced author biography offers more information on the life of the author as well as Holt's interactive resources pertaining to the author.

go.hrw.com H12-1415 Go

Comparing Resources

Unit 6 Resources, on-level practice and assessment, p. 256

PowerNotes, interactive lesson presentations with activities

Teacher One Stop™, on-level lesson plans and all print resources

Holt Audio Library

Holt Audio Library: Selections and Summaries in Spanish

UA: Holt Interactive Reader, p. 385

UA: Differentiating Instruction, modified lesson plans and leveled assessment, p. 318

UA: Supporting Instruction in Spanish, selection summary

UA: Resources for Teaching Advanced Students, lesson plans, p. 213

ThinkCentral Online Assessment, Selection Standards Check

ThinkCentral Online Remediation

Teacher Preparation

Selection Plot Summary

On a hot afternoon in India, several children decide to play hide-and-seek. All the children scatter and hide except Raghu, who is "it." A boy named Ravi finds a hiding place in a dark, spooky shed filled with discarded household goods. Ravi spends hours in the shed, anticipating the thrill of winning the game. At twilight he finally emerges, expecting victory and acclamation, only to discover that the others have long since forgotten him and have gone on to other pursuits. Devastated, Ravi refuses to rejoin the others. He withdraws, overwhelmed by the "terrible sense of his insignificance."

Direct Teach

Think About/Talk About

Read with a Purpose Have students read the Read with a Purpose statement and consider the connotations of the word *twilight.*

Comprehension

B Reading Focus

Possible response: *Images such as bloated red faces, stifling hot stillness, stuffed lungs and noses, and the choking sensation the children felt help readers to visualize the scene and imagine the children's feelings.*

Analysis

A Literary Focus

Possible responses: *Sight: tea, red, curtained, shuttered, light, sun. Hearing: burst. Touch: washed, brushed, cool, bloated, stuffed, cotton wool, dust, air, choke. Taste: tea, cotton wool. Smell: dust. These images help readers to picture exactly what is happening.*

SHORT STORY

Games at Twilight

by Anita Desai

Read with a Purpose
Read to find out what happens during games played at twilight.

Build Background
The story is set not long after India gained its independence from Britain in 1947. During the long British rule, many upper-class Indian families had adopted Western values, behaviors, customs, and leisure pastimes.

It was still too hot to play outdoors. They had had their tea, they had been washed and had their hair brushed, and after the long day of confinement in the house that was not cool but at least a protection from the sun, the children strained to get out. Their faces were red and bloated with the effort, but their mother would not open the door, everything was still curtained and shuttered in a way that stifled the children, made them feel that their lungs were stuffed with cotton wool and their noses with dust and if they didn't burst out into the light and see the sun and feel the air, they would choke. **A** **B**

"Please, ma, please," they begged. "We'll play in the veranda and porch—we won't go a step out of the porch."

"You will, I know you will, and then——"

"No—we won't, we won't," they wailed so horrendously that she actually let down the bolt of the front door so that they burst out like seeds from a crackling, overripe pod into the veranda, with such wild, maniacal yells that she retreated to her bath and the shower of talcum powder and the fresh sari that were to help her face the summer evening.

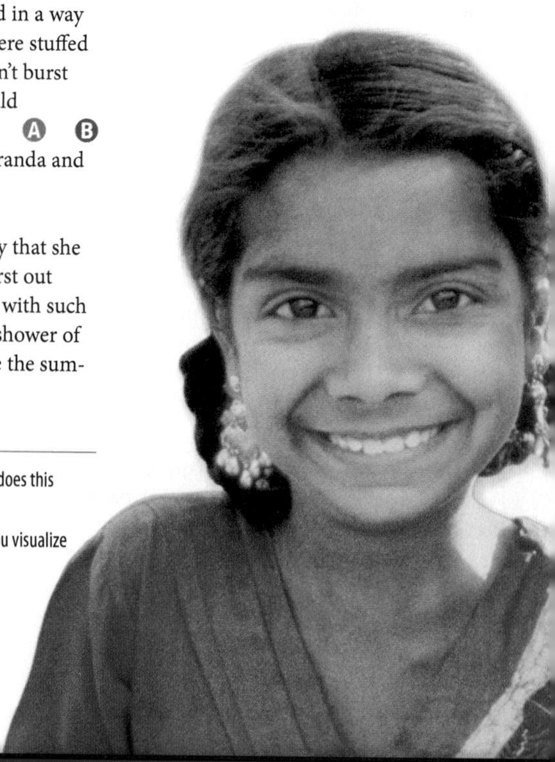

A Literary Focus **Imagery** Identify the images in this passage. How does this imagery work to stimulate readers' senses?

B Reading Focus **Analyzing Details** What words and details help you visualize this scene and imagine the children's feelings?

Vocabulary **maniacal** (muh NY uh kuhl) *adj.:* crazed; wildly enthusiastic.

Universal Access

English Learners

English for Academic Success Point out that Desai paints her scenes with carefully chosen, specific words and rarely uses vague or general diction. Encourage students to list difficult words. Then, ask them to think of a concrete object or an experience to which they can relate each word. Suggest that they confer with other students and check their associations in the dictionary.

✔ See **UA: Differentiating Instruction** for strategies for teaching English learners.

Struggling Readers

Guide students in analyzing details. Direct students to the paragraph that begins, "The children, too, felt released." Point out that the children "began tumbling, shoving, pushing . . . frantic to start." Have students note this detail in their chart. Tell students to ask themselves, "What does this detail tell me about the characters?" Students should note that the characters are boisterous, familiar with one another, and anxious to start playing. Tell students that this detail should help them visualize disorderly kids pushing and falling over each other.

They faced the afternoon. It was too hot. Too bright. The white walls of the veranda glared stridently in the sun. The bougainvillea[1] hung about it, purple and magenta, in livid balloons. The garden outside was like a tray made of beaten brass, flattened out on the red gravel and the stony soil in all shades of metal—aluminum, tin, copper, and brass. No life stirred at this arid time of day—the birds still drooped, like dead fruit, in the papery tents of the trees; some squirrels lay limp on the wet earth under the garden tap. The outdoor dog lay stretched as if dead on the veranda mat, his paws and ears and tail all reaching out like dying travelers in search of water. He rolled his eyes at the children—two white marbles rolling in the purple sockets, begging for sympathy—and attempted to lift his tail in a wag but could not. It only twitched and lay still. Ⓒ

Then, perhaps roused by the shrieks of the children, a band of parrots suddenly fell out of the eucalyptus tree, tumbled frantically in the still, sizzling air, then sorted themselves out into battle formation and streaked away across the white sky.

The children, too, felt released. They too began tumbling, shoving, pushing against each other, frantic to start. Start what? Start their business. The business of the children's day which is—play.

"Let's play hide-and-seek."

"Who'll be It?"

"You be It."

"Why should I? You be——"

"You're the eldest——"

"That doesn't mean——"

The shoves became harder. Some kicked out. The motherly Mira intervened. She pulled the boys roughly apart. There was a tearing sound of cloth, but it was lost in the heavy panting and angry grumbling, and no one paid attention to the small sleeve hanging loosely off a shoulder.

"Make a circle, make a circle!" she shouted, firmly pulling and pushing till a kind of vague circle was formed. "Now clap!" she roared, and, clapping, they all chanted in melancholy unison: "Dip, dip, dip—my blue ship——" and every now and then one or the other saw he was safe by the way his hands fell at the

1. **bougainvillea** (boo guhn VIHL ee uh): woody, tropical vine with showy, purplish bracts, or modified leaves.

Ⓒ **Literary Focus** **Imagery** What images does Desai use to create the impression of oppressive heat?

Vocabulary **stridently** (STRY duhnt lee) *adv.:* harshly; sharply.

Two young girls in Rajasthan, India.

Think About/Talk About

Analysis

Ⓒ Literary Focus

Possible response: *Images include references to how "the white walls . . . glared stridently in the sun," the "livid balloons" of the flowers, the garden "like a tray made of beaten brass," the limp squirrels, and the dog stretched out as if dead, "his paws and ears and tail all reaching out like dying travelers in search of water."*

Extend the Discussion

Breaking Down Difficult Text What is happening in the last two paragraphs on p. 1417? What clues in the text reveal what is happening? ***Possible responses:*** *The children are playing a game but are having some difficulty organizing themselves. The "motherly Mira" takes charge and organizes the circle game. The details about Mira's behavior make the action clear.*

Evaluating Do the language and behavior of the children seem realistic to you? Explain. ***Possible response:*** *The interruptions, rough play, self-centered words and actions, and give-and-take seem convincing and realistic.*

Vocabulary: Own the Word

- **maniacal:** Tell students that *maniacal* is the adjective form of the noun *maniac.* A *maniac* is a person who behaves wildly or acts crazy. If someone laughs *maniacally* (adverb form), they laugh in a crazy, wild way. Ask students to explain how they might react if they encountered a *maniacal* man on the street.
- **stridently:** In the selection, *stridently* means "harshly"; its antonym is *softly.* Have students use both words in a sentence. ***Possible response:*** *The wind blew stridently in the middle of the day, but by evening time it was just wafting softly.*

Advanced Learners

Enrichment Suggest that students research the work of another Indian writer, Ruth Prawer Jhabvala, and compare it with that of Anita Desai. Jhabvala's works include the novel *Heat and Dust* (1983); a superb collection of short stories, *Out of India* (1987); and numerous highly acclaimed screenplays, including *The Remains of the Day,* the film version of Kazuo Ishiguro's novel.

✔ See **UA: Resources for Teaching Advanced Students** for strategies for teaching advanced learners.

Students with Disabilities

To help students notice images that appeal to the senses, have them create a chart with five columns for each of the five senses. Then, guide them in finding the imagery in each paragraph. For example, you might say: "In the second to last paragraph on p. 1417, I notice imagery that appeals to touch, hearing, and sight. Which details in this paragraph can you find that appeal to these senses?" Have students record their answers in their charts.

Model the Skill

- Tell students that the purpose of **imagery** is to create a mood and help readers visualize a scene. When students analyze imagery, they need to think about the author's word choice and the overall impression the images create.
- Read aloud the first sentence that begins the final paragraph on p. 1418. Model for students how to analyze the first main clause ("Ravi had never . . . animal life"). For example, you might say, "I first notice the adjectives *dark* and *depressing*. I am very struck by the next few words. Desai calls the shed a 'mortuary of defunct household goods.' I immediately get a sense of this place as lonely, mysterious, and spooky. Then, Desai writes that the shed is 'seething' with animal life. I can sense the creatures moving around."

Guided Practice: Apply

Read-Talk-Write Have students work with a partner to read and analyze the rest of the paragraph. Then, have them write their impressions of the overall mood of the passage in their **Reader/Writer Notebooks**.

crucial moment—palm on palm, or back of hand on palm—and dropped out of the circle with a yell and a jump of relief and jubilation.

Raghu was It. He started to protest, to cry "You cheated—Mira cheated—Anu cheated——" but it was too late, the others had all already streaked away. There was no one to hear when he called out, "Only in the veranda—the porch—Ma said—Ma *said* to stay in the porch!" No one had stopped to listen, all he saw were their brown legs flashing through the dusty shrubs, scrambling up brick walls, leaping over compost heaps and hedges, and then the porch stood empty in the purple shade of the bougainvillea, and the garden was as empty as before; even the limp squirrels had whisked away, leaving everything gleaming, brassy, and bare. **D**

Only small Manu suddenly reappeared, as if he had dropped out of an invisible cloud or from a bird's claws, and stood for a moment in the center of the yellow lawn, chewing his finger and near to tears as he heard Raghu shouting, with his head pressed against the veranda wall, "Eighty-three, eighty-five, eighty-nine, ninety . . ." and then made off in a panic, half of him wanting to fly north, the other half counseling south. Raghu turned just in time to see the flash of his white shorts and the uncertain skittering of his red sandals, and charged after him with such a bloodcurdling yell that Manu stumbled over the hosepipe, fell into its rubber coils, and lay there weeping, "I won't be It—you have to find them all—all—All!"

"I know I have to, idiot," Raghu said, superciliously kicking him with his toe. "You're dead," he said with satisfaction, licking the beads of perspiration off his upper lip, and then stalked off in search of worthier prey, whistling spiritedly so that the hiders should hear and tremble.

Ravi heard the whistling and picked his nose in a panic, trying to find comfort by burrowing the finger deep—deep into that soft tunnel. He felt himself too exposed, sitting on an upturned flowerpot behind the garage. Where could he burrow? He could run around the garage if he heard Raghu come—around and around and around—but he hadn't much faith in his short legs when matched against Raghu's long, hefty, hairy footballer legs. Ravi had a frightening glimpse of them as Raghu combed the hedge of crotons and hibiscus, trampling delicate ferns underfoot as he did so. Ravi looked about him desperately, swallowing a small ball of snot in his fear.

The garage was locked with a great heavy lock to which the driver had the key in his room, hanging from a nail on the wall under his workshirt. Ravi had peeped in and seen him still sprawling on his string cot in his vest and striped underpants, the hair on his chest and the hair in his nose shaking with the vibrations of his phlegm-obstructed snores. Ravi had wished he were tall enough, big enough to reach the key on the nail, but it was impossible, beyond his reach for years to come. He had sidled away and sat dejectedly on the flowerpot. That at least was cut to his own size.

But next to the garage was another shed with a big green door. Also locked. No one even knew who had the key to the lock. That shed wasn't opened more than once a year, when Ma turned out all the old broken bits of furniture and rolls of matting and leaking buckets, and the white anthills were broken and swept away and Flit sprayed into the spider webs and rat holes so that the whole operation was like the looting of a poor, ruined, and conquered city. The green leaves of the door sagged. They were nearly off their rusty hinges. The hinges were large and made a small gap between the door and the walls—only just large enough for rats, dogs, and, possibly, Ravi to slip through.

Ravi had never cared to enter such a dark and depressing mortuary of defunct household goods seething with such unspeakable and alarming animal life but, as Raghu's whistling grew angrier and sharper and his crashing and storming in the hedge wilder, Ravi suddenly slipped off the flowerpot and through the crack and was gone. He chuckled aloud with

D **Reading Focus** **Analyzing Details** How does Desai use language to suggest physical action? Explain.

Vocabulary **superciliously** (soo puhr SIHL ee uhs lee) *adv.*: disdainfully; scornfully.

Universal Access

EL English Learners

English for Academic Success Model for students how to recognize the powerful, active verbs Desai uses in the selection. Point out that at the top of p. 1418, Raghu protested loudly while the others "streaked away." Remind students that the verb *streaked* means "to run rapidly." Tell them that instead of *walk* or *run,* the use of the verb *streaked* helps them visualize the children running at high speed away from Raghu, rushing to find a hiding place. Ask students as they continue reading to note how the strong verbs help to visualize the movement of the children.

Students with Disabilities

Students may struggle filling in the graphic organizer. Have students use the details on p. 1418 to make an observation about a character. Tell them to create a web diagram with their observation in the center circle and details on the lines of the web. For example, students might note that Raghu is a bully. Students might record on the web that he kicks helpless Manu and calls him an "idiot."

✔ See **UA: Differentiating Instruction** for strategies for teaching students with disabilities.

SPORTS LINK

Cricket match near Rajabai Tower (c. 2003).

Games in India

Many of the games played in India, such as chess, were developed in that country: Kite flying, wrestling, hunting, and polo are all traditional Indian games. When the British colonized India, they introduced other games, such as soccer, field hockey, and track and field. Cricket, by far the most popular English athletic import, is a summer game similar to baseball. The first recorded cricket game in India was a match played by a group of sailors in 1721. In 1926, India joined the Imperial Cricket Conference, which allowed the national team to play against England and a select group of other colonies. The king of England (then emperor of India) attended the country's first match against England along with 24,000 spectators. Some historians believe facing the English in cricket was a turning point in India's struggle for independence. Today, cricket remains an obsession throughout India, and cricket players are some of the nation's wealthiest and most famous people.

Ask Yourself

In what ways has the British culture influenced the children in the story and their games? Support your answer with details and examples from the story.

astonishment at his own temerity so that Raghu came out of the hedge, stood silent with his hands on his hips, listening, and finally shouted, "I heard you! I'm coming! *Got* you——" and came charging round the garage only to find the upturned flowerpot, the yellow dust, the crawling of white ants in a mud hill against the closed shed door—nothing. Snarling, he bent to pick up a stick and went off, whacking it against the garage and shed walls as if to beat out his prey.

Ravi shook, then shivered with delight, with self-congratulation. Also with fear. It was dark, spooky in the shed. It had a muffled smell, as of graves. Ravi had once got locked into the linen cupboard and sat there weeping for half an hour before he was rescued. But at least that had been a familiar place, and even smelled pleasantly of starch, laundry, and, reassuringly, of his mother. But the shed smelled of rats, anthills, dust, and spider webs. Also of less definable, less recognizable horrors. And it was dark. Except for the white-hot cracks along the door, there was no light. The roof was very low. Although Ravi was small, he felt as if he could reach up and touch it with his fingertips. But he didn't stretch. He hunched himself into a ball so as not to bump into anything, touch or feel anything. What might there not be to touch him and feel him as he stood there, trying to see in the dark? Something cold, or slimy—like a snake. Snakes! He leapt up as Raghu whacked the wall with his stick—then, quickly realizing what it was, felt almost relieved to hear Raghu, hear his stick. It made him feel protected. **E**

But Raghu soon moved away. There wasn't a sound once his footsteps had gone around the garage and disappeared. Ravi stood frozen inside the shed.

E **Literary Focus** **Imagery** Identify the similes that Desai uses in this passage to suggest death.

Vocabulary **temerity** (tuh MEHR uh tee) *n.:* reckless boldness.

Think About/Talk About

Comprehension

D Reading Focus

Possible response: *The words* flashing, scrambling, *and* leaping *create a sense of action as Raghu runs, stopping abruptly at the empty veranda. The lengthy sentence and use of repetition add to the sense of continuous action.*

Analysis

E Literary Focus

Possible response: *In the simile, the shed is said to have "a muffled smell, as of graves." The metaphor in the previous paragraph compares the shed to "a mortuary" of "defunct" items.*

Extend the Discussion

Finding Details Why does Ravi decide to hide in the shed? ***Possible response:*** *He feels nervous and exposed out in the yard. He would have liked to hide in the garage but it was locked. Raghu's intense pursuit gives him little choice but to hide in the dark, depressing shed.*

Interpreting How do Ravi's emotions change while he is in hiding? How realistic is his experience? ***Possible responses:*** *In the beginning, he is delighted and proud of himself. After some time, the mysteries of the shed begin to make him feel afraid. The emotions he feels are very realistic for a child his age.*

Vocabulary: Own the Word

- **superciliously:** Ask students: "Have you ever gotten in trouble for acting *superciliously,* in other words, for being disrespectful and insulting? Explain what happened, when it happened, and how you acted *superciliously.*"
- **temerity:** Write *temerity* in a center circle on the board and provide a definition: "nerve." Draw spider legs from the center as students add concepts and attributes. ***Possible responses:*** *boldness, gall, doing something risky*

Reaching Reluctant Readers

To engage reluctant readers in the text, help them connect to Ravi's experience by asking the following questions:

- When was the longest time you have stayed hidden during a game of hide-and-seek? How long would you stay hidden in a dark shed that smelled of dust, rats, and spider webs? How would you react if you felt something crawling on you in the dark?
- Do you sympathize with Ravi for having to put up with a challenging situation, or do you think he is trying too hard to prove himself? Explain.

Sports Link

Ask Yourself

Possible response: *The games played in the story are almost universal among children. However, some aspects of their particular versions of the games, such as Raghu's counting up rather than down, seem to be based on British models. Raghu himself is described as "that hirsute, hoarse-voiced football champion." In this story, "football" refers to a European game introduced to India and similar to soccer in the United States.*

Model the Skill

- Provide students with a copy of the Reading Skills Focus graphic organizer for "Games at Twilight." (See **Unit 6 Resources**.)
- Tell students that when **analyzing details**, they must combine major and minor details to understand the story's depth and meaning.
- Read aloud the first paragraph on p. 1420. Tell students to pay attention to the details.
- Next, model how the detailed imagery helps readers visualize the scene. For instance, you might say: "I appreciate why Ravi waited before lifting his hand. In the dark, he has no idea what kind of insect landed on his neck. Is it a spider, as he suspects? It could be something else with lots of tiny legs. He was brave to squash it. I understand that the tickling on his skin must have been uncomfortable."

Details/ Imagery	What I Learn about the Characters and the Scene
It took him a while to pick up the courage to lift his hand and explore.	Ravi can be afraid, but he takes action.

Guided Practice: Apply

Read-Talk-Write Have students read the next paragraph ("There was nothing now. . . ."), discuss it with a partner, and add information about details and imagery to their graphic organizers.

Then he shivered all over. Something had tickled the back of his neck. It took him a while to pick up the courage to lift his hand and explore. It was an insect—perhaps a spider—exploring *him.* He squashed it and wondered how many more creatures were watching him, waiting to reach out and touch him, the stranger. **F**

There was nothing now. After standing in that position—his hand still on his neck, feeling the wet splodge of the squashed spider gradually dry—for minutes, hours, his legs began to tremble with the effort, the inaction. By now he could see enough in the dark to make out the large solid shapes of old wardrobes, broken buckets, and bedsteads piled on top of each other around him. He recognized an old bathtub —patches of enamel glimmered at him, and at last he lowered himself onto its edge. **G**

He contemplated slipping out of the shed and into the fray. He wondered if it would not be better to be captured by Raghu and be returned to the milling crowd as long as he could be in the sun, the light, the free spaces of the garden, and the familiarity of his brothers, sisters, and cousins. It would be evening soon. Their games would become legitimate. The parents would sit out on the lawn on cane basket chairs and watch them as they tore around the garden or gathered in knots to share a loot of mulberries or black, teeth-splitting *jamun*[2] from the garden trees. The gardener would fix the hosepipe to the water tap, and water would fall lavishly through the air to the ground, soaking the dry yellow grass and the red gravel and arousing the sweet, the intoxicating scent of water on dry earth—that loveliest scent in the world. Ravi sniffed for a whiff of it. He half-rose from the bathtub, then heard the despairing scream of one of the girls as Raghu bore down upon her. There was the sound of a crash, and of rolling about in the bushes, the shrubs, then screams and accusing sobs of "I touched the den——" "You did not——" "I did——" "You liar, you did *not*" and then a fading away and silence again.

Ravi sat back on the harsh edge of the tub, deciding to hold out a bit longer. What fun if they were all found and caught—he alone left unconquered! He had never known that sensation. Nothing more wonderful had ever happened to him than being taken out by an uncle and bought a whole slab of chocolate all to himself, or being flung into the soda man's pony cart and driven up to the gate by the friendly driver with the red beard and pointed ears. To defeat Raghu—that hirsute,[3] hoarse-voiced football champion—and to be the winner in a circle of older, bigger, luckier children—that would be thrilling beyond imagination. He hugged his knees together and smiled to himself almost shyly at the thought of so much victory, such laurels.

There he sat smiling, knocking his heels against the bathtub, now and then getting up and going to the door to put his ear to the broad crack and listening for sounds of the game, the pursuer and the pursued, and then returning to his seat with the dogged determination of the true winner, a breaker of records, a champion.

It grew darker in the shed as the light at the door grew softer, fuzzier, turned to a kind of crumbling yellow pollen that turned to yellow fur, blue fur, gray fur. Evening. Twilight. The sound of water gushing, falling. The scent of earth receiving water, slaking its thirst in great gulps and releasing that green scent of freshness, coolness. Through the crack Ravi saw the long purple shadows of the shed and the garage lying still across the yard. Beyond that, the white walls of the house. The bougainvillea had lost its lividity, hung in dark bundles that quaked and twittered and seethed with masses of homing sparrows. The lawn was shut

2. ***jamun*** (JAH muhn): plumlike fruit.

3. **hirsute** (HUR soot): hairy; shaggy.

F **Literary Focus** **Imagery** In this passage, find examples of imagery that appeals to multiple senses. To which sense does each image appeal?

G **Reading Focus** **Analyzing Details** What details does Desai use to make the shed seem creepy and scary?

Vocabulary **intoxicating** (ihn TAHK suh kay tihng) *v.* used as *adj.:* causing wild excitement, often beyond the point of self-control.
dogged (DAWG ihd) *adj.:* stubbornly persistent.

Word-Attack Skills Mini-Lesson

English for Academic Success On the chalkboard, write the selection word *maniacal* and compare the two related nouns *mania* and *maniac*. Help students realize that in *mania* and *maniac*, the primary stress is on the first syllable and *i* has the sound /ee/ (MAY nee uh), (MAY nee ak). When the suffix *–al* is added to form the adjective *maniacal*, the second syllable becomes the one with the primary stress, and the sound of *i* becomes /y/ (muh NY uh kuhl). Similarly, explore the effect of the suffix *–al* in the word *sepulchral*. In the base word *sepulcher*, the stress is on the first syllable (SEH puhl kur). When the suffix *–al* is added to form the adjective, the second syllable becomes the one with the heaviest stress: (seh PUHL kruhl).

Activity Have students compare the pronunciations of these related words and identify the syllable that is stressed the most heavily in each word.

1. sequence	sequential
2. octagon	octagonal
3. family	familial
4. liturgy	liturgical
5. horizon	horizontal

off from his view. Could he hear the children's voices? It seemed to him that he could. It seemed to him that he could hear them chanting, singing, laughing. But what about the game? What had happened? Could it be over? How could it when he was still not found? **H**

It then occurred to him that he could have slipped out long ago, dashed across the yard to the veranda, and touched the "den." It was necessary to do that to win. He had forgotten. He had only remembered the part of hiding and trying to elude the seeker. He had done that so successfully, his success had occupied him so wholly, that he had quite forgotten that success had to be clinched by that final dash to victory and the ringing cry of "Den!"

With a whimper he burst through the crack, fell on his knees, got up, and stumbled on stiff, benumbed legs across the shadowy yard, crying heartily by the time he reached the veranda so that when he flung himself at the white pillar and bawled, "Den! Den! Den!" his voice broke with rage and pity at the disgrace of it all, and he felt himself flooded with tears and misery.

Out on the lawn, the children stopped chanting. They all turned to stare at him in amazement. Their faces were pale and triangular in the dusk. The trees and bushes around them stood inky and sepulchral, spilling long shadows across them. They stared, wondering at his reappearance, his passion, his wild animal howling. Their mother rose from her basket chair and came toward him, worried, annoyed, saying, "Stop it, stop it, Ravi. Don't be a baby. Have you hurt yourself?" Seeing him attended to, the children went back to clasping their hands and chanting, "The grass is green, the rose is red. . . ." **I**

But Ravi would not let them. He tore himself out of his mother's grasp and pounded across the lawn into their midst, charging at them with his head lowered so that they scattered in surprise. "I won, I won, I won," he bawled, shaking his head so that the big tears flew. "Raghu didn't find me. I won, I won——"

It took them a minute to grasp what he was saying, even who he was. They had quite forgotten him. Raghu had found all the others long ago. There had been a fight about who was to be It next. It had been so fierce that their mother had emerged from her bath and made them change to another game. Then they had played another and another. Broken mulberries from the tree and eaten them. Helped the driver wash the car when their father returned from work. Helped the gardener water the beds till he roared at them and swore he would complain to their parents. The parents had come out, taken up their positions on the cane chairs. They had begun to play again, sing and chant. All this time no one had remembered Ravi. Having disappeared from the scene, he had disappeared from their minds. Clean.

"Don't be a fool," Raghu said roughly, pushing him aside, and even Mira said, "Stop howling, Ravi. If you want to play, you can stand at the end of the line," and she put him there very firmly.

The game proceeded. Two pairs of arms reached up and met in an arc. The children trooped under it again and again in a lugubrious circle, ducking their heads and intoning

> "The grass is green,
> The rose is red;
> Remember me
> When I am dead, dead, dead, dead. . ." **J**

And the arc of thin arms trembled in the twilight, and the heads were bowed so sadly, and their feet tramped to that melancholy refrain so mournfully, so helplessly, that Ravi could not bear it. He would not follow them, he would not be included in this funereal game. He had wanted victory and triumph—not a funeral. But he had been forgotten, left out, and he would not join them now. The ignominy of being forgotten—how could he face it? He felt his heart go heavy and ache inside him unbearably. He lay down full length on the damp grass, crushing his face into it, no longer crying, silenced by a terrible sense of his insignificance.

H Reading Focus **Analyzing Details** Does Ravi actually wait a long time, or does he just feel that it has been a long time? How do you know?

I Literary Focus **Imagery** What visual imagery does Desai use in this paragraph to help you picture the children? How does the imagery help you understand Ravi's emotions at this moment?

J Reading Focus **Analyzing Details** How do the words of the song relate to Ravi's experience?

Vocabulary **lugubrious** (loo GOO bree uhs) *adj.:* solemn or mournful, especially in an excessive way.
ignominy (IHG nuh mihn ee) *n.:* shame; disgrace.

California Standards, pp. 1422–1424

(For a full text of the standards, see pp. A48–A55.)

- **Reading Standard 1.3** Meaning of analogies.
- **Reading Standard 3.3** Effects of irony, tone, mood, and style.
- **Grades 9–10 Review Reading Standard 3.3** Interactions between characters.
- **Grades 9–10 Review Reading Standard 3.7** Literary devices.
- **Writing Standard 2.1c** Narratives: sensory details.
- **Writing Standard 2.2a** Responses to literature: significant ideas.
- **Writing Standard 2.3a** Reflective compositions: personal experiences.

Think About/Talk About

Comprehension

G Reading Focus

Possible response: *Details that make the shed seem creepy are "the wet splodge of the squashed spider," the shapes of the furniture, and the glimmering bathtub."*

H Reading Focus

Possible responses: *He waits a long time. The light coming through the door gets darker. He hears the gardener watering the grass, which would happen later in the day.*

J Reading Focus

Possible response: *The song's theme, nature's indifference to death, echoes the way the children have forgotten Ravi.*

Analysis

F Literary Focus

Possible response: *"footsteps" (sound); "shivered," "squashed" (touch); "creatures were watching" (sight)*

I Literary Focus

Possible responses: *The other children stare in wonderment at him when he reappears. He is howling wildly. The mother reacts by saying, "Don't be a baby." This helps the reader understand why Ravi is "flooded with tears."*

Vocabulary: Own the Word

- **intoxicating:** Have students name things that they find *intoxicating.*
- **dogged:** *Dogged* means "strong-willed"; an antonym is *weak-willed.* Have students name jobs in which people must be *dogged.* ***Possible responses:*** *detective, police officer*
- **lugubrious:** Demonstrate the demeanor of someone who is listening to *lugubrious* music. Ask students to demonstrate.
- **ignominy:** Ask students to applaud to indicate the degree to which they would like to be associated with *ignominy.* ***Possible response:*** *Students do not applaud to show they do not want to feel shame.*

Check for Understanding

Independent Practice

Reading Skills Focus

Possible responses:

1. *During a game of hide-and-seek, Ravi hides and waits. As it starts to get dark, Ravi goes to the den and claims victory. The children hardly notice Ravi's absence.*
2. *The mood at the end is somber, dark, and unsettling, as was the shed that Ravi hid in.*
3. *The irony is that he hides so well that he is forgotten about.*
4. *Some students may be familiar with these games. Some may find them completely foreign.*
5. *Students' responses should include sensory details.*

Literary Skills Focus

Possible responses:

6. *Everyone assumed that the game was over.*
7. *They are playing a funeral game, which is appropriate for the ending of the day.*
8. *He learns that his personal concerns are of no importance to others. The last line states that he has been "silenced by a terrible sense of his insignificance."*
9. *The theme is the pain of recognizing the world's indifference. The word "games" in the title suggests the need to learn the "rules" of life. "Twilight" suggests the end of innocence.*
10. *The children's self-centeredness makes them seem very realistic.*
11. *The fading of daylight, the response of the plants and animals to the heat, Ravi's isolation in the tomblike shed, the cast-off objects, the squashed spider, and the funereal song during the children's game all suggest death.*
12. *Ravi is the protagonist because we focus our attention on him. The other children are the antagonists because they destroy Ravi's sense of his own significance by not noticing he was gone.*

Applying Your Skills

Reading Standard 3.3; **Grades 9–10 Review Reading Standard** 3.3, 3.7 (see pages A48–A50)
Writing Standard 2.3a (see pages A51–A52)

Games at Twilight

Literary Response and Analysis

Reading Skills Focus

Quick Check

1. Briefly summarize the main events in this story.
2. How do Ravi's experiences in the shed contribute to the mood of the story?
3. What is ironic about the end of the story? (Consider what Ravi originally wanted to do and what actually ends up happening.)

Read with a Purpose

4. Are the children's games described in the story similar to or different from games you played when you were a child? Explain.

Reading Skills: Analyzing Details

5. Review the details and images you recorded in your graphic organizer. Which were most vivid to you? If you had to draw one picture to illustrate the story, what would you draw?

Literary Skills Focus

Literary Analysis

6. **Draw Conclusions** Why is everyone surprised to see Ravi when he finally emerges from his hiding place?
7. **Infer** What kind of game are the children playing at twilight? Why might the time of day be significant?
8. **Interpret** What has Ravi learned by the end of the story? Cite a passage from the story that supports your answer.
9. **Analyze** What is the **theme** of this story; that is, what truth or insight about life does it reveal? How does the story's title reinforce its theme?
10. **Evaluate** Are the children in this story and childhood itself realistically portrayed? Give examples to support your view.

Literary Skills: Imagery

11. **Analyze** Which images in the story suggest loss and death? What mood do these images create?

Literary Skills Review: Protagonist and Antagonist

12. **Make Judgments** A **protagonist** is the hero of the story, the person we focus our attention on or the person who sets the conflict in motion. The **antagonist** is the person or force that blocks the protagonist. Who is the story's protagonist? How can you tell? Who or what is the story's main antagonist? Why do you think so?

Writing Skills Focus

Think as a Reader/Writer

Use It in Your Writing Review your list of strong, precise verbs. Write a short essay describing an activity, such as a sport or game, and then analyze the verbs you used. Can you choose more precise verbs to strengthen your description? Look for adverbs—you can often replace a verb-adverb combination with a more effective verb. For example, rather than say, "She ran quickly through the woods," you might say, "She darted through the woods."

What Do You Think Now? How do you think Ravi's childhood experience will shape his view of the world? Many people have similar experiences. How do you think these experiences might affect people's worldviews differently?

Universal Access

Struggling Writers

Some students may need additional scaffolding to complete the Writing Skills Focus activity. Suggest that students write about a game or sporting event they have seen recently. After students have finished, have them look over the essay and circle or highlight all the action verbs or verb combinations. Then, have them review each highlighted verb or verb combination and replace it with a stronger, more urgent verb. Have students share their revised verbs with a partner and provide feedback to each other on whether the verb is effective or not.

What Do You Think Now?

To help students answer this question, have them think about their own maturation process. Point out that most teenagers have had to come to terms with the realization that they are not the center of the universe. Ask students how gaining that knowledge and developing a realistic view of one's own importance is a necessary part of the transition from child to adult.

Reading Standard 1.3 (see pages A48–A50)

Vocabulary Development

Vocabulary Check

State whether each Vocabulary word is paired with its synonym or antonym.

1. lugubrious	cheerful
2. temerity	recklessness
3. intoxicating	boring
4. dogged	persistent
5. maniacal	crazed
6. stridently	gently
7. ignominy	honor
8. superciliously	scornfully

Vocabulary Skills: Analogies

In a word analogy, the relationship between the first pair of words is the same as the relationship between the second pair. Some relationships expressed in analogies are part and whole; action and related object; and performer and related action.

Part and Whole

CHAPTER : BOOK :: fender : car

A *chapter* is part of a *book*, as a *fender* is part of a *car*.

Action and Related Object

BOIL : EGG :: throw : ball

You *boil* an *egg*; you *throw* a *ball*.

Performer and Related Action

AUTHOR : WRITE :: chef : cook

An *author* is one who *writes*; a *chef* is one who *cooks*.

Steps for Solving Analogy Questions

- Identify the relationship between the capitalized pair of words, and note the part of speech of each word.
- Look for the same relationship and the same part of speech in the pairs of words in the answer choices.
- Choose the pair whose relationship and word order most closely match those of the capitalized pair.

Your Turn

For each numbered item, choose the pair of words that expresses a relationship that is most similar to the relationship between the pair of capitalized words.

1. PALM : HAND ::

a. eye : face
b. steeple : church
c. fingernail : finger
d. sole : foot

2. PURSUER : CHASE ::

a. pilot : fly
b. hunter : stalk
c. shallow : deep
d. instruct : teacher

3. WASH : CAR ::

a. climb : ladder
b. garden : lettuce
c. garage : clean
d. polish : shoe

Language Coach

Pronunciation Look back at the Vocabulary words on page 1415. Use the pronunciation key to say aloud each of the words. What is surprising about the pronunciation of *dogged?*

Academic Vocabulary

Talk About

Like many postcolonial writers, Desai is considerably influenced by her cultural perspective. In a small group, discuss whether a writer can "escape" his or her background. Is it inevitable that cultural heritage will inform a writer's work?

Learn It Online

For more about synonyms and antonyms, visit *WordSharp.*

go.hrw.com H12-1423 Go

Independent Practice

Vocabulary Development

Vocabulary Check

1. *antonyms*
2. *synonyms*
3. *antonyms*
4. *synonyms*
5. *synonyms*
6. *antonyms*
7. *antonyms*
8. *synonyms*

Your Turn

1. *d (location, part-whole)*
2. *b (performer and related action)*
3. *d (action and related object)*

English for Academic Success

Language Coach

Possible response: *The stress remains on the first syllable.*

English for Academic Success

Academic Vocabulary

Possible response: *Yes, it is inevitable that a writer's cultural heritage will inform his or her work. Everybody, including writers, learn to adapt to their culture, so a writer's work will exhibit characteristics of the writer's own culture.*

Universal Access: Vocabulary Development

EL English Learners

English for Academic Success Give students more practice with pronouncing difficult words through the following exercise. Have them work in pairs to discuss which pronunciation in each pair is correct for the given word. Correct answers are underlined.

- lugubriousness: (loo GOO bree uhs nihs) (loo goo bree UHS nihs)
- intoxicate: (IHN tahk suh kayt) (ihn TAHK suh kayt)
- doggedly: (DAWG ihd lee) (DAW jihd lee)
- maniacally: (muh NY uh kuhl ee) (muh ny uh KUHL ee)
- strident: (stry DUHNT) (STRY duhnt)
- ignominies: (IHG nuh mihn ees) (IHG noh mihn ees)
- supercilious: (soo puhr SIHL ee uhs) (soo puhr sihl EE uhs)

✔ See the **Academic and Selection Vocabulary Builder** in **UA: Differentiating Instruction.**

Learn It Online

WordSharp: An Interactive Vocabulary Tutor provides additional support for vocabulary development. Multimedia tutorials show students how to apply vocabulary skills to unfamiliar words—and how to make those words their own.

go.hrw.com H12-1423 Go

Independent Practice

Grammar Link

Your Turn

1. *Motherly and self-assured, Mira prods the children to form a circle.*
2. *Frightened by Raghu's shouting, Manu dashes away.*
3. *A tropical plant, bougainvillea, thrives in the heat.*
4. *Careless of Ravi's feelings, the children ignore him.*

Choices: Evaluation Criteria

Review: Homework
Write with Imagery

- The paragraph describes a real or imaginary shared experience.
- The paragraph contains imagery that appeals to each of the five senses.

Connect: Timed Writing 40–50 Minutes

- The essay takes a clear position on whether Desai's story relates a universal childhood experience.
- The essay clearly describes the kind of experience that Desai's story recounts.
- The essay states why Desai's story is memorable.

Extend: Homework
Design a Web Page

- The Web page is about children's games around the world.
- The Web page identifies and explains what these games have in common.

Applying Your Skills

Writing Standard 2.1c, 2.2a (see pages A51–A52)

Games at Twilight

Grammar Link

Effective Sentences: Variety

Desai crafts lively prose not only by using rich imagery and details but also by varying sentence structures. One way to vary your sentences is to vary the beginnings. Instead of starting with the subject, rearrange some of your sentences to begin with modifiers.

SUBJECT FIRST	*Ravi, ordinary and small, yearns to triumph over Raghu.*
SINGLE-WORD MODIFIERS FIRST	*Ordinary and small, Ravi yearns to triumph over Raghu.*
SUBJECT FIRST	*The children, not noticing Ravi's absence, continue their games.*
PARTICIPIAL PHRASE FIRST	*Not noticing Ravi's absence, the children continue their games.*
SUBJECT FIRST	*Raghu, a hefty football player, intimidates the other children.*
APPOSITIVE PHRASE FIRST	*A hefty football player, Raghu intimidates the other children.*

Your Turn

Rewrite the following sentences so that they do not start with the subject.

1. Mira, motherly and self-assured, prods the children to form a circle.
2. Manu, frightened by Raghu's shouting, dashes away.
3. Bougainvillea, a tropical plant, thrives in the sun.
4. The children, careless of Ravi's feelings, ignore him.

Writing Application Re-read a paragraph you wrote recently in your *Reader/Writer Notebook.* Look for ways to diversify sentence structure by varying the beginnings of at least two sentences.

CHOICES

As you respond to the Choices, use these **Academic Vocabulary** words as appropriate: perspective, considerably, adapt, exhibit, inevitable.

REVIEW

Write with Imagery

With five classmates, think of an experience you can all imagine that involves your five senses, such as sledding or going to the beach. Have each group member relate a different sensory perspective: The first member describes what he or she would see; the second describes what he or she would hear; the third describes what he or she would taste; the fourth describes what he or she would smell; and the fifth describes what he or she would feel. Combine your input into one imagery-rich paragraph.

CONNECT

Describe a Memory

Timed Writing In her review of *Games at Twilight,* Victoria Glendinning calls the title story a "jewel." She believes that it "recounts something that has happened in one way or another to nearly everyone in childhood.... Mrs. Desai is a writer's writer in that anyone who has ever set pen to paper must ask himself just what it is about the writing that makes it so memorable, and there is, naturally, no simple answer to the question." In a brief essay, discuss the following questions: Do you agree that Desai is recounting something "that has happened... to nearly everyone in childhood"? How would you describe that experience? What makes Desai's story memorable?

EXTEND

Design a Web Page

TechFocus Design a Web page about children's games around the world, using the notes you took as you read as well as any additional research you did on the Internet. What, if anything, do many of the games have in common?

Universal Access: Grammar Link

English Learners

English for Academic Success Tell students that when they start a sentence with a participial phrase, they must be sure not to create a *dangling participle*—one that has no word to modify—or a *misplaced modifier*—one that modifies the wrong word in the sentence. Give these examples:

- *dangling participle:* Hiding in the shed, it was dark.
- *misplaced modifier:* Crawling down his neck, Ravi felt the spider.

To fix a dangling participle, be sure there is a word in the sentence for it to modify: Hiding in the shed, we noticed how dark it was. (modifies *we*)

To fix a misplaced modifier, reword the sentence: Ravi felt the spider crawling down his neck. (modifies *spider*)

✔ For more practice with sentence variety, see **Warriner's Handbook, GrammarNotes,** and **Language Handbook Worksheets.**

COMPARING TEXTS
Wrap Up

Writing Standard 2.2a–e, 2.3a–c (see pages A51–A52)

from Omeros / B. Wordsworth / *from* Sir Vidia's Shadow / A Writer's Influence / Games at Twilight

Writing Skills Focus

Analyzing Postcolonial Literature

Postcolonial literature provides readers with many avenues for reflection and analysis. Below you will find three different writing assignments to challenge and synthesize your thinking about the issues and the voices of the period.

Postcolonial Traditions

Think about what makes Walcott's, Naipaul's, and Desai's texts representative of postcolonial literature. How does each reflect the influence of colonialism? Remember that a work can be influenced by colonialism in two ways:

- The work may reflect the influence of colonialism in its **content** (what the work is about). For instance, it may describe traditions and behaviors that come from the region's colonizers.
- The work may reflect the influence of colonialism in its **form** (the structure of the work). For instance, an author might borrow a form, such as the sonnet, which comes from the colonizer's literary tradition.

Choose one of these approaches to write a comparison-contrast analysis of these writers and their works. Decide on the **content** or the **form** that you want to focus on for your analysis, and then determine how each text exhibits the content or form relevant to your analysis. Use ample evidence from each text to support your thesis.

The Role of a Mentor for Writers

Think about the thematic relationship among the three selections "from *Sir Vidia's Shadow*," the cartoon "A Writer's Influence" on page 1412, and "B. Wordsworth." All three explore the role of a mentor in a writer's life. What do the three have in common? How do they differ? How do they approach the subject similarly and differently?

Write a comparison-contrast essay in which you use the **block method** of organization to address what each has to say about mentoring. In the block method, each of your body paragraphs addresses one text. Since the cartoon is unique from the other two, begin with it for your first body paragraph. Then proceed to develop a body paragraph for the other two selections. Remember to keep your focus on how each one addresses the idea of a mentor. In each body paragraph, address the similarities and differences among the three. Use ample examples from the texts to support your points about each one.

Writing a Personal Reflection

Now that you have read the three selections "from *Sir Vidia's Shadow*," "B. Wordsworth," and the cartoon "A Writer's Influence" on page 1412, you may be thinking about the role of a mentor in your own life. Who serves as a mentor for you? How is that role enacted? How has the mentor affected your life? How was this accomplished? How are you different now? Is the change positive or negative?

Write an essay that explains how a mentor has influenced your life. Be specific as you describe the process and the effect the mentor has had on your life.

What Do You Think Now? Now that you have read these postcolonial works, how do you think the experience of colonialism has shaped the way citizens of colonized countries view the world?

Independent Practice

What Do You Think Now?

To help students answer this question, have students review what they learned from the selections about colonialism and how it affected the characters' lives.

Assess

Unit 6 Resources, Selection Standards Check, pp. 241, 247, 253, 259

go.hrw.com **ThinkCentral Online Assessment,** Selection Standards Check

Teacher One Stop™, editable Selection Standards Check

Reteach

go.hrw.com **ThinkCentral Online Remediation**

Universal Access

Struggling Writers

Some students may need additional scaffolding to complete the Writing Skills Focus activity on Postcolonial Traditions. Have them create a graphic organizer in groups of three or four and brainstorm ideas for either the content approach or for the form approach. Suggest that they choose two works to address in their analysis. Have them use the information in the graphic organizer to individually write an outline of the essay before writing their actual essay.

California Standards, p. 1425

- **Writing Standard 2.2** Write responses to literature: **a.** Demonstrate a comprehensive understanding of the significant ideas in works or passages. **b.** Analyze the use of imagery, language, universal themes, and unique aspects of the text. **c.** Support important ideas and viewpoints through accurate and detailed references to the text and to other works. **d.** Demonstrate an understanding of the author's use of stylistic devices and an appreciation of the effects created. **e.** Identify and assess the impact of perceived ambiguities, nuances, and complexities within the text.
- **Writing Standard 2.3** Write reflective compositions: **a.** Explore the significance of personal experiences, events, conditions, or concerns by using rhetorical strategies (e.g., narration, description, exposition, persuasion). **b.** Draw comparisons between specific incidents and broader themes that illustrate the writer's important beliefs or generalizations about life. **c.** Maintain a balance in describing individual incidents and relate those incidents to more general and abstract ideas.

Standards Focus

Objectives

Students will learn prewriting, drafting, and revising techniques for writing a biographical narrative.

Preteach

Write with a Purpose Read aloud the essentials of a good biographical narrative to guide students' understanding of this type of writing. Also, refer students to the scoring guide on p. 1434 for more information on biographical narratives that they can use throughout the workshop.

Direct Teach

Model the Skill

Think as a Reader/Writer Use the professional model on this page and others in the unit to provide examples of the elements of a good biographical narrative. Point out how the Boswell model uses concrete details to describe his subject's peculiarities.

Think About the Model

Possible responses:

1. *Boswell justifies his conclusions by describing a time when he personally witnessed Johnson's movements.*
2. *Through the descriptions of Johnson's peculiar habits, Boswell presents him as a person of oddities.*

Writing Workshop

Biographical Narrative

Write with a Purpose

Write a biographical narrative about a person you know well from personal experience or research. Your **purpose** is to communicate information about the individual. Your **audience** comprises others who want to know this individual better.

A Good Biographical Narrative

- focuses on an individual that you know well from experience or research
- provides essential context or background information
- communicates a controlling impression of the individual
- uses concrete narrative and descriptive details to locate scenes and incidents in specific places
- explains the significance of the individual

See page 1434 for a complete scoring guide.

Reader/Writer Notebook

Use your **RWN** to complete the activities for this workshop.

Think as a Reader/Writer

In this unit, you have seen how writers use different techniques to reveal the personalities of interesting people. Before you write your own **biographical narrative,** read the following excerpt from *The Life of Samuel Johnson* (page 646) and note how Boswell describes the subject of his biography.

. . . Talking to himself was, indeed, one of his singularities ever since I knew him. I was certain that he was frequently uttering pious ejaculations; for fragments of the Lord's Prayer have been distinctly overheard. His friend, Mr. Thomas Davies, of whom Churchill says, "That Davies hath a very pretty wife," when Dr. Johnson muttered, "lead us not into temptation," used with waggish and gallant humor to whisper [to] Mrs. Davies, "You, my dear, are the cause of this."

← Boswell cites an example to support his claim in the previous sentence.

He had another particularity. . . . It appeared to me some superstitious habit, which he had contracted early, and from which he had never called upon his reason to disentangle him. This was his anxious care to go out or in at a door or passage by a certain number of steps from a certain point, or at least so as that either his right or his left foot (I am not certain which) should constantly make the first actual movement when he came close to the door or passage. Thus I conjecture: For I have, upon innumerable occasions, observed him suddenly stop, and then seem to count his steps with a deep earnestness; and when he had neglected or gone wrong in this sort of magical movement, I have seen him go back again, put himself in a proper posture to begin the ceremony, and, having gone through it, break from his abstraction, walk briskly on, and join his companion.

← He speculates on the origin of another of Johnson's "particularities."

← He describes an observation that led to a particular interpretation of Johnson's behavior.

Think About the Professional Model

1. How does Boswell justify his conclusions about Johnson?
2. What image of Johnson is Boswell conveying through this description?

California Standards, pp. 1426–1434

- **Writing Standard 1.1** Demonstrate an understanding of the elements of discourse (e.g., purpose, speaker, audience, form) when completing narrative, expository, persuasive, or descriptive writing assignments.
- **Writing Standard 1.9** Revise text to highlight the individual voice, improve sentence variety and style, and enhance subtlety of meaning and tone in ways that are consistent with the purpose, audience, and genre.
- **Writing Standard 2.1** Write fictional, autobiographical, or biographical narratives. **a.** Narrate a sequence of events and communicate their significance to the audience. **b.** Locate scenes and incidents in specific places. **c.** Describe with concrete sensory details the sights, sounds, and smells of a scene and the specific actions, movements, gestures, and feelings of the characters; use interior monologue to depict the characters' feelings. **d.** Pace the presentation of actions to accommodate temporal, spatial, and dramatic mood changes. **e.** Make effective use of descriptions of appearance, images, shifting perspectives, and sensory details.

Writing Workshop Resources

UA: Holt Interactive Writer and Speaker, practice and assessment, p. 105

UA: Differentiating Instruction, modified lesson plans, p. 328

Writing Notes, interactive lesson presentations with activities

GrammarNotes, interactive lesson presentations with activities

Writing and Research in a Digital Age, interactive lesson presentations with activities

Writing Standard 1.1, 1.9, 2.1a–e (see pages A51–A52)
Language Conventions Standard 1.1, 1.2, 1.3 (see page A53)

Prewriting

Gather Ideas

As you think about a subject for your biographical narrative, make a list of the people that are significant to you. A biographical narrative can be about someone you know personally or it can be someone that you find fascinating that you have "met" through the media, your own research, or information from school. Think about what makes these individuals **significant** to you. Has the person been a role model or mentor to you? Has the person influenced others? Has the individual changed history or impacted popular culture? Make a list of these individuals, and include notes about one or two **incidents** that illustrate their unique qualities. An incident is an example or experience that you can relate that illustrates something important about the individual.

Who	Significance	Incidents
William Butler Yeats	Wrote poems that celebrated nation's culture during a time of transition	Incorporated elements of ancient myths and traditions in political works Helped Lady Gregory start Irish Literary Theatre

Choose a Subject

Review your list of individuals and think about the **significance** of each one. When choosing *one* for the subject of your biographical narrative, ask yourself if the significance will be meaningful to the audience as well as yourself. If the answer is "yes," then you have chosen a good subject for a biographical narrative.

Think About Purpose and Audience

As you think about your experience, keep your **purpose** and **audience** in mind. Your **purpose** in writing a biographical narrative is to inform your readers and explain the significance of your subject to them. Your **audience** may be your family, friends, fellow students, or readers in a much wider audience.

Idea Starters

- a favorite relative
- a good friend
- a mentor
- a major influence
- a significant contributor

Peer Review

Share your chart with another student. Discuss why each individual is **significant.** Ask your partner which person is most interesting as a subject for a biographical narrative. Repeat this process with your partner's chart. Make certain you both choose an individual for your biographical narrative.

Your Turn

Get Started Free-write in your **RWN** for ten minutes on the individual you have chosen. Although you will be able to add information from research and experience, you should have a good working knowledge about this person. Be sure that you can explain why this individual is significant. Keep your purpose and audience in mind as you write.

Learn It Online
To see how one writer completed this assignment, see the model biographical narrative online.
go.hrw.com H12-1427 Go

Teacher One Stop™, on-level lesson plans and all print resources

Holt Six Traits for Writing, rubrics, prompts, and sample papers

Language and Sentence Skills Practice

UA: Developmental Language and Sentence Practice

Language Handbook Worksheets, pp. 117–118, 128–129

Formal Assessment, End-of-Year Summative Test

ThinkCentral Online Assessment, Writing Workshop Test

ThinkCentral Online Remediation

Holt Online Essay Scoring

Guided Practice: Apply

Choose a Subject

Suggest that students break into pairs and brainstorm people they might be interested in writing about. They should consider subjects they have studied in class and individuals who have made a significant impact on their lives.

Think About Purpose and Audience

To reinforce the importance of keeping the purpose and audience in mind, have students turn to a partner and verbally express in their own words the purpose of their biographical narrative and their audience. If students are not sure about who their audience will be, specify it for them.

Your Turn

Get Started Tell students to free write interesting information about their subject that may appeal to their audience. Ask them to consider which qualities about their subject they wish to highlight and why these qualities make the subject significant. Have them write conclusions they might make about their subject.

Guided Practice: Apply

Identify the Individual's Significance

Inform students that, when developing a thesis statement, they should be sure they are making an assertion that will arouse their audience's interest.

Gather Concrete Details

Tell students that in order to support their opinion, they need to provide specific details about their subject. Remind students that their evidence will be a combination of narrative and descriptive details.

Your Turn

Have students complete the **Your Turn** as independent practice. Encourage students to review the facts and incidents involving the subject before answering the questions. Remind students that each paragraph in their biographical narrative should support the thesis statement.

Identify the Individual's Significance

Unlike a biography, a biographical narrative does not relate the entire life of an individual. You must decide on the most significant aspect of the individual you have chosen and convey that aspect throughout the composition. Ask yourself the following questions to discover the significant observation you want to make about the individual. The answer to these questions will become the basis for your **thesis statement.** Notice how one student writer analyzed the subject of her biographical narrative in order to create an effective thesis statement.

What is unique about the individual?

What has the individual contributed to myself or others?

Are there incidents and examples I can use to illustrate these observations and their significance?

Thesis statement: ______________________

A good thesis statement in a biographical narrative provides an interesting perspective about the individual. Each paragraph then explains how the actions and events in the individual's life contribute to the person's significance.

Use Facts and Incidents

A biographical narrative is based on facts and incidents that you have either learned or personally experienced. **Facts** can be verified by research, and **incidents** are experiences that reveal vital information about the individual. Both are important to illustrate and support the thesis statement as well as prove the individual's significance. Keep your readers' interests in mind as you choose information to convey.

Gather Concrete Details

Narrative and **descriptive** details provide specific information about your subject. Narrative details tell what happened and occur in a sequence. Descriptive details include specific information about the places described in the essay as well as the appearance and actions of the subject. Add imagery to your information to create **sensory details** that help the reader better understand the incidents you are relating. **Imagery** is language that appeals to the five senses (taste, touch, smell, hearing, sight). Although imagery is especially important in poetry, which usually relies on a few words or a single phrase to evoke a full, provocative picture in the mind of the reader, it can be used to enrich any type of writing. Imagery in a biographical narrative helps convey a full sense of the subject's appearance, personality, and experiences.

Your Turn

In your **Reader/Writer Notebook,** answer the questions in the table above to determine the significance of the individual about which you have chosen to write.

Biographical Narrative

Students can choose their own biographical narrative idea or use one of the following prompts to write a biographical narrative.

Language Arts Write a biographical narrative about your favorite author. Research the author's background and character to explore what makes the author unique among others.

History Choose a figure whom you believe has made a huge impact in history. Describe a key incident in the subject's life that conveys interesting qualities that most people are not aware of.

Fine Arts Choose your favorite musician or artist in the past or the present. As you research biographical information about the subject, think about which qualities make the individual memorable and significant. Write about this significance in a biographical narrative.

Drafting

Organize and Draft Your Narrative

Biographical narratives usually unfold in **chronological** order—showing the events as they happened over time—in order to control the reader's impression of the individual. They also **explain** the significance of the individual; therefore, there is a logical progression to the information as well. Use the following basic structure in your biographical narrative.

Framework of Biographic Narrative		
Introduction	**Body**	**Conclusion**
• Begin with an intriguing fact or incident about the individual. • Provide necessary background information. • State the significance of the individual and the thesis statement.	• Narrate incidents, facts or examples that reveal the impression you want to convey and that support your thesis. • Explain the relationship between the information and the thesis. • Include sensory details and specific information that inform the reader. • Organize and pace your narrative logically.	• Restate the significance of the individual. • Elaborate on the significance of the individual.

Grammar Link Punctuating Nonessential Clauses

A biographical narrative provides ample information about an individual as the writer attempts to convince the reader of the subject's significance. Both facts and incidents are included and are often embedded in complex sentences that contain phrases and clauses. Some of this information is interesting, yet it is not necessary to the meaning of the sentence. That information is called "nonessential" and is separated from the sentence by commas.

Notice how Boswell uses nonessential clauses in his biographical narrative of Samuel Johnson.

> It appeared to me some superstitious habit, which he had contracted early, and from which he had never called upon his reason to disentangle him.

Because "which he had contracted early" is not necessary to the sentence's meaning, it is set off by commas.

Writing Tip

Remember to vary your sentence structure to prevent your writing from sounding stilted or monotonous. Begin sentences with introductory phrases or clauses to diversify paragraph structure.

Your Turn

Organize and Draft Your Narrative As you draft the biographical narrative, use facts and incidents with concrete details to explain logically the significance of your subject. As you convey the information, remember to use some nonessential and some essential clauses.

Real Issues, Real Experts

*Holt author **Carol Jago** offers strategies for writing a biographical narrative.*

Samuel Johnson (1709-1784) wrote that "Fame like all other things which are supposed to give or to increase happiness, is dispensed with the same equality of distribution. He that is loudly praised will be clamorously censured: he that rises hastily into fame will be in danger of sinking suddenly into oblivion."

I have had a lot of fun asking twelfth-grade students to write a biographical narrative of someone who has risen to fame quickly and soon after fallen into either disrepute or oblivion. I invite them to consider sports figures, politicians, actors or actresses, musicians, and American Idols.

The assignment provides students an opportunity to practice their Internet research skills. I require that the essays include citations from at least three sources. With some classes I ask that they print the Web pages and attach them to their essays. Along with meeting the demands of the California writing standard on Biographical Narratives, the assignment invites students to reflect on the fleeting nature of fame.

Guided Practice: Apply

Organize and Draft Your Narrative

Ask students to refer to the basic structure of the introduction, body, and conclusion, organize their information and notes on the subject under each category, and then use their organized notes to start drafting their narrative.

Introduction

Tell students that the introduction of their narratives should captivate the interest of the audience. Suggest that students start with a startling fact or interesting but brief anecdote. Have students state their thesis at the end of the introduction.

Body

Inform students that as they narrate an incident about the subject, the narrative should move at a logical pace. Tell students to avoid any gaps of information between any two sentences and make sure each fact or detail flows to the next. Remind students that the body may consist of more than one paragraph.

Conclusion

Remind students not to include minor details in this section. They should only restate their thesis in a different way and expand upon this significance.

Grammar Link

For practice, have students write three sentences related to their subject using nonessential clauses.

Warriner's Handbook, Sixth Course, p. 338

Your Turn

Organize and Draft Your Narrative

Ask students to complete the **Your Turn** as independent practice. Suggest that students use every other line as they write their drafts so they can more easily revise drafts later.

Model the Skill

- Using a student draft on a transparency, model how to use the questions, tips, and revision techniques suggested in the chart. You might use a student's biographical narrative or a biographical narrative of your own creation to evaluate and revise using the steps in the chart.
- Ask volunteers to explain to the rest of the class how they plan to use each of the steps on their own biographical narratives.

Peer Review

Before students meet with their partners, have them make a list of the questions they want answered about their drafts. For example, they might ask, "Do you think I included enough evidence to support my thesis statement?" or "Did I use transitions that make my essay clear?"

Holt Six Traits for Writing, rubrics, prompts, and sample papers

Peer Review

Double space your biographical narrative on the computer, or skip lines if you are writing by hand. The extra space will allow for peer review comments and suggested revisions when you work on revising your draft with a partner.

Evaluating and Revising

Exchange biographical narratives with a peer. Use the chart below to help you evaluate and revise the drafts.

Biographical Narrative: Guidelines for Content and Organization

Evaluation Question	Tip	Revision Technique
1. Does the introduction provoke interest in the subject and hint at the subject's significance?	**Underline** the introduction of the subject. **Double underline** any hint of the subject's significance.	**Replace** the opening sentences with a striking or intriguing view of the individual. Add a hint about the subject's significance.
2. Do all facts and incidents contribute to the thesis statement and the significance of the individual?	**Star** each sentence that begins a separate incident or fact. Determine if they are related to the thesis.	**Delete** incidents that do not support the thesis. **Add** relevant facts and incidents.
3. Are concrete sensory details used to describe all people and places?	**Highlight** all sensory details.	**Add** specific details about people, places, and actions in the anecdotes.
4. Are incidents and facts organized both logically and sequentially?	**Number** the incidents. Are they organized logically and sequentially?	**Rearrange** events into a logical, narrative order.
5. Does the essay contain transitions to link the narrative and expository structure effectively?	**Bracket** the transitional statements that link the incidents and facts into a coherent whole.	**Add** transitional statements to link the facts and incidents in both a narrative and logical presentation of information.
6. Does the conclusion reinforce the individual's significance and support the thesis?	**Box** sentences that add to the significance of the subject. Add information and commentary about significance.	**Add** a final comment that clarifies the subject's significance.

Real Issues, Real Experts

Holt Professional Learning for Language Arts

To watch videos on teaching **revision, grammar,** and **on-demand writing skills** featuring Linda Rief, Amy Benjamin, and Leila Christenbury, go to this page in **ThinkCentral, Teacher Access.**

Universal Access

EL English Learners

English for Academic Success Review the types of transitions students can use to link incidents and facts in their essay.

- Addition: besides, moreover, next, furthermore
- Emphasis: indeed, certainly, in fact, importantly
- Example: as an illustration, for instance, in this case, on this occasion
- Sequence: thereafter, then, next, immediately, after a short while

Read this student draft and the comments on its strengths and suggestions for improvement.

Student Draft

One Poet, Many Lives

by Joanna Wren, Hexam High School

By the age of twenty-four in 1889, William Butler Yeats was already an accomplished poet. His literary career continued, however, and his writing was profoundly affected by a series of political and personal events. Indeed, Yeats was a different poet as a young man than he was as a middle-aged adult. His love affair with Maud Gonne, his changing attitudes toward the Irish Independence movement, and his new wife and family shaped his evolution as a man and an artist.

← Joanna provides background information that supports her thesis statement.

Early in life, Yeats garnered an appreciation for Irish folktales from his mother. Yeats's first poetry collection, The Wanderings of Oisin and Other Poems, is in part a response to the mythological tales and folklore he heard as a child. Many of his poems expressed his homesickness for his native country and revolved around themes of romantic love and mysticism.

← The writer supports the thesis and uses chronological order as she explains early influences.

Yeats was forever changed by his relationship to the activist and actress Maud Gonne. Admiring her political aspirations and passionate personality, he regarded her as the epitome of female beauty. Yeats proposed to Gonne multiple times, but she rejected him and ultimately married an Irish patriot. The unrequited love affair contributed to the less carefree tone of Yeats's later writing.

← Joanna comments on the influence of Gonne, but she does not do so with specific information.

MINI-LESSON **How to Revise for Specificity**

Joanna revises her third paragraph because it lacks specific information to support the paragraph about the impact of Maude Gonne on Yeats's life and is vague in its description of tone.

Joanna's Revision of Paragraph Three

. . . beauty. Yeats proposed to Gonne multiple times, but she rejected him and ultimately married an Irish patriot, ^Major John MacBride in 1903. Their marriage inspired Yeats's poem "No Second Troy." The unrequited love affair ~~contributed to the less carefree~~ ^influenced the melancholy tone of Yeats's later writing.

Your Turn

Read your draft to discover if there is specific information in the form of names, places, and dates that will improve your biographical narrative. Add the specific information.

Guided Practice: Apply

Student Draft

Explain that the Student Draft on this page is the first half of a biographical narrative written by the student. Model reading the draft and the annotations in blue, and explain that the yellow highlighting illustrates the student's language choices. Explain that a mini-lesson follows with helpful information about ways to improve this draft as well as their own.

Mini-Lesson

How to Revise for Specificity

- Explain that the student writer has revised her paragraph by adding specific information to make the paragraph stronger.
- Remind students to avoid using vague descriptions and general information.

Your Turn

As students complete the **Your Turn,** tell them to find two places in their drafts where specific details can be interwoven into their sentences. Remind students to use the **Grammar Link** on p. 1429 to help them transition correctly.

Struggling Writers

Instruct students to read through their drafts and highlight places where specific dates, names, or titles of works could be inserted so that they have specific information. For example, if their subject was a musician, they might consider mentioning specific works and compositions or specific names of people who influenced the subject.

To make their essay sound more effective, have students replace their weaker descriptions with more specific words. For example, "He wrote about nature" can be revised to "He wrote essays about the magnificent California redwoods." Encourage students to work with a partner in pointing out which phrases and sentences in their essay can be strengthened by adding more specific details.

Guided Practice: Apply

Student Draft

- Explain that the Student Draft is continued and completed on this page. Again, the draft is annotated and highlighted for the students.
- Read the draft and annotations aloud. Ask students to point out where the writer adds specific information about her subject.

Mini-Lesson

How to Show the Subject's Significance

- Tell students to make sure they explain the significance of their subject in the conclusion. Inform students that an effective conclusion contributes to the overall effectiveness of the essay as a whole.
- Explain to students that while their thesis statement can hint at the significance by revealing key incidents and facts, the conclusion should discuss the significance of the subject in detail. Tell students that the sentences explaining the significance should answer the questions, "So what?" and "What is the point of all this information about the subject?"

Your Turn

As students work independently to complete the **Your Turn,** suggest that they discuss how and where their subject made an impact.

Student Draft *continues*

The writer adds **specific information** in paragraph four to **support** both the significance of Yeats and her own thesis statement.

Yeats' friendship with Lady Augusta Gregory, his patron and benefactor, caused his later work to have a more overt cultural agenda. Yeats wrote nationalist drama that was performed by the Irish Literary Theatre. His political involvement led to his appointment in 1922 to the Irish Senate. He eventually married Georgie Hyde Lees, a much younger woman with whom he had two children. In his final years, Yeats composed poetry such as "The Wild Swans at Coole" reflecting the parallel changes he saw in himself and in his country.

Joanna **concludes** the biographical narrative with a **final statement.**

Yeats witnessed and influenced the revival of Irish culture. His contributions to literature reflect the diverse personal influences as well as the political influence of Irish Nationalism.

MINI-LESSON How to Show the Subject's Significance

Joanna has provided interesting information about William Butler Yeats in her biographical narrative, but she misses an opportunity to emphasize his significance in the concluding paragraph. She decides to revise the last paragraph in order to add information and explanation about his significance. Note how she broadens Yeats's significance by adding the specific detail about the Nobel Prize in Literature. Joanna also adds a transitional phrase, "During the course of his lifetime," to begin the revised paragraph. This too expresses his significant contributions and prepares the reader for the conclusion.

Joanna's Revision of Paragraph Five

During the course of his lifetime, Yeats witnessed and influenced the revival of Irish culture. *Winning the Nobel Prize in Literature in 1923 marked his worldwide recognition. The evolution of his personal and professional life combined with the changing political landscape* ~~His contributions to literature reflect the diverse personal influences as well as the political influence~~ of Irish Nationalism *contributed to a body of remarkable drama and poetry that have had a lasting impact on Irish literature.*

Your Turn

Re-read your biographical narrative to determine if you have emphasized the **significance** of the subject of your writing. Add at least one sentence, including specific information that will add proof about the significance of your subject.

Universal Access

AAVE Students Who Use African American Vernacular English

English for Academic Success Point out to students that in the first sentence of the last body paragraph, the student correctly indicates the possessive by adding an apostrophe and an *s* at the end of *Yeats.* Remind students that they should add an apostrophe and an *s* to singular nouns to form the possessive. Tell them that there are a few singular nouns that only take the apostrophe: *Moses', Jesus',* and names ending in *–es* (eez), such as *Xerxes'.* Have students correct the following sentence: Nancy essay explored the themes of most of Shakespeare plays.

✔ For additional instruction strategies, see **ThinkCentral, Teacher Access.**

Proofreading and Publishing

Proofread

Proofread your paper before you prepare a final copy for publishing. Find and eliminate errors in grammar, mechanics, and usage.

Grammar Link Identifying and Punctuating Singular Possessives

When you write about a significant individual, you will probably use the singular possessive to show relationships and ownership. This becomes more challenging when the proper name of the individual ends in *s* as in the case of Yeats. To indicate the singular possessive, you must add an *'s* as in the phrase "Yeats's accomplishments." When you are proofreading, be sure to determine if you need to use the possessive form of the proper noun or the singular form only. Joanna found and corrected the following examples in the fourth paragraph of her draft.

> Yeats's friendship with Lady Augusta Gregory, his patron and benefactor, caused his later work to have a more overt cultural agenda.

Publish

One way to publish your biographical narrative is to print your composition, mount each page on a display board, and add photographs that illustrate points in your biographical narrative. You could download these photographs from online resources. Readers are usually interested in visual images that complement the information. Add a time line with pertinent dates to the display board and mount the board in your classroom, the school library, or a public library.

Reflect on the Process Reflecting on how you wrote your biographical narrative will help you with future writing. In your **RWN**, write short responses to the following questions.

1. How did writing this biographical narrative help you to appreciate the subject of your narrative?
2. Which is your favorite line or passage in the biographical narrative? Why?
3. Do you think you have conveyed the significance of the individual? Why or why not?

Proofreading Tip

Writing about an individual usually involves proper names and places. Be sure that you capitalize all specific names and places.

Your Turn

Proofread and Publish
Proofread your biographical narrative carefully, particularly looking for singular possessives that you may confuse with plurals or proper nouns. Then make a final copy of your biographical narrative so that you can publish it.

Guided Practice: Apply

Proofreading

Integrating with Grammar, Usage, and Mechanics If students make errors in using punctuating singular possessives as they are proofreading, send them to the Punctuation chapters in **Warriner's Handbook.**

Grammar Link

- Tell students to circle all the singular possessives in their biographical narratives.
- Tell students to add an apostrophe and *s* to indicate the singular possessive.

Publishing

Brainstorm with students additional ways to publish their biographical narratives.

Reflect on the Process

Have students reflect on their writing process as well as their final product. Challenge them to reflect metacognitively about how they can improve and apply what they have learned about.

Your Turn

Proofread and Publish Have students highlight or underline the revisions and submit their drafts with their final biographical narratives so that you can check to make sure they are following the revision guidelines on p. 1430.

Struggling Writers

Benchmark Students To help students proofread their essay, tell them that an effective method is reading their essay aloud, word for word. Have students work with a partner and take turns reading aloud their essay. As one person reads slowly, the partner should listen attentively and stop the person when something does not sound right. Then, they should work together in improving any phrase or sentence to clear up confusing phrases or correct grammatical errors.

Students with Disabilities

To help students construct a sentence on the significance of the subject, have them choose one of the following sentence patterns:

- The works of ______ have made a lasting impact on ______.
- ______ will be forever known as the ______.
- The works and contributions of ______ will always serve as powerful inspirations for ______.

Guided Practice: Apply

Scoring Guide

- Tell students that the best way to understand scoring guides is to use them to score actual writing.
- Have students use the scoring guide to evaluate the final copy of the biographical narratives they wrote in the Writing Workshop. Ask students to score their essays and then write a brief paragraph using the language of the scoring guide to explain the reasons for the score.

Holt Six Traits for Writing, rubrics, prompts, and sample papers

Assess

UA: Holt Interactive Writer and Speaker, literary analysis analytical scales and rubrics, p. 105

ThinkCentral Online Assessment, Writing Workshop Test

Teacher One Stop™, editable Writing Workshop Test

Reteach

ThinkCentral Online Remediation

Scoring Guide

Use the scoring guide below to evaluate your biographical narrative from the Writing Workshop or your response to the on-demand writing prompt on page 1435.

	Biographical Narrative	Organization and Focus	Sentence Structure and Vocabulary	Language Conventions
4	• develops a *meaningful* narrative that is responsive to the writing task.	• *thoroughly* develops the narrative with *specific* details and examples. • demonstrates a *clear* sense of audience. • demonstrates a consistent tone and focus, and illustrates a *purposeful* control of organization.	• provides a *variety* of sentence types and uses *precise, descriptive* language.	• contains *few, if any, errors* in the conventions of the English language. (Errors are generally first-draft in nature.)
3	• develops a narrative that is *responsive* to the writing task.	• develops the narrative with details and examples. • demonstrates a *general* sense of audience. • demonstrates a consistent tone and focus; and illustrates a control of organization.	• provides a *variety of* sentence types and uses *some descriptive* language.	• may contain *some errors* in the conventions of the English language. (Errors do **not** interfere with the reader's understanding of the essay.)
2	• develops a narrative that is *related* to the writing task.	• develops the narrative with *limited* details and/or examples. • demonstrates *little* or **no** sense of audience. • demonstrates an *inconsistent* tone and focus; and illustrates *little, if any* control of organization.	• provides *few, if any,* sentence types, and basic, *predictable* language.	• may contain *several errors* in the conventions of the English language. (Errors **may** interfere with the reader's understanding of the essay.)
1	• *may* develop a *weak* narrative that is related to the writing task.	• *fails* to develop the narrative with details and/or examples. • may demonstrate **no** sense of audience. • demonstrates a *lack of* tone and focus; and illustrates **no** control of organization.	• may provide **no** sentence variety and uses *limited* vocabulary.	• may contain *serious errors* in the conventions of the English language. (Errors interfere with the reader's understanding of the essay.)

California Standards, pp. 1434–1435

- **Writing Standards 1.1** Demonstrate an understanding of the elements of discourse (e.g. purpose, speaker, audience, form) when completing narrative, expository, persuasive or descriptive writing assignments.
- **Writing Standard 1.9** Revise text to highlight the individual voice, improve sentence variety and style, and enhance subtlety of meaning and tone in ways that are consistent with the purpose, audience, and genre.
- **Writing Standard 2.1** Write fictional, autobiographical, or biographical narratives: **a.** Narrate a sequence of events and communicate their significance to the audience. **b.** Locate scenes and incidents in specific places. **c.** Describe with concrete sensory details the sights, sounds, and smells of a scene and the specific actions, movements, gestures, and feelings of the characters; use interior monologue to depict the characters' feelings. **d.** Pace the presentation of actions to accommodate temporal, spatial, and dramatic mood changes. **e.** Make effective use of descriptions of appearance, images, shifting perspectives, and sensory details.

Biographical Narrative Writing Prompts

Students can use the writing prompt in the Student Edition or one of the following prompts:

- Have students write a biographical narrative about a historical figure that is not well known but deserves to be celebrated because of his or her significant impact on history.
- Suggest that students write about a sports figure in a biographical narrative and include details regarding physical appearance, athletic abilities, personality, and future potential.

Preparing for Timed Writing

Biographical Narrative

Writing Standard 1.1, 1.9, 2.1a–e
(see pages A51–A52)

When responding to an on-demand prompt requiring a biographical narrative, use the models you have read, what you have learned from writing your own biographical narrative, the scoring guide on page 1434, and the steps below.

Writing Prompt

Some critics have observed recently that we have a "culture of celebrity" in this country. Think about a celebrity that you know well from media coverage and additional research who serves as a role model for others. Write an essay in which you discuss what it is that makes this person a role model. Use details and examples to support your ideas.

Study the Prompt

Begin by reading the prompt carefully. Circle or underline key words: *celebrity, positive role model, explain.* The word *celebrity* means a famous person from sports, media, entertainment, politics or other pursuits. Your purpose is to explain, using specific information, what makes a particular celebrity a role model for others. The most important step is to choose a celebrity role model that you can discuss with specific details and anecdotes. **Tip:** Spend about five minutes studying the prompt.

Plan Your Response

You will need to know some basic facts about the celebrity: name, age, field, and accomplishments. You will also need to explain how his or her actions have a positive impact on others.

This assertion will become your thesis statement and the controlling impression that you convey about the individual. The essay is organized around specific examples of the celebrity's actions that make that person a role model for others. These actions are explained in anecdotes that all convey a similar controlling impression of the individual. Organizing the anecdotes in chronological order helps show how the celebrity assumed this role over time. **Tip:** Spend about ten minutes planning your response.

Respond to the Prompt

Using your thesis statement and your notes, draft your essay. Follow these suggestions:

- The introduction should clearly identify the celebrity. One creative way to begin your essay is with an interview of your chosen celebrity. Basic information could be revealed in a brief dialogue of questions and answers.
- The body of the essay should include specific examples of the celebrity's actions that make him or her a role model. Use sensory details, both narrative and descriptive, within these anecdotes.
- Put the anecdotes in sequence so that your reader can follow the celebrity's development as a role model. Then explain how the actions led you to consider this person a role model. Remember to pace the presentation of actions to accommodate changes in time and mood.
- In the conclusion, restate the assertion and convey the impression you have of the celebrity.

Tip: Spend about twenty minutes writing your draft.

Improve Your Response

Revising Return to the key aspects of the prompt. Does your response identify the celebrity with specific information? Do you include anecdotes that support your assertion that the celebrity is a role model? Is your essay logically and effectively organized?

Proofreading Spend a few minutes identifying and correcting any errors in grammar, spelling, punctuation, and capitalization. Make sure your edits are neat and your paper is legible.

Checking Your Final Copy Before turning in your paper, read it one more time to catch any errors you may have missed. **Tip:** Save ten minutes to improve your paper.

Universal Access

English Learners

Encourage students to research key words in the dictionary. Then, give students the option of working with advanced learners to organize their thoughts into an outline. Advanced learners should assist English learners in proofreading for errors in grammar, spelling, punctuation, and capitalization.

Struggling Writers

Tell students that when drafting their work they should ask themselves: Did I include enough background information? Is there anything I need to explain so my essay will make sense to all readers? Where would the explanation fit best?

Standards Focus

Objectives

Students will learn the elements of writing a biographical narrative.

Direct Teach

Study the Prompt

Before students begin writing, encourage them to answer the following questions:

1. What is my time limit?
2. What are the key skills assessed in the scoring guide?
3. Who is my audience?
4. What is my purpose?

Plan Your Response

Remind students that the biographical narrative scoring guide emphasizes the focus on a consistent, clear thesis. Tell students that they should ask themselves these questions to evaluate their writing as they work on their drafts: Have I focused on a consistent thesis? Have I clearly stated my position? Are my ideas reasonable?

Improve Your Response

Point out that the scoring guide also emphasizes effective organization. Remind students to focus on organizing their main ideas and transitioning smoothly from one point to the next.

Assess

Use the scoring guide on p. 1434 to assess students' essays.

Standards Focus

Objectives

Students will
- analyze media messages
- evaluate credibility and appropriateness of sources

Preteach

Listen and View with a Purpose
Ask students to think about the methods different media outlets use to influence their audience. Ask them how newspapers and magazines use words to catch a reader's attention, and how television and electronic media sources, such as the Internet, use images and sound to convey their message.

Direct Teach

Model the Skill

Analyzing Media
Ask students to think about why the informational media on the World Wide Web is not always a reliable and objective source.

Guided Practice: Apply

Have students find an example of a reliable source on the Web and an example of an unreliable Web source. Ask them to explain why each example is or is not a reliable source.

Media Workshop

Analyzing Media

Listen and View with a Purpose
Analyze how various media influence your perspective; then, create and deliver your own multimedia presentation using words, images, and sounds.

Think as a Reader/Writer You can often choose what you read. Today, however, you are bombarded by information, images, and sounds beyond your control. Television, advertisements, the Internet, and other media of the digital age have made it increasingly important to understand how media messages work. This workshop will show you how to apply analytical skills to the media that surround you and how to combine media into a presentation of your own.

Analyzing Media

It is difficult to imagine a day without e-mail, the Internet, television, radio, books, or newspapers; indeed, receiving and decoding media messages are part of daily life. These messages reach their intended audiences through two categories of **media sources.**

- **Print media sources** include books, newspapers, magazines, pamphlets, advertising fliers, billboards, and posters.
- **Electronic media sources** include radio, television, videos, the Internet, blogs, and podcasts.

In the twenty-first century, many digital media combine several kinds of information, not to mention multiple modes of delivery. For example, consider today's cell phone. Unlike traditional telephones, which transmit voices over telephone wires, the cell phone accomplishes several functions wirelessly. It can provide phone service, voice mail, text messaging, e-mail, digital photography, digital video clips, digital music, video games, and more.

Media for the Twenty-First Century

To function successfully in today's world, you must be able to read and analyze three kinds of media:

- **Informational media** Advances in computer technology have led to an information explosion. Using the Internet, you can access search engines, online databases, newspaper Web sites, blogs, and hundreds of thousands of other Web-based resources when you need information. Much of what is available on the Web, however, is unreliable.
- **Commercial advertisements** Every day, you are exposed to a flood of commercial images. Learning how advertisements work can help you make informed choices.
- **Political advertisements** Our political process is shaped, in large part, by the advertising media. Understanding such political advertising can help you to participate effectively in the political process.

Reader/Writer Notebook
Use your **RWN** to complete the activities for this workshop.

California Standards, pp. 1436–1443
(For a full text of the standards, see pp. A48–A55.)
- **Reading Standard 2.1** Rhetorical devices.
- **Reading Standard 2.2** Clarify meaning.
- **Reading Standard 2.3** Verify and clarify facts.
- **Writing Standard 1.8** Integrate databases, graphics, and spreadsheets into documents.
- **Writing Standard 2.6** Deliver multimedia presentations.
- **Listening and Speaking Standard 1.1** Recognize media strategies.
- **Listening and Speaking Standard 1.2** Analyze impact of the media.
- **Listening and Speaking Standard 1.3** Evaluate ways information is presented.
- **Listening and Speaking Standard 1.7** Rehearsal strategies.
- **Listening and Speaking Standard 1.10** Using different effects.
- **Listening and Speaking Standard 1.11** Critique a speaker's diction and syntax.
- **Listening and Speaking Standard 1.12** Identify logical fallacies.
- **Listening and Speaking Standard 1.13** Types of persuasive speech.
- **Listening and Speaking Standard 1.14** Analyze media techniques.
- **Listening and Speaking Standard 2.4** Historical investigations.

Writing Workshop Resources

UA: Holt Interactive Writer and Speaker, practice and assessment, p. 142

UA: Differentiating Instruction, modified lesson plans, p. 330

WritingNotes, interactive lesson presentations with activities

GrammarNotes, interactive lesson presentations with activities

Writing and Research in a Digital Age, interactive lesson presentations with activities

Reading Standard 2.1, 2.2, 2.3 (see pages A48–A50)
Writing Standard 1.8, 2.6a–d (see pages A51–A52)
Listening and Speaking Standard 1.1, 1.2, 1.3, 1.7, 1.10, 1.11, 1.12, 1.13, 1.14, 2.4a–e (see pages A53–A55)

Media Literacy

Critical readers and viewers use media literacy concepts to analyze, interpret, and evaluate media messages. The left column of the following chart will help you understand basic media literacy concepts. The suggestions in the right column will help you analyze the media messages you receive.

Media Literacy Concepts

Concept	Application
1. People—alone or in groups—write, edit, select, illustrate, or compose every media message.	When you look at a Web page, try to determine who is responsible for the information on the page—the name of the individual or group. Always be on the alert for bias in the media you encounter.
2. Like a story or poem, a media message reflects a particular point of view—sometimes a combined point of view.	When you see an eyewitness account on televised news, remember that it reflects at least three points of view: the witness speaking in the video clip, the technician who edited the original video footage, and the television station airing it.
3. Your interpretation of a media message is based on your knowledge.	Discover as much as you can about the media that shape your world. As you learn more about how media work, you will be a more effective citizen of the digital age.
4. Regardless of whether a media message informs, entertains, or both, its purpose is always to persuade.	As you observe media messages, always look for a persuasive purpose and the persuasive methods that support the purpose.
5. Media producers shape messages according to the characteristics of the medium in use.	Remember that even the most versatile cell phone is limited by its size.

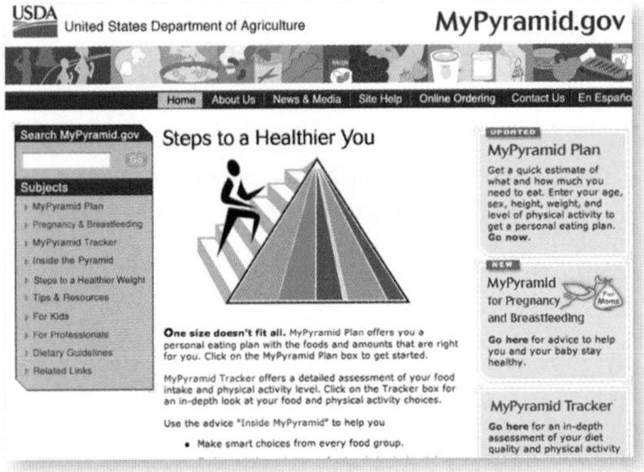

Web page for USDA Food Pyramid.

A Good Media Analysis

- identifies the medium and its message
- considers the creator of the message and his or her purpose
- discerns how the form or style of the medium affects its message
- recognizes the strategies used in creating or expressing the message
- infers what may have been excluded from the message and why
- evaluates the effectiveness of the message

Learn It Online
Analyze Web pages and more at MediaScope.

go.hrw.com H12-1437 Go

Guided Practice: Apply

Media Literacy

- Remind students that a major purpose of many media messages is to persuade the person receiving the message. Ask students to think about how a media message can be both entertaining and persuading. In addition, how can it be both informative and persuading?
- Have students look at a local newspaper and a national newspaper from the same day. Ask students to note the differences in the type of stories covered as well as variations in the way two outlets cover the same story. Have them indicate which media literacy concept can explain those differences.

Learn It Online
If students need help adding multimedia features to their projects, send them to the **MediaScope** mini-site, where students can work through an interactive tutorial on creating multimedia.

go.hrw.com H12-1437 Go

Teacher One Stop™, on-level lesson plans and all print resources

Holt Six Traits for Writing, rubrics, prompts, and sample papers

Language and Sentence Skills Practice

UA: Developmental Language and Sentence Practice

Formal Assessment, Progress Monitoring End-of-Unit Summative Test

ThinkCentral Online Assessment, Writing Workshop Test

ThinkCentral Online Remediation

Guided Practice: Apply

Media Strategies

Discuss with students the persuasive strategies commonly used in mass media. For practice, have students use their **Reader/Writer Notebooks** identify which persuasive media strategy is used in each of the following media messages:

- "Brookstone cookies are high in fiber, low in fat, and enriched with calcium, and they taste great too!" [*cardstacking*]
- "More than 90 percent of local teachers agree." [*facts and figures*]
- "Our new on-the-go packaging allows you to enjoy our product anywhere—whether you're skydiving or enjoying a rock concert." [*transfer*]
- "It's the type of luxury only a select few can afford." [*snob appeal*]
- "'This is my favorite sports drink. I drink a bottle before every game,' says Joe Athlete." [*testimonial*]
- "We're strengthening our communities, one family at a time." [*glittering generalities*]
- "A party is just not a party without Fizz Cola." [*bandwagon*]
- "Senator Johnson supported a bill to raise taxes. She does not care about the needs of the middle class." [*ad hominem attack*]
- "The right suit can help you get the right job that gives you and your family the life you deserve." [*false causality*]
- "Our motorized skateboard has passed numerous safety tests." [*weasel words*]

Recognizing Propaganda

Media producers use the techniques of propaganda to achieve their purposes and to shape their messages for their intended audiences. To be an effective media consumer, you must be able to analyze and evaluate the use of these methods. The following chart describes some of the most common propaganda strategies in use today.

Presentation Tip

Ensure a successful multimedia presentation by learning as much as you can about how today's media work. Before you choose a topic, examine as many print and televised ads as possible, looking for the propaganda methods presented in this workshop. If time allows, use the Internet to research other persuasive methods used by advertisers in the digital age.

Media Strategies

Strategy	Examples
Ad Hominem Attack Also known as name-calling, this approach is common in political advertising, in which one candidate or group tries to persuade voters by smearing the reputation of another candidate or group.	In a common variation on the political attack ad, a disapproving voice repeats the name of a candidate and, with each repetition, names something supposedly negative the candidate has done or supported. Attack ads present heavily edited evidence, almost always out of context.
Bandwagon This technique appeals to the human desire to belong by suggesting that all the right people use a particular product or support a particular candidate.	Advertisements for a particular food or drink will picture a crowd of happy, attractive people consuming the product in a particularly pleasant setting. The implicit message: Purchase the product and you will be popular.
Card Stacking Advertisers stack the cards when they emphasize the appealing aspects of their product—or their candidate—and leave out any negative traits.	A snack-food ad might trumpet that the product is low in fat, and neglect to mention the high sugar content.
Facts and Figures Propaganda exploits our tendency to see data as proof, selecting facts and figures to make the favored candidate—or product—look appealing.	"Nine out of ten doctors recommend" product X.
False Causality Suggesting that one event caused another because they occurred in sequence is a trick of advertising and political propaganda.	Advertisements regularly suggest that purchasing the "right" product will lead to success or happiness.
Glittering Generalities Abstract words with a positive emotional appeal give propaganda persuasive power.	Ads in favor of a particular candidate use phrases such as "truth, justice, and the American way." Attack ads use words and phrases that have the reverse effect.

Universal Access

EL English Learners

English for Academic Success Introduce students to following vocabulary words related to media strategies:

- **propaganda**—misleading information used to promote a point of view, product, or political cause
- **testimony**—a formal written or spoken statement believed to be truthful
- **exploit**—to make full use of, usually in a selfish way
- **smearing**—damaging a person's reputation with false or exaggerated statements

Struggling Learners

Help students understand the purpose behind different media strategies by choosing which strategies would be best suited to a particular commercial product. Ask students to think about what strategy a car company would use if they wanted customers to think their cars were luxurious status symbols. Have them consider the possible strategies a cereal company could use to hide the fact that its product is high in sugar. Have students create their scenario and question a partner about it.

Plain Folks / Snob Appeal Variations on the bandwagon method, Plain Folks appeals to the ordinary citizen in you, while Snob Appeal exploits the desire to be part of a select group.	Commercials for fast-food products often picture ordinary people, sometimes even in rural settings. By contrast, ads for expensive designer luggage feature rich and exclusive-looking settings.
Testimonial This method uses the testimony of a well-known person to support a product, a cause, or a candidate.	Rock stars, movie stars, and famous athletes are everywhere in the world of advertising.
Transfer When advertisers create an exciting scene and place their product in it, they rely on viewers to transfer their desire for excitement from the scene to the product.	Think Carribbean vacations, white-water rapids, and gorgeous views—as depicted in television ads for beverages, chewing gum, and other products.
Weasel Words Propaganda can use words to soften a harsh truth or to create the illusion of substance where none exists.	When an ad says the product has been "clinically tested," the advertiser has weaseled out of telling you what you really need to know to make an informed choice.

"Got Milk" print ad with Mia Hamm. © 1999 America's Dairy Farmers and Milk Processors.

Analyzing Visuals

Connecting to the Text This advertisement counts on viewers to recognize the slogan and the milk mustache common to a series of advertisements for milk. What elements of the advertisement make it visually appealing? With a partner, examine the ad closely and identify at least two strategies presented in the adjacent chart. If time allows, share your ideas with the whole class.

Model the Skill

- Explain to students that more than one media strategy can be used at once. Advertisers often use multiple strategies to deliver their message. Present students with this example: A well-known movie actress appears in a cosmetic advertisement and says "I love this new super glossy lipstick—in fact, it's Hollywood's best-kept secret of the stars." Note that this example combines three techniques: a testimonial, snob appeal, and the bandwagon technique.
- Remind students that when evaluating media strategies, they must think about the advertiser's purpose. They should consider what the advertiser wants them to do or buy, what the ad encourages them to feel, and what information is unclear or omitted.

Guided Practice: Apply

Have students work in pairs to create their own print advertisement. Suggest they combine two or more propaganda techniques to ensure their ad's effectiveness. As pairs share with the class, have the other students identify which propaganda strategies were used.

Analyzing Visuals

Connecting to the Text: *This ad relies on the strategies of bandwagon and testimonial. The ad presents the question, "got milk?" to suggest that everybody drinks milk and that the viewer should then join the crowd. The ad also employs the image of a successful soccer player, which suggests how successful and health-conscious people consume the product advertised.*

Advanced Learners

Enrichment Have students consider the differences between the ways print media, television, and the Internet are used by advertisers. Have students choose one media strategy and compare and contrast the way each of these media outlets would apply the same strategy.

Students with Disabilities

Have students work in small groups to look through periodicals and find text or images that show the listed media strategies in action. Focus students' efforts by having them search for one or two of the most common strategies, such as the use of facts and figures or celebrity testimonials. Have students place the ads on a poster board to create an image collage. Students can also use the Internet to search for images and paste them in a file to create a digital collage. Ask students to present their collages to the class and explain what strategy each image represents.

Model the Skill

Select Words, Images, and Sound

- Explain to students that a successful media presentation balances text, images, and sounds. Inform students that they do not want to overstimulate their audience with too many scattered images or excessive use of sound. Point out that it is also important to avoid boring their audience with overly dense text.
- Explain that the chart on this page lists students' various options for presenting their content in different formats.

Guided Practice: Apply

Have students create a similar chart to help them organize their multimedia presentation. Inform students that they might need to revise their charts later based on the availability and knowledge of equipment.

Preparing a Multimedia Analysis

Now that you have studied strategies common to the propaganda of advertising, you will analyze a commercial advertisement or a group of related commercial advertisements and shape your analysis into a multimedia presentation, using words, images, and sound. In choosing a suitable subject, consider your own interests, as well as the kinds of advertising that are prominent at the time of your presentation. You might wish to choose print and television ads for a single product.

Presentation Tip

Before planning your multimedia presentation, check with your campus library or media center to see what kind of presentation equipment is available to you. Many schools also make training and support available to students. In addition, you can take advantage of interactive training software that is available for presentation software and for presentational equipment such as LCD projectors.

Select Words, Images, and Sound You will use words to present the major ideas in your analysis, images to illustrate your ideas, and sound to enhance what your words and images convey. Use the following chart to help you assemble the components of your presentation.

Media	Content	Format
Text	• the major points of your presentation • important facts, figures, or quotations	• Use presentation software or a similar approach to present major points in large lettering, attractively formatted. • An LCD projector will display the text of your presentation on a large screen. • A document camera will enlarge facts, figures, and quotations and display them on a large screen.
Images	• color reproductions of still images from the advertisement(s) your presentation analyzes • video clips from the advertisement(s) your presentation analyzes	• You can use presentation software to project still images and even video clips. • You can also use an LCD projector, a video projector, or a document camera to project images.
Sound	• video clips with sound—for advertisements that have a soundtrack • your own voice to conduct the presentation	• The methods listed above can be used to project sound. • Use speakers appropriate for the size of the room and your audience. • Practice projecting your voice; if appropriate, use a microphone and speakers.

Analyzing Media Presentation Prompts

Students can choose their own presentation subject or use one of the following prompts to create a presentation.

School Analyze propaganda used by or seen around your school. This could be a promotion for a social event or a flyer that encourages students to get good grades or follow school rules.

Music Consider how music is used in advertisements today. Analyze an ad in which a company and a recording artist combine efforts to boost the sale of a product as well as album sales.

Science Analyze the way a pharmaceutical company advertises prescription drugs. Think about the motivation behind the company that produces the product.

History Choose a piece of political propaganda from World War II or another historical era. Analyze the media strategies used to gain support for the war or for a particular political administration.

Research Your Topic Remember the purpose of your presentation—to analyze the persuasive methods at work in a commercial or political advertisement. You may choose to analyze a print or televised ad. If time allows, you might wish to analyze a group of related ads. Once you have chosen an advertisement, analyze it thoroughly, looking for the media strategies presented on pages 1438–39. After you identify your ad's primary methods of persuasion, do some more research on these methods so that you can explain them effectively when you make your presentation.

Consider Your Audience As you prepare your presentation, think about the characteristics and needs of your audience. The following questions will help you analyze your audience:

- What will my audience know about my chosen subject?
- What will my audience want to know?
- What methods can I use to capture and hold my audience's attention?
- What media would work best in presenting my topic?
- What combination of media will my audience find most interesting?

Maximize Your Impact The most appropriate text, image, or sound effect might be ineffective and even distracting if it is not designed properly. Pay close attention to the quality of the material you choose. Think carefully about how to incorporate it into your presentation. Use the following design principles to create the maximum impact on your audience.

- **Text** Limit the amount of text that you expect your audience to read. For each screen or slide, display information in list form, if possible. Present three to five listed items per slide—or one impressive quotation. Choose a plain, non-serif font in a size that your audience will be able to read from the back of the presentation area. If you begin with a list of major points, consider repeating the slide with this list, as needed, for emphasis.
- **Images** Since your purpose is to analyze the persuasive techniques at work in print or televised advertising, high-quality slides or video clips are essential. Be sure images are large enough and clear enough to be seen by everyone in the presentation area. Consider a four-step process for any image or video you analyze: (1) Introduce the image or clip. (2) Show your audience the image or clip without commenting. (3) Show and briefly discuss a slide listing the points you want to make about the image or clip. (4) Show the image or clip again, and point out the features you want your audience to notice. Use a wand-shaped pointer about the length of a yardstick to pinpoint details in any advertisement you share with your audience.
- **Sound** If you present televised advertising, be certain that your equipment is loud enough for your presentation area. Use speakers if necessary. Practice projecting your voice to the back of the presentation area. If possible, use a microphone and speakers.

A Good Multimedia Presentation

- effectively combines text with images and sound
- presents a clear thesis and evidence that supports it
- organizes information and ideas in a logical way
- considers the needs of the audience

Presentation Tip

Consider the **purpose** and **audience** when selecting a topic. When you know why and for whom you are writing, you should be better able to focus your thoughts and establish a direction for your presentation. In this workshop, your purpose is to inform, and your audience will be your teachers and classmates.

Learn It Online
Plan your multimedia presentation online with MediaScope.
go.hrw.com H12-1441 Go

Guided Practice: Apply

Consider Your Audience

Remind students that they can capture their audience's attention by stating their purpose clearly and presenting a corresponding image or sound that will pique their audience's interest. Whatever subject they choose to analyze, they should keep their purpose and audience in mind as they develop their presentations.

Maximize Your Impact

Encourage students to consider the space in which they will deliver their presentations. If the space is large, the audience's ability to see small text or images may become a problem. If the space is small, the student's ability to use multiple media sources may be limited. Allow students to rearrange the room, if possible, to maximize their ability to interact with the audience as well as the audience's ability to observe the presentation comfortably.

English for Academic Success

Remind students to use formal English when delivering their presentations. They should use informal English only when quoting an advertisement.

Universal Access

EL English Learners

English for Academic Success Provide students with additional guidance when preparing their multimedia presentations.

- Pair students with a more proficient English speaker. Have the proficient speaker read over the student's text and help them simply and organize the text into a bulleted list to make it easier for the audience to read and understand.
- Ask students to identify any words that are not sure how to pronounce. Have them work with their partner to determine the words' pronunciations.
- Have students practice presenting their images to their partners using the four-step process. Remind students to point to their image to highlight certain features they address in their presentation.

Learn It Online
If students need help adding multimedia features to their projects, send them to the **MediaScope** mini-site, where students can work through an interactive tutorial on creating multimedia.
go.hrw.com H12-1441 Go

Model the Skill

Develop a Thesis Statement

Explain that to students that a thesis statement should summarize the point they intend to prove. In this case, the thesis statement will identify which persuasive strategies are used in the advertisement(s) analyzed. Tell students to make sure their thesis statement is clear and direct.

Guided Practice: Apply

Suggest students share their thesis statement with a partner to inquire whether the main points are understandable and explicit.

Teaching Tip

Organize your Presentation

Remind students that while presenting their analysis, it is important for them to address the audience and not read directly from their slides or notes. Encourage students to organize their presentations in a way that allows them time to speak freely to the audience. For instance, students may wish to conclude their presentation with a brief question-and-answer session.

Develop a Thesis Statement The thesis statement for your presentation will identify the most important persuasive strategies at work in the advertisement or group of advertisements you have chosen to analyze. For the sake of your audience, consider presenting your thesis statement as a list of bulleted points—on a single slide or screen, using large, non-serif letters, clearly visible from the back of the presentation area.

Organize Your Presentation To help ensure that the audience can easily follow your presentation, plan its organization carefully. Follow the steps in the chart below to combine effectively the spoken content and the multimedia support you have chosen.

Organizing a Multimedia Presentation
1. Compose your thesis statement and create a single slide or screen presenting the major points of your thesis as a bulleted list.
2. Create a single slide or screen for each of the major points listed on your thesis slide or screen. Each of these screens will introduce a major part of your presentation.
3. Plan the visual back-up for each major point in your presentation. What image or video clip will you show your audience? How will you point out the persuasive strategy you want to highlight at this point in your presentation?
4. Plan the textual support for each major point in your presentation. Set up one or more slides or screens to display the information and ideas you want your audience to remember.
5. If it would be useful to remind your audience of any major point or points, make duplicate slides or screens of these to insert in your presentation, as appropriate.
6. Plan your conclusion. Consider repeating your thesis slide. If time allows, consider showing your audience a new advertisement that uses the techniques your presentation analyzed. Ask members of the audience to identify these techniques.
7. Plan how you will integrate the components of your analysis—words, images, and sound—into a seamless presentation. Make an outline, chart, or storyboard to consult as you rehearse.

Universal Access

EL English Learners

Allow students to use note cards during their presentation. While students practice, have them note any words they have trouble pronouncing or statements they find difficult to express. Have students highlight those words and statements in their notes and refer to them when needed.

Struggling Learners

Hold a mock-presentation day for students who struggle with their presentation skills. Have each students present a preview of their presentation for thirty seconds. Students might present and talk about one image. Then, have the rest of the class give feedback on the strengths and weaknesses of each performance.

Practice Your Presentation In the course of planning and developing your presentation, you have probably seriously considered the effect it will have on your intended audience. Now, it is time to determine whether all of the elements work together as planned. Gather a group of friends or family members, and rehearse your presentation. Deliver it exactly as you would for the intended audience of your final presentation. If you need to use the school's audiovisual equipment, arrange a rehearsal before or after school.

As you rehearse, express interest in and enthusiasm for your topic. Indeed, your delivery holds the whole presentation together. Speak confidently, enunciate, and avoid vocalized pauses, such as "um" or "ah." Use nonverbal behavior—eye contact, facial expressions, and gestures—to your advantage. Be familiar with your presentation equipment, and do not turn your back on the audience when using it. After your rehearsal, use the questions in the chart below to ask your audience for feedback.

Audience Feedback
Which section of the spoken part of the presentation was most memorable? Why did it succeed?
Which of the multimedia elements of the presentation were most effective? Why did you think so?
How well did the presentation combine spoken words with text, images, and sounds? Explain.
What parts of the multimedia presentation, if any, did you find confusing? Why?
How did the delivery itself affect the presentation? Explain.
What did you learn about propaganda techniques in advertising? Where in the presentation would you like more information?

Revise Your Presentation Adjust the content and delivery of your presentation according to the responses of your rehearsal audience. Do further research, if indicated, to strengthen the content of your analysis. If necessary, revise slides or screens for greater clarity or adjust the way you present still images or video clips. Then, practice delivering your presentation for a second time to ensure all problems have been eliminated. Check and double-check your presentation equipment. The effectiveness of an excellent presentation depends on your efficient management of your equipment. Because a multimedia presentation coordinates so many different parts, anticipate possible challenges and be prepared for emergencies.

Viewing Tip

As a viewer of media, do not ignore or discount your instinctual reaction to an image, but also use your head. Think about why you reacted to the image in such a manner. Ask yourself these questions:

- What made me react that way?
- Is my reaction the one the image maker wanted me to have? Why might he or she have tried to evoke a particular reaction?
- How does my reaction to the image affect my understanding of the issue or story the image accompanies?

Model the Skill

Practice Your Presentation

- Demonstrate effective delivery and ineffective delivery. Model delivering a presentation full of *um*'s and *ah*'s, speaking extremely nervously, not enunciating, never looking at the audience, and not gesturing. Ask students to point out how the presentation can be improved. Then, model an effective presentation that does not include any *um*'s or *ah*'s, makes frequent eye contacts, uses gestures, and speaks confidently and clearly to the audience.
- Remind students that unless the presenter has fun in delivering the presentation confidently, the audience will be just as nervous and bored as the presenter.

Guided Practice: Apply

- Have students work on their oral presentation skills at home in front of a mirror. Instruct students to practice at least three times.
- After each speech, students should self-assess their performance on a scale of 1–5 in the areas of speech rate, eye contact, use of nonverbal techniques, and overall comfort.
- Tell students to continue practicing until they see improvement in their performance.

Assess

Independent Practice

Use the Analyzing and Using Media analytical scale and rubric to evaluate students' presentations. See **Workshop Resources**.

Advanced Learners

Acceleration Ask student volunteers who are familiar and skilled with most or all of the presentational equipment to give a basic fifteen-minute demonstration of how to use one or two pieces of equipment. Students might opt to demonstrate how to use the equipment as a group. Have the rest of the class ask questions at the end of the demonstration about anything that is still confusing for them.

Students with Disabilities

To help students address their audience while presenting, have students try different forms of notes. Some students may prefer index cards; others might create an outline or a flow chart. Some students may find they can give a presentation effectively while referring only occasionally to notes. Encourage students to use the method that works best for them.

Standards Focus

Objectives

Students will understand, analyze, and compare poetry from different cultures and literary periods.

Literary Skills Review

Review

If necessary, use the following questions to guide students in their reading before they answer the questions at the end of the review.

Theme

Which Romantic themes can you find in "The Lorelei"? ***Possible response:*** *Nature is seen as a mirror of human emotions; the poem is strongly influenced by the speaker's imagination.*

Compare and Contrast

How does the point of view in "The Lorelei" differ from the "Siren Song"? ***Possible response:*** *"The Lorelei" retells the story from the point of view of the male speaker, who identifies with the Lorelei's victim; Atwood tells her story from the point of view of the female predator, the siren.*

Test-Taking Tip

Advise students to read all the questions first and quickly answer those they are certain of. Then, have them go back to the most puzzling questions and try to rephrase them in their own words to facilitate understanding.

California Standards, pp. 1444–1445

- **Reading Standard 3.7** Analyze recognized works of world literature from a variety of authors: **a.** Contrast the major literary forms, techniques, and characteristics of the major literary periods (e.g., Homeric Greece, medieval, romantic, neoclassic, modern).

STANDARDS REVIEW

Literary Skills Review

Comparing Literature **Directions:** Read the poems below, and answer the questions that follow.

The Lorelei

by **Heinrich Heine**
translated by **Louis Untermeyer**

I cannot tell why this imagined
Despair has fallen on me;
The ghost of an ancient legend
That will not let me be:

The air is cool, and twilight
Flows down the quiet Rhine;
A mountain alone in the high light
Still holds the faltering shine.

The last peak rosily gleaming
Reveals, enthroned in air,
A maiden, lost in dreaming,
Who combs her golden hair.

Combing her hair with a golden
Comb in her rocky bower,°
She sings the tune of an olden
Song that has magical power.

The boatman has heard; it has bound him
In throes of a strange, wild love;
Blind to the reefs that surround him,
He sees but the vision above.

And lo, hungry waters are springing—
Boat and boatman are gone. . . .
Then silence. And this, with her singing,
The Lorelei has done.

14. bower: enclosed place or retreat, usually a lady's bedroom or private room; a natural enclosure.

Siren Song

by **Margaret Atwood**

This is the one song everyone
would like to learn: the song
that is irresistible:

the song that forces men
to leap overboard in squadrons
even though they see the beached skulls

the song nobody knows
because anyone who has heard it
is dead, and the others can't remember.

Shall I tell you the secret
and if I do, will you get me
out of this bird suit?

I don't enjoy it here
squatting on this island
looking picturesque and mythical

with these two feathery maniacs,
I don't enjoy singing
this trio, fatal and valuable.

I will tell the secret to you,
to you, only to you.
Come closer. This song

is a cry for help: Help me!
Only you, only you can,
you are unique

at last. Alas
it is a boring song
but it works every time.

Resources for Skills and Standards Review

Unit 6 Resources, Unit Standards Mastery, Unit Vocabulary Review, p. 269

UA: Differentiating Instruction, below-level Unit Standards Mastery

Teacher One Stop™, editable Unit Standards Mastery

Focus on Standards with CAHSEE Support

Preparing for the SAT and ACT

ThinkCentral Online Assessment, Unit Standards Mastery

ThinkCentral Online Remediation

Holt Online Essay Scoring

Reading Standard 3.7a (see pages A48–A50)

1. In lines 1–4 of "The Lorelei," the speaker
   - **A** is pursued by a real ghost.
   - **B** finds comfort in a legend.
   - **C** experiences real love for the first time.
   - **D** feels a compelling connection to a legend.

2. The **mood** in lines 5–8 of "The Lorelei" could *best* be described as
   - **A** fearful.
   - **B** joyful.
   - **C** romantic.
   - **D** reckless.

3. What has occurred in the final stanza of "The Lorelei"?
   - **A** The speaker betrays the Lorelei.
   - **B** The boatman has gone away with the woman.
   - **C** The boatman has drowned.
   - **D** The speaker expresses envy of the boatman.

4. The **tone** of "Siren Song" is *best* described as
   - **A** cynical.
   - **B** romantic.
   - **C** sorrowful.
   - **D** joyful.

5. What do lines 13–16 of "Siren Song" suggest about the speaker's attitude?
   - **A** She finds her situation ridiculous.
   - **B** She enjoys being mythical and powerful.
   - **C** She is proud of her beauty.
   - **D** She does not want to find true love.

6. Who is the speaker of "Siren Song"?
   - **A** a siren wearing a bird suit
   - **B** Margaret Atwood
   - **C** a sailor
   - **D** a bitter woman

7. What implied **theme** is contained in the last two lines of "Siren Song"?
   - **A** Help is available for those who ask.
   - **B** Women are rarely taken seriously.
   - **C** Men cannot be manipulated.
   - **D** Attraction follows a predictable pattern.

8. How does the overall **imagery** in "Siren Song" differ from that in "The Lorelei"?
   - **A** The imagery in "The Lorelei" is romantic, while the imagery in "Siren Song" is jarring.
   - **B** The imagery in "The Lorelei" is violent, while the imagery in "Siren Song" is soothing.
   - **C** The imagery in "The Lorelei" is powerful, while the imagery in "Siren Song" is understated.
   - **D** The imagery in "The Lorelei" is playful, while the imagery in "Siren Song" is naive.

9. The sirens in "The Lorelei" and "Siren Song" are alike in that they both
   - **A** are mermaids.
   - **B** regret their actions.
   - **C** call men to their deaths.
   - **D** feel unattractive.

Timed Writing

10. Briefly contrast the concluding stanzas of "The Lorelei" and "Siren Song," focusing on tone. Use specific evidence from the poems to support your response.

Word-Attack Skills Mini-Lesson

English for Academic Success Review Use the activities below to check students' grasp of the word-attack skills taught in this unit.

Activity Have students identify the syllable that is said with the greatest stress in each word. Answers are underlined.

1. parentage
2. parental
3. concert
4. disconcerted
5. illustration
6. illustrative
7. parasite
8. parasitic
9. malefactor
10. malevolent

Activity Have students identify the word in each of the following pairs that has a silent *h*.

a. vehement, behemoth [*vehement*]
b. antihistamine, annihilate [*annihilate*]
c. exhaust, exhale [*exhaust*]
d. inhibitions, prohibitions [*prohibitions*]

Assess

Answers and Explanations

1. ***D*** *Students can eliminate A, since the ghost is a legend, and B and C, since the speaker feels despair rather than comfort or love.*
2. ***C*** *Students can eliminate A, B, and D, since the imagery suggests a serene, enchanting image.*
3. ***C*** *The phrase "hungry waters" makes it clear that the boatman drowns.*
4. ***A*** *Diction determines tone. The term "bird suit" is deliberately ridiculous (A), not romantic (B) or sorrowful (C). The speaker doesn't "enjoy it here," so D is incorrect.*
5. ***A*** *The speaker does not see any purpose in her position. She is not concerned with power, beauty, or love (B) (C) (D).*
6. ***A*** *The title identifies the speaker as the siren.*
7. ***D*** *A song that "works every time" is predictable (D).*
8. ***A*** *The imagery in "The Lorelei" is romantic, not violent, powerful, or playful, and the imagery in "Siren Song" is jarring, not soothing, understated, or naïve.*
9. ***C*** *A can be eliminated since neither the siren nor the Lorelei is described as fish-like. Neither woman regrets her actions (B), and both know they can attract men to their deaths (D).*

Timed Writing

10. ***Possible response:*** *"The Lorelei" has a very melancholy tone in the last stanza, and the "Siren Song" is cynical. However, both poems are pragmatic about the men dying.*

Reteach

go.hrw.com ThinkCentral Online Remediation

Vocabulary Skills Review

Assess

Answers and Explanations

1. **C** *An impetuous person does things quickly and without thought.*
2. **A** *An impediment is a hindrance, so it would not make a good architectural feature, law, or plea.*
3. **D** *To use guile means to be sly or deceitful.*
4. **B** *An implacable person would be relentless.*
5. **B** *Ignominy is public disgrace.*
6. **C** *A person looking reproachfully would be disapproving and blaming, not admiring.*
7. **A** *To have allure is to be attractive.*

Academic Vocabulary

8. **B** *If something is inevitable, it is unavoidable.*
9. **D** *A person's perspective is his or her point of view. Although context, period, and anxiety affect someone's perspective, they are not synonymous with perspective.*

go.hrw.com **WordSharp: An Interactive Vocabulary Tutor**

Reteach

go.hrw.com **ThinkCentral Online Remediation**

California Standards, p. 1446

- **Grades 9–10 Review Reading Standard**
  1.1 Identify and use the literal and figurative meanings of words and understand word derivations.

STANDARDS REVIEW

Vocabulary Skills Review

Grades 9–10 Review Reading Standard 1.1 (see pages A48–A50)

Synonyms **Directions:** Words that have similar meanings are called **synonyms.** For example, *benign* and *benevolent* are synonyms meaning "kind." In the sentences below, choose the word or phrase that is closest to the meaning of the italicized word.

1. An *impetuous* person is
A overly helpful.
B dangerously manipulative.
C extremely impulsive.
D unreasonably stubborn.

2. An *impediment* is
A an obstacle.
B an architectural feature.
C a commandment.
D a plea.

3. *Guile* is the same as
A innocence.
B bitterness.
C awe.
D deceit.

4. Someone who is *implacable* is
A fearful.
B relentless.
C attentive.
D confused.

5. *Ignominy* means
A ignorance.
B disgrace.
C aggression.
D retaliation.

6. Someone who looks at you *reproachfully* is
A studying you.
B admiring you.
C blaming you.
D recognizing you.

7. An object with *allure* is
A fascinating.
B flattering.
C repulsive.
D threatening.

Academic Vocabulary

Directions: Choose the word or phrase that is closest to the meaning of the italicized word.

8. If something is *inevitable*, it is
A enviable.
B unavoidable.
C inedible.
D not edited correctly.

9. Your *perspective* is your
A context.
B historical period.
C anxiety level.
D point of view.

Vocabulary Review

Use this activity to assess whether students have retained the unit Vocabulary. Ask students to fill in the blanks below with a boxed Vocabulary word.

conspicuous	monotonous	annulled
heedless	forsaken	

1. Although the widow remarried, she vowed that her late husband's memory would not be _____. [*forsaken*]
2. The contract between the two parties was _____ because a judge found the document to be invalid. [*annulled*]
3. Several students fell asleep in class because the professor's lecture was long and _____. [*monotonous*]
4. To avoid being _____ around predators, a chameleon changes color to blend in with its environment. [*conspicuous*]
5. Jamie's _____ action of leaving the stove on resulted in the house catching fire. [*heedless*]

STANDARDS REVIEW

Writing Skills Review

Writing Standard 2.1a–c (see pages A51–A52)

Edit a Biographical Narrative **Directions:** The following passage is a rough draft. It may contain errors in grammar, punctuation, sentence structure, and organization. Read the passage below, and answer the questions that follow.

Rough Draft

(1) Like many young girls that grew up in the Victorian era, Woolf was educated at home rather being sent away to school. (2) At an early age, other domestic influences caused Woolf to realize that society had certain expectations for women and female writers. (3) Both her mother and her father were heavily connected in London's literary circles, and renowned writers and editors such as George Eliot and Henry James often visited their home. (4) As a child, Woolf listened to discussions between these famous people on important academic and literary issues. (5) She also read many books from her house's extensive library and formed an early appreciation of classic literature. (6) Woolf learned that many people expected women to be only good wives and mothers. (7) Because women were often not given the same opportunities or encouragement as men, they found it hard to do other things. (8) Later in life Woolf included these and other thoughts in a essay titled "A Room of One's Own." (9) This piece of writing is now considered a very important work of feminist criticism that is read by students all over the world.

1. The writer's main purpose in writing this essay is to explain
   - **A** why Woolf received an incomplete education.
   - **B** how Woolf's childhood shaped her development as an author.
   - **C** that Victorian girls found it difficult to learn.
   - **D** Woolf's contribution to Modernism.

2. Which sentence could serve as the best transition between sentences 1 and 2?
   - **A** Woolf was especially good at geography.
   - **B** Many academics considered boarding school a waste of money.
   - **C** Although the instruction she received from her father was valuable, most of Woolf's education occurred outside the classroom.
   - **D** Woolf's parents kept to themselves.

3. Which sentence in the essay states the thesis?
   - **A** sentence 2
   - **B** sentence 1
   - **C** sentence 3
   - **D** sentence 6

4. Which evidence could the writer have added to support the idea in sentence 4?
   - **A** a list of some books considered to be classic literature
   - **B** a statistic about child literacy rates in Victorian England
   - **C** a quote from a critic discussing Woolf's reading interests
   - **D** a quote from Virginia Woolf describing her love of good books

5. Which of the following would be the MOST precise way to restate the underlined passage in the sentence labeled 7?
   - **A** to manage successful households
   - **B** to keep up with other women
   - **C** to fulfill vocational and professional ambitions
   - **D** to understand current events

Writing Skills Review

Assess

Answers and Explanations

1. ***B*** *The writer details how Woolf was exposed to the literary work and how it influenced her.*
2. ***C*** *The best transition between the first two sentences should mention her education and other influences.*
3. ***D*** *The details of her childhood influences and her adult works support sentence 6 as the thesis.*
4. ***D*** *Woolf's own declaration of her love for good books in general would best support sentence 4.*
5. ***C*** *"Other things" would most likely refer to vocational and professional ambitions, not household affairs (A), other women (B), or current events (D).*

Reteach

go.hrw.com **ThinkCentral Online Remediation**

Application Homework
Public Service Announcement

Have students practice delivering multimedia presentations by having small groups write and produce public service announcements. Possible subjects include anti-drug messages or an ad supporting a local food bank. Groups should choose an appropriate subject and elements they can combine in producing a brief (thirty seconds to one minute) videotaped or audiotaped piece. Groups can then present their announcements to the class.

Extension
Media Watch Dog

Have students write an essay comparing two newspaper or magazine articles that address the same event or issue. Students may refer to print or online periodicals. Students should evaluate each source for its accuracy, objectivity, and depth in addition to noting overall similarities and differences between the two sources' approaches. Ask students to present their analysis to the class.

California Standards, p. 1447

- **Writing Standard 2.1** Write fictional, autobiographical, or biographical narratives. **a.** Narrate a sequence of events and communicate their significance to the audience. **b.** Locate scenes and incidents in specific places. **c.** Describe with concrete sensory details the sights, sounds, and smells of a scene and the specific actions, movements, gestures, and feelings of the characters; use interior monologue to depict the characters' feelings.

Read On

If students enjoyed the themes and topics explored in this unit, you might recommend these titles for independent reading.

Assessment Options

The following projects can help you evaluate and assess your students' outside work. Videotapes or audiotapes of completed projects may be included in students' portfolios.

Create a Utopia

Just as Aldous Huxley creates a Utopian world in his novel *Brave New World,* have students imagine their own Utopia, or ideal place. Ask students to write a short essay describing their "new world." Then, have students consider what steps would need to take place to achieve this perfection and what problems might occur in the process. Have students address these issues in a continuation of their essay. Have students think about the issues that arise in Huxley's book when assessing their Utopia.

Create a Family Tree

As Gabriel García Márquez traces his family history through many centuries, have students keep track of his family members by creating a family tree. Ask students to list three defining details about each person whose name they add to the tree. Then, have students present their trees to the class and highlight the main characters in the story and their connection to the other family members. Ask that students also summarize the events that affect the personal relationships between family members.

Read On

For Independent Reading

FICTION

The Inimitable Jeeves

To say that P. G. Wodehouse is a hilarious writer is an understatement. In the course of his long career, Wodehouse wrote over ninety humor books, many of which chronicle the hijinks of Bertie Wooster and Bingo Little. Bertie's valet, Jeeves, deftly rescues Bertie from his entanglements and provides sardonic commentary on his foppish employer's antics. This volume contains several classic stories, including "The Metropolitan Touch," "The Delayed Exit of Claude and Eustace," and "The Purity of the Turf," which some consider to be the funniest story ever written by Wodehouse.

FICTION

Brave New World

Imagine a society that is perfectly harmonious, a community where everyone gets along. How terrible would it be? In his science fiction novel, Aldous Huxley presents a terrifying vision of a Utopian world gone wrong. "Community, Identity, Stability" is the motto of this future state envisioned by Huxley, and to achieve its totalitarian ideals, the government uses pleasure to subdue its citizens. It seems that everyone should be happy, yet the protagonist, Bernard Marx, feels empty and attempts to find fulfillment through love—a subversive emotion.

FICTION

One Hundred Years of Solitude

Stories about our origins are fascinating to storytellers and writers. In his prize-winning novel, Gabriel García Márquez invents a mythical Colombian village called Macondo and recounts the history of its founding family, the Buendías. In tracing several generations over the course of a century, he weaves together reality and fantasy, exploring the development of his country's unique culture and illuminating the wonder and strangeness of life.

FICTION

Things Fall Apart

The rise and fall of powerful people and societies inevitably makes for a compelling story, one that Chinua Achebe tells particularly well in this novel. His portrayal of Nigerian tribal life before and after the arrival of Europeans in Africa centers on the protagonist Okonkwo, a successful man who loses everything and is exiled from the tribe. How will he handle the change, both as a man and as a leader? Losing all hope as his homeland is transformed and modernized, Okonkwo, in his downfall, becomes a poignant symbol of colonial Africa.

Word Counts and Readabilities of Read On Books

Fiction	Estimated Word Counts	Readability
The Inimitable Jeeves	67,787	Accessible
Brave New World	257,100	Easily Accessible
One Hundred Years of Solitude	159,500	Challenging
Things Fall Apart	161,700	Easily Accessible
A Passage to India	99,771	Accessible
Waiting for the Barbarians	65,462	Accessible

FICTION

A Passage to India

E. M. Forster's most famous novel depicts culture clashes and racial tension in British India just after the turn of the twentieth century. Adela Quested and Mrs. Moore (the mother of Adela's fiancé) come to the city of Chandrapore and befriend Dr. Aziz, who suggests that they all visit the mysterious Marabar Caves. This seemingly innocuous proposal is their undoing: In the darkness of the caves, Adela believes Aziz has assaulted her, and Mrs. Moore becomes panic-stricken. Aziz is arrested, and the British and Indian communities seem even more hopelessly divided.

NONFICTION

Churchill: A Life

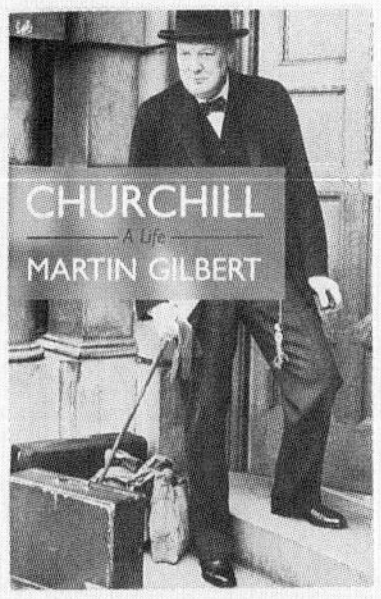

That this 1,000-page biography is merely a condensed version of Martin Gilbert's eight-volume opus on Winston Churchill should give you an idea of how famous and fascinating Churchill was as both a public figure and private person. Filled with anecdotes, excerpts from letters and conversations, and comments from Churchill's family and friends, this biography traces Churchill's life as a schoolboy undergoing floggings, a soldier writing war dispatches and escaping from capture during the Boer War, a prime minister keeping Britain rallied during World War II, and a writer winning the Nobel Prize in Literature.

FICTION

Waiting for the Barbarians

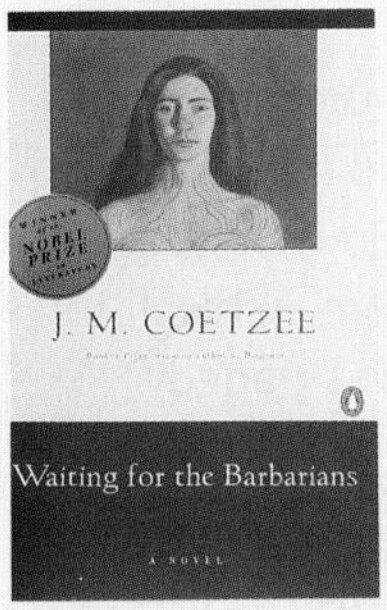

Set in an unnamed Empire, in a remote, unnamed village overseen by an unnamed bureaucrat, this tale grapples with notions of power and justice. The Magistrate has long ignored rumors of insurgency by the natives, or "barbarians," living outside the village. He, the villagers, and the natives live peacefully together until the Empire's military arrives and the soldiers brutally and unjustly persecute the barbarians. J. M. Coetzee's fable of the misuse of power will leave you contemplating which people, after all, are really the barbarians.

NONFICTION

Unbowed

When Maathai was born in 1940, the land around her village in Kenya was lush and fertile. Thirty years later, ill-advised agricultural practices had deforested the valley, displaced food crops, and led to erosion and malnutrition. Maathai began a grass-roots movement to restore the land and improve the lives of the people. Read about why she was beaten and jailed for her work, but also about how her efforts have led to the planting of twenty million trees, an accomplishment that won Maathai a seat in Parliament—and the Nobel Peace Prize.

Learn It Online
Go online to find tips for choosing, reading, and studying books.
go.hrw.com H12-1449 Go

Nonfiction	Estimated Word Counts	Readability
Churchill: A Life	442,241	Challenging
Unbowed	32,922	Accessible

Assessment Options

Compare and Contrast

Inform students that although E. M. Forster's work *A Passage to India* is fiction, it addresses real issues that occurred in British India. Have students research information on the British occupancy of India. Ask them to compare and contrast in an essay the historical information regarding social tensions and government policy found in Forster's book with the information they find in a nonfiction reference.

Award a Nobel Peace Prize

Have students answer the question addressed in Maathai's introduction on this page, "Why was an environmentalist awarded the Nobel Peace Prize?" by writing a speech directed toward the Nobel nominating committee citing reasons why Maathai should receive the award. Have students use evidence from Maathai's memoir to support their argument. Students can present this speech in a written form or in an audiotape.

Become Churchill

After students read Martin Gilbert's biography of Winston Churchill, ask them to give an oral report on the book by assuming the voice of Winston Churchill in their presentation. Have students address various events from both Churchill's public and private lives. Students may choose to address subjects such as common misconceptions, political influences, or famous quotes.

Learn It Online
The **NovelWise Mini-Site** site offers students interactive instruction on choosing, reading, and considering novels; it also links to a catalogue of books and associated study guides, teaching guides, and **NovelNotes** presentations.
go.hrw.com H12–1449 Go

Reteaching Lessons

Public Documents

Reading Standard 2.1 Analyze both the features and the rhetorical devices of different types of public documents (e.g., policy statements, speeches, debates, platforms) and the way in which authors use those features and devices.

Objective: To analyze the way authors use the features and rhetorical devices of public documents.

Direct Teaching: Share the following information with students.

What does a political speech have in common with a television commercial? They are both trying to sell you something. While the commercial is selling a product or service, the speech is selling ideas, perhaps in order to receive votes, raise money, or gather support for a law or policy. Political leaders are promoters of ideas and actions, and their speeches, platforms, and policy statements are written with the purpose of persuading you to support their ideas and adopt their programs. For example, when the president of the United States delivers his annual State of the Union speech, he is not just giving the nation a progress report but is touting his past achievements and looking for support for his current proposals. In short, most political speeches are trying to sell an idea or course of action, and the devices their authors use are common to all documents whose purpose is to persuade. Therefore, when you read or listen to a political speech, keep in mind that it is designed to impress, move, and convince you. The writers of these documents achieve their aims by the use of repetition, parallelism, figurative language, and appeals to emotion. Parallelism, or parallel structure, is the repetition of words and phrases with similar grammatical structures in a sentence or longer passage of prose. Such repetition creates a pleasing rhythm, calls attention to important ideas, and helps readers or listeners remember a message. Emotionally charged and figurative language is designed to get your attention, create vivid images in your mind, and stir your sympathies—or in some cases, anger or indignation. Very often, an emotional appeal—say to people's patriotism, to their hope for the future, or to their fear of violence—is more effective in persuading an audience than an appeal to reason alone.

Guided Practice: Analyzing rhetorical devices. Review figurative language with students, especially the use of metaphor. Remind them that a metaphor defines one experience in terms of another, quite different experience. For example, to speak of "the birth of a nation" is to speak metaphorically, since a nation is not actually born in the same way a person is. However, since nations do have beginnings, comparing the formation of a nation to a human birth makes an abstract concept easier to imagine and care about. Also, if you think students need a further review of parallelism, direct them to the Handbook of Literary and Historical Terms and review the definition and examples given there. Then, read aloud the following excerpt from the opening of "The Noble Mansion of Free India" (p. 1155), as students follow along in their books.

"Long years ago we made a tryst with destiny, and now the time comes when we shall redeem our pledge, not wholly or in full measure, but very substantially. At the stroke of the midnight hour, when the world sleeps, India will awake to life and freedom."

Remind students that this speech was given by Jawaharlal Nehru to the Indian Parliament on the eve of Indian independence. Point out that although Nehru at this point did not need to convince the majority of Indians that independence was desirable, he was addressing an anxious audience. The independence movement was coinciding with a wrenching partition of the nation into two states: India and Pakistan. Discuss with students the figurative and emotional language Nehru uses in these two sentences, why he may have chosen those words, and what effects he inspires in his audience. For example, the words *tryst, destiny,* and *pledge* suggest a bethrothal or romantic attachment, which equates the pact between citizen and nation with that between lovers. This has the effect of heightening the audience's emotional involvement in what is more a political than a personal event. It arouses feelings of warmth, hope, and loyalty. The metaphorical language "when the world sleeps" and "India will awake" also stirs powerful emotions of excitement and hope. It equates colonial India with a sleeping person, while independent India is compared to an awake and fully aware person.

Have students read the rest of the speech and look for other passages in which Nehru uses powerful persuasive devices to reach his audience. Draw on the chalkboard a chart like the one below, and fill it in with examples of persuasive passages that students identify. Or, if you prefer, provide them with the passage and have them identify the persuasive device that Nehru uses and its effect on the audience. (Possible responses appear in brackets.)

Passage	Device	Effect
["when we step out . . . , when an age ends, and when the soul of a nation . . ."]	[parallelism]	[underscores the importance of the occasion; creates a memorable rhythm, which holds the audience's attention]
["At the dawn of history, India started on her unending quest . . . has never lost sight of that quest or forgotten the ideals which gave her strength. . . . India discovers herself again."]	[figurative and emotional language]	[appeals to patriotism and idealism; acknowledges past suffering and offers hope for a better future]
["Before the birth of freedom we have endured all the pains of labor . . . ."]	[metaphor]	[links a political experience to a highly personal experience (giving birth), stirring emotions of joy, hope, and identification]
["to wipe every tear from every eye"]	[emotional language and parallelism]	[stirs feelings of sympathy and solidarity; creates a pleasing, musical rhythm]
["so is freedom, so is prosperity now, and so also is disaster in this One World. . . ."]	[parallelism]	[emphasizes important ideas; balances good and bad experiences, thereby appealing to reason and emotion]
["We have to build the noble mansion of free India. . . ."]	[metaphor]	[equates the new nation with high-mindedness, spaciousness, beauty, and wealth; appeals to feelings of pride, hope, and idealism]

Independent Practice: Evaluating rhetorical devices. Assign students in small groups to locate recent speeches made by local or national politicians, such as the most recent State of the Union address by the president. Ask groups to read the speech or sections of it and identify the speaker's purpose. Ask, "What does he or she want to convince the audience to think or do?" Then, have students work together to identify and evaluate the rhetorical devices the speaker uses to try to persuade the audience. Encourage students to organize their ideas on a chart like the one in the Guided Practice. When they have completed their charts, have a class discussion about the effective use of persuasive devices and the relative power of appeals to reason and emotion. Urge students to support their opinions with examples from their group work.

Clarity of Meaning

Reading Standard 2.2 Analyze the way in which clarity of meaning is affected by the patterns of organization, hierarchical structures, repetition of the main ideas, syntax, and word choice in the text.

Objective: To analyze the way in which clarity of meaning is affected by patterns of organization, syntax, and word choice in the text.

Direct Teaching: Share the following information with students.

> **When writers sit down to write, their thoughts don't instantly flow onto the page in clear and easy-to-understand sentences and paragraphs. On the contrary, good writers work hard to present their ideas in organized patterns that readers can recognize and follow. For example, writers can organize events, actions, or steps in a process in chronological order, the order in which the events or steps occurred. Writers also can present events and actions in cause-and-effect order: Event A brings about Event B, or Event B is the result of Event A. When writers are presenting ideas, they are likely to organize their presentation around a main idea that is followed by supporting details. These supporting details can take the form of reasons, facts, or examples. This type of organization is often used when a writer is making an assertion or advancing an argument and wishes to convince the reader of his or her opinion.**
>
> **Writers also seek to make their ideas clear and memorable by repeating key words and phrases. Parallel structure is a very polished form of repetition in which grammatically similar words, phrases, clauses, or sentences are repeated for emphasis or emotional effect. Lincoln's formulation "government of the people, by the people, for the people" is a famous example of parallel structure. Word choice also affects clarity. A precise word makes meaning instantly clear; a vague one obscures it. In general, specific words have greater impact than general ones, and figurative and sensory language make a stronger impression than literal or abstract word choices. For example, "a summer soldier" or "sunshine patriot" is a far more powerful choice of words than "an unreliable participant."**

Guided Practice: Analyzing patterns of organization and word choice. Have a volunteer read aloud the first passage from Margaret Cavendish's "Female Orations" (p. 377). Ask the class, "What is the purpose of the passage?" Help them to see that as a participant in a fictional debate, the speaker is trying to convince her listeners to adopt her point of view on women's position in society. Next, work with students to identify the speaker's assertions and the support she offers for those opinions in the form of reasons, facts, or examples. As students volunteer assertions, write them in the first column of a chart like the one on p. 1449E. If the class is having difficulty, you may want to provide the assertions and have students find the supporting details. (Possible responses appear in brackets.)

When students have finished analyzing the patterns of assertion and support, ask them to look again at the passages they identified for examples of effective sentence structure and vivid word choice. Write these in the third column of the chart, and discuss with students how these words and sentences make the speaker's ideas clearer and more convincing. If students are having trouble appreciating Cavendish's use of repetition and figurative language, rephrase some of her passages in less rhythmic and more abstract prose so they can hear the difference.

Assertion	Support	Sentence Structure and Word Choice
["I have been industrious to assemble you together"]	[Reason: "that we may unite in prudent counsels, to make ourselves as free, happy, and famous as men"]	[Parallel structure: "free, happy, and famous"]
["for men are happy, and we women are miserable"]	[Examples: "they possess all the ease, rest, pleasure, wealth, power, and fame; whereas women are restless with labor, easeless with pain, melancholy for want of pleasures, helpless for want of power, and die in oblivion, for want of fame."]	[Parallel structure: "women are restless with labor, easeless with pain, melancholy for want of pleasures, helpless for want of power, and die in oblivion, for want of fame."]
[". . . men are so unconscionable and cruel against us that they . . . bar us of all sorts of liberty"]	[Examples: "will not suffer us freely to associate amongst our own sex . . . would fain bury us in their houses or beds, as in a grave . . . we live like bats or owls, labor like beasts, and die like worms."]	[Figurative language and parallel structure: "bury us in their houses or beds, as in a grave (simile); . . . we live like bats or owls, labor like beasts, and die like worms (similes)."]

Independent Practice: Analyzing writing for clarity. Have individual students continue studying Cavendish's patterns of organization, sentence structure, and word choice by applying the same technique of analysis begun in the Guided Practice to the remaining passages from "Female Orations." Have them organize their ideas on a chart and bring their charts to class for a general discussion of Cavendish's methods. Also, encourage students to consider alternative patterns of organization that Cavendish or another speaker might have used to make clear and convincing arguments about the position of women.

As an alternative, have students read and analyze John Donne's sermon Meditation 17 (p. 297), charting how Donne makes use of assertion and support, parallel structure, rhetorical questions, figurative language, and other powerful word choices. Ask students to use their charts to write a brief essay on Donne's organizational patterns, sentence structure, and word choice, explaining how these contributed to the clarity and effectiveness of his argument.

Making Assertions

Reading Standard 2.4 Make warranted and reasonable assertions about the author's arguments by using elements of the text to defend and clarify interpretations.

Objective: To make reasonable assertions about an author's arguments by using elements of the text to defend interpretations.

Direct Teaching: Share the following ideas with students.

Whether you are reading fiction or nonfiction, reading is not a passive task. When reading fiction, you will need to activate your imagination to make the characters, setting, and events come alive. To get the most out of reading nonfiction, you will need to question and evaluate the ideas presented to you. One of the best ways to evaluate informative or persuasive prose is first to identify the author's main idea and then find the evidence, reasoning, or examples the author uses to support this idea. The next step is to form opinions, make inferences, and draw conclusions about the case the writer has made for the main idea or argument. You can apply this process by using these questions:

- **What assertions, or statements, can I make about the writer's arguments?**

- **How can I support these assertions with direct quotations, paraphrases, or other evidence from the text itself?**

Reader assertions include generalizations characterizing the writer's point of view, such as a statement declaring that a writer's ideas are too pessimistic. An assertion may also take the form of an overall evaluation of the writer's persuasiveness, such as a conclusion that the support is insufficient to prove the point.

Guided Practice: Analyzing an author's arguments. If needed, review the process of finding the main idea and identifying supporting details. Remind students that an author's main idea or argument is sometimes stated directly in a sentence somewhere near the beginning or end of the text. Just as often, however, the main idea is not summed up in any one statement in the text and must be inferred from the overall weight of the evidence presented. Be sure students understand that to assert an idea, they must express it in a clear and positive statement. To be convincing, an assertion about an author's argument—whether in the form of an evaluation, an opinion, or a conclusion—must be supported with facts, examples, or other evidence from the text.

Have students read the excerpt from Virginia Woolf's "A Room of One's Own" (p. 1163). After students have reviewed the entire selection, ask them to identify the purpose of Woolf's essay. [to persuade] Next, have a volunteer read the first column of text aloud while students listen for the sentence in which Woolf sums up her main idea or argument. Draw on the chalkboard a flowchart like the one on p. 1449G, and fill in student responses as the discussion progresses. (Possible responses appear in brackets.) When students have located Woolf's main idea, ask them to discuss the kind of support she offers to persuade readers to accept her argument. Guide students to see that Woolf primarily offers inferences or suppositions about the life of a hypothetical sister of Shakespeare. Her inferences, however, are based on known facts about women's lives in Shakespeare's day. Then, have students provide examples of Woolf's supporting arguments and write these on the chart. Finally, help students to make an assertion about the nature or effectiveness of the case Woolf makes to support her main idea.

Main Idea

["It would have been impossible, completely and entirely, for any woman to have written the plays of Shakespeare in the age of Shakespeare."]

Support

[Shakespeare's sister would not have received any formal education.]

[Her days would have been filled with tiring domestic duties.]

[She probably would have had to write secretly and would have hidden or destroyed her writing.]

[She would have been forced to marry very young or run away to London.]

[In London, she would have been unable to support herself and would have been taken advantage of by men.]

[A gifted female, without any outlet for her talent, she would have ended up frustrated, maybe mentally ill, or even suicidal.]

Reader Assertion

[Woolf convincingly supports her argument because the imagined life she creates for Shakespeare's sister is based on known facts about women's lives in the sixteenth century and is presented in such vivid, lively, and plausible detail that readers find it believable.]

You may want to continue the class discussion by raising this question: Do you think Virginia Woolf makes a convincing case that women writers in her day face difficulties like those of "Shakespeare's sister"? Ask students to look at the selection to see how Woolf supports this assertion, and have them discuss the effectiveness of her reasoning. Remind students that they should assess Woolf's effectiveness in supporting her ideas, not express their own views on the struggles of women writers.

Independent Practice: Analyzing an author's arguments. Have students read Joseph Chamberlain's speech "I Believe in a British Empire" (p. 1152). Then, have them work in pairs to identify Chamberlain's main idea and the arguments he presents to support his thesis, using direct quotations from or paraphrases of the text. Next, have them evaluate the effectiveness of the case Chamberlain makes for his main idea or claim and assert their evaluation in a formal statement. To organize their ideas, encourage students to use a flowchart like the one in the Guided Practice. (Possible responses appear in brackets on the chart that follows.)

Alternatively, students may want to work in pairs to prepare a rebuttal to Chamberlain's main idea. Remind them that they will have to assert a counterargument and support it with reasons, facts, inferences, or appeals to logic and emotion. They may want to imagine themselves as editorial writers for a London newspaper or as members of the opposition party in Parliament in the early 1900s, preparing to speak out against Chamberlain's view of the empire.

Main Idea

["I believe in a British Empire, in an Empire which, though it should be its first duty to cultivate friendship with all the nations of the world, should yet, even if alone, be self-sustaining and self-sufficient, able to maintain itself against the competition of all its rivals."]

Support

[The old isolationism "went very far to dry and even to sap the loyalty of our colonial brethren."]

["The Empire is in its infancy . . . we can mold [it and] . . . decide its future destinies."]

["I want you to consider the infinite importance of this not only to yourselves but to your descendants."]

["think what it means to your power and influence as a country . . . to your position among the nations of the world . . . to your trade and commerce. . . ."]

["if we were . . . face to face some day . . . with some great coalition of hostile nations . . . there is nothing within the power of these self-governing colonies they would not do to come to our aid."]

Reader Assertion

[Chamberlain's reasons for advocating a strong Empire are unconvincing because they are based more on appeals to narrow self-interest and wishful thinking about the loyalty and self-government of the colonies than on hard evidence.]

Philosophical Assumptions and Beliefs

Reading Standard 2.5 Analyze an author's implicit and explicit philosophical assumptions and beliefs about a subject.

Objective: To analyze an author's implicit and explicit philosophical assumptions and beliefs about a subject.

Direct Teaching: Share the following information with students.

Like all of us, authors have beliefs, values, and opinions that shape the way they think and the way they view the world. Their beliefs are a result of their personal experience; their political and social affiliations; and their religious, cultural, and ethnic backgrounds. Naturally, what writers believe affects what they write, and smart readers keep that in mind when they read. Sometimes, what a writer believes about a topic is stated explicitly, or directly, in the text. Phrases such as *I believe* or *in my opinion* are signals that the writer is stating beliefs directly. Sometimes, however, writers express their beliefs implicitly in what they write—that is, the beliefs are implied or suggested but not stated outright. In that case, a reader must be like a detective and look for clues in the stated ideas for what is unstated. Readers should also consider what they know from biographical and historical sources about a writer's experience and society and keep this information in mind when looking for the unstated beliefs and convictions. For example, if you know that a writer has been a victim of racial discrimination, you will understand why opposition to social stereotyping is an important theme in his or her work.

Guided Practice: **Analyzing explicit and implicit beliefs.** Have students read Lady Chudleigh's poem "To the Ladies" (p. 677). On the chalkboard, draw a chart like the one at the top of p. 1449J. Ask students to look for examples in the poem that reveal the speaker's beliefs on the subjects of marriage, the position of wives, and the position of husbands. Write students' responses on the chart, and for each example, ask them to determine if the speaker's beliefs are explicit or implicit. Also, have students rephrase in their own words the speaker's beliefs. Students should be able to see that nearly every line of the poem is either an explicit or implicit statement of the speaker's beliefs about marriage and its effects on men and women.

Next, have students consider how Lady Chudleigh arrived at her beliefs about marriage. [Possible responses: from her own experience; from her observations of married people around her; from some political or social organization to which she belonged.] Then, ask students what stance or plan of action the speaker believes women should take regarding marriage. ["Then shun, oh! shun that wretched State"] Remind students that to be valid these inferences would have to be supported with some verifiable biographical facts. Ask students if there are any other conclusions they can draw about Lady Chudleigh's beliefs from what she (or her speaker) says either directly or indirectly in this poem. [Possible response: The last two lines of the poem and even the fact that Lady Chudleigh wrote poetry suggests that she believes in education and self-expression for women, as well as in women's independence from men.]

Examples	Explicit/Implict	Beliefs
["Wife and Servant are the same, / But only differ in the Name"]	[explicit]	[There is no difference between a wife and a servant.]
["And Man by Law supreme has made"]	[explicit]	[Men are considered superior beings.]
["When she the word obey has said, / And Man by Law supreme has made"]	[implicit; inferred from her statement that after the marriage ceremony "all that's kind is laid aside"]	[Before marriage, women are treated more fairly.]
[Value your selves, and Men despise, / You must be proud, if you'll be wise."]	[both explicit and implicit]	[The only way for women to survive is to value themselves and not let the law or men color their judgment.]

Independent Practice: Identifying explicit and implicit beliefs. As homework, ask students to read George Orwell's "Shooting an Elephant" (p. 1142) and to find examples in the text where Orwell reveals his philosophical beliefs. Have students list these examples on a chart like the one below. Then, ask students to categorize the examples as explicitly or implicitly stated beliefs and to write Orwell's views in their own words. Have students share their charts with the class. (Possible responses appear in brackets on the chart.)

Examples	Beliefs
["For at that time I had already made up my mind that imperialism was an evil thing. . . ."]	[explicit; Orwell believes that imperialism is unjust.]
["As for the job that I was doing, I hated it more bitterly than I can perhaps make clear."]	[implicit; Orwell was opposed to the tyrannical aspects of British rule.]
["Theoretically—and secretly, of course—I was all for the Burmese and all against their oppressors, the British."]	[explicit; Orwell believed that the Burmese had the right to be free from British rule.]
["And it was at this moment . . . that I first grasped the hollowness, the futility of the white man's dominion in the East."]	[explicit; Orwell believed that the Burmese will of the people would ultimately overcome Britain's imperialistic rule.]

Critiquing Public Documents

Reading Standard 2.6 Critique the power, validity, and truthfulness of arguments set forth in public documents; their appeal to both friendly and hostile audiences; and the extent to which the arguments anticipate and address reader concerns and counterclaims (e.g., appeal to reason, to authority, to pathos and emotion).

Objective: To critique the validity, appeal, and truthfulness of arguments in public documents.

Direct Teaching: Share the following ideas with students.

Many public documents—such as speeches, debates, and policy statements—are prepared for political purposes. Although they provide information, they are basically statements of opinion or calls to action, designed to win audience support for the author's ideas and plans. Politicians almost always have a persuasive purpose when they address people. Therefore, when we read or listen to political statements or speeches, whether from the past or present, it is important to decide exactly what the writer or speaker wants the audience to believe or do. Then, we can go on to examine how he or she goes about trying to convince the audience. We can expect to find appeals to the minds and hearts of listeners in every persuasive message, and these techniques can be either effective or ineffective, depending on the soundness of the reasoning and the power of the emotional appeal. We also find many appeals to authority, status, or expertise. The opinions of experts and authorities generally carry more weight than those of the untrained and undistinguished. Also, effective persuaders often try to anticipate and address what they know to be the doubts and concerns of their audience and to counter the objections opponents are likely to raise. For example, a speaker who is trying to persuade voters to support an increase in the local school budget may counter fears of increased property taxes by assuring listeners that a better school system will increase the resale value of their homes.

Guided Practice: Critiquing public documents. Review with students the difference between logical and emotional appeals. Remind them that emotional appeals often carry charged or heightened language, which is designed to stir the audience to feelings of affection, loyalty, patriotism, fear, or pity. Speakers can also appeal to an audience's desire for reward or their fear of punishment or hardship. Remind students that the most effective persuaders foresee and address the concerns of their audience, giving a sense that they understand the immediate and long-range effects of what they are proposing and the impact their proposals will have on the interested parties.

Now, have students read Queen Elizabeth I's "Tilbury Speech" (p. 380). Explain that the speech was delivered in 1588 just before news of the defeat of the Spanish fleet (which was attempting to invade England) was received. Make sure students understand that Elizabeth was expecting an invasion and that her purpose was to rally the army and the people for a vigorous defense of the nation. Ask students what kinds of concerns the English people might have had on the eve of the supposed invasion. [Possible responses: whether the queen, a woman, was ready for leading the nation in a time of war; who would be called on to fight and die; why any subject should risk his or her life for queen and country; how aware the queen was of the effects of her call to arms on her subjects.] Write the concerns on the chalkboard as students offer them, and ask them if and how these concerns are addressed in the "Tilbury Speech."

After students have read the speech, draw on the chalkboard a chart like the one on p. 1449L. Read aloud each excerpt in the first column. Next, discuss with students whether the passage appeals to logic, emotion, authority, or all three, and what, if any, audience concern or objection the passage addresses. Work with students to be as specific as possible in identifying Elizabeth's persuasive techniques. (Possible responses appear in brackets.)

Passage	Persuasive Techniques
"My loving people . . ."	[appeals primarily to listeners' emotions—their sense of affection and loyalty to the queen as an individual and a symbol of the nation]
"We have been persuaded by some that are careful of our safety to take heed how we commit ourself to armed multitudes for fear of treachery, but I assure you I do not desire to distrust my faithful and loving people."	[a subtle appeal to both logic and emotion, calling attention to the queen's personal courage and trust in her subjects in order to persuade her audience to show similar courage and trust in her]
"Let tyrants fear. I have always so behaved myself that, under God, I have placed my chiefest strength and safeguard in the loyal hearts and goodwill of my subjects."	[appeals to logic, emotion, and authority, reminding the audience of the queen's exemplary conduct as a monarch and her subjection to God, the highest authority, with the implication that her subjects now owe her their complete loyalty]
"I know I have the body but of a weak and feeble woman, but I have the heart and stomach of a king—and of a king of England too—and think foul scorn that Parma, or Spain, or any prince of Europe should dare to invade the borders of my realm. . . . I myself shall take up arms, I myself will be your general, judge, and rewarder. . . ."	[appeals to emotion by stirring up the audience's feelings of patriotism, indignation, and fear in the face of an invasion; addresses the subjects' doubts on the fitness and resolve of their female monarch and warns would-be invaders that they shall face opposition]
"I know already for your forwardness you have deserved rewards and crowns, and we do assure you, in the word of a prince, they shall be duly paid to you."	[appeals to the audience's desire for rewards and to the people's respect for the queen's authority to make good on her promises; reveals the queen's understanding of the practical concerns of her people, which she addresses by promising material rewards for their loyal service]

After discussing the persuasive appeals of particular passages, lead students in a general discussion of the overall effectiveness of Queen Elizabeth's speech. Ask questions like the following:

- Do you think most of the queen's audience would have supported her call to arms?
- Which of her appeals do you think would have been most effective?
- What factors beyond the persuasiveness of this particular speech would have played a part in her audience's response to her message?
- How would the speech of the president of a contemporary democracy facing invasion be similar to or different from Queen Elizabeth's speech?

Ask students to explain their responses. Help them to see that much of the force of Queen Elizabeth's arguments was based on her personal record as a benign monarch and on the general respect for the monarchy that existed in England in her day. A contemporary president might appeal less to personal loyalty and affection and more to the self-interest and nationalism of the citizens.

Independent Practice: Critiquing public documents. Have students working in pairs read aloud Winston Churchill's speech "Blood, Sweat and Tears" (p. 1110). Then, ask them to identify the policy or course of action that Churchill is asking his audience to support. [Possible response: As prime minister, Churchill is seeking government and popular support for his plans to wage all-out war to save the British Empire.] Next, have the pairs work together to prepare an oral report in which they critique Churchill's persuasive techniques and compare and contrast them with those of Queen Elizabeth I in the "Tilbury Speech." (They may want to organize their analysis of Churchill's techniques in a chart like the one used for the Guided Practice.) Suggest that students pay attention not only to what Churchill and Elizabeth I say but also to how they deliver their message—that is, their use of language. Remind students that although the two speeches were inspired by similar circumstances (the threat of war and invasion), one was given by a hereditary monarch in the sixteenth century and the other by an elected leader of a democratic nation four centuries later.

Theme and Meaning

Reading Standard 3.2 Analyze the way in which the theme or meaning of a selection represents a view or comment on life, using textual evidence to support the claim.

Objective: To analyze the way in which the theme of a selection represents a comment on life, using evidence from the text to support your claim.

Direct Teaching: Share the following information with students.

> **The theme of a literary work is its central idea or general comment on human life and experience. A work's theme expresses the insights of the author, but it also may offer clues to the views or values of the culture or period to which the author belongs. The theme is not the same as the subject or topic of a selection. For example, friendship may be the subject of many stories and poems, but writers' insights into the meaning of friendship will differ from work to work. Writers rarely state their themes directly in their stories and poems. Rather, they leave it to readers and critics to weigh all the literary elements in a work and come up with a generalization that summarizes the writer's take on the subject. Such a generalization is called a theme statement. "Friendship is more enduring than romance because it is based on reason, not passion" is an example of a theme statement on the subject of friendship. To determine this statement, a reader would have to look at how individual literary elements—like characterization, setting, symbolism, conflict, and resolution—combine and interact in a work to suggest this general meaning. Discovering the theme, then, is a process of reflection and integration, which requires careful reading and often re-reading of the text.**

Guided Practice: Analyzing themes. Ask students to form small reading groups and read Guy de Maupassant's "The Jewels" (p. 1034). On the chalkboard draw a web like the one at the bottom of this page. Use the web to help students gather and organize evidence from the story that will help them to develop a theme statement for "The Jewels." (Possible responses appear in brackets on the web.) Begin by asking students to identify the subject of the story. Write their responses on the web. Follow up with discussions of the story's main character, setting, symbolism, conflict, and resolution.

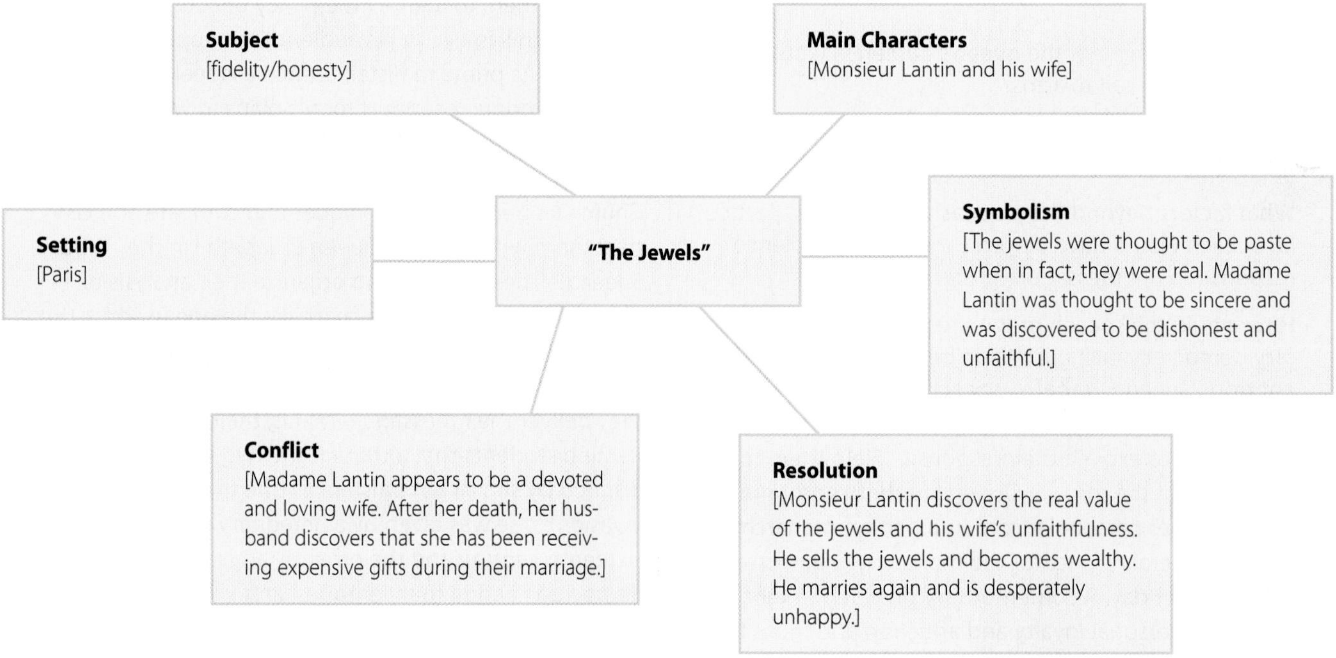

When you have filled in the web with all the evidence they have gathered from the story, ask students to reflect on what they have discovered and discuss what comment on human experience they think de Maupassant is making in this story. Tell them that there is more than one way to state de Maupassant's theme and that various interpretations are valid as long as they can be supported with evidence from the text. Then, write several student theme statements on the chalkboard. [Possible theme statements: People often are not what they appear to be. Ignorance of deception is bliss. Knowledge is not always happiness.] Ask students to evaluate each one, referencing the story and their own prior knowledge.

Independent Practice: Analyzing themes. Have students working in pairs read A. E. Housman's poem "To an Athlete Dying Young" (p. 982) or another poem in the Student Edition. Then, have them work together to gather evidence from the poem that will help them to discover the comment on life that the poet is making. Encourage them to organize their evidence on a web like the one below. (Possible responses appear in brackets.) Ask the partners to use their charts to write a short essay, stating the writer's theme as they see it and explaining the process they used to arrive at their conclusion. Have them share their essays with students who analyzed the same poem and compare and contrast the various theme statements. [Possible theme statements: It is better to die young when success and happiness are fresh than to grow old, stale, and disillusioned; all human achievement ends in death, so it matters little whether we die young or old.]

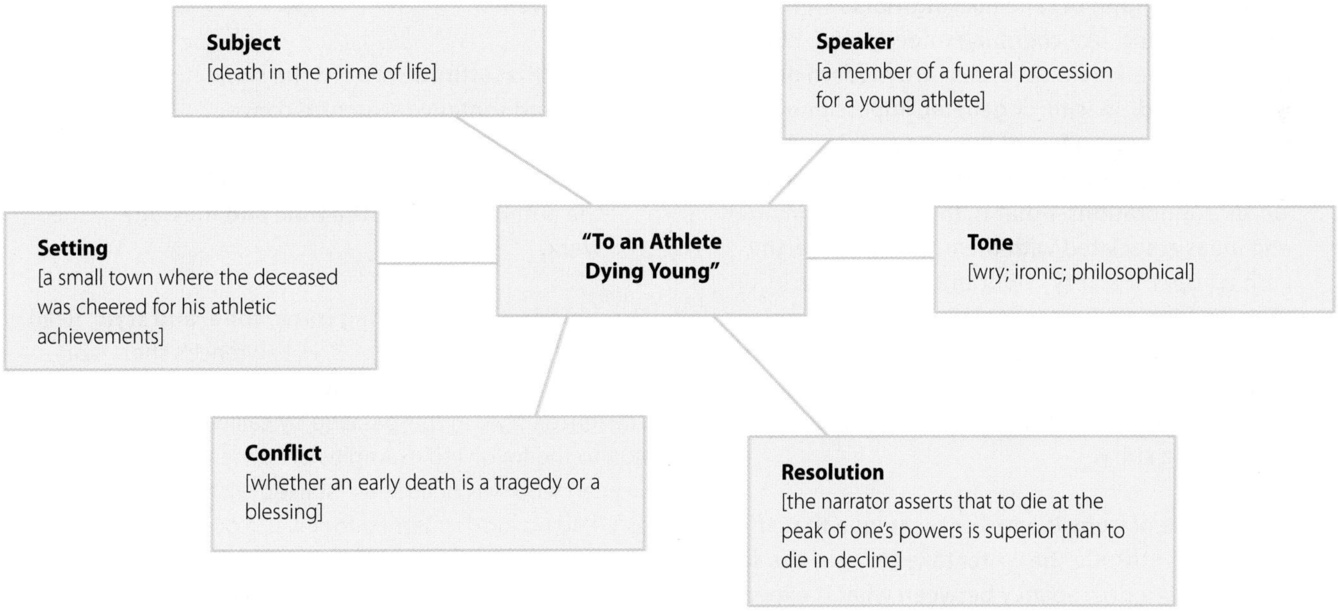

Irony, Tone, and Author's Style

Reading Standard 3.3 Analyze the ways in which irony, tone, mood, the author's style, and the "sound" of language achieve specific rhetorical or aesthetic purposes or both.

Objective: To analyze the ways irony, tone, and the author's style achieve specific purposes.

Direct Teaching: Share the following ideas with students.

When we talk about an author's style we mean the way in which he or she writes, rather than what he or she writes about. Style is the distinctive manner in which writers present their ideas—their way with words. Diction—the choice of words—is one way a writer creates a style. For example, a writer can choose a plain, everyday word like *pleasant* to describe a house (as D. H. Lawrence does in the second paragraph of "The Rocking-Horse Winner") or a fancier one, like *charming* or *delightful*. Writers can choose between words that are modern or old-fashioned, specific or general, impassioned or cool, to name just a few of the many choices open to them. Writers confronting these choices consider words' connotations—that is, the emotions, images, and ideas associated with them. For example, the verb *whisper* is a very important word choice in "The Rocking-Horse Winner." It carries connotations of secrecy, shame, and menace that words like *say, speak,* or even *murmur* would not convey. *Whisper* is the perfect choice to convey the dark mystery at the heart of the story.

The use of irony is another technique that affects the tone or attitude the writer takes toward the subject. Irony is a discrepancy between what is expected and what actually happens or between what is true and what appears to be true.

Sentence structure is another important component of style. The unique rhythm—the pattern of repeated sounds—of a passage is created by the way its words, phrases, and clauses are strung together. Sequences of short, simple sentences, for example, create one effect while strings of long, complex sentences create another.

As you read, pay careful attention to the writer's word choices and to the rhythm created by the sentence structure. Look to see if the words and sentences create an overall tone or attitude. A tone can be described in words such as *lighthearted, mournful, detached, disillusioned.* To assess style, ask yourself questions like these:

- **Are most of the words simple or elaborate, formal or slangy, restrained or extravagant?**
- **Does the writer create irony through word choices or through the depiction of characters and events?**
- **What attitude toward the subject do the words and sentence structure convey?**

The responses will help you evaluate the impact of the author's style on the tone and message of the work.

Guided Practice: **Analyzing irony, tone, and style**. Read aloud the first paragraph of D. H. Lawrence's short story "The Rocking-Horse Winner" (p. 1310). Begin an analysis of Lawrence's style in this passage by calling students' attention to the following examples of Lawrence's diction: "a woman who was beautiful"; "started with all the advantages"; "had no luck"; "married for love"; "love turned to dust"; and "felt the center of her heart go hard." Ask students how they would describe these word choices. [Possible responses: plain, straightforward, understated, unadorned.] If students are having difficulty characterizing the diction, give them some alternatives such as "a woman who was as brilliant as summer lightning" or "love curdled like sour milk." These examples should help them to see that Lawrence makes little use of figurative or flowery language.

Next, review irony with students. Encourage them to consult the Handbook of Literary and Historical Terms for detailed definitions of verbal, dramatic, and situational irony. Guide them to study the examples provided in the handbook. Then, draw on the chalkboard a chart like the one below. Write in the chart the following instances of irony from Lawrence's first paragraph. Work with students to identify the type of irony in each example and to explain the nature of the ironic contrast. Write students' responses on the chart. (Possible responses appear in brackets.)

Ask students to look at the sentence structure of the first paragraph. Point out that the passage consists of a series of compound and compound-complex sentences that seem to go on and on without much subordination of one idea to the next. Everything seems of equal importance. Ask students what effect this kind of sentence structure creates. Guide them to see that the sentence structure in the first paragraph creates a sense of confusion or mystification—no one, certainly not the reader, seems to know exactly what is going on in this family.

Examples of Irony	Type of Irony
"started with all the advantages, yet she had no luck"	[situational: what happens is the opposite of what is expected]
"She married for love, and the love turned to dust."	[situational: what happens is the opposite of what is expected]
"She had bonny children . . . and she could not love them."	[situational: what happens is the opposite of what is expected]
"And hurriedly she felt she must cover up some fault in herself. Yet what it was that she must cover up she never knew."	[dramatic: the reader knows something the character doesn't]
"In her manner she was all the more gentle and anxious for her children, as if she loved them very much."	[situational: a contrast between what the character does and what she feels]
"Everybody else said of her: 'She is such a good mother. She adores her children.'"	[verbal: a contrast between what is said and what is known to be true; may also be construed as dramatic irony, since one character, the mother, and the audience know that what is being said is untrue, even if the people saying it believe it to be true]

Independent Practice: Analyzing style and tone. When students have finished working with you on the Guided Practice, ask them to read the entire text of "The Rocking-Horse Winner" as homework and use what they have learned about Lawrence's diction, use of irony, and sentence structure in the first paragraph to analyze the rest of the story. Have them write a short essay or oral report on the overall style and tone of Lawrence's story. You may also want to challenge some students by asking them to compare Lawrence's style and tone with that of Nadine Gordimer in "Once upon a Time" (p. 1370) or V. S. Naipaul in "B. Wordsworth" (p. 1398).

Poetic Devices

Reading Standard 3.4 Analyze ways in which poets use imagery, personification, figures of speech, and sounds to evoke readers' emotions.

Objective: To analyze the ways poets use imagery, personification, figures of speech, and sounds.

Direct Teaching: Share the following ideas with students.

When someone mentions the word poetry, what do you think of? Do you think of a lullaby or nursery rhyme, the words to your favorite song, a Shakespearean sonnet, or a humorous limerick? All of these are poetry. What sets poetry apart from ordinary prose is its ability to excite readers with new sensations, ideas, and feelings and make the familiar seem fresh and alive again. What is even more amazing is that poets achieve these effects with words alone, by making use of a variety of poetic devices. These devices include imagery, figures of speech, and various sound effects. Imagery is the use of words to make vivid sense impressions on readers' imaginations. Imagery makes it possible for readers to see, hear, smell, and feel what the writer wants them to experience. Figurative language links objects or experiences that seem at first to have no similarity but turn out to be connected in some unexpected and revealing way. T. S. Eliot, for example, linked fog and cats in "The Love Song of J. Alfred Prufrock" when he wrote that a yellow fog "rubs its back upon the window-panes" and "Curled once about the house, and fell asleep." Sound effects—like alliteration, assonance, and rhyme—are what give poetry its musical quality. Imagery, figures of speech, and sound effects all work together to stir readers' emotions and imaginations at levels deeper than ordinary prose can reach.

Guided Practice: Identifying poetic devices. Review with students the definitions of the terms *simile, metaphor, personification, alliteration, assonance,* and *rhyme* in the Handbook of Literary and Historical Terms. Go over the provided examples with students, and ask them to offer additional examples from their favorite poems. Remind them that poems are meant to be read aloud and listened to carefully and that more than one reading is usually needed to notice many of their devices. Then, have volunteers read aloud John Donne's "Death be not proud" (p. 301) and William Wordsworth's "Composed upon Westminster Bridge" (p. 762). As the volunteers are reading the poems, draw on the chalkboard charts like the one below and the one on p. 1449R. Explain that the first column of the charts includes examples of the use of poetic devices from the two poems they have just heard. Have students take turns identifying the device(s) used in each passage. Be sure to tell them that many passages display more than one of the devices you have been discussing. Write their responses in the second column of the charts. (Responses appear in brackets.)

"Death be not proud"

Passage from Poem	Poetic Device	Emotional Effect
"Die not, poor Death, nor yet canst thou kill me."	[personification (of Death); alliteration ("Die not, poor Death . . . canst thou kill me")]	[makes Death seem real rather than abstract; alliteration adds emphasis and a tone of determination]
"Thou art slave to fate, chance, kings, and desperate men"	[personification (of death); assonance ("slave to fate")]	[assonance emphasizes the feeling of inevitability]
"One short sleep past, we wake eternally"	[metaphor (sleep and death are linked); alliteration ("short sleep . . . we wake")]	[stirs feelings of promise and hope]

"Composed upon Westminster Bridge"		
Passage from Poem	**Poetic Device**	**Emotional Effect**
"This City now doth, like a garment, wear / The beauty of the morning; silent, bare"	[imagery (visual, auditory); personification (City wears a garment); alliteration (city / silent, beauty / bare); end rhyme]	[helps one to imagine a quiet city just before dawn]
"Never did sun more beautifully steep / In his first splendor, valley, rock, or hill"	[imagery (visual); personification (of the sun); alliteration (sun / steep / splendor)]	[creates a picture of sun-drenched nature and stirs feelings of joy and elation]
"the very houses seem asleep; / and all that mighty heart is lying still!"	[personification (of house); metaphor (city is compared to a slumbering organism); assonance (mighty / lying)]	[creates a picture of power in repose and stirs feelings of both peace and excitement]

Independent Practice: **Analyzing poetic devices' emotional effects**. Add a third column to the chart as shown on this page. For each example, have student pairs discuss how the poetic devices make them feel or help them imagine an experience in the poem. (Possible responses appear in brackets.) When partners have finished their discussions, have students regroup as a class and compare and contrast their responses.

For further practice, ask students to read Tu Fu's "Jade Flower Palace" (p. 874). For homework, have them find examples of the poetic devices they have been studying and analyze them, using a three-column chart like the one in this lesson. When they have completed their charts, ask them to write a short essay on the emotional effects that Tu Fu creates by means of his poetic devices.

Archetypes

Reading Standard 3.6 Analyze the way in which authors through the centuries have used archetypes drawn from myth and tradition in literature, film, political speeches, and religious writings (e.g., how the archetypes of banishment from an ideal world may be used to interpret Shakespeare's tragedy Macbeth).

Objective: To analyze archetypes drawn from myth and tradition.

Direct Teaching: Share the following information with students.

The English word archetype comes from a Greek word meaning "original," which in turn came from the Greek root word for "stamp" or "model. " A literary archetype, then, is a pattern, which becomes the model for many different but related versions of a character, plot, setting, or object. Since myths, religious texts, and folk tales are among the earliest forms of literature, they are the source for many of the archetypal patterns on which so much later literature is based. Archetypes are also used in political speeches, films, television shows, and advertisements. The larger-than-life hero of the Greek myths is an example of an archetypal character and his or her quest to overcome evil or regain a lost paradise is an archetypal plot. This same character and plot structure recur in the literature and popular culture of many nations, times, and places. The details change, but the core remains the same, suggesting that human beings everywhere share the same concerns and use their imaginations in similar ways.

Guided Practice: Identifying archetypes. Draw on the chalkboard a web like the one below. Help students to think of examples of the four kinds of archetypes, and write their examples in the web. (Possible responses appear in brackets.) Remind students that archetypes are still being used in movies, such as fantasy or science fiction films, and in other forms of popular media, such as television series, music videos, and advertisements. Give them a few examples to start them off.

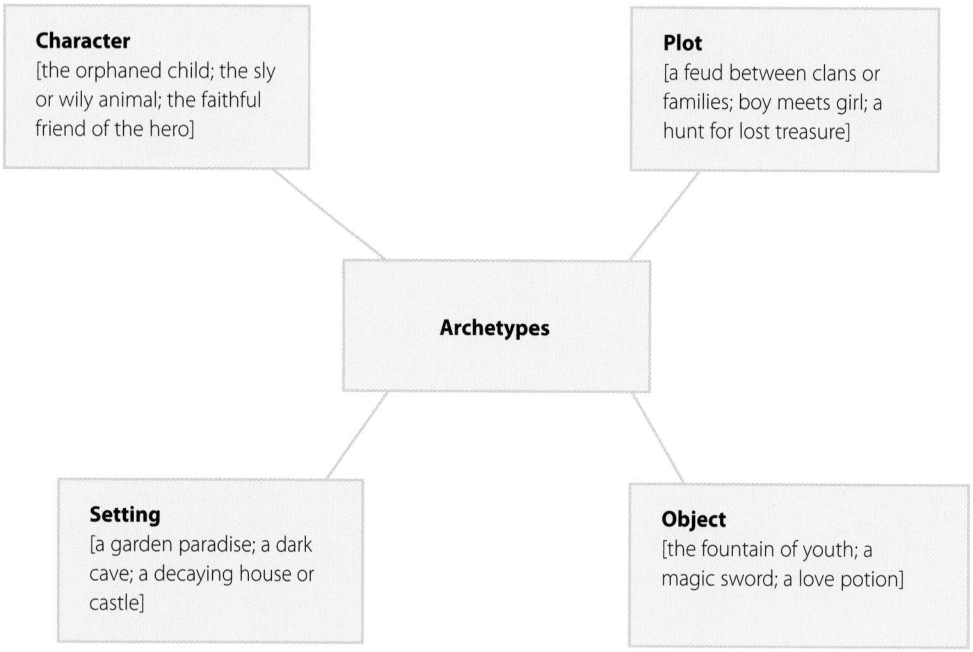

Have students read the excerpt from *Sir Gawain and the Green Knight* (p. 196). Ask students to keep the four kinds of archetypes in mind as they read and look for examples of each. Draw another web for the Gawain selection like the one on this page, and write in any appropriate examples of archetypes that students identify. (Possible responses appear in brackets.)

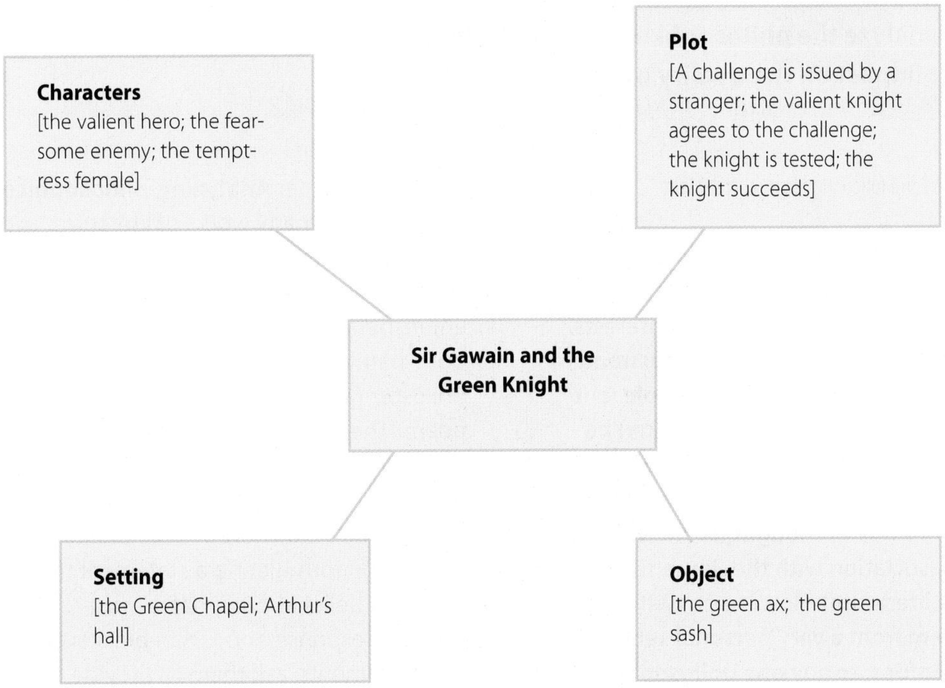

After you have completed the web, lead students in a general discussion of the role of archetypes in literature by asking questions such as these:

- Was the story of Gawain more or less interesting because it was based on archetypal patterns? Explain.
- What other stories, movies, or television programs do you know based on similar patterns?
- Why do you think these patterns keep reappearing in texts from different authors, times, and cultures?
- What have you learned or could you learn from such stories?

Help students understand that archetypes recur because human beings everywhere face similar problems, devise similar solutions, and have similar feelings in the face of adversity.

Independent Practice: Analyzing archetypes. Have students read "The Battle with Grendel" or "The Monster's Mother" (p. 22). Next, assign partners to read the same excerpt from *Beowulf* and work together to identify archetypes in the text. [Possible responses: the superhuman hero, the good king, the man-eating monster, the monster's lair, the battle between good and evil, the magic sword, the descent to the underworld, the hidden treasure.] Have students compare and contrast the *Beowulf* excerpt with the *Gawain* excerpt and prepare an oral report to be given in class. Encourage partners to use a two-column chart or a Venn diagram to organize their analysis of the works' similarities and differences. Students can refer to their charts or diagrams when giving their reports. Then, lead a class discussion of why these archetypal battles between heroes and monsters keep recurring and how cultural or religious differences may account for some of the variations in the basic plot. Be sure students give examples of contemporary movies and television shows that dramatize these epic battles between the good brave hero and the evil monster or villain.

Philosophical Approach to Literature

Reading Standard 3.9 Analyze the philosophical arguments presented in literary works to determine whether the authors' positions have contributed to the quality of each work and the credibility of the characters. (Philosophical approach)

Objective: To analyze the philosophical arguments in literary works and their impact on the quality of each work.

Direct Teaching: Share the following ideas with students.

The ideas that form the foundation of a writer's work come from many sources. Writers draw from their own knowledge, experiences, and interests. Their writing also reflects what they understand and believe about the world and the people in it. This overall pattern of beliefs and values can be thought of as their philosophy of life. Often a writer's philosophy coincides with a particular religious, scientific, or literary body of thought (such as William Wordsworth's association with the Romantic movement in English literature). However, a writer's philosophy may stem from a very personal set of beliefs, which do not conform to any one philosophical system (such as the ideas of William Blake). Writers' philosophies affect how they write about issues, such as war, materialism, self-sacrifice, and the importance of art or spirituality in human life. Careful readers will look to see if writers have successfully integrated their philosophical beliefs into their works and will evaluate whether characters and other details "ring true" or function merely as mouthpieces for the writers' philosophical positions.

Guided Practice: Analyzing philosophical positions. Tell students that many works of literature, both in poetry and prose, pose the question, "What is really important in life?" Different authors in different times and places have different responses—from human love to faith in the unseen—but whatever response they offer will reflect their personal philosophy and values. Read aloud William Wordsworth's poem "The World Is Too Much with Us" (p. 764), and review with students the tenets of the Romantic movement, as presented in the introduction to Unit 4 (p. 708). Draw on the chalkboard a chart like the one on p. 1449V, and guide students in formulating a statement that expresses the speaker's belief about what is most important in life. (A possible response appears in brackets.) As students volunteer statements, ask them to provide details from the poem that support their conclusions, and write these at the bottom of the chart. Keep the discussion going until all agree on a single statement of the speaker's highest value.

Next, ask students if they think William Wordsworth, through his speaker, made a good case for his philosophical point of view. Tell students that they do not have to accept a belief in order to judge whether a writer has made a convincing case for it. Rather, they need only evaluate the strength of the evidence—in this case, the power of Wordsworth's diction and imagery.

"The World Is Too Much with Us"

Subject

[conflict between the "civilized" world and the pleasures of nature]

Philosophical Position

[Communion with nature is more important than any progress the industrialized world or modern thinking has to offer.]

Detail	Detail	Detail	Detail	Detail
["The world is too much with us"]	["Getting and spending, we lay waste our powers"]	["We have given our hearts away"]	[". . . we are out of tune; / It (nature) moves us not"]	[". . . I'd rather be / a Pagan suck-led in a creed outworn; / . . . so might I / Have glimpses that would make me less forlorn"]

Independent Practice: **Analyzing philosophical positions in literature**. Ask students to read Leo Tolstoy's "How Much Land Does a Man Need?" (p. 1010). Have pairs work together to discover how the author, through his characters and plot, answers the question "What is most important in life?" To gain insight into the author's background and general philosophy of life, urge students to read the biographical information on the author that precedes the selection Then, ask the partners to make a chart for their story like the one used in the Guided Practice. They can use it to write a short essay that explains what they have learned from the story about the author's philosophy and values. Remind students that authors do not necessarily agree with the actions or choices of all their characters, but they often reveal their beliefs by the way they work out their plots. Therefore, it is important for students to identify what the values of the main characters are, how far the characters are willing to go to get what they want, and what the outcomes of their choices are. [Possible responses: Tolstoy values life and freedom over material wealth, since Pahom dies as a result of his obsessive greed.] Finally, conduct a class discussion of partners' conclusions about the Tolstoy's values. Remind students to consider whether the fate of the main character seems believable in the context of the story or merely contrived for the purpose of emphasizing the author's philosophical points.

Resource Center

Reading Matters Strategy Lessons by Kylene Beers

Reading Standard 2.1, 2.2, 2.3, 2.4, 2.5, 2.6
(see pages A48–A50)

Introduction

The reading you did in first, second, and third grades probably involved big print, easy words, and relatively short texts. In high school, however, the texts you read often have small print, long chapters, and complicated plots or topics. You may also now find yourself reading diverse materials—anything from a driver's education handbook to college and job applications, to e-mail and e-zines, to classics and comics. Doing something every day that you find difficult and tedious is not much fun—and that includes reading. This section of this book is designed to show you what to do when you encounter difficult or challenging texts. We will begin by examining some reading matters.

How to Use This Section

- **This section is designed with you in mind.** Turn to this section whenever you need reminders about what to do when the text gets tough. Do not wait for your teacher to assign this section: It is your handbook, so use it when you see fit.
- **Read the relevant sections.** It may not be necessary for you to read every word of this section. Skim the headings to locate the information relevant to your work.
- **Use this section to help you read for other classes.** The instruction in this section does not just pertain to the reading you do in this book but to any challenging reading you may encounter.
- **Do not hesitate to *re-read* the information in Reading Matters.** The best readers constantly re-read information.
- **If you need more help, check the index.** The index will direct you to other pages in this book with information on reading skills and strategies.

Reading Strategies

Improving Your Comprehension

This lesson, the heart of Reading Matters, gives students strategies for improving comprehension of literary and informational texts. Assure students that these reading strategies will help them understand the types of texts—for example, college or job applications—that will play a crucial part in their lives.

Your Turn

1. A fork-in-the-road sign might mark a point where the text has two levels of meaning.
2. A dead-end sign might indicate a point at which the reader is confused by the text.
3. A winding road sign might indicate that the text requires special attention.
4. A no-U-turn sign might indicate a point where the reader resists temptation to re-read and continues with the hope of understanding the text better after finishing it.
5. A yield sign might indicate a point in the text where the writer's ideas run contrary to the reader's beliefs.
6. A U-turn sign might indicate a point in the text where the reader has to re-read the text to improve comprehension.
7. A falling-rocks sign might signal difficult vocabulary, unfamiliar allusions, or complex ideas.
8. A stop sign might indicate a point where the reader pauses to summarize the text or to note questions or comments.
9. A person-working sign might indicate a point where the reader thinks the writer needs to clarify some aspect of the text.
10. A railroad-crossing sign might indicate a point that requires re-reading.

Improving Your Comprehension

Understanding What You Read

Comprehension—your ability to understand what you read—is a critical part of the reading process. Many different factors can affect your comprehension. Think about each of the following texts, and rate your comprehension of each type from 1 (*never understand*) to 5 (*always understand*):

A. notes from friends

B. e-mail messages from friends

C. college applications

D. job applications

E. magazines

F. computer manuals

G. Internet sites

H. school textbooks

I. novels you choose

J. novels your teachers choose for you

You probably did not rate yourself the same for each type of text. Factors such as your interest level and the text's vocabulary level will cause your ratings to differ. Now return to items H, I, and J. How did you rate yourself with regard to those texts? If you think your comprehension of those materials is low, then you will want to study the next few pages carefully. They are filled with tips to help you improve your comprehension.

Your Turn Monitoring Your Comprehension

Skilled readers often pay more attention to what they do not understand rather than to what they readily comprehend. Below are some symbols you could put on positional notes to be placed on texts so that you can remember those elements that confuse you. Decide how you would use each symbol. What reading problem could each sign indicate?

Using Reading Matters

Reading Matters is a handbook of strategies designed to improve students' reading comprehension and reading rate. Because it is a handbook, the lessons can be read in any order and referred to as often as needed. You may choose to introduce the strategies in class or have students use the handbook independently.

At the beginning of the school year, orient students with Reading Matters.

- Preview the section, noting the lesson content, headings, and Your Turn boxes.
- Model each reading strategy in class.
- Emphasize that the lessons and strategies apply to both literary and informational texts.

Throughout the school year, you might use a particular reading strategy as preteaching instruction for a selection or chapter, or you may choose to target only those students who need reteaching and remediation.

Visualizing the Text

The ability to visualize—or see in your mind—what you are reading is important for comprehension. To understand how visualizing makes a difference, try this quick test. At home, turn on a television program you enjoy. Then turn your back to the television set. You are probably not inclined to keep "watching" the program in that position because you would soon become bored if you were unable to see what was happening. The same is true of reading: If you cannot see in your mind's eye what is happening on the page, then you are likely to tune out quickly. You can improve your ability to visualize a text by practicing the following strategies:

1. **Read a few sentences; then pause, and describe what is happening on the page.** Forcing yourself to describe the scene will initially take some time, but doing so will benefit your comprehension in the long term.
2. **On a sheet of paper or an adhesive note, make a graphic representation of what is happening as you are reading.** For instance, if two characters are talking, draw two stick figures with arrows pointing between them to indicate their conversation.
3. **Discuss a scene or a part of a chapter with a partner.** Talk about what you "saw" as you were reading.
4. **Read aloud.** You might be having trouble visualizing the text because you are not "hearing" it. Try reading a portion of your text aloud, using good expression and phrasing. As you hear the words, you may find it easier to see the scenes.

Your Turn Visualizing What You Read

Read the following excerpt from "from Le Morte d'Arthur" (see page 208), and discuss what you "see":

> Then, on the night of Trinity Sunday, Arthur was vouchsafed a strange dream:
>
> He was appareled in gold cloth and seated in a chair which stood on a pivoted scaffold. Below him, many fathoms deep, was a dark well, and in the water swam serpents, dragons, and wild beasts. Suddenly the scaffold tilted and Arthur was flung into the water, where all the creatures struggled toward him and began tearing him limb from limb.
>
> Arthur cried out in his sleep and his squires hastened to waken him.

Reading Strategies

Visualizing the Text

The Visualizing the Text strategy applies to literary texts, biographies, autobiographies, and informational essays, as well as some science and nature writing. All of these texts contain sensory details and images that students can visualize. Emphasize that this strategy applies to all kinds of sensory details, not just those that appeal to the sense of sight.

Have students work with a partner or in a small group to practice the four numbered strategies. When they have finished reading, ask them to describe how well the strategies worked.

Your Turn

As students read the passage from "Le Morte d'Arthur," have them jot down details that appeal to the senses. ***Possible responses:*** *Sight—"appareled in gold cloth"; "a chair which stood on a pivoted scaffold"; "dark well." Sound—"cried out."*

California Standards, pp. 1451–1465

- **Reading Standard 2.1** Analyze both the features and the rhetorical devices of different types of public documents (e.g., policy statements, speeches, debates, platforms) and the way in which authors use those features and devices.
- **Reading Standard 2.2** Analyze the way in which clarity of meaning is affected by the patterns of organization, hierarchical structures, repetition of the main ideas, syntax, and word choice in the text.
- **Reading Standard 2.3** Verify and clarify facts presented in other types of expository texts by using a variety of consumer, workplace, and public documents.
- **Reading Standard 2.4** Make warranted and reasonable assertions about the author's arguments by using elements of the text to defend and clarify interpretations.
- **Reading Standard 2.5** Analyze an author's implicit and explicit philosophical assumptions and beliefs about a subject.
- **Reading Standard 2.6** Critique the power, validity, and truthfulness of arguments set forth in public documents; their appeal to both friendly and hostile audiences; and the extent to which the arguments anticipate and address reader concerns and counterclaims (e.g., appeal to reason, to authority, to pathos and emotion).

Reading Strategies

Evaluating Your Metacognition

When it comes to movies and TV, students choose to watch fast-moving, action-packed drama, so it is no wonder that when they are required to read literary texts with a slow-moving plot, their attention is likely to wander. Older literary texts with long sentences, difficult syntax, and a heavy vocabulary load present special problems in maintaining attention. For some students the difficulty arises mainly while reading informational texts, such as textbooks, reference books, and newspaper and magazine articles.

You might review this lesson before students read the excerpt from "Le Morte d'Arthur" (p. 208) or any of the Renaissance poems in Chapter 3.

Go over the two numbered activities in class. The first activity advises students to take notes as they read; the second advises that they stop to review and summarize the paragraphs they have just read.

Your Turn

This survey is designed to help students measure how well they pay attention to what they read.

Point out that students' responses to the survey will vary according to the type of text they are reading. For example, students' attention may never wander when they are reading a poem by their favorite writer, but it may wander a lot when they are reading their science textbook to prepare for an exam. Suggest that students complete the survey for each type of text they read during the school year.

Evaluating Your Metacognition

Sometimes, as you are reading, your attention momentarily wanders, but your eyes keep moving from word to word. After a few minutes, you realize you are several pages beyond the last point at which you can remember actively thinking about what you were reading. Then you know you need to back up and begin again. This ability to think about your thinking—or, in this case, your lack of thinking—is called **metacognition.**

Metacognition refers to your ability to analyze what you are doing as you try to make sense of texts. A critical part of metacognition is paying attention to what you are reading. It is normal to find that your mind *sometimes* wanders while reading; however, if you are constantly finding it difficult to pay attention, then try one of the following activities: (1) Keep paper and pen close, and record notes as you read; (2) read for a set amount of time (five minutes), and then stop and review what has happened since the last time you stopped. Lengthen this amount of time as you find yourself able to focus longer. Take the following quiz to evaluate your metacognition level.

Your Turn Measuring Your Attention Quotient

Respond to items A through E below by choosing the number (1, 2, or 3) that best describes your attention when you read. Determine your score by adding together the numbers. The lower the score, the less you pay attention to what you are reading. The higher the score, the more you pay attention.

When I read, I

A. allow my mind to wander

1	2	3
most of the time	sometimes	almost never

B. forget what I am reading

1	2	3
most of the time	sometimes	almost never

C. become (and stay) confused or do not even realize I am confused

1	2	3
most of the time	sometimes	almost never

D. discover I have turned many pages but do not understand what I have read

1	2	3
most of the time	sometimes	almost never

E. rarely finish whatever I am supposed to be reading

1	2	3
most of the time	sometimes	almost never

Thinking Aloud

Comprehension problems appear not only after you *finish* reading but also *as* you read. For that reason, do not wait until you complete your reading assignment to attempt to understand the text; instead, work on comprehending while reading by becoming an active reader.

Active readers **predict, connect, clarify, question,** and **visualize** as they read. If you do not already practice these active-reading skills, you need to pause while you read to

- make **predictions**
- make **connections**
- **clarify** in your own thoughts what you are reading
- **question** what you do not understand
- **visualize** the text

One Student's Think-Aloud
Here is Steve's Think-Aloud for Shakespeare's Sonnet 130 (page 398):

After reading the entire sonnet once: I don't get it. This is like he's saying the woman he loves is ugly. Why would he say these things? **(Question)**

After reading sonnet a second time: He isn't saying very nice things about her. At the end he still says his love is rare, so I think he does love her. **(Comment/Clarification)**

After reading sonnet a third time: You know, maybe this is a joke about love: like, it's always supposed to be perfect, you know—coral red lips and eyes like the sun—but even if she doesn't have those things, he still loves her. I think it's those last two lines that are important, you know, showing that someone you love doesn't have to be perfect. This is like realizing that even if your car isn't the coolest car in the lot, it's your car, and so you still love it. **(Connection)**

Your Turn Using the Think-Aloud Strategy

Use the Think-Aloud strategy to practice your active-reading skills. To implement this strategy effectively, begin by reading a selection of text aloud to a partner. As you read, pause to make comments and ask questions. Your partner's job is to tally your comments and classify each one according to the list at the top of this page.

Reading Strategies

Thinking Aloud

The Think-Aloud strategy requires that students monitor their understanding of a text and, as a result, helps them stay focused as they read. Some students will have difficulty classifying their partner's comments. Emphasize that such classification is not essential. The purpose of the Think-Aloud strategy is to help students become active readers, who are aware of their thoughts, responses, and questions.

You may wish to model a Think-Aloud in class by reading aloud a challenging poem or prose passage, making comments as you read. Be sure to demonstrate a wide variety of Think-Aloud comments, and point out that it is not necessary to comment on every sentence or line.

Your Turn

Draw students' attention to the student's model Think-Aloud. Tell students that Steve's comments about Shakespeare's Sonnet 130 (p. 398) are only a sample of the many comments and questions that he could have recorded. Point out that Steve read the sonnet three times (using the Re-reading strategy—see p. 1457) and that each re-reading led to a deeper understanding of the sonnet.

You might ask students to work with a partner to try out the Think-Aloud strategy with a challenging text, such as John Milton's "The Fall of Satan" from *Paradise Lost* (p. 351) or the excerpt from John Bunyan's *The Pilgrim's Progress* (p. 368).

Reading Strategies

Questioning the Text

Questioning the Text combines aspects of the Metacognition (p. 1454) and Think-Aloud (p. 1455) strategies but is much more analytic. This reading strategy focuses on elements of literature students are used to discussing.

Your Turn

The questions in the Your Turn section will seem familiar to students because they resemble the questions that follow the literary selections in the Student Edition. Advise students that they can use these questions to analyze any unfamiliar short story, novel, or play.

The questions in the Your Turn section do not apply to poetry, nonfiction, or informational material. If you have time, suggest that students work with a partner to develop a list of analytical questions for a different type of writing, such as poetry, essays, biographies and autobiographies, or informational materials. See whether groups working on the same genre can reach a consensus on important questions to ask.

Questioning the Text

This scenario may be familiar: You have just finished reading one of the selections in this book. You then look at the questions to be discussed tomorrow in class. Realizing you do not know the answers, you give up on the questions in frustration.

While giving up is certainly one way to deal with the problem, it is not the best approach. What you should do is focus *more* on questions as you read the text instead of just at the end. This is not to say that you should memorize study questions before you read so that as you are reading you are thinking only about those questions. Rather, you should be continuously asking yourself questions about characters, plot, point of view, setting, conflict, and even vocabulary while reading. You will find that the more you question the text as you read, the more prepared you will be to answer the questions at the end of the text.

Your Turn Asking Questions While You Read

Here is a list of questions you can use as you read literary selections. You should copy this list on note cards and keep it close as you read.

Character Questions

1. Who is the central character? Is this character the narrator? What are the greatest strengths and greatest weaknesses of this character? What does this character discover by the story's end? Has he or she changed?
2. Is the narrator telling the story as it is happening or is he or she recounting the story as a past event? Is the narrator trustworthy? What if the narrator were a different character? How would the story change? What is the narrator's point of view (first-person, limited-third-person, omniscient) and how does that point of view affect the narrator's authority?
3. Who are the other characters? What makes them important to the central character? What do their actions reveal about their personalities? How do your thoughts about the characters change as you read the story? Can you find specific points in the text where your feelings about characters shift? Is it possible that any characters were omitted from the story?
4. Which character do you like the best? What do you have in common with this character?

Plot, Setting, and Conflict Questions

1. What are the major events in the plot? Which events are necessary for the story's conclusion? What prior knowledge do you need to understand the plot?
2. How does the setting affect the story? Would the story be the same (or nearly the same) if you altered the location or the historical context? How does the author situate the reader in the setting? Is the setting believable?
3. What event creates the conflict? How does the central character react to the conflict? How do other characters react? How is the conflict resolved?

Re-reading and Rewording

The best way to improve your comprehension is simply to **re-read.** When you first read something, you usually understand the basic idea of the text. The next time you read that same text, you revise your understanding. Think of your first reading as a sort of draft, similar to the first draft of an essay. As you revise your essay, you are improving your writing; as you revise your reading, you are improving your comprehension.

Sometimes, as you re-read, you find some specific sentences or even passages that you do not understand. In those instances, you should spend some time closely studying those sentences. One effective way to tackle tough text is to **reword** the text:

1. On a piece of paper, write down the sentences that are confusing you.
2. Leave a few blank lines between each line that you write.
3. Then, choose the difficult words, and reword them in the space above.

While rewording every line of a long difficult text is impractical, this technique is a good way to augment your understanding of individual key sentences.

Your Turn Rewording the Text

Thomas tried rewording some of "The Fall of Satan" (page 351, lines 1–6). Because the word order is as confusing as the word choice, Thomas combined reordering with rewording. Read the original lines on page 351 of your book. Then, examine Thomas's changes below. Note that he has combined a Think-Aloud (see page 1455) with his rewording. Finally, explain why you Think Thomas's evaluation is or is not effective.

> This first part seems backwards. Look, I think he's asking this muse—what's a muse? OK, the sidenote says it's a muse of poetry; I think this is like a Greek mythology character—so I think he's asking this muse to sing—not a real song, but just to tell him something. So it really could start by saying Heavenly Muse, tell me about "man's first disobedience, and the fruit of that forbidden tree." Well, that would be in the Garden of Eden. So he's saying to the Muse,
>
> Tell me about when man first sinned in the Garden of Eden by eating the apple that brought death to the world and all our problems because now we don't live in Eden, until Christ brings us back to that blissful—that would be like perfect—seat.

Reading Strategies

Re-reading and Rewording

The difference between the Re-reading strategy and an ordinary second reading of a text lies in the level of the reader's awareness. When readers apply the Re-reading strategy, they focus on passages, sentences, or words that puzzle them, and they actively try to untangle these puzzles. Re-reading is an easy strategy and works well with all types of literary and informational texts.

Suggest that students consult a college dictionary and a thesaurus when they set out to apply the Rewording strategy. For students who need occasional practice with rewording, you might assign short passages from informational or literary texts that contain difficult words, complex ideas, or both.

Your Turn

Point out that the first part of the Your Turn activity presents Thomas's Think-Aloud on ll. 1–6 of John Milton's "The Fall of Satan" (p. 351); his rewording is the final paragraph in the Your Turn section. You might ask students to compare carefully Thomas's rewording with the original text and then to apply the Rewording strategy to another passage from Milton's poem.

Reading Strategies

Summarizing Narrative Text

The SWBS (Somebody Wanted But So) strategy helps students clarify and organize their thinking about a narrative text, such as a story, novel, or play. Remind students that long, complex narratives often require several SWBS statements to summarize the plot adequately. As students read the numbered steps for writing an SWBS statement, point out that they are focusing on a single character and his or her conflict.

Your Turn

The following is a sample SWBS statement from the point of view of one of the merchants in the excerpt from *The Pilgrim's Progress* (p. 368): *Somebody*—merchants. Wanted—to sell their vanities to the pilgrims. *But*—the pilgrims did not care to buy the vanities. So—a great hubbub ensued.

For further practice, have students use the SWBS strategy with any of the stories or the play excerpt in the Student Edition.

Summarizing Narrative Text

Understanding a long piece of text is easier if you can summarize sections of it separately. If you are reading a **narrative,** or a story (including a biography or an autobiography), then use a strategy called **Somebody Wanted But So (SWBS)** for help writing a summary of what you are reading.

SWBS is a powerful way to think about the characters in a narrative and to note what each one does, what conflict each faces, and what resolution (if any) occurs. As you write an SWBS statement for different characters or subjects within the same narrative, you are forcing yourself to rethink the narrative from different **points of view.**

Here are the steps for writing SWBS statements:

1. Write the words *Somebody, Wanted, But,* and *So* across the top of four columns.
2. Under the "Somebody" column, write a character's name.
3. Then, under the "Wanted" column, write what that character wanted to do.
4. Next, under the "But" column, explain what happened that kept the character from doing what he or she wanted.
5. Finally, under the "So" column, explain the eventual outcome.

If you are making an SWBS chart for a long story or novel, you might need to write several SWBS statements at different points in the story.

Your Turn Using SWBS to Summarize

Read this SWBS statement of the excerpt from *The Pilgrim's Progress* (page 368). This statement includes information up through the break on page 371. Try writing an SWBS statement from the point of view of one of the merchants at Vanity Fair.

Somebody	Wanted	But	So
Christian	did not want to buy the merchandise at Vanity Fair,	but the merchants kept pushing wares on him,	so he was taken to prison and put on trial.

Summarizing Expository Text

If summarizing the information in a text is difficult, try a strategy called GIST.

1. Choose three or four sections of text you want to summarize.
2. Read the first section of text.
3. Draw twenty blank lines on a sheet of paper.
4. Write a summary of the first section of text using exactly twenty words—one word for each blank.
5. Read the next section of text.
6. Now, in your next set of twenty blanks, write a new summary statement that combines your first summary with whatever you want to add from this second section of text. You still have only twenty blanks to fill, not forty.

Repeat this process one or two more times, depending on how many more sections of text you have to read. When you are finished, you will have a twenty-word statement that gives you the gist, or overall idea, of the entire text.

Your Turn Using GIST to Summarize

Study the GIST statements for Joseph Chamberlain's speech "I Believe in a British Empire" found on page 1152. Then, try your hand at creating the third GIST.

GIST 1 (for the first paragraph of text on page 1152)

Despite some mutual alienation, Great Britain and its colonies can still be firmly united in their support of the Empire.

GIST 2 (adding the second, third, and fourth paragraphs of text on pages 1153–1154)

White citizens of Great Britain should appreciate the importance of cultivating the colonies and maintaining profitable ties with their peoples.

GIST 3 (adding the fifth and sixth paragraphs of text on page 1154)

____ ____ ____ ____ ____ ____ ____ ____

Reading Strategies

Summarizing Expository Text

The GIST (Generating Interactions between Schemata and Text) strategy requires that students write a summary statement that is exactly twenty words long—not an easy task. Each GIST statement summarizes the main idea of its section and all preceding sections.

Tell students that they will probably have to try out many different GIST statements until they find one that is both accurate and the right length.

Your Turn

Have students turn to p. 1154 to read the fifth and sixth paragraphs and invite students to create a third GIST for Chamberlain's speech. Have students share their responses with the class. ***Possible response:*** *Great Britain's relationship to its colonies is vital in wartime and helps the country be self-sufficient and successfully competitive internationally.*

The GIST strategy works well for nonfiction selections or informational material. You might have students practice this strategy on one of the selections in Comparing Texts: Views on Education and Equality (p. 373) in Chapter 3 or on the excerpt from Mary Wollstonecraft's *A Vindication of the Rights of Woman* (p. 668) in Chapter 6.

Reading Strategies

Using Question Maps

The Question Maps strategy is intended to guide dependent readers through the process of independently answering the questions that confront them as they read a difficult text. Readers generate a list of questions, figure out how to answer the questions, and then answer them—without relying on others to do the answering for them.

Many students already read independently and do not need to make question maps, but encourage everyone to practice the strategy at least once. Students will find question maps particularly useful with older literary texts, such as those in Chapters 1 and 2.

Your Turn

In class, go over Denise's question map for "The Mark of the Beast" (p. 994). If students have already read this selection, ask them to continue reading the question map, adding their own questions and answers. To practice this strategy, students might make a question map for the next selection they are assigned to read.

Using Question Maps

Most readers at some point will struggle with a text. Some readers find reading poetry difficult but can breeze through computer magazines; others are stumped by the technical language in computer magazines but read poetry easily. It is not important what types of text challenge you; what matters is what you *do* when you find yourself struggling.

If you are an independent reader, then you know how to find, on your own, the answers to whatever causes you to struggle. If you are a dependent reader, you expect others to explain difficult concepts to you. Dependent readers often say, "I don't get it," and give up. Independent readers, by contrast, recognize what they do not understand, then figure out how to surmount that misunderstanding.

If you think you are a dependent reader, try using a question map like the one below. As you complete the chart, you will map your way toward independent reading.

1. In the first column, **list your questions** as you are reading.
2. In the second column, **make notes about each question.** For instance, record what made you think about the question or what page you are on in the text.
3. In the third column, **list possibilities for finding answers.** Remember that re-reading the text is always a good idea. Other places to find answers include dictionaries (especially if you have questions about vocabulary), your own mind (sometimes the text gives you part of the information, and you must figure out the rest), or other parts of the book (especially if you are reading a science, math, or history book).
4. In the final column, **record answers to your questions** only after you have made notes about them and thought out where to find answers. If you cannot answer your questions at this point, then it is time to see your teacher.

Your Turn Using Question Maps

Here is a part of Denise's question map for "The Mark of the Beast" (page 994):

Questions	Notes	Places to find answers	Answers
1. Why is *Providence* capitalized?	p. 994, 4th line	ask teacher	to make luck seem like a person
2. Who is Hanuman?	p. 995, 3rd paragraph, line 3	dictionary or encyclopedia	a god in Hindu mythology

Now, try creating your own question map for a portion of "The Mark of the Beast." Use Denise's question map only as a guide for your map; be certain to compose as many original questions, notes, answer sources, and solutions as needed.

Talking and Writing About Literature

It is sometimes the case that you understand what you have read, but you cannot discuss the plot, characters, theme, or author's writing style when it is time to talk about or write about the selection. Here is a list of words and phrases that can serve as a springboard to discussion. They are beginning points—you still must be able to explain why you chose those words or phrases.

Words and Phrases to Describe the Plot

Positive	Negative
realistic	unrealistic
good pace from scene to scene	plodding
suspenseful	predictable
well-developed ideas	sketchy ideas

Words and Phrases to Describe the Characters

Positive	Negative
original	stereotyped
well-rounded	flat
dynamic; able to change	static; unable to change

Words to Describe the Theme

Positive	Negative
subtle	obvious
unique	overworked
powerful	trivial

Words and Phrases to Describe the Author's Style of Writing

Positive	Negative
descriptive; filled with figurative language	boring; lacking imagery
original	filled with clichés
lively; full of action	plodding; slow-moving
poetic; lyrical	stilted

Your Turn Choosing Your Words

Choose one of the stories you have read in *Holt Literature and Language Arts* this semester and, using some of the words and phrases in the above list, describe the plot, characters, theme, and author's writing style. Remember to support your word choices with examples from the story.

Reading Strategies

Talking and Writing About Literature

The Talking and Writing About Literature strategy provides students with vocabulary that is critical to their evaluation of literary texts. Students will find the words useful when they write about or discuss literary texts. Note that the first two sections, "Words and Phrases to Describe the Plot" and "Words and Phrases to Describe the Characters," apply only to fiction and drama. The second two sections, "Words to Describe the Theme" and "Words and Phrases to Describe the Author's Style of Writing," can be applied to both fiction and nonfiction.

These word lists are not exhaustive. Ask students to suggest other words to add to each list. You might also assign small groups the task of creating additional lists of words and phrases for evaluating poems or informational material.

Your Turn

Before students begin this exercise, you might have them bring to class a critical review of a novel—a review they have written or a review they have found in a newspaper or magazine or on the Internet. As they go over their review with a partner, have them keep track of the words the writer uses to evaluate the novel. Ask students to determine whether the review is favorable or unfavorable. Also, have students identify the words and phrases that reveal the writer's opinion.

Reading Strategies

Improving Your Reading Rate

Review this brief lesson early in the school year so that students have ample time to benefit from improving their reading rate. You might ask everyone to do a base-line reading-rate score to retest themselves several times throughout the year. Stress that reading speed varies with the kind of text and the reader's purpose. Ask students to identify some kinds of texts they read quickly (for example, e-mail, a sports or entertainment magazine, a murder mystery) and some types of texts they read much more slowly (a physics textbook, an encyclopedia article, a difficult poem, technical directions).

Improving Your Reading Rate

Varying Your Reading Rate

If your concerns about reading stem more from getting through the words than comprehending their individual meanings, then this part of Reading Matters is for you.

Reading can seem overwhelming if you are a relatively slow reader. With practice, however, you can change your **reading rate,** that is, the pace at which you read. The point of working on your reading rate is not to read so that you just rush over words—the Iamgoingtoreadsofastthatallthewordsruntogether approach. Instead, the goal is to find a pace that keeps you moving comfortably through the pages. Why is it important to establish a good reading rate? A simple math exercise demonstrates why your silent-reading rate counts.

MATH PROBLEM!
If you read 40 words per minute (wpm) and there are 400 words on a page, how long will it take you to read 1 page? 5 pages? How long will it take if you read 80 wpm? 100 wpm? 200 wpm?

Now, assume that with literature homework, science homework, and social studies homework, you have a total of forty pages to read in one night. If you are reading at 40 wpm, you are spending more than six *hours* just reading the information; but at 100 wpm, you spend only two hours and forty minutes. At 200 wpm, you would finish in one hour and twenty minutes.

Words per Minute (wpm)	1 page @ 400 words/page	5 pages @ 400 words/page	10 pages @ 400 words/page
40 wpm	10 minutes	50 minutes	100 minutes
80 wpm	5 minutes	25 minutes	50 minutes
100 wpm	4 minutes	20 minutes	40 minutes
200 wpm	2 minutes	10 minutes	20 minutes

Reading Rate Reminders

1. **Make sure you are not reading one word at a time with a pause between each word.** For instance, read the following rhyme. The first time you read it, pause between each word; the second time, pause only where you see the slash marks. Do you hear the difference the phrasing makes?

Mary had a little lamb, / Its fleece was white as snow. / Everywhere that Mary went, / The lamb was sure to go.

Word-at-a-time reading is much slower than phrase reading. If you are reading a word at a time, you will want to practice reading by phrases.

2. **Make sure you are actually reading *silently*.** As you read, avoid moving your lips or reading aloud softly. Also, do not use your finger to point to words as you read. Instead, use a bookmark to stay on the correct line while you practice your phrase reading.
3. **As you practice your fluency, remember that the single best way to improve your reading rate is simply to read more.** You will not get better at that which you never do. Also, always remember that your rate will vary as your purpose for reading varies. Do not rush to read quickly if that means understanding less.

Your Turn Determining Your Reading Rate

To determine your silent-reading rate, you will need three things: a watch or clock with a second hand, a book, and someone to act as a timekeeper. Then, complete the following steps:

1. Have your friend time you as you begin reading to yourself.
2. Read at your normal rate. Do not read faster because you are being timed.
3. Stop when your friend tells you that one minute has passed.
4. Count the number of words you read in that minute. Write down that number.
5. Repeat this process several more times, using different passages.
6. Then, add the number of words together, and divide by the number of times you timed yourself to determine the average number of words you read per minute.

Example

1st minute	180 words
2nd minute	215 words
3rd minute	190 words
	585 words ÷ 3 = 195 wpm

Reading Rate Reminders

In class, review the three steps to faster reading. If any of your students have the bad reading habits described in items 1 and 2, assure them that they can change; others have done it. Whenever they read, they need to try consciously to stop reading one word at a time, sounding words aloud, and pointing to each word. You might suggest that they keep a reading log to record their efforts and successes.

Your Turn

Select a long passage from the Unit 2 Key Concepts essay (p. 254), and have students read for one minute. Caution students not to sacrifice comprehension for speed; they need to pay attention to what they are reading. Have them figure out their own reading rates, and ask a few Reading Check questions about the content, such as:

- Who was Henry VIII?
- What questions interested the humanist thinkers?
- What social and economic developments during the Renaissance fostered a growing interest in reading and learning?

Reading Strategies

Vocabulary Development

Emphasize to students that a familiarity with the Latin and Greek roots, prefixes, and suffixes with give them an advantage when taking standardized tests. Point out that when they encounter a word they have never seen—in a difficult selection that tests reading comprehension, for example—they can figure out the meaning using context clues together with their knowledge of the roots, prefixes, and suffixes. This knowledge can help students answer difficult analogy questions.

Vocabulary Development

Fluency, reading rate, and comprehension are all connected to how quickly you recognize words and know what they mean. No matter how many words you study in school, you cannot learn all the words you will ever encounter. You need to understand how words work—what *prefixes, suffixes,* and *roots* mean—so that when you encounter new words, you use their components to determine their meanings.

LATIN AND GREEK PREFIXES, ROOTS, AND SUFFIXES

Prefixes	Meaning	Examples
ad–	to	adapt, addict, adhere, admit
amphi–	both; around	amphibian, amphitheater
an–	without	anarchy, anesthesia, anonymous, anorexia
auto–	self	autobiography, autograph, automatic, automobile
co–	together	coauthor, cognate, coincide, cooperate
de–	opposite	deactivate, deform, degrade, deplete, descend
dis–	opposite	disagree, disarm, discontinue, disgust, dishonest
for–	not	forbid, forget, forgo
il–	not	illegal, illegible, illegitimate, illiterate, illogical
im–	not	imbalance, immaculate, immature
in–	not	inaccurate, inactive, inadvertent, incognito
ir–	not	irreconcilable, irregular, irresponsible
mal–	bad	maladjusted, malaise, malevolent, malice
pro–	before	progeny, prognosis, program, prologue
pro–	forward	proceed, produce, proficient, progress
re–	again	reappear, redistribute, redo, repaint, rewrite
sub–	under	subcontract, subject, submarine, subordinate
trans–	across	transatlantic, transcend, transcribe, transfer
un–	not	unable, uncertain, uncomfortable, unhappy

LATIN AND GREEK ROOTS, PREFIXES, AND SUFFIXES *(continued)*

Roots	Meaning	Examples
-act-	do	action, actor, enact, react, transact
-aud-	hear	audible, audience, audition, auditorium
-cred-	believe	credit, credulous, discredit, incredible
-dic-	speak	contradict, dictate, diction, predict, verdict
-graph-	write	autograph, paragraph, phonograph, photograph
-loc-	place	allocate, dislocate, locate, location
-man-	hand	manipulate, manual, manufacture, manuscript
-mot-	move	demote, motion, motor, promote
-ped-	foot	pedal, pedestal, pedestrian
-pop-	people	populace, popular, population
-port-	carry	export, import, portable, porter, transport
-sign-	mark	insignia, signal, signature, significant
-spec-	see	inspect, respect, spectacle, spectator, suspect
-tract-	pull; drag	attract, contract, detract, subtract, traction, tractor
-vid-	see	evidence, provide, providence, video
-volve-	roll	evolve, involve, revolution, revolve, revolver

Suffixes	Meaning	Examples
-ade	action or process	blockade, escapade, parade
-age	action or process	marriage, pilgrimage, voyage
-ant	one who	assistant, defendant, immigrant, merchant, servant
-cle	small	corpuscle, cubicle, particle
-dom	state or quality of	boredom, freedom, martyrdom, wisdom
-ent	one who	parent, resident, regent, superintendent
-ful	full of	careful, fearful, joyful, thoughtful
-ic	relating to	comic, historic, poetic, public
-less	without	ageless, careless, thoughtless, tireless
-let	small	islet, leaflet, owlet, rivulet
-ly	resembling	fatherly, helpfully, motherly, scholarly
-ly	every	daily, monthly, weekly, yearly
-ment	action or process	development, embezzlement, government
-ment	state or quality of	amazement, amusement, predicament
-ment	product or thing	fragment, instrument, ornament
-or	one who	actor, auditor, doctor, donor

Handbook of Literary and Historical Terms

ALEXANDRINE **A line of poetry comprising six iambs**—that is, a line written in iambic hexameter. The following alexandrine is from Lord Byron's *Childe Harold's Pilgrimage* (Chapter 8):

> Without a grave, unknelled, uncoffined, and
> unknown.

See page 813.

ALLEGORY **A story in which the characters, settings, and events stand for abstract or moral concepts.** Allegories thus have two meanings: a literal meaning and a symbolic meaning. Allegories were a popular literary form during the Middle Ages. The best-known English allegory is John Bunyan's *The Pilgrim's Progress* (Chapter 3), which recounts the adventures of a character named Christian. The hero's journey to the Celestial City brings him up against many trials that symbolize the pitfalls facing the Christian traveling through this world toward the spiritual world.

See pages 216, 217, 325, 367, 1009.

ALLITERATION **The repetition of consonant sounds in words that are close to one another.** Alliteration occurs most often at the beginning of words, as in "rough and ready." However, consonants within words sometimes alliterate, as in "baby blue." The echoes that alliteration creates can increase a poem's rhythmic and musical effects and make its lines especially memorable. In this line from Shakespeare's Sonnet 30 (page 393), the /w/ sounds emphasize the melancholy tone:

> And with old woes new wail my dear time's
> waste.

Alliteration is an essential feature of Anglo-Saxon poetry; in most lines, two or three of the four stressed syllables alliterate.

See pages 50, 767, 957, 1205.

"Basil, do you think the center is going to hold?

ALLUSION **A reference to a statement, person, place, event, or thing that is known from literature, history, religion, mythology, politics, sports, science, or popular culture.** The concluding lines of Wilfred Owen's poem "Dulce et Decorum Est" (Chapter 11) are *"Dulce et decorum est / Pro patria mori."* ("It is sweet and proper to die for one's country"). These lines allude to a line from an ode by the Latin poet Horace. The title of William Faulkner's *The Sound and the Fury* is an allusion to a line from Shakespeare's *Macbeth* (Chapter 4). The cartoon above alludes to William Butler Yeats's poem "The Second Coming" (Chapter 12).

See pages 294, 345, 363, 667, 763, 1189, 1204.

ANALOGY **A comparison of two things to show that they are alike in certain respects.** Writers often make analogies to show how something unfamiliar is like something well-known or widely experienced. For example, people often draw an analogy between creating a work of art and giving birth to a child.

See page 563.

ANECDOTE **A brief and sometimes witty story that focuses on a single interesting incident or event, often in order to make a point or teach a moral lesson.** Sometimes an anecdote reveals the character of a famous person. Taoists, Zen Buddhists, and Sufis, among others, use anecdotes to convey indirectly the teachings of their philosophies.

See pages 81, 340.

ANIMISM **A belief that spirits or souls are present in all living things.** This belief was at the heart of the ancient Celtic religion, and it can be found in many other ancient religions.

See page 5.

ANTAGONIST **The character or force that opposes or blocks the protagonist, or main character, in a narrative.** Usually the antagonist is human, like Sir Modred, the villainous rebel who destroys the Round Table in Sir Thomas Malory's *Le Morte d'Arthur* (Chapter 2) or the schoolgirls who mercilessly taunt the Kelvey sisters in Katherine Mansfield's "The Doll's House" (Chapter 13). Sometimes the antagonist is supernatural, like Satan, who opposes God in John Milton's *Paradise Lost* (Chapter 3).

ANTICLIMAX See *Climax*.

ANTITHESIS **A contrast of ideas expressed in a grammatically balanced statement.** In the following line from Canto III of *The Rape of the Lock* (Chapter 6), Alexander Pope balances noun against noun and verb against verb:

> And wretches hang that jurymen may dine.

See page 615.

APHORISM **A concise, sometimes witty saying that expresses a principle, truth, or observation about life.** Alexander Pope's poetry contains some of the most famous aphorisms in the English language, as in this heroic couplet from *An Essay on Criticism* (Chapter 6):

> To err is human, to forgive, divine.

APOSTROPHE **A figure of speech in which a speaker directly addresses an absent or dead person, an abstract quality, or something nonhuman as if it were present and capable of responding.** Apostrophe was a popular device with the Romantic poets: Wordsworth, for example, apostrophizes the river Wye in his "Tintern Abbey" (Chapter 7). Among the second-generation Romantics, Shelley apostrophized the west wind; Byron apostrophized the ocean; and Keats apostrophized a nightingale and a Greek urn (all in Chapter 8).

See pages 313, 813.

ARCHETYPE **A pattern that appears in literature across cultures and is repeated through the ages. An archetype can be a character, a plot, an image, or a setting.** All stories or myths that contain a quest, for example, share certain features, suggesting that each quest-story has been formed from a master pattern. Similarly, all epic heroes have a number of common characteristics, though each one also has culturally specific characteristics. Ignoring the culturally specific characteristics of a particular epic hero will allow you to perceive the archetype of the epic hero.

See pages 17, 21, 88, 600.

ASIDE **Private words that a character in a play speaks to the audience or to another character and that are not supposed to be overheard by others onstage.** Stage directions usually tell when a speech is an aside.

ASSONANCE **The repetition of similar vowel sounds followed by different consonant sounds in words that are close together.** Assonance differs from exact rhyme in that it does not repeat the consonant sound following the vowel. The words *face* and *base* rhyme, while the words *face* and *fade* are assonant. Like alliteration, assonance can create musical and rhythmic effects. In this line from Alfred, Lord Tennyson's "The Lady of Shalott" (Chapter 9), the repetition of the short /a/ sounds creates a rhythmic effect that mimics the action being described:

> An abbot on an ambling pad,

See pages 774, 957, 1205.

ATMOSPHERE **The mood or feeling in a literary work.** Atmosphere is usually created through descriptive details and evocative language.

See page 1322.

AUGUSTAN **Similar to the reign of Emperor Augustus (63 B.C.–A.D. 14) or having qualities or tastes that are associated with classical Rome.** In English literary history the Augustan Age dates from the Restoration to the middle of the eighteenth century. Perhaps more than anyone else, Alexander Pope (Chapter 6) exhibits Augustan literary tastes in his poetry.

AUTOBIOGRAPHY **A written account of the author's own life.** Unlike **diaries, journals,** and letters, autobiographies are unified narratives usually prepared for a public audience. And unlike **memoirs,** which often focus on famous events and people, autobiographies are usually quite introspective. George Orwell's "Shooting an Elephant" (Chapter 11) is a well-known autobiographical essay.

See page 1093.
See also *Memoir.*

BALLAD **A song or songlike poem that tells a story.** Most ballads have a regular pattern of **rhythm** and **rhyme,** and they use simple language with a great deal of repetition. Ballads generally have a **refrain**—lines or words that are repeated at regular intervals. They usually tell sensational stories of tragedy, adventure, betrayal, revenge, and jealousy. **Folk ballads** are composed by anonymous singers and are passed down orally from generation to generation before they are written down (often in several different versions). "Lord Randall" (Chapter 2) is an example of a folk ballad. **Literary ballads,** on the other hand, are composed and written down by known poets, usually in the style of folk ballads. Samuel Taylor Coleridge's *The Rime of the Ancient Mariner* (Chapter 7) is a famous literary ballad.

The typical ballad stanza is a quatrain with the rhyme scheme *abcb.* The first and third lines have four stressed syllables, and the second and fourth lines have three. The number of unstressed syllables in each line may vary, but often the meter is primarily **iambic.**

See pages 184–185.

BIOGRAPHY **An account of a person's life written by another person.** The *Life of Samuel Johnson* by James Boswell (Chapter 6) is one of the most famous biographies ever written.

BLANK VERSE **Poetry written in unrhymed iambic pentameter.** "Blank" means that the poetry is unrhymed. "Iambic pentameter" means that each line contains five iambs, or metrical feet, each consisting of an unstressed syllable followed by a stressed syllable (˘´). Blank verse is the most important metrical form used in English dramatic and epic poetry. It is the verse line used in Shakespeare's plays and John Milton's *Paradise Lost* (Chapter 3). One of the reasons blank verse has been so popular, even among modern poets, is that it combines the naturalness of unrhymed verse with the structure of metrical verse. Except for **free verse,** it is the poetic form that sounds the most like natural speech. It also lends itself easily to slight variations within the basic pattern. Like most of the English Romantic poets, William Wordsworth made extensive use of blank verse, as in these lines from "Tintern Abbey" (Chapter 7):

> And nŏw, wĭth gleams ŏf hălf-extĭnguĭshed
> thought,
> Wĭth many recŏgnĭtions dĭm and faint,
> And sŏmewhat ŏf ă sad perplexity,
> The pĭcture ŏf the mind revives again:

CADENCE **The natural rise and fall of the voice.** Poets who write in **free verse** try to imitate the cadences of spoken language.

See pages 350, 439, 747.
See also *Rhythm.*

CAESURA **A pause or break within a line of poetry, usually indicated by the natural rhythm of the language.** A midline, or medial, caesura is a characteristic of Anglo-Saxon poetry; it divides the four-beat line in half. Later poets use the caesura less predictably, as in the following lines from Wilfred Owen's "Dulce et Decorum Est" (Chapter 11). Here, the caesuras are indicated by the symbol ||.

> Bent double, || like old beggars under sacks,
> Knock-kneed, || coughing like hags, || we
> cursed through sludge

See page 51.

CANTO **A subdivision in a long poem, corresponding to a chapter in a book.** Poems divided into cantos include Pope's *The Rape of the Lock* (Chapter 6) and Byron's *Childe Harold's Pilgrimage* (Chapter 8). Not all major subdivisions of long poems are called cantos: Milton's *Paradise Lost* (Chapter 3) is divided into books, and Coleridge's *The Rime of the Ancient Mariner* (Chapter 7) into parts.

The word *canto* comes from a Latin word for "song" and originally designated a section of a narrative poem that a minstrel could sing in one session.

See page 622.

CAPITALISM **An economic philosophy that advocates the idea that the means of production and distribution should be owned and controlled by private individuals.** Adam Smith, an eighteenth-century economist, is one of the great theorists of capitalism, a system which helped to foster the conditions that produced the Industrial Revolution in England and the technological advances of the nineteenth and twentieth centuries.

See also *Laissez Faire.*

CARPE DIEM **A Latin phrase that literally means "seize the day"—that is, "make the most of present opportunities."** The *carpe diem* theme is common in seventeenth-century English poetry, as in this famous line from Robert Herrick's "To the Virgins, to Make Much of Time": "Gather ye rosebuds while ye may." The theme is also forcefully expressed in Andrew Marvell's "To His Coy Mistress" (both in Chapter 3).

See page 283.

CHARACTER **An individual in a story or play.** A character always has human traits, even if the character is an animal, like the ravens in "The Twa Corbies" (Chapter 2); or a god, as in the *Iliad* (Chapter 1); or a monster, as in *Beowulf* (Chapter 1). A character may also be a human with superhuman powers, like Gilgamesh (Chapter 1). Most characters, however, are ordinary human beings, like Geoffrey Chaucer's colorful pilgrims in *The Canterbury Tales* (Chapter 2) and the boy in James Joyce's "Araby" (Chapter 13).

The process by which the writer reveals the personality of a character is called **characterization.** A writer can reveal a character in the following ways:

1. by telling us directly what the character is like: humble, ambitious, vain, easily manipulated, etc.
2. by describing how the character looks and dresses
3. by letting us hear the character speak
4. by revealing the character's private thoughts and feelings
5. by revealing the character's effect on other people—showing how other characters feel or behave toward the character
6. by showing the character's actions

The first method of revealing a character is called **direct characterization.** When a writer uses this method, we do not have to figure out what a character's personality is like—the writer tells us directly. The other five methods of revealing a character are known as **indirect characterization.** When a writer uses these methods, we have to exercise our own judgment, putting clues together to figure out what a character is like—just as we do in real life when we are getting to know someone.

Characters can be classified as static or dynamic. A **static character** is one who does not change much in the course of a story. A **dynamic character,** on the other hand, changes in some important way as a result of the story's action. Characters can also be classified as flat or round. **Flat characters** have only one or two personality traits. They are one-dimensional—they can be summed up by a single phrase. In contrast, **round characters** have more dimensions to their personalities—they are complex, solid, and multifaceted, like real people.

See pages 161, 1309.

CHIVALRY **The system of ideals and social codes governing the behavior of knights and gentlewomen in feudal times.** The ideal knight was meant to be brave, honorable, and courteous; gentlewomen were meant to be chaste. The code of chivalry is reflected in medieval romance literature, particularly in Malory's *Le Morte d'Arthur* (Chapter 2).

See page 122.

CLASSICISM **A movement in art, literature, and music that advocates imitating the principles manifested in the art and literature of ancient ("classical") Greece and Rome.** Classicism emphasizes reason, clarity, balance, harmony, restraint, order, and universal themes. Classicism is often placed in direct opposition to **Romanticism,** with its emphasis on unrestrained emotions and personal themes. However, this opposition should be approached with caution, as it is sometimes exaggerated for effect. Classicism was particularly admired in art in the eighteenth century and is exemplified in Alexander Pope's mock heroic epic, *The Rape of the Lock* (Chapter 6).

See also *Neoclassicism, Romanticism.*

CLICHÉ **An expression that was fresh and apt when it was first coined but is now so overused that it has become hackneyed and stale.** "Busy as a bee" and "fresh as a daisy" are two examples. Clichés are often likened to dead metaphors—figures of speech ("leg of a chair," "mouth of a river") whose power to surprise has now been completely lost.

CLIMAX **The point of greatest emotional intensity or suspense in a plot when the outcome of the conflict becomes known.** In Shakespeare's plays, the climax usually occurs in the last act, just before the final scene. Following the climax, the story is **resolved,** or closed.

Some critics talk of more than one climactic moment in a long work (though usually the greatest climax occurs near the end of the plot). In drama, one such climactic moment is called the turning point, or **crisis.** At the **turning point,** something happens that seals the fate of the hero. In Shakespeare's plays, this moment usually occurs in the third act. At the turning point the hero's fortunes begin to decline or improve. All the action leading up to this turning point is **rising action,** and all the action following it is **falling action.** The turning point in Guy de Maupassant's "The Jewels" (Chapter 10) occurs when Madame Lantin dies, leaving her husband alone and ravaged by grief. From that point onward, it is downhill for Monsieur Lantin—everything goes wrong, culminating in the story's climax, when Lantin, attempting to sell his wife's necklace, discovers that she has been deceptive. The sale of the jewels brings about the ironic resolution of the story: Lantin becomes wealthy and remarries, choosing a wife who is virtuous but makes him very unhappy.

In contrast, when something trivial or comical occurs at the point in a narrative when one expects something important or serious, the accompanying deflation is called an **anticlimax.** James Joyce's "Araby" (Chapter 13) contains such an anticlimactic moment.

See page 203.
See also *Plot.*

COMEDY **In general, a story that ends happily.** The hero of a comedy is usually an ordinary character who overcomes a series of obstacles that block what he or she wants. Often a comedy pits two young people who wish to marry against parental blocking figures who want to prevent the marriage. The wedding that concludes these comedies suggests the formation of a new society and a renewal of life. Comedy is distinct from **tragedy,** in which a great person comes to an unhappy or disastrous end, usually through some lapse in judgment or character flaw. Comedies are often, but not always, intended to make us laugh. Two famous comedies are Oscar Wilde's play *The Importance of Being Earnest* and George Bernard Shaw's *Pygmalion.* Even though it contains some of the darker elements of tragedy, Shakespeare's *The Tempest* is considered a comedy because harmony and reconciliation are achieved by the end of the play.

See also *Farce, Tragedy.*

COMMUNISM **A philosophy that advocates the creation of a classless and stateless society in which economic goods are distributed equally.** The most famous communist government is, of course, the now dissolved Soviet Union, a country which one could say perverted the ideals of communism, since it had a ruling class which was better off than the working class. Human nature seems to prevent people from bringing into being a perfect communist society. George Orwell's novel *Animal Farm* satirizes the ideals of communism, showing the ruination of a farm which has been taken over by radical animal reformers.

CONCEIT **A fanciful and elaborate figure of speech that makes a surprising connection between two seemingly dissimilar things.** A conceit may be a brief metaphor, or it may form the framework of an entire poem. Two particularly important types of conceits are the **Petrarchan conceit** and the **metaphysical conceit.**

Petrarchan conceits get their name from the fourteenth-century Italian poet Petrarch (page 400), who developed their use in his influential sonnet sequence. Poets influenced by Petrarch used these conceits to describe the beauty of the lady for whom they wrote. She invariably had hair of gold, lips of cherry red, and teeth of oriental pearl. In Sonnet 130 (Chapter 4), Shakespeare ridicules the use of such conceits. Petrarchan conceits were also used to describe a paradoxical state.

The metaphysical conceit is so called because it was widely used by the seventeenth-century metaphysical poets. This type of conceit is especially startling, complex, and ingenious. A famous example is John Donne's comparison of separated lovers to the legs of a compass in "A Valediction: Forbidding Mourning" (Chapter 3).

See pages 291, 398.

CONFLICT **A struggle or clash between opposing characters, forces, or emotions.** In an **external conflict,** a character struggles against some outside force: another character, society as a whole, or some natural force. An **internal conflict,** on the other hand, is a struggle between opposing needs, desires, or emotions within a single character. Many works, especially longer ones, contain both internal and external conflicts. In Doris Lessing's "No Witchcraft for Sale" (Chapter 13), the conflict between Gideon and the scientist reflects larger cultural conflicts.

See pages 307, 993.
See also *Plot.*

CONNOTATIONS **All the meanings, associations, or emotions that have come to be attached to a word.** For example, an expensive restaurant might prefer to advertise its "delicious cuisine" rather than its "delicious cooking." *Cuisine* and *cooking* have the same literal meaning—"prepared food." But *cuisine* has connotations of elegance and sophistication, while *cooking* does not. The same restaurant would certainly not describe its food as "great grub."

Notice the difference between the following pairs of words: *young/immature, ambitious/cutthroat, uninhibited/shameless, lenient/lax.* We might describe ourselves using the first words but someone else using the second ones. The English philosopher Bertrand Russell once gave a classic example of the different connotations of words: "I am firm. You are obstinate. He is a pigheaded fool."

See pages 315, 657, 667, 1216.
See also *Denotation.*

CONSONANCE **The repetition of final consonant sounds after different vowel sounds.** The words *east* and *west, dig* and *dog, turn* and *torn,* and Shakespeare's famous *"struts* and *frets"* (from *Macbeth,* in Chapter 4) are examples of consonance. The term is also sometimes used to refer to repeated consonant sounds in the middle of words, as in *solemn stillness.* (Consonance, when loosely defined, can be a form of **alliteration.** Strictly speaking, however, alliteration is the repetition of initial consonant sounds.) Like **assonance,** consonance is one form of **approximate rhyme.**

See also *Alliteration, Assonance.*

COUPLET **Two consecutive lines of poetry that rhyme.** The couplet has been widely used since the Middle Ages, especially to provide a sense of closure. A couplet that presents a completed thought is called a closed couplet. Shakespeare used closed couplets to end his sonnets, as in this example from Sonnet 29 (Chapter 4):

> For thy sweet love remembered such wealth brings
> That then I scorn to change my state with kings.

A couplet written in **iambic pentameter** is called a **heroic couplet.** Although the heroic couplet has been used in English literature since Chaucer, it was perfected during the eighteenth century. Here is an example from Pope's *An Essay on Man* (Chapter 6):

> Ălíke ĭn ĭgnórănce, hĭs réasŏn súch,
> Whĕthér hĕ thínks tŏo líttlĕ, ór tŏo múch:

See pages 824, 843, 981, 1273.

COURTLY LOVE **A conventional medieval code of behavior that informed a knight of the proper way to treat his lady.** The code was first developed by the troubadours (lyric poets) of southern France and extensively employed in European literature from the twelfth century throughout the medieval period.

DEISM **The belief that God, after creating the universe, ceased to interfere with the laws of nature and society.** Influenced by Newton's description of the universe as a great clock that was set in motion by the Creator, the deists of the mid-eighteenth century argued that people could only gain an understanding of the laws of nature and society by using their reason.

DENOTATION **The literal, dictionary definition of a word.** For example, a denotation, or dictionary definition, of the word *star* (as in "movie star") is an "eminent actor or actress," but the **connotation** is that of an actor or actress who is adored by fans and who leads a fascinating and glamorous life.

See also *Connotation.*

DENOUEMENT See *Plot.*

DEUS EX MACHINA **Any artificial or contrived device used at the end of a plot to resolve or untangle the complications.** The term is Latin and means "god from a machine." The phrase refers to a device used in ancient Greek and Roman drama: At the conclusion of the play, a god would be lowered onto the stage by a mechanical device so that he could save the hero and end the story happily. The term now refers to any device that resolves a plot in a forced or implausible way: An orphan finds that he has inherited a fortune just as he is being packed off to the poorhouse; a hero is saved because the villain has forgotten to load his gun. Oscar Wilde's *The Importance of Being Earnest* and Charles Dickens's *Oliver Twist* both contain examples of *deus ex machina.*

DIALECT **A way of speaking that is characteristic of a particular region or group of people.** A dialect may have a distinct vocabulary, pronunciation system, and grammar. In the Middle Ages, when Latin was the "literary" language of Europe, writers such as Geoffrey Chaucer (Chapter 2) began writing for middle-class audiences in their own regional languages, or what are now interchangeably called **dialects** or **vernaculars.** Today one dialect usually becomes accepted as the standard for a country or culture. In the United States, the dialect used in formal writing and spoken by most TV and radio announcers is known as standard English.

Writers often use other dialects, however, to establish character or to create local color. For example, V. S. Naipaul (Chapter 13) has used the dialect spoken by Trinidad's Asian Indian population in many of his works. The East London cockney dialect, and the lower-class background it betrays, are at the very heart of George Bernard Shaw's famous play *Pygmalion.* In this excerpt from the play, Henry Higgins, with his friend Colonel Pickering in attendance, begins to instruct the flower girl Eliza Doolittle in how to speak "proper" English:

> **Higgins.** Say your alphabet.
> **Liza.** I know my alphabet. Do you think I know nothing? I dont need to be taught like a child.
> **Higgins.** (*thundering*). Say your alphabet.
> **Pickering.** Say it, Miss Doolittle. You will understand presently. Do what he tells you; and let him teach you in his own way.
> **Liza.** Oh well, if you put it like that—Ahyee, beyee, ceyee, deyee—
> **Higgins.** (*with the roar of a wounded lion*). Stop. Listen to this, Pickering. . . . (*To Eliza*) Say A, B, C, D.
> **Liza.** (*almost in tears*). But I'm saying it. Ahyee, Bee, Ce-ee—

See page 721.

DIALOGUE **Conversation between two or more people.** Writers use dialogue to advance the action of a plot, to present an interplay of ideas and personalities, and to reveal the background, occupation, or social level of the characters through **tone** and **dialect.**

DICTION **A writer's or speaker's choice of words.** Speakers and writers use different types of words depending on the audience they are addressing, the subject they are discussing, and the effect they are trying to produce. For example, slang that would be suitable in a casual conversation with a friend ("He's a total nerd") would be unsuitable in a political debate. Similarly, the language that a nutritionist would use to describe a meal would be different from the language that a restaurant reviewer or a novelist would use.

Diction is an essential element of a writer's **style.** A writer's diction can be simple or flowery (*shop/boutique*), modern or old-fashioned (*pharmacy/apothecary*), general or specific (*sandwich/grilled cheese on rye*). Notice that the **connotations** of words (rather than their strict, literal meanings, or **denotations**) are an important aspect of diction.

See pages 315, 548, 837, 1181, 1223.

DIDACTIC LITERATURE **Literary works that are meant to instruct, give advice, or convey a philosophy or moral message.** Much didactic literature derives from religious teaching, as is the case with "The Parable of The Prodigal Son" (Chapter 3) and the Taoist Anecdotes (Chapter 3). Secular works such as fables, folk tales and maxims are also didactic in intent.

See page 332.
See also *Fable, Parable.*

DISSONANCE (DIHS·uh nuhns) **A harsh, discordant combination of sounds.** The opposite of **euphony** (YOO fuh nee), a pleasant, harmonious combination of sounds, dissonance is usually created by the repetition of harsh consonant sounds. Dissonance is often used in poetry to communicate energy. Dissonance is also called **cacophony** (kuh KAHF uh nee).

DRAMATIC MONOLOGUE **A poem in which a character addresses one or more listeners who remain silent or whose replies are not revealed.** The occasion is usually a critical one in the speaker's life. Tennyson's "Ulysses" and Browning's "My Last Duchess" (Chapter 9) are famous dramatic monologues.

See page 943.

DRAMATIC SONG **A poem found in a play that serves to establish mood, reveal character, or advance action.** The songs in Shakespeare's plays are the best songs of this kind. Employing a variety of techniques and forms and relying heavily on **onomatopoeia,** Shakespeare wrote songs that can be read alone, but which are best understood within the context of the plays in which they appear.

See pages 387, 400.

ELEGY **A poem that mourns the death of a person or laments something lost.** Elegies may lament the passing of life and beauty, or they may be meditations on the nature of death. A type of **lyric,** an elegy is usually formal in language and structure and solemn or even melancholy in tone. Much of English poetry is elegiac, from the Anglo-Saxon lyric "The Seafarer" (Chapter 1) to A. E. Housman's "To an Athlete Dying Young" (Chapter 10) and Dylan Thomas's "Do Not Go Gentle into That Good Night" (Chapter 12).

See pages 61, 613, 657, 931, 1235.

END-STOPPED LINE **A line of poetry in which the meter and the meaning conclude with the end of the line.** Often the end-of-line pause is marked with punctuation, though it need not be. These lines from Alexander Pope's *An Essay on Man* (Chapter 6) are end-stopped:

> Know then thyself, presume not God to scan;
> The proper study of mankind is man.

See also *Run-on line.*

ENLIGHTENMENT; THE AGE OF REASON
Names historians have applied to the eighteenth century. The period has been called the Enlightenment and the Age of Reason because at that time, people began to rely on reason and experience, rather than superstition and church authority, to gain an understanding of the world.

EPIC **A long narrative poem that relates the great deeds of a larger-than-life hero who embodies the values of a particular society.** Most epics include elements of myth, legend, folklore, and history. Their tone is serious and their language grand. Most **epic heroes** undertake quests to achieve something of tremendous value to themselves or their society. Homer's *Odyssey* and *Iliad* (Chapter 1) and Virgil's *Aeneid* are the best-known epics in the Western tradition. The two most important English epics are the Anglo-Saxon poem *Beowulf* (Chapter 1) and John Milton's *Paradise Lost* (Chapter 3).

Many epics share standard characteristics and formulas known as **epic conventions,** which the oral poets drew upon to help them recall the stories they were recounting and which the writers of literary epics draw upon to establish the epic quality of their poems. The conventions include an **invocation,** or formal plea for aid, to a deity or some other spiritual power; action that begins ***in medias res*** (literally "in the middle of things") and then **flashes back** to events that take place before the narrative's current time setting; **epic similes,** or elaborately extended comparisons relating heroic events to simple, everyday events; a consistently predictable **metrical structure;** and **stock epithets,** or descriptive adjectives or phrases used repeatedly with—or in place of—a noun or proper name.

See pages 17–18, 1391.
See also *Literary Epic.*

EPIGRAM **A brief, clever, and usually memorable statement.** Alexander Pope's writings are **epigrammatic** in style. Here is an example from his *Essay on Criticism:*

> We think our fathers fools, so wise we grow,
> Our wiser sons, no doubt, will think us so.

See also *Maxim, Proverb.*

EPIPHANY **In a literary work, a moment of sudden insight or revelation that a character experiences.** The word comes from the Greek and can be translated as "manifestation" or "showing forth." The term has religious meanings that have been transferred to literature by modern writers. James Joyce first gave the word its literary meaning in an early draft of *A Portrait of the Artist as a Young Man*. In Joyce's story "Araby" (Chapter 13), the narrator experiences an epiphany at the end of the story when he recognizes the cheap vulgarity of the bazaar and the emptiness of his dream.

See page 1325.

EPITAPH **An inscription on a tombstone or a commemorative poem written about a person who has died.** Epitaphs range from the solemn to the farcical. Ben Jonson's "On My First Son" (Chapter 3) contains a famously poignant epitaph.

EPITHET **An adjective or other descriptive phrase that is regularly used to characterize a person, place, or thing.** Phrases such as "Peter the Great," "Richard the Lion-Hearted," and "America the Beautiful" are epithets. Homer created so many descriptive epithets in his *Iliad* (Chapter 1) and *Odyssey* that his name has been permanently associated with a type of epithet. The **Homeric epithet** consists of a compound adjective that is regularly used to modify a particular noun. Famous examples are "the wine-dark sea," "the gray-eyed goddess Athena," and the "rosy-fingered dawn."

See also *Kenning.*

ESSAY **A short piece of nonfiction prose that examines a single subject from a limited point of view.** There are two major types of essays. **Informal essays** (also called **personal essays**) generally reveal a great deal about the personalities and feelings of their authors. They tend to be loosely structured, conversational, sometimes even humorous, in tone; and usually highly subjective. **Formal essays** (also called **traditional essays**) are usually serious and impersonal in tone. Because they are written to inform or persuade, they are expected to be factual, logical, and tightly organized.

In the European literary tradition the essay began in France with Michel de Montaigne, who sought to test his own judgment by analyzing it in a series of short prose pieces, which he called *essais,* a common sixteenth-century spelling of the French word *assay,* which means "trial" or "attempt." Sir Francis Bacon, who published his *Essays* (see "Of Studies," Chapter 3) in the late sixteenth and early seventeenth century, brought the form into England and pioneered what we now call the formal essay. Notable twentieth-century English essayists include Virginia Woolf and George Orwell (both in Chapter 11).

See page 1162.

EXAGGERATION See *Hyperbole.*

FABLE **A very brief story in prose or verse that teaches a moral, or a practical lesson about life.** The characters in most fables are animals that behave and speak like humans. Some of the most popular fables are those attributed to Aesop, who was supposed to have been a slave in ancient Greece. Several of the pilgrims' tales in Geoffrey Chaucer's *The Canterbury Tales* (Chapter 2) also contain fables. Other popular and widely influential fables include those collected in the Panchatantra, like "Right-Mind and Wrong-Mind."

See also *Parable.*

FALLING ACTION See *Climax.*

FARCE **A type of comedy in which ridiculous and often stereotyped characters are involved in far-fetched, silly situations.** The humor in farce is based on crude physical action, slapstick, and clowning. Characters may slip on banana peels, get pies thrown in their faces, and knock one another on the head with ladders. The movies featuring Abbott and Costello, Laurel and Hardy, and the Marx brothers are all examples of farces.

The word *farce* comes from a Latin word for "stuffing," and in fact farces were originally used to fill in the waiting time between the acts of a serious play. Even in tragedies, farcical elements are often included to provide **comic relief,** or a break from the pervading tension. Shakespeare frequently lets his "common" characters engage in farcical actions.

FASCISM **A nationalistic philosophy that advocates rule by a single charismatic dictator.** Fascism properly speaking refers to the philosophy of Benito Mussolini's political party, which was founded in 1919 to oppose communism in Italy. The word, however, was soon used to describe the philosophies of similar repressive, nationalistic political parties in other countries. The German Nazis were fascists. The regimes of Francisco Franco in Spain and Juan Peron in Argentina were fascistic.

See pages 1066, 1140.

FEUDALISM **The economic, political, and social system of medieval Europe.** This system was basically composed of three classes: the feudal lords, who were powerful landowners; vassals, who did work or military service for the feudal lords in exchange for land; and serfs, who were servants to the lords and vassals and who were bound to their masters' land.

See page 7.

FIGURE OF SPEECH **A word or phrase that describes one thing in terms of another, dissimilar thing, and is not meant to be understood on a literal level.** Some 250 different types of figures of speech have been identified, but the most common are the **simile** ("My love is like a red, red rose"), the **metaphor** ("The Lord is my shepherd"), and **personification** ("Death, be not proud"). These involve a comparison between unlike things, but not all figures of speech involve comparison. When one refers to the king using the word *crown,* one is not comparing the crown to the king, but associating the crown with the king.

See pages 99, 282, 291, 313, 761, 811, 1075.
See also *Hyperbole, Metaphor, Metonymy, Oxymoron, Personification, Simile, Symbol.*

FLASHBACK **A scene in a movie, play, short story, novel, or narrative poem that interrupts the present action of the plot to "flash backward" and tell what happened at an earlier time.** "The Demon Lover" by Elizabeth Bowen (Chapter 11) includes a flashback that describes Mrs. Drover's farewell to her fiancé twenty-five years before the main action of the story takes place.

See page 1117.

FOIL **A character who sets off another character by strong contrast.** This contrast emphasizes the differences between two characters, bringing out each's distinctive qualities. In *Gilgamesh* (Chapter 1), Enkidu is a foil to Gilgamesh.

See pages 89, 477.

FORESHADOWING **The use of clues to hint at what is going to happen later in the plot.** Foreshadowing arouses the reader's curiosity and builds up **suspense.** Foreshadowing occurs in Elizabeth Bowen's "The Demon Lover" (Chapter 11) when Mrs. Drover imagines "spectral glitters in the place of" her fiancé's eyes, and when we learn that she made an "unnatural promise" to him—that she "could not have plighted a more sinister troth."

See pages 214, 1124, 1309.
See also *Suspense.*

FRAME STORY **An introductory narrative within which one or more of the characters proceed to tell individual stories.** Perhaps the best-known example of stories contained in a frame story is the Persian collection called *The Thousand and One Nights.* In English literature, Geoffrey Chaucer's *The Canterbury Tales* (Chapter 2) uses a frame story involving a group of people on a pilgrimage; within the narrative frame, each of the pilgrims then tells his or her own story.

See pages 118, 121.

FREE VERSE **Poetry that has no regular meter or rhyme scheme.** Free verse usually relies on the natural **rhythms** of ordinary speech. Poets writing in free verse may use **alliteration, internal rhyme, onomatopoeia,** and other musical devices to achieve their effects. They may also place great emphasis on **imagery.** Matthew Arnold's "Dover Beach" (Chapter 10) is an early example of free verse, and T. S. Eliot's poems, including "The Hollow Men" (Chapter 12), are especially fine and famous examples.

GOTHIC **A term used to describe literary works that contain primitive, medieval, wild, mysterious, or natural elements.** Such elements were frowned upon by eighteenth-century neoclassicists but hailed by the Romantic writers of the following era. The **Gothic novel,** a genre popular in the late eighteenth and early nineteenth centuries, is chiefly characterized by gloomy settings and an atmosphere of terror and mystery. Mary Wollstonecraft Shelley's *Frankenstein* is one of the most widely known Gothic novels.

See page 658.

HAIKU **A brief, unrhymed, three-line poem developed in Japan in the 1600s.** The first and third lines of a traditional haiku have five syllables each, and the middle line has seven. Haiku generally juxtapose familiar images and present them in a compressed form, forcing the reader to make an imaginative leap to understand the connection between them.

See pages 867, 868, 870, 871.

HUMANISM **An intellectual movement of the Renaissance that restored the study of the classics and focused on examining human life here and now.** Though humanists were still interested in theology and religious questions, the focus of their interest expanded to include earthly matters as well. Famous humanists include Sir Thomas More and Erasmus.

See page 267.

HYPERBOLE **A figure of speech that uses exaggeration to express strong emotion or create a comic effect.** While hyperbole (also known as **overstatement**) does not express the *literal* truth, it is often used in the service of truth to capture a sense of intensity or to emphasize the essential nature of something. For instance, if you claim that it was 250 degrees in the shade, you are using hyperbole to express the truth that it was miserably hot.

See pages 287, 289.

IAMBIC PENTAMETER **A line of poetry composed of five iambs.** An **iamb** is a metrical foot, or unit of measure, consisting of an unstressed syllable followed by a stressed syllable (˘´). The word *suggest,* for example, is made up of one iamb. *Pentameter* derives from the Greek words *penta* (five) and *meter* (measure). Here are two lines from John Keats's "Ode to a Nightingale" (Chapter 8) that are written in iambic pentameter:

> Forlorn the very word is like a bell
> To toll me back from thee to my sole self!

Iambic pentameter is by far the most common verse line in English poetry. Shakespeare's sonnets and plays, for example, are written primarily in this meter. Many modern poets, such as W. H. Auden (Chapter 12), have continued to use iambic pentameter. Other than **free verse,** it is the poetic meter that sounds the most like natural speech.

See pages 385, 813.
See also *Blank Verse.*

IMAGERY Language that appeals to the senses. Most images are visual—that is, they appeal to the sense of sight. Imagery can also appeal to the senses of hearing, touch, taste, or smell. While imagery is an element in all types of writing, it is especially important in poetry.

See pages 99, 271, 289, 291, 324, 868, 877, 917, 1081, 1265.

INCREMENTAL REPETITION A device widely used in ballads whereby a line or lines are repeated with slight variations from stanza to stanza. Each repetition advances the plot of the narrative. Incremental repetition is used in the folk ballad "Lord Randall" (Chapter 2).

INDUSTRIAL REVOLUTION The period of social and economic change following the replacement of hand tools by machines and power tools, which allowed manufacturers to increase their production and save money. The perfection of the steam engine in the last half of the eighteenth century signaled the arrival of the age of the machine. The Industrial Revolution began on a small scale among textile manufacturers in the middle of the eighteenth century, but soon spread rapidly. Most textile products were produced by steam-engine-powered machines by the early nineteenth century. As the nineteenth century progressed, other industries began to use steam engines to produce their goods. George Eliot used the Industrial Revolution as the backdrop for *Silas Marner* (1861), and Charles Dickens satirizes its social effects in *Hard Times* (1854).

See page 711.

IN MEDIAS RES **The technique of starting a story in the middle and then using a flashback to tell what happened earlier.** *In medias res* is Latin for "in the middle of things." Epics traditionally begin *in medias res.* For example, John Milton's *Paradise Lost* (Chapter 3) opens with Satan and his cohorts in Hell, after the war in Heaven and their fall, events that are recounted later in a flashback.

IRONY A contrast or discrepancy between expectation and reality—between what is said and what is really meant, between what is expected and what really happens, or between what appears to be true and what really is true.

Verbal irony occurs when a writer or speaker says one thing but really means something quite different—often the opposite of what he or she has said. If you tell your friend that you "just love being kept waiting in the rain," you are using verbal irony. A classic example of verbal irony is Jonathan Swift's suggestion in *A Modest Proposal* (Chapter 5) that the Irish solve their poverty and overpopulation problems by selling their babies as food to their English landlords.

Situational irony occurs when what happens is the opposite of what is expected or appropriate. In James Joyce's story "Araby" (Chapter 13), the boy hears about a bazaar called Araby and imagines that it will be a splendid, exotic place, yet when he arrives, he finds that the bazaar is cheap and commonplace.

Dramatic irony occurs when the audience or the reader knows something important that a character in a play or story does not know. Dramatic irony occurs in Elizabeth Bowen's "The Demon Lover" (Chapter 11), when Mrs. Drover is riding in the taxi. The reader suspects that the taxi driver is the demon lover even though Mrs. Drover does not. Dramatic irony is a powerful device in William Blake's "The Chimney Sweeper" from *Songs of Innocence* (Chapter 7). The speaker is a child who believes what he has been told—that "if all do their duty they need not fear harm." However, the reader, who is not so innocent, knows this is not so.

See pages 149, 359, 565, 580, 819, 1033, 1141, 1239, 1295.

KENNING In Anglo-Saxon poetry, a metaphorical phrase or compound word used to name a person, place, thing, or event indirectly. *Beowulf* (Chapter 1) includes the kennings "whale-road" for the sea and "shepherd of evil" for Grendel.

See page 35.
See also *Epithet.*

LAISSEZ FAIRE (LEHS ay FAIR) **An economic policy based on the idea that economic forces should be allowed to operate freely and without government regulation.**

See page 718.

LITERARY EPIC Literary epics are epics that have been composed by individual writers, often following earlier models. Unlike an **oral epic** or a **primary epic,** which is performed by generations of anonymous storytellers and modified slightly with each retelling, a literary epic is the product of a single imagination working within the epic tradition.

See page 348.
See also *Epic.*

LYRIC POETRY **Poetry that focuses on expressing emotions or thoughts, rather than on telling a story.** Most lyrics are short, and they usually imply rather than directly state a single strong emotion. The term *lyric* comes from the Greek. In ancient Greece, lyric poems were recited to the accompaniment of a stringed instrument called the lyre. Today, poets still try to make their lyrics melodious, but they rely only on the musical effects they can create with words (such as rhyme, **rhythm, alliteration,** and **onomatopoeia**). Samuel Taylor Coleridge's "Kubla Khan," William Wordsworth's "Tintern Abbey" (both in Chapter 7), and Matthew Arnold's "Dover Beach" (Chapter 10) are all lyric poems.

See page 309.

MAGIC REALISM **A literary style that combines incredible events with realistic details and relates them all in a matter-of-fact tone.** Magic realism originated in Latin America, where writers such as Gabriel García Márquez and Julio Cortázar drew on elements of surrealism and local folklore to create a style that is both timeless and innovative.

MATERIALISM **A belief that nothing exists except matter and that the operations of everything, including thought, will, and feeling, are caused by material agencies.**

MAXIM **A brief, direct statement that expresses a basic rule of human conduct or a general truth about human behavior.** "It is better to give than to receive" is an example of a well-known maxim.

See page 338.
See also *Epigram, Moral Tale, Proverb.*

MEMOIR **A type of autobiography that usually focuses on a single time period or historical event.** *Survival in Auschwitz* by Primo Levi (Chapter 11) is a memoir about the author's experience at the death camp in 1944–1945.

See pages 1073, 1093.

METAPHOR **A figure of speech that makes a comparison between two seemingly unlike things without using a connective word such as *like, as, than,* or *resembles.*** You are using a metaphor if you say you are "at the end of your rope" or describe two political candidates as "running neck and neck."

Some metaphors are **directly** stated, like Percy Bysshe Shelley's comparison "My soul is an enchanted boat." (If he had written, "My soul is *like* an enchanted boat," he would have been using a **simile.**) Other metaphors are **implied,** like John Suckling's line "Time shall molt away his wings." The words *molt* and *wings* imply a comparison between time and a bird shedding its feathers.

An **extended metaphor** is a metaphor that is extended, or developed, over several lines of writing or even throughout an entire poem.

A **dead metaphor** is a metaphor that has become so common that we no longer even notice that it is a figure of speech. Our everyday language is filled with dead metaphors, such as *foot of the bed, bone of contention,* and *mouth of the river.*

A **mixed metaphor** is the incongruous mixture of two or more metaphors. Mixed metaphors are usually unintentional and often conjure up ludicrous images: "If you put your money on that horse, you'll be barking up the wrong tree."

See pages 275, 852, 937, 1212, 1261, 1279.

METAPHYSICAL POETRY **A term applied to the poetry of John Donne, Andrew Marvell, and other seventeenth-century poets who wrote in a difficult and abstract style.** Metaphysical poetry is intellectual and detached. It is characterized by ingenious, obscure imagery, philosophical meditation, verbal wit. It often uses rough-sounding meter.

See page 289.

METER **A generally regular pattern of stressed and unstressed syllables in poetry.** When we want to indicate the metrical pattern of a poem, we mark the stressed syllables with the symbol ´ and the unstressed syllables with the symbol ˘. Indicating the metrical pattern of a poem in this way is called **scanning** the poem, or **scansion.** Here is how to scan these lines from William Blake's "The Tyger" (Chapter 7):

> Týgĕr! Týgĕr! búrnĭng bríght
> Ín thĕ fórests ŏf thĕ níght,

Meter is measured in units called feet. A **foot** usually consists of one stressed syllable and one or more unstressed syllables. The basic metrical feet used in English poetry are the **iamb** (as in *cŏnvínce*), the **trochee** (as in *bórrŏw*), the **anapest** (as in *cŏntrădíct*), the **dactyl** (as in *áccŭrăte*), and the **spondee** (as in *séawéed*). A poem is described as iambic, trochaic, anapestic, dactylic, or spondaic according to what kind of foot appears most often in its lines.

A complete description of a metrical line indicates both the type and number of feet the line contains. For example, a line of iambic pentameter consists of five iambs, while a line of trochaic tetrameter consists of four trochees.

See pages 289, 657, 745, 747, 757.

METONYMY (muh TAHN uh mee) **A figure of speech in which something closely related to a thing or suggested by it is substituted for the thing itself.** You are using metonymy if you call the judiciary "the bench," the king "the crown," the president (or presidential staff) "the White House," or the race track "the turf."

See also *Synecdoche.*

MOCK EPIC **A comic narrative poem that parodies the epic by treating a trivial subject in a lofty, grand manner.** A mock epic uses dignified language, elaborate figures of speech, and supernatural intervention. The style of the mock epic is called **mock heroic** (and short mock epics are often called mock heroics). Alexander Pope's *The Rape of the Lock* (Chapter 6) is considered the supreme mock epic in the English language.

MODERNISM **A broad trend in literature and other arts, from approximately 1890 to 1940, that reflected the impact of works like Sigmund Freud's writings on psychology.** In general, modernist writers rejected the forms and values of the past and sought new forms to reflect the fragmentation and uncertainty that they felt characterized modern life. Many modern poets, for example, rejected traditional poetic meters and wrote **free verse.** Novelists such as James Joyce employed a technique called **stream of consciousness** to record the randomness and free associations of their characters' thoughts.

See page 1065.

MONOLOGUE **A long, formal speech made by a character in a play.** A monologue may be directed at another character or the audience. Shakespeare's soliloquies (Chapter 4) can also be called monologues.

See also *Soliloquy.*

MOOD See *Atmosphere.*

See pages 502, 873, 965.

MORAL TALE **A tale that teaches a lesson about life.** Several of the pilgrims' tales in Geoffrey Chaucer's *The Canterbury Tales* (Chapter 2) are moral tales.

MOTIF **In literature, a word, a character, an object, an image, a metaphor, or an idea that recurs in a work or in several works.** The rose is a motif that runs through many love poems. *Beowulf* (Chapter 1) contains many of the traditional motifs associated with heroic literature from all over the world, including a hero who does great deeds in battle or undertakes an extraordinary journey and a supernatural or fantastic being that takes part in the action. These motifs, along with others common to heroic literature, also appear in epics such as the *Iliad* (Chapter 1) and Milton's *Paradise Lost* (Chapter 3). A motif almost always bears an important relationship to the **theme** of a work of literature.

See page 20.

MOTIVATION **The reasons for or forces behind the action of a character.** Motivation is revealed through a combination of the character's desires and moral nature with the circumstances in which he or she is placed. In James Joyce's "Araby" (Chapter 13), the narrator's crush on Mangan's sister and his romanticized view of the world combine to provide his motivation for attending the bazaar.

See page 1030.
See also *Character.*

MYTH **An anonymous traditional story, rooted in a particular society, that usually serves to explain the mysteries of nature and a society's beliefs and customs.** Most myths grew out of religious rituals, and almost all of them involve the exploits of gods and heroes. Myths helped people to understand and cope with things beyond human control. Every culture has its own **mythology,** but in the Western world the most important myths have been those of ancient Greece and Rome. In twentieth-century literature, **allusions** to myths are often **ironic,** intended to reveal how diminished humanity has become in comparison with grand mythological figures.

NARRATOR **One who tells, or narrates, a story.** In fiction the narrator occupies any one of a variety of relations to the events described: from the center of the action to a distant, even objective, observer. A narrator may also be reliable or unreliable—if unreliable, the reader is made aware that the narrator's perceptions and interpretations of the action are different from those of the author. Such unreliable narrators can be deceitful or bumbling, but are often just naive or highly impressionable characters. The narrator at the beginning of James Joyce's "Araby" (Chapter 13), for example, is an impressionable boy, and the story is, in part, about how the boy's point of view changes and becomes more reliable.

See pages 161, 557.
See also *Point of View.*

NEOCLASSICISM **The revival of classical standards and forms during the late seventeenth and eighteenth centuries.** The neoclassicists valued the classical ideals of order, reason, balance, harmony, clarity, and restraint. In particular, they studied and tried to emulate the Latin poets Horace and Virgil. Alexander Pope (Chapter 6) is one of the most celebrated English neoclassical poets.

NOVEL **A long fictional prose narrative, usually of more than fifty thousand words.** In general, the novel uses the same basic literary elements as the short story: **plot, character, setting, theme,** and **point of view.** The novel's length usually permits these elements to be more fully developed than they are in the short story. However, this is not always true of the modern novel. Some modern novels are basically character studies, with only the barest plot structures. Others reveal little about their characters and concentrate instead on setting or tone or even the language of the novel itself.

Some of the greatest novels ever written are *Tom Jones* by Henry Fielding, *Pride and Prejudice* by Jane Austen, *Jane Eyre* by Charlotte Brontë, *Bleak House* and *Great Expectations* by Charles Dickens, *The Brothers Karamazov* by Fyodor Dostoyevsky, *Madame Bovary* by Gustave Flaubert, *Middlemarch* by George Eliot, *Jude the Obscure* by Thomas Hardy, *War and Peace* by Leo Tolstoy, *Lord Jim* by Joseph Conrad, *Sons and Lovers* by D. H. Lawrence, *Ulysses* by James Joyce, and *One Hundred Years of Solitude* by Gabriel García Márquez.

See pages 541–542.

OCTAVE **An eight-line stanza or poem or the first eight lines of an Italian, or Petrarchan, sonnet.** The usual rhyme scheme of the octave in this type of sonnet is *abbaabba.* The octave, which is sometimes called the **octet,** is followed by a six-line **sestet** with the rhyme scheme *cdecde* or *cdcdcd.*

See pages 745, 1075.
See also *Sonnet.*

ODE **A complex, generally long lyric poem on a serious subject.** In English poetry, there are basically two types of odes. One is highly formal and dignified in style and is generally written for ceremonial or public occasions. This type of ode derives from the choral odes of the classical Greek poet Pindar. The other type of ode derives from those written by the Latin poet Horace, and it is much more personal and reflective. In English poetry, it is exemplified by the intimate, meditative odes of such Romantic poets as Wordsworth, Keats, and Shelley (Chapters 7 and 8).

See pages 809, 824.

ONOMATOPOEIA (ahn uh mat uh PEE uh) **The use of a word whose sound imitates or suggests its meaning.** Many familiar words, such as *clap, squish, sizzle,* and *wheeze* are onomatopoeic. In poetry, onomatopoeia can reinforce meaning while creating evocative and musical effects. The word "lapping," in the following lines from W. B. Yeats's "The Lake Isle of Innisfree" (Chapter 12), is onomatopoeic.

I will arise and go now, for always night and
    day
I hear lake water lapping with low sounds by
    the shore;

See pages 299, 309.

OTTAVA RIMA **An eight-line stanza in iambic pentameter with the rhyme scheme *abababcc.*** The form was developed in Italy and was popularized by the fourteenth-century Italian poet Giovanni Boccaccio. The most famous example of ottava rima in English poetry is Lord Byron's *Don Juan.* William Butler Yeats's "Sailing to Byzantium"(Chapter 12) is another notable example.

OXYMORON **A figure of speech that combines apparently contradictory or incongruous ideas.** "Bittersweet," "cruel kindness," and "eloquent silence" are oxymora. The classic oxymoron "wise fool" is almost a literal translation of the term from the Greek—*oxys* means "sharp" or "keen," and moros means "foolish." A famous oxymoron in literature is John Milton's description of Hell in Paradise Lost (Chapter 3):

> No light, but rather darkness visible. . .

See pages 359, 1075.

PARABLE A short, allegorical story that teaches a moral or religious lesson about life. The most famous parables in Western literature are those like "The Parable of the Prodigal Son" (Chapter 3) told by Jesus in the Gospels of the Bible.

See pages 325, 336.

PARADOX An apparent contradiction that is actually true. A paradox may be a statement or a situation; as a statement, it is a figure of speech. The metaphysical poets of the seventeenth century (Chapter 3) made brilliant use of paradoxes, as in this famous example from John Donne's "Death be not proud" (Chapter 3):

> One short sleep past, we wake eternally,
> And death shall be no more; Death, thou shalt
> die.

The speaker in the cartoon does not understand the famous series of paradoxes that open *A Tale of Two Cities* by Charles Dickens.

"I wish you would make up your mind, Mr. Dickens. Was it the best of times or was it the worst of times? It could scarcely have been both."

See pages 275, 300, 359, 1335.

PARALLELISM The repetition of words, phrases, or sentences that have the same grammatical structure or that restate a similar idea. Parallelism is often used in literature meant to be spoken aloud, such as poetry, drama, and speeches, because it can help make lines emotional, rhythmic, and memorable. It is also one of the most important techniques used in Biblical poetry. The parallelism in the following lines from Psalm 23 (Chapter 3) heightens the emotional effect and enacts a meditative tone:

> He maketh me to lie down in green pastures:
> He leadeth me beside the still waters.
> He restoreth my soul:
> He leadeth me in the paths of righteousness for
> his name's sake.

See pages 321, 374, 737.

PARODY The imitation of a work of literature, art, or music for amusement or instruction. Parodies usually use exaggeration or inappropriate subject matter to make a serious style seem ridiculous. Alexander Pope's *The Rape of the Lock* (Chapter 6) is a parody of such serious and sweeping epics as the *Iliad* (Chapter 1) and the Aeneid. Cervantes' *Don Quixote* (Chapter 5) is a parody of medieval romances.

See pages 205, 603.

PASTORAL A type of literature that depicts country life in idyllic, idealized terms. The term *pastoral* comes from the Latin word for shepherd, and originally, pastorals were about shepherds, nymphs, and rural life. Today, the term has a looser meaning and refers to any literary work that portrays an idyllic rural setting or that expresses nostalgia for an age or place of lost innocence. The most famous traditional English pastoral is Christopher Marlowe's "The Passionate Shepherd to His Love," which is satirized in Sir Walter Raleigh's "The Nymph's Reply to the Shepherd" (both in Chapter 3).

See page 277

PERSONIFICATION **A kind of metaphor in which a nonhuman or nonliving thing or quality is talked about as if it were human or had life.** In these lines, from William Wordsworth's "The World Is Too Much with Us" (Chapter 7), the sea is given human form and the wind is given a voice:

> This Sea that bares her bosom to the moon;
> The winds that will be howling at all hours,

See pages 282, 761, 915.
See also *Apostrophe, Figure of Speech, Metaphor.*

PLOT **The series of related events that comprise a story or drama.** The plot is the underlying structure of a story. Most plots are built on these "bare bones"; a **basic situation,** or **exposition,** introduces the characters, setting, and, usually, the story's major **conflict.** Out of this basic situation, **complications** develop that intensify the conflict. **Suspense** mounts until a **climax**—the tensest or most exciting part of the plot—is reached, where something happens to determine the outcome of the conflict. Finally, all the problems or mysteries of the plot are unraveled in the **resolution,** or **denouement.**

See page 1383.
See also *Climax.*

POINT OF VIEW **The vantage point from which a writer tells a story.** There are three main points of view: **first person, limited third person,** and **omniscient third person.**

In the **first-person point of view,** the narrator is a character in the story. Using the pronoun *I,* this narrator tells us his or her own experiences but cannot reveal the private thoughts of other characters. When we read a story told in the first person, we hear and see only what the narrator hears and sees. We may have to interpret what this narrator says because a first-person narrator may or may not be objective, honest, or perceptive. For example, in James Joyce's "Araby" (Chapter 13), the narrator is a boy who is, in the beginning of the story, a youth whose point of view is romantic, and the story is about his giving up this view.

In the **limited-third-person point of view,** the narrator is outside the story—like an omniscient narrator—but tells the story from the vantage point of only one character. The narrator can enter the mind of this chosen character but cannot tell what any other characters are thinking except by observation. This narrator also can go only where the chosen character goes. For example, "In the Shadow of War" by Ben Okri is told entirely from the point of view of Omovo, the main character. We experience the stupefying summer heat, the mysteriousness of the veiled woman, and the horror of the gruesome river scene through Omovo's eyes alone.

In the **omniscient** (or **"all-knowing"**) **point of view,** the person telling the story knows everything that's going on in the story. This omniscient narrator is outside the story, a godlike observer who can tell us what all the characters are thinking and feeling, as well as what is happening anywhere in the story. For example, in "The Rocking-Horse Winner" by D. H. Lawrence (Chapter 13), the narrator enters into the thoughts and secrets of every character, revealing both the "hard little place" in the mother's heart and Paul's determination to "compel her attention" by being lucky.

See page 1176.
See also *Narrator, Stream of Consciousness.*

POSTMODERNISM **A trend in art and philosophy that reflects the late-twentieth-century distrust in the idea that there is a legitimate and true system of thought that can be used to understand the world and our place in it.** Postmodernists, like the modernists, see contemporary life as fragmentary, but rather than regard the fragmentary condition of our world with horror, as for instance T. S. Eliot had done in "The Hollow Men" (Chapter 12), postmodernists look upon the fragments as materials that can be plundered and combined in new ways to create works of art. Postmodern writing typically experiments with nontraditional forms and allows for multiple meanings. The lines between real and imaginary worlds are often blurred, as is the boundary between fiction and nonfiction. Other characteristics of postmodern literature are cultural diversity and an often playful self-consciousness; that is, an acknowledgment that literature is not a mirror that accurately reflects the world, but a created world unto itself. Gabriel García Márquez's *One Hundred Years of Solitude,* in which reality and fantasy are blended, is an exemplary postmodern novel.

See page 1067.

PROTAGONIST **The main character in fiction, drama, or narrative poetry.** The protagonist is the character on whom we focus our attention—the person whose conflict sets the plot in motion. (The character or force that blocks the protagonist is called the **antagonist.**) In *Beowulf* (Chapter 1), the title character is the protagonist and the monster Grendel his antagonist. Most protagonists are **rounded, dynamic**

characters who change in some important way by the end of the story. Whatever the protagonist's weaknesses, we still usually identify with his or her conflict and care about how it is resolved.

See page 541.

PROVERB **A short saying that expresses a common truth or experience, usually about human failings and the ways that people interact with one another.** Proverbs often incorporate such literary elements as **metaphor, alliteration, parallelism,** and **rhyme.**

See page 342.
See also *Epigram, Maxim.*

PUN **A play on the multiple meanings of a word or on two words that sound alike but have different meanings.** Many jokes and riddles are based on puns. ("Why was Cleopatra so negative? Answer: Because she was the queen of denial.") Shakespeare was one of the greatest punsters of all time. Dylan Thomas uses a pun in his poem, "Do Not Go Gentle into That Good Night" (Chapter 12):

> Do not go gentle into that good night,
> Old age should burn and rave at the close of
> day;
> Rage, rage against the dying of the light.

The casual farewell "good night" also means death.

QUATRAIN **A four-line stanza or poem or a group of four lines unified by a rhyme scheme.** The quatrain is the most common verse unit in English poetry. This quatrain from John Donne's "A Valediction: Forbidding Mourning" (Chapter 3) has the rhyme scheme *abab:*

> As virtuous men pass mildly away,
> And whisper to their souls, to go,
> Whilst some of their sad friends do say,
> The breath goes now, and some say, no:

See page 1075.

RATIONALISM **A philosophy that advocates the idea that one should use reason rather than emotion when one is attempting to discover the truth.** Rationalists believe that one must follow reason to determine what opinions are correct and what course of action one should take in any given situation. Opposed to rationalism is Romanticism, which places emphasis on the value of intuition and emotion in arriving at truth.

REALISM **In literature and art, the attempt to depict people and things as they really are, without idealization.** Realism as a movement developed during the mid–nineteenth century as a reaction against Romanticism. Realist writers believed that fiction should truthfully depict the harsh, gritty reality of everyday life without beautifying, sentimentalizing, or romanticizing it. The Norwegian playwright Henrik Ibsen was among the first to introduce realism to the stage. The English novelists Charles Dickens, George Eliot, Thomas Hardy, and Joseph Conrad are also considered realists.

See pages 961–962.
See also *Romanticism.*

REFRAIN **A repeated word, phrase, line, or group of lines.** While refrains are most common in poetry and songs, they are sometimes used in prose, particularly speeches. Refrains are used to create rhythm, build suspense, or emphasize important words or ideas.

See pages 185, 1257.

REFORMATION **The break from Catholicism and the authority of the pope that resulted in the establishment of the Protestant churches in the sixteenth century.** Most scholars date the beginning of the Reformation to 1517, the year Martin Luther nailed his *Ninety-five Theses* to the door of a church in Wittenburg, Germany. The *Theses* criticized the Catholic Church's abuse of indulgences and called for reform. In response the Church leaders condemned Luther, and he was forced to break from the Catholic Church and begin his own religious movement.

RENAISSANCE **A French word meaning "rebirth," used to designate the period in European history beginning in Italy in the fourteenth century and ending in the seventeenth century when scientific truths began to challenge long-accepted religious beliefs.** The Renaissance was characterized by a renewal of interest in classical learning and a focus on the study of human life on earth, not only on God and eternity.

See page 267.

RESOLUTION See *Plot.*

RHYME **The repetition of accented vowel sounds and all sounds following them in words that are close together in a poem.** *Park* and *bark* rhyme, as do *sorrow* and *borrow*. The most common type of rhyme, **end**

rhyme, occurs at the ends of lines. **Internal rhyme** occurs within lines. Both types are used throughout *The Rime of the Ancient Mariner* by Samuel Taylor Coleridge (Chapter 7), contributing to the poem's bouncy, song-like rhythm:

> The fair breeze blew, the white foam flew,
> The furrow followed free;
> We were the first that ever burst
> Into that silent sea.

When words sound similar but do not rhyme exactly, they are called **approximate rhymes** (or **half rhymes, slant rhymes,** or **imperfect rhymes**).

The pattern of rhymed lines in a poem is called its **rhyme scheme.** A rhyme scheme is indicated by giving each new rhyme a new letter of the alphabet. For example, the rhyme scheme of Coleridge's lines is *abcb.*

See pages 267, 309, 757, 1235.

RHYTHM **The alternation of stressed and unstressed syllables in language.** Rhythm occurs naturally in all forms of spoken and written language. The most obvious kind of rhythm is produced by **meter,** the regular pattern of stressed and unstressed syllables found in some poetry. Writers can also create less structured rhythms by using rhyme, repetition, pauses, and variations in line length and by balancing long and short words or phrases. (Poetry that is written without any regular meter or rhyme scheme is called **free verse.**)

See pages 309, 774.
See also *Free Verse, Meter.*

ROMANCE **Historically, a medieval verse narrative chronicling the adventures of a brave knight or other hero who must undertake a quest and overcome great danger for love of a noble lady or high ideal.** Such a heroic character is bound by the code of **chivalry,** which emphasizes loyalty to his lord and ready service to the oppressed. He also must adhere to the philosophy of **courtly love,** an idealized view of the relationship between the sexes in which a knight performs brave deeds to win the approval of his lady.

Today the term *romance* has come to mean any story that presents a world of wish-fulfillment, a world that is happier, more perfect, or more heroic than the real world. Characters in romances "live happily ever after" in a world where good always triumphs over evil. Many of today's most popular novels, movies, TV shows, and even cartoons are essentially romances. *Sir Gawain and the Green Knight* and Sir Thomas Malory's *Le Morte d'Arthur* (Chapter 2) are famous English romances.

See pages 114, 194, 195.

ROMANTICISM **A literary, artistic, and philosophical movement that developed as a reaction against neoclassicism in the late eighteenth century and dominated the early nineteenth century.** While classicism and neoclassicism emphasize reason, order, harmony, and restraint, Romanticism emphasizes emotion, imagination, intuition, freedom, personal experience, the beauty of nature, the primitive, the exotic, and even the grotesque. However, many critics feel that the traditional opposition between Romanticism and classicism is all too often forced and exaggerated.

In English literature, William Blake, Samuel Taylor Coleridge, William Wordsworth, Percy Bysshe Shelley, John Keats, Lord Byron, Mary Wollstonecraft Shelley and Sir Walter Scott are the leading Romantic writers.

RUN-ON LINE **A line of poetry that does not contain a pause or conclusion at the end, but rather continues on to the next line.** Run-on lines force the reader on to the next line. Only with the next line do they form a grammatical unit and thus make complete sense. Such lines are said to exhibit **enjambment** (French for "striding over"). The following lines from Margaret Atwood's "Siren Song" (page 1444) are run-on lines:

> This is the one song everyone
> would like to learn: the song
> that is irresistible:

See page 1083.
See also *End-stopped Line.*

SARCASM **A kind of particularly cutting irony, in which praise is used tauntingly to indicate its opposite in meaning.** The speaker's tone of voice can be an important clue in understanding this kind of irony. When a mud-soaked, windblown friend arrives for dinner, one might say sarcastically, "Why, don't you look lovely!"

SATIRE **A kind of writing that ridicules human weakness, vice, or folly in order to bring about social reform.** Satires often try to persuade the reader to do or believe something by showing the opposite view as absurd or—even more forcefully—vicious and inhumane. Among the most brilliant satirists in English literature are Geoffrey Chaucer, Alexander Pope, John Dryden, Jonathan Swift, Jane Austen, George Bernard Shaw, and Evelyn Waugh.

See pages 146, 565, 577, 595, 1385.

SCANSION See *Meter.*

SCOP **An Anglo-Saxon minstrel or poet.** Scops are the Anglo-Saxon equivalents to the ancient Celtic bards.

SESTET **A six-line stanza or poem or the last six lines of an Italian, or Petrarchan, sonnet.** The usual rhyme scheme of the sestet in an Italian sonnet is *cdecde* or *cdcdcd.* It follows an eight-line **octave** with the rhyme scheme *abbaabba.*

See pages 745, 1075.

SETTING **The time and place of a story or play.** Usually the setting is established early in a story. It may be presented immediately through descriptive details, as in Anita Desai's "Games at Twilight" (Chapter 13), or it may be revealed more gradually, as in Rudyard Kipling's "The Mark of the Beast" (Chapter 10). Setting often contributes greatly to a story's emotional effect. The exotic setting of V. S. Naipaul's "B. Wordsworth" (Chapter 13) sets the tone for its eccentric characters, while the green valley in William Wordsworth's "Tintern Abbey" (Chapter 7) creates a contemplative calm. Setting may also play a role in a story's conflict, as the fortress-like suburban houses do in Nadine Gordimer's "Once upon a Time" (Chapter 13). Two of the most important functions of setting are to reveal character and to suggest a theme, as the setting of blitzed London does in Graham Greene's "The Destructors" (Chapter 11).

See pages 81, 963, 1099, 1127, 1397.
See also *Atmosphere.*

SHORT STORY **A brief work of fiction.** The short story generally has a simpler plot than a novel and often reveals character through significant moments, or **epiphanies,** rather than through the accretion of many incidents or detailed descriptions.

See pages 1007, 1300.

SIMILE **A figure of speech that makes a comparison between two seemingly unlike things by using a connective word such as *like, than,* or *resembles.*** The following simile, from Lord Byron's "She Walks in Beauty" (Chapter 8), is one of the most famous in English literary history:

> She walks in beauty, like the night
> Of cloudless climes and starry skies;

An **epic simile,** also called a **Homeric simile,** is an extended simile in which many parallels are made between two dissimilar things.

See pages 99, 811.
See also *Figure of Speech, Metaphor.*

SOCIAL DARWINISM **The notion that, in society, only the fittest will survive.** This idea is an extension of Darwin's scientific theories of natural selection—though Darwin was not involved in its development. Social Darwinism was used to justify rigid class distinctions, indifference to social ills, and doctrines of racial superiority.

SOCIALISM **A political movement that advocates the idea that the ownership and operation of the means of production and distribution should be owned by the community rather than by private individuals.** This political movement is related to communism in that it seeks to eliminate class distinctions within society.

SOLILOQUY **A long speech in which a character who is usually alone onstage expresses his or her private thoughts or feelings.** The soliloquy is an old dramatic convention that was particularly popular in Shakespeare's day. Perhaps the most famous soliloquy is the "To be, or not to be" speech in Shakespeare's play *Hamlet.* Another major soliloquy occurs in *Macbeth,* when Macbeth bewails his wife's death in the celebrated "Tomorrow, and tomorrow, and tomorrow" speech (Chapter 4).

See also *Monologue.*

SONNET **A fourteen-line lyric poem, usually written in iambic pentameter, that has one of several rhyme schemes.** There are two major types of sonnets. The oldest sonnet form is the **Italian sonnet,** also called the **Petrarchan sonnet** (after the fourteenth-century Italian poet Petrarch, who popularized the form). The Petrarchan sonnet is divided into two parts: an eight-line **octave** with the rhyme scheme *abbaabba* and a six-line **sestet** with the rhyme scheme *cdecde* or *cdcdcd.* The octave usually presents a problem, poses a question, or expresses an idea, which the sestet then resolves, answers, or drives home. The transition from octave to sestet is known as the **turn.** Louise Labé's Sonnet 23, Elizabeth Barrett Browning's Sonnet 43 (Chapter 9), and John Keats's "On First Looking into Chapman's Homer" (Chapter 8) are written in the Petrarchan form.

The other major sonnet form, which was widely used by Shakespeare, is called the **Shakespearean sonnet,** or the **English sonnet** (Chapter 4). It has three four-line units, or **quatrains,** followed by a concluding two-line unit, or **couplet.** The organization of thought in the Shakespearean sonnet usually corresponds to this structure. The three quatrains often express related ideas or examples, while the couplet summarizes the poet's conclusion or message found in the first three. The turn in the Shakespearean sonnet usually occurs during the transition from the third quatrain to the couplet. The rhyme scheme of the Shakespearean sonnet is *abab cdcd efef gg.*

A third type of sonnet, the **Spenserian sonnet,** was developed by Edmund Spenser. Like the Shakespearean sonnet, the Spenserian sonnet is divided into three quatrains and a couplet, but it uses a rhyme scheme that links the quatrains: *abab bcbc cdcd ee.*

A group of sonnets on a related theme is called a **sonnet sequence** or a **sonnet cycle.**

See pages 267, 268, 385, 390, 745, 843, 953, 1077, 1263, 1291.

SPEAKER **The imaginary voice, or persona, assumed by the author of a poem.** This voice is often not identified immediately or directly. Rather, the reader gradually comes to understand that a unique voice is speaking and that this speaker's characteristics must be interpreted as they are revealed. This process is an especially important part of reading a **lyric poem.**

SPEECH **A more or less formal address delivered to an audience or assembly, or the written or printed copy of this address.** The use of the word *speech* to designate an address to an audience seems to have entered into the English language in the sixteenth century.

Speeches are most commonly delivered by politicians, political activists, and other public figures.

SPENSERIAN STANZA **A nine-line stanza with the rhyme scheme *ababbcbcc.*** The first eight lines of the stanza are in iambic pentameter, and the ninth line is an **alexandrine**—that is, a line of iambic hexameter. The form was created by Edmund Spenser for his long poem *The Faerie Queene.* Several English Romantic poets have used the Spenserian stanza, including John Keats, Percy Bysshe Shelley, Lord Byron (all in Chapter 8), and Robert Burns.

See page 809.

SPRUNG RHYTHM **A term coined by Gerard Manley Hopkins (Chapter 9) to designate his unconventional use of poetic meter.** Instead of the regular, musical **meter** of most poetry, Hopkins uses sounds that impede smooth reading and echo the sound of Anglo-Saxon poetry, which greatly influenced him. Sprung rhythm is based on the stressed syllables in a line without regard for the number of unstressed syllables; it also makes frequent use of **alliteration** and inverted syntax.

See page 956.

STANZA **A group of consecutive lines in a poem that form a single unit.** A stanza in a poem is something like a paragraph in prose: It often expresses a unit of thought. A stanza may consist of only one line or of any number of lines beyond that. The word *stanza* is Italian for "stopping place" or "place to rest."

STREAM OF CONSCIOUSNESS **A writing style that tries to depict the random flow of thoughts, emotions, memories, and associations running through a character's mind.** The term *interior monologue* is often used interchangeably with "stream of consciousness." James Joyce (Chapter 13) and Virginia Woolf (Chapter 11) were among the first to experiment with the stream-of-consciousness style in their novels.

STYLE **The manner in which writers or speakers say what they wish to say.** An author's style simultaneously expresses his or her ideas and reveals his or her unique way of expressing them. Style is closely connected to **diction,** or word choice, and, depending on what the author wants to communicate, can be formal or casual, plain or ornate, abstract or concrete, as well as comic, poetic, forceful, journalistic, and so on. Sir Francis Bacon (Chapter 3) and James Joyce (Chapter 13) are both often studied for their styles.

See pages 315, 350, 595, 820, 821, 944, 1172.
See also *Diction.*

SUSPENSE **The uncertainty or anxiety we feel about what is going to happen next in a story.** Writers often create suspense by dropping hints or clues that something—especially something bad—is going to happen. In "The Demon Lover" by Elizabeth Bowen (Chapter 11), we begin to feel suspense when Mrs. Drover receives a mysterious letter that makes her lips "go white"; our anxiety increases sharply when the flashback reveals that the letter writer is her old fiancé; and our suspense reaches a climax when she escapes into a taxi and we discover who the driver is.

SYMBOL **A person, place, thing, or event that stands both for itself and for something beyond itself.** Many symbols have become widely recognized: A lion is a symbol of power; a dove is a symbol of peace. These established symbols are sometimes called **public symbols.** Writers also often invent new, personal symbols whose meaning is revealed in their work. For example, the old house in Graham Greene's "The Destructors" (Chapter 11) is a symbol of civilization and beauty.

See pages 730, 829, 871, 1040, 1113, 1148, 1208, 1215, 1267, 1288, 1306, 1369.

SYMBOLISM **A literary movement that began in France during the late nineteenth century and advocated the use of highly personal symbols to suggest ideas, emotions, and moods.** The French symbolists believed that emotions are fleeting, individual, and essentially inexpressible—and that the poet is, therefore, forced to suggest meaning rather than directly express it. Many twentieth-century writers were influenced by the symbolists, including T. S. Eliot, William Butler Yeats, James Joyce, Dylan Thomas, and Virginia Woolf (Chapter 11, 12, and 13).

SYNECDOCHE (sih NEHK duh kee) **A figure of speech in which a part represents the whole.** The capital city of a nation, for example, is often spoken of as though it were the government: "Washington is claiming popular support for its position." Another example is "our daily bread" meaning food. Synecdoche is closely related to **metonymy.**

See also *Metonymy.*

SYNESTHESIA (sihn ehs THEE zhuh) **In literature, a term used for descriptions of one kind of sensation in terms of another.** For example, color may be described as sound (a "loud" yellow), sound as taste (how "sweet" the sound), odor as tangible (a "sharp" smell), and so on.

See page 847.

TANKA **A traditional five-line form of Japanese poetry.** The tanka follows a strict form: The first and third lines have five syllables each, and the second, fourth, and fifth lines each have seven syllables.

See pages 864, 866, 869.

TERCET **A triplet, or stanza of three lines, in which each line ends with the same rhyme.** It is also either of the two three-line groups forming the sestet of a **sonnet.**

TERZA RIMA **An interlocking, three-line stanza form with the rhyme scheme *aba bcb cdc ded* and so on.** Terza rima is an Italian verse form originally devised by Dante for *The Divine Comedy.* Among the many English poems that borrowed the form, Shelley's "Ode to the West Wind" (Chapter 8) is one of the most famous.

See page 824.

THEME **The central idea or insight about human experience revealed in a work of literature.** A theme is not the same as the subject of a work, which can usually be expressed in a word or two: old age, ambition, love. The theme is the idea the writer wishes to convey about that subject—the writer's view of the world or revelation about human nature. For example, one theme of James Joyce's "Araby" (Chapter 13) might be stated this way: One of the painful aspects of growing up is that some of our dreams turn out to be illusions.

A theme may also be different from a **moral,** which is a lesson or rule about how to live. The theme of "Araby" stated above, for example, would not make sense as a moral.

While some stories, poems, and plays have themes that are directly stated, most themes are **implied.** It is up to the reader to piece together all the clues the writer has provided about the work's total meaning.

See pages 42, 73, 296, 302, 325, 742, 984, 1009, 1079, 1200, 1243, 1285, 1023, 1223, 1357.

TONE **The attitude a writer takes toward the reader, a subject, or a character.** Tone is conveyed through the writer's choice of words and details. For example, Jonathan Swift's *A Modest Proposal* (Chapter 5) is satiric in tone, while the tone of "Pied Beauty" by Gerard Manley Hopkins (Chapter 9) might be described as awed.

See pages 85, 161, 203, 273, 277, 296, 297, 298, 299, 404, 496, 562, 588, 620, 621, 667, 839, 931, 1021, 1069, 1181, 1331, 1407.

TOTALITARIANISM **A system of government that advocates the rule of an absolute dictator or a single political party.** Totalitarian governments forbid any opposition to the government party or ruler to emerge within the state. Consequently, free speech and other liberties guaranteed in democracies are denied to those living under a totalitarian government. George Orwell's *Animal Farm* explores the consequences of a totalitarian regime.

See page 1140.

TRAGEDY **A play, novel, or other narrative depicting serious and important events, in which the main character comes to an unhappy end.** In a tragedy, the main character is usually dignified, courageous, and often high ranking. This character's downfall may be caused by a **tragic flaw**—an error in judgment or a character weakness—or the downfall may result from forces beyond his or her control. The **tragic hero** usually wins some self-knowledge and wisdom, even though he or she suffers defeat, possibly even death. Tragedy is distinct from **comedy,** in which an ordinary character overcomes obstacles to get what he or she wants. *Beowulf* (Chapter 1), Shakespeare's *Macbeth* (Chapter 4), and John Milton's *Paradise Lost* (Chapter 3) are all tragedies.

See page 404.
See also *Comedy.*

TURN See *Sonnet.*

See pages 267, 385, 1075, 1291.

UNDERSTATEMENT **A figure of speech that consists of saying less than what is really meant or saying something with less force than is appropriate.** Understatement is the opposite of **hyperbole** and is a form of **irony.** You are using understatement if you come in from a torrential downpour and say, "It's a bit wet out there," or if you describe a Great Dane as "not exactly a small dog." Understatement can be used to create a kind of deadpan humor, but it can also function as a sustained ironic tone throughout a work, as in Wole Soyinka's "Telephone Conversation" (Chapter 13).

See also *Hyperbole, Irony.*

VERNACULAR See *Dialect.*

See page 8.

VILLANELLE **A nineteen-line poem divided into five tercets (three-line stanzas), each with the rhyme scheme *aba,* and a final quatrain with the rhyme scheme *abaa.*** Line 1 is repeated entirely to form lines 6, 12, and 18, while line 3 is repeated as lines 9, 15, and 19. Thus, there are only two rhymes in the poem, and the two lines used as **refrains** (lines 1 and 3) are paired as the final couplet. The villanelle was originally used in French pastoral poetry. Dylan Thomas's "Do Not Go Gentle into That Good Night" (Chapter 12) is an example of a modern villanelle.

See page 1235

WIT **A quality of speech or writing that combines verbal cleverness with keen perception, especially of the incongruous.** The definition of wit has undergone dramatic changes over the centuries. In the Middle Ages it meant "common sense"; in the Renaissance it meant "intelligence"; and in the seventeenth century it meant "originality of thought." The modern meaning of *wit* began to develop during the seventeenth and eighteenth centuries with the writings of John Dryden and Alexander Pope (Chapter 6). In his *Essay on Criticism,* Pope said:

> True wit is Nature to advantage dressed:
> What oft was thought, but ne'er so well
> expressed

Perhaps the best examples of more modern wit can be found in the works of Oscar Wilde and George Bernard Shaw.

The World of Work

The ability to read critically and write effectively is your driver's license to navigating today's world. Without strong reading and writing skills, you will feel as frustrated and powerless as you do in a traffic jam. A future college student must be able to write application essays and understand scholarship guidelines. A mechanic must be able to read instruction manuals to use new equipment. A renter must understand a lease before getting an apartment. A supervisor must be able to write an effective memo to present ideas. In your life and in the world of work, you will rely on reading and writing skills to learn new information, communicate effectively, and achieve the results you want.

Reading

To avoid becoming stranded in life and in the world of work, you will need to learn to read **informative documents** and **persuasive documents.**

Informative Documents

Informative documents are like road maps: They provide facts and information. They can also be good places to check when you want to verify or clarify information from other sources. If a friend writes down directions that you are uncertain about, you consult a map to verify the directions. Likewise, if you read on a Web site an angry customer's complaint about repairs on a computer you just bought, you could review the warranty to see if the information is valid. Two kinds of common informative documents are consumer documents and workplace documents.

CONSUMER DOCUMENTS You have probably already made thousands of buying decisions in your life. As you grow older, however, buying decisions often carry bigger consequences. Should you sign a six- or a twelve-month apartment lease? Should you buy or lease a car? Being informed about the details of major purchases can help you avoid costly mistakes. This information can be found in **consumer documents,** such as warranties, contracts, product information, and instruction manuals.

- **Warranties** describe what happens if the product does not work properly or breaks down. Warranties note how long the product is covered for repair or replacement, which repairs the warranty does and does not cover, and how to receive repair service.

> The SureFocus digital camera is guaranteed to be free of defects in material or workmanship under normal use for a period of one (1) year from the date of purchase. Equipment covered by the warranty will be repaired by SureFocus Repair Members WITHOUT CHARGE, except for insurance, transportation, and handling charges. A copy of this warranty card and proof of purchase must be enclosed when returning equipment for warranty service. The warranty does not apply in the following cases:
>
> - the camera has been damaged through abuse
> - leaking batteries or other liquids have caused damage to the camera
> - unauthorized repair technicians have attempted to service the camera

Reading Standard 2.3 (see pages A48–A50)
Writing Standard 1.8, 2.5a-d (see pages A51–A52)

- **Contracts** provide details about an agreement that a buyer enters into with a company. A lease for an apartment or a car is a contract that defines the terms of the lease, including how long it lasts, what the responsibilities of the customer—also known as the lessee—and the landlord or car company are, how to end the lease, and what the penalties for breaking the lease are. A lease always includes a space for the customer's signature, which signifies agreement with the terms of the contract. Below is a portion of a typical apartment lease.

This apartment lease is entered into by Althea Brown, hereinafter "Lessee," and Sun Valley Apartments.

1. **Grant of Lease:** Sun Valley Apartments does hereby lease unto Lessee Apartment #B-2, located at 101 Saguaro Drive, El Cajon, CA.
2. **Term of Lease:** This lease shall begin on the first day of August, 2008, and extend until the first day of August, 2009, after which the lessee can extend the lease month to month until terminated according to the terms described below.
3. **Rental Payments:** Lessee agrees to pay as rent the sum of $800 per month each month during the term of this lease before the fifth day of each month.

- **Product information** describes the basic features and materials of a product. A suit label would tell whether the suit is 100 percent wool or a blend of materials and would give cleaning instructions. Product information on the box of a cordless telephone would list the frequency, number of channels, and features such as automatic redial, memory, caller ID, voice-mail indicator light, and other features.

- **Instruction manuals** tell the owner how to set up, operate, and troubleshoot problems with a product. Instruction manuals also include safety precautions, diagrams, and descriptions of the product's features.

WORKPLACE DOCUMENTS Two common workplace documents—**procedure manuals** and **memoranda**—can tell you how to do your job and how to stay informed so you are both knowledgeable and effective.

- **Procedure manuals** are the step-by-step directions that tell employees how to serve customers, operate machinery, report problems, request vacation, or do anything that the company wants performed in a certain way. Procedure manuals are often used to train new employees and to clarify procedures for existing employees. As you read a procedure manual, pay attention to the specific instructions so you know exactly how to carry out the procedures.

- **Memoranda** —or memos—are the standard form of communication in many businesses. Memos are concise messages, generally covering only one topic. For example, an employee might send a memo to a supervisor reporting on the status of a project, or a supervisor might send a brief summary of discussions and decisions made in a meeting. To read a memo effectively, first check the subject line at the top to learn the topic of the memo. As you read, notice the pattern of organization in the body of the memo. Headings or bullets may indicate the main ideas. Pay attention to the purpose of the memo to decide whether and how to respond. Is the memo summarizing information, requesting action, or providing facts, such as dates and prices?

Persuasive Documents

While informative documents are like road maps, persuasive documents are like travel brochures, trying to influence a reader's destination. Persuasive documents try to persuade readers to believe or act in a certain way. It is important for you to be able to distinguish between informative and persuasive public documents. For example, a policy statement from a county commission about recycling might quote facts, but its primary purpose is to influence citizens to support the commission's position. By critically reading persuasive public documents, you can evaluate whether you agree or disagree. Persuasive public documents include **policy statements, political platforms, speeches,** and **debates.**

- A **policy statement** outlines a person's or group's position on an issue and sometimes provides the rationale for that position. For example, the mayor might issue a policy statement explaining why she supports or opposes a tax increase for school construction. The policy statement gives the main points for the mayor's position and may provide facts or use rhetorical devices to support the position. A policy statement may also include a **call to action,** or a request for readers to take a specific action. Some organizations issue policy statements to endorse specific legislation, hoping to win the support of the voting public or of the lawmakers who can create the legislation.
- A **political platform** outlines a political candidate's position on a variety of issues so voters know where the candidate stands. It may also set forth the candidate's goals and describe the beliefs that guide his or her positions. The positions and goals are known as the *planks* of the platform. The audience for a political platform is usually friendly to the candidate, and the platform is intended to rouse support and to persuade undecided voters. Sometimes a platform will also address and rebut opposing viewpoints. Below is an excerpt from the political platform of a city council candidate about the issue of noise pollution.

> Rocky Mount is a quiet and peaceful place that does not need more intrusion from the local government to reduce noise levels. We are not close to a major airport, so we do not hear the regular drone of airplanes. Concertgoers hear Beethoven and Mozart, not the loud rock groups that play in larger cities. Noise pollution is an occasional, not regular or excessive, problem that can be handled without more city ordinances. Therefore, I do not support the development of laws to address the nonexistent issue of noise pollution.

- A **persuasive speech** is designed to change an audience's attitudes or beliefs or to move an audience to action. A speaker may make persuasive arguments and address audience counterclaims by using reasoning and rhetorical devices, such as repetition. (For more on **persuasive speaking,** see page 692.)
- A **debate** involves two teams who take turns discussing a controversial topic. The topic under discussion is called the proposition. One side argues for the proposition, and the other side argues against it. Each side also refutes, or argues against, its opponent's case.

CRITIQUING PERSUASIVE DOCUMENTS Persuasive documents use logical, emotional, and ethical appeals to be convincing. Notice how these appeals are used to help you critique a document's validity and truthfulness.

- **Logical appeals** are based on reasons and supporting evidence. As you read, notice whether the evidence is based on reliable facts that can be confirmed through other, unbiased sources. If you are unsure, consult informative public documents, such as state laws, to verify the evidence. Notice whether the appeal makes sense and avoids fallacies, such as **hasty generalizations** or **circular reasoning.** A hasty generalization is a conclusion based on insufficient evidence. Circular reasoning occurs when the reason for an opinion is simply the opinion stated in different words.
- **Emotional appeals** rely on strong feelings to persuade readers. The writer may use examples that tug on heartstrings or arouse anger. Vivid language may make either positive or negative associations with the topic. Evaluate emotional appeals based on all of the evidence. If an argument is based primarily on emotion, the case may be weak. Watch out for signs of bias and stereotypes—including words such as *always* and *never*—that suggest the reasoning is unsound.
- **Ethical appeals** rely on the reader's sense of right and wrong. For example, a writer might persuade an audience to share a certain view by implying that the opposing position is unpatriotic or selfish.

Critique a persuasive document by seeing how fairly the writer treats the topic. Does the writer use credible evidence? Does he or she know enough about the topic to be believed?

Your Turn Choose a persuasive public document, and critique its effectiveness and validity. Identify the appeals and the call to action, if any. Consult at least one informative public document to verify information presented in the persuasive document.

Writing

Writing is your passport to exciting places in life. A powerful résumé can win you the job of your dreams. A memo proposing cost-saving measures can earn you a promotion. A letter to your city council can lead to a new soccer field for a recreational league. Clear, effective writing is one of the best skills you can have as you enter the world of work.

Job Applications and Résumés

One of the first places you will use writing beyond school will be in a job application or résumé. To fill out a **job application** completely and accurately, first read the instructions carefully. Type or write neatly in blue or black ink. Include all information requested. If a question does not apply to you, write *N/A* or *not applicable* in the blank. Proofread your completed form and neatly correct any errors. Finally, submit the form to the correct person.

A **résumé** summarizes your skills, education, achievements, and work experience. Prepare a résumé to use when you apply for a job or when you seek admission to a college or special program. Keep in mind that a résumé should be tailored to match the target audience. Select and highlight the skills and experiences that would most appeal to the employer or college reading the résumé. For a college or academic program, for example, you would highlight a strong GPA, successful class projects, and involvement in school clubs. The language would create a sophisticated, but not artificial, tone. For an employer, on the other hand, you would highlight work experience, both paid and volunteer, and the skills you learned on the job, using clear and direct language.

Here are some more tips to help you create a résumé:

- Give complete information about work experience, including job title, dates of employment, company, and location.
- Do not use *I;* instead, use short, parallel phrases that describe duties and activities.
- Proofread carefully. Mistakes on a résumé make the writer seem careless—not a positive quality for an employee.

Workplace Documents

Memos are the standard form of communication in many businesses. To write a concise, easy-to-understand memo, you must first understand your main purpose for writing. Are you writing to provide information or to make a request? Memos should provide all essential information—*who, what, when, where, why,* and *how*—and get quickly to the point. If you are asking for action and information, include a deadline. Memos follow a standard format that includes, at the top of the document, the date, the recipient, the sender, and the subject. Notice how the following memo gets right to the point and communicates information clearly and directly.

Date:	February 25, 2008
To:	Sophia Cervenka
From:	Cole Hurley
Subject:	Computer Training

Training on the new software will begin Monday, March 10, 2008. Members of your department who are interested in receiving training should call me at extension 4390 by Friday, March 7, to sign up. Training will last from 8:00 A.M.–3:00 P.M. The next training session will be held on March 18.

Word-Processing Features

A clear message is essential in workplace communication, but the appearance of workplace documents also counts. Learn to use word-processing features to your advantage by making documents that are easy on both the eyes and the mind.

- **Margins** are the space that surrounds the text on a page. Most word-processing programs automatically set side and top margins. You can adjust these default margins to suit your purpose.
- A **font** is a complete set of characters (including letters, numbers, and punctuation marks) in a particular size and design. For most workplace documents, use a font that is businesslike and easy to read. (For more on **fonts,** see page 1503.)
- **Line spacing** is the white space between lines of text. Most letters and memos are single-spaced to conserve space, but longer reports are often double-spaced to allow room for handwritten edits and comments.

INTEGRATING DATABASES, GRAPHICS, AND SPREADSHEETS Workplace documents often integrate databases, graphics, and spreadsheets into text. For example, a pie chart or a spreadsheet can show budget expenses, or a list of customers in a specific ZIP Code might be integrated from a database into a report. Add features such as these to communicate your ideas more effectively. Place a graphic close to the related text, and explain the graphic's context. For help with integrating visuals and other components into documents, consult the Help section of your word-processing program or ask your teacher to help you.

RÉSUMÉ FORMAT Word-processing features can help you create an attractive format for your résumé. Here are some guidelines to remember:

- **Make sure the résumé is not cluttered. Use wide margins for the top, bottom, and sides, and use double-spacing between sections to make the résumé easy to scan for information.**
- **Consider using a different font, boldface, and a larger point size for your name and for headings. Be sure all the fonts are easy to read.**

The following résumé was written by a student interested in a sales job. He highlighted skills and experiences that show his interpersonal skills and initiative and used an attractive, easy-to-read format.

MIGUEL GUERRERO
1902 Greig Street
Santa Rosa, CA 95403
(707) 555-0085
E-mail: mguerrero@fhs.k12.ca.us

EDUCATION

Senior, Forsythe High School
Grade-point average: 3.3 (B)

WORK EXPERIENCE

Summer 2007–present

Waiter, Starlite Restaurant

- Serve customers quickly and efficiently
- Train new employees in effective customer service
- Twice awarded Star Employee

Summer 2006

Campaign Volunteer, Antonio Suarez Campaign for Mayor

- Assisted in door-to-door campaigns
- Collected and input data for mailing list
- Organized teen volunteers to distribute flyers

SKILLS

Communication: Telephone sales, oral presentations
Computers: Word processing, Web design

ACTIVITIES

Debate team, soccer team, student government representative

REFERENCES

Janet Matteson, Owner
Starlite Restaurant
(707) 555-0146

David Cho, Principal
Forsythe High School
(707) 555-0013

Your Turn Create a résumé for your dream job. Think about what experiences and skills you have that would appeal to a potential employer. Present this information in a clear, concise, and eye-catching way.

Writer's Handbook

The Writing Process

Effective writing involves a process. The steps in this process, called a **recursive** process because you may repeat them several times, are like those of a spiral staircase—you must travel around and around, yet with each revolution you ascend toward your goal. While each writer's process is slightly different, most effective writers follow the steps below.

Stages of the Writing Process	
Prewriting	• Identify your purpose and audience. • Choose a topic and an appropriate form. • Formulate your thesis, or main idea, about the topic. • Gather information about the topic. • Organize information in a preliminary plan.
Drafting	• Draft an introduction that seizes your readers' attention and provides necessary background information. • State your thesis clearly and assertively. • Develop body paragraphs that elaborate on key ideas. • Follow an organizational plan. • Draft a conclusion that restates your thesis and leaves readers with something to think about.
Evaluating and Revising	• Evaluate your draft. • Revise to improve its content, organization, and style.
Proofreading and Publishing	• Proofread your draft, and correct errors in spelling, punctuation, grammar, and usage. • Share your final draft with readers. • Reflect on your writing experience.

Throughout the writing process, make sure you do the following:

- **Keep your ideas coherent and focused.** Keep your specific purpose in mind to help you present a tightly reasoned argument. Evaluate every idea to make sure it will focus your readers on your main point, and make that point clear in your thesis statement.
- **Share your own perspective.** You bring your own ideas to every piece you write. Share not only information you have gathered but also your viewpoint on your topic. Let your natural voice shine through to readers.

- **Keep your audience in mind.** Consider your readers' backgrounds and interests. If your form is not assigned, choose a form that will grab your readers, such as a song, editorial, screenplay, or letter.
- **Plan to publish.** Labor over every piece as though it will be published or shared with an audience. Enlist the help of a classmate when you proofread a finished piece. Use the following questions to guide you.

Questions for Proofreading
1. Is every sentence complete, not a fragment or run-on?
2. Are punctuation marks used correctly?
3. Are the first letters of sentences, proper nouns, and proper adjectives capitalized?
4. Does each verb agree in number with its subject? Are verb forms and tenses used correctly?
5. Are subject and object forms of personal pronouns used correctly? Does every pronoun agree with a clear antecedent in number and gender?

When revising and proofreading, use the symbols below.

Symbols for Revising and Proofreading

Symbol	Example	Meaning of Symbol
≡	805 Linden avenue	Capitalize a lowercase letter.
/	the First of May	Lowercase a capital letter.
∧	one of my friends	Insert a missing word, letter, or punctuation mark.
∧ ⎯	at the onset ~~beginning~~	Replace a word.
ℓ	Give me a a number	Delete a word, letter, or punctuation mark.
∽	beleive	Change the order of letters.
¶	¶"Yes," she answered.	Begin a new paragraph.

Paragraphs

The Parts of a Paragraph

Paragraphs can be as different as oak trees are from pines. Some paragraphs are a single word; others run several pages. Their uses differ, too: A paragraph may present a main idea, connect one idea to another, emphasize an idea, or simply give the reader's eyes a rest in a long passage.

Many paragraphs in essays and other types of nonfiction, including workplace writing, develop one main idea. A main-idea paragraph is often built from a **topic sentence, supporting sentences,** and a **clincher sentence.**

Parts of a Paragraph	
Topic Sentence	• is an explicit statement of the paragraph's main idea or central focus • is often the first or second sentence in a paragraph, but may appear at the end to emphasize or summarize
Supporting Sentences	• provide elaboration by supporting, building, or proving the main idea • often include details of the following types: *sensory details:* information about sight, sound, taste, smell, and texture *facts:* details that can be proved true *examples:* specific instances that illustrate a general idea *anecdotes:* brief stories about people or events that illustrate a main idea *analogies:* comparisons between familiar ideas and unfamiliar concepts
Clincher Sentence	• may restate the topic sentence, summarize supporting details, offer a final thought, or help readers refocus on the main idea of a long paragraph

Tip Not every paragraph needs a clincher sentence. Use one for a strong or dramatic touch or for renewing a main idea in a lengthy or complicated paragraph.

Tip Not every paragraph has, or needs, a topic sentence. In fiction, paragraphs rarely have topic sentences. Paragraphs presenting time sequences (how-to instructions or histories, for example) may also lack topic sentences—the steps or events themselves focus the reader's mind. Finally, a paragraph may imply, or suggest, its main idea without directly stating it in a topic sentence. In your school writing, however, topic sentences are a help: They keep you focused on each paragraph's topic.

PUTTING THE PARTS TOGETHER You can clearly see the parts of a paragraph in the following example. Notice that its topic sentence expresses the paragraph's main idea and that the clincher sentence re-emphasizes it.

> The arrival of printing in England was to be of far more importance than any of the changes of ruler during the Wars of the Roses. Up until this time books had been copied out by hand by scribes in monasteries or other workshops, a long and laborious process. As a result books were rare and very costly. Printing by machine meant that they could be cheap and plentiful. The knowledge books contained could also be spread far wider, reaching new audiences, as more people than ever before learned to read. When William Caxton set up his printing presses in the precincts of Westminster Abbey in 1476, it was to be a landmark in the history of the English language and literature, daily life, and culture.
>
> Sir Roy Strong, *The Story of Britain*

Topic Sentence

Supporting Sentences

Clincher Sentence

Qualities of Paragraphs

Think about trees again. Each type is so distinct: a pine with its needles and cones, a magnolia with its glossy leaves and huge blossoms. While different, each is a pleasing whole. Paragraphs achieve this wholeness, too, through two major qualities: **unity** and **coherence**.

UNITY Unity means that all of a paragraph's supporting sentences really fit the main idea—no pine cones should poke out among the magnolia blooms. In other words, all of the supporting sentences must work together and stay on the topic. Unity is achieved when

- all sentences relate to the paragraph's main idea, whether it is stated in a topic sentence or implied, or
- all sentences relate to a sequence of events.

COHERENCE When a paragraph has coherence, the ideas are arranged in an order that makes sense so that the reader moves easily from one idea to another. The paragraph flows; it does not bounce readers around or befuddle them. You can create coherence in a paragraph by paying attention to

- the order you use to arrange ideas
- the connections you make between ideas to show readers how the ideas are related.

To create coherence through the arrangement of your ideas, choose the type of order that best fits your purpose. The chart on the next page explains how to use the four main types of order.

Types of Order		
Order	**When to Use**	**How It Works**
Chronological	• to tell a story or relate an event • to explain a process • to show cause and effect	• presents events in the order they happen • shows how things change over time
Spatial	• to describe individual features • to create a complete visual picture	• arranges details by location in space—top to bottom, left to right, near to far, center to edge, and so on
Order of Importance	• to inform • to persuade	• arranges ideas and details from most important to least, or vice versa • places emphasis where the writer thinks it is most effective
Logical	• to inform or to persuade, often by classifying: defining, dividing a subject into parts, or comparing and contrasting	• groups ideas or details together in ways that illustrate the relationships between them; for example, as parts of a whole

Tip The types of order can overlap or can be used in combination. For example, to explain an effect, you might move **chronologically** through its causes, describing the first cause, which leads to the second cause, and so on. However, suppose that three simultaneous causes produce a single effect. You could discuss those causes in **order of importance.**

Guide readers through your clearly arranged ideas by pointing out the connections among them. Show connections by using **direct references** (repetition of ideas), **transitional expressions,** and **parallelism**. The chart on the next page details how you can use these three types of connections to add to the coherence of your writing.

Connecting Ideas

Type of Connection	How to Use It
Direct References, or Repetition of Ideas	• Refer to a noun or pronoun used earlier in the paragraph. • Repeat a word used earlier. • Substitute synonyms for words used earlier.
Transitional Expressions	• Compare ideas (*also, and, another, in the same way, just, like, likewise, moreover, similarly, too*). • Contrast ideas (*although, but, however, in spite of, instead, nevertheless, on the other hand, still, yet*). • Show cause and effect (*accordingly, as a result, because, consequently, for, since, so, so that, therefore*). • Indicate time (*after, at last, before, early, eventually, first, later, next, then, thereafter, until, when, while*). • Show place (*above, across, adjacent, behind, beside, beyond, down, here, in, near, over, there*). • Show importance (*first, last, less significant, mainly, more important, to begin with*).
Parallelism	• Use the same grammatical forms or structures to balance related ideas in a sentence. • Sparingly, use the same sentence structures to show connections between related ideas in a paragraph or composition.

Your Turn **Develop two paragraphs on a single topic that interests you. First, choose two primary methods of organizing ideas on the topic (keeping in mind that you may use a combination of orders). Then, plan a topic sentence, a variety of supporting details, and a clincher sentence for each of your two paragraphs. Finally, draft your paragraphs, clearly organizing and connecting ideas and eliminating any ideas that detract from your focus.**

The Writer's Language

Revising often focuses on a piece's content and organization. However, to communicate ideas effectively, you must work just as carefully to revise a piece's **style**—how you express those ideas. When revising your style, fine-tune your writing's **sound, word choice,** and **sentence variety,** and use **rhetorical devices** to grab reader attention and make your ideas clear and interesting.

A SOUND STYLE Keep your **audience** and **purpose** in mind to help you choose a suitable **voice, tone,** and **level of formality** for a piece of writing.

Voice In writing, voice is your unique personality on paper. Just as you recognize a friend's spoken voice, you can recognize the work of favorite writers by the unique way they express ideas. To evaluate your own writing voice, read your work out loud. If your writing does not sound natural, revise it to bring your personality to life.

Tone Tone reveals your attitude toward a topic and audience. Always use an appropriate tone for your audience and purpose. For example, if your purpose is to persuade readers to share your view on an important issue, your tone should be serious and respectful.

Level of Formality You would not don formal wear for a beach party, and neither should you use a casual, informal style for a serious essay on a subject about which you care deeply. Match the level of formality to your subject, your audience, and your purpose. Look at these examples.

INFORMAL	Some people shouldn't own pets. Period.
FORMAL	Certain people should not own pets under any circumstances.

WORD CHOICE Make sure your words express the ideas you want them to express. Every word should help create a clear, vivid picture of what you mean and communicate the connotation you want.

Precise Language Replace vague language in your writing with words that are distinct and strong. For example, you might describe a big boulder you saw on a hike as being *as huge as a car* or *as mammoth as a double-decker bus.* You could mention that the boulder *rumbled* down the hill or *squatted* by the path. Using **precise verbs, nouns,** and **adjectives** like these will make your writing clearer and more interesting.

Connotations As you choose words, notice their **connotations**—the emotional effects they create. For instance, the word *cheap* means "economical," but it also has the negative connotation of being poor in quality. The word *inexpensive* expresses the same idea as *cheap* but in a more positive way. Choose words carefully by considering their effects.

SENTENCE VARIETY Readers can become bored with writing that uses the same types of sentences over and over. Create variety by varying the beginnings of your sentences and mixing simple, compound, and complex sentences.

RHETORICAL DEVICES To give your ideas a greater impact, use the rhetorical devices of **parallelism, repetition,** and **analogy.**

Parallelism Just as a train stays on its tracks because they are parallel, readers will stay on track if your written ideas are grammatically parallel.

NOT PARALLEL	More lives are saved when **drivers wear seat belts** and **motorcyclists are wearing helmets.**
PARALLEL	More lives are saved when **drivers wear seat belts** and **motorcyclists wear helmets.**

You can also use parallelism for effect by using similar sentence structures to express related ideas.

Repetition Repeating important words or phrases can create an emotional response or underscore their significance. Use this technique sparingly to make your key ideas resonate with readers.

Analogy An analogy illustrates an idea by comparing it to something with similar characteristics. For example, you could say, "The politician worked the crowd as if he were selling the Fountain of Youth."

A STYLISH MODEL Read the following passage, noting the writer's sound, word choice, sentence variety, and rhetorical devices.

A Writer's Model

Credit cards are a ticket to an unpleasant lesson for college freshmen. One in five college students will rack up $10,000 in credit card debt by graduation. That's right—$10,000! Some people use credit as recklessly as play money. Unfortunately, the consequences for misusing credit cards are staggering. A $5,000 credit card debt can take up to 30 years and $15,000 to pay off—three times the value of the items purchased. Credit cards only look good until the bill comes due. I encourage students to stand firm and refuse the temptations dangled before them by credit card companies.

Voice/tone

Repetition
Analogy
Connotation

Precise verbs

Your Turn **Revise the paragraph below to improve its style. Add your own ideas as appropriate.**

I think students should be allowed to bring cell phones to school. What if we need to call someone? Students have rights too. I think the school staff should quit treating us like babies. This rule just isn't fair and should be changed.

Designing Your Writing

A document must be designed to convey information in a way that is easy to understand and remember. In other words, the text arrangement and appearance and any visuals must support the content. You can create effective design and visuals by hand, or you can use advanced publishing software and graphics programs to design pages and to integrate other features into your word-processed documents.

Page Design

LAY IT ON THE LINE If you want your documents to catch readers' attention, you must design them to be visually appealing and easy to read. Use the following design elements to improve readability.

- **Columns** arrange text in separate sections printed vertically side by side. Text in reference books and newspapers usually appears in columns. A **block** is a rectangle of text shorter than a page. The text in advertisements is usually set in blocks so that it may be read quickly. Blocks and columns are separated from each other by white space.
- A **bullet** (•) is a symbol used to highlight information in a text. Bullets separate information into lists like this one. Bullets attract attention and help readers remember information.
- A **heading** appears at the beginning of a section of text to tell readers what that section is about. A **subheading** indicates a smaller section within a heading. Headings and subheadings may be set off from other text in large, **boldface**, or *italic* type or in a different font.
- **White space** is any area on a page where there is little or no text or graphics. Usually, white space is limited to the margins and the spaces between words, lines, and columns. Advertisements usually have more white space than do books or articles.
- A **caption** appears under a photograph or illustration to explain its meaning and connect it to the text. Captions may appear in italics or in a smaller type size than the main text.
- **Contrast** refers to the balance of light and dark areas on a page. Dark areas contain blocks of text or graphics. Light areas have little type. A page with high contrast, or roughly balanced light and dark areas, is easier to read than a page with low contrast.
- **Emphasis** is how a page designer indicates to a reader which information on a page is most important. Because readers' eyes are drawn naturally to color, large and bold print, and graphics, these elements are commonly used to create emphasis.

Type

LETTER PERFECT The basic material of your document is the type. Your choice of different **cases** and **fonts** can pull the reader into the text, provide emphasis, and make your document easy to read.

Case The two cases of type are uppercase, or capital, letters and lowercase, or small, letters. You can vary case in these ways:

- **Uppercase letters** Text in all uppercase letters attracts readers' attention and may be used in headings or titles. Because text in all capital letters can be difficult to read, use all capitals only for emphasis, not for large bodies of text.
- **Small caps** Small caps are uppercase letters that are reduced in size. They are used in abbreviations of time, such as 9:00 A.M. and A.D. 1500. Small caps may be combined with capital letters for an artistic effect.

Font A font is one complete set of characters (such as letters, numbers, and punctuation marks) of a given size and design. The three types of fonts are explained in the chart below.

Categories of Fonts

Category	Explanation	Uses
decorative, or **script,** fonts	elaborately designed characters that convey a distinct mood or feeling	Decorative fonts are difficult to read and should be used in small amounts for an artistic effect.
serif fonts	characters with small strokes (serifs) at each end	Because the strokes on serif characters help guide the reader's eyes from letter to letter, serif type is often used for large bodies of type.
sans serif fonts	characters such as these, formed of straight lines with no serifs	Sans serif fonts are easy to read and are used as headings, subheadings, and captions.

- **Font size** The size of the type in a document is called the font size or point size. In general, newspapers and textbooks use type measured at 12 points. Type for headings and headlines is larger, while captions are usually smaller.
- **Font style** Most text is set in roman (not slanted) style. *Italic,* or slanted, style is used for captions or book titles. Underscored or boldface type can be used for emphasis.

Visuals

Tip Consider copying and pasting information from databases into your documents. For example, if you were writing a letter to your school administration proposing a senior class trip to a national park, you could paste information from a database comparing costs and available activities at several parks in your area. (Always give credit to your sources for such data.)

SHOW, DON'T TELL If you wanted to tell about the weekly expenses and income from your summer lawn-care business, it would be more effective to show the information in a table than to list it in a paragraph. Visuals, or graphics, such as this must be accurate and appropriate. You can create visuals by hand or by using technology, such as advanced computer software and graphics programs. You can also add to a document's impact by integrating a database or spreadsheet into it. Here are some useful visuals.

- **Graphs** present numeric information and can show trends or changes over time or how one thing changes in relation to another. A **bar graph** can also compare quantities at a glance or note the parts of a whole. A **line graph** can compare trends or show how two or more variables interact, as in this example.

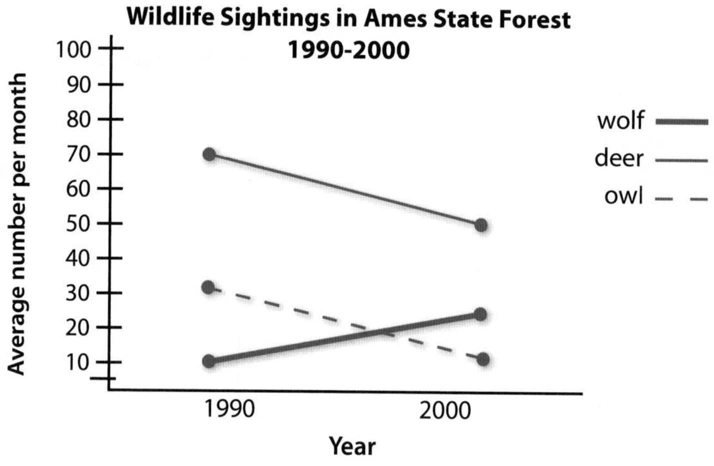

- **Tables** use rows and columns to provide detailed information arranged in an accessible way. A **spreadsheet** is a special kind of table created on a computer. The cells of a spreadsheet are associated with mathematical equations. Spreadsheets are especially useful for budgets or schedules in which the numbers are variables in an equation. In the spreadsheet below, the last column of each row calculates the average of the figures to the left of it.

First Quarter Grades

Name	Essay	Test	Speech	Project	Average
Cooper, L.	84	78	81	92	84
Nguyen, H.	90	86	88	95	90
Torres, B.	88	94	91	90	91
Watt, K.	96	90	93	88	92

- **Pictures,** such as drawings and photographs, can show how something works, what something or someone looks like, or something new, unfamiliar, or indescribable. You can scan a copyright-free picture on the computer or paste it manually into your document. Place it near the reference in the text, and include a caption.
- **Charts** show relationships among ideas or data. A **flowchart** uses geometric shapes linked by arrows to show the sequence of events in a process. A **pie chart** is a circle divided into wedges. Each wedge represents a certain percentage of the total, as in this example.

How Energy Is Used Worldwide

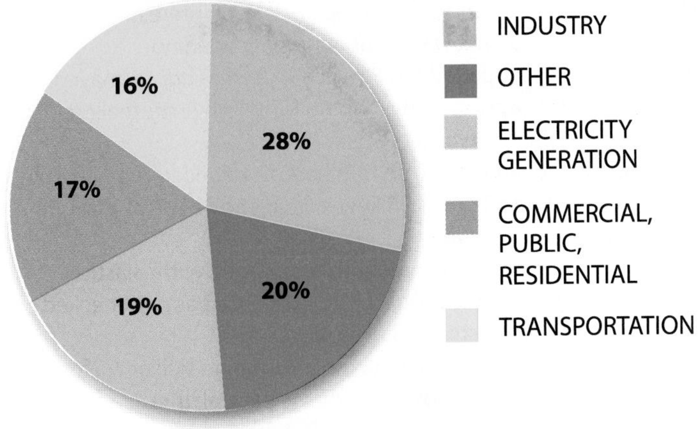

- **Time lines** identify the events that have taken place over a given period of time. (For an example of a time line, see page 2.)

Your Turn **Choose and create the visual you think would most effectively communicate the following information using the guidelines in this section.**

The estimated expenses for the Sanger High senior class trip are as follows: bus rental, $1,000; gas, $200; hotel, ten rooms at $45 per room for five days, or $2,250; food, $30 a day per person (ten people for five days), or $1,500. The total trip cost is $4,950

Glossary

The glossary that follows is an alphabetical list of words found in the selections in this book. Use this glossary just as you would use a dictionary—to find out the meaning of unfamiliar words. (Some technical, foreign, and more obscure words in this book are not listed here but instead are defined for you in the footnotes that accompany many of the selections.)

Many words in the English language have more than one meaning. This glossary gives the meanings that apply to the words as they are used in the selections in this book. Words closely related in form and meaning are usually listed together in one entry (for instance, cower and cowered), and the definition is given for the first form.

The following abbreviations are used:

adj.	adjective
adv.	adverb
n.	noun
v.	verb

Each word's pronunciation is given in parentheses. For more information about the words in this glossary or for information about words not listed here, consult a dictionary.

A

abated (uh BAYT ihd) *v.* used as *adj.* lessened.
abides (uh BYDZ) *v.* endures.
abominable (uh BAHM uh nuh buhl) *adj.* disgusting; hateful.
abstain (ab STAYN) *v.* refrain.
accommodate (uh KAHM uh dayt) *v.* provide room for.
advance (ad VANS) *v.* promote; accelerate growth or progress of.
adversary (AD vuhr sehr ee) *n.* enemy; opponent.
aesthetics (ehs THEHT ihks) *n.* principles of beauty.
affectation (af ehk TAY shuhn) *n.* artificial behavior designed to impress others.
affinity (uh FIHN uh tee) *n.* kinship; bond.
affliction (uh FLIHK shuhn) *n.* suffering; something that causes pain or distress.
aggrieved (uh GREEVD) *v.* used as *adj.* offended.
altruistic (al tru IHS tihk) *adj.* unselfish.
ambitious (am BIHSH uhs) *adj.* aiming at a goal that is hard to reach.
anarchy (AN uhr kee) *n.* disorder and confusion.
animosities (an ih MAHS uh teez) *n.* hostilities; violent hatreds or resentments.
annals (AN uhlz) *n.* records, organized by year, that tell someone or something's history.
annihilate (uh NY uh layt) *v.* destroy; make nonexistent.
annulled (uh NUHLD) *v.* erased; canceled.
antique (an TEEK) *adj.* ancient.
apathy (AP uh thee) *n.* lack of interest.
apertures (AP uhr churz) *n.* openings.
appalled (uh PAWLD) *v.* used as *adj.* dismayed.
apprehensive (ap rih HEHN sihv) *adj.* feeling anxious; worried.
arable (AR uh buhl) *adj.* fit to be farmed or cultivated.
archive (AHR kyv) *n.* collection of documents or other data.
ardent (AHR duhnt) *adj.* eager; enthusiastic.
arrested (uh REHST ihd) *v.* used as *adj.* checked or stopped in motion.
artifice (AHR tuh fihs) *n.* human skill or craft, as opposed to what is natural; trickery; deception.
ascended (uh SEHND ihd) *v.* went up.
aspire (uh SPYR) *v.* reach upward to a goal.
assent (uh SEHNT) *n.* acceptance.
asserted (uh SURT ihd) *v.* declared.
assuage (uh SWAYJ) *v.* ease; calm.
audaciously (aw DAY shuhs lee) *adv.* boldly.
austere (aw STIHR) *adj.* spare; very plain.
avarice (AV uhr ihs) *n.* uncontrolled desire for wealth.

B

bawling (BAWL ihng) *v.* used as *adj.* crying loudly.
benign (bih NYN) *adj.* kind; gracious.
bequest (bih KWEHST) *n.* a gift left through a will.
bibliophile (BIHB lee uh fyl) *n.* one who loves books.
bid (bihd) *v.* demanded; asked.
blanched (blancht) *v.* used as *adj.* made white or pale.
blithe (blyth) *adj.* happy and cheerful.
botanical (buh TAN uh kuhl) *adj.* of plants or plant life; relating to the science of botany.
boundless (BOWND lihs) *adj.* limitless.
brandishing (BRAN dihsh ihng) *v.* used as *adj.* shaking in a threatening way.
brazen (BRAY zuhn) *adj.* made of brass.
buoyancy (BOY uhn see) *n.* lightness of spirit; cheerfulness.
burnished (BUR nihsht) *v.* used as *adj.* made bright and smooth.

C

cadence (KAY duhns) *n.* beat of a repetitive motion; sound that rises and falls.
candor (KAN duhr) *n.* honesty; directness, openness.
caprice (kuh PREES) *n.* sudden notion or desire.
carefree (KAIR free) *adj.* without worry; happy.
caste (kast) *n.* social class.
celestial (suh LEHS chuhl) *adj.* heavenly.
censure (SEHN shuhr) *v.* express disapproval of.
certitude (SUR tuh tood) *n.* feeling of sureness.
chaste (chayst) *adj.* pure, decent, or modest in nature and behavior.
clambered (KLAM buhrd) *v.* climbed clumsily.
clamorous (KLAM uhr uhs) *adj.* loud and noisy.
clinical (KLIHN uh kuhl) *adj.* objective; without emotion.
coarse (kawrs) *adj.* of low quality; rough.
coherently (koh HIHR uhnt lee) *adv.* clearly and logically.
colossal (kuh LAHS uhl) *adj.* magnificently huge.
combustible (kuhm BUHS tuh buhl) *adj.* easy to set on fire; fast-burning.
commendable (kuh MEHN duh buhl) *adj.* deserving of admiration.
commiserate (kuh MIHZ uh rayt) *v.* feel sorrow or pity for; sympathize.
compatible (kuhm PAT uh buhl) *adj.* able to exist or work together.
complemented (KAHM pleh mehnt ihd) *v.* accompanied with; made more complete by adding something.
compulsive (kuhm PUHL sihv) *adj.* driven by an irresistible impulse.
compulsory (kuhm PUHL suhr ee) *adj.* required; enforced.
concealed (kuhn SEELD) *v.* used as *adj.* hidden.
conceding (kuhn SEED ihng) *v.* admitting as true.
conception (kuhn SEHP shuhn) *n.* the originating of something.
concocted (kahn KAHKT ihd) *v.* prepared (food or drink) by mixing a variety of ingredients.
condemned (kuhn DEHMD) *v.* doomed.
confounded (kahn FOWN dihd) *v.* used as *adj.* confused.
congealed (kuhn JEELD) *v.* used as *adj.* thickened.
conjectured (kuhn JEHK chuhrd) *v.* reasoned; guessed.
connoisseur (kahn uh SUR) *n.* person with highly informed and refined taste.
consecrate (KAHN suh krayt) *v.* make honorable and sacred.
consequently (KAHN suh kwehnt lee) *adv.* as a result of something.
conspicuous (kuhn SPIHK yoo uhs) *adj.* attracting attention.
constancy (KAHN stuhn see) *n.* faithfulness; loyalty.
consumption (kahn SUHMP shuhn) *n.* use.
contemplation (kahn tuhm PLAY shuhn) *n.* deep thought; meditation.
contemporaries (kuhn TEM puh rehr eez) *n.* people living during the same time period; peers.
contemptuous (kuhn TEHMP choo uhs) *adj.* showing strong dislike; scornful.
contention (kuhn TEHN shuhn) *n.* struggle.
contortion (kuhn TAWR shuhn) *n.* twisted shape or motion.
convey (kuhn VAY) *v.* communicate; express.
conviction (kuhn VIHK shuhn) *n.* firm belief or certainty.
copious (KOH pee uhs) *adj.* plentiful; abundant.
corporeal (kawr PAWR ee uhl) *adj.* of the body.
cosmopolitan (kahz muh PAHL uh tuhn) *adj.* worldly; sophisticated.
countenance (KOWN tuh nuhns) *n.* facial appearance.
countenances (KOWN tuh nuhns ehz) *v.* extends approval to; favors.
courtiers (KAWR tee uhrz) *n.* palace attendants.
covetousness (KUHV uh tuhs nihs) *n.* desire for what belongs to others.
credible (KREHD uh buhl) *adj.* believable.
creed (kreed) *n.* the essential points of religious belief.
cultivate (KUHL tuh vayt) *v.* develop; promote.
cursory (KUR suhr ee) *adj.* hasty; superficial.

D

daunted (DAWNT ihd) *v.* used as *adj.* made to lose courage; intimidated.
decay (dih KAY) *n.* wasting away; rotting; decline in quality.
decreed (dih KREED) *v.* ordered; commanded.
defiant (dih FY uhnt) *adj.* rebellious; disobedient.
defiled (dih FYLD) *v.* made unclean.
deities (DEE uh teez) *n.* gods and goddesses.
delusion (dih LOO zhuhn) *n.* false belief.
demeanor (dih MEE nuhr) *n.* the way in which a person behaves.
demolition (dehm uh LIHSH uhn) *n.* destruction.
derives (dih RYVZ) *v.* comes from a certain source.
desolate (DEHS uh liht) *adj.* uninhabited; barren; dreary.
desolation (dehs uh LAY shuhn) *n.* grief; loneliness.

desperate (DEHS puhr iht) *adj.* driven by hopelessness; moved to use extreme means to try to escape frustration and loss.
deviate (DEE vee ayt) *v.* turn aside from a way, norm, or truth.
diabolic (dy uh BAHL ihk) *adj.* of or having to do with evil or the devil.
diffusive (dih FYOO sihv) *adj.* spread out; not concentrated in one place.
digressed (dy GREHSD) *v.* wandered away from the subject.
diligence (DIHL uh juhns) *n.* carefulness.
diminishes (duh MIHN ihsh ehz) *v.* makes smaller; lessens; reduces.
discerning (dih SURN ihng) *v.* used as *adj.* displaying good judgment; perceptive.
discomfiture (dihs KUHM fih chuhr) *n.* frustration; embarrassment.
disconcerted (dihs kuhn SUR tihd) *v.* used as *adj.* confused.
discord (DIHS kawrd) *n.* conflict.
discourse (DIHS kawrs) *n.* conversation or speech.
disillusionment (dihs ih LOO zhehn muhnt) *n.* being disenchanted, or freed from a false idea.
dismal (DIHZ muhl) *adj.* gloomy.
dismayed (dihs MAYD) *v.* upset; alarmed.
disparaged (dihs PAR ihjd) *v.* belittled; spoke negatively of.
dispassionately (dihs PASH uh niht lee) *adv.* without emotion; impartially.
disperses (dihs PURS ihz) *v.* breaks up and scatters.
displaced (dihs PLAYST) *v.* moved from its usual location.
disposition (dihs puh ZIHSH uhn) *n.* natural qualities of personality.
dissuade (dih SWAYD) *v.* advise against.
distend (dihs TEHND) *v.* expand; swell.
distill (dihs TIHL) *v.* draw out the essence of.
distorting (dihs TAWRT ihng) *v.* used as *adj.* misshaping; deforming.
distraught (dihs TRAWT) *adj.* extremely agitated.
divine (dih VYN) *adj.* of or like God or a god; given or inspired by God.
doctrine (DAHK truhn) *n.* teachings of the church.
dogged (DAWG ihd) *adj.* stubbornly persistent.
dread (drehd) *adj.* inspiring fear and awe.
dreadful (DREHD fuhl) *adj.* terrible; causing fear.
dregs (drehgz) *n.* sediment.

E

ecstatic (ehk STAT ihk) *adj.* extremely joyful; showing great pleasure.
efficacious (ehf uh KAY shuhs) *adj.* effective or useful.
efficacy (EHF uh kuh see) *n.* ability to produce a desired effect.
emanated (EHM uh nayt id) *v.* flowed; came forth.
embers (EHM buhrz) *n.* glowing remains of a fire.
embrace (ehm BRAYS) *v.* accept readily; take up or adopt.
embroidered (ehm BROY duhrd) *v.* used as *adj.* ornamented with needlework or as if with needlework.
eminence (EHM uh nuhns) *n.* high rank or position.
eminent (EHM uh nuhnt) *adj.* great; high-standing.
encampment (ehn KAMP muhnt) *n.* gathering of people who have set up temporary shelter.
endowed (ehn DOWD) *v.* used as *adj.* provided with.
endure (ehn DOOR) *v.* undergo; bear.
endured (ehn DOORD) *v.* suffered; put up with.
engagements (ehn GAYJ muhnts) *n.* military battles.
enmity (EHN muh tee) *n.* hostility.
enticing (ehn TYS ihng) *adj.* attracting by arousing hopes or desires; tempting.
epilogue (EHP uh lawg) *n.* short section at the end of a literary work that often tells what happened after the end of the story.
epithet (EHP uh theht) *n.* descriptive expression.
erect (ih REHKT) *adj.* upright.
erupted (ih RUHPT ihd) *v.* burst forth.
eternal (ih TUR nuhl) *adj.* forever; everlasting.
ethereal (ih THIHR ee uhl) *adj.* light and delicate; unearthly.
exhilaration (ehg zihl uh RAY shuhn) *n.* excitement; high spirits.
expedient (ehk SPEE dee uhnt) *n.* way of getting something; a means for achieving an end.
expire (ehk SPYR) *v.* die; come to an end.
exploit (EHKS ployt) *n.* daring act.
extolled (ehk STOHLD) *v.* praised.

F

fancy (FAN see) *n.* liking for something or someone.
fastidious (fas TIHD ee uhs) *adj.* picky; overly fussy.
fawning (FAWN ihng) *v.* used as *adj.* cringing and pleading.
fervor (FUR vuhr) *n.* intense emotion.
feverishly (FEE vuhr ihsh lee) *adv.* in an agitated manner.
fickleness (FIHK uhl nuhs) *n.* changeableness.

fidelity (fy DEHL uh tee) *n.* loyalty; faithfulness.
flaccid (FLAS ihd) *adj.* limp; flabby.
flagged (flagd) *v.* declined; lost strength or interest.
flinging (FLIHNG ihng) *v.* used as *adj.* throwing forcefully.
foliage (FOH lihj) *n.* leafy plants.
folly (FAHL ee) *n.* foolishness.
forlorn (fawr LAWRN) *adj.* hopeless; wretched.
formidable (FAWR muh duh buhl) *adj.* hard to surmount.
forsaken (fawr SAY kuhn) *adj.* forlorn; abandoned.
fragrant (FRAY gruhnt) *adj.* sweet-smelling.
frame (fraym) *v.* shape.
frivolous (FRIHV uh luhs) *adj.* silly or unimportant.
frugal (FROO guhl) *adj.* thrifty; careful with money.

G

gallant (GAL uhnt) *adj.* noble; brave.
garrulous (GAR uh luhs) *adj.* talkative.
gaudy (GAW dee) *adj.* overly bright or colorful.
genial (JEEN yuhl) *adj.* friendly.
ghastly (GAST lee) *adj.* dreadful; ghostly.
girdled (GUR duhld) *v.* used as *adj.* enclosed or circled around.
glade (glayd) *n.* small open space in a forest.
gleaned (gleend) *v.* gathered little by little or gradually.
glimmer (GLIHM uhr) *n.* faint, unsteady light.
gloat (gloht) *v.* feel or express great, often malicious, self-satisfaction or pleasure.
goblet (GAHB liht) *n.* drinking vessel, often ornate.
gourd (gawrd) *n.* vegetable with a hard rind that can be dried, hollowed out, and used as a bowl.
grievous (GREE vuhs) *adj.* outrageous; horrible.
groveling (GRAHV uhl ihng) *v.* used as *adj.* crawling; begging; humiliating oneself.
guile (gyl) *n.* sly dealings; skill in deceiving.

H

habitual (huh BIHCH oo uhl) *adj.* regular; steady.
haggled (HAG uhld) *v.* argued about a price.
heedless (HEED lihs) *adj.* careless; thoughtless.
hoard (hawrd) *v.* save or store, often in secret.
hoarding (HAWR dihng) *v.* storing; accumulating.
hulking (HUHLK ihng) *adj.* big and clumsy.
hydraulic (hy DRAW lihk) *adj.* operated by fluid that is under pressure.

I

idyll (YD uhl) *n.* short work of prose or poetry about an idealized country scene.
ignoble (ihg NOH buhl) *adj.* shameful; degrading.
ignominy (IHG nuh mihn ee) *n.* shame; disgrace.
immobility (ihm oh BIHL uh tee) *n.* lack of movement.
impaired (ihm PAIRD) *v.* marred; weakened.
impassively (ihm PAS ihv lee) *adv.* calmly; indifferently.
impediment (im PEHD uh muhnt) *n.* obstacle; obstruction.
impels (ihm PEHLZ) *v.* forces; causes to move.
impersonality (ihm pur suh NAL uh tee) *n.* lack of human connection.
imperturbable (ihm puhr TUR buh buhl) *adj.* calm; impassive.
impetuous (ihm PEHCH oo uhs) *adj.* forceful; violent.
impinge (ihm PIHNJ) *v.* strike; touch.
implacable (ihm PLAK uh buhl) *adj.* impossible to please, satisfy, or change; unyielding.
impotence (IHM puh tuhns) *n.* helplessness.
improvised (IHM pruh vyzd) *v.* used as *adj.* made for the occasion with whatever is handy.
impute (ihm PYOOT) *v.* attribute to someone or something, usually negatively.
incapacitated (ihn kuh PAS uh tayt ihd) *v.* disabled; deprived of power.
incessant (ihn SEHS uhnt) *adj.* constant; never ending.
incoherent (ihn koh HIHR uhnt) *adj.* confused; rambling.
inconstancy (ihn KAHN stuhn see) *n.* changeability or changeableness, specifically, a shift in loyalties; variability.
incurred (ihn KURD) *v.* brought upon oneself.
indiscriminately (ihn dihs KRIHM uh niht lee) *adv.* without making careful distinctions; randomly.
indivisible (ihn duh VIHZ uh buhl) *adj.* unable to be divided or separated.
industrious (ihn DUHS tree uhs) *adj.* hardworking.
infallible (ihn FAL uh buhl) *adj.* unable to fail or be wrong.
infect (ihn FEHKT) *v.* spread a disease to.
infernal (ihn FUR nuhl) *adj.* hellish; fiendish.
ingenuity (ihn juh NOO uh tee) *n.* cleverness; inventiveness.
ingrained (ihn GRAYND) *adj.* deeply and firmly fixed in one's nature or being.
ingratiate (ihn GRAY shee ayt) *v.* try to gain another's favor or goodwill.
innumerable (ih NOO muhr uh buhl) *adj.* too many to count.
inspiration (ihn spuh RAY shuhn) *n.* influence of thought and strong feelings on actions, especially good actions.
insufficient (ihn suh FIHSH uhnt) *adj.* not enough.
intensity (ihn TEHN suh tee) *n.* great vigor.

intermittent (ihn tuhr MIHT uhnt) *adj.* starting and stopping; periodic.
intoxicating (ihn TAHK suh kay tihng) *v.* used as *adj.* causing wild excitement, often beyond the point of self-control.
intrudes (ihn TROODZ) *v.* pushes in; interrupts.
iridescent (ihr ih DEHS uhnt) *adj.* showing rainbowlike colors.
itinerant (y TIHN uhr uhnt) *adj.* migratory.

K

keenly (KEEN lee) *adv.* strongly and clearly.

L

lament (luh MEHNT) *v.* mourn or grieve for.
lamentable (luh MEHN tuh buhl) *adj.* deserving of or inspiring sorrow; regrettable; unfortunate.
languor (LANG guhr) *n.* lack of interest or enthusiasm.
lechery (LEHCH uhr ee) *n.* indulgence in lust.
leisurely (LEE zhuhr lee) *adv.* without hurry; taking plenty of time.
lethal (LEE thuhl) *adj.* deadly.
lilting (LIHLT inhg) *v.* used as *adj.* singing or speaking with a gentle rhythm.
linger (LIHNG guhr) *v.* stay a long while.
livid (LIHV ihd) *adj.* pale; grayish.
loath (lohth) *adj.* unwilling or reluctant.
loathsome (LOHTH suhm) *adj.* very hateful; disgusting.
lugubrious (loo GOO bree uhs) *adj.* solemn or mournful, especially in an excessive way.

M

majesty (MAJ uh stee) *n.* grandeur.
malice (MAL ihs) *n.* active ill will; spite.
maniacal (muh NY uh kuhl) *adj.* crazed; wildly enthusiastic.
manifest (MAN uh fehst) *adj.* evident; obvious.
martyrdom (MAHR tuhr duhm) *n.* death of a martyr, someone who dies for his or her beliefs.
meandering (mee AN duhr ihng) *v.* used as *adj.* wandering with no clear direction.
melancholy (MEHL uhn KAHL ee) *adj.* sad or causing sadness.
melodious (muh LOH dee uhs) *adj.* producing pleasant sounds; tuneful.
mingle (MIHNG guhl) *v.* mix.
minuscule (mih NUHS kyool) *adj.* extremely small.
misanthropy (mih SAN thruh pee) *n.* hatred for humankind.
misery (MIHZ uh ree) *n.* wretchedness; suffering.
momentum (moh MEHN tuhm) *n.* the force with which an object moves.
monotonous (muh NAHT uh nuhs) *adj.* unvarying.
moorline (MOOR lyn) *n.* edge of a heath or wasteland.
multitudes (MUHL tuh toodz) *n.* crowds; great numbers.
munificence (myoo NIHF uh suhns) *n.* generosity.
murmurous (MUHR muhr uhs) *adj.* making consistent soft, low sounds.
mute (myoot) *adj.* not speaking; silent.

N

native (NAY tihv) *adj.* belonging to a person because of birth.
nestled (NEHS uhld) *v.* snugly settled, as in a nest.
nocturnal (nahk TUR nuhl) *adj.* occurring at night.
notorious (noh TAWR ee uhs) *adj.* well known because of something bad; having a bad reputation.
noxious (NAHK shuhs) *adj.* very harmful, often poisonous.

O

object (AHB jihkt) *n.* goal or purpose.
oblivious (uh BLIHV ee uhs) *adj.* unaware or paying no attention to.
obscure (uhb SKYOOR) *adj.* little known.
obstinate (AHB stuh niht) *adj.* unreasonably stubborn.
obtained (uhb TAYND) *v.* got; acquired.
odious (OH dee uhs) *adj.* hateful; offensive.
officious (uh FIHSH uhs) *adj.* eager to give unwanted help.
oppressive (uh PREHS ihv) *adj.* hard to bear.
overwrought (oh vuhr RAWT) *adj.* overly excited.

P

pagan (PAY guhn) *n.* person who believes in many gods or no god.
pallor (PAL uhr) *n.* paleness.
parallel (PAIR uh lehl) *adv.* in line with, but without meeting.
passion (PASH uhn) *n.* strong emotion.
pastoral (PAS tuhr uhl) *adj.* of simple or peaceful rural life.
pathos (PAY thohs) *n.* feeling of sadness or melancholy often brought on by a work of art.
patronize (PAY truh nyz) *v.* be a customer of.
pedantic (peh DAN tihk) *adj.* showing an exaggerated concern for books, learning, and rules.
pensive (PEHN sihv) *adj.* reflective; thoughtful.
perfunctory (puhr FUHNGK tuhr ee) *adj.* halfhearted; disinterested. —**perfunctorily** *adv.*

perpetual (puhr PEHCH oo uhl) *adj.* lasting forever.
perplexed (puhr PLEHKST) *v.* troubled with doubt; puzzled.
perplexes (puhr PLEHKS uhz) *v.* confuses.
perplexing (puhr PLEHK sihng) *v.* used as *adj.* confusing.
persevered (puhr suh VIHRD) *v.* persisted despite difficulty or opposition.
pervades (puhr VAYDZ) *v.* spreads throughout.
perversely (puhr VURS lee) *adv.* disagreeably; contrarily.
pestilence (PEHS tuh luhns) *n.* plague.
piety (PY uh tee) *n.* devotion to religion; holiness.
pilgrimage (PIHL gruh mihj) *n.* journey, especially to a sacred place.
piqued (peekt) *v.* used as *adj.* provoked; resentful.
piteous (PIHT ee uhs) *adj.* deserving of pity.
plagued (playgd) *v.* used as *adj.* afflicted.
pledge (plehj) *n.* promise or vow.
pledge (plehj) *v.* solemnly promise; drink a toast to.
posthumous (PAHS choo muhs) *adj.* happening after death.
potency (POH tuhn see) *n.* strength; power.
precautions (prih KAW shuhnz) *n.* care taken in advance; safeguards.
precipitately (prih SIHP uh tiht lee) *adv.* suddenly.
predominant (prih DAHM uh nuhnt) *adj.* having superior influence; prevailing.
prescribe (prih SKRYB) *v.* limit by rules or laws; order.
presumptuous (prih ZUHMP choo uhs) *adj.* going beyond the proper bounds.
pretense (prih TEHNS) *n.* weakly supported claim.
pretext (PREE tehkst) *n.* excuse.
prevailed (prih VAYLD) *v.* gained the desired effect.
prodding (PRAHD ihng) *v.* poking; jabbing.
prodigious (proh DIHJ uhs) *adj.* huge; very great.
profane (proh FAYN) *adj.* irreverent; not associated with religious matters.
profuse (pruh FYOOS) *adj.* very abundant.
propensity (pruh PEHN suh tee) *n.* natural inclination.
propitious (pruh PIHSH uhs) *adj.* favorable.
proportion (pruh POHR shuhn) *n.* ratio; relative amount.
prosaic (proh ZAY ihk) *adj.* ordinary; dull.
prosperity (prahs PEHR uh tee) *n.* wealth or good fortune.
prostrate (PRAHS trayt) *adj.* lying flat.
protracted (proh TRAK tihd) *v.* used as *adj.* drawn out over time.
prowess (PROW ihs) *n.* outstanding ability.
prudence (PROO duhns) *n.* cautious management.
punctiliousness (puhngk TIHL ee uhs nuhs) *n.* care for following rules and traditions exactly.
punctual (PUHNGK choo uhl) *adj.* prompt; on time.

Q

quarantine (KWAWR uhn teen) *n.* enforced isolation of ill people so they do not spread their illness to others.
quell (kwehl) *v.* bring under control by subduing.
quench (kwehnch) *v.* put out; extinguish.

R

radiant (RAY dee uhnt) *adj.* shining with beams of light.
rapture (RAP chuhr) *n.* bliss; profound joy.
rash (rash) *adj.* foolhardy.
ravenous (RAV uh nuhs) *adj.* very hungry.
realms (rehlmz) *n.* kingdoms.
rebuffed (rih BUHFD) *v.* rejected with disdain.
reckon (REHK uhn) *v.* estimate; consider; judge.
reckoning (REHK uh nihng) *n.* calculation, accounting.
recompense (REHK uhm pehns) *n.* payment or compensation in return for something lost.
redress (REE drehs) *n.* payment or action that serves to remedy an injustice or injury.
reed (reed) *n.* a kind of tall grass with a hollow, jointed stalk that grows in wet places.
reeks (reeks) *v.* has a strong, bad smell.
reiterate (ree IHT uh rayt) *v.* repeat.
relentlessly (rih LEHNT lihs lee) *adv.* unyielding; without pity.
remonstrated (rih MAHN strayt ihd) *v.* protested.
rendered (REHN duhrd) *v.* made; caused to be.
rendering (REHN duh rihng) *v.* causing to be or become; making.
renounce (rih NOWNS) *v.* formally give up; reject.
renown (rih NOWN) *n.* fame; celebrity.
reparation (rehp uh RAY shuhn) *n.* payment to make up for a wrong or injury.
replenish (rih PLEHN ihsh) *v.* fill again; renew.
reprisal (rih PRY zuhl) *n.* punishment in return for an injury.
reproachfully (rih PROHCH fuhl ee) *adv.* accusingly.
reputation (rehp yoo TAY shuhn) *n.* people's opinion of a person.
respite (REHS piht) *n.* postponement; reprieve.
resume (rih ZOOM) *v.* begin again.
revelation (rehv uh LAY shuhn) *n.* act of making known; something revealed.
reverence (REHV uhr uhns) *n.* feeling of great respect and awe.

reverently (REHV uhr uhnt lee) *adv.* with great respect or awe, as for something sacred.
righteous (RY chuhs) *adj.* morally right.
rigor (RIHG uhr) *n.* severity.
rite (ryt) *n.* formal ceremony.
ritualistic (rihch yoo uh LIHS tihk) *adj.* relating to a formal ceremony.

S

sanguine (SANG gwihn) *adj.* reddish in color; red-faced from effort.
satiety (suh TY uh tee) *n.* feeling of disgust or weariness caused by excess.
schism (SKIHZ uhm) *n.* division.
scorn (skawrn) *v.* refuse; reject by showing contempt.
scourge (skurj) *n.* punish severely, usually with a whip.
scrupulous (SKROO pyoo luhs) *adj.* extremely careful in deciding what is right or wrong.
scurry (SKUR ee) *v.* run away quickly.
secular (SEHK yuh luhr) *adj.* not belonging to a religious order; worldly.
sensual (SEHN shoo uhl) *adj.* appealing to bodily senses rather than to the mind.
sepulchral (suh PUHL kruhl) *adj.* deep and gloomy.
sequestered (sih KWEHS tuhrd) *v.* used as *adj.* set apart from; isolated.
serenely (suh REEN lee) *adv.* calmly; peacefully.
serrated (SEHR ay tihd) *v.* used as *adj.* marked along the edge with jagged, sawlike notches.
servile (SUR vuhl) *adj.* like a slave; submissive.
shied (shyd) *v.* shrank or flinched away.
sinews (SIHN yooz) *n.* powerful, tough connective tissues.
singularities (sihng gyoo LAR uh teez) *n.* characteristics that make a person unique.
singularly (SIHNG gyuh luhr lee) *adv.* extraordinarily; unusually.
sinuous (SIHN yoo uhs) *adj.* winding; twisted.
sloth (slawth) *n.* laziness; idleness.
slovenly (SLUHV uhn lee) *adj.* untidy.
sneer (snihr) *n.* proud, unkind facial expression.
somber (SAHM buhr) *adj.* gloomy.
sordid (SAWR dihd) *adj.* filthy; foul.
specious (SPEE shuhs) *adj.* showy but false.
splendor (SPLEHN duhr) *n.* great brightness; brilliant light.
spontaneous (spahn TAY nee uhs) *adj.* caused by natural impulse; not forced.
squalid (SKWAHL ihd) *adj.* foul; dirty.
squall (skwawl) *n.* brief, violent storm.
stealthy (STEHL thee) *adj.* secret; sly.
stratagems (STRAT uh juhmz) *n.* clever plans to achieve a goal.
stridently (STRY duhnt lee) *adv.* harshly; sharply.
sublime (suh BLYM) *adj.* awe inspiring due to majesty or nobility.
successive (suhk SEHS ihv) *adj.* following in consecutive order.
succor (SUHK uhr) *v.* help in time of distress.
summon (SUHM uhn) *v.* call.
superciliously (soo puhr SIHL ee uhs lee) *adv.* disdainfully, scornfully.
supplant (suh PLANT) *v.* replace; displace.
supplement (SUHP luh muhnt) *n.* something added to make complete or to enrich.
supplication (suhp luh KAY shuhn) *n.* humble plea.
suppressed (suh PREHST) *v.* used as *adj.* kept from being known.
surly (SUR lee) *adj.* bad-tempered; unfriendly.
surreptitiously (sur uhp TIHSH uhs lee) *adv.* in a secret or sneaky manner.
sustenance (SUHS tuh nuhns) *n.* food or provisions needed to support life.

T

taciturn (TAS uh turn) *adj.* not talkative.
teeming (TEEM ihng) *v.* used as *adj.* full of; alive with; fruitful.
temerity (tuh MEHR uh tee) *n.* reckless boldness.
temperate (TEHM puhr iht) *adj.* moderate.
temporal (TEHM puhr uhl) *adj.* limited to this world; not spiritual.
thatched (thacht) *v.* used as *adj.* covered with straw, leaves, or similar materials.
torment (TAWR mehnt) *n.* great pain.
tortuous (TAWR choo uhs) *adj.* characterized by twists and turns.
traditions (truh DIHSH uhnz) *n.* customs, values, or ideas handed down from generation to generation.
transgress (trans GREHS) *v.* sin against; violate a limit.
transitory (TRAN suh tawr ee) *adj.* not permanent.
treachery (TREHCH uhr ee) *n.* breaking of faith; betrayal of trust.
tremulous (TREHM yuh luhs) *adj.* quivering; wavering
tribulation (trihb yuh LAY shuhn) *n.* great trouble or misery.
tribute (TRIHB yoot) *n.* something done to show respect.
tumult (TOO muhlt) *n.* great noise; agitation.

tuneful (TOON fuhl) *adj.* musical; melodious.
turbid (TUR bihd) *adj.* cloudy; confused.
turmoil (TUR moyl) *n.* state of agitation or commotion.
tyrannous (TIHR uh nuhs) *adj.* harsh; oppressive.

U

uncanny (uhn KAN ee) *adj.* strange; eerie; weird.
uncouth (uhn KOOTH) *adj.* unsophisticated; awkward.
underfoot (uhn duhr FUT) *adv.* between the feet and the ground.
undeterminable (uhn dih TUR muh nuh buhl) *adj.* not able to be measured or decided.
unendurable (uhn ehn DOOR uh buhl) *adj.* more than can be tolerated.
unpremeditated (uhn pree MEHD uh tay tihd) *adj.* not planned in advance.
unpretentious (uhn prih TEHN shuhs) *adj.* modest.

V

vain (vayn) *adj.* of no use; producing no good result.
valiant (VAL yuhnt) *adj.* brave; courageous.
vanquish (VANG kwihsh) *v.* defeat in battle or conflict.
vehemently (VEE uh muhnt lee) *adv.* with strong feeling; passionately.
veneer (vuh NIHR) *n.* surface appearance or show.
vexed (vehkst) *v.* troubled or disturbed.
vie (vy) *v.* compete.
vile (vyl) *adj.* evil; disgusting.
virtuous (VUR choo uhs) *adj.* moral; righteous.
vivacity (vy VAS uh tee) *n.* liveliness; energetic spirit.

W

wan (wahn) *adj.* faint or weak in a way suggesting sadness, sickness, or weariness.
waning (WAYN ihng) *v.* fading gradually.
welded (WEHLD ihd) *v.* used as *adj.* joined; sealed.
whetting (HWEHT ihng) *v.* used as *adj.* act of sharpening a blade on a stone made for the purpose.
whimsical (HWIHM zuh kuhl) *adj.* fanciful.
withered (WIHTH uhrd) *v.* used as *adj.* dried up.
withers (WIHTH uhrz) *v.* fades; dries up.
wrenched (rehncht) *v.* used as *adj.* anguished; grief-stricken.
wretched (REHCH ihd) *adj.* miserable; unhappy.
writhing (RY thihng) *v.* used as *adj.* twisting and turning, as in pain.

Z

zeal (zeel) *n.* eager enthusiasm.
zealously (ZEHL uhs lee) *adv.* fervently; devotedly.
zenith (ZEE nihth) *n.* highest point.

Spanish Glossary

A

abarrotar *v.* llenar con algo.
abatido *adj.* desalentado; afligido.
abolir *v.* anular; cancelar.
abominable *adj.* desagradable; odioso.
aborrecible *adj.* detestable; ofensivo.
abrazar *v.* aceptar gustosamente; adoptar.
absolver *v.* perdonar; librar de culpas.
abstener *v.* no hacer algo.
acaparar *v.* guardar o almacenar, a menudo en secreto.
acongojado *v.* abatir.
acopiar *v.* amontonar; acumular.
admitir *v.* reconocer que algo es cierto.
adular *v.* arrastrarse y suplicar.
adversario *sust.* enemigo; oponente.
afectación *sust.* comportamiento artificial planeado para impresionar a otras personas.
afilar *v.* hacer más filosa una cuchilla usando una piedra que sirve para esa función.
afinidad *sust.* similitud; lazo.
aflicción *sust.* sufrimiento; algo que causa dolor o preocupación.
agraviado *adj.* sentirse herido o maltratado.
ajeno *adj.* que no es conciente o no presta atención a algo.
alojar *v.* dar lugar.
altaneramente *adv.* con desprecio.
altruista *adj.* que no es egoísta.
amainar *v.* disminuir.
ambicioso *adj.* que aspira a un objetivo muy difícil de alcanzar.
amilanar *v.* intimidar.
anales *sust.* registros, organizados por año, que cuentan la historia de alguien o algo.
anarquía *sust.* desorden y confusión.
anidar *v.* ubicarse cómodamente, como en un nido.
animosidad *sust.* hostilidad; resentimiento u odio violento.
aniquilar *v.* destruir; hacer que algo deje de existir.
antiguo *adj.* viejo.
apatía *sust.* falta de interés.
apertura *sust.* abertura.
apesadumbrado *adj.* angustiado; afligido.
aplacar *v.* controlar.
aprensivo *adj.* ansioso y preocupado.
apuro *sust.* condición o situación poco prometedora.
arable *adj.* que puede cultivarse.
archivo *sust.* conjunto de documentos y otros datos.
ardiente *adj.* entusiasta.
ardor *sust.* emoción intensa.
armónico *adj.* musical; melodioso.
arraigado *adj.* firmemente establecido en uno mismo o en la propia naturaleza.
artificio *sust.* destreza u oficio humano, opuesto a lo natural.
artificio *sust.* trampa; engaño.
ascender *v.* subir.
ascua *sust.* restos de una fogata que está por extinguirse.
aséptico *adj.* objetivo; sin sentimiento.
aspirar *v.* tratar de alcanzar un objetivo.
astucia *sust.* uso de métodos maliciosos; habilidad para engañar.
atribular *v.* afligir.
atroz *adj.* espantoso; terrible.
atroz *adj.* terrible; horrible.
aturdido *adj.* confundido.
aturdido *v.* used as *adj.* confundido.
audazmente *adv.* con atrevimiento.
austero *adj.* sobrio; muy sencillo.
avaricia *sust.* deseo incontrolable de riquezas.
azotar *v.* castigar violentamente, en general con un látigo.

B

bajo los pies *loc. adv.* entre los pies y el piso.
benigno *adj.* amable; gentil.
berrear *v.* llorar en voz muy alta.
bibliófilo *sust.* persona a la que le encantan los libros.
blandir *v.* sacudir de modo amenazante.
blanquear *v.* hacer que algo se vuelva blanco o pálido.
bordado *adj.* decorado con aplicaciones de hilo o como si tuviera aplicaciones de hilo.
botánico *adj.* relativo a las plantas o la flora; que tiene que ver con la ciencia botánica.
bruñir *v.* hacer que algo luzca brillante y liso.
burdo *adj.* poco sofisticado; ordinario.

C

cadencia *sust.* ritmo de un movimiento repetitivo; sonido que se eleva y cae.

cadencioso *adj.* caracterizado por un ritmo moderado.

cáliz *sust.* recipiente para beber, a menudo ornamentado.

campamento *sust.* conjunto de personas que establecen un alburgue de forma temporal.

candor *sust.* honestidad; sinceridad.

candor *sust.* honestidad; sinceridad.

capricho *sust.* idea o deseo repentino.

casta *sust.* clase social.

casto *adj.* puro, decente o modesto de carácter y comportamiento.

celestial *adj.* relativo al cielo.

celosamente *adv.* fervientemente; devotamente.

cenit *sust.* el punto más alto.

censurar *v.* expresar desaprobación.

certeza *sust.* sentimiento de seguridad.

charlatán *adj.* conversador.

chillón *adj.* demasiado brillante o colorido.

circundar *v.* rodear o cercar.

cisma *sust.* división.

claro *sust.* pequeño espacio abierto en un bosque.

codicia *sust.* deseo de tener lo que pertenece a otros.

coherentemente *adv.* clara y lógicamente.

colosal *adj.* extraordinariamente grande.

combate *sust.* batalla militar.

combinar *v.* mezclar.

combustible *adj.* que arde con facilidad.

compadecer *v.* sentir pena o dolor por algo o alguien.

compatible *adj.* que puede existir o funcionar con otra cosa.

complementar *v.* cosa que completa a otra.

compromiso *sust.* promesa o juramento.

compulsivo *adj.* causado por un impulso irresistible.

cómputo *sust.* cálculo, cuenta.

concepción *sust.* el origen de algo.

condenar *v.* sentenciar.

conducta *sust.* forma en la que se comporta una persona.

congraciar *v.* intentar obtener el favor o la aprobación de otra persona.

conjeturar *v.* razonar; adivinar.

conmoción *sust.* estado de agitación o alteración.

consagrar *v.* hacer honorable y sagrado.

consecuentemente *adv.* como resultado de algo.

consentimiento *sust.* aceptacón.

conspicuo *adj.* que llama la atención.

consternado *adj.* extremadamente agitado.

contienda *sust.* lucha.

consumo *sust.* uso.

contemporáneo *sust.* y *adj.* personas que vivien durante la misma época; compañeros.

contorsión *sust.* movimiento o forma retorcido.

conturbar *v.* preocupar; alarmar.

convertir *v.* hacer que algo sea de determinada manera.

convertir *v.* causar; hacer que algo o alguien sea otra cosa.

convicción *sust.* seguridad o creencia firme.

convicción *sust.* creencia firme.

convocar *v.* llamar.

copioso *adj.* abundante; cuantioso.

copioso *adj.* abundante; cuantioso.

corpóreo *adj.* relativo al cuerpo.

corromper *v.* hacer que algo sea impuro.

cortesano *sust.* miembro del séquito de un palacio.

cosmopolita *adj.* de mucho mundo; sofisticado.

credo *sust.* puntos esenciales de una creencia religiosa.

cuarentena *sust.* aislamiento forzado de una persona enferma para que no contagie su enfermedad a otros.

cultivar *v.* desarrollar; promover.

D

deambular *v.* caminar sin rumbo definido.

decretar *v.* ordenar; mandar.

deidad *sust.* dios.

demandar *v.* ordenar; pedir.

demolición *sust.* destrucción.

denigrar *v.* arrastrarse; suplicar; humillarse.

deplorable *adj.* que inspira pena.

deplorable *adj.* lamentable; desafortunado.

derivar *v.* provenir de determinada fuente.

derrotar *v.* ganarle a alguien en una batalla o conflicto.

desafiante *adj.* rebelde; desobediente.

desaliñado *adj.* desordenado.

desapasionadamente *adv.* sin emoción; imparcialmente.

descomunal *adj.* grande y torpe.

desconcertar *v.* preocupar con dudas; confundir.

desconcertar *v.* confundir.

desconcertar *v.* confundir.

desdén *sust.* expresión orgullosa y poco amable.

desdicha *sust.* desgracia; sufrimiento.

desencanto *sust.* desilusión o abandono una idea falsa.

desesperado *adj.* dominado por la desesperanza; impulsado a emplear medios extremos para intentar escapar a la frustración y la pérdida.
desestimar *v.* rechazar con desdén.
desierto *adj.* abandonado.
desolación *sust.* tristeza; soledad.
desolación *sust.* desdicha absoluta; soledad extrema.
desolado *adj.* inhabitado; árido; deprimente.
desorientar *v.* confundir.
despectivo *adj.* despreciativo.
despectivo *adj.* que muestra gran disgusto o es muy irrespetuoso.
desplazar *v.* mover de su ubicación habitual.
despreciar *v.* no aceptar; rechazar con desdén.
despreocupado *adj.* sin preocupaciones; feliz.
destilar *v.* extraer la esencia de algo.
desventurado *adj.* desgraciado; infeliz.
desviar *v.* apartar de un camino, norma o verdad.
deterioro *sust.* consumición, podredumbre; disminución de la calidad.
diabólico *adj.* relacionado con el mal o el demonio.
difuso *adj.* esparcido; que no está concentrado en un solo lugar.
dilatar *v.* expandir; hinchar.
diligencia *sust.* cuidado.
discordia *sust.* conflicto.
discurso *sust.* conversación o habla.
disminuir *v.* hacer más pequeño; rebajar; reducir.
disparar *v.* correr muy rápido.
dispersar *v.* separar y desparramar.
distorsionar *v.* deformar.
disuadir *v.* aconsejar en contra de algo.
divagar *v.* alejarse del asunto que se trata.
divino *adj.* similar a Dios o a un dios, o relativo a él; brindado o inspirado por Dios.
doctrina *sust.* enseñanzas de la iglesia.
dotar *v.* equipar con algo.

E

eficacia *sust.* capacidad de producir el efecto deseado.
eficaz *adj.* efectivo o útil.
elaborar *v.* preparar (comida o bebida) mezclando una variedad de ingredientes.
emanar *v.* fluir; aparecer.
embelesar *v.* causar gran excitación, a menudo más allá del autocontrol.
eminencia *sust.* alto rango o posición.
eminente *adj.* excelente, grandioso.
empajar *v.* cubrir con paja, hojas o materiales similares.
enchapado *adj.* que tiene una capa de algo en la superficie.
encomiar *v.* alabar.
enemistad *sust.* hostilidad.
engaño *sust.* falsa creencia.
engañoso *adj.* que parece cierto pero es falso.
engarabitar *v.* trepar con torpeza.
entendido *sust.* persona de gusto muy refinado que sabe mucho sobre un tema.
epílogo *sust.* sección corta al final de una obra literaria que a menudo cuenta qué pasó después del final del relato.
epíteto *sust.* expresión descriptiva.
erecto *adj.* derecho.
escandaloso *adj.* famoso por algo negativo; que tiene mala reputación.
escandaloso *adj.* famoso por su mala reputación.
escrupuloso *adj.* extremadamente cuidadoso en decidir qué está bien y qué está mal.
espantoso *adj.* terrible; que causa temor.
esplendor *sust.* brillo fuerte; luz brillante.
espontáneo *adj.* causado por un impulso natural; que no es forzado.
estallar *v.* explotar.
estética *sust.* conjunto de principios de la belleza.
estimar *v.* considerar; juzgar.
estratagema *sust.* plan inteligente para alcanzar un objetivo.
estrepitoso *adj.* ruidoso.
estridentemente *adv.* con severidad; con dureza.
etéreo *adj.* suave y delicado; de otro mundo.
exaltado *adj.* demasiado agitado.
excepcionalmente *adv.* particularmente; extraordinariamente.
expediente *sust.* modo de obtener algo; medio para alcanzar un objetivo.
expirar *verbo.* morir; terminar.
extasiado *adj.* extremadamente alegre; que demuestra gran placer.
éxtasis *sust.* alegría; felicidad absoluta.
extravagante *adj.* fuera de lo normal sin razón aparente.

F

famélico *adj.* que tiene mucha hambre.
fascinación *sust.* atracción por algo o por alguien.
febrilmente *adv.* con agitación o excitación.
fervor *sust.* entusiasmo y ansiedad.
fidelidad *sust.* lealtad.
flácido *adj.* flojo; blando.
flaquear *v.* disminuir; perder fuerza o interés.

follaje *sust.* plantas con muchas hojas.
formidable *adj.* difícil de manejar o soportar.
fragante *adj.* que tiene un aroma agradable.
frecuentar *v.* aquí, ser cliente de alguien.
frenar *v.* detener el movimiento.
frívolo *adj.* superficial o poco importante.
frívolo *adj.* superficial; que no tiene seriedad.
furtivo *adj.* secreto; disimulado.

G

gallardo *adj.* noble; valiente.
genial *adj.* simpático, agradable.
güira *sust.* fruto de cáscara dura que puede ser secado, ahuecado y usado como recipiente.

H

habitual *adj.* frecuente, constante.
hastío *sust.* sensación de disgusto o cansancio provocada por un exceso.
heder *v.* tener mal olor.
hosco *adj.* malhumorado; poco amable.
hosco *adj.* grosero o poco amistoso.
hidráulico *adj.* que se opera mediante un fluido bajo presión.

I

idilio *sust.* texto corto en prosa o verso sobre una escena ideal relacionada con el campo.
impávidamente *adv.* calmadamente; indiferentemente.
impedimento *sust.* obstáculo; dificultad.
impedimento *sust.* obstáculo; estorbo.
impeler *v.* incitar; estimular.
impersonalidad *sust.* falta de relación con los pensamientos, sentimientos, etc. de una persona.
impertinente *adj.* que sobrepasa los límites de lo correcto.
imperturbable *adj.* calmo, sereno.
impetuoso *adj.* enérgico; violento.
implacable *adj.* imposible de complacer, satisfacer o cambiar; que no cede.
importunar *v.* molestar; interrumpir.
impotencia *sust.* desesperanza.
improvisar *v.* no planificar.
improvisar *v.* hacer en el momento, con lo que se tiene a mano.
imprudente *adj.* insensato.
impulso *sust.* fuerza por la cual se mueve un objeto.
imputar *v.* atribuir algo a alguien.
incapacitar *sust.* inhabilitar, quitar el poder.
incesante *adj.* constante; que nunca termina.
incoherente *adj.* confuso; ilógico.
inconstancia *sust.* cambio o transformación, especialmente un cambio en la lealtad hacia otra persona; variabilidad.
incurrir *v.* atraer algo sobre uno mismo.
indemnización *sust.* pago en compensación por un mal o un daño hecho.
indeterminable *adj.* que no se puede medir o determinar.
indiscriminadamente *adv.* sin hacer distinciones cuidadosas, al azar.
indivisible *adj.* que no se puede separar.
inexorablemente *adv.* inflexiblemente; sin piedad.
infalible *adj.* que no falla ni se equivoca.
infernal *adj.* relativo al infierno; endemoniado.
infinito *adj.* que no tiene límites.
ingenio *sust.* inteligencia; creatividad.
inmovilidad *sust.* falta de movimiento.
innato *adj.* que pertenece a una persona de nacimiento.
innoble *adj.* vergonzoso.
innumerable *adj.* que son tantos que no se pueden contar.
inquietante *adj.* extraño; asombroso; raro.
inspiración *sust.* influencia del pensamiento y de fuertes sentimientos sobre las acciones, especialmente buenas acciones.
insuficiente *adj.* que no alcanza.
insufrible *adj.* que no se puede tolerar.
intermitente *adj.* que empieza y se detiene a intervalos; periódico.
intimidar *v.* lograr que otra persona pierda el coraje.
irisado *adj.* que muestra colores similares a los del arco iris.
irreflexivo *adj.* descuidado; desconsiderado.
itinerante *adj.* que viaja.

J

jovialidad *sust.* ligereza de ánimo; alegría.
júbilo *sust.* ánimo; alegría.
juicioso *adj.* que muestra buen juicio, perceptivo.
junco *sust.* tipo de pasto alto con un tallo hueco que crece en lugares húmedos.
jurar *v.* prometer solemnemente.

L

laborioso *adj.* trabajador.
lamentar *v.* sentir pena o dolor por algo.
languidez *sust.* falta de interés o de entusiasmo.
lánguido *adj.* débil de una manera que expresa tristeza, enfermedad o cansancio.

precaución *sust.* medida de cuidado que se toma de antemano.
precipitadamente *adv.* de repente.
precipitado *adj.* rápido.
predominante *adj.* que tiene una influencia superior; que prevalece.
prescribir *v.* limitar por medio de reglas y leyes; ordenar; determinar.
pretensión *sust.* reclamo débilmente respaldado.
pretexto *sust.* excusa.
prevalecer *v.* lograr el efecto deseado.
proclamar *v.* declarar.
prodigioso *adj.* extraordinario; maravilloso.
prodigioso *adj.* enorme.
proeza *n.* acto de valentía.
profano *adj.* irrespetuoso; que no se relaciona con asuntos religiosos.
profuso *adj.* muy abundante.
prolongar *v.* alargar en el tiempo.
promover acelerar el crecimiento o el progreso de algo o alguien.
propagar *v.* contagiar una enfermedad.
propagar *v.* expandirse por todos lados.
propensión *sust.* inclinación o tendencia natural.
propicio *dj.* favorable.
proporción *sust.* razón; cantidad relativa.
prórroga *sust.* postergación; retraso.
prosaico *adj.* ordinario; aburrido.
prosperidad *sust.* riqueza o buena fortuna.
prudencia *sust.* comportamiento cuidadoso.
puntilloso *adj.* manático; demasiado exigente.
puntual *adj.* sin demora; a tiempo.
punzar *v.* pinchar; clavar.

R

radiante *adj.* que irradia luz.
reacio *adj.* que no está dispuesto a hacer algo.
reanudar *v.* continuar.
recluir *v.* separar; incomunicar.
recolectar *v.* juntar de a poco o gradualmente.
recompensa *sust.* pago o compensación a cambio de algo que se había perdido y se ha encontrado.
recto *adj.* moralmente correcto.
reflexión *sust.* pensamiento profundo; meditación.
regatear *v.* discutir por un precio.
regodearse *v.* sentir o expresar gran placer y satisfacción, a menudo maliciosamente.
reino *sust.* territorio dominado por un rey.
reiterar *v.* repetir.
reiterar *v.* repetir.
renombre *sust.* fama; celebridad.
renunciar *v.* rendirse formalmente; rechazar.
reponer *v.* volver a llenar; renovar.
represalia *sust.* castigo en respuesta a una agresión u ofensa.
reproche *sust.* acusación.
repugnante *adj.* odioso; desagradable.
reputación *sust.* la buena opinión que tiene la gente sobre una persona.
resarcimiento *sust.* compensación o pago por una pérdida.
resarcimiento *sust.* pago o acción que sirve como remedio de una injusticia o de un daño.
resentirse *v.* sentir rencor o despecho.
respingar *v.* encogerse o estremecerse.
retorcer *v.* moverse o sacudirse por dolor.
revelación *sust.* acto de dar algo a conocer.
revelación *sust.* algo que se descubre.
reverencia *sust.* sentimiento de respeto o veneración.
reverencia *sust.* respeto profundo.
reverencialmente *adv.* con veneración y respeto.
reverencialmente *adv.* con gran respeto, como el que se tiene por algo sagrado.
rigor *sust.* firmeza.
risueño *adj.* feliz y despreocupado.
rito *sust.* ceremonia formal.
ritualista *adj.* relativo a una ceremonia formal.
rivalizar *v.* competir.
robusto *adj.* pesado; corpulento.

S

saciar *v.* aliviar; calmar.
sancionar *sust.* aprobar; autorizar.
sanguíneo *adj.* rojizo.
secular *adj.* que no pertenece a ninguna orden religiosa; mundano.
seducir *v.* atraer despertando esperanzas y deseos; tentar.
semblante *sust.* expresión en la cara de una persona.
sensual *adj.* relativo a los cinco sentidos.
sensual *adj.* que apela a los sentidos del cuerpo en vez de a la mente.
sepulcral *adj.* profundo y oscuro.
serenamente *adv.* calmadamente; pacíficamente.
serrado *adj.* que tiene dientes como los de una sierra a lo largo del borde.
servil *adj.* dedicado ciegamente.
servil *adj.* como un esclavo; obediente.
sinuoso *adj.* con muchas curvas; torcido.
socorrer *v.* ayudar en caso de peligro o necesidad.
sofocar *v.* apagar; extinguir.
soldar *v.* unir; sellar.

precipitadamente *adv.* de repente.
precipitado *adj.* rápido.
predominante *adj.* que tiene una influencia superior; que prevalece.
prescribir *v.* limitar por medio de reglas y leyes; ordenar; determinar.
pretensión *sust.* reclamo débilmente respaldado.
pretexto *sust.* excusa.
prevalecer *v.* lograr el efecto deseado.
proclamar *v.* declarar.
prodigioso *adj.* extraordinario; maravilloso.
prodigioso *adj.* enorme.
proeza *n.* acto de valentía.
profano *adj.* irrespetuoso; que no se relaciona con asuntos religiosos.
profuso *adj.* muy abundante.
prolongar *v.* alargar en el tiempo.
promover *v.* acelerar el crecimiento o el progreso de algo o alguien.
propagar *v.* contagiar una enfermedad.
propagar *v.* expandirse por todos lados.
propensión *sust.* inclinación o tendencia natural.
propicio *dj.* favorable.
proporción *sust.* razón; cantidad relativa.
prórroga *sust.* postergación; retraso.
prosaico *adj.* ordinario; aburrido.
prosperidad *sust.* riqueza o buena fortuna.
prudencia *sust.* comportamiento cuidadoso.
puntilloso *adj.* manático; demasiado exigente.
puntual *adj.* sin demora; a tiempo.
punzar *v.* pinchar; clavar.

R

radiante *adj.* que irradia luz.
reacio *adj.* que no está dispuesto a hacer algo.
reanudar *v.* continuar.
recluir *v.* separar; incomunicar.
recolectar *v.* juntar de a poco o gradualmente.
recompensa *sust.* pago o compensación a cambio de algo que se había perdido y se ha encontrado.
recto *adj.* moralmente correcto.
reflexión *sust.* pensamiento profundo; meditación.
regatear *v.* discutir por un precio.
regodearse *v.* sentir o expresar gran placer y satisfacción, a menudo maliciosamente.
reino *sust.* territorio dominado por un rey.
reiterar *v.* repetir.
renombre *sust.* fama; celebridad.
renunciar *v.* rendirse formalmente; rechazar.
reponer *v.* volver a llenar; renovar.
represalia *sust.* castigo en respuesta a una agresión u ofensa.
reproche *sust.* acusación.
repugnante *adj.* odioso; desagradable.
reputación *sust.* la buena opinión que tiene la gente sobre una persona.
resarcimiento *sust.* compensación o pago por una pérdida.
resarcimiento *sust.* pago o acción que sirve como remedio de una injusticia o de un daño.
resentirse *v.* sentir rencor o despecho.
respingar *v.* encogerse o estremecerse.
retorcer *v.* moverse o sacudirse por dolor.
revelación *sust.* acto de dar algo a conocer.
revelación *sust.* algo que se descubre.
reverencia *sust.* sentimiento de respeto o veneración.
reverencia *sust.* respeto profundo.
reverencialmente *adv.* con veneración y respeto.
reverencialmente *adv.* con gran respeto, como el que se tiene por algo sagrado.
rigor *sust.* firmeza.
risueño *adj.* feliz y despreocupado.
rito *sust.* ceremonia formal.
ritualista *adj.* relativo a una ceremonia formal.
rivalizar *v.* competir.
robusto *adj.* pesado; corpulento.

S

saciar *v.* aliviar; calmar.
sancionar *sust.* aprobar; autorizar.
sanguíneo *adj.* rojizo.
secular *adj.* que no pertenece a ninguna orden religiosa; mundano.
seducir *v.* atraer despertando esperanzas y deseos; tentar.
semblante *sust.* expresión en la cara de una persona.
sensual *adj.* relativo a los cinco sentidos.
sensual *adj.* que apela a los sentidos del cuerpo en vez de a la mente.
sepulcral *adj.* profundo y oscuro.
serenamente *adv.* calmadamente; pacíficamente.
serrado *adj.* que tiene dientes como los de una sierra a lo largo del borde.
servil *adj.* dedicado ciegamente.
servil *adj.* como un esclavo; obediente.
sinuoso *adj.* con muchas curvas; torcido.
socorrer *v.* ayudar en caso de peligro o necesidad.
sofocar *v.* apagar; extinguir.
soldar *v.* unir; sellar.
solidificar *v.* espesar.
sombrío *adj.* lúgubre.
someramente *adv.* mecánicamente; sin cuidado.
somero *adj.* poco entusiasta; indiferente.
soportar *v.* resistir.

sórdido *adj.* sucio; repugnante; desagradable.
sublime *adj.* impresionante por ser noble o majestuoso.
subrepticiamente *adv.* en secreto o a escondidas.
sucesivo *adj.* que sigue en orden consecutivo.
suplantar *v.* reemplazar; desplazar.
suplemento *sust.* algo agregado a una dieta, a menudo para compensar una deficiencia.
súplica *sust.* humilde ruego.
suprimir *v.* evitar que se conozca.
sustento *sust.* comida o provisiones necesarias para vivir.
susurrante *adj.* que produce un ruido suave y continuo.

T

taciturno *adj.* callado.
temeridad *sust.* atrevimiento tonto o impulsivo; insensatez.
templado *adj.* moderado.
temporal *adj.* limitado a este mundo; que no es espiritual.
tendón *sust.* tejido fibroso y fuerte de gran poder conector.
térmico *adj.* relacionado con el calor.
tirano *adj.* severo; opresivo.
tolerar *v.* soportar.
tolerar *v.* sufrir; tolerar.
tormento *sust.* gran angustia.
tortuoso *adj.* lleno de vueltas o curvas.
tosco *adj.* de baja calidad; áspero.
tradición *sust.* costumbres, valores o ideas que se pasan de generación en generación.
traición *sust.* deslealtad; abuso de confianza.
transgredir *v.* ir en contra de algo; violar un límite impuesto.
transitorio *adj.* que no es permanente.
transmitir *v.* comunicar; expresar.
trastornar *v.* inquietar o perturbar.
trémulo *adj.* que tiembla o se tambalea.
tribulación *sust.* gran preocupación o pena.
tributo *sust.* algo hecho en honor a alguien.
tumulto *sust.* ruido grande; agitación.
turbación *sust.* frustración; vergüenza.
turbio *adj.* empañado; confuso.
turbión *sust.* tormenta violenta y breve.

V

valeroso *adj.* valiente; que tiene coraje.
vano *adj.* inútil; que no produce ningún resultado bueno.
vehementemente *adv.* violentamente.
vehementemente *adv.* con gran sentimiento; apasionadamente.
velado *v.* oculto.
verosímil *adj.* creíble.
vigor *sust.* gran intensidad.
vil *adj.* malvado, desagradable.
vil *adj.* desagradable.
virtuoso *adj.* moral; recto.
vislumbre *sust.* luz débil y temblorosa.
vivacidad *sust.* animación; espíritu energético.
vivamente *adv.* con fuerza y claridad.
volubilidad *sust.* capacidad de cambio.
vulnerar *v.* golpear; afectar.

Academic Vocabulary Glossary

The Academic Vocabulary Glossary in this section is an alphabetical list of the academic vocabulary words found in this textbook. Use this glossary just as you would use a dictionary—to find out the meanings of words used in your literature class, to talk about and write about literary and informational texts, and to talk about and write about concepts and topics in your other academic classes.

For each word, the glossary includes the pronunciation, part of speech, and meaning. A Spanish version of the glossary immediately follows the English version. For more information about the words in the Academic Vocabulary Glossary, please consult a dictionary.

ENGLISH

A

adapt (uh DAPT) *v.* adjust for a new purpose.
approach (uh PROHCH) *n.* way of addressing something.
attribute (uh TRIHB yoot) *v.* regard as being caused by something.

B

benefit (BEHN uh fiht) *n.* anything that is for the good of a person or thing.

C

complex (kuhm PLEHKS) *adj.* hard to understand; complicated.
concept (KAHN sehpt) *n.* notion or idea.
considerably (kuhn SIHD uhr uh blee) *adv.* by a large amount.
controversies (KAHN truh vur seez) *n.* lengthy disagreement.
convince (kuhn VIHNS) *v.* persuade; cause to believe.

D

device (dih VYS) *n.* something made for a particular purpose.
differentiate (dihf uh REHN shee ayt) *v.* distinguish; identify differences.
diverse (duh VURS) *adj.* varied.
dominate (DAHM uh nayt) *v.* hold a commanding position.

E

emphasis (EHM fuh sihs) *n.* stress; importance.
enhance (ehn HANS) *v.* improve the quality of.
ensure (ehn SHOOR) *v.* make certain.
established (ehs TAB lihsht) *v.* set up; caused to happen.
exhibit (ehg ZIHB iht) *v.* show, demonstrate.

F

function (FUNGK shuhn) *n.* action for which a person or thing is specially fitted; purpose.

I

inevitable (ihn EHV uh tuh buhl) *adj.* unavoidable.
inherent (ihn HIHR uhnt) *adj.* existing in something as a fixed, essential quality.

P

participate (par TIHS uh payt) *v.* take part in.
perspective (puhr SPEHK tihv) *n.* particular way of looking at something.
publish (PUHB lihsh) *v.* print and issue for the public.

R

respond (rih SPAHND) *v.* react.

S

statistics (stuh TIHS tihks) *n.* numerical facts.
status (STAT uhs) *n.* social or professional rank.

T

technique (tehk NEEK) *n.* method; way of using skills.

W

widespread (WYD SPREHD) *adj.* occurring over a wide area.

SPANISH

A

adaptar *v.* ajustar a un nuevo propósito.
artefacto *sust.* algo construido para un fin específico.
atribuir *v.* considerar que es la causa de algo.

B

beneficio *sust.* algo que sea para el bien de una persona o cosa.

C

complejo *adj.* difícil de entender; complicado.
concepto *sust.* noción o idea.
considerablemente *adv.* por gran cantidad.
controversia *sust.* desacuerdo o discusión prolongada.

D

diferenciar *v.* distinguir; reconocer lo que es distinto.
diverso *adj.* variado.
dominar *v.* tener poder.

E

énfasis *sust.* hincapié; importancia.
enfoque *v.* modo de considerar algo.
estadística *sust.* datos numéricos.
estatus *sust.* rango social o profesional.
exhibir *v.* mostrar, demostrar.

F

función *sust.* acción para la que una persona está especialmente capacitada; propósito.

G

generalizado *adj.* que ocurre en un área amplia.

I

ineludible *adj.* inevitable.
inherente *adj.* que existe como una cualidad natural e inseparable de algo.
instaurar *v.* establecer; permitir que algo ocurra.

P

participar *v.* formar parte de algo.
perfeccionar *v.* mejorar la calidad de algo.
perspectiva *sust.* modo particular de ver algo.
persuadir *v.* convencer; hacer que alguien crea algo.
publicar *v.* imprimir algo y distribuirlo al público.

R

ratificar *v.* dar certeza.
reaccionar *v.* responder.

T

técnica *sust.* método; modo de usar las destrezas.

ACKNOWLEDGMENTS

For permission to reproduce copyrighted material, grateful acknowledgment is made to the following sources:

"B. Wordsworth" from *Miguel Street* by V. S. Naipaul. Copyright © 1959 by V. S. Naipaul. Reproduced by permission of **Aitken Alexander Associates Ltd.**

"Raven doth to raven fly" from *Alexander Pushkin: Collected Narrative and Lyrical Poetry,* translated by Walter Arndt. Copyright © 1984 by Walter Arndt. Reproduced by permission of **Ardis Publishers.**

"Soneto LXXIX" from *Cien sonetos de amor* by Pablo Neruda. Copyright © 1959 by Pablo Neruda and Fundación Pablo Neruda; copyright © renewed 2007 by Fundación Pablo Neruda. Reproduced by permission of **Agencia Literaria Carmen Balcells.**

From *Walking to Canterbury* by Jerry Ellis. Copyright © 2003 by Jerry Ellis. Reproduced by permission of **Ballentine Books, a division of Random House, Inc., www.randomhouse.com.**

From "The Second Teaching: Philosophy and Spiritual Decline" from *The Bhagavad-Gita,* translated by Barbara Stoler Miller. Translation copyright © 1986 by Barbara Stoler Miller. Reproduced by permission of **Bantam Books, a division of Random House, Inc.** and electronic format by permission of **The Estate of Barbara Stoler Miller.**

From "Introduction" to *The Life and Times of Chaucer* by John Gardner. Copyright © 1977 by Boskydell Artists, Ltd. Reproduced by permission of **Georges Borchardt, Inc.**

"The Diary of Samuel Pepys and Eyewitness" (retitled "Diary of Samuel Pepys Weblog") by Tom Regan from *The Christian Science Monitor* Web site, December 18, 2003, accessed February 11, 2008, at http://www.csmonitor.com/2003/1218/p25s01-stin.html. Copyright © 2003 by **The Christian Science Monitor.** Reproduced by permission of the publisher.

"Another Renaissance?" by Gary Fisher from *Electronic Engineering Times,* October 28, 1996. Copyright © 1996 by **CMP Media Inc.** Reproduced by permission of the publisher.

From "Games at Twilight" from Games *at Twilight and Other Stories* by Anita Desai. Copyright © 1978 by Anita Desai. Reproduced by permission of **Anita Desai c/o Rogers, Coleridge & White Ltd., 20 Powis Mews, London W11 1JN.**

"Marriage is a Private Affair" from *Girls at War and Other Stories* by Chinua Achebe. Copyright © 1972, 1973 by Chinua Achebe. Reproduced by permission of **Doubleday, a division of Random House, Inc.** and electronic format by permission of **Harold Ober Associates Incorporated.**

"A morning-glory vine" by Kobayashi Issa from *An Introduction to Haiku,* translated by Harold G. Henderson. Copyright © 1958 by Harold G. Henderson. Reproduced by permission of **Doubleday, a division of Random House, Inc.,www.randomhouse.com.**

From "Le Morte D'Arthur" from *Le Morte D'Arthur* by Sir Thomas Malory, translated by Keith Baines. Copyright © 1962 by Keith Baines; copyright renewed © 1990 by Francesca Evans. Introduction copyright © 1962 by Robert Graves; copyright renewed © 1990 by Beryl Graves. Reproduced by permission of **Dutton Signet, a division of Penguin Group (USA) Inc.**

From *Beowulf,* translated by Burton Raffel. Translation copyright © 1962 and renewed © 1991 by Burton Raffel. Reproduced by permission of **Dutton/Signet, a division of Penguin Group (USA) Inc.** and electronic format by permission of **Russell & Volkening as agents for the author.**

From "The Unfed Dervish," "Information and Knowledge," "The Elephant-Keeper," "Safety and Riches," and "The Fox and the Camels" by Saadi of Shiraz from *The Way of the Sufi* by Idries Shah. Copyright © 1968 by Idries Shah. Reproduced by permission of **Dutton Signet, a division of Penguin Group (USA) Inc.** and electronic format by permission of **The Octagon Press Ltd., London.**

From *WIT* by Margaret Edson. Copyright © 1993, 1999 by Margaret Edson. Reproduced by permission of **Faber and Faber, Inc., an affiliate of Farrar, Straus and Giroux, LLC.**

"The Wife's Lament" from *A Choice of Anglo-Saxon Verse,* translated by Richard Hamer. Translation copyright © 1970 by Richard Hamer. Reproduced by permission of **Faber and Faber Ltd.**

"Once upon a Time" from *Jump and Other Stories* by Nadine Gordimer. Copyright © 1991 by Felix Licensing, B.V. All rights reserved. Reproduced by permission of **Farrar, Straus and Giroux, LLC** and electronic format by permission of **Russell & Volkening, Inc., as agents for Nadine Gordimer.**

"Digging" from *Selected Poems 1966–1987* by Seamus Heaney. Copyright © 1990 by Seamus Heaney. All rights reserved. Reproduced by permission of **Farrar, Straus and Giroux, LLC.**

"The Horses" from *Collected Poems* by Ted Hughes. Copyright © 2003 by The Estate of Ted Hughes. All rights reserved. Reproduced by permission of **Farrar, Straus and Giroux, LLC** and electronic format by permission of **Faber and Faber Ltd.**

"The Explosion" from *Collected Poems* by Philip Larkin. Copyright © 1988, 2003 by the Estate of Philip Larkin. All rights reserved. Reproduced by permission of **Farrar, Straus and Giroux, LLC** and electronic format by permission of **The Society of Authors as the Literary Representative of the Estate of Philip Larkin.**

From Chapter LXIV, Section 1 from *Omeros* by Derek Walcott. Copyright © 1990 by Derek Walcott. Reproduced by permission of **Farrar, Straus and Giroux, LLC.**

"The Virgins" from *Sea Grapes* by Derek Walcott. Copyright © 1976 by Derek Walcott. All rights reserved. Reproduced by permission of **Farrar, Straus and Giroux, LLC.**

From "Dear Smitty" (retitled "Saving Creatures Great and Small") by Timothy Foote from *Smithsonian* Magazine, September 2001. Copyright © 2001 by **Timothy Foote.** Reproduced by permission of the author.

From *Reason for Hope* by Jane Goodall and Phillip Berman. Copyright © 1999 by Soko Publications Ltd. with Phillip Berman. All rights reserved. Reproduced by permission of **Grand Central Publishing.**

Come and Go from *Collected Shorter Plays* by Samuel Beckett. Copyright © 1968, 1984 by Samuel Beckett. Reproduced by permission of **Grove/Atlantic Inc.**

From "That's All" from *Complete Plays: Three* by Harold Pinter. Copyright © 1966 by H. Pinter Ltd. Reproduced by permission of **Grove/Atlantic, Inc.**

"After 14 days trapped underground, Australian miners walk to safety" (retitled "Trapped Australian Miners Rescued") by Duncan Campbell, Alex Kumi and Agencies from *The Guardian* Web site, May 9, 2006, accessed February 11, 2008 at http://www.guardian.co.uk/australia/story/0,,1770790,00.html. Copyright © 2006 by **Guardian Newspapers Limited.** Reproduced by permission of the publisher.

Slightly adapted from "Private Twice Rescued Colleagues While Under Heavy Fire in Iraq: Soldier Wins First VC Since Falklands" (retitled "Under Heavy Fire in Iraq") by Richard Norton-Taylor from *The Guardian,* March 18, 2005. Copyright © 2005 by **Guardian News & Media Limited.** Reproduced by permission of the publisher.

"The Hollow Men" from *Collected Poems* 1909–1962 by T. S. Eliot. Copyright 1936 by **Harcourt, Inc.;** copyright © 1963, 1964 by T. S. Eliot. Reproduced by permission of the publisher

"Shooting an Elephant" from *Shooting an Elephant and Other Essays* by George Orwell. Copyright 1950 by Sonia Brownell Orwell; copyright renewed © 1978 by Sonia Pitt-Rivers. Reproduced by permission of **Harcourt, Inc.** and electronic format by permission of **Bill Hamilton as the Literary Executor of the Estate of Sonia Brownell Orwell and Secker & Warburg Ltd.**

"Lot's Wife" from *View with a Grain of Sand* by Wislawa Szymborska, translated by Stanislaw Baranczak and Clare Cavanaugh. Copyright © 1993 by Wislawa Szymborska. English translation copyright © 1995 by **Harcourt, Inc.** Reproduced by permission of the publisher and electronic format by permission of **Stanislaw Baranczak.**

Letter No. 1454: "To Lytton Strachey, March 21st 1924" from *The Letters of Virginia Woolf, Volume III: 1923–1928.* Copyright ©1977 by Quentin Bell and Angelica Garnett. All rights reserved. Reproduced by permission of **Harcourt, Inc.** and electronic format by permission of **The Hogarth Press.**

"A Haunted House" from *The Complete Shorter Fiction of Virginia Woolf* by Susan Dick. Copyright © 1985 by Quentin Bell and Angelica Garnett. Reproduced by permission of **Harcourt, Inc.**

From *A Room of One's Own* by Virginia Woolf. Copyright 1929 by Harcourt, Inc; copyright renewed © 1957 by Leonard Woolf. Reproduced by permission of **Harcourt, Inc.** and **The Society of Authors** as the Literary Representative of the Estate of Virginia Woolf.

From *The Civilization of the Middle Ages* by Norman F. Cantor. Copyright © 1963, 1968, 1974 and 1993 by Norman F. Cantor. Reproduced by permission of **HarperCollins Publishers, Inc.**

"# 8 The supreme good is like water" from *Tao Te Ching by Lao Tzu, A New English Version,* translated by Stephen Mitchell. Translation copyright © 1988 by **Stephen Mitchell.** Reproduced by permission of **HarperCollins Publishers, Inc.** and electronic format by permission of the translator.

"Never Shall I Forget" from *Night* by Elie Wiesel, translated by Marion Wiesel. Copyright © 1972, 1985 by Elie Wiesel; translation copyright © 2006 by Marion Wiesel. All rights reserved. Reproduced by permission of **Hill and Wang, a division of Farrar, Straus and Giroux, LLC** and electronic format by permission of **Georges Borchardt, Inc. for the author.**

From *The Collected Beowulf* by Gareth Hinds. Copyright © 1999–2000 by **Gareth Hinds.** Reproduced by permission of the artist.

"Mushrooms" from *Selected Poems II: 1976–1986* by Margaret Atwood. Copyright © 1987 by Margaret Atwood. All rights reserved. Reproduced by permission of **Houghton Mifflin Company** and electronic format by **Margaret Atwood and the Larmore Literary Agency.**

"Siren Song" from *Selected Poems, 1965–1975* by Margaret Atwood. Copyright © 1976 by Margaret Atwood. Reproduced by permission of **Houghton Mifflin Company** and electronic format by permission of **Margaret Atwood and Larmore Literary Agency.**

From *Gilgamesh: A Verse Narrative* translated by Herbert Mason. Copyright © 1970 by Herbert Mason. All rights reserved. Reproduced by permission of **Houghton Mifflin Company, www.hmco.com.**

From *Sir Vidia's Shadow* by Paul Theroux. Copyright © 1998 by Paul Theroux. All rights reserved. Reproduced by permission of **Houghton Mifflin Company, www.hmco.com.**

From *The Two Towers* by J.R.R. Tolkien. Copyright © 1954, 1965, 1966 by J.R.R. Tolkien; copyright renewed © 1982 by Christopher R. Tolkien, Michael H.R. Tolkien, John F.R. Tolkien and Priscilla M.A.R. Tolkien. 1965/1966 editions copyright renewed © 1993, 1994 by Christopher R. Tolkien, John F. R. Tolkien and Priscilla M.A.R. Tolkien. All rights reserved. Reproduced by permission of **Houghton Mifflin Company**

"Telephone Conversation" by Wole Soyinka from *Reflections: Nigerian Prose and Verse,* edited by Frances Ademola. Copyright © 1962, 1990 by Wole Soyinka. Reproduced by permission of **Melanie Jackson Agency, L.L.C.**

"The Demon Lover" from *The Collected Stories of Elizabeth Bowen.* Copyright © 1981 by Curtis Brown Ltd., Literary Executors of the Estate of Elizabeth Bowen. Reproduced by permission of **Alfred A. Knopf, a division of Random House, Inc.** and electronic format by permission of **Curtis Brown Ltd., on behalf of the Estate of Elizabeth Bowen.**

"The Doll's House" from *The Short Stories of Katherine Mansfield.* Copyright 1923 by Alfred A. Knopf, a division of Random House, Inc.; copyright renewed 1951 by John Middleton Murry. Reproduced by permission of **Alfred A. Knopf, a division of Random House, Inc., www.randomhouse.com.**

From speech by Jawaharlal Nehru, August 14, 1947. Reproduced by permission of **Jawaharlal Nehru Memorial Fund.**

"Not Waving But Drowning" from *Collected Poems of Stevie Smith.* Copyright © 1972 by Stevie Smith. Reproduced by permission of **New Directions Publishing Corporation.**

"Fern Hill" from *The Poems of Dylan Thomas.* Copyright 1945 by The Trustees for the Copyrights of Dylan Thomas. Reproduced by permission of **New Directions Publishing Corporation** and electronic format by permission of **Harold Ober Associates Incorporated.**

"Do Not Go Gentle into That Good Night" from *The Poems of Dylan Thomas.* Copyright 1945 by The Trustees for the Copyrights of Dylan Thomas. Reproduced by permission of **New Directions Publishing Corporation** and electronic format by permission of **Harold Ober Associates Incorporated.**

"Jade Flower Palace" by Tu Fu from *One Hundred Poems from the Chinese,* translated by Kenneth Rexroth. Copyright © 1971 by Kenneth Rexroth. Reproduced by permission of **New Directions Publishing Corporation.**

"Dulce et Decorum Est" from *The Collected Poems of Wilfred Owen.* Copyright © 1963 by Chatto & Windus, Ltd. Reproduced by permission of **New Directions Publishing Corporation.**

From Nobel Lecture: "The Poet and the World" by Wislawa Szymborska. Copyright © 1996 by **The Nobel Foundation.** Reproduced by permission of the publisher.

"Atlantis—A Lost Sonnet" from *Domestic Violence* by Eavan Boland. Copyright © 2007 by Eavan Boland. Reproduced by permission of **W. W. Norton & Company, Inc.**

From *Beowulf: A New Verse Translation* by Seamus Heaney. Translation copyright © 2000 by Seamus Heaney. Reproduced by permission of **W. W. Norton & Company, Inc.**

"I love you as I love..." from *The Flowers of Evil* by Charles Baudelaire, translated by James McGowan. Translation copyright © 1993 by James McGowan. Reproduced by permission of **Oxford University Press (UK).**

From *The Meaning of Everything: The Story of the Oxford English Dictionary* by Simon Winchester. Copyright © 2003 by Simon Winchester. Reproduced by permission of **Oxford University Press (UK).**

From *African Proverbs,* compiled by Charlotte and Wolf Leslau. Copyright © 1962, 1985 by **Peter Pauper Press, Inc.** Reproduced by permission of the publisher.

"Even stones in streams" by Uejima Onitsura from *Haiku Harvest: Japanese Haiku, Series IV,* translated by Peter Beilenson and Harry Behn. Copyright © 1962 by **Peter Pauper Press, Inc.** Reproduced by permission of the publisher.

"Caedmon of Whitby" from *A History of the English Church and People by Bede,* translated by Leo Sherley-Price, revised by R. E. Latham (Penguin Classics 1955, Revised edition 1968). Translation copyright © 1955, 1968 by Leo Sherley-Price. Reproduced by permission of **Penguin Books Ltd.**

From Introduction by Nevill Coghill from *The Canterbury Tales* by Geoffrey Chaucer, translated by Nevill Coghill (Penguin Classics 1951, Fourth Revised Edition 1977). Copyright © 1951, 1958, 1960, 1975, 1977 by Nevill Coghill. Reproduced by permission of **Penguin Books Ltd.** and electronic format by permission of **Curtis Brown Group Ltd.**

"The Pardoner's Prologue and Tale" from *The Canterbury Tales* by Geoffrey Chaucer, translated by Nevill Coghill (Penguin Classics 1951, Fourth Revised Edition 1977). Copyright © 1951, 1958, 1960, 1975, 1977 by Nevill Coghill. Reproduced by permission of **Penguin Books Ltd.** and electronic format by permission of **Curtis Brown Group Ltd.**

From "The Prologue" from *The Canterbury Tales* by Geoffrey Chaucer, translated by Nevill Coghill (Penguin Classics 1951, Fourth Revised Edition 1977). Copyright © 1951, 1958, 1960, 1975, 1977 by Nevill Coghill. Reproduced by permission of **Penguin Books Ltd.** and electronic format by permission of **Curtis Brown Group Ltd.**

From "The Wife of Bath's Prologue and Tale" from *The Canterbury Tales* by Geoffrey Chaucer, translated by Nevill Coghill (Penguin Classics 1951, Fourth Revised Edition 1977). Copyright © 1951, 1958, 1960, 1975, 1977 by Nevill Coghill. Reproduced by permission of **Penguin Books Ltd.** and electronic format by permission of **Curtis Brown Group Ltd.**

"Night" from *The Koran,* translated by N. J. Dawood (Penguin Classics 1956, Fifth Revised Edition 1990). Copyright © 1956, 1959, 1966, 1968, 1974, 1990 by N. J. Dawood. Reproduced by permission of **Penguin Books Ltd.**

"Question and answer among the mountains" by Li Po from *The Penguin Book of Chinese Verse,* translated by Robert Kotewall and Norman L. Smith (Penguin Books, 1962). Translation copyright © 1962 by N. L. Smith and R. H. Kotewall. Reproduced by permission of **Penguin Books Ltd.**

"Quiet Night Thoughts" and "Letter to His Two Small Children" by Li Po, and "Night Thoughts Afloat" by Tu Fu from *Li Po and Tu Fu,* translated by Arthur Cooper (Penguin Classics, 1973). Copyright © 1973 by Arthur Cooper. Reproduced by permission of **Penguin Books Ltd.**

"The Jewels" from *Selected Short Stories* by Guy de Maupassant, translated by Roger Colet (Penguin Classics, 1971). Copyright © 1971 by Roger Colet. Reproduced by permission of **Penguin Books Ltd.**

"A Clever Judge" by Chang Shih-nan from *Chinese Fairy Tales and Fantasies,* translated and edited by Moss Roberts. Copyright © 1979 by Moss Roberts. Reproduced by permission of **Pantheon Books, a division of Random House, Inc., www.randomhouse.com.**

"Gold, Gold" by Lieh Tzu from *Chinese Fairy Tales and Fantasies,* translated and edited by Moss Roberts. Copyright © 1979 by Moss Roberts. Reproduced by permission of **Pantheon Books, a division of Random House, Inc., www.randomhouse.com.**

Sonnet (retitled "Spacecraft Voyager 1 has boldly gone...") from *Woods etc.* by Alice Oswald. Copyright © 2005 by Alice Oswald. All rights reserved. Reproduced by permission of **The Peters Fraser & Dunlop Group Ltd.**

From *William Shakespeare's Macbeth: The Graphic Novel,* adapted by Arthur Byron Cover, illustrated by Tony Leonard Tamai. Copyright 2005 by Byron Preiss Visual Publications. All rights reserved. Reproduced by permission of **Puffin Books, a division of Penguin Young Readers Group, a member of Penguin Group (USA), www.penguin.com, 345 Hudson Street, New York, NY 10014.**

"Musée des Beaux Arts" from *W. H. Auden: Collected Poems,* edited by Edward Mendelson. Copyright 1940 and renewed © 1968 by W. H. Auden. Reproduced by permission of **Random House, Inc.** and electronic format by permission by **Curtis Brown, Ltd.**

"The Night-Soil Men" from *Ghost Map* by Steven Johnson. Copyright © 2006 by Steven Johnson. Reproduced by permission of **Riverhead Books, an imprint of Penguin Group (USA) Inc, www.penguin.com.**

Number 17 from Book II, numbers 15 and 21 from Book VII, and number 23 from Book XV from *The Analects of Confucius,* translated by Arthur Waley. Copyright 1938 George Allen & Unwin, Ltd. Reproduced by permission of **Scribner, an imprint of Simon & Schuster Adult Publishing Group** and electronic format by permission of **The Estate of Arthur Waley.**

"Sailing to Byzantium" from *The Collected Works of W. B. Yeats, Volume I: The Poems, Revised,* edited by Richard J. Finneran. Copyright 1928 by The Macmillan Company; copyright renewed © 1956 by Georgie Yeats. Reproduced by permission of **Scribner, an imprint of Simon & Schuster Adult Publishing Group** and electronic by permission of **A.P. Watt, Ltd. on behalf of Michael B. Yeats.**

From *Memoirs: Autobiography* by W.B. Yeats, edited by Denis Donoghue. Copyright © 1972 by Michael Butler Yeats and Anne Yeats. All rights reserved. Reproduced by permission of **Scribner, an imprint of Simon & Schuster Adult Publishing Group** and electronic format by permission of **A P Watt, Ltd. on behalf of Gráinne Yeats.**

"No Witchcraft for Sale" from *African Stories* by Doris Lessing. Copyright 1951 by Doris Lessing. Reproduced by permission of **Simon & Schuster Adult Publishing Group** and electronic format by permission by **Jonathan Clowes Ltd., London, on behalf of Doris Lessing.**

From *1 Dead in Attic-After Katrina* by Chris Rose. Copyright © 2006, 2007 by the Times-Picayune Publishing Corp. Reproduced by permission of **Simon and Schuster Adult Publishing Group.**

"I waited and I," by Princess Nukada, "The end of my journey" by ōshikōchi Mitsune, "Now, I cannot tell" by Ki Tsurayuki, "How helpless my heart!" by Ono Komachi, and "Every single thing" by Priest Saigyo from *The Penguin Book of Japanese Verse,* translated by Geoffrey Bownas and Anthony Thwaite (Penguin Classics, 1964). Translation copyright © 1964 by Geoffrey Bownas and Anthony Thwaite. Reproduced by permission of **Anthony Thwaite.**

"The First Principle," "The Gates of Paradise," "The Moon Cannot Be Stolen," and "Temper" from *Zen Flesh, Zen Bones: A Collection of Zen and Pre-Zen Writings,* compiled by Paul Reps. Copyright © 1957 by **Charles E. Tuttle Co., Inc., Boston, MA, and Tokyo, Japan.** Reproduced by permission of the publisher.

From "Sir Gawain and the Green Knight" from *The Complete Works of the Gawain-Poet,* translated by John Gardner. Copyright © 1965 by **The University of Chicago.** Reproduced by permission of the publisher.

"Sonnet 79/Soneto 79" from *100 Love Sonnets/Cien sonetos de amor* by Pablo Neruda, translated by Stephen Tapscott. Copyright © 1959 by Pablo Neruda and Fundación Pablo Neruda; translation copyright © 1986 by **The University of Texas Press.** Reproduced by permission of the publisher.

"The Lorelei" from *Heinrich Heine: Paradox and Poet* by Louis Untermeyer. Copyright 1937 by Louis Untermeyer. Reproduced by permission of **Laurence S. Untermeyer on behalf of The Estate of Louis Untermeyer, Norma Anchin Untermeyer c/o Professional Publishing Services Company.**

From "The Book of Sand" from *Collected Fictions* by Jorges Luis Borges, translated by Andrew Hurley. Copyright © 1998 by Maria Kodama; translation copyright © 1998 by Penguin Putnam Inc. Reproduced by permission of **Viking Penguin, a division of Penguin Group (USA). Inc.** and electronic format by permission of **The Wylie Agency, Inc.**

"The Destructors" from *Collected Stories of Graham Greene.* Copyright © 1955, 1983 by Graham Greene. Reproduced by permission of **Viking Penguin, a division of Penguin Group (USA) Inc., www.penguin.com.**

"The Death of Hector" from *The Iliad* by Homer, translated by Robert Fagles. Copyright © 1990 by Robert Fagles. Reproduced by permission of **Viking Penguin, a division of Penguin Group (USA) Inc.** and electronic format by permission of **Georges Borchardt, Inc.**

"The Rocking-Horse Winner" from *Complete Short Stories of D. H. Lawrence.* Copyright 1933 by the Estate of D. H. Lawrence; copyright renewed © 1961 by Angelo Ravagli and C.M. Weekley, Executors of the Estate of Frieda Lawrence Ravagli. Reproduced by permission of **Viking Penguin, a division of Penguin Group (USA) Inc.** and electronic format by permission by **Pollinger Limited and the Estate of Frieda Lawrence Ravagli.**

"On the Bottom" from *If This Is a Man (Survival in Auschwitz)* by Primo Levi, translated by Stuart Woolf. Copyright © 1958 by Giulio Einaudi Editore S.P.A.; copyright © 1959 by Orion Press, Inc. Reproduced by permission of **Viking Penguin, a division of Penguin Group (USA) Inc.** and electronic format by permission of **Giulio Einaudi Editore S.P.A.**

From *Don Quixote* by Miguel de Cervantes Saavedra, translated by Samuel Putnam. Copyright 1949 by The Viking Press, Inc. Reproduced by permission of **Viking Penguin, a division of Penguin Group (USA) Inc., www.penguin.com.**

"When Elements Go Extreme" by Jason La Canfora from *The Washington Post,* August 2, 2006. Copyright © 2006 by **The Washington Post.** Reproduced by permission of the publisher.

"Pronunciation Key" from *World Book Online Reference Center* at www.worldbook.com. Reproduced by permission of **World Book, Inc.**

"Fear" from *Selected Poems of Gabriela Mistral: A Bilingual Edition,* translated by Doris Dana. Copyright © 1961, 1964, 1970, 1971 by Doris Dana. Published by The Johns Hopkins University Press, Baltimore, 1971. Reproduced by permission of **Writers' House, Inc., as agent for the proprietor.**

"To a Mosquito" from *Present Company* by W. S. Merwin. Copyright © 2005 by W. S. Merwin. Reproduced by permission of **The Wylie Agency, Inc.**

"The Seafarer" from *Poems and Prose from the Old English,* translated by Burton Raffel. Copyright © 1960, 1964, 1998 by Burton Raffel. Reproduced by permission of **Yale University Press.**

Riddles 1, 14, and 32 from *Poems and Prose from the Old English,* translated by Burton Raffel. Copyright © 1960, 1964, 1998 by Burton Raffel. Reproduced by permission of **Yale University Press.**

"The Wanderer" from *Poems and Prose from the Old English,* translated by Burton Raffel. Copyright © 1960, 1964, 1998 by Burton Raffel. Reproduced by permission of **Yale University Press.**

Sources Cited:
Parable of the Prodigal Son from *The New Oxford Annotated Bible*. Published by Oxford University Press, New York, NY, 1946.

PICTURE CREDITS

The illustrations and photographs on the Contents pages are picked up from pages in the textbook. Credits for those can be found either on the textbook page on which they appear or in the listing below.

Picture Credits: iii (all), Sam Dudgeon/HRW Photo; **iv** (bl, bc, br), Sam Dudgeon/HRW Photo; (tl), Courtesy of Hector Rivera; (tr), Courtesy of Eric Cooper; **v** (l, cl), Sam Dudgeon/HRW Photo; (cr), Courtesy of Margaret McKeown; (r), Courtesy of Mabel Rivera; **vi** (all), Sam Dudgeon/HRW Photo; **A4,** CM Dixon/HIP/The Image Works; **A5,** Nik Wheeler/Corbis; **A6-A7,** Private Collection/Bridgeman Art Library; **A9,** Bridgeman Art Library; **A11** (b), PCL/Alamy; (br), Private Collection/Ken Welsh/Bridgeman Art Library; **A13,** Bridgeman Art Library; **A14,** Pictorial Press, Ltd/Alamy; **A15,** Dover Publications; **A17,** Dennis Cox/ChinaStock; **A18,** Art Resource, NY; **A21,** Bridgeman Art Library; **A23** (tl), Private Collection/Bridgeman Art Library; (br), Private Collection/Bridgeman Art Library; **A48** (bkgd), Joe Ginsberg/Photodisk/Getty Images; (t), VisionsofAmerica/Joe Sohm/Digital Vision/Getty Images; (tc), Rubberball Productions/Getty Images; (c), Somos/Veer/Getty Images; (b), Image100/Alamy; **A49** (tl), Tony Hopewell/Taxi/Getty Images; (cr), Meiko Arquillos/UpperCut Images/Getty Images; (br bkgd), Skye Chalmers/Iconica/Getty Images; **1,** Bridgeman Art Library; **2** (tr), Bridgeman Art Library, NY; (cl), Art Resource, NY; (cr), Werner Karrasch; **3** (cl), Private Collection/Bridgeman Art Library; (cr), Bridgeman Art Library; (br), Paolo Aguilar/EPA/Corbis; **4,** Getty Images/Guy Edwardes; **5,** Bridgeman Art Library; **8** (tr), Corbis; **8-9** (c), Scala/Art Resource, NY; **10-11** (c), R.G. Ojeda/Reunion des Musees Nationaux/Art Resource, NY; **12-13, 14,** New Line/The Everett Collection; **16,** Erich Lessing/Art Resource, NY; **17,** AKG-Images; **18,** Bridgeman-Giraudon/Art Resource, NY; **22,** Scala/Art Resource, NY; **28,** HIP/Art Resource, NY; **31** (cr), Bridgeman Art Library; **32,** Gareth Hinds, 2007; **35,** Max Morse/Reuters; **40,** Werner Forman/Art Resource, NY; **43** (b), Eirik Irgens Johnsen; **44,** Michael Holford; **47,** CM Dixon/HIP/The Image Works; **54-58** (all), Gareth Hinds, 2007; **63,** Gary Cook/Alamy; **64,** The Art Archive; **65,** Werner Forman/Corbis; **67,** David Lyons/Alamy; **69,** David Hancock/Alamy; **71,** Hans Strand/Corbis; **75** (cr), Art Resource, NY; **76,** Art Resource, NY; **87,** Mary Evans Picture Library; **88** (bkgd), Nik Wheeler/Corbis; (bl), Erich Lessing/Art Resource, NY; **90-91,** Nik Wheeler/Corbis; **92,** Dagli Orti/The Art Archive; **94,** Art Resource, NY; **98,** Dagli Orti/The Art Archive; **100-101,** Warner Brothers/The Everett Collection; **102,** Bridgeman Art Library; **104,** Dagli Orti/The Art Archive; **107,** Erich Lessing/Art Resource, NY; **108,** Ronald Sheridan/Ancient Art & Architecture Collection Ltd.; **109,** Ancient Art and Architecture Collection/Bridgeman Art Library; **112,** Bridgeman Art Library; **114,** Private Collection/Bridgeman Art Library; **116** (bkgd), QT Luong/Terra Galleria Photography; **117,** Bridgeman Art Library; **118-119,** Private Collection/Bridgeman Art Library; **120,** Bridgeman Art Library; **124,** Private Collection/Bridgeman Art Library; **125** (br), Private Collection/Bridgeman Art Library; **126-133** (all), Private Collection/Bridgeman Art Library; **135, 137** (all), Bridgeman Art Library; **138-140** (all), Private Collection/Bridgeman Art Library; **141, 142-143,** Bridgeman Art Library; **144,** Private Collection/Bridgeman Art Library; **150,** Private Collection/Harry Mileham/Bridgeman Art Library; **151,** Bridgeman Art Library; **157,** Mary Evans Picture Library; **165,** Private Collection/Bridgeman Art Library; **166-167,** Nigel Norrington/Arena Pal; **170,** ©Bettmann/CORBIS; **177,** DLILLC/Corbis; **179,** Colin Edwards/Alamy; **181** (tl), Fine Art Photographic Library/Corbis; (cl), AA World Travel Library/Alamy; (both cr), Bridgeman Art Library; (br), David Noble Photography/Alamy; **184,** Dagli Orti/The Art Archive; **187** (br), J. Garcia/Photocuisine/Corbis; **189,** Art Resource, NY; **191,** HIP/Art Resource, NY; **193,** Mario Perez/ABC/The Everett Collection; **194,** Private Collection/Photo ©Christie's Images/Bridgeman Art Library; **197,** Blue Lanterns Studio/Corbis; **198,** Clive Barda/The Arena Pal; **200,** Blue Lanterns Studio/Corbis; **202,** Clive Barda/The Arena Pal; **206,** Dagli Orti/The Art Archive; **208-209,** Touchstone/The Everett Collection; **210-211,** Jonathan Hession/Touchstone/Bureau L.A. Collection/Corbis; **213,** Touchstone Pictures/Jerry Bruckheimer Films/The Kobal Collection; **216,** Bridgeman Art Library; **218** (c), Han Klaus Techt/Epa/Corbis; **225,** Erich Lessing/Art Resource, NY; **228,** Mary Evans Picture Library/The Image Works; **236,** HRW; **248** (tl), "Jacket Cover" copyright ©1971, from Grendel by John Gardner. Used by permission of Alfred A. Knopf, a division of Random House, Inc.; (br), Cover from Mythology: The Voyage of the Hero by David Adams Leeming. ©1988 by David Adams Leeming. Used by permission of Oxford University Press; **249,** From The Hobbit by J.R.R. Tolkien, ©1982. Used by permission of Ballantine Books, a division of Random House, Inc.; **250-251,** Erich Lessing/Art Resource, NY; **252** (cl, cr), Art Resource, NY; (br), HIP/Art Resource, NY; **253** (c), Donald Cooper/Photo Stage; (cr), Bridgeman Art Library; (bl), Superstock, Inc.; **254,** Chris George/Alamy; **255,** Bridgeman Art Library; **256,** Bridgeman-Giraudon/Art Resource, NY; **257,** Private Collection/Philip Mould Ltd, London/Bridgeman Art Library; **258** (bl), Bridgeman Art Library; (br), Cristian Peña; **259,** AKG-Images; **260** (t), Lebrecht Music and Arts Photo library/Alamy; (br), Art Resource, NY; **262** (b), AKG-Images; **263** (c), Erich Lessing/Art Resource, NY; **264** (br), Fredrick Naumann/Panos Pictures; **265** (tl), F. Hoffman-La Roche, Ltd. Basel Switzerland; **266,** Scala/Art Resource, NY; **268,** Visual Art Library, London/Alamy; **270** (bc), Kingston Lacy, Dorset, UK/National Trust Photographic Library/Derrick E. Witt/Bridgeman Art Library; **279,** Bridgeman Art Library; **284,** Christie's Images/Bridgeman Art Library; **286,** Giraudon/Bridgeman Art Library; **288,** Lebrecht Music and Arts Photo Library/The Image Works; **290,** Rolf Richardson/Alamy; **293,** Art Resource, NY; **295,** Bridgeman Art Library; **297,** Angelo Hornak/Corbis; **298,** Bridgeman Art Library; **301,** Jeremy Pardoe/Alamy; **303,** HIP/Art Resource, NY; **306,** The Kobal Collection; **308** (bkgd), The Bridgeman Art Library; **310** (bkgd), Paul Watts/Cornish Picture Library; (br), Private Collection/Christie's Images/Bridgeman Art Library; **311** (cr), Fine Art Photographic Library, London/Private Collection/Art Resource; (br), Paul Watts/Cornish Picture Library; **313,** Julia Engelhardt; **316, 317,** Bridgeman Art Library; **320** (bkgd), Art Resource, NY; (bl), Erich Lessing/Art Resource, NY; **322** (br), Dagli Orti/Corbis; **322-323** (bkgd), Nik Wheeler/Corbis; **326-327** (bkgd), Nik Wheeler/Corbis; **327,** ©Scala/Art Resource, NY; **328** (bkgd), Nik Wheeler/Corbis; Michael S. Quinton/National Geographic Image Collection; **330,** Art Resource, NY; **331,** Art Resource, NY; **336,** B.S.P.I./CORBIS; **338,** Vanni/Art Resource, NY; **339,** Archives Charmet/Bridgeman Art Library; **340,** Bridgeman Art Library; **342,** Bridgeman Art Library; **347,** Private Collection/Photo ©Bonhams, London, UK/Bridgeman Art Library; **348,** Rick Stafford ©President and Fellows of Harvard College; **353,** Private Collection/Christopher Wood Gallery, London/Bridgeman Art Library; **356,** Charles Walker/

Topham/The Image Works; **364,** Private Collection/©Cider House Galleries, Ltd., Bletchingley, Surrey, UK/Bridgeman Art Library; **366,** British Library, London, UK/Bridgeman Art Library; **369,** Private Collection,Bridgeman Art Library; **371,** The Everett Collection; **373,** Erich Lessing/Art Resource, NY; **375,** Private Collection/Bridgeman Art Library; **376,** Dagli Orti/The Art Archive; **378,** Courtesy of Vintage, Random House, NY; **380,** Giles Keyte/©HBO/The Everett Collection; **381** (tl), Bridgeman Art Library; **381** (tr), Ray T/Rex Features/The Everett Collection; **384,** PCL/Alamy; **387,** Nathan Benn/Corbis; **388** (bl), Private Collection/Ken Welsh/Bridgeman Art Library; (bc), Chris Cole/ The Image Bank/Getty Images; **389** (t), Private Collection/Ken Welsh/Bridgeman Art Library; (bc), Bridgeman Art Library; (br), Shakespeare Birthplace Trust Records Office; **391** (cr), Private Collection/c Christopher Wood Gallery, London/Bridgeman Art Library; (br), Charles Gullung/Photonica/Getty Images; **392-393** (bkgd), Bridget Webber/Photonica/Getty Images; **392** (br), Art Resource, NY; **393** (br), Giraudon/Bridgeman Art Library; **395,** Steve Frost/Alamy; **396-397** (t), Richard Green/Photonica/Getty Images; **397** (tl), Photograph ©1984 The Metropolitan Museum of Art; **398,** Bridgeman Art Library; **402,** Art Resource, NY; **403,** Erich Lessing/Art Resource, NY; **405** (bkgd), Roger Holmes/ Photonica/Getty Images; (b), Sara Krulwich/The New York Times/ Redux; **406,** David Robertson/Alamy; **410,** Donald Cooper/ Photostage; **411,** (tr) Roger Holmes/Photonica/Getty Images; **417,** Donald Cooper/Photostage; **418,** Dale Jorgensen/ Superstock; **421,** Ben Graville/PhotoNews Service LTD.; **428,** Steve Mackins; **429,** David Gowans/Alamy; **430,** Cromwell/ Lamancha/Grampian TV/ The Kobal Collection; **432,** Steve Mackins; **437,** Bridgeman Art Library, NY; **438,** David Sanger Photography/Alamy; **442,** Donald Cooper/Photostage; **444,** Steve Mackins; **447,** Vittoriano Rastelli/Corbis; **449** (bkgd), Roger Holmes/Photonica/Getty Images; (b), Donald Cooper/ Photostage; **454** (bkgd), Roger Holmes/Photonica/Getty Images; (c), Donald Cooper/Photostage; **458,** Donald Cooper/ Photostage; **461** (bkgd), Roger Holmes/Photonica/Getty Images; (b), Donald Cooper/Photostage; **462,** Robbie Jack/ Corbis; **465,** Robert Holmes/Corbis; **466,** Clive Barda/ArenaPal; **469,** Robert Harding Picture Library Ltd./Alamy; **471** (tr), Roger Holmes/Photonica/Getty Images; **472,** Vittoriano Rastelli/Corbis; **479** (bkgd), Roger Holmes/Photonica/Getty Images; (b), Paul Ridgeway/PhotoNews Service, LTD; **481,** Matti Kolho/Lebrecht Music & Arts; **484,** Steve Mackins; **486,** Private Collection/Pace Wildenstein Gallery, New York; **487,** (tr) Roger Holmes/ Photonica/Getty Images; **488,** David Sanger/Alamy; **491,** ©Columbia Pictures/Photofest, NY; **497-501,** (all) Penguin Group USA Inc; **511,** HRW Photo; **524** (bl), Book cover from Zen And The Art Of Motorcycle Maintenance by Robert Pirsig. Copyright ©1974 by Robert M. Pirsig. Reprinted by permission of HarperCollins Publishers. William Morrow; **525** (tl), The Tragedy of Hamlet by William Shakespeare. Cover, ©HRW. Cover art by Joe Melomo; (br), Photodisc/Getty Images; **526-527,** Skyscan Photolibrary/Alamy; **528** (cl), Private collection/ Archives Charmet/Bridgeman Art Library; (br), National Trust/Art Resource, NY; **529** (cl), Bildarchiv Preussischer Kulturbesitz/Art Resource, NY; (cr), Archives Charmet/Bridgeman Art Library; (br), Bridgeman Art Library; **530,** Guildhall Art Gallery, City of London/Bridgeman Art Library; **532,** Alen Lauzan Falcon/Cagle Cartoons, Inc; **533,** Historical Picture Archive/Corbis; **534,** Jon Arnold Images/Alamy; **535,** HIP/Art Resource, NY; **537** (t), Jerry Grayson/Helifilms Australia PTY Ltd./Getty Images; (cl), AKG Images; **540,** Erich Lessing/Art Resource, NY; **542,** The Everett Collection; **543,** Courtesy of the Warden and Scholars of New College, Oxford/Bridgeman Art Library; **544** (bkgd), AKG Images; (bl), National Portrait Gallery, London/Bridgeman Art Library; **547,** Yale Center for British Art, Paul Mellon Collection/ The British Art Library; **551** (br), Jonathan Blair/Corbis; **552,** Private Collection/Bridgeman Art Library; **553,** John Miller/ Robert Harding Picture Librray, Ltd/Alamy; **558-559** (bkgd), Private Collection/Bridgeman Art Library; **559** (cr), Private Collection/Bridgeman Art Library; **560** (bkgd), Private Collection/Bridgeman Art Library; **561** (bkgd), Private Collection/Bridgeman Art Library; **564** (bl), National Portrait Gallery, London; **567,** The Everett Collection; **569,** The Everett Collection; **572-573,** The Everett Collection; **575,** Alex Bailey/ Corbis Sygma; **585** (bkgd), The Illustrated London News Picture Library; (bl), The Illustrated London News Picture Library; **591,** Richard Melloul/Sygma/Corbis; **592,** ©Burstein Collection/ Corbis; **593,** Petar Pismestrovic/Artizan; **594** (bkgd), Achim Bednorz; (bl), Lauros/Giraudon//Bridgeman Art Library; **596** (t), Achim Bednorz; (b), Donald Cooper/Photostage; **598** (br), Donald Cooper/Photostage; **602** (bkgd), Hans Georg Roth/ Corbis; (bl), Private Collection/Bridgeman Art Library; **604,** Hans Georg Roth/Corbis; **606,** Thorsten Indra/Alamy; **612, 617,** Bridgeman Art Library; **618,** David Levenson/Alamy; **620,** Bridgeman Art Library; **622** (bkgd), iStockphoto; (br), Bridgeman Art Library; **625,** Visual Arts Library, London/Alamy; **632,** Private Collection/Bridgeman Art Library; **634,** AP Photo/Adam Butler; **638** (bl), Scott Eells/Getty Images; **642,** Rob Howard/Corbis; **644** (bkgd), Bridgeman Art Library; (bl), Bridgeman Art Library; **646** (bkgd), Bridgeman Art Library; (b), ©Michael Nicholson/Corbis; **650-651,** Bridgeman Art Library; **656** (bkgd), Thomas Dobner/ Alamy; **659,** Thomas Dobner/Alamy; **661,** Christopher Weil Photography/StoryCorps; **662-663,** Alan Novelli/Alamy; **665** (c), Private Collection/Gemalde Mensing/Bridgeman Art Library; **668,** Bridgeman Art Library; **671,** Mark Atkinson/JupiterImages/ Comstock; **672,** Bridgeman Art Library; **675,** Art Resource, NY; **677,** Bridgeman Art Library; **686,** HRW Photo; **698** (tl), The Misanthrope and Tartuffe by Moliere. Cover illustration by Mark English. Used by permission of Harcourt Publishers; **700-701,** Fine Art Photographic Library, London/Art Resource, NY; **702** (tr), Bridgeman Art Library; (cl), Jochen Remmer/Bildarchiv Preussischer Kulturbesitz/Art Resource, NY; (bl), Reunion des Musees Nationaux/Art Resource, NY; (br), Wim Wiskerke/Alamy; **703** (t), Ann Ronan Picture Library, London/HIP/Art Resource, NY; (cl), Private Collection/Bridgeman Art Library; (cr), The British Library, London/Bridgeman Art Library; (b), Bridgeman Art Library; **706,** Lauros/Giraudon/Bridgeman Art Library; **707,** Everett Collection; **709,** Alex Segre/Alamy; **711** (tr), Bridgeman Art Library; (b), Hugo Van Lawick; **713,** Michael Nichols/National Geographic Image Collection; **716,** Bridgeman Art Library; **719,** Tate Picture Library, London; **720** (bkgd), Anna Grossman/ Photonica/Getty Images; **722** (t), Anna Grossman/Photonica/ Getty Images; **723** (bkgd), Anna Grossman/Photonica/Getty Images; (br), The Maas Gallery, London, UK/Bridgeman Art Library; **725,** Herve Lewandowski/Reunion des Musees Nationaux/Art Resource, NY; **726,** Peter Arnold, Inc./Alamy; **728** (bkgd), Art Resource, NY; **729,** Jarrold Publishing/The Art Archive; **732** (cr), Bridgeman Art Library; **736** (cr), Randy Wells/ Corbis; (br), Moodboard/Corbis; **738,** INSADCO Photography/ Alamy; **739** (br), Bettmann/Corbis; **740,** Bridgeman Art Library; **746** (bkgd), Pictorial Press Ltd./Alamy; **749,** Neil Setchfield/ Alamy; **750,** Pictorial Press, Ltd/Alamy; **753,** AA World Travel Library/Alamy; **758,** Erich Lessing/Art Resource, NY; **759,** Art

Resource, NY; 762 (t), Frank Rothe/Photonica/Getty Images; (br), John Miller/Robert Harding World Imagery/Corbis; **766** (bkgd), Bridgeman Art Library; **775,** Bridgeman Art Library; **778, 783,** Dover Publications; **787** (all), Momatiuk-Eastcott/Corbis; **789, 791, 798,** Dover Publications; **803,** Bridgeman Art Library; **804-805,** (bkgd) Art Wolfe/Photo Researchers Inc.; **804** (cl), Art Wolfe/Photo Researchers, Inc.; **805** (tl), Kevin Schafer/Corbis; (cr), David Hosking/Photo Researchers, Inc.; (bc), Eric Hosking/ Photo Researchers, Inc.; **808,** Bridgeman Art Library; **809,** Art Resource, NY; **810,** Sotheby's Library, London; **812,** Private Collection/Bridgeman Art Library; **814** (br), Sharon Montrose/ Stone/Getty Images; **814-815** (bkgd), Farhad J. Parsa/ Photonica/Getty Images; **818,** Bridgeman Art Library; **820,** Michael Juno/Alamy; **823,** World Pictures/Alamy; **825,** Terry Deroy Gruber/Photonica/Getty Images; **826-827,** Amelia P. Schaffner; **831,** Andrew Darrington/Alamy; **834,** David Tipling/ Alamy; **836,** Stephanie Young Merzel/Just This Moment Photography; **838,** Eye of Science/Photo Researchers, Inc.; **839,** Jeff Faerber; **841** (cr), DLILLC/Corbis; (bc), Martin Harvey/Gallo Images/Corbis; **842** (bkgd), Tom Mackie/Alamy; (bl), Bridgeman Art Library; **844, 845,** Erich Lessing/Art Resource, NY; **850,** Reunion des Musees Nationaux/Art Resource, NY; **853,** Erich Lessing/Art Resource, NY; **854** (cr), Reunion des Musees Nationaux/Art Resource; (br), Bildarchiv Preussincher Kulturbesitz/Art Resource, NY; **863,** Dennis Cox/ChinaStock; **864,** Judy Mundy/Alamy; **865** (cr), Dennis Cox/Alamy; (bl), View Stock/Alamy; **866,** Pacific Press Service/Alamy; **867** (bkgd), Chris Porter/Alamy; (br), Bridgeman Art Library; **869,** Darby Sawchuk/ Alamy; **870,** Golden Gate Images/Alamy; **872,** B.S.P.I./Corbis; **875,** Dennis Cox/ChinaStock; **879,** Panorama Media (Beijing) Ltd./Alamy; **886,** HRW Photo; **898** (tl), Frankenstein, Or the Modern Prometheus by Mary Shelley. Cover ©HRW, illustration by Cliff Nielsen ©Philippe Weisbecker. Used by permission of Riley Illustration; (tl), ©HRW; **899** (tl), Book cover from Days of The French Revolution by Christopher Hibbert. Reprinted by permission of Harper Collins Publishers; **900-901,** Art Resource, NY; **902** (tr), Private Collection/Bridgeman Art Library; (cr), Archives Charmet/Bridgeman Art Library; **903** (tl), Private Collection/Bridgeman Art Library; (tr), Pictorial Press Ltd./Alamy; (cr), Bettmann/Corbis; **904,** Bridgeman Art Library; **907** (cr), Bridgeman Art Library; (bc), Stefan Schuetz/Zefa RF/Alamy; **908,** Private Collection/Whitford & Hughes, London/Bridgeman Art Library; **909,** Private Collection/Bridgeman Art Library; **911** (cr), Roger Bamber/Alamy; **912** (cr), Ed Maynard/Alamy; (b), Neil McAllister/Alamy; **914,** Tate Collection, London; **915,** Christie's Images/Corbis; **919,** Art Resource, NY; **921** (tr), Everett Collection, NY; (cr), Bettmann/Corbis; **927** (t), Erich Lessing/Art Resource, NY; **929,** Erich Lessing/Art Resource, NY; **933,** Bridgeman Art Library, NY; **936,** Private Collection/Bridgeman Art Library, NY; **938,** Steve Hawkins Photography/Alamy; **940,** Mary Evans Picture Library; **945,** Alinari/Bridgeman Art Library; **948,** Digital Image/licensed by Scala/Art Resource, NY; **954,** National Trust Photographic Library/Derrick E. Witty/Bridgman Art Library; **956,** Mary Evans/Jeffrey Morgan Collection/The Image Works; **958,** Roger Camp/Images.com; **960,** Bridgeman Art Library; **961,** Private Collection/Bridgeman Art Library; **963,** NMPFT/SSPL/The Image Works; **967,** Art Resource, NY; **972** (bkgd), William Leaman/Alamy; (bl), Bridgeman Art Library, NY; **974,** William Leaman/Alamy; **977,** Private Collection/Photo ©Bonhams, London, UK/Bridgeman Art Library, NY; **980,** Mary Evans Picture Library; **983,** Michael Steele/Getty Images; **985,** Brigitte Sporrer/Zefa/Corbis; **989,** Robert Llewellyn/Image State/Alamy; **990,** Simon Bruty/Sports Illustrated; **994,** Walter Crump/Corbis; **995,** Tibor Bognar/Corbis; **997,** Kazuyoshy Nomachi/Corbis; **998,** Atlantide Phototravel/Corbis; **1001** (tr), Bridgeman Art Library; (cr), Cyril Ruoso/JH Editorial/Minden Pictures; **1003,** ©Lindsay Hebberd/Woodfin Camp & Associates; **1006,** Everett Collection; **1007,** Bridgeman Art Library; **1008,** Michael Nicholson/Corbis; **1010-1011,** Library of Congress Prints and Photographs Division; **1014-1015,** Corbis; **1018,** AKG London; **1022,** Bridgeman Art Library, NY; **1025,** Scala/Art Resource, NY; **1027,** Bridgeman Art Library, NY; **1032,** Stefano Bianchetti/Corbis; **1034-1035** (b), Corbis; **1035** (tc), Newmann/ Zefa/Corbis; **1046,** HRW Photo; **1058** (br), The Importance of Being Earnest by Oscar Wilde. Cover ©HRW, photo by Scott Van Osdol; **1059** (tl), Reprinted with permission of Scribner, an imprint of Simon & Schuster Adult Publishing Group from What Jane Austen Ate and Charles Dickens Knew by Daniel Poole. (New York: Simon & Schuster, 1993); (br), Lawrence Manning/ Corbis; **1060-1061,** Dominic Burke/Alamy; **1062** (tr, c), Everett Collection; (cr), Corbis; (br), Private Collection/Topham Picturepoint/Bridgeman Art Library; **1063** (tl), Donald Cooper/ Photostage; (cr), Donald Cooper/Photostage; (br), David Magnus/Rex Features/the Everett Collection; **1064,** Mike Booth/ Alamy; **1065,** Private Collection/Bridgeman Art Library; **1067** (t), Gavin Whitelaw Collection/Hulton Archive/Getty Images; (cr), Picture Post/Hulton Archive/Getty Images; **1068,** Bill Pierce/ Time Life Pictures/Getty Images; **1069,** Mark Boulton/Alamy; **1071,** NASA Glenn Research Center ImageNet; **1072,** Digital Image/Licensed by Scala/Art Resource, NY; **1073,** Laurie Platt Winfrey Inc.; **1074** (bkgd), Michael Busselle/Stone/Getty Images; (bl), Time Life Pictures/Mansell/Time Life Pictures/Getty Images; **1076,** Popperfoto/Alamy; **1078,** Michael Busselle/Stone/Getty Images; **1080, 1082,** Hulton Deutsch Collection/Corbis; **1085,** BOP/Popperfoto/Classicstock; **1087,** Jack Sullivan/Alamy; **1089,** Fiona Hanson/WPA Pool/AP Photo; **1092,** Jerry Bauer; **1095,** Bildarchiv Preussischer Kulturbesitz/Art Resource, NY; **1097,** Private Collection//Roger Perrin/Bridgeman Art Library; **1102,** William Coupon/Corbis; **1104,** Les Gibbon/Alamy; **1105,** Iain Masterton/Alamy; **1108,** Estate of Robert Elliot; **1111,** NMPFT/ Daily Herald Archive/SSPL/The Image Works; **1112,** AP Photos; **1116,** Hulton-Deutsch Collection/Corbis; **1119,** Private Collection/Bridgeman Art library; **1120-1121,** Private Collection/Connaught Brown, London/Bridgeman Art Library; **1122,** Bridgeman Art Library; **1126,** AFP/Agence France Presse/ Getty Images; **1129,** Hulton-Deutsch Collection/Corbis; **1135,** Bridgeman Art Library; **1142** (bkgd), Vivian kereki/Veer/Corbis; (br), Hulton Archive/Getty Images; **1145,** Christophe Boisvieux/ Corbis; **1150** (bl), Hulton-Deutsch Collection/Corbis; **1153,** Time Life Pictures/Mansell/Getty Images; **1155,** Paul Almasy/Corbis; **1159** (c), Cordaiy Photo Library Ltd./Corbis; **1160** (cl), AP Photos; **1161** (bc), Paramount/The Everett Collection; **1165,** Permission of Angelica Garnett/Sotheby's Library, London; **1166,** Michael Boys/Corbis; **1174-1175,** Bridgeman Art Library; **1179,** Private Collection/Bridgeman Art Library; **1186,** Private Collection/ Bridgeman Art Library; **1188,** Topham/The Image Works; **1193,** Digital Image/Licensed by Scala/Art Resource, NY; **1197** (bkgd), Stefano Amantini/Atlantide Phototravel/Corbis; (c), Pictorial Press Ltd./Alamy; **1198** (bl), Roy Hewson; (br), Geray Sweeney/ Corbis; **1199,** Private Collection/Bridgeman Art Library; **1201,** Jim Zuckerman/Corbis; **1204,** Vanni Archive/Corbis; **1206,** Michael Foyle/Alamy; **1209,** Private Collection/Bridgeman Art Library; **1210,** Envision/Corbis; **1213,** Danny Lehman/Corbis; **1214,** Cameraphoto Arte, Venice/Art Resource, NY; **1217,** Liam White/Alamy; **1218,** World History Archive/Alamy; **1222,** Mary Evans Picture Library/Alamy; **1228,** Bridgeman Art Library; **1231,** Jeff Towns/Dylan Bookstore; **1234,** Sigrid Olsson/ PhotoAlto/Alamy; **1236,** Private Collection/Bridgeman Art

Library; **1238,** Hulton-Deutsch Collection/Corbis; **1240,** Stefan Schuetz/Zefa/Corbis; **1242,** Topham Picturepoint/The Image Works; **1244,** Rheinisches Blidarchiv/Stadt Köln; **1246,** AP Photo/Czarek Sokolowski; **1249,** Patrick Robert/Sygma/Corbis; **1252** (bkgd), AP Photo/Alastair Grant; (bl), AP Photo/Filip Miller; **1256,** Bettmann/Corbis; **1258,** Rheinisches Blidarchiv/Stadt Köln; **1260,** AP Photo/Michael Lipchitz; **1262,** Look Photography/Beateworks/Corbis; **1264,** Estate of Fay Godwin; **1266,** Charles Hewitt/Hulton Archive/Getty Images; **1269** (cr), Ian Waldie/AP Photo; (bl), Ian Waldie/EPA/Corbis; **1272,** Jane Bown/Camera Press; **1274, 1275,** Photolink/Getty Images; **1278,** Johnny Eggitt/AFP/Getty Images; **1280,** Nicholas Devore III/Bruce Coleman, Inc.; **1282,** Paul A. Souders/Corbis; **1284,** Sophie Bassouls/Corbis; **1286,** Lew Robertson/Corbis; **1287,** Keith Shuttlewood/Alamy; **1292,** Oriol Alamany & E. Vicens/ Corbis; **1294,** Digital Image/licensed by Scala/Art Resource, NY; **1300,** Erich Lessing/Art Resource, NY; **1301,** Nadia Mackenzie/ National Trust Photographic Library/Bridgeman Art Library; **1303,** Steve Allen/The Image Bank/Getty Images; **1304,** Bridgeman Art Library; **1308,** Hulton-Deutsch Collection/Corbis; **1310-1311** (t), Glyn Kirk/Action Plus/Alamy; **1310** (br), Stockbyte/Alamy; **1311** (tr), Everett Collection; **1313, 1314,** Stockbyte/Alamy; **1317** (tl), Leo Mason/Alamy; (tr), Everett Collection; **1321,** Bert Hardy/Picture Post/Getty Images; **1323,** Private Collection/Bridgeman Art Library; **1324,** Roy Hewson; **1334,** Arici Graziano/Grazia Neri; **1338,** Christopher Zacharow/ Images.com/Corbis; **1342,** Hulton-Deutsch Collection/Corbis; **1344** (all), Donald Cooper/Photostage; **1347,** Donald Cooper/ Photostage; **1349,** Lee M. Rose and Jenny Moore; **1350,** Popperfoto/Alamy; **1352,** Cornell Capa/Magnum Photos; **1356,** MC Pherson Colin/Corbis Sygma; **1358,** John King/Alamy; **1361,** Juhan Kuus/SIPA Press; **1362, 1364,** John King/Alamy; **1367,** Peter Titmuss/Alamy; **1368,** Ed Bailey/AP Photo; **1370-1371** (bkgd), Kolvenbach/Alamy; **1371** (dogs), Gideon Mendel/Corbis; **1372-1373,** Kolvenbach/Alamy; **1374,** Kolvenbach/Alamy; **1376,** Reuters/Ralph Orlowski ROR/CMC; **1379,** Private Collection/Bridgeman Art Library; **1381,** Don Cole; **1384,** Ira Wyman/Corbis Sygma; **1387,** Private Collection/Bridgeman Art Library; **1389,** Tim Graham/Alamy; **1390,** Sophie Bassouls/ Corbis Sygma; **1393,** June Kelly Gallery, NY; **1396,** MC Pherson Colin/Corbis Sygma; **1406,** David Levenson/Getty Images; **1408,** Jeremy Young; **1412,** Andrew Toos/Cartoon Stock; **1414,** Paolo Della Corte/Rex USA; **1416-1417,** Jon Hicks/eStock Photo; **1416** (t), Smari/Photographer's Choice/Getty Images; **1419,** Christophe Boisvieux/Corbis; **1430,** HRW Photo; **1437,** USDA; **1448,** (tr) Brave New World by Aldous Huxley. ©1932, 1946 by Aldous Huxley. Cover design ©Marc Cohen. Cover photo ©Jeffery Zaruba/Photonica/Getty; (bl) Book cover from One Hundred Years of Solitude by Gabriel Garcia Marquez. Translated by Gregory Rabassa. English translation copyright ©1970 by Harper & Row Publishers, Inc. Reprinted by permission of Harper Collins Publishers; (br) Things Fall Apart by Chinua Achebe. Cover, ©HRW, art by Earl Keleny; **1451,** BananaStock/age Fotostock.

INDEX OF SKILLS

The Index of Skills is divided into the following categories:

LITERARY SKILLS

INFORMATIONAL TEXT SKILLS

READING SKILLS

VOCABULARY SKILLS

STANDARDS REVIEW

LANGUAGE (GRAMMAR, USAGE, AND MECHANICS) SKILLS

LISTENING AND SPEAKING SKILLS

READ ON: For Independent Reading

INDEX OF AUTHORS AND TITLES

Page numbers in italics refer to the pages on which author biographies appear.

ACKNOWLEDGMENTS:

From *Medieval Europe: A Short History, 3rd Edition,* by C. Warren Hollister. Copyright © 1964, 1968, 1974 by John Wiley & Sons, Inc. Reproduced by permission of **The McGraw-Hill Companies.**

For permission to reprint copyrighted material, grateful acknowledgment is made to the following sources:

From "V.S. Naipaul, Man Without a Society" from *Words and Their Masters* by Israel Shenker. Copyright © 1974 by V. S. Naipaul. Reproduced by permission of **Gillon Aitken Associates Ltd.**

From "Letter to Rolf Gardiner, 18 December 1927" from *The Letters of D. H. Lawrence,* vol. V-VI. Copyright 1932 by the Estate of D. H. Lawrence; copyright 1934 by Frieda Lawrence; copyright 1933, 1948, 1953, 1954, © 1956, 1957, 1958, 1959, 1960, 1961, 1962, 1967, 1969 by Stefano Ravagli and R. G. Seaman, executors of the Estate of Frieda Lawrence Ravagli; copyright © 1987 by the Estate of Frieda Lawrence Ravagli. Published by Cambridge University Press. Reproduced by permission of **Pollinger Limited and the Estate of Frieda Lawrence Ravagli.**

Sources Cited

From *Morning Yet on Creation Day: Essays* by Chinua Achebe. Published by Anchor Books, New York, 1975.

From "Revolution and the Rule of Law" by Christopher Harvie from *The Oxford Illustrated History of Britain,* edited by Kenneth O. Morgan. Published by Oxford University Press, Oxford, 2001.

PHOTOGRAPHY CREDITS:

Abbreviations used: c-center, b-bottom, t-top, l-left, r-right, bkgrd-background.

All images HRW Photo unless otherwise noted.
All Teacher-to-Teacher photos courtesy of the Teachers.

Page ix (t) ©2009 Jupiter Images Corporation; formerly Comstock; **T2** (bkgd) Radius Images/Punchstock, (bl) Blend Images/Punchstock, (br) BananaStock/Jupiter Images; **T3** (bl) ©Emely/zefa/Corbis; (br) Eric Audras/ Photo Alto/Getty Images; **T33** (br) Image Source/Corbis; **T36** (cr) Photodisc, (bc) PhotoObjects.net/Jupiter Images; **T37** (pencil) Brand X/Jupiter Images; **T38** Stockbyte; **T39** Digital Vision/Getty Images; **250E** (all), ©2009 Jupiter Images; **700E** (girl at computer), ©2009 Jupiter Images; **1060G** (audio-boy), © 2009 JupiterImages; **1060G** (audio-girl), ©Blend Images/Punchstock; **1060G** (girl at computer), ©2009 Jupiter Images.

Teacher's Edition